Everyman's
Dictionary of music

Everyman's
DICTIONARY
OF
MUSIC

COMPILED BY ERIC BLOM

REVISED BY SIR JACK WESTRUP

Professor of Music, University of Oxford

with the collaboration of
John Caldwell, Edward Olleson
and R. T. Beck

ST. MARTIN'S PRESS

NEW YORK

AFFILIATED PUBLISHERS: Macmillan & Company, Limited,
London – also at Bombay, Calcutta, Madras and Melbourne
– The Macmillan Company of Canada, Limited, Toronto

Preface

This edition, which has been reset in a bolder type, differs from its predecessors in three respects:

1 The system of abbreviations has been simplified: a list of those used will be found on p. vii.
2 Music examples have been included to illustrate technical terms.
3 Living performers are not excluded.

In addition to these changes there has been extensive revision. Apart from several thousand minor alterations and corrections, many entries have been rewritten, a few have been omitted and several new ones have been added. The general plan of the book, however, remains the same; so does its purpose, which is to provide the maximum amount of information possible in a limited space.

It is obvious that a work of this kind has to be selective. Not all musicians can be included, nor can lists of works, in most cases, be complete. To define a single principle of selection is not easy; and even if the attempt were made its application could easily be challenged. Nothing is easier than to ask, 'If A is included, why not B?'; and the questioner is rarely satisfied with the answer that the line has to be drawn somewhere. It may be relevant, however, to quote what Eric Blom wrote in his preface to the original edition: 'The contents of the Dictionary are uncritical; the inclusion of any composer or work does not imply approbation any more than the exclusion of any subject, which may be due to one of a variety of other reasons, suggests disapproval.'

One of the difficulties that face a compiler, and equally a reviser, is to achieve consistency, not so much in matters of detail, such as the use of abbreviations, as in presentation in general – particularly in the relative amount of space allotted to individual entries. Here again there is likely to be more than one opinion: the reader who thinks that X is twice as important as Y will observe with disfavour that the space allotted to each is approximately equal. All that can be said here is that the attempt has been made to avoid any glaring discrepancy. It will presumably be generally accepted that composers like Bach, Beethoven and Mozart should be treated at some length.

Another difficulty, which fortunately occurs less frequently, is to discover whether musicians who are not as well known as they were are still alive. Here recent dictionaries have been helpful, and also periodicals, particularly *Notes*, which now publishes an annual necrology. It should not be assumed, however, that anyone who appears to be over ninety must in fact be dead. Musicians are just as likely to live to an advanced age as anyone else, and several of them have done so.

A note should be added here about the alphabetical arrangement, which remains the same as in previous editions. As Eric Blom explained in his preface, 'all entries consisting of more than one word are ranged in such a way as to make the first word alone the key to their place in the alphabet'; thus, 'Lero Viol' comes before 'Leroux', and so on. A hyphened word is treated as if it were two separate words. Christian names in brackets are ignored in assigning an alphabetical order to persons with the same surname.

I should not have been able to attempt such an extensive revision without the aid of my three collaborators, to whom I am more than grateful. Each of us has dealt with a particular area of the dictionary; but we have also offered advice and criticism to each other, and we have all read the proofs. This is not, unfortunately, a guarantee of complete accuracy, but it has meant the elimination of a number of errors that might have escaped a single pair of eyes. I must also express my gratitude to the printers, who have dealt expertly with an intractable mass of material, and to the publishers, who have patiently kept a watchful eye on the progress of this book.

JACK WESTRUP

Oxford
January 1971

Abbreviations

abbr.	abbreviated; abbreviation	Aus.	Austria; Austrian
abl.	ablative	Austral.	Australia; Australian
Acad.	Academy	autobiog.	autobiographical; autobiography
accomp.	accompanied; accompaniment; accompany	b.	born
Add. MSS.	Additional Manuscripts	B.B.C.	British Broadcasting Corporation
addit.	addition; additional	B.Mus.	Bachelor of Music
adj.	adjective	Bavar.	Bavaria; Bavarian
Alsat.	Alsatian	Beds.	Bedfordshire
altern.	alternate; alternating	Belg.	Belgian; Belgium
Amer.	America; American	Bibl.	Bibliothek; Bibliothèque
anag.	anagram	bibliog.	bibliographer; bibliography
Angl.	Anglican	biog.	biographer; biography
anon.	anonymous		
app.	appointed; appointing	Boh.	Bohemia; Bohemian
appar.	apparently	Brazil.	Brazilian
appt.	appointment	Brit.	British
appts.	appointments	Brit. Mus.	British Museum
Arg.	Argentine; Argentinian	Bulg.	Bulgaria; Bulgarian
arr.	arranged; arrangement; arranger	c.	*circa* (about)
		C.B.	Companion of the Bath
assoc.	associated; association	C.B.E.	Commander of the British Empire
asst.	assistant; assisted	C.B.S.	Columbia Broadcasting System
attrib.	attributed		

Calif.	California	Dan.	Danish
Cantuar.	Canterbury	ded.	dedicated; dedication
cent.	century		
cf.	*confer* (compare)	Den.	Denmark
charact.	characteristic; characterized	dept.	department
		do.	ditto
Ches.	Cheshire		
Chin.	Chinese	E.	East
clar.	clarinet	e.g.	*exempli gratia* (for example)
Co.	Company; County		
co-ed.	co-editor	eccles.	ecclesiastical
Coll.	College	ed.	edited; edition; editor
comp.	composed; composer; composing; composition	educ.	educated; education
		Encyc. Brit.	Encyclopaedia Britannica
cond.	conducted; conducting; conductor	Eng.	England; English
		esp.	especially
Conn.	Connecticut	estab.	establish; established; establishing; establishment
Cons.	Conservatoire; Conservatorio; Conservatorium; Conservatory		
		Eur.	Europe; European;
		ex.	example
contemp.	contemporary	fem.	feminine
contrib.	contributed; contribution; contributor	Fin.	Finland; Finnish
		fl.	flute
Ct.	Canton	Fla.	Florida
Cz.	Czech; Czechoslovakia	Flem.	Flemish
		foll.	followed; following
		Fr.	France; French
d.	died		
D.B.E.	Dame of the British Empire	G.S.M.	Guildhall School of Music
D. Mus.	Doctor of Music	Gael.	Gaelic

Ger.	German; Germany	lit.	literally; literary
Gk.	Greek	Litt.D.	Doctor of Letters
Glam.	Glamorganshire		
Glos.	Gloucestershire		
Gvt.	Government	M.Mus.	Master of Music
		maj.	major
		masc.	masculine
hist.	historian; historical; history	Mass.	Massachusetts
Hol.	Holland	Me.	Maine
hon.	honorary	Metropol.	Metropolitan
Hung.	Hungarian; Hungary	Mex.	Mexican; Mexico
		min.	minor
		Minn.	Minnesota
I.M.S.	International Musical Society	Miss.	Mississippi
I.S.C.M.	International Society for Contemporary Music	Mo.	Missouri
		Morav.	Moravian
		MS.	manuscript
Ill.	Illinois	munic.	municipal
Imp.	Imperial	mus.	music; musical
incid.	incidental	Mus.B.	Bachelor of Music
incl.	include; included; includes; including	Mus.D.	Doctor of Music
		N.	North
Inst.	Institute	N.B.C.	National Broadcasting Corporation
intro.	introduce; introduced; introducing; introduction		
		N.C.	North Carolina
Ir.	Ireland; Irish	N.F.	Newfoundland
It.	Italian; Italy	N.H.	New Hampshire
		N.J.	New Jersey
Jap.	Japanese	N.S.W.	New South Wales
		N.Y.	New York
Lancs.	Lancashire	nat.	national
Lat.	Latin	Neapol.	Neapolitan
lib.	libretto	no.	number

Northants.	Northamptonshire	prin.	principal; principle
Norw.	Norway; Norwegian	prob.	probably
Notts.	Nottinghamshire	prod.	produced; producer; producing; production
nr.	near		
		prof.	professor
ob.	oboe	Prov.	Provençal
obs.	oboes; obsolete	prov.	province; provincial
Okla.	Oklahoma	Prus.	Prussia; Prussian
onomat.	onomatopœic	pseudo.	pseudonym
Ont.	Ontario	pub.	publication; published; publisher publishing
op.	opus		
orch.	orchestra; orchestrated; orchestration		
org.	organ		
orig.	original; originally	q.v.	quod vide (which see)
		R.A.M.	Royal Academy of Music
P.I.	Philippine Islands		
partic.	particular; particularly	R.C.M.	Royal College of Music
perc.	percussion	Rect.	Rector
perf.	performance; performed; performer	ref.	reference; referring
		repres.	represented; representing
pf.	pianoforte		
Phil.	Philharmonic	repro.	reproduced; reproduction
plur.	plural		
Pol.	Poland; Polish	repub.	republished
Pom.	Pomerania	Rest.	Restoration
Port.	Portugal; Portuguese	Rom.	Roman
		Rum.	Rumania; Rumanian
poss.	possibly	Rus.	Russia; Russian
posth.	posthumous		
prec.	preceded; preceding	S.	South
Pres.	President	S.C.	South Carolina

S.I.M.	Société Internationale de Musicologie	U.S.A.	United States of America
		unaccomp.	unaccompanied
Salop.	Shropshire	Univ.	University
Scand.	Scandinavia; Scandinavian	unpub.	unpublished
Scot.	Scotland; Scottish	Va.	Virginia
sec.	secretary	var.	variety; various
sep.	separate	Venez.	Venezuela; Venezuelan
Som.	Somerset		
Span.	Spanish	vla.	viola
Swed.	Sweden; Swedish	vln.	violin
Switz.	Switzerland	vol.	volume
symph.	symphonic; symphony		
		W.	West
		W. Va.	West Virginia
		Wilts.	Wiltshire
T.C.M.	Trinity College of Music	Wis.	Wisconsin
theol.	theological; theology	Yorks.	Yorkshire
theoret.	theoretical		
Thur.	Thuringia; Thuringian	4tet	quartet
		5tet	quintet
trans.	translated; translation; translator	6tet	sextet
		7tet	septet
		8tet	octet
tpt.	trumpet	8ve	octave
tromb.	trombone		

The Dictionary

A

A, the 6th note, or submediant, of the scale of C major. The note

to which an orch. tunes, is estab. by international agreement at a pitch of 440 cycles a second.

A battuta (It. = at the beat, with the beat), a direction indicating that after a free passage the strict time is to be resumed.

A cappella (Its.), also **Alla cappella** (lit. at or in the chapel), a term used now only to designate unaccomp. mus. for a vocal ensemble.

A due (It.) = in 2 parts; generally written '*a* 2'. The term is also used in the opposite sense in orchestral scores where pairs of instruments are to play in unison.

A. E. (George William Russell) (1867–1935), Ir. poet. *See* **Busch** (songs).

A la manière de . . . (*In the Manner of . . .*), 2 sets of pf. pieces by Casella and Ravel imitating the styles of Wagner, Fauré, Brahms, Debussy, R. Strauss, Franck, Borodin, d'Indy, Chabrier and Ravel. Only the Borodin and Chabrier pieces are by Ravel.

A piacere (It. = at pleasure), a direction indicating that a passage may be played or sung in any way the perf. desires, esp. in regard to tempo.

A.R.C.M. (abbr.), Associate of the Royal College of Music (London).

A tempo (It. = in time), a direction indicating a return to the principal pace of a comp. after a temporary alteration.

Aaron (Aron), Pietro (b. Florence, *c.* 1490; d. Venice, 1545), It. monk and contrapuntist. Wrote on hist. and science of mus. and founded a school in Rome *c.* 1516.

Aavik, Juhan (b. Estonia, 29. I. 1884), Estonian cond. and comp. Studied at the St. Petersburg Cons. and became a cond. at Wanemuine in 1911, later director of the Dorpat Cons. and choral cond. at Reval. Settled in Swed. in 1944.

Works incl. cantata *Homeland*; unaccomp. choruses; pf. sonata in C min.; songs, etc.

Abaco, Evaristo and Joseph dall'. *See* **Dall' Abaco.**

Abba-Cornaglia, Pietro (b. Alessandria, Piedmont, 20. III. 1851; d. Alessandria, 2. V. 1894), It. comp. Studied at the Milan Cons. and later became a teacher and mus. historian.

Works incl. operas *Isabella Spinola, Maria di Warden, Una partita di scacchi;* Requiem; chamber mus., etc.

Abbatini, Antonio Maria (b. Tiferno, now Città di Castello, *c.* 1595; d. Tiferno, 1679), It. comp. and church musician. Held various posts at churches in Rome.

Works incl. 3 operas, Masses, motets, psalms, madrigals, etc.

Abbellimenti (It. lit. embellishments) = Ornaments, esp. florid passages introduced into vocal mus.

Abbey, John (b. Whilton, Northants., 22. XII. 1785; d. Versailles, 19. II. 1859), Eng. org. builder. Worked in Paris from 1826 and built many orgs. in Fr. and S. America.

Abbott, Emma (b. Chicago, 9. XII. 1850; d. Salt Lake City, 5. I. 1891), Amer. soprano. Studied with Achille Errani in N.Y., later in Milan and Paris, with Mathilde Marchesi and others. She 1st appeared at Covent Garden in London, 1876, and formed an operatic co. in Amer., managed by Eugene Wetherell, whom she had married in 1875.

Abegg Variations, Schumann's Op. 1, for pf., a set of variations on a theme constructed on the notes A. B(♭). E. G. G. and bearing the ded. 'à Mlle. Pauline, Comtesse d'Abegg', who did not exist, though there was such a family with whom Schumann was, or pretended to be, on friendly terms. The work was comp. in 1830 and pub. in 1832.

Abeille, Johann Christian Ludwig (b. Bayreuth, 20. II. 1761; d. Stuttgart, 2. III. 1838), Ger. comp., pianist and organist. In the service of the Duke of Württemberg in Stuttgart.

Works incl. *Singspiele*, songs and keyboard music.

Abel, Carl Friedrich (b. Cöthen, 22. XII. 1723; d. London, 20. VI. 1787), Ger. harpsichord and vla. da gamba player. Worked under Hasse at Dresden 1748–58. From 1759 resident in London, where he was app. chamber musician to Queen Charlotte. A. was joint promoter with Johann Christian Bach of the Bach-Abel Concerts (1765–82). Comp. a large quantity of instrumental mus., of which the works for vla. da gamba are perhaps the most notable.

Abel, Christian Ferdinand (b. ?; d. ?), Ger. cellist and vla. da gamba player, father of prec. Served at Cöthen under J. S. Bach, whose unaccomp. cello suites were probably written for him.

Abel, Leopold August (b. Cöthen, 24. III. 1718; d. Ludwigslust, 25. VIII. 1794), Ger. violinist and comp., son of prec.

Abélard, Pierre (b. Pallet nr. Nantes, 1079; d. Saint-Marcel nr. Châlon-sur-Saône, 21. IV. 1142), Fr. scholar and musician. Comp. songs for his beloved, Héloïse, Lat. Lamentations, etc. *See* **Hutchings** (*O quanta qualia*).

Abell, John (b. Aberdeenshire, 1653; d.

1

Cambridge, 1724), Scot. counter-tenor and lutenist. Possibly a boy chorister at the Chapel Royal in London, of which he became a Gentleman in 1679. Married Frances Knollys, sister of the Earl of Banbury, travelled much abroad, was intendant at Cassel, 1698–9, and returned to Eng. as a stage singer. Pub. some collections of songs.

Abencérages, Les, ou L'Étendard de Grenade (*The Abencerrages, or The Standard of Granada*), opera by Cherubini (lib. by Victor Joseph Étienne de Jouy, based on a novel by Jean-Pierre de Florian), prod. Paris, Opéra, 6. IV. 1813.

Abendmusik(en) (Ger. = evening music[s]), mus. evening perfs. of semi-sacred character estab. by Tunder at Lübeck in the 1640s and becoming so famous there that they were imitated by other N. Ger. towns, esp. Hamburg. They were held mainly during Advent.

Abenteuer des Casanova (*Casanova's Adventures*), opera by Andreae (lib. by Ferdinand Lion, based on Casanova's memoirs), prod. Dresden, 17. VI. 1924.

Abert, Hermann (b. Stuttgart, 25. III. 1871; d. Stuttgart, 13. VIII. 1927), Ger. musicologist of Cz. descent. Prof. of mus. at Leipzig Univ. in succession to Riemann from 1920 and at Berlin from 1923. Wrote many hist. works, incl. a greatly enlarged ed. of Jahn's *Mozart*.

Abert, Johann Joseph (b. Kochovice, 20. IX. 1832; d. Stuttgart, 1. IV. 1915), Cz. double bass player, cond. and comp., father of prec.

Abgesang (Ger. = after-song). *See* **Bar.**

Abingdon, Henry. *See* **Abyngdon.**

Abondante, Giulio (b. ?; d. ?). It. 16th-cent. lutenist and comp. Pub. several books of lute pieces.

Abos, Girolamo (b. Valetta, 16. XI. 1715; d. Naples, 1760), Maltese (?) comp. principally of Italian opera and church mus.

Abraham, Gerald (b. Newport, Isle of Wight, 9. III. 1904), Eng. musicologist. Apart from pf. lessons he is self-taught and studied Rus. in order to specialize in Rus. mus. His 1st book was on Borodin, and others followed, incl. some in collaboration with Calvocoressi, whose posthumous vol. on Mussorgsky he finished; other works incl. a study of Chopin. Ed. of a series of books on comps. with chapters by var. authors. From 1947 to 1962 he was Prof. of Mus. at Liverpool Univ. and from 1962 to 1967 Assistant Controller of Mus., B.B.C. He is ed. of vols. iv, viii and ix of the *New Oxford History of Music* and co-ed. of vol. iii.

Abramsky, Alexander (b. Moscow, 22. I. 1898), Rus. comp. Studied at the Moscow Cons. He turned to Soviet ideology by writing an opera on the subject of life on a collective farm.

Works incl. opera *Song of Friendship*; choral works; chamber mus., etc.

Ábrányi, Emil (b. Budapest, 22. IX. 1882), Hung. cond. and comp. Cond. of the Opera at Budapest since 1911. His operas, prod. there, incl. *Monna Vanna* (after Maeterlinck), *Paolo and Francesca* (after Dante) and *Don Quixote* (after Cervantes).

Ábrányi, Kornél (b. Szentgyörgy-Ábrány, 15. X. 1822; d. Budapest, 20. XII. 1903), Hung. critic, father of prec. Part-founder of the mus. paper *Zenészeti Lapok*, 1860, and prof. at Budapest Acad. of Mus. from 1875. Wrote the lib. for his son's *Monna Vanna*.

Abreise, Die, opera by d'Albert (lib. by Ferdinand von Sporck, based on a play by August von Steigentesch), prod. Frankfurt, 20. X. 1898.

Absil, Jean (b. Péruwelz, Hainault, 23. X. 1893), Belg. comp. Studied at the Brussels Cons., where he became prof. in 1931, after being app. director of the Mus. Acad. at Etterbeek in 1923.

Works incl. opera *Peau d'âne*; ballet *Le Miracle de Pan*; radio opera *Ulysse et les Sirennes*; 5 symphs.; 4 string 4tets; 3 string trios and other chamber mus.

Absolute Music, broadly speaking, any mus. not set to words and not based on any kind of literary, pictorial, descriptive or other extra-mus. subject or idea.

Absolute Pitch. Those who can identify by ear any note heard without ref. to mus. are said to possess the faculty of A. P.

Abt, Franz (b. Eilenburg, 22. XII. 1819; d. Wiesbaden, 31. III. 1885), Ger. comp. and cond. Studied at St. Thomas's and Univ., Leipzig; later cond. at Bernburg, Zürich and Brunswick. Comp. an enormous number of songs and part-songs.

Abu Hassan, opera by Weber (lib. by Franz Carl Hiemer), prod. Munich, 4. VI. 1811.

Abyngdon, Henry (b. *c.* 1418; d. *c.* 1497), Eng. musician. In the service of the Duke of Gloucester, 1445; app. succentor of Wells Cathedral, 1447; Master of the Children of the Chapel Royal, 1456; was the 1st to receive a mus. degree, namely B.Mus. at Cambridge, 1463; master of St. Catherine's Hospital, Bristol, 1478, in which year he was succeeded by Gilbert Banastre at the Chapel Royal.

Abzug (Ger.). *See* **Ornaments.**

Academic Festival Overture (*Akademische Fest-Ouvertüre*), an overture by Brahms, Op. 80, comp. in 1880 and 1st perf. at Breslau, 4. I. 1881. It was Brahms's acknowledgment of the hon. degree of doctor of philosophy, conferred on him by Breslau Univ. in 1879. The thematic material is taken from Ger. students' songs. The *Tragic Overture* was written as a companion-piece.

Academie (or **Akademie**), 18th-cent. Ger. term for a concert.

Académie de Musique, the official title o the Paris Opéra, though never actually called so after 1671. It was first so sty ed in letters-patent granted by Louis XIV, 28. VI. 1669. It became the Académie des Opera [*sic*] in 1671 and the Académie Royale de Musique in 1672 until the Revolution more than a cent. later; after that, at various times, according to the political situation: Théâtre de l'Opéra, Opéra National, Théâtre des Arts, Théâtre de la République et des Arts, Théâtre Impérial de l'Opéra, Théâtre de la Nation, Académie Nationale de Musique, Théâtre National de l'Opéra.

Accademia (It. = academy, from Plato's *Academia*), a type of It. society for the encouragement and furtherance of science and/or the arts. An 'A. di Platone' was founded, on Plato's model, at the Medici court of Florence in 1470. The earliest A. of any importance devoted primarily to mus. was the 'A. Filarmonica' of Verona (1543); later ones included the 'A. di Santa Cecilia' at Rome (1584) and the 'A. Filarmonica' at Bologna (1666). In France the movement began with the foundation of the 'Académie de poésie et de musique' by Baïf and Thibaut at Paris in 1570, with the aim of promoting the ideals of *musique mesurée*.

Accelerando (It.) = accelerating; quickening the pace.

Accent (Fr.). *See* **Ornaments.**

Accents. A.s have much the same function in mus. as in prosody, being the metrical or rhythmic stresses of mus. Normally the main A. is on the 1st beat after the bar-line, and in any mus. divided into bars of more than 3 beats there is usually a secondary A., less strongly stressed. But A.s are frequently displaced by being marked on a weak beat, transferred by syncopation or omitted on the main beat by the replacement of a rest for a note or chord. Strong accents are marked by the sign > or by the abbreviations *sf* (*sforzando*) or *fz* (*forzando*).

Acciaccatura (It., from *acciaccare* = to crush), an ornament in old keyboard mus. consisting of a discordant note struck together with that immediately above, but at once released while the principal note is held on, e.g.:

Bach, *Partita No.3*

The term is now generally used for the short Appoggiatura.

Accidentals, the signs by which notes are chromatically altered by being raised or lowered by a semitone or whole tone. The ♯ raises and the ♭ (flat) lowers the note by a semitone: the × (double sharp) raises and the ♭♭ (double flat) lowers it by a whole tone; the ♮ (natural) contradicts a ♯ or ♭ in the key signature or restores a note previously sharpened or flattened to its orig. position.

Accompagnato. *See* **Recitativo accompagnato.**

Accompanied Recitative. *See* **Recitativo accompagnato.**

Accompaniment, the instrumental part or parts forming a background to the melodic line of a solo voice or instrument, generally played by a keyboard instrument or by the orch. The A. may also be improvised or ed. by the setting out of additional parts where the comp.'s harmony has been left incomplete or indicated only by a figured bass.

Accord (Old Eng.), harmony, harmoniousness, being in tune.

Accordance (Old Eng.), the tuning of string instruments in certain intervals.

Accordatura (It.), the notes to which a string instrument is tuned.

Accordion, an instrument prod. its sound by means of tuned reeds through which wind is driven by pleated bellows opened and closed by the player's hands. The reeds speak when opened by the pressing of buttons and sometimes by the playing of one hand on a keyboard similar to that of the pf.

Achille, It. opera by Paer (lib. by Giovanni di Gamera), prod. Vienna, Kärntnertortheater, 6. VI. 1801. Contains a funeral march said to have been admired by Beethoven.

Achille et Polyxène, opera by Lully and Colasse (lib. by Jean Galbert de Campistron), prod. Paris, Opéra, 7. XI. 1687. Left unfinished at Lully's death and completed by his pupil Colasse.

Achille in Sciro (*Achilles in Scyros*), opera by Caldara (lib. by Metastasio), prod. Vienna, Burgtheater, 13. II. 1736.

Opera by Naumann (lib. do.), prod. Palermo, 5. IX. 1767.

Numerous other settings.

Achron. *See* **Akhron.**

Aci, Galatea e Polifemo, It. serenata by Handel, comp. Naples, 1708. *See also* following.

Acis and Galatea, masque for soloists, chorus and orch. by Handel (lib. by John Gay, with additions by Hughes, Pope and Dryden), comp. *c*. 1718, perf. Cannons, nr. Edgware; 1st public perf. London, Lincoln's Inn Theatre, 13. III. 1731. A composite, bilingual version of this and the prec. It. serenata (1708) received several perfs. in 1732.

Acis et Galatée (*Acis and Galatea*), opera

3

by Lully (lib. by Jean Galbert de Campistron), prod. at Anet at an entertainment given for the Dauphin by the Duke of Vendôme, 6. IX. and 1st perf. Paris, 17. IX. 1686.

Acoustic Bass, a 32-ft. org. stop, the tone of which is given by the beats prod. from the playing of 5ths on 16-ft. pedals.

Acoustics, the physical science of all matters pertaining to sound, esp. the generation and reception of sound-waves; also, more loosely, the properties of sound-transmission in the interior of buildings.

Act Tune (obs.), a term used in 17th-cent. Eng. for a mus. Intermezzo or Entr'acte perf. between the acts of a play.

Action, the mechanism intervening between the player and an instrument, esp. in stringed keyboard instruments, orgs. and harps (in the last case pedals only).

Action musicale (Fr.), a term used by d'Indy for some of his operas, evidently on the model of Wagner's 'Handlung für Musik'.

Acute. *See* **Ornaments.**

Acute Mixture, an org. stop in which overtones are actually sounded by additional pipes, tuned slightly sharp.

Ad lib. (abbr. of Lat. *ad libitum* = at pleasure), a direction indicating that a passage may be played freely according to the perf.'s fancy. The term also applies to an instrumental part that may be added or omitted in the perf. of a work.

Adagietto (It. lit. a little Adagio), a tempo direction indicating a pace slightly quicker than *adagio*.

Adagio (It. *ad agio* = at ease, comfortably) = at a slow pace. The word is also used as a noun for a slow piece or movement.

Adam (b. ?; d. ?), 15th-cent. comp. Three *rondeaux* by him are in the Oxford MS. Canonici misc. 213.

Adam, Adolphe (Charles) (b. Paris, 24. VII, 1803; d. Paris, 3. V. 1856), Fr. comp. Allowed to study at the Paris Cons. only as an amateur. Prod. an operetta, *Pierre et Catherine,* at the Opéra-Comique in 1829 and his first opera, *Danilowa,* in 1830. Comp. a great deal for the stage and in 1847 started a new operatic venture, the Théâtre National. Member of the Institut, 1844, and prof. of comp. at the Cons., 1849.

Works incl. operas *Le Châlet, Le Postillon de Longjumeau, La Poupée de Nuremberg, Si j'étais roi, Falstaff, Richard en Palestine* (after Scott), etc.; ballets *Faust, Giselle,* etc.

Adam, Jean Louis (b. Mütterscholtz, 3. XII. 1758; d. Paris, 8. IV. 1848), Alsat. pianist, comp. and teacher. Prof. at Paris Cons., 1797–1842.

Adam de la Halle. *See* **La Halle.**

Adam de St. Victor. *See* **St. Victor.**

Adam und Eva, opera by Theile (lib. by Christian Richter), prod. Hamburg, at the opening of the 1st estab. Ger. opera house, Theater beim Gänsemarkt, 12. I. 1678.

Adam von Fulda. *See* **Fulda.**

Adam Zero, ballet by Bliss (scenario by Michael Benthall, choreography by Robert Helpmann), prod. London, Covent Garden, 8. IV. 1946.

Adamberger, Valentin (b. Munich, 6. VII. 1743; d. Vienna, 24. VIII. 1804), Ger. tenor. Studied and sang in It., appeared in London in 1777 and went to Vienna, becoming a member of the Ger. opera in 1780 and of the Imperial Chapel in 1789. Sang Belmonte in the 1st perf. of Mozart's *Entführung.*

Adams, Charles (b. Charlestown, Mass., 9. II. 1843; d. Charlestown, 4. VII. 1900), Amer. tenor. Between 1867 and 1876 1st tenor at the Opera in Vienna; made his 1st real success in U.S.A. in 1877.

Adams, Thomas (b. London, 5. IX. 1785; d. London, 15. IX. 1858), Eng. organist and comp. for his instrument. Held various church posts in London, but was known chiefly as a virtuoso.

Added Sixth, a term invented by Rameau (*sixte ajoutée*) to describe the addition of a 6th from the bass to a submediant chord when it is followed by the tonic chord, e.g. in the key of C major:

Addinsell, Richard (b. Oxford, 13. I. 1904), Eng. comp. Studied law at Hertford Coll., Oxford, but became interested in theatre mus. and studied for a short time at the R.C.M. in London. In 1929–32 he studied abroad, mainly in Berlin and Vienna; in 1933 visited U.S.A. and wrote film mus. at Hollywood.

Works incl. incid. mus. for films, theatre (incl. plays by Clemence Dane) and radio. His greatest success was mus. for the film *Dangerous Moonlight,* which incl. the *Warsaw* concerto for pf. and orch. He has also written light mus. and revue songs, etc.

Addison, John (b. London, *c.* 1766; d. London, 30. I. 1844), Eng. double bass player and comp. His wife (*née* Willems) sang at Vauxhall Gardens in London; then both went to Liverpool and Dublin, returning to London in 1796 and proceeding to Bath, Dublin and Manchester. From 1805, when he wrote mus. for Skeffington's *Sleeping Beauty,* he had a number of stage successes in London.

Addison, Joseph (1672–1719), Eng. essayist and poet. *See* **Conte Caramella** (Galuppi), **Festing** (*Ode for St. Cecilia's Day*), **Paisiello** (*Tamburo*), **Rosamond** (Arne and Clayton), **Stanton** (*Spacious Firmament*).

Additional Accompaniments, amplifying orchestral parts added to old oratorios and other works left by the comps. in an incomplete state, to be amplified orig. by the continuo player at the org. or harpsichord. The most familiar exs. are Mozart's A. A.s for Handel's *Messiah*.

Adélaïde (ballet, Ravel). *See* **Valses nobles.**

Adelaide, song by Beethoven to words by Friedrich von Matthisson, comp. in 1795 or 1796 and ded. to the poet.

'Adélaïde' Concerto, a vln. concerto ed. by Marius Casadesus in the early 1930s from a sketch supposedly written by Mozart and ded. to Princess Adélaïde of Fr. in 1766. Its authenticity is doubtful.

Adelboldus (b. nr. Liège, ?; d. ?), Flem. 10th-cent. ecclesiastic and musician. Bishop of Utrecht; wrote a treatise, *Ars musica*, between 990 and 1003.

Adenez (Adam Le Roy) (b. ?; d. ?), Fr. 13th-cent. minstrel. Lived at the court of Henry III, Duke of Brabant; sang troubadour romances, some of which are preserved.

Adhémar, Guillaume (b. ?; d. ?), Fr. 13th-cent. minstrel and juggler. Some of his troubadour songs are extant.

Adieux, l'absence et le retour, Les (*Farewell, Absence and Return*), Beethoven's own title for his pf. sonata in E♭ maj., Op. 81a, comp. in 1809–10 and ded. to the Archduke Rudolph to commemorate his absence from Vienna during the occupation by the Fr.

Adler, Guido (b. Eibenschütz, Moravia, 1. XI. 1855; d. Vienna, 15. II. 1941), Cz.-Ger. musicologist and ed. Studied in Vienna; app. prof. of musicology at Prague Univ., 1885, and prof. in Vienna, 1898, in succession to Hanslick. Wrote many books on mus. and ed. a *Handbuch der Musikgeschichte*, 1924.

Adler, Larry (Lawrence) (b. Baltimore, 10. II. 1914), Amer. harmonica virtuoso. Won a competition aged 13, and has since travelled widely, incl. command perfs. before King George VI, King Gustav of Sweden, Presidents Roosevelt and Truman. Learned to read mus. in 1940 and studied with Toch. Many comps. have written for him, incl. Milhaud and Vaughan Williams.

Adlgasser, Anton Cajetan (b. Inzel, Bavaria, 1. X. 1729; d. Salzburg, 21. XII. 1777), Ger. organist and comp. A pupil of Eberlin in Salzburg, he was 1st organist of the cathedral there from 1750. His church mus. was highly valued by Mozart.

Adlung, Jakob (b. Bindersleben, nr. Erfurt, 14. I. 1699; d. Erfurt, 5. VII. 1762), Ger. organist and scholar. Organist in Erfurt from 1727, and prof. at the *Gymnasium* there from 1741. Author of important mus. treatises.

Admeto, rè di Tessaglia (*Admetus, King of Thessaly*), opera by Handel (lib. by Nicola Francesco Haym or Paolo Antonio Rolli), prod. London, King's Theatre, Haymarket, 31. I. 1727.

Adolfati, Andrea (b. Venice, 1711; d. Genoa, *c.* 1760), It. comp. Pupil of Galuppi at Venice. Held church posts there and wrote several operas, incl. *Artaserse, Arianna, Adriano in Siria* and *La clemenza di Tito.*

Adorno, Theodor Wiesengrund (b. Frankfurt, 11. IX. 1903; d. Geneva, 6. VIII. 1969), Ger. writer on mus. Studied with Sekles in Frankfurt and Alban Berg in Vienna. Mus. critic in Frankfurt and taught at the univ. Emigrated to U.S.A. in 1934, working in connection with radio research at Princeton (1938–41). In 1950 returned to Frankfurt and became prof. at the univ. His writings, which have influenced the younger generation of comps., include *Philosophie der neuen Musik* (1949), *Klangfiguren* (1959).

Adrastus (b. Philippi, Macedonia, ?; d. ?), Gk. 4th-cent. B.C. philosopher. Pupil of Aristotle; wrote a treatise on acoustics, *Harmonicon biblia tria.*

Adriaensen, Emmanuel (b. Antwerp, ?; d. ?), Flem. 16th-cent. lutenist. Pub. books of lute pieces. Also known as Hadrianus.

Adriana Lecouvreur, opera by Cilèa (lib. by Arturo Colautti, based on the play *Adrienne Lecouvreur* by Scribe and Ernest Legouvé), prod. Milan, Teatro Lirico, 6. XI. 1902.

Adriani, Francesco (b. Sanseverino, Ancona, *c.* 1539; d. Rome, 16. VIII. 1575), It. comp. *Maestro di cappella* at St. John Lateran in Rome towards the end of his life. Wrote madrigals and other vocal works.

Adriano in Siria (*Hadrian in Syria*), opera by Pergolesi (lib. by Metastasio), prod. Naples, Teatro San Bartolommeo, with the intermezzi *Livietta e Tracollo*, 25. X. 1734.

Adson, John (b. ?; d. London *c.* 1640), Eng. musician and comp. He was a member of Charles I's household and pub. *Courtly Masquing Ayres* for var. instruments in 1611.

Aegidius de Murino. *See* **Murino.**

Aegyptische Helena (Strauss). *See* **Ägyptische Helena.**

Aeolian Harp, an instrument played by no human performer, but by currents of air blown across its strings when it is hung up in the open. It was first recorded in the 17th cent., but the principle dates back to antiquity.

Aeolian Mode, the scale represented by the white keys of the pf. beginning on the note A. *See also* **Ionian Mode.**

Aeoliphone. *See* **Wind Machine.**

Aerophor (or **Aerophon**), a Ger. instrument invented by Bernhard Samuel and patented in 1911, with the aid of which wind instruments can sustain notes indefinitely. R. Strauss used it in the *Alpensinfonie* and *Festliches Praeludium*.

Aeschylus (525–456 B.C.), Gk. dramatist. *See* **Emmanuel** (*Prométhée* and *Salamine*), **Halévy** (*Prometheus*), **Hauer** (do.), **Honegger** (*Prometheus* and *Suppliants*), **Lambert** (**L.**) (*Prometheus*), **Leroux** (*Persians*), **Meyerbeer** (*Eumenides*), **Milhaud** (*Agamemnon*, *Choéphores* and *Euménides*), **Mulè** (*Choephori* and *Seven against Thebes*), **Oresteia** (Taneiev), **Orestes** (Weingartner), **Parry** (**H.**) (*Agamemnon*), **Pizzetti** (do.), **Prométhée** (Fauré), **Schillings** (*Orestes*), **Siccardi** (*Prometheus*), **Stanford** (*Eumenides*), **Wallace** (**W.**) (do.), **Whittaker** *Choephorae*).

Aesop (*c.* 620–*c.* 560 B.C.), Gk. fabulist. *See* **Reed** (W. H.) (symph. poem).

Aetherophone (from Gk.), an electrophonic instrument invented by Lev Theremin of Leningrad in 1924, prod. notes from the air the pitch of which was determined by movements of the hand but could not be definitely fixed according to the normal chromatic scale, the transitions between the notes producing a sliding wail like that of a siren. But *see* **Theremin**.

Affektenlehre (Ger., doctrine of affections), 18th-cent. aesthetic theory, associated partic. with J. J. Quantz and C. P. E. Bach, according to which mus. should be directly expressive of partic. emotions. *See* **Empfindsamer Stil**.

Affettuoso (It.) = affectionate, feeling (adv. *affettuosamente*).

Affilard, Michel d' (b. ?; d. ?), Fr. 17th–18th cent. tenor and teacher, app. to the Sainte Chapelle in Paris, 1679, and to the royal chapel, 1696–1708. In 1691 he pub. a treatise on sight-singing in which he used a system of regulating the speed of mus. by a pendulum.

Affligem, John of. *See* **Cotton.**

Held various church posts in Rome, but returned to Siena in 1630 as *maestro di cappella* of the cathedral.
Works incl. pastoral *Eumelio*, madrigals, Masses and other church mus., etc.

Aggházy, Károly (b. Budapest, 30. X. 1855; d. Budapest, 8. X. 1918), Hung. pianist and comp. Pupil of Liszt, Bruckner and Volkmann.
Works incl. opera *Maritta*, cantata *Rakoczy*, etc.

Agincour, d'. *See* **Dagincourt.**

Agitato (It.) = agitated, precipitate, restless.

Agnelli, Salvatore (b. Palermo, 1817; d. Marseilles, 1874), It. comp. Pupil of Donizetti and Zingarelli at Naples. He worked at Marseilles and Paris in later life.
Works incl. operas, ballets, church mus., etc.

Agnes von Hohenstaufen, opera by Spontini (lib. by Ernst Raupach), prod. Berlin, Opera, 12. VI. 1829.

Agnese di Fitz-Henry, opera by Paer (lib. by Luigi Buonavoglia, based on Amelia Opie's novel *Father and Daughter*), prod. Ponte d'Altaro nr. Parma, X. 1809.

Agnesi, Luigi (real name Louis Ferdinand Léopold Agniez) (b. Erhent, Namur, 17. VII. 1833; d. London, 2. II. 1875), Belg. bass. Made his 1st appearance in Merelli's It. opera company in Ger. and Hol. and went to the Théâtre Italien in Paris, 1864, and to London in 1865. After his successes in It. opera he also became a concert singer in Eng., 1871–4.

Agnew, Roy (b. Sydney, 23. VIII. 1893; d. Sydney, 12. XI. 1944), Austral. comp. Taught at the Sydney Cons. Director of Austral. Radio, 1938–43.
Works incl. Poem for voice and orch.; pf. sonatas and pieces, etc.

Agnus Dei (Lat. 'Lamb of God'), the 5th and last item of the Ordinary of the Mass. Orig, a part of the Litany, it was

AGNUS DEI

Affrettando (It.) = urging, hastening. The term is often used to indicate emotional pressure as well as increase in speed.

Afranio Albonese (b. Pavia, *c.* 1480; d. ? Ferrara, *c.* 1560), It. priest. Canon at Ferrara, inventor of the Phagotus.

Africaine, L' (*The African Girl*; orig. title *Vasco da Gama*), opera by Meyerbeer (lib. by Scribe), prod. Paris, Opéra, 28. IV. 1865, after the comp.'s death.

Agazzari, Agostino (b. Siena, 2. XII. 1578; d. Siena, 10. IV. 1640), It. comp.

1st intro. into the Rom. Mass towards the end of the 7th cent. It is not present in the Ambrosian rite. Its text is tripartite in structure, and its mus., in its simplest form, consists of three statements of the same melody (*see* illustration).

More complex plainsong settings exist, and in the later Middle Ages numerous additional melodies were comp. The A. is naturally incl. in polyphonic settings of the Mass Ordinary, and in later settings of the same series of texts. *See* **Mass.**

Agostini, Ludovico (b. Ferrara, 1534; d. Ferrara, 20. IX. 1590), It. priest, comp. and poet. *Maestro di cappella* to Alfonso II, Duke of Este. Wrote madrigals and other vocal works.

Agostini, Paolo (b. Valerano, 1593; d. Rome, 3. X. 1629), It. comp. Pupil and son-in-law of B. Nanini in Rome. After var. posts in Rome, he became master of the Vatican chapel in 1627. Comp. Masses and other church mus.

Agostini, Pietro Simone (b. Rome, *c.* 1650; d. ?), It. comp. *Maestro di cappella* to the Duke of Parma. Wrote 5 operas, incl. *Il ratto delle Sabine*, oratorios, church mus., etc.

Agrell, Johan Joachim (b. Löth, 1. II. 1701; d. Nuremberg, 19. I. 1765), Swed. comp. Studied at Linköping and Uppsala, was app. court musician at Cassel in 1723 and mus. director at Nuremberg in 1746.
Works incl. harpsichord concertos, sonatas, etc.

Agréments (Fr. obs. *Agrémens*) = Ornaments.

Agricola, Alexander (Alexander Ackerman) (b. 1446; d. nr. Valladolid, 1506), Flem. composer. His epitaph (printed by Rhaw in 1538) states that he d. at the age of 60, the date of death being estab. by his disappearance from the court rolls of Philip the Handsome, Duke of Austria, (Philip I of Spain from 1504). He served at the court of Galeazzo Maria Sforza, Duke of Milan, during the early 1470s, as well as with Lorenzo the Magnificent in Florence. After a brief period at Mantua he returned to the Low Countries, his name appearing in the Accounts of Cambrai Cathedral for 1475–6. After a 2nd visit to Italy he entered in 1500 the service of Philip, whom he accomp. on journeys to Paris and Spain. During his 2nd visit to Spain Philip died of fever, A. apparently dying at the same time.
Works include 9 Masses, 2 Credos, 25 motets and 93 secular pieces. Stylistically he resembles his precursor Okeghem.

Agricola, Johann Friedrich (b. Dobitz, Saxony, 4. I. 1720; d. Berlin, 2. XII. 1774), Ger. comp. Studied with Bach at Leipzig, afterwards with Hasse at Dresden and Quantz and Graun in Berlin. Director of the Hofkapelle there from 1759 to his death. Married the singer Benedetta Molteni in 1751.
Works incl. operas, psalms, hymns and other church mus., It. secular cantatas, etc.

Agricola, Martin (Martin Sore) (b. Schwiebus, 6. I. 1486; d. Magdeburg, 10. VI. 1556), Ger. theorist and comp. His most important treatise was a work on mus. instruments, *Musica instrumentalis deudsch* (1528, based on Virdung's *Musica getutscht* of 1511, but in verse), and he contributed 3 pieces to Georg Rhaw's *Newe deudsche geistliche Gesenge* (1544).

Agricola, Rudolph (real name Huessmann) (b. Baffeln nr. Groningen, 1442; d. Heidelberg, 25. X. 1485), Dutch lutenist, comp. and scholar. He returned from It. in 1477 and was sent to the court of the Ger. emperor. In 1479 he helped to build the great org. at Groningen and in 1482 he became prof. at Heidelberg.
Works incl. Dutch part-songs.

Agrippina, opera by Handel (lib. by Vincenzo Grimani), prod. Venice, Teatro San Giovanni Crisostomo, 26. XII. 1709.

Aguado y Garcia, Dionisio (b. Madrid, 8. IV. 1784; d. Madrid, 29. XII. 1849), Span. guitar player and comp. Wrote a method and studies for his instrument.

Aguiar, Alexandra de (b. Oporto, ?; d. nr. Talavéra, 12. XII. 1605), Port. lutenist and poet. In the service of King Sebastian and later of Philip II of Spain.
Works incl. Lamentations for Holy Week.

Aguiar, Luiza Rosa d'. *See* Todi.

Aguiari (Agujari), Lucrezia (b. Ferrara, 1743; d. Parma, 18. V. 1783), It. soprano. Made her 1st appearance at Florence in 1764. In a letter of 24. III. 1770 Mozart wrote down a remarkably high and florid passage he heard her sing. She married the comp. and cond. Giuseppe Colla in 1780.

Aguilera de Heredia, Sebastián (b. Huesca, Aragon, *c.* 1565; d. ?), Span. organist and comp. For many years from 1603 organist at the old cathedral of Saragossa.
Works incl. Magnificats and other church mus.

Aguirre, Julián (b. Buenos Aires, 28. I. 1868; d. Buenos Aires, 13. VIII. 1924), Arg. pianist and comp. Studied at the Madrid Cons. and became director of the Buenos Aires Cons.
Works incl. chamber mus.; pf. works; songs, etc.

Ägyptische Helena, Die (*The Egyptian Helen*), opera by R. Strauss (lib. by Hugo von Hofmannsthal), prod. Dresden, 6. VI. 1928.

Ahle, Johann Georg (b. Mühlhausen, Thuringia, VI. 1651; d. Mühlhausen, 2. XII. 1706), Ger. comp. Organist at the church of St. Blasius, Mühlhausen. Like his father, he wrote hymn tunes.

Ahle, Johann Rudolph (b. Mühlhausen, Thuringia, 24. XII. 1625; d. Mühlhausen, 9. VII. 1673), Ger. organist and comp., father of prec. App. cantor at Erfurt in 1646 and organist at Mühlhausen from or before 1654.

Åhlström, Olof (b. Vårdinge, 14. VIII. 1756; d. Stockholm, 11. VIII. 1835), Swed. organist and comp. Organist at St. James's Church in Stockholm from 1729. As a pub. he held from 1788 to 1823 the monopoly for mus.-printing in Sweden. Comp. of operas, songs, instrumental mus., and co-ed. of a collection of Swed. folksongs.

Aiblinger, Johann Kaspar (b. Wasserburg, Bavaria, 23. II. 1779; d. Munich, 6. V. 1867), Ger. comp. and cond. Mus. director of the Munich opera, 1819–23, but as a comp. devoted mainly to church mus.

Aich, Arnt von (Arnt of Aachen) (b. ?1474; d. Cologne, 1530), Ger. mus. pub. His *Liederbuch* (Cologne, *c.* 1510) contained 75 4-part songs, sacred and secular, and is possibly the 1st printed ed. of its kind.

Aichinger, Gregor (b. Regensburg, 1564; d. Augsburg, 21. I. 1628), Ger. priest and musician. Organist to the Fugger family at Augsburg, pub. books of sacred mus. at Venice in 1590 and 1603 and visited Rome for further mus. study in 1599.

Aida, opera by Verdi (lib. by Antonio Ghislanzoni, based on a scenario by François Auguste Ferdinand Mariette and outlined in Fr. by Camille Du Locle), prod. Cairo, 24. XII. 1871; 1st perf. in It., Milan, Teatro alla Scala, 8. II. 1872.

Aiglon, L' (*The Eaglet*), opera by Honegger and Ibert (lib. by Henri Cain, based on Rostand's play), prod. Monte Carlo, 11. III. 1937.

Aimeric de Belenoi. *See* Belenoi.

Aimeric de Péguilhan. *See* Péguilhan.

Aimon (Pamphile Léopold) François (b. L'Isle nr. Avignon, 4. IX. 1779; d. Paris, 2. II. 1866), Fr. cellist and comp. He cond. at Marseilles in his youth and in Paris from 1821.
Works incl. *Jeux floraux, Michel et Christine, Les Sybarites de Florence* and 4 others; chamber mus., etc.

Air à boire (Fr.) = Drinking-Song, cultivated esp. in the 16th and 17th cents. and sung in parts.

Air de Cour (Fr. = court air), a courtly type of Fr. song originating in the 16th cent., written either for a vocal ensemble or for a single voice with lute or harpsichord accomp.

Akademie. *See* Academie.

Akeroyde, Samuel (b. Yorkshire, ?; d. ?), Eng. 17th-cent. comp. Musician in Ordinary to James II in 1687 and later to William and Mary. Contrib. many songs to var. collections and to the 3rd part of Durfey's *Don Quixote* in 1696, the mus. to the 1st 2 of which had been written by Purcell the year before his death.

Akhron, Joseph (b. Losdzieje, Poland, 13. V. 1886; d. Hollywood, 29. IV. 1943), Rus. (Americanized) violinist and comp. Studied at Warsaw and at the St. Petersburg Cons., where Auer taught him vln. and Liadov comp. Toured much as a soloist and in 1913 joined the staff of the Kharkov Cons. In 1925 he settled in U.S.A.
Works incl. incid. and film mus.; *Golem Suite* for small orch.; 3 vln. concertos; *Sinfonietta* for string 4tet, etc.

Akimenko, Feodor Stepanovich (b. Kharkov, 20. II. 1876; d. Paris, 8. I. 1945), Rus. comp. Pupil of Balakirev and Rimsky-Korsakov in St. Petersburg. Taught in the court choir, where he had been a chorister, but lived in Fr. from 1903 to 1906 and settled there after the Rus. Revolution. He was Stravinsky's first comp. teacher.
Works incl. opera, *The Queen of the Alps*; orchestral and chamber mus.; sonatas; numerous pf. works incl. *Sonate fantastique*, etc.

Al (It. masc. = 'at the', 'to the'). The word is used in var. combinations with nouns, as below.

Al fine (It.) = 'to the end'. The term is used in cases where an earlier portion of a comp. is to be repeated (*da capo*) and indicates that it is to be played over again to the end, not to some earlier place, which would otherwise be marked with a special sign, the appropriate direction being then *al segno*.

Al rovescio. *See* Rovescio.

Ala, Giovanni Battista (b. Monza, 1580; d. ?, 1612), It. comp. Organist of the church of the Servitori at Milan and comp. of canzonets, madrigals, etc.

Alabev, Alexander Alexandrovich (b. Tobolsk, 15. VIII. 1787; d. Moscow, 6. III. 1851), Rus. comp. He was an army officer and cultivated mus. as an amateur.
Works incl. opera *A Moonlit Night*; vaudevilles; *c.* 100 drawing-room songs, incl. *The Nightingale*, etc.

Aladdin, opera by Bishop (lib. by George Soane), prod. London, Drury Lane Theatre, 29. IV. 1826. It was commissioned as a counter-attraction to Weber's *Oberon* at Covent Garden, but failed.

Alain, Jean. *See* Aleyn, John.

Alain, Jehan (Ariste) (b. Saint-Germain-en-Laye, 3. II. 1911; d. Saumur, 20. VI. 1940), Fr. comp. Studied at the Paris Cons., org. with Dupré and comp. with Dukas and Roger-Ducasse. He became a church organist in Paris in 1936, but served in World War II and was killed in action.
Works incl. numerous choral comps., mainly sacred; 3 dances for orch.; chamber mus.; pf. and org. works; songs, etc.

Alalá, a Span. folksong of Galicia, set to vocalized syllables and sung in free time.

Alaleona, Domenico (b. Montegiorgio, Piceno, 16. XI. 1881; d. Montegiorgio, 28. XII. 1928), It. comp. and organist. Became organist in his native town at the age of 10, but later went to Rome for study, afterwards cond. choral and orchestral societies at Leghorn and Rome. Best known as a writer of theoret. books, esp. on modern mus.
Works incl. opera *Mirra*, Requiem, orchestral works, a string 4tet and songs.

Alanus, Johannes. *See* Aleyn, John.

Alarcón, Pedro Antonio de (1833–91),

Span. novelist. *See* **Corregidor** (H. Wolf), **Manuel Venegas** (do.), **Rung** (*Three-Cornered Hat*), **Sombrero de tres picos** (Falla).

Alard, (Jean) Delphin (b. Bayonne, 8. III. 1815; d. Paris, 22. II. 1888), Fr. violinist and comp. Student at the Paris Cons., where he succeeded Baillot as prof. Formed a string 4tet. Comp. mainly for his instrument.

Alba, type of troubadour-trouvère song, in which the singer watches for daybreak on behalf of two lovers (e.g. *Reis glorios*, by Guiraut de Bornelh). As used by the Minnesinger it was called *Tagelied*.

Albanese, Licia (b. Bari, 23. VII. 1909), Amer. soprano of It. origin. Studied in Milan and made her first stage appearance at the Teatro Lirico there in 1935, followed in the same year by an appearance at the Scala. From 1940 she was a member of the Metropolitan Opera, N.Y. She was chosen by Toscanini for his recorded broadcasts of *La Bohème* and *La Traviata*.

Albanesi, Carlo (b. Naples, 22. X. 1856; d. London, 21. IX. 1926), It. pianist and comp. Settled in Eng. from 1882 and app. prof. of pf. at the R.A.M. in 1893, when he married the novelist E. Maria Albanesi. His daughter Meggie was a gifted actress in the 1920s, but died at an early age.'

Works incl. pf. pieces, chamber mus. and songs.

Albani (orig. Lajeunesse), **(Marie Louise Cécile) Emma** (b. Chambly nr. Montreal, 1. XI. 1847; d. London, 3. IV. 1930), Canadian soprano. Studied with Duprez in Paris and Lamperti at Milan. 1st stage appearance at Messina, 1870, and 1st in London at Covent Garden, 1872. Lived and taught there, but toured widely. D.B.E. 1925.

Albéniz, Isaac (b. Camprodón, Catalonia, 29. V. 1860; d. Cambo-les-Bains, Pyrenees, 18. V. 1909), Span. comp. He made his appearance as an infant prodigy both as pianist and comp. at Barcelona, a *pasodoble*, written at the age of 7, being played by a military band there. Later he appeared in Paris as a child-pupil of Marmontel and afterwards studied at the Madrid Cons., where he received a grant from the king to enable him to go to Brussels. There he studied comp. with Gevaert and pf. with Brassin, and later went to Liszt at Weimar for pf. and to Jadassohn and Reinecke at Leipzig for comp. After touring successfully, he settled as pf. teacher 1st at Barcelona and then at Madrid, from *c.* 1880, but left before long and spent the rest of his life mainly in London and Paris. He had married in 1883. In London he prod. operas and began a trilogy on Arthurian legends to a libretto by Francis Money-Coutts (Lord Latymer), who financed him, but did not progress far.

Works incl. operas *The Magic Opal*, *Henry Clifford*, *Pepita Jiménez*, *San Antonio de la Florida*, *Merlin* (unfinished 1st part of Arthurian cycle); zarzuelas *Cuanto más viejo*, *Los Catalanes en Grecia*; contribution to Millöcker's operetta *Der arme Jonathan* for the London prod.; *Catalonia*, orch. with the aid of Dukas; *c.* 250 pf. pieces, incl. *Catalonia*, *La Vega*, *Navarra*, *Azulejos*; the cycle of 12 entitled *Iberia*; 13 songs, etc.

Albéniz, Mateo Pérez de (b. *c.* 1755; d. San Sebastian, 23. VI. 1831), Span. comp. of church mus. and keyboard mus. *Maestro de capilla* at Logroño and San Sebastian.

Albéniz, Pedro (b. Logroño, 14. IV. 1795; d. Madrid, 12. IV. 1855), Span. pianist and comp., son of prec. He was organist at var. towns from the age of 13 and in 1830 became prof. of pf. at Madrid Cons. and 1st organist at the royal chapel in 1834. App. pf. teacher to Queen Isabella and the Infanta Maria Luisa in 1841. Wrote a method for pf., *c.* 70 pf. works and some songs.

Albergati, Pirro Capacelli, Count (b. Bologna, 20. IX. 1663; d. Bologna, 22. VI. 1735), It. nobleman and amateur comp..

Works incl. operas *Gli amici*, *Il principe selvaggio*; oratorios *Giobbe*, *L'innocenza di Santa Eufemia*, *Il convito di Baldassare*; church mus.; comps. for var. instruments, etc.

Albert de Sisteron (b. Gapençois, ?; d. Sisteron, ?), Fr. 12th–13th-cent. troubadour, *c.* 20 of whose songs exist.

Albert, Eugen (Eugène Francis Charles) d' (b. Glasgow, 10. IV. 1864; d. Riga, 3. III. 1932), Fr.-Eng. (later Germanized) pianist and comp., son of C. L. N. d'A. Although born in Scotland, he came from Newcastle-on-Tyne, and after being well taught by his father as a very precociously gifted child, he went as Newcastle scholar to the Nat. Training School in London (later the R.C.M.), where he learnt pf. from Pauer and theory from Stainer, Prout and Sullivan. He appeared with great success as pianist and comp. in London and later went to Vienna for further study, finishing with a course under Liszt. In 1892 he married Teresa Carreño, but they were divorced in 1895, and d'A. married 5 times more. In 1907 he succeeded Joachim as director of the Hochschule für Musik in Berlin. During World War I he repudiated his Brit. birth, declaring himself to be entirely Ger. Of his 20 operas, only *Tiefland* (1903) has had any real success. The rest of his considerable output has largely fallen into neglect.

Works incl. operas *Der Rubin* (after Hebbel), *Ghismonda*, *Gernot*, *Die Abreise*, *Kain*, *Der Improvisator*, *Tiefland*, *Flauto solo*, *Tragaldabas* (*Der geborgte Ehemann*), *Izeyl*, *Die verschenkte Frau*, *Liebesketten*,

Die toten Augen, Der Stier von Olivera, Revolutionshochzeit, Scirocco, Mareike von Nymwegen, Der Golem, Die schwarze Orchidee, Die Witwe von Ephesus, Mister Wu (unfinished, completed by Blech); *Der Mensch und das Leben*, choral work in 6 parts; symph. in F maj.; overtures *Esther* and *Hyperion*; 2 pf. concertos, cello concerto; 2 string 4tets; pf. suite and sonata, etc.

Albert, Heinrich (b. Lobenstein, Saxony, 8. VII. 1604; d. Königsberg, 6. X. 1651), Ger. poet, organist and comp. Studied mus. at Dresden with Schütz, who was his uncle. His parents, however, compelled him to read law at Leipzig Univ.; but in 1626 he set out for Königsberg, was taken prisoner by the Swedes, and at last reached that city in 1628, resuming mus. studies with Stobäus. In 1631 he was app. organist at the Old Church there, and became member of the Königsberg school of poets.

Works incl. Te Deum, many hymns to words of his own, secular songs, etc.

Albert Herring, opera by Britten (lib. by Eric Crozier, based on Maupassant's story *Le Rosier de Madame Husson*), prod. Glyndebourne, 20. VI. 1947.

Alberti Bass, a conventional broken-chord accomp. common in 18th-cent. keyboard mus., taking its name from Do-

d. Rome—or Warsaw?—IV. 1811), It. comp., resident much of his life in Pol. Works include 2 Pol. operas, *Don Juan* and *Kapelmajster Polski*, also It. and Ger. operas.

Albertus, Magister, Parisian comp. of early 12th cent. A *Benedicamus Domino* trope, *Congaudeant catholici*, is ascribed to him in the Codex Calixtinus of Compostela (*c.* 1125), and is the earliest known 3-part comp.

Albicastro, Enrico (It. from Hainz Weissenburg), (b. ?; d. ?), Swiss 17th-cent. comp. He was a captain of the Swiss horse, serving in the Span. war in the Netherlands as a mercenary. Works incl. 8 op. nos. of solo and trio sonatas and 1 of concertos.

Albinoni, Tommaso (b. Venice, 8. VI. 1671; d. Venice, 17. I. 1750), It. violinist and comp. Wrote operas and instrumental mus. Bach used some of his themes.

Works incl. 55 operas, 9 op. nos. for instrumental chamber combinations, etc.

Albion and Albanius, opera by Grabu (lib. by Dryden), prod. London, Duke's Theatre, 3. VI. 1685.

Alboni, Marietta (b. Città di Castello, 6. III. 1823; d. Ville d'Avray, 23. VI. 1894), It. contralto. Pupil of Rossini; 1st appearance 1843, at the Scala, Milan. Sang with much success in Paris and London.

Mozart, *Piano Sonata K.545*

ALBERTI BASS

menico Alberti, who made much use of it. Many familiar examples of the device can be found in the works of Haydn, Mozart and Beethoven, e.g. the opening of Mozart's little C maj. sonata (*see* illustration).

Alberti, Domenico (b. Venice, *c.* 1710; d. Rome, *c.* 1740), It. singer, harpsichordist and comp., pupil of Lotti. The charact. left-hand accomp. figuration in his keyboard mus. has given his name to the 'Alberti Bass'.

Alberti, Giuseppe Matteo (b. Bologna, 1685; d. Bologna, II. 1751), It. violinist and comp. Wrote mainly for strings.

Alberti, Innocenzo di (b. Tarvisio, *c.* 1545; d. ?), It. comp. In the service of Alfonso, Duke of Ferrara. In 1568 he ded. a book of 46 madrigals to Henry, Earl of Arundel.

Works incl. madrigals, penitential psalms, secular songs, etc.

Albertini, Gioacchino (b. Pesaro, 1751;

Alborada (Span., from *alba* = dawn) = morning song, in the same sense that a serenade is an evening song; *cf.* Fr. *aubade*. Orig. the A. is a popular instrumental piece of NW. Spain, usually played on bagpipes.

Alborada del gracioso (Span., *The Jester's Morning Song*), a pf. piece by Ravel, No. 4 of the set entitled *Miroirs*, comp. 1905.

Albrechtsberger, Johann Georg (b. Klosterneuburg nr. Vienna, 3. II. 1736; d. Vienna, 7. III. 1809), Aus. theorist, comp. and teacher. Court organist in Vienna and *Kapellmeister* of St. Stephen's Cathedral. Renowned as a contrapuntist, he was for a short time Beethoven's teacher. Prolific comp. of church mus. and instrumental mus., much of it in a contrapuntal style.

Albrici, Bartolomeo (b. ? Rome, ?; d. ?), It. 17th-cent. organist. In the service of Queen Christina of Swed., organist at

Dresden until 1663, in the service of Charles II from 1664 and James II from 1685. Also active as a private teacher in London.

Albrici, Vincenzo (b. Rome, 26. VI. 1631; d. Prague, 8. VIII. 1696), It. comp. and organist, brother of prec. Pupil of Carissimi. Director of the Queen of Swed.'s It. musicians, 1652–4; *Kapellmeister* at Dresden from 1654; in the service of Charles II in London, 1664–7; returned to Dresden, 1667; organist of St. Thomas's, Leipzig, 1681–2; finally *Kapellmeister* at Prague. Works incl. Masses, psalms, concertos and madrigals.

Albumblatt (Ger. = album leaf), the title often given to a short piece, usually for pf., suggesting an inscription in an autograph album.

Alceste. *See also* **Alkestis.**

Opera by Gluck (lib. by Ranieri Calzabigi), It. version prod. Vienna, Burgtheater, 26. XII. 1767. Fr. version, revised by the comp. (lib. by François Louis Gand Lebland du Roullet), prod. Paris, Opéra, 23. IV. 1776.

Opera by Schweitzer (lib. by Wieland), prod. Weimar, at court, 28. V. 1773. The 1st Ger. opera in the manner of Metastasio.

Opera by Strungk (lib. by Paul Thiemich, based on Aurelio Aureli's *Antigona delusa da Alceste*), prod. Leipzig, 18. V. 1693. Written for the opening of the Leipzig opera-house.

Incid. mus. by Handel (later used for *The Choice of Hercules*) to a play by Tobias Smollett, comp. for a prod. in London, Covent Garden Theatre, in 1750, which did not take place.

Alceste, ou Le Triomphe d'Alcide, opera by Lully (lib. by Quinault), prod. Paris, Opéra, 19. I. 1674.

Alchemist, The, incid. mus. by Handel, partly adapted from *Rodrigo,* for a revival of Ben Jonson's play, prod. London, Drury Lane Theatre, 7. III. 1732.

Opera by Cyril Scott (lib. by comp.), prod. in Ger. trans., Essen, 28. V. 1925.

Alchymist, Der, opera by Spohr (lib. by Karl Pfeiffer, based on a story by Washington Irving), prod. Cassel, 28. VII. 1830.

Alcina, opera by Handel (lib. by Antonio Marchi), prod. London, Covent Garden Theatre, 16. IV. 1735.

Alcione, opera by Marais (lib. by Antoine Houdar de la Motte), prod. Paris, Opéra, 18. II. 1706.

Alcock, John (b. London, 11. IV. 1715; d. Lichfield, 23. II. 1806), Eng. organist and comp. Organist at var. parish churches in London and Warwicks., and for a time at Lichfield Cathedral. D. Mus. Oxford, 1761. Works incl. church mus., glees and catches, harpsichord mus., etc.

Alcoke (Alcock), Philip (b. ?; d. ?), Eng.

mid 16th-cent. comp. of a *Salve Regina* (c. 1555).

Alcôve, L', operetta by Offenbach (lib. by Philippe Auguste Alfred Pittaud de Forges and Adolphe de Leuven), prod. Paris, Salle de la Tour d'Auvergne, 24. IV. 1847. Offenbach's 1st operetta.

Alcuin (b. ? York, c. 753; d. Tours, 19. V. 804), poet, statesman, musician and adviser to Charlemagne. He is the putative author of a *Musica* containing the 1st mention of a system of church modes.

Alder (Alderinus), Cosmos (b. Baden, c. 1497, d. Bern, 7. XI. 1550), Ger. comp. He wrote hymns and motets to Ger. and Lat. texts.

Aldomar (b. ?; d, ?), Span. 16th-cent. comp. Contrib. villancicos for several voices to var. collections.

Aldrich, Henry (b. London, 1647; d. Oxford, 14. XII. 1710), Eng. comp., theologian and architect. Educ. at Westminster School and Christ Church, Oxford, where he became a canon in 1681 and dean in 1689. Vice-Chancellor of the univ., 1692–5. He designed Peckwater quadrangle and All Saints' Church. Collected material for a large treatise on harmony.

Works incl. church and other mus. (catch *Christ Church Bells*), etc.

Aldrich, Richard (b. Providence, Rhode Island, 31. VII. 1863; d. Rome, 2. VI. 1937), Amer. mus. critic. After var. activities he became mus. ed. of the *New York Times.* His work incl. 2 Wagnerian guide-books.

Aleatory (from Lat. *alea,* a die, plur. *aleae,* dice), a term applied to mus. in which the details of perf. or the actual notes are left wholly or in part to the players or singers.

Aleko, opera by Rakhmaninov (lib. by Vassili Ivanovich Nemirovich-Danchenko, based on Pushkin's novel *The Gypsies*), prod. Moscow, 8. V. 1893.

Alembert, Jean Le Rond d' (b. Paris, 16. XI. 1717; d. Paris, 29. X. 1783), Fr. author, philosopher and mathematician. His books incl. many studies of mus. subjects, incl. acoustics, opera, the theories of Rameau, etc., and he contrib. mus. articles to the *Encyclopédie.* One of the adherents of Gluck against Piccinni.

Alen, William (b. ?; d. ?), Eng. 16th-cent. comp. His *Gaude virgo mater Christi* is in Cambridge, Peterhouse part-books (1540–7).

Alessandrescu, Alfred (b. Bucharest, 14. VIII. 1893; d. Bucharest, 18. II. 1959), Rum. cond. and comp. Studied at Bucharest and with Vidal and d'Indy in Paris. Later he became cond. of the Royal Opera at Bucharest and mus. director of the Rum. radio service. From 1926 to 1940 he was cond. of the Bucharest Phil. Orch.

Works incl. Rum. Fantasy, symph. poem *Actéon,* overture *Didona* for orch.;

11

Crépuscule d'automne for string 4tet and other chamber mus.; songs, etc.

Alessandri, Felice (b. Rome, 24. XI. 1747; d. Casalbino, 15. VIII. 1798), It. cond. and comp. Studied at Naples and 1st worked in Turin and Paris; prod. his 1st opera at Venice in 1767 and went to London the following year, and in 1786 to St. Petersburg in search of a court app., which he failed to secure. From 1789 to 1792 he was 2nd *Kapellmeister* at the Berlin Opera.

Works incl. *c.* 35 operas, an oratorio, several symphs., sonatas, etc.

Alessandro, opera by Handel (lib. by Paolo Antonio Rolli), prod. London, King's Theatre, Haymarket, 5. V. 1726.

Alessandro della Viola. See **Merlo.**

Alessandro nell' Indie (*Alexander in India*). See also **Cleofide** and **Poro.**

Opera by Johann Christian Bach (lib. by Metastasio), prod. Naples, Teatro San Carlo, 20. I. 1762.

Opera by Francesco Corselli (*c.* 1700–78) (lib. do.), prod. Madrid, Palacio Real Buen Retiro, 9. V. 1738, at the wedding of Charles IV of Naples and Princess Maria Amalia of Saxony. The 1st It. opera prod. there.

Opera by Galuppi (lib. do.), prod. Mantua, Carnival 1738.

Opera by Pérez (lib. do.), prod. Genoa, Teatro Sant' Agostino, 26. XII. 1745.

Opera by Piccinni (lib. do.), prod. Naples, Teatro San Carlo, 12. I. 1774.

Opera by Sacchini (lib. do.), prod. Venice, Teatro San Salvatore, spring 1763.

Opera by Vinci (lib. do.), prod. Rome, Teatro delle Dame, 26. XII. 1729. (This was the 1st setting of the lib.)

Alessandro Romano. See **Merlo.**

Alessandro Severo, opera by Lotti (lib. by Apostolo Zeno), prod. Venice, Teatro San Giovanni Crisostomo, 26. XII. 1716.

Alessandro Stradella, opera by Flotow (lib., in Ger., by Friedrich Wilhelm Riese, pseud. 'W. Friedrich'), prod. Hamburg, 30. XII. 1844. It deals with doubtful incidents in the life of Stradella, and is based on a play with mus., some by Flotow, by Philippe Auguste Alfred Pittaud de Forges and Paul Dupert.

Alessandro vincitor di se stesso (*Alexander, Victor over himself*), opera by Cavalli (lib. by Francesco Sbarra), prod. Venice, Teatro Santi Giovanni e Paolo, prob. 20. I. 1651.

Alexander Balus, oratorio by Handel (lib. by Thomas Morell), prod. London, Covent Garden Theatre, 23. III. 1748.

Alexander der Wilde (b. ?; d. ?), Ger. 13th-cent. Minnesinger, 6 of whose songs have been preserved.

Alexander's Feast, Dryden's ode set to m. by Handel (words arr. and added to by Newburgh Hamilton), prod. London, Covent Garden Theatre. 19. II. 1736.

Alexandrov, Alexander Vassilievich (b. Plakhino nr. Riazan, 1. IV. 1883; d. Berlin, 8. VII. 1946), Rus. cond. and comp. He came of peasant stock, was a choir-boy and later choral cond. in St. Petersburg, where he studied under Rimsky-Korsakov and Glazunov at the Cons.; later with Vassilenko at the Moscow Cons., where he became prof.

Works incl. opera, *Water Nymph*; symph. in E♭ maj., symph. poem *Death and Life*; the Soviet hymn, patriotic cantatas, Red Army songs, etc.

Alexandrov, Anatol Nicolaievich (b. Plakhino, 25. V. 1888; d. Berlin, 8. VII. 1946), Rus. comp. Studied under Taneiev and at the Moscow Cons., later comp. under Vassilenko and Ilyinski. Prof. at Moscow Cons.

Works incl. operas *Two Worlds* and *The Forty-First*; incid. mus. for Maeterlinck's *Ariane et Barbe-bleue*, Scribe's *Adrienne Lecouvreur*, etc.; mus. for film *Thirteen*; overture on popular Rus. themes and 2 suites for orch.; string 4tet; 8 pf. sonatas, pf. pieces; *Three Goblets* for baritone and orch.; songs, folksong arrs., etc.

Alexis, Willibald (Georg Häring) (1798–1871), Ger. novelist. See **Leoncavallo** (*Roland*).

Aleyn (Alanus), John (b. ?; d. ?), Eng. 14th–15th-cent. comp. whose identity is uncertain, possibly a canon of Windsor who d. in 1373 or a minor canon of St. Paul's who d. in 1437. A motet praising the skill of Eng. musicians in MS. 1047 of the Musée Condé, Chantilly, is ascribed to Johannes Alanus, while a *Gloria* in the Old Hall MS. is ascribed to A. A Jean Alain was one of John of Gaunt's musicians in 1396, together with three Fr. minstrels.

Alfano, Franco (b. Posilipo, 8. III. 1876; d. San Remo, 26. X. 1954), It. comp. Studied 1st at the Naples Cons. and afterwards at that of Leipzig, under Jadassohn. He had some pf. pieces pub. in Ger. before the end of the cent. and in 1896 wrote his 1st opera, *Miranda*, on a subject from Fogazzaro. The ballet *Napoli*, prod. Paris, 1901, was his first big success, and was followed by the still greater success of his 3rd opera, *Risurrezione*, prod. 1904, a work in the *verismo* tradition. His first symph. was perf. at San Remo in 1910. In 1919 he was app. director of the Liceo Musicale Rossini at Bologna and in 1923 of the Cons. at Turin. After Puccini's death in 1924 he completed the unfinished *Turandot*, finishing the final scenes from Puccini's sketches.

Works incl. operas *Miranda*, *La fonte Enschir*, *Risurrezione* (based on Tolstoy), *Il principe Zilah*, *L'ombra di Don Giovanni*, *Sakuntala* (after Kalidasa), *L'ultimo Lord*, *Cyrano de Bergerac* (after Rostand), *Il dottor Antonio*; ballet *Napoli*; 2 symphs., *Suite romantica* for orch.; pf. 5tet, 2 string 4tets; sonata for cello and pf.; songs incl. 3 settings of Tagore and a cycle *Dormiveglia*.

Alferaky, Achilles Nicholaievich (b. Taganrog, 3. VII. 1846; d. Leningrad, 1920), Rus. comp. Wrote mainly pf. pieces and songs.

Alfieri, Pietro (b. Rome, 29. VI. 1801; d. Rome, 12. VI. 1863), It. priest and musicologist. For many years prof. of Gregorian mus. at the Eng. Coll. in Rome; wrote a number of books on var. aspects of church mus., ed. old masters and wrote a life of Jommelli.

Alfieri, Vittorio, Count (1749–1803), It. dramatist. *See* **Bazzini** (*Saul*), **Virginia** (Mercadante).

Alfonso X (King of Castile and Leon, 1252–84), known as *El Sabio* (the Wise). He assembled a collection of 400 songs in Galician-Port., known as the *Cantigas de Santa Maria*.

Alfonso und Estrella, opera by Schubert (lib. by Franz von Schober), comp. 1821–2, but never perf. in Schubert's lifetime; prod. Weimar, by Liszt, 24. VI. 1854.

Alford, John (b. ?; d. ?), Eng. 16th-cent. lutenist. He lived in London and in 1568 pub. a trans. of Adrien Le Roy's book on the lute. *A Briefe and Easye Instruction to learne . . . the Lute.*

Alfred, masque by Arne (words by James Thomson and David Mallet), perf. at Cliveden, Bucks., the residence of Frederick, Prince of Wales, 1. VIII. 1740. It contains 'Rule, Britannia'.

Alfvén, Hugo (b. Stockholm, 1. V. 1872; d. Uppsala, 8. V. 1960), Swed. violinist and comp. Studied under Lindegren at the Stockholm Cons., and began his career as violinist in the court orch. From 1910 to 1939 he was mus. director at the Univ. of Uppsala.

Works incl. 5 symphs., 2 symph. poems and Swed. rhapsody *Midsommarvaka* and 2 others for orch.; *Sten Sture* for chorus and orch.; *The Bells* for solo voice and orch.; a cantata; 2 marches; pieces for pf. and for vln.; songs; etc.

Algarotti, Francesco, Count (b. Venice, 11. XII. 1712; d. Pisa, 3. V. 1764), It. scholar. Among many learned works he wrote a treatise on the reform of opera, *Saggio sopra l'opera in musica*, pub. 1755.

Algarotti, Giovanni Francesco (b. Novara, c. 1536; d. ?), It. comp. Pub. books of madrigals at Venice in 1567 and 1569.

Alghisi, Paris Francesco (b. Brescia, 2. VI. 1666; d. Brescia, 29. III. 1743), It. comp. Studied under Polarolo and was engaged for some time at the Pol. court. Two operas were prod. at Venice: *Amor di Curzio per la patria*, 1690, and *Il trionfo della continenza*, 1691. He also wrote several oratorios and other works.

Ali Baba, ou Les Quarante Voleurs (. . ., *or The Forty Thieves*), opera by Cherubini (lib. by Scribe and Anne Honoré Joseph Mélesville), prod. Paris, Opéra, 22. VII. 1833. A new version of *Koukourgi*, comp. 1793, but not perf.

Aline, Reine de Golconde, opera by Berton (lib. by Jean Baptiste Charles Vial and Étienne Guillaume François de Favières, based on Sedaine's older lib.), prod. Paris, Opéra-Comique, 2. IX. 1803.

Opera by Monsigny (lib. by Jean Michel Sedaine), prod. Paris, Opéra, 15. IV. 1766.

Alió, Francisco (b. Barcelona, 21. III. 1862; d. Barcelona, 31. III. 1908), Span. comp. Wrote many pf. pieces and songs in a Span. nat. idiom.

Aliquot Parts (from Lat. *aliquot* = some), parts contained by the whole, integral factors: in mus. the parts of a fundamental note vibrating separately as Overtones.

Aliquot Scaling ⎫
Aliquot Strings ⎭ additional strings, vibrating with those struck by the hammers, introd. into the upper registers of Blüthner's pfs., evidently on the old principle of the sympathetic strings in bowed string instruments.

Alison, Richard. *See* **Allison.**

Alkan (actually Charles Henri Valentin Morhange) (b. Paris, 30. XI. 1813; d. Paris, 29. III. 1888), Fr. pianist and comp. He was so precocious as a player as to be admitted to the Paris Cons. at the age of 6. After a visit to London in 1833, he settled in Paris as teacher of the pf. In his comps. he cultivated an advanced, immensely difficult and often very modern technique.

Works incl. 2 pf. concertos; pf. trio; pf. sonatas, numerous pf. studies (incl. 1 for the right hand and 1 for the left), charact. pieces; 4 op. nos. of pieces for pedal pf., etc.

Alkestis, opera by Boughton (lib. taken from Gilbert Murray's Eng. trans. of the tragedy by Euripides), prod. Glastonbury, 26. VIII. 1922.

Opera by Wellesz (lib. by Hugo von Hofmannsthal, after Euripides), prod. Mannheim, 20. III. 1924.

All' ottava (It. = at the octave), a direction that a passage, so far as it is marked by a dotted line over it, is to be played an octave higher than it is written; it is usually represented by the symbol 8*va.* If the dotted line is below it means an octave lower.

All' unisono (It.) = in unison.

Alla (It. fem. = 'at the', in the manner of, = Fr. *à la*). The word is used in var. ways in combination with nouns, e.g. *alla marcia* = march-like, *alla francese* = in the Fr. manner, etc. (also abbr. *all'* with nouns beginning with a vowel).

Alla breve (It. = with the breve [as unit of the beat, instead of the semibreve]), a term used for a tempo direction indicating that the time is twice as fast as the note-values would suggest, though not necessarily a rapid tempo. The normal *alla breve* time-signature is 𝄵. See **A cappella.**

Alla cappella. *See* **A cappella.**

Allargando. (It.) = becoming broader, slowing down.

Allegranti, Maddalena (b. Florence, *c*. 1750; d. ? Ireland, *c*. 1802), It. soprano. Made her 1st appearance in Venice in 1770. Later appeared in Ger. and Eng. as well as It.

Allegretto (It. dim. of *allegro*) = a little fast, i.e. not as fast as *allegro*.

Allegri, Domenico (b. Rome, 1585; d. Rome, 5. IX. 1629), It. comp. *Maestro di cappella* at Santa Maria Maggiore in Rome, 1610–29. Works incl. motets and mus. for voices and strings.

Allegri, Gregorio (b. Rome, 1582; d. Rome, 17. II. 1652), It. priest and comp. Pupil of the Nanini brothers in Rome, where he sang tenor in the Papal Chapel from 1629. His famous *Miserere* is still sung there; Mozart, as a boy of 14, wrote it down from memory after hearing it in Rome. A. also wrote Magnificats, motets and other church mus.

Allegro (It. lit. cheerful, sprightly). In mus. the term, although orig. doubtless describing the character of a piece, now indicates merely speed: a fast but not very fast pace.

Allegro, il Penseroso ed il Moderato, L' (*The Cheerful, the Thoughtful and the Moderate Man*), oratorio by Handel (lib. Parts i and ii by Milton, Part iii by Charles Jennens), prod. London, Lincoln's Inn Fields Theatre, 27. II. 1740.

Alleluia, the 3rd chant of the Proper of the Mass, sung immediately after the Gradual. The word is Hebrew (= praise ye Jehova), and was sung in many contexts in Jewish life, but especially in connection with the singing of the Psalms. It was taken over unchanged by the Christian Church and sung both alone and as an addition to chants of various kinds, especially during the Easter season. As a Mass-chant of the Roman rite it was originally sung alone, at first during Eastertide only and, after the time of Gregory I, during the whole year except from Septuagesima to Easter. At some time before 750 one or more verses were added, in which form it became a responsorial chant, the choir singing the A. at the beginning and end, and the soloists the verse or verses in between. The exact form as sung since the Middle Ages may be illustrated from the A. for the 1st Sunday of Advent (*see* illustration).

The A. of the Ambrosian chant, possibly retaining more of its original oriental characteristics, is even more florid in character.

Allemande (Fr. fem. = German) (1) A dance in moderate 4–4 time, divided into 2 sections, each repeated, and usually beginning with a short upbeat. It occurs in most classical suites, where it takes 1st place unless they open with a prelude. (2) = Deutscher Tanz.

Allen, Henry Robinson (b. Cork, 1809; d. London, 27. XI. 1876), Ir. baritone. He first became known in London *c*. 1842 and made a great reputation as an operatic artist, but retired early to devote himself to teaching and the comp. of songs, incl. 'When we two parted'.

Allen, Hugh P(ercy). (b. Reading, 23. XII. 1869; d. Oxford, 20. II. 1946), Eng. mus. scholar. He was organist at var. churches, went to Cambridge Univ. later and took the D. Mus. at Oxford in 1889. Organist at New Coll. there from 1901, from which time he took an active share in the univ.'s mus. life. In 1918 he succeeded Parry as director of the R.C.M. in London and Parratt as Prof. of Mus. at Oxford. Knighted in 1920.

Allende, Pedro Humberto (b. Santiago, 29. VI. 1885), Chilean comp. and educationist. Studied at the Nat. Cons. of Chile. Works incl. *Tres Tonadas, Escenas campesinas chilenas* and *La voz de la calle,* for orch.; concertos for vln., cello and pf.

Allison (Alison, Aloyson), Richard (b. ?; d. ?), Eng. 16th–17th-cent. comp. He first appeared as a contrib. to East's *Whole Book of Psalms* in 1592 and pub. a collec-

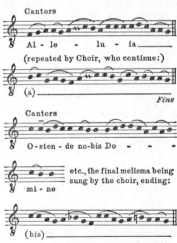

D.C. al Fine, but *without* the repetition of the first section by the choir.

ALLELUIA

tion of church melodies set for voices and instruments, *The Psalmes of David in Meter*, in 1599. Other works incl. lute mus. and 24 songs for voices and instruments, *An Howres Recreation . . .*, pub. in 1606.

Allwood, Richard. *See* **Alwood.**

Almahide, opera by ? Giovanni Bononcini (lib. by ?, after Dryden's *Almanzor and Almahide*), prod. London, Queen's Theatre, Haymarket, 10. I. 1710. According to Burney, the 1st opera performed in Eng. wholly in It.

Almain (Middle Eng. adj. = German), one of the names given to the 'Allemande' in the 16th cent.

Almand (Old Eng.) = Allemande.

Almaviva (Rossini). *See* **Barbiere di Siviglia.**

Almeida, Fernando de (b. Lisbon, ? 1618; d. Thomar, 21. III. 1660), Port. monk and comp. Pupil of Lobo; entered the monastery of Thomar in 1638; wrote Masses and other church mus.

Almeida, Francisco Antonio de (b. ?; d. ?), Port. 18th-cent. comp. Prob. studied in Rome and was the 1st Port. to write It. operas, incl. *La Spinalba* and *La pazienza di Socrate.*

Almeida, Ignacio Antonio de (b. Guimarães, 18. II. 1760; d. S. Pedro de Penedono, 25. X. 1825), Port. priest and comp. His works incl. a Requiem, a *Stabat Mater* and other church mus.

Almérie, a kind of lute invented in the 18th cent. by Jean Lemaire, on whose name its own is an anagram.

Almira, opera by Handel (lib. by Friedrich Christian Feustking), prod. Hamburg, Theater beim Gänsemarkt, 8. I. 1705.

Almond (Old Eng.) = Allemande.

Alnaes, Eyvind (b. Frederiksstad, 29. IV. 1872; d. Oslo, 24. XII. 1932), Norw. organist, cond. and comp. Studied at Christiania and Berlin and later became organist and choral cond. at Drammen. Works incl. 2 symphs.; pf. concerto; songs, etc.

Alpaerts, Flor (b. Antwerp, 12. IX. 1876; d. Antwerp, 5. X. 1954), Belg. cond. and comp. Studied with Benoit and Blockx at the Antwerp Cons., in 1903 became prof. there and in 1934–41 was its director. In 1919 he also became cond. of the Antwerp Zoo Orch. and in 1922–3 he directed the Royal Flem. Opera.

Works incl. opera *Shylock* (after Shakespeare); incid. mus. for plays; church mus.; *Spring* symph., symph. poem *Psyche* and other orchestral works; vln. concerto; chamber mus.; pf. works; songs, etc.

Alpenkönig und Menschenfeind (*Alpine King and Misanthrope*), opera by Blech (lib. by Richard Batka, based on Ferdinand Raimund's play), prod. Dresden, 1. X. 1903.

Alpensinfonie, Eine (*An Alpine Symph.*), symph. by R. Strauss, Op. 64, 1st perf. Berlin, 28. X. 1915.

Alphabetical Music. *See* **Letters.**

Alphorn (Ger. *Alpenhorn*), a primitive wind instrument, often *c.* 8 ft. long, with a raucous and powerful tone, used by cowherds in Switz. and other mountainous countries. Having no keys, it can prod. only the natural harmonics.

Alpine Symphony (R. Strauss). *See* **Alpensinfonie.**

Also sprach Zarathustra (*Thus spake Zoroaster*), symph. poem by R. Strauss, Op. 30, based on Nietzsche, comp. 1896, 1st perf. Frankfurt, 27. XI. 1896.

Alt, In (from Lat. 'in alto' = high up), a term used for notes above the stave in mus. written in the treble clef.

Altenburg, Michael (b. Alach nr. Erfurt, 27. V. 1584; d. Erfurt, 12. II. 1640), Ger. theologian and church musician. Comp. hymn tunes, psalms, motets, sacred pieces for voices and instruments, intradas for instruments, etc.

Alternatim (Lat.), a manner of performance in which singers or players are heard in alternation, e.g. between two sides of a choir, between choir and org., etc. It can also be applied to alternation between mus. styles, e.g. plainsong and polyphony.

Alternativo (It.), a contrasting section, much the same as the trio in a minuet or scherzo, but often in a piece of a different character, and there may be more than one A. in a single piece. Familiar exs. appear in Schumann.

Althorn. *See* **Saxhorn.**

Altissimo, In (It. = at the highest), a term used for notes in the octave above that described as 'in alt'.

Altmann, Wilhelm (b. Adelnau, 4. IV. 1862; d. Hildesheim, 25. III. 1951), Ger. mus. critic and ed. Director of the mus. dept. of the State Library in Berlin, 1915–1927. Ed. of classical mus. and of mus. catalogues.

Altnikol, Johann Christoph (b. Berna, Silesia, XII. 1719; d. Naumburg, VII. 1759), Ger. harpsichordist, organist and comp. Pupil of Bach in Leipzig from 1744. App. organist at Niederwiesa nr. Greifenberg early in 1748, and later the same year at Naumburg. Married Bach's daughter Elisabeth Juliane Friderike (1726–81) in 1749.

Alto (It. = high). (1) Properly an extension of the highest male-voice register, prod. by Falsetto, used in Angl. church choirs and in male-voice 4tets and choral societies, partic. in glees and part-songs. (2) = Contralto. (3) (Fr.) = Viola. (4) As a prefix to an instrument = a size larger than the soprano, e.g. alto saxophone.

Alto Bassoon. *See* **Caledonica** and **Dolcian.**

Alto Clef, the C clef so used as to indicate that middle C stands on the central line of the stave; now obs. in vocal mus., but still in use for the vla.:

Alto Rhapsody (Brahms). *See* **Rhapsodie.**

Alva, Luigi (Luis) (b. Lima, 10. IV. 1927), Peruvian tenor. Began his career with Radio Lima and in 1953 went to It., singing at La Scala in 1954. He specializes in operatic lyric roles, and has sung at most of the great opera-houses and festivals.

Alwood (Allwood), Richard (b. ?; d. ?), Eng. 16th-cent. priest and comp. He wrote a Mass, 'Praise him praiseworthy', and 7 keyboard pieces, one of which, called 'In nomine', is based on the same 5-note motive as the Mass.

Alwyn, William (b. Northampton, 7. XI. 1905), Eng. comp. Entered the R.A.M. in London as a student for fl., pf. and comp., studying the last under McEwen and obtaining the Costa Scholarship. Later he became prof. of comp. there, was elected to the Collard Fellowship of the Worshipful Co. of Musicians in 1937 and became an Hon. Freeman of that Co. in 1940

Works incl. mus. for films, *Our Country*, *The Lost Illusion*, and many others; 5 preludes, concerto grosso, overture to a masque. and 4 symphs. for orch.; pf. concerto, vln. concerto, *Pastoral Fantasia* for vla. and strings; mus. for films *Desert Victory*, *World of Plenty*, *The Way Ahead*, etc.; string 4tets., Rhapsody for pf. 4tet.; Sonata-Impromptu for vln. and vla., sonatina for vla. and pf.; pf. pieces; Divertimento for solo fl., etc.

Alypios, 4th-cent. Gk. theorist to whom our knowledge of ancient Gk. notation is due.

Alzira, opera by Verdi (lib. by Salvatore Cammarano, based on Voltaire's play *Alzire*), prod. Naples, Teatro San Carlo, 12. VIII. 1845.

Amadei, Filippo (b. Reggio, *c.* 1670; d. ?, after 1729), It. cellist and comp. His 1st opera, *Teodosio il giovane*, was prod. in Rome in 1711. *See also* **Mattei (F.).**

Amadei, Michele Angelo (b. ?; d. ?), It. 16th–17th-cent. comp. 2 books of his motets were pub. at Venice in 1614–15.

Amadigi di Gaula (*Amadis of Gaul*), opera by Handel (lib. adapted from Antoine Houdar de la Motte's *Amadis de Grèce*, set by Destouches, 1699), prod. London, King's Theatre, Haymarket, 25. V. 1715.

Amadis, opera by Lully (lib. by Quinault, based on the old Span. or Port. romance *Amadis de Gaula*), prod. Paris, Opéra, 18. I. 1684.

Amadis de Gaule opera by J. C. Bach

(lib. do., altered by Alphonse Marie Denis de Vismes), prod. Paris, Opéra, 14. XII. 1779.

Amadori, Giuseppe (b. ?; d. ?), It. 17th–18th-cent. comp. *Maestro di cappella* in Rome, where his oratorio, *Il martirio di Sant' Adriano*, was prod. in 1702. He also wrote Masses and other church mus.

Amahl and the Night Visitors, opera in 1 act by Menotti (lib. by the comp., after Bosch's painting *The Adoration of the Magi*), prod. on N.B.C. Television 24. XII. 1951. It is the 1st opera esp. written for television.

Amalarius of Metz (b. *c.* 780; d. *c.* 850), liturgist and mus. theorist. In 831 or 832 he travelled to Rome in order to obtain an authentic Antiphonary.

Amat, Juan Carlos (b. Monistrol nr. Barcelona, ?; d. ?), Span. 16th-cent. scientist and author. He wrote *Guitarra española* . . ., the earliest known treatise on the subject, pub. prob. 1586.

Amati, It. 16th–17th-cent. family of vln. makers at Cremona.:

Andrea A. (b. *c.* 1535; d. *c.* 1611).

Antonio A. (b. 1550; d. 1638).

Girolamo (or Geronimo) A. (b. 1551; d. 1635).

Nicolo A. (b. 3. XII. 1596; d. 12. IV. 1684).

Girolamo A. (b. 26. II. 1649; d. 21. II. 1740).

Amato, Pasquale (b. Naples, 21. III. 1878; d. Jackson Heights, Long Island, N.Y., 12. VIII. 1942), It. baritone. Made his 1st appearance in Eng. in 1904 and later had much success in opera in U.S.A.

Amato, Vincenzo (b. Ciminna, Palermo 6. I. 1629; d. Palermo, 29. VII, 1670), It. priest and comp. Wrote Masses, psalms, sacred concertos and an opera, *L'Isauro*, prod. at Palermo in 1664.

Amber Witch, The, opera by Wallace (lib. by Henry Fothergill Chorley, based on Lady Duff-Gordon's trans. of Johann Wilhelm Meinhold's novel *Maria Schweidler, die Bernsteinhexe*), prod. London, Her Majesty's Theatre, 28. II. 1861.

Ambiela, Miguel (b. Aragon, 1665; d. Toledo, 23. III. 1733), Span. priest and comp. Mus. director of the new cathedral at Saragossa, 1700–7, and *maestro de capilla* at Toledo, 1710–33.

Works incl. Masses, *Stabat Mater* and other church mus.

Ambleto (*Hamlet*), opera by Gasparini (lib. by Apostolo Zeno and Pietro Pariati), prod. Venice, Teatro San Cassiano, Carnival 1705.

Opera by D. Scarlatti (lib. do.), prod. Rome, Teatro Capranica, Carnival 1715.

Ambros, August Wilhelm (b. Vysoké Myto, 17. XI. 1816; d. Vienna, 28. VI. 1876), Cz. (Germanized) musicologist. Studied at Prague Univ. His life's work was a hist. of mus. which at his death reached only the 4th vol. and the early 17th cent. He also comp. a Cz. opera, *Bratislav and Jitka*, overtures to Shakespeare's *Othello* and Calderón's *Mágico prodigioso*, etc.

Ambrose, John (b. ?; d. ?), Eng. 15th–16th-cent. comp. of an untitled keyboard piece (Oxford, Christ Church MS. 1034) and a wordless canon in Brit. Mus. Roy. App. 58. An 'Ambros' was a clerk of King's College, Cambridge, 1481–2.

Ambrosian Chant, the mus. of the Milanese rite associated with St. Ambrose (340–397), Bishop of Milan from 374. The mus. as we now have it is mostly preserved in late medieval MSS. and probably differs considerably from that heard in Ambrosian times; nor can any of the extant tunes to the few authentic hymns of St. Ambrose be definitely considered to be of the same date. The rite itself belongs to the Gallican family, containing oriental features not preserved in that of Rome; while the chant, even in its present form, shows Eastern influences to a greater degree than 'Gregorian' chant.

Ambrosio, Alfredo d' (b. Naples, 13. VI. 1871; d. Nice, 29. XII. 1914), It. violinist and comp. Studied at Naples and Paris; wrote mainly light vln. pieces.

Amelia al Ballo (*Amelia goes to the Ball*), opera by Menotti (lib. by the comp.), prod. Philadelphia, 1. IV. 1937.

Amener (Fr., prob. from *à mener* = to lead), a Fr. dance of the 17th cent. in triple time and moderate pace, with charact. 6-bar phrases. It occurs in Fr. instrumental suites and thence passed to some extent into Ger. and It. mus.

Amerbach, Elias Nikolaus. *See* **Ammerbach.**

America, epic rhapsody by Bloch (1. 1620; 2. 1861–5; 3. 1926), comp. 1926–7. 1st perf. 20. XII. 1928 and then on 21. XII. 1928 simultaneously in 7 Amer. cities. It won the £3,000 prize offered by *Mus. America* for the best Amer. symph. work.

American Organ, an instrument similar to the Harmonium, differing from the latter in some details, partic. in sucking in the wind through its reeds instead of expelling it. Its principle was discovered by a workman attached to Jacob Alexandre (1804–1876), an instrument maker in Paris, but he took it to Amer. and the 1st important instruments of the kind were made by Mason & Hamlin of Boston *c.* 1860.

Ames, John (Carlovitz) (b. Westbury-on-Trym nr. Bristol, 8. I. 1860; d. Torquay, 21. VII. 1924), Eng. pianist and comp. Wrote an opera, *The Last Inca*, incid. mus. to Shakespeare's *Richard II*, 2 pf. concertos, choral works and chamber mus.

Amfiparnaso, L' (*The Amphi-Parnassus*), madrigal opera by Orazio Vecchi, prod. Modena, 1594, and pub. Venice, 1597,

described as a *commedia harmonica*. It consists of 3 acts and a prologue, and the characters are the stock figures of the *commedia dell' arte*, but the mus. setting of their speech is in the form of madrigals for mixed voices. It has been supposed that the action was prod. in dumb-show while the madrigals were sung behind the scenes, but a passage in the text which says that 'the spectacle is to enter by the ear, not by the eye', gives good reason to doubt this. The same subject was treated earlier in a smaller form by Lassus.

Amicis, Anna Lucia de (b. Naples, *c.* 1740; d. Naples, 1816), It. soprano, pupil (?) of Tesi-Tramontini. In 1772 sang the leading role in *Lucio Silla* by Mozart, who thought highly of her.

Amico Fritz, L', opera by Mascagni (lib. by P. Suardon, based on Erckmann-Chatrian's novel *L'Ami Fritz*), prod. Rome, Teatro Costanzi, 31. X. 1891.

Amid Nature (or *In Nature's Realm*), concert overture by Dvořák, Op. 91, comp. 1891 and forming with *Carnival* and *Othello*, a cycle with thematic connections, orig. called *Nature, Life and Love*.

Amitié á l'épreuve, L' (*Friendship on Trial*), opera by Grétry (lib. by Charles Simon Favart and Claude Henri Fusée de Voisenon, based on a story by Marmontel), prod. Fontainebleau, at court, 13. XI. 1770; 1st Paris perf., Comédie-Italienne, 24. I. 1771.

Amleto (*Hamlet*), opera by Faccio (lib. by Boito, after Shakespeare), prod. Genoa, Teatro Carlo Felice, 30. V. 1865.

Ammerbach (Amerbach), Elias Nikolaus (b. Naumberg, *c.* 1530; d. Leipzig, I. 1597), Ger. organist and comp. Was organist of St. Thomas, Leipzig, from 1560 and pub. 2 books of mus. in org. tablature containing important explanations of ornaments and modes of perf.

Ammon (Amon), Blasius (b. Imst, Tyrol, *c.* 1560; d. Vienna, VI. 1590), Aus. monk and comp. Studied in Vienna and entered the Franciscan monastery there. Wrote much church mus.

Amner, John (b. Ely, 1579; d. Ely, 1641), Eng. organist and comp. He became organist and choirmaster at Ely Cathedral in 1610; wrote services, anthems and *Sacred Hymns.*

Amon, Blasius. *See* **Ammon.**

Amon, Johann Andreas (b. Bamberg, 1763; d. Wallerstein, Bavaria, 29. III. 1825), Ger. horn player, cond. and comp. Toured in Fr. and Ger. and had comp. lessons from Sacchini in Paris in 1781; became mus. director at Heilbronn in 1789 and *Kapellmeister* to the Prince of Oettingen-Wallerstein in 1817.

Works incl. 2 *Singspiele*, Masses, symphs., chamber mus., etc.

Amor brujo, El (*Love, the Wizard*), ballet

17

by Falla, comp. 1913–14, 1st perf. Madrid, Teatro de Lara, 15. IV. 1915.

Amor vuol sofferenza (*Love means Suffering*), opera by Leo (lib. by Gennaro Antonio Federico), prod. Naples, Teatro Nuovo, autumn 1739.

Amore artigiano, L' (*Love among the Artisans*), opera by Gassmann (lib. by Goldoni), prod. Vienna, Burgtheater, 26. IV. 1767.

Opera by Latilla (lib. do.), prod. Venice, Teatro Sant' Angelo, 26. XII. 1760.

Amore di tre re, L' (*The Love of Three Kings*), opera by Montemezzi (lib. by Sem Benelli, from his play of the same title), prod. Milan, Teatro alla Scala, 10. IV. 1913.

Amorevoli, Angelo (b. Venice, 16. IX. 1716; d. Dresden, 15. XI. 1798), It. tenor. Spent most of his time at the court of Dresden, but sang in London in 1741–3.

Amoroso (It. = amorous), a direction indicating an emotional and tender manner of perf.

Amours d'Antoine et de Cléopâtre, Les (*The Loves of A. and C.*), ballet by R. Kreutzer (choreography by Jean Pierre Aumer, based on Shakespeare), prod. Paris, Opéra, 8. III. 1808.

Amy, Gilbert (b. Paris, 29. VIII. 1936), Fr. comp. of advanced tendencies. Studied with Milhaud, Messiaen and Boulez. Director of the Concerts du Domaine Musical, specializing in new mus. His comps. show influences of oriental mus., total serialism and also aleatory techniques. Works incl. *Mouvements* for chamber orch.; *Alpha-Beth* for 6 wind instruments; *Cycles* for perc.; *Epigrammes* for pf.

Amy Robsart, opera by Isidore de Lara (lib. by Augustus Henry Glossop Harris, based on Scott's *Kenilworth*), prod. in Fr. (trans. by Paul Milliet), London, Covent Garden Theatre, 20. VII. 1893.

An die ferne Geliebte (*To the Distant Beloved*), song cycle by Beethoven (6 songs), Op. 98, to poems by A. Jeitteles, comp. 1816. It is prob. the 1st Ger. set of songs intended to form a connected cycle.

Ana, Francesco d' (b. ?; d. Venice, c. 1503), It. comp. At St. Mark's, Venice, 1490; comp. *frottole*, Lamentations, etc.

Anacreon (c. 560–c. 476 B.C.), Gk. poet. *See* Gotovac (odes), Maconchy (*Garland*), Renvoysy (odes), Roussel (A.) (do.), Smyth (do.).

Anacréon, ou L'Amour fugitif, opera-ballet by Cherubini (lib. by R. Mendouze), prod. Paris, Opéra, 4. X. 1803.

Anacrusis, in prosody an unstressed syllable at the beginning of a verse or line; in mus. the literary term is borrowed as a synonym for Upbeat.

Analysis. *See* Programme Notes.

Ancelot, Jacques (1794–1854), Fr. playwright. *See* Puritani di Scozia (Bellini),

Roberto Devereux (Donizetti), **Roi malgré lui** (Chabrier).

Ancerl, Karel (b. Tučapy, Bohemia, 11. IV. 1908), Cz. cond. Studied with Křička and Alois Hába at the Prague Cons. (1925–1929). Ass. to Scherchen in Berlin (1929–1931). His public career began in 1931 as a theatre cond. and with Cz. radio. Imprisoned in World War II, he resumed his career in 1945, becoming prof. at the Academy of Mus. Arts in Prague (1950). He is a champion of modern mus., esp. Cz.

Anches (Fr. = Reeds). The Fr. name for the reed stops of the org.

Anchieta, Juan de (b. Azpeitia nr. San Sebastián 1462; d. Azpeitia, 30. VII. 1523), Span. comp. He became a court musician in 1489 and a canon of Granada 10 years later. From 1504 he was rector of the parish church in his native place. Wrote church mus. and secular songs.

Ancina, Giovenale (b. Fossano, 19. X. 1545; d. Saluzzo, 31. VIII. 1604), It. priest and comp. He 1st studied medicine, then theology and became one of St. Philip Neri's oratorians. He wrote var. essays on mus. and instruments and in 1599 compiled a collection of sacred songs, *Tempio armonico della Beata Vergine*, incl. some of his own.

Anda, Géza (b. Budapest, 19. XI. 1921), Hung. pianist. Studied at the Royal Mus. Acad. in Budapest with Dohnányi, winning the Liszt Prize. Left Hung. in World War II and now lives in Switz. He is best known as an exponent of Brahms, Liszt and Bartók.

Andamento (It.) = a fugue subject of more than usual length and often in 2 contrasted sections.

Andante (It. = going), a tempo direction indicating a 'walking pace', i.e. a moderate tempo.

Andantino (It. dim. of prec.), orig. intended to indicate a slower pace than *andante*, i.e. a dim. of 'walking'; but since *andante* is now taken to mean a slow pace, the dim. suggests an only moderately slow, i.e. slightly quicker tempo.

Ander, Aloys (b. Libice nad Doubravkou, 13. X. 1817; d. Sedmihorky, 11. XII. 1864), Boh. tenor. Made his 1st appearance in Vienna, 1845.

Anders, Peter (b. Essen, 1. VII. 1908; d. Hamburg, 10. IX. 1954), Ger. tenor. Made his début in Berlin in 1931 and from 1936 to 1948 sang at the Berlin State Opera. He made his Eng. début in 1950. He was killed in a car crash.

Andersen, Hans (Christian) (1805–75), Dan. poet and fairy-tale writer. *See* Arregui, Bruden fra Lammermoor (Bredal), Enna (*Little Match Girl*), Farjeon, Français (*Roi nu*), Hamerik (E.) (*Rejsekammeraten*), Hartmann (J. P. E.) (*Liden Kirsten*), Høffding (*Emperor's New Clothes*), Klenau

18

(*Little Ida's blomster*), **Maconchy** (*Little Red Shoes*), **Nightingale** (*Stravinsky*), **Rogers** (**Bernard**), **Rota** (N.) (*Principe porcaro*), **Toch** (*Prinzessin auf der Erbse*), **Travelling Companion** (Stanford), **Veretti** (*Favola di A.*), **Wagner-Régeny** (*Nackte König*), **Weissberg** (*Little Mermaid*).

Anderson, Emily (b. Galway, Ir., 17. III. 1891; d. London, 26. X. 1962), Eng. musicologist. Although employed in the Foreign Office, she ed. and trans. the complete letters of Mozart and his family (2 vols., 1938) and those of Beethoven (3 vols., 1962).

Anderson Lucas, Mary. *See* **Lucas.**

Anderson, W(illiam). R(obert). (b. Blackburn, 7. XII. 1891), Eng. mus. author, critic and ed. Trained as an organist, took the B.Mus. at Durham and var. other mus. degrees, was ed. of the *Music Teacher* in 1920–5 and later broadcasting critic to the *Observer* and *Musical Times*. Author of *Music as a Career*, with H. D. McKinney of *Discovering Music, Music in History* and *The Challenge of Listening*, etc.

Andrade, Francisco d' (b. Lisbon, 11. I. 1859; d. Berlin, 8. II. 1921), Port. baritone. Made his 1st appearance in 1882; sang all over Eur.

André, Johann (b. Offenbach, 28. III. 1741; d. Offenbach, 18. VI. 1799), Ger. mus. pub. and comp. Prod. his first successful *Singspiel* in 1773 and set Goethe's *Erwin und Elmire* in 1775. Estab. his mus. pub. firm in 1774. His opera *Belmont und Constanze* of 1781 preceded Mozart's *Entführung*, on the same subject.

André, Johann Anton (b. Offenbach, 6. X. 1775; d. Offenbach, 6. IV. 1842), Ger. mus. pub., violinist, pianist and comp., son of prec. He followed his father in business, acquired Mozart's MSS. from Constanze in 1799 and with Senefelder applied the principle of lithography to mus. pub.

Andrea Chénier, opera by Giordano (lib. by Luigi Illica), prod. Milan, Teatro alla Scala, 28. III. 1896.

Andrea da Firenze. *See* **Firenze.**

Andrea de Antiquis. *See* **Antiquis.**

Andreae, Volkmar (b. Berne, 5. VII. 1879; d. Zürich, 18. VI. 1962), Swiss comp. and cond. Studied at Berne and Cologne, in 1900 became asst. cond. at the Munich Opera, in 1902 choral cond. at Zürich and Winterthur, later cond. of the Zürich symph. concerts. From 1914 to 1916 he lectured at Zürich Univ. and from 1914 to 1939 was director of the Zürich Cons.

Works incl. operas *Ratcliff* (based on Heine's tragedy) and *Abenteuer des Casanova*; 2 symphs.; several concertos; choral works; chamber mus., etc.

Andrée, Elfrida (b. Visby, 19. II. 1841; d. Stockholm, 11. I. 1929), Swed. organist and comp. She was organist at Stockholm in 1861 and at Göteborg Cathedral in 1867;

wrote a Swed. Mass, org. symphs., chamber mus., etc.

Andreiev, Leonid Nikolaievich (1871–1919), Rus. novelist and playwright. *See* Rebikov (*Abyss*) Sessions (*Black Maskers*), Tcherepnin (A.) (*Ol-Ol*).

Andreozzi, Gaetano (b. Naples, 1763; d. Paris, 21. XII. 1826), It. comp. Pupil and relation of Jommelli; wrote 45 operas, 3 oratorios, chamber mus. and songs.

Andrevi, Francisco (b. nr. Lérida, 16. XI. 1786; d. Barcelona, 23. XI. 1853), Span. comp. of It. descent. He held var. church posts in Spain and Fr.; wrote 2 oratorios, a Requiem, a *Stabat Mater* and other church mus.

Andrico, Michel (b. Bucharest, 22. IX. 1894), Rum. comp. Studied at the Bucharest Cons. and later became prof. at the Royal Acad. there, gaining the Enesco Prize for comp. in 1924. From 1926 to 1959 he was prof. at the Bucharest Cons.

Works incl. ballet *Taina*; 9 symphs., 8 sinfoniettas, suite, serenade, 3 *Tableaux symphoniques*, *Suite pittoresque*, *Suite brève*, Poem, etc., for orch.; string 4tet, *Novellettes* for pf. 5tet and other chamber mus.; sonatina, *Suite lyrique* and other pf. works, etc.

Andriessen, Hendrik (b. Haarlem, 17. IX. 1892), Dutch organist and comp. Studied under Zweers at the Amsterdam Cons. Later became director of the Utrecht Cons. and choirmaster at the Rom. Catholic cathedral there.

Works incl. 8 Masses and *Te Deum*; 3 symphs., variations for orch.; songs for voice and orch.; chamber mus.; cello and pf. sonata; org. works, etc.

Andriessen, Willem (b. Haarlem, 25. X. 1887; d. Amsterdam, 30. III. 1964), Dutch pianist and comp. Studied at the Amsterdam Cons., of which he became director in 1937 in succession to Dresden, after teaching at The Hague and Rotterdam.

Works incl. Mass for solo voices, chorus and orch.; scherzo for orch.; pf. concerto; pf. sonata, etc.

Andrieu Contredit d'Arras. *See* **Arras.**

Andrieu, F. (b. ?; d. ?), Fr. 14th-cent. comp. He set a double *ballade* by Eustace Deschamps on the death of Machaut.

Andromaque (*Andromache*), opera by Grétry (lib. by Louis Guillaume Pitra, based on Racine's tragedy), prod. Paris, Opéra, 6. VI. 1780.

Androt, Albert Auguste (b. Paris, 1781; d. Rome, 19. VIII. 1804), Fr. comp. Student at the Paris Cons., where he was the 1st winner of the Prix de Rome at its institution in 1803 and was sent to It., making further studies with Guglielmi in Rome. There he wrote a Requiem and another sacred work with such success that he was asked to comp. an opera, but died as soon as it was finished.

Anerio, Felice (b. Rome, *c.* 1560; d. Rome, 27. IX. 1614), It. comp. Chorister in the Papal Chapel as a boy, later *maestro di cappella* at the Eng. Coll. in Rome, which he left for the service of Cardinal Aldo-brandini. App. comp. to the Papal Chapel on the death of Palestrina in 1594.

Works incl. Masses, motets, hymns and other church mus.; madrigals, canzonets, etc.

Anerio, Giovanni Francesco (b. Rome, *c.* 1567; d. Graz, VI. 1630), It. comp., brother of prec. In the service of Sigismund III of Poland about 1609, then *maestro di cappella* at the cathedral of Verona and, about 1613, app. mus. instructor at the Seminario Romano and *maestro di cappella* of the church of the Madonna de' Monti in Rome.

Works incl. Masses, Requiem, Te Deum and other church mus.

Anet, Jean-Baptiste (b. ?, *c.* 1661; d. Lunéville 14. VIII. 1755), Fr. violinist and comp. He travelled in Fr. and It., studying with Corelli in Rome, and made a great reputation. He retired to the court of the ex-king of Pol., Stanislas Leszcsinski, at Lunéville. Wrote sonatas and other works for his instrument.

Anfossi, Pasquale (b. Taggia nr. Naples, 25. IV. 1727; d. Rome, II. 1797), It. comp. Pupil of Piccinni at Naples. Wrote operas from 1763, but had his 1st real success with *L'incognita perseguitata* (Rome, 1773). Later prod. operas in Paris, London, Berlin and Prague. In 1792 he became *maestro di cappella* of St. John Lateran in Rome.

Works incl. operas *La donna fedele*, *L'incognita perseguitata*, *La finta giardiniera*, *Il geloso in cimento*, *L'avaro*, *La vera costanza*, *Il curioso indiscreto*, *I viaggiatori felici*, *Le gelosie fortunate*, church mus., etc.

Angecourt, Perrin d' (b. ?; d. ?), Fr. 13th-cent. troubadour. He was at the court of Charles of Anjou. 53 of his songs have survived.

Angeles, Victoria de los. *See* Los Angeles.

Angelina, an alternative title for Rossini's opera *La Cenerentola*, used esp. in Ger. and Aus.

Angiolina, ossia Il matrimonio per susurro (*Angiolina, or The Marriage by Noise*), opera by Salieri (lib. by Carlo Prospero Defranceschi, based on Ben Jonson's *Epicoene*). prod. Vienna, Kärntnertortheater, 22. X. 1800.

Anglaise (Fr.), a dance-form similar to that of the country dance, which in Fr. became the *contredanse* in the 18th cent., when the name of A. was sometimes given to it instead to show its Eng. origin unmistakably.

Anglebert, Jean Henri d' (b. Paris, 1635; d. Paris, 23. IV. 1691), Fr. harpsichordist and comp. Pupil of Chambonnières. Be-

came organist to the Duke of Orleans in 1661 and chamber musician to Louis XIV in 1664. He wrote harpsichord and org. pieces and arr. many instrumental pieces from Lully's operas for harpsichord.

Anglès, Higini (b. Maspujols, Catalonia, 1. I. 1888; d. Rome, 8. XII. 1969), Span. musicologist. Pupil of Pedrell at Barcelona. App. librarian of the mus. dept. of the Catalan Library there, and after further studies in Ger., prof. of mus. hist. at the Cons. From 1947 he was Pres. of the Pontificio Istituto di Musica Sacra in Rome. He pub. a great deal of old Span. music and wrote extensively on it.

Anglican Chant. *See* Chant.

Ängstlich (Ger. = anxiously, apprehensively). Beethoven used the term as a direction for the singing of the recitative in the 'Agnus Dei' section of his *Missa solemnis*.

Animato (It. = animated), a direction orig. intended to suggest a spirited perf., but later generally the quickening of a passage.

Animuccia, Giovanni (b. Florence *c.* 1500; d. Rome, 25. III. 1571), It. comp. Studied under Goudimel in Rome; *maestro di cappella* at the Vatican from 1555 until his death. A friend of St. Philip Neri, for whom he comp. a series of *Laude*. He also wrote Masses, other church mus. and madrigals.

Animuccia, Paolo (b. ? Florence, ?; d. Rome, 1563), It. comp., brother of prec. *Maestro di cappella* at the Lateran in Rome 1550–2, before Lassus. Wrote madrigals and church mus.

Aniuta, Rus. opera adapted from mus. by Piccinni, Grétry and others, prod. St. Petersburg, 1772. Formerly wrongly attr. to Fomin.

Anna Amalia, Princess of Prussia (b. Berlin, 9. XI. 1723; d. Berlin, 30. III. 1787), sister of Frederick the Great and amateur musician. With her *Kapellmeister* Kirnberger she was a champion of the works of Bach and Handel in Berlin, and collected a valuable library of old mus. She was also a comp.

Anna Bolena (*Anne Boleyn*), opera by Donizetti (lib. by Felice Romani), prod. Milan, Teatro Carcano, 26. XII. 1830.

Anna Karenina, opera by Hubay (lib., in Hung., by Sandor Góth, based on Tolstoy's novel), prod. Budapest, 10. XI. 1923.

Années de pèlerinage, 4 sets of pf. pieces by Liszt, mainly recording his travels in Switz. and It.—*1re Année: En Suisse*, comp. 1835–6, pub. 1855: 1. *Chapelle de Guillaume Tell.* 2. *Au Lac de Wallenstadt.* 3. *Pastorale.* 4. *Au Bord d'une source.* 5. *Orage.* 6. *Vallée d'Obermann* (inspired by Senancour's *Obermann*; the valley is an imaginary or unidentified one in the canton of Valais). 7. *Eglogue.* 8. *Le Mal du* *pays*. 9. *Les Cloches de Genève*. (Nos. 1, 2, 4, 6 and 9 orig. formed part of an *Album d'un voyageur* for pf. pub. in 1836: they were revised for the pub. of the *A. d. p.* in 1855.—*2me Année: In Italie*, comp. 1838–9, pub. 1846: 1. *Sposalizio* (after Raphael's picture in the Brera at Milan). 2. *Il pensieroso* (after Michelangelo's statue of Giuliano dei Medici in the Medici mausoleum at San Lorenzo, Florence). 3. *Canzonetta del Salvator Rosa*. 4. *Sonetto No. 47 del Petrarca*. 5. *Sonetto No. 104 del Petrarca*. 6. *Sonetto No. 123 del Petrarca* (Nos. 4–6 are transcriptions of settings of these Petrarch sonnets for voice and pf.). 7. *Après une lecture du Dante: Fantasia quasi Sonata*.—*3me Année*, comp. 1872–7, pub. 1883: 1. *Angelus: Prière aux anges gardiens*. 2. *Aux Cyprès de la Villa d'Este*. 3. do.: *Thrénodie*. 4. *Les Jeux d'eau de la Villa d'Este*. 5. *'Sunt lacrymae rerum' en mode hongrois*. 6. *Marche funèbre* (in memory of the Emperor Maximilian I of Mex., d. 19. VI. 1867). 7. *Sursum corda.*—Supplement to Vol. II: *Venezia e Napoli*, comp. 1859, pub. 1861: 1. *Gondoliera* (on a canzona by Cavaliere Peruchini). 2. *Canzone* (on the gondolier's song in Rossini's *Otello*). 3. *Tarantella* (on some canzoni by Guillaume Louis Cottrau). (This set is partly a revision of an earlier one of the same title comp. in 1840, but not pub.)

Annibale (Il Padovano) (b. Padua, 1527; d. Graz, III. 1575), It. contrapuntist and comp. Organist at St. Mark's, Venice, 1552–66, and then *maestro di cappella* to the Archduke Carl at Graz. Wrote church and org. mus., madrigals, etc.

Annibali, Domenico (b. Macerata, *c.* 1705; d. ? Rome, 1779), It. male soprano. He 1st appeared at Rome in 1725 and later went to Dresden, where he remained till 1764, singing the soprano lead in many of Hasse's operas. He sang for Handel in London in 1736–7.

Annunzio, Gabriele d' (1863–1938), It. poet novelist, dramatist and politician. *See* **Boulanger** (N.) (*Città morta*), **Fedra** (Pizzetti), **Francesca da Rimini** (Zandonai), **Franchetti** (*Figlia di Jorio*), **Honegger**

(*Phaedre*), **Leva** (*Gioconda*), **Martyre de Saint Sébastien** (*Debussy*), **Nave** (Montemezzi and Pizzetti), **Parisina** (Mascagni), **Pizzetti** (*Pisanella* and *Cabirio*), **Pugno** (*Città morta*), **Scontrino** (*Francesca da Rimini*), **Toselli** (*Fuoco*).

Ansani, Giovanni (b. Rome, 11. II. 1744; d. Florence, 15. VII. 1826), It. tenor. Sang with great success in Copenhagen and London, as well as It., and retired to Naples at the age of 50 to teach singing.

Anschlag
Anschlagend } (Ger.). *See* **Ornaments.**

Ansermet, Ernest (b. Vevy, 11. XI. 1883; d. Geneva, 20. II. 1969), Swiss cond. Originally a prof. of mathematics, 1906–10, he studied mus. with Bloch, Mottl and Nikisch. From 1915 to 1923 he was assoc. with Diaghilev's ballet company. In 1918 he founded the Orchestre de la Suisse Romande, which he cond. until 1967. He pub. a book criticizing certain aspects of modern, esp. serial, mus. in 1961. A. was well known for his perfs. of Stravinsky's earlier mus.

Anson, Hugo (Vernon) (b. Wellington, N.Z., 18. X. 1894; d. London, 4. VIII. 1958), Brit. comp. Studied at the R.C.M. and Trinity Coll., Cambridge. In 1922 he became director of mus. at Alleyn's School, Dulwich, from 1925 to 1939 he taught at the R.C.M. and in 1939 he was app. Registrar there.

Works incl. incid. mus. for Euripides' *Alkestis*; *Saadabad* (Flecker) for baritone, chorus and orch.; church mus.; concerto for 2 pfs. and orch.; string 4tet; suites for vln. and pf. and fl. and pf.; instrumental pieces; *Saint-Tropez Suite* for 2 pfs.; pf. pieces; songs, part-songs, etc.

Ansorge, Conrad (b. Buchwald, Silesia, 15. X. 1862; d. Berlin, 13. II. 1930), Ger. pianist and comp. Studied at the Leipzig Cons. and under Liszt at Weimar. Wrote a Requiem, pf. concerto, chamber mus., pf. works, songs, etc.

Answer, in Fugue the 2nd entry of the subject, brought in while the 1st entry continues with a counterpoint to it (*see* illustration).

Answer

Subject

Bach, '48', Bk. I, no. 1

ANSWER

Antar, a programme symph. by Rimsky-Korsakov, Op. 9, based on Senkovsky's oriental story of that name, comp. 1868 as '2nd Symph.', rev. 1875 and 1st perf. St. Petersburg, Rus. Mus. Soc., I. 1876, repub. in 1903 as 'symph. suite'. The titles of the movements are I. Introduction; II. 'Joy of Revenge'; III. 'Joy of Power'; IV. 'Joy of Love'.

Antegnati, Costanzo (b. Brescia, 1549; d. Brescia, 16. XI. 1624), It. comp. and member of a family of org.-builders famous in N. It. from 1470 to 1642. He wrote Masses, motets and madrigals, and org. and other instrumental mus.

Antheil, George (b. Trenton, N.J., 8. VII. 1900: d. N.Y., 12. II. 1959), Amer. comp. Studied with Bloch, later in Europe. His mus. of the 1920s is aggressively 'modern' (the *Ballet mécanique* of 1924 incl. 8 pianos, aeroplane propellers, motor horns, anvils, etc.) but his later work is much more restrained and classical in character. In 1939 he became associated with the film industry at Hollywood.

Works incl. operas *Transatlantic, Helen Retires* and *Volpone*; ballets *Ballet mécanique* and *Dreams*; 6 symphs., *Zingaresca, Capriccio* and *Archipelago* for orch.; 3 string 4tets; 2 vln. and pf. sonatas, etc.

Anthem, a comp. for church choir, with or without solo voices and accomp., sung in the course of Morning or Evening Service in the Angl. Church. There are 2 kinds of A.; the Full A. is a species sung by the choir throughout, the Verse A. is written for solo voices, with or without sections for the choir.

Anthony, Cristofferus (b. ?; d. ?), 15th-cent. comp., probably Eng., of a Magnificat and other pieces from the Trent Codices.

Anticipation, the occurrence of a note or notes from a chord before the rest of the chord is sounded, e.g.:

Beethoven, *Piano Sonata, Op. 27, No. 2*

Antico. *See* **Antiquis.**

Antigonae, play with mus. by Orff (text by Johann Christian Friedrich Hölderlin, after Sophocles), prod. Salzburg, 9. VIII. 1949.

Antigone, incid. mus. to Sophocles' tragedy by Mendelssohn, prod. at the New Palace, Potsdam, 28. X. 1841, and repeated at the Berlin Opera, 13. IV. 1842.

Opera by Honegger (lib. by Jean Cocteau, after Sophocles), prod. Brussels, Théâtre de la Monnaie, 28. XII. 1927.

Opera by Zingarelli (lib. by Jean François Marmontel), prod. Paris, Opéra, 30. IV. 1790.

Antigono, opera by Gluck (lib. by Metastasio), prod. Rome, Teatro Argentina, 9. II. 1756.

Opera by Hasse (lib. do.), prod. Hubertusburg nr. Dresden, 10. X. 1743.

Antinori, Luigi (b. Bologna, *c.* 1697; d. ?), It. tenor. First appeared in London, 1725.

Antiphon (Gk. = 'answering sound'), in Gregorian chant a refrain sung before and after a psalm, and orig. between verses as well. Its name prob. derives from its use in connection with antiphonal, or alternate, choir singing. The earliest A.s are often merely a single verse of the psalm itself, which in that case is not necessarily repeated. The canticle *Nunc dimittis* is still sung on 2 Feb. with the A. *Lumen ad revelationem*, its own 4th verse, sung between verses:

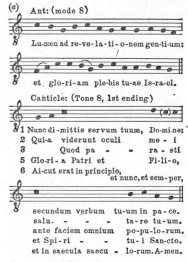

(The antiphon 'Lumen' is repeated after each verse.)

The tone of the psalm always corresponds numerically to the mode of the A., while its ending is chosen to link up with the beginning of the A. The bulk of the repertory consists of biblical texts set to nonpsalmodic melodies. A basic repertory of nearly 50 themes in the 8 modes is used for many thousands of texts. Their structure is often quite regular, and they may even have been sung metrically (*see* illustration *b*).

Works incl. operas *Un duello a Palermo*, *Amina*, etc.

ANTIPHON

The Introit and Communion of the Mass are A.s, orig. sung with a complete psalm. The final stage in its history occurs when the A. becomes an independent piece in its own right (e.g. votive and processional A.s). Originally they were borrowed from A.s to psalms, but later they were newly comp. and often achieved considerable complexity, e.g. Hermannus Contractus' *Alma redemptoris mater*:

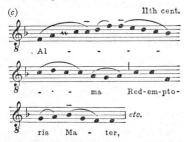

Antiquis, Andrea de (Andrea Antico) (b. ?; d. ?), It. comp. and mus. pub. who worked mainly in Rome and then Venice during the 1st half of the 16th cent. His most important pub. was probably *Frottole intabulate da sonar organi* (Rome, 1517), the first known printed ed. of keyboard mus. in Italy.

Antiquis, Giovanni de (b. ?; d. ?), It. 16th-cent. comp. Mus. director at the church of San Niccolo at Bari; ed. 2 books of *Villanelle alla napolitana* by musicians of Bari, incl. himself, pub. at Venice, 1574.

Antoine de Bertrand. *See* **Bertrand.**

Antonella da Caserta. *See* **Caserta.**

Antoni, Antonio d' (b. Palermo, 25. VI. 1801; d. Trieste, 18. VIII. 1859), It. cond. and comp. Prod. a Mass at the age of 12 and became cond. at the Palermo Theatre in 1817; settled at Trieste and founded the Società Filarmonica there, 1829.

Antonii, Pietro degli (b. Bologna, *c.* 1645; d. Bologna, *c.* 1720), It. comp. *Maestro di cappella* at var. Bologna churches. Wrote 3 operas, 3 oratorios, Masses, motets and instrumental works.

Antonio da Cividale del Friuli. *See* **Cividale.**

Antonio e Cleopatra, opera by Malipiero (lib. by comp., based on Shakespeare), prod. Florence, Teatro Comunale, 4. V. 1938.

Antony and Cleopatra. *See* **Amours d'Antoine et de Cléopâtre; Antonio e Cleopatra; Barber (S.)** (opera).

Anvil, an orch. perc. instrument imitating the sound of a blacksmith's anvil, but constructed of small steel bars struck by a mallet of wood or metal. It can be so made as to prod. notes of definite pitch, as in Wagner's *Rheingold*, but is usually indeterminate in sound.

Anzengruber, Ludwig (1839–89), Aus. novelist and playwright. *See* **Prohaska** (*Vierte Gebot*).

Ap Rhys, Philip (b. ?; d. ?), Eng. 16th-cent. comp. and organist. In 1547 he resigned his position as organist of St. Mary-at-Hill, London, to become master of the choristers at St. Paul's Cathedral. His works consist of org. mus. for the Lat. Liturgy, including an org. Mass.

Apel, Nikolaus (b. Königshofen, ?; d. Leipzig, 1537), compiler of a large MS. in choirbook form (Leipzig, Univ. Bibl. 1494) containing sacred and secular music of the late 15th and early 16th cents. It has been pub. in full by Rudolf Gerber (*Das Erbe deutscher Musik*, xxxii–xxxiv).

Apel, Willi (b. Konitz, 10. X. 1893), Ger. (now Amer.) musicologist. Studied mathematics at Bonn, Munich and Berlin Univs., and also pf. under Edwin Fischer, Martienssen and others. Settled in the U.S.A. in 1936. Taught at the Longy School of Music, Cambridge, Mass., 1936–43, and Harvard Univ., 1938–42. Prof. at Indiana Univ., 1950–63. His pubs.

23

incl. *The Notation of Polyphonic Music* (5th ed. 1961), *Harvard Dictionary of Music* (rev. ed., 1969) and *Gregorian Chant* (1958). Joint ed. (with A. T. Davison) of *Historical Anthology of Music* (2 vols., 1946 and 1960).

Aperto (It., lit. open, frank, straightforward). Mozart used the adj. in conjunction with *allegro* in some early works. The meaning is not clear, but may be taken to suggest an energetic delivery strictly in time.

Apiarius, Matthias (b. Berchingen, *c.* 1500, d. Bern, 1554), Ger. mus. pub. He worked in partnership with Peter Schöffer in Strasbourg, 1543–7, and independently in Bern, 1537–54.

ApIvor, Denis (b. Collinstown, Ir., 14. IV. 1916), Ir. comp. of Welsh stock. Was chorister at Hereford Cathedral, later at Christ Church, Oxford, and studied comp. with Patrick Hadley and Rawsthorne.

Works incl. opera *She Stoops to Conquer* (after Goldsmith); *The Hollow Men* (T. S. Eliot) for baritone, chorus and orch.; pf. concerto; Chaucer songs with string 4tet, sonata for clar., pf., and perc., vln. and pf. sonata; songs with words by F. García Lorca and others, etc.

Apollinaire, Guillaume (Wilhelm Apollinaris Kostrowitski) (1880–1918), Fr. poet of Pol. descent. *See* **Durey** (*Bestiaire*), **Poulenc** (do., *Les Mamelles de Tirésias*, *Banalités*).

Apollo et Hyacinthus, Lat. intermezzo by Mozart, K.38 (lib. by Rufinus Widl), prod. Salzburg Univ., 13. V. 1767.

Apollo Lyre. *See* **Lyre-Guitar.**

Apollonicon, a large organ playable both by hand and mechanically by barrels, built by Flight & Robson in London and exhib. by them in 1817.

Apostel, Hans Erich (b. Karlsruhe, 22. I. 1901), Aus. comp. of Ger. birth. Entered Karlsruhe Cons. in 1916, there coming into contact with Schönberg's mus. He later studied with Schönberg and Berg in Vienna, where he has lived since 1921. In 1937 his *Requiem* won the Hertzka Prize.

Works incl. *Requiem* (text by Rilke) for 8-part chorus and orch.; *Variations on a theme of Haydn* for orch.; pf. concerto; 2 string 4tets; songs with pf. or orch. on texts by Trakl and Hölderlin.

Apostles, The, oratorio by Elgar, Op. 49 (lib. compiled from the Bible by the comp.), Part I of a trilogy of which II *is The Kingdom* and III was never completed. Prod. Birmingham Festival, 14. X. 1903.

Appalachia, variations for orch. with chor. by Delius, comp. 1902, 1st perf. Elberfeld, 1904. The title is the old Red Indian name for N. Amer.; the theme is a Negro folksong.

Appassionata (It. = impassioned), the name commonly used for Beethoven's F

min. pf. sonata of 1804–5, Op. 57, but not authorized by himself.

Appassionato (It.) = impassioned, to be played or sung in a passionate manner.

Appenzeller, Benedictus (b. ?; d. ?), Flem. 16th-cent. comp. Pupil of Josquin des Prés. In the service of Mary of Hung., dowager regent of the Netherlands, with whom he went to Spain in 1551; later (?) choirmaster at Lille.

Works incl. *chansons*, church mus., a *Nenia* on the death of Josquin, etc.

Appleby, Thomas (b. ? Lincoln, 1488; d. Lincoln, *c.* 1562), Eng. organist and comp. App. organist of Lincoln Cathedral in 1538, the next year organist at Magdalen Coll., Oxford, but returned to Lincoln in 1541; was succeeded by Byrd there in 1563. Comp. church mus.

Applicatio (Lat.), a term formerly used for fingering in Ger.

Applicatur (Lat.-Ger.), sometimes used for fingering in Ger.

Appoggiatura (It., from *appoggiare* = to lean), a note of varying length, dissonant with the harmony against which it is heard but resolving on to a harmony note. Var. symbols have been used in the past to indicate it, the commonest of which is a note in smaller type, e.g.:

played approximately:

Where the A. is short it may in certain contexts occur before the beat.

Apprenti sorcier, L' (*The Sorcerer's Apprentice*), sherzo for orch. by Dukas on Goethe's ballad *Der Zauberlehrling*; 1st perf. Paris, Société Nationale de Musique, 1897.

Après-midi d'un faune (Debussy). *See* **Prélude à L'Après-midi d'un faune.**

Aprile, Giuseppe (b. Martina Franca, Apulia, 29. X. 1732; d. Martina Franca, 11. I. 1813), It. male alto and singing teacher. He 1st appeared in 1763 and was later a teacher of Cimarosa.

Apuleius (*c.* 125–?), Gk. philosopher. *See* **Bentzon** (J.) (*Saturnalia*).

Arabella, opera by R. Strauss (lib. by Hugo von Hofmannsthal, based on his story *Lucidor*), prod. Dresden, 1. VII. 1933. Hofmannsthal's last lib. for S.

Arabeske (Ger.) } orig. a term applied
Arabesque (Fr.) } to ornamentation in Arabic or Moorish architecture; used by some comps. (e.g. Schumann, Debussy) for pieces prob.

meant to be regarded as decorative rather than emotionally expressive.

Arabian Nights, The (*Thousand and One Nights*), Arabian cycle of stories of (?) the 10th cent., partly of Persian and prob. Indian origin. *See* **Dobroven** (opera), **Gerhard** (*Shaharazada*), **Mârouf** (Rabaud), **Sekles** (*Schahrazade*), **Shahrazad** (Rimsky-Korsakov), **Weisberg** (*Gulnara*).

Aragonaise (Fr.), a Span. dance of Aragon, i.e. the *Jota aragonesa*.

Araia (Araja), Francesco (b. Naples, 25. VI. 1709; d. Bologna, c. 1770), It. comp. He prod. his 1st opera in 1729. From 1735 he was for 24 years opera director to the Rus. court in St. Petersburg, where he prod. several of his own works. His setting of Metastasio's *La clemenza di Tito* in a translation by Feodor Grigorievich Volkov (prod. 1751) was the 1st opera in Rus. Another was *Cephalus and Procris*.

Aranaz, Pedro (b. Tudela, 1742; d. Cuença, 1821), Span. priest and comp. App. *maestro de capilla* at Saragossa Cathedral in 1766, having been a choir-boy there. After a year at Zamora he went to Cuença Cathedral in 1769.
Works incl. church mus. with orchestral accomp., secular songs (*tonadillas* and *villancicos*), etc.

Arbeau, Thoinot (anag. on real name of Jehan Tabourot) (b. Dijon, 1519; d. Langres, 1595), Fr. priest and author. Wrote a book on dancing, *Orchésographie*, pub. 1589, containing a large number of dance tunes current in 16th-cent. Fr.

Arbore di Diana, L' (*Diana's Tree*), opera by Martín y Soler (lib. by Lorenzo da Ponte), prod. Vienna, Burgtheater, 1. X. 1787.

Arbós, (Enrique) Fernández (b. Madrid, 24. XII. 1863; d. San Sebastian, 2. VI. 1939), Span. violinist and cond. Studied at Cons. of Madrid and Brussels, also with Joachim; toured and returned to Madrid to teach at the Cons.; prof. of vln. at R.C.M. in London, 1894–1916, and cond. of the Madrid Symph. Orch. from 1904.

Arbre enchanté, L', ou Le Tuteur dupé (*The Enchanted Tree, or The Tutor Duped*), comic opera by Gluck (lib. by Jean Joseph Vadé), prod. Vienna, Schönbrunn Palace, at court, 3. X. 1759.

Arcadelt, Jacob (b. ?, c. 1505; d.? Paris, 14. X. 1568), Flem. comp. Became a singer at the court of the Medici at Florence before 1539, in which year he was app. singing-master to the boys at St. Peter's in Rome, entering the coll. of papal singers the following year. Many of his madrigals were pub. in his lifetime.
Works incl. Masses, motets, madrigals, etc. (The *Ave Maria* attributed to him is a spurious adaptation of a 3-part *chanson, Nous voyons que les hommes Font tous vertu d'aimer*.)

Arcadia in Brenta, L', opera by Galuppi (lib. by Goldoni), prod. Venice, Teatro Sant' Angelo, 14. V. 1749. The 1st comic opera by Galuppi written in collaboration with Goldoni.

'Archduke' Trio, the name sometimes given to Beethoven's pf. trio in B♭ maj., Op. 97, comp. in 1811 and ded. to the Archduke Rudolph of Aus.

Archlute, a large Lute of the theorbo type with 2 sets of strings, the pegs of which were set at different distances in the double neck; the longer bass strings had no fingerboard and could therefore not be altered in pitch during perf.

Arciliuto (It.) = Archlute.

Arco (It. = bow), a direction (sometimes **col arco**) in mus. for bowed string instruments, indicating that the bow is to be resumed after a passage of plucked notes.

Arden muss sterben (*Arden must die*), opera by A. Goehr (lib. by Erich Fried, after the anon. Elizabethan play *Arden of Faversham*), prod. Hamburg, 5. III. 1967.

Arditi, Luigi (b. Crescentino, 22. VII. 1822; d. Hove, 1. V. 1903). It. comp. and cond. Educ. at Milan Cons. Cond. in var. It. towns, went on tour with Bottesini in 1846, cond. in U.S.A. and settled in London in 1858. Of his comps. only the popular waltz song *Il bacio* is now remembered.

Arensky, Anton Stepanovich (b. Novgorod, 11. VIII. 1861; d. Terioki, Finland, 25. II. 1906), Rus. comp. Pupil of Rimsky-Korsakov for a time, but belonged to the eclectic rather than the nationalist school. App. prof. at the Moscow Cons. in 1882.
Works incl. operas *A Dream on the Volga* (on Ostrovsky's *Voyevoda*), *Raphael, Nal and Damayanti*; ballet *Egyptian Night*; incid. mus. for Shakespeare's *Tempest*; 2 symphs.; pf. concerto; chamber mus.; numerous pf. pieces; choruses, songs, church mus., etc.

Argentine Composers. *See* **Aguirre, Bautista, Berutti, Buchardo, Castro (J. J.), Castro (J. M.), Drangosch, Faleni, Gianneo, Gilardi, Ginastera, Morillo, Paz, Siccardi, Ugarte, Williams (A.).**

Aria (It. = air), a vocal piece, esp. in opera or oratorio, formally more highly organized than a song: in the late 17th and early 18th cent. as a rule in 3 sections, the 3rd being a repetition of the 1st and the 2nd a contrasting strain (*da capo* A.); later often var. modifications of the instrumental sonata form. In the late 18th cent. arias were conventionally classified as follows:

A. all' unisono, an A. in which the voice and instrumental parts have the tune in octave unison, without harmony, at any rate so far as the comp.'s writing went, though chords may have been added by the *continuo* player at the harpsichord.

A. cantabile, an A. with a slow, sustained melody.

A. concertata, an A. making a feature of an elaborate instrumental solo part in the accomp.

A. d'agilità = *A. di bravura.*

A. d'imitazione, an A. in which either the voice or some instruments, or both, gave a more or less realistic imitation of some other mus. or non-mus. sounds.

A. di bravura, an A. containing a more than usual amount of brilliant and difficult passages.

A. di mezzo carattere, an A. 'of indeterminate character' which could be almost anything that could not be classified under any other species, but had as a rule an elaborate accomp.

A. di portamento, an A. requiring a slow and full-toned delivery and laying great stress on the display of a beautiful voice at the expense of the accomp.

A. parlante, an A. of a declamatory kind, intended less to display the voice than the singer's verbal eloquence and dramatic expression.

A. senza accompagnamento. A wholly unaccomp. A., which was very rarely used. *See also* Parable Aria.

Ariadne. *See also* **Ariane, Arianna.**

Ariadne auf Naxos, play with music (melodrama) by G. Benda (text by Johann Christian Brandes), prod. Gotha, 27. I. 1775.

Opera by R. Strauss (lib. by Hugo von Hofmannsthal), orig. a 1-act opera played after a shortened version of Molière's *Le Bourgeois gentilhomme*, with incid. mus. by S., prod. Stuttgart, 25. X. 1912; 2nd version, with a new operatic 1st act, prod. Vienna, Opera, 4. X. 1916.

Ariane et Barbe-bleue (*A. and Bluebeard*), opera by Dukas (lib. Maeterlinck's play with slight alterations), prod. Paris, Opéra-Comique, 10. V. 1907.

Ariane, ou Le Mariage de Bacchus, opera by Grabu (lib. by Pierre Perrin, previously set by Cambert), prod. London, Drury Lane Theatre, 30. III. 1674.

Arianna, opera by Marcello (lib. by Vincenzo Cassani, comp. 1727, never perf. in Marcello's lifetime; ed. by Oscar Chilesotti, 1885, prod. Venice, Liceo Benedetto Marcello, 27. IV. 1913.

Opera by Handel (lib. adapted from Pietro Pariati's *Arianna e Teseo*), prod. London, King's Theatre, Haymarket, 26. I. 1734.

Arianna, L', opera by Monteverdi (lib. by Ottavia Rinuccini), prod. Mantua, at the ducal court, for the wedding of the Hereditary Prince Francesco Gonzaga with Margherita, Princess of Savoy, 28. V. 1608.

Arianna e Teseo (*Ariadne and Theseus*), opera by Porpora (lib. by Pietro Pariati), prod. Vienna, 1. X. 1714.

Aribo Scholasticus (b. ?; d. ?), Flem. (?) 11th-cent. monk and mus. theorist. His treatise *De Musica* is important in the development of modal theory in the W., with its emphasis on melodic formulae as well as scales in the definition of mode.

Arienzo, Nicola d' (b. Naples, 23. XII. 1842; d. Naples, 25. IV. 1915), It. comp. Studied law, and secretly mus., at Naples. He first wrote operas in the Neapolitan dialect and later several others which gained a wider currency.

Arietta (It. = little air), a shorter and simpler kind of Aria, usually of a lighter character.

Ariette (Fr. = little aria or air). Now the same as an *arietta*, but in early 18th-cent. Fr. opera an elaborate aria (sometimes with Italian words) and in late 18th-cent. *opéra comique* a song introduced into a scene in dialogue. *See also* **Debussy** (*Ariettes oubliées*).

Ariodante, opera by Handel (lib. by Antonio Salvi, based on Ariosto's *Orlando furioso*), prod. London, Covent Garden Theatre, 8. I. 1735.

Arioso (It. = song-like), a vocal or instrumental piece or passage of a declamatory or recitative character, to be sung or played in a melodic manner.

Ariosti, Attilio (b. Bologna, 5. XI. 1666; d. ?, c. 1740), It. comp. Prod. his 1st opera at Venice in 1696. Court comp. in Berlin, 1697–1703. Later visited Vienna, London and Bologna.

Works incl. operas *La più gloriosa fatica d'Ercole, Amor tra nemici, La fede ne' tradimenti, Caio Marzio Coriolano, Vespasiano, Artaserse, Dario, Lucio Vero*, etc.; oratorio *Nabucodonosor*, Passion oratorio and others, cantatas, lessons for vla. d'amore, etc.

Ariosto, Lodovico (1474–1533), It. poet. *See* **Ariodante** (*Orlando furioso*, Handel), **Holmès** (do.), **Orlando** (Handel), **Purcell (D.)** (*Orlando f.*), **Roussel** (*Enchantements d'Alcine*), **Vivaldi** (*Orlando*).

Aristophanes (5th cent. B.C.), Gk. playwright. *See* **Arundell** (*Peace*), **Auric** (*Birds*), **Bantock** (*Frogs*), **Broman** (*Lysistrata*), **Commer** (*Frogs*), **Delannoy** (*Peace*), **Diepenbrock** (*Birds*), **Glière** (*Lysistrata*), **Humperdinck** (do.), **Lajtha** (do.), **Leigh** (*Frogs*), **Mohaupt** (*Lysistrata*), **Ornstein** (do.), **Paine** (*Birds*), **Parry (H.)** (do., *Frogs, Clouds* and *Acharnians*), **Sabata** (*Lysistrata*), **Vaughan Williams** (*Wasps*), **Verschworenen** (Schubert), **Vögel** (Braunfels), **Walliser** (*Clouds*).

Aristoxenus of Tarentum, Gk. philosopher of 4th cent. B.C. His treatise on *Harmonics* (i.e. acoustics and mus. theory) has the merit of being based on the mus. practice of his day rather than being purely speculative.

Arkwright, Godfrey (Edward Pellew) (b.

Norwich, 10. IV. 1864; d. Highclere, 16. VIII. 1944), Eng. mus. ed. and musicologist. Educ. at Eton and Oxford. Brought out a collection of early Eng. mus. *Old Eng. Ed.*, 1889–1902; ed. Purcell's church mus. for the complete ed., *The Musical Antiquary* and the mus. catalogue of Christ Church library, Oxford.

Arlecchino, opera in 1 act by Busoni (lib. by the comp.), prod. Zürich, 11. V. 1917.

Arlesiana, L' (*The Girl from Arles*), opera by Cilèa (lib. by Leopoldo Marenco, based on Daudet's play, *L'Arlésienne*), prod. Milan, Teatro Lirico, 27. XI. 1897.

Arlésienne, L' (*The Girl from Arles*), incid. mus. by Bizet for Alphonse Daudet's play, prod. Paris, 1. X. 1872. Bizet afterwards extracted an orchestral suite from it. (The 2nd suite was arr. by Guiraud.)

Armenian Chant, the mus. of the Church in Armenia from its estab. in 303. It pursued an independent path after the separation from the Gk. Church in 536. Its original, alphabetical notation was replaced in the 12th cent. by a neumatic system (in which the only MSS. have survived), which cannot now be deciphered. The Church's collection of hymns (the *Sharakan*) is arr. according to the 8 modes or *echoi*, apparently defined by melodic formulae rather than by scale.

Armida, opera by Anfossi (lib. by Jacopo Durandi, based on Tasso's *Gerusalemme liberata*) prod. Turin, Teatro Regio, Carnival 1770.

Opera by Dvořák (lib. by Jaroslav Vrchlický, based on his Cz. trans. of Tasso), prod. Prague, Cz. Theatre, 25. III. 1904.

Opera by Haydn (lib. by Jacopo Durandi), prod. Esterház, 26. II. 1784.

Opera by Mysliveček (lib. by Giovanni Ambrogio Migliavacca, an It. version of Quinault), prod. Milan, Teatro alla Scala, 26. XII. 1779.

Opera by Naumann (lib. by Giovanni Bertati, based on Tasso), prod. Padua, VI. 1773.

Opera by Rossini (lib. by Giovanni Schmidt, after Tasso), prod. Naples, Teatro San Carlo, 11. XI. 1817.

Opera by Sacchini (lib. by Giovanni de Gamerra), prod. Milan, Teatro Regio Ducal, Carnival 1772.

Opera by Salieri (lib. by Marco Coltellini, based on Tasso), prod. Vienna, Burgtheater, 2. VI. 1771.

Opera by Traetta (lib. by Count Giacomo Durazzo, based on Quinault), prod. Vienna, Burgtheater, 3. I. 1761.

Armide, opera by Gluck (lib. by Quinault, based on Tasso's *Gerusalemme liberata*), prod. Paris, Opéra, 23. IX. 1777.

Opera by Lully (lib. do.), prod. Paris, Opéra, 15. II. 1686.

Arminio, opera by Handel (lib. by

Antonio Salvi), prod. London, Covent Garden Theatre, 12. I. 1737.

2 operas by Hasse: I. (lib. by Giovanni Claudio Pasquini), prod. Dresden, at court, 7. X. 1745; II. (lib. by Antonio Salvi), prod. Milan, 28. VIII. 1730.

Opera by A. Scarlatti (lib. by Salvi), prod. Villa Medici, Pratolino, IX. 1703.

Armonica, an instrument also called Glass Harmonica, the notes of which are prod. by friction on a series of tuned glasses, either with the fingers or mechanically.

Armourer of Nantes, The, opera by Balfe (lib. by John Vipon Bridgeman, based on Victor Hugo's *Marie Tudor*), prod. London, Covent Garden Theatre, 12. II. 1863.

Armstrong, Thomas (Henry Wait) (b. Peterborough, 15. VI. 1898), Eng. organist, cond., teacher and comp. Studied under Keeton at Peterborough Cathedral, where he became asst. organist in 1913. Subsequently at Keble Coll., Oxford (1916), Manchester Cathedral (1922), St. Peter's Eaton Sq., London (1923) and Exeter Cathedral (1928). From 1933 to 1955 he was organist of Christ Church, Oxford. Principal of the R.A.M. in London 1955–68. Knighted, 1958.

Works incl. church mus., songs, part-songs, etc.

Arnaut, Henricus of Zwolle. *See* **Zwolle.**

Arne, Michael (b. London, 1741; d. London, 14. I. 1786), Eng. singer and comp., illegitimate (?) son of Thomas Augustine A. He made his first appearance as a singer in 1750, and a collection of songs, *The Flow'ret*, was pub. the same year. In 1761 he prod. his 1st opera, *Edgar and Emmeline*. He also collaborated with other comps. in the prod. of works for the stage, e.g. *A Midsummer Night's Dream* (with Burney and others, 1763) and *Almena* (with Battishill, 1764). He married the singer Elizabeth Wright on 5. XI. 1766, and the next year wrote the mus. for Garrick's *Cymon*, his most successful work. In 1771–2 he toured Ger., where he cond. the first Ger. perf. of *Messiah*. He was also interested in alchemy, his search for the 'philosophers' stone' twice ruined him.

Arne, Susanna Maria (b. London, II. 1714; d. London, 30. I. 1766), Eng. singer and actress, sister of Thomas Augustine A. First appeared on the London stage in 1732. Married Theophilus Cibber in 1734, and sang under her married name.

Arne, Thomas Augustine (b. London, 12. III. 1710; d. London, 5. III. 1778), Eng. comp. He was educ. at Eton and intended for the law, but practised secretly on a muffled harpsichord and learnt the vln. from Festing, until his father at length allowed him to make music his career. He also taught his sister Susanna singing, and she appeared in his first opera, a setting of

Addison's *Rosamund*, in 1733. Many successful works for the stage followed, incl. *Alfred*, containing 'Rule, Britannia', which was prod. at the residence of Frederick, Prince of Wales, at Cliveden in 1740. He married the singer Cecilia Young in 1736. In 1742–4 he and his wife worked successfully in Dublin, which they twice revisited in the 1750s. In 1745 A. was app. comp. to Vauxhall Gardens. D.Mus. Oxford, 1759. In 1760, after a quarrel with Garrick, he gave up his post as comp. to Drury Lane Theatre and went over to Covent Garden, where in 1762 he prod. his opera *Artaxerxes*, trans. by himself from Metastasio and comp. in the It. manner. Two years later he set the same librettist's *Olimpiade* in the orig. language.

Works incl. operas and plays with mus.: *Rosamond, The Opera of Operas, or Tom Thumb the Great* (adapted from Fielding), *Love and Glory, The Fall of Phaeton, An Hospital for Fools, The Blind Beggar of Bethnal Green, Eliza, Britannia, The Temple of Dullness, King Pepin's Campaign, Harlequin's Incendiary, or Columbine, The Triumph of Peace, Henry and Emma* (after M. Prior), *Don Saverio, The Prophetess, Thomas and Sally, Artaxerxes, Love in a Village, The Birth of Hercules, The Guardian Outwitted, L'Olimpiade, The Ladies' Frolic, The Fairy Prince, Squire Badger* (later *The Sot*), *The Cooper, The Rose, Achilles in Petticoats, May Day, Phoebe at Court*; masques *Dido and Aeneas, Comus* (Milton adapted by Dalton), *The Judgment of Paris, Alfred*; incid. mus. to Aaron Hill's *Zara*, Shakespeare's *As You Like It, Twelfth Night, The Merchant of Venice, The Tempest, Romeo and Juliet, Cymbeline*, Mason's *Elfrida* and *Caractacus*; oratorios *The Death of Abel* and *Judith*; *Ode on Cheerfulness, Ode to Shakespeare*; *c.* 25 books of songs; Masses and motets; 8 overtures for orch.; 6 concertos for keyboard (org. or harpsichord); 7 sonatas for 2 vlns. and bass; 8 harpsichord sonatas, etc.

Arneiro, José Augusto Ferreira Veiga d' (b. Macao, China, 22. XI. 1838; d. San Remo, VII. 1903), Port. comp.

Works incl. operas *Elisir di giovinezza, La derelitta* (after Ann Radcliffe) and *Don Bibas*; ballet *Gina*; Te Deum and other church mus., etc.

Arnell, Richard (Anthony Sayer) (b. London, 15. IX. 1917), Eng. comp. Studied with John Ireland at the R.C.M. in London and took the Farra Prize in 1938. From 1939 to 1947 he lived in N.Y., where he was consultant to the B.B.C.'s N. Amer. service, composed much and pub. some comps.

Works incl. ballets *Punch and the Child, Harlequin in April* and *The Great Detective* (after Conan Doyle); film mus.; 5 symphs.,

symph. poem *Lord Byron* and other orchestral mus.; vln. concerto; 2 string 4tets; pf. and org. mus., etc.

Arnold, F(ranck). T(homas). (b. Rugby, 6. IX. 1861; d. Bath, 24. IX. 1940), Eng. musicologist. Educ. at Rugby and Cambridge; app. lecturer in Ger. at Cardiff Univ. Made a special study of the practice of writing and playing from thorough-bass, on which he wrote for var. periodicals and pub. a large treatise in 1931.

Arnold, J(ohn). H(enry). (b. London, 29. V. 1887; d. Stanmore, 19. VI. 1956), Eng. scholar and organist. Educ. at Dulwich Coll. and studied mus. with M. Shaw and Harvey Grace. He was organist at 2 London churches and made a special study of plainsong and its application to the service of the Church of Eng. He wrote papers and books on the subject, ed. services and wrote org. accomps. to plainsong.

Arnold, Malcolm (Henry) (b. Northampton, 21. X. 1921), Eng. trumpeter and comp. Studied at the R.C.M. in London with a scholarship, 1938–41, then joined the London Phil. Orch. becoming 1st trumpet in 1942. In 1945 he became 2nd trumpet of the B.B.C. Symph. Orch., rejoining the London Phil. Orch. as principal in 1946. He has since taken up the career of a full-time comp. Hon. D. Mus., Exeter, 1970.

Works incl. ballet *Solitaire*; incid. mus. for Shakespeare's *Tempest*; overture *Beckus the Dandipratt* for orch.; symph. for strings; 4 symphs.; concertos for horn, clar., ob., pf. duet and mouth organ; vln. and pf. sonata, vla. and pf. sonata; pf. works, etc.

Arnold, Matthew (1822–88), Eng. poet and critic. *See* **Barber** (*Dover Beach*), **Somervell** (*Forsaken Merman*), **Vaughan Williams** (*Oxford Elegy*).

Arnold, Samuel (b. London, 10. VIII. 1740; d. London, 22. X. 1802), Eng. comp. Chorister at the Chapel Royal under Gates and Nares; was engaged by Beard as comp. to Covent Garden Theatre in 1765, where he prod. the *pasticcio, The Maid of the Mill*, that year. Ed. a collection of *Cathedral Music* and the works of Handel. D.Mus., Oxford, 1773, and organist of the Chapel Royal, 1783. Founder of the Glee Club with Callcott in 1787. Organist of Westminster Abbey, 1793.

Works incl. operas and plays with mus.: *The Maid of the Mill, The Portrait, The Castle of Andalusia, Gretna Green, Peeping Tom of Coventry, Inkle and Yarica, The Enraged Musician* (on Hogarth's picture), *The Surrender of Calais, Harlequin, Dr. Faustus, The Mountaineers, The Shipwreck, Obi, or Three-fingered Jack* and many others; oratorios *Elisha, The Cure of Saul, The Resurrection, The Prodigal Son*; church mus.; overture for orch.; odes for chorus; harpsichord mus; songs, etc.

Arnold von Bruck. *See* **Bruck.**

Arnoldson, Sigrid (b. Stockholm, 20. III. 1861; d. Stockholm, 7. II. 1943), Swed. soprano. Daughter of the tenor Oscar A. Studied with Maurice Strakosch and Désirée Artôt-Padilla, made her 1st stage appearance at Prague, 1885, and 1st appeared in London, 1887.

Arnould, Madeleine Sophie (b. Paris, 14. II. 1740; d. Paris, 18. X. 1802), Fr. soprano and actress. She made her début in 1757. Sang Iphigenia in the first perf. of Gluck's *Iphigénie en Aulide* in Paris, 1774, and Eurydice in the Fr. version of his *Orfeo* the same year.

Arnt von Aich. *See* **Aich.**

Aron, Pietro. *See* **Aaron.**

Arpeggio (It. *arpeggiare*, to play the harp), the notes of a chord played in rapid succession, either in regular time (as in instrumental and vocal exercises) or freely as an interpretation of the foll. sign:

played approximately:

Arpeggione, a 6-stringed instrument invented by G. Staufer of Vienna in 1823; a hybrid between a cello and a guitar, played with a bow and with a fretted fingerboard. Schubert wrote a sonata for it in 1824.

Arpicordo (It. = Harpsichord), another and much rarer It. name for the harpsichord.

Arquimbau, Domingo (b. ?; d. Seville, 1829), Span. comp. Mus. director of Seville Cathedral, 1795–1829. Wrote a Mass, motets and sacred *villancicos*.

Arrangement, an adaptation of a mus. work for some other medium than that orig. intended by the comp.

Arras, Andrieu Contredit d' (b. Arras, *c.* 1180; d. Arras, 1284), troubadour poet and musician, 18 of whose songs survive.

Arrau, Claudio (b. Chillan, 6. II. 1903), Chilean pianist. First played in public aged 5, and in 1910 was sent to study in Berlin, where he settled from 1925 to 1940. Since 1941 he has lived in the U.S.A. He is best known for his perfs. of the classical pf. repertory.

Arregui Garay, Vicente (b. Madrid, 3. VII. 1871; d. Madrid, 2. XII. 1925), Span. comp. Studied at Madrid, Rome and Paris. Later mus. critic of *El Dabete* in Madrid.
Works incl. opera *Yolanda* (after Hertz's

King René's Daughter); oratorio *San Francisco*; symph. poem, *Historia de una madre* (after Hans Andersen) and *Sinfonia vasca* for orch.; string 4tet., pf. sonata, etc.

Arresti, Giulio Cesare (b. Bologna, 1617; d. Bologna, 1692), It. organist and comp. Pupil of Vernizzi at Bologna Cathedral, where he was afterwards organist and *maestro di cappella*. Wrote church and chamber mus.

Arriaga y Balzola, Juan Crisóstomo Antonio (b. Bilbao, 27. I. 1806; d. Paris, 17. I. 1826), Span. violinist and comp. Played and comp. as a child and was sent to the Paris Cons. in 1821. His early death cut short a remarkable career.

Arrieta y Corera, (Pascual Juan) Emilio (b. Puente la Reina, Navarre, 21. X. 1823; d. Madrid, 11. II. 1894), Span. comp. Studied under Vaccai at the Milan Cons. and prod. his 1st opera there in 1845, returning to Spain the following year. Prof. of comp. at the Madrid Cons. from 1857 and director from 1868.

Works incl. It. operas *Ildegonda*, *La conquista di Granada*, *Isabella la catolica*; zarzuelas *El dómino azul*, *El grumete*, *La Estrella de Madrid*, *Marina* and *c.* 50 others, etc.

Arrigoni, Carlo (b. Florence, 5. XII. 1697; d. Florence, 19. VIII. 1744), It. lutenist and comp. Gave concerts with Sammartini in London 1732–3, and pub. *10 Cantate da camera* there in 1732.

Arrigoni, Giovanni Giacomo (b. ?; d. ?), It. 17th-cent. organist and comp. Organist at the Viennese court under Ferdinand II and III. Wrote vocal chamber concertos, madrigals and church mus.

Arroyo, João (Marcellino) (b. Oporto, 4. X. 1861; d. Quinta de Casal, 18. V. 1930), Port. comp. Studied at Oporto and Coimbra and was minister of arts and public educ. under King Manoel. Works incl. operas *O amor de Perdição* and *Leonor Tellez*; *Poème symphonique* for orch., etc.

Ars antiqua (Lat. = old art), mus. of the late 12th and 13th cents., before the intro. of the *ars nova* in the 14th cent. A term originally used by 14th-cent. writers of the mus. immediately preceding their own time.

Ars nova (Lat. = new art), the title of a treatise ascribed to Philippe de Vitry (1291–1361). It is now applied to all 14th-cent. mus., both Fr. and It., which was characterized by a greater freedom of rhythm and the increasing use of smaller note-values.

Arsinoë, Queen of Cyprus, opera or pasticcio ? by Clayton (lib. by Peter Anthony Motteux from the It. by Tommaso Stanzani), prod. London, Drury Lane Theatre, 16. I. 1705.

Arsis. *See* **Metre.**

Art of Fugue, The. *See* **Kunst der Fuge.**

Artamene, opera by Albinoni (lib. by

Bartolomeo Vitturi), prod. Venice, Teatro di Sant' Angelo, 26. XII. 1740.

Opera by Gluck (lib. do.), prod. London, King's Theatre, Haymarket, 4. III. 1746.

Artaria, Viennese firm of mus. pubs. Prominent in the pub. of works by Haydn, Mozart and Beethoven.

Artaserse (*Artaxerxes*), opera by Abos (lib. by Metastasio), prod. Venice, Teatro di San Giovanni Crisostomo, Carnival 1746.

Opera by Gluck (lib. do.), prod. Milan, Teatro Regio Ducal, 26. XII. 1741. Gluck's 1st opera.

Opera by Graun (lib. do.), prod. Berlin, Opera, 2. XII. 1743.

Opera by Hasse (lib. do.), prod. Venice, Teatro San Giovanni Crisostomo, II. 1730.

Opera by Jommelli (lib. do.), prod. Rome, Teatro Argentina, 4. II. 1749.

Opera by Terradellas (lib. do.), prod. Venice, Teatro San Giovanni Crisostomo, Carnival 1744.

Opera by Vinci (lib. do.), prod. Rome, Teatro delle Dame, 4. II. 1730.

Artaxerxes, opera by Arne (lib. by comp., trans. from Metastasio's *Artaserse*), prod. London, Covent Garden Theatre, 2. II. 1762.

Arteaga, Esteban (b. Moraleja (Segovia), 26. XII. 1747; d. Paris, 30. X. 1799), Span. scholar. He was a Jesuit priest, but after the suppression of the Order went to It. where he worked for many years with Padre Martini in Bologna. 5 treatises on mus. survive, the most important of them being that on opera, *Rivoluzioni del teatro musicale italiano*, pub. 1733–8.

Arthur, Fanny. *See* Robinson, Joseph.

Arthurian Legends, the epic 12th–13th-cent. cycle of Brit. tales, written in medieval Fr. *See* Albéniz (I.), Boughton, Draeseke (*Merlin*), Ladmirault (*Tristan et Iseult*), Lancelot and Elaine (MacDowell), Martin (F.) (*Vin herbé* on *Tristram and Yseult*), Marty (*Merlin enchanté*), Sessions (*Lancelot and Elaine*), Steggall (*Elaine*), Tristan und Isolde (Wagner).

Artôt, (Marguerite Joséphine) Désirée (Montagney) (b. Paris, 21. VII. 1835; d. Berlin, 3. IV. 1907), Belg. mezzo-soprano. Pupil of Pauline Viardot-García. First sang at concerts in Belg., Hol. and Eng., but joined the Paris Opéra in 1858. Later appeared in It., Ger. and Rus. Married Mariano Padilla in 1869.

Arts Council of Great Britain, a nat. organization formed in 1940 as the Council for the Encouragement of Mus. and the Arts (CEMA), whose charter was renewed under the new title, 9. VIII. 1946.

Artsibushev, Nikolai Vassilievich (b. Tsarskoie Selo, 7. III. 1858; d. Paris, 15. IV. 1937), Rus. comp. and lawyer. Pupil of Rimsky-Korsakov and from 1920 Paris director of Belaiev's mus. pub. firm.

Works incl. *Valse-Fantasia* for orch.;

serenade for string 4tet.; pf. mus., songs, etc.

Artusi, Giovanni Maria (b. *c.* 1540; d. Bologna, 18. VIII. 1613), It. comp. and theorist. His 4-part canzonets appeared in 1598, and his *L'Arte del Contrapunto* in 1586–9. Apart from his polemical works against Zarlino, Galilei and Bottrigari, his *L'Artusi, overo delle Imperfettioni della musica moderna* (1600) singles out 9 as yet unpub. madrigals by Monteverdi for special attack, to which the comp. replied in the preface to his 5th book of madrigals (1605). Here he promised a treatise, never completed, to be entitled *Seconda Prattica overo delle perfettioni della moderna musica*, in contradistinction to the 'Prima prattica' of the conservatives. The controversy was continued in two more works by A., pub. under a pseud. (1606 and 1608), and by Monteverdi's brother Giulio Cesare in the preface to the *Scherzi musicali* of 1607.

Arundell, Dennis (b. London, 22. VII. 1898), Eng. actor, producer and comp. Educated at Tonbridge School and Cambridge, he prod. many operas and mus. plays, trans. several It. and Fr. libs. and wrote a book on Purcell (1927).

Works incl. operas *Ghost of Abel* (after Blake) and *A Midsummer Night's Dream* (after Shakespeare); mus. plays *The Scarlet Pimpernel* (after d'Orczy); incid. mus. for Sophocles, *Electra*, Aristophanes, *Peace*, Shakespeare, *Tempest*, Congreve, *Love for Love*, Sheridan, *St. Patrick's Day*, Shaw, *St. Joan*, Flecker, *Don Juan*, A. P. Herbert, *King of the Castle*, and Priestley, *Ever since Paradise*; film and broadcast mus., etc.

Asbjørnsen, Peter Christen (1812–85), Dan. folklore collector and author. *See* Delius (*Eventyr*).

Ascanio in Alba, opera by Mozart (lib. by Giuseppe Parini), prod. Milan, Teatro Regio Ducal, 17. X. 1771.

Ashton, Algernon (Bennet Langton) (b. Durham, 9. XII. 1859; d. London, 10. IV. 1937), Eng. comp. Son of a lay clerk at Durham Cathedral. He entered the Leipzig Cons. in 1875 and studied with Raff at Frankfurt in 1880–1. Prof. of pf. at the R.A.M. in London, 1885–1910. Comp. a vast amount, esp. chamber mus.

Ashwell, Thomas (Ashewell, Hashewell) (b. ?; d. ?), Eng. comp. In 1508 he was appointed *informator choristarum*, Lincoln Cathedral, and in 1513 to the equivalent post in Durham. His surviving works consist of four Masses, two (*God save King Henry* and *Sancte Cuthberte*) in a fragmentary state and two (*Ave Maria* and *Jesu Christe*) complete.

Asioli, Bonifazio (b. Correggio, 30. VIII. 1769; d. Correggio, 18. V. 1832), It. mus. scholar and comp. Worked in his native town at the beginning and end of his career, but in between was at Turin, Venice, Milan and Paris. Wrote much church, stage, vocal and instrumental mus. and several theoret. treatises.

Asola, Giovanni Matteo (b. Verona, *c.* 1560; d. Venice, 1. X. 1609), It. priest and comp. *Maestro di cappella* successively at Treviso (1578) and Vicenza (1581). Wrote church mus., madrigals, etc.

Aspelmayr, Franz (b. Vienna, 1728; d. Vienna, 29. VII. 1786), Aus. comp. attached to the Viennese court.
Works incl. melodrama *Pygmalion* (after Rousseau), *Singspiele*, ballets, symphs., chamber mus., etc.

Aspiration (Fr.). *See* **Ornaments.**

Asproys (Hasprois), Johannes (b. ?; d. ?), Fr. comp., one of the singers of the antipope at Avignon in 1394. Some of his *chansons* are in an early 15th-cent. MS now at Oxford, Bodleian Library, Canonici misc. 213.

Assafiev, Boris Vladimirovich (b. St. Petersburg, 29. VII. 1884; d. Moscow, 27. I. 1949), Rus. comp. and critic. Studied philosophy at St. Petersburg Univ. and mus. at the Cons., where he later became prof. Author of numerous books on comps., incl. Glinka, Tchaikovsky, Skriabin and Stravinsky, on Rus. and Cz. mus., etc., written under the name of Igor Glebov.
Works incl. 9 operas, e.g. *Cinderella*, *The Treasurer's Wife* (after Lermontov), *The Storm* (after Ostrovsky), *A Feast in Time of Plague* (Pushkin), *The Brass Horseman* (Pushkin); 27 ballets incl. *Solveig* (based on Grieg), *The Fountain of Bakhchisserai* (after Pushkin), *Lost Illusions* (after Balzac), *The Beauty is happy* (after Gorky's story *Makar Chudra*), *Christmas Eve* (after Gogol); incid. mus. to Shakespeare's *Macbeth*, *Merchant of Venice* and *Othello*, Tirso de Molina's *Seducer of Seville* (*Don Juan*), Sophocles' *Oedipus Rex*, Schiller's *Fiesco* and *Don Carlos*; 4 symphs., sinfonietta for orch., Suvarov Suite for wind instruments; pf. concerto; string 4tet; vla. solo sonata, sonata for tpt. and pf.; 6 Arias for cello and pf.; pf. works; choruses; songs, etc.

Assai (It.) = much, very.

Assmayr, Ignaz (b. Salzburg, 11. II. 1790; d. Vienna, 31. VIII. 1862), Aus. organist and comp. Held several organist's posts at Salzburg and Vienna, was cond. of the Vienna Mus. Society and wrote oratorios and much church and other mus.

Astaritta, Gennaro (b. Naples, *c.* 1745; d. ?, 1803), It. comp. of *c.* 40 operas, 1765–93, incl. the popular *Circe ed Ulisse*.

Astarto, opera by G. Bononcini (lib. by Paolo Antonio Rolli, based on one by Zeno and Pietro Pariati), prod. London, King's Theatre, Haymarket, 19. XI. 1720.

Aston, Hugh (b. ?, *c.* 1480; d. ?, 1549 or after), Eng. comp. He took the B.Mus. at Oxford, 1510, and was *magister choristarum* at Newarke College, Leicester, 1525–1548. His works include 6 votive antiphons and 2 Masses, the 'Hornepype' for keyboard, and possibly other keyboard mus. also. There are comps. on a ground bass of his by Whytbroke (for viols) and Byrd (for keyboard).

Astorga, Emanuele (Gioacchino Cesare Rincón) d' (b. Augusta, Sicily, 20. III. 1680; d. Lisbon or Madrid, 1757), It. nobleman and comp. of Span. descent. His only opera, *Dafni*, was prod. in Genoa and Barcelona in 1709. His most famous work is a *Stabat Mater*. He also comp. a number of chamber cantatas. From *c.* 1721 he seems to have lived mainly in Spain and Port.

Astuzie femminili, Le (*Women's Wiles*), opera by Cimarosa (lib. by Giovanni Palomba), prod. Naples, Teatro del Fondo, 16. VIII. 1794.

At the Boar's Head, opera by Holst (lib. by comp., drawn from Shakespeare's *Henry IV*), prod. Manchester, 3. IV. 1925.

At the Old Bleaching-Ground (*Na Starém Bělidle*), opera by Kovařovic (lib. by Karel Šipek, based on Božena Němcová's novel *Babička*), prod. Prague, Cz. Theatre, 22. XI. 1901. An opera on the same subject, *Babička* (*Grandmother*), by Antonín Horák (1875–1910), was prod. at the same theatre, 3. III. 1900.

Atalanta, opera by Handel (lib. adapted from *La caccia in Etolia* by Belisario Valeriani), prod. London, Covent Garden Theatre, 12. V. 1736.

Atfield, John (b. ?; d. ?), Eng. 18th-cent. comp. Wrote songs pub. between 1735 and 1750.

Athalia, oratorio by Handel (words by Samuel Humphreys), prod. Oxford, 10. VII. 1733.

Athalie, incid. mus. for Racine's tragedy by Mendelssohn, Op. 74; choruses comp. 1843, overture 1844–5, prod. Charlottenburg, 1. XII. 1845.
The choruses were also set by Moreau (Saint-Cyr, 5. I. 1691), Gossec (1785), Vogler (1786), J. A. P. Schulz (1786) and Boïeldieu (1836).
See also **Clément (Félix)** and **Cohen.**

Atonality, a modern term for mus. not written in a specific key.

Attacca (It. imper. = attack, begin), a direction placed at the end of a movement indicating that the next movement is to be started without a pause.

Attacco (It. = attack), a short mus. figure or phrase treated by imitation.

Attaingnant, Pierre (b. ?; d. Paris, 1552), Fr. 16th-cent. mus. printer. He pub. many important mus. books between 1525 and his death, and his widow (*née* Pigouchet), whose father he had succeeded, continued after 1553.

Attaque du moulin, L' (*The Attack on the Mill*), opera by Bruneau (lib. by Louis Gallet, based on Zola's story in *Soirées de Médan*), prod. Paris, Opéra-Comique, 23. XI. 1893.

Attenhofer, Karl (b. Wettingen, Aargau, 5. V. 1837; d. Zürich, 22. V. 1914), Swiss cond. and comp. Studied at the Leipzig Cons. and later became a choral cond. at Rapperswil and Zürich and organizer of nat. singing festivals. Joint director with Hegar of the Zürich Cons. from 1896. Wrote numerous popular part-songs for male and mixed voices, also some church and chamber mus.

Atterberg, Kurt (Magnus) (b. Göteborg, 12. XII. 1887), Swed. comp. and cond. First trained as a civil engineer, he studied mus. at the R.A.M. in Stockholm under Hallén, and later at Munich, Berlin and Stuttgart. Mus. critic of *Stockholms Tidningen* since 1919. Has cond. much in Swed., Fr. and Ger.

Works incl. 5 operas; pantomime-ballets; incid. mus. for plays; Requiem, *Järnbäraland* (*The Land of Iron-Carriers*), for chorus and orch.; 9 symphs. (1 in memory of Schubert), 9 suites, *Swed. Rhapsody*, symph. poem *Le Fleuve, Rondeau rétrospectif* and *The Song* for orch.; symph. poem for baritone and orch.; concertos for vln., cello, pf. and horn; 3 string 4tets; cello and pf. sonata, etc.

Atterbury, Luffman (b. ? London, ?; d. London, 11. VI. 1796), Eng. comp. Orig. a carpenter; became musician to George III. He wrote many glees and catches, also an oratorio, *Goliath*, prod. in 1773.

Attey, John (b. ?; d. ?), Eng. comp. His vol. of 'Ayres' (1622) marks the virtual end of the lute-song in Eng.

Attila, opera by Verdi (lib. by Temistocle Solera), prod. Venice, Teatro La Fenice, 17. III. 1846.

Attwood, Thomas (b. London, 23. XI. 1765; d. London, 24. III. 1838), Eng. organist and comp. He was a chorister at the Chapel Royal; later studied in Naples and Vienna, where he was a pupil of Mozart 1785–7. Organist of St. Paul's Cathedral and comp. to the Chapel Royal from 1796 to his death. One of the orig. members of the Phil. Society in 1813, and a prof. at the R.A.M. on its foundation in 1823. He was also a friend of Mendelssohn, whose 3 Preludes and Fugues for org., Op. 37, were dedicated to him.

Works incl. over 30 dramatic comps.; coronation anthems for George IV and William IV, service settings, anthems and other church mus.; songs, etc. His harmony and counterpoint exercises for Mozart also survive, with Mozart's corrections.

Atys, opera by Lully (lib. by Philippe Quinault), prod. at Saint-Germain, 10. I., and 1st perf. Paris, IV. 1676.

Opera by Piccinni (lib. do., altered by Jean François Marmontel), prod. Paris, Opéra, 22. II. 1780.

Aubade (Fr. from *aube* = dawn) = morning song, in the same sense that a serenade is an evening song; cf. Span. *Alborada*.

Auber, Daniel François Esprit (b. Caen, 29. I. 1782; d. Paris, 12. V. 1871), Fr. comp, Began to comp. early, but went to London as a young man to follow a commercial career. He attracted attention with his songs, however, and on his return to Paris in 1804 wrote cello concertos for the cellist Lamarre and a vln. concerto for Mazas. In 1805 he appeared with a comic opera, *L'Erreur d'un moment*, the lib. of which had previously been set by Dezède, but did not prod. an opera in public until 1813 (*Le Séjour militaire*) and had no real success until 1820 (*La Bergère châtelaine*). In 1842 he became director of the Paris Cons. and in 1857 of the Imp. chapel.

Works incl. nearly 50 operas incl. *Emma, Leicester, Le Maçon, La Muette de Portici* (*Masaniello*), *La Fiancée, Fra Diavolo, Le Dieu et la Bayadère, Le Philtre, Le Serment, Gustave III, Le Cheval de bronze* (2 versions), *Actéon, L'Ambassadrice, Le Domino noir, Les Diamants de la couronne, La Part du diable, Haydée, Marco Spada* (with a later ballet version), *Jenny Bell, Manon Lescaut, La Circassienne*, etc.

Aubert, Jacques (b. 30. IX. 1689; d. 17 or 18. V. 1753), Fr. violinist and comp. Pupil of Senaillé; member of the king's 24 vlns. from 1727 and of the Paris Opéra orch. from 1728. Wrote numerous vln. concertos, concert suites and other instrumental works.

Aubert, Louis (b. Paris, 15. V. 1720; d. ? Paris, *c.* 1800), Fr. violinist and comp., son of prec. He was violinist and 2nd cond. at the Paris Opéra, 1731–74. Wrote sonatas and other works for his instrument.

Aubert, Louis (François Marie) (b. Paramé, Ille-et-Vilaine, 19. II. 1877; d. Paris, 10. I. 1968), Fr. pianist, comp., critic and teacher. Studied at the Paris Cons., finally under Fauré.

Works incl. opera *La Forêt bleue*; ballets *La Momie* and *Chrysothémis*; incid. mus. for Jean Bertheroy's *La Moisson*; some church mus.; symph. poem *Habanera*; *Fantaisie* for pf. and orch.; *Suite brève* for 2 pfs. (later orch.); pf. suite *Sillages*; song cycle *Crépuscules d'automne*, etc.

Aubin, Tony (Louis Alexandre) (b. Paris, 8. XII. 1907), Fr. comp. Studied at the Paris Cons., where Dukas was his comp. master. Took the Prix de Rome in 1930. In 1939 he was app. head of the mus. dept. of

the Paris-Mondial radio station and in 1946 prof. at the Paris Cons.
Works incl. suite *Cressida* for solo voices, chorus and orch.; cantata *Actéon*; *Symphonie romantique* and *Le Sommeil d'Iskander* for orch.; string 4tet; sonata and *Prélude, Récitatif et Final* for pf.; 6 Verlaine songs, etc.

Aubry, Pierre (b. Paris, 14. II. 1874; d. Dieppe, 31. VIII. 1910), Fr. musicologist and orientalist. Lectured on mus. hist. at the École des Hautes Études Sociales in Paris; wrote several works on medieval mus., esp. that of the troubadours.

Aucassin et Nicolete, a 13th-cent. Fr. narrative in prose and verse. Its verse sections show a technique similar to that employed in the *chanson de geste*, in that each pair of lines is sung to the same tune constantly repeated, each section being rounded off by a single line sung to a different tune. Its alternation between prose and verse, however, classifies it as a *chante-fable*.

Aucassin et Nicolette, ou Les Mœurs du bon vieux temps, opera by Grétry (lib. by Jean Michel Sedaine, based on the Fr. 13th-cent. tale), prod. Versailles, at court, 30. XII. 1779, 1st Paris perf., Comédie-Italienne, 3. I. 1780.
See also **Fickenscher, Le Flem, Lyon, Parker (C.), Rossellini.**

Aucassin og Nicolette, opera by Enna (lib. in Dan., by Sophus Michaelis, based on the Fr. 13th-cent. tale), prod. Copenhagen, 2. II. 1896.

Audefroi le Bastart (b. ?; d. ?), N. Fr. poet and musician of the 12th and 13th cents., 10 of whose love-songs and 6 of whose romances have come down to us.

Auden, W(ystan). H(ugh). (b. 1907), Eng. poet. *See* Britten (*Paul Bunyan, Ascent of F.6, Ode to St. Cecilia, Our Hunting Fathers* and *On this Island*), **Henze** (*Elegy for Young Lovers*), **Stravinsky** (*Rake's Progress*).

Audran, Edmond (b. Lyons, 11. IV. 1842; d. Tierceville, 17. VIII. 1901), Fr. comp. Studied at Niedermeyer's school in Paris and 1st made his mark as a church organist and comp. at Marseilles and Paris, prod. a Mass; but later with operettas, the 1st of which, *L'Ours et le Pacha*, was prod. at Marseilles in 1862. The 1st prod. in Paris (1879) was *Les Noces d'Olivette*. Others incl. *La Mascotte, Gillette de Narbonne* (based on Boccaccio), *La Cigale et la Fourmi* (based on La Fontaine), *La Poupée, Monsieur Lohengrin*, etc.

Auer, Leopold (b. Veszprém, 7. VI. 1845; d. Loschwitz, 17. VII. 1930), Hung. violinist. Pupil of Dont in Vienna and Joachim at Hanover. Prof. at the St. Petersburg Cons. from 1868. Went to U.S.A. after the Rus. Revolution.

Aufforderung zum Tanz (*Invitation to the Dance*), a pf. piece by Weber, Op. 65, which he calls a *rondeau brillant*, in waltz form with a slow intro. and epilogue, comp. in 1819.

Aufgesang (Ger. = Fore-song). *See* **Bar.**

Aufstieg und Fall der Stadt Mahagonny (*Rise and Fall of the City of Mahagonny*), opera by Weill (lib. by Brecht), prod. Leipzig, 9. III. 1930.

Auftakt (Ger.) = Upbeat.

Auftrittslied (Ger. = entry song), a song or air in a mus. play or opera, esp. a Ger. *Singspiel*, by which a character introduces and describes himself to the audience, either directly or by addressing another character or characters; e.g. Papageno's 1st song in Mozart's *Die Zauberflöte*.

Augenarzt, Der (*The Oculist*), opera by Gyrowetz (lib. by Johann Emanuel Veith), prod. Vienna, Kärntnertortheater, 1. X. 1811.

Augmentation, the enlargement of a mus. figure or phrase by lengthening, usually doubling, the note-values.

Augmented, said of intervals normally 'perfect' (4ths, 5ths, 8ves) or 'major' (2nds, 3rds, 6ths, 7ths) which have been made wider by a semitone:

Perfect 4th   Augmented 4th

Major 6th   Augmented 6th

Aulen, Johannes (b. ?; d. ?), Ger. 15th-cent. comp. of a motet printed by Petrucci in 1505 and of a Mass, called 'Officium Auleni' in some MSS.

Auletta, Pietro (b. Sant' Angelo a Scala nr. Avellino, 1698; d. Naples, 1771), It. comp. He made his début as an opera comp. at Naples in 1725 with *Il trionfo d'amore*, in which year he also received the title of *maestro di cappella* to the Prince of Belvedere. Several comic and then some serious operas followed. His most popular work, *Orazio* (1737), eventually became debased into a pasticcio by the addition of mus. by other comps., and was pub. in Paris as *Il maestro di musica* in 1753 under the name of Pergolesi.

Aulin, Tor (b. Stockholm, 10. IX. 1866; d. Stockholm, 1. III. 1914), Swed. violinist, cond. and comp. He founded a string 4tet in 1887 and became leader of the Royal Opera orch. at Stockholm in 1889. Wrote 3 vln. concertos, many smaller pieces for vln. and miscellaneous works.

Aulos, an ancient Gk. double-reed instrument, the equivalent of the Lat.

tibia and akin to the modern ob. The double A. often seen in pictures and sculpture would have enabled the melody to be accompanied by a drone.

Aurelian of Réomé. *See* **Réomé.**

Aureliano in Palmira, opera by Rossini (lib. by Felice Romani), prod. Milan, Teatro alla Scala, 26. XII. 1813. The overture was afterwards used for *Elisabetta regina d'Inghilterra*, and later for *Il barbiere di Siviglia*. Other parts of the mus. also appear in the latter work.

Auric, Georges (b. Lodève, Hérault, 15. II. 1899), Fr. comp. Studied at the Paris Cons. and the Schola Cantorum. Member of the group of 'Les Six' and influenced by Satie and later by Stravinsky.

Works incl. comic opera *Sous le masque* (lib. by Louis Laloy); ballets *Les Noces de Gamache* (from *Don Quixote*), *Les Matelots*, *La Pastorale*, *La Concurrence*, *Les Imaginaires*; incid. mus. to *Les Fâcheux* (Molière), *The Birds* (Aristophanes), *Volpone* (Ben Jonson), *Le Mariage de Figaro* (Beaumarchais), *Le 14 Juillet* (Rolland), with 9 others; film mus. *À nous la liberté* (René Clair), *Caesar and Cleopatra* (after Bernard Shaw), etc.; symph., suite, overture, *Fox-trot* and *Nocturne* for orch.; pf. concerto; pf. sonata and sonatina, *3 Pastorales* for pf.; *Chandelles romaines* for pf. duet; trio for ob., clar. and bassoon; vln. and pf. sonata; several song cycles, etc.

Aus Italien (*From Italy*), symph. by R. Strauss, Op. 16, comp. 1885–6 during and after a visit to It., 1st perf. Munich, 2. III. 1887. The 4 movements are entitled *On the Campagna*, *The Ruins of Rome*, *On the Shore of Sorrento* and *Neapolitan Folk Life*, and the last contains a quotation of Denza's *Funiculì, funiculà*, which Strauss took for a folksong.

Austin, Alfred (1835–1913), Eng. poet and dramatist. *See* **Pitt** (*Flodden Field*).

Austin, Ernest (b. London, 31. XII. 1874; d. Wallington, Surrey, 24. VII. 1947), Eng. comp. After a business career he took up comp., with no formal mus. training, at the age of 33.

Works incl. variations on *The Vicar of Bray* for string orch.; 12 tone-poems for org. on Bunyan's *Pilgrim's Progress*; numerous chamber and pf. works.

Austin, Frederic (b. London, 30. III. 1872; d. London, 10. IV. 1952), Eng. baritone and comp. Began his career as organist and mus. teacher at Liverpool, but came out as a singer in 1902 and in opera at Covent Garden Theatre, London, in 1908. Artistic director of the B.N.O.C. from 1924. He arr. *The Beggar's Opera* for the revival at the Lyric Theatre, Hammersmith, London, in 1920, and the sequel, *Polly*, for that at the Kingsway Theatre, in 1922.

Works incl. symph. in E maj.; symph. poems *Spring* and *Palsgaard*; incid. mus. to Capek's *Insect Play*, Congreve's *The Way of the World*, Beaumont and Fletcher's *The Knight of the Burning Pestle*; *Pervigilium Veneris* for chorus and orch. etc,

Austral (real name Wilson), **Florence** (b. Melbourne, 26. IV. 1894; d. Newcastle, N.S.W., 16. V. 1968), Austral. soprano. Entered Melbourne Cons. in 1914 and in 1918 studied in N.Y. She made her début at Covent Garden in 1922. She was known as a leading Wagner singer, touring both Europe and Amer.

Australian Composers. *See* **Agnew, Banks, Benjamin, Clutsam, Glanville-Hicks, Grainger, Sculthorpe, Williamson.**

Authentic Cadence. *See* **Perfect Cadence.**

Authentic Modes. *See* **Modes.**

Auxcousteaux, Artus (or **Arthur**) (b. ?; d. ?, 1656), Fr. singer and comp. He was a singer in Louis XIII's chapel *c.* 1613–27 and (?) at Noyon; later mus. master at the cathedral of Saint-Quentin and singer in the Sainte-Chapelle in Paris, becoming chaplain, precentor and canon at later dates.

Works incl. Masses, Magnificats, *Noëls* and other church mus.

Avere (Avery). *See* **Burton.**

Averkamp, Antonius Josephus (b. Cabouw nr. Willinge Langerak, 18. II. 1861; d. Bussum, 1. VI. 1934), Dutch cond., musicologist and comp. Studied at Amsterdam, Berlin and Munich and later founded a choral society at Amsterdam, for which he ed. much old Dutch and other mus. Director of the Utrecht School of Mus.

Works incl. a symph., many songs, etc.

Avison, Charles (b. Newcastle-on-Tyne, 1709; d. Newcastle, 10. V. 1770), Eng. organist and comp. Pupil of Geminiani. He is chiefly remembered for his treatise *An Essay on Musical Expression* (1752), but also wrote a quantity of instrumental mus., principally concertos, and (with John Garth) edited Marcello's Psalms in 1757.

Avolio (Avoglio), Signora (b. ?; d. ?), It. 18th-cent. soprano, who sang in the 1st perf. of *Messiah*.

Avondano, Pedro Antonio (b. Lisbon, ?; d. Lisbon, 1827), Port. violinist and comp. of It. descent.

Works incl. comic operas *Berenice* and *Il mondo della luna*; sacred dramas *Il voto di Jefte* and *Adamo ed Eva*; *Sinfonia* for strings; ? church mus. and harpsichord pieces destroyed in the Lisbon earthquake of 1755.

Axman, Emil (b. Rataje, Moravia, 3. VI. 1887; d. Prague, 25. I. 1949), Cz. comp. Studied at Prague Univ. and was a comp. student of Novák.

Works incl. melodrama *Just Once*; cantatas and other choral works; 6 symphs., symph. poem *Sorrow and Hope*; suite, sinfonietta, suite *From the Beskides*, Morav. dances for orch.; vln. concerto; 4 string 4tets, pf. trio; vln. and pf. sonata, cello and pf. sonata; 3 pf. sonatas, sonatina and other pf. works, etc.

Axur (Salieri). *See* **Tarare.**

Aylward, Theodore (b. ?, 1730; d. London, 27. II. 1801), Eng. organist and comp. Organist at several London churches. D.Mus. Oxford; app. Prof. of Mus. at Gresham Coll., London, 1771.

Works incl. incid. mus. for Shakespeare's *Cymbeline* and *Midsummer Night's Dream* (with M. Arne, Battishill and Burney); lessons for org.; canzonets for 2 voices; glees, catches and songs, etc.

Ayre (Old Eng.), a 16th–17th-cent. song with predominantly melodic, as distinct from harmonic or contrapuntal, interest.

Ayrton, Edmund (b. Ripon, 1734; d. London, 22. V. 1808), Eng. organist and comp. Studied with Nares at York Minster, became organist and choirmaster at South-well Minster in 1754, vicar-choral at St. Paul's Cathedral in London, 1767, and lay clerk at Westminster Abbey in 1780, also Master of the Children at the Chapel Royal. Mus.D., Cambridge, 1784. Comp. services and anthems.

Ayrton, William (b. London, 24. II. 1777; d. London, 8. III. 1858), Eng. writer on mus., son of prec. Lived in London. Ed. of the *Harmonicon*, mus. contrib. to the *Morning Chronicle* and the *Examiner*, married a daughter of Arnold; one of the founders of the Phil. Society in 1813.

Azione sacra (It. = sacred action), a 17th–18th-cent. term for a sacred drama with mus. or acted oratorio.

Azione teatrale (It. = theatrical action), a 17th-cent. term for an opera or mus. festival play.

Azzaiolo, Filippo (b. ?; d. ?), It. 16th-cent. comp. of *villote*, popular madrigal-like part-songs. His popular *Chi passa* was arranged as a keyboard piece by Byrd.

B

B, the 7th note, or leading note, of the scale of C major. In Ger. B = B♭, and B♮ is repres. by H.

B.A.C.H., a mus. theme formed of the notes B♭, A, C, B♮, in Ger. nomenclature (*see* above) and used by var. comps. as a ref. to Bach, who was himself the 1st to use it. Here are some exs.:

Albrechtsberger, Fugue for org.

Bach, one of the subjects of the final fugue (unfinished) in *The Art of Fugue* (4 org. fugues are prob. spurious).

Bach, J. C., Fugue for clavier or org.

Barblan, Passacaglia for org.

Busoni, *Fantasia contrappuntistica* for pf.

Casella, *Ricercari sul nome di Bach* for pf.

Eisler, Trio on the 12-note scale.

Honegger, *Prélude, Arioso et Fughette* for strings.

d'Indy, *Beuron* in *Tableaux de voyage* for pf.

Karg-Elert, *Basso ostinato* in org. pieces *Semplice*, Op. 42; Passacaglia and Fugue, Op. 150. for org.; Sonata, B♭ min., Op. 46, for Kunstharmonium.

Koechlin, *Offrande musicale* for org. and orch.

Liszt, Fantasy and Fugue for org.

Nielsen (R.), Ricercare, Chorale and Toccata for pf.

Piston, Chromatic Study for org.

Reger, Fantasy and Fugue for org.

Rimsky-Korsakov, Fugue in *Chopsticks* Vars. for pf. by var. comps.; 6 variations for pf., Op. 10.

Schönberg, Variations for orch., Op. 31.

Schumann, 6 Fugues for org. or pedal pf.

Varvoglis, Prelude, Chorale and Fugue for strings.

B.B.C. *See* **British Broadcasting Corporation.**

B-la-F Quartet, a string 4tet on the name of Belaiev by Rimsky-Korsakov, Liadov, Borodin and Glazunov, perf. on M. P. Belaiev's 50th birthday, 22. II. 1886. It is constructed on the notes B♭, A, F.

B minor Mass. Bach's great setting of the' Lat. text begins in B min., but as a whole centres on D maj. The work was not comp. in one piece, however, but in four sections, probably intended for separate perf. The *Kyrie* and *Gloria* (comprising in themselves a complete Lutheran short Mass) were written in 1733, and used to support Bach's application for the title of Court Comp. to the Elector of Saxony; the *Symbolum Nicenum* (Creed) ? 1732; *Sanctus c.* 1736; finally, the movements from *Osanna* to *Dona nobis pacem c.* 1738–1739. Several of the movements were adapted from earlier works, viz. church cantatas Nos. 11, 12, 29, 46, 120 and 171

and the secular cantata *Preise dein Glücke.*

B.N.O.C. *See* **British National Opera Company.**

Baaren, Kees van (b. Enschede, 22. X. 1906), Dutch comp. Studied with Pijper. B. is a leading Dutch exponent of serial mus., and also very active as a teacher. Since 1957 he has been director of the Royal Cons. in The Hague.

Works incl. *The Hollow Men* (words by T. S. Eliot), cantata for chorus and orch.; *Variazioni per Orchestra*; a string 4tet and a wind 5tet (*Sovraposizione I and II*).

Babán, Gracián (b. ?; d. ?), Span. 17th-cent. comp. *Maestro de capilla* at Valencia Cathedral from 1657 for nearly 20 years. Comp. Masses, psalms, Lamentations and other church mus.

Babbitt, Milton (b. Philadelphia, 10. V. 1916), Amer. comp. Studied at univs. of New York and Princeton, and also privately with Sessions. In 1938 he was app. to the mus. faculty at Princeton, where from 1943 to 1945 he also taught mathematics. His early work is much influenced by Webern, and later he turned to total serialism and electronic mus.

Works incl. *Composition for 12 instruments*; *Composition for 4 instruments*; *Composition for vla. and pf.*; *Composition for Synthesizer*; *Vision and Prayer* (words by Dylan Thomas) with electronic tape accomp.; *Du*, a song cycle; var. electronic and film scores.

Babell, William (b. ?, *c.* 1690; d. London, 23. IX. 1723), Eng. harpsichordist, violinist and comp. Member of the royal band in London and for some years organist at All Hallows Church.

Works incl. chamber mus.; harpsichord pieces, airs from operas arr. for harpsichord, etc.

Babini, Matteo (b. Bologna, 19. II. 1754; d. Bologna, 22. IX. 1816), It. tenor. Began his career in the service of Frederick the Great and Catherine II of Rus.; afterwards sang in Vienna, London, It. and again in Berlin.

Baborák, a Cz. folk dance with alternating sections of 2–4 and 3–4 time.

Baby Grand (Piano), a grand pf. of the smallest size.

Bacarisse, Salvador (b. Madrid, 12. IX. 1898; d. Paris, 7. VIII. 1963), Span. comp. Studied at the Madrid Cons., Conrado del Campo being his comp. master. He became mus. director of the Unión Radio in Madrid, 1925. After the Span. Civil War he settled in Fr. in 1939.

Works incl. opera *Charlot*; ballet *Corrida de feria*; *Tres marchas burlescas*, *Heraldos*, *Concertino*, *Música sinfónica*, *Serenata*, *Impromptu* for orch.; choral symph. *La nave de Ulises*; pf. concerto, cello concerto; 2 string 4tets; trio-sonata for fl., cello and harp; *Tres nanas* for voice and chamber orch.; *Ofrenda a Debussy, Tres canciones* and other songs; pf. pieces, etc.

Baccaloni, Salvatore (b. Rome, 14. IV. 1900; d. N.Y., 31. XII. 1969), It. bass. Sang as a boy in the choir of the Sistine Chapel. Studied with Kaschmann. As an adult made his 1st appearance in opera in Rome in 1922. A member of the opera co. at La Scala, Milan, from 1927. He sang also at Covent Garden, Glyndebourne and the Metropolitan Opera, N.Y. He specialized in *buffo* roles.

Bacchantinnen, Die (*The Bacchantes*), opera by Wellesz (lib. by comp., based on Euripides), prod. Vienna, Opera, 20. VI. 1931.

Baccusi, Ippolito (b. Mantua, *c.* 1550; d. Verona, 1609), It. comp. His works incl. madrigals, Masses, motets, psalms and Magnificats.

Bacewicz, Grażyna (b. Łódź, 5. V. 1909; d. Warsaw, 17. I. 1969), Pol. comp. and violinist. She studied composition at the Warsaw Cons. under Sikorski and later in Paris with Nadia Boulanger. Taught at Łódź Cons. 1934–5, returning to Paris in 1945. Her 4th string 4tet won 1st prize at the International Competition, Liège, in 1951.

Works incl. 4 symphs.; 4 vln. concertos; cello concerto; pf. concerto; concerto for string orch.; 6 string 4tets.; pf. 5tet; 6 vln. sonatas and various vln. pieces.

Bach, Ger. 16th–18th-cent. family of musicians:

1. Hans B. (b. ?, *c.* 1520; d. Wechmar nr. Gotha, ?).
2. Veit B. (b. ? Wechmar, ?; d. Wechmar, 8. III. 1619), ? son of prec.
3. Lips (Philippus) (b. Wechmar, ?; d. ? Wechmar, 10. X. 1620), son of prec.
4. Johannes (Hans) B. (b. Wechmar, ?; d. Wechmar, 1626), brother of prec.
5. Johannes B. (b. Wechmar, 26. XI. 1604; d. ? Erfurt, 13. V. 1673), son of prec.
6. Christoph B. (b. Wechmar, 19. IV. 1613; d. Arnstadt, 12. IX. 1661), brother of prec.
7. Heinrich B. (b. Wechmar, 16. IX. 1615; d. Arnstadt, 10. VII. 1692), brother of prec.
8. Johann Christian B. (b. Erfurt, 25. VIII. 1640; d. Erfurt, 11. VI. 1682), son of 5.
9. Georg Christoph B. (b. Erfurt, 6. IX. 1642; d. Schweinfurt, 24. IV. 1697), son of 6.
10. Johann Christoph B. (b. Arnstadt, 8. XII. 1642; d. Eisenach, 31. III. 1703), son of 7.
11. Johann Aegidius B. (b. Erfurt, 9. II. 1645; d. Erfurt, 1716), son of 5, brother of 8.
12. Johann Christoph B. (b. Erfurt, 22. II. 1645; d. Arnstadt, 25. VIII. 1693), son of 6.

13. Johann Ambrosius B. (b. Erfurt, 22. II. 1645; d. Eisenach, 20. II. 1695), son of 6, twin brother of 12, father of 26.
14. Johann Michael B. (b. Arnstadt, 6. VIII. 1648; d. Gehren, V. 1694), son of 7, father of 25.
15. Johann Günther B. (b. Arnstadt, 17. VII. 1653; d. Arnstadt, 8. IV. 1683), son of 7.
16. Johann Nikolaus B. (b. Eisenach, 10. X. 1669; d. Jena, 4. XI. 1753), son of 10.
17. Johann Christoph B. (b. Erfurt, 16. VI. 1671; d. Ohrdruf, 22. II. 1721), son of 13, brother of 26.
18. Johann Christoph B. (b. Eisenach, 29. VIII. 1674; d. ? London, 1740), son of 10.
19. Johann Friedrich B. (b. Eisenach, *c.* 1675; d. Mühlhausen, 1730), brother of prec.
20. Johann Michael B. (b. Eisenach, *c.* 1676; d. ?), brother of prec.
21. Johann Bernhard B. (b. Erfurt, 23. XI. 1676; d. Eisenach, 11. VI. 1749), son of 11.
22. Johann Ludwig B. (b. ? 1677; d. ? Meiningen, *c.* 1710), descendant of 3.
23. Johann Jakob B. (b. Eisenach, 9. II. 1682; d. ? Stockholm, ? 1722), son of 13, brother of 26.
24. Johann Ernst B. (b. Arnstadt, 8. VIII. 1683; d. Arnstadt, 21. III. 1739), son of 12.
25. Maria Barbara B. (b. Gehren, 20. X. 1684; d. Cöthen, VII. 1720), daughter of 14, 1st wife of 26.
26. Johann Sebastian B. (b. Eisenach, 21. III. 1685; d. Leipzig, 28. VII. 1750), son of 13, husband of 25 and 29.
27. Johann Christoph B. (b. Erfurt, 15. VIII. 1685; d. Erfurt, *c.* 1740), son of 11.
28. Johann Lorenz B. (b. ?, 10. IX. 1695; d. Lahm, 14. XII. 1773), grandson of 9.
29. Anna Magdalena B. (*née* Wilcken) (b. 22. IX. 1701; d. 27. II. 1760), 2nd wife of 26.
30. Johann Elias B. (b. ?, 12. II. 1705; d. Schweinfurt, 30. XI. 1755), grandson of 9, brother of 28.
31. Samuel Anton B. (b. Meiningen, *c.* 1710; d. ?, 1781), son of 22.
32. Johann Ernst B. (b. Eisenach, 1. IX. 1722; d. Eisenach, 28. I. 1777), son of 21.
33. Johann Michael B. (b. Schweinfurt, 1754; d. ?), son of 30.

Children of Johann Sebastian Bach (26) by 25:

34. Catharina Dorothea B. (b. Weimar, 29. XII. 1708; d. 14. I. 1774).
35. Wilhelm Friedemann B. (b. Weimar, 22. XI. 1710; d. Berlin, 1. VII. 1784).
36. Johann Christoph B. (b. and d. Weimar, 23. II. 1713). Twin.
37. Maria Sophie B. (b. and d. Weimar, 23. II. 1713). Twin.

38. **Carl Philipp Emanuel B.** (b. Weimar, 8. III. 1714; d. Hamburg, 15. XII. 1788).

39. **Johann Gottfried Bernhard B.** (b. Weimar, 11. V. 1715; d. Jena, 27. V. 1739).

40. **Leopold Augustus B.** (b. Cöthen, 15. XI. 1718; d. Cöthen, 28. IX. 1719).

Children of Johann Sebastian Bach (26) by 29:

41. **Christiane Sophie Henrietta B.** (b. Cöthen or Leipzig, 1723; d. Leipzig, 29. VI. 1726).

42. **Gottfried Heinrich B.** (b. Leipzig, 26. II. 1724; d. Naumburg, 12. II. 1763).

43. **Christian Gottlieb B.** (b. Leipzig, 14. IV. 1725; d. 21. IX. 1728).

44. **Elisabetha Juliane Frederica B.** (b. Leipzig, 5. IV. 1726; d. Naumburg, 25. VII. 1759), married Johann Christoph Altnikol.

45. **Ernestus Andreas B.** (b. Leipzig, 30. X. 1727; d. Leipzig, 1. XI. 1727).

46. **Regine Johanne B.** (b. Leipzig, 10. X. 1728; d. Leipzig, 24. IV. 1733).

47. **Christiane Benedicta B.** (b. Leipzig, 31. XII. 1729; d. Leipzig, 4. I. 1730).

48. **Christiane Dorothea B.** (b. Leipzig, 18. III. 1731; d. Leipzig, 31. VIII. 1732).

49. **Johann Christoph Friedrich B.** (b. Leipzig, 21. VI. 1732; d. Bückeburg, 26. I. 1795).

50. **Johann August Abraham B.** (b. Leipzig, 4. XI. 1733; d. Leipzig, 6. XI. 1733).

51. **Johann Christian B.** (b. Leipzig, 5. IX. 1735; d. London, 1. I. 1782).

52. **Johanne Caroline B.** (b. Leipzig, 30. X. 1737; d. 16. VIII. 1781).

53. **Regine Susanna B.** (b. Leipzig, 22. II. 1742; d. 14. XII. 1809).

Bach, Carl Philipp Emanuel (b. Weimar, 8. III. 1714; d. Hamburg, 15. XII. 1788), Ger. harpsichordist and comp. (38 above), 2nd son of J. S. and Maria Barbara B. (26 and 25 above). Educ. at St. Thomas's School, Leipzig, and at the univs. of Leipzig (1731–4) and Frankfurt-on-Oder (1734–8), where he studied law. His mus. training, according to himself, he received entirely from his father. He was connected with the household of the Crown Prince of Prussia from 1738, and in 1740, on the latter's accession as King Frederick II, he was app. harpsichordist to the court at Berlin and Potsdam. In 1744 he married Johanna Maria Dannemann, and in 1747 his father visited him at court. His most important comps. at this time were keyboard pieces, which contributed much to the estab. of a more homophonic style and modern formal procedures. His treatise on keyboard playing (*Versuch über die wahre Art das Clavier zu spielen*, 1753 and 1762) is a valuable guide to contemporary practice. B. found Berlin restricting, partly because his duties involved only harpsi-

chord playing, partly because of the stiff-necked conservatism of the king, and in 1768 he moved to Hamburg as municipal director of mus. at the 5 principal churches. Burney visited him there in 1772, and commented on his remarkable improvising. In Hamburg B. had wider scope, directing concerts, etc., with great success, and there he wrote most of his mus. for large forces, e.g. oratorios.

Works incl. oratorios *Die Israeliten in der Wüste* and *Die Auferstehung und Himmelfahrt Jesu*; Magnificat, *Heilig* (*Sanctus*) for double choir, Passions and other church mus.; 19 symphs.; 50 keyboard concertos; *c.* 200 keyboard pieces (sonatas, fantasias, rondos, etc.), odes, songs, etc.

Bach, Johann Ambrosius (b. Erfurt, 22. II. 1645; d. Eisenach, 20. II. 1695), Ger. organist and comp. (13 above). Born as the twin of Johann Christoph B. (12 above) and taught by his father Christoph B. (6 above). He became town musician at Erfurt in 1667, marrying Elisabeth Lämmerhirt there on 8. IV. 1668. In 1671 he was app. town musician at Eisenach. His wife d. on 3. V. 1694, and he married Barbara Margaretha Keul on 27. XI., but d. himself 2 months later.

Bach, Johann (John) Christian (b. Leipzig, 5. IX. 1735; d. London, 1. I. 1782), Ger. clavier player and comp. (51 above), youngest son of J. S. and Anna Magdalena B. (26 and 29 above). Pupil of his father and, after the latter's death in 1750, of his brother Carl Philipp Emanuel (38 above) in Berlin. In 1756 he went to Italy, studying under Padre Martini in Bologna; embraced Roman Catholicism, wrote much Lat. church mus., and in 1760 was app. organist of Milan Cathedral. His 1st opera, *Artaserse*, was prod. at Turin in 1761. The following year he went to London, where he remained for the rest of his life. In 1763 he prod. his 1st opera for London, *Orione*, and was app. mus. master to Queen Charlotte. With C. F. Abel he founded in 1764 a series of subscription concerts which continued till 1781, and in the same year befriended the young Mozart on his visit to London. B. visited Mannheim in 1772 and 1776, and Paris in 1778, where his last opera was prod. in 1779. His popularity in London declined in his last years.

Works incl. operas *Artaserse*, *Catone in Utica*, *Alessandro nell' Indie* (all Metastasio), *Orione ossia Diana vendicata*, *Zanaida*, *Adriano in Siria*, *Carattaco*, *Temistocle*, *Lucio Silla*, *La Clemenza di Scipione*, *Amadis de Gaule*; oratorio *Gioas rè di Giuda*; church mus.; over 90 symphs. and similar works for orch.; *c.* 40 concertos and over 30 sonatas for clavier; chamber mus.; Eng. and It. cantatas, arias, songs, etc.

Bach, Johann Christoph (b. Arnstadt, 8. XII. 1642; d. Eisenach, 31. III. 1703), Ger. organist and comp. (10 above). Became organist at Eisenach in 1665 and remained there to the end of his life. Comp. motets, church cantatas, chorale preludes for org. and harpsichord mus.

Bach, Johann Christoph (b. Erfurt, 16. VI. 1671; d. Ohrdruf, 22. II. 1721), Ger. organist (17 above). Pupil of Pachelbel at Erfurt. In X. 1694 he married Dorothea von Hof, and the next year he took his young brother Johann Sebastian (26 above) into his house after their parents' death.

Bach, Johann Christoph Friedrich (b. Leipzig, 21. VI. 1732; d. Bückeburg, 26. I. 1795), Ger. comp. (49 above), son of J. S. and Anna Magdalena B. (26 and 29 above). Educ. at St. Thomas's School and Leipzig Univ., where he studied law. Received his mus. training from his father, and in 1750 was app. chamber musician to Count Wilhelm of Schaumburg-Lippe in Bückeburg, where he remained for the rest of his life, becoming *Konzertmeister* in 1758. He married the court singer Elisabeth Münchhausen in 1755. In 1778 he visited his brother Johann Christian in London.

Among his most notable comps. are the oratorios on words by Johann Gottfried Herder (attached to the court at Bückeburg 1771–4), *Die Kindheit Jesu* and *Die Auferweckung Lazarus*; a third oratorio and an opera, *Brutus*, both on words by the same poet, are lost. Other works incl. Passion oratorio *Der Tod Jesu* (words by Ramler); cantatas (some with Herder); 14 symphs., keyboard concertos and sonatas, chamber mus., etc.

Bach, Johann Michael (b. Arnstadt, 6. VIII. 1648; d. Gehren, V. 1694), Ger. organist, instrument maker and comp. (14 above). Organist and parish clerk at Gehren from 1673. Comp. motets, sacred arias, etc.

Bach, Johann Sebastian (b. Eisenach, 21. III. 1685; d. Leipzig, 28. VII. 1750), Ger. organist and comp. (26 above). After his father's death in 1695 he was a pupil of his brother Johann Christoph in Ohrdruf. At 15 he became a chorister in Lüneburg, where he may have had org. lessons from Böhm. App. violinist in the court orch. of the Duke of Weimar in 1703, but left the same year to become organist in Arnstadt, from where in 1705 he took leave to travel to Lübeck, to hear Buxtehude play. In 1707 moved to Mühlhausen, where he married his cousin Maria Barbara B. A year later returned to Weimar as court organist, remaining there for nine years. In 1717 app. *Kapellmeister* to the court of Prince Leopold of Anhalt-Cöthen. His wife died in 1720, and he married Anna Magdalena Wilcken in 1721. At Cöthen B. had little opportunity for church mus., and there he

wrote mainly instrumental works, but in 1723 he returned to church work when he succeeded Kühnau as Cantor of St. Thomas's in Leipzig, where he remained for the rest of his life. In 1747, with his eldest son, Wilhelm Friedemann, he visited the court of Frederick the Great at Potsdam, where his second son, Carl Philipp Emanuel, was court harpsichordist. Two years later his eyesight failed; an operation in 1750 was unsuccessful, and he spent his last months totally blind.

Works incl. choral mus.: Passions according to St. John and St. Matthew, Mass in B minor, Christmas Oratorio, over 200 cantatas, 6 motets, etc.; orch. and chamber mus.: 6 'Brandenburg' concertos, concertos for solo instrument(s), 4 orchestral suites, 6 sonatas and partitas for unaccomp. vln., 6 suites for unaccomp. cello, sonatas, etc., for various instruments and continuo, *Musicalisches Opfer*; keyboard mus. (except org.): *Das wohltemperirte Clavier* ('the 48'—2 sets of preludes and fugues in every maj. and min. key), 7 partitas, 7 toccatas, 6 Fr. and 6 Eng. suites, 2- and 3-part inventions, Italian concerto, Goldberg variations, *Kunst der Fuge* (? for keyboard); org. mus.: 6 sonatas, 143 chorale preludes, toccatas, fantasias, preludes and fugues, etc.

Bach Trumpet, a special brass wind instrument of the tpt. type invented by Kosleck of Berlin and improved by Walter Morrow of London, so devised as to be capable of playing the high Clarino parts in the works of Bach and his contemporaries and forerunners; first heard at Eisenach in 1884.

Bach, Wilhelm Friedemann (b. Weimar, 22. XI. 1710; d. Berlin, 1. VII. 1784), Ger. organist and comp. (35 above), eldest son of J. S. and Maria Barbara B. (26 and 25 above). Educ. at St. Thomas's School and Leipzig Univ.; received his mus. training from his father. App. organist of St. Sophia's, Dresden, in 1723, and in 1746 succeeded Zachau as organist of St. Mary's, Halle. Married Dorothea Elisabeth Georgi in 1751. He resigned his post in Halle in 1764, and never held another permanent position, living an unsettled life and supporting his family mainly by teaching. In 1770 he moved to Brunswick, and in 1774 finally to Berlin. There his remarkable org. playing could still arouse astonishment, but his last years were spent in increasing poverty.

Works incl. cantatas and other church mus.; 9 symphs.; keyboard concertos; 9 sonatas, 12 fantasias and other works for keyboard; org. mus., etc.

Bachauer, Gina (b. Athens, 21. V. 1913), Gk. pianist of Aus. parentage. Won Medal of Honour at an international competition in Vienna, 1933, and from 1933 to 1935 took occasional lessons with Rachmaninov. Made her professional début in Athens in 1935.

Bache, Francis Edward (b. Birmingham, 14. IX. 1833; d. Birmingham, 24. VIII. 1858), Eng. pianist and comp. Studied with Sterndale Bennett in London and came out early as a gifted player and comp.

Bache, Walter (b. Birmingham, 19. VI. 1842; d. London, 26. III. 1888), Eng. pianist, brother of prec. Lived in London. Pupil and disciple of Liszt.

Bachelet, Alfred (Georges) (b. Paris, 26. II. 1864; d. Nancy, 10. II. 1944), Fr. comp. Took the Prix de Rome at the Paris Cons. in 1890. App. head of the Cons. in Nancy in 1919, and in 1939 elected a member of the Académie des Beaux Arts. Prod. the opera *Scemo* at the Paris Opéra in 1914, another, *Quand la cloche sonnera*, at the Opéra-Comique in 1922 and *Un Jardin sur l'Oronte* at the Opéra in 1932. He also wrote orchestral mus. and songs.

Bachmann, Sixtus (b. Kettershausen, 18. VII. 1754; d. ? Marchtal, 1818), Aus. priest, organist and comp. Wrote symphs., church and chamber mus. when living in retirement at the monastery of Marchtal.

Bachofen, Johann Caspar (b. Zürich, 26. XII. 1695; d. Zürich, 23. VI. 1755), Swiss comp. Cantor of the grammar school in Zürich, 1720, and of the *Grossmünster*, 1742. He compiled and partly comp. several books of hymns and sacred songs, and in 1759 wrote a setting of the Passion oratorio by Brockes.

Bachrich, Sigismund (b. Zsambokreth, 23. I. 1841; d. Vienna, 16. VII. 1913), Hung. violinist and comp. Studied at the Vienna Cons. Played and cond. in Vienna and Paris, became prof. at the Vienna Cons. and played vla. in the Phil. and Opera Orch. and with the Rosé 4tet.

Works incl. operas *Muzzedin* and *Heini von Steier*, operetta *Der Fuchs-Major*; ballet *Sakuntala* (after Kalidasa), etc.

Bäck, Sven-Erik (b. Stockholm, 16. IX. 1919), Swed. comp. and violinist. Studied comp. with Rosenberg at the Stockholm Cons., 1940–4, and later at the Schola Cantorum, Basle.

Works incl. *Ett Spel om Maria*; a scenic oratorio; vln. concerto; 2 string 4tets; string 5tet; songs and pf. mus.

Backer-Grøndahl, Agathe (Ursula) (b. Holmestrand, 1. XII. 1847; d. Ormøen nr. Oslo, 4. VI. 1907), Norw. pianist and comp. Pupil of Kjerulf and later of Kullak in Berlin and Bülow at Florence. She wrote many pf. pieces and songs.

Backer-Lunde, Johan (b. Le Havre, 6. VII. 1874; d. 4. XI. 1958), Norw. pianist and comp. Pupil of Agathe Backer-Grøndahl at Oslo and Busoni in Berlin. Comp. much pf. mus.

Backfall = Appoggiatura (taken from the note above).

Backhaus, Wilhelm (b. Leipzig, 26. III. 1884; d. Villach, 5. VII. 1969), Ger. pianist. Studied at the Leipzig Cons. under A. Reckendorf until 1899, and then with d'Albert in Frankfurt. In 1905 he taught at the Royal Manchester Coll. of Mus., winning the Rubinstein Prize in the same year. He then began his professional concert career. B. excelled in the classical repertory, esp. the sonatas of Beethoven.

Bacon, Ernst (b. Chicago, 26. V. 1898), Amer. pianist, cond. and comp., studied mus. at Chicago and in Vienna, later in the U.S.A. with Bloch and Eugene Goossens. In 1925 he was app. pf. prof. at the Eastman School of Mus., Rochester, N.Y.; in 1945 director of the mus. school of the Univ. of Syracuse, N.Y.

Works incl. mus. comedy *Take your Choice*; mus. play *A Tree on the Plains*; cantatas *Ecclesiastes* and *From Emily's Diary* (Emily Dickinson); 2 symphs., 2 suites and other orchestral mus.; settings of Dickinson and Whitman for voice and orch.; pf. 5tet, etc.

Badajoz (? Garci Sánchez de) (b. ?, 1460; d. ?, 1526), Span. organist and comp. Was for a time in the service of John III of Port. Wrote songs for several voices, incl. one in Gil Vicente's play *Dom Duardos*.

Badiali, Cesare (b. Imola, ?; d. Imola, 17. XI. 1865), It. bass. Made his 1st appearance at Trieste in 1837. Sang in Madrid, Vienna and London as well as It.

Badinage (Fr., lit. teasing, playfulness). *See* **Badinerie**.

Badinerie (Fr., lit. teasing, frivolity, playfulness), a title given, sometimes as *Badinage*, by Fr. and Ger. comps. of the 18th cent. to light, playful pieces in quick 2–4 time (e.g. the final movement of Bach's B min. Overture [suite] for fl. and strings).

Badings, Henk (Hendrik Herman) (b. Bandoeng, Java, 17. I. 1907), Dutch comp. Began his career as a mining engineer, but studied mus. with Pijper and in 1935 abandoned science entirely for mus. Married the violinist Olly Folge Fonden. Prof. at the Mus. Lyceum, Amsterdam, and the Rotterdam Cons. Director of the Royal Cons. at The Hague, 1941.

Works incl. opera *The Night Watch* (after Rembrandt), ballets and incid. mus. for plays; a cantata; 10 symphs.; symph. variations; *Heroic Overture*; vln. concerto, cello concerto, concerto for 2 vlns. and orch.; recitations with orch.; 2 string 4tets; vln. and cello sonatas; pf. pieces; since 1956 electronic mus., incl. 2 operas with electronic accomp.

Bagatelle (Fr. = trifle). A short piece, generally of a light or humorous character.

Bagatelles. Beethoven pub. 3 sets of Bs.:

7, Op. 33, comp. 1802; 11, Op. 119, comp. 1820-2; 6, Op. 126, comp. 1823.

Bagpipe, an instrument prod. its sound by wind stored up in a bag filled by the player through a mouthpiece; the melody is fingered on a pipe attached to that bag, called the chanter, while a drone-bass is sounded continually by 2 or 3 additional pipes giving out fixed notes. In some types the wind was supplied by bellows.

Bahr-Mildenburg, Anna (b. Vienna, 29. XI. 1872; d. Vienna, 27. I. 1947), Aus. soprano, made her 1st appearance at Hamburg in 1895 and became a noted Wagner and Strauss singer. She sang in London between 1906 and 1913.

Bai, Tommaso (b. Crevalcuore nr. Bologna, 1650; d. Rome, 22. XII. 1714), It. tenor and comp. Sang in the Vatican choir; wrote Masses, motets and a famous *Miserere*.

Baildon, Joseph (b. ?, c. 1727; d. London, IV. 1774), Eng. singer, organist and comp. Lay-vicar at Westminster Abbey and organist at 2 other London churches. Wrote catches, glees and songs.

Bailey, Lilian (June) (b. Columbus, Ohio, 18. I. 1860; d. London, 4. XI. 1901), Amer. soprano. 1st appeared at Boston in 1876, where she married Henschel in 1881.

Baillot, Pierre (Marie François de Sales) (b. Passy nr. Paris, 1. X. 1771; d. Paris, 15. IX. 1842), Fr. violinist. Studied in Rome and later under Catel, Cherubini and Reicha in Paris; joined Napoleon's private band, 1802, and began to give chamber concerts in 1814. Was prof. at the Cons. and comp. works for his instrument and chamber mus.

Baines, William (b. Horbury, Yorks., 26. III. 1899; d. York, 6. XI. 1922), Eng. comp. Although self-taught, he developed remarkably early, but d. before he had attained full mus. maturity.

Works incl. symph., Fantasy for string 4tet; pf. sonata, several sets of pf. pieces, etc.

Baini, Giuseppe (b. Rome, 21. X. 1775; d. Rome, 21. V. 1844), It. priest, singer and writer on mus. Sang at the Pontifical Chapel in Rome; comp. a *Miserere*, prod. there, 1821. He wrote a biog. of Palestrina.

Bainton, Edgar L(eslie) (b. London, 14. II. 1880; d. Sydney, 8. XII. 1956), Eng. comp. Studied at the R.C.M. in London and in 1901 was app. prof. of pf. and comp. at the Cons. of Newcastle-on-Tyne, of which he became principal in 1912. In 1934 he went to Australia as director of the State Cons. at Sydney.

Works incl. opera *Oithona* (after Ossian); *Before Sunrise* (Swinburne), for contralto solo, chorus and orch.; *The Blessed Damozel* (Rossetti) for solo voices, chorus and orch.; Symph. in B♭ maj., symph. poem *Paracelsus* (after Browning); Concerto-

Fantasia for pf. and orch.; string 4tet; vla. and pf. sonata; songs, part-songs, pf. pieces, etc.

Baird, Tadeusz (b. Grodzisk Masowiecki, 26. VII. 1928), Pol. comp. Studied at Łódź Cons. Imprisoned in World War II. His mus. is influenced by serialism, esp. by Berg.

Works incl. 2 symphs.; *Cassation for Orch.*; *4 Essays for Orch.*; *Expressions* for vln. and orch.; pf. concerto; and other orchestral mus.

Bairstow, Edward C(uthbert). (b. Huddersfield, 22. VIII. 1874; d. York, 1. V. 1946), Eng. organist, cond. and comp. After var. organist's posts he took the D.Mus. at Durham in 1901 and became organist and choirmaster at York Minster in 1913. Ed. *The Eng. Psalter* and wrote *The Evolution of Mus. Form* and (with Plunket Greene) *Singing learnt from Speech*. Prof. of Mus. at Durham Univ., 1929-46. Knighted 1932.

Works incl. services, anthems; org. mus.; Vars. for 2 pfs., etc.

Baiser et la quittance, Le (*The Kiss and the Receipt*), opera by Boïeldieu, Isouard, R. Kreutzer and Méhul (lib. by Louis Picard, Michel Dieulafoy and Charles de Longchamps), prod. Paris, Opéra-Comique, 18. VI. 1803.

Baker, Janet (Abbott) (b. 21. VIII. 1933), Eng. mezzo-soprano. Made her 1st appearance in opera at Oxford in 1956. Since then has acquired an international reputation as a concert and opera singer.

Bakfark, Balint Valentin (b. Brasso [Kronstadt], 1507; d. Padua, 13. VIII. 1576), Hung., later Pol., lutenist and comp. also known by name of Greff. He went into royal service, learnt the lute, later lived in France and in 1549-66 was at the Pol. court. He pub. a lute book with Moderne of Lyons in 1552 and a second with Andreae of Cracow in 1565.

Balakirev, Mily Alexeievich (b. Nizhny-Novgorod, 2. I. 1837; d. St. Petersburg, 29. V. 1910), Rus. comp. He was taught mus. by his mother, but learnt most of what he knew as a youth in the house of Ulibishev, on whose estate he was able to use the mus. library and gain experience with the private orch. At 18 he went to St. Petersburg, full of enthusiasm for nat. mus., and won the approval of Glinka. In 1861 he began to form the group of nationalist musicians of which he became the leader, although he was not the eldest. Cui became his 1st disciple, Mussorgsky, Rimsky-Korsakov and Borodin foll. later, and he even influenced Tchaikovsky to some extent at first. In 1862 he helped to estab. the Free School of Mus. with the choral cond. Lomakin, and in connection with it cond. progressive symph. concerts.

In 1871 he had a grave nervous break-down and withdrew from public life, feeling that he had been defeated by the 'official' musicians; he was forced to become a min. railway official to earn a modest living and he turned to religious mysticism. Not till 1876 did he begin to take some interest in mus. life and comp. again, but only in 1883, when he was app. director of the Imp. Chapel, did he fully emerge once more. He retired in 1895 with a pension and took up comp. anew, but again lived in seclusion and was almost wholly forgotten by his former friends.

Works incl. incid. mus. for Shake-speare's *King Lear*; 2 symphs., symph. poems *Russia* and *Tamara*, overtures on a Span. march, on 3 Rus. themes, to *King Lear* and on Cz. themes; pf. concerto (finished by Liapunov); many pf. works, incl. sonata in B♭ min., *Islamey* fantasy, scherzos, mazurkas, nocturnes, waltzes, etc.; 43 songs; 2 books of folk-songs; 6 anthems for unaccomp. chorus; cantata for the unveiling of the Glinka monument.

Balalaika, a Rus. instrument similar to the guitar, but as a rule with a triangular body. It is made in var. sizes, so that bands of instruments ranging from treble to bass can be organized.

Balbi, Lodovico (b. Venice, 1545; d. Venice, XII. 1604), It. monk, singer and comp. Pupil of Porta; singer at St. Mark's, Venice, *c*. 1570; later at Verona Cathedral. Afterwards worked at Venice and Padua, and retired to the Minorite monastery at Venice.

Works incl. Masses, motets and other church mus.; madrigals, etc.

Baldassari, Benedetto (b. ?; d. ?), It. 18th-cent. tenor. Appeared in London, 1719–22.

Baldwin, John (b. ?; d. London, 28. VIII. 1615), Eng. singer and comp. At var. times singer in St. George's Chapel, Windsor, and a gentleman of the Chapel Royal in London. He copied out much mus., esp. into a book for his own use, which pre-serves many valuable works and incl. instrumental pieces and sacred and secular works for several voices. He also com-pleted the Sextus part-book of the Forrest-Heyther collection of Tudor Masses, and wrote out 'My Lady Nevells Booke', a beautifully copied anthology of keyboard mus. by Byrd, dated 1591.

Baldwyn, John (b. ?; d. ?), Eng. 15th-cent. musician. Took the Mus.B. at Cam-bridge, 1470 or 1471; prob. the composer of a Magnificat (lost) in the Eton Choir-book.

Balfe, Michael (William) (b. Dublin, 15. V. 1808; d. Rowney Abbey, Herts., 20. X. 1870), Ir. comp. Son of a dancing-master, who removed to Wexford in 1810. There B. had vln. lessons and he soon played for his father's classes; at 7 he comp. and scored a

polacca. On the death of his father in 1823, he was sent to London as a pupil of C. E. Horn; there he appeared as a violinist and played in the orch. at Drury Lane Theatre. Next he studied comp. with C. F. Horn and came out as a singer in the 1st perf. in Eng. of Weber's *Freischütz* at Norwich. In 1825 Count Mazzara became his patron and took him to It., where he introduced him to Cherubini. He took comp. lessons from Paer in Rome and Federici at Milan, and improved his singing under Filippo Galli. A ballet, his 1st stage work, was prod. there. Next he went to Paris, met Rossini, and in 1827 appeared as Figaro in that comp.'s *Barbiere* at the Théâtre Italien.

Three years later he sang at Palermo and prod. his 1st opera there, *I rivali di se stessi*. At Milan he sang with Malibran and at Bergamo he met the Hung. singer Lina Rosa, whom he married. Early in 1833 he returned to London and appeared at con-certs. His 1st Eng. opera, *The Siege of Rochelle*, was prod. at Drury Lane in 1835 and the next year Malibran sang in *The Maid of Artois*. In 1842 he went to live in Paris for some years and worked there with great success, though in 1843 he returned for a time to prod. *The Bohemian Girl* in London. Triumphant visits to Berlin in 1849 and St. Petersburg in 1852 followed, and in 1854 he prod. *Pittore e Duca* at Trieste. That year he finally returned to Eng., though a Fr. version, with some new mus., of *The Bohemian Girl* was brought out in Paris, 1869. He had bought property in Hertfordshire, where he took to farming.

Works incl. 29 operas, among which are *Un avvertimento ai gelosi*, *The Siege of Rochelle*, *The Maid of Artois*, *Joan of Arc*, *Falstaff* (It.), *Le Puits d'amour*, *The Bo-hemian Girl*, *Les Quatre Fils Aymon*, *The Bondman*, *The Maid of Honour*, *The Sicilian Bride*, *The Rose of Castile*, *Sata-nella*, *The Armourer of Nantes*, *Il Talis-mano*; operetta *The Sleeping Queen*; ballet *La Pérouse*; 3 cantatas, incl. *Mazeppa*; many songs, etc.

Balino. *See* **Fabri**.

Ballabene, Gregorio (b. Rome, 1720; d. Rome, *c*. 1803), It. comp. One of the latest adherents of the *stile antico*, wrote un-accomp. church mus., often of consider-able complexity, incl. a 48-part Mass.

Ballabile (It. = in a dancing manner, accent on 2nd syll.). A term applicable to any piece in the form or character of a dance.

Ballad, a narrative song either tradi-tional or written in traditional style. Applied in the late 19th and early 20th cents. to a sentimental, drawing-room song.

Ballad Opera, an Eng. light operatic entertainment the fashion for which was set by John Gay's *The Beggar's Opera* in 1728 and continuing its vogue until the

1760s. The most distinctive feature of its mus. is that it consists mainly of short songs interspersed with dialogue and that they are not specially comp. for the piece, but chosen from popular songs of the day.

Ballade (Fr.). (1) A form of medieval Fr. verse, often set to mus. by trouvères and 14th-cent. comps., in which a refrain occurs at the end of each stanza. (2) In the 19th and 20th cents. an instrumental piece, often of a lyrical and romantic character.

Ballard, Fr. 16th–18th-cent. family of mus. printers. The founder was Guillaume Le Bé, 1540, and the chief members were:
1. Robert B. (b. ?; d. Paris, 1606), son-in-law of Le Bé.
2. Lucrèce B. (*née* Le Bé), (b. ?; d. ?), his wife, who continued after his death.
3. Pierre B. (b. Paris, *c.* 1600; d. Paris, *c.* 1640), their son.
4. Robert B. (b. ?; d. Paris, 1679), son of 3.
5. Christophe B. (b. ?; d. Paris, 1715), son of 4.
6. Jean-Baptiste Christophe B. (b. ?; d. Paris, 1750), son of 5.
7. Christophe Jean François B. (b. ?; d. Paris, 1765), son of 6.
8. Pierre Robert Christophe B. (b. ?; d. Paris, ? 1788), son of 7.

Ballata (It.), a 14th-cent. verse form, often set to mus., in which the refrain precedes and follows each stanza. The term implies an association with dancing.

Ballet (*see also* **Ballett**), a stage entertainment consisting entirely of dancing and therefore requiring exclusively instrumental mus. from the comp., although vocal features have been intro. by some modern musicians and were a feature in Fr. B. of the 18th cent., where the term was often short for *opéra-ballet* and the B. proper was called *ballet-pantomime*.

Ballet comique de la royne, stage entertainment perf. in Paris, 15. X. 1581, at the marriage of the Duc de Joyeux and Mlle. de Vaudemont, under the supervision of Balthasar de Beaujoyeulx. The verse was by the Sieur de la Chesnaye, the scenery by Patin, and the mus. by the bass singer Lambert de Beaulieu, Jacques Salmon and others. It is in effect the 1st of the *ballets de cour*.

Ballet de Cour (Fr. = court ballet), a 16th–17th-cent. Fr. stage entertainment with mus. developing from the older tourneys and masquerades, containing vocal and dance movements specially comp. Guédron and Boësset were its chief exponents. The species developed later into the opera-ballet and the opera.

Ballet-pantomime. *See* **Ballet.**

Ballett (or **Ballet**), a type of 16th–17th-cent. comp. for several voices, resembling a madrigal, but in a lighter, more dance-like style.

Balletti (It.), pieces of mus. intended for dancing, esp. on the stage.

Balling, Michael (b. Heidingsfeld, 28. VIII. 1866; d. Darmstadt, 1. IX. 1925), Ger. cond. Associated with the Wagner festivals at Bayreuth and cond. of the Hallé Orch., Manchester, 1912–14.

Ballo (It. = dance), usually used in comb., e.g. *tempo di ballo*.

Ballo in maschera, Un (*A Masked Ball*), opera by Verdi (lib. by Antonio Somma, based on Scribe's *Gustave III* set by Auber), prod. Rome, Teatro Apollo, 17. II. 1859.

Balmer, Luc (b. Munich, 13. VII. 1898), Swiss comp. and cond., son of a painter, Wilhelm B., of Basle. Studied with Huber at the Basle Cons. and with Busoni in Berlin. Prof. of harmony at the Berne Cons., cond. of concerts at Lucerne and opera at Berne, where from 1935 he also cond. the popular symph. concerts. From 1938 attached to Radio Berne.

Works incl. incid. mus. for plays; Petrarch's Sonnet 103 for chorus and orch.; symph., symph. fragment, serenade and symph. variations for orch.; pf. concerto, cello concerto; 2 string 4tets and other chamber mus., etc.

Baltazarini. *See* **Beaujoyeulx.**

Baltic Composers. *See* **Aavik, Erdmann, Lopatnikov, Medinš, Wihtol, Wilm, Wolfurt.**

Baltzar, Thomas (b. Lübeck, *c.* 1630; d. London, VII. 1663), Ger. or Swed. violinist. In the service of Queen Christina of Swed. 1653–5 and violinist to Charles II from 1661.

Balzac, Honoré de (1799–1850), Fr. novelist. *See* **Assafiev** (*Lost Illusions*), **Leoncavallo** (*Serafita*), **Levadé** (*Peau de chagrin*), **Massimilla Doni** (Schoeck), **Nouguès** (*Auberge rouge*), **Shostakovich** (*Human Comedy*), **Waltershausen** (*Oberst Chabert*).

Bamboula, a Negro drum and a Negro dance accomp. by it, orig. in the West Indies. Coleridge-Taylor's 'rhapsodic dance' for orch., Op. 75, is entitled *Bamboula*.

Banchieri, Adriano (b. Bologna, 3. IX. 1568; d. Bologna, 1634), It. organist, theorist and comp. Learnt mus. as a chorister at Lucca Cathedral. Afterwards at St. Mark's, Venice; organist at Imola, 1600–7, and at the monastery of San Michele in Bosco (Monte Oliveto) nr. Bologna. He founded the Accademia de' floridi at Bologna, *c.* 1623, and wrote theoret. works, esp. on figured bass.

Works incl. Masses; sacred symphs. and concertos; comic intermezzi for the stage; org. works, etc.

Bancroft, Richard (1544–1610), Eng. archbishop and author. *See* **Paisible** (*King Edward III*).

Banda (It. = band), a military band, in particular a band used on the stage or behind the scene in an opera, e.g. in Verdi's *Macbeth*.

Bandora. *See* **Pandora.**

Bandurria (Span. = Pandora), a string instrument of the Cittern type, with 6 double strings which are plucked with the fingers or with a plectrum.

Banestre, Gilbert (b. ?, *c.* 1445; d. London, VIII. 1487), Eng. comp. Master of the Children in the Chapel Royal in succession to Abyngdon, 1478; wrote sacred and secular vocal mus.

Banister, John (b. ?, 1630; d. London, 3. X. 1679), Eng. violinist and concert promoter. Lived in London; sent to Fr. by Charles II in 1661. Leader of the King's vlns., 1662–7. Comp. mus. for Davenant's *Circe* and Wycherley's *Gentleman Dancing-Master* and contrib. songs to var. collections.

Banister, John (b. ?; d. London, 1735), English violinist and teacher of his instrument, son of prec. Comp. for the stage.

Banjo, an Amer. Negro string instrument of the Guitar type with a hollow body covered with stretched parchment and 5 strings, which are plucked with the fingers; the neck is fretted. The 5-stringed instrument is now the normal type but previously there were up to 9 strings.

Bánk-Bán, opera by Erkel (lib. by Béni Egressy, based on a play by József Katona), prod. Budapest, 9. III. 1861.

Banks, Don (b. Melbourne, 25. X. 1923), Austral. comp. Studied at Melbourne Cons. and later (1950) with Seiber in London and Dallapiccola in Florence (1953). Settled in London.

Works incl. horn concerto; divertimento for fl. and string trio; *Duo* for vln. and cello; vln. sonata; 3 studies for cello and pf.; 3 Episodes for fl. and pf.; film mus.

Bänkelsänger (Ger.), a singer of ballads, esp. at fairs, a chapman singing the songs he sold.

Banti (*née* **Giorgi**), **Brigitta** (b. Crema, 1757; d. Bologna, 18. II. 1806), It. soprano. She sang in the streets of Venice and the cafés of Paris at first, but was engaged for the Paris Opéra in 1776 and had much success in London.

Bantock, Granville (b. London, 7. VIII. 1868; d. London, 16. X. 1946), Eng. comp. Son of a doctor; educ. for the civil service, but entered the R.A.M. in 1889, where some of his earliest works were perf., and Lago prod. the opera *Cædmar* at the Olympic Theatre in 1892. After some experience in theatrical cond. he gave a concert of modern Eng. mus. in 1896. The next year he was app. cond. at the Tower, New Brighton, where he introd. much contemp. mus. In Feb. 1900 he gave a concert of new Brit. mus. at Antwerp and in Sept. was app. principal of the Birmingham and Midland Inst. School of Mus. He

remained in Birmingham until 1933, and became Prof. of Mus. at the Univ. in 1908, succeeding Elgar. Knighted in 1930.

Works incl. operas *Cædmar, Pearl of Iran, The Seal Woman*; 5 ballets; incid. mus. for Sophocles' *Electra*, Shakespeare's *Macbeth*, Wilde's *Salome*, etc.; orchestral works: *Processional* and *Jaga-Naut* (from 24 projected symph. poems on Southey's *Curse of Kehama*), *Helena* variations, comedy overtures *The Pierrot of the Minute* (after Ernest Dowson) and *Circus Life*, orchestral ballad *The Sea Reivers*, *Overture to a Gk. Tragedy*, symph. poem *Dante and Beatrice*, *Fifine at the Fair* (after Browning), overture to *The Frogs* (Aristophanes), *Hebridean Symph.*, *A Pagan Symph.*; serenade *From the Far West, Scenes from the Scottish Highlands, The Land of Gael* for string orch.; *Elegiac Poem, Sapphic Poem, Celtic Poem* for cello and orch.; chorus and orch. (with or without solo voices): *The Fire-Worshippers, The Time-Spirit, Sea Wanderers, Christ in the Wilderness, Omar Khayyám* (setting of FitzGerald's trans. in 3 parts), *Gethsemane, The Great God Pan, Song of Songs*, oratorio *The Pilgrim's Progress* (Bunyan); unaccomp. chorus: choral symphs. *Atalanta in Calydon* (Swinburne) and *Vanity of Vanities* (Ecclesiastes), suite *A Pageant of Human Life* and many smaller works and part-songs; numerous songs incl. cycles *Songs of the East* (6 vols.), *Songs of the Seraglio, Six Jester Songs, Five Ghazals of Hafiz, Ferishtah's Fancies* (Browning), *Sappho, Songs from the Chinese Poets* (8 sets); sonatas for vln. and pf. and vla. and pf.; *Poem* for cello and pf.; pf. pieces, etc.

Banville, Théodore de (1823–91), Fr. poet. *See* Scontrino (*Gringoire*), Terrasse (*Matinées poétiques*), Vidal (P.) (*Baiser*).

Bar (Eng.). (1) Orig. the line drawn through the mus. stave or staves to indicate the metrical divisions of a comp., now called 'bar-line' in Eng. (2) The space between two bar-lines, called 'measure' in Amer.

Bar (Ger.), a medieval Ger. musical form (*Barform*) of song, used by the Minnesinger and Meistersinger. It consists of two similar phrases or members (*Stollen*, together called the *Aufgesang*), followed by a different but relevant one (*Abgesang*).

Baranovič Krešimir (b. Šibenik, 25. VII. 1894), Yugoslav cond. and comp. Studied at the Zagreb and Vienna Conss., and in 1915 became cond. at the Zagreb theatre. He was cond. of the Nat. Theatre at Belgrade in 1927–9, but returned to Zagreb as opera cond.

Works incl. operas *Clipped-mowed* and *The Turks go on*; ballets *The Cake Heart* and *Imbrek with the Nose*; Symph. Scherzo and *Poème balcanique* for orch.; *From my*

Mountains for voice and orch.; chamber mus.; songs, etc.

Barbaia, Domenico (old spelling Barbaja) (b. Milan, 1778; d. Posilipo, 16. X. 1841), It. impresario. Was 1st a waiter, then a circus proprietor and finally the most popular of operatic managers. In 1821–8, coming from the Teatro San Carlo at Naples, he managed the Kärntnertortheater and the Theater an der Wien in Vienna.

Barbé, Anton (b. ?; d. Antwerp, 2. XII. 1564), Flem. comp. and 1st of a line of Antwerp musicians. From 1527 to 1562 he was *Kapellmeister* at Antwerp Cathedral. He pub. Masses, motets and *chansons*, and contributed a Dutch song to Susato's *Het ierste musyck boexken* (1551).

Barbe-bleue (*Bluebeard*), operetta by Offenbach (lib. by Henri Meilhac and Ludovic Halévy), prod. Paris, Théâtre des Variétés, 5. II. 1866.

Barbella, Emanuele (b. Naples, 14. IV. 1718; d. Naples, 1. I. 1777), It. violinist and comp. Studied at Naples and wrote sonatas and duets for vln., trio-sonatas, also an opera in collaboration with Logroscino, *Elmira generosa* (Naples, 1753).

Barber of Baghdad, The (Cornelius). *See* **Barbier von Bagdad.**

Barber of Seville, The (Paisiello, Rossini). *See* **Barbiere di Siviglia.**

Barber, Robert (b. ?; d. ?), Eng. 16th-cent. comp. *Informator choristarum*, Winchester Coll., 1541–2. A *Dum transisset sabbatum* is in the Gyffard part-books.

Barber, Samuel (b. West Chester, Pa., 9. III. 1910), Amer. comp. Entered Curtis Institute of Mus. in 1924, winning a prize with a vln. sonata in 1928. In the following years he won several more prizes, incl. the American *Prix de Rome*, 1935. In 1964 he was commissioned to write an opera for the opening of the new Metropolitan Opera House, and prod. *Antony and Cleopatra*.

Works incl. operas, *Vanessa, A Hand of Bridge* and *Antony and Cleopatra* (after Shakespeare); 2 symphs., 2 Essays, overture to Sheridan's *School for Scandal*, mus. for a scene from Shelley for orch.; Adagio for strings; vln. concerto, cello concerto, pf. concerto; *Capricorn Concerto* for fl., ob., tpt. and strings; 2 string 4tets; cello and pf. sonata; vln. and pf. sonata, pf. sonata; *Dover Beach* (Matthew Arnold) for baritone and string 4tet; works for unaccomp. chorus to words by Helen Waddell, Emily Dickinson, James Stephens and Stephen Spender; song cycle from James Joyce's *Chamber Music* and songs to words by James Stephens, A. E. Housman, Gerard Manley Hopkins, Yeats, etc.; *Excursions* for pf., etc.

Barberiis, Melchiore de (b. ?; d. ?), It. 16th-cent. lutenist. Lived at Padua and

pub. several books of pieces in lute tablature, 1546–9.

Barbetta, Giulio Cesare (b. ? Padua, ?; d. ? Padua, ?), It. 16th-cent. lutenist. Lived at Padua and pub. 4 books of mus. in lute tablature, 1569–1603.

Barbi, Alice (b. Modena, 1. VI. 1862; d. Rome, 4. IX. 1948), It. mezzo-soprano and violinist. Made her 1st appearance as singer in 1882 at Milan. She toured widely and became a favourite interpreter of Brahms.

Barbier von Bagdad, Der (*The Barber of B.*), opera by Cornelius (lib. by comp.), prod. Weimar, 15. XII. 1858.

Barbiere di Siviglia, Il, ossia La precauzione inutile (*The Barber of Seville, or Vain Precaution*; orig. title: *Almaviva, ossia L'inutile precauzione*), opera by Rossini (lib. by Cesare Sterbini, based on Beaumarchais' *Le Barbier de Séville*), prod. Rome, Teatro Argentina, 20. II. 1816.

Barbiere di Siviglia, Il, ovvero La precauzione inutile (*The Barber of Seville, or Vain Precaution*), opera by Paisiello (lib. by Giuseppe Petrosellini, based on Beaumarchais' *Le Barbier de Séville*), prod. St. Petersburg, Hermitage, at court, 26. IX. 1782.

Barbieri, Francisco (Asenjo) (b. Madrid, 3. VIII. 1823; d. Madrid, 19. II. 1894), Span. comp. Studied pf. with P. Albéniz and comp. with Carnicer at the Madrid Cons. He made at 1st a poor living as clarinettist in a military band, pianist in cafés, chorus singer, copyist, etc. Having deputized as an opera singer, he took to the stage and made his 1st success with the comic opera *Jugar con fuego* in 1851. As a scholar he did valuable work in ed. the *Cancionero musical* containing secular Span. vocal mus. of the 15th and 16th cents.

Comic operas incl. *Gloria y peluca, Tramoya, Jugar con fuego, Los diamantes de la corona, Pan y toros, El barberillo de Lavapiés,* etc.

Barbion, Eustachius (b. ?; d. Kortrijk, VI. 1556), Flem. comp. From 12. IV. 1543 he was *Kapellmeister* of the church of Notre-Dame at Kortrijk. His works consist of motets and *chansons*.

Barbireau, Jacques (b. ? Mons, *c.* 1408; d. Antwerp, 8. VIII. 1491), Flem. comp. Was choirmaster of Antwerp Cathedral from 1448 until his death. Wrote Masses and other church mus., also songs for 3 and 4 voices.

Barbirolli, John (b. London, 2. XII. 1899; d. London, 28. VII. 1970), Eng. cond. Studied at Trinity College, London (1911–12) and the R.A.M. (1912–17). He made his début as a cellist, aged 11, and joined the Queen's Hall Orch. in that capacity in 1915. Achieved recognition as a cond. in 1926, later succeeding

Toscanini as chief cond. of the New York Phil. in 1937. He returned to England in 1943, where he took over the Hallé Orch. In 1949 he was knighted and in 1950 received the Royal Phil. Society's gold medal. He was married to the oboist Evelyn Rothwell (1939). B. excelled in the classical repertory, esp. the symphs. of Bruckner.

Barblan, Otto (b. Scanfs, Engadine, 22. III. 1860; d. Geneva, 20. XII. 1943), Swiss organist, cond. and comp. Studied at the Stuttgart Cons. After teaching and cond. at Chur, he became organist at Geneva Cathedral in 1887. Taught at the Cons. there and cond. the Société de Chant Sacré.

Works incl. mus. for a festival play, *Ode patriotique* and cantatas for solo voices, chorus and orch.; Passion according to St. Luke; Psalm cxvii for double chorus; Passacaglia on B.A.C.H. for orch.; org. works, pf. pieces, part-songs, etc.

Barcarolle (Fr. from It. *barcaruola*), a boating-song, esp. of the type sung by the gondoliers at Venice. A piece or song in that style, generally in 6–8 time and a moderate tempo with a swaying rhythm.

Barcroft, George (b. Ely, ?; d. Ely, ?), Eng. 16th–17th-cent. organist and comp. Studied at Cambridge and was min. canon and organist at Ely Cathedral, 1579–1610. Comp. church mus.

Barcroft, Thomas (b. ?; d. Ely, ?), Eng. 16th-cent. organist and comp., ? father of prec. Organist at Ely. Wrote church mus.

Bardi, Giovanni, Count of Vernio (b. Florence, 5. II. 1534; d. Rome, *c.* 1614), It. nobleman and amateur musician. Patron of the *camerata* at Florence. Works by Caccini, Galilei, Peri and others were perf. at his house. He comp. madrigals himself.

Bärenhäuter, Der (*Lazy-bones*), opera by Siegfried Wagner (lib. by comp.), prod. Munich, 21. I. 1899.

Bargiel, Woldemar (b. Berlin, 3. X. 1828; d. Berlin, 23. II. 1897), Ger. comp. Studied under Dehn in Berlin and at Leipzig Cons. Later taught in Berlin, Cologne and Amsterdam, where he also cond.

Works incl. a symph., orchestral overtures; psalm for chorus and orch.; much chamber mus.; pf. pieces, etc.

Barham, Richard (1788–1845), Eng. clergyman and author. *See* **Lady Rohesia** (Hopkins).

Baring, Maurice (1874–1945), Eng. novelist and essayist. *See* **Edmunds** (*Blue Harlequin*), **Fête galante** (Smyth).

Bariolage (Fr.), the playing of high notes on a string instrument in high positions on the lower strings to obtain a different tone-colour or to facilitate the perf. of rapid high passages without changing to lower positions. Also the alternation of the same note on an open string and a stopped string.

Baritone (from Gk. *barutonos* = deep-sounding). (1) A male voice midway between tenor and bass, with approximately the foll. compass:

(2) A brass instrument of the Saxhorn family, of the same pitch as the Euphonium but with a smaller bore and only 3 valves.

(3) Applied to instruments of moderately low compass, e.g. baritone ob., baritone saxophone.

Baritone Clef, the F clef on the 3rd line of the stave, now obs.:

Barkworth, John (Edmund) (b. Beverley, 20. V. 1858; d. Geneva, 18. XI. 1929), Eng. comp. Educ. at Rugby, Oxford and the R.C.M. His chief work is an opera on Shakespeare's *Romeo and Juliet*, prod. Middlesbrough, 7. I. 1916.

Bärmann, Heinrich Joseph (b. Potsdam, 14. II. 1784; d. Munich, 11. VI. 1847), Ger. clarinettist. Member of the court orch. at Munich. Weber wrote several works for him.

Barnard, John (b. ?; d. ?), Eng. 17th-cent. musician. Min. canon at St. Paul's Cathedral in London; pub. the 1st printed collection of Eng. cathedral mus. in 1641.

Barnby, Joseph (b. York, 12. VIII. 1838; d. London, 28. I. 1896), Eng. cond., organist and comp. Held various organist's posts in London; precentor at Eton Coll. 1875–92, then principal of G.S.M. Distinguished as choral cond. Knighted 1892.

Barnett, John (b. Bedford, 15. VII. 1802; d. nr. Cheltenham, 16–17. IV. 1890), Eng. comp. of Ger. descent (orig. name Beer: Meyerbeer's family). Was a stage singer as a child and studied with C. E. Horn. In 1825 he prod. his 1st stage piece, which was followed by a large number of others, incl. *The Mountain Sylph*, prod. 25. VIII. 1834.

Barnett, John Francis (b. London, 16. X. 1837; d. London, 24. XI. 1916), Eng. comp. and pianist, nephew of prec. Studied in London and Leipzig, where he appeared at the Gewandhaus.

Works incl. symph. in A min., overture to Shakespeare's *A Winter's Tale*; cantatas *The Ancient Mariner* (Coleridge), *Paradise and the Peri* (Moore) and others; 2 oratorios; pf. concerto; chamber mus.; pf. pieces, etc.

Baron, Ernst Gottlieb (b. Breslau, 17. II. 1696; d. Berlin, 12. IV. 1760), Ger. author, lutenist and comp., pupil of Weiss. Travelled widely as a lutenist, wrote several theoretical works on the lute, and comp. for his instrument.

Baroness, The. *See* **Lindelheim.**

Baroni, It. 17th-cent. family of singers and lutenists:

1. **Adriana B.** (*née* Basile) (b. ?; d. ?). She worked at Mantua and was eulogized in a book of verses in 1623.

2. **Leonora B.** (b. Mantua, XII. 1611; d. Rome, IV. 1670), daughter of 1. Also played vla. da gamba and comp. Milton met her in Rome in 1638 and wrote 3 poems on her and her mother.

3. **Catarina B.** (b. Mantua, after 1620; d. ?), sister of 2. Also played the harp and wrote poetry.

Barraine, Elsa (b. Paris, 13. II. 1910), Fr. comp. Studied at the Paris Cons., Dukas being among her masters, and gained the Prix de Rome in 1929. In 1939–44 she gave up comp. to devote herself wholly to the Fr. resistance movement.

Works incl. ballet *Le Mur*; incid. mus. for Shakespeare's *King Lear* and other plays; *Avis* (Éluard) for chorus and orch.; 3 symphs., symph. poem *Pogromes*, *Fête des colonies* and variations *Le Fleuve rouge* for orch.; wind 5tet; variations and *Marche du printemps sans amour* for pf.; Chin. songs, Jewish songs, songs to words by Tagore, etc.

Barraqué, Jean (b. Paris, 17. I. 1928), Fr. comp. Studied with Jean Langlais and Messiaen, later working in the experimental laboratories of the Radiodiffusion Française in Paris.

Works incl. *Sequence* for soprano and chamber ensemble; *Le Temps restitué* for voices and orch.; *Au delà du hasard* (based on Hermann Broch) for voices and instrumental groups; *Chant après chant* for perc.; pf. sonata.

Barraud, Henry (b. Bordeaux, 23. IV. 1900), Fr. comp. Studied 1st at Bordeaux and later at the Paris Cons. with Caussade, Dukas and Aubert. In 1937 he was in charge of the mus. at the Paris World Fair and then joined the radio service, where he rose to the post of head of the national programme in 1948.

Works incl. operas *La Farce du Maître Pathelin*, *Numance* and *Lavinia*; ballets *La Kermesse* and *L'Astrologue dans le puits*; film and radio mus.; oratorio *Les Mystères des Saints Innocents*, cantatas and other choral works; 3 symphs.; pf. concerto; woodwind trio, string trio, string 4tet, vln. and pf. sonata; pf. mus.; songs, etc.

Barré (Fr. lit. barred). A chord on string instruments with fretted fingerboards is said to be played B. when a finger is laid horizontally across the whole fingerboard, thus raising all the strings in pitch by the same interval's distance from the fundamental tuning.

Barre, Antonio (b. ?; d. ? Rome, ?), It.

16th-cent. singer, mus. printer and comp. Alto in the choir of St. Peter's in Rome in the middle of the cent. Wrote madrigals and pub. them, with those of many other comps., in 7 books printed by his own press, 1st in Rome and after 1564 at Milan.

Barré (or **Barri**), **Léonard** (b. Limoges, ?; d. ?), Fr. comp. Pupil of Willaert and singer in the Papal Choir in Rome, 1537–1552. He attended the Council of Trent in 1545 to give advice on church mus. His works incl. motets and madrigals.

Barrel Organ, a popular mechan. instrument prod. mus. by the mere turning of a handle, but sometimes actuated by clockwork. A cylinder (barrel) moves tongue-shaped keys by means of pins or studs arranged in such order that its turning prod. an ordered piece of mus. The keys control pipes similar to those of the org., but restricted to a single range of tone-colour and limited in compass. B. O.s were formerly used in small village churches that could not maintain an org. and organist, and they mechan. played a number of hymn tunes. The B. O. is often wrongly called Hurdy-gurdy, which is a totally different instrument.

Barrett, John (b. ?, *c*. 1674; d. ?, *c*. 1735), Eng. organist, teacher and comp. Wrote incid. mus. for plays, many popular songs, etc.

Barrett, Thomas. *See* **Stuart, Leslie.**

Barrie, James (Matthew) (1860–1937), Scot. playwright and novelist. *See* **Bax** (*Truth about the Rus. Dancers*), **Davies** (Walford) (*Peter Pan* 4tet), **Mackenzie** (*Little Minister*), **O'Neill** (*Mary Rose* and *Kiss for Cinderella*), **Skilton** (*Mary Rose*).

Barrière, Théodore (1823–77), Fr. playwright. *See* **Offenbach** (*Gascon*).

Barrios, Ángel (b. Granada, 4. I. 1882; d. Madrid, 27. XI. 1964), Span. guitarist and comp.

Works incl. comic operas, *Granada mia*, etc., an opera with a Goya setting, *El Avapiés*, in collab. with C. del Campo, and works for his own instrument.

Bartered Bride, The (*Prodaná Nevěsta*) opera by Smetana (lib. by Karel Sabina), prod., 1st version, Prague, Cz. Theatre, 30. V. 1866; rev. version, 29. I. 1869; final version (with recitatives), 25. IX. 1870.

Barth, Hans (b. Leipzig, 25. VI. 1897; d. Jacksonville, Florida, 9. XII. 1956), Ger. pianist and comp. who emigrated to the U.S.A. in 1907. A meeting with Busoni encouraged him to experiment with new scales, and in 1928 he invented a ¼-tone pf., for which he composed a number of works. He also composed ¼-tone chamber and instrumental mus., as well as more normal pieces.

Barthélémon, François Hippolyte (b. Bordeaux, 27. VII. 1741; d. London, 20. VII. 1808), Fr. violinist and comp. Settled in London, 1765. A year later prod. *Pelopida*, the 1st of several successful dramatic works, and married the singer Mary Young, daughter of Charles Young and niece of Mrs. Arne and Mrs. Lampe. Comp. stage pieces for Garrick and visited Fr., Ger. and It. with his wife, who sang there. A friend of Haydn during the latter's visits to London, B. is said to have suggested the subject of *The Creation*.

Works incl. oratorio *Jefte in Masfa*; symphs.; concertos, sonatas, duets for vln., etc.

Bartholomew, Ann. *See* **Mounsey.**

Bartleman, James (b. London, 19. IX. 1769; d. London, 15. IV. 1821), Eng. bass. Educ. at Westminster School and Abbey; a distinguished boy treble, he first appeared as a bass in 1788.

Bartlet, John (b. ?; d. ?), Eng. 16th–17th-cent. lutenist and comp. Prob. in the service of Lord Hertford. Pub. a *Booke of Ayres* for voices and instruments in 1606.

Bartók, Béla (b. Nagyszentmiklós, 25. III. 1881; d. New York, 26. IX. 1945), Hung. comp. Son of a director of agriculture. His mother, a school-teacher, was a musician and taught him from an early age. He appeared as public pianist at the age of 10. Studied under Laszlo Erkel at Pozsony (Pressburg) until 1899 and then the pf. under István Thomán and comp. under Koessler at the Budapest Cons. About 1905 he began to collect folk tunes and to discover that the true Magyar mus. differed greatly from that of the Hung. gypsies so far regarded as the only Hung. folk mus. App. prof. of pf. at Budapest Cons. in 1907. After the war of 1914–18 he began to be known in Eur. and Amer., and in 1922 was made an hon. member of the I.S.C.M. In 1940 emigrated to the U.S.A. where he taught briefly at Columbia Univ. and Harvard. B. is one of the foremost comps. of the 20th cent. Much influenced by Hung. folk mus., he never imitated it, but incorporated its rhythms and melodic characteristics into complex, subtle and effective forms.

Works incl. opera *Bluebeard's Castle* (1911); mime plays *The Wooden Prince* (1916), *The Miraculous Mandarin* (1919); orchestral mus.: *Kossuth* symph., 2 suites, *Two Portraits, Two Pictures, Dance Suite*, concerto for orch. (1944), 3 pf. concertos (1926, 1931, 1945), 2 rhapsodies for vln. and orch., 1 for pf. and orch., 2 vln. concertos (No. 2, 1938); *Music for Strings, Percussion and Celesta* (1936); *Divertimento* for strings (1939); sonata for 2 pfs. and perc. (1937); chamber mus.: 6 string 4tets (1908, 1917, 1927, 1928, 1934, 1939); 2 sonatas for vln. and pf.; *Contrasts* for vln., clar. and pf.; sonata for solo vln. (1944); much pf. mus., incl. *Mikrokosmos* (153 progressive pieces); sonata (1926); sona-

tina; *Allegro barbaro*; *Rumanian Dances*, etc.; vocal mus., incl. *Cantata Profana* for solo voices, chorus and orch. (1930) and many arrs. of Hung., Slovak, and Rumanian folksongs, etc.

Bartolino da Padua. *See* **Padua.**

Bartoš, František (b. Mlatcová, Moravia, 16. III. 1837; d. Mlatcová, 11. VI. 1906), Morav. musicologist. Ed. 3 collections of Morav. folk mus.

Bartoš, Josef (b. Vysoké Mýto, 4. III. 1887; d. Prague, 27. X. 1952), Cz. critic. Author of biogs. of Dvořák, Fibich and J. B. Foerster.

Baryton, an obs. string instrument of the bass viol type with sympathetic strings which can be plucked by the hand. It was cultivated mainly in Ger. and Aus. Haydn's patron, Prince Nicolas Esterházy, played it and Haydn wrote nearly 200 works for it.

Bas-dessus (Fr. lit. low above), an obs. term for a mezzo-soprano.

Base (Eng. obs.). The old Eng. word for Bass.

Basili (or **Basily), Francesco** (b. Loreto, 3. II. 1767; d. Rome, 25. III. 1850), It. singer and comp. Became dir. of the Milan Cons. in 1827. *Maestro di cappella* at St. Peter's in Rome from 1837.

Works incl. operas *La locandiera, Achille nell' assedio di Troia, Ritorno d'Ulisse, Antigona, Achille, L'orfana egiziana*; oratorio *Sansone*; Requiem for Jannaconi; several Misereres; symphs., etc.

Basilius (*Der königliche Schäfer, oder Basilius in Arcadien: The Royal Shepherd, or Basil in Arcady*), opera by Keiser (lib. by Friedrich Christian Bressand), prod. Hamburg, Theater beim Gänsemarkt, ? spring 1694.

Basiron, Philippe (Baziron, Philippon) (b. ?; d. ?), 15th–16th-cent. Fr. or Flem. comp. Comp. Masses, motets and *chansons*.

Basoche, La (*The Corporation of Lawyers*), opera by Messager (lib. by Albert Carré), prod. Paris, Opéra-Comique, 30. V. 1890.

Basque Composer. *See* **Usandizaga.**

Bass. (1) The lowest adult male voice, with approximately the foll. compass:

(2) Abbr. for Double Bass.

(3) Applied to instruments of a low compass, e.g. Bass Trumpet.

(4) The lowest part of a vocal or instrumental ensemble, often used as an abbr. for *Basso continuo*.

Bass Clarinet, a clar. with a range an octave lower than the ordinary instrument.

Bass Clef, the F clef on the 4th line of the stave:

Bass Drum, the largest of the drums not prod. notes of definite pitch. It is placed upright and struck sideways, prod. a dull thud. It is used both in the orch. and in military bands, and in the latter it is played in conjunction with the Cymbals, one of which is placed on it while the other is held in the player's hand not used to hold the drumstick.

Bass Flute, a fl. with a range a fourth lower than that of the ordinary instrument. It is a transposing instrument in G. Also an 8-ft. org. pedal stop.

Bass Horn. *See* **Ophicleide.**

Bass Trumpet, a tpt. invented by Wagner, with a written compass an octave below that of the normal orchestral instrument.

Bass Viol. *See* **Viola da gamba.**

Bassani, Giovanni Battista (b. Padua, *c.* 1657; d. Bergamo, 1. X. 1716), It. violinist and comp. Organist at Ferrara and later in charge of the cathedral mus. at Bologna; returned to Ferrara as *maestro di cappella* in 1683. Comp. 12 oratorios, prod. 11 operas and brought out a large amount of church and instrumental mus.

Bassano, Giovanni (b. ?; d. ?), Venetian comp. of the late 16th cent. Comp. instrumental mus., incl. ornamented transcriptions of vocal works by Gabrieli, Marenzio, etc.

Basse chantante (Fr. = singing-bass), a bass voice esp. suited to melodic delivery and lyrical parts.

Basse chiffrée (Fr.) = Figured Bass, Thorough-bass.

Basse-Contre (Fr.), low bass, whether a voice, an instrument or an org. stop.

Basse Danse, a Fr. dance of the 15th–

16th cent. So called because the feet were kept low, not thrown up in the air as in some other dances. The illustration below is a 16th-cent. ex.

Basset Horn, an alto instrument of the clar. family, with an extra key controlling notes below the normal range of instruments of this family. Mozart frequently wrote for it.

Bassi, Luigi (b. Pesaro, 5. IX. 1766; d. Dresden, 13. IX. 1825), It. baritone. Appeared in soprano parts at the age of 13 and went to Prague in 1784, where he made a great reputation. He was Mozart's 1st Don Giovanni there in 1787.

Basso cantante (It. = singing-bass), a bass voice esp. suited to melodic delivery and lyrical parts.

Basso continuo (It. = continuous bass). *See* **Thorough-Bass.**

Basso ostinato (It., lit. obstinate bass) = Ground Bass, a bass part in a comp. continually tracing the same melodic outline.

Bassoon, a double-reed instrument dating from the 16th cent. The normal compass is:

though a few higher notes are possible. Also a 16-ft. org. reed stop.

Bastardella, La, the nickname given to the singer Lucrezia Aguiari, who was the illegitimate daughter of an It. nobleman.

Bastien und Bastienne, *Singspiel* by Mozart, K. 50 (lib. by Friedrich Wilhelm Weiskern and Andreas Schachtner, based on Favart's parody of Rousseau's *Le Devin du Village*), prod. Vienna, at the house of Anton Mesmer, the hypnotist, IX. or X. 1768.

Baston, Josquin (b. ?; d. ?), Flem. 16th–

Anon, 16th cent.

BASSE DANSE

cent. comp. Prob. worked in It. Wrote motets and songs for several voices.

Bataille, Gabriel (b. ?, 1575; d. Paris, 17. XII. 1630), Fr. lutenist and comp. Contrib. mus. to ballets danced at the court of Louis XIII. Between 1608 and 1623 he pub. many lute pieces and songs.

Bate, Stanley (b. Plymouth, 12. XII. 1911; d. London, 19. X. 1959), Eng. comp. Studied with Vaughan Williams at the R.C.M. in London and later, with the aid of scholarships, with Hindemith in Ger., and Nadia Boulanger in Paris. On his return to London he was engaged in var. theatre and ballet activities. He married Peggy Glanville-Hicks, who had been his fellow student, in 1939, toured Australia with her in 1941, and both emigrated to U.S.A. After the war B. returned to England.

Works incl. incid. mus. for *The Patriots*; 8 ballets incl. *Dance Variations*; mus. for documentary film *The Fifth Year*; 4 symphs., 2 sinfoniettas, ballet suite *Perseus* for orch.; 3 pf. concertos, concerto for 2 pfs., 2 vln. concertos, concertante for pf. and strings, concertino for pf. and chamber orch., *Haneen* for fl., gong and strings; *Incantations* for voice and orch.; 4 string 4tets and 5 pieces for string 4tet, trio for fl., cello and pf.; sonatas for vln. and pf. and fl. and pf., sonatina for recorder and pf.; 3 pieces, ballet suite *Cap over Mill* and overture for Rus. War Relief for 2 pfs.; sonata, 9 sonatinas, concert suite, *Romance and Toccata* and *6 Studies for an Infant Prodigy* for pf., etc.

Bates, Joah (b. Halifax, III. 1741; d. London, 8. VI. 1799), Eng. organist, scholar and cond. Cond. the Concert of Ancient Mus. in London from its foundation in 1776.

Bates, William (b. ?; d. ?), Eng. 18th-cent. comp. Worked in London, where he prod. several stage pieces and wrote songs for the pleasure gardens, glees, catches, etc.

Bateson, Thomas (b. ? Cheshire, *c.* 1570; d. Dublin, III. or IV. 1630), Eng. organist and comp. Prob. organist at Chester Cathedral until 1609, when he became vicar-choral and organist at Trinity Cathedral, Dublin. 2 books of madrigals by him were pub. in 1604 and 1618.

Bath, Hubert (b. Barnstaple, 6. XI. 1883; d. Harefield, Middlesex, 24. IV. 1945), Eng. cond., educationist and comp. Studied at the R.A.M. in London.

Works incl. opera *Trilby* (after G. du Maurier) and others; incid. mus. to Hauptmann's *Hannele*; film mus. for *Love Story*, incl. *Cornish Rhapsody* for pf. and orch.; orchestral variations and suites; cantatas, songs, etc.

Bathe, William (b. Ireland, 2. IV. 1564; d. Madrid, 17. VI. 1614), Ir. priest and mus. scholar. In state service at first, he went to

Spain and became a Jesuit priest in 1599. He wrote *Briefe Introductions to the True Art of Musick and the Skill of Song*, also *Janua linguarum*.

Batistin. *See* **Stuck.**

Baton (Fr.), the stick used by the cond. in orchestral and choral perfs. It orig. from a roll of mus. used in the 15th cent. and passed through a phase of a heavy stick beaten on the floor in the 17th cent. (e.g. Lully).

Battaglia di Legnano, La (*The Battle of L.*), opera by Verdi (lib. by Salvatore Cammarano), prod. Rome, Teatro Argentina, 27. I. 1849.

Battement (Fr.) = Mordent.

Batten, Adrian (b. ?; d. London, ? 1637), Eng. organist and comp. Chorister at Winchester Cathedral as a boy. In 1614 he came to London as vicar-choral at Westminster Abbey and in 1624 became organist at St. Paul's Cathedral.

Works incl. 11 services, *c.* 50 anthems and other church mus.

Batterie (Fr.). An 18th-cent. term for rapid broken accomp. figures. Also a collective term for the group of perc. instruments in the orchestra.

Battery (Eng. obs.) = Arpeggio.

Battishill, Jonathan (b. London, V. 1738; d. London, 10. XII. 1801), Eng. harpsichordist, organist and comp. Chorister at St. Paul's Cathedral. About 1762 became harpsichordist to Covent Garden Theatre, where he prod. in 1764 the opera *Almena*, written jointly with M. Arne. About the same time he became organist of 3 city churches, and began to write church mus. His best-known pieces are the anthems *Call to remembrance* and *O Lord, look down from heaven*. Other works incl. mus. for the stage, glees, catches, songs, etc.

Battistini, Mattia (b. Rome, 27. II. 1856; d. Colle Baccaro nr. Rieti, 7. XI. 1928), It. baritone. Made his 1st appearance in opera in Rome, 1878.

Battle of Prague, The, a descriptive pf. piece with vln., cello and drum *ad lib.* by Franz Koczwara, comp. 1788, of no mus. value, but very popular in the early 19th cent.

Battle of the Huns (Liszt). *See* **Hunnenschlacht.**

Battle of Vittoria, The, Beethoven's 'Battle Symph.', Op. 91, orig. entitled *Wellingtons Sieg oder die Schlacht bei Vittoria*, first perf. 8. XII. 1813. An extravagantly descriptive piece, orig. intended for a mechanical instrument, it contains quotations from nat. songs, incl. *Rule, Britannia*.

Batton, Désiré (Alexandre) (b. Paris, 2. I. 1798; d. Versailles, 15. X. 1855), Fr. comp. Studied at the Paris Cons. and gained the Prix de Rome in 1817; went to Rome and travelled after prod. his 1st comic opera, *La Fenêtre secrète*, in 1818.

Works incl. operas *Ethelwina, Le Prisonnier d'état, Le Champ du drap d'or*; church mus.; symph., etc.

Battuta (It.) = Beat, often used loosely in the plur. (e.g. *ritmo di 3 battute*) to indicate a change in the metrical scheme of bars — not beats — grouped in unexpected numbers.

Baudelaire, Charles (1821–67), Fr. poet. *See* Berg (A.)(*Wein*), Bréville (*Cloche fêlée*), Charpentier (G.)(*Fleurs du mal*), Debussy (5 poems and *Préludes*, i. 4), Dieren (van) (recitations), Lutyens (*Bienfaits de la lune*), Morawski (*Fleurs du mal*), Préludes (Debussy, i. 4), Sorabji (songs), Tommasini (*Hymne à la Beauté*).

Baudrier, Yves (b. Paris, 11. II. 1906), Fr. comp. Originally a law student, he formed the group of 'La Jeune France' with Jolivet, Lesur and Messiaen in 1936.

Works incl. *Agnus Dei* for soprano, chorus and orch.; symph., symph. poem *Le Grand Voilier*; string 4tet; pf. pieces, songs, etc.

Bauer, Harold (b. London, 28. IV. 1873; d. Miami, Florida, 12. III. 1951), Anglo-Amer. pianist. Studied in Eng. and had some lessons from Paderewski. In 1893 he appeared in Paris and Russia, then toured all over Eur. and in 1900 he 1st visited U.S.A., where he settled *c.* 1914.

Baulduin, Noël (b. ?; d. Antwerp, *c.* 1530), Flem. comp. *Maître de chapelle* of Notre Dame at Antwerp, 1513–18, ? living some time in it. Wrote motets and other church mus.

Baumgartner, Wilhelm (b. Rorschach, 15. XI. 1820; d. Zürich, 17. III. 1867), Swiss pianist, cond. and comp. Studied in Switz. and Berlin, later settled at Zürich as pf. teacher and choral cond.

Works incl. many songs, incl. the patriotic 'O mein Heimatland' to words by Gottfried Keller; pf. pieces, etc.

Bautista, Julián (b. Madrid, 21. IV. 1901; d. Buenos Aires, 8. VII. 1961), Span.-Arg. comp. Studied at the Madrid Cons. Pupil of Conrado del Campo. He gained 2 nat. prizes for comp. in 1923 and 1926 and became prof. of harmony at the Madrid Cons. Some of his works were destroyed in the Span. Civil War, when he left Spain (1940), settling in Buenos Aires.

Works incl. opera *Interior* (lost); ballet-pantomime *Juerga*; 3 *Jap. Preludes* for orch.; *Suite all' antica* for strings; *Tres Ciudades* for soprano and orch.; *La Flûte de jade* for voice and chamber orch.; 3 string 4tets (2 lost); *Colores* and *Preludio y danza* for pf.; songs, etc.

Bax, Arnold (Edward Trevor) (b. London, 8. XI. 1883; d. Cork, 3. X. 1953), Eng. comp. Entered the R.A.M. in 1900, studying pf. with Matthay and comp. with F. Corder. Stayed frequently in Ir. and travelled in Rus. He never held any official mus. position until he was app. Master of the King's Mus. in 1942. Knighted in 1937.

Works incl. ballet *The Truth about the Rus. Dancers* (James Barrie); film mus. for *Malta G.C.* (documentary) and *Oliver Twist* (after Dickens); choral works incl. *Enchanted Summer, Fatherland, I sing of a Maiden, Mater ora Filium, St. Patrick's Breastplate, This Worlde's Joie, To the Name above every Name*; Te Deum and Nunc Dimittis for chorus and org.; 7 symphs., *Sinfonietta*, symph. poems *November Woods, The Garden of Fand, The Happy Forest, Tintagel*, overture *Work in Progress, Overture to a Picaresque Comedy, Legend*, 2 *Northern Ballads* and other orchestral works; concertos for vln. and orch., and for cello and orch., symph. variations and *Winter Legends* for pf. and orch.; chamber mus., incl. nonet, 8tet, 5tets for pf. and strings, ob. and strings, strings and harp, strings, 3 string 4tets, pf. 4tet, trios for vln., vla. and pf., vln., cello and pf., and fl., vla. and harp; 3 sonatas for vln. and pf., sonata for vla. and pf., sonata for cello and pf., sonata for clar. and pf.; 4 pf. sonatas and numerous pf. pieces; sonata and 5 other works for 2 pfs.; many songs and a number of folksong arrs., etc.

Bax, Clifford (1886–1962), Eng. poet and dramatist, brother of prec. *See* Gibbs (C. A.) (*Midsummer Madness*), Shaw (M.) *Mr. Pepys*.

Bayer, Joseph (b. Vienna, 6. III. 1852; d. Vienna, 12. III. 1913), Aus. cond. and comp. Studied at the Vienna Cons., played the vln. at the Court Opera and from 1885 was director of the ballet mus. there.

Works incl. operettas *Der Chevalier von San Marco, Mr. Menelaus, Fraulein Hexe, Der Polizeichef* and others; ballets *Die Puppenfee* and many others, etc.

Bayreuth, the small town in Bavaria where Wagner built the festival theatre for the perf. of his works, opened in 1876 with the 1st prod. of the *Ring*.

Bazin, Emmanuel (Joseph François) (b. Marseilles, 4. IX. 1816; d. Paris, 2. VII. 1878), Fr. cond. and comp. Won the Prix de Rome at the Paris Cons. in 1840 and was later a prof. there. 7 of his operas were prod. at the Opéra-Comique between 1846 and 1865.

Baziron, Philippe. *See* Basiron.

Bazzini, Antonio (b. Brescia, 11. III. 1818; d. Milan, 10. II. 1897), It. violinist and comp. Toured in many countries, prod. an opera at Milan in 1867 and became prof. of comp. at the Cons. there in 1873; director in 1882.

Works incl. opera *Turanda* (after Gozzi's *Turandot*); concert overtures to Alfieri's *Saul* and Shakespeare's *King Lear*; 2 cantatas; 6 string 4tets and other chamber mus.; *Ronde des lutins* for vln. and pf., etc.

Beach (*née* **Cheney**), **Amy Marcy** (b. Henniker, New Hampshire, 5. IX. 1867; d. New York, 27. XII. 1944), Amer. pianist and comp., known as Mrs. Henry Beach. Works incl. Mass in E maj.; *Christ in the Universe* for chorus and orch.; *Gaelic Symph.* (1896, the first symph. work by an Amer. woman); pf. concerto; string 4tett pf. trio; numerous songs, stc.

Beak Flute (= Ger. *Schnabelflöte*) = **Recorder.**

Beale, William (b. Landrake, 1. I. 1784; d. London, 3. V. 1854), Eng. comp. Choirboy at Westminster Abbey in London; joined the Navy; Gentleman of the Chapel Royal, 1816–20; organist of Trinity Coll., Cambridge, 1820–1, and of var. London churches later. Wrote glees and so-called madrigals.

Bear, The, nickname (*L'Ours*) of the 1st of Haydn's 'Paris' symphs., No. 82 in C maj., comp. 1786.
Opera by Walton (lib. by Paul Dehn and the comp., based on Tchekhov), prod. Aldeburgh, 3. VI. 1967.

Bearbeitung (Ger. = working with or working upon), the process, either in playing or writing down, of developing given material; also that of arranging mus. for another than its orig. medium.

Beard, John (b. London, *c.* 1717; d. Hampton, 5. II. 1791), Eng. tenor. Chorister of the Chapel Royal under Gates, he later sang in the 1st perfs. of many of Handel's oratorios. The tenor parts in *Israel in Egypt, Messiah, Samson, Judas Maccabeus* and *Jephtha* were comp. for him.

Beat. (1) The unit of measurement in mus., indicated in choral and orchestral mus. by the cond. It is not necessarily synonymous with accent. (2) An Old Eng. name for a variety of ornaments.

Béatitudes, Les, oratorio by Franck for solo voices, chorus and orch. (words from the Bible), comp. 1869–79, 1st perf. privately by the comp.'s pupils at his house, and in public only after his death, Paris, 1893.

Beatrice di Tenda, opera by Bellini (lib. by Felice Romani), prod. Venice, Teatro La Fenice, 16. III. 1833.

Béatrice et Bénédict (*Beatrice and Benedick*), opera by Berlioz (lib. by comp., based on Shakespeare's *Much Ado about Nothing*), prod. Baden-Baden, 9. VIII. 1862.

Beats, in acoustics the clashing of soundwaves of slightly different frequencies prod., for ex., by 2 pf. strings for the same note not perfectly in tune with each other, or certain org. stops using 2 pipes for each note purposely kept slightly out of tune to prod. that wavering effect. Sensitive ears perceive B. as slight periodical swellings of the tone on sustained notes, and pf. tuners

rely on B. to tell them whether the strings of any one note are in tune or not.

Beaucé, Delphine. *See* Ugalde.

Beaujoyeulx, Balthasar de (Baldassare da Belgioioso, Baltazarini) (b. ?; d. *c.* 1587), It. violinist, sent to Fr. *c.* 1555 with a large band of string players by the Maréchal de Brissac to form the orch. of Catherine de' Medici. He supervised the perf. of the *Ballet comique de la royne.*

Beaulieu, (Marie) Désiré (family name Martin-Beaulieu) (b. Paris, 11. IV. 1791; d. Niort, 21. XII. 1863), Fr. comp. and scholar. Won the Prix de Rome at the Paris Cons. in 1810 and settled at Niort, where he founded mus. societies for the perf. of chamber and esp. choral works. He wrote several theoret. books.
Works incl. operas *Anacréon* and *Philadelphie*; Requiem for Méhul; 3 oratorios; Masses and other church mus.; orchestral works, etc.

Beaulieu, Eustorg (b. Beaulieu-sur-Menoire, 1495–1500; d. Basle, 8. I. 1552), Fr. poet and musician. He wrote a few *chansons*, but is better known for his verse, incl. a collection of early Protestant song texts.

Beaumarchais, Pierre Augustin Caron de (1732–99), Fr. author and min. musician. He sang and played the fl. and harp, teaching the latter to the daughters of Louis XV. His comedy, *Le Barbier de Séville*, was at 1st to be a comic opera with mus. arr. by B. from Span. songs and dances. *See also* Auric (*Mariage de Figaro*), **Barbiere di Siviglia** (Paisiello and Rossini), **Benda (F. L.)** (*Barbier von Sevilla*), **Dittersdorf** (*Hochzeit des F.*), **Glière** (*Figaro*), **Morlacchi** (*Barbiere di S.*), **Nozze di Figaro** (Mozart), **Paer** (*Nuovo Figaro*), **Portugal** (*Pazza giornata*), **Ricci (L.)** (do. and *Nozze di F.*), **Schulz** (*Barbier de Séville*), **Shaporin** (*Marriage of Figaro*), **Shield** (do.), **Tarare** (Salieri).

Beaumont, Francis (1584–1616) and **Fletcher, John** (1579–1625), Eng. poets and dramatists. *See* Austin (F.) (*Knight of the Burning Pestle*), Confalonieri (F.'s *Faithful Shepherdess*), Cooper (J.) (masque), Glanville-Hicks (Fletcher), Johnson (R. ii) (F.'s *Valentinian* and *Mad Lover*), Pastoral (Bliss: F.), Prophetess (Purcell), Purcell (*Bonduca* and *Double Marriage*, F.'s *Fool's Preferment* and *Rule a Wife*), Rawsthorne (F. 2 songs).

Bebung (Ger. = Trembling), an effect of tone-vibration obtainable on the Clavichord by letting the finger oscillate on the key much as string players do in prod. *Vibrato.*

Bécarre (Fr.) = Natural: the sign ♮.

Beck, Conrad (b. Lohn, Schaffhausen, 16. VI. 1901), Swiss comp. After studying engineering, he became a student at the Zürich Cons. under Andreae and others;

later in Berlin and Paris, where he lived in 1923–32 and was closely in touch with Roussel and Honegger. Awarded important prizes for comp. in 1954, 1956 and 1964.

Works incl. opera *La Grande Ourse*; incid. mus. for Goethe's *Pandora* and other plays; oratorios *Angelus Silesius* and *Der Tod zu Basel*; Requiem; *Der Tod des Oedipus* for chorus and orch.; *Lyric Cantata* (Rilke) for female voices and orch.; chamber cantata (sonnets by Louise Labé); 7 symphs., *Sinfonietta, Innominata* and *Ostinato* for orch.; concerto for string 4tet and orch., *Konzertmusik* for ob. and strings, concerto, concertino and rhapsody for pf. and orch., cello concerto; 4 string 4tets; org. and pf. works; *Liederspiel* cycle and other songs, etc.

Beck, Franz (b. Mannheim, ? 15. II. 1723; d. Bordeaux, 31. XII. 1809), Ger. violinist and comp. A member of the Mannheim school of symphonists and a pupil of Johann Stamitz. He is said to have fled from Mannheim as the result of a duel, went to It. and later settled in Fr.

Works incl. *c*. 30 symphs., *Stabat Mater*, keyboard mus., etc.

Becken (Ger., sing. and plur.), lit. basin[s], bowl[s] = Cymbal[s].

Becker, Albert (Ernst Anton) (b. Quedlinburg, 13. VI. 1834; d. Berlin, 10. I. 1899), Ger. comp. Studied under Dehn in Berlin; later taught there and became director of the cathedral choir in 1891.

Works incl. Mass in B♭ min.; oratorio *Selig aus Gnade*; psalms, motets and other sacred mus.; symph. in G min.; chamber mus., songs, etc.

Becker, Cornelius (b. Leipzig, 24. X. 1561; d. Leipzig, 25. V. 1604), Ger. Lutheran pastor and theologian. His rhymed version of the psalms was set by Seth Calvisius (1605), Heinrich Grimm (1624) and Heinrich Schütz (1628, 2nd ed. 1661).

Beddoes, Thomas Lovell (1803–49), Eng. physiologist, poet and dramatist. *See* **Busch** (songs), **Dieren (van)** (do.), **Ireland (J.)** (*If there were dreams*), **Warlock** (*Sorrow's Lullaby*).

Bedford, Herbert (b. London, 23. I. 1867; d. London, 13. III. 1945), Eng. comp., author and painter. Largely self-taught in mus. Married Liza Lehmann in X. 1894.

Works incl. opera *Kit Marlowe*; love scene from *Romeo and Juliet* for contralto, baritone and orch.; masque *The Daughters of Dawn*; many miscellaneous works, incl. mus. for military band and unaccomp. songs.

Bédier, Joseph (1864–1938), Fr. lit. scholar. *See* **Martin (F.)** (*Vin herbé*).

Bedyngham, John (b. ?; d. ?), Eng. 15th-cent. comp. Wrote Masses, motets and

other church mus.; known on the Continent as well as in Eng. He provided additional parts to Dunstable's *O rosa bella*.

Bee's Wedding, The. The Eng. nickname of Mendelssohn's Song without Words in C maj., Op. 67 No. 4, the Ger. being *Spinnerlied* (spinning-song).

Beecham, Thomas (b. St. Helens, Lancs., 29. IV. 1879; d. London, 8. III. 1961), Eng. cond. He was educated at Rossall School and Wadham Coll., Oxford. After cond. the Hallé Orch. at a concert at St. Helens in 1899 he studied comp. with Charles Wood, intending to be a comp. but turned his attention to cond. and first appeared in London in 1905. From that time he rapidly became one of the most original and versatile Eng. conds. From 1909 up to the 1914–1918 war, and also during the war, he was responsible for introd. a number of unfamiliar operas to the public. In 1929 he gave a festival of Delius's mus. in London, and in 1932 founded the London Phil. Orch. During the 1939–45 war he was active as a cond. in Australia, Canada and U.S.A. He founded the Royal Phil. Orch. in 1947. While excelling in Mozart, he was also passionately interested in the works of Romantic comps., and particularly Delius. He was knighted in 1914 and succeeded to his father's baronetcy in 1916.

Beecke (or Becké), Ignaz von (b. Wimpfen im Tal, 28. X. 1733; d. Wallerstein, 2. I. 1803), Ger. pianist, cond. and comp. Officer in a Württemberg regiment, where he was adjutant and mus. director to the Prince of Oettingen-Wallerstein.

Works incl. *Singspiele*, among them Goethe's *Claudine von Villa Bella*; oratorio *Die Auferstehung*; symphs.; chamber mus.; keyboard mus., etc.

Beer, Jakob Liebmann. *See* **Meyerbeer.**

Beerbohm, Max (1872–1956). Eng. essayist, novelist and caricaturist. *See* **Addinsell** (*Happy Hypocrite*), **Elwell** (do.), **Rawsthorne** (do.), **Tranchell** (*Zuleika*).

Beethoven, Ludwig van (b. Bonn, 16. XII. 1770; d. Vienna, 26. III. 1827), Ger. comp. of Flem. descent. Son and grandson of musicians in the service of the Elector of Cologne in Bonn. Pupil of C. G. Neefe. In 1783 was harpsichordist in the court orch., and the same year pub. 3 pf. sonatas. 2nd organist at court 1784, and 1789 also vla. player. A visit to Vienna in 1787 to study with Mozart was cut short after only a few weeks by his mother's fatal illness, but in 1792 he returned to be a pupil of Haydn, whom he had met in Bonn. He remained in Vienna for the rest of his life, scarcely leaving the city or its suburbs. Tuition with Haydn was not a success, and he took lessons from Schenk, Albrechtsberger and Salieri. Made his first public appearance as a pianist and comp. in 1795, and lived by playing and teaching, later increasingly by the pub. of his works.

He refused to accept regular employment under the old system of patronage, but received support from the aristocracy: in 1808, for instance, 3 noblemen agreed to pay him an unconditional annuity. The deafness which had threatened from as early as *c.* 1795 increased, and his despair gave rise to the suicidal 'Heiligenstadt Testament' in 1802; by 1808 he was forced to abandon public perf. altogether. Prod. his only opera in 1805 under the title *Leonore* (rev. 1806 and again 1814, now as *Fidelio*). In 1815, after his brother's death, became guardian to his nephew Karl, a task he took seriously and which caused him constant worry. By 1819 he was totally deaf, and communication with him was possible only in writing. He never recovered from an infection caught in 1826, and his death the following year was due to dropsy.

Works incl. choral mus.: 2 Masses (in C maj. and *Missa Solemnis* in D maj.); oratorio *Christus am Ölberg*; also finale of 9th symph. and choral fantasia; dramatic works: opera *Fidelio*; incid. mus. to Goethe's *Egmont*, *Die Ruinen von Athen*, *König Stephan*; ballet *Prometheus*; orchestral works: 9 symphs.; 5 pf. concertos; vln. concerto; concerto for pf., vln. and cello; overtures, etc.; chamber mus.: 7tet; string 5tet; 16 string 4tets and *Grosse Fuge* for 4tet; 6 pf. trios, 4 string trios; 10 vln. sonatas, 5 cello sonatas, etc.; pf. mus.: 32 sonatas, 22 sets of variations, 3 sets of Bagatelles, miscellaneous pieces; songs, incl. song cycle *An die ferne Geliebte*, etc.

Beffroy de Reigny, Louis Abel (b. Lâon, 6. XI. 1757; d. Paris, 18. XII. 1811), Fr. play-. wright and comp. Known as 'Cousin Jacques', under which name he wrote satirical operettas popular during the Revolution, incl. *Nicodème dans la lune*, *Nicodème aux enfers* and *La Petite Nanette*.

Beggar's Opera, The, ballad opera, prod. London, Theatre in Lincoln's Inn Fields, 29. I. 1728, consisting of a play by John Gay interspersed with songs. The mus., popular tunes of the day but for the most part not folksongs, was arr. by John Christopher Pepusch, who also comp. the overture.

Begleiten (Ger.) = To accompany.

Begleitung (Ger.) = Accompaniment.

Begnis, Giuseppe de (b. Lugo, 1793; d. N.Y., VIII. 1849), It. bass. Choir-boy at Lugo; made his 1st operatic appearance at Modena in 1813, and went to Paris and London with his wife, 1819 and 1822.

Begnis (*née* Ronzi), **Giuseppina de** (b. Milan, 11. I. 1800; d. Florence, 7. VI. 1853), It. soprano, wife of prec. Made her 1st appearance in Paris in 1819 and in London in 1822.

Beheim (Behaim), Michel (b. Sulzbach, 1416; d. Sulzbach, 1474), Ger. Meistersinger. Active as soldier and singer in the service of Ger., Dan. and Hung. princes. 11 of his melodies survive.

Behn (*née* Johnston), **Aphra** (1640–89), Eng. dramatist and novelist. *See* **Courteville** (*Oroonoko*), **Paisible** (do.), **Purcell** (do. and *Abdelazer*).

Beiden Freunde von Salamanka, Die. *See* **Freunde von Salamanka**.

Beinum, Eduard van (b. Arnhem, 3. IX. 1901; d. Amsterdam, 13. IV. 1959), Dutch cond. Studied with his brother and comp. with Sem Dresden. After a post in Haarlem (1926) he became 2nd cond. of the Concertgebouw Orch. of Amsterdam (1931–8), an associate to Mengelberg in 1938 and his successor in 1945. He toured Europe and America, and in 1956 became cond. of the Los Angeles Phil., but resigned and returned to Europe, where he died.

Bekker, Paul (b. Berlin, 11. IX. 1882; d. N.Y., 7. III. 1937), Ger. writer on mus. Studied in Berlin and was at 1st a violinist in the Phil. Orch. there. In 1906 he began to devote himself to mus. journalism and became critic to several papers, later operatic manager at Cassel and Wiesbaden. The Nazi regime drove him to the U.S.A. Wrote on Beethoven, Wagner, Mahler, opera and modern comps.

Beklemmt (Ger. = oppressed), a term used by Beethoven in the Cavatina of the string 4tet, Op. 130.

Bel canto (It., lit. beautiful song), singing in the traditional It. manner, with beautiful tone, perfect phrasing, clean articulation, etc. The art of B. c. culminated in It. in the 19th cent.

Belaiev, Mitrofan Petrovich (b. St. Petersburg, 22. II. 1836; d. St. Petersburg, 10. I. 1904), Rus. timber merchant and mus. amateur. Founded a pub. firm for the propagation of Rus. mus. in 1885.

Belaiev, Victor Mikhailovich (b. Uralsk, 6. II. 1888; d. Moscow, 17. II. 1968), Rus. critic. He wrote mainly on mus. in var. Soviet countries, esp. Turkmenistan and Uzbekistan.

Belasco, David (1859–1931), Amer. playwright. *See* **Fanciulla del West** (Puccini), **Madama Butterfly** (do.).

Belcari, Feo (1410–84), It. poet and dramatist. *See* **Pizzetti** (*Sacra rappresentazione di Abraam ed Isacco*).

Beldemandis, Prosdocimo de (b. Padua, *c.* 1375; d. Padua, 1428), It. mus. scholar. Prof. of mathematics and astronomy at Padua in 1422. Wrote treatises on mus. pub. between 1404 and 1413.

Belenoi, Aimeric de (b. Lespare, Bordelais, ?; d. Catalonia, ?), Fr. 13th-cent. troubadour, 22 of whose songs have been preserved.

Belfagor, opera by Respighi (lib. by

Claudio Guastalla, based on a comedy by Ercole Luigi Morselli), prod. Milan, Teatro alla Scala, 26. IV. 1923.

Belgian (excl. earlier Flemish) Comps. See Absil, Benoit, Bériot, Blockx, Campenhout, Dupuis (2), Eeden (van den), Franck, Gevaert, Gilson, Goovaerts, Gossec, Gregoir (2), Grétry, Grisar, Hasselmans, Hullebroek, Huybrechts, Jongen, Lassen, Le Borne, Lekeu, Lemmens, Maleingreau, Mathieu, Mermet, Quinet, Radoux (2), Ryelandt, Servais (F.), Timmermans, Tinel, Urhan, Verheyen, Vieuxtemps, Vreuls, Ysaÿe (2).

Beliczay, Gyula de belicz (b. Komárom, 10. VIII. 1835; d. Budapest, 30. IV. 1893), Hung. theorist and comp. Trained as an engineer at first, but studied mus. in Vienna and became prof. at the Nat. Mus. Acad. at Budapest. Pub. a book on comp., 1891.

Works incl. Mass in F maj., *Ave Maria* for contralto, chorus and orch.; 2 symphs., pieces for string orch.; 3 string 4tets; pf. pieces; songs, etc.

Belin, Julien (b. Le Mans, *c.* 1530; d. ?), Fr. lutenist and comp. Pub. a book of lute pieces in tablature, 1556.

Belisario, opera by Donizetti (lib. by Salvatore Cammarano), prod. Venice, Teatro La Fenice, 4. II. 1836.

'Bell Anthem', the familiar name of Purcell's anthem *Rejoice in the Lord alway*, comp. *c.* 1682–5. The instrumental introd. contains descending scales resembling the ringing of church bells.

Bell Gamba, an 8-ft. org. stop similar to the Gamba stop, but with the pipes surmounted by a 'bell' or cone.

Bell, W(illiam). H(enry). (b. St. Albans, 20. VIII. 1873; d. Cape Town, 13. IV. 1946), Eng. comp., cond. and teacher. Studied at the R.A.M. in London and under Stanford. In 1912 became principal of the S. African Coll. of Mus. at Capetown.

Works incl. operas *Hippolytus* (after Euripides), *Isabeau* and Japanese Nohplay *Tsuneyo*; incid. mus. for Ben Jonson's masque *A Vision of Delight*; *Maria Assumpta* for chorus; 2 symphs., *Walt Whitman Symph.*, symph. variations for orch., several symph poems; vln. and vla. sonatas, etc.

Bella, Jan Levoslav (b. Liptovský Sväty Mikuláš, 4. IX. 1843; d. Bratislava, 25. V. 1936), Slovak priest and comp. Studied at Levoča and Vienna and entered the priesthood. Wrote Masses on Slovak folk tunes and other religious works. Prod. an opera, *Veland the Smith,* based on Wagner's sketched lib. for *Wieland der Schmied,* at Bratislava in 1926. Other works incl. a symph. poem, a string 4tet and Slovak folksong arrs.

Bellaigue, Camille (b. Paris, 24. V. 1858; d. Paris, 4. X. 1930), Fr. critic and pianist. Attached to the *Revue des Deux Mondes*

from 1885. Author of a number of books on mus. and musicians.

Bellanda, Lodovico (b. ? Verona, ?; d.? Verona, ?), It. 16th–17th-cent. comp. Lived at Verona; wrote sacred vocal pieces, madrigals, canzonette for 3 voices and songs.

Bellasio, Paolo (b. Verona, 20. V. 1554; d. Rome, 10. VII. 1594), It. comp. Lived in Rome for a time and wrote 6 books of madrigals.

Bellazzi, Francesco (b. Vigevano, ?; d. ? Venice, ?), It. monk and comp. Pupil (?) of G. Gabrieli at Venice. 6 books of Masses, motets and other sacred works of his were pub. between 1618 and 1628.

Belle Hélène, La (*The Fair Helen*), operatta by Offenbach (lib. by Henri Meilhac and Ludovic Halévy), prod. Paris, Théâtre des Variétés, 17. XII. 1864.

Bellermann, Ger. fam. of mus. scholars:
1. Johann Joachim B. (b. Erfurt, 23. IX. 1754; d. Berlin, 25. X. 1842). Wrote on Rus., incl. mus.

2. Johann Friedrich B. (b. Erfurt, 8. III. 1795; d. Berlin, 5. II. 1874), son of prec. Wrote on ancient Gk. mus.

3. Johann Gottfried Heinrich B. (b. Berlin, 10. III. 1832; d. Potsdam, 10. IV. 1903), son of prec. Wrote on mensural notation and counterpoint. He was also a comp.

Bellerofonte, Il, opera by Mysliveček (lib. by Giuseppe Bonechi), prod. Naples, Teatro San Carlo, 20. I. 1767.

Opera by Terradellas (lib. by Francesco Vanneschi), prod. London, King's Theatre, Haymarket, 24. III. 1747.

Bellérophon, opera by Lully (lib. by Thomas Corneille with (?) Bernard de Fontenelle and Boileau), prod. Paris, Opéra, 31. I. 1679.

Belletti, Giovanni Battista (b. Sarzana, 17. II. 1813; d. Sarzana, 27. XII. 1890), It. baritone. Studied at Bologna and made his 1st stage appearance at Stockholm in 1838 under the patronage of the sculptor Byström, and then sang with Jenny Lind.

Bell'haver, Vincenzo (b. ?; d. Venice, IX. 1587), It. comp. From 30. XII. 1586 he was 2nd organist of St. Mark's Venice, in succession to Andrea Gabrielli. His works incl. Magnificats, motets and madrigals.

Belli, Domenico (b. ?; d. ?), It. 16th–17th-cent. comp. Prob. in the service of the Duke of Parma, and teacher at the church of San Lorenzo at Florence, 1610–13. Pub. a book of airs for 1 and 2 voices with chitarrone accomp, and another of 5 interludes for Tasso's *Aminta.*

Belli, Girolamo (b. Argenta nr. Ferrara, 1552; d. ?), It. comp. Pupil of Luzzaschi; in the service of the Duke of Mantua; in Rome in 1582. Pub. several books of madrigals as well as Masses, psalms and *Sacrae cantiones.*

Belli, Giulio (b. Longiano, *c.* 1560; d. ? Imola, ?), It. monk and comp. Held var. church apps. at Imola, Venice, Montagnana, Osimo, Forli and Padua. He returned to Imola in 1611. Wrote madrigals and other secular vocal works at first, but (?) only church mus. later, incl. numerous Masses, motets, psalms, etc.

Bellincioni, Gemma (b. Como, 18. VIII. 1864; d. Naples, 23. IV. 1950), It. mezzo-soprano. Made her 1st appearance at Naples in 1881 and sang with great success in It. and on tour in Eur. In 1895 she 1st visited Eng. and in 1899 S. Amer.

Bellini, Vincenzo (b. Catania, Sicily, 3. XI. 1801; d. Puteaux nr. Paris, 23. IX. 1835), It. comp. His father, an organist, was enabled with the help of a Sicilian nobleman to send him to study with Zingarelli at the Naples Cons., where he met Donizetti and Mercadante. In 1825 his 1st opera was prod., while he was still a student, and attracted the attention of Barbaia, who commissioned him to write a 2nd, which he prod. at the San Carlo Theatre in 1826. Its success induced Barbaia to ask for another opera (*Il pirata*) for the Scala Theatre at Milan, which was prod. there in 1827 with Rubini in the cast. It was also successfully perf. in Paris, and 3 other operas followed, at Milan, Parma and Venice, before he attained full maturity in *La sonnambula*, brought out at Milan in 1831. *Norma* followed in December of the same year, with Pasta in the title-part. In 1833 B. went to London and Paris, where Rossini advised him to write a work for the Théâtre Italien. This was *I Puritani*, prod. there in 1835, with Giulia Grisi, Rubini, Tamburini and Lablache in the cast. It was brought to London the same year for Grisi's benefit perf. B. went to stay with an Eng. friend at Puteaux, at whose house he was taken ill and died.

Works incl. operas *Adelson e Salvina, Bianca e Gernando, Il pirata, La straniera, Zaira, I Capuletti ed i Montecchi* (based on Shakespeare's *Romeo and Juliet*), *La sonnambula, Norma, Beatrice di Tenda, I Puritani*; church mus.; songs; symphs., etc.

Belloc, (Joseph) Hilaire (Pierre) (1870–1953), Eng. man of letters of Fr. descent. *See* Williams (G.) (songs).

Belloc, Teresa Giorgi (b. San Benigno nr. Turin, 2. VII. 1784; d. San Giorgio Cavanese, 13. V. 1855), It. soprano of Fr. descent. Made her 1st appearance at the Teatro Regio, Turin, in 1801.

Belly, the surface of string instruments, also sometimes the sound-board of the pf.

Belmont und Constanze, oder Die Entführung aus dem Serail, opera by André (lib. by Christoph Friedrich Bretzner, based on Isaac Bickerstaffe's *The Captive*), prod. Berlin, 25. V. 1781.
Opera by Christian Ludwig Dieter

(1757–1822) (lib. do.), prod. Stuttgart, 27. VIII. 1784.
For Mozart's opera on this subject *see* **Entführung.**

Belshazzar, oratorio by Handel (words by Charles Jennens), prod. London, King's Theatre, Haymarket, 27. III. 1745.

Belshazzar's Feast, cantata by William Walton (words from the Bible arr. by Osbert Sitwell), prod. Leeds Festival, 8. X. 1931.

Bely, Victor (b. Berditchev, Ukraine, 14. I. 1904), Rus. comp. Studied vln. and comp. at the Kharkov and Moscow Conss., pupil of Miaskovsky at the latter. Later prof. at Moscow Cons. and folksong expert. In 1925 he organized the Procoll society for the promotion of Soviet Mus. with Davidenko and Shekhter.

Works incl. incid. mus. for *Salute to Spain* and other plays and films; suite on Tchuvash themes for orch.; poem for vla. and pf.; 3 pf. sonatas, sonatina, preludes and other pf. works; oratorio for 25th anniversary of the Oct. Revolution, *Hunger March* for chorus and orch., choral works, mass songs, etc.

Bemberg, Herman (b. Paris, 29. III. 1859; d. Berne, 21. VII. 1931), Fr. comp. Pupil of Dubois and Massenet at the Paris Cons.

Works incl. operas *Le Baiser de Suzon* and *Elaine*; cantata *La Mort de Jeanne d'Arc*; recitation with accomp. *La Ballade du désespéré*; many songs incl. *Aime-moi* and *Chant hindou*, etc.

Bémol (Fr.)
Bemolle (It.) $\left. \right\}$ = Flat; the sign $\flat$.

Benavente y Martínez, Jacinto (1866–1954), Span. dramatist. *See* **Rosenberg** (*Marionettes*).

Benda. Bohemian family of musicians:

1. **Franz** (**František**) **B.** (b. Stáre Benátzky, 25. XI. 1709; d. Potsdam, 7. III. 1786), violinist and comp. After being a chorister in Prague he travelled widely in his youth until in 1733 he joined the service of the Crown Prince of Prussia. He succeeded J. G. Graun as *Konzertmeister* to the same patron, now Frederick II, in 1771. His daughter Juliane married Reichardt.

Works incl. trio-sonatas; concertos; sonatas, studies, etc., for vln.

2. **Johann** (**Jan**) **Wenzl B.** (b. Stáre Benátzky, 16. IV. 1713; d. Potsdam, 1752), violinist and comp., brother of prec. In the service of Frederick II in Potsdam.

3. **Georg** (**Jiří**) **Antonín B.** (b. Stáre Benátzky, VI. 1722; d. Köstritz, 6. XI. 1795), harpsichordist, oboist and comp., brother of prec. Entered the service of Frederick II of Prussia in 1742, app. *Kapellmeister* to the Duke of Gotha 1750. He retired in 1778. His most influential comps. were the melodramas (spoken words to instrumental music) *Ariadne auf*

Naxos, Medea and *Pygmalion*. Other works incl. *Singspiele*: *Der Dorfjahrmarkt, Romeo und Julia, Walder, Der Holzhauer*, etc.; symphs.; concertos; keyboard mus., etc.

4. Joseph B. (b. Stáre Benátzky, 7. III. 1724; d. Berlin, 22. II. 1804), violinist, brother of prec. Succeeded his brother Franz (1 above) as *Konzertmeister* to the Prussian court in 1786.

5. Friedrich Wilhelm Heinrich B. (b. Potsdam, 15. VII. 1745; d. Postdam, 19. VI. 1814), violinist and comp., son of Franz (1 above). In the service of the Prussian court, 1765–1810, and comp. *Singspiele*, concertos, sonatas, etc.

6. Friedrich Ludwig B. (b. Gotha, 1746; d. Königsberg, 20. III. 1792), violinist and comp., son of Georg (3 above). Director of mus. in Hamburg 1780–2, *Konzertmeister* at Königsberg from 1789.

Works incl. opera *Der Barbier von Seville* (based on Beaumarchais) and 2 others; oratorio; cantatas; instrumental mus.

7. Ernst Friedrich B. (b. Berlin, 1747; d. Berlin, 1785), violinist and harpsichordist, son of Joseph (4 above). One of the founders of the Berlin amateur concerts in 1770.

8. Karl Hermann Heinrich B. (b. Potsdam, 2 or 21. V. 1784; d. 15. III. 1836), violinist and comp., son of Franz (1 above). Comp. little, mainly chamber mus.

Bender, Paul (b. Driedorf, Westerwald, 28. VII. 1875; d. Munich, 25. XI. 1947), Ger. bass. Made a great reputation at the Munich Opera, 1st visited London in 1914 and again, after World War I, in 1924 and onwards. Afterwards he became a leading bass at the Metrop. Opera in N.Y., but returned to Munich to teach at the State School of Mus.

Bendix, Victor Emanuel (b. Copenhagen, 17. V. 1851; d. Copenhagen, 5. I. 1926), Dan. cond. and comp. Pupil of Gade. Cond. choral and orchestral concerts.

Works incl. 4 symphs., pf. concerto; psalm with orch.; pf. trio; pf. sonata; songs, etc.

Bendl, Karel (b. Prague, 16. IV. 1838; d. Prague, 20. IX. 1897), Boh. comp. and cond. After var. posts in foreign countries as a cond. he worked in Prague from 1865 to 1878 and from 1881. He gave much encouragement to Dvořák. His works, partly in a traditional style and partly influenced by Smetana, incl. 11 operas, choral and orchestral works, church and chamber mus.

Benedict, Julius (b. Stuttgart, 27. XI. 1804; d. London, 5. VI. 1885), Engl. cond. and comp. of Ger. birth. Pupil of Hummel and Weber, with the latter of whom he met Beethoven in Vienna in 1823, when he was app. cond. at the Kärntnertortheater. Next he went to Naples, where he prod. his

1st It. opera in 1829. In 1835 he went to Paris and to London, where he remained for the rest of his life. He cond. a great deal in London, both opera and concerts and was cond. of the Norwich Festival, 1845–1878, and of the Liverpool Phil. Soc., 1876–1880. Knighted in 1871.

Works incl. operas *Giacinta ed Ernesto, I Portoghesi in Goa, Un anno ed un giorno, The Gypsy's Warning, The Brides of Venice, The Crusaders, The Lily of Killarney, The Bride of Song*; 2 symphs.; 2 pf. concertos; 5 cantatas, etc.

Benedictus de Opitiis. *See* **Opitiis.**

Benelli, Antonio Peregrino (b. Forli, 5. IX. 1771; d. Börnichen, Saxony, 16. VIII. 1830), It. tenor and comp. Pupil of Mattei in Bologna, 1st appeared as a singer in 1790 in Naples, where his opera *Partenope* was prod. in 1798. Other works incl. church mus. and a treatise on singing.

Benet, John (b. ?; d. ?), Eng. 15th-cent. comp. Wrote Masses and other church mus.

Benevoli, Orazio (b. Rome, 19. IV. 1605; d. Rome, 17. VI. 1672), It. comp. Held appts. at the churches of San Luigi de' Francesi and Santa Maria Maggiore in Rome, the former with an interruption in 1644–6, when he was at the Aus. court in Vienna. In 1646 he became *maestro di cappella* at the Vatican.

Works incl. Masses, motets and other church mus., much of it for several choirs in a large number of parts, up to 56 voices.

Benjamin, Arthur (b. Sydney, 18. IX. 1893; d. London, 9. IV. 1960), Austral. pianist and comp. Educ. at Brisbane and studied mus. at the R.C.M. in London, where later he became prof. After fighting in the 1914–18 war, he returned to Austral. to teach pf. at the Sydney Cons. in 1919–21, but having developed as a comp., settled in London, but from 1930 to 1936 lived at Vancouver.

Works incl. operas *The Devil take her, Prima Donna, A Tale of Two Cities* (after Dickens), *Tartuffe*; film mus. incl. *An Ideal Husband* (after Oscar Wilde); symph., suite *Light Mus.* and *Overture to an It. Comedy* for orch.; *Romantic Fantasy* for vln., vla. and orch., vln. concerto, concertino for pf. and orch., *Elegy, Waltz and Toccata* for vla. and orch.; *Pastoral Fantasy* for string 4tet, clar. 5tet; sonatina for vln. and pf., vla. and pf. sonata; sonata, suite and pieces for pf.; songs, etc.

Benlowes, Edward (? 1633–76), Eng. poet. *See* **Jenkins** (*Theophila*).

Bennet, John (b. ? Lancashire, ?; d. ?), Eng. 16th–17th-cent. comp. Pub. a book of madrigals in 1599 and contrib. others to collections, incl. *The Triumphes of Oriana*.

Bennett (Enoch) Arnold (1867–1931), Eng. novelist and dramatist. *See* **Don Juan de Mañara** (Goossens), **Judith** (do.).

Bennett, Joseph (b. Berkeley, Glos., 29. XI. 1831; d. Purton, 12. VI. 1911), Eng. critic and author. Lived in London and was for many years mus. critic of the *Daily Telegraph*. Wrote libs. for J. F. Barnett, Bottesini, Cowen, Mackenzie and Sullivan (*The Golden Legend*).

Bennett, Richard Rodney (b. Broadstairs, Kent, 29. III. 1936), Eng. comp. Studied at the R.A.M. with Lennox Berkeley and Howard Ferguson, and in Paris with Boulez. Influenced by Bartók, he also uses serial techniques.

Works incl. operas *The Ledge*, *The Mines of Sulphur*, *A Penny for a Song*, *Victory* (after Conrad); symph.; *Aubade* for orch.; pf. concerto; 4 string 4tets; *Calendar* for chamber ensemble; vocal mus., film, radio and television mus., etc.

Bennett, Robert Russell (b. Kansas City, 15. VI. 1894), Amer. pianist, cond. and comp. Studied with his parents and later with Nadia Boulanger in Paris. He played in his father's orch. as a youth and earned a living as arranger and orchestrator.

Works incl. opera *Maria Malibran*; film mus. *Sights and Sounds*, *Abraham Lincoln*; symph., *Charleston Rhapsody*, etc. for orch.; March for 2 pfs. and orch., etc.

Bennett, William Sterndale (b. Sheffield, 13. IV. 1816; d. London, 1. II. 1875), Eng. pianist and comp. Chorister at King's Coll., Cambridge and student at the R.A.M. in London. He then went to Leipzig, where he made friends with Mendelssohn. Schumann ded. his *Études symphoniques* for pf. to him. Prof. of Mus. at Cambridge Univ., 1856–75. Principal of the R.A.M., 1866–75. Knighted 1871.

Works incl. incid. mus. to Sophocles' *Ajax*; cantata *The May Queen*, odes for the Internat. Exhib. (Tennyson) and the Cambridge Installation of a Chancellor (Kingsley); anthems; symph. in G min., overtures *The Naiads* and *The Wood-Nymphs*, fantasy-overture on Moore's *Paradise and the Peri*; 4 pf. concertos; pf. pieces, songs, etc.

Benoît, Camille (b. Roanne, Loire, 7. XII. 1851; d. Paris, 1. VII. 1923), Fr. writer on mus. and comp. Pupil of Franck. On the staff of the Louvre museum and curator from 1895.

Works incl. opera *Cléopâtre*; symph. poem *Merlin l'enchanteur*; *Eleison* for solo voices, chorus and orch.; Épithalamium for Anatole France's *Noces corinthiennes*, etc.

Benoit, Peter (Léonard Léopold) (b. Harlebeke, 17. VIII. 1834; d. Antwerp, 8. III. 1901), Belg. comp. Pupil of Fétis at the Brussels Cons. He became cond. at a Flem. theatre and was keenly interested in Flem. nat. mus. as distinct from that influenced by Fr. comps. He travelled in Ger. and visited

Paris, but tended more and more towards an indigenous type of mus. His 1st opera was prod. in 1857.

Works incl. Fr. opera *Le Roi des aulnes* (on Goethe's *Erl King*), Flem. operas *The Mountain Village, Isa, Pompeja*; incid. mus. to Flem. plays; Te Deum, *Messe solennelle*, Requiem; oratorios *Lucifer* and *The Scheldt*; *Petite Cantate de Noël* and many Flem. cantatas, etc.

Benserade, Isaac de (1612–91), Fr. poet and dramatist. *See* **Festes de l'Amour** (Lully).

Bentzon, Jørgen (b. Copenhagen, 14. II. 1897; d. Hørsholm, 9. VII. 1951), Dan. comp. Studied law at first, but became a comp. pupil of Nielsen in 1915 and in 1920–1921 was at the Leipzig Cons. President of the Dan. schools of mus. He began the folk mus. school movement in Den.

Works incl. opera *Saturnalia* (after Apuleius); 2 symphs. (No. 1 on Dickens), overture and variations for orch.; 5 string 4tets, *Racconti* and *Variazioni interrotti* for wind and strings, sonatina for wind instruments, intermezzo for fl., clar. and vln., etc.

Bentzon, Nils Viggo (b. Copenhagen, 24. VIII. 1919), Dan. comp. Studied pf. with his mother and comp. with Jeppesen.

Works incl. opera *Faust II* (after Goethe); 4 symphs.; pf. concerto; much chamber mus., incl. chamber concerto for 11 instruments, a chamber symph. sonata for solo cello; 4 pf. sonatas, *Propostae Novae* for 2 pfs.; vocal mus., incl. *Bonjour Max Ernst*, cantata for chorus and orch.

Benucci, Francesco (b. Florence, c. 1745; d. Florence, 5. IV. 1824), It. bass. He was engaged for Vienna in 1783, and was Mozart's orig. Figaro there in 1786.

Benvenuto Cellini, opera by Berlioz (lib. by Léon de Wailly and Auguste Barbier, based on Cellini's autobiog.), prod. Paris, Opéra, 10. IX. 1838.

Béranger, Pierre Jean de (1780–1857), Fr. poet. *See* **Monpou** (*Si j'étais petit oiseau*).

Berceuse (Fr.) = Cradle Song. Although strictly speaking a song, a B. may just as well be an instrumental piece.

Berchem, Jachet de (b. ? Berchem, ?; d. ? Ferrara, ?), Flem. 16th-cent. comp. Prob. organist to the ducal court at Ferrara in 1555. Wrote church mus., madrigals for 4 and 5 voices, Fr. *chansons*, etc. Not to be confused with Jachet of Mantua.

Berenguier de Palazol. *See* **Palazol**.

Berenice, opera by Handel (lib. by Antonio Salvi), prod. London, Covent Garden Theatre, 18. V. 1737.

Opera by Perti (lib. do.), prod. Villa Pratolino nr. Florence, IX. 1709.

Berenstadt, Gaetano (b. ?; d. ?), It. 17th–18th-cent. bass singer of Ger. descent. The

1st record of his appearing in London dates from 1717.

Berezovsky, Maximus Sosnovich (b. Glukhov, 1745; d. St. Petersburg, 1777), Rus. comp. Pupil at the academy in Kiev, later a singer in the service of the court. In 1765 went to It. to study under Martini. On his return to Rus., unable to secure an appointment, he finally shot himself. His most important contrib. was to church mus.; he also wrote an opera, *Demofoonte*, and other works.

Berezovsky, Nikolai (b. St. Petersburg, 17. V. 1900; d. N.Y., 27. VIII. 1953), Rus. (Americanized) violinist and comp. Learnt mus. in the Imperial Chapel at St. Petersburg, became violinist in the opera orchs. at Saratov and Moscow and cond. at the School of Modern Art there; but emigrated to U.S.A. in 1922, continued his studies there, played in the N.Y. Phil. Orch., became a member of the Coolidge 4tet and appeared as concert and broadcasting cond.

Works incl. 4 symphs., *Sinfonietta* and *Hebrew Suite* for orch.; waltzes for string orch.; vln. concerto, Fantasy for 2 pfs. and orch., *Concerto lirico* for cello and orch., *Toccata, Variations and Finale* for string 4tet and orch.; 2 string 4tets, 2 woodwind 5tets, 6tet for clar., pf. and strings, suite for 7 brass instruments, etc.

Berg, Alban (b. Vienna, 9. II. 1885; d. Vienna, 24. XII. 1935), Aus. comp. Self-taught from the age of 15, he became a pupil of Schönberg from 1904 to 1910. Schönberg's influence on him was profound and B. continued a devoted admirer to the end. The nature of this influence may be measured as B. passes from the extended tonality of his early works to atonality and, later, serialism. B.'s use of serial technique is distinctive in that he does not avoid tonal references (e.g. the vln. concerto). He was also a gifted writer. In 1911 he married Helene Nahowski.

Works incl. operas *Wozzeck* (1917–21, after Büchner) and *Lulu* (1929–35, after Wedekind, unfinished); 3 pieces for orch. (1914); vln. concerto (1935); string 4tet (1910), *Lyric Suite* for string 4tet (1925–6); chamber concerto for pf., vln. and 13 wind players (1923–5); 4 pieces for clar. and pf. (1913); sonata for pf. (1907–8); vocal mus.: *Der Wein*, concert aria (1929, after Baudelaire); 5 songs for voice and orch. (1912, Altenberg); many early songs with piano, etc.

Berg, (Carl) Natanael (b. Stockholm, 9. II. 1879; d. Stockholm, 15. X. 1957), Swed. comp. Studied at the Stockholm Cons. and in Paris and Vienna.

Works incl. operas *Leila* (after Byron's *Giaour*), *Engelbrekt*, *Judith* (after Hebbel's drama), *Birgitta*, *Genoveva*; 5 symphs.; symph. poems; vln. concerto; pf. concerto; 2 string 4tets, pf. 5tet, etc.

Bergamasca, an It. dance from Bergamo, at least as old as the 16th cent., called Bergomask by Shakespeare.

Berger, Arthur (b. New York, 15. V. 1912), Amer. comp. Studied with Piston at Harvard Univ., with Pirro at the Sorbonne in Paris, also with P. Lalo and Paul Valéry there, and comp. with Nadia Boulanger. He became mus. ed. of the N.Y. *Sun*.

Works incl. *Slow Dance* for strings; serenade for chamber orch.; 3 pieces for string 4tet, wind 4tet, 2 movements for vla. and cello; ballet *Entertainment Piece* and other works for pf.; *Words for Mus.*, *Perhaps* (Yeats) and other songs, etc.

Berger, Erna (b. Dresden, 19. X. 1900), Ger. soprano. Studied singing and pf. at the Dresden Cons., making her début at the Dresden Opera in 1926, and later joining the Berlin State Opera. She was esp. well known as a Mozart singer.

Bergère châtelaine, La (*The Shepherdess as Lady of the Manor*), opera by Auber (lib. by François Antoine Eugène de Planard), prod. Paris, Opéra-Comique, 27. I. 1820.

Bergerette (Fr. from *berger* = shepherd), a light Fr. song of an artificially pastoral character fashionable in the 18th cent.

In the 15th cent. a form similar to the Virelai but with only one stanza. In the 16th cent. a dance in quick triple time.

Berggreen, Andreas Peter (b. Copenhagen, 2. III. 1801; d. Copenhagen, 9. XI. 1880), Dan. organist, teacher and comp. He prod. the opera *Billedet og Busten* (*The Picture and the Bust*) in 1832. Among his pupils was Gade.

Works incl. collections of nat. songs, psalm tunes, etc.

Bergholz, Lucas (b. Plauen, after 1520; d. ?), Ger. comp. His works consist of 4-part settings of psalms in Ger.

Bergknappen, Die (*The Miners*), opera by Umlauf (lib. by Paul Weidmann), prod. Vienna, Burgtheater, on the opening of its career as a nat. Ger. opera, 17. II. 1778.

Bergman, Valentina Semenovna. *See* Serov.

Bergmann, Carl (b. Ebersbach, Saxony, 11. IV. 1821; d. N.Y., 16. VIII. 1876), Ger. cellist and cond. Went to U.S.A. in 1850 and did much to estab. orchestral mus. there. He was cond. of the N.Y. Phil. Society from 1862..

Bergomask. *See* **Bergamasca.**

Bergonzi, It. family of vln. makers:

1. Carlo B. (b. Cremona, *c.* 1683; d. Cremona, 1747). He began to work independently about 1716.

2. Michelangelo B. (b. Cremona, 1722; d. Cremona, *c.* 1770), son of 1.

3. Nicola B. (b. Cremona, ?; d. ?), son of 2.

4. Zosimo B. (b. Cremona, ?; d. ?), brother of 3.

5. Carlo B. (b. Cremona, ?, d. ?), brother of 4.

Bergsma, William (b. Oakland, Calif., 1. IV. 1921), Amer. comp. Studied at Stanford Univ. and the Eastman School of Mus. under Hanson and Bernard Rogers, and after winning many awards became teacher of comp. at the Juilliard School of Mus.

Works incl. opera *The Wife of Martin Guerre*; ballets *Paul Bunyan* and *Gold and the Señor Commandante*; choral symph;. choral works; symph. for chamber orch. 2 string 4tets; songs, etc.

Berio, Luciano (b. Oneglia, 24. X. 1925), It. comp. Studied with Ghedini in Milan and with Dallapiccola in U.S.A. He is one of the most active comps. of electronic mus.

Works incl. opera *Allez, hop!*; ballet *Mimusique n.2*; variations and *Nones* for Orch.; string 4tets; electronic comps. *Mutazioni* and *Perspectives*; *Allelujah I, II* for 6 and 5 instrumental groups; *Circles* for woman's voice, harp and perc. (after E. E. Cummings); *Sequenza* for solo fl., harp, voice, pf., tromb.

Bériot, Charles (Auguste) de (b. Louvain, 20. II. 1802; d. Brussels, 8. IV. 1870), Belg. violinist and comp. Played in public at the age of 9, but 10 years later went to Paris to perfect himself under Viotti and Baillot. He had a brilliant success in Paris and was app. chamber musician to the king. In 1826 he visited London for the 1st time. He travelled much in the company of Malibran, whom he married after her divorce from her 1st husband; but after her early death in 1836 he retired to Brussels until 1840, when he travelled again and married Marie Huber in Vienna. Prof. of vln. at the Brussels Cons., 1843–52.

Works incl. 10 vln. concertos, variations and studies for vln., pf. trios, etc.

Berkeley, Lennox (Randal Francis) (b. Oxford, 12. V. 1903), Eng. comp. Did not study mus. until he left Oxford (Merton Coll.) in 1926, when he went to Paris until 1933 as a pupil of Nadia Boulanger. Works of his were heard at the I.S.C.M. festivals at Barcelona and London, 1936 and 1938, and at the Leeds and Worcester festivals, 1937–8. Hon. D. Mus., Oxford. 1970.

Works incl. operas *Nelson*, *A Dinner Engagement* and *Ruth*: ballet *The Judgment of Paris*; incid. mus. for Shakespeare's *Tempest*; mus. for film *Hotel Reserve*; oratorio *Jonah*; psalm *Donimi est terra* for chorus and orch.; *Missa brevis*; overture *Nocturne* and divertimento for orch.; pf. concerto, vln. concerto; 2 string. 4tets; 2 vln. and pf. sonatas, sonata and pieces for pf.; *Polka* for 2 pfs., etc.

Berlijn, Anton (b. Amsterdam, 2. V. 1817; d. Amsterdam, 18. I. 1870), Dutch comp. Wrote 9 operas, 7 ballets, oratorio *Moses*, symphs., etc.

Berlin (real name Balin), **Irving** (b. Temum, 11. V. 1888), Amer. comp. of Rus. origin. He had no formal musical training and was unable to read mus., but became one of the most successful comps. of popular songs.

Works incl. mus. for plays and revues, incl. *Music Box Revues*; popular songs, e.g. *Alexander's Ragtime Band*; film mus., etc.

Berlioz (Louis)-, Hector (b. Côte-Saint-André, Isère, 11. XII. 1803; d. Paris, 8. III. 1869), Fr. comp. Son of a doctor who taught him the fl., but wished him to study medicine. As a boy he also learnt the guitar and picked up theoret. knowledge from books. Sent to the École de Médecine in Paris, 1821, he found the studies so distasteful that he decided to give them up for mus. His parents made great difficulties, but Lesueur accepted him as a pupil in 1823, when he at once set to work on an opera and an oratorio, a Mass following the next year. Entered the Cons. in 1826, but failed several times to gain the Prix de Rome, obtaining it at last in 1830. In the meantime he had fallen in love with the Ir. actress Harriet Smithson and expressed his disillusion in her in the *Fantastic Symph.* Then, on the point of going to Rome, he became engaged to the pianist, Marie Moke, who during his absence married Camille Pleyel.

He wrote much in Rome and returned to Paris in 1832, this time meeting Harriet and marrying her in October 1833. To add to his income he became a mus. critic. In 1938 Paganini sent him 20,000 francs to enable him to devote all his time to comp. Separation from Harriet in 1842 and liaison with the singer Marie Recio. Much travelling with her during the next few years, to Ger., Vienna, Prague, Budapest, Rus. and London. Death of Harriet and marriage to Marie, 1854; meanwhile he had resumed his journalistic work. Death of Marie, 1862. He suffered much ill health during the 1860s and was greatly depressed by the death of his son Louis in 1867. After another visit to Rus. he had a bad fall at Nice, where he had gone for his health in 1868, and he grew gradually worse. He wrote 7 books, incl. *Traité de l'instrumentation* and *Mémoires.*

Works incl. operas *Benvenuto Cellini*, *Les Troyens* (2 parts) and *Béatrice et Bénédict* (after Shakespeare's *Much Ado about Nothing*); the programme symphs., *Symphonie fantastique*, *Harold en Italie* (with solo vla.), *Roméo et Juliette* (with voices) and *Symphonie funèbre et triomphale* (for military band, strings and chorus); 6 concert overtures; 2 marches for orch.; 25 choral works incl. *Messe des morts* (Requiem), *La Damnation de Faust*, *Te Deum* and *L'Enfance du Christ*; 6 smaller vocal works with orch. or pf.; 28 songs incl. the cycle *Nuits d'été*; *Lélio, ou Le Retour à*

Bermudo

Bernhard

la vie, a lyric monodrama intended as a sequel to the *Fantastic Symph.,* etc.

Bermudo, Fray Juan (b. Ecija nr. Seville, ?; d.?), Span. 16th-cent. friar and mus. theorist. Friend of Morales. He wrote 3 mus. treatises, pub. 1549–55.

Bernabei, Ercole (b. Caprarola, *c.* 1620; d. Munich, XII. 1687), It. comp. Pupil of Benevoli in Rome, where he worked successively at the Lateran chapel, the church of San Luigi de' Francesi and the Julian chapel. In 1674 he entered the service of the Elector of Bavaria at Munich, where he was *Kapellmeister* for the rest of his life.

Works incl. 5 operas; Masses, motets and other church mus., etc.

Bernabei, Giuseppe Antonio (b. Rome, *c.* 1649; d. Munich, 9. III. 1732), It. comp., son of prec. He went to Munich as asst. to his father in 1677 and succeeded him in January 1688.

Works incl. 15 operas; Masses, motets and other church mus., etc.

Bernac (real name Bertin), **Pierre** (b. 12. I. 1899), Fr. baritone. Since 1936 he has specialized in recitals, frequently in association with Poulenc, many of whose songs he introduced.

Bernacchi, Antonio (b. Bologna, VI. 1685; d. Bologna, III. 1756), It. castrato and teacher. 1st heard in London in 1716.

Bernard, Robert (b. Geneva, 8. X. 1900), Swiss critic and comp. Studied at Geneva, where he founded the Nouvelle Société d'Art in 1918, but settled in Paris in 1926 and later became prof. at the Conus. Internat. and the Schola Cantorum. Became asst. ed. to Prunières of the *Revue musicale* and in 1935 ed., and wrote several works on modern Fr. mus.

Works incl. *Hymne à la divinité* for solo voices, chorus and orch.; *Psalm CL* for chorus, strings and org.; incid. mus. to plays, incl. Samain's *Polyphème*; *Prélude au cimetière marin* (after Paul Valéry) and other orchestral works; pf. concerto, divertissement for vln. and orch.; chamber mus. etc.

Bernard, Tristan (actually Paul) (1866–1947), Fr. playwright. *See* Terrasse (*Femme de Loth*).

Bernardi, Bartolomeo (b. Bologna, *c.* 1660; d. Copenhagen, V. 1732), It. violinist and comp. Left It. *c.* 1700 and entered the service of the Dan. court at Copenhagen. He prod. an opera, *Libussa,* at Prague in 1703.

Works incl. vln. sonatas and trio sonatas.

Bernardi, Francesco. *See* Senesino.

Bernardi, Steffano (b. Verona, *c.* 1580; d. ? Salzburg, prob. 1637), It. priest and comp. Chaplain at Verona Cathedral, studied in Rome later and became *maestro di cappella* of the church of the Madonna dei Monti. In 1611 he became *maestro di*

cappella at Verona Cathedral, and in 1622 went into the service of the Archduke Karl Josef, Bishop of Breslau, and soon afterwards to Salzburg Cathedral, which he helped to inaugurate by cond. Benevoli's 52-part Mass and prod. a Te Deum for 12 choirs of his own. He also wrote many Masses, motets, psalms, madrigals and instrumental works.

Bernart de Ventadorn. *See* Ventadorn.

Bernasconi, Andrea (b. Marseilles, 1706; d. Munich, I. 1784), It. comp., *Kapellmeister* in Munich from 1755. He was stepfather of Antonia B. (below), who was his pupil.

Works incl. *c.* 25 operas, one oratorio and a large quantity of church mus.

Bernasconi, Antonia (b. Stuttgart, 1741; d. 1803), Ger. soprano, stepdaughter of prec. She sang the title role in the 1st prod. of Gluck's *Alceste* (Vienna, 1767), also Aspasia in Mozart's *Mitridate* (Milan, 1770).

Berneker, Constanz (b. Darkehmen, E. Prus., 30. X. 1844; d. Königsberg, 9. VI. 1906), Ger. cond. and comp. Studied in Berlin and cond. there and later at Königsberg, where he also lectured at the Univ. and taught at the Cons.

Works incl. oratorio *Judith*; *The Song of Solomon* for chorus and orch.; incid. mus. to Schiller's *Bride of Messina*; church mus., songs, etc.

Berners, Lord (Gerald Hugh Tyrwhitt-Wilson) (b. Arley Park nr. Bridgnorth, 18. IX. 1883; d. London, 19. IV. 1950), Eng. comp., painter and author. In the diplomatic service at first, he studied mus. at Dresden and Vienna, also sought the advice of Stravinsky and Casella. His operatic setting of Mérimée's comedy, *Le Carrosse du Saint-Sacrement,* was prod. in Paris in 1924, and the ballet *The Triumph of Neptune* in London in 1926; another, with words by Gertrude Stein, *The Wedding Bouquet,* at Sadler's Wells Theatre, London, in 1937, with settings designed by himself.

Works incl. opera *Le Carrosse du Saint-Sacrement;* ballets *The Triumph of Neptune, Luna Park, The Wedding Bouquet* (words by Gertrude Stein), *Cupid and Psyche;* 3 pieces (*Chinoiserie, Valse sentimentale, Kasatchok*), *Fantaisie espagnole* and *Fugue* for orch.; *Variations, Adagio and Hornpipe* for string orch.; *Le Poisson d'or, Trois Petites Marches funèbres* and *Fragments psychologiques* for pf.; *Valses bourgeoises* for pf. duet; songs incl. 3 sets in the Ger., Fr. and Eng. manners, etc.

Bernhard, Christoph (b. Danzig, 1627; d. Dresden, 14. XI. 1692), Ger. comp. The son of a poor sailor, he picked up mus. instruction precariously, but was sent to Schütz at Dresden by a patron and there

Berni   Berutti

sang so well that the Elector of Saxony sent him to It. in 1649. He studied with Carissimi and attracted attention by his comps.; returned to Dresden in 1655 and became vice-*Kapellmeister*; was ousted by the Its. at court and went to Hamburg as cantor, 1664–74, but returned to Dresden as *Kapellmeister*.

Works incl. Masses and other church mus., some in many elaborately contrapuntal parts, etc.

Berni, Francesco (1497–1536), It. poet. *See* **Malipiero** (sonnets).

Bernier, Nicolas (b. Mantes, 28. VI. 1664; d. Paris, 5. IX. 1734), Fr. comp. Studied in Rome. *Maître de chapelle* at Chartres and at the church of Saint-Germain-l'Auxerrois in Paris; then mus. master at the Sainte Chapelle there, 1704–26.

Works incl. 8 books of cantatas, 3 of motets, church mus., etc.

Berno von Reichenau. *See* **Reichenau.**

Bernstein, Leonard (b. Lawrence, Mass., 25. VIII. 1918), Amer. cond. and comp. of Rus. descent. Studied pf. and comp. at Harvard Univ. and graduated in 1939, later attended the Curtis Inst. of Mus. in N.Y. In 1941 he became Kussevitsky's asst. cond. of the Boston Symph. Orch. and in 1943 made his 1st important appearance with the N.Y. Phil. Symph. Orch. As a comp. his greatest success has been the musical *West Side Story*, which was also filmed.

Works incl. ballets *Fancy Free* and *Facsimile*; symphs. *The Age of Anxiety* and *Jeremiah*; oratorio *Kaddisch*; string 4tet; vln. and pf. sonata; 6 anti-fascist songs, etc.

Berselli, Matteo (b. ?; d. ?), It. 18th-cent. tenor. Went to London with Senesino in 1720.

Bertali, Antonio (b. Verona, III. 1605; d. Vienna, 1. IV. 1669), It. violinist and comp. Played in the court chapel in Vienna from 1637 and became *Kapellmeister* in 1649. His opera *L'inganno d'amore* was prod. at the Diet of Regensburg in 1653.

Works incl. several operas; equestrian ballet; 2 oratorios; Masses and other church mus., etc.

Berté, Heinrich (b. Galgócz, 8. V. 1858; d. Vienna, 25. VIII. 1924), Aus.-Hung. comp.

Works incl. operettas *Die Schneeflocke, Die Millionenbraut, Der Märchenprinz, Das Dreimäderlhaus (Lilac Time*, on mus. by Schubert) and others; ballets *Das Märchenbuch, Amor auf Reisen* and others, etc.

Bertheaume, Isidore (b. Paris, c. 1752; d. St. Petersburg, 20. III. 1802), Fr. violinist and comp. Appeared at the Concert spirituel in Paris, 1761, and became cond. in 1783, but left at the Revolution, going 1st to Eutin and then to St. Petersburg, where he joined the Imp. band.

Works incl. 2 symphs.; vln. concerto and

several for 2 vlns.; sonatas for pf. with vln. accomp.; vln. duets, etc.

Bertin, Louise Angélique. *See* **Fausto.**

Bertini, Henri (b. London, 28. X. 1798; d. Meylan, 1. X. 1876), Fr. pianist and comp. Pupil of his brother, Benoît Auguste B. (b. 1780). Went on a continental tour at the age of 12, lived in Eng. and Scot., but settled in Paris in 1821. Wrote much for his instrument, incl. studies.

Bertoldo, Bertoldino e Cacasenno (also **Bertoldo** or **Bertoldo alla corte**), comic opera by Ciampi (lib. by Goldoni), prod. Venice, Teatro San Moisè, 27. XII. 1748.

Bertoletti, Gasparo di. *See* **Salò.**

Bertolli, Francesca (b. ?; d. ?), It. 18th-cent. contralto. 1st heard in London in 1729.

Berton, Henri-Montan (b. Paris, 17. IX. 1767; d. Paris, 22. IV. 1844), Fr. violinist and comp. Violinist at the Paris Opéra from 1782, prof. at the Cons. from 1795 and cond. at the Opéra-Comique from 1807. The 1st of his 48 operas was prod. in 1787.

Works incl. operas *Les Promesses de mariage, Les Rigueurs du cloître, Ponce de Léon, Montano et Stéphanie, Le Délire, Le Grand Deuil, Le Concert intérrompu, Aline, Reine de Golconde, Les Maris garçons, Virginie*, etc.; oratorios *Absalon*, etc.; ballets; cantatas; instrumental mus.; also theoret. works.

Berton, Pierre-Montan (b. Maubert-Fontaines, 7. I. 1727; d. Paris, 14. V. 1780), Fr. comp. and cond., father of prec. App. cond. at the Paris Opéra in 1759 and of the Concert spirituel in 1773.

Bertoni, Ferdinando Giuseppe (b. Salò, Lake Garda, 15. VIII. 1725; d. Desenzano, Lake Garda, 1. XII. 1813), It. comp. Pupil of Martini at Bologna. Organist at St. Mark's, Venice, from 1752 and choirmaster at the Cons. dei Mendicanti from 1757. He prod. his 1st opera at Florence, 1745. In 1776 prod. his *Orfeo*, on the lib. by Calzabigi already set by Gluck in 1762. He visited London to prod. operas in 1778–80 and 1781–3. In 1785 he succeeded Galuppi as *maestro di cappella* at St. Mark's, Venice.

Works incl. operas *Cajetto, Orazio Curiazo, Tancredi, Orfeo ed Euridice, Quinto Fabio* and over 40 others; oratorios and Lat. cantatas; string 4tets; keyboard mus., etc.

Bertrand, Antoine de (b. Fontanges, c. 1545; d. Toulouse, 1581), Fr. comp. In some of his settings of Ronsard's *Amours* he experimented with quarter-tones. Altogether he published 3 vols. of *chansons*, and a vol. of *Airs spirituels* appeared posthumously in 1582.

Bertrand, Aloysius (1807–42), Fr. poet. *See* **Ravel** (*Gaspard de la nuit*).

Bertrand de Born. *See* **Born.**

Berutti, Arturo (b. San Juan, 27. III.

1862; d. Buenos Aires, 3. I. 1938), Arg. comp. Studied at the Leipzig Cons. and in Paris and Milan, settling at Buenos Aires in 1896.

Works incl. operas *Vendetta, Evangelina, Taras Bulba* (after Gogol), *Pampa, Yupanki, Khrysé, Horrida nox* and *Los heroes*.

Berwald, Franz Adolf (b. Stockholm, 23. VII. 1796; d. Stockholm, 3. IV. 1868), Swed. violinist and comp. Comp. several works before he studied in Berlin. He twice visited Vienna, where he had more success than at home, but settled at Stockholm in 1849 as director of mus. at the univ. and court *kapellmästare*.

Works incl. operas *Leonida, The Traitor, Estrella di Soria, The Queen of Golconda*; operettas *I Enter a Convent, The Milliner, A Rustic Betrothal in Swed.*; incid. mus. to plays; 6 symphs. (one lost); vln. concerto, pf. concerto; orchestral works incl. *Recollections of the Norw. Alps*; 3 string 4tets, 2 pf. 5tets and other chamber mus.; songs, etc.

Besard (Besardus), Jean-Baptiste (b. Besançon, *c.* 1567; d. ? Augsburg, *c.* 1625), Fr. lutenist and comp. Studied law at the Univ. of Dôle, then the lute with Lorenzini in Rome. Later lived at Cologne and Augsburg. Pub. theoret. works and collections of lute mus. incl. his own.

Besseler, Heinrich (b. Hörde nr. Dortmund, 2. IV. 1900; d. Leipzig, 25. VII. 1969), Ger. musicologist. Studied at Freiburg i/B., Vienna and Göttingen, where later he became lecturer at the univ. Prof. at Jena, 1949, and at Leipzig from 1956. Wrote on medieval and Renaissance mus.

Best, W(illiam). T(homas). (b. Carlisle, 13. VIII. 1826; d. Liverpool, 10. V. 1897), Eng. organist. Studied at Liverpool, where he lived most of his life as organist at St. George's Hall, where he gave recitals that made him famous all over the world. He made many org. arrs. of famous works.

Béthune, Conon de (b. ?; d. ?), Fr. 12th-cent. trouvère. 10 of his poems, 9 with mus., are preserved.

Bettelstudent, Der (*The Beggar-Student*), operetta by Millöcker (lib. by F. Zell and Richard Genée), prod. Vienna, Theater an der Wien, 6. XII. 1882. There was an earlier opera of this name by Winter (1785).

Betterton, Thomas (*c.* 1635–1710), Eng. actor and playwright. *See* Prophetess (Purcell).

Betz, Franz (b. Mainz, 19. III. 1835; d. Berlin, 11. VIII. 1900), Ger. baritone. Made his 1st appearance at Hanover in 1856, was Wagner's 1st Hans Sachs at Munich in 1868, and the 1st Wotan at Bayreuth.

Bevin, Elway (b. ?; d. ?), Eng. 16th–17th-cent. organist and comp. of Welsh descent. Pupil of Tallis, Vicar-choral at Wells

Cathedral, 1575–84, and organist at Bristol Cathedral after that. He wrote a *Brief and Short Introduction to the Art of Musicke* (1631). Comp. services, anthems and other church mus. Possibly identical with 'Edward Bevin', comp. of keyboard mus.

Bevis (or **Beves**) **of Hampton** (or **Hamtoun**), Anglo-Norman 13th-cent. romance. *See* Buovo d'Antona (Traetta).

Beydts, Louis (Antoine Hector Désiré) (b. Bordeaux, 29. VI. 1895; d. Bordeaux, 16. IX. 1953), Fr. comp. Studied at Bordeaux.

Works incl. operettas *Moineau, Canards Mandarins, La S.A.D.M.P.* and *Le Voyage de Tchong-Li* (both libs. by Sacha Guitry); incid. mus. to Musset's *Il ne faut jurer de rien*; suite for 14 instruments, *A travers Paris*; film mus. incl. *La Kermesse héroïque*; many songs with orch. and with pf.; instrumental pieces; pf. works, etc.

Beyle, Henri. *See* Stendhal.

Bianca e Falliero, ossia Il consiglio di tre (. . ., or *The Council of Three*), opera by Rossini (lib. by Felice Romani, from Manzoni's tragedy *Il conte di Carmagnola*), prod. Milan, Teatro alla Scala, 26. XII. 1819.

Bianca e Fernando, opera by Bellini (lib. by Domenico Gilardoni), prod. Naples, Teatro San Carlo, 30. V. 1826. B.'s 1st opera heard in public.

Bianca und Giuseppe, oder Die Franzosen vor Nizza (. . ., or *The French before Nice*), opera by Johann Friedrich Kittl (lib. by Wagner), prod. Prague, 19. II. 1848. Wagner had written the lib. for himself in 1836; it is based on a novel by Heinrich König.

Bianchi, Francesco (b. Cremona, *c.* 1752; d. London, 27. XI. 1810), It. comp. *Maestro al cembalo* at the Comédie Italienne in Paris 1775, where he worked under Piccinni and prod. 2 operas. In 1778 went to Florence, and in 1783 was app. 2nd *maestro di cappella* at Milan Cathedral. His most successful opera, *La villanella rapita*, was prod. the same year in Venice. In 1795 he went to London as comp. to the King's Theatre, and 3 years later to Dublin. He returned to London in 1801, where he remained till his death.

Works incl. *c.* 60 operas, oratorios, church mus., trio-sonatas, etc.

Biber, Heinrich Ignaz Franz von (b. Wartenberg, Boh., 12. VIII. 1644; d. Salzburg, 3. V. 1704), Boh. violinist and comp. He was high steward and cond. at the archbishop's court at Salzburg.

Works incl. opera *Chi la dura la vince*; church mus., several sets of vln. sonatas, partitas for 3 instruments; vespers for voices, strings and trombs., etc.

Bibi. *See* Pianette.

Bicinium (Lat.) = a song or instrumental piece in 2 parts.

Bickerstaffe, Isaac (*c.* 1735–?1812), Eng. playwright and librettist. *See* **Belmont und Constanze** (André and Dieter), **Ephesian Matron** (Dibdin), **Judith** (Arne), **Lionel and Clarissa** (Dibdin), **Love in a Village** (Arne), **Maid of the Mill** (Arnold), **Padlock** (Dibdin), **Thomas and Sally** (Arne).

Bie, Oscar (b. Breslau, 9. II. 1864; d. Berlin, 21. IV. 1938), Ger. writer on mus. Studied at Leipzig and Berlin. Taught at the Berlin Hochschule für Musik from 1921. Wrote books on opera, dance music, hist. of the pf., R. Strauss, etc.

Biely, Victor. *See* **Bely.**

Bierbaum, Otto Julius (1865–1910), Ger. poet and playwright. *See* **Mottl** (*Pan im Busch*), **Thuille** (*Lobetanz* and *Gugeline*).

Bierey, Gottlob Benedikt (b. Dresden, 25. VII. 1772; d. Breslau, 5. V. 1840), Ger. comp. Succeeded Weber as cond. at the opera of Breslau in 1808. He wrote numerous operas, operettas and mus. plays, incl. *Rosette, das Schweizer Hirtenmädchen* and *Wladimir, Fürst von Novgorod.*

Bigot (*née* **Kiene**), **Marie** (b. Colmar, 3. III. 1786; d. Paris, 16. IX. 1820), Alsat. pianist, wife of the librarian to Count Rasumovsky in Vienna and a friend of Haydn and Beethoven. In 1809 she and her husband went to Paris, but he was taken prisoner at Milan in the war of 1812 and she had to give poorly paid lessons. Mendelssohn was her pupil in 1816.

Bihari, János (b. Nagyabony, X. 1764; d. Pest, 26. IV. 1827), Hung. violinist and comp. Of gypsy stock, he learnt the vln. early and acquired great virtuosity. After his marriage to a daughter of Banyák, a cimbalom player, he soon took up the leadership of his father-in-law's band. It travelled throughout Hung. and repeatedly visited Vienna. As a comp. B. cultivated the *verbunkos* style with great success.

Billet de loterie, Le (*The Lottery Ticket*), opera by Isouard (lib. by Augustin François Creuzé de Lesser and Jean François Roger), prod. Paris, Opéra-Comique, 14. IX. 1811.

Billings, William (b. Boston, Mass., 7. X. 1746; d. Boston, 26. IX. 1800), Amer. tanner and amateur comp. Wrote many hymn tunes and patriotic songs.

Billington (*née* **Weichsel**), **Elizabeth** (b. London, *c.* 1765; d. nr. Venice, 25. VIII. 1818), Eng. soprano, daughter of Carl Weichsel, a Ger. oboist settled in London. She was a pupil of J. C. Bach, and first appeared as a child pianist in 1774. Married the double-bass player James B. in 1783. Made her début as a singer in Dublin, and subsequently sang with great success in London, Paris and Naples. On her return to London in 1801 she continued to be in great demand until her retirement in 1811.

Billy Budd, opera by Britten (lib. by

E. M. Forster and Eric Crozier, on Herman Melville's story), prod. London, Covent Garden, 1. XII. 1951.

Billy the Kid, ballet by Copland, prod. N.Y., 24. V. 1939.

Binary. A song or piece in 2 distinct sections is said to be in B. form. The sections are dependent on each other because the 1st does not close and the 2nd does not open in the principal key, so that each by itself would fail to give an impression of completeness. They are also usually based on the same or similar thematic material—alike but not identical. The dances in Bach's suites are exs. of B. form.

Binchois, Gilles (or **Egidius**) (b. Mons, *c.* 1400; d. ? Mons, 20. IX. 1460), Flem. comp. Chaplain to Philip, Duke of Burgundy, until 1437, when he became a canon at Mons. In 1452 he returned to the Burgundian court. He comp. Mass-movements, Magnificats and other liturgical works in a severely functional style; but his most charact. works are his *chansons,* mostly in 3 parts and in the form of *rondeau* or *ballade.*

Binenbaum, Janco (b. Adrianople, 28. XII. 1880; d. Chevreuse, Fr., 4. II. 1956), Bulg. comp. Studied at Munich and cond. opera at var. Ger. theatres, but later retired to Chevreuse and comp. much mus. which he wished to see neither perf. nor pub.

Works incl. an opera; a ballet; 3 symphs.; 2 vln. concertos; 5 string 4tets and other chamber mus.; sonatas, etc.

Binet, Jean (b. Geneva, 17. X. 1893; d. Trélex-sur-Nyon, Switz., 24. II. 1960), Swiss comp. Studied at the Jaques-Dalcroze Inst. at Geneva and with Barblan, Templeton Strong, Bloch and others. Lived in U.S.A. and Brussels for a time.

Works incl. 3 psalms for chorus and orch., *Cantate de Noël* for chorus and org.; ballet *Die Strasse*; suites on Swiss and Eng. themes and dances for orch.; concertino for chamber orch.; string 4tet and other chamber mus., songs, part-songs, etc.

Biniou (Fr.), a small bagpipe used in Brittany.

Binyon, (Robert) Laurence (1869–1943), Eng. poet. *See* **Rootham** (*For the Fallen*), **Shaw** (M.) (*Sursum corda*), **Spirit of England** (Elgar), **Stanford** (*Attila*).

Bioni, Antonio (b. Venice, 1698; d. after 1739), It. comp. Pupil of Porta. Prod. his 1st opera at Chioggia in 1721; worked at Breslau and Prague, 1726–34.

Works incl. *c.* 25 operas, e.g. *Climene, Issipile*; serenata *La pace fra la virtù e la bellezza* (Metastasio); also church mus.

Birmingham, George (James Owen Hannay) (1865–1950), Eng. novelist. *See* **Nicholson** (S.) (*Mermaid*).

Birthday Odes, works for soli, chorus and orch. written by Eng. comps. from the

Restoration onwards to commemorate royal birthdays. Purcell wrote 6 for Queen Mary, consort of William III, as follows: 1. *Now does the glorious day appear* (1689), 2. *Arise my Muse* (1690), 3. *Welcome, welcome, glorious morn* (1691), 4. *Love's goddess sure was blind* (1692), 5. *Celebrate this festival* (1693), 6. *Come ye sons of art away* (1694).

Birtwistle, Harrison (b. Accrington, Lancs., 15. VII. 1934), Eng. comp. Studied at the Royal Manchester Coll. of Mus. and later at the R.A.M., London. As a comp. he combines delicate sonorities with a strictly controlled serial technique.

Works incl. one-act opera *Punch and Judy*; *Refrains and Choruses* for wind 5tet; *Monody for Corpus Christi* for soprano, fl., vln., horn; *The World is discovered*, instrumental motet; *Précis* for pf.

Bis (Lat. = twice). In Fr. = Encore!

Bisbigliando } (It. = whispering, whis-
Bisbigliato } pered), a direction used esp. for the harp, where it indicates a rapid, soft repetition of notes.

Bishop (*née* Rivière), Ann (b. London, 9. I. 1810; d. N.Y., 18. III. 1884), Eng. soprano. Taught singing by her father and pf. by Moscheles, also studied at the R.A.M., where she met Bishop, whom she married in 1831. She made her 1st public appearance that year, but in 1839 went on a tour with Bochsa and soon afterwards eloped with him, never to return to her husband.

Works incl. over 100 pieces for the stage, e.g. *The Corsair*, *The Circassian Bride*, *Guy Mannering* (after Scott), *The Burgomaster of Saardam*, *The Heart of Midlothian* (after Scott), *Montrose* (after Scott), *The Law of Java*, *Maid Marian*, *Clari*, *Cortez*, *Faustus*, *Aladdin*, *The Fortunate Isles*; incid. mus. for 3 tragedies, for adapts. of Scott's *Kenilworth* and *Waverley*, for Byron's *Manfred* and for Shakespeare's *Midsummer Night's Dream*, *Comedy of Errors*, *Twelfth Night*, *2 Henry IV*, *Two Gentlemen of Verona*, *As You Like It*, *Hamlet*, *Love's Labour's Lost*; oratorio *The Fallen Angel*; cantata *The Seventh Day*; *Triumphal Ode* and Installation Ode for the chancellor of Oxford Univ.; 3 vols. of nat. melodies with words by Moore and other collections of arrs., etc.

Bispham, David (Scull) (b. Philadelphia, 5. I. 1857; d. N.Y., 2. X. 1921), Amer. baritone. Studied with Vannuccini and Lamperti at Milan and with Wm. Shakespeare in London, where he made his 1st concert appearance in 1890, and his 1st on the stage in 1891. 5 years later he 1st came out in N.Y., at the Metropolitan Opera.

Bisser (Fr. verb from Lat. *bis* = twice) = to encore.

Bitonality, the writing of mus. in 2 keys at once, e.g. the fanfare in Stravinsky's *Petrushka*, played simultaneously in C maj. and F♯ maj., or the following (*see* illustration).

Ravel, *L'Enfant et les Sortilèges*

BITONALITY

Bishop, Henry (Rowley) (b. London, 18. XI. 1786; d. London, 30. IV. 1855), Eng. cond. and comp. Studied under Bianchi and prod. *Angelina* (comp. with Lanza) at Margate in 1804 and the ballet *Tamerlan et Bajazet* at the King's Theatre in London, 1806. From that time on he brought out one or more stage pieces almost each year until 1840. In 1813 he was one of the founders of the Phil. Society and became one of its conds. Knighted in 1842; D.Mus. at Oxford in 1853. Prof. of mus. at Oxford, 1848. He was twice married to singers: Sarah Lyon on 30. IV. 1809 and Ann Rivière on 9. VII. 1831.

Bittner, Julius (b. Vienna, 9. IV. 1874; d. Vienna, 10. I. 1939), Aus. comp. A lawyer at first, studied mus. with Josef Labor and Bruno Walter.

Works incl. operas *Die rote Gret*, *Der Musikant*, *Der Bergsee*, *Der Abenteurer*, *Das höllisch Gold*, *Die Kohlhaymerin*, *Das Rosengärtlein*, *Mondnacht*, *Das Veilchen*; ballets *Der Markt der Liebe*, *Die Todestarantella*; *Missa Austriaca* for solo voices, chorus and orch.; chamber mus.; pf. pieces; songs, etc.

Bizet, Georges (actually Alexandre César Léopold) (b. Paris, 25. X. 1838; d. Bougival nr. Paris, 3. VI. 1875), Fr. comp.

His father, a teacher of singing, gave him his 1st instruction in mus. and at the age of 9, being exceptionally gifted, he was admitted to the Paris Cons., studying pf. under Marmontel, org. under Benoist and comp. under Zimmermann. In 1853, when Zimmermann d., he became a pupil of Halévy, having already taken a 1st prize for pf. In 1857 he won the Prix de Rome, but before he went to Rome he had already gained a prize in a competition for an operetta, *Le Docteur Miracle*, sponsored by Offenbach. He tied with Lecocq, whose setting was prod. alternately with his own at the Théâtre des Bouffes-Parisiens.

He wrote several works in Rome and on his return to Paris in 1860 he set out to capture the operatic stage; but although the Opéra-Comique accepted his 1-act opera, *La Guzla de l'Émir*, he withdrew it, destroying it later. The Théâtre Lyrique prod. his next work, *Les Pêcheurs de perles*, in 1863; *Ivan le Terrible*, written in 1865, said to have been burnt by him, was recovered in 1944 and perf. in Ger., at Mühringen Castle, Württemberg. In 1869 Pasdeloup for the 1st time gave him the chance to appear with an orchestral work, *Souvenirs de Rome*, perf. 28. II., which he later entitled *Roma*. The same year he married Geneviève Halévy, his former master's daughter.

In 1872 he was commissioned to write. incid. mus. for Daudet's play, *L'Arlésienne*, prod. at the Vaudeville on 1. X. In 1874 Pasdeloup prod. his overture *Patrie* (unconnected with Sardou's play), but he had set to work before that on *Carmen*, which was prod. at the Opéra-Comique, with spoken dialogue, on 3. III. 1875 and received 37 perfs., but on the day of the 31st B. d., before the work had won through prejudice to a decided success.

Works incl. operas *Don Procopio, Les Pêcheurs de perles, La Jolie Fille de Perth* (after Scott), *Djamileh, Carmen* (after Mérimée); operetta *Le Docteur Miracle*; incid. mus. to Daudet's *L'Arlésienne*: cantatas *David* and *Clovis et Clotilde*; completion of Halévy's opera *Noë*; symph. in C maj., suite *Roma*, overture *Patrie, Petite Suite* (*Jeux d'enfants*) and *Marche funèbre* for orch.; *Vasco de Gama*, symph. ode with chorus; pf. pieces: *Chasse fantastique, Chants du Rhin, Trois Esquisses, Marine, Premier Nocturne, Variations chromatiques*; *Jeux d'enfants* suite for pf. duet; *Chanson du rouet* for vocal solo and chorus, *Le Golfe de Bahia* for solo voices and chorus; *Saint Jean de Pathmos* for unaccomp. male chorus, 4 vocal duets; a number of songs incl. *Feuilles d'album*, etc.

Björkander, Nils (Frank Fredrik) (b. Stockholm, 28. VI. 1893), Swed. comp. and teacher. Founder of a school of mus. in Stockholm.

Works incl. for the most part numerous pf. pieces, also a concert fantasy for pf. and orch., chamber mus., etc.

Björling, Johan ('Jussi') Jonaton (b. Stors Tuna, Kopparbergs län, 2. II. 1911; d. Stockholm, 9. IX. 1960), Swed. tenor. Studied with his father at the Stockholm Cons., and at the Royal Opera School in Stockholm. 1st appeared as Don Ottavio in *Don Giovanni*, Stockholm, 1930. He also sang at Covent Garden and the N.Y. Metropolitan, both before and after the war.

Bjørnson, Bjørnstjerne (1832–1910), Norw. poet, novelist and dramatist. *See* **Grieg** (*Sigurd Jorsalfar, Bergliot* and songs), **Hulda** (Franck, C.), **Kjerulf** (songs), **Nordraak** (*Mary Stuart, Sigurd Slembe* and Norw. nat. anthem), **Olav Trygvason** (Grieg), **Svendsen** (*Sigurd Slembe*).

Blacher, Boris (b. China, 3. I. 1903), Ger. comp. Studied in Berlin and began his career under great difficulties during the Nazi rule, but later became very successful as a comp. of the vanguard, developing a system of variable metres following arithmetical progressions, upon which many of his works are based. In 1953 he became director of the Berlin High School for Mus.

Works incl. opera *Fürstin Tarakanova*, chamber operas *Die Flut* and *Romeo und Julia* (after Shakespeare); several ballets; scenic oratorio *Der Grossinquisitor* (after Dostoievsky); symph., symph. poem *Hamlet* (after Shakespeare), variations on theme by Paganini and other orchestral works; 2 pf. concertos, vla. concerto; 4 string 4tets and other chamber mus; pf. mus.; songs; etc.

Black, Andrew (b. Glasgow, 15. I. 1859; d. Sydney, N.S.W., 15. IX. 1920), Scot. baritone. At first an organist, but studied singing in London and Milan. Appeared in Scot. with success and 1st sang in London in 1887.

'Black Key' Study. Chopin's pf. Study in G♭ maj., Op. 10, No. 5, written *c*. 1831–2 and pub. in 1833. So called because the right hand plays only on the black keys throughout.

Black Knight, The, cantata for chorus and orch. by Elgar, Op. 25, a setting of Longfellow's trans. of Uhland's ballad *Der schwarze Ritter*, prod. Worcester Festival, 1893.

Blackmore, Richard (Doddridge) (1825–1900), Eng. novelist and poet. *See* **Nevin** (A.) (*Lorna Doone*).

Blackwood, Algernon (1869–1951), Eng. novelist. *See* **Elgar** (*Starlight Express*).

Bladder Pipe, a primitive bagpipe with an animal's bladder used for the bag

Blaise le savetier (*B. the Cobbler*), opera by Philidor (lib. by Jean Michel Sedaine, after La Fontaine), prod. Paris, Opéra-Comique, 9. III. 1759.

Blake, William (1757–1827), Eng. poet and painter. *See* **Arundell** (*Ghost of Abel*), **Britten** (*Songs and Proverbs*), **Busch** (songs), **Fogg** (*Seasons*), **Job** (Vaughan Williams), **Lucas** (**M. A.**) (*Book of Thil*), **Parry** (*Jerusalem*), **Poldowski** (songs), **Stevens** (**B.**) (choral work), **Tate** (songs), **Tippett** (*Song of Liberty*).

Blamont, François Colin de (b. Versailles, 22. XI. 1690; d. Versailles, 14. II. 1760), Fr. comp. Pupil of his father, who was in the royal band, and later of Lalande. In 1719 he became superintendent of the royal mus. and after Lalande's death in 1726 master of the chamber mus.

Works incl. stage pieces (mostly ballets and ballet-operas) *Les Festes grecques et romaines*, *Le Retour des dieux sur la terre* (for the marriage of Louis XV), *Le Caprice d'Érato*, *Endymion*, *Les Caractères de l'Amour*, *Les Amours du printemps*, *Jupiter vainqueur des Titans*, *Les Festes de Thétis*; cantata *Circé* and 3 books of *Cantates françaises* for solo voice; motets with orchestral accomp., etc.

Blanchard, Esprit Joseph Antoine (b. Perne [now Vaucluse], 29. II. 1696; d. Versailles, 10. IV. 1770), Fr. comp. Held a number of church and cathedral apps. at Aix, Marseilles, Toulon, Besançon and Amiens and in 1738 was app. to one of the 4 subordinate mus.-masters' posts at the royal chapel in Paris and Versailles. Wrote motets and other church mus.

Blanchard, Henri Louis (b. Bordeaux, 7. II. 1778; d. Paris, 18. XII. 1858), Fr. violinist, comp., mus. critic and playwright. Studied vln. under R. Kreutzer and comp. under Méhul and others. Was cond. and theatre director in Paris. Wrote 3 operas, chamber mus. and airs for vaudevilles.

Blanchet, Émile (Robert) (b. Lausanne, 17. VII. 1877; d. Pully, Vaud, 27. III. 1943), Swiss pianist and comp. Studied at the Cologne Cons. and with Busoni at Weimar.

Works incl. *Conzertstück* for pf. and orch., numerous pf. works, etc.

Bland (*née* **Romanzini**), **Maria Theresa** (b. ? Italy, 1769; d. London, 15. I. 1838), Eng. ballad singer of It. extraction. Sang with great success, esp. at Vauxhall and other London pleasure gardens as well as in opera. Married Bland, a brother of Mrs. Jordan, the actress.

Blangini, (Giuseppe Marco Maria) Felice (b. Turin, 18. XI. 1781; d. Paris, 18. XII. 1841), It. tenor and comp. Sang at Turin Cathedral as a child and learnt mus. there. In 1799 he went to Paris, where he finished an opera left incomplete by a comp. named Della Maria and prod. one of his own. In 1809 he was called to Cassel as mus. director to King Jérôme; but he returned to Paris in 1814 and 2 years later became prof. of singing at the Cons.

Works incl. over 30 operas, e.g. *La Fausse Duègne* (finished by him), *Chimère et réalité*, *Nephtali, ou Les Ammonites*, *Encore un tour de Caliphe*, *Inez de Castro*, *Les Fêtes lacédémoniennes*, *Le Sacrifice d'Abraham*; contrib. to *La Marquise de Brinvilliers*; cantata *Die letzten Augenblicke Werthers* (after Goethe); 174 songs, etc.

Blaník (Smetana). *See* **Má Vlast**.

Blankenburg, Quirijn Gerbrandt van (b. Gouda, 1654; d. The Hague, *c.* 1740), Dutch organist and comp. Studied philosophy and medicine at Leyden, was organist there and later at The Hague. Wrote theoret. books, pub. harpsichord and org. accomps. to psalms and hymns, and in honour of the betrothal of the Prince of Orange in 1677 wrote pieces in 2 parts to be sung normally or upside down, forwards or backwards.

Blaramberg, Pavel Ivanovich (b. Orenburg, 26. IX. 1841; d. Nice, 28. III. 1907), Rus. comp. Was a civil servant and amateur musician, but studied for a short time with Balakirev.

Works incl. operas *Mary of Burgundy* (after Victor Hugo), *The Mummer*, *The Russalka Maiden*, *Tushino* (based on Ostrovsky's play); incid. mus to Ostrovsky's *The Voyevoda*; cantata on Lermontov's *The Demon*; symph. in B min.; songs, etc.

Blas de Castro, Juan (b. Aragon, *c.* 1560; d. Madrid, 6. VIII. 1631), Span. comp. In the 1590s he was private musician to the Duke of Alba at Salamanca and in 1605 musician and usher to Philip III. Lope de Vega and Tirso de Molina mentioned him in their works. Only 20 songs for 3 and 4 voices survive.

Bläser (Ger. = blowers), wind instruments and their players.

Blasinstrumente (Ger.) = wind instruments.

Blasmusik (Ger. = blown mus.) = mus. for wind instruments.

Blauwaert, Émile (b. St. Nikolaas, 13. VI. 1845; d. Brussels, 2. II. 1891), Belg. bass. Studied at the Brussels Cons.; made his 1st appearance in 1866; sang at Bayreuth in 1889.

Blavet, Michel (b. Besançon, 13. III. 1700; d. Paris, 28. X. 1768), Fr. flautist and comp. Works incl. *opéra comique Le Jaloux corrigé* (1752), ballets, sonatas and duets for fl., etc.

Blaze. *See* **Castil-Blaze**.

Blech (Ger.) = Brass, an abbr. often used in scores for *Blechinstrumente*.

Blech, Leo (b. Aachen, 21. IV. 1871; d. Berlin, 24. VIII. 1958), Ger. cond. and comp. Pupil of Bargiel and Humperdinck; cond. in his native town, 1892–8; later at Prague and in 1906–37 cond. of the Berlin Opera.

Works incl. operas *Aglaja, Cherubina, Versiegelt, Das war ich, Aschenbrödel, Alpenkönig und Menschenfeind* (after Raimund); 3 symph. poems; choral works with orch., etc.

Blechinstrumente (Ger.) = brass instruments.

Blechmusik (Ger.) = mus. for brass instruments.

Blessed Damozel, The (Debussy). *See* Damoiselle élue.

Bleyle, Karl (b. Feldkirch, Vorarlberg, 7. V. 1880), Ger. comp. Studied at Stuttgart and Munich, last under Thuille. Comp. orchestral and choral works, a vln. concerto, pf. pieces, etc.

Blind Octaves, a trick in pf. writing: figures in 8ves rapidly alternating between the 2 hands where the thumbs trace a continuous melodic line while the outer notes fly off at broken intervals.

Bliss, Arthur (b. London, 2. VIII. 1891), Eng. comp. Educ. at Rugby and Pembroke Coll., Cambridge, where he studied mus. under C. Wood. Entered the R.C.M. in London, 1913, studying with Stanford, Vaughan Williams and Holst, but joined the army in 1914, serving all through the war until 1918. Prof. of comp. at R.C.M. in 1921, but took wholly to comp. the next year, never holding any official post until he was app. mus. director of the B.B.C. in 1941, an appt. he resigned to Hely-Hutchinson in 1945. He was knighted in 1950 and succeeded Bax as Master of the Queen's Music in 1953.

Works incl. operas *The Olympians* (lib. by J. B. Priestley) and *Tobias and the Angel* (C. Hassall); ballets *Checkmate, Miracle in the Gorbals* and *Adam Zero*; incid. mus. for Shakespeare's *Tempest*; film mus. for *Things to Come* (H. G. Wells), *Conquest of the Air, Caesar and Cleopatra* (G. B. Shaw); *Morning Heroes* for orator, chorus and orch., *Pastoral* for mezzo-soprano, chorus, fl., strings and drums, *Mary of Magdala*; *A Colour Symph., Introduction and Allegro, Hymn to Apollo, Meditations on a Theme by John Blow* and other orchestral works; march *Phoenix* for the liberation of Fr.; *Mus. for Strings; Serenade* for baritone and orch.; concertos for pf. and for 2 pfs.; concerto for pf., tenor and chamber orch., *Rout* for voice and chamber orch., *Madam Noy* for voice and 6 instruments; *Conversations* for fl., ob., vln., vla. and cello; 2 string 4tets, ob. 5tet, clar. 5tet; sonatas for vln. and pf. and vla. and pf.; several song cycles with var. instruments or pf., incl. 5 *Amer. Songs* (Edna St. Vincent Millay), etc.

Blitheman, William (b. ?; d. Whitsunday, 1591), Eng. organist and comp. Choirmaster at Christ Church, Oxford, in 1564; became organist of the Chapel Royal in London in 1585.

Works incl. motets and 6 *In Nomines* for virginal.

Blitzstein, Marc (b. Philadelphia, 2. III. 1905; d. Port-de-France, Martinique, 22. I. 1964), Amer. pianist and comp. Appeared as solo pianist at the age of 15; studied comp. with Scalero in N.Y., Nadia Boulanger in Paris and Schönberg in Vienna; also pf. with Siloti in Amer. His 1st great success was the light opera *The Cradle will rock*, prod. in N.Y., 1937.

Works incl. operas *Triple Sec, Parabola and Circula, The Harpies, The Cradle will rock*; ballet *Cain*; incid. mus. for Shakespeare's *Julius Caesar*; film mus. for *Surf and Seaweed, The Spanish Earth, No for an Answer, Chesapeake Bay Retriever*; choral opera *The Condemned*; radio song-play *I've got the Tune*, Children's Cantata, *The Airborne* for orch., chorus and narrator; *Romantic Piece, Jigsaw* ballet suite and variations for orch.; pf. concerto; string 4tet and serenade for string 4tet; pf. sonata and *Percussion Music* for pf., etc.

Bloch, Ernest (b. Geneva, 24. VII. 1880; d. Portland, Oregon, 15. VII. 1959), Swiss (Americanized) comp. Pupil of Jaques-Dalcroze at first, then of Ysaÿe and Rasse at the Brussels Cons., and afterwds. at the Hoch Cons. at Frankfurt where Iwan Knorr was his comp. master. His last teacher was Thuille at Munich, and he then went to live in Paris, where he began the opera *Macbeth* on a Fr. lib. by Edmond Fleg, having already written several important works. It was prod. in Paris in 1910, but he had in the meantime returned to Switz. to cond. subscription concerts at Lausanne and Neuchâtel. From 1911 to 1915 he was prof. of mus. aesthetics at the Geneva Cons. In 1917 he went to the U.S.A. and settled in N.Y. as prof. at the David Mannes School of Mus. A second opera *Jézabel*, begun there in 1918, was unfinished.

From 1920 to 1925 B. was director of the Cleveland Inst. of Mus. In 1930 he retired to Switz. and lived quietly in remote places. Some interest was shown in his work in Eng. and a good deal in It., where his *Sacred Service* was prod. (at Turin) and *Macbeth* was revived in an It. trans. at Naples, 5. III. 1938. But the anti-Semitic movement encouraged by the Fascists put an end to this appreciation. As an Amer. citizen he could no longer remain absent from U.S.A. without losing his adopted nationality, and he returned there at the end of 1938.

Works incl. opera *Macbeth*; *Sacred Service* (*Avodath Hakdesh*) for baritone solo, chorus and orch.; *Israel* symph. for 5 voices and orch.; symph. in C♯ min., symph. poems *Hiver—Printemps, Trois Poèmes juifs* for orch., *America*, epic rhapsody for orch., *Helvetia*, symph. fresco, *Evo-*

cations, symph. suite, suite: *Overture, Passacaglia and Finale*; vln. concerto.; *Concerto symphonique* for pf. and orch., *Schelomo* for cello and orch., *Concerto grosso* for pf. and strings, *Voice in the Wilderness* for cello and orch.; *Four Episodes* for chamber orch.; 5 string 4tets; 2 vln. and pf. sonatas, vla. and pf. suite, pf. 5tet, *Three Nocturnes* for pf. trio, *In the Mountains, Night, Three Landscapes* and *Recueillement* (prelude) for string 4tet; *Poèmes d'automne* and 3 Psalms for voice and orch.; *Enfantines*, 5 *Sketches in Sepia, In the Night, Nirvana, Poems of the Sea* and sonata for pf.; *Baal Shem* (3 pieces), *Melody, Exotic Night* and *Abodah* for vln. and pf.; *From Jewish Life* (3 pieces) and *Méditation hébraïque* for cello and pf., song cycle *Historiettes au crépuscule* and other songs, etc.

Block Harmony, a term used for a type of harmonic accomp. in which all the notes of the chords move simultaneously in 'blocks' without being made to depart from one another by means of figuration or counterpoint.

Blockflöte (Ger. lit. block fl.; actually Fipple Fl.) = Recorder.

Blockx, Jan (b. Antwerp, 25. I. 1851; d. Antwerp, 26. V. 1912), Belg. comp. Learnt mus. as a choir-boy and went to the Antwerp School of Mus., later to the Leipzig Cons. In 1886 he became prof. and in 1901 director of the Antwerp Cons., succeeding Benoit, whom he followed as a Flem. mus. nationalist. Most of his operas and all his cantatas for solo voices, chorus and orch. are set to Flem. words.

Works incl. operas *Jets vergeten, Maître Martin, Herbergprinses, Thyl Uilenspiegel, De Bruid der Zee, De Kapel, Baldie*; ballet *Milenka*; cantatas *Op den Stroom, Een Droom van't Paradijs, Vredeszang, Klokke Roeland, De Scheldezang*; overture *Rubens*; Romance for vln. and orch. etc.

Blodek, Vilém (b. Prague, 3. X. 1834; d. Prague, 1. V. 1874), Cz. flautist, teacher and comp. Prod. the nat. operas *In the Well* and *Zitek* at Prague in 1867–8.

Blok, Alexander (1880–1921), Rus. poet and dramatist. *See* **Gnessin** (*Rose and the Cross* and songs), **Mossolov** (songs), **Weissberg** (*The Twelve*).

Blom, Eric (Walter) (b. Berne, 20. VIII. 1888; d. London, 11. IV. 1959), Eng. critic, of Dan. origin. He was educated privately and 1st became known in England as assistant to Rosa Newmarch in providing programme notes for the Promenade concerts in 1919. He was London mus. critic of the *Manchester Guardian* from 1923 to 1931, mus. critic of the *Birmingham Post* from 1931, and mus. critic of the *Observer* from 1949 to 1953. He also ed. *Music & Letters* from 1937 to 1950 and 1954 to 1959. His books incl. *The Limitations of Music, Mozart, Beethoven's Sonatas Dis-*

cussed and *Music in England*. He also trans. several foreign books and ed. the 5th ed. of Grove's *Dictionary of Music and Musicians*. He was made C.B.E. and Hon. D.Litt. of Birmingham Univ. in 1955.

Blomdahl, Karl-Birger (b. Växjö, 19. X. 1916; d. Växjö, 17. VI. 1968), Swed. comp. Studied at Stockholm under var. masters, incl. Rosenberg and Wöldike. In 1960 he was app. prof. at the Stockholm Cons.

Works incl. opera *Aniara* (a space-ship drama); incid. mus.; 3 symphs., symph. dances, concert overture, *Concerto grosso* for orch.; vln. concerto; vla. concerto; chamber concerto for pf., wind and perc.; string 4tet, string trio, woodwind trio; suites for cello and pf. and bassoon and pf.; pf. pieces; trios for women's voices, etc.

Blondel de Nesle. *See* **Nesle.**

Blow, John (b. Newark, II. 1649; d. London, 1. X. 1708), Eng. organist and comp. He became one of the children in the Chapel Royal in London as soon as it was re-established after the Restoration (1660) and was taught by H. Cooke. He wrote 3 anthems in 1663 and took a share with Humfrey and Turner in the 'Club Anthem' c. 1664. About the same time he set Herrick's 'Go, perjur'd man' in the style of Carissimi at Charles II's request. Hingston and C. Gibbons also had a share in B.'s mus. educ. In 1668 he became organist at Westminster Abbey in succession to Albert Bryne; in III. 1674 he was sworn a Gentleman of the Chapel Royal and the following July became Master of the Children following Humfrey. In November he married Elizabeth Braddock. Mus.D. at Canterbury, 1677. In 1679 he was followed in the Westminster organist's post by Purcell, returning as organist after Purcell's death in 1695. In 1687 he succeeded Wise as almoner and choirmaster at St. Paul's Cathedral (as yet unfinished). James II app. him a member of the royal band and confirmed a previous app. as Comp. in Ordinary. Towards the end of the cent. he bought a property at Hampton, but still retained a house at Westminster, where he d.

Works incl. *c.* 12 services; over 100 Eng. anthems, 15 Lat. anthems; masque *Venus and Adonis*; Act Songs for Oxford Univ.; at least 16 Welcome Songs, 5 for St. Cecilia's Day, odes on the death of Queen Mary and of Purcell; 3 coronation anthems for James II, 1 for William and Mary; anthem for the opening service at St. Paul's Cathedral (1697); sonata for 2 vlns. and bass; harpsichord lessons, suites and pieces; some org. pieces; song collection *Amphion Anglicus*; songs and catches, etc.

Blue Bird, The (Maeterlinck). *See* **Oiseau bleu.**

Blue Notes, a device in Blues, the playing of certain notes, esp. the 3rd and 7th of the scale, deliberately out of tune, between maj. and min.

Bluebeard. *See* **Ariane et Barbebleue; Barbe-bleue; Ritter Blaubart.**

Bluebeard's Castle (*A Kékszakállú Herceg Vára*), opera by Bartók (lib. by Béla Balázs), prod. Budapest, 24. V. 1918.

Blues, an Amer. dance stemming from the Foxtrot, the speed of which it reduced and into which it brought a deliberately contrived dismal atmosphere.

Bluette (Fr. = flash, spark). In mus. the equivalent of an epigram, a light, graceful short piece; a trifle.

Blume, Friedrich (b. Schlüchtern, Hesse, 5. I. 1893), Ger. musicologist. Studied at Munich, Leipzig and Berlin. He was a prisoner in England for 3 years during the 1914–18 war. After teaching in Berlin from 1921 he became prof. at Kiel Univ. from 1934 to 1958. He has been ed.-in-chief of the complete works of M. Praetorius and the series *Das Chorwerk*, and is ed. of the encyclopaedia *Die Musik in Geschichte und Gegenwart*. His books incl. a history of Protestant church mus.

Blumenfeld, Felix Mikhailovich (b. Kovalevka, 19. IV. 1863; d. Moscow, 21. I. 1931), Rus. pianist, cond. and comp. Studied at the St. Petersburg Cons. and taught there from 1885 to 1918. Cond. of the Imp. opera from 1898 to 1912.

Works incl. symph.; *Allegro de Concert* for pf. and orch.; numerous pf. works incl. 24 preludes and sonata-fantasy; songs, etc.

Blumenthal, Jacob (b. Hamburg, 4. X. 1829; d. London, 17. V. 1908), Ger. pianist and comp. Settled in London in 1848 and became pianist to Queen Victoria. Wrote many light pf. pieces and songs.

Blunden, Edmund (b. 1896), Eng. poet and critic. *See* **Finzi** (St. Cecilia Ode).

Blüthner, Julius Ferdinand (b. Falkenhain, 11. III. 1824; d. Leipzig, 13. IV. 1910), Ger. pf. manufacturer. Founded his firm at Leipzig in 1853.

Boabdil, der letzte Maurenkönig (*B., the Last Moorish King*), opera by Moszkowski (lib. by Carl Wittkowsky), prod. Berlin, Opera, 21. IV. 1892.

Boatswain's Mate, The, comic opera by Ethel Smyth (lib. by comp., based on a story by William Wymark Jacobs), prod. London, Shaftesbury Theatre, 28. I. 1916.

Boccabadati, Luigia (b. Modena, 1800; d. Turin, 12. X. 1850), It. mezzo-soprano. Made her 1st appearance at Parma in 1817. Her 3 daughters were also singers.

Boccaccio, Giovanni (1313–75), It. poet and novelist. *See* **Delannoy** (*Ginevra*), **Delvincourt** (*Boccacerie*), **Kreutzer** (R.) (*Imogène*), **Nakhabin** (*Burgess of Tuscany*).

Boccherini, Luigi (b. Lucca, 19. II. 1743; d. Madrid, 28. V. 1805), It. cellist and comp. Pupil of his father, a double-bass

player, who sent him to Rome for further study in 1757. On his return to Lucca in 1761 he played cello in the theatre orch. With the violinist Manfredi he travelled widely on concert tours in Aus. and Fr. Particularly successful in Paris (1767–8), he pub. there his first chamber mus. In 1769 he went to Madrid and settled there, being first in the service of the Infante Don Luis until 1785, when the latter died. In 1787 B. was app. court comp. to Frederick William II of Prussia, who had the exclusive right to his works, but seems to have maintained his residence in Madrid. After the king's death in 1797 he was apparently without a permanent post, for he spent his last years in increasing poverty.

Works incl. oratorios *Giuseppe riconosciuto* and *Gioas, rè di Giuda*; *Stabat Mater*, Mass, cantatas, motets, etc.; opera *La Clementina*; concert arias, etc.; 20 symphs.; 4 cello concertos and one each for fl., vln. and harpsichord; 102 string 4tets, 60 string trios, 125 string 5tets, 12 piano 5tets, 18 5tets for wind and strings, 16 6tets, 2 8tets; 27 vln. sonatas, 6 cello sonatas, etc.

Bochsa, Robert Nicolas Charles (b. Montmédy, 9. VIII. 1789; d. Sydney, N.S.W., 6. I. 1856), Fr. harpist, cond. and comp. Began as a comp. of opera, oratorio and ballet at Lyons and Bordeaux; entered the Paris Cons. in 1806; made a great name as harpist and opera comp., but fled to Eng. in 1817 when discovered in forgeries. Although condemned, he was able to live in London, where he made the harp extremely popular and became prof. of the instrument on the foundation of the R.A.M., but in 1827 had to leave owing to scandals. In 1839 he ran away with Bishop's wife, Ann Rivière, and they went on a world tour together, during which he d.

Works incl. opera *Trajan* and 8 others; a ballet; oratorio *Le Déluge universel*; 2 Requiems (1 for Louis XVI); many pieces for harp, etc.

Bockelmann, Rudolf (**August Louis Wilhelm**) (b. Bodenteich, nr. Lüneburg, 2. IV. 1890; d. Dresden, 10. X. 1958), Ger. bass-baritone. He studied with Oscar Lassner and 1st appeared in *Lohengrin* at Leipzig, 1921. He sang Wagnerian parts regularly at Bayreuth and frequently in London. After the 1939–45 war he settled as a teacher in Hamburg.

Bocklet, Carl Maria von (b. Prague, 1801; d. Vienna, 15. VII. 1881), Boh. pianist and violinist. Settled in Vienna in 1820. Friend of Beethoven and Schubert.

Bockshorn, Samuel (**Friedrich**) (**Capricornus**) (b. Žeřžice nr. Mlada Boleslav, 21. XII. 1628; d. Stuttgart, 10. XI. 1665), Boh. comp. Mus. director at Pressburg, Nuremberg and Stuttgart.

Works incl. dramatic cantata *Raptus*

Proserpinae; sacred and secular works for voices and instruments; vocal table mus.; songs, etc.

Bockstriller (Ger. = goat's trill), a kind of vocal shake of no artistic value, prod. by a rapid, bleating repetition of a single note. Wagner asks for this kind of shake from the tailors' chorus in the 3rd act of *The Mastersingers*.

Bodanzky, Artur (b. Vienna, 16. XII. 1877; d. N.Y., 23. XI. 1939), Aus. cond. Studied at the Vienna Cons. and after some min. apps. became asst. cond. to Mahler at the Imp. Opera. After several engagements at Ger. opera houses, he became cond. of the Ger. operas at the Metropolitan Opera in N.Y., 1915.

Bodenschatz, Erhard (b. Lichtenberg, 1576; d. Gross-Osterhausen, 1636), Ger. theologian and musician. Ed. of var. collections of sacred mus., notably the *Florilegium Portense*, pub. in 2 parts (1603 and 1621).

Boehm, Theobald (b. Munich, 9. IV. 1794; d. Munich, 25. XI. 1881), Ger. flautist and inventor. He wrote mus. for his instrument and made important changes in its fingering and mechanism.

Boehme, Kurt (b. Dresden, 5. V. 1908), Ger. bass. He was a leading singer at the Dresden opera from 1930, specializing in *buffo* roles. From 1950 he sang at the Munich State Opera, and from 1955 in Vienna.

Boëllmann, Léon (b. Ensisheim, 25. IX. 1862; d. Paris, 11. X. 1897), Fr. (Alsatian) organist and comp. Pupil of Gigout at Niedermeyer's school in Paris, later organist at the church of Saint-Vincent-de-Paul there.

Works incl. symph. in F maj.; *Fantaisie dialoguée* for org. and orch., *Variations symph.* for cello and orch.; pf. 4tet, pf. trio; cello and pf. sonata; church mus.; org. works incl. 2 suites (1st *Gothique*).

Boëly, Alexandre (Pierre François) (b. Versailles, 19. IV. 1785; d. Paris, 27. XII. 1858), Fr. pianist, organist and comp. Organist at the church of Saint-Germain-l'Auxerrois, 1840–51, where he cultivated Bach's org. mus.

Works incl. chamber mus.; org. works; vln. and pf. sonatas; numerous pf. works incl. sonatas, caprices, studies, preludes and fugues, etc.

Boelza, Igor Fedorovich (b. Kielce, Poland, 8. II. 1904), Rus. mus. scholar and comp. Studied at the Kiev Cons., where he taught later, settled at Moscow in 1941; did much work for film mus. in 1930–8, and in the 1940s began a hist. of Eng. mus.

Works incl. film mus.; 5 symphs.; overture, *Lyric Poem*, etc. for orch.; concertos for pf. and for org.; string 4tet, pf. trio; 5 pf. sonatas; instrumental pieces; songs, etc.

Boësset, Fr. 16th–17th-cent. family of musicians:

1. Antoine B., Sieur de Villedieu (b. Blois, *c.* 1585; d. Paris, 8–9. XII. 1643). Became Master of the King's Music to Louis XIII through his marriage to Guédron's daughter and held other important posts at court. Wrote 24 ballets and pub. many of them in several books of *Airs de cour* in 4 and 5 parts; also comp. Masses and motets, etc.

2. Jean-Baptiste B., Seigneur de Dehault (b. ?, *c.* 1613; d. Paris, 27. XII. 1685), son of prec. Succeeded his father in 1644. Wrote ballets, incl. *La Mort d'Adonis*, with words by Perrin, *Ballet du Temps*, *Triomphe de Bacchus* and *Alcidiane*; also vocal chamber mus., etc.

3. Claude Jean-Baptiste B., Seigneur de Launay (b. ?, VII. 1664; d. Paris, *c.* 1701), brother of prec. Held some of his father's posts and titles from 1686, but was replaced by 1696 by Lully's son Jean-Baptiste and by Colasse.

Works incl. *Fruits d'automne*, etc.

Boethius, Anicius Manlius Severinus (b. ? Rome, *c.* 480; d. Pavia, 524), Roman consul and senator, and philosopher. His most important work is the *De consolatione philosophiae* (some verses from which were set to mus. in Carolingian times), but he is also, in his *De institutione musica*, the interpreter of ancient Gk. mus. theory to the Western world. In spite of some misconceptions and the irrelevancy of much of the Gk. system, his work remained the fundamental basis of almost all medieval and Renaissance mus. theory.

Bogatirev, Anatoly Vassilevich (b. Vitebsk, 13. VIII. 1913), Rus. comp. Studied at the Minsk Cons. under Zolotarev. Later studied folksong and became deputy director of the Cons. at Minsk.

Works incl. operas *The Two Foscari* (after Byron) and *In the Thick Woods of Polesye*; incid. mus. for Romashev's *Stars cannot be dimmed*; *The Tale of a Bear* for solo voices, chorus and orch., cantata *To the People of Leningrad*; string 4tet, pf. trio; *Manfred* suite (after Byron) and variations for pf.; choruses, songs, folksong arrs., etc.

Bohème, La (*The Bohemians*), opera by Leoncavallo (lib. by comp., based on Murger's novel *Scènes de la vie de Bohème*), prod. Venice, Teatro La Fenice, 6. V. 1897. Comp. at the same time as Puccini's work.

Opera by Puccini (lib. by Giuseppe Giacosa and Luigi Illica, based on Murger), prod. Turin, Teatro Regio, 1. II. 1896.

Bohemian (incl. Moravian) Composers. *See* (also Czech for later names) Benda (2), Bendl, Biber, Brixi, Černohorsky, Dušek, Dussek, Finger, Foerster (J.), Gassmann, Gelinek, Gläser, Gluck (?), Gyrowetz, Kalliwoda, Kittl, Kotzwara, Kozeluch,

Kraft (2), Krommer, Krumpholz (2), Miča, Moscheles, Mraczek, Mysliveček, Pichel, Reicha, Richter (F. X.), Schack, Sechter, Seegr, Škroup, Skuherský, Stamitz (4), Stich, Tomašek, Tuczek, Tuma, Walter (I.), Wanhal, Weber (D.), Worzischek, Wranitzky, Zelenka.

Bohemian Girl, The, opera by Balfe (lib. by Alfred Bunn, based on a ballet-pantomime, *La Gypsy*, by Jules Henri Vernoy de Saint-Georges), prod. London, Drury Lane Theatre, 27. XI. 1843.

Böhm, Georg (b. Hohenkirchen nr. Ohrdruf, 2. IX. 1661; d. Lüneburg, 18. V. 1733), Ger. comp. Organist at Hamburg before 1698, then at St. John's Church, Lüneburg. As comp. and organist an important forerunner of Bach; his works incl. a Passion, songs, org. and harpsichord mus., etc.

Böhm, Karl (b. Graz, 28. VIII. 1894), Aus. cond. Studied mus. and law in Vienna. He has held posts in many of the chief European opera houses, incl. Dresden (1934–43) and Vienna (1943–5, 1954–6). B. is esp. well known for his perfs. of Mozart and R. Strauss.

Bohnen, Michael (b. Cologne, 2. V. 1887; d. Berlin, 26. IV. 1965), Ger. bass-baritone. Made his début in Düsseldorf in 1910 and then sang at the Berlin Hofoper from 1913 to 1921. From 1922 to 1932 he sang at the Metropolitan Opera in N.Y. and in Berlin again from 1933 to 1945.

Boieldieu, François Adrien (b. Rouen, 16. XII. 1775; d. Jarcy, 8. X. 1834), Fr. comp. Studied under Broche, the organist of Rouen Cathedral, and in 1793 brought out his 1st opera, *La Fille coupable*, there, with a lib. by his father, who was secretary to the archbishop. He also wrote many songs at that time, some of which were pub. in Paris. Having failed to estab. a school of mus. at Rouen on the model of the Paris Cons., he left for the capital, where in 1797 he prod. his 1st opera away from home, *La Famille suisse*, which was so successful that he brought out 4 more within 2 years. He also became pf. prof. at the Cons. in 1798. Being reproached by Cherubini for having attained too easy a success on very slender gifts, he placed himself under that master for a course in counterpoint. In 1802 he married the dancer Clotilde Mafleuray, with disastrous results, and in 1803 he left for St. Petersburg as cond. of the Imp. Opera. There he prod. 9 operas between 1804 and 1810. He returned to Paris in 1811 and had a greater success than before because there was less competition and he did better work.

He collaborated by turns with Cherubini, Catel, Isouard, R. Kreutzer, Hérold, Berton, Paer and Auber, also with some of these and Batton, Blangini and Carafa in *La Marquise de Brinvilliers* of 1831; but his best works are among those he did alone. In *La Dame blanche*, to match the lib. from Scott, he used some Scot. folksongs. Soon after he began to suffer from consumption contracted in Rus. and his fortune declined until he was granted a state pension. In 1827 he was married for the 2nd time, to the singer Jenny Philis-Bertin, with whom he had long been living and by whom he had a son, Adrien Louis Victor, in 1815, who also became a comp. B. lived at Geneva for a time not long before his death.

Works incl. operas *Le Calife de Bagdad, Ma Tante Aurore, Aline, Reine de Golconde, La Jeune Femme colère, Télémaque, Rien de trop, Jean de Paris, La Fête du village voisin, Le Petit Chaperon rouge, La Dame blanche, Les Deux Nuits* and others; incid. mus. for Racine's *Athalie*; pf. concerto; pf. trio and other chamber mus.; duets for vln. and pf. and harp and pf., 6 pf. sonatas, etc.

Boileau(-Despreaux), Nicolas (1636–1711), Fr. critic and poet. *See* (?) **Bellérophon** (Lully), **Dieren (van)** (songs).

Boisdeffre, (Charles Henri) René (Le Mouton) de (b. Vesoul, 3. IV. 1838; d. Vézelise, Meurthe-et-Moselle, 25. XI. 1906), Fr. comp. Gained a prize for chamber mus. in 1883.

Works incl. symph. in A min., *Scènes champêtres* for orch.; *Messe solennelle*, cantata *Cantique des cantiques*; pf. 6tet, 2 pf. 5tets, pf. 4tet, 2 pf. trios; pf. sonatas, etc.

Boismortier, Joseph Bodin de (b. Perpignan, c. 1691; d. Paris, 1755), Fr. comp. Wrote 3 opera-ballets, cantatas, over 50 instrumental works incl. many for musette and vielle.

Boito, Arrigo (b. Padua, 24. II. 1842; d. Milan, 10. VI. 1918), It. poet and comp. Studied at the Milan Cons. and prod. his Faust opera, *Mefistofele*, at the Teatro alla Scala there in 1868. Wrote libs. for several comps. as well as for himself, incl. those of Verdi's *Otello* and *Falstaff*. His *Nerone* was not prod. until after his death. He also comp. the opera, *Ero e Leandro*, but destroyed the mus. (the lib. was set by Bottesini and later by Mancinelli) and he wrote a lib. on *Hamlet* for Faccio.

Bolero, a Span. dance in 3–4 with a characteristic rhythm that usually has a triplet on the 2nd half of the 1st beat.

Bolero, an orchestral work by Ravel, commissioned as a ballet by Ida Rubinstein and 1st perf. by her in Paris, 22. XI. 1928. It consists entirely of a single theme of Span. character, repeated over and over again with different orch. and in a gradually rising *crescendo*.

Bolivian Composer. *See* **Velasco Maidana.**

Bologna, Jacopo da (Jacobus de Bononia) (b. ?; d. ?), It. 14th-cent. comp. He belongs to the earliest generation of *trecento* comps.: all his known works are madrigals, and nearly all are for two voices. There is also a short treatise, *L'arte del biscanto misurato*.

Bombard, the bass instrument of the obs. family of the Shawm, a double reed wind instrument prec. the ob., the B. thus being a forerunner of the bassoon.

Bombarde, a 16-ft. reed org. pedal stop, similar to the Bombardon, but with more powerful tone.

Bombardon (Fr.; *see also* **Saxhorn**), the name of a brass instrument of the Tuba variety, derived from Bombard (or Ger. *Pommer*), previously applied to var. instruments of the ob. and bassoon family. The B. takes the lowest bass parts in military and brass bands. Also a bass org. stop for 16-ft. reed pipes.

Bomtempo, João Domingos (b. Lisbon, 28. XII. 1775; d. Lisbon, 18. VIII. 1842), Port. comp. Settled in Paris in 1802, but returned to Lisbon in 1815, founding a Phil. Society there in 1820 and became director of the Cons. in 1833.

Works incl. It. opera *Alessandro in Efeso*; Mass for the promulgation of the Port. Constitution (1821), Requiems for Maria I, Pedro IV and Camões; 6 symphs.; 4 pf. concertos; pf. 5tet; variations on a fandango and on *God Save the King* for pf., etc.

Bona, Valerio (b. Brescia, c. 1560; d. ? Verona, after 1619), It. comp. and Franciscan friar. *Maestro di cappella* at var. churches, incl. Vercelli, Milan, Brescia and Verona.

Works incl. Masses, motets and other church mus.; madrigals, canzonets and instrumental canzonas.

Bonadies, Johannes (b. ?; d. ?), It. 15th-cent. comp. and copyist. He is chiefly remembered for his insertions in the Faenza Codex (also known as the Bonadies Codex) consisting of works by himself, John Hothby, Johannes de Erfordia and others.

Bondeville, Emmanuel (b. Rouen, 29. X. 1898), Fr. organist and comp. Studied at Rouen and was app. organist of the church of Saint-Nicaise there in 1915, but held important broadcasting posts in Paris from 1935.

Works incl. operetta *L'École des maris*; opera *Madame Bovary* (after Flaubert); *Le Bal des pendus*, *Lara*, *Ophélie*, *Marine* for orch.; pf. sonata; songs; etc.

Boni, Guillaume (b. Saint-Fleur, ?; d. ?), Fr. 16th-cent. comp. *Maître de chapelle* at the church of Saint-Étienne at Toulouse. Comp. 2 books of sonnets by Ronsard, 1 of quatrains by Pibrac, *Psalmi Davidici*, etc.

Bonini, Severo (b. Florence, 1582; d. Florence, 5. XII. 1663), It. comp. Organist at Forlì. Set Rinuccini's *Lamento d'Arianna* in recitative style and wrote madrigals and spiritual canzonets for a single voice with

continuo accomp. He also wrote 3-part motets and *Affetti spirituali* for 2 voices in the same style.

Bonnal, Joseph (Ermand) (b. Bordeaux, 1. VII. 1880; d. 1944), Fr. organist and comp. Studied at the Paris Cons. Held several organist's appts. at Paris churches, and in 1921 at Saint-André at Bayonne where he became director of the school of mus.

Works incl. 2 ballets; *Poèmes franciscains*, *Le Tombeau d'Argentina* and *Petite Suite basque* for orch.; 2 string 4tets and other chamber mus.; symph., *Paysages euskariens* and many other works for org., etc.

Bonne Chanson, La, cycle of 9 songs by Fauré, set to poems from Verlaine's vol. of that name, comp. 1891–2.

Symph. poem by Loeffler, on the same source, comp. 1901 and perf. Boston, 12. IV. 1902.

Bonner, Eugene (MacDonald) (b. Washington, N.C., 1889), Amer. critic and comp. Studied at the Peabody Cons. of Baltimore and in Eng., where he lived in 1911–17. Having served in the war of 1914–18, he settled in Paris until 1927, studying with Albert Wolff. On his return to the U.S.A. he became mus. critic in N.Y.

Works incl. operas *Barbara Frietchie*, *Celui qui épousa une femme muette*, *The Venetian Glass Nephew* and *The Gods of the Mountain*; incid. mus. to *The Young Alexander*; prelude *White Nights* for orch.; *Whispers of Heavenly Death* (Whitman) for voice and orch.; pf. 5tet; *Flutes* for voice and 4 instruments; *Suite sicilienne* for vln. and pf., etc.

Bonno, Giuseppe (b. Vienna, 29. I. 1710; d. Vienna, 15. IV. 1788), Aus. comp. of It. extraction. Studied in Naples 1726–37. In 1739 app. comp. to the Aus. court, and in 1774 succeeded Gassmann as *Kapellmeister*.

Works incl. over 20 operas; 3 oratorios, incl. *Il Giuseppe riconosciuto*; Masses, Requiems and other church mus.

Bononcini (or **Buononcini**). It. 17th–18th-cent. family of musicians:

1. Giovanni Maria B. (b. Montecorone nr. Modena, 23. IX. 1642; d. Modena, 18. XI. 1678), chief musician to the Duke of Modena, *maestro di cappella* there of the church of San Giovanni in Monte and later of the cathedral. He wrote a treatise, *Il musico prattico*.

Works incl. cantatas, sonatas, suites, etc.

2. Giovanni B. (b. Modena, 18. VII. 1670; d. Vienna, 9. VII. 1747), son of prec. Pupil of Colonna and of his father, whom he succeeded at San Giovanni in Monte at Modena. He prod. his 1st opera in Rome in 1692. Lived in Vienna, 1698–1711, in It., 1711–20, in London, 1720–32, later in Fr. and Vienna.

Works incl. operas *Tullo Ostilio*, *Xerse*,

Astarto, Crispo, Erminia, Farnace, Calfurnia, Astianatte, Griselda and many others, incl. an act in *Muzio Scevola* with Handel and Amadei; 7 oratorios; funeral anthem for Marlborough; mus. for the Peace of Aix-la-Chapelle; Masses, Te Deum, psalms, *Laudate pueri*; chamber cantatas and duets, etc.

3. Antonio Maria B. (b. Modena, 18. VI. 1677; d. Modena, 8. VII. 1726), brother of prec. Became *maestro di cappella* to the Duke of Modena in 1721.

Works incl. *c.* 20 operas, oratorios, etc.

Bonporti, Francesco Antonio (b. Trent, VI. 1672; d. Padua, 19. XII. 1749), It. comp. Trained for the priesthood in Rome from 1691 and studied mus. with Pitoni and Corelli. On his ordination he returned to Trent, and spent the next 40 years in hope of a canonry. He retired disappointed to Padua in 1740.

Works incl. motets; trio sonatas; concertos; 'Inventions' for solo vln., etc.

Bontempi-Angelini, Giovanni Andrea (b. Perugia, *c.* 1624; d. Perugia, 1. VI. 1705), It. castrato, theorist and comp. He took the name of a patron, Cesare Bontempi, and sang in St. Mark's, Venice, from 1643. At the end of the 1640s he went to Dresden, where he became asst. cond. to Schütz in 1666, but devoted himself to science and architecture the next year. He returned to It. in 1669 and after another visit to Dresden in 1671 settled down in his birthplace. He wrote 3 theoret. books.

Works incl. It. operas *Paride*, etc., Ger. operas (with Marco Giuseppe Peranda), *Daphne, Io*, etc.

Boogie-woogie, in jazz mus. a special type of Blues for pf. solo with a continuous *ostinato* bass for the left hand over which the right prod. varied melodic formations, often by improvisation.

Borck, Edmund von (b. Breslau, 22. II. 1906; d. nr. Nettuno, It., 16. II. 1944), Ger. cond. and comp. Studied at the Hochschule für Musik in Berlin. After cond. at Frankfurt he became prof. at the Berlin Cons. in 1939.

Works incl. opera *Napoleon* (based on C. D. Grabbe's play): 5 pieces, prelude and fugue, concerto, and theme, variations and finale for orch.; 6tet for fl. and strings and other chamber mus., etc.

Borde, Jean de la. *See* **La Borde.**

Bordes, Charles (b. La Roche-Corbon nr. Vouvray, 12. V. 1863; d. Toulon, 8. XI. 1909), Fr. pianist, comp. and scholar. Pupil of Marmontel for pf. and of Franck for comp. As *maître de chapelle* 1st at Nogent-sur-Marne and from 1890 at the church of Saint-Gervais in Paris, he devoted himself to research into old polyphonic mus. and gave perfs. with the Chanteurs de Saint-Gervais cond. by him. In 1899–90 he explored Basque folk mus.

and in 1884 was one of the founders of the Schola Cantorum.

Works incl. unfinished opera *Les Trois Vagues*; Fantasy on a Basque theme for pf. and orch.; motets and spiritual dialogues; pf. works; choruses; 33 songs, etc.

Bordes-Pène (*née* **Pène**), **Léontine Marie** (b. Lorient, Finistère, 25. XI. 1858; d. Rouen, 24. I. 1924), Fr. pianist. Studied at the Paris Cons. and married a brother of Charles Bordes. She took a great interest in contemp. Fr. mus.

Bordoni, Faustina (b. Venice, 1700; d. Venice, 4. XI. 1781), It. mezzo-soprano, pupil of Gasparini. 1st appeared in Venice in 1716. For 2 seasons, 1726–8, sang for Handel in London. Her rivalry with Cuzzoni at this time was satirized in *The Beggar's Opera*. Married the comp. Hasse in 1731 and sang at Dresden.

Bore, the width of the tubing of wind instruments, which affects the character of their tone.

Boree, one of the old Eng. names for the Bourrée, others being Borea, Bore and Borry.

Borgomastro di Saardam, Il (*The Burgomaster of Saardam*), comic opera by Donizetti (lib. by Domenico Gilardoni, based on a Fr. play by Anne Honoré Joseph Mélesville, Jean Toussaint Merle and Eugène Cantiran de Boirie), prod. Naples, Teatro del Fondo, 19. VIII. 1827. The subject is that of Lortzing's *Zar und Zimmermann*.

Boris Godunov, opera by Mussorgsky (lib. by comp. based on Pushkin's drama and Nikolai Mikhailovich Karamazin's *History of the Russian Empire*), comp. 1868–9; enlarged and revised 1871–2; this later version cut and prod. St. Petersburg, Imp. Opera, 8. II. 1874, the orig. having been rejected in 1870. Rimsky-Korsakov's ed. prod. St. Petersburg, Imp. Opera, 10. XII. 1896. Further revision by Rimsky-Korsakov, 1908. The orig. prod. Leningrad, 16. II. 1928.

Born, Bertrand de (b. ?; d. ?, *c.* 1215), Fr. troubadour. 46 poems and 1 tune of his songs have been preserved.

Borne, Fernand Le. *See* **Le Borne.**

Bornelh, Guiraut de (b. ?; d. ?, *c.* 1220), Fr. troubadour. He was regarded as the master of his calling. More than 80 poems and 4 tunes of his songs are extant.

Bornier, Henri, Vicomte (1825–1901), Fr. dramatist. *See* **Coquard** (*Agamemnon*).

Borodin, Alexander Porphyrevich (b. St. Petersburg, 11. XI. 1833; d. St. Petersburg, 28. II. 1887), Rus. scientist and comp. Illegitimate son of Prince Gedeanov, who registered him as the son of one of his serfs. He tried to compose at the age of 9 and was given mus. lessons. In his studies at the Acad. of Medicine he distinguished himself esp. in chemistry, and while studying in Germany he met the pianist Ekaterina Protopopova, whom he married in 1863. The prec. year, having so far been self-taught in comp., he began to take lessons from Balakirev, who cond. his 1st symph. in 1869. He lectured on chemistry at the School of Medicine for Women from 1872 to his death and wrote important treatises on his subject.

Works incl. opera *Prince Igor* (unfinished); 3 symphs. (3rd unfinished); *In the Steppes of Central Asia* and Scherzo for orch.; 2 string 4tets; *Serenata alla spagnuola* for string 4tet; *Serenade de quatre galants à une dame* for male-voice 4tet; *Petite Suite* for pf.; 13 songs, etc.

Borosini, Francesco (b. Modena, *c*. 1690; d. ?), It. tenor. He sang at Prague in 1723 and went to London the following year, singing in Handel's and Ariosti's operas in 1724–5.

Borosini (*née* d'Ambreville), **Rosa** (b. Modena, 27. VI. 1698; d. ?), It. soprano, wife of prec. Made her début in 1713. Sang in Prague in 1723, and married Francesco B., prob. after his return from London in 1725.

Borren, Charles (Jean Eugène) van den (b. Brussels, 17. XI. 1874; d. Brussels, 14. I. 1966), Belg. musicologist. Studied law and practised for 8 years, but later devoted himself to mus. hist., esp. of the old Netherland school. App. librarian to the Brussels Cons. in 1920, succeeding Wotquenne. His works incl. many valuable studies, e.g. on Eng. virginal mus., the Eng. madrigal, the origins of Netherland keyboard mus., the beginnings of mus. in Venice, Lassus, Dufay, etc.

Børresen, Hakon (Axel Einar) (b. Copenhagen, 2. VI. 1876; d. Copenhagen, 6. X. 1954), Dan. comp. Pupil of Svendsen, he took a comp. prize in 1901. Later he held many important administrative posts in the mus. life of Copenhagen.

Works incl. operas *The Royal Guest* and *Kaddara*; ballet *Tycho Brahe's Dream*; incid. mus. for plays; several symphs. and other orchestral works; chamber mus.; songs, etc.

Borry, Eng. corruption of the Fr. *bourrée* found in 17th-cent. mus., e.g. Purcell.

Bortkievich, Sergei Eduardovich (b. Kharkov, 28. II. 1877; d. Vienna, 25. X. 1952), Rus. comp. Studied law at St. Petersburg and comp. under Liadov, later at Leipzig. Lived in Berlin until 1914, when he joined the Rus. army, and at Constantinople after World War I.

Works incl. opera *Acrobats*; 2 symphs.; symph. poem *Othello*; 4 pf. concertos (1 for the left hand), 2 vln. concertos, cello concerto; pf. sonatas and pieces; songs, etc.

Bortniansky, Dimitri Stepanovich (b. Glukhov, Ukraine, 1752; d. St. Petersburg,

7. X. 1825), Rus. comp. Studied at Moscow and in St. Petersburg under Galuppi, whom he followed to It. in 1768 with a grant from Catherine II. He made further studies at Bologna, Rome and Naples. He wrote motets and operas at Venice in 1776 and at Modena in 1778. In 1779 he returned to Rus. and became director of the Imp. church choir, which he reformed and turned into the Imp. Chapel in 1796.

Works incl. operas *Le Faucon, Le Fils rival, Creonte* and *Quinto Fabio*; 35 sacred concertos, 10 concertos for double choir, Mass, chants, etc.

Borwick, Leonard (b. London, 26. II. 1868; d. Le Mans, 15. IX. 1925), Eng. pianist. Pupil of Clara Schumann in 1883–9 at Frankfurt, where he made his 1st appearance, playing in London for the 1st time in 1890, at a Phil. Society concert. He also appeared in Vienna, frequently played with the most eminent artists in chamber mus. at the London St. James's Hall and gave many recitals with Plunket Greene.

Boschi, Giuseppe (b. ? Viterbo, ?; d. ?), It. 17th–18th-cent. bass. Member of St. Mark's, Venice; (?) sang Polyphemus in Handel's *Aci* at Naples in 1709. 1st appeared in London in 1710 and subsequently sang in many of Handel's operas.

Boschot, Adolphe (b. Fontenay-sous-Bois, Seine, 4. V. 1871; d. Neuilly, nr. Paris, 1. VI. 1955), Fr. critic. Was attached to var. Paris newspapers and reviews and wrote a number of books on mus., particularly a biog. of Berlioz in 3 vols.

Bösendorfer, Ignaz (b. Vienna, 28. VII. 1796; d. Vienna, 14. IV. 1859), Aus. pf. manufacturer. Founded his firm in Vienna in 1828 and was succeeded in it by his son Ludwig (1835–1919) in 1859.

Bosio, Angiolina (b. Turin, 22. VIII. 1830; d. St. Petersburg, 12. IV. 1859), It. soprano. Studied at Milan under Cataneo and made her 1st appearance there in 1846. After many tours she 1st went to London in 1852.

Bossi, (Marco) Enrico (b. Salò, 25. IV. 1861; d. at sea, 20. II. 1925), It. organist and comp. Studied at the Liceo Musicale of Bologna and at the Milan Cons. After var. organist's and teaching apps. he became director of the principal mus. schools at Venice, Bologna and Rome in succession. Meanwhile he had become very famous as a concert organist, and it was when returning from a tour in U.S.A. that he d.

Works incl. operas *Paquita, Il veggente* and *L'angelo della notte*; oratorios *Il Paradiso perduto* (after Milton) and *Giovanna d'Arco*; Masses, motets and sacred cantatas; secular choral works with orch. or org. incl. *Il cieco, Inno di gloria* and *Cantico dei cantici*; orchestral works; concerto for org. and orch.; chamber mus.; *c.* 50 org. works incl. suite *Res severa magnum gaudium*; pf. pieces; songs, etc.

Bossi, Renzo (b. Como, 9. IV. 1883; d. Milan, 2. IV. 1965), It. comp., son of prec. Studied under his father at the Liceo Benedetto Marcello in Venice and took a comp. prize in 1902, when he went to Leipzig, where he continued studying pf., org. and cond., the last under Nikisch. He was cond. of more than 1 Ger. opera house before he went to Milan as asst. cond. at La Scala. Prof. of comp. at Parma from 1913 and Milan from 1916.

Works incl. operas *Rosa rossa* (after Oscar Wilde), *Passa la ronda!, La notte del mille*, *Volpino il calderaio* (after Shakespeare's *Taming of the Shrew*) and *Proserpina*; symph., *Sinfoniale, Fantasia sinfonica* and *Bianco e nero* for orch.; vln. concerto; chamber mus., etc.

Bossuet, Jacques-Bénigne (1627–1704), Fr. bishop, orator and author. *See* **Thomson (V.)** (*Oraison funèbre*).

Boston, a slow type of waltz, also called Valse Boston, coming into vogue in Amer. ballrooms *c.* 1910. Compared with the ord. waltz it has a certain complexity of rhythm and accomp. which later allied it to Jazz.

Botstiber, Hugo (b. Vienna, 21. IV. 1875; d. Shrewsbury, 15. I. 1941), Aus. musicologist. Pupil of Adler, R. Fuchs and Zemlinsky. Held several important mus. administrative posts in Vienna, ed. old mus., wrote books on the orchestral overture, on the symph. since Berlioz, etc., and completed Pohl's biog. of Haydn.

Bottesini, Giovanni (b. Crema, 22. XII. 1821; d. Parma, 7. VII. 1889), It. double bass player, cond. and comp. Was engaged at Havana, Paris, Palermo, Barcelona and Cairo.

Works incl. operas *Marion Delorme* (after Victor Hugo), *Ali Baba* and *Ero e Leandro*; double bass concertos with orch.; much mus. for double bass and pf., etc.

Bottrigari (Bottrigaro), **Hercole**, (b. Bologna, 24. VIII. 1531; d. San Alberto, 30. IX. 1612), It. theorist. His *Il Desiderio* (1594) deals with the problems of combining instruments of different families. From 1600 to 1604 he was involved in a controversy with Artusi.

Boucher, Alexandre (Jean) (b. Paris, 11. IV. 1778; d. Paris, 29. XII. 1861), Fr. violinist. Appeared in public at the age of 6, was court violinist at Madrid, 1787–1805, and toured Eur. from 1820 to 1844 with sensational success.

Boucicault, Dion (1820–90), Ir. actor and playwright. *See* **Lily of Killarney** (Benedict).

Bouffons. *See* **Guerre des Bouffons.**

Boughton, Rutland (b. Aylesbury, 23. I. 1878; d. London, 25. I. 1960), Eng. comp. Studied at the R.C.M. in London under Stanford and Walford Davies. But he left very soon, and prod. some early orchestral works, cond. for a time at the Haymarket Theatre, had a hard struggle and accepted a teaching engagement at the Midland School of Mus. in Birmingham in 1904, remaining there until 1911, at the same time lecturing and cond., and prod. the choral work *Midnight* to words from Edward Carpenter's *Towards Democracy* at the Birmingham Festival of 1909. Idealizing Wagner, he determined to found an Eng. centre of opera on the same lines as Bayreuth and began in a very modest way at Glastonbury with a series of mus. dramas on the Arthurian legends, but in 1914 1st prod. *The Immortal Hour.* A special theatre was to be built at Glastonbury, but the project had to be abandoned. In 1922 *The Immortal Hour* had a long run in London, and *Alkestis* was prod. there by the B.N.O.C. in 1924.

Works incl. mus. dramas *The Birth of Arthur, The Immortal Hour, Bethlehem, The Round Table, Alkestis, The Queen of Cornwall, The Lily Maid*; ballets *Choral Dances, Snow White, The Moon Maiden*; dramatic scene *Agincourt* from Shakespeare's *Henry V*; works for chorus and orch.; *The Skeleton in Armour* (Longfellow), *The Invincible Armada* (Schiller), *Midnight* (Edward Carpenter), *Song of Liberty*; unaccomp. chorus, choral variations on folksongs, motet *The City*, 4 *Festival Choruses* (Drinkwater); 2 string 4tets; songs with string 4tet; vln. and pf. sonata; songs, etc.

Bouhy, Jacques (Joseph André) (b. Pepinster, 18. VI. 1848; d. Paris, 29. I. 1929), Belg. baritone. Studied at Liège and Paris, where he made his 1st appearance at the Opéra in 1871. Director of N.Y. Cons., 1885–9. Lived and taught in Paris from 1907. The 1st Escamillo in Bizet's *Carmen.*

Bouilly, Jean-Nicolas (1763–1842), Fr. writer. Administrator of a dept. nr. Tours during the Terror. Wrote libs. for a number of operas (*see* **Rescue Opera**) for var. comps., incl. Cherubini and Gaveaux. The lib. of Beethoven's *Fidelio* is based on his book for Gaveaux's *Léonore.*

Boulanger, Lili (Juliette Marie Olga) (b. Paris, 21. VIII. 1893; d. Mézy, Seine-et-Oise, 15. III. 1918), Fr. comp. Pupil of her sister Nadia at first, then at the Paris Cons. Gained the Prix de Rome in 1913 (the 1st woman ever to do so), but suffered much ill health.

Works incl. incid. mus. for Maeterlinck's *La Princesse Maleine*; 2 poems for orch.; cantata *Faust et Hélène* (after Goethe); psalms with orch., etc.

Boulanger, Nadia (Juliette) (b. Paris, 16. IX. 1887), Fr. comp. and teacher, sister of prec. Student at the Paris Cons., where she taught later, as well as at the École Normale de Musique and the Amer. Cons. at Fontainebleau. She went to U.S.A. after the outbreak of war in 1939, returning in 1946. Many distinguished comps. in var. countries have been her pupils. Hon. D. Mus., Oxford, 1968.

Works incl. incid. mus. to d'Annunzio's *La città morta* (with Pugno); cantata *La Sirène*; orchestral works; instrumental pieces, songs, etc.

Boulevard Solitude, opera by Henze (lib. by the comp. and Grete Weil), prod. Hanover, 17. II. 1952.

Boulez, Pierre (b. Montbrison, 26. III. 1925), Fr. comp. and cond. After abandoning studies in mathematics, he studied with Messiaen at the Paris Cons. and later took a course in serial technique with Leibowitz (1946). In 1946 he worked for the Renaud-Barrault theatre co. and in 1953–4 founded the 'Domaine Musical' with Barrault, which specialized in new mus. As a comp., he belongs to the *avant-garde*, writing in a style which has its roots in Debussy and Webern, and also in the ideas of James Joyce and Mallarmé. He is one of the pioneers of total serialism, but later intro. freer elements into his mus. B. is also a leading cond. of advanced new mus. He became principal cond. of the B.B.C. Symph. Orch. in 1970.

Works incl. *Pli selon pli* for soprano and orch. (after Mallarmé, 1958–62); *Poésie pour pouvoir* for orch. and electronic tape (after Michaux, 1958); *Figures for Doubles-Prismes* for orch. (1963–6); *Le Soleil des eaux* for solo voices, chorus and orch. (after Char); *Le Marteau sans maître* for alto and 6 instruments (after Char); fl. sonatine; 3 pf. sonatas (1946, 1948, 1957); *Structures* I, II, for 2 pianos (1952, 1961); *Livre* for string 4tet, etc.

Boult, Adrian Cedric (b. Chester, 8. IV. 1889), Eng. cond. Educ. at Westminster School and Christ Church, Oxford, where he received a D.Mus. He then went to Leipzig to study cond. with Nikisch (1912–1913), also taking lessons from Reger. In 1914 he joined Covent Garden, making his début as an orchestral cond. in 1918. B. taught at the R.C.M. in 1919 and from 1924 to 1930 was cond. of the Birmingham Symph. Orch. He later became cond. of the B.B.C. Symph. Orch., from which he retired in 1950, being then appointed cond. of the London Phil. Orch. In 1937 he was knighted. B. is best known for his perfs. of the classical repertoire, although he has helped to further the cause of modern (esp. Eng.) mus. He is also the author of a useful book on cond.

Bourdon (Fr. = Drone), an org. stop with 16-ft tone, stopped diapason.

Bourgault-Ducoudray, Louis (Albert) (b. Nantes, 2. II. 1840; d. Vernouillet, 4. VII. 1910), Fr. comp. A lawyer at first, he entered the Paris Cons. late and took a comp. prize in 1862. In 1869 he founded a choral society in Paris with which he gave perfs. of unfamiliar works. Collected and pub. Gk. and Breton folksongs. Lectured on hist. of mus. at the Cons. from 1878.

Works incl. operas *L'Atelier de Prague*, *Michel Colomb*, *Bretagne*, *Thamara*, *Myrdhin*; satiric play *La Conjuration des fleurs*; *Stabat Mater*, *Symphonie religieuse* for unaccomp. chorus; *Fantaisie en Ut mineur*, *Carnaval d'Athènes*, *Rapsodie cambodgienne*, *L'Enterrement d'Ophélie* (after Shakespeare) for orch., etc.

Bourgeois gentilhomme, Le (*The Bourgeois as Gentleman*), comedy-ballet by Molière with mus. by Lully, prod. Chambord, 14. X. 1670.

Incid. mus. by R. Strauss to a shortened version of Molière's comedy trans. by Hugo von Hofmannsthal, prec. the 1-act opera *Ariadne auf Naxos*, prod. Stuttgart, 25. X. 1912. Strauss afterwards dropped it for a new operatic 1st act and made a concert suite for orch. of the incid. mus., adding a minuet by Lully.

Bourgeois, Louis (b. Paris, *c.* 1510; d. Paris, *c.* 1561), Fr. musician. A Protestant, he went to Geneva to join Calvin's church, taking the place of Franc, who had gone to Lausanne, and working with Guillaume Fabri. He contrib. to the Genevan Psalter by selecting and harmonizing tunes. He also composed secular *chansons*.

Bourgeois, Louis Thomas (b. Fontaine-l'Évêque, Hainault, 24. X. 1676; d. Paris, I. 1750), Fr. singer and comp. Choirmaster at Strasbourg 1703, alto at the Paris Opéra 1706–11, when he left to devote himself to comp. App. *maître de chapelle* at Toul *c.* 1716.

Works incl. opera-ballets, solo cantatas, motet *Beatus vir*, etc.

Bournonville, Jean-Valentin de (b. Noyon, *c.* 1580; d. ?, *c.* 1640), Fr. organist and comp. Worked successively at Rouen, Évreux, Saint-Quentin, Abbeville and Amiens Cathedral. Wrote Masses and other church mus.; org. mus., etc.

Bourrée (Fr.), a Fr. dance in quick 2–2 time beginning with an upbeat (in 17th-cent. Eng. 'borry') (*see* illustration opposite).

Boutade (Fr. = whim, frolic), an 18th-cent. dance, or sometimes a whole ballet, in a style described by the title; also sometimes an instrumental piece of the same character.

Boutique fantastique, La (*The Fantastic Toyshop*), ballet by Respighi, arr. from mus. by Rossini (choreography by Leonid Fedorovich Massin), prod. London, Alhambra Theatre, 5. VI. 1919. The mus. consists mainly of small pieces written by Rossini in his retirement for the amusement of his friends.

Boutmy, Flem. family of musicians.
1. Jacques Adrien B. (b. Ghent, 16. I.

78

1683; d. Brussels, 6. IX. 1719), organist. Followed his father, Jacques B., as organist of St. Nicholas, Ghent, and in 1711 was app. organist of the collegiate church of Ste. Gudule in Brussels.

2. Josse B. (b. Ghent, 12. II. 1697; d. Brussels, 27. XI. 1779), organist, harpsichordist and comp., brother of prec. Went to Brussels early, entered the service of Prince Thurn and Taxis in 1736, taught at court and was app. organist of the royal chapel in 1744. Works incl. a cantata and 4 books of harpsichord pieces.

3. Guillaume B. (b. Brussels, 15. VI. 1723; d. Brussels, 22. I. 1791), comp., son of prec. Also served Prince Thurn and Taxis from 1752 and in 1760 was app. keeper of keyboard instruments at court. Comp. sonatas for harpsichord.

4. Jean-Baptiste Joseph B. (b. Brussels, 29. IV. 1725; d. Cleves, ?), harpsichordist, organist and comp., brother of prec. Went to Ghent early, taught the harpsichord there and in 1757 was app. organist at St. Baafs. In 1764 he settled at The Hague and after 1775 at Cleves. Works incl. 6 *Divertissements* for harpsichord with vln. *ad lib.*, and concertos for harpsichord and orch.

5. Laurent François B. (b. Brussels, 19. VI. 1759; d. Brussels, 3. XI. 1838), harpsichordist, organist and comp., brother of prec. Deputized for his ageing father, but failed to succeed him and in 1779 settled at Rotterdam. In 1789 he went to Fr., but soon after returned to Brussels, and again in 1815, after taking refuge in London from the Fr. occupation. Works incl. var. pf. pieces, some with vln. or fl., vocal works with var. accomps., etc.

Bouvet, Charles (René Clément) (b. Paris, 3. I. 1858; d. Paris, 19. V. 1935), Fr. musicologist. He was at first a violinist in the Cons. orch., but from 1903 to 1911 was in charge of the Fondation J. S. Bach, from

of Antoine Bovy, a stamp engraver. Studied at home at first, but at the age of 15 was sent to Paris to study the pf. with Chopin and comp. with Belaire. Later he became prof. at the Geneva Cons.

Works incl. opera *La Fille du carillonneur*; pf. sonata *L'Absence*, studies, nocturnes, waltzes, barcarolles, caprices, etc., for pf., etc.

Bow, the stick with horsehair stretched over it with which instruments of the viol and vln. family are played.

Bowen, York (b. London, 22. II. 1884; d. London, 23. XI. 1961), Eng. pianist, violinist, horn player and comp. Studied at the R.A.M. in London.

Works incl. 3 symphs., *Symph. Fantasia* for orch.; 3 pf. concertos., vln. and vla. concertos; sonata for vla. and pf.; numerous pf. works, etc.

Bowles, Paul (Frederic) (b. New York, 30. XII. 1910), Amer. comp. Pupil of Aaron Copland, Virgil Thomson and Nadia Boulanger. He lived by turns in Spain, Mexico, Guatemala and N. Africa, but later returned to U.S.A. In 1949 he published a novel, *The Sheltering Sky*, which established him as a writer.

Works incl. operas *The Wind Remains* and *Denmark Vesey*; ballets *Patorela, Yankee Clipper, Colloque sentimentale, Dance Ballet* and *Johnny A.*; film and incid. mus.; cantata *Par le détroit*; Suite for orch.; pf. concerto, concerto for 2 pfs.; *Romantic Suite* for 9 instruments, *Mediodia* for 11 instruments, *Mus. for a Farce* for clar., tpt. pf. and perc., *Scènes d'Anabase* for tenor, ob. and pf., pf. trio; sonatas for ob. and clar., fl. and pf. and vln. and pf.; 2 sonatinas, *Huapango* Nos. 1 and 2, 2 *Portraits, Aria, Chorale and Rondo, La Femme de Dakar, Café sin nombre* and other works for pf.; *El Bejuco, Sayula, Nocturne, Caminata*, sonata and suite for 2 pfs.; song

BOURRÉE

1924 of the library and museum at the Opéra and in 1920–7 he was sec. of the Société française de Musicologie. He ed. old mus. and wrote books on the Couperin family, on Tartini, Massenet, Spontini, etc.

Bovy-Lysberg, Charles Samuel (b. Lysberg, Ct. Berne, 1. III. 1821; d. Geneva, 14. II. 1873), Swiss pianist and comp. Son

cycles *Memnon* (Jean Cocteau), *Green Songs*, 4 Span. songs, *Danger de mort*, 6 *Songs, Letter to Freddy* (Gertrude Stein) and a number of other songs; part-songs, etc.

Bowman, Henry (b. ?; d. ?), Eng. 17th-cent. comp. Lived (?) at Oxford.

Works incl. a Miserere and a vol. of

songs for 1–3 voices to words by Cowley and others.

Boyarina Vera Sheloga (Rimsky-Korsakov). *See* **Pskovitianka.**

Boyce, William (b. London, *c.* 1710; d. London, 7. II. 1779), Eng. organist and comp. Chorister at St. Paul's Cathedral and a pupil of Greene, whom he succeeded as Master of the King's Mus. in 1755. Meanwhile he held var. org. posts in London, was app. comp. to the Chapel Royal in 1736, and cond. of the Three Choirs Festival the foll. year. From 1758 he was organist of the Chapel Royal. Deafness forced him to give up much of his work during his later years.
Works incl. stage entertainments *The Chaplet* and *The Shepherd's Lottery*; masque *Peleus and Thetis* and Dryden's *Secular Masque*; incid. mus. for Shakespeare's *Tempest*, *Cymbeline* and *Romeo and Juliet*; pantomime *Harlequin's Invasion* (with M. Arne and Aylward, and containing the song *Heart of Oak*); service settings and anthems; cantatas and odes; 20 symphs. and overtures; 12 trio-sonatas; keyboard mus.; songs, etc. He also completed a notable collection of church mus. begun by Greene (pub. under the title *Cathedral Music* in 3 vols., 1760–73).

Brabançonne, La. *See* **National Anthems: Belgium.**

Brace, a bracket connecting the 2 staves, e.g. in pf. and harp mus., or a greater number of staves in a score.

Brack, Georg (Jörg) (b. ?; d. ?), Ger. 15th-cent. comp. His part-songs were pub. in collections printed by Schöffer (1513?), Arnt von Aich (1519) and others.

Brade, William (b. ?, *c.* 1560; d. Hamburg, 26. II. 1630), Eng. violist and comp. Worked by turns at the court of Christian IV of Den., in the service of the Margraves of Brandenburg and the Duke of Schleswig-Gottorp, and at Halle, Berlin and Hamburg. Pub. instrumental mus. in several parts, incl. pavans, galliards and other dances, *canzone*, concertos and fancies in 6 books at Hamburg, Lübeck, Antwerp and Berlin, 1609–21.

Bradford, Hugh (St. John) (b. St. John's, N.F., 10. III. 1900), Brit. comp. Studied with Charles Wood at the R.C.M. in London, but became an Anglican clergyman.
Works incl. ballet *The Jackdaw and the Pigeons*; *Paysage* and *Fugal March* for orch.; variations on a Popular Theme and 7 Charact. Pieces for pf., *Song without Words* for 2 pfs., etc.

Braga, Gaetano (b. Giulianova, 9. VI. 1829; d. Milan, 21. XI. 1907), It. cellist and comp. Studied at the Naples Cons., toured Eur. and lived mainly in Paris and London.
Works incl. opera *La Reginella* and 7 others; cantata; cello concerto; instrumental pieces incl. *Serenata*, etc.

Braham (real name Abraham), **John** (b. London, 20. III. 1777; d. London, 17. II. 1856), Eng. tenor and comp. 1st appeared as a treble at Covent Garden Theatre in 1787. When his voice broke he taught the pf., but reappeared at Rauzzini's concerts at Bath in 1794 and in London in 1796. In 1798–1801 he appeared in Paris, It. and Ger. He then became attached to Covent Garden for many years and often interpolated his own songs, which became very popular, in operas. He also contrib. to operas prod. at the Lyceum and Drury Lane Theatres, incl. one on Shakespeare's *Taming of the Shrew*. Towards the end of his career he was the 1st Huon in Weber's *Oberon*.

Brahms, Johannes (b. Hamburg, 7. V. 1833; d. Vienna, 3. IV. 1897), Ger. comp. Son of a double bass player, from whom he learnt the rudiments of mus. as a child. Although intended for an orch. player, he made such progress on the pf. that his parents decided to make a prodigy perf. of him when about 11; but his teachers wisely opposed this. He soon afterwards began to comp., but had to play in sailors' taverns and dancing-saloons at night to supplement his parents' earnings. He gave 2 concerts in 1848–9, but did not free himself from drudgery of playing and teaching until he went on a concert tour with Reményi in 1853, when he met Joachim, Liszt and other musicians of importance, partic. Schumann and Clara S., who took much interest in him. In 1857–60 he was intermittently engaged at the court of Lippe-Detmold, travelled as pianist and worked at Hamburg between, cond. a ladies' choir there.
1st visited Vienna in 1862 and settled there for good the following year. Entirely devoted to comp. from 1864, except for some concert tours, on which he played mainly his own works. His success as a comp. was firmly estab. during the 1860s, and he became known abroad; but he did not write his 1st symph. until 1875, aged 42. He wrote much during summer holidays in Aus., Ger. or Switz., but hardly visited other countries except It. In 1877 he refused the Cambridge Mus.D. because he did not wish to go to receive it in person. bnt accepted the Ph.D. from Breslau in 1879. The later years were uneventful except for the growing importance of his work. In 1896 he began to suffer seriously from cirrhosis of the liver, the disease from which he died.
Works incl. *Ein deutsches Requiem* (see *German Requiem*) for soprano, baritone, chorus and orch., *Schicksalslied* (Hölderlin), *Triumphlied*, *Nänie* (Schiller) and *Gesang der Parzen* (from Goethe's *Iphigenie auf Tauris*) for chorus and orch., *Rinaldo* (Goethe) for tenor, male chorus and orch.,

Rhapsodie (Goethe) for contralto, male chorus and orch.; 4 symphs., 2 Serenades, variations on a theme by Haydn (also 2 pfs.), *Academic Festival* and *Tragic* overtures for orch.; 2 pf. concertos, vln. concerto, double concerto for vln. and cello; 3 string 4tets, 2 string 5tets, clar. 5tet, 2 string 6tets, 5 pf. trios (1 with clar., 1 with horn), 3 pf. 4tets, pf. 5tet; 3 vln. and pf. sonatas, 2 cello and pf. sonatas, 2 clar. and pf. sonatas, movement of a vln. and pf. sonata (with Schumann and Dietrich); 3 sonatas, 5 sets of variations (1 with fugue on theme by Handel), Ballads, Rhapsodies, Capricci, Intermezzi, Scherzo, etc. for pf.; pf. duets incl. 2 sets of *Liebeslieder* with vocal 4tet *ad lib.*; sonata (from pf. 5tet) and Haydn Variations for 2 pfs.; 12 chorale preludes and 2 fugues for org.; over 100 part-songs for chorus or solo 4tet; 25 vocal duets; 190 songs; 7 vols. of arrs. of Ger. folksongs, etc.

Brain, Dennis (b. London, 17. V. 1921; d. Hatfield, 1. IX. 1957), Eng. horn player. Studied under his father, Aubrey B., played in orchs., formed a wind chamber-mus. group and became the most brilliant soloist on his instrument. He was killed in a car accident on his way home from the Edinburgh Festival.

Brall, an old Eng. name for the Branle, a variant of 'Brawl'.

Bramston, Richard (b. ?; d. 1552–3), Eng. comp. He was instructor of the choristers and organist at Wells Cathedral, 1507–31, though apparently *in absentiis* from 1508 on. An antiphon, *Mariae virginis fecunda viscera*, survives.

Branco, Luiz Freitas \ *See* **Freitas**
Branco, Pedro Freitas / **Branco.**

Brand, Max (b. Lwów, 26. IV. 1896), Aus.-Pol. comp. Studied in Vienna under Schreker and Hába. Settled in U.S.A. His opera (1st perf. 1929) is one of the outstanding works of the 'machinist' period of the 1920s. He also experimented with mus. films.

Works incl. opera *Maschinist Hopkins*; scenic oratorio *The Gate*, symph. poems, chamber mus., etc.

Brand, Michael. *See* **Mosonyi.**

Branden (Ger. plur.) = Branles.

Brandenburg Concertos, a series of 6 orchestral concertos by Bach, ded. in 1721 to the Margrave Christian Ludwig of Brandenburg: I, F maj., for 3 obs., 2 horns, bassoon, *violino piccolo*, strings and continuo; II, F maj., for recorder, ob., tpt., vln., strings and continuo; III, G maj., for 3 vlns., 3 vlas., 3 cellos, bass and continuo; IV, G maj., for 2 recorders, vln., strings and continuo; V, D maj., for fl., vln., harpsichord, strings and continuo; VI, B♭ maj., for 2 vlas., 2 bass viols, cello, bass and continuo.

Brandenburgers in Bohemia, The (*Brani-*

boři v Čechách), opera by Smetana (lib. by Karel Sabina), prod. Prague, Cz. Theatre, 5. I. 1866.

Brandts-Buys, Jan (b. Zutphen, 12. IX. 1868; d. Salzburg, 8. XII. 1933), Dutch comp. He won a state prize as a youth and studied at Frankfurt. Most of his operatic successes were Ger. works prod. in Ger. and Aus.

Works incl. operas *Das Veilchenfest, Le Carillon, Die Schneider von Schoenau, Der Eroberer, Mi-carême, Der Mann im Mond, Traumland, Ulysses; Oberon Romancero* for orch.; 3 pf. concertos; suite for strings, harp and horn; string 4tets, 5tet for fl. and strings, pf. trios; pf. works, songs, etc.

Brandukov, Anatol Andreievich (b. Moscow, 6. I. 1859; d. Moscow, 15. II. 1930), Rus. cellist. Studied at the Moscow Cons., where he taught from 1920; travelled much as a virtuoso.

Brangill (Eng. obs.) = Branle.

Branle, a Fr. dance in 2–2 or 3–2 time, dating from the 15th cent. and cultivated until the 18th, called Brawl in Eng. (*see* illustrations *a* and *b* overleaf).

Brannigan, Owen (b. Annitsford, Northumberland, 10. III. 1908), Eng. bass. Studied at the Guildhall School of Mus. 1934–42, winning the G.S.M. Gold Medal in 1942. From 1940 to 1947 he was principal bass at Sadler's Wells, and from 1947 to 1949 he sang at Glyndebourne. He has also sung at Covent Garden and at many important festivals throughout Eng.

Branson, David (b. King's Lynn, 13. VII. 1909), Eng. pianist and comp. He studied comp. with Ireland and pf. with Harold Samuel at the R.C.M., appeared in London as a child pianist, later broadcast frequently and joined the Cecilia Hansen Trio.

Works incl. *Paraphrases* for string orch.; Pavane and Toccata for pf. and orch.; pf. pieces; songs.

Brant, Henry Dreyfus (b. Montreal, 15. IX. 1913), Amer. comp. Studied in Montreal and later at the Juilliard School of Mus. in N.Y., also taking lessons from Antheil. B. concentrates on exploring unusual sonorities and instrumental combinations.

Works incl. ballet *The Great American Goof*; concertos for clar., saxophone, double bass; *Angels and Devils* for fl. and fl. orch.; *Millenium No. 2* for brass and perc., etc.

Brant, Jobst vom (b. Waldersdorf, 28. X. 1517; d. Brand, 22. I. 1570), Ger. comp. Contrib. songs to var. collections and also wrote psalms and Ger. songs for several voices.

Brass Band, a band consisting solely of brass instruments (apart from percussion), as distinct from the military band, which contains woodwind instruments as well.

Brassart, Johannes (de Leodio) (b. Liège,

(a)

(b)

16th Cent.

BRANLE

?; d. ?), Flem. 15th-cent. singer and comp. Sang in the Papal choir in Rome until 1431 and later worked at Liège and Tongern. Wrote church mus.

Brätel, Ulrich (b. ?, 1495; d. Stuttgart, 1544 or 1545), Ger. comp. He wrote Ger. sacred and secular part-songs, and Lat. motets and psalms.

Bratsche (Ger.) = Viola, a corruption from the It. *vla. da braccio.*

Braunfels, Walter (b. Frankfurt 19. XII. 1882; d. Cologne, 19. III. 1954), Ger. pianist and comp. Studied at the Hoch Cons. at Frankfurt, later in Vienna and Munich.

Works incl. operas *Prinzessin Brambilla* (after a story by E. T. A. Hoffmann), *Till Eulenspiegel, Die Vögel, Don Gil von den grünen Hosen, Der gläserne Berg, Galatea*; incid. mus. to Shakespeare's *Twelfth Night* and *Macbeth*; Mass, Te Deum; orchestral variations and other works; pf. mus.; songs, etc.

Brautwahl, Die (*The Choice of a Bride*), opera by Busoni (lib. by comp., based on a story by E. T. A. Hoffmann), prod. Hamburg, 13. IV. 1912.

Bravura (It., lit. courage, bravery, swagger). In mus. the term refers to passages in a comp. or feats in a perf. calling for virtuosity.

Brawl (Eng. obs.) = Branle.

Brazilian Composers. *See* **Fernandez** (O. L.), **Gomes, Guarnieri** (C.), **Huizar, Levy, Mignone, Nepomuceno, Siqueira, Villa-Lobos.**

Break, the change in tone-quality between different registers of voices and of wind instruments, a natural defect which may be more or less successfully corrected by technical means.

Breaking, the 17th-cent. practice of varying a theme by dividing it into figura-

tions of smaller note-values, as in Divisions (variations). Breaking the Ground was the same process if the theme was on a ground-bass.

Bream, Julian (b. London, 15. VII. 1933), Eng. guitarist and lutenist. Studied guitar with his father, also going to the R.C.M. in London, where he studied pf. and cello as well. He was encouraged by Segovia, whose protégé he became. A brilliant perf. on many stringed instruments, B. specializes in the mus. of the 16th, 17th and 18th cents., and is also an able musicologist.

Brecht, Bert(olt) (1895–1956), Ger. poet and playwright. *See* **Lehrstück** and **Weill.**

Brechung (Ger.). *See* **Ornaments.**

Brehme, Hans (b. Potsdam, 10. III. 1904; d. Stuttgart, 10. XI. 1957), Ger. comp. Pupil of Robert Kahn in Berlin, he 1st attracted attention at the Bremen mus. festival.

Works incl. *Triptychon* (variations on a theme by Handel) and *Concerto sinfonico* for orch.; pf. concerto; partita for string 4tet, etc.

Breitengraser, Wilhelm (b. Nuremberg, *c.* 1495; d. Nuremberg, 23. XII. 1542), Ger. comp. He wrote Ger. part-songs and Masses.

Breitkopf & Härtel, pub. firm at Leipzig, founded 1719 by Bernhardt Christoph Breitkopf (1695–1777). A branch was estab. at Wiesbaden in 1945, becoming independent in 1947.

Brema, Marie (real name Minny Fehrmann) (b. Liverpool, 28. II. 1856; d. Manchester, 22. III. 1925), Eng. mezzo-soprano of Ger.-Amer. descent. 1st appearance at Bremen, 1891. Sang at Covent Garden in London, Bayreuth, N.Y. and in many Eur. capitals, both in opera and concerts. Prof. of singing at Manchester R.C.M.

Brendel, Karl (Franz) (b. Stolberg, 26. XI. 1811; d. Leipzig, 25. XI. 1868), Ger. mus. critic, ed. and author. Settled at Leipzig and ed. the *Neue Zeitschrift für Musik*, founded by Schumann, from 1845. He advocated modern mus. and wrote several books.

Brenet, Michel (real name Antoinette Christine Marie Bobillier) (b. Lunéville, 12. IV. 1858; d. Paris, 4. XI. 1918), Fr. musicologist. Lived in Paris from 1871. Her books incl. studies of Okeghem, Palestrina, Handel, Haydn, Grétry and Berlioz, hists. of the symph., of the lute, of the musicians of the Sainte-Chapelle, and of concerts and mus. libraries in Fr.

Brent, Charlotte (b. London, c. 1735; d. London, 10. IV. 1802), Eng. soprano. Pupil of Arne, in whose opera *Eliza* she made her 1st appearance, at Dublin in 1755.

Bret, Gustave (b. Brignoles, Var, 30. VIII. 1875; d. 1969), Fr. organist, critic and comp. Studied at the Paris Cons, with Lavignac and Widor, also comp. with d'Indy and org. with Guilmant. He did much work on behalf of Bach and Franck and cond. orchs. in Paris, Ger. and Cz. Mus. critic of *L'Intransigeant* from 1900. Works incl. oratorio *Les Pèlerins d'Emmaüs*; unaccomp. choral works; org. mus.; songs, etc.

Bretón, Tomás (b. Salamanca, 29. XII. 1850; d. Madrid, 2. XII. 1923), Span. comp. Director of Madrid Cons. from 1901. Works incl. operas *Guzman el Bueno*, *Garin*, *Raquel*, *Farinelli*, *El certamen de Cremona*, *Tabaré* and *Don Gil*, zarzuelas *Los amantes de Teruel*, *La Dolores*, *La verbena de la paloma* and c. 30 others; oratorio *Apocalipsia*; *Las escenas andaluzas*, *Salamanca*, *En la Alhambra* for orch.; vln. concerto; 3 string 4tets, pf. 5tet, 6tet for wind, pf. trio, etc.

Bréval, Lucienne (real name Berthe Agnès Lisette Schilling) (b. Berlin, 4. XI. 1869; d. Neuilly-sur-Seine, 15. VIII. 1935), Fr. soprano of Swiss descent. Studied at the Conss. of Geneva and Paris. Made her 1st appearance at the Paris Opéra in 1892 and remained there for nearly 30 years. She excelled partic. in Wagner.

Breve (Lat. *brevis* = short), a square note equalling 2 semibreves in value: ▭. So called because it was originally a short note having one half or one third of the value of a Long (Lat. *longa*).

Bréville, Pierre (Onfroy) de (b. Bar-le-Duc, 21. II. 1861; d. Paris, 24. IX. 1949), Fr. comp. Was intended for the diplomatic service, but allowed to study with Dubois at the Paris Cons. He decided to devote himself to comp. and became a pupil of Franck. Later became prof. at the Schola Cantorum, a mus. critic and member of the committee of the Société Nationale de Musique.

Works incl. opera *Éros vainqueur*; incid. mus. for Maeterlinck's *Sept Princesses* and overture for his *La Princesse Maleine*; Mass and motets; *La Cloche fêlée* (after Baudelaire) for orch.; 2 vln. and pf. sonatas; cello and pf. sonata; sonata and other works, incl. *Portraits de Maîtres*, *Stamboul*, *Prélude et Fugue*, for pf.; instrumental pieces; songs, etc.

Brewer, Thomas (b. London, 1611; d. ?), Eng. comp. In the service of Sir Nicholas Lestrange.

Works incl. fancies for viols, songs for several voices, rounds and catches.

Brian, Havergal (b. Dresden, Staffs., 29. I. 1876), Eng. comp. and writer on mus. Mainly self-taught as a comp., he became an organist and mus. teacher in Staffordshire and wrote criticism at Manchester from 1905. Later he moved to London, where he made a precarious living under great difficulties.

Works incl. opera *The Tigers*; setting of Heine's *Pilgrimage to Kevlaar* for chorus and orch.; 18 symphs.; 3 *English Suites*, *Hero and Leander*, overtures *For Valour* (Whitman) and *Dr. Merryheart*, *Festal Dance*, *Fantastic Variations on Old Rhymes*, symph. poem *In Memoriam* for orch.; *By the Waters of Babylon*, *The Vision of Cleopatra* and a setting from Shelley's *Prometheus* for chorus; songs; part-songs, etc.

Bride of Dionysus, The, opera by Tovey (lib. by Robert Calverley Trevelyan), prod. Edinburgh, 9. IV. 1929.

Bride of Lammermoor. See **Bruden fra Lammermoor, Lucia di Lammermoor**.

Bride of Messina, The (*Nevěsta Messinská*), opera by Fibich (lib. by Otakar Hostinský, based on Schiller's drama *Die Braut von Messina*), prod. Prague, Cz. Theatre, 28. III. 1884.

Bridge, the support over which the strings are stretched and kept away from the belly of string instruments.

Bridge, Frank (b. Brighton, 26. II. 1879; d. Eastbourne, 10. I. 1941), Eng. comp. Student at the R.C.M., where Stanford was his comp. master. He also learnt the vln., vla. and cond. Later played vla. in var. 4tets and gained varied experience as operatic and concert cond. Won Cobbett Prizes for chamber mus. in 1905–15 and honourable mention for the E min. string 4tet at Bologna in 1906. He was well known as a teacher; one of his pupils was Britten.

Works incl. symph. poem *Isabella*, suite *The Sea*, rhapsody *Enter Spring*, tone-poem *Summer* for orch.; Lament for strings *There is a willow grows aslant a brook* (on a passage in *Hamlet*); *Phantasm* for pf. and orch., *Oration* for cello and orch.; 4 string 4tets, 2 pf. trios, Fantasy 4tet and several smaller pieces for string 4tet, pf. 5tet, Fantasy Trio and 4tet for pf.

and strings, string 6tet, Rhapsody for 2 vlns. and vla., *Divertimenti* for wind instruments, vln and pf. sonata, cello and pf. sonata; numerous pf. works incl.sonata, 4 *Characteristic Pieces*, suite *A Fairy Tale*, 3 Improvisations for the left hand; vln., vla., cello and org. pieces; choruses; songs, etc.

Bridge Passage, a transitional passage in a comp., esp. the transition between 1st and 2nd subjects in a sonata-form movement.

Bridges, Robert (1844–1930), Eng. poet. *See* **Finzi** (7 part-songs), **Holst** (*Choral Fantasy*), **Parry** (**H.**) (*Invocation to Music, Song of Darkness and Light, Chivalry of the Sea* and *Eton Memorial Ode*), **Stanford** (*Eden* and songs), **Swain** (songs).

Bridie, James (O. H. Mavor) (1888–1951), Scot. dramatist. *See* **Davie.**

Bridgetower, George (Augustus Polgreen) (b. ?, *c.* 1779; d. London, 29. II. 1860), mulatto violinist, son of an African father and Ger. or Pol. mother. Met Beethoven in Vienna and Teplice and played the 'Kreutzer' sonata with him in 1803.

Briegel, Wolfgang Carl (b. Nuremberg, 1626; d. Darmstadt, 19. XI. 1712), Ger. comp. Organist at Schweinfurt and Gotha; from 1671 to his death mus. director at Darmstadt. Wrote sacred works for several voices, pieces for 3 and 4 instruments, convivial and funeral songs for several voices, hymns, etc.

Briganti, I (*The Brigands*), opera by Mercadante (lib. by Jacopo Crescini, based on Schiller's drama *Die Räuber*), prod. Paris, Théâtre Italien, 22. III. 1836.

Brigg Fair (i.e. the fair at Brigg, Lincs.), rhapsody for orch. by Delius on a Lincs. folksong, actually a set of variations, or a kind of passacaglia, comp. 1907, perf. London, 1908.

Brighenti, Maria. *See* **Giorgi-Righetti, Geltrude,** for the singer's correct name.

Bright, Dora (Estella) (b. Sheffield, 16. VIII. 1863; d. London, XII. 1951), Eng. pianist and comp. Studied at the R.A.M. in London. She was the 1st pianist to give a recital of Eng. mus. and the 1st woman comp. invited to write a work for the Phil. Society. She also played in Berlin.

Works incl. 3 operas; *c.* 12 ballets incl. *The Dryad*; 2 pf. concertos; instrumental pieces; songs, etc.

Brillant (Fr.) }
Brillante (It.) } = Brilliant, used either as an adj. in titles or as a direction showing how a partic. passage is to be perf.

Brimley, John (b. ?; d. ?), Eng. comp. He was a cantor at Durham Cathedral in 1536–7, and remained there as organist and choirmaster under the New Foundation until *c.* 1576. Some Eng. church mus. has survived.

Brindisi (It. = a toast), drinking of some-

one's health, a drinking song esp. in opera, e.g. in Donizetti's *Lucrezia Borgia*, Verdi's *Macbeth*, *Traviata* and *Otello* or Mascagni's *Cavalleria rusticana*.

Brio (It. = spirit, fire, brilliance). The word is often used in the direction *con* (with) *b.*

Brisé (Fr. = broken), an arpeggio in keyboard or harp mus.; détaché bowing in string mus.; for an earlier meaning *see* **Ornaments.**

Bristol Musical Festival, founded in 1873 and held triennially until 1888, afterwards less regularly until 1912.

British Broadcasting Corporation, founded as the British Broadcasting Company Ltd. in 1922 and incorporated under a Royal Charter in 1927, when it took its present name, now always known by its abbreviation, B.B.C.

British Council, The, an organization estab. in 1935 to further non-materialistic Brit. interests in foreign countries, incl. educ. and the arts. During the 1st decade of its existence its mus. dept. formed 57 libraries of Brit. printed and recorded mus. in 44 countries, among the largest being those at Buenos Aires, Cairo, Stockholm and Trinidad. The B. C. also assists eminent Brit. artists to perf. abroad, and gramophone records of a number of important Brit. orchestral and choral works have been made under its auspices.

British National Opera Company, founded in 1922 by members of the company that had previously appeared under the direction of Sir Thomas Beecham. It went into liquidation in 1929.

Britten, (Edward) Benjamin (b. Lowestoft, 22. XI. 1913), Eng. comp. Educ. at Gresham School, Holt, and studied pf. with Harold Samuel and comp. with Frank Bridge; later, with a scholarship, at the R.C.M. in London under Benjamin and Ireland. He was represented at the I.S.C.M. festivals of 1934, 1936 and 1938. During the early war years he was in the U.S.A. His talent showed itself early, and his first international success was the *Variations on a theme of Frank Bridge*, played at the Salzburg Festival of 1937. This was followed by a number of works which estab. him as the leading Eng. composer of the day, esp. the stark *Sinfonia da Requiem* (1940) and the *Serenade* (1943). In 1945 his 2nd opera, *Peter Grimes*, estab. him as a dramatist, and was succeeded by further operas, incl. the chamber opera *The Turn of the Screw* (1955). Much of B.'s best mus. is inspired by words, as shown by the many song cycles, the *Spring Symphony* (1949) and the *Nocturne* (1958). One of his most successful works is the *War Requiem*, which combines the liturgical text with poems by Wilfred Owen and was composed to mark the opening of the new Coventry Cathedral

(1962). B. is an accomplished cond. and accomp., performing his own mus. and that of others with great distinction. He was one of the founders of the Aldeburgh Festival, 1948.

Works incl. operas *Paul Bunyan* (W. H. Auden), *Peter Grimes* (after Crabbe), *The Rape of Lucretia* (Ronald Duncan), *Albert Herring* (Eric Crozier, after Maupassant), *Let's Make an Opera* (on Blake's poem *The Chimney Sweep*), *Billy Budd* (after Melville), *Gloriana* (William Plomer), *The Turn of the Screw* (Myfanwy Piper, after James) and *A Midsummer Night's Dream* (Shakespeare); *Noye's Fludde*; church parables: *Curlew River, The Burning Fiery Furnace* and *The Prodigal Son*; ballet *The Prince of the Pagodas*; incid. mus. for Webster's *Duchess of Malfi*, Priestley's *Johnson over Jordan*, Auden and Isherwood's *Ascent of F.6* and *On the Frontier*, Duncan's *This Way to the Tomb*; choral works incl. *Hymn to St. Cecilia* (Auden), *A Ceremony of Carols*, cantatas *Rejoice in the Lamb* (Christopher Smart) and *Saint Nicholas* (Crozier), *Spring Symphony, Cantata Academica, War Requiem, Cantata Misericordium*; orchestral works incl. variations on a theme by Frank Bridge for strings, *Sinfonia da Requiem*, Prelude and Fugue for strings, *The Young Person's Guide to the Orch.*, concertos for pf. and for vln., *Diversions for pf.* (left hand) and orch., *Scot. Ballad* for 2 pfs. and orch., cello symph.; *Our Hunting Fathers* (Auden) for high voice and orch., *Les Illuminations* (Arthur Rimbaud) for high voice and strings, *Serenade* (var. poets) for tenor, horn and strings, *Nocturne*; 2 string 4tets, cello sonata, 2 suites for solo cello; *Lacrymae* on song by Dowland for vla. and pf.; 6 *Metamorphoses of Ovid* for solo ob.; *Holiday Diary* and 2 *Comps.* for pf.; Prelude and Fugue on a theme by Victoria for org.; song cycles *On this Island* (Auden), 7 *Sonnets of Michelangelo, The Holy Sonnets of John Donne, A Charm of Lullabies* (var. poets), *Winter Words* (Hardy), 6 *Hölderlin-Fragmente, Songs and Proverbs of William Blake, The Poet's Echo* (Pushkin).

Britton, Thomas (b. Rushden nr. Higham Ferrers, 14. I. 1644; d. London, 27. IX. 1714), Eng. coal dealer and mus. amateur. Began very poorly as a hawker, but acquired much knowledge in mus. and science and estab. weekly concerts in a room over his shop in London which soon had a great following.

Brixi, Franz Xaver (b. Prague, 2. I. 1732; d. Prague, 14. X. 1771), Boh. organist and comp. After var. church posts he became *Kapellmeister* of Prague Cathedral in 1756.

Works consist largely of church mus.: 105 Masses; 263 offertories, hymns and motets; 5 Requiems; 24 Vespers; Litanies,

etc.; also org. pieces (incl. 3 concertos), a sinfonia, etc.

Broadwood, Brit. family of pf. manufacturers and mus. eds.:

1. John B. (b. Cockburnspath, 1732; d. London, 1812), worked with Shudi, married his daughter Barbara in 1769 and was sole proprietor of Shudi & Broadwood from 1782.

2. James Shudi B. (b. London, 1772; d. London, 1851), son of prec., was taken into partnership in 1795, when the firm became John B. & Son.

3. Thomas B. (b. ?; d. ?), brother of prec., was taken into partnership in 1807 and the name became John B. & Sons.

4. Henry Fowler B. (b. London 1811; d. London, 1893), son of 2.

5. John B. (b. ?; d. ?), brother of prec. One of the earliest folksong collectors.

6. Henry John Tschudi B. (b. ?; d. London, 8. II. 1911), grandson of 4.

7. Lucy B. (b. ?; d. 22. VIII. 1929), daughter of 4. Collector and ed. of folksongs.

Brockes (Barthold) Heinrich (1680–1747), Ger. poet. *See* **Handel** (Passion), **Telemann** (do.).

Brockway, Howard (b. Brooklyn, 22. XI. 1870; d. N.Y., 20. II. 1951), Amer. pianist and comp. Studied in N.Y. and Berlin, taught privately in N.Y. from 1895 and in 1903 joined the Peabody Cons. at Baltimore. Returning to N.Y. in 1910 he taught comp. there privately and at the David Mannes Mus. School.

Works incl. symph. in D maj., Ballad, Scherzino, *Sylvan Suite* for orch.; *Cavatina and Romanza* for vln. and orch., suite in E min. for cello and orch.; vln. and pf. sonata in G min.; pf. pieces, etc.

Brodsky, Adolf (b. Taganrog, 21. III. 1851; d. Manchester, 22. I. 1929), Rus. violinist. Pupil of Hellmesberger in Vienna; successively cond. at Kiev, prof. at the Leipzig Cons., leader of the Hallé Orch. in Manchester and principal of the R.C.M. there from 1895.

Broken Consort, in old Eng. mus. a mixed team of instruments of different families, as distinct from a consort of viols.

Broman, Sten (b. Uppsala, 25. III. 1902), Swed. vla. player, critic and comp. Studied in Prague, Stockholm, Fribourg (Switz.) and Berlin, and in 1927 took a degree in mus. hist. at Lund Univ. He became mus. critic to the *Sydsvenska Dagbladet*.

Works incl. incid. mus. to Aristophanes' *Lysistrata*; fantasy for chorus and orch.; Acad. Festival Overture, Chorale Fantasy and concerto for orch.; prelude, *Gothic Suite* and Litany for string orch.; suite for vla. and strings; 2 string 4tets, suite for vln., vla. and pf.; sonatas and suites for vla. and pf. and vla. and org.; pf. and org. works; unaccomp. choral works, etc.

Brome, Richard (?–?1652), Eng. play-wright. *See* Wilson (J.) (*Northern Lass*).

Bronsart, Ingeborg von. *See* Starck.

Bronwen (Holbrooke). *See* Cauldron of Annwen.

Brooke, Rupert (Chawnor) (1887–1915), Eng. poet. *See* Hughes (G.) (songs).

Broqua, Alfonso (b. Montevideo, 11. XII. 1876; d. Paris, 24. XI. 1946), Uru-guayan comp. Studied at Montevideo and after 1900 in Belg. and under d'Indy at the Schola Cantorum in Paris. He 1st appeared as a comp. at Montevideo in 1910.

Works incl. opera *Cruz del Sur*; ballets *Thelen et Nagouëy* and *Isabelle*; *Tabaré* for voice and orch; songs *Trois Chants de l'Uruguay* and *Chants du Paraná*; *Trois Préludes pampéens* for pf.; *Evocaciones criollas* for guitar, etc.

Bros, Juan (b. Tortosa, 5. V. 1776; d. Oviedo, 12. III. 1852), Span. comp. Mus. director by turns at the cathedrals of Málaga, León and Oviedo. Wrote church mus.

Broschi, Carlo. *See* Farinelli.

Brossard, Sébastien de (b. Dompierre, IX. 1655; d. Meaux, 10. VIII. 1730), Fr. comp. Studied philosophy and theol. at Caen and was self-taught in mus. He lived there until 1683, when he went to Paris and worked at Notre-Dame, later at Stras-bourg. In 1689 he became *maître de chapelle* at the cathedral there and in 1698 mus. director at Meaux Cathedral. Author of a dictionary of mus. (1703).

Works incl. 2 books of *Élévations et Motets* and other church mus.; lute pieces; *Airs sérieux et à boire*; *Symphonie pour la nuit de Noël*; cantatas, sonatas for 2 vlns. and bass, etc.

Brouwenstijn, Gre (Gerda Demphina) (b. Den Helder, 26. VIII. 1915), Dutch soprano. Studied under various teachers from childhood, becoming a leading singer at the Amsterdam opera. She has since sung all over Eur., both in lyric and dramatic roles.

Brown, Earle (b. Lunenburg, Mass., 26. XII. 1926), Amer. comp. of the *avant-garde*. Much influenced by the ideas of John Cage, and also by the visual arts (Calder, Pollock), he has developed a method of notating controlled improvisa-tion by graphical means.

Works incl. *Available Forms I*; *Available Forms II* for 98 players and 2 cond.; 2 8tets for 8 magnetic tapes; *Light Music* for electric lights, electronic equipment and instruments, etc.

Browne, John (b. ?, *c.* 1426; d. London, II. 1498), Eng. comp. Scholar (?) at Eton and King's Coll., Cambridge.

Works incl. a part-song *Margarit meke*; Latin antiphons and Magnificats, esp. from the Eton Choirbook, and hymns, etc.

Browning, an Eng. form of fancy for viols, similar to the 'In Nomine', but based on a folk-tune instead of a plainsong theme.

Browning, Elizabeth Barrett (1806–61), Eng. poet. *See* Carse (*Lay of Brown Rosary*), Castelnuovo-Tedesco (*Sonnets from the Portuguese*), Sea Pictures (Elgar).

Browning, Robert (1812–89), Eng. poet, husband of prec. *See* Bainton (*Paracelsus*), Bantock (*Ferishtah's Fancies*), Davies (Walford) (*Hervé Riel*), Fifine at the Fair (Bantock), Franco (songs), Greenwood (*Pippa passes*), Morris (H.) (*Prospice*), Parry (H.) (*Pied Piper of Hamelin*), Somer-vell (*James Lee's Wife* and *Broken Arc*), Stanford (*Cavalier Songs*), Walthew (*Pied Piper*).

Brownlee, John (Donald Mackenzie) (b. Geelong, 7. I. 1900; d. N.Y., 10. I. 1969), Austral. baritone. Educated at Geelong College, he was persuaded by Melba to take up singing seriously. He made his début at her farewell concert in 1926, and in 1927 joined the Paris Opéra. In 1956 he became director of the Manhattan School of Mus.

Bruch, Max (b. Cologne, 6. I. 1838; d. Friedenau nr. Berlin, 2. X. 1920), Ger. comp. Learnt mus. as a child from his mother, a singer, later, with a scholarship, from Hiller, Reinecke and Breuning. He visited Leipzig, Munich and other mus. centres to gain further experience and in 1863 prod. his opera *Loreley* at Mannheim, having obtained permission from Geibel to use the lib. orig. written for Mendelssohn. After 2 appts. at Coblenz and Sonders-hausen, he lived 1st in Berlin and then at Bonn, wholly devoted to comp. From 1880 to 1883 he was cond. of the Liverpool Phil. Society, and in 1881 he married the singer Clara Tuczek. From 1883 to 1890 he cond. at Breslau and in 1891 he became prof. of comp. at the Hochschule in Berlin, retiring to Friedenau in 1910.

Works incl. operas *Scherz, List und Rache* (Goethe), *Die Loreley* and *Hermione* (after Shakespeare's *Winter's Tale*); works for solo voices, chorus and orch.: *Frithjof-Scenen* (after Tegnér), *Schön Ellen, Odysseus* (after Homer), *Das Lied von der Glocke* (Schiller), *Achilleus* (after Homer), *Das Feuerkreuz* (after Scott's *Lay of the Last Minstrel*), *Moses, Gustav Adolf Damajanti, Die Macht des Gesanges* (Schiller); 3 symphs.; 2 vln. concertos; *Scottish Fantasia* for vln., harp and orch.; *Kol Nidrei* and *Ave Maria* for cello and orch.; Marfa's scene from Schiller's *Demetrius* for mezzo-soprano and orch.; 2 string 4tets, pf. trio; many choruses; instrumental pieces; pf. mus.; songs, etc.

Bruck, Arnold van (b. Bruges, *c.* 1490; d. ? Linz, *c.* 1554), Netherlands comp. 1st *Kapellmeister* to the emperor and dean of the Abbey of Laibach. Wrote motets and other church mus., sacred and secular songs, esp. Ger. songs, etc.

Brucken-Fock, Gerard von (b. Middelburg, 28. XII. 1859; d. Heemstede, 15. VIII. 1935), Dutch comp. and painter. Studied mus. at Utrecht and Berlin, but was mainly self-taught.

Works incl. Requiem, oratorio *De wederkomst van Christus*, bibl. cantata; 2 symphs., suites for orch.; many preludes and other works for pf.; songs, etc.

Bruckner, Anton (b. Ansfelden, 4. IX. 1824; d. Vienna, 11. X. 1896), Aus. comp. Son of a country schoolmaster intended for the same calling and receiving little mus. educ. On the early death of his father in 1837 he was taken in as a choir-boy by the monastery of St. Florian. There he learnt the org. and was app. organist in 1845. By this time he had begun to comp., but was dissatisfied with his poor technique and went to study counterpoint with Sechter in Vienna, 1855. Cathedral organist at Linz, 1855–68, where he comp. much in his spare time and became an ardent Wagnerian on visiting Munich for the prod. of *Tristan* in 1865. App. prof. at the Vienna Cons. in 1868 and remained in the capital for the rest of his life, but visited Nancy, Paris and London as org. virtuoso in 1869 and 1871. He was pensioned in 1891 and received an hon. doctor's degree from the univ.

Works incl. 9 symphs. (last unfinished), 2 early symphs.; overture in G min.; 4 Masses; Requiem; Te Deum, Psalm cl; 3 secular choral works; string 5tet, etc.

Bruden fra Lammermoor (*The Bride of Lammermoor*), opera by Ivar Frederik Bredal (1800–64) (lib., in Dan., by Hans Christian Andersen, based on Scott's novel), prod. Copenhagen, 5. V. 1832.

Brudieu, Jean (or **Juan** or **Joan**) (b. nr. Limoges, *c.* 1520; d. Urgell, Catalonia, 1591), Fr. (Hispanicized) singer and comp. He visited Urgell in the Pyrenees to sing there at Christmas in 1538 and remained there as choirmaster until the 1570s, when he was at the church of Santa Maria del Mar at Barcelona, where he pub. a book of madrigals in 1585. He had returned to Urgell in 1578. Comp. church mus. as well as madrigals, incl. a *Missa defunctorum* (Requiem).

Bruhns, Nikolaus (b. Schwabstedt, Slesvig, *c.* 1665; d. Husum, 1697), Dan. organist, string player and comp. 1st employed in Copenhagen, then town organist at Husum, Slesvig-Holstein. Wrote cantatas, motets with orch. and org. mus.

Brulé, Gace (b. ?; d. ?), Fr. 12th-cent. trouvère. 90 songs are attrib. to him, but only some 30 are accepted as authentic.

Brüll, Ignaz (b. Prossnitz, Moravia, 7. XI. 1846; d. Vienna, 17. IX. 1907), Aus. pianist and comp. Studied in Vienna, where

his family settled when he was 3, played there, toured, and prod. a number of comps. Later he taught the pf.

Works incl. operas *Die Bettler von Samarkand*, *Das goldene Kreuz*, *Der Landfriede*, *Bianca*, *Königin Mariette*, *Gloria*, *Das steinerne Herz*, *Gringoire*, *Schach dem König*, *Der Husar*; ballet *Champagnermärchen*; symph.; overture to Shakespeare's *Macbeth*, serenade for orch.; 2 pf. concertos; vln. concerto; pf. trio and other chamber mus.; sonata for 2 pfs.; pf. mus.; songs, etc.

Brumel, Antoine (b. *c.* 1460; d. Ferrara, ?), Fr. 15th–16th-cent. comp. Choirmaster at Chartres Cathedral in 1483, canon at Laon in 1498, and from that year to 1501 choirmaster at Notre-Dame in Paris. Went to the court of the Duke of Ferrara in 1505, where he may have died. Wrote Masses, motets, Fr. *chansons*, etc.

Brun, Fritz (b. Lucerne, 18. VIII. 1878; d. Grosshöchstetten, 29. XI. 1959), Swiss cond. and comp. Studied under Mengelberg, who was cond. at Lucerne in 1892–5, later at the Cologne Cons. and in Berlin and London. In 1903 he became pf. prof. at the Berne School of Mus., at whose periodical students' concerts he showed himself an exceptional cond. In 1909 he was app. cond. of both the male and mixed choral societies as well as of the symph. concerts.

Works incl. 10 symphs.; *Verheissung* (Goethe) for chorus, orch. and org.; *Aus dem Buch Hiob* for orch.; pf. concerto, cello concerto; 4 string 4tets; 2 vln. and pf. sonatas; male-voice choruses, songs, etc.

Bruneau, (Louis Charles Bonaventure) Alfred (b. Paris, 3. III. 1857; d. Paris, 15. VI. 1934), Fr. comp. and mus. critic. Son of a painter; learnt mus. incl. cello from his parents, who played vln. and pf., and took a cello prize at the Paris Cons. as a pupil of Franchomme. Afterwards studied comp. with Massenet and played in Pasdeloup's orch. In 1887 he prod. his 1st opera; the next 2 were based on works by Zola, who himself wrote the libs. for the next 3 stage works. The 1st of these, however, failed in 1897 because B. and Zola were ardent supporters of Dreyfus. After Zola's death B. wrote his own libs., some still based on Zola's work.

Works incl. operas *Kérim*, *Le Rêve* and *L'Attaque du moulin* (after Zola), *Messidor*, *L'Ouragan* and *L'Enfant-roi* (libs. by Zola), *Lazare*, *Naïs Micoulin* and *Les Quatre Journées* (after Zola), *Le Tambour*, *Le Roi Candaule*, *Angélo, tyran de Padoue*, *Virginie*; ballets *Les Bacchantes* (after Euripides) and *Le Jardin de Paradis*; incid. mus. to his dram. adapt. of Zola's *La Faute de l'Abbé Mouret*; Requiem; choral symphs. *Léda*, *La Belle au bois dormant* and *Penthésilée*; cantata *Geneviève de Paris*;

Ouverture héroïque for orch.; vocal duets; songs *Chansons à danser* and 2 books of *Lieds de France* (all words by Catulle Mendès).

Brunelli, Antonio (b. Bagnorea nr. Orvieto, *c.* 1575; d. ?), It. organist, mus. scholar and comp. Worked at Florence, both at churches and at the Tuscan court. Wrote 2 learned theoret. books.

Works incl. Masses, Requiems, sacred songs, psalms; a ballet; canzonets, madrigals, etc.

Brunette (Fr. lit. a dark-haired girl), a light love-song of a type current in 17th–18th-cent. Fr., orig. so called because of the association of the words with dark girls.

Brunetti, Gaetano (b. Pisa, *c.* 1740; d. Madrid, 1808), It. violinist and comp. Pupil of Nardini in Florence. Spent most of his life in Spain, in the service of the court and of the Duke of Alba, and there worked with Boccherini.

Works incl. symphs., serenades, 6tets, 5tets, trio sonatas, vln. duets, etc.

Brunetti, Giovanni Gualberto (b. Naples, *c.* 1715; d. Pisa, 1808), It. comp. Succeeded Clari as *maestro di cappella* of Pisa Cathedral in 1754.

Works incl. 6 operas; Masses and other church mus., etc.

Bruscantini, Sesto (b. 10. XII. 1919), It. bass-baritone. Having originally studied law, he turned to singing and made his début at La Scala, Milan, in 1949. He is principally known as a *buffo* singer. In 1953 he married the singer Sena Jurinac.

Brusselmans, Michel (b. Paris, 12. II. 1886), Belg. comp. Pupil of Gilson at the Brussels Cons. In 1922 he settled in Paris as a member of mus. pub. house of Jamin.

Works incl. *Kermesse flamande, Rapsodie, Ouverture fériale, Hélène de Sparte, Les Néréides*; sonatas for vln. and pf. and cello and pf.; org. pieces; songs, etc.

Brussilovsky, Evgeny (b. Rostov-on-Don, 12. XI. 1905), Rus. comp. Having lost both his parents he joined the army at 16, but was released in 1922 in order to develop his mus. talent at the Moscow Cons. He was expelled in 1924 for non-attendance, due to serious illness, but although very poor, managed to go to Leningrad and induced Steinberg to teach him at the Cons. there. In 1933 he was commissioned to do mus. research in Kazakh folk mus. and went to live at Alma-Ata, the capital of Kazakhstan. There he wrote operas in the nat. idiom.

Works incl. operas *Kiz-Ji-Bek, Er-Targhin* and *Jalbir*; 3 symphs.; instrumental pieces; pf. pieces; songs, etc.

Brustad, Bjarne (b. Oslo, 4. III. 1895), Norw. violinist, violist and comp. Studied at the Oslo Cons., later under Carl Flesch, and became active as violinist and cond. in the Norw. capital.

Works incl. symph. poem *Atlantis*, suite for orch.; *Nature morte* for string orch.; 2 vln. concertos, *Rhapsody* for vln. and orch., Concertino for vln. and chamber orch.; string 4tet; suite for unaccomp. vln., suite for vla. and pf.; vln., vla. and pf. pieces, etc.

Brygeman, William (b. ?; d. ?), Eng. 16th-cent. comp. Singer (?) at Eton, 1503–1504; 'conduct' (i.e. singer) (?) at King's Coll., Cambridge, 1513–15. A fragmentary *Salve Regina* is in the Eton Choirbook.

Bryllupet ved Como-Søen (*The Wedding by Lake Como*), opera by Franz Gläser (1798–1861) (lib. by Hans Christian Andersen, based on Manzoni's novel, *I promessi sposi*), prod. Copenhagen, 29. I. 1849.

Bryne, Albert (or Albertus Bryan) (b. ? London, ?; d. London, ? 1668), Eng. organist and comp. Organist of St. Paul's Cathedral in London from 1638 and again after the Restoration. After the fire of London in 1666 he became organist of Westminster Abbey, a post in which he was succeeded by Blow in 1668. Wrote services, anthems, dances, etc.

Bryson, (Robert) Ernest (b. Liverpool, 31. III. 1867; d. St. Briavels, Glos., 20. IV. 1942), Eng. amateur comp. living at Liverpool.

Works incl. opera *The Leper's Flute*; choral comps. *The Cloak, the Boat and the Shoes* (Yeats) and *Drum Taps* (Whitman); 2 symphs., *Voices* study for orch.; *Vaila* for string orch.; 2 string 4tets, etc.

Brzezinski, Franciszek (b. Warsaw, 6. XI. 1867; d. Warsaw, 6. VIII. 1944), Pol. critic and comp. Studied at Leipzig with Reger and others and became mus. critic to 2 Warsaw papers in succession.

Works incl. *Polonaise-Ballad*, waltz, etc. for orch.; pf. concerto; vln. and pf. sonata; pf. pieces, etc.

Buccina. The Roman bugle horn, used in the army for signalling.

Bucenus, Paulus (b. Holstein, ?; d. ? Riga, II. 1586), Dan. comp. Worked as church musician at Riga.

Works incl. a St. Matthew Passion, Masses, motets, *Sacrae Cantiōnes*, etc.

Buchanan, George (1506–82), Scot. histor. and trans. *See* Olthoff (psalms).

Buchardo, Carlos (b. Buenos Aires, 12. X. 1881), Arg. comp. Studied in Buenos Aires and with Roussel in Paris. On returning to Arg. he became director of the Nat. Cons. of Buenos Aires.

Works incl. opera *El sueño de Alma*; *Escenas argentinas* for orch.; pf. pieces; songs, etc.

Büchner, Georg (1813–37), Ger. poet and playwright. *See* Einem (*Dantons Tod*), Gurlitt (M.) (*Wozzeck*), Müller-Hartmann (*Leonce und Lena*), Syberg (do.), Wagner-Regeny (*Günstling*), Weismann (do.), Wozzeck (A. Berg and M. Gurlitt).

Buchner, Johann (Hans von Constantz) (b. Ravensburg, Württemberg, 26. X. 1483; d. ?, c. 1538), Ger. comp. Prob. pupil of Hofhaimer. Worked at Constance Cathedral, but left in 1526 because of its growing Protestantism, (?) for Zürich. Wrote sacred and secular songs, org. pieces, etc. His *Fundamentum* is a didactic work incorporating org. mus. for the liturgical year.

Buck, Dudley (b. Hartford, Conn., 10. III. 1839; d. Orange, N.J., 6. X. 1909), Amer. comp. and organist. Studied in his native town and at Leipzig and Dresden. Held many org. posts until 1903 and wrote a large variety of mus. as well as some books on the art.

Works incl. comic opera *Deseret*; numerous choral works incl. *Voyage o, Columbus, The Golden Legend* (Longfellow), *The Light of Asia*, Psalm xlvi; symph. overture *Marmion* (after Scott); anthems and other church mus., etc.

Buck, Percy (Carter) (b. London, 25. III. 1871; d. London, 3. X. 1947), Eng. mus. scholar and educationist. Studied at the R.C.M. in London; M.A. and D.Mus., Oxford, 1897; organist at Wells and Bristol Cathedrals, 1896–1901, then mus. director at Harrow School. Prof. of Mus. at Univ. of Dublin, 1910, and London, 1915. Knighted 1937. Author of several books on mus.

Buckingham, Duke of. *See* **Villiers, George.**

Budashkin, Nikolai (b. Liubakhovka nr. Mosalsk, 6. VIII. 1910), Rus. comp. Pupil of Miaskovsky.

Works incl. symph., Festival Overture, Sonatina for pf.; songs, etc.

Buffa. *See* **Opera buffa.**

Buffo (It. 'comic', also 'comedian'), in mus. a singer of comic parts, used esp. as adj.; *tenore buffo, basso buffo.*

Bugle, a treble brass instrument with a wide conical bore, used mainly in the armed forces. Having no valves it can prod. only the natural harmonics. *See also* **Key Bugle.**

Bühnenweihfestspiel (Ger., from *Bühne* = stage, *Weihe* = consecration, *Fest* = festival, *Spiel* = play), the description given by Wagner to *Parsifal*, which he did not wish to call an 'opera' or a 'mus.-drama'.

Bukofzer, Manfred (b. Oldenburg, 27. III. 1910; d. Oakland, Calif., 7. XII. 1955), Ger.-Amer. musicologist. Studied at Heidelberg, Berlin and Basle, and went to U.S.A. in 1939, where after var. appts. he became prof. at Calif. Univ. He specialized in medieval, partic. Eng. mus. and edited the complete works of Dunstable. His most important book is *Studies in Medieval and Renaissance Music.*

Bulg. (abbr.) = Bulgaria, Bulgarian.

Bulgarian Composers. *See* **Binenbaum, Vladigerov.**

Bull, John (b. ?, c. 1562; d. Antwerp, 12–13. III. 1628), Eng. comp. He was a choirboy in the Chapel Royal in London under Blitheman and became organist of Hereford Cathedral in 1582. On Blitheman's death in 1591 he became organist of the Chapel Royal. Mus.D., Cambridge, before 1592, and Oxford that year. In 1596 app. 1st Prof. of Mus. at Gresham Coll. In 1601 he travelled abroad, Thomas Byrd, son of William Byrd, acting as his deputy at Gresham Coll. Married Elizabeth Walter in 1607 and gave up his professorship, which could be held only by single men. In 1613 he left Eng., apparently to escape punishment for some misdemeanours, and became organist at the archducal chapel in Brussels. In 1617 he was app. organist at Antwerp Cathedral, where he remained to his death.

Works incl. anthems, incl. the 'Star' anthem *Almighty Lord*; secular vocal works for several voices; canons; a laud for the Blessed Virgin in Flem.; numerous org. and virginal pieces; some works for viols, etc.

Bull, Ole (Borneman) (b. Bergen, 5. II. 1810; d. Lysø nr. Bergen, 17. VIII. 1880), Norw. violinist and comp. Was largely self-taught, his father insisting on his studying theol. In 1829 he visited Spohr at Cassel and in 1832 1st made his mark as a public player in Paris. He married a Fr. girl there, appeared with Chopin and Ernst, and visited It. with great success. Went to Brit. 1st in 1836 and to U.S.A. in 1843. Founded the Norse Theatre at Bergen in 1850. In 1870 he was married a 2nd time, to an Amer. Wrote 2 concertos and many other works for the vln., etc.

Bülow, Hans (Guido) von (b. Dresden, 8. I. 1830; d. Cairo, 12. II. 1894), Ger. pianist and cond. 1st husband of Cosima Wagner (*née* Liszt). Studied law at Leipzig Univ. and pf. with Wieck there. At first exclusively a Wagnerian as a cond., but after his divorce in 1869 became equally enthusiastic about Brahms without abandoning Wagner. Made many tours both as cond. and pianist.

Bumbass. *See* **Drone.**

Bungert, August (b. Mühlheim on Ruhr, 14. III. 1845; d. Leutesdorf, 26. X. 1915), Ger. comp. Studied at Cologne Cons. and in Paris. Prod. his 1st (comic) opera at Leipzig in 1884. His ambition was to build a special theatre for the prod. of his tetralogy on the model of Bayreuth.

Works incl. operas *Die Studenten von Salamanka*, tetralogy *Homerische Welt* (*Kirke, Nausicaa, Odysseus' Heimkehr, Odysseus' Tod*), 'mystery' *Warum? Woher? Wohin?*; incid. mus. to Goethe's *Faust*; symph. *Zeppelins erste grosse Fahrt; Tasso, Hohes Lied der Liebe, Auf der Wartburg* for orch.; pf. 4tet; pf. pieces; songs, etc.

Bunning, Herbert (b. London, 2. V. 1863;

d. Thundersley, Essex, 26. XI. 1937), Eng. cond. and comp. Educ. at Oxford and began a military career, but later studied mus. in Fr. and It. In 1892 he became mus. director of the Lyric Theatre in London.
Works incl. opera *Princess Osra*; incid. mus. for plays; overtures for orch.; songs. etc.

Bunyan, John (1628–88), Eng. author. For works based on *The Pilgrim's Progress* see **Austin (E.), Bantock, Kelley, Pilgrim's Progress** (Vaughan Williams).

Buona figliuola, La (*The Good Girl*), also *La Cecchina*, opera by Piccinni (lib. by Goldoni, based on Richardson's *Pamela*), prod. Rome, Teatro delle Dame, 6. II. 1760.

Buonamente, Giovanni Battista (b. ?; d. Assisi, 1643), It. violinist and comp. Imp. court musician from 1622; *maestro di cappella* at the Franciscan monastery of Assisi in 1636. Wrote sonatas for 2 vlns. and bass, mus. for mixed teams of instruments, etc.

Buonamici, Giuseppe (b. Florence, 12. II. 1846; d. Florence, 18. III. 1914), It. pianist, cond. and mus. ed. Studied at home at first, then at the Munich Cons., pf. with Bülow and comp. with Rheinberger. Prof. there from 1870, but returned to Florence in 1873 as pf. prof., choral cond. and founder of a pf. trio. He did much to cultivate serious mus.

Buononcini. *See* **Bononcini.**

Buovo d'Antona (*Bevis of Hampton*), opera by Traetta (lib. by Goldoni, based on the Anglo-Norman 13th-cent. romance), prod. Venice, Teatro San Moisè, 27. XII. 1758.

Burbero di buon cuore, Il (*The Good-hearted Grumbler*), opera by Martín y Soler (lib. by Lorenzo da Ponte, based on Goldoni's Fr. comedy *Le Bourru bienfaisant*), prod. Vienna, Burgtheater, 4. I. 1786. Mozart wrote 2 extra arias for it when it was revived, Vienna, 9. XI. 1789, and Haydn an addit. duet for its prod. in London, 1794.

Burbure de Wesembeek, Léon (Philippe Marie) de (b. Termonde, 16. VIII. 1812; d. Antwerp, 8. XII. 1889), Belg. musicologist and comp. Graduated at Ghent Univ. and studied old Netherland mus., of which he wrote many studies. Comp. sacred vocal works, orchestral mus., etc.

Burchiello, Il (Domenico di Giovanni) (1404–49), It. poet. *See* **Malipiero** (sonnets).

Burck, Joachim à (Joachim Moller von Burck) (b. Burg, 1546; d. Mühlhausen, 24. V. 1610), Ger. organist and comp. Organist at var. towns in Thuringia.
Works incl. 3 Passions, psalms; odes, songs, etc.

Bürde-Ney (*née* Ney), **Jenny** (b. Graz, 21. XII. 1826; d. Dresden, 17. V. 1886), Aus. soprano. Made her 1st appearance on the

stage of Olomouc in 1847 and was a member of the opera co. at Dresden from 1853 to 1867.

Burden, in old vocal mus. the refrain sung at the end of each verse.

Burell, John (b. ?; d. ?), Eng. 15th-cent. comp. He is named as a clerk of the Royal Chapel, 1413–21. Mus. by him for the Mass is in the Old Hall MS.

Bürger, Gottfried August (1747–94), Ger. poet. *See* **Chasseur maudit** (Franck), **Duparc** (*Lénore*), **Paradies** (*Lenore*), **Raff** (do.), **Zumsteeg** (do.).

Burgmein. *See* **Ricordi.**

Burgmüller, (August Joseph) Norbert (b. Düsseldorf, 8. II. 1810; d. Aachen, 7. V. 1836), Ger. comp. Studied under his father, mus. director at Düsseldorf, later under Spohr and Hauptmann at Cassel. A weak constitution led to his early death.
Works incl. 2 symphs., an overture; pf. pieces and studies, etc.

Burian, Emil František (b. Plzen, 11. IV. 1904; d. Prague, 9. VIII. 1959), Cz. singer, actor, author, stage manager and comp. Studied at the Prague Cons., joined the Dada Theatre in Prague and was director of the dramatic studio of the Brno Nat. Theatre in 1929–30; also founded a voice band, which sang to given rhythms without definite pitch, accomp. by perc.
Works incl. operas *Alladine and Palomides* (after Maeterlinck), *Before Sunset*, *Bubu de Montparnasse*, *Mr. Ipokras*, *Fear*; ballets *Bassoon and Flute*, *Manège*, *Autobus*; choruses; chamber mus., songs, etc.

Burian, Karel (b. Rousinov nr Rakovnik, 12. I. 1870; d. Senomaty, 25. IX. 1924), Cz. tenor. 1st appeared at Brno in 1891. Sang at Bayreuth and in many Eur. capitals, but chiefly at Dresden.

Burkhard, Willy (b. Évilard-sur-Bienne, 17. IV. 1900; d. Zürich, 18. VI. 1955), Swiss comp. Studied at the Berne School of Mus., at Leipzig with Karg-Elert and Teichmüller and at Munich with Courvoisier, later in Paris. Became pf. prof. at the Berne Cons. and cond. choirs and an amateur orch. Settled at Davos in 1937 to devote himself entirely to comp.
Works incl. opera *Die schwarze Spinne* (after Gotthelf); oratorios *Musikalische Uebung* (Luther) and *Das Gesicht Jesajas*, Te Deum, choral suite *Neue Kraft*, festival cantata *Le Cantique de notre terre*, cantata *Das Jahr* and others, Psalm xciii for chorus and org.; *Christi Leidensverkündung* for tenor, chorus and org.; 2 symphs., *Ulenspiegel* variations for orch.; Fantasy, Little Serenade and Concerto for string orch.; vln. concerto, org. concerto; 2 string 4tets, pf. Trio, 2 trio-sonatas; Variations and Fantasy for org.; song-cycles *Frage* and one on poems by Rilke, 6 poems by Morgenstern, etc,

Burla (It. = jest, trick, practical joke),

in mus. a humorous piece, rather more boisterous than a scherzo.

Burleigh, Cecil (b. Wyoming, N.Y., 17. IV. 1885), Amer. violinist and comp. Studied in U.S.A., Berlin and finally at Chicago. After touring frequently and teaching in var. places, he settled down as vln. prof. at Wisconsin Univ.

Works incl. symph. poem *Evangeline*, *Mountain Pictures*, etc. for orch.; 3 vln. concertos; 2 vln. and pf. sonatas *The Ascension* and *From the Life of St. Paul*; numerous vln. pieces, etc.

Burleigh, Henry T(hacker). (b. Erie, Pa., 2. XII. 1866; d. Stamford, Conn., 12. IX. 1949), Amer. Negro singer and comp. Pupil of Dvořák at the Nat. Cons. in N.Y., where he introd. Negro tunes to his master.

Works incl. arrs. of Negro tunes, songs, etc.

Burlesca (It.) = Burla.

Burlesque, another name sometimes used for the Burletta in Eng.

Burletta (It. = a little joke), a form of light comic opera or operetta in 18th- and 19th-cent. Eng.

Burmeister, Joachim (b. Lüneburg, *c.* 1566; d. Rostock, 5. V. 1629), Ger. mus. theorist. In treatises pub. in 1599, 1601 and 1606 he codified as *figurae* the various technical and expressive devices used by 16th-cent. comps.

Burmester, Willy (b. Hamburg, 16. III. 1869; d. Hamburg, 16. I. 1933), Ger. violinist. Pupil of Joachim, but afterwards a virtuoso who travelled extensively as an exponent of his instrument rather than an interpreter of great mus. He wrote a few comps. and arr. mus. for vln.

Burney, Charles (b. Shrewsbury, 7. IV. 1726; d. Chelsea, 12. IV. 1814), Eng. organist, mus. hist. and comp. Pupil of Arne, held org. posts in London (1749–51) and King's Lynn (1751–60). D.Mus., Oxford, 1769. Travelled extensively on the Continent 1770–2, collecting material for his 4-vol. *General History of Music* (pub. 1776–89). He also pub. those parts of his travel diaries relating to mus. He was father of the novelist Fanny Burney, and a friend of Dr. Johnson, Reynolds, Garrick, etc. On his travels he made the acquaintance of many of the leading musicians of his day. His works incl. an Eng. version of Rousseau's *Le Devin du Village* under the title *The Cunning Man*, songs for a revival of *A Midsummer Night's Dream* (with M. Arne, Aylward and Battishill) and a quantity of instrumental music.

Burns, Robert (1759–96), Scot. poet. *See* **Chadwick** (*Tam o' Shanter*), **Drysdale** (do. and *To Edinburgh*), **Goossens** (*Tam o' S.*), **Jensen** (songs), **Khrennikov** (songs), **Mackenzie** (*Cottar's Sat. Night* and *Tam o' S.*), **Scott** (F. G.) (songs), **Swain** (songs).

Burton, Avery (b. ?; d. ?), Eng. 15th–

16th-cent. comp. On 29. XI. 1494 he was paid 20*s.* for composing a Mass; in 1509 he became a Gentleman of the Chapel Royal. On 20. VI. 1513 he went to France with the Chapel Royal, a Te Deum of his being sung after Mass at Tournai on 17. IX.; in VI. 1520 he was present at the Field of the Cloth of Gold. His name disappears from the records of the Chapel Royal after 1542. He is known as the composer of a Mass, *Ut re mi fa sol la*, in the Forrest-Heyther part-books (this is prob. not the Mass of 1494) and of a Te Deum for org.

Burton, John (b. Yorkshire, 1730; d. Naples, *c.* 1. IX. 1782), Eng. harpsichordist, organist and comp. Pupil of Keeble. Became a very famous player and had a great success in Ger. in 1754. Comp. concertos for both his instruments, sonatas, It. canzonets, etc.

Busby, Thomas (b. London, XII. 1755; d. London, 28. V. 1838), Eng. organist and comp. Sang at Vauxhall as a boy with great success, later became a pupil of Battishill. Worked at a mus. dictionary with Arnold, was app. church organist *c.* 1786. Mus.D. at Cambridge in 1801. Wrote several books on mus.

Works incl. incid. mus. for Cumberland's *Joanna of Montfaucon* (an Eng. version of Kotzebue's *Johanna von M.*), Holcroft's *Tale of Mystery*, Anna Maria Porter's *Fair Fugitives* and Lewis's *Rugantino*; oratorios *The Prophecy* (from Pope's *Messiah*) and *Britannia*; settings of odes by Pope and Gay.

Busch, Adolf (b. Siegen, Westphalia, 8. VIII. 1891; d. Guildford, Vermont, 9. VI. 1952), Ger. violinist and comp. Studied at the Cologne Cons. and comp. with Hugo Grüters at Bonn. In 1918 he became vln. prof. at the Berlin High School for Mus. In 1919 he formed a string 4tet with which he toured all over the world, and he was also famous as an interpreter of vln. and pf. sonatas with Rudolf Serkin. In 1933 he renounced Ger. citizenship as a protest against the Nazi rule.

Works incl. choral, orchestral and much chamber mus.

Busch, Fritz (b. Siegen, Westphalia, 13. III. 1890; d. London, 14. IX. 1951), Ger. cond., brother of prec. Studied at the Cologne Cons. and after gaining experience at var. Ger. theatres and with orchs., he became cond. of the Stuttgart Opera in 1918 and mus. director of the Dresden State Opera in 1922. Like his brother he renounced Ger. citizenship, went to Buenos Aires in 1933, conducted the Glyndebourne Opera from 1934 to his death and lived in Copenhagen as cond. of the State Radio.

Busch, Wilhelm (1832–1908), Ger. comic versifier and cartoonist. *See* **Goldschmidt** (A.) (*Fromme Helene*), **Mraczek** (*Max und Moritz*).

Busch, William (b. London, 25. VI. 1901; d. Woolacombe, Devon, 30. I. 1945), Eng. pianist and comp. Educ. in N.Y., London and Berlin, studied pf. with Backhaus, Petri and others, and comp. with Leichtentritt, Ireland and van Dieren. Made his 1st appearance as pianist in London, 1927. Later he became mus. master at Highgate School in London.

Works incl. Prelude for orch.; pf. concerto, cello concerto; pf. 4tet, *Ode to Autumn* for voice and string 4tet; 4 pieces for cello and pf.; *Theme, Variations and Fugue, Nicholas Variations, Allegretto quasi pastorale, Gigue, Prelude and Fugue* for pf.; songs to poems by Campion, Blake, Beddoes, 'A.E.' and James Stephens, etc.

Bush, Alan (Dudley) (b. London, 22. XII. 1900), Eng. comp. Studied at the R.A.M. in London and Berlin Univ., later with John Ireland. He also studied the pf. with Schnabel. He became prof. at the R.A.M., cond. of the London Labour Choral Union and in 1936 chairman of the Workers' Mus. Assoc.

Works incl. operas *The Press-Gang, Wat Tyler, The Spell* and *Men of Blackmoor*; incid. mus. for Shakespeare's *Macbeth*, Sean O'Casey's *The Star Turns Red* and Patrick Hamilton's *The Duke in Darkness*; choral work *The Winter Journey* (Randall Swingler) and others; 2 symphs. (No. 2 'Nottingham') and other orch. mus.; pf. concerto with chorus (Swingler), vln. concerto, *Concert Suite* for cello and orch.; string 4tet, pf. 4tet, *Dialectic* for string 4tet; instrumental pieces with pf.; pf. and org. mus.; songs, etc.

Bush, Geoffrey (b. London, 23. III. 1920), Eng. comp. Became a choir-boy at Salisbury Cathedral in 1928, went to Lancing Coll. in 1933 and later to Balliol Coll., Oxford, where he gained the Nettleship Scholarship in mus. comp. B.Mus., Oxford, 1940, D.Mus. 1946. His studies were interrupted by war service at a hostel for abnormal evacuee children. He is mainly self-taught in comp., but had much valuable advice from his masters at Salisbury and Lancing, also from John Ireland and others later.

Works incl. opera *Spanish Rivals*; *12th Night* entertainment for chorus and orch.; overtures *In Praise of Salisbury* and *The Rehearsal* for orch., Divertimento for string orch.; concerto for pf. and strings, *Sinfonietta concertante* for cello and chamber orch., ob. concerto, rhapsody for clar. and string 4tet; sonatas for vln. and pf. and tpt. and pf.; 2 pf. sonatinas; *Portraits* and *La Belle Dame sans merci* (Keats) for unaccomp. chorus; songs, etc.

Busnois, Anthoine (b. ?; d. Bruges, 6. XI. 1492), Fr. comp. Pupil of Okeghem and later in the service of the Burgundian court until 1481, when (?) he became mus.

director at the church of Saint-Sauveur at Bruges.

Works incl. Masses, motets, Magnificats; secular vocal pieces; songs, etc.

Busoni, Ferruccio (Benvenuto) (b. Empoli, 1. IV. 1866; d. Berlin, 27. VII. 1924), It. pianist and comp. Appeared as pianist in public at the age of 7; studied at Graz and Leipzig. Taught at the Helsinki Cons. in 1889 and there married the Swed. Gerda Sjöstrand; taught at Moscow in 1890 and in Amer., 1891–4. Settled in Berlin for good in 1894, but travelled widely as a pianist and during the war of 1914–18 lived 1st at Bologna as director of the Cons. and then at Zürich. At Bologna he hoped to influence It. mus. and to prove that he was himself an It. comp., but was disappointed. His opera *Doktor Faust* was completed by Jarnach and 1st perf. in 1925. His ideas on aesthetics, esp. his *Sketch of a New Aesthetic of Music*, are of interest.

Works incl. operas, *Die Brautwahl, Turandot, Arlecchino* and *Doktor Faust*; 4 suites for orch., *Nocturne symphonique, Rondo arlecchinesco, Comedy Overture* and other works for orch.; *Konzertstück, Indian Fantasy* and *Romanza e Scherzoso* for pf. and orch.; concerto for pf., orch. and male-voice chorus; vln. concerto; several vocal works with orch.; 2 string 4tets; 2 vln. and pf. sonatas; many pf. solo works, incl. Sonata in F min.; *4 Ballettszenen*, 24 Preludes, 7 Elegies, *Indianisches Tagebuch, Fantasia contrappuntistica*, 6 sonatinas; songs, etc.

Büsser, (Paul) Henri (b. Toulouse, 16. I. 1872), Fr. cond. and comp. Pupil of Guiraud at the Paris Cons. Gained the Prix de Rome in 1893. Successively organist at Saint-Cloud, cond. of the choral class at the Cons. and director of Niedermeyer's school. App. prof. of comp. at the Cons. in 1921.

Works incl. operas *Jane Grey, Daphnis et Chloé, Colomba* (after Mérimée), *Les Noces corinthiennes, La Pie borgne, Le Carrosse du Saint-Sacrement* (Mérimée); Masses and motets; *Hercule au jardin des Hespérides, Suite funambulesque* and other orchestral works; choruses, songs, etc.

Bussotti, Sylvano (b. Florence, 1. X. 1931), It. comp. Studied mus. in Florence and painting in Paris. After prod. some early works in a relatively traditional style, he turned to a graphical manner of composing which is influenced by Cage and attempts to suggest the type of improvisation required.

Works incl. *Torso* for voice and orch.; *Fragmentations* for harp; *5 pf. pieces for David Tudor; Pour clavier* for pf.; *Pearson Piece* for baritone and pf.; cantata *Memoria*.

Bustini, Alessandro (b. Rome, 24. XII. 1876), It. comp. Studied at the Acc. di

Santa Cecilia in Rome, where he became prof. later.

Works incl. operas *Maria Dulcis* (based on a story in Berlioz's *Soirées de l'orchestre*), *La città quadrata* and *L'incantesimo di Calandrino*; funeral Mass for Victor Emmanuel II; 2 symphs., symph. poem *Le tentazioni*; string 4tet; sonatas for vln. and pf. and vla. and pf., pf. pieces, etc.

Buths, Julius (b. Wiesbaden, 7. V. 1851; d. Düsseldorf, 12. III. 1920), Ger. pianist and cond. Worked at Düsseldorf from 1890, director of the Cons. there and cond. of the Lower Rhine Festival, where he introd. Elgar's *Dream of Gerontius* in 1901.

Butler, Samuel (b. Langar nr. Bingham, Notts., 4. XII. 1835; d. London, 18. VI. 1902), Eng. author, critic, biologist, painter and amateur comp. He was a passionate admirer of Handel and wrote 2 cantatas, *Narcissus* and *Ulysses*, in imitations of Handel's oratorio style.

Butt, Clara (b. Southwick, Sussex, 1. II. 1873; d. North Stoke, Oxon, 23. I. 1936), Eng. contralto. Studied at R.C.M. in London, and in Paris. Made her 1st concert and stage appearance in 1892. A great voice made her very popular, and having placed it at the disposal of war charities, she received the D.B.E. in 1920.

Butterfly (Puccini). *See* **Madama Butterfly.**

'Butterfly' (or **'Butterfly's Wing'**) **Study,** a nickname sometimes given to Chopin's pf. Study in G♭ maj., Op. 25 No. 9.

Butterworth, George (Sainton Kaye) (b. London, 12. VII. 1885; d. Pozières, 5. VIII. 1916), Eng. comp. Educ. at Eton and Oxford, studied mus. briefly at the R.C.M. in London. He collected folksongs, cultivated folk dancing and comp., but enlisted on the outbreak of war and was killed in action.

Works incl. Rhapsody *A Shropshire Lad* and Idyll *The Banks of Green Willow* for orch.; 2 song cycles on Housman's *Shropshire Lad*; Sussex folksongs arr.; carols set for chorus; a few other choral pieces and songs, etc.

Butting, Max (b. Berlin, 6. X. 1888), Ger. comp. Studied at Munich.

Works incl. unfinished Mass; 6 symphs., chamber symph.; cello concerto; 4 string 4tets and other chamber mus.; songs with small orch., etc.

Buttstett, Johann Heinrich (b. Bindersleben nr. Erfurt, 25. IV. 1666; d. Erfurt, 1. XII. 1727), Ger. organist and comp. Pupil of Pachelbel. Organist of 2 Erfurt churches from 1684 and of the cathedral from 1691. Wrote Masses, a vol. of keyboard mus. *Musikalische Clavierkunst,* etc.

Buus, Jachet (Jacques) (b. ? Bruges, ?; d. ? Vienna, VIII. 1565), Flem. organist and comp. 1st pub. some work in Fr., but went to It. and in 1541 became organist at St Mark's in Venice, succeeding Baldassare da Imola. He went to Vienna on leave in 1550, but never returned and became organist at the court of Ferdinand I.

Works incl. motets, madrigals; Fr. chansons; ricercari for org., etc.

Buxheimer Orgelbuch, large Ger. MS. of keyboard mus. (not all of it necessarily for org.) dateable c. 1470. It contains mostly ornamented arrangements of sacred and secular vocal works; also several versions of the *Fundamentum organisandi* by Paumann and some liturgical org. mus. The upper part is written on a staff of (usually) 7 lines, the lower part(s) in letters. In some pieces the use of pedals is indicated.

Buxtehude, Dietrich (orig. **Diderik**) (b. Oldesloe, 1637; d. Lübeck, 9. V. 1707), Dan. comp. and organist. Settled in Den. and from 1668 organist of St Mary's Church, Lübeck. An important forerunner of Bach as org. comp.

Works incl. concerted mus. works for chorus and orch. (*Abendmusiken*); church cantatas; sonatas for strings; org. mus., incl. chorale preludes; suites for harpsichord, etc.

Buysine (or **Buzine**), in the early Middle Ages a large horn. From the 13th cent. a long tpt., Saracen in origin, which survived till the 16th cent. as a ceremonial instrument.

Byrd, William (b. ? Lincoln, 1543; d. ? Stondon, Essex, 4. VII. 1623), Eng. comp. After prob. studying under Tallis as one of the children of the Chapel Royal in London, he was app. organist of Lincoln Cathedral in 1563, at an unusually early age. He married Juliana Birley there, 14. IX. 1568, and on 22. II. 1569 was elected a Gentleman of the Chapel Royal, but continued his duties at Lincoln until 1572, when he became organist of the Chapel Royal jointly with Tallis. In 1575 Queen Elizabeth granted the 2 an exclusive licence for printing and selling mus., and they dedicated to her their *Cantiones sacrae* pub. that year. B. married a 2nd time about 1587. In 1593 he bought Stondon Place nr. Stapleford-Abbott, Essex, where he remained for the rest of his life, as often as his duties in town would let him. He was frequently involved in litigation and was several times prosecuted for recusancy as a Rom. Catholic, but remained in favour with the queen. He wrote impartially and with equal genius for his own and the Angl. Church.

Works incl. 3 Masses; 17 Lat. motets in the *Cantiones sacrae* by Tallis and B.; 61 Lat. motets in 2 books of *Cantiones sacrae*; 99 Lat. motets in 2 books of *Gradualia; c.* 50 motets in MS.; 5 Anglican services (1 incomplete); 61 anthems; some miscellaneous Eng. church mus.; *Psalmes, Sonets and Songs* (18 Nos.); *Songs of Sundrie*

Natures (47 Nos.); *Psalmes, Songs and Sonnets* (32 Nos.); 4 sep. madrigals (others are in those 3 books); 31 songs; 32 canons; 6 rounds; 14 fantasies for strings, 8 In Nomines for strings, 9 pieces for strings on plainsong tunes, some miscellaneous mus. for strings; *c.* 120 virginal pieces, etc.

Byron, George Gordon, Lord (1788–1824) Eng. poet. *See* **Arnell** (symph. poem), **Berg (N.)** (*Leila*), **Bishop** (*Manfred*), **Bogatirev** (*Two Foscari* and *Manfred*), **Corsaire** (Berlioz), **Corsaro** (Verdi), **Due Foscari** (Verdi), **Harold en Italie** (Berlioz) **Hedy** (*Don Juan*, Fibich), **Hiller (F.)** (*Hebrew Melodies*), **Holbrooke** (*Ode to Victory*), **Holstein** (*Marino Faliero*), **Lacombe** (*Manfred*), **Lebrun (P.)** (*Fiancée d'Abydos*), **Mackenzie** (*Manfred*), **Maillart** (*Lara*), **Manfred** (incid. mus., Schumann; symph. Tchaikovsky), **Mario Faliero** (Donizetti), **Mussorgsky** (*Destruction of Sennacherib*), **Nathan** (*Hebrew Melodies*), **Novák** (*Corsair* and *Manfred*), **Parisina** (Donizetti), **Poniatowski** (*Sposa d'Abido*), **Praeger** (*Manfred*), **Reinecke** (*König Manfred*), **Roslavets** (*Heaven and Earth*), **Rytel** (*Corsair*), **Schönberg** (*Ode to Napoleon*), **Starck** (*Manfred*), **Steinberg** (*Heaven and Earth*), **Tasso** (Liszt), **Vavrinecz** (*Bride of Abydos*), **White (M. V.)** (songs), **Williams (G.)** (do.). *See also* **Vampyr** (Lindpainter and Marschner; subject attrib. to Byron, but actually from a story by John William Polidori).

Byttering (b. ?; d. ?, his name formerly misread as Gyttering), Eng. 14th–15th-cent. comp. represented in the Old Hall MS.

Byzantine Chant, the name given to the Christian chant of the Gk.-speaking Orthodox Church. In 330 Constantine the Great made Byzantium (henceforth Constantinople) capital of the Roman Empire; but only in 527, with the coronation of Justinian I as Emperor, did B. liturgy, art and mus. gain supremacy throughout the Empire. Other important dates are 726–843 (the iconoclastic age), 1054 (the final break from Roman Catholicism), and 1453 (the sack of Constantinople by the Turks). During the course of the 11th cent. the introduction of new hymns was forbidden, and the power of the B. Empire was broken with the estab. of the Lat. Empire (1204–1261). However, the restoration of the Eastern Empire in 1261 led to a renaissance which lasted for a century, followed by a gradual deterioration until the end of the Empire.

B. mus. and liturgy was dominated by its hymns, which adorned the Offices rather than the Mass. The *troparion* (later *sticheron*) was an intercalation between the verses of a psalm. The *kontakion* was a sermon in verse, sung after the reading of the Gospel at the Morning Office. At the end of the 7th cent. it was replaced by the *kanon*, consisting of 9 odes of 9 stanzas each: each ode had its own melody. Finally acclamations to the Emperor were sung throughout the period; unlike mus. actually sung in church, these were accompanied by instruments, esp. the org.

B. mus., notated in neumes, is based on a system of eight modes (*echoi*), defined by charact. melodic formulas as well as by tonality. Like the verse itself (scanned by stress, not quantity) it is Semitic in origin. The comparative simplicity of earlier and middle B. mus. gave way, at the end of the period, to a highly embellished style in which the balance between verse and music tended to be destroyed. The foll. short extract is a *heirmos* (model stanza) for the second ode of a *kanon* for the feast of the Purification by Andrew of Crete (*c.* 660–*c.* 740), the 1st writer of *kanons*:

C

C, the keynote, or tonic, of the scale of C maj.

C Clef, the clef, derived from an ornamental letter C, which indicates that the line on which it is placed =

In the past it has been placed on all 5 lines of the stave (*see* illustration below). (The last of these has the same effect as the Baritone Clef, q.v., using the F clef.) Only two C clefs are in use today: the Alto, for the viola, and the Tenor, for

Soprano   Mezzo-soprano   Alto   Tenor

C CLEF

the tenor trombone and the upper register of the bassoon, cello and double bass.

Cabaletta (It. corrupt. from *cavatinetta,* dim. of *cavatina*), the quick and usually brilliant final section of an aria consisting of more than one movement.

Cabanilles, Juan (Bautista José) (b. Algemesí, Valencia, IX. 1644; d. Valencia, 20. IV. 1712), Span. organist and comp. In 1665 he was app. organist of Valencia Cathedral, a post he held till his death. He is one of the great representatives of org. comp. of his time.

Cabell, James Branch (1879–1958), Amer. author. *See* **Taylor (Deems)** (*Jurgen*).

Cabezón, Antonio de (b. Castrillo de Matajudíos, nr. Burgos, *c.* 1500; d. Madrid, 26. III. 1566), Span. organist and comp. Although (?) blind from birth, he studied with Tomás Gómez at Palencia and became chamber organist and harpsichordist to Charles V, remaining at court under Philip II, (?) accomp. him to Eng. on his marriage to Mary I. Comp. org., vihuela and other mus.

Cabezón, Hernando (b. Madrid, ?; d. Valladolid, 1. V. 1602), Span. organist and comp., son of prec. Studied under his father, whom he succeeded at court and whose works he ed. in 1578. Wrote org. mus.

Cable, George Washington (1844–1925), Amer. novelist. *See* **Gilbert (H. F.)** (*Dance in Place Congo*), **Koanga** (Delius).

Cabo, Francisco Javier (b. Nájara,

Valencia, 1768; d. Valencia, 21. XI. 1832), Span. organist and comp. After some min. posts he was app. cantor at Valencia Cathedral in 1810, 1st organist in 1816 and *maestro de capilla* in 1830, succeeding Andreví.

Works incl. church mus., vocal mus. with org. or orch., org. pieces, etc.

Cabrette (Fr. dialect for *chevrette* = shekid), a variety of musette from the Auvergnat region in Fr.

Caccia (It. = hunt), a 14th-cent. It. comp. in which 2 voices, with or without a supporting instrument, sang in canon. The texts, though always lively, were not confined to hunting. The corresponding form in Fr. was called *chace.*

Caccini, Francesca (b. Florence, 18. IX. 1587; d. ? Lucca, *c.* 1640), It. singer and comp. Pupil of her father.

Works incl. opera, *La liberazione di Ruggiero*; ballets *Il ballo delle zigane* and *Rinaldo innamorato* (after Tasso); sacred and secular cantatas for 1 and 2 voices, etc.

Caccini, Giulio (b. Rome, *c.* 1545; d. Florence, XII. 1618), It. singer, lutenist and comp., father of prec. Entered the service of the Medici at Florence in 1564. Visited Paris with his daughter in 1604–5. He wrote short vocal pieces in recitative style and sang them to the theorbo, which led to larger essays of the kind, set to scenes by Count Bardi, and eventually to Rinuccini's lib. for the opera *Euridice*, 1st set by Peri and immediately afterwards by C. in 1600.

Works incl. operas *Euridice* and *Il rapimento di Cefalo*; *Nuove musiche* containing madrigals and arias for voice and thorough-bass.

Cachucha (Span.), an Andalusian dance in quick, energetic 3–4 time.

Cadéac, Pierre (b. ?; d. ?), 16th-cent. Fr. comp. He was master of the choir-boys at Auch (near Toulouse) in 1556. He comp. Masses, motets and *chansons*, incl. perhaps the *Je suis désheritée* ascribed to him by Attaingnant in 1539 (but to 'Lupus' by the same pub. in 1533). This famous piece was used as the basis of numerous Masses in the 16th cent., incl. one by Palestrina.

Cadence (from Lat. *cado* = I fall). (1) The fall of a melody to its final note.

(2) The harmonization of such a fall.

Cadence

Traditional forms are, in the key of C major:

(a) Perfect (in Amer. Authentic): dominant to tonic:

Perfect:

(b) Plagal: subdominant to tonic:

Plagal:

(c) Imperfect: tonic to dominant:

Imperfect:

(d) Interrupted (in Amer. Deceptive): dominant to a chord other than the tonic:

Interrupted:

The so-called Phrygian C., where the 'fall' is in the lowest part:

Phrygian:

derives its name from the Phrygian Mode. Apart from these traditional forms any harmonic progression which suggests finality, if only temporarily, is technically a C.

Cadence (Fr.) = Shake.

Cadence appuyée (Fr.). *See* **Ornaments.**

Cadence-Phrase, the final group in the exposition of a sonata movement, leading to the close in a key other than the tonic.

Cadence sans tremblement (Fr.). *See* **Ornaments.**

Cadent. *See* **Ornaments.**

Cadenza (It. = Cadence). Orig. the C. was simply a cadence; but the custom gradually estab. itself of creating a feeling of suspense between the chords of a cadence by interpolating brilliant passages of greater or less extent and at the same time giving

Cage

the perf. a chance to display technical gifts and inventiveness in improvisation. C.s in concertos are now rarely improvised, but supplied either by the comp. himself or some other musician.

'Cadet Roussel' Variations, a series of vocal variations on the Fr. folksong by Arnold Bax, Frank Bridge, Eugene Goossens and John Ireland, comp. *c.* 1917.

Cadi dupé, Le (*The Cadi Duped*), opera by Gluck (lib. by Pierre René Lemonnier), prod. Vienna, Burgtheater, XII. 1761.

Opera by Monsigny (lib. do.), prod. Paris, Opéra-Comique, 4. II. 1761.

Cadman, Charles Wakefield (b. Johnstown, Pa., 24. XII. 1881; d. Los Angeles, 30. XII. 1946), Amer. comp. Studied at Pittsburgh and became organist, chorus cond. and critic there. He explored Amer.-Indian mus. and used it in some of his comps. After a visit to Eur. in 1910 he became organist at Denver and later settled at Los Angeles.

Works incl. operas *The Garden of Mystery, The Land of Misty Water, The Garden of Death, Shanewis* (*The Robin Woman*), *A Witch of Salem, The Willow Tree*; cantatas for mixed and male voices; *Thunder-bird* suite, *Oriental Rhapsody, Dark Dancers of the Mardi Gras* for orch.; *Amer. Suite* and *To a Vanishing Race* for string orch.; string 4tet; pf. trio; vln. and pf. sonata; sonata, suite *Omar Khayyám, Idealized Indian Themes* and other works for pf.; *Four Indian Songs,* song cycles, *From Wigwam and Tepee, Birds of Flame, White Enchantment, Sayonara* (Jap.), *The Willow Wind* (Chin.) and *c.* 300 separate songs, etc.

Cadmus et Hermione, opera by Lully (lib. by Philippe Quinault), prod. Paris, Opéra, 27. IV. 1673.

Caduta de' giganti, La (*The Fall of the Giants*), opera by Gluck (lib. by Francesco Vanneschi), prod. London, King's Theatre, Haymarket, 7. I. 1746.

Cafaro, Pasquale (b. San Pietro in Galantina nr. Lecce, *c.* 1715; d. Naples, 23. or 25. X. 1787), It. comp. Pupil of Leo in Naples, app. director of the Conservatorio della Pietà in 1759, and supernumerary *maestro di cappella* to the court in 1770.

Works incl. operas *Ipermestra, La Disfatta di Dario,* etc.; oratorios *Il Figlio prodigo, Il trionfo di Davidde,* etc.; *Stabat Mater,* Masses, motets and other church mus.

Caffarelli (real name **Gaetano Majorano**) (b. Bitonto, 12. IV. 1710; d. Naples, 31. I. 1783), It. castrato alto. Pupil of Porpora, made his operatic début in Rome, 1724. Sang for Handel in London, 1738.

Cage, John (b. Los Angeles, 5. IX. 1912), Amer. comp. Studied pf. in Los Angeles and Paris and comp. with, among others, Cowell, Schönberg and Varèse. C. is the most prominent pioneer and exponent of such 'experimental' concepts as indeterminacy, chance, silence, etc., his ideas having had a very considerable influence in both Amer. and Eur. He has invented the 'prepared piano', in which different objects are inserted between the strings, altering the tone and the sound produced. C. has also explored electronic mus.

Works incl. pf. concerto; *Music of changes* for pf.; *Winter Music* for 1–20 pfs.; *Music for Amplified Toy Piano*; *Radio Music* for 1–8 radios; *Amores* for prepared pf.; *Imaginary Landscape No. 5* for electronic tape; *4′ 33″*, silent piece for different combinations. C. has also pub. *Silence*, a collection of his writings and ideas on mus.

Cagnoni, Antonio (b. Godiasco, Voghera, 8. II. 1828; d. Bergamo, 30. IV. 1896), It. comp. Studied at the Milan Cons., 1842–7. *Maestro di cappella* at Vigevano, 1856–63, then at Novara Cathedral, and from 1887 at the church of Santa Maria Maggiore at Bergamo.

Works incl. operas *Don Bucefalo*, *Il testamento di Figaro*, *Amori e trappole*, *Giralda*, *La valle d'Andorra*, *Il vecchio della montagna*, *La tombola*, *Un capriccio di donna*, *Papa Martin*, *Francesca da Rimini* (after Dante), etc.; motets and other church mus.

Cahen, Albert (b. Paris, 8. I. 1846; d. Cap d'Ail, 23. II. 1903), Fr. comp. Pupil of Franck for comp.

Works incl. operas *Le Bois*, *La Belle au bois dormant*, *Le Vénitien*, *La Femme de Claude*; ballet *Fleur de neiges*; *Jean le Précurseur* and *Endymion* for chorus and orch.; song cycle *Marines*, etc.

Caietain, Fabrice Marin (b. ?; d. ?), 16th-cent. Fr. comp. *Maître de chapelle* at Toul Cathedral in 1571; he comp. motets and *chansons*, etc.

Caimo, Gioseppe (b. Milan, 1540; d. Milan, 1584), It. comp. Organist of Milan Cathedral, 1580 until his death. He wrote canzonets and madrigals, some of the latter employing the extremes of chromaticism favoured by Gesualdo.

Caine, (Thomas Henry) Hall (1853–1931), Eng. novelist and playwright. *See* Mascagni (*Eternal City*).

Caisse (Fr.) *See* Grosse Caisse.

Caisse claire (Fr.) = Side Drum.

Caisse roulante ⎫
    or   ⎬ (Fr.) = Tenor Drum.
Caisse sourde ⎭

Caix d'Hervelois, Louis de (b. Paris, *c.* 1670; d. Paris, *c.* 1760), Fr. vla. da gamba player. In the service of the Duke of Orleans. A son and 3 daughters of his were chamber musicians at court. Wrote many pieces for vla. da gamba, duets for viols and fl. sonatas.

Calando (It. = lowering, decreasing, calming down), a direction similar to

diminuendo and *rallentando*, capable of expressing both at once, i.e. weakening in tone as well as slowing down.

Calascione (It.). *See* Colascione.

Calata (It.), an It. lute dance of the early 16th cent., similar to the Fr. *basse danse*. It was written in duple time, but had a triple rhythm of 3-bar groups.

Caldara, Antonio (b. Venice, 1670; d. Vienna, 28. XII. 1736), It. comp. Pupil of Legrenzi at Venice. After travelling much and working in Rome and Madrid, he settled in Vienna as vice-cond. under Fux in 1716.

Works incl. *c.* 100 operas and other stage works, e.g. *Ifigenia in Aulide*, *Lucio Papirio*, *Gianguir*, *Don Chisciotte*, *La pazienza di Socrate con due moglie* (with Reutter), *Il Demetrio*, *Sancio Panza*, *Achille in Sciro*; church mus.; oratorios cantatas, madrigals, canons; trio sonatas 4tets, septet, etc.

Calderón de la Barca, Pedro (1600–81),, Span. dramatist. *See* Ambros (*Mágico prodigioso*), Casal Chapí, Celos aun del ayre matan (Hidalgo), Courvoisier, Ferreira, Fierrabras (Schubert), Friedenstag (R. Strauss), Hidalgo, Křenek (*Vida es sueño*), Laserna, Lassen (*Circe*), Opieński (*Príncipe constante*), Peyro (*Jardin de Falerina*), Raff (*Dame Kobold*), Reinecke (do.), Rheinberger (*Mágico p.*), Rietz (J.) (incid. mus. for plays), Soler (incid. mus. for plays), Tommasini (*Life is a Dream*), Umlauf (I.) (*Oberamtmann und die Soldaten*), Weingartner (*Dame Kobold*), Wolfurt (do.).

Caledonica, an alto bassoon invented by the Scot. bandmaster Meik, *c.* 1820. It was played with a clar. reed mouthpiece.

Calife de Bagdad, Le, opera by Boïeldieu (lib. by Claude Godard d'Aucour de Saint-Just), prod. Paris, Opéra-Comique, 16. IX. 1800.

Calinda (or **Calenda**), a negro dance intro. into the W. Indies and later cultivated in the southern states of U.S.A., orig. an African ritual dance accomp. by drums, which remained a feature of its mus. Delius makes use of it in *Koanga*.

Calino casturame. *See* Callino casturame.

Callas, Maria (real name Calogeropoulos) (b. N.Y., 3. XII. 1923), Amer. soprano of Gk. descent. Aged 13, she went to Greece, where she studied at the Athens Cons., returning to N.Y. in 1945. She made her début at Verona in 1947. Although she has sung many types of role, C. is most famous for her perfs. in 19th- and early 20th-cent. romantic It. operas. In 1949 she married the It. industrialist G. B. Meneghini.

Callcott, John (Wall) (b. London, 20. XI. 1766; d. Bristol, 15. V. 1821), organist and comp. Son of a bricklayer, he had no regular mus. teaching, but picked up much knowledge from Arnold and Cooke.

Having obtained a deputy organist's post, he found time to compose and in 1785 gained 3 of the 4 prizes offered by the Catch Club. Two years later he took part in founding the Glee Club. When Haydn came to Eng. he studied instrumental writing under him, but he continued to write glees and catches with great success. D.Mus., Oxford, 1800. In 1809 he went insane.

Works incl. setting of Joseph Warton's *Ode to Fancy*; anthem for Arnold's funeral; scena on the death of Nelson; a book of psalms ed. with Arnold, with some new tunes; numerous glees, catches and canons, etc.

Callino casturame (corrupt. from Ir. 'Cailín ó chois tSiúire mé' = 'I am a girl from beside the [river] Suir'), a tune mentioned in Shakespeare's *Henry V* (IV. iv) and contained in the *Fitzwilliam Virginal Book*.

Calm Sea and Prosperous Voyage (Beethoven and Mendelssohn). *See* **Meeresstille**.

Calvé, Emma (Rose Emma Calvet) (b. Décazeville, 15. VIII. 1858; d. Millau, 6. I. 1942), Fr. soprano. 1st appeared at Nice and came out in Brussels in 1882 and Paris in 1884. She was famous as an interpreter of the role of Carmen.

Calvisius, Seth (b. Gorsleben, Thuringia, 21. II. 1556; d. Leipzig, 24. XI. 1615), Ger. scholar and musician. Cantor of St. Thomas's School and mus. director of its church from 1594, and thus a predecessor of Bach. Wrote several learned books on mus., compiled collections of vocal mus. and comp. motets, hymns, etc.

Calvocoressi, M(ichael). D(imitri). (b. Marseilles, 2. X. 1877; d. London, 1. II. 1944), Eng. mus. critic of Gk. descent. Studied in Paris, partic. mus. and languages, lectured there on mus. at the École des Hautes Études Sociales, 1905–14, and then settled in London, becoming naturalized. His books incl. studies of mus. criticism, Mussorgsky, etc.

Calzabigi, Ranieri da (1714–95), It. lit. critic and author. Lived in Paris and Vienna for a time. Wrote the libs. for Gluck's *Orfeo*, *Alceste* and *Paride ed Elena*. *See also* **Finta giardiniera** (Anfossi and Mozart), **Orfeo ed Euridice** (Bertoni) and **Orpheus und Euridike** (Naumann).

Cambert, Robert (b. Paris, *c*. 1628; d. London, *c*. II. 1677), Fr. comp. Studied harpsichord with Chambonnières, was organist at the church of Saint-Honoré in Paris and superintendent of the queen's mus. He was ousted by Lully and went to live in London in 1673. His *Pomone* (1671) was the 1st Fr. opera to be staged in public. Most of his mus. is lost.

Works incl. comedy with mus. *La Muette ingrate*; a pastoral perf. at Issy and another, *Les Peines et les plaisirs de l'amour*; operas *Ariane, ou Le Mariage de Bacchus, Pomone*;

a trio for Brécourt's *Jaloux invisible*; *Airs à boire*, etc.

Cambiale di matrimonio, La (*The Marriage Contract*), opera by Rossini (lib. by Gaetano Rossi, based on a comedy by Camillo Federici), prod. Venice, Teatro San Moisè, 3. XI. 1810. Rossini's 1st opera to be perf.

Cambiare (It. = to change). The word is sometimes used in place of *mutare*, e.g. *cambia in Re* (change to D), *cambiano in La* (they change to A), etc.

Cambiata. *See* **Nota Cambiata.**

Cambini, Giovanni Giuseppe (b. Leghorn, 13. II. 1746; d. Bicêtre nr. Paris, 29. XII. 1825), It. violinist and comp. Pupil of Martini at Bologna. In 1770 he settled in Paris, where at first he had great success as both comp. and cond. Later his fortunes declined, and he d. in poverty.

Works incl. 19 operas, ballets, an oratorio, 60 symphs., 144 4tets and 5tets, church mus., etc.

Camera, Concerto da ⎫ (It. = chamber
Camera, Sonata da ⎭ concerto or sonata), a secular work written for perf. at home or at concerts, as distinct from a concerto or sonata *da chiesa* = for the church.

Camerata (It. = society), a group of intellectuals meeting for cultural exchanges, in particular one at Florence working together just before and after 1600 and evolving the form of opera, incl. the musicians Caccini, Cavalieri, V. Galilei and Peri, the poet Ottavio Rinuccini and the amateur patrons Counts Bardi and Corsi.

Cameriera (It. = chambermaid), a term used in It. opera, esp. of the 17th and 18th cents., in the same way as *servetta* (servant-girl), for soubrette parts.

Camilla (Bononcini). *See* **Trionfo di C.**

Camões, Louis Vaz de (1524–80), Port. poet. *See* **Branco** (L.F.) (madrigals), **Machado** (*Lusiads*), **Viana da Mota** (do.).

Campagnoli, Bartolomeo (b. Cento di Ferrara, 10. IX. 1751; d. Neustrelitz, 7. XI. 1827), It. violinist and comp. Pupil of Nardini; worked in It., Ger. and Paris; wrote concertos, sonatas, duets, etc. for vln.; fl. mus., Caprices for vla., etc.; also an important work on vln. playing, *Metodo per violino*.

Campane (It. plur.) = Bells.

Campanella, La, the 3rd of Liszt's *Études d exécution transcendante d'après Paganini* for pf., comp. in 1838, already used by him in 1831–2 for the *Grande Fantaisie de bravoure sur la Clochette*. The theme is that of the finale of Paganini's vln. concerto in B. min., Op. 7, a rondo in which harmonics are combined with a bell.

Campanelli (It. plur.) = Chime Bells, *Glockenspiel*.

Campanini, Cleofonte (b. Parma, 1. IX. 1860; d. Chicago, 19. XII. 1919), It. cond.

Made his 1st appearance at Parma in 1883 and the same year went to U.S.A., where he spent most of his life, apart from visits to It., Eng. and S. Amer. Cond. Manhattan Opera, N.Y., 1906–9; Chicago Opera Co., 1910–19. Married Eva Tetrazzini, the sister of Louisa T.

Campbell, Thomas (1777–1844), Scot., poet. *See* MacCunn (*Lord Ullin's Daughter*).

Campenhout, François van (b. Brussels, 5. II. 1779; d. Brussels, 24. IV. 1848), Belg. tenor and comp. Sang in Belg., Hol. and Fr. until 1827. During the 1830 revolution he wrote the Belg. nat. anthem, *La Brabançonne*.

Works incl. operas *Grotius, Le Passepartout, L'Heureux Mensonge*; church mus.; choruses; songs, etc.

Campian (or Campion), **Thomas** (b. London, 12. II. 1567; d. London, 1. III. 1620). Eng. physician, poet and comp. Was sent to Cambridge in 1581 and being a lawyer at 1st entered Gray's Inn in 1586; (?) took part in the siege of Rouen in 1591 and soon afterwards practised medicine in London. He pub. a 1st collection of airs to the lute with Rosseter in 1601 and 4 more followed between *c.* 1613 and 1617, all the words of the songs being his own. In 1613 he pub. a book on counterpoint, and wrote the poetry for *Songs of Mourning* on the death of Prince Henry, set by John Cooper. He also pub. poems and a book on poetry. His poem *Neptune's Empire* was comp. for chorus and orch. by Ernest Walker. Poems set as songs by Wm. Busch.

Works incl. 5 books of airs to the lute (over 100) and 3 separate earlier songs; songs for the prod. of 4 masques, 1607–13, incl. *The Mask of Flowers.*

Campioli (real name **Antonio Gualandi**) (b. Germany, ?; d. ?), It. castrato alto. Made his operatic début in Berlin, 1708, and sang in Handel's operas in London, 1731–2.

Campion, Thomas. *See* **Campian.**

Campioni, Carlo Antonio (b. Leghorn, *c.* 1720; d. Florence, 1793), It. comp. In the service of the Grand Duke of Tuscany at Florence and the King of Sardinia.

Comp. a Requiem and other church mus., trio sonatas, duets for 2 vlns. and for vln. and cello; keyboard mus., etc.

Campo, Conrado del (b. Madrid, 28. X. 1876; d. Madrid, 16. III. 1953), Span. comp. Student and later prof. at the Madrid Cons.

Works incl. operas *Dies irae, Los amantes de Verona* (*Romeo and Juliet*), *El final de Don Alvaro, La flor del agua* and (with Barrios) *El Avapiés*; choral works *La dama de Amboto* and *La divina commedia* (after Dante); symph. poems *Ante las ruinas* and *Granada y Galicia*; 8 string 4tets; vln. and pf. sonata; *Paisajes de Granada* for pf.; songs, etc.

Camporese, Violante (b. Rome, 1785; d. Rome, 1839), It. soprano. Sang in Paris and Milan before she made her 1st stage appearance in London, in 1817.

Campra, André (b. Aix-en-Provence, XII. 1660; d. Versailles, 29. VI. 1744), Fr. comp. of It. descent. He held var. provincial organist's posts and settled in Paris in 1694, when he was app. mus. director at Notre-Dame, where his motets soon attracted large congregations; but he became equally famous as a stage comp.

Works incl. operas and opera-ballets *L'Europe galante, Le Carnaval de Venise, Hésione, Tancrède, Iphigénie en Tauride* (with Desmarets), *Alcine, Hippodamie, Les Festes vénitiennes, Idoménée, Le Jaloux trompé, Achille et Déidamie*, etc.; pasticcios *Fragments de Lully* and *Télémaque* (the latter with pieces by Charpentier, Colasse, Desmarets, Marais and Rebel sen.); entertainments *Amaryllis, Les Festes de Corinthe, Le Génie de la Bourgogne, Les Noces de Vénus*, etc.; a Mass, cantatas, motets and psalms.

Canadian Composers. *See* Lavallée, Willan.

Canary (Eng.), also Canarie or Canaries, a dance in quick triple time with a dotted rhythm, now obs., poss. originating from the Canary Islands.

Cancan, a dance of a rather disreputable nature fashionable in Paris from *c.* the

CANCRIZANS   Scheidt

middle of the 19th cent. It is in very animated 2–4 time.

Cancel (Amer.) = Natural, ♮.

Canción (Span.) = Song.

Cancionero (Span.), a song-book.

Cancrizans (from Lat. *cancer* = crab) = crab-wise, a term used for the device of repeating a mus. phrase or theme backwards, note for note. 'Canon cancrizans' is a canon in which one part or more proceed normally while another one or more go backwards (*see* illustration previous page).

Candeille, Amélie-Julie (b. Paris, 31. VII. 1767; d. Paris, 4. II. 1834), Fr. actress, singer, pianist and comp. Made her début as a singer at the Paris Opéra in 1782, but left to become an actress. 10 years later sang in her 1st opera, for which she had written both words and mus.

Works incl. operas *La Belle Fermière*, *Bathilde ou le Duc* and *Ida ou l'Orpheline*; chamber mus.; piano mus.; songs, etc.

Candeille, Pierre Joseph (b. Estaires, 8. XII. 1744; d. Chantilly, 24. IV. 1827), Fr. singer and comp., father of prec.

heim, XII. 1731; d. Frankfurt, 20. I. 1798), Ger. violinist, cond. and comp. Pupil of Stamitz in Mannheim and Jommelli in Rome, became *Konzertmeister* of the Mannheim orch. in 1758 and director of instrumental mus. in 1774. From 1778 he worked in Munich. His cond. was admired by Mozart, who taught his daughter Rosa C. in 1777 and wrote a pf. sonata for her.

Works incl. operas, ballets, symphs., chamber mus., etc.

Cannon, Philip (b. Paris, 21. XII. 1929), Eng. comp. Studied with Imogen Holst and later at the R.C.M. with Gordon Jacob (comp.) and Pierre Tas (vln.). This was followed by some study with Hindemith. After a period of lecturing at Sydney Univ. he returned to the R.C.M. in 1952.

Works incl. 2 string 4tets and other chamber mus., vocal and choral mus., and pf. comps.

Canon (Gk. *kanōn* = rule), a polyphonic comp., or section of a comp., in which one part is imitated by one or more others which enter successively, so that the entries overlap (*see* illustration (*a*)).

Clementi, *Piano Sonata in G Major*

CANON

Wrote operas, incl. *Castor et Pollux*, ballets, pantomime, incid. mus., etc.

Candia, Cavaliere di. *See* **Mario.**

Canis, Corneille (Cornelis de Hond) (b. ? Antwerp, ?; d. Ghent, *c.* 1556), Flem. comp. Choirmaster of Charles V's imp.

If the imitation is exact the C. is termed 'strict'; if it is modified by the addition or omission of accidentals it is 'free as to intervals'. A C. may proceed (1) by inversion, with one part going up where the other goes down and *vice versa* (*see* illustration

Purcell, *Sonata No. 6*

CANON

chapel in the Netherlands from 1548, later chaplain to the Emperor Ferdinand in Prague. Wrote church mus., *chansons*, etc.

Cannabich, (Johann) Christian (b. Mann-

(*c*)); (2) by augmentation, with one part in notes, twice or more the length of the other (*see* illustration (*b*)); (3) by diminution, with one part in notes half or less the length of the other; (4) by retrograde motion (*canon cancrizans*), with one part going backwards while the other goes forward. Var. combinations of these forms are also possible. A C. may be accomp. by one or more independent parts. Two or more C.s can occur simultaneously.

Stanford (lib. by Gilbert Arthur à Beckett, after Chaucer), prod. London, Drury Lane Theatre, 28. IV. 1884. *See also* **Dyson, Koven.**

Cantigas (Span. = canticles), Span. sacred songs for a single voice of the 13th cent., mostly in honour of the Virgin Mary, allied in form to the Fr. Virelai and the It. Lauda.

CANON   Clementi

Cantabile (It. = song-like, songful, singable). The direction is usually placed against phrases in instrumental rather than vocal mus., where the comp. desires an expressive delivery.

Cantata (It. = a sung piece). The definition has become narrowed in modern times to short vocal works, sacred or secular and for single voices or chorus, with instrumental accompaniment.

Cantatore (It.) = male singer.

Cantatrice (Fr. and It.) = female singer.

Cante flamenco (Span. lit. 'flamingo song' or 'Flem. song'), a form of *cante hondo* modernized in the 19th cent. by the gypsies in a rather debased form.

Cante hondo (or jondo) (Span. lit. 'deep song'), a traditional form of Andalusian song with guitar accomp., ornate in melody, using intervals smaller than the semitone on some notes and expressing moods of dejection, misery or even tragedy.

Cantelli, Guido (b. Novara, 27. IV. 1920; d. Paris, 24. XI. 1956), It. cond. Studied at the Milan Cons. and, after escaping from a Ger. prison camp and a Fascist prison hospital, began to cond. concerts with the Scala orch. in Milan. He then quickly made his way in It. and abroad as a cond. whose gifts were second only to Toscanini's. He was killed in an air accident.

Canteloube de Malaret, (Marie) Joseph (b. Annonay, Ardèche, 21. X. 1879; d. Paris, 4. XI. 1957), Fr. comp. Studied with d'Indy at the Schola Cantorum in Paris. In 1900 he began to collect and study Fr. folksong, particularly of Auvergne, of which he pub. several collections. Lecturer on Fr. mus. and folksong from 1923.

Works incl. operas *Le Mas* and *Vercingétorix*; symph. poems *Vers la princesse lointaine* and *Lauriers*; *Pièces françaises* for pf. and orch.; *Poème* for vln. and orch.; *Dans la montagne* for vln. and pf.; songs with orch. and with pf., etc.

Canterbury Pilgrims, The, opera by

Cantilena (It.) = a sustained, flowing melodic line, esp. when sung *legato* or played in the manner of such singing.

Cantillation, chanting in unison in the Jewish synagogue service.

Cantino (It.), the E string of the vln.

Cantiones Sacrae (Lat. = Sacred Songs), a title often given to collections of Lat. motets in the 16th and 17th cents.

Canto (It. = song), in instrumental as much as in vocal mus. usually the part of a comp. which has the chief melody. The direction *marcato il canto* indicates that such a melody is to be emphasized.

Canto carnascialesco (It. carnivalesque song), a Florentine part-song of the 15th–16th cents. with secular, often ribald, words, sung in carnival processions, with the tune in the tenor part.

Canto fermo (It.). *See* **Cantus firmus.**

Cantor (Lat. = singer), a church singer, esp. the leader or director of a church choir in a Lutheran church (e.g. Bach at Leipzig) or a synagogue.

Cantoris. In Eng. cathedrals and in churches where the choir is divided, the C. side is that on the north of the chancel, near the stall of the cantor or precentor, the other being the *Decani* side.

Cantus firmus (Lat. lit. 'fixed song'), a pre-existing melody chosen by a comp. to envelop in contrapuntal parts of his own, either for exercise or for the prod. of a comp. In old Masses popular tunes were commonly used in this way, being sung in long notes in the tenor part.

Canzone (It. = song, ballad). (1) A part-song in the style of a madrigal but lighter in character and less elaborately polyphonic.

(2) An instrumental piece in a polyphonic style, orig. *canzone francese*.

Canzonet (from It. *canzonetta* = little song), light songs written in Eng. round about 1600, either for several voices with or without insts. or for a single voice with lute accomp. Later simply a song in Eng., e.g. Haydn's Eng. C.s.

Canzonetta (It. = little song), often synonymous with Canzone in 16th–17th-cent. It.; later a light song or short and simple air in an opera, etc.

Çanzoniere (It.), a song-book.

Čapek, Karel (1890–1938), Cz. novelist and dramatist. *See* **Austin (F.)** (*Insect Play*), **Makropoulos Case** (Janáček).

Capella, Martianus (b. Madaura, N. Africa, ?; d. ?), 4th–5th-cent. philosopher. His *De musica* is the ninth and last book of his *De nuptiis Mercurii et Philologiae*. His treatise, deriving in part from Varro and Quintilian, had considerable influence on later medieval theorists.

Capell, Richard (b. Northampton, 23. III. 1885; d. London, 21. VI. 1954), Eng. critic. His career of mus. critic to the *Daily Mail* in London was interrupted by the 1914–18 war, in which he served and received the Military Medal. In 1933 he became chief mus. critic of the *Daily Telegraph*. On the outbreak of World War II in 1939 he volunteered to serve as correspondent, 1st in Fr., later in N. Africa and Greece. O.B.E., 1946. He wrote a book on Schubert's songs and trans. songs by var. comps. and R. Strauss's *Friedenstag*.

Capet, Lucien (b. Paris, 8. I. 1873: d. Paris, 18. XII, 1928), Fr. violinist and comp. Studied at the Paris Cons. Formed a string 4tet in 1893. He left vln., chamber and other mus.

Caplet, André (b. Le Havre, 23. XI. 1878; d. Paris, 22. IV. 1925), Fr. cond. and comp., much influenced by Debussy, of several of whose works he completed the orch.

Works incl. symph. study *Le Masque de la Mort rouge* (after Poe); *Épiphanie* for cello and orch.; Mass for unaccomp. voices; *Le Miroir de Jésus* for voices, string 5tet and harp; *Le Pie Jésus* for voice and org.; *Suite persane* for 10 wind instruments; *Conte fantastique* (after Poe) for harp and string 4tet; *Sonata da chiesa* for vln. and org.; children's suite for pf. duet; song cycles *Prières*, *La Croix douloureuse*, *3 Fables de La Fontaine*, *5 Ballades françaises*, etc.

Capocci, Filippo (b. Rome, 11. V. 1840; d. Rome, 25. VII. 1911), It. organist and comp. Studied under his father, whom he succeeded as master of the Lateran Chapel in Rome, 1898. Wrote 6 sonatas and much other mus. for the org.

Capocci, Gaetano (b. Rome, 16. X. 1811; d. Rome, 11. I. 1898), It. organist and comp., father of prec. After var. studies and appts. he became master of the Lateran Chapel in 1855. Wrote Masses, motets, psalms and other church mus.

Capotasto (It. = master fret), a device on fretted string instruments by which the strings can be all simultaneously shortened without retuning, so that a piece can be played in a different key and the instrument becomes temporarily a transposing one.

Capriccio (It. = whim), a name given to var. types of comp. at different times: in the 17th & 18th cent. to animated pieces in a fugal style, but not strictly fugues in form; by Bach to a harpsichord piece in several movements on the departure of his brother Johann Jakob; c. from the middle of the 18th cent. to studies for the vln. (e.g. Paganini's); later still to fantasies for pf. on well-known themes; last of all to short pieces in a humorous or whimsical manner.

Capriccio, opera by R. Strauss (lib. by Clemens Krauss and the comp.), prod. Munich, State Opera, 28. X. 1942.

Capriccio espagnol (*Span. C.*), orchestral work by Rimsky-Korsakov, written as a display piece for the St. Petersburg Orch., finished 4. VIII. and perf. St. Petersburg, 17. XII. 1887. It contains brilliant solo parts for most of the principal instruments and for the brass in groups. It was orig. intended to be for vln. and orch., a companion-piece to Rimsky-Korsakov's *Rus. Fantasy*.

Capriccio italien (*It. C.*), orchestral work by Tchaikovsky, comp. during a visit to Rome in 1880 and 1st perf. Moscow, 18. XII.

Caproli (or **Caprioli**), **Carlo** (b. ?; d. ?), It. 17th-cent. violinist and comp. Was brought to Paris by Cardinal Mazarin and prod. the opera *Le nozze di Peleo e Teti* there in 1654. He wrote the oratorio *Davidde prevaricante* in 1683.

Capuleti ed i Montecchi, I (*The Capulets and Montagues*), opera by Bellini (lib. by Felice Romani, based on Shakespeare's *Romeo and Juliet*), prod. Venice, Teatro La Fenice, 11. III. 1830.

Cara, Marchetto (b. Verona, ?; d. ? Mantua, after 1525), It. lutenist and comp. In service at the ducal court of Mantua, 1495–1525. Wrote *frottole* and other songs.

Caractacus, cantata for solo voices, chorus and orch. by Elgar, Op. 35 (lib. by H. A. Acworth), comp. in 1898 and prod. Leeds Festival, 1899.

Mus. by Arne for a dramatic poem by William Mason (pub. 1759), perf. London, Covent Garden Theatre, 6. XII. 1776.

Caradori-Allan (*née* **de Munck**), **Maria** (**Caterina Rosalbina**) (b. Milan, 1800; d. Surbiton, Surrey, 15. X. 1865). It.-Alsat. soprano. Was taught mus. entirely by her mother, whose name she took, and after a tour in Fr. and Ger. made her 1st stage appearance in London in 1822. She married in Eng. and appeared also at concerts and festivals, incl. the 1st perf. of Mendelssohn's *Elijah* in 1846.

Carafa (di Colobrano), Michele Enrico (b. Naples, 17. XI. 1787; d. Paris, 26. VII. 1872), It. comp. On the failure of his 1st opera he enlisted in the bodyguard of Murat, then king of Naples, took part in the Rus. campaign in 1812 and was decorated by Napoleon, after whose fall he returned to mus. He prod. operas not only in It. but in

Vienna and Paris, where he settled in 1827 and became very popular. Prof. of comp. at the Paris Cons., 1840–58.

Works incl. *c.* 35 operas, e.g. *Il fantasma, Il vascello d' occidente, Gabriella di Vergy, Ifigenia, Berenice, Le Solitaire, La Violette, La Fiancée de Lammermoor* and *Elisabetta in Derbyshire* (after Scott), *Masaniello* (competing with Auber's *Muette de Portici*), *La Prison d' Édimbourg* (after Scott's *Heart of Midlothian*), *Jeanne d' Arc* (after Schiller), etc.

Cardew, Cornelius (b. Winchcombe, Glos., 1936), Eng. comp. and pianist. Studied at the R.A.M. with, among others, Howard Ferguson (comp.). In 1958 he went to Cologne to study electronic mus., also working with Stockhausen until 1960. C. belongs to the *avant-garde* school whose ideas are much influenced by Cage. His works have been widely perf. in Europe.

Works incl. *Octet 1959*; *Autumn 60* for orch.; *A Bun* for orch.; pf. mus., etc.

Cardillac, opera by Hindemith (lib. by Ferdinand Lion, based on E. T. A. Hoffmann's story *Das Fräulein von Scudéri*), prod. Dresden, 9. XI. 1926.

Cardoso, Manuel (b. Fronteira nr. Estremoz, III. 1571; d. Lisbon, 24. XI. 1650), Port. monk, organist and comp. Studied at the seminary of Evora and became choirmaster at the cathedral there. Joined the Carmelite monastery at Lisbon in 1588 and became its mus. director.

Works incl. Masses, motets, Magnificats and other church mus.

Carducci, Giosuè (1836–1907), It. poet. See **Pratella** (*Chiesa di Polenta*).

Cardus, Neville (b. Manchester, 2. IV. 1889), Eng. critic. Began to write for the *Daily Citizen* at Manchester in 1913 and in 1917 joined the *Manchester Guardian* as asst. critic to Samuel Langford, whom he succeeded in 1927. He wrote on cricket as well as mus., but not on the latter in London until 1931, ed. Langford's writings and pub. a book on *Ten Composers* as well as several on cricket. In 1939–47 he lived in Australia. In 1948 he settled in London.

Carestini, Giovanni (b. Ancona, *c.* 1705; d. ?, *c.* 1760), It. castrato alto. 1st appeared in Rome, 1721, and sang in Handel's operas in London, 1733–5.

Carew, Thomas (?1598–?1639), Eng. poet. *See* **Georges** (songs).

Carey, Henry (b. ?, *c.* 1687; d. London, 4. X. 1743), Eng. poet, comp. and dramatist. Pupil of Roseingrave and Geminiani. Wrote libs. for Lampe's operas *The Dragon of Wantley, Margery* and *Amelia*; also both words and mus. of *Sally in our alley* (though this is now commonly sung to a traditional tune). The attribution of *God save the King* to him is unfounded.

Comps. incl. cantatas and songs to his own words; ballad operas *The Contrivances,*

A Wonder or the Honest Yorkshireman, Nancy, or the Parting Lovers, etc.; songs for Vanbrugh and Cibber's *The Provok'd Husband,* etc.

Carillon, a set of bells hung in a church steeple or specially built tower, controlled by a keyboard below and played like an org. on manuals and pedals. C.s are found partic. in the Netherlands. Also an org. stop controlling steel bars, gongs or bells.

Carissimi, Giacomo (b. Marino nr. Rome, IV. 1605; d. Rome, 12. I. 1674), It. comp. *Maestro di cappella* at Assisi in 1628–9; then went to Rome, where he held a similar post at the church of Sant' Apollinare attached to the Ger. Coll. He cultivated the oratorio and cantata in their early stages.

Works incl. Masses, motets; *Lauda Sion* and *Nisi Dominus* for 8 voices; oratorios *History of Job, Baltazar, Abraham and Isaac, Jephtha, The Last Judgment, Jonah*; sacred cantatas; vocal duets, etc.

Carl Rosa Opera Company, The Royal, founded by Carl Rosa in 1873 for the perf. of opera in Eng.

Carlton, Nicholas (I) (b. ?; d. ?), Eng. 16th-cent. comp. Two keyboard works are in the Mulliner Book.

Carlton, Nicholas (II) (b. ?; d. Beoley, Worcs., 1630), Eng. comp. and friend of Thomas Tomkins. A few keyboard works survive, one of which is an *In nomine* for keyboard duet (four hands at one keyboard).

Carlton, Richard (b. ?, *c.* 1558; d. ?, *c.* 1638), Eng. comp. Educ. at Cambridge; became vicar at St. Stephen's Church, Norwich, and min. canon at the cathedral. Pub. a book of madrigals in 1601 and contrib. to *The Triumphes of Oriana.*

Carmen, opera by Bizet (lib. by Henri Meilhac and Ludovic Halévy, based on the story by Mérimée), prod. Paris, Opéra-Comique, 3. III. 1875.

Carmen, Johannes (b. ?; d. ?), ? Fr. 15th-cent. comp. (whose name is known only in its Lat. form). Wrote motets, etc.

Carmen Sylva (Queen Elizabeth of Rum.) (1843–1916), Rum. poet of Ger. birth. *See* Hallström (*Neaga*), **Otesco** (*Ilderim*), **Sommer** (*Sappho*).

Carmina Burana, a 13th-cent. collection of Lat. poems and other material, of Bavarian origin. Some of the poems have been provided with mus., but the notation is in neumes which cannot be read except by comparing them with other MSS.

A setting of the poems by Carl Orff for chorus, orch. and soloists (1937), 1st perf. 8. VI. 1937, Frankfurt.

Carnaval (Schumann). *See* **Carnival.**

Carnaval des animaux, Le (*The Animals' Carnival*), suite ('grand zoological fantasy') by Saint-Saëns for chamber orch. with 2 pfs., privately perf. and not intended by the comp. to be pub. It contains a number of humorous mus. allusions (*see* **Quotations**).

Carnaval romain, Le (*The Roman Carnival*), concert overture by Berlioz, Op. 9, written in 1843 on material from the opera *Benvenuto Cellini* of 1834–8, and 1st perf., Paris, 3. II. 1844.

Carner, Mosco (b. Vienna, 15. XI. 1904), Eng. critic and cond. of Aus. origin. Studied at the New Vienna Cons. and musicology at the univ. under Adler, taking a Ph.D. degree there in 1928. He then became opera cond. in Vienna, Troppau and Danzig until 1933, when he settled in London, later becoming naturalized. He has worked as critic, mus. correspondent to foreign journals and cond. and has pub. books, incl. *A Study of 20th-cent. Harmony, Of Men and Music*, *Puccini, a Critical Biography*, chapters on Schubert, Dvořák, etc.

Carneyro, Claudio (b. Oporto, 27. I. 1895; d. Oporto, 18. X. 1963), Port. comp. Studied with Lucien Lambert at the Oporto Cons. and later with Widor in Paris. With several interruptions, incl. study with Dukas in Paris in 1935, he served as prof. of comp. at the Oporto Cons.

Works incl. ballet *Nau Catrineta*; choral, orchestral and chamber-orch. comps.; 2 string 4tets, pf. trio, pf. 4tet; vln. and pf. sonata, pf. mus.; songs, etc.

Carnicer, Ramón (b. Tárrega nr. Lérida, 24. X. 1789; d. Madrid, 17. III. 1855), Span. comp. Choir-boy at Urgel Cathedral, later went to Barcelona and in 1808 fled to Minorca when Spain was invaded by Fr. Later managed the It. opera at Barcelona and wrote It. works for it, into which he intro. Span. songs. In 1827 he was called by royal command to dir. the opera at Madrid.

Works incl. operas *Adele di Lusignano*, *Elena e Constantino*, *Don Giovanni Tenorio, ossia Il convitato di pietra*, *Elena e Malvina*, *Cristoforo Colombo*, *Eufemio di Messina*, *Ismalia*; *Missa solemnis*, 2 Requiems; symphs., etc.

Carnival.(1) Concert overture by Dvořák, Op. 92, comp. 1891 and forming, with *Amid Nature* and *Othello*, a cycle with thematic connections orig. called *Nature, Life and Love.*

(2) Suite of pf. pieces on the notes A. S. (Ger. Es = E♭; also As = A♭) C. H. (Ger. = B♮) by Schumann, Op. 9, the letters representing the only mus. ones in Schumann's surname and the town of Asch in Bohemia, the home of Ernestine von Fricken, with whom he was in love in 1834–5, when he wrote the work. She is alluded to in the piece entitled *Estrella*; other persons referred to are Clara Wieck in *Chiarina*, Chopin and Paganini under their own names, and Schumann himself in his 2 different imaginary characters of *Florestan* and *Eusebius.*

(3) Ballet on Schumann's mus., orch. by Glazunov and others (choreography by Mikhail Mikhailovich Fokin), prod. Paris, Opéra, 4. VI. 1910.

Carol, orig. a round dance from Fr. (*carole*), in which the participants sang a burden (formally a separate refrain) while dancing in a circle, alternating with stanzas sung by the leader while they remained still. In 15th-cent. Eng. it lost its orig. dance associations and became a polyphonic form, still charact. by the alternation of stanzas and burden, but frequently with a sacred text. It was only after the Reformation that the word lost its specifically formal connotation and became primarily a Christmas song, though even today common usage admits the possibility of secular carols and carols celebrating seasons other than Christmas.

Caron, Philippe (b. ?; d. ?), Fr. or Flem. 15th-cent. comp., ? pupil of Binchois and Dufay; ? chorister at Cambrai Cathedral. Wrote Masses and other church mus., *chansons*, etc.

Caron (*née* Meuniez), **Rose-Lucile** (b. Monerville, Seine-et-Oise, 17. XI. 1857; d. Paris. 9. IV. 1930), Fr. soprano. Studied at the Paris Cons. where she became prof. of singing in 1902. Made her 1st stage appearance at Brussels in 1884.

Caroubel, Pierre-Francisque (b. ?; d. Paris, before 1619), Fr. violinist and comp., in the service of Henri III of Anjou from 1576. He wrote and harmonized numerous dance-tunes, including 78 from *Terpsichore musarum* by Michael Praetorius (1612).

Carpani, Giuseppe (Antonio) (b. Villalbese, nr. Como, 28. I. 1752; d. Vienna, 22. I. 1825), It. poet and writer on mus. Settled in Vienna. Friend and biog. of Haydn.

Carpenter, Edward (1844–1929), Eng. poet. *See* Boughton (*Midnight*).

Carpenter, John Alden (b. Chicago, 28. II. 1876; d. Chicago, 26. IV. 1951), Amer. comp. Learnt mus. privately and studied with Paine while a student at Harvard Univ., and with Elgar in Rome in 1895, later at Chicago with Bernard Ziehn. Although a business man, he comp. much.

Works incl. ballets *Krazy-Kat*, *Skyscrapers* and *The Birthday of the Infanta* (after Wilde); *Song of Faith* for chorus and orch.; symph., *Adventures in a Perambulator* and *Sea Drift* (after Whitman) for orch.; concertino for pf. and orch., vln. concerto; string 4tet, pf. 5tet; many songs incl. *Gitanjali* cycle (Tagore).

Carpentras. *See* Genet.

Carreño, Teresa (b. Caracas, 22. XII. 1853; d. N.Y., 12. VI. 1917), Venez. pianist. Studied in N.Y. and Paris, later under A. Rubinstein; made her 1st public appearance in N.Y. aged 9, later became an opera singer for a time, reappearing as pianist in

1889. She married Émile Saurat in 1872; later Giovanni Tagliapietra, d'Albert and her second husband's brother; cond. opera in Venez.

Carrillo, Julián (b. San Luis Potosi, 28. I. 1875; d. Mexico City, 9. IX. 1965), Mex. comp. Studied at the Nat. Cons. at Mex. City, gained a vln. prize and made further studies at the Leipzig and Ghent Conss. Returning to Mex. in 905, he was active as violinist and cond. as well as comp. He experimented in his later works with mus. sing small fractional divisions of the scale.
Works incl. operas *Mathilda*, *Ossian*, *Xulitl* and *Mexico in 1810*; 2 Masses, Requiem; 6 symphs., 3 suites, overture *8 de Septiembre*, symph. poem *Xochimilco* for orch.; Fantasy for pf. and orch., concerto for fl., vln. and cello; 4 string 4tets, pf. 5tet, string 6tet; 4 vln. and pf. sonatas; *c.* 40 works in fractional scales, incl. *Ave Maria* for chorus, *Fantasía Sonido 13* for chamber orch., *Preludio a Cristobál Colón* for soprano, fl., vln. and guitar, etc.

Carroll, Lewis (Charles Lutwidge Dodgson) (1832–98), Eng. mathematician and children's author. *See* Head (*Jabberwocky*), **Kelley** (*Alice in Wonderland*), **Taylor** (Deems) (*Through the Looking-Glass*).

Carrosse du Saint-Sacrement, Le (*The Coach of the Holy Sacrament*), opera by Lord Berners (lib. from Mérimée's play), prod. Paris, Théâtre des Champs-Élysées, 24. IV. 1924.

Carse, Adam (b. Newcastle-on-Tyne, 19. V. 1878; d. Gt. Missenden, 2. XI. 1958), Eng. mus. scholar and comp. Studied in Ger. and at the R.A.M. Asst. mus. master at Winchester Coll., 1909–22 and prof. at the R.A.M. from 1923. He made a special study of instruments and orch.
Works incl. ballad *Judas Iscariot's Paradise* for baritone, chorus and orch., cantata *The Lay of the Brown Rosary* (E. B. Browning); variations on *Barbara Allen* for string orch. and other small orchestral works; *Norw. Fantasy* for vln. and orch.; instrumental pieces; songs, etc.

Cartan, Jean (Louis) (b. Nancy, 1. XII. 1906; d. Bligny, 26. III. 1932), Fr. comp. Studied at the Paris Cons., where his comp. master was Dukas.
Works incl. cantata *Pater* for solo voices, chorus and orch., *Hymne à Dante* for chorus and orch.; 2 string 4tets, *Introduction and Allegro* for wind instruments and pf., sonatina for fl. and clar.; Psalm xxii for voice and pf. and other songs incl. *Trois Chants d'été* and settings of poems by Tristan Klingsor, Villon and Mallarmé, etc.

Carter, Charles Thomas (b. Dublin, *c.* 1735; d. London, 12. X. 1804), Ir. comp. Choir-boy at Christ Church Cathedral, Dublin, and organist at St. Werburgh's

Church there, 1751–69. He became very popular as a song-writer and settled in London in 1770. Prod. a comic opera, *Just in Time*, in 1792 and wrote lighter stage pieces, etc.

Carter, Elliot (b. N.Y., 11. XII. 1908), Amer. comp. Educ. at Harvard Univ., where he studied mus. with Piston; later a pupil of Nadia Boulanger in Paris. From 1960 to 1962 he was prof. of comp. at Yale Univ. and in 1960 was awarded the Pulitzer Prize.
Works incl. 2 ballets; incid. mus.; oratorio *The Bridge* and other choral works; symph.; concerto for Eng. horn; concerto for pf. and harpsichord; 2 string 4tets; sonata for fl. and pf., etc.

Cartier, Antoine (b. ?; d. Paris, after 1580), Fr. comp., organist of Saint-Séverin, Paris, from 1558. His surviving works consist entirely of *chansons* for 3 and 4 voices.

Cartier, Jean-Baptiste (b. Avignon, 28. V. 1765; d. Paris, 1841), Fr. violinist and comp. Pupil of Viotti; held posts at court before and after the Revolution, during which he played in the Opéra orch. Comp. 2 operas, 2 symphs., vln. mus. and other works.

Cartwright, William (1611–43), Eng. playwright. *See* Lawes (H.).

Caruso, Enrico (b. Naples, 25. II. 1873; d. Naples, 2. VIII. 1921), It. tenor. Made his 1st public appearance at Naples in 1894 and began to become famous when he sang in the prod. of Giordano's *Fedra* at Milan in 1899. He 1st sang in London, with Melba, in 1902, and in Amer. in 1903.

Caruso, Luigi (b. Naples, 25. IX. 1754; d. Perugia, 1822), It. comp. Pupil of Sala at Naples. *Maestro di cappella* at Perugia Cathedral from 1790. Comp. nearly 60 operas, Masses, oratorios, cantatas, etc.

Carvalho, João de Sousa (b. Estremoz, 22. II. 1745; d. ? Borba, 1798), Port. comp. Studied at Naples; taught at Lisbon on his return.
Works incl. 15 It. operas, e.g. *Perseo*, *Testoride Argonauta*, *Penelope*, *L'Endimione*; Masses and other church mus. with orch.; harpsichord sonatas, etc.

Carvalho, Marie (Caroline Félix Miolan-) (b. Marseilles, 31. XII. 1827; d. Puys, 10. VII. 1895), Fr. soprano. Studied under her father and at the Paris Cons.; 1st appeared in 1849 and was engaged by the Opéra-Comique in 1850. There she married in 1853 Léon Carvalho (1825–97), who later became manager of that theatre.

Carver, Robert (b. ? 1487; d. after 1546), Scot. monk and comp. Canon of Scone Abbey.
Works incl. Masses (1 in 10 parts), motets (1 in 19 parts) and other church mus.

Cary, Annie Louise (b. Wayne, Me., 22. X. 1842; d. Norwalk, Conn., 3. IV. 1921), Amer. contralto. Studied at Milan

107

and later with Pauline Viardot. Made her début in Copenhagen. Made her 1st appearance in London and the 1st important one in U.S.A. in 1870.

Caryll, Ivan (actually Félix Tilkin) (b. Liège, 1861; d. N.Y., 28. XI. 1921), Belg.-Amer. comp. Studied at the Liège Cons. Works incl. operettas *The Duchess of Dantzig, The Earl and the Girl, Our Miss Gibbs*, etc.

Casadesus, Robert Marcel (b. Paris, 7. IV. 1899), Fr. pianist and comp. Coming from a very mus. family, he showed precocious ability. He studied at the Paris Cons., where he won prizes in 1913, 1919, 1921. He began his career as a concert pianist in 1922, and on the outbreak of World War II went to the U.S.A., where he taught and lectured at Princeton Univ. From 1935 he was prof. at the Amer. Cons. at Fontainebleau, of which he became director in 1945. He has comp. much for the pf., and is also a noted exponent of Fr. pf. mus.

Casal Chapí, Enrique (b. Madrid, 15. I. 1909), Span. comp., grandson of Chapí. Self-taught at first, he entered the Madrid Cons. in 1928, studying comp. under Conrado del Campo. Cond. at the Teatro Escuela de Arte in Madrid from 1933 to 1937. Now lives in Uruguay.

Works incl. incid. mus. to plays by Lope de Vega, Calderón, Georg Kaiser, etc.; *Fantasía sinfónica, Final para una sinfonía imaginaria* and other works for orch.; songs with orch.; pf. works, etc.

Casali, Giovanni Battista (b. Rome, *c.* 1715; d. Rome, 6. VII. 1792), It. comp. *Maestro di cappella* of St. John Lateran, 1759–92. Wrote much church mus.; also operas, e.g. *Candaspe* and *Antigona*; oratorios, e.g. *Santa Firmina, La Benedizione di Giacobbe*; etc.

Casals, Pau (b. Vendrell, 29. XII. 1876), Catalan cellist, cond. and comp. He studied at the Madrid Cons. and first appeared as a soloist in Paris in 1898. In 1905 he joined the pf. trio founded by Cortot. In 1919 he founded the Orquesta Pau Casals in Barcelona. After the Spanish Civil War he left Catalonia and made his home at Prades, in the Fr. Pyrenees, where he held an annual festival from 1950. He now lives in Puerto Rico. His first wife was the Port. cellist Guilhermina Suggia.

Works incl. oratorios *La Visión de Fray Martín* and *El Pesebre*; church mus.; works for cello and pf., vln. and pf., etc.

Casanova, opera by Rózicky (lib., in Pol., by Juliusz Krzewinski), prod. Warsaw, 3. VI. 1923.

Casanova, André (b. Paris, 12. X. 1919), Fr. comp. Studied the 12-note technique with Leibowitz. Works incl. trio for fl., vla. and horn, pf. pieces, songs, etc.

Casanova (de Seingalt), Giovanni Jacopo (1725–98), It. adventurer and author, son of

an opera singer (Giovanna C.), author and trans. of some libs., acquainted with many singers and comps., friend of Lorenzo da Ponte, etc. *See* **Abenteuer des Casanova** (Andreae), **Casanova** (Rózycky), **Pick-Mangiagalli** (ballet).

Cascia, Giovanni da (Giovanni da Firenze) (b. ?; d. ?), one of the earlier 14th-cent. It. madrigal comps.

Casella, Alfredo (b. Turin, 25. VII. 1883; d. Rome, 5. III. 1947), It. comp. Was sent to the Paris Cons. in 1896 to study pf. under Diémer and comp. under Fauré. He lived there until the 1914–18 war, when he went to Rome and taught pf. at the Accademia di Santa Cecilia. In 1924 he founded, with d'Annunzio and Malipiero, an assoc. for the propagation of modern It. mus.

Works incl. operas *La donna serpente* (after Gozzi), *La favola d' Orfeo, Il deserto tentato*; ballets *Il convento veneziano* and *La giara* (after Pirandello); 3 symphs., suite *Italia, Elegia eroica, Pagine di guerra, Introduzione, aria e toccata, Concerto* for orch.; *A notte alta, Partita* and *Scarlattiana* for pf. and orch.; concertos for vln., cello, org. and orch.; *Notte di maggio* for voice and orch.; concerto and 5 pieces for string 4tet and other chamber mus.; cello and pf. sonata; many pf. works incl. sonatina and *Sinfonia, arioso e toccata*; 2 suites for pf. duet; numerous songs, etc.

Caserta, Antonello da (b. ?; d. ?), 15th-cent. It. comp. of madrigals and *ballate*; a Filippo da C. is also mentioned in the MSS.

Casimiri, Rafaele (Casimiro) (b. Gualdo Tadino, Umbria, 3. XI. 1880; d. Rome, 15. IV. 1943), It. musicologist, cond. and comp. Studied at Padua and in 1899 became master of the Schola Cantorum in Rome, and after var. appts. as choirmaster, master at the Lateran there. He wrote a book on Palestrina, ed. the journal *Note d'archivio* and comp. much church mus.

Cassa (It.) = Drum.

Cassadó, Gaspar (b. Barcelona, 30. IX. 1897; d. Madrid, 24. XII. 1966), Span. cellist, son of the comp. Joaquín C. He made his 1st public appearance aged 9, and later studied with, among others, Casals. He has also comp., mostly for strings and pf.

Cassandra, opera by Gnecchi (lib. by Luigi Illica), prod. Bologna, Teatro Comunale, 5. XII. 1905. In 1909 the It. critic Giovanni Tebaldini created a sensation by pointing out that R. Strauss's *Elektra*, which did not appear until that year, contained passages strikingly resembling Gnecchi's music.

Cassation, an 18th-cent. term, similar to divertimento and serenade, for a work in several movements suitable for open-air perf. The derivation of the word is uncertain.

Casse-Noisette (Tchaikovsky). *See* **Nutcracker.**

Cassiodorus, Flavius Magnus Aurelius (b. *c.* 487; d. *c.* 580). Rom. senator, ecclesiastical hist. and theologian. He wrote no specifically mus. work, but the mus. theory contained in his *Institutiones* (*c.* 560), deriving largely from Aristoxenus, caused him to be regarded, with Boethius and Isidore of Seville, as one of the three founding fathers of medieval mus. theory.

Castanets (from Span. *castañetas*), a perc. instrument, doubtless orig. made of chestnut wood (*castaña*), held between the fingers and made to strike against each other by motions of the hand. So used mainly by Span. dancers, but a simplified form is made for use in orchs. and bands.

Castel, Louis Bertrand (b. Montpellier, 11. XI. 1688; d. Paris, 11. I. 1757), Fr. scientist. He made a study of the relationships between the 7 notes of the mus. scale and the 7 colours of the spectrum, wrote on the subject and constructed a 'Clavecin oculaire'.

Castelnuovo-Tedesco, Mario (b. Florence, 3. IV. 1895; d. Hollywood, 16. III. 1968), It. comp. Studied at the Istituto Musicale Cherubini at Florence and later with Pizzetti. At the age of 15 he wrote *Cielo di settembre* for pf. (later orch.) and in 1925 he gained a prize for his opera *La Mandragola* (after Machiavelli). He settled in U.S.A. in 1939, at 1st at Larchmont, N.Y., and then at Los Angeles.

Works incl. operas *La Mandragola*, *Bacco in Toscana*, *Aucassin et Nicolette*, *The Merchant of Venice*, *All's Well that Ends Well* (both after Shakespeare), *The Importance of being Earnest* (after Wilde); 7 Shakespearian concert overtures: *The Taming of the Shrew*, *The Merchant of Venice*, *Twelfth Night*, *Julius Caesar*, *A Winter's Tale*, *A Midsummer Night's Dream*, *King John*; 2 pf. concertos, *Concerto italiano*, symph. variations and *The Prophets* for vln. and orch., concerto for cello and orch., concerto for guitar and orch.; concertino for harp and 7 instruments, string 4tet, pf. trio; *Sonata quasi una fantasia* and suite on themes by Donizetti for vln. and pf., cello and pf. sonata; 6 illustrations for Voltaire's *Candide* and other pf. pieces; settings of all the songs in Shakespeare's plays (in Eng.) for voice and pf., *Sonnets from the Portuguese* (Elizabeth Barrett Browning) and other songs, etc.

Castéra, René de (b. Dax, 3. IV. 1873; d. Angoumi nr. Dax, 9. X. 1955), Fr. comp. Pupil of d'Indy at the Schola Cantorum in Paris. In 1902 he founded the Édition Mutuelle for the pub. of works by pupils and assocs. of the Schola.

Works incl. ballet-pantomime *Nausicaa*; 2 choruses for Shakespeare's *As You Like It*; *Jour de fête au pays basque*

for orch.; concerto for fl., clar., cello and pf., pf. trio; pf. pieces; songs, etc.

Castiglioni, Niccolo (b. Milan, 17. VII. 1932), It. comp. and pianist. Studied with Ghedini at the Milan Cons. He has also pursued a career as a concert pianist. His music is eclectic in style, influenced by Debussy, Messiaen, Webern and Cage, and remarkable for its frequently delicate textures.

Works incl. *Impromptus I–IV* for orch.; *Rondels* for orch.; *Movimento continuato* for pf. and small ensemble; *Gymel* for fl. and pf.; *Inizio di movimento* for pf.; *A Solemn Music II* for soprano and chamber orch.

Castil-Blaze (François Henri Joseph Blaze) (b. Cavaillon, 1. XII. 1784; d. Paris, 11. XII. 1857), Fr. critic, comp., trans. of opera libs. and author of books on mus. Critic of the *Journal des Débats* before Berlioz.

Works incl. 3 operas, church mus. and chamber mus.

Castileti, Johann (Jean Guyot) (b. Chatelet nr. Liège, *c.* 1512; d. Liège, 8. III. 1588), Flem. comp. He comp. Masses, motets and *chansons*, and added a further 6 voices to Josquin's 6-part motet *Benedicta es caelorum regina*.

Castillo, Bernardo Clavijo del (b. ?; d. Madrid, 1. II. 1626), Span. organist and comp. Comp. motets and org. mus.

Castillon (de Saint-Victor, Marie) Alexis de, Vicomte (b. Chartres, 13. XII. 1838; d. Paris, 5. III. 1873), Fr. comp. After training for a military career at Saint-Cyr, he studied in Paris with Massé and Franck. He served in the war of 1870–1 and lost his health, but before his death served as the 1st secretary of the Société Nationale de Musique.

Works incl. a symph., *Esquisse symph.* and overture *Torquato Tasso* for orch.; pf. concerto; Psalm for solo voices, chorus and orch.; string 4tet, pf. 4tet, 2 pf. trios; vln. and pf. sonata; pf. works; songs, etc.

Castor et Pollux, opera by Rameau (lib. by Pierre Joseph Justin Bernard), prod. Paris, Opéra, 24. X. 1737.

Castore e Polluce (*Castor and Pollux*), opera by Vogler (lib. based on one by Carlo Innocenzio Frugoni), prod. Munich, 12. I. 1787. Weber wrote variations for pf. on an air from it, Op. 5.

Castrati (It.), male singers of the 17th and 18th cents., mainly but not exclusively in It., who were mutilated in boyhood to prevent the breaking of their voices and to supply male sopranos and contraltos to the churches and theatres of the time. They eventually became fashionable and made their greatest and most sensational successes on the operatic stage. The last famous castrato was Velluti (1781–1861).

Castro, Jean de (b. Evreux, ?; d. ?),

Fr. 16th-cent. comp. of Span. or Port. descent. Worked at Antwerp, Vienna, Cologne, etc. Wrote Masses, motets, madrigals, *chansons.*

Castro, José Maria (b. Avellaneda, Buenos Aires, 17. XI. 1892; d. Buenos Aires, 10. VIII. 1964), Arg. cond. and comp. Studied at Buenos Aires and joined his brother's 5tet as cellist, also became cond. of the Asociación del Profesorado Orquestal and was one of the founders of the Grupo Renovación of progressive musicians.

Works incl. ballet *Georgia;* concerto grosso and Overture for a Comic Opera for orch.; pf. concerto; *Sonata de primavera* for pf., etc.

Castro, Juan (José) (b. Avellaneda, Buenos Aires, 7. III. 1895; d. Buenos Aires, 3. IX. 1968), Arg. cond. and comp., brother of prec. Studied in Buenos Aires and with d'Indy in Paris. On his return he formed a 5tet with himself as violinist and his brother as cellist, and in 1928 a chamber orch. In 1930–43 he was cond. at the Teatro Colón.

Works incl. ballet *Mekhano;* 3 symphs., *Sinfonia Argentina* and *Sinfonia Biblica,* symph. poems *Dans le jardin des morts, A una madre* and *La Chellah,* etc. for orch.; *Suite brève* for chamber orch.; pf. concerto; songs, etc.

Castrucci, Pietro (b. Rome, 1679; d. Dublin, 29. II. 1752), It. violinist, comp. and comp. Studied with Corelli in Rome and went to Eng. with Lord Burlington in 1715. He became leader in Handel's opera orch., but was replaced by Festing in 1737. In 1750 he settled at Dublin.

Works incl. 12 *Concerti grossi* and 3 books of vln. sonatas.

Castrucci, Prospero (b. Rome, ?; d. ? London, 1760), It. violinist, brother of prec. Prob. also studied with Corelli and went to Eng. with his brother or later. He is the orig. of Hogarth's 'Enraged Musician'. In 1739 he pub. 6 vln. sonatas.

Casulana. *See* **Mezari.**

'Cat's Fugue, The', popular name for D. Scarlatti's G min. harpsichord sonata (No. 30 in Kirkpatrick's list). Its bizarre subject has been taken to represent a cat picking its way along a keyboard. Experiment suggests that no cat would hit upon this particular succession of intervals.

Catalani, Alfredo (b. Lucca, 19. VI. 1854; d. Milan, 7. VIII. 1893), It. comp. Studied 1st with his father, an organist, and prod. a Mass at the age of 14. Went to the Paris Cons. in 1871 and then taught at the Milan Cons.

Works incl. operas *La Falce, Elda, Dejanice, Edmea, Loreley* and *La Wally;* Mass; symph. poem *Ero e Leandro,* etc.

Catalani, Angelica (b. Sinigaglia, 10. V. 1780; d. Paris, 12. VI. 1849), It. soprano.

1st appearance, Teatro La Fenice, Venice, 1795. Went to Port. in 1804, to London in 1806 and was manager of the It. Opera in Paris, 1814–17, after which she resumed her career as a singer.

Catch, a part-song, in vogue in Eng. from the early 17th to the 19th cent., in which the voices follow each other in the manner of a canon or round, with the difference in the most characteristic examples that the words, thus mixed up, acquire new and ludicrous meanings, often of an indecent nature in the 17th cent.

Catch Club, a society named The Noblemen and Gentlemen's C. C., founded in London in 1761 for sociable gatherings and the singing of catches. It still exists.

Catel, Charles Simon (b. L'Aigle, Orne, 10. VI. 1773; d. Paris, 29. XI. 1830), Fr. comp. Pupil of Sacchini and Gossec in Paris. After working as teacher, he became chief musician with Gossec of the Garde Nationale, for which he wrote much military mus., and accompanist at the Opéra in 1790. App. prof. of harmony at the Cons. on its foundation in 1795, and pub. a treatise on the subject in 1802.

Works incl. operas *Sémiramis, L'Auberge de Bagnières, Les Bayadères,* etc.; *De Profundis, Hymn of Victory;* symphs. for wind instruments; choral pieces; chamber mus.; songs, etc.

Catgut Strings. Although still often so called, such strings are not made of the bowels of cats but of sheep.

Catleen ⎱ the old Eng. names for the
Catling ⎰ top string of a lute, connected with cat (catgut).

Catoire, George Lvovich (b. Moscow, 27. IV. 1861; d. Moscow, 21. V. 1926), Rus. comp. of Fr. descent. Pupil of Klindworth in Berlin for pf. and Liadov at St. Petersburg for comp. App. prof. of comp. at the Moscow Cons. in 1917.

Works incl. symph. in C min., symph. poem *Mtsyri* (after Lermontov); pf. concerto in A♭ maj.; chamber mus.; sonatas and other pf. works, etc.

Catterall, Arthur (b. Preston, Lancs., 1883; d. London, 28. XI. 1943), Eng. violinist. Studied in Manchester, became a member of the Queen's Hall Orch. in London in 1909, later of the Hallé Orch. in Manchester and in 1929 of the B.B.C. Orch., which he left in 1936. He founded a string 4tet in 1910.

Caturla, Alejandro García (b. Remedios, 7. III. 1906; d. Remedios, 12. XI. 1940), Cuban comp. Studied at Havana and with Nadia Boulanger in Paris. He married a Negress and was much influenced by Afro-Cuban folk mus. He was assassinated.

Works incl. 3 *Danzas cubanas,* symph. poem *Yamba-O, La Rumba* for orch.; *Bembé* suite for 14 instruments, *Primera*

Suite cubana for 6 wind instruments and pf., sonata and prelude for pf.; songs, etc.

Cauldron of Annwen, The, operatic trilogy by Holbrooke (lib. by Thomas Evelyn Ellis = Lord Howard de Walden).
I. **The Children of Don,** prod. London Opera House, 15. VI. 1912.
II. **Dylan, Son of the Wave,** prod. London, Drury Lane Theatre, 4. VII. 1914.
III. **Bronwen,** prod. Huddersfield, 1. II. 1929.

Caurroy, (François) Eustache du, Sieur de Saint-Frémin (b. Gerberoy nr. Beauvais, 1549; d. Paris, 7. VIII. 1609), Fr. comp. Went to Paris *c.* 1569 as a singer in the royal chapel, where he became master of the children in 1583. He became a canon in the Sainte-Chapelle and the title of Surinten-dant de la Musique du Roy was created for him in 1599.
Works incl. Requiem, motets, psalms, noëls, 2 books of *Preces ecclesiasticae*; instrumental fantasies on sacred and secular tunes, etc.

Causton, Thomas (b. ?; d. London, 28. X. 1569), Eng. comp. Gentleman of the Chapel Royal in London. Comp. services, anthems, psalms, and contrib. to Day's *Certaine Notes*.

Cavaccio, Giovanni (b. Bergamo, *c.* 1556; d. Bergamo, 11. VIII. 1626), It. comp. *Maestro di cappella* at Bergamo Cathedral in 1583 and later at the church of Santa Maria Maggiore there. Wrote a Requiem, Magnificats, psalms, madrigals, etc. and contrib. psalms to a collection ded. to Palestrina.

Cavalieri, Catharina (b. Währing nr. Vienna, 19. II. 1760; d. Vienna, 30. VI. 1801), Aus. soprano. Pupil of Salieri in Vienna, where she made her operatic début in 1775. Mozart wrote for her the role of Constanze in *Die Entführung*, specially designing the virtuoso part, as he wrote to his father, for her 'flexible gullet'.

Cavalieri, Emilio de' (b. Rome, *c.* 1550; d. Rome, 11. III. 1602), It. comp. He was long in the service of Ferdinando de' Medici at Florence, where he was in close touch with the *Camerata*, and with them worked towards the evolution of opera, though his own works were still dramatic pieces to be perf. in concert form. They are the following, all set to words by Laura Guidiccioni: *Il satiro*, *La disperazione di Fileno* and *Il giuoco della cieca*, and *La rappresentazione di anima e di corpo*, an allegory prod. in 1600, the words of which are by Agostino Manni.

Cavalieri, Lina (b. Viterbo, 25. XII. 1874; d. Florence, 8. II. 1944), It. soprano. Born of humble parents, she 1st sang in cafés, but later studied seriously and made her 1st appearance in opera at Lisbon in 1901. 1st visited Eng. in 1908, but made her

greatest successes in U.S.A. She was killed in an air raid.

Cavalleria rusticana (*Rustic Chivalry*), opera by Mascagni (lib. by Guido Menasci and Giovanni Targioni-Tozzetti, based on Giovanni Verga's play), prod. Rome, Teatro Costanzi, 17. V. 1890.

Cavalli (orig. **Caletti-Bruni**), **(Pietro) Francesco** (b. Crema, 14. II. 1602; d. Venice, 14. I. 1676), It. comp. Became a singer under Monteverdi at St. Mark's, Venice, in 1617, 2nd organist of that church in 1640, 1st organist in 1665 and *maestro di cappella* in 1668. His 1st opera was prod. in 1639, and in 1660 he was called to Paris to perform his *Serse* at Louis XIV's marriage. He wrote operas for the 5 theatres of Venice.
Works incl. operas *Le nozze di Teti e di Peleo*, *Gli amori di Apollo e di Dafne*, *La Didone*, *L'Egisto*, *Il Giasone*, *L'Oristeo*, *Serse*, *Il Ciro*, *L'Erismena*, *L'Hipermestra*, *Ercole amante*, *Scipione Africano*, *Mutio Scevola*, *Il Coriolano* and *c.* 20 others; Masses, motets, psalms, antiphons, vespers, a Requiem, etc.

Cavata (It. lit. a thing carved or engraved, e.g. an epitaph), in mus. a short Arioso following a recitative, esp. in the early 18th cent.

Cavatina (It. poss. from *cavata*), in the 18th cent. a song in an opera less elaborate than an aria. Now normally used of a short, sustained piece or air.

Cavazzoni, Girolamo (b. ? Urbino, *c.* 1506; d. after 1577), It. organist and comp. Organist of Mantua Cathedral, 1523–56, and in the service of the Duke of Mantua (including duties as organist of the ducal church of S. Barbara) until at least 1577. His two books of org. mus. (1543 and before 1549) contain *ricercari*, *chanson* arrangements (*canzoni*), hymns, Magnificats and Masses.

Cavazzoni, Marco Antonio (da Bologna, d'Urbino) (b. ? Urbino, before 1490; d. ? Venice, after 1559), It. comp. father of prec. The 2 *ricercari* from his *Recerchari, Motetti, Canzoni* for org. (Venice, 1523) are toccata-like pieces designed as preludes to the 2 motet arrs.; the *canzoni* are arrs. of Fr. *chansons* and the forerunners of the It. instrumental *canzona*. There is also a choral *Missa Domini Marci Antonii* which may be his.

Cavendish, Michael (b. ? Cavendish Overhall, Suffolk, *c.* 1565; d. London, 5. VII. 1628), Eng. comp. Belonging to a noble family, he seems to have held no appts. He contrib. to East's *Whole Booke of Psalmes* in 1592 and pub. a vol. of his own comps., ded. to Lady Arabella Stuart, his 2nd cousin, in 1598, containing 20 airs to the lute, or with 3 other voices, and 8 madrigals. He also contrib. a madrigal to *The Triumphes of Oriana*.

Caverne, La (*The Cave*), opera by Lesueur

(lib. by P. Dercy, from an episode in
Lesage's *Gil Blas*), prod. Paris, Théâtre
Feydeau, 16. II. 1793.

Cavos, Catterino (b. Venice, 1775; d.
St. Petersburg, 10. V. 1840), It. comp.
Assisted his father, who was cond. at the
Teatro La Fenice, later cond. at Padua and
taught at Venice. In 1800 he went to Rus.
with Astaritta's opera co., and in 1803
became director of the It. and Rus. operas
there, for which he had to write works in
both languages, as well as some in Fr. His
Rus. opera, *Ivan Susanin*, prod. in 1815, was
very successful.

Cazzati, Maurizio (b. Guastalla, *c.*
1620; d. Mantua, 1677), It. organist and
comp. Held successive posts at Mantua,
Ferrara, Bergamo and Bologna. Comp.
secular vocal and instrumental mus. as well
as works for the church.

Ce qu'on entend sur la montagne (*What
is heard on the Mountain*), symph. poem by
Liszt, based on a poem by Victor Hugo,
comp. 1848–9, 1st perf. Weimar, II.
1850.

Cebell, a dance occurring in Eng.
17th-cent. mus., similar to the Gavotte.

Cecchina, La (Piccinni). *See* **Buona
figliuola.**

Čech, Svatopluk (1846–1908), Cz. novelist
and dramatist. *See* **Janáček** (*Excursions of
Mr. Brouček*), **Kovařovic** (do.).

Cecilia, Saint (b. ?; d. Sicily, *c.* 178),
the patron saint of mus. and the blind.
She is said to have suffered martyrdom
under Marcus Aurelius with her husband
and other friends she had converted to
Christianity and to have praised God by
vocal and instrumental mus. Her festival is
22. XI.

Cédez (Fr. imper., lit. cede, give, surrender) = hold back, a direction used by
Debussy and some other Fr. comps. to
indicate a *ritenuto.*

Celesta, a keyboard instrument brought
out by Mustel of Paris in the 1880s. The
tone is prod. by hammers struck upon steel
plates.

Celestina, a 4-ft. org. stop of delicate tone.

Celestina, La, opera by Pedrell (lib.
by ?, based on an anon. 15th–16th-cent.
Span. dialogue novel, *La comedia de
Calisto y Melibia,* sometimes attrib. to
Fernando de Rojas), not prod.

Celibidache, Sergiu (b. Rome, 26. VI.
1912), Rum. cond. He studied musicology
and cond. in Berlin, 1939–45, becoming
resident cond. of the Berlin Phil. Orch. in
1948. In 1948 he shared the orch. with
Fürtwängler on a tour of the U.S.A. He has
also comp. 4 symphs. and written a book on
Josquin des Prés.

Cellier, Alfred (b. London, 1. XII.
1844; d. London, 28. XII. 1891), Eng. comp.
Having been a choir-boy in the Chapel
Royal, he held var. organist's appts., was

cond. at Belfast and theatre cond. at Manchester and London.
Works incl. numerous operettas, e.g.
*The Sultan of Mocha, Nell Gwynne, The
Foster-Brothers, Dorothy, The Mountebanks* (lib. by Gilbert); opera *The Masque
of Pandora* (lib. by Longfellow); Gray's
Elegy for chorus and orch.; *Suite symphonique* for orch.; pf. pieces; songs, etc.

Cellini, Benvenuto (1500–71), It. sculptor,
craftsman and autobiog. *See* **Benvenuto
Cellini** (Berlioz), **Lachner** (F.).

Cello (It. dim. ending), the colloquial
name of the Violoncello.

Cellone (It. lit. big cello). A modern cello
of large size made by Stelzner of Dresden,
capable of being played seated and intended
to supply a double bass instrument for
chamber mus. It has 4 strings tuned in
perfect 5ths 2 octaves below the vln.

Celos aun del ayre matan (*Jealousy,
even of the air, is deadly*), opera on the subject of Cephalus and Procris by Juan
Hidalgo (lib. by Calderón), prod. Madrid,
Buen Retiro, 5. XII. 1660. The 1st Span.
opera.

Cembalist. Harpsichord player. *See also*
Maestro al cembalo.

Cembalo (It. abbr. for clavicembalo,
accent on 1st syll.) = Harpsichord; also
used to designate a Thorough-bass *continuo*
part.

Cendrillon (*Cinderella*), opera by Isouard
(lib. by Charles Guillaume Étienne, after
Perrault), prod. Paris, Opéra-Comique, 22.
II. 1810.
Opera by Laruette (lib. by Louis An-
seaume, after Perrault), prod. Paris, Opéra-
Comique, 21. II. 1759.
Opera by Massenet (lib. by Henri Cain,
after Perrault), prod. Paris, Opéra-Comique
24. V. 1899.
Opera by Steibelt (lib. by Étienne),
prod. St. Petersburg, 26. X. 1810.

Cenerentola (*Cinderella*), opera by Wolf-
Ferrari (lib. by Maria Pezzè-Pescolato, after
Perrault), prod. Venice, Teatro La Fenice,
22. II. 1900.

**Cenerentola, La, ossia La bontà in
trionfo** (*Cinderella, or The Triumph of
Goodness*), opera by Rossini (lib. by Jacopo
Ferretti, based on Étienne's), prod. Rome,
Teatro Valle, 25. I. 1817.

Cent, in acoustics the unit by which mus.
intervals are measured, a C. being a hun-
dredth part of a semitone in a tempered scale.

Central American Composers. *See* **Mexican, Nicaraguan.**

Céphale et Procris, opera by Grétry
(lib. by Marmontel), prod. Versailles, at
court, 30. XII. 1773; 1st Paris perf., Opéra,
2. V. 1775.

Cephalus and Procris, opera by Araia
(lib., in Rus., by Alexander Petrovich
Sumarokov), prod. St. Petersburg, at
court, 10. III. 1755.

Cerha, Friedrich (b. Vienna, 17. II. 1926), Aus. comp. and violinist. He studied musicology at Vienna Univ. and also comp. with Alfred Uhl. In 1958, with Kurt Schwertsik, he founded *Die Reihe*, an organization devoted to the perf. of new mus. He became director of the electronic studios of the Vienna Mus. Academy 1960. Works incl. *Espressioni Fondamentali* for orch.; *Relazioni Fragile* for harpsichord and chamber orch.; *Intersecazioni* for vln. and orch.; *Spiegel I–VI*.

Černohorský, Bohuslav Matěj (b. Nymburk, Boh., 16. II. 1684; d. Graz, 1. VII. 1742), Boh. comp., theorist and friar. Held church apps. at Padua and Assisi, where Tartini was his pupil. From 1739 he was director of mus. at St. James's Church in Prague. He was a highly valued comp. of church and org. mus., but most of his works were destroyed by fire in 1754.

Certon, Pierre (b. ? Melun, ?; d. Paris, 23. II. 1572), Fr. comp. He was in the Sainte-Chapelle in Paris, 1532, and became choirmaster there before 1542 and chaplain in 1548. As a canon of Notre-Dame at Melun he founded an annual service there. Works incl. Masses, *c.* 50 motets, psalms, canticles, *c.* 200 *chansons*, etc.

Cervantes, Miguel de (1547–1616), Span. novelist and dramatist. For operas, etc. based on *Don Quixote see* **Abrányi (E.)**, **Akeroyde**, **Auric** (ballet), **Caldara** (*Don Chisciotte*), **Champein, Clay, Conti (F. B.)**, **Courteville, Don Chisciotte** (2 operas), **Don Quichotte** (Massenet), **Don Quixote** (Kienzl and R. Strauss, symph. poem), **D. Q., The Comical History of** (Purcell and others), **Esplá, Generali, Gerhard** (ballet and radio play), **Henze** (*Wundertheater*, opera), **Hervé, Heuberger, Hochzeit des Gamacho** (Mendelssohn), **Ibert** (film), **Khrennikov** (incid. mus.), **Lalande** (*Folies de Cardenio*), **Lattuada** (*Caverna di Salamanca*), **Leo** (*Fantastico*), **Macfarren (G.), Mackenzie, Martini (G. B.), Marawski** (symph. poem), **Paisiello** (*Don Chisciotte della Mancia*), **Paumgartner** (*Höhle von Salamanca*), **Pessard, Petrassi** (*Ritratti di Don Chisciotte*), **Ravel** (*Don Quichotte à Dulcinée*), **Reeve** (*Harlequin Q.*), **Retablo de Maese Pedro** (Falla), **Rubinstein (A.)** (mus. portrait), **Sancho Pança dans son île** (Philidor), **Sancho Panza** (Jaques - Dalcroze), **Sancio Panza** (Caldara), **Serrano y Ruiz** (*Primera salida*), **Treu, Weinberger** (orchestral work). Other works *see* **Padlock** (Dibdin), **Preciosa** (Weber).

Cervelat (Fr., from *cervelas*, a kind of sausage). *See* **Sausage Bassoon.**

Cervetto (real name **Giacomo Bassevi**) (b. ?, 1682; d. London, 14. I. 1783), It. cellist and comp. Settled in London in 1728 and played in the orch. at Drury Lane, where he was later theatre manager. Wrote sonatas, etc. for his instrument, chamber mus., etc.

Cervetto, James (b. London, 1747; d. London, 5. II. 1837), Eng. cellist and comp. of It. descent, son of prec. Pupil of his father. Comp. mus. for his instrument.

Cesaris, Johannes (b. ?; d. ?), early 15th-cent. Fr. or Flem. organist and comp. Mentioned (with Carmen and Tapissier) by Martin le Franc in his poem *Le Champion des dames* (1441–2) as having 'astonished all Paris' in the recent past. Composed motets, Mass movements and *chansons*.

Cesti, (Pietro) Antonio (b. Arezzo, VIII. 1623; d. Florence, 14. X. 1669), It. comp. After serving as a choir-boy at Arezzo he became a Minorite friar in 1637. He was a pupil of Carissimi in Rome, and in 1645 was app. *maestro di cappella* at Volterra Cathedral. In 1653, having previously become a priest, he entered the service of the court at Innsbruck and remained there, with a brief interval as tenor in the papal chapel, for 13 years. From 1666 to 1669 he was vice-*Kapellmeister* in Vienna, where his spectacular opera *Il pomo d'oro* was perf. in 1667.

Works incl. operas *L'Orontea, Il Cesare amante, Alessandro il vincitor di se stesso, L'Argia, La Dori, Tito, Nettuno e Fiora festeggianti, Il pomo d'oro, Semiramide, Le disgrazie d'Amore*; motets; cantatas, etc.

Cetera (It.) = Cittern.

Chabrier, (Alexis) Emmanuel (b. Ambert, Puy-de-Dôme, 18. I. 1841; d. Paris, 13. IX. 1894), Fr. comp. Studied law and was employed at the Ministry of the Interior, but cultivated mus. as a gifted amateur. Having prod. 2 operettas in 1877 and 1879, he devoted himself entirely to comp. After the prod. of *Le Roi malgré lui*, the run of which was interrupted by the fire of 25 May 1887 at the Opéra-Comique, he came under the influence of Wagner.

Works incl. operas *Le Roi malgré lui, Gwendoline* and *Briséis* (unfinished); operettas *L'Étoile* and *L'Éducation manquée*; rhapsody *España* and *Joyeuse Marche* for orch.; *La Sulamite* for mezzo-soprano, chorus and orch.; 10 *Pièces pittoresques, Habanera* and *Bourrée fantasque*, etc. for pf.; 3 *Valses romantiques* for 2 pfs.; songs, etc.

Chace (old Fr. = *chasse* = chase, hunt), a 14th-cent. term for Canon, because the parts 'chase' each other.

Chaconne (Fr.), orig. a dance, prob. of Span. provenance. Now a comp., generally in 3–4 time, on an unvarying ground-bass which goes on throughout the piece and over which, at each reappearance, the upper parts are freely varied in different ways. This definition applies even to Bach's Chaconne for unaccomp. vln., since the bass is always implied even when not actually heard.

Chacony (Eng., obs.) = Chaconne.

Chadwick, George (Whitefield) (b. Lowell, Mass., 13. XI. 1854; d. Boston, 4. IV. 1931), Amer. comp. Studied at Boston, Leipzig and Munich, in the last place under Rheinberger. Returned to Amer. in 1880, became organist at Boston, then prof. at the New Eng. Cons. and its director in 1897.

Works incl. operas *Tabasco, Judith, The Padrone*, etc.; choral and orchestral works *The Viking's Last Voyage, The Song of the Viking, Lovely Rosabel, The Lily Nymph, Phoenix expirans*, etc.; 3 symphs., symph. poems *Cleopatra, Aphrodite, Angel of Death, Tam o' Shanter* (after Burns), overtures *Rip van Winkle, Thalia, Melpomene, Adonis* (after Shelley), *Euterpe*, etc., *Symph. Sketches, Sinfonietta, Suite symphonique*; 5 string 4tets, pf. 5tet; songs with orch. and with pf.; pf. and org. works; church mus.; part-songs, etc.

Chagrin, Francis (b. Bucharest, 15. XI. 1905), Anglo-Rum. comp. Studied at Zürich, Bucharest and, with Dukas and Nadia Boulanger, in Paris; later with Seiber in London, where he joined the Fr. section of the B.B.C. Overseas Service in 1941. In 1943 he founded the Committee for the Promotion of New Music.

Works incl. incid. mus. for Shaw's *Heartbreak House* and Gozzi's *Re cervo*; mus. for films and broadcasts; *Prelude and Fugue* and suites for orch.; pf. concerto; chamber mus.; pf. pieces; over 100 songs, etc.

Chair Organ = Choir Organ.

Chalet, Le, opera by Adam (lib. by Eugène Scribe and Anne Honoré Joseph Mélesville), prod. Paris, Opéra-Comique, 25. IX. 1834.

Chaliapine. *See* **Shaliapin.**

Chalumeau (Fr. = chanter). The pipe of the bagpipes on which the melody is played. The Fr. name is also given to a single-reed wind instrument, the forerunner of the clar., and sometimes to a double-reed one which preceded the ob. (shawm). C. is also the name for the lowest register of the clar.

Chamber Music, properly mus. played in a private room, consisting of works assigning individual parts to a few players (more rarely singers).

Chamber Opera, a type of opera written for few singers without chorus and a small orch. often consisting entirely of solo instruments.

Chamber Orchestra, a small orch. designed for the perf. of table mus., serenades, etc. in domestic surroundings or small concert halls.

Chamber Organ, a small org. with 1 or 2 manuals, suitable for playing figured-bass accomps. or 18th-cent. solo concertos.

Chamber Pitch. *See* **Kammerton.**

Chamber Sonata. *See* **Sonata da camera.**

Chamberlain, Houston Stewart (b. Portsmouth, 9. IX. 1855; d. Bayreuth, 9. I. 1927), Eng. writer, mainly on Wagner. Educ. at Cheltenham and in Switz. Married Wagner's daughter Eva in 1908 and became a naturalized Ger. Great champion of Wagner and propagandist of Pan-Ger. theories.

Chambonnières, Jacques Champion de (b. ? Brie district, *c*. 1602; d. Paris, *c*. 1672), Fr. harpsichordist and comp. In the service of Louis XIII and XIV, also for a time in Swed. He taught several of the later harpsichordists and pub. 2 books of harpsichord pieces.

Chaminade, Cécile (Louise Stéphanie) (b. Paris, 8. VIII. 1857; d. Monte Carlo, 18. IV. 1944), Fr. pianist and comp. Studied with var. masters, incl. Godard for comp. Began to comp. at the age of 8, and at 18 gave her 1st concert. Toured widely in Fr. and Eng.

Works incl. comic opera *La Sévillane*; ballet *Callirhoë*; *Symphonie lyrique* for chorus and orch.; suites for orch.; *Concertstück* for pf. and orch.; 2 pf. trios; numerous light pf. pieces; songs, etc.

Chamisso, Adelbert von (1781–1838), Ger. poet and novelist of Fr. descent. *See* **Frauenliebe und Leben** (Schumann), **Jensen** (*Tränen*), **Palmgren** (*Peter Schlemihl*), **Reznicek** (do.).

Champein, Stanislas (b. Marseilles, 19. XI. 1753; d. Paris, 19. IX. 1830), Fr. comp. Went to Paris *c*. 1775 and prod. a comic opera in 1780, which was followed by some 50 other works for the stage, incl. (?) a setting of a Fr. prose trans. of Sophocles' *Electra*, rehearsed at the Opéra, but prohibited.

Works incl. operas *La Mélomanie, Le Nouveau Don Quichotte*, etc.; Masses and other church mus., etc.

Chandos Anthems, 11 anthems by Handel, comp. *c*. 1717–20 for the Earl of Carnarvon, later Duke of Chandos, for perf. in his private chapel at Canons nr. Edgware.

Chanson (Fr. = song). In a special technical sense the C. is an old Fr. part-song cultivated in Fr. before and during the period when the madrigal occupied the comps. of the Netherlands, It. and Eng. Though it is often polyphonic in construction, many exs. approximate more closely to the lighter type of the canzonet. Many such Cs. were arranged for solo voice and lute.

Chanson de geste (Fr. = song of deeds, epic or heroic song), 11th–13th-cent. verse-chronicle recited to music by Jongleurs. The subject-matter might be secular or religious. In form it consisted of verse-paragraphs (*laisses*) of unequal length, the mus. being the same for each line of verse except the last.

Chanson de toile (Fr. = cloth song),

a Fr. medieval song which tells its story or
perf. its actions with reference to a female,
not a male, character. Hence the name, which
doubtless referred to spinning or weaving.

Chant, in Catholic church mus. the singing of psalms, canticles, Masses, etc. in
plainsong to Lat. words; in Angl. church
mus. the singing of the psalms to harmonized and measured tunes, the rhythm of
which may, however, be modified or obscured by the necessity to fit longer or
shorter psalm verses.

Chant-Fable (Fr. = song-fable), a 13th-
cent. narrative interspersed with songs.

Chantavoine, Jean (François Henri) (b.
Paris, 17. V. 1877; d. Mussy-sur-Seine, 16.
VII. 1952), Fr. musicologist. Studied mus.
and philosophy at the univs. of Paris and
Berlin. Mus. critic of the *Revue hebdoma-
daire* 1903–20 and *Excelsior* 1911–20, and
contrib. to mus. journals. Wrote books on
Beethoven, Liszt, mus. and poetry, Fr.
mus., etc., and trans. Beethoven's letters as
well as a number of operas and songs by
Mozart, Brahms, Wagner, R. Strauss, etc.

Chanter, the pipe of the bagpipes on
which the melody is played.

Chanterelle (Fr. lit. the singing one),
the E string of the vln. or (less often) the
highest string of any stringed instrument.

Chanty. *See* **Shanty.**

Chapeau chinois (Fr. = Chin. hat) =
Chinese Pavilion.

Chapel Royal, the Eng. court chapel,
incl. not only the building but the whole
institution, dating back to the 12th cent. at
the latest.

Chapí y Lorente, Ruperto (b. Villena nr.
Alicante, 27. III. 1851; d. Madrid, 25. III.
1909), Span. comp. Studied at the Madrid
Cons. and in 1872 was given a mus. post in
the artillery. Lived in Rome for a time from
1873.

Works incl. operas *Margarita la Tornera,
La serenata, Roger de Flor, Circe* and 4
others, 30 zarzuelas; oratorio *Los Angeles,
Veni Creator* for double chorus and orch.;
symph. in D min., Moorish fantasy *La
corte de Granada,* legend *Los gnomos de la
Alhambra* and other orchestral works; *Jota*
for vln. and orch.; 4 string 4tets, pf. trio;
pf. pieces; songs, etc.

Chaplet, The, mus. stage entertainment
by Boyce (lib. by Moses Mendez), prod.
London, Drury Lane Theatre, 2. XII.
1749.

Chapuis, Auguste (Paul Jean-Baptiste)
(b. Dampierre-sur-Sâlon, 20. IV. 1858; d.
Paris, 6. XII. 1933), Fr. organist and comp.
Studied at the Paris Cons. under Dubois,
Massenet and Franck. He became organist
at 2 Paris churches and prof. of harmony at
the Cons., also mus. inspector of schools
and examiner of military bands and choral
cond.

Works incl. operas *Enguerrande* and *Les*

Demoiselles de Saint-Cyr; *Tableaux fla-
mands* for orch.; sonatas for vln. and pf.
and cello and pf.; songs, etc.

Char, René (b. 1907), Fr. poet. *See* **Boulez**
(*Le Visage Nuptial, Le Soleil des eaux, Le
Marteau sans maître*).

Charakterstück (Ger. = character or
characteristic piece), a short instrumental
piece outlining some definite mood,
human character or literary conception.

Charles V (Křenek). *See* **Karl V.**

Charleston, an Amer. dance stemming
from the Foxtrot, of which it is a debased
form.

Charpentier,   Gustave   (b. Dieuze,
Meurthe, 25. VI. 1860; d. Paris, 18. II.
1956), Fr. comp. Went into business at
Tourcoing at the age of 15, but studied mus.
at the Lille and Paris Conss., gaining at the
latter the Prix de Rome as a pupil of
Massenet in 1887. In 1902 he founded the
Cons. de Mimi Pinson, providing free
instruction in mus. for working-class girls.

Works incl. operas *Louise* and *Julien*;
cantata *Didon*; symph. drama for solo
voices, chorus and orch., *La Vie du poète*
(afterwards used in *Julien*); orch. suite
*Impressions d'Italie; Fête du couronnement
de la Muse* (later used in *Louise*); *Impressions fausses* (Verlaine) and *Sérénade à
Watteau* for voice and orch.; *Poèmes
chantés* and 5 poems from Baudelaire's
Fleurs du mal for voice and pf., etc.

Charpentier, Marc-Antoine (b. Paris,
1634; d. Paris, 24. II. 1704), Fr. comp. Pupil
of Carissimi in Rome. On his return he
became domestic musician to Mlle. de Guise
and comp. to the Comédie-Française,
where he worked with Molière and continued after M.'s death. In 1679 he was
app. church comp. to the Dauphin; later
mus. master to a Jesuit coll. and comp.
teacher to the Duke of Orleans. In 1698 he
became *maître de chapelle* at the Sainte-
Chapelle.

Works incl. operas *Les Amours d'Acis
et Galatée, La Descente d'Orphée aux enfers,
Endimion, Médée* and *c.* 12 others; incid.
mus. for Molière's *La Comtesse d'Escarbagnas* and *Le Malade imaginaire,* for P.
Corneille's *Polyeucte* and *Andromède,* T.
Corneille's *La Pierre philosophale,* T.
Corneille and Visé's *Circé* and *L'Inconnu*
and Visé's *Les Amours de Vénus et d'Adonis;*
ballets, etc.; *c.* 10 Masses, Requiem,
motets, psalms and other church mus.,
some with orch.; *Histoires sacrées,
Tragédies spirituelles;* vocal chamber mus.,
Airs sérieux et à boire; instrumental pieces,
etc.

Charton-Demeur (*née* Charton), Anne
Arsène (b. Saujon, 5. III. 1824; d. Paris, 30.
XI. 1892), Fr. soprano. Made her 1st
appearance at Bordeaux in 1842. She sang
the part of Dido in Berlioz's *Les Troyens à
Carthage* in 1863.

Chartreuse de Parme, La (*The Carthusian Monastery of Parma*), opera by Sauguet (lib. by Armand Lunel, based on Stendhal's novel), prod. Paris, Opéra, 16. III. 1939.

Chase, Gilbert (b. Havana, 4. IX. 1906), Amer. mus. critic. Studied in N.Y. and Paris, where he lived in 1929–35 as mus. critic to the *Daily Mail*. In 1936 he settled in N.Y. Made a special study of Span. mus. and wrote *The Mus. of Spain*.

Chasse. *See* Chace.

Chasse, La (*The Hunt*). Nickname of Haydn's symph. No. 73, in D maj., comp. in 1781; also of his string 4tet in B♭ maj., Op. 1 No. 1, written *c*. 1755.

Chasseur maudit, Le (*The Accursed Huntsman*), symph. poem by Franck, based on a ballad by Bürger, comp. 1882. 1st perf. Paris, Soc. Nat., 31. III. 1883.

Chastelain de Couci, Le. *See* Couci.

Chateaubriand, François René, Vicomte de (1768–1848), Fr. poet and novelist. *See* Franck (C.) (songs), Lenepveu (*Velléda*), Pedrell (F.) (*Ultimo Abencerraje*), Setaccioli (*Ultimo degli Abenceragi*).

Chaucer, Geoffrey (?1340–1400). Eng. poet. *See* Aplvor (songs with string 4tet), Canterbury Pilgrims (Stanford), Dyson (*Canterbury Pilgrims*), Fée Urgèle (Duni), Fricker (*Canterbury Prologue*), Koven (*Canterbury Pilgrims*), Pleyel (I.) (*Fée Urgèle*), Walton (*Troilus and Cressida*).

Chausson, Ernest (b. Paris, 20. I. 1855; d. Limay, 10. VI. 1899), Fr. comp. Pupil of Massenet at the Paris Cons., then of Franck. He never held an official app., but helped to found the Société Nationale de Musique and was its sec. 1889–99. He d. after a bicycle accident.

Works incl. operas *Le Roi Arthus, La Légende de Sainte Cécile*, etc.; incid. mus. to Shakespeare's *Tempest*; symph. in B♭ maj., symph. poem *Viviane*; *Poème de l'amour et de la mer* for voice and orch.; string 4tet (unfinished), concerto for vln. and pf. with string 4tet, pf. trio, pf. 4tet, *Chanson perpétuelle* for voice, string 4tet and pf.; pf. and org. pieces; 10 op. nos. of songs, etc.

Chauvet, Charles Alexis (b. Marines, Seine-et-Oise, 7. VI. 1837; d. Argentan, Orne, 28. I. 1871), Fr. organist and comp. Studied org. under Benoist and comp. under A. Thomas at the Paris Cons. and after filling var. posts was app. organist at the church of the Trinité there, 1869. He wrote much for org. and pf.

Chávez, Carlos (b. Mexico City, 13. VI. 1899), Mex. comp. of mixed Indian and Span. descent. He was taught mus. as a child by his brother and 2 casual teachers, but later went to Eur. and N.Y. to gain experience. In 1928 he founded a Mex. symph. orch., of which he later became cond., and the same year he became director of the Nat. Cons. A post in the Dept. of

Fine Arts enabled him to do still more for the country's mus. reorganization, and he did much to explore Mex. folk mus.

Works incl. ballets *El fuego nuevo, Los cuatros soles* and *H.P.*; *Energía, Sinfonía de Antigona, Sinfonía proletaria* and *Sinfonía India* for orch.; concertos for harp and for pf. and orch.; *El sol* for chorus and orch.; 3 string 4tets; sonata for 4 horns; pf. pieces, etc.

Checkmate, ballet by Bliss (choreography by Ninette de Valois), prod. by Sadler's Wells Ballet, Paris, Théâtre des Champs-Élysées, 15. VI. 1937; 1st London perf., Sadler's Wells Theatre, 5. X. 1937.

Chef d'attaque (Fr.), the leader of an orch., so called because great importance was always attached in Fr. to unanimity of bowing and attack in orchestral string playing.

Chef d'orchestre (Fr. = chief of the orch.) = Conductor.

Chekhov. *See* Tchekhov.

Chekker, a 14th–16th-cent. keyboard instrument used in Eng., Fr. and Spain, in which latter countries it was called *échiquier* and *exaquir* (and similar names). Its Ger. name is properly *Schachtbrett*, from the old Flem. word *Schacht* (spring or quill), and has nothing to do with the modern *Schachbrett* (chessboard). The instrument is clearly a forerunner of the harpsichord.

Chelard, Hippolyte (André Jean Baptiste) (b. Paris, 1. II. 1789; d. Weimar, 12. II. 1861), Fr. cond. and comp. Studied at the Paris Cons., vln. under R. Kreutzer and comp. under Gossec, Méhul and Cherubini. Gained the Prix de Rome in 1811, studied church mus. in Rome under Baini and Zingarelli, afterwards opera with Paisiello and Fioravanti at Naples, where he prod. an It. comic opera in 1815. In 1816 he became violinist at the Paris Opéra, where he prod. *Macbeth* in 1827. After the 1830 Revolution he settled at Munich and remained in Ger. to the end of his life. In 1832 and 1833 he cond. Ger. opera in London, with Schröder-Devrient and Haitzinger as the chief singers. From 1835 to 1840 he was employed as cond. at Augsburg, finally becoming court mus. director at Weimar.

Works incl. operas *La casa da vendere, Macbeth* (in Fr., lib. by Rouget de l'Isle), *La Table et le logement* (later Ger. version *Der Student*), *Mitternacht, Die Hermannschlacht*, etc.

Chemineau, Le (*The Tramp*), opera by Leroux (lib. by Jean Richepin), prod. Paris, Opéra-Comique, 6. XI. 1907.

Chénier, Joseph (1764–1811), Fr. poet and dramatist. *See* Méhul (*Timoléon*).

Cherkassky, Shura (b. Odessa, 7. X. 1911), Rus. pianist. He studied 1st with his mother and later with Josef Hofmann. As a child prodigy, he played before President Hoover in the U.S.A. in 1923.

Cherubini, Luigi (Carlo Zanobi Salvatore Maria) (b. Florence, 14. IX. 1760; d. Paris, 15. III. 1842), It. comp. Studied 1st under his father, a musician at the Teatro della Pergola at Florence, then under var. min. masters. At the age of 16 he had written an oratorio, Masses, etc. About 1778, with a grant from the Grand Duke, he went to study with Sarti at Venice and in 1780 he prod. his 1st opera, *Quinto Fabio*. In 1785 and 1786 he prod. *La finta principessa* and *Giulio Sabino* in London and was app. Composer to the King, but left for Paris in the latter year. After a brief return to It. he settled in Paris for good in 1788 and prod. his 1st Fr. opera, *Démophon*, there, to a lib. by Marmontel. He soon became very busy cond. and comp. opera, but was not very successful. In 1795 he married Cécile Tourette. In 1806 he prod. *Faniska* in Vienna, where it had been specially commissioned, and met Beethoven, who admired his work and whose *Fidelio* was influenced by it. On his return to Fr. he lived retired and embittered at the Prince de Chimay's country residence and there wrote church mus. as well as more operas. In 1816 he and Lesueur became attached to the royal chapel with large salaries and in 1822 he became director of the Cons.

Works incl. operas *Armida abbandonata*, *Alessandro nell' Indie*, *Demetrio*, *Artaserse*, *Ifigenia in Aulide*, *Lodoïska* (Fr.), *Médée*, *Les Deux Journées* (*The Water Carrier*), *Anacréon, ou L'Amour fugitif*, *Faniska*, *Pimmalione*, *Les Abencérages*, *Bayard à Mézières*, *Ali Baba, ou Les Quarante Voleurs*; ballet-pantomime *Achille à Scyros*; 10 Masses and 2 coronation Masses, 2 Requiems (1 for male voices) and other choral works; symph. in D maj. and overture for orch.; 6 string 4tets, string 5tet; songs, etc.

Chest of Viols, a set of (usually 6) viols of var. sizes in a cupboard or chest, an article of furniture which was often found in the households of well-to-do Eng. families of the 16th and 17th cents.

Chest Voice, one of the so-called 'registers' in singing, used or said to be used for the lower notes of the singer's range, and so called because its resonance gives the sensation of being lodged in the chest, not in the head, as in the case of the Head Voice.

Chester Musical Festival, opened in 1772 and continued irregularly until 1829; a 2nd series began in 1879 and was given triennially until 1900.

Chesterton, G(ilbert). K(eith). (1874–1936), Eng. essayist, novelist and poet. *See* **Wordsworth** (*Hymn of Dedication*).

Cheval de bronze, Le (*The Bronze Horse*), opera by Auber (lib. by Eugène Scribe), prod. Paris, Opéra-Comique, 23. III. 1835.

Chevalet (Fr.), vln. bridge.

Chevillard, (Paul Alexandre) Camille (b. Paris, 14. X. 1859; d. Chatou, 30. V. 1923), Fr. cond. and comp. Pupil of Chabrier and son-in-law of Lamoureux, whose concerts he cond. after L.'s retirement.

Works incl. incid. mus. for E. Schuré's play *La Roussalka*, *Ballade symphonique*, symph. poem *Le Chêne et le Roseau* and *Fantaisie symphonique* for orch.; string 4tet, pf. 5tet, 4tet and trio; sonatas for vln. and pf. and cello and pf.; variations and *Étude chromatique* for pf.; vln. and cello pieces, etc.

Cheville (Fr.), vln. peg.

Chevreuille, Raymond (b. Watermael, 17. XI. 1901), Belg. comp. Mainly self-taught, although he took some courses at the Brussels Cons. He has written works of all kinds in a harmonically advanced idiom.

Works incl. chamber opera *Atta Troll*; 3 ballets; symph. with vocal 4tet, *Évasions* for soprano and chamber orch., *Saisons* for baritone and chamber orch.; concerto for 3 woodwind instruments, cello concerto; 6 string 4tets, etc.

Chevroté (Fr.). *See* **Ornaments.**

Chézy (*née* von Klencke), **Wilhelmine** (or **Helmina**) **von** (1783–1856), Ger. dramatist and novelist. Wrote the lib. of Weber's *Euryanthe* and the play *Rosamunde* for which Schubert provided incid. mus.

Chiavetta (It. lit. little key, actually little clef). Chiavette (plur.) were clefs other than those normal in 16th and early 17th cent. vocal mus., used either to avoid leger-lines or to indicate transposition, e.g. the tenor clef might be used for a bass part, the treble clef for a soprano part, and so on.

Child, William (b. Bristol, 1606; d. Windsor, 23. III. 1697), Eng. comp. and organist. Educ. at Bristol Cathedral and app. one of the organists at St. George's Chapel, Windsor, in 1632. At the Restoration he received a court appt. and in 1663 he took the D.Mus. degree at Oxford.

Works incl. *c.* 25 services, *c.* 50 anthems, motet *O bone Jesu*, 20 psalms for 3 voices with thorough-bass, chants, *Magnificat* in *Gamut*, Te Deum and Jubilate and other church mus.; secular vocal pieces, catches and ayres; 2 suites of dances for viols, etc.

Childe, Ann. *See* **Seguin, Arthur.**

Childhood of Christ (Berlioz). *See* **Enfance du Christ.**

Children of Don, The (Holbrooke). *See* **Cauldron of Annwen.**

Children's Corner, a set of pf. pieces, with Eng. titles, by Debussy, comp. in 1906–8, ded. to his daughter Claude-Emma D. (Chouchou): 1. *Doctor Gradus ad Parnassum*; 2. *Jimbo's Lullaby*; 3. *Serenade for the Doll*; 4. *Snow is dancing*; 5. *The Little Shepherd*; 6. *Golliwog's Cake-Walk*.

Chilean Composer. *See* **Allende.**

Chilesotti, Oscar (b. Bassano, 12. VII. 1848; d. Bassano, 23. VI. 1916), It. musicologist. Studied law at Padua Univ. Ed. much old It. mus. and wrote several hist. works.

Chime-Bells. *See* **Glockenspiel.**

Chinese Block (or **Temple Block**), a perc. instrument in the shape of a hollow wooden box on which a dry, rapping sound is prod.

Chinese Pavilion, an instrument shaped like a tree or pagoda and hung with brass plates and small bells, shaken to make a jingling noise and used in military bands, esp. in the 18th cent. It was popularly called 'Jingling Johnny' or 'Turkish Crescent'.

Chirbury, Robert (b. ?; d. ?), early 15th-cent. Eng. comp., represented in the Old Hall MS. He was a clerk of the Chapel Royal, 1421–7, and Dean of St. Mary's, Warwick, 1443.

Chiroplast, Logier's apparatus invented in the early years of the 19th cent. to facilitate pf. practice by mechanically making the hands flexible.

Chishko, Oles. *See* **Tchishko.**

Chisholm, Erik (b. Glasgow, 4. I. 1904; d. Cape Town, 7. VI. 1965), Scot. pianist, organist, cond. and comp. Studied comp. under Tovey and in 1934 took the D.Mus. degree at Edinburgh Univ. After touring in Canada he returned to Glasgow as organist and cond., founded a society for the propagation of modern mus. in 1930 and became cond. of the Glasgow Grand Opera Co., with which he gave interesting perfs., partic. of Berlioz's operas. In 1945 he went to Singapore as cond. of the Symph. Orch. and in 1947 he became principal of the Cape Town School of Mus.

Works incl. opera *Isle of Youth* (lib. by comp.); ballets *The Forsaken Mermaid* and *The Pied Piper of Hamelin*; 2 symphs.; overture *The Friars of Berwick*; 2 pf. concertos, *Straloch Suite* for pf. and strings; double trio for wind and strings, etc.

Chitarrone (It. lit. big guitar, from *chitarra* with augment. ending), a very large double-necked lute or theorbo, used as a bass to the lute family in It. in the 17th cent.

Chladni, Ernst (Florens Friedrich) (b. Wittenberg, 30. XI. 1756; d. Breslau, 3. IV. 1827), Ger. scientist. After studying both law and medicine he devoted himself to physics, made important researches into acoustics and wrote numerous books on the subject.

Chlubna, Osvald (b. Brno, 22. VII. 1893), Cz. comp. Pupil of Janáček and later prof. at the Brno Cons.

Works incl. operas *Catullus's Vengeance*, *Alladine and Palomides* (after Maeterlinck), *Nura* and *The Day of Beginning*; cantatas *Lord's Prayer*, *Minstrel's Child* and others; *Symph. of Life and Love*, symph. poems *Dreams*, *Before I go dumb*, *Two Fairy Tales*, *Song of my Longing*; overture *Fairy Land*, 2 suites for orch.; Sinfonietta for chamber orch.; 3 string 4tets, ballad for string 4tet, Andante and Scherzo for pf. trio; Elegy for cello and pf.; sonatina and other pf. works; songs, part-songs, etc.

Chocolate Soldier, The (*Der tapfere Soldat*), operetta by Oscar Straus (lib. by Leopold Jacobson and Rudolf Bernauer, based on Bernard Shaw's *Arms and the Man*), prod. Vienna, Theater an der Wien, 14. XI. 1908.

Choirbook, a large book in which the parts of a polyphonic comp., though written out separately, were collected together on the open page so that they could be read simultaneously by all the perfs. (If a piece was too long for one 'opening' the parts were copied so that the turn came simultaneously in all of them.) The format was first employed in motet MSS. of the 13th cent. (superseding score arr. to save space), was common in Eng. in the 15th and early 16th cents. (*see* **Eton Choirbook**), and was also used for chamber mus. and lute songs in Eng. in the later 16th and early 17th cents., the parts now being arranged so that the book could be placed flat on a table and the perfs. seated around it.

Choir Organ, formerly often a small instrument set apart from the principal org. in a church and used separately to accomp. the choir. It is now the name given to the lowest manual of an organ with three or more manuals, of which it forms an integral part.

Chopin, Frédéric (François) (orig. **Fryderyk Franciszek**) (b. Zelazowa Wola, 1. III. 1810; d. Paris, 17. X. 1849), Pol. comp. of Fr. descent. The family moved to Warsaw later in 1810, C.'s father becoming prof. of Fr. there. C. took pf. lessons at the age of 6, played at a mus. evening at 7 and in public at 8; took comp. lessons with Elsner from 1822, made great progress in comp. and improvisation, and 1st pub. a work, a Polonaise in G min., at the age of 7. Left Warsaw Cons. in 1827 and played in Vienna in 1829. On his return he fell in love with the singer Konstancja Gladkowska, who appeared at the 3rd of his public concerts in 1830; but he left Pol. that year, playing in Vienna and Munich and visiting Stuttgart, where he heard of the taking of Warsaw by the Russ. Went to Paris in X. 1831 and decided to remain there. He appeared frequently in public and gave private lessons, esp. in Fr. and Pol. aristocratic circles.

Met Marya Wodzińska at Dresden in 1835 and Marienbad in 1836, fell in love with and became secretly engaged to her, but the engagement was broken off by her family. In 1838 he visited George Sand at Nohant, where she held house-parties in the summer, and although she was 6 years older an intimacy developed between them. She took him to Majorca in XI for his health, but the stay, until II. 1839, was spoilt by bad weather and primitive living conditions. Most summers spent at Nohant until 1847, when a family quarrel between G. Sand and her children led to one with C., and they parted. He suffered from consumption of the throat and gave his last public concert in II. 1848, but continued to teach and play at private houses. His pupil Jane Stirling took him to Scot. in VIII. 1848 for a rest at the country house of her brother-in-law, Lord Torphichen. He afterwards played in Manchester, Glasgow, Edinburgh, and returned to London in XI. In I. 1849 he was back in Paris in a critical state of health and finance, but was supported by wealthy friends until his death.

Works (nearly all for pf. solo) incl. 2 concertos; 4 other works with orch.; over 50 Mazurkas, 27 Studies, 26 Preludes (24 in all keys), 19 Nocturnes, 14 Waltzes, 16 Polonaises, 4 Ballades, 4 Impromptus, 4 Scherzos, 3 Rondos, 3 sonatas, *Barcarolle*, *Berceuse*, *Bolero*, *Fantasy* in F min., *Tarantella* and other miscellaneous pf. pieces; pf. trio; cello and pf. sonata.

Chopsticks, a childish little waltz played on the pf. by children with the forefingers of each hand, to which the name refers by analogy with the 2 sticks with which the Chin. eat their food.

'Chopsticks' Variations, a set of variations for pf. (3 hands, the 2nd player playing a variant in 2–4 time of the above with 1 hand) by Borodin, Cui, Liadov and Rimsky-Korsakov, written before 1880, when a 2nd ed. appeared and Liszt contrib. a new variation of his own.

Choragus, a post established by William Heather at Oxford Univ. in 1627. The duties were to conduct vocal and instrumental practices, but these soon fell into disuse and the C. came to be known as Prof. At a later date the office was revived, and in fact still exists, but there are no longer any statutory duties attached to it and only a nominal stipend.

Choral (Ger.), **Chorale** (Eng.), Lutheran hymn. The Ger. word was orig. used to mean the choral parts of Lat. chant, and by extension plainsong in general, a meaning which it still bears today. At the Reformation it took on the secondary meaning of the monophonic congregational singing of the Lutheran liturgy, many of the melodies being adaptations from the plainsong itself; hence the term *Choralbearbeitung* (chorale arr.) to denote any kind of setting of such melodies. The Eng. word is simply an adaptation of the Ger. in its Lutheran sense, the final 'e' being added to make the pronunciation clear and to avoid confusion with the adj. 'choral'.

'Choral Symphony', popular name for Beethoven's 9th symph. in D min., Op. 125, on account of its last movement, a setting of Schiller's ode *An die Freude* ('To Joy') for solo 4tet, chorus and orch. Comp. *c*. 1817–1824, first perf. Vienna, 7. V. 1824.

Chorale. *See* Choral.

Chorale Cantata, term used for a form of church cantata, esp. by Bach, which draws on the text and, usually, mus. of a Lutheran hymn. The chorale words and melody may (rarely) be present in each movement of the cantata (e.g. in *Christ lag in Todesbanden*), or some verses may be replaced by free paraphrases of the text or completely new material set as recitatives, arias, etc. Treatment varies from the simple harmonizations found as the last movement of many cantatas to the complexity of the massive fantasia-like chorus which opens *Ein' feste Burg*.

Chorale Fantasy, a type of org. comp. in which a hymn-tune is freely treated.

Chorale Prelude, a type of org. piece for church use repres. with partic. distinction by Bach; introducing the tune of the hymn about to be sung by the congregation and artistically elaborating it by contrapuntal treatment or by the provision of an orig. accomp.

Chord, properly the sounding together of 3 or more notes, though 2 notes may imply others.

Chording, a term used to designate either the spacing of the notes in a chord in comp. or the perf. of them strictly in tune in relation to each other.

Choreography, the invention, design and stage management of the dancing in a ballet.

Chorley, Henry F(othergill). (b. Blackley Hurst, Lancs., 15. XII. 1808; d. London, 16. II. 1872), Eng. mus. critic, librettist and author, contrib. to the *Athenaeum* from 1830.

Choron, Alexandre (Étienne) (b. Caen, 21. X. 1772; d. Paris, 28. VI. 1834), Fr. mus. scholar and comp. Among his books are a mus. encyclopaedia and treatises on mus. study, part-writing, plainsong, etc.

Comps. incl. a Mass, a *Stabat Mater*, psalms, hymns, etc.

Chorton (Ger. lit. choir-pitch), the pitch to which church orgs. in Ger. were tuned in the 17th–18th cent. It was higher, usually by a whole tone, than *Kammerton* (chamber-pitch), and it is for this reason that Bach transposed the wood-wind parts in his cantatas up, or alternatively transposed the org. parts down. The strings could, if necessary, play at either pitch.

Chouquet, (Adolphe) Gustave (b. Le Havre, 16. IV. 1819; d. Paris, 30. I. 1886), Fr. musicologist. Lived in N.Y. in 1840–56, settled in Paris in 1860 and became curator of the Cons. museum of mus. instruments in 1871. He pub. its catalogue and *Histoire de la Musique dramatique en France*.

Christmas Concerto, Corelli's Concerto grosso Op. 6. No 8.

Christmas Eve (*Notch Pered Rozhdestvom*), opera by Rimsky-Korsakov (lib. by comp., based on Gogol's story), prod. St. Petersburg, 10. XII. 1895.
See also **Vakula the Smith.**

Christmas Oratorio, a series of six cantatas by Bach (1734) designed for separate perf. between Christmas and Epiphany. Not orig. intended for perf. as one composite work.

Christmas Symphony (Haydn). *See* **Lamentatione.**

Christoff, Boris (b. Sofia, 18. V. 1918), Bulg. bass-baritone. Initially a law student, he later studied singing in Rome and Salzburg, making his début in Rome in 1946. He excels in the Russian repertory (esp. *Boris Godunov*) and has also given numerous recitals.

Christophe Colomb (*Christopher Columbus*), opera by Milhaud (lib. by Paul Claudel), prod., in Ger., Berlin, Opera, 5. V. 1930. The work makes use of cinematographic films.

Christus, oratorio by Liszt (words from the Bible and the Roman Catholic liturgy), comp. 1855–66, 1st perf. Weimar, 29. V. 1873.

Oratorio by Mendelssohn (words by Chevalier Bunsen), begun 1844, resumed 1847, but left unfinished.

Christus am Oelberge (*Christ at the Mount of Olives*), oratorio by Beethoven, Op. 85 (lib. by Franz Xaver Huber), prod. Vienna, 5. IV. 1803.

Chromatic (from Gk. *chrōmatikos* = coloured). The C. scale is one proceeding entirely by semitones, i.e. taking in all the notes available in normal western mus. (*see* illustration). C. harmony consists of

strings for all the notes of the chromatic scale. They are not all strung parallel, but slightly crossed, so that except where they actually intersect they stand away from each other in 2 ranges, one repres. the diatonic scale of C maj., the other the sharps or flats, like the white and black notes on the pf.

Chromatic Madrigal. (1) A madrigal making free use of chromatic harmony.

(2) In 16th-cent. It. a *madrigale cromatico* was one using black notes as the basis of measurement and hence moving at a brisk speed.

Chrotta. *See* **Crwth.**

Chrysander, (Karl Franz) Friedrich (b. Lübtheen, Mecklenburg, 8. VII. 1826; d. Bergedorf nr. Hamburg, 3. IX. 1901), Ger. mus. scholar and ed. Lived in Eng. for some time to research into material for his great biog. of Handel, pub. 1858–67, never completed. He also ed. Handel's complete works. Other works of his on old mus. are valuable, but he was violently opposed to all 'modern', i.e. post-Handelian, mus.

Chueca, Federico (b. Madrid, 5. V. 1846; d. Madrid, 20. VI. 1908), Span. comp. Studied the mus. of the Span. people in var. parts of the country and reprod. it in many of his light operas. He organized a street band for his own amusement and attracted Barbieri's attention with a set of waltzes for orch., which B. conducted with success.

Works incl. light operas *Cádiz, Caramelo, La alegría de la huerta, La caza del oso, Pobre chica, El caballero de gracia, La gran vía* (with Valverde) and others; waltzes, etc.

Church Modes. *See* **Modes.**

Church Sonata. *See* **Sonata da chiesa.**

Churchill, Sir Winston (Leonard Spencer) Rt. Hon. (1874–1965), Eng. politician. *See* **Gundry** (passages from a speech).

Chute (Fr.). *See* **Ornaments.**

CHROMATIC

chords using notes not included in the scale of the prevailing key and thus, in notation, involving the use of many accidentals.

Chromatic Fantasy and Fugue. A keyboard work in D min. by Bach, written *c.* 1720–3. The adj. refers to the Fantasy, but there is also some chromaticism in the Fugue.

Chromatic Harp, a Fr. type of harp which, instead of being tuned to the scale of C♭ maj., like the normal harp, where each string can be raised in pitch by a semitone or a whole tone with the aid of pedals, has

Chute de la Maison Usher, La (*The Fall of the House of Usher*), opera by Debussy (lib. by himself, based on Edgar Allan Poe's story), worked at between 1908 and 1918, but never completed.

Chybiński, Adolf (b. Cracow, 29. III. 1880; d. Poznan, 31. X. 1952), Pol. musicologist. Studied at Cracow Univ. and Munich. App. prof. of harmony at the Lwów Cons. in 1916, lecturer at the univ. there in 1917 and prof. of mus. in 1921. He ed. old Pol. mus. and wrote on the subject and on others in Pol. and Ger.

Ciacona (It.). *See* **Chaconne.**

Ciaia, A. B. della. *See* **Della Ciaia.**

Ciampi, Vincenzo Legrenzio (b. Piacenza, 1719; d. Venice, 30. III. 1762), It. comp. Pupil of Durante. He was resident in London 1748–60, and from the latter year to his death *maestro di cappella* at the Ospizio degli Incurabili in Venice.
Works incl. 22 operas, e.g. *Bertoldo, Bertoldino e Cacasenno* and *Il negligente*; 4 oratorios; church mus., chamber mus., etc.

Cibber, Colley (1671–1757), Eng. actor and playwright of Dan. descent. *See* **Carey** (*The Provoked Husband*), **Finger** (*Love makes a Man*), **Franck** (**J. W.**) (*Love's Last Shift*), **Paisible** (2 plays), **Pepusch** (*Myrtillo*), **Purcell** (**D.**) (*Love's L. S.* and *Love makes a Man*), **Weldon** (*She would*).

Cibber, Susanna Maria. *See* **Arne.**

Ciconia, Johannes (b. Liège, *c.* 1340; d. after 142), Flem. comp. He was active in Padua and Venice from about 1400, returning to Liège *c.* 1413. He wrote Mass movements, motets, a canon and secular pieces to Fr. and It. words. There is also a treatise, *Nova musica.*

Cid, Der, opera by Cornelius (lib. by comp., based on Corneille's drama), prod. Weimar, 21. V. 1865.

Cid, Le, opera by Massenet (lib. by Adolphe Philippe d'Ennery, Louis Gallet and Édouard Blau, based on Corneille's drama), prod. Paris, Opéra, 30. XI. 1885.

Cifra, Antonio (b. Rome, 1584; d. Loreto, 2. X. 1629), It. comp. Pupil of G. B. Nanini in Rome. He was *maestro di cappella* of the Ger. Coll. there in 1609, at Loreto from 1609 to 1622 and at the church of St. John Lateran, Rome, from 1622 to 1625, returning to Loreto in 1626.
Works incl. Masses, motets, psalms, madrigals, etc.

Cigale et la Fourmi, La (*The Grasshopper and the Ant:* in Eng. known as *La Cigale*), operetta by Audran (lib. by Henri Charles Chivot and Alfred Duru, the title alluding to La Fontaine's fable), prod. Paris, Théâtre de la Gaîté, 30. X. 1886.

Cikker, Jan (b. Banska Bystrica, 29. VII. 1911), Cz. comp. Studied comp. with J. Křička and Novák. He became prof. at Bratislava Cons. in 1951. His chief interest is in theatre comp., writing in an atonal, though romantically inclined, idiom.
Works incl. operas *Beg Bejazid, Resurrection* (after Tolstoy), *Mr. Scrooge* (after Dickens).

Cilea, Francesco (b. Palmi, Calabria, 26. VII. 1866; d. Varazze, 20. XI. 1950), It. comp. Studied at Naples and while still at the Cons. prod. his 1st opera there in 1889. The pub. Sonzogno then commissioned a second, prod. at Florence in 1892. Prof. at the Reale Istituto Musicale at Florence, 1896–1904.
Works incl. operas *Gina, La Tilda, L'Arlesiana* (after Daudet), *Adriana Lecouvreur* (after Scribe), *Gloria*; cello and pf. sonata; numerous pf. works, etc.

Cimador(o), Giovanni Battista (b. Venice, 1761; d. Bath, 27. II. 1805), It. comp. Successfully prod. dramatic works *Ati e Cibeli, Il ratto di Proserpina* and 'scena lyrica' *Pimmalione* in It., but settled in London *c.* 1791. Other works incl. concerto for double bass, vocal pieces, etc.

Cimarosa, Domenico (b. Aversa nr. Naples, 17. XII. 1749; d. Venice, 11. I. 1801), It. comp. Studied at Naples, among his masters being Sacchini and Piccinni, and prod. his 1st opera there in 1772. Later lived in Rome and Naples by turns, became famous with several operas, travelled much and in 1787 went to the court of Catherine II at St. Petersburg. In 1791 the Emperor Leopold II invited him to Vienna, to succeed Salieri as court *Kapellmeister.* There he prod. his most successful opera, *Il matrimonio segreto*, in 1792. His engagement in Vienna ended the same year, when, on the death of Leopold, Salieri was re-app. C. returned to Naples, becoming *maestro di cappella* to the king. He was imprisoned because of his involvement in the Neapolitan rising of 1799. On his release he set out for St. Petersburg, but d. at Venice on the way.
Works incl. over 60 operas, e.g. *Le stravaganze del conte, L'Italiana in Londra, Il pittore parigino, La ballerina amante, L'Olimpiade, Artaserse, L'impresario in angustie, Cleopatra, Idalide, Il matrimonio segreto, Le astuzie femminili, Il marito disperato, L'impegno superato, Gli Orazi ed i Curiazi, Penelope, Achille all' assedio di Troia*; Masses, oratorios, cantatas, etc.

Cimbalo (Span.) = Cymbal.

Cimbalom, a Hung. nat. instrument, descendant of the dulcimer, with strings stretched over a horizontal sound-board which are struck by hammers.

Cimbasso (It.) = Bass tuba.

Cinderella. *See* **Cendrillon, Cenerentola.**

Cinelli (It.) = Cymbals (more often called *piatti*).

Cinesi, Le (*The Chinamen*), opera by Caldara (lib. by Metastasio), prod. Vienna, at court, Carnival 1735.
Opera by Gluck (lib. do.), prod. Schlosshof nr. Vienna, at court, 24. IX. 1754.

Cinquepace (from Fr. *cinq pas* = 5 steps; also colloq. 'Sink-a-pace') a dance of the 16th cent. in quick 3–4 time and requiring movements in groups of 5 paces. The name was used both for the Galliard following the Pavan and for the Tordion concluding the Basse Danse. Shakespeare makes a pun on it in *Much Ado about Nothing.*

Cinquième (Fr. = fifth), an obsolete name for the vla., also known as *taille*.

Cinti-Damoreau, Laure (Cinthie Montalant) (b. Paris, 6. II. 1801; d. Paris, 25. II. 1863), Fr. opera singer. Studied at the Paris Cons. 1st appearance at the Théâtre Italien at the age of 18 and at the Opéra in 1826. She remained there until 1835 and the following year joined the Opéra-Comique.

Ciphering, the escape of sound from org. pipes by a fault in or damage to the mechanism.

Circassian Bride, The, opera by Bishop (lib. by Charles Ward), prod. London, Drury Lane Theatre, 23. II, 1809.

Circe and Penelope, 2 parts of a cyclic opera, *Ulysses,* by Keiser (lib. by Friedrich Christian Bressand), prod. Brunswick, II. 1696.

Circolo mezzo (It.) = Turn.

Circular Canon, a canon whose tune, instead of coming to an end, returns to the beginning and may be repeated *ad infinitum.* The round, e.g. *Three blind mice,* is a familiar example.

Ciro in Babilonia, o sia La caduta di Baldassarre (*Cyrus in Babylon, or The Fall of Belshazzar*), opera by Rossini (lib. by Francesco Aventi), prod. Ferrara, 14. III. 1812.

Cirullo, Giovanni Antonio (b. Andria, ?; d. Andria, ?), It. 16th–17th-cent. comp. Lived at Andria nr. Bari. Pub. 6 books of madrigals and contrib. to Phalèse's collection *Il Helicone* in 1616.

Cithara. *See* **Kithara.**

Citole (Fr.), medieval ancestor of the Cittern.

Cittern (or **Cithren, Cither, Cythern,** etc.), an obs. string instrument of the guitar type, a descendant of the medieval citole. It usually had 4 pairs of wire strings tuned either: or:

The finger-board was fretted and the strings were played either with the fingers or with a plectrum. The back was flat. The modern Ger. and Aus. *Zither* derives its name from it, but is a different instrument.

Cividale del Friuli, Antonio da (Antonius de Civitate Austriae) (b. ?; d. ?), It. 14th–15th-cent. comp. active at Florence as well as in N. It. 5 motets, 3 Mass movements, 4 *chansons* and one *ballata* survive.

Clairon (Fr.) = Bugle.

Clapisson, Antoine Louis (b. Naples, 15. IX. 1808; d. Paris, 19. III. 1866), Fr. violinist and comp. Violinist at the Paris Opéra, 1832–8, after which he made a great success with songs and comic operas. His collection of old instruments is in the Paris Cons.

Works incl. operas *La Figurante, Le Code noir, Gibby la Cornemuse, La Promise, La Fanchonnette, Madame Grégoire,* etc.

Clapp, Philip Greeley (b. Boston, Mass., 4. VIII. 1888; d. Iowa City, 9. IV. 1954), Amer. comp. Graduated at Harvard Univ. and studied with Schillings at Stuttgart, and in London. After several scholastic appts. he became Prof. of Mus. at Iowa Univ.

Works incl. cantata *A Chant of Darkness* (Helen Keller); 12 symphs., symph. poem *A Song of Youth,* prelude *Summer, An Academic Diversion, Overture to a Comedy, Prologue to a Tragedy* for orch.; *Norge* for pf. and orch., pf. concerto in B min., Fantasy on an Old Plainchant for cello and orch., *Dramatic Poem* for tromb. and orch.; songs with orch.; Fanfare Prelude for 20 brass instruments; Suite for brass 6tet, Concert Suite for 4 trombs., Prelude and Finale for woodwind 5tet; string 4tet in C min.; vln. and pf. sonata; sonatina for pf.; 20 songs; anthem 'O Gladsome Light' with org.; part-songs, etc.

Clarabella. *See* **Claribel.**

Claretie, Jules (1840–1913), Fr. novelist and dramatist. *See* **Navarraise** (Massenet).

Clari, Giovanni Carlo Maria (b. Pisa, 27. IX. 1677; d. Pisa, 16. V. 1754), It. comp. *Maestro di cappella* successively at Pistoia (*c.* 1712), Bologna (1720) and Pisa (1736). 5 of his vocal duets were used by Handel in *Theodora.*

Works incl. opera *Il Savio delirante;* 11 oratorios; Masses, *Stabat Mater* and other church mus., etc.

Clari, or The Maid of Milan, opera by Bishop (lib. by John Howard Payne, based on Marmontel's story, *Laurette*), prod. London, Covent Garden Theatre, 8. V. 1823. It contains the song *Home, sweet home,* not only as a song, but as a kind of *Leitmotiv* or theme-song occurring in var. forms.

Claribel (or **Clarabella** or **Claribel Flute**), an 8-ft. org. stop of wooden flues.

Clarichord (Eng., obs.), a corruption, prob. from Lat. *clarus,* of Clavichord.

Clarinet. A woodwind instrument with a single reed made in var. pitches, the most current being C.s in A and in B♭ (there is also a smaller C. in E♭). It came into use later than the other woodwind instruments still current, and did not estab. itself regularly in the orch. until after the middle of the 18th cent. The sounding compass of the A C. is:

8ve higher

of the B♭:

8ve higher

of the E♭:

Other members of the family are the **Basset Horn**, the **Clarinette d'amour**, the **Bass Clarinet** and the **Contrabass** (or **Pedal**) **Clarinet** (with a compass 2 octaves below the ordinary C.). Also an 8-ft reed org. stop reproducing the tone of the C.

Clarinet Quintet, the technical term for a 5tet for clar. and string 4tet.

Clarinette d'amour (Fr. = love clar.), an obs. instrument a maj. 3rd or 4th lower than the clar. in C.

Clarino (It. = clarion), the name given to the tpt. in the 17th and 18th cents., also the name of the highest register of the instrument, from C above middle C upwards, which was regularly used for florid passages in the works of Bach and his contemporaries.

As a name for the instrument it = Tromba. In the early 18th cent. it sometimes = Clarinet, for which the normal It. term was *clarinetto*.

Clarion. *See* **Clarino**. C. may also be a 4-ft. reed stop on the org.

Clarion Mixture, an org. stop with Mixtures prod. by flue-pipes.

Clarionet (obs.). *See* **Clarinet**.

Clarionet Flute, a stopped diapason org. stop with 8-ft. tone.

Clarke, Jeremiah (b. ? London, *c*. 1673; d. London, 1. XII. 1707), Eng. comp. Pupil of Blow at the Chapel Royal, organist at Winchester Coll., 1692–5, and of St. Paul's Cathedral in London from 1695. Sworn Gentleman-extraordinary of the Chapel Royal in 1700 and organist in 1704. He committed suicide.

Works incl. anthems; odes on the Assumption of the Blessed Virgin, in praise of Barbadoes and *O Harmony*; setting of Dryden's *Alexander's Feast*; operas *The Island Princess* (with D. Purcell and Leveridge), *The World in the Moon* (Settle, with D. Purcell); incid. mus. for Shakespeare's *Titus Andronicus*, Sedley's *Antony and Cleopatra* and other plays; harpsichord lessons, many songs, etc.

Clarke, Rebecca (b. Harrow, 27. VIII. 1886), Eng. vla. player and comp. Studied at the R.A.M. in London. In a competition in U.S.A. in 1919 for a work for vla. and pf. she won the prize with a sonata, 2nd only to Ernest Bloch's Suite. She settled in N.Y. in 1944 and married James Friskin.

Works incl. Psalm for chorus; pf. trio; vla. and pf. sonata, Rhapsody for cello and pf., duets for vla. and cello; songs for voice and vln. and for voice and pf.; instrumental pieces, etc.

Clarone (It.) = Bass Clarinet (also called *clarinetto basso*), earlier sometimes the name for the Basset Horn.

Clarseach (Gael.), the old Celtic harp, formerly used in Ir., Wales and Scot. and revived in the last-named region early in the 20th cent. for the accomp. of the rediscovered Gaelic folksongs.

Classical, a term commonly used to denote the period of Haydn, Mozart and Beethoven, as opposed to the late Romantic period.

Claudel, Paul (1868–1955), Fr. poet and dramatist. *See* **Christophe Colomb** (Milhaud), **Homme et son désir** (do.), **Honegger** (*Danse des morts, Soulier de satin*, 3 songs), **Jeanne d'Arc au bûcher** (Honegger), **Milhaud** (*Protée, Annonce faite à Marie*, Aeschylus transs. and songs).

Claudine von Villa Bella, play for mus. by Goethe.

Mus. by Ignaz von Beeck (1733–1803), prod. Vienna, Burgtheater, 13. VI. 1780.

Mus. by Johann Christoph Kienlen (1784–*c*. 1830), prod. Munich, 9. IX. 1810.

Mus. by Reichardt, prod. Charlottenburg, Schlosstheater, at court, 29. VII. 1789; perf. Berlin, Opera, 3. VIII. 1789.

Mus. by Claus Schall (1757–1837) (lib. a Dan. translation of Goethe's play by Niels Henrik Weinwich), prod. Copenhagen, 29. I. 1787.

Claudio da Correggio. *See* **Merulo.**

Claudius, Matthias (1740–1815), Ger. poet. *See* **Schoeck** (*Wandsbecker Liederbuch*), **Siegi** (*Grosse Hallelujah*). 12 songs by **Schubert.**

Clausula, an interpolation in regular rhythm into 12th- and 13th-cent. organum, without words, but either sung to the syllable of the text immediately preceding it or played by instruments or both together. The lowest (tenor) part, which in the main portions of the music is in very long notes, here moves at a quicker speed, the notes being arranged in a rhythmical pattern. Numerous Cs. were also designed apparently as independent pieces. In later usage the term meant 'cadential formula'.

Clavecin (Fr.) = Harpsichord (old spelling sometimes *clavessin*).

Clavecin oculaire. *See* **Castel** and **Colour Music.**

Clavel, Antoinette. *See* **Saint-Huberty.**

Clavicembalo (It.) = Harpsichord. The abbr. *cembalo* is often used.

Clavichord, a stringed keyboard instrument which differs in its tone-production from the harpsichord. The strings are not plucked, but struck by a tangent which presses against them as long as the key is held down by the finger and prod. a very faint note which can be made to vibrate by a gentle shaking of the finger. The pitch of the note is determined by the place at which the string is struck by the tangent, so that the same string can be used for 2 adjacent notes, which then can never be sounded simultaneously. Such instruments are called 'fretted' Cs.; those which have a separate string for each note are 'fretless'.

Clavicymbal (Eng., obs.), the name sometimes given in Eng. to the harpsichord, from the It. *clavicembalo*.

Clavicytherium (Lat.), a harpsichord whose wing-shaped body stood upright instead of being placed horizontally as in the grand pf.

Clavier (Fr. and Ger. = keyboard; Ger. also = harpsichord or pf.). In Eng. the word may be used to designate any stringed keyboard instrument, esp. the harpsichord, clavichord and early pf. in cases where it is doubtful which was used in perf. or where the choice was at the player's discretion.

Clavierübung (Ger. lit. 'keyboard practice'). A collection of keyboard mus. by Bach, pub. in 4 parts: I (1731), 6 partitas; II (1735), It. concerto and 'Fr. overture' (partita in B min.); III (1739), org. prelude and fugue in E♭ maj. framing 21 chorale preludes on the catechism and 4 harpsichord *duetti*; IV (1742), 'Goldberg' variations.

Clavijo del Cartillo, Bernardo. *See* Cartillo.

Clavilux. *See* Colour Music.

Claviorganum, an instrument combining harpsichord and org. mechanisms, dating from the late 16th cent. and made in var. forms until the 18th.

Clay, Frederic (b. Paris, 3. VIII. 1838; d. Great Marlow, 24. XI. 1889), Eng. comp. Pupil of Molique and of Hauptmann at Leipzig. He began by writing light operas for amateurs, 1859–60, but prod. *Court and Cottage* at Covent Garden Theatre in London in 1862.

Works incl. light operas *Princess Toto*, *Don Quixote*, *The Merry Duchess*, *The Golden Ring*, etc.; incid. mus. for Shakespeare's *Twelfth Night*; cantatas *The Knights of the Cross* and *Lalla Rookh* (Moore), the latter incl. 'I'll sing thee songs of Araby'; songs 'She wandered down the mountainside', *The Sands of Dee*, etc.

Clayton, Thomas (b. ? London, *c.* 1670; d. ? London, *c.* 1730), Eng. comp. and adapter. He set Addison's opera lib. of *Rosamond*, which proved a complete failure, in 1707. *Arsinoë*, prod. as his own opera in 1705, was a pasticcio of It. songs. In 1711 he prod. a setting of an altered version of Dryden's *Alexander's Feast*.

Clef, the sign in front of the key and time signatures at the beginning of a comp. and repeated on each stave, determining the position of the notes shown on the stave; e.g. the C clef placed on the 3rd line indicates that the note on that line is middle C.

Clemenceau, Georges (1841–1929), Fr.

statesman and author. *See* Fauré (*Voix du bonheur*, incid. mus.).

Clemens non Papa (Lat. = Clement, not Papa). *See* Clément, Jacques.

Clément, Félix (b. Paris, 13. I. 1822; d. Paris, 23. I. 1885), Fr. musicologist, ed. and comp. Wrote largely on and ed. church mus. Comps. incl. choruses for Racine's *Athalie* and *Esther*.

Clement, Franz (Joseph) (b. Vienna, 17. XI. 1780; d. Vienna, 3. XI. 1842), Aus. violinist. 1st appeared at the age of 7; leader of the orch. at the Theater an der Wien in Vienna in 1802–11 and 1817–21. Beethoven wrote his vln. concerto for him.

Clément, Jacques (called **Jacobus Clemens non Papa**) (b. Ypres, *c.* 1500; d. ? Dixmude, *c.* 1556), ? Flem. comp. Worked at Bruges, (?) at Antwerp Cathedral and at the cathedral of 's Hertogenbosch. His nickname was long said to have distinguished him from Pope Clement VII, but it did not appear on pubs. until 14 years after that pope's death. There was a poet at Ypres named Jacobus Papa, to whom C.'s 'non Papa' may refer.

Works (over 400) incl. Masses, motets, psalms in Flem., *chansons*, etc.

Clementi, Muzio (b. Rome, 23. I. 1752; d. Evesham, 10. III. 1832), It. pianist, comp., pub. and pf. manufacturer. Showed early promise, and had comp. several works by the age of 14, when Peter Beckford took him to Eng. to complete his education. Pub. his 1st pf. sonatas in 1773, and appeared with spectacular success as virtuoso pianist and comp. He was cond. of the It. Opera in London 1777–80, after which he toured extensively on the Continent, in 1781 playing before the Viennese court in competition with Mozart (who thought little of him). Back in London, Cramer and John Field were his pupils. He was associated with the mus. pubs. and pf. manufacturers Longman & Broderip, upon whose bankruptcy in 1798 he re-estab. the firm in partnership with Longman. His interest in the co. (trading under a constantly changing variety of names) continued to his death. He was again on tour in Europe 1802–10, taking Field with him to St. Petersburg, where the latter remained. In 1807 he met Beethoven in Vienna. From 1810, apart from occasional further travels, he remained in England.

Works incl. several symphs.; *c.* 60 pf. sonatas; 100 progressive pf. studies entitled *Gradus ad Parnassum*; capriccios and other pf. pieces; sonatas for various instruments and pf.; chamber mus., etc.

Clemenza di Scipione, La (*The Clemency of Scipio*), opera by J. C. Bach (lib. by ?), prod. London, King's Theatre, Haymarket, 4. IV. 1778.

Clemenza di Tito, La (*The Clemency of Titus*). *See also* Tito Vespasiano.

Opera by Gluck (lib. by Metastasio), prod. Naples, Teatro San Carlo, 4. XI. 1752.

Opera by Mozart (lib. do., altered by Caterino Mazzolà), prod. Prague, to celebrate the coronation of the Emperor Leopold II as King of Boh., 6. IX. 1791.

Cleofide, opera by Hasse (lib. by M. A. Boccardi, based on Metastasio's *Alessandro nell'Indie*), prod. Dresden, at court, 13. IX. 1731.

Cleopatra (*Die betrogene Staats-Liebe, oder Die unglückselige Cleopatra, Königin von Egypten*), opera by Mattheson (lib. by Friedrich Christian Feustking), prod. Hamburg, Theatre beim Gänsemarkt, 20. X. 1704.

Cleopatra e Cesare, opera by Graun (lib. by Giovanni Gualberto Bottarelli, based on Corneille's *La Mort de Pompée*), prod. Berlin, Opera, 7. XII. 1742. Written for the inauguration of that theatre.

Cleopatra's Night, opera by H. K. Hadley (lib. by Alice Leal Pollock, based on Théophile Gautier's *Une Nuit de Cléopâtre*), prod. N.Y., Metropolitan Opera, 31. I. 1920.

Cléopâtre, opera by Massenet (lib. by Louis Payen), prod. Monte Carlo, 23. II. 1914.

Clérambault, Louis Nicolas (b. Paris, 19. XII. 1676; d. Paris, 26. X. 1749), Fr. organist and comp. Pupil of André Raison. Organist at var. Paris churches. Wrote cantatas and pieces for org. and for harpsichord.

Cleve, Johannes de (b. ? Cleve, *c.* 1529; d. Augsburg, 14. VII. 1582), Flem. comp. Sang tenor in the imp. chapel in Vienna under Ferdinand I, 1553–64. He wrote Masses, motets and settings of Ger. Protestant texts.

Cliff (Eng., obs.) = Clef.

Clifford, James (b. Oxford, 1622; d. London, IX. 1698), Eng. divine and musician. Chorister at Magdalen Coll., Oxford, 1632–42; app. min. canon at St. Paul's Cathedral in London, 1661. Pub. a collection of the words of *Divine Services and Anthems*, 1663.

Clive (*née* Raftor), Catherine (Kitty) (b. London, 1711; d. Twickenham, 6. XII. 1785), Eng. actress and stage singer. Attached to Drury Lane Theatre in London, 1728–41.

Cloches de Corneville, Les (*The Bells of C.*), operetta by Planquette (lib. by Clairville and Charles Gabet), prod. Paris, Folies-Dramatiques, 19. IV. 1877.

Clochette, La (*The Little Bell*), opera by Duni (lib. by Louis Anseaume), prod. Paris, Comedie-Italienne, 24. VII. 1766.

Clochette, La, ou Le Diable page (*The Little Bell, or Devil as Page*), opera by Hérold (lib. by Emmanuel Guillaume Théaulon de Lambert), prod. Paris,

Opéra-Comique, 18. X. 1817. Schubert wrote 2 songs for the Vienna prod. in 1821.

'Clock Symphony', the nickname of Haydn's symph. No. 101, in D maj. (No. 9 of the 'Salomon' symphs.), written for London in 1794. The name derives from the ticking motion of the accomp. figuration in the slow movement.

Close Shake. *See* Vibrato.

Closed Horn, an 8-ft. reed org. stop.

Closson, Ernest (b. Saint-Josse-ten-Noode nr. Brussels, 12. XII. 1870; d. Brussels, 21. XII. 1950), Belg. musicologist. Attached to the Conss. of Brussels and Mons and mus. critic to *L'Indépendance belge* from 1920. Wrote several books on mus., esp. Belg. folksong.

Clough, Arthur Hugh (1819–61), Eng. poet. *See* Gatty (odes).

Club Anthem, an anthem comp. jointly by Blow, Humfrey and Wm. Turner *c.* 1664, when they were choir-boys at the Chapel Royal. It is a setting of the words 'I will always give thanks'.

Club Works. *See* Collective Works.

Cluer, John (b. ?; d. London, 1728), Eng. mus. pub. Worked in London early in the 18th cent. and was succeeded by his widow and later her 2nd husband, Thomas Cobb. He pub. some of Handel's operas.

Clutsam, George (b. Sydney, N.S.W., 26. IX. 1866; d. London, 17. XI. 1951), Austral. pianist and comp. Settled in London after touring as pianist in New Zealand and Asia, and was mus. critic to the *Observer*, 1908–18.

Works incl. operas *A Summer Night* and *After a Thousand Years*; cantata *The Quest of Rapunzel*; symph. idyll *The Lady of Shalott* (Tennyson); mus. comedies, etc. He also prod. a Ger. opera, *König Harlekin*, in Berlin in 1912. He is responsible for the Eng. version of the Schubert pasticcio *Lilac Time* and other similar things.

Cluytens, André (b. Antwerp, 26. III. 1905), Belg. cond. Studied pf. at Antwerp Cons. He 1st worked for his father as a chorus trainer at the Théâtre Royal in Antwerp, where he later cond. opera. Since then he has held numerous posts in France, incl. director of the Paris Opéra.

Coates, Albert (b. St. Petersburg, 23. IV. 1882; d. Milnerton nr. Cape Town, 11. XII. 1953), Eng. cond. and comp. (mother Rus.). Sent to school in Eng. and entered Liverpool Univ., returned to Rus. to enter his father's business, but was sent to Leipzig Cons. on showing mus. gifts. Studied cond. with Nikisch and cond. opera at several Ger. theatres before he was engaged at St. Petersburg. He fled to Eng. during the Revolution in 1919 and settled in London for good.

Works incl. operas *Assurbanipal, Samuel Pepys, Pickwick, Gainsborough's Duchess*;

symph. poem *The Eagle*, Rus. Suite for orch.; pf. pieces, etc.

Coates, Eric (b. Hucknall, Notts., 27. VIII. 1886; d. Chichester, 21. XII. 1957), Eng. comp. Studied at the R.A.M. in London and became a vla. player in a 4tet and in the Queen's Hall Orch., but later devoted himself to the comp. of light and popular mus.

Coates, Henry (b. London, 28. III. 1880; d. East Preston, 28. XII. 1963), Eng. writer on mus., teacher and lecturer. Took the degrees of M.A. (Cantab.) and Ph.D. (London); teacher in the Faculty of Mus., London Univ., fellow and member of the board of Trinity Coll. of Mus., where he was teacher and examiner, as also at the G.S.M., lecturer to the London County Council, etc. He was the author of a book on Palestrina, and also ed. of Franck's and other org. mus.

Coates, John (b. Girlington nr. Bradford, 29. VI. 1865; d. Northwood nr. London, 16. VIII. 1941), Eng. tenor. He was trained for and began to make a career as a bariton_, but made his 1st appearance as a _nor in 1899. He became equally famous in opera and oratorio, and later in life was one of the finest song recitalists.

Cobbett, W(alter). W(illson). (b. Blackheath, 11. VII. 1847; d. London, 22. I. 1937), Eng. mus. amateur and ed. A wealthy business man, he did much valuable work for chamber mus. by offering prizes for new works by Brit. comps., esp. 1-movement fantasies, and he ed. a *Cyclopaedic Survey of Chamber Music* pub. in 1929.

Cobbold, William (b. Norwich, 5. I. 1560; d. Beccles, 7. XI. 1639), Eng. organist and comp. Organist at Norwich Cathedral, 1599–1608. He was one of the 10 musicians who harmonized the tunes in East's Psalter of 1592 and he contrib. a madrigal to *The Triumphes of Oriana* in 1601. Another madrigal and an anthem are preserved.

Cocchi, Claudio (b. Genoa, ?; d. ?), It. 17th-cent. comp. Worked in Ger. for a time and later at Trieste Cathedral and San Francesco at Milan.

Works incl. Masses; books of vocal mus. entitled *Armonici concentus* and *Ghirlanda sacra*, etc.

Cocchi, Gioacchino (b. ? Naples, *c.* 1715; d. Venice, 1804), It. comp. Worked at Naples, Rome and Venice until 1757, when he went to London as comp. to the King's Theatre, remaining there till 1773. He was also cond. of Mrs. Cornely's subscription concerts.

Works incl. over 40 operas, e.g. *La Maestra, Li Matti per Amore, Demetrio re di Siria*, etc.

Coccia, Carlo (b. Naples, 14. IV. 1782; d. Novara, 13. IV. 1873), It. comp. Pupil of Paisiello. He prod. many operas in It. between 1807 and 1820, when he went 1st

to Lisbon and then to London. He became cond. of the Opera there, also prof. of comp. at the R.A.M., and stayed until 1828, returning in 1833, but eventually settling at Novara as *maestro di cappella* in succession to Mercadante, 1840.

Works incl. *c.* 40 operas, e.g. *Il matrimonio per cambiale, Donna Caritea, Maria Stuarda, Il lago delle fate*, 2 cantatas, etc.

Coccia, Maria Rosa (b. Rome, 4. I. 1759; d. Rome, XI. 1833), It. comp. At the age of 16 she passed a severe examination at the Accademia di Santa Cecilia in Rome with brilliant success and an account of it was pub. In 1780 another eulogy of her was issued with letters from Martini, Metastasio and Farinelli.

Works incl. Magnificat for voices and org., written at 15, *Dixit Dominus* and a cantata, but most are lost.

Cochlaeus, Johannes (Johann Dobnek) (b. Wendelstein nr. Nuremberg, 10. I. 1479; d. Breslau, 10. I. 1552), Ger. cleric and mus. scholar. He was a Roman Catholic and an opponent of Luther, in office at Cologne, Worms, Mainz and Frankfurt. Wrote a treatise on mus. and comp. odes, etc.

Cockaigne (In London Town), concert overture by Elgar, Op. 40, comp. 1900 and 1st perf. London, Phil. Society, 20. VI. 1901.

Coclico (Coclicus), Adrien Petit (b. ? Hainault, *c.* 1500; d. Copenhagen, 1563), Flem. comp. Pupil of Josquin des Prés. He was in Rome as a member of the Papal chapel, but was imprisoned for moral laxity, went to Wittenberg in 1545 and became a Protestant. After var. posts in Ger. he went to the Dan. court at Copenhagen. Pub. a treatise entitled *Compendium musices* and *Musica reservata* (psalm settings).

Cocteau, Jean (1891–1963), Fr. critic and author. *See* Antigone (Honegger), **Bowles** (*Memnon*), **Mariés de la Tour d'Eiffel** (Les Six), **Markevitch** (cantata), **Milhaud** (songs), **Poulenc** (*Cocardes*).

Coda (It. = tail), the part of a mus. comp. which forms a peroration, where it can be regarded, from the structural point of view, as a distinct and separate section. It is thus most clearly marked, for ex., in sonata form, where it appears as a 4th division after the exposition, working-out and recapitulation, or in a minuet or scherzo with trio, where it rounds off the movement after the restatement of the 1st section, usually with material based either on that or on the trio.

Codetta (It. = little tail), a small form of coda, not appearing as a rule at the end of a movement, but rather rounding off a section of such a movement, or a theme or group of themes, thus assuming the function of a bridge-passage.

Coelho, Ruy (b. Alcácer do Sal, 3. III. 1891), Port. comp. Studied at Lisbon and later with Humperdinck in Berlin. Became mus. critic of the *Diario de Noticias* at Lisbon and in 1924 won a prize with his 2nd opera.

Works incl. operas *Ines de Castro, Belkiss, Crisfal, Entre gestas, Tá-Mar*; symph. poems *Sinfonia camoniana, Promenade d'été*, etc.; chamber mus., pf. pieces, songs, etc.

Coerne, Louis (Adolphe) (b. Newark, N.J., 27. II. 1870; d. Boston, Mass., 11. IX. 1922), Amer. cond. and comp. Studied in Ger., Fr. and at Harvard Univ. After filling an organist's post at Buffalo and cond. there and at Columbus, he became assoc. prof. at Smith Coll., Northampton, Mass., and also taught at Harvard. Later he held other distinguished teaching posts and visited Ger., where some of his works were perf.

Works incl. operas *A Woman of Marblehead, Zenobia* and *Sakuntala* (after Kalidasa); incid. mus. to Euripides' *Trojan Women*; 6-part Mass; symph. poem *Hiawatha* (after Longfellow) and other works for orch.; vln. concerto; string 4tet in C min., 3 pf. trios in canon; Swed. sonata for vln. and pf.; pf. pieces; songs, partsongs, etc.

Cœuroy, André (actually Jean Bélime) (b. Dijon, 24. II. 1891), Fr. critic and musicologist. Studied mus. privately with Reger in Ger. Became mus. critic of *Paris-Midi* and founder, with Prunières, of the *Revue musicale* in 1920. He has ed. books on mus. and written works on modern mus., the relationships between mus. and literature, trans. old and modern operas from Ger., etc.

Coffee Cantata ('Schweiget stille, plaudert nicht'), a secular cantata by Bach for solo voices, chorus and orch., comp. *c.* 1732.

Coffey, Charles (?–1745), Ir. playwright. Author of the early ballad operas *The Devil to pay* (1731) and *The Merry Cobbler* (1735).

Cohen, Harriet (b. London, 2. XII. 1895; d. London, 13. XI. 1967), Eng. pianist. Studied at the R.A.M. and with T. Matthay, making her début, aged 13, at the Queen's Hall, London. She did much for Eng. mus., esp. that of Bax, and also pub. a book, *Music's Handmaid*, on pf.-playing and interpretation. In 1937 she was awarded the C.B.E.

Cohen, Jules (Émile David) (b. Marseilles, 2. XI. 1835; d. Paris, 13. I. 1901), Fr. comp. Studied at the Paris Cons., where he was prof. later.

Works incl. operas *Maître Claude, José Maria, Les Bleuets*, etc.; incid. mus. for Racine's *Athalie* and *Esther*, etc.

Coke, Roger Sacheverell (b. Derbyshire 20. X. 1912), Eng. pianist and comp. Educ. at Eton Coll. First appeared as pianist and comp. in 1932.

Works (some withdrawn) incl. opera *The Cenci* (after Shelley); 3 symphs., *The Lotos Eaters* and 3 other symph. poems; 6 pf. concertos, 3 vocal concertos for soprano and orch.; chamber mus.; 3 cello and pf. sonatas; 3 pf. sonatas, variations and other works for pf.; *c.* 80 songs, etc.

Col legno (It. = 'with the wood'), a direction indicating that a passage for a string instrument or a group of such instruments is to be played by striking the strings with the stick of the bow.

Colachon ⎱ an obs. instrument of the
Colascione ⎰ lute type used esp. in S. It., very large in size, but having only 2 or 3 strings.

Colasse, Pascal (b. Rheims, I. 1649; d. Versailles, 17. VII. 1709), Fr. comp. Studied at the Maîtrise de Saint-Paul and the Collège de Navarre in Paris, and *c.* 1677 obtained an appt. at the Opéra from Lully, in whose works he wrote some of the subordinate parts. In 1683 he became one of the 4 superintendents of the royal chapel, each of whom had to direct the mus. for 3 months in the year, and 2 years later he shared with Lalande the appt. of royal chamber musician. *Maître de musique de chambre* from 1696.

Works incl. operas *Achille et Polyxène* (with Lully), *Thétis et Pélée, Énée et Lavinie, Jason, La Naissance de Vénus, Polyxène et Pyrrhus*, etc.; motets, *Cantiques spirituels* and other church mus., etc.

Colbran, Isabella (Ángela) (b. Madrid, 2. II. 1785; d. Bologna, 7. X. 1845), Span. mezzo-soprano. Made her 1st appearance in It. in 1806; married Rossini in 1822; comp. songs.

Coleman, Charles (b. ?; d. London, before 9. VII. 1664), Eng. comp. Chamber musician to Charles I and after the Civil War mus. teacher in London. Mus.D., Cambridge, 1651; app. comp. to Charles II, 1662. With Cooke, Hudson, H. Lawes and Locke he contrib. mus. to Davenant's *Siege of Rhodes* (entertainment at Rutland House), 1656.

Coleman, Edward (b. ?; d. Greenwich, 29. VIII. 1669), Eng. singer, lutenist and comp., son of prec. Both he and his wife sang in *The Siege of Rhodes* in 1656. He became a Gentleman of the Chapel Royal on its re-estab. in 1660 and succeeded Lanier in the royal band in 1662. Comp. incid. mus. to Shirley's *Contention of Ajax and Achilles* in 1653, contrib. songs to *Select Musicall Ayres and Dialogues* the same year, and pieces of his appeared in Playford's *Musical Companion* in 1672.

Coleridge, Samuel Taylor (1772–1834), Eng. poet, critic and philosopher. *See* **Barnett** (J. F.) (*Ancient Mariner*), **Coleridge-Taylor** (*Kubla Khan*), **Griffes** (do.).

Coleridge-Taylor, Avril (b. London, 8.

III. 1903), Eng. cond. and comp., daughter of Samuel C.-T. Studied at the G.S.M.

Works incl. *Wyndore* and *Hist. Episode* for chorus and orch.; *Sussex Landscape, From the Hills, To April, In Memoriam R.A.F.* for orch.; pf. concerto; instrumental pieces; songs, etc.

Coleridge-Taylor, Samuel (b. London, 15. VIII. 1875; d. Croydon, 1. IX. 1912), Brit. comp., father of prec. Son of a Negro doctor and an Eng. mother. Sang at a church at Croydon as a boy and entered the R.C.M. as a vln. student in 1890, but also studied comp. under Stanford. He had works perf. while still at coll. and in 1899 he was represented at the N. Staffordshire Festival at Hanley. App. cond. of the Handel Society in 1904, and visited U.S.A. that year, as well as in 1906 and 1910; but otherwise devoted all his time to comp. and private teaching, with some teaching activity at the G.S.M. in the last years of his life.

Works incl. opera *Thelma*; settings for solo voices, chorus and orch. of portions from Longfellow's *Hiawatha* (3 parts), Coleridge's *Kubla Khan*, Noyes's *A Tale of Old Japan*; 5 Choral Ballads (Longfellow), *Sea Drift* (Whitman) for chorus; oratorio *The Atonement*; incid. mus. for Shakespeare's *Othello* and Stephen Phillips's *Herod, Ulysses, Nero* and *Faust* (after Goethe); symph. in A min.; *Ballade, African Suite, Scenes from an Everyday Romance*, overture *Toussaint l'Ouverture*, concert march *Ethiopia saluting the Colours, Symph. Variations on an African Air* and *Bamboula* rhapsody for orch.; vln. concerto in G min.; nonet for strings and wind, pf. 5tet, clar. 5tet, string 4tet in D min. and other chamber mus.; vln. and pf. sonata in D min.; many pf. pieces; songs; anthems; part-songs, etc.

Colette, Sidonie Gabrielle Claudine (1873–1954), Fr. novelist and critic. *See* **Enfant et les sortilèges** (Ravel).

Colin Muset. *See* Muset.

Colin, Pierre (b. ?; d. ?), Fr. 16th-cent. comp. 1st chaplain of the *Chapelle des Enfants de France*, 1532–6; master of the children, Autun, 1550. Wrote numerous motets, Masses and *chansons*.

Colinda (Rum.), a Rum. Christmas folksong.

Colla, Giuseppe (b. Parma, 4. VIII. 1739; d. Parma, 16. III. 1806), It. comp. *Maestro di musica* to the court at Parma, 1766, and to Ferdinand of Bourbon, 1785. He married the singer Lucrezia Aguiari in 1780.

Works incl. operas *Adriano in Siria, Andromeda* and 10 others; also church mus.

Colla parte (It. = 'with the part'), a direction indicating that the accomp. to a vocal or instrumental solo part is to follow the soloist in a passage perf. without strict adherence to the tempo.

Collective Works, mus. comps. in which more than one comp. had a hand. *See*
A la manière de . . .
Aiglon, L'
B-la-F Quartet
Baiser et la quittance, Le
Brahms, Dietrich and Schumann, vln. and pf. sonata
'Cadet Rousselle' Variations
Chopsticks Variations
Club Anthem
Don Quixote, The Comical History of
Ernst and Heller, Pensées fugitives
Éventail de Jeanne, L'
Franchomme and others, duos on operatic airs
Garland for the Queen
Hexameron
Hillemacher brothers
In questa tomba oscura
Jour de fête
Joyce Book
Leighton, Teares and Lamentacions
Liberté
Mariés de la Tour Eiffel
Marquise de Brinvilliers, La
Mlada
Mouvements du cœur
Muzio Scevola
Quatorze Juillet (Rolland)
Rebel and Francœur
Requiem for Rossini
Ricci, F. and L. (4 operas)
Siege of Rhodes, The
Triumphes of Oriana, The
Triumphs of Peace, The
Variations on a Rus. Theme
Variations on a Theme by Goossens
Vaterländischer Künstlerverein
Vendredis, Les

Collegium Musicum (Lat. = mus. fraternity), an assoc. for the perf. of chamber and orch. mus. in var. Ger. towns in the 18th cent. Now used in Ger. and Amer. univs.

Colles, H(enry). C(ope). (b. Bridgnorth, 20. IV. 1879; d. London, 4. III. 1943), Eng. mus. critic and scholar. Educ. at Oxford and the R.C.M. in London. Asst. mus. critic to Fuller Maitland on *The Times* until 1911, when he became chief critic, and lecturer at the R.C.M. from 1919. Pub. var. books on mus., incl. *Brahms, The Growth of Music, Voice and Verse*, etc., the 7th vol. of the *Oxford History of Music*, and ed. the 3rd and 4th eds. of Grove's *Dictionary of Music and Musicians*.

Collet, Henri (b. Paris, 5. XI. 1885; d. Paris, 27. XI. 1951), Fr. musicologist and comp. He made a special study of Span. mus. and wrote *Le Mysticisme musical espagnol au XVIe siècle, Victoria, Albéniz et Granados* and *L'Essor de la musique espagnole au XXe siècle*.

Comps. incl. symph. poem *El Escorial*; chamber mus.; songs in the Span. manner, etc.

Collin, Heinrich Joseph von (1771–1811), Aus. poet. His chief connection with mus. is the drama *Coriolan* for which Beethoven wrote an overture. Stadler wrote incid. mus. for his tragedy *Polyxena*.

Collingwood, Lawrance (b. London, 14. III. 1887), Eng. cond. and comp. Chorister at Westminster Abbey and org. scholar at Exeter Coll., Oxford; lived in Rus. for a time and worked with Albert Coates at the St. Petersburg Opera; married there and returned to Eng. during the Revolution. Principal cond. of the Sadler's Wells Opera, 1931–46.

Works incl. opera *Macbeth*, symph. poem for orch., 2 pf. sonatas, etc.

Collins, William (1721–59), Eng. poet. *See* **Cooke (B.)** (*The Passions*), **Cowen** (do.), **Sanderson (J.)** (*Ode to the Passions*), **Smith (A. M.)** (do.).

Collodi, Carlo (C. Lorenzini) (1826–90), It. author. *See* **Toch** (*Pinocchio*).

Colman, George, jun. (1762–1836), Eng. playwright. *See* **Inkle and Yarico** (Arnold), **Kelly** (*Love laughs at Locksmiths*), **Storace (S.)** (*Iron Chest*).

Colman, George, sen. (1732–94), Eng. playwright. *See* **Gast** (*Heimliche Ehe*), **Matrimonio segreto** (Cimarosa).

Colomba, opera by Mackenzie (lib. by Francis Hueffer, based on Mérimée's story), prod. London, Drury Lane Theatre, 9. IV. 1883.

Colombani, Orazio (b. Verona, ?; d. ?, after 1595), It. comp. Pupil of Porta; *maestro di cappella* at Vercelli Cathedral and from 1584 at the monastery of San Francesco, Milan. Later at Venice, Padua and Urbino.

Works incl. Magnificats, Te Deum, psalms; madrigals, etc.

Colombe, La (*The Dove*), opera by Gounod (lib. by Jules Barbier and Michel Carré, after La Fontaine), prod. Baden-Baden, 3. VIII. 1860.

Colombian Composer. *See* **Uribe-Holguin.**

Colonna, Giovanni Paolo (b. Bologna, 16. VI. 1637; d. Bologna, 28. XI. 1695), It. comp. Studied in Rome with Carissimi, Abbatini and Benevoli. Became organist of San Petronio at Bologna in 1659 and *maestro di cappella* in 1674.

Works incl. opera *Amilcare di Cipro* and some others; Masses, motets, psalms, litanies; oratorios, etc.

Colonne, Édouard (actually Judas) (b. Bordeaux, 23. VII. 1838; d. Paris, 28. III. 1910), Fr. violinist and cond. Founder of the Concerts Colonne. He was the 1st to popularize Berlioz and was well known for his perfs. of Wagner, Tchaikovsky and other comps. then unknown in Fr.

Color (Lat.), in medieval mus. = melodic figuration in general. Also a melodic unit repeated in the context of an isorhythmic structure. *See* **Isorhythmic.**

Coloratura (It. lit. colouring), florid singing, esp. in soprano parts containing elaborately decorative passages.

Colour, a word frequently used metaphorically for the different qualities of tone prod. by var. instruments and combinations of instruments. 'Tone-colour' is now generally current.

Colour Music, var. attempts have been made to trans. mus. into colour effects, e.g. by Castel with his 'Clavecin oculaire', Rimington with the 'Colour Org.', Thomas Wilfrid with the 'Clavilux', Skriabin with the 'Tastiera per luce' in the score of his *Prometheus* and Adrian Bernard Klein with an improved 'Colour Org.' exhibited in London in 1932. Comps. referring to or using colour (light):

Bantock, *Atalanta in Calydon*, during the perf. of which the concert-room is to be lighted in a different colour for each movement.

Bliss, *Colour Symph.*, each movement of which bears the name of a colour as title.

Schönberg, *Die glückliche Hand*, in which coloured light plays a part, as noted in the score.

Skriabin, *Prometheus*, which contains an optional part for the *tastiera per luce*, designed to throw differently coloured lights.

Colporteur, Le, ou L'Enfant du bûcheron (*The Pedlar, or The Woodcutter's Child*), opera by Onslow (lib. by François Antoine Eugène de Planard), prod. Paris, Opéra-Comique, 22. XI. 1827.

Coltellini, Celeste (b. Leghorn, 26. XI. 1760; d. Capodimonte nr. Naples, 24. VII. 1828), It. mezzo-soprano. 1st appeared in 1780. Attached to the Teatro dei Fiorentini in Naples 1781–91, but made frequent appearances in Vienna. Paisiello wrote *Nina* for her.

Colum, Padraic (b. 1881), Ir. poet. *See* **Hughes** (songs).

Combarieu, Jules (Léon Jean) (b. Cahors, 3. II. 1859; d. Paris, 7. VII. 1916), Fr. musicologist. Studied with Spitta in Berlin, settled in Paris, founded the *Revue musicale* in 1904 and ed. it until 1912. His books incl. a hist. of mus. in 3 vols. and studies of the relations of mus. to poetry, rhythm, etc.

Combe, William (1741–1823), Eng. author. *See* **Walton** (*Dr. Syntax*).

Combination Tones, the secondary sounds prod. by intervals of 2 notes struck at the same time. There are 2 kinds of C.T.: Difference Tones, prod. by the difference between the 2 generating notes, which consequently sound below the generators, and Summation Tones, prod. by the sum of these 2 notes, which sound above. All C. T. are faint, and some are virtually inaudible. Tartini was the first to observe Difference Tones.

Come prima (It. = as at first), a direction indicating that the opening section of a movement is to be played again exactly as before, or that a passage is to be treated in the same manner as before.

Come sopra (It. = as above), a direction asking the player to repeat the manner of perf. of a passage heard earlier.

Come, thou monarch of the vine, song by Schubert, from Shakespeare's *Antony and Cleopatra*, trans. by Ferdinand von Mayerhofer as *Trinklied*, '*Bacchus*' and comp. in Ger. in 1826.

Comédie lyrique (Fr.), an 18th-cent. Fr. name for comic opera.

Comes. *See* ~~D~~ and **Comes.**

Comes, Juan Bautista (b. Valencia, 29. II. 1568; d. Valencia, 5. I. 1643), Span. comp. *Maestro de capilla* at Lérida at first, later mus. director at Valencia Cathedral from 1613 and again from 1632, with an appt. at the royal chapel in Madrid and another at the Colegio del Patriarca at Valencia in between.

Works incl. much church mus. on a large scale; sacred mus. with Span. words, etc.

Commedia per musica (It. = comedy for mus.), a Neapol. term of the 18th cent. for comic opera.

Commer, Franz (b. Cologne, 23. I. 1813; d. Berlin, 17. VIII. 1887), Ger. organist, ed. and comp. Organist at the Cologne Carmelite Church, 1828–32, then in var. posts in Berlin. Ed. old vocal and org. mus. and comp. a number of works incl. mus. for Aristophanes' *The Frogs* and Sophocles' *Electra*.

Commodo (It.). *See* **Comodo.**

Common Chord, the non-technical term for the maj. or min. triad.

Common Time, a loose but widely current term for 4–4 time.

Communion, the last item of the Proper of the Rom. Mass. Orig. a psalm with antiphon before and after each verse, only the antiphon is now retained. In general style the C. resembles the Introit (*see* illustration).

the unrehearsed perf. by large gatherings of people of folk and popular songs familiar to all.

Comodo (It. = easy, convenient). As a mus. direction the word means leisurely; it is frequently misspelt *commodo* by non-It. comps.

Compass. The range of notes covered by a voice or instrument.

Compenius, Ger. family of org.-builders who also worked in Denmark:

1. Heinrich C. the elder (b. *c.* 1525; d. Nordhausen, 2. V. 1611).

2. Esaias C. (b. ? Eisleben, 1560; d. Frederiksborg, nr. Copenhagen, 1617), son of prec.

3. Heinrich C. the younger (b. Eisleben, 1565; d. Halle, 22. IX. 1631), brother of prec.

4. Ludwig C. (b. ? Halle, *c.* 1603; d. Erfurt, 11. II. 1671), son of prec.

Heinrich C. the elder was also a theorist and comp. The org. at Frederiksborg Castle, rebuilt by Esaias C. in 1616, is still playable. His treatise, *Orgeln Verdingnis* (1615–16), was finished by Michael Praetorius (*c.* 1619).

Compère, Loyset (b. ? Saint-Quentin, *c.* 1455; d. Saint-Quentin, 16. VIII. 1518), Fr. comp. At first a chorister, later a canon and chancellor of Saint-Quentin Cathedral. Pupil of Okeghem (?).

Works incl. motets and other church mus.; sacred and secular vocal comps.; part-songs with It. words, etc.

Competition Festival, an institution in Eng. based on the Eisteddfod in Wales, begun by J. S. Curwen (London) and Mary Wakefield (Kendal) in 1882–5, giving opportunities to bodies of singers and players, or individual perfs., mainly amateurs or learners, to perf. in friendly rivalry and to be judged by professional adjudicators.

Complainte (Fr. = complaint, plaint), an ancient form of Fr. song, esp. a religious ballad.

Composer, the creative mus. artist who

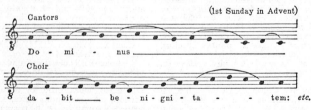

(1st Sunday in Advent)

Cantors

Do — mi — nus _____

Choir

da — bit _____ be — ni — gni — ta — — tem: *etc.*

COMMUNION

Community Singing, a form of popular mus.-making, in favour partic. during and after the war of 1914–18, which consists of

expresses himself through the medium of mus. invented, constructed and written down by himself.

Composition, the act of writing down mus. originated by his own imagination by the comp.

Compound Intervals, any Intervals exceeding the compass of an 8ve, so called, as distinct from Simple Is., because they differ from the latter only in width, not in character: e.g. a maj. 10th is essentially the same as a maj. 3rd, etc.

Compound Time, any mus. metre in which the beats can be subdivided into three, e.g. 6–8, 9–8, 12–8, where there are respectively 2, 3 and 4 beats in the bar, each divisible into 3 quavers. In Simple Time, on the other hand, the beats are divisible into 2.

Comte Ory, Le (*Count O.*), opera by Rossini (lib. by Eugène Scribe and Charles Gaspard Delestre-Poirson), prod. Paris, Opéra, 20. VIII. 1828. The only Fr. opera by Rossini apart from *Guillaume Tell.*

Comus, masque by Milton, with mus. by Henry Lawes, prod. Ludlow Castle, 29. IX. 1634.

The same with alterations by Dalton and mus. by Arne, prod. London, Drury Lane Theatre, 4. III. 1738.

Con (It.) = with. The prep. is often used in directions indicating the manner of perf. of a piece or movement, e.g. *con brio* = with dash, *con molta espressione* = with much expression, etc.

Con amore (It. = with love, with affection), indicating an enthusiastic manner of perf.

Concento (It. = union, agreement), the playing of the notes of a chord exactly together.

Concert, orig., as in the Eng. 'consort', the singing or playing together under any conditions; now a public perf. of mus., except that of an opera or as a rule that given by a single perf., which is more often called a Recital.

Concert spirituel, a mus. institution founded in Paris by A. Philidor in 1725 for the prod. of sacred works, but afterwards widening its scope to incl. secular mus., esp. symphs. and concertos. It lasted until 1791, but was later replaced by similar organizations.

Concertante (It. = concertizing), **concertant** (Fr.), an adj. used to designate instrumental or more rarely vocal parts in a comp. which are designed largely for the display of virtuosity. A *sinfonia concertante,* for ex., is a work with a prominent and brilliant solo part or several such parts.

Concertato (It. = concerted), a work or portion of a comp. written for several persons to perf. together.

Concerted Music, any mus. written for several soloists to perf. together. Any chamber mus. or a 4tet or other ensemble in an opera or oratorio is C. M., but the opera or oratorio itself is not, neither is, for ex., a symph. or a choral part-song.

Concertgebouw (Dutch = Concert Building) a concert hall at Amsterdam opened in 1888.

Concertina, an instrument, patented in 1829, similar to the accordion, prod. its sound by means of metal reeds set vibrating by wind driven by pleated bellows opened and closed by the player's hands.

Concertino (It. = little concert or little concerto). In the former sense the C. is a group of solo instruments playing alternately with the orchestra (*ripieno*) in a work of the *Concerto grosso* type; in the latter a C. is a concerto for a solo instrument formally on a smaller scale.

Concertmaster (Amer.), the term used in U.S.A. for the leader of an orch., derived from the Ger. *Konzertmeister.*

Concerto (It. = concert or consort), a comp. formerly for orch. with or without solo instruments; now normally a work for 1 or more solo instruments, with orch., designed for display of the individual perf.'s technical powers, but also, in the best exs., to be valuable as a work of art.

Concerto grosso (It. = grand or big concert), an orch. work of the 17th–18th cent. played by an orch. in which generally a group of solo instruments take a more or less prominent part. The group of soloists was called the *concertino* and the main orch. (*tutti*) the *ripieno.* Bach's Brandenburg Concertos are works of the C. g. type, although Nos. 3 and 6 contain no *concertino* parts.

Concertstück (Ger., also *Konzertstück* = concerto piece), a title sometimes given to works of the concerto type for solo instrument and orch. which are not fully developed concertos. C.'s are often in 1 movement or in several connected sections. Although Ger., the title has been used by comps. in other countries, e.g. Chaminade and Piernéi n Fr., Cowen in Eng., etc.

Conchita, opera by Zandonai (lib., in Fr., by Maurice Vaucaire, trans. into It. by Carlo Zangarini, based on Pierre Louÿs's novel, *La Femme et le pantin*), prod. Milan, Teatro dal Verme, 14. X. 1911. The lib. was orig. written for Puccini.

Concitato (It.) = Excited, agitated.

Concone, Giuseppe (b. Turin, 12. IX. 1801; d. Turin, 6. VI. 1861), It. teacher of singing. Worked in Paris for a time, but during the 1848 Revolution returned to Turin, where he became organist at the royal chapel. He pub. numerous useful vocal exercises and wrote 2 operas.

Concord, the sounding together of notes in harmony that satisfies the ear as being final in itself and requiring no following chord to give the impression of resolution.

Concrete Music, a new kind of mus., or near-mus., invented by Pierre Schaeffer in Paris, so called because, unlike composed mus., which is 'abstract', it consists of pre-existing elements.

Conductorless Orchestra. *See* **Persymfans.**

Conductus, a 12th–13th-cent. vocal comp. originally processional in character and written for 1 or more voices. The basic melody of a C. was generally a tune specially comp. A. C. *cum cauda* was a polyphonic comp. ending with an elaborate tail-piece without words (*cauda*, Lat. = tail). In the polyphonic C. the parts normally move in the same rhythm.

Confalonieri, Giulio (Melian) (b. Milan, 23. V. 1896), It. comp. Studied at Milan and was a pupil of Alfano at Bologna.

Works incl. incid. mus. to Fletcher's *Faithful Shepherdess*; symph. poem *Una notte sul monte Imetto*; 2 vln. and pf. sonatas; *Preludi al mattino* for pf.; 4 *Melodie per Cloti* for voice and pf., etc.

Congreve, William (1670–1729), Eng. dramatist and poet. *See* Arundell (*Love for Love*), **Austin (F.)** (*The Way of the World*), **Eccles (J.)** (do., *Love for Love, Semele* and *Ode for St. Cecilia's Day*), **Finger** (*Love for Love* and *Mourning Bride*), **Judgment of Paris** (J. Eccles, Finger, D. Purcell and Weldon), **Philidor (8)** (*Ode for St. C.'s D.*), **Purcell** (*Double Dealer* and *Old Bachelor*), **Sammartini (G.)** (*Judgment of P.*), **Semele** (Handel), **Wellesz** (*Incognita*).

Conjunct Motion. *See* **Motion.**

Conon de Béthune. *See* **Béthune.**

Conrad, Joseph (1857–1924), Eng. (orig. Pol.) novelist. *See* Joubert (*Under Western Eyes*), **Victory** (Bennett, R. R.).

Conradi, Johann Georg (b. ?; d. ?), Ger. 17th-cent. comp. Mus. director at Ansbach, 1683–6, and director of the Hamburg opera from 1690–3. One of the earliest comps. of Ger. operas, which incl. *Ariadne, Diogenes, Numa Pompilius, Der tapfere Kaiser Carolus, Jerusalem, Pygmalion*, etc.

Consecration of the House (Beethoven). *See* **Weihe des Hauses.**

Consecutive, an adj. used to describe the progression of intervals of the same kind in similar motion.

Conseil, Jean (Johannes Consilium) (b. Paris, 1498; d. Rome, 11. I. 1535), Fr. comp. He joined the papal chapel in 1513 or 1514, where he remained with intervals until his death. Comp. motets and *chansons*.

Consequent, another term for the Answer in a Fugue.

Conservatoire de Musique, the chief school of mus. in Paris, opened in 1795 with Sarrette as director, having grown out of the École Royale du Chant, estab. in 1784 under the direction of Gossec. Later directors were Cherubini, Auber, A. Thomas, Dubois, Fauré, Rabaud, Delvincourt, M. Dupré and Loucheur.

Conservatorio (It.), later Conservatoire (Fr.), Conservatorium (Ger.), Conservatory (Eng., esp. Amer.), a school of mus., orig. in It., esp. Venice and Naples, an orphanage where children were 'conserved' to become useful citizens and at the same time trained as musicians.

Console, the part of an org. which is directly under the control of the player's hands and feet.

Consonance, the purely intoned sounding together of notes capable of prod. concord.

Consort (Eng., obs.), in mus. formerly the equivalent of 'concert', i.e. instruments playing together. A 'whole consort' was an ensemble of instruments of the same kind, e.g. viols. A 'broken consort' included a variety of instruments.

Constantinescu, Paul (b. Ploesti, 30. VI. 1909; d. Bucharest, 20. XII. 1963), Rum. comp. Studied at Bucharest and Vienna, and later became director of broadcasting at Bucharest.

Works incl. opera *The Stormy Night*; ballet *The Wedding in the Far End of Moldavia*; Liturgy in the Byzantine style; choral works; sinfonietta, suite, *Four Fables* etc. for orch.; sonatina for vln. and pf.; Rum. song-cycle, etc.

Constantz, Hans von. *See* **Buchner.**

Consul, The, opera by Menotti (lib. by the composer), prod. Philadelphia, 1. III. 1950.

Contano (It. = they count; accent on 1st syll.), an obs. direction in a vocal or instrumental part of a work where the perfs. have a prolonged rest, warning them to count bars during that rest in order to make sure of coming in again at the proper moment.

Conte Caramella, Il, opera by Galuppi (lib. by Goldoni, partly based on Addison's comedy *The Drummer, or The Haunted House*), prod. Verona, 18. XII. 1749.

Contes d'Hoffmann, Les (*The Tales of Hoffmann*), opera by Offenbach (lib. by Jules Barbier and Michel Carré, based on a play of their own and farther back on stories by E. T. A. Hoffmann), prod. Paris, Opéra-Comique, 10. II. 1881, after the comp.'s death. He did not finish it; the scoring is partly by Guiraud.

Contesa dei numi, La (*The Contest of the Gods*), opera by Gluck (lib. by Metastasio), prod. Copenhagen, at court, 9. IV. 1749, to celebrate the birth of Prince Christian, later Christian VII.

Opera by Vinci (lib. do.), prod. Rome, Cardinal Polignac's palace, 26. XI. 1729, to celebrate the birth of the Dauphin, son of Louis XV.

Conti, Carlo (b. Arpino, 9. X. 1796; d. Arpino, 10. VII. 1868), It. comp. Pupil of Zingarelli, later prof. at the Naples Cons., where he deputized as director in 1862 when Mercadante became blind.

Works incl. operas *Olimpia* and *Giovanna*

Shore (after Rowe); 6 Masses, 2 Requiems, etc.

Conti, Francesco Bartolomeo (b. Florence, 20. I. 1682; d. Vienna, 20. VII. 1732), It. lutenist and comp. Theorbo player to the Aus. court in Vienna, 1701–5 and again from 1708; court comp. from 1713.

Works incl. operas *Alba Cornelia, Clotilda, Il trionfo dell' Amore, I satiri in Arcadia, Don Chisciotte in Sierra Morena, L'Issipile, Pallade trionfante*, etc., stage serenades; oratorios, cantatas, etc.

Continental Fingering, the fingering of pf. mus. now in universal use, with the fingers marked 1–5 from the thumb. This system has displaced the so-called Eng. Fingering, marked + for the thumb and 1–4 for the other fingers, which however was by no means in use throughout the whole hist. of Eng. keyboard mus.

Contino, Giovanni (b. Brescia, *c.* 1513; d. *c.* 1574), It. comp. Active at Trent, perhaps teacher of Marenzio. From 1561 *maestro di cappella* to the Mantuan court. Composed Masses, Lamentations and motets.

Continuo (It. abbr. for *basso continuo*). *See* **Thorough-Bass.**

Contra (Lat. = against), a prefix used for org. stops denoting that the stop indicated by the word following it sounds an 8ve lower.

Contrabass. *See* **Double Bass.**

Contrabass (Ger.) ⎱ = Double Bass.
Contrabasso (It.) ⎰

Contrabassoon. *See* **Double Bassoon.**

Contrafactum (L. = counterfeit), a vocal comp. in which the orig. words have been replaced by new ones, either secular words substituted for sacred, or vice versa. In the 16th cent. the Reformation was responsible for several changes of this kind, esp. from Lat. to vernacular words in the conversion of plainsong melodies to hymn-tunes.

Contrafagotto (It.) = Double Bassoon.

Contralto, the lowest woman's voice, frequently abbreviated to *alto*, though this term is also used for the highest (falsetto) male voice,

Contrapunctus (Lat.), counterpoint.

Contrapuntal, the adj. derived from 'counterpoint'.

Contrary Motion. *See* **Motion.**

Contratenor, a 2nd tenor part in vocal comps. of the 14th and 15th cents., often instrumental in character.

Contrebasse (Fr.) = Double Bass.

Contredanse (Fr.). *See* **Country Dance.**

Conus. *See* **Konius.**

Converse, Frederick (Shepherd) (b. Newton, Mass., 5. I. 1871; d. Westwood, Mass., 8. VI. 1940), Amer. comp. Although intended for a commercial career, he studied mus. at Harvard Univ. under Paine. Later he studied pf. with Carl Baermann and

comp. with Chadwick at Boston, and took a finishing course at Munich. After his return to U.S.A. he held var. teaching posts at Boston and Harvard until 1907. From 1917 to 1919 he served in the army and in 1930 became Dean of the New England Cons., a post which he held until 1938.

Works incl. operas *The Pipe of Desire, The Sacrifice, The Immigrants* and *Sinbad the Sailor; Job* for solo voices, chorus and orch., Psalm for male voices, brass and org.; 6 symphs., tone-poems *Endymion's Narrative, The Mystic Trumpeter* (after Whitman), *Ormazd, Ave atque vale, Song of the Sea, Euphrosyne* overture; Fantasy *Flivver Ten Million and The Festival of Pan* for orch.; *Night and Day* for pf. and orch. (after Whitman); *Hagar in the Desert* for contralto and orch., *La Belle Dame sans merci* (Keats) for baritone and orch.; 3 string 4tets; pf. trio; sonata and concerto for vln. and pf.; pf. pieces; songs.

Convitato di pietra, Il (*The Stone Guest*), opera by Fabrizi (*c.* 1765–?) (lib. by G. B. Lorenzi), prod. Rome, 1787.

Convitato di pietra, Il, o sia Il dissoluto, opera by Righini (lib. by ?), prod. Vienna, Kärntnertortheater, 21. VIII. 1777.

Cook, Thomas (Aynsley) (b. London, VII. 1831 or 1836; d. Liverpool, 16. II. 1894), Eng. bass. Studied with Staudigl at Munich and sang at var. Bavar. theatres before he made his 1st stage appearance in Eng., at Manchester in 1856. The maternal grandfather of E. and L. Goossens.

Cooke, Arnold (b. Gomersal, Yorks., 4. XI. 1906), Eng. comp. Educ. at Repton School and Caius Coll., Cambridge, where he took the Mus.B. degree in 1929. From that year to 1932 he was a pupil of Hindemith at the State High School for Mus. in Berlin, then succeeded Walter Leigh as mus. director to the Cambridge Festival Theatre and in 1933 was app. prof. of harmony and comp. at the Royal Manchester Coll. of Mus. In 1938 he settled in London and in 1941 joined the Royal Navy for the duration of World War II, serving as liaison officer on foreign ships.

Works incl. cantata *Holderneth* for baritone, chorus and orch.; concert overture for orch.; Passacaglia, Scherzo and Finale for string orch.; pf. concerto; 4 Shakespeare sonnets for voice and orch.; 2 string 4tets, variations for string 4tet, pf. trio, 4tet for fl., vln., vla. and cello, 5tet for fl., clar., vln., cello and harp; duo for vln. and vla.; sonatas for vln. and pf., vla. and pf., cello and pf.; sonata for 2 pfs.; pf. sonata and suite, etc.

Cooke, Benjamin (b. London, 1734; d. London, 14. IX. 1793), Eng. organist and comp. Pupil of Pepusch, whom he succeeded in 1752 as cond. to the Academy of Ancient Mus. In 1757 he was app. choirmaster at Westminster Abbey in succession to Gates.

Mus.D., Cambridge, 1775, and Oxford, 1782, when he became organist of St. Martin-in-the-Fields in London.

Works incl. services, anthems (some for special occasions), psalms, chants and hymns; ode for Delap's tragedy *The Captives*; *Ode on the Passions* (Collins), odes for Christmas Day, on Handel, on Chatterton and for the king's recovery, ode *The Syren's Song to Ulysses*; glees, catches and canons; orchestral concertos; org. pieces; harpsichord lessons, etc.

Cooke, Deryck (b. Leicester, 14. IX. 1919), Eng. musicologist. Studied privately and at Cambridge. From 1947 to 1959 he worked for the B.B.C., devoting much time to writing and broadcasting. His best known works incl. the book *The Language of Music* and his reconstruction of Mahler's 10th symph.

Cooke, Henry (b. Lichfield, *c.* 1616; d. Hampton Court, 13. VII. 1672), Eng. bass and comp. Pupil of the Chapel Royal; was a captain in the Duke of Northumberland's army during the Civil War. App. singer and Master of the Children at the Chapel Royal at the Restoration. With Charles Coleman, Hudson, H. Lawes and Locke he contrib. to Davenant's *Siege of Rhodes* (entertainment at Rutland House), 1656, and sang in it. His daughter married Humfrey.

Works incl. coronation mus., hymn for the installation of Knights of the Garter, anthems, songs for 1 and more voices, etc.

Cooke, John (b. ?; d. 1433), Eng. comp., clerk of the Chapel Royal from 1413 until his death. His surviving works are in the Old Hall MS. There are records of several other English musicians of this name, one of whom (spelt 'Cuk') has left a Mass, *Veni dilectus meus*, dating from the last quarter of the 15th cent.

Cooke, Thomas (Simpson) (Tom), (b. Dublin, 1782; d. London, 26. II. 1848), Ir. tenor, violinist and comp. Learnt mus. from his father, Bartlett C., an oboist, played a vln. concerto in public at 7, learnt comp. from Giordani, was leader of the Crow Street Theatre orch. at 15 and kept a mus. shop in 1806–12. In 1813 he appeared in London with great success and settled there. For *c.* 20 years he not only sang at Drury Lane Theatre, but led the orch., played 9 different instruments, managed the house and provided mus. stage pieces for it. He also taught singing with success.

Works incl. stage pieces *Frederick the Great*, *The Wager*, *The Brigand*, *Peter the Great*, *King Arthur and the Knights of the Round Table*; songs for Shakespeare's *Midsummer Night's Dream*; songs, glees, catches, etc.

Coolidge, Elizabeth Sprague (b. Chicago, 20. X. 1864; d. Cambridge, Mass., 4. XI. 1953), Amer. mus. patron. In 1918 she

estab. the Berkshire Festivals of Mus., and in 1925 created a foundation (named after her) to produce concerts, mus. festivals, to make awards, etc. She instituted the award of a gold medal (also named after her) for distinguished services to chamber mus. in 1932. The comps. from whom she commissioned works incl. Schönberg, Webern, Stravinsky, Bartók, Prokofiev, Malipiero, Casella, Piston, etc.

Cooper, Gerald M(elbourne). (b. London, 13. IX. 1892; d. London, 17. XI. 1947), Eng. musicologist, author and ed. Wrote numerous articles, mainly on old Eng. mus., organized series of old and modern mus. and of classical chamber mus. in London in 1922–30, and again from 1942. Hon. sec. of the Purcell Society and ed. of a popular ed. of extracts from its complete ed. of Purcell's works. Hon. sec. of the Royal Phil. Society 1929–32. On the death of Edwin Evans in 1945 he succeeded him as chairman of the London Contemporary Mus. Centre (Brit. section of the I.S.C.M.).

Cooper, James Fenimore (1789–1851), Amer. novelist. *See* Genée.

Cooper, John. *See* Coperario.

Cooper, Martin (Du Pré) (b. Winchester, 17. I. 1910), Eng. writer on mus. Educ. at Winchester Coll. and Oxford, studied mus. with Wellesz in Vienna. His work incl. books on Gluck, Bizet and Beethoven. He is chief mus. critic of *The Daily Telegraph* and was ed. of *The Mus. Times* from 1953 to 1956.

Coperario, John (b. ?, *c.* 1575; d. London, 1626), Eng. lutenist, violist and comp. Studied in It. and on his return, *c.* 1604, adopted the Italianized name of Coperario or Coprario. He taught the children of James I and was the master of W. and H. Lawes.

Works incl. *The Masque of the Inner Temple and Gray's Inn* (Francis Beaumont), *The Masque of Flowers*; *Funeral Teares* on the death of the Earl of Devonshire, *Songs of Mourning* on the death of Prince Henry (words by Campian); anthems; works for viols and for viols and org.; fancies for the org. based on It. madrigals; lute mus.; songs, etc.

Copland, Aaron (b. Brooklyn, N.Y., 14. XI. 1900), Amer. comp. Began to learn the pf. at the age of 13 and studied theory with Rubin Goldmark; later went to Fr. and became a pupil of Nadia Boulanger at the Fontainebleau School of Mus. In 1924 a Guggenheim scholarship enabled him to spend 2 more years in Eur. He was represented for the 1st time at an I.S.C.M. festival at Frankfurt in 1927 and won a prize in Amer. with his *Dance Symphony* in 1930. He has since done much propaganda work for Amer. mus., and writes and lectures on mus.

Works incl. opera *The Tender Land*;

ballets *Billy the Kid, Rodeo, Appalachian Spring*; school opera *The Second Hurricane*; mus. for films incl. *Of Mice and Men*; orchestral works: symph. for org. and orch., 3 symphs., *Mus. for the Theatre, Symph. Ode, A Dance Symph., Statements, El Salón Mexico, Mus. for the Radio, An Outdoor Overture, Quiet City, Letter from Home, Danzon Cubano; Portrait of Abraham Lincoln* for orator and orch.; pf. concerto, clar. concerto; *The House on the Hill* and *An Immorality* for female chorus; 2 pieces for string 4tet; 6tet for clar., strings and pf.; pf. 4tet; nonet; vln. and pf. sonata; pf. sonata, pieces, etc.

Coppard, A(lfred). **E**(dgar). (1878–1957), Eng. poet and novelist. *See* **Swain** (songs).

Coppée, François (1843–1908), Fr. poet and dramatist. *See* **Hubay** (*Luthier de Crémone*), **Mascagni** (*Zanetto*), **Paladilhe** (*Passant*), **Svendsen** (do.), **Widor** (*Jacobites*).

Coppélia, ou La Fille aux yeux d'émail (*C., or The Girl with Enamel Eyes*), ballet by Delibes (scenario by Charles Nuitter and A. Saint-Léon; choreography by Louis Mérante), prod. Paris, Opéra, 25. V. 1870.

Coppola, Pier Antonio (b. Castro-giovanni, Sicily, 11. XII. 1793; d. Catania, 13. XI. 1877), It. comp. Studied at Naples and prod. his 1st opera, *Il figlio del bandito*, there in 1816. He was at Lisbon in 1839–42 as cond. of the San Carlos Theatre and again in 1850–71.

Works incl. operas *La pazza per amore* (*Eva* in Fr.), *Gli Illinesi, Inès de Castro*, etc.; Masses, litanies and other church mus., etc.

Coprario, Giovanni. *See* **Coperario.**

Coptic Chant, the mus. of the Christian Church in Egypt, which from the middle of the 5th cent. has been Monophysite. There was a primitive system of notation by the 10th cent., but nothing definite is known about the chant in its orig. form. It still flourishes today, and is charact. by the use of perc. instruments.

Coq d'or (Rimsky-Korsakov). *See* **Golden Cockerel.**

Coquard, (Joseph) Arthur (b. Paris, 26. V. 1846; d. Noirmoutier, 20. VIII. 1910), Fr. comp. Studied law in Paris and took harmony lessons from Franck. He gave up the idea of becoming a musician at first and in 1870 became secretary to a member of the Senate; but later Franck encouraged him to further mus. studies. He became a mus. critic and lecturer at the Institution for the Blind.

Works incl. operas *L'Épée du roi, Le Mari d'un jour, La Jacquerie* (left un-finished by Lalo), *Jahel, La Troupe Joli-cœur*; incid. mus. for Racine's *Esther*, Bornier's *Agamemnon* and other plays; scenes for voice and orch. *Le Chant des épées, Cassandre, Héro et Léandre*,

Christophe Colomb, Andromaque; symph. poem on Ossian; sacred trilogy *Jeanne d'Arc*, etc.

Cor anglais. *See* **English Horn.** Also an 8-ft. reed org. stop reproducing that instrument's tone.

Cor-de-Nuit, an 8-ft. closed metal flue stop on the org.

Cor-Oboe, an 8-ft. flue org. stop.

Corant (Eng.) = **Courante.**

Coranto (It.). *See* **Courante.**

Corbett, William (b. ?; d. ? London, 7. III. 1748), Eng. violinist and comp. At var. times leader of the orch. at the King's Theatre, Haymarket, director of Lincoln's Inn Fields Theatre, member of the royal band; lived for some time in It., where he toured as a violinist and collected instruments.

Works incl. incid. mus. to plays, e.g. Shakespeare's *Henry IV*, orch. concertos and sonatas for var. instruments.

Cordatura (It.), the notes to which a string instrument is tuned, e.g. G, D, A, E for the vln. Any change in the normal tuning made temporarily is called *scordatura*.

Corder, Frederick (b. London, 26. I. 1852; d. London, 21. VIII. 1932), Eng. teacher, cond. and comp. Studied at the R.A.M. in London and under F. Hiller at Cologne. Prof. of comp. at R.A.M. from 1888. 1st Eng. trans. of Wagner's *Ring*.

Works incl. opera *Nordisa*, cantatas *The Bridal of Triermain* (after Scott) and *The Sword of Argantyr*, overture *Prospero* (after Shakespeare's *Tempest*), Elegy for 24 vlns. and org.; recitations with mus.; songs, part-songs, etc.

Cordier, Baude (b. ?; d. ?), early 15th-cent. Fr. comp. famous for two *chansons*: a *rondeau, Belle, bonne*, written out in the form of a heart, and a canon, *Tout par compas suy composes*, in the form of a circle. Other *chansons*, mostly charact. by some rhythmical or notational complexity, or both, also survive.

Corelli, Arcangelo (b. Fusignano, Imola, 17. II. 1653; d. Rome, 8. I. 1713), It. violinist and comp. Studied at Bologna, settled in Rome *c.* 1685 and pub. his 1st vln. sonatas. He lived at the palace of his patron, Cardinal Pietro Ottoboni. Visited Modena and Naples, cond. at the Roman residence of Christina of Swed., collected pictures and taught many vln. pupils, incl. Geminiani and Locatelli.

Works incl. a set of Concerti grossi; 5 sets of chamber sonatas, etc.

Coriolan, Beethoven's overture to the play of that name by Heinrich von Collin, Op. 62, comp. in 1807 and prod. with the play in March of that year. Apart from its subject the play has no connection with Shakespeare's *Coriolanus*.

Corkine, William (b. ?; d. ?), Eng.

16th–17th-cent. lutenist and comp. Pub. 2 books of airs to the lute and bass viol, followed by dances and other instrumental pieces; an anthem is also preserved. The 2nd book of airs contains settings of Donne's 'Go and catch a falling star'; *Break of Day:* "Tis true, 'tis day'; *The Bait:* 'Come live with me, and be my love'.

Cornago, Johannes (b. ?; d. ?), 15th-cent. Span. Franciscan friar and comp. He was at the Neapol. court of Alfonso V and his son Ferrante I. His *Missa de la mapa mundi* has a *cantus firmus* with the text 'Ayo visto lo mappamundo'. His other works include a motet, and secular pieces to Span. words.

Corneille, Pierre (1606–84), Fr. poet and dramatist. *See* **Charpentier (M.-A.)** (*Polyeucte* and *Andromède*), **Cid** (Cornelius and Massenet), **Cleopatra e Cesare** (Graun), **Dukas** (*Polyeucte* overture), **Flavio** (Handel), **Gouvy** (*Cid*), **Holmes (A.)** (do.), **Lully** (*Œdipe*), **Lunssens** (*Cid*, symph. poem), **Martyres** (Donizetti), **Nottara** (*Polyeucte*), **Poliuto** (Donizetti), **Polyeucte** (Gounod), **Rieti** (*Illusion comique*), **Roberto Devereux** (Donizetti), **Sacchini** (*Gran Cid*), **Tiersot** (*Andromède*), **Tinel** (*Polyeucte*), **Tito Vespasiano** (Caldara and Hasse), **Wagenaar (J.)** (*Cid*).

Corneille, Thomas (1625–1709), Fr. poet and dramatist, brother of prec. *See* **Bellérophon** (Lully), **Charpentier (M.-A.)** (*Pierre philosophale* and 2 plays with Visé), **Médée** (M.-A. Charpentier), **Psyché** (Lully).

Cornelius, Peter (b. Mainz, 24. XII. 1824; d. Mainz, 26. X. 1874), Ger. comp. and author. Studied mus. after failing as an actor, 1st with Dehn in Berlin, 1845–50, and from 1852 with Liszt at Weimar, where he joined the new Ger. group of musicians and wrote eloquently about them in Schumann's *Neue Zeitschrift*, without however succumbing to Wagnerian influence in his own work. But he sought out Wagner in Vienna in 1858 and followed him to Munich in 1865.

Works incl. operas *Der Barbier von Bagdad, Der Cid* and *Gunlöd* (unfinished); choral works *Trauerchöre* and *Vätergruft*; duets for soprano and baritone; songs incl. cycles *Liedercyclus, Weihnachtslieder, Brautlieder,* etc.

Cornelys (*née* **Imer**), **T(h)eresa** (b. Venice, 1723; d. London, 19. VIII. 1797), It. singer, married to the dancer Pompeati, but assumed the name of C. when at Amsterdam. She made her 1st appearance in London in 1746 as Signora P., in Gluck's *Caduta de' giganti*, and in 1760 began to give mus. entertainments at Carlisle House in Soho Square, continuing until 1771, when she was indicted for keeping it for immoral purposes, poss. at the instigation of jealous rivals.

Cornemuse (Fr.) = Bagpipe.

Cornet, a brass wind instrument derived from the coiled post-horn and fitted with valves to enable it to prod. all the chromatic notes within its compass. It is a regular member of the military band and the treble instrument of the brass band. It is also used in the orchestra as an addition to the tpts., less often as a substitute. C.s are usually in A or Bb and transpose accordingly; a smaller C. in Eb is standard in brass bands. Also an org. mixture stop.

To be distinguished from Cornett.

Cornet à pistons (Fr. = C. with valves), the Fr. name of the Cornet.

Cornett (Eng.), the name of a wind instrument made of wood or ivory in the shape of a long, thin, slightly tapering tube, either straight or slightly curved, and covered with leather. C.'s were often used as treble instruments with sackbuts (trombs.), frequently in church. The Serpent belongs to the same family.

Cornetta (It.) = Cornet.

Cornetto (It.) = Cornett.

Corno (It.) = Horn.

Corno di bassetto (It.) = Basset Horn. (In 1888–9 Bernard Shaw wrote mus. criticism for *The Star* under the pseudonym of C. di B.) Also an 8-ft. org. stop with clar. tone and a bass register.

Corno dolce, an 8-ft. metal org. stop with soft tone.

Corno inglese (It.) = English Horn.

Corno torto. *See* **Lyzarden.**

Cornopean, an 8-ft. reed org. stop.

Cornyshe, John (b. ?; d. ?), Eng. 16th-cent. comp. He was a member of the Chapel Royal from 1504. His only surviving comp. is a setting of *Dicant nunc Judei*.

Cornyshe, William (b. ? London, *c.* 1468; d. ? Hylden, Kent, *c.* X. 1523), Eng. comp. Attached to the courts of Henry VII and Henry VIII, not only as musician, but as actor and prod. of interludes and pageants. Gentleman of the Chapel Royal from *c.* 1496; succeeded Newark as Master of the Children in 1509. He wrote mus. for the court banquets and masques and officiated in Fr. at the Field of the Cloth of Gold in 1520.

Works incl. motets, Magnificats, *Ave Maria*; secular songs, some with satirical words, for instruments and voices, incl. a setting of (?) Skelton's *Hoyda, Jolly Rutterkin.*

A William C. senior, not to be confused with this comp., was the 1st recorded master of the choristers at Westminster Abbey (*c.* 1480–90).

Coronach (Gael. = 'crying together'), a funeral cry, or in its more cultivated mus. form a dirge.

Coronation Anthems, 4 anthems by Handel comp. for the coronation of George II and perf. at the ceremony in Westminster Abbey, 11. X. 1727. 1. 'Zadok the Priest,'

2. 'The King shall rejoice,' 3. 'My heart is inditing,' 4. 'Let thy hand be strengthened.' A number of other comps., from H. Cooke in the 17th cent. to Vaughan Williams in the 20th, have written anthems for coronations in Eng.

'Coronation' Concerto, the nickname of Mozart's pf. concerto in D maj., K. 537 (dated 24. II. 1788) and perf. by him at Frankfurt at the coronation festivities for Leopold II, 15. X. 1790.

'Coronation' Mass (Haydn). See **'Nelson' Mass.**

'Coronation' Mass, Mozart's Mass in C maj., K. 317 (dated 23. III. 1779), so called because it is said to have been written to commemorate the crowning in 1751 of a miraculous image of the Virgin Mary.

Correggio, Claudio da. See **Merulo.**

Corregidor, Der (*The Magistrate*), opera by Wolf (lib. by Rosa Mayreder, based on Pedro Antonio de Alarcón's story *El sombrero de tres picos = The Three-cornered Hat*), prod. Mannheim, 7. VI. 1896.

Corrente (It.) = **Courante.**

Corri, Domenico (b. Rome, 4. X. 1746; d. London, 22. V. 1825), It. cond., pub. and comp. Pupil of Porpora. Settled at Edinburgh in 1771 as cond. of the Mus. Society, pub. and singing-master. He failed in business and settled in London *c.* 1790, where he set up in partnership with Dussek, who married his daughter Sophia in 1792. Works incl. operas *Alessandro nell' Indie* and *The Travellers*; instrumental sonatas, rondos and other pieces; songs incl. *Six Canzones dedicated to Scots Ladies*, etc. He also wrote theoret. works, incl. a mus. dictionary.

Corri, Sophia. See **Dussek.**

Corsaire, Le, overture by Berlioz, Op. 21, comp. in It., 1831, rewritten in Paris, 1844 and 1855, 1st perf. Paris, 19. 1. 1845, as *La Tour de Nice*; final revision Paris, 1. IV. 1855.

Corsaro, Il (*The Corsair*), opera by Verdi (lib. by Francesco Maria Piave, based on Byron's poem), prod. Trieste, 25.X.1848.

Corsi, Jacopo (b. ? Florence, *c.* 1560; d. Florence, 1604), It. nobleman and amateur comp. Took part in the initiation of opera at Florence. Peri's *Dafne* was prod. at his house and he took some share in its comp.

Corteccia, Francesco di Bernardo (b. Arezzo, VII. 1504; d. Florence, 7. VI. 1571), It. organist and comp. Organist at the church of San Lorenzo from 1531 and *maestro di cappella* from 1539 to Cosimo I de' Medici, for the marriage of whose son Francesco to Joanna of Aus. in 1565 he wrote mus., with Striggio, for Cini's intermezzo *Psiche ed Amore.*

Works incl. hymns in 4 parts, canticles and responses, madrigals, pieces for 4–8 voices and instruments.

Cortellini, Camillo (b. Bologna, ?; d. Bologna, *c.* 1621), It. violinist and comp. Worked at Bologna from *c.* 1583. Wrote Masses (incl. some concerted ones with prominent instrumental parts), psalms, litanies, madrigals, etc.

Corthol (Eng., obs.) = **Curtal(l).**

Cortot, Alfred (Denis) (b. Nyon, Switz., 26. IX. 1877; d. Lausanne, 15. VI. 1962), Fr. pianist and cond. He studied at the Paris Cons., where he gained the *premier prix* in 1896. After serving as a *répétiteur* at Bayreuth he founded the Société des Festivals Lyriques at Paris and gave the first perf. in Fr. of *Götterdämmerung.* In 1905 he formed a pf. trio with Jacques Thibaud and Pau Casals. From 1907 to 1917 he taught at the Paris Cons. and in 1918 was joint founder of the École Normale de Musique. In addition to his continuous activity as a pianist and cond. he gave many lectures on pf. technique and interpretation and collected a valuable library of rare works.

Cosa rara (Martín y Soler). See **Una cosa rara.**

Così fan tutte, o sia La scuola degli amanti (*All women do it, or The School for Lovers*), opera by Mozart (lib. by Lorenzo da Ponte), prod. Vienna, Burgtheater, 26. I. 1790.

Costa, Michele (Michael Andrew Agnus) (b. Naples, 4. II. 1808; d. Hove, 29. IV. 1884), It. (anglicized) cond. and comp., of Span. descent. Studied in Naples and prod. his 1st 2 operas at the Cons. there in 1826–7, and wrote a Mass, 3 symphs. and other works. In 1829 he was sent to Birmingham by Zingarelli to cond. a work by that comp. at the Festival, but by a mistake was made to sing tenor instead. He then settled in London, comp. many ballets and operas and perfected the orch. at the Opera; in 1846 he was app. cond. of the Philh. Society and Covent Garden opera, and he became the most important festival cond. Knighted in 1869.

Works incl. operas *Il delitto punito, Il sospetto funesto, Il carcere d'Ildegonda, Malvina, Malek Adhel* (on Marie Cottin's novel, for Paris), *Don Carlos* (London); ballets *Kenilworth* (after Scott), *Une Heure à Naples, Sir Huon*; oratorios *La passione, Eli, Naaman*; Mass for 4 voices, *Dixit Dominus*; symphs.; vocal 4tet *Ecco il fiero istante*, etc.

Costanza e Fortezza (*Constancy and Fortitude*), opera by Fux (lib. by Pietro Pariati), prod. Prague, Hradžin Palace, at the coronation of the Emperor Charles VI as king of Bohemia, and birthday of the Empress Elizabeth Christina, 28. VIII. 1723.

Costeley (Cauteley), Guillaume (b. ? Pont-Audemer, Normandy, 1531; d. Évreux, 1. II. 1606), Fr. organist and comp. He was organist to Henri II and Charles IX. 1st president of the St. Cecilia society at Évreux estab. in the 1570s. Wrote *chansons* for several voices, instrumental pieces, etc.

Cosyn, Benjamin (b. ?; d. ?), Eng. 16th–17th cent. organist and comp. Organist at Dulwich Coll., 1622–4 and

crusade which was to lead to the estab. of the Lat. Empire in Constantinople (*see* **Byzantine Chant**). He was a *trouvère*, 15 of his poems with their mus. having come down to us.

Coulé (Fr.). *See* **Ornaments.**

Council of Trent, an eccles. council held at Trent (It. Trento, Ger. Trient) in S.

COUNTER SUBJECT   Bach, '48', *Bk. II, no. 16*

afterwards at the Charterhouse. Wrote church mus. and collected a book of virginal pieces by var. comps.

Cottin, Marie (1770–1807), Fr. novelist. *See* **Costa** (*Malek Adhel*).

Cotton, John (also known as John of Affligem) (b. ?; d. ?), Eng. or Flem. 12th-cent. mus. scholar. Author of a Lat. treatise on mus. which seems to have been widely distributed in MS.; 6 copies are preserved in Fr., It., Belg., Ger. and Aus.

Couci, Le Chastelain de (Gui II) (b. ?; d. 1203), castellan, 1186–1201, of the Château de Coucy, N. of Soissons. He d. in the

Tyrol between 1545 and 1563 in 3 different periods each incl. a number of sessions. It was intended to intro. counter-reforms into the Roman Catholic Church to make the Reformation appear superfluous to Catholics who inclined to embrace Protestantism. Mus. reforms were not discussed in detail until near the end, esp. at the meeting of 11. XI. 1563. They incl. the abolition of all Sequences except 4 (*Dies irae, Veni Sancte Spiritus, Victimae Paschali* and *Lauda Sion*), the expunging of all tunes with impious or lascivious associations used as *canti fermi*, the simplifying of polyphony to make the words clearly audible (some members advocating the use of plainsong alone), correspondence between the mus. and the meaning of the words, etc. The opening of a Roman seminary for the training of priests was also decided, and this was opened in 1565 with Palestrina as mus. master.

Counter (verb), to perf. improvised variations on a tune in the 16th–17th cents.

Counter Subject, the name for a theme in a fugue which continues in the 1st voice at the point where the 2nd voice enters with the subject (*see* illustration opposite). A regular C. S. recurs from time to time in association with the subject in the course of the comp.

Counterpoint, the art of combining 2 or more independent melodic lines. The general practice of C. as a mode of comp. is called Polyphony. Double (or Invertible) C. is the term used where the top-and-bottom position of 2 melodies combined in C can be reversed (*see* illustration).

Counter-tenor, properly a high-pitched type of male voice which is prod. naturally in contrast to the *falsetto* of the male alto.

off of the breath-stream. It is effective as an inflection and insisted on as a point of good technique by many singing-masters, while others consider it harmful to the voice.

Couperin. Fr. 17th–18th cent. family of musicians:

1. Louis C. (b. Chaumes-en-Brie, *c.* 1626; d. Paris, 29. VIII. 1661).

2. François C., Sieur de Crouilly (b. Chaumes-en-Brie, *c.* 1631; d. Paris, *c.* 1701), brother of prec.

3. Charles C. (b. Chaumes-en-Brie, 7–8. IV. 1638; d. Paris, I. 1679), brother of prec.

4. François C. (b. Paris, 10. XI. 1668; d. Paris, 12. IX. 1733), son of prec.

5. Marguerite-Louise C. (b. Paris, 1676 or 1679; d. Versailles, 30. V. 1728), daughter of 2.

6. Marie-Anne C. (b. Paris, 11. XI. 1677; d. ?), sister of prec.

7. Nicolas C. (b. Paris, XII. 1680; d. Paris, 25. VII. 1748), brother of prec.

8. Marie-Madeleine (Cécile) C. (b. Paris, 11. III. 1690; d. Maubuisson, 16. IV. 1742), daughter of 4.

9. Marguerite-Antoinette C. (b. Paris, 19. IX. 1705; d. Paris, *c.* 1778), sister of prec.

Inversion:

Bach

COUNTERPOINT

Country Dance, an Eng. dance which became very popular in Fr. in the 18th cent. and was called *Contredanse* there, having appeared as *Contredanse anglaise* in a pub. as early as 1699. It spread to other countries, being called *Contratanz* or *Kontretanz* in Ger. and Aus. It lost not only its rustic name but also its rustic nature on the Continent, where it was used for ballroom dancing and cultivated by comps. of distinction, incl. Mozart and Beethoven.

Coup d'archet (Fr. = stroke of the bow), the bow attack in string playing.

Coup de glotte (Fr. = stroke of the glottis), a trick in singing whereby vowel sounds are preceded by a kind of click in the throat prod. by a momentary cutting

10. Armand-Louis C. (b. Paris, II. 1725; d. Paris, 2. II. 1789), son of 7.

11. Pierre-Louis C. (b. Paris, 14. III. 1755; d. Paris, 10. X. 1789), son of prec.

12. Gervais-François C. (b. Paris, 22. V. 1759; d. Paris, 11. III. 1826), brother of prec.

13. Céleste C. (b. Paris, 1793 or 1794; d. Belleville, 14. II. 1860), daughter of 12.

Couperin, Charles (b. Chaumes-en-Brie, 7–8. IV. 1638; d. Paris, I. 1679), Fr. organist and comp. (3 above). Succeeded his brother Louis as organist at the church of Saint-Gervais in Paris in 1661.

Couperin, François (b. Paris, 10. XI. 1668; d. Paris, 12. IX. 1733), Fr. comp., harpsichordist and organist, son of prec.

(4 above). The greatest member of a large mus. family. Learnt mus. from his father and from Jacques-Denis Thomelin, organist of the king's chapel. App. organist at the church of Saint-Gervais in 1685, where he remained until his death. In 1693 he succeeded Thomelin as one of the organists to the king, and in 1717 received the title of Ordinaire de la Musique de la chambre du Roi. He had been connected with the court before and taught the royal children. In wider circles, too, he was famous as harpsichord teacher and laid down his system in the treatise *L'Art de toucher le clavecin*, pub. in 1716. He married Marie-Anne Ansault *c.* 1689, and they had 2 daughters, the 2nd of whom, Marguerite-Antoinette (9 above), became a distinguished harpsichordist.

Works incl. 4 books of harpsichord pieces (*c.* 230); 42 org. pieces; 4 *Concerts royaux* for harpsichord, strings and wind instruments; 10 chamber concertos *Les Goûts-réunis*; 4 suites for strings and harpsichord *Les Nations*; chamber sonatas *Le Parnasse, ou l'Apothéose de Corelli* and *L'Apothéose . . . de Lully*; 2 suites of pieces for viols with figured bass; some miscellaneous chamber works; 12 songs for 1, 2 or 3 voices; church mus. incl. *Laudate pueri Dominum, Leçons de Ténèbres*, a number of motets, etc.

Coupler, an appliance whereby 2 manuals of an org. or a manual and the pedals can be so connected that while only 1 is being played the stops controlled by the other are brought into action. Special C.'s can also be used to double the notes played automatically an octave above or below.

Couplet (Fr.), lit. a verse or stanza in a poem. In mus. a strophic song, generally of a light and often of a humorous type, in which the same mus. recurs for each verse. Also the forerunner of the Episode in the Rondo form, occurring in the Fr. Rondeau as cultivated by Couperin and others, where a main theme returns again and again after statements of var. *couplets* between.

Coupleux Organ, an electrophonic org. prod. its notes from the air, 1st installed at the Paris radio station and in one of the churches in 1932.

Courante (Fr.). (1) A dance in 3–2 time popular esp. in the 17th cent., whose name ('the running one', from *courir* = to run) suggests some affinity with the Eng. 'running set'. It has 2 parts of equal length, each repeated, and its special feature is the rhythmic modification of the last bar of each section, where the notes appear in 2 groups of 3 instead of 3 groups of 2, as in the rest of the piece. (2) An It. dance (*corrente*) in brisk 3–4 or 3–8 time, with running passages.

Exs. of both types occur in Bach's suites and partitas.

Courses, sets of strings in instruments of the lute type used in pairs and prod. the same note, usually in unison, but sometimes in 8ves.

Courteville, Eng. family of musicians, (?) of Fr. descent:

1. Raphael C. (b. ?; d. ? London, 28. XII. 1675), Gentleman of the Chapel Royal under Charles I and again under Charles II after the Restoration.

2. Ralph (or Raphael) C. (b. ? London, ?; d. ? London, *c.* 1735), son of prec. Educ. in the Chapel Royal. App. organist of the church of St. James, Westminster, in 1691.

Works incl. incid. mus. for Southerne's dramatic version of Aphra Behn's *Oroonoko* and for Part III of Durfey's *Don Quixote*; sonatas for 2 fls.; hymn-tune *St. James*; many songs.

3. Raphael C. (b. ? London, ?; d. London, VI. 1772), son of prec., whom (?) he succeeded at St. James's Church, though he was active mainly as a political writer.

Courtly Style. *See* **Galant.**

Courtois, Jean (b. ?; d. ?), Fr. or Flem. 16th-cent. comp. *Maître de chapelle* at Cambrai Cathedral. Wrote Masses, motets, *chansons* in several parts, canons, etc.

Courvoisier, Walter (b. Riehen nr. Basle, 7. II. 1875; d. Locarno, 27. XII. 1931), Swiss comp. Initially studied medicine, taking his doctorate in 1900 and practising until 1902 in a Basle hospital. Later he became a pupil of Thuille at Munich and later his son-in-law. He became teacher at the Munich Acad. of Mus. in 1910 and prof. in succession to Klose in 1919.

Works incl. operas *Lanzelot und Elaine, Die Krähen* and *Der Sünde Zauberei* (after Calderón); *Totenfeier* (*Auferstehung*) for solo voices, chorus and orch.; symph. prologue to Spitteler's *Olympischer Frühling*; choruses, pf. pieces, songs, etc.

Cousin Jacques. *See* **Beffroy de Reigny.**

Coussemaker, Charles (Edmond Henri) de (b. Bailleul, 19. IV. 1805; d. Bourbourg, 10. I. 1876), Fr. musicologist. He was destined for the law, but played pf., vln. and cello well at an early age and went to Paris to study comp. under Reicha in 1825, later turned to mus. research. He became a judge, but continued to cultivate musicology and wrote more than a dozen books on old mus.

Cousser. *See* **Kusser.**

Covent Garden Theatre, London, 1st house opened 7. XII. 1732, burnt down 19. IX. 1808; 2nd opened 18. IX. 1809, burnt down 5. III. 1856; 3rd opened 15. V. 1858. The theatre did not become a regular opera house until 1847, though opera had long been perf. in it (e.g. Handel's 1st season there in 1734 and Weber's *Oberon* in 1826). The 1st work in 1847 was Rossini's *Semiramide*. It became the Royal Opera in 1892 and ran annual seasons, wholly in It. at first, but later in Fr. and Ger. also, until 1914, and again between the 2 world wars from 1919 to 1939. After being used as a dance hall from 1940 to 1945 it re-opened as a national opera house in 1946.

Coward, Henry (b. Liverpool, 26. XI. 1849; d. Sheffield, 10. VI. 1944), Eng. choir-trainer and choral cond. Trained to become a cutler at Sheffield, he picked up what educ. he could, left his trade at the age of 22, became a schoolmaster and in 1876 founded the Sheffield Tonic Sol-fa Assoc. Took the D.Mus. at Oxford and was knighted in 1926. He cond. much at festivals and abroad.

Cowell, Henry (Dixon) (b. Menlo Park, Cal., 11. III. 1897; d. Shady, N.Y., 10. XII. 1965), Amer. comp. and writer on mus. Studied in N.Y., at California Univ. and in Berlin. Toured in Eur. and Amer. as pianist, lectured on mus. at univs. and colls. in U.S.A. and contrib. to many mus. papers. As early as 1912–13 he developed a technique using tone-clusters, played by striking the keyboard with the fist, forearm or elbow. He used these devices in, among other works, his pf. concerto (1929). He also employed sounds produced by plucking or stroking the strings inside the pf. With Lev Theremin he invented the Rhythmicon, an instrument allowing accurate performance of different, conflicting rhythms.

Works incl. opera *O'Higgins of Chile*; ballets *The Building of Banba* and *Atlantis*; 19 symphs., *Synchrony, Reel, Hornpipe, Sinfonietta, Scherzo*, etc. for orch.; 10 'tunes', *Hymn and Fuguing Tune, Exultation* and *Four Continuations* for strings; pf. concerto; 5 string 4tets; Toccata for soprano (wordless), fl., cello and pf.; other chamber mus.; many pf. works, etc.

Cowen, Frederic (Hymen) (b. Kingston, Jamaica, 29. I. 1852; d. London, 6. X. 1935), Eng. comp. and cond. Studied in London, Leipzig and Berlin. Cond. by turns of the London Phil. Society, at Liverpool and Manchester. Knighted 1911.

Works incl. operas *Pauline, Thorgrim, Signa* and *Harold*; operettas and incid. mus.; oratorios *The Deluge, St. Ursula, Ruth, The Veil*, etc.; cantatas *The Corsair, The Sleeping Beauty, St. John's Eve, Ode to the Passions* (Collins), *John Gilpin* (Cowper); jubilee (1897) and coronation (1902) odes; cantatas for female voices, anthems, part-songs; 6 symphs. (No. 3 *Scandinavian*, No. 4 *Welsh*, No. 6 *Idyllic*); 4 concert overtures, *Sinfonietta, Indian Rhapsody* and other works for orch.; concerto and *Concertstück* for pf. and orch.; string 4tet, pf. trio; many pf. pieces; *c.* 300 songs, etc.

Cowley, Abraham (1618–67), Eng. poet. *See* **King (W.)** (songs).

Cowper, Robert (b. ? 1474; d. ? 1541), Eng. comp. Clerk of King's Coll., Cambridge, 1492–6. Comp. sacred pieces and carols, esp. in *XX songes ix of iiii partes and xi of thre partes* (1530).

Cowper, William (1731–1800), Eng. poet. *See* **Cowen** (*John Gilpin*), **Dunhill** (do.), **Latrobe** (airs).

Cox and Box, operetta by Sullivan (lib. by Francis Cowley Burnand, based on John Maddison Morton's farce *Box and Cox*), prod. London, Adelphi Theatre, 11. V. 1867.

Crab Canon. *See* **Cancrizans**.

Crabbe, George (1754–1832), Eng. poet. *See* **Peter Grimes** (Britten).

Cracovienne. *See* **Krakowiak**.

Craigie (*née* **Roberts**), **Pearl Mary Theresa** (John Oliver Hobbes) (1867–1906), Amer. novelist and playwright. *See* **Parry (H.)** (*Repentance*).

Cramer, Johann Baptist (b. Mannheim, 24. II. 1771; d. London, 16. IV. 1858), Ger. (anglicized) pianist, cond. and comp. Was taken to London at the age of 1, taught by his father and later went to Clementi for pf. study; 1st appeared in public in 1781. In 1824 he estab. a mus. pub. business. He lived abroad from 1835 to 1845.

Works incl. 7 pf. concertos; pf. 4tet and 5tet; 105 pf. sonatas, 2 vols. of 42 studies each, 16 later studies, 100 daily exercises, etc.

Cramer, Wilhelm (b. Mannheim, 1745; d. London, 5. X. 1799), Ger. violinist, father of prec. Member of the Mannheim Orch., 1757–72. Settled in London in 1772; leader of the royal band and of many important concert organizations. Comps. incl. 3 vln. concertos and chamber mus.

Cras, Jean (Émile Paul) (b. Brest, 22. V. 1879; d. Brest, 14. IX. 1932), Fr. naval officer and comp. He never abandoned his sailor's career and reached the rank of rear-admiral, but after some comp. lessons from Duparc and org. from Guilmant, he went on comp. whenever time allowed.

Works incl. opera *Polyphème* (lib. by Albert Samain); *Le Songe d'Acis et Galathée*, suite *Âmes d'enfants* and *Journal de bord* for orch.; string 4tet, pf. 5tet, *La Flûte de Pan* for voice, fl., vln. and cello; cello and pf. sonata; *Élégies* and *Offrande lyrique* (Tagore) for voice and orch.; songs incl. several cycles; pieces for pf. and for harp, etc.

Crashaw, Richard (? 1612–49), Eng. poet. *See* **Finzi** (festival anthem).

Crassia, B. de. *See* **Vacqueras**.

Creation Mass (Haydn). *See* **Schöpfungsmesse**.

Creation, The (*Die Schöpfung*), oratorio by Haydn (lib. by Gottfried van Swieten after an Eng. model, now lost, based on Genesis and Milton's *Paradise Lost*), prod. Vienna, Schwarzenberg Palace, 29. IV. 1798.

Credo (Lat., 'I believe'), the 3rd item of the Ordinary of the Mass. Its text dates from

the Council of Nicea (325), and its use was ordered in the Mozarabic and Gallican liturgies in 589. It was not introduced into the Roman liturgy until 1071. The example shows (i) the Mozarabic, (ii) the Gallican and (iii) the Roman forms of the chant (*see* illustration).
Later medieval melodies are also known.

1731), It. harpsichord maker. Worked 1st at Padua and then at Florence. Inventor of the pf., the 1st specimens of which he made in the earliest years of the 18th cent.

Critic, The, or An Opera Rehearsed, opera by Stanford (lib. by Lewis Cairns James, adapted from Sheridan's play), prod. London, Shaftesbury Theatre, 14. I. 1916.

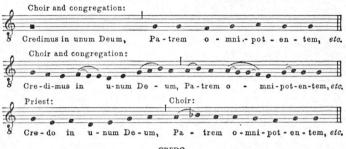

CREDO

Cremona, another name for the Clar. org. stop, orig. a corrupt. of Cromorne.

Créquillon, Thomas (b. ?; d. Béthune, 1557), Flem. comp. Choirmaster in Charles V's imperial chapel in the Netherlands. Wrote Masses, motets, Lamentations, *chansons*, etc.

Crescendo (It. = growing), increasing in loudness.

Crescentini, Girolamo (b. Urbania nr. Urbino, 2. II. 1762; d. Naples, 24. IV. 1846), It. male soprano. Made his 1st appearance in Rome in 1783; sang in London in 1785–7.

Crespin, Régine (b. Marseille, 23. III. 1927), Fr. soprano. Studied at the Paris Cons. After making her début in the provinces, she appeared at the Paris Opéra in 1951.

Creston, Paul (real name **Joseph Guttovegio**) (b. N.Y., 10. X. 1906), Amer. comp. and teacher of It. stock. Studied pf. and org., but is self-taught in harmony, theory and comp. He has also done research in musicotherapy, aesthetics, acoustics and the history of mus. In 1938 he was awarded a Guggenheim Fellowship. His mus. uses jazzy rhythms and a rich orch. palette. Works incl. 5 symphs., a number of concertos, a large amount of orch. mus. and choral works often based on texts by Whitman, chamber mus., songs, etc.

Cricket on the Hearth, The. *See also* **Heimchen am Herd.**
Opera by Mackenzie (lib. by Julian Russell Sturgis, based on Dickens's story), prod. London, R.A.M., 6. VI. 1914.

Cristofori, Bartolommeo di Francesco (b. Padua, 4. V. 1655; d. Florence, 27. I.

Crivelli, Gaetano (b. Bergamo, 1774; d. Brescia, 10. VII. 1836), It. tenor. Appeared in It. at a very early age and 1st went to Paris in 1811 and London in 1817.

Croce, Giovanni (b. Chioggia nr. Venice, c. 1557; d. Venice, 15. V. 1609), It. priest and comp. Pupil of Zarlino, at Venice, where he worked at St. Mark's and succeeded Donati as *maestro di cappella* in 1603. Wrote motets, psalms, madrigals, *capricci* for voices, etc.

Croche (Fr.) = Quaver.

Croche, Monsieur, an imaginary character under whose name Debussy pub. a selection of his critical articles in 1917, the book being entitled *Monsieur Croche, antidilettante.*

Crociato in Egitto, Il (*The Crusader in Egypt*), opera by Meyerbeer (lib. by Giacomo Rossi), prod. Venice, Teatro La Fenice, 7. III. 1824.

Croesus (*Der hochmütige, gestürzte und wieder erhabne Croesus*), opera by Keiser (lib. by Lucas von Bostel after the It. of Niccolò Minato), prod. Hamburg, Theater beim Gänsemarkt, ? Carnival, 1711.

Croft, William (b. Nether Ettington, Warwicks., XII. 1678; d. Bath, 14. VIII. 1727), Eng. organist and comp. Chorister of the Chapel Royal under Blow. Organist of St. Anne's, Soho, from 1700 and, with Clarke, of the Chapel Royal from 1704. Master of the Children there and organist of Westminster Abbey from 1708, succeeding Blow. D.Mus. Oxford, 1713. His most famous comp. is his setting of the Burial Service, which is still in use. Much other church mus. survives, incl. 2 vols. of anthems pub. under the title *Musica Sacra* in 1724.

Other works incl. theatrical pieces, keyboard mus., etc.

Croiza, Claire (b. Paris, 14. IX. 1882; d. Paris, V. 1946), Fr. mezzo-soprano. Although attached to the Opéra-Comique in Paris and appearing periodically at the Théâtre de la Monnaie in Brussels, she was known mainly as a singer of modern Fr. songs. In 1934 she became prof. of singing at the Paris Cons.

Croma (It.) = Quaver.

Crommelynck, Fernand. *See* **Goldschmidt (B.)** (*Gewaltige Hahnrei*).

Cromorne. *See* **Crumhorn.**

Crook, a detachable piece of tubing that can be fitted into brass wind instruments, esp. horns, to alter the length of the tube and thus change the tuning.

Crosdill, John (b. London, 1751; d. Eskrick, Yorks., X. 1825), Eng. cellist. The best Eng. player of his time, attached to the Concert of Ancient Mus., the Chapel Royal, etc. Chamber musician to Queen Charlotte.

Cross Fingering, a method of fingering woodwind instruments which omits intermediate holes. It is often necessary for high notes and ᴍay also be convenient as an alternative.

Cross-Rhythm, the device in comp. of making the accentuation of a theme or melody conflict with (*a*) the normal strong beats of the bar or (*b*) the accents of another tune combined with it. For ex. a melodic shape in groups of 3 crotchets to the bar would be in C.-R. if it occurred in a piece with the key-signature of 6–8.

Crossley, Ada (b. Tarraville, Austral., 3. III. 1874; d. London, 17. X. 1929), Austral. contralto. Studied at Melbourne, with Santley in London and Mathilde Marchesi in Paris; made her 1st London appearance in 1895.

Crotch, William (b. Norwich, 5. VII. 1775; d. Taunton, 29. XII. 1847), Eng. comp. Played the org. in London at the age of 4, went to Cambridge at 11 to assist Randall at the orgs. of Trinity and King's Colls. and prod. an oratorio *The Captivity of Judah* there in 1789, having removed the prec. year to Oxford for theological studies. He turned to mus. finally in 1790 and was app. organist at Christ Church there. D.Mus., Oxford, 1799, having already succeeded Hayes as prof. in 1797. On the estab. of the R.A.M. in London in 1822 he became its 1st principal.

Works incl. oratorios *Palestine* and *The Captivity of Judah* (2 settings); *Ode to Fancy* (Joseph Warton) and ode for the installation of Lord Grenville as Chancellor of Oxford Univ., ode for the accession of George IV; funeral anthem for the Duke of York; anthems and chants, motet *Methinks I hear*; glees; concertos and fugues for org., etc.

Crotchet, a note or rest taking half the time of a minim and forming the unit of any time-signature of which the lower figure is 4, also that marked C (= 4–4).

Crouch, Frederick (Nicholls) (b. London, 31. VII. 1808; d. Portland, Me., 18. VIII. 1896), Eng. cellist and comp. Studied at the R.A.M. in London and held var. apps. after 2 years at sea. He went to U.S.A. in 1849 and worked in var. cities, incl. N.Y., Boston and Baltimore.

Works incl. operas *Sir Roger de Coverley* and *The Fifth of November*, songs *Echoes of the Lakes* containing *Kathleen Mavourneen*, etc.

Crowd. *See* **Crwth.**

Crowder (obs.), a player on the Crwth.

Crowne, John (? 1640–1703), Eng. playwright. *See* **Humfrey** (*Charles VIII*), **King (R.)** (*Sir Courtly Nice*), **Purcell** (*Married Beau* and *Regulus*), **Staggins** (*Calisto*).

Crüger, Johann (b. Gross-Breese, Prus., 9. IV. 1598; d. Berlin, 23. II. 1662), Ger. theorist and comp. Cantor at St. Nicholas's Church, Berlin, from 1622. Wrote several chorales afterwards used by Bach.

Works incl. *Praxis pietatis melica* containing hymn-tunes with bass, *Geistliche Kirchen-Melodien* containing hymn-tunes prescribed by Luther set for 4 voices with instruments, Magnificats; secular songs, etc.

Crumhorn (or Cromorne), a woodwind instrument made of wood and bent, played with a double reed enclosed in a cap.

Cruvelli (Crüwell), Johanne (Jeanne) Sophie Charlotte (b. Bielefeld, 12. III. 1826; d. Monte Carlo, 6. XI. 1907), Ger. soprano. Made her 1st stage appearance at Venice in 1847; 1st sang in Paris in 1851 and was engaged for the Opéra in 1854.

Cruz, Ivo (b. Cidade de Corumba, Braz., 19. V. 1901), Port. cond. and comp. Studied mus. and law at Lisbon, where later he founded the review *Renascimento musical*, resuming his mus. studies at Munich in 1924. On his return he founded a choral society in 1930 and a chamber orch. in 1933. App. director of the Lisbon Cons. in 1938.

Works incl. *Nocturnos da Lusitania* and *Motivos lusitanos* for orch., *Vexilla regis* for soprano and orch., sonatina for vln. and pf., pf. mus., songs, etc.

Crwth (Welsh = Crowd, also called Cruit, Crot, Crotta, Crotte or Rotte), an ancient bowed string instrument, ancestor of the vln. family.

Crystal Palace, London, the enormous iron and glass structure built in Hyde Park for the 1851 Exhibition and re-erected at Sydenham in 1854, 1st used for concerts in 1855, when Manns was engaged as cond. It was destroyed by fire in 1936.

Csárdás (Hung.), a Hung. dance consisting of a slow movement called *Lassú* and a quick one called *Friss*.

Csermák, Antal György (b. ?, 1774; d. Veszprém, 25. X. 1822), Hung. violinist and comp. He became leader in a Budapest theatre orch., visited many noble houses and under the influence of Bihari began to cultivate a nat. style, esp. that of the *verbunkos*.

Cuban Composers. *See* **Caturla, Roldán, Sánchez de Fuentes.**

Cuckoo, a toy instrument. *See* **Toy Symphony.**

Cuclin, Demetre (b. Galatz, 5. IV. 1885), Rum. comp. Studied at the Bucharest Cons. and later with Widor at the Cons. and d'Indy at the Schola Cantorum in Paris. In 1922–30 he taught in N.Y., but returned to Rum. to become prof. at the Bucharest Cons.

Works incl. operas *Soria, Agamemnon, Trajan* and *Bellerophon*; overture for chorus and orch., sacred and secular choruses; 9 symphs., symph. Scherzo for orch.; vln. concerto; pf. trio; vln. and pf. sonatas, suites for vln. and pf. and cello and pf.; pf. pieces; songs, etc.

Cucuel, Georges (b. Dijon, 14. XII. 1884; d. Grenoble, 28. X. 1918), Fr. musicologist. Made a special study of Fr. 18th-cent. mus. Wrote books on Fr. chamber and orchestral mus. of that period, and on comic opera, also a number of learned articles.

Cue, a few notes printed in small mus. type in instrumental or vocal parts of a mus. work, serving as a guide to show where the perf. is to come in after a lengthy rest.

Cui, César Antonovich (b. Wilno, 18. I. 1835; d. St. Petersburg, 24. III. 1918), Rus. comp. of Fr. descent. Educ. at the High School of Wilno, where his father, a Fr. officer left behind in the retreat from Moscow in 1812, was prof. of Fr. He had some lessons in mus. from Moniuszko, but was sent to the School of Military Engineering at St. Petersburg in 1850, where he became sub-prof. in 1857. He became an authority on fortifications and remained an amateur in mus. But he joined Balakirev's circle of Rus. nationalist comps. and became one of the 'Kutchka' group, though the least exclusively Rus. among them. He became a critic in 1864 and did much literary work for the cause.

Works incl. operas *The Mandarin's Son, The Captive in the Caucasus* (after Pushkin), *William Ratcliff* (after Heine), *Angelo* (after Hugo), *Le Flibustier* (lib. by Jean Richepin), *The Saracen* (after Dumas sen.), *A Feast in Time of Plague* (Pushkin), *Mam'zelle Fifi* (after Maupassant), *Matteo Falcone* (after Mérimée) and *The Captain's Daughter*; works for chorus with and without orch.; 4 suites and other works for

orch.; string 4tet in C min.; 15 op. nos. of pf. pieces, 3 pieces for 2 pfs.; var. instrumental pieces; *c.* 25 op. nos. of songs incl. settings of Pushkin, Lermontov, Nekrassov, Richepin and Mickiewicz.

Cuivré (Fr. lit. 'coppery') = brassy, brazen, a term used by Fr. and other comps. to indicate that the clanging tone prod. by stopped horns is required.

Cumberland, Richard (1732–1811), Eng. novelist and playwright. *See* **Busby** (*Joanna of Montfaucon*).

Cummings, Edward Estlin (1894–1962), Amer. poet. *See* **Berio** (*Circles*).

Cundell, Edric (b. London, 29. I. 1893; d. London, 19. III. 1961), Eng. cond. and comp. Studied at Trinity Coll. of Mus. in London, where he became a prof. later. Cond. amateur orchs. and founded a chamber orch. of his own, and in 1938 became principal of the G.S.M. in succession to Ronald. He won the *Daily Telegraph* prize with a string 4tet in 1933.

Works incl. *Hymn to Providence* for chorus and orch., Mass for unaccomp. chorus; symph. in C min., symph. poem *Serbia*; 2 string 4tets, string 6tet; *Our Dead*, sonnet for tenor and orch., etc.

Cunningham, Allan (1784–1842), Scot. poet, novelist and biog. *See* **Jensen** (songs), **Scott** (F. G.) (songs).

Cunningham, G(eorge). D(orrington). (b. London, 2. X. 1878; d. Birmingham, 14. VIII. 1948), Eng. organist. Studied at the R.A.M. in London. In 1901 he became organist at the Alexandra Palace there. He also held some church apps., but was active mainly as a brilliant concert perf. In 1924 he became City and Univ. organist at Birmingham, where he also cond. the City Choir.

Cupid and Death, masque by James Shirley with mus. by Locke and C. Gibbons, perf. London, before the Port. ambassador, Leicester Fields, 26. III. 1653.

Curioso indiscreto, Il (*Indiscreet Curiosity*), opera by Anfossi (lib. by ?), prod. Rome, Teatro delle Dame, II. 1777. Mozart wrote 2 extra soprano arias for this when it was prod. in Vienna, 30. VI. 1783.

Curschmann, Karl Friedrich (b. Berlin, 21. VI. 1804; d. Langfuhr nr. Danzig, 24. VIII. 1841), Ger. comp. Pupil of Spohr and Hauptmann. Remembered only for his songs, of which 92 are pub. incl. 9 duets and trios.

Curtain Tune (obs.), an old term sometimes used in the place of 'Act tune' for an Intermezzo or Entr'acte in the incid. mus. for a play.

Curtal(l), the 16th–17th-cent. Eng. name for the bassoon.

Curwen, Eng. family of mus. educationists and mus. pubs.:
1. John C. (b. Heckmondwike, Yorks.,

14. XI. 1816; d. Manchester, 26. V. 1880), founded the Tonic Sol-fa method of mus. teaching, estab. the Tonic Sol-fa Assoc. in 1853 and the pub. firm in London in 1863.

2. John Spencer C. (b. London, 30. IX. 1847; d. London, 6. VIII. 1916), son of prec., studied at the R.A.M. under Macfarren, Sullivan and Prout, carried on his father's work and began the competition festival movement in Eng. with the Stratford (E. London) Festival in 1882.

3. Annie (Jessy), *née* Gregg (b. Dublin, 1. IX. 1845; d. Matlock, 22. IV. 1932), wife of prec., studied at the R.Ir.A.M., married in 1877 and wrote a number of books on a mus.-teaching method of her own.

Curzon, Clifford (b. London, 18. V. 1907), Eng. pianist. Entered R.A.M. in 1919, winning 2 scholarships and the Macfarren Gold Medal. He made his début, aged 16, at the Queen's Hall, London. In 1926 he was appointed prof. at the R.A.M. and in 1928 went to Berlin to study with Schnabel for 2 years. He later studied with Landowska and Nadia Boulanger, resigning his post at the R.A.M. in 1932 to devote himself to concert work. He married in 1931. His great sensitivity and mus. intelligence make him one of the finest pianists of the day, esp. in the work of Schubert and Brahms.

Curzon, (Emmanuel) Henri (Parent) de (b. Le Havre, 6. VII. 1861; d. Paris, 25. II. 1942), Fr. musicologist. Archivist of the Archives Nationales, 1882–1926. Mus. critic to var. Paris papers, last of the *Journal des Débats*, and librarian at the Opéra-Comique from 1926. Trans. Mozart's letters into Fr. and wrote var. books on mus.

Cusins, William (George) (b. London, 14. X. 1833; d. Remonchamps, Ardennes, 31. VIII. 1893), Eng. pianist, violinist, organist, cond. and comp. Studied under Fétis at the Brussels Cons. and at the R.A.M. in London. Was active in var. mus. organizations in London and at court. Knighted 1892.

Works incl. oratorio *Gideon*; *Royal Wedding Serenata*; overture to Shakespeare's *Love's Labour's Lost*; pf. concerto in A min., etc.

Cutting, Thomas (b. ?; d. ?), Eng. 16th–17th-cent. lutenist. In the service of Lady Arabella Stuart until 1607, then of Christian IV of Den. at Copenhagen until 1611, when he returned and entered Prince Henry's private band.

Cuzzoni, Francesca (b. Parma, *c.* 1700; d. Bologna, 1770). It. soprano. Made her operatic début in 1716. and sang 1723–8 in Handel's operas in London, where her rivalry with Faustina Bordoni became notorious.

Cycle of Songs. *See* Song Cycle.

Cyclic Form. The form of a mus. work in several movements, usually a symph. or chamber work, in which one or more themes appear in at least 2 movements and lend organic unity to the whole.

Cyclic Mass. A misleading term for a setting of the Ordinary of the Mass in which there is some kind of thematic connection between the movements.

Cymbalom. *See* Cimbalom.

Cymbals. Plate-shaped brass percussion instruments a pair of which is struck together or 1 of which is made to sound in var. ways by being touched with hard or soft drum-sticks. They have no fixed pitch, but there are ancient C.s of smaller size which give out definite notes.

Cymon, opera by Michael Arne (lib. by David Garrick, based on Dryden's *Cymon and Iphigenia*), prod. London, Drury Lane Theatre, 2. I. 1767.

Cyrano, opera by W. Damrosch (lib. by William James Henderson, based on Rostand's play, *Cyrano de Bergerac*), prod. N.Y., Metropolitan Opera, 27. II. 1913.

Cyrano de Bergerac, opera by Alfano (lib. by Henri Cain, based on Rostand's play), prod. in It., trans., Rome, Teatro Reale, 22. I. 1936.

Cythare (Fr.) = Cittern.

Cythère assiégée, La (*Cytherea Besieged*), opera by Gluck (lib. by Charles Simon Favart, based on Longus's *Daphnis and Chloe*), prod. Schwetzingen nr. Mannheim and Vienna, summer 1759.

Cythern. *See* Cittern.

Czaar und Zimmermann (Lortzing). *See* Zar und Zimmermann.

Czakan. A woodwind instrument, prob. originating from Transylvania but very fashionable in Vienna *c.* 1830, of the fl. type, but made in the shape of a walking-stick and often used as such.

Czanyi, Cornelia. *See* Schmitt, Aloys.

Czardas (incorrect spelling). *See* Csárdás.

Czech Composers. *See also* Bohemian for earlier names. Bella, Blodek, Dreyschock, Dvořák, Ernst, Fibich, Figuš-Bystrý, Finke, Foerster (J. B.), Hába, Hoffmeister, Janáček, Jeremiaš, Ježek, Jirák, Jiránek, Kafenda, Kaprálova, Karel, Klička, Kovařovic, Křicka, Kunc, Kvapil, Lichard, Mahler, Martinů, Nápravnik, Navrátil, Nedbal, Nešvera, Neumann, Novák, Ostrčil, Petyrek, Pick-Mangiagalli, Roskošný, Schulhoff (2), Skroup, Smetana, Štěpan, Stiastný, Stransky, Suk (2), Vomáčka, Vycpálek, Weinberger, Weiss (K.), Zich, Zvonař.

Czernohorsky. *See* Černohorský.

Czerny, Carl (b. Vienna, 20. II. 1791; d. Vienna, 15. VII. 1857), Aus. pianist, teacher and comp. He was 1st taught the pf. by his father, played brilliantly at the age of

10 and became a pupil of Beethoven about that time; he also took advice from Hummel and Clementi. Not liking to appear in public, he took to teaching and soon had an enormous following of pupils, among which he chose only the most gifted. This left him enough leisure for comp., which he cultivated so assiduously as to prod. almost 1,000 works.

Works incl. 24 Masses, 4 Requiems, 300 graduals and offertories; many symphs., overtures; concertos; string 4tets and trios; choruses; songs and, most numerous of all, masses of pf. music, incl. studies, exercises, preludes and fugues in all the keys and endless arrs. of other comps'. works.

Czibulka, Alphons (b. Szepes-Várallya, 14. V. 1842; d. Vienna, 27. X. 1894), Hung. comp. He became a military bandmaster in Vienna and wrote 6 operettas and much dance and popular light mus.

D

D, the 2nd note, or supertonic, of the scale of C major.

d, the Tonic note in any key in Tonic Sol-fa notation, pronounced Doh.

d', Fr. names with the prefix *de* abbr. to *d'* before a vowel appear under the principal surnames: e.g. Vincent d'Indy as Indy, Vincent d'.

D.C. (It. abbr.). *See* **Da capo.**

Da capo (It. = 'from the beginning'), a direction indicating that from the point at which it is marked the performer is to turn back to the beginning of the comp.

Da capo al fine (It. = 'from the beginning to the end'), as with the simple *da capo*, the perf. is asked to go back to the beginning, but the comp. is not in this case to be repeated as a whole, but only to the point where the word *fine* (end) appears.

Da capo Aria, a distinctive type of vocal piece for a single voice (though duets and other ensemble pieces may be in the same form) consisting of 3 sections, the 3rd of which is a repetition of the 1st, while the middle section is a contrast based sometimes on similar and sometimes on wholly different thematic material. The D. c. A. was cultivated in the 2nd half of the 17th and 1st half of the 18th cent. (up to the earlier works of Gluck), notably by A. Scarlatti, Handel, Bach, Hasse, Jommelli, etc.

Da Ponte, Lorenzo. *See* **Ponte, Lorenzo da.**

Dafne, opera by Schütz (lib. by Martin Opitz, partly trans. from Rinuccini), prod. Torgau, Hartenfels Castle, at the wedding of Georg, Landgrave of Hesse, and Sophia Eleonora, Princess of Saxony, 23. IV. 1627. The mus. has not survived.

Dafne, La, opera by Gagliano (lib. by Ottavio Rinuccini), prod. Mantua, at the ducal court, I. 1608.

Opera by Peri (lib. do.), prod. Florence, Palazzo Corsi, Carnival 1597. The 1st It. opera and 1st opera on record anywhere.

Dafni, opera by Astorga (lib. by Eustachio Manfredi), prod. Genoa, Teatro Sant' Agostino, 21. IV. 1709.

Dagincourt (or **d'Agincour), François** (b. Rouen, ? 1684; d. Paris, 18. VI. 1758), Fr. organist and comp. App. organist to the royal chapel in Paris, 1714. Wrote org. and harpsichord pieces.

Dahn, Felix (1834–1912), Ger. hist., and novelist. *See* **Scharwenka (X.)** (*Mataswintha*), **Strauss (R.)** (*Schlichte Weisen*).

Dal Monte, Toti (orig. name **Antonietta Meneghal**) (b. Mogliano, Veneto, 27. VI. 1898), It. soprano. Took up singing after her pf. studies had been interrupted by an accident. She made her début at La Scala, Milan, in 1916.

Dal segno . . . (It. = 'from the sign . . .'), a direction indicating that where a comp. is to be perf. over again from an earlier point, it is to be resumed, not at the beginning, as in an ordinary *da capo*, but from where a certain sign or 'signal' has been placed by the composer. The sign normally used is ·*S*·.

Dalayrac (orig. **d'Alayrac), Nicholas** (b. Muret, 8. VI. 1753; d. Paris, 27. XI. 1809), Fr. comp. He was 1st intended for the law, then in 1774 sent to Versailles to embark on a military career. But his main interest was mus., and he took lessons from Langlé. In 1777 he pub. 6 string 4tets, and 2 small operas were perf. privately in 1781. The following year he made his début with *L'Éclipse totale* at the Théâtre Italien. He changed his name from its aristocratic form during the Revolution.

Works incl. *c.* 60 operas, e.g. *Nina ou la Folle par amour*, *Les Deux petits Savoyards*, *Camille*, *Adolphe et Clara*, *Maison à vendre* etc.; string 4tets, etc.

Dale, Benjamin (b. London, 17. VII. 1885; d. London, 30. VII. 1943), Eng. comp. Studied at the R.A.M. in London, where he later became prof. of comp. and warden.

Works incl. cantatata *Before the Paling of the Stars* and *Song of Praise* for chorus and orch.; vln. and pf. sonata; Suite and Fantasy for vla. and pf.; *Introd. and Andante* for 6 vlas.; pf. sonata in D min.; 2 songs from Shakespeare's *Twelfth Night*, etc.

Dalibor, opera by Smetana (lib. in Ger., by Joseph Wenzig, trans into Cz. by Ervin Spindler), prod. Prague, Cz. Theatre, 16. V. 1868.

Dall' Abaco, Evaristo Felice (b. Verona, 12. VII. 1675; d. Munich, 12. VII. 1742), It. violinist and comp. Worked at Modena, Munich and Brussels; wrote chiefly string mus. Like Torri, he followed the Elector Max Emanuel into exile at Brussels.

Dall' Abaco, Joseph Clemens Ferdinand (b. Brussels, 1710; d. nr. Verona, 31. VIII. 1805), It.-Ger. cellist and comp., son of prec. Worked at Bonn and played in London, Vienna, etc. Comp. sonatas for his instrument.

Dallam, Thomas (b. ?; d. ?), 17th-cent. Eng. org.-builder. Built orgs. for King's Coll., Cambridge, and Worcester Cathedral. Travelled to Constantinople in 1599–1600 with a mechanical org., a present from Queen Elizabeth I to the Sultan. Robert D. (1602–65), Ralph D. (d. 1673) and George D., also org.-builders, were prob. members of the same family.

Dall' Occa, Sophie. *See* **Schoberlechner.**

Dallapiccola, Luigi (b. Pisino, Istria,

3. II. 1904), It. comp. For political reasons his family were moved to Graz in 1917, where his decisive first contacts with mus. (esp. opera) were made. The family returned to It. in 1921, where D. studied at the Florence Cons. and in 1931 became prof. In 1956 he was app. prof. at Queen's Coll., N.Y., D.'s mature mus., while using serial techniques, modifies them to allow for a more lyrical style than is usual, not avoiding tonal references, thematic structures and harmonic progressions.

Works incl. operas *Volo di notte* (after Saint-Exupéry, 1937–9), *Il prigioniero*|(1944–1948); ballet *Marsia*; voices and orch.: *Canti di prigionera* (1941), *Canti di liberazione* (1955), *Parole di San Paolo* (1964), *Dalla mia terra*, *Laudi* (Jacopone da Todi), 2 lyrics from the *Kalevala*, 3 studies, rhapsody, *I cori di Michelangelo Buonarroti il giovane*, *Tre laudi*; partita for orch.; *Piccolo concerto* for pf. and orch.; mus. for 3 pfs.; *Liriche anacreontiche Roncevals*, cycle of Gk. and other songs, etc.

Dallier, Henri (b. Rheims, 20. III. 1849; d. Paris, 23. XII. 1934), Fr. organist and comp. Organist at Rheims Cathedral from 1865, went to Paris in 1872 and studied under Franck and Bazin at the Cons. App. organist at Saint-Eustache there in 1879 and at the Madeleine in 1905, when Fauré left to become director of the Cons.

Works incl. much org. mus.; string 4tet, pf. trio, pf. 5tet; pf. pieces, songs, etc.

Daman (or Damon), William (b. Liège, c. 1540; d. London, 1591), Walloon (anglicized) comp. He was brought to Eng. by Lord Brockhurst in the 1560s. Harmonized 2 books of psalm tunes and wrote anthems, motets, etc.

Damascene, Alexander (b. ?; d. London, 14. VII. 1719), ? Fr. comp. of ? It. descent. Settled in London, comp. to William III and Gentleman of the Chapel Royal after Purcell's death in 1695. Contrib. songs to several collections.

Dame blanche, La (*The White Lady*), opera by Boïeldieu (lib. by Scribe, based on Scott's *Guy Mannering* and *The Monastery*), prod. Paris, Opéra-Comique, 10. XII. 1825. It contains some Scot. tunes.

Damett, Thomas (b. ?; d. 1437), Eng. comp. At the Chapel Royal, 1413–31; canon of Windsor, 1431 until his death. Works are incl. in the Old Hall MS.

Damnation de Faust, La, dramatic cantata by Berlioz (words by comp. and Almire Gandonnière, based on Goethe's drama), comp. 1846, incorporating the *Huit Scènes de Faust* of 1828; 1st perf. Paris, Opéra-Comique, 6. XII. 1846; prod. as an opera, Monte Carlo, 18. II. 1893.

Damoiselle élue, La (*The Blessed Damozel*), cantata for solo voice, chorus and orch. by Debussy, set to a Fr. trans.

by Gabriel Sarrazin of Rossetti's poem in 1887–8.

Damoreau, Laure Cinthie Montalant. *See* Cinti-Damoreau.

Dämpfer (Ger. = damper). *See* Mute.

Damping Pedal, the so-called 'soft' P. of the pf., which on a grand pf. so shifts the hammers of the instrument that they touch only a single string for each note, instead of 2 or 3, for which reason its use is often indicated by the words *una corda* (1 string).

Damrosch, Leopold (b. Posen, 22. X. 1832; d. N.Y., 15. II. 1885), Ger. cond., violinist and comp. Studied medicine in Berlin, but gave it up for mus. Appeared as violinist and became leader in the Weimar court orch. under Liszt. Having cond. at Breslau from 1850–71, he went to N.Y., where he did much to advance orchestral mus. and opera at the Metropolitan Opera House.

Damrosch, Walter (Johannes) (b. Breslau, 30. I. 1862; d. N.Y. 22. XII. 1950), Amer. cond. and comp., son of prec. Studied in Ger. and settled in U.S.A. in 1871; became cond. of the N.Y. Oratorio and Symph. Societies in 1885. Director of the Damrosch Opera Co., 1894–9.

Works incl. operas *The Scarlet Letter* (after Hawthorne), *Cyrano de Bergerac* (after Rostand), *The Dove of Peace*, *The Man without a Country*; incid. mus. to Euripides' *Electra*, *Iphigenia in Aulis* and *Medea*; *Abraham Lincoln's Song* for baritone solo, chorus and orch.; Te Deum; vln. and pf. sonata; songs, etc.

Danae's Love (R. Strauss). *See* Liebe der Danae.

Danaïdes, Les, opera by Salieri (lib. by François Louis Lebland du Roullet and Louis Théodore de Tschudy, partly based on and trans. from Calzabigi's *Ipermestra* intended for Gluck, comp. by Millico), prod. Paris, Opéra, 26. IV. 1784.

Danckerts, Ghiselin (b. Tholen, Zeeland, ?; d. ? Rome, ?), Netherlands 16th-cent. comp. Singer in the Papal Chapel in Rome, 1538–65. He acted as judge in the dispute between Vicentino and Lusitano. Wrote motets and madrigals.

Dancla, (Jean Baptiste) Charles (b. Bagnères-de-Bigorre, 19. XII. 1817; d. Tunis, 9. XI. 1907), Fr. violinist. Pupil of Baillot at the Paris Cons., where he later became vln. prof. He comp. much mus., incl. educ. works for vln.

Danco, Suzanne (b. Brussels, 22. I. 1911), Belg. soprano. Studied at Brussels Cons., where she won prizes not only for singing, but also pf. and hist. of mus. In 1936 she won an international singing competition in Venice. Her repertoire is a wide one, incl. a number of modern comps., and she is a noted exponent of Ravel and Debussy.

Dandelot, Georges (Édouard) (b. Paris,

Dandrieu Daphne

2. XII. 1895), **Fr.** comp. Studied at the
Paris Cons. and in 1919 became prof. of
comp. at the École Normale de Musique
there.
  Works incl. oratorio *Pax*; pf. concerto;
Trio en forme de suite, string 4tet; waltzes
for 2 pfs.; *Bilitis*: 17 songs (Pierre Louÿs),
etc.
  Dandrieu (or **d'Andrieu**), **Jean François**
(b. Paris, 1682; d. Paris, 17. I. 1738), Fr.
organist and comp. Became organist of the
church of Saint-Barthélemy in Paris in
succession to his uncle, Pierre D., and in
1704 of that of Saint-Merry; member of the
royal chapel in 1721; wrote a book on
harpsichord accomp.
  Works incl. a set of symphs. *Les
Caractères de la guerre*; trios for 2 vlns.
and bass; vln. sonatas; org. pieces; 3 vols.
of harpsichord pieces, etc.
  Dane, Clemence (Winifred Ashton) (d.
1965), Eng. playwright. *See* **Addinsell**
(*Adam's Opera*, *Come of Age*, etc.).
  Danican, Michel (b. Dauphiné, ?; d.
Paris, *c.* 1659), Fr. oboist in the service of
Louis XIII, who bestowed on him the
name of Philidor after the great oboist
Filidori of Siena. (For all other members of
the family *see* **Philidor**.)
  Daniel, John. *See* **Danyel.**
  Daniel, Play of (*Danielis Ludus*), a
medieval liturgical mus. drama dealing
with the story of Daniel in the lions' den.
It was written by students of Beauvais be-
tween 1227 and 1234 and intended almost
certainly for perf. after matins on the feast
of the Circumcision (1 Jan.).
  Danish Composers. *See* **Bendix, Bentz-
zon (J.), Bentzon (N. V.), Berggreen,
Børresen, Bruhns, Bucenus, Buxtehude,
Danning, Enna, Gade, Gram, Hamerik** (2),
Hartmann (3), **Heise, Henriques, Høffding,
Holmboe, Horneman, Hyllested, Jeppesen,
Klenau, Kuhlau, Lange-Müller, Lassen,
Lumbye** (3), **Malling, Nielsen** (3), **Paulli,
Pedersøn, Riisager, Rung, Schytte, Siboni**
(E.), Syberg, Tarp, Weyse.
  Dankerts, Ghiselin. *See* **Danckerts.**
  Danning, Sophus Christian (b. Copen-
hagen, 16. VI. 1867; d. Odense, 7. XI.
1925), Dan. cond. and comp. Studied in
Copenhagen, Sondershausen and Leipzig.
Travelled in It., Fr. and Ger., lived for a
time in Fin., then taught at Copenhagen
and in 1899 went to Norw. as theatre
cond. at Bergen. In 1907–11 he was cond.
at Oslo.
  Works incl. operas *Gustav Adolf,
Elleskudt* and *Kynthia*, operetta *Columbine*; incid. mus. to Oehlenschläger's
Aladdin and other plays; symphs. (incl.
Dante) and overtures for orch.; cantatas;
vln. concerto; ⌐f. pieces, songs, etc.
  Dannreuther, E ⌐ward (**George**) (b. Strasbourg, 4. XI. 1844; d. Hastings, 12. II.
1905), Ger.-Eng. pianist, teacher and

critic. Studied at Leipzig and went to live
in London in 1863. Prof. at the R.A.M.
from 1895 and author of a valuable work
on ornamentation.
  Dante Alighieri (1265–1321), It. poet.
See **Abrányi (E.)** (*Paolo and Francesca*),
Cagnoni (*Francesca da Rimini*), **Campo**
(*Divina commedia*), **Danning** (sym.), **Dante
Sonata** (Liszt), **Dante Symphony** (Liszt),
Davies (Walford) (Fantasy), **Foote** (*Fran-
cesca da R.*), **Foulds, Francesca da Rimini**
(operas, Goetz, Nápravnik, Rakhmaninov,
Zandonai; symph. fantasy, Tchaikovsky),
Françoise de Rimini (opera, A. Thomas),
Frank (*Francesca da R.*), **Galilei** (*Conte
Ugolino*), **Generali** (*Francesca da R.*), **Gilson**
(do.), **Hernried** (do.), **Klenau** (*Inferno*),
Lourié (*Canzona*), **Morlacchi** (*Fran-
cesca da R.* and *Narration of Ugolino*),
Ollone (*Amants de Rimini*), **Paolo e
Francesca** (Mancinelli), **Tommasini** (chor.
work), **Trittico** (*Gianni Schicchi*, Puccini),
Volbach (*Hymne an Maria*), **Wallace (W.)**
(*Passing of Beatrice*), **Wolf-Ferrari** (*Vita
nuova*), **Weyrsch** (Prologue to *Divina
commedia*).
  Dante and Beatrice, symph. poem by
Bantock, 1st perf. London, Mus. Festival,
1911.
  Dante Sonata, a 1-movement sonata by
Liszt, entitled *Après une lecture du Dante*,
in the It. vol. of his *Années de pèlerinage*,
comp. 1837–9, revised 1849. Liszt called it
a *sonata quasi fantasia*.
  Dante Symphony, a symph. by Liszt
based on Dante's *Divina commedia*, comp.,
1855–6, 1st perf. Dresden, 7. XI. 1857.
There are 2 movements, *Inferno* and
Purgatorio.
  Dantons Tod (*Danton's Death*), opera by
Einem (lib. by Boris Blacher and comp.,
based on Georg Büchner's drama), prod.
Salzburg, 6. VIII. 1947.
  Danyel (or **Daniel**), **John** (b. ? nr.
Taunton, *c.* 1565; d. ? London, *c.* 1630),
Eng. lutenist and comp., brother of the
poet Samuel D. When his brother d. in
1619 he succeeded him as inspector of the
Children of the Queen's Revels and later
joined the royal company of musicians
for the lutes. Pub. a book of 20 songs
with lute and bass in 1606.
  Danzi, Franz (b. Mannheim, 15. V.
1763; d. Carlsruhe, 13. IV. 1826), Ger.
cellist and comp. Pupil of Vogler; was a
member of the court band at Mannheim
and, from 1778, at Munich. *Kapellmeister*
to the court of Württemberg at Stuttgart,
and later at Carlsruhe. A minor member of
the Mannheim school of symphonists.
  Works incl. operas *Die Mitternachts-
stunde*, *Turandot* (after Gozzi); church
mus.; symphs.; chamber mus.; etc.
  Daphne, opera by R. Strauss (lib. by
Joseph Gregor), prod. Dresden, 15. X.
1938.

151

Daphnis et Alcimadure, pastoral by Mondonville (lib., in the Languedoc dialect, by the comp.), prod. Fontainebleau, at court, 29. X. 1754, 1st Paris perf., Opéra, 29. XII. 1754.

Daphnis et Chloé, ballet by Ravel (scenario after Longus, choreography by Mikhail Mikhailovich Fokin), prod. Paris, Théâtre du Chatelet, 8. VI. 1912.

Daquin (or d'Aquin), Louis Claude (b. Paris, 4. VII. 1694; d. Paris, 15. VI. 1772), Fr. organist, harpsichordist and comp. Pupil of Marchand. He played before Louis XIV as a child prodigy at the age of 6, and at 12 was app. organist of Petit St. Antoine in Paris. In 1727 he was Rameau's successful rival for the post of organist of St. Paul, and in 1739 succeeded Dandrieu at the Chapel Royal.

Works incl. cantata *La Rose*; harpsichord pieces incl. *Le Coucou*; *Noëls* for org. or harpsichord.

Dardanus, opera by Rameau (lib. by Charles Antoine Leclerc de La Bruère), prod. Paris, Opéra, 19. XI. 1739.

Opera by Sacchini (lib. do., altered by Nicolas François Guillard), prod. Versailles, at court, 18. IX. 1784; 1st Paris perf., Opéra, 30. XI. 1784.

Dargason, an Eng. country dance and folksong at least as old as the 16th cent. Holst used it in his *St. Paul's Suite.*

Dargillières, Parisian family of instrument makers:

1. Anthoine D. (b. ?; d. 1572), 'faiseur d'orgues de la Chapelle du roi'; built various church orgs. in Paris.

2. Jehan D. (b. ?; d. ?), prob. son of prec.

3. Gabriel D. (b. ?; d. ?). Worked in various places near Paris; brother of prec.?

4. Roch D. (b. 27. I. 1559; d. ?), another son of Anthoine; built numerous orgs. in the Paris neighbourhood, incl. those at Rouen (St. Michael) and Chartres (cathedral).

Dargomizhsky, Alexander Sergeievich (b. Tula, 14. II. 1813; d. St. Petersburg, 17. I. 1869), Rus. comp. Studied mus. as an amateur at St. Petersburg and after retiring from 4 years' government service in 1835 led the life of a dilettante. In 1833 he met Glinka, who lent him his notes taken during his studies with Dehn in Berlin, and he set to work on his 1st opera. After the next stage attempt he devoted himself mainly to songs between 1856 and 1860, incl. many of a satirical nature anticipating those of Mussorgsky. In 1864 he visited western Eur., but was able to gain a hearing only in Belg., where he perf. his orch. fantasies. On his return he assoc. himself with Balakirev's nationalist group, without actually joining it. He set Pushkin's *Stone Guest* as an opera word for

word; it was orchestrated by Rimsky-Korsakov.

Works incl. operas *Esmeralda* (after Hugo), *The Russalka* (after Pushkin), *Rogdana* (unfinished). *The Stone Guest* (Pushkin): ballet *Bacchus's Feast*: a duet for an opera *Mazeppa*; orchestral fantasies *Kazatchok*, *Baba-Yaga* and *Mummers' Dance*; *Tarantelle slave* for pf. duet; *c*. 90 songs, vocal duets, trios, 4tets, choruses, etc.

Darke, Harold (Edwin) (b. London, 29. X. 1888), Eng. organist and comp. Studied org. with Parratt and comp. with Stanford at the R.C.M. in London. Organist at St. Michael's, Cornhill, from 1916 to 1966.

Works incl. *The Kingdom of God* for soprano, chorus and orch., *Ring out ye crystal spheres* (Milton) for chorus, org. and orch., other chor. works incl. *O Lord Thou art my God, Hymn of Heavenly Beauty* (Spenser); church mus.; org. works, songs, etc.

Darnton, (Philip) Christian (b. Leeds, 30. X. 1905), Eng. comp. Educ. at Cambridge. Studied mus. with Rootham there, at the R.C.M. in London and under Butting in Berlin.

Works incl. *Cantilena* for string orch., sinfonietta for chamber orch., 3 symphs., 5 orch. pieces; 2 pf. concertos, vla. concerto; string 4tet, 8tet for wind and strings, suite for fl., vla. and harp; *Duo concertante* for 2 pfs.; duet for 2 vlns.; *Swansong* (Robert Nichols) for soprano and orch., etc.

Dart, (Robert) Thurston (b. London, 3. IX. 1921; d. London, 6. III. 1971), Eng. musicologist and harpsichordist. Studied at the R.C.M. and London Univ. After further studies with C. van den Borren in Brussels he became lecturer in mus. at Cambridge in 1947 and prof. in 1962. Prof. of Mus., London Univ. (King's Coll.) 1964–71. He was an expert continuo player and soloist on the harpsichord; author of *The Interpretation of Music* as well as learned articles.

Daser, Ludwig (b. Munich, *c*. 1525; d. Stuttgart, 27. III. 1589), Ger. comp. He was *Kapellmeister* to the Bavarian court at Munich, 1552–9, when Lassus succeeded him, and held a similar post at the court of Württemberg at Stuttgart from 1572 to his death. Wrote Masses, motets, a Passion, org. mus., etc.

Daudet, Alphonse (1840–97), Fr. novelist. *See* **Arlesiana** (Cilea), **Arlésienne** (Bizet), **Pessard** (*Tartarin sur les Alpes*), **Porrino** (*Tartarin de Tarascon*), **Sapho** (Massenet).

Daughter of the Regiment (Donizetti). *See* **Fille du Régiment.**

Dauvergne, Antoine (b. ? Clermont-Ferrand, 3. X. 1713; d. Lyons, 11. II.

1797), Fr. violinist and comp. Pupil of his father, Jacques D.; played at Clermont-Ferrand and went to Paris in 1739 as violinist in the court chamber mus. and in 1744 at the Opéra. In 1762 he became one of the directors of the Concert spirituel and later manager of the Opéra.

Works incl. over 20 operas and other stage works, e.g. *Les Troqueurs, Les Amours de Tempé*; motets; symphs., divertimenti; vln. sonatas; etc.

Davenant (or D'Avenant), William (1606–1668), Eng. poet and playwright. *See* Banister (*Circe*), Lawes (W.) (*Triumph of the Prince d'Amour* and *Unfortunate Lovers*), Locke (*Macbeth*), Pepys ('Beauty retire'), **Siege of Rhodes** (Locke, H. Lawes, H. Cooke, Coleman and Hudson).

Davico, Vincenzo (b. Monaco, 14. I. 1889; d. 1970), It. comp. Studied at Turin and with Reger at Leipzig.

Works incl. opera *La dogaressa*; Requiem, oratorio on Flaubert's *La Tentation de Saint Antoine*; orchestral works *La principessa lontana, Impressioni romani, Poema erotico* and *Polifemo*, etc.

David, Félicien (César) (b. Cadenet, Vaucluse, 13. IV. 1810; d. Saint-Germain-en-Laye, 29. VIII. 1876), Fr. comp. Entered the Paris Cons. in 1830, having been a chorister at Aix Cathedral and afterwards cond. at the theatre. In 1833 he travelled in the nr. E., returned in 1835, lived nr. Igny for a time on finding that Paris neglected him, but settled in the capital in 1841 and made a great success with his oriental descriptive symph. *Le Désert* in 1844.

Works incl. operas *La Perle du Brésil, La Fin du monde, Herculanum, Lalla-Roukh* (after Moore), *Le Saphir* and *La Captive* (withdrawn); oratorio *Moïse au Sinaï*; mystery *Eden*; motets and hymns; descriptive symphs. *Le Désert* and *Christophe Colomb*; 2 symphs.; string 4tet, 24 string 5tets, 2 nonets for wind; *Mélodies orientales* for pf.; songs, etc.

David, Ferdinand (b. Hamburg, 19. VI. 1810; d. Klosters, Switz., 19. VII. 1873), Ger. violinist and comp. Studied with Spohr and Hauptmann and made his 1st appearance at the Leipzig Gewandhaus in 1825, where he became leader under Mendelssohn in 1836. Wrote 5 concertos and many other works for the vln., chamber mus., etc.

David, Johann Nepomuk (b. Eferding, 30. XI. 1895), Aus. comp. He was choir-boy at St. Florian and studied at the Vienna Academy. He has taught comp. successively at Leipzig, Salzburg and Stuttgart, and has published analytical studies of classical comps.

Works incl. 8 symphs., 2 partitas for orch., 2 concertos for string orch.; fl. concerto, 2 vln. concertos; *Requiem chorale* for soli, chorus and orch.; 3 string 4tets, 5 string trios and other chamber mus.; 3 cello sonatas; chorale preludes and other works for org., etc.

David, Karl Heinrich (b. St. Gall, 30. XII. 1884; d. Nervi, 17. V. 1951), Swiss cond. and comp. Studied at the Cologne and Munich Conss. Cond. at var. theatres, became prof. at the Basle Cons. in 1910 and settled at Zürich in 1917. Ed. of the *Schweizerische Musikzeitung*.

Works incl. operas *Der Sizilianer* (after Molière), *Traumwandel; Aschenpüttel* play with mus., Youth Festival Play; *Das hohe Lied Salomonis* for solo voices, chorus and orch.; festival drama for the Berne Exhib. of 1914; choral works with solo voices; concertos for vln., vla., cello and pf.; 5 string 4tets, string 5tet, 2 string 6tets; songs, etc.

Davidde penitente (*The Penitent David*), cantata by Mozart, K. 469 (lib. ? by Lorenzo da Ponte), made up in III. 1785, mainly from portions of the unfinished C min. Mass, K. 427, of 1782–3. Only 2 arias are new.

Davide, Giacomo (b. Presezzo nr. Bergamo, 1750; d. Presezzo, 31. XII. 1830), It. tenor. After many triumphs in It. he 1st sang in Paris in 1785 and London in 1791.

Davide, Giovanni (b. Naples, 15. IX. 1790; d. St. Petersburg, *c*. 1851), It. tenor and bass, son and pupil of prec. Made his 1st appearance at Brescia in 1810.

Davidenko, Alexander Alexandrovich (b. Odessa, 1. IV. 1899; d. Moscow, 1. V. 1934), Rus. comp. Studied with Glière at the Moscow Cons.

Works incl. opera *The Year 1905* (with Shekhter); pf. sonata *Tchetchensk*; mass songs; songs, etc.

Davidov, Charles (b. Goldingen, Courland, 17. III. 1838; d. Moscow, 25. II. 1889), Rus. cellist and comp. Made his 1st appearance at the Leipzig Gewandhaus in 1859 and later became 1st cellist in its orch. and prof. at the Cons. In 1862 he was app. to a similar post at the St. Petersburg Opera and was director of the Cons. there in 1876–86. Wrote 4 cello concertos and many other works for his instrument, etc.

Davidsbund (Ger. = League of David), an assoc. formed in 1834 by Schumann and his friends to combat the mus. 'Philistines'.

Davidsbündler (Ger.), the members of the above. They appear in the title of Schumann's *Davidsbündlertänze* and in the finale of his *Carnival* in a 'marche contre les Philistins'.

Davidsbündlertänze (*Dances of the David Leaguers*), a set of 18 pf. pieces by Schumann, Op. 6, comp. in 1837, the title alluding to the above.

Davie, Cedric Thorpe (b. Blackheath, 30. V. 1913), Scot. organist and comp.

Student at the Scot. Nat. Acad. of Mus., Glasgow, the R.A.M. in London and later the R.C.M. there, where he was a pupil of R. O. Morris, Vaughan Williams and Gordon Jacob, gaining the Cobbett and Sullivan Prizes in 1935. He also studied pf. with Egon Petri in Ger., and comp. with Kodály at Budapest and Kilpinen at Helsinki. Head of music at St. Andrews Univ. since 1945.

Works incl. opera *Gammer Gurton's Needle*, ballad opera *The Forrigan Reel* (James Bridie); *Dirge for Cuchullin* (Ossian); 3 anthems for chorus and orch.; incid. mus. for Bridie's *The Anatomist* and *The Switchback* and for Neil Gunn's *Sun and Moon*; *Fantasy on 4 Scot. Folk Tunes* for orch.; concerto for pf. and strings; string 4tet; vln. and pf. sonata, sonatinas for cello and pf. and fl. and pf.; *8 Little Songs*, etc.

Davies, Ben(jamin Grey) (b. Pontardawe, nr. Swansea, 6. I. 1858; d. Bath, 28. III. 1943), Welsh tenor. Studied at the R.A.M. in London; made his 1st concert appearance at Dublin in 1879 and 1st sang in opera at Birmingham in 1881.

Davies, Cecilia (b. ? London, *c*. 1750; d. London, 3. VII. 1836), Eng. soprano. Sang at Dublin in 1763 and 1st appeared in London in 1767. The following year she went to Paris and Vienna with her sister Marianne (1744-?), a fl., harpsichord and harmonica player, where they had a great success, Hasse writing an ode for them to words specially provided by Metastasio; and in 1771-3 they were in It., where C. became famous as 'L'Inglesina'.

Davies, Fanny (b. Guernsey, 27. VI. 1861; d. London, 1. IX. 1934), Eng. pianist. Studied at Leipzig and under Clara Schumann at Frankfurt, making her 1st London appearance in 1885.

Davies, (Albert) Meredith (b. Birkenhead, 30. VII. 1922), Eng. cond. and organist. Studied at the R.C.M., graduating in 1938, and then Keble Coll., Oxford, taking his B.Mus. in 1946. He took the post of organist at St. Albans Cathedral in 1947 and Hereford in 1949, also conducting at the Three Choirs Festival. From 1956 to 1959 he was organist of New Coll., Oxford. He has since conducted frequently in Britain and abroad.

Davies, Peter Maxwell (b. Manchester, 8. IX. 1934), Eng. comp. Studied at the Royal Manchester Coll. of Mus. and in 1957 with Petrassi in Rome. From 1959 to 1962 he taught mus. at Cirencester Grammar School, and in 1962 went to the U.S.A. to study with Sessions at Princeton Univ. His mus. is strongly influenced by medieval techniques, which he uses in combination with serial devices.

Works incl. 2 fantasies based on Taverner's *In Nomine*, *Prolation*, *St.*

Thomas Wake (foxtrot), *Worldes Blis* for orch.; *St. Michael* sonata for 17 wind instruments, *Alma Redemptoris Mater* for wind 6tet; *O Magnum Mysterium*, cycle of carols and instrumental sonatas, *Veni Sancte Spiritus* for soloists, chorus and orch., 5 motets for soloists, chorus and instruments, settings of Leopardi for soprano, alto and chamber ensemble; *Revelation and Fall* and *8 Songs for a Mad King* for voice and chamber ensemble, etc.

Davies, (Henry) Walford (b. Oswestry, 6. IX. 1869; d. Wrington, Som., 11. III. 1941), Eng. organist, educationist and comp. Educ. at St. George's Chapel, Windsor, under Parratt, and at the R.C.M. in London, where Stanford was his comp. master. Held var. organist's apps., took the Cambridge Mus.D. degree in 1898, when he was app. organist and choirmaster at the Temple Church. Prof. of Mus. at the Univ. of Wales, Aberystwyth, from 1919. Knighted 1922. He resigned from the Temple in 1923 and became organist at St. George's, Windsor, in 1927 and Master of the King's Mus. in succession to Elgar in 1934.

Works incl. comps. for solo voices, chorus and orch.: *Hervé Riel* (Browning), *Everyman*, *Ode on Time* (Milton), *Noble Numbers* (Herrick), *Dante Fantasy* (from the *Divine Comedy*), *High Heaven's King* (Spenser), *Christ in the Universe* (Alice Meynell); symph. in G maj., *Festal Overture*, *Parthenia* and *Memorial* suites, suite after Wordsworth for orch.; *Solemn Melody* for org. and strings; *Conversations* for pf. and orch.; many services and anthems; *Peter Pan* suite for string 4tet; pf. 5tet, 2 vln. and pf. sonatas; several works for voices with chamber mus. and with pf.; many songs, part-songs, etc.

Davies, W(illiam). H(enry). (1871-1940), Eng. poet. *See* Head (*Songs of the Countryside*), Tate (songs).

Davis, Colin (b. Weybridge, 25. IX. 1927), Eng. cond. Studied at the R.C.M. From 1957 to 1959 he was assistant cond. of the B.B.C. Scot. Orch., becoming principal cond. at Sadler's Wells in 1960; he was also their mus. director, 1961-5. From 1967 to 1971 he was principal cond. of the B.B.C. Symph. Orch. and from 1971 of Covent Garden. He was awarded the C.B.E. in 1965. A versatile musician, he is esp. known for his perfs. of Mozart and Stravinsky.

Davis, J(ohn). D(avid). (b. Birmingham, 22. X. 1867; d. Estoril, Port., 20. XI. 1942). Eng. comp. Studied at the Raff Cons. at Frankfurt, and at the Brussels Cons. Taught at the Midland Inst. School of Mus., Birmingham, 1893-1904.

Works incl. opera *The Zaporogues*; symph. ballad *The Cenci* (after Shelley), prelude to Maeterlinck's *L'Intruse*, *Miniatures* for small orch.; chamber mus.; pf. pieces; songs, etc.

Davison, James William (b. London, 5. X. 1813; d. Margate, 24. III. 1885), Eng. critic. attached to *The Times*, 1846–1879. Married the pianist Arabella Goddard.

Davy, John (b. Upton Helions, nr. Exeter, 23. XII. 1763; d. London, 22. II. 1824), Eng. comp. Pupil of Jackson at Exeter. Played in the Covent Garden orch. in London and wrote mus. for many plays, incl. Shakespeare's *Tempest*. His song *The Bay of Biscay* became famous.

Davy, Richard (b. *c*. 1467; d. *c*. 1516), Eng. 15th–16th-cent. comp. Educ. at Magdalen Coll., Oxford, where he was organist and choirmaster in 1490–2. Chaplain to Anne Boleyn's grandfather and father in 1501–15. Comp. motets, Passion mus. for Palm Sunday, partsongs, etc.

Day, John (b. Dunwich, Suffolk, 1522; d. Walden, Essex, 23. VII. 1584), Eng. printer. Estab. in London *c*. 1547. His mus. pubs. incl. *Certaine notes* (mus. for matins, communion and evensong, 1560, re-issued as *Mornyng and Evenyng prayer*, 1565) and *The whole psalmes* (*c*. 1563).

De. The prefix 'De' or 'de' appears in this work as an initial only in the case of Eng. names, with some exceptions (e.g. De Lara).

De la Mare, Walter (1873–1956), Eng. poet. *See* Dyson (*Won't you look out of your window?*), Gibbs (C. A.) (*Crossings* and songs).

De Quincey, Thomas (1785–1859), Eng. essayist. *See* Dieren (van) (*Murder as One of the Fine Arts* and songs).

Dean, Winton (Basil), (b. Birkenhead, 18. III. 1916), Eng. writer on mus., son of the producer Basil Dean. Educ. at Harrow and King's Coll., Cambridge; read classics and Eng., but studied mus. privately, trans. choruses, etc. from Aristophanes' *Frogs* for Walter Leigh and Weber's *Abu Hassan*. His books incl. Bizet and *Handel's Dramatic Oratorios*, and he has written numerous articles and reviews.

'Death and the Maiden' Quartet, Schubert's string 4tet in D min., begun III. 1824, finished or revised I. 1826 and 1st perf. Vienna, 1. II. 1826. It is so called because the 2nd movement is a set of variations on the introduction and the 2nd half of his song, *Der Tod und das Mädchen*, which consists of Death's quiet and re-assuring answer to the girl's agitated plea to be spared.

Death and Transfiguration (Strauss). *See* **Tod und Verklärung.**

Debora e Jaele (*Deborah and Jael*),

opera by Pizzetti (lib. by comp.), prod. Milan, Teatro alla Scala, 16. XII. 1922.

Deborah, oratorio by Handel (words by Samuel Humphreys), prod. London, King's Theatre, Haymarket, 17. III. 1733.

Debussy, (Achille) Claude (b. Saint-Germain-en-Laye nr. Paris, 22. VIII. 1862; d. Paris, 25. III. 1918), Fr. comp. Son of a shopkeeper, took his 1st pf. lessons at the age of 7, and from 1870 was taught for 3 years by Mme. Mauté de Fleurville, a former pupil of Chopin. Entered the Paris Cons. in 1873, studying with Lavignac and Marmontel, later with Émile Durand. At 17 he failed to win a pf. prize, but entered a comp. class in 1880. For the next 2 summers became domestic musician to Nadezhda von Meck, Tchaikovsky's former patroness, whose children he taught and who took him to Switz. and It. the 1st time and to Rus. the 2nd. Gained 1st Prix de Rome in 1884 and went to Rome the next year, but left in 1887 before the statutory 3 years were completed. Began to comp. seriously in the new manner for which he became known with a Fr. trans. of Rossetti's *Blessed Damozel*, finished 1888. Influenced by Satie in 1891 and perf. his 1st important mature work, the prelude to Mallarmé's poem *L'Après-midi d'un faune*, in 1894. Married a dressmaker, Rosalie (Lili) Texier, in 1899; became mus. critic for the *Revue blanche* in 1901; prod. his only finished opera, a setting of Maeterlinck's *Pelléas et Mélisande*, 30. IV. 1902. Left his wife in 1904 for Mme. Emma Bardac; divorced 1905 and married to Mme. B. Growing success, abroad as well as in Fr., during the last 10 years, but *c*. 1909 he began to suffer from cancer.

Works incl. opera *Pelléas et Mélisande*; incid. mus. to d'Annunzio's *Le Martyre de Saint Sébastien*; ballets *Jeux* and *Khamma*; cantatas *L'Enfant prodigue* and *La Damoiselle élue*; 3 *Chansons de France* (Charles d'Orléans) for unaccomp. chorus; *Printemps*, *Prélude à l'Après-midi d'un faune*, 3 *Nocturnes*, *La Mer* and 3 *Images* for orch.; *Fantaisie* for pf. and orch.; *Danse sacrée et danse profane* for harp and strings; string 4tet; sonatas for cello and pf., fl., vla. and harp and vln. and pf., and some smaller chamber works for saxophone, clar. and fl.; many pf. pieces incl. *Suite bergamasque*, suite *Pour le Piano*, 3 *Estampes*, *Masques*, *L'Île joyeuse*, 2 sets of 3 *Images*, suite *Children's Corner*, 2 sets of 12 *Préludes* and 12 *Études*; *Petite Suite*, *Marche écossaise*, *Six Épigraphes antiques* (on Pierre Louÿs's *Chansons de Bilitis*), etc. for pf. duet; *Lindaraja* and *En blanc et noir* for 2 pfs.; *c*. 70 songs incl. sets *Cinq Poèmes de Baudelaire*, *Ariettes oubliées* (Verlaine), 2 sets of *Fêtes galantes* (Verlaine), *Proses lyriques* (Debussy), 3 *Ballades de Villon*, *Chansons de Bilitis* (Pierre Louÿs), *Le Promenoir des deux amants* (Tristan Lhermite), *Trois Poèmes de Stéphane Mallarmé*, etc.

Decani. In Eng. cathedrals and in churches where the choir is divided, the D. side is that on the south of the chancel. near the dean's stall, the other being the *Cantoris* side.

Deceptive Cadence (Amer. from Ger. **Trugschluss**). *See* **Cadence.**

Decius, Nikolaus (b. Hof, *c.* 1485; d. ?, after 1546), Ger. Lutheran pastor and theologian. He wrote the words and comp. or adapted the mus. of 3 chorales, anticipating even Luther in this field.

Declamation with Music. *See* **Recitations.**

Decrescendo (It. = waning, decreasing), synonym of *diminuendo*, which is now more frequently used.

Dedekind, Constantin Christian (b. ? Reinsdorf, Anhalt, 2. IV. 1628; d. Dresden, 2. IX. 1715), Ger. poet and comp. Studied at Dresden and in 1654 became a member of the Saxon court chapel and *Konzertmeister* in 1666. He arr. words for sacred mus. dramas.

Works incl. psalms, sacred and secular vocal mus., concertos for voices and instruments, etc.

Dedekind, Heinrich (or Enricius) (b. Neustadt, Bavaria, 1554; d. Lüneburg, 1619), Ger. clergyman and comp. Cantor at St. John's Church, Lüneburg. Wrote psalms and other sacred vocal works.

Dedekind, Henning (b. Neustadt, 30. XII. 1562; d. Gebsee, Thuringia, 28. VII. 1626). Ger. comp., brother of prec. Held posts as cantor and preacher at Langensalza and Gebsee.

Works incl. Mass; secular vocal mus., etc.

Deering. *See* **Dering.**

Defesch, William (b. Alkmaar, VIII. 1687; d. London, 3. I. 1761), Flem. organist, violinist and comp. Organist and later choirmaster at Antwerp Cathedral until 1731, when he settled in London.

Works incl. Mass; oratorios *Judith* and *Joseph*; concertos and sonatas for var. instruments; cello pieces; songs, etc.

Defoe, Daniel (? 1661–1731), Eng. novelist and journalist. *See* **Linley (1)** (*Robinson Crusoe*), **Rieti** (*Robinson and Friday*), **Robinson Crusoé** (Offenbach).

Degtiarev, Stephan Anikievich (b. ?, 1766; d. nr. Kusk, 5. V. 1813), Rus. comp. Pupil of Sarti at St. Petersburg.

Works incl. church mus., choral works *Minin and Pozharsky*, *The Liberation of Moscow* and *Napoleon's Flight* (unfinished), many concertos, etc.

Dehmel, Richard (1863–1920), Ger. poet. *See* **Knab** (songs), **Melcer** (songs with orch.), **Verklärte Nacht** (Schönberg), **Zilcher** (*Fitzebutze*).

Dehn, Siegfried (Wilhelm) (b. Altona, 25. II. 1799; d. Berlin, 12. IV. 1858), mus. author, ed. and teacher. Librarian of the mus. section of the Royal Library in Berlin, ed. of the periodical *Caecilia*, author of theoretical books, ed. of Lassus, Bach and other old composers and teacher of mus. theory.

Deidamia, opera by Handel (lib. by Paolo Antonio Rolli), prod. London, Theatre Royal, Lincoln's Inn Fields, 10. I. 1741. Handel's last opera.

Del Mar, Norman (René) (b. London, 31. VII. 1919), Eng. cond. Studied at the R.C.M. with R. O. Morris and Vaughan Williams. In 1944 he founded the Chelsea Symph. Orch., and in 1947 became conductor of the Croydon Symph. Orch. In the same year he was appointed assistant to Beecham with the Royal Phil. Orch. He is esp. noted as a performer of complex modern scores, and has written a 3-vol. study of the mus. of Richard Strauss.

Del Monaco, Mario (b. Florence, 27. VII. 1915), It. tenor. Studied at the Pesaro Cons. and made his début in Milan in 1941, but later served in the It. army during World War II. From 1951 to 1959 he sang with the Metropolitan Opera in N.Y. A dramatic singer, one of his finest roles is that of Verdi's Otello.

Delage, Maurice (Charles) (b. Paris, 13. XI. 1879; d. Paris, 19. IX. 1961), Fr. comp. Pupil of Ravel. He travelled to the E. and incorporated exotic elements into his mus.

Works incl. overture to a ballet *Les Bâtisseurs de ponts* (after Kipling), symph. poem *Conté par la mer* and other orchestral works; pf. pieces; songs, etc.

Delannoy, Marcel (François Georges) (b. Ferté-Alais, 9. VII. 1898; d. Nantes, 14. IX. 1962), Fr. comp. A painter and architect at first, he was mainly self-taught in mus.

Works incl. operas *Le Poirier de misère*, *Philippine*, *Fête de la danse*, *Ginevra*; ballet-cantata *Le Fou de la dame*, ballets *La Pantoufle de vair* and *L'Éventail de Jeanne* (with others); incid. mus. for Aristophanes' *Peace* and other plays; symph. and *Figures sonores* for orch.; *Sérénade concertante* for vln. and orch.; string 4tets; many songs, etc.

Delatre, Claude Petit Jean (b. ? ; d. ?), 16th-cent. Fr. or Flem. comp. Wrote Lamentations and *chansons*.

Delbos, Claire. *See* **Messiaen.**

Deldevez, Édouard (Marie Ernest) (b. Paris, 31. V. 1817); d. Paris, 5. XI. 1897), Fr. violinist, cond. and comp. Studied at the Paris Cons. Later played in and cond. var. orchs. Wrote several theoret. books.

Works incl. ballet *Lady Henriette* (with Burgmüller and Flotow, the latter's opera

Martha being later based on it); 3 symphs., concert overtures; chamber mus., etc.

Delgadillo, Luis (b. Managua, 26. VIII. 1887). Nicaraguan comp. Studied at the Milan Cons. and on his return home travelled extensively collecting Central and S. Amer. folk mus. Later became director of the Nat. Cons. of Panama. Works incl. *Las sietes palabras de Cristo, Escenas pastoriles,* Mex. suite *Teotihuacán, Sinfonía incaica, Sinfonía serrana, Fantasía tropical panameña* for orch., etc.

Delibes, (Clément Philibert) Léo (b. Saint-Germain-du-Val, 21. II. 1836; d. Paris, 16. I. 1891), Fr. comp. Studied at the Paris Cons., where Adam was his comp. master. He became accompanist at the Théâtre Lyrique in 1853 and was organist successively at 2 churches. Later he became accompanist and chorus master at the Opéra and in 1881 prof. of comp. at the Cons.

Works incl. operas *Maître Griffard, Le Jardinier et son seigneur, Le Roi l'a dit, Jean de Nivelle, Lakmé, Kassya* (unfinished); ballets *La Source* (with Minkus), *Coppélia* (on E. T. A. Hoffmann's story *Olympia*), *Sylvia, Le Pas des fleurs*; divertissement for Adam's ballet *Le Corsaire*; incid. mus. for Hugo's *Le Roi s'amuse*; operettas *Deux Sous de charbon, Deux Vieilles Gardes, L'Omelette à la Follembûche, Le Serpent à plumes, L'Écossais de Chatou* and others; Mass; cantata *Alger*; dramatic scene *La Mort d'Orphée*; songs; children's choruses, etc.

Delius, Frederick (b. Bradford, 29. I. 1862; d. Grez-sur-Loing, 10. VI. 1934), Eng. comp. of Ger. descent. His father was a well-to-do business man and wished him to follow a commercial career; but mus. was cultivated in the home and although D. had little systematic teaching until he went to Florida as an orange planter in 1884 and came under the influence of Thomas Ward, organist at Jacksonville, he worked steadily at mus. by himself. In 1886, after some teaching in U.S.A., he went to the Leipzig Cons. for a short time, but found its conservative teaching uncongenial. In 1887 he visited Norw. and made friends with Grieg, who persuaded his father to let him devote himself to comp. From 1889 he lived in Fr., mainly Paris, and in 1897 he married Jelka Rosen, a Ger. painter of Dan. descent, and they settled at Grez-sur-Loing nr. Fontainebleau. A concert of his works was given in London in 1899 and he became known here and there in Ger. In 1922 he was attacked by paralysis, which gradually increased until 4 years later he was helpless and totally blind. In 1928 Eric Fenby volunteered to live in his house and act as amanuensis.

Works incl. operas *Irmelin, The Magic Fountain, Koanga, A Village Romeo and Juliet, Margot-la-Rouge, Fennimore and Gerda*; incid. mus. for Heiberg's *Folkeraadet* and Flecker's *Hassan*; orchestral works: *Florida* suite, *Over the Hills and Far Away, Paris, Life's Dance, Brigg Fair, In a Summer Garden,* 2 *Dance Rhapsodies, On hearing the first Cuckoo in Spring* and *Summer Night on the River, N. Country Sketches, Eventyr* (after Asbjørnsen's fairy-tales), *A Song before Sunrise*; concertos for pf., vln., cello and vln. and cello; 2 string 4tets; 3 vln. and pf. sonatas; sonata for cello and pf.; works for chorus and orch.: *Appalachia, Sea Drift, A Mass of Life, Songs of Sunset, Arabesk, A Song of the High Hills, Requiem, A Poem of Life and Love*: some part-songs; songs with orch. incl. cycle from Tennyson's *Maud,* 7 Dan. songs, Dowson's *Cynara; c.* 40 songs; 2 pieces for pf. and 1 for harpsichord, etc.

Della Casa, Lisa (b. Burgdorf, Bern, 2. II. 1919), Swiss soprano. Studied at the Bern Cons. and in Zürich, beginning her career at the Salzburg Festival of 1947. She has become known as one of the outstanding Mozart and Strauss singers of the day, also doing much to further the cause of Swiss mus.

Della Ciaia, Azzolino Bernardino (b. Siena, 21. III. 1671; d. Pisa, 15. I. 1755), It. organist and comp. He was a knight of the order of San Stefano and presented an org. to its church at Pisa, not only designed by himself but partly built by his own hands.

Works incl. Masses, motets, *Salmi concertati; Cantate da camera*; harpsichord sonatas, etc.

Delle Sedie, Enrico (b. Leghorn, 17. VI. 1822; d. Paris, 28. XI. 1907), It. baritone. After fighting as a volunteer in the war against Aus. he studied singing with Orazio Galeffi at Leghorn and made his 1st appearance at Pistoia in 1851. In 1867 he became prof. at the Paris Cons.

Deller, Alfred (b. Margate, 30. V. 1912), Eng. counter-tenor. Entirely self-trained, he became a lay clerk at Canterbury Cathedral in 1940 and in 1947 joined the choir of St. Paul's Cathedral. He is widely known as a soloist of outstanding musicianship, also frequently singing with the Deller Consort, which he formed in 1948.

Dello Joio, Norman (b. New York, 24. I. 1913), Amer. comp. Studied comp. at the Juillard Graduate School in N.Y., with Wagenaar, later with Hindemith at Yale School of Mus. He joined the teaching staff of Sarah Lawrence Coll.

Works incl. opera *The Ruby*; symph. ballet *On Stage; Western Star* for solo voices, narrator, chorus and orch.; sinfonietta, ballet suite *Duke of Sacra-*

mento, symph. movement *Silvermine* for orch.; concertos for pf., 2 pfs., harp and fl.; 4tet and trio for woodwind, trio for fl., cello and pf.; vln. and pf., sonata, *Duo concertante* for cello and pf., sonatina for cello solo; suite and *Duo concertante* for 2 pfs.; 2 sonatas, suite and 2 preludes for pf., etc.

Delmas, Marc (Marie Jean Baptiste) (b. Saint-Quentin, 28. III. 1885; d. Paris, 30. XI. 1931), Fr. comp. Studied at the Paris Cons. and took the Prix de Rome in 1919.

Works incl. operas *Iriam, Camille, Le Dieu sans couronne, Le Masque, Cyrca, Le Giaour*; symph. poem *Les Deux Routes*; chamber mus.; pf. pieces; songs, etc.

Delvincourt, Claude (b. Paris, 12. I. 1888; d. Obertello nr. Grosseto, It., 5. IV. 1954), Fr. comp. Studied at the Paris Cons. under Caussade and Widor. Took the Prix de Rome in 1913. He was wounded in the 1914–18 war and incapacitated for 8 years, but became director of the Versailles Cons. in 1932 and of the Paris Cons. in 1941 in succession to Rabaud. During World War II he helped the students to join the Maquis and to escape service in Ger.

Works incl. operas *La Femme à barbe* and *Lucifer*; *Boccacerie, L'Offrande à Siva, Bal vénitien* and *Prélude chorégraphique* for orch.; trio for ob., clar. and bassoon; vln. and pf. sonata; *Heures juvéniles* and *Images pour les contes du temps passé* for pf.; pf. duets and solo pieces; songs, etc.

Demelli, Francesco. *See* **Suppé.**

Demetrio (*Demetrius*), lib. by Metastasio.

Opera by Caldara, prod. Vienna, at court, 4. XI. 1731.

Opera by Gluck, prod. Venice, Teatro San Samuele, 2. V. 1746.

Opera by Hasse, prod. Venice, Teatro San Giovanni Crisostomo, I. 1732.

Opera by Jommelli, prod. Parma, spring 1749.

Opera by Pérez, prod. Venice, Teatro San Samuele, 13. VI. 1741.

Opera by Pescetti, prod. Florence, Teatro della Pergola, 26. XII. 1732.

Demeur. *See* **Charton-Demeur.**

Demisemiquaver, a note or rest of the value of a quarter of a quaver.

Demofoonte, rè di Tracia (*Demophoon, King of Thrace*), lib. by Metastasio.

Opera by Caldara, prod. 4. XI. 1733.

Opera by Gluck, prod. Milan, Teatro Regio Ducal, 26. XII. 1742.

Opera by Graun, prod. Berlin, Opera, 17. I. 1746. 3 airs are by Frederick II of Prus.

Opera by Hasse, prod. Dresden, at court, 9. II. 1748.

Opera by Jommelli, prod. Padua, 13. VI. 1743.

Opera by Leo, prod. Naples, Teatro San Bartolommeo, 20. I. 1735.

Opera by Portugal, prod. Milan, Teatro alla Scala, 8. II. 1794.

Demon, The, opera by A. Rubinstein (lib., in Rus., by Pavel Alexandrovich Viskovatov, based on Lermontov's poem), prod. St. Petersburg, 25. I. 1875.

Démophoon, opera by Cherubini (lib. by Marmontel, based on Metastasio's *Demofoonte*), prod. Paris, Opéra, 5. XII. 1788. Cherubini's 1st Fr. opera.

Demuth, Norman (b. London, 15. VII. 1898; d. Chichester, 21. IV. 1968), Eng. comp. and author. Educ. as a choir-boy at St. George's Chapel, Windsor, and at Repton School. Studied mus. at the R.C.M. in London and became prof. of comp. at the R.A.M. there in 1930. His books include studies of Franck, Ravel and Roussel.

Works incl. ballets *The Flame* and *Planetomania*, choreographic symph. *Night Mus. for a dancer*; 5 symphs., *Intro. and Allegro*, partita, nocturne *Paris, Serenata, Prelude for a Drama, Cortège, Notturno e Scherzo, The Dance of Life, Fantasy and Fugue* for orch.; *Pastoral* for strings; vln. concerto, vla. concerto; 3 vln. and pf. sonatas and pieces; sonatina for fl. and pf.; *Prelude, Air and Toccata* for harpsichord; *Mus. for Dancing* and other pf. works; part-songs, etc.

Dent, Edward J(oseph). (b. Ribston, Yorks., 16. VII. 1876; d. London, 22. VIII. 1957), Eng. musicologist and comp. Educ. at Eton and Cambridge, Prof. of Mus. there from 1926 to 1941. President of the I.S.C.M. from its foundation in 1922 until 1938. A governor of Sadler's Wells Opera, for which he trans. many works. His books incl. works on A. Scarlatti, Mozart's operas, Eng. opera, Handel and Busoni, and his comps. polyphonic motets and a version of *The Beggar's Opera*. He was a member of the Editorial Board of the *New Oxford History of Music*.

Denza, Luigi (b. Castellammare di Stabia, 24. II. 1846; d. London, 26. I. 1922), It. singing-teacher and comp. Studied at the Naples Cons. Settled in London in 1879, made a success with many of his light songs, esp. *Funiculì, funiculà*, and was prof. of singing at the R.A.M. from 1898.

Works incl. an opera on Schiller's *Wallenstein*, over 500 songs, etc.

Deprés. *See* **Josquin.**

Dering, Lady. *See* **Harvey, Mary.**

Dering (or Deering), Richard (b. ?, *c.* 1580; d. London, III. 1630), Eng. organist and comp. Became a Catholic and went to Brussels in 1617 as organist to the convent of Eng. nuns, but returned again to become organist to Henrietta Maria on her marriage to Charles I in 1625.

Works incl. *Cantiones sacrae* for several voices, motets, anthems; canzonets for 3 and 4 voices, quodlibets on street cries; fancies and other pieces for viols, etc.

Des Prés. *See* **Josquin.**

Desbordes-Valmore, Marceline (1785–1859), Fr. poet. *See* **Franck (C.)** (songs).

Descant. (1) A melodic line added to an existing melody, hence in general = counterpoint and was so used by older Eng. writers.
(2) The upper part of a polyphonic comp., whether vocal or instrumental; hence D. Recorder, D. Viol.
(3) In modern usage the addition of a treble part to a well-known tune, either by a comp. or by improvisation: the word Faburden (or Fauxbourdon) is often used as an equivalent.

Descant Mass, a term borrowed from the Ger. *Diskantmesse* to designate 15th-cent. Masses in which the principal part is not the tenor but the treble or descant.

Descant Viol. *See* **Treble Viol.**

Descartes, René (b. La Haye, 31. III. 1596; d. Stockholm, 11. II. 1650), Fr. philosopher. Wrote a book on mus., *Compendium musicae.*

Deschamps, Émile (1791–1875), Fr. poet. *See* **Niedermeyer** (songs).

Déserteur, Le, opera by Monsigny (lib. by Jean Michel Sedaine), prod. Paris, Comédie-Italienne, 6. III. 1769.

Désir, Le (a waltz attrib. to Beethoven). *See* **Trauerwalzer.**

Desmarets, Henri (b. Paris, *c.* 1662; d. Lunéville, 7. IX. 1741), Fr. comp. Educ. at the court of Louis XIV. At the end of the cent. he secretly married the daughter of a dignitary at Senlis and fled to Spain, becoming mus. superintendent to Philip V in 1700. In 1708 he became mus. director to the Duke of Lorraine at Lunéville.
Works incl. operas *Didon, Circé, Théagène et Chariclée* (on Heliodorus's *Aethiopica*), *Les Amours de Momus, Vénus et Adonis, Les Fêtes galantes, Iphigénie en Tauride* (with Campra) and *Renaud ou La Suite d'Armide*; motet and Te Deum for the marriage of Princess Élisabeth Thérèse to the King of Sardinia; church mus. comp. early in his career under the name of Goupillier, etc.

Désormière, Roger (b. Vichy, 13. IX. 1898; d. Paris, 25. X. 1963), Fr. cond. Studied at the Paris Cons. and in 1924 became cond. of the Swed. ballet. From 1925 to 1929 he worked with the Ballet Russe and from 1936 to 1944 cond. at the Opera Comique. He became seriously ill in 1950 and was forced to give up his career.

Dessau, Paul (b. Hamburg, 19. XII. 1894), Ger. comp. From 1910 he studied at the Klindworth-Scharwenka Cons. in Berlin and later in Hamburg, where in 1913 he became a coach at the opera. He cond. all over Ger., but was forced to leave and in 1939 went to N.Y. He returned to E. Ger. in 1948.
Works incl. opera *Das Verhör des Lukullus*; children's operas *Das Eisenbahnspiel, Tadel der Unzuverlässigkeit*; concertino for solo fl., clar., horn and vln.; a pf. sonata; much vocal and orchestral mus., film and incid. mus., etc.

Dessus (Fr. = above, top), treble, whether voice or instrument. In particular, in the 17th cent., the 1st vln. in a string ensemble.

Dessus de viole (Fr. = top of the viols), the treble viol.

Destinn (*née* **Kittl**) (later known as **Destinnova**), **Emmy** (b. Prague, 26. II. 1878; d. České Budějovice, 28. I. 1930), Cz. soprano. Made her 1st appearance in Berlin in 1898; 1st visited London (Covent Garden) in 1904. She wrote poems and novels.

Destouches, André(-Cardinal) (b. Paris, IV. 1672; d. Paris, 7. II. 1749), Fr. comp. A sailor at first, and then a musketeer, he studied with Campra and prod. his 1st stage work, *Issé*, in 1697. He held var. court apps. and was director of the Opéra in 1728–31.
Works incl. operas *Amadis de Grèce, Marthésie, Omphale, Callirhoé, Télémaque et Calypso, Sémiramis, Les Stratagèmes de l'Amour*; heroic pastoral *Issé*; comedy-ballet *Le Carnaval et la folie*; ballet *Les Éléments* (with Lalande); cantatas *Œnone* and *Sémélé*, etc.

Détaché (Fr. = detached, separated), a bowing style in string playing. In quick passages the bow changes direction so that each note is clearly separated, but without the sound being perceptibly interrupted, as in *staccato*.

Dettingen Te Deum, a Te Deum comp. by Handel to celebrate the victory of Dettingen won on 26. VI. 1743. 1st perf. London, Chapel Royal, 27. XI. 1743.

Deuteromelia, the 2nd part of a collection of canons, rounds and catches pub. by Ravenscroft in London in 1609, the 1st part being *Pammelia.*

Deutsch, Otto Erich (b. Vienna, 5. IX. 1883; d. Vienna, 23. XI. 1967), Aus. mus. biog. and bibliog. Made a special study of 1st eds. and of Schubert and other classics. After the *Anschluss* he took refuge in Eng. and settled at Cambridge, but returned to Vienna in 1954. His pubs. incl. the complete Schubert, Handel and Mozart documents, a thematic catalogue of Schubert's works, a study of Mozart eds. (with C. B. Oldman), Leopold Mozart's later letters (with B. Paumgartner), the Harrow Replicas of var. old pubs., etc.

Deutsche Tänze (Ger. plur. = Ger. Dances), not an equivalent of the Allemande, but a type of country dance in 3–4 (slow waltz) time, cultivated by Mozart, Beethoven, Schubert and others. The adj. 'Deutsche' was frequently used alone in titles.

Deutsches Requiem (Brahms). *See* German Requiem.

Deux Avares, Les (*The Two Misers*), opera by Grétry (lib. by Charles Georges Fenouillot de Falbère), prod. Fontainebleau, at court, 27. X. 1770; 1st Paris perf., Comédie-Italienne, 6. XII. 1770.

Deux Chasseurs et la Laitière, Les (*The Two Huntsmen and the Milkmaid*), opera by Duni (lib. by Louis Anseaume, after La Fontaine), prod. Paris, Comédie-Italienne, 21. VII. 1763.

Deux Journées, Les (*The Two Days*: better known as *The Water-Carrier*), opera by Cherubini (lib. by Jean Nicolas Bouilly), prod. Paris, Théâtre Feydeau, 16. I. 1800.

Deux Petits Savoyards, Les (*The Two Little Savoyards*), opera by Dalayrac (lib. by Benoît Joseph Marsollier), prod. Paris, Comédie-Italienne, 14. I. 1789.

Development. *See* Working-Out.

Devil and Kate, The (*Čert a Káča*), opera by Dvořák (lib. by Adolf Wenig), prod. Prague, Cz. Theatre, 23. XI, 1899.

Devil to Pay, The, or The Wives Metamorphos'd, ballad opera (lib. by Charles Coffey), prod. London, Drury Lane Theatre, 6. VIII. 1731.

Devil's Opera, The, opera by Macfarren (lib. by George Macfarren, the comp.'s father, a satire on the diabolic elements in works like Weber's *Freischütz*, Meyerbeer's *Robert le Diable*, Marschner's *Vampyr*, etc.), prod. London, Lyceum Theatre, 10. IX. 1838.

Devil's Trill (Tartini). *See* Trillo del Diavolo.

Devil take her, The, opera by Benjamin (lib. by Alan Collard and John B. Gordon), prod. London, R.C.M., XII. 1931.

Devin du village, Le (*The Village Soothsayer*), opera by Rousseau (lib. by comp.), prod. Fontainebleau, at court, 18. X. 1752, with overture and recitatives by Pierre de Jélyotte (1713–87) and Francœur; Paris, Opéra, 1. III. 1753, with mus. all by Rousseau.

Devisenarie (Ger. = device aria), a type of aria of the 17th and 18th cents. in which the 1st word or words occur separately in the voice-part, as though the singer were announcing a title, before the 1st line of the text or more is sung continuously, often after a further instrumental passage.

Devrient, Eduard (Philipp) (b. Berlin, 11. VIII. 1801; d. Carlsruhe, 4. X. 1877), Ger. baritone and actor. A close friend of Mendelssohn, to whom he devoted a vol. of memoirs, and librettist of Marschner's *Hans Heiling* and other operas.

Devrient, Wilhelmine. *See* Schröder-Devrient.

Dezède, Nicolas (b. ?, *c.* 1745; d. Paris, 11. IX. 1792), Fr. comp. (?) of It. descent. He did not know what his parentage was, but received a handsome allowance on condition that he should not try to find out, and it was stopped when he persisted in his inquiries. He then began to prod. light operas.

Works incl. operas *Julie*, *L'Erreur d'un moment*, *Les Trois Fermiers*, *Blaise et Babet*, *Alexis et Justine*, etc.

Diabelli, Anton (b. Mattsee nr. Salzburg, 6. IX. 1781; d. Vienna, 7. IV. 1858), Aus. mus. pub. and comp. Educ. for the priesthood, but studied mus. with M. Haydn. Went to Vienna as pf. and guitar teacher and joined Peter Cappi in his pub. firm in 1818; it became D. & Co. in 1824.

Works incl. operetta *Adam in der Klemme*; Masses; many pf. pieces, incl. the little waltz on which Beethoven wrote the 33 variations, Op. 120, etc.

'Diabelli' Variations. *See above* and Vaterländischer Künstlerverein.

Diable à quatre, Le, ou La Double Métamorphose, ballad opera with airs arr. by Philidor (lib. by Jean Michel Sedaine, based on Coffey's *Devil to Pay*), prod. Paris, Opéra-Comique, 19. VIII. 1756.

Diable dans le beffroi, Le (*The Devil in the Belfry*), opera by Debussy (lib. by himself, based on Edgar Allan Poe's story), worked at in 1903 but not completed.

Diabolus in Musica (Lat. = the devil in mus.), a medieval warning against the use of the Tritone—the interval of the augmented 4th (e.g. C–F♯ or F–B), which was looked at askance as a melodic progression.

Diaghilev, Sergey Pavlovich (b. Government of Novgorod, 19. III. 1872; d. Venice, 19. VIII. 1929), Rus. impresario. Studied law and mus. at St. Petersburg, founded an art review there in 1899, prod. Rus. mus. in Paris from 1907 and in 1909 organized the Rus. Ballet there, which 1st visited London in 1911. He encouraged many comps. to write for his co., incl. Stravinsky, Ravel, Debussy, Prokofiev, R. Strauss, de Falla, Poulenc, Milhaud, etc., and was thus directly responsible for some of the most important mus. of the 20th cent.

Dialogue, a type of 17th-cent comp. for 2 or more voices where distinct personages are represented.

Dialogues des Carmélites, Les, opera by Poulenc (lib. by G. Bernanos), prod. Milan (La Scala), 26. I. 1957.

Diamants de la Couronne, Les (*The Crown Diamonds*), opera by Auber (lib. by Scribe and Jules Henri Vernoy de Saint-Georges), prod. Paris, Opéra-Comique, 6. III. 1841.

Diamond, David (Leo) (b. Rochester, N.Y., 9. VII. 1915), Amer. comp. of Aus. descent. Studied at the Eastman School of Mus. at Rochester and later at Fontaine-bleau with Nadia Boulanger. After his return to Amer. he was awarded several comp. prizes.

middle of the 18th cent., for the divisions of mus. into sections or phrases.

Diatessaron (Gk.), the interval of the 4th.

Diatonic. The D. scale is, in a maj. key, one involving no accidentals (*see* illustration). In a min. key the D. scale has two forms, (*a*) melodic, (*b*) harmonic (*see*

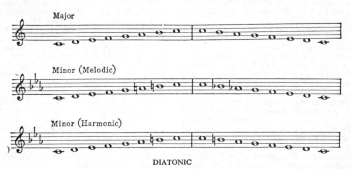

Major

Minor (Melodic)

Minor (Harmonic)

DIATONIC

Works incl. 8 symphs., sinfonietta, serenade, variations, *Psalm*, *Elegy in Memory of Ravel* and ballet suite *Tom* for orch.; concerto and *Rounds* for string orch.; vln. concerto, *Hommage à Satie* and ballade for chamber orch., concertos for pf., cello and vln. (2) with chamber orch.; *A Night Litany* (Ezra Pound) for chorus and 3 madrigals (James Joyce); 6 string 4tets, string trio; sonatina for vln. and pf., cello and pf. sonata, partita for bassoon and pf.; sonata and sonatina for pf. etc.

Diana, Paolo. *See* Spagnoletti.

Diapason (from Gk. = through all [the notes], hence interval of an octave; Fr. = a tuning-fork and hence pitch). The normal modern Eng. use of the term designates the foundation stops of the org., which produce the instrument's most distinctive and characteristic tone. There are 2 kinds of D. pipes: open and stopped. The 4-ft. D. is generally called Principal (or Octave) on Eng. orgs.

Diapente (Gk.), the interval of the 5th. In old mus. canons at the 5th were called Epidiapente when answered in the 5th above and Subdiapente when answered below.

Diaphone, a powerful valvular reed org. stop which may embrace 8-ft., 16-ft. and 32-ft. pipes.

Diaphony (or Lat. **Diaphonia**), in Lat. 'dissonance', as distinct from *symphonia* = 'consonance'. Also the name given by some medieval theorists to early Organum.

Diastole (from Gk. = distinction, differentiation), an old term, in use to the

illustrations). D. harmony is the opposite of chromatic harmony, using the notes proper to the prescribed maj. or min. scale only, without deviations to those marked with additional accidentals. D. discords are those that occur in D. harmony.

Diaz, Gabriel (b. ?, *c.* 1590; d. Madrid, after 1631), Span. comp. Worked at the Span. court and later at Larma, Granada and Córdoba.

Works incl. church mus., a Requiem, secular vocal mus., etc.

Dibdin, Charles (b. Southampton, III. 1745; d. London, 25. VII. 1814), Eng. singer, author and comp. Chorister at Winchester Cathedral, went to London at the age of 15. Made his stage début in 1762, and shortly afterwards was engaged as a singing actor at Covent Garden, where his pastoral *The Shepherd's Artifice* was prod. in 1764. Over 100 dramatic works followed. In 1778 app. comp. to Covent Garden Theatre, and during the 1780s dabbled in theatrical management with variable success. A projected journey to India came to nothing, but the fund-raising travels which were to have financed it provided material for his *Musical Tour* (1788). In 1789 he began his series of 'Table Entertainments', in which he was author, comp., narrator, singer and accompanist. One of the most successful, *The Oddities*, contained the song *Tom Bowling*. Many other sea-songs achieved great popularity. Towards the end of his life a pub. venture made him bankrupt, and he was saved from destitution by a public subscription. He also wrote an account of his professional life and other literary works.

Works incl. over 100 dramatic pieces, e.g. *Lionel and Clarissa, The Padlock, The Ephesian Matron, The Captive, The Ladle, The Trip to Portsmouth, The Seraglio, Rose and Colin, The Touchstone, The Milkmaid, Tom Thumb, Harvest Home*; over 30 table entertainments containing innumerable songs, etc.

Dichterliebe (*Poet's Love*), song cycle by Schumann, Op. 48 (16 poems by Heine), comp. in 1840.

Dickens, Charles (1812–70), Eng. novelist. *See* Bax (*Oliver Twist*, film), Benjamin (*Tale of Two Cities*), Bentzon (J.) (symph.), Cikker (*Mr. Scrooge*), Cricket on the Hearth (Mackenzie), Edwards (J.) (*Dolly Varden*), Gál (*Pickwickian Overture*), Heimchen am Herd (Goldmark), Holbrooke (*Pickwick Club* 4tet), O'Neill (*Pickwick*) Pickwick (A. Coates), Préludes (Debussy, II. 9), Schmidt (G.) (*Christmas Carol*), Sutermeister (*Drei Geister*), Vaughan Williams (*On Christmas Night*), Village Coquettes (Hullah), White (F.) (*D. Notebook*), Wood (C.) (*Pickwick Papers*), Zandonai (*Grillo sul focolare*).

Dickinson, Emily (1830–86), Amer. poet. *See* Bacon (cantata and songs with orch.), Barber (choruses).

Diction, the popular but inaccurate term for enunciation of the words in singing.

Dido and Aeneas, opera by Purcell (lib. by Nahum Tate, after Virgil), prod. Chelsea, London, Josias Priest's boarding school ('by young gentlewomen'), ? XII. 1689.

Dido, Königin von Carthago, opera by Graupner (lib. by Heinrich Hinsch), prod. Hamburg, Theater beim Gänsemarkt, spring 1707.

Didon (*Dido*), opera by Piccinni (lib. by Marmontel), prod. Fontainebleau, at court, 16. X. 1783, 1st Paris perf., Opéra, 1. XII. 1783.

Didone abbandonata (*Dido Forsaken*), lib. by Metastasio:

Opera by Hasse, prod. Hubertusburg nr. Dresden, 7. X. 1742.

Opera by Jommelli, prod. Rome, Teatro Argentina, 28. I. 1747.

Opera by Sarro, prod. Naples, Teatro San Bartolommeo, 5. II. 1724.

Opera by Traetta, prod. Venice, Teatro San Moisè, autumn 1757.

Didone, La (*Dido*), opera by Cavalli (lib. by Giovanni Francesco Busenello), prod. Teatro San Cassiano, Carnival 1641.

Diémer, Louis (b. Paris, 14. II. 1843; d. Paris, 21. XII. 1919), Fr. pianist and comp. Studied with Marmontel, Bazin and A. Thomas at the Paris Cons. In 1888 he became pf. prof. there.

Works incl. pf. concerto, *Concertstück* for pf. and orch., another for vln. and orch.; chamber mus., etc.

Diepenbrock, Alphons (b. Amsterdam, 2. IX. 1862; d. Amsterdam, 5. IV. 1921), Dutch comp. At first a philologist, self-taught in mus.

Works incl. incid. mus. for Aristophanes' *The Birds,* Sophocles' *Electra,* Goethe's *Faust,* Vondel's *Gysbrecht van Amstel; Stabat Mater,* Te Deum for solo voices, chorus and orch., Mass; songs with orch.; chamber mus.; songs, etc.

Dieren, Bernard van (b. Rotterdam, 27. XII. 1884; d. London, 24. IV. 1936), Dutch (anglicized) comp. Educ. for science, he had little mus. experience, apart from vln. playing, before the age of 20, when he began to comp. In 1909 he settled in London as correspondent to foreign papers, after making serious mus. studies, which he continued in Ger. in 1912, when his real creative career began. He also prod. a book on the sculptor Epstein and a vol. of mus. essays, *Down among the Dead Men.*

Works incl. opera *The Tailor* (Robert Nichols); symph. on Chin. poems for solo voices, chorus and orch., *Les Propous des beuveurs* (Rabelais) for chorus and orch.; *Beatrice Cenci,* orchestral epilogue to Shelley's drama, overture *Anjou;* serenade for small orch., overture for chamber orch.; *Diafonia* for 17 instruments and baritone (Shakespeare sonnets), *Fayre eies* (Spenser) for baritone and chamber orch.; 6 string 4tets; 3 unaccomp. choruses; sonata and 3 studies for unaccomp. vln., vln. and pf. sonata; songs for baritone and string 4tet (Shelley and De Quincey), 2 recitations with string 4tet (Baudelaire and Villon); *Marginalia* from De Quincey's *Murder as One of the Fine Arts* for baritone, vocal 4tet and pf.; 6 sketches, toccata, 3 studies, prelude, 12 variations for pf.; songs to words by Shakespeare, Nash, Beddoes, Keats, Landor, Joyce, Goethe, Heine, Mörike, Verlaine, Charles d'Orléans, Ronsard, Boileau, Hugo, Villiers de l'Isle Adam, etc.

Dies irae (*Day of wrath*), the sequence from the Mass for the Dead orig. assoc. with a distinct plainsong theme which has been frequently used or quoted by var. comps., e.g.:

Bantock, Witches' Dance in incid. mus. to *Macbeth.*

Berlioz, Witches' Sabbath in *Fantastic Symph.* and Requiem.

Dallapiccola, *Canti di prigionia.*

Davies (Maxwell), *St. Michael.*

Kraft, Fantasia *Dies irae* for org.

Liszt, *Totentanz* for pf. and orch.

Miaskovsky, symph. No. 6.

Pierres, *Litany for the Day of Human Rights.*

Rakhmaninov, Rhapsody on a Theme by Paganini for pf. and orch. and Symph. Dances, Op. 45.

Dièse   Diruta

Respighi, *Impressioni brasiliane*.
Saint-Saens, *Danse macabre* for orch.
Schelling, *Victory Ball* for orch.
Séverac, *En Languedoc*.
Sorabji, variations for pf. and *Sequentia cyclica*.
Stevenson (Robert), *Passacaglia on DSCH*.
Tchaikovsky, Theme and Variations in Suite No. 3 for orch. and song *In Dark Hell*.
Vaughan Williams, *Five Tudor Portraits* for chorus and orch. (lament for Philip Sparrow).

Dièse (or **Dièze**) (Fr.) = Sharp; the sign ♯.

Diesis (Gk.), in ancient Greece either the interval between a fourth and 2 'maj.' tones or a quarter-tone. In modern acoustics (*a*) the Great D. is the difference between 4 min. thirds and an octave; (*b*) the Enharmonic D. is the difference between an octave and 3 maj. thirds.

Dietrich, Albert (Hermann) (b. Golk nr. Meissen, 28. VIII. 1829; d. Berlin, 20. XI. 1908), Ger. comp. and cond. Court mus. director at Oldenburg from 1861. Wrote a vln. and pf. sonata jointly with Schumann and Brahms, 1853.
Works incl. opera *Robin Hood*; incid. mus. to Shakespeare's *Cymbeline*; symph. in D min.; choral and orchestral works; horn concertos; chamber mus., etc.

Dietrich, Sixt (b. Augsburg, *c.* 1491; d. St. Gall, 21. X. 1548), Ger. comp. Studied at the Univs. of Freiburg i/B. and Wittenberg, holding appts. at Strasbourg and Constance between. Wrote Magnificats, antiphons and other vocal mus.

Dietsch, Pierre Louis Philippe (b. Dijon, 17. III. 1808; d. Paris, 20. II. 1865), Fr. cond. and comp. He comp. an unsuccessful opera to the orig. Fr. lib. of Wagner's *Flying Dutchman*, *Le Vaisseau fantôme*, prod. at the Paris Opéra in 1842. Cond. the disastrous perfs.of Wagner's *Tannhäuser* in 1861. Works incl. church and org. mus.

Dieupart, Charles (b. France, ?; d. London, *c.* 1740), Fr. violinist, harpsichordist and comp. Settled in London *c.* 1700 and was involved in the promotion of It. opera there. Later abandoned opera, gave concerts and taught the harpsichord. Comp. suites, etc., for harpsichord.

Dièze. See **Dièse.**

Diferencias (Span. lit. differences) = Variations.

Difference Tones. *See* **Combination Tones.**

Dima, Gheorge (b. Brasov, 10. X. 1847; d. Cluj. 4. VI. 1925), Rum. comp. Studied at Carlsruhe, Vienna, Graz and Leipzig, and on returning to Rum. became choral cond. at Brasov and mus. director of the church of St. Nicholas, also of the cathedral at Sibiu.

Works incl. oratorio *The Mother of Stephen the Great*; church liturgies; cantatas; songs, etc.

Diminished, said of intervals normally 'perfect' (4ths, 5th, 8ves) or 'minor' (2nds, 3rds, 6ths, 7ths) which have been made a semitone narrower, e.g.:

Diminished 7th Chord, a chord of 3 superimposed min. 3rds, e.g.:

Diminuendo (It. = waning, lessening), a direction to decrease the sound of a note, chord or phrase, synonymous with *decrescendo* and now more frequently used.

Diminution, a shortening of a mus. figure or phrase by its reduction to smaller note-values.

Dimitri, opera by Dvořák (lib. by Maria Červinková-Riegerová), prod. Prague, Cz. Theatre, 8. X. 1882. The subject is the 'false Dimitri', the pretender who also figures in Mussorgsky's *Boris Godunov*.

Dinorah (Meyerbeer). *See* **Pardon de Ploërmel.**

Dioclesian (Purcell). *See* **Prophetess.**

Direct, a sign used in plainsong notation and often in old mus. in staff notation, indicating at the end of the stave the position of the first note at the beginning of the following one.

Dirge, a funeral comp., usually vocal, perf. at a burial or more rarely on a memorial occasion. The word derives from the Lat. *Dirige Domine*, the opening words of an antiphon from the Office for the Dead.

Diruta, Agostino (b. Perugia, ?; d. Rome, ?), It. 16th–17th-cent. organist and comp, Organist at Venice, 1617, Asolo, 1620–2. and Rome, 1630–47.
Works incl. Masses, motets, psalms, *Sacrae cantiones*, canticles and other vocal mus.

Diruta, Girolamo (real name **Mancini**) (b. Deruta nr. Perugia, 1561; d. ? after 1628), It. Franciscan monk, organist and comp., uncle and master of prec. Pupil of Zarlino, Porta and Merulo. Organist at Chioggia and Gubbio Cathedrals. He was a famous player and wrote a treatise on org. playing. *Il Transilvano*, ded. to the Prince of Transylvania, Sigismund Bathori. Comp. org. mus.

163

Discant. See **Descant.**

Discord, the opposite of concord: the sounding together of notes that do not satisfy the ear as being final in themselves and require a following chord to give the impression of resolution.

Disjunct Motion. See **Motion.**

Diskantmesse (Ger.). See **Descant Mass.**

Dissoluto punito, Il (Mozart). See **Don Giovanni.**

Dissonance, the sounding together of notes which produces Discord.

Distler, Hugo (b. Nuremberg, 24. VI. 1908; d. Berlin, 1. XI. 1942), Ger. organist and comp. Studied at Leipzig, became organist and cantor at Lübeck in 1921 and prof. of comp. at the Stuttgart Cons. in 1937. He d. by committing suicide.

Works incl. 52 motets entitled *Jahrkreis*, a Passion, oratorio *Nativity*; org. works; harpsichord concerto.

Distratto, Il, nickname of Haydn's symph. No. 60 in C maj., so called on account of its being an adaptation of the incid. mus. to *Der Zerstreute* (1775), a Ger. version of Regnard's *Le Distrait*.

Dital Harp. See **Harp Lute.**

Dittersdorf, Karl Ditters von (orig. simply **Karl Ditters**) (b. Vienna, 2. XI. 1739; d. Neuhof, Pilgram, Boh., 24. X. 1799), Aus. violinist and comp. Educ. in the household of Prince Hildburghausen in Vienna, studied comp. with Bonno. Played in the orch. of the Imp. Opera in Vienna, 1761–3, when he travelled to Italy with Gluck, winning great success as a violinist. In 1765 succeeded Michael Haydn as *Kapellmeister* to the Bishop of Grosswardein, and from 1769 to 1795 served the Prince Bishop of Breslau in the same capacity. But much of his time was spent in Vienna, where his most popular opera, *Doctor und Apotheker*, was prod. in 1786. He was ennobled in 1773, henceforth calling himself von D. Kelly's *Reminiscences* contain an account of D. playing string 4tets with Haydn, Mozart and Vanhal. During his last years he was in the service of Baron Stillfried at Rothlhotta. His autobiography, dictated shortly before his death, was pub. in 1801.

Works incl. over 40 operas, e.g. *Amore in musica, Betrug durch Aberglauben, Doctor und Apotheker, Hieronimus Knicker, Das rothe Kaeppchen, Die Hochzeit des Figaro* (after Beaumarchais), etc.; oratorios *Isacco, Davidde Penitente, Esther, Giobbe*; Masses and other church mus.; over 100 symphs., incl. 21 on Ovid's *Metamorphoses*; concertos; divertimenti, chamber mus., etc.

Divertimento, a work for instrumental ensemble in several movements akin to the suite and predominantly light-hearted in character.

Divertissement, mainly a term connected with ballet, where it means a set of varied dances with no partic. plot. In mus. a suite, partic. of arrs. or pieces based on familiar tunes, an entertaining piece of any kind or a fantasy of a lighter sort, such as Schubert's *Divertissement à la hongroise*. In 18th-cent. Fr. usage a dance interlude, with or without songs, in a play or opera; also sometimes a short play with dances and songs.

Divisi (It. plur. = divided), a direction found in orchestral scores where string parts are intended to be distributed in such a way as to play in 2 or more parts within a single group of instruments which would normally play in unison.

Division Viol, a bass viol of moderate size on which divisions were often played in the 17th cent. Simpson, for ex., wrote a work for it.

Divisions, a term used in 17th-cent. Eng. for variations. It became current because variations then usually consisted of breaking up the melody of the theme into notes of smaller value.

Divitis, Antonius (van Rijcke, Le Riche, etc.) (b. Louvain, *c*. 1475; d. ?, after 1526), Flem. comp. In the service of Philip the Handsome, Duke of Burgundy, and Louis XII of France, and possibly a member of the choir at St. Peter's, Rome. 2 Masses, 2 Magnificats, some motets and a *chanson* are extant.

Djamileh, opera by Bizet (lib. by Louis Gallet, based on Musset's *Namouna*), prod. Paris, Opéra-Comique, 22. V. 1872.

Djinns, Les (*The Genii*), symph. poem by Franck for pf. and orch., based on verses from Hugo's *Les Orientales*, comp. 1884.

Dmitri (Dvořák). See **Dimitri.**

Do, the old name for the note C (*see* **Solmization**), still used in Lat. countries. In Tonic Sol-fa notation the Tonic note in any key, represented by the symbol **d**, pronounced Doh.

Dobroven, Issay Alexandrovich (b. Nizhny-Novgorod, 27. II. 1894; d. Oslo, 9. XII. 1953), Rus. cond. and comp. Studied with Taneiev and others at the Moscow Cons. and later took a pf. course with Godowsky in Vienna. He became prof. at the Moscow Cons. in 1917 and cond. of the Opera in 1919. Later he cond. Rus. opera on tour in Ger. and in 1927–8 he was cond. of the Bulg. State Opera at Sofia. In the 1930s he cond. extensively in U.S.A. and Palestine.

Works incl. opera *A Thousand and One Nights*; incid. mus. to Verhaeren's *Philip II*; pf. concerto; vln. concerto; sonata and *Fairy Tales* for vln. and pf.; 2 sonatas, studies and pieces for pf.; songs, etc.

Docteur Ox, Le, opéra-bouffe by Offenbach (lib. by Philippe Gille and Arnold Mortier, based on a Jules Verne story), prod. Paris, Théâtre des Varietés, 26. I. 1877.

Doctor und Apotheker (*Doctor and Apothecary*), opera by Dittersdorf (lib. by Gottlieb Stephanie, jun.), prod. Vienna, Kärntnertortheater, 11. VII. 1786.

Dog Waltz, one of the nicknames given to Chopin's Waltz in D♭ maj., Op. 64 No. 1, another being 'Minute Waltz'. It is supposed to illustrate George Sand's dog chasing its tail.

Doh, the name for the Tonic note in any key in Tonic Sol-fa, so pronounced, but in notation represented by the symbol **d**.

Dohnányi, Ernö (or **Ernst von**) (b. Pozsony = Pressburg, 27. VII. 1877; d. New York, 11. II. 1960), Hung. pianist and comp. Studied under Carl Forstner, the cathedral organist at his native town, until 1893, when he went to the R. Hung. Acad. at Budapest, where he studied pf. under Stephan Thomán and comp. under Koessler. In 1897 he had some lessons from d'Albert and appeared as pianist in Berlin and Vienna. He visited Eng. in 1898 and U.S.A. in 1899, made many tours later, but eventually became better known as a comp. From 1908 to 1915 he was prof. of pf. at the Hochschule in Berlin and in 1919 became cond. of the Budapest Phil. Orch. and director of the city's Cons. As a pianist his powers were prodigious, while as a comp. he drew upon the classical Ger. tradition, esp. Brahms.

Works incl. operas *Aunt Simona*, *The Tower of Voivod* and *The Tenor*; ballet *Pierrette's Veil*; symphs. in F min., D min. and E maj., suite in F♯ min. and *Suite en valse* for orch.; concerto and *Variations on a Nursery Song* for pf. and orch., vln. concerto, *Concertstück* for cello and orch.; 2 string 4tets, pf. 5tet, 6tet for vln., vla., cello, clar., horn and pf., serenade for string trio; sonatas for vln. and pf. and cello and pf.; *c*. 12 op. nos. of pf. mus., incl. a passacaglia, 4 rhapsodies, *Humoresques in form of a Suite*, *Ruralia hungarica*; songs, etc.

Doina (Rum. = lament), a Rum. type of folksong. The term was formerly used for var. kinds of songs, but is now properly restricted to laments.

Doktor Faust, opera by Busoni (lib. by comp. based on Goethe's drama), left unfinished at Busoni's death and completed by Jarnach; prod. Dresden, 21. V. 1925.

Dolby, Charlotte. *See* **Sainton-Dolby**.

Dolcan, an 8-ft. metal org. stop of soft tone, also called Dolce.

Dolce (It. = sweet), a direction indicating a suave and ingratiating perf., usually but not necessarily in a soft tone.

Dolce, Lodovico (1508–68), It. poet and playwright. *See* **Merulo** (*Troiano*).

Dolcian, an early form of bassoon.

Doles, Johann Friedrich (b. Steinbach, Saxe-Meiningen, 23. IV. 1715; d. Leipzig,

7. II. 1797), Ger. organist and comp. Pupil of Bach at Leipzig from 1739. Cantor of St. Thomas's School there from 1756 in succession to Harrer. Perf. Bach's motet *Singet dem Herrn* for Mozart, when the latter visited Leipzig in 1789.

Works incl. Passions, Masses, motets, cantatas and other church mus.

Dollarprinzessin, Die (*The Dollar Princess*), operetta by Fall (lib. by Alfred Maria Willner and Fritz Grünbaum), prod. Vienna, Theater an der Wien, 2. XI. 1907.

Dolly, suite of 6 children's pieces for pf. duet by Fauré, Op. 56, comp. in 1893, orch. for a ballet by Rabaud in 1896. It is ded. to the daughter of Mme. Emma Bardac, later Debussy's 2nd wife. As in the case of Debussy's *Children's Corner*, the title and 2 of the sub-titles seem to suggest some Eng. association: 1. *Berceuse*; 2. *Mi-a-ou*; 3. *Le Jardin de Dolly*; 4. *Kitty-Valse*; 5. *Tendresse*; 6. *Le Pas espagnol*.

Dolmetsch, Arnold (b. Le Mans, 24. II. 1858; d. Haslemere, 28. II. 1940), Swiss (anglicized) musicologist, instrument maker and perf. on old instruments. B. in Fr., he studied vln. under Vieuxtemps at Brussels, but turned his interests to old mus. and instruments. Worked with the pf. firm of Chickering at Boston, 1902–9, and then with that of Gaveau in Paris until 1914, when he went to live in Eng. and set up his own workshop for harpsichords, viols, lutes, recorders, etc. at Haslemere, where he arr. periodical festivals of old mus. and brought up a family to take part in it with var. instruments. He ed. old mus. and wrote a book on interpretation.

Domaine Musical, founded by Jean-Louis Barrault, Madeleine Renaud and Pierre Boulez in 1954 to promote concerts of new mus., with Boulez as mus. director. The group had as its headquarters the Petit Marigny theatre.

Domestic Symphony (R. Strauss). *See* **Symphonia domestica**.

Dominant. (1) The 5th note of the maj. or min. scale above the tonic or keynote, or the 4th below it. In classical harmony the D. is the most conspicuous note in the scale apart from the tonic.

(2) The name often given to the reciting note of a psalm-tone or mode. *See* **Modes**.

Domino noir, Le (*The Black Domino*), comic opera by Auber (lib. by Scribe) prod. Paris, Opéra-Comique, 2. XII. 1837.

Domp(e). *See* **Dump**.

Domra, a Rus. lute with a long neck, used in the 16th and 17th cents.

Don Carlos, opera by Verdi (lib. by François Joseph Méry and Camille Du Locle, based on Schiller's drama), prod. Paris, Opéra, 11. III. 1867. Verdi's 2nd Fr. opera.

Don Chisciotte in corte della duchessa (*Don Quixote at the Duchess's Court*), opera by Caldara (lib. by Giovanni Claudio Pasquini, based on Cervantes), prod. Vienna, 6. II. 1727.

Don Chisciotte in Sierra Morena (*Don Quixote in the S. M.*), opera by Conti (lib. by Zeno and Pietro Pariati, based on Cervantes), prod. Vienna, 11. II. 1719.

Don Giovanni (*Don Juan*), opera by Lattuada (lib. by Arturo Rossato, based on a Span. drama by José Zorilla), prod. Naples, 18. V. 1929.

Opera by Mozart (1st title: *Il dissoluto punito, o sia Il D. G.*: *The Rake Punished, or Don Juan*) (lib. by Lorenzo da Ponte), prod. Prague, 29. X. 1787. In Vienna, with additions, Burgtheater, 7. V. 1788.

Don Giovanni di Mañara (Alfano). *See* **Ombra di Don Giovanni.**

Don Giovanni Tenorio, ossia Il convitato di pietra (*Don Juan Tenorio, or The Stone Guest*), opera by Carnicer (lib. by ?), prod. Barcelona, Teatro Principal, 20. VI. 1822. The 1st Don Juan opera by a Span. comp., but set to It. words.

Opera by Gazzaniga (lib. by Giovanni Bertati, based on Tirso de Molina), prod. Venice, Teatro San Moisè, 5. II. 1787.

Don Juan. *See also* **Convitato di pietra; Don Giovanni; Ombra di Don Giovanni; Stone Guest.**

Symph. poem by R. Strauss, Op. 20, based on Lenau's poem, comp. 1887–8, 1st perf. Weimar, 11. XI. 1889.

Don Juan de Mañara, opera by Goossens (lib. by Arnold Bennett), prod. London, Covent Garden Opera, 24. VI. 1937.

Don Juan legend. For mus. treatments *see* **Albertini, Alfano** (*L'ombra di Don Giovanni*), **Assafiev** (*The Seducer of Seville*), **Carnicer, Convitato di pietra** (Fabrizi and Righini), **Dargomizhsky** (*Stone Guest*), **Don Giovanni** (Lattuada and Mozart), **Don G. Tenorio** (Carnicer and Gazzaniga), **Don Juan** (R. Strauss), **D. J. de Mañara** (Goossens), **D. Js. letztes Abenteuer** (Graener), **Enna** (*D. J. Mañara*), **Ferreira, Koreshtchenko, Lattuada, Ombra di Don Giovanni** (Alfano), **Purcell** (Shadwell's *Libertine*), **Salazar** (*D. J. en los infiernos*), **Schulhoff** (E.) (opera), **Shebalin** (*Stone Guest*). *See also* **Byron.**

Don Juans letztes Abenteuer (*Don Juan's Last Adventure*), opera by Graener (lib. by Otto Anthes), prod. Leipzig, 11. VI. 1914.

Don Pasquale, comic opera by Donizetti (lib. by comp. and ?, based on Angelo Anelli's *Ser Marcantonio*, comp. by Pavesi in 1810), prod. Paris, Théâtre Italien, 3. I. 1843.

Don Quichotte, opera by Massenet (lib. by Henri Cain, based on Cervantes and Jacques Le Lorrain's comedy, *Le Chevalier de la longue figure*), prod. Monte Carlo, 19. II. 1910.

Don Quixote. *See also* **Don Chisciotte; Retablo de Maese Pedro; Sancio Panza; Sancho Panza.**

Opera by Kienzl (lib. by comp., based on Cervantes), prod. Berlin, Opera, 18. XI. 1898.

Symph. poem by R. Strauss, Op. 35, based on Cervantes, comp. 1897, 1st perf. Cologne, 8. III. 1898. The work is described as 'Fantastic Variations' and contains important solo parts for cello (Don Q.) and vla. (Sancho Panza).

Don Quixote, The Comical History of, play by Thomas Durfey, based on Cervantes, with mus. by Purcell and others, comp. Parts i and ii, 1694, by Purcell and Eccles; Part iii, 1695, by Akeroyde, Courteville, Pack, Morgan and D. Purcell. i. prod. London, Dorset Gardens, V. 1694; ii. do. VI. 1694; iii. London, Drury Lane Theatre, XI. 1695.

Don Sébastien, Roi de Portugal (*Dom Sebastian, King of Portugal*), opera by Donizetti (lib. by Scribe), prod. Paris, Opéra, 13. XI. 1843.

Donati, Ignazio (b. Casalmaggiore nr. Cremona, *c.* 1585; d. Milan, 1638), It. organist and comp. *Maestro di cappella* and organist in succession at var. It. cities, incl. Milan Cathedral.

Works incl. Masses, motets, psalms, eccles. concertos, etc.

Donato (or **Donati**), **Baldassare** (b. ? Venice, *c.* 1530; d. Venice, 1603), It. organist, singer and comp. App. to St. Mark's at Venice in 1550, he remained there in var. capacities all his life, becoming *maestro di cappella* in succession to Zarlino in 1590. He also taught singing at the seminary attached to St. Mark's.

Works incl. motets, psalms; madrigals, *villanelle, canzoni*, etc.

Doni, Giovanni Battista (b. Florence, *c.* 1594; d. Florence, 1. XII. 1647), It. scholar, musicologist and antiquarian. He travelled to France and Spain and held important secretarial and professional posts in Rome and Florence; pub. treatises on ancient mus. and on opera.

Donington, Robert (b. Leeds, 4. V. 1907), Eng. mus. antiquarian, instrumentalist and musicologist. Educ. at St. Paul's School, London, and Oxford, he studied old instruments and interpretation of ancient mus. with Dolmetsch at Haslemere. He has ed. old mus., written learned articles, perf. with various teams on old instruments and prod. books on instruments and ornaments, incl. *The Interpretation of Early Music*. He has also pub. *Wagner's Ring and its Symbols.*

Donizetti, Gaetano (Domenico Maria) (b. Bergamo, 29. XI. 1797; d. Bergamo, 8. IV. 1848), It. comp. Studied at Bergamo and at the Liceo Filarmonico at Bologna. He entered the army to avoid following his father's trade and while at Venice in 1818 prod. his 1st opera, *Enrico di Borgogna*, there. After that, except in 1821, he prod. operas annually until 1844, when *Catarina Cornaro* came out as the last at Naples and his reason began to fail. In 1839–40 and 1843 he visited Paris and prod. operas there. He became paralysed in 1845.

Works incl. more than 70 operas, among them *Emilia di Liverpool*, *Olivo e Pasquale*, *Il burgomastro di Saardam*, *La regina di Golconda*, *Il castello di Kenilworth* (after Scott), *Anna Bolena*, *Fausta*, *L'elisir d'amore*, *Torquato Tasso*, *Lucrezia Borgia* (after Hugo), *Rosmonda d'Inghilterra*, *Buondelmonte* (*Maria Stuarda*), *Marino Faliero* (after Byron), *Lucia di Lammermoor* (after Scott), *Maria di Rudenz*, *La Fille du régiment*, *La Favorita*, *Linda di Chamounix*, *Don Pasquale*, *Maria di Rohan*, *Don Sébastien*, etc.

Donna ancora è fedele, La (*The Lady is still Faithful*), opera by Pasquini (lib. by Domenico Filippo Contini), prod. Rome, Palazzo Colonna, 19. IV. 1676.

Donna del lago, La (*The Lady of the Lake*), opera by Rossini (lib. by Andrea Leone Tottola, based on Scott's poem), prod. Naples, Teatro San Carlo, 24. IX. 1819.

Donna Diana, opera by Rezniček (lib. by comp., based on Moreto's comedy), prod. Prague, Ger. Theatre, 16. XII. 1894.

Donna serpente, La (*The Serpent-Woman*), opera by Casella (lib. by Cesare Lodovici, based on Gozzi's comedy), prod. Rome, Teatro Reale, 17. III. 1932. Wagner's *Die Feen* was on the same subject.

Donne curiose, Le (*The Inquisitive Ladies*), opera by Wolf-Ferrari (lib. by Luigi Sugano, based on Goldoni's comedy), prod. Munich, in Ger., 27. XI. 1903.

Donne, John (1571–1631), Eng. divine and poet. *See* Britten (sonnets), **Corkine** (3 songs), **Hilton** (J. ii) (hymn from *Divine Poems*), **Křenek** (choruses and songs), **Maconchy** (motets), **Wordsworth** (sacred sonnets).

Donneau de Visé, Jean. *See* Visé.

Donzelli, Domenico (b. Bergamo, 2. II. 1790; d. Bologna, 31. III. 1873), It. tenor. Made his 1st appearance in It., 1816, in Vienna, 1822, in Paris, 1824, and in London, 1829.

Doppelschlag (Ger.) = **Turn.**

Dopper, Cornelius (b. Stadskanaal nr. Groningen, 7. II. 1870; d. Amsterdam, 18. IX. 1939), Dutch cond. and comp. Studied at the Leipzig Cons., cond. opera in Hol. and U.S.A. and became asst. cond. to Mengelberg at the Amsterdam Concertgebouw in 1908. Comp. operas, choral works, 7 symphs., etc.

Doppio (It.) = double.

Doppio movimento (It. = double movement), a direction indicating that a new tempo is to be exactly twice as fast as the one it displaces.

Doppler. Pol.-Hung. family of musicians: 1. Albert Franz D. (b. Lwów, 16. X. 1821; d. Baden nr. Vienna, 27. VII. 1883), flautist and comp. Taught at Pest and comp. operas, incl. *Judith*, a ballet, overtures, fl. concertos, etc.

2. Karl D. (b. Lwów, 12. IX. 1825; d. Stuttgart, 10. III. 1900), flautist, cond. and comp., brother of prec. Toured widely and became cond. at the Pest Nat. Theatre. Wrote operas, incl. *Erzébeth* with Albert D. and Erkel, ballets, fl. mus., etc.

3. Arpad D. (b. Pest, 5. VI. 1857; d. Stuttgart, 13. VIII. 1927), pianist and comp., son of prec. Studied and taught at Stuttgart, and for a time in N.Y. Wrote a mus. play *Halixula*, orchestral works, pf. mus., songs, etc.

Dorati, Antal (b. Budapest, 9. IV. 1906), Hung. cond. Studied at the Budapest Acad. of Mus. with Bartók and Kodaly. He first cond. at the age of 18. In 1947 he became an Amer. citizen and in 1948 cond. of the Minneapolis Symph. Orch. From 1963 to 1967 he was chief cond. of the B.B.C. Symph. Orch. He has also comp. and made a number of successful arrs. (e.g. *Graduation Ball*, after J. Strauss).

Doret, Gustave (b. Aigle, Vaud, 20. IX. 1866; d. Lausanne, 19. IV. 1943), Swiss comp. Studied vln. in Ger. with Joachim and comp. in Paris with Massenet. App. cond. of the Société Nationale there, and lived alternately in Paris and nr. Lausanne.

Works incl. plays with mus. *Henriette, Aliénor, La Nuit des Quatre-Temps, Tell, Davel*; operas *En Prison, Maedeli, Les Armaillis, Le Nain du Hasli, La Tisseuse d'orties*; incid. mus. for Shakespeare's *Julius Caesar*; cantata *La Fête des vignerons* and hymns; orchestral works; many songs, part-sóngs, etc.

Dorfbarbier, Der (*The Village Barber*), comic opera by Schenk (lib. by Joseph and Paul Weidmann), prod. Vienna, Burgtheater, 30. X. 1796.

Dori, La, ovvero La schiava fedele (*Doris, or The Faithful Slave*), opera by Cesti (lib. by Apollonio Apolloni), prod. Florence, Teatro dei Sorgenti, Carnival 1661.

Dorian Mode, the scale represented by the white keys on the pf. beginning on the note D.

'Dorian' Toccata and Fugue, org. work in D min. by Bach, so called on account of its notation without key-signature, the B♭ being inserted where necessary as an accidental.

Dorn, Heinrich (Ludwig Egmont) (b. Königsberg, 14. XI. 1804; d. Berlin, 10. I. 1892), Ger. comp., teacher and

cond. Pupil of Zelter in Berlin, teacher of
Schumann at Leipzig, opera cond. at Hamburg and Riga, where he succeeded
Wagner in 1839. Finally cond. at the Royal
Opera and prof. in Berlin.
Works incl. operas, e.g. *Die Rolands-*
knappen, Die Nibelungen, etc.; ballet
Amors Macht; Requiem; cantatas; orch-
estral works; pf. mus.; songs, etc.
Dornel, Louis Antoine (b. ?, *c.* 1685;
d. Paris, 1765), Fr. organist, harpsi-
chordist and comp. Worked in Paris and
was famous as a keyboard player.
Works incl. motets, psalms, harpsi-
chord pieces, trios, instrumental sonatas,
etc.
Dorothy, operetta by Cellier (lib. by
Benjamin Charles Stephenson), prod.
London, Gaiety Theatre, 25. IX. 1886.
Dostoievsky, Feodor Mikhailovich
(1821–81), Rus. novelist. *See* **Blacher**
(*Grossinquisitor*), **Janáček** (*From the House
of the Dead*), **Jeramiáš** (*Brothers Karamazov*), **Maréchal** (*Crime and Punishment*),
Pedrollo (*Delitto e castigo*), **Prokofiev**
(*Gambler*), **Sutermeister** (*Raskolnikov*).
Dot. (1) Above or under a note normally indicates *staccato*. Uses other than
this are: (*a*) in 18th-cent. vln. mus. a
series of dots with a slur indicates notes to
be detached without changing the bow; (*b*)
in 18th-cent. clavichord mus. a series of
dots with a slur above or under a single
note indicates repeated pressure on the
key; (*c*) in older Fr. mus. dots above or
under a succession of quavers or semi-
quavers could mean the observance of
equal note-values (*notes égales*), as opposed to the current fashion of lengthening
or shortening such notes alternately (*notes
inégales*).
(2) A D. to the right of a note normally
lengthens it by half. *See* **Dotted Notes.**
Dot-Way, a 17th-cent. system of notation for recorders, with staves each line
of which repres. a fingerhole, while dots
placed over the lines showed which fingers
were to be kept down for each note.
Dotted Notes, notes with a dot placed
on their right, with the effect of prolonging them by half their orig. value. A
double dot has the effect of adding another half of the smaller value to the orig.
note, which is thus lengthened by three-
quarters of its value. Double dots were
intro. by Leopold Mozart, before whose
time their effect could not be precisely
indicated in notation, though it was often
prod. at will by the interpreter, esp. in
slow movements written in singly dotted
rhythm, such as the slow intros. in Lully's
and Handel's overtures.
Dotzauer, (Justus Johann) Friedrich (b.
Hildburghausen, 20. VI. 1783; d. ?
Dresden, 6. III. 1860), Ger. cellist. Played
1st in the court orch. at Meiningen, then

at Leipzig, Berlin and Dresden. Wrote an
opera, *Graziosa*, a symph., chamber mus.
and many cello works.
Double (Fr.), the old Fr. name for a
type of variation that was merely a more
highly ornamented version of a theme
previously played in plainer notes.
Doublé (Fr.) = Turn.
Double Bar, a pair of bar-lines placed
very close together and marking off a
principal section of a comp., such as the
end of the exposition and beginning of
the working-out in a sonata or symph. It
may be prec. or followed by repeat signs,
or both, in which case the mus. before
and/or after it must be repeated.
Double Bass, the largest instrument of
the vln. family, the bass of the string
section in the orch. and occasionally in
chamber music. It had 3 strings formerly,
but now usually 4, tuned

8ve lower ⌐_____⌐

or

8ve lower ⌐_____⌐

The first of these is the one in general use.
The range can be artificially extended
either by tuning down the bottom string
or by the addition of a 5th string. In the
latter case the instrument is normally
tuned

8ve lower ⌐_____⌐

If the C string is tuned down to B, this
will continue the tuning in 4ths.
Double Bass Viol. *See* **Violone.**
Double Bassoon, a bassoon with a
range an 8ve lower than that of the ordi-
nary instrument.
Double Cadence (Fr.) = Turn. *See*
Ornaments.
Double Chant, a chant in 2 sections used
in the Angl. Church and covering 2 verses
of a psalm.
Double Concerto, a concerto for 2 solo
instruments: e.g. Bach's D min. for 2 vlns.,
Mozart's E♭ maj. for 2 pfs., Brahms's A
min. for vln. and cello, etc.
Double Counterpoint. *See* **Counterpoint.**
Double croche (Fr.) = Semiquaver.
Double Dots. *See* **Dotted Notes.**
Double Flat, an accidental, ♭♭, lowering
the note before which it stands by a whole
tone.
Double Fugue. (1) A fugue on 2 subjects which appear simultaneously.

(2) A fugue in which a 2nd subject appears in the course of the comp.

Double Sharp, an accidental, ×, raising the note before which it stands by a whole tone.

Double Stopping, the prod. of 2 notes simultaneously on any string instrument.

Doucemelle (Fr.), a keyboard instrument of c. the 15th cent.; a forerunner of the pf. Also = Dulcimer.

Douglas, Roy (b. Tunbridge Wells, 1907), Eng. pianist and comp. Assoc. as orch. pianist with ballet, orchestral and broadcast perfs. He has arr. much mus. for dancing and films, etc. Works incl. film mus.; suites for orch.; 2 4tets with harp, trio with fl., wind 5tet; songs, etc.

Dowland, John (b. ? London, 1563; d. ? London, 20–21. I. 1626), Eng. lutenist and comp. He entered the service of the Eng. ambassador, Sir Henry Cobham, in Paris c. 1580, and was from 1583 in that of his successor, Sir Edward Stafford. He became a Rom. Catholic, returned to Eng. soon after and married. In the 1590s he sought a place at Elizabeth's court, but was not admitted, and went to Ger. in the service of the Duke of Brunswick, then entered that of the Landgrave of Hesse and travelled to It., returning home towards the end of the cent. and turning to Protestantism again. In XI. 1598 he went to Den. as court musician to Christian IV, returning in 1601 to buy mus. instruments for the king and living in London again for a time in 1603, finally settling there in 1606 on being dismissed from Copenhagen. He complained of neglect after his successes abroad, but from 1612 to 1618 he was employed in var. ways at court. Works incl. 3 vols. of songs to the lute; a book of instrumental pavans entitled *Lachrymae*; a book of songs with lutes and viols, *A Pilgrimes Solace*; lute, viol and vocal mus. contrib. to Leighton's *Teares and Lamentacions*, East's Psalter and to a number of foreign collections, incl. Füllsack's and Fuhrmann's.

Dowland, Robert (b. ? London, c. 1586; d. ? London, 1641), Eng. lutenist and comp., son of prec. App. lutenist to Charles I on his father's death in 1626. Comp. lessons for the lute, etc. and pub. a book of airs by Eng., Fr., It. and Span. comps.

Down Bow, the movement of the bow in the playing of string instruments in the direction from the heel to the point.

Downbeat, the downward motion of the cond.'s baton indicating the stressed beats of any bar. The corresponding upward motion is called the Upbeat.

Dowson, Ernest (1867–1900), Eng. poet. *See* **Bantock** (*Pierrot of the Minute*), **Delius** (*Cynara*).

Doyle, Arthur Conan (1859–1930), Eng. novelist. *See* **Arnell** (*Great Detective*, ballet).

Drachman, Holger (1846–1908), Dan. poet and dramatist. *See* **Halvorsen** (*Gurre*), **Rangström** (*Medeltida*), **Rung** (*1001 Nights*).

Draeseke, Felix (August Bernhard) (b. Coburg, 7. X. 1835; d. Dresden, 26. II. 1913), Ger. comp. Studied at the Leipzig Cons. and with Liszt at Weimar, later taught at Dresden, Lausanne, Munich and Geneva, and finally settled at Dresden in 1876, becoming prof. of comp. at the Cons. in 1884.

Works incl. operas *Gudrun, Herrat* and *Merlin*; Requiem, trilogy of oratios *Christus*, Easter scene from Goethe's *Faust* for solo voices, chorus and orch.; 4 symphs., overtures for orch. incl. *Penthesilea* (after Kleist); concertos for pf., vln. and cello; 3 string 4tets, string 5tet; many pf. works incl. a sonata, etc.

Drag, a stroke on the side-drum preceded by a group of grace-notes, usually 3 or 4.

Draghi, Antonio (b. Rimini, 1635; d. Vienna, 16. I. 1700), It. comp. Began his career as a singer at Venice. Went to Vienna to take up a court app. in 1658, and app. *Hofkapellmeister* in 1682. He was also a librettist for other comps., incl. Bertali, Ziani and the Emperor Leopold I. Works incl. 67 operas, 116 smaller stage pieces, c. 40 oratorios, cantatas, hymns, etc.

Draghi, Giovanni Battista (b. ?, c. 1640; d. ?), It. harpsichordist and comp. Settled in London; mus. master to the Princesses Mary and Anne and organist to Catherine of Braganza, wife of Charles II. Set Dryden's Ode for St. Cecilia's Day, 1687, contrib. mus. to Durfey's *Wonders in the Sun*, 1706, and comp. many harpsichord lessons and songs.

Dragon of Wantley, The, burlesque opera by Lampe (lib. by Carey), prod. London, Little Theatre, Haymarket, 16. V. 1737.

Dragonetti, Domenico (b. Venice, 7. IV. 1763; d. London, 16. IV. 1846), It. double bass player and comp. He was admitted to the opera orchs. at Venice from the age of 13 and soon began to comp. concertos, sonatas and other works for his instrument. His 1st appearance abroad was in 1794 in London, where he spent most of the rest of his life with the cellist Lindley as partner.

Dragoni, Giovanni Andrea (b. Mendola, c. 1540; d. Rome, 1598), It. comp., pupil of Palestrina. Wrote mainly madrigals and motets.

Dragons de Villars, Les (*The Dragoons of Villars*), opera by Maillart (lib. by Joseph Phillippe Lockroy and Eugène Cormon), prod. Paris, Opéra-Comique, 19. IX. 1856.

Drame lyrique, a modern Fr. term for a serious opera.

Dramma giocoso (It. = jocular drama), name occasionally used for *opera buffa* in the later 18th cent. Mozart's orig. designation of *Don Giovanni.*

Dramma (per musica) (It. = drama [for mus.]), 18th-cent. It. term for opera; actually plays written especially for the purpose of being set to mus.

Drangosch, Ernesto (b. Buenos Aires, 22. I. 1882; d. Buenos Aires, 26. VI. 1925), Arg. comp. Studied with Alberto Williams and Aguirre in Buenos Aires and later with Bruch and Humperdinck in Berlin. Returning home in 1905, he devoted himself to comp. and teaching.

Works incl. *Overtura criolla* for orch., suite *Sueños de un baile* for strings; pf. concerto; vln. and pf. sonata; *Fantasia quasi Sonata,* 6 concert studies, dances in the nat. manner and other works for pf.; songs, etc.

Drátenik (*The Tinker*), opera by Škroup (lib. by Josef Krasoslav Chmelenský), prod. Prague, 2. II. 1826. The 1st Cz. opera.

Drdla, František (b. Žďár, Moravia, 28. XI. 1868; d. Gastein, Aus., 3. IX. 1944), Cz. violinist and comp. Studied at the Prague and Vienna Conss., played vln. in the Vienna Court Opera orch. and toured Eur. as a virtuoso.

Works incl. operettas *The Golden Net* and *The Shop Countess*; many vln. pieces; pf. pieces; songs, etc.

Dream of Gerontius, The, oratorio by Elgar, Op. 38 (words selected from Cardinal Henry Newman's poem), prod. Birmingham Festival, 3. X. 1900.

Drei Pintos, Die (*The Three Pintos*), unfinished opera by Weber (lib. by Theodor Hell, based on Carl Ludwig Seidel's story *Der Brautkampf*), partly comp. 1821; prod. in an ed. completed by Mahler, Leipzig, 20. I. 1888.

Dreigroschenoper, Die (*The Three Groats' Opera*), operetta by Weill (lib. by Bert Brecht, based on Elisabeth Hauptmann's Ger. version of Gay's *Beggar's Opera*), prod. Berlin, Theater am Schiffbauerdamm, 31. VIII. 1928.

Dresden, Sem (b. Amsterdam, 20. IV. 1881; d. The Hague, 31. VII. 1957), Dutch cond. and comp. Studied under Zweers at the Copenhagen Cons. and with Pfitzner in Ger. He became a choral cond., cultivating partic. motets and madrigals in Hol. Director of the Amsterdam Cons., 1924–37, and then of that at The Hague, in succession to Wagenaar. He was compelled to withdraw from public life during the Ger. occupation of Hol., but comp. much during that period. He wrote a book on *Dutch Music since 1880.*

Works incl. *Chorus tragicus* for chorus

and orch.; variations for orch.; vln. concerto; *Symphonietta* for clar. and orch.; string 4tet, 6tet for strings and pf., 3 6tets for wind and pf.; sonatas for vln. and pf., cello and pf. and fl. and harp; duo for 2 pfs.; pf. pieces; songs, etc.

Dressler, Ernst Christoph (b. Greussen, Thuringia, 1734; d. Cassel, 6. IV. 1779), Ger. comp. and singer. Worked as secretary and singer at Bayreuth and Gotha, later *Kapelldirektor* to Prince Fürstenberg at Wetzlar, finally opera singer in Vienna and Cassel. Beethoven's 1st pub. work was a set of variations (1782) on a march by D.

Dressler, Gallus (b. Nebra, 16. X. 1533; d. Zerbst, *c.* 1585), Ger. comp. Wrote Lutheran psalms and hymns as well as Lat. church mus.

Dreyschock, Alexander (b. Žak. 15. X. 1818; d. Venice, 1. IV. 1869), Cz. pianist and comp. Pupil of Tomašek in Prague. Travelled widely from 1838 and in 1862 was app. prof. of pf. at the St. Petersburg Cons. and court pianist. Comp. mainly for his instrument.

Drigo, Riccardo (b. Padua, 30. VI. 1846; d. Padua, 1. X. 1930), It. cond. and comp. He became ballet cond. at the St. Petersburg Court Opera.

Works incl. ballet *Harlequin's Millions*; many drawing-room pieces, etc.

Drinkwater, John (1882–1937), Eng. actor, dramatist and poet. *See* **Boughton** (festival choruses), **Filippi** (*Robert E. Lee*).

Drone, the 3 lower pipes of the bagpipe which prod. a fixed chord above which the melody is played on the chanter. The name was also given to a bowed instrument with a single string stretched on a stick over a bladder; this was also called Bumbass.

Drone Bass, an unvaryingly sustained bass in any mus. comp. resembling the drone of a bagpipe.

Drum Mass (Haydn). *See* **Paukenmesse.**

'Drum-Roll' Symphony (Ger. *S. mit dem Paukenwirbel*), nickname of Haydn's symph. No. 103 in E♭ maj. (comp. for London, 1795), so called because it opens with a timpani roll.

Drummond, William (1585–1649), Scot. poet. *See* **Finzi** (3 Elegies), **Paine** (*Phoebus arise*), **Scott** (F. G.) (songs).

Drums, percussion instruments on which the sound is prod. by beating a skin stretched tightly over a hollow space left open by a framework of var. patterns. *See* **Bass Drum, Kettledrums, Side Drum, Tabor, Tambourine, Tenor Drum.**

Drumslade (Eng. obs., also 'dromslade'), a drum-beat, prob. a corrupt. from Ger. *Trommelschlag,* also used by false analogy for a drum in the 17th cent. and for a drummer in the 18th.

Dryden, John (1631–1700), Eng. poet, dramatist and satirist. *See* **Acis and**

Galatea (Handel), **Albion and Albanius** (Grabu), **Alexander's Feast** (Handel), **Almahide** (G. Bononcini), **Boyce** (*Secular Masque*), **Clarke (J.)** (*Alexander's Feast*), Clayton (do.), **Cymon** (M. Arne), **Draghi (G. B.)** (*Ode for St. Cecilia's Day*), **Eccles (J.)** (*Spanish Friar*), **Humfrey** (*Conquest of Granada* and *Indian Emperor*), **Indian Queen** (Purcell), **King Arthur** (do.), **Marcello** (*Timoteo*), **Ode for St. Cecilia's Day** (Handel), **Purcell** (*Amphitryon, Aureng-Zebe, Cleomenes, Love Triumphant, Spanish Friar, Tyrannic Love* and *Oedipus*), **Staggins** (*Conquest of G.* and *Marriage à la Mode*).

Drysdale, Learmont (b. Edinburgh, 3. X. 1866; d. Edinburgh, 18. VI. 1909), Scot. comp. Studied at R.A.M.

Works incl. operas *Fionn and Tera, Red Spider, The Plague, Hippolytus* (Euripides, trans. by Gilbert Murray); cantatas *The Kelpie, Tamlane, To Edinburgh* (Burns), *The Lay of Thora, The Scottish Tribute to France, The Proud Damozel, Barbara Allen*; orch. works: concert overtures *Tam o' Shanter* (after Burns) and *Herondean*, Overture to a Comedy, ballad *The Spirit of the Glen*, prelude *Thomas the Rhymer*, tone-poem *Border Romance*; pf. pieces; songs, part-songs, etc.

Du Mage, Pierre (b. ? ; d. ?), Fr. 17th-18th-cent. organist and comp. Pupil of Marchand in Paris, organist of the collegiate church at Saint-Quentin in 1703–1713. He played at the inauguration of the new org. at Notre Dame in Paris. Pub. a vol. of org. pieces in 1708.

Du Maurier, George (Louis Palmella Busson) (1834–96), Eng. novelist and black-and-white artist of Fr. descent. *See* Bath (*Trilby*), Holländer (V.) (do.), Peter Ibbetson (Taylor, Deems).

Du Puy, (Jean Baptiste) Édouard (b. Corcelles, Neuchâtel, 1770–1; d. Stockholm, 3. IV. 1822), Swiss baritone, violinist, pianist and comp. Studied vln. with Chabran and pf. with Dussek in Paris and became a member of the orch. of Prince Henry of Prus. at Rheinsberg in 1785 and leader in 1787. In 1793 he settled at Stockholm, but was expelled in 1799, when he went to sing in opera at Copenhagen and taught singing to the wife of the future Christian VIII, with whom he was exiled for a love affair in 1809. In 1811 he returned to Stockholm and became court cond. and prof.

Works incl. operas *Ungdom og Galskab* (a Dan. version of the lib. of Méhul's *Une Folie*) and *Felicie*; several ballets; incid. mus. for plays; funeral mus. for Charles XIII, etc.

Düben, Ger.-Swed. family of musicians:
1. **Andreas D.** (b. Lützen, 27. V. 1558; d. Leipzig, 19. IV. 1625), organist at St. Thomas's Church, Leipzig.

2. **Andreas D.** (b. ? Leipzig, *c.* 1590; d. Stockholm, 7. VII. 1662), organist and comp., son of prec. Pupil of Sweelinck at Amsterdam, 1614–20, went to Swed. in 1621, became organist at the Ger. church in Stockholm in 1625 and court mus. director in 1640. Comp. dances for viols, etc.

3. **Gustaf D.** (b. Stockholm, 1624; d. Stockholm, 19. XII. 1690), organist and comp., son of prec. Succeeded his father in both his posts.

Works incl. church mus., *concerti grossi,* symphs. and dances for strings, etc.

4. **Gustaf D.** (b. Stockholm, 6. VIII. 1659; d. Stockholm, 5. XII. 1726), son of prec., whom he succeeded as court mus. director.

5. **Andreas D.** (b. Stockholm, 28. VIII. 1673; d. Stockholm, 23. VIII. 1738), son of prec., whom he succeeded.

Dubois, (François Clément) Théodore (b. Rosnay, Marne, 24. VIII. 1837; d. Paris, 11. VI. 1924), Fr. comp. Studied at Rheims and then at the Paris Cons., where he took the Prix de Rome in 1861. Returning to Paris in 1866, he was active as organist and teacher, at last succeeding Saint-Saëns as organist at the Madeleine in 1877. From 1896 to 1905 he was director of the Cons.

Works incl. operas *La Guzla de l'Émir, Le Pain bis, Aben-Hamet, Xavière*; ballet *La Farandole*; Requiem, *Messe de la Délivrance* and other Masses, motets and other church mus.; oratorios, *Les Sept Paroles du Christ* and *Paradis perdu*; orchestral works: *Divertissement, Pièces d'orchestre, Suite d'orchestre, Scènes symphoniques,* overture *Frithjof* (after Tegnér), symph. poem *Notre-Dame de la mer,* etc.

Dubourg, Matthew (b. London, 1703; d. London, 3. VII. 1767), Eng. violinist, pupil of Geminiani. Lived much of his life in Dublin, where he played in the first perf. of *Messiah* in 1742. He also comp.

Ducasse, Roger. *See* **Roger-Ducasse.**

Duchess of Dantzic, The, operetta by Caryll (lib. by Henry Hamilton, based on Sardou's comedy, *Madame Sans-Gêne*), prod. London, Lyceum Theatre, 17. X. 1903.

Ducis, Benedictus (b. nr. Constantz, ? ; d. Schalckstetten, nr. Ulm, 1544), Ger. comp. and Lutheran pastor. Wrote Lutheran psalms and hymns, Lat. church mus. and Ger. part-songs.

Due Foscari, I (*The Two Foscari*), opera by Verdi (lib. by Francesco Maria Piave, based on Byron's drama), prod. Rome, Teatro Argentina, 3. XI. 1844.

Due litiganti (Sarti). *See* **Fra due litiganti.**

Duenna, The, or The Double Elopement, opera by Thomas Linley, father and son (lib. by Sheridan), prod. London, Covent

171

Garden Theatre, 21. XI. 1775. Sheridan was son-in-law of Linley sen.

Duet, a comp. in 2 parts for voices or instruments. A D. may be in 2 single melodic parts only, or it may be accomp. by instruments in fuller harmony or it may be itself for 2 harmonic instruments or a single such instrument for 2 players (e.g. pf. D.).

Duettino (It.) = little duet.

Dufay, Guillaume (b. ? Hainault, *c.* 1400; d. Cambrai, 27. XI. 1474), Flem. comp. He learnt mus. as a chorister at Cambrai Cathedral, became a singer in the Papal choir in Rome, 1428–37, and afterwards became a canon both of Cambrai and of Mons, but (?) lived for some time in Savoy, and some time in the 1440s he was in the service of Philip the Good, Duke of Burgundy, as mus. master to his son, Charles, Comte de Charolais.

He wrote several motets in the old isorhythmic style, other motets, Mass movements, complete Masses, and secular songs in Fr. and It. His hymns and other pieces 'à faux bourdon' were written out in two parts but were to be sung in three by improvising a middle part a 4th below the upper part throughout; they are among the earliest known examples of this convention. He pioneered the style whereby the tenor and contratenor, though still having the same range, were no longer at the bottom of the texture, being underpinned by a bass part, thus anticipating the modern S.A.T.B. arrangement (see esp. his last two Masses, *Ecce ancilla domini,* and *Ave regina caelorum*).

Dugazon (*née* Lefèbvre), **Louise Rosalie** (b. Berlin, 18. VI. 1755; d. Paris, 22. IX. 1821), Fr. mezzo-soprano. Trained as a dancer, made her début at the age of 12. Her voice was discovered by Grétry, in whose *Sylvain* she 1st appeared as a singer in 1774. Married the actor Dugazon in 1776.

Dukas, Paul (b. Paris, 1. X. 1865; d. Paris, 17. V. 1935), Fr. comp. Studied at the Paris Cons., among his masters being Dubois and Guiraud. Prof. of comp. there from 1913 to his death. From 1909 he taught orch. at the Paris Cons. and from 1913 comp. In 1926 he also began teaching at the École Normale. His best-known piece is the brilliant orch. scherzo *L'Apprenti sorcier* (1897), and his opera *Ariane et Barbe-bleue* (1907) is among the finest Fr. operas of its day.

Works incl. opera *Ariane et Barbe-bleue* (Maeterlinck); ballet *La Péri*; symph. in C maj., overture to Corneille's *Polyeucte, L'Apprenti sorcier* (on Goethe's poem *Der Zauberlehrling*); sonata in E♭ min., *Variations on a theme by Rameau, Prélude élégiaque* on the name of Haydn and *La Plainte, au loin, du faune* in memory of

Debussy for pf.; *Sonnet de Ronsard* and *Vocalise* for voice and pf.; *Villanelle* for horn and pf., etc. (incl. unpub. overtures to Shakespeare's *King Lear* and Goethe's *Götz von Berlichingen*).

Duke, Vernon. *See* Dukelsky.

Dukelsky, Vladimir (b. Parfianovka nr. Pskov, 10. X. 1903; d. Santa Monica, 17. I. 1969), Rus.-Amer. comp. Studied at Moscow and Kiev, Glière being among his masters. Went to live in Constantinople in 1920 and settled in N.Y. in 1922. Under the influence of Gershwin he wrote light mus. under the name of Vernon Duke, but cultivated an advanced modern style under his own name. In 1924 Diaghilev heard his pf. concerto and commissioned him to write a work for the Rus. Ballet.

Works incl. operetta *Yvonne*; ballets *Zéphire et Flore* and *Public Gardens*; oratorio *The End of St. Petersburg*; 2 symphs., *Dédicaces* for soprano, pf. and orch., pf. concerto; string 4tet; vln. sonata; song cycle *Triolets of the North* (Feodor Sologub); 3 Chin. songs and other songs, etc.

Dulce Melos (Lat. = sweet melody), another name for the Chekker.

Dulciana, an open Diapason org. stop of delicate tone. It may embrace 4-ft., 8-ft. or 16-ft. pipes.

Dulciana Mixture, an organ Mixture stop of Dulciana pipes.

Dulcimer, an instrument akin to the psaltery, with a set of strings stretched over a sound-board which are struck by hammers. The Hung. Cimbalom is a descendant of it.

Dulcitone, a keyboard instrument prod. its sound on a set of tuning-forks, similar to the Celesta.

Dulichius, Philipp (b. Chemnitz, 18. XII. 1562; d. Stettin, 25. III. 1631), Ger. comp. Took the D.Phil. degree at Chemnitz and went to Stettin as mus. teacher at the Pädagogium in 1587.

Works incl. sacred and secular comps. for several voices, etc.

Dumanoir, Guillaume (b. Paris, 16. I. 1615; d. Paris, *c.* 1690), Fr. violinist and comp. As 'Roi des Violons' he came into conflict with the dancing-masters, whom he wished to compel to contribute to the violinists' guild of Saint-Julien, and being unsuccessful he wrote the abusive pamphlet *Le Mariage de la musique avec la danse* in 1664. He comp. dance mus. which was liked by Louis XIV, who app. him ballet master of the royal pages.

Dumanoir, Guillaume (Michel) (b. Paris, ?; d. ? Paris, 1697), Fr. violinist and comp., son of prec. Succeeded his father as head of the Confrérie de Saint-Julien and renewed the quarrel with the dancing-masters, resigning in 1685. Before that he had quarrelled with Lully over the privilege of training orch. musicians and lost a law-suit against him in 1673. Comp. dance mus.

Dumas, Alexandre, jun. (1824–95), Fr. dramatist and novelist. *See* **Fauré** (*Caligula*), **Traviata** (Verdi), **Varney (P.)** (*Chant des Girondins*), **Vlad** (*Dama delle camelie*).

Dumas, Alexandre, sen. (1803–70), Fr. novelist. *See* **Cui** (*Saracen*), **Enna** (*Gloria Arsena*), **Franck (C.)** (songs), **Gemma di Vergy** (Donizetti), **Salvayre** (*Dame de Monsereau*), **Trois Mousquetaires** (Lara).

Dumka (Pol., Rus. and Cz.), a lament, which in mus. takes the form of a slow piece alternating with more animated sections, as e.g. in Dvořák's *Dumky* Trio.

Dumky, plur. of Dumka.

'Dumky' Trio, a pf. Trio by Dvořák, Op. 90, based on mus. of the type of the above, comp. in 1891.

Dump (Eng., obs.), a name sometimes used for a doleful piece in the 17th and 18th cents. Also Domp or Dompe.

Dunayevsky, Isaac (b. Lokhvitsy nr. Poltava, 30. I. 1900; d. Moscow, 25. VII. 1955), Rus. comp. Studied at the Kharkov Cons.

Works incl. incid. mus. for plays; mus. for many films; operettas, ballets *Rest of a Faun* and *Mursilka*; 2 suites for orch.; Rhapsody on People's Songs and *The Music Shop* for jazz-band; string 4tet; instrumental pieces; songs for massed voices, etc.

Dunbar, William (? 1465–? 1530), Scot. poet. *See* **Dyson** (*In Honour of the City of London*), **Parry (H.)** (*Ode on the Nativity*), **Scott (F. G.)** (*7 Deadly Sins, Ballad of Kynd Kittok* and songs), **Walton** (*In Honour of the C. of L.*).

Duncan, Ronald (b. 1914), Eng. poet and dramatist. *See* **Britten** (*This Way to the Tomb*), **Oldham** (do).

Dunhill, Thomas (Frederick) (b. London, 1. II. 1877; d. Scunthorpe, Lincs., 13. III. 1946), Eng. comp. Entered the R.C.M. in 1893, Stanford being his comp. master. He was asst. mus. master at Eton Coll. in 1899–1908 and organized concerts for chamber mus. and for the promotion of contemp. Brit. mus. in London during the early years of the cent. Prof. of comp. at the R.C.M. His 2nd ballet was prod. at Hamburg in 1937.

Works incl. operas *The Enchanted Garden, Tantivy Towers* (A. P. Herbert) and *Happy Families*; ballets *Dick Whittington* and *Gallimaufry*; symph. in A min., *Elegiac Variations* in memory of Parry and overture *Maytime* for orch.; *Triptych* for vla. and orch.; pf. 4tet, 2 pf. trios, 5 5tets and other chamber mus.; vln. and pf. sonata in D min., variations for cello and pf.; many songs incl. *The Cloths of Heaven* (Yeats); children's cantatas incl. *John Gilpin*, part-songs, incl. *Song of the*

King's Men from Hardy's *Dynasts* for male voices, etc.

Duni, Egidio Romoaldo (b. Matera nr. Naples, 9. II. 1709; d. Paris, 11. VI. 1775), It.-Fr. comp. Pupil of Durante in Naples, where he prod. his 1st opera in 1731. Travelled widely, and settled in Paris in 1757, becoming a leading comp. of *opéra comique*.

Operas incl. *Nerone, Le Caprice amoureux, Le Peintre amoureux de son modèle, L'Isle des fous, Le Milicien, Les Deux Chasseurs et la laitière, La Fée Urgèle, La Clochette, Les Moissonneurs, Les Sabots,* etc.

Dunstable, John (b. ?; d. ? London, 24. XII. 1453), Eng. mathematician, astrologer, and comp. Prob. connected with St. Albans Cathedral, (?) visited the Netherlands, Fr., Spain and It., where he was certainly famous in his lifetime.

Works incl. motets, hymns and other church mus.; 3-part songs incl. *O Rosa bella*, etc.

Duo (It.) = Duet.

Duodrama, a mus. stage work for 2 solo singers, an opera with a cast of 2. The outstanding ex. is G. Benda's *Ariadne auf Naxos*, prod. in 1775, which is also a Melodrama, i.e. a spoken play with mus.

Duparc, Elizabeth (b. ?; d. ?, 1778), Fr. soprano. She appeared in It. in her youth, where she was given the nickname of La Francesina, under which name she sang in many of Handel's operas and oratorios in London from 1738.

Duparc, (Marie Eugène) Henri (Fouques-) (b. Paris, 21. I. 1848; d. Mont de Marsan, 13. II. 1933), Fr. comp. Was taught the pf. as a child by Franck at the Jesuit Coll. of Vaugirard in Paris, and later became a comp. pupil of that master. He never took any share in official mus. life, but continued to comp. at intervals until 1885, when he began to suffer from an incurable nervous complaint and retired to Switz.

Works incl. symph. poem *Lénore* (on Bürger's poem) and nocturne *Aux Étoiles*; motet *Benedicat vobis Dominus*; 15 songs incl. *Phydilé* and *Invitation au voyage*; and several afterwards destroyed.

Duple Time, 2 beats in a bar, e.g. 2–4 or 6–8.

Duplet, a group of 2 notes occupying the time of 3.

Dupont, Gabriel (b. Caen, 1. III. 1878; d. Vésinet, 2. VIII. 1914), Fr. comp. Son of the organist Achille D. of the church of Saint-Pierre at Caen and pupil of Widor at the Paris Cons. He took the Sonzogno Prize at Milan with his 1st opera. Owing to ill health he never held an official mus. post.

Works incl. operas *La Cabrera, La Glu* (after Richepin), *La Farce du cuvier* and

Duport   Durey

Antar; symph. poems *Hymne à Aphrodite* and *Chant de la destinée*; string 4tet; pf. pieces incl. *Les Heures dolentes*; songs incl. cycle *Poème d'automne*, etc.

Duport, Jean Louis (b. Paris, 4. X. 1749; d. Paris, 7. IX. 1819), Fr. cellist. Made his 1st appearance at the Concert spirituel in Paris in 1768. He went to the Prus. court in Berlin at the outbreak of the Revolution and there Beethoven played with him (or with his brother) his 2 cello sonatas, Op. 5. He returned to Paris, 1806.

Duport, Jean Pierre (b. Paris, 27. XI. 1741; d. Berlin, 31. XII. 1818), Fr. cellist, brother of prec. Made his 1st appearance at the Concert spirituel in Paris in 1761, visited Eng. in 1769 and Spain in 1771, and in 1773 went to the court of Frederick II of Prus. in Berlin. Mozart wrote pf. variations on a minuet of his (K. 573).

Dupré, Marcel (b. Rouen, 3. V. 1886; d. near Paris, 30. V. 1971), Fr. organist and comp. Played Bach from memory at the age of 10, in 1898 was app. organist of the church of Saint-Vivien at Rouen and prod. an oratorio in 1901. After that he studied pf., org. and comp. at the Paris Cons. and gained the Prix de Rome in 1914 as a pupil of Widor. Organist at Notre-Dame in 1916–22 during the illness of Vierne. App. prof. of org. at the Paris Cons. in 1926 and organist at Saint-Sulpice in 1936, succeeding Widor. From 1954 to 1956 he was director of the Cons.

Works incl. oratorio *Le Songe de Jacob*, motets and *De Profundis*; 2 symphs.; concerto for org. and orch.; vln. and pf. sonata; cello pieces; songs; many org. works incl. *Symphonie-Passion*, 79 chorales, *Le Chemin de la Croix*, etc.

Duprez, Gilbert (Louis) (b. Paris, 6. XII. 1806; d. Paris, 23. IX. 1896), Fr. tenor and comp. 1st appeared at the Théâtre de l'Odéon in Paris, 1825. Prof. at the Cons., 1842–50.

Dupuis, Albert (b. Verviers, 1. III. 1877), Belg. comp. Studied at the Verviers mus. school, under d'Indy and Guilmant at the Schola Cantorum in Paris and at the Brussels Cons., where he gained the Belg. Prix de Rome in 1903. Later he became director of the Verviers school of mus.

Works incl. operas *L'Idylle*, *Bilitis*, *Jean-Michel*, *Martylle*, *Fidelaine*, *La Chanson d'Halewyn*, *Le Château de la Bretèche*, *La Passion*, *La Délivrance*, *La Victoire*, *Hassan*, biblical drama *La Captivité de Babylone*; cantatas *Les Cloches nuptiales*, *Œdipe à Colone* (after Sophocles); symph. and other orchestral works; concertos for pf., vln., cello and horn; string 4tet, pf. trio; pf. sonata, songs, etc.

Dupuis, Sylvain (b. Liège, 9. X. 1856; d. Bruges, 28. IX. 1931), Belg. cond. and comp. Studied at the Liège Cons., where he gained the Belg. Prix de Rome in

1881 and became prof. in 1886. He cond. choral and orch. concerts there, became cond. of the Théâtre de la Monnaie in Brussels, 1900–11, and then returned to Liège as director of the Cons.

Works incl. operas *Coûr d'Ognon* and *Moïna* (after Ossian); cantatas; symph. poem on Shakespeare's *Macbeth*, overture and 2 suites for orch.; concertino for ob.; pf., org., vln. and cello pieces, etc.

Dur (Ger., from Lat. *durus* = hard), the Ger. word for Major, because *B durum* meant B♮.

Durand, (Marie) Auguste (b. Paris, 18. VII. 1830; d. Paris, 31. V. 1909), Fr. mus. pub., organist and comp. Studied at the Paris Cons., was organist at var. churches and was a partner in the pub. firm of Durand & Fils. He wrote drawing-room mus. for pf., incl. popular waltzes.

Durand (Duranowski), Auguste Frédéric (b. Warsaw, 1770; d. Strasbourg, 1834), Pol.-Fr. violinist and comp. He was sent to Paris in 1787 to study under Viotti, travelled much in Ger. and It., joined the Fr. army and settled at Strasbourg in 1814. Wrote much superficial concert mus. for his instrument.

Durante, Francesco (b. Fratta Maggiore nr. Naples, 31. III. 1684; d. Naples, 13. VIII. 1755), It. comp. Educ. at Naples, where he later became *maestro di cappella* at the Cons. di S. Maria (1742) and S. Onofrio (1745). His pupils incl. Traetta, Paisiello, Sacchini, Pergolesi, Piccinni, etc. Unusually for a Neapol. comp., he wrote no operas. His works consist largely of church mus.; also sonatas, toccatas, etc., for harpsichord.

Durastanti, Margherita (b. ?, *c.* 1685; d. ?), It. soprano. Visited London in 1720 and again in 1733, singing in several of Handel's operas.

Durazzo, Count Giacomo (b. Genoa, 27. IV. 1717; d. Venice, 15. X. 1794), It. nobleman. He was director of the Imp. Theatres in Vienna 1754–64, and played an influential role in the reform of mus. drama, particularly in connection with Gluck's *Orfeo*.

Durchführung (Ger. lit. through-leading), the Ger. term for the development or working-out section of a movement in sonata form.

Durchkomponiert (Ger. lit. set throughout). A song is said in Ger. to be *durchkomponiert* if the words are set to mus. continuously, not strophically with the same mus. repeated for each verse.

Durey, Louis (b. Paris, 27. V. 1888), Fr. comp. He did not study mus. until the age of 22, and in 1914 he enlisted on the outbreak of war. In 1916, during leave, he came under the influence of Satie and joined the group of 'Les Six', but was the 1st to secede from it in 1921, and in

174

1923 he went to live in seclusion in the S. of Fr., writing very little.

Works incl. opera on Mérimée's *L'Occasion*; incid. mus. to Hebbel's *Judith*; *Éloges* for solo voices, chorus and orch.; *Pastorale* for orch. (all these unpub.); 2 string 4tets, pf. trio, string trio; song cycles with chamber mus. or pf. *Offrande lyrique* (Tagore), *Images à Crusoé*, *Épigrammes de Théocrite*, *Trois Poèmes de Pétrone*, *Le Bestiaire* (Guillaume Apollinaire); songs to words by Verlaine, Francis Jammes, André Gide; *Carillon* and *Neige* for pf. duet, etc.

Durezza (It. = hardness). Up to the 17th cent. the term was used for discord in It.; it is now used in the direction *con durezza* to indicate that a harsh or unyielding manner of perf. is required.

Durfey (D'Urfey), Thomas (1653–1723), Eng. playwright and poet. *See* **Akeroyde** (*Don Quixote*), **Courteville** (do.), Don Quixote, The Comical History of (Purcell and others), **Draghi (G. B.)** (*Wonders in the Sun*), **Eccles (J.)** (*Don Q.*), **Locke** (*Fool turned Critic*), **Purcell (D.)** (*Cynthia and Endymion*), **Purcell** (*Fool's Preferment, Marriage-Hater Matched, Richmond Heiress, Sir Barnaby Whigg* and *Virtuous Wife*), **Turner (Wm.)** (*Fond Husband* and *Madam Fickle*).

Durón, Sebastián (b. Brihuega, Castile, *c.* 1650; d. ? Cambó, Pyrenees, after VIII. 1716), Span. comp. Was organist at Las Palmas, Canary Islands, and in 1691 became *maestro de capilla* at the court of Madrid until 1702. Not having supported the Bourbon succession, he seems to have gone into exile. He was an early exponent of Span. opera.

Works incl. operas *Muerte en amor es la ausencia, Apolo y Dafne, Selva encantada de Amor, Las nuevas armas de Amor, La guerra de los gigantes, Salir el amor del mundo*; incid. mus. for a comedy, *Jupiter*; 2 ballets, etc.

Duruflé, Maurice (b. Louviers, Eure, 11. I. 1902), Fr. organist and comp. Learnt mus. in the choir-school of Rouen Cathedral, 1912–18, and then studied at the Paris Cons. under Vierne, Tournemire and Dukas. App. organist at the church of Saint-Étienne-du-Mont in 1929.

Works incl. Requiem for chorus and orch.; chorale on *Veni Creator*, suite and many other works for org.; *Prelude, Recitative and Variations* for fl., vla. and pf.; 3 dances for orch., etc.

Dušek. *See also* **Dussek** and **Tuczek.**

Dušek, Franz (František Xaver) (b. Chotěborky, 8. XII. 1731; d. Prague, 12. II. 1799), Boh. pianist and comp. Pupil of Wagenseil in Vienna; taught in Prague, master of many famous pupils. He and his wife were friends of Mozart, who worked on *Don Giovanni* at their home in Prague.

Dušek (née Hambacher), Josefa (b. Prague, 6. III. 1754; d. Prague, 8. I. 1824), Boh. soprano, wife of prec. She travelled in Aus. and Ger. Mozart wrote the concert aria *Bella mia fiamma* (K. 528) for her.

Dusík. *See* **Dussek.**

Dusk of the Gods, The (Wagner). *See* Ring des Nibelungen.

Dussek (or Dušek, Dusík), Jan Ladislav (b. Čáslav, 12. II. 1760; d. St. Germain-en-Laye, Paris, 20. III. 1812), Boh. pianist and comp. Educ. at the Jesuit Coll. in Jihlav and Prague Univ., where he read theology. He had shown early mus. promise, and *c.* 1779 went to the Netherlands, holding org. posts at Malines and Bergen-op-Zoom. He gave up his organist's career *c.* 1782, and won great success in Amsterdam and The Hague as a pianist and comp. Concert tours took him to Hamburg (where he studied with C. P. E. Bach), Berlin and St. Petersburg, where he entered the service of Prince Radziwill, spending the next 2 years on the latter's estate in Lithuania. He played before Marie Antoinette in Paris in 1786, and after a visit to It. returned there in 1788. At the Revolution he fled to London, where he 1st appeared at one of Salomon's concerts in 1790. He married the singer and pianist Sophia Corri in 1792, and joined his father-in-law's firm of mus. pubs. The business failed, and he went to Hamburg to escape his creditors in 1800. More travels followed. He was with Prince Louis Ferdinand of Prus. 1803–6, then in the service of the Prince of Isenburg and, finally, Talleyrand.

Works incl. incid. mus. for *The Captive of Spilburg* and Sheridan's *Pizarro* (both with Kelly); 3 overtures and serenade for orch.; (?) Mass; 3 string 4tets, 2 pf. 4tets, pf. 5tet, *c.* 20 pf. trios; *c.* 12 sonatas for pf. duet, sonata for 2 pfs.; pf. mus.: *c.* 18 concertos, *c.* 32 sonatas, *c.* 25 rondos, *c.* 20 sets of variations, var. miscellaneous pieces; *c.* 65 sonatas with vln. or fl., etc.

Dussek (or Dusík, Dušek), Sophia Giustina (b. Edinburgh, 1. V. 1775; d. ? London, 1847), Eng. soprano of It. descent. Daughter of Domenico Corri and wife of prec. Pupil of her father, she appeared as a pianist at Edinburgh at a very early age, and came out as a singer in London when the family moved there in 1788. She married in 1792.

Dutch (excl. early Netherland) Composers. *See* Agricola (R.), Andriessen, Averkamp, Baaren, Badings, Berlijn, Blankenburg, Brandts-Buys, Bruck-en-Fock, Diepenbrock, Dieren (van), Dopper, Dresden-Enthoven, Felderhof, Franco, Gilse (van), Hol, Hollander, Hutschenruyter (2), Ingen, hoven, Ketting, Koeberg, Landré (2), Lange (3), Lier (van), Mengelberg, Mon-

nikendam, Nicolai (W.), Noordt, Otterloo,
Pijper, Roos, Ruygrok, Ruyneman, Schäfer,
Schwindl (?), Sigtenhorst-Meyer, Silas,
Verhulst, Voormolen, Wagenaar (2), Zag-
wijn, Zweers.

Dutilleux, Henri (b. Angers, 22. I. 1916),
Fr. comp. Studied at the Paris Cons.,
winning the Prix de Rome in 1938. In
1944 he began working for Fr. Radio.
Works incl. ballet *La Belle Époque*;
2 symphs.; *Métaboles* for orch.; sonata for
fl. and pf.; pf. sonata; incid. and film mus.,
etc.

Duval, François (b. ?, c. 1673; d. Versailles, 27. I. 1728), Fr. violinist and comp.
He was a member of Louis XIV's '24
violons du roi' and wrote vln. sonatas in
the It. style and pub. as the 1st of the kind
in 1704. Wrote numerous books of
sonatas for vln. and bass and 2 vlns. and
bass.

Duvernoy, Victor Alphonse (b. Paris,
30. VIII. 1842; d. Paris, 7. III. 1907), Fr.
pianist and comp. Pupil at the Paris
Cons. where later he became pf. prof.
Works incl. operas *Sardanapale* and
Hellé; ballet *Bacchus*; lyric scene *Cléopâtre*;
La Tempête for solo voices, chorus and
orch.; overture to Hugo's *Hernani* and
other orchestral works; numerous pf.
pieces, etc.

Dux and Comes (Lat. = leader and companion), the names formerly used for the
subject and answer in a fugue.

Dvořák, Antonín (b. Nelahozeves, 8.
IX. 1841; d. Prague, 1. V. 1904), Cz. comp.
Son of a village innkeeper and butcher.
He heard only popular and simple church
mus. as a child, but developed remarkable
gifts. Sent to the org. school at Prague in
1857, began to comp. 2 years later and
joined an orch. as violinist; later vla. in
the orch. at the Cz. nat. theatre, under
Smetana. In 1873 he married Anna
Čermaková. The next year he received for
the 1st time the Aus. state prize for comp.
and became a friend of Brahms, who was
on the committee and intro. him to his
pub., Simrock. 1st visit to Eng. in 1884 to
cond. the *Stabat Mater* in London. In
1885 he bought the country estate of
Vysoká, which remained his home. Hon.
Mus.D. at Cambridge in 1891, when he
was app. prof. at Prague Cons., of which
he became director in 1901. In 1892–5 he
was director of the new Nat. Cons. in N.Y.,
and spent some holidays at the Cz. colony
of Spillville, Iowa. In 1896 he paid the
last of his many visits to Eng., where
he had prod. several works at the mus.
festivals.
Works incl. operas *Alfred* (unpub.,
lib. by Körner), *King and Collier*, *The
Pigheaded Peasants*, *Wanda*, *The Peasant
a Rogue*, *Dimitri*, *The Jacobin*, *The Devil
and Kate*, *Russalka*, *Armida*; 9 symphs.

(incl. 2 posthumously pub.); 5 symph·
poems *The Water-Sprite*, *The Noon-day
Witch*, *The Golden Spinning-Wheel*, *The
Wood-Dove*, *Hero's Song*; 7 concert overtures incl. *Husitská* and the cycle *Amid
Nature*, *Carnival* and *Othello*; var. orch.
works incl. *Czech Suite*, 3 *Slavonic Rhapsodies*, *Scherzo capriccioso*, *Symph. Variations*; 2 sets of Slavonic Dances; *Serenade*
and *Notturno* for string orch.; concertos
for pf., vln. and cello; 4 smaller pieces for
solo instruments and orch.; 8 string 4tets
and some early exs. pub. later; 3 string
5tets; string 6tet; 4 pf. trios; pf. 4tet; pf.
5tet; *Bagatelles* for 2 vlns., cello and
harmonium; *Terzetto* for 2 vlns. and vla.;
works for chorus and orch. (some with
solo voices): *Stabat Mater*, *The Spectre's
Bride*, *St. Ludmilla*, Psalm cxlix, Mass in
D maj., Requiem; *The American Flag*,
Te Deum; smaller choral works: *The
Heirs of the White Mountain*, *Song of the
Czechs*, *Hymn of the Czech Peasants*,
Hymnus, *Festival Song*; several sets of part-
songs; 4 sets of vocal duets; 68 songs; 14
op. nos. of pf. pieces, incl. Theme and
Variations, *Poetic Tone-Pictures*, Suite and
Humoresques, also some separate pf.
pieces; 6 sets of pf. duets, incl. Slavonic
Dances, *Legends* and *From the Bohemian
Forest*; sonata, sonatina and smaller
pieces for vln. and pf.; rondo, etc. for
cello and pf. etc.

Dvorsky, Michel. *See* **Hofmann, Josef.**

Dyck, Ernest (Marie-Hubert) van (b.
Antwerp, 2. IV. 1861; d. Berlaer-les-
Lierre, 31. VIII. 1923), Belg. tenor. After
studying law and working as a journalist,
he learnt singing and made his 1st appearance in Paris in 1883. In 1887 he sang
the 1st of the Wagnerian parts with which
he was afterwards chiefly assoc., Lohengrin in Paris, and the following year he was
1st engaged as Parsifal at Bayreuth. He
also sang in Wagner's operas in Paris,
Brussels, N.Y., etc.

Dygon, John (b. ? Canterbury, c. 1485;
d. ?, 1541), Eng. cleric and comp. Took the
B.Mus. at Oxford in 1512, (?) in 1521 went
to Louvain to study with the Span.
humanist Juan Luis Vives, and became a
prior at St. Austin's Abbey, Canterbury. A
motet of his is preserved and a treatise on
proportions in Trinity Coll. library,
Cambridge.

Dykes, John Bacchus (b. Hull, 10. III.
1823; d. Ticehurst, Sussex, 22. I. 1876),
Eng. church musician. Learnt mus. from
an organist at Hull, graduated at Cambridge, where he studied mus. under
Walmisley, and became curate at Malton
Yorks., becoming precentor and min.
canon at Durham Cathedral in 1849–62.
Wrote services, anthems and esp. many
hymn-tunes, and took part in the compilation of *Hymns A. & M.*

Dylan (Holbrooke). *See* **Cauldron of Annwen.**

Dynamics, the gradations of loudness and softness in mus.

Dyphone. *See* **Mace, Thomas.**

Dyson, George (b. Halifax, 28. V. 1883; d. Winchester, 29. IX. 1964), Eng. comp. Studied at the R.C.M. in London and became mus. director at Winchester Coll. in 1924, having already held the appts. of mus. master at Osborne, Marlborough, Rugby and Wellington, serving in the 1914–18 war between. In 1937 he was app. director of the R.C.M. in succession to Hugh Allen, retiring in 1952. Knighted in 1941.

Works incl. comps. for solo voices, chorus and orch.: *The Canterbury Pilgrims* (setting of Chaucer's prologue), *St. Paul's Voyage to Melita, Nebuchadnezzar, Quo vadis*; chorus and orch.: *In Honour of the City of London* (Dunbar), *The Blacksmiths*; symph., *Siena* and suite *Won't you look out of your window?* (after Walter de la Mare) for orch.; *Prelude, Fantasy and Chaconne* for cello and orch.; 3 rhapsodies for string 4tet; church mus., pf. pieces, songs, part-songs, etc.

Dzerzhinsky, Ivan (b. Tambov, 21. IV. 1909), Rus. comp. Studied at the Gnessin School of Mus. at Moscow and at the Leningrad Cons.

Works incl. operas *Quiet flows the Don, Ploughing the Fallows* (both after novels by Mikhail Sholokhov), *In the Days of Volochaiev, The Storm* (after Ostrovsky), *The Blood of the People*; incid. mus. for plays; film mus.; *Spring, Poem of the Dnieper* and *Rus. Overture* for orch.; 2 pf. concertos, pf. pieces; song cycles, etc.

E

E, The third note, or mediant, of the scale of C maj.

E.N.S.A. *See* ENSA.

Eadie, Noel (b. Paisley, 10. XII. 1901; d. London, 11. IV. 1950), Scot. soprano. Studied pf. at first, then singing with Esta d'Argo in London. She 1st appeared in London, at Covent Garden, in 1931, joined the B.N.O.C. and after an engagement at the Chicago Opera sang Constanze and the Queen of Night in the Mozart perfs. at Glyndebourne in 1935–6.

Eagles, Solomon. *See* Eccles.

Ear Training, the development of the sense of pitch, the ready distinction of intervals, identification of var. types of chords, etc.

Early Reign of Oleg, The, Rus. 'opera' or play with mus. (lib. by Catherine II), mus. by Pashkeievich, Canobbio and Sarti, prod. St. Petersburg, at court, Hermitage Theatre, 26. X. 1790.

Easdale, Brian (b. Manchester, 10. VIII. 1909), Eng. comp. Educ. at the Westminster Abbey choir-school and the R.C.M. in London.

Works incl. operas *Rapunzel, The Corn King* and *The Sleeping Children*; incid. mus. for Eugene O'Neill's *Mourning Becomes Electra*; film mus. *The Red Shoes*; *Missa Coventrensis, Dead March, Tone Poem, Six Poems* for orch.; pf. concerto; string trio; pieces for 2 pfs.; song cycles, etc.

East, Michael (b. ? London, *c.* 1580; d. ? London, 1648), Eng. comp. He was apparently in the service of Lady Hatton in London early in the 17th cent. and later organist of Lichfield Cathedral.

Works incl. Evening Service, anthems; 6 books of madrigals (some with anthems) and a madrigal contrib. to *The Triumphes of Oriana*; mus. for viols, etc.

East, Thomas (b. ?; d. London, I. 1609), Eng. pub., ? father of prec. He worked in London and brought out several works by Byrd and the Elizabethan madrigalists.

Easter Music-Drama. *See* Liturgical Drama.

Ebeling, Johann Georg (b. Lüneburg, 8. VII. 1637; d. Stettin, 4. XII. 1676), Ger. comp. Mus. director at the Nicolai Church in Berlin in 1662 and prof. of mus. at Stettin in 1668. He ed. the hymns of Paul Gerhardt and other mus. Comp. church mus., esp. chorales.

Eberhard von Freising. *See* Freising.

Eberl, Anton (b. Vienna, 13. VI. 1765; d. Vienna, 11. III. 1807), Aus. pianist and comp. Friend and possibly pupil of Mozart, he toured as a pianist and from 1796 to 1800 was *Kapellmeister* in St. Petersburg. Works incl. operas *La Marchande des modes, Die Königen der schwarzen Inseln,* etc.; melodrama *Pyramus und Thisbe*; symphs.; pf. concertos; chamber mus.; sonatas, variations, etc. for pf.; songs, etc.

Eberlin, Johann Ernst (b. Jettingen, 27. III. 1702; d. Salzburg, 19. VI. 1762), Ger. organist and comp. Settled in Salzburg in 1724, where he became organist to the court and cathedral in 1729, and *Kapellmeister* in 1749. He was esteemed as a comp. of church mus.

Works incl. over 50 Masses; 12 Requiems; offertories, etc.; several oratorios; org. mus., etc.

Eberst, Jakob Levy. *See* Offenbach.

Eberwein, Traugott Maximilian (b. Weimar, 27. X. 1775; d. Rudolstadt, 2. XII. 1831), Ger. violinist and comp. Son of a member of the Weimar court band, in which he played as a child. Through Zelter's influence he was much esteemed by Goethe. He went into the service of the Prince of Schwarzburg-Rudolstadt in 1797 and became mus. director there in 1817.

Works incl. operas *Claudine von Villa Bella* and *Der Jahrmarkt von Plundersweilen* (libs. by Goethe), *Preciosa* (P. A. Wolff) and 8 others; Mass; 3 cantatas; concertos, *Sinfonia concertante* for wind instruments; vocal 4tets; songs, etc.

Eccard, Johann (b. Mühlhausen, Thuringia, 1553; d. Berlin, 1611), Ger. comp. Pupil of David Köler in the choir-school attached to the Weimar court chapel, 1567–71, and (?) of Lassus at Munich. In the service successively of Jacob Fugger at Augsburg, at Königsberg, of the Margrave of Brandenburg-Ansbach and of the Elector Joachim Friedrich of Brandenburg in Berlin and his successor, Johann Sigismund.

Works incl. motets, chorales (some harmonized, some newly comp. by him); sacred songs; secular Ger. songs for several voices, wedding songs, odes, festival songs, etc.

Eccles (Eagles), Eng. family of musicians:

1. **Solomon E.** (b. ? 1618, d. London, 11. II. 1683), descendant of a mus. family, teacher of virginals and viols. He embraced Quakerism *c.* 1660 and burnt all his mus. and instruments, but in 1667 pub. a book arguing for and against the moral justification of mus. He went to the West Indies with George Fox to estab. Quakerism in 1671, was in New Eng. in 1672 and was prosecuted for sedition at Barbados in 1680.

2. **Solomon E.** (b. ?; d. ?), violinist and comp., (?) son of prec., musician at the courts of James II and William and Mary. Works incl. mus. for plays by Aphra Behn and Otway.

3. **John E.** (b. London, 1668; d. Kingston-upon-Thames, 12. I. 1735), comp.,

son of prec. Pupil of his father. Began to write mus. for the theatres *c.* 1690. He became a member of the King's Band in 1694 and its Master in 1700 on the death of Staggins, and the same year gained the 2nd prize in a contest for the best comp. of Congreve's masque *The Judgment of Paris*, Weldon being 1st and D. Purcell and Finger 3rd and 4th. For *c.* a quarter of a cent. he lived in retirement at Kingston, devoted mainly to fishing, though he continued to write odes for the royal household.

Works incl. mus. for many plays, e.g. *The Spanish Friar* (Dryden), *Love for Love* (Congreve), *Don Quixote* (Durfey, with Purcell), *The Stage Coach* (Farquhar), *Macbeth* (Shakespeare), *Europe's Revels for the Peace, Rinaldo and Armida, The Way of the World* and *Semele* (both Congreve), *The Biter* (Rowe); mus. for Queen Anne's coronation; Congreve's *Ode for St. Cecilia's Day*; many songs; etc.

4. Henry E. (b. London, *c.* 1670; d. ? Paris, ? 1742), violinist and comp., brother of prec. Member of the King's Band, 1689–1710, but went to Paris, considering himself neglected at home, and joined the royal band there. Wrote sonatas for vln. and for viol.

5. Thomas E. (b. London, *c.* 1672; d. *c.* 1745), violinist, son of 2. Pupil of his brother Henry (4), although highly gifted, secured no app., being a wastrel, but made such a living as he could by playing at taverns.

Échappée (Fr., short for *note échappée* = escaped note), a progression between 2 adjacent notes which deviates by at 1st taking a step in the opposite direction and then taking the 2nd note aimed at by an interval of a 3rd, e.g.:

Échelle de soie, L' (*The Silken Ladder*), opera by Gaveaux (lib. by François Antoine Eugène de Planard), prod. Paris, Opéra-Comique, 22. VIII. 1808. The orig. of Rossini's *Scala di seta*.

Échiquier. *See* **Chekker.**

Echo. In comp. var. echo effects have been used in many ways at all times; e.g. Lassus's madrigal *Olà, che buon eco,* the witches' chorus in Purcell's *Dido and Aeneas,* the *Echo* piece in Bach's B min. clavier partita, the *Scène aux champs* in Berlioz's *Fantastic Symph.,* the 2nd act of Humperdinck's *Hänsel and Gretel,* etc.

Écho et Narcisse, opera by Gluck (lib. by Louis Théodor de Tschudy), prod. Paris, Opéra, 24. IX. 1779.

Echo Organ, a set of pipes placed at some distance from the main body of an org. and controlled either by a separate manual or by stops assigned to one of the usual manuals, generally the Solo.

Eck, Franz (b. Mannheim, 1774; d. Strasbourg, 1804), Ger. violinist. Pupil of his brother Johann. Played in the court band at Munich as a youth, then travelled much and took Spohr to Rus. with him as his pupil.

Eck, Johann Friedrich (b. Mannheim, 1766; d. Bamberg, *c.* 1809), Ger. violinist, cond. and comp., brother of prec. In the service of the court at Munich from 1778, *Konzertmeister* 1788, later opera cond. there. Left Munich *c.* 1801 and settled in France.

Works incl. 6 vln. concertos, *Concertante* for 2 vlns., etc.

Eckardt, Johann Gottfried (b. Augsburg, 21. I. 1735; d. Paris, 24. VII. 1809), Ger. pianist, comp. and miniature painter. Settled in Paris, 1758. Wrote sonatas, variations, etc. for pf.

Eckert, Carl (Anton Florian) (b. Potsdam, 7. XII. 1820; d. Berlin, 14. X. 1879), Ger. pianist, violinist, cond. and comp. Pupil of Mendelssohn at Leipzig. Accompanist at the Théâtre Italien in Paris and to Henriette Sontag in the U.S.A., then cond. at the same theatre in Paris, director of the Court Opera in Vienna, *Kapellmeister* at Stuttgart in succession to Kücken, and successor of Dorn in Berlin.

Works incl. operas *Das Fischermädchen, Wilhelm von Oranien;* oratorios *Ruth* and *Judith;* church mus.; symph.; cello concerto; pf. pieces; songs; etc.

École d'Arcueil, a group of Fr. comps. gathered round Satie in his later years at his home in the Arcueil suburb of Paris, formed in 1923 and incl. Henri Cliquet-Pleyel, Roger Désormière, Maxime Jacob, Henri Sauguet and others.

Écorcheville, Jules (Armand Joseph) (b. Paris, 18. III. 1872; d. Perthes-les-Hurlus, 19. II. 1915), Fr. musicologist. Pupil of Franck and Riemann, co-founder of the Fr. section of the I.M.S., whose publications he ed. He did much research, and pub. the results, on old Fr. lute and vln. mus., mus. bibliography, etc. He was killed in battle.

Écossaise (Fr. fem. = lit. Scot. one), a dance long supposed to be of Scot. origin, but no longer considered so. As a fashionable ballroom dance in the early 19th cent. it was in fairly animated 2–4 time, about half way between the polka and the galop in speed. Among the comps. who cultivated it were Beethoven, Schubert and Chopin. The Ger. *Schottisch* (usually written [in the plur.] *Schottische* in Eng.) is the same thing.

Edelmann, Johann Friedrich (b. Strasbourg, 6. V. 1749; d. Paris, 17. VIII. 1794), Alsat. pianist and comp. He became famous in Paris through the patronage of his pupil, Baron Dietrich. He was a friend of Gluck, and Mozart thought well of his pf. comps. He apparently played a discreditable part during the Fr. Revolution, and died on the guillotine.

Works incl. operas *Ariane dans l'île de Naxos*, *La Bergère des Alpes* and *Diane et l'Amour*; symphs.; keyboard concertos and sonatas, etc.

Edelmann, Otto (b. Vienna, 5. II. 1917), Aus. bass-baritone. Studied at the Vienna State Acad. of Mus. His career was interrupted by World War II, but in 1947 he joined the Vienna State Opera, and in 1951 sang at Bayreuth.

Edgar, opera by Puccini (lib. by Ferdinando Fontana, based on Musset's *La Coupe et les lèvres*), prod. Milan, Teatro alla Scala, 21. IV. 1889.

Edgcumbe, Richard. See **Mount-Edgcumbe.**

Edmunds, Chris(topher Montague). (b. Birmingham, 26. XI. 1899), Eng. comp. and organist. Pupil of Bantock at the Birmingham and Midland School of Mus., later prof. of comp. there, and principal from 1945 to 1957 in succession to Allan K. Blackall. Mus.D., Manchester, 1935. Organist at Aston parish church.

Works incl. opera *The Blue Harlequin* (after Maurice Baring); symph. in D maj. (No. 2), symph. for strings (No. 1); romance for pf. and orch.; many chamber works; pf. mus., etc.

Eduardo e Cristina, opera by Rossini (lib. by Giovanni Schmidt, written for Pavesi, altered by Andrea Leone Tottola and Gherardo Bevilacqua-Aldovrandini), prod. Venice, Teatro San Benedetto, 24. IV. 1819.

Edwards, Julian (b. Manchester, 11. XII. 1855; d. Yonkers, N.Y., 5. IX. 1910), Anglo-Amer. comp. Pupil of Oakley and Macfarren, became a theatre cond. in 1877 and in 1888 settled in U.S.A.

Works incl. operas *Jupiter*, *King René's Daughter* (on Hertz's play) and *The Patriot*; operettas *Brian Boru*, *Princess Chic*, *Dolly Varden* (on Dickens's *Barnaby Rudge*), *When Johnny comes marching home*, *Friend Fritz* (after Erckmann-Chatrian), *The Belle of London Town*, *The Maid o, Plymouth*, *The Land of Heart's Desire* (W. B. Yeats) and others; 4 sacred cantatas, secular cantata *The Mermaid*; songs, etc.

Edwards, Richard (b. nr. Yeovil, *c.* 1522; d. London, 31. X. 1566), Eng. comp. Pupil of the musician, physician and Gk. scholar George Etheridge of Thame, entered Corpus Christi Coll., Oxford in 1540, and transferred to Christ Church on its foundation in 1546. App. Master of the Children of the Chapel Royal in London

in 1561. He was also a playwright, prod. *Palamon and Arcite* before Queen Elizabeth and also writing *Damon and Pithias*, etc., and a poet, compiling and contributing to a book of verse, *The Paradise of Dainty Devices*.

Works incl. mus. to his own *Damon and Pithias*; part-songs *In going to my naked bed* and *O the silly man*, etc.

Eeden, Gilles (or Heinrich) van den (b. ?; d. Bonn, VI. 1782), ? Flem., Dutch or Ger. organist and comp. 2nd court organist at Bonn. One of Beethoven's early teachers.

Eeden, Jean-Baptiste van den (b. Ghent, 24. XII. 1842; d. Mons, 4. IV. 1917), Belg. comp. Studied at Ghent and Brussels Conss. In 1878 he became director of the School of Mus. at Mons.

Works incl. operas *Numance* and *Rhéna*; oratorio *Le Jugement dernier*; cantatas; orchestral works; songs, part-songs, etc.

Egge, Klaus (b. Gransherad, Telemark, 19. VII. 1906), Norw. comp. Studied under Valen and in Ger. He ed. *Tonekunst* in 1935–38.

Works incl. 2 symphs., 2 pf. concertos, trio for vln., cello and pf., vln. and pf. sonatas, etc.

Egiazarov, Grigory (b. Ikdir, Rus. Armenia, 23. X. 1908), Rus. comp. After being an army bandsman, 1921–9, he studied at the Moscow Cons. under Glière, Miaskovsky and others.

Works incl. ballet *A Drop of Mead*; string 4tet; scherzo for bassoon and pf.; dances for pf., mostly based on Tartar, Armenian and Kurd folk mus., etc.

Egidius de Murino. See **Murino.**

Egisto, L' (*Aegisthus*), opera by Cavalli (lib. by Giovanni Faustini), prod. Venice, Teatro San Cassiano, autumn 1643.

Egk, Werner (b. Auchsesheim, Bavar., 17. V. 1901), Ger. comp. Mainly self-taught and spent some time in It. He began to comp. to broadcasting commissions. Settled nr. Munich and succeeded Graener as head of the faculty o comp. in the Reichsmusikkammer. From 1936 to 1940 he cond. at the Berlin State Opera and from 1950 to 1953 was director of the Hochschule für Musik in Berlin.

Works incl. operas *Die Zaubergeige*, *Irische Legende* (after Yeats), *Der Revisor* (after Gogol), *Die Verlobung in San Domingo*, *Peer Gynt* (after Ibsen); ballets *Joan de Zarissa* and *Abraxas*; radio opera *Columbus*; dance suite *Georgica* for orch.; vln. concerto, etc.

Egli, Johann Heinrich (b. Seegraben nr. Zürich, 4. III. 1742; d. Zürich, 19. XII. 1810), Swiss comp. Pupil of Pastor Schmiedli at Wetzikon nr. Zürich and later mus. teacher at Zürich.

Wrote many songs of which he pub. several books.

Egmont, incid. mus. by Beethoven for Goethe's tragedy of that name, Op. 84, written in 1809–10 for a revival at the Burgtheater in Vienna on 15. VI. 1810.

Egyptian Helen, The (R. Strauss). *See* **Ägyptische Helena.**

Ehlert, Ludwig (b. Königsberg, 13. I. 1825; d. Wiesbaden, 4. I. 1884), Ger. pianist, critic and comp. Pupil of Mendelssohn at the Leipzig Cons. and afterwards studied in Vienna. Worked in Berlin, Florence and at the court of Meiningen. He wrote several books on comps. and mus. life in It. and Ger.

Works incl. *Spring Symph.*, overture *Hafiz* and *A Winter's Tale* (Shakespeare); Requiem for a child; Romantic Sonata and pieces for pf.; songs, etc.

Eichendorff, Joseph von (1788–1857), Ger. poet and novelist. *See* **Fröhlich** (**F. T.**) (song from *Aus dem Leben eines Taugenichts*), **Knab** (songs), **Lothar** (*Freier*), **Paumgartner** (*Aus dem Leben e. T.*), **Pfitzner** (*Von deutscher Seele*), **Schoeck** (*Schloss Dürande, Wandersprüche* and songs), **Schumann** (*Liederkreis*); 6 songs by **Brahms**, 16 by **Schumann**, 28 (incl. 8 early) by **H. Wolf.**

Eichheim, Henry (b. Chicago, 3. I. 1870; d. Montecito, Cal., 22. VIII. 1942), Amer. violinist and comp. Studied at the Chicago Mus. Coll. and became violinist in Theodore Thomas's orch., where his father was a cellist. Later he played in the Boston Symph. Orch., 1890–1912. He then devoted himself to comp. and to travel in Asia, esp. Japan, where he studied eastern mus.

Works incl. ballets *Chinese Legend, Burmese Pwe* and *The Moon, my Shadow and I*; *Oriental Impressions, Chinese Legend, Burma, Java* and *Malay Mosaic* for orch. with oriental instruments, etc.

Eighteen-Twelve Overture (Tchaikovsky). *See* **Year 1812.**

Eighth Note (Amer.) = Quaver.

Eilen (Ger.) = to hurry. *Nicht eilen* = do not hurry.

Eimert, Herbert (b. Bad Kreuznach, 8. IV. 1897), Ger. comp. and critic. Studied mus. and musicology at Cologne Cons. and Univ. (1927–33). Worked for Ger. radio and from 1936 to 1945 ed. the *Kölnische Zeitung*. In 1951 he founded an electronic studio at the Cologne branch of W. Ger. Radio and since 1955 has edited *Die Reihe*. He has written extensively on modern mus.

Works incl. *Glockenspiel; Etuden über Tongemische; Requiem für Aikichi Kuboyama*; choral and chamber mus. and electronic pieces.

Ein musikalischer Spass (Mozart). *See* **Musikalischer Spass.**

Eine kleine Nachtmusik (Mozart). *See* **Kleine Nachtmusik.**

Einem, Gottfried von (b. Berne, 24. I. 1918), Aus. comp. Son of a military attaché at the Aus. embassy to Switz. The family moved to Plön in Holstein, where he went to school, and he 1st learned mus. from a pupil of Lamond. He worked at the Wagner theatre at Bayreuth and the State Opera in Berlin, studied further in London and Vienna. A plan to become Hindemith's pupil was frustrated by the latter's suspension by the Nazis in 1938, and E. and his mother were themselves arrested by the Gestapo. After his release he studied with Boris Blacher, with whom he wrote the lib. for his 1st opera. In 1948 he was invited to help to direct the festival at Salzburg, where he now lives.

Works incl. operas *Dantons Tod* (on Büchner's drama) and *Der Prozess* (after Franz Kafka); ballet *Prinzessin Turandot* (after Gozzi); *Capriccio* and concerto for orch.; 'Philadelphia' symph.; pf. concerto; pf. pieces; Hafiz songs, etc.

Einleitung (Ger.) = Introduction.

Einstein, Alfred (b. Munich, 30. XII. 1880; d. El Cerrito, Calif., 13. II. 1952), Ger. musicologist. Pupil of Sandberger, took his doctor's degree in 1903. Became ed. of the *Zeitschrift für Musikwissenschaft* in 1918, was mus. critic of the *Berliner Tageblatt* from 1929, in 1933 went into exile from Ger., settling 1st in London, then at Florence and lastly in Northampton, Mass., where he was prof. at Smith Coll. He revised Riemann's *Musiklexicon* and Köchel's Mozart catalogue and wrote works on Ger. vla. da gamba mus., on Gluck and Mozart, a short hist. of mus. and in partic. specialized in the study of the It. madrigal, on which he wrote a monumental book.

Eisler, Hanns (b. Leipzig, 6. VII. 1898; d. Berlin, 6. IX. 1962), Ger. comp. Studied with Schönberg in Vienna and gained a comp. prize in 1924. In 1925–33 he taught in Berlin, but emigrated to U.S.A. when a price was put on his head for being interested in mus. for the proletariat and in anti-Nazi activities. He was app. prof. at the New School of Social Research there. He left the U.S.A. in 1948, living first in Vienna and then in E. Berlin.

Works incl. operas *Goliath* and *Johannes Faustus*, didactic plays *Mother* (after Gorky's novel), *Hangmen also die, For whom the bell tolls, The Roundheads and the Pointedheads* and others; mus. for numerous films; *Ger. Symph.* for solo voices, chorus and orch., cantatas, choral ballads, proletarian songs, etc.; orchestral suites on Rus. and Jewish folksongs; wind 5tet; chamber cantata *Palmström* for speech-song, fl., clar., vln. and cello;

Zeitungsausschnitte for voice and pf., etc.

Eisteddfod (Welsh, plur. Eisteddfodau = a sitting of the learned), an annual gathering, now taking the form of a mainly mus. festival, but formerly a triennial assembly of Welsh bards, dating back to the 7th cent. at latest.

Eitner, Robert (b. Breslau, 22. X. 1832; d. Templin nr. Berlin, 2. II. 1905), Ger. musicologist and bibliog. Founder of the Gesellschaft für Musikforschung in 1868, ed. of the *Monatshefte für Musikgeschichte*, compiler of the *Quellen-Lexicon* (a catalogue of the contents of mus. libraries) and other bibliog. works, etc.

Electrochord, an electrophonic pf. invented by Vierling of Berlin in 1929–33, prod. its notes by the conversion of electrical waves into audible sounds.

Electronde, an electrophonic instrument, invented by Martin Taubman of Berlin in 1929, prod. notes from the air graded according to the chromatic scale by means of a switch, not indeterminate in pitch like those of the Aetherophone or Theremin.

Electrone, an electrophonic org. brought out by the Compton Org. Co. of London in 1939, prod. its notes by electrostatic methods and capable of imitating the sound of var. org. stops and mixtures.

Electronic Music, mus. which is produced entirely by electrophonic instruments without living players.

Electrophonic Instruments, modern instruments of var. kinds prod. their sound by high-frequency oscillations of radio vacuum tubes or by electro-magnetic agencies.

Elegy (from Gk. *elegeia*), in poetry a piece of sorrowful and usually commemorative character; in mus. either a vocal setting of such a poem or an instrumental piece suggesting the mood awakened by it.

Elegy for Young Lovers, opera by Henze (lib. by W. H. Auden and Chester Kallman), prod. Schwetzingen, Schlosstheater, 22. V. 1961; first Eng. prod. Glyndebourne, 19. VII. 1961.

Elektra, opera by R. Strauss (lib. by Hugo von Hofmannsthal, a much modernized re-interpretation of Sophocles), prod. Dresden, Royal Opera, 25. I. 1909.

Elgar, Edward (William) (b. Broadheath nr. Worcester, 2. VI. 1857; d. Worcester, 23. II. 1934), Eng. comp. Son of a Worcester mus. dealer and organist at St. George's Rom. Catholic Church. Self-taught as a comp. Wrote mus. for a little domestic play, *The Wand of Youth*, at the age of 12. Sent to a solicitor's office at 15, but preferred to help at his father's shop; joined a wind 5tet as bassoonist and the Worcester Glee Club, and at 17 became an orch. violinist. In 1879 he became cond. ⌐ the Worcester Glee Club and of the bar at the county lunatic asylum, for which he arr. much mus. Also played org. at his father's church and became member of Stockley's orch. at Birmingham, which gave the 1st public perf. of a work of his, the *Sérénade mauresque*. Married Caroline Alice Roberts in 1889 and went to live in London.

In 1890 the Three Choirs Festival (at Worcester that year) for the 1st time played a work of his, the *Froissart* overture. Choral works, incl. *King Olaf* and *Caractacus*, were heard at festivals, and the *Enigma* variations for orch., were prod. by Hans Richter in VI. 1899. Setting of Cardinal Newman's *Dream of Gerontius* prod. at Birmingham Festival, 3. X. 1900 and, in Ger., at the Lower Rhine Festival, Düsseldorf, in 1901 and 1902. Elgar Festival at Covent Garden Theatre in London, III. 1904, brought him greater recognition, and he was knighted on 5. VII. that year. Prof. of Mus. at Birmingham Univ., 1905–6. 1st symph. prod. by Richter, Manchester and London, XII. 1908, and vln. concerto by Kreisler, XI. 1910. During the war of 1914–18 he wrote much topical mus. and afterwards 3 chamber works. After the death of his wife in 1920 he wrote only some small pieces and incid. mus. At his death he left unfinished a 3rd symph. and an opera, *The Spanish Lady*, based on Ben Jonson's *The Devil is an Ass*.

Works incl. incid. mus. for Yeats and George Moore's *Grania and Diarmid*, Algernon Blackwood's *The Starlight Express* and other plays; 2 symphs.; concert overtures *Froissart, Cockaigne, In the South, Polonia*; many miscellaneous orchestral works, incl. 2 suites from *The Wand of Youth*, serenade for strings, *Enigma* variations, *Introduction and Allegro* for strings, symph. study *Falstaff, Dream Children* (after Lamb) for small orch., *Nursery Suite*; vln. concerto, cello concerto; cantatas *The Black Knight, King Olaf, The Banner of St. George, Caractacus, The Music Makers*; oratorios *The Light of Life, The Dream of Gerontius, The Apostles, The Kingdom*; string 4tet, E min., pf. 5tet, A min., vln. and pf. sonata, E min.; numerous smaller choral pieces and part-songs; songs for solo voice, incl. cycle *Sea Pictures* with pf. or orch.; *Severn Suite* for brass band, etc.

Elijah (Ger. *Elias*), oratorio by Mendelssohn (words from the Old Testament), prod. 1st in the Eng. version at the Birmingham Festival, 26. VIII. 1846; 1st Ger. perf., Hamburg, 7. X. 1847.

Eliot, T(homas). S(tearns). (1888–1965), Eng. poet. *See* Ap Ivor (*Hollow Men*), Baaren (do.), Pizzetti (*Assassinio nella*

Porter (Q.) (*Sweeney Shaw* (M.) (*Rock*).

pera by Fux (lib., in It., by riati), prod. at court at Laxen-ace nr. Vienna, 25. VIII. 1719.

..etta regina d'Inghilterra (*Elizabeth, ..n of England*), opera by Rossini (lib. ..y Giovanni Schmidt), prod. Naples, Teatro San Carlo, 4. X. 1815. The overture was taken from *Aureliano in Palmira* and afterwards used for *Il barbiere di Siviglia*.

Elisir d'amore, L' (*The Love Potion*), opera by Donizetti (lib. by Felice Romani, based on Scribe's *Le Philtre*, comp. by Auber), prod. Milan, Teatro della Canobbiana, 12. V. 1832.

Elizalde, Federico (b. Manila, P.I., 12. XII. 1907), Span. cond. and comp. Educ. at Stanford Univ., California, and Cambridge; studied mus. with Pérez Casas in Madrid, Alfred Hertz and Bloch at San Francisco and E. Halffter in Paris.

Works incl. opera *Paul Gauguin*; overture *La pájara pinta*; sinfonia concertante for pf. and orch.; mus. for 15 solo instruments, etc.

Ella, John (b. Leicester, 19. XII. 1802; d. London, 2. X. 1888), Eng. violinist and writer on mus. Estab. the chamber concerts of the Mus. Union in London and ran them for 35 years.

Elman, Mischa (b. Stalnoye, 20. I. 1891; d. N.Y., 5. V. 1967), Rus. violinist. Began serious studies at the age of 6 and in 1902 was accepted by Auer for his master class. He made his début in 1904 in Berlin, later touring Europe and Amer.

Elmendorff, Karl (b. Düsseldorf, 25. I. 1891; d. 21. X. 1962), Ger. cond. After studying philology he entered the Cologne Cons. in 1913. He held var. cond. appts., incl. Berlin State Opera, Munich, Wiesbaden, Cassel, Mannheim and Dresden. From 1927–42 he was a regular guest cond. at Bayreuth.

Elsner, Ksawery Józef (b. Grotków, Silesia, 29. VI. 1768; d. Warsaw, 18. IV. 1854), Pol. comp. of Swed. descent. Being intended for medicine, he had little mus. teaching in his youth, but learnt the vln. and some harmony at Breslau and studied more assiduously on going to Vienna. In 1791 he became violinist at the Brno theatre and the next year cond. at Lwów. He went to Warsaw as theatre cond. in 1799, estab. a mus. society there in 1815 and became the 1st director of the Cons. opened in 1821. Among his pupils there was Chopin.

Works incl. 27 operas (22 in Pol., e.g. *Krol Lokietek*), ballets and melodramas; *Stabat Mater*, church mus.; 3 symphs.; 6 string 4tets; instrumental pieces, etc.

Éluard, Paul (1895–1952), Fr. poet. *See* **Barraine** (*Avis*), **Poulenc** (*Chansons vil-*

lageoises, *Tel jour, telle nuit*, and *Figure humaine*).

Elvey, George (Job) (b. Canterbury, 27. III. 1816; d. Windlesham, 9. XII. 1893), Eng. organist and comp. Received his mus. educ. at Canterbury Cathedral and at the R.A.M. in London under Potter and Crotch. Organist at St. George's Chapel, Windsor, 1835–82; D.Mus., Oxford, 1840; knighted 1871.

Works incl. oratorios *The Resurrection and Ascension* and *Mount Carmel*; services, anthems, festival anthems for Gloucester and Worcester; wedding march for Princess Louise; org. mus., etc.

Elwart, Antoine (Aimable Élie) (b. Paris, 18. XI. 1808; d. Paris, 14. X. 1877), Fr. comp., mus. scholar and author of Pol. descent. Studied at the Paris Cons. under Fétis and Lesueur and gained the Prix de Rome in 1834. He taught at the Cons., cond. concerts, wrote books on var. subjects and gave much time to comp.

Works incl. opera *Les Catalans*; oratorios *Noé* and *La Naissance d'Ève*; incid. mus. for Euripides' *Alcestis*; *Omaggio alla memoria di Bellini*; Masses and other church mus.; symphs., overtures; chamber mus. etc.

Elwell, Herbert (b. Minneapolis, 10. V. 1898), Amer. comp. Educ. at Minnesota Univ. and studied mus. with Bloch in N.Y., Nadia Boulanger in Paris and at the Amer. Acad. in Rome. Settled at Cleveland on his return to U.S.A. in 1932 as critic and teacher.

Works incl. ballet *The Happy Hypocrite* (after Max Beerbohm); cantata; Sketches for orch.; 2 string 4tets, pf. 5tet, Divertimento for string 4tet; vln. and pf. sonata; sonata and other works for pf. etc.

Elwes, Gervase (Cary) (b. Northampton, 15. XI. 1866; d. nr. Boston, U.S.A., 12. I. 1921), Eng. tenor. Studied in Vienna, Munich, Paris and London. In Brit. diplomatic service, 1891–5. Made his 1st professional appearance in 1903.

Embouchure (Fr., but used in Eng.), the position of the lips on the mouthpiece in wind instrument playing.

Emerald Isle, The, unfinished operetta by Sullivan, completed by German (lib. by Basil Hood), prod. London, Savoy Theatre, 27. IV. 1901.

Emicon, an electrophonic instrument appearing in U.S.A. in 1931, prod. notes from the air graded according to the chromatic scale by means of a keyboard, not indeterminate in pitch like those of the Aetherophone or Theremin.

Emma di Resburgo (*Emma of Roxburgh*), opera by Meyerbeer (lib. by Gaetano Rossi), prod. Venice, Teatro San Benedetto, 26. VI. 1819.

Emmanuel, (Marie François) **Maurice** (b. Bar-sur-Aube, 2. V. 1862; d. Paris,

14. XII. 1938), Fr. musicologist and comp. Student at the Paris Cons. and pupil of Gevaert at Brussels. After var. appts. as hist. and musician he became prof. of mus. hist. at the Cons. in succession to Bourgault-Ducoudray in 1907 and retained the post until 1936. He wrote several learned books on the mus. idiom, Gk. mus., modal accomp., Burgundian folksong, etc. Works incl. operas *Prométhée enchaîné* and *Salamine* (both after Aeschylus); operetta *Pierrot peintre*; incid. mus. for Plautus's *Amphitryon*; 2 symphs., *Suite française*, *Ouverture pour un conte gai*, *Zingaresca* for orch.; *3 Odelettes anacréontiques* for voice, fl. and pf.; vln. and pf. and cello and pf. sonatas; *Sonate bourguignonne* and 6 sonatinas for pf.; *In memoriam matris* and *Musiques* for voice and pf., etc.

'Emperor' Concerto, nickname for Beethoven's E♭ maj. pf. concerto, Op. 73, known only in Brit. and U.S.A., prob. invented by J. B. Cramer. There is nothing to justify it, though it suits the majestic work well enough.

Emperor Jones, opera by Gruenberg (lib. by Kathleen de Jaffa, based on Eugene O'Neill's play), prod. N.Y., Metrop. Opera, 7. I. 1933.

'Emperor' Quartet. *See* **Emperor's Hymn.**

Emperor's Hymn, The, *Gott erhalte Franz den Kaiser* (words by Lorenz Leopold Haschka), comp. by Haydn and first sung to celebrate the Emperor's birthday, 12. II. 1797. Also used by Haydn as a theme for variations in the string 4tet Op. 76 No. 3 (known as the 'Emperor' 4tet). Later adopted as the Aus. nat. anthem. Well-known in England as a hymn-tune.

Empfindsamer Stil (Ger., sensitive style), term applied to mus. by some Ger. 18th-cent. comps., esp. C. P. E. Bach, Quantz, etc., who sought to make their mus. directly expressive of feeling. *See* **Affektenlehre.**

En Saga (Sibelius). *See* **Saga, A.**

Encina, Juan del (b. nr. Salamanca, 12. VII. 1468; d. León, 1529), Span. poet, playwright and comp. Studied at Salamanca Univ., entered the service of the Duke of Alba at Toledo, was app. archdeacon of Málaga in 1509, went to Rome in 1514 and to the Holy Land in 1519, and became prior of León. Prod. the *Farsa de Placida e Vittoriano* in Rome and comp. many songs for his own plays. His poems were pub. at Salamanca, 1496. Over 60 of his songs are contained in a MS. at Madrid, the *Cancionero Musical de Palacio*. He cultivated esp. the *villancico*, a form resembling the French *virelai*.

Enée et Lavinie (*Aeneas and Lavinia*), opera by Colasse (lib. by Bernard de Fontenelle, after Virgil), prod. Opéra, 16. XII. 1690.

Opera by Dauvergne (lib. do.), ⊦ Paris, Opéra, 14. II. 1758.

Enesco, Georges (b. Dorohoiû, 19. VI. 1881; d. Paris, 4. V. 1955), Rum. violinist and comp. Studied at the Vienna Cons., 1888–93, and then went to Paris to finish his vln. studies with Marsick and comp. with Massenet, Gedalge and Fauré. In 1899 he began his career as a virtuoso violinist and teacher of the instrument. Works incl. opera *Œdipe* (after Sophocles); 3 symphs., *Poème roumain, Rumanian Rhapsodies*, suites and intermezzi, etc. for orch.; mus. for string and for wind combinations; vln. and pf. sonatas; suites and other works for pf.; songs, etc.

Enfance du Christ, L' (*The Childhood of Christ*), oratorio by Berlioz, Op. 25, for solo voices, chorus and orch., comp. in 1850–4, 1st perf. Paris, 10. XII. 1854.

Enfant et les sortilèges, L' (*The Child and the Witcheries*), opera in 1 act by Ravel (lib. by Colette), prod. Monte Carlo, 21. III. 1925.

Enfant prodigue, L' (*The Prodigal Son*), lyric scene by Debussy (lib. by Édouard Guinand), written for the Prix de Rome and pub. 1884; prod. as an opera, London, Covent Garden Theatre, 28. II. 1910.

Pantomime by Wormser (scenario by M. Carré, jun.), prod. Paris, Cercle Funambulesque, 14. VI., and Bouffes-Parisiens, 21. VI. 1890.

Engel, Carl (b. Thiedewiese nr. Hanover, 6. VII. 1818; d. London, 17. XI. 1882), Ger. musicologist who wrote on mus. in Eng. After studying the org. at Hanover and the pf. with Hummel at Weimar and being for some time attached to the household of a Pomeranian nobleman, he went to Eng. *c.* 1845, settling 1st at Manchester, then in London. He wrote on mus. archaeology, instruments, folk mus., etc. and compiled the catalogue of the mus. instruments in the Victoria and Albert Museum.

Engel, Carl (b. Paris, 21. VII. 1883; d. New York, 6. V. 1944), Amer. musicologist of Ger. descent. Studied at Strasbourg and Munich and settled in U.S.A. in 1905. App. chief of the mus. division of the Library of Congress at Washington in 1922 and succeeded Sonneck as ed. of the *Musical Quarterly* in 1929. One of the organizers and in 1937–8 president of the Amer. Musicological Society. He pub. many articles and books on mus., also some comps.

Engführung (Ger. lit. 'close conduct') = Stretto.

English Fingering, an obs. system of fingering of pf. mus. according to the principle that the human hand has 4 fingers and a thumb, the former being thus

and the latter +. E. F. has
Eng~~~~olly displaced by Continental
where the thumb is marked 1,
~ering continuing to the little
~ich thus becomes 5. This system
fact, in use in early Eng. virginal
~. F. was a later fashion.
~glish Flute, an obs. name for the
~rder.

~nglish Folk Dance and Song Society,
~ amalgamation of the Folksong Society,
.ounded in 1898, and the Eng. Folk Dance
Society, founded by Cecil Sharp in 1911,
the aim of both being the collection, study
and practice of old folksongs and dances,
the pub. of a *Journal* and the holding of
annual festivals with the collaboration of
visiting foreign singers and dancers.

English Horn (from Fr. *cor anglais*, a
term which has not been satisfactorily
explained), a woodwind instrument with
double reed, belonging to the ob. family,
played exactly like that instrument but
standing a 5th lower in pitch and written
for as a transposing instrument. Its tone is
nasal, like that of the ob., but darker in
quality.

English Suites, 6 keyboard suites by
Bach, comp. at Cöthen. In what respect
they are 'Eng.' has never been fully
explained.

Enharmonic (adj.). In Gk. mus. there
were 3 *genera*: the diatonic, the chromatic
and the E., and the last had divisions into
degrees smaller than semitones. In modern
usage the word E. is applied to modulations
made by means of changes of a note or
notes between sharps and flats, e.g. C♯
becoming D♭, E♭ becoming D♯, etc. On
the pf. or other instrument using the
tempered scale these notes actually
remain the same, but in string instruments
there is, at least to the player's feeling, a
minute difference between them.

Enigma Canon, a Canon written down
in a single part with no indication where
the subsequent entries of the other parts
are to occur, the perfs. being left to guess
how the mus. fits by solving a riddle.

'Enigma' Variations, a set of orchestral
variations by Elgar, Op. 36, entitled
Variations on an Original Theme, comp.
1898, 1st perf. London, 19. VI. 1899.
Each variation is a mus. portrait of some
person indicated only by initials or by a
nickname, all of whom have, however,
been identified. The word 'Enigma'
appears over the theme. *See also* **Potter.**

Enigmatic Scale (Verdi's). *See* **Scala
enigmatica.**

Enna, August (b. Nakskov, 13. V.
1860; d. Copenhagen, 3. VIII. 1939),
Dan. comp. of It. descent. The son of a
cobbler, he was almost entirely self-
taught. The family moved to Copenhagen
in 1870. In 1888 Gade helped him to study

in Ger. for a year. He had already prod. an
operetta by that time and become a
provincial cond.
Works incl. operas *Heksen* (*The Witch*),
*Cleopatra, Aucassin and Nicolette, The
Little Match-Seller* and *The Princess on the
Pea* (both after Andersen), *Komedianter*
(*The Jesters*) (after Hugo), *Gloria Arsena*
(after Dumas *père*), *Don Juan Mañara*,
etc.; operetta, *A Village Tale*; ballets;
choral work *Mother-Love*; 2 symphs.,
Festival Overture, symph. pictures; vln.
concerto, etc.

ENSA (abbr.). Entertainments Nat.
Service Assoc.: an organization estab.
during World War II (1939–45) to provide
entertainment for troops and factory
workers.

Ensalada (Span. lit. salad), a kind of
burlesque madrigal cultivated in Spain
in the 16th cent., in dramatic form, like
Vecchi's *Amfiparnaso*, not intended for
stage perf. Also a Quodlibet.

Ensemble (Fr. = together). The word
is used in Eng. for concerted singing or
playing, esp. in critical descriptions of such
singing or playing.

Entführung aus dem Serail, Die (*The
Elopement from the Harem*, known in Eng.
as *The Seraglio*, in It. as *Il ratto dal
serraglio*). *See also* **Belmont und Constanze.**
Opera by Mozart (lib. by Christoph
Friedrich Bretzner [*Belmont und Constanze*]
altered by Gottlieb Stephanie, jun.), prod.
Vienna, Burgtheater, 16. VII. 1782.

Enthoven, Henri Émile (b. Amsterdam,
18. X. 1903; d. N.Y. 27. XII. 1950), Dutch
comp. Pupil of Wagenaar at Amsterdam
and Schreker in Berlin. Asst. to Weingartner at the Basle theatre and later
lecturer and mus. critic at Leyden and
Amsterdam.
Works incl. incid. mus. for plays; 3
symphs., 4 suites and other orchestral
works; Fantasy for vln. and orch.; Festival
Prelude for wind instruments and org.; pf.
mus.; songs; etc.

Entr'acte (Fr.). *See* **Intermezzo.**

Entrata (It.). *See* **Intrada.**

Entrée (Fr. = entrance, entry). In the
17th and 18th cents. a piece of mus. in a
stately rhythm accomp. the entry of
processions, etc. in ballets and other stage
pieces; also, more generally, an intro. or
prelude to any work, but more esp. a
ballet or opera where it accomp. the rise of
the curtain; an E. could also be the
beginning of each new scene in a ballet.

Entries, the appearances of the subject
in the different parts of a fugue.

Entry, a 17th–18th-cent. Eng. term for
Prelude.

Enunciation. *See* **Diction.**

Enzina, Juan del. *See* **Encina.**

Éolides, Les, symph. poem for orch. by
Franck, on a poem of the same name by

Leconte de Lisle; comp. 1876, 1st perf. Paris, 13. V. 1877.

Éoliphone (Fr.). *See* Aeoliphone.

Ephesian Matron, The, comic serenata by Dibdin (lib. by Isaac Bickerstaffe), prod. London, Ranelagh House, 12. V. 1769.

Epidiapente (from Gk. *See also* Diapente), a 5th higher. The term is used esp. for canons at the 5th.

Epidiatessaron (from Gk.), a 4th higher.

Épine, Francesca Margherita de l'. *See* L'Épine.

Épinette (Fr.) = Spinet.

Episcopius, Ludovicus (b. Mechlin, *c.* 1520; d. Straubing, 29. IV. 1595), Flem. comp. Works incl. motets, a Mass, and part-songs to Dutch texts.

Episode, an incid. passage in a comp. that may be described as a digression from the main theme or themes. It may or may not be derived from the chief thematic material: in a fugue it usually is so derived, whereas in a rondo it is as a rule an entirely new idea placed between 2 recurrences of the subject, but may assume the function of a 2nd subject, as in sonata form.

Equal Temperament, the tuning of an instrument, esp. the pf. or org., by dividing the 8ve into 12 semitones all divided by exactly the same ratio of vibrations, as distinct from Just Intonation, where the intervals vary slightly and the sharps and flats are not precisely the same in pitch.

Equal Voices. A vocal comp. written for more than 1 voice of similar compass, e.g. 2 sopranos or 3 tenors (also, more loosely, for such combinations as 2 contraltos and 2 basses—because they are all low voices), is said to be for E. V.

Equale (It., plur. *Equali* = equals), a term used for instrumental pieces, esp. trombs. (e.g. Beethoven's E.), written for a group of similar instruments.

Equivoci, Gli (*The Doubles*), opera by Storace (lib. by Lorenzo da Ponte, based on Shakespeare's *Comedy of Errors*), prod. Vienna, Burgtheater, 27. XII. 1786.

Equivoci nel sembiante, Gli (*Dissimilarity in Similarity*), opera by A. Scarlatti (lib. by Domenico Filippo Contini), prod. Rome, Teatro Capranica, II. 1679. Scarlatti's 1st opera.

Érard, Pierre (b. Paris, 1796; d. Passy nr. Paris, 18. VIII. 1855), Fr. pf. and harp maker. Joined his uncle Sébastien É. in business.

Érard, Sébastien (b. Strasbourg, 5. IV. 1752; d. nr. Passy, 5. VIII. 1831), Fr. pf. and harp maker, uncle of prec., founder of the firm estab. *c.* 1777.

Erba, Dionigi (b. ?; d. ?), It. 17th-cent. comp. *Maestro di cappella* at the church of San Francesco, Milan, in 1692. Wrote a

Magnificat for double choir from which Handel borrowed for *Israel in Egypt.*

Erckmann-Chatrian (Émile E., 1822–99; Alexandre C., 1826–90), Fr. novelists. *See* Amico Fritz (Mascagni), Edwards (J.) (*Friend Fritz*), Fourdrain (*Rantzau*), Juif polonais (C. Erlanger), Maréchal (*Ami Fritz*), Mascagni (*Ranizau*), Roland-Manuel (*Ami F.*), Walthew (*Friend F.*), Weiss (K.) (*Polish Jew*).

Ercole amante (*Hercules as Lover*), opera by Cavalli (lib. by Francesco Buti), prod. Paris, Tuileries, 7. II. 1662. The only opera specially written for Paris by Cavalli. The ballet mus. was by Lully. The title alludes to the marriage of Louis XIV.

Erdmann, Eduard (b. Tseziz, Latvia, 5. III. 1896; d. Hamburg, 21. VI. 1958), Baltic-Ger. pianist and comp. Educ. at Riga and studied pf. with Ansorge and comp. with Tiessen in Berlin. Toured as pianist from 1919 and propagated modern mus.; prof. of comp. at Cologne from 1925 and prof. of pf. at the Hamburg Hochschule für Musik from 1950. Works incl. 2 symphs., pf. concerto; sonata for unaccomp. vln.; pf. works; songs, etc.

Erdmannsdörfer, Max von (b. Nuremberg, 14. VI. 1848; d. Munich, 14. II. 1905), Ger. cond. and comp. Studied at the Leipzig Cons. Became director of the Imp. Rus. Mus. Society in Moscow, 1882. Director of the Phil. concerts in Bremen, 1889–95. *Hofkapellmeister* in Munich, 1897–8. Comp. choral works, chamber mus., etc.

Erich, Daniel (b. ?; d. ?), Ger. 17th–18th-cent. organist and comp. Pupil of Buxtehude and later organist at Güstrow, Mecklenburg. Works incl. org. preludes.

Erk, Ludwig Christian (b. Wetzlar, 6. I. 1807; d. Berlin, 25. XI. 1883), Ger. organist, cond. and ed. Studied under his father, organist at Wetzlar, and André at Offenbach. Became a mus. educationist and choral cond., from 1836 in Berlin, and ed. a collection of old Ger. songs and so-called folksongs, *Deutscher Liederhort.*

Erkel, Ferenc (b. Békésgyula, 7. XI. 1810; d. Budapest, 15. VI. 1893), Hung. comp. As a pianist and cond. he organized mus. life at Kolozsvar in his early days. In 1835 he became mus. director of the Hung. theatre in Buda, in 1836 asst. cond. of the Ger. theatre in Pest, and in 1838 cond. of the Nat. Theatre. In 1845 he gained the prize in a competition for a Hung. nat. anthem. He founded the Budapest Phil. Society in 1853 and was director of the Acad. of Mus. in 1875–89. His operas were very popular for their patriotic subjects and nat. mus.
Works incl. operas *Bátori Mária,*

Hunyadi László, Bánk Bán, Dózsa György, Brankovics György, Névtelen Hősök, István Király (*King Stephen*); pf. mus.; songs, etc.

Erlanger, Camille (b. Paris, 25. V. 1863; d. Paris, 24. IV. 1919), Fr. comp. Studied at the Paris Cons. and gained the Prix de Rome in 1888.

Works incl. operas *Saint Julien l'Hospitalier* (after Flaubert), *Kermaria, Le Juif polonais* (after Erckmann-Chatrian), *Aphrodite, Bacchus triomphant, La Sorcière, Le Fils de l'étoile* and *La Forfaiture*; cantata *Velléda*; *Sérénade carnavalesque* for orch.; pf. pieces; *Poèmes russes* and other songs, etc.

Erlanger, Frédéric d' (b. Paris, 29. V. 1868; d. London, 23. IV. 1943), Fr. (anglicized) banker and comp. He had only private lessons in mus. and was largely self-taught. Settled in London and became naturalized, but retained the Fr. title of Baron.

Works incl. operas *Jehan de Saintré, Inez Mendo* and *Tess* (after Hardy's *Tess of the d'Urbervilles*): Requiem; *Suite symphonique* for orch.; *Concerto symphonique* for pf. and orch., vln. concerto; string 4tet, pf. 5tet; songs, etc.

Erlkönig (*Erl* [actually Alder] *King*), a ballad by Goethe, set by Schubert in 1815 at the age of 18, 1st sung in public by Johann Michael Vogl, Vienna, 7. III. 1821, pub. as Op. 1 that year.

Ermelinda Talèa Pastorella Arcada. *See* **Maria Antonia Walpurga.**

Ernani, opera by Verdi (lib. by Francesco Maria Piave, based on Victor Hugo's drama *Hernani*), prod. Venice, Teatro La Fenice, 9. III. 1844. The 1st of Verdi's operas prod. outside Milan.

Ernelindo, Princesse de Norvège, opera by Philidor (lib. by Antoine Alexandre Henri Poinsinet), prod. Paris, Opéra, 24. XI. 1767.

Ernst, Heinrich Wilhelm (b. Brno, 6. V. 1814; d. Nice, 8. X. 1865), Morav. violinist and comp. Pupil of Böhm, Seyfried and Mayseder in Vienna. Lived in Paris from 1832 to 1838.

Works incl. concertos, fantasies, variations, an *Elégie*, etc. for vln., also, with Heller, *Pensées fugitives* for vln. and pf.

Ernste Gesänge (Brahms). *See* **Vier ernste Gesänge.**

Ero e Leandro (*Hero and Leander*), opera by Bottesini (lib. by Boito, 1st intended for himself), prod. Turin, Teatro Regio, 11. I. 1879.

Opera by Mancinelli (lib. do.), 1st prod. as a cantata, in Eng., Norwich Festival, 8. X. 1896; 1st stage prod. Madrid, Teatro Real, 30. XI. 1897.

Eroe cinese, L' (*The Chinese Hero*), opera by Bonno (lib. by Metastasio), prod. Vienna, Schönbrunn Palace, at court, 13. V. 1752.

'Eroica' Symphony, Beethoven's symph. No. 3 in E♭ maj., comp. 1803–4. It was to have been entitled *Bonaparte,* but on hearing that Napoleon had declared himself hereditary Emperor Beethoven renamed it *Sinfonia eroica, composta per festeggiare il sovvenire di un grand' uomo* (Heroic symphony, composed to celebrate the memory of a great man).

'Eroica' Variations, Beethoven's pf. variations and fugue, Op. 35 (comp. 1802), so called because they use the same theme as the finale of the 'Eroica' symph. The theme, however, was taken from one of Beethoven's dances, and the variations were written before the symph.

Erreur d'un moment, L', ou La Suite de Julie (*The Error of a Moment, or The Sequel to Julie*), opera by Dezède (lib. by Jacques Marie Boutet de Monvel), prod. Paris, Comédie-Italienne, 14. VI. 1773.

Errico, Corrado (15th–16th cent.), It. poet. *See* Pizzetti (*Rappresentazione di Santa Uliva*).

Erwartung, monodrama by Schönberg (lib. by Maria Pappenheim), comp. 1909 but 1st prod. Prague, 6. 1st prod. 1924.

Esclarmonde, opera by Massenet (lib. by Édouard Blau and Louis de Gramont), prod. Paris, Opéra-Comique, 15. V. 1889.

Escobar, Pedro (b. ?; d. Seville, 1514), Span. comp., *maestro de capilla* at Seville early in the 16th cent. Comp. church mus. and secular pieces for 3 and 4 voices.

Escobedo, Bartolomeo (b. Zamora, *c.* 1515; d. Segovia, 1563), Span. comp. Entered the Papal Chapel in Rome in 1536, acted as judge in a dispute between Vicentino and Lusitano in 1551. In 1554 he returned to Spain as *maestro de capilla* at Segovia. Wrote Masses, motets, Magnificats, Miserere, etc.

Escribano, Juan (b.? *c.* 1480; d. Rome, 7. X. 1558), Span. singer and comp. Sang in the Papal Chapel in Rome, 1507–39. Wrote church mus., *chansons* for several voices, etc.

Escudier, Léon (b. Castelnaudary, Aude, 17. IX. 1821; d. Paris, 22. VI. 1881) and **Escudier, Marie** (b. Castelnaudary, Aude, 29. VI. 1819; d. Paris, 17. IV. 1880), Fr. writers on mus., brothers, who did most of their work jointly. It incl. biogs. of singers and of Rossini, a mus. dictionary, etc., and they ed. *La France musicale.* L. was director of the Théâtre Italien in 1876.

Eslava (y Elizondo, Miguel) Hilarion (b. Burlada, Navarre, 21. X. 1807; d. Madrid, 23. VI. 1878), Span. comp. and ed. App. *maestro de capilla* at Burgo de Osma in 1828, at Seville in 1832, where he took holy orders, and at Madrid in 1847. Ed. *Lira sacrohispana,* a collection of Span. church mus. in 10 vols., and the *Gaceta musical de Madrid.* App. prof. at

the Real Cons. de Música in Madrid, 1854 and director, 1866.
Works incl. operas *Il solitario, La trequa di Ptolemaide* and *Pedro el cruel*; Miserere for Seville Cathedral, Masses, motets, psalms and other church mus.; org. works.

Esmeralda, opera by Fabio Campana (1815–82) (lib. by Giorgio Tommaso Cimino, based on Victor Hugo's novel, *Notre-Dame de Paris*), prod. St. Petersburg, 30. XII. 1869.
Opera by Dargomizhsky (lib. by comp., trans. from Victor Hugo's lib. based on his *Notre-Dame de Paris*, and written for Louise Angélique Bertin (1805–77) for her opera prod. Paris, 1836), prod. Moscow, 17. XII. 1847.
Opera by G. Thomas (lib. by Theophilus Julius Henry Marzials and Alberto Randegger, based on Hugo), prod. London, Drury Lane Theatre, 26. III. 1883.

España, rhapsody for orch. by Chabrier on Span. tunes collected by the comp. during a visit to Spain in 1882–3; comp. 1883 and 1st perf. Paris, XII. 1883. Waldteufel later made a ballroom waltz of it.

Espinosa, Juan de (b. ?; d. ?), Span. 15th–16th-cent. comp., by whom a few part-songs are extant. He may be identical with the theorist of the same name, whose 3 treatises were pub. in Toledo in 1514 and 1520 (2).

Esplá, Oscar (b. Alicante, 5. VIII. 1886), Span. comp. Studied civil engineering and took the degree of doctor of philosophy, but also worked at mus. and took a prize for an orchestral suite in Vienna in 1909. Settled at Brussels in 1936.
Works incl. ballets *El contrabandista* and *Ciclopes*; symph. poems *El sueño de Eros, La vela de armas de Don Quixote* and *Los Cumbres, Poema de niños, Ambito de la danza* and *Levantine Suite* for orch.; 5tet; vln. and pf. sonata; sonata, scherzo and other works for pf., etc.

Esposito, Michele (b. Castellamare nr. Naples, 29. IX. 1855; d. Florence, 23. XI. 1929), It. pianist and comp. Studied at the Naples Cons., lived in Paris in 1878–82 and was then app. prof. of pf. at R. Ir. Acad. at Dublin, where in 1899 he estab. the Dublin Orchestral Society, which he cond.
Works incl. operetta *The Postbag*; incid. mus. for Douglas Hyde's *The Tinker and the Fairy*; cantata *Deirdre*; Ir. Symph., overture to Shakespeare's *Othello*; string 4tet; sonatas for vln. and pf. and cello and pf., etc.

Esquivel, Juan (b. Ciudad-Rodrigo, c. 1565; d. after 1613), Span. comp. He was *maestro de capilla* at Salamanca Cathedral (1608) and at Ciudad-Rodrigo (1611–13). His Masses and motets were

pub. (in 2 vols.) in 1608, and a vol. of miscellaneous sacred works in 1613. An *Officium pro defunctis* survives in MS.

Essential Discord, a chord which is dissonant according to acoustic theory, but whose notes belong to the key in which a comp. or passage is written and has become sufficiently current to be intro. without preparation.

Essipova, Anna Nikolaievna (b. St. Petersburg, 1. II. 1851; d. St. Petersburg, 18. VIII. 1914), Rus. pianist and teacher. Studied at the St. Petersburg Cons., esp. under Leschetizky, whom she married in 1880, separating in 1892. She toured widely and taught many pianists.

Estampes (*Engravings*), a set of 3 pf. pieces by Debussy, comp. 1903; 1. *Pagodes*, 2. *Soirée dans Grenade*, 3. *Jardins sous la pluie*.

Estampida (Provençal), **Estampie** (Fr.), an instrumental dance form of the 13th and 14th cents. related to the troubadour/ trouvère repertory. Its form consisted of several *puncta* (sections), each played twice, with 1st- and 2nd-time endings, called *ouvert* and *clos*. Frequently the *ouvert* and *clos* endings, which often comprised the greater part of each *punctum*, were the same throughout the piece, resulting in a great deal of repetition.

Esteban, Fernando (b. Seville, c. 1375; d. ?), Span. mus. theorist and sacristan at the chapel of St. Clement in Seville. His *Reglas de canto plano é de contrapunto é de canto de órgano* (the last expression meaning 'mensural polyphonic music') was written in 1410.

Esther, oratorio by Handel. Orig. perf. as a masque entitled *Haman and Mordecai* (lib. prob. by Pope and Arbuthnot, after Racine), Canons, nr. Edgware, c. 1720. Subsequently recast, with additional words by Samuel Humphreys, and perf. as an oratorio in London, at 1st privately to celebrate Handel's birthday and then at King's Theatre, Haymarket, 2. V. 1732.

Estinto (It. = extinct, dead), a direction indicating that a passage is to be perf. in a toneless manner.

Estompé (Fr. lit. stumped, shaded off) = damped, muffled, a direction frequently used by Debussy where he asks for a veiled or dull tone.

Estonian Composers. *See* **Baltic Composers.**

Estrée, Jean d' (b. ?; d. Paris, 1576), Fr. comp. and instrumentalist. His *Livre de danseries* was pub. in 1559.

Etheredge, George (1635–? 91), Eng. playwright. *See* **Staggins** (*Man of Mode*).

Ethiopian Chant, the name given to the Christian chant of Abyssinia. It was much influenced by Coptic chant and today exhibits similar features.

Étoile du Nord, L' (*The North Star*),

opera by Meyerbeer (lib. by Scribe), prod. Paris, Opéra-Comique, 16. II. 1854.

Eton Choirbook (Eton Coll. Library, MS. 178), the most important source of English church mus. of the late 15th cent., containing works by John Browne, William Cornyshe, Walter Lambe, Richard Davy, Robert Fayrfax, and many others. The repertory reflects the statutes of the coll., which prescribed the singing of a polyphonic antiphon to the Virgin every evening (in Lent, the *Salve Regina*). The MS. orig. contained 67 antiphons to the Virgin and other saints (including 15 settings of the *Salve Regina*), 24 Magnificats, the St. Matthew Passion by Davy, and a setting of the Apostles' Creed in the form of a 13-part round by Robert Wylkynson. The settings, except for this last, are for from 4 to 9 voices. About half the orig. contents are now lost, although some works can be recovered from other sources. The MS. is pub. in *Musica Britannica*, vols. x–xii. For the format, *see* **Choirbook**.

Étouffé (Fr. = stifled, smothered), a direction to deaden the tone on instruments where it is liable to vibrate after being sounded, as on the harp or the kettledrums.

Étranger, L' (*The Stranger*), opera by d'Indy (lib. by comp.), prod. Brussels, Théâtre de la Monnaie, 7. I. 1903.

Ettinger, Max (b. Lwów, Pol., 27. XII. 1874; d. Basle, 19. VII. 1951), Ger. comp. Studied in Berlin and Munich and lived at both places until 1933, when he went into exile in It. Switz.

Works incl. operas *Clavigo* (after Goethe), *Judith* (after Hebbel), *Frühlingserwachen* (after Frank Wedekind), *Juana* (after Georg Kaiser), *Dolores*; oratorio *Königin Esther*; *Old English Suite* (from virginal pieces), *Suite of Old Dances*, *3 Traumbilder*, *An den Wassern Babylons* for orch.; oratorio *Moses, Weisheit des Orients* (from Omar Khayyám) for solo voices, chorus and orch.; string 4tet; sonatas for vln. and pf. and cello and pf., suite for vla. and pf., songs, etc.

Étude (Fr. = study), a technical exercise for an instrumental (more rarely a vocal) perf., which may be as much an exercise in expression as in technique.

Études symphoniques, a set of 12 concert studies for pf. by Schumann, Op. 13, at first entitled *Études en forme de variations*, comp. in 1834. They are variations on a theme by the father of Ernestine von Fricken, with whom Schumann was in love at that time, but they are ded. to Sterndale Bennett, in whose honour Schumann intro. into the finale a theme from Marschner's *Ivanhoe* opera *Der Templer und die Jüdin*: a song in praise of Eng.

Etwas (Ger. = somewhat, rather).

Eugene Onegin, opera by Tchaikovsky (lib. by comp. and Konstantin S. Shilovsky,

based on Pushkin's poem-novel), prod., by students of the Cons., Moscow, 29. III. 1879.

Eulenburg, a pub. firm founded in Leipzig in 1874 by Ernst E. (1847–1926). In 1892 the firm took over the series of miniature scores issued by Albert Payne and extended its scope to cover a wide repertory of oratorios, operas, orchestral works and chamber mus. The firm is now owned by Schott.

Eunuch Flute, an obs. wood-wind instrument with a mouthpiece containing a membrane vibrating when the player sang into it. It dates back to the 16th cent. at least, but was never much more than a toy. *See also* **Mirliton**.

Eunuch Singers. *See* **Castrati**.

Euphonium (*see also* **Saxhorn**), a four-valved brass instrument of the Tuba family, used chiefly in military and brass bands. The compass is:

Euphony, suavity and harmoniousness of sound, the opposite of Cacophony.

Eurhythmics, a system of teaching mus., esp. rhythmic, perception by means of bodily movements, invented by Jaques-Dalcroze.

Euridice, L', opera by Caccini (lib. by Ottavio Rinuccini), prod. Florence, Palazzo Pitti, 5. XII. 1602.

Opera by Peri (lib. do.), prod. Florence, Palazzo Pitti, 6. X. 1600.

Euripides (*c.* 484–406 B.C.), Gk. dramatist. *See* **Alkestis** (Boughton and Wellesz), **Anson** (*Alkestis*), **Bachantinnen** (Wellesz), **Bell** (*Hippolytus*), **Bruneau** (*Bacchantes*), **Coerne** (*Trojan Women*), **Damrosch** (W.) (*Electra, Iphigenia in Aulis, Medea*), **Drysdale** (*Hippolytus*), **Elwart** (*Alcestis*), **Foulds** (*Trojan Women*), **Ghedini** (*Baccanti, Ifigenia in Tauride*), **Gray** (C.) (*Trojan W.*), **Ifigenia in Aulide** (Caldara, Cherubini, Graun, Zingarelli), **Ifigenia in Tauride** (Galuppi, Maio and Traetta), **Iphigénie en Aulide** (Gluck), **Iphigénie en Tauride** (Campra, Gluck and Piccinni), **Karyotakis** (*Trojan W.* and *Iphigenia in A.*), **Lloyd** (C. H.) (*Alcestis*), **Mulè** (*Bacchae, Medea, Cyclops, Hippolytus, Iphigenia in A.* and *in T.*), **Nottara** (*Hecuba*), **Pijper** (*Cyclops* and *Bacchantes*), **Riadis** (*Hecuba*), **Salviucci** (*Alcestis*), **Schürmann** (*Getreue Alceste*), **Senilov** (*Hippolytus*), **Slonimsky** (*Orestes*), **Taubert** (*Medea*), **Thomson** (V.) (do.), **Toch** (*Bacchantes*), **Walker** (R.) (*Rhesus* and *Hymn to Dionysus*), **Wood** (C.) (*Ion* and *Iphigenia in T.*).

Europe galante, L' (*Love in Europe*),

opera-ballet by Campra (lib. by Antoine Houdar de la Motte), prod. Paris, Opéra, 24. X. 1697.

Euryanthe, opera by Weber (lib. by Helmine von Chézy), prod. Vienna, Kärntnertortheater, 25. X. 1823.

Eusebius, one of the 2 imaginary characters, Florestan and E., used by Schumann as pseudo. for his critical writings and also intro. into his mus. (*Carnaval, Davidsbündlertänze*) to personify what he felt to be his dual character as an artist. F. repres. him as an impetuous romantic and E. as a dreamer.

Euterpe, the Muse of lyric poetry in Gk. mythology, and since such poetry was sung, also the Muse of mus., which had no separate patroness among the 9 Muses, doubtless because in ancient Greece it had no separate existence as an art.

Evangelimann, Der (*The Gospel Man*), opera by Kienzl (lib. by comp., based on a story by Leopold Florian Meissner), prod. Berlin, Opera, 4. V. 1895.

Evans, Edwin (b. London, 1. IX. 1874; d. London, 3. III. 1945), Eng. mus. critic. App. critic to the *Pall Mall Gazette* in 1912 and the *Daily Mail* in 1933. President of the I.S.C.M. in succession to Edward Dent in 1938. He wrote much on behalf of modern mus.

Evans, Geraint (Llewellyn) (b. Pontypridd, Glamorgan, 16. II. 1922), Welsh baritone. Studied at the Guildhall School of Mus. and later in Hamburg, Geneva and in Italy. He made his début at Covent Garden in 1948, and since then has sung all over Europe, incl. La Scala, Milan, in 1960 and the Vienna State Opera in 1961. Knighted in 1970.

Eve of St. John, The, opera by Mackenzie (lib. by Eleanor Farjeon, based on Scott's ballad), prod. Liverpool, 16. IV. 1924.

Éventail de Jeanne, L' (*Joan's Fan*), ballet by Auric, Delannoy, Ferroud, Ibert, Milhaud, Poulenc, Ravel, Roland-Manuel, Roussel and Schmitt (choreography by Alice Bourgat), prod. Paris, in private, 16. VI. 1927; Opéra, 4. III. 1929.

Everyman, incid. mus. for Hugo von Hofmannsthal's Ger. version of the 15th-cent. Eng. morality play, *Jedermann*, by Sibelius, Op. 83, comp. 1916.

Setting of the morality play for solo voices, chorus and orch. by Walford Davies, prod. Leeds Festival, 1904. *See also* **Lehmann (L.).**

Evesham, Walter of. *See* **Odington.**

Evirati (It.). *See* **Castrati.**

Évocations, 3 symph. poems by Roussel, comp. 1910–12: 1. *Les Dieux dans l'ombre des cavernes*; 2. *La Ville rose*; 3. *Aux bords du fleuve sacré*; 1st perf. Paris, Société Nat., 18. V. 1912.

Exaquir. *See* **Chekker.**

Exaudet, Joseph (b. Rouen, *c.* 1710; d. Paris, *c.* 1763), Fr. violinist and comp. Played at the Rouen Acad. concerts and joined the Paris Opéra orch. in 1749. Works incl sonatas for vln. and bass and trios for 2 vlns. and bass.

Excetre, John (b. ?; d. ?), Eng. comp. at the Chapel Royal 1374–96. Comps. are in the Old Hall MS.

Eximeno, Antonio (b. Valencia, 26. IX. 1729; d. Rome, 9. VI. 1808), Span. Jesuit and mus. theorist. Studied at Salamanca Univ. and became prof. of mathematics and mus. at the military acad. of Segovia. Settled in Rome when the Jesuits were expelled from Spain. Wrote a treatise *Dell' origine e delle regole della musica* and a novel *Don Lazarillo Vizcardi* dealing with a mus. adventurer on the model of Don Quixote.

Expert, Henri (b. Bordeaux, 12. V. 1863; d. Tourrettes-sur-Loup, 18. VIII. 1952), Fr. musicologist. Studied, and later taught, at Niedermeyer's school in Paris, and was also a pupil of Franck and Gigout. Prof. of mus. at the École des Hautes Études Sociales and librarian of the Cons. library. Ed. series of old Fr. mus., *Les Maîtres musiciens de la renaissance française* and *Monuments de la musique française*, of settings of Ronsard's poetry, old songs, church and harpsichord mus., etc.

Exposition, the 1st setting forth of thematic material in a comp. In a fugue the E. is the statement of the subject by its 1st entry in each voice; in a rondo the statement of the subject up to the 1st episode; in a sonata-form movement the whole 1st section up to the point at which the development (or working-out) section begins.

Expression Marks, all the indications by which the comp. indicates his wishes as to the manner of perf. of a work, esp. from the dynamic point of view (*forte, piano, crescendo, diminuendo*); but they may extend also to matters of speed and rhythm (e.g. *rallentando, rubato, acceleran-do*, etc.). E. M.s were little used before the 18th cent. and hardly at all before the 17th.

Expressionism, a term properly belonging to painting, esp. in Ger. in the 1910s, but loosely applied to comps. who aimed at a similar kind of interpretation, not of outward and visible things, but of moods and states of mind.

Extemporization. *See* **Improvisation.**

Extravaganza (corrupt. from It. *stravaganza*), a word sometimes used for a comp. of a freakish nature, esp. for a light and fantastic stage piece with mus., e.g. Gilbert and Sullivan's *Trial by Jury.*

Eybler, Joseph Leopold von (b. Schwechat nr. Vienna, 8. II. 1765; d. Vienna, 24. VII. 1846), Aus. comp. Pupil of Albrechtsberger and, after holding var.

apps. in Vienna, chief *Kapellmeister* to the Aus. court from 1824 to 1833.

Works incl. opera *Das Zauberschwert* and others; oratorio *Die vier letzten Dinge*, Requiem in C min., cantata *Die Hirten bei der Krippe*, 7 Te Deums, 32 Masses, offertories, graduals and other church mus.; symphs.; chamber mus.; pf. pieces, etc.

Ezio (*Aetius*). Lib. by Metastasio:

Opera by Gluck, prod. Prague, Carnival 1750.

Opera by Handel, prod. London, King's Theatre, Haymarket, 15. I. 1732.

Opera by Hasse, prod. Dresden, at court, 20. I. 1755.

Opera by Jommelli, prod. Bologna, Teatro Malvezzi, 29. IV. 1741.

F

F, the 4th note, or subdominant, of the scale of C major.

f, the subdominant note in any key in Tonic Sol-fa notation, pronounced Fah.

f (abbr.), the symbol commonly employed in mus. to indicate a loud (*forte*) tone. Progressively even louder dynamics are marked *ff*, *fff*, etc.

f Holes (or *ff* Holes), the sound-holes of instruments of the vln. family, so called because of their shape.

F.R.C.O. (abbr.) = Fellow of the Royal College of Organists.

Fa, the old name for the note F (*see* Solmization), still used in Lat. countries, and in Tonic Sol-fa notation the subdominant note in any key represented by the symbol f, pronounced Fa.

Fa-La, a light 16th–17th-cent. Eng. comp. for several voices of the ballett type. Its name derives from the syllables to which the refrain was sung.

Faa, Orazio (b. ?; d. ?), It. 16th-cent. comp. Pub. 2 books of madrigals in 1569 and 1571, set psalms to mus. and comp. other church mus.

Faber, Gregor (b. Lützen, *c.* 1520; d. ?), Ger. mus. theorist. His *Musices Practicae Erotematum Libri II* was pub. in Basle, 1553.

Faber, Heinrich (b. Lichtenfels, ?; d. Olsnitz, 26. II. 1552), Ger. theorist and comp., author of a *Compendiolum musicae pro incipientibus* (Brunswick, 1548), which ran into numerous eds. There is some church mus. to Lat. and Ger. texts.

Fabliau (old Fr. = fable), a Troubadour ballad with narrative words, distinct from the love songs sung by the Troubadours.

Fabre, Henri (1823–1915), Fr. entomologist and author. *See* Festin de l'araignée (Roussel).

Fabre (d'Eglantine), Philippe (François Nazaire) (1750–94), Fr. dramatist, revolutionist and amateur comp. (song 'Il pleut, il pleut, bergère'). *See* Godard (*Jeanne d'Arc*).

Fabri, Annibale Pio (b. Bologna, 1697; d. Lisbon, 12. VIII. 1760), It. tenor. Pupil of Pistocchi. Sang in Handel's operas in London, 1729–31.

Fabricius, Werner (b. Itzehoe, Holstein, 10. IV. 1633; d. Leipzig, 9. I. 1697), Ger. organist and comp. Studied under his father, Albert F., organist at Flensburg and under Selle and Scheidemann at the Hamburg Gymnasium. After pursuing other studies at Leipzig Univ., incl. law, he became mus. director at St. Paul's Church there in 1656 and, in addition, at St. Nicolas' Church in 1658. He was also public notary.

Works incl. motets, hymn tunes; sacred and secular songs for several voices; suites for viols and other instruments, etc.

Fabritius, Albinus (b. Görlitz, after 1550; d. ? Bruck an der Murr, 19. XII. 1635), Ger. comp. Wrote motets, 25 of which were pub. in his lifetime in 1595, many of them reissued in var. collections.

Faburden (Eng.). *See* Fauxbourdon.

Façade, diversion by Walton (poems by Edith Sitwell), privately prod. London, Chenil Gallery, Chelsea; 1st public perf. London, Aeolian Hall, 12. VI. 1923. 2 concert suites arr. later for enlarged orch. and for pf. duet. Prod. as a ballet (choreography by Frederick Ashton), London, Cambridge Theatre, 26. IV. 1931.

Faccio, Franco (b. Verona, 8. III. 1840; d. Monza, 21. VII. 1891), It. cond. and comp. Studied at the Milan Cons., prod. his 1st opera there and the 2nd at the Teatro alla Scala in 1863. App. prof. of harmony at the Cons. in 1868 and later cond. at the Carcano and Scala theatres. He was Verdi's cond. for *Aida* and *Otello* at Milan, 1872 and 1887.

Works incl. operas *Le sorelle d'Italia*, *I profughi fiamminghi*, *Amleto* (after Shakespeare's *Hamlet*); symph. in F maj., etc.

Fachiri (*née* d'Aranyi), Adila (b. Budapest, 26. II. 1888; d. Florence, 15. XII. 1962), Hung. violinist, a great-niece of Joachim, with whom she studied. She settled in London and appeared frequently as a soloist, often in double concertos with her sister, Jelly d'Aranyi (1895–1966).

Fackeltanz (Ger.) = Torch Dance.

Fadinho } (Port.), a type of popular
Fado } song perf. in Port. towns, in the streets and cafés, accomp. by the guitar and enlivened by dancing.

Faenza Codex (Faenza, Bib. Comm., MS. 117), a large MS. of keyboard music from the late 14th or early 15th cent., containing ornamented transcriptions of Fr. and It. secular vocal works (incl. some by Machaut and Landini), and some liturgical organ mus. The notation is on two staves with regular barring. In the mid-15th cent. parts of the orig. contents were erased by Bonadies (q.v.) to make room for sacred vocal works by himself and others.

Fage. *See* La Fage.

Fago, Nicola (b. Taranto, 26. II. 1677; d. Naples, 18. II. 1745), It. comp., nicknamed Il Tarantino after his birthplace. Educ. at the Cons. della Pietà dei Turchini in Naples. *Maestro di cappella* at the Cons. di S. Onofrio, 1704–8, and at the Cons. della Pietà, 1705–40. His comps. consist mainly of church mus., but he also wrote 4 or more operas, oratorios, etc.

Fagott (Ger.) = Bassoon.

Fagottino (It. lit. little bundle) = Tenoroon.

Fagotto (It. lit. fagot or bundle) = Bassoon; also a 16-ft. reed org. stop prod. bassoon tone.

Faignient, Noël (b. Cambrai, ?; d. ?), Flemish 16th-cent. comp. From 1561 he lived in Antwerp. Wrote *chansons*, madrigals, songs to Dutch texts, and sacred Lat. works.

Fair Maid of Perth (Bizet). *See* **Jolie Fille de Perth**.

Fair Maid of the Mill (Schubert). *See* **Schöne Müllerin**.

Fair Melusina (Mendelssohn). *See* **Schöne Melusine**.

Fair of Sorotchintsy (Mussorgsky). *See* **Sorotchintsy Fair**.

Fairchild, Blair (b. Belmont, Mass., 23. VI. 1877; d. Paris, 23. IV. 1933), Amer. comp. Studied at Harvard Coll. under Paine and Spalding and later at Florence under Buonamici. Was in the U.S.A. diplomatic service 1901–3 and in the latter year settled in Paris for the rest of his life.

Works incl. ballet-pantomime *Dame Libellule*; symph. poems *East and West*, *Zál*, *Shah Feridoun*; *Légende* and *Étude symphonique* for vln. and orch.; string 4tet, pf. 5tet, pf. trio and other chamber mus.; 2 vln. and pf. sonatas; choral works; song cycle *Stornelli toscani* and others, etc.

Fairies, The, opera by John Christopher Smith (lib. by comp., based on Shakespeare's *A Midsummer Night's Dream*), prod. London, Drury Lane, 3. II. 1755.

Fairy Queen, The, opera by Purcell (lib. adapted from Shakespeare's *A Midsummer Night's Dream* ? by Elkanah Settle), prod. London, Dorset Gardens Theatre, IV. 1692.

Faisst, Immanuel (Gottlob Friedrich) (b. Esslingen nr. Stuttgart, 13. X. 1823; d. Stuttgart, 5. VI. 1894), Ger. organist and comp. Studied theology at Tübingen Univ., but gave it up, on Mendelssohn's advice, for mus., in which he was self-taught. He travelled as organist and settled at Stuttgart, where he founded an org. school in 1847 and a society for the study of church mus., and was one of the founders of the Cons. He wrote on and ed. mus.

Works incl. cantata *Des Sängers Wiederkehr*, choral setting of Schiller's *Die Macht des Gesanges*; double fugue for pf.; org. works; vocal 4tets, etc.

Falchi, Stanislao (b. Terni, 29. I. 1851; d. Rome, 14. XI. 1922), It. comp. Director of the Liceo Musicale di Santa Cecilia in Rome, 1902–15.

Works incl. operas *Lorhélia*, *Giuditta*, *Il trillo del diavolo*; Requiem; overture to Shakespeare's *Julius Caesar*; chamber mus., etc.

Falcon, (Marie) Cornélie (b. Paris, 28. I.

1812; d. Paris, 25. II. 1897), Fr. soprano. Student at the Paris Cons. and pupil of Nourrit for operatic acting. 1st appearance 1832, at the Opéra. She lost her voice in 1838.

Falconi, Placido (b. Asola, *c.* 1530; d. Monte Cassino, after 1600), It. comp. He became a Benedictine at Brescia in 1549 and later a monk at Monte Cassino. Wrote church mus.

Falconieri, Andrea (b. Naples, 1586; d. Naples, 29. VII. 1656), It. comp. Lived successively at Parma, Florence, Rome and Modena, and visited Spain. *Maestro di cappella* at Naples from 1650.

Works incl. motets, madrigals, instrumental pieces, etc.

Faleni, Arturo (b. Chieti, It., 1877; d. Buenos Aires, 1942), Arg. comp. of It. descent. Studied at Genoa. In 1897 he settled at Buenos Aires and became an Arg. citizen. He founded a mus. acad. named after Verdi and wrote several educ. works on mus.

Works incl. overture in D maj., fantasy, fugue, symph. poem *The Earthquake* for orch.; pf. pieces; songs, etc.

Fall, a Cadence (e.g. 'dying fall' in Shakespeare). *See also* **Backfall**, **Forefall**.

Fall, Leo (b. Olomouc, 2. II. 1873; d. Vienna, 16. IX. 1925), Aus. comp. Studied at the Vienna Cons. and became cond. at Berlin, Hamburg and Cologne. Wrote *c.* 25 works for the stage, chiefly operettas, incl. *Die Dollarprinzessin*, *Eternal Waltz*, *Die geschiedene Frau* (*The Girl in the Train*), *Der liebe Augustin* (*Princess Caprice*), *Madame Pompadour*, etc.

Falla, Manuel de (b. Cádiz, 23. XI. 1876; d. Alta Gracia, Arg., 14. XI. 1946), Span. comp. Began to study the pf. in Madrid at the age of 8 and prod. a *zarzuela*, *Los amores de Inés*, written with very little tuition in comp. in 1902. This had no success, and he studied comp. with Pedrell, 1902–4. In 1905 he gained 2 prizes, for pf. playing and for his opera *La vida breve*. In 1907–14 he lived in Paris, becoming friendly with Debussy, Ravel and Dukas, but returned to Spain and settled in Madrid on the outbreak of war. The prod. of *La vida breve* at Nice and Paris in 1913 and of the ballet *The Three-cornered Hat* in London in 1919 spread his reputation. In 1921 he moved to Granada and became more exclusively a nationalist comp. again; but had later works perf. in Eng., Paris and N.Y. During the Span. Civil War he settled in S. Amer. and remained there.

Works incl. operas *La vida breve*, *Fuego fatuo* (based on Chopin's mus.), *El retablo de maese Pedro* (for puppets after Cervantes's *Don Quixote*), *La Atlantida* (posth., completed by Ernesto Halffter); ballets *El amor brujo*, *El sombrero de tres picos* (on Alarcón's story); *Noches en los jardines de España* for pf. and orch.; *Psyché* for mezzo-soprano, fl., vln., vla., cello and harp; concerto for harpsichord, fl., ob., clar., vln. and cello; 4 Span. pieces, *Fantasía baetica* and *Pour le tombeau de Paul Dukas* for pf.; *Homenaje: pour le tombeau de Debussy* for guitar; 3 songs (Gautier), 7 popular Span. songs, *A Cordoba* (Góngora), for voice and harp, etc.

False Relations, the simultaneous or closely adjacent occurrence in a comp. in several parts of 2 notes a semitone apart, at least 1 of which is foreign to the key of the passage in question. They often arise as a result of the independent movement of parts. 16th-cent. and early 17th-cent. comps. readily accepted simultaneous F.Rs. and they were still being used by Eng. comps. in the latter half of the 17th cent., partly as a result of tradition and partly as a means of expression.

Falsetto (It.), the tone-prod. of male singers resulting in notes above their normal pitch and sounding like those of an unbroken voice. F. is the voice normally cultivated by male altos.

Falsobordone (It.). See **Fauxbourdon.**

Falstaff. *See also* **At the Boar's Head; Lustigen Weiber von Windsor; Sir John in Love.**

Opera by Balfe (lib., in It., by S. Manfredo Maggioni, based on Shakespeare's *Merry Wives of Windsor*), prod. London, Her Majesty's Theatre, 19. VII. 1838.

Opera by Verdi (lib. by Boito, based on Shakespeare's *Merry Wives of Windsor* and *King Henry IV*), prod. Milan, Teatro alla Scala, 9. II. 1893.

Symph. study by Elgar, Op. 68 (based on Shakespeare's *King Henry IV* & refs. to Falstaff in *King Henry V*), comp. 1913, perf. Leeds Festival, 2. X. 1913.

Falstaff, ossia Le tre burle (*Falstaff, or The Three Jests*), opera by Salieri (lib. by Carlo Prospero Defranceschi, after Shakespeare), prod. Vienna, Kärntnertortheater, 3. I. 1799.

Famintsin, Alexander (Sergeievich) (b. Kaluga, 5. XI. 1841; d. St. Petersburg, 6. VII. 1896), Rus. critic and comp. Studied at St. Petersburg Univ. and mus. under Hauptmann, Richter and Riedel at Leipzig. Prof. of mus. hist. at the St. Petersburg Cons., 1865–72. He wrote some valuable books on mus. hist. but fiercely attacked the new nat. school headed by Balakirev.

Works incl. operas *Sardanapalus* and *Uriel Acosta* (after Gutzkow); *Rus. Rhapsody* for vln. and orch.; 3 string 4tets, pf. 5tet, etc.

Fanciulla del West, La (*The Girl of the [Golden] West*), opera by Puccini (lib. by Guelfo Civinini and Carlo Zangarini,

based on David Belasco's play), prod. N.Y., Metrop. Opera, 10. XII. 1910.

Fancy, the old Eng. term equivalent to the It. *fantasia*, i.e. a polyphonic comp. for a consort of viols or broken consort or keyboard instrument. F.s had no definitely determined form, but always made considerable use of counterpoint and were generally divided into a number of sections, played without a break but not thematically connected.

Fandango, a Span. dance in lively triple time, prob. S. Amer. in origin, with guitar and castanets prominent in the accomp. A slower, Basque, form also exists, which was adopted by Gluck in the ballet *Don Juan,* and subsequently by Mozart in *Figaro.*

Fandanguillo (Span.), an Andalusian folksong.

Fanelli, Ernest (b. Paris, 29. VI. 1860; d. Paris, 24. XI. 1917), Fr. comp. Studied with Alkan and Delibes at the Paris Cons., but was too poor to make his way as a comp. and became perc. player in an orch. Works incl. *Tableaux symphoniques* (on Gautier's *Roman de la momie*), *Suite rabelaisienne, Impressions pastorales, Les Humoresques* for orch.; string 5tet, etc.

Fanfare, a flourish of tpts., in Fr. also a brass band. F.s have also been written for other instruments, though usually wind and mainly brass, or imitated in any medium (e.g. strings in Purcell's *Dido and Aeneas* or pf. in Debussy's *Feux d'artifice* prelude). In opera F.s have frequently served as an excellent scenic effect (e.g. in Beethoven's *Fidelio,* Bizet's *Carmen,* Verdi's *Otello,* etc.).

Faniska, play with mus. by Cherubini (lib., in Ger., by Josef Sonnleithner), prod. Vienna, Kärntnertortheater, 25. II. 1806.

Fantaisie (Fr.)
Fantasia (It.)　　*See* **Fancy; Fantasy.**
Fantasie (Ger.)

Fantasiestück (Ger. = Fantastic Piece). A short instrumental piece of a free or fantastic character, rather less extended as a rule than a fantasy and keeping to a single movement and mood, whereas the latter is usually in several connected sections.

Fantasio, opera by Ethel Smyth (lib. by comp. based on Musset's play), prod. in Ger., Weimar, 24. V. 1898.

Fantastic Symphony (Berlioz). *See* **Symphonie fantastique.**

Fantasy, an instrumental comp. of a free or fantastic character, in no particular form, usually in a number of linked-up but not thematically connected sections. A F. may also be a comp. based on a chosen mus. theme from another comp.'s work, a folksong, a popular tune, an operatic air, etc.

Faramondo, opera by Handel (lib. by Apostolo Zeno, altered), prod. London, King's Theatre, Haymarket, 3. I. 1738.

Farandole (Fr.), a dance of Provence, prob. of Gk. orig. It is danced by large groups of people in procession through the streets and accomp. by pipe and tabor. The mus. is in 6–8 time, so that the ex. in Bizet's *Arlésienne* mus. is not traditionally correct, though very evocative.

Farce (Eng. and Fr., from Lat. *farcire* = to stuff, to lard). In earlier Eng. the verb had the meaning it still has in Fr. of stuffing food with seasoning, and in mus. it was used for the practice of interpolating words in the *Kyrie eleison*. In 18th-cent. opera, a comic scene introduced into a serious work. Hence a complete comic opera so interpolated, or simply a comic opera in 1 act (It. *farsa*). The modern sense of the term in Eng. (an absurdly comic play) is derived from this.

Farewell, Absence and Return (Beethoven). *See* **Adieux, l'absence et le retour.**

'Farewell' Symphony, nickname of Haydn's symph. No. 45 in F♯ min., comp. in 1772 as a hint to Prince Esterházy that the orch. would welcome leave of absence. In the finale the players leave one by one until only 2 vlns. remain.

Farinelli (real name **Carlo Broschi**) (b. Andria, 24. I. 1705; d. Bologna, 15. VII. 1782), It. male soprano. Pupil of Porpora, in whose *Eumene* he made his début in Rome in 1721. Sang with great success in many Eur. cities, incl. Vienna and London. In the service of the Span. court 1737–59, then retired to Bologna.

Farjeon, Harry (b. Hohokus, New Jersey, 6. V. 1878; d. London, 29. XII. 1948), Eng. comp. Pupil in London of Landon Ronald and others, and later at the R.A.M. where Corder was his comp. master. He taught harmony and comp. there later.
Works incl. opera *Floretta*, operettas *The Registry Office, A Gentleman of the Road; Hans Andersen* suite for small orch.; pf. concerto; string 4tets; vln. and pf. sonatas; suites, preludes and other works for pf.; song cycles and other songs, etc.

Farkas, Ferenc (b. Nagykanizsa, 15. XII. 1905), Hung. comp. Studied at the Budapest Cons. and with Respighi in Rome. After travelling to enlarge his experience and holding 2 posts at provincial schools of mus., he became prof. of comp. at the Acad. of Dramatic Art in Budapest in 1948.
Works incl. opera *Csinom Palkó*; ballet *Three Vagabonds*; incid. mus. (incl. Shakespeare's *Timon of Athens, As You Like It* and *Romeo and Juliet*); cantata *Fountain of St. John*; symph. and other orchestral works, chamber mus., pf. mus., songs, etc.

Farkas, Ödön (b. Jászmonostor, 1851; d. Kolozsvár, 11. IX. 1912), Hung. cond. and comp. Studied at the Acad. of Mus. in Budapest and in 1880 became director of

the Kolozsvár Cons. He had great influence as a teacher.
Works incl. 7 operas, an operetta; church mus., choral and orchestral works, 5 string 4tets and other chamber mus., pf. mus., songs etc.

Farmer, Henry G(eorge). (b. Birr, 17. I. 1882; d. Law, 30. XII. 1965), Ir. mus. scholar. Educ. at Glasgow Univ. He graduated as a scholar in Arabic and hist. and wrote much on Arabian mus. and instruments, ancient Scot. mus., military mus., etc.

Farmer, John (b. ?; d. ?), Eng. 16th–17th-cent. comp. He was (?) in the service of Edward de Vere, Earl of Oxford, and organist from 1595 of Christ Church Cathedral at Dublin until 1599, when he went to London. He wrote a treatise on the polyphonic setting of plainsong tunes.
Works incl. psalm tunes set for 4 voices contrib. to East's Psalter; madrigals; instrumental pieces, etc.

Farnaby, Giles (b. *c.* 1565; d. London, XI. 1640), Eng. comp. He lived in London, where he married in 1587, and took the B.Mus. at Oxford in 1592.
Works incl. 20 canzonets for 4 and 1 for 8 voices, madrigals; psalm tunes set for 4 voices in East's Psalter; over 50 virginal pieces, etc.

Farnaby, Richard (b. London, *c.* 1594; d. ?), Eng. comp., son of prec. In 1608 he became apprentice to Sir Nicholas Saunderson of Fillingham, Lincs.; in 1614 he married. 4 keyboard pieces were incl. in the Fitzwilliam Virginal book (q.v.), compiled by Francis Tregian, who d. in 1619.

Farquhar, George (1678–1707), Ir. dramatist. *See* **Eccles** (*Stage Coach*), **Finger** (*Sir Harry Wildair*), **Leveridge** (*Constant Couple, Recruiting Officer, Love and a Bottle*), **Purcell (D.)** (*Beaux's Stratagem, Constant Couple, Inconstant*).

Farrant, John (b. ?; d. ?), Eng. organist and comp. Organist of Ely Cathedral from 1567 to 1572, when he married Margaret Andras at Salisbury, where he became lay clerk and choirmaster at the cathedral. In 1587 he was app. organist but he was expelled in 1592 for an attack made on the dean. He then became organist of Hereford Cathedral, but lost that post too in 1593 because of his ungovernable temper. Wrote church mus.

Farrant, John (b. Salisbury, IX. 1575; d. Salisbury, 1618), Eng. organist and comp., son of prec. He became a choir-boy at the cathedral under his father, and later organist, holding the post in 1598–1606 and 1611–16, prob. without any interruption between. Wrote church mus.

Farrant, Richard (b. ?; d. Windsor or Greenwich, 1581), Eng. organist and comp. Gentleman of the Chapel Royal in London until 1564, when he became organist and choirmaster at St. George's Chapel, Windsor.

Works incl. Service in A min. (usually sung in G min.), anthems *Call to remembrance* and *Hide not Thou Thy face* and other church mus.; songs for plays prod. by him with the choir-boys before Queen Elizabeth; keyboard pieces in the Mulliner Book (q.v.), etc.

Farrar, Geraldine (b. Melrose, Mass., 28. II. 1882; d. Ridgefield, Conn., 11. III. 1967), Amer. soprano. Studied first in Boston and later in Paris and Berlin, making her début in 1901. From 1906 to 1922 she sang at the N.Y. Metropolitan Opera, and on retiring became a concert singer. Her most famous role was that of Madame Butterfly.

Farrenc (*née* Dumont), **Louise** (b. Paris, 31. V. 1804; d. Paris, 15. IX. 1875), Fr. pianist and comp., wife of Jacques Hippolyte Aristide Farrenc (1794–1865), flautist, writer on mus. and pub. Pupil of Reicha, Hummel & Moscheles, she married in 1821, toured with her husband and was prof. of pf. at the Paris Cons. 1842–73. Ed. the *Trésor des pianistes* with her husband, and her pf. works were favourably noticed by Schumann.

Works incl. 3 symphs., 3 overtures; chamber mus.; vln. and cello sonatas; studies, sonatas, etc. for pf., etc.

Farsa (or **Farsa per musica**) (It. = farce [for mus.]), an It. term of the early 19th cent. for a type of comic opera in 1 act, e.g. Rossini's *La cambiale di matrimonio*.

Farthyng, Thomas (b. ?; d. ?), Eng. 15th–16th-cent. comp. At King's Coll., Cambridge as chorister, 1477–83, and as clerk, 1493–9. At the Chapel Royal, 1511–20. Comp. church mus. and secular songs.

Farwell, Arthur (b. St. Paul, 23. IV. 1872; d. N.Y., 20. I. 1952), Amer. comp. and educationist. Studied engineering, but afterwards went to Ger. as a pupil of Humperdinck and Pfitzner and to Guilmant in Paris. On returning to U.S.A. in 1899 he began to collect Indian folk mus., and became a mus. lecturer, critic and pub. Prof. in the mus. dept. of the Michigan State Coll., 1927–39.

Works incl. masque *Caliban* for the Shakespeare tercentenary; symph., Symbolistic Studies (No. 3 based on Whitman), suite *The Gods of the Mountain, Prelude to a Spiritual Drama* and other orch. works; symph. song suite *Mountain Song* and other choral works; string 4tet; pf. 5tet; sonatas for vln. solo and for vln. and pf.; vln. pieces; pf. works, etc.

Fasch, Carl Friedrich (Christian) (b. Zerbst, 18. XI. 1736; d. Berlin, 3. VIII. 1800), Ger. harpsichordist and comp. Pupil of his father and later of Hertel at Strelitz. App. 2nd harpsichordist (with

C. P. E. Bach) to the court of Frederick the Great in 1756, but the outbreak of the Seven Years War (1756–63) cost him his position and forced him to live by teaching. Cond. of the court opera in Berlin 1774–6. In 1791 he founded the Berlin *Singakademie*, the choral society which he cond. until his death.

Works incl. oratorio *Giuseppe riconosciuto*, Mass for 16 voices, cantatas, psalms and other church mus.; also some instrumental mus.

Fasch, Johann Friedrich (b. Büttelstedt nr. Weimar, 15. IV. 1688; d. Zerbst, 5. XII. 1758), Ger. organist and comp., father of prec. Pupil of Kuhnau at St. Thomas's School, Leipzig. He founded the 'Collegium musicum' at Leipzig, travelled after 1714, held var. posts at Gera, Greitz and in the service of Count Morzin at Lukaveč, Boh., and in 1722 was app. *Kapellmeister* at Zerbst.

Works incl. 3 operas; Masses, a Requiem, church cantatas, motets, a Passion; overtures; trios, sonatas, etc.

Fasolo, Giovanni Battista (b. Asti, ?; d. ?), It. 17th-cent. monk, organist and comp. He became a Franciscan *c.* 1645 and in 1659 was app. *maestro di cappella* to the Archbishop of Monreale at Palermo.

Works incl. *Arie spirituali*, cantatas, ariettas, sacred and secular songs; org. works; guitar pieces, etc.

Faugues, Guillermus (also **Vincent F.**) (b. ?; d. ?), Fr. or Flem. 15th-cent. comp. Of his 3 surviving Masses one is based on 'L'Homme armé', and another is described as 'super basse dance'.

Fauré, Gabriel (Urbain) (b. Pamiers nr. Foix, 12. V. 1845; d. Paris, 4. XI. 1924), Fr. comp. Studied at Niedermeyer's school of mus. in Paris, 1854–66, and became church organist at Rennes in the latter year. Returned to Paris in 1870, became organist 1st at Saint-Sulpice and then at Saint-Honoré, and choirmaster at the Madeleine in 1877, being app. organist there in 1896, a post he held until 1905, when he became director of the Cons., where he had been prof. since 1896. He resigned in 1920. He had many distinguished comp. pupils.

Works incl. mus.-drama *Prométhée*, opera *Pénélope*; incid. mus. *Caligula* (Dumas), *Shylock* (*Merchant of Venice*: Shakespeare), *La Voix du bonheur* (G. Clemenceau), *Pelléas et Mélisande* (Maeterlinck); *Pavane*, suite *Masques et bergamasques*, etc. for orch; symph. (unpub.); *Ballade & Fantaisie* for pf. and orch., *Romance* for vln. and orch.; 2 pf. 5tets, 2 pf. 4tets; string 4tet; pf. trio; 2 sonatas for vln. and pf., 2 sonatas for cello and pf.; pieces for vln. and pf., cello and pf. and fl. and pf.; *Cantique de Racine* and *Les Djinns* (Hugo) for chorus and orch.; *La Naissance*

Faure Favart

de Venus for solo voices, chorus and orch.;
Madrigal for vocal 4tet; Requiem for solo
voices, chorus and orch.; *Messe basse* for
fem. voices and org.; 11 miscellaneous
religious vocal pieces; 34 op. nos. of pf.
mus. incl. 3 *Romances sans paroles*, 5
Impromptus, 13 Barcarolles, 4 Valses-
caprices, 8 Nocturnes, Theme and Variations, 8 *Pièces brèves*, 9 Preludes; *Dolly*, 6
pieces for pf. duet; 96 songs incl. cycles
Poème d'un jour, 5 *Mélodies de Verlaine*, *La
Bonne Chanson* (Verlaine), *La Chanson
d'Ève* (Charles van Lerberghe), *Le Jardin
clos* (do.), *Mirages*, *L'Horizon chimérique*,
etc.

Faure, Jean-Baptiste (b. Moulins, 15.
I. 1830; d. Paris, 9. XI. 1914), Fr. baritone.
Studied at the Paris Cons. Made his 1st
appearance at the Opéra-Comique in 1852
and from 1861 was attached for many
years to the Opéra.

Faust. *See also* **Adam (A.)** (ballet),
Arnold (S.) (*Harlequin Dr. Faustus*),
Damnation de Faust (Berlioz), **Doktor
Faust** (Busoni), **Goethe; Lenau; Marlowe;
Mefistofele** (Boito), **Petit Faust** (Hervé),
Reutter (H.) (*Doktor F.*), **Szenen aus
Goethes 'Faust'** (Schumann).

Ballet by Costa, Panizza and Bajetti
(choreography by Jules Perrot), prod.
Milan, Teatro alla Scala, 12. II. 1848.

Episodes from Lenau's *Faust*: 2 orch.
pieces by Liszt, *Night Procession* and
Dance in the Village Inn (1st *Mephisto
Waltz*), comp. *c.* 1860, 1st perf. Weimar,
8. III. 1861.

Opera by Gounod (lib. by Jules Barbier
and Michel Carré, based on Goethe's
drama), prod. Paris, Théâtre Lyrique, 19.
III. 1859.

Opera by Spohr (lib. by Joseph Karl
Bernard, founded on the Faust legend
without ref. to Goethe's work, not completed at that time), prod. Prague, 1. IX.
1816.

Opera by Zöllner (lib. by comp., based
on Goethe's drama), prod. Munich, 19.
X. 1887.

Overture by Wagner, not for Goethe's
drama, but a kind of symph. poem on it,
comp. Paris, XI. 1839–40 after hearing
Beethoven's symphs. at the Cons.; 1st
perf. Dresden, 22. VII. 1844; rewritten
1854–5 and perf. at Zürich, 23. I. 1855.

Faust-Symphonie, Eine, symph. by Liszt,
based on Goethe's drama, 'in 3 character
pictures': 1. *Faust*; 2. *Gretchen*; 3. *Mephis-
topheles*, with final chor. 'Alles Vergäng-
liche ist nur ein Gleichnis'; finished
without the chorus, 19. X. 1854, chorus
added 1857 and revised 1880; 1st perf.
Weimar, Court Theatre, 5. IX. 1857, on
the occasion of the unveiling of the Goethe-
Schiller monument. The work is ded. to
Berlioz.

Fausta (i.e. Empress F., wife of Con-

stantine I), opera by Donizetti (lib. by
Domenico Gilardoni), prod. Naples,
Teatro San Carlo, 12. I. 1832.

Fausto (*Faust*), opera by Louise Angélique Bertin (1805–77) (lib., in It., by
comp., based on Goethe's drama), prod.
Paris, Théâtre Italien, 8. III. 1831. The 1st
It. *Faust* opera and the only one by a
woman. B. was the daughter of Berlioz's
ed. of the *Journal des Débats*: he may have
had a hand in the work; at any rate he
almost certainly suggested the subject.

Faut (= Fa ut). *See* **Gamut**.

Fauvel, Roman de, a satirical poem
written in two parts (1310 and 1314) by
Gervais de Bus. One MS. (Paris, Bibl. Nat.,
fr. 146) incorporates mus. interpolations
inserted by Chaillou de Pesstain in 1316.
The most important of these are 33 motets
in 2 and 3 parts, but there are numerous
other pieces, sacred and secular, polyphonic and monophonic.

Faux Lord, Le (*The False Lord*), opera
by Piccinni (lib. by Giuseppe Maria
Piccinni, the comp.'s son), prod. Paris,
Comédie-Italienne, 6. XII. 1783.

Fauxbourdon (Fr.), **Faburden** (Eng.),
Falsobordone (It.), lit. 'false bass', name
given to a wide variety of technical procedures in the 15th–16th cents., usually
involving improvisation. As originally used
by Dufay and others, the term implied the
use of chains of 6–3 chords, the middle
part being 'improvised' by doubling the
top part a 4th lower throughout; later,
different techniques were employed to
achieve the same effect. The Eng. used
their version of the word for a similar
process, the 3 parts being improvised
straight from plainsong (at first in the
middle, later in the top part). The F. itself
(i.e. the lowest part) was also used as the
basis of entirely new compositions.

In the later 15th and early 16th cents. the
use of the term in both Fr. and Eng. was
enormously extended to include techniques
in which the idea of 6–3 chords was
entirely lost. It is to this final stage in its
hist. that the It. use of the term belongs,
meaning initially a kind of F. in 4 parts
with the 'true' bass supplied beneath the
false one, and ultimately nothing more than
simple declamatory comp. in note-against-
note style.

Favart, Charles Simon (1710–92). Fr.
playwright and librettist. *See* **Bastien und
Bastienne** (Mozart), **Cythère assiégée**
(Gluck), **Lottchen am Hofe** (J. A. Hiller),
Moissonneurs (Duni), **Rosina** (Shield),
Süssmayr (*Soliman II*).

Favart (*née Duronceray*), **Marie Justine
Benoiste** (b. Avignon, 15. VI. 1727; d.
Paris, 21. IV. 1772), Fr. dancer, actress and
singer, wife of prec. After making her
début as a dancer in 1744, she married
Favart in 1745 and in 1751 joined the

Favola d'Orfeo

Félix

Comédie-Italienne. In 1753 she appeared in her own *Bastien et Bastienne* (the direct model for Mozart's little opera), a parody of Rousseau's *Devin du village* with popular tunes in the style of a ballad opera.

Favola d'Orfeo, La (*The Story of Orpheus*), opera by Casella (lib. by Angelo Ambrogini = Poliziano, prod. Mantua, ducal court, 18. VII. 1472, with mus. by one Germi), prod. Venice, Teatro Goldoni, 6. IX. 1932.
Opera by Monteverdi (lib. by Alessandro Striggio), prod. Mantua, at the court of the Hereditary Prince Francesco Gonzaga, Carnival 1607.

Favola per musica (It. = story for mus.), an early It. term for opera of a legendary or mythological character; actually a story of that kind in dramatic form written for the purpose of being set to mus.

Favorite, La, opera by Donizetti (lib., in Fr., by Alphonse Royer and Gustave Vaëz, with Scribe's assistance), prod. Paris, Opéra, 2. XII. 1840.

Fawkyner (b. ?; d. ?), Eng. 15th–16th-cent. comp. repres. in the Eton Choirbook (q.v.).

Faydit, Gaucelm (b. Uzerche, Limousin, *c.* 1150; d. *c.* 1216), Fr. troubadour. He went to the Holy Land with Richard Cœur de Lion.

Fayrfax, Robert (b. *c.* 1465; d. St. Albans, 24. X. 1521), Eng. comp. Lived for a time (?) at Bayford, Herts., and became organist and choirmaster at St. Albans Cathedral before 1502, when he took the D.Mus. degree at Oxford. On the accession of Henry VIII in 1509 he was a Gentleman of the Chapel Royal, with which he attended at the Field of the Cloth of Gold in 1520.
Works incl. Masses, motets, Magnificats, *Stabat Mater*; songs for several voices, etc.

Feast at Solhaug, The, incid. mus. for Ibsen's play by H. Wolf for a prod. of a Ger. trans. by Emma Klingenfeld, Vienna, 1891.

Fedé, Jehan (b. Douai, ?; d. ?), 15th-cent. Fr. comp. He was vicar of Douai, 1439–40, a papal singer, 1443–5; at the Sainte Chapelle, 1449; at the court of Charles VII, 1452–3; at St. Peter's, Rome, 1466; and a member of Louis XI's chapel, 1473–4. He wrote sacred and secular mus.

Fedele. *See* **Treu, Daniel Gottlieb.**

Federici, Camillo (1749–1802), It. actor and playwright. *See* **Cambiale di matrimonio** (Rossini).

Fedora, opera by Giordano (lib. by Arturo Colautti, based on Sardou's play), prod. Milan, Teatro Lirico, 17. XI. 1898.

Fedra (*Phaedra*), opera by Pizzetti (lib. Gabriele d'Annunzio's tragedy), prod. Milan, Teatro alla Scala, 20. III. 1915.
Opera by Romani (lib. by Alfredo

Lenzoni), prod. Rome, Teatro Costanzi, 3. IV. 1915.

Fée Urgèle, La, ou Ce qui plaît aux dames (*The Fairy U., or What Pleases the Ladies*), opera by Duni (lib. by Charles Simon Favart, based on a story by Voltaire founded on Chaucer's *Tale of the Wife of Bath*), prod. Fontainebleau, at court, 26. X. 1765; 1st perf. Paris, Comédie-Italienne, 4. XII. 1765.

Feen, Die (*The Fairies*), opera by Wagner (lib. by comp., based on Gozzi's comedy, *La Donna serpente*), comp. 1833 and not staged in Wagner's lifetime; prod. Munich, 29. VI. 1888.

Feinberg, Samuel Evgenievich (b. Odessa, 26. V. 1890; d. Moscow, 23. X. 1962), Rus. pianist and comp. Studied at the Moscow Cons. under Skriabin and Miaskovsky.
Works incl. 3 pf. concertos, 11 pf. sonatas, 2 fantasies and other pf. pieces, songs, etc., to words by Pushkin and others, folksong arrs., etc.

Feis Ceoil. An Ir. mus. festival founded in 1897 on the model of the Welsh Eisteddfod, held annually, generally at Dublin.

Fel, Marie (b. Bordeaux, 24. X. 1713; d. Chaillot nr. Paris, 2. II. 1794), Fr. soprano. Made her 1st appearance at the Paris Opéra and at the Concert spirituel in 1734.

Felderhof, Jan (b. Bussum, 25. IX. 1907), Dutch comp.
Works incl. opera *Serenade on St. John's Night*; symph., 2 sinfoniettas, *Dance Rhapsody* for orch.; Rhapsody for ob. and orch.; 3 string 4tets, 1 pf. trio; 2 vln. and pf. sonatas, cello and pf. sonata, suite for fl. and pf., etc.

Feldman, Morton (b. New York, 12. I. 1926), Amer. comp. Studied with Stefan Wolpe and Wallingford Riegger. Influenced by abstract expressionist painting, he intro. the element of chance into his mus., indicating often only an approximation of what is to be played.
Works incl. *Durations I–V*; *Extensions I–V*; *Vertical Thoughts I–V*; *Two Instruments* for cello and horn; *For Franz Kline* for soprano, vln., cello, horn, chimes and pf.; *De Kooning* for pf., cello, vln., horn and perc.; ballet *Ixion*; *The Swallows of Salangan* for chorus and 76 instruments.

Feldpartie
or ⎬ (Ger. lit. field suite), an old
Feldpartita
Ger. term for suites written for wind instruments and played in the open on military or war-like occasions.

Felis, Stefano (b. Bari, *c.* 1550; d. ? Bari, after 1603), It. comp. Wrote Masses, motets, madrigals, *villanelle*, etc.

Félix, ou L'Enfant trouvé (*Felix, or The Foundling*), opera by Monsigny (lib. by Jean Michel Sedaine), prod. Fontainebleau, at court, 10. XI. 1777; 1st Paris perf., Comédie-Italienne, 24. XI. 1777. Monsigny's last opera.

Fellerer, Karl (Gustav) (b. Freising, Bavaria, 7. VII. 1902), Ger. mus. scholar. Studied at the Ratisbon School of Church Mus. and at Munich and Berlin. Lecturer at the Univ. of Münster in 1927 and now prof. of mus. at Cologne Univ. Has written esp. on Catholic church mus.

Fellowes, Edmund H(orace). (b. London, 11. XI. 1870; d. Windsor, 21. XII. 1951), Eng. clergyman and musicologist. Educ. at Winchester Coll. and Oxford. Attached to St. George's Chapel, Windsor, as minor canon from 1900. Hon. Mus.D., Dublin, 1917 and Oxford, 1938. Author of books on the Eng. madrigal, Byrd and O. Gibbons; ed. of *The Eng. Madrigal School*, Eng. lutenist songs, Byrd's works and co-ed. of *Tudor Church Mus.*

Felsztynski, Sebastian (b. Felsztyn nr. Przemysl, *c*. 1490; d. ?, *c*. 1544), Pol. comp. Studied at Cracow Univ. He compiled a hymn-book for Sigismund I in 1522. Comp. church mus.

Felton, William (b. Drayton, 1715; d. Hereford, 6. XII. 1769), Eng. organist and comp. Educ. at Manchester and Cambridge, he became a clergyman, vicarchoral and later minor canon at Hereford Cathedral. He became famous as perf. on the organ and harpsichord, for which he wrote concertos and lessons. The celebrated *Felton's Gavotte* was a set of variations in one of the concertos.

Feminine Cadence, a cadence in which the conclusive tonic chord is reached on a weak beat of the bar.

Fenby, Eric (William) (b. Scarborough, 22. IV. 1906), Eng. comp. Became an organist at the age of 12 and studied mus. with A. E. Keeton. From 1928–34 he acted voluntarily as amanuensis to Delius, who was living blind and paralysed at Grez-sur-Loing, and helped him to commit his last works to paper until his death.

Works incl. symph., overture *Rossini on Ilkla Moor*, etc.

Fénelon, François (de Salignac de La Mothe) (1651–1715), Fr. archbishop, moralist and author. *See* Schürmann (*Télémaque*).

Fenney, William (b. Birmingham, 21. V. 1891; d. Epsom, *c*. VII. 1957), Eng. comp. Pupil of Bantock at the Birmingham and Midland School of Mus.

Works incl. *Avon Romance, Dawn, In Shadow, Vision of Ancient Empire* for orch.; suite for strings; 2 string 4tets, pf. trio; sonatina for vln. and pf.; instrumental pieces; songs, part-songs, etc.

Fennimore und Gerda, opera by Delius (lib., in Ger., by comp., based on Jens Peter Jacobsen's novel *Niels Lyhne*), prod. Frankfurt, 21. X. 1919.

Fenton (real name **Beswick**), **Lavinia** (b. London, 1708; d. Greenwich 24. I. 1760), Eng. soprano and actress. Made her 1st appearance at the King's Theatre in London in 1726 and was the 1st Polly in *The Beggar's Opera* in 1728. She retired at the end of the season and became the mistress of the Duke of Bolton, who married her on the death of his wife in 1751.

Feo, Francesco (b. Naples, 1691; d. Naples, 28. I. 1761), It. comp. Pupil of Gizzi and Fago at the Cons. della Pietà della Turchini in Naples, and later of Pitoni in Rome. Prod. his first opera in Naples, 1713. *Maestro di cappella* of the Cons. St. Onofrio, 1723–8, and of the Cons. dei Poveri, 1739–43. Jommelli and Pergolesi were among his pupils.

Works incl. operas *L'Amor tirannico, Siface, Ipermestra* and others; Masses and other church mus., etc.

Feragut (or **Feraguti**), **Beltrame** (or **Bertrand**) (b. ?; d. ?), Fr. 15th-cent. comp., who travelled in Burgundy and It. His motet *Excelsa civitas Vincencia* was written in honour of a new bishop of Vicenza, Francesco Malipiero, in 1433. A few other sacred works survive.

Feramors, opera by A. Rubinstein (lib., in Ger., by Julius Rodenberg, based on Moore's *Lalla Rookh*), prod. Dresden, 24. II. 1863.

Ferguson, Howard (b. Belfast, 21. X. 1908), Ir. comp. Educ. at Westminster School and the R.C.M. in London as a pupil of R. O. Morris.

Works incl. ballet *Chaunteclear*; partita and 4 *Diversions on Ulster Airs* for orch.; concerto for pf. and strings; octet; 2 vln. and pf. sonatas, 4 pieces for clar. and pf.; sonata and 5 bagatelles for pf.; 2 ballads for baritone and orch.; 3 *Medieval Carols* for voice and pf., etc.

Fermata (It.) = pause, indicated by the sign ⌒, prolonging a note or rest beyond its normal length. For very short pauses a square sign was invented by Vincent d'Indy, but this device never found general acceptance.

In *da capo* arias the F. sign over the final chord of the 1st section indicates where the aria is to end after the repeat.

In a chorale, or a chorale prelude, it indicates the end of a line.

Fernand Cortez, ou La Conquête de Mexique (*Hernán Cortés, or The Conquest of Mexico*), opera by Spontini (lib. by Joseph Alphonse Esménard and Victor Joseph Étienne de Jouy, based on a tragedy by Piron), prod. Paris, Opéra, 28. XI. 1809.

Fernandez, Oscar Lorenzo (b. Rio de Janeiro, 4. XI. 1897; d. Rio de Janeiro, 26. VIII. 1948), Braz. comp. He studied pf. as well as comp. at Rio and won a comp. prize in 1924. App. director of the Braz. Cons. in 1936.

Works incl. opera *Malazarte*; Symph. Suite on popular themes, Indian poem *Imbapara* and *Reisado do pastoreio* for orch.; suite for wind 5tet; *Trio brasileiro* for vln., cello and pf.; over 100 pf. pieces; songs, etc.

Fernando, operetta by Schubert (lib. by Albert Stadler), comp. 1815; never perf. in Schubert's lifetime; prod. Magdeburg, 18. VIII. 1918.

Ferne Klang, Der (*The Far-off Sound*), opera by Schreker (lib. by comp.), prod. Frankfurt, 18. VIII. 1912.

Ferrabosco, Eng. family of musicians, later members:

1. Alfonso F. (b. ? Greenwich, *c.* 1620; d. ? London, before 1660), son of Alfonso, jun. Violist and wind player at court.

2. Henry F. (b. ? Greenwich, *c.* 1623; d. ? Jamaica, *c.* 1658), brother of prec. Succeeded his father as comp. to the King's Mus.

3. John F. (b. ? Greenwich, 1626; d. ? London, X. 1682), brother of prec. Wind player at court; app. organist at Ely Cathedral in 1662. Comp. services and anthems.

4. Elizabeth F. (b. Greenwich, 1640; d. ?), singer, daughter of 1.

Ferrabosco, Alfonso (b. Bologna, I. 1543; d. Bologna, 12. VIII. 1588), It. comp. Settled in London before 1562; left the service of Queen Elizabeth in 1569 and returned to It. on leave, which he extended until 1572. In 1578 he left Eng. for good and entered the service of the Duke of Savoy at Turin.

Works incl. motets, madrigals, etc.

Ferrabosco, Alfonso (b. Greenwich, *c.* 1575; d. Greenwich, III. 1628), Eng. comp. of It. descent, son of prec. He was left behind, being prob. illegitimate, when his father left Eng. in 1578. Trained in mus. (?) at Queen Elizabeth's expense, he became one of James I's court musicians.

Works incl. masques (Ben Jonson) *The Masque of Blackness*, *Hymenaei*, *The Masque of Beauty*, *The Hue and Cry after Cupid*, *The Masque of Queens*, *Love freed from Ignorance and Folly*; fancies for viols; lessons for lyra viol; ayres with lute and bass viol.; contribs. to Leighton's *Teares or Lamentacions*, etc.

Ferrabosco, Domenico Maria (b. Bologna, ? 14. XI. 1513; d. Bologna, ? II. 1574), It. comp., grandfather of prec. *Maestro di cappella* of the church of San Petronio at Bologna. App. to a similar post at the Vatican basilica in Rome, 1546; was a singer in the Papal Chapel there, 1550–5.

Works incl. motets, madrigals, etc.

Ferrarese del Bene (*née* **Gabrieli**), **Adrianna** (b. Ferrara, *c.* 1755; d. ? Venice, after 1798), It. soprano. Pupil of the Ospedaletto at Venice, married to one Del Bene and called La Ferrarese. Appeared in

London in 1785–6 and in Vienna in 1788–1791. The 1st Fiordiligi in Mozart's *Così fan tutte*, 1790.

Ferrari, Benedetto (b. Reggio, 1597; d. Modena, 22. X. 1681), It. theorbist, playwright and comp. Lived at Venice, where he began to prod. mus. dramas with words and mus. of his own in 1637. In 1645 he went to the court of Modena, where he remained until 1662, except for a visit to Vienna in 1651–3. He was then dismissed, but app. again in 1674.

Works incl. operas *Armida*, *La ninfa avara*, *Il pastor regio*, *Proserpina rapita* and others; oratorio *Sansone*; 3 books of *Musiche varie a voce sola*, etc.

Ferrari, Domenico (b. Piacenza, *c.* 1722; d. Paris, 1780), It. violinist. Pupil of Tartini. Won great acclaim on concert tours as one of the leading players of his time. Worked in Vienna and Stuttgart, and finally settled in Paris. Pub. 36 vln. sonatas, trio-sonatas, etc.

Ferrari, Gustave (b. Geneva, 28. IX. 1872; d. Geneva, 29. VII. 1948), Swiss pianist, writer on mus. and comp. Settled in London in 1901. Accompanist to Yvette Guilbert. Wrote incid. mus. for Shakespeare's *Hamlet* for Irving's prod. in 1905, songs, etc.

Ferreira, Manuel (b. ?; d. ?), Span. 18th-cent. comp. and cond. Attached to a Madrid theatre for which he wrote incid. mus. for plays and light operas which are early exs. of *tonadillas*.

Works incl. opera *El mayor triunfo de la mayor guerra*, numerous light operas, incid. mus. to plays by Calderón, Moreto, etc., incl. Antonio de Zamora's *Don Juan* play.

Ferretti, Giovanni (b. *c.* 1540; d. Loreto, *c.* 1605), It. comp. and priest. Apart from a few sacred works, he specialized in the lighter types of madrigal, publishing 5 books of *Canzoni alla Napolitana* (1573–1585).

Ferri, Baldassare (b. Perugia, 9. XII. 1610; d. Perugia, 8. IX. 1680), It. castrato. In 1625 he went to the court of Pol. and later to that of the Emperors Ferdinand III and Leopold I.

Ferrier, Kathleen (b. Higher Walton, Lancs., 22. IV. 1912; d. London, 8. X. 1953), Eng. contralto. Studying the pf. at 1st and taking a diploma for it, she turned to singing in 1940 and sang in factories during the war. Made her operatic début in Britten's *Rape of Lucretia* at Glyndebourne in 1946 and sang Gluck's Orpheus there and in Amsterdam and U.S.A. She toured very extensively, sang at the Edinburgh and Salzburg Festivals, and gave song recitals accomp. by Bruno Walter. Received the C.B.E. and sang in *Orfeo* again at Covent Garden on 20. II. 1953, but was by then so ill that she had to withdraw.

Ferroud, Pierre (Octave) (b. Chasselay, Rhône, 6. I. 1900; d. Debrecen, Hung., 17. VIII. 1936), Fr. comp. and critic. Pupil of Ropartz and Florent Schmitt. He was killed in a motor accident. Works incl. opera *Chirurgie*; ballets *Jeunesse* and *Le Porcher*; symph. in A maj., *Foules, Au Parc Monceau* and *Types* for orch.; trio for wind instruments; sonatas for vln. and pf. and cello and pf.; *Trois Chansons de fou* for voice and orch.; choruses for female voices; pf. pieces, songs, etc.

Fervaal, opera by d'Indy (lib. by comp., based on and altered from Tegnér's *Axel*), prod. Brussels, Théâtre de la Monnaie, 12. III. 1897.

Fesca, Friedrich Ernst (b. Magdeburg, 15. II. 1789; d. Carlsruhe, 24. V. 1826), Ger. violinist and comp., ? of It. descent. Works incl. operas *Cantemira* and *Leila*; *De profundis*; 3 symphs.; 19 string 4tets, etc.

Fesch, Willem de (b. Alkmaar, 1687; d. London, 3. I. 1761), Dutch violinist and comp. *Maître de chapelle* at Antwerp Cathedral 1725–30, settled in London 1732, where he became known as a vln. teacher and comp. of oratorios. Works incl. operetta *The London 'Prentice*, serenata *Love and Friendship*; oratorios *Judith* and *Joseph*; sonatas for cello(s) and a large quantity of other chamber mus.

Festa, Costanzo (b. Piedmont, *c.* 1490; d. Rome, 10. IV. 1545), It. comp. Became a member of the Papal choir in Rome, 1517, and later *maestro di cappella* at the Vatican. Comp. Masses, Magnificat, Litanies, motets, Te Deum; madrigals, etc.

Festa teatrale (It. = theatrical feast or festival), an 18th-cent. type of opera of a festive kind, esp. one expressly written for an occasion, such as a royal or princely patron's wedding. The subject of the lib. was usually mythological and allegorical.

Festes. *See also* **Fêtes.**

Festes de l'Amour et de Bacchus, Les (*The Feasts of Cupid and Bacchus*), pastorale by Lully (lib. by Quinault, with Molière and Isaac de Benserade), prod. Paris, Opéra, 15. XI. 1672.

Festes de Thalie, Les (*Thalia's Feasts*), opera-ballet by Mouret (lib. by Joseph de Lafont), prod. Paris, Opéra, 19. VIII. 1714.

Festes vénitiennes, Les (*The Venetian Feasts*), opera by Campra (lib. by Antoine Danchet), prod. Paris, Opéra, 17. VI. 1710.

Festin de l'araignée, Le (*The Spider's Feast*), ballet by Roussel (choreography by Gilbert de Voisins, based on Henri Fabre's *Souvenirs entomologiques*), prod. Paris, Théâtre des Arts, 3. IV. 1913.

Festing, Michael (Christian) (b. ?, 1680; d. London, 24. VII. 1752), Eng. violinist and comp., ? of Ger. birth or descent. Pupil of Geminiani in London. Made his 1st appearance there about 1724 and became a member of the King's Band in 1735. Mus. director of the It. Opera in 1737 and of Ranelagh Gardens from 1742. Works incl. Paraphrase of the 3rd chapter of Habakkuk, Milton's *Song on May Morning*, Addison's Ode for St. Cecilia's Day and other odes, cantatas; symphs., concertos and sonatas for var. instruments; songs, etc.

Festschrift (Ger. = festival writing[s]), a vol. containing musicological essays written by various authors as a tribute to an eminent colleague or master on some anniversary occasion.

Fête galante, opera by Ethel Smyth (lib. by Edward Shanks, based on a story by Maurice Baring), prod. Birmingham Repertory Theatre, 4. VI. 1923.

Fêtes. *See also* **Festes.**

Fêtes d'Hébé, Les, ou Les Talens lyriques (*Hebe's Feasts, or The Lyrical Gifts*), opera-ballet by Rameau (lib. by Antoine Gautier de Montdorge), prod. Paris, Opéra, 21. V. 1739.

Fétis, François Joseph (b. Mons, 25. III. 1784; d. Brussels, 26. III. 1871), Belg. musicologist. App. prof. at the Paris Cons., 1821, and librarian, 1827. Director of the Brussels Cons. from 1833. Author of a *Biographie universelle des musiciens*, an *Histoire générale de la musique* and many theoret. works. He also comp. several operas.

Feuermann, Emanuel (b. Kolomyja nr. Lwów, 22. XI. 1902; d. New York, 25. V. 1942), Aus. cellist. Made his 1st appearance as a boy in 1914, later travelled and studied with Klengel at Leipzig and became prof. at the Cologne Cons., at 16. In 1929–33 prof. in Berlin, in succession to Hugo Becker; driven to U.S.A. by the Nazi régime.

Feuersnot (*The Dearth of Fire*), opera by R. Strauss (lib. by Ernst von Wolzogen), prod. Dresden, 21. XI. 1901.

Feuillet, Octave (1821–90), Fr. novelist and dramatist. *See* **Petrella** (*Contessa d'Amalfi*).

Fevin, Antoine de (b. ? Arras, *c.* 1474; d. Blois, I. 1512), Fr. comp. Wrote Masses, motets, Magnificats, Lamentations, etc.

Fevin, Robert de (b. Cambrai, ?; d. ?), Fr. 15th–16th-cent. comp. In the service of the Duke of Savoy early in the 16th cent. Wrote Masses, etc.

Février, Henri (b. Paris, 2. X. 1875; d. Paris, 8. VII. 1957), Fr. comp. Studied under Massenet and Fauré at the Paris Cons. Works incl. operas *Monna Vanna* (after Maeterlinck), *Ghismonda, La Damnation de Blanchefleur, La Femme nue, L'Île* *désenchantée*, operetta *Sylvette* (with Delmas); comic operas *Le Roi aveugle*, *Agnès dame galante*, *Carmosine* (after Musset); songs, etc.

ff (abbr.) = *fortissimo* = loudest. Although the sign indicates a superlative, it can be further multiplied to demand even greater loudness of tone.

ff **Holes (or *f* Holes),** the Sound-holes of instruments of the vln. family, so called because of their shape.

Ffrangcon-Davies, David (Thomas) (b. Bethesda, Carnarvon, 11. XII. 1855; d. London, 13. IV. 1918), Welsh baritone. Studied at G.S.M., London, and made his 1st appearance with the Carl Rosa Opera Co. in 1890, but later became mainly a concert singer.

Fiati (It., from *fiato* = breath), wind instruments.

Fibich, Zdeněk (b. Šerbořice nr. Čáslav, 21. XII. 1850; d. Prague, 15. X. 1900), Cz. comp. Very precociously gifted, he studied at the Leipzig Cons. under Carl Richter and Jadassohn, also Moscheles for the pf. Later in Paris and Mannheim. After teaching in Pol. for a time, he returned to Cz. in 1874 and cond. at the Nat. Theatre in Prague. He soon retired to devote himself entirely to comp. and wrote over 600 works of var. kinds.

Works incl. operas *Bukovín*, *Blaník*, *The Bride of Messina* (after Schiller), *The Tempest* (after Shakespeare), *Hedy* (after Byron's *Don Juan*), *Šárka*, *Pad Arkuna*; melodramas *Christmas Eve*, *Eternity*, *The Water-Sprite*, *Queen Emma*, *Haakon* and the trilogy *Hippodamia*; incid. mus. to Vrchlický's comedy *A Night at Karlstein*; 3 symphs., overtures, symph. poems *Othello* and *The Tempest* (both after Shakespeare) and 4 others; 2 string 4tets, pf. 4tet, pf. trio, 5tet for pf., vln., cello, clar. and horn; pf. sonata, 350 pieces *Moods, Impressions and Memories* for pf.; songs, vocal duets, etc.

Fickenscher, Arthur (b. Aurora, Ill., 9. III. 1871; d. San Francisco, 15. IV. 1954), Amer. comp. Studied at the Munich Cons. Taught in Berlin, where he patented his Polytone (which divided the octave into 60 parts) in 1912, and settled at San Francisco in 1914. In 1920 he became head of the mus. dept. of the Univ. of Virginia.

Works incl. *The Chamber Blue* and *Aucassin and Nicolette* for solo voices, chorus and orch.; *Willowwave and Wellaway*, *Day of Judgment* and *Out of the Gay Nineties* for orch.; *Visions* for voice and orch.; *Variations on a Theme in Medieval Style* for strings; pf. 5tet; church mus.; part-songs, songs etc.

Fiddle, a colloquial generic term for instruments of the vln. family.

Fidelio, oder Die eheliche Liebe (*Fidelio, or Wedded Love*), opera by Beethoven (lib.

by Josef Sonnleithner, based on Bouilly's lib. of *Léonore, ou L'Amour conjugal* written for Gaveaux), prod. Vienna, Theater an der Wien, 20. XI. 1805, with the overture *Leonora No. 2*; revised version, with overture *Leonora No. 3*, same theatre, 29. III. 1806; overture *Leonora No. 1* written for the 1st perf. but abandoned as unsuitable; 2nd revision prod. Vienna Kärntnertortheater, 23. V. 1814, with *Fidelio* overture in E maj.

Field, John (b. Dublin, 26. VII. 1782; d. Moscow, 23. I. 1837), Ir. pianist and comp. Son of a violinist at the Dublin theatre, he was taught mus. and the pf. by his grandfather, an organist. Having removed to Bath and then to London, his father apprenticed him to Clementi, who taught him and at whose pf. warehouse he was employed to show off the instruments by improvisation. He made his 1st public appearance at Giordani's concerts at Dublin in 1792 and in London in 1794. In 1802 Clementi took him to Paris, Ger. and Rus., leaving him behind at St. Petersburg in 1803, where he settled down as pf. teacher. He married Mlle. Percheron in 1808. In 1822 he settled down at Moscow, where he had as great a success as he had had in the new capital. He travelled much as pianist, visited London in 1832, afterwards Paris, Belg., Switz. and It. At Naples he was taken ill and lay in hospital for months until a Rus. family took him back to Moscow, where he d. soon after his return.

Works incl. 7 pf. concertos; 20 nocturnes, 4 sonatas and many rondos, fantasies, variations, etc., for pf.; pf. 5tet and other chamber mus.; works for pf. duet, etc.

Fielding, Henry (1707–54), Eng. novelist and dramatist, author of ballad operas *The Intriguing Chambermaid*, *The Lottery*, *Miss Lucy in Town*, *Don Quixote in England* and others. *See* Arne (T. A.), Monro (*Temple Beau*), Tom Jones (German and Philidor, 8).

Fielitz, Alexander von (b. Leipzig, 28. XII. 1860; d. Salzungen, 29. VII. 1930), Ger. comp. and cond. Studied comp. under Kretschmer at Dresden and cond. under Nikisch at Leipzig. After 10 years spent in It. for his health he held posts as cond. and teacher in Berlin, Chicago from 1906, and Berlin again from 1908 as prof. and from 1915 director of Stern's Cons.

Works incl. operas *Vendetta* and *Das stille Dorf*; 2 suites for orch.; pf. pieces; song cycle *Eliland* and other songs, etc.

Fierrabras (Span. *Fierabrás* = *The Braggart*), opera by Schubert (lib. by Joseph Kupelwieser, after Calderón, taken from A. W. von Schlegel's *Spanisches Theater*), comp. 1823, but not perf. during Schubert's lifetime; prod. Carlsruhe, 9. II. 1897.

Fiesco, Giulio (b. Ferrara, *c.* 1519; d. ? Modena, *c.* 1586), It. lutenist and comp. In the service of the Dukes of Modena, Ercole II and Alfonso II. Wrote madrigals for 4 and 5 voices, *Musica nova* for 5 voices, songs, etc.

Fifara (It.), 17th-cent. name for the transverse flute.

Fife, a simple and now obs. form of small transverse fl. with finger-holes and without keys, generally used in military bands in connection with drums. The name is now used for a military fl. in B♭ with six finger-holes and several keys, used in drum and fife bands.

Fifine at the Fair, orchestral fantasy by Bantock on Browning's poem, 1st perf. Birmingham Mus. Festival, 1912.

Fifteenth, a 2-ft. org. stop prod. notes 2 8ves. above those played on the keyboard.

Fifth, an interval covering 3 whole tones and a semitone, in which case it is a perfect F., e.g. D–A. If either of these notes is sharpened or flattened, the result is an augmented or a diminished F. D♭–A or D–A♯ is an augmented F., D♯–A or D–A♭ a diminished F.

Figaro (Mozart). *See* **Nozze di Figaro.**

Figlia del reggimento. *See* **Fille du Régiment.**

Figuration, the persistent use of decorative or accomp. figures of similar type throughout a piece of mus.

Figure, a short mus. phrase, esp. one that assumes a distinctive character in the course of a comp.

Figured Bass. *See* **Thorough-Bass.**

Figured Chorale, a hymn-tune setting, esp. for org., in which the plain notes of the melody are surrounded by more rapid patterns of notes, usually all of the same kind of formation.

Figuš-Bystrý, Viliam (b. Bánská Bystrica, 28. II. 1875; d. Bánská Bystrica, 11. V. 1937), Slovak comp. As the child of poor parents he made his way with difficulty, but taught at var. places until he returned to Bánská in 1907 as teacher and organist. He took great interest in the folk mus. of his country, which was then under Hung. rule, and refused a professorship at Budapest in order to collect folksongs at home, which he pub. in 5 books.

Works incl. opera *Detvan* (in Slovak); *The Cricket and the Glow-worm* and *Songs of Rest, Love and Peace* for women's voices and pf., cantata *Slovak Songs* for solo 4tet and chorus; pf. 4tet, etc.

Filar la voce (It.)
Filar il tuono (It.)　　⎱ spin the voice
Filer la voix (Fr.)　　⎰　　(tone),
Filer le son (Fr.)

sustaining the voice in singing on a long-drawn soft note, without *crescendo* or *diminuendo*.

Fileuse (Fr. fem. = spinner, from *filer* = to spin), the name of a special type of instrumental piece with rapid figurations of var. kinds suggesting the motion of a spinning-wheel and often, in its melody, a spinning-song. There are familiar exs. by Raff and Fauré (in the latter's incid. mus. for *Pelléas et Mélisande*), and Mendelssohn's Song without Words, Op. 67 No. 4, although not so entitled, conforms to the type, being in fact nicknamed *Spinnerlied* in Ger., though called *The Bee's Wedding* in Eng. The prototype of the F. was vocal, e.g. the spinning-choruses in Haydn's *Seasons* (Winter) and Wagner's *Flying Dutchman*, Schubert's song *Margaret at the Spinning-Wheel*, etc.

Filippi, Amadeo de (b. Ariano, 1900), Amer. cond. and comp. of It. birth. Was taken to U.S.A. at the age of 5 and studied in N.Y. Later became theatre cond.

Works incl. operas *The Green Cockatoo* and *Malvolio* (on Shakespeare's *Twelfth Night*); ballets *Les Sylphides* and *Carnival*; incid. mus. for John Drinkwater's *Robert E. Lee*; mus. for films; symph., suite, concerto and *5 Arabian Songs* for orch.; serenade for strings; sonnet for contralto and chamber orch.; choral works; string 4tet, pf. 5tet; sonata and Dance Suite for vln. and pf.; sonata, 6 sonatinas, *Prelude, Passacaglia* and *Toccata,* partita for pf., etc.

Fille de Madame Angot, La (*Mme A.'s Daughter*), operetta by Lecocq (lib. by Clairville, Paul Siraudin and Victor Koning, based on a vaudeville by Maillot, *Madame Angot, ou La Poissarde parvenue,* of 1796), prod. Brussels, Théâtre Alcazar, 4. XII. 1872.

Fille du Régiment, La (*The Daughter of the Regiment*), opera by Donizetti (lib. by Jules Henri Vernoy de Saint-Georges and Jean François Alfred Bayard), prod. Paris, Opéra-Comique, 11. II. 1840. Donizetti's 1st Fr. opera.

Film Music. Silent cinematographic films were variously accomp. by ready-made mus. played on anything from a pf. to (esp. in U.S.A.) a full orch.; but the invention of the sound-track led to the mechanical reprod. of more elaborate mus. and to the commission of special scores, often from the most distinguished comps. of the day. This kind of mus. has been esp. cultivated in U.S.A., Fr., Ger., Rus. and Eng. from the 1930s onwards.

Filosofo di campagna, Il (*The Country Philosopher*), opera by Galuppi (lib. by Goldoni), prod. Venice, Teatro San Samuele, 26. X. 1754.

Filtz, Anton (Antonín Fils) (b. ? Boh., *c.* 1730; d. Mannheim, 1760), ? Boh. cellist and comp. Entered the orch. at Mannheim in 1754 and became one of the early symphonists attached to that court.

Wrote *c*. 40 symphs., overtures, a Mass, trios, etc.

Final, the Tonic note of the Modes on which the scales of the authentic modes begin and end, whereas in the case of the plagal modes the F. is on the 4th above the starting-note. *See* Modes.

Final (Fr.) = Finale.

Finale, the last movement of any instrumental work in several movements, also the last number in any act of an opera where the mus. is divided into more or less distinctly separated pieces, provided that this number is on a large scale (e.g. the great ensemble piece at the end of Act II of Mozart's *Figaro* is a F., but the aria at the end of Act I is not).

Finck, Heinrich (b. Bamberg, 1445; d. Vienna, 9. VI. 1527), Ger. comp. Educ. in the court chapel at Warsaw and (?) at Leipzig Univ. and held apps. at the Pol. court *c*. 1492–1506; then at the Court of Württemberg at Stuttgart until *c*. 1519. Later he lived at the Scot. monastery in Vienna.

Works incl. Masses, motets, hymns and other church mus., sacred and secular songs for several voices, songs to the lute, etc.

Finck, Henry T(heophilus). (b. Bethel, Mo., 22. IX. 1854; d. Rumford Falls, Me., 1. X. 1926), Amer. critic. Studied under Paine at Harvard Univ., also in Berlin, Heidelberg and Vienna. Mus. critic of the N.Y. *Evening Post* 1881–1924. Wrote books on Chopin, Wagner, Grieg, etc.

Finck, Hermann (b. Pirna, Saxony, 21. III. 1527; d. Wittenberg, 28. XII. 1558), Ger. comp. and theorist. Studied at the Univ. of Wittenberg, where he taught mus. later. In 1557 he was app. organist, but he d. the following year at the age of 31. He wrote a theoret. book, *Practica musica* in 5 vols. Comps. incl. motets, sacred songs and wedding songs for several voices, etc.

Findeisen, Nikolai Feodorovich (b. St. Petersburg, 5. VII. 1868; d. Leningrad, 20. IX. 1928), Rus. musicologist and critic. Studied at the St. Petersburg Cons. and in 1894 founded the *Russian Musical Gazette*. He also ed. *Musical Antiquity* in 1903–12 and collected much material on Rus. instruments and for the biogs. of the 19th-cent. Rus. comps., some of which he pub., as well as a hist. of early Rus. mus.

Fine (It. = end). The word is often set by comps. at the close of a work, but serves no purpose unless it occurs at some intermediate point, e.g. in a piece where an earlier portion is to be repeated to form the closing section.

Fingal's Cave (also called **Hebrides**), concert overture by Mendelssohn, Op. 26, comp. in recollection of a visit to the Hebrides in 1829, Rome, XII. 1830; revised version, London, summer 1832. The 1st score was entitled *Die einsame Insel* (*The Solitary Island*).

Finger, Gottfried (or Godfrey) (b. Olomouc, *c*. 1660; d. after 1723), Morav. comp. Nothing is known of his career until he went to London *c*. 1685, working under the patronage of James II. He left in 1702, piqued at having gained only the 4th prize after Weldon, Eccles and D. Purcell for the comp. of Congreve's masque *The Judgment of Paris*, and went into the service of the Queen of Prus., Sophia Charlotte, in Berlin. Later he lived in the Palatinate and wrote some operas for Neuburg and Heidelberg.

Works incl. operas *The Virgin Prophetess* (Settle), *Sieg der Schönheit über die Helden*, *L'amicizia in terzo* (in part); masques *The Loves of Mars and Venus* (Motteux, with Eccles) and *The Judgment of Paris* (Congreve); incid. mus. (some with D. Purcell) for Lee's *Rival Queens*, *The Wive's Excuse*, *Love for Love* and *The Mourning Bride* (both Congreve), *Love at a Loss*, *Love makes a Man* (Cibber), *The Humours of the Age* (Southerne), *Sir Harry Wildair* (Farquhar) and *The Pilgrim* (Vanbrugh); concertos and sonatas for var. instruments; pieces for vln. and fl. (with Banister), etc.

Fingerboard, the part of the neck of a string instrument to which the strings are pressed by the fingers in order to change their length and thus prod. different notes.

Fingered Tremolo. *See* Tremolo.

Fingering, the use of the fingers on any instrument to prod. the notes in var. ways; also the figures written above the notes indicating which finger is to be used to prod. this or that note.

Finite Canon, a Canon sung through once, without repetition of its phrases.

Finke, Fidelio (b. Josefstal, Boh., 22. X. 1891; d. Dresden, VI. 1968), Ger.-Cz. comp. Studied at the Prague Cons. with his uncle Romeo F. and with Novák for comp. He taught there from 1915, became inspector of the Ger. mus. schools in Cz. in 1920 and director of the Ger. Acad. of Mus. in Prague in 1927.

Works incl. opera *Die Jacobsfahrt*; *Pan* symph., overture and other works for orch., suite for strings; pf. concerto; 2 string 4tets, pf. 5tet, pf. trio and other chamber mus.; sonatas for vln. and pf., cello and pf. and fl. and pf.; numerous pf. works; many pieces for recorder; choral works with pf. and with wind instruments, unaccomp. choral works; songs, etc.

Finlandia, symph. poem for orch. by Sibelius, Op. 26, comp. in 1899 (rev. 1900). It has become a work for nat. celebrations in Fin., being based on material sounding like Fin. patriotic songs, the whole of which, however, is the comp.'s own invention, not folk mus.

Finney, Ross Lee (b. Wells, Minnesota,

23. XII. 1906), Amer. comp. Educ. at Carleton Coll., Minn., and studied mus. at Minn. Univ. and later in Paris and Vienna with Nadia Boulanger and Alban Berg, also with Sessions at Harvard Univ. Prof. of Mus. and resident comp. at Univ. of Michigan.

Works incl. Overture to a Social Drama for orch.; 3 symphs.; pf. concerto, vln. concerto; *John Brown* for tenor, male chorus and chamber orch.; 7 string 4tets, pf. trio; vln. and pf. sonata; 4 pf. sonatas; 8 Poems for soprano, tenor and pf., etc.

Finnish Composers. *See* **Furuhjelm, Hannikainen, Järnefelt, Kilpinen, Klami, Klemetti, Krohn, Kuula, Launis, Linko, Madetoja, Melartin, Merikanto (2), Pacius, Palmgren, Raito, Ranta, Schantz, Sibelius, Törne, Wegelius.**

Finot, Dominique. *See* **Phinot.**

Finta giardiniera, La (*The Pretended Garden-Girl*), opera by Anfossi (lib. by Ranieri de Calzabigi), prod. Rome, Teatro delle Dame, Carnival 1774.

Opera by Mozart (lib. do.), prod. Munich, 13. I. 1775.

Finta semplice, La (*The Pretended Simpleton*), opera by Mozart (lib. by Marco Coltellini), comp. for Vienna, 1768, but not perf. there; prod. Salzburg, 1. V. 1769.

Finte gemelle, Le (*The Pretended Twins*), opera by Piccinni (lib. by Giuseppe Petrosellini), prod. Rome, Teatro Valle, 2. I. 1771.

Finto Stanislao, Il (*The False Stanislas*), opera by Gyrowetz (lib. by Felice Romani), prod. Milan, Teatro alla Scala, 5. VIII. 1818. The lib. was used by Verdi in 1840.

Opera by Verdi. *See* **Giorno di regno.**

Finzi, Gerald (b. London, 14. VI. 1901; d. Oxford, 27. IX. 1956), Eng. comp. Private pupil of Bairstow and R. O. Morris; prof. of comp. at the R.A.M. in London, 1930–3, and afterwards went to live in the country to give his whole time to comp.

Works incl. incid. mus. for Shakespeare's *Love's Labour's Lost*; festival anthem (Crashaw), *Intimations of Immortality* (Wordsworth) and *For St. Cecilia* (Edmund Blunden) for chorus and orch.; 3 Elegies (Drummond) and 7 part-songs (Robert Bridges) for unaccomp. chorus; *New Year Music* for orch., *Romance* for strings; *Introit* for vln. and small orch., concerto for clar. and strings, cantata *Dies Natalis* (Traherne) for high voice and orch., *Farewell to Arms* (Ralph Knevet and George Peele) for tenor and small orch., 2 Sonnets by Milton for do.; *Interlude* for ob. and string 4tet, Prelude and Fugue for string trio; 5 Bagatelles for clar. and pf.; Thomas Hardy song cycles, *A Young Man's Exhortation, Earth and Air and Rain* and *Before and After Summer*,

5 Shakespeare songs, *Let us Garlands Bring*, etc.

Fiocco. It.-Belg. family of musicians.

1. Pietro Antonio F. (b. Venice, *c.* 1650; d. Brussels, 3. IX. 1714), cond. and comp. He went to Brussels late in the 17th cent. and was app. cond. of the court band. Comp. prologues for several of Lully's operas; Masses, motets; *Sacri concerti*; cantata *Le Retour du printemps*, etc.

2. Jean Joseph F. (b. Brussels, XII. 1686; d. Brussels, 30. III. 1746), cond., son of prec. Succeeded his father as cond. in 1714.

3. Joseph Hector F. (b. Brussels, 20. I. 1703; d. Brussels, 22. VI. 1741), cond., harpsichordist and comp., brother of prec. He was cond. at Brussels in 1729, became choirmaster at Antwerp Cathedral in 1731 and at Sainte-Gudule at Brussels in 1737. Comp. harpsichord pieces, church mus., etc.

Fioravanti, Valentino (b. Rome, 11. IX. 1764; d. Capua, 16. VI. 1837), It. comp. Pupil of Sala at one of the Naples Conss. Prod. his 1st opera in Rome in 1784. Cond. at Lisbon from 1803 and visited Paris in 1807, returning to It. to become *maestro di cappella* at St. Peter's in Rome.

Works incl. operas *Le avventure di Bertoldino, Le cantatrici villane, I virtuosi ambulanti, Ogni eccesso è vizioso* and *c.* 50 others; church mus., etc.

Fiorillo, Federico (b. Brunswick, V. 1755; d. ?, after 1823), It.-Ger. violinist and comp. Pupil of his father. Travelled on concert tours, and in 1782 was app. *Kapellmeister* in Riga. Visited Paris in 1785, and from 1788 to 1794 lived in London, where he appeared mostly as a vla. player.

Works incl. a large quantity of vln. mus., incl. 36 *Caprices* (studies); string 4tets, 5tets and other chamber mus., etc.

Fiorillo, Ignazio (b. Naples, 11. V. 1715; d. Fritzlar, Hesse, VI. 1787), It. comp., father of prec. Pupil of Leo and Durante at Naples. Prod. his 1st opera, *Mandane*, at Venice in 1736; became court *Kapellmeister* at Brunswick in 1754 and at Cassel in 1762, retiring in 1780.

Works incl. 21 operas; oratorio; Requiem, 3 Te Deums; symphs.; sonatas, etc.

Fioriture (It. lit. flowerings, flourishes, decorations), ornamental figures elaborating a plainer melodic passage, either according to the comp.'s notation or improvised according to the perf.'s fancy.

Fipple Flute, a generic term for a woodwind instrument held vertically and blown into through a mouthpiece in which the air is diverted by an obstructive block called the 'fipple'. The recorder (Ger. *Blockflöte*) is the chief member of the family.

Fire Symphony, the nickname of a

symph. by Haydn, No. 59, in A maj., comp. *c.* 1766–8.

Firebird, The (*Zhar Ptitsa*), ballet by Stravinsky (choreography by Mikhail Mikhailovich Fokin), prod. Paris, Opéra, 25. VI. 1910.

Firenze, Andrea da (b. ?; d. ?), 14th-cent. It. comp. of madrigals, *ballate*, etc.

Firenze, Ghirardello da (b. ?; d. ?), 14th-cent. It. comp., famous esp. for his *caccia* (canonic hunting-song) 'Tosto che l'alba del bel giorno appare'.

Firenze, Giovanni da. *See* Cascia.

Fireworks Music. Handel's *Music for the Royal Fireworks*, a suite of pieces originally for wind band, was comp. for the celebrations of the Peace of Aix-la-Chapelle, perf. London, Green Park, 27. IV. 1749.

Firkušný, Rudolf (b. Napajedlá, Morav., 11. II. 1912), Cz. pianist and comp. Studied at Brno Cons. with Vilem Kurz (pf.) and Janáček for comp. Later he studied with Suk and Schnabel. His comps. incl. a pf. concerto and many pf. solos.

First-movement Form. The term is sometimes used for 'sonata form', but does not serve well, since there are some 1st sonata movements in other forms (e.g. variations) while there are any number of slow movements and still more of finales in regular sonata form.

First Subject. *See* Sonata.

Fischer, Edwin (b. Basle, 6. X. 1886; d. Zürich, 24. I. 1960), Swiss pianist and cond. Studied at the Basle Cons., where he taught for several years. He returned to Switzerland in 1942. In addition to his activities as a soloist he also cond. orchs. in Lübeck and Munich. He ed. a number of old keyboard works and wrote books on Bach and on Beethoven's pf. sonatas.

Fischer, Johann (b. Augsburg, 25. IX. 1646; d. Schwedt, Pomerania, *c.* 1716), Ger. violinist and comp. Studied with Bockshorn at Stuttgart and went to Paris, where he became copyist to Lully. Later he travelled, worked for a time at Augsburg and Schwerin, in Den. and Swed., and finally became *Kapellmeister* to the Margrave of Schwedt.

Works incl. *Feld und Helden Musik* describing the battle of Hochstadt, table mus., overtures, dances and other pieces for vln. and for vla., some with *scordatura*.

Fischer, Johann Caspar Ferdinand (b. ?, *c.* 1665; d. Rastatt, 27. III. 1746), Ger. comp. *Kapellmeister* to the Margrave of Baden in Schlackenwerth (Bohemia) and Rastatt from 1692. His keyboard mus. includes *Ariadne musica* (1715), a series of 20 preludes and fugues, each in a different key, and thus a precursor of Bach's *Wohltemperirtes Clavier*.

Other works incl. *Musicalisches Blumen-Büschlein* (a collection of keyboard suites in the French style), *Musicalischer Par-*

nassus (9 suites named after the Muses), *Blumenstrauss* (organ preludes and fugues on the 8 modes), *Le Journal de Printemps* (suite for orch. with tpts. *ad lib.*), church mus., etc.

Fischer, Johann Christian (b. Freiburg, Breisgau, 1733; d. London, 29. IV. 1800), Ger. oboist and comp. In the service of the Saxon court at Dresden, 1760–4. Concert tours took him in 1768 to London, where he settled, marrying Gainsborough's daughter in 1780. Played frequently at the concerts promoted by J. C. Bach and Abel, and was a member of the queen's band. He was again on tour on the Continent, 1786–90. Mozart, hearing him in Vienna in 1787, thought little of his playing, though he had already (1774) comp. pf. variations on a minuet by F., K. 179.

Works incl. 10 ob. concertos, divertimenti for 2 fls., fl. sonatas and 4tets, etc.

Fischer, Ludwig (b. Mainz, 18. VIII. 1745; d. Berlin, 10. VII. 1825), Ger. bass, the original Osmin in Mozart's *Die Entführung*.

Fischer, Michael Gotthard (b. Albach nr. Erfurt, 3. VI. 1773; d. Erfurt, 12. I. 1829), Ger. organist and comp. Pupil of Kittel at Erfurt and later organist of the Franciscan church there. Wrote org. mus., symphs., string 4tets, pf. sonatas, songs, etc.

Fischer-Dieskau, Dietrich (b. Berlin, 28. V. 1925), Ger. baritone. Studied in Berlin with Georg Walter and with Weissenborn. Made his début in 1947 and his first stage appearance in 1948. He has since sung at most of the great opera houses and mus. centres of the world. An equally fine *Lieder* and opera singer, he is a musician of great intelligence, with a fine voice of remarkable range and flexibility and a perfect technique.

Fischietti, Domenico (b. Naples, *c.* 1720; d. Salzburg, *c.* 1810), It. comp. Pupil of Durante and Leo in Naples, where he prod. his first opera in 1742. Worked as cond. in Prague, then became *Kapellmeister* at Dresden 1766–72, and at Salzburg Cathedral 1772–9.

Works incl. operas *Lo speziale* (with V. Pallavicini), *Il signor dottore*, *Il mercato di Malmantile*, *La ritornata di Londra* (all on libs. by Goldoni) and *c.* 20 others; church mus., etc.

Fisher, John Abraham (b. London, 1744; d. ? London, V. 1806), Eng. violinist and comp. Pupil of Pinto, made his début as a violinist in 1765. His marriage in 1770 brought him a part-share in Covent Garden Theatre, and over the next ten years he comp. many dramatic works. On the death of his wife in 1780 he went on tour on the Continent. Married the singer Nancy Storace in Vienna in 1784, but his ill-treatment of her caused him subsequently to be banished from Austria. Later he spent some years in Dublin.

Works incl. oratorio *Providence*; incid. mus. for Shakespeare's *Macbeth*; pantomimes; songs for Vauxhall Gardens, etc.; symphs. and other intrumental mus.

Fistoulari, Anatole (b. Kiev, 20. VIII. 1907), Rus. cond. Studied with his father and cond. Tchaikovsky's 6th symph. at the age of 8. From 1933 he was in Paris and in 1940 he settled in Eng.

Fitelberg, Grzegorz (b. Dinaburg, Livonia, 18. X. 1879; d. Katowice, 10. VI. 1953), Pol. cond. and comp. App. cond. of the Warsaw Phil. concerts in 1908 and returned there after cond. at the Vienna Opera and at Leningrad, identifying himself with the nat. Pol. mus. movement.

Works incl. 2 symphs., *Pol. Rhapsody* for orch.; chamber mus.; songs, etc.

Fitelberg, Jerzy (b. Warsaw, 20. V. 1903; d. N.Y., 25. IV. 1951), Pol. comp., son of prec. He played perc. in his father's orch. as a boy and studied comp. at the Warsaw Cons. and under Schreker in Berlin; settled in Paris in 1933 and in N.Y. in 1940.

Works incl. Concert Pieces, *Sinfonietta, Pol. Pictures, Nocturne* and 2 suites for orch., symph. for strings, pf., harp and perc., concerto for strings.; 2 pf. concertos, 2 vln. concertos, cello concerto; 5 string 4tets, string trio, woodwind 5tet; Suite for vln. and pf., sonatina for 2 vlns., duo for vln. and cello, sonata for cello solo; pf. sonata and pieces, etc.

FitzGerald, Edward (1809–83), Eng. poet and translator. *See* **Omar Khayyám**.

Fitzwilliam, Viscount (Richard Wentworth) (1745–1816), Eng. collector and founder of the Fitzwilliam Museum at Cambridge, which houses his collection of MS. and printed mus., among other things left by him, incl. the old It. church mus. pub. as *Fitzwilliam Music* by Vincent Novello in 1825 and Eng. virginal mus. ed. as the *Fitzwilliam Virginal Book* by J. A. Fuller-Maitland and W. Barclay Squire in 1899.

Fitzwilliam Virginal Book, a large MS. of keyboard mus. written between 1609 and 1619 by Francis Tregian while in Fleet Prison, now in the Fitzwilliam Museum, Cambridge. It is an important source of pieces by Byrd, Bull and Giles Farnaby.

'Five, The'. *See* **Kutchka**.

Five Tudor Portraits, choral suite by Vaughan Williams on poems by Skelton. I. Ballad, *The Tunning of Elinor Rumming*; II. Intermezzo, *My Pretty Bess*; III. Burlesca, *Epitaph on John Jayberd of Diss*; IV. Romanza, *Jane Scroop: her Lament for Philip Sparrow*; V. Scherzo, *Jolly Rutterkin*. For mezzo-soprano, baritone, chorus and

orch. 1st perf. Norwich Festival, 25. IX. 1936.

Flackton, William (b. Canterbury, 1709; d. Canterbury, 5. I. 1798). Eng. organist and comp. He was a book-seller, but played the org. and vln., taught and comp. harpsichord and string mus., including works for vla.

Flageolet. A woodwind instrument similar to the recorder, with 2 of its fingerholes on the under side, to be stopped by the thumbs. It belongs to the Fipple Flute family. Also a soft 2-ft. flue org. stop.

Flageolets (Fr. plur.) ⎫
Flageolette (Ger. plur.) ⎬ = Harmonics.

Flagstad, Kirsten (Malfrid) (b. Hamar, 12. VII. 1895; d. Oslo, 7. XII. 1962), Norw. soprano. She 1st appeared in opera at the Oslo Nat. Theatre in 1913 and continued to sing in Norw. (incl. operetta) until 1930. In 1933 she sang for the first time at Bayreuth and in 1934 sang Sieglinde and Gutrune there. For the next 17 years she enjoyed an international reputation as a Wagnerian soprano. She also appeared as Dido in Purcell's *Dido and Aeneas* in 1951. From 1958–60 she was director of the Norw. State Opera.

Flam, a double stroke, as distinct from a roll, on the Side Drum.

Flamenco. *See* **Cante flamenco**.

Flat, the sign ♭, which lowers a note by a semitone. Also an adj. describing out-of-tune intonation on the F. side.

Flatté (Fr.). *See* **Ornaments**.

Flatterzunge (Ger.) *See* **Flutter-Tonguing**.

Flaubert, Gustave (1821–80), Fr. novelist. *See* Bondeville (*Mme. Bovary*), Davico (*Tentation de Saint Antoine*), Erlanger (C.) (*Saint Julien l'Hospitalier*), Gilbert (H. F.) (*Salammbô*), Giuliano (Zandonai), Gray (C.) (*Temptation of St. Anthony*), Hauer (*Salammbô*), Hérodiade (Massenet), Kabalevsky (*Mme. Bovary*), Navrátil (*Salammbô*), Salammbô (Mussorgsky and Reyer), Schmitt (F.) (*Salammbô*), Tiessen (do.).

Flautando (It. = fluting), a flute-like tone prod. on the vln. by drawing the bow lightly over the strings near the end of the fingerboard.

Flautina, a 2-ft. org. stop like the Fifteenth, but with softer tone, prod. notes 15 diatonic degrees above those played.

Flautino (It. = little fl.), a small recorder, either the descant recorder or the flageolet, also called *flauto piccolo* in the early 18th cent. (e.g. in Handel's *Rinaldo*).

Flautist, the Eng. word for flute-player, der. from It. *flauto* and *flautista*.

Flauto (It.) = Flute, also in the 17th cent. = Recorder.

Flauto piccolo (It. = little flute). *See* Flautino, Piccolo.

Flauto traverso (It.), the transverse fl.,

distinguished from the Recorders and similar fls. played vertically; also a 4-ft. org. stop with fl. tone.

Flautone (It. = big fl.) = Bass Flute.

Flavio, rè de' Longobardi (*Flavius, King of the Lombards*), opera by Handel (lib. by Nicola Francesco Haym, partly based on Corneille's *Cid*), prod. London, King's Theatre, Haymarket, 14. V. 1723.

Flavius Bertaridus, König der Longobarden (*F.B., King of the Lombards*), opera by Telemann (lib. by Christian Gottlieb Wendt), prod. Hamburg, Theater beim Gänsemarkt, 23. XI. 1729.

Flebile (It.; accent on 1st syll.), plaintive, mournful.

Flecha, Mateo (b. Prades, Tarragona, 1481; d. Poblet, *c.* 1553), Span. monk and comp. Pupil of Juan Castelló at Barcelona, *maestro de capilla* to the Infantas of Castile, later became a Carmelite and settled in the monastery of Poblet.

Flecha, Mateo (b. Prades, 1530; d. Solsona, Lérida, 20. II. 1604), Span. monk and comp., nephew of prec. Pupil of his uncle. In the service of the Emperor Charles V until 1558 and of Philip II, then in Prague in that of the Emperor Maximilian, after whose death in 1576 he remained there until 1599, when he went to the abbey of Solsona as a Franciscan monk. A stage work of his, *El Parnaso*, (?) was perf. at Madrid in 1561.

Works by the 2 Fs. (not always distinguishable) incl. church mus., madrigals, *ensaladas* (burlesque madrigals), etc.

Flecker, James Elroy (1884–1915), Eng. poet and dramatist. *See* Anson (*Saadabad*), Arundell (*Don Juan*), Delius (*Hassan*), Wood (T.) (*Ballad of Hampstead Heath*).

Fledermaus, Die (*The Flittermouse, The Bat*), operetta by J. Strauss, jun. (lib. by Carl Haffner and Richard Genée, based on a Fr. vaudeville, *Le Réveillon*, by Henri Meilhac and Ludovic Halévy, taken from a Ger. comedy, *Das Gefängnis*, by Roderich Benedix), prod. Vienna, Theater an der Wien, 5. IV. 1874.

Flem, Paul Le. *See* Le Flem.

Flesch, Carl (b. Moson, 9. X. 1873; d. Lucerne, 14. XI. 1944), Aus.-Hung, violinist and teacher. Studied in Vienna and Paris, where he was a pupil of Marsick with Kreisler. Made his 1st public appearance in Vienna, 1895, toured widely and taught by turns at Bucharest, Amsterdam, Philadelphia and Berlin. In 1934 he settled in London. Wrote books on vln. playing and comp. vln. studies.

Fletcher, John. *See* Beaumont and Fletcher.

Fleury, André (b. Neuilly-sur-Seine, 25. VII. 1903), Fr. organist and comp. He studied at the Paris Cons. under Gigout and Dupré and privately with Marchal and Vierne, also comp. with Vidal. In 1930 he became organist of St. Augustin in Paris and after a period of illness during World War II, of Dijon Cathedral, also prof. at the Cons. there. His works are almost entirely for the org.

Fleury, Louis (b. Lyons, 24. V. 1878; d. Paris, 11. VI. 1925), Fr. flautist. Studied at the Paris Cons. From 1905 until his death he was head of the Société Moderne d'Instruments à Vent. It was for him that Debussy comp. *Syrinx*.

Flicorno, an It. brass instrument used in military bands corresponding to the Saxhorn and Flügelhorn.

Fliegende Holländer, Der (*The Flying Dutchman*), opera by Wagner (lib. by comp., based on Heine's *Memoiren des Herrn von Schnabelewopski,* ? Marryat's novel *The Phantom Ship* and other sources), prod. Dresden, 2. I. 1843.

Flood, W(illiam). H(enry). Grattan (b. Lismore, Co. Waterford, 1. XI. 1859; d. Enniscorthy, 7. VIII. 1928), Ir. organist and musicologist. Educ. for the priesthood, he became a musician and organist at Belfast, Thurles and Enniscorthy Cathedrals successively. Comp. church mus. and wrote a number of books on Ir. and early Eng. mus.

Floquet, Étienne Joseph (b. Aix-en-Provence, 23. XI. 1748; d. Paris, 10. V. 1785), Fr. comp. He received his mus. educ. at the church of Saint-Sauveur at Aix, wrote a motet at the age of 10 and went to Paris *c.* 1769. In 1774, having come into conflict with Gluck's partisans, he went to Naples, where he studied under Sala, and to Bologna, where he sought further instruction from Martini, but returned to Paris in 1777.

Works incl. operas *Hellé, Le Seigneur bienfaisant, La Nouvelle Omphale* and *Alceste* (Quinault); opera-ballets *L'Union de l'Amour et des Arts* and *Azolan*; 2 Requiems, ode *La Gloire du Seigneur* (J. B. Rousseau), etc.

Florence (actually **Houghton**), **Evangeline** (b. Cambridge, Mass., 12. XII. 1873; d. London, 1. XI. 1928), Amer. soprano. Made her 1st appearance at Boston in 1891. Later continued her studies in London and appeared much in Eng.

Florestan, one of the 2 imaginary characters, F. and Eusebius, used by Schumann as pseudos. for his critical writings and also intro. into his mus. (*Carnaval, Davidsbündlertänze*) to personify what he felt to be his dual character as an artist, F. repres. him as an impetuous romantic and E. as a dreamer.

Flori, family of Ger. 16th-cent. musicians:

1. **Franz (I) F.** (b. ?; d. Munich, 1588);
2. **Franz (II) F.** (b. ?; d. Innsbruck, 1583), ? son of prec.;

3. Johann F. (b. *c.* 1546; d. ?), son of Franz (I);

4. Georg F. (b. *c.* 1558; d. ?), son of Franz (I);

5. Jacob F. (b. ?; d. ?), son of Franz (I). The comps. by Franz (I) and Franz (II) are not always distinguishable: they incl. a Mass based on a Flem. song. Johann and Georg both wrote Masses and It. madrigals; Jacob confined himself largely to church music.

Florian, Jean-Pierre (Claris) de (1755–94), Fr. novelist and poet. *See* **Abencérages** (Cherubini), **Franck (C.)** (songs).

Florid, a term used for any decorative passages, but more partic. those which elaborate a theme or motif 1st stated in a simpler form. Variations are most apt to use the device of F. writing.

Floridante, Il, opera by Handel (lib. by Paolo Antonio Rolli), prod. London, King's Theatre, Haymarket, 9. XII. 1721.

Florimo, Francesco (b. San Giorgio Morgeto, Calabria, 12. X. 1800; d. Naples, 18. XII. 1888), It. mus. hist. and comp. Studied under Zingarelli and others at Naples and later became librarian of the Real Collegio di Musica there. Friend of Bellini and later of Wagner, on both of whom he wrote, also on the Neapol. school of comps.

Works incl. church mus.; choral works; Funeral Symph. on the death of Bellini; vocal 4tets and duets, songs, etc.

Flothuis, Marius (b. Amsterdam, 30. X. 1914), Dutch comp. Studied with Hans Brandts-Buys.

Works incl. concertos for fl., horn, vln., chamber orch.; *Sinfonietta Concertante* for clar., saxophone and chamber orch.; cello sonata.

Flotow, Friedrich von (b. Teutendorf, Mecklenburg-Schwerin, 26. IV. 1812; d. Darmstadt, 24. I. 1883), Ger. comp. Son of a nobleman. Went to Paris in 1827 and studied mus. under Reicha and others. Began to prod. operas at aristocratic houses and wrote incid. mus. for the play *Alessandro Stradella* (enlarged into an opera, 1844) at the Palais-Royal in 1837. The next 2 years he contrib. mus. numbers to Grisar's operas *Lady Melvill* and *L'Eau merveilleuse*, and in 1839 he made his 1st public stage success with *Le Naufrage de la Méduse*. He was intendant of the court theatre at Schwerin in 1856–63. He then returned to Paris, but went to live nr. Vienna in 1868.

Works incl. Fr., Ger. and It. operas, e.g. *La Duchesse de Guise*, *L'Esclave de Camoëns*, *Stradella*, *L'Âme en peine*, *Martha*, *Rübezahl*, *L'Ombre*, *Il fior d'Harlem*, *Rob Roy* (after Scott); ballets *Lady Henriette* (with Burgmüller and Deldevez, on which *Martha* was based later), *Die Libelle* and *Tannkönig*; incid.

mus. to Shakespeare's *Winter's Tale*; *Fackeltanz*, overtures, etc. for orch.; chamber mus.; songs, etc.

Flourish, lit., in old Eng., a Fanfare, but in modern mus. terminology a short figure used as an embellishment rather than as a theme.

Flue Stops, org. stops which control pipes resembling whistles and fls. in being mere tubes with an open mouthpiece, as distinct from the Reed Stops, which have vibrating metal tongues.

Flügel (Ger. lit. wing), the Ger. name for the grand pf., which is wing-shaped.

Flügelhorn (Ger. lit. wing horn), a brass wind instrument akin to the keyed bugle and alto Saxhorn, still called by its Ger. name in Eng. though spelt 'flugelhorn' (generally abbr. to 'flugel'). It is made in 3 pitches, soprano, alto and tenor, and used in military and brass bands. In Eng. only the middle size (in B♭) is used, and normally only in brass bands.

Flute, a woodwind instrument played horizontally (*see also* **Bass Flute, Piccolo**). It is played through an open mouth-hole without reeds and the notes are controlled by keys, many more being obtainable, however, by overblowing and cross-fingering. It has the following compass:

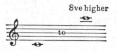

In the 17th cent. F. normally meant Recorder, sometimes called the Eng. F. Also an org. stop of 4-ft. or 8-ft. open or stopped pipes with fl. tone.

Flûte à bec (Fr. = beak fl.) = Fipple Fl., Flageolet, Recorder.

Flûte à cheminée, an org. stop of metal pipes with 8-ft. tone with a tube or 'chimney' in the stopper.

Flute Bass, sometimes the name of the Bass Fl. org. stop.

Flûte d'amour, a soft flue org. stop with 4-ft. or 8-ft. pipes; also an obs. fl. standing a min. 3rd lower than the common fl.

Flûte douce (Fr. lit. sweet fl.) = Recorder.

Flute, Harmonic, a 4-ft. or 8-ft. org. stop of open metal pipes of double speaking length.

Flutter-Tonguing, a special kind of tone-prod. used mainly in playing the fl. and clar., i.e. rolling an R while playing.

Fluyd, John, *See* **Lloyd, John.**

Flying Dutchman. *See* **Fliegende Holländer, Vaisseau-fantôme.**

Fock, Gerard van Brucken. *See* **Brucken Fock.**

Fodor-Mainvielle, Joséphine (b. Paris, 13. X. 1789; d. Saint-Genis nr. Lyons, 14.

VIII. 1870), Fr. soprano, daughter of the violinist and comp. Joseph Fodor (1751–1828). 1st appeared at the Opéra-Comique in Paris, 1814. She retired in 1833.

Foerster. *See also* **Förster.**

Foerster, Josef (b. Osenice, 22. II. 1833; d. Prague, 3. I. 1907), Boh. comp. and organist. Wrote mainly church mus. Organist at Prague Cathedral from 1887 and prof. at the Cons.

Foerster, Josef Bohuslav (b. Dětenice, 30. XII. 1859; d. Nový Vestec nr. Stará Boleslav, 29. V. 1951), Cz. comp. son of prec. Studied at Prague Org. School. Mus. teacher and critic at Hamburg, 1893–1903, and Vienna, 1903–18. Returned to Prague and was app. prof. at the Cons., and director in 1922.

Works incl. operas *Deborah, Eva, Jessica* (on Shakespeare's *Merchant of Venice*), *The Invincibles, The Heart, The Fool*; incid. mus. for Vrchlický's *Samson*, Strindberg's *Journey of Fortunate Peter*, Schiller's *Maria Stuart* and other plays; *Stabat Mater* and other works for chorus and orch.; 4 symphs., 6 suites, 4 symph. poems and 2 overtures for orch.; 2 vln. concertos; 3 string 4tets, 3 pf. trios, 5tet for wind instruments; 2 vln. and pf. sonatas, cello and pf. sonata; works for pf., org. and harmonium; 10 recitations with pf. accomp.; songs, part-songs, etc.

Fogazzaro, Antonio (1842–1911), It. novelist. *See* **Alfano** (*Miranda*).

Fogg, Eric (b. Manchester, 21. II. 1903; d. London, 19. XII. 1939), Eng. comp. Studied mus. with his parents and as choir-boy at Manchester Cathedral, later with Bantock. Worked for the B.B.C. at Manchester and later in London.

Works incl. ballets *Hänsel and Gretel* and *The Golden Butterfly; The Hillside* (Tagore) and *The Seasons* (Blake) for chorus and orch.; suite *The Golden Valley* and *Sea-Sheen* for orch.; overture to Shakespeare's *Comedy of Errors* for small orch.; bassoon concerto; string 4tet in Ab maj., *Dance Fantasy* for pf. 5tet; Poem for cello and pf.; pf. pieces; *Three Chinese Songs* and a song-cycle *Songs of Love and Life* (Tagore); songs, part-songs, etc.

Foggia, Francesco (b. Rome, c. 1604; d. Rome, 8. I. 1688), It. comp. Studied under Cifra, Nanini and Agostini; went into the service of the Elector of Cologne and Bavaria and the Archduke Leopold of Aus. in turn and after his return held var. church apps. in It., including St. John Lateran in Rome 1636–61, and Santa Maria Maggiore there from 1677.

Works incl. Masses, motets and other church mus.

Fogliano, Giacomo (b. Modena, 1468; d. Modena, 10. IV. 1548), It. comp. of madrigals and *frottole*.

Fogliano, Ludovico (b. Modena, ?; d.

after 1538), brother (?) of prec. His *Musica Theorica* was pub. in 1529, and a single *frottola* was incl. in Petrucci's 9th book (1508).

Foldes, Andor (b. Budapest, 21. XII. 1913), Hung. pianist. Studied at Budapest Mus. Acad. with Dohnányi, winning the international Liszt Prize in 1933. He toured Eur. until 1939, when he went to the U.S.A., becoming a citizen in 1948. He is well known as a performer of Bartók's mus. and for his playing of the classical repertory.

Foli (Foley), Allan James (b. Cahir, Tipperary, 7. VIII. 1835; d. Southport, 20. X. 1899), Ir. bass. Studied at Naples and made his 1st appearance at Catania in 1862; in London in 1865. He sang regularly in oratorio as well as in opera.

Folksong (*see also* **Volkslied**), a traditional song of often great but indeterminate antiquity the origins and comp. of which are unknown, but which has been preserved by being handed down aurally from generation to generation, often in several different versions or corruptions.

Folksong Society. *See* **English Folk Dance and Song Society.**

Folquet de Marseille (b. Marseilles, ?; d. Toulouse, 25. XII. 1231), Fr. troubadour. He entered the Church at the end of the 12th cent. and d. as Bishop of Toulouse. 27 poems and 13 tunes of his songs are extant.

Fomin, Evstigney Ipatovich (b. St. Petersburg, 16. VIII. 1761; d. St. Petersburg, IV. 1800), Rus. comp. Studied under Martini at Bologna and later became cond. in St. Petersburg.

Works incl. operas *Boyeslav, The Wizard, the Soothsayer and the Marriage-Broker, Orpheus, Clorinda and Milo, The Americans, The Golden Apple*, etc.

Fontaine, Pierre (b. ? Rouen, ?; d. ?, c. 1450), Fr. singer and comp. Sang in the Papal Chapel in Rome c. 1420. Wrote *chansons*.

Fontana, Giovanni Battista (b. Brescia, ?; d. Padua, 1631), It. violinist and comp. Wrote sonatas for his instrument.

Fontane, Theodor (1819–98), Ger. poet and novelist. *See* **Loewe (K.).**

Fontanelli, Alfonso, Count (b. Reggio d'Emilia, 15. II. 1557; d. Rome, 11. II. 1622), It. comp. Was in the service of the Duke of Modena at the end of the 16th cent. and in 1605 settled in Rome. Comp. madrigals.

Foote, Arthur (William) (b. Salem, Mass., 5. III. 1853; d. Boston, 8. IV. 1937), Amer. organist and comp. Studied at the New Eng. Cons. at Boston and later with Paine. For many years held org. apps. at Boston.

Works incl. cantatas on Longfellow's

The Farewell of Hiawatha, The Wreck of the Hesperus and *The Skeleton in Armour*; overture *In the Mountains*, prologue to *Francesca da Rimini* and 3 suites for orch.; cello concerto; 3 string 4tets, pf. 4tet, pf. 5tet, 2 pf. trios; choral works; org. and pf. pieces; songs etc.

Ford, Thomas (b. ?, c. 1580; d. London, XI. 1648), Eng. lutenist and comp. He was in the service of Henry, Prince of Wales, in 1611 and app. one of the musicians to Charles I in 1626.

Works incl. airs to the lute (also to be perf. in 4 vocal parts), catches and rounds; 2 anthems contrib. to Leighton's *Teares and Lamentacions* and others; dances for lute, etc.

Ford, Walter (Armitage Justice) (b. London, 20. III. 1861; d. Padworth, 21. VIII. 1938), Eng. baritone and teacher. Educ. at Repton and Cambridge. He taught at Wellington Coll. and then studied singing in Berlin and Milan. He sang much in London and was app. prof. of singing at the R.C.M. in 1895 and Reading Coll. in 1915.

Forefall = Appoggiatura (from below).

Forest (b. ?; d. ?), Eng. comp., poss. the John F. who was canon and later dean of Wells, dying there in 1446. His motet *Qualis est dilectus tuus* was incl. (together with the beginning of *Ascendit Christus*, ascribed to Dunstable in a continental MS.), among the latest additions to the Old Hall MS. (q.v.). Other sacred mus. survives in continental sources.

Forêt bleue, La (*The Blue Forest*), opera by Aubert (lib. by Jacques Chenevière, based on a tale by Perrault), prod. Geneva, 7. I. 1913.

Forkel, Johann Nikolaus (b. Meeder, 22. II. 1749; d. Göttingen, 20. III. 1818), Ger. organist and mus. hist. Studied law at Göttingen, where he was director of mus. at the Univ. from 1779 to his death. Among his many writings his biog. of Bach (1802) is part. notable—the first biog. of Bach and an important contrib. to the awakening interest in his mus.

Forlana (or **Furlana**) (It.), an old It. dance in 6–8 time. A classical ex. of its use is in Bach's Overture (Suite) in C for orch. and a modern one in Ravel's *Tombeau de Couperin* (*see* illustration opposite).

Form. The F. of a mus. comp. is the course it is planned to take from beginning to end in such a way as to unfold itself logically. *See* **Fugue, Rondo, Sonata, Suite, Symphony, Variations**.

Formé, Nicolas (b. Paris, 26. IV. 1567; d. Paris, 27. V. 1638), Fr. comp. He was a clerk and singer in the Sainte-Chapelle in Paris, 1587–92, then became a counter-tenor in the royal chapel and succeeded Eustache du Caurroy as choirmaster and comp. there in 1609. Although dismissed

from the Sainte-Chapelle for not conforming to the eccles. rules, he returned there in 1626 and, as a favourite musician of Louis XIII, enjoyed special privileges.

Works incl. Masses motets, Magnificat and other church mus.

Forqueray, Fr. family of vla. da gamba players:

1. **Antoine F.** (b. Paris, IX. 1672; d. Nantes, 28. VI. 1745), pupil of his father. He played before Louis XIV at the age of 5. In 1689 he became a royal chamber musician.

2. **Jean Baptiste Antoine F.** (b. Paris, 3. IV. 1699; d. Paris 15. VIII. 1782), son of prec. His father's pupil. In the service of the Prince of Conti.

Forrest-Heyther Part-Books, a set of 6 books in the Bodleian Library, Oxford (Mus. Sch. e. 376–81) containing 18 Masses of the early Tudor period. They belonged to a William Forrest in 1530 and subsequently to William Heyther, who may have written down the 3 Eng. anthems which the books also contain. The last part of the 6th book is in the hand of John Baldwin.

Förster, (Emanuel) Aloys (b. Niederstein, Silesia, 26. I. 1748; d. Vienna, 12. XI. 1823), Ger. oboist and comp. After 2 years as a military bandsman, 1766–8, he lived as a freelance teacher and comp., first in Prague, then, from 1779, in Vienna. Author of a treatise on thorough-bass. Beethoven acknowledged his debt to F. in the comp. of string 4tets.

Works incl. 48 string 4tets; 4 string 5tets; 6 pf. 4tets, and other chamber mus.; pf. concertos, sonatas, variations etc.

Forster, E(dward). M(organ). (1879–1970). *See* **Billy Budd**.

Forster, Georg (b. Amberg/Oberpfalz, c. 1510; d. Nuremberg, 12. XI. 1568), Ger. mus. pub. and comp. He pub. 5 sets of Ger. songs, 1539–56, some of which are by himself; he also comp. sacred and Lat. works.

Forster, Josef (b. Trofaiach, Styria, 20. I. 1838; d. Vienna, 23. III. 1917), Aus. comp.

Works incl. operas *Die Wallfahrt der Königin, Die Rose von Pontevedra, Evanthia* and *Der dot Mon* (Hans Sachs); 2 ballets; symph. in C min., etc.

Forsyth, Cecil (b. Greenwich, 30. XI. 1870; d. New York, 7. XII. 1941), Eng. violist, comp. and writer on mus. Studied at Edinburgh Univ. and the R.C.M. in London. Author of books on orch., *Mus. and Nationalism* and, with Stanford, a hist. of mus.

Works incl. operas *Westward Ho!, Cinderella; The Last Supper* for baritone, chorus and orch.; 2 Masses; vla. concerto.

Forte (It. lit. strong) = loud. Generally abbr. by the symbol *f*.

Bach, *Suite No. 1*

Ravel, *Le Tombeau de Couperin*

FORLANA

Fortepiano (It. lit. loud-soft), the early It. name for the pf., given to the instrument because, unlike the harpsichord, it was capable of having var. intensities of tone prod. by the player's touch.

Fortissimo (It. superl., lit. strongest) = loudest. Abbr. by *ff*.

Fortner, Wolfgang (b. Leipzig, 12. X. 1907), Ger. comp. Studied with Hermann Grabner. From 1931 to 1954 he taught theory and comp. at the Evangelical Church Mus. Inst. in Heidelberg, where he founded and cond. a chamber orch. In 1954 he became prof. of comp. at the N.W. Ger. Mus. Acad. in Detmold, and in 1957 succeeded Genzmer at the Musik-hochschule in Freiburg-im-Breisgau. His

mus. shows the influence of Reger and Hindemith. He also uses serial techniques in a personal way.

Works incl. operas *Die Witwe von Ephesus, Der Wald* and *Die Bluthochzeit* (both after Lorca, later revised and prod. under the title *In seinem Garten liebt Don Pimperlin Belison*); ballet *Die weisse Rose* (after Wilde); *Deutsche Liedmesse, Marianische Antiphonen* for unaccomp. chorus; symph., *Sinfonia concertante* for chamber orch.; concertos for var. instruments and small orch.; 3 string 4tets, etc.

Forty-Eight (Preludes and Fugues) (Bach). *See* **Wohltemperierte Clavier.**

Forza d'amor paterno, La (*The Force of Paternal Love*), opera by Stradella (lib.

by ?), prod. Genoa, Teatro del Falcone, Carnival 1678.

Forza del destino, La (*The Force of Destiny*), opera by Verdi (lib. by Francesco Maria Piave, based on the drama by Angelo Pérez de Saavedra, Duke of Rivas, *Don Alvaro, o La fuerza de sino*), prod. St. Petersburg, 10. XI. 1862; 1st perf. in It., Rome, Teatro Apollo, 7. II. 1863.

Foss, Hubert J(ames). (b. London, 2. V. 1899; d. London, 27. V. 1953), Eng. pianist, writer on mus., ed., and comp. Educ. at Bradfield Coll., joined the Oxford Univ. Press in 1921, formed a mus. dept. and remained until 1941, when he became active in the nat. organization of mus. educ. He wrote *Music in my Time* and ed. 3 vols., *The Heritage of Music*. Comps. incl. settings of poems by Thomas Hardy for voice and pf.

Foss (orig. **Fuchs**), **Lukas** (b. Berlin, 15. VIII. 1922), Ger., later Amer. comp. Studied in Berlin with Julius Goldstein and from 1933 in Paris with Lazare Lévy (pf.) and Noel Gallon (comp.). In 1937 he went with his parents to the U.S.A., studying at the Curtis Institute in Philadelphia. Later he studied with Hindemith at Yale Univ. In 1945 he won a Guggenheim Fellowship and in 1950 a Fulbright Fellowship. He became prof. of comp. at California Univ. in 1953. He has composed much, in more recent years using an aleatory style. He was app. conductor of the Buffalo Phil. Orch. in 1964.

Works incl. operas *The Jumping Frog of Calaveras County* (after Mark Twain), *Griffelkin* (television opera), *Introductions and Goodbyes* (lib. by Foss and Menotti); ballet *Gift of the Magi*; cantata *The Prairie* (after Carl Sandberg); oratorio *A Parable of Death* (Rilke); 2 pf. concertos; 2 symphs.; concerto for cello, ob. and clar.; string 4tet; incid. mus. to *The Tempest*, etc.

Fossa, Johannes de (b. ?; d. Munich, 1603), Ger. or Flem. comp. He wrote 6 Masses and other sacred works.

Foster, Arnold (Wilfred Allen) (b. Sheffield, 6. XII. 1898; d. London, 30. IX. 1963), Eng. comp. After serving in the 1914–18 war, he studied pf., horn and comp. at the R.C.M. in London, the last under Vaughan Williams. Mus. master at Westminster School, 1926–61, and director of mus. at Morley Coll., 1928–40.

Works incl. ballets *Midsummer Eve* and *Lord Bateman*; *Autumn Idyll* and other works for small orch.; suite on Eng. folk airs for strings; pf. concerto on country-dance tunes; Fantasy pf. 4tet; vln. and pf. pieces; pf. mus.; many folksong arrs. for orch., pf., chorus and voice and pf., etc.

Foster, Muriel (b. Sunderland, 22. XI. 1877; d. London, 23. XII. 1937), Eng. contralto. Studied at the R.C.M., London,

made her 1st appearance at Bradford in 1896, and sang extensively in Eng., on the Continent and in Amer. until her marriage in 1906.

Foster, Stephen (Collins) (b. nr. Pittsburgh, 4. VII. 1826; d. N.Y., 13. I. 1864), Amer. comp. Almost wholly self-taught in mus., pub. his 1st song as early as 1842. He wrote *c.* 175 popular songs, incl. *Old Folks at Home, My Old Kentucky Home, Massa's in the cold, cold ground,* etc.

Foulds, John (Herbert) (b. Manchester, 2. XI. 1880; d. Calcutta, 24. IV. 1939), Eng. cond. and comp. He joined a theatre orch. in Manchester at the age of 14 and the Hallé Orch. in 1900. Later he worked at var. opera-houses abroad, gave concerts for the forces during the 1914–18 war, and later cond. var. mus. societies in London.

Works incl. incid. mus. for Kalidasa's *Sakuntala*, Euripides' *Trojan Women* and several others; *A Vision of Dante* (concert opera), *A World Requiem* for solo voices, chorus and orch.; *Epithalamium, Keltic Suite* and *Suite fantastique* for orch.; *Holiday Sketches, Suite française* and *Gaelic Dream Song* for small orch.; *Idyll* for string orch.; *Mood Pictures* for vln. and pf.; *Variations* and *Essays in the Modes* for pf., etc.

Fouqué, Friedrich (Heinrich Karl), Baron de la Motte (1773–1843), Ger. poet and novelist. *See* Lvov (*Undine*), Perfall (do.), **Smart (H.)** (*Undine*), **Strong** (*Sintram and Undine*), **Undine** (Girschner, Hoffmann [E. T. A.] and Lortzing).

Four Saints in Three Acts, opera by Virgil Thomson (lib. by Gertrude Stein), prod. in concert form at Ann Arbor, Mich., 20. V. 1933 and on the stage at Hartford, Conn., 8. II. 1934.

Four Serious Songs (Brahms). *See* Vier ernste Gesänge.

Fourdrain, Félix (Alfred) (b. Nice, 3. II. 1880; d. Paris, 23. X. 1923), Fr. comp. Pupil of Widor at the Paris Cons.

Works incl. operas *La Légende du pont d'Argentan, La Glaneuse, Vercingétorix, Madame Roland, Les Contes de Perrault* and *La Griffe*; operettas *Cadet-Roussel, Le Secret de Polichinelle* and *Dolly*; incid. mus. for Erckmann-Chatrian's *Les Rantzau*, George Sand's *Claudie* and *La Mare au Diable*, etc.

Fourestier, Louis (Félix André) (b. Montpellier, 31. V. 1892), Fr. cond. and comp. Pupil of Leroux, Gédalge, Vidal and d'Indy at the Paris Cons., and a follower of Dukas; took the Prix de Rome in 1925. He cond. much in Paris and also took charge of concerts at Angers, Cannes and Vichy, being app. cond. of the Paris Opéra in 1938.

Works incl. cantata *La Mort d'Adonis*; symph. poem *Polynice* and *À Saint-Valéry* for orch.; *Orchestique* (Paul Valéry),

Edward and 4 poems by Tagore for voice and orch.; string 4tets, etc.

Fournier, Pierre (b. Paris, 24. VI. 1906), Fr. cellist. Studied at the Paris Cons., making his début in 1925. He has toured widely and is now prof. of cello at the Paris Cons.

Fourniture, the Fr. name of the Furniture org. stop.

Fourth, an interval which, if perfect, embraces 4 degrees of the diatonic scale, e.g.:

Perfect

It may be augmented or diminished, e.g:

Augmented　Diminished

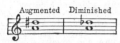

Fox Strangways A(rthur). H(enry). (b. Norwich, 14. IX. 1859; d. Dinton nr. Salisbury, 2. V. 1948), Eng. musicologist, critic and ed. Educ. at Wellington Coll. and Balliol Coll., Oxford and studied mus. in Berlin. After teaching at Dulwich and Wellington Colls. until 1910, and visiting India, on the mus. of which he wrote a book, *The Music of Hindostan*, he became asst. critic of *The Times* in London in 1911 and chief critic of the *Observer* in 1925. Founded *Music & Letters* in 1920 and ed. it until 1936. He also wrote a biog. of Cecil Sharp and trans. many songs (some with Steuart Wilson) by Schubert, Brahms, Wolf, etc.

Fox, The, dance scene by Stravinsky (lib. by comp., based on Rus. folk tales, Fr. trans., *Renard*, by Charles Ferdinand Ramuz), prod. Paris, Opéra, 3. VI. 1922.

Foxtrot, an Amer. dance dating from 1912 and cultivated mainly by the jazz bands. It gradually developed into 2 forms, quicker and slower, the former merging into the Charleston and the latter into the Blues.

Fra Diavolo, ou L'Hôtellerie de Terracine (*Brother Devil, or the Inn at Terracina*), opera by Auber (lib. by Scribe), prod. Paris, Opéra-Comique, 28. I. 1830.

Fra due litiganti il terzo gode (*Between Two Litigants the Third makes Profit*), opera by Sarti (lib. altered from Goldoni's *Le nozze*), prod. Milan, Teatro alla Scala, 14. IX. 1782. Mozart quotes a tune from it in the second-act finale of *Don Giovanni*: it was 1st perf. in Vienna 28. V. 1783.

Franc, Guillaume Le. *See* Le Franc.

Françaix, Jean (b. Le Mans, 23. V. 1912), Fr. comp. Studied under his father, director of the Le Mans Cons. and Nadia Boulanger in Paris.

Works incl. ballets *Beach* and *Le Roi nu* (after Hans Andersen); symph., *Suite concertante* and *Le Diable boiteux* (after Lesage) for orch.; *Divertissement* for string trio and orch.; pf. concerto and concertino, fl. concerto, Fantasy for cello and orch.; *Petit Quatuor* for strings, 5tet for fl., harp and strings, etc.

France, Anatole (A. Thibault) (1844–1924), Fr. poet, novelist and essayist. *See* Benoît (C.) (*Noces corinthiennes*), Jongleur de Notre-Dame (Massenet), Levadé (*Rôtisserie de la Reine Pédauque*), Thaïs (Massenet).

Francesca da Rimini. *See also* Françoise de Rimini; Paolo e Francesca.

Opera by Generali (lib. by Paolo Pola, based on Dante), prod. Venice, Teatro La Fenice, 26. XII. 1829.

Opera by Nápravník (lib. by O. O. Paleček and E. P. Ponomarov, based on a play by Stephen Phillips, *Paolo and Francesca*, and farther back on Dante), prod. St. Petersburg, 9. XII. 1902.

Opera by Rakhmaninov (lib. taken from scenes of Pushkin's play, with additions by Modest Ilich Tchaikovsky, based on Dante), prod. Moscow, 24. I. 1906.

Opera by Zandonai (lib. by Tito Ricordi, based on d'Annunzio's tragedy, and farther back on Dante), prod. Turin, Teatro Regio, 19. II. 1914.

Symph. fantasy by Tchaikovsky, Op. 32 (based on Dante), comp. 1876, 1st perf. Moscow, 9. III. 1877.

Unfinished opera by Goetz, completed by Ernst Frank (lib. by comp.), prod. Mannheim, 30. IX. 1877.

Francescatti, Zino (b. Marseilles, 9. VIII. 1905), It. violinist. Made his début aged 5 and played the Beethoven vln. concerto aged 10. In 1926 he toured England with Ravel.

Francescina, La. *See* Duparc, Elisabeth.

Francesco Canova da Milano (b. ? Monza, 18. VIII. 1497; d. ?, 1543), It. lutenist and comp. In the service 1st of the Duke of Mantua, *c.* 1510, and then of Pope Paul III from 1535. Pub. and contrib. to several books of lute pieces.

Franchetti, Alberto (b. Turin, 18. IX. 1860; d. Viareggio, 4. VIII. 1942). It. comp. Studied 1st in It., then with Draeseke at Dresden and at the Munich Cons. under Rheinberger. Director of the Cherubini Cons., Florence, 1926–8.

Works incl. operas *Asrael*, *Cristoforo Colombo*, *Fior d'Alpe*, *Signor di Pourceaugnac* (after Molière), *Germania*, *La figlia di Jorio* (after d'Annunzio), *Notte di leggenda*, *Glauco* and (with Giordano) *Giove a Pompei*; symph. in E min., etc.

Franchois, Johannes ('de Gemblaco') (b. ? Gembloux, ?; d. ?), 15th-cent. Flem. comp., not to be confused with Franchois Lebertoul. His extant works include

Mass-sections, a motet, *Ave virgo*, and *chansons*.

Franchomme, Auguste (Joseph) (b. Lille, 10. IV. 1808; d. Paris, 21. I. 1884), Fr. cellist. Studied at the Paris Cons. He played in var. theatre orchs. and had much success as solo and 4tet player. Prof. at the Cons. from 1846. Chopin, whose friend he was, wrote the Polonaise for cello and pf., Op. 3, for him, and F. collaborated with him, as well as with Bertini and Osborne, in duos on operatic airs, Chopin's choice being Meyerbeer's *Robert le Diable*. He was the cellist in Alard's 4tet. Chopin's cello sonata is ded. to him.

Francis of Assisi (1181 or 2–1226), It. saint and poet. *See* Inghelbrecht (*Cantique des créatures*), Loeffler (*Canticum*), Pierné (*Fioretti*), Sigtenhorst Meyer (*Hymn to the Sun*), Suter (*Laudi*).

Francisque, Antoine (b. Saint-Quentin, *c.* 1570; d. Paris, X. 1605), Fr. lutenist and comp. He lived at Cambrai in 1596 and was married there, but went to Paris not long after, pub. a book of lute pieces, *Le Trésor d'Orphée*, some comp. by himself, others arr. from popular dances.

Franck, César (Auguste) (b. Liège, 10. XII. 1822; d. Paris, 8. XI. 1890), Belg. comp. Precociously gifted, esp. as a pianist, he made a concert tour in Belg. at the age of 11. Sent to Paris in 1835 to study, he entered the Cons. in 1837. There he won var. prizes each year until he left in 1842. He returned to Belg., but settled permanently in Paris in 1844. In 1848 he married a young actress and was app. organist at the church of Saint-Jean-Saint-François in 1851. In 1853 he became choirmaster and in 1858 organist at Sainte-Clotilde. App. prof. of the org. at the Cons. in 1872. He became a chevalier of the Legion of Honour in 1885 and 2 years later, 30. I. 1887, a festival of his mus. was held. 6 months before his death he was involved in a street accident.

Works incl. operas *Le Valet de ferme* (unpub.), *Hulda*, *Ghisèle*; symph. in D min.; symph. poems, *Les Éolides*, *Le Chasseur maudit* (after Burger), *Psyché* (with chorus); *Les Djinns* and *Variations symphoniques* for pf. and orch.; 4 pf. trios, pf. 5tet, string 4tet; sonata for vln. and pf.; works for chorus and orch. (some with solo voices): *Ruth*, *La Tour de Babel*, *Les Béatitudes*, *Rédemption*, *Rébecca*, Psalm cl; *Paris: chant patriotique* for tenor and orch.; *Messe solennelle* for bass and org.; Mass for 3 voices, org., harp, cello and double bass; 3 motets, 3 offertories and other small sacred vocal works; *c.* 16 works for pf., incl. *Prélude, Choral et Fugue* and *Prélude, Aria et Final*; 9 works for org., incl. 6 *Pièces pour Grand Orgue*, 44 *Petites Pièces*, 3 *Pièces pour Grand*

Orgue, 3 *Chorals*; 5 works for harmonium; songs to poems by Chateaubriand, Hugo, Musset, Dumas, sen., Sully-Prudhomme, Joseph Méry, Jean-Pierre de Florian, Jean Reboul, Marceline Desbordes-Valmore, etc.

Franck, Johann Wolfgang (b. Unterschwaningen, VI. 1644; d. ? London, *c.* 1710), Ger. comp. *Kapellmeister* at Ansbach between 1673 and 1679, when he killed a musician of the chapel and wounded his wife from jealousy and fled to Hamburg, where he prod. 14 operas in 1679–86. After 1690 he lived in London for some years, giving concerts with Robert King, contrib. songs to the *Gentleman's Journal* and writing one for Colley Cibber's *Love's Last Shift*, also mus. for a masque by Motteux added to Shadwell's adaptation of Shakespeare's *Timon of Athens*.

Franck, Melchior (b. Zittau, 1573; d. Coburg, 1. VI. 1639), Ger. comp. Worked at Augsburg and briefly at Nuremberg, and in 1603 became *Kapellmeister* to the Duke of Coburg.

Works incl. *Melodiae sacrae* for 3 to 12 voices, *Paradisus musicus* for 4 voices, church mus., hymn-tunes; songs with instrumental accomp.; madrigals; instrumental pieces etc.

Franckenstein, Clemens von (b. Wiesentheid, Bavaria, 14. VII. 1875; d. Hechendorf, Bavaria, 19. VIII. 1942), Ger. comp. Studied in Vienna and later at Munich with Thuille and at Frankfurt with Knorr. After a visit to U.S.A. he cond. the Moody-Manners Opera Co. in Eng., 1902–7, then worked at the court theatres of Wiesbaden and Berlin, and in 1912 became general intendant of the Munich court theatres.

Works incl. operas *Griseldis*, *Rahab* and *Des Kaisers Dichter*; ballet *Die Biene*; orchestral works: variations on a theme by Meyerbeer, Dance Suite, Serenade, Rhapsody, Praeludium, Symph. Suite, *Das alte Lied*, 4 Dances, *Festival Prelude*; chamber mus.; pf. works; songs, etc.

Franco of Cologne (b. ?; d. ?), 13th-cent. mus. theorist, author of an *Ars cantus mensurabilis* surviving in 7 MSS. It expounds the system of notation in his day, now called 'Franconian'. An anon. monk of Bury St. Edmunds, writing of Parisian mus. in the 13th cent., refers also to a 'Franco primus', apparently a Parisian, who also wrote on the same subject.

Franco, Johan (b. Zaandam, 12. VII. 1908), Dutch, now Amer., comp. Pupil of Pijper. Settled in U.S.A. in 1936.

Works incl. 4 symphs., symph. poem *Péripétie*; *In Memoriam* for string orch.; *Concertino lirico* for vln. and orch., *Introduzione e scherzo* for clar. and orch.; vln. concerto, 2 works for pf. and orch., 5 string 4tets, string trio; 2 vln. sonatas; Christmas oratorio *The Stars look down*;

songs with orch.; 2 pf. sonatas; songs to poems by Browning, etc.

Francœur, François (b. Paris, 8. IX. 1698; d. Paris, 5. VIII. 1787), Fr. violinist and comp. Pupil of his father, Joseph F., he joined the Opéra orch. at the age of 15 and there met Rebel, with whom he worked for the rest of his life. In 1720 he pub. his 1st vln. sonatas, and in 1723 went with Rebel to Prague for the coronation of Charles VI. After his return to Paris in 1726 he gradually rose to the highest positions in Fr. mus.: comp. to the court 1727; member of the king's band 1730; 1743 Inspector, 1757 Director of the Opéra, 1760 Superintendent of the king's mus. (the last three jointly with Rebel). His nephew, Louis Joseph F. (1738–1804), was also a violinist and comp., and for a time Director of the Opéra.

Works incl. operas (comp. jointly with Rebel), ballets, vln. sonatas, etc.

Françoise de Rimini (*Francesca da R.*), opera by A. Thomas (lib. by Jules Barbier and Michel Carré, based on Dante), prod. Paris, Opéra, 14. IV. 1882.

Francs-Juges, Les (*The Judges of the Secret Court*), unfinished opera by Berlioz (lib. by Humbert Ferrand), comp. 1827–8; 1st perf. of the overture Paris, 26. V. 1828. The rest discarded or used elsewhere, e.g. in the *Symphonie fantastique*.

Frangipani, Cornelio (16th cent.), It. poet and playwright. *See* Merulo (*Tragedia*).

Frank, Ernst (b. Munich, 7. II. 1847; d. Oberdöbling nr. Vienna, 17. VIII. 1889), Ger. cond and comp. Studied at Munich Univ. and mus. under Franz Lachner. Cond. successively at Würzburg, Vienna, Mannheim, Frankfurt and Hanover. He finished Goetz's opera *Francesca da Rimini* and trans. operas by Stanford and Mackenzie.

Works incl. operas *Adam de la Halle*, *Hero* (after Grillparzer) and *Der Sturm* (after Shakespeare's *Tempest*); vocal duets from Kate Greenaway's *Under the Window*; songs, part-songs, etc.

Frankel, Benjamin (b. London, 31. I. 1906), Eng. comp. His father was a synagogue beadle and, unable to give him a mus. educ., sent him to the City to work at warehouses and as a watchmaker's apprentice. But Victor Benham insisted on giving him pf. lessons and he managed to secure 6 months' study in Ger. thanks to the favourable exchange after the 1914–18 war. At 17 he returned to London and picked up a precarious living as mus. teacher, café pianist and jazz-band violinist. But he managed to attend the G.S.M. in the daytime and eventually gained a comp. scholarship there, studying with Orlando Morgan. He gradually improved his living as orchestrator and

theatre cond., finally succeeding as cond. and comp. of film mus.

Works incl. mus. for many films, incl. some sponsored by the Ministry of Information and the British Council (e.g. 'shorts' from Shakespeare's *Julius Caesar* and *Macbeth*); film mus. *Mine Own·Executioner*, etc.; *Pezzo sinfonico* for orch., *Solemn Speech and Discussion* and *Mus. for Young Comrades* for string orch., *The Aftermath* (Robert Nichols) for tenor, strings, tpt. and drums; 7 symphs; vln. concerto; 4 string 4tets, *3 Sketches* for string 4tet, string trio, trio for clar., cello and pf., *Early Morning Pieces* for ob., clar. and bassoon; vln. and pf. sonata, sonatas for unaccomp. vln. and vla., *Sonata ebraica* for cello and harp, *Élégie juive* for cello and pf.; Passacaglia for 2 pfs.; pf. pieces, etc.

Franz (orig. **Knauth**), **Robert** (b. Halle, 28. VI. 1815; d. Halle, 24. X. 1892), Ger. comp. After much parental opposition he became a pupil of Schneider at Dessau in 1835, and after 2 years returned home, devoting himself to study and comp. without being able to secure a mus. post. He became one of the best exponents of Ger. songs, the 1st of which he pub. in 1843 and which attracted the attention of Schumann, Mendelssohn, Liszt and others. He then became a church organist and choral cond., also lecturer at Halle Univ. Much troubled by increasing deafness and a nervous complaint, he had to retire in 1868, but did much work in ed. the older choral classics.

Works incl. more than 350 songs, church mus., part-songs, etc.

Frappé (Fr.). *See* Ornaments.

Fraschini, Gaetano (b. Pavia, 1815; d. Naples, 24. V. 1887), It. tenor. Made his 1st appearance as a church and opera singer at Pavia in 1837. 1st appearance in London, 1847.

Fraser, Marjory Kennedy (b. Perth, 1. X. 1857; d. Edinburgh, 22. XI. 1930), Scot. singer and folksong collector, daughter of David Kennedy. Studied under her father and Mathilde Marchesi in Paris and began to visit the Hebrides to collect folksongs in 1905. Pub. several collections of these songs and wrote the lib. for Bantock's opera *The Seal Woman*.

Frasi, Giulia (b. ?; d. ?), It. singer. Made her London début in 1743, the same year sang in *Roxana, or Alexander in India* (an adaptation of Handel's *Alessandro*), and subsequently in several of Handel's oratorios.

Frau ohne Schatten, Die (*The Woman without a Shadow*), opera by R. Strauss (lib. by Hugo von Hofmannsthal), prod. Vienna, Opera, 10. X. 1919.

Frauenliebe und Leben (*Woman's Love and Life*), song cycle by Schumann, Op.

42 (8 poems by Adelbert von Chamisso), comp. in 1840.

Frauenlob (Heinrich von Meissen) (b. Meissen, ?; d. Mainz, 1318), Ger. *Minnesänger*. His songs belong to the end of the tradition of the *Minnesinger*, and in some ways foreshadow those of the *Meistersinger*.

Fredegunda, opera by Keiser (lib. by Johann Ulrich König, from the It. by Francesco Silvani), prod. Hamburg, Theater beim Gänsemarkt, III. 1715.

Frederick II (Frederick the Great) (b. Berlin, 24. I. 1712; d. Potsdam, 17. VIII. 1786), king of Prus., flautist and comp. Learnt mus. from Gottlob Hayn, the Berlin Cathedral organist, and in 1728 had fl. lessons from Quantz. In 1734 he estab. a private band at his castle at Rheinsberg and on his accession in 1740 a court band at Berlin and Potsdam. Graun, Quantz and C. P. E. Bach were in his service.

Works incl. part of the opera *Il rè pastore* (Metastasio) and contribs. to others; over 120 instrumental works, many with prominent fl. parts, etc.

Frege (*née* **Gerhard**), **Livia** (b. Gera, 13. VI. 1818; d. Leipzig, 22. VIII. 1891), Ger. soprano. Made her 1st appearance at the Leipzig Gewandhaus in 1832 at a concert given by Clara Wieck.

Freischütz, Der (lit. *The Freeshooter*), opera by Weber (lib. by Friedrich Kind, based on a story in Apel and Laun's *Gespensterbuch*), prod. Berlin, Schauspielhaus, 18. VI. 1821.

Freising, Eberhard von (Eberhardus Frisingensis) (b. ?; d. ?), 9th-cent. author of a short treatise on the measurement of org. pipes.

Freitas Branco, Luiz (b. Lisbon, 12. X. 1890; d. Lisbon, 27. XI. 1955), Port. comp. Studied at Lisbon, with Humperdinck in Berlin, and in Paris. Taught score-reading at the Lisbon Cons. from 1916 and in 1930 took charge of the master-class in comp.

Works incl. oratorio, cantata; 5 symphs., 2 Port. suites for orch.; vln. concerto, Ballad for pf. and orch.; songs with orch.; string 4tet; 2 vln. and pf. sonatas, cello and pf. sonata; pf. pieces; songs; madrigals to words by Camoens, etc.

Freitas Branco, Pedro (b. Lisbon, 31. X. 1896; d. Lisbon, 24. III. 1963), Port. cond. and comp., brother of prec. Studied under his brother and others, founded a Port. opera company in 1926, symph. concerts at Lisbon in 1928 and cond. the State Symph. Orch. from 1934. Married the Fr. pianist Marie-Antoinette de Lévêque (b. 1903).

Works incl. 2 string 4tets, pf. trio, songs, etc.

Freitas, Frederico de (b. Lisbon, 15. XI. 1902), Port. cond. and comp. Studied at the Lisbon Cons. He visited Brazil,

Fr., Spain and Hol. as cond. and became broadcasting cond. at Lisbon.

Works incl. opera *Luzdor*; ballets *Ribatejo* and *Nazeré*; cantata *The Seven Words of Our Lady*; symph. poems *Lenda dos bailarins* and *Suite colonial*; poem on an eclogue by Virgil and prelude on a Lisbon street-cry for string orch.; *Quarteto Concertante* for 2 vlns., 2 cellos and string orch.; sonata for vln. and cello; instrumental works; pf. pieces; songs, etc.

Fremsted, Olive (b. Stockholm, 14. III. 1871; d. Irvington, N.Y., 21. IV. 1951), Swed. soprano. Adopted by an Amer. couple, who took her to Minnesota, she studied pf. in Minneapolis and then singing in N.Y. in 1890. In 1893 she studied in Berlin with Lilli Lehmann, making her début in 1895, in Cologne. She later sang at Bayreuth, Munich, Vienna and London, becoming a leading soprano at the N.Y. Metropolitan Opera from 1903 to 1914. An outstanding Wagner singer, she also excelled in It. opera.

French Horn. *See* Horn.

French Overture. *See* Overture.

French Sixth, a form of the chord of the augmented 6th, which incl. a maj. 3rd with a maj. 2nd above it, e.g.:

French Suites, 6 keyboard suites by Bach, comp. at Cöthen *c.* 1722. The name is said to refer to their Fr. style. They differ from the Eng. Suites in having no preludes.

Frescobaldi, Girolamo (b. Ferrara, IX. 1583; d. Rome, 1. III. 1643), It. comp. and organist. Studied at Ferrara under the cathedral organist Luzzaschi. Visited Brussels, 1607–8. App. organist at St. Peter's in Rome, 1608. He was given leave of absence from 1628 to 1633, during which time he served as organist to Ferdinand II, Duke of Tuscany.

Works incl. *ricercari, canzoni*, toccatas, etc. for org. and for harpsichord; fantasies for instruments in 4 parts; madrigals, etc.

Frets, the small strips of gut, wood or metal fixed on the fingerboard on certain string instruments (incl. the lute, viols, guitar, mandoline, banjo, ukelele and the Rus. balalaika), enabling the player to play in tune with certainty, the string being stopped by the finger at exactly the right spot, determined by the F.

Freunde von Salamanka, Die (*The Friends of Salamanca*), operetta by Schubert (lib. by Johann Mayrhofer), comp. 1815, but never perf. in Schubert's lifetime; prod., with a new lib. by Günther Ziegler, Halle, 6. V. 1928.

Frey, Emil (b. Baden, Aargau, 8. IV. 1889; d. Zürich, 20. V. 1946), Swiss pianist and comp. Studied at the Geneva and Paris Conss., at the latter with Fauré and Widor. After living as pianist in Berlin, he became pf. prof. at the Moscow Cons., 1912–17, when he settled at Zürich. He toured widely as pianist in Eur. and Amer.

Works incl. Mass and Psalms c and ciii for solo voices, chorus, orch. and org., Psalm cxxi for soprano, chorus and org.; 2 symphs.; Symph. Concert Piece for pf. and orch.; string 4tet; chamber mus.; instrumental sonatas and pieces; pf. works; songs (incl. some in Swiss dialects), etc.

Freytag, Gustav (1816–95), Ger. novelist. See **Vollerthun** (*Freikorporal*).

Frezzolini, Erminia (b. Orvieto, 27. III. 1818; d. Paris, 5. XI. 1884), It. soprano. Made her 1st appearance in 1838 at Florence. Sang in Vienna, London, St. Petersburg, Madrid, Paris and the U.S.A.

Friberth, Karl (b. Wullersdorf, Lower Aus., 7. VI. 1736; d. Vienna, 6. VIII. 1816), Aus. tenor, author and comp. Studied with Bonno and Gassmann in Vienna and in 1759 joined the Esterházy household under Haydn, for whom he wrote the lib. of *L'incontro improviso*. Returned to Vienna as *Kapellmeister* to the Jesuits and Minorites in 1776. Comp. mainly church mus.

Fricassée (Fr.), a term now used only in cookery, but in the 16th cent. for a Quodlibet or var. tunes sung together, often in different languages.

Fricker, Peter Racine (b. London, 5. IX. 1920), Eng. comp., partly of Fr. descent. He studied at the R.C.M. in London and later with Seiber. His wind 5tet won the Clements Prize in 1947 and his 1st symph. the Kussevitsky Award.

Works incl. radio opera *The Death of Vivien*; ballet *Canterbury Prologue* (after Chaucer); oratorio *A Vision of Judgment*; 3 symphs., *Prelude, Elegy and Finale* for strings; vln. and vla. concertos, *Concertante* for 3 pfs. and strings; wind 5tet, string 4tet; vln. and pf. sonata; org. sonata, etc.

Fricsay, Ferenc (b. Budapest, 9. VIII. 1914; d. Basle, 20. II. 1963), Hung. cond. He studied with Bartók and Kodály at the Budapest Academy, and was successively cond. at the Szeged Opera 1934–44, the Budapest Opera, 1945, and the Vienna State Opera, 1947. From 1948 to 1952 he was director of the Berlin City Opera, and from 1956 to 1959 of the Munich State Opera. He appeared frequently as a guest cond. in Eng., It., Holland and Amer., and made a large number of gramophone records.

Friderici, Daniel (b. Eichstedt, Querfurt, 1584; d. Rostock, 23. IX. 1638), Ger. comp. Cantor at St. Mary's Church, Rostock,

from 1618 to his death. Pub. Morley's 3-part madrigals with Ger. words in 1624. Works incl. madrigals, Ger. songs for 3–8 voices, etc.

Friedemann Bach, opera by Graener (lib. by Rudolf Lothar), prod. Schwerin, 13. XI. 1931.

Friedenstag (*Peace Day*), opera by R. Strauss (lib. by Joseph Gregor, who 1st suggested it to Stefan Zweig, based on Calderón's play *La redención de Breda* and Velázquez's picture illustrating that), prod. Munich, 24. VII. 1938.

Friedheim, Arthur (b. St. Petersburg, 26. X. 1859; d. N.Y., 19. X. 1932), Rus. pianist of Ger. descent. Pupil of Liszt. He taught at Leipzig and at the R.C.M., Manchester, and settled in N.Y. in 1915.

Friedlaender, Max (b. Brieg, Silesia, 12. X. 1852; d. Eichkamp nr. Berlin, 2. V. 1934), Ger. baritone and writer on mus. Studied under García in London and Stockhausen at Frankfurt. Taught in Berlin and at Harvard Univ. Ed. songs by Schubert and Schumann, Gluck's odes and Ger. folksongs and wrote books on Ger. song and Brahms's songs.

Friedman, Ignacy (b. Cracow, 14. II. 1882; d. Sydney, 26. I. 1948), Pol. pianist and comp. Studied pf. at Cracow and with Leschetizky in Vienna, and comp. with Adler there and Riemann at Leipzig. He toured very extensively and wrote nearly 100 works, mainly for pf., but incl. chamber mus.

Frigel, Pehr (b. Kalmar, 2. IX. 1750; d. Stockholm, 24. XI. 1842), Swed. comp. He studied at Uppsala and took to comp. after retirement from a government post in 1801.

Works incl. operas *Arsène, Zemir och Azor* and *Zoroaster*; oratorio *The Redeemer on Mt. Olivet*; church cantatas, 2 symphs., etc.

Friml, Rudolf (b. Prague, 2. XII. 1879), Cz. comp. and pianist. Studied at the Prague Cons. with Juranek (pf.) and Foerster (comp.). Toured for some time as accompanist to Jan Kubelík, remaining in Amer. after a tour in 1906. He appeared as a soloist with many orchs.

Works incl. operettas *The Firefly, High Jinks, Katinka, Rose Marie, The Vagabond King* and many others. He also comp. some light pf. mus.

Friskin, James (b. Glasgow, 3. III. 1886; d. N.Y., 16. III. 1967), Scot. pianist and comp. Studied at the R.C.M. in London. In 1914 he went to N.Y. and became pf. prof. at the Inst. of Mus. Art. He married Rebecca Clarke in 1944.

Works incl. 2 motets on Scot. psalm tunes; suite for orch.; pf. 5tet in C min.; phantasy string 4tet; cello and pf. sonata, etc.

Friss. See **Csárdás**.

Froberger   Fuentes

Froberger, Johann Jacob (b. Stuttgart,
V. 1616; d. Héricourt nr. Montbéliard, 7.
V. 1667), Ger. organist and comp. Studied
under his father, who was a singer, and
later *Kapellmeister* at Stuttgart. App. court
organist in Vienna on the accession of
the Emperor Ferdinand III in 1637,
remaining there until 1657, but spending
1637–41 in It. as a pupil of Frescobaldi. In
1662 he went to London, where he is said
to have arrived destitute, having been twice
robbed on the way. In later years he lived
in the house of Sibylla, Dowager Duchess
of Württemberg, at her retreat at Héricourt.
Works incl. harpsichord suites, many
pieces for org. and harpsichord incl.
toccatas, *ricercari*, etc.

'Frog' Quartet, the nickname of
Haydn's string 4tet in D maj., Op. 50
No. 6, the finale of which is supposed to
have a 'croaking' theme.

Fröhlich, Aus. family of musicians, 4
sisters, friends of Schubert:
1. **Anna (Nanette)** F. (b. Vienna, 19.
IX. 1793; d. Vienna, 11. III. 1880), pianist
and soprano. Pupil of Hummel, Hauss and
Siboni, singing teacher at the Vienna
Cons. 1819–54. She gave the 1st perf. of
several of Schubert's works.
2. **Barbara** F. (b. Vienna, 30. VIII.
1797; d. Vienna, 30. VI. 1879), contralto
and painter. Married Ferdinand Bogner,
prof. of fl. at the Vienna Cons.
3. **Katharina** F. (b. Vienna, 10. VI.
1800; d. Vienna, 3. III. 1879), intimate
friend of Grillparzer, who lived in the
sisters' house until his death in 1872.
4. **Josephine** F. (b. Vienna, 12. XII.
1803; d. Vienna, 7. V. 1878), soprano.
Pupil of her sister Anna, made her 1st
appearance in 1821, later went to Copenhagen to study under Siboni and sang
with success in Scand., also, c. 1829–31,
in It.

Fröhlich, Friedrich Theodor (b. Brugg,
25. II. 1803; d. Aarau, 16. X. 1836), Swiss
comp. Pupil of Zelter and Klein in Berlin.
Taught and cond. at Aarau.
Works incl. pf. mus.; popular songs,
e.g. Eichendorff's 'Wem Gott will rechte
Gunst erweisen', etc.

Froissart, concert overture by Elgar,
Op. 19, comp. in 1890 and prod. at the
Worcester Festival of that year.

Froissart, Jean (1338–1404), Fr. hist.
See above.

'From Bohemia's Fields and Groves'
(Smetana). *See* **Má Vlast.**

'From the New World' (Dvořák). *See*
'New World' Symphony.

Fromm, Andreas (b. Pänitz, Brandenburg, 1621; d. Strahov, Prague, 16. X.
1683), Ger. comp. He was cantor and prof.
at the Pädagogium of Stettin in the middle
of the cent.
Works incl. oratorio (one of the earliest

known in Ger.) *Vom reichen Mann und
Lazarus; Dialogus Pentecostalis,* etc.

Frosch (Ger. = frog), the heel of the
vln. bow. The direction 'am F.' found in
Ger. scores means that a passage is to be
bowed near the heel of the bow.

Frottola, an early 16th-cent. It. song,
originating in Milan, for several voices or
for solo voice and instruments, forerunner
of the madrigal but less polyphonically
elaborate.
The term is used in a general sense to
cover numerous different forms: *strambotto, oda, capitolo,* etc., and also in a
partic. sense, to mean a song in several
stanzas with a refrain or burden (*ripresa*)
sung complete at the beginning and
(usually) curtailed, but often with a mus.
extension, after each stanza; the same
mus. serves for both refrain and stanza.

Frumerie, Gunnar de (b. Nacka nr.
Stockholm, 20. VII. 1908), Swed. pianist
and comp. His teachers incl. Erwin Stein
in Vienna and Alfred Cortot in Paris.
Works incl. 2 pf. concertos; Variations
and Fugue for pf. and many other pf.
works incl. chaconne, suite, *Six Pieces*;
songs, Persian and gypsy poems, etc.

Fry, William Henry (b. Philadelphia, 10.
VIII. 1813; d. Santa Cruz, Virgin Islands,
21. IX. 1864), Amer. comp. and critic.
He was mainly self-taught. Lived in Eur.
in 1846–52 as mus. correspondent of the
New York Tribune, of which he later
became mus. critic.
Works incl. operas *Leonora* (after
Bulwer-Lytton's *Lady of Lyons*) and *Notre-
Dame de Paris* (after Hugo); *Stabat Mater*;
cantatas; 4 programme symphs., overtures;
pf. pieces, songs, etc.

Frye, Walter (b. ?; d. ?), 15th-cent. Eng.
comp. who apparently lived abroad for
much of his life. He wrote 3 Masses,
chansons and antiphons; his *Ave regina
caelorum mater regis* was copied into 13
continental MSS. and is found in 3 arrs.
for keyboard in the *Buxheimer Orgelbuch*
(q.v.).

Fuchs, Robert (b. Frauenthal, 15. II.
1847; d. Vienna, 19. II. 1927), Aus. comp.
Prof. at the Vienna Cons. from 1875 to
1912.
Works incl. 2 operas; Mass; symph. in
C maj., 5 Serenades (4 for strings); pf.
concerto; chamber mus., etc.

Fuenllana, Miguel de (b. Naval-
carnero, Madrid, c. 1500; d. ?), Span.
lutenist and comp. Although blind, he
became a great player, and in 1554 he pub.
a book of mus. for *vihuela* and similar
instruments, incl. comps. of his own and
many arrs. of works by Guerrero, Morales,
Arcadelt, Verdelot and others.

Fuentes, Pascual (b. Albaida, Valencia,
?; d. Valencia, 26. IV. 1768), Span. comp.
Maestro de capilla at the church of S.

222

Andrea at Valencia and from 1757 of the cathedral. Wrote church and secular vocal mus.

Fuga (It. = flight) = Fugue; in earlier times one of the It. terms for Canon, another being Caccia.

Fuga ricercata. *See* Ricercare.

Fugato (It. = fugued), a passage written in the manner of a fugue, occurring merely incidentally in a comp.; or a piece in fugal style that cannot be considered to be in the form of a fugue.

Fugère, Lucien (b. Paris, 22. VII. 1848; d. Paris, 15. I. 1935), Fr. baritone. Having failed as a sculptor and made a living as a commercial traveller, he appeared at the Ba-ta-clan café-concert in Paris in 1870 with Planquette's marching-song *Le Régiment de Sambre-et-Meuse* and made his 1st stage appearance at the Bouffes-Parisiens in 1874. 1st sang at the Opéra-Comique in 1877 and continued singing until he was 80.

Fughetta (It. = little fugue). Unlike a *fugato*, a F. is formally a proper fugue, but much more condensed.

Fugue, a contrapuntal comp. in 2 or more parts, based on a 'subject', short or long, which is intro. successively in imitation at the beginning and recurs in the course of the piece. The 2nd entry of the subject, generally at a level a 5th higher or a 4th lower (but sometimes a 4th higher or a 5th lower), is called the Answer. It does not necessarily imitate the subject exactly: it may be modified to preserve the tonality of the piece or to facilitate a 3rd entry. A 3rd entry is often deferred for a few bars, the intervening space being occupied by a Codetta.

The answer is accomp. by a counterpoint which, if it also recurs in the course of the piece, is called the Countersubject. After all the initial entries of the subject and answer there is generally an Episode, derived from the material already heard or completely independent, leading to a further entry of the subject. The remainder of the F. is made up of an alternation of episodes and entries, which may incl. treatment of the subject in Canon. The foll. ex. shows the beginning of one of Bach's F.s (*see* illustration overleaf).

A F. may have more than one subject and more than one countersubject. It may be written for instruments or voices or for both combined and may occur as part of a large-scale work, such as a symph., opera or oratorio.

Fuhrmann, Georg Leopold (b. ?; d. ?), Ger. 16th–17th cent. lutenist, engraver and bookseller. Worked at Nuremberg, where in 1615 he pub. a book of lute pieces, *Testudo Gallo-Germanica*, incl. some by J. and R. Dowland.

Fulda, Adam of (b. ?, c. 1445; d. Witten-

berg, 1505), Ger. monk, theorist and comp. Wrote a tract on mus. and comp. motets, etc.

Fuleihan, Anis (b. Kyrenia, Cyprus, 2. IV. 1900), Amer. (naturalized) pianist and comp. Educ. at the Eng. School in Cyprus and studied mus. in U.S.A., where he settled in 1915. Toured much in U.S.A. and the E., and lived at Cairo for 2 years. After his return to Amer. in 1928 he cond. and comp.

Works incl. opera *Vasco*; several ballets; symph., suite *Mediterranean* and *Preface to a Child's Story-Book* for orch.; suite for chamber orch.; 3 pf. concertos, cello concerto, 2 vln. concertos, concerto for Theremin, Fantasy for vla. and orch.; 5 string 4tets, clar. 5tet, horn 5tet; sonatas for vln., vla. and cello; 11 pf. sonatas.

Full Anthem. *See* Anthem.

Full Score. *See* Score.

Fuller, Donald (b. Washington, D.C., 1. VII. 1919), Amer. comp. Graduated at Yale Univ. and studied mus. in U.S.A. with Wagenaar, Copland and Milhaud.

Works incl. symph.; trio for clar., cello and pf., sonatina for ob., clar. and pf.; sonata for 2 pfs.; sonata, sonatina and pieces for pf.; songs, etc.

Fuller-Maitland J(ohn). A(lexander). (b. London, 7. IV. 1856; d. Carnforth, Lancs., 30. III. 1936), Eng. critic, ed. and writer on mus. Educ. at Westminster School and Cambridge. Studied mus. with Stanford, Dannreuther and Rockstro, became a mus. critic in London and was from 1889 to 1911 chief critic of *The Times*. Ed. old mus., esp. for the harpsichord, incl. the *Fitzwilliam Virginal Book* with W. Barclay Squire, and was ed. of the 2nd ed. of Grove's Dict. Among his books is the 4th vol. of the *Oxford Hist. of Music*.

Füllsack, Zacharias (b. ?; d. 1616), Ger. 16th–17th-cent. lutenist and trombonist. Worked at Hamburg until 1612 and later in the court chapel at Dresden. In 1607, with Christoph Hildebrand, he pub. a book of *Auserlesene Paduanen und Galliarden*, incl. many pieces by Eng. comps.

Fundamental Bass, an imaginary harmonic phenomenon expounded by Rameau. The F. B. is the Root bass of any chord occurring in a comp., and according to Rameau no comp. was aesthetically satisfying unless that bass, either actually present or implied, was in each chord used, proceeding from the one before it to the one after it in accordance with definite rules of mus. logic.

Fundamental Tones. *See* Partials.

Funeral March. *See* March.

Funeral Ode (Bach). *See* Trauer-Ode.

Furiant (Cz.), a lively Cz. dance in 3–4 time with a characteristic effect of cross-rhythm, often used in place of a scherzo by

FUGUE

Dvořák and other Cz. comps. of the nat. school.

Furlana. *See* **Forlana.**

Furlong, an old Eng. name for the Forlana.

Furniture, an org. Mixture stop.

Fürstenau, Anton Bernhard (b. Münster, 20. X. 1792; d. Dresden, 18. XI. 1852), Ger. flautist and comp. In the court orch. at Dresden from 1820. Wrote 2 methods and many pieces for his instrument. He accomp. Weber to London in 1826.

Furtwängler, Wilhelm (b. Berlin, 25. I. 1886; d. Baden-Baden, 30. XI. 1954), Ger. cond. Studied at Munich with Rheinberger and Schillings, and early began gaining experience as cond. of concerts and opera. After an engagement at Mannheim he followed Nikisch at the Leipzig Gewandhaus, and in 1922 he became cond.-in-chief of the Berlin Phil. Orch. He toured infrequently but with great success, including Bayreuth and London (Covent Garden and concerts), etc. He was also active as a comp., prod. 2 symphs., a pf. concerto, a Te Deum and some chamber mus.

Furuhjelm, Erik (b. Helsinki, 6. VII. 1883), Fin. critic and comp. Studied at the Helsinki Cons. and later in Vienna, Munich and Paris. After his return to Fin. he became prof. at the Helsinki Cons. and mus. critic to 2 newspapers. He wrote a biog. of Sibelius.

Works inc. 2 symphs., overture and

suites for orch.; *Concertstück* for vln. and orch.; chamber mus., etc.

Fux, Johann Joseph (b. Hirtenfeld, Styria, 1660; d. Vienna, 14. II. 1741), Aus. theorist and comp. Became organist to the Schottenstift in Vienna in 1696, court comp. 1698, 2nd *Kapellmeister* at St. Stephen's Cathedral 1705 and 1st in 1712, vice-*Kapellmeister* to the court 1713, *Kapellmeister* 1715. His *Gradus ad Parnassum* (1725) was for many years the standard treatise on counterpoint, and was studied by Haydn and Beethoven among others.

Works incl. 18 operas, e.g. *Costanza e fortezza*; 11 oratorios; 70 Masses and quantities of other church mus.; 38 trio sonatas; partitas, etc., for orchestra; keyboard mus., etc.

fz. (abbr. for It. *forzando*), a direction which, placed against a note or chord, indicates that it should be strongly accentuated. The more usual word is *sforzando*, marked *sf*.

G

G, the 5th note, or dominant, of the scale of C major.

G.P. (abbr.), General Pause. Used formerly to indicate that all the performers had a rest at the same time.

G.S.M. (abbr.), Guildhall School of Music (London).

Gabrieli, Andrea (b. Venice, c. 1520; d. Venice, 1586), It. comp. Pupil of Willaert at St. Mark's in Venice, where he became a member of the Doge's choir in 1536, 2nd organist in succession to Merulo in 1566 and later 1st organist. He was a famous teacher and had many distinguished pupils, It. and foreign, incl. his nephew Giovanni G.

Works incl. Masses, motets and other church mus. with instruments; spiritual songs; madrigals, etc. for several voices; choruses for Sophocles' *Oedipus Tyrannus*; *ricercari* for org., etc.

Gabrieli, Giovanni (b. Venice, c. 1555; d. Venice, 12. VIII. 1612), It. comp., nephew of prec. Pupil of his uncle, musician (?) to the Duke of Bavar. in his youth; became 1st organist at St. Mark's in Venice in 1585 in succession to Andrea G., like whom he had many famous It. and foreign pupils.

Works incl. church mus. for voices and instruments, often laid out antiphonally for choral and orchestral groups; *Sacrae symphoniae* in many vocal and instrumental parts; instrumental pieces of var. kinds; org. mus., etc.

Gabrielli, Catterina (b. Rome, 12. XI. 1730; d. Rome, 16. II. 1796), It. soprano. Pupil of Garcia and Porpora, made her 1st appearance at Lucca in 1747.

Gabrilovich, Ossip Salomonovich (b. St. Petersburg, 7. II. 1878; d. Detroit, 14. IX. 1936), Rus.-Amer. pianist, cond. and comp. Studied pf. with A. Rubinstein, later at the St. Petersburg Cons., where Liadov and Glazunov were among his masters, and finished his pf. studies with Leschetizky in Vienna, 1894–6, making his 1st appearance in Berlin in the latter year. He toured much in Eur. and U.S.A., married the contralto Clara Clemens (b. 1874), daughter of Mark Twain, in 1909 and settled in N.Y. as an Amer. citizen in 1914. App. cond. of the Detroit Symph. Orch. in 1918.

Works incl. Overture-Rhapsody for orch.; Elegy for cello and pf.; many pf. pieces; songs, etc.

Gade, Niels Vilhelm (b. Copenhagen, 22. II. 1817; d. Copenhagen, 21. XII. 1890), Dan. comp. Pupil of Berggreen, Weyse and others. He learnt var. instruments and became a violinist in the royal

orch.; and having gained a comp. prize with the *Ossian* overture in 1841, was enabled to go to Leipzig for further study with a royal grant. There he came into touch with Mendelssohn, who prod. his 1st symph. in 1843 and engaged him to cond. the Gewandhaus concerts in his absence. He returned to Copenhagen in 1848 and worked as organist, cond. and teacher, becoming court mus. director in 1861.

Works incl. opera *Mariotta*; cantatas *Baldurs Drom*, *Comala*, *Erl King's Daughter*, *Zion*, *The Crusaders*, *Den Bjaergtagne*, *Psyche*, etc.; 8 symphs., overtures *Echoes from Ossian*, *In the Highland*, *Hamlet* (after Shakespeare), *Michelangelo*, etc., suite *Holbergiana* for orch.; string 4tet, 5tet, string 8tet, pf. trios and other chamber mus.; 4 vln. and pf. sonatas; instrumental pieces; pf. sonata in E min. and pieces for pf. solo and duet; songs, part-songs, etc.

Gadski, Johanna (b. Anclam, Pom., 15. VI. 1872; d. Berlin, 23. II. 1932), Ger. soprano. Made her 1st appearance in Berlin in 1889.

Gadzhibekov, Uzeir Abdul Hussein Ogli (b. Agzhabad nr. Shusha, Azerbaijan, 17. IX. 1885; d. Baku, 23. XI. 1948), Rus. (Azerbaijan) comp. Educ. at a teacher's training coll. at Gori, Georgia, later studied mus. at Baku, Moscow and St. Petersburg. He became director of the Baku Cons. and studied Azerbaijan folk mus., on which his work is based.

Works incl. 7 Azerbaijan nat. operas and 1 operetta; folksong arrs., etc.

Gafori, Franchino (b. Lodi, 14. I. 1451; d. Milan, 25. VI. 1522), It. priest, comp. and writer on mus. *Maestro di cappella* at Monticello and Bergamo, and from 1484 attached to Milan Cathedral. Wrote several theoret. books, incl. *Practica musicae* (1496), and comp. Masses and other church mus.

Gagliano (actually **Zenobi**), **Giovanni Battista da** (b. Gagliano nr. Florence, c. 1585; d. Florence, c. 1650), It. comp. Instructor at the church of San Lorenzo at Florence in 1613 in succession to his brother and later musician to the Grand Duke of Tuscany.

Works incl. motets, psalms and other church mus., etc.

Gagliano, Marco da (Zenobi) (b. Gagliano nr. Florence, c. 1575; d. Florence, 24. II. 1642), It. comp., brother of prec. Studied org. and theorbo under Luca Bati at the church of San Lorenzo at Florence, where he became instructor in 1602 and *maestro di cappella* in 1608. In 1607 he founded the Accademia degl' Elevati for the cultivation of mus. and c. 1610 became *maestro di cappella* to the Grand Duke of Tuscany. He was also in touch with the ducal family of Gonzaga at Mantua, where

his opera *Dafne*, a setting of Rinuccini's lib., was prod. *c*. I. 1608. He stayed till VI. and wrote mus. for the wedding of the duke's son.
Works incl. operas *Dafne*, *La Flora*, *Il Medoro* (mus. lost); oratorio *La regina Santa Orsola* (mus. lost); Masses, Offices for the Dead, *Sacrae cantiones*; madrigals, etc.

Gagliarda (It.) = Galliard.

Gaigerova, Varvara (b. Orekhovo-Zuevo, 4. X. 1903), Rus. comp. She was a pupil of Miaskovsky at the Moscow Cons. Works incl. 3 symphs., symph. suite on Caucasian themes; 2 string 4tets; pf. sonatas; songs to words by Pushkin, etc.

Gailhard, Pierre (b. Toulouse, 1. VIII. 1848; d. Paris, 12. X. 1918), Fr. baritone. Studied at the Toulouse and Paris Conss. and made his 1st appearance in 1867, at the Opéra-Comique. He 1st appeared in London in 1879. From 1884 to 1891, 1893 to 1899 and 1900 to 1905 he was joint manager of the Opéra, and from 1899 to 1900 and 1905 to 1908 sole manager.

Gaillarde. *See* Galliard.

Gál, Hans (b. Brunn, nr. Vienna, 5. VIII. 1890), Aus. comp. and musicologist. Pupil of Mandyczewski in Vienna and lecturer at the Univ. there from 1918; later director of the Mus. Acad. at Mainz. After the *Anschluss* he took refuge at Edinburgh, where he was lecturer at the Univ. from 1945 to 1957.
Works incl. operas *Der Fischer*, *Der Arzt der Sobeide*, *Ruth*, *Die heilige Ente*, *Das Lied der Nacht*, *Die beiden Klaus*, *Der Zauberspiegel*; *Requiem für Mignon* (from Goethe's *Wilhelm Meister*) for chorus and orch. and other choral works; *Sinfonietta*, *Ballet Suite*, *Pickwickian Overture* (after Dickens), etc. for orch.; serenade for strings; pf. concerto, vln. concerto; 2 string 4tets, 5 Intermezzi for string 4tet, serenade for string trio; pf. works, etc.

Galant (Fr. and Ger. = courtly), an adj. used to designate a special mus. style of the 18th cent., esp. that of C. P. E. Bach and the Mannheim school. Its main characts. are elegance, a certain superficiality of feeling, formality (the 1st approaches towards sonata form) and profuse ornamentation.

Galanterien (Ger.) } (lit. courtesies),
Galanteries (Fr.) }
the extra dances or other pieces added to those which were normal in the classical Suite or Partita (Allemande, Courante, Sarabande and Gigue). The most frequently used Gs. were Bourrées, Minuets, Passepieds, Chaconnes and, among pieces other than dances, Airs.

Galatea, La, opera by Schürer (lib. by Metastasio), prod. Dresden, at court, 8. XI. 1746.

Galilei, Vincenzo (b. Santa Maria in

Monte nr. Florence, *c*. 1520; d. Florence, VI. 1591), It. comp., lutenist and theorist. Studied under Zarlino at Venice. He took part in the discussions which led the Florentine *camerata* to opera after his death and wrote theoret. books, becoming involved in controversy with Zarlino. Father of the astronomer Galileo Galilei.
Works incl. cantata *Il Conte Ugolino* from Dante, a setting of the Lamentations of Jeremiah (both lost, and both among the earliest mus. for a single voice with accomp.); 2 books of madrigals; pieces for 2 viols; a lute book in tablature; *Dialogo della musica antica et della moderna* (1581), etc.

Galimat(h)ias (Fr. = gallimaufry, farrago, gibberish). In mus. the term is found in Mozart's *Galimathias musicum* (K. 32) written by him at The Hague in 1766, at age of 10, for the coming of age of William of Orange. It contains the Dutch nat. air 'Wilhelmus van Nassouwe'.

Gallenberg, Wenzel (Robert) von, Count (b. Vienna, 28. XII. 1783; d. Rome, 13. III. 1839), Aus. amateur comp. Studied with Albrechtsberger and married Countess Giulietta Guicciardi, the pupil of Beethoven.
Works incl. *c*. 50 ballets, 3 overtures, 8 pieces for wind band, dances for orch. and for pf., contributions to periodical pubs., etc.

Galli, Antonius (b. ?; d. ?), Flem. 16th-cent. comp., active in Bruges, 1544–50. Wrote much church mus. and a few *chansons*.

Galli, Caterina (b. ?, 1727; d. London, 1804), It. mezzo-soprano. Lived in London from *c*. 1742 and sang leading parts in several of Handel's oratorios.

Galli, Filippo (b. Rome, 1783; d. ? Paris, 3. VI. 1853), It. bass, at 1st a tenor. Made his 1st appearance as a tenor at Bologna in 1804 and as a bass at Venice in 1812.

Galli-Curci, Amelita (b. Milan, 18. XI. 1882; d. La Jolla, Calif., 26. XI. 1963), It. soprano. Studied pf. at Milan Cons. but mainly self-taught as a singer. She made her début at Trani in 1906. She joined the Chicago Opera Co. in 1916 and sang subsequently in N.Y. and London (though not in opera). She retired through illness in 1930.

Galli-Marié, Marie (Célestine Laurence) (b. Paris, XI. 1840; d. Vence nr. Nice, 22. IX. 1905), Fr. mezzo-soprano. Pupil of her father; made her 1st appearance at Strasbourg in 1859. She was the 1st Mignon (A. Thomas) and Carmen (Bizet).

Galliard (Eng., from Fr. *Gaillarde* and It. *Gagliarda*), a sprightly dance dating from the early 16th cent., orig. in 3–2 time but later also in 2–2 time; often used in mus. as a contrast to the Pavan and fre-

GALLIARD

Byrd

quently based on the same mus. material (*see* illustration).

Galliard, Johann Ernst (John Ernest) (b. Celle, *c.* 1680; d. London, 1749), anglicized oboist and comp. of Fr.-Ger. origin. Pupil of J. B. Farinelli and Steffani, settled in Eng. *c.* 1706 as oboist to Prince George of Denmark. Later active as a comp., esp. for the theatre, and also trans. Tosi's treatise on singing under the title *Observations on the Florid Song* (1742). Works incl. operas *Calypso and Telemachus*, *Pan and Syrinx* and *Oreste e Pilade* (unfinished); several pantomimes and other stage entertainments; choruses for the Earl of Buckingham's *Julius Caesar*; *The Hymn of Adam and Eve* from Milton's *Paradise Lost*; church mus.; instrumental mus., incl. piece for 24 bassoons and 4 double basses.

Gallican Chant, the Provençal plainsong in use in Fr. until the intro. of the Rom. ritual in the 8th cent.

Galliculus (? Hähnel, Hähnlein), Joannes (b. ?; d. ?), Ger. 16th-cent. theorist and comp. Worked at Leipzig (?) as a teacher; wrote a theoret. work *Isagoge* (later *Libellus*) *de compositione cantus* and comp. a Passion according to St. Mark, 2 Magnificats, a psalm, liturgical works for Easter and Christmas, etc.

Galloway, Lady, Scot. author. *See* McQuaid (*Witch Lady*).

Gallus, Jacobus. *See* Handl.

Gallus, Johannes (Jehan Le Cocq) (b. ?; d. ?), Fr. or Flem. 16th-cent. comp. not to be confused with Handl (Jacobus Gallus). Comp. *chansons.*

Galop (Fr. = gallop), a quick ballroom dance in 2–4 time 1st appearing under that name in Paris in 1829, but of older

Ger. origin, its Ger. name (now *Galopp*) having been *Hopser* (hopper) or *Rutscher* (glider).

Galoubet (Prov.), a small wind instrument, the Pipe used with the accomp. Tabor (Fr. *tambourin*).

Galpin, Francis W(illiam). (b. Dorchester, 25. XII. 1858; d. Richmond, Surrey, 30. XII. 1945), Eng. clergyman and mus. scholar. Educ. at Sherborne School and Cambridge, where he studied the org. and played the clar. in the Univ. orch. Canon of Chelmsford in 1917 and Litt.D. Cambridge, 1938. He made a collection of old mus. instruments and wrote several books and many articles on the subject.

Galpin Society, a society for the investigation of the hist. of mus. instruments, founded in 1946 in memory of Francis W. Galpin (1858–1945), hist. and collector. In 1948 the society began the pub. of a *Journal,* which has since appeared annually.

Galsworthy, John (1867–1933), Eng. novelist and playwright. Made a trans. of Bizet's *Carmen.*

Galuppi, Baldassare (b. Burano nr. Venice, 18. X. 1706; d. Venice, 3. I. 1785), It. comp. Pupil of his father and later, after the failure of his first opera in 1722, of Lotti in Venice. His operatic career proper began in 1728, after which he comp. a vast quantity of works. His *opere serie* met with indifferent success, but his comic operas are notable, esp. those on libretti by Goldoni, the most famous being *Il filosofo di campagna* (1754). Visited London 1741–3, where he prod. several operas. App. 2nd *maestro di cappella* at St. Mark's, Venice, 1748; 1st *maestro* and

Director of the Ospitale degl' Incurabili, 1762. Visited St. Petersburg 1765. Thereafter comp. few operas, and devoted himself chiefly to oratorios for the Incurabili. Works incl. operas *Alessandro nell' Indie, L'Olympiade, L'Arcadia in Brenta, Il Conte Caramella, Il mondo della luna, Il mondo alla roversa, La calamita de cuori, Il filosofo di campagna, Le nozze, L'amante di tutte, Le tre amanti ridicoli, Il Marchese Villano, Ifigenia in Tauride*, etc. (over 90 in all); 27 oratorios; church mus.; instrumental mus., etc.

Gamba (abbr., *see* **Viola da gamba**), also an open metal org. stop imitating the tone of the vla. da gamba, ranging over 4-ft., 8-ft. and 16-ft. pipes.

Gamma (Gk. = Letter *Γ*), the name of the lowest note of the mus. scale known to medieval theory, G on the bottom line of the bass stave. Where the Hexachord was based on it, it received the name of 'gamma-ut' (hence 'Gamut'), and in Fr. the name of the scale is still *gamme*.

Gammer Gurton's Needle, Eng. comedy by ? (poss. John Bridges, Dean of Salisbury, or William Stevenson), written *c.* 1560, pub. 1575. *See* **Davie** (opera).

Gamut, old Eng. term for the scale or key of G, whether major or minor, and hence for a scale or range in general. It derives from the combination of *gamma* (Gk. = G) and *ut*, the name given in medieval theory to the note:

See **Hexachord, Solmization.**

Gamut-Way, a 17th-cent. term for mus. written in ordinary notation, as distinct from tablature.

Ganascione (It.), a large It. lute.

Ganassi, Silvestro di (b. Fontego nr. Venice, 1492; d. Venice, ?), It. theorist, who pub. tutors for the recorder and the viol.

Ganne, Louis (Gaston) (b. Buxière-les-Mines, Allier, 5. IV. 1862; d. Paris, 14. VII. 1923), Fr. comp. Pupil of Dubois and Franck. He cond. the Opéra balls in Paris and orchs. at Royan and Monte Carlo, and became very popular as a comp. of ballets and operettas. Works incl. operettas *Rabelais, Les Colles des femmes, Les Saltimbanques* and *Hans le joueur de flûte*; ballet *La Source du Nil* and several others; popular songs including *La Marche Lorraine* and *Le Père la Victoire*; dances *La Tsarine*, etc.

Gänsbacher, Johann (b. Sterzing, Tyrol, 8. V. 1788; d. Vienna, 13. VII. 1844), Aus. comp. Pupil of Vogler and Albrechtsberger. Became *Kapellmeister* of St. Stephen's Cathedral in Vienna, 1823. Works incl. incid. mus. to Kotzebue's *Die Kreuzfahrer*; 35 Masses, 8 Requiems and other church mus.; a symph.; pf. mus.; songs, etc.

Gänsbacher, Joseph (b. Vienna, 6. X. 1829; d. Vienna, 4. VI. 1911), Aus. teacher of singing and cellist, son of prec. Prof. at the Vienna Cons.

Gapped Scales, any scales containing less than 7 notes, e.g. the Pentatonic scale, which has 5.

Garat, Pierre Jean (b. Bordeaux, 26. IV. 1762; d. Paris, 1. III. 1823), Fr. tenor-baritone. Pupil of Beck at Bordeaux. He became the favourite singer of Marie Antoinette, went to Hamburg and London during the Revolution and in 1796 became prof. of singing at the Paris Cons. He wrote some popular songs.

Garay, János (1812–53), Hung. poet. *See* **Háry János** (Kodály).

Garborg, Arne (1851–1925), Norw. poet. *See* **Grieg** (*Haugtussa*).

Garcia, Span. family of singers:

1. Manuel (del Popolo Vicente) G. (b. Seville, 22. I. 1775; d. Paris, 9. VI. 1832), tenor, teacher and comp. Was a chorister at Seville Cathedral and became well known as singer, cond. and comp. in his teens. In 1808 he made his 1st appearance in Paris and in 1811 in It. At Naples he prod. an opera, *Il Califfo di Bagdad*, not the 1st of a number of works for the stage. He now sang much in Paris and London, in 1825 brought the 1st It. opera co., incl. himself, his son (2) and elder daughter (3), to N.Y., and in 1826–8 was in Mex.

2. Manuel (Patricio Rodríguez) G. (b. Madrid, 17. III. 1805; d. London, 1. VII. 1906), singing teacher, son of prec. Pupil of his father and of Fétis in mus. theory. He appeared early in opera, but in 1829 retired to devote himself to teaching only. App. prof. at the Paris Cons. in 1842 and at the R.A.M. in London in 1848, where he remained to the end of his long life, retiring in 1895. He was the inventor of the laryngoscope.

3. Maria Felicità G. (b. Paris, 24. III. 1808; d. Manchester, 23. IX. 1836), sister of prec. *See* **Malibran.**

4. (Michelle Ferdinande) Pauline G. (b. Paris, 18. VII. 1821; d. Paris, 17–18. V. 1910, sister of prec. *See* **Viardot-Garcia.**

5. Gustave G. (b. Milan, 1. II. 1837; d. London, 12. VI. 1925), baritone, son of 2. Appeared as an opera singer in London and then sang at Milan, but settled in London as teacher, at the R.A.M. from 1880 and was prof. at the R.C.M. from 1883.

García Robles, José (b. Olot, 2. VII. 1835; d. Barcelona, 28. I. 1910), Span. comp. Teacher at Barcelona, where he helped to found the Orfeó Català. Works incl. opera *Julio César* (after

230

Shakespeare); *Catalonia* for chorus and orch. and other choral works; chamber mus., etc.

Gardano, Antonio (b. ?; d. Venice, *c.* 1570), It. mus. printer, estab. at Venice from 1538. His sons Cipriano and Annibale continued the business, as well as 2 other relatives, Angelo and Alessandro G., until 1619.

Garden, Mary (b. Aberdeen, 20. II. 1877; d. Aberdeen, 3. I. 1967), Scot. soprano. Went to America as a child and first studied singing in Chicago. In 1895 she went to Paris, where she continued her studies under various teachers, making her début in 1900. She created the role of Debussy's Mélisande and many others. In 1910 she joined the Chicago Opera and from 1919–20 was its director.

Garden of Fand, The, symph. poem by Bax, comp. 1913, 1st perf. Chicago, 29. X. 1920. (Fand is a heroine of Ir. legend, but in this work the garden of F. is simply the sea, charged with Ir. legendry).

Gardiner, H(enry). Balfour (b. London, 7. XI. 1877; d. Salisbury, 28. VI. 1950), Eng. comp. Educ. at Charterhouse School and Oxford, and studied mus. under Knorr at Frankfurt. Became mus. master at Winchester Coll. for a short time, then devoted himself wholly to comp.

Works incl. *News from Wydah* (Masefield) for chorus and orch.; symph. in D maj., *English Dance*, Fantasy and *Shepherd Fennel's Dance* (after Hardy) for orch.; string 4tet, string 5tet and other chamber mus.; *Noel*, 5 pieces, etc. for pf.; partsongs, etc.

Gardiner, William (b. Leicester, 15. III. 1770; d. Leicester, 16. XI. 1853), Eng. manufacturer, mus. amateur, writer and ed. Admirer of Haydn, to whom he sent 6 pairs of silk stockings with themes from Haydn's works woven into them. He adapted to Eng. words mus. by Haydn, Mozart and Beethoven.

Gardner, John (Linton) (b. Manchester, 2. III. 1917), Eng. comp. Educated at Wellington and Oxford, became mus. master at Repton School in 1939, and after doing war service app. coach at Covent Garden Opera in London. Chamber mus. of his was heard in London and Paris in the 1930's, but his first great success was the perf. of the 1st symph. at the Cheltenham Festival of 1951.

Works incl. opera *The Moon and Sixpence* (after Somerset Maugham); symph. and Variations on a Waltz by Nielsen for orch.; pf. concerto; string 4tet, ob. 5tet; 2 pf. sonatas; *Intermezzo* for org.; choruses, songs, etc.

Gargantua, opera by Mariotte (lib. by Armory, based on Rabelais), prod. Paris, Opéra-Comique, 17. II. 1935.

Garland for the Queen, a set of songs for mixed voices ded. to Queen Elizabeth II on her coronation in 1953, with contribs. by Bax, Berkeley, Bliss, Finzi, Howells, Ireland, Rawsthorne, Rubbra, Tippett and Vaughan Williams.

Garlandia, Johannes de (b. ?; d. ?), Eng. 13th-cent. scholar and writer on mus. Studied at Oxford and Paris, where he later opened a school, *c.* 1215. In 1229 he helped to found the Univ. of Toulouse, where he remained until 1232, returning to Paris. Wrote treatises on plainsong and mensurable mus. Two further treatises are apparently the work of a younger author of the same name (*c.* 1300).

Garnett, Richard (1835–1906), Eng. essayist, biog. and poet. *See* **Sea Pictures** (Elgar).

Garrick, David (1717–79), Eng. actor and playwright. *See* **Cymon** (M. Arne), **Gast** (*Heimliche Ehe*), **Matrimonio segreto** (Cimarosa), **Vernon** (2 plays).

Garrigues, Malwina (b. Copenhagen, 7. XII. 1825; d. Carlsruhe, 8. II. 1904), Ger. soprano. Was engaged for the Opera at Carlsruhe, where she met the tenor Ludwig Schnorr von Carolsfeld, whom she married. In 1860 they were engaged by the Dresden Court Opera. In 1865 she was Wagner's 1st Isolde in the Munich prod. of *Tristan und Isolde*, to the Tristan of her husband, who d. the following month.

Garsi, Santino (b. ?; d. Parma, 1604), It. comp., lute-player at the court of Parma from 1594 until his death. Wrote dance mus. for lute.

Gasco, Alberto (b. Naples, 3. X. 1879; d. Rome, 11. VII. 1938), It. comp. Pupil of Terziani and d'Indy. Mus. critic of *La Tribuna* in Rome.

Works incl. opera *La leggenda delle sette torri* (after Rossetti's water-colour *The Tune of Seven Towers*); oratorio *San Francesco*; *Presso al Clitunno, Preludio pastorale, Preludio giocoso, Buffalmacco* and *Scherzo orgiastico* for orch.; string 4tet *Venere dormiente* (after Giorgione's picture); vln. and pf. sonata *La visione di Sant' Orsola* (after Carpaccio's picture); *Le danzatrici di Jodhpur* (after Besnard's picture) for pf., etc.

Gascongne, Matthieu (b. ?; d. ?), Fr. 16th-cent. comp., priest in the diocese of Cambrai; he is mentioned in a document of 1518. Wrote numerous Masses, motets and *chansons*.

Gaspar van Weerbeke. *See* **Weerbeke.**

Gasparini, Francesco (b. Camaiore nr. Lucca, 5. III. 1668; d. Rome, 22. III. 1727), It. comp. Pupil of Corelli and Pasquini; choirmaster at the Ospedale della Pietà, Venice; app. *maestro di cappella* of St. John Lateran, Rome, 1725. Author of *L'armonico pratico al cimbalo* (1708).

Works incl. 61 operas, e.g. *Il più fedel fra i vassalli*, *La fede tradita e vendicata*, *Ambleto* (on Shakespeare's *Hamlet*); oratorios *Mosè liberato dal Nilo*, *La nascita di Cristo* and *Le nozze di Tobia*; church mus.; cantatas, etc.

Gasparini, Quirino (b. Bergamo, 1721; d. Turin, 23. IX. 1778), It. cellist and comp., pupil of Padre Martini in Bologna. *Maestro di cappella* to the court at Turin 1749–70, and of the cathedral from 1776. Works incl. operas, instrumental mus., church mus., etc.

Gasparo da Salò. *See* Salò.

Gassenhauer (Ger. lit. street-beater), a 16th-cent. term for a popular dance, which was very soon used to mean a popular song. It survived till the 20th cent. The modern term is *Schlager.*

Gassier, Édouard (b. ? Paris, 30. IV. 1820; d. Havana, 18. XII. 1872), Fr. baritone. Studied at the Paris Cons. and made his 1st appearance at the Opéra-Comique there in 1845.

Gassier (*née* **Fernandez**), **Josefa** (b. Bilbao, 1821; d. Madrid, 8. XI. 1866), Span. soprano, wife of prec. Made her 1st appearance in London in 1846.

Gassmann, Florian Leopold (b. Brüx, 3. V. 1729; d. Vienna, 20. I. 1774), Boh. comp., pupil of Padre Martini in Bologna. Settled in Vienna as a ballet comp. in 1763. In 1771 he was instrumental in founding the *Tonkünstlersocietät* (a sort of musicians' benevolent fund). App. court *Kapellmeister* in succession to Reutter in 1772.

Works incl. 25 operas, e.g. *Gli uccellatori*, *L'amore artigiano*, *La notte critica*, *La contessina*; oratorio, *La Betulia liberata*; 54 symphs.; much church mus., chamber mus., etc.

Gast, Peter (actually **Johann Heinrich Köselitz**) (b. Annaberg, 10. I. 1854; d. Annaberg, 15. VIII. 1918), Ger. comp. Studied at the Leipzig Cons. and later went to Basle as a friend and disciple of Nietzsche, some of whose mus. works he revised. Afterwards he lived at Venice and Weimar.

Works incl. operas *Wilbram*, *Orpheus und Dionysos*, *König Wenzel*, *Die heimliche Ehe* (based on the lib. of Cimarosa's *Matrimonio segreto* and farther back on Colman and Garrick's *Clandestine Marriage*); festival play *Walpurgis*; *Hosanna* for chorus and orch.; symph., symph. poem *Helle Nächte* and other orchestral works; string 4tet, 7tet, songs, etc.

'Gastein' Symphony, a symph. in C maj. supposed to have been written by Schubert during a visit to Gastein in VIII.–IX. 1825, of which no trace is left. It has been suggested that it is identical with the Grand Duo for pf. duet, Op. 140, or with the 'Great' C maj. symph. (1828).

Gastoldi, Giovanni Giacomo (b. Caravaggio, ?; d. ?, 1622), It. comp. *Maestro di cappella* at the church of Santa Barbara at Mantua from 1582 to his death. Works incl. a Magnificat and other church mus.; madrigals; *balletti* and *canzoni* for voices and instruments, etc.

Gastoué, Amédée (b. Paris, 13. III. 1873; d. Paris, 1. VI. 1943), Fr. musicologist and organist. Prof. of plainsong at the Schola Cantorum and the Institut Catholique in Paris and author of several books on the subject, on old Fr. mus., the hist. of the org., etc.

Gates, Bernard (b. London, 1685; d. North Aston nr. Oxford, 15. XI. 1773), Eng. theorist, singer and comp. Gentleman of the Chapel Royal from 1708 and Master of the Children some time before 1732. Works incl. Service in F maj.; songs, etc.

Gatti, Guido M(aria). (b. Chieti, 30. V. 1892), It. critic. Founder of the review *Il Pianoforte* (later *La Rassegna Musicale*) in 1920 and promoter of concerts. His books incl. studies of Schumann, Bizet, Fr. mus. and esp. modern It. mus.

Gatty, Nicholas (Comyn) (b. Bradfield nr. Sheffield, 13. IX. 1874; d. London, 10. XI. 1946), Eng. critic and comp. Studied at Cambridge and at the R.C.M. in London, under Stanford. Having taken the Mus.D. degree, he went to Covent Garden Opera as mus. ass. and in 1907 became mus. critic to the *Pall Mall Gazette.*

Works incl. operas *Greysteel*, *Duke or Devil*, *Prince Ferelon*, *The Tempest* and *Macbeth* (both Shakespeare), *King Alfred and the Cakes*; *Ode on Time* (Milton) and 3 *Short Odes* (Clough and Shelley) for chorus and orch.; *King Cole Variations*, comedy overture and other works for orch., *Haslemere Suite* for string orch.; variations for string 4tet, pf. trio; vln. and pf. sonata; instrumental pieces; songs, etc.

Gaubert, Philippe (b. Cahors, 3. VII. 1879; d. Paris, 8. VII. 1941), Fr. flautist, cond. and comp. Studied at the Paris Cons. and became principal flautist in the leading Paris orchs. and fl. prof. at the Cons. in 1919. Later he became known chiefly as a cond. of the Cons. concerts and from 1920 at the Paris Opéra.

Works incl. opera *Naïla*; 3 ballets; 3 symph. poems; vln. concerto; fl. sonata and sonatina, etc.

Gaudentios, 2nd-cent. A.D. Gk. theorist, the first to formulate a system of 8 *tonoi* (modes in the scalic sense) based on the idea of joining the interval of a 4th to that of a 5th with one note common to both.

Gaul, Alfred (Robert) (b. Norwich, 30. IV. 1837; d. Birmingham, 13. IX. 1913), Eng. organist and comp. Studied under Z. Buck as a chorister at Norwich Cathe-

Gaultier

dral and later became organist at var. churches at Birmingham.

Works incl. oratorios *Hezekiah, Ruth, The Holy City, Joan of Arc, The Ten Virgins, Israel in the Wilderness, Una*; Psalms, Passion mus., hymns, chants; part-songs; pf. pieces, etc.

Gaultier, the name of several Fr. lutenists of the 17th cent.:

1. Ennemond G. (b. ? Lyons, c. 1575; d. Villette, Dauphiné, 17. XII. 1651), taught Queen Marie de' Medici and Richelieu. Wrote lute pieces.

2. Jacques G. (b. ?; d. ?), ? unrelated to prec. Fled to London, c. 1617 and was attached to the court until 1647. Visited Hol. and Spain and comp. lute pieces and songs.

3. Denis G. (b. ? Marseilles, c. 1603; d. Paris, I. 1672), nephew or cousin of 1. Wrote a large number of lute pieces.

4. Pierre G. (b. Orléans, ?; d. ?), ? unrelated to the prec. He was in Rome in 1638 and pub. lute pieces there.

Gautier, Théophile (1811–72), Fr. poet and novelist. *See* **Cleopatra's Night** (H. K. Hadley), **Falla** (songs), **Fanelli** (*Tableaux symphoniques*), **Giselle** (Adam), **Pessard** (*Capitaine Fracasse*), **Reyer** (*Sélam*), **Terrasse** (*Matinées poétiques*), **Tcherepnin** (N.) (*Romance of a Mummy*).

Gavazzeni, Gianandrea (b. Bergamo, 25. VII. 1909), It. comp. Studied in Rome and Milan, and later became a comp. Pupil of Pizzetti and Pilati. He has also been active as a cond. and a critic.

Works incl. opera *Paolo e Virginia* (after Saint-Pierre); oratorio *Canti per Sant' Alessandro*; choral triptych; Symph. Prelude, *Three Episodes*, etc. for orch.; concertos for vln. and for cello; interludes to Tasso's *Aminta* for baritone and orch.; pf. trio; sonatas for vln. and pf. and cello and pf.; sonata and other works for pf.; songs, etc.

Gaveau, Étienne (b. Paris, 7. X. 1872; d. Paris, 26. V. 1943), Fr. pf. manufacturer. Followed his father, Joseph G. (1824–1903) and built a factory at Fontenay-sous-Bois in 1896 and a concert hall (Salle G.) in Paris in 1907.

Gaveaux, Pierre (b. Béziers, VIII. 1761; d. Paris, 5. II. 1825), Fr. tenor and comp.

Gaztambide y Garbayo

Pupil of Beck at Bordeaux, where he appeared as an opera singer.

Works incl. operas *Les Deux Suisses, L'Amour filial, La Famille indigente, Le Petit Matelot, Léonore, ou L'Amour conjugal, Un Quart-d'heure de silence, Le Bouffe et le tailleur, Monsieur Deschalumeaux, L'Enfant prodigue*; revolutionary hymn *Le Réveil du peuple*; It. canzonets and Fr. romances for voice and pf., etc.

Gaviniès, Pierre (b. Bordeaux, 11. V. 1728; d. Paris, 8. IX. 1800), Fr. violinist and comp. Made his 1st appearance in Paris in 1741, at the Concert spirituel, of which he was cond. in 1773–7. Prof. of vln. at the Cons. from its foundation in 1795.

Works incl. opera *Le Prétendu*; vln. concertos; sonatas for vln. and bass, vln. and pf., 2 vlns. and unaccomp. vln.; studies *Les Vingt-quatre Matinées*, vln. pieces incl. the *Romance de G.*, etc.

Gavot, the old Eng. name of the Gavotte.

Gavotte (Fr.), a Fr. dance in moderately

GAVOTTE

Bach, *French Suite, No.5*

animated 2–2 time, generally beginning on the 2nd beat, in 2 sections, each of which is repeated, the 1st ending usually in the dominant (*see* illustration).

It often occurs in suites, but is not a regular constituent of them. It may have an alternative or trio section, sometimes in the character of a Musette.

Gay, John (1685–1732), Eng. poet and playwright. *See* **Acis and Galatea** (Handel), **Beggar's Opera**, **Busby** (odes), **Dreigroschenoper** (Weill), **Polly.**

Gay, María (b. Barcelona, 13. VI. 1879; d. New York, 29. VII. 1943), Span. mezzo-soprano. Studied sculpture and vln. as a girl, but was self-taught in singing. In 1902 Pugno engaged her to sing at his and Ysaÿe's concerts in Brussels and she appeared as Carmen at the Théâtre de la Monnaie at 5 days' notice. She 1st appeared in Eng. in 1906. In 1913 she married the tenor Giovanni Zenatello.

Gaztambide y Garbayo, Joaquín (Romualdo) (b. Tudela, Navarre, 7. II. 1822; d. Madrid, 18. III. 1870), Span. cond. and comp. Studied at Pamplona and the Madrid Cons. After a stay in Paris he became theatre manager and cond. in Madrid.

Works incl. 44 *zarzuelas*, e.g. *La mensajera*, *El estreno de una artista*, *El valle de Andorra*, *Catalina*, *Los Magyares*, *El juramento*, *La conquista de Madrid*, etc.

Gazza ladra, La (*The Thievish Magpie*), opera by Rossini (lib. by Giovanni Gherardini, based on the Fr. melodrama, *La Pie voleuse*, by Jean Marie Théodore Baudouin d'Aubigny and Louis Charles Caigniez); prod. Milan, Teatro alla Scala, 31. V. 1817.

Gazzaniga, Giuseppe (b. Verona, X. 1743; d. Crema, 1. II. 1818), It. comp., pupil of Porpora and Piccinni in Naples, where his first opera was prod. in 1768. Later lived chiefly in Venice, until his app. as *maestro di cappella* at Crema Cathedral in 1791. Of his 44 operas, *Don Giovanni o sia Il convitato di pietra* (1787) was an immediate forerunner of Mozart's opera with the same title (prod. later the same year in Prague). Other works incl. oratorios, a symph. and 3 pf. concertos.

Gebel, Georg (sen.) (b. Breslau, 1685; d. Breslau, *c*. 1750), Ger. organist and comp., pupil of Tiburtius Winckler in Breslau. App. organist in Brieg in 1709, but in 1713 returned to Breslau, where he became director of mus. at St. Christophori the following year.

Works incl. Mass for double chorus; motets; cantatas; Passion oratorio; concertos; org. and harpsichord mus., etc.

Gebel, Georg (jun.) (b. Brieg, 25. X. 1709; d. Rudolstadt, 24. IX. 1753), Ger. organist, harpsichordist and comp., son of prec. Pupil of his father, app. 2nd organist of St. Mary Magdalen in Breslau in 1729. After apps. in Oels, Warsaw and Dresden, he became *Konzertmeister* to the court in Rudolstadt in 1747, and *Kapellmeister* 3 years later.

Works incl. over 12 operas (none extant), and large quantities of cantatas, symphs., chamber mus., keyboard mus., etc.

Gebel, Georg Sigismund (b. Breslau, *c*. 1715; d. Breslau, 1775), Ger. organist, harpsichordist and comp., brother of prec. Orgst. of several churches at Breslau. Comp. org. mus. and cantatas.

Gebrauchsmusik (Ger. lit. utility mus.), a termi nvented by Hindemith for a species of work written for practical use, and best trans. as 'workaday mus.', since no work of art can be intended strictly for pure usefulness. Hindemith's pub. works of the kind (several are unpub.) are: *Spielmusik* for strings, fls. and obs.; 4 3-part *Songs for Singing Groups*; an educ. work for concerted vlns. in 1st position; *Music to Sing or Play* (5 Nos. for var. vocal or instrumental combinations); *Lesson* for 2 male voices, narrator, chorus, orch., a dancer, clowns and community singing; *Let's Build a Town*, a mus. game for children; *Plöner Musiktag* (4 Nos. for var. vocal and

instrumental combinations). Some other comps., e.g. Milhaud in Fr., Copland in U.S.A., and Weill and Orff in Ger., have done similar work.

Gedackt (sometimes **Gedact,** Ger. properly 'gedeckt' = covered), an adj. used for stopped Diapason org. stops prod. a muted 8-ft. tone.

Gédalge, André (b. Paris, 27. XII. 1856; d. Paris, 5. II. 1926), Fr. comp. Studied at the Paris Cons., where he became prof. of counterpoint and fugue in 1905. Author of the 1st vol. of a *Traité de la fugue*.

Works incl. operas *Le Petit Savoyard*, *Pris au piège*, *Sita*, *La Farce du Cadi* and *Hélène*; 3 symphs.; concertos; chamber mus.; songs, etc.

Gedämpft (Ger., lit. damped) = muted, muffled (drums).

Gedda, Nicolai (b. Stockholm, 11. VII. 1925), Swed. tenor of Russian parentage. Studied in Stockholm, making his début there in 1952. In 1953 he sang in Paris and London, and in 1957 at the N.Y. Metropolitan Opera.

Geibel, Emanuel von (1815–84), Ger. poet. *See* **Jensen** (*Spanisches Liederbuch*), **Loreley** (Bruch and Mendelssohn), **Schumann** (*Vom Pagen und der Königstochter*), **Spanisches Liederbuch** (H. Wolf), **Volbach** (*Vom Pagen und der K.*).

Geige (Ger. = fiddle), the familiar Ger. name of the vln.

Geigen Principal, an 8-ft. open Diapason org. stop prod. an imitation of vln. tone.

Geijer, Erik Gustaf (b. Ransäter nr. Karlstad, 12. I. 1783; d. Stockholm, 23. IV. 1847), Swed. hist., philosopher, poet and comp. As a musician he became popular with many simple songs that have become the common property of the Swed. people.

Geiser, Walther (b. Zofingen, 16. V. 1897), Swiss comp. Studied in Basle with Hermann Suter and in Berlin with Busoni. From 1924 he taught at the Basle Cons.

Works incl. cantata *Inclyta Basilea* for soloists, chorus and orch.; a symph., 3 Fantasies for orch.; vln. concerto; 2 string 4tets, etc.

Geisha, The, operetta by Sidney Jones (lib. by Owen Hall and Harry Greenbank), prod. London, Daly's Theatre, 25. IV. 1896.

Geisslerlieder (Ger. = flagellants' songs), sacred Ger. monophonic songs of the Middle Ages, the equivalent of the It. *laude* and particularly cultivated during the plague of the Black Death in 1349. The chief MS. is the *Chronikon* of Hugo von Reutlingen, which also describes how the singing was accomp. by penitential rites perf. by the *Geissler* (flagellants).

Gelinek, Joseph (b. Selč, 3. XII. 1758; d. Vienna, 13. IV. 1825), Boh. priest, pianist and comp. Studied mus. and theology in Prague, was ordained there and later had lessons in comp. from Albrechtsberger. He became famous as a pf. teacher and improviser and in 1795 entered the service of Prince Esterházy.

Works incl. variations, fantasies, etc. for pf.

Gellert, Christian Fürchtegott (1715–1769), Ger. poet. *See* **Hiller (J. A.)** (odes and songs), **Quantz** (hymns).

Gelosie fortunate, Le (*The Fortunate Jealousies*), opera by Anfossi (lib. by Filippo Livigni), prod. Venice, Teatro San Samuele, autumn 1786. Mozart added an aria to it on its prod. in Vienna, 2. VI. 1788.

Gelosie villane, Le (*The Rustic Jealousies*), opera by Sarti (lib. by Tommaso Grandi, based on a comedy by Goldoni), prod. Venice, Teatro San Samuele, XI. 1776.

Gemel. *See* **Gymel.**

Gemellum (*see also* **Gymel**). In the 15th and 16th cents. the term G. ('twin-song') was used to indicate the division of a single voice-part temporarily into 2 parts, like the modern *divisi*; the return to a single part was marked *semellum*.

Geminiani, Francesco Saverio (b. Lucca, *c*. 1680; d. Dublin, 17. IX. 1762), It. violinist and comp., pupil of Corelli in Rome. Went to Eng. in 1714, where he had great success as a virtuoso. Apart from periods of residence in Dublin (1733–40 and 1759–62) and Paris, he remained there for the rest of his life. His teaching intro. modern vln. technique to Eng., and his *Art of Playing on the Vln.* was one of the earliest tutors on vln.-playing. He also wrote several other theoretical works.

Comps. incl. *concerti grossi*, vln. sonatas, cello sonatas, trio sonatas, keyboard pieces, etc.

Gemma di Vergy, opera by Donizetti (lib. by Emanuele Bidera, based on the elder Dumas's play, *Charles VII chez ses grands vassaux*), prod. Milan, Teatro alla Scala, 26. XII. 1834.

Gemshorn (Ger. = chamois horn), a 4-ft. open org. stop of soft, rather nasal tone.

Genée, (Franz Friedrich) Richard (b. Danzig, 7. II. 1823; d. Baden nr. Vienna, 15. VI. 1895), Ger. cond. and comp. Studied medicine at first, but took to mus. and became cond. successively at Reval, Riga, Cologne, Aachen, Düsseldorf, Danzig, Mainz, Schwerin, Amsterdam, Prague and Vienna. He wrote or collaborated in many libs. for operettas by other Viennese comps.

Works incl. operettas *Der Geiger aus Tirol, Der Musikfeind, Die Generalprobe, Rosita, Der schwarze Prinz, Am Runenstein* (with Flotow), *Der Seekadett, Nanon, Im Wunderlande der Pyramiden, Die letzten*

Mohikaner (after Fenimore Cooper), *Nisida, Rosina, Die Zwillinge, Die Piraten, Die Dreizehn*; part-songs incl. the comic *Italienischer Salat*, etc.

General Pause. *See* **G.P.**

Generalbass (Ger. lit. general bass) = Thorough-Bass.

Generali (real name **Mercandetti**), **Pietro** (b. Masserano, 23. X. 1773; d. Novara, 3. XI. 1832), It. comp. Studied under Giovanni Massi in Rome and in 1802 prod. his 1st opera there. In 1817–21 he cond. opera at Barcelona, and later became *maestro di cappella* at Novara Cathedral.

Works incl. *c.* 60 operas, e.g. *Gli amanti ridicoli, Il Duca Nottolone, La villana in cimento, Le gelosie di Giorgio, Pamela nubile* (after Richardson, *via* Goldoni's comedy), *La calzolaia, Misantropia e pentimento* (after Kotzebue), *Gli effetti della somiglianza, Don Chisciotte* (after Cervantes), *Orgoglio ed umiliazione, L'idolo cinese, Lo sposo in bersaglio, Le lagrime di una vedova, Adelina, La moglie giudice del marito, I baccanti di Roma, Francesca da Rimini* (after Dante); Masses and other church mus.; cantata *Roma liberata*, etc.

Generalpause (Ger. = general pause). *See* **G.P.**

Genet, Elzéar (Carpentras) (b. Carpentras, *c.* 1470; d. Avignon, 14. VI. 1548), Fr. comp. He was a papal singer to Julius II in 1508 and *maestro di cappella* under Leo X from 1513, as well as being at the court of Louis XII some time between those dates. He wrote secular works to both It. and Fr. texts, and numerous sacred works (Masses, motets, hymns, Magnificats, etc.).

Genlis, Stéphanie Félicité de, Countess (1746–1830), Fr. educationist and novelist. *See* **Siege of Rochelle** (Balfe).

Genoveva, opera by Schumann (lib. by comp. altered from one by Robert Reinick based on the dramas by Tieck and Hebbel), prod. Leipzig, 25. VI. 1850.

Gentle Shepherd, The, ballad opera (lib. by Allan Ramsay), prod. Edinburgh, Taylor's Hall, 29. I. 1729. It was published in 1725 as a pastoral comedy, and is therefore not, as is sometimes said, the 1st ballad opera, *The Beggar's Opera* having appeared earlier.

Genzmer, Harald (b. Blumental, nr. Bremen, 9. II. 1909), Ger. comp. Studied 1st in Marburg and later with Hindemith in Berlin. From 1946 to 1957 he was prof. of comp. at the Hochschule für Musik in Freiburg-im-Breisgau, and from 1957 prof. at the Hochschule für Musik in Munich.

Works incl. cantata *Racine*; Mass in E; symph. no. 1, *Bremen* symph.; concertos for pf., cello, ob., fl. (2), trautonium (2);

string 4tet; sonatas for vln., fl. and other chamber mus.

George, Stefan (1868–1933), Ger. poet. *See* Berg (A.) (*Wein*), **Knab** (songs), **Maler** (cantata), **Schönberg** (*Buch der hängenden Gärten*), **Webern** (songs and chor.).

Georges, Alexandre (b. Arras, 25. II. 1850; d. Arras, 18. I. 1938), Fr. organist and comp. Studied at the École Niedermeyer in Paris and qualified as an organist and choirmaster.

Works incl. operas *Le Printemps, Balthazar, Charlotte Corday, Miarka* (Jean Richepin), *La Passion, La Marseillaise, Myrrha, Sangre y sol*; incid. mus. for Villiers de l'Isle-Adam's *Le Nouveau Monde* and *Axel* and other plays; symph. poems *Léïla, La Naissance de Vénus, Le Paradis perdu* (after Milton); *Chansons de Miarka* for voice and orch.; 3 *Chansons anglaises, Chansons de Leïlah, Poèmes d'amour,* etc.

Gerber, Ernst Ludwig (b. Sondershausen, 29. IX. 1746; d. Sondershausen, 30. VI. 1819), Ger. lexicographer and organist. His most important work was the dictionary of musicians, *Historisch-biographisches Lexicon der Tonkünstler* (2 vols., 1790–2), later much expanded as *Neues historisch-biographisches Lexicon* (4 vols., 1812–14).

Gerber, Heinrich Nicolaus (b. Wenigen-Ehrich, 6. IX. 1702; d. Wenigen, 6. VIII. 1775), Ger. organist and comp., father of prec. Studied at Leipzig Univ. and became a disciple of Bach there. Court organist at Sondershausen from 1731. Improved and invented instruments, incl. the *Strohfiedel*.

Works incl. a hymn-book with figured basses; variations on chorales for org.; mus. for harpsichord, org., harp, etc.

Gerbert, Martin (b. Horb on Neckar, 12. VIII. 1720; d. St. Blasien, 13. V. 1793), Ger. mus. hist. Entered the Benedictine monastery of St. Blasien in 1737, ordained priest 1744, abbot 1764. Pub. a hist. of church mus. in 1774 under the title *De cantu et musica sacra*, and a collection of medieval mus. treatises in 1784.

Gerhard, Roberto (b. Valls, Catalonia, 25. IX. 1896; d. Cambridge, 5. I. 1970), Span. pianist and comp. Although a choir-boy and a tentative pianist and comp. from an early age, he began serious mus. studies late, owing to parental opposition. But after 2 years' commercial studies in Fr. Switz., he studied pf. with Granados and comp. with Pedrell at Barcelona in 1915–22 and then comp. with Schönberg in Vienna in 1923–8. In 1929–38 he lived and taught at Barcelona, was in charge of the mus. dept. of the Catalan Library, for which he ed. mus. by 18th-cent. Catalan comps., trans. var. mus. treatises into Span. and contrib. to

the literary weekly *Mirador*. Pedrell intro. him as a comp. and he began to make his way in Spain and Lat. Amer. After the downfall of the Span. Republic he emigrated to Eng. and in 1939 settled at Cambridge with a research scholarship from King's Coll.

Works incl. opera *The Duenna* (Sheridan); ballets *Ariel, Soirées de Barcelone, Don Quixote* (after Cervantes), *Alegrías* and *Pandora*; oratorio *The Plague* (after Camus); mus. for radio plays *Cristobal Colón* and *Adventures of Don Quixote* (Eric Linklater after Cervantes); 4 symphs.; *Collages* for orch. and magnetic tape; concerto for orch.; *Epithalamion* for orch.; vln. concerto; *Cancionero de Pedrell, Serranillas* and *Cançons i Arietes* for voice and orch.; *Hymnody* for 11 players; *Concert for 8*; nonet, 2 string 4tets, pf. trio, wind 5tet; *Gemini* for vln. and pf.; cantata for solo voices, chorus and orch.; song cycle *L'infantament meravellós de Shaharazada* and other songs; var. arrs. of old Span. mus. etc.

Gerhardt, Elena (b. Leipzig, 11. XI. 1883; d. London, 11. I. 1961), Ger. mezzosoprano. Studied at the Leipzig Cons. with Marie Hedmont, making her début in 1903. She owed much to the encouragement of Artur Nikisch, who accomp. her at many of her recitals. She excelled in the interpretation of Ger. songs. In 1933 she left Ger. and settled in London, where she was active in later years as a teacher.

Gerhardt, Paul (? 1606–76), Ger. hymnwriter. *See* Ebeling (hymns).

Gerle, Hans (b. Nuremberg, c. 1500; d. Nuremberg, 1570), Ger. 16th-cent. lutenist, violist and lute-maker. Son of Conrad Gerle (d. 1521), also a lute-maker. He pub. a book on viol and lute playing and a collection of lute pieces in tablature.

German, Edward (orig. **Edward German Jones**) (b. Whitchurch, Salop., 17. II. 1862; d. London, 11. XI. 1936), Eng. comp. Educ. at Chester. On his return home he organized and cond. a band and learnt the vln. Later he studied at Shrewsbury and the R.A.M. in London. He became an orchestral violinist and in 1888 mus. director of the Globe Theatre, writing incid. mus. for Richard Mansfield's prods. In 1901 he completed *The Emerald Isle*, left unfinished by Sullivan. Knighted in 1928.

Works incl. light operas *The Rival Poets, Merrie England, The Princess of Kensington, Tom Jones* (after Fielding), *Fallen Fairies* (W. S. Gilbert); incid. mus. for Shakespeare's *Richard III, Henry VIII, Romeo and Juliet, As You Like It, Much Ado about Nothing*, Anthony Hope's *Nell Gwynn*, etc.; 2 symphs., symph. suite in D min., symph. poem *Hamlet*, symph. suite *The Seasons, Welsh Rhapsody, Theme and 6 Diversions* and other orchestral works; Coronation March and Hymn for George V, etc.

German Flute, the name for the transverse fl. in Eng. in the 18th cent.

German Requiem, A, work for chorus, soprano and baritone solo and orch. by Brahms, Op. 45, comp. in 1866–9. The orig. name, *Ein deutsches Requiem,* means that Brahms did not set the liturgical Lat. text, but a choice of his own from Luther's trans. of the Bible.

German Sixth, in harmony a chord, the 2 outer notes of which are an augmented 6th, e.g.:

Germani, Fernando (b. Rome, 5. IV. 1906), It. organist and comp. Pupil of Respighi and others. He has taught at the Curtis Inst. in Philadelphia, in Siena and at the Rome Cons., and has been organist at St. Peter's, Rome, since 1948. He has travelled widely as a soloist and has pub. a *Metodo per organo* and an ed. of works by Frescobaldi, as well as org. comps. of his own.

Gernsheim, Friedrich (b. Worms, 17. VII. 1839; d. Berlin, 10. IX. 1916), Ger. pianist, cond. and comp. Studied at the Leipzig Cons. and in Paris. Cond. in var. cities, incl. Rotterdam, and later taught in Berlin.

Works incl. *Salamis, Hafis, Preislied, Nornenlied, Phöbus Apollo, Agrippina,* etc. for chorus and orch.; 4 symphs. and other orchestral mus.; concertos for pf. and for vln.; 2 string 4tets, string 5tet, pf. 4tets and trios and other chamber mus.; 3 vln. and pf. sonatas, etc.

Gero, Jhan (b. ?, *c.* 1518; d. ?, *c.* 1583), ? Flem. comp. Went to It. and became *maestro di cappella* at Orvieto Cathedral. Comp. motets and other sacred mus., madrigals, *canzoni,* etc.

Gérold, (Jean) Théodore (b. Strasbourg, 26. X. 1866; d. Allenwiller, Alsace, 15. II. 1956), Fr. musicologist. Studied theology, hist. of mus. and singing. Lecturer at Strasbourg Univ., 1919–37. Author of several important books on medieval and Renaissance mus., Bach, Schubert, etc.

Gershwin, George (b. Brooklyn, N.Y., 26. IX. 1898; d. Hollywood, 11. VII. 1937), Amer. comp. Wrote a popular song at the age of 14, studied the pf. and had lessons in theory from R. Goldmark. From 1914 to 1917 he worked as pianist in a mus. pub.'s office and wrote songs and a mus. comedy. Aged 20, he was comissioned to write incid. mus. for George White's play *Scandals,* and in 1923, at the invitation of Paul Whiteman, he wrote the *Rhapsody in Blue.*

Works incl. opera *Porgy and Bess*;

many mus. comedies incl. *Lady, be good* and *Of Thee I sing*; mus. for several films; *An American in Paris* and *Cuban Overture* for orch.; *Rhapsody in Blue* and concerto for pf. and orch.; a large number of popular songs.

Gerster, Etelka (b. Kassán, Hung., 25. VI. 1855; d. Pontecchio nr. Bologna, 20. VIII. 1920), Hung.-Ger. soprano. Studied with Mathilde Marchesi in Vienna and made her 1st stage appearance at Venice in 1876. She married the It. cond. Carlo Gardini.

Gerster, Ottmar (b. Braunfels nr. Wetzlar, 29. VI. 1897; d. Leipzig, 31. VIII. 1969), Ger. comp. Studied at Hoch's Cons. at Frankfurt and became vla. in the symph. orch. there. Later he taught at Essen.

Works incl. opera *Enoch Arden* (after Tennyson) and 3 others; 2 ballets; choral and orchestral works; concertos for pf., vln. and cello; chamber mus., etc.

Gertler, André (b. Budapest, 26. VI. 1907), Hung., now Belg., violinist. Studied with Hubay and Kodály. In 1928 he settled in Belg., and formed his own string 4tet in 1931. Since 1940 he has been a prof. at the Brussels Cons. He is esp. well known as a perf. of modern music.

Gervais, Claude (b. ?; d. ?), 16th-cent. Fr. musician who comp. a considerable amount of dance mus. for var. instruments, and var. books of *chansons,* 1541–57.

Gervais, Terence White (d'Olbert) (b. London, 22. V. 1913), Eng. critic, organist, cond. and comp., partly of Ir., Fr. and African descent. Studied at the R.C.M. and became a solo organist and contrib. to mus. periodicals. He at first wrote as Terence White, but from 1946 did so under his mother's name.

Works incl. 3 operas; ballets; religious works for chorus and orch.; 2 symphs.; 3 string 4tets; org. and pf. works; songs, etc.

Gervasius de Anglia (Jervays) (b. ?; d. ?), early 15th-cent. Eng. comp. about whom nothing certain is known. A *Gloria* survives in the Old Hall MS.; other pieces ascribed in continental MSS. to 'de Anglia' or 'Anglicus' are not necessarily by him.

Geschöpfe des Prometheus, Die (*The Creatures of Prometheus*), ballet by Beethoven (choreography by Salvatore Vigano), prod. Vienna, Burgtheater, 28. III. 1801.

Gese (or Gesius), Bartholomäus (or **Barthel Göss**) (b. Müncheberg nr. Frankfurt o/O., *c.* 1555; d. Frankfurt o/O., 1613), Ger. theologian and comp. Cantor at Frankfurt o/O.

Works incl. Masses (1 on themes by Lassus), motets, psalms, hymns, sacred songs, etc., all for the Lutheran Church; Passion according to St. John; wedding and funeral mus., etc.

Gesellschaft der Musikfreunde (Ger. lit. Society of the Friends of Music = Phil. Society), a society formed in Vienna in 1813 for the promotion, perf. and collection of mus.

Gesius. *See* **Gese.**

Gestalt (Ger. = shape, formation), a word that has gained currency as a mus. term in Ger.-speaking countries recently, used in mus. analysis and in philosophical or pseudo-philosophical discussions on mus. to designate a mus. idea as it comes from the comp.'s mind in what is supposed to be a kind of primeval or pre-existing form.

Gestopft (Ger. = stopped up, obstructed), notes on the horn played with the hand inserted into the bell to prod. an altered sound; formerly to obtain extra notes not in the series of natural harmonics, a device made unnecessary by the valve horn.

Gesualdo, Carlo, Prince of Venosa (b. Naples, *c.* 1560; d. Naples, 8. IX. 1613), It. amateur comp. In spite of his position, he took his mus. studies seriously in his youth and became a very accomplished lutenist. He married a noble Neapol. lady in 1586, but had her assassinated with her lover in 1590. In 1594 he went to the court of Ferrara and married Eleonora d'Este there, but returned to his estate at Naples soon after Duke Alfonso d'Este II's death in 1597.

Works incl. 7 books of madrigals (the last posth.); 2 books of *Sacrae cantiones*, responds for 6 voices, etc.

Getreue Alceste, Die (*The Faithful Alcestis*), opera by Schürmann (lib. by Johann Ulrich König), prod. Brunswick, II. 1719.

Gevaert, François Auguste (b. Huysse nr. Oudenarde, 31. VII. 1828; d. Brussels, 24. XII. 1908), Belg. mus. hist., theorist and comp. Studied at Ghent and worked as organist there; later travelled in Spain, It. and Ger. Director of mus. at the Paris Opéra, 1867–70; of the Brussels Cons. from 1871. He wrote several treatises on hist., plainsong and theory.

Works incl. operas *Hugues de Zomerghem, La Comédie à la ville, Georgette, Le Billet de Marguerite, Les Lavandières de Santarem, Quentin Durward* (after Scott), *Le Diable au moulin, Château Trompette, La Poularde de Caux, Les Deux Amours, Le Capitaine Henriot*; Requiem for male voices and orch., Christmas cantata, psalm *Super flumina*, cantatas *De nationale verjaerdag* and *Le Retour de l'armée*; orchestral *Fantasia sobre motivos espanoles*, etc.

Gewandhaus (Ger. = Cloth Hall), orig. the hall of the clothmakers' guild at Leipzig, used for concerts from 1781 and rebuilt espec. as a concert hall in 1884. It was destroyed in World War II.

Ghedini, Giorgio Federico (b. Cuneo' Piedmont, 11. VII. 1892; d. Nervi, 25. III. 1965), It. comp. Studied at Turin and Bologna, at first intended to be a cond., later taught at the conss. of Turin, Parma and Milan, but eventually devoted himself to comp.

Works incl. 8 operas incl. *Le baccanti* (after Euripides) and *Billy Budd* (after Melville); incid. mus. for Euripides' *Iphigenia in Tauris*; 2 Masses and var. choral works; *Partita*, symph., *Concerto dell' Albatro* (after Melville's *Moby Dick*) for orch.; concertos for pf., 2 pfs., 2 cellos and vln.; concerto for vln. and fl. with chamber orch.; wind 5tet, pf. 4tet, string 4tet and other chamber mus.; vln. and pf. sonata; pf. works; songs, etc.

Gherardello. *See* **Firenze, Ghiradello da.**

Gherardeschi, Filippo Maria (b. Pistoia, 1738; d. Pisa, 1808), It. comp., pupil of Padre Martini at Bologna, 1756–61. *Maestro di cappella* at the cathedrals of Volterra and Pistoia, and finally, from *c.* 1766 to his death, at S. Stefano in Pisa. Also mus. director to the court of the Grand Duke of Tuscany.

Works incl. 7 operas, church mus., keyboard mus., etc.

Gheyn, Matthias van den (b. Tirlemont, 7. IV. 1721; d. Louvain, 22. VI. 1785), Flem. harpsichordist, organist, carillonneur and comp. Son of a bell founder. The family moved to Louvain in 1725 and in 1741 G. became organist at the church of Saint-Pierre there, having been (?) a pupil of Déodat Raick. In 1745 he was app. carillonneur to the city. Wrote org., harpsichord and carillon mus.

Ghimel. *See* **Gymel.**

Ghiradello da Firenze. *See* **Firenze.**

Ghiselin, Jean (b. ?; d. ?, *c.* 1535), Flem. comp. Petrucci of Venice pub. several of his works between 1501 and 1542. Comp. Masses, motets, songs, etc.

Ghisi, Federico (b. Shanghai, 25. II. 1901), It. musicologist and comp. He studied at Pavia Univ. and the Turin Cons., and was a lecturer at Florence Univ. from 1937 to 1940. He has travelled widely as a lecturer and pub. a number of studies of It. mus. from the 14th to the 17th cent., as well as eds. of old It. mus.

Works incl. opera-ballet *Piramo e Tisbe* (after Shakespeare's *Midsummer Night's Dream*), 2 television operas; *Vita, morte e miracoli di Sant' Alessio* for chorus and orch. and other choral works: *Sinfonia italiana, Sinfonia per due orchestre da camera* and other orchestral works; chamber mus.; songs, etc.

Ghislanzoni, Antonio (b. Lecco, 25. XI. 1824; d. Caprino Bergamasco, 16. VII. 1893), It. baritone, novelist, mus. ed. and librettist. He ed. the *Gazzetta musicale* of Milan and wrote the lib. for Verdi's *Aida* on a scenario by Mariette and a Fr. draft by Camille du Locle.

Ghizzolo, Giovanni (b. Brescia, ?; d. Novara, ? 1625), It. comp, ? pupil of Costanzo Porta. Wrote madrigals, motets and Masses.

Ghizzolo, Stefano. *See* **Pasino.**

'Ghost' Trio, the nickname given to Beethoven's pf. trio in D maj., Op. 70 No. 1, on account of its slow movement in D min., which has a mysterious, gloomy and haunting theme, accomp. frequently by string tremolos.

Ghro (or **Groh**), **Johann** (b. Dresden, *c.* 1575; d. ?, 1627), Ger. 16th–17th-cent. organist and comp. Organist at Meissen in 1604–12 and later mus. director at Wesenstein.

Works incl. *intradas*, pavans, galliards and other pieces for several instruments, etc.

Giacobbi, Girolamo (b. Bologna, *c.* 1567; d. Bologna, II. 1629), It. comp. *Maestro di cappella* at San Petronio at Bologna.

Works incl. operas *Andromeda, L'Aurora ingannata, Amor prigioniero, La selva dei mirti, Il Reno sacrificante*; intermezzi, etc.; motets, psalms and other church mus., etc.

Giacomelli, Geminiano (b. Piacenza, *c.* 1692; d. Loreto, 25. I. 1740), It. comp. Pupil of Capelli at Parma and later of A. Scarlatti. *Maestro di cappella* at Parma, 1719–27 and 1732–7; at Piacenza, 1727–1732; at Loreto from 1738.

Works incl. operas *Ipermestra, Cesare in Egitto* and 16 others; psalm for 2 tenors and bass; concert arias, etc.

Giacometti, Paolo (1816–82), It. dramatist. *See* **Judith** (Serov).

Gianneo, Luis (b. Buenos Aires, 9. I. 1897), Arg. comp. Studied with Drangosch and others at Buenos Aires and in 1923 settled as teacher and cond. at Tucumán. He studied native folk mus. and in 1932 joined the Grupo Renovación.

Works incl. *Sinfonietta* (homage to Haydn), *Obertura para una comedia infantil*, symph. poem *Turay-Turay, El Tarco en flor* for orch.; vln. concerto; chamber mus.; pf. pieces; songs, etc.

Giannettini, Antonio (b. prob. Fano, 1648; d. Munich, 12. VII. 1721), It. comp. App. *maestro di cappella* at the ducal court of Modena in 1686. Prod. his 1st opera, *Medea in Atene*, at Venice in 1675.

Works incl. operas, oratorios, cantatas, motets, psalms, etc.

Gianni Schicchi (Puccini). *See* **Trittico.**

'Giant' Fugue, the nickname of Bach's fugal chorale prelude on 'Wir glauben all', in Part III of the *Clavierübung*, so named because of a striding figure in the pedals.

Giardini, Felice de (b. Turin, 12. IV. 1716; d. Moscow, 17. XII. 1796), It. violinist and comp. Choir-boy at Milan Cathedral and later pupil of Somis at

Turin. Played in the opera orchs. at Rome and Naples, in 1748 visited Ger. and then settled in London, becoming leader of the opera orch. in 1752, succeeding Festing. He played and taught there until 1784, when he retired to It., but he reappeared in London in 1790 and d. during a tour in Rus.

Works incl. operas *Enea e Lavinia, Il rè pastore* and others; incid. mus. for Wm. Mason's *Elfrida*; oratorio *Ruth* (with Avison); 12 vln. concertos; 21 string 4tets, 6 string 5tets, 7 sets of string trios; sonatas for vln. and pf.; vln. duets, etc.

Giasone (*Jason*), opera by Cavalli (lib. by Giacinto Andrea Cicognini), prod. Venice, Teatro San Cassiano, prob. 5. I. 1649.

Gibbons, Eng. family of musicians:

1. **William G.** (b. Oxford, *c.* 1540; d. Cambridge, X. 1595), singer and/or player. Lived at Cambridge from 1567, but returned to Oxford *c.* 1579 and went back to Cambridge *c.* 1587.

2. **Edward G.** (b. Cambridge, III. 1568; d. ? Exeter, *c.* 1650), organist and comp., son of prec. Graduated Mus.B. at Cambridge and later (1592) at Oxford. Lay clerk at King's Coll. chapel, Cambridge, and from *c.* 1606 held an appt. at Exeter Cathedral.

Works incl. anthems, Kyrie and Creed; In Nomine in 5 parts, etc.

3. **Ellis G.** (b. Cambridge, XI. 1573; d. ? Cambridge, V. 1603), comp., brother of prec.

Works incl. madrigals, etc.

4. **Ferdinando G.** (b. Oxford, 1581; d. ?), singer, brother of prec. Lived at Lincoln.

5. **Orlando G.** (b. Oxford, XII. 1583; d. Canterbury, 5. VI. 1625), brother of prec. Brought up at Cambridge, where he took the Mus.B. in 1606. Oxford conferred the D.Mus. on him in 1622. App. organist at Westminster Abbey in 1623. He d. suddenly at Canterbury while waiting to officiate at Charles I's marriage service, for which he had comp. mus.

Works incl. Angl. church mus. (4 services, 13 full anthems, 25 verse anthems); 20 madrigals; *Cries of London* for voices and strings, 30 fantasies for strings, 4 *In Nomine* for strings, 2 pavans and 2 galliards for strings; 16 keyboard fantasies, 6 sets of variations for keyboard and other keyboard pieces.

6. **Christopher G.** (b. London, VIII. 1615; d. London, 20. X. 1676), comp., son of prec. Pupil of his father in the Chapel Royal, but (?) was adopted by his uncle Edward G. at Exeter on Orlando's death. App. organist at Winchester Cathedral in 1638. In 1646 he married Mary Kercher, who d. in 1662, and later Elizabeth Ball. On the Restoration in 1660 he was app.

private organist to Charles II, also organist at the Chapel Royal and Westminster Abbey. D.Mus., Oxford, 1663.

Works incl. mus. for Shirley's masque *Cupid and Death* (with Locke); anthems; many fantasies for strings, etc.

Gibbs, C(ecil). Armstrong (b. Great Baddow, nr. Chelmsford, 10. VIII. 1889; d. Chelmsford, 12. V. 1960), Eng. comp. Educ. at Winchester Coll. and Trinity Coll., Cambridge, where he studied mus. with Dent, and later at the R.C.M. in London, where he became a prof. of comp.

Works incl. incid. mus. to school play *Crossings* (W. de la Mare) and Maeterlinck's *The Betrothal*; comic opera *The Blue Peter* (A. P. Herbert); play with mus. *Midsummer Madness* (Clifford Bax); Nativity play *The Three Kings*; cantata *The Birth of Christ*, Passion according to St. Luke, choral symph. *Odysseus*; *La Belle Dame sans merci* (Keats), *The Highwayman* (Alfred Noyes) and *Deborah and Barak* for chorus and orch.; 3 Psalm Motets for unaccomp. chorus; *Cantate Domino, Deus misereatur*, anthem *I, then the prisoner* and other church mus.; symph. in E maj., *A Westmorland Symph.* for orch.; *Prelude, Andante and Finale* for strings; concertino for pf. and strings; string 4tet in A maj. and other chamber mus.; songs (many to poems by Walter de la Mare), etc.

Gibbs, Joseph (b. ? Dedham, 23. XII. 1699; d. Ipswich, 12. XII. 1788), Eng. organist and comp. Organist at various Essex churches, finally from 1748 to his death at St. Mary-le-Tower in Ipswich. His only works to survive complete are a set of 8 vln. sonatas, pub. *c.* 1746.

Gibbs, Richard (b. ?; d. ?), Eng. 17th-cent. organist and comp. Organist at Norwich Cathedral *c.* 1622–35. Wrote services, anthems, etc.

Gide, André (1869–1951), Fr. novelist, essayist, poet and dramatist. *See* **Durey** (songs), **Honegger** (*Saül*), **Perséphone** (Stravinsky), **Reutter (H.)** (*Verlorene Sohn*).

Gieseking, Walter (b. Lyons, 5. XI. 1895; d. London, 26. X. 1956), Ger. pianist. Studied privately and at the Hanover Cons., and 1st appeared in 1915. He won great fame by his sensitive perfs., esp. of modern Fr. mus.

Giga (It.). *See* **Jig.**

Gigault, Nicolas (b. ? Paris, *c.* 1625; d. Paris, 20. VIII. 1707), Fr. organist and comp. Organist at var. Paris churches from 1646. Pub. a book of org. pieces in 1685.

Gigg (obs.). *See* **Jig.**

Gigli, Beniamino (b. Recanati, 20. III. 1890; d. Rome, 30. XI. 1957), It. tenor. Of humble parentage, he began to make his way with difficulty, but gained a scholarship to the Rome Liceo Musicale and in 1914 made his 1st stage appearance. He

won world-wide fame and was considered the successor of Caruso.

Gigout, Eugène (b. Nancy, 23. III. 1844; d. Paris, 9. XII. 1925), Fr. organist and comp. Studied mus. at Nancy Cathedral and the École Niedermeyer in Paris. He was a pupil of Saint-Saëns there and often deputized for him as organist at the Madeleine. Married one of Niedermeyer's daughters and became prof. at his school. App. organist of Saint-Augustin Church in 1863 and travelled much as org. virtuoso. In 1885 he founded an org. school.

Works incl. church mus.; Meditation for vln. and orch.; pf. sonata; *c.* 50 org. works for concert use and *c.* 400 smaller org. pieces with pedals *ad lib.* for the church.

Gigue (Fr.). *See* **Jig.**

Gilardi, Gilardo (b. San Fernando, 25. V. 1889; d. Buenos Aires, 16. I. 1963), Arg. comp. Studied with Berutti at Buenos Aures, began to comp. early and in 1923 prod. his 1st opera. He was one of the founders of the Grupo Renovación in 1929, but left it in 1932.

Works incl. operas *Ilse* and *La leyenda del Urutaû*; suite on Arg. airs, *Firmeza, Noviando* and *Evocación quichua* for orch.; vln. and pf. sonata; pf. pieces; songs; etc.

Gilbert, Henry (Franklin Belknap) (b. Somerville, Mass., 26. IX. 1868; d. Cambridge, Mass., 19. V. 1928), Amer. comp. Studied mus. and Fr. lit. at Boston and became a business man, but later devoted himself to comp. He often used Negro tunes for his thematic material.

Works incl. ballet *The Dance in Place Congo* (after G. W. Cable); symph. prologue to Synge's *Riders to the Sea*; *Salammbô's Invocation to Tanith* (after Flaubert) for soprano and orch.; *Indian Sketches* and *Hymn to America* for chorus and orch.; *Americanesque, Comedy Overture on Negro Themes*, 3 *American Dances, Negro Rhapsody, Legend* and *Negro Episode* for orch.; *The Island of Fay* (after Poe), *Indian Scenes* and *Negro Dances* for pf.; *Pirate Song* (Stevenson) for voice and pf.; ed. of 100 folksongs, etc.

Gilbert, W(illiam). S(chwenck). (1836–1911), Eng. playwright and librettist. Libs. *see* **Cellier** (*Mountebanks*), **Gondoliers** (Sullivan), **Grand Duke** (do.), **H.M.S. Pinafore** (do.), **Iolanthe** (do.), **Mikado** (do.), **Patience** (do.), **Pirates of Penzance** (do.), **Princess Ida** (do.), **Ruddigore** (do.), **Sorcerer** (do.), **Thespis** (do.), **Trial by Jury** (do.), **Utopia Limited** (do.), **Yeomen of the Guard** (do.).

Gilchrist, Anne (Geddes) (b. Manchester, 8. XII. 1863; d. nr. Lancaster, 24. VII. 1954), Eng. folksong expert. She collected and studied folksongs and in 1906 joined the ed. committee of the *Journal of* *the Folk Song Society*, to which she contrib. regularly.

Gilels, Emil (b. Odessa, 19. X. 1916), Rus. pianist. Studied in Odessa and made his début there in 1929. At the age of 16 he won 1st prize in the Soviet Pianists Competition and in 1936 2nd prize in the international pf. competition in Vienna. In 1938 he won 1st prize in the Brussels international pf. competition.

Giles, Nathaniel (b. Worcestershire, *c.* 1558; d. Windsor, 24. I. 1634), Eng. organist and comp. Organist of Worcester Cathedral, 1581–5, when he became organist and choirmaster of St. George's Chapel, Windsor, and also, in 1596, of the Chapel Royal in London, where he took the official titles of Gentleman and Master of the Children on the death of Hunnis in 1597. D.Mus., Oxford, 1622.

Works incl. 4 services, 32 anthems, 5 motets; madrigal *Cease now, vain thoughts*, etc.

Gilly, Dinh (b. Algiers, 19. VII. 1877; d. London, 19. V. 1940), Fr.-Algerian baritone. Pupil of Cotogni. Made his 1st appearance in London, at Covent Garden, in 1911. Married the contralto Edith Furmedge.

Gilman, Lawrence (b. Flushing, N.Y., 5. VII. 1878; d. Franconia, N.H., 8. IX. 1939), Amer. critic. Self-taught in mus., he wrote for var. papers at first and in 1923 became mus. critic to the *New York Herald-Tribune* in succession to Krehbiel. Wrote books on MacDowell, Wagner, modern mus., etc., and was a well-known programme annotator and radio commentator.

Gilse, Jan van (b. Rotterdam, 11. V. 1881; d. Leyden, 8. IX. 1944), Dutch cond. and comp. Studied at the Cologne Cons. and with Humperdinck. Cond. of the Utrecht Municipal Orch., 1917–22; app. director of the Cons. there in 1933. He lost 2 sons and d. during the Ger. occupation of Hol.

Works incl. operas *Frau Helga von Stavern* and *Thyl*; *A Mass of Life* and *Circle of Life* for chorus and orch.; 5 symphs. and *Prologus brevis* for orch.; *Dansschetseis* for pf. and orch.; songs with orch., etc.

Gilson, Paul (b. Brussels, 15. VI. 1865; d. Brussels, 3. IV. 1942), Belg. comp. Pupil of Gevaert and others, he gained the Belg. Prix de Rome in 1889. App. prof. of harmony at the Cons. of Brussels in 1899 and of Antwerp in 1904. He was also mus. critic of *Le Soir*, 1906–14, and then of *Le Midi*.

Works incl. operas *Prinsess Zonneschijn* and *Zeevolk*; ballets *La Captive* and *Daphne*; oratorio *Le Démon* (after Lermontov); *Francesca da Rimini* (after Dante) for solo voices, chorus and orch.;

cantata *Sinaï* and one for the Brussels Exhibition of 1897; *La Mer* for recitation and orch.; Fantasy on Canadian Themes, Scot. Rhapsody, etc., for orch.; *Humoresque* and other works for wind instruments; chamber mus.; many songs with orch. or pf., etc.

Gimel. *See* **Gymel.**

Ginastera, Alberto (b. Buenos Aires, 11. IV. 1916), Arg. comp. Studied with Athos Palma at the Nat. Cons. of Buenos Aires and graduated in 1938.

Works incl. opera *Don Rodrigo*; ballets *Panambí* and *Estancia*; psalms for chorus and orch.; *Sinfonía porteña* for orch.; vln. concerto; *Concierto argentino* for pf. and orch.; *Impresiones de la Puna* for fl. and string 4tet, *Cantos del Tucumán* for soprano, fl., vln., harp and drums; *Pampeana*, Nos. 1, 2 and 3 for vln. and pf., cello and pf., and orch.; string 4tet; 2 cantatas; pf. pieces; songs, etc.

Gines Pérez, Juan (b. Orihuela, X. 1548; d. ? Orihuela, 1612), Span. comp. He held a church appt. in his native town at the age of 14, in 1581–95 was *maestro di cappella* and director of the choir school at Valencia, and *c.* 1600 returned home as canon at Orihuela Cathedral.

Works incl. motets, psalms; secular Span. songs; mus. contrib. to the Mystery play perf. annually at Elche nr. Alicante, etc.

Ginguené, Pierre Louis (b. Rennes, 25. IV. 1748; d. Paris, 16. XI. 1816), Fr. writer. In the controversy between the partisans of Gluck and Piccinni he sided with the latter and wrote his biog. Also pub. a mus. dictionary and other works on mus.

Gintzler, Simon (b. *c.* 1490; d. after 1550), Ger. comp. His collection of lute mus. was published in Venice, 1547, and he also contrib. to Hans Gerle's *Eyn Newes . . . Lautenbuch* (Nuremberg, 1552).

Gioconda, opera by Ponchielli (lib. by Boito, based on Victor Hugo's *Angelo*), prod. Milan, Teatro alla Scala, 8. 1V. 1876.

Giocoso (It.) = playful, joking, humorous.

Gioielli della Madonna, I (*The Jewels of the Madonna*), opera by Wolf-Ferrari (lib. by Enrico Golisciani and Carlo Zangarini), prod., in Ger., Berlin, Kurfürsten-Oper, 23. XII. 1911.

Gioioso (It., formerly *giojoso*) = joyous, joyful.

Giordani, It. family of musicians:

1. Carmine G. (b. Cerreto Sannita, nr. Benevento, *c.* 1685; d. Naples, 1758), singer and comp. Prod. an opera, *La vittoria d'amor coniugale* at Naples in 1712. Other works incl. cantata for soprano, *Versetti* for org., etc.

2. Giuseppe G. (called Giordanello) (b.

Naples, 9. XII. 1743; d. Fermo, 4. I.
1798), comp., ? son of prec. Studied mus.
at the Cons. di Loreto at Naples and
brought out his 1st opera there in 1771.
He became *maestro di cappella* at Fermo
Cathedral in 1791.

Works incl. over 30 operas, e.g. *L'astuto
in imbroglio, La disfatta di Dario,* etc.;
oratorios *La fuga in Egitto, La morte
d'Abele,* etc. The *canzonetta* 'Caro mio
ben' is attrib. to him, but many of the
works formerly supposed to be his are by
Tommaso G.

Giordani, Tommaso (b. Naples, *c.* 1730;
d. Dublin, II. 1806), It. comp., unrelated
to the above family. Son of a travelling
opera impresario, prod. his first opera
with his father's co. in London in 1756.
Subsequently lived chiefly in London and
Dublin, comp. a large number of theatrical
works for both capitals.

Works incl. operas *La comediante fatta
cantatrice, L'eroe cinese, Il padre e il figlio
rivali, Artaserse, Il re pastore, Love in
Disguise, Phyllis at Court* and others,
c. 50 in all; songs for Sheridan's *The Critic*;
oratorio *Isaac*; church mus.; concertos
for pf. and other instruments; string
4tets, trios; pf. sonatas, etc.

Giordano, Umberto (b. Foggia, 27. VIII.
1867; d. Milan, 12. XI. 1948), It. comp.
Son of an artisan, he was allowed to learn
mus. as best he could, but in the end
studied at the Naples Cons. under Serrao.
He attracted the attention of the pub.
Sonzogno with the opera *Marina* and soon
became very successful with a series of
stage works.

Works incl. operas *Marina, Mala vita,
Regina Diaz, Andrea Chénier, Fedora*
(after Sardou), *Siberia, Marcella, Mese
Mariano, Madame Sans-Gêne* (after Sardou
and Moreau), *Giove a Pompei* (with
Franchetti), *La cena delle beffe, Il rè.*

Giorgi-Righetti, Geltrude (b. Bologna,
1792; d. ?), It. mezzo-soprano. Made her
1st appearance at Bologna in 1814 and
was Rossini's 1st Rosina in *Il Barbiere di
Siviglia* in 1816. She pub. her reminiscences
of Rossini in 1823.

**Giorno di regno, Un, ossia Il finto
Stanislao** (*A Day's Reign, or The False
Stanislas*), opera by Verdi (lib. by Felice
Romani, used earlier by Gyrowetz, *see
Finto Stanislao*), prod. Milan, Teatro alla
Scala, 5. IX. 1840. V.'s only comic opera
except *Falstaff.*

Giornovichi, Giovanni (Mane) (known as
Jarnowick) (b. Palermo, *c.* 1740; d. St.
Petersburg, 21. XI. 1804), It. violinist and
comp. Pupil of Lolli, made his 1st appearance at the Concert spirituel in Paris
in 1770. Having lived in Paris, Berlin, Aus.,
Pol., Rus. and Swed., he went to London
in 1791, but left for Han burg in 1796,
whence he went to St. Petersburg in 1802.

He wrote *c.* 20 vln. concertos, 3 string
4tets and much mus. for the vln.

Giovane, Joan Domenico del. *See* **Nola.**

Giovanna d'Arco (*Joan of Arc*), opera
by Verdi (lib. by Temistocle Solera,
based on Schiller's drama *Die Jungfrau
von Orleans*), prod. Milan, Teatro alla
Scala, 15. II. 1845.

Giovanna di Guzman (Verdi). *See*
Vêpres siciliennes.

Giovannelli, Ruggiero (b. Velletri nr.
Rome, *c.* 1560; d. Rome, 7. I. 1625), It.
comp. After holding var. church apps.
in Rome, he followed Palestrina at St.
Peter's in 1594 and became a member of
the Sistine Choir in 1599. At the request of
Pope Paul V he undertook a new ed. of the
Gradual.

Works incl. Masses, Miserere and other
church mus.; 6 books of madrigals, 1 of
canzonette and *villanelle*, etc.

Giovanni da Cascia. *See* **Cascia.**

Giovanni da Firenze. *See* **Cascia.**

Giovanni de Antiquis. *See* **Antiquis.**

Giovannini, ? de (b. ?; d. ?, 1782), It.
comp. The customary identification of G.
with the Comte de St. Germain remains
without proof. The only works extant
under the name G. are a handful of songs
(incl. 'Willst du dein Herz mir schenken'
in Bach's Anna Magdalena Notebook)
and 8 vln. sonatas.

Giove in Argo (*Jupiter in Argos*), opera
by Lotti (lib. by Antonio Maria Lucchini),
prod. Dresden, Redoutensaal, 25. X.
1717, the new opera-house not being ready.
The latter was opened with the same work
3. IX. 1719. (An Eng. adaptation of the
same lib., under the title *Jupiter in Argos,*
was set by Handel, prod. London, King's
Theatre, 1. V. 1739).

Gioventù di Enrico V, La (*The Youth
of Henry V*), opera by Pacini (lib. by
Jacopo Ferretti, partly based on Shakespeare's *Henry IV*), prod. Rome, Teatro
Valle, 26. XII. 1820.

Gipps, Ruth (b. Bexhill, 20. II. 1921),
Eng. comp., pianist, cond. and oboist. She
played the pf. in public at the age of 4 and
pub. a pf. piece, *The Fairy Shoemaker,*
when she was 8. Pupil of her mother, Mrs.
Bryan G., at the Bexhill School of Mus. and
later at the R.C.M. in London. In 1944–5
she was in the City of Birmingham Orch.
as 2nd ob. and Eng. horn.

Works incl. ballet *Sea Nymph*; 2 symphs.,
symph. poems *Knight in Armour* and
Death on the Pale Horse (after Blake),
overture to Rostand's *Chantecler*, Variations on a theme by Byrd for orch.; vln.
concerto, clar. concerto, ob. concerto;
string 4tet *Sabrina*; 5tet for ob., clar. and
strings, trio for ob., clar. and pf., *Flax
and Charlock* for Eng. horn, vln., vla. and
cello, *Brocade* for pf. 4tet, Rhapsody for
clar. and string 4tet; sonata and suites for

ob. and pf.; *Jane Grey* for vla. and pf.;
Ducks for soprano, fl., cello and pf.;
Rhapsody without words for soprano and
small orch.; *Chamois* for 2 vlns. and pf.;
instrumental pieces; pf. pieces; songs, etc.

Giraffe, an obs. 19th-cent. species of pf.,
like a grand pf. the body of which stands
up on end, the bass strings on the left
encased in an elongated box not unlike
the neck of a G. in appearance.

Girardeau (*née* ? **Calliari**), **Isabella**
(b. ?; d. ?), It. 17th–18th-cent. soprano,
Fr. by marriage. Made her 1st appearance
in London *c*. 1710.

Giraud, Albert (1860–1929), Belg. poet.
See **Pierrot lunaire** (Schönberg), **Vrieslander** (*Pierrot l.*).

Giraudoux, Jean (1882–1944), Fr. poet,
novelist and dramatist. *See* **Honegger**
(*Sodôme et Gomorrhe*), **Liebermann** (cantata), **Rieti** (*Électre*).

Girdlestone, C(uthbert). M(orton). (b.
Bovey-Tracey, 17. IX. 1895), Eng. scholar.
Educ. at the Sorbonne in Paris and
Cambridge, where he became lecturer in Fr.
Prof. of Fr. at King's Coll., Newcastle-
on-Tyne, 1926–61. Author of *Mozart et ses
concertos pour piano* and *Jean-Philippe
Rameau.*

Girelli Aguilar, Antonia Maria (b. ?;
d. ?), It. 18th-cent. soprano. She sang in
Mozart's *Ascanio in Alba* at Milan in
1771 and the following year appeared in
London, succeeding Grassi.

Girl of the Golden West (Puccini). *See*
Fanciulla del West.

Giroflé-Girofla, operetta by Lecocq (lib.
by Albert Vanloo and Eugène Leterrier),
prod. Brussels, Théâtre Alcazar, 21. III.
1874.

Giselle, ou Les Willis, ballet by Adam
(choreography by Jean Coralli, on a story
by Heine, adapted by Théophile Gautier),
prod. Paris, Opéra, 28. VI. 1841.

Gismondi, Celeste (b. ?; d. London,
28. X. 1735), It. mezzo-soprano. Made her
1st appearance in London in 1732. She
married an Englishman named Hempson.

Gittern, the medieval guitar with 4
strings, played with a plectrum. It survived
in Eng. until the late 17th cent.

Giuliano, opera by Zandonai (lib. by
Arturo Rossato, based on Flaubert's
Saint Julien l'Hospitalier), prod. Naples,
Teatro San Carlo, 4. II. 1928.

Giulietta e Romeo (*Juliet and Romeo*).
opera by Vaccai (lib. by Felice Romani,
after Shakespeare), prod. Milan, Teatro
della Canobbiana, 31. X. 1825.

Opera by Zandonai (lib. by Arturo
Rossato, after Shakespeare), prod. Rome,
Teatro Costanzi, 14. II. 1922.

Opera by Zingarelli (lib. by Giuseppe
Maria Foppa, after Shakespeare), prod.
Milan, Teatro alla Scala, 30. I. 1796.

Giulini, Carlo Maria (b. Barletta, 9. V.

1914), It. cond. Studied at the Acad. of
Santa Cecilia in Rome, vla. and cond.
(Bustini). Later he studied cond. further
with Casella and B. Molinari. From
1946 to 1951 he worked for It. Radio, in
1950 becoming cond. of Radio Milan.
He made his début at La Scala, Milan,
during the 1951–2 season. G. is most
famous as a cond. of It. opera, especially
Verdi, although he can also excel in mus.
by Ger. comps.

Giulio Cesare, opera by Malipiero (lib.
by comp., based on Shakespeare's *Julius
Caesar*), prod. Genoa, Teatro Carlo Felice,
8. II. 1936.

Giulio Cesare in Egitto (*Julius Caesar
in Egypt*), opera by Handel (lib. by Nicola
Francesco Haym), prod. London, King's
Theatre, Haymarket, 20. II. 1724.

Giulio Sabino, opera by Sarti (lib. by
Pietro Giovannini), prod. Venice, Teatro
San Benedetto, I. 1781.

Giuramento, Il (*The Vow*), opera by
Mercadante (lib. by Giacomo Rossi,
based on Victor Hugo's *Angelo*), prod.
Milan, Teatro alla Scala, 10. III. 1837.

Giusti, Giuseppe (1809–50), It. poet.
See **Nielsen (R.)** (satires).

Giustini, Lodovico (b. Pistoia, 12. XII.
1685; d. ?), It. 18th-cent. comp. Pub. in
1732 a book of sonatas, prob. the 1st pub.
mus. specifically written for the pf., as
distinct from mus. for keyboard instruments in general.

Giustiniana (It.), a type of It. song similar to the *villanella*, but always set to a
love poem, current in the 15th and 16th
cents. and so named after Leonardo
Giustiniani. *See also* **Justiniana.**

Giustiniani, Girolamo (17th–18th cent.),
It. poet. *See* **Marcello** (psalms).

Giustiniani, Leonardo (*c*. 1385–1446), It.
poet. He wrote love poems for mus.
settings, some of which he provided himself, which were called after him as late as
the 16th cent.

Giustino, opera by Handel (lib. altered
by ? from Nicolo Beregani), prod. London,
Covent Garden Theatre, 16. II. 1737.

Giusto (It. = just, strict, suitable), a
direction used, generally as an adj. with
tempo, to indicate that a movement is to be
taken at a suitable or reasonable pace.

Gizziello (so called after his teacher
Domenico Gizzi, real name Gioacchino
Conti) (b. Arpino nr. Naples, 28. II. 1714;
d. Rome, 25. X. 1761), It. male soprano.
1st appeared in Rome, 1730, and in
London, 1736.

Gjellerup, Karl (1857–1919), Dan. dramatist. *See* **Schjelderup** (*Offerildene*).

Glanville-Hicks, Peggy (b. Melbourne,
29. XII. 1912), Austral. comp. Studied at
the Melbourne Cons. and from the age of
19 under Vaughan Williams, Gordon
Jacob and R. O. Morris at the R.C.M. in

London. She gained a scholarship in 1932 and another in 1935, which enabled her to travel and to study further with Wellesz in Vienna and Nadia Boulanger in Paris. In 1938 her choral suite was perf. at the I.S.C.M. festival in London and in 1939 she married Stanley Bate, with whom she went to U.S.A., settling in N.Y.

Works incl. operas *Cædmon, The Glittering Gate, Nausicaa*; Sinfonietta, *Prelude* and *Scherzo, Span. Suite* and *Mus. for Robots* for orch.; choral suite (Fletcher) for women's voices, ob. and strings; pf. concerto, fl. concerto; *Concertino da camera* for fl., clar., bassoon and pf.; *Aria concertante* for tenor, ob., gong, pf. and 4 women's voices; sonatina for recorder (or fl.) and pf.; sonata and sonatina for pf.; 6 Housman songs, 5 modern Chin. songs and others, etc.

Glareanus, Henricus (real name **Heinrich Loris**) (b. Mollis, Glarus, VI. 1488; d. Freiburg i/B., 28. III. 1563), Swiss theorist. Studied mus. at Berne and Cologne, taught at Basle from 1515 and again from 1522, after holding a professorship in Paris from 1517 on the recommendation of Erasmus of Rotterdam. In 1529 he moved to Ger., settling at Freiburg. He studied the relationship between the Gk. and the church modes and wrote 2 treatises, *Isagoge in musicen* and *Dodecachordon*.

Glasenapp, Carl Friedrich (b. Riga, 3. X. 1847; d. Riga, 14. IV. 1915), Ger. biog. Author of the 1st large biog. of Wagner and of var. other works on him.

Gläser, Franz (b. Horní Jiřetín, Obergeorgental, 19. IV. 1798; d. Copenhagen, 29. VIII. 1861, Boh. comp. Studied in Prague; app. cond. at the Leopoldstadt Theatre in Vienna, 1817, at the Josephstadt Theatre, 1822, and at the Theater an der Wien, 1827. Later in Berlin and Copenhagen. Wrote mainly operas, e.g. *Des Adlers Horst, Bryllupet ved Como-Søen* (after Manzoni's *Promessi sposi*) and 2 other Dan. operas.

Glass Harmonica. *See* **Harmonica.**

Glastonbury. The mus. connection of the ancient town in Somerset is the festival theatre planned there and partly carried into practice by Rutland Boughton in 1914–27.

Glazunov, Alexander Konstantinovich (b. St. Petersburg, 10. VIII. 1865; d. Paris, 21. III. 1936), Rus. comp. After being taught mus. at home as a child, he studied with Rimsky-Korsakov from 1880 and finished his course in 18 months, having a 1st symph. ready for perf. early in 1882. Belaiev arr. a concert of his works in 1884 and began to pub. them. App. director of the St. Petersburg Cons. in 1905 and wrote little after that to augment his enormous earlier output. He left Rus. in 1928 and settled in Paris.

Works incl. ballets, *Raymonda, Les Ruses d'amour* and *The Seasons*; incid. mus. for Romanov's play, *The King of the Jews*; 8 symphs.; 5 concert overtures incl. 2 on Gk. themes and *Carnival*, symph. poems *Stenka Razin, The Sea, The Kremlin*; suite *From the Middle Ages*, 2 serenades, fantasy *The Forest, Introduction and Salome's Dance* (after Oscar Wilde), many miscellaneous orchestral works; vln. concerto, 2 pf. concertos, concerto for saxophone; 7 string 4tets, string 5tet, *Novelettes* and suite for string 4tet; 17 works for pf. incl. 2 sonatas and Theme and Variations; suite for 2 pfs.; var. small instrumental pieces; 21 songs; 3 cantatas; *Hymn to Pushkin* for female voices, etc.

Glebov, Igor. *See* **Assafiev.**

Glee, a part-song, usually for male voices, in not less than 3 parts, much cultivated by Eng. comps. in the 18th and early 19th cents. The word is derived from the Anglo-Saxon *gliw* = entertainment, partic. musical entertainment. Webbe, Stevens, Callcott, Horsley, Attwood, Battishill, Cooke and others cultivated the G.

Glee Club, a club formed in London in 1783 and existing until 1857, for the performance of glees, madrigals, motets, canons and catches at table after dinner at a member's house or in a tavern or coffeehouse.

Gleichnisarie (Ger.) *See* **Parable Aria.**

Glière, Reinhold Moritzovich (b. Kiev, 11. I. 1875; d. Moscow, 23. VI. 1956), Rus. comp. of Belg. descent. Learnt the vln. as a child, but soon began to comp. and was sent to the Kiev School of Mus. and later to the Moscow Cons., where he was a pupil of Arensky, Taeiev and Ippolitov-Ivanov. Taught at the Gnessin School of Mus. in Moscow and at the Kiev Cons., of which he became director in 1914, but settled at Moscow in 1920. He made research into Azerbaijan, Uzbek and Ukrainian folksong and based some of his later works on it. In 1939 he became chairman of the Organizing Committee of U.S.S.R. comps.

Works incl. operas *Shakh-Senem, Leili and Medjun, Rachel* (after Maupassant's *Mlle. Fifi), Ghulsara*; ballets *The Red Poppy, 1905*; incid. mus. for Sophocles' *Oedipus Rex*, Aristophanes' *Lysistrata*, Beaumarchais's *Marriage of Figaro*, etc.; 3 symphs. (No. 3, *Ilia Muromets*), 3 symph. poems, 5 concert overtures; harp concerto, concerto for soprano and orch.; fantasy for wind instruments; 4 string 4tets, 3 string 6tets, string 8tet; many instrumental pieces; 18 op. nos. of pf. mus.; 22 op. nos. of songs, etc.

Glinka, Mikhail Ivanovich (b. Novospasskoye, Government of Smolensk, 1. VI. 1804; d. Berlin, 15. II. 1857), Rus. comp. The son of a wealthy landowner, he was sent

Glissando   Gluck

to school at St. Petersburg, 1817–22. He took some pf. lessons from Field and others, also studied vln. and theory. At his father's wish he worked in the Ministry of Communications in 1824–8, but not being obliged to earn a living and wishing to devote himself to mus. he gave it up. He visited It., 1830–3, where he had lessons from Basili at Milan, and afterwards Vienna and Berlin, studying under Dehn in the latter city. On his father's death he returned to Rus., settled in St. Petersburg and married in 1835. There he worked at *A Life for the Tsar* and succeeded in having it prod. in 1836. *Russlan and Ludmilla* was delayed by domestic troubles and the separation from his wife in 1841. It was prod. in 1842. In 1844 he visited Paris and Spain, in 1848 Warsaw, and Fr. again in 1852–4. It was during a visit to Berlin, 1856–7, that he d.

Works incl. operas *A Life for the Tsar* (now *Ivan Sussanin*) and *Russlan and*

Glock, William (b. 3. V. 1908), Eng. pianist and mus. critic. Studied with Boris Ord and Edward Dent at Cambridge in 1926–30 and with Schnabel in Berlin in 1930–3. He joined the *Observer* in 1934 and succeeded Fox Strangways as chief mus. critic in 1940, resigning in 1945. In 1948 he founded a summer school for advanced courses in mus. which is now held at Dartington Hall, Devon. He was app. B.B.C. Controller of Music in 1959 and knighted in 1970.

Glockenspiel (Ger. = play of bells), a set of tuned steel bars played either with 2 hammers held one in each hand or with a pf. keyboard (e.g. Papageno's bells in Mozart's *Magic Flute*). In the former case not more than 2 notes can be struck together.

Glogauer Liederbuch, an extensive MS. collection in 3 part-books of Lat. pieces, Ger. songs and instrumental pieces, dating from c. 1480 and now in Berlin.

GLORIA

Ludmilla; incid. mus. to Count Kukolnik's *Prince Kholmsky*; orchestral works: *Jota aragonesa, A Night in Madrid, Kamarinskaya, Valse-Fantaise*; string 4tet in F maj.; trio for clar., bassoon and pf.; 6tet for pf. and strings; c. 40 pf. pieces; Pol. hymn and *Memorial Cantata* for chorus; c. 85 songs; some vocal duets and 4tets, etc.

Glissando (It. from Fr. *glisser* = to glide, slide), a direction for rapid scales played on the pf. or harp, not by fingering, but by sliding over the keys or strings. On the pf. only the C maj. and pentatonic scales can thus be played (on white and black keys respectively), and this applies also to the chromatic harp with its crossed strings, where however a chromatic scale can be played in addition if the strings are touched at the point of intersection. A G. effect can also be obtained on string instruments by sliding the finger along the string or by a voice by scooping, but in both cases the direction for this is more properly *portamento*. Trombs. can play G. passages by not interrupting the breath while the slide is brought to another position.

Gloria (Lat., *Gloria in excelsis Deo* = 'Glory to God in the highest'), the 2nd item of the Ordinary of the Mass, following immediately upon the Kyrie. Although the Ambrosian G. is sung to an even simpler tone, the melody printed with Mass XV of the Vatican ed. is probably the oldest, and bears a striking resemblance to the Mozarabic *Pater noster* (*see* illustration).

Gloriana, opera by Britten (lib. by William Plomer), prod. London, Covent Garden Theatre, 8. VI. 1953.

Glosas (Span. = glosses), ornamentations by which passages in old vocal or instrumental mus. were elaborated.

Gloucester Festival. *See* **Three Choirs Festival.**

Gluck (*née* Fiersohn), **Alma** (b. Bucharest, 11. V. 1884; d. N.Y., 27. X. 1938), Rum.-Amer. soprano. Was taken to U.S.A. as a child and worked as a stenographer in N.Y. until her marriage to Bernard G. in 1906, when she began to study singing, making her 1st appearance in 1909 at the Metropolitan Opera. In 1914 she married the violinist Efrem Zimbalist.

245

Gluck, Christoph Willibald (b. Erasbach, Upper Palatinate, 2. VII. 1714; d. Vienna, 15. XI. 1787), Boh.-Ger. comp. Son of a forester, he left home in face of parental opposition to mus., and matriculated at Prague Univ. in 1731. In Vienna *c.* 1735 entered the service of Prince Melzi, with whom he went to It. For 4 years a pupil of Sammartini in Milan, where he made his début as an opera comp. in 1741 with *Artaserse.* A number of operas followed, all in the conventional It. form. Went to Eng. with Prince Lobkowitz in 1745, possibly visiting Paris on the way. In London, where he met Handel, prod. 2 operas and appeared as a perf. on the glass harmonica. In *c.* 1747 joined the Mingotti touring opera company, of which he subsequently became *Kapellmeister,* and travelled widely. Married in 1750, he settled in Vienna 2 years later, being connected with the court from 1754, though without official title (only in 1774 was he app. court comp.). Under the management of Count Durazzo the Viennese theatre moved away from conventional *opera seria,* and G. comp. a number of Fr. *opéras-comiques.* Dramatic ballet *Don Juan,* embodying Noverre's ideas on modern dance, prod. 1761. Finally in *Orfeo* (1762) G. and his librettist Calzabigi realized in opera the current demands for greater dramatic truth in the theatre. The aims of this 'reform' were set out in the prefaces to *Alceste* (1767) and *Paride ed Elena* (1770). In many ways, e.g. prominent use of chorus and ballet, these works adopted features of Fr. opera, and G. now turned to Paris, where *Iphigénie en Aulide* was prod. in 1774, followed by Fr. versions of *Orfeo* and *Alceste* (1774 and 1776) and *Armide* (1777). G. was reluctantly involved in a squabble between his supporters and the partisans of Piccinni, but this was decisively closed by the triumph of his *Iphigénie en Tauride* (1779). His last opera for Paris, *Écho et Narcisse,* was unsuccessful, and he returned to Vienna, remaining there till his death.

Apart from a number of symphs., 7 trio sonatas, a fl. concerto, a setting of *De profundis* for chorus and orch., and settings of Klopstock's *Odes,* G.'s works are almost entirely for the theatre, viz. *opere serie: Artaserse, Demetrio, Demofoonte, Il Tigrane, La Sofonisba, Ipermestra, La caduta de' giganti, Artamene, Le nozze d'Ercole e d'Ebe, Semiramide riconosciuta, La Contesa dei numi, Ezio, La clemenza di Tito, Le Cinesi, Antigono, Il re pastore, Il Telemaco,* etc.; Fr. *opéras-comiques: L'Isle de Merlin, La Cythère assiégée, L'Arbre enchanté, L'Yvrogne corrigé, Le Cadi dupé, La Rencontre imprévue,* etc.; 'reform' operas: *Orfeo, Alceste, Paride ed Elena;* Fr. operas for Paris: *Iphigénie en Aulide,*

Orphée et Euridice and *Alceste* (both Fr. versions of the earlier It. operas), *Armide, Iphigénie en Tauride, Écho et Narcisse;* ballets: *Don Juan, Semiramide,* etc.

Glückliche Hand, Die (*The Lucky Hand*), opera by Schönberg (lib. by comp.), comp. 1913, prod. Vienna, Volksoper, 14. X. 1924.

Glyndebourne Opera, a private opera theatre opened by John Christie on his estate of Glyndebourne, Sussex, in 1934, for the perf. of opera in beautiful surroundings with an internat. company of singers. Until World War II the repertory was devoted almost wholly to Mozart, the only exceptions being Verdi's *Macbeth* and Donizetti's *Don Pasquale.* Since 1946 it has been considerably extended.

Gnecchi, Vittorio (b. Milan, 17. VII. 1876; d. Milan, 5. II. 1954), It. comp. Studied mus. at Milan. His 1st opera at Bologna in 1905 aroused great controversy in 1909, when Strauss's *Elektra* appeared and showed var. striking similarities to G.'s mus.

Works. incl. operas *Cassandra* (after Homer's *Iliad*) and *La Rosiera;* heroic poem for orch. *Notte nel campo di Holoferne,* etc.

Gnecco, Francesco (b. Genoa, 1769; d. Milan, 1810), It. comp. Pupil (?) of Mariani and Cimarosa. *Maestro di cappella* at Savona Cathedral.

Works incl. 26 operas, e.g. *Carolina e Filandro* and *La prova d'un opera seria,* etc.

Gnessin, Mikhail Fabianovich (b. Rostov-on-Don, 2. II. 1883; d. Moscow, 5. V. 1957), Rus. comp. Studied with Rimsky-Korsakov and Liadov at the St. Petersburg Cons. and in Ger. from 1911 to 1914. Settled at Rostov in 1914, at Moscow in 1923 and became prof. at the Leningrad Cons. in 1936. His work is influenced by Jewish mus.

Works incl. operas *Youth of Abraham* and *The Maccabees;* incid. mus. for plays, incl. Sophocles' *Antigone* and *Oedipus Rex,* Gogol's *The Revisor,* Blok's *The Rose and the Cross,* etc.; *1905–17* for solo voices, chorus and orch.; *Symph. Fragment* (after Shelley), *The Conqueror Worm* (after Poe), *Song of Adonis* and *Fantasia in the Jewish Style* for orch.; *Requiem* for pf. 5tet, *Variations on Jewish Themes* and *Azerbaijan Folksongs* for string 4tet, 6tet *Adygeya;* vln. and pf. sonata in G min., *Sonata-Ballade* for cello and pf.; songs with orch.; song cycles to words by Alexander Blok, Sologub, etc.; Jewish folksong arrs., etc.

Gobbi, Tito (b. Bassano del Grappa, 24. X. 1915), It. baritone. Orig. studied law, but later singing in Rome with Crimi, making his début in Rome in 1938. He first appeared at La Scala, Milan in 1942. G. has a huge repertory of some 100 roles, and is especially outstanding as a Verdi and Puccini singer. He is also a fine actor and has made some 26 films.

God save the Queen (or King), the Brit. nat. anthem. A tune of possibly remote but uncertain ancestry, 1st appearing in very nearly its present form in 2 eds. of the *Thesaurus Musicus* in London, 1744–5. In the latter year it became very popular as a royalist song attacking the Young Pretender. The tune has been adopted in several other countries.

Godard, Benjamin (Louis Paul) (b. Paris, 18. VIII. 1849; d. Cannes, 10. I. 1895), Fr. comp. Studied vln. and comp. at the Paris Cons. He became a vla. player in chamber mus. In 1878 he tied with Dubois in gaining the prize in a competition organized by the municipality of Paris with the dramatic symph. *Le Tasse* for solo voices, chorus and orch. In 1885 he estab. a series of 'modern concerts' without success.

Works incl. operas *Pedro de Zalamea*, *Jocelyn*, *Le Dante*, *La Vivandière*, *Les Guelfes*; incid. mus. to Shakespeare's *Much Ado about Nothing* and Fabre's *Jeanne d'Arc*; *Scènes poètiques*, dramatic poem *Diane*, *Symphonie-Ballet*, *Symphonie gothique*, *Symphonie orientale* and *Symphonie légendaire* for orch.; 2 vln. concertos, pf. concerto; 3 string 4tets, pf. trio; 3 vln. and pf. sonatas; pf. pieces; over 100 songs, etc.

Goddard, Arabella (b. Saint-Servan, Saint-Malo, 12. I. 1836; d. Boulogne, 6. IV. 1922), Eng. pianist. Pupil of Kalkbrenner in Paris and later of Thalberg in Eng. Made her 1st public appearance in London in 1850. She studied the classics with Davison, whom she married in 1859.

Goddard, Scott (b. Ore, Sussex, 25. IX. 1895; d. 4. XI. 1965), Eng. critic. Studied in London under Walford Davies at the Temple Church, where he became a pupil-asst., and at the R.C.M. in 1913. In 1915–18 he worked among Belg. refugees in Hol. and in 1918 returned to the R.C.M. as a pupil of Stanford, Charles Wood and Parratt. In 1921–7 he was mus. master at Leighton Park School, Reading, then became critic to var. London papers, finally (1938) the *News Chronicle*.

Godfrey, Dan(iel Eyers) (b. London, 20. VI. 1868; d. Bournemouth, 20. VII. 1939), Eng. cond. Son of the bandmaster Daniel G. (1831–1903). Studied at the R.C.M. in London and 1st cond. a military band and opera, and in 1892 became cond. of a small seaside orch. at Bournemouth, which in time he raised to a full symph. orch. He was knighted in 1922 and retired in 1934.

Godowsky, Leopold (b. Wilno, 13. II. 1870; d. N.Y., 21. XI. 1938), Pol. (Americanized) pianist and comp. Very precociously gifted, he appeared in public at the age of 9, made a tour of Pol. and Ger., and then entered the Hochschule für Musik in Berlin, studying with Bargiel and Rudorff. He 1st visited the U.S.A. in 1884, where he settled in 1901 and later became director of the Chicago Cons. In 1909–14 he taught in Vienna. He made many arrs. for pf. and comp. studies, concert pieces, etc.

Goedicke, Alexander Feodorovich (b. Moscow, 4. III. 1877; d. Moscow, 9. VIII. 1957), Rus. pianist and comp. Studied under Pabst, Arensky, Safonov and others at the Moscow Cons., where he became prof. in 1903.

Works incl. operas *Virinea*, *Driving the Railway Engine*, *The Jacquerie* and *Moving Through*; cantata *Glory of the Soviet Pilots*; 3 symphs. and other orchestral works; string 4tets, pf. 5tet, pf. trio; vln. and pf. sonata; Rus. folksongs for voice, pf. and cello; pf. pieces; songs, etc.

Goehler (Karl) Georg (b. Zwickau, 29. VI. 1874; d. Lübeck, 4. III. 1954), Ger. cond. and comp. Studied under Kretzschmar at Leipzig Univ. Cond. the Riedelverein there in 1879–1913 and later was operatic, choral and orchestral cond. at Hamburg, Lübeck and Halle, but retired to devote himself to comp. in 1932. He was also a writer on mus. and trans. operas by Verdi.

Works incl. opera *Prinz Nachtwächter*; 5 symphs., suite and other orchestral works; concertos for pf., vln. (2) and cello; cantatas with orch. on poems by Leopardi; 2 string 4tets and other chamber mus.; 24 Bagatelles for pf.; male voice choruses; *c.* 200 songs, etc.

Goehr, Alexander (b. Berlin, 10. VIII. 1932), Eng. comp. son of Walter G. Studied at the Royal Manchester Coll. of Mus. and at the Paris Cons. with Messiaen. He comps. frequently in a free serial technique. Prof., Leeds Univ., 1971.

Works incl. opera *Arden muss sterben* (Erich Fried); cantatas *The Deluge*, *Sutter's Gold*, *Hecuba's Lament*; fantasia for orch.; *Little Symph.* for orchestra; vln. concerto; *Little Music* for strings; *Fantasias* for clar. and pf.; *4 Songs from the Japanese* for soprano and orch., etc.

Goes, Damião de (b. Alemquer, 1502; d. Alemquer, 30. I. 1572), Port. hist., explorer and musician.

Works incl. motets and songs for several voices, etc.

Goethe, Johann Wolfgang von (1749–1832), Ger. poet, novelist, dramatist and philosopher. *See* André (J.) (*Erwin und Elmire*), Apprenti sorcier (Dukas), Beeke (*Claudine von Villa Bella*), Benoit (P.) (*Roi des aulnes*), Bentzon (N.V.) (*Faust II*), Blangini (*Letzten Augenblicke Werthers*), Brahms (*Gesang der Parzen* and *Rinaldo*), Brun (*Verheissung*), Claudine von Villa Bella (4 comps.), Dieren (van) (songs), Dukas (*Apprenti sorcier* and *Götz von Berlichingen*), Eberwein (*Claudine von V. B.* and

247

Jahrmarkt von Plundersweilen), **Egmont** (Beethoven), **Erlkönig** (Schubert), **Ettinger** (*Clavigo*), **Gál** (*Requiem für Mignon*), **Goldmark (C.)** (*Götz von B.* and *Meeresstille und glückliche Fahrt*), **Hoffmann (E. T. A.)** (*Scherz, List und Rache*), **Hüttenbrenner (A.)** (*Erlkönig*), **Istel** (*Satyros*), **Jery und Bätely** (Reichardt and Seckendorff), **Kienlen** (*Claudine von V. B.* and *Scherz, L. und R.*), **Koechlin** (*Nuit de Walpurgis classique*), **Křenek** (*Triumph der Empfindsamkeit*), **Lassen** (*Pandora*), **Loewe (K.)** (*Erlkönig*), **Marx (A. B.)** (*Jery und B.*), **Mathieu** (ballads), **Medtner** (songs), **Meeresstille** (Beethoven and Mendelssohn), **Mendelssohn (A.)** (*Werther*), **Mendelssohn** (*Erste Walpurgisnacht*), **Mignon** (A. Thomas), **Moser (R.)** (*Fischerin*), **Pugnani** (*Werther* symph.), **Rauzzini (V.)** (*Werther*), **Reichardt** (*Claudine von V. B.*, *Erwin und E.* and *Jery und B.*), **Rhapsodie** (Brahms), **Rietz (J.)** (*Jery und B.* and incid. mus. for plays), **Rinaldo** (Brahms), **Rubinstein (A.)** (*Wilhelm Meister*), **Scherz, List und Rache** (Bruch), **Schoeck** (*Erwin und Elmire*, *Dithyrambe* and songs), **Scholz** (*Iphigenie*), **Schröter (C.)** (*Fischerin, Neue Amadis* and *Erlkönig*), **Schubert** (*Claudine von V. B.*), **Schumann** (*Requiem für Mignon*), **Schweizer** (*Clavigo* and *Erwin und E.*), **Starck** (*Jery und B.*), **Stegmann** (*Erwin und E.*), **Stiehl** (*Jery und B.*), **Streicher (T.)** (*Mignons Exequien*), **Suter** (*Erste Walpurgisnacht*), **Tasso** (Liszt), **Tomášek** (songs), **Trunk** (male choruses), **Unger (H.)** (*Gott und Bajadere*), **Valen** (songs), **Veilchen** (Mozart), **Vogler** (*Erwin und E.*), **Vrieslander** (songs), **Wallace (W.)** (*Anvil or Hammer*), **Webern** (2 choral songs), **Wellesz** (*Scherz, L. und R.*), **Werther** (Massenet), **Winter** (*Scherz, L. und R.* and *Jery und B.*), **Wolf (E. W.)** (*Erwin und E.*), **Zagwijn** (*Sorcerer's Apprentice*), **Zelter** (songs), **Zumsteeg** (*Clavigo*).

5 songs by Brahms, 1 by Mozart (*Veilchen*), 71 by Schubert, 19 by Schumann, 60 (incl. 9 early) by Wolf.

Faust see **Adam (A.)** (ballet), **Boulanger (L.)** (*F. et Hélène*), **Bungert** (incid. mus.), **Coleridge-Taylor** (do.), **Damnation de Faust** (Berlioz), **Diepenbrock** (incid. mus.), **Doktor Faust** (Busoni), **Draeseke** (*Easter Scene*), **Faust** (ballet, Costa etc.; operas, Gounod and Zöllner; orchestral works. Liszt and Wagner), **Fausto** (Bertin), **Gregoir (J. M. J.)** (cantata), **Gretchen am Spinnrade** (song, Schubert), **Hatton** (incid. mus.), **Höffer** (do.), **Lassen** (do.), **Lazzari** (do.), **Lindpaintner** (do.), **Liszt** (symph.), **Lortzing** (incid. mus.), **Mefistofele** (Boito), **Meyer-Lutz** (opera), **Mihalovich** (overture), **Paumgartner** (incid. mus.), **Petit Faust** (parody-operetta, Hervé), **Pierson** (incid. mus.), **Radziwill** (do.), **Rubinstein (A.)** (mus. portrait), **Salmhofer** (incid. mus.), **Schillings** (do.), **Schulz-**

Beuthen (2 scenes), **Streicher (T.)** (monologues), **Szenen aus G.s F.** (Schumann), **Tomášek** (incid. mus.), **Wagner** (overture and 7 songs), **Walter (I.)** (opera), **Weingartner** (incid. mus.), **Wolfurt** (Rhapsody).

Separate settings of songs, etc. in 'Faust' incl. *Der König in Thule* by Schubert; *Gretchen* (prayer, 'Ach neige') by Schubert (unfinished); 'Song of the Flea' by Beethoven and Mussorgsky.

Goetz. *See* **Götz.**

Gogol, Nikolai Vassilievich (1809–52), Rus. novelist. *See* Assafiev (*Christmas Eve*), Berutti (*Taras Bulba*), Christmas Eve (Rimsky-Korsakov), Egk (*Revisor*), Gnessin (do.), Janáček (*Taras B.*), Kashperov (do.), Lissenko (do.), Marriage (Mussorgsky), May Night (Rimsky-Korsakov), Rousseau (M.) (*Taras B.*), Searle (*Diary of a Madman*), Serov (*Christmas Eve Revels*), Shostakovich (*Nose*), Sokalsky (P.) (*Night in May* and *Taras B.*), Soloviev (*Vakula the Smith*), Sorotchintsy Fair (Mussorgsky), Vakula the Smith (Tchaikovsky), Weiss (K.) (*Revisor*), Zanella (do.).

Göhringer, Franzilla. *See* **Pixis.**

Goldberg, Johann Gottlieb (b. Danzig, 14. III. 1727; d. Dresden, 13. IV. 1756), Ger. harpsichordist, pupil of W. F. and J. S. Bach. The latter apparently wrote for him (aged only 15) the 'Goldberg Variations' in 1742.

'Goldberg Variations' (Bach). *See above.*

Golden Cockerel, The (*Zolotoy Petushok*), opera by Rimsky-Korsakov, (lib. by Vladimir Ivanovich Bielsky, based on Pushkin's satirical fairy-tale), prod. Moscow, 7. X. 1909, after Rimsky-Korsakov's death. It is his last opera.

Golden Legend, The, oratorio by Sullivan (on Longfellow's poem), prod. Leeds Festival, 1886.

'Golden Sonata', the nickname given to the 9th (F maj.) of Purcell's 10 *Sonatas of IV Parts* for 2 vlns., cello and continuo, pub. posthumously in 1697.

Goldene Kreuz, Das (*The Golden Cross*), opera by Brüll (lib. by Salomon Hermann Mosenthal, based on a Fr. play, *Cathérine*, by Ann Honoré Joseph Mélesville and Nicolas Brazier), prod. Berlin, Royal Opera, 22. XII. 1875.

Goldmark, Carl (b. Keszthely, 18. V. 1830; d. Vienna, 2. I. 1915), Aus.-Hung. comp. Son of a poor Jewish cantor, who managed to enter him at the Sopron school of mus. in 1842. He studied vln. and made such rapid progress that he was sent to Vienna the next year and entered the cons. in 1847. During the 1848 Revolution he played at the theatre at Györ in Hung. and was nearly shot as a rebel. In 1850 he returned to Vienna, where he eventually settled as a teacher.

Works incl. operas *Die Königin von Saba, Merlin, Das Heimchen am Herd* (after Dickens's *Cricket on the Hearth*), *Die Kriegsgefangene*, *Götz von Berlichingen* (after Goethe) and *Ein Wintermärchen* (after Shakespeare's *Winter's Tale*); symphs. *Rustic Wedding* and E♭ maj., 2 Scherzos for orch. and overtures *Sakuntala* (after Kalidasa), *Penthesilea* (after Kleist), *Im Frühling*, *Der gefesselte Prometheus*, *Sappho*, *In Italien* and *Aus Jugendtagen*, symph. poem *Zrinyi*; *Meeresstille und glückliche Fahrt* (Goethe) for male chorus and horns and other choral works; 2 vln. concertos; string 4tet, pf. 5tet, 3 pf. trios and other chamber mus.; 2 suites and sonata for vln. and pf., cello and pf. sonata; pf. pieces; songs, etc.

Goldmark, Rubin (b. New York, 15. VIII. 1872; d. N.Y., 6. III. 1936), Amer. comp. of Aus.-Hung. descent, nephew of prec. Studied at the Vienna Cons. and the Nat. Cons. in N.Y., where Dvořák was his comp. master. He was director of the Colorado Coll. Cons. in 1895–1901, but returned to N.Y. in 1902 and settled as private pf. and comp. teacher, until in 1924 he was app. to the Juilliard Graduate School there.

Works incl. *Hiawatha* (after Longfellow), *Samson*, *Requiem* (on Lincoln's address at Gettysburg), *Negro Rhapsody* and *The Call of the Plains* for orch.; string 4tet in A maj., pf. trio in D min.; vln. and pf. sonata; vln. pieces; pf. mus.; songs; choruses, etc.

Goldoni, Carlo (1707–93), It. playwright and librettist. *See* **Amore artigiano** (Gassmann and Latilla), **Arcadia in Brenta** (Galuppi), **Buovo d'Antona** (Traetta), **Burbero di buon cuore** (Martín y Soler), **Conte Caramella** (Galuppi), **Donne curiose** (Wolf-Ferrari), **Filosofo di campagna** (Galuppi), **Fischietti** (4 operas), **Fra due litiganti** (Sarti), **Gelosie villane** (Sarti), **Generali** (*Pamela nubile*, after Richardson), **Isola disabitata** (G. Scarlatti), **Jeppesen** (opera), **Lottchen am Hofe** (J. A. Hiller), **Malipiero** (3 operas), **Mondo alla roversa** (Galuppi), **Mondo della luna** (do. and Haydn), **Paisiello** (*Ciarlone*), **Pallavicini** (V.) (*Speziale*), **Pescatrici** (Bertoni), **Piccinni** (*Vittorina*), **Quattro rusteghi** (Wolf-Ferrari), **Scarlatti** (6) (*Portentosi effetti*), **Scholz** (*Mirandolina*), **Sinigaglia** (*Baruffe chiozzotte*), **Speziale** (Haydn), **Tigrane** (Gluck), **Uccellatori** (Gassmann), **Usiglio** (*Donne curiose*), **Vendemmia** (Gazzaniga), **Wagenaar (J.)** (*Philos. Princess*), **Wolf (E. W.)** (*Dorfdeputierten*).

Goldschmidt, Adalbert von (b. Vienna, 5. V. 1848; d. Vienna, 21. XII. 1906), Aus. comp. He devoted himself as an amateur to the comp. of large-scale works, the 1st of which, prod. in Berlin in 1876, showed remarkable affinities with Wagner's *Ring*, not heard until later in the year at Bayreuth.

Works incl. mus.-dramas *Die sieben*

Todsünden, *Helianthus*, *Gaea* (trilogy), opera *Die fromme Helene* (after Wilhelm Busch); symph. poem; *c.* 100 songs, etc.

Goldschmidt, Berthold (b. Hamburg, 18. I. 1903), Eng. cond. and comp. of Ger. birth. Studied in Berlin, became asst. cond. there in 1926 and cond. at the Darmstadt Opera in 1927. In 1931–3 he cond. on the Berlin radio and was artistic adviser to the munic. Opera there. But the Nazi régime drove him to Eng.

Works incl. operas *Der gewaltige Hahnrei* (after Crommelynck) and *Beatrice Cenci* (after Shelley); ballet *Chronica*; overture to Shakespeare's *Comedy of Errors*, symph. and other orchestral works; vln., cello and harp concertos, chamber mus., etc.

Goldschmidt, Hugo (b. Breslau, 19. IX. 1859; d. Wiesbaden, 26. XII. 1920), Ger. musicologist. Studied singing with Stockhausen at Frankfurt, but later took up mus. hist. One of the directors of the Scharwenka-Klindworth Cons. in Berlin and later prof. of mus. hist. there. Wrote several works on the hist. of singing, one on 17th-cent. It. opera, etc.

Goldschmidt, Otto (b. Hamburg, 21. VIII. 1829; d. London, 24. II. 1907), Ger. pianist and comp. Studied at the Leipzig Cons. under Mendelssohn and in 1848 went to Paris to study with Chopin. In 1849 he went to London, where he settled in 1858. Accompanist and husband of Jenny Lind. Founder of the Bach Choir.

Works incl. oratorio *Ruth*; cantata *Music* for soprano and female voices; pf. concerto; pf. trio; 2 duets for 2 pfs.; studies and pieces for pf.; songs etc.,

Goldsmith, Oliver (1728–74), Eng. novelist, poet, dramatist and essayist. *See* **ApIvor** (*She Stoops*), **Lehmann (L.ii)** (*Vicar of Wakefield*), **She Stoops to Conquer** (G. Macfarren), **Torrance** (*Captivity*), **Vento** (*Threnodia Augustalis*), **White (F.)** (*Deserted Village*).

Golenishtchev-Kutuzov, Arseny, Count (1848–1913), Rus. amateur poet, distant relative of Mussorgsky. *See* **Songs and Dances of Death** (Mussorgsky), **Sunless** (do.).

Golestan, Stan (b. Vaslui, 26. V. 1875; d. Paris, 22. IV. 1956), Rum. comp. Studied at the Schola Cantorum and the Cons. in Paris under d'Indy, Roussel and Dukas. Mus. critic of *Le Figaro*. As a comp. he cultivated a Rum. nat. style.

Works incl. symph., *Rapsodie Dambovitza* and *Rumanian Rhapsody*; *Concerto roumain* for vln. and orch., *Concerto moldave* for cello and orch.; pf. concerto, *Sur les cîmes carpathiques*, *Intermezzo et Siciliennes* for harp and orch., *Oriental Fantasy* for bassoon and orch.; 2 string 4tets, *Divertissement* for ob., clar. and bassoon; vln. and pf. sonata, fl. and pf.

sonatina; Theme and Variations for pf.; pieces for wind instruments; 10 Rum. folksongs, etc.

Golinelli, Stefano (b. Bologna, 26. X. 1818; d. Bologna, 3. VII. 1891), It. pianist and comp. Pupil of Benedetto Donelli for pf. and of Vaccai for comp. Prof. at the Liceo musicale at Bologna, 1840–70.

Works (all for pf.) incl. 5 sonatas, 12 studies, 3 sets of 24 preludes, 3 toccatas and others in c. 200 op. nos.

Goltermann, Georg (Eduard) (b. Hanover, 19. VIII. 1824; d. Frankfurt, 29. XII. 1898), Ger. cellist, cond. and comp. Studied at Munich and began to tour as a cello virtuoso in 1850. In 1853 he became 2nd and in 1874 1st cond. at the Frankfurt theatre. Comp. a symph.; a cello concerto and many pieces for that instrument.

Golubev, Evgeny (b. Moscow, 16. II. 1910), Rus. comp. Studied at the Moscow Cons. He went to the Ukraine in 1937 to study its folk mus.

Works incl. oratorio *The Return of the Sun*; 4 symphs. and Double Fugue for orch.; 3 string 4tets; Poem for vln. and pf.; 3 sonatas and *Ukrainian Rhapsody* for pf., etc.

Gombert, Nicolas (b. c. 1500; d. ? Tournai, c. 1556), Flem. comp. Pupil of Josquin des Prés. He was in service at the Emperor Charles V's chapel in Flanders from 1520 and became *maître de chapelle* in 1530; later he became a canon at Tournai and in 1537 went to Spain with 20 singers and held a post in the imp. chapel in Madrid.

Works incl. Masses, motets, psalms; *chansons*, etc.

Gombosi, Otto (Johannes) (b. Budapest, 23. X. 1902; d. Lexington, Mass., 17. II. 1955), Hung.-Amer. musicologist. Studied in Budapest and Berlin. He was a mus. critic in Berlin from 1929 to 1935, moving to Rome in 1935, to Basle in 1936, and finally to the U.S.A., where he held in succession univ. apps. at Seattle, Michigan State Coll. and Harvard. He wrote a number of works on medieval and Renaissance mus. and pub. modern eds.

Gomes, (Antônio) Carlos (b. Campinas, 11. VII. 1836; d. Belém, 16. IX. 1896), Braz. comp. of Port. descent. Studied with Lauro Rossi in Milan. In 1895 he was app. director of the Cons. at Pará, but he was delayed at Lisbon by illness and d. soon after his arrival.

Works incl. operas *A noite do castello*, *Joanna di Flandres*, *Il Guarany*, *Fosca*, *Salvator Rosa*, *Maria Tudor* (on Victor Hugo's play), *Lo schiavo*, *Condor*; revues *Se sa minga* and *Nella luna*; ode *Il saluto del Brasil* (Philadelphia Exhibition, 1876) and cantata *Colombo* (Columbus Festival, 1892), etc.

Gomis, José Melchior (b. Onteniente,

Valencia, 6. I. 1791; d. Paris, 26. VII. 1836), Span. comp. Bandmaster at Barcelona, moved to Madrid c. 1817 and in 1823 went to Paris for political reasons. In 1826–9 he taught singing in London, where he pub. many Span. songs, and then returned to Paris, where he prod. comic operas.

Works incl. Span. monodrama *Sensibilidad y prudencia*, *ó La Aldeana*, Fr. comic operas *Le Diable à Séville*, *Le Revenant* (after Scott), *Le Portefaix* and *Rock le barbu*; *L'inverno* for 4 voices and orch.; songs, etc.

Gondoliers, The, or The King of Barataria, operetta by Sullivan (lib. by W. S. Gilbert), prod. London, Savoy Theatre, 7. XII. 1889.

Gong, an oriental bronze disc with turned-down rims. It is struck with a mallet covered with var. materials according to the quality of sound required.

Góngora y Argote, Luis de (1561–1627), Span. poet. *See* Falla (*A Córdoba*).

Gonzaga, Guglielmo, Duke of Mantua (b. Mantua, 1538; d. Mantua, 1587). He succeeded to the duchy in 1550, became a great patron of mus. and was himself a comp., pub. anonymously a book of madrigals and 1 of *Sacrae cantiones*.

Good-Humoured Ladies, The, ballet by Tommasini on mus. by D. Scarlatti (choreography by Leonid Fedorovich Massin), prod. Rome, Teatro Costanzi, 12. IV. 1917.

Goossens, Eugene (b. London, 26. V. 1893; d. Hillingdon, 13. VI. 1962), Eng. cond. and comp. of Belg. descent, grandson of Eugène G. (1845–1906) and son of Eugène G. (1867–1958), both conds. of the Carl Rosa Opera Co. He was sent to the Bruges Cons. in 1903, to the Liverpool Coll. of Mus. in 1906 and later studied vln. with Rivarde and comp. with Stanford at the R.C.M. in London, with pf. as 2nd study. He played vln. in the Queen's Hall Orch., 1911–15, and then, until 1920, cond. some of Beecham's operatic prods. After that he formed an orch. of his own, which had a brief season in 1921, and cond. the Rus. Ballet and the Symph. Orch. at Rochester, U.S.A. In 1931 he was app. cond. of the Cincinnati Symph. Orch. and continued to live there until he was app. cond. of the Sydney Orch. and director of the Cons. there (1947–56). Knighted in 1955.

Works incl. operas *Judith* and *Don Juan de Mañara*; ballet *L'École en crinoline*; incid. mus. to Verhaeren's *Philip II*, Somerset Maugham's *East of Suez* and Margaret Kennedy's *The Constant Nymph*; 2 symphs., sinfonietta, symph. poem *The Eternal Rhythm*, symph. prelude to a poem by Ossian, scherzo *Tam o' Shanter* (after Burns), Overture for Jubilee of

Cincinnati Orch.; Miniature Fantasy and Concertino for string orch.; *Silence* for chorus and orch.; Fantasy Concerto for pf. and orch., ob. concerto, vln. concerto; 2 string 4tets, Fantasy and 2 Sketches for string 4tet, pf. 5tet, string 6tet, suite for fl., vln. and harp, *Impressions of a Holiday* for fl., cello and pf. and other chamber mus.; vln. and pf. sonata, Rhapsody for cello and pf.; *Kaleidoscope, Four Conceits, Nature Poems, Ships,* etc. for pf.; *The Cowl* (Barbor) for recitation and pf.; many songs in Eng. and Fr., etc.

Goossens, Leon (b. Liverpool, 12. VI. 1897), Eng. oboist, brother of prec. Studied at the R.C.M. From 1913 to 1924 he was 1st ob. of the Queen's Hall Orch., afterwards playing with the Royal Phil. Orch. and with Covent Garden Opera. He has taught at the R.A.M. and the R.C.M.

Goovaerts, Alphonse (Jean Marie André) (b. Antwerp, 25. V. 1847; d. Brussels, 25. XII. 1922), Belg. comp. and writer on mus. Studied at the Jesuit Coll. of Antwerp and at the age of 15 was obliged by financial losses to take a commercial career; but he studied mus. thoroughly by himself and in 1866 obtained a post at the Antwerp town library. In 1869 his *Messe solennelle* was perf. In 1874 he was app. mus. secretary to Antwerp Cathedral and he estab. a special choir for which he copied a vast quantity of old motets of var. schools. He began to write on the reform of church mus. and in 1898 was app. keeper of the royal archives in Brussels.

Works incl. motets, *Petite Messe, Messe solennelle* and other church mus.; songs, part-songs, etc.

Gopak (or Hopak), a Rus. folk dance with mus. of a lively character in quick 2–4 time.

Gorczycki, Grzegorz (b. ?, *c.* 1664; d. Cracow, 30. IV. 1734), Pol. comp. *Magister capellae* at Cracow Cathedral. Comp. motets and other church mus. from 1698.

Gordigiani, Luigi (b. Florence, 12. VI. 1806; d. Florence, 30. IV. 1860), It. comp. Pupil of his father, Antonio G., who d. when he was 14, so that he had to make a living by writing pf. pieces under Ger. names. The Rus. Prince Nikolai Demidov and the Pol. Prince Joseph Poniatowski discovered his great gifts and patronized him, the latter providing him with the lib. for his opera *Filippo,* prod. at Florence in 1840.

Works incl. 10 operas; *Canzonette, Canti popolari* and other songs (*c.* 300 in all); duets for female voices; Tuscan airs with pf. accomp., etc.

Gordon, Adam Lindsay (1833–70) Austral. poet. *See* **Sea Pictures** (Elgar).

Gordon, Gavin (Muspratt) (b. Ayr, 24. XI. 1901; d. 18. XI. 1970). Scot. singer,

actor and comp. Educ. at Rugby and studied mus. at the R.C.M. in London.

Works incl. ballets *A Toothsome Morsel, Regatta, The Scorpions of Ysit* and *The Rake's Progress* (after Hogarth), etc.

Górecki, Henryk (b. Czernica, 6. XII. 1933), Pol. comp. Studied with Szabelski in Katowice. He tends toward strict serialism, but is also influenced by neo-classicism.

Works incl. cantata *Epitafium; Symph. 1959; Scontri* for orch.; *Instrumental Ensemble* for 15 instruments; toccata for 2 pfs.; sonata for 2 vlns. etc.

Gorgia (It. = throat), the practice of improvised embellishments in the solo vocal mus. of the 16th and 17th cents.

Gorky, Maxim (Alexei Maximovich Peshkov) (1868–1936), Rus. novelist. *See* **Assafiev** (*Makar Chudra*), **Eisler** (*Mother*), **Zhelobinsky** (do.).

Görner, Johann Gottlieb (b. Penig, Saxony, IV. 1697; d. Leipzig, 15. II. 1778), Ger. organist and comp. Educ. in Leipzig and held various org. posts there: St. Paul (1716), St. Nikolai (1721) and St. Thomas (1729). In 1723 he founded a Collegium Musicum. Comp. church mus.

Gorzanis, Giacomo (b. Apulia, *c.* 1525; d. ? Trieste, after 1575), It. comp. He pub. 4 books of lute mus., incl. numerous dance-suites in 2 or 3 movements. One of these, consisting of a *passo e mezzo* and *padovana* (1561), is the earliest known work to be called *sonata.*

Göss, Barthel. *See* **Gese, Bartholomäus.**

Goss, John (b. Fareham, Hants., 27. XII. 1800; d. London, 10. V. 1880), Eng. organist and comp. Studied under his father, organist at Fareham, then under J. S. Smith at the Chapel Royal in London and finally under Attwood. After holding several org. apps., he succeeded Attwood as organist of St. Paul's Cathedral in 1838 and in 1856 became one of the comps. to the Chapel Royal in succession to Knyvett. Knighted in 1872 and Mus.D., Cambridge, in 1876.

Works incl. services, anthems, chants, psalms; orchestral pieces; glees; songs, etc.

Gossec, François Joseph (b. Vergnies, Hainault, 17. I. 1734; d. Passy nr. Paris, 16. II. 1829), Belg.-Fr. comp. Chorister at Antwerp Cathedral, went to Paris in 1751, where with Rameau's help he obtained a post in La Pouplinière's private orch. in 1754. Later mus. director to the Prince of Condé. Founded the Concert des Amateurs in 1770, and in 1773 took over the direction of the Concert spirituel. On the foundation of the Paris Cons. in 1795 he became one of its directors and prof. of comp. As one of the leading comps. of the Fr. Revolution he wrote many works for public ceremonies, often

251

using vast forces. After 1800 he comp. little.

Works incl. operas *Le Tonnelier, Le Faux Lord, Les Pêcheurs, Toinon et Toinette, Le Double Déguisement, Sabinus, Alexis et Daphné, Philémon et Baucis, Hilas et Silvie, La Fête de village, Thésée, Rosine*, etc.; ballets *Les Scythes enchaînés, La Reprise de Toulon, Mirsa* and *Callisto*; incid. mus. for Racine's *Athalie* and Rochefort's *Électre*; oratorios *La Nativité, Saül* and *L'Arche d'alliance*; Requiem, *Dixit Dominus, Exaudiat, Dernière Messe des vivants*, motets, etc.; funeral mus. for Mirabeau, *Le Chant du 14 juillet, L'Offrande à la liberté, Le Triomphe de la République* and other mus. for the Revolution; over 30 symphs., overtures and other orchestral works; 12 string 4tets, trios and other chamber mus., etc.

Gosswin, Antonius (b. *c.* 1540; d. *c.* 1594), Flem. comp., a pupil of Lassus in Munich. Wrote Ger. songs, madrigals, motets and Masses.

Gostena, Giovanni Battista dalla (b. Genoa, *c.* 1540; d. Genoa, XII. 1598), It. comp. Pupil of Philippe de Monte, *maestro di cappella* at Genoa Cathedral from 1584 to 1598, when his nephew, Molinaro, succeeded him.

Works incl. motets and other church mus.; 2 books of madrigals, 1 of *canzonette*; 25 fantasies for lute, etc.

Gostling, John (b. East Malling, Kent, *c.* 1650; d. ? London, 17. VII. 1733), Eng. cleric and bass. Became a Gentleman of the Chapel Royal in London, 1679, and later held var. clerical posts in and out of the capital. Purcell's anthems afford evidence of his remarkable compass.

Gotovac, Jakov (b. Split, 11. X. 1895), Yugoslav cond. and comp. Studied at his home town, at Zagreb and in Vienna. In 1923 he became cond. of the Croatian Opera at Zagreb, also of a Balkan choral society, with which he travelled in the East.

Works incl. operas *Morana* and *Ero from the Other World*; incid. mus. for pastoral play *Dubravka*; choral works; *Symph. Kolo* and *The Ploughers* for orch.; songs with orch. (incl. 2 odes by Anacreon); string 4tet; songs with pf., etc.

Götterdämmerung (*The Dusk of the Gods*, Wagner). *See* **Ring des Nibelungen.**

Gotthelf, Jeremias (Albrecht Bitzius) (1797–1854), Swiss novelist. *See* Burkhard (*Schwarze Spinne*), Hauer (do.), Mendelssohn (A.) (*Elsi*), Sutermeister (*Schwarze S.*).

Göttin der Vernunft, Die (*The Goddess of Reason*), operetta by J. Strauss, jun. (lib. by Alfred Maria Willner and Bernhard Buchbinder), prod. Vienna, Theater an der Wien, 13. III. 1897. Strauss's last operetta.

Götz, Hermann (b. Königsberg, 7. XII. 1840; d. Hottingen nr. Zürich, 3. XII.

1876), Ger. comp. At first he studied mus. only incidentally when a student at Königsberg Univ., but later went to the Stern Cons. in Berlin. In 1863 he went to Switz. as organist at Winterthur and in 1867 he settled at Zürich. From 1870 he devoted himself wholly to comp.

Works incl. operas *Der Widerspänstigen Zähmung* (on Shakespeare's *Taming of the Shrew*) and *Francesca da Rimini* (unfinished); *Nänie* (Schiller) and Psalm lxxxvii for solo voices, chorus and orch.; cantata for male voices and orch.; symph. in F maj., *Spring* overture for orch.; vln. concerto in G maj., pf. concerto in B♭ maj.; pf. 5tet, pf. 4tet, pf. trio; sonata for pf. duet; sonatina, *Genrebilder* and other works for pf.; songs, etc.

Goudimel, Claude (b. Besançon, *c.* 1514; d. Lyons, 28. VIII. 1572), Fr. comp. 1st appeared as comp. in Paris in 1549. About 1557, having become a Huguenot, he went to live at Metz with the Protestant colony there, but about 10 years later left for Besançon, and afterwards for Lyons, where he d. in the massacre of the Huguenots.

Works incl. Masses, Magnificats, psalms in motet form and other works for the Catholic Church; psalms, incl. a complete psalter, for the Protestant Church; sacred songs and numerous secular *chansons* for several voices, etc.

Gould, Glen (b. Toronto, 25. IX. 1932), Canadian pianist. Studied at the Royal Cons. of Mus. in Toronto, graduating at the age of 12, the youngest ever to do so. Made his début in Toronto, aged 14, and his Eur. début (under Karajan) in 1957.

Gounod, Charles (François) (b. Paris, 18. VI. 1818; d. Saint-Cloud, 18. X. 1893), Fr. comp. Son of a painter. His mother, a good pianist, taught him mus. from an early age and he was educ. at the Lycée Saint-Louis and in mus. at the Paris Cons., where his masters incl. Halévy, Paer and Lesueur. He gained the Prix de Rome in 1839 and spent the statutory 3 years in Rome, studying old It. church mus. After a tour in Aus. and Ger. he returned to Paris and was app. organist at the church of the Missions étrangères. Intending to become a priest, he did not prod. any important mus. until his opera *Sapho* appeared in 1851. In 1852–60 he cond. the united choral societies named Orphéon. In 1870–5 he lived in London, where he founded what became the Royal Choral Society.

Works incl. operas *Sapho, La Nonne sanglante, Le Médecin malgré lui* (on Molière), *Faust* (after Goethe), *Philémon et Baucis, La Reine de Saba, Mireille* (after Mistral), *La Colombe, Roméo et Juliette* (after Shakespeare), *Cinq-Mars* (after Alfred de Vigny), *Polyeucte* (after Corneille), *Le Tribut de Zamora*; incid. mus. for Ponsard's *Ulysse*, Legouvé's *Les Deux Reines* and Barbier's *Jeanne d'Arc*; oratorios *La Rédemption*, *Mors et Vita*, *Tobie*; 8 cantatas; 9 Masses, 3 Requiems, *Stabat Mater*, *Te Deum*, *De profundis*, *Ave verum corpus*, *Pater noster*, Magnificat and other sacred vocal pieces; 3 symphs.; some pf. comps. incl. the *Funeral March for a Marionette*; *Méditation sur le Prélude de Bach* for soprano, vln. pf., and org.; some smaller choral works; many songs, etc.

Gouvy, (Louis) Théodore (b. Goffontaine nr. Saarbrücken, 2. VII. 1819; d. Leipzig, 21. IV. 1898), Ger. comp. of Fr. parentage. Studied law at Metz and Paris, but turned to mus., which he learnt under Elwart in Paris and in Berlin and It.

Works incl. opera *Der Cid* (after Corneille); *Missa brevis*, Requiem, *Stabat Mater*, cantatas and dramatic scenas; 7 symphs., sinfonietta, symph. paraphrases, overtures, etc. for orch.; 5 string 4tets, 8tet for wind, 6tet for fl. and strings, pf. 5tet, 5 pf. trios; instrumental sonatas; pf. solos; songs, etc.

Gow, Scot. family of musicians:
1. Niel G. (b. Strathbrand, Perthshire, 22. III. 1727; d. Inver nr. Dunkeld, 1. III. 1807), violinist. Intended to become a weaver, he made his fame by playing Scot. dance tunes at balls in Scot. cities and even in London.
2. Donald G. (b. Inver nr. Dunkeld, *c.* 1730; d. ?), cellist, brother of prec.
3. William G. (b. ?; d. ?, 1791), violinist, son of 1. Leader of the Edinburgh Assembly orch. until his death.
4. Nathaniel G. (b. Inver nr. Dunkeld, 28. V. 1763; d. Edinburgh, 19. I. 1831), trumpeter, violinist and pub., brother of prec. At 16, when living at Edinburgh, he was app. royal trumpeter, learnt the vln. from Mackintosh, became leader of the Edinburgh Assembly orch. on the death of his brother and provided dance mus. by playing, comp. and after 1796 pub. it. He wrote songs, pieces descriptive of Edinburgh street cries (incl. 'Caller Herrin'', at first an instrumental piece and not fitted with words by Lady Nairne until *c.* 20 years later), etc.
5. Neil G. (b. Edinburgh, *c.* 1795; d. Edinburgh, 7. XI. 1823), comp., son of prec. He joined his father in the pub. business in 1818. Wrote songs, incl. 'Flora Macdonald's Lament', 'Cam' ye by Athol', etc.

Goyescas, opera by Granados (lib., in Span., by Fernando Periquet y Zuaznabar), prod. N.Y., Metropolitan Opera, 28. I. 1916. Much of the material is taken from G.'s pf. work below.
2 sets of pf. pieces by Granados inspired by etchings of Span. scenes by Goya, 1st

perf. Paris, 4. IV. 1914: I. *Los requiebros* (*The Compliments*), *Coloquio en la reja* (*Colloquy at the Grilled Window*), *El fandango del candil* (*The F. of the Lantern*), *Quejas, ó La maja y el ruiseñor* (*Plaints, or The Maja and the Nightingale*); II. *El Amor y la Muerte* (*Love and Death*), *Epílogo: la serenata del espectro* (*Epilogue: the Spectre's Serenade*). (A *maja* is the fem. counterpart of *majo* = a fop, a masher). G. also wrote a separate *escena goyesca* for pf.: *El pelele* (a puppet or straw-man tossed in a blanket).

Gozzi, Carlo (1722–1806), It. dramatist, *See* Chagrin (*Re cervo*), Danzi (*Turandot*), Donna serpente (Casella), Einem (*Turandot*), Feen (Wagner), Hartmann (J. P. E.) (*Ravnen*), Himmel (*Sylphen*), Jensen (*Turandot*), Joachim (A.) (overture on 2 comedies), Lachner (V.) (*Turandot*), Liuzzi (*Augellin bel verde*), Love for Three Oranges (Prokofiev), Paumgartner (*Turandot*), Reissiger (do.), Romberg (A.) (*Rabe* and *Blaue Ungeheuer*), Romberg (B.) (*Wiedergefundene Statue*), Schweitzer (*Segreto pubblico*), Sessions (*Turandot*), Stenhammar (*Turandot*), Turanda (Bazzini), Turandot (incid. mus., Weber; operas, Busoni, Løvenskjold and Puccini), Vesque von Püttlingen (*Turandot*).

Grabbe, Christian Dietrich (1801–36), Ger. dramatist. *See* Borck (*Napoleon*), Lortzing (*Don Juan und Faust*), Tiessen (do.).

Grabu (or Grabut, Grebus), Louis (b. ?; d. ?), Fr. 17th-cent. violinist and comp. App. comp. to Charles II in 1665 and Master of the King's Mus. from 1666–74.
Works incl. operas *Ariane, ou le mariage de Bacchus*, 1674 and *Albion and Albanius* (lib. by Dryden), 1685.

Grace, Harvey (b. Romsey, 25. I. 1874; d. Bromley, Kent, 15. II. 1944), Eng. organist, educationist, mus. ed. and writer. Studied mus. under the organist of Southwark Cathedral in London and later held var. organists posts, the last being that of Chichester Cathedral. He often adjudicated at mus. festivals, succeeded W. G. McNaught as ed. of the *Mus. Times* in 1918 and wrote books on org. playing and choral conducting and on Bach's and Rheinberger's org. mus.

Grace Notes
or   } = Ornaments.
Graces

Gracioso (Span. = jester, buffoon). The word appears in the title of one of Ravel's *Miroirs* for pf., *Alborada del gracioso* (*The Jester's Morning Song*).

Gradual (Lat. *gradus*, a step), the 2nd item of the Proper of the Mass. It is a responsorial chant following the reading of the epistle. Formerly the respond was always repeated after the solo verse. In the following ex. there is a clear distinction

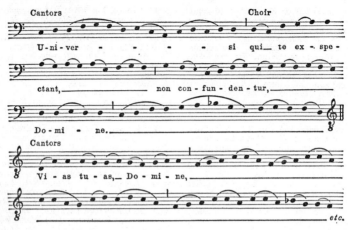

GRADUAL

between the low-pitched, freely melodic respond, and the higher, more melismatic and yet clearly psalmodic verse (*see* illustration).

Gradus ad Parnassum (Lat. = steps to Parnassus). (I) a treatise on counterpoint by Fux, pub. in 1725; (II) a series of 100 instructive and progressive pf. pieces by Clementi, pub. in 1817. The 1st piece in Debussy's *Children's Corner* for pf. alludes to Clementi's collection.

Graener, Paul (b. Berlin, 11. I. 1872; d. Salzburg, 13. XI. 1944), Ger. comp. Was a choir-boy in Berlin Cathedral and at 16 entered Veit's Cons., but soon began to teach himself, leading a wandering life, cond. at var. theatres and comp. a number of immature works. In 1896–1908 he was in London as teacher at the R.A.M. and cond. at the Haymarket Theatre, and was then app. director of the New Cons. in Vienna and in 1910 of the Mozarteum at Salzburg. After some years in Munich he succeeded Reger as prof. of comp. at the Leipzig Cons., but resigned in 1924. In 1930 he became director of Stern's Cons. in Berlin and under the Nazi régime vice-president of the Reichsmusikkammer, being succeeded by Egk in 1941.

Works incl. operas *Der vierjährige Posten* (Körner), *Das Narrengericht, Don Juans letztes Abenteuer, Theophano* (By-zanz), *Schirin und Gertraude, Hanneles Himmelfahrt* (after Gerhart Hauptmann), *Friedemann Bach, Der Prinz von Homburg* (after Kleist); choral works; symph. (*Schmied Schmerz*), *Romantic Fantasy, Variations on a Rus. folksong* and other orchestral works; 6 string 4tets, 3 pf. trios

and other chamber mus.; sonata and suite for vln. and pf., suite for cello and pf.; pf. pieces; over 100 songs, etc.

Graf (or **Graff**), **Friedrich Hartmann** (b. Rudolstadt, 1727; d. Augsburg, 19. VIII. 1795), Ger. flautist and comp. Travelled widely as a fl. virtuoso, and was app. mus. director in Augsburg in 1772. Later visited Vienna, and 1783–4 was cond. of the Professional Concerts in London.

Works incl. oratorios, cantatas, symphs., concertos, chamber mus., etc.

Grahame, Kenneth (1859–1932), Eng. author. See **Thompson (R.)** (*Wind in the Willows*).

Grainger, Percy (Aldridge) (b. Melbourne, 8. VII. 1882; d. N.Y., 20. II. 1961), Austral.-Amer. pianist and comp. Studied under his mother and Louis Pabst at Melbourne, later in Ger. with Kwast, Knorr and Busoni. He lived in London in 1900–15 and became interested in Eng. folk mus. ; toured Scand. in 1909 and settled in U.S.A. in 1914, later becoming naturalized.

Works incl. comps. for chorus and orch. with and without solo voices: *Marching Song of Democracy, The Bride's Tragedy* (Swinburne), *Father and Daughter* (Faroe folksong), *Sir Eglamore, We have fed our seas* (Kipling), *Tribute to Foster, Bridal Song,* etc.; part-songs *Brigg Fair, Morning Song of the Jungle* (Kipling), etc.; pieces for small orch.: *Molly on the Shore, Colonial Song, Shepherd's Hey, Mock Morris, Irish Tune from County Derry* (Londonderry Air), clog dance *Handel in the Strand*; suite *In a Nutshell* for 2 pfs.;

4 Ir. dances on themes by Stanford, *Walking Tune*, etc. for pf.; songs, etc.

Gram, Peder (b. Copenhagen, 25. XI. 1881; d. Copenhagen, 4. II. 1956), Dan. cond. and comp. Studied at Copenhagen Univ. and mus. at the Leipzig Cons., cond. under Nikisch. In 1908 he became cond. and prof. at Copenhagen. He visited Fr. and Ger. as cond.; held var. official posts and in 1937 became director of mus. of the Dan. broadcasting organization.

Works incl. 2 symphs., overtures; concertos. for vln. and for cello; songs, etc.

Gramophone (formerly Phonograph, and still so called in Amer.), an instrument invented in its primitive form by Edison. The mus. is now recorded on magnetic tape, afterwards transferred to a disc of some kind of hard shellac mixture. The sound-waves of the mus. are reproduced thereon in a continuous groove. In perf. the disc revolves, a static needle is brought into contact with the groove, and the 'frozen' sound-waves are released and electrically amplified.

Gran Cassa (It. lit. great case, great box) = Bass Drum.

Gran Mass ('Graner Messe'), a Mass by Liszt for solo voices, chorus, orch. and org., comp. in 1855 for the inauguration of a church at Gran (Esztergom) in Hung. and perf. there 31. VIII. 1856.

Granados, Enrique (b. Lérida, 27. VII. 1867; d. at sea, 24. III. 1916). Span. comp. Studied comp. with Pedrell at Barcelona and pf. in Paris. Returning to Madrid in 1889, he became a well-known pianist and in 1900 he founded the Sociedad de conciertos clásicos there, which he cond. After a visit to N.Y. for the prod. of *Goyescas* in the operatic version in I. 1916, he went down in the *Sussex*, torpedoed by a Ger. submarine in the Eng. Channel.

Works incl. operas *María del Carmen*, *Gaziel*, *Goyescas* (based on the pf. work), *Petrarca*, *Picarol*, *Follet*, *Liliana*; symph. poem *La nit del mort*, 4 suites etc. for orch.; *Cant de las Estrelles* for chorus, org. and pf.; pf. trio, *Oriental* for ob. and strings; *Goyescas* (2 vols.), 12 Span. Dances, 6 pieces on Span. folksongs, *Escenas románticas*, *Escenas poéticas*, *Libro de horas*, Impromptus, children's pieces for pf.; songs *Escritas en estilo antiguo* and a collection of *tonadillas*, etc.

Grand Bourdon (Fr.), an org. pedal stop of 32-ft. tone.

Grand Chœur (Fr. lit. great choir) = Full Org., a direction that the org. is to be used with all the registers.

Grand Duke, The, or The Statutory Duel, operetta by Sullivan (lib. by W. S. Gilbert), prod. London, Savoy Theatre, 7. III. 1896. Gilbert's last lib. for S.

Grand Jeu (Fr. lit. great play) = Grand Chœur; also used for a harmonium stop

that brings the whole instrument into play.

Grand Piano. *See* Pianoforte.

Grand Prix de Rome. *See* Prix de Rome.

Grande-Duchesse de Gérolstein, La, operetta by Offenbach (lib. by Henri Meilhac and Ludovic Halévy), prod. Paris, Théâtre des Variétés, 12. IV. 1867.

Grandi, Alessandro (b. Sicily, ?; d. Bergamo, *c.* 1630), It. comp. Pupil of (?) G. Gabrieli at Venice, *maestro di cappella* of the church of the Santo Spirito at Ferrara, 1610–17, and then at St. Mark's, Venice, until 1628, when he became choirmaster at the church of Santa Maria Maggiore at Bergamo.

Works incl. Masses, motets, psalms; madrigals; arias for solo voice, etc.

Grandioso (It. = grandiose), a direction asking for perf. in a dignified manner.

Graner Messe (Liszt). *See* Gran Mass.

Grania and Diarmid, incid. mus. by Elgar, Op. 42, for the play by George Moore and William Butler Yeats, comp. in 1902.

Graphophone, an obs. name for the Gramophone.

Gräser, Wolfgang (b. Zürich, 7. IX. 1906; d. Nikolassee nr. Berlin, 13. VI. 1928), Swiss mathematician, physicist, philologist and writer on mus. He wrote a book on Bach's *Art of Fugue* and scored it for orch.

Grassi, Cecilia (b. Naples, *c.* 1740; d. ?), It. soprano. Went to London in 1766, where she married J. C. Bach.

Grassi, Eugène (Cinda) (b. Bangkok, 5. VII. 1887; d. Paris, 8. VI. 1941), Fr. comp. Studied with d'Indy and Bourgault-Ducoudray in Paris, then returned to Siam to study native mus., and settled in Paris in 1913.

Works incl. *5 Mélodies siamoises* and *Poème de l'Univers* for orch.; *3 Poèmes bouddhiques* for chorus and orch.; *Les Équinoxes* for pf.; *Chanson nostalgique* for voice and pf., etc.

Grassini, Josephina (b. Varese, 8. IV. 1773; d. Milan, 3. I. 1850), It. contralto. Studied singing at Milan and made her 1st appearance there in 1794. She 1st sang in Paris in 1800 and London in 1804.

Graun, Ger. family of musicians:

1. **August Friedrich G.** (b. Wahrenbrück, Saxony, 1699; d. Merseburg, 5. V. 1765), cantor at Merseburg from 1729.

2. **Johann Gottlieb G.** (b. Wahrenbrück, 1703; d. Berlin, 27. X. 1771), violinist and comp., brother of prec. Pupil of Pisendel and, in It., of Tartini; played in the Dresden court orch. until 1726, when he became orch. leader at Merseburg. In 1732 he went into the service of the Crown Prince of Prus. at Rheinsberg and followed him to Berlin when he became Frederick II, becoming cond. of the court orch.

Works incl. symphs.; concertos for
harpsichord and for org.; trio sonatas
with 2 fls.; vln. sonatas, etc.

3. Carl Heinrich G. (b. Wahrenbrück,
1703 or 1704; d. Berlin, 8. VIII. 1759),
tenor and comp., brother of prec. Chorister
at Dresden, went in 1725 to Brunswick,
first as a singer, later as comp. and vice-
Kapellmeister (1727). In 1735 he joined his
brother (2) at Rheinsberg, and on the
accession of Frederick II in 1740 was app.
court *Kapellmeister*, with responsibility
for the Berlin opera. His opera *Cleopatra e
Cesare* opened the new opera house in
1742. His most famous comp. is the
Passion oratorio to words by Ramler,
Der Tod Jesu (1755), perhaps the most
popular continental oratorio of the 18th
cent.

Works incl. operas *Sancio und Sinilde,
Iphigenia in Aulis* (Ger.), *Polidorus,
Scipio Africanus, Lo specchio della fedeltà,
Pharao Tubaetes, Rodelinda, regina de'
Longobardi, Cleopatra e Cesare, Artaserse,
Demofoonte, Ifigenia in Aulide* (It.), *Silla,
Montezuma, Merope,* etc.; several Passion
cantatas incl. *Der Tod Jesu,* Te Deum;
funeral mus. for the Duke of Brunswick
and for Frederick William I of Prus.;
pf. concertos; trios, etc.

Graupner, Christoph (b. Kirchberg,
Saxony, 13. I. 1683; d. Darmstadt, 10. V.
1760), Ger. comp. Pupil of Schelle and
Kuhnau at St. Thomas's, Leipzig, he was
harpsichordist at the Hamburg opera
under Keiser 1707–9, and there prod. his
1st operas. In 1709 entered the service of
the Landgrave Ernst Ludwig of Hesse-
Darmstadt as vice-*Kapellmeister*, becoming
Kapellmeister in 1712 on the death of
Briegel. Elected cantor of St. Thomas's
Leipzig, in 1722/3, he was unable to obtain
his release from Darmstadt, so that the
post fell to Bach.

Works incl. operas *Dido, Antiochus und
Stratonica, La costanza vince l'inganno,*
etc.; over 1,400 church cantatas; 113
symphs.; 87 overtures; 50 concertos;
quantities of chamber mus., keyboard
mus., etc.

Grave (It. = heavy, serious), a direction
indicating a slow tempo.

Grave Mixture, a Mixture org. stop
sounding the lower ranges of the harmonics
with the fundamental notes, unlike the
Sharp M., which sounds the higher partials.

Gravicembalo (It.) = Clavicembalo, of
which it is a perversion.

Gray, Alan (b. York, 23. XII. 1855; d.
Cambridge, 27. IX. 1935), Eng. organist,
educationist and comp. Studied with E. G.
Monk, was mus. director at Wellington
Coll., 1883–92, and organist at Trinity
Coll., Cambridge, 1892–1930, also cond.
of the Cambridge Univ. Mus. Society.

Works incl. Festival Te Deum, Easter

Ode, cantatas *Arethusa, The Vision of
Belshazzar, A Song of Redemption* for
chorus and orch.; Coronation March;
chamber mus.; org. pieces, etc.

Gray, Cecil (b. Edinburgh, 19. V. 1895;
d. Worthing, 9. IX. 1951), Scot. writer on
mus. and comp. Studied mus. privately.
In 1920 he became joint ed. of the *Sackbut*
with Philip Heseltine, with whom he also
wrote a book on Gesualdo, and whose
biog. as a comp. (Peter Warlock) he pub.
Other books are a *History of M.,* essays
Predicaments and *Contingencies,* and 2
works on Sibelius.

Comps. incl. operas *Deirdre, The Temptation of St. Anthony* (after Flaubert) and *The
Trojan Women* (after Euripides).

Gray, Thomas (1716–71), Eng. poet.
See **Cellier** (*Elegy*), **Randall** (*Installation
Ode*), **Stanford** (*Bard*).

Grazia, Con (It. = with grace) =
grazioso.

Graziani, Tommaso (b. Bagnacavallo,
Ravenna, *c.* 1553; d. Bagnacavallo, III.
1634), It. monk and comp. Pupil of Porta.
Maestro di cappella of Ravenna, Porto
Gruaro (Lombardy) and several churches
at Milan at var. times.

Works incl. Masses, psalms and other
church mus.

Grazioli, Giovanni Battista (b. Bogliaco,
Lake Garda, 6. VII. 1746; d. Venice, *c.*
1820), It. organist and comp. Pupil of
Bertoni, he was app. 2nd organist of St.
Mark's, Venice, in 1782, 1st organist 1785.

Works incl. 12 harpsichord sonatas,
6 sonatas for vln. and harpsichord,
church mus., etc.

Grazioso (It. = graceful), an adj. sometimes used alone to indicate the character
of a piece or passage and more often in
combination with a tempo indication, e.g.
allegro grazioso, andantino grazioso, etc.

Great Fugue (Beethoven). *See* **Grosse
Fuge.**

Great Organ, the principal manual
keyboard of the org.

Great Quint, another name for the
Quint org. stop.

Greaves, Thomas (b. ?; d. ?), Eng.
16th–17th-cent. lutenist and comp. In the
service of Sir Henry Pierpoint, whose wife
was a cousin of Michael Cavendish. In
1604 he pub. a book of *Songs of Sundrie
Kindes* containing 15 songs to the lute, 6
songs for voice and viols and 6 madrigals.

Greber, Jakob (b. ?; d. ?), Ger. 17th–
18th-cent. comp. Went to London *c.* 1702
with Margherita de l'Épine and stayed
there until *c.* 1706. In Vienna or Innsbruck
in the service of the Emperor Charles VI,
c. 1708, and in the Palatinate (Heidelberg,
etc.) in 1717–23.

Works incl. opera *The loves of Ergasto*
(*The Temple of Love* attrib. to him is by
Saggione), shorter stage pieces, serenatas,

etc.; cantata for solo voice and var. instruments, etc.

Grebus. *See* **Grabu, Louis.**

Grechaninov. *See* **Gretchaninov.**

Greco, Gaetano (b. Naples, *c.* 1657; d. Naples, *c.* 1728), It. comp. Pupil of A. Scarlatti at Naples. Taught for many years at the Cons. dei Poveri di Gesù there. Wrote harpsichord mus., etc.

Greef, Arthur de (b. Louvain, 10. X. 1862; d. Brussels, 29. VIII. 1940), Belg. pianist and comp. Pupil of Brassin at the Brussels Cons. and of Liszt at Weimar. He began his career about the age of 20 and became pf. prof. at the Brussels Cons. in 1887. He toured widely in Eur. and frequently visited Eng.

Works incl. symph., *4 Old Flemish Folksongs* for orch.; Ballad for string orch.; Concerto & Fantasy for pf. and orch., *Menuet varié* for pf. and strings; *Chants d'amour* for voice and orch.; sonata for 2 pfs.; pf. pieces; songs, etc.

Greek Composers. *See* **Kalomiris, Karyotakis, Kazasoglou, Lavranga, Levidis, Petridis, Samara, Skalkottas, Varvoglis, Xenakis, Xyndas.**

Greenaway, Kate (Catherine) (1846–1901), Eng. painter and illustrator. *See* **Frank** (*Under the Window*).

Greene, Harry Plunket (b. Old Connaught House, Co. Wicklow, 24. VI. 1865; d. London, 19. VIII. 1936), Ir. baritone. Studied at Stuttgart, Florence and London, where he made his 1st appearance in 1888. Wrote *Interpretation in Song.*

Greene, Maurice (b. London, *c.* 1695; d. London, 1. XII. 1755), Eng. organist and comp. Son of a clergyman, he was a chorister at St. Paul's Cathedral, studied the org. there under Richard Brind, and after holding church posts was app. organist of St. Paul's in 1718. On Croft's death in 1727 he became organist and comp. of the Chapel Royal, and in 1730 succeeded Tudway as prof. at Cambridge Univ. App. Master of the King's Music in 1735. An inheritance in 1750 enabled him to devote time to a collection of Eng. church mus., which after his death was completed by Boyce and pub. under the title *Cathedral Music.*

Works incl. numerous anthems, the most notable pub. in *Forty Select Anthems* (1743), and other church mus.; oratorios *Jephtha* and *The Force of Truth*; pastorals *Florimel, or Love's Revenge, The Judgment of Hercules* and *Phoebe*; Odes for St. Cecilia's Day and other occasions; miscellaneous songs, catches, etc.; overtures; org. voluntaries; harpsichord mus., etc.

Greenwood, John (b. London, 1889), Eng. comp. Learnt pf. and vla. from his parents and at 18 entered the R.C.M. to study vla. and horn, also comp. under Stanford.

Works incl. ballet; incid. mus. for Shakespeare's *Merchant of Venice* and *Midsummer Night's Dream*; film mus. for *Man of Aran* and many others; Psalm cl for chorus and orch.; 2 symphs., symph. poems *Pippa passes* (after Browning) and *Punchinello, Salute to Gustav Holst* for orch.; *La Belle Dame sans merci* (Keats) for tenor and orch.; fl. and pf. sonata; pf. sonata, etc.

Greff. *See* **Bakfark.**

Grefinger, Wolfgang (b. ?; d. after 1515), Ger. organist and comp. He was a pupil of Hofhaimer and (?) successor to Grimpeck as organist at the Hung. court. Wrote Lat. church mus. and secular Ger. songs.

Greghesca. A type of 16th-cent. *villanella* for 3 voices to words that are a mixture of Gk. and Venetian dialect, written by the Levantine Venetian Antonio Molino.

Gregoir, Édouard (Georges Jacques) (b. Turnhout, 7. XI. 1822; d. Wijneghem nr. Antwerp, 28. VI. 1890), Belg. comp. and writer on mus. Studied at Biberich together with his brother and later prod. works of his in London, Amsterdam and Paris. He settled at Antwerp in 1850. He wrote a hist of the org. and other books.

Works incl. operas *Marguerite d'Autriche, Willem Beukels* and *La Belle Bourbonnaise*; incid. mus. for *De Belgen in 1848* and *Leicester*; oratorios *La Vie* and *Le Déluge*; hist. symph. *Les Croisades*, etc.

Gregoir, Jacques Mathieu Joseph (b. Antwerp, 18. I. 1817; d. Brussels, 29. X. 1876), Belg. pianist and comp., brother of prec. Appeared in public as a child pianist and studied with Herz in Paris, later, together with his brother, under Rummel at Biberich. He taught at Brussels and for a year at Bruges and toured widely.

Works incl. *Le Gondolier de Venise; Lauda Sion*, cantata *Faust* (after Goethe); concerto; numerous pf. works; duets for vln. and pf. (with Léonard and Vieuxtemps) and for cello and pf. (with Servais).

Gregorian Chant, the official repertory of plainsong traditionally assoc. with the name of Pope (St.) Gregory (*c.* 540–604) who is said to have been the first to supervise its organization.

Gregorian Tones, the chants of the Gregorian psalmody sung in groups corresponding to the 8 church modes (4 authentic and 4 plagal).

Greiter, Matthias (b. Aichach, Bavaria, *c.* 1500; d. Strasbourg, 20. XII. 1550), Ger. singer, poet and comp. He was a monk and a chorister in Strasbourg Cathedral, but became a Lutheran in 1524. In 1549 he founded a Protestant choir school. He wrote words and (?) mus. of hymns and comp. Ger. songs for 4 and 5 voices.

Grell, (August) Eduard (b. Berlin, 6. XI.

1800; d. Steglitz nr. Berlin, 10. VIII. 1886), Ger. organist and comp. Pupil of Zelter and others. Vice-cond. under Rungenhagen of the Berlin Singakademie from 1832 and cond. from 1853; organist of the court cathedral from 1839. Works incl. oratorio *Die Israeliten in der Wüste*, unaccomp. Mass in 16 parts, Te Deum, psalms, motets; cantatas; songs, duets, etc.

Grenon, Nicolas (b. ?; d. ?), early 15th-cent. Fr. comp., active at the Burgundian court under John the Fearless and Philip the Good. Wrote sacred Lat. mus. and *chansons*.

Gresham, Thomas (1519–79), founder of Gresham Coll. in London. Knighted 1559. The Coll. was provided for by his will and among the professorships was one for mus., which has continued to the present day. The 1st prof. app. in 1596 was Bull.

Gretchaninov, Alexander Tikhonovich (b. Moscow, 25. X. 1864; d. N.Y., 3. I. 1956), Rus. comp. Although the son of small, semi-literate shop-keepers, he managed to study the pf. at the Moscow Cons. under Safonov, but in 1890 he went to that of St. Petersburg as a comp. pupil of Rimsky-Korsakov. He settled in Paris, *c.* 1925 and later in U.S.A.

Works incl. operas *Dobrinya Nikitich* and *Sister Beatrice* (after Maeterlinck's play), incid. mus. for plays; much mus. for the Rus. Church, incl. 2 complete liturgies; Catholic church mus., incl. 3 Masses and 6 motets; choral works; 5 symphs., Elegy for orch.; concertos for cello, vln. and fl.; 4 string 4tets; *Mus. Pictures* for bass solo, chorus and orch.; vln. pieces; pf. mus.; many songs, incl. 'The Dreary Steppe', etc.

Gretchen am Spinnrade (*Margaret at the Spinning-Wheel*). Schubert's setting of Gretchen's song in Goethe's *Faust*, Part I, comp. 1814 at the age of 17, pub. as Op. 2 in 1821.

Grétry, André Ernest Modeste (b. Liège, 11. II. 1741; d. Montmorency nr. Paris, 24. IX. 1813), Belg. comp. Chorister at St. Denis's, Liège, received his initial training from his father (a violinist) and local church musicians. By 1759 he had already comp. some symphs. and church mus., which won him a scholarship to study in Rome, where he remained till 1766, producing there in 1765 the intermezzo *Le vendemmiatrice*. After a time in Geneva he went to Paris in 1767 to make his way as an opera comp. From 1768 he prod. a continuous stream of *opéras-comiques*, the most popular being *Richard Cœur-de-Lion* (1784), an early ex. of a 'rescue opera'. He was made an inspector of the Paris Cons. on its foundation in 1795, and the same year became one of the

orig. members of the Institut de France. He pub. his memoirs in 3 vols. 1789–97, and wrote other lit. works.

Works incl. operas *La vendemmiatrice, Isabelle et Gertrude, Le Huron, Lucile, Le Tableau parlant, Silvain, Les Deux Avares, L'Amitié à l'épreuve, Zémire et Azor, L'Ami de la maison, Le Magnifique, La Rosière de Salency, La Fausse Magie, Les Mariages samnites* (several versions), *Matroco, Le Jugement de Midas, Les Fausses Apparences, ou L'Amant jaloux, Les Événements imprévus, Aucassin et Nicolette, Thalie au Nouveau Théâtre, Théodore et Paulin* (later *L'Épreuve villageoise*), *Richard Cœur-de-Lion, Les Méprises par ressemblance, Le Comte d'Albert, Le Prisonnier anglais* (later *Claire et Belton*), *Le Rival confident, Raoul Barbebleue, Pierre le Grand, Guillaume Tell, Basile, Les Deux Couvents, Joseph Barra, Callias, Lisbeth, Le Barbier de village, Elisca*: all comic operas; prod. at the Opéra: *Céphale et Procris, Les Trois Âges de l'Opéra, Andromaque, La Double Épreuve, ou Colinette à la cour, L'Embarras des richesses, La Caravane du Caire, Panurge dans l'île des lanternes* (after Rabelais), *Amphitryon, Aspasie, Denys le Tyran, La Fête de la Raison, Anacréon chez Polycrate, Le Casque et les Colombes, Delphis et Mopsa*, etc. (some in MS.).

Grétry, Lucile (b. Paris, 16. VII. 1772; d. Paris, 25. VIII. 1790), Fr. comp., daughter of prec. At the age of 15 she comp. the opera *Le Mariage d'Antonio* which, scored by her father, was successfully prod. in 1786 at the Comédie Italienne, followed by *Toinette et Louis* a year later.

Greville, Fulke (Lord Brooke) (1554–1628), Eng. statesman and poet. *See* Peerson (*Caelica*).

Grew, Sydney (b. Birmingham, 13. VIII. 1879; d. Birmingham, 24. XII. 1946), Eng. writer on mus. Studied at the Midland Ins. School of Mus. and ed. the *British Musician* from 1926. Pub. books on the player-pf., on comps. and perfs. and, with his wife, Eva Mary G., a work on Bach.

Grieg, Edvard (Hagerup) (b. Bergen, 15. VI. 1843; d. Bergen, 4. IX. 1907), Norw. comp. of Scot. descent (orig. Greig). Son of a merchant. He was taught the pf. by his mother from 1849. Ole Bull persuaded his parents to send him to Leipzig for study in 1858, and he entered the Cons. there. In 1863 he went to live in Copenhagen and studied with Gade. In 1864 he met Rikard Nordaak, who fired his enthusiasm for Norw. nat mus., and became engaged to his cousin Nina Hagerup, whom he married in 1867. Settled as teacher and cond. at Christiania in 1867. In 1874 Ibsen invited him to write incid. mus. for his *Peer Gynt*, which was prod. on 24. II. 1876. In 1888–9 he and his wife appeared in London, Paris and Vienna, and in 1894 he was made hon. Mus.D. by Cambridge Univ. and hon. D.Mus. by Oxford Univ. in 1906.

Works incl. incid. mus. for Ibsen's *Peer Gynt* and Bjørnson's *Sigurd Jorsalfar*; concert overture *In Autumn*; *Holberg Suite* for string orch.; pf. concerto in A min.; works for solo voices, chorus and orch.: *Before the Cloister Gate*, *Land-sighting*, *Olaf Trygvason*; *Bergliot* (Bjørnson) for declamation and orch.; 4 Psalms for mixed voices unaccomp.; a set of part-songs for male voices; *Den bergtekne* (*The Solitary*) for baritone solo, strings and 2 horns; string 4tet in G min.; 3 sonatas for vln. and pf.; sonata for cello and pf.; 22 op. nos. of pf. pieces, incl. 10 vols. of *Lyric Pieces*, sonata in E min., Ballad in variation form, arrs. of Norw. folk tunes; 4 works for pf. duet; old Norw. melody with variations for 2 pfs.; 143 songs, incl. *Haugtussa* cycle (Garborg), settings of Ibsen, Bjørnson, etc.

Grieg (*née* Hagerup), **Nina** (b. Bergen, 24. XI. 1845; d. Copenhagen, 9. XII. 1935), Norw. singer, cousin and wife of Edvard Grieg, most of whose songs she was the 1st to sing both at home and on their tours abroad.

Griffes, Charles T(omlinson). (b. Elmira, N.Y., 17. IX. 1884; d. N.Y., 8. IV. 1920), Amer. comp. Studied in Berlin and taught there for a time. Returned to U.S.A. in 1907, and became mus. teacher at a boys' school at Tarrytown, N.Y., until his early death, brought about by ill-health and overwork.

Works incl. Jap. mime play *Schojo*; dance drama *The Kairn of Koridwen*; *The Pleasure Dome of Kubla Khan* (after Coleridge) for orch.; Poem for fl. and orch.; *These things shall be* (J. A. Symonds) for unison chorus; Sketches on Indian themes for string 4tet; pf. sonata and pieces; songs, etc.

Grigny, Nicolas de (b. Rheims, 8. IX. 1672; d. Rheims, 30. XI. 1703), Fr. organist and comp. Son of Louis de G. (*c.* 1646–1709), organist at Notre-Dame of Rheims. Studied under his father and in Paris, was organist of Saint-Denis Abbey in 1693–5 and then of Rheims Cathedral. Wrote org. mus. which Bach knew and copied in his early years.

Grillparzer, Franz (1791–1872), Aus. poet and dramatist. Friend of Beethoven and Schubert. Wrote funeral oration for the former and sketched incription for the latter's gravestone.

For works used by comps. *see* **Frank** (*Hero*), **Hummel** (J. N.) (*Ahnfrau*), **Kreutzer** (C.) (*Libussa* and *Melusine*) **Mraczek** (*Traum*), **Sappho** (Kaun), **Schöne**

Melusine (Mendelssohn and K. Kreutzer), **Schulz-Beuthen** (*Meeres und der Liebe Wellen*), **Seyfried** (*Ahnfrau* and *König Ottokar*), **Straus** (O.) (*Traum ein Leben*).

Grimaldi. *See* Nicolini.

Grimm, Friedrich Melchior von, Baron (1723–1807), Ger. littérateur. Lived in Paris from 1750 to the Revolution and during the 'Guerre des bouffons' in 1752 took the part of the Its. He wrote several pamphlets on mus. matters, incl. a satire on Stamitz, *Le Petit Prophète de Boemisch-Broda*.

Grimm, Jacob (Ludwig Carl) (1785–1863) and **Wilhelm (Carl)** (1786–1859), brothers, Ger. philologists, mythologists and authors. *See* Hänsel und Gretel (Humperdinck), Schoeck (*Vom Fischer und syner Fru*).

Grimm, Julius Otto (b. Pernau, Livonia, 6. III. 1827; d. Münster, Westphalia, 7. XII. 1903), Ger. pianist and comp. Studied at the Leipzig Cons. Worked at Göttingen at first and in 1860 was app. choral cond. at Münster.

Works incl. ode for chorus and orch., *An die Musik*; symph. in D min. and other orchestral works; suite in canon-form for strings; pf. works; songs, etc.

Grimmelshausen, Hans Jakob Christoffel von (*c.* 1625–76), Ger. novelist. *See* Mohaupt (*Gaunerstreiche der Courasche*).

Grisar, Albert (b. Antwerp, 26. XII. 1808; d. Asnières, 15. VI. 1869), Belg. comp. He was intended for a business career and sent to Liverpool, but ran away to Paris to study mus. in 1830; became a pupil of Reicha, but was driven to Antwerp by the Revolution; prod. *Le Mariage impossible* at Brussels in 1833, returned to Paris, where he made further operatic successes, studied with Mercadante at Naples in 1840 and returned to Paris in 1848.

Works incl. operas *Sarah* (after Scott), *L'An 1000*, *Lady Melvill* and *L'Eau merveilleuse* (both with Flotow), *Le Naufrage de la Méduse* (with Flotow and Pilati), *Les Travestissements*, *L'Opéra à la cour* (with Boïeldieu, jun.), *Gilles Ravisseur*, *Les Porcherons*, *Bonsoir M. Pantalon*, *Le Carillonneur de Bruges*, *Les Amours du diable*, *Le Chien du jardinier*, *Voyage autour de ma chambre* (after Xavier de Maistre), *La Chatte merveilleuse*, *Bégaiements d'amour*, *Douze innocentes*, etc.

Grisi, Giuditta (b. Milan, 28. VII. 1805; d. Robecco nr. Cremona, 1. V. 1840), It. mezzo-soprano. Studied at the Milan Cons., and made her 1st appearance in Vienna in 1826.

Grisi, Giulia (b. Milan, 28. VII. 1811; d. Berlin, 29. XI. 1869), It. soprano, sister of prec. Pupil of her sister, Boccabadati, Guglielmi and others. Made her 1st appearance in 1828 and was engaged for Milan in 1829. In 1832 she 1st sang in Paris and in 1834 in London.

Grocheo, Johannes de (b. ?; d. ?), mus. theorist of uncertain nationality who worked in Paris *c*. 1300. His *De musica* survives in two MSS. and is important for the light it throws on the secular mus. of his day and how it was perf.

Groh, Johann. *See* **Ghro.**

Groll, Sophie. *See* **Tomasini, 3.**

Gröndahl, Agathe. *See* **Backer-Gröndahl.**

Groot, Cor de (b. Amsterdam, 7. VII. 1914), Dutch pianist and comp. Studied at the Amsterdam Cons. and in 1936 won the international pf. competition in Vienna. He has toured widely in Europe.

Works incl. ballet *Vernisage*; 2 pf. concertos, pf. concertino, concerto for 2 pfs., and a number of pf. pieces.

Groppo (It.) = **Turn.**

Grosse Caisse (Fr. lit. great case or chest) = Bass Drum.

Grosse Fuge (*Great Fugue*), a work for string 4tet by Beethoven, Op. 133, in a fugal form 'tantôt libre, tantôt recherchée', written in 1825 as the finale of the Bb maj. string 4tet, Op. 130, and 1st perf. with it, Vienna, 21. III. 1826. Beethoven realized that it was too long, difficult and abstruse for that purpose and subsequently wrote the new finale now part of Op. 130.

Grossi, Carlo (b. Modena, ?; d. ?), It. 17th-cent. singer and comp. Worked as singer and *maestro di cappella* successively at Reggio, Vicenza, Venice and Mantua.

Works incl. 4 operas; Masses and other church mus.; sacred concertos; sonatas; songs, etc.

Grossi, Giovanni Francesco. *See* **Siface.**

Grossi, Lodovico. *See* **Viadana.**

Grossi, Tommaso (1791–1853), It. poet and novelist. *See* **Lombardi alla prima crociata** (Verdi).

Grossin (Grossim), Estienne (b. ?; d. ?), Fr. comp., chaplain at St. Merry, Paris, 1418, and *clerc de matines* at Notre Dame, 1421. Wrote church mus. and *chansons*, incl. a Mass (without *Agnus*) with a part for tpt.

Grossvater-Tanz (Ger. = grandfather's dance), a 17th-cent. Ger. dance, with words referring to a grandfather's wooing, sung and danced at weddings and later used as the final dance at balls and therefore called 'Kehraus' (sweep-out). Schumann used it both in *Papillons*, Op. 2, and *Carnaval*, Op. 9, in the latter to stand for the 'Philistines' in the finale.

Grosz, Wilhelm (b. Vienna, 11. VIII. 1894; d. N.Y., 10. XII. 1939), Aus. comp. Pupil of Adler for theory and Schreker for comp. Cond. at Mannheim Opera in 1921, but returned to Vienna in 1922 to make a living as pianist and comp.; worked with a gramophone company in Berlin from 1928, cond. the Kammerspiele in Vienna,

1933–4, when he became a refugee in London and N.Y.

Works incl. operas *Sganarell* and *Achtung, Aufnahme*; play with mus. *St. Peters Regenschirm*; ballets *Der arme Reinhold* and *Baby in der Bar*; incid. mus. to Werfel's *Spiegelmensch* and Hauptmann's *Die versunkene Glocke*; mus. for films and radio; Symph. Variations, serenade, suite, overture to an opera buffa, etc. for orch.; Symph. Dance for pf. and orch.; string 4tet; 2 vln. and pf. sonatas; 3 pf. sonatas, variations on a theme by Grieg and other pf. works; suite for 2 pfs.; several song cycles, etc.

Ground, a comp. built on a Ground Bass.

Ground Bass, a melodic figure used as a bass in a comp., constantly repeated without change, except sometimes by way of transposition, while the upper structure of the mus. is developed freely at the comp.'s will.

Grove, George (b. London, 13. VIII. 1820; d. London, 28. V. 1900), Eng. civil engineer, biblical scholar and writer on mus. Sec. to the Crystal Palace Co., 1852–1875; director of R.C.M. 1883–94. Ed. of the 1st edition of the *Dictionary of Music and Musicians* and author of a book on Beethoven's symphs. Knighted in 1883.

Grovlez, Gabriel (Marie) (b. Lille, 4. IV. 1879; d. Paris, 20. X. 1944), Fr. cond., pianist and comp. Studied at the Paris Cons., later taught pf. at the Schola Cantorum and in 1939 became prof. of chamber mus. at the Cons. Cond. at Lisbon, Chicago and Paris, from 1914 at the Opéra.

Works incl. operas *Cœur de rubis* and *Psyche*; *conte lyrique*, *Le Marquis de Carabas*; 3 ballets incl. *Maïmouna*; symph. poems *Dans le Jardin*, *Madrigal lyrique*, etc.; cello and pf. sonata; pieces for wind instruments; *Almanach aux images*, *Le Royaume puéril*, 2 Impressions, etc. for pf.; 3 *Ballades françaises* and other songs, etc.

Gruenberg, Louis (b. Brest-Litovsk, 3. VIII. 1884; d. Los Angeles, 9. VI. 1964), Amer. pianist and comp. of Rus. descent. He was taken to U.S.A. at the age of 2. Studied in Berlin and Vienna, pf. pupil of Busoni; 1st appeared as pianist in Berlin in 1912 and then began to travel, but from 1919 remained in U.S.A. to devote himself wholly to comp.

Works incl. operas *The Bride of the Gods*, *The Dumb Wife*, *Jack and the Beanstalk*, *Emperor Jones* (after Eugene O'Neill), *Helena's Husband*; children's opera *The Witch of Brocken*; radio opera *Green Mansions* (after W. H. Hudson); 5 symphs., *Hill of Dreams*, *Enchanted Isle*, *Vagabondia*, *Jazz Suite*, *Moods*, *Serenade*, *Music to an Imaginary Pantomime* for

orch.; vln. concerto; *The Daniel Jazz*
(Vachell Lindsay), *Animals and Insects*
and *The Creation* for voice and chamber
orch.; *4 Indiscretions* for string 4tet;
2 string 4tets; 2 sonatas and *Jazzettes* for
vln. and pf.; Poem for cello and pf.;
Jazzberries and *Impressions* for pf.;
numerous songs, etc.

Grümmer, Elisabeth (b. Diedenhofen,
Alsace-Lorraine, 31. III. 1911), Ger.
soprano. After 3 years as an actress she
made her singing début in 1941. Since
then she has sung in many of the leading
Eur. opera houses, incl. Covent Garden in
1951. She is esp. well known for her
singing of Mozart and R. Strauss.

Grünewald, Gottfried (b. Eywau, Lusatia,
1675; d. Darmstadt, 19. XII. 1739), Ger.
singer and comp. Sang at Hamburg 1703–
1704, where 2 of his operas *Germanicus* and
Der ungetreue Schäfer Cardillo, were prod.
App. vice-*Kapellmeister* in Weissenfels
1709, and settled in Darmstadt as vice-
Kapellmeister under Graupner *c.* 1712.

Gruppo (It.) = Trill, Turn.

**Grützmacher, Friedrich (Wilhelm Lud-
wig)** (b. Dessau, 1. III. 1832; d. Dresden,
23. II. 1903), Ger. cellist and comp.
Studied at Leipzig, where he became 1st
cellist at the Gewandhaus in 1849 and later
teacher at the Cons. In 1860 he became
chamber virtuoso to the King of Saxony at
Dresden. Comp. mainly concertos and
studies for cello, but also orchestral and
chamber works, songs, etc.

Guadagni, Gaetano (b. Lodi or ?
Vicenza, *c.* 1725; d. Padua, XI. 1792),
It. castrato alto. Made his 1st appearance
prob. at Parma in 1747 and went to
London in 1748. Later sang in Dublin,
Paris, Lisbon, It. and Vienna, where he
was the 1st Orpheus in Gluck's *Orfeo*
in 1762.

Guadagnini, It. family of vln. makers:
1. Lorenzo G. (b. ? Piacenza, before 1695;
d. Piacenza, *c.* 1745), ? pupil of Stradivari,
worked at Piacenza.
2. Giovanni Battista G. (b. ? Piacenza,
1711; d. Turin, 19. IX. 1786), son of prec.
Worked at Piacenza, Milan, Parma and
Turin.
3. Giuseppe G. (b. ?, *c.* 1736; d. ?, *c.*
1805), cousin of prec. Worked at Como,
Pavia and Turin.

Guajira, a Cuban dance with changes of
time from 6–8 to 3–4 or 2–4. It is known in
Fr. as Guarache.

Guami, Francesco (b. Lucca, *c.* 1544; d.
Lucca, 1601), It. comp. and organist. At the
Munich court, 1568–80; *maestro di
cappella* at San Marciliano, Venice, from
1593. Wrote madrigals, church mus.,
instrumental mus.

Guami, Gioseffo (b. Lucca, *c.* 1535; d.
Lucca, 1611), It. organist and comp.,
brother of prec. He was at Munich with

Francesco G., and organist of St. Mark's,
Venice, from 1588. Wrote numerous madrigals, church mus. and instrumental mus.
Bull wrote a fantasia for keyboard on a
theme from his instrumental canzona *La
Guamina*. Of his 5 sons Domenico (*c.* 1560–
1631) and Valerio (1567–1615) are known as
comps. Vincenzo (b. ?; d. 1615) was for a
short time from 1613 organist at the chapel
of the Archduke Albert at Antwerp. About
Pietro and Gugliemo nothing is known.

Guarache (Fr.) *See* Guajira.

Guarducci, Tommaso (b. Montefiascone,
c. 1720; d. ?), It. singer. Pupil of Bernacchi
at Bologna. Made his 1st appearance *c.*
1745 and went to London in 1766.

Guarini, Giovanni Battista (1537–1612),
It. poet. *See* Pastor fido (Handel), Rossi (S.)
(*Idropica*), Settle (*Pastor fido*).

Guarneri, It. family of vln. makers:
1. Andrea G. (b. ?, *c.* 1626; d. Cremona,
7. XII. 1698). Pupil of Amati.
2. Pietro Giovanni G. (b. Cremona, 18.
II. 1655; d. Mantua, 26. III. 1720), son of
prec. Worked at Mantua.
3. Giuseppe Giovanni Battista G. (b.
Cremona, 25. XI. 1666; d. Cremona, *c.*
1740), brother of prec.
4. Pietro G. (b. Cremona, 14. IV. 1695;
d. Venice, 7. IV. 1762), nephew of 2.
Worked at Venice.
5. Giuseppe Antonio G. (b. Cremona,
21. VIII. 1698; d. Cremona, 17. X. 1744),
son of 3. Worked at Cremona and is
known as Giuseppe G. del Gesù.

Guarnieri, (Mozart) Camargo (b. Tietê,
1. II. 1907), Braz. comp. Pupil of Koechlin
in Paris. Cond. of the Orquestra Sinfônica
Municipal, São Paulo.
Works incl 3 symphs.; 2 pf. concertos,
2 vln. concertos; chamber mus.; cello and
pf. sonata, etc.

Gudehus, Heinrich (b. Altenhagen nr.
Celle, 30. III. 1845; d. Dresden, 9. X.
1909), Ger. tenor. Studied with Malwina
Schnorr von Carolsfeld at Brunswick and
Gustav Engel in Berlin; made his 1st
appearance there in 1871, sang Parsifal at
Bayreuth in 1882 and 1st went to London
in 1884.

Güden, Hilda (b. Vienna, 15. IX. 1917),
Aus. soprano. Studied at the Vienna Cons.,
making her début in Zürich in 1939. In
1946 she joined the Vienna State Opera,
becoming an Aus. *Kammersängerin* in
1950.

Gudenian, Haig (b. Caesaria, Asia
Minor, 19. V. 1886), Armen. violinist and
comp. Studied mus. at Brussels and Prague,
collected folksongs in the E., in 1918 visited
the U.S.A. and married the pianist
Katherine Lowe, with whom he toured in
Eur. and Amer., where he settled. His
comps. are based on nr.-eastern mus.

Guédron, Pierre (b. ? Châteaudun, *c.*
1565; d. ? Paris, *c.* 1621), Fr. singer and

comp. He was a chorister in the chapel of the Cardinal de Guise and later of Henri IV. In 1601 he was app. comp. to the king in succession to Claude Le Jeune and held var. other posts at court, finishing as Surintendant de la Musique under Louis XIII in 1613. His daughter Jeanne married Boësset, with whom, as well as Bailly, Maudit and Bataille, he collaborated in the comp. of court ballets. He also contrib. airs with lute accomp. (*airs de cour*) to var. collections.

Guerre des Bouffons (Fr., lit. War of the Buffoons), the quarrel that broke out in Paris in 1752 between the adherents of Fr. mus., esp. opera, and the imported art of the Its., who prod. or revived several exs. of *opera buffa* in the Fr. capital that year.

Guerrero, Francisco (b. Seville, 1527 or 1528; d. Seville, 8. XI. 1599), Span. comp. Pupil of his brother Pedro G. and of Fernández de Castilleja at Seville Cathedral, where he was a chorister; he also had some lessons from Morales as a child. App. to the cathedral of Jaén in 1545 and after the death of Morales to that of Málaga, though he never resided there, filling posts at Seville Cathedral until he succeeded Castilleja as *maestro de capilla* in 1574. Visited Lisbon, Rome (twice), Venice and the Holy Land.

Works incl. Masses, motets, psalms, vespers, Magnificats, Te Deum, spiritual songs, etc.

Geurrero, Pedro (b. Seville, *c.* 1515; d. ?), Span. comp., brother of prec.; (?) visited It. early in life and (?) d. there. Wrote church mus., lute songs, etc.

Guevara, Luis Vélez de (1579–1644), Span. novelist and dramatist. *See* Hidalgo (*Celos hacen estrellas*), **Una cosa rara** (Martín y Soler).

Guglielmi, Pietro (b. Massa Carrara, 9. XII. 1728; d. Rome, 19. XI. 1804), It. comp. Pupil of Durante in Naples, he prod. his first opera there in 1757, and thereafter had great success throughout It. and abroad. He was in Eng. intermittently 1767–72, and also visited Brunswick and Dresden. In 1793 he was app. *maestro di cappella* at St. Peter's, Rome.

Works incl. *c.* 100 operas, e.g. *Il ratto della sposa, La sposa fedele, La villanelle ingentilata, I finti amori, La virtuosa in Mergellina, L'inganno amoroso, La pastorella nobile, La bella pescatrice*, etc.; 9 oratorios, e.g. *La morte d'Abele, La Betulia liberata*, etc.; church mus.; symphs.; chamber mus.; keyboard mus., etc.

Guglielmi, Pietro Carlo (b. ? Naples, *c.* 1763; d. Naples, 28. II. 1817), It. comp., son of prec. Studied at the Cons. di Santa Maria di Loreto in Naples, prod. the first of many successful operas in 1794 in Madrid. Also visited London, Lisbon and Paris.

Works incl. almost 50 operas, e.g. *Amor tutto vince, Guerra aperta, Paolo e Virginia*, etc.

Guglielmo Ebreo da Pesaro (b. ?; d. ?), 15th-cent. Jewish-It. dancing-master and theorist. His book, *De pratica seu arte tripudii vulgare opusculum* (*c.* 1460), incl. both tunes and choreography.

Guglielmo Ratcliff (*William R.*), opera by Mascagni (lib. by comp., based on Heine's tragedy), prod. Milan, Teatro alla Scala, 16. II. 1895. An earlier work than *Cavalleria rusticana*, although prod. later.

Gui, Vittorio (b. Rome, 14. IX. 1885), It. cond. and comp. Student at the Liceo di Santa Cecilia in Rome. App. cond. at the Teatro Adriano there and later cond. opera at Turin, Naples and Milan. In 1928 he founded the Stabile Orchestrale at Florence.

Works incl. opera *La fata Malerba*; symph. poems; chamber mus., etc.

Guida (It. = guide), the leading part of a canon, into which the other voices subsequently drop with the same tune one by one.

Guidetti, Giovanni (b. Bologna, XII. 1530; d. Rome, 30. XI. 1592), It. priest. Pupil of Palestrina, whom he assisted in compiling the revised church services commissioned by Pope Gregory XIII, the *Directorium chori* (pub. 1582), in 1576–81.

Guidiccioni, Laura (16th cent.), It. poet. *See* Cavalieri (E.).

Guido d'Arezzo (b. Arezzo, *c.* 990; d. Pomposa, *c.* 1050), It. Benedictine monk and mus. theorist. Went to Fr. and (?) Eng. and worked at the Abbey of Saint-Maur-des-Fossés. He returned to It. later. He greatly advanced Solmization and Mutation by adapting the syllables Ut, Re, Mi, Fa, Sol, La to the Hexachord and by demonstrating the hexachordal positions on the fingers by the use of the 'Guidonian hand'. He is also, rather doubtfully, credited with the invention of the mus. stave, the use of which he certainly encouraged. His chief theoret. work is entitled *Micrologus de musica*.

Guignon, Jean-Pierre (Giovanni Petro Ghignone) (b. Turin, 10. II. 1702; d. Versailles, 30. I. 1774), It.-Fr. violinist and comp., a champion of the It. style of playing in Fr. In 1733 app. at court, and received in 1741 the title of *Roi des violons et des ménétriers*, being the last to hold the position.

Works incl. sonatas, concertos, etc. for vln., trio sonatas, etc.

Guilbert, Yvette (b. Paris, 20. I. 1867; d. Aix-en-Provence, 2. II. 1944), Fr. diseuse. Trained as an actress and café singer, but cultivated Fr. folksong and popular songs of the past, of which she became a great exponent.

Guildhall School of Music, a mus. school

established in 1880 to serve the City of London and housed in a new building in 1887. Its principal is Allen Percival.

Guilelmus Monachus (b. ?; d. ?), 15th-cent. theorist of uncertain nationality who lived in It. but may possibly have been Eng. His treatise *De praeceptis artis musicae* contains references to the Eng. use of 'faulxbourdon' and 'gymel'.

Guillaume Tell (*William Tell*), opera by Grétry (lib. by Jean Michel Sedaine), prod. Paris, Comédie-Italienne, 9. IV. 1791.

Opera by Rossini (lib. by Victor Joseph Étienne de Jouy and Hippolyte Louis Florent Bis, based on Schiller's drama), prod. Paris Opéra, 3. VIII. 1829. Rossini's last opera.

Guillemain, (Louis) Gabriel (b. Paris, 15. XI. 1705; d. Paris, 1. X. 1770), Fr. violinist and comp. App. to the court in Versailles in 1737, comp. sonatas, etc. for vln., chamber mus., etc.

Guilmant, (Félix) Alexandre (b. Boulogne-sur-Mer, 12. III. 1837; d. Meudon, 29. III. 1911), Fr. organist and comp. Pupil of his father, an organist at Boulogne, where he afterwards held several church appts., studying briefly in Brussels with Lemmens in 1860 and removing to Paris in 1871, where he was organist at the Trinité Church until 1901. He toured widely with great success and was prof. of org. at the Schola Cantorum, which he had helped Bordes and d'Indy to found, and at the Cons.

Works incl. 2 symphs. for org. and orch.; 8 sonatas and 25 sets of pieces for org., org. mus. for church use, etc.

Guimbarde (Fr.) = Jew's Harp.

Guimerá, Angel (1849–1924), Span. (Catalan) dramatist. *See* **Tiefland** (d'Albert).

Guiraud, Ernest (b. New Orleans, 23. VI. 1837; d. Paris, 6. V. 1892), Fr. comp. Son of a musician. Studied at the Paris Cons. and gained the Prix de Rome in 1859. He became prof. at the Cons. in 1876, following Massé at the head of the advanced comp. class in 1880. Debussy was one of his pupils.

Works incl. operas *Sylvie*, *En Prison*, *Le Kobold*, *Madame Turlupin*, *Piccolino*, *Galante Aventure*, *Le Feu*, *Frédégonde* (unfinished, completed by Saint-Saëns); ballet *Gretna Green*; overture *Arteveld*, *Chasse fantastique* (after Hugo's *Beau Pécopin*), and suite for orch.; Caprice for vln. and orch., etc. Recitatives for Bizet's *Carmen* and orch. of Offenbach's *Contes d'Hoffmann*.

Guiraut de Bornelh. *See* **Bornelh.**

Guitar, a string instrument of great antiquity. Its back is flat, its belly has a waist, as though to allow for the playing with a bow, but the strings are plucked with the fingers. The sound-hole in the

sound-board is often very decoratively carved. There are 6 strings, tuned:

The finger-board is fretted.

Guitar Violoncello. *See* **Arpeggione.**

Guitry, Sacha (1885–1957), Fr. actor and playwright. *See* **Beydts** (*La S.A.D.M.P.* and *Voyage de Tchong-Li*), **Hahn** (*Mozart*), **Honegger** (*Oiseau bleu*).

Gulda, Friedrich (b. Vienna, 16. V. 1930), Aus. pianist. Studied with Bruno Seidlhofer, winning 1st prize in the Geneva International Pianists' Competition in 1946. Toured Eur. in 1947–8, and made his Amer. début in 1950. Outside the classical repertory he is also well known as a jazz pianist.

Gumpeltzhaimer, Adam (b. Trostberg, Bavaria, *c.* 1559; d. Augsburg, 3. XI. 1625), Ger. comp. Studied at the monastery of St. Ulric at Augsburg and in 1575 went into the service of the Duke of Württemberg at Stuttgart. In 1581–1621 he was cantor at the church of St. Anna at Augsburg. He pub. a treatise, *Compendium musicae latinum-germanicum* in 1591.

Works incl. psalms, hymns, sacred songs, etc.

Gundry, Inglis (b. London, 8. V. 1905), Eng. comp. Educ. at Oxford, where he read law, but turned to literature, writing poems and a novel, *The Countess's Penny*, and studied mus. at the R.C.M. in London under Vaughan Williams, Gordon Jacob and R. O. Morris. In 1940 he enlisted in the Navy, his ship, H.M.S. *Welshman*, was sunk, he was promoted warrant officer and went as schoolmaster to the Royal Marines at Chatham. In 1944 he became instructor Lieutenant and mus. adviser to the Admiralty educ. dept., for which he ed. a *Naval Song Book*.

Works incl. operas *Naaman: the Leprosy of War*, *The Return of Odysseus* (after Homer), *The Sleeping Beauty* and *Partisans*; ballet *Sleep*; naval suite *Five Bells* and *Choral Overture 1940* (words from a speech by Winston Churchill) for chorus and orch.; suite *Heyday*, *Freedom*, Variations on an Indian theme and overture *Per mare, per terram* for orch.; Comedy Overture for small orch.; *Sostenuto and Vivace* for strings; Fantasy string 4tet, Duo for clar. and vla.; 3 Chin. Pictures for baritone, clar. and pf.; 5 Homeric songs and a duet, 3 *Songs from a Medieval Bestiary*, etc.

Gungl, Joseph (b. Zsámbék, 1. XII. 1810; d. Weimar, 31. I. 1889), Aus.-Hung. bandmaster and comp. Entered the Aus. army and later made tours with a military band of his own. In 1849 he visited the

U.S.A., becoming mus. director to the King of Prus. on his return and in 1858 to the Aus. Emperor. In 1864 he went to live at Munich and in 1876 at Frankfurt. He wrote hundreds of marches and dances.

Gunn, Neil (b. 1891), Scot. dramatist. See **Davie.**

Günther von Schwarzburg, opera by Holzbauer (lib. by Anton Klein), prod. Mannheim, at court, 5. I. 1777.

Guntram, opera by R. Strauss (lib. by comp.), prod. Weimar, 10. V. 1894. Strauss's 1st opera.

Gura, Eugen (b. Pressern nr. Saatz, 8. XI. 1842; d. Aufkirchen, Bavar., 26. VIII. 1906), Boh.-Ger. baritone. After technical and art studies in Vienna, he studied singing at the Munich Cons. and made his 1st stage appearance there in 1865. In 1876 he appeared in the prod. of Wagner's *Ring* at Bayreuth.

Guridi, Jesús (b. Vitoria, 25. IX. 1886; d. Madrid, 7. IV. 1961), Span. comp. of Basque race. Studied at the Schola Cantorium in Paris, also at Brussels and Cologne. His mus. is based on Basque themes.

Works incl. operas *Mirentxu* and *Amaya, zarzuela El caserío*; orchestral and org. mus.; 4 string 4tets; settings of Basque folksongs, etc.

Gurlitt, Cornelius (b. Altona, 10. II. 1820; d. Altona, 17. VI. 1901), Ger. pianist, organist and comp. App. church organist at Altona in 1864.

Works incl opera *Scheik Hassan,* 2 operettas; choral mus.; sinfonietta for orch.; chamber mus.; numerous pf. pieces, mostly educational, etc.

Gurlitt, Manfred (b. Berlin, 6. IX. 1890), Ger. cond. and comp. Studied comp. with Kaun and Humperdinck, cond. with Muck and pf. with Breithaupt in Berlin. After var. operatic appts. he was general mus. director at Bremen in 1914–27. Later he appeared as guest opera cond. in Ger. and Spain.

Works incl. operas *Die Heilige, Wozzeck* (Georg Büchner's drama), *Soldaten, Nana* (after Zola), *Seguidilla bolero, Feliza*; incid. mus. for 2 Span. plays; mus. for films; *Goya* symph., *Shakespeare* symph.; cello concerto; chamber concertos for pf. and vln.; pf. 5tet in C. min.; pf. sonata; songs with chamber orch., etc.

Gurlitt, Wilibald (b. Dresden, 1. III. 1889; d. Freiburg i/B., 15. XII. 1963), Ger. musicologist, great-nephew of Cornelius G. above and son of Cornelius G., an authority on painting. Prof. at Freiburg i/B., 1920–37 and from 1945, and founded a Collegium Musicum there for the perf. of old mus. He wrote works on M. Praetorius, Johann Walther, Schütz, Bach, etc.

Gurney, Ivor (Bertie) (b. Gloucester, 28.

VIII. 1890; d. Dartford, Kent, 26. XII. 1937), Eng.. comp. and poet. He was a choir-boy at Gloucester Cathedral and later studied at the R.C.M. in London with a scholarship. He suffered much from ill-health and during the 1914–18 war was badly wounded and shell-shocked. He struggled for a time against poverty, but in 1922 lost his reason, and he d. of tuberculosis.

Works incl. *The Apple Orchard* and *Scherzo* for vln. and pf.; 2 sets of pf. pieces; song cycles *Ludlow and Teme* (A. E. Housman) and *The Western Playland,* many songs, some to his own poems (27 pub.). 2 vols. of poetry, *Severn and Somme* and *War's Embers.*

Gussly, a Rus. string instrument of the psaltery type.

Gustave III, ou Le Bal masqué (*Gustavus III, or The Masked Ball*), opera by Auber (lib. by Scribe), prod. Paris, Opéra, 27. II. 1833. *See also* **Ballo in maschera.**

Gutiérrez, Antonio García (1812–84), Span. dramatist. *See* **Simon Boccanegra** (Verdi), **Trovatore** (do.).

Gutmann, Adolph (b. Heidelberg, 12. I. 1819; d. Spezia, 27. X. 1882), Ger. pianist and comp. Pupil and friend of Chopin. Wrote numerous pf. works, incl. 10 *Études caractéristiques.*

Gutzkow, Karl (Ferdinand) (1811–78), Ger. novelist and dramatist. *See* **Famintsin** (*Uriel Acosta*), **Rathaus** (do.), **Serov** (do.), by V. S. Bergman).

Guyon, Jean (b. *c.* 1514; d. after 1574), Fr. comp., first a choir-boy (from 1523) and later canon (from 1543) of Chartres Cathedral. Wrote 2 Masses, a motet and several *chansons.*

Guyot. *See* **Castileti.**

Guy-Ropartz (Joseph Guy Marie Ropartz) (b. Guingamp, Côtes du Nord, 15. VI. 1864; d. Lanloup, 22. XI. 1955), Fr. comp. He 1st studied law, but went to the Paris Cons. as a pupil of Dubois, Massenet and Franck. In 1894 he became director of the Nancy Cons. and in 1919 of that of Strasbourg. Later he retired to Brittany, where he was b. and to which he belonged by race.

Works incl. operas *Le Diable couturier, Marguerite d'Écosse, Le Miracle de Saint-Nicolas, Le Pays*; ballet *L'Indiscret*; incid. mus. for a stage version of Pierre Loti's *Pêcheur d'Islande* and for Sophocles' *Oedipus at Colonus; Messe de Sainte-Odile, Messe de Saint-Anne,* Requiem, Psalm cxxxvi, motets and other church mus.; 5 symphs., *Petite Symphonie, Paysage de Bretagne, Les Landes, Dimanche breton, La Cloche des morts, Concert en ré majeur* and other orchestral works; *Rhapsodie* for vln. and orch.; 5 string 4tets, string trio, pf. trio; 2 vln. and pf. sonatas, 2 cello and pf. sonatas; *Ouverture, Variations et*

Final, Choral varié, Dans l'ombre de la montagne, Musique au jardin, 3 Nocturnes, *Croquis d'été, Croquis d'automne, Jeunes Filles* and other works for pf.; org. works; songs *4 Poèmes, Veilles de départ, Le Rêve sur le sable, 4 Odelettes*, etc.

Guzla, a bowed string instrument of a primitive kind used in Dalmatia and Serbia. It has a single string made of horsehair and played with a bow, stretched over a belly covered with skin or parchment and with a round back.

Gwendoline, opera by Chabrier (lib. by Catulle Mendès) prod. Brussels, Théâtre de la Monnaie, 10. IV. 1886.

Gwynneth, John (b. *c*. 1500; d. *c*, 1562), Eng. or Welsh comp., contrib. to the anthology *XX Songes*, pub. 1530.

Gyffard Part-Books, a set of 4 books containing sacred Lat. works, written down *c*. 1555 but incl. works written earlier, such as John Taverner's Mass *The Western Wind*. It once belonged to a Dr. Philip Gyffard.

Gymel (from Lat. *gemellum* = a 'twinsong'), vocal mus. in 2 parts, both of the same range. A characteristic feature is the use of parallel 3rds. The term 1st occurs in the 15th cent., when it usually refers to a divided voice-part in a polyphonic composition, but examples are found as early as the 13th cent.

Gyrowetz (Jírovec), Adalbert (Vojcěch) (b. Budějovice, 19. II. 1763; d. Vienna, 19. III. 1850), Boh. comp. Learnt mus. from his father, a choirmaster; later studied law in Prague, but continued to work at mus. As private secretary to Count Franz von Fünfkirchen, he was expected to take part in the domestic mus. He then went to It. for study under Sala at Naples and later visited Paris, where symphs. of his had been perf. under the name of Haydn. In 1789 the Revolution drove him to London, where the score of his opera *Semiramis* was burnt in the fire of the Pantheon in 1792. He returned to Vienna soon after, and in 1804 was app. cond. at the court theatres, where he prod. many works until 1831.

Works incl. It. operas *Federica ed Adolfo* and *Il finto Stanislao*, Ger. operas *Agnes Sorel, Ida die Büssende, Der Augenarzt, Robert, oder Die Prüfung, Helene, Felix und Adele, Hans Sachs, Die Junggesellen-Wirtschaft, Der Sammtrock, Aladin* (after Oehlenschläger), *Das Ständchen*, etc.; ballet *Die Hochzeit der Thetis* and others; melodramas *Mirina* and others; comic cantata *Die Dorfschule*; over 60 symphs., serenades, overtures and other orchestral works; *c*. 60 string 4tets, 5tets, numerous trios; *c*. 40 vln. and pf. sonatas; instrumental pieces, dances, etc.

Gyterne
Gythorne } *See* **Gittern.**

H

H, the Ger. symbol for the note B♮.

H.M.S. Pinafore, operetta by Sullivan (lib. by W. S. Gilbert), prod. London, Opéra Comique, 25. V. 1878. The 1st work by Gilbert and Sullivan to make a world-wide success.

Haas, Joseph (b. Maihingen, Bavaria, 19. III. 1879; d. Munich, 31. III. 1960), Ger. comp. Pupil of Reger at Munich and then at the Leipzig Cons. Teacher of comp. at Stuttgart from 1911 and Munich from 1921.

Works incl. opera *Tobias Wunderlich*; choral works; serenade for orch.; 2 string 4tets, divertimento for string trio, trio for 2 cellos and pf. and other chamber mus.; sonata and sonatina for vln. and pf.; many pf. works; org. pieces; songs, etc.

Haas, Robert (Maria) (b. Prague, 15. VIII. 1886; d. Vienna, 4. X. 1960), Aus. musicologist. Took the Ph.D. at Prague Univ. and became asst. to Adler. Later lecturer at Vienna Univ. and director of the mus. dept. of the State Library there. Part ed. of the orig. versions of Bruckner's works, etc., author of books on baroque mus., Gluck, Mozart, Bruckner, etc.

Hába, Alois (b. Vizovice, Morav., 21. VI. 1893), Cz. comp. Picked up a knowledge of folk mus. before he studied at the Prague Cons. under Novák; later a pupil of Schreker in Vienna and Berlin. App. prof. at the Prague Cons. in 1924. He became interested in the division of the scale into quarter-tones, on which much of his later work is based.

Works incl. opera *Matka (Mother)*; Overture and Symph. Mus. for orch.; Fantasy for pf. and orch.; vln. concerto; 13 string 4tets and other chamber mus.; pf. sonata and other works (some for quarter-tone pf.); works for string instruments, etc.

Hába, Karel (b. Vizovice, 21. V. 1898), Cz. violinist and comp., brother of prec. Studied vln. under Karel Hoffmann, comp. under Křička, Foerster and Novák, and 4ter-tone mus. with his brother. He played vla. in the Cz. Phil. Orch. in 1929–36 and in 1949 became head of the educ. section of the Cz. Radio.

Works incl. opera *Jánošík*; 2 symphs.; vln. and cello concertos; 3 string 4tets, 7tet; pf. mus.; songs, etc.

Habanera, a dance, with words to be sung, intro. into Spain from Africa via Cuba. It is a moderate 2–4 time and has a basic rhythm of 4 quavers, the 1st of which is dotted. The most famous ex. by a comp. is that in the 1st act of Bizet's *Carmen*.

Habeneck, François Antoine (b. Mézières, 22. I. 1781; d. Paris, 8. II. 1849),

Fr. violinist and cond. of Ger. descent. Pupil of Baillot. Founder of the Société des Concerts du Cons. in Paris; cond. at the Opéra 1824–47. The 1st cond. to cultivate Beethoven in France.

Haberl, Franz Xaver (b. Ober Ellenbach, Bavaria, 12. IV. 1840; d. Regensburg, 5. IX. 1910), Ger. priest and musicologist. Worked at Passau, Rome and Regensburg, where he was *maestro di cappella* of the cathedral, 1871–82, and devoted much time to the study of Catholic church mus., about which he wrote extensively. Ed. Palestrina's complete works, etc.

Habermann, Franz Wenzel (b. Königswart [Lázně Kynžvart], 20. IX. 1706; d. Eger, 7. IV. 1783), Boh. comp. Pub. 6 Masses in 1747, which Handel drew upon for his *Jephtha* of 1751.

Hackbrett (Ger. lit. 'chopping-board'), the Ger. name for the Dulcimer.

Hacomblene (Hacomplaynt), Robert (b. London, c. 1456; d. Cambridge, 1528), Eng. comp. He was scholar of Eton, 1469–72, and of King's Coll., Cambridge, from 1472. He was a Fellow there, 1475–93, and Provost from 1509 until his death. A *Salve Regina* is in the Eton Choirbook.

Haddon Hall, operetta by Sullivan (lib. by Sydney Grundy), prod. London, Savoy Theatre, 24. IX. 1892.

Hadley, Henry (Kimball) (b. Somerville, Mass., 20. XII. 1871; d. N.Y., 6. IX. 1937), Amer. cond. and comp. Studied with his father, with Chadwick at Boston and Mandyczewski in Vienna. Cond. opera in U.S.A. and Ger., and in 1909 became cond. of the symph. orch. at Seattle, of that of San Francisco in 1911–15 and from 1920 lived in N.Y.

Works incl. operas *Safié, Azora, Daughter of Montezuma, Bianca, Cleopatra's Night* and *Mirtil in Arcadia*; *Music, The New Earth* and *Resurgam* for solo voices, chorus and orch.; 4 symphs., overtures *In Bohemia, Herod* and to Shakespeare's *Othello*, Symph. Fantasy, tone-poems *Salome, Lucifer* and *The Ocean*, etc.

Hadley, Patrick (Arthur Sheldon) (b. Cambridge, 5. III. 1899), Eng. comp. Educ. at Winchester Coll. and Cambridge Univ., and studied mus. at the R.C.M. in London, where in 1925 he joined the teaching staff. Mus.D. Cambridge in 1938, app. lecturer at the univ. and Prof. of Mus. in succession to Dent from 1946 to 1962.

Works incl. incid. mus. to Sophocles' *Antigone*; symph. for baritone and chorus *The Trees so high, La Belle Dame sans merci* (Keats) for tenor, chorus and orch., *My Beloved spake* (Song of Solomon) for chorus and orch., cantata *The Hills* for soprano, tenor, bass, chorus and orch., and *Travellers; Ephemera* (Yeats) and *Mariana* (Tennyson) for voice and chamber orch.; string 4tet in C maj., fantasy for 2 vlns. and pf.; songs with orch. and with pf.; part-songs, etc.

Hadow, (William) Henry (b. Ebrington, Glos., 27. XII. 1859; d. London, 8. IV. 1937), Eng. educationist and mus. scholar. Educ. at Malvern Coll. and Oxford, where later he lectured on mus., having studied at Darmstadt and under C. H. Lloyd. Principal of Armstrong Coll., Newcastle-on-Tyne, 1909–19, and Vice-Chancellor of Sheffield Univ., 1919–30. He ed. the *Oxford History of Music* and wrote vol. v and other pubs., incl. *Studies in Modern Music*, *English Music*, etc. He also comp. chamber mus. and songs. Knighted in 1918.

Hadrianus. *See* **Adriaensen.**

Haessler, Johann Wilhelm (b. Erfurt, 29. III. 1747; d. Moscow, 29. III. 1822), Ger. pianist, organist and comp. Pupil of the organist Kittel, a pupil of Bach. Travelled much, estab. concerts at Erfurt in 1780, visited London and St. Petersburg in 1790–4, when he settled at Moscow.

Works incl. pf. sonatas, *Grande Gigue* in D min. and many other works for pf., org. works; songs, etc.

'Haffner' Serenade, Mozart's Serenade in D maj., K. 250, written at Salzburg in VII. 1776 for the marriage of Elisabeth Haffner, daughter of the late burgomaster Sigmund Haffner, celebrated on 22. VII.

'Haffner' Symphony, Mozart's symph. in D maj., K. 385, comp. in Vienna in VII–VIII. 1782 for the Haffner family, probably on the occasion of the ennoblement of Sigmund Haffner, jun., on 29. VII. 1782.

Hafiz (Shams-ud-din Mohammed) (14th cent.), Pers. poet. *See* **Bantock** (5 *ghazals*), **Einem** (songs), **Gernsheim** (choral work), **Henschel** (songs), **Huber** (do.), **Schoeck** (do.), **Szymanowski** (love songs).

Häfliger, Ernst (b. Davos, 6. VII. 1919), Swiss tenor. Studied in Zürich and later in Vienna with Patzak and in Prague with Carpi. He made his début in Salzburg in 1949 and since 1953 has sung in Berlin. He appeared in Glyndebourne in 1956. He is esp. noted as a Mozart singer, Evangelist in the Bach Passions and also as a perf. of modern mus.

Hageman, Richard (b. Leeuwarden, 9. VII. 1882; d. Beverly Hills, Calif., 6. III. 1966), Dutch-Amer. cond. and comp. Studied at the Amsterdam Cons., of which his father was director, and later at the Brussels Cons. He was app. cond. of the Amsterdam Opera and in 1907 settled in U.S.A., where he cond. opera and concerts in var. cities. From 1908 to 1922 he cond. at the Metropolitan Opera in N.Y.

Works incl. opera *Caponsacchi*; many songs, incl. *At the Well*, etc.

Hahn, Reynaldo (b. Caracas, Venezuela, 9. VIII. 1875; d. Paris, 28. I. 1947), Fr. cond. and comp. Was sent to the Paris Cons. at the age of 11, where he studied under var. masters, incl. Massenet. In 1934 he was app. mus. critic of *Le Figaro*, and in 1945 became mus. director of the Paris Opéra.

Works incl. operas *L'Île du rêve*, *La Carmélite*, *La Colombe de Bouddha*, *Nausicaa*, *Le Pauvre d'Assise*, *La Reine de Saba*, *Le Temps d'aimer*, *Brummell*, *Le Marchand de Venise* (after Shakespeare), many operettas incl. *Ciboulette*; ballets *La Fête chez Thérèse* and *Le Dieu bleu*; incid. mus. for Shakespeare's *Much Ado*, Rostand's *Le Bois sacré*, Sacha Guitry's *Mozart*, etc.; ode *Prométhée* for solo voices, chorus and orch.; symph. poem *Nuit d'amour bergamasque*; string 4tet and other chamber mus.; pf. pieces; songs incl. cycles *Chansons grises*, *Chansons latines*, *Chansons espagnoles*, etc.

Hainlen, Paul. *See* **Heinlein.**

Hairpins, the colloq. word for *crescendo* and *diminuendo* marks shown by the conventional signs < and >.

Haitink, Bernard (b. Amsterdam, 4. III. 1929), Dutch cond. Initially an orchestral violinist, in 1955 he became cond. of the Radio Orch. in Amsterdam. He was guest cond. of the Concertgebouw Orch. on their Amer. tour of 1961, becoming their permanent cond. when they returned to Hol. and subsequently also cond. of the London Phil. Orch.

Haitzinger, Anton (b. Wilfersdorf, Lichtenstein, 14. III. 1796; d. Vienna, 31. XII. 1869), Aus. tenor. Made his 1st appearance at the Theater an der Wien in Vienna in 1821. Sang later in Paris, London and St. Petersburg.

Hale, Adam de la. *See* **La Halle.**

Hale, Philip (b. Norwich, Vermont, 5. III. 1854; d. Boston, Mass., 30. XI. 1934), Amer. mus. critic. Studied in U.S.A., Ger. and Paris, and settled as critic at Boston in 1889 and for many years wrote programme notes for the orchestral concerts there.

Halévy (actually **Lévy**), **(Jacques François) Fromental (Elias)** (b. Paris, 27. V 1799; d. Nice, 17. III. 1862), Fr. comp. Studied at the Paris Cons. under Berton and Cherubini from 1809 and, after twice taking a 2nd prize, gained the Prix de Rome in 1819. He continued to study in It., and on his return to Paris tried to gain a foothold on the operatic stage, for which he had already written more than one work. He succeeded with *L'Artisan* in 1827, after which he prod. an enormous number of operas. He became prof. of harmony and accomp. at the Cons. in 1827, of counterpoint and fugue in 1833 and of comp. in 1840.

Works incl. *c.* 40 operas, e.g. *La Dilettante d'Avignon*, *Ludovic* (begun by Hérold), *La Juive*, *L'Éclair*, *Guido et Ginevra*, *Le Shérif*, *Le Guitarréro*, *La Reine de Chypre*,

Charles VI, Les Mousquetaires de la reine, Le Val d'Andorre, La Fée aux roses, La Tempesta (in It., after Shakespeare), *La Dame de Pique* (after Mérimée), *Le Jui, errant* (after Sue), *Jaguarita l'Indienne, La Magicienne,* etc.; ballets *Yella, Manon Lescaut* (after Prévost); incid. mus. to *Prométhée enchaîné* (trans. from Aeschylus); cantatas *Les Derniers Moments du Tasse, La Mort d'Adonis* and *Herminie*; funeral march and *De profundis* on the death of the Duc de Berry, etc.

Halewijn, opera by Pijper (lib., in Dutch, by Emmy van Lokhorst, based on a Flem. story by Charles de Coster), prod. Amsterdam, I.S.C.M. festival, 13. VI. 1933.

Half-Close, an imperfect cadence, i.e. one in which the dominant chord is preceded by the tonic, e.g.:

Half Fall. See **Ornaments.**

Half Note (Amer.) = **Minim.**

Halffter, Cristóbal (b. Madrid, 24. III. 1930), Span. comp. Nephew of Ernesto and Rodolfo H. Studied with Conrado del Campo and Alexandre Tansman. In 1962 he became prof. of comp. at Madrid Cons. His mus. tends toward total serialism. Works incl. *Cantata in Expectatione Resurectionis Domini*; concertino for string orch.; *Sinfonia* for 3 instrumental groups; *Cinco microformas* for orch.; *Dos movimientos* for timpani and string orch.; *Espejos* for 4 percussionists and tape; ballet *Saeta*; *Misa ducal*; *Tres piezas* for string 4tet.; *Formantes* for 2 pfs.; *Trespiezas* for solo fl.; sonata for solo vln.; *Antífona pascual* for soloists, chorus and orch., etc.

Halffter Escriche, Ernesto (b. Madrid, 16. I. 1905), Span. cond. and comp., Cond. of the Orquesta Bética de Cámera. After the Span. war he settled in Port. Works incl. *Dos retratos, Dos bocetos, Rapsodia portuguesa* for orch.; *Suite ancienne* for wind instruments; 2 string 4tets, etc.

Halffter, Rodolfo (b. Madrid, 30. X. 1900), Span. comp., brother of prec. Like his brother, he was self-taught in comp. H. began to write mus. at the age of 24. In 1939 he left Spain and settled in Mexico, having fled after the fall of the Republic and lost some of his works in an air-raid during his escape to Fr. on foot. Works incl. ballets *Don Lindo de Almeria* and *The Baker's Morning*; *Obertura concertante* for pf. and orch., vln. concerto; pf. pieces, etc.

Halíř, Karel (b. Hohenelbe, Boh., 1. II. 1859; d. Berlin, 21. XII. 1909), Cz. violinist. Educ. at the Prague Cons., and under Joachim, of whose 4tet he became a member, besides leading one of his own.

Halka, opera by Moniuszko (lib., in Pol., by Wlodzimierz Wolski, based on a story by Kazimierz Wladyslaw Wójcicki), prod. Wilno, 1. I. 1848, rev. version Warsaw, 1. I. 1858. The chief Pol. nat. opera. Wallek-Walewski's opera *Jontek's Revenge* is a sequel to it.

Hall, Henry (b. New Windsor, c. 1655; d. Hereford, 30. III. 1707), Eng. organist and comp. He was a choir-boy in the Chapel Royal in London under Cooke. App. organist at Exeter Cathedral in 1674 and at Hereford Cathedral in 1688. Works incl. Te Deum in E♭ maj., Benedicite in C min., *Cantate Domino* and *Deus misereatur* in B♭ maj., anthems and other church mus.; songs, duets, catches, etc.

Hall, Marie (b. Newcastle-on-Tyne, 8. IV. 1884; d. Cheltenham, 11. XI. 1956), Eng. violinist. Taught the harp by her father, she decided to take up the vln. and studied with Elgar, Wilhelmj, at the R.A.M. in London and with Ševčík in Prague, where she 1st appeared in 1902; in Vienna and London in 1903.

Halle (or Hale), Adam de la. See **La Halle.**

Hallé, Charles (orig. Carl Halle) (b. Hagen, Westphalia, 11. IV. 1819; d. Manchester, 25. X. 1895), Ger.-Engl. pianist and cond. Studied 1st under his father, an organist, then at Darmstadt and Paris, where he had pf. lessons from Kalkbrenner. Settled in Eng. in 1848 and founded the Hallé concerts at Manchester. He cond. many concerts and festivals elsewhere in the country as well and frequently appeared as pianist. His 2nd wife was the violinist Wilma Neruda, whom he married in 1888, when he was knighted.

Hallé, Lady. See **Neruda.**

Hallé Orchestra. Founded by Charles Hallé at Manchester in 1857. The present cond. is James Loughran.

Hallén, (Johan) Andreas (b. Göteborg. 22. XII. 1846; d. Stockholm, 11. III. 1925), Swed. cond., critic and comp. Studied at Leipzig, Munich and Dresden and later worked mainly at Göteborg and Stockholm. Works incl. operas *Harold der Wiking* (in Ger.), *Hexfällan* (later revised as *Valborgsmässan*) and *Valdemarsskatten*; ballads for solo voices, chorus and orch.; symph. suite *Gustaf Vasas Saga*, symph. poems *The Island of the Dead* (after Böcklin's picture), *Sounds of the Spheres, Autumn* and *A Summer Saga*, 2 rhapsodies for orch.; instrumental pieces; songs, etc.

Halling, a Norw. dance originating from the Hallingdal between Oslo and

Bergen. It is usually in 2–4 time and goes at a moderately quick pace. In its primitive form, as distinct from that cultivated by Grieg and other comps., its mus. is played on the Hardanger Fiddle.

Hallström, Ivar (b. Stockholm, 5. VI. 1826; d. Stockholm, 11. IV. 1901), Swed. pianist and comp. Had private mus. lessons and studied law at Uppsala Univ. There he met Prince Gustaf, with whom he wrote an opera, which was prod. at Stockholm in 1847. After the prince's death he became librarian to Prince Oscar, later Oscar II, and in 1861 he was app. director of Lindblad's mus. school, where he had taught the pf.

Works incl. operas *Hvita frun på Drottningholm* (with Prince Gustaf), *Den bergtagna*, *Hertig Magnus och sjöjungfrun*, *Vikingarne*, *Neaga* (lib. by Carmen Sylva), *Liten Karin*; operettas *Den förtrollade katten*, *Mjölnarvargen*, *Per Svinaherde*; ballets *En dröm*, *Ett äventyr i Skottland*; cantatas; songs, etc.

Halvorsen, Johan (August) (b. Drammen, 15. III. 1864; d. Oslo, 4. XII. 1935), Norw. violinist and comp. Pupil of Lindberg and Nordquist at the Stockholm Cons., later of Brodsky at Leipzig and César Thomson at Liège for vln. and A. Becker in Berlin for comp. Became cond. of the symph. concerts at Bergen and later of the Nat. Theatre at Oslo. He married a niece of Grieg.

Works incl. incid. mus. for Drachman's *Gurre*, Hamsun's *Dronning Tamara*, etc.; coronation cantata for King Haakon; 3 symphs.; symph. poem; vln. concerto; 3 suites for vln. and pf., etc.

Haman and Mordecai (Handel). *See* **Esther**.

Hambourg, Mark (b. Boguchar, 31. V. 1879; d. Cambridge, 26. VIII. 1960), Eng. pianist of Rus. origin. A pupil of Leschetizky, he 1st app. in Moscow in 1888. With his brothers Jan H. (1882–1947) and Boris H. (1885–1954) he formed a pf. trio, but in later years devoted himself entirely to solo perf. He lived in London for most of his life.

Hamboys, *See* **Hanboys**.

Hambraeus, Bengt (b. Stockholm, 29. I. 1928), Swed. comp. and musicologist. Studied musicology at the Univ. of Uppsala from 1947 to 1956, and from 1957 worked for Swed. Radio, at the same time teaching at Uppsala Univ. He participated in the Darmstadt courses, being chiefly influenced by the work of Webern, Stockhausen and Boulez.

Works incl. *Rota* for 3 orchs., perc. and electronic tape; *Constellation I* for org.; *Constellation II* for recorded tape; *Constellation III* derived from nos. I and II; *Doppelrohr II*, an electronic piece; *Introduzione-Sequenze-Coda,* etc.

Hamel, Margarete Luise. *See* **Schick.**

Hamerik (orig. Hammerich), **Asger** (b. Copenhagen, 8, IV. 1843; d. Frederiksborg, 13. VII. 1923), Dan. comp. of Ger. descent. Pupil of Gade at Copenhagen, later of Bülow in Berlin for pf. and of Berlioz in Paris for orch. In 1872–98 he was in U.S.A. as director of the Cons. of the Peabody Inst. at Baltimore.

Works incl. operas *Tovelille*, *Hjalmar og Ingeborg*, *La vendetta* and *Den Rejsende*; Requiem, 2 choral trilogies; 6 symphs., the last for strings, 5 *Northern Suites* and other orchestral works, etc.

Hamerik, Ebbe (b. Copenhagen, 5. IX. 1898; d. Copenhagen, 15. VIII. 1951), Dan. cond. and comp., son of prec. Pupil of his father and Frank van der Stucken. Cond. of the royal theatre at Copenhagen, 1919–22, and of the Musikforeningen there, 1927–30. He then went to live in Aus., but returned home in 1934. He was drowned in the Kattegat.

Works incl. operas *Stepan, Leonardo da Vinci, Marie Grubbe* (after Jacobsen) and *Rejsekammeraten* (*The Travelling Companion*, after Andersen); 5 symphs., *Quasi Passacaglia e Fuga*, Variations on an old Dan. folk-tune; 2 string 4tets; suite for contralto and chamber orch.; pf. pieces; org. works; songs etc.

Hamilton, Iain (Ellis) (b. Glasgow, 6. VI. 1922), Scot. pianist and comp. Studied at the R.A.M. in London, where var. works of his were introd. and he won the Royal Phil. Society prize for his clar. concerto and the Kussevitsky Award for his 2nd symph.

Works incl. ballet *Clerk Saunders*; 2 symphs., Variations for strings; clar. 5tet, string 4tet, fl. 4tet; Variations for solo vln.; vla. and pf. sonata; pieces for wind instruments and pf.; pf. sonata; vln. concerto; 8tet for strings, etc.

Hamilton, Patrick (b. 1904), Eng. playwright. *See* Bush (A.) (*Duke in Darkness*).

Hamlet. *See also* **Ambleto**; **Amleto**; **Shakespeare**.

Incid. mus. for Shakespeare's tragedy by Tchaikovsky, Op. 67a, incl. 16 numbers and an abridged version of the *Hamlet* fantasy-overture, Op. 67, 1st perf. St. Petersburg, 17, XI. 1888; the play 1st perf. with Tchaikovsky's mus., St. Petersburg, 21. II. 1891.

Opera by Aristide Hignard (1822–98) (lib. by Pierre de Garal, after Shakespeare), pub. 1868, but not then prod. on account of A. Thomas's rival opera; prod. Nantes, 21. IV. 1888.

Opera by Searle (text of Shakespeare's play), prod. (in Ger.) Hamburg, 5. III. 1968.

Opera by A. Thomas (lib. by Jules Barbier and Michel Carré, after Shakespeare), prod. Paris, Opéra, 9. III. 1868.

Symph. poem by Liszt, comp. 1858 as a prelude to Shakespeare's tragedy; 1st concert perf. Sondershausen, 2. VII. 1876.

Hammerclavier, obs. Ger. name (lit. 'hammer keyboard instrument') used to distinguish the piano from the (plucked) harpsichord. Beethoven designated his sonatas Op. 101 and 106 as 'für das H.', and the word is now used (for no good reason) as a nickname for the latter sonata.

Hammerich. *See* Hamerik.

Hammerschmidt, Andreas (b. Brüx, 1612; d. Zittau, 8. XI. 1675), Boh. comp. Taken to Freiberg, Saxony, in 1626. Became organist there, 1635, and at Zittau, 1639. Wrote much Lutheran church mus. Works incl. sacred concertos and madrigals for several voices, sacred dialogues for 2 voices, odes, motets and hymns, 17 short Lutheran Masses; thanksgiving for 8 voices for the Saxon victory at Liegnitz; dances for viols., etc.

Hammond Organ, an electrophonic org. invented by Laurens Hammond of Chicago in 1934, prod. its notes by means of electromagnets and offering a choice of tone colours by the selection and combination of the appropriate harmonics.

Hampshire, Richard (b. *c.* 1465; d. ? 1499), Eng. comp. He was a chorister of Windsor, 1474, scholar and clerk of King's Coll. Cambridge, 1484 and 1486, and clerk of Windsor, 1489–99, being master of the choristers there from 1495. He is repres. in the Eton Choirbook.

Hampton, John (b. ?; d. ? 1522), Eng. comp. Master of the choristers at Worcester Priory, 1484–1522. He is repres. in the Eton Choirbook.

Hamsun, Knut 1859 – 1952), Norw. novelist and dramatist. *See* Halvorsen (*Dronning Tamara*), Karel (*Game of Life*).

Hanboys, John (b. ?; d. ?), Eng. Franciscan friar and mus. theorist of the 15th cent. His treatise *Summa . . . super musicam* is a commentary on Franco of Cologne.

Handbassl (Aus. & S. Ger. dialect = little hand bass), Leopold Mozart's name for the violoncello piccolo.

Handel, George Frideric (orig. Händel, Georg Friedrich) (b. Halle, 23. II. 1685; d. London, 14. IV. 1759), Ger.-Eng. comp. After initial opposition from his father, a barber-surgeon, he studied mus. with Zachow in Halle, and in 1702 matriculated at the univ. there to read law, at the same time holding the probationary post of organist at the Domkirche. The next year he left for Hamburg, where he played vln., later harpsichord, at the opera under Keiser, and had the operas *Almira* and *Nero* prod. in 1705. Travelled in It. 1706–9, visiting the principal cities and meeting the leading comps. *Agrippina* was successfully prod. at Venice in 1709, and he also made a great reputation as a harpsichordist.

Other works comp. in It. incl. the oratorios *La resurrezione* and *Il trionfo del tempo*, solo cantatas, chamber duets, etc. With the support of Steffani he was app. to succeed the latter as *Kapellmeister* to the Elector of Hanover in 1710, but left almost immediately on leave of absence for London, where *Rinaldo* was prod. with great success the next year. Again in London on leave in 1712, he settled there, never returning to his post in Hanover. Between 1712 and 1715 he prod. 4 operas, and in 1713 comp. a *Te Deum* and *Jubilate* to celebrate the Peace of Utrecht, receiving a life pension of £200 from Queen Anne. On her death in 1714 the Elector of Hanover succeeded to the throne as George I, but apparently took a lenient view of his former *Kapellmeister*'s truancy, for H.'s pension was soon doubled. As mus. director to the Earl of Carnavon (later Duke of Chandos) 1717–20, H. comp. the *Chandos Anthems*, *Acis and Galatea* and the masque *Haman and Mordecai*.

With the founding of the R.A.M. in 1720 began H.'s most prolific period as an opera comp., and over the next 20 years he prod. more than 30 works. Difficulties arose from the formation of partisan factions round himself and his rival Bononcini, and were aggravated by internal strife between his 2 leading ladies, Faustina and Cuzzoni. The popular success of *The Beggar's Opera* in 1728 made matters worse, and in that year the R.A.M. went bankrupt. H. continued to prod. operas, acting as his own impresario in partnership with Heidegger, but rival factions, now of a political nature, again undermined his success, and in the 1730s he increasingly turned to oratorio. *Esther* (a revision of the masque *Haman and Mordecai*), 1732, was followed by *Deborah*, *Saul* and *Israel in Egypt*. His last opera was prod. in 1741, after which he devoted his time chiefly to oratorio, *Messiah* being perf. in Dublin in 1742, followed by 12 more. He continued to appear in public as a cond. and organist, playing concertos between the parts of his oratorios, but his health declined and he spent his last years in blindness.

Works incl. operas *Almira, Nero, Rodrigo, Agrippina, Rinaldo, Il pastor fido, Teseo, Silla, Amadigi di Gaula, Radamisto, Muzio Scevola, Floridante, Ottone, Flavio, Giulio Cesare, Tamerlano, Rodelinda, Scipione, Alessandro, Admeto, Riccardo Primo, Siroe, Tolomeo, Lotario, Partenope, Poro, Ezio, Sosarme, Orlando, Arianna, Ariodante, Alcina, Atalanta, Arminio, Giustino, Berenice, Faramondo, Serse, Imeneo, Deidamia*; incid. mus. to Ben Jonson's *The Alchemist* and Smollett's *Alceste*; 2 Ger. Passions; oratorios *La resurrezione, Esther, Deborah, Athalia, Saul, Israel in Egypt, Messiah, Samson,*

Joseph and his Brethren, Belshazzar, Occasional Oratorio, Judas Maccabaeus, Joshua, Alexander Balus, Susanna, Solomon, Theodora, Jephtha, The Triumph of Time and Truth; secular choral works *Acis and Galatea, Alexander's Feast, Ode for St. Cecilia's Day, L'Allegro, il Penseroso ed il Moderato* (after Milton), *Semele, Hercules, The Choice of Hercules*; 11 'Chandos' Anthems, anthems for the coronation of George II, funeral anthem for Queen Caroline, Utrecht *Te Deum* and *Jubilate*, Dettingen *Te Deum* and other church mus.; numerous It. cantatas, chamber duets etc.; sonatas for various instruments and continuo, trio sonatas, etc.; 12 *concerti grossi* for strings, 'oboe concertos', org. concertos, *Water Music, Fireworks Music*, etc.; keyboard mus., incl. organ fugues and harpsichord suites, etc.

Handl, Jacob (Latinized Jacobus Gallus) (b. Reifnitz, Carniola, ? 31. VII. 1550; d. Prague, 18. VII. 1591), Aus. comp. *Kappellmeister* to the Bishop of Olomouc in 1579 and later cantor in Prague. Wrote Masses, motets, Te Deum and other church mus.

Handle-Piano. *See* **Piano-Organ.**

Handlo, Robert de (b. ?; d. ?), Eng. 14th-cent. writer on mus. His treatise *Regulae cum maximis Magistri Franconis* (1326) is a commentary on Franco of Paris.

Hannikainen, Ilmari (b. Jävaskylä, 19. X. 1892; d. Helsinki, 25. VII. 1955), Fin. pianist and comp. Studied at the Helsinki Cons., also in Vienna, Leningrad, Berlin, Paris, Antwerp and London. With his brothers Arvo and Tauna, a violinist and a cellist, he founded a pf. trio and toured Eur. widely with them.

Works incl. opera *Talkootanssit*; pf. concerto; pf. 4tet; pf. mus.; songs, etc.

Hans Heiling, opera by Marschner (lib. by Eduard Devrient, orig. written for Mendelssohn), prod. Berlin, Opera, 24. V. 1833.

Hans Sachs, opera by Lortzing (lib. by comp. and Philipp Reger, based on a play by Johann Ludwig Ferdinand Deinhardstein), prod. Leipzig, 23. VI. 1840. An earlier opera on the subject of Wagner's *Meistersinger*, which was also used before that by Gyrowetz.

Hänsel und Gretel, opera by Humperdinck (lib. by Adelheid Wette, Humperdinck's sister, from a tale by the Brothers Grimm), prod. Weimar, 23. VII. 1893.

Hanslick, Eduard (b. Prague, 11. IX. 1825; d. Baden nr. Vienna, 6. VIII. 1904), Aus. mus. critic. Wrote for the *Neue freie Presse* in Vienna and was lecturer on mus. hist. at the Univ. A fierce opponent of Wagner and ardent partisan of Brahms. His books incl. *Vom Musikalisch-Schönen (Of the Beautiful in Music).*

Hanson, Howard (b. Wahoo, Neb., 28. X. 1896), Amer. comp. of Swed. descent. Studied mus. in N.Y. and at Evanston, Ill. Univ. After var. appts., he gained the Amer. Prix de Rome, and after his stay in It. was director of the Eastman School of Mus. at Rochester, N.Y., 1924–64.

Works incl. opera *Merry Mount* (after Hawthorne); choral work *The Lament for Beowulf*; 5 symphs., symph. poems *North and West, Lux aeterna* and *Pan and the Priest* for orch.; string 4tet, pf. 5tet, concerto for pf. 5tet; pf. pieces; songs, etc.

Hardanger Fiddle (Norw. *Hardangerfelen*), a primitive Norw. vln. with 4 strings and 4 sympathetic strings used for playing folk dances.

Harding, James (b. *c.* 1560; d. 1626), Eng. comp. and instrumentalist. Wrote 2 keyboard fancies and instrumental dance mus.

Hardy, Thomas (1840–1928), Eng. novelist and poet. *See* **Dunhill** (*Song of the King's Men* from *The Dynasts*), **Finzi** (30 songs), **Gardiner** (H. B.) (*Shepherd Fennel's Dance* from *Wessex Tales*), **Holst** (*Egdon Heath* from *The Return of the Native*), **Milford** (*Dark Thrush*), **Queen of Cornwall** (Boughton), **Shaw** (M.) (*Budmouth Dears*), **Tess** (d'Erlanger), **Tranchell** (*Mayor of Casterbridge*).

Poems set as songs by Austin (F.) (3), Bax (3), Britten (8), Cochran (1), Finzi (3: 2 cycles), Foss (H.) (7), Gardiner (H. B.) (1: mus. arr. from Hardy's own), Gibbs (C. A.) (2), Hale (Alfred) (12: incl. 2 cycles), Harrison (Sydney) (1), Head (Michael) (2), Holst (2), Ireland (6, incl. cycle), Lane (Edgar) (2), Le Fleming (Christopher) (4), Milford (5), Parish (F. Wilson) (1), Sarson (May) (1), Scott (Cyril) (1), Serell (Alys F.) (1), Sheldon (Mary) (4), Slater (Gordon) (1), Speyes (Charles A.) (2), Stewart (D. M.) (1), Tate (Phyllis) (1).

Harington, Henry (b. Kelston, Som., 29. IX. 1727; d. Bath, 15. I. 1816), Eng. physician and amateur musician. Studied 1st theology and then medicine at Oxford and settled in practice at Bath. Comp. glees, catches, rounds, songs, etc. The popular setting of Ben Jonson's 'Drink to me only with thine eyes' is attrib. to him.

Hark, hark, the lark, song by Schubert from Shakespeare's *Cymbeline*, trans. by A. W. Schlegel as *Ständchen aus 'Cymbeline'* and comp., in Ger., in 1826.

Harmonic, a prefix denoting org. pipes prod. harmonic notes from pipes of double, triple or quadruple speaking-length. *See also* **Harmonics.**

Harmonic Bass, another name for the Acoustic Bass org. stop.

Harmonic Flute. *See under* **Flute, Harmonic.**

Harmonic Minor, the min. scale conforming to the key signature, with the exception of the leading-note (*see* illustration).

studying H. is to master the principles of succession.

Harold en Italie, a descriptive symph. by

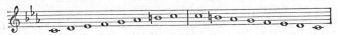

HARMONIC MINOR

Harmonic Series, the composite series of notes that can be prod. by a vibrating substance or air column (*see* illustration).

Berlioz, Op. 16, for solo vla. and orch., based on Byron's *Childe Harold*, comp. in 1834 and 1st perf. Paris, 23. XI. It was

1   2   3   4   5   6   7   8   9   10   11   12   13   14   15   16

HARMONIC SERIES

Those marked *x* are not in tune with the normal scale. The members of the series have a proportional relation to each other which can be deduced from the numbers given above.

Harmonica, a modern term for the mouth organ. For the Glass Harmonica *see* **Armonica.**

Harmonics, a commonly used term for (upper) partial tones (overtones) in the notes of a mus. inst. Also a technical term for notes prod. by touching a bowed string at suitable (nodal) points, or similarly by making a hole in an open org. pipe. In acoustics, compound elements of a periodic vibration. The corresponding elements in the vibration of a bell or a drum are 'inharmonic'. *See* **Harmonic Series.**

Harmonie der Welt, Die (*The Harmony of the World*), opera by Hindemith (lib. by the composer) in 5 acts, prod. Munich, 11. VIII. 1957.

Harmoniemusik (Ger.), mus. for a combination of woodwind and brass instruments, with or without perc., i.e. for military band.

Harmonious Blacksmith, The, name given to the Air and Variations in Handel's E maj. harpsichord suite (Book I, No. 5, pub. 1720). Despite the traditional story that Handel comp. the piece after hearing a blacksmith singing at his work, the nickname is of 19th-cent. origin.

Harmonium, a keyboard instrument, the sound of which is prod. by reeds played by wind coming from bellows worked by the player's feet. It dates from the early 19th cent. The American Organ is similar to it, except that there the wind is sucked into instead of driven out through the reeds.

Harmony, composite sounds heard either singly or in succession. The purpose of

suggested by Paganini, but not played by him.

Harp, an instrument dating from prehistoric times, so shaped that the strings stretched parallel across its frame are graded in length and thus prod. the different notes of a mus. scale. Old Hs. had comparatively few strings and their notes were fixed; the modern concert H. has a range of 6½ 8ves and the strings represent the diatonic scale of C♭ maj.; but each note can be raised individually throughout all the octaves at once by a semitone and by a whole tone at will by means of a set of pedals at the base of the instrument. Thus the H. can be tuned in a moment to any diatonic scale. The chromatic scale is available only on the Chromatic Harp (q.v.).

Harp Lute, an obs. instrument sometimes called Dital Harp, invented early in the 19th cent. It was derived from instruments of the lute type, but had a larger number of strings held by pegs in the harp-shaped head, *c.* half of them changeable in pitch by a finger-board, the others remaining open and thus capable of playing only a single fixed note.

'Harp' Quartet, the nickname given to Beethoven's string 4tet in E♭ maj., Op. 74, comp. in 1809, because it contains several arpeggios divided between the instruments.

Harpègement. *See* **Ornaments.**

Harper, Heather (Mary) (b. Belfast, 8. V. 1930), Eng. (N. Ir.) soprano. Studied at Trinity Coll. of Mus., London, and privately. First appeared in opera at Oxford, 1954. She has sung at Bayreuth and elsewhere and has also made a reputation as a concert singer. Hon. D.Mus., Queen's Univ., Belfast, 1966.

Harpsicall ⎫ Old Eng. terms, corrup-
Harpsicon ⎭ tions of 'Harpsichord'.

Harpsichord, a keyboard instrument shaped usually in the wing form of a grand pf. and played by means of a similar keyboard, but prod. its notes by plucking the strings with plectra, not striking them with hammers. The square-shaped Virginal and the Spinet are instruments of the same type but smaller. H.s often have 2 keyboards, each controlling a different set of quills, harder and softer, and there are frequently stops by which yet other ranges of quills can be set into action; but the tone cannot be controlled by the player's fingers.

Harpway, the special tuning of the Bass Viol or Lyra Viol in the 17th cent., not in the usual way, but to the notes of a common chord, either maj. (H. sharp) or min. (H. flat).

Harrer, Johann Gottlob (b. Görlitz, 1703; d. Leipzig, 9. VII. 1755), Ger. comp. and collector of mus. Succeeded Bach as cantor at St. Thomas's Church, Leipzig, in 1750.
Works incl. oratorios., Passion mus.; 24 symphs.; instrumental concertos; harpsichord sonatas, etc.

Harris, Clement (Hugh Gilbert) (b. London, 8. VII. 1871; d. Pentepagadia, Turkey, 23. IV. 1897), Eng. pianist and comp. Educ. at Harrow, studied mus. at Frankfurt and became a pupil of Clara Schumann. He was travelling in Greece when the Greco-Turkish war broke out, fought voluntarily on the Gk. side and was killed in battle.
Works incl. symph. poem *Paradise Lost* (after Milton); Romances for vln. and pf. and clar., cello and pf.; 4 concert studies, Ballade, *Il Pensieroso* and *L'Allegro* (after Milton), etc. for pf.; songs, etc.

Harris, Joel Chandler (1848–1908), Amer. author. *See* Jacob (G.) (*Uncle Remus*).

Harris, Renatus (b. ?; d. ?), Eng. 17th–18th-cent., org. builder. Worked in London. Built many famous orgs. and enlarged that made by his grandfather for Magdalen Coll., Oxford.

Harris, Roy (actually Leroy Harris) (b. Lincoln Co., Okla., 12. II. 1898), Amer. comp. His father was a farmer who migrated to California during H.'s boyhood, and at 18 H. had a farm of his own. In 1916 he enlisted in the World War I, returning to U.S.A. in 1918 and becoming a mus. student at the Univ. of California, driving a dairy cart to earn a living. Next he studied under Arthur Farwell for 2 years and prod. an Andante for strings with the N.Y. Phil. Orch. in 1926, when he went to Paris for a further 2 years' study with Nadia Boulanger with a Guggenheim scholarship. He returned to U.S.A. in 1929 and later held posts at the Westminster Choir school at Princeton, N.J., Cornell Univ.,

Colorado, Logan (Utah), Nashville and Pittsburgh.
Works incl. 10 symphs., *Folksong Symph.*, *Farewell to Pioneers*, *Three Symph. Essays*, *Memories of a Child's Sunday* and other works for orch.; *Chorale* and *Prelude and Fugue* for string orch.; concerto for vln. and orch.; symph. for chorus and orch., *Whitman Suite* and *Second Suite* for women's chorus and 2 pfs., *Song for Occupation*, *Story of Noah* and *Symph. for Voices* for 8-pt. unaccomp. chorus; 3 string 4tets, 6tet and 5tet for wind and pf., string 6tet, pf. 5tet, pf. trio, *Variations on a Theme* for string 4tet, *4 Minutes 20 Seconds* for fl. and string 4tet, concerto for pf. clar. and string 4tet; vln. and pf. sonata; pieces for vln. and vla. and pf.; pf. works, incl. sonatas and *Children's Suite*, etc.

Harrison, Frank Llewellyn (b. Dublin, 29. IX. 1905), Ir. musicologist and educationist. Studied at the R.Ir.A.M. and Trinity Coll., Dublin, and subsequently under Schrade and Hindemith at Yale Univ. He was mus. director at Queen's Univ., Kingston (Canada), from 1935 to 1946, and Prof. of Mus. at Colgate Univ., Hamilton (N.Y.), from 1946 to 1947 and at Washington Univ., St. Louis, from 1947 to 1952. From 1952 to 1970 he was a lecturer in mus., subsequently reader, at Oxford Univ. App. Prof. of Ethnomusicology at Amsterdam Univ., 1970. He has specialized in the study of Eng. medieval mus., and has ed. *The Eton Choirbook* (3 vols.) and pub. *Music in Medieval Britain* (1958). He is general ed. of the series *Early English Church Music*.

Harrison, Julius (b. Stourport, Worcs., 26. IIII 1885; d. 5. IV. 1963), Eng. cond. and comp. Studied under Bantock at the Midland Inst., Birmingham. Cond. opera under Beecham's management and with the B.N.O.C. and from 1930 to 1940 was mus. director at Hastings.
Works incl. Mass for solo voices, chorus and orch.; Requiem Mass; suite *Worcestershire Pieces* for orch.; *Troubadour Suite* for strings, harp and 2 horns; string 4tet *Widdicombe Fair* and other chamber mus.; vla. and pf. sonata; pf. works, instrumental pieces; songs, etc.

Harrison, Lou (b. Portland, Oregon, 14. V. 1917), Amer. comp. Studied with Cowell and Schönberg from 1937 to 1940. He then taught at Mills College and at the Univ. of California in 1942. From 1945 to 1948 he was a mus. critic for the *New York Herald-Tribune*. H. has experimented with new sonorities, incl. novel scales and methods of tuning.
Works incl. opera *Rapunzel*; ballets *Solstice*, *The Perilous Chapel*, *Almanac of the Seasons*, *Johnny Appleseed*, *Changing World* and others; Prelude and Saraband for orch., symph. in G maj., 3 suites; *Four*

Strict Songs for 8 baritones and orch. in pure intonation; *Recording Piece* for perc.; *Simfony I*; vln. concerto with perc. orch.; string trio; suite for cello and harp; pf. mus., etc.

Harsányi, Tibor (b. Magyarkanizsa, 27. VI. 1898; d. Paris, 19. IX. 1954), Hung. comp. Studied at the Budapest Cons. under Kodály and later settled in Paris in 1923. Works incl. operas *Illusion, Les Invités*; ballets *The Last Dream* and *Shota Roustaveli* (with Honegger and A. Tcherepnin); Christmas Cantata for chorus and strings; suite, *Suite hongroise*, *Ouverture symphonique*, *La Joie de vivre* for orch.; *Concertstück* for pf. and orch., Divertimento No. 1 for 2 vlns. and orch.; *Aria and Rondo* for cello and orch., Divertimento No. 2 for tpt. and strings; *The Story of the Little Tailor* for 7 instruments and perc.; 3 string 4tets, pf. trio, concertino for pf. and string 4tet, nonet for wind and string 4tet; sonatas for vln. and pf. and cello and pf.; pf. pieces; songs; etc.

Harte, Francis Bret (1839–1902), Amer. humorous writer. *See* **James** (overture), **Weinberger** (*Outcasts of Poker Flat*).

Hartleben, Otto Erich (1864–1905), Ger. poet and dramatist. *See* **Pierrot lunaire** (Schönberg).

Hartmann, Ger.-Dan. family of musicians:

1. **Johann Ernst H.** (b. Glogau, Silesia, 24. XII. 1726; d. Copenhagen, 21. X. 1793), Ger. violinist, cond. and comp. Worked at Breslau and Rudolstadt before he settled in Copenhagen, where he became leader of the royal orch. in 1768.
Works incl. opera *The Fishermen*, containing the song *Kong Christian* by D. L. Rogert, now the Dan. nat. anthem, etc.

2. **August Wilhelm H.** (b. Copenhagen, 6. XI. 1775; d. Copenhagen, 15. XI. 1850), organist, son of prec. Organist at the Garrison Church in Copenhagen from 1800.

3. **Johann Peter Emilius H.** (b. Copenhagen, 14. V. 1805; d. Copenhagen, 10. III. 1900), comp., son of prec. Succeeded his father as organist of the Garrison Church in Copenhagen in 1824, app. organist of the cathedral 1843. Prof. at Copenhagen Cons., he became one of its directors in 1867.
Works incl. operas *Ravnen, Korsarerne, Liden Kirsten* (after Andersen); melodrama *Guldhornene*; incid. mus. for plays; ballets; 2 symphs.; sonatas, etc., for pf., etc.

4. **Emil H.** (b. Copenhagen, 21. II. 1836; d. Copenhagen, 18. VII. 1898), organist and comp., son of prec. Pupil of his father and Gade, who was his brother-in-law. Organist at var. churches in 1861–73 and cond. of the Mus. Society from 1891 to 1892, succeeding Gade.
Works incl. operas *En Nat mellem Fjaeldene, Elverpigen, Korsikaneren* and *Ragnhild*; ballet *Fjeldstuen*; cantata *Winter*

and Spring; 3 symphs., *Northern Folk Dances* and overture *A Northern Campaign*; concertos for vln. and for cello; serenade for clar., cello and pf.; songs, etc.

Hartmann, Karl Amadeus (b. Munich, 2. VIII. 1905; d. Munich, 5. XII. 1963), Ger. comp. Studied with Josef Haas at the Munich Acad. and later with Scherchen. Began comp. late in life, but destroyed his early works and turned to serialism under the influence of Webern. After World War II he organized the important 'Musica Viva' concerts in Munich to propagate new mus. In 1952 he was elected to the Ger. Acad. of Fine Arts and in 1953 became president of the German section of the I.S.C.M.
Works incl. chamber opera *Des Simplicius Simplicissimus Jugend*; 8 symphs.; concerto for pf., wind and perc.; *Musik der Trauer* for vln. and strings; concerto for vla., pf., strings and perc.; 2 string 4tets, etc.

Hartmann, Thomas de (b. Moscow, 21. IX. 1885; d. Princeton, N.J., 26. III. 1956), Rus. comp. Went to live in St. Petersburg, where he studied with Arensky and S. Taneiev, but was unable to devote himself entirely to mus. from the first. Later he went to Tiflis, where he was assoc. with N. Tcherepnin and gave lectures on Armen. mus. and studied oriental mus. In 1921 he left Rus. for Constantinople, where he estab. an orch., and he afterwards settled in Paris.
Works incl. opera *Esther* (Racine's tragedy); ballets *The Purple Flower, Plastic Dances* and 3 others; 3 symphs. and other orch. works; concertos for pf., vln., cello, double bass and harp; chamber mus.; cello and pf. sonata; *Paysages tristes* (Verlaine), 6 *Mus. Commentaries on James Joyce's 'Ulysses'* and *Fragment tiré de 'A l'ombre des jeunes filles en fleurs'* (Proust) for voice and pf., etc.

Harty, (Herbert) Hamilton (b. Hillsborough, Ir., 4. XII. 1879; d. Hove, 19. II. 1941), Ir. cond. and comp. Studied pf., vla. and comp. under his father and became an organist at the age of 12. Later organist at Belfast and Dublin, where he studied further under Esposito. In 1900 he settled in London as accompanist and comp. and married the soprano Agnes Nicholls. He then took to cond. and after much experience in London was app. cond. to the Hallé Orch. at Manchester in 1920, retiring in 1933. Knighted and Mus.D. Dublin, 1925.
Works incl. Ir. Symph., *Comedy Overture*, symph. poem *With the Wild Geese* for orch.; vln. concerto; cantata *The Mystic Trumpeter* (Whitman); *Ode to the Nightingale* (Keats) for soprano and orch.; many songs, etc.

Harvey, Mary (Lady Dering) (b. ?, VIII. 1629; d. ?, 1704), Eng. amateur comp. Daughter of Daniel Harvey of Folkestone and Combe (Surrey), married Sir Edward Dering, a member of a Kentish family, 1648. Pupil of H. Lawes, in whose *Second Book of Select Ayres and Dialogues* 3 of her songs appeared.

Harwood, Basil (b. Woodhouse, Olveston. Glos., 11. IV. 1859; d. Oxford, 3. IV. 1949), Eng. organist and comp. Educ. at Charterhouse and Oxford, studied mus., at Bristol, Oxford and the Leipzig Cons. Organist 1st in London, then at Ely Cathedral, 1887–92, and Christ Church, Oxford, 1892–1909, and choragus of the univ.

Works incl. psalms and motets with orch.; services, anthems and other church mus.; *Ode on a May Morning* (Milton) for chorus and orch., cantata *Love Incarnate*; org. concerto with orch.; 2 sonatas and other works for org., etc.

Háry János, ballad opera by Kodály (lib. by Béla Paulini and Zsolt Harsányi, based on a poem by János Garay), prod. Budapest, 16. X. 1926. It contains popular Hung. tunes and begins with an orchestral imitation of a sneeze.

Hashewell. *See* **Ashwell.**

Haskil, Clara (b. Bucharest, 7. I. 1895; d. Brussels, 7. XII. 1960), Rum. pianist. Made her début aged 7 in Vienna, then entered the Paris Cons., where she studied with Cortot and Fauré and won a prize at the age of 14. She later studied with Busoni on his invitation. She was esp. well known as a perf. of Mozart and Beethoven.

Hasprois. *See* **Asproys.**

Hasse, Faustina. *See* **Bordoni.**

Hasse, Johann Adolf (b. Bergedorf nr. Hamburg, 23 or 24. III. 1699; d. Venice, 16. XII. 1783), Ger. comp. Sang tenor at the Hamburg Opera under Keiser, 1718–19, then at Brunswick, 1719–22, where his first opera, *Antioco*, was prod. in 1721. Went to It. in 1722, and studied with Porpora and A. Scarlatti. After many successful operas for Naples, became *maestro di cappella* at the Cons. degli Incurabili in Venice in 1727. Married the singer Faustina Bordoni in 1730, and in 1734 went to Dresden as *Kapellmeister* to the Saxon Court, a post he held for 30 years. But he was allowed generous leave of absence, and travelled widely, incl. a visit to London in 1734, becoming the most successful *opera seria* comp. of his generation. In 1764, after the death of the Saxon Elector, he moved to Vienna, then in 1773 to Venice, where he lived for the rest of his life.

Works incl. operas *Antioco, Il Sesostrate, Tigrane, Artaserse, Cleofide, Cajo Fabricio, Il Demetrio, Siroe, rè di Persia, Tito Vespasiano, Lucio Papirio, Didone abbandonata, Antigono, Semiramide riconosciuta, Arminio, Leucippo, Demofoonte, Attilio Regolo, Il Ciro riconosciuto, Solimano,*

Ezio, Olimpiade, Alcide al Bivio, Il trionfo di Clelia, Partenope, Piramo e Tisbe, Ruggiero, and many others; oratorios *I Pellegrini al sepolcro, Sant' Elena al calvario, La Conversione di Sant' Agostino,* etc.; Masses and other church mus.; concertos for fl., vln., etc.; solo sonatas, trio sonatas, harpsichord pieces, etc.

Hasselbeck, Rosa. *See* **Sucher.**

Hasselmans, Alphonse (Jean) (b. Liège, 5. III. 1845; d. Paris, 19. V. 1912), Belg., naturalized Fr., harpist and comp. Settled early in Paris and became harp prof. at the Cons. in 1884. Appeared frequently as a virtuoso and comp. *c.* 50 works for the harp, incl. *Patrouille* and *L'Orientale.*

Hassler, Hans Leo (b. Nuremberg, 25–26. X. 1564; d. Frankfurt, 8. VI. 1612), Ger. organist and comp. Pupil of his father, Isaac H. (*c.* 1530–91) and, after an appt. at Nuremberg, was sent to Venice for further study under A. Gabrieli. Organist to Octavian Fugger at Augsburg, 1585–1600. Having returned to Nuremberg as organist of the church of Our Lady, he married and went to live at Ulm in 1604, but soon went into the service of the Emperor Rudolph in Prague. In 1608 he became organist to the Elector of Saxony at Dresden, but suffered from consumption and d. during a visit with the elector to Frankfurt.

Works incl. Masses, Magnificats, hymntunes, motets (incl. 2 collections *Sacrae cantiones* and *Sacri concentus*), fugal psalms and Christian songs; It. canzonets for 4 voices, It. and Ger. madrigals, *Lustgarten neuer teutscher Gesäng* (32 Ger. songs for 4–8 voices); *ricercari,* toccatas, etc. for org., etc.

Hassler, Jacob (b. Nuremberg, 17–18. XII. 1569; d. ?, *c.* 1622), Ger. organist and comp., brother of prec. Studied under his father and at Venice, became organist to Christoph Fugger at Augsburg and then to Prince Eitel-Fritz of Hohenzollern at Hechingen, and in 1602–12 was in the service of the court in Prague.

Works incl. Masses and other church mus.; It. madrigals; org. works, etc.

Hassler, Kaspar (b. Nuremberg, VIII. 1562; d. Nuremberg, VIII. 1618), Ger. organist and comp., brother of prec. Studied under his father and (?) at Venice. Organist at the church of St. Laurence at Nuremburg. Ed. collections of motets, incl. some by his brother Hans Leo H.

Hatton, John (Liptrott) (b. Liverpool, 12. X. 1809; d. Margate, 20. IX. 1886), Eng. comp. He was almost wholly self-taught in mus. In 1832 he settled in London, in 1842 became attached to Drury Lane Theatre as comp. and in 1844 visited Vienna to prod. his opera *Pascal Bruno.* In 1848 he went to U.S.A. and later became mus. director of the Prince's Theatre in London, where he wrote much incid. mus. for Kean's prods.

Works incl. operas *Pascal Bruno* and *Rose, or Love's Ransom*, operetta *The Queen of the Thames*; incid. mus. for Shakespeare's *Macbeth, Henry VIII, Richard II, King Lear, The Merchant of Venice* and *Much Ado About Nothing*, Sheridan's *Pizarro*, an adaptation of Goethe's *Faust* and other plays; Mass, 2 services, 8 anthems; oratorio *Hezekiah*; cantata *Robin Hood*; over 150 songs, incl. *To Anthea* (Herrick); many part-songs, etc.

Haubenstock-Ramati, Roman (b. Cracow, 27. II. 1919), Pol., later Israeli, comp. Studied comp. in Cracow and Lwow from 1937 to 1940. From 1947 to 1950 he was mus. director of Radio Cracow and then emigrated to Israel, where he became director of the mus. library in Tel-Aviv. In 1957 he moved to Paris, living also in Vienna, where he worked for the Universal Edition. His early works are conservative in idiom, but his mature mus. uses serial and experimental techniques.

Works incl. opera *Ameri ka* (after) Kafka; *La Symphonie des timbres* for orch.; *Vermutungen über ein dunkles Haus* for 3 orchs.; *Papageno's Pocket-size Concerto* for glockenspiel and orch.; *Recitativo and Aria* for cembalo and orch.; *Sequences* for vln. and orch.; *Petite Musique de nuit*, mobile for orch.; *Blessings* for voice and 9 players; *Mobile for Shakespeare* for voice and 6 players; *Jeux* for 6 perc. groups; *Interpolation*, mobile for solo fl.; *Ricercari* for string trio.

Hauch, Johannes Carsten (1790–1872), Dan. poet and dramatist. *See* Heise (*Marsk Stig*).

Hauer, Josef (Matthias) (b. Wiener-Neustadt, 19. III. 1883; d. Vienna, 22. IX. 1959), Aus. comp. Pub. a series of pamphlets on comp. according to a 12-note system of his own, different from that of Schönberg, his mus. material being based on groups of notes he called *Tropen*, derived from the combinations of the 12 notes of the chromatic scale allowed by the agreement of their overtones.

Works (all based on this system) incl. opera *Salammbô* (after Flaubert); play with mus. *Die schwarze Spinne* (after Jeremias Gotthelf); Mass for chorus, org. and orch.; cantata *Wandlungen*; mus. for Aeschylus's *Prometheus Bound* and tragedies by Sophocles: *Vom Leben*, recitation with singing voices and chamber orch. for broadcasting; Sinfonietta, 8 suites, 7 Dance Fantasies, Concert Piece, *Apocalyptic Fantasy, Kyrie*, etc. for orch.; symph. for strings, harmonium and pf.; vln. concerto, pf. concerto; 6 string 4tets, 5tet for clar., vln., vla., cello and pf.; many pf. pieces incl. 2 sets of Studies and pieces on Hölderlin titles; *c.* 87 *Zwölftonspiele* for

different instruments and instrumental combinations; 6 song-cycles to poems by Hölderlin and other songs, etc.

Haug, Hans (b. Basle, 27. VII. 1900; d. Lausanne, 15. IX. 1967), Swiss cond. and comp. Studied at Basle and Munich and became orch. and chorus cond. of var. Swiss towns and prof. at the Lausanne Cons.

Works incl. operas *Don Juan in der Fremde, Madrisa, Tartuffe* (after Molière), *E liederlieg Kleeblatt* (in Swiss dialect), *Ariadne*; Te Deum; oratorio *Michelangelo*; symph. and other orchestral works; vln. concerto, pf. concerto; chamber mus., incl. 3 string 4tets; part-songs, arrs. of Swiss folksongs, songs with pf.; film and radio mus., etc.

Hauk, Minnie (orig. Mignon) (b. N.Y., 16. XI. 1851; d. Triebschen, Lucerne, 6. II. 1929), Amer. mezzo-soprano of Ger. descent. Made her 1st stage appearance at Brooklyn in 1866 and her Eur. début in London, at Covent Garden, in 1868.

Haunted Tower, The, opera by Storace (lib. by James Cobb), prod. London, Drury Lane Theatre, 24. XI. 1789.

Hauptmann, Gerhart (1862–1946), Ger. dramatist. *See* Bath (*Hannele*), Graener (*Hanneles Himmelfahrt*), Grosz (*Versunkene Glocke*), Krehl (*Hannele*), Lendvai (*Elga*), Tcherepnin (A.) (*Hannele*), Ullrich (*Hanneles H.*), Unger (H.) (*Hannele*), Versunkene Glocke (Respighi and Zöllner), Weisberg (*Rautendelein*), Zilcher (*Goldene Harfe*).

Hauptmann, Moritz (b. Dresden, 13. X. 1792; d. Leipzig, 3. I. 1868), Ger. theorist, writer on mus. and comp. Studied at Dresden and began to work there, lived in Rus. in 1815–19, played vln. in Spohr's orch. at Cassel from 1822 and was cantor at St. Thomas's Church in Leipzig from 1842 to his death. Wrote on acoustics, harmony, fugue, etc.

Works incl. opera *Mathilde*; 2 Masses, motets and psalms; choruses and part-songs; 3 sonatas for vln. and pf., vln. duets; songs, etc.

Hausegger, Siegmund von (b. Graz, 16. VIII. 1872; d. Munich, 10. X. 1948), Aus. cond. and comp. Studied under his father, a Wagnerian critic, and others. After cond. at Graz, he shared the conductorship of the Kaim Orch. at Munich with Weingartner. Later in charge of concerts at Frankfurt, Glasgow and Edinburgh (Scot. Orch.) and Hamburg, and at Munich again in 1920–38.

Works incl. opera *Zinnober*; *Barbarossa* and *Natursinfonie, Dionysische Phantasie, Wieland der Schmied* and *Aufklänge* for orch.; Mass and Requiem; choral works, part-songs, etc.

Hauser, Franz (b. Krasovice nr. Prague, 12. I. 1794; d. Freiburg i/B., 14. VIII. 1870), Boh.-Ger. baritone. Pupil of Tomašek and successful opera singer until 1837, when he began to teach in Vienna. In 1846 he became director of the Munich Cons.

Hauser, Miska (b. Pozsony, 1822; d. Vienna, 9. XII. 1887), Hung. violinist. He studied in Vienna and made his 1st appearance on a tour undertaken at the age of 12. Travelled much and wrote *Lieder ohne Worte* for vln.

Hausmann, Robert (b. Rottleberode, Harz, 13. VIII. 1852; d. Vienna, 18. I. 1909), Ger. cellist. Studied at the Hochschule für Musik in Berlin and with Piatti in London and It. He joined the Joachim 4tet in 1879.

Haussman, Valentin (b. ?; d. c. 1612), Ger. 16th–17th cent. organist and comp. He was organist and town councillor at Gerbstädt nr. Merseburg. Ed. vocal pieces by Marenzio, Vecchi, Gastoldi and Morley with Ger. words.

Works incl. Ger. secular songs for 4–8 voices, instrumental dances, incl. *Venusgarten* containing 100 dances, mostly Pol., etc.

Hautboy (from Fr. *hautbois* = lit. 'loud wood'), the old Eng. name for the ob., sometimes spelt 'hoboy'. Also an 8-ft. reed org. stop reprod. the tone of the ob.

Haute-contre (Fr.), alto or high tenor, whether voice or instrument. Hence one of the old names for the alto or tenor viol and the vla.

Hawaiian Guitar. *See* Ukelele.

Hawkins, John (b. London, 30. III. 1719; d. London, 21. V. 1789), Eng. mus. hist. Devoted at first to architecture and then to law, he gradually became interested in lit. and mus. Having married a wealthy wife in 1753, he was able to retire and to undertake, in addition to minor works, his *General History of the Science and Practice o, Music*, pub. in 5 vols. in 1776, the same year as the 1st vol. of Burney's similar work. Knighted in 1772.

Hawley, Stanley (b. Ilkeston, 17. V. 1867; d. Ilkeston, 13. VI. 1916), Eng. pianist and comp. Studied at the R.A.M. in London and later became hon. sec. to the Phil. Society.

Works incl. mus. for Poe's *The Bells, The Raven* and other pieces for recitation with accomp., etc.

Hawte, William (b. Canterbury, c. 1435; d. ? Canterbury, before 1498), Eng. comp. Wrote 4 settings of the *Benedicamus Domino* (Cambridge, Magdalene Coll., Pepys MS. 1236) and a processional antiphon, *Stella caeli*.

Hawthorne, Nathaniel (1804–64), Amer. novelist. *See* Hanson (*Merry Mount*), **Scarlet Letter** (W. Damrosch).

Hay (Country Dance). *See* **Hey.**

Haydn, Franz Joseph (b. Rohrau, Lower Aus., 31. III. 1732; d. Vienna, 31. V. 1809), Aus. comp. Son of a wheelwright, he went at the age of 8 as a chorister to St. Stephen's Cathedral in Vienna under Georg Reutter (jun.). On leaving the choirschool c. 1749 he lived at first as a freelance, playing vln. and org., teaching, etc. He was for a time pupil-manservant to Porpora, but in comp. he was largely self-taught, studying the works of C. P. E. Bach, Fux's *Gradus ad Parnassum*, etc. From these years date his earliest comps., esp. church mus., incl. 2 Masses. His first string 4tets were written c. 1755 for Baron Fürnberg, through whom he obtained the post of mus. director to Count Morzin in 1759. The next year he contracted what was to prove an unfortunate marriage, and in 1761 entered the service of the Esterházy family, in 1766 succeeding Franz Gregor Werner as *Kapellmeister*, a post he held for the rest of his life. At Esterház, the magnificent palace in the Hung. marshes completed in 1766, where the household now spent the greater part of the year, H. was responsible for all the mus. entertainment, and there wrote the majority of his instrumental mus. and operas. Though he was isolated in Esterház, his fame spread; his works were pub. abroad, and he received invitations to travel, which, however, his duties obliged him to refuse. In 1786 he was commissioned to comp. 6 symphs. for the Concert de la Loge Olympique in Paris.

On the death of Prince Nicolaus in 1790 the Esterházy musicians were disbanded and H., though retaining his title and salary, was free to accept an invitation from the violinist and impresario J. P. Salomon to go to Eng. His first visit to London, 1791–2, for which he comp. an opera (never prod.) and 6 symphs., was a great success, and was followed by another in 1794–5, for which a further 6 symphs. were written. In 1792 he received the honorary degree of D.Mus. at Oxford. On the accession of Prince Nicolaus II in 1795 the Esterházy mus. estab. was revived, but H.'s duties were light, chiefly involving the comp. of a Mass each year for the princess's name-day, and giving rise to the 6 great Masses of 1796–1802. Inspired by the works of Handel he had heard in London, he comp. *The Creation* (1798) and *The Seasons* (1801). From 1803 he comp. little, living in retirement in Vienna.

Works (many still unpub.) incl. over 20 operas, e.g. *Lo speziale, Le pescatrici, L'infedeltà delusa, L'incontro improviso, Il mondo della luna, La vera costanza, L'isola disabitata, La fedeltà premiata, Orlando Paladino, Armida, L'anima del filosofo* (*Orfeo*), etc.; incid. mus. to *Der Zerstreute* (after Regnard), *Alfred* (after Alexander Bicknell), etc.; oratorios *Il ritorno di Tobia, The Seven Last Words* (choral version, arr. 1796, of the orig. orchestral work), *The Creation, The Seasons;*

14 Masses (1 lost), *Stabat Mater*, settings of the *Te Deum, Salve Regina*, etc., and other church mus.; miscellaneous cantatas, etc.; 107 symphs. (1 lost) and *sinfonia concertante*; numerous concertos, incl. one each for cello and tpt., 2 for horn, etc.; *The Seven Last Words* (orig. orch. version comp. for Cadiz, 1784); 78 string 4tets (Op. 3, formerly attrib. to H., has been shown to be spurious), 31 piano trios, 125 baryton trios and other chamber mus.; 52 sonatas, 5 sets of variations, etc., for piano; solo songs, partsongs, arrs. of Scot. and Welsh folksongs, etc.

Haydn, (Johann) Michael (b. Rohrau, Lower Aus., 14. IX. 1737; d. Salzburg, 10. VIII. 1806), Aus. comp., brother of prec. Chorister at St. Stephen's Cathedral in Vienna under Reutter from *c.* 1745. App. *Kapellmeister* to the Archbishop of Grosswardein (Hung.) in 1757, and became *Konzertmeister* to the Archbishop of Salzburg in 1762, where he was cathedral organist from 1781. Apart from occasional visits to Vienna, he remained in Salzburg till his death, in 1801 refusing the post of vice-*Kapellmeister* (under his brother Joseph H.) to Prince Esterházy.

Works incl. 32 Masses, 2 Requiem Masses, 8 Ger. Masses, 6 *Te Deum* settings, 117 Graduals, 45 Offertories, 27 Holy Week Responsories, etc.; opera *Andromeda e Perseo*, Ger. *Singspiele* and other mus. for the stage, oratorios; cantatas; 46 symphs.; 5 concertos; 6 string 5tets; 9 string 4tets; keyboard mus., etc.

'Haydn' Quartets, the familiar name of Mozart's 6 string 4tets ded. to Haydn: G maj., K. 387 (1782), D min., K. 421 (1783), E♭ maj., K. 428 (1783), B♭ maj., K. 458 (1784), A maj., K. 464 (1785), C maj., K. 465 (1785).

'Haydn' Variations, a set of variations by Brahms for orch., Op. 56a, or for 2 pfs., Op. 56b, on a theme called the 'St. Anthony Chorale' from a Divertimento for wind instruments, attrib. formerly to Haydn, where it is also treated in variation form. 1st perf. of the orchestral version, Vienna, 2. XI. 1873.

Hayes, Catherine (b. Limerick, 25. X. 1825; d. London, 11. VIII. 1861), Ir. soprano. Studied under Antonio Sapio at Dublin, where she made her 1st appearance in 1840. Later she studied with García in Paris and Ronconi at Milan, where she sang at the Scala in 1845, after a début at Marseilles. After many successes in It. and Vienna, she 1st appeared in London in 1849.

Haym, Nicola Francesco (b. Rome, *c.* 1679; d. London, 11. VIII. 1729), It. cellist, librettist and comp. of Ger. descent. Went to London in 1702, and with Dieupart and Clayton was active in estab. It. opera there. From 1713 wrote several libretti for Handel,

also for Bononcini and Ariosti. His own works incl. a Lat. oratorio and a serenata, anthem *The Lord is King*, 2 sets of trio sonatas, etc.

Hayne van Ghizeghem (b. ?; d. ?), Flem. comp. Wrote many *chansons*, of which those published by Petrucci in his collection *Canti B* (1501), incl. 'De tous bien plaine', are the best known.

Hayward, Marjorie (Olive) (b. Greenwich, 14. VIII. 1885; d. London, 10. I. 1953), Eng. violinist. Studied with Sauret at the R.A.M. and with Ševčik in Prague (1903–6). In 1924 she became vln. prof. at the R.A.M. She led the Eng. String Quartet and the Virtuoso Quartet, also played in the Eng. Ensemble Pf. Quartet and the Kamaran Trio

Head, Michael (Dewar) (b. Eastbourne, 28. I. 1900), Eng. singer, pianist and comp. Gave up the study of mechanical engineering for mus., which he studied at the R.A.M. in London, incl. comp. under Corder. In 1927 he became pf. prof. there. He has given many song recitals and broadcasts, playing his own accomps., and toured widely in the Brit. Commonwealth.

Works incl., Tone Poem and Scherzo for orch.; *Jabberwocky* (Lewis Carroll) for chorus; pf. concerto; *c.* 60 songs incl. cycles *Songs of the Countryside* (W. H. Davies), *Over the Rim of the Moon*, part-songs, etc.

Heath, John (b. ?; d. ?), Eng. 16th-cent. comp. His morning and communion services were printed by John Day (1560), but had already been in use in Edwardian times (*c.* 1548). There is also an anthem and a part-song, and a keyboard piece in the Mulliner Book (*q.v.*) is almost certainly his. He is not to be confused with his namesake of Rochester (d. 1668), possibly his grandson, who wrote Eng. church mus.

Heather, William. *See* **Heyther.**

Hebbel, (Christian) Friedrich (1813–1863), Ger. poet and dramatist, *See* d'Albert (*Rubin*), Durey (*Judith*), Ettinger (do.), Genoveva (Schumann), Holofernes (Rezniček), Judith (N. Berg), Lassen (*Nibelungen*), Mottl (*Agnes Bernauer*), Rathaus (*Herodes und Mariamne*), Schillings (*Moloch*), Schoeck (songs), Stephan (*Liebeszauber*).

Hebenstreit, Pantaleon (b. Eisleben, 1667; d. Dresden, 15. XI. 1750), Ger. dulcimer player. At 1st a violinist and dancing-master at Leipzig, he made his name as a virtuoso on the dulcimer towards the end of the 17th cent. and had such a success in Paris in 1705 that Louis XIV named his instrument after him, and it was long called 'Pantaleon'. In 1714 it was intro. into the court band at Dresden, with him as player.

'Hebrides' Overture (Mendelssohn). *See* **Fingal's Cave.**

Heckel, Wolff (b. Munich, c. 1515; d. ?), Ger. lutenist and comp. His lute-book (incl. some pieces for 2 lutes) was pub. in 1556 at Strasbourg.

Heckelclarina, the name of a special instrument created by the firm of Heckel at Biberich for the playing of the shepherd's pipe part in Act III of Wagner's *Tristan*.

Heckelphone, a double-reed instrument invented by the Ger. instrument maker Heckel. The standard type has a compass an 8ve lower than the ob. There are also smaller members of the family.

Heding (or Hedine), Jacques de (b. Picardy, ?; d. ?, c. 1270), Fr. troubadour, 2 of whose songs are preserved.

Hedley, Arthur (b. Newcastle-on-Tyne, 12. XI. 1905; d. Birmingham, 8. XI. 1969), Eng. writer on mus. Studied at Durham Univ. (Armstrong Coll., now Newcastle Univ.), 1st-class honours in Fr. and mus. with W. G. Whittaker, later at the Sorbonne in Paris, where he joined the Chopin Society. He learnt Pol., visited Warsaw in 1936, made special studies in Chopin and in 1946 became Eng. correspondent of the Chopin Inst. at Warsaw. Author of a book on Chopin.

Hedy (*Haidée*), opera by Fibich (lib. by Anežka Schulzová, based on an episode in Byron's *Don Juan*), prod. Prague, Cz. Theatre, 12. II. 1896.

Hegar, Friedrich (b. Basle, 11. X. 1841; d. Zürich, 2. VI. 1927), Swiss cond. and comp. Studied at Zürich and at the Leipzig Cons. After working in Pol. and Alsace, he went to Zürich, where he did much useful work as concert, operatic and esp. choral cond., and was given an hon. doctor's degree by the univ. in 1885.

Works incl. numerous choral works with and without solo voices or orch., many for male voices; vln. concerto, cello concerto; string 4tet; vln. and pf. sonata; pf. pieces; songs, etc.

Hegedüs, Ferencz (b. Pécs, 26. II. 1881; d. London, 12. XII. 1944), Hung. violinist. Pupil of Hubay and others at the Budapest Cons. Began to tour Eur. in 1901, 1st visiting Eng. Later he lived at Zürich.

Heger, Robert (b. Strasbourg, 19. VIII. 1886), Ger. cond. and comp. Studied at Zürich and Munich, Schillings being his chief master. He has cond. opera in many Ger. cities, also in Vienna and London.

Works incl. operas *Ein Fest zu Haderslev*, *Der Bettler Namenlos* (from Homer's *Odyssey*), *Der verlorene Sohn*; melodrama *Die Jüdin von Worms*; *Ein Friedenslied* for solo voices, chorus, orch. and org.; 3 symphs., symph. poem *Hero und Leander*; vln. concerto in D maj.; pf. Trio, etc.

Heiberg, Johan Ludvig (1791–1860), Dan. critic and poet. *See* **Delius** (*Folkeraadet*), **Kuhlau** (*Elverhoj*).

Heifetz, Jascha (b. Vilna, 2. II. 1901),

Rus.-Amer. violinist. First played in public aged 5, having learned from his father, and at the age of 6 played the Mendelssohn concerto. In 1910 he entered the St. Petersburg Cons., soon becoming a pupil of Auer. In 1912 he played in Berlin with great success. After the Revolution of 1917 he went to Amer. His perfect technical mastery, allied with fine musicianship, make him one of the outstanding violinists of the cent.

Heiller, Anton (b. Vienna, 15. IV. 1923), Aust. comp. and organist. After studying org. and comp. privately, he entered the Vienna Cons. from 1941 to 1942. In 1945 he was app. prof. of org. at the Vienna Acad. of Mus. In 1952 he won 1st prize at an international org. competition in Haarlem, Hol.

Works incl. *Symphonie Nordique*; *Psalmen-Kantate*; *Te Deum*; 5 Masses; *Tentatio Jesu* for soloists, chorus and 2 pfs.; toccata for 2 pfs.; much org. mus., etc.

Heimchen am Herd, Das (*The Cricket on the Hearth*), opera by Goldmark (lib. by Alfred Maria Willner, based on Dickens's story), prod. Vienna, Opera, 21. III. 1896.

Heimkehr aus der Fremde, Die (*The Return from Abroad*, better known as *Son and Stranger*), operetta by Mendelssohn (lib. by Karl Klingemann), prod. Leipzig, 10. IV. 1851.

Heine, Heinrich (1797–1856), Ger. poet. *See* **Brian** (*Pilgrimage to Kevlaar*), **Dichterliebe** (Schumann), **Dieren (van)** (songs), **Fliegende Holländer** (Wagner), **Giselle** (Adam), **Guglielmo Ratcliff** (Mascagni), **Humperdinck** (*Wallfahrt nach Kevlaar*), **Jirák** (*Tragi-Comedy*), **Klose** (*Wallfahrt nach K.*), **Leroux** (*William Ratcliff*), **Lesur** (songs with string 4tet), **Medtner** (songs), **Meyer-Helmund** (*Heines Traumbilder*), **Ratcliff** (Andreae), **Schoeck** (songs), **Schumann** (*Liederkreis*), **Schwanengesang** (Schubert), **Shebalin** (songs), **Shtcherbatchev (N. V.)** (songs), **Silcher** (*Loreley*), **Stanford** (*Wallfahrt nach K.*), **Stucken** (*Wm. Ratcliff*), **Vavrinecz** (do.), **White (M. V.)** (5tet *Du bist wie eine Blume* and songs), **William Ratcliff** (operas, Cui, Dopper and Pizzi).

6 songs by Brahms, 6 by Schubert, 39 by Schumann.

Heinichen, Johann David (b. Krössuln nr. Weissenfels, 17. IV. 1683; d. Dresden, 16. VII. 1729), Ger. comp. and theorist. Pupil of Schelle and Kuhnau in Leipzig, first practised as a lawyer in Weissenfels, but in 1709 returned to Leipzig, as an opera comp. The following year he went to It. to study, remaining there till 1716. In 1717 app. *Kapellmeister* to the Elector of Saxony in Dresden, where he lived till his death. Wrote 2 important treatises on figured bass.

Works incl. operas, numerous Masses, motets and other church works, cantatas, symphs., orchestral suites, solo and trio sonatas, etc.

Heinlen, Paul (b. Nuremberg, 11. IV. 1626; d. Nuremberg, 6. VIII. 1686), Ger. organist, wind player and comp. Studied with a town musician at Nuremberg and in 1646–9 in It. App. to var. Nuremberg churches in 1655–8, finishing as organist at St. Sebald's Cathedral. Wrote church mus. and set many sacred poems by contemporary authors.

Heinrich von Meissen. *See* Frauenlob.

Heinrich von Müglin (b. ?; d. ?), Ger. 14th-cent. song comp.

Heise, Peter Arnold (b. Copenhagen, 11. II. 1830; d. Ny Taarback, 12. IX. 1879), Dan. comp. Pupil of Berggreen at Copenhagen and Hauptmann at Leipzig.

Works incl. *Paschaens Datter* and *Drot og Marsk*; incid. mus. for many plays, incl. Oehlenschläger's *Palnatoke* and Hauch's *Marsk Stig*; *Rusk Cantata* and cantata *Tornerose (Sleeping Beauty)*; symph.; pf. trio; numerous songs, etc.

Hekking, André (b. Bordeaux, 30. VII. 1866; d. Paris, 15. XII. 1925), Fr. cellist. Pupil of his uncle Charles H. Began his concert career with a tour in Spain, settled in Paris in 1909 and in 1919 became prof. of cello at the Cons.

Heldenleben, Ein (*A Hero's Life*), symph. poem by R. Strauss, comp. VIII.–XII. 1898, 1st perf. Frankfurt, 3. III. 1899. The work is autobiographical.

Heldentenor (Ger. = heroic tenor), one of the Ger. categories of operatic voices: a tenor capable of sustaining parts of a heroic as distinct from lyrical type; equivalent to the It. *tenore robusto*.

Hèle, Georges de la. *See* La Hèle.

Helicon, a brass wind instrument playing the bass in military bands, similar to the Bombardon, but made in a circular form so that it may be carried over the player's shoulder when marching.

Heliodorus (?–?), Gk. author. *See* Desmarets (*Théagène et Chariclée*).

Heller, Stephen (b. Pest, 15. V. 1813 or 1814; d. Paris, 14. I. 1888), Hung. pianist and comp. Studied with Anton Halm in Vienna and made his 1st public appearance at Pest in his teens and later went on tour in Ger. He lived at Augsburg in 1830–8 after a long illness, working quietly at comp., and settled in Paris in 1838. He visited Eng. in 1850 and 1862.

Works (nearly all for pf.) incl. 4 sonatas, a very large number of studies, variations and fantasies on operatic tunes, 5 Tarantellas, Caprice on Schubert's *Trout*, several sets entitled *Im Walde, Promenades d'un solitaire* (after Rousseau's letters on botany), *Blumen-, Frucht- und Dornenstücke* (after Jean Paul), *Dans le bois, Nuits blanches*, etc. With Ernst he wrote vln. and pf. pieces entitled *Pensées fugitives*.

Hellinck, Joannes Lupus (b. ? *c.* 1496; d. Bruges, I. 1541), Flem. comp., (?) choirmaster at Cambrai and Bruges at different times.

Works incl. Masses, motets; Ger. sacred songs; Fr. *chansons*, etc.

Hellmesberger. Aus. family of musicians:

1. **Georg H.** (b. Vienna, 24. IV. 1800; d. Neuwaldegg, 16. VIII. 1873), violinist, cond. and comp. Studied in Vienna and became in 1821 asst. teacher and in 1833 prof. of the vln. at the Cons. In 1829 he was app. cond. of the court Opera. Wrote many works for his instrument.

2. **Joseph H.** (b. Vienna, 23. XI. 1828; d. Vienna, 24. X. 1893), violinist and cond., son of prec. Pupil of his father. Appeared as an infant prodigy and was app. vln. prof. at the Cons. in 1851, and cond. of the Gesellschaft concerts. He resigned the latter post to Herbeck in 1859, but retained that of director of the Cons. He also held posts at the Opera and the court concerts, and led a string 4tet from 1849 to 1887.

3. **Georg H.** (b. Vienna, 27. I. 1830; d. Hanover, 12. XI. 1852), violinist and comp., brother of prec. Studied with his father and toured with him and his brother Joseph in Ger. and Eng. In 1850 he was app. leader of the opera orch. at Hanover, where he wrote the operas *Die Bürgschaft* (after Schiller, not prod.) and *Die beiden Königinnen*.

4. **Joseph H.** (b. Vienna, 9. IV. 1855; d. Vienna, 26. IV. 1907), violinist and comp., son of 2. Pupil of his father, in whose 4tet he played 2nd vln. until 1887, when he succeeded him as leader. Solo violinist at the Opera and court chapel and vln. prof. at the Cons. from 1878. App. court *Kapellmeister* in 1890.

Works incl. 22 operettas and 6 ballets.

Helmholtz, Hermann (Ludwig Ferdinand) von (b. Potsdam, 31. VIII. 1821; d. Berlin, 8. IX. 1894), Ger. scientist. After holding 3 professorships in physiology he turned to physics, of which he became prof. at Berlin Univ. in 1871. He specialized in acoustics and in 1863 pub. his *Lehre von den Tonempfindungen als physiologische Grundlage für die Theorie der Musik.*

Hely-Hutchinson, (Christian) Victor (b. Cape Town, 26. XII. 1901; d. London, 11. III. 1947), Eng. pianist and comp. Educ. at Eton and Balliol Coll., Oxford, and became lecturer in mus. at Cape Town Univ. in 1922. In 1926 he returned to Eng. and joined the staff of the B.B.C. 1st in London and then as regional director of mus. at Birmingham, where he became prof. of mus. at the univ. in 1934. He resigned in 1944 to take up the app. of mus. director of the B.B.C.

Works incl. *A Carol Symph.* and variations for orch.; pf. 5tet, string 4tet;

choral works; songs, incl. settings of Edward Lear; film mus., etc.

Hemans (*née* **Browne**), **Felicia Dorothea** (1793–1835), Eng. poetess. *See* **Jensen** (songs).

Heming, Percy (b. Bristol, 6. IX. 1887; d. London, 11. I. 1956), Eng. baritone. Studied at the R.A.M. in London and early began to specialize in opera. He sang a great variety of parts with great distinction.

Hemiolia (or **Hemiola**) (Gk. lit. the proportion 3 : 2), a change of rhythm effected by the substitution of 3 beats where 2 would be normal, e.g. by writing 3 minims instead of 2 dotted minims in a bar of 6–4, or over 2 bars of 3–4.

Hemmel, Sigmund (b. ?; d. 1564), Ger. comp. He comp. the first complete polyphonic metrical psalter in Ger. (pub. Tübingen, 1569). He also wrote Ger. and Lat. sacred songs, and a Mass.

Hempel, Frieda (b. Leipzig, 26. VI. 1885; d. 7. X. 1955), Ger. soprano. Studied at the Cons. of Leipzig and Berlin, and made her 1st appearance at the Berlin Royal Opera in 1905. She won worldwide fame and after her 1st appearance in N.Y. she settled in U.S.A.

'Hen' Symphony (Haydn). *See* **Poule**.

Henderson, W(illiam). J(ames). (b. Newark, N.J., 4. XII. 1855; d. N.Y., 5. VI. 1937), Amer. mus. critic. After some general journalistic work he became mus. critic to the *N.Y. Times* in 1887 and the *N.Y. Sun* in 1902. In 1904 he was app. lecturer at the Inst. of Mus. Art in N.Y. His books incl. studies of the hist. and practice of singing, aesthetics, the evolution of mus., Wagner, early It. opera, etc.

Henkemans, Hans (b. The Hague, 23. XII. 1913), Dutch comp. and pianist. Studied pf. with Sigtenhorst-Meyer and comp. with Pijper. Made his début, aged 19, in his own pf. concerto. He later studied medicine and for some time practised as a psychiatrist, before devoting himself entirely to mus.

Works inc. symph.; 2 pf. concertos; concertos for fl., vln., vla., harp; 3 string 4tets; sonatas for cello, vln., 2 pfs.

Henley, W(illiam). E(rnest). (1849–1903), Eng. poet and critic. *See* **Stanford** (*Last Post*).

Henriques, Fini (Valdemar) (b. Copenhagen, 20 XII. 1867; d. Copenhagen, 27. X. 1940), Dan. violinist and comp. Among his masters were Joachim for vln. and Svendsen for comp. He played at the Dan. royal chapel and in the Copenhagen State Orch., where he was leader.

Works incl. several operas; ballets, e.g. *Den lille Havfrue*; incid. mus. for plays; 2 symphs., symph. poems; 2 string 4tets and other chamber mus.; vln. and pf. sonata in G min.; pf. pieces; songs, etc.

Henry IV (b. Bolingbroke Castle, 3. IV.

1367; d. Westminster, 20. III. 1413), King of Eng., 1399–1413. He is a more likely candidate than his son Henry V as comp. of the pieces ascribed to 'Roy Henry' in the Old Hall MS. (*q.v.*).

Henry V (b. Monmouth, VIII. 1387; d. Bois de Vincennes, 31. VIII. 1422), King of Eng., 1413–22. *See* **Henry IV**.

Henry VIII (b. Greenwich, 28. VI. 1491; d. Windsor, 28. I. 1547), King of Eng., 1509–47. He comp. or arr. several songs found in a MS. (Brit. Mus., Add. 31,922) dating from his reign, and a 3-part motet *Quam pulchra es*.

Henry VIII, opera by Saint-Saëns (lib. by Léonce Détroyat and Paul Armand Silvestre, based on Shakespeare), prod. Paris, Opéra, 5. III. 1883.

Henschel, (Isidor) Georg (later **George**) (b. Breslau, 18. II. 1850; d. Aviemore, Inverness, 10. IX. 1934), Ger. (naturalized Brit). baritone, cond., pianist and comp. Appeared as pianist in Berlin in 1862 and at Hirschberg as singer in 1866. After studying at the Leipzig and Berlin Conss. he appeared at the Lower Rhine Festival in 1874 and for the 1st time in Eng. in 1877. He remained there until 1881, when he married the Amer. soprano Lillian Bailey and became cond. of the new Boston Symph. Orch. In 1884 he settled in London and organized var. orchestral and choral concerts, also cond., the Scot. Orch. in 1893–5. His wife d. in 1901 and he married Amy Louis in 1907. He sang again, in Eng. and on the Continent, often accompanying himself, until he gave his last recital in London in 1914, when he was knighted.

Works incl. operas *Friedrich der Schöne* and *Nubia*; operetta *A Sea Change*; incid. mus. for Shakespeare's *Hamlet*; Eng. Mass for 8 voices, Te Deum, Stabat Mater, Requiem, Psalm cxxx, anthems; Festival March for orch.; Ballade for vln. and orch.; string 4tet in B♭ maj.; many pf. works; numerous songs (some with orch.) incl. 2 cycles from Scheffel's *Trompeter von Säckingen*, 4 poems by Hafiz, 3 songs from Kingsley's *Water Babies*, ballad *Young Dietrich*; *Serbisches Liederspiel* for 1–4 voices; 5 vocal 4tets to poems from Rus.; part-songs, etc.

Hensel (*née* **Mendelssohn-Bartholdy**), **Fanny (Cécile)** (b. Hamburg, 14. XI. 1805; d. Berlin, 17. V. 1847), Ger. pianist and amateur comp., elder sister of Mendelssohn, with whom she was brought up musically. She married the painter Wilhelm Hensel in 1829.

Works incl. pf. trio; 4 books of pf. pieces; 2 of songs; part-songs *Gartenlieder*, etc. (6 of her songs were pub. as her brother's.)

Henselt, Adolf von (b. Schwabach, Bavar., 9. V. 1814; d. Warmbrunn, Silesia, 10. X. 1889), Ger. pianist and comp. Pupil of Hummel at Weimar and Sechter in

Henze

Vienna. He toured Ger. in 1836 and settled in St. Petersburg in 1838. He was app. court pianist and teacher to the Tsar's children.

Works incl. pf. concerto in F min.; pf. trio; much pf. solo mus., comprising 2 sets of Studies (e.g. *Si oiseau j'étais*), *Frühlingslied*, *Wiegenlied*, impromptu in C min., *La Gondola*, etc.; transcriptions of Cramer, Weber, etc.

Henze, Hans Werner (b. Gütersloh, 1. VII. 1926), Ger. comp. Studied with Fortner at Heidelberg and Leibowitz in Paris. He is influenced by Schönberg, though not strictly a 12-note comp., and has also done much to further the ballet in Ger.; in 1950–2 he was ballet adviser to the Wiesbaden Opera.

Works incl. operas *Das Wundertheater* (after Cervantes), *Boulevard Solitude* (after Prévost's *Manon Lescaut*), *Der Prinz von Homburg*, *Elegy for Young Lovers*, *Der junge Lord* (after Hauff), *Die Bassariden*; ballets *Jack Pudding*, *Variations*, *Rosa Silber* and *Ondine*; oratorio *Das Floss der Medusa*; cantata *Novae de infinito Laudes*; *Cantata della Fiaba Estrema*; 6 symphs.; vln. and pf. concertos, string 4tet, chamber cantata (Whitman); vln. and fl. sonatas; pf. sonata and variations, etc.

Heptachord (from Gk.), a scale of 7 notes.

Her Foster-Daughter (*Jeji Pastorkyna*; also called *Jenufa*), opera by Janáček (lib. by comp., based on a story by Gabriela Preissová), prod. Brno, 21. I. 1904.

Herbeck, Johann (Franz) von (b. Vienna, 25. XII. 1831; d. Vienna, 28. X. 1877), Aus. cond. and comp. Lived in Vienna; app. cond. of the Gesellschaft concerts in 1859 and director of the Court Opera in 1871.

Works incl. 2 Masses; symph. in D min., symph. variations and other orch. mus.; 2 string 4tets; songs, part-songs, etc.

Herbert, A(lan). P(atrick). (b. 1890), Eng. author and statesman. *See* **Arundell** (*King of the Castle*), **Dunhill** (*Tantivy Towers*), **Gibbs** (C. A.) (*Blue Peter*), **Tate** (*Policeman's Serenade*), **Toye** (G.) (*Red Pen*).

Herbert, George (1593–1633), Eng. poet. *See* **Vaughan Williams** (*5 Mystical Songs*).

Herbert, Victor (b. Dublin, 1. II. 1859; d. N.Y., 26. V. 1924), Ir.-Amer. cellist, cond. and comp. Studied in Ger. and toured Eur.; settled in N.Y. in 1886. Director of the Pittsburgh Symph. Orch., 1898–1904.

Works incl. operas *Natoma* and *Madeleine*, operettas *The Wizard of the Nile*, *Babes in Toyland* and over 30 others; cantata *The Captive*; symph. poem *Hero and Leander* and 3 suites for orch.; Serenade for string; songs, etc.

Herbst, Johann Andreas (b. Nuremberg,

Hero's Life

9. VI. 1588; d. Frankfurt, 26. I. 1666), Ger. comp. He was *Kapellmeister* at var. places, incl. Darmstadt, Nuremberg and Frankfurt. Pub. 4 theoret. works.

Works incl. Ger. and Lat. madrigals; motets; settings of hymn-tunes, etc.

Hercules, secular oratorio by Handel (lib. by Thomas Broughton), prod. London, King's Theatre, Haymarket, 5. I. 1745.

Herder, Johann Gottfried von (1744–1803), Ger. philos., philologist and author. *See* **Bach** (J. C. F.) (*Brutus*, oratorios and cantatas), **Jensen** (*Stimmen der Völker*), **Prometheus** (Liszt), **Reichardt** (*Morning Hymn*), **Schröter** (C.) (songs), **Wolf** (E. W.) (*Easter Cantata*).

Heredia, Pedro de (b. ?; d. Rome, 1648), It. comp. of Span. descent. Choirmaster at Vercelli in his early days and later in the service of the Vatican.

Works incl. Masses, motets; a madrigal, etc.

Hereford Festival. *See* **Three Choirs Festival.**

Héritier, Jean l'. *See* **L'Héritier.**

Héritte-Viardot, Louise (Pauline Marie) (b. Paris, 14. XII. 1841; d. Heidelberg, 17. I. 1918), Fr. contralto, teacher and comp. Daughter of Louis V. and Pauline V.-García. Studied with her mother and later taught at St. Petersburg Cons., the Hoch Cons. at Frankfurt and in Berlin. She married the Fr. consul-general H. in 1862.

Hermann von Salzburg (b. ?; d. ?), 14th-cent. Aus. monk and comp. He belonged to the tradition of the *Minnesinger* but also wrote a few polyphonic pieces in a primitive style.

Hermannus Contractus (Hermann the Cripple) (b. Sulgen, 18. VII. 1013; d. Alleshausen nr. Biberach, 24. IX. 1054), Ger. mus. scholar and comp. Studied in Switz. at the monastery of Reichenau and became a Benedictine monk. Wrote mus. treatises and comp. hymns, sequences, etc.

Hermione, opera by Bruch (lib. by Emil Hopffer, based on Shakespeare's *Winter's Tale*), prod. Berlin, Opera, 21. III. 1872.

Hernried, Robert (b. Vienna, 22. IX. 1883; d. Detroit, 3. IX. 1951), Amer. scholar and comp. of Aus. birth. Studied in Vienna and after a career as opera cond. in 1908–14 he held var. teaching-posts and professorships in Ger. and U.S.A., whither he emigrated in 1934. In 1946 he was app. prof. at Detroit Univ. He wrote several books and over 300 articles.

Works incl. operas *Francesca da Rimini* (after Dante) and *The Peasant Woman*; Mass; over 60 choral works; concert overture for orch.; pieces for fl., vln. and horn and orch.; instrumental pieces with pf.; 58 songs, etc.

Hero and Leander. *See* **Ero e Leandro.**

Hero's Life (R. Strauss). *See* **Heldenleben.**

Hérodiade (*Herodias*), opera by Massenet (lib. by Paul Milliet and 'Henri Grémont' = Georges Hartmann, based on a story by Flaubert), prod. Brussels, Théâtre de la Monnaie, 19. XII. 1881.

Hérold, (Louis Joseph) Ferdinand (b. Paris, 28. I. 1791; d. Paris, 19. I. 1833), Fr. comp. Studied under his father, the pianist François Joseph H. (1755–1802), and later under Fétis, Louis Adam, Catel and Méhul, and took the Prix de Rome in 1812. In Rome and Naples, where he became pianist to Queen Caroline, he comp. several instrumental works, also a comic opera *La Jeunesse de Henri V*. Returning to Paris in 1816, he collaborated with Boïeldieu in *Charles de France* and in 1817 began to prod. operas of his own. He was accompanist at the Théâtre Italien from 1820 to 1827, when he married Adèle Élise Rollet and became choirmaster at the Opéra. About this time he began to suffer seriously from consumption, from which he d.

Works incl. operas *Les Rosières, La Clochette, Le Premier Venu, Les Troqueurs, L'Amour platonique, L'Auteur mort et vivant, Le Muletier, Lasthénie, Le Lapin blanc, Vendôme en Espagne* (with Auber), *Le Roi René, Marie, L'Illusion, Emmeline, L'Auberge d'Auray* (with Carafa), *Zampa, Le Pré aux Clercs, Ludovic* (unfinished, completed by Halévy); ballets *Astolphe et Joconde, Le Sonnambule, Lydie, La Fille mal gardée, La Belle au bois dormant* (after Perrault); incid. mus. for Ozaneaux's *Dernier Jour de Missolonghi*; 2 symphs.; cantata *Mlle. de la Vallière, Hymne sur la Transfiguration*; 3 string 4tets; 2 sonatas, variations, rondos, etc. for pf., etc.

Heroldt, Johannes (b. Jena, *c.* 1550; d. Weimar, IX. 1603), Ger. comp. His works incl. a setting of the St. Matthew Passion for 6 voices, pub. Graz, 1594.

Herrick, Robert (1591–1674), Eng. poet. *See* **Davies (Walford)** (*Noble Numbers*), **Horn (C. E.)** (*Cherry ripe*), **Hughes (G.)** (songs), **Lawes (H.)** (*Hesperides*), **Murrill** (songs), **Quilter** (*To Julia*), **White (M. V.)** (songs), **Williams (W.)** (do.).

Herrmann, Bernard (b. N.Y., 29. I. 1911), Amer. comp. and cond. After winning a comp. prize at the age of 13, he began studying with Phillip James at N.Y. Univ. and later at the Juilliard Graduate School of Mus. He then became a radio cond. with C.B.S., later living in Hollywood where he comp. many film scores.

Works incl. opera *Wuthering Heights*; cantatas *Moby Dick, Johnny Appleseed*; symph. poem *City of Brass*; *Fiddle Concerto*; symph.; string 4tet; film scores incl. *Citizen Kane*.

Herrmann, Hugo (b. Ravensburg, 19. IV. 1896; d. Stuttgart, 7. IX. 1967), Ger. organist and comp. Studied at Stuttgart and Berlin, Schreker being among his masters.

Organist at Ludwigsburg 1919–23, then at Detroit until 1925, when he left the U.S.A.,becoming choral cond. at Reutlingen and in 1930 at Weimar; organist again from 1931. Director of the Mus. School at Trossingen from 1935.

Works incl. opera *Vasantasena*, chamber opera *Das Gazellenhorn*, 2 school operas; oratorio *Jesus und seine Jünger* and several other choral works; 5 symphs., Concert Mus. I and II, etc., for orch.; vln. concerto; symph. for chamber orch.; 4 string 4tets, etc.

Hertoghs. *See* **Ducis.**

Hertz, Henrik (1797–1870), Dan. poet and dramatist. For works on *King René's Daughter see* **Arregui, Edwards (J.), Iolanta** (Tchaikovsky), **Smart (H.).**

Hertzka, Emil (b. Budapest, 3. VIII. 1869; d. Vienna 3. V. 1932), mus. pub. Studied chemistry at the Univ. of Vienna, and also mus. In 1901 he joined Universal Ed., founded that year, becoming director in 1907 until his death. He did great service to modern mus., pub. the work of such comps. as Bartók, Berg, Křenek, Schönberg, Webern, Weill and others. He also encouraged many other young comps.

Hervé (real name Florimond Ronger) (b. Houdain, Pas de Calais, 30. VI. 1825; d. Paris, 4. XI. 1892), Fr. comp. Studied mus. as a choir-boy, then with Elwart and Auber. Organist at var. Paris churches, incl. Saint-Eustache; later theatre manager, operetta singer, librettist, cond., etc.

Works incl. more than 80 operettas, e.g. *Don Quixote et Sancho Pança* (after Cervantes), *Le Hussard persécuté, La Fanfare de Saint-Cloud, Les Chevaliers de la Table Ronde, L'Œil crevé, Chilpéric, Le Petit Faust, Les Turcs* (parody of Racine's *Bajazet*), *La Belle Poule, Le Nouvel Aladin, Frivoli*; ballets *Dilara, Sport, La Rose d'Amour, Cléopâtre, Les Bagatelles*; symph. *The Ashanti War* for solo voices and orch.; many light songs, etc.

Hervelois. *See* **Caix d'Hervelois.**

Herz, Henri (Heinrich) (b. Vienna, 6. I. 1803; d. Paris, 5. I. 1888), Aus. pianist and comp. Pupil of his father and of Hünten, entered the Paris Cons. in 1816 and settled there, becoming a fashionable teacher. App. pf. prof. at the Cons. in 1842. Toured U.S.A., Mex. and the W. Indies in 1845–51, making a fortune with which to begin a pf. manufacture, and built a concert hall.

Works incl. 8 pf. concertos and some 200 works for pf. solo: variations, studies, fantasies, etc.

Herzogenberg, Heinrich von (Baron v. H.-Peccaduc) (b. Graz, 10. VI. 1843; d. Wiesbaden, 9. X. 1900), Aus. comp. and cond. Studied at the Vienna Cons. and settled at Leipzig in 1872. Cond. the Bach society there in 1875–85 and then became prof. of comp. at the Berlin Hochschule für Musik. Husband of Elisabeth von H. (1842–92), a fine amateur pianist and pupil of Brahms.

Works incl. Mass, Requiem, psalms; oratorios *Die Geburt Christi* and *Die Passion*, cantata *Columbus*; 2 symphs., symph. poem *Odysseus*; 5 string 4tets, 2 pf. trios, 2 string trios; 2 vln. and pf. sonatas, cello and pf. sonata; 2 sets of variations for 2 pfs., many pf. pieces and duets; fantasies for org.; songs, vocal duets, part-songs, etc.

Hesdin, Nicolle des Celliers d' (b. ?; d. Beauvais, 21. VIII. 1538), Fr. comp. He was a choir-boy at Beauvais Cathedral, but little more is known of him. He has been confused with Pierre H., singer in the Fr. Royal Chapel, 1547–59. He wrote 2 Masses and various motets and *chansons*.

Heseltine, Philip (Peter Warlock), (b. London, 30. X. 1894; d. London, 17. XII. 1930), Eng. musicologist and comp. who pub. under both names. Educ. at Eton, where he studied mus. in partic., and later influenced by Delius and van Dieren. Founded the *Sackbut*, a combative mus. paper, wrote numerous articles, ed. old Eng. mus., esp. of the lutenist school and pub. books on the Eng. ayre, Delius and (with Cecil Gray) Gesualdo.

For comps. *see* **Warlock.**

Hess, Myra (b. London 25. II. 1890; d. London 25. XI. 1965), Eng. pianist. Studied at the Royal Acad. of Mus. with Matthay, making her début in 1907 under Beecham in London. Her success was immediate and she toured widely. In 1941 she received the D.B.E. for her work in organizing the Nat. Gallery wartime concerts. She was especially noted for her playing of Mozart.

Hess, Willy (b. Mannheim, 14. VII. 1859; d. Berlin, 17. II. 1939), Ger. violinist. Studied with his father, a pupil of Spohr, was taken to U.S.A. as a child, played in T. Thomas's orch. there and made his 1st appearance as a soloist in Hol. in 1872. Later studied with Joachim in Berlin, became prof. at Rotterdam, leader of the Hallé Orch. at Manchester, and worked by turns at Cologne, London, Boston and Berlin.

Hesse, Adolf Friedrich (b. Breslau, 30. VIII. 1809; d. Breslau, 5. VIII. 1863), Ger. organist and comp. Studied org. and pf. at Breslau and was sent by the city authorities on a tour to play his own org. works. In 1831 he was app. organist to the church of the Bernhardins at Breslau, where he remained until his death, also cond. the symph. concerts. Wrote numerous org. works and much other mus., incl. oratorio *Tobias*; 6 symphs.; pf. concerto; 2 string 4tets, etc.

Hessenberg, Kurt (b. Frankfurt, 17. VIII. 1908), Ger. comp. Studied with Günther

Raphael at Leipzig and then taught comp. there. In 1933 he became prof. of comp. at Hoch's Cons. at Frankfurt.

Works incl. incid. mus. for Shakespeare's *Tempest*; cantata (Matthias Claudius) and other choral works; 3 symphs., *Concerto grosso*, etc for orch.; harpsichord and pf. concertos; 4 string 4tets, pf. 4tet; 2 vln. sonatas, cello sonata; pf. mus.; songs, etc.

Heterophony (from Gk. = other sound), the use of two parts to be simultaneously perf. in different versions, one more elaborate than the other .

Heuberger, Richard (Franz Josef) (b. Graz, 18. VI. 1850; d. Vienna, 28. X. 1914), Aus. mus. critic and comp. Studied engineering at first, but at the age of 26 devoted himself to mus., becoming a chor. cond. in 1878 and a critic in 1881.

Works incl. operas *Abenteuer einer Neujahrsnacht, Manuel Venegas, Miriam* (later *Das Maifest*), *Barfüssele*; operettas *Der Opernball, Ihre Excellenz, Der Sechsuhrzug, Das Baby, Der Fürst von Düsterstein, Don Quixote* (after Cervantes); ballets *Die Lautenschlägerin* and *Struwwelpeter*, etc.

Heugel, Johannes (Heigel, Hegel, etc.), (b. Degendorf, before 1500; d. Cassel, I. 1585), Ger. comp. He wrote numerous Lat. motets.

Heure espagnole, L' (*The Spanish Hour*), opera by Ravel (lib. by Franc-Nohain, based on his own comedy), prod. Paris, Opéra-Comique, 19. V. 1911.

Heward, Leslie (Hays) (b. Liversedge, Yorks, 8. XII. 1897; d. Birmingham, 3. V. 1943), Eng. cond. and comp. Began to learn mus. from his father, an organist, and became a chorister at Manchester Cathedral, having been discovered at the Morecambe Festival by Sydney H. Nicholson. In 1914 he was given an organist's post, but in 1917 he went as asst. mus. master to Eton, studying at the R.C.M. in London at the same time. He then taught at Westminster School, became theatre cond., and coach and occasional cond. with the B.N.O.C. on its tours. In 1924 he went to Cape Town as mus. director to the S. African Broadcasting Corporation and cond. of the Cape Town Orch., but returned to Eng. in 1927 and rejoined the B.N.O.C. In 1930 he succeeded Boult as cond. of the City of Birmingham Orch.

Works incl. opera on Ibsen's *Peer Gynt* (unfinished); mus. for film *The Loves of Robert Burns*; church mus.; *S. African Patrol, Revel, Quodlibet*, etc. for orch.; string 4tet in A min.; songs with orch. and with pf., part-songs, etc.

Hewlett, Maurice (1861–1923), Eng. novelist. *See* Křička (*Hypolita*).

Hexachord (from Gk. = six strings), a scale of 6 notes, which Guido d'Arezzo in the 11th cent. named Ut, Re, Mi, Fa, Sol, La. There were 3 hexachords, beginning respectively on G, C and F, and the same names were used for the notes of each. Since the hexachords overlapped every note after the first three could have 2 or more names:

Hexachordum durum:

Hexachordum naturale:

Hexachordum molle:

The G hexachord was called hard (*durum*), the C natural (*naturale*) and the F soft (*molle*). (*Durum* and *molle* are the origins of the Ger. words for major and minor.) *See* **Solmization.**

Hexachord Fantasy, a type of comp. cultivated partic. by 16th–17th-cent. Eng. comps., a piece based on the 1st 6 notes of the scale, ascending or descending. The pieces were often entitled 'Ut, re, mi, fa, sol, la'.

Hexameron, a collective pf. work, pub. in 1837, consisting of bravura variations on the march in Bellini's *Puritani* by Liszt, Thalberg, Pixis, Herz, Czerny and Chopin, with an intro., finale and connecting passages by Liszt.

Hey, an old country dance similar to the Reel and prob. to the Canarie.

Heyden, Sebald (b. Bruck, near Erlangen, 8. XII. 1499; d. Nuremberg, 9. VII. 1561), Ger. theologian and mus. theorist. He is particularly valuable for his explanations of the mus. notation of his time.

Heyns, Cornelius (b. ?; d. ?), Flem. 15th-cent. comp. He was succentor at St. Donatian in Bruges in 1452–3 and 1462–5. His Mass *Pour quelque paine* has also been attrib. to Okeghem.

Heyse, Paul (Johann Ludwig) (1830–1914), Ger. poet and novelist. *See* **Italienisches Liederbuch** (H. Wolf), **Jensen** (*Spanisches Liederbuch*). **Spanisches Liederbuch** (H. Wolf).

Heyther (Heather), William (b. Harmondsworth, *c.* 1563; d. ?, VII. 1627), Eng. singer, from 1586 to 1615 at Westminster Abbey and from 1615 in the Chapel Royal. He founded the chair of mus. at Oxford Univ. in Feb. 1627 and presented the Mus. School with instruments and mus.

Heywood, John (b. ? London, 1497; d. ? Mechlin, 1587), Eng. musician. He was player of the virginals' to Henry VIII,

succentor of St. Paul's Cathedral and a friend of Thomas Mulliner. He was also a playwright and may have collaborated with Redford in the prod. of mus. plays. After the death of Mary in 1558 he fled to Mechlin on account of his Catholicism.

Hiawatha, 3 cantatas for solo voices, chorus and orch. by Coleridge-Taylor, a setting of parts of Longfellow's poem: I. *Hiawatha's Wedding Feast*, II. *The Death of Minnehaha*, III. *Hiawatha's Departure*, 1st perf. as a whole, London, 22. III. 1900.

Hichens, Robert (Smythe) (1864–1950), Eng. novelist. *See* **Ronald** (*Garden of Allah*).

Hidalgo, Juan (b. ?; d. Madrid, 1685), Span. 17th-cent. comp. Harpist in the royal chapel at Madrid. Said to have invented an instrument called the *claviharpa*.

Works incl. operas *Celos aun del aire matan* (lib. by Calderón) and *Los celos hacen estrellas* (lib. by Guevara); incid. mus. to var. plays by Calderón incl. *Ni Amor se libra de Amor*, etc.

Hidden Fifths
Hidden Octaves } the movement of 2 parts in the same direction to a 5th or an 8ve. Such a progression was at one time held to imply consecutive 5ths or 8ves.

Hieronymus de Moravia. *See* **Moravia.**

Highland Fling, A Scot. dance-step, rather than the dance itself, although that is often so called. The mus. is that of the Strathspey and the step is a kick of the leg backwards and forwards.

Hignard, (Jean Louis) Aristide (b. Nantes, 20. V. 1822; d. Vernon, 20. III. 1898), Fr. comp. Pupil of Halévy at the Paris Cons., where he gained the 2nd Prix de Rome in 1850.

Works incl. operas *Hamlet* (after Shakespeare), *Le Colin-Maillard*, *Les Compagnons de la Marjolaine* and *L'Auberge des Ardennes* (all on libs. by Jules Verne and Michael Carrol) and 8 others; choruses; *Valses concertantes* and *Valses romantiques* for pf. duet; songs, etc.

Hildegard, Saint (b. Böckelheim, 1098; d. Rupertsberg, nr. Bingen, 1179), Ger. abbess and musician. Educ. at the Benedictine nunnery of Disisbodenberg, where she became abbess in 1136. She wrote monophonic mus. for the church which shows some departures from traditional plainsong style.

Hill, Aaron (1685–1750), Eng. playwright. *See* **Arne** (T. A.) (*Zara*), **Rinaldo** (Handel).

Hill, Edward Burlingame (b. Cambridge, Mass., 9. IX. 1872; d. Francestown, N.H., 9. VII. 1960), Amer. comp. and teacher. Studied at Harvard Univ., where he became a teacher in 1908 and prof. of mus. in 1928. Wrote a book on modern Fr. mus.

Works incl. 2 ballets; 3 symphs., 2 suites *Stevensoniana*, sinfonietta, symph.

Hill   Himmel

poem *Lilacs* for orch.; sinfonietta and
suite for string orch.; concertino for pf.
and orch., Mus. for Eng. horn and orch.;
vln. concerto; string 4tet in C. maj., 6tet for
wind and pf.; clar. and pf. sonata and pieces;
songs, etc.

Hill, Joseph (b. ?, 1715; d. London,
1784), Eng. vln. maker. He worked in
London, where the house of his descendants,
W. E. Hill and Sons, still exists.

Hill, Ralph (b. Watford, 8. X. 1900; d.
London, 20. X. 1950), Eng. critic, studied
cello under his father, a prof. at the G.S.M.
in London. Having been engaged in mus.
pub. and ed. from 1920, he became mus. ed.
of the *Radio Times* in 1933, also asst. mus.
critic to the *Daily Mail*, where he was app.
chief critic in 1945 in succession to Edwin
Evans. In 1946 he became ed. of the *Penguin
Mus. Magazine*, He also did much lecturing
and broadcasting. His books incl. *An
Outline of Mus. Hist.*, studies of Brahms
and Liszt and var. essays.

Hillemacher, Paul (Joseph Wilhelm) (b.
Paris, 29. XI. 1852; d. Versailles, 13.
VIII. 1933) and **Lucien (Joseph Édouard)**
(b. Paris, 10. VI. 1860; d. Paris, 2. VI.
1909), Fr. comps., brothers who wrote all
their works in collaboration. Studied at the
Paris Cons., where P. gained the Prix de
Rome in 1876 and L. in 1880.

Works incl. operas *Saint-Mégrin, La
Légende de Sainte Geneviève, Une Aventure
d'Arlequin, Le Régiment qui passe, Le
Drac, Orsola, Circé*; mimed dramas *One
for Two* and *Fra Angelico*; incid. mus. for
Haraucourt's *Héro et Léandre* and for
George Sand's *Claudie*; symph. legend
Loreley and other orchestral works;
chamber mus., songs, part-songs, etc.

Hiller, Ferdinand (b. Frankfurt, 24. X.
1811; d. Cologne, 10. V. 1885), Ger. pianist,
cond. and comp. Was taught mus. privately
as a child and appeared as pianist at the age
of 10. In 1825 he went to Weimar to study
under Hummel. After a brief return to
Frankfurt he lived in Paris from 1828 to
1835, where he taught and gave concerts.
He prod. his 1st opera at Milan in 1839 and
his 1st oratorio at Leipzig in 1840, then
studied with Baini in Rome, lived at Frankfurt, Leipzig and Dresden, became cond. at
Düsseldorf in 1847 and at Cologne in 1850,
where he remained and founded the Cons.

Works incl. operas *Romilda, Die
Katakomben, Der Deserteur*; oratorios *Die
Zerstörung Jerusalems* and *Saul*; cantatas
Nala und Damajanti, Prometheus, Rebecca
and others, incl. one from Byron's *Hebrew
Melodies*; 4 symphs., 4 overtures (e.g. to
Schiller's *Demetrius*) and other orchestral
works; 2 pf. concertos, vln. concerto; 3
string 4tets, 3 pf. 4tets, 5 pf. trios; vln. and
cello sonata; sonata, 24 studies, *Modern
Suite* and many other works for pf.; songs,
part-songs, etc.

Hiller, Johann Adam (b. Wendisch-
Ossig nr. Görlitz, 25. XII. 1728; d. Leipzig,
16. VI. 1804), Ger. comp. Chorister under
Homilius in Dresden, studied law at Leipzig Univ. After a short period in the service
of Count Brühl, he returned to Leipzig,
working as flautist, singer, conductor, etc.
In 1763 he estab. subscription concerts
on the model of the Paris Concert spirituel,
these becoming the Gewandhaus concerts
in 1781. He also prod. a mus. weekly
(*Wöchentliche Nachrichten*, 1766–70) and
was one of the originators of the Ger.
Singspiel, of which he prod. many successful examples, 1766–82. Left Leipzig in
1785, but after some short-term posts
returned to succeed Doles as municipal
mus. director and Cantor of St. Thomas's.

Works incl. *Singspiele: Der Teufel ist
los* (after Coffey's *The Devil to Pay*),
*Lisuart und Dariolette, Lottchen am Hofe,
Die Muse, Die Liebe auf dem Lande, Die
Jagd, Der Dorfbalbier, Der Aerndtekranz,
Der Krieg, Die Jubelhochzeit, Das Grab
des Mufti, Das gerettete Troja*; settings of
Gellert's odes and other choral comps.;
cantatas; 100th Psalm; instrumental mus.
etc.; also many theoret. and critical writings
on mus.

Hillern, Wilhelmine von (1836–1916),
Ger. novelist. *See* **Jaques-Dalcroze** (*Fille au
vautour*), **Wally** (Catalani).

Hilton, John (b. ?; d. Cambridge, III.
1608), Eng. organist and comp. App.
organist to Trinity Coll., Cambridge, in
1594. Comp. anthems, madrigals, etc.

Hilton, John (b. ? Oxford, 1599; d.
London, III. 1657), Eng. organist and
comp., (?) son of prec. Took the Mus.B.
degree at Cambridge in 1626 and 2 years
later became organist at St. Margaret's
Church, Westminster.

Works incl. services and anthems;
madrigals, *Ayres, or Fa La's* for 3 voices;
Elegy on the death of Wm. Lawes for 3
voices and bass; collection of catches,
rounds and canons *Catch that catch can*;
songs, fantasies for viols, hymn 'Wilt
Thou forgive that sin where I begun' from
Donne's *Divine Poems*, etc.

Himmel, Friedrich Heinrich (b. Treuenbrietzen, Brandenburg, 20. XI. 1765; d.
Berlin, 8. VI. 1814), Ger. harpsichordist,
pianist and comp. Read theology at Halle
Univ., but later under the patronage of
Frederick William II of Prus. studied mus.
at Dresden under Naumann and in It.,
where he prod. 2 operas. App. court
Kapellmeister in Berlin in 1795, he was still
able to travel and visited Rus., Scand.,
Paris, London and Vienna.

Works incl. operas *Il primo navigatore,
La morte di Semiramide, Alessandro, Vaso
di Gama, Frohsinn und Schwärmerei,
Fauchon das Leyermädchen, Die Sylphen,
Der Kobold*; oratorio *Isacco*; funeral

cantata for the King of Prussia; Masses, Te Deum, motets, psalms and other church mus.; instrumental mus., songs, etc.

Hindemith, Paul (b. Hanau, 16. XI. 1895; d. Frankfurt, 28. XII. 1963), Ger. comp. He was taught the vln. as a child and entered the Hoch Cons. at Frankfurt, where he studied under Arnold Mendelssohn and Sekles. Later he played in the Frankfurt Opera orch. and was leader there in 1915–23; and in 1921 he founded a string 4tet with the Turkish violinist Licco Amar (Amar-Hindemith 4tet) in which he played vla. Works of his were heard at the Donaueschingen festival in 1921 and at the I.S.C.M. festival at Salzburg in 1922, and from that time he became known abroad. From 1927 he taught comp. at the Berlin Hochschule für Musik, but the Nazis proscribed his works as degenerate art. His opera *Mathis der Maler* was therefore prod. in Switz., at Zürich, in 1938. For some years after 1933 he was at Ankara in an official capacity to reorganize Turkish mus. educ. In 1939 he emigrated to U.S.A., where he taught at Yale Univ., but in 1946 he returned to Eur. and was active for several years as a cond.

Works incl. operas *Mörder, Hoffnung der Frauen* (Kokoschka), *Das Nusch-Nuschi* (for Marionettes), *Sancta Susanna*, *Cardillac* (after E. T. A. Hoffmann), *Neues vom Tage*, *Mathis der Maler*, *Harmonie der Welt*, *The Long Christmas Dinner*; revue sketch *Hin und zurück*; ballets *Der Dämon*, *Nobilissima Visione*, *Cupid and Psyche*, *Mirror before Me* (after Mallarmé's *Hérodiade*); incid. mus. for Christmas play on Immermann's *Tulifäntchen*; oratorio *Das Unaufhörliche*, for solo voices, chorus, boys' chorus and orch.; symph. in E maj., Concert Mus. for strings and brass, *Philharmonic Concerto*, symph. from *Mathis der Maler*, concerto for orch., *Philharmonic Dances*, symph. metamorphosis on themes by Weber; pf. concerto, cello concerto, clar. concerto, variations for pf. and strings; for chamber orch.: *Kammermusik* nos. 1–6 for var. instruments, *Merry Sinfonietta* (unpub.), concerto for org. and chamber orch., *Der Schwanendreher* for vla. and small orch., *Trauermusik* for vla. and strings; *Concert Music* for wind orch. and for pf., brass and harp; 6 string 4tets; 2 string trios; var. other chamber works; 16 sonatas for var. instruments; some pieces for solo instruments and pf.; 3 sonatas, *1922 Suite*, *Ludus tonalis*: 12 fugues with prelude and postlude, and some other works for pf.; 7 waltzes for pf. duet (unpub.); sonata for 2 pfs.; 3 org. sonatas; 8 songs and songcycle, *Das Marienleben* (Rilke); *Die junge Magd*, 6 songs for contralto with fl., clar. and string 4tet; *Die Serenaden* for soprano with ob., vla. and cello; sonatas for fl., ob.,

Eng. horn, clar., bassoon, horn, tpt., tromb., harp, etc.; 3 sets of part-songs, *chansons* (Rilke) for unaccomp. chorus; several works for 'workaday mus.' (*see* **Gebrauchsmusik**).

Hingston, John (b. ?; d. London, XII. 1683), Eng. organist, violinist and comp. Pupil of O. Gibbons. Musician to Charles I and later to Cromwell, in whose household he was organist at Hampton Court and played on the org. removed from Magdalen Coll., Oxford. He taught Cromwell's daughters. At the Restoration in 1660 he became violinist in the royal band and keeper of the orgs. at court, in which he was succeeded by Purcell.

Hinton, Arthur (b. Beckenham, Kent, 20. XI. 1869; d. Rottingdean, 11. VIII. 1941), Eng. comp. Educ. at Shrewsbury School and later studied mus. at the R.A.M. in London, afterwards with Rheinberger at Munich. Married the pianist Katherine Goodson (1872–1958).

Works incl. opera *Tamara*; children's operettas *The Disagreeable Princess* and *St. Elizabeth's Rose*; 2 symphs., fantasy *The Triumph of Caesar*, suite *Endymion* for orch.; pf. concerto in D min., *Chant des vagues* for cello and orch.; pf. 5tet, pf. trio; sonata and suite for vln. and pf.; *Summer Pilgrimage in the White Mountains*, 4 Bagatelles, etc. for pf., etc.

Hippolyte et Aricie (*Hippolytus and Aricia*). See also **Ippolito ed Aricia.**
Opera by Rameau (lib. by Simon Joseph de Pellegrin), prod. Paris, Opéra, 1. X. 1733.

Histoire du soldat (*The Soldier's Tale*), action for a narrator, actors and dancers by Stravinsky (lib. by Charles Ferdinand Ramuz), prod. Lausanne, 28. IX. 1918.

Hobday, Alfred C(harles). (b. Faversham, 19. IV. 1870; d. Tankerton, Kent, 23. II. 1942), Eng. vla. player. Studied at the R.A.M. in London, became principal vla. in the Phil. and London Symph. Orchs. and excelled in chamber mus. Married the pianist Ethel Sharpe (1872–1947) in 1895. His brother Claude (1872–1954) was a double bass player.

Hoboe (Ger.), an earlier Ger. spelling of Oboe.

Hoboy. See Hautboy.

Hobrecht, Jacob. See Obrecht.

Hochzeit des Camacho, Die (*Camacho's Wedding*), opera by Mendelssohn (lib. by Carl August Ludwig von Lichtenstein, based on Cervantes' *Don Quixote*), prod. Berlin, Schauspielhaus, 29. IV. 1827.

Hocket, a word similar to 'hiccup' and derived from the Fr. equiv. *hoquet*. It is used for a device in medieval vocal and instrumental mus., consisting of phrases when broken up by rests, in such a way that when one part is silent another fills the gap. Also a piece written in this style.

Hoddinott, Alun (b. Bargoed, Glam., 11. VIII. 1929), Welsh comp. He studied at the Univ. Coll. of S. Wales, Cardiff, where he was app. Prof. of Music in 1968. Works incl. 3 symphs., Sinfonietta, *Variants*, *Night Music* for orch., clar. concerto, ob. concerto, 3 pf. concertos, org. concerto; choral mus.; clar. 4tet, string 4tet, string trio; 5 pf. sonatas, etc.

Hoesslin, Franz von (b. Munich, 31. XII. 1885; d. off Site, 28. IX. 1946), Ger. cond. and comp. Pupil of Mottl for cond. and Reger for comp. After engagements at var. theatres in Ger. and Switz he became cond. at the Volksoper in Berlin from 1922 to 1923, later cond. at Dessau and Breslau and for 6 years at Bayreuth. Works incl. orch. and choral mus.; chamber mus.; songs, etc.

Høffding, (Nils) Finn (b. Copenhagen, 10. III. 1899), Dan. comp. Pupil of Jeppesen in Copenhagen and J. Marx in Vienna. App. prof. at the Royal Dan. Cons. in 1931, where he started the Copenhagen Folk Mus. School with Jørgen Bentzon. Author of several theoret. books. Works incl. operas *The Emperor's New Clothes* (after Andersen), etc.; 3 symphs. (1 with chorus); 2 string 4tets; duet for ob. and clar.; pf. pieces; songs, etc.

Höffer, Paul (b. Barmen, 21. XII. 1895; d. Berlin, 31. VIII. 1949), Ger. comp. He was trained as a pianist in the 1st place, at Cologne, and later studied comp. with Schreker in Berlin, where he became prof. of pf. at the High School for Mus. in 1923 and prof. of comp. in 1930. He was app. director in 1948, but died of a heart attack. Works incl. operas *Borgia* and *Der falsche Waldemar*, 3 children's operas; incid. mus. for Shakespeare's *Coriolanus*, Goethe's *Faust*, etc.; 4 oratorios and other choral works; symph., 2 serenades, etc. for orch.; var. concertos; 3 string 4tets, clar. 5tet, wind 6tet. etc.

Hoffheimer. *See* Hofhaimer.

Hoffmann, Ernst Theodor Amadeus (orig. Wilhelm) (b. Königsberg, 24. I. 1776; d. Berlin, 25. VI. 1822), Ger. novelist and comp. He changed his 3rd name to Amadeus in homage to Mozart. He is the hero of Offenbach's *Tales of Hoffmann*.

Comps incl. operas (mostly lost) *Der Renegat*, *Faustine*, *Die lustigen Musikanten* (Brentano), *Der Kanonikus von Mailand*, *Liebe und Eifersucht* (after Calderón), *Der Trank der Unsterblichkeit*, *Das Gespenst*, *Aurora*, *Undine* (after Fouqué), *Julius Sabinus* (unfinished); ballet *Harlekin* (unfinished); incid. mus. to Goethe's *Scherz*, *List und Rache* and other plays; 2 Masses; symph., etc.

For mus. works based on his writings *see* **Braunfels** (*Prinzessin Brambilla*), **Brautwahl** (Busoni), **Cardillac** (Hindemith),

Contes d'Hoffmann (Offenbach), **Delibes** (*Coppélia*), **Kreisleriana** (Schumann), **Malipiero** (*Capricci di Callot*), **Nutcracker** (Tchaikovsky), **Offenbach** (*Goldsmith of Toledo*).

Hoffmann, Heinrich, Ger. writer and illustrator, author of *Struwwelpeter*. *See* **Heuberger** (*Strewwelpeter*), **Maconchy** (*Great Agrippa*).

Hoffmann, Karel (b. Smichov, Prague, 12. XII. 1872; d. Prague, 30. III. 1936), Cz. violinist. Studied at the Prague Cons. and founded the Boh. 4tet with Suk, Nedbal and Berger in 1892. App. vln. prof. at the Cons. in 1922.

Hoffmann, Leopold (b. Vienna, c. 1730; d. Vienna, 17. III. 1793), Aus. comp. *Kapellmeister* at St. Stephen's Cathedral in Vienna from 1772. He belongs to the Viennese school of symphonists. Works incl. church mus., symphs., concertos, chamber mus., etc.

Hoffmeister, Karel (b. Liblice, 26. V. 1868; d. Hluboká, 23. IX. 1952), Cz. teacher, writer on mus. and comp. Studied in Prague, where, after some years at Ljubljana, he was app. prof. at the Cons. in 1898. He was pianist of the Cz. Trio and wrote books on Smetana, Dvořák and pf. mus.

Comps. incl. song-cycles *At Twilight*, *Unhappy Love*, *Legend of May* and others, etc.

Hofhaimer (Hoffheimer), Paul (b. Radstadt, 25. I. 1459; d. Salzburg, 1537), Aus. organist and comp. In the service of the Emperor Maximilian at Innsbruck, c. 1480–1519, and was organist to the Archbishop of Salzburg from 1526 to his death. Works incl. setting of odes by Horace *Harmoniae poeticae* for 4 voices, Ger. songs for 3 and 4 voices, org. mus., etc.

Hofmann, Heinrich (Karl Johann) (b. Berlin, 13. I. 1842; d. Gross-Tabarz, Thur., 16. VII. 1902), Ger. pianist and comp. Was a chorister at the cathedral in Berlin and studied at Kullak's acad. He taught pf. and played much in public. Works incl. operas *Cartouche*, *Der Matador*, *Armin*, *Aennchen von Tharau*, *Wilhelm von Oranien*, *Donna Diana* (Moreto); *Hungarian Suite*, *Fritdjof* symph. (after Tegnér), suite *Im Schlosshof*, scherzo *Irrlichter und Kobolde*, etc. for orch.; cantatas *Die schöne Melusine*, *Aschenbrödel*, *Editha*, *Prometheus*, *Waldfräulein*, *Festgesang*; several works for voices and orch.; cello concerto; pf. 4tet, pf. trio, string 6tet, octet; pf. pieces; songs, duets, etc.

Hofmann, Josef (Casimir) (b. Cracow, 20. I. 1876; d. Los Angeles, 16. II. 1957), Pol.-Amer. pianist and comp. Studied early with his elder sister and his father, the pianist and cond. Casimir H., and made his 1st public appearance at the age of 6. At 9 he toured Eur. and in 1887 paid his 1st visit to U.S.A., where after further study and success in Eur. he settled in 1898 and became naturalized in 1926. His comps. appeared for a time under the pseud. of Michel Dvorsky.

Works incl. symph. in E maj., symph. narrative *The Haunted Castle*; 5 pf. concertos and *Chromaticon*, for pf. and orch.; numerous pf. works; nocturne for vln. and pf.; *God's Hand* for voice and pf., etc.

Hofmannsthal, Hugo von (1874–1929), Aus. poet and dramatist. *See* **Ägyptische Helena** (R. Strauss), **Alkestis** (Wellesz), **Arabella** (R. Strauss), **Ariadne auf Naxos** (do.), **Bourgeois gentilhomme** (do.), **Elektra** (do.), **Everyman** (Sibelius), **Frau ohne Schatten** (R. Strauss), **Legend of Joseph** (do.), **Martin (F.)** (*Jedermann*), **Reuss** (*Tor und der Tod*), **Rosenkavalier** (R. Strauss), **Tcherepnin (A.)** (*Hochzeit der Sobeide*), **Unger (H.)** (*Tod und der Tor*), **Wagner-Régeny** (*Bergwerk zu Falun*), **Wellesz** (*Alkestis, Lied der Welt* and *Leben, Traum und Tod*).

Hogarth, George (b. Carfrae Mill nr. Oxton, Berwickshire, 1783; d. London, 12. II. 1870), Scot. critic and writer on mus. Studied law in Edinburgh, but learnt cello and comp. as an amateur. Settled in London in 1830 and became critic to the *Morning Chronicle*. In 1836 his daughter Catherine married Charles Dickens, who became ed. of the *Daily News* in 1846 and engaged H. as mus. critic. He wrote several books, mainly chronicles of opera, festivals and concerts.

Hogg, James (1770–1835), Scot. poet. *See* **McCunn** (*Bonny Kilmeny* and *Queen Hynd*).

Hohl Flute, an 8-ft. org. stop similar to the Claribel, but having the mouth on the wider side of the square pipes.

Hohlflöte (Ger. = hollow flute), the name sometimes used for the Hohl Flute.

Hol, Richard (b. Amsterdam, 23. VII. 1825; d. Utrecht, 14. V. 1904), Dutch organist, cond. and comp. Studied at Amsterdam and became cond. of a male-voice choral society there in 1856. In 1862 he went to Utrecht as mus. director to the town, became cathedral organist in 1869 and director of the mus. school in 1875. He wrote a book on Sweelinck.

Works incl. operas *Floris V* and *Uit de branding*; Masses and cantatas; oratorio *David*; 4 symphs., overtures and other orchestral works; chamber mus.; songs, etc.

Holberg, Ludvig (1684–1754), Norw. dramatist and satirist. *See* **Gade** (suite), **Grieg** (do.), **Nielsen (C.)** (*Maskarade*), **Riisager** (*Erasmus Montanus*), **Schoeck** (*Don Ranudo*), **Weismann** (*Pfiffige Magd*).

Holborne, Antony (b. ?; d. ? London,

1602), Eng. musician and comp. in the service of Queen Elizabeth I. He pub. a vol. of mus. for strings or wind in 1599 and in 1597 *The Cittharn Schoole*, which incl. 3-part songs by his brother William.

Holbrooke, Joseph (or **Josef**) (b. Croydon, Surrey, 6. VII. 1878; d. London, 5. VIII. 1958), Eng. comp. Studied at the R.A.M. After a hard struggle as pianist and cond. he came under the patronage of Lord Howard de Walden, who wrote the libs. for his dramatic trilogy. He engaged in much militant propaganda on behalf of some Brit. comps.

Works incl. operas *Pierrot and Pierrette, The Snob, The Wizard, The Stranger* and the trilogy *The Cauldron of Annwen* (*The Children of Don, Dylan* and *Bronwen*); ballets *The Red Mask* (after Poe), *The Moth and the Flame, Coromanthe*, etc.; *Dramatic Choral Symph.* and *The Bells* for chorus and orch. (both after Poe); symph. poems *The Raven, Ulalume, The Masque of the Red Death* (all after Poe), *The Viking, Ode to Victory* (Byron), *The Skeleton in Armour* (Longfellow), *Queen Mab* (Shakespeare), *Apollo and the Seaman*, with chor. (Herbert Trench); variations for orch. on *Three Blind Mice, Auld Lang Syne* and *The Girl I left behind me*; pf. concerto *The Song of Gwyn ap Nudd*, vln. concerto; 6 string 4tets (incl. *Pickwick Club* after Dickens), 3 trios, 4 4tets, 5 5tets, 4 6tets for var. instruments, sinfonietta for chamber orch. and other chamber mus.; pf. pieces; songs, etc.

Holcroft, Thomas (1745–1809), Eng. playwright. *See* **Busby** (*Tale of Mystery*).

Holden, John (b. ? Glasgow, ?; d. Glasgow, ?, Scot. 18th-cent. scholar and comp. Pub. an *Essay towards a Rational System of Music*, and a collection of church mus.

Holden, Smollett (b. ?; d. Dublin, ?), Ir. 18th–19th-cent. mus. dealer, pub. and comp. He kept a mus. shop at Dublin and pub. 2 vols. of Ir. airs, also Welsh mus., etc., and wrote military mus.

Hölderlin, Johann Christian Friedrich (1770–1843), Ger. poet. *See* **Apostel** (songs), **Britten** (songs), **Hauer** (pf. pieces and songs), **Schicksalslied** (Brahms), **Strauss (R.)** (3 hymns).

Hole, William (b. ?; d. 15. IX. 1624) and **Robert** (b. ?; d. ?), Eng. mus. engravers and pubs. William H. produced *Parthenia* for keyboard, the first mus. ever engraved on copper plates in England, in 1612 or 1613, and Robert H. produced its successor, *Parthenia in-violata*, apparently in 1624 or 1625.

Holland, Theodore (Samuel) (b. London, 25. IV. 1878; d. London, 29. X. 1947), Eng. teacher and comp. Studied at the R.A.M. in London, later in Berlin. In 1927 he was app. prof. of comp. at the R.A.M., a post he held till his death. He was chair-

Hollander   Holmès

man of the Royal Phil. Society from 1933 to 1946 and treasurer of the Mus. Assoc. from 1931 to 1947.
Works incl. children's operetta, mus. play; cantata and part-songs; *Cortège* for orch. of cellos, orchestral works; 2 string 4tets, 2 pf. trios; instrumental pieces; pf. works; songs, etc.

Hollander, Benno (Benoit) (b. Amsterdam, 8. VI. 1853; d. London, 27. XII. 1942), Dutch (anglicized) violinist and comp. Studied at the Paris Cons. with Massart, later comp. with Saint-Saëns. After a tour in Eur. he settled in London in 1876. He played vla. in Auer's 4tet and led several important orchs., later estab. one of his own.
Works incl. opera *Mietje*; symph. *Roland*, symph. poem *Pompeii*, orchestral pieces *Drame* and *Comédie*; 2 concertos and *Pastoral Fantasy* for vln. and orch.; 2 string 4tets, 7tet for pf., strings and horns, pf. trio, string trio; 2 vln. and pf. sonatas; pf. sonata, etc.

Hollander, Christian Janszon (b. ?; d. Innsbruck, 1568 or 1569), Flem. singer and comp. App. choirmaster at St. Walburg's Church at Oudenarde in 1549 and from 1559 was a singer in the Imp. Chapel in Vienna.
Works incl. many motets, sacred songs for several voices, secular Ger. songs, etc.

Holländer, Gustav (b. Leobschütz, Silesia, 15. II. 1855; d. Berlin, 4. XII. 1915), Ger. violinist, teacher and comp. Studied with David at Leipzig and Joachim in Berlin and became 4tet player, orch. leader and prof. of vln. at Cologne and Berlin. Director of the Stern Cons. in Berlin from 1895.
Works incl. 4 vln. concertos, 1 for students, etc.

Holländer, Victor (b. Leobschütz, Silesia, 20. IV. 1866; d. Hollywood, Calif., 24. X. 1940), Ger. pianist and comp., brother of prec. Pupil of Kullak in Berlin, where he taught and cond. after var. appts. at Hamburg, Budapest, Marienbad, U.S.A. and London. He emigrated to California in 1934.
Works incl. operas *San Lin* and *Trilby* (on G. du Maurier's novel), comic operas *Die Primanerliebe*, *Carmosinella*, *The Bey of Morocco*, *Der Sonnenvogel* and *Der Regimentspapa*; pantomime *Sumurun*; pf. mus., etc.

Höller, Karl (b. Bamberg, 25. VII. 1907), Ger. comp. Studied at Munich under Josef Haas. Taught at the Musikhochschule in Frankfurt in 1937–49, and became President of the Musikhochschule in Munich in 1954.
Works incl. orch. and solo concertos, symph. fantasy on a theme by Frescobaldi, *Gregorianische Hymnen*; concertos for org., vlns. (2) and cello (2); 6 string 4tets, 8 vln.

sonatas, cello sonatas; pf. and org. works, etc.

Holliger, Heinz (b. Langenthal, 21. V. 1939), Swiss oboist and comp. Studied ob. and pf. in Berne and Paris, and comp. with Veress in Berne and Boulez in Paris. He has won several prizes for his ob. playing.
Works incl. cantata *Himmel und Erde* for tenor and chamber group; *Studie* for soprano, ob. and cello with harpsichord; *Improvisation* for ob., harp and 12 string instruments; sonata for ob. and pf.; sonata for ob. solo.

Hollins, Alfred (b. Hull, 11. IX. 1865; d. Edinburgh, 17. V. 1942), Eng. organist and comp. for his instrument. Although blind, held var. organist's appts. and toured widely in Austral., S. Africa and U.S.A.

Holm, Richard (b. Stuttgart, 3. VIII. 1912), Ger. tenor. Made his début in Kiel in 1936. In 1948 he joined the Munich State Opera and first sang at Covent Garden in 1953. A fine Wagner singer, he also excels in Mozart.

Holmboe, Vagn (b. Horsens, Jutland, 20. XII. 1909), Dan. comp. Studied with Jeppesen and Hoffding in Copenhagen and Toch in Berlin. With his wife, the Rum. pianist Meta Graf, he explored Rum. for folk mus.
Works incl. opera *Fanden og Borgmesteren*; ballet *Den galsindede Tyrk*; 10 symphs., 13 chamber concertos, 2 vln. sonatas, etc.

Holmes, Alfred (b. London, 9. XI. 1837; d. Paris, 4. III. 1876), Eng. violinist and comp. With very little regular instruction he became a famous violinist, playing duets with his brother Henry (1839–1905) and later touring widely with him in Eur. He settled in Paris in 1864.
Works incl. opera *Inez de Castro*: symphs. *Jeanne d'Arc*, *The Youth of Shakespeare*, *Robin Hood*, *The Siege of Paris*, *Charles XII* and *Romeo and Juliet* (after Shakespeare); overtures *The Cid* (after Corneille) and *The Muses*.

Holmès (orig. Holmes), **Augusta (Mary Anne)** (b. Paris, 16. XII. 1847; d. Paris, 28. I. 1903), Ir., naturalized Fr., pianist and comp. Although her Ir. parents were against her taking up mus., she played the pf. and sang as a child prodigy and began to comp. under the name of Hermann Zenta. She then studied with the organist Lambert at Versailles and had already written much when in 1875 she went to Franck for more solid study.
Works incl. operas *Héro et Léandre*, *La Montagne noire*, *Astarté*, *Lancelot du Lac*; choral works *Les Argonautes* (on Homer's *Iliad*), psalm *In exitu*, ode *Ludus pro patria* and *Ode triomphale*; symphs. on Ariosto's *Orlando furioso*, *Lutèce* and

291

Pologne, symph. poem *Irlande*; song-cycle *Les Sept Ivresses*, etc.

Holmes, Edward (b. ?, 1797; d. London, 28. VIII. 1859), Eng. author and critic. He wrote *A Ramble among the Musicians of Germany* (1828) and the 1st Eng. biography of Mozart (1845).

Holmes, George (b. ?; d. Lincoln, 1721), Eng. organist and comp. At 1st organist to Bishop of Durham, he was app. organist of Lincoln Cathedral in 1704. Wrote anthems, burial sentences for Lincoln Cathedral, Ode for St. Cecilia's Day, catches, etc.

Holmes, Henry (b. London, 7. XI. 1839; d. San Francisco, 9. XII. 1905), Eng. violinist and comp., brother of Alfred H., whose career he largely shared. After parting with Alfred in Paris in 1865, he went to Den. and Swed. and later gave chamber concerts in London and was vln. prof. at the R.C.M., but retired to California in 1894.

Works incl. 4 symphs.; vln. concerto, etc.

Holmes, John (b. ?; d. Winchester, 1602), Eng. organist and comp. He was organist at Winchester Cathedral. Wrote church mus. and contrib. a madrigal to *The Triumphes of Oriana* in 1601.

Holofernes, opera by Rezniček (lib. by comp., based on Hebbel's drama *Judith*), prod. Berlin, Deutsches Opernhaus, 27. X. 1923.

Holst, Gustav (Theodore) (b. Cheltenham, 21. IX. 1874; d. London, 25. V. 1934), Eng. comp. of Swed. descent. The family had been in Eng. since 1807. His father was a mus. teacher and his mother a pianist, and he was intended to follow their career; he also had early experience as organist and choral and orchestral cond. in a small way. In 1893 he was sent to the R.C.M. in London, but disliked the keyboard instruments and wished to take to comp., which he studied under Stanford. Suffering from neuritis, he took up the tromb. instead of the pf., and on leaving played in the orch. of the Carl Rosa Opera Co. and later in the Scot. Orch. In 1903 he became mus. master at a school in south London, in 1905 at St. Paul's Girls' School, where he remained to his death, and in 1907 was app. director at Morley Coll. for Working Men and Women. From 1919 he taught comp. at the R.C.M. and in 1919–23 at Reading Coll.

Works incl. operas *The Idea, The Wandering Scholar, Sāvitri, The Perfect Fool, At the Boar's Head* (on Shakespeare's *Henry IV*); ballets *The Golden Goose* and *The Morning of the Year* with chorus and orch.; choral hymns from the *Rig Veda* with orch., 2 psalms for chorus, strings and org., *The Hymn of Jesus* for chorus and orch., Festival Te Deum, *Ode to Death*

(Whitman) for chorus and orch., choral symph. (Keats) for soprano, chorus and orch., choral fantasy (Bridges) for chorus, org., strings, brass and perc.; 2 motets for unaccomp. chorus, *Ave Maria* for fem. voices, part-songs and arrs. for folksongs for unaccomp. chorus; *A Somerset Rhapsody, Beni Mora* suite, *The Planets, Jap. Suite, Fugal Overture, Egdon Heath* (after Thomas Hardy) for orch.; *St. Paul's* suite for strings; *Fugal Concerto* for fl., ob. and strings, concerto for 2 vlns. and orch.; 2 suites for military band: *A Moorside Suite* for brass band; 9 hymns from the *Rig Veda* for voice and pf., 12 songs (Humbert Wolfe) for voice and pf., 4 songs for voice and vln.; a few pf. pieces, etc.

Holst, Imogen (b. Richmond, Surrey, 12. IV. 1907), Eng. pianist and comp., daughter of prec. Studied with her father and at the R.C.M. in London and became mus. mistress at several schools, did much work for the Eng. Folk Dance Society and wrote books on Holst, Purcell and Britten.

Works incl. overture for orch., pf. pieces, folksong arrs., etc.

Holstein, Franz (Friedrich) von (b. Brunswick, 16. II. 1826; d. Leipzig, 22. V. 1878), Ger. comp. Although trained for the army, he studied mus. under Griepenkerl. When he had written 2 operas, Moritz Hauptmann persuaded him in 1852 to take entirely to mus. and gave him further instruction.

Works incl. operas *Zwei Nächte in Venedig, Waverley* (after Scott), *Der Haideschacht, Der Erbe von Morley, Die Hochländer* and *Marino Faliero* (after Byron); overtures *Loreley* and *Frau Aventiure*; vocal scene from Schiller's *Braut von Messina* and another, *Beatrice*.

Holtei, Karl Eduard von (1798–1880), Ger. actor and dramatist. *See* Rietz (J.) (*Lorbeerbaum und Bettelstab*).

Hölty, Ludwig (Heinrich Christoph) (1748–76), Ger. poet. *See* Tomašek (*Elegie auf eine Rose*).

6 songs by Brahms, 21 by Schubert.

Holz, Carl (b. Vienna, 1798; d. Vienna, 9. XI. 1858), Aus. amateur violinist. Lived in Vienna, where he became a member of Schuppanzigh's 4tet in 1824. A devoted friend of Beethoven.

Holzbauer, Ignaz (b. Vienna, 17. IX. 1711; d. Mannheim, 7. IV. 1783), Aus. comp. Originally intended for the law, he was largely self-taught in mus., and visited It. to complete his studies. Director of the court opera in Vienna intermittently 1742–1750, he was app. *Kapellmeister* in Stuttgart in 1751, and 2 years later to the court of the Elector Palatine in Mannheim, where the orch. under Johann Stamitz was the most famous of the time. During visits to It. on leave of absence he prod. several operas, and in Mannheim prod. the Ger. opera *Günther von Schwarzburg*. As a comp. of symphs. he belongs to the 'Mannheim School'.

Works incl. operas *Il figlio delle selve, L'isola disabitata, Nitetti, Alessandro nell' Indie, Tancredi, Günther von Schwarzburg*, etc.; oratorios *La Passione, Isacco, La Betulia liberata*, etc.; Masses, motets and other church mus.; 65 symphs.; concertos, chamber mus., etc.

Holzbläser (Ger. lit. woodblowers) = woodwind instruments.

Holzblasinstrumente (Ger.) = woodwind instruments.

Holztrompete (Ger. = wooden tpt.), an instrument designed for use in the 3rd act of Wagner's *Tristan*, actually a revival of the Cornett, but provided with a valve.

Homer (?-? B.C.), Gk. poet. *See* **Bruch** (*Achilles* and *Odysseus*), **Gnecchi** (*Cassandra*), **Gundry** (*Return of Odysseus* and songs), **Heger** (*Bettler Namenlos*), **Herzogenberg** (*Odysseus* symph.), **Holmes** (*Argonautes*), **Homerische Welt** (Bungert), **Morning Heroes** (Bliss).

Homer, Sidney (b. Boston, 9. XII. 1864; d. Winter Park, Fla., 10. VII. 1953), Amer. comp. Studied with Chadwick at Boston and Rheinberger at Munich. Became lecturer at Boston until 1900 and then moved to N.Y. Married the contralto Louise Beatty (1871–1947) in 1895. Wrote many popular songs.

Homerische Welt (*Homeric World*), operatic tetralogy by Bungert (lib. by comp., based on Homer's *Odyssey*).

I. *Kirke* (*Circe*), prod. Dresden, 29. I. 1898.

II. *Nausikaa* (*Nausicaa*), prod. Dresden, 20. III. 1901.

III. *Odysseus' Heimkehr* (*The Return of Ulysses*), prod. Dresden, 12. XII. 1896.

IV. *Odysseus' Tod* (*The death of Ulysses*), prod. Dresden, 30. X. 1903.

Bungert's attempt to create a Wagnerian cycle, but based, like Berlioz's *Troyens* and Taneiev's *Oresteia*, on classical Gk. subjects.

Homilius, Gottfried August (b. Rosenthal, Saxony, 2. II. 1714; d. Dresden, 5. VI. 1785), Ger. comp. app. and organist. Pupil of Bach at Leipzig, app. organist of the church of Our Lady, Dresden, 1742, and mus. director of the 3 principal churches there, 1755.

Works incl. 32 motets, a Passion cantata, Christmas oratorio, several settings of the Passions, a book of 167 hymns; 6 Ger. arias; org. mus., etc.

Homme armé, L' (Fr. = the armed man), the name of an old Fr. secular song the tune of which was often used by comps. of the 15th and 16th cents. as *cantus firmus* for their Masses, which were then designated by that name.

Homme et son désir, L' (*Man and his Desire*), ballet by Milhaud (words, 'plastic poem', by Paul Claudel, choreography by Jean Borlin), prod. Paris, Théâtre des Champs-Élysées, 6. VI. 1921.

Homophonic (from Gk., lit. alike-sounding), applied to mus. in which the individual lines making up the harmony have no independent significance.

Honauer, Leontzi (b. ? Strasbourg, c. 1735; d. ?), Ger. comp. Settled in Paris c. 1760 and pub. 3 sets of harpsichord sonatas, some movements of which were later arr. as concerto movements in Mozart's K. 37, 40 and 41.

Hond, Cornelis de. *See* **Canis.**

Honegger, Arthur (b. Le Havre, 10. III. 1892; d. Paris, 27. XI. 1955), Swiss comp. Was 1st taught by the organist R. C. Martin at his birthplace, then sent to the Zürich Cons., 1909–11, and, his parents still living at Le Havre, studied at the Paris Cons. 1911–13. After that he became a private pupil of Widor and d'Indy and in 1914 began to comp. Though always in touch with Switz., he belonged mainly to the Fr. school, and he joined the group which c. 1920 became known as 'Les Six'. He married the comp. Andrée Vaurabourg, who was also attached to it, though not as a member.

Works incl. operas *Antigone* (after Sophocles), *L'Aiglon* (with Ibert) and *Charles le Téméraire*; stage oratorios *Le Roi David, Judith, Cris du monde, Jeanne d'Arc au bûcher* (Paul Claudel) and *Nicolas de Flue*; ballets *Horace victorieux, Sémiramis* (Paul Valéry), *Amphion* (Valéry), *Un oiseau bleu s'est envolé* (Sacha Guitry), *Shota Roustaveli* (with A. Tcherepnin and Harsányi); incid. mus. for *Le Dit des jeux du monde, La Mort de Sainte Alméenne* (Max Jacob), *Saül* (André Gide), *Fantasio* (Musset), *Phædre* (d'Annunzio), *Les Suppliantes* (Aeschylus), *La Mandragora* (Machiavelli), *Le Soulier de satin* (Claudel), *Sodôme et Gomorrhe* (Jean Giraudoux), *Hamlet* (Shakespeare), *Prométhée* (Aeschylus), *Oedipe-Roi* (Sophocles); radio and film mus.; *La Danse des morts* (Claudel) for solo voices, chorus and orch. (on Holbein); prelude to Maeterlinck's *Aglavaine et Sélysette, Chant de joie*, prelude to Shakespeare's *Tempest, Mouvements symphoniques: Pacific 231, Rugby* and No. 3, 5 symphs., *Prélude, Arioso et Fugue* on B.A.C.H., suite *Jour de fête suisse, Suite archaïque* for orch., *Pastorale d'été* and *Sérénade à Angélique* for chamber orch.; concertino for pf. and orch., cello concerto; 5 Poems by Guillaume Apollinaire for voice and orch.; 3 string 4tets and other chamber mus., 2 vln. and pf. sonatas, sonatas for vla. and pf., cello and pf., clar. and pf.; pf. and org. mus.; songs to poems by Apollinaire, Paul Fort, Jean Cocteau, Claudel, Giraudoux and others, etc.

Hood, Thomas (1799–1845), Eng. humorist and poet. *See* **Tate** (songs).

Hook, James (b. Norwich, 3. VI. 1746; d. Boulogne, 1827), Eng. organist and comp. Studied under Garland, the Norwich Cathedral organist. He made a success in London in early manhood and in 1769 became organist and comp. to Marylebone Gardens, and acted in the same posts at Vauxhall in 1774–1820. He married Miss Madden *c.* 1766 and wrote mus. for her play, *The Double Disguise*, in 1784. In 1795 and 1797 he did the same for 2 libretti by his son James, *Jack of Newbury* and *Diamond cut Diamond*, and from 1805 for several works by his 2nd son, Theodore Edward. Of his vast output of songs for Vauxhall, some are still remembered, e.g. 'The Lass of Richmond Hill'.

Works incl. mus. plays *Love and Innocence, Country Courtship, The Lady of the Manor, Too civil by half, The Triumph of Beauty, The Peruvian, The Soldier's Return, The Siege of St. Quintin*, Hannah Moore's *The Search after Happiness*, etc.; odes, cantatas, catches, etc.

Hook, James (1772–1828), Eng. divine and author, son of prec. *See* **Hook (J. i)** (*Jack of Newbury* and *Diamond cut Diamond*).

Hook, Theodore (Edward) (1788–1841), Eng. novelist, playwright and wit, brother of prec. *See* **Hook (J. i)**.

Hooper, Edmund (b. Halberton, Devon, c. 1553; d. London, 14. VII. 1621), Eng. organist and comp. After being (?) a chorister at Exeter Cathedral he went to London and joined the Westminster Abbey choir, becoming a Gentleman of the Chapel Royal in 1604 and organist of the abbey in 1606. He contrib. harmonizations of hymn tunes to East's and Ravenscroft's Psalters, also 2 vocal pieces to Leighton's *Teares or Lamentacions* and 1 to Myriell's *Tristitiae remedium*.

Works incl. services and anthems; secular mus. for several voices; virginal mus., etc.

Hopak. *See* **Gopak.**

Hope, Anthony (A. Hope Hawkins) (1863–1933), Eng. novelist and playwright. *See* **German** (*Nell Gwynn*).

Hopekirk, Helen (b. Edinburgh, 20. V. 1856; d. Cambridge, Mass., 19. XI. 1945), Scot.-Amer. pianist and comp. Studied at Edinburgh, at the Leipzig Cons. and with Leschetizky in Vienna. Made her 1st appearance at the Gewandhaus, Leipzig, in 1878, and in 1882 married William Wilson, a Scot. merchant, with whom she settled in U.S.A. in 1883. She lived in Vienna, 1887–91, and taught at the New Eng. Cons. at Boston in 1897–1901, later at Brookline, Mass.

Works incl. orchestral mus.; concerto and *Konzertstück* for pf. and orch.; 2 vln.

and pf. sonatas; many pf. works; over 100 songs, etc.

Hopf, Hans (b. Nuremberg, 2. VIII. 1916), Ger. tenor. Made his début in 1936 and in 1949 joined the Munich Opera. He has also sung at Bayreuth and Salzburg. He is best known as a heroic tenor, esp. in the operas of Wagner.

Hopkins, Antony (Antony Reynolds) (b. London, 21. III. 1921), Eng. comp. His father d. when the family was in It. in 1925 and he was adopted by a schoolmaster at Berkhamsted School, where he was educ., and whose name he took by deed-poll. In 1938 he went to Bromsgrove School as student-teacher for 2 terms and in 1939 to Oxford with an org. scholarship. The next 4 years were spent at the R.C.M. in London, where he studied pf. with Cyril Smith and comp. with Gordon Jacob. After that he joined the mus. staff at Morley Coll. and worked further under Tippett.

Works incl. opera *Lady Rohesia* (from the *Ingoldsby Legends*), mus. for Dorothy Sayers's Lichfield Cathedral Festival play (1946) *The Just Vengeance*, incid. mus. for Marlowe's *Faustus*, Sophocles' *Oedipus Rex*, Shakespeare's *Antony and Cleopatra*, etc., mus. for radio plays by Louis Mac-Neice and others; cantata *Crown of Gold*; vla. and pf. sonata; 3 sonatas and 5 Preludes for pf., cantata *A Humble Song to the Birds* for high voice and pf., *Nocturne* for voice and pf., etc.

Hopkins, Edward John (b. London, 30. VI. 1818; d. London, 4. II. 1901), Eng. organist and comp. Was a chorister in the Chapel Royal and studied with T. F. Walmisley. After var. appts. became organist of the Temple Church in 1843, remaining for 55 years. He received the degree of Mus.D. from the Archbishop of Canterbury in 1882.

Works incl. services, anthems, chants, hymns; vocal duets and trios, etc.

Hopkins, Gerard Manley (1844–89), Eng. poet. *See* **Barber** (songs), **Maconchy** (*Leaden Echo and Golden Echo*), **Tippett** (*Windhover*), **Wellesz** (*Leaden Echo and Golden Echo*).

Hopkinson, Francis (b. Philadelphia, 21. IX. 1737; d. Philadelphia, 9. V. 1791), Amer. lawyer, politician and amateur musician, commonly regarded as the first Amer. comp. Wrote a number of songs, incl. 'Beneath a weeping willow's shade', and the 'oratorical entertainment' *The Temple of Minerva*. Also developed some mechanical improvements for keyboard instruments, etc.

Hopser. *See* **Galop.**

Hoquegan. *See* **Okeghem.**

Hoquet (Fr.) = Hocket.

Horace (Quintus Horatius Flaccus) (65–8 B.C.), Rom. poet. *See* **Moser (R.)** (odes), **Parry (H.)** (*Persicos odi*), **Philidor**

(8) (*Carmen saeculare*), Thompson (R.) (odes), Tritonius (do.).

Horák, Antonin. See At the Old Bleaching-Ground.

Horenstein, Jascha (b. Kiev, 6. V. 1898), Rus. cond. Went with his family to Ger. as a child. Studied with Max Brode in Königsberg and with Adolph Busch in Vienna, also studying comp. with Schrecker in Berlin. He was app. cond. of the Düsseldorf Opera, settled in the U.S.A. in 1933 and later toured widely.

Horn, a brass wind instrument with its tube bent in a circular form. In its early stages it could prod. only the natural harmonics and was used mainly for hunting fanfares. When comps. began to write for it in the early 18th cent. they were still restricted to the natural harmonics; but by the invention of a series of crooks which could be inserted the length of the tube could be altered and the instrument played in a variety of keys. Some extra notes, of rather uncertain quality, could also be obtained by inserting the hand into the bell. It was only by the intro. of valves about the 1830s that the full chromatic scale could be played on a single instrument.

The modern H. is built in F and high B♭, with 4 valves, one of which transposes the instrument from the lower to the higher pitch. The normal compass is:

with one or two higher and lower notes possible.

Also an 8-ft. reed org. stop of powerful tone.

Horn, Charles Edward (b. London, 21. VI. 1786; d. Boston, Mass., 21. X. 1849), Eng. tenor-baritone singer and comp. of Ger. descent. He studied under his father, Karl Friedrich H., and had singing lessons from Rauzzini at Bath in 1808, making his 1st stage appearance in London in 1809. He then began to comp. theatrical pieces, starting with *The Magic Bride* in 1810. In 1823 he visited Dublin and brought Balfe back with him as a pupil. Having been mus. director at the Olympic Theatre in 1831–2, he went to U.S.A. in 1833, became a mus. teacher and pub. at Boston, where after a brief return to Eng. he settled for good in 1847, becoming cond. of the Handel and Haydn Society.

Works incl. stage pieces *Lalla Rookh* (after Moore), *The Beehive*, *Rich and Poor*, *Peveril of the Peak* (after Scott), *Honest Frauds* and many others, some with Blewitt, Braham, T. Cooke or Reeve; overture to Thomas Moore's *M.P., or The Blue Stocking*; songs in Shakespeare's *Merry Wives of Windsor* (with Webbe, jun. and

Parry); oratorios *The Remission of Sin* (later *Satan*) and *Daniel's Prediction*; glees, canzonets and many songs, incl. 'Cherry ripe' (Herrick), etc.

Horn Diapason, an 8-ft. open Diapason org. stop.

Horn, Karl Friedrich (b. Nordhausen, Thuringia, 13. IV. 1762; d. Windsor, 5. VIII. 1830), Ger. organist and comp., father of C. E. H. Pupil of C. G. Schröter, settled in Eng. 1782, where under the patronage of Count Brühl he quickly rose to become mus.-teacher to Queen Charlotte and her daughters. In 1810 he pub. with S. Wesley the first Eng. edn. of Bach's *Wohltemperirtes Clavier*. He was app. organist of St. George's Chapel, Windsor, in 1824.

Works incl. sonatas for pf. and fl. or vln., divertimenti for piano and vln., divertimenti for military band, etc.

Horn Signal, Symphony with the, nickname of Haydn's symph. No. 31 in D maj., comp. 1765, so called because of the horn fanfares at the beginning and end.

Hornbostel, Erich (Moritz) von (b. Vienna, 25. II. 1877; d. Cambridge, 28. XI. 1935), Aus. musicologist. Studied physics and philosophy at Vienna and Heidelberg, and in 1906 became head of the gramophone archives in Berlin for the recording of the mus. of primitive peoples, on which he wrote several learned works. In 1933 he went to N.Y. and the following year to London and Cambridge.

Horneman, Christian (Frederik Emil) (b. Copenhagen, 17. XII. 1841; d. Copenhagen, 8. VI. 1906), Dan. comp. Studied with his father and at the Leipzig Cons. On his return to Copenhagen he founded a concert society and in 1880 a mus. school.

Works incl. opera *Aladdin* (Oehlenschläger); overture *A Hero's Life*; pf. pieces; songs, etc.

Hornpipe, an Eng. dance, so called because it was at first accomp. on a pipe of the same name, made from an animal's horn. It did not always have nautical assocs., and up to the time of Handel, who has such an ex. in one of his Concerti grossi, it was in 3–2 time. The later form is in 2–4.

Horowitz, Vladimir (b. Kiev, 1. X. 1904), Rus., later Amer., pianist. Studied in Kiev with Felix Blumenfeld and made his début in Kharkov, aged 17. Later he went to Paris and in 1928 made his Amer. début under Beecham. In 1933 he married Toscanini's daughter Wanda. From 1938 to 1939 he lived in Switz. and in 1940 settled in America. He retired from concert life for 12 years, returning in 1965. H. ranks as one of the most technically gifted and musicianly pianists of the day.

Horsley, Charles Edward (b. London, 16. XII. 1822; d. New York, 28. II. 1876),

Eng. pianist, organist and comp. Studied under his father, William H., and Moscheles, later with Hauptmann at Cassel and Mendelssohn at Leipzig. In 1845 he returned to London and became organist at St. John's Church, Notting Hill, comp. several works for provincial festivals, etc. In 1862 he went to Austral. and in the early 1870s to U.S.A.

Works incl. oratorios *David, Joseph* and *Gideon*; setting of Milton's *Comus*; ode *Euterpe* for the opening of Melbourne Town Hall; pf. trio, etc.

Horsley, William (b. London, 15. XI. 1774; d. London, 12. VI. 1858), Eng. organist and comp., father of prec. Studied mus. privately, but had some advice from Callcott. He became organist of Ely Chapel, Holborn, in 1794, asst. Callcott as organist at the Asylum for Female Orphans and succeeded him in 1802. Later he held several other appts. He was one of the founders of the Phil. Society in 1813. His family were close friends of Mendelssohn's.

Works incl. anthem *When Israel came out of Egypt*, hymn and psalm tunes; 3 symphs.; many glees, etc.

Horwood, William (b. ?; d. ? 1484), Eng. comp. He became master of the choristers at Lincoln Cathedral in 1477. His mus., consisting of Lat. antiphons and a Magnificat, is included in the Eton Choirbook (*q.v.*); a fragmentary *Kyrie* has also survived.

Hostinský, Otakar (b. Martinoves, 2. I. 1847; d. Prague, 19. I. 1910), Cz. critic and librettist. Studied at Prague Univ. and became prof. of aesthetics there. Critic to several newspapers, author of books on Cz. and other mus. and librettist of Fibich's *Bride of Messina* and Rozkošný's *Popelka*.

Hoteterre. *See* **Hotteterre.**

Hothby, John (b. ?; d. ?, 6. XI. 1487), Eng. Carmelite, mus. scholar, comp. and doctor of theology. Graduated at Oxford and lectured there in 1435. Travelled (?) in Spain, Fr. and Ger., settled *c.* 1440 (?) at Florence and also (?) lived at Ferrara. He was called Giovanni Ottobi in It. and spent *c.* 1468–86 at Lucca. He taught there, but was recalled to Eng. by Henry VII. Wrote a number of theoret. treatises. Some sacred and secular comps. were entered in the Faenza Codex (*q.v.*).

Hotter, Hans (b. Offenbach-am-Main, 19. I. 1909), Ger. bass-baritone. Initially an organist and choirmaster, studying church mus., he later turned to opera. After studying with Roemer, a pupil of De Reszke, he made his début in 1929. In 1940 he became a member of the Munich and Vienna operas. He is one of the leading Wagner singers of his day and also an impressive actor. Both these qualities are seen at their best in his Wotan.

Hotteterre, Fr. family of wind instrument players:

1. **Loys de H.** (b. ?; d. La Couture-Boussey, *c.* 1620).

2. **Louis H.** (b. La Couture-Boussey, ?; d. La Couture-Boussey, *c.* 1670), son of prec.

3. **Jean H.** (b. La Couture-Boussey, ?; d. La Couture-Boussey, *c.* 1691), brother of prec.

4. **Nicolas H.** (b. La Couture-Boussey, ?; d. ?, 1693), brother of prec.

5. **Pierre H.** (b. ?; d. Paris, 1665), brother of prec.

6. **Jean H.** (le jeune) (b. ?; d. ?, 1669), brother of prec.

7. **Martin H.** (b. ?; d. ?, 1712), son of 3.

8. **Jacques Martin H.** (b. Paris, *c.* 1680; d. Paris, *c.* 1761), son of prec.

9. **Jean H.** (b. ?; d. ?, II. 1720), brother of prec.

House of the Dead, The (*Z Mrtvého Domu*), opera in 3 acts by Janáček (lib. by the comp. after Dostoievsky), prod. Brno, 12. IV. 1930.

Housman, A(lfred). E(dward). (1859–1936, Eng. poet and Lat. scholar. Poems from *A Shropshire Lad* (S.L.) and *Last Poems* (L.P.) set to mus.:

Barber, Samuel, S.L. LIV.
Bax, L.P. XXIII, S.L. XIII, LII.
Butterworth, S.L. II, VI, XIII, XV, XX, XXI, XXIII, XXV, XXVII, XLIX, LIV.
Cripps, A. Redgrave, S.L. V, XIII, XV, XVI, XXII, XXIII, XXVII, XXIX, XXXV, XL, XLIX, LII, LIV, LVII.
Douglas, Keith, L.P. XI.
Foss, Hubert, S.L. XXXIV.
Gardiner, S.L. III. XIII.
Gibbs, Armstrong, S.L. XIII.
Glanville-Hicks, 6 songs.
Gurney, S.L. II, IV, VII, X, XIII, XVI, XVII, XXIII, XXVI, XXVII, XXIX, XXXV, XXXIX, XL, LII, LIV.
Hamilton, Janet, S.L. II, XXI, XXXIX, LIV.
Herbert, Muriel, S.L. II.
Ireland, L.P. Pref., XXXII, S.L. X, XVII, XXII, XXIX, XXXIII, XXXIX, LI, LVII.
Johnson, Ora Agatha, S.L. XIII.
Lambert, Frank, S.L. XXII.
Ley, Henry G., S.L. XXXVI, LII.
Lutyens, Elisabeth, *The Deserter*.
Manson, Willie B., S.L. II. XLIX, LVIII
Mi ain, Hilda, S.L. XXIX.
Moeran, S.L. II. VII, VIII, XXIII, XXIV, XXXXIX, LII.
Orr. C. W., S.L. II. V. VI, VII, VIII, XI. XII, XIII, XVIII, XX, XXIII, XXV, XXVI, XXVII, XXIX, XXXIX, XL, XLVII, LIV, LV, LIX, LXI.
Peele, Graham, S.L. II, IV, VI, XXI, XXII, XXIV.

Priestley-Smith, Hugh, S.L. XXXII, XXXVI, XL, XLIX.

Procter-Gregg, Humphrey, S.L. II, XL.

Rose, Edwin, C., S.L. XL.

Searle, Humphrey, 2 songs.

Somervell, S.L. II, XIII, XIV, XXI, XXII, XXIII, XXXV, XXXVI, XL, XLIX.

Stewart, D. M., L.P. Pref., XXIII, XXVII, XXXIV.

Swain, S.L. XX, XXI, XXXVI, XXXIX, LII.

Taylor, E. Kendal, S.L. XXXVI.

Vaughan Williams, L.P. Pref., XXIII, XXVI, XXVII, LXI; S.L. XVIII, XXI, XXVI, XXVII, XXXI, XXXII, L, LIV.

Young, Dalhousie, S.L. XXI.

Housman, Laurence (1865–1959), Eng. author, *See* **Lehmann (Liza)** (*Sergeant Brue*).

Hove, Joachim van den (b. Antwerp, ?; d. ?), Flem. 16th–17th-cent. lutenist and comp. Pub. a book of songs for 2 voices and lute, 1 of songs and dances arr. for lute and 1 of preludes for lute and viol.

Hoven. *See* **Vesque von Püttlingen.**

Hovhaness, Alan (b. Somerville, Mass., 8. III. 1911), Amer. comp. of Armen. descent. Studied pf. with Heinrich Gebhard and comp. with Converse and Martinů. He is much influenced by Indian and other oriental mus. He has composed much, but destroyed a great deal of it in 1940.

Works incl. 17 symphs., 2 *Armen. Rhapsodies* for strings; *Elibris* for fl. and strings; *Lousadzak* for pf. and strings; concerto for tpt. and strings; *Sosi* for vln., pf., perc. and strings; *Arekeval* for orch.; concerto for orch.; *Ad Lyram* for orch.; chamber mus., etc.

Howard, Robert (1625–98), Eng. playwright. *See* **Indian Queen** (Purcell).

Howard, Samuel (b. ?, 1710; d. London, 13. VII. 1782), Eng. organist and comp. Pupil of Croft at the Chapel Royal and later of Pepusch. App. organist at the churches of St. Clement Danes and St. Bride. Mus.D., Cambridge, in 1769. He asst. Boyce in compiling his *Cathedral Music.*

Works incl. anthems and other church mus.; pantomimes, *The Amorous Goddess, or Harlequin Married* and *Robin Goodfellow, or The Rival Sisters*; cantatas; songs, incl. vols. *The British Orpheus*, etc.

Howard, Walter (b. Leipzig, 8. V. 1880), Swiss mus. scientist and teacher of Ger. birth and Eng. descent. Studied at Leipzig and Jena, devoted himself to teaching of pf. and mus. theory on a scientific basis of acoustics, psychology and physiology. He lectured and taught in Berlin until 1935, when the Nazis induced him to retire to Switz., and he settled in Hol. in 1937. He wrote numerous books on his theories.

Howard-Jones, Evelyn (b. London, 1877; d. London, 4. I. 1951), Eng. pianist.

Studied at the R.C.M. in London and with d'Albert in Berlin. He specialized in Brahms but had a comprehensive repertory.

Howe, John (b. ?; d. London, III. 1571), Eng. org.-builder. His father, John H., had followed the same trade, and he was asst. by his son Thomas from 1548. His first known assignment was the org. at Holy Trinity, Coventry, in 1526, and he was responsible for the building or renewing of 26 orgs. of which records survive.

Howell, Dorothy (b. Birmingham, 25. II. 1898), Eng. pianist and comp. Studied comp. under McEwen and pf. under Tobias Matthay at the R.A.M. in London.

Works incl. ballet *Koong Shee*; symph. poem *Lamia* (after Keats), overture *The Rock*; pf. concerto; chamber mus.; pf. mus., etc.

Howells, Herbert (Norman) (b. Lydney, Glos., 17. X. 1892), Eng. comp. Pupil of Herbert Brewer at Gloucester Cathedral and later under Stanford at the R.C.M. in London, where he became prof. of comp. later, having been 1st sub-organist at Salisbury Cathedral and living a retired life in 1917–20 owing to poor health. Mus. Director at St. Paul's Girls' School from 1936, in succession to Holst. D.Mus., Oxford, 1937. He was Prof. of Mus. at London Univ. from 1952 to 1962 and was created C.B.E. in 1953.

Works incl. ballet *Penguinski*; *Sine Nomine, A Kent Yeoman's Song* and *Hymnus Paradisi* for soli, chorus and orch.; *Procession, Pastoral Rhapsody, Paradise Rondel, Merry-Eye,Puck's Minuet, King's Herald* for orch.; *Lady Audrey's Suite* for string orch.; *Pageantry* for brass band; 2 pf. concertos; song cycle *In Green Ways* with orch.; fantasy string 4tet, string 4tet *In Gloucestershire*, clar. 5tet; 3 vln. and pf. sonatas, 2 org. sonatas; ob. sonata, clar. sonata; *Lambert's Clavichord* and *Howells' Clavichord* for clavichord; pf. pieces; much church mus.; songs, etc.

Howes, Frank (b. Oxford, 2. IV. 1891), Eng. mus. critic. Educ. at St. John's Coll., Oxford. He joined *The Times* as asst. mus. critic in 1925, became lecturer at the R.C.M. in 1938 and was chief *Times* critic in succession to Colles from 1943 to 1960. His books incl. a life of Byrd, studies of Vaughan Williams and Walton, of mus. appreciation, psychology, opera, the orch., etc.

Hubay, Jenö (orig. Eugen Huber) (b. Budapest, 15. IX. 1858; d. Budapest, 12. III. 1937), Hung. violinist and comp. Pupil of his father Karl Huber, he appeared as a prodigy at the age of 11, but later went to study with Joachim in Berlin. He travelled much, ed. and completed some of Vieuxtemps's works and became vln. prof. at the Brussels Cons. in 1882 and at the Budapest Cons. in 1886, of which he was director from 1919 to 1934.

Works incl. operas *Alienor*, *A Cremonai Hegedüs* (after Coppée's *Luthier de Crémone*), *A Falu Rossza*, *Karenina Anna* (after Tolstoy), *Az Álarc*, etc.; 4 symphs.; 4 vln. concertos; *Sonate romantique* for vln. and pf.; many vln. pieces, studies, etc.

Huber, Ferdinand (Fürchtegott) (b. St. Gall, 31. X. 1791; d. St. Gall, 9. I. 1863), Swiss trumpeter, organist, cond. and comp. Studied mus. at Stuttgart and held var. appts. as organist, cond. and teacher at Berne and St. Gall. Studied Swiss folk mus. and adapted some of it as part-songs. Works incl. instrumental works; pf. mus.; songs, part-songs, etc.

Huber, Hans (b. Eppenberg, Solothurn, 28. VI. 1852; d. Locarno, 25. XII. 1921), Swiss comp. After attending an eccles. seminary at Solothurn, he studied mus. under Carl Munzinger there and later at the Leipzig Cons. After teaching in Alsace, he settled at Basle in 1877. In 1889 he became prof. at the Cons. there and succeeded Selmar Bagge as its director in 1896, retiring in 1918.

Works incl. operas *Weltfrühling*, *Kudrun*, *Simplicius*, *Die schöne Bellinde*, *Frutta di mare*, *Der gläserne Berg* (unfinished); oratorio *Mors et Vita* (unfinished); Masses, cantatas, etc.; 8 symphs. (No. 2 on pictures by Böcklin) and other orchestral works *Sommernächte*, Serenade, *Carneval* and *Römischer Carneval*; 4 pf. concertos, vln. concerto; much chamber mus.; pf. mus.; songs, incl. Hafiz cycle, etc.

Huber, Klaus (b. Bern, 30. XI. 1924), Swiss comp. Studied with Willy Burkhard at the Zürich Cons. and with Blacher in Berlin. From 1950 he taught vln. in Zürich and from 1960 mus. hist. at the Lucerne Cons.

Works incl. cantata for voice and 4 instruments *Des Engels Anredung an die Seele*; oratorio *Mechthildis* for alto voice and chamber orch. *Auf die ruhige Nacht-Zeit* for soprano and chamber group; *Soliloquia* for soloists, chorus and orch.; *Sonata da chiesa* for vln. and org.; *Concerto per la Camerata*.

Huberman, Bronislaw (b. Czestochowa, 19. XII. 1882; d. Nant-sur-Corsier, Switz., 15. VI. 1947), Pol. violinist. Studied at the Warsaw Cons., in Paris and Berlin, played in public at the age of 7 and later toured the world.

Hubert, Anton. *See* **Uberti, Antonio.**

Hubert, Nikolai Albertovich (b. St. Petersburg, 19. III. 1840; d. Moscow, 8. X. 1888), Rus. mus. scholar, fellow-pupil with Tchaikovsky at the St. Petersburg Cons.; became prof. of theory at the Moscow Cons. and succeeded N. Rubinstein as its head, 1881–3.

Hucbald (b. ?, *c.* 840; d. Saint-Amand, 20. VI. 930), Fr. monk and musician. Lived at the monastery of Saint-Amand. Wrote the treatise *De harmonica institutione*, mainly on the Gamut and the Modes.

Hudson, George (b. ?; d. ?), Eng. 17th-cent. violinist and comp. Worked in London. Took part, with Coleman, sen., Cooke, H. Lawes and Locke, in providing mus. for Davenant's *Siege of Rhodes* (entertainment at Rutland House) in 1656; member of the King's Band from 1661 and comp. to the king.

Hudson, W(illiam). H(enry). (1841–1922), S. Amer.-Brit. naturalist, traveller and author. *See* Gruenberg (*Green Mansions*), Tippett (*Boyhood's End*).

Hüe, Georges (Adolphe) (b. Versailles, 6. V. 1858; d. Paris, 7. VI. 1948), Fr. comp. Studied at the Paris Cons., where he obtained the Prix de Rome in 1879. Member of the Académie des Beaux-Arts in 1922 in succession to Saint-Saëns.

Works incl. operas *Les Pantins*, *Le Roi de Paris*, *Le Miracle*, *Titania* (after Shakespeare), *Dans l'ombre de la cathédrale*, *Riquet à la Houppe* (after Perrault); ballets *Siang Sin* and *Nimba*, pantomime *Cœur brisé*; incid. mus. to Rostand's *Les Romanesques*, Kalidasa's *Sakuntala*, etc.; symph., symph. legend *Rübezahl*, and other orchestral works; songs, etc.

Hueffer, Francis (orig. Franz) (b. Münster, 22. V. 1843; d. London, 19. I. 1889), Ger. (anglicized) mus. critic. Studied in Ger., Paris and London, where he settled, became mus. critic to several periodicals and wrote and lectured on the troubadours, Wagner and other subjects. Wrote libs. for Mackenzie and Cowen.

Hugh the Drover, or Love in the Stocks, opera by Vaughan Williams (lib. by Harold Child), prod. London, R.C.M., 4. VII. 1924.

Hughes, Anselm (b. London, 15. IV. 1889), Eng. mus. scholar and Angl. Benedictine, Prior of Nashdom Abbey. Part-ed. of the pub. of the Old Hall MS. of 15th-cent. Eng. church mus., preserved at Ware. He is a member of the Ed. Board of the *New Oxford History of Music*, ed. of Vol. II and joint ed. of Vol. III.

Hughes, Gervase (b. Birmingham, 1. IX. 1905), Eng. comp. Studied under Frank Shera, Ernest Walker, W. H. Harris, Thomas Wood and Armstrong Gibbs, and took the B.Mus. at Oxford in 1927. In 1926 he joined the mus. staff of the B.N.O.C. and later cond. at var. theatres. In 1933 he left the mus. profession, but after World War II took to comp. again.

Works incl. opera *Imogen's Choice*, operettas *Castle Creevy* and *Venetian Fantasy*; symph. in F min., *Overture for a Mus. Comedy* for orch.; instrumental pieces; pf. mus.; songs to words by Herrick, R. L. Stevenson and Rupert Brooke, etc.

Hughes, Herbert (b. Belfast, 16. III.

1882; d. Brighton, 1. V. 1937), Ir. critic and comp. Studied at the R.C.M. in London, collected Ir. folksongs and was for many years attached as mus. critic to the *Daily Telegraph*. Ed. *Irish Country Songs* and comp. *Rhymes, Parodies*, songs to poems by Padraic Colum, etc.

Hughes, John (1677–1720), Eng. playwright. *See* Acis and Galatea (Handel), Pepusch (*Alexis*, etc.).

Hugo, Victor (1802–85), Fr. poet, novelist and dramatist. *See* Armourer of Nantes (Balfe), Blaramberg (*Mary of Burgundy*), Bottesini (*Marion Delorme*), Ce qu'on entend . . . (Liszt), Cui (*Angelo*), Dargomizhsky (*Esmeralda* and *Notre-Dame de Paris*), Delibes (*Le Roi s'amuse*), Dieren (van) (songs), Djinns (Franck), Duvernoy (*Hernani* overture), Enna (*Komedianter*), Ernani (Verdi), Esmeralda (Campana, Dargomizhsky and G. Thomas), Fauré (*Djinns*), Franck (C.) (songs), Fry (*Notre-Dame de P.*), Gioconda (Ponchielli), Giuramento (Mercadante), Guiraud (*Chasse fantastique*), Kashperov (*Mary Tudor*), Lange (D. de) (*Hernani*), Lucrezia Borgia (Donizetti), Maillart (*Gastibelza*), Maria Tudor (Gomes) Mazeppa (Liszt), Mazzucato (A.) (*Esmeralda*), Monpou (songs), Niedermeyer (songs), Nielsen (L.) (*Lola*), Pedrell (F.) (*Quasimodo*), Pedrollo (*L'uomo che ride*), Pedrotti (*Marion Delorme*), Ponchielli (do.), Poniatowski (*Ruy Blas* and *Esmeralda*), Prévost (*Esmeralda*), Rigoletto (Verdi), Ruy Blas (Glover, Marchetti and Mendelssohn), Schmidt (F.) (*Notre-Dame*), Simon (A.) (*Esmeralda* and *Fishers*), Strunz (*Ruy Blas*), Wagner-Régeny (*Günstling*), White (M. V.) (songs).

Huguenots, Les, opera by Meyerbeer (lib. by Scribe and Émile Deschamps), prod. Paris, Opéra, 29. II. 1836.

Huizar, Candelario (b. Jérez, 2. II. 1888), Mex. comp. of Indian orig. Studied at the Cons. Nacional in Mexico, where he later taught.

Works incl. 4 symphs. on native tunes; string 4tet, etc.

Hulda, opera by C. Franck (lib. by Charles Grandmougin, based on a play by Bjørnson), not perf. in Franck's lifetime; prod. Monte Carlo, 8. III. 1894.

Hullah, John (Pyke) (b. Worcester, 27. VI. 1812; d. London, 21. II. 1884), Eng. cond., teacher and comp. Had mus. lessons from Wm. Horsley in London and studied singing at the R.A.M. In 1836 he became known as the comp. of Dickens's opera, *The Village Coquettes*. After a stay in Paris he taught singing in London, esp. at a school opened at Exeter Hall in 1841 for the instruction of schoolmasters. In 1847 his friends opened St. Martin's Hall for him, and he gave concerts there until 1860, when the hall was burnt down. Later he held a number of mus. appts. and wrote

several books, mainly on singing and vocal mus.

Works incl. operas *The Village Coquettes, The Outpost* and *The Barbers of Bassora*; numerous songs, etc.

Hullebroeck, Emiel (b. Ghent, 20. II. 1878), Belg. pianist, singer and comp. A promoter of community singing in Flem. and Dutch, and comp. of a large number of Flem. songs that have become very popular.

Works incl. opera *Het Meisje van Zaventhem*; oratorio *Kunstvisionen*; cantatas; instrumental mus., etc.

Hüllmandel, Nicolas Joseph (b. Strasbourg, 1751; d. London, 19. XII. 1823), Alsat. harpsichordist, pianist and comp. Pupil of C. P. E. Bach. He appeared in London in 1771 and settled there in 1790 after a visit to It. and residence in Paris. Wrote a treatise on pf. playing.

Works incl. numerous sonatas for harpsichord and later for pf., many with vln. accomp., etc.

Hume, Tobias (b. ?; d. London, 16. IV. 1645), Eng. vla. da gamba player and comp. He was an army captain and towards the end of his life a pensioner in the Charterhouse. Comp. dances for vla. da gamba, songs to the lute, etc., pub. in *Musicall Humours* and *Poeticall Musicke*, etc.

Humfrey, Pelham (b. ? London, 1647; d. Windsor, 14. VII. 1674), Eng. comp. Entered the re-estab. Chapel Royal in London in 1660 under Cooke, joined Blow and Turner in the comp. of the so-called 'club anthem' and was sent abroad for study by Charles II in 1664. Returned in 1667 from Fr. and It. and became a Gentleman of the Chapel Royal, where he succeeded Cooke as Master of the Children in 1672.

Works incl. mus. to Shakespeare's *Tempest*, Dryden's *Conquest of Granada* and *The Indian Emperor*, Crowne's *Hist. of Charles VIII* and Wycherley's *Love in a Wood*; anthems; odes, sacred songs, airs for 1 and 2 voices, etc.

Hummel, Ferdinand (b. Berlin, 6. IX. 1855; d. Berlin, 24. IV. 1928), Ger. pianist, harpist and comp. After playing pf. and harp in public as a child, he studied at Kullak's Cons. in Berlin and later had a success with realistic operas.

Works incl. operas *Mara, Angla, Ein treuer Schelm, Assarpai, Sophie von Brabant, Die Beichte, Die Gefilde der Seligen*; incid. mus. for 14 plays by Wildenbruch and others; symph., overture; pf. concerto, fantasy for harp and orch.; choral works; chamber mus.; pf. pieces, etc.

Hummel, Johan Nepomuka (Johann Nepomuk) (b. Pozsony, 14. XI. 1778; d. Weimar, 17. X. 1837), Hung. pianist and comp. Learnt mus. at first from his father, the cond. Joseph H., who went to Vienna in 1785 as cond. of the Theater auf der Wieden. By that time he was already a brilliant pianist and Mozart took him as a pupil for 2 years. In 1787 he went to tour in Ger., Hol., Scot. and Eng. and had further lessons from Clementi in London, where he stayed until 1792. In 1793 he was back in Vienna, studying comp. with Albrechtsberger, Haydn and Salieri. In 1803 he visited Rus. and from 1804–11 he was mus. director to Prince Esterházy. In 1816–19 he held a similar post at the court of Württemberg at Stuttgart and in 1819–22 and 1833–7 at that of Weimar, undertaking extensive concert tours in between, spending much time in London. He married the singer Elisabeth Röckl (1793–1883).

Works incl. operas *Die Rückfahrt des Kaisers* and *Mathilde von Guise*; ballets *Hélène et Paris*, *Das belebte Gemälde*, *Sappho*; pantomime *Der Zauberring*; incid. mus. to Grillparzer's *Die Ahnfrau*; Masses and other church mus.; 7 pf. concertos; chamber mus.; sonatas for pf. with another instrument; pf. sonatas, rondos, variations, etc.

Humoreske (Ger.) ⎫
Humoresque (Fr.) ⎬ a piece (or in
Schumann a series of movements) of capricious or fantastic rather than humorous character.

Humperdinck, Engelbert (b. Siegburg, 1. IX. 1854; d. Neustrelitz, 27. IX. 1921), Ger. comp. Studied under F. Hiller at the Cologne Cons. and later with F. Lachner and Rheinberger at Munich. In 1879 he met Wagner in It. and acted as his asst. at Bayreuth in 1880–1. Later he travelled in Fr., It. and Spain and taught at the Barcelona Cons. in 1885–7. In 1890–6 he taught at the Hoch Cons. at Frankfurt and was for a time mus. critic of the *Frankfurter Zeitung*. In 1900 he became director of the Meisterschule for comp. in Berlin.

Works incl. operas *Hänsel und Gretel*, *Dornröschen*, *Die Heirat wider Willen*, *Königskinder*, *Die Marketenderin*, *Gaudeamus*; play with mus. *Königskinder* (an earlier version of the opera); spectacular pantomime *The Miracle*; incid. mus. to Shakespeare's *Merchant of Venice*, *Winter's Tale*, *The Tempest* and *Twelfth Night*, Maeterlinck's *The Blue Bird*, Aristophanes' *Lysistrata*; choral works *Das Glück von Edenhall* (Uhland), *Die Wallfahrt nach Kevlaar* (Heine); *Humoreske* and *Maurische Rhapsodie* for orch.; part-songs, songs, etc.

Humphrey, Pelham. *See* Humfrey.

Humphries, John (b. ?, *c.* 1707; d. ?, *c.* 1745), Eng. comp. Pub. 6 solos for vln. and bass and 2 sets of concertos. He is possibly identical with J. S. H., who *c.* 1733 pub. a set of sonatas for 2 vlns.

Humstrum, a primitive and now obs.

vln. with 4 wire strings and a tin canister for a soundbox.

Huneker, James (Gibbons) (b. Philadelphia, 31. I. 1857; d. N.Y. 9. II. 1921), Amer. critic. Studied the pf. in Paris and N.Y. and later became a teacher at the Nat. Cons. there. He wrote essays on the arts and became art and mus. critic to var. newspapers in Philadelphia and N.Y., the last being the *N.Y. World*. His books incl. vols. on Chopin and Liszt and collected essays.

Hungarian Composers. *See* Abrányi, Aggházy, Bartók, Beliczay, Berté, Bihari, Cousser, Csermák, Czibulka, Dohnányi, Doppler, Erkel, Farkas (F.), Farkas (Ö.), Goldmark, Gungl, Hrisányi, Heller, Hubay, Hummel, Jemnitz, Joachim, Kéler-Béla, Kodály, Lajtha, Lavotta, Lehár, Lendvai, Liszt, Mihalovich, Molnár, Moór, Mosonyi, Nováček, Poldini, Radnai, Raimann, Seiber, Siklós, Sucher, Szábados, Szábo, Szántó, Székely, Szendy, Vavrinecz, Veress, Wagner-Régeny, Weiner, Zador, Zichy.

Hunnenschlacht (*Battle of the Huns*), symph. poem by Liszt inspired by Kaulbach's fresco, comp. 1857; 1st perf. Weimar, 29. XII. 1857.

Hunnis, William (b. ?; d. London, 6. VI. 1597), Eng. comp. Gentleman of the Chapel Royal in the reigns of Edward VI, Mary I and Elizabeth, though dismissed as a Protestant in Mary's time. He became Master of the Children in 1566.

Works incl. metrical psalms and other portions of the Bible versified by himself.

Hunt, Arabella (b. ?; d. London, 26. XII. 1705), Eng. singer and lutenist. Mus. teacher of Princess (later Queen) Anne and a favourite of Queen Mary. Blow and Purcell wrote many songs for her. Congreve wrote an ode on her and Kneller painted her portrait.

'Hunt' Quartet, the familiar nickname of Mozart's B♭ maj. string 4tet, K. 458, because the opening suggests hunting-horns.

Hünten, Franz (b. Coblenz, 26. XII. 1793; d. Coblenz, 22. II. 1878), Ger. pianist and comp. Pupil of his father, the organist Daniel H., and later of Pradher for pf. and Reicha and Cherubini for comp. at the Paris Cons. Taught there for some years and made pf. arrs. of var. mus. He wrote a method of pf. playing and comp. a *Trio concertante* for vln., cello and pf., many pf. works, songs, etc.

Hunyady László, opera by Erkel (lib. by Beni Egressy), prod. Budapest, 27. I. 1844. The chief Hung. nat. opera.

Huon de Bordeaux, medieval Fr. romance. *See* Oberon (Weber and Wranitzky).

Hurdy-Gurdy (onomat.), the Eng. name for the medieval *organistrum*. Its strings, usually 6, are set vibrating by a wheel

300

turned with a handle. The tune is played on the top string by means of a keyboard, the lower strings remaining unchanged in pitch and thus acting as a drone.

Huré, Jean (b. Gien, Loiret, 17. IX. 1877; d. Paris, 27. I. 1930), Fr. organist and comp. He became organist of the church of Saint-Augustin in Paris in succession to Gigout in 1925 and ed. a journal *L'Orgue et les Organistes*.

Works incl. opera *Le Bois sacré*; incid. mus. to Musset's *Fantasio*; Te Deum and other church mus.; 3 symphs.; vln. concerto, saxophone concerto; 2 string 4tets and other chamber mus.; vln. and pf. sonata, 3 cello and pf. sonatas; org. works, etc.

Hurlebusch, Heinrich Lorenz (b. Hanover, 8. VII. 1666; d. Brunswick, ?), Ger. organist and comp. Wrote org. works.

Hurlebusch, Conrad Friedrich (b. Brunswick, 1696; d. Amsterdam, 16. XII. 1765), Ger. organist and comp., son of prec. Travelled much as a virtuoso, visiting It. and Swed., holding brief offices at Brunswick and Hamburg, and finally settling at Amsterdam.

Works incl. operas, cantatas, hymns, overtures, harpsichord pieces, songs, etc.

Hurlstone, William (Yeates) (b. London, 7. I. 1876; d. London, 30. V. 1906), Eng. pianist and comp. Studied at the R.C.M. in London, having already pub. waltzes for pf. at the age of 9. Prof. of counterpoint at the R.C.M. from 1905 to his early death.

Works incl. Fantasy-Variations on a Swed. Air and suite *The Magic Mirror* for orch.; pf. concerto; string 4tet in E min., pf. and wind 5tet, pf. 4tet, Fantasy string 4tet; sonatas for vln. and pf., cello and pf., bassoon and pf., suite for clar. and pf., etc.

Hüsch, Gerhard (b. Hanover, 2. II. 1901), Ger. baritone. Made his début in Osnabrück in 1924 and then sang at the Cologne Opera from 1927 to 1930 and in Berlin from 1930 to 1942. In addition to being a fine opera-singer he was also a distinguished *Lieder*-singer.

Husitská, concert overture by Dvořák, Op. 67, comp. 1883, 1st perf. Prague, reopening of the Nat. Theatre, 13. XI. 1883. Based on the 10th-cent. St. Vaclav chorale and the 15th-cent. Hussite hymn.

Huss, Henry Holden (b. Newark, N.J., 21. VI. 1862; d. N.Y., 17. IX. 1953), Amer. pianist and comp. 1st studied with his father and others at home, later at Munich, his comp. master being Rheinberger.

Works incl. pf. concerto in B maj., Rhapsody for pf. and orch., vln. concerto in C min.; 2 string 4tets; 2 vln. and pf. sonatas, cello and pf. sonata; pf. pieces; songs, etc.

Hussey, Dyneley (b. Deolali, India, 27. II. 1893), Eng. mus. critic. Educ. at Oxford,

joined the staff of *The Times* and became critic 1st to the *Saturday Review* and then to the *Spectator*. During World War II he joined the Admiralty. His books incl. vols. on Mozart and Verdi and *Eurydice, or The Nature of Opera*.

Hutchings, Arthur (James Bramwell) (b. Sunbury-on-Thames, 14. VII. 1906), Eng. writer on mus. and comp. Contrib. to mus. periodicals since the age of 19 and author of books on Schubert, Mozart's pf. concertos, Delius and the Baroque concerto. In 1947 he followed Bairstow as Prof. of Mus. at Durham Univ., becoming prof. at Exeter Univ. from 1968 to 1971.

Works incl. *O quanta qualia, or Heart's Desire* (Abélard) for double chorus, orch., brass band and org.; motets and other church mus.; works for string orch., etc.

Hutschenrijter, Wouter (b. Rotterdam, 28. XII. 1796; d. Rotterdam, 18. XI. 1878), Dutch violinist, cond. and comp. Studied vln. and horn, and later cond var. mus. societies at Rotterdam and Schiedam.

Works incl. opera *Le Roi de Bohème*; Masses, cantatas and other choral works; 4 symphs., 2 overtures; cello and pf. sonata; songs, etc.

Hutschenrijter, Wouter (b. Rotterdam, 15. VIII. 1859; d. The Hague, 24. XII. 1943), Dutch cond., comp. and writer on mus., grandson of prec. Cond. at Amsterdam and Utrecht, and in 1917–25 director of the Mus. School at Rotterdam. His books incl. studies of Chopin, Wagner, Brahms, Mahler and R. Strauss, and his comps. orchestral and chamber mus.

Hüttenbrenner, Anselm (b. Graz, 13. X. 1794; d. Ober-Andritz nr. Graz, 5. VI. 1868), Aus. comp. Pupil of Salieri and friend of Schubert, whose unfinished symph. he withheld from the world until 1865.

Works incl. operas *Die Einquartierung*, *Ödipus auf Kolonos* (Sophocles), *Armella* and *Lenore*; incid. mus. for several plays; 6 Masses, 3 Requiems and other church mus.; 6 symphs.; 2 string 4tets; songs incl. a setting of Goethe's *Erlkönig*, etc.

Huybrechts, Albert (b. Dinant, 12. II. 1899; d. Brussels, 21. II. 1938), Belg. critic and comp. Studied at the Brussels Cons., Jongen being among his masters.

Works incl. 2 symph. poems, *David* and *Chant d'angoisse*; concertino for cello and orch.; string 4tet; vln. and pf. sonata; songs, etc.

Huygens, Constantin (b. The Hague, 4. IX. 1596; d. The Hague, 28. III. 1687), Dutch official, physicist, poet, writer, linguist and musician. He was military secretary at The Hague from 1625 to his death. He was a lutenist and also played viol and the keyboard instruments, paying 3 visits to Eng. and others to Ger., It. and Fr. He collected a mus. library and wrote on the use of the org. in church and other mus. subjects. One of his sons, Christian H. (1629–95), was also a musician as well as a mathematician.

Hyde, Douglas (1860–1949), Ir. philologist and author, President of Eire from 1938 to 1945. *See* **Esposito** (*Tinker and Fairy*).

Hydraulis, the water org. invented in Egypt by Ctesibius in the 3rd cent. B.C. The pipes were played by wind forced through them by the pressure of water.

Hygons, Richard (b. ?; d. ? 1508), Eng. comp. He was one of the organists at Wells Cathedral, 1461–2, and master of the choristers there, 1479–1508, when he was succeeded by John Clausy. His only complete surviving work, a 5-part *Salve regina,* is in the Eton Choirbook.

Hyllested, August (b. Stockholm, 17. VI. 1858; d. Blairmore, Argyll, 5. IV. 1946), Dan. pianist and comp. Studied at the Copenhagen Cons. and toured Scand. as a pianist, was cathedral organist in Copenhagen, 1876–9, then went to finish

his studies in Berlin and with Liszt at Weimar. From 1886 to 1894 he taught in Chicago.

Works incl. symph. poem *Elizabeth* for chorus and orch.; *Suite romantique, Marche triomphale* and other works for orch.; 2 pf. trios; *Scand. Dances, Variations, sérieuses, Suite de ballet,* etc. for pf., etc.

Hymn, a metrical song in praise of God. Many medieval H.s survive with plainsong melodies, which should properly be sung unacc. The Protestant churches in the 16th cent. adopted the practice of harmonizing H.-tunes. *See* **Choral.**

Hymn of Praise (Lobgesang), Mendelssohn's symph. cantata, Op. 52, in which three movements of a symph. precede the choral portion; prod. Leipzig, St. Thomas's Church, 25. VI. 1840; in Eng., Birmingham Festival, 23. IX. 1840.

Hymn of the Nations (Verdi). *See* **Inno delle nazioni.**

Hypo- (prefix). *See* **Modes.**

Hyslop, James (1798–1827), Scot. poet, *See* **MacCunn** (*Cameronian's Dream*).

Images

I

I.S.C.M. (abbr.) = International Society for Contemporary Music.

Iberia, 4 sets of pf. pieces by I. Albéniz, representing different parts of Spain, comp. at var. times before 1909; I. *Evocación, El Puerto, Fête-Dieu à Séville*; II. *Triana, Almeria, Rondeña*; III. *El Albaicin, El Polo, Lavapiés*; IV. *Málaga, Jérez, Eritaña.*

Ibéria (Debussy). See **Images pour Orchestre.**

Ibert, Jacques (François Antoine) (b. Paris, 15. VIII. 1890; d. Paris, 5. II. 1962), Fr. comp. Studied at the Paris Cons. and gained the Prix de Rome in 1919. He became director of the Fr. Acad. in Rome in 1937 and returned there after World War II. From 1955 to 1957 he was director of the Opéra-Comique in Paris.

Works incl. operas *Angélique, Persée et Andromède, On ne saurait penser à tout, Le Roi d'Yvetot, Gonzague* and (both with Honegger) *L'Aiglon* (after Rostand), *Le Petit Cardinal*; radio opera *Barbe-bleue*; ballets *Les Rencontres, Diane de Poitiers* and contrib. to *L'Éventail de Jeanne*; incid. mus. to Labiche's *Le Chapeau de paille d'Italie* and other plays, also (with 6 others) for Rolland's *Le 14 Juillet*; film mus. incl. *Don Quichotte*; cantata *Le Poète et la Fée*; symph. poem *La Ballade de la geôle de Reading* (after Wilde); suites *Escales* and *Paris, Scherzo féerique, Nationale* (for Paris Exhib., 1937), *Jeux, Donogoo, Ouverture pour une fête,* all for orch.; *Divertissement* for chamber orch ; concertos for pf., for saxophone and for cello and wind; string 4tet; pf. works, incl. *Pièces romantiques, Noël de Picardie, Le Vent dans les ruines, Matin sur l'eau, Le Petit Âne blanc,* etc.; 5 pieces for harp; pieces for pipes and pf., etc.

Ibsen, Henrik (1828–1906), Norw. dramatist. See **Egg** (*Peer Gynt*), **Feast at Solhaug** (incid. mus., H. Wolf), **Grieg** (songs), **Heward** (*Peer Gynt*), **O'Neill** (*Pretenders*), **Paz** (*Julian the Emperor*), **Peer Gynt** (Grieg), **Pfitzner** (*Feast at S.*), **Rangström** (*Brand*), **Schjelderup** (do.), **Steinberg** (do.), **Stenhammar** (*Feast at S.*), **Ullmann** (*Peer Gynt*), **Wallace (W.)** (*Lady from the Sea*).

Ideale, Die (*The Ideals*), symph. poem by Liszt, based on a poem by Schiller, comp. 1857, 1st perf. Weimar, 5. IX. 1857 at the unveiling of the Goethe-Schiller monument.

Idée fixe, Berlioz's term for a theme (e.g. in the *Fantastic Symph.*) which recurs in varying forms in the course of a comp. as an allusion to some definite idea.

Idoménée (*Idomeneus*), opera by Campra (lib. by Antoine Danchet), prod. Paris, Opéra, 12. I. 1712.

Idomeneo, rè di Creta, ossia Ilia ed Idamante (*Idomeneus, King of Crete, or Ilia and Idamantes*), opera by Mozart (lib. by Giovanni Battista Varesco, based on the Fr. lib. by Antoine Danchet), prod. Munich, 29. I. 1781.

Iernin, opera by George Lloyd (lib. by William Lloyd, the comp.'s father), prod. Penzance, 6. XI. 1934.

Ifigenia, L', opera by Jommelli (lib. by Mattia Verazi), prod. Rome, Teatro Argentina, 9. II. 1751.

Ifigenia in Aulide (*Iphigenia in Aulis*), opera by Caldara (lib. by Apostolo Zeno), prod. Vienna, 4. XI. 1718.

Opera by Cherubini (lib. by Ferdinando Moretti), prod. Turin, Teatro Regio, II. 1788.

Opera by Graun (lib. by Leopoldo de Villati, after Racine's *Iphigénie en Aulide*), prod. Berlin, Royal Opera, 13. XII. 1748. Frederick II of Prus. prob. collaborated.

Opera by Zingarelli (lib. by Ferdinando Moretti), prod. Milan, Teatro alla Scala, 27. I. 1787. (All libs. based ultimately on Euripides.)

Ifigenia in Tauride (*Iphigenia in Tauris*), opera by Galuppi (lib. by Marco Coltellini), prod. St. Petersburg, at court, 2. V. 1768.

Opera by Maio (lib. by Mattia Verazi), prod. Mannheim, at court, 4. XI. 1764.

Opera by Traetta (lib. by Marco Coltellini), prod. Vienna, Schönbrunn Palace, at court, 4. X. 1763. (Libs. based on Euripides.)

See also **Iphigénie.**

Ileborgh, Adam (b. ?; d. ?), 15th-cent. Ger. priest and musician. He compiled and owned a collection of keyboard mus., now in the Curtis Inst. of Mus., Philadelphia. It bears the date 1448 and contains early exs. of preludes for org., incl. pedals.

Ilyinsky, Alexander Alexandrovich (b. Tsarskoye Selo, 24. I. 1859; d. Moscow, 23. II. 1920), Rus. pianist and comp. Studied pf. under Kullak and comp. under Bargiel in Berlin. Returning to Rus. in 1885, he became prof. at the Phil. Society's School of Mus. in Moscow.

Works incl. opera *The Fountain of Bakhchiserai* (after Pushkin); cantatas *Strekozi* and *Russalka*; incid. mus. to Sophocles' *Oedipus Rex* and *Philoctetes*, overture to A. Tolstoy's *Tsar Feodor*; symph., 3 orchestral suites (No. 2 *A Village Holiday*, No. 3 *Noor and Anitra*), symph. scherzo, Croatian dances for orch.; string 4tet; vln. pieces; pf. mus.; songs, etc.

Images, 2 sets of pf. pieces by Debussy: 1st series comp. 1905, *Reflets dans l'eau, Hommage à Rameau, Mouvement*; 2nd series, comp. 1907, *Cloches à travers les feuilles, Et la lune descend sur le temple qui fut, Poissons d'or.*

Images pour Orchestre, 3 symph. pieces by Debussy: *Gigues* (orig. *Gigues tristes*), comp. 1906–11; *Rondes de printemps*, comp. 1909; *Ibéria (Par les rues et par les chemins, Les Parfums de la nuit* and *Le Matin d'un jour de fête*), finished 1908.

Imareta, Tirso. *See* **Yriarte.**

Imbert, Hugues (b. Moulins-Engilbert, Nièvre, 11. I. 1842; d. Paris, 15. I. 1905), Fr. critic and writer on mus. He had a general educ. and became an official, but did much mus.-lit. work. His books incl. sketches of var. comps. and special studies of Wagner, Brahms, Gounod, Bizet, etc.

Imitation, a device in comp. whereby a mus. figure is repeated after its 1st statement, either exactly or with some change, such as displacement to a higher or lower position, augmentation, diminution, rhythmic distortion, elaboration, simplification, etc. Such an I. may either be deferred until the 1st statement has been completed or made to overlap with it.

Imitations, mus. comps. or parts thereof where a comp. deliberately writes in the manner of some other comp. Here are some exs.:

Bréville, *Portraits de Maîtres* for pf. (Franck, d'Indy, Chausson, Fauré).

Casella and Ravel, *À la manière de ...* for pf. (Wagner, Fauré, Brahms, Debussy, R. Strauss, Franck, d'Indy, Ravel, Borodin, Chabrier; only the last 2 by Ravel).

Grieg, *Gade* (*Lyric Pieces* for pf.).

Holbrooke, *Les Hommages* for orch. (Wagner, Grieg, Dvořák, Tchaikovsky).

Holst, parodies of Wagner and Verdi, in *The Perfect Fool.*

Hopkins, Anthony, var. parodies in *Lady Rohesia.*

d'Indy, *Schumanniana* for pf., Op. 30.

Karg-Elert, *Intarsien* for org., Op. 76: No. 5, *Vor dem Bildnis Griegs*; 33 *Portraits* for harmonium, Op. 101 (imitations of comps. from Palestrina to Schönberg).

Mason, D. G., *Variations on Yankee Doodle* for pf. (Grieg, Tchaikovsky, Brahms, Debussy, MacDowell, Dvořák, Liszt).

Mozart, overture (suite) in Handel's style for pf. (K. 399).

Mussorgsky, satirical song, *The Peepshow* (var. styles).

Ravel, *La Valse* for orch. (in the manner of Viennese waltzes of the J. Strauss period).

Ries, sonata in Mozart's style for pf.

Rimsky-Korsakov, var. passages in the opera *Mozart and Salieri.*

Rossini, *Capriccio offenbachique* (orch. by Respighi for *La Boutique fantasque*).

Schumann, *Chopin* and *Paganini* movements in *Carnaval* for pf.; *Erinnerung*

(Mendelssohn) in *Album für die Jugend* for pf.

Spohr, 1st 3 movements of *Historical Symph.* (Haydn, Mozart, Beethoven).

Strauss, R., waltzes in *Der Rosenkavalier* in the style of Johann Strauss; also tenor aria in Act I, imitating 18th-cent. It. opera style. S.'s *Ariadne auf Naxos* contains var. incidents in different styles.

Tchaikovsky, divertissement in Act II of *The Queen of Spades* in the style of Mozart; *Un poco di Chopin* and *Un poco di Schumann* for pf.; *Alla Schumann* in Variations on an orig. theme for pf.

Vaughan Williams, *The Poisoned Kiss*, opera, parodies of var. styles.

Immermann, Karl Leberecht (1796–1840), Ger. novelist and dramatist. *See* **Hindemith** (*Tulifäntchen*), **Rietz (J.)** (incid. mus. for plays), **Tiessen** (*Merlin*).

Immortal Hour, The, opera by Boughton (lib. by comp. adapted from plays and poems by Fiona Macleod), prod. Glastonbury, 26. VIII. 1914.

Imperfect Cadence. *See* **Half-Close.**

Impériale, L', nickname of Haydn's symph. No. 53 in D maj., comp. *c.* 1775 (?).

Impresario in angustie, L' (*The Impresario in Distress*), opera by Cimarosa (lib. by Giuseppe Maria Diodati, similar to that of Mozart's *Schauspieldirektor*), prod. Naples, Teatro Nuovo, X. 1786.

Impresario, The (Mozart). *See* **Schauspieldirektor.**

Impressionism, a term properly belonging to painting but transferred, more or less loosely, to comps. (esp. Fr.) contemporary with the school of impressionist painters. Debussy, although he disapproved, was designated as the leader of mus. I. One of the chief aims of I. is to interpret artistically a momentary glimpse of things rather than their permanent state.

Impromptu (from Lat. *in promptu* = in readiness), a piece of mus. suggesting, or intended to suggest, that it resembles an improvisation.

Improvisation (or **Extemporization**), the art of playing or singing mus. not written down by a comp. but proceeding straight from the player's imagination. Improvised cadenzas were expected of singers and instrumental soloists in the 17th–18th cents. and survived, to a limited extent, in the 19th cent. Improvisation is an essential part of the educ. of an organist.

In Nature's Realm (Dvořák). *See* **Amid Nature.**

In Nomine, an instrumental piece of the later 16th cent. for viols or keyboard, similar to the Fancy or Fantasia, but based on a plainsong melody used as a *cantus firmus.* The melody is that of 'Gloria tibi Trinitas', an antiphon for Trinity Sunday, which was used by

Taverner as the *cantus firmus* of a Mass with the title *Gloria tibi Trinitas*. Part of the *Benedictus* of this Mass, beginning at the words 'In nomine Domini', was arranged as an instrumental piece, and this seems to have suggested to other comps. the idea of writing orig. instrumental pieces on the same *cantus firmus*. The last comp. to write In N.s was Purcell.

In questa tomba oscura, a collective work, of which only Beethoven's song remains known today. In 1808 comps. were invited to set this poem by Giuseppe Carpani, probably at the invitation of Countess Rzewuska in Vienna. Among the 63 comps. who responded were, apart from Beethoven, Asioli, Cherubini, Czerny, Paer, Reichardt, Righini, Salieri, Tomašek, Weigl and Zingarelli.

In the South, concert overture by Elgar, Op. 50, comp. during a visit to It. in 1903 and pub. in 1904.

Incalzando (It.) = persuading, urging forward, *i.e.* accelerating the pace.

Incidental Music, songs and instrumental mus. intro. into spoken drama, either in the form of preludes or interludes or as an essential part of the action, e.g. marches, dances, etc.

Incledon, Charles (Benjamin) (b. St. Keverne, Cornwall, I. or II. 1763; d. London, 18. II. 1826), Eng. tenor. Chorister at Exeter Cathedral, he joined the Navy at the age of 16, but on his return to Eng. in 1783 became a professional singer. Made his London début at Vauxhall Gardens in 1790.

Incognita, opera by Wellesz (lib. by Elizabeth Mackenzie, on Congreve's story), prod. Oxford, 5. XII. 1951.

Incontro improviso, L' (*The Unforeseen Meeting*), opera by Haydn (lib. by Karl Friberth, trans. into. It. from Dancourt's *La Rencontre imprévue*, comp. by Gluck), prod. Esterház, 29. VIII. 1775.

Incoronazione di Poppea, L' (*The Coronation of Poppaea*), opera by Monteverdi (lib. by Giovanni Francesco Busenello, based on Tacitus), prod. Venice, Teatro SS. Giovanni e Paolo, autumn 1642.

Indes galantes, Les (*Love in the Indies*), opera-ballet by Rameau (lib. by Louis Fuzelier), prod. Paris, Opéra, 23. VIII. 1735.

Indian Queen, The, play by Dryden and Robert Howard, prod. 1664; adapted as an 'opera' with mus. by Purcell, prod. London, Drury Lane Theatre, 1695.

Indigo und die vierzig Räuber (*I. and the Forty Robbers*), operetta by J. Strauss, jun. (lib. by Maximilian Steiner), prod. Vienna, Theater an der Wien, 10. II. 1871. Strauss's 1st operetta.

Indy, (Paul Marie Théodore) Vincent d' (b. Paris, 27. III. 1851; d. Paris, 2. XII. 1931), Fr. comp. Although b. in Paris, he belonged to a noble family of the Ardèche district in the Vivarais. His mother d. at his birth and he was brought up by his paternal grandmother, a good musician. At the age of 11 he was sent to Diémer for the pf. and Lavignac for theory, and later studied pf. under Marmontel. In 1870 he pub. his 1st comps. and served in the defence of Paris against the Prus. army. To please his family he studied law, but was determined to be a musician and went for advice to Franck, who offered to teach him. He also joined Colonne's orch. as timpanist to gain experience. Pasdeloup gave the 1st perf. of one of his works, the overture to Schiller's *Piccolomini*, afterwards part of his *Wallenstein* trilogy. Next to Franck he admired Liszt, with whom he spent 2 months at Weimar in 1873, and Wagner, whose 1st *Ring* cycle he attended at Bayreuth in 1876. In 1894 he joined Charles Bordes, together with Guilmant, in founding the Schola Cantorum; he taught there until his death and had many pupils of the highest distinction. From 1912 he also directed the orchestral class at the Cons.

Works incl. operas *Attendez-moi sous l'orme* (after Regnard), *Le Chant de la cloche*, *Fervaal*, *L'Étranger*, *La Légende de Saint Christophe*, *La Rêve de Cinyras*; incid. mus. for Catulle Mendès's *Médée*; 2 symphs., *Jean Hunyade* and *De bello gallico*, symph. trilogy *Wallenstein* (after Schiller), symph. variations *Istar*, *Jour d'été à la montagne*; *Symphonie sur un chant montagnard français* (*Symph. cévenole*) for pf. and orch.; 3 string 4tets, string 6tet, pf. 4tet and pf. 5tet, trios for pf., clar. and cello and pf., vln. and cello, suite for tpt., 2 fls. and string 4tet, and some other chamber works; sonatas for vln. and pf. and cello and pf.; 18 op. nos. of pf. works, incl. *Poèmes des montagnes*, *Tableaux de voyage*, sonata in E maj., *Thème varié*, *Fugue et Chanson*; 3 org. works; 10 songs; 90 *Chansons populaires du Vivarais* arr.; 12 Fr. folksongs for unaccomp. chorus; var. vocal works with and without orch., etc.

Inez de Castro, opera by Persiani (lib. by Salvatore Cammarano), prod. Naples, Teatro San Carlo, 28. I. 1835. It was written for Malibran.

Infantas, Fernando de las (b. Córdoba, 1534; d. ? Paris, after 1609), Span. comp., descendant of the Fernández family of Córdoba, known by that name because one of his ancestors conveyed the infantas Constanza and Isabella to Bayonne, occupied by the Eng. in the 14th cent., before their marriage to John of Gaunt and Edmund Langley. His comps. attracted the attention of the Bishop of Córdoba, the Archduke Charles of Austria. He settled in Rome c. 1559, but took holy orders in 1584 and went (?) to Paris.

Works incl. motets, some for special occasions, such as the death of the Emperor Charles V (1558) and the battle of Lepanto (1571), a setting of Psalm xcix, etc.

Infinite Canon, a canon contrived to make the end overlap with the beginning, so that it can be repeated to infinity.

Inganno (It. = deception), the It. name for the Interrupted Cadence.

Inganno felice, L' (*The Happy Deceit*), opera by Rossini (lib. by Giuseppe Maria Foppa), prod. Venice, Teatro San Moise, 8. I. 1812.

Ingegneri, Marc Antonio (b. Verona, *c.* 1545; d. Cremona, 1. VII. 1592), It. comp. Learnt mus. from V. Ruffo at Verona Cathedral and *c.* 1570 became *maestro di cappella* at Cremona Cathedral. Monteverdi was his pupil there.

Works incl. 2 books of Masses, 3 books of motets, 1 of hymns and 8 of madrigals; also 27 responsories for Holy Week (long attrib. to Palestrina).

Ingenhoven, Jan (b. Breda, 19. V. 1876; d. Hoenderloo, 20. V. 1951), Dutch cond. and comp. He was a choral cond. before he had any systematic mus. educ., but studied later with Brandts-Buys and with Mottl at Munich, where he cond. both orchestral and choral concerts, as he did later both in Hol. and abroad. He also sang tenor and played the pf. and clar.

Works incl. 3 symph. pieces for orch.; symph. fantasy on Nietzsche's *Zarathustras Nachtlied* and ballad *Klaus Tink* for voice and orch.; 4 string 4tets; vln. and pf. sonata in C maj., cello and pf. sonata in G maj.; choruses and vocal 4tets; songs, etc.

Inghelbrecht, D(ésiré-). É(mile). (b. Paris, 17. IX. 1880; d. Paris, 14. II. 1965), Fr. cond. and comp. Cond. many concerts of modern mus. in Paris, also the Swed. Ballet in Paris and London.

Works incl. operas *La Nuit vénitienne* (after Musset) and *La Chêne et le tilleul*; 2 operettas; ballets *El Greco* and *Le Diable dans le beffroi*; Requiem; *Cantique des créatures de Saint François* for chorus and orch.; *Sinfonia breve*; string 4tet; sonata for fl. and harp; 5tet for strings and harp; *Suite Petite-Russienne* and other pf. works; *La Nursery* for pf. duet (3 books); songs, etc.

Inglesina, L'. *See* Davies, Cecilia.

Ingoldsby, Thomas. *See* Barham.

Inharmonic. *See* Harmonics.

Inkle and Yarico, opera by Arnold (lib. by George Colman, jun., based on a story by Steele), prod. London, Little Theatre, Haymarket, 4. VIII. 1787.

Innig (Ger. = inward, intimate, heartfelt), a term frequently used by Ger. romantic comps., esp. Schumann, where profound feeling is required in perf.

Inno delle nazioni (Hymn of the Nations),

cantata by Verdi written for the International Exhibition in London, but prod. at Her Majesty's Theatre, 24. V. 1862. It intro. nat. airs in contrapuntal combination.

Innocenza giustificata, L' (*Innocence Vindicated*), opera by Gluck (lib. by Giacomo Durazzo, with words for the airs by Metastasio), prod. Vienna, Burgtheater, 8. XII. 1755.

Insanguine, Giacomo (b. Monopoli, Bari, 22. III. 1728; d. Naples, 1. II. 1795), It. comp. Studied at the Cons. di Sant' Onofrio at Naples, where he taught from 1767, eventually becoming *maestro di cappella*. Between 1756 and 1782 he prod. 21 operas. Other works incl. Masses and other church mus., cantatas, arias, etc.

Instrumentation, the art of writing for instruments in a manner suited to their nature, also Orchestration.

Intavolatura (It.), Tablature. In the 16th and 17th cents. the term was used for pubs. issued for keyboard instruments and written on 2 staves, as distinct from instrumental mus. printed in score or in separate parts.

Intendant (Ger.), the manager or director of an opera-house or other theatre in Ger., esp. one attached to a court in former times.

Interdominant, a useful term to describe temporary dominants in the keys in which episodes may appear in the course of a comp., other than the dominant of the prescribed key. The same as the Ger. *Zwischendominante*.

Interlude, a piece of mus. played or (more rarely) sung between 2 others or forming a bridge between 2 distinct sections of a large-scale comp.; also a mus. piece perf. between parts of some other perf. or function, such as certain liturgical portions of a church service, acts or scenes of a play, dances at a ball or courses of a dinner, etc. Act-tunes (*entr'actes*) in a theatre are, properly speaking, I.s.

Intermède (Fr.) = Interlude, Intermezzo.

Intermedio. *See* **Intermezzo.**

Intermezzo (It. = interlude), in the 16th cent. (*intermedio*) a series of vocal and instrumental pieces interpolated in a festival play or other dramatic entertainment.

In the 18th cent. a comic operatic piece, usually in 2 scenes and for 2 or 3 characters, 1 of whom could be a 'mute', played as an interlude between the acts of a serious opera in 18th-cent. It., esp. Naples. The most famous ex. is Pergolesi's *La serva padrona*.

In general any mus. piece played between the parts of a larger work, mus. or theatrical. Also a short concert piece, not necessarily designed for any purpose implied by the name, e.g. Brahms's Intermezzi for pf.

Intermezzo, opera by R. Strauss (lib. by comp.), prod. Dresden, 4. XI. 1924. The material of the lib. is autobiographical.

International Society for Contemporary Music, an organization formed after a mus. festival held at Salzburg in 1922 for the furtherance of modern mus. and the holding of annual festivals in var. mus. centres.

panying the entry of the ministers. Orig. a complete psalm with antiphon before and after each verse, it was reduced in the Middle Ages to its present form of antiphon, psalm-verse, *Gloria Patri* and repeat of antiphon. The antiphon is a freely-comp. melody, the psalm being sung to a slightly ornate psalm-tone (*see* illustration).

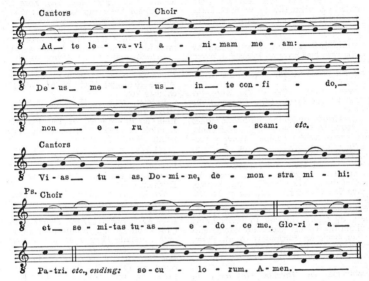

INTROIT

Interpretation, the presentation of a mus. work to an audience according to the perf.'s idea of what was in the comp.'s mind.

Interrupted Cadence. *See* **Cadence.**

Interval, the distance in pitch between 2 notes, whether struck simultaneously or successively.

Intonation, the way in which mus. is sung or played according to the ear's perception of what is or is not in tune; also the act of Intoning.

Intonazione (It., lit. Intonation), a 16th-cent. term for a prelude, esp. one for org. used in church to precede a service.

Intoning, in plainsong, the singing of the opening phrase by a singer in authority to ensure that the right melody will be sung and at the proper pitch.

Intrada (It., now *entrada*; lit. entrance, entry) = Introduction, Prelude.

Introit (Lat. *introitus* = entrance), the 1st item of the Proper of the Mass, accom-

Inventions, the title given to Bach's 2 sets of short keyboard pieces written strictly in 2 and 3 parts respectively, and prob. designed as technical studies. He called the 3-part set 'symphonies', but there is no essential difference between them and the 2-part I.s in character.

Inversion. (1) Of an interval. The I. of a 5th is a 4th.

(2) Of a melody. Writing a melody upside-down, i.e. the intervals remain the same but go in the opposite direction.

(3) Of a chord. A 3-note chord has 2 possible I.s, e.g.:

'Root' position 1st inversion 2nd inversion

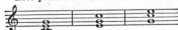

A 4-note chord has 3 possible I.s, and so on.

(4) Of counterpoint. *See* **Counterpoint.**

Invertible Counterpoint. *See* **Counterpoint.**

Invitation to the Dance (Weber). *See* **Aufforderung zum Tanz.**

Iolanta, opera by Tchaikovsky (lib. by Modest Ilich Tchaikovsky, Tchaikovsky's brother, based on Hertz's play *King René's Daughter*), prod. St. Petersburg, 18. XII. 1892.

Iolanthe, or The Peer and the Peri, operetta by Sullivan (lib. by W. S. Gilbert), prod. London, Savoy Theatre, 25. XI. 1882, and N.Y., Standard Theatre, same date.

Ione (old It. spelling *Jone*), opera by Petrella (lib. by Giovanni Peruzzini, based on Bulwer-Lytton's novel *The Last Days of Pompeii*), prod. Milan, Teatro alla Scala, 26. I. 1858.

Ionesco, Eugène (b. 1912), Rum.-Fr. dramatist. *See* Searle (*The Photo of the Colonel*).

Ionian Mode, one of the 2 authentic modes recognized by Glareanus in the 16th cent., the other being the Aeolian Mode. Represented by the white keys of the pf. beginning from C, it corresponds exactly to the modern C maj. scale. *See* **Modes.**

Ipermestra (*Hypermnestra*), opera by Gluck (lib. by Metastasio), prod. Venice, Teatro San Giovanni Cristostomo, 21. XI. 1744.

Iphigénie en Aulide (*Iphigenia in Aulis*), opera by Gluck (lib. by François Louis Lebland du Roullet, based on Racine and further back on Euripides), prod. Paris, Opéra, 19. IV. 1774. Gluck's 1st opera for the Paris stage, though not his 1st Fr. work.

Iphigénie en Tauride (*Iphigenia in Tauris*), opera by Desmarets and Campra (lib. by Joseph François Duché and Antoine Danchet), prod. Paris, Opéra, 6. V. 1704.

Opera by Gluck (lib. by Nicolas François Guillard), prod. Paris, Opéra, 18. V. 1779.

Opera by Piccinni (lib. by Alphonse Du Congé Dubreuil), prod. Paris, Opéra, 23. I. 1781.

(All libs. based on Euripides.)
See also Ifigenia.

Ippolito ed Aricia (*Hippolytus and Aricia*), opera by Traetta (lib. by Carlo Innocenzio Frugoni, trans. from Simon Joseph de Pellegrin's lib. for Rameau's *Hippolyte et Aricie*, 1733), prod. Parma, 9. V. 1759.

Ippolitov-Ivanov, Mikhail Mikhailovich (b. Gatchina nr. St. Petersburg, 19. XI. 1859; d. Moscow, 28. I. 1935), Rus. comp. Studied under Rimsky-Korsakov at the St. Petersburg Cons. In 1884 he was app. cond. of the Imp. opera at Tiflis, and in 1893 prof. at the Moscow Cons., of which he was director from 1906 to 1922.

Works incl. operas *Ruth, Azra, Assia* (after Turgenev's story), *Treachery, Ole from Norland, The Last Barricade,* also completion of Mussorgsky's *Marriage*; *Hymn to Labour* for chorus and orch.; 2 symphs., *Caucasian Sketches, Iberia, Armenian Rhapsody, Mtsyri* (after Lermontov), *From Ossian, Episode from Schubert's Life, Turkish Fragments, Mus. Scenes from Uzbekistan, The Year 1917, Catalonian Suite,* etc. for orch.; 2 string 4tets, *An Evening in Georgia* for harp and wind instruments; vln. and pf. sonata; pf. and other instrumental pieces; cantatas for chorus and pf.; 116 songs, etc.

Ireland (real name Hutcheson), **Francis** (b. Dublin, 13. VIII. 1721; d. Dublin, 1780), Ir. physician and amateur comp. Wrote madrigal 'Return, return', glees, catches, etc.

Ireland, John (b. Bowdon, Ches., 13. VIII. 1879; d. Sussex, 12. VI. 1962), Eng. comp. Studied at the R.C.M. in London in 1893–1901, his comp. master being Stanford. Apart from 1 or 2 organist's appts., and his later comp. professorship at the R.C.M., he devoted himself entirely to creative work. In 1932 he received the hon. D.Mus. degree from Durham Univ.

Works incl. film mus. *The Overlanders; Greater Love Hath no Man,* motet for chorus, orch. and org., Morning and Evening Services; *These Things shall be* (John Addington Symonds) for chorus and orch.; prelude *The Forgotten Rite,* symph. rhapsody *Mai-Dun, A London Overture, Epic March* and overture on Petronius's *Satyricon* for orch.; *Concertino pastorale* for string orch.; concerto in E♭ maj. and *Legend* for pf. and orch.; *A Downland Suite* for brass band; *Maritime Overture* for military band; 3 pf. trios; 2 vln. and pf. sonatas, cello and pf. sonata, fantasy-sonata for clar. and pf.; sonata, sonatina, *Decorations, Rhapsody,* 4 Preludes, *London Pieces, Leaves from a Child's Sketchbook, The Towing Path, Equinox, February's Child, Month's Mind, Green Ways* and many other pieces for pf.; some vln. and pf. and org. pieces; song cycles *Songs of a Wayfarer, Marigold, The Cost, Mother and Child* (Christina Rossetti), *The Land of Lost Content* (A. E. Housman), 3 and 5 Thomas Hardy songs, 5 16th-cent. songs, *Songs Sacred and Profane,* etc.; c. 30 separate songs, incl. *Bed in Summer, Earth's Call, Hawthorn Time* (Housman), *Hope the Hornblower, If there were dreams to sell* (Beddoes), *Sea Fever* (Masefield), *Spring Sorrow, The Adoration, The Heart's Desire* (Housman); c. 20 part-songs, etc.

Iris, opera by Mascagni (lib. by Luigi Illica), prod. Rome, Teatro Costanzi, 22. XI. 1898.

Irish Composers. *See* **Balfe, Carter, Cooke**

(T.), Ferguson, Field, Holden (S.), Holmes, Hughes, Ireland (F.), Kelly, Levey, Maconchy, Moorhead, O'Neill, Rooke, Stanford, Stevenson (J. A.), Stewart, Torrance, Wallace (V.), Wood (C.), Woodward.

Irish Symphony, Stanford's 3rd symph., in F min., Op. 28, comp. 1887 and 1st perf. London, 27. VI.

Irmelin, opera in 3 acts by Delius (lib. by comp.), prod. Oxford, 4. V. 1953.

Irving, Washington (1783–1859), Amer. author. *See* **Alchymist** (Spohr), **Koven** (*Rip van Winkle*), **Planquette** (do.).

Isaac, Henricus (Heinrich) (b. Brabant or E. Flanders, *c.* 1450; d. Florence, 1517), Flem. comp. In *c.* 1484, when he seems to have been at Innsbruck and in touch with Hofhaimer there, he went *via* Ferrara to Florence as musician to the Medici family. He became organist at the chapel of San Giovanni there, visited Rome in 1489 and married Bartolomea Bello, the daughter of a wealthy butcher. Lorenzo de' Medici having d. in 1492 and his successor, Pietro, keeping a less lavish household, I. accepted an invitation from the Emperor Maximilian, who visited Pisa in 1496, to join the Imp. court, just then about to be transferred from Augsburg to Vienna; but he seems to have visited Innsbruck again to be formally app. and possibly Augsburg too. His duties were not arduous, so that he was able to live by turns in Vienna, Innsbruck, Constance (all connected with the court) and It. He also spent much time at the court of Ercole d'Este, Duke of Ferrara, and during his last years he remained at Florence.

Works incl. many Masses, *c.* 50 motets, sequences, Lamentation *Oratio Jeremiae,* 58 4-part settings of the offices under the title *Choralis Constantinus*; 4-part Monodia on the death of Lorenzo de' Medici (words by Poliziano); many Ger., It., Fr. and Lat. songs (incl. 'Innsbruck, ich muss dich lassen', which may not be his own tune), 58 instrumental pieces in 3–5 parts, 29 domestic pieces in 2–5 parts, etc.

Isidor of Seville (b. Carthage, *c.* 560; d. Seville, 4. IV. 636), philosopher and theologian. He was Archbishop of Seville from 599. His contrib. to mus. theory is contained in book III of his *Etymologiae* (largely a summary of Cassiodorus), and he deals with practical matters of church mus. in *De Ecclesiasticis Officiis.*

Isis, opera by Lully (lib. by Quinault), prod. Saint-Germain, 5. I. 1677 and 1st perf. Paris, IV. 1677.

Isle de Merlin, L', ou Le Monde renversé (*Merlin's Island or the World Upside-down*), opera by Gluck (lib. by Louis Anseaume), prod. Vienna, Schönbrunn Palace, at court, 3. X. 1758.

Isola disabitata, L' (*The Desert Island*),

opera by Bonno (lib. by Metastasio), prod. Aranjuez, at the Span. court, spring 1754, and Schlosshof nr. Vienna, before the Aus. court, 23. IX. 1754.

Opera by Haydn (lib. do.), prod. Esterház, 6. XII. 1779.

Opera by G. Scarlatti (lib. by Goldoni), prod. Venice, Teatro San Samuele, 20. XI. 1757.

Opera by Traetta (lib. by Metastasio), prod. Bologna, Teatro Comunale, ? 26. IV. 1768.

Isometric (from Gk. = equally metrical), a manner of writing vocal mus. in several parts mainly in block chords, i.e. in the same rhythm.

Isorhythmic (from Gk. = equally rhythmic), a modern term for a method of construction used by comps. of polyphonic mus. in the 14th and 15th cents. One or more of the parts were arr. in a rhythmic pattern several bars long which was repeated throughout the piece, sometimes with changes of tempo (indicated by the use of smaller note-values).

Isouard, Nicolò (also known as Nicolò di Malta, or just Nicolò) (b. Malta, 6. XII. 1775; d. Paris, 23. III. 1818), Maltese comp. of Fr. descent. Educ. at a military acad. in Paris, he had to leave Fr. at the Revolution, and after a time in Malta studied mus. in Palermo and in Naples under Sala and Guglielmi. Made his début as an opera comp. in Florence with *L'avviso ai maritati* in 1794. The following year he was app. organist to the Order of St. John of Malta in Valetta, and later became *maestro di cappella* there. Leaving Malta in 1799 he settled in Paris, where he prod. many operas and also appeared as a pianist.

Works incl. over 40 operas, e.g. *L'avviso ai maritati, Artaserse, Le Tonnelier, Michel-Ange, Cendrillon, Le Billet de loterie, Joconde, Jeannot et Colin, Aladin ou La Lampe merveilleuse,* etc.; Masses, motets, cantatas and other vocal works, etc.

Israel in Egypt, oratorio by Handel (words from the Bible and the Prayer Book version of the psalms), comp. 1738, perf. London, King's Theatre, Haymarket, 4. IV. 1739.

'Israel' Symphony, a symph. by Bloch, comp. 1912–16, 1st perf. N.Y., 3. V. 1916.

Issé, opera by Destouches (lib. by Antoine Houdar de la Motte), prod. Fontainebleau, at court, 7. X. 1679, 1st Paris perf., Opéra, 30. XII. 1697.

-issimo (It. superl. ending), e.g. *pianissimo* = softest; *fortissimo* = loudest, etc.

Istar, symph. variations by d'Indy, Op. 42, 1st perf. Brussels, 10. I. 1897. The work is based on the Babylonian legend of Ishtar's descent into limbo and illustrates her disrobing at the 7 stations of her progress by the devices of presenting the variations 1st, in diminishing complexity, and stating the theme only at the end, in bare 8ve unison.

Istel, Edgar (b. Mainz, 23. II. 1880; d. Miami, Florida, 17. XII. 1948), Ger. musicologist and comp. Studied at Munich, comp. with Volbach and Thuille and musicology with Sandberger. He lived and taught there until 1913, when he went to Berlin as lecturer on mus. In 1920 he was in Madrid and later went to the U.S.A. His books incl. works on Wagner, Cornelius, Paganini and esp. on var. aspects of opera.

Comps. incl. operas *Der fahrende Schüler, Des Tribunals Gebot* and others; incid. mus. for Goethe's *Satyros*, etc.; *Hymn to Zeus* and other choral works; *Singspielouvertüre* for orch., etc.

Istesso tempo, L' (It. from *lo stesso tempo* = the same pace), a direction given where a change is indicated in the time-signature, but the comp. wishes the mus. to continue at the same pace or beat in the new rhythm. The change is thus merely one of metre, not of movement.

Italian Concerto, a harpsichord work in 3 movements by Bach, pub. (together with the 'French Overture') in the second part of the *Clavierübung* in 1735. The 2 manuals of the harpsichord are used to reproduce the contrast between *concertino* and *ripieno* characteristic of the *concerto grosso*.

Italian Overture. *See* **Overture.**

Italian Sixth, a three-note form of the chord of the augmented 6th with a maj. 3rd above its lowest note, e.g.:

'Italian' Symphony, Mendelssohn's 4th symph., Op. 90, in A maj. and min., begun in It. in 1831 and finished in Berlin, 31. III. 1833; 1st perf. London, 13. V. 1833, cond. by the comp.

Italiana in Algeri, L' (*The Italian Girl in Algiers*), opera by Rossini (lib. by Angelo Anelli), prod. Venice, Teatro San Benedetto, 22. V. 1813.

Italiana in Londra, L' (*The Italian Girl in London*), opera by Cimarosa (lib. by Giuseppe Petrosellini), prod. Rome, Teatro Valle, 28. XII. 1778.

Italienisches Liederbuch (*Italian Song Book*), H. Wolf's settings of It. poems in Ger. trans. by Paul Heyse, comp. (22 nos.) IX. 1890–XII. 1891 and (24 nos.) III–IV. 1896.

Iturbi, José (b. Valencia, 28. XI. 1895), Span. pianist and cond. Studied as a child in Barcelona, and afterwards played in cafés to earn money. Later he studied in Paris at the Cons. and graduated in 1912.

He began teaching at the Geneva Cons. in 1919 and in 1923 began his career as a concert pianist.

Ivan le Terrible, opera by Bizet (lib. by Arthur Leroy and Henri Trianon, 1st offered to Gounod and abandoned by him), comp. in 1865 and accepted for prod. by the Théâtre Lyrique in Paris, but withdrawn by the comp. The 1st perf. took place at Mühringen (Württemberg) in 1946.

Ivan Sussanin, opera by Cavos (lib. by Prince Alexander Alexandrovich Shakhovskoy), prod. St. Petersburg, 31. X. 1815. The subject is that on which Glinka's *Life for the Tsar* was based in 1836.

The title given to Glinka's *Life for the Tsar* in Soviet Rus.

Ivan the Terrible (Rimsky-Korsakov). *See* **Pskovitianka.**

Ivanhoe, opera by Sullivan (lib. by Julian Russell Sturgis, based on Scott's novel), prod. London, Royal Eng. Opera House (now Palace Theatre), 31. I. 1891.

Ivanov, Mikhail Mikhailovich (b. Moscow, 23. IX. 1849; d. Rome, 20. X. 1927), Rus. critic and comp. Studied with Tchaikovsky and others at the Moscow Cons., lived mainly in Rome in 1870–6 and then became mus. critic to the *Novoie Vremya*.

Works incl. operas *Potemkin's Feast, Zabava Putiatishna, The Proud Woman* and *Woe to the Wise*; ballet *The Vestal*; Requiem; symph., symph. prologue *Savonarola, Suite champêtre* for orch.; pf. pieces; songs, etc.

Ivanov-Radkevich, Nikolai Pavlovich (b. Krasnoyarsk, Siberia, 10. II. 1904; d. Moscow, 4. II. 1962), Rus. comp. He was exceptionally gifted as a child, but did not study until 1923, when he went to Vassilenko and Glière at the Moscow Cons. Later he became prof. of orch. there.

Works incl. a ballet and incid. mus. for plays; 4 symphs. and *Dance Suite* for orch.; instrumental sonatas, etc.

Ive (or Ives), Simon (b. Ware, VII. 1600; d. London, 1. VII. 1662), Eng. singer, organist and comp. Vicar-choral at St. Paul's Cathedral in London; singing-master during the Commonwealth, returned to St. Paul's in 1661. In 1633 he took part with W. Lawes in the comp. of Shirley's masque *The Triumph of Peace.* Other works incl. elegy on the death of W. Lawes, catches and rounds; fancies and other instrumental works, etc.

Ives, Charles (Edward) (b. Danbury, Conn., 20. X. 1874; d. N.Y., 19. V. 1954), Amer. comp. Pupil of H. Parker and D. Buck. Engaged in business, but wrote much mus., some in a polytonal idiom employing intervals smaller than the semitone. In addition, he experimented with conflicting rhythms, dissonant harmony and counterpoint, chord clusters and the spatial presentation of mus. He also made frequent use of hymn and folk tunes. I. is now recognized as the real founder of Amer. mus.

Works incl. 5 symphs., *3 Places in New England* for orch.; string 4tet; 5 vln. and pf. sonatas; *Aeschylus and Socrates* for voice, pf. and string 4tet; choral works; 2 sonatas and other mus. for pf.; org. works; over 200 songs; marches, dances, etc.

Ivrea Codex, a large collection of 14th-cent. mus., and an important source of mus. by Philippe de Vitry and Machaut. It is housed in the cathedral of the city.

Ivrogne corrigé, L' (*The Reformed Drunkard*), opera by Gluck (lib. by Louis Anseaume on a fable by La Fontaine), prod. Vienna, Burgtheater, IV. 1760.

Opera by Laruette (lib. do.), prod. Paris, Opéra-Comique, 24. VII. 1759.

Ivry, Richard d', Marquis (b. Beaune, 4. II. 1829; d. Hyères, 18. XII. 1903), Fr. amateur comp. who wrote under the name of Richard Yrvid.

Works incl. operas *Fatma, Quentin Matsys, La Maison du docteur, Omphale et Pénélope, Les Amants de Vérone* (on Shakespeare's *Romeo and Juliet*) and *Persévérance d'amour.*

Jadin

J

Jaches de Wert. See **Wert.**
Jachet Buus. See **Buus.**
Jachet da Mantova (Jaquet ?) (b. Vitré, ?; d. Mantua, 1559), Flem. singer and comp. Attached to San Pietro Cathedral at Mantua in 1527–58. Wrote Masses, Magnificats, motets, psalms, hymns, etc.
Jachet de Berchem. See **Berchem.**
Jack, the mechanism in the virginal, harpsichord and similar instruments by which the strings are plucked.
Jackson, William (b. Exeter, 29. V. 1730; d. Exeter, 5. VII. 1803), Eng. organist and comp. Learnt mus. as a choir-boy in Exeter Cathedral, then studied in London, became mus. teacher at Exeter and from 1777 held var. appts. at the cathedral there.
Works incl. operas *The Lord of the Manor* and *The Metamorphosis*; a stage piece *Lycidas* (based on Milton); Te Deum, services, anthems and other church mus.; setting of Pope's ode *The Dying Christian*; var. vocal pieces and songs; harpsichord sonatas, etc.
Jackson, William (b. Masham, Yorks., 9. I. 1815; d. Bradford, 15. IV. 1866), Eng. organist and comp. Mainly self-taught, he was so gifted as to be app. church organist at the age of 16. Having been a tallow-chandler for some years, he went to Bradford as mus. dealer, organist and choirmaster.
Works incl. oratorio *The Deliverance of Israel from Babylon*, Psalm ciii for solo voices, chorus and orch., cantata *The Year*; services, anthems, a Mass, etc.; part-songs, glees; songs, etc.
Jacob, Gordon (Percival Septimus) (b. London, 5. VII. 1895), Eng. comp. and cond. Studied under Stanford and C. Wood at the R.C.M., where later he became prof. of orchestration. D. Mus., London, 1935.
Works incl. ballets *The Jew in the Bush* and *Uncle Remus* (after J. C. Harris); mus. for films; sinfonietta, variations on an air by Purcell and on an orig. theme for orch., *Passacaglia on a Well-known Theme* ('Oranges and Lemons') for orch.; 2 symphs. and *Denbigh* suite for strings, Divertimento for small orch.; concertos for pf., vln., vla., ob., bassoon and horn; suite for military band; 4tets for ob. and strings and clar. and strings and other chamber mus.; instrumental pieces, etc.
Jacob, Max (1876–1944), Fr. dramatist. See **Honegger** (*Mort de Sainte Alméenne*), **Poulenc** (*Bal masqué*).
Jacob, Maxime (b. Bordeaux, 13. I. 1906), Fr. comp. Pupil of Koechlin and Milhaud and later a member of Satie's

'École d'Arcueil'. He became a Benedictine monk in 1930.
Works incl. comic opera *Blaise le savetier*; orch. mus.; sonatas for vln. and cello; org. mus.; pf. pieces; songs, etc.
Jacobi, Frederick (b. San Francisco, 4. V. 1891; d. N.Y., 24. X. 1952), Amer. cond. and comp. Pupil of Bloch and others in U.S.A. and of Juon in Berlin. Asst. cond. at Metropolitan Opera in N.Y., 1913–17, later studied mus. of the Pueblo Indians in Mex. and Arizona. Prof. of comp. in N.Y. from 1924. Taught at the Juilliard School of Mus., 1936–50.
Works incl. opera *The Prodigal Son*; 2 symphs., *Indian Dances*, *The Eve of St. Agnes* (after Keats), etc. for orch.; concertos for pf., vln. and cello; concerto for pf. and strings; Sabbath Evening Service; *Two Assyrian Prayers* and *The Poet in the Desert* for voice and orch.; 2 string 4tets, pf. 5tet *Hagiographia*, scherzo for wind instruments, etc.
Jacobs, W(illiam). W(ymark). (1863–1941), Eng. novelist. See **Boatswain's Mate** (Smyth).
Jacobsen, Jens Peter (1847–85), Dan. poet and novelist. See **Fennimore und Gerda** (Delius), **Hamerik (E.)** (*Marie Grubbe*), **Schönberg** (*Gurrelieder*).
Jacobson, Maurice (b. London, 1. I. 1896), Eng. pianist and comp. Studied at the R.C.M. in London under Stanford and Holst. He was a director of the mus. pub. house of Curwen and frequently adjudicates at mus. competition festivals.
Works incl. ballet *David*; incid. mus. for Shakespeare's *Antony and Cleopatra*, *Hamlet*, *Julius Caesar* and *Macbeth*; mus. for broadcast *The Woman of Samaria* (after Rostand's *La Samaritaine*) and for 6 biblical broadcast plays, *Men of God*; *The Lady of Shalott* (Tennyson) for chorus and orch.; suite for fl., cello and pf.; Theme and Variations and numerous pf. works; songs, etc.
Jacopo da Bologna. See **Bologna.**
Jacques, Gheert and **Jacques, Jean** } See **Turnhout.**
Jacquet, Élizabeth. See **La Guerre.**
Jadassohn, Salomon (b. Breslau, 13. VIII. 1831; d. Leipzig, 1. II. 1902), Ger. comp., cond. and teacher. Studied at the Leipzig Cons. and under Liszt at Weimar. Became cond. at Leipzig and later prof. at the Cons. He wrote several theoret. works.
Comps. incl. psalms and cantatas; 4 symphs., overtures and serenades (1 in canon) for orch.; 2 pf. concertos; 2 string 4tets, pf. trios, 4tets, 5tets and 6tet, etc.
Jadin, Louis Emmanuel (b. Versailles, 21. IX. 1768; d. Paris, 11. IV. 1853), Fr. comp., son of the violinist and comp. Jean J. Worked as accompanist at the

315

Théâtre de Monsieur in Paris from 1789 and became pf. prof. at the Cons. in 1802.

Works incl. opera *Joconde* and *c.* 40 others; vocal and instrumental works for the Revolution festivals; *La Bataille d'Austerlitz* for orch.; chamber mus.; works for 1 and 2 pfs., etc.

Jagd, Die (*The Hunt*), opera by J. A. Hiller (lib. by Christian Felix Weisse, based on Jean Michel Sedaine's lib. for Monsigny's *Le Roi et le fermier*), prod. Weimar, 29. I. 1770.

Jahn, Otto (b. Kiel, 16. VI. 1813; d. Göttingen, 9. IX. 1869), Ger. philologist, archaeologist and writer on art and mus. Studied at Kiel, Leipzig and Berlin, became prof. at Greifswald and later at Bonn. His numerous writings on mus. include the 1st large-scale work written on Mozart.

Jaleo, a Span. dance in moderate 3–8 time, accomp. by castanets.

James, Philip (b. Jersey City, N.J., 17. V. 1890), Amer. cond., organist, teacher and comp. Studied in N.Y. and became prof. at Columbia and N.Y. Univs.

Works incl. *Missa imaginum, Stabat Mater* and other choral works; 2 symphs., overtures on Fr. Noëls and *Bret Harte*, Welsh rhapsody *Gwallia, Station WGZBX*, for orch.; suite for string orch.; pf. 4tet, woodwind 5tet, string 4tet, etc.

Jammes, Francis (1868–1938), Fr. poet and novelist. *See* **Durey** (songs), **Roos** (*5 Quatrains*).

Janáček, Leoš (b. Hukvaldy, Morav., 3. VII. 1854; d. Morava-Ostrava, 12. VIII. 1928), Cz. comp. Son of a poor schoolmaster; became choir-boy at the monastery of the Austin Friars at Brno; later earned his living as mus. teacher and went to the Org. School in Prague for study. Cond. var. choral societies, made some desultory studies at Leipzig and Vienna, and in 1881 returned to Brno to found an org. school there, where he taught until it was taken over by the state in 1920, when he became prof. of a master class at the Prague Cons. Made close studies of folksong and speech, which he applied to his vocal mus.

Works incl. operas *The Beginning of a Novel, Fate, Her Stepdaughter* (*Jenufa*), *The Excursions of Mr. Brouček* (after Čech), *Káta Kabanová, The Cunning Little Vixen, Sárka, The Makropoulos Case* (on a play by Čapek), *From the House of the Dead* (after Dostoievsky); *The Eternal Gospel* and *Glagolitic Mass* for solo voices, chorus and orch., *The Wandering Madman* (Tagore) for soprano and male-voice chorus, numerous choral works, many for male voices; *Šumařovo Dítě*, rhapsody *Taras Bulba* (on Gogol), *The Ballad of Blanik*, sinfonietta for orch.; 2 string 4tets

(1 on Tolstoy's *Kreutzer Sonata*), wind 6tet *Youth,* suite for 2 vlns., vla., cello and double bass; vln. and pf. sonata; pf. sonata, variations, etc.; org. works; *The Diary of a Vanished One* for voice and pf., Morav. folksongs for voice and pf., etc.

Janiewicz, Felix (b. Vilna, 1762; d. Edinburgh, 21. V. 1848), Pol. violinist. Studied in Vienna, where he met Haydn and Mozart, and in It. Appeared in Paris and London later and settled 1st at Liverpool and then at Edinburgh.

Janissaries, Turkish infantry forming a bodyguard for the sultan. Their mus. made use of special perc. instruments incl. the Turkish Crescent or Jingling Johnny, imitated by western comps., as in Haydn's 'Military' Symph. (No. 100) and Mozart's *Entführung*. Brahms playfully called the 3rd movement of his 4th symph. 'janissaries' mus.'.

Jannacom, Giuseppe (b. Rome, 1741; d. Rome, 16. III. 1816), It. comp. Studied in Rome, where in 1811 he became *maestro di cappella* at St. Peter's in succession to Zingarelli.

Works incl. 30 Masses, 42 psalms, motets and other church mus., some for several antiphonal choirs, etc.

Jannequin, Clément (b. Châtelleraut, *c.* 1475; d. Paris, *c.* 1560), Fr. comp. Pupil (?) of Josquin des Prés. He may have become a Huguenot in the course of his long life.

Works incl. Masses on his own songs *La Bataille* and *L'Aveugle Dieu,* motet *Congregati sunt, Proverbes de Salomon, Psaumes de David* (both to Fr. rhymed versions); numerous *chansons* for 4 voices, many of which contain imitative and descriptive passages, etc.

Janotha, Nathalie (b. Warsaw, 8. VI. 1856; d. The Hague, 9. VI. 1932), Pol. pianist. Studied in Berlin, also with Clara Schumann, Brahms and others, and made her 1st appearance at Leipzig in 1874.

Japart, Johannes (b. ?; d. ?), 15th–16th-cent. comp., many of whose *chansons* were printed by Petrucci in Venice.

Jaques-Dalcroze, Émile (b. Vienna, 6. VII. 1865; d. Geneva, 1. VII. 1950), Swiss teacher and comp. Studied with Delibes in Paris, with Bruckner and Fuchs in Vienna and at the Geneva Cons., where in 1892 he became prof. of harmony. There he invented a system of teaching mus. by co-ordination with bodily movement, known as Eurhythmics. In 1910 he founded an inst. for this purpose at Hellerau nr. Dresden.

Works incl. operas *Le Violon maudit, Janie, Sancho Panza* (after Cervantes), *Le Bonhomme Jadis, Les Jumeaux de Bergame, La Fille au vautour* (after W. von Hillern's *Die Geier-Wally*), festival play *La Fête de la jeunesse et de la joie*; choral

Jarnach
'Jena' Symphony

works *La Veillée, Festival vaudois*; suite for orch.; 2 vln. concertos; 3 string 4tets; pf. pieces; many collections of popular and children's songs, *Chansons de route, Rondes enfantines, Chansons de gestes,* etc.

Jarnach, Philipp (b. Noisy, Fr., 26. VII. 1892), Franco-Span. comp. Studied pf. with Risler and comp. with Lavignac in Paris, went to Switz. in 1914 and taught counterpoint at the Zürich Cons. in 1918–1921, when he settled in Berlin and continued to study with Busoni, whose unfinished opera *Doktor Faust* he completed.

Works incl. prelude to *Prometheus*, suite *Winterbilder, Prologue to a Tournament, Sinfonia brevis, Morgenklangspiel,* Prelude No. 1, *Musik mit Mozart* for orch.; string 4tet and 5tet; vln. and pf. sonata, 2 sonatas for unaccomp. vln.; *Konzertstück* for org.; sonatina and other works for pf.; songs with orch. and with pf., etc.

Järnefelt, Armas (b. Viborg, 14. VIII. 1869; d. Stockholm, 23. VI. 1958), Fin. cond. and comp. Studied at Helsinki, Berlin and Paris, cond. at var. Ger. theatres and from 1898 to 1903 at Helsinki. App. cond. of the Opera there in 1903 and at Stockholm 1907–32.

Works incl. incid. mus. to *The Promised Land*; choral works; orchestral mus. incl. *Praeludium* and *Berceuse* for small orch.; songs, etc.

Järnefelt-Palmgren (*née* **Pakarinen**), **Maikki** (b. Joensuu, 26. VIII. 1871; d. Turku, 4. VII. 1929), Fin. soprano, wife, 1st of prec., then of Palmgren. Studied at Helsinki and in Paris, Berlin and It. She married Järnefelt in 1893 and in 1895 began to appear in opera in Ger. After a divorce she married Palmgren in 1910 and lived in U.S.A. with him for several years.

Jarnowick. *See* **Giornovichi.**

Jazz, Amer. dance mus. of the early 20th cent. developed out of Ragtime and relying for its effects mainly on syncopations and rhythmic displacement of accents; and on a special combination of instruments, incl. plucked string instruments and saxophones, made to play abnormally for the most part, e.g. *pizzicato* double bass, muted brass, etc. J. has influenced certain comps., e.g. Stravinsky in *Ragtime*, Milhaud in *La Création du monde* and *Le Bœuf sur le toit*, Křenek in *Jonny spielt auf*, Gershwin in the *Rhapsody in Blue*, Copland in the ballet *Billy the Kid*, Blitzstein in his operas, etc., Hindemith in *Kammermusik No. 1*, Lambert in *The Rio Grande*, Weill in *Mahagonny* and *Dreigroschenoper*, etc.

Jean de Paris, opera by Boïeldieu (lib. by Claude Godard d'Aucour de Saint-Just), prod. Paris, Opéra-Comique, 4. IV. 1812.

Jean Paul. *See* **Richter, J. P.**

Jeanie Deans, opera by MacCunn (lib.

by Joseph Bennett, based on Scott's *Heart of Midlothian*), prod. Edinburgh, 15. XI. 1894.

Jeanne d'Arc au bûcher (*Joan of Arc at the Stake*), dramatic oratorio by Honegger (lib. by Paul Claudel), prod. Basle, 12. V. 1938.

Jeans, James (Hopwood) (b. London, 11. IX. 1877; d. Dorking, 16. IX. 1946), Eng. astronomer and physicist. Wrote a book on acoustics, *Science and Music.* Knighted 1928.

Jeffries, George (b. ?; d. ?, 1685), Eng. comp. Steward to Lord Hatton of Kirby, Northants., member of the Chapel Royal, organist to Charles I at Oxford in 1643 during the Civil War.

Works incl. services, anthems, over 120 motets, sacred solos and duets, carols; mus. for masques and plays; secular songs, duets, etc.; fancies for strings and virginals, etc.

Jeffries, Matthew (b. ?; d. ?), Eng. 16th-17th-cent. comp. Vicar-choral at Wells Cathedral. Comp. services, anthems, etc.

Jelmoli, Hans (b. Zürich, 17. I. 1877; d. Zürich, 6. V. 1936), Swiss pianist, cond., critic and comp. Studied with Humperdinck and others at Frankfurt, and after cond. opera in Ger. settled at Zürich as teacher and critic.

Works incl. operas *Sein Vermächtnis, Prinz Goldhaar, Die Schweizer, Die Badenerfahrt, Das Gespenst auf dem Petersturm;* incid. mus. to Wiegand's *Marignano* and other plays; cantata to words from *Des Knaben Wunderhorn;* pf. pieces; choruses; songs, etc.

Jélyotte, Pierre de (b. Lasseube, Basses-Pyrénées, 13. IV. 1713; d. Estos, Basses-Pyrénées, 11. IX. 1787), Fr. tenor, guitarist and comp. Orig. intended for the priesthood, he made his operatic début in Paris in 1733. He was also guitar-teacher to the king, and as a comp. prod. the opera-ballet *Zelisca.*

Jemnitz, Alexander (b. Budapest, 9. VIII. 1890; d. Balatonfüred, 8. VIII. 1963), Hung. comp. and critic. Studied at the Budapest Cons., then with Reger at Leipzig and lastly with Schönberg in Berlin, where he also taught. Later he returned to Budapest.

Works incl. ballet *Divertimento;* Prelude and Fugue, 7 *Miniatures* for orch.; choral mus.; string 4tet, 2 string trios, trios for var. other instruments, Partita for 2 vlns., 3 vln. and pf. sonatas, sonatas for vla. and cello, saxophone and banjo; Passacaglia and Fugue for org.; 4 pf. sonatas, unaccomp. sonatas for vln., cello, double bass, harp and tpt., etc.

'Jena' Symphony, a symph. in C maj. discovered at Jena in 1910 and attrib. to Beethoven because it bears the inscription 'par L. van Beethoven' in an unidentifiable hand; it is now known to be by Friedrich Witt (1771–1837). Ed. by Fritz Stein and 1st perf. by him, Jena, 17. I. 1910.

Jenkins, John (b. Maidstone, 1592; d. Kimberley, Norfolk, 27. X. 1678), Eng. comp., lutenist and string player. He lived under the patronage of the gentry and nobility, esp. Sir Hamon L'Estrange in Norfolk and Lord North, whose sons, incl. Roger, he taught mus. His last patron was Sir Philip Wodehouse at Kimberley.

Works incl. fancies and consorts for viols and vlns. with org.; anthems and psalms; Elegy on the death of W. Lawes, *Theophila, or Love's Sacrifice* (Benlowes), *A Divine Poem* for voices; rounds, songs, etc.

Jensen, Adolf (b. Königsberg, 12. I. 1837; d. Baden-Baden, 23. I. 1879), Ger. pianist and comp., grandson of the organist and comp. Wilhelm J. (d. 1842), prof. of mus. at Königsberg Univ. A. J. studied under var. masters, visited Rus. and Copenhagen, where he made friends with Gade, was back at Königsberg in 1860–6, taught the pf. in Berlin for the next 2 years and then lived at Dresden, Graz and elsewhere for his health.

Works incl. opera *Die Erbin von Montfort* (adapted to a new lib. based on Gozzi's *Turandot* by Kienzl after his death); cantatas *Jephthas Tochter, Der Gang der Jünger nach Emmaus, Donald Caird* (Scott) and *Adonisfeier*; concert overture and *Geistliches Tonstück* for orch.; *c.* 25 op. nos. of pf. mus. incl. *Innere Stimmen, Romantische Studien*, sonata in F♯ min., *Deutsche Suite, Erotikon, Ländler aus Berchtesgaden; Hochzeitsmusik, Abendmusik, Lebensbilder, Silhouetten, Ländliche Festmusik*, etc., for pf. duet; song for baritone and orch. *Alt Heidelberg*; *c.* 30 sets of songs incl. 2 from Geibel and Heyse's *Spanisches Liederbuch, Liebeslieder, Dolorosa* (from Chamisso's *Tränen*), *Gaudeamus* (Scheffel), *Romanzen und Balladen* and songs from Burns, Scott, Moore, Allan Cunningham, Tennyson, Mrs. Hemans and Herder's *Stimmen der Völker*; part-songs, etc.

Jensen, Johannes (Vilhelm) (1873–1950), Dan. poet, novelist and dramatist. *See* **Riisager** (*Darduse*).

Jenůfa (Janáček). *See* **Her Fosterdaughter**.

Jephta's Gelübde (*Jephtha's Vow*), opera by Meyerbeer (lib. by Alois Schreiber), prod. Munich, 23. XII. 1812. Meyerbeer's 1st opera.

Jephté (*Jephtha*), opera by Montéclair (lib. by Simon Joseph de Pellegrin), prod. Paris, Opéra, 28. II. 1732.

Jephtha, oratorio by Handel (lib. by Thomas Morell), prod. London, Covent Garden Theatre, 26. II. 1752.

Jeppesen, Knud (b. Copenhagen, 15. VIII. 1892), Dan. musicologist and comp.

Studied with Nielsen and Thomas Laud at Copenhagen and later with Adler and Robert Lach in Vienna. Member of the board of the Cons. and prof. of mus. science at the Univ. of Aarhus. His books incl. studies of Palestrina, vocal polyphony, the It. *laudi*, etc.

Works incl. opera *Rosaura* on a play by Goldoni; *Te Deum Danicum* for chorus and orch., *Lave og Jon* (old Dan. folksong) for men's chorus and orch., motets and cantatas; symph., horn concerto; songs, etc.

Jeremiáš, Bohuslav (b. Řestoky nr. Chrudim, 1. V. 1859; d. Budějovice, 18. I. 1918), Cz. organist, choral cond. and comp. Having held var. other posts, he was in 1906 app. director of the mus. school at Budějovice.

Jeremiáš, Jaroslav (b. Písek, 14. VIII. 1889; d. Budějovice, 16. I. 1919), Cz. comp., son of prec. Pupil of Novák and others at the Prague Cons.

Works incl. opera *The Old King*; mystery play *Rimoni*; oratorio *Jan Hus*; symph. idyll *A Summer's Day*, etc.

Jeremiáš, Otakar (b. Písek, 17. X. 1892; d. Prague, 5. III. 1962), Cz. comp., brother of prec. Pupil of Novák at the Prague Cons. Succeeded his father at Budějovice.

Works incl. operas *The Brothers Karamazov* (after Dostoievsky), *Till Eulenspiegel*; 2 symphs., etc.

Jeritza (real name Jedlitzka), **Maria** (b. Brno, 6. X. 1887), Cz. soprano. Studied in Brno and first appeared in the chorus of the Brno Opera. She made her début as a soloist at Olmütz in 1910 and was a member of the Vienna State Opera from 1913 to 1932. She also sang at the N.Y. Metropolitan Opera from 1921 to 1932.

Jérusalem, the title of the Fr. version of Verdi's opera *I Lombardi alla prima crociata*.

Jervays. *See* **Gervasius**.

Jervis-Read, H(arold). V(incent). (b. Powyke, Worcs., 14. III. 1883; d. Salisbury, 15. XII. 1945), Eng. comp. Prof. of comp. at the R.A.M. in London.

Works incl. Concertino da camera for 2 vlns. and chamber orch.; chamber mus.; sonata, Poems and pieces for pf., etc.

Jery und Bätely, play with mus. by Reichardt (text by Goethe), prod. Berlin, Opera, 30. III. 1801.

Play with mus. by Carl Siegmund von Seckendorff (text do.), prod. Weimar, at court, 12. VII. 1780.

Jessonda, opera by Spohr (lib. by Eduard Heinrich Gehe, based on Lemierre's tragedy *La Veuve de Malabar*), prod. Cassel, 28. VII. 1823.

Jeté (Fr. = thrown), a style of bowing on string instruments. The upper part of the bow is made to fall lightly on the

Jeu de clochettes   Jochum

string so that it rebounds several times
during the downward motion and repeats
notes in a rapid *staccato*.

Jeu de clochettes ⎫ Fr. names for the
Jeu de timbres ⎭
Chimebells (*Glockenspiel*).

Jeune France, La, a group of young Fr.
comps. formed in 1936 by Baudrier,
Jolivet, Lesur and Messiaen.

Jeune Henri, Le (*The Young Henry*),
opera by Méhul (lib. by Jean Nicolas
Bouilly, orig. intended for Grétry and
called *La Jeunesse de Henri IV*), prod.
Paris, Opéra-Comique, 1. V. 1797. The
overture called *La Chasse du jeune Henri*
was known as a concert piece long after
the opera was forgotten.

Jeune Sage et le vieux fou, Le (*The Wise
Youth and the Old Fool*), opera by Méhul
(lib. by François Benoît Hoffman), prod.
Paris, Opéra-Comique, 28. III. 1793.

Jeux, ballet by Debussy (choreography
by Vaslav Nizhinsky), comp. in 1912 and
prod. Paris, Théâtre du Châtelet, 13.
V. 1913.

Jeux d'enfants, suite for pf. duet by
Bizet, Op. 22, comp. 1871; *Petite Suite* for
orch. arr. from 5 pieces of it, 1872, 1st perf.
Paris, 2. III. 1873.

Jew's Harp, an ancient and primitive
instrument consisting of a metal frame held
between the player's teeth and a vibrating
metal tongue set in motion by the fingers
and emitting a note which can be varied by
changes in the cavity of the mouth.

Jewels of the Madonna (Wolf-Ferrari).
See **Gioielli della Madonna.**

Jewess, The (Halévy). *See* **Juive, La.**

Ježek, Jaroslav (b. Prague, 25. IX.
1906; d. N.Y., 31. XII. 1941), Cz. comp.
Born of poor parents and became all but
totally blind at the age of 8. With great
difficulty he contrived to study at the
Prague Cons. and later estab. an independent theatre with 2 young actors. He fled
to U.S.A. before the 1939–45 war, being in
danger of his life because of his anti-Nazi
songs.

Works incl. string 4tet, pf. sonata, many
popular and patriotic songs incl. *The
World in Dark Blue, Marching against
the Wind, The Song of the Violin*, etc.

Jhan, ? (called **Maître J.**) (poss. identical with Gero) (b. ?; d. ?), ? Fr. or
Flem. 16th-cent. comp. He was *maestro di
cappella* to Ercole d'Este, Duke of Ferrara.
Comp. motets, psalms, sacred songs for
several voices, madrigals, etc.

Jig, an old dance in binary form in
some kind of animated duple time, usually
6–8 or 12–8; the It. *giga* and Fr. *gigue*. It
was the 4th of the dances regularly found
in the classical suite. The 2nd half was
often built on an inversion of the theme of
the 1st.

Jingling Johnny. *See* **Chinese Pavilion.**

Jirák, Karel Boleslav (b. Prague, 28. I.
1891), Cz. cond. and comp. Studied with
Novák in Prague and was later influenced
by J. B. Foerster. Cond. at the Hamburg
Opera in 1915–18, but returned to Prague
and cond. the Hlahol choral society on a
tour in Yugoslavia, 1920–1.

Works incl. opera *Apollonius of Tyana*
(later called *Woman and the God*); 5
symphs., overture to a Shakespearian
comedy; 7 string 4tets, string 6tet; sonatas
for vln. and pf. and cello and pf.; song-
cycles *Tragi-Comedy* (Heine), *Meditations,
Brief Happiness, 3 Songs of Home, Evening
and the Soul*; *Suite in the Old Style* for pf.,
etc.

Jiránek, Josef (b. Ledec, 24. III. 1855;
d. Prague, 5. I. 1940), Cz. pianist, teacher
and comp. Pupil of Smetana. Prof. of pf.
at Kharkov in 1877–91 and from 1927 at
the Prague Cons.

Works incl. ballad and *Scherzo fantastique* for orch.; pf. trio, pf. 5tet; songs,
choruses, etc.

Jírovec. *See* **Gyrowetz.**

Joachim, Amalie. *See* **Weiss.**

Joachim, Joseph (b. Kittsee nr. Pozsony,
28. VI. 1831; d. Berlin, 15. VIII. 1907),
Hung. (Germanized) violinist, comp. and
cond. Made his 1st appearance at the age
of 7. Studied at the Vienna Cons. and in
Leipzig, where he came under the influence
of Mendelssohn. Leader of the orch. at
Weimar, 1849–53, and at Hanover, 1853–
1868. App. director of the Berlin Hochschule für Musik, 1868. Founded the
Joachim 4tet, 1869.

Works incl. overtures for orch. to
Shakespeare's *Hamlet* and *Henry IV*, in
commemoration of Kleist and on 2
comedies by Gozzi; 3 vln. concertos
(incl. 'Hung.'), variations for vln. and
orch.; variations for vla. and pf.; vln. and
pf. pieces; Marfa's scene from Schiller's
Demetrius for contralto and orch., etc.

Joan of Arc. *See* **Giovanna d'Arco,
Jeanne d'Arc au bûcher, Maid of Orleans.**

Job, masque for dancing by Vaughan
Williams (choreography by Ninette de
Valois, settings by Gwendolen Raverat,
based on Blake's illustrations to the Book
of Job), prod. London, Cambridge
Theatre, 5. VII. 1931.

Oratorio by Parry (words from the Book
of Job), prod. Gloucester Festival, 1892.

Jocelyn, opera by Godard (lib. by Paul
Armand Silvestre and Victor Capoul,
based on Lamartine's poem), prod.
Brussels, Théâtre de la Monnaie, 25.
II. 1888. It contains the popular *Berceuse
de Jocelyn*.

Jochum, Eugen (b. Babenhausen, 1. XI.
1902), Ger. cond. Studied pf. and org. at
Augsburg Cons. (1914–22) and comp. at
the Munich Acad. of Mus. (1922–4).
After some time as a *répétiteur* in Munich

and Kiel, he cond. at Mannheim and Duisburg, becoming mus. director of the Hamburg State Opera from 1934 to 1945. From 1949 he was cond. of the Munich Radio Orch.

Johannes de Garlandia. *See* **Garlandia.**

Johannes de Grocheo. *See* **Grocheo.**

Johannes de Limburgia. *See* **Limburgia.**

Johannes de Muris. *See* **Muris.**

Johansen, David Monrad (b. Vefsn, 8. XI. 1888), Norw. comp. and critic. Studied at Oslo and Berlin, Humperdinck being among his masters. He became mus. critic of 2 Norw. papers in succession and ed. of the *Norsk Musikblad*, and has written a life of Grieg.

Works incl. symph. fantasy for orch.; large choral works, unaccomp. choruses; vln. and pf. sonata; 5 suites for pf., etc.

Johnny plays (Křenek). *See* **Jonny spielt auf.**

Johnson, Edward (b. ?; d. ?), Eng. 16th–17th-cent. comp. ? in the service of Lord Hertford at Elvetham, where (?) he contrib. mus. to an entertainment given to Queen Elizabeth in 1591. Mus.B., Cambridge, 1594.

Works incl. madrigals, viol mus., virginal pieces, etc.

Johnson, John (b. ?, *c.* 1540; d. ?, 1595), Eng. lutenist and comp. Attached to Queen Elizabeth's court and (?) to the household of Sir Thomas Kitson at Hengrave Hall, Suffolk, and in London, 1572–4. Took part in Leicester's entertainments at Kenilworth Castle in 1575. Wrote lute pieces, songs to the lute, etc.

Johnson, Robert (b. Duns, *c.* 1490; d. ?, *c.* 1565), Scot. priest and comp. Fled to Eng. as a heretic and (?) settled at Windsor. Wrote Lat. motets, Eng. services and prayers, In Nomines for instruments, songs, etc.

Johnson, Robert (b. ?, *c.* 1583; d. London, 1633), Eng. lutenist and comp., son of John J. Was taught mus. at the expense of Sir George Carey, husband of Sir Thomas Kitson's granddaughter, in whose household he was brought up, and was app. lutenist to James I in 1604; taught Prince Henry and remained in his post under Charles I.

Works incl. songs for several voices; songs to the lute; catches; pieces for viols; also songs in Shakespeare's *Tempest*, in Fletcher's *Valentinian* and *The Mad Lover.*

Joio, Norman dello. *See* **Dello Joio.**

Jókai, Mór (or **Maurus**) (1825–1904), Hung. novelist. *See* **Zigeunerbaron** (J. Strauss).

Jolie Fille de Perth, La (*The Fair Maid of Perth*), opera by Bizet (lib. by Jules Henri Vernoy de Saint-Georges and Jules Adenis, based on Scott's novel), prod. Paris, Théâtre Lyrique, 26. XII. 1867.

Jolivet, André (b. Paris, 8. VIII. 1905), Fr. comp. Pupil of Le Flem and Varèse. He formed the group of 'La Jeune France' with Baudrier, Lesur and Messiaen in 1936.

Works incl. opera *Dolorès*; 2 ballets; oratorio *La Vérité de Jeanne*; 2 symphs.; concertos for tpt. (2), fl., pf., harp, bassoon and Ondes Martenot; string 4tet; sonata and suite *Mana* for pf., songs, etc.

Jommelli, Niccolò (b. Aversa nr. Naples, 10. IX. 1714; d. Naples, 25. VIII. 1774), It. comp. Pupil of Durante, Feo and Leo in Naples, made his début as an opera comp. there in 1737, and soon became famous throughout It. and in Vienna. *Kapellmeister* to the Duke of Württemberg at Stuttgart 1753–69, he then returned to Naples, but was unable to recapture his old success in It.

Works incl. over 50 extant operas, e.g. *Ricimero, Ezio, Semiramide, Sofonisba, Artaserse, Ifigenia in Aulide, Talestri, Attilio Regolo, Fetonte, La clemenza di Tito, Pelope, Il matrimonio per concorso, La schiava liberata, Armida, Ifigenia in Tauride*; oratorios *Isacco, Betulia liberata, Santa Elena al Calvario,* etc.; Passion oratorio, *Miserere,* Masses and other church mus.; cantatas; symphs. and other instrumental mus., etc.

Jonas, Émile (b. Paris, 5. III. 1827; d. Saint-Germain, 22. V. 1905), Fr. comp. Studied at the Paris Cons., prof. of Solfège there in 1847–65, director of mus. at the Port. synagogue and bandmaster in the Garde Nationale. Prod. his 1st operetta, *Le Duel de Benjamin,* in 1855.

Works incl. numerous operettas, e.g. *Avant la Noce, Les Deux Arlequins, Le Canard à trois becs, Cinderella the Younger* (*Javotte*), *Le Premier Baiser*; collection of Hebrew tunes, etc.

Joncières, Victorin de (actually Félix Ludger Rossignol) (b. Paris, 12. IV. 1839; d. Paris, 26. X. 1903), Fr. comp. Began by studying painting, but set a friend's adaptation of Molière's *Le Sicilien* as a comic opera with such success that he entered the Cons. He left again after a disagreement about Wagner, whom he admired, and studied privately. In 1871 he became mus. critic to *La Liberté.*

Works incl. operas *Sardanapale, Le Dernier Jour de Pompéi* (after Bulwer-Lytton), *Dimitri, La Reine Berthe, Le Chevalier Jean, Lancelot,* incid. mus. to Shakespeare's *Hamlet*; *La Mer,* symph. ode for mezzo-soprano, chorus and orch.; suite for orch. *Les Nubiennes, Sérénade hongroise,* overture, marches and other orchestral mus.; vln. concerto, etc.

Jone (Petrella). *See* **Ione.**

Jones, Daniel (b. Pembroke, 7. XII. 1912), Welsh comp. Studied at Univ. Coll., Swansea, where he read Eng., and later at the Royal Acad. of Mus. in

London. He studied cond. with Sir Henry Wood and comp. with Harry Farjeon. He began comp. at a very early age and has since produced a large quantity of mus.

Works incl. 4 symphs.; symph. poems *Cystuddiau Branwen*, *Cloud Messenger*; concertino for pf. and orch.; 8 string 4tets, string 5tet, 5 string trios, vln. sonata, cello sonata, pf. sonata, sonata for kettle-drums, wind septet, wind nonet, etc.

Jones, Edward (b. Llanderfel, Merioneth, 2. IV. 1752; d. London, 18. IV. 1824), Welsh harpist and song collector. Taught the harp by his father, he went to London in 1775 and was app. bard to the Prince of Wales in 1783. Pub. several collections of Welsh and other nat. airs.

Jones, John (b. ?, 1728; d. London, 17. II. 1796), Eng. organist and comp. App. organist of the Middle Temple in 1749, of Charterhouse, succeeding Pepusch, in 1753 and of St. Paul's Cathedral in 1755. Wrote chants, harpsichord lessons, etc.

Jones, Robert (b. ?, *c*. 1485; d. ?, *c*. 1536), Eng. comp. He was a Gentleman of the Chapel Royal from 1513. He composed a song, 'Who shall have my fair lady', a Mass, *Spes nostra*, and a Magnificat.

Jones, Robert (b. ?, *c*. 1570; d. ?, *c*. 1617), Eng. lutenist and comp. He worked for several patrons and took the B.Mus. degree at Oxford in 1597. In 1610, with Rosseter and others, he obtained a patent to train children for the queen's revels, and in 1615 they were allowed to erect a theatre in Blackfriars, but its opening was subsequently prohibited.

Works incl. madrigals, 5 books of *Songs and Ayres* to the lute, anthems, etc.

Jones, Sidney (b. London, 17. VI. 1861; d. Kew, 29. I. 1946), Eng. cond. and comp. At first a bandmaster and cond. of a travelling opera, he became cond. of the Empire Theatre in London in 1905. Wrote a number of operettas, incl. *The Geisha*, *San Toy*, *The Greek Slave*, *My Lady Molly*, etc.

Jongen, Joseph (b. Liège, 14. XII. 1873; d. Sart-lez-Spa nr. Liège, 12. VII. 1953), Belg. comp. Studied at the Liège Cons. Gained a prize from the Académie Royale in 1893 and the Belg. Prix de Rome in 1897. After teaching for a short time at the Liège Cons., he went to Rome and later travelled in Ger. and Fr., taking up a professorship at Liège in 1903. In 1914–18 he was in Eng. as a war refugee, but returned to Liège until 1920, when he became prof. at the Brussels Cons., of which he was later app. director.

Works incl. ballet *S'Arka*; symph., *Fantaisie sur deux Noëls wallons*, symph. poem *Lalla Rookh* (after Thomas Moore), *Impressions d'Ardennes*, *Tableaux pittoresques*, *Passecaille et Gigue* for orch.; *Pièce symphonique* for pf. and wind orch., vln. concerto, harp concerto, suite for vla. and orch., *Symphonie concertante* for org. and orch., concerto for wind 5tet; 3 string 4tets, 2 serenades for string 4tet, pf. trio; 2 vln. and pf. sonatas, cello sonata; *Sonata eroica* for org.; Intro. and Dance for vla. and pf. and other instrumental pieces; *Suite en forme de sonate* and other pf. works; songs, etc.

Jongleur (Fr. = juggler), a medieval wandering minstrel, one of whose accomplishments was juggling, but who also sang and played.

Jongleur de Notre Dame, Le (*Our Lady's Juggler*), opera by Massenet (lib. by Maurice Léna on a story by Anatole France in *L'Étui de nacre*, based on a medieval miracle play), prod. Monte Carlo, 18. II. 1902.

Jonny spielt auf (*Johnny plays*), opera by Křenek (lib. by comp.), prod. Leipzig, Munic. Opera, 10. II. 1927.

Jonson, Ben(jamin) (1573–1637), Eng. poet and dramatist. *See* **Alchemist** (Handel), **Angiolina** (Salieri), **Auric** (*Volpone*), **Bell** (*Vision of Delight*), **Ferrabosco** (A. ii) (masques), **Harington** ('Drink to me only'), **Lanier** (*Lovers made Men* and *Vision of Delight*), **Lothar** (*Lord Spleen*), **Pastoral** (Bliss), **Schweigsame Frau** (R. Strauss), **Spanish Lady** (Elgar), **Vaughan Williams** (*Pan's Anniversary*).

Joseffy, Rafael (b. Hunfalu, 3. VII. 1852; d. N.Y., 25. VI. 1915), Hung. pianist. Studied at Budapest, Leipzig and Berlin, also with Liszt at Weimar; made his 1st public appearance in 1872, at Berlin; settled in N.Y. in 1879 and taught at the Nat. Cons. there from 1888 to 1906.

Joseph, opera by Méhul (lib. by Alexandre Duval), prod. Paris, Opéra-Comique, 17. II. 1807. Weber wrote pf. variations, Op. 28, on a romance from it and Ethel Smyth used a tune in *Entente cordiale*.

Joseph and his Brethren, oratorio by Handel (lib. by James Miller), perf. London, Covent Garden Theatre, 2. III. 1744.

Josephslegende (R. Strauss). *See* **Legend of Joseph**.

Joshua, oratorio by Handel (lib. by Thomas Morell), perf. London, Covent Garden Theatre, 23. III. 1748.

Josquin Desprez (or des Prés) (b. ?, *c*. 1440; d. ? Condé, 27. VIII. 1521), Flem. or Fr. comp., apparently a native of Hainaut. He was (?) a choir-boy at St. Quentin, and worked in It. (Milan, Rome and Ferrara) between 1459 and 1503. Later he became *maître de chapelle* to Louis XII until the death of the king in 1515, and finally canon of St. Gudule in Brussels and provost of Condé.

He excelled in all branches of comp.

Josten Judith

then practised. His 20 complete Masses incl. exs. of the canonic, *cantus firmus*, paraphrase and so-called 'parody' types. His numerous motets and psalm-settings are remarkable for their careful adherence to the spirit of the words. In his *chansons* he abandons the old *formes fixes*: *rondeau*, *virelai* and *ballade*. Except in some of the Masses, his work is largely free of pedantry or constructional rigidity.

Josten, Werner (b. Elberfeld, 12. VI. 1885; d. N.Y., 6. II. 1963), Ger.-Amer. comp. Studied in Munich, Geneva (with Jaques-Dalcroze) and Paris. In 1918 he became asst. cond. at the Munich Opera, but in 1920 emigrated to U.S.A. App. prof. at Smith Coll., Northampton, Mass., in 1923.
Works incl. ballets *Jungle*, *Batouala*, *Joseph and his Brethren*, *Endymion*; *Crucifixion* for bass solo and chorus, *Hymnus to the Quene of Paradys* for contralto solo, women's chorus, strings and org., *Ode for St. Cecilia's Day* for solo voices, chorus and orch.; symph. in F maj., serenade, symph. movement *Jungle* (on Henri Rousseau's picture 'Forêt exotique'), etc. for orch.; symph. and 2 *Concerti sacri* for strings and pf., etc.

Jota, Span. dance, esp. of Aragon and Navarre. It dates from the 12th cent. and is said to derive its name from the Moor Aben Jot. It is in quick 3–4 time. The mus. is played on instruments of the guitar type and often accomp. by castanets and other perc.

Joteyko, Tadeusz (b. Potsuiky nr. Kiev, 1. IV. 1872; d. Cieszyn, 19. VIII. 1932), Pol. comp., critic and teacher. Studied with Gevaert at Brussels and Noskowski at Warsaw. There he cond. the Phil. Orch. in 1914–18 and was app. prof. at the State Cons.
Works incl. operas *The Minstrel*, *Zygmunt August*, *The Fishermen*, *Queen Jadwiga*, *Kilinski*; *The Phantom*, *Peasant Wedding* and *Suite of the Legions* for chorus; symph., Pol. Overture, Pol. Suite, *Le Doute et la foi*, *Christmas*, *Esquisses maritimes* and *Tatra* suite for orch., etc.

Joubert, John (b. Cape Town, 20. III. 1927), S. African comp. Studied at Cape Town Univ. and the R.A.M. in London. Lecturer at Hull Univ., 1950–62, at Birmingham Univ. since 1962.
Works incl. operas *Antigone*, *In the drought*, *Silas Marner*, *Under Western Eyes*; cantatas *The Leaves of Life and Urbs beata*; 3 motets; symph. prelude, 2 symphs., *In Memoriam, 1820* for orch.; vln. concerto, pf. concerto; string 4tet and other chamber mus.; choral works; songs, etc.

Jour de Fête, a collective work for string 4tet: 1. *Les Chanteurs de Noël* (Glazunov); 2. *Glorification* (Liadov); 3. *Chœur dansé russe* (Rimsky-Korsakov).

Journet, Marcel (b. Grasse, 25. VII. 1867;

d. Vittel, 5. IX. 1933), Fr. bass. Studied at the Paris Cons. and made his 1st appearance at Béziers in 1891. He was a well-known figure at the Paris Opéra, the Teatro alla Scala in Milan, Covent Garden Opera in London and the Metropolitan Opera in N.Y.

Joyce Book, a collection of settings of poems by James Joyce by George Antheil, Arnold Bax, Arthur Bliss, Edgardo Carducci, Bernard van Dieren, Eugene Goossens, Herbert Howells, Herbert Hughes, John Ireland, E. J. Moeran, C. W. Orr, Albert Roussel and Roger Sessions, ed. by Herbert Hughes, pub. in 1932.

Joyce, James (1882–1941), Ir. novelist and poet. *See* **Barber** (*Chamber M.*), **Diamond**, **Dieren (van)** (songs), **Hartmann** (**T. de**) (*Ulysses*), **Joyce Book**, **Moeran** (songs), **Orr (C. W.)** (songs), **Roussel** (**A.**) ('A flower given to my daughter'), **Searle** (*Riverrun*), **Seiber** (*Ulysses*), **Sessions** (songs), **Szymanowski** (songs).

Jubel-Ouvertüre (*Jubilee Overture*), a concert overture by Weber, Op. 59, comp. in 1818 as a companion-piece to the *Jubel-Cantate* for the 50th anniversary of the accession of the King of Saxony, Frederick Augustus, and perf. Dresden, 20. IX. It concludes with the tune of 'God save the King'.

Jubilus (Lat. = jubilation), the Lat. name given to the florid extension of the melody of the Alleluia in the Mass, in the form of a wordless melisma. The J. was of eastern origin. *See also* **Sequence**.

Judas Maccabaeus, oratorio by Handel (lib. by Thomas Morell), comp. 9. VII.–11. VIII. 1746, prod. London, Covent Garden Theatre, 1. IV. 1747.

Judenkünig, Hans (b. ?; d. ? Vienna, c. 4. III. 1526), Ger. or Aus. lutenist. Lived in Vienna and wrote and arr. pieces for his instrument.

Judgment of Paris, The, masque by Congreve, for the comp. of which a prize was advertised in the *London Gazette* in 1700, the 1st 4 prizes being won by Weldon, Eccles, D. Purcell and Finger in 1701. Eccles's setting prod. London, Dorset Gardens Theatre, 21. III. and Finger's 27. III. 1701. The lib. was later set by G. Sammartini, prod. Cliveden, Bucks., 1. VIII. 1740, and by Arne, prod. Drury Lane, London, 12. III. 1742.

Judith. *See also* **Ettinger**, **Holofernes**, **Klughardt**.
Opera by Natanael Berg (1879–1957), (lib., in Swed., by comp., based on Hebbel's drama), prod. Stockholm, 22. II. 1936.
Opera by Goossens (lib. by Arnold Bennett), prod. London, Covent Garden Theatre, 25. VI. 1929.
Opera by Serov (lib., in Rus., by comp. and Apollon Nikolaievich Maikov, based

322

on Paolo Giacometti's drama *Giuditta*), prod. St. Petersburg, 28. V. 1863.

Oratorio by Arne (lib. by Isaac Bickerstaffe), perf. London, Drury Lane Theatre, 27. II. 1761.

Oratorio by Parry (lib. from the Bible), perf. Birmingham Festival, 1888.

Play with mus. by Honegger (lib. by René Morax), prod. Mézières, Swi., open-air Théâtre du Jorat, 13. VI. 1925; operatic version, Monte Carlo, 13. II. 1926.

Juif polonais, Le (*The Polish Jew*), opera by C. Erlanger (lib. by Henri Cain and Pierre Barthélemy Gheusi, based on Erckmann-Chatrian's novel), prod. Paris, Opéra-Comique, 11. IV. 1900. The subject is that of the play *The Bells*, in which Irving made his greatest popular success.

Juive, La (*The Jewess*), opera by Halévy (lib. by Scribe), prod. Paris, Opéra, 23. II. 1835.

Julie, opera by Dezède (lib. by Jacques Marie Boutet de Monvel), prod. Paris, Comédie-Italienne, 28. IX. 1772. Mozart wrote pf. variations (K. 264) on the air 'Lison dormait' in 1778.

Julien, ou La Vie du poète (*Julian, or The Poet's Life*), opera by G. Charpentier, sequel to *Louise* (lib. by comp.), prod., Paris, Opéra-Comique, 4. VI. 1913.

Julius Caesar (Handel and Malipiero). *See* Giulio Cesare.

Jullien, (Jean Lucien) Adolphe (b. Paris, 1. VI. 1845; d. Chaintreauville, 30. VIII. 1932), Fr. critic. Studied law at first, and mus. with a retired prof. of the Cons. He began to write for the mus. papers and to champion Berlioz, Wagner, Schumann and modern mus. App. mus. critic to *Le Français* in 1872 and the *Journal des Débats* in 1873. His books incl. studies of 18th-cent. opera, Berlioz, Wagner, Goethe and mus., etc.

Jullien (orig. Julien), **Louis Antoine** (b. Sisteron, 23. IV. 1812; d. Paris, 14. III. 1860), Fr. cond. Son of a bandmaster, he studied unsuccessfully at the Paris Cons., became a cond. of dance mus. and compiler of quadrilles on popular operas. Went to London *c.* 1840 and made sensational successes with promenade concerts, quadrille bands, etc., due as much to his eccentric behaviour as to his superficial mus. gifts.

Junge Lord, Der (*The Young Lord*), opera by Henze (lib. by Ingeborg Bachmann, after Wilhelm Hauff), prod. Berlin, Deutsche Oper, 7. IV. 1965.

Jungfernquartette (Ger. = Maiden 4tets), another nickname for Haydn's 6 string 4tets, Op. 33, also known as 'Rus. 4tets' and more generally as 'Gli Scherzi'.

Juon, Paul (b. Moscow, 8. III. 1872; d. Vevey, Switz., 21. VIII. 1940), Rus. comp. Studied with Taneiev and Arensky in Moscow and with Bargiel in Berlin, where he settled and was later app. prof. at the Hochschule für Musik by Joachim.

Works incl. ballet *Psyche*; 2 symphs., serenade and other works for orch.; 2 vln. concertos, *Épisodes concertantes* for vln., cello and pf. and orch.; chamber symph., 5 pieces for string orch.; 3 string 4tets, 6tet for pf. and strings, 2 pf. 5tets, 2 pf. 4tets, 3 pf. trios, Divertimento for wind and pf., do. for clar. and 2 vlas.; instrumental pieces; *Satyrs and Nymphs, Preludes* and *Capriccios*, etc. for pf., etc.

'Jupiter' Symphony, nickname (not the comp.'s own) given to Mozart's last symph., K. 551 in C maj., finished 10. VIII. 1788.

Jurinac, Sena (b. Travnik, 24. X. 1921), Yugoslav soprano. Studied singing in Zagreb, making her début there in 1942. Since 1944 she has been a member of the Vienna State Opera. She has also sung at Glyndebourne and Covent Garden, and is esp. noted for her singing of Mozart and R. Strauss.

Just Intonation, singing or instrumental playing in what is said to be the pure natural scale, not that artificially fixed on keyboard instruments by Equal Temperament.

Justiniana, a type of 16th-cent. *villanella* for 3 voices the words of which satirized the Venetian patricians. There is no connection between the J. and the *villanella* set to poetry of the type originated by L. Giustiniani (*see* **Giustiniana**).

Kalevala

K

K. (abbr.) = **Köchel**, the thematic catalogue of Mozart's works ed. by Ludwig von Köchel. Mozart's works are identified by the sign 'K.', followed by catalogue numbers instead of by op. numbers.

Kabalevsky, Dimitri Borisovich (b. Leningrad, 30. XII. 1904), Rus. comp. Entered the Skriabin School of Mus. at Moscow when the family settled there in 1918, studying pf. and becoming a comp. pupil of Vassilenko and Catoire, afterwards of Miaskovsky. Later became prof. of comp. there.
Works incl. operas *The Golden Spikes*, *The Craftsman of Clamecy* (after Romain Rolland's novel *Colas Breugnon*), *Before Moscow* and *Nikita Vershinin*; incid. mus. for Shakespeare's *Measure for Measure*, Sheridan's *School for Scandal* and an adaptation of Flaubert's *Madame Bovary*; film mus.; *Poem of Struggle, Our Great Fatherland* and *People's Avengers* for chorus and orch.; 4 symphs. (No. 3 *Requiem for Lenin*); 3 pf. concertos, vln. concerto, cello concerto; 2 string 4tets; 3 sonatas, 2 sonatinas and other pf. mus.; Requiem; songs, etc.

Kabeláč, Miloslav (b. Prague, 1. VIII. 1908), Cz. comp. Studied comp. at the Prague Cons. with K. B. Jirák from 1928 to 1931 and later also the pf. at the Master School. In 1932 he joined the staff of Czech Radio.
Works incl. 6 symphs,; cantatas *Mystery of Time, Do not retreat*; 2 overtures; wind 6tet; suite for saxophone and pf.; vln. and pf. pieces; choral mus., etc.

Kade, Otto (b. Dresden, 6. V. 1819; d. Doberan nr. Rostock, 19. VII. 1900), Ger. musicologist. Studied at Dresden and went to It. for research in old mus., in which he specialized, esp. the Flem., Ger. and Span. schools. He also cond. the ducal chapel choir at Mecklenburg-Schwerin.

Kafenda, Frico (b. Mošovce, 2. XI. 1883), Slovak comp. and cond. Studied at the Leipzig Cons. and in 1920 became prof. at the Mus. School at Bratislava.
Works incl. church mus., choral works, *Ave Maria* for soprano and org.; string 4tet; sonatas for vln. and pf. and cello and pf.; songs, etc.

Kafka, Franz (1883–1924), Ger. novelist. *See* **Einem** (*Prozess*), **Haubenstock-Ramati** (*Amerika*), **Ruyneman** (*Prozess*).

Kagel, Mauricio (b. Buenos Aires, 24. XII. 1931), Arg. comp. of advanced tendencies. Studied in Buenos Aires, settling in Cologne in 1957. He has evolved a very complex style employing serial and aleatory techniques, permutations of different languages, light effects, etc.

Works incl. *Anagrama* for 4 soloists, speaking chorus and chamber ensemble; *Sur scène*, theatrical piece in 1 act for speaker, mime, singer and 3 instruments; *The Women*, dramatic scene for 3 female voices, 3 actresses, a dancer, chorus of women, and electronic tapes; *Match* for 3 players; *Diaphony* for chorus, orch. and 2 projectors; *Transición I* for electronic sounds; *Transición II* for pf., perc. and 2 tapes; *Hetrophonie* for an orch. of solo instruments; string 6tet.

Kahn, Robert (b. Mannheim, 21. VII. 1865; d. Biddenden, Kent, 29. V. 1951), Ger. comp. Studied at Mannheim, Berlin and (with Rheinberger) at Munich. In 1890–3 he cond. a women's choir at Leipzig and was prof. at the Hochschule für Musik in Berlin from 1897 to 1930. He settled in Eng. in 1937.
Works incl. string 4tet, pf. 5tet, 3 pf. 4tets, 3 pf. trios, clar. trio; 3 sonatas and suite for vln. and pf., 2 cello and pf. sonatas; many women's choruses; pf. pieces; songs, etc.

Kaiser, Georg (1878–1945), Ger. dramatist. *See* **Casal y Chapí, Ettinger** (*Juana*), **Wagner-Régeny** (*Bürger von Calais*), **Weill** (*Protagonist, Silbersee* and *Zar lässt sich photographieren*).

Kaiser Quartett (Haydn). *See* **Emperor Quartet**.

Kajanus, Robert (b. Helsinki, 2. XII. 1856; d. Helsinki, 6. VII. 1933), Fin. cond. and comp. Studied at the Helsinki and Leipzig Conss., also comp. with Svendsen in Paris. Founded the orch. of the Helsinki Phil. Society in 1882, with which later he paid several important visits to foreign countries. Director of mus. at Helsinki Univ., 1897–1926.
Works incl. symph. *Aino* (on an incident from the *Kalevala*), etc.

Kalafaty, Vassily Pavlovich (b. Eupatoria, Crimea, 10. II. 1869; d. Leningrad, 30. I. 1942), Rus. comp. Pupil of Rimsky-Korsakov. In 1900 he was app. prof. of comp. at the St. Petersburg Cons., where he had Stravinsky and Prokofiev among his pupils.
Works incl. symph. and other orchestral works; chamber mus.; pf. pieces; songs, etc.

Kalbeck, Max (b. Breslau, 4. I. 1850; d. Vienna, 4. V. 1921), Ger. critic and writer on mus. Worked in Vienna. Trans. opera libs. and wrote the 1st full Brahms biog.

Kalcher, Johann Nepomuk (b. Freising, Bavar., 1766; d. Munich, 1826), Ger. organist and comp. Studied at Munich, where he became court organist in 1798. Weber was one of his pupils. Wrote Masses, symphs., org. mus., songs, etc.

Kalevala, The, Fin. nat. epic. *See* **Dallapiccola, Kajanus** (*Aino*), **Klami** (suite), **Launis** (*Kullervo*), **Lemminkäinen's Home-**

325

Faring (Sibelius), **Merikanto (A.)** (*Abduction of Kyllikö*), **Pohjola's Daughter** (Sibelius), **Schantz** (*Kullervo*), **Sibelius** (do.), **Swan of Tuonela** (Sibelius), **Tapiola** (do.).

Kalidasa (?– ?), Indian (Sanskrit) dramatist. Works based on *Sakuntala, see* Bachrich (ballet), **Coerne, Foulds, Goldmark (C.), Hüe, Paderewski, Perfall, Sacountala** (Reyer), **Sakuntala** (Weingartner), **Scharwenka (P.).**

Kalinnikov, Vassily Sergeyevich (b. Vony, 13. I. 1866; d. Yalta, 11. I. 1901), Rus. comp. He was educ. at a seminary, where he cond. the choir. In 1884 went to Moscow and, in spite of great poverty, obtained a mus. educ. at the Phil. Society Mus. School. After cond. It. opera for the 1893–4 season, he was found to suffer from consumption and lived mainly in the Crimea, devoted to comp.

Works incl. incid. mus. to Alexey Tolstoy's *Tsar Boris*; cantatas *St. John Chrysostom* and *Russalka*; 2 symphs., suite, 2 Intermezzi and 2 sketches for orch.; string 4tets; pf. pieces; songs, etc.

Kalisch, Alfred (b. London, 13. III. 1863; d. London, 17. V. 1933), Eng. critic of Ger. descent. Educ. at Oxford for law, but became a mus. journalist in 1894. Translator of R. Strauss's operas.

Kalkbrenner, Friedrich (Wilhelm Michael) (b. on a journey between Cassel and Berlin, XI. 1785; d. Enghien-les-Bains, 10. VI. 1849), Ger. pianist, teacher and comp. Studied under his father, Christian K. (1755–1806) and at the Paris Cons. Made his 1st public appearance in Vienna in 1803, returning to Paris in 1806. Lived in London as teacher and perf. in 1814–23 and then settled in Paris as a member of the pf. firm of Pleyel, but continued to teach and perf.

Works incl. 4 pf. concertos, concerto for 2 pfs.; pf. 7tet, 6tet and 5tet; pf. school with studies appended, sonatas, variations and numerous other works for pf.

Kalliwoda, Johan Vaclav (b. Prague, 21. II. 1801; d. Carlsruhe, 3. XII. 1866), Boh. violinist and comp. Studied at the Prague Cons. in 1811–17 and played in the orch. in 1817–22. He then became mus. director to Prince Fürstenberg at Donaueschingen until his retirement in 1866.

Works incl. opera *Blanka*; 7 symphs.; concertinos for vln., for clar. and other instruments; string 4tets; vln. duets, vln. pieces; songs, etc.

Kalomiris, Manolis (b. Smyrna, 26. XII. 1883; d. Athens, 3. IV. 1962), Gk. comp. Studied in Athens, Constantinople and Vienna. He taught at Kharkov in 1906–10 and then settled in Athens as prof. at the Cons. From 1919 he was director of the Hellenic Cons. there, but in 1926 he founded the Nat. Cons. and became its director.

Works incl. operas *The Master Builder*

(after N. Kazantzakis), *The Mother's Ring* (after J. Kambyssis), *Anatoli* and *The Haunted Waters* (after Yeats); incid. mus.; 2 symphs., symph. poems, etc., for orch.; chamber mus.; pf. works; songs, etc.

Kamarinskaya, fantasy for orch. on 2 Rus. themes by Glinka, comp. 1848 and known only in an ed. revised by Rimsky-Korsakov and Glazunov.

Kamieński, Lucjan (b. Gniezno, 7. I. 1885), Pol. comp. and musicologist. Studied at Breslau and Berlin, became mus. ed. of a paper at Königsberg in 1909, was app. 2nd director of the Poznan Cons. in 1920 and prof. at the univ. there from 1922 to 1939. From 1949 to 1957 he taught at the Mus. School at Toruń and then settled in Canada.

Works incl. opera *Ladies and Hussars*; *Silesia sings* for orch.; *Symphonia paschalis* and 2 poems from *Des Knaben Wunderhorn* for chorus and orch.; vln. and pf. sonata; *Fantasy on Pol. Christmas Song, Early Pol. Suite*, etc. for pf.; songs with chamber orch., with cello and pf. and several song cycles with pf., etc.

Kamieński, Maciej (b. Sopron, 13. X. 1734; d. Warsaw, 25. I. 1821), Hung.-Pol. comp. Studied in Vienna and settled at Warsaw in c. 1760. He prod. the 1st Pol. opera there on 11. V. 1778.

Works incl. opera *Happiness in Unhappiness* and 5 others in Pol. and 2 in Ger.; church mus.; cantata for the unveiling of the Sobieski monument, etc.

Kaminski, Heinrich (b. Tiengen nr. Waldshut, 4. VII. 1886; d. Ried, Bavar., 14. VI. 1946), Ger. comp. of Pol. descent. Studied at Heidelberg and Berlin, then lived nr. Munich devoted to comp., which he later taught for a short time in Berlin.

Works incl. opera *Jürg Jenatsch* (after Conrad Ferdinand Meyer); Psalm lxix, Magnificat and *Introit and Hymn* for solo voices, chorus and orch.; concerto for orch., *Concerto grosso*; string 5tet; string 4tet; *Triptychon* for voice and org., etc.

Kammerton (Ger., lit. chamber-pitch), the pitch to which orch. instruments in Ger. were tuned in the 17th–18th cent. It was lower, by a whole tone or more, than the *Chorton* (choir-pitch) used for church orgs., and it was for this reason that Bach, in his Leipzig cantatas, transposed the org. parts down a tone in order to make them agree with the orch. The transposition applied only to the org. parts: the orchestral parts could be used as they stood.

Kantele, a Fin. obs. instrument of the Psaltery type.

Kapelle (Ger. = chapel), orig. the mus. estab. of a king's or prince's chapel; later, by transfer, an orch.

Kapellmeister (Ger.), orig. choirmaster; later also cond.

Kapellmeistermusik (Ger. = conductor's

mus.), a contemptuous term for a mus. work which betrays creative weakness and has no merit but that of a knowledge of rules and glib craftsmanship.

Kapp, Julius (b. Steinbach, Baden, 1. X. 1883; d. Hinang bei Alstädten-im-Allgau, 18. III. 1962), Ger. writer on mus. Studied chemistry and then became a literary ed. In 1921 he ed. the paper of the Berlin State Opera and in 1923 he became dramatic director there and adapted a number of works for its stage. He ed. Wagner's letters and his books incl. studies of Liszt, Wagner, Berlioz, Weber, Meyerbeer, R. Strauss, etc.

Kaprálová, Vitězslava (b. Brno, 24. I. 1915, d. Montpellier, 16. VI. 1940), Cz. comp. Studied with her father, Vaclav Kaprál (b. 1889), Novák and others.

Works incl. *Military Sinfonietta*; pf. concerto; string 4tet; pf. works; songs, etc.

Kapsberger, Johann Hieronymus (b. *c.* 1575; d. Rome, *c.* 1650), Ger. lutenist and comp. Lived in Venice and pub. 3 books of mus. for chitarrone in tablature. He also wrote vocal *villanelle* with that instrument, motets, an epithalamium, an apotheosis of Ignatius Loyola, etc.

Karajan, Herbert von (b. Salzburg, 5. IV. 1908), Aus. cond. Studied at Salzburg Mozarteum and in Vienna. Made his début at Ulm in 1928, remaining there until 1933. From 1934 to 1938 he was at Aachen and from 1938 to 1945 at the Berlin State Opera. After Furtwängler's death in 1954 he took over the Berlin Phil. Orch. and in 1956 became director of the Vienna State Opera, resigning in 1964. One of the best-known conds. of the day, K. is esp. noted for his perf. of Mozart, Wagner, Bruckner and R. Strauss.

Karamzin, Nikolai Mikhailovich (1765–1826), Rus. hist., novelist and poet. *See* **Boris Godunov** (Mussorgsky).

Karatyghin, Viatcheslav Gavrilovich (b. Pavlovsk, 17. IX. 1875; d. Leningrad, 23. XII. 1925), Rus. critic and comp. Wrote on Skriabin and Mussorgsky and pub. a number of his own songs.

Karel, Rudolf (b. Plzeň [Pilsen], 9. XI. 1880; d. Terezín, 6. III. 1945), Cz. comp. Studied comp. under Dvořák at the Prague Cons. In 1914, on holiday in Rus., he was interned as an Aus. subject, then taught at Taganrog and Rostov-on-Don, fled to Siberia and eventually escaped to Cz., where he became prof. at the Prague Cons. He d. tragically at a concentration camp.

Works incl. operas *Ilsa's Heart* and *Godmother Death*; incid. mus. to Knud Hamsun's *The Game of Life*; *Awakening*, symph. for solo voices, chorus and orch.; 3 symphs., symph. poems *The Ideals* and *Demon*, suite, fantasy, Slavonic dances,

etc. for orch.; vln. concerto, 3 string 4tets, pf. 4tet, pf. trio; vln. and pf. sonata; sonata, *Tema con variazioni* and other pf. works; choruses, etc.

Karg-Elert (real name Karg), **Sigfrid** (b. Oberndorf-am-Neckar, 21. XI. 1877; d. Leipzig, 9. IV. 1933), Ger. organist, pianist and comp. Studied at the Leipzig Cons. and became prof. at those of Magdeburg and Leipzig, was a brilliant pianist, but was persuaded by Grieg to devote himself to comp.

Works incl. a symph.; string 4tet; vln. and pf. sonatas; sonata and other works for pf.; over 100 songs; pieces for harmonium and many org. works, incl. 66 chorale improvisations, 24 preludes and postludes, Sonatina, passacaglia, fantasy and fugue in D maj., *Chaconne, Fugue-Trilogy and Chorale*, 10 characteristic pieces, 3 symph. chorales, 7 *Pastels from Lake Constance*, 6 *Cathedral Windows*, 54 variation-studies *Homage to Handel*, etc.

Karl V, opera by Křenek (lib. by comp.), prod. Prague, Ger. Opera, 15. VI. 1938.

Karlowicz, Miecyslaw (b. Wiszniezwo, 11. XII. 1876; d. Zakopane, 10. II. 1909), Pol. comp. The son of a noble family, he travelled much as a child and learnt the vln. in Prague, Dresden and Heidelberg, and soon played chamber mus. with his parents, a cellist and a pianist. Later studied at Warsaw, where his comp. teacher was Noskowski, and afterwards with Urban in Berlin, also cond. with Nikisch at Leipzig. Settled at Zakopane in the Tatra mountains in 1908 and was killed by an avalanche there.

Works incl. incid. mus. to *Biala Golabka*; symph. in E min., symph. poems *Returning Waves, The Sad Story* (*Preludes to Eternity*), *Stanislas and Anna Oswiecim, An Episode of the Masquerade,* serenade, *Lithuanian Rhapsody* for orch.; vln. concerto; songs, etc.

Karyotakis, Theodore (b. Argos, 21. VII. 1903), Gk. comp. Studied under Mitropoulos and Varvoglis in Athens.

Works incl. ballet *Prometheus*; incid. mus. for Euripides' *Ion*; orchestral works; chamber mus.; vln. and fl. sonatas, pf. mus., etc.

Kasanli. *See* **Kazanly.**

Kashin, Daniel Nikitich (b. Moscow, *c.* 1769; d. Moscow, 22. XII. 1841), Rus. comp. Pupil of Sarti. Orig. a serf, he cond. a serfs' orch. in Moscow from 1790 to 1800. Pub. a collection of Rus. folksongs with pf. accomp.

Works incl. operas *Natalia, Fair Olga* and *The One-day Reign of Nourmahal* (on Moore's *Lalla Rookh*); cantatas and other choral works; patriotic songs, etc.

Kashkin, Nikolai Dmitrievich (b. Voronezh, 9. XII. 1839; d. Moscow, 15. IV. 1920), Rus. mus. critic and teacher. Prof.

at the Moscow Cons. from its foundation in 1866 to 1896. Critic of the *Russky Vedomosti* and author of a vol. of reminiscences of Tchaikovsky.

Kashperov, Vladimir Nikitich (b. Simbirsk, 1827; d. Romantsevo, 8. VII. 1894), Rus. comp. Studied with Henselt in St. Petersburg and later in Berlin and It. Prof. of singing at the Moscow Cons. from 1866 to 1872.

Works incl. operas *The Gypsies*, *Mary Tudor* (after Hugo), *Rienzi* (after Bulwer-Lytton), *Consuelo* (after George Sand), *The Storm* (after Ostrovsky), *Taras Bulba* (after Gogol), etc.

Kashtchey the Immortal (*K. Bessmertny*), opera by Rimsky-Korsakov (lib. by comp.), prod. Moscow, 25. XII. 1902. Kashtchey is the wizard of Rus. fairy lore who appears also in Stravinsky's *Firebird* ballet.

Kasprowicz, Jan (1860–1926), Pol. poet. *See* **Szymanowski** (songs).

Kassern, Tadeusz Zygfryd (b. Lwów, 19. III. 1904; d. N.Y., 2. V. 1957), Pol. comp. Studied at the Poznan Cons. while reading law at the univ. there, and settled there later.

Works incl. operas *The Anointed*, *Sun-up* and *Comedy about the Dumb Wife*; Children's Cantata for soprano, chorus and orch.; symph. poem *Dies irae* in memory of Marshal Pilsudski, *Sinfonietta giocosa*; concerto for string orch.; concertos for soprano, for double bass and for fl.; concertino for fl., clar. and bassoon; 2 sonatas, sonatina, mazurkas and preludes for pf.; *Naïve Songs* and other songs; choruses, etc.

Kastalsky, Alexander Dmitrievich (b. Moscow, 28. XI. 1856; d. Moscow, 17. XII. 1926), Rus. comp. Studied under Tchaikovsky and Taneiev at the Moscow Cons. He taught the pf. at the Synodal School there from 1887 and became its director in 1910. After the Revolution he took part in the reform of Rus. church mus. and wrote liturgical works; he also helped to estab. people's theatres and centres for the cultivation of Rus. folksongs, many of which he ed.

Works incl. opera *Clara Milich* (after Turgenev's tale); *Requiem for Fallen Heroes* and other choral works: *Epic Tale*, *Glory*, *Russia*, *Hymn to the Proletariat*, *Hymn for the First of May*, cantata *1905*; *The Railway Train* for chorus, pf., tpt. and perc.; *Symph. of the Tilling of the Soil*, *Georgian Suite*, etc. for orch., etc.

Kastner, Jean Georges (Johann Georg) (b. Strasbourg, 9. III. 1810; d. Paris, 19. XII. 1867), Alsat. comp. and theorist. Studied theology at home, but prod. an opera *Die Königin der Sarmaten* and was sent by the Strasbourg town council to study with Berton and Reicha at the Paris Cons. He wrote a treatise on orchestration,

a manual on military mus., and methods for var. instruments.

Works incl. operas *Die Königin der Sarmaten*, *Gustav Wasa*, *Oskars Tod*, *Der Sarazene*, *Beatrice*, *La maschera*, *Le Dernier Roi de Juda*, *Les Nonnes de Robert le Diable*; cantatas *La Résurrection*, *Sardanapale*, *Cantate alsacienne*; scenes for voice and pf.; songs, part-songs, etc.

Kastner, Santiago (Macario) (b. London, 15. X. 1908), Anglo-Port. musicologist and comp. Studied at Amsterdam, Leipzig and with Anglès at Barcelona. He writes on Span. and Port. mus. and has ed. a collection of old Span. and Port. keyboard mus. Comps. incl. *Kraviastas portugueses*; 5 *Tentos* by Manoel Rodrigues Coelho, etc.

Káta Kabanová, opera by Janáček (lib. by Vincenc Červinka, based on Alexander Nikolaievich Ostrovsky's play *Groza*), prod. Brno, 23. X. 1921.

Katchen, Julius (b. Long Branch, N.J., 15. VIII. 1926; d. Paris, 29. IV. 1969), Amer. pianist. Studied in New York with David Saperton, making his début in 1937. He toured widely.

Katona, József (1792–1830), Hung. dramatist. *See* **Bánk-Bán** (Erkel).

Katuar. *See* **Catoire.**

Kauer, Ferdinand (b. Dyjákovičky, Morav., 18. I. 1751; d. Vienna, 13. IV. 1831), Aus. comp. Studied at Znaim and Vienna, where he was app. leader and 2nd cond. at the Leopoldstadt Theatre, for which he wrote mus. for *c.* 100 pantomimes, farces, etc. as well as operettas and operas.

Works incl. operas *Das Donauweibchen*, *Das Waldweibchen*; oratorio *Die Sündflut*; trio *Nelsons grosse See-Schlacht*, etc.

Kaun, Hugo (b. Berlin, 21. III. 1863; d. Berlin, 2. IV. 1932), Ger. comp. He had written over 150 works before he was 1 and studied with Kiel at the Berlin Acad. of Arts. In 1884 he went to U.S.A. as pianist, but had to give up that career owing to an injury; and in 1887 settled at Milwaukee, but returned to Berlin in 1901, teaching comp. 1st at the Acad. and from 1922 at the Klindworth-Scharwenka Cons.

Works incl. operas *Der Pietist*, *Sappho*, *Der Fremde* and *Menandra*; several choral works; 3 symphs., *Minnehaha und Hiawatha* (after Longfellow), symph. prologue *Marie Magdalene*, humoresque *Falstaff* (after Shakespeare) and other orchestral works; 4 string 4tets, pf. 5tet, 2 pf. trios, 8tet; vln. and pf. sonata, etc.

Kazanly, Nikolai Ivanovich (b. Tiraspol, 17. XII. 1869; d. Petrograd, 5. VIII. 1916), Rus. comp. and cond. Studied with Rimsky-Korsakov at the St. Petersburg Cons.

Works incl. opera *Miranda*; symph.; sinfonietta, symph. poem *Villa by the Sea* (on Böcklin's picture); songs, etc.

Kazasoglou, George (b. Athens, 13. XII.

1910), Gk. comp. Studied under Lavranga, Kalomiris and Varvoglis in Athens and devoted himself particularly to the comp. of incid. mus.

Works incl. 3 ballets; incid. mus. for *Andromache*, *Medea* and *Orestes* (Euripides), *Ajax* and *Antigone* (Sophocles), *The Clouds* (Aristophanes), *As You Like It* and *Richard III* (Shakespeare), *Hellas* (Shelley), *Penthesilea* (Kleist), *The Pretenders* (Ibsen); symph. and other orchestral works; vln. and pf. sonatas, etc.

Kazuro, Stanisław (b. Teklinopol nr. Wilno, 1. VIII. 1882; d. Warsaw, 30. XI. 1961), Pol. comp. and cond. Studied at the Warsaw Cons. and the Accademia di Santa Cecilia in Rome. App. prof. at the Warsaw Cons. and trained and cond. several choral societies.

Works incl. operas *The Fairy Tale* and *The Return*; oratorios *The Sun*, *The Flight* and *The Sea*; miscellaneous choral works; symph. poem *Youth*; songs, incl. children's songs and It. and Pol. folksongs, etc.

Keats, John (1795–1821), Eng. poet. *See* Converse (*Belle Dame sans merci*), Dieren (van) (songs), Gibbs (C. A.) (*Belle dame s. m.*), Greenwood (do.), Hadley (P.) (do.), Harty (*Ode to Nightingale*), Holst (*Choral Symph.*), Howell (*Lamia*), Jacobi (*Eve of St. Agnes*), MacDowell (*Lamia*), Mackenzie (*Belle Dame s. m.*), Miles (*Ode to Autumn*), Paine (*Realm of Fancy*), Parry (H.) (*Proserpine*), Riegger (*Belle Dame s. m.*), Rubbra (do.), Scott (C.) (do.), Valen (*To Hope*), Walker (*Ode to Nightingale*), Walthew (do.).

Keeners, professional singers of lamentations for the dead in Ir.

Kehraus (Ger. = clear-out or sweep-out). *See* Grossvater-Tanz.

Keil, Alfredo (b. Lisbon, 3. VII. 1850; d. Hamburg, 4. X. 1907), Port. comp. of Ger. descent. Studied at Nuremberg and prod. his 1st stage work, the operetta *Susana*, at Lisbon in 1883.

Works incl. operas *Donna Bianca*, *Irene*, *Serrana*; symph. poems *Uma caçada na corte* and *Orientães*; cantatas *Patria* and *Primavera*; song 'A Portugueza', which became the nat. anthem in 1911, etc.

Keilberth, Joseph (b. Karlsruhe, 19. IV. 1908; d. Munich, 21. VII. 1968), Ger. cond. From 1935 to 1940 he cond. at the Karlsruhe State Opera and from 1940 to 1945 was cond. of the Berlin Phil. Orch. He cond. at Dresden from 1945 to 1951 and at Bayreuth from 1952 to 1956. He was best known as a cond. of R. Strauss's operas.

Keirnine, a small Ir. harp.

Keiser, Reinhard (b. Teuchern nr. Weissenfels, Saxony, 9. I. 1674; d. Hamburg, 12. IX. 1739), Ger. comp. A pupil of Schelle at St. Thomas's School, Leipzig, worked at Brunswick from 1692 under

Kusser, whom he succeeded as chief comp. to the Hamburg Opera in 1695. There he comp. over 100 operas, making Hamburg the most distinguished operatic centre in Ger. App. *Kapellmeister* to the Dan. Court in Copenhagen in 1723, returned to Hamburg as Cantor of the cathedral, 1728.

Works incl. operas *Basilius*, *Circe*, *Penelope*, *Der geliebte Adonis*, *Augustus*, *Orpheus*, *La forza della virtù*, *Stoertebecker und Joedge Michaels*, *Die verdammt Staat-Sucht*, *Nebucadnezar*, *Octavia*, *Masagniello furioso*, *Desiderius*, *Croesus*, *Fredegunda*, *Die grossmüthige Tomyris*, *Ulysses*, *Der lächerliche Printz Jodelet*, etc.; Passion oratorios *Der für die Sünde der Welt gemartete und sterbende Heiland Jesus* (text by Brockes), *Der blutige und sterbende Jesus* (Hunold), etc.; cantatas; motets; instrumental mus.; etc.

Kelemen, Milko (b. Podravska, Slatina, 30. III. 1924), Croatian comp. Studied at the Zagreb Cons. with Šulek. His mature style employs serial and aleatory techniques.

Works incl. opera *State of Siege*; *Koncertantne Improvizacije* for strings; *Concerto giocoso* for chamber orch.; concertos for vln. and bassoon; concertino for double bass and strings; *Symphonic Music 57*; *Games* song cycle; pf. sonata.

Kéler Béla (Adalbert von Kéler) (b. Bártfa, Hung., 13. II. 1820; d. Wiesbaden, 20. XI. 1882), Hung. violinist and comp. After studying law and taking up agriculture, he studied mus. in Vienna, where he became a violinist at the Theater an der Wien. In 1854 he became cond. of Gungl's band in Berlin, but returned to Vienna and took over Lanner's band in 1855. The next year he became an infantry bandmaster and in 1870 cond. of the Spa orch. at Wiesbaden. He wrote innumerable light pieces, esp. overtures, dances and marches.

Keller, Gottfried (1819–90), Swiss poet and novelist. *See* Baumgartner ('O mein Heimatland'), Romeo und Julia auf dem Dorfe (Delius), Schoeck (*Gesangfest im Frühling*, *Lebendig begraben*, *Gaselen*, *Unter Sternen*, *Sommernacht* and songs), Vrieslander (songs), Zemlinsky (*Kleider machen Leute*).

6 of his poems set by Hugo Wolf.

Kelley, Edgar Stillman (b. Sparta, Wis., 14. IV. 1857; d. N.Y., 12. XI. 1944), Amer. comp. and writer on mus. Studied at Chicago and Stuttgart, and on his return to U.S.A. became organist and critic in Calif., where he also made a study of Chin. mus. He then taught at Yale Univ., in Berlin and, from 1910, at the Cincinnati Cons.

Works incl. operetta *Puritania*; incid. mus. for Shakespeare's *Macbeth* and for a dramatic version of Wallace's *Ben Hur*; orchestral suite on Chin. themes, *Aladdin*, *Gulliver* symph. (after Swift), *New England*

Symph., suite *Alice in Wonderland* (after Lewis Carroll); cantata *Pilgrim's Progress* (after Bunyan), *Wedding Ode* for tenor, male chorus and orch.; *My Captain* (Whitman) and *The Sleeper* (Poe) for chorus; variations for string 4tet, string 4tet, pf. 5tet; pf. pieces; songs, etc.

Kellner, Johann Peter (b. Gräfenroda, Thuringia, 28. IX. 1705; d. Gräfenroda, 22. IV. 1772), Ger. organist and comp. App. Cantor at Frankenhain in 1725, he returned in a similar capacity to his home town in 1728, a post which he held till his death. He knew Bach and Handel personally.

Works incl. cantatas, an oratorio, org. and harpsichord mus., etc.

Kellogg, Clara Louise (b. Sumterville, S.C., 12. VII. 1842; d. New Hartford, Conn., 13. V. 1916), Amer. soprano. Studied in N.Y. and made her 1st stage appearance there in 1861.

Kelly, Michael (b. Dublin, 25. XII. 1762; d. Margate, 9. X. 1826), Ir. tenor, actor and comp. Pupil of M. Arne and others, went to Naples in 1779 to study with Fenaroli and Aprile, and there made his operatic début in 1781. At the Court Opera in Vienna, 1784–7, he was the first Basilio and Curzio in Mozart's *Figaro* (1786). Returned to London in 1787, and 2 years later prod. the first of over 60 theatrical comps. His entertaining *Reminiscences* (pub. 1826), though not fully reliable, contain valuable information on his contemporaries, esp. Mozart.

Works incl. dramatic works *A Friend in Need*, *The Castle Spectre*, *Blue Beard*, *Pizarro* (Sheridan), *The Gipsy Prince*, *Love laughs at Locksmiths*, *Cinderella*, *Polly*, etc.

Kellyk, Hugh (b. ?; d. ?), Eng. 15th-cent. comp. Nothing is known of his life. An antiphon, *Gaude flore virginali*, and a Magnificat are in the Eton Choirbook.

Kelterborn, Rudolf (b. Basle, 3. IX. 1931), Swiss comp. Studied with J. Handschin and Willy Burkhard, Blacher and Fortner. In 1960 he became an instructor at the Detmold Mus. Acad. In his mus. he tends toward total serialism.

Works incl. *Metamorphosen* for orch.; concertino for vln. and chamber orch., concertino for pf. and chamber orch.; suite for woodwind, perc. and strings; sonata for 16 solo strings; *Cantata Profana* for baritone, chorus and 13 instruments; cantata *Ewige Wiederkehr* for mezzosoprano, fl. and string trio; cello concerto; chamber mus. for var. instrumental groups incl. *5 Fantasien* for fl., cello and harpsichord; *7 Bagatellen* for wind 5tet; *Metamorphosen* for pf.; *Meditation* for 6 wind instruments.

Kelway, Joseph (b. ? Chichester, *c.* 1702; d. ? London, ? V. 1782), Eng. organist

and harpsichordist. Pupil of Geminiani, he was organist of St. Michael's Cornhill, London, 1730–6, then of St. Martin-in-the-Fields. Made a great reputation as a player, was teacher to Queen Charlotte, and often deputized for Handel at the org. Comp. harpsichord mus.

Kelway, Thomas (b. Chichester, *c.* 1695; d. Chichester, 21. V. 1744), Eng. organist and comp., elder brother of prec. Chorister at Chichester Cathedral under John Reading, whom he succeeded as organist in 1733. Comp. church mus.

Kemble, Adelaide (b. London, 1814; d. Warsash House, Hants., 4. VIII. 1879), Eng. soprano, daughter of the actor Charles Kemble. She 1st appeared in London and at the York Festival in 1835, then went to Ger. and It. for further study, last with Pasta. In 1839 she appeared as Norma in Venice, toured widely in It. and returned to London for an appearance in the same part in 1841.

Kempe, Rudolf (b. Nieder-Poyritz, nr. Dresden, 14. VI. 1910), Ger. cond. Studied ob., becoming 1st ob. in the Leipzig Gewandhaus Orch. in 1929. Began cond. in 1936 and from 1949 to 1952 was mus. director of the Dresden State Opera, and from 1952 to 1954 of the Munich State Opera. From 1954 to 1956 he cond. at the N.Y. Metropolitan Opera. He has cond. at many of the great opera houses of the world, including many appearances at Covent Garden, and is at present mus. director of the Royal Phil. Orch.

Kempff, Wilhelm (b. Jüterborg, 25. XI. 1895), Ger. pianist and comp. Studied pf. with H. Barth and comp. with R. Kahn. After winning both the Mendelssohn Prizes in 1917, he took up the career of a concert pianist. From 1924 to 1929 he was head of the Hochschule für Musik in Stuttgart. He is best known as one of the finest and most thoughtful interpreters of the classical pf. repertory, esp. the mus. of Beethoven.

His comps. incl. the operas *König Midas* and *Die Familie Gozzi*; several symphs. and ballets; concertos for pf. and vln.; string 4tets; and many pieces for solo pf. and org.

Kendale, Richard (b. ?; d. 1431), Eng. grammarian and mus. theorist. A short mus. treatise by him is incl. in the MS. written down by John Wylde, precentor of Waltham Holy Cross Abbey, *c.* 1460 (Brit. Mus., Lans. 763).

Kenilworth. *See* Amy Robsart, Leicester.

Kennedy, David (b. Perth, 15. IV. 1825; d. Stratford, Ont., 12. X. 1886), Scot. singer. He 1st sang in church as precentor and was an apprentice and later master house-painter. He studied singing in Edinburgh, and in 1859 made his 1st concert appearance at Liverpool. He began to tour widely, 1st in Scot. and Eng. and later in the Brit. colonies and U.S.A. One of his daughters was Marjory Kennedy-Fraser; another was Jessie, who married Tobias Matthay.

Kennedy-Fraser, Marjory. *See* **Fraser.**

Kent Bugle. *See* **Key Bugle.**

Keraulophon, an 8-ft. org. stop of the Gamba type.

Kerl (or Kerll), Johann Caspar (b. Adorf, Saxony, 9. IV. 1627; d. Munich, 13. II. 1693), Ger. organist and comp. Settled early in Vienna as a pupil of Valentini; then studied in Rome under Carissimi and prob. the org. under Frescobaldi. In the service of the Elector of Bavar. in Munich, 1656–74. Again went to Vienna, as private teacher, and was app. court organist there in 1677, but returned to Munich in 1684.

Works incl. operas *Oronte, Erinto, Le pretensioni del sole, I colori geniali*; Masses, motets and other church mus.; sonatas for 2 vlns. and bass; toccatas, *ricercari* and other works for org., etc.

Kerle, Jacob van (b. Ypres, *c.* 1531; d. Prague, 7. I. 1591), Flem. comp. He spent some time in It., partly in Rome in the service of Otto von Truchsess, Cardinal-Archbishop of Augsburg, in whose service he was in 1562–75, with whom he was also at Augsburg at times, and with whom he (?) attended the Council of Trent in 1562–3. Later he became canon of Cambrai, but was often in Vienna and Prague attending on the Emperor Rudolf.

Works incl. Masses, motets, Te Deums, Magnificats, hymns, *Sacrae cantiones*, etc.

Kern, Jerome (David) (b. N.Y., 27. I. 1885; d. N.Y., 11. XI. 1945), Amer. comp. Pupil of Paolo Gallico and Alexander Lambert in N.Y. He turned to the comp. of mus. comedy and other light mus.

Works incl. mus. comedies *Sunny, Show Boat, Mus. in the Air* and others; film mus., etc.

Kersey, Eda (b. Goodmayes, Essex, 15. V. 1904; d. Ilkley, 13. VII. 1944), Eng. violinist. Studied in London, but was partly self-taught, made her 1st appearance at the age of 16 and began to broadcast in 1925.

Ketting, Piet (b. Haarlem, 29. XI. 1905), Dutch pianist and comp. Studied with Pijper and later became prof. at the Rotterdam Cons.

Works incl. symph.; choral mus.; string 4tets, trio for fl., clar. and bassoon and other chamber mus., sonatas for fl., bass clar. and pf. and fl., ob. and pf., partita for 2 fls.; 4 sonatinas, fugue, etc., for pf.; songs, incl. Shakespeare sonnets, etc.

Kettledrums, drums with a single head of skin stretched over a cauldron-shaped receptacle. They produce notes of definite pitch which can be altered by the turning of screws at the rim of the 'kettle', thus

tightening or relaxing the skin. A mechanical device now widely used enables the player to increase or relax the tension by means of a pedal. The modern orch. has at least 3 K.s of different sizes, and more may be demanded by the comp., in which case 1 player may not be sufficient. A variety of sticks covered with different materials can be used to prod. a harder or softer impact.

Keuchenthal, Johannes (b. Ellrich am Harz, *c.* 1522; d. St. Andreasberg, 1583), Ger. clergyman and musician. Pub. *Kirchengesang, lateinisch und deutsch*, a collection of mus. for the Lutheran Church, incl. a setting of the Passion, at Wittenberg in 1573, etc.

Keussler, Gerhard von (b. Schwanenburg, 5. VII. 1874; d. Niederwartha nr. Dresden, 21. VIII. 1949), Ger. comp. and cond. Orig. a botanist, he did not study mus. until 1900, when he went to the Leipzig Cons. He became cond. and lecturer in Prague in 1906, and in 1918 cond. of the Hamburg Singakademie. Later he cond. in var. places, incl. Prague again and Austral. in 1932–5, and in 1939 he was app. head of the comp. class at the Berlin Acad. of Art.

Works incl. operas *Wandlungen, Gefängnisse* and *Die Geisselfahrt*; oratorios *Jesus aus Nazareth, Die Mutter, Zebaoth, In jungen Tagen*; symphs. in D min. and C maj.; symph. works *Auferstehung und jüngstes Gericht, Morgenländische Phantasie, An den Tod, Das hohe Lied, Australia*; many songs, etc.

Key. (1) The levers by means of which notes are prod. on keyboard instruments by being pressed down or struck. Also those on wind instruments stopping the note-holes which cannot be reached directly by the fingers.

(2) The tonality of a piece of mus. which is based on a particular maj. or min. scale and accepts harmonic relationships deriving from the notes of those scales. The 1st note of the scale (or Tonic) gives its name to the K., e.g. K. of D maj., K. of E♭ min.

Key Bugle (also **Kent Bugle**), an instrument invented in the early 19th cent.; a bugle with side-holes covered with keys similar to those used on woodwind instruments.

Key Relationships. These may be close or remote, e.g. in the key of C maj. the relation of the tonic chord (C) with the dominant (G) is close:

The relation of C min. with E♭ maj. (its relative major) is also close:

whereas the relation of C maj. with E♭ maj. is less close:

Transference from one key to another may be abrupt or may be effected by Modulation.

Key Signature, the sharps and flats which occur in the key of a given comp., written at the beginning of each stave. The signatures are as opposite.

Keys with 5 to 7 sharps or flats overlap enharmonically; in the tempered scale of the pf. they are identical as follows: B maj. and G♯ min. = C♭ maj. and A♭ min.; F♯ maj. and D♯ min. = G♭ maj. and E♭ min.; C♯ maj. and A♯ min. = D♭ maj. and B♭ min.

Keyboard, the array of levers on instruments of the pf. type and on the org., also on such instruments as the Hurdy-gurdy and the Accordion, by means of which the fingers, and on the org. also the feet, control the sound.

Keyes, Sidney (1922–43), Eng. poet. *See* **Tate** (*Nocturne*).

Keynote, the Tonic: the note on which the scale begins and ends, which determines the key of a piece of mus. in maj. or min. and after which that key is named.

Khatchaturian, Aram Ilich (b. Tiflis, 6. VI. 1903), Rus. comp. His father, a poor workman, was able to send him to Moscow only after the Revolution; he entered the Gnessin School of Mus. there and studied under that master in 1923; in 1929 he went to the Moscow Cons. as a pupil of Vassilenko and afterwards of Miaskovsky. Studied the folksongs of Rus. Armen. and other southern regions, which have influenced his comps.

Works incl. ballets *Happiness* and *Gayaneh*, incid. mus. for Shakespeare's *Macbeth*, Lope de Vega's *Widow of Valencia*, Pogodin's *Kremlin Chimes*,

Maj. Min.

KEY SIGNATURE

Kron's *Deep Drilling*, Lermontov's *Masquerade*, etc.; film mus.; *Song of Stalin* for chorus and orch.; 2 symphs., *Dance Suite* and *Solemn Overture*, '*To the End of the War*' for orch.; marches and pieces on Uzbek and Armen. themes for wind band; concertos for pf., vln., cello and vln. and cello.; string 4tet, trio for clar., vln. and pf.; sonata and pieces for vln. and pf.; pf. mus., part-songs; songs for the Rus. army, etc.

Khorovod (Rus.), a type of ancient Rus. folksong sung in chorus of 2 or more parts in a primitive kind of counterpoint. It was sung mainly at religious and family festivals and on seasonal occasions.

Khovanshchina, unfinished opera by Mussorgsky (lib. by comp. and Vladimir Vassilievich Stassov), prod., as completed and scored by Rimsky-Korsakov after Mussorgsky's death, St. Petersburg, 21. II. 1886.

Khrennikov, Tikhon Nikolaievich (b. Elets, 10. VI. 1913), Rus. comp. He was taught mus. at home, but entered the Gnessin School of Mus. at Moscow in 1929 and the Cons. in 1932 as a pupil of Shebalin.

Works incl. operas *The Brothers* (*In the Storm*); incid. mus. for Shakespeare's *Much Ado about Nothing*, an adaptation of Cervantes's *Don Quixote*, etc., film mus. for *The Pigs and the Shepherd*; 2 symphs.; pf. concerto; pf. pieces; songs to words by Pushkin and Burns; war songs; etc.

Kidson, Frank (b. Leeds, 15. XI. 1855; d. Leeds, 7. XI. 1926), Eng. musicologist and folksong collector. He became an authority on Eng. folksong and dance, also on the popular mus. of the 18th cent. Collected and pub. country dances and other traditional tunes and wrote on Eng. mus. printers, engravers and pubs., on ballad opera, etc.

Kiel, Friedrich (b. Laasphe, Westphalia, 7. X. 1821; d. Berlin, 13. IX. 1885), Ger. comp. and teacher. He made his way as a violinist at first, but studied theory with Dehn in Berlin from 1843 and became attached to the court of Frederick William IV of Prus. In 1869 he joined the council of the Berlin Acad. of Arts, and he was app. prof. of comp. at the Hochschule für Musik there.

Works incl. *Missa solemnis*, 2 Requiems; oratorio *Christus*; pf. concerto; 2 pf. 5tets, 2 string 4tets, 3 pf. 4tets, 7 pf. trios; 4 vln. sonatas, *Reisebilder* for cello and pf.; *Canons and Fugues, Variations and Fugue*, etc., for pf., etc.

Kielflügel (Ger., lit. quill-wing) = Harpsichord, so named from the quills that pluck the strings and the wing shape of the instrument's body.

Kienlen, Johann Christoph (b. Ulm, XII. 1783; d. Dessau, 7. XII. 1829), Ger. comp. He appeared as singer and pianist at the age of 7 and was later sent to Paris to study with Cherubini. After being mus. director at Ulm he went to Vienna in 1811, where he taught, and in 1823 he became singing-master to the Berlin opera.

Works incl. operas, e.g. *Claudine von Villa Bella* (Goethe: 2 versions); a symph.; additions to E. T. A. Hoffmann's incid. mus. for Goethe's *Scherz, List und Rache*; 2 pf. sonatas; many songs, etc.

Kienzl, Wilhelm (b. Waizenkirchen, Styria, 17. I. 1857; d. Vienna, 19. X. 1941), Aus. comp. His father, a lawyer, became mayor of Graz in 1861 and the family settled there. He studied there under W. Mayer, who also taught Weingartner and Busoni, later went to Prague and Vienna for further study. Jensen and Liszt encouraged him to comp. and he came into close touch with Wagner at Bayreuth for a time. He was an opera cond. at Amsterdam, Krefeld, Hamburg and Munich (till 1893).

Works incl. operas *Urvasi, Heilmar der Narr, Der Evangelimann, Don Quixote, In Knecht Rupprechts Werkstatt, Der Kuhreigen, Das Testament, Hassan der Schwärmer, Sanctissimum*; orch., choral and chamber works; *Dichterreise* and many other pf. works; *Tanzbilder* for pf. duet; over 100 songs, etc. He adapted Jensen's opera *Die Erbin von Montfort* to a new lib. based on Gozzi's *Turandot*.

Kiladze, Grigory Varfelomeyevich (b. Batum, 6. XII. 1903; d. Tbilisi, 3. IV. 1962), Rus. comp. He earned his living as a manual worker and later as a film mechanic, but studied vln. and entered the Tiflis Cons., later that of St. Petersburg, returning to Tiflis to teach at the Cons. He studied the folk mus. of Georgia.

Works incl. opera *Lado Ketskhovelli*; incid. and film mus.; symph. poem *The Hermit* and suites for orch.; massed choruses incl. *Song of Stalin*, etc.

Kilpinen, Yrjö (b. Helsinki, 4. II. 1892; d. Helsinki, 2. III. 1959), Fin. comp. Had a few lessons in theory at the Helsinki Cons. and in Berlin and Vienna, but was otherwise self-taught. In receipt of a small government grant, he devoted himself entirely to comp.

Works incl. cello sonata, vla. da gamba sonata; pf. sonatas; over 500 songs on Fin., Swed. and Ger. poems, etc.

Kindertotenlieder (*Songs of Dead Children*), cycle of 5 songs by Mahler, with orch. or pf., to poems by Rückert, comp. 1902.

King and Collier (or **Charcoal-Burner**) (*Král a Uhliř*, opera by Dvořák (lib. by Bernhard Guldener), prod. Prague, Cz. Theatre, 24. XI. 1874. D.'s 1st opera to be perf.

King Arthur, or The British Worthy, opera by Purcell (lib. by Dryden), prod. London, Dorset Gardens Theatre, V. or VI. 1691.

King Charles II, opera by Macfarren (lib. by Michael Desmond Ryan, based on a play by John Howard Payne), prod. London, Princess's Theatre, 27. X. 1849.

King, Charles (b. Bury St. Edmunds, 1687; d. London, 17. III. 1748), Eng. singer, organist and comp. Chorister under Blow at St. Paul's Cathedral, where he succeeded his father-in-law Clarke as Almoner and Master of the Children in 1708. Comp. church mus.

King Christian II, incid. mus. for Adolf Paul's play by Sibelius, Op. 27, comp. 1898.

King Lear. *See also* **Re Lear.** Verdi worked at the Shakespearian subject for many years, but never brought the opera anywhere near completion, and his sketches were destroyed after his death, by his own wish.

Incid. mus. for Shakespeare's tragedy by J. André, prod. Berlin, 30. XI. 1778.

Incid. mus. by Balakirev, prod. St. Petersburg, 1861.

Incid. mus. by Haydn, written *c.* 1776–80, for a perf. at Esterhàz.

Incid. mus. by Stegmann, prod. Hamburg, 17. VII. 1778.

Overture by Berlioz, Op. 4, comp. in It., 1831, 1st perf. Paris, 9. XI. 1834.

King, Matthew (Peter) (b. London, 1773; d. London, I. 1823), Eng. comp. Studied under C. F. Horn.

Works incl. many stage pieces (some with Braham, Kelly and others); oratorio *The Intercession*; 4 sets of pf. sonatas; solo cantatas, glees, songs, etc.

'King of Prussia' Quartets (Mozart). *See* **'Prussian' Quartets.**

King Olaf, cantata for solo voices, chorus and orch. by Elgar, Op. 30, set to words by Longfellow altered by H. A. Acworth, prod. at the N. Staffs. Festival, Hanley, 1896.

King Priam, opera in 3 acts by Tippett (lib. by comp.), prod. Coventry, 29. V. 1962.

King, Robert (b. ?; d. ?), Eng. 17th–18th-cent. comp. He joined the royal band in 1680 on the death of Banister, received a licence to give concerts in 1689 and took the Mus.B. at Cambridge in 1696.

Works incl. incid. mus. for Crowne's *Sir Courtly Nice* and many other plays; Shadwell's Ode on St. Cecilia's Day, Motteux's Ode for John Cecil, Earl of Exeter; many songs for one and more voices, etc.

King Stephen (Beethoven). *See* **König Stephan.**

King, William (b, Winchester, 1624; d. Oxford, 17. XI. 1680), Eng. organist and comp., son of George K., organist of Winchester Cathedral (d. 1665). He went to Oxford as a clerk of Magdalen Coll. in 1648, took the B.A. there in 1649, became a chaplain at the coll. in 1652, went to All Souls' Coll. as probationer-fellow in 1654 and became organist of New Coll. in 1664.

Works incl. a service, a litany, anthems; songs to a thorough-bass for theorbo, harpsichord or bass viol to poems by Cowley, etc.

Kingdom, The, oratorio by Elgar, Op. 51 (lib. compiled from the Bible by the comp.), Part II of a trilogy of which I is *The Apostles* and III was never completed. Prod. Birmingham Festival, 3. X. 1906.

King's Henchman, The, opera by Deems Taylor (lib. by Edna St. Vincent Millay), prod. N.Y., Metropolitan Opera, 17. II. 1927.

Kingsley, Charles (1819–75), Eng. novelist and poet. *See* **Bennett (W. S.)** (installation ode), **Henschel** (*Water Babies*), **Macfarren (G.)** (songs), **Miles** (*Westward Ho!*).

Kinkeldey, Otto (b. New York, 27. XI. 1878; d. 19. IX. 1966), Amer. musicologist. After a general academic educ. in N.Y. and Berlin, he studied mus. with MacDowell in 1900–2 while he was a schoolmaster and chapel organist. After further studies at the univ. and acad. for church mus. in Berlin, he became org. teacher at a similar institution at Breslau, and later lecturer and prof. in musicology. Returning to U.S.A. in 1914, he was alternately chief of the mus. division of the N.Y. Public Library and prof. at Cornell Univ. He wrote a dissertation on 16th-cent. keyboard mus. and many valuable contribs. to mus. periodicals, ed. old mus., etc.

Kinsky, Georg (b. Marienwerder, W, Prus., 29. IX. 1882; d. Berlin, 7. IV. 1951), Ger. mus. scholar and ed. Self-taught in mus., he worked at first at the Prus. State Library in Berlin and then became curator until 1927 of the Heyer Museum of mus. instruments, of which he compiled a valuable catalogue. From 1921 he was also active at the Cologne Cons., from which he retired in 1932. His books, which incl. a *History of Music in Pictures*, are mainly on instruments and on orig. eds. of important works.

Kipling, Rudyard (1865–1936), Eng. poet and novelist. *See* **Delage** (songs), **Grainger** (*We have fed our seas* and *Morning Song of the Jungle*), **Koechlin** (*Bandar-Log*, *Course de printemps*), **Scott (C.)** (*Jungle Book*), **Sullivan** (*Absent-minded Beggar*), **Thompson (R.)** (*Solomon and Balkis*).

Kipnis, Alexander (b. Zhitomir, 1. II. 1891), Rus. bass. Studied cond. at the Warsaw Cons. and later singing in Berlin, making his début in 1915. From 1918 to 1925 he sang in Berlin, in Chicago from 1923 to 1932 and at the N.Y. Metropolitan Opera from 1939 to 1946. In 1934 he became an Amer. citizen.

Kirbye, George (b. ? Suffolk, *c.* 1565; d. Bury St. Edmunds, X. 1634). He 1st appeared as the most copious contrib., except Farmer, to East's Psalter. In 1598 he married Anne Saxye, and he seems to have lived at that time at Rushbrooke nr. Bury St. Edmunds as domestic musician at the residence of Sir Robert Jermyn, to whose daughters he ded. his book of 24 madrigals in 1597. In 1601 he contrib. a madrigal to *The Triumphes of Oriana.*

Works incl. motets, a hymn; madrigals; a pavan for viols, etc.

Kircher, Athanasius (b. Geisa nr. Fulda, 2. V. 1602; d. Rome, 28. XI. 1680), Ger. mathematician, philosopher and mus. scholar. He was prof. at the Jesuit Coll. of Würzburg, but was driven from Ger. by the 30 Years War in 1633, going to Avignon, Vienna and in 1637 to Rome, where he settled for the rest of his life. His chief mus.-literary work is *Musurgia universalis* (1650).

Kirchhoff, Gottfried (b. Mühlbeck nr. Bitterfeld, 15. IX. 1685; d. Halle, 21. I. 1746), Ger. organist and comp. Pupil of Zachow at Halle, whom he succeeded, after some other apps., as organist of the church of Our Lady there in 1714. He comp. much for the org.

Kirchner (Fürchtegott), Theodor (b. Neukirchen nr. Chemnitz, 10. XII. 1823; d. Hamburg, 18. IX. 1903), Ger. comp. Studied under C. F. Becker at Leipzig and went to Switz. in 1843 to become organist at Winterthur. In 1862 he went to Zürich as cond. and teacher, but returned to Ger. in 1873 to become director of the mus. school at Würzburg. In 1875 he moved to Leipzig, in 1883 to Dresden and in 1890 to Hamburg.

Works incl. a string 4tet, 3 works for pf. trio; vln. and cello pieces; *c.* 100 op. numbers of pf. pieces; songs, etc.

Kirkby Lunn, Louisa. *See* Lunn.

Kirkman, Eng. family of harpsichord and later pf. makers:

1. Jacob K. (orig. Kirchmann) (b. Bischweiler, 1710; d. Greenwich, 1792), was a Ger. by birth, settled in London early in the 18th cent., working for Tabel, a Flem. maker, whose widow he married.

2. Abraham K. (b. Bischweiler, 1737; d. London, IV. 1794), nephew of prec.

3. Joseph K. (b. ?; d. London, ?), son of prec.

4. Joseph K. (b. ?, 1790; d. London, 1877), son of prec.

5. Henry K. (b. London, ?; d. London, ?), son of prec.

Kirkpatrick, Ralph (b. Leominster, Mass., 10. VI. 1911), Amer. harpsichordist and musicologist. Studied pf. at home and theory at Harvard, later with Nadia Boulanger in Paris. In Paris he took harpsichord lessons with Landowska, also working with Arnold Dolmetsch in Haslemere. He received a Guggenheim Fellowship in 1937 and toured Europe studying old

MSS., etc. In 1940 he was app. to Yale Univ. He has pub. a number of scholarly eds. incl. Bach's *Goldberg Variations* and an important book on D. Scarlatti.

Kirnberger, Johann Philipp (b. Saalfeld, Thuringia, IV. 1721; d. Berlin, 27. VII. 1783), Ger. theorist and comp. Pupil of Bach in Leipzig, 1739–41, after var. posts he entered the service of Frederick the Great as a violinist in 1751. App. *Kapellmeister* and teacher of comp. to Princess Amalia of Prussia in 1758, he increasingly abandoned perf. and comp. to devote his time to theoret. writings. Among many treatises the most important is *Die Kunst des reinen Satzes.*

Comps. incl. cantatas, motets, instrumental mus., etc.

Kiss, The (*Hubička*), opera by Smetana (lib. by Eliška Krásnohorská, based on a story by Karolina Světlá), prod. Prague, Cz. Theatre, 7. XI. 1876.

Kistler, Cyrill (b. Grossaitingen nr. Augsburg, 12. III. 1848; d. Kissingen, 1. I. 1907), Ger. comp. He learnt mus. as a choir-boy and was taught the fl. as a child. After a period of schoolmastering, he went to the Munich Cons. in 1876, and F. Lachner taught him privately for a time afterwards. After teaching mus. for 2 years at Sondershausen, he settled at Kissingen, where he ran a private mus. school.

Works incl. operas *Kunihild, Eulenspiegel, Arm Elslein, Röslein im Hag, Der Vogt auf Mühlstein, Baldurs Tod, Die deutschen Kleinstädter* (after Kotzebue); orchestral and choral works; org. pieces; songs, etc.

Kit, a diminutive vln., now obs., formerly used by dancing-masters, who on account of its small size and narrow shape were able to carry it in the long pockets of their tail-coats. Its Fr. name is therefore *pochette* and its Ger. *Taschengeige.*

Kitezh (Rimsky-Korsakov). *See* **Legend of the Invisible City of Kitezh.**

Kithara, a plucked string instrument of ancient Greece. *See* Lyre.

Kitson, Charles Herbert (b. Leyburn, Yorks., 13. XI. 1874; d. London, 13. V. 1944), Eng. theorist. Studied theology at Cambridge, but was also an org. scholar there and decided to devote himself to mus. He took the D.Mus. at Oxford in 1902. In 1913–20 he lived at Dublin as organist and choirmaster of Christ Church Cathedral and prof. at Univ. Coll. He then returned to Eng. to become prof. of harmony and counterpoint at the R.C.M. in London, but also accepted the appt. of prof. of mus. at Dublin Univ., which did not require continuous residence. He wrote many books on theoret. subjects.

Kittel, Johann Christian (b. Erfurt, 18. II. 1732; d. Erfurt, 18. V. 1809), Ger. organist and comp. Pupil of Bach in the last years at Leipzig, organist at Erfurt from 1756.

Works incl. preludes and other org. mus.; 6 sonatas for keyboard instruments and a fantasy, etc.

Kittel, Kaspar (b. Lauenstein, 1603; d. Dresden, 9. X. 1639), Ger. 16th-cent. lutenist, organist and comp. Studied under Schütz and in 1624–8 in It. at the expense of the Elector of Saxony. He taught theorbo at Dresden from 1630 and 2 years later became inspector of instruments. He wrote arias and cantatas in the style of Caccini.

Kittl, Johann Friedrich (b. Vorlík, Boh., 8. V. 1806; d. Lissa, Pol., 20. VII. 1868), Boh. comp. Pupil of Tomašek in Prague, where he gave a 1st concert in 1836. In 1843 he succeeded Dionys Weber as director of the Prague Cons.

Works incl. operas *Bianca und Giuseppe, oder Die Franzosen vor Nizza* (lib. by Wagner, orig. written for himself), *Die Waldblume* and *Die Bilderstürmer*; *Jagdsymphonie* for orch., etc.

Kjerulf, Halfdan (b. Christiania, 17. IX. 1815; d. Grefsen nr. Christiania, 11. VIII. 1868), Norw. comp. At his father's desire he studied law at Christiania Univ., but on the death of his father in 1840 he decided to devote himself to mus. He taught, and pub. some songs, even before he had done much in the way of theoret. study. About 1850 he received a government grant to study at Leipzig for a year, and on his return he tried to estab. classical subscription concerts, with little success. He became a friend of Bjørnson, who wrote many poems esp. for him to set.

Works incl. choruses and 4tets for male voices; pf. pieces; over 100 songs, etc.

Klabund, Ger. man of letters. *see* **Liebermann** (2 solo cantatas), **Zemlinsky** (*Kreidekreis*).

Klafsky, Katharina (b. Szt. János, 19. IX. 1855; d. Hamburg, 22. IX. 1896), Hung. mezzo-soprano, later soprano. Daughter of a poor shoemaker, she had to beg for her living at Sopron, but went to Vienna as a nursery maid, and her employers had her taught singing. After singing in an opera chorus she attracted Hellmesberger's attention by her voice and he induced Mathilde Marchesi to teach her free. After her 1st marriage at Leipzig she appeared in small parts there, but gradually made a repertory of the most important parts, esp. Wagner's, and she visited London, Paris and the U.S.A. with great distinction.

Klami, Uuno (Kalervo) (b. Virolahti, 20. IX. 1900; d. Helsinki, 29. V. 1961), Fin. comp. Studied at the Helsinki Cons., 1920–4, with Ravel in Paris, 1924–5, and Bruno Walter in Vienna. He became mus. critic to the *Helsingin Sanomat* and in 1938 received a government grant for comp.

Works incl. psalm for solo voices, chorus and orch.; 2 symphs., 2 symph. poems, *Karelian Rhapsody, Pictures of the Sea, Kalevala* suite for orch.; 2 pf. concertos, vln. concerto, fantasy for cello and orch; pf. 4tet; pf. pieces, etc.

Klaviatur (Ger.) = Keyboard.

Klavier (Ger.) = Pianoforte (but *see also* Clavier).

Klebe, Giselher (b. Mannheim, 28. VI. 1925), Ger. comp. Studied at the Berlin Cons. with Kurt von Wohlfurt and later with Josef Rufer and Blacher. From 1946 to 1949 he worked for Berlin Radio. His mus. follows the traditions of Schönberg and Webern.

Works incl. operas *Die tödlichen Wünsche, Alkmene, Figaro lässt sich scheiden* and *Die Rauber* (after Schiller); *Con moto* for orch.; symph., symph. for 42 strings; *Divertissement joyeux* for chamber orch., *Zwitschermaschine* for orch. (after Paul Klee); concerto for vln., cello and orch.; ballet *Pas de trois*; *Geschichte der lustigen Musikanten* for tenor, chorus and 5 instruments; wind 5tet, 2 sonatas for solo vln., vla. sonata; string 4tet.

Kleber, Leonhard (b. ?, Wiesensteig, *c.* 1495; d. Pforzheim, 4. III. 1556), Ger. comp. and organist. He compiled a tablature, dated 1524, containing mus. by himself and others and arrs. by himself of vocal mus.

Kleeberg, Clotilde (b. Paris, 27. VI. 1866; d. Brussels, 7. II. 1909), Fr. pianist. Studied at the Paris Cons. and made her 1st appearance in her early teens; 1st visited Eng. in 1883.

Kleiber, Erich (b. Vienna, 5. VIII. 1890; d. Zürich, 27. I. 1956), Aus. cond. Studied in Prague, where he became chorus master at the Ger. Opera. After various appts. he became director of the State Opera in Berlin in 1923, but he left in 1935 as a protest against the Nazis and lived mainly in Buenos Aires. He was internationally famous.

Klein, Bernhard (b. Cologne, 6. III. 1793; d. Berlin, 9. IX. 1832), Ger. comp. Studied in Paris, became attached to Cologne Cathedral on his return and settled in Berlin in 1819 as teacher at the Inst. for Church Mus. and mus. director at the univ.

Works incl. operas *Dido, Kenilworth* (after Scott), *Ariadne* and *Irene*; oratorios *Job, Jephthah* and *David*; Mass in D maj., Magnificat and much other church mus., etc.

Kleine Nachtmusik, Eine (Ger. = *A Little Serenade*), Mozart's own title for his serenade in G maj. for strings, K.525, finished 10. VIII. 1787.

Kleinknecht, Ger. family of musicians:

1. **Johannes K.** (b. Ulm, XII. 1676; d. Ulm, VI. 1751), violinist and organist.

Studied in Venice, 2nd organist of Ulm Cathedral from 1712.

2. **Johann Wolfgang K.** (b. Ulm, 17. IV. 1715; d. Ansbach, 20. II. 1786), violinist and comp., son of prec. Entered the service of the court at Stuttgart in 1733, from 1738 to his death *Konzertmeister* at Bayreuth.

3. **Jakob Friedrich K.** (b. Ulm, IV. 1722; d. Ansbach, 11. VIII. 1794), flautist, violinist and comp., brother of prec. Entered the service of the court at Bayreuth in 1743, and rose to *Kapellmeister*.

Works incl. *Sinfonia concertata*, fl. sonatas, trio sonatas, etc.

4. **Johann Stephan K.** (b. Ulm, 17. IX. 1731; d. Ansbach, after 1806), flautist, brother of prec. Toured as a fl. virtuoso, entered the service of the court at Bayreuth in 1754.

Kleinmichel, Richard (b. Posen, 31. XII. 1846; d. Charlottenburg, 18. VIII. 1901), Ger. pianist, teacher and comp. Studied under his father, the cond. Friedrich K. (1817–94), and at the Leipzig Cons. 1st settled at Hamburg, but was later operatic cond. at Leipzig, Danzig and Magdeburg. He made simplified pf. scores of Wagner's operas.

Works incl. operas *Schloss de l'Orme* (after Prévost's *Manon Lescaut*), *Der Pfeifer von Dusenbach*; 2 symphs.; much pf. mus., etc.

Kleist, (Bernd) Heinrich (Wilhelm) von (1777–1811), Ger. poet, novelist and dramatist. *See* Draeseke (*Penthesilea* overture), Goldmark (C.) (do.), Graener (*Prinz von Homburg*), Henze (do.), Joachim (commemoration overture), Klenau (*Michael Kohlhaas*), Lux (*Käthchen von Heilbronn*), Marschner (*Prinz von H.*), **Penthesilea** (Schoeck), Pfitzner (*Käthchen von H.*), Reinthaler (do.), Unger (H.) (*Penthesilea*), Vesque von Püttlingen (*Käthchen von H.*), Wagenaar (J.) (*Amphitryon*), Wagner-Régeny (*Zerbrochene Krug*), Wolf (H.) (*Penthesilea*).

Klemetti, Heikki (b. Kuortane, 14. II. 1876; d. Helsinki, 26. VIII. 1953), Fin. comp. and cond. Studied at Helsinki, Berlin and in Fr., It. and Scand. Cond. of a students' choir, 1898–1927 and of the mixed choir Suomen Laulu, 1900–42.

Works incl. opera *Vallis gratiae*; *Lyric Overture* for orch.; church mus.; choral works; songs, etc.

Klemperer, Otto (b. Breslau, 14. V. 1885), Ger. cond. Learned the rudiments of mus. from his mother and then studied in Frankfurt and later Berlin, where his teachers included Ph. Scharwenka, J. Kwast and Pfitzner. In 1907, on Mahler's recommendation, he was app. cond. at the Ger. Nat. Theatre in Prague. He later cond. at the opera houses of Hamburg (1910–14), Strasbourg (1914–17), Cologne (1917–24), Wiesbaden (1924–7) and Berlin (1927–33),

including both the Kroll and State Operas. He was a champion of much new mus. and a fine exponent of the classical repertory. From 1933 to 1939 he cond. in the U.S.A., and from 1947 to 1950 at the Budapest Opera. He is now best known for his interpretations of Beethoven and Wagner and is chief cond. of the New Philharmonia Orch. of London.

Klenau, Paul von (b. Copenhagen, 11. II. 1883; d. Copenhagen, 31. VIII. 1946), Dan. cond. and comp., ? of Ger. descent. Studied vln. and comp., the latter with Malling, at Copenhagen, and after 1902 with Bruch in Berlin and Thuille in Munich. When app. operatic cond. at Stuttgart in 1908 he studied further with Schillings. In 1914 he returned home and estab. the Phil. Society, at which he intro. many modern orchestral works; he also cond. orchestral and choral concerts in Vienna.

Works incl. operas *Sulamith*, *Kjartan and Gudrun* (revised as *Gudrun in Iceland*), *The School for Scandal* (after Sheridan), *Michael Kohlhaas* (after Kleist), *Rembrandt van Rijn*; ballet *Lille Ida's blomster* (after Andersen); 3 symphs., 3 orchestral fantasies on Dante's *Inferno*, *Bank-Holiday Souvenir of Hampstead Heath* for orch.; oratorio *Job*, *The Song of the Love and Death of Cornet Christof Rilke* for baritone solo, chorus and orch.; *Dialogues with Death* for contralto and orch., *Ebbe Skammalsen* for baritone and orch.; string 4tet in E min.; pf. pieces, etc.

Klengel, August (Alexander) (b. Dresden, 27. I. 1783; d. Dresden, 22. XI. 1852), Ger. organist and comp. Pupil of Clementi, with whom he travelled from 1803 onwards. He visited Rus., Paris and London, and in 1816 was app. court organist at Dresden.

Works incl. pf. concertos; pf. 5tet; much pf. mus., incl. esp. canons and fugues, etc.

Klengel, Julius (b. Leipzig, 24. IX. 1859; d. Leipzig, 27. X. 1933), Ger. cellist and comp. Studied cello with Emil Hegar and comp. with Jadassohn, joined the Leipzig Gewandhaus orch. at the age of 15, began to travel as virtuoso in 1875 and in 1881 became leading cellist in the orch. and prof. of cello at the Cons.

Works incl. cello concertos, double concertos for vln. and cello and 2 cellos, *Hymnus* for 12 cellos; *Caprice in form of a Chaconne* for cello solo, many cello pieces and studies, etc.

Klengel, Paul (b. Leipzig, 13. V. 1854; d. Leipzig, 24. IV. 1935), Ger. violinist, pianist, cond. and comp., brother of prec. Studied at the Leipzig Cons. and became choral and orchestral cond. in Leipzig, Stuttgart and N.Y.

Works incl. 2 suites for vln. and pf.; songs, etc.

Klenovsky, Nikolai Semenovich (b. Odessa, 1857; d. Petrograd, 6. VII. 1915),

Rus. comp. and cond. Studied at the Moscow Cons., Tchaikovsky being among his masters, cond. the 1st perf. of the latter's *Eugene Onegin*; later cond. of the univ. orch. and asst. cond. at the Imp. Opera. Collected and ed. folksongs with Melgunov. App. director of the school of mus. at Tiflis, 1893, and asst. director of the Imp. Chapel at St. Petersburg, 1902.

Works incl. several ballets; incid. mus. to Shakespeare's *Antony and Cleopatra* and other plays; *Georgian Liturgy* for unaccomp. chorus; cantatas, etc.

Klenovsky, Paul, a comp. invented by Sir Henry Wood to shoulder his orchestral arr. of Bach's D min. Toccata and Fugue.

Kletzki, Paul (b. Lodz, 21. III. 1900), Pol. cond. Studied the vln. and played in the Lodz Phil. Orch. Later (1921–33) he studied and cond. in Berlin. From 1935 to 1938 he taught comp. in Milan, while continuing as a cond. Between 1958 and 1961 he was cond. of the Dallas Symph. Orch.

Klička, Josef (b. Klatovy, 15. XII. 1855; d. Klatovy, 28. III. 1937), Cz. organist, cond. and comp. Studied at the Org. School in Prague, was asst. cond. at the Cz. Theatre, 1878–81, choirmaster of the Hlahol choir, 1890–7, and app. org. prof. at the Prague Cons. in 1920.

Works incl. Masses; choral cantatas and humorous choruses; sonata, concert fantasies and other works for org.; chamber mus., etc.

Klindworth, Karl (b. Hanover, 25. IX. 1830; d. Stolpe, 27. VII. 1916), Ger. pianist and cond. Pupil of Liszt; arranger of mus. for his instrument, incl. vocal scores of Wagner's works. He lived in London as pianist, cond. and teacher in 1854–68, then became pf. prof. at the Moscow Cons., but returned to Ger. in 1884 and opened a school of mus. in Berlin, 1893. His adopted daughter Winifred Williams (b. 1897) married Siegfried Wagner.

Klingsor, Tristan (Léon Leclère) (1874–1966), Fr. poet. *See* **Cartan, Shéhérazade** (Ravel).

Klopstock, Friedrich (1724–1803), Ger. poet. *See* **Bach** (C. P. E.) (*Morgengesang am Schöpfungstage*), **Gluck** (odes), **Lesueur** (*Mort d'Adam*), **Mahler** (*Auferstehung* in 2nd symph.), **Meyerbeer** (sacred cantatas), **Schröter** (C.) (songs), **Schwenke** (odes), **Spohr** (*Vater unser*), **Stadler** (*Frühlingsfeier*), **Wolfrum** (*Grosse Hallelujah*).

13 songs by Schubert.

Klose, Friedrich (Karl Wilhelm) (b. Karlsruhe, 29. XI. 1862; d. Ruvigliana nr. Lugano, 24. XII. 1942), Swiss comp. Studied with V. Lachner at Karlsruhe, Adolf Ruthardt at Geneva and finally with Bruckner in Vienna. He lived in these 3 cities until 1906, when he was app. prof. at the Basle Cons., which he left in 1907

for a professorship at Munich. In 1919 he retired to Switz., living 1st at Thun and then in the Ticino.

Works incl. Mass in D min.; oratorio *Der Sonne-Geist, Ein Festgesang Neros* for tenor solo, chorus, orch. and org., *Die Wallfahrt nach Kevlaar* (Heine) for recitation, chorus, orch. and org.; dramatic symph. *Ilsebill*, symph. poem *Das Leben ein Traum*; prelude and double fugue for org. and wind; string 4tet in Eb maj.; male-voice choruses; songs, etc.

Klotz, Ger. 17th–18th-cent. family of vln. makers in Mittenwald, incl.:

1. **Matthias K.** (b. II. VI. 1653; d. 16. VIII. 1743). He worked for a time at Florence and Cremona, but returned to Mittenwald *c.* 1683.

2. **Georg K.** (b. 31. III. 1687; d. 31. VIII. 1737), son of prec.

3. **Sebastian K.** (b. 18. I. 1696; d. 20. I. 1775), brother of prec.

4. **Johann Carl K.** (b. 29. I. 1709; d. 25. V. 1769), brother of prec.

At least 18 members of succeeding generations are known.

Klughardt, August (Friedrich Martin) (b. Cöthen, 30. XI. 1847; d. Dessau, 3. VIII. 1902), Ger. cond. and comp. Began his career as a theatre cond. and became court mus. director at Weimar, 1869, Neustrelitz, 1873, and Dessau, 1882. At Weimar he came under Liszt's influence.

Works incl. operas *Miriam, Iwein, Gudrun, Die Hochzeit des Mönchs (Astorre), Judith* (after Hebbel's drama); incid. mus. for Calderón's *La vida es sueño*; oratorios *Die Grablegung Christi, Die Zerstörung Jerusalems, Judith*; 2 psalms for solo voices and chorus; 5 symphs., 5 overtures, 2 orchestral suites; ob., vln. and cello concertos; chamber mus., etc.

Knab, Armin (b. Neu-Schleichach, Franconia, 19. II. 1881; d. Wörishofen, 23. VI. 1951), Ger. comp. Studied at Würzburg and began his career as a lawyer, but devoted all his leisure to mus. In 1934 he was app. prof. at the High School for Church Mus. in Berlin.

Works incl. Christmas play *Das Lebenslicht*; incid. mus. to var. plays; cantatas *Maria Geburt* and *Till Eulenspiegel*; unaccomp. cycles of mixed, male and female choruses, unison choruses. with instruments; chamber mus.; *c.* 12 song cycles incl. 2 of children's songs and others on poems from *Des Knaben Wunderhorn* and by Stefan George, Dehmel, Eichendorff, etc.

Knaben Wunderhorn, Des (*The Youth's Magic Horn*), Ger. anthology of old folk poetry. *See* **Jelmoli** (cantata), **Kamieński** (L.) (choruses), **Knab** (songs), **Mahler** (songs, 9 with pf., 13 with orch.), **Trunk** (male choruses), **Vrieslander** (songs).

Knappertsbusch, Hans (b. Elberfeld, 12.

III. 1888; d. Munich, 26. X. 1965), Ger. cond. Studied at the Cologne Cons. with Steinbach and Lohse (1909–12) and then took var. positions as an opera cond. In 1922 he became cond. at the Munich State Opera, where he remained until 1938, in which year he became director of the Vienna State Opera. He was best known for his perfs. of Wagner, esp. *Parsifal*.

Knecht, Justin Heinrich (b. Biberach, 30. IX. 1752; d. Biberach, 1. XII. 1817), Ger. organist and comp. Worked as organist and cond. in Biberach from 1771, and was vice-*Kapellmeister* in Stuttgart, 1806–8.

Works incl. a symph. entitled *Le Portrait musical de la nature* (*c.* 1784) which has a programme similar to that of Beethoven's 'Pastoral' Symph.

Kneisel, Franz (b. Bucharest, 26. I. 1865; d. N.Y., 26. III. 1926), Cz. violinist, whose father, a bandmaster, came from Olomouc in Morav. He studied at the Vienna Cons. and made his 1st appearance in 1882. In 1885 he went to U.S.A. as leader of the Boston Symph. Orch. and founded the K. 4tet there in 1885.

Knevet, Ralph (1600–71), Eng. poet. See **Finzi** (*Farewell to Arms*).

Kniegeige (Ger. = knee fiddle) = Viola da gamba.

Knight, Robert (b. ?; d. ?), Eng. 16th-cent. comp. A 5-part motet *Propterea maestum* is possibly his.

Knight, Thomas (b. ?; d. ?), Eng. 16th-cent. comp. Organist and vicar-choral of Salisbury Cathedral for 5 or 10 years from 1535.

Works incl. Magnificat and (?) Mass, motets, evening canticles, etc., some of which may be by Robert K.

Knipper, Lev Constantinovich (b. Tiflis, 16. XII. 1898), Rus. comp. Self-taught as pianist and comp. at first; but after 5 years' military service he entered the Gnessin School of Mus. at Moscow as a comp. pupil of Glière and others. About 1930 he made research into the folksongs of Tadjskistan, which has influenced his work, and in 1932 he became mus. instructor to the Red Army and Navy.

Works incl. operas *North Wind* and *Maria*; opera-ballet *Candide* (after Voltaire); ballets *Satanella* and *The Little Negro Sebi*; incid. and film mus.; 14 symphs., sinfonietta, *The Legend of the Plaster Buddha*, *Miniatures* for children, *Maku*, *Vanteh* and other suites, studies and sketches for orch.; *Radif for* string orch.; vln. concerto; *A Poem to Horses*, for chorus and orch.; string 4tet; songs; army songs, etc.

Knittl, Karel (b. Polná, 4. X. 1853; d. Prague, 17. III. 1907), Cz. cond. and teacher. Studied at the Org. School in Prague and became prof. at the Cons., of

which he became the administrative director in 1901, acting in that capacity when Dvořák was nominal director. He cond. the Hlahol choral society and was also a critic.

Knöfel, Johann (b. Lauban, Silesia, *c.* 1530; d. ? Prague, after 1592), Ger. comp. He wrote church mus. and a collection, *Newe Teutsche Liedlein*, 1581.

Knorr, Iwan (b. Mewe, W. Prus., 3. I. 1853; d. Frankfurt, 22. I. 1916), Ger. comp. and teacher. Studied at the Leipzig Cons. after having lived in var. small Rus. towns in 1857–68. He returned to Rus. and became prof. at Kharkov in 1874, but settled at Frankfurt in 1883, where he became director of the Hoch Cons. in 1908. He had a number of Eng. pupils, incl. C. Scott and H. Balfour Gardiner.

Works incl. operas *Dunja*, *Die Hochzeit* and *Durchs Fenster*; symph. fantasy for orch.; pf. 4tets, variations on a theme by Schumann for pf. trio; *Ukrainian Love-Songs* for vocal 4tet and pf.; pf. works for 2 and 4 hands; songs, etc.

Knot, the ornamental fretwork sound-hole of many flat-bellied string instruments and keyboard instruments, more generally called Rose.

Knüpfer, Paul (b. Halle, 21. VI. 1866; d. Berlin, 4. XI. 1920), Ger. bass. Studied at the Cons. of Sondershausen and made his 1st stage appearance there in 1885. He 1st sang at Bayreuth in 1901 and in London in 1904 and was leading bass at the Berlin Opera, 1898–1920.

Knyvett, Eng. family of musicians:

1. **Charles K.** (b. ? London, 22. II. 1752; d. London, 19. I. 1822), alto and organist. App. Gentleman of the Chapel Royal, 1786, and one of the organists, 1796. Estab. the Vocal Concerts with Samuel Harrison in 1791.

2. **Charles K.** (b. London, 1773; d. London, 2. XI. 1859), organist, teacher and comp., son of prec. Pupil of Samuel Webbe. App. organist of St. George's, Hanover Square, 1802, and pub. a *Selection of Psalm Tunes*, 1823.

3. **William K.** (b. London, 21. IV. 1779; d. Ryde, 17. XI. 1856), alto and comp., brother of prec. App. Gentleman of the Chapel Royal, 1797, and comp. to it in succession to Arnold, 1802. He sang and cond. much at concerts and festivals, and comp. anthems, glees, songs, etc.

4. **Deborah K.**, *née* Travis (b. Shaw nr. Oldham, ?; d. ? London, 10. II. 1876), singer, wife of prec. Studied under Greatorex and made her 1st appearance in 1815.

Koanga, opera by Delius (lib. by Charles Francis Keary, based on George Washington Cable's novel *The Grandissimes*), prod. Elberfeld, in Ger., 30. III. 1904.

Koch, Erland von (b. Stockholm, 26. IV. 1910), Swed. comp. Studied at the Stockholm Cons. and later in London, Paris and Dresden.

Works incl. 4 symphs.; symph. poem *A Tale from the Wilderness, Symph. Episode, Symph. Dance*; pf. concerto; vln. concerto; suite for chamber orch.; string 4tet, string trio; vln. and pf. sonata; pf. works; songs, etc.

Kochanski, Pawel (b. Odessa, 14. IX. 1887; d. New York, 12. I. 1934), Pol. violinist. Studied with Mlynarski and at 14 joined the Phil. Orch. at Warsaw; later studied with Thomson at Brussels and became vln. prof. at the Warsaw Cons. in 1907 and at that of St. Petersburg in 1913 in succession to Auer. In the 1920s he settled in U.S.A.

Köchel, Ludwig (Alois Friedrich) von, Ritter (b. Stein nr. Krems, 14. I. 1800; d. Vienna, 3. VI. 1877), Aus. naturalist and mus. bibliog. He lived at Salzburg in 1850–63 for the purpose of compiling his thematic catalogue of Mozart's works, pub. in 1862 (6th ed. 1964).

Koczwara. *See* Kotzwara.

Kodály, Zoltán (b. Kecskemét, 16. XII. 1882; d. Budapest, 6. III. 1967), Hung. comp. Learnt the vln. in his childhood, sang in a cathedral choir and tried to comp. without systematic instruction. In 1900, after living in small provincial towns, he entered the Univ. of Budapest for science, but also became a pupil at the Cons. Studied Hung. folksong and in 1906 wrote his univ. thesis on it, afterwards collecting songs in collaboration with Bartók. App. prof. at the Cons. that year and deputy director in 1919. He was often from the first (1923) repres. at the I.S.C.M. festivals. In 1945 he became president of the newly founded Hung. Arts Council, and in 1967 was awarded the Gold Medal of the Royal Phil. Society. Hon. D. Mus., Oxford, 1960.

Works incl. plays with mus. *Háry János* and *Székely Fonó*; symph. in C maj., *Summer Evening, Ballet Music, Theatre Overture, Dances of Galánta, Marosszék Dances,* concerto for orch.; 2 string 4tets; duo for vln. and cello, serenade for 2 vlns. and vla.; sonatas for cello solo and for cello and pf.; *Meditation on a motif by Debussy, Valsette*, 9 pieces (Op. 3), 7 pieces (Op. 11) for pf.; 21 songs, *Énekszó* (16 songs on folk words); 57 folksong arrs.; 21 works for chorus with and without orch., incl. *Psalmus Hungaricus, Jesus and the Traders, Budavari Te Deum, Bicinia Hungarica* (60 children's songs), *Missa brevis,* etc.

Koeberg, Frits Ehrhardt Adrian (b. The Hague, 6. VII. 1876; d. The Hague, 9. VI. 1961), Dutch violinist, pianist, cond. and comp. Studied at The Hague Cons. and in Berlin. Played vln. in var. Ger. orchs. and toured as pianist, but returned to Hol. as comp. and cond. of a students' mus. society at Leyden and an orch. at The Hague, where he also became prof. of comp. at the Cons.

Works incl. opera *Bloemenkind*; open-air plays *Ydylle, Bloemensproke, Plato, Alianora, Middelburg's Overgang in 1574, Koninginne Kantate*; 3 symphs., symph. poems *Zeelandia, Zevenzot, Zonneweg, Zotskap, Zelma, Minone, Kolma,* overtures; choruses; string 4tet; vln. pieces, pf. pieces; songs, etc.

Koechlin, Charles (b. Paris, 27. XI. 1867; d. Canaden, Var, 31. XII. 1950), Fr. (Alsat.) comp. Studied at the Paris Cons., finally under Fauré. He never appeared as an executive musician or held any official appt., but devoted himself wholly to comp. and the writing of some theoret. books as well as studies of Debussy and Fauré.

Works incl. ballet *La Divine Vesprée*; incid. mus. to Rolland's *14 Juillet* (with 6 others); 2 symphs., orchestral cycles *La Forêt* and *Les Saisons, Seven Stars Symph.* (on film stars), *Les Bandar-Log* (after Kipling) and other orchestral works: *En Mer la nuit, Études antiques, Nuit de Walpurgis classique* (after Goethe), *Rapsodie sur des chansons françaises, Les Heures persanes, La Course de printemps* (after Kipling's *Jungle Book*); 3 *Chorals* for org. and orch., *Ballade* for pf. and orch.; 3 string 4tets, pf. 5tet, trio for fl., clar. and bassoon, pieces for pf., vln. and horn, suite for pf., vla. and fl.; sonatas for vln., vla., cello, fl., ob., clar., bassoon and horn, all with pf., sonata for 2 fls.; sonatinas, *Esquisses, Pastorales, Petites Pièces*, etc. for pf., suites and *Sonatines françaises* for pf. duet and 2 pfs.; choruses, songs, etc.

Koessler, Hans (b. Waldeck, Bavar. 1. I. 1853; d. Ansbach, 23. V. 1926), Ger. comp. and teacher. Studied with Rheinberger at Munich and at the Dresden Cons. After cond. at Dresden and Cologne, he went to Budapest as prof. of comp. at the Nat. Acad. of Mus., where Dohnányi, Bartók and Kodály were among his pupils.

Works incl. opera *Der Münzenfranz*; Mass and psalms; choral works; 2 symphs., symph. variations; vln. concerto, cello concerto; 2 string 4tets, string 5tet, string 6tet; sonata for vln. and pf. and cello and pf.; pf. suite; songs with pf. and with chamber mus., etc.

Koffler, Józef (b. Stryj, 28. XI. 1896; d. Warsaw, 1943), Pol. comp. Studied comp. with Grädener and musicology with Adler in Vienna, where he came under the influence of Schönberg and began to cultivate the 12-note system. Later he became prof. at the Lwów State Cons. Works incl. ballet *Alles durch M.O.W.*; 3 symphs. and *Pol. Suite* for orch., 15 variations for string orch.; string 4tet, string trio, cantata *Die Liebe* for voice, vla., cello and clar.; pf. mus. 40 *Pol. Folksongs*, *Musique de ballet*, *Musique quasi una sonata*, sonatina, etc.; 4 poems for voice and pf., etc.

Kogan, Leonid (b. Dniepropetrovsk, 14. XI. 1924), Rus. violinist. Studied first with his father and later with Abram Yampolsky at the Moscow Cons., graduating in 1948 and becoming a teacher there. In 1951 he won 1st prize at an international competition in Brussels. He is married to the sister of Emil Gilels.

Köhler, (Christian) Louis (Heinrich) (b. Brunswick, 5. IX. 1820; d. Königsberg, 16. II. 1886), Ger. pianist, teacher and comp. Studied in Vienna and became a theatre cond. before he settled at Königsberg in 1847.

Works incl. opera *Maria Dolores*; ballet *Der Zauberkomponist*; numerous pf. works, incl. studies and other educ. mus.

Kokoschka, Oskar (b. 1886), Ger. poet, playwright and painter. *See* **Hindemith** (*Mörder, Hoffnung der Frauen*), **Orpheus und Eurydike** (Křenek).

Kolb, Carlmann (b. Kösslarn, Lower Bavar., I. 1703; d. Munich, 15. I. 1765), Ger. priest, organist and comp. In 1729 was ordained priest and became organist of Ansbach Abbey, but later spent much of his time as mus.-tutor to a noble household in Munich. Comp. organ mus. for liturgical use.

Kolberg, Oskar (b. Przysucha nr. Radom, 22. II. 1814; d. Warsaw, 3. VI. 1890), Pol. folksong collector and comp. Studied in Berlin and in 1840 began to collect Pol. songs. Comp. Pol. dances and an opera *The Shepherd King*.

Kolenda (Pol.), a type of Pol. folksong (carol) sung at Christmas, some specimens dating back to the 13th cent.

Köler, David (b. Zwickau, *c.* 1532; d. Zwickau, 25. VII. 1565), Ger. comp. After working at Altenburg and Güstrow in Mecklenburg, he was recalled to Zwickau to become cantor at St. Mary's Church.

Works incl. 10 psalms for 4–6 voices, Mass on a motet by Josquin des Prés, sacred songs, etc.

Kolisch, Rudolf (b. Klamm, Austria, 20. VI. 1896), Aus. violinist. Studied at the Mus. Acad. and the Univ. in Vienna, graduating in 1913. He also studied the vln. with Ševcik and comp. with Schönberg. In 1922 he founded the Kolisch 4tet, who were esp. well known for their perfs. of modern mus. In 1942 K. became leader of the Pro Arte 4tet.

Kollmann, August Friedrich Christoph (b. Engelbostel, Hanover, 21. III. 1756; d. London, 19. IV. 1829), Ger. organist, theorist and comp. Held a post at Lüne nr. Lüneburg, but in 1782 went to London, where he was app. sacristan and cantor of the Ger. Chapel, St. James's. Wrote many theoret. works, and also comp. a pf. concerto, chamber mus., etc.

Kolo, a Serbian dance in quick 2–4 time. The 15th of Dvořák's *Slavonic Dances* for pf. duet is a K.

Kondracki, Michal (b. Poltava, 4. X. 1902), Pol. comp. Studied with Szymanowski at Warsaw and with Dukas and Nadia Boulanger in Paris, returning to Pol. in 1931.

Works incl. opera *Popieliny*; ballet *Legend of Cracow*; *Cantata ecclesiastica* and humorous cantata *Krasula*; orchestral works *Little Mountain Symph.*, symph. action *Metropolis*, toccata and fugue, symph. picture *Soldiers march past*, *Match*, partita for small orch., nocturne for chamber orch.; pf. concerto, etc.

König Stephan, incid. mus. by Beethoven, Op. 117, for Kotzebue's play written for the opening of the new theatre at Pest and perf. there 9. II. 1812.

Königin von Saba, Die (*The Queen of Sheba*), opera by C. Goldmark (lib. by Salomon Hermann Mosenthal), prod. Vienna, Opera, 10. III. 1875.

Königskinder (*King's Children*), opera by Humperdinck (lib. by Ernst Rosmer), prod. as a play with accompanying mus., Munich, 23. I. 1897; the operatic version prod. N.Y., Metropolitan Opera, 28. XII. 1910.

Königsperger, Marianus (b. Roding, Bavar., 4. XII. 1708; d. Prüfening nr. Regensburg, 9. X. 1769), Ger. priest, organist and comp. He was educ. and took his vows at the Benedictine abbey of Prüfening, where he was organist and choirmaster all his life.

Works incl. Masses, offertories, Litanies, etc.; symph. and sonatas for var. instruments with org.; preludes, fugues and other works for org., etc.

Konius (Conus), Georgey Edvardovich (b. Moscow, 30. IX. 1862; d. Moscow, 29. VIII. 1933), Rus. comp. and teacher. Studied under S. I. Taneiev and Arensky at the Moscow Cons. and was prof. there in 1891–9, later at the Moscow Phil. Society mus. school and director of the Saratov Cons. After the Revolution he returned to the Moscow Cons. He wrote on mus. form and harmony.

Works incl. ballet *Daita*; suite *From Child Life* for chorus and orch.; 2 symph. poems; vln. concerto; pf. pieces, songs, etc.

Kontrabass (Ger.) = Double Bass.

Kontrafagott (Ger.) = Double bassoon.

Konwitschny, Franz (b. Fulnek, 14. VIII.

1901; d. Belgrade, 27. VI. 1962), Ger. cond. Studied in Leipzig and Brünn, playing vln. and vla. in var. orchs. His cond. career began at Stuttgart in 1926. He later cond. in many of the leading Ger. opera houses and in 1959 cond. *The Ring* at Covent Garden.

Konzertmeister (Ger. = concert master), the leader of an orch.

Konzertstück. See **Concertstück.**

Kopylov, Alexander Alexandrovich (b. St. Petersburg, 14. VII. 1854; d. nr. St. Petersburg, 20. II. 1911), Rus. comp. He was educ. musically in the Imp. chapel and later became vocal instructor there. Works incl. symph. in C maj., scherzo, concert overture for orch.; 2 string 4tets and Andantino for string 4tet; *Souvenir de Peterhof* for vln. and pf.; pf. pieces; choruses, songs, etc.

Koreshtchenko, Arseny Nikolaievich (b. Moscow, 18. XII. 1870; d. Kharkov, 3. I. 1921), Rus. pianist and comp. Studied pf. with Arensky and comp. with Taneiev at the Moscow Cons., where he later became a prof. Works incl. operas *Belzhazzar's Feast*, *The Angel of Death* (after Lermontov), *The Ice Palace*; ballet *The Magic Mirror*; incid. mus. to Euripides' *The Trojan Women* and *Iphigenia in Aulis* and Shakespeare's *Twelfth Night*; symph., 2 *Symph. Sketches*, *Armen. Suite*, *Scènes nocturnes* and other works for orch.; concert fantasy for pf. and orch.; string 4tet; pieces for vln. and for cello; pf. pieces; *c.* 80 songs, etc.

Körner, (Karl) Theodor (1791–1813), Ger. poet. See Dvořák (*Alfred*), Graener (*Vierjährige Posten*), Reinecke (do.), Vierjährige Posten (Schubert).

Korngold, Erich (Wolfgang) (b. Brno, Morav., 29. V. 1897; d. Hollywood, 29. XI. 1957), Aus. comp. Son of Julius K. (1860–1945), mus. critic of the *Neue Freie Presse* in Vienna, thanks to whose influence he had his pantomime *The Snowman* prod. at the Court Opera at the age of 13. He studied with Fuchs, Grädener and Zemlinsky. App. cond. at the Hamburg Opera, 1919, and prof. at the Vienna State Acad., 1927. After the *Anschluss* he emigrated to U.S.A. Collaborated with Max Reinhardt at his Theatre School at Hollywood. Works incl. operas *Der Ring des Polycrates*, *Violanta*, *Die tote Stadt*, *Das Wunder der Heliane*, *Die Katrin*; ballet-pantomime *Der Schneemann*; incid. mus. to Shakespeare's *Much Ado about Nothing*; film mus. *Sea Hawk*; symphonietta, symph.-overture, overture to a play; pf. concerto for the left hand; string 4tet, pf. trio, pf. 5tet, 6tet; vln. and pf. sonata; 3 pf. sonatas and pieces; songs, etc.

Kortchmarev, Klementy Arkadievich (b. Verkhni Udinsk, 3. VII. 1899), Rus. comp. Pupil of Malishevsky at the Odessa Cons. Works incl. operas *Ivan the Soldier* and *Ten Days that Shook the World*; ballet *The Serf Ballerina*; incid. mus. for plays; vocal symph. on his 2nd opera; 2 pf. sonatas, etc.

Kossenko, Victor (b. St. Petersburg, 23. XI. 1896; d. Kiev, 3. X. 1938), Rus. comp. Studied pf. under his sister at first, but in 1914 entered the St. Petersburg Cons., continuing pf. studies and becoming a comp. pupil of Sokolov and Steinberg. In 1918 he went to live in the Ukraine, settling at Zhitomir, and in 1929 to Kiev as prof. at the Cons. Works incl. *Heroic Overture* and *Moldavian Poem* for orch.; pf. concerto, vln. concerto; string trio; sonatas for vln., vla. and cello and pf.; 3 pf. sonatas and other works for pf.; songs; Ukrainian folksong arrs., etc.

Kotter, Johannes (b. Strasbourg, *c.* 1480; d. Bern, 1541), Ger. organist and comp., a pupil of Hofhaimer. He compiled a tablature in the form of an instruction book in org.-playing and comp.

Kotzebue, August (Friedrich Ferdinand) von (1761–1819), Ger. playwright. See Busby (*Johanna von Montfaucon*), Generali (*Misantropia e pentimento*), Kistler (*Deutschen Kleinstädter*), König Stephan (Beethoven), Lortzing (*Wildschütz*), Reichardt (*Kreuzfahrer*), Ritter (P.) (*Eremit auf Formentara*), Ruins of Athens (Beethoven), Salieri (*Hussiten vor Naumburg*), Süssmayr (*Wildfang*), Teufels Lustschloss (Schubert), Walter (I.) (*Spiegelritter*), Wessely (C. B.) (*Sonnenjungfrau*), Wildschütz (Lortzing), Wolf (E. W.) (*Eremit auf Formentara*), Wranitzky (mus. for plays).

Kotzwara (Koczwara), Franz (František) (b. Prague, 1730; d. London, 2. IX. 1791), Boh. comp. Settled in London in the 1780s, visited Ir. in 1788 and played in the King's Theatre Orch. in London, 1790. Works incl. *The Battle of Prague* for pf. with vln., cello and drums ad lib.; songs, etc.

Koukourgi (Cherubini). See **Ali Baba.**

Koussevitzky. See **Kussevitsky.**

Koval, Marian (b. Pristan-Voznessenya nr. Olonets, 17. VIII. 1907), Rus. comp. Studied at St. Petersburg and Nizhny-Novgorod. In 1925 he became a comp. pupil of Gnessin at the Moscow Cons. and in 1930 a private pupil of Miaskovsky. Works incl. operas *The Manor House* (after Pushkin) and *Emilian Pugatchev*, children's opera *The Wolf and the Seven Goats*; incid. mus.; 2 suites and symph. poem *Tale of a Partisan* for orch.; oratorios *The People's Sacred War* and *Tchkalov*, cantata *Fighting in Moscow* for chorus and orch.; several song cycles to poems by Pushkin, Nekrasov, etc., ballad for cello and pf.; battle songs, etc.

Kovařovic, Karel (b. Prague, 9. XII. 1862; d. Prague, 6. XII. 1920), Cz. cond. and comp. Studied clar. and harp at the Prague Cons., became an orchestral harpist in 1885 and then studied comp. with Fibich. He toured as accompanist with the violinist Ondříček. Cond. at Brno and Plzeň, 1885–8, in 1895 cond. at the Ethnographic Exhibition in Prague, and from 1900 to 1920 chief cond. at the Nat. Opera there.

Works incl. operas *The Peasants' Charter*, *At the Old Bleaching-House*, comic operas *The Bridegrooms*, *The Way through the Window*, *The Night of Simon and Jude*; ballets *Hashish* and *A Tale of Luck Found*; incid. mus. to Tyl's *Wood Nymph*, Čech's *The Excursions of Mr. Brouček* and other plays; symph. poem *The Rape of Persephone*, dramatic overture in C min.; pf. concerto in F min.; 3 string 4tets; choral pieces, songs, etc.

Koven, (Henry Louis) Reginald de (b. Middletown, Conn., 3. IV. 1859; d. Chicago, 16. I. 1920), Amer. comp. Graduated at Oxford in 1879 and then studied mus. on the Continent. He was mus. critic for several Amer. papers.

Works incl. operas *The Begum*, *Robin Hood* (*Maid Marian*) and *Rob Roy* (both after Scott), *The Canterbury Pilgrims* (after Chaucer), *Rip van Winkle* (after Washington Irving), many operettas and ballets; orchestral works; pf. sonata and pieces; c. 400 songs, etc.

Kozeluch (Kotzeluch, Koželuh), Leopold (b. Welwarn, 9. XII. 1752; d. Vienna, 7. V. 1818), Boh. comp. Pupil of his cousin Johann Anton K. (1738–1814), studied law at Prague Univ., but devoted himself entirely to comp. from 1771. Went to Vienna in 1778 and succeeded Mozart as Imp. comp. in 1792.

Works incl. operas *Didone abbandonata*, *Judith*, *Deborah*, etc.; oratorio *Moisé in Egitto*; 24 ballets and 3 pantomimes; c. 30 symphs.; 13 pf. concertos and several for other instruments; chamber mus.; pf. sonatas, etc.; folksong arrs., etc.

Kraft, Anton (b. Rokitzan nr. Plzeň, 30. XII. 1752; d. Vienna, 28. VIII. 1820), Boh. cellist and comp. Originally intended for the law, he was engaged by Prince Esterházy as principal cellist in 1778, remaining till 1790 and receiving tuition in comp. from Haydn. Subsequently in the service of Prince Grassalkovich and (from 1795) Prince Lobkowitz.

Works incl. concertos, sonatas, etc. for cello, duets for 2 cellos, etc. Haydn's D maj. cello concerto, sometimes ascribed to K., is by Haydn.

Kraft, Nicolaus (b. Esterház, 14. XII. 1778; d. Stuttgart, 18. V. 1853), Boh.

cellist and comp., son of prec. Pupil of his father, with whom he travelled. Settled in Vienna, 1790, and became chamber musician to Prince Lobkowitz in 1796. In 1801 he had further lessons with Duport in Berlin. In 1809 he became a member of the Vienna Court Orch., and in 1814 went to Stuttgart as a member 1st of the Court Opera and then of the Court Chapel.

Works incl. cello concertos, *Scène pastorale* for cello and orch.; fantasy for cello and string 4tet; duets and divertissements for 2 cellos, etc.

Krakowiak, a Pol. dance from the region of Cracow, sometimes intro. into ballets and ballrooms in the 19th cent. under the name of *Cracovienne*. In its orig. form it was danced by all the assembled couples and sometimes words were sung to it. It is in quick 2–4 time.

Krasner, Louis (b. Cherkassy, 21. VI. 1903), Rus. violinist. As a small child he was taken to the U.S.A., studying at the New Eng. Cons. and graduating in 1923. He then studied abroad, where his teachers incl. Flesch, Lucien Capet and Ševčík. After a period as leader of the Minneapolis Symph. Orch., he became prof. at Syracuse Univ. He commissioned Berg's vln. concerto, giving its world *première* in 1936, and also gave the 1st perf. of Schönberg's vln. concerto in 1940.

Kraus, Joseph Martin (b. Miltenberg nr. Mainz, 20. VI. 1756; d. Stockholm, 15. XII. 1792), Ger.-Swed. comp. Studied law and philosophy at Mainz, Erfurt and Göttingen, also comp. with Vogler. He accomp. a Swed. friend to Stockholm and remained there as theatre cond., becoming mus. director in 1781. In 1782–7 he travelled with a grant from the King of Swed., visiting Ger., Fr., It. and Eng.. In 1788 he succeeded Uttini as *Kapellmeister*.

Works incl. operas *Soliman II*, *Aeneas at Carthage* and 2 others; church mus.; symphs. and overtures; string 4tets, etc.

Kraus, Otokar (b. Prague, 10. XII. 1909), Cz., later Eng., baritone. Studied in Prague and later in Milan with Fernando Carpi, making his début in Brno in 1935. He came to Eng. in World War II, joining the Eng. opera group in 1946. He sang in the 1st performance of Britten's *Rape of Lucretia* and also created the role of Nick Shadow in Stravinsky's *Rake's Progress* in 1951. A fine Wagner singer, he is esp. noted for his Alberich.

Krauss, Clemens (b. Vienna, 31. III. 1893; d. Mex. City, 16. V. 1954), Aus. cond. Studied with Grädener and Heuberger at the Vienna Cons. and from 1912 cond. at var. provincial opera-houses in Ger. and Aus. In 1922 he became cond. at the Vienna State Opera and in 1924 Opera intendant and cond. of the Museum concerts at Frankfurt. In 1929–34 he was director of the Vienna and in 1934–6 of the Berlin State Opera, after which he directed the Opera at Munich. He was closely assoc. with Richard Strauss as cond. and, in the case of *Capriccio*, as librettist. He married the singer Viorica Ursuleac.

Krauss, (Marie) Gabrielle (b. Vienna, 24. III. 1842; d. Paris, 6. I. 1906), Aus. soprano. Studied at the Vienna Cons. and with Mathilde Marchesi; after singing at concerts she made her 1st stage appearance at the Vienna Opera in 1859 and in Paris, at the Théâtre des Italiens, in 1867; in 1875–88 she was a member of the Opéra almost continuously.

Krebs, Johann Ludwig (b. Buttelstedt, Thuringia, 10. X. 1713; d. Altenburg, 1. I. 1780), Ger. organist, harpsichordist and comp. Pupil of Bach at Leipzig from 1726, organist at Zwickau, Zeitz and Altenburg.

Works incl. Magnificat, settings of Sanctus; trios; sonatas, suites, fugues, choruses, with variations, etc., for clavier; fl. sonatas, org. mus., etc.

Krebs, Johann Tobias (b. Heichelheim, 7. VII. 1690; d. Buttstädt, 11. II. 1762), Ger. organist and comp., father of prec. Pupil of Walther, later of Bach, app. organist at Buttstädt in 1721. Comp. org. mus.

Krehbiel, Henry (Edward) (b. Ann Arbor, Mich., 10. III. 1854; d. N.Y., 20. III. 1923), Amer. mus. critic and author. After studying law at Cincinnati, he became mus. critic to the *Cincinnati Gazette*, 1874, and to the *N.Y. Tribune*, 1880. He ed. Thayer's life of Beethoven, collected and wrote on Negro folksongs and wrote many books incl. studies of opera, of Wagner and of Amer. mus. life.

Krehl, Stephan (b. Leipzig, 5. VII. 1864; d. Leipzig, 7. IV. 1924), Ger. theorist and comp. Studied at the Leipzig and Dresden Conss., taught at Carlsruhe and Leipzig, and became director of the Cons. at the latter in 1921. He wrote several theoret. books.

Works incl. cantata *Tröstung*; symph. prelude to Hauptmann's *Hannele*; string 4tet, suite for string 4tet, clar. 5tet; cello and pf. sonata, etc.

Krein, Alexander Abramovich (b. Nizhny-Novgorod, 20. X. 1883; d. Staraya Ruza, nr. Moscow, 21. IV. 1951), Rus. comp. Son of a violinist and folksong collector, went to the Moscow Cons. in 1897 to study cello and comp. He became prof. there in 1912.

Works incl. opera *Zagmuk*; ballets *Laurencia* (after Lope de Vega's *Fuente Ovejuna*) and *Tatiana*, choral ballet *Othello and Desdemona* (after Shakespeare); incid. mus. to many plays; film mus.; *Kaddish* symph. cantata for solo voice, chorus and orch., trilogy *The*

Soviet Shock Brigade for chorus and orch.; symph. in F♯ min., symph. poem *Salome* (after Wilde) and other orchestral works; *Poem* for string 4tet, 2 suites of *Jewish Sketches* for clar. and string 4tet, *Elegy* for pf. trio; many instrumental pieces; pf. sonata, *Dance Suite* and other pf. pieces; song cycle *From Balkaria's Mountains*, 16 op. nos. of songs; Jewish folksong arrs., etc.

Krein, Grigory Abramovich (b. Nizhny-Novgorod, 18. III. 1879; d. Komoravo, 6. I. 1955), Rus. comp., brother of prec. Studied with Glière at Moscow and Reger at Leipzig.

Works incl. 3 symph. episodes *Lenin*; vln. concerto; string 4tet, pf. 4tet; sonata and *Poem* for vln. and pf., etc.

Krein, Julian Grigorievich (b. Moscow, 5. III. 1913), Rus. comp., son of prec. Studied with Dukas in Paris. He returned to Rus. in 1933.

Works incl. *Spring Symph.*, 2 ballads for orch., symph. prelude *Destruction*, 3 symph. poems; *Lyric Poem* for pf. and orch.; cello concerto; suite for cello and pf.; 4 string 4tets; vln. pieces; *Tango*, *Nocturne et Bal* for pf., other pf. works, etc.

Kreisler, Fritz (b. Vienna, 2. II. 1875; d. N.Y., 29. I. 1962), Aus. violinist and comp. Appeared as an infant prodigy at the age of 7. Studied at the Vienna Cons. under Hellmesberger and J. Auber, and at the Paris Cons. under Massart and Delibes, winning the gold medal at the age of 12. After touring in U.S.A. in 1889 he returned to Aus. to study medicine. After his military service and a period of intense study he reappeared as a soloist in Berlin in 1899 and again toured in U.S.A. After 3 months' service in the Aus. army in 1914 he was discharged on account of wounds and returned to U.S.A., where he eventually made his home. He made frequent tours in Eur. and gave the 1st perf. of Elgar's vln. concerto. His comps. incl. a string 4tet and an operetta (*Apple Blossoms*) and a number of vln. solos, some of which were orig. pub. as the work of 18th-cent. comps.

Kreisleriana, a cycle of pf. pieces by Schumann, Op. 16, comp. in 1838 and ded. to Chopin. The title is borrowed from the musician Kreisler in E. T. A. Hoffmann's stories *Fantasiestücke in Callots Manier*.

Kreissle von Hellborn, Heinrich (b. Vienna, 19. I. 1822; d. Vienna, 6. IV. 1869), Aus. lawyer and state official, 1st biog. of Schubert, on whom he pub. *F. Schubert: eine biographische Skizze*, 1861, and *Franz Schubert*, 1865.

Krejčí, Iša (b. Prague, 10. VII. 1904), Cz. comp. Pupil of Novák and Jirák. After working for some time at Bratislava he returned to Prague and joined the radio service.

Křenek

Works incl. opera *Confusion at Ephesus* (on Shakespeare's *Comedy of Errors*), operatic scene *Antigone* (after Sophocles); sinfonietta for orch.; *Little Ballet* for chamber orch.; string 4tet in D maj., nonet, trios for ob., clar. and bassoon and clar., double bass and pf.; sonatina for clar. and pf.; songs, etc.

Křenek, Ernst (b. Vienna, 23. VIII. 1900), Aus. (now Amer.) comp. Pupil of Schreker in Vienna and Berlin. In the 1920s he appeared at several of the smaller festivals in Ger. and in 1925–7 he was cond. at the operas of Cassel, Wiesbaden and other smaller towns in order to gain experience in operatic stage-craft. His 1st wife was Anna Mahler, the comp.'s daughter. After the prod. of *Jonny spielt auf* at Leipzig in 1927 his success was assured, but he later worked in 12-note mus. as a disciple of Schönberg. In 1933, when the Nazi régime gained the upper hand, he settled in Vienna and worked on behalf of progressive Aus. comps., but was interfered with by the Fascist party; left Aus. for U.S.A. in 1937, where he later became Dean of the School of Fine Arts and director of the Mus. Dept. at Hamline Univ., St. Paul, 1942–7. His book, *Über neue Musik*, is a defence of the 12-note system.

Works incl. operas *Der Sprung über den Schatten*, *Orpheus und Eurydike*, *Jonny spielt auf*, *Leben des Orest*, *Karl V*, *Tarquin*, also 3 1-act operas; cantatas *Die Jahreszeiten* and *Von der Vergänglichkeit des Irdischen*; ballets *Mammon*, *Der vertauschte Cupido*; incid. mus. to Shakespeare's *Midsummer Night's Dream*, Goethe's *Triumph der Empfindsamkeit* and Calderón's *La vida es sueño*; choruses to poems by John Donne, *Cantata for Wartime* (Herman Melville), Lat. choral works; *The Seasons* for unaccomp. chorus; 5 symphs. and *Little Symph.*, 2 *Concerti grossi*, variations on *I wonder where I wander* for orch.; *Symph. Elegy* for strings; 4 pf. concertos, 2 vln. concertos; cello concerto; theme and 13 variations for orch.; 7 string 4tets; vln. and pf. sonata, sonata for solo vla.; 6 pf. sonatas; *c.* 25 songs, song cycles *Reisebuch aus den österreichischen Alpen*, *Fiedellieder*, *Gesänge des späten Jahres*, *Poems by John Donne*, etc.

Kretschmer, Edmund (b. Ostritz, Saxony, 31. VIII. 1830; d. Dresden, 13. IX. 1908), Ger. organist and comp. Studied at Dresden, where he became church organist in 1854 and court organist in 1863. He founded and cond. choral societies.

Works incl. operas *Die Folkunger*, *Heinrich der Löwe*, *Der Flüchtling*, *Schön Rotraut*; 4 Masses; cantatas *Die Geisterschlacht*, *Pilgerfahrt*, *Sieg im Gesang*; *Musikalische Dorfgeschichten* for orch., etc.

Kreutzer

Kretzschmar, (August Ferdinand) Hermann (b. Olbernhau, Saxony, 19. I. 1848; d. Nikolassee nr. Berlin, 10. V. 1924), Ger. musicologist. Studied at Dresden and the Leipzig Cons., where he became a prof. in 1871. After several appts. as cond. elsewhere, he returned as mus. director to Leipzig Univ. in 1887 and cond. var. organizations there. In 1909 he succeeded Joachim as director of the Berlin Hochschule für Musik. He wrote on many subjects, incl. old notation, the hist. of opera and of Ger. song, and pub. a collection of analytical notes on a var. of works, *Führer durch den Konzertsaal*.

Kreusser, Georg Anton (b. Heidingsfeld, 31. XII. 1743; d. Aschaffenburg, 3. XI. 1810), Ger. violinist and comp. Studied in Fr. and It., entered the service of the court at Mainz in 1773, app. *Konzertmeister* 1774.

Works incl. Passion oratorio *Der Tod Jesu* (Ramler); symphs.; chamber mus., etc.

Kreutzer, Conradin (b. Messkirch, Baden, 22. XI. 1780; d. Riga, 14, XII. 1849), Ger. cond. and comp. He 1st learnt mus. as a choir-boy, went to Freiburg i/B. to study law, but gave it up for mus., travelled in Switz. as pianist and singer and in 1804 went to Vienna to study comp. with Albrechtsberger. After cond. at the court of Stuttgart and Donaueschingen, he returned to Vienna and became cond. at the Kärntnertortheater for 3 periods between 1822 and 1840 and of the Josefstadttheater in 1833–40. Later he worked at Cologne and Paris, and again in Vienna.

Works incl. operas *Conradin von Schwaben*, *Die Alpenhütte*, *Libussa* (lib. by Grillparzer), *Melusina* (lib. do.), *Das Nachtlager von Granada*, *Cordelia* and *c.* 25 others; incid. mus. to plays incl. Raimund's *Der Verschwender*; oratorio *Sendung Moses*; church mus.; chamber mus.; pf. works; male-voice part-songs; songs, etc.

Kreutzer, Rodolphe (b. Versailles, 16. XI. 1766; d. Geneva, 6. VI. 1831), Fr. violinist and comp. He was taught mainly by his father and at the age of 16 was app. by Marie Antoinette 1st vln. in the royal chapel, where he learnt much from hearing Mestrino and Viotti. Later he became leader at the Théâtre Italien, where he began to prod. operas of his own. He toured much and became vln. prof. at the Paris Cons. in 1795. In 1798 he went to Vienna in the suite of Bernadotte and made friends with Beethoven. He often played vln. duets with Rode, on whose departure to Rus. in 1801 K. became leader at the Opéra, and later he held court appts. under both Napoleon I and Louis XVIII. He compiled a *Méthode de violon* with Baillot.

Works incl. operas *Jeanne d'Arc à Orléans*, *Paul et Virginie* (after Saint-Pierre), *Lodoïska*, *Imogène, ou La Gageure indiscrète* (after Boccaccio), *Astyanax*, *Aristippe*, *La Mort d'Abel*, *Mathilde* and many others; ballets *Paul et Virginie*, *Le Carnaval de Venise*, *Clari* and others; 19 vln. concertos, 3 *Symphonies concertantes*; 15 string 4tets, 15 trios; sonatas, caprices, studies, airs with variations, etc., for vln., etc.

'Kreutzer' Sonata, the nickname of Beethoven's A maj. vln. and pf. sonata, Op. 47, comp. in 1803 and ded. to R. Kreutzer. The work is the subject of Tolstoy's novel *The Kreutzer Sonata*, in which it has a disastrous effect on the characters.

Křička, Jaroslav (b. Kelč, Morav., 27. VIII. 1882), Cz. comp. Studied at the Prague Cons., 1902–5, and came under the influence of Novák, enlarged his experience in Berlin, and then went to Rus., teaching at the mus. school of Ekaterinoslav. On his return to Prague in 1909 he became cond. of the Hlahol choral society. Director of the Prague Cons., 1942–5.

Works incl. operas *Hypolita* (after one of Maurice Hewlett's *Little Novels of Italy*) and *The Gentleman in White* (after Wilde's *Canterville Ghost*); choral works *The Temptation in the Wilderness* and many others with and without orch.; symph. in D min., symph. poems *Faith*, overture to Maeterlinck's *Blue Bird*, *Polonaise* and *Elegy on the Death of Rimsky-Korsakov*, *Children's Suite* for small orch., *Nostalgia* for string orch.; 3 string 4tets; vln. and pf. sonata; *Intimate Pieces*, *Lyric Suite*, etc., for pf.; song cycles *Northern Lights*, *Of Love and Death*, *Songs of Parting*, *3 Legends*, etc.

Krieger, Adam (b. Driesen, Prus., 7. I. 1634; d. Dresden, 30. VI. 1666), Ger. organist, comp. and poet. Pupil of Scheidt, organist of St. Nicholas's Church at Leipzig and afterwards court organist at Dresden.

Works incl. arias for voice and bass, songs for 1–5 voices and instruments, etc.

Krieger, Johann (b. Nuremberg, 28. XII. 1651; d. Zittau, 18. VII. 1735), Ger. organist and comp. Pupil of his brother; court organist at Bayreuth, 1671–7, and later organist and town mus. director at Zittau.

Works incl. plays with mus.; sacred and secular songs for several voices with instruments; org. works; 6 partitas, preludes, fugues, etc., for clavier, etc.

Krieger, (Johann) Philipp (b. Nuremberg, 25. II. 1649; d. Weissenfels, 7. II. 1725), Ger. organist and comp., brother of prec. Travelled in It. and studied under Rosenmüller at Venice; entered the service of the Duke of Saxe-Weissenfels, was chamber musician and organist at Halle from 1677 and mus. director at Weissenfels from 1712.

Works incl. opera *Der grossmütige Scipio* and others; plays with mus.; church mus.; arias for 1–4 voices with instruments; sonatas for vln. and vla. da gamba; *Partien* for wind instruments, etc.

Krilov, Ivan Andreievich (1769–1844), Rus. fabulist. *See* Rebikov (*Fables*).

Krips, Josef (b. Vienna, 8. IV. 1902), Aus. cond. Studied in Vienna with Mandyczewski and Weingartner and became a violinist in the Volksoper there. In 1924 he began his career as a cond. and from 1926 to 1933 was general mus. director at Karlsruhe. In 1933 he became a cond. at the Vienna State Opera and in 1935 prof. at the Vienna Acad. of Mus. During World War II he lost these positions, but rejoined the Vienna State Opera in 1945. From 1950 to 1954 he was cond. of the London Symph. Orch.

Krizhanovsky, Ivan Ivanovich (b. Kiev, 8. III. 1867; d. Leningrad, 9. XII. 1924), Rus. comp. He took mus. lessons at Kiev while studying medicine, and in 1896–1900 was a pupil of Rimsky-Korsakov in St. Petersburg. He returned to medicine and became prof. at St. Petersburg Univ., but continued to comp. in his spare time.

Works incl. cantata *Paradise and the Peri* (Thomas Moore); several orchestral works; pf. concerto, vln. concerto; string 4tet, pf. trio; vln. and pf. sonata, cello and pf. sonata; org. and pf. mus.; songs, etc.

Křížkovský, Pavel (christened Karel) (b. Holasovice, 9. I. 1820; d. Brno, 8. V. 1885), Cz. monk and comp. His father was so poverty-stricken a musician that he would not allow his son to take up mus.; but he picked up much knowledge at the church of Opava and was eventually admitted to the choir-school; later he took a degree at Brno Univ. and entered the Augustinian community of St. Thomas, became prof. of divinity, collected and arr. folksongs, and was sent to Prague for 6 months for mus. study. He succeeded Bohumir Rieger (1764–1855) as mus. director of the Austin Friars' church and cond. concerts of sacred mus. at Brno.

Works incl. cantata *SS. Cyril and Methodius*, funeral song with tromb. accomp.; many choral works for male voices, often based on folk material; songs, etc.

Krohn, Ilmari (b. Helsinki, 8. XI. 1867; d. Helsinki, 25. IV. 1960), Fin. musicologist and comp. Studied at Helsinki and Leipzig Conss., app. lecturer in mus. at Helsinki Univ. 1900, and prof., 1918. He coll. and ed. Fin. folksongs and wrote several books incl. a study of old Fin. sacred songs and a theoret. handbook.

Comps. incl. opera *The Deluge*; oratorios *Eternal Treasures* and *Victors*; church cantatas; org. and pf. mus., etc.

Krommer, Franz (orig. Kramář, František Vincenc) (b. Kamenice, 27. XI. 1759; d. Vienna, 8. I. 1831), Morav. violinist, organist and comp. Having been an organist from 1776 to 1784, he went to Hung. and later became mus. director to Prince Grassalkovich in Vienna. In 1818 he succeeded Kozeluch as court mus. director.

Works incl. Masses; mus. for wind band; symphs.; 69 string 4tets and 5tets, fl. 4tets and 5tets, etc.

Kronke, Emil (b. Danzig, 29. XI. 1865; d. Dresden, 16. XII. 1938), Ger. pianist and comp. Studied at the Leipzig and Dresden Conss. and settled at Dresden as concert pianist and teacher. Ed. Chopin's works.

Works incl. symph. variations, *Carnival* suite and *Ballad* for orch.; pf. concerto; horn 4tets and other chamber mus.; suites for vln. and pf., cello and pf., fl. and pf., etc.; var. instrumental pieces; concert variations and numerous pieces for pf., etc.

Kroyer, Theodor (b. Munich, 9. IX. 1873; d. Cologne, 12. I. 1945), Ger. musicologist. Studied with Rheinberger and Sandberger at Munich. Prof. of mus. at Munich, 1907, Heidelberg, 1920, at Leipzig, where he succeeded Abert, 1923, and Cologne, 1932, where he estab. an institute for mus. research. He wrote on the It. madrigal and other subjects, and ed. works by Machault, Okeghem, Senfl, Aichinger, Marenzio, etc.

Krug, Arnold (b. Hamburg, 16. X. 1849; d. Hamburg, 4. VIII. 1904), Ger. comp. Studied with var. masters and at the Leipzig Cons. In 1872–7 he taught at Stern's Cons. in Berlin, then visited Fr. and It., and in 1878 settled at Hamburg, where he cond. choral concerts and became prof. at the Cons. in 1885.

Works incl. a number of cantatas; symph., suite *Aus der Wanderzeit*, prelude to Shakespeare's *Othello*, *Italienische Reiseskizzen* for orch.; *Liebesnovelle* and serenade for strings; vln. concerto; string 4tet, pf. 4tet, pf. trio, string 6tet; pieces for vln. and for cello; pf. works, etc.

Krummhorn. *See* **Crumhorn.**

Krumpholz, Johann Baptist (b. Zlonice nr. Prague, *c.* 1745; d. Paris, 19. II. 1790), Boh.-Fr. harpist and comp. He grew up in Paris, travelled as a virtuoso, and was in the service of Prince Esterházy, 1773–6, receiving tuition in comp. from Haydn. After further travels he settled in Paris, and was responsible for some notable improvements to his instrument. On the desertion of his wife he drowned himself.

Works incl. 8 concertos, 32 sonatas for

harp; 2 symphs. for harp and small orch.; harp duets, etc.

Krumpholz, Wenzel (b. ?, *c.* 1750; d. Vienna, 2. V. 1817), Boh.-Fr. violinist, mandoline player and comp., brother of prec. He was a member of Prince Esterházy's orch. under Haydn, and in 1796 entered the service of the court in Vienna. He was friendly with Beethoven, who wrote a mandoline sonata for him. Comp. vln. mus.

Krylov. *See* **Krilov.**

Kryzhanovsky. *See* **Krizhanovsky.**

Kubelík, Jan (b. Michle nr. Prague, 5. VII. 1880; d. Prague, 5. XII. 1940), Cz. violinist. He was taught by his father, a gardener and good mus. amateur, and made his 1st public appearance in Prague in 1888. In 1892 he entered the Cons. as a pupil of Ševčík and began his real career with a concert in Vienna, 1898.

Kubelík, Rafael (b. Býchory, nr. Kolín, 29. VI. 1914), Cz. cond., son of prec. Studied at the Prague Cons., making his début with the Cz. Phil. Orch. in 1934. From 1939 to 1941 he was cond. of the National Theatre in Brno and from 1942 to 1948 of the Cz. Phil. Orch. Between 1948 and 1950 he was much in Eng. and in 1950 was app. principal cond. of the Chicago Symph. Orch. He returned to Eur. in 1953 and became mus. director at Covent Garden (1955–8). In 1961 he became cond. of the Bavar. Radio Orch. He has also comp.; his works incl. the opera *Veronika*, a choral symph., concertos for vln. and cello, a Requiem and some chamber mus.

Kubik, Gail (b. Coffeyville, Okla., 5. IX. 1914), Amer. violinist and comp. Studied at the Eastman School of Mus., Rochester, N.Y., and gained several comp. prizes.

Works incl. ballet *Frankie and Johnnie* for dance band and folk singer; *In Praise of Johnny Appleseed* (Vachel Lindsay) for baritone, chorus and orch.; 3 symphs.; suite for orch.; vln. concerto, *American Caprice* for pf. and 32 instruments; 2 *Sketches* for string 4tet, pf. trio, wind 5tet, *Trivialities* for fl., horn and string 4tet, etc.

Kücken, Friedrich Wilhelm (b. Bleckede, Hanover, 16. XI. 1810; d. Schwerin, 3. IV. 1882), Ger. cond. and comp. His father, a landed proprietor, was against his taking up mus., but he was helped by his brother-in-law, Lührss, who was mus. director and organist at Schwerin, where he played var. instruments in the ducal orch. He began to comp. songs, some of which became very popular, but in 1832 he went to Berlin for further study, and later still studied counterpoint with Sechter in Vienna and orchestration with Halévy in Paris. In 1851 he became court cond. at Stuttgart with Lindpaintner, and alone after the latter's death in 1856.

Works incl. operas *Die Flucht nach der Schweiz* and *Der Prätendent*; sonatas for vln. and for cello and pf.; a vast number of songs, some of which became so popular that the Gers. mistook them for folksongs, e.g. 'Ach, wie wär's möglich dann', etc.

Kufferath, Hubert Ferdinand (b. Mühlheim, 10. VI. 1818; d. Brussels, 23. VI. 1896), Ger. violinist, pianist and comp. Studied under his brother Johann K. at Utrecht, also at Dessau and at the Leipzig Cons. In 1844 he settled at Brussels, where he founded chamber concerts with Léonard and Servais, became court pianist to Leopold I and prof. at the Cons., 1872.

Works incl. symph.; pf. concerto, capriccio for pf. and orch.; string 4tet, pf. trio; pf. pieces; songs, etc.

Kufferath, Maurice (b. Brussels, 8. I. 1852; d. Brussels, 8. XII. 1919), Belg. writer on mus., son of the prec. Studied law and philology at Brussels Univ. and was on the staff of *L'Indépendance belge* until 1900, when he became joint director of the Théâtre de la Monnaie with Guillaume Guidé. He wrote on Berlioz, Schumann, Vieuxtemps and Wagner, and made Fr. trans. of some of Wagner's writings and operas.

Kugelmann, Hans (b. ? Augsburg, ?; d. Königsberg, 1542), Ger. trumpeter and comp. He was trumpeter in the service of the Emperor Maximilian at Innsbruck in 1519 and afterwards at the ducal court of Königsberg, where he became mus. director. In 1540 he pub. a Lutheran service book, containing a Mass, a Magnificat and hymns, some comp. by himself.

Kuhlau, (Daniel) Frederik (Rudolph) (b. Ülzen, Hanover, 11. IX. 1786; d. Copenhagen, 12. III. 1832), Dan. comp. of Ger. origin. A child of poor parents, he picked up mus. knowledge at Brunswick and Hamburg. During the Fr. occupation he went to Den. to escape conscription and became flautist in the court orch. at Copenhagen. In 1825 he visited Vienna and met Beethoven, who comp. a punning canon on his name.

Works incl. operas *Røverborgen, Trylleharpen, Lulu* and several others; incid. mus. for Heiberg's *Elverhøj*; pf. works; fl. pieces, etc.

Kühmstedt, Friedrich (b. Oldisleben, Saxe-Weimar, 20. XII. 1809; d. Eisenach, 10. I. 1858), Ger. organist and comp. Studied at Weimar Univ. and mus. under Rinck at Darmstadt. His playing was marred by paralysis of the hand, but he became mus. director and prof. at the seminary of Eisenach in 1836.

Works incl. operas; oratorios *Die*

Auferstehung and *Triumph des Göttlichen*; symphs.; many org. pieces, incl. preludes, fugues, *Gradus ad Parnassum* preparatory to the works of Bach, *Fantasia eroica*, etc.

Kuhnau, Johann (b. Geising, Saxony, 6. IV. 1660; d. Leipzig, 5. VI. 1722), Ger. organist, harpsichordist, comp. and writer on mus. Cantor at Zittau, went to Leipzig in 1682, became organist at St. Thomas's Church in 1684, mus. director of the univ. and the churches of St. Nicholas and St. Thomas in 1700, and cantor of St. Thomas's in 1701, in which post he preceded Bach. His biblical sonatas for harpsichord are early exs. of programme mus.

Other works incl. motets on hymntunes and other church mus.; partitas and other pieces for harpsichord, incl. 7 sonatas entitled *Frische Clavier-Früchte*, etc.

Kühnel, August (b. Delmenhorst, 3. VIII. 1645; d. ?), Ger. vla. da gamba player and comp. He was in the court chapel of Zeitz, 1661–81, visited Fr. in 1665 to study the players there, played at var. Ger. courts on his return, visited London in 1685 and was subsequently *Kapellmeister* at the court of Cassel. He wrote sonatas for his instrument.

Kuhreigen
or   } *See* **Ranz des Vaches.**
Kuhreihen

Kujawiak, a Pol. dance in 3–4 time, a variant of the Mazurka.

Kullak, Theodor (b. Krotoschin, Posen, 12. IX. 1818; d. Berlin, 1. III. 1882), Ger. pianist and comp. He was intended for a lawyer and at some time studied medicine, but in 1842 decided definitely in favour of mus. and went to Vienna to finish his pf. studies with Czerny. In 1846 he became court pianist to the King of Prus. and settled in Berlin, founding a Cons. with Stern and Marx there, 1850, and one of his own in 1855.

Works incl. pf. concerto in C min.; pf. trio; duets for pf. and vln.; a vast number of pf. pieces, studies, etc.

Kummer, Friedrich August (b. Meiningen, 5. VIII. 1797; d. Dresden, 22. VIII. 1879), Ger. cellist, oboist and comp. Pupil of Dotzauer at Dresden, where he hoped to enter the court orch. as a cellist, but did so as an oboist, finding no vacancy for the former post, 1814. In 1817, however, he changed to the cello again and also travelled as a virtuoso.

Works incl. concertos, fantasies and numerous other works for the cello; interludes for the Dresden theatre, etc.

Kunc, Jan (b. Doubravice, Morav., 27. III. 1883), Cz. cond., teacher and comp. Pupil of Janáček at the Org.

School of Brno, and later of Novák and Kovařovic at the Prague Cons. He became a critic, toured with his wife, a singer, and in 1919–20 was cond. at the Cz. theatre in Prague. Later he went to the Brno Cons., of which he became director in 1923.

Works incl. symph. poem *Song of Youth*; *Seventy Thousand* for chorus and orch., many other choral works with and without orch.; Cz. Mass for soprano and org.; 2 string 4tets, pf. trio; sonata in C min., *Moods* and *Miniatures* for pf.; many songs, etc.

Kunst der Fuge, Die (*The Art of Fugue*), Bach's last work, left unfinished at his death in 1750. A series of exs. of the art of fugal and canonic writing, all based on the same theme.

Kunz, Erich (b. Vienna, 20. V. 1909), Aus. bass-baritone. Studied in Vienna and made his début in 1933 in Breslau. He sang in the Glyndebourne chorus in 1935 and in 1947 in Vienna. From 1952 to 1954 he sang at the N.Y. Metropolitan Opera. He is one of the finest *buffo* baritones of the day, Mozart's Figaro and Papageno being among his most famous roles.

Kunz, Ernst (b. Berne, 2. VI. 1891), Swiss cond. and comp. Studied at Munich and cond. at theatres there and at Rostock. In 1919 he returned to Switz. and became mus. director at Olten and to the canton of Solothurn, cond. choral and orchestral concerts, also a choral society at Zürich.

Works incl. operas *Der Fächer*, *Vreneli ab em Guggisberg*, *Die Bremer Stadtmusikanten*; Christmas Oratorio, Requiem; *Huttens letzte Tage* (C. F. Meyer) for solo voices, male chorus and orch., other choral works; 5 symphs.; concertos; 3 string 4tets and other chamber mus.; org. and pf. works; songs, etc.

Kunzen, Friedrich Ludwig Aemilius (b. Lübeck, 24. IX. 1761; d. Copenhagen, 28. I. 1817), Ger. cond. and comp. Pupil of his father, Adolph Karl K. (1720–81). Having given up legal studies, he went to the Copenhagen Opera, where he prod. his 1st work. After a period in Berlin, where he ed. a mus. journal with Reichardt, he went as cond. to Frankfurt, 1792, and Prague, 1794, prod. his only Ger. opera at the former city. He returned to Copenhagen 1795 as director of the Opera.

Works incl. operas *Holger Danske*, *Ossians Harfe*, *Hemmeligheden*, *Dragedukken*, *Erik Ejegod*, *Min Bedstemoder*, *Kærlighed paa Landet*, *Stormen* (on Shakespeare's *Tempest*), etc.

Kurpiński, Karol (Kasimir) (b. Wloszakowice, 6. III. 1785; d. Warsaw, 18. IX. 1857), Pol. violinist, cond. and comp. Taught by his father, a village organist, he took part in private string 4tet perfs.

and in 1810 succeeded in securing a post as violinist at the Boguslawski Theatre at Warsaw. He later became cond. and finally co-director with Elsner.

Works incl. operas *Two Huts*, *Jadwiga*, *The New Cracovians*, *The Castle of Czorstzyn* and many others; ballets; church mus.; overtures, etc.

Kurth, Ernst (b. Vienna, 1. VI. 1886; d. Berne, 2. IV. 1946), Aus. musicologist. Studied under Adler in Vienna and after holding a post in Thuringia went to Switz., settling as teacher at Berne, 1912, and becoming prof. of mus. at the univ. in 1920. His books incl. studies of Gluck's operas, of harmonic theory, of linear counterpoint based on Bach's works and of romantic harmony based on Wagner.

Kurz, Selma (b. Bielitz, Silesia, 15. XI. 1874; d. Vienna, 10. V. 1933), Aus. coloratura soprano. Studied with Pless, making her début at the Frankfurt opera. In 1899 Mahler engaged her at the Vienna Court Opera and she remained with that co. until 1926. She 1st sang in London in 1904.

Kuss der Danae, Der (*Danae's Kiss*) (R. Strauss). *See* Liebe der Danae. The opera was 1st reported under the title of this entry, but this was changed later.

Kusser (or Cousser), Johann Sigismund (b. Pressburg = Pozsony, 13. II. 1660; d. Dublin, 1727), Ger. cond. and comp. Pupil of Lully in Paris, where he lived from 1674 to 1682. He was one of the directors of the Hamburg Opera from 1694 to 1696, and *Kapellmeister* at Stuttgart from 1700 to 1704. He went to London in 1705, and later to Dublin, where he became director of mus. to the viceroy.

Works incl. operas *Erindo*, *Porus*, *Pyramus und Thisbe*, *Scipio Africanus*, *Jason* and *Ariadne*; serenade for the king's birthday; ode on the death of Arabella Hunt; suites (with overtures) for strings; collection of opera overtures and airs, etc.

Kussevitsky, Sergey (b. Tver, 26. VII. 1874; d. Boston, Mass., 4. VI. 1951), Rus. cond. Studied in Moscow and became a double bass player in the Imp. Orch., later specialized as a soloist on the instrument and toured Europe. He then formed an orch. of his own and took to cond. In 1924 he was app. cond. of the Boston Symph. Orch.

Kutchka (Rus. = handful; short for *mogutchaya kutchka* = the mighty handful), the group of 5 Rus. comps. who under the leadership of Balakirev began a conscious campaign in favour of nationalist mus. based on folk mus. The other members of the group were Borodin, Cui, Mussorgsky and Rimsky-Korsakov.

Kuula, Toivo (b. Vaasa, 7. VII. 1883;

Kvapil   Kyrie

d. Viipuri, 18. V. 1918), Fin. comp.
Studied with Wegelius, Järnefelt and
Sibelius at the Helsinki Cons., also with
Busoni at Bologna and Labey in Paris.
App. cond. of the orch. at Uleaaborg,
1910, and asst. cond. of the Helsinki
Municipal Orch. under Kajanus, 1911.
In 1915 he became cond. of the orch. at
Viipuri.

Works incl. *Stabat Mater, Song of
the Sea* for chorus and orch.; symph.,
symph. poem *Son of a Slave,* 2 *East Both-
nian Suites* for orch.; pf. trio; vln. and pf.
sonata; pf. pieces; songs, etc.

Kvapil, Jaroslav (1868–1950), Cz. poet and
dramatist. *See* **Ostrčil** (*Orphan*).

of pf. and comp. at the Cons. and cond.
of the Phil. Society.

Works incl. 4 symphs., variations and
fugue for orch.; cantata for baritone solo,
chorus and orch.; 6 string 4tets, pf. 5tet,
pf. trio; 2 vln. and pf. sonatas, cello and pf.
sonata; pf. sonata and pieces; songs, etc.

Kyrie (Gk., *Kyrie eleison* = 'Lord, have
mercy'). The 1st item of the Ordinary
of the Mass. Orig. it was not part of the
Mass but of var. Litanies, at the head of
which it still stands. In the Mass it has a
9-fold structure, and the simplest melodic
form consisted of 8 repetitions of a simple
melody followed by a quite different
melody for the 9th clause (*see* illustration).

KYRIE

Kvapil, Jaroslav (b. Fryšták, Morav.,
21. IV. 1892; d. Brno, 18. II. 1958), Cz.
comp. Studied with Janáček at Brno and
was later app. prof. of org. and counterpoint at the Org. School there. In 1911–13
he continued studying at the Leipzig Cons.,
and on his return to Brno became prof.

This melody closely resembles that still
used for the Litany Kyries for Rogationtide and Holy Saturday. Other mus.
forms in common use were: *aaa bbb aaa'*;
aaa bbb ccc'; and *aba cdc efe'* (a stroke
represents an extended form of the phrase
concerned).

L

l, the submediant note in any key in Tonic Sol-fa notation, pronounced Lah.
L. H. (abbr.) = Left Hand, often used in pf. mus., also in Ger. (*Linke Hand*).
L.R.A.M. (abbr.), licentiate of the Royal Academy of Music (London).
La, the old name for the note A (*see* **Solmization**), still used in Lat. countries, and in Tonic Sol-fa notation the submediant note in any key, repres. by the symbol **l,** pronounced Lah.
La Borde, Jean Benjamin de (b. Paris, 5. IX. 1734; d. Paris, 22. VII. 1794), Fr. author and amateur comp. Pupil of Rameau for comp., chamberlain to Louis XV. He d. on the scaffold during the Revolution.
Works incl. 32 operas, songs with vln. and bass, songs with pf. He wrote books incl. an *Essai sur la musique ancienne et moderne*.
La Cruz, Ramón de (1731–94), Span. dramatist. *See* **Rodríguez de Hita** (var. operas).
La Fage, (Juste) Adrien (Lenoir de) (b. Paris, 30. III. 1805; d. Charenton, 8. III. 1862), Fr. writer on mus. and comp. Pupil of Choron in Paris and Baini in Rome. He held church appts. in Paris and paid 2 more long visits to It. Comp. a comic opera, *I creditori*, church mus., instrumental works, etc., and wrote books on plainsong hist., bibliog., etc.
La Fontaine, Jean de (1621–95), Fr. poet. *See* **Blaise le savetier** (Philidor), **Caplet, Cigale et la Fourmi** (Audran), **Colombe** (Gounod), **Deux Chasseurs** (Duni), **Gluck** (*Ivrogne corrigé*), **Laruette** (do.), **Philidor (8)** (*Jardinier et son seigneur*), **Pierné** (*Coupe enchantée*), **Poulenc** (*Animaux modèles*).
La Grotte, Nicolas de (b. *c.* 1530; d. *c.* 1600), Fr. comp. and keyboard-player. He pub. settings of Ronsard and examples of *musique mesurée à l'antique*.
La Guerre (*née* **Jacquet**), **Elisabeth Claude de** (b. Paris, ? 1664; d. Paris, 27. VI. 1729), Fr. harpsichordist and comp. A pupil of her father, she showed early promise and attracted the patronage of Louis XIV and later Mme. de Montespan. She married the comp. Marin La Guerre in 1687.
Works incl. opera *Céphale et Procris*; cantatas; *Te Deum* and other church mus.; vln. sonatas, trio sonatas, harpsichord mus., etc.
La Guerre, Michel de (b. Paris, *c.* 1605; d. Paris, 13. XI. 1679), Fr. organist and comp., father-in-law of prec. Organist of the Sainte-Chapelle in Paris, 1633–79. His 2 sons, Jérôme (*c.* 1654–?) and Marin

(1658–1704) were both organists and comps.; the latter married Elisabeth Jacquet.
Works incl. opera *Le Triomphe de l'Amour sur des bergers et bergères*; airs de cour, etc.
La Halle (or La Hale), Adam de (b. ? Arras, *c.* 1230; d. Naples, before 1288), Fr. poet and comp. Educ. for the priesthood, but fell in love and married a young girl, whom he left to retire to Douai in 1263 (?) to rejoin the Church. In 1282 he went to Naples with the Comte d'Artois.
Works incl. stage pieces *Le Jeu d'Adam, ou de la feuillée* and *Le Jeu de Robin et de Marion*; motets; *chansons*, etc.
La Hèle (or Helle), Georges de (b. Antwerp, 1547; d. Madrid, 19. II. 1587), Flem. comp. Chorister at the royal chapel in Madrid in his youth. Choirmaster at Tournai Cathedral in 1578, but prob. back in Spain by 1580. He obtained 2 prizes at the Puy de Musique at Évreux in 1576.
Works (some destroyed in a fire at Madrid in 1734) incl. Masses, motets; *chansons*, etc.
La Laurencie, Lionel de (b. Nantes, 24. VII. 1861; d. Paris, 21. XI. 1933), Fr. musicologist. While studying law in Paris he also attended the Cons. In 1898 he decided to devote himself entirely to mus. and became lecturer at the École des Hautes Études Sociales. He wrote much for mus. journals and pub. books on Rameau, Fr. vln. mus., lutenists, etc., as well as library catalogues.
La Mara (actually Marie Lipsius) (b. Leipzig, 30. XII. 1837; d. Leipzig, 2. III. 1927), Ger. author and ed. Wrote, under the pen-name of La Mara, var. books on comps., mainly of a romantically biog. character, and ed. letters of Liszt and Berlioz.
La Pouplinière (or Poupelinière), Alexandre Jean Joseph le Riche de (b. Chinon, 29. VII. 1693; d. Paris, 5. XII. 1762), Fr. mus. patron. He was farmer-general of taxes and amassed a huge fortune. He kept a private orch., had Rameau living in his house for several years and studied under him, and patronized a number of other comps. and perfs.
La Presle, Jacques (Paul Gabriel Sauville) de (b. Versailles, 5. VII. 1888; d. Paris, 1969), Fr. comp. Studied at the Paris Cons. both before and after the 1914–18 war, in which he served. In 1921 he gained the Prix de Rome, in 1930 became mus. director of Radio-Paris and in 1937 prof. of harmony at the Cons.
Works incl. oratorio *L'Apocalypse de Saint Jean*; cantata *Hermione* and *2 Chœurs de printemps* for chorus and orch.; *Album d'images* for orch.; pf. concerto; *Le vent* and *Impressions* for voice and orch.;

suite in G maj. for string 4tet; vln. and pf. sonata; *Parade fantasque* for pf.; songs, etc.

La Rue, Pierre de (b. ? Tournai, ?; d. Courtrai, 20. XI. 1518), Flem. comp. Pupil of Okeghem, in the service by turns of the court of Burgundy, Charles V and Margaret of Aus. when governor of the Netherlands. He was app. prebendary of Courtrai and later of Namur.

Works incl. 31 Masses, Requiem, 38 motets; *chansons*, etc.

La Tombelle, (Antoine Louis Joseph Gueyrand) Fernand (Fouant) de (b. Paris, 3. VIII. 1854; d. Château de Fayrac, Dordogne, 13. VIII. 1928), Fr. organist and comp. Began to study with his mother, a pupil of Liszt and Thalberg, later entered the Paris Cons. and finished his studies with Saint-Saëns. From 1878 he shared the org. concerts at the Trocadéro with Guilmant. From 1896 to 1904 he was prof. at the Schola Cantorum.

Works incl. operetta *Un Rêve au pays du bleu*; Mass, motets and other church mus.; oratorios *Crux, Les Sept Paroles de notre Seigneur*; suite *Impressions matinales* for orch.; string 4tet in E maj., pf. vln. and pf. sonata; org. and harmonium pieces; songs, etc.

Labé, Louise (*c.* 1525–66), Fr. poet. *See* Beck (sonnets).

Labey, Marcel (b. Le Vésinet nr. Paris, 6. VIII. 1875; d. Nancy, 21. XI. 1968), Fr. cond. and comp. Studied at the Schola Cantorum in Paris, d'Indy being among his masters. Later he cond. the orch. class there and in 1931 became vice-director, also pf. prof. 1907–14. Sec. and organizer of the Société Nationale de Musique.

Works incl. opera *Bérengère*; 3 symphs., *Fantaisie, Suite champêtre, Ouverture pour un drame* for orch.; string 4tet, pf. 5tet, 2 pf. trios; 2 vln. and pf. sonatas; choruses; pf. pieces; songs, etc.

Labialstimme(n) (Ger. lit. labial voice), the Flue Stop(s) of the org.

Labiche, Eugène (1815–88), Fr. playwright. *See* Ibert (*Chapeau de paille d'Italie*), Shaporin (*It. Straw Hat*), Thompson (R.) (do.).

Lablache, Luigi (b. Naples, 6. XII. 1794; d. Naples, 23. I. 1858), It. bass, of Fr. descent. Made his 1st stage appearance at the Teatro San Carlo, Naples; later became famous all over Eur.

Labroca, Mario (b. Rome, 22. XI. 1896), It. critic and comp. Pupil of Respighi and Malipiero. Critic of *Il Lavoro fascista* and *L'Idea nazionale*, superintendent of the Teatro Vittorio Emanuele at Florence and organizer of the *Maggio musicale*.

Works incl. *Stabat Mater, Il lamento dei mariti e delle mogli* for 6 voices and small orch.; symph. for pf. and small

orch.; 2 string 4tets, pf. trio; sonatina for vln. and pf., suite for vln. and pf.; pieces; songs, etc.

Labuński, Feliks Roderyk (b. Ksawerynowo, 27. XII. 1892), Pol. comp. Studied at Warsaw and with Dukas and Nadia Boulanger in Paris. He founded a society of Pol. musicians there and later went to live in U.S.A.

Works incl. symph. and *Pastoral Triptych* for orch.; concertino for pf. and orch.; string 4tet; divertimento for fl. and pf.; *Olympic Hymn* for chorus and orch., *The Birds* for voice and orch., Pol. Cantata, for solo voices and chorus; pf. pieces; songs, etc.

Lac des cygnes (Tchaikovsky). *See* Swan Lake.

Lach, Robert (b. Vienna, 29. I. 1874; d. Mondsee, 11. IX. 1958), Aus. musicologist and comp. Studied at the Vienna Cons. and graduated in Prague, 1902. In 1911 he was app. director of the mus. dept. of the Vienna State Library, in 1915 teacher and in 1920 prof. at the univ. His writings incl. studies of folksong, oriental and western melody, the dance, Mozart, Schubert, Wagner and Brahms.

Comps. incl. 2 operas; 8 Masses, Requiem, 3 cantatas; 10 symphs.; chamber mus., incl. 25 string 4tets; choruses; songs, etc.

Lächerliche Prinz Jodelet, Der (*The Ridiculous Prince J.*), opera by Keiser (lib. by Johann Phillipp Praetorius, based on Paul Scarron's comedy, *Jodelet, ou Le Maître valet*), prod. Hamburg, Theater beim Gänsemarkt, 1726.

Lachmann, Robert (b. Berlin, 28. XI. 1892; d. Jerusalem, 8. V. 1939), Ger. musicologist. Studied philology in London and Berlin, and later, becoming interested in the exotic songs of African and Asiatic war prisoners, studied mus. science under Carl Stumpf and Johannes Wolf in Berlin. In 1927 he became an official in the mus. dept. of the Prus. State Library, but emigrated to Palestine in 1935 as lecturer at the Hebrew Univ. at Jerusalem. He wrote several books on exotic mus.

Lachner, Ger. family of musicians:

1. **Theodor L.** (b. Rain, Bavaria, 1798; d. Munich, 22. V. 1877), organist and cond. He was the eldest son and pupil of an organist at Rain o/Lech and became organist at Munich, also chorus-master at the court theatre.

2. **Thekla L.** (b. Rain, *c.* 1800; d.? Augsburg, ?), organist, sister of prec. Pupil of her father, became organist at Augsburg.

3. **Franz L.** (b. Rain, 2. IV. 1803; d. Munich, 20. I. 1890), cond. and comp., brother of prec. Pupil of his father and later of Stadler and Sechter in Vienna, where he became a friend of Schubert.

App. asst. cond. at the Kärntnertor-theater there, 1826, and succeeded Weigl as chief cond., 1827. In 1834 he went to Mannheim as opera cond. and in 1836 to Munich as court mus. director.

Works incl. operas *Die Bürgschaft* (on Schiller's poem), *Alidia, Catarina Cornaro* and *Benvenuto Cellini*; oratorios *Moses* and *Die vier Menschenalter*; Requiem, 3 Masses; cantatas and other choral works; 8 symphs.; harp and bassoon concertos; 5 string 4tets, nonet for wind instruments, trios and other chamber mus.; pf. pieces; songs, etc.

4. **Christiane L.** (b. Rain, 1805; d. Rain, ?), organist, sister of prec. She studied under her father and succeeded him as organist at Rain o/Lech.

5. **Ignaz L.** (b. Rain, 11. IX. 1807; d. Hanover, 24. II. 1895), cond. and comp., brother of prec. Studied under his father and at Augsburg, joined his brother Franz in Vienna, 1824, became asst. cond. at the Kärntnertortheater there, 1825, app. court mus. director at Stuttgart, 1831, and at Munich, 1842, jointly with Franz. Later he filled var. posts at Hamburg, Stockholm and Frankfurt.

Works incl. operas *Der Geisterturm, Die Regenbrüder* and *Loreley*; ballets and melodramas; Masses; symphs.; string 4tets; pf. mus.; songs, etc.

6. **Vincenz L.** (b. Rain, 19. VII. 1811; d. Carlsruhe, 22. I. 1893), cond. and comp., brother of prec. Studied with his father and at Augsburg. He became organist in Vienna, 1834, and was court mus. director at Mannheim, 1836–73. He retired to Karlsruhe, where he taught at the Cons.

Works incl. incid. mus. to Schiller's adaptation of Gozzi's *Turandot*; part-songs, songs, etc.

Lacombe, Louis (Trouillon) (b. Bourges, 26. XI. 1818; d. Saint-Vaast-la-Hougue, 30. IX. 1884), Fr. pianist and comp. Studied at the Paris Cons. and, after a tour with his sister, with Czerny, Sechter and Seyfried in Vienna. He settled in Paris in 1839.

Works incl. operas *L'Amour, La Madone, Winkelried, Le Tonnelier de Nuremberg, Korrigane*; dramatic symphs. with solo voices and chorus *Manfred* (after Byron) and *Arva*, melodrama with choruses *Sapho*; 5tet for pf., vln., ob., cello and bassoon, 2 pf. trios and other chamber mus.; pf. pieces and studies, etc.

Lacombe, Paul (b. Carcassonne, 11. VII. 1837; d. Carcassonne, 5. VI. 1927), Fr. comp. Studied with the organist François Teysserre and from 1866 by correspondence with Bizet.

Works incl. 3 symphs., *Ouverture symphonique*; suite for pf. and orch.; string 4tet, 3 pf. trios; 3 sonatas for vln. and pf.,

sonata for cello and pf.; numerous pf. works; songs, etc.

Lacy, John (?–1681), Eng. playwright. See Purcell (D.) (*Sawny the Scot*).

Lacy, John (b. ?; d. Devonshire, *c.* 1865), Eng. bass. Pupil of Rauzzini at Bath. He sang in London with success at an early age and went to It., settling in London afterwards, except for a period spent at Calcutta, 1818–26, with his wife.

Lacy, Michael Rophino (b. Bilbao, 19. VII. 1795; d. London, 20. IX. 1867), Ir. violinist. Learnt mus. as a child in Spain, was sent to school at Bordeaux, 1802, and in 1803 went to Paris to finish his training with R. Kreutzer. He 1st appeared in Paris, 1804, and London, 1805. He played with success for many years there as well as at Liverpool, Edinburgh, Glasgow, Dublin, etc., and made a number of tasteless adaptations of operas and oratorios by var. comps. He was an early Handel scholar and collab. with Schoelcher.

Ladmirault, Paul (Émile) (b. Nantes, 8. XII. 1877; d. Camoël, Morbihan, 30. X. 1944), Fr. comp. Studied at home and later at the Paris Cons. He became prof. at the Nantes Cons.

Works incl. operas *Gilles de Retz* and *Myrdhin*; ballet *La Prêtresse de Korydwen*; incid. mus. to *Tristan et Iseult*; *Messe brève, Tantum ergo* and other sacred works; symph., symph. poems *En Forêt, La Brière, La Jeunesse de Cervantes* for orch.; variations on a chorale for pf. 5tet; vln. and pf. sonata, modal fantasy *De l'ombre à la clarté* for vln. and pf.; *Esquisses, 2 Danses bretonnes*, etc. for pf.; *Variations sur des airs de biniou trécorois, Rapsodie gaëlique* for pf. duet; *Triolets à Catherine, Chansons écossaises, Chansons bretonnes* and other songs; part songs, etc.

Lady Macbeth of the Mtsensk District (*L. M. Mtsenskago Uyezda*), opera by Shostakovich (lib. by A. Preis and comp., based on a novel by Nikolai Semenovich Leskov), prod. Moscow, 22. I. 1934. Very successful at first, but afterwards discountenanced as decadent by the Soviet Government.

Lady of the Lake, The, songs by Schubert set to Ger. transs. from Scott's poem by P. A. Storck in 1825 and pub. in 1826 as Op. 52. 1. Ellen's 1st song, 'Soldier, rest!'; 2. Ellen's 2nd song, 'Huntsman, rest!'; 3. Ellen's 3rd song, 'Ave Maria'; 4. Norman's song, 'The heath this night'; 5. Lay of the Imprisoned Huntsman, 'My hawk is tired'. Op. 52 contains 2 more poems from Scott's work, *Boating Song* for male chorus and *Coronach* for female chorus.

Lady Rohesia, 'operatic frolic' by Antony Hopkins (lib. by comp., based on Barham's *Ingoldsby Legends*), prod.

London, Sadler's Wells Theatre, 17. III. 1948.

Lafont, Charles Philippe (b. Paris, 1. XII. 1781; d. nr. Tarbes, 23. VIII. 1839), Fr. violinist, singer and comp. He was at 1st taught by his mother, a sister of the violinist Berthaume, and he travelled to Ger. with his uncle as a child, playing there with success. Later he studied with R. Kreutzer in Paris, appeared as a ballad singer at the Théâtre Feydeau, completed his vln. studies with Rode and went on tour in 1801–8. In 1808–15 he was solo violinist to the Tsar in St. Petersburg, and then received a similar appt. from Louis XVIII. In 1831–9 he made long tours with Herz, cut short by a carriage accident that caused his death.

Works incl. 2 operas; 7 vln. concertos; duets for vln. and pf. written with Kalkbrenner, Herz and others; more than 200 songs, etc.

Lafontaine. *See* **La Fontaine.**

Lagerlöf, Selma (1858–1940), Swed. novelist. *See* **Vittadini** (*Nazareth*), **Zandonai** (*Cavalieri di Ekebù*).

Lah, the name for the submediant note in any key in Tonic Sol-fa, so pronounced, but in notation represented by the symbol l.

Lahee, Henry (b. London, 11. IV. 1826; d. London, 29. IV. 1912), Eng. organist and comp. Pupil of Sterndale Bennett, Goss and Potter. Organist of Holy Trinity Church, Brompton, 1847–74.

Works incl. cantatas *The Building of the Ship* (Longfellow) and *The Sleeping Beauty* (Tennyson); madrigals and glees, etc.

Lai (Fr., later Eng. *lay*), a medieval lyrical poem in pairs of stanzas in different metrical forms; also the mus. set to such poems.

Laidlaw, Robena Anna (b. Bretton, Yorks., 30. IV. 1819; d. London, 29. V. 1901), Eng. pianist. Pupil of Herz and L. Berger. Played with much success on the Continent. App. court pianist to the Queen of Hanover, 1840. Schumann ded. his *Fantasiestücke*, Op. 12, to her.

Lajtha, László (b. Budapest, 30. VI. 1892; d. Budapest, 17. II. 1963), Hung. folksong expert and comp. Studied at the Mus. High School at Budapest, specialized in folk mus. and joined the folklore dept. of the Nat. Museum in 1913. Prof. at the Budapest Cons., 1919–49.

Works incl. 3 ballets; 2 Masses and other choral works; 9 symphs.; vln. concerto; 8 string 4tets and other chamber mus.; sonatas for vln., cello and pf., etc.

Lakmé, opera by Delibes (lib. by Edmond Gondinet and Philippe Gille), prod. Paris, Opéra-Comique, 14. IV. 1883.

Lalande, Henriette-Clémentine. *See* **Méric-Lalande.**

Lalande, Michel (Richard) de (b. Paris, 15. XII. 1657; d. Versailles, 18. VI. 1726), Fr. organist and comp. He learnt mus. as a chorister at the church of Saint-Germain-l'Auxerrois in Paris and taught himself the vln., bass viol and harpischord. On being refused admission to Lully's orch., he took to the org. and secured organist's appts. at 3 churches. He failed to obtain the post of court organist, but was given charge of the princesses' mus. educ. and in 1683 was app. one of the superintendents of the royal chapel. He became master of the royal chapel in 1704. In 1684 he married the court singer Anne Rebel, who d. in 1722, and in 1723 he married again, Mlle. de Cury, daughter of one of the court surgeons.

Works incl. ballets and opera-ballets *Ballet de la jeunesse, Le Palais de Flore, Adonis, Myrtil et Mélicerte, Les Fées, L'Amour fléchi par la Constance, L'Hymen champêtre, Ballet de la Paix, Les Folies de Cardenio* (from Cervantes's *Don Quixote*), *Ballet de l'inconnu, Les Élémens* (with Destouches), *L'Amour berger, Églogue, ou Pastorale en musique, Les Fontaines de Versailles;* 42 motets with orchestral accomp.; cantata *Le Concert d'Esculape; 3 Leçons des Ténèbres,* Miserere for solo voice; mus. for the royal table, etc.

Lalla-Roukh, opera by F. David (lib. by Hippolyte Lucas and Michel Carré, based on Moore's *Lalla Rookh*), prod. Paris, Opéra-Comique, 12. V. 1862.

Lallouette, Jean François (b. Paris, 1651; d. Paris, 31. VIII. 1728), Fr. violinist and comp. He studied vln. with Guy Leclerc and comp. with Lully. From 1668 to 1677 he was violinist and cond. at the Opéra, but Lully dismissed him for claiming collaboration in his *Isis,* which may have been true, for he was said to have often assisted Lully. In 1693 he became *maître de chapelle* at Rouen Cathedral, in 1695 at Notre-Dame at Versailles, and in 1700 at Notre Dame in Paris.

Works incl. dramatic interludes and ballets; Masses, motets, Misereres, etc.

Lalo, (Victor Antoine) Édouard (b. Lille, 27. I. 1823; d. Paris, 22. IV. 1892), Fr. comp. of Span. descent. He 1st studied vln. and cello at the Lille Cons. and then vln. at that of Paris, taking comp. lessons privately at the same time. In 1855 he became vla. in the Armingaud-Jacquard 4tet. He wrote little until 1865, the year of his marriage to Mlle. Bernier de Maligny, who sang his songs in public. Gradually his success grew both in the opera-house and the concert-room.

Works incl. operas *Fiesque* (after Schiller), *Le Roi d' Ys, La Jacquerie* (unfinished, completed by Coquard); pantomime with choruses *Néron;* ballet *Namouna;* symph. in G min., *Divertissement,*

Lalo   Lamond

Rapsodie norvégienne and scherzo for
orch., 2 aubades for small orch., concerto,
Symphonie espagnole, *Fantaisie norvégienne*,
Romance-Sérénade and *Concerto russe* for
vln. and orch., concertos for pf. and for
cello; string 4tet (later revised as No. 2),
3 pf. trios; vln. and pf. sonata and a
number of pieces, cello and pf. sonata and
pieces; *La Mère et l'enfant* for pf. duet;
over 30 songs and 2 vocal duets; church
mus., etc.
    Lalo, Pierre (b. Puteaux, 6. IX. 1866;
d. Paris, 9. VI. 1943), Fr. mus. critic, son
of prec. He became mus. critic to *Le
Temps* in 1898 and also wrote for the
Journal des Débats.
    Laloy, Louis (b. Grey, Haute Saône,
18. II. 1874; d. Dôle, 3. III. 1944), Fr.
musicologist and critic. Initially studied
philosophy in Paris, becoming Dr.-ès-
lettres in 1904. Studied at the Schola
Cantorum, became a mus. critic, lecturer
at the Sorbonne, 1906, sec. to the Opéra,
1914, and prof. of mus. hist. at the Paris
Cons., 1936. His works incl. studies
of ancient and Chin. mus., Rameau,
Debussy, etc.
    Lamartine, Alphonse de (1790–1869), Fr.
politician and poet. *See* Jocelyn (Goddard),
Massé (*Fior d'Aliza*), Niedermeyer (songs),
Préludes (Liszt).
    Lamb, Charles (1775–1834), Eng.
essayist. *See* Elgar (*Dream Children*).
    Lambe, Walter (b. Salisbury, c. 1452;
d. ?, c. 1500), Eng. comp. He was King's
Scholar at Eton in 1467 (aged 15), and
clerk at St. George's, Windsor, from 1479
to 1499 or later, acting as master of the
choristers (at first jointly with William
Edmunds), 1480–4. His known mus. was
all incl. in the Eton Choirbook: it consists
of a Magnificat and 5 votive antiphons (a
6th can be completed from another MS.;
another is partially lost and 4 more
completely so).
    Lambert, Constant (b. London, 23. VIII.
1905; d. London, 21. VIII. 1951), Eng.
comp., cond. and critic. Son of the painter
George Washington L. Studied at the
R.C.M. in London. Diaghilev commissioned a ballet from him when he was still
a student and prod. it at Monte Carlo in
1926. He began to make his mark as a
cond. of ballet with the Camargo Society
and was later engaged to cond. ballet at
Sadler's Wells Theatre, with which he
appeared in Paris in 1937, having already
cond. at the I.S.C.M. Festival at Amsterdam, 1933. He also became a concert
cond., was for a time mus. critic to the
Referee and pub. a book of criticism,
Music Ho!
    Works incl. ballets *Romeo and Juliet*,
Pomona, *Horoscope*; incid. mus. for
Shakespeare's *Hamlet*; mus. for films
Merchant Seamen and *Anna Karenina*

(after Tolstoy); *Summer's Last Will and
Testament* (Nash), masque for baritone
solo, chorus and orch.; *The Rio Grande*
for pf., orch. and chorus; dirge in Shakespeare's *Cymbeline* for voices and orch.;
Mus. for Orch., *Aubade héroïque* for small
orch.; concerto for pf. and chamber
orch.; pf. sonata; 4 poems by Li-Po for
voice and pf., etc.
    Lambert, Lucien (b. Paris, 5. I. 1858; d.
Oporto, 21. I. 1945), Fr. pianist and comp.
Studied pf. under his father and toured
successfully in Eur. and U.S.A. He then
studied comp. with Massenet and Dubois
in Paris.
    Works incl. operas *Brocéliande*, *Le
Spahi* (lib. by Loti), *La Flamenca*, *Penti-
cosa*, *La Sorcière*, *La Marseillaise*; ballet
La Roussalka; incid. mus. to A. Alexandre's *Sire Olaf*; lyric scene *Prométhée
enchaîné* (after Aeschylus); *Tanger le soir*,
Moorish rhapsody for orch.; *Andante
et Fantaisie tzigane* for pf. and orch.; pf.
pieces; songs, etc.
    Lambert, Michel (b. Vivonne, Poitou,
c. 1610; d. Paris, 29. VI. 1696), Fr. lutenist,
singer and comp. He was master of the
royal chamber mus. and in 1663 became
master of the children in the royal chapel.
Lully married his daughter Madeleine. He
wrote songs to the lute.
    Lambertini, Giovanni Tommaso (b.
Bologna, ?; d. ?), It. 16th–17th cent.
priest and comp. Singer at San Petronio
at Bologna, (?) 1556–1628, and sometime
treasurer there.
    Works incl. penitential psalms and other
church mus.; madrigals, *villotte*, etc.
    Lamentatione, name (apparently authen-
tic) given to Haydn's symph. No. 26 in
D min., comp. c. 1768, on account of the
use it makes of a chant assoc. with the
Lamentations of Jeremiah.
    Lamentations, the L.s of Jeremiah used
in the Rom. Catholic service at matins on
Thur., Fri. and Sat. of Holy Week; orig.
sung in plainsong and still surviving in
that form, but from the early 16th cent. also
used in polyphonic settings.
    Lamento (It. = lament), a plaintive aria
in early 17th-cent. It. opera conventionally
placed before the tragic culmination of the
plot.
    Lamm, Pavel Alexandrovich (b. Mos-
cow, 27. VII. 1882; d. Moscow, 5. V. 1951),
Rus. pianist and mus. ed. Studied at the
Moscow Cons. and began his career as
pianist. Later became director of the Rus.
State Pub. Dept., where among other
things he ed. the critical ed. of Mussorgsky's complete works in the orig.
form.
    Lämmlein. *See* Lemlin.
    Lamond, Frederic (b. Glasgow, 28. I.
1868; d. Stirling, 21. II. 1948), Scot.
pianist. Studied pf., org. and vln. at

357

home and after becoming a church organist went to the Raff Cons. at Frankfurt in 1882. Although he wished to become a comp., he studied pf. further with Bülow and Liszt, making his début in Berlin in 1885. In Brit. he first played in 1886, at Glasgow and London. He toured widely, but mainly in Ger., and from 1904, when he married the actress Irene Triesch, he had his home in Berlin. It was not until the 1939–45 war that he settled in London.

Lamoureux, Charles (b. Bordeaux, 28. IX. 1834; d. Paris, 21. XII. 1899), Fr. violinist and cond. Studied vln. and theory at the Paris Cons., joined a theatre orch., then played at the Opéra, in 1860 helped to found a chamber mus. society for the intro. of new works, cond. choral works by Bach, Handel and others in the 1870s, became cond. at the Opéra and in 1881 founded the Concerts L., at which he made a great deal of orchestral mus., incl. Wagner, known to a wide public.

Lampe, Johann Friedrich (John Frederick) (b. Saxony, 1703; d. Edinburgh, 25. VII. 1751), Ger. bassoonist and comp. Went to Eng. from Brunswick about 1725 and settled in London, but went to Dublin in 1748 and to Edinburgh in 1750. Married Isabella Young, sister of T. A. Arne's wife.

Works incl. burlesque operas *The Dragon of Wantley* and *Margery, or A Worse Plague than the Dragon* (libs. by Carey), mock opera *Pyramus and Thisbe* (from Shakespeare's *Midsummer Night's Dream*), masque *The Sham Conjurer*; mus. for Carey's *Amelia*; *c.* 10 other stage works; cantata to celebrate the suppression of the Stuart rebellion; songs, etc.

Lamperti, Francesco (b. Savona, 11. III. 1813; d. Como, 1. V. 1892), It. teacher of singing. Master of many eminent singers and author of vocal studies and a treatise on singing.

Lampugnani, Giovanni Battista (b. Milan, 1706; d. Milan, 1781), It. comp. Studied in Naples, and made his début as an opera comp. there in 1732. Successful throughout It., he went to London in 1743 to take over from Galuppi the opera at the King's Theatre, but later returned to Milan. From 1779 he was *maestro al cembalo* at the Teatro alla Scala.

Works incl. *c.* 30 operas, e.g. *Semiramide, Rossane, Tigrane, Artaserse, Siroe, L'amor contadino*, etc.; also trio sonatas, church mus., etc.

Lancelot and Elaine, symph. poem No. 2 by MacDowell, Op. 25, based on the Arthurian legend, comp. 1888.

Lancers. *See* **Quadrille.**

Länderer. *See* **Ländler.**

Landi, Stefano (b. Rome, *c.* 1590; d. Rome, *c.* 1655), It. singer and comp. He

was *maestro di cappella* at Padua about 1620 and in Rome from 1624, and sang alto in the Papal Chapel from 1630.

Works incl. operas *La morte d'Orfeo* and *Il S. Alessio*; Masses and psalms; madrigals and cantatas; arias for 1 voice, etc.

Landini (or Landino), Francesco (b. ? Fiesole, *c.* 1335; d. Florence, 2. IX. 1397), It. organist, lutenist and comp. Although blind from early childhood, he perfected himself on var. instruments and became organist of the church of San Lorenzo at Florence. He is one of the chief exponents of the It. Ars nova.

Works incl. madrigals, *ballate*, etc.

Landini Sixth, a cadence in mus. of the 14th and 15th cents. named after the prec., of whose vocal works it is a feature, e.g.:

The idiom is not confined to It. mus., nor is there any evidence to suggest that Landini invented it.

Ländler, an Austrian country dance having the character of a slow waltz. Mozart, Beethoven and Schubert left many exs.

Landon, H(oward). C(handler). Robbins (b. Boston, Mass., 6. III. 1926), Amer. musicologist and comp. He studied at Swarthmore Coll. and Boston Univ. Since 1947 he has lived in Eur. He has devoted himself particularly to the study of late 18th-cent. mus. and has pub. a number of articles and books, incl. *The Symphonies of Joseph Haydn* and *The Collected Correspondence and London Notebooks of Joseph Haydn*, as well as eds. of numerous works by Haydn, incl. several operas and the complete symphs.

Works incl. incid. mus. to *The Taming of the Shrew*, Requiem for soli, chorus and orch., 2 orchestral overtures, cello sonata, etc.

Landor, Walter Savage (1775–1864), Eng. poet and man of letters. *See* Dieren (van) (songs).

Landormy, Paul (Charles René) (b. Issy, 3. I. 1869; d. Paris, 17. XI. 1943), Fr. musicologist and critic. After teaching philosophy at var. provincial schools, he went to Paris in 1892 to study singing and mus. science. He organized lectures with Rolland at the École des Hautes Études Sociales and directed his own laboratory for the study of mus. physics, 1904–7. In 1918 he became critic to *La Victoire* and also wrote on mus. for *Le Temps* and mus. journals. Sec. to the mus. section of the International Exhibition in Paris, 1937.

His books on mus. incl. studies of hist., the great masters, Schubert, etc.

Landowska, Wanda (b. Warsaw, 5. VII. 1877; d. Lakeville, Conn., 16. VIII. 1959), Pol. harpsichordist, pianist and mus. research scholar. She toured widely and settled in Fr., where in 1927 she opened a school for the study of old mus. at Saint-Leu-la-Forêt nr. Paris. From 1941 she lived in the U.S.A. Her lit. work incl. books and articles on var. aspects of old mus.

Landré, Guillaume (b. The Hague, 24. II. 1905; d. Amsterdam 16. X. 1968), Dutch lawyer and comp. Studied law at Utrecht Univ. and mus. under his father and Pijper.

Works incl. light opera *The Pike*; mus. for the open-air play *Cortez*; chamber symph. for 13 instruments; concertos for vln., cello and clar.; 4 symphs., sinfonietta and other orchestral works; chamber mus., incl. 3 string 4tets; part-songs, etc.

Landré, Willem (b. Amsterdam, 12. VI. 1874; d. Eindhoven, 1. I. 1948), Dutch critic and comp., father of prec. Mus. ed. of the *Nieuwe Rotterdamsche Courant*, 1906–37.

Works incl. operas *De roos van Dekama* and *Beatrijs*; Requiem for solo voices, chorus and orch.; Nocturne and other works for orch.; cantata for pf. and orch.; *Illegale Liederen* for baritone and orch.; chamber mus., etc.

Lang, Paul H(enry). (b. Budapest, 28. VIII. 1901), Amer. musicologist of Hung. birth. In 1924 he went to the Univ. of Paris and 4 years later, with a scholarship, to U.S.A. He became prof. of musicology at Columbia Univ. in N.Y. in 1939. In 1945 he became ed. of the *Music Quarterly*. Among his writings are *Music in Western Civilization* and *George Frideric Handel*.

Lang, Walter (b. Basle, 19. VIII. 1896; d. Baden, 17. III. 1966), Swiss pianist and comp. Studied in his native town at first and afterwards with Jaques-Dalcroze both at Hellerau nr. Dresden and at Geneva. Klose at Munich and Andreae and Walter Frey at Zürich were among his later teachers. As a pianist he was chiefly interested in chamber mus., and he founded a trio.

Works incl. *Sonata festiva* for string orch., *Bulgarian Folksongs* for chamber orch.; variations on a Siberian convict song for vla. and orch.; string 4tet, string trio; sonatas for var. instruments; pf. sonatas and pieces, etc.

Lange, de., Dutch family of musicians:
1. Samuel de L. (b. Rotterdam, 9. VI. 1811; d. Rotterdam, 15. V. 1884), organist, teacher and comp. Organist at the church of St. Lawrence at Rotterdam and comp. of org. mus.
2. Samuel de L. (b. Rotterdam, 22. II.

1840; d. Stuttgart, 7. VII. 1911), cond. and comp., son of prec. Pupil of his father and of Verhulst, and later studied in Vienna. He travelled in Pol., lived at Lwów in 1859–63 and then returned to Rotterdam as organist, teacher and cond. Later he worked at Basle, Cologne, The Hague and Stuttgart, where he succeeded Faisst as prof. at the Cons., of which he became director in 1900.

Works incl. oratorio *Moses*: 3 symphs.; *Conzertstück* for cello and orch., pf. concerto; 3 string 4tets, 5tet, pf. trio; 4 vln. and pf. sonatas, 2 cello and pf. sonatas; 8 org. sonatas; male-voice part-songs, etc.

3. Daniel de L. (b. Rotterdam, 11. VII. 1841; d. Point Loma, Calif., 31. I. 1918), cellist, pianist, organist and comp., brother of prec. Studied under his father and Verhulst, also cello under Servais. He followed his brother to Lwów, 1860–3, then went to Paris for further study and remained there as organist until 1870, when he returned to Hol. and settled at Amsterdam, cond. choral societies and teaching at the Cons., of which he became director in 1895.

Works incl. opera *De val van Kuilenburg*; incid. mus. to Hugo's *Hernani*; Psalm xxii for solo voices, chorus and orch., Mass, Requiem; cantatas; 2 symphs., overture *Willem van Holland*; cello concerto, etc.

Lange-Müller, Peter (Erasmus) (b. Frederiksborg, 1. XII. 1850; d. Copenhagen, 25. II. 1926), Dan. comp. Studied at the Copenhagen Cons.

Works incl. operas *Tove*, *Spanske Studenter* and *Vikingeblod*; incid. mus. to plays; 2 symphs. and other orchestral works; vln. concerto; *c.* 200 songs, etc.

Langford, Samuel (b. Manchester, 1863; d. Manchester, 8. V. 1927), Eng. mus. critic. He was brought up to succeed his father as a nursery gardener, but turned to mus. and studied with Reinecke at Leipzig, 1896–1900. In 1905, he became mus. critic to the *Manchester Guardian*, a post he held until his death.

Langlais, Jean (b. La Fontenelle, Ille-et-Vilaine, 15. II. 1907), Fr. organist and comp. He was educ. at an inst. for the blind and studied org. under André Marchal, also blind, later with Dupré at the Paris Cons., where he also studied comp. with Dukas. He held several organist's appts. at Paris churches, lastly at Sainte-Clotilde, and teaches org. and comp. at the Inst. des Jeunes Aveugles. His best-known works are for org., but he has written many others.

Lanier (or **Laniere**), **Nicholas** (b. London, IX. 1588; d. London, II. 1666), Eng. painter, flautist, singer and comp. of Fr. descent (? Lanière). He was prob. a pupil of his father, John Lanier (or Lanyer), a sackbut player. In 1613, with Coperario and others, he comp. a masque for the marriage of the Earl of Somerset and in 1617 he not only set Ben Jonson's *Lovers made Men*, but sang in it and painted the scenery. In 1625 he was sent to It. to collect pictures for the royal collection. App. Master of the King's Mus. in 1626. Lived in the Netherlands during the Commonwealth, but resumed his post at the Restoration. Several other members of the family were musicians in the royal service.

Works incl. masques, e.g. *Lovers made Men* and *The Vision of Delight* (Jonson); cantata *Hero and Leander*, New Year's songs; vocal dialogues, songs, etc.

Lanner, Joseph (Franz Karl) (b. Vienna, 12. IV. 1801; d. Oberdöbling nr. Vienna, 14. IV. 1843), Aus. violinist and comp. Son of a glove-maker, he taught himself the vln. Anxious to cond. an orch. he began by getting together a string 4tet, in which J. Strauss, sen., played vla. They played at var. taverns selections from favourite operas arr. by him. He soon turned to the comp. of country dances and waltzes, in which he was to be Strauss's greatest rival. He was engaged to cond. the orch. at dances, visited prov. cities with his own band and finally cond. the court balls in turn with Strauss.

Works incl. over 200 waltzes, country dances, quadrilles, polkas, galops, marches, etc.

Lantins, Arnold de (b. ?; d. ?), early 15th-cent. Flem. comp. from the diocese of Liège. He was in Venice in 1428 and was incl. (with Dufay) in a list of papal singers in 1431. He comp. *chansons*, motets and a Mass, *Verbum incarnatum*.

Lantins, Hugo de (b. ?, d. ?), Flem. comp., possibly brother of prec. Like Arnold he visited Italy, and in 1420 wrote an epithalamium for Cleofe Malatesta di Pesaro. Two of his 5 motets connect him with Venice (1423) and Bari respectively. He also wrote numerous *chansons*.

Laparra, Raoul (b. Bordeaux, 13. V. 1876; d. nr. Paris, 4. IV. 1943), Fr. comp. Studied at the Paris Cons.

Works incl. operas *Peau d'âne*, *La Habanera*, *La Jota*, *Le Joueur de viole*, *Las Toreras*, *L'Illustre Fregona*; *Un Dimanche basque* for pf. and orch.; string 4tet; songs, etc.

Lapicida, Erasmus (b. c. 1445–50; d. Vienna, 19. XI. 1547), Ger. comp. Towards the end of his life he is found in the Imp. court, described as being 'in extreme old age'. He wrote church mus., a *frottola* (the latter and much of the former pub. by Petrucci) and Ger. songs.

Lara (actually Cohen), **Isidore de** (b. London, 9. VIII. 1858; d. Paris, 2. VIII. 1935), Eng. amateur comp. Studied comp.

with Mazzucato and singing with Lamperti at the Milan Cons., later went to Lalo in Paris. He returned to London and became well known in wealthy drawing-rooms as a song comp. and perf. Later he came under the patronage of the Princess of Monaco, which enabled him to have his operas staged in the grand manner.

Works incl. operas *The Light of Asia*, *Amy Robsart* (after Scott's *Kenilworth*), *Moïna*, *Messaline*, *Soléa*, *Sanga*, *Naïl*, *Les Trois Masques*, *The Three Musketeers* (after Dumas) and others; cantata *The Light of Asia* (1st version of the opera); many songs, etc.

Largamente (It. = broadly, spaciously), an indication that a movement or phrase is to be played in a broad manner.

Large, the largest note-value in the medieval system of measured notation. It was known in Lat. as *duplex longa* or *maxima*, and was divisible into 2 Longs.

Larghetto (It. lit. little *largo*), a tempo indication for a slow movement, less slow than a Largo.

Largo (It. = large, broad, wide, spacious), a tempo indication for a slow movement denoting a broad style as much as a slow pace. *See also* **Larghetto**.

'Largo', the popular name for the aria 'Ombra mai fù' ('Shade never was') from Handel's opera *Serse* (*Xerxes*), more gen. known as an instrumental piece pub. in all kinds of arrs. The familiar title is not even the original tempo indication, which is *Larghetto*.

Larigot, a soft org. stop sounding 2 8ves. and a 5th above normal pitch.

Lark Ascending, The, romance for vln. and orch. by Vaughan Williams, comp. 1914, 1st perf. London, Queen's Hall, 14. VI. 1921.

'Lark' Quartet, a nickname sometimes given to Haydn's string 4tet in D maj., Op. 64 No. 5 on account of the exposed high 1st-vln. passage at the opening.

Laroche, Herman Augustovich (b. St. Petersburg, 25. V. 1845; d. St. Petersburg, 18. X. 1904), Rus. mus. critic. Fellow-student with Tchaikovsky at the St. Petersburg Cons.; prof. at the Moscow Cons. from 1867 to 1872 and 1883 to 1886, and at St. Petersburg from 1872 to 1879 and from 1886. Critic of many leading Rus. newspapers.

Larsen, Jens Peter (b. Copenhagen, 14. VI. 1902), Dan. musicologist. Studied at Copenhagen Univ. and taught there from 1928, becoming prof. in 1945. Organist at Vangede Church, 1930–45. Ed. of several works by Haydn and other comps., and author of *Die Haydn-Überlieferung*, *Drei Haydn Kataloge* and *Handel's 'Messiah'*.

Larsson, Lars-Erik (b. Åkarp nr. Lund, 15. V. 1908), Swed. cond. and

Laruette

Latrobe

comp. Studied at the R.A.M. at Stockholm, and later in Leipzig and Vienna, where he was a pupil of Berg. In 1937 he was app. to a mus. post in the Stockholm broadcasting service.

Works incl. opera *The Princess of Cyprus*; incid. mus. to Shakespeare's *Winter's Tale*; 2 symphs., 2 concert overtures, lyric suite for orch.; sinfonietta for strings, divertimento for chamber orch.; saxophone concerto, etc.

Laruette, Jean Louis (b. Toulouse, 27. III. 1731; d. Toulouse, I. 1792), Fr. actor, singer and comp. He appeared at the Opéra-Comique and the Comédie-Italienne in Paris.

Works incl. operas *Cendrillon, L'Ivrogne corrigé* (after La Fontaine) and 8 others, operettas, etc.

Las Huelgas Codex, an important MS., *c.* 1325, containing monophonic and polyphonic mus., the latter incl. *conductus*, motets and settings of the Mass Ordinary. It is housed in the monastery of Las Huelgas nr. Burgos in N. Spain.

Las Infantas, Fernando de. *See* **Infantas.**

Laserna, Blas (b. Corella, Navarre, II. 1751; d. Madrid, 8. VIII. 1816), Span. comp. He became official comp. to several Madrid theatres in 1779.

Works incl. numerous *tonadillas*, comic opera *La gitanilla por amor*; incid. mus. for plays by Calderón, Lope de Vega, Moreto, Ramón de la Cruz's *El café de Barcelona* and others, lyric scene *Idomeneo*, etc.

Lassalle, Jean Louis (b. Lyons, 14. XII. 1847; d. Paris, 7. IX. 1909), Fr. baritone. He was intended to follow his father in the business of a silk merchant, but went to Paris, 1st to study painting and then singing at the Cons. and privately. He made his 1st public appearance at Liège in 1868.

Lassen, Eduard (b. Copenhagen, 13. IV. 1830; d. Weimar, 15. I. 1904), Dan.-Belg. cond. and comp. Was taken to Brussels at the age of 2 and studied at the Cons. there, and took the Belg. Prix de Rome in 1851. Unable to get his 1st opera staged at Brussels, he took it to Liszt at Weimar, who prod. it in 1857. He was mus. director there from 1858 and cond. of the opera from 1860.

Works incl. operas *Landgraf Ludwigs Brautfahrt, Frauenlob, Le Captif*; incid. mus. to Sophocles' *Oedipus*, Goethe's *Faust* and *Pandora*, Calderón's *Circe*, Hebbel's *Nibelungen*; festival cantata, Te Deum; *Biblische Bilder* for voices and orch.; 2 symphs., *Beethoven* and *Festival* overtures, etc.

Lasso, Orlando di. *See* **Lassus.**

Lassú. *See* **Csárdás.**

Lassus, Orlande de (Orlando di Lasso) (b. Mons, prob. 1532; d. Munich, 14. VI. 1594), Flem. comp. He seems to have gone

to It. as a boy, and he travelled there and served in var. noble households, in Sicily, Naples and Milan. In 1553–4 he was choirmaster at St. John Lateran in Rome, after which he returned home and settled for 2 years at Antwerp, where in 1555–6 he began to pub. his 1st works. In 1556 he went to Munich and entered the service of the Duke of Bavaria. There he married Regina Weckinger in 1558, and in 1563 became chief *Kapellmeister* in succession to Daser. Visit to Venice, 1567, to find musicians for Munich, and to Ferrara. In 1570 he was ennobled by the Emperor Maximilian. After a visit to Paris in 1571 Charles IX offered him a post as chamber musician, but he returned to Munich after the king's death in 1574. That year he went to Rome to present Pope Gregory XIII with a vol. of Masses and received the order of the Golden Spur. In spite of an offer from Dresden, he remained attached to the Bavar. court to the end. His Lat. motets were collected and pub. in 1604 by his sons Ferdinand and Rudolph under the title *Magnum opus musicum.*

Works incl. some 1,250 comps.: Masses, Requiem, motets, *Sacrae cantiones*, psalms (incl. 7 penitential psalms); madrigals, It. *canzoni*, Fr. *chansons*, Ger. songs for several voices, etc.

Last Days of Pompeii. *See* **Ione** and **Ultimo giorno di Pompei.**

Last Judgment, The, the Eng. title of Spohr's oratorio *Die letzten Dinge*, prod. Cassel, 25. III. 1826.

Latilla, Gaetano (b. Bari, 12. I. 1711; d. Naples, 15. I. 1788), It. comp. Chorister at Bari Cathedral, he studied with Prota and Feo at the Cons. di Sant'Onofrio in Naples, where his first opera was prod. in 1732. App. vice-*maestro di cappella* at Santa Maria Maggiore, Rome, in 1738, he returned to Naples in 1741 for health reasons. Later choirmaster at the Cons. della Pietà in Venice (1756) and vice-*maestro di cappella* at St. Mark's (1762). Retired to Naples 1772.

Works incl. *c.* 50 operas, e.g. *Li marite a forza, Gismondo, Madame Ciana, Romolo, Siroe*, etc.; oratorio *Omnipotenza e misericordia divina*; church mus.; instrumental mus., etc.

Latrobe, Christian Ignatius (b. Leeds, 12. II. 1757; d. Manchester, 6. V. 1836), Eng. clergyman and comp. Studied at the coll. of the Morav. Brethren at Niesky in Upper Lusatia and in 1795 became secretary of the Eng. branch. Ded. 3 sonatas to Haydn, with whom he made friends during the latter's visits to Eng. Ed. Morav. hymn-tunes and 6 vols. of Ger. and It. church mus.

Works incl. *Dies irae*, Te Deum, Miserere, anthems and other church mus.;

instrumental sonatas; airs to poems by Cowper and Hannah More, etc.

Lattuada, Felice (b. Caselle di Morimondo nr. Milan, 5. II. 1882; d. 2. XI. 1962), It. comp. Studied at the Milan Cons.

Works incl. operas *La Tempesta* (after Shakespeare), *Sandha*, *Le preziose ridicole* (after Molière), *Don Giovanni* (after Zorrilla's *Don Juan Tenorio*), *La caverna di Salamanca* (after Cervantes), *Caino*; choral works; orchestral mus., etc.

Latvian Composers. *See* **Baltic Composers.**

Laub, Ferdinand (b. Prague, 19. I. 1832; d. Gries nr. Bozen, 17. III. 1875), Cz. violinist. Studied at the Prague Cons. and in Vienna. Travelled much and succeeded Joachim as leader of the court orch. at Weimar in 1853. Prof. at Stern's Cons. in Berlin and from 1866 at the Moscow Cons.

Lauber, Joseph (b. Ruswil, Lucerne, 25. XII. 1864; d. Geneva, 28. V. 1952), Swiss comp. Studied at Zürich and later with Rheinberger at Munich and Massenet in Paris. After teaching at the Zürich Cons. he became director of that of Geneva.

Works incl. opera *Hexe*, festival play *Neuchâtel Suisse*; oratorios *Ad gloriam Dei* and *Weltendämmerung*, 4 cantatas; 5 symphs., symph. poems *Sur l'Alpe*, *Chant du soir* and *Le Vent et la vague*, suites and overtures for orch., divertimento for small orch.; 2 pf. concertos, 2 vln. concertos; chamber mus.; songs, etc.

Laúd (Span.) = Lute.

Lauda Sion, a sequence sung at Mass on the Feast of Corpus Christi in the Rom. Church, words by St. Thomas Aquinas, *c.* 1264.

Cantata by Mendelssohn written for a festival at Liège and perf. here on 11. VI. 1846.

Laudi spirituali, It. sacred songs of the 13th cent. and later, with words in the vernacular, at first for single voice and later in parts. Their centre of origin was Florence.

Laudon Symphony, nickname of Haydn's symph. No. 69 in C maj., comp. *c.* 1778 and ded. to Field-Marshal Baron Gideon Ernst von Laudon.

Launis, Armas (Emanuel) (b. Tavastehus, 22. IV. 1884; d. 1959), Fin. musicologist and comp. Studied at Helsinki and Berlin, also mus. hist. with Krohn at Helsinki Univ., where he lectured, 1918–22. Ed. Fin. folksongs.

Works incl. operas *The Seven Brothers*, *Kullervo* (from the *Kalevala*), *Aslak Hetta*, *The Song of the Magician*, etc.

Laurencie, Lionel de la. *See* **La Laurencie.**

Lautenclavicymbel. *See* **Lute-Harpsichord.**

Lauterbach, Johann Christoph (b. Culmbach, Bavar., 24. VII. 1832; d. Dresden, 28. III. 1918), Ger. violinist. Studied at the Brussels Cons. and later held appts. as Munich and Dresden, where he was leader of the orch. and prof. at the Cons.

Lavallée, Calixa (b. Verchères, Quebec, 28. XII. 1842; d. Boston, Mass., 21. I. 1891), Canadian pianist and comp. Studied at the Paris Cons. and later toured as pianist in N. Amer.

Works incl. opera *The Widow*; symphs.; string 4tets; nat. air 'O Canada,' etc.

Lavignac, (Alexandre Jean) Albert (b. Paris, 21. I. 1846; d. Paris, 28. V. 1916), Fr. musicologist. Studied at the Paris Cons., where he became prof. in 1882 Founder and 1st ed. of the *Encyclopédie de la musique*; also wrote many technical treatises, a study of Wagner, etc.

Lavoix, Henri (Marie François) (b. Paris, 26. IV. 1846; d. Paris, 27. XII. 1897), Fr. musicologist. Studied at the Sorbonne in Paris and in 1865 became librarian of the Bibliothèque Nationale. Wrote books on mus. hist., medieval mus., Fr. mus., Shakespeare and mus., orch., singing, etc.

Lavolta, or (It.) *Volta* or (Fr.) *Volte*, an old dance in 3–2 time, prob. of It. orig., since the jump that was a feature of it retained the It. word *volta*.

Lavotta, János (b. Pusztafödémes, 5. VII. 1764; d. Tallya, 11. VIII. 1820), Hung. violinist and comp. He was of noble birth, but left home on his father's remarriage and became a professional musician, at the same time following a legal career. He became very fashionable in Vienna and Pest, cond. at var. theatres, but took to drink and ended in decay. As a comp. he was one of the outstanding exponents of *verbunkos* mus.

Lavrangas, Denis (b. Argostoli, Cephalonia, 17. X. 1864; d. Razata, Cephalonia, 18. VII. 1941), Gk. cond. and comp. He studied at Naples and Paris, became a cond. in Fr., later in It., and in 1894 became director of the Phil. Society in Athens. He wrote 7 operas, 3 operettas, choral and orchestral works, etc.

Lawes, Henry (b. Dinton, Wilts., 5. I. 1596; d. London, 21. X. 1662), Eng. comp. Pupil of Coperario, app. gentleman of the Chapel Royal in 1626. Having supplied mus. for Thomas Carew's masque *Coelum Britannicum*, prod. at court, 18. II. 1634, he was commissioned by the Earl of Bridgewater to set Milton's *Comus* for perf. at Ludlow Castle, 29. IX. 1634. He was the subject of a sonnet by Milton, 1646. He was re-app. to the court service on the Restoration in 1660 and wrote a coronation anthem for Charles II.

Works incl. opera *The Siege of Rhodes* (with Locke, Cooke, Colman and Hudson);

masques (as above); coronation anthem *Zadok the Priest*, anthems, psalm-tunes; elegy on the death of his brother William; songs in plays by William Cartwright, Christmas songs in Herrick's *Hesperides*; airs, dialogues and songs for 1 and more voices, etc.

Lawes, William (b. Salisbury, IV. 1602; d. Chester, 1645), Eng. comp., brother of prec. Studied with Coperario and became a musician at Charles I's court. He joined the Royalist army during the Civil War and was killed by a shot during the siege of Chester.

Works incl. mus. for Shirley's masque *The Triumph of Peace* (with Ive) and Davenant's *The Triumph of the Prince d'Amour* and *The Unfortunate Lovers*; anthems and psalms; mus. for consorts of viols; airs for vln. and bass; catches and canons; airs and dialogues for 1 and more voices, etc.

Lawrence, D(avid). H(erbert). (1885–1930), Eng. novelist and poet. *See* **Williams** (G.) (songs), **Wordsworth** (*Houseless Dead*).

Lay. *See* **Lai.**

Layolle, François de (Francesco dell' Aiolle) (b. Florence, *c.* 1475; d. Lyons, *c.* 1540), Fr. organist and comp. He was Benvenuto Cellini's mus. teacher. His son Aleman L. afterwards taught Cellini's daughter and became organist at Lyons for for a time.

Works incl. Masses, motets; *canzoni*, madrigals, etc.

Lays (or **Lay, Laï** or **Lais**), **François** (b. La Barthe-de-Nesthes, Gascony, 14. II. 1758; d. Ingrande nr. Angers, 30. III. 1831), Fr. singer. He learnt mus. at the monastery of Guaraison, but left to become a public singer and made his 1st appearance at the Paris Opéra in 1780. He also sang at court, at the Concert spirituel, etc., and on the foundation of the Cons. in 1795 became prof. of singing there.

Lazarus, Daniel (b. Paris, 13. XII. 1898), Fr. pianist and comp. Studied at the Paris Cons.

Works incl. 3 ballets; incid. mus. for Rolland's *14 Juillet* (with 6 others); *Symphonie avec Hymne* for orch. and chorus; fantasy for cello and orch.; vln. and pf. sonata; pf. pieces, etc.

Lazarus, Henry (b. London, 1. I. 1815; d. London, 6. III. 1895), Eng. clarinettist. Studied under var. masters and after playing in theatre and concert orchs. was app. 1st clar. at the Opera in London, 1840, prof. at the R.A.M., 1854, and at Kneller Hall, 1858.

Lazzari, Sylvio (b. Bozen, 31. XII. 1857; d. Paris, 18. VI. 1944), Aus.-It. comp., later belonging to the Fr. school and naturalized Fr. Studied at Innsbruck,

Munich and the Paris Cons., where Franck was one of his masters.

Works incl. operas *Armor*, *La Lépreuse*, *Le Sautériot*, *Melaenis*, *La Tour de feu*; incid. mus., for Goethe's *Faust*; symph. in E♭ maj., orchestral suite in F maj., symph. tableau *Effet de nuit* (after Verlaine), *4 Tableaux maritimes*, *Ophélie* (after Shakespeare), *Rapsodie espagnole*, *Impressions d'Adriatique*, etc.; *Concertstück* for pf. and orch., *Rapsodie* for vln. and orch.; string 4tet, pf. trio, octet for wind instruments; vln. and pf. sonata; pieces for vln., cello, pf. etc.; *c.* 50 songs; choruses, etc.

Le Bègue, Nicolas (Antoine) (b. Laon, 1631; d. Paris, 6. VII. 1702), Fr. organist and comp. Organist of 2 Paris churches and succeeded Joseph La Barre as organist to the king in 1678.

Works incl. 2 books of harpsichord and 3 of org. pieces.

Le Bel, Firmin (b. Noyon, ?; d. Rome, 18. XI. 1573), Fr. cleric and musician. Worked in the diocese of Noyon, but in 1540 succeeded Mallapert as *maestro di cappella* at Santa Maria Maggiore in Rome and later occupied a similar post at San Luigi dei Francesi, eventually becoming, in 1561, a singer in the Papal choir.

Le Borne, Fernand (b. Charleroi, 10. III. 1862; d. Paris, 15. I. 1929), Belg. comp. Pupil of Franck, Massenet and Saint-Saëns in Paris. He was later a mus. critic.

Works incl. operas *Daphnis et Chloé*, *Hedda*, *Mudarra*, *Les Girondins*, *La Catalane*, *Cléopâtre*, *Néréa*, *Le Maître*; 2 ballets; incid. mus.; Mass in A maj., motets; *Symphonie dramatique* and other orchestral works; *Symphonie-Concerto* for pf., vln. and orch.; string 4tet, pf. trio; sonatas for vln., cello, ob., clar. and fl.; pf. pieces; songs, etc.

Le Brun, Jean (b. ?; d. ?), Fr. priest and comp. of the 2nd half of the 15th cent. He wrote motets and *chansons*.

Le Cocq, Jehan. *See* **Gallus. Johannes.**

Le Couppey, Félix (b. Paris, 14. IV. 1811; d. Paris, 5. VII. 1887), Fr. pianist and teacher. Studied at the Paris Cons., where later he was pf. prof. He wrote many studies for his instrument and several books on its perf.

Le Fanu, Joseph Sheridan (1814–73), Ir. novelist and poet. *See* **Shamus O'Brien** (Stanford), **Stanford** (*Phaudrig Crohoore*).

Le Flem, Paul (b. Lézardrieux, Côtes-du-Nord, 18. III. 1881), Fr. comp. and critic. Pupil of d'Indy and Roussel, among others, later prof. at the Schola Cantorum, chor. master at the Opéra-Comique, cond. of the Chanteurs de Saint-Gervais and critic for *Comoedia*.

Works incl. operas *Le Rossignol de*

Saint-Malo and *Dahut*; choreographic drama on Shakespeare's *Macbeth*; cantata *Aucassin et Nicolette*; symph. in A maj., *Triptyque symphonique* for orch.; fantasy for pf. and orch.; chamber mus.; vln. and pf. sonata; pf. works; choral mus., etc.

Le Franc, Guillaume (b. Rouen, ?; d. Lausanne, VI. 1570), Fr. comp. Fled to Switz. (?) as a Protestant, settled at Geneva in 1541 and estab. a school of mus., becoming master of the children and singer at the cathedral the next year, and ed. Calvin's Genevan Psalter, in which Bourgeois and Marot also had a hand; but in 1545 he left for the cathedral of Lausanne. In 1565 he issued a new Psalter there with some tunes of his own.

Le Jeune, Claude (or **Claudin**) (b. Valenciennes, *c.* 1530; d. Paris, IX. 1600), Fr.-Flem. comp. Worked most of his life in Paris. Having turned Huguenot, he tried (?) to escape from Paris during the siege of 1588, and his MSS. were (?) saved from seizure by the Catholic soldiers by his colleague Mauduit, himself a Catholic. Later L. became chamber musician to the king. Like Baïf and Mauduit, he was an exponent of *musique mesurée*.

Works incl. motets, psalms set to rhymed versions in measured mus. and also to tunes in the Genevan Psalter set for 3 voices; *chansons*, madrigals; instrumental fantasies, etc.

Le Maistre, Matthieu (b. ? Liège, *c.* 1505; d. Dresden, 1577), Flem. comp. He succeeded Walther as *Kapellmeister* to the Saxon court at Dresden in 1554, a post from which he retired with a pension in 1568.

Works incl. Masses, motets; Lat. and Ger. sacred songs, setting of the Lutheran catechism in Lat.; Ger. secular songs, etc.

Le Roy, Adrien (b. ?; d. Paris, 1589), Fr. singer, lutenist, mus. pub. and comp. He worked in Paris and assoc. himself with Ballard (1) in 1552, having married his sister the prec. year. Lassus visited him in 1571 and he pub. some works of his. He pub. an instruction book for the lute and another for the cittern. Some of the airs with lute and *chansons* for 4 voices were comp. by himself.

Lead. *See* **Ornaments.**

Leader, the usual Eng. name for the principal 1st violin in an orch. or of a string 4tet or other chamber mus. team. In Amer., esp. in journalism, the cond. is often called 'leader', the usual term for the leading 1st orchestral vln. there being Concertmaster, from Ger. *Konzertmeister.*

Leading Motif. *See* **Leitmotiv.**

Leading-Note, the seventh note of a maj. or ascending min. scale 'leading' to the tonic by a semitonal step.

Lear, Edward (1812–88), Eng. artist and author. *See* Hely-Hutchinson (songs).

Lebègue. *See* **Le Bègue.**

Leben des Orest (*The Life of Orestes*), opera by Křenek (lib. by comp.), prod. Leipzig, 19. I. 1930.

Lebertoul, Franchois (b. ?, d. ?), early 15th–cent. Fr. or Flem. comp. He was at Cambrai when Dufay was a choir-boy there, around 1409. His surviving works are a motet and four *chansons*.

Lebrun (*née* **Danzi**), **Franziska** (b. Mannheim, III. 1756; d. Berlin, 14. V. 1791), Ger. soprano and comp. of It. descent, daughter of a cellist at the court of Mannheim, sister of Franz D. and wife of Ludwig L. She made her 1st appearance in 1771, was engaged by the court opera, and later sang in It. and Eng. Comp. sonatas.

Lebrun, Jean (b. Lyons, 6. IV. 1759; d. Paris, 1809), Fr. horn player. Pupil of Punto in Paris. Played in the Paris Opéra orch., 1786–92, and later worked in London and Berlin. He is said to have invented the mute for the horn.

Lebrun, Louis (**Sébastien**) (b. Paris, 10. XII. 1764; d. Paris, 27. VI. 1829), Fr. tenor and comp. He sang at the Paris Opéra and Opéra-Comique and was Napoleon's *maître de chapelle.*

Works incl. operas *Marcelin, Le Rossignol* and many others; a Te Deum, etc.

Lebrun, Ludwig (**August**) (b. Mannheim, V. 1752; d. Berlin, 16. XII. 1790), Ger. oboist and comp. of Fr. descent. He was oboist at the Mannheim court, which he followed to Munich in 1778, and toured all over Eur. with his wife, Francesca L.

Works incl. 7 ob. concertos; 12 trios with ob. parts, etc.

Lebrun, Paul (**Henri Joseph**) (b. Ghent, 21. IV. 1861; d. Louvain, 4. XI. 1920), Belg. comp. Studied at the Ghent Cons., took the Belg. Prix de Rome in 1891, became prof. at his Cons. and in 1913 director of the mus. school at Louvain.

Works incl. opera *La Fiancée d'Abydos* (after Byron); cantata *Andromède*, ode *Ons Belgie vrij*; symph. in E min., symph. poem *Sur la montagne, Marche jubilaire* for orch.; string 4tet, etc.

Lechner, Leonhard (b. Etsch valley, before 1550; d. Stuttgart, 9. IX. 1606), Aus. comp. Pupil of Lassus in the court chapel at Munich, became a schoolmaster at Nuremberg in 1570 and in 1579 began to pub. a revised ed. of Lassus's works. In 1584–5 he was mus. director to Count Eitel Friedrich of Hohenzollern at Hechingen and in 1587 was app. to a similar post at the court of Württemberg at Stuttgart.

Works incl. Masses, motets, Magnificat, psalms, introits, wedding motet for the Elector Johann Georg I of Saxony; sacred and secular Ger. songs for 2–5 voices, etc.

Leclair, Jean-Marie (b. Lyons, 10. V. 1697; d. Paris, 22. X. 1764), Fr. violinist and comp. Began his career as a dancer, and in 1722 was ballet master in Turin, but while there turned to the vln., studying with Somis. In 1728 he settled in Paris, having great success as a player and comp. Member of the royal orch. 1734–6, he then went to Hol., returning to Paris after various travels in 1743. For a time in the service of Don Philip of Spain at Chambéry, he joined the orch. of the Duke of Gramont in 1748. He met his death at the hand of an unknown murderer.

Works incl. opera *Scylla et Glaucus*; ballets and 'divertissements'; 12 vln. concertos; 48 vln. sonatas; vln. duets; trio sonatas, etc.

Lecocq, (Alexandre) Charles (b. Paris, 3. VI. 1832; d. Paris, 24. X. 1918), Fr. comp. Studied at the Paris Cons., 1849–54, and prod. his 1st operetta, *Le Docteur Miracle*, in 1857, having tied with Bizet in a competition organized by Offenbach. He did not make a great success until he prod. *Fleur de thé* in 1868 and until then supplemented his income by teaching and org. playing. After that he made a fortune with his many operettas.

Works incl. opera *Plutus*, operettas *Les Cent Vierges*, *La Fille de Madame Angot*, *Giroflé-Girofla*, *La Petite Mariée*, *Le Petit Duc*, *Camargo*, *Ninette*, *Barbe-bleue* and about 40 others; orchestral works; vln. and pf. sonata; sacred songs for women's voices *La Chapelle au couvent*; instrumental pieces; pf. works; songs, etc.

Leçon (Fr.). *See* **Lesson.**

Leçons des Tenèbres (Fr.), settings of the Lamentations of Jeremiah for perf. at matins on the last 3 days of Holy Week. *See* Lamentations.

Leconte de Lisle, Charles (1818–94), Fr. poet. *See* **Éolides** (Franck), **Massenet** (*Érynnies*), **Préludes** (Debussy, I. 8.).

5 songs by Fauré.

Ledger Lines. *See* **Leger Lines.**

Leduc, Simon (b. Paris, *c.* 1748; d. Paris, I. 1777), Fr. violinist, comp. and mus. pub. A pupil of Gaviniès, he was joint director (with the latter and Gossec) of the Concert spirituel from 1773. As a pub. he issued from 1767 works by himself and other comps.

Comps. incl. 3 vln. concertos; 3 symphs. and 2 *symphonies concertantes*; vln. sonatas and duets; trio sonatas, etc.

Ledwidge, William. *See* **Ludwig.**

Lee, Nathaniel (? 1653–92), Eng. playwright. *See* **Finger** (*Rival Queens*), **Galliard** (*Oedipus*), **Purcell** (*Oedipus*, *Massacre of Paris*, *Sophonisba* and *Theodosius*), **Staggins** (*Gloriana*).

Leeds Musical Festival, a triennial mus.

festival estab. at Leeds, on the opening of the new town hall, in 1858.

Leero Viol. *See* **Lyra Viol.**

Lees, Benjamin (b. Harbin, Manchuria, 8. I. 1924), Amer. comp. of Rus. parentage, brought to the U.S.A. as a child. He studied pf. in San Francisco and Los Angeles. After serving in the U.S. Army from 1942 to 1945, he studied at the Univ. of S. California, Los Angeles, theory, harmony and comp. with Halsey Stevens, Ingolf Dahl and Ernst Kanitz, also taking private lessons from George Antheil. In 1955 he won a Guggenheim Fellowship and in 1956 a Fulbright Fellowship.

Works incl. 3 symphs. (no. 3 for string 4tet and orch.); concertos for vln., ob. and pf. (2); *Profile* for orch., concerto for orch., *Declamations* for string orch. and pf.; *Visions of Poets*, a dramatic cantata; string 4tet, vln. sonata; pf. mus., etc.

Leeuw, Ton de (b. Rotterdam, 16. XI. 1926), Dutch comp. Studied comp. in Paris with Messiaen and Thomas de Hartmann. He became interested in mus. folklore and in 1961 toured India to collect material. His chief interest is in experimental mus.

Works incl. opera *De Droom* (*The Dream*); oratorio *Job*; 2 symphs. *Ombres* for orch. and perc.; concertos for pf. and vln.; concerto grosso for strings; string 4tet, string 6tet; sonatas for vln. and fl.; pf. mus., etc.

Lefébure-Wély, Louis (James Alfred) (b. Paris, 13. XI. 1817; d. Paris, 31. XII. 1869), Fr. organist and comp. Studied at the Paris Cons., but had already appeared as an infant prodigy before he entered it. He was organist of the Madeleine in 1847–57 and of Saint-Sulpice from 1863 to his death, but made his living mainly as a concert player.

Works incl. opera *Les Recruteurs*; Masses, canticles, offertories and *O Salutaris*; much org. mus.; pf. and harmonium pieces, etc.

Lefebvre, Charles (Édouard) (b. Paris, 19. VI. 1843; d. Aix-les-Bains, 8. IX. 1917), Fr. comp. Studied at the Paris Cons. and took the Prix de Rome in 1870. After his stay in Rome he travelled in the E. and in 1895 succeeded Godard as prof. of the ensemble class at the Cons.

Works incl. operas *Le Trésor*, *Zaïre*, *Djelma* and 2 others; 4 cantatas; symph. in D maj., *Ouverture dramatique* and *Toggenburg* overture, orchestral scenes *Dalila*; suite for wind instruments and other chamber mus., etc.

Left Hand, Pianoforte Works for. Such works have been written mainly as exercises for the L.H The right hand has not been thus cultivated by comps. because the left is more in need of practice, and also because it has the advantage of commanding the bass region of the pf., the notes of which can be sustained by the pedal while the hand moves on to play passages above. The following are exs. of L.H. pf. mus.:

Alkan, study.
Bortkievich, concerto, Op. 28.
Brahms, arr. of Bach's vln. chaconne.
Bridge (Frank), 3 improvisations.
Britten, diversion on a theme, with orch.
Brun, concerto.
Czerny, studies, Op. 399.
Gál, pf. 4tet.
Korngold, concerto.
Lipatti, 3 nocturnes and sonatina.
Pauer, E., suite, Op. 72.
Ravel, concerto.
Reger, 4 studies.
Rheinberger, 6 studies, Op. 113.
Saint-Saëns, 6 studies, Op. 135.
Skriabin, prelude and nocturne, Op. 9.
Strauss (R.) parergon to the *Symphonia Domestica*, with orch.
Tappert, 50 studies.
Walker (E.), variations with clar. and string trio.
Zichy, concerto in E♭, sonata and 6 studies.

Legato (It. = bound, tied). In mus. the word is used to designate a sustained manner of singing or playing, one note leading smoothly to the next.

Legend of Joseph, The, ballet by R. Strauss (scenario by Hugo von Hofmannsthal and Harry Kessler, choreography by Mikhail Mikhailovich Fokin), prod. Paris Opéra, 14. V. 1914.

Legend of the Invisible City of Kitezh and the Maiden Fevronia (*Skazhanie o nevidimom gradie Kitezh i dieve Fevronie*), opera by Rimsky-Korsakov (lib. by Vladimir Ivanovich Bielsky), prod. St. Petersburg, 20. II. 1907.

Legend of Tsar Saltan, The (*Skazka o Tsarie Saltanie*), opera by Rimsky-Korsakov (lib. by Vassily Ivanovich Bielsky, after Pushkin), prod. Moscow, 2. XI. 1900.

Légende de Saint Christophe, La, opera by d'Indy (lib. by comp.), prod. Paris, Opéra, 6. VI. 1920.

Legende von der heiligen Elizabeth, Die (*The Legend of St. Elizabeth of Hungary*), oratorio by Liszt (words by Otto Roquette), 1st perf., in Hung., Budapest, 15. VIII. 1865; 1st prod. as an opera, Weimar, 23. X. 1881.

Leger Lines, the short strokes drawn through or between those notes which go above or below the stave in mus. notation.

Leggenda di Sakuntala, La, opera by Alfano (lib. by comp., based on Kalidasa's play), prod. Bologna, Teatro Comunale, 10. XII. 1921.

Leggermente (It.), adv. of leggero.
Leggero, Leggiero (It.) = light, swift.
Leggiadro (It.) = elegant, graceful.

Leggieramente. *See* **Leggermente.** The word under this entry is used by Beethoven and others, but is not It.
Leggiero. *See* **Leggero.**
Legno. *See* **Col legno.**
Legouvé, Ernest (1807–1903), Fr. playwright. *See* **Adriana Lecouvreur** (Cilèa), **Gounod** (*Deux Reines*).
Legrant, Guillaume (b. ?, d. ?), Fr. or Flem. comp. Between 1419 and 1421 he was a member of the papal chapel. He wrote 3 *chansons*, a florid org. piece without title, and a very chromatic *Gloria-Credo* pair.
Legrant, Johannes (b. ?, d. ?), Fr. or Flem. composer, possibly a younger brother of prec. Nothing is known of his life, but several *chansons* and a little church mus. survive.
Legrenzi, Giovanni (b. Clusone nr. Bergamo, VIII. 1626; d. Venice, 26. V. 1690), It. comp. Organist at his birthplace, then *maestro di cappella* at Ferrara. In 1672 he became director of the Cons. dei Mendicanti at Venice and in 1685 *maestro di cappella* of St. Mark's there.
Works incl. operas *Achille in Sciro, Eteocle e Polinice, La divisione del mondo, Germanico sul Reno, Totila, I due Cesari, Il Giustino, Pertinace* and *c.* 10 others; Masses, motets, psalms and other church mus.; orchestral works; church sonatas, etc.
Legros, Joseph (b. Monampteuil nr. Laon, 7. IX. 1739; d. La Rochelle, 20. XII. 1793), Fr. tenor and concert manager. Made his operatic début in 1764 in Paris, and later became Gluck's principal tenor there. Forced by corpulence to abandon the stage in 1783, he turned to concert management.
Lehár, Ferencz (Franz) (b. Komárom, 30. IV. 1870; d. Ischl, 24. X. 1948), Hung. comp. Studied at the Prague Cons. and became a military bandmaster. Later he devoted himself entirely to the successful comp. of operettas. During his last years he lived in retirement at Ischl.
Works incl. opera *Kukuška* (later called *Tajana*), operettas *The Merry Widow, The Count of Luxembourg, Gypsy Love, The Three Graces, Pompadour, Springtime, Frasquita, Clo Clo, The Blue Mazurka, Frederica, The Land of Smiles* and many others; symph. poem *Fieber,* 3 comedy scenes for orch., etc.
Lehmann, Lilli (b. Würzburg, 24. XI. 1848; d. Berlin, 16. V. 1929), Ger. soprano. Studied under her mother, the singer and harpist Marie Loew, appeared at Prague as the 1st genie in Mozart's *Magic Flute* at an early age, was engaged at Danzig in 1868, at Leipzig in 1869, and made her 1st appearance in Berlin in 1870. In 1876 she 1st sang at the Wagner performances at Bayreuth and in 1880 1st visited London.

Lehmann, Liza (Elizabetta Nina Mary Frederika) (b. London, 11. VII. 1862; d. Pinner, Middlesex, 19. IX. 1918), Eng. singer and comp. Studied 1st with her mother, Amelia Chambers, an accomplished amateur comp. and later at Rome, Wiesbaden and at home with MacCunn, also singing with Randegger. In 1885 she made her 1st appearance as a singer at St. James's Hall, where she sang for the last time in 1894, when she married Herbert Bedford. The composer David Bedford is her grandson.
Works incl. light opera *The Vicar of Wakefield* (after Goldsmith), mus. comedy *Sergeant Brue* (L. Housman); incid. mus. for *Everyman* and other plays; ballads for voice and orch.; song cycles *In a Persian Garden* (Omar Khayyám), *In Memoriam* (Tennyson), *The Daisy-Chain, More Daisies, Songs of Love and Spring*; pf. pieces; songs, etc.

Lehmann, Lotte (b. Perleberg, 27. II. 1888), Ger. soprano. Studied in Berlin with Erna Tiedke, Eva Reinhold and Mathilde Mallinger, making her début in Hamburg in a small role. She soon estab. herself and in 1914 was engaged at the Vienna State Opera, where R. Strauss selected her to sing the Composer in *Ariadne auf Naxos* and Octavian in *Der Rosenkavalier*. Later she also sang the Marschallin in the latter opera, one of her greatest roles. She was a great Wagner singer and made her Amer. début in the role of Sieglinde in *Die Walküre*. In 1938 she settled in the U.S.A., living mostly in California. She has pub. a novel, an autobiog. and other writings on mus.

Lehrstück (Ger. = didactic piece, educational play), a small form of mus. drama cultivated in Ger. in the 1920s–1930s by Eisler, Hindemith, Weill and other comps., the chief literary exponent being Bert Brecht. It was cultivated mainly by the working classes in Ger. at first, though later the influence spread to other Eur. countries and to U.S.A. The L. makes use of hist. material and dialectical discussion for the purpose of enlightening the masses, and it was for a time a counteragent to the Nazi movement until its exponents were forced to emigrate.

Leibowitz, René (b. Warsaw, 17. II. 1913). Fr.-Pol. comp. Settled in Paris in 1926 and in 1930–3 studied in Ger. and Aus. with Schönberg and Webern. He destroyed all his works written up to 1937, incl. 6 string 4tets., and devoted himself entirely to 12-note mus. He cond. works of that school in U.S.A. in 1947–8. He is known as a leading teacher of 12-note comp. and has pub. *Schönberg et son école* and *Introduction à la musique de douze sons*.
Works incl. mus.-drama *La Nuit close*;

4 unaccomp. choruses; symph. and variations for orch.; chamber symph. for 12 instruments, chamber concerto for vln., pf. and 17 instruments, *Tourist Death* for soprano and chamber orch. *L'Explication des métaphores* for speaker, 2 pfs., harp and perc.; string 4tet, 10 canons for ob., clar. and bassoon, wind 5tet; vln. and pf. sonata; sonata and pieces for pf.; songs, etc.

Leicester, ou Le Château de Kenilworth, opera by Auber (lib. by Scribe and Anne Honoré Joseph Mélesville, based on Scott's *Kenilworth*), prod. Paris, Opéra-Comique, 25. I. 1823.

Leich (Ger., obs. = lay), a medieval type of Ger. song similar to the Fr. Lai.

Leichtentritt, Hugo (b. Pleszow, Posen, 1. I. 1874; d. Cambridge, Mass., 13. XI. 1951), Ger. musicologist. Studied with Paine at Harvard Univ. and later at the Hochschule für Musik in Berlin, where he became prof. at the Klindworth-Scharwenka Cons. In 1933 he left Ger. as a refugee from the Nazi régime and returned to U.S.A. to join the staff of Harvard Univ. His books incl. studies of Keiser, Handel, Chopin, Busoni, the motet, etc.

Leigh, Walter (b. London, 22. VI. 1905; d. nr. Tobruk, Libya, 12. VI. 1942), Eng. comp. Studied at Cambridge and with Hindemith in Berlin. In 1932 a work of his was perf. at the I.S.C.M. festival in Vienna. He joined up during World War II and was killed in action.
Works incl. comic operas *The Pride of the Regiment, The Jolly Roger*; pantomime *Aladdin*; revues *Nine Sharp* and *Little Revue, 1939*; incid. mus. to Aristophanes' *Frogs*, Shakespeare's *Midsummer Night's Dream*; overture *Agincourt, Mus. for String Orch.*, *3 Pieces for Amateur Orch.*; concertino for harpsichord and strings; 3 movements for string 4tet, trio for fl., ob. and pf. and sonatina for vla. and pf.; songs, etc.

Leighton, Kenneth (b. Wakefield, 2. X. 1929), Eng. comp. Studied at Queen's Coll., Oxford, and after winning the Mendelssohn Scholarship in 1951 with Petrassi in Rome. He has won several prizes for comp. Lecturer at Edinburgh Univ. 1956–68, and at Oxford Univ., 1968–70. Prof. at Edinburgh Univ. from 1970.
Works incl. symph. for strings; 3 pf. concertos, vln. concerto, cello concerto; string 4tet, 2 vln. sonatas; 3 pf. sonatas; choral works, etc.

Leighton, Sir William (b. ?; d. ?, 1616), gentleman pensioner under Elizabeth and James I. He pub. in 1614 a collection of airs for voices and instruments entitled *The Teares or Lamentacions of a Sorrowfull Soule* with contributions by Bull, Byrd,

Coperario, Dowland, A. Ferrabosco (jun.), Ford, O. Gibbons, Giles, Hooper, Robert Johnson, Robert Jones, Kindersley, Leighton, T. Lupo, John Milton (sen.), Peerson, Pilkington, John Ward, Weelkes and Wilbye.

Leila, opera by Bendl (lib., in Cz., by Eliška Krásnohorská, based on Bulwer-Lytton's novel), prod. Prague, Cz. Theatre, 4. I. 1868.

Leinsdorf, Erich (b. Vienna, 4. II. 1912), Aus., later Amer., cond. Studied with Paul Emerich and Hedwig Kammer-Rosenthal at the Vienna Gymnasium. In 1934 he became asst. to Bruno Walter and Toscanini at the Salzburg Festival and later appeared as a cond. in It., Fr. and Belg. In 1938 he was engaged as an asst. cond. at the N.Y. Metropolitan Opera, becoming chief cond. from 1939 to 1943. He served in the U.S. Army from 1944 and returned to the Metropolitan Opera, 1958–62.

Leite, Antonio da Silva. *See* **Silva Leite.**

Leitgeb. *See* **Leutgeb.**

Leitmotiv (Ger. lit. leading motif, plur. *Leitmotive*), a short theme assoc. with a personage, object or idea in an opera or other work, quoted at appropriate moments or worked up symphonically. Its chief exponent is Wagner, but it was not his invention, for it occurs in earlier comps. *See also* **Clari.**

Lekeu, Guillaume (b. Heusy nr. Verviers, 20. I. 1870; d. Angers, 21. I. 1894), Belg. comp. Studied with Franck and d'Indy in Paris. In 1891 he obtained the 2nd Belg. Prix de Rome with the lyric scene *Androméde.*

Works incl. symph. study on Shakespeare's *Hamlet, Fantaisie sur deux airs populaires angevins* for orch.; Adagio for string 4tet and orch.; Intro. and Adagio for brass; *Chant lyrique* for chorus and orch.; pf. 4tet (completed by d'Indy), pf. trio; vln. and pf. sonata, cello and pf. sonata (completed by d'Indy); 3 pf. pieces; *3 Poèmes* for voice and pf., etc.

Lélio, or Le Retour à la Vie (*L., or The Return to Life*), 'lyric monodrama' by Berlioz for an actor, solo voices, chorus, pf. and orch., Op. 14bis, comp. in 1831 as a sequel to the *Symphonie fantastique* and 1st perf. with the latter, Paris Cons., 9. XII. 1832.

Lemare, Edwin (Henry) (b. Ventnor, Isle of Wight, 9. IX. 1865; d. Los Angeles, 24. IX. 1934), Eng. organist and comp. Studied at the R.A.M. in London and after var. church apps. became organist of St. Margaret's, Westminster. In 1900 he toured in U.S.A., having by that time become a very successful concert organist. He was attached to the Carnegie Inst. at Pittsburg from 1902–15, was municipal

organist at San Francisco, 1917–21, and at Portland, Maine, from 1921.

Works incl. 2 symphs. for org. and a vast amount of other concert mus. for his instrument.

Lemierre, Antoine Marin (1723–93), Fr. poet and dramatist. *See* **Jessonda** (Spohr).

Lemlin (or **Lämmlein**), **Lorenz** (b. Eichstätt, Bavar. *c.* 1495; d. ? Heidelberg, ?), Ger. 16th-cent. singer and comp. He studied at Heidelberg Univ. and became singer and *Kapellmeister* to the elector palatine there.

Works incl. Lat. motets, Ger. songs, e.g. 'Ein Gutzgauch auf dem Zaune sass,' etc.

Lemmens, Nicolas Jacques (b. Zoerle-Parwijs, Westerloo, 3. I. 1823; d. Linterpoort nr. Malines, 30. I. 1881), Belg. organist, pianist and comp. Studied at the Brussels Cons. and with Hesse at Breslau. In 1849 he became org. prof. at the Brussels Cons., but after 1857, when he married Helen Sherrington, he lived much in Eng..

Works incl. sonata, offertories and other concert mus. for org., a treatise for accomp. of plainsong, etc.

Lemmens-Sherrington (*née* **Sherrington**), **Helen** (b. Preston, 4. X. 1834; d. Brussels, 9. V. 1906), Eng. soprano, wife of prec. Studied with Verhulst at Rotterdam and at the Brussels Cons., and made her 1st appearance in London in 1856.

Lemminkainen's Home-Faring, symph. legend by Sibelius, Op. 22, one of 4 on subjects from the *Kalevala,* comp. in 1893–5, 1st perf. Helsinki, 1896. The best known of the other three is *The Swan of Tuonela.*

Lemnitz, Tiana (b. Metz, 26. X. 1897), Ger. soprano. Studied in Metz and then at the Hoch Cons. in Frankfurt. She made her début in 1921 and from 1922 to 1929 sang at Aachen. From 1929 to 1933 she was the leading soprano at Hanover, and from 1934 to 1957 at the Berlin State Opera. She sang at Covent Garden in 1936 and 1938.

Lemoyne, Jean Baptiste (b. Eymet, Périgord, 3. IV. 1751; d. Paris, 30. XII. 1796), Fr. cond. and comp. Having cond. in the provinces, he went to Berlin to study with Graun, Kirnberger and Schulz, and was there app. 2nd *Kapellmeister* by Frederick the Great. But after visiting Warsaw he returned to Fr. and prod. in 1782 the opera *Électre* in the style of Gluck, whose pupil he claimed to be. When Gluck denied this, he joined the partisans of Piccinni .

Works incl. operas *Électre* (after Sophocles), *Phèdre* (after Racine), *Les Prétendus, Nephté,* etc.; ballets, etc.

Lenau, Nikolaus (Franz Niembsch von Strehlenau) (1802–50), Hung. poet who

wrote in Ger. *See* **Don Juan** (R. Strauss),
Liszt (*Faust*), **Rabaud** (*Procession nocturne*),
Schoeck (*Postillon* and songs).

Lendvai, Erwin (b. Budapest, 4. VI. 1882;
d. London, 31. III. 1949), Hung. comp.
Studied under Koessler at Budapest and
with Puccini at Milan, where he gained a
state prize. From 1913 he taught at Jaques-
Dalcroze's school at Hellerau nr. Dresden
and from 1919 to 1922 at the Klindworth-
Scharwenka Cons. in Berlin, later at
Hamburg, Munich, etc.

Works incl. opera *Elga* (after G.
Hauptmann); *Stimmen der Seele* for double
chorus, *Nippon* for female chorus, cycle
for male-voice chorus and baritone solo;
symph. in D maj., orch. scherzo *Masken*,
Archaic Dances for small orch.; string 4tet
in E min., 3 string trios, 5tet for wind
instruments; 4 pieces for cello and pf.; pf.
pieces; *Minnelieder* and other songs, etc.

Lenepveu, Charles (Ferdinand) (b. Rouen,
4. X. 1840; d. Paris, 16. VIII. 1910), Fr.
comp. 1st studied law in Paris, but after a
success with a cantata at Caen decided to
enter the Cons., where he worked under A.
Thomas. He won the Prix de Rome in
1865 and after his stay in Rome resumed
studies with the organist Charles Chauvet.
In 1880 he became teacher of harmony at
the Cons. and in 1894 prof. of comp.

Works incl. operas *Le Florentin* and
Velléda (after Chateaubriand's *Les
Martyrs*), lyric drama *Jeanne d'Arc* (for
perf. in Rouen Cathedral); 2 Requiems;
cantatas for the Société d'Agriculture et
de Commerce of Caen and *Renaud dans
les jardins d'Armide* (after Tasso); funeral
march for Henri Régnault, etc.

Lengyel, Menyhért (b. 1880), Hung.
playwright. *See* Bartók (*Miraculous Mandarin*), Szántó (*Typhoon*).

'Leningrad' Symphony, Shostakovich's
7th symph., Op. 60, awarded the Stalin
Prize in 1942 and 1st perf. Kuibishev, by
the evacuated Bolshoy Theatre Orch. of
Moscow, 5. III. 1942.

Lenormand, René (b. Elbeuf, 5. VIII.
1846; d. Paris, 3. XII. 1932), Fr. comp.
Intended for a commercial career, but
studied mus. with his mother and from
1868 with Damcke in Paris. He founded
a society for the cultivation of songs of all
nations and wrote a book on modern
harmony (with almost exclusively Fr. exs.).

Works incl. opera *Le Cachet rouge*;
mimed drama *La Nuit de juillet*; cantata
Souvenirs du Valais; *Le Voyage imaginaire*
and *2 Esquisses* on Malay themes for orch.;
Le Lahn de Mabed for vln. and orch.;
string 4tet, pf. trio; vln. pieces; pf. mus.;
c. 150 songs, etc.

Lento (It..) = slow.

Lenton, John (b. ?, 1656; d. London,
? *c.* 1719), Eng. violinist and comp. He
was a musician at court under Charles

II, William and Mary and Anne, pub.
an instruction book for the vln. containing airs of his own, revised the tunes
for Durfey's *Wit and Mirth* and contrib.
songs for var. collections.

Works incl. incid. mus. for Shakespeare's *Othello*, Otway's *Venice Preserved*,
Rowe's *Tamerlane* and *The Fair Penitent*
and other plays, etc.

Lenz, Wilhelm von (b. Riga, 1. VI. 1809;
d. St. Petersburg, 31. I. 1883), Latvian
statesman and writer on mus. Councillor
at St. Petersburg. Pub. 2 books on Beethoven, *Beethoven et ses trois styles* and
Beethoven: eine Kunststudie, as well as
studies of contemporary pf. virtuosi.

**Leo, Leonardo (Lionardo Oronzo Salva-
tore de)** (b. San Vito degli Schiavi, nr.
Brindisi, 5. VIII. 1694; d. Naples, 31. X.
1744), It. comp. Pupil of Provenzale and
Fago in Naples at the Cons. della Pietà dei
Turchini, 1709–13, where his first oratorio
was perf. in 1712. App. supernumerary
organist to the court in 1713, he rose to
become royal *maestro di cappella* just
before his death. As a teacher at the Cons.
della Pietà (from 1715, *maestro* 1741) and
the Cons. S. Onofrio (from 1725, *maestro*
1739) he incl. among his pupils Piccinni
and Jommelli.

Works incl. operas *Sofonisba*, *Lucio
Papirio*, *Caio Gracco*, *La 'mpeca scoperta*
(in Neapol. dialect), *Timocrate*, *Il trionfo di
Camilla*, *La semmeglianza di chi l'ha fatta*,
Il Cid, *Catone in Utica*, *La clemenza
di Tito*, *Demofoonte*, *Farnace*, *Siface*, *Ciro
riconosciuto*, *L'amico traditore*, *La sim-
patia del sangue*, *L'Olimpiade*, *Vologeso*,
Amor vuol sofferenza (*La finta Frascatana*),
Achille in Sciro, *Scipione nelle Spagne*,
Il fantastico (*Il nuovo Don Chisciotte*,
after Cervantes) and *c.* 40 others; oratorios
Il trionfo della castità di S. Alessio, *Dalla
morte alla vita*, *La morte di Abele*, *S.
Elena al Calvario*, *S. Francesco di Paola
nel deserto* and others; Masses, motets,
psalms and other church mus.; concerto
for 4 vlns., 6 cello concertos; harpischord
pieces, etc.

Léonard, Hubert (b. Bellaire, Belg., 7.
IV. 1819; d. Paris, 6. V. 1890), Belg.
violinist. Studied at the Paris Cons.
under Habeneck, made his 1st appearance
on tour in Ger., 1844, later became vln.
prof. at the Brussels Cons. and retired to
Paris in 1867.

Leonel. *See* **Power, Leonel.**

Leoncavallo, Ruggiero (b. Naples, 8.
III. 1858; d. Montecatini nr. Florence,
9. VIII. 1919), It. comp. Studied pf.
privately at first and then entered the
Naples Cons., which he left in 1876 with
a master diploma. He went to Bologna to
attend Carducci's lectures in lit. There he
was on the point of prod. his 1st opera,
Chatterton, but was swindled and found

himself penniless. He made a precarious living by lessons and playing the pf. at cafés, but later managed to travel as café pianist to Eng., Fr., Hol., Ger. and Egypt. He then began a trilogy on the It. Renaissance, *Crepusculum*, with *I Medici*, but never prod. the 2 following works, *Savonarola* and *Cesare Borgia*. In the meantime he made an enormous success with *Pagliacci* at Milan in 1892 and soon all over It. *La Bohème* at Venice in 1897 suffered from the appearance of Puccini's work on the same subject, and in spite of a commission for a Ger. opera for Berlin, *Der Roland von Berlin*, in 1904, he never repeated his *Pagliacci* success. He wrote all his own libs. and some for other comps.

Works incl. operas *Chatterton* (after Alfred de Vigny), *I Medici*, *Pagliacci*, *La Bohème* (after Murger), *Zaza*, *Der Roland von Berlin* (after Willibald Alexis), *Maia*, *Gli zingari*, *Goffredo Mameli*, *Edipo rè* (after Sophocles), *Tormenta* (unfinished); operettas *A chi la giarettiera*, *Il primo bacio*, *Malbruk*, *La reginetta delle rose*, *Are you there?*, *La candidata* and *Prestami tua moglie*; ballet *La vita d'una marionetta*; symph. poem *Serafita* (after Balzac's novel), etc.

Leoni, Leone (b. ?; d. Vicenza, ?), It. 16th–17th-cent. comp. *Maestro di cappella* of Vicenza Cathedral from c. 1588. Works incl. Masses, motets (some in many parts with instruments), *Sacrae cantiones*, psalms, Magnificats and other church mus.; sacred and secular madrigals, etc.

Léonin (Leoninus), Fr. comp. (late 12th cent.) at Notre Dame, Paris. He is the reputed author of a *Magnus Liber* containing Organa. He was succeeded by Pérotin.

Leonora, ossia L'amore conjugale (*Leonora, or Wedded Love*), opera by Paer (lib. by ? Giacomo Cinti, based on Bouilly's lib. for Gaveaux), prod. Dresden, 3. X. 1804.

Leonora Overtures (Beethoven). *See Fidelio.*

Léonore, ou L'Amour conjugal (*Leonora, or Wedded Love*), opera by Gaveaux (lib. by Jean Nicolas Bouilly, based on a real event), prod. Paris, Théâtre Feydeau, 19. II. 1798. A forerunner and model of Beethoven's *Fidelio*.

Leonova, Daria (Mikhailovna) (b. Vyshny-Volotchok, 9. III. 1829; d. St. Petersburg, 6. II. 1896), Rus. contralto. Pupil of Glinka; made her 1st appearance at St. Petersburg in his *Life for the Tsar* in 1852. She helped Mussorgsky towards the end of his life by engaging him as pianist on a tour in S. Rus. and at her singing-school at St. Petersburg.

Leopardi, Giacomo (1798–1837), It.

poet. *See* **Davies (P. M.)** (motets), **Goehler** (cantatas), **Malipiero** (*Commiato*).

Leopold I (1640–1705), emperor, comp. an opera, *Apollo deluso*, to a lib. by his court musician Antonio Draghi, 1669, and contrib. to numerous other operas by the same comp.

Leopolita, Martinus (Marcin Lwowczyk) (b. Lwów, c. 1540; d. Lwów, 1589), Pol. comp. Member of the Coll. of Roratists and court comp. at Cracow from 1560. Works incl. Masses (e.g. *Missa Paschalis*), motets; secular songs for several voices, etc.

Lepetit, Nino (Ninot) (b. ?, d. ?), 15th-cent. Fr. comp. His sacred and secular mus. appears in the pubs. of Petrucci as well as in MSS. He wrote *chansons* and motets.

L'Épine, (Francesca) Margherita de (b. ?; d. ?, 9–10. VIII. 1746), Fr. or Fr.-It. soprano. She settled in Eng. in 1692, and married Pepusch in 1718.

Lermontov, Mikhail Yurevich (1814–1841), Rus. poet and novelist. *See* Assafiev (*The Treasurer's Wife*), Blaramberg (*Demon*), Catoire (*Mtsyrí*) Cui (songs), Demon (Rubinstein), Gilson (*Demon*), Ippolitov-Ivanov (*Mtsyrí*), Khatchaturian (*Masquerade*), Koreshtchenko (*Angel of Death*), Mossolov (songs), Nápravník (*Tamara* and *Demon*), Rogowski (*Tamara*), Senilov (*Mtsyrí*), Shebalin (*Masquerade*), Spendiarov (*3 Palm Trees*), Tamara (*Balakirev*).

Lero Viol. *See* **Lyra Viol.**

Leroux, Xavier (Henri Napoléon) (b. Velletri, It., 11. X. 1863; d. Paris, 2. II. 1919), Fr. comp. Studied at the Paris Cons., among his masters being Massenet, and gained the Prix de Rome in 1885. He became harmony prof. there in 1896 and ed. the periodical *Musica*.

Works incl. operas *Évangeline*, *Astarté*, *La Reine Fiammette* (after Catulle Mendès), *William Ratcliff* (after Heine), *Théodora*, *Le Chemineau*, *Le Carillonneur*, *La Fille de Figaro*, *Les Cadeaux de Noël*, *1814*, *Nausithoé*, *La Plus Forte*, *L'Ingénu*; incid. mus. to Sardou and Moreau's *Cléopâtre*, Aeschylus's *The Persians* and Richepin's *Xantho chez les courtisanes*; cantatas *Endymion* and *Vénus et Adonis*; overture *Harald*; Mass with orch.; motets; numerous songs, etc.

Lesage, Alain René (1668–1747), Fr. novelist. *See* Caverne (Lesueur). **Françaix** (*Diable boiteux*), **Rencontre imprévue** (Gluck), **Satanella** (Balfe), **Semet** (*Gil Blas*).

Leschetizky, Theodor (b. Łańcut, Pol., 22. VI. 1830: d. Dresden, 14. XI. 1915), Pol.-Aus. pianist, teacher and comp. Pupil of Czerny and Sechter in Vienna. He was pf. prof. at St. Petersburg Cons., 1852–78, and then settled in Vienna as an

independent teacher of many famous pupils, incl. Paderewski.
Works incl. opera *Die erste Falte,* many pf. pieces, etc.

L'Escurel, Jehannot de (b. ?; d. prob. 1303), Fr. comp. His 34 secular works, all but one of which are monophonic, were incorporated into the *Roman de Fauvel* (*see* Fauvel).

Leskov, Nikolai Semenovich (1831–95), Rus. novelist. *See* Lady Macbeth of the Mtsensk District (Shostakovich).

Lessel, Franz (Franciszek) (b. Puławy, *c.* 1780; d. Piotrków, 26. XII. 1838), Pol.-Aus. comp. Studied medicine in Vienna, but became a pupil of Haydn, whom he looked after until his death. He then returned to Pol. and lived with Prince Czartoryski's family until they were driven away by the Revolution. The rest of his life was unsettled.
Works incl. Masses, Requiem and other church mus.; symphs.; pf. concerto; chamber mus.; pf. sonatas and fantasies, etc.

Lesson, a 17th–18th-cent. term for a keyboard piece, generally of an instructive character.

Lesueur, Jean François (b. Drucat-Plessiel nr. Abbeville, 15. II. 1760; d. Paris, 6. X. 1837), Fr. comp. He 1st learnt mus. as a choir-boy at Abbeville, then held church appts. at Amiens and Paris. After 1781 he became *maître de chapelle* successively at Dijon Cathedral, Le Mans, Tours, SS. Innocents, Paris, 1784, and Notre-Dame, Paris, 1786. He was allowed to use a full orch. at Mass and to open the proceedings with an overture. This aroused a controversy which led to his resignation, and he spent 1788–92 in the country, devoted to the comp. of operas. In 1793 he was app. prof. at the school of the Nat. Guard and in 1795 one of the inspectors at the newly opened Cons. In 1804 he succeeded Paisiello as *maître de chapelle* to Napoleon, after whose fall he was app. superintendent and comp. to the chapel of Louis XVIII. In 1818 he became prof. of comp. at the Cons., where his pupils incl. Berlioz and Gounod.
Works incl. operas *Télémaque, La Caverne, Paulin et Virginie* (after Saint-Pierre), *Ossian, ou Les Bardes, Le Triomphe de Trajan* (with Persuis), *La Mort d'Adam* (after Klopstock) and some others; Mass and Te Deum for Napoleon's coronation, 3 Solemn Masses, *Stabat Mater,* motets, psalms and other church mus.; oratorios *Messe de Noël, Debora, Rachel, Ruth et Noémi, Ruth et Boaz;* cantatas, etc.

Lesur, Daniel (b. Paris, 19. XI. 1908), Fr. organist and comp. Pupil of Tournemire, Caussade and others. In 1938 he became prof. of counterpoint at the

Schola Cantorum in Paris. He was also app. organist at the Benedictine abbey, and with Baudrier, Jolivet and Messiaen formed the group known as 'La Jeune France'.
Works incl. *Suite française* for orch.; *Passacaille* for pf. and orch.; suite for string trio and pf.; 3 Heine songs for voice and string 4tet; *Noëls* and suite *Le Carillon* for pf.; *La Vie intérieure* for org.; songs, etc.

Letters, Music based on. Comps. have sometimes amused themselves by turning names or other words into notes representing in mus. nomenclature the letters of which they are formed, or as many as can be thus used. In Eng. the letters A to G can be thus represented; in Ger. H (= B♮) and S (Es = E♭) can be added, and in Fr. and It. the syllables Do, Re, Mi, Fa, Sol, La, Si may be used. In Fr. a system was devised for the works on the names of Fauré and Haydn listed below, whereby the notes A to G were followed by further 8ves named from H onwards. Here are some exs.:

Abegg (supposed friends of Schumann's): Schumann, *Variations on the Name of A.* for pf., Op. 1.

Asch (the birthplace of Ernestine von Fricken): Schumann, *Carnaval* for pf. Op. 9.

Bach. *See* B.A.C.H., *also* Faber *below.*

Bamberg (the maiden name of Cui's wife): Cui, scherzo for pf. duet (on B. A. B. E. G. and C. C. = César Cui).

Belaiev: Borodin, Glazunov, Liadov and Rimsky-Korsakov, string 4tet on 'B-la-F.'

Faber: canon in 7 parts by Bach, dated 1. III. 1749, sung over a Ground or *Pes* on the notes F. A. B(♭). E. and marked 'F A B E Repetatur,' thus forming the name Faber, which may be a Lat. form of some Ger. surname derived from some kind of manual labour. The canon also bears an inscription in Lat. containing the following acrostics on the names of Faber and Bach: 'Fidelis Amici Beatum Esse Recordari' and 'Bonae Artis Cultorem Habeas.' *See also* B.A.C.H.

Fauré: pieces by Aubert, Enesco, Koechlin, Ladmirault, Ravel, Roger-Ducasse and Schmitt contrib. to a Fauré number of the *Revue musicale* in 1924.

Gade: Schumann's pf. piece so entitled in *Album für die Jugend.* Rheinberger, fughetta for org.

Gedge: Elgar, allegretto for vln. and pf. on G.E.D.G.E., ded. to the Misses Gedge.

Haydn: Ravel, *Menuet sur le nom d'Haydn* for pf.

Sacha: Glazunov, *Suite sur le thème du nom diminutif russe* for pf., Op. 2.

Schumann (letters S. C. H. A. only): Schumann, *Carnaval* (inversion of the letters A. S. C. H.).

Leutgeb (or Leitgeb), Ignaz (b. ?; d. Vienna, 27. II. 1811), Aus. horn-player. He was 1st horn in the orch. of the Archbishop of Salzburg, then settled in Vienna as a cheese merchant. Mozart wrote his 4 horn concertos and the horn 5tet for him.

Leva, Enrico de (b. Naples, 19. I. 1867; d. Naples, 28. VII. 1955), It. comp. and singing-teacher. Studied at the Naples Cons. and in 1907 became director of the Istituto dei SS. Giuseppe e Lucia there.

Works incl. opera *La Camargo*; settings of poems from d'Annunzio's *Gioconda*; serenade *A Capomonte* and a very large number of light and popular songs in the Neapol. folksong manner.

Levadé, Charles Gaston (b. Paris, 3. I. 1869; d. Paris, 27. X. 1948), Fr. comp. Studied under Massenet at the Paris Cons.

Works incl. operas *L'Amour d'Héliodore*, *Les Hérétiques*, *La Rôtisserie de la Reine Pédauque* (after Anatole France), *La Peau de chagrin* (after Balzac); pantomime *Cœur de Margot*; suites, *Prélude religieux* etc. for orch.; chamber mus.; pf. pieces; songs; etc.

Levasseur, Nicolas (Prosper) (b. Bresles, Oise, 9. III. 1791; d. Paris, 6. XII. 1871), Fr. bass. Studied at the Paris Cons. and made his 1st stage appearance in 1813.

Levasseur, Rosalie (Marie Claude Josephe) (b. Valenciennes, 8. X. 1749; d. Neuwied-on-Rhine, 6. V. 1826), Fr. soprano. Sang at the Paris Opéra from 1766, and in the 1770s had great success in Gluck's Paris operas.

Leveridge, Richard (b. London, *c.* 1670; d. London, 22. III. 1758), Eng. bass and comp. He appeared as a singer mainly in pantomimes etc., but also in It. opera, his career extending from 1695 to 1751. As a comp. he is remembered for his songs.

Works incl. incid. mus. for Shakespeare's *Macbeth*, Farquhar's *The Recruiting Officer*, *Love and a Bottle* and (with D. Purcell) *The Constant Couple*, Vanbrugh's *Aesop* and other plays; masque *Pyramus and Thisbe* (after Shakespeare); songs, e.g. 'The Roast Beef of Old England', etc.

Levey (actually O'Shaughnessy), **Richard Michael** (b. Dublin, 25. X. 1811; d. Dublin, 28. VI. 1899), Ir. violinist, cond. and comp. He entered the orch. of the Theatre Royal at Dublin in 1826, for which he comp. 50 overtures and arr. mus. for 44 pantomimes. He was one of the founders of the R.Ir.A.M. in 1850.

Levi, Hermann (b. Giessen, 7. XI. 1839; d. Munich, 13. V. 1900) Ger. cond. Studied with V. Lachner at Munich and at the Leipzig Cons. After var. appts. he became director of the Munich court theatre, 1872–96. Cond. the 1st perf. of Wagner's *Parsifal* at Bayreuth.

Levidis, Dimitri (b. Athens, 8. IV. 1886; d. Athens, 30. V. 1951), Gk. comp. Studied at the Athens Cons., at the Munich Acad. and with Dénéréaz in Switz. He settled in Fr. and became naturalized in 1929. Some of his comps. make use of the Ondes Musicales invented by Martenot.

Works incl. ballet *Le Pâtre et la nymphe*; *Roubayyat Persans* (after Omar Khayyám) and *Sirène* for orch.; *Poème* for pf., vln. and orch.; symph. poem for O. M.; *De profundis* for voice and 2 O. M., etc.

Levitsky, Misha (b. Krementchug, 25. V. 1898; d. Avon-by-the-Sea, N.J., 2. I. 1941), Rus. pianist and comp. Studied at Warsaw, went to U.S.A. in 1906 and continued his studies under Stojowski in N.Y., later with Dohnányi in Berlin, 1911–15.

Works incl. many pf. pieces, cadenza for Beethoven's C min. pf. concerto, etc.

Levy, Alexandre (b. São Paulo, 10. XI. 1864; d. São Paulo, 17. I. 1892), Brazil. pianist and comp. Pupil of E. Durand in Paris.

Works incl. *Suite brasileira* for orch., Variations on a Brazil. theme for pf., etc.

Lewis, Anthony (Carey) (b. Bermuda, 2. III. 1915). Eng. musicologist and comp. Educ. at Wellington Coll. and Cambridge, he studied mus. at the latter, at the R.C.M. in London and with Nadia Boulanger in Paris. He was on the mus. staff of the B.B.C. in 1935–47 (except during his war service in 1939–45), organizing var. series of mus. incl. finally the mus. on the 3rd Programme. From 1947 to 1968 he was Prof. of Mus. at Birmingham Univ. and in 1968 was app. principal of the R.A.M. in London.

Works incl. *Choral Overture* for unaccomp. voices; *Elegy and Capriccio* for tpt. and orch.; horn concerto, etc.

Lewis, C(ecil). Day (b. 1904), Eng. poet. *See* Rawsthorne (*Enemy Speaks*).

Lewis, Matthew Gregory (1775–1818), Eng. novelist and playwright. *See* Busby (*Rugantino*), Kelly (*Castle Spectre*).

Lewis, Richard (b. Manchester, 10. V. 1914), Eng. tenor. Studied privately with T. W. Evans at the Royal Manchester Coll. of Mus. and later at the R.A.M. with Norman Allin. He made his début in the Glyndebourne chorus in 1947. In the same year he also sang at Covent Garden. He has a wide range of roles, both modern and classical.

Ley, Henry G(eorge). (b. Chagford, Devon, 30. XII. 1887; d. 24. VIII. 1962), Eng. organist and cond. Studied at Keble Coll., Oxford, and was app. organist at Christ Church Cathedral there in 1909. Later taught org. at the R.C.M. in London. Director of mus. at Eton Coll. from 1926 to 1945.

Works incl. church mus.; variations on a theme by Handel for orch.; chamber mus.; org. mus.; songs, etc.

L'Héritier, Jean (b. ?; d. ?), Fr. comp. Pupil of Josquin Desprez. Wrote Masses, motets, etc.

Lhermite, Tristan (orig. François) (*c.* 1601–55), Fr. poet. See **Debussy** (*Promenoir des deux amants*).

Lhévinne, Josef (b. Orel, 13. XII. 1874; d. N.Y., 2. XII. 1944), Rus. pianist. After some study at home he entered the Moscow Cons. and studied with Safonov, playing Beethoven's 5th piano concerto at the age of 15. He graduated in 1891 and in 1895 won the Rubinstein Prize. From 1900 to 1902 he taught at the Tiflis Cons. and in 1902–6 at the Cons. in Moscow. He made many tours and from 1907 to 1919 lived mostly in Berlin. He went to the U.S.A. in 1919 and taught at the Juilliard Graduate School. He had an impeccable technique and a profound understanding of mus.

L'Homme armé. See **Homme armé.**

Lhotka, Fran (b. Vožice, 25. XII. 1883; d. Zagreb, 26. I. 1962), Yugoslav comp. Studied at the Prague Cons. with Dvořák, Janáček and others, and went to Rus. as prof. at the Cons. of Ekaterinoslav. He then joined the Opera at Zagreb and later became prof. and in 1948 director of the Acad. of Mus. there, also cond. of a choral society.

Works incl. operas *Minka* and *The Sea*; ballets *The Devil at the Village* and *A Medieval Love*; symph., scherzo, Yugoslav capriccio and *Reveille of the Trenks Soldiers* for orch.; vln. concerto; chamber mus.; choruses; songs. etc.

Li-Tai-Po (or **Li-Po**) (705–62), Chin. poet. See **Lambert (C.)** (songs), **Lied von der Erde** (Mahler), **Morning Heroes** (Bliss).

Liadov, Anatol (Constantinovich) (b. St. Petersburg, 11. V. 1855; d. Novgorod, 28. VIII. 1914), Rus. comp. Studied under his father and later with Rimsky-Korsakov at the St. Petersburg Cons., where he became a teacher in 1878. The Imp. Geographical Society commissioned him, with Balakirev and Liapunov, to collect folksongs in var. parts of the country.

Works incl. symph. poems *Baba Yaga*, *The Enchanted Lake*, *Kikimora*, 2 orch. scherzos, *The Inn-Mazurka*, Polonaise in Memory of Pushkin for orch.; choral settings from Schiller's *Bride of Messina* and Maeterlinck's *Sœur Béatrice*, 3 choral works for female voices; *c.* 40 op. nos. of pf. pieces, incl. *Birulki* (*Spillikins*), ballads *From Days of Old*, *Marionettes*, *Musical Snuff-Box*, variations on a theme by Glinka and on a Pol. song, *From the Book of Revelation*, studies, preludes, mazurkas, etc.; songs, folksong settings, etc.

Liapunov, Sergey Mikhailovich (b. Yaroslav, 30. XI. 1859; d. Paris, 8. XI. 1924), Rus. pianist and comp. Studied at Nizhny-Novgorod and at the Moscow Cons. In 1893 the Imp. Geographical Society commissioned him, with Balakirev and Liadov, to collect folksongs. From 1891 to 1902 he was asst. director of the Imp. Chapel, and from 1910 prof. at the St. Petersburg Cons. He took refuge in Paris from the Revolution.

Works incl. 2 symphs., *Ballad, Solemn Overture*, Polonaise and symph. poem *Hashish* for orch.; 2 pf. concertos, rhapsody on Ukrainian themes for pf. and orch.; numerous pf. pieces, incl. suite *Christmas Songs*, etc.; folksong settings, etc.

Liatoshinsky, Boris Nikolaievich (b. Zhitomir, 16. I. 1895), Rus. comp. He played pf. and vln. and attempted comp. as a child and in 1913 was sent to the Kiev Cons., where he studied with Glière, remaining until 1918, having studied law at the univ. at the same time. From 1920 he was prof. of comp. at Kiev and Moscow.

Works incl. operas *The Golden Hoop* and *Shtchors*; film mus.; solemn cantata for chorus and orch. for Stalin's 60th birthday; 3 symphs., overture on Ukrainian themes, *Fantastic March* and other orchestral works; 4 string 4tets, pf. trio; vln. and pf. sonata; 2 pf. sonatas and other pf. works; songs, Ukrainian folksong arrs., etc.

Liberati, Antimo (b. Foligno, 3. IV. 1617; d. Rome, 24. II. 1692), It. singer, organist and comp. Pupil of Allegri and Benevoli in Rome, where in 1661 he became a singer in the Papal Chapel (and later *maestro di cappella*) and organist at 2 churches. He wrote a letter giving particulars for Palestrina's biog. and another defending a passage in Corelli.

Works incl. oratorios, madrigals, arias, etc.

Libert, Henri (b. Paris, 15. XII. 1869; d. Paris, 14. I. 1937), Fr. organist and comp. Studied at the Paris Cons., where Franck, Widor and Massenet were among his masters. He was app. organist at the church of Saint-Denis and prof. at the Amer. Cons. at Fontainebleau.

Works incl. motets; *Variations symphoniques, Chorals, Préludes et Fugues* and many other org. works; pf. pieces, etc.

Liberté, '14 tableaux inspirés par l'histoire du peuple de France,' mus. by Delannoy, Honegger, Ibert, Lazarus, Milhaud, Roland-Manuel, Rosenthal, Tailleferre and others, prod. Paris, Théâtre des Champs-Élysées, V. 1937.

Librettist, the author of a lib.

Libretto (It. = booklet), the text of an opera or other vocal work in dramatic form.

Libuše, opera by Smetana (lib., in Ger.,

by Joseph Wenzig, Cz. trans. by Ervín Špindler), prod. Prague, Cz. Theatre, 11. VI. 1881.

Licenza (It., plur. *licenze*) = licence, freedom, liberty, e.g. the direction *con alcune licenze* = 'with some freedom' (in form, style or perf.); up to the 18th cent., a cadenza or ornament inserted at the perf.'s discretion and not written down by the comp.; also, in 17th-cent. opera, esp. in Vienna, a mus. epilogue to a stage perf. with special reference to the occasion (royal birthday, wedding, etc.).

Lichard, Milan (b. Uhorská Skalica, Slovakia, 24. II. 1853; d. Užhorod, 21. IV. 1935). Cz. comp. While under Hung. rule he worked as a railway official, but cultivated mus. as best he could. Later took to comp. and folksong collecting. For a time he was imprisoned as a rebel.

Works incl. *The Lark, Praise to Thee*, 2 funeral odes, etc., for chorus; rhapsody for orch.; songs; folksong arrs. incl. *Garlands of Popular Song*, etc.

Lichfild, Henry (b. ?; d. ?), Eng. 16th–17th-cent. (? amateur) comp. He was in some capacity in the household of Lord, and later Lady, Cheney at Toddington House nr. Luton. Wrote madrigals.

Lickl, Johann Georg (b. Korneuburg, 11. IV. 1769; d. Pécs, 12. V. 1843), Aus. comp. He wrote several mus. plays for Schikaneder's theatre.

Works incl. plays with mus.; Masses, motets; chamber mus., etc.

Lidarti, Christian Joseph (b. Vienna, 23. II. 1730; d. Pisa, after 1793), Aus.-It. comp. Pupil of his uncle, Bonno, in Vienna and later of Jommelli in It. In the service of the Cavalieri di S. Stefano in Pisa, 1757–1784.

Works incl. trio sonatas, catches and glees, etc.

Lidholm, Ingvar (b. Jönköping, 24. II. 1921), Swed. comp. Studied at the Stockholm Cons. with, among others, Hilding Rosenberg and Tor Mann. Later he studied in It., Fr. and Switz., and also with Seiber. From 1947 to 1956 he was cond. of the Örebro Symph. Orch.

Works incl. concerto for string orch., *Toccata e canto* for chamber orch., *Ritornell* for orch.; concertino for fl., cor anglais, ob. and bassoon; *Cantata* for baritone and orch.; string 4tet, 4 pieces for cello and pf., sonata for solo fl.

Lidl, Andreas (b. Vienna, *c.* 1740; d. ? London, ?), Aus. barytone virtuoso and comp. He increased the strings on his instrument, travelled much on the Continent and 1st appeared in London in 1778.

Works incl. chamber mus.; pieces for the barytone, etc.

Lie-Nissen, Erika (b. Kongsvinger, 17. I. 1845; d. Christiania, 27. X. 1903), Norw. pianist. Pupil of Kjerulf at Christiania,

Kullak in Berlin and Tellefsen in Paris. She was app. prof. of pf. at the Copenhagen Cons. in 1870, but 4 years later married Dr. Oscar Nissen and settled at Christiania.

Lie, Sigurd (b. Drammen, 23. V. 1871; d. Vestre Aker, 30. IX. 1904), Norw. cond., violinist and comp. Studied at the Leipzig Cons. and in 1894 became choral and theatre cond. at Bergen. After further study in Berlin he became choral cond. at Christiania.

Works incl. symph. in A min., *Orientalisk Suite*, *Marche symphonique* for orch.; cantatas and other choral works; pf. 5tet; songs, etc.

Liebe der Danae, Die (*Danae's Love*), opera by R. Strauss (lib. by Josef Gregor), intended for prod. at the Salzburg Festival, 1. VIII. 1944, but postponed owing to war; prod. there 14. VIII. 1952. The title was orig. *Der Kuss der Danae* (*D.'s Kiss*).

Liebe im Narrenhaus, Die (*Love in the Madhouse*), opera by Dittersdorf (lib. by Gottlieb Stephanie, jun.), prod. Vienna, Kärntnertortheater, 12. IV. 1787.

Liebenthaler, Marie. *See* Wilt.

Liebermann, Rolf (b. Zürich, 14. IX. 1919), Swiss comp. Studied cond. with Scherchen and comp. with Vladmir Vogel at Zürich, and was later app. to the staff of Radio-Zürich. Some of his work is based on the 12-note system.

Works incl. operas *Leonore 40/45*, *Penelope* and *School for Wives* (after Molière); incid. mus., film mus.,; cantata *Streitlied zwischen Leben und Tod*; polyphonic studies and folksong suite for orch.; concerto for jazz band and orch.; solo cantatas *Une des fins du monde* (Giraudoux), *Chinesische Liebeslieder* (Klabund) and *Chinesisches Lied* (do.), pf. sonata, etc.

Liebert, Reginaldus (b. ?, d. ?), early 15th-cent. Fr. comp. He prob. succeeded Grenon at Cambrai in 1424. His main work is a complete Mass (Ordinary and Proper) of the Blessed Virgin Mary for 3 voices. A Gautier Liebert, composer of 3 *rondeaux*, was a papal singer in 1428.

Liebeslieder (*Love Songs*), a set of waltzes by Brahms for pf. duet with solo vocal quartet *ad lib.*, Op. 52, comp. in 1869. There is a 2nd set of *Neue Liebeslieder*, Op. 65, written in 1874.

Liebesverbot, Das, oder Die Novize von Palermo (*The Love-Ban, or The Novice of P.*), opera by Wagner (lib. by comp., based on Shakespeare's *Measure for Measure*), prod. Magdeburg, 29. III. 1836.

Lieblich Flute (*lieblich*, Ger. = lovely, sweet), a 4-ft. org. stop, the upper range of Lieblich gedackt.

Lieblich gedackt (Ger. lit. 'lovely and covered', earlier *gedact* or *gedakt*), an old name for an 8-ft. org. stop, used in Eng.

Lied

as well as Ger., governing a range of stopped diapason pipes.

Lied (Ger.) = Song.

Lied von der Erde, Das (*The Song of the Earth*), symph. for mezzo-soprano, tenor and orch. by Mahler (so called by the comp., but not numbered among his other symphs.). The words are from Hans Bethge's anthol. of Ger. transs. of Chin. poetry, *Die chinesische Flöte*: 1. (Li-Tai-Po). *Das Trinklied vom Jammer der Erde* (*The Drinking-Song of Earth's Misery*); 2. (Tchang-Tsi) *Der Einsame im Herbst* (*The Lonely One in Autumn*); 3. (Li-Tai-Po) *Von der Jugend* (*Of Youth*): 4. (do.) *Von der Schönheit* (*Of Beauty*); 5. (do.) *Der Trunkene im Frühling* (*The Toper in Spring*); 6. (Mong-Kao-Yen and Wang-Wei) *Der Abschied* (*The Farewell*). Comp. in 1908; 1st perf. Munich, 20. XI. 1911, after Mahler's death.

Lieder ohne Worte, 36 pf. pieces by Mendelssohn in the form and character of songs exploiting the principle of accomp. melody rather than polyphonic textures. Vol. I, Op. 19, Nos. 1–6 (1830–2); II, Op. 30, 7–12 (1833–7); III, Op. 38, 13–18 (1836–7); IV, Op. 53, 19–24 (1841); V. Op. 62, 25–30 (1842–3); VI, Op. 67, 31–6 (1843–5). The only titles which are Mendelssohn's own are those of the 3 *Venezianische Gondellieder* (*Venetian Barcarolles*), Nos. 6, 12 and 29, the *Duetto*, No. 18, and the *Volkslied*, No. 23.

Liederkreis (Ger.). *See Song Cycle.*

Liederspiel (Ger. lit. 'song-play'), a play with songs similar to the *Singspiel*. The term was 1st used by Reichardt in 1800. It may also mean 'song cycle', e.g. Schumann's *Spanisches L.*

Liedertafel (Ger. lit. 'song-table' or 'singing-table'), a male-voice choral assoc. doubtless deriving its name from early gatherings seated round a table drinking and singing.

Lier, Bertus van (b. Utrecht, 10. IX. 1906), Dutch cellist, cond., critic and comp. Studied at the Amsterdam Cons., Pijper being his comp. master, and later learnt cond. from Scherchen at Strasbourg. Became mus. critic at Amsterdam, cond. of amateur orchs. and prof. at the Utrecht Cons.

Works incl. incid. mus. to Sophocles' *Ajax* and *Antigone*; 3 symphs.; concertino for cello and chamber orch.; bassoon concerto; chamber mus.; unaccomp. choruses; declamation with orch. *The Duke*, etc.

Lieto (It.) = joyous, joyful.

Life for the Tsar, A (*Zhizn za Tsaria*; now *Ivan Sussanin*), opera by Glinka (lib. by Georgy Fedorovich Rosen), prod. St. Petersburg, 9. XII. 1836.

Ligature(s), a group of 2 or more notes in medieval and Renaissance mus. Also the var. signs, originating in plain-

Lilien

song notation, by which such groups are indicated, e.g.:

Modern equivalent

Ligeti, György (b. Dicsöszentmarton, Transylvania, 28. V. 1923), Hung. comp. Studied comp. with Sándor Veress and Ferenc Farkas at the Budapest Mus. Acad. (1945–9), becoming an instructor there from 1950 to 1956. In 1956 he went to the Studio for Electronic Mus. at Cologne, and in 1959 was app. instructor at the International Courses for New Mus. at Darmstadt. In 1961 he was visiting prof. of comp. at the Stockholm Mus. Acad., and eventually settled in Vienna. His mature mus. is experimental in nature.

Works incl. *Artikulation* for electronic sounds; *Apparitions* for orch.; *Atmospheres* for large orch.; *Poème symphonique* for 100 metronomes; *Aventures* for soprano, alto and baritone with 7 instruments; *Nouvelles Aventures*, for soprano and 7 instruments; Requiem for soloists, chorus and orch.; *Lux aeterna* for 16 solo voices; cello concerto; 2 string 4tets, 2 wind 5tets, etc.

Lilac Time, the Eng. version, made by Clutsam in 1922, of the operetta *Das Dreimäderlhaus* by Berté (lib. by Willner and Reichert), prod. (Ger. orig.) Vienna, Raimund-Theater, 15. I. 1916; *L. T.* prod. London, 22. XII. 1922.

Lilien, Ignace (b. Limburg, 29. V. 1897), Dutch comp. Studied in Hol. and with Suk in Prague.

Works incl. operas *Beatrix* (in Flem.) and *Die grosse Katharina* (in Ger., based on Shaw's *Great Catherine*); symph.; pf. concerto; chamber mus.; songs, etc.

Liliencron, Rochus von (b. Plön, Holstein, 8. XII. 1820; d. Coblenz, 5. III. 1912), Ger. theologian, philologist and musicologist. He was successively prof. at Kiel and Jena, later lived at Munich and afterwards became prelate of the St. John's foundation at Schleswig. His mus. writings incl. studies of old Ger. song, Lutheran church mus. and 16th-cent. Ger. settings of Horace's odes.

Lilliburlero, a satirical song sung in Ir. after the appt. of General Talbot to the lord-lieutenancy in 1687. It is not likely that the attribution of the tune to Purcell is justified: it was prob. a popular melody merely arr. by him, much as *The Prince of Denmark's March* was arr. by J. Clarke.

Lily of Killarney, The, opera by Benedict (lib. by John Oxenford and Dion Boucicault, based on the latter's play, *The Colleen Bawn*), prod. London, Covent Garden Theatre, 8. II. 1862.

Lima, Jeronymo Francisco de (b. Lisbon, 30. IX. 1741; d. Lisbon, 19. II. 1822), Port. comp. He was elected to the Brotherhood of St. Cecilia, visited It., and in 1798 became cond. of the Royal Opera at Lisbon.

Works incl. opera *Le nozze d'Ercole e d'Ebe* and 5 others (all It.); church mus.; cantatas, etc.

Limburgia, Johannes de (b. ?; d. ?), late 14th- and early 15th-cent. comp. from N. Fr. His 50 or so comps. (all church mus.) incl. a complete Mass (3 and 4 voices) and 16 motets.

Lincke, Josef (b. Trachenberg, Prus. Silesia, 8. VI. 1783; d. Vienna, 26. III. 1837), Ger. cellist and comp. He settled in Vienna in 1808, becoming a member of Rasumovsky's quartet and later 1st cellist at the Vienna opera. He wrote concertos, variations, etc. for the cello.

Lincoln, Abraham (1809–65), Amer. statesman and president. *See* Copland (speeches), **Damrosch (W.), Goldmark (R.)** (address at Gettysburg).

Lincoln Portrait, A, a work by Copland for orch. and a speaker, who declaims portions of Lincoln's speeches, 1st perf. by Cincinnati Symph. Orch., 14. V. 1942.

Lind, Jenny (b. Stockholm, 6. X. 1820; d. Malvern, 2. XI. 1887), Swed. soprano. 1st appeared at Stockholm, 1838; studied with Garcia in Paris; sang much in Ger.; went to Eng. in 1847 and settled in London permanently. Distinguished in opera in her early years, but afterwards mainly as a concert singer. She made many extensive tours. Married Otto Goldschmidt in 1852. She was called 'The Swed. Nightingale'.

Linda di Chamounix, opera by Donizetti (lib. by Gaetano Rossi, after a vaudeville,

La Grâce de Dieu), prod. Vienna, Kärntnertortheater, 19. V. 1842.

Lindberg, Oskar Fredrik (b. Gagnef, 23. II. 1887; d. Stockholm, 10. IV. 1955), Swed. organist and comp. Studied at the Stockholm Cons. and at Sondershausen. In 1906 he was app. organist at a Stockholm church and in 1919 prof. at the Cons. Works incl. Requiem and cantata for solo voices, chorus and orch.; symph. in F maj.; *3 Pictures from Dalarne,* 3 overtures, symph. poems *Wilderness, Flor and Blancheflor* and *From the Great Forests,* suite *Travel Memories* for orch.; pf. pieces; songs with orch. and with pf., etc.

Lindblad, Adolf Fredrik (b. Skänninge nr. Stockholm, 1. II. 1801; d. Linköping, 23. VII. 1878), Swed. comp. and singing-teacher. Studied with Zelter in Berlin and in 1827 settled at Stockholm as teacher of singing. Jenny Lind was among his pupils.

Works incl. opera *Frondörerna;* 2 symphs.; duo for vln. and pf.; vocal duets, trios and 4tets; numerous songs, etc.

Lindblad, Otto Jonas (b. Karlstorp, 31. III. 1809; d. Ny Mellby, 24. I. 1864), Swed. comp. Learnt the org. while studying theology, which he afterwards abandoned in order to study mus., mainly by himself, though he had a few lessons at Copenhagen. Having learnt the vln. he joined a touring opera company, took part in a mus. festival at Hamburg in 1841 and founded a students' choral society at Lund.

Works incl. numerous choruses, vocal 4tets, trios and duets, songs, etc.

Lindelheim (?), Johanna Maria (b. ?; d. ?), Ger. (?) singer, sometimes wrongly identified with Maria Margherita Gallia. Made her London début in 1703 and later seems to have appeared under the name of 'the Baroness'.

Lindeman, Ludvig Mathias (b. Trondhjem, 28. XI. 1812; d. Christiania, 23. V. 1887), Norw. organist and comp. Studied theology at first and mus. afterwards. App. organist at Our Saviour's Church at Christiania in 1840, teacher of singing at the Theological Seminary in 1849 and estab. a mus. school with his son Peter L. (1858–1930) in 1883. Collected Norw. folksongs and ed. a book of them, also a hymn-book.

Works incl. *Dream Chant* for chorus; hymn-tunes; org. fugues, etc.

Lindley, Robert (b. Rotherham, 4. III. 1776; d. London, 13. VI. 1855), Eng. cellist and comp. Learnt vln. and cello from his father, then studied the latter under Cervetto, played at the Brighton theatre, and in 1794–1851 was principal cellist at the Opera in London. He wrote concertos and other works for cello.

Lindner, Friedrich (b. Liegnitz, Silesia, *c.* 1540; d. Nuremberg, IX. 1597), Ger.

comp. and ed. He was a choir-boy in the electoral chapel at Dresden and later studied at Leipzig Univ., became musician to the Margrave of Brandenburg and in 1574 cantor at St. Giles's Church at Nuremberg. He ed. several books of It. church mus. and madrigals, and comp. 2 Passions.

Lindpaintner, Peter Joseph von (b. Coblenz, 9. XII. 1791; d. Nonnenhorn, Lake of Constance, 21. VIII. 1856), Ger. cond. and comp. Studied at Augsburg and (?) with Winter at Munich, where in 1812 he became cond. at a minor theatre. In 1819 he went to Stuttgart as court *Kapellmeister*. In 1853–4 he visited London to cond. the New Phil. concerts.

Works incl. operas *Der Bergkönig*, *Der Vampyr*, *Die Genueserin*, *Lichtenstein* and 24 others; ballet *Joko* and 2 others; incid. mus. to Goethe's *Faust*; *Stabat Mater*, 6 Masses; oratorios *Abraham* and others; cantatas *The Widow of Nain*, Schiller's *Lied von der Glocke*; symphs. and overtures; concertos; chamber mus.; over 50 songs, etc.

Lindsay, (Nicholas) Vachel (1879–1931), Amer. author. *See* **Gruenberg** (*Daniel Jazz*), **Kubik** (*In Praise of Johnny Appleseed*), **Palmer (R.)** (*Abraham Lincoln Walks at Night*).

Linear Counterpoint, a term for a kind of counterpoint in 20th-cent. mus. which regards the individuality of melodic lines as more important than the harmony they prod. in combination.

Lingual Stops. *See* **Reed Stops.**

Linke, Joseph. *See* **Lincke.**

Linklater, Eric (b. 1899), Scot. novelist. *See* **Gerhard** (*Adventures of Don Quixote*).

Linko, Ernst (b. Tammerfors, 14. VII. 1889), Fin. comp. Studied at Helsinki Cons. and Stern's Cons. in Berlin, also in Paris and St. Petersburg. In 1915 he became prof. at and in 1936 director of the Helsinki Cons.

Works incl. 4 pf. concertos; 3 sonatinas and other works for pf., songs, etc.

Linley, Eng. family of musicians:

1. Thomas L. (b. Badminton, 17. I. 1733; d. London, 19. XI. 1795), singing-master and comp. Studied with Thomas Chilcot, organist of Bath Abbey, and with Paradisi in London; settled at Bath as singing-teacher and concert promoter. From 1774 he managed the oratorios at Drury Lane Theatre in London jointly with Stanley and from 1786 with Arnold. Sheridan having become his son-in-law in 1773, he and his son Thomas (3) wrote mus. for Sheridan's play *The Duenna* in 1775. In 1776 he moved to London and bought Garrick's share in Drury Lane Theatre, where he managed the mus. and wrote mus. for var. pieces.

Works incl. opera *The Royal Merchant*;

mus. for Sheridan's *Duenna* and *School for Scandal* (the song 'Here's to the maiden'), *The Carnival of Venice*, *The Gentle Shepherd*, *Robinson Crusoe* (pantomime by Sheridan, after Defoe), *The Triumph of Mirth*, *The Spanish Rivals*, *The Strangers at Home*, *Love in the East* and other plays; adaptations from Grétry: *Selima and Azor* and *Richard Cœur de Lion*; accomps. for *The Beggar's Opera*; mus. for Sheridan's monody on the death of Garrick; 6 elegies for 3 voices; 12 ballads; cantatas, madrigals, etc.

2. Elizabeth Ann L. (b. Bath, 5. IX. 1754; d. Bristol, 28. VI. 1792), soprano, daughter of prec. Pupil of her father, she 1st sang in his concerts in Bath. Made her London début in 1770 but after her marriage to Sheridan in 1773 retired from singing.

3. Thomas L. jun. (b. Bath, 5. V. 1756; d. Grimsthorpe, Lincs., 5. VIII. 1778), violinist and comp., brother of prec. Pupil of his father and of Boyce, later of Nardini in Florence, where he struck up a friendship with the young Mozart in 1770. On his return to Eng. he played in his father's concerts, and collaborated with him in the comp. of *The Duenna* in 1775. He was drowned in a boating accident.

Works incl. opera *The Cadi of Bagdad*; mus. for Shakespeare's *The Tempest* and Sheridan's *The Duenna* (with his father); oratorio *The Song of Moses*; *Ode on the Witches and Fairies of Shakespeare*; anthem 'Let God arise'; vln. concerto, several elegies, etc.

4. Mary L. (b. Bath, 4. I. 1758; d. Clifton, Bristol, 27. VII. 1787), singer, sister of prec. Pupil of her father, sang at festivals, oratorios, etc., but retired on her marriage to Richard Tickell, commissioner of stamps and dramatist (wrote *The Carnival of Venice* for his father-in-law and altered Ramsay's *Gentle Shepherd* for him).

5. Maria L. (b. Bath, autumn 1763; d. Bath, 5. IX. 1784), singer, sister of prec. Pupil of her father, sang at concerts and oratorios, but d. young, (?) of consumption.

6. Ozias Thurston L. (b. Bath, VIII. 1765; d. London, 6. III. 1831), clergyman and organist, brother of prec. Pupil of his father, entered the church, but resigned his living on becoming fellow and organist at Dulwich Coll. in 1816.

7. William L. (b. Bath, II. 1771; d. London, 6. V. 1835), government official and comp., brother of prec. Pupil of his father and Abel, he held official posts in India, but in between was Sheridan's partner in the management of the Drury Lane Theatre, for which he comp. some unsuccessful works. Settled in London in 1806 as writer and comp.

Works incl. pantomimes, etc. *Harlequin*

Captive, The Honey Moon, The Pavilion,
etc.; songs to Shakespeare's plays; glees,
etc.

Linstead, George (Frederick) (b. Melrose, 24. I. 1908), Scot. critic, organist and
comp. Studied with F. H. Shera at Sheffield,
also comp. with Sir Edward Bairstow and
pf. with James Ching. He took the D.Mus.
degree at Durham. App. organist and
choirmaster at Walkley Parish Church,
Sheffield, in 1933, and mus. critic to the
Sheffield Daily Telegraph in 1940.

Works incl. opera *Eastward in Eden*;
symph. movement, suite *Cadmus et Hermione* (after Lully) and In Nomine for
orch.; 2 concertinos for pf. and orch.;
folksong arrs. for orch. and for military
band; string 4tet; vln. and pf. sonata;
sonatina, *4 Moods, Le Babil, Une Brioche,*
5 2-part inventions for pf., etc.

'Linz' Symphony, Mozart's symph. in
C maj., K. 425, comp. at the house of
Count Thun at Linz, where Mozart and
his wife stayed on their return from Salzburg to Vienna, and perf. there 4. XI. 1783.

Lioncourt, Guy de (b. Caen, 1. XII.
1885; d. Paris, 24. XII. 1961), Fr. musicologist and comp. Studied under d'Indy
at the Schola Cantorum in Paris and later
taught there. In 1918 he gained a prize
with a mus. fairy-tale, *La Belle au bois
dormant* (after Perrault).

Other works incl. opera *Jean de la
lune*, liturgical drama *Le Mystère d'Emmanuel*; church mus.; cantata *Hyalis le
petit faune* (Samain) and sacred cantatas;
chamber mus., etc.

Lionel and Clarissa, opera by Dibdin
(lib. by Isaac Bickerstaffe), prod. London,
Covent Garden Theatre, 25. II. 1768.

Lipatti, Dinu (b. Bucharest, 19. III. 1917;
d. Geneva, 2. XII. 1950), Rum. pianist
and comp. Studied at the Bucharest Cons.
and with Cortot, Dukas and Nadia Boulanger in Paris. He made a very brilliant
career, but owing to ill health had soon to
cancel engagements.

Works incl. symph. suite *Satrarii*; concertino for pf. and orch.; *Symphonie concertante* for 2 pfs. and strings; 3 nocturnes
and sonatina for pf., left-hand; 3 Rum.
dances for 2 pfs., etc.

Lipiński, Karol Józef (b. Radzyń, 30.
X. 1790; d. Urlow nr. Lwów, 16. XII.
1861), Pol. violinist and comp. Travelled
widely and became leader of the court
orch. at Dresden, 1839. Ed. a collection of
Pol. and Ruthenian folksongs with the
poet Zalewski. Schuman's *Carnaval* was
ded. to him.

Works incl. opera *The Siren of the
Dnieper; Polonaise guerrière* for orch.; 4
vln. concertos; string trio; vln. pieces, etc.

Lipp, Maria Magdalena (b. ?; d.?, 1827),
Aus. singer. Married Michael Haydn at
Salzburg in 1768.

Lipsius, Marie. *See* **La Mara.**
Lira (It.), a generic name given to var.
old bowed string instruments, such as the
Rebec and Crwth in earlier times.

Lira da braccio (It., lit. 'arm lyre'), a
bowed string instrument current in the 16th
and early 17th cents. It had 7 strings, 2
or more of which served as drones. As the
name implies, it was played on the arm.

Lira da gamba (It., lit. 'leg lyre'), a
larger version of the *lira da braccio*,
played between the legs. The number of
strings, incl. drones, varied from 11 to 15.

Lira organizzata. *See* Vielle organisée.
Lisinki, Vatroslav (b. Zagreb, 8. VII.
1819; d. Zagreb, 31. V. 1854), Yugoslav
comp. Studied at Zagreb and with Kittl
in Prague. Although he comp. much, he
lived in obscurity and d. in poverty.

Works incl. operas *Love and Malice*
and *Porin* (in Croatian); *Evening* for
small orch., 7 orchestral overtures; numerous dances, choruses, songs, etc.

Lisle, Charles Leconte de. *See* Leconte
de Lisle.

Lisle, Rouget de. *See* Rouget de Lisle.
Lisley, John (b. ?; d. ?), Eng. 16th–17th-
cent. comp. One of the contribs. to the
madrigal coll. *The Triumphes of Oriana* of
1601, of whom nothing is otherwise known.

Lissenko, Nikolai Vitalievich (b. Grilky,
Government of Poltava, 22. III. 1842; d.
Kiev, 6. XI. 1912), Rus. comp. Studied
natural science, but while making researches
in ethnography he became interested in
Ukrainian folksong, specimens of which he
began to collect. He then studied at the
Leipzig Cons. and later with Rimsky-
Korsakov at St. Petersburg. He settled at
Kiev.

Works incl. operas *Taras Bulba* (after
Gogol), *Sappho, The Aeneid* (after Virgil)
and others; operettas; cantatas and other
choral works; *Ukrainian Rhapsody* for
vln. and pf.; pf. pieces; songs, settings of
Ukrainian folksongs, etc.

Listov, Constantin (b. Odessa, 19. VIII.
1900), Rus. comp. Although of poor
parentage and without advantages, he
showed mus. talent as a child and in 1914
was sent to the Tsaritsin (Stalingrad)
Cons.; but left in 1917 to join the army,
for which he wrote songs. Severely
wounded, he was enabled by the army
command to continue his mus. studies at
Saratov, 1919–21.

Works incl. mus. comedies, mus. for
reviews, incid. mus. for plays incl. Molière's
Le Bourgeois Gentilhomme; many army and
battle songs, etc.

Liszt, Ferencz (more commonly **Franz**)
(b. Raiding, Hung., 22. X. 1811; d.
Bayreuth, 31. VI. 1886), Hung. pianist
and comp. His father, a steward of the
Esterházy family's property, was Hung.,
his mother Aus. At the age of 9 he gave

a concert at Sopron and in 1823 he had advanced so amazingly that his father took him to Vienna and Paris, where he had an immense success. In Vienna he studied briefly with Salieri and Czerny. In 1824–5 he paid 2 visits to Eng. and another in 1827. At 14 he came out as a comp. as well, prod. his opera *Don Sanche* in Paris. His father d. in 1827 and he was taken to Paris by his paternal grandmother, who looked after his educ. there. He remained there and after a period of religious mysticism under the influence of Lamennais and great success as a pianist, he began a love affair with the Comtesse d'Agoult in 1833. They went to live at Geneva in 1835, where a daughter, Blandine, was b., followed by another, Cosima (later Wagner's 2nd wife) at Como in 1837. A son, Daniel, was b. in Rome, 1839.

He travelled widely as pianist and made much money. In 1840 he collected funds for the Beethoven memorial at Bonn, and he often played for charitable purposes organized on a large scale. In 1840–1 he paid further visits to Eng., playing before Queen Victoria, and in 1842–4 he toured in Rus., Turkey, Den., etc. After a break with the countess in the latter year, he went to Spain and Port. in 1845; 2 years later, at Kiev, he met Princess Caroline Sayn-Wittgenstein, the wife of a wealthy Rus. landowner, who fell violently in love with him and in 1848 left with him for Weimar, where he was engaged as cond. and mus. director to the grand-ducal court for certain periods of the year. He prod. many new operas there, incl. Wagner's *Lohengrin* and Berlioz's *Béatrice et Bénédict*, and settled down to cultivate comp. of a var. of works, some on a very large scale, having previously confined himself almost exclusively to pf. mus.

He retired to Rome in 1861, and in 1865 took minor orders. He continued, however, to visit Weimar and also Budapest as a teacher.

Works incl. a vast number of pf. comps. incl. 3 vols. of *Années de pèlerinage*, 12 *Études d'exécution transcendante*, 2 *Légendes* (*Saint François d'Assise prédicant aux oiseaux* and *Saint François de Paule marchant sur les flots*), *Liebesträume* (3 nocturnes, orig. songs), sonata in B min., 20 Hung. Rhapsodies; innumerable transcriptions for pf. incl. *c.* 50 operatic pieces and fantasies, *c.* 40 works by var. comps. (Beethoven's symphs., Berlioz's *Symph. fantastique*, 6 caprices by Paganini, 9 waltzes by Schubert [*Soirées de Vienne*], etc., *c.* 150 songs incl. many by Schubert); *Faust* and *Dante* symphs.; 14 symph. poems for orch.; other orchestral works incl. 2 Episodes from Lenau's *Faust*; 2 pf.

concertos, Hung. fantasy, *Malédiction*, *Totentanz* and fantasy on Beethoven's *Ruins of Athens* for pf. and orch.; oratorios *St. Elizabeth* and *Christus*; *Gran Mass* for solo voices, chorus and orch., Hung. Coronation Mass and 2 other Masses, 3 psalms and a number of other choral works; 55 songs; 6 recitations with pf.; fugue on B. A. C. H., fantasy and fugue on *Ad nos, ad salutarem undam* and a few other org. works, etc.

Litaniae Lauretanae (Lat. = Litanies of Loreto), a litany sung in honour of the Virgin Mary in the Rom. church, dating prob. from the 13th cent. It has its own plainsong melody, but has also been set by comps., incl. Palestrina, Lassus and Mozart.

Litany, a supplicatory chant consisting of a series of petitions with an infrequently changing response to each. The best-known L.s in the Rom. Church are the Litany of the Saints, sung on Holy Saturday and during Rogationtide, and the 13th-cent. *Litaniae Lauretanae* (*see above*). The reformed churches have also adopted the L., excluding refs. to the saints, as in Cranmer's L. still used in the Angl. Church.

Literes, Antonio (b. Artá, Majorca, *c.* 1670; d. Madrid, 18. I. 1747), Span. bass viol. player and comp. (often confused with his son, also called Antonio, who was a well-known organist). Member of the royal band in Madrid from 1693.

Works incl. operas *Júpiter y Danae*, *Los Elementos*, *Dido y Eneas*; zarzuela *Coronis*; 14 psalm settings; 8 Magnificat settings; etc.

Lithuanian Composers. See Baltic Composers.

Litinsky, Heinrich (b. Lipovets, Ukraine, 17. III. 1901), Rus. comp. Studied with Glière at the Moscow Cons.

Works incl. 2 symphs.; pf. concerto, vln. concerto; 11 string 4tets; unaccomp. sonatas for vln., vla. and cello, etc.

Litolff, Henry (Charles) (b. London, 6. II. 1818; d. Bois-les-Combes nr. Paris, 6. VIII. 1891), Anglo-Alsat. comp., pianist and mus. pub. His father was Alsat., his mother Eng. As a boy of 13 he became a pupil of Moscheles for pf., made his 1st appearance in 1832 and at 17 left for Fr., having married against his parents' wish. He travelled widely as concert pianist until 1851, when he acquired a mus. pub. business at Brunswick, marrying as his 2nd wife the widow of the former owner. But he soon left his adopted son Theodor L. in charge and settled in Paris, where later he married again, a Comtesse de la Rochefoucauld. He prod. his best opera at Brussels in 1886.

Works incl. opera *Les Templiers* and several others; oratorios *Ruth and Boaz*;

pf. concs., vln. concerto; overture *Robespierre* and others; chamber mus.; pf. works, etc.

'Little - Russian' Symphony, Tchaikovsky's 2nd symph. in C min., Op. 17, also called 'Ukrainian' symph., comp. VI.–X. 1872, perf. Moscow, 18. I. 1873.

Liturgical Drama, a medieval church representation of Bible and other stories. It originated, prob. in Fr., in a 10th-cent. trope to the Introit for Easter Day, which takes the form of a dialogue for the Angel and the Marys at the sepulchre. In the second half of the cent. it was transferred to Matins. The mus. was originally an extension of plainsong but in course of time came to consist of original comps. Later subjects treated include the Walk to Emmaus, the Nativity, Epiphany, the Massacre of the Innocents, Old Testament stories and the lives of the saints. The texts were generally in Lat. but sometimes also in the vernacular.

Lituus (Lat.), the Rom. cavalry tpt. In the 18th-cent. the word was occasionally used to mean 'horn'.

Litvinne (actually Litvinova), **Felia** (b. St. Petersburg, 1861; d. Paris, 12. X. 1936), Rus. soprano. Studied with Maurel and others in Paris and made her 1st appearance there in 1880. She was partic. successful in Wagnerian roles.

Liuto (It.) = Lute.

Liuzzi, Fernando (b. Senigallia, 19. XII. 1884; d. Florence, 6. X. 1940), It. musicologist and comp. Studied with Fano and later with Reger and Mottl at Munich. He became prof. of harmony at the Conss. of Parma and of Florence successively, and prof. of mus. hist. at Rome Univ. in 1927–8. He ed. old It. *laudi,* arr. perfs. of Vecchi's *Amfiparnaso* and of Sophocles' *Oedipus Rex* with A. Gabrieli's mus., wrote books on the *laudi,* on It. musicians in Fr. and a vol. of critical studies *Estetica della musica,* also numerous learned articles.

Works incl. puppet opera *L'augellin bel verde* (after Gozzi); incid. mus. to Pirandello's *Scamandro;* oratorios *La Passione, Laudi Francescane* and *Le vergini savie e le vergini folli;* Neapol. impression *Giaola e Marecchiaro* for orch.; vln. and pf. sonata and 2 pieces; org. mus.; 5 sets of songs, incl. It., Gk. and Serbian folksongs, etc.

Livietta e Tracollo, intermezzi by Pergolesi (lib. by Tommaso Mariani), prod. Naples, Teatro San Bartolommeo, between the acts of Pergolesi's serious opera *Adriano in Siria,* 25. X. 1734.

Livonian Composers. *See* **Baltic Composers.**

Livy (Titus Livius) (59 B.C.–A.D. 17), Rom. historian. *See* **Rape of Lucretia** (Britten).

Lizard. *See* **Lyzarden.**

Lloyd, Charles Harford (b. Thornbury, Glos., 16. X. 1849; d. Slough, 16. X. 1919), Eng. organist and comp. Educ. at Oxford; D.Mus. there in 1892. App. organist at Gloucester Cathedral, 1876, and Christ Church, Oxford, 1882; precentor at Eton Coll., 1892–1914, then organist at Chapel Royal, London.

Works incl. services and anthems; motet *The Souls of the Righteous;* cantatas *Hero and Leander, Song of Balder, Andromeda, The Longbeards' Saga, A Song of Judgment, Sir Ogie and Lady Elsie;* incid. mus. to Euripides' *Alcestis;* sonata, concerto, and other works for org.; madrigals and part-songs, etc.

Lloyd, Edward (b. London, 7. III. 1845; d. Worthing, 31. III. 1927), Eng. tenor. Choir-boy at Westminster Abbey in London until 1860 and one of the Gentlemen of the Chapel Royal from 1869. 1st important public appearance at Gloucester Festival, 1871.

Lloyd, George (b. St. Ives, Cornwall, 28. VI. 1913), Eng. comp. Studied vln. with Albert Sammons and comp. with Harry Farjeon, then briefly attended Trinity Coll. of Mus. in London. His father wrote the libs. for his 2 operas, the 1st of which was prod. at Penzance in 1934 and the 2nd in London in 1938. He was severely wounded in the 1939–45 war.

Works incl. operas *Iernin* and *The Serf;* 5 symphs., etc.

Lloyd (also Floyd), John (b. ?, d. 1523), Eng. comp. He sang at the funeral of Prince Henry in 1511 and was present at the Field of the Cloth of Gold in 1520. He comp. a Mass *O quam suavis,* preceded by an antiphon, *Ave regina,* bearing the inscription 'Hoc fecit iohannes maris' (*mare* = sea = flood = Floyd or Lloyd).

Lloyd, Ll(ewelyn). S(outhworth). (b. Cheadle Hulme, Ches., 20. IV. 1876; d. Birmingham, 14. VIII. 1956), Brit. physicist and writer on acoustics. Educ. at King William's Coll., Isle of Man, and Christ's Coll., Cambridge. He became an inspector of schools and later asst. sec. to the Dept. of Scientific and Industrial Research. He wrote articles on acoustics, esp. intonation, for scientific and mus. periodicals and pub. books *The Musical Ear, Music and Sound,* etc. He was created C.B. in 1921.

Lloyd, Robert (1733–64), Eng. poet and dramatist. *See* **Giordani (T. G.)** (*Capricious Lovers*), **Stanley** (*Arcadia* and *Tears and Triumphs of Parnassus*).

Lobe, Johann Christian (b. Weimar, 30. V. 1797; d. Leipzig, 27. VII. 1881), Ger. flautist, comp. and writer on mus. Studied at the expense of the Grand Duchess of Weimar, Maria Pavlovna, appeared as fl. soloist at Leipzig in 1811, and then joined the court orch. at Weimar, where his 5 operas were prod. He left in 1842 and 4 years later became ed. of the *Allgemeine Musik-Zeitung* at Leipzig; he also pub. several books on mus.

Works incl. operas *Wittekind, Die Flibustier, Die Fürstin von Granada, Der rote Domino* and *König und Pächter*: 2 symphs., overtures; pf. 4tets, etc.

Lobgesang. *See* Hymn of Praise.

Lobo (also called **Lopez** or **Lupus**), **Duarte** (b.? Alcáçovas, IX. 1565; d. Lisbon, 24. IX. 1646), Port. comp. Studied under Mendes at Evora and later became choirmaster there. Afterwards he went to Lisbon with an appt. to the Royal Hospital and became *maestro di cappella* at the cathedral *c.* 1590.

Works incl. Masses, offices for the dead, canticles, motets and much other church mus.

Locatelli, Pietro (b. Bergamo, 3. IX. 1695; d. Amsterdam, 1. IV. 1764), It. violinist and comp. Pupil of Corelli in Rome. Travelled widely as a virtuoso and settled down at Amsterdam, where he estab. public concerts.

Works incl. concertos, sonatas, studies, caprices, etc. for vln.

Lochamer (also **Locheimer**) **Liederbuch,** a Ger. 15th-cent. songbook, now in Berlin. It contains 44 Ger. and 3 Lat. songs, mostly monophonic and all anon. It dates *c.* 1455–65. Also bound with the book is a copy of Paumann's *Fundamentum Organisandi*.

Locke (or **Lock**), **Matthew** (b. Exeter, 1622; d. London, VIII. 1677), Eng. comp. He was a choir-boy at Exeter Cathedral under Edward Gibbons. He visited the Netherlands in 1648, and having returned to London collaborated in Shirley's masque *Cupid and Death*, perf. before the Port. ambassador in 1653. In 1656 he wrote the *Little Consort* for viols in 3 parts for William Wake's pupils and the same year he was one of the comps. who took part in the setting of Davenant's *Siege of Rhodes*. He was Comp. in Ordinary to the King and for Charles II's coronation in 1661 he wrote instrumental mus. for the procession. In 1663, having turned Rom. Catholic, he became organist to Queen Catherine. He was a vigorous and acrimonious defender of 'modern mus.', writing in 1666 a pamphlet defending his church mus. and in 1672 opening a controversy with Thomas Salmon. Purcell wrote an elegy on his death.

Works incl. operas, Davenant's *The Siege of Rhodes* (with Coleman, Cooke, Hudson and H. Lawes), *Psyche* (with G. B. Draghi); masque, Shirley's *Cupid and Death* (with C. Gibbons); incid. mus. to Stapylton's *The Stepmother*, (?) Shake-

speare's *Macbeth* altered by Davenant and containing material from Middleton's *The Witch*, and for Shadwell's version of Shakespeare's *Tempest*, song in Durfey's *The Fool turned Critic*; Kyrie, Credo, anthems, Lat. hymns; consorts for viols in 3 and 4 parts; songs in 3 parts, duets; airs and songs for 1 voice with accomp., etc.

Lockey, Charles (b. Thatcham nr. Newbury, 23. III. 1820; d. Hastings, 3. XII. 1901), Eng. tenor. Made his 1st important appearance in the prod. of Mendelssohn's *Elijah* at Birmingham Festival, 1846.

Lockspeiser, Edward (b. London, 21. V. 1905), Eng. critic. Studied with Nadia Boulanger in Paris and at the R.C.M. in London. Author of *Debussy: His Life and Mind* and trans. of Prunières's hist.

Loco (It. = place, sometimes *al loco* = to the place), a direction indicating that a passage is to be played in the normal position indicated by the written notes, often given for greater safety after a passage shown to be played an 8ve higher or lower.

Loder, Edward (James) (b. Bath, 1813; d. London, 5. IV. 1865), Eng. comp. He 1st learnt mus. from his father, John David L. (1788–1846), a violinist and mus. pub., and in 1826–8 studied with F. Ries at Frankfurt. After a 2nd period of study there he settled in London and was induced by Arnold to set an opera, *Nourjahad,* for the New Eng. Opera House, under which name the Lyceum Theatre opened with it in 1834. He was theatre cond. in London and later at Manchester. About 1856 began to suffer from a disease of the brain.

Works incl. operas and plays with mus., *Nourjahad, The Dice of Death, Francis I* (a concoction from his songs), *The Foresters, The Deerstalker, The Night Dancers, Robin Goodfellow, The Sultana, The Young Guard, Raymond and Agnes,* etc.; masque *The Island of Calypso*; string 4tets; numerous songs, incl. *12 Sacred Songs, The Diver, The Brave old Oak, Invocation to the Deep* and *The Brooklet* (a trans. of Wilhelm Müller's *Wohin* set by Schubert in *The Fair Maid of the Mill*).

Loder, Kate (Fanny) (b. Bath, 21. VIII. 1825; d. Headley, Surrey, 30. VIII. 1904), Eng. pianist and comp., cousin of the prec. Studied at the R.A.M. in London, where she later became prof. of harmony; made her 1st appearance in 1844. The 1st perf. in Eng. of Brahms's Requiem took place at her house in 1871, the accomp. being played on the piano by herself and C. Potter.

Works incl. opera *L'elisir d'amore*, etc.

Lodizhensky, Nikolai Nikolaievich (b. St. Petersburg, 1. I. 1843; d. St. Petersburg, 15. II. 1916), Rus. comp. Studied for a diplomatic career, but comp. as an amateur and about 1866 joined the Bala-

kirev circle. He went to the Balkans and later to N.Y. in the diplomatic service, but returned to Rus. in 1907.
Works incl. opera *Dimitri the Usurper*; cantata *Russalka*; several symphs. (all unfinished); 6 songs, etc.

Lodoïska, opera by Cherubini (lib. by Claude François Fillette-Loraux), prod. Paris, Théâtre Feydau, 18. VII. 1791.
Opera by R. Kreutzer (lib. by Jean Claude Bédéno Dejaure), prod. Paris, Comédie-Italienne, 1. VIII. 1791.

Lodoïska, opera by Mayr (lib. by Francesco Gonella), prod. Venice, Teatro La Fenice, 26. I. 1796.

Loeffler, Charles Martin (Tornow) (b. Mulhouse, 30. I. 1861; d. Medfield, Mass., 19. V. 1935), Alsat.-Amer. comp. Before Alsace was lost to Fr. in the 1870–1 war, L., whose father was an agricultural chemist and an author who wrote under the name of 'Tornow', was taken to Smela nr. Kiev, and it was there that he was 1st given vln. lessons. The family later moved to Debreczin in Hung. and about 1873 to Switz. There he decided to become a violinist and went to Berlin to study with Rappoldi, Kiel, Bargiel and lastly Joachim. Later he had a period of study with Massart and Guiraud in Paris, joined the Pasdeloup Orch. and that of a wealthy amateur, where he remained until 1881. That year he went to U.S.A., played in Damrosch's orch., in 4tets and with touring companies. In 1882 he joined the Boston Symph. Orch., where he remained, sharing the 1st desk with the leader, until 1903. In 1887 he became a naturalized Amer.
Works incl. psalm *By the waters of Babylon* for women's voices and instruments, *Beat! Beat! Drums!* (from Whitman's *Drum Taps*) for male voices and orch., *Evocation* for women's voices and orch., *For one who fell in battle* for unaccomp. chorus; dramatic poem for orch. and vla. *La Mort de Tintagiles* (after Maeterlinck), fantasy for orch. and org. *La Villanelle du Diable*, *A Pagan Poem* (after Virgil) for orch. with pf., Eng. horn and 3 tpts., *Poem* and *Memories of my Childhood* for orch.; *Canticum Fratris Solis* (St. Francis) and 5 Ir. fantasies for voice and orch.; 2 rhapsodies for ob., vla. and pf., 5tet for 3 vlns., vla. and cello, mus. for string 4tet; partita for vln. and pf., vln. studies; 4 songs with vla. and pf.; 3 sets of songs, incl. *The Wind among the Reeds* (Yeats), etc.

Lœillet, Jean-Baptiste (b. Ghent, XI. 1680; d. London, 19. VII. 1730), Flem. flautist, oboist and comp. He made an early success as a perf., went to Paris in 1702 and to London in 1705, where he joined the orch. of the King's Theatre in the Haymarket. He retired in 1710 and

made a living by teaching and giving concerts in his house in Hart Street (now Floral Street), Covent Garden.
Works incl. sonatas for 1, 2 and 3 fls., for ob. or vln., etc.

Loeschhorn, Albert (b. Berlin, 27. VI. 1819; d. Berlin, 4. VI. 1905), Ger. pianist, teacher and comp. Studied in Berlin, where he taught from 1851 and became prof. in 1858.
Works incl. 4tets; sonatas and esp. studies and other instructive works for pf., etc.

Loewe. *See also* **Löwe.**

Loewe, (Johann) Carl (Gottfried) (b. Löbejün nr. Halle, 30. XI. 1796; d. Kiel, 20. IV. 1869), Ger. comp. He was a choirboy at Cöthen, and in 1809 went to the grammar-school at Halle. Encouraged by Jérôme Bonaparte, then king of Westphalia, he devoted himself to comp., to further mus. studies, to the learning of Fr. and It. and later, at Halle Univ., the study of theology. The flight of Jérôme in 1813 deprived him of his income, but he managed to make a living and in 1820 became prof. and cantor at Stettin, and in 1821 mus. director and organist. He visited Vienna in 1844, London in 1847, Swed. and Norw. in 1851 and Fr. in 1857. In 1864 he suffered from a 6 weeks' coma and was asked to resign in 1866, when he went to live at Kiel. He d. there after a similar attack.
Works incl. opera *Die drei Wünsche* and 4 others; oratorios *Die Zerstörung Jerusalems, Palestrina, Hiob, Die Auferweckung des Lazarus* and 12 others; symphs.; concertos; pf. solos and duets; numerous songs and ballads, incl. Goethe's *Erlkönig*, Fontane's Ger. versions of *Archibald Douglas, Tom the Rhymer*, etc.

Loewenberg, Alfred (b. Berlin, 14. V. 1902; d. London, 29. XII. 1949), Eng. mus. bibliog. of Ger. origin. Studied at Jena Univ. and graduated there in 1925. The Nazi régime drove him from Ger. in 1934, and he settled in London, where he compiled *Annals of Opera*, containing details of c. 4,000 operas in chronological order.

Loewenstern, Matthaeus (Apelles) von (b. Neustadt, Silesia, 20. IV. 1594; d. Bernstadt nr. Breslau, 16. IV. 1648), Ger. poet and comp. Studied (?) at the Univ. of Frankfurt o/O. Having been schoolmaster and cantor at Leobschütz, he entered the service of the Duke of Oels-Bernstadt.
Works incl. choruses for Opitz's tragedy *Judith*; Lat. and Ger. motets; sacred concertos; book of 30 sacred songs to words of his own entitled *Frühlings-Mayen*, etc.

Logier, Johann Bernhard (b. Cassel, 9. II. 1777; d. Dublin, 27. VII. 1846), Ger. musician of Fr. descent. Pupil of his father. He settled in Eng. as a boy after his parents' death and soon went to Ir., settling finally at Dublin in 1809 as band-master and mus. dealer. He invented the Chiroplast, an appliance used in learning the pf., spent 3 years in Berlin, returned to Dublin, and comp. and arr. pf. mus. In 1809 he prod. an ode on the 50th year of George III's reign.

Logroscino, Nicola (b. Bitonto, X. 1698; d. Palermo, after 1765), It. comp. Pupil at the Cons. di Santa Maria di Loreto, 1714–27, he held an org. post in Conza, 1728–31. He was chiefly a comp. of *opera buffa*, though his first known opera was not written till 1738. From 1747 taught counterpoint at the Cons. in Palermo.

Works incl. operas *Inganno per inganno*, *L'Inganno felice*, *Ciommetella correvata*, *Il Governadore*, *Giunio Bruto*, *Leandro*, *Li zite*, *Don Paduano*, *La Griselda*, *Le finte magie* and many others; oratorio *La spedizione di Giosué*; 2 settings of the *Stabat Mater*; church mus., etc.

Lohengrin, opera by Wagner (lib. by comp.), prod. Weimar, Court Theatre, by Liszt, 28. VIII. 1850.

Lohet, Simon (b. Liège, *c.* 1550; d. Stuttgart, VII. 1611), Ger. organist and comp. App. organist to the court of Württemberg at Stuttgart in 1571. Works incl. pieces in fugal style, *canzoni* and hymn-tune fantasies for org., etc.

Lolli, Antonio (b. Bergamo, *c.* 1730; d. Palermo, 10. VIII. 1802), It. violinist and comp. In the service of the court of Württemberg at Stuttgart, 1758–74, and of Catherine II of Rus. in St. Petersburg, 1774–83, he nevertheless spent most of his time as a touring virtuoso. Of his many works for vln. (concertos, sonatas, etc.), prob. only the solo parts are by L.

Lombardi alla prima crociata, I (*The Lombards at the First Crusade*), opera by Verdi (lib. by Temistocle Solera, founded on a romance by Tommaso Grossi), prod. Milan, Teatro alla Scala, 11. II. 1843.

Lombardini, Maddalena. *See* Sirmen.

London (real name Burnstein), George (b. Montreal, 30. V. 1920), Canadian bass-baritone. Studied in Los Angeles with Richard Lert and made his début in 1941. Later he studied in N.Y. and toured the U.S.A. He was engaged to sing at the Vienna State Opera in 1949 and in 1951 sang at the N.Y. Metropolitan Opera.

London Philharmonic Orchestra. Founded in 1932 by Sir Thomas Beecham and assoc. with the Royal Phil. Society for its concerts in London, also with the Covent Garden Opera. During World War II it became a self-governing co.

London Symphony, Haydn's symph. No. 104, in D maj. (No. 12 of the 'Salomon' symphs.), written for perf. in London in 1795.

London Symphony, A, the 2nd symph. by Vaughan Williams, comp. 1912, perf.

London, 27. III. 1914; revised version, London, Queen's Hall, 4. V. 1920.

London Symphony Orchestra, founded in 1904 from the bulk of players of the 1st Queen's Hall Orch., who left Henry J. Wood, since he insisted on abolishing the system of sending deputies to rehearsals and concerts.

Long, the name of a note-value in old mensural notation, half the value of the Large and equal to either 2 or 3 Breves.

Long, John Luther (1861–1927), Amer. novelist. *See* Madama Butterfly (Puccini).

Longas, Federico (b. Barcelona, 18. VIII. 1895), Span. pianist and comp. Studied with Granados and others, founded a pf. school at Barcelona, married the singer Margarita Salvi and later settled in Paris. Works incl. pf. pieces, songs, etc.

Longfellow, Henry Wadsworth (1807–1882), Amer. poet. *See* Black Knight (Elgar), Boughton (*Skeleton in Armour*), Buck (D.) (*Golden Legend*), Cellier (*Masque of Pandora*), Coerne (*Hiawatha*), Coleridge-Taylor (do. and *Choral Ballads*), Foote (*Hiawatha*, *Wreck of the Hesperus* and *Skeleton in Armour*), Golden Legend (Sullivan), Goldmark (R.) (*Hiawatha*), Hiawatha (Coleridge-Taylor), Holbrooke (*Skeleton in A.*), Kaun (*Hiawatha*), King Olaf (Elgar), Lahee (*Building of the Ship*), MacCunn (*Wreck of the H.*).

Longo, Alessandro (b. Amantea, 30. XII. 1864; d. Naples, 3. XI. 1945), It. pianist and ed. He became prof. of pf. at the Naples Cons., but later moved to Bologna, where he founded the Cercolo Scarlatti and the Società del Quartetto. He ed. the journal *L'arte pianistica* and brought out eds. of old It. keyboard mus., incl. the sonatas of D. Scarlatti.

Longueval, Antoine de (b. ?; d. ?), N. Fr. 15th-cent. comp. about whom very little is known. He wrote 3 motets, a *chanson*, and a Passion, formerly attrib. to Obrecht, based on all four gospels.

Longus (5th cent.), Gk. author. *See* Cythère assiégée (Gluck), Daphnis et Chloé (Ravel).

Loosemore, George (b. Cambridge, ?; d. ? Cambridge, ? 1682), Eng. organist and comp. Studied under his father, Henry L., as a chorister at King's Coll. Chapel, Cambridge, and in 1660 became organist of Trinity Coll. there. Works incl. anthems, etc.

Loosemore, Henry (b. ?; d. Cambridge, 1670), Eng. organist and comp., father of prec. He learnt mus. as a choir-boy at Cambridge and became organist of King's Coll. Chapel there in 1627. Works incl. Service in D min., anthems, 2 Lat. litanies; a piece for 3 viols and org., etc.

Lopatnikov, Nikolai Lvovich (b. Reval, 16. III. 1903), Estonian-Rus. pianist and comp. Studied at the St. Petersburg Cons., left for Fin. during the 1917 Revolution and in 1920 settled in Ger., studying pf. with Willi Rehberg and comp. with Toch in Berlin. In 1933 he returned to Fin. and sought the advice of Sibelius. Settled in U.S.A. in 1939 and became an Amer. citizen in 1944. App. prof. of composition at Carnegie Inst. of Technology, Pittsburgh, 1945.

Works incl. opera *Danton* (after Rolland's play); 2 symphs., variations, concertino and *Intro. and Scherzo* for orch.; 2 pf. concertos, concerto for 2 pfs., vln. concerto; 3 string 4tets; vln. and pf. sonata (with side-drum *ad lib.*), 3 pieces for vln. and pf.; cello sonata, etc.

Lope de Vega. *See* **Vega.**

López de Velasco, Sebastián (b. Segovia, ?; d. ? Madrid, *c.* 1650), Span. comp. He may have been a pupil of Victoria, whose post as *maestro de capilla* he was given later by the Infanta Juana at the convent of the Descalzas Reales in Madrid.

Works incl. Masses, motets, psalms, Magnificats and other church mus.

Lopez, Duarte. *See* **Lobo.**

Loqueville, Richard de (b. ?; d. Cambrai, 1418), Fr. comp. He was in the service of Duke Robert of Bar in 1410 and *maître de chant* at Cambrai Cathedral from 1413 until his death. He wrote church mus. and *chansons* in the Burgundian style of his day.

Lorca, Federico Garcia (1899–1936), Span. poet and dramatist. *See* **ApIvor** (songs), **Fortner** (*Wald, Bluthochzeit*).

Loreley. *See also* **Lurline.**

Opera by Bruch (lib. by Emanuel Geibel, orig. written for Mendelssohn), prod. Mannheim, 14. VI. 1863.

Unfinished opera by Mendelssohn (lib. by Emanuel Geibel). Only the 1st-act finale, an *Ave Maria* and a chorus of vintners exist.

Lorenz, Alfred (Ottokar) (b. Vienna, 11. VII. 1868; d. Munich, 20. XI. 1939), Aus. cond. and writer on mus. After var. other appts. he became cond. at Coburg-Gotha in 1898; but he retired, took a degree in 1922, became lecturer at Munich Univ., 1923, and prof. 1926. He ed. Wagner's literary works and Weber's early operas, and wrote several books on the form of Wagner's mus.-dramas, on the hist. of western mus. and on A. Scarlatti's early operas.

Lorenzani, Paolo (b. Rome, 1640; d. Rome, 28. X. 1713), It. comp. Pupil of Benevoli in Rome. In 1675 he went to Sicily and became *maestro di cappella* at the cathedral of Messina. In 1678 the Fr. viceroy, Marshal de Vivonne, induced him to go to Paris. From 1679 to 1683 he was one of the superintendents of the queen's mus. After her death he became

maître de chapelle at the Theatine monastery, where he wrote motets. His opera *Orontée* was prod. at Chantilly in 1687 by order of the Prince de Condé. He returned to Rome as *maestro di cappella* of the Papal chapel in 1694.

Works incl. operas *Nicandro e Fileno* and *Orontée*; motets and Magnificats; cantatas; It. and Fr. airs, etc.

Loris, Heinrich. *See* **Glareanus.**

Lortzing, (Gustav) Albert (b. Berlin, 23. X. 1801; d. Berlin, 21. I. 1851), Ger. cond., singer, comp. and librettist. He had some lessons with Rungenhagen in Berlin as a child, but his parents being wandering actors, he had to obtain his general and mus. educ. as best he could. He learnt the pf., vln. and cello and studied such theoret. works as he could pick up. He married in 1823 and found it very difficult to make a living in a travelling opera co. His 1st stage work, *Ali Pascha von Janina*, was prod. at Münster in 1828 and repeated at Cologne, Detmold and Osnabrück. In 1833–4 he was able to lead a more settled life, being engaged as tenor and actor at the Leipzig municipal theatre. The 1st 2 comic operas he wrote there were very successful, and so was his adaptation from Kotzebue, *Der Wildschütz*, in 1842, when he gave up acting. 2 short terms as cond. at Leipzig and Vienna were unsuccessful. He had a large family by this time and fell upon more and more difficult times. The conductorship at a suburban theatre in Berlin in 1850 merely humiliated him without doing much to relieve the situation.

Works incl. operas *Die beiden Schützen, Zar und Zimmermann, Hans Sachs, Casanova, Der Wildschütz* (after Kotzebue), *Undine* (after de La Motte Fouqué), *Der Waffenschmied, Zum Grossadmiral, Rolandsknappen, Regina* and others; operettas *Ali Pascha von Janina, Die Opernprobe, oder Die vornehmen Dilettanten*; oratorio *Die Himmelfahrt Christi*; incid. mus. for plays incl. Goethe's *Faust*, Grabbe's *Don Juan und Faust*, Scribe's *Yelva*; plays with mus. *Der Pole und sein Kind, Der Weihnachtsabend, Szenen aus Mozarts Leben* (with mus., adapted from Mozart); partsongs, songs, etc.

Los Angeles, Victoria de (real name Victoria Gomez Cima). (b. Barcelona, 1. XI. 1923), Span. mezzo-soprano. She made her début in Madrid in 1944 and in 1947 won an international contest at Geneva. In 1949 she toured Eur. and S. Amer. and appeared at the Salzburg Festival in 1950. She married in 1948.

Lotario, opera by Handel (lib. by ?, based on Antonio Salvi's *Adelaide*, not, as Burney says, on Matteo Noris's *Berengario*), prod. London, King's Theatre, Haymarket, 2. XII. 1729.

Lothar, Mark (b. Berlin, 23. V. 1902), Ger. comp. He studied at the Berlin Musikhochschule with Schreker (comp.), Juon (harmony) and Krasselt (cond.). Later he had lessons with Wolf-Ferrari and others. After appts. as director of mus. at 2 Berlin theatres, he was in charge of the mus. at the Bav. Staatstheater in Munich from 1945 to 1955.

Works incl. operas *Tyll*, *Lord Spleen* (after Ben Jonson's *Epicoene*), *Münchhausen* and *Schneider Wibbel*; incid. mus. for Eichendorff's *Die Freier* and other plays; *Narrenmesse* for male chorus; *Orchesterstücke* and suite for orch.; serenade for chamber orch.; mus. for film and radio; pf. trio; pf. pieces; songs, etc.

Loti, Pierre (Julien Viaud) (1850–1923), Fr. novelist. *See* **Lambert (L.)** (*Spahi*), **Messager** (*Mme. Chrysanthème*), **Préludes** (Debussy, II. 7), **Rawsthorne** (*Mme. Chrysanthème*, ballet), **Ropartz** (*Pêcheur d'Islande*), **Taylor (D.)** (*Ramuntcho*).

Lottchen am Hofe (*Lottie at Court*), opera by J. A. Hiller (lib. by Christian Felix Weisse, after Goldoni and Charles Simon Favart), prod. Leipzig, 24. IV. 1767.

Lotti, Antonio (b. ? Venice, *c.* 1667; d. Venice, 5. I. 1740), It. comp. Pupil of his father and of Legrenzi in Venice. App. singer at St. Mark's 1687, and rose to become 2nd organist (1692), 1st organist (1704), finally *maestro di cappella* (1736). Prod. his first opera, *Il trionfo dell' innocenza* in Venice in 1692 (*Giustino*, 1683, commonly ascribed to him, is by Legrenzi). Visited Dresden 1717–19 as an opera comp., but after his return to It. devoted himself entirely to church mus.

Works incl. operas *Porsenna*, *Irene Augusta*, *Polidoro*, *Alessandro Severo*, *Constantino* (for Vienna, 1716, with Fux and Caldara), *Giove in Argo*, *Ascanio*, *Teofane*, etc.; oratorios *Il voto crudele*, *L'umilità coronata in Esther*, *Gioa*, *Giuditta*; Masses, Requiems, Misereres, motets and other church mus., etc.

Loucheur, Raymond (b. Tourcoing, 1. I. 1899), Fr. comp. Studied with Henry Woollett at Le Havre and afterwards at the Paris Cons., where he took the Prix de Rome in 1928. In 1938, after teaching mus. in Paris schools, he was made inspector of mus. educ. there, rising later to the post of inspector-general.

Works incl. ballet *Hop-Frog*; Psalm xxxix for chorus and orch.; 2 symphs., *Défilé*, *Pastorale*, *Nocturne*, *En Famille*, *Apothéose de la Seine* for orch.; string 4tet; vocal duets, songs, etc.

Loud Pedal, the popular name for the Sustaining Pedal of the pf.

Louis Ferdinand of Prussia, Prince (b. Friedrichsfelde nr. Berlin, 18. XI. 1772; d. Saalfeld 10. X. 1806), Ger. amateur comp. and pianist. Beethoven praised his

playing and ded. to him the C min. pf. concerto. From 1804 Dussek was in his service as his companion and teacher. He fell in the battle of Saalfeld. Comp. pf. trios, pf. 4tets and 5tets and other chamber mus., pf. pieces, etc.

Louise, opera by G. Charpentier (lib. by comp.), prod. Paris, Opéra-Comique, 2. II. 1900.

Loure (Fr.), orig. a special type of bagpipe, found esp. in Normandy; later the name of a dance in fairly slow 6–4 time.

Louré (Fr.), past participle from the following, sometimes found as a direction in vln. mus., but more often indicated by the notation.

Lourer (Fr.), verb der. from *loure*, indicating a *legato* style of playing with a slight accent or *sostenuto* effect on each note of a group.

Lourié, Arthur (Vincent) (b. St. Petersburg, 14. V. 1892), Rus. comp. of Fr. descent. Studied for a short time at the St. Petersburg Cons., but was self-taught later. App. director of the mus. section of the Ministry of Public Instruction in 1918, but left in 1921. He settled in Fr. and in 1941 in the U.S.A., where he became an Amer. citizen.

Works incl. operas *A Feast in Time of Plague* (after Pushkin) and *The Blackamoor of Peter the Great*; ballet *Le Masque de neige* and others; 2 symphs.; *Sonate liturgique* for orch., pf. and chorus; *Ave Maria*, *Salve Regina* and other church mus.; *Regina coeli* for contralto, ob. and tpt., *Improperium* for baritone, 4 vlns. and double bass; *Canzona di Dante* for chorus and strings; Jap. Suite for voice and orch.; 3 string 4tets; sonata for vln. and double bass; 3 pf. sonatinas; songcycles *Elysium* (Pushkin) and *Alphabet* (A. Tolstoy).

Louvet de Couvray, Jean-Baptiste (1760–1797), Fr. author. *See* **Luigini** (*Faublas*).

Louÿs, Pierre (1870–1925), Fr. novelist and poet. *See* **Conchita** (Zandonai), **Dandelot** (*Bilitis*), **Debussy** (do., 2 works), **Dupuis (A.)** (do.), **Maciejewski** (do.).

Love for Three Oranges, The (*Liubov k trem Apelsinam*), opera by Prokofiev (lib. by comp., based on Gozzi's comedy *Fiaba dell' amore delle tre melarancie*), prod., in Fr. trans., Chicago, Auditorium, 30. XII. 1921. The March from it has become popular.

Love in a Village, opera by Arne (lib. by Isaac Bickerstaffe), prod. London, Covent Garden Theatre, 8. XII. 1762. Partly a ballad opera and pasticcio, Arne having intro. popular songs and airs by Handel, Galuppi, Geminiani and others.

Love of Three Kings (Montemezzi). *See* **Amore di tre re**.

Löwe. *See also* **Loewe**.

Lowe, Edward (b. Salisbury, *c.* 1610;

d. Oxford, 11. VII. 1682), Eng. organist and comp. Chorister at Salisbury Cathedral; became organist of Christ Church, Oxford, about 1630. App. one of the organists at the Chapel Royal in London, 1660. Wrote on the perf. of cathedral mus. and comp. anthems.

Löwe, Ferdinand (b. Vienna, 19. II. 1865; d. Vienna, 6. I. 1925), Aus. cond. Studied at the Vienna Cons. and taught there, 1884–97. From 1896 to 1898 he cond. the Wiener Singakademie, and from 1900 to 1904 the Gesellschaft concerts. He held further posts in Munich, Budapest and Berlin and was director of the Vienna Acad. of Mus. from 1919 to 1922.

Löwe, Johann Jakob (b. Vienna, VII. 1629; d. Lüneburg, IX. 1703), Ger. organist and comp. Pupil of Schütz at Dresden; held appts. at Wolfenbüttel from 1655 and Zeitz from 1663, became organist of St. Nicholas's Church at Lüneburg in 1682.

Works incl. operas *Amelinde, Andromeda* and *Orpheus aus Thracien*; ballets; symphs., etc.

Lowe, Thomas (b. ?; d. London, 1. III. 1783), Eng. tenor. Made his 1st appearance at Drury Lane Theatre, London, in 1740. He sang in many Handel oratorios.

Lualdi, Adriano (b. Larino, 22. III. 1885), It. comp. and mus. critic. Studied with Wolf-Ferrari at Venice, became critic to the *Secolo* at Milan and in 1936 to the *Giornale d'Italia* in Rome. Later he became director of the Naples Cons.

Works incl. operas *Le nozze di Haura, La figlia del rè, Le furie di Arlecchino, Il diavolo nel campanile* (after Poe), *La Granceola*; ballet *Lumawig e la Saetia*; choral pieces; *La leggenda del vecchio marinaio, Suite adriatica*, colonial rhapsody *Africa*, 3 folk-tunes *Samnium* for orch.; *Sire Halewyn* for soprano and orch., *La rosa di Saron* for tenor and orch.; string 4tet in E. maj.; vln. and pf. sonata; passacaglia for org.; songs, etc.

Lübeck, Vincenz (b. Padingbüttel, Hanover, IX. 1654; d. Hamburg, 9. II. 1740), Ger. organist and comp. Organist at Stade until 1702, when he was app. organist to St. Nicholas's Church at Hamburg.

Works incl. cantatas, chorale-preludes and other org. mus., etc.

Lucas, Charles (b. Salisbury, 28. VII. 1808; d. London, 30. III. 1869), Eng. cellist, organist, cond. and comp. Choir-boy at Salisbury Cathedral, 1815–23 studied cello and comp. at the R.A.M. in London, of which, after a number of appts. as cond., cellist and organist, he became principal in 1859, succeeding Potter.

Works incl. opera *The Regicide* anthems; 3 symphs.; string 4tets; songs, etc.

Lucas, Leighton (b. London, 5. I. 1903), Eng. dancer, cond. and comp. He studied mus. by himself while engaged in the career of a dancer and at 19 became a theatre cond. He served in the R.A.F. during the 1939–45 war.

Works incl. ballets *Orpheus* and *The Horses*, masques (tragic) *The Wolf's Bride* and (Japanese) *Kanawa, the Incantation*; film mus. for *Target for To-night*; *Missa pro defunctis* for solo voices, chorus and orch.; *Masque of the Sea* for chorus and orch.; passacaglia, chaconne and Litany for orch.; sonnets for pf. and orch.; *La Goya*, 2 dance impressions for chamber orch.; partita for pf. and chamber orch., *Eurhythmy* for vln. and strings., 4 divertissements for vln. and chamber orch., pf. trio in F maj.; songs, etc.

Lucas, Mary Anderson (b. London, 24. V. 1882; d. London, 14. I. 1952), Eng. comp. Studied, with pf. as principal study, at the Dresden Cons. and the R.A.M. in London, then comp. with R. O. Morris, Herbert Howells and Maurice Jacobson.

Works incl. ballets *Undine, Cupid and Death* and *Sawdust*; masque on Blake's *Book of Thil*; *Circus Suite* for orch., variations on theme by Purcell for strings; concertino for fl. and chamber orch.; 6 string 4tets, trio for clar., vla. and pf., rhapsody for fl., cello and pf., clar. and pf. sonata, etc.

Lucca, Pauline (b. Vienna, 25. IV. 1841; d. Vienna, 28. II. 1908), Aus. soprano of It. origin. Studied in Vienna, joined the Opera chorus and made her 1st stage appearance at Olomouc in 1859. In 1863 she 1st visited London. She was a member of the Vienna opera from 1874 to 1889.

Lucia di Lammermoor, opera by Donizetti (lib. by Salvatore Cammarano, based on Scott's *Bride of Lammermoor*), prod. Naples, Teatro San Carlo, 26. IX. 1835.

Lucia, Fernando de (b. Naples, 11. X. 1860; d. Naples, 21. II. 1925), It. tenor. Studied at Naples and made his 1st stage appearance there in 1883. His 1st visit to Eng. was in 1887. Later in life he was prof. of singing at the Naples Cons.

Lucio Papiro, opera by Caldara (lib. by Apostolo Zeno), prod. Vienna, 4. XI. 1719.

Opera by Hasse (lib. do.), prod. Dresden, at court, 18. I. 1742.

Lucio Silla, opera by J. C. Bach (lib. by Giovanni de Gamerra, with alterations by Metastasio), prod. Mannheim, at court, 4. XI. 1774.

Opera by Mozart (lib. do.), prod. Milan, Teatro Regio Ducal, 26. XII. 1772.

Lucio Vero, opera by Pollarolo (lib. by Apostolo Zeno), prod. Venice, Teatro San Giovanni Crisostomo, 1700.

Opera by Sacchini (lib. do.), prod. Naples, Teatro San Carlo, 4. XI. 1764.

Lucrezia Borgia, opera by Donizetti (lib. by Felice Romani, based on Victor Hugo's tragedy). prod. Milan, Teatro alla Scala, 26. XII. 1833.

Ludford, Nicholas (b. *c*. 1485; d. London, *c*. 1557), Eng. comp. He was for long active at the Royal Chapel of St. Stephen, Westminster. He wrote 6 festal Masses, motets, a Magnificat, and a set of 7 Masses for the daily Mass of Our Lady which is unique. A John L., comp. of a Mass *Dame sans pere*, belonged to the previous generation: nothing is known of his life.

Ludovic, opera by Hérold, left unfinished and completed by Halévy (lib. by Jules Henri Vernoy de Saint-Georges), prod. Paris, Opéra-Comique, 16. V. 1833. Chopin wrote pf. variations on an air from it, Op. 12.

Ludwig, Christa (b. Berlin, 16. III. 1924), Ger. mezzo-soprano. Studied mus. with her mother and with Felice Hüni-Mihaček, making her début in 1946. After appearing in a number of Ger. opera houses she sang at the Salzburg Festival in 1954, and was engaged by the Vienna State Opera in 1955. She is married to the baritone Walter Berry.

Ludwig, Friedrich (b. Potsdam, 8. V. 1872; d. Göttingen, 3. X. 1930), Ger. musicologist. Studied at Marburg and Strasbourg Univs. He became a lecturer at Strasbourg in 1905 and prof. at Göttingen in 1911, where he was later app. Rector. He specialized in the study of medieval mus. and pub. in 1910 the 1st vol. of a catalogue of Organa entitled *Repertorium organorum*.

Ludwig, Otto (1813–65), Ger. novelist and dramatist. *See* **Mottl** (*Agnes Bernauer*), **Rubinstein (A.)** (*Maccabees*).

Ludwig (actually Ledwidge), **William** (b. Dublin, VII. 1847; d. London, 25. XII. 1923), Ir. baritone. Studied at Dublin, joined the Gaiety Theatre in London as a chorister, gradually appeared in small parts and made his 1st important stage appearance with the Carl Rosa Opera Co. in 1877.

Lugg (or Lugge), John (b. ?, *c*. 1587; d. ?), Eng. 17th-cent. organist and comp. He was vicar-choral and organist at Exeter.

Works incl. services, anthems, motets; org. voluntaries; canons; jig for harpsichord, etc.

Lugg (or Lugge), Robert (b. Exeter, 6. XI. 1620; d. ?), Eng. organist and comp., son of prec. B. Mus. Oxford, 1638, and organist at St. John's Coll. He became a Rom. Catholic and went abroad.

Works incl. services, anthems, etc.

Luigini, Alexandre (Clément Léon Joseph) (b. Lyons, 9. III. 1850; d. Paris 29. VII. 1906), Fr. violinist, cond. and comp. Studied at the Paris Cons., became leader at the Grand Théâtre of Lyons in 1869 and cond. in 1877. In 1897 he became cond. of the Opéra-Comique in Paris.

Works incl. operas *Faublas* (after Louvet de Couvray) and *Les Caprices de Margot*; ballets; cantata *Gloria victis*; *Ballet égyptien*, *Ballet russe*, *Carnaval turc* and other light works for orch., etc.

Luineag ⎱ a Gaelic labour song sung in
or ⎰ chorus, mainly by women.
Luinig ⎰

Luisa Miller, opera by Verdi (lib. by Salvatore Cammarano, based on Schiller's drama *Kabale und Liebe*), prod. Naples, Teatro San Carlo, 8. XII. 1849.

Lully, Jean Baptiste (orig. Giovanni Battista Lulli) (b. Florence, 28. XI. 1632; d. Paris, 22. III. 1687), It.-Fr. comp. Son of a miller, he had little educ. and learnt guitar and vln. without much guidance. At first joined strolling players, but in 1646 was discovered by the Chevalier de Guise and taken to Fr., where he entered the household of Mlle. de Montpensier, the king's cousin, as a scullion; but when she found that he was mus. she made him a personal servant and leader of her string band. In 1652 he passed into the service of Louis XIV, who was then 14. L. became ballet dancer, violinist in the king's '24 vlns.' and comp. In 1658 he began to comp. ballets of his own, having contrib. to some since 1653, in which the king himself danced. In 1661 he became a naturalized Frenchman and Comp. to the King's Chamber Mus. and in 1662 Mus. Master to the Royal Family.

His 1st opera, *Cadmus et Hermione*, appeared in 1673, when he obtained a royal patent granting him the monopoly of operatic prod. and annulling a previous patent given to Perrin and Cambert. The Académie Royale de Musique, as the Opéra was 1st called, was opened in 1672 with a pasticcio from earlier works of his, *Les Festes de l'Amour et de Bacchus*. His last complete opera was *Acis et Galatée* in 1686. In 1687 he injured his foot with the stick with which he cond. a Te Deum to celebrate the king's recovery and d. of blood poisoning. The opera *Achille et Polyxène*, left unfinished by him, was completed by Colasse.

Works incl. operas *Cadmus et Hermione*, *Alceste*, *Thésée*, *Atys*, *Isis*, *Psyché*, *Bellérophon*, *Proserpine*, *Persée*, *Phaéton*, *Amadis de Gaule*, *Roland*, *Armide et Renaud*, *Acis et Galatée*, *Achille et Polyxène*; comedy-ballets (all with Molière) *Les Fâcheux*, *Le Mariage forcé*, *L'Amour médecin*, *La Princesse d'Élide*, *Le Sicilien*, *George Dandin*, *Monsieur de Pourceaugnac*, *Les Amants magnifiques*, *Le Bourgeois Gentilhomme*; pastorals and divertissements *Les

Plaisirs de l'île enchantée, La Pastorale comique, L'Églogue de Versailles (or *La Grotte de Versailles*, words by Quinault), *L'Idylle sur la paix* (or *Idylle des Sceaux*, words by Racine); ballets (some poss. by Boësset and others) *Ballet d'Alcidiane, B. de la raillerie, B. de Xerxès* (for Cavalli's opera), *B. de l'impatience, B. des saisons, B. de l'Ercole amante, B. des arts, B. des noces de village, B. des amours déguisés, La Naissance de Vénus, B. des gardes, Le Triomphe de Bacchus dans les Indes, B. des Muses, Le Carnaval ou Mascarade de Versailles, B. de Flore, B. des ballets, Le Triomphe de l'Amour, Le Temple de la paix;* incid. mus. to Corneille's *Œdipe;* church mus. *Miserere, Plaude laetare,* Te Deum, *De profundis, Dies irae* and Benedictus, 5 *Grands Motets,* 12 *Petits Motets,* motets for double chorus; dances for var. instruments, *Suites de trompettes, Suites de symphonies et trios,* etc.

Lulu, unfinished opera by Berg. (lib. by comp., based on Frank Wedekind's plays *Erdgeist* and *Die Büchse der Pandora*), Acts I and II and a fragment of III prod. Zürich, 2. VI. 1937.

Lumby, Herbert (Horace) (b. Birmingham, 8. X. 1906), Eng. violinist, violist, pianist and comp. Studied with Bantock and others at the Birmingham and Midland Institute School of Mus. and joined the City of Birmingham Orch. as vla. Later studied comp. with Edmunds and left the orch. in 1944.

Works incl. symph. in A min., *Ankerdine* and *Summer Pastoral* for orch., *The Lovely Rosalind* and *Pastoral* for string orch.; 2 pf. trios; vln. and pf. sonata in E min.; pieces for vla and pf.; prelude and rondo for 2 pfs.; variations, *Rhapsody-Ballade* and other works for pf.; songs, etc.

Lumbye, Dan. family of musicians:
1. Hans Christian L. (b. Copenhagen, 2. V. 1810; d. Copenhagen, 20. III. 1874), cond. and comp. Cond. a light orch. at the Tivoli in Copenhagen from 1848 and wrote much dance and other light mus. for it.
2. Carl Christian L. (b. Copenhagen, 9. VII. 1841; d. Copenhagen, 10. VIII. 1911), cond. and comp., son of prec. He succeeded his father in 1865 and also comp. dances, marches, etc.
3. Georg August L. (b. Copenhagen, 26. VIII. 1843; d. Oringe, 29. X. 1922), cond. and comp., brother of prec. Wrote chiefly for the stage, incl. the opera *The Witch's Flute.*

Lund, Signe (b. Christiania, 15. IV. 1868; d. Oslo, 6. IV. 1950), Norw. comp. Studied with W. Berger in Berlin and later in Copenhagen and Paris. She then lived in U.S.A. for *c.* 20 years.

Works incl. Norw.-Amer. cantata,

mus. for the Bjørnson memorial at Chicago, 1910, and *The Road to France* for Amer.'s entry into World War I; orchestral pieces; pf. works; songs, etc.

Lunn, (Louisa) Kirkby (b. Manchester, 8. XI. 1873; d. London, 17. II. 1930), Eng. mezzo-soprano. Studied under the organist J. H. Greenwood at Manchester and with Visetti at the R.C.M. in London. In 1893–4 she appeared at the R.C.M.'s students' perfs. of Schumann's *Genoveva* and Delibes's *Le Roi l'a dit,* and in the latter year she was engaged by Augustus Harris to begin her career in opera. Later she appeared with the Carl Rosa Opera Co., at concerts and from 1901 in important parts at Covent Garden.

Lunssens, Martin (b. Molenbeek-Sant-Jean, 16. IV. 1871; d. Etterbeek, 1. II. 1944), Belg. comp. Studied with Gevaert and others at the Brussels Cons., gained the Belg. Prix de Rome in 1895, travelled for 3 years in Fr., It. and Ger., and became leader of the orch. at the Lyric Theatre of Antwerp in 1901. In 1911 he was app. prof. of harmony at the Brussels Cons. and in 1924 director of that of Ghent.

Works incl. incid. mus. for *Saint Amand* (Delbeke); cantatas *Callirhoë* and *Jubilaire, Ode to Mus.* for chorus and orch.; 4 symphs., symph. poems on Shakespeare's *Romeo and Juliet, Timon of Athens* and *Julius Caesar* and on Corneille's *Cid,* overture to Racine's *Phèdre,* concert overture for orch.; chamber mus.: songs with orch., etc.

Lupi, Johannes (Jean Leleu) (b. Cambrai, *c.* 1506; d. Cambrai, 20. XII. 1539), Fr. comp. He was assoc. with Cambrai Cathedral from 1526. He wrote church mus. and *chansons.* A different Johannes L. was organist at Nivelles in 1502, possibly the comp. of a lament on the death of Okeghem (d. 1495); the name is also found in the records of Antwerp Cathedral in 1548. It is often impossible to be certain to which of these comps. to assign var. names. Lupus Hellinck (*q.v.*) is again a distinct comp., as was Didier Lupi of Lyons.

Lupo, 16th–17th-cent. family of musicians, of It. origin but active at the Eng. court:
1. Lupus Italus (? = Ambrose de Milan, d. ? London, ? 1591).
2. Joseph (d. ? London, ? 1615), violist.
3. Peter (also Pietro, Petro) (d. ? London, ? 1608), ? brother of 2.
4. Thomas (d. ? London, before June 1628), son of 2, singer, violist, lutenist, comp.
5. Thomas (d. ? London, before 1660), son of 3.
6. Horatio (d. ? London, ? 1626).

Luprano

Of the mus. ascribed to Thomas some may be by 4 and some by 5, and some by a 3rd Thomas whose existence is doubtful. But it seems likely that 4 comp. most of the numerous fancies for viols which survive.

Luprano, Filippo de (b. ?; d. ?), It. 15th–16th-cent. comp. Works incl. *frottole*, etc.

Lupus, Eduardus. *See* **Lobo.**

Lupus, Joannes. *See* **Hellinck.**

Lur or **Lure** a primitive horn found among prehistoric remains in Scand.

Lurline, opera by V. Wallace (lib. by Edward Fitzball), prod. London, Covent Garden Theatre, 23. II. 1860. The subject is that of the Ger. legend of the Loreley.

Luscinius (real name Nachtgall or Nachtigall), **Othmar,** (b. Strasbourg, *c.* 1480; d. Freiburg i/B., 1537), Ger. organist and comp. Pupil of Hofhaimer. He was organist at Strasbourg, but left for Freiburg in 1523, owing to the Reformation, and settled at a Carthusian monastery. He wrote mus. treatises and comp. org. mus., etc.

Lusingando or **Lusinghiero** (It. = wheedling, coaxing), a direction to perf. a piece or passage in a charming, alluring manner.

Lusitano, Vicente (b. ? Olivença, ? ; d. ?, after 1553), Port. theorist and comp. He was known as Vicente de Olivença in Port., but was called L. ('the Port.') in Rome, where he settled about 1550. In 1551 he had a learned dispute with Vicentino, which was settled in his favour, with Danckerts and Escobedo as judges. He pub. a treatise on *cantus firmus* in 1553.

Works incl. motets *Epigrammata*, etc.

Lussan, Zélie de (b. Brooklyn, N.Y., 21. XII. 1862; d. London, 18. XII. 1949), Amer. mezzo-soprano of Fr. origin. After some parental opposition, she was trained by her mother and made her stage début at Boston in 1886. In 1888 she went to London and sang Carmen at Covent Garden, which became her great part. She also sang soprano parts and commanded Fr., It. and Eng. with equal ease. She appeared all over the world, but on her marriage in 1907 retired and settled in London.

Lustige Krieg, Der (*The Merry War*), operetta by J. Strauss, jun. (lib. F. Zell and Richard Genée), prod. Vienna, Theater an der Wien, 25. XI. 1881.

Lustige Witwe, Die (*The Merry Widow*), operetta by Lehár (lib. by Victor Léon and Leo Stein), prod. Vienna, Theater an der Wien, 30. XII. 1905.

Lustigen Weiber von Windsor, Die (*The Merry Wives of W.*), comic opera

Lutosławski

by Nicolai (lib. by Solomon Hermann Mosenthal, after Shakespeare), prod. Berlin, Opera, 9. III. 1849.

Lute, a plucked string instrument with a pear-shaped body. Its orig. is eastern. It gained currency in Eur. in medieval times and was still very popular in the 17th cent., but declined in the 18th. In the 16th cent. there were 5 pairs of strings, 2 to each note, and one single string. The tuning was:

Other tunings were adopted in the 17th cent. Music for the lute is played from a tablature of letters or figures.

Lute-Harpsichord, an instrument made for Bach in 1740, called *Lautenclavicymbel,* with gut strings and a keyboard.

Lutenist, a lute-player, also a singer to the lute and often a comp. for the instrument.

Luther, Martin (b. Eisleben, 10. XI. 1483; d. Eisleben, 18. II. 1546), Ger. reformer and amateur musician. The mus. relevant facts of his biog. are that his reforms of the church service, begun in 1522, incl. the much greater scope given to singing by the congregation and the consequent necessity to sing in the vernacular, instead of in Lat. He arranged a Ger. Mass in 1524 and he had the assistance of Walther and of Conrad Rupff, mus. director to the Elector of Saxony, in compiling a Ger. hymn-book, with tunes selected by him, some adapted from Lat. and earlier Ger. hymns and some possibly invented by himself.

For literary works set by other comps. *see* Burkhard (*Musikalische Uebung*), Otto (hymn 'Ein' feste Burg'), Walther (J.) (sacred songs).

Luthier (Fr.), orig. a lute-maker, later, by transference, a maker of string instruments in general.

Lutosławski, Witold (b. Warsaw, 25. 1. 1913), Pol. comp. Studied at the Warsaw Cons. with Maliszewski (theory and comp.) and Lefeld (pf.), graduating in 1937. At the same time he studied mathematics at Warsaw Univ. His earlier mus. is influenced by Bartók and Stravinsky, and also by Pol. folk mus., but during recent years he has adopted a more advanced, aleatory technique.

Works incl. 2 symphs., *Symph. Variations, Concert for Orch., Venetian Games* for small orch., *Musique funèbre* for strings (in memory of Bartók), *5 Dance Preludes* for clar., strings, harp and perc.; cello concerto; *Trois Poèmes d'Henri Michaux* for wind instruments, 2 pfs., perc. and 20-part chorus; *Silesian Tryptich* for soprano and orchestra, *Paroles tissées* for voice and orch., string 4tet; *Variations* on a theme of Paganini for 2 pfs., etc.

Lutyens, Elisabeth (b. London, 9. VII. 1906), Eng. comp. Daughter of the architect Sir Edwin Lutyens. Studied vla. and comp. at the R.C.M. in London, the latter with Harold Darke, and later with Caussade in Paris. She married the B.B.C. cond. Edward Clark. Her more recent work is generally, though not invariably, written in 12-note technique.

Works incl. ballet *The Birthday of the Infanta* (after Oscar Wilde); chamber cantata *Winter the Huntsman* (Osbert Sitwell), *Bienfaits de la lune* (Baudelaire) and other choral works; 3 symph. preludes, *Petite Suite*, *Divertissement* and other orchestral works; vla. concerto, *Lyric Piece* for vln. and orch.; 6 chamber concertos; 6 string 4tets, string trio, *Suite gauloise* for wind octet; *Aptote* for solo vln., sonata for solo vla.; pf. mus.; suite for org.; *O saisons, o chateâux* (Rimbaud) and other works for voice and chamber mus.; songs, etc.

Lux, Friedrich (b. Ruhla, 24. XI. 1820; d. Mainz, 9. VII. 1895), Ger. cond. and comp. Pupil of his father and of F. Schneider at Dessau, where he cond. in the Court Opera in 1841–50. He then became opera cond. at Mainz and also cond. choral societies.

Works incl. operas *Käthchen von Heilbronn* (on Kleist's play), *Der Schmied von Ruhla* and *Die Fürstin von Athen*; choral symph. *Durch Nacht zum Licht* and other choral works; scene from Shakespeare's *Coriolanus* for voices and orch.; orchestral works; string 4tets, pf. trio; org. and pf. pieces; songs, etc.

Luyton, Karel (b. Antwerp, *c.* 1556; d. Prague, VIII. 1620), Flem. organist and comp. He was in the service of the Emperor Maximilian II at Prague in 1576, when that monarch d., and was app. to the Emperor Rudolf II in the same capacity.

Works incl. Masses, motets, Lamentations, *Sacrae cantiones*; It. madrigals; *Fuga suavissima* and *Ricercare* for org., etc.

Luzzaschi, Luzzasco (b. Ferrara, 1545; d. Ferrara, 11. IX. 1607), It. organist and comp. Pupil of Rore at Ferrara and afterwards organist and *maestro di cappella* to Duke Alfonso II. Among his org. pupils was Frescobaldi.

Works incl. motets, *Sacrae cantiones*; madrigals; org. mus., etc.

Lvov, Alexis Feodorovich (b. Reval, 6. VI. 1799; d. Romanovo nr. Kovno, 28. XII. 1870), Rus. comp. Studied with his father, Feodor L., an authority on church mus. and folksong, who succeeded Bortniansky as director of the Imp. Chapel in

1825. His son, who rose to high rank in the army and became adjutant to Nicholas I, succeeded him there from 1837 to 1861. He was a good violinist and founded a string 4tet at St. Petersburg. He became deaf and retired in 1867.

Works incl. operas *Bianca e Gualtiero*, *Undine* (after Fouqué) and *The Bailiff*; much church mus.; vln. concerto; fantasy *The Duel* for vln. and cello; Rus. Imp. hymn 'God save the Tsar', etc.

Lydian Mode, one of the old eccles. modes with semitones between the 4th and 5th and 7th and 8th notes of the scale, represented by the scale beginning on F on the white notes of the pf. keyboard.

Lyne, Felice (b. Slater, Miss., 28. III. 1887; d. Allentown, Pa., 1. IX. 1935), Amer. soprano. Studied in Paris and made her 1st appearance in opera in London, 1911.

Lyon, James (b. Manchester, 24. X. 1872; d. Australia, 25. VIII. 1949), Eng. comp. He was mainly self-taught, but took the Mus.D. degree in 1905 and later taught comp. at the Midland Inst. School of Mus. at Birmingham.

Works incl. operas *The Palace of Cards*, *Stormwreck*, *Fiammetta*, *La sirena*; melomimes *Toinette*, *The Necklace*, *Madame s'amuse*; 4 suites, *Gwalia*, *Poem on Manx Tunes*, prelude *Aucassin and Nicolette* for orch.; *Idyll* for strings; ballade for vln. and orch.; fantasy string 4tet, pf. trio; org. and pf. pieces; songs, etc.

Lyra (1) = Lira.

(2), a percussion instrument with tuned steel bars or plates which are played with hammers, similar to the Stahlspiel, used in Eng. military bands and made for them in the shape of a lyre.

Lyra viol, a small bass viol, tuned in various ways and played from a tablature. It was in use in Eng. *c.* 1650–1700; also variously called 'Lero Viol', 'Leero Viol' or 'Viol Lyra Way'.

Lyre, the most important instrument of ancient Greece, of eastern orig. The number of strings varied. They were stretched on a framework with a hollow sound-box at the bottom and plucked, like those of a harp, with both hands, but only the left used the finger-tips, while the right played with a plectrum. The large instrument of the type was called Kithara, a name from which the modern word 'guitar' derives.

Lyre-Guitar, or Apollo Lyre, a string instrument prod. in Fr. near the end of the 18th cent., built to suggest the shape of the ancient Gk. lyre, but with a fretted finger-board. It had 6 strings.

Lysard. *See* Lyzarden.

Lysberg, Charles Samuel. *See* Bovy-Lysberg.

Lytton, Edward George Earle Lytton Bulwer-, Baron Lytton (1803–73), Eng. novelist. *See* **Fry** (*Lady of Lyons*), **Ione** (Petrella), **Joncières** (*Dernier Jour de Pompéi*), **Kashperov** (*Rienzi*), **Leila** (Bendl), **Pauline** (Cowen), **Perosi (M.)** (*Pompei*), **Rienzi** (Wagner).

Lyzarden or **Lyzardyne** } the old Eng. name for the bass Cornett or Corno torto, the predecessor of the Serpent, which latter came into use in the 17th cent. Also sometimes called Lizard or Lysard.

M

M'. For names with this prefix *see* **Mac...**

ᵐ⌐. The Mediant note in any key in Tonic Sol-fa notation, pronounced Me.

M.D. (abbr. Fr. *main droite*, It. *mano destra*) = Right Hand, often used in pf. mus.

M.G. (abbr. Fr. *main gauche*) = Left Hand, often used in pf. mus.

M.S. (abbr. It. *mano sinistra*) = Left Hand, often used in pf. mus.

Ma Mère l'Oye (*Mother Goose*), suite by Ravel, written for pf. duet in 1908 and pub. in 1910, scored for orch. and prod. as a ballet, Paris, Opéra, 11. III. 1915, scenario by Louis Laloy, choreography by L. Staats. The movements are based on tales by Perrault: 1. *Pavan of the Sleeping Beauty*; 2. *Hop-o'-my-Thumb*; 3. *Little Ugly, Empress of the Pagodas*; 4. *Colloquy between the Beauty and the Beast*; 5. *The Fairy Garden*.

Má Vlast (*My Country*), cycle of 6 symph. poems by Smetana, comp. 1874–9 and containing programme works on var. aspects of Cz. hist. and geography: 1. *Vyšehrad* (the citadel of Prague); 2. *Vltava* (the river); 3. *Šarka* (the Cz. Amazon); 4. *From Bohemia's Fields and Groves*; 5. *Tabor* (the city); 6. *Blanik* (the mountain).

Maag, Peter (b. St. Gallen, 10. V. 1919), Swiss cond. Studied pf. and theory with Marek and cond. with Fr. v. Hoesslins and Ansermet. After a number of lesser posts became 1st cond. of Düsseldorf Opera, 1952–4, and then mus. director of Bonn Opera, specializing in the perf. of lesser-known works.

Maas, Joseph (b. Dartford, 30. I. 1847; d. London, 16. I. 1886), Eng. tenor. He was a choir-boy at Rochester Cathedral, and after working as a clerk in Chatham dockyard he went to Milan in 1869 to study singing under San Giovanni. He 1st appeared at a concert in London, taking Sims Reeves's place, in 1871, and on the stage in 1872.

Maazel, Lorin (b. Paris, 6. III. 1930), Amer. cond. of Fr. birth. Brought to U.S.A. as a child, and soon displayed great mus. ability, cond. N.Y. Phil. aged 9. At 15 formed his own string 4tet. and also appeared as vln. soloist. He became a member of the Pittsburgh Symph. Orch. and its cond. in 1949. He has since appeared with all the great Eur. orchs., incl. the Vienna Phil., Vienna Symph., at Salzburg, Bayreuth and La Scala, Milan. Since 1965 he has been mus. director of the Ger. Opera in Berlin and chief cond. of the Berlin Radio Symph. Orch., and from 1971 assoc. cond. of the new Philharmonia Orchestra.

Mabellini, Teodulo (b. Pistoia, 2. IV.

1917; d. Florence, 10. III. 1897), It. cond. and comp. Studied at the Istituto Reale Musicale at Florence and prod. his 1st opera there at the age of 19. After further study with Mercadante at Novara, he settled at Florence, became cond. of the Società Filarmonica in 1843 and of the Teatro della Pergola in 1848. In 1860–87 he was prof. at the Istituto.

Works incl. operas *Matilda a Toledo*, *Rolla*, *Ginevra degli Almieri*, *Il conte di Lavagna*, *I Veneziani a Constantinopoli*, *Maria di Francia*, *Il venturiero*, *Baldassare* and *Fiammetta*; oratorios *Eudossio e Paolo* and *L'ultimo giorno di Gerusalemme*; cantatas *La caccia*, *Il ritorno*, *Elegiaca*, *Rafaelle Sanzio* and *Lo spirito di Dante*; much church mus., etc.

Macbeth, incid. mus. by (?) Locke for Davenant's version of Shakespeare's play, prod. London, Dorset Gardens Theatre, summer 1674. There were later prods. with mus. by D. Purcell, Eccles, Leveridge, etc.

Opera by Bloch (lib. by Edmond Fleg, after Shakespeare), prod. Paris, Opéra-Comique, 30. XI. 1910.

Opera by Chelard (lib. by Rouget de Lisle, after Shakespeare), prod. Paris, Opéra, 29. VI. 1827.

Opera by Collingwood (lib. by comp., chosen from Shakespeare), prod. London, Sadler's Wells Theatre, 12. IV. 1934.

Opera by Taubert (lib. by Friedrich Eggers, after Shakespeare), prod. Berlin, Royal Opera, 16. XI. 1857.

Opera by Verdi (lib. by Francesco Maria Piave and Andrea Maffei, after Shakespeare), prod. Florence, Teatro della Pergola, 14. III. 1847; revised version (Fr. lib. by Charles Nuitter and A. Beaumont) prod. Paris, Th. Lyrique, 21.IV.1865.

Overture by Spohr, Op. 75.

Symph. poem by R. Strauss, Op. 23, comp. 1886–7, revised 1890, 1st perf. Weimar, 13. IX. 1890.

Macbeth, Allan (b. Greenock, 13. III. 1856; d. Glasgow, 25. VIII. 1910), Scot. cond., organist, teacher and comp. Studied at the Leipzig Cons., and was cond. of the Glasgow Choral Union in 1880–7. He was organist at var. churches at Glasgow and Edinburgh and in 1890 became director of the mus. school of the Glasgow Athenaeum.

Works incl. operetta *The Duke's Doctor*; incid. mus. for *Bruce, Lord of the Isles*, a dramatic adaptation from Scott; cantata *The Land of Glory* and others; orchestral pieces; chamber mus.; many pf. pieces; songs; part-songs, etc.

McBride, Robert (b. Tucson, Arizona, 20. II. 1911), Amer. comp. Studied and took the Mus.B. at Arizona Univ. and obtained the Guggenheim Fellowship in 1937. Later he joined the faculty of Bennington Coll.

Works incl. ballet *Show Piece*; *Mexican Rhapsody* and *Prelude to a Tragedy* for orch.; Fugato for 25 instruments, *Workout* for 15 instruments; prelude and fugue for string 4tet; sonata *Depression* for vln. and pf., *Workout* for ob. and pf., *Swing Music* for clar. and pf.; dance suite for pf., etc.

McCormack, John, Count (b. Athlone, 14. VI. 1884; d. Dublin, 16. IX. 1945), Ir. tenor. Began as chorister in Dublin Rom. Catholic Cathedral. Without previous training won the gold medal at the Ir. Festival, Dublin, 1902. In 1905 went to It. to study with Sabbatini at Milan. Made his 1st concert appearance in London in Il. 1907 and was engaged for opera by Covent Garden in the autumn. He soon sang in It., U.S.A., etc., and made a great reputation, but in later years made popularity rather than serious mus. interest his chief concern. His title was a papal one.

McCracken, James (b. Gary, Indiana, 16. III. 1926), Amer. tenor. Appeared as light entertainer before making his début at the N.Y. Metropolitan Opera in 1953. He has frequently sung in Eur. and is best known for his 'Otello' (Verdi).

MacCunn, Hamish (b. Greenock, 22. III. 1868; d. London, 2. VIII. 1916), Scot. cond. and comp. Studied with Parry and Stanford at the R.C.M. in London and had an overture *Cior Mhor* perf. at the Crystal Palace at the age of 17. He married a daughter of the painter John Pettie in 1889 and soon afterwards cond. the Carl Rosa Opera Co. for some time, also German's light operas at the Savoy Theatre.

Works incl. operas *Jeanie Deans* (after Scott), *Diarmid* and *Breast of Light* (unfinished), light operas *The Golden Girl* and *Prue*; mus. for *The Masque of War and Peace* and *Pageant of Darkness and Light*; cantatas *The Moss Rose*, *Lord Ullin's Daughter* (Thomas Campbell), *The Lay of the Last Minstrel* (after Scott), *Bonny Kilmeny* (James Hogg), *The Cameronian's Dream* (James Hyslop), *Queen Hynde of Caledon* (Hogg), *The Death of Parcy Reed*, *The Wreck of the Hesperus* (Longfellow) and others; Psalm viii for chorus and org.; overture *The Land of the Mountain and the Flood*; ballads *The Ship o' the Fiend* and *The Dowie Dens o' Yarrow*, 3 descriptive pieces *Highland Memories* for orch.; 3 pieces for cello and pf.; *Scotch Dances* and other pieces for pf.; *c.* 80 songs; part-songs etc.

McDonald, Harl (b. nr. Boulder, Colorado, 27. VII. 1899; d. Princeton, N.J., 30. III. 1955), Amer. pianist, scientist and comp. Studied at home, at California Univ., and the Leipzig Cons. He toured as a pianist in Eur. and U.S.A., settled at Philadelphia as teacher and cond. and in 1930–3 studied physics in re-

lation to acoustic problems with a Rockefeller grant and wrote a book on *New Methods of Measuring Sound*.

Works incl. 84th Psalm and *Missa ad Patrem* for chorus and orch.; 4 symphs. (No. 1 *The Santa Fé Trail*, No. 2 *Rhumba*), 2 suites and 3 Poems on Aramaic Themes for orch.; 2 pf. concertos; string 4tet on Negro themes, pf. trio; pf. works; songs; etc.

MacDowell, Edward (Alexander) (b. N.Y., 18. XII. 1861; d. N.Y. 23. I. 1908), Amer. comp. and pianist. Learnt the pf. at home at first, was taken to the Paris Cons. in 1876, where he studied pf. under Marmontel and theory under Savard; afterwards worked with Louis Ehlert at Wiesbaden, 1878, and entered the Frankfurt Cons. in 1879, where Raff taught him comp. In 1881 he became pf. prof. at the Darmstadt Cons. and the next year played his 1st pf. concerto at Zürich at Liszt's invitation. Returned to U.S.A. in 1884 and married Marian Nevins, who had been his pupil at Frankfurt, 21. VII. After another period at Frankfurt and Wiesbaden, he went home for good and settled at Boston in 1888, making his 1st public appearance in U.S.A. there, 19. XI. In 1896 he was app. head of the new mus. dept. at Columbia Univ. in N.Y. and became hon. Mus.D. at Princeton Univ. Resigned in 1904, but continued to teach and comp. In 1905 his mind became affected and soon broke down completely.

Works incl. symph. poems *Hamlet and Ophelia* (after Shakespeare), *Lancelot and Elaine*, *Lamia* (after Keats), 2 suites (No. 2 *Indian*) for orch.; 2 pf. concertos; 6 orchestral works; 26 op. nos. of pf. solos, incl. 4 sonatas, 2 *Modern Suites*, 24 studies, *Woodland Sketches*, *Sea Pieces*, *Fireside Tales*, *New England Idylls*, also 2 books of technical exercises; 2 sets of pieces for pf. duet; 42 songs; 26 part-songs, etc.

Mace, Thomas (b. Cambridge, *c.* 1613; d. ? Cambridge, ? 1709), Eng. writer on mus. Clerk of Trinity Coll., Cambridge; pub. *Musick's Monument* in 1676. He invented a 'table org.' for use with a consort of viols and in 1672 a lute with 50 strings which he called the 'Dyphone', designed to serve him when he was becoming deaf. His comps. incl. an anthem 'I heard a voice'.

McEwen, John (Blackwood) (b. Hawick, 13. IV. 1868; d. London, 14. VI. 1948), Scot. mus. educationist and comp. Studied at Glasgow Univ. and, after being choirmaster at 2 churches there, entered the R.A.M. in London, 1893. In 1895 he returned to Scot. to become choirmaster at Greenock and prof. of pf. at the school of mus. attached to the Glasgow Athenaeum; but he came back to the R.A.M. as prof. of harmony and comp. in 1898 and succeeded Mackenzie as its principal in 1924, retiring in 1936. He received the hon. D.Mus. from Oxford Univ. in 1926 and was knighted in 1931.

Works incl. incid. mus. for *Empire Pageant* (1910); symphs. (incl. *Solway Symph.*); border ballad *Grey Galloway* and prelude for orch.; vla. concerto; 16 string 4tets (incl. *Biscay* 4tet), string 5tet; choral works; pf. pieces, etc.

Macfarren, George (Alexander) (b. London, 2. III. 1813; d. London, 31. X. 1887), Eng. mus. educationist and comp. Pupil of C. Lucas from 1827, entered the R.A.M. in 1829, of which he became a prof. in 1834 and principal in 1876. In 1845 he married the Ger. contralto and translator Natalia Andrae (1828–1916). He ed. works by Purcell and Handel. In the 1870s his eyesight began to fail and he eventually became blind, but he continued to work at comp. and to teach. Knighted in 1883.

Works incl. operas *The Devil's Opera, The Adventures of Don Quixote* (after Cervantes), *King Charles II, Robin Hood, Jessy Lea, She Stoops to Conquer* (after Goldsmith), *The Soldier's Legacy, Helvellyn*; masque *Freya's Gift*; oratorios *St. John the Baptist, The Resurrection, Joseph, King David*; cantatas *Emblematical Tribute on the Queen's Marriage* (1840), *The Sleeper Awakened, Lenora, May Day, Christmas, The Lady of the Lake* (after Scott); much church mus.; symph. in F min. and others, overtures, to Shakespeare's *Hamlet, Romeo and Juliet* and *The Merchant of Venice*, Schiller's *Don Carlos*, overture *Chevy Chase* and other orchestral works; vln. concerto; string 4tets and other chamber mus.; sonatas for var. instruments; pf. sonatas and pieces; *Shakespeare Songs* for 4 voices; *Songs in a Cornfield* and numerous other songs, incl. settings of Tennyson and Kingsley, etc.

Macfarren, Walter (Cecil) (b. London, 28. VIII. 1826; d. London, 2. IX. 1905), Eng. pianist, cond. and comp., brother of prec. Choir-boy at Westminster Abbey and student at the R.A.M., where he became prof. of pf. in 1846.

Works incl. symph. in B♭ maj., overtures to Shakespeare's *Winter's Tale, Taming of the Shrew, Henry V* and *Othello* and other overtures; pf. concerto; sonatas for var. instruments; pf. sonatas and pieces; church mus.; madrigals and partsongs; songs, etc.

M'Gibbon, William (b. Edinburgh, *c.* 1690; d. Edinburgh, 3. X. 1756), Scot. violinist and comp. Pupil of his father, the oboist Matthew M'G., and of Corbett in London, on his return to Edinburgh he became leader of the orch. in the Gentlemen's Concerts. Comp. overtures, vln. concertos, vln. sonatas, etc., and pub. 3 vols. of Scot. tunes.

M'Guckin, Barton (b. Dublin, 28. VII. 1852; d. Stoke Poges, Bucks., 17. IV. 1913), Ir. tenor. Choir-boy at Armagh Cathedral, became a singer at St. Patrick's Cathedral, Dublin, and made his 1st concert appearance there in 1874. The next year he came out in London, then studied briefly at Milan, and afterwards took to opera. In 1887–8 he appeared in U.S.A.

Machado, Augusto (b. Lisbon, 27. XII. 1845; d. Lisbon, 24. III. 1924), Port. comp. Studied in Lisbon and at the Paris Cons. Director of the San Carlos Opera from 1892 to 1908, and of the Lisbon Cons. 1901–10.

Works incl. It. operas *Lauriana, I Doria, Mario Wetter* (lib. by Leoncavallo) and *La Borghesina*; Port. operettas; cantata *Camões e os Lusiadas*, etc.

Machaut (or Machault), Guillaume de (b. at or nr. Rheims, *c.* 1300; d. Rheims, 1377), Fr. poet and comp. He became secretary, *c.* 1323, to John of Luxemburg, King of Boh., and went with him to Pol., Lithuania and It. On the king's death in 1346 M. went into the service of his daughter, the Duchess of Normandy, and on her death in 1349 into that of Charles, King of Navarre; later into that of the dauphin (afterwards Charles V) and his brother Jean, Duc de Berry. He became canon of Rheims Cathedral in 1333. An exponent of the *Ars nova* in Fr.

Works incl. Mass for 4 voices, motets, vocal ballades and *rondeaux*, *chansons balladées*, *lais*, etc.

Machiavelli, Niccolo (1469–1527), It. politician and author. *See* **Mandragola** (Castelnuovo-Tedesco), Honegger (*Mandragola*), Ullrich (do.), Waghalter (do.).

Machicotage (Fr.)   a kind of ornaor   mentation once **Macicotaticum** (Lat.) used in plainsong in Fr. but now discredited, extraneous notes being inserted between those prescribed by the notation. It was normally reserved for soloists.

Machl, Tadeusz (b. Lwow, 22. X. 1922), Pol. comp. Studied comp. in Cracow with Malawski and org. with Rutkowski.

Works incl. 4 symphs., 3 concertos for org. and orch., harpsichord concerto, *Lyric Suite* for orch.; chamber mus., songs, etc.

Maciejewski, Roman (b. Berlin, 1910), Pol. pianist and comp. Studied pf. at the Poznan Cons. and comp. with Sikorski at the Warsaw Cons. He went to live in Paris in 1934 and in Eng. in 1938.

Works incl. concerto for 2 pfs. and orch.; mazurkas, *Dances of the Highlander*, etc., for pf.; *Songs from Kurpie*, *Songs of Bilitis* (Pierre Louÿs), etc.

Macintyre, Margaret (b. India, *c.* 1865; d. ?, IV. 1943), Brit. soprano. Made her 1st appearance in London, at Covent Garden, in 1888.

Mackay, Angus (b. ?; d. nr. Dumfries, 21. III. 1859), Scot. bagpiper and folksong collector. Piper to Queen Victoria. Pub. a collection of old bagpipe tunes and a book on bagpipe playing.

Mackenzie, Alexander (Campbell) (b. Edinburgh, 22. VIII. 1847; d. London, 28. IV. 1935), Scot. comp. Studied in Ger. and at the R.A.M. in London, of which, after 14 years as violinist and teacher at Edinburgh and some years at Florence, he became principal in 1888. Knighted 1895.

Works incl. operas *Colomba, The Troubadour, The Cricket on the Hearth* (after Dickens) and *The Eve of St. John*; incid. mus. for *Marmion* and *Ravenswood* (plays based on Scott), Shakespeare's *Coriolanus*, Byron's *Manfred* and Barrie's *The Little Minister*; oratorios *The Rose of Sharon, Bethlehem, The Temptation* (after Milton); cantatas *The Bride, Jason, The Story of Sayid, The Witch's Daughter, The Sun-God's Return*; *The Cottar's Saturday Night* (Burns) for chorus and orch.; suite, Scot. Rhapsody, Canadian Rhapsody, ballad *La Belle Dame sans merci* (after Keats), *Tam o' Shanter* (after Burns), overtures *Cervantes, Twelfth Night* (Shakespeare), *Britannia* and *Youth, Sport and Loyalty* for orch.; concerto, Scot. Concerto, suite and *Pibroch* suite for vln. and orch.; string 4tet; pf. 4tet, pf. trio; vln. and pf. pieces; org. and pf. mus.; songs, part-songs, etc.

Mackerras, Charles (b. Schenectady, N.Y., 17. XI. 1925), Austral. cond., b. in Amer. Taken to Sydney aged 2. Studied at Sydney Cons. and then became 1st ob. of Sydney Symph. Orch. and began his career as a cond. Came to Eng. in 1946 and from 1947 to 1948 studied with V. Talich in Prague. On his return to Eng. he was engaged by Sadler's Wells Opera and has since cond. throughout the world with considerable success. Now principal cond. of Sadler's Wells Opera.

Mackintosh, Robert (b. Tullymet, Perthshire, 1745; d. London, II. 1807), Scot. violinist and comp. Settled at Edinburgh as vln. teacher and concert organizer, but went to live in London in 1803. He comp. and arr. reels, strathspeys, minuets, gavottes, etc.

Maclean, Alick (Alexander Morvaren) (b. Eton, 20. VII. 1872; d. London, 18. V. 1936), Eng. cond. and comp. Educ. at Eton Coll. He became cond. at Wyndham's Theatre in 1899 and of the Scarborough orch. in 1911.

Works incl. operas *Petruccio* (after Shakespeare's *Taming of the Shrew*), *Die Liebesgeige, Maître Seiler, Quentin Dur-*

ward (after Scott), *The King's Price, Die Waldidylle*; incid. mus. for Rostand's *Cyrano de Bergerac*, etc.

Maclean, Charles (Donald) (b. Cambridge, 27. III. 1843; d. London, 23. VI. 1916), Eng. mus. scholar and comp., father of prec. Educ. at Shrewsbury School and Exeter Coll., Oxford, studied mus. with Hiller at Cologne and was mus. director at Eton Coll., 1871–5. After 22 years in the Indian Civil Service, he ed. the pubs. of the I.M.C. and became its gen. secretary in 1908. Comp. a large number of works. esp. for orch.

Macleod, Fiona (William Sharp) (1856–1902), Scot. poet. *See* **Immortal Hour** (Boughton).

M'Leod, Peter (b. West Calder, 8. V. 1797; d. Bonnington, nr. Edinburgh, 10. II. 1859), Scot. comp. Pub. several vols. of songs to words by Scot. poets.

McNaught, William (Gray) (b. London, 30. III. 1849; d. London, 13. X. 1918), Eng. mus. educationist and ed. Studied at the R.A.M., became a choral cond., an inspector of mus. for the Board of Educ., adjudicator at mus. festivals and in 1909 ed. of the *Musical Times*.

McNaught, William (b. London, 1. IX. 1883; d. London, 9. VI. 1953), Eng. mus. critic and ed., son of prec. Educ. at Univ. Coll. School and Worcester Coll., Oxford. He was critic to var. London newspapers, asst. his father and Harvey Grace in ed. the *Musical Times* and followed the latter as ed. in 1944.

MacNeice, Louis (b. 1907), Eng. poet. *See* **Britten** (*Dark Tower*), **Hopkins** (A.) (radio plays), **Walton** (*Christopher Columbus*).

MacNeil, Cornell (b. Minneapolis, 24. IX. 1907), Amer. baritone. Became well known after appearing in Menotti's *The Consul* and joined N.Y. City Opera Co. Has also sung in Eur., appearing at La Scala, Milan, in 1959.

Maçon, Le (*The Mason*), opera by Auber (lib. by Scribe and Germain Delavigne), prod. Paris, Opéra-Comique, 3. V. 1825.

Maconchy, Elizabeth (b. Broxbourne, Herts., 19. III. 1907), Eng. comp. of Ir. descent. Studied comp. under Vaughan Williams and pf. under Arthur Alexander at the R.C.M. in London; later in Prague. Several of her works were perf. at the I.S.C.M. festivals abroad and were successful in Belg., Cz., Hung. and Pol. She married Wm. Le Fanu, who trans. poems by Anacreon for her.

Works incl. ballets *Great Agrippa* (from Hofmann's *Shock-headed Peter*) and *The Little Red Shoes* (after Andersen); 2 motets for double chorus (Donne); *The Leaden Echo and the Golden Echo* (Gerard Manley Hopkins) for chorus and chamber orch.; symph. and suites for orch. *The*

Land (on a poem by V. Sackville-West) and *Puck*; pf. concerto, vln. concerto, concertino for clar.; *Samson at the Gates of Gaza* for voice and orch.; 8 string 4tets, string trio, *Prelude Interlude* and *Fugue* for 2 vlns.; song-cycle *The Garland* (Anacreon), etc.

McPhee, Colin (b. Montreal, 15. III. 1901; d. Los Angeles, 7. I. 1964), Canadian-Amer. comp. Studied at Peabody Cons., Baltimore, with Strube and graduated in 1921. Studied pf. with Friedheim at the Canadian Acad. of Mus., where he played a pf. concerto of his own in 1924. Then studied comp. in Paris with Paul le Flem and pf. with I. Philipp. Meetings with Varèse from 1926 much influenced his own mus. From 1934 to 1939 he spent much time in Bali and Mex.

Works incl. 2 symphs., concerto for pf. and 8 wind instruments, *Tabuh-Tabuhan* for 2 pfs. and orch.; *Balinese Ceremonial Music* for 2 pfs., and other pf. mus.; *4 Iroquois Dances* for orch. Also a number of books on Bali and its mus.

Macpherson, Charles (b. Edinburgh, 10. V. 1870; d. London, 28. V. 1927), Scot. organist and comp. At the age of 9 he became a choir-boy at St. Paul's Cathedral in London and in 1890 entered the R.A.M. After holding 2 private appts., he became sub-organist in 1895 and organist in 1916 of St. Paul's.

Works incl. Psalm cxxxvii for chorus and orch.; anthems and other church mus.; *Highland* and *Hallowe'en* suites and overture *Cridhe an Ghaidhil* for orch.; pf. 4tet; *Gaelic Melodies* for voice, strings and harp, etc.

Macpherson, James (1736–96), Scot. poet, alleged trans. of 'Ossian'. For mus. works *see* Ossian.

Macpherson, Stewart (b. Liverpool, 29. III. 1865; d. London, 27. III. 1941), Eng. mus. educationist and comp. Studied at the R.A.M. in London and later became a prof. there. He also held organist's and cond.'s posts, acted as examiner and wrote a number of theoret. books.

Works incl. Mass in D maj.; symph. in C maj., 2 overtures and other orch. works; *Concerto alla fantasia* for vln. and orch.; church mus.; pf. pieces; songs, etc.

MacQuaid, John (b. Lochgelly, Fifeshire, 14. III. 1909), Scot. comp. Educ. at Glasgow (St. Mungo's Acad. and Univ.) and in Fr., he studied mus. with Chisholm at Glasgow, where for a short time he was asst. mus. master at his old school. He did war service in 1941–6 and afterwards studied Scot. mus. of the 16th and 17th cents. at Edinburgh Univ. with a Carnegie grant.

Works incl. ballet for Lady Galloway's play *The Witch Ladye*; symph. and symph study for orch.; *African Melodies* for ob.,

vln., cello and pf.; suite *The Sea, Elegy* and *Impromptu* for pf., etc.

Macque, Giovanni de (b. Valenciennes, *c.* 1551; d. Naples, IX. 1614), Flem. comp. Pupil of Philippe de Monte. He went to It., living in Rome, 1576–82, and at Naples from 1586, where he became choirmaster of the royal chapel.

Works incl. motets, madrigals and keyboard mus.

Madama Butterfly, opera by Puccini (lib. by Giuseppe Giacosa and Luigi Illica, based on David Belasco's dramatic version of a story by John Luther Long), prod. Milan, Teatro alla Scala, 17. II. 1904.

Madeira (orig. Browning), **Jean** (b. Centralia, Illinois, 14. XI. 1924), Amer. contralto. Studied pf. with her mother and appeared with St. Louis Symph. Orch. aged 12. Studied singing in St. Louis, N.Y. and Vienna, making her début in 1943. In 1948 she became a member of the N.Y. Metropolitan Opera and since 1955 of the Vienna State Opera.

Mademoiselle Fifi, opera by Cui (lib. by ?, in Rus., based on Maupassant's story), prod. Moscow, 15. XII. 1903.

Maderna, Bruno (b. Venice, 21. IV. 1920), It. comp. and cond. Studied vln. and pf., and comp. with Bustini at Acad. of St. Cecilia in Rome, and then took comp. and cond. lessons with Malipiero and Scherchen. He has since cond. throughout Eur., specializing in modern mus.

Works incl. concertos for pf., 2 pfs., fl., ob.; *Introduzione e Passacaglia* for orch.; *Musica su due Dimensioni* for fl., perc. and electronic tape; instrumental works incl. *Composizione in tre tempi, Improvvisazione I, II, Serenata I, II* for 11 and 13 instruments; *Studi per il Processo di Fr. Kafka* for speaker, soprano and chamber orch.; electronic mus. incl. *Notturno, Syntaxis, Continuo, Dimensioni.*

Madetoja, Leevi (Antti) (b. Uleaaborg, 17. II. 1887; d. Helsinki, 6. X. 1947), Fin. cond., critic and comp. Studied at the Cons. of his native town and later with Järnefelt and Sibelius at Helsinki; afterwards with d'Indy in Paris and Fuchs in Vienna. In 1912–14 he cond. the Helsinki orch., afterwards that of Viborg; became mus. critic at Helsinki in 1916 and teacher at the Cons., and in 1926 at the univ.

Works incl. operas *Pohjalaisia* and *Juha*; ballets; 3 symphs., symph. poems and overtures; *Stabat Mater*; 8 cantatas; pf. trio; vln. and pf. sonata; *Lyric Suite* for cello and pf.; pf. pieces; songs, etc.

Madrigal, a comp. for several voices cultivated in the 16th cent. and continuing until the early 17th. Among its special features were a richly polyphonic style and its assoc. with poetry of high value. The texts were secular, except where they were otherwise designated (e.g. *madrigali spiri-tuali*), and the mus. showed a tendency to keep a definite melody in the top part; indeed Ms. were often sung by a single voice, the lower parts being played by instruments; and sometimes the whole perf. was instrumental. The M. was cultivated partic. by Flem., It. and Eng. comps. In the 14th cent. the word was used for a poetic form and its mus.

Madrigal Comedy (*see also* **Amfiparnaso**), a sequence of madrigals in a quasi-dramatic form. The most famous but not the earliest ex. is Orazio Vecchi's *L'Amfiparnaso*, and similar works of his are *La selva di varie ricreazioni* (*The Forest of Multifarious Delights*), *Il convito musicale* (*The Musical Banquet*) and *Le veglie di Siena* (*The Vigils of Siena*). A similar work, Simone Balsamino's *Novellette*, based on Tasso's *Aminta*, appeared the same year as *L'Amfiparnaso* (1594), but there were earlier ones, notably Striggio's *Il cicalamento delle donne al bucato* (*The Cackling of Women at the Wash*), and later Vecchi was imitated by Banchieri and others.

Madrileñe, a Span. dance from the city or province of Madrid.

Maessins, Pieter (b. Ghent, *c.* 1505; d. Vienna, prob. X. 1563), Flem. comp. Chief *Kapellmeister* in Vienna, 1546–60. Comp. Lat. motets.

Maestoso (It. lit. 'majestic') = stately, dignified.

Maestrale. *See* **Stretto maestrale.**

Maestro (It. = master), a title given by Its. to a distinguished musician, whether comp., perf. or teacher.

Maestro al cembalo (It. lit. 'master at the harpsichord'), in the late 17th and 18th cents. the harpsichord player who not only played continuo in the orch. but also acted as asst. to the cond. and helped to coach singers.

Maestro de capilla (Span.) = Maestro di cappella.

Maestro di cappella (It.), director of mus. in a cathedral, a royal or princely chapel, or any similar mus. estab.

Maeterlinck, Maurice (1862–1949), Belg. dramatist and essayist. *See* Abrányi (E.) (*Monna Vanna*), Alexandrov (A. N.) (*Ariane et Barbe-bleue*), Ariane et Barbe-bleue (Dukas), Boulanger (L.) (*Princesse Maleine*), Bréville (do. and *Sept Princesses*), Burian (E.) (*Aladina und Palomid*), Chlubna (do.), Davis (J. D.) (*Intruse*), Février (*Monna Vanna*), Gibbs (C. A.) (*Betrothal*), Gretchaninov (*Sœur Béatrice*), Honegger (*Aglavaine et Sélysette*), Humperdinck (*Blue Bird*), Křička (do.), Liadov (*S. Béatrice*), Loeffler (*Mort de Tintagiles*), Marqués (*Sor Beatriz*), Monna Vanna (Février), Netchaiev (*Seven Princesses*), Nouguès (*Mort de Tintagiles*), Oiseau bleu (Wolff), O'Neill (*Blue Bird*), Pelléas et Mélisande

(Debussy, Fauré, Schönberg and Sibelius), Salmhofer (*Intruse*), Santoliquido (*Morte di Tintagiles*), Séverac (songs), Steinberg (*Princesse Maleine*), Szeligowski (*Blue Bird*), Tocchi (*Destino*), Tovey (*Aglavaine et Sélysette*).

Magadizing (from Gk. *magadis*) = playing or singing in 8ves.

Magalhães, Filippe de (b. Azeitão nr. Lisbon, ?; d. Lisbon, after 1648), Port. 16th–17th-cent. comp. Pupil of Mendes at Evora. *Maestro de capilla* of the Misericordia at Lisbon and from 1614 of the royal chapel there under the Span. king, Philip III.
Works incl. Masses, canticles to the Blessed Virgin, chants, etc.

Magaloff, Nikita (b. St. Petersburg, 26. I. 1912), Rus. pianist. Studied pf. with I. Philipp at the Paris Cons., and comp. with Prokofiev. Began his career as accompanist to Szigeti, later turning to solo concert perfs. In 1949 he succeeded Lipatti as prof. of pf. at the Geneva Cons.

Mage, Pierre du. *See* **Du Mage.**

Magelone Romances, a cycle of 15 songs by Brahms, settings of poems from Ludwig Tieck's *Story of the Fair Magelone*, Op. 33, comp. in 1861–6.

Maggiore (It.) = major. The word is sometimes explicitly stated at a point in a comp. where the maj. key returns after a prolonged section in min., esp. in variations, to prevent the perf. from overlooking the change of key.

Magic Flute (Mozart). *See* **Zauberflöte.**

Magic Opal, The, opera by I. Albéniz (lib. by Arthur Law), prod. London, Lyric Theatre, 19. I. 1893.

Magic Opera, a species of opera not unlike the Eng. pantomime, popular partic. on the Viennese stage at the end of the 18th and opening of the 19th cent., where it was called *Zauberoper*. It consisted of dialogue and mus. numbers, had a fairy-tale subject with incidents of low comedy, and contained numerous scenic effects. The outstanding ex. is Mozart's *Zauberflöte*; others are Müller's *Zauberzither*, Wranitzky's *Oberon*, Süssmayr's *Spiegel von Arkadien*, Schubert's *Zauberharfe*; the Eng. work nearest to it in character is Weber's *Oberon*.

Magnard, (Lucien Denis Gabriel) Albéric (b. Paris, 9. VI. 1865; d. Baron, Oise, 3. IX. 1914), Fr. comp. Studied at the Paris Cons. and in 1888 became a private pupil of d'Indy. As the son of Francis M., ed. of *Le Figaro*, he was comfortably off and never held any official posts. He retired to Baron to devote himself to comp., pub. his works himself and never took any trouble to have them perf., though some were brought out by enthusiastic friends. During the very first days of the 1914–18

war he fired on the Gers. from his window, was killed as a sniper, and his house, incl. several of his MSS., was burnt down.
Works incl. operas *Yolande* (destroyed), *Guercœur* (partly destroyed) and *Bérénice*; 4 symphs., *Suite dans le style ancien, Chant funèbre*, overture *Hymne à la Justice* and *Hymne à Vénus* for orch.; string 4tet, pf. trio, pf. and wind 5tet; vln. and pf. sonata, cello and pf. sonata; pf. pieces; songs, etc.

Magnetton (Ger. = magnet tone), an electrophonic instrument invented by Stelzhammer of Vienna in 1933, prod. its notes by means of electro-magnets and capable of imitating var. instruments.

Magnificat, the song of the Blessed Virgin, regularly sung as a Vesper canticle in the Rom. Catholic Church and as part of the evening service in the Ang. Church; also, more rarely, in a form better suited to concert perf., e.g. Bach, Vaughan Williams, etc.

Mahabharata, The, Hindu epic, in Sanskrit. *See* **Sāvitri** (Holst), **Zumpe** (*Sawitri*).

Mahillon, Victor (b. Brussels, 10. III. 1841; d. Saint-Jean, Cap Ferrat, 17. VI. 1924), Belg. mus. scholar. Son of the instrument maker Charles M. (1813–87). Studied at the Brussels Cons., where he became curator of the museum of mus. instruments. He wrote on accoustics and instruments.

Mahler, Fritz (b. Vienna, 16. VII. 1901), Aus. cond. and comp. A nephew of the comp. Gustav M., he studied comp. with Berg and Schönberg and musicology with Guido Adler (1920–4) at Vienna Univ. After cond. at the Vienna Volksoper he was in charge of the Radio Orch. in Copenhagen from 1930 to 1935, emigrating to the U.S.A. in 1936. He taught at the Juilliard Summer School from 1947 to 1953, when he became cond. of the Hartford Symph. Orch.

Mahler, Gustav (b. Kalište, Boh., 7. VII. 1860; d. Vienna, 18. V. 1911), Cz.-Aus. comp. and cond. Son of a Jewish shopkeeper. He showed great talent as a pianist in his childhood, and in 1875 his family, who had removed to Jihlava (Iglau) soon after his birth, succeeded in entering him at the Vienna Cons. His pf. prof., Julius Epstein, seeing his real gifts, advised him to study comp. and cond. He remained at the Cons. until 1878 and also attended Bruckner's lectures at the univ. He began his career as a cond. at a small summer theatre at Hall, in 1881 at Ljubljana and in 1882–3 at Olomouc. His outstanding gifts advanced him to more and more important posts: Cassel, 1884; Prague, 1885; Leipzig, 1886–8; Budapest, 1888-91; Hamburg, 1891–7; and Vienna, Imp. Opera, 1897–1907, where he

became artistic director after a few months. In 1902 he married Alma Maria Schindler, 10. III. In 1892 he cond. Ger. opera at Covent Garden, London, and in 1907, when he was already suffering from heart disease, at the Metropolitan Opera in N.Y. From 1908 to his death he was cond. of the N.Y. Phil. Society, but spent the summers in Aus. composing.
Works incl. 10 symphs. (the last unfinished), some with vocal parts; *Das Lied von der Erde*, symph. for mezzo-soprano and tenor solo and orch.; cantata *Das klagende Lied*; song-cycles *Lieder eines fahrenden Gesellen, Kindertotenlieder*; 3 books of early songs, 5 songs to words by Rückert, many other songs, incl. settings from *Des Knaben Wunderhorn*, etc.

Mahu, Stephan (b. *c.* 1485; d. ?, 1541), Ger. comp. From 1529 he was employed at the court of Ferdinand I as vice-*Kapellmeister* and trombonist. Comp. Lat. motets, and Ger. sacred and secular works.

Mai-Dun, symph. rhapsody by Ireland, inspired by Mai-Dun, now called Maiden Castle, the prehist. earth-works in Dorset; comp. 1919, 1st perf. London, Queen's Hall Promenade concerts, 1921.

Maichelbeck, Franz Anton (b. Reichenau nr. Constance, VII. 1702; d. Freiburg i/B., 14. VI. 1750), Ger. organist and comp. Studied mus. in Rome, 1725–7, and on his return to Freiburg became organist at the Minster (1728) and prof. of It. at the univ. (1730). Comp. chiefly keyboard mus.

Maid Marian, or The Huntress of Arlingford, opera by Bishop (lib. by James Robinson Planché, based on Thomas Love Peacock's novel), prod. London, Covent Garden Theatre, 3. XII. 1822.

Maid of Artois, The, opera by Balfe (lib. by Alfred Bunn), prod. London, Drury Lane Theatre, 27. V. 1836. Written for Malibran.

Maid of Honour, The, opera by Balfe (lib. by Edward Fitzball, based on the same subject as Flotow's *Martha*), prod. London, Drury Lane Theatre, 20. XII. 1847.

Maid of Orleans, The (*Orleanskaya Dieva*), opera by Tchaikovsky (lib. by comp., based on Vassily Andreievich Zhukovsky's trans. of Schiller's drama), prod. St. Petersburg, 25. II. 1881.

Maid of the Mill, The, opera by Arnold (lib. by Isaac Bickerstaffe, based on Richardson's *Pamela*), prod. London, Covent Garden Theatre, 31. I. 1765.

Maikov, Apollon Nikolaievich (1821–1897), Rus. poet and dramatist. *See* **Judith** (Serov).

Maillard, Jean (b. ?; d. ?), Fr. 16th-cent. comp. Pupil (?) of Josquin des Prés. Wrote Masses, motets, Magnificats, *chansons*, etc.

Maillart

Maillart, Aimé (actually Louis) (b. Montpellier, 24. III. 1817; d. Moulins, Alliers, 26. V. 1871), Fr. comp. Studied vln. and comp. at the Paris Cons., Halévy being among his masters. He gained the Prix de Rome in 1841.

Works incl. operas *Gastibelza* (on Hugo's ballad *Guitare*), *Le Moulin des tilleuls*, *La Croix de Marie*, *Les Dragons de Villars*, *Les Pêcheurs de Catane* and *Lara* (after Byron); cantatas *Lionel Foscari*, *La Voie sacrée* and *Le 15 Août*, etc.

Mainardi, Enrico (b. Milan, 19. V. 1897), It. cellist. Studied cello and comp. at Milan Cons. until 1920 and then cello with H. Becker in Berlin. In 1933 he was appointed prof. of cello at the Acad. of St. Cecilia in Rome.

Works incl. cello concerto, suite for cello and pf. and some chamber mus.

Maine, Basil (b. Norwich, 4. III. 1894), Eng. critic, novelist and biog. Studied at Cambridge, and after school-mastering and acting became mus. critic to the *Daily Telegraph* in London, 1921, and the *Morning Post*, 1926. Later in his career he took orders in the Church of Eng. His mus. books incl. a large biog. of Elgar, *The Glory of English Music*, var. essays, etc.

Maison à vendre (*House for Sale*), opera by Dalayrac (lib. by Alexandre Duval), prod. Paris, Opéra-Comique, 23. X. 1800.

Maistre, Matthieu Le. *See* Le Maistre.

Maistre, Xavier de (1763–1852), Fr. novelist. *See* **Grisar** (*Voyage autour de ma chambre*).

Maître de chapelle (Fr.) = Maestro di cappella (*q.v.*).

Maîtrise (Fr. = mastership), the former Fr. name for the whole estab. of the choir at cathedrals and collegiate churches, incl. not only all that appertained to their perf. in church, but also to their accommodation and maintenance. The M.s were actually schools of mus.

Majo, Gian Francesco di (b. Naples, 24. III. 1732; d. Naples, 17. XI. 1770), It. comp. Pupil of his father, Giuseppe di M. (1697–1771), *maestro di cappella* at the court at Naples, and later of Padre Martini in Bologna. App. 2nd organist at court in 1750, but lived chiefly as an opera comp.

Works incl. 20 operas, e.g. *Ricimero, rè dei Goti, Astrea Placata, Cajo Fabricio, Ifigenia in Tauride, Eumene* (unfinished at his death, completed by Errichelli and Insanguine), etc.; 8 oratorios; 5 Masses and other church mus.; cantatas, etc.

Major, one of the 2 predominant scales (the other being Minor) of the tonal system. *See* **Scale**. A M. key is one based on the M. scale. *See also* **Major Interval**.

Major Bass, a 32-ft. open pedal org. stop.

Major Interval. 2nds, 3rds, 6ths and 7ths can be M.I.s. If the upper note of a M.I. is flattened (or the lower note is sharp-

Malcużyński

ened) it becomes a min. I. If the upper note of a M.I. is sharpened (or the lower note is flattened) it becomes an augmented I. e.g.:

Makarova, Nina (b. Yurin-on-Volga, 12. VIII. 1908), Rus. comp. She studied at the School of Mus. at Gorky (Nizhny-Novgorod) from 1923 and at the Moscow Cons. from 1927 to 1935. She married Khatchaturian.

Works incl. opera *Courage*; mus. for films; symph. in D min.; cantata for Molotov for solo voices, chorus and orch.; vln. and pf. sonata; instrumental pieces; pf. sonata & pieces; song cycles (Pushkin, etc.), choral songs, etc.

Maklakiewicz, Jan Adam (b. Chojnaty nr. Warsaw, 24. XI. 1899; d. Warsaw, 7. II. 1954), Pol. organist and comp. Studied at the Chopin High School of Mus. and the Cons. at Warsaw, later with Dukas in Paris. In 1932 he became organist at the church of the Holy Cross at Warsaw and gained the Pol. State Mus. Prize for comp. He was also a teacher and critic.

Works incl. mus. for plays and films; church mus.; symph. *Holy God* and Prelude to *Lilla Weneda* for solo voices, chorus and orch.; symph. variations, *Lyric Poem, Song of the Daily Bread, Span. Impressions*, suite of Pol. dances, *The Last Drum in memory of Marshal Pilsudski* for orch. (some with voices); concerto for pf., voice and orch., vln. and cello concertos; vln. and cello pieces; 4 Jap. songs with orch.; *Les Vierges au crépuscule* for 2 voices, fl., vla. and harp; 7 songs *Preludes*, other songs; folksong arrs., etc.

Makropulos, Case, The (*Več Makropulos*), opera by Janáček (lib. based on Karel Čapek's play), prod. Brno, 18. XII. 1926.

Malagueña, a Span. (Andalusian) song whose place of orig. is Málaga. It also appears often as an instrumental piece. It begins and ends on the dominant of its key.

Malbecque, Guillermus (b. ?; d. ?), Fr. comp., member of the papal chapel, 1431–8. Comp. 3-part *chansons*.

Malcużyński, Witold (b. Warsaw, 10. VIII. 1914), Pol. pianist. Studied at Warsaw Cons. with Turczyski, and then with Paderewski in Switz. In 1939 he married the Fr. pianist Colette Gaveau and moved to Paris. He has played in all parts of the world and is esp. well known as an interpreter of Chopin.

Malczewski, Antoni (1793–1826), Pol. poet. *See* **Melcer** (*Maria*), **Opieński** (do.), **Soltys** (do.), **Statkowski** (do.).

Maldere, Pierre van (b. Brussels, 16. X. 1729; d. Brussels, 1. XI. 1768), Belg. violinist and comp. Travelled as a virtuoso, 1752–8, visiting Dublin, Paris and Vienna, and on his return to Brussels entered the service of the Duke of Lorraine. Director of the Brussels Opera, 1763–6.

Works incl. operas *Le Déguisement pastoral*, *Les Précautions inutiles*, *La Bagarre*, etc.; symphs., concertos, sonatas, etc.

Male Alto, an artificial extension of the highest male-voice register, prod. by falsetto, used in Angl. church choirs and in male-voice 4tets and choral societies, partic. in glees and part-songs.

Male Contralto } *See* **Castrati.**
Male Soprano }

Maleingreau (properly Malengreau), **Paul de** (b. Trélon-en-Thiérache, 23. XI. 1887; d. Brussels, 9. I. 1956), Belg. organist and comp. Entered the Brussels Cons. in 1905, studying comp. under Tinel. He became prof. of harmony there and acquired fame as an org. recitalist.

Works incl. *Symphonie de Noël*, *Symphonie de la Passion*, 2 *Opus sacrum*, *Préludes à l'Introit*, *Triptyque pour la Noël*, etc. for org.; *Prélude, Choral et Fugue*, suite, sonatina, *Les Angelus de printemps*, etc. for pf.; cello and pf. sonata, etc.

Maler, Wilhelm (b. Heidelberg, 21. VI. 1902), Ger. comp. Studied with var. masters, incl. Jarnach, and was influenced by Hindemith. He was app. prof. of comp. at Cologne Cons. in 1925 and later also taught at Bonn Univ.

Works incl. oratorio *Der ewige Strom*, cantata on poems by Stefan George; *Concerto grosso* and *Rondo on an Old Flem. Dance Ballad* for orch.; pf. concerto, harpsichord concerto, vln. concerto; string 4tet; mus. for Youth Movement, games, etc.

Malherbe, Charles Théodore (b. Paris, 21. IV. 1853; d. Cormeilles, Eure, 5. X. 1911), Fr. musicologist. Studied law and literature in Paris, but turned to mus. and became asst. archivist at the Opéra in 1896 and archivist, in succession to Nuitter, in 1899. He made a great collection of mus. autographs, which he left to the Paris Cons. His books incl. studies of *opéra-comique*, Wagner, Donizetti (catalogue), Auber, Tchaikovsky, etc.

Malheurs d'Orphée, Les (*The Miseries of Orpheus*), opera by Milhaud (lib. by Armand Lunel), prod. Brussels, Théâtre de la Monnaie, 7. V. 1926.

Malibran (*née* García), **Maria (Felicità)** (b. Paris, 24. III. 1808; d. Manchester, 23. IX. 1836), Span. soprano. Studied under her father, Manuel García. After much travelling in It., etc., and appearing in a child's part in Paer's *Agnese* at Naples in 1814, she made her 1st concert appearance in Paris in 1824, and on the stage in London in 1825. In 1826 she married Malibran, an elderly Frenchman, but left him when he went bankrupt in 1827, and in 1830 she formed an attachment with Bériot, whom she married as soon as she had obtained her divorce, shortly before her sudden death.

Malinconia (noun) }
Malinconico (adj.) } (It.) = melancholy.

Malipiero, (Gian) Francesco (b. Venice 18. III. 1882), It. comp. In 1898 he began studying vln. at the Vienna Cons., but on failing an examination turned to comp., returning to Venice in 1899. Graduated from Bologna Liceo Musicale in 1904. In 1913 he went to Paris. From 1921 to 1923 he was prof. of comp. at Parma Univ. and from 1939 to 1953 was director of the Liceo Musicale Benedetto Marcello in Venice. He is the ed. of the complete ed. of Monteverdi's works.

Works incl. operatic trilogy *L'Orfeide* (*La morte delle maschere, Sette canzoni, Orfeo*), operas *Tre commedie goldoniane* (Goldoni's plays *La bottega da caffè, Sior Todero Brontolon, Le baruffe chiozzotte*), *Filomela e l'infatuato, Merlino mastro d'organi, Il mistero di Venezia* (*Le aquile Aquileia, Il finto Arlecchino, I corvi di San Marco*), *Torneo notturno, La favola del figlio cambiato* (lib. by Pirandello), *Giulio Cesare* and *Antonio e Cleopatra* (both after Shakespeare), *Ecuba, I capricci di Callot* (after E. T. A. Hoffmann), *L'allegra brigata, La vita è sogno, Santa Eufemia*; ballets *La mascherata delle principesse prigioniere, Pantea*; *Virgilii Aeneis* for solo voices, chorus and orch., *Li sette peccati mortali* (7 sonnets by Fazio degli Uberti) for chorus and orch.; for orch.: *Sinfonia del mare, Sinfonia del silenzio e della morte, Ditirambo tragico, Impressioni dal vero* (3 sets), *Per una favola cavalleresca, Pause del silenzio, Concerti, Inni, Invenzioni, Sinfonia in quattro tempi come le quattro stagioni, Sinfonia elegiaca, Sinfonie delle campane* and others; 4 pf. concertos, *Variazioni senza tema* for pf. and orch., vln. concerto, cello concerto; *Il commiato* (Leopardi) for baritone and orch.; oratorios *San Francesco d'Assisi, La cena, La passione, Missa pro mortuis*; 7 string 4tets, incl. *Rispetti e strambotti, Stornelli e ballate* and *Canzoni alla madrigalesca*; *Sonata a tre* for vln., cello and pf., *Sonata a cinque* for fl., harp, vln., vla. and cello, *Ricercari* and *Ritrovari* for 11 instruments, *Le sette allegrezze d'amore* for voice and 14 instruments and other chamber mus.; many pf. works: *Preludi autunnali, Poemi asolani, Barlumi, Maschere che passano*, etc.; songs *Tre poesie di Angelo Poliziano*, *Quattro sonetti del Burchiello*, *Due sonetti del Berni*, *Le stagioni italiche*, etc.

Maliszewski, Witold (b. Mohylev, Podolia, 20. VII. 1873; d. Warsaw, 18. VII. 1939), Pol. violinist, pianist and comp. In his youth the family lived in the Caucasus and he studied at Tiflis, but in 1891 went to St. Petersburg to study medicine; however, he later entered the Cons. as a pupil of Rimsky-Korsakov, and in 1908–21 was director of the Odessa school of mus. He then left for Warsaw, where he taught at the Cons. and the Chopin School of Mus. In 1931 he became director of the art dept. of the Ministry of Educ., and gained the State Mus. Prize. In 1933 he founded the Chopin Inst. in Warsaw.

Works incl. opera-ballets *Syrena* and *The Legend of Boruta*; Requiem and *Missa Pontificalis Papae Pii XI*; 4 symphs., 2 symph. pictures, *Merry Overture* and overture on themes by Schubert; pf. concerto, fantasy for pf. and orch., suite for cello and orch.; 3 string 4tets, string 5tet; pf. pieces; songs, etc.

Malko, Nikolai (Andreievich) (b. Brailov, 4. V. 1883; d. Roseville, Sydney, 22. VI. 1961), Rus. cond. He studied at St. Petersburg with Rimsky-Korsakov, Glazunov and N. Tcherepnin, and at Carlsruhe with Mottl. After teaching in Moscow and Leningrad he became cond. of the Leningrad Phil. Orch. in 1926, but left. Rus. in 1928 for Denmark and U.S.A. He was cond. of the Yorkshire Symph. Orch. from 1954 to 1956 and was app. cond. of the Sydney Symph. Orch. in 1957.

Mallarmé, Stéphane (1842–98), Fr. poet. *See* **Boulez** (*Pli selon pli*), **Cartan**, **Debussy** (3 poems), **Hindemith** (*Mirror before me*), **Prélude à l'Après-midi d'un faune** (Debussy), **Ravel** (3 poems).

Mallet (orig. Malloch), **David** (1705–65), Scot. poet and essayist. *See* **Alfred** (Arne, incl. 'Rule, Britannia').

Malling, Otto (Valdemar) (b. Copenhagen, 1. VI. 1848; d. Copenhagen, 5. X. 1915), Dan. comp. Studied in Copenhagen and abroad, became choral cond. in Copenhagen in 1872, church organist in 1878 and director of the Cons. in 1899.

Works incl. symph. and other orchestral comps.; pf. concerto; choral works; chamber mus.; songs, etc.

Mallinger (*née* Lichtenegger), **Mathilde** (b. Zagreb, 17. II. 1847; d. Berlin, 19. IV. 1920), Ger.-Croatian soprano. Studied 1st with her father, then at the Prague Cons. and in Vienna; made her 1st stage appearance at Munich in 1866 and created the part of Eva in Wagner's *Meistersinger* in 1868.

Mallinson, (James) Albert (b. Leeds, 13. XI. 1870; d. Helsingør, Den., 5. IV.

1946), Eng. organist and comp. He studied mainly abroad and married the Ger. singer Anna Steinhauer, who sang his songs on her tours with him in Ger. and Den. In 1904 he was app. organist of the Eng. church at Dresden.

Works incl. over 300 songs, etc.

Malten (actually Müller), **Therese** (b. Insterburg, 21. VI. 1855; d. Neu-Zschieren nr. Dresden, 2. I. 1930), Ger. soprano. Studied with Gustav Engel in Berlin and made her 1st stage appearance at Dresden in 1873, remaining attached to the Court Opera there.

Malvezzi, Cristoforo (b. Lucca, 28. VI. 1547; d. Florence, 25. XII. 1597), It. comp. Wrote mus. for the Florentine stage performances of 1589 and 1591.

Mälzel, Johann Nepomuk (b. Regensburg, 15. VIII. 1772; d. at sea, 21. VII. 1838), Ger. inventor. Settled in Vienna in 1792 and invented var. mechanical instruments, incl., in 1814, the Metronome. Later he lived in Paris and from 1826 in U.S.A. Beethoven's *Battle of Victoria* was orig. written for M.'s 'Panharmonicon'.

Mamelles de Tirésias, Les (*The Breasts of Tiresias*), *opéra-bouffe* in 2 acts by Poulenc. (lib. by Guillaume Apollinaire), prod. Paris, Opéra-Comique, 3. VI. 1947.

Manara, Francesco (b. ?; d. ?), It. 16th-cent. comp. In 1555 he was in the service of Alfonso II of Ferrara. Wrote madrigals and some church mus.

Manchicourt, Pierre de (b. Béthune, *c.* 1510; d. Madrid, 5. X. 1564), Fr. or Flem. comp. He worked at Tournai, *c.* 1540, Arras, *c.* 1555 and (?) Antwerp later.

Works incl. Masses, motets; *chansons*, etc.

Mancinelli, Luigi (b. Orvieto, 5. II. 1848; d. Rome, 2. II. 1921), It. cond. and comp. Studied at Florence, incl. the cello, and joined the orch. at the Teatro della Pergola there. In 1874 he went to the Teatro Apollo in Rome, where he deputized for a cond. so successfully that he made operatic cond. his future career. In 1876 he appeared as comp. of incid. mus. and in 1884 prod. his 1st opera. From 1881 to 1886 he was director of the Liceo Musicale at Bologna, as well as *maestro di cappella* at San Petronio and cond. of the Teatro Comunale there, and he organized orchestral and chamber mus. Later he appeared as a cond. in London, Madrid and N.Y. From 1906 to 1912 he was principal cond. at the Teatro Colón in Buenos Aires.

Works incl. operas *Isora di Provenza*, *Ero e Leandro*, *Paolo e Francesca* (after Dante), *Tizianello*, *Sogno di una notte d'estate* (after Shakespeare); incid. mus. to Pietro Cossa's *Messalina* and *Cleopatra*; oratorio *Isaias*, cantata *St. Agnes*; 2 Masses, etc.

Mancini, Francesco (b. Naples, 16. I. 1672; d. Naples, 22. IX. 1737), It. comp. Pupil of Provenzale and Ursino at the Cons. della Pietà dei Turchini in Naples, entered the service of the court and rose to become *maestro di cappella* 1708 and from 1725 till his death. Director of the Cons. S. Maria di Loreto from 1720.

Works incl. operas *L'Idaspe fedele* (orig. title *Gli Amanti generosi*), *Trajano*, and *c.* 20 others; 6 oratorios; cantatas; vln. sonatas; keyboard mus., etc.

Mancinus (real name Mencken), **Thomas**, (b. Schwerin, 1550; d. Schwerin, *c.* 1612), Ger. comp. Cantor at the cathedral school of Schwerin, 1572–8, and then in the service of the Duke of Brunswick at Wolfenbüttel.

Works incl. Passions according to St. Matthew and St. John, Lat. and Ger. motets and madrigals, secular Ger. songs for several voices, etc.

Mandolin(e), a string instrument related to the lute, but with a more rounded back and metal strings, which are played with a plectrum. The fingerboard is fretted to facilitate fingering and intonation.

Mandore, a small string instrument of the lute family, now obs.

Mandragola, La (*The Mandrake*), opera by Castelnuovo-Tedesco (lib. based on Machiavelli's comedy), prod. Venice, Teatro La Fenice, 4. V. 1926.

Mandyczewski, Eusebius (b. Czernowitz [Cernauti], 18. VIII. 1857; d. Vienna, 13. VII. 1929), Aus. musicologist. Studied at the Vienna Cons. In 1887 he became keeper of the archives of the Vienna Phil. Society and in 1897 prof. at the Cons. Co-ed. of the complete Schubert and Brahms eds. and of that of Haydn's works (now abandoned).

Manelli, Francesco (b. Tivoli, *c.* 1595; d. Parma, IX. 1667), It. bass and comp. Singer at Tivoli Cathedral, 1605–24, and *maestro di cappella* there, 1627–9. He then went to Rome, married a singer, and about 1636 settled at Venice, where his wife ed. his collected non-operatic works. From about 1645 he was in the service of the Duke of Parma, Ranuccio II.

Works incl. operas *L'Andromeda, La maga fulminata, L'Alcate, La Licaste* and others; cantatas, *canzonets, chaconnes,* etc.

Manén, Joan (b. Barcelona, 14. III. 1883), Span. violinist and comp. Studied with his father and later with Jean Alard in Paris. He toured widely and eventually settled in Berlin. Ed. of complete works of Paganini.

Works incl. operas *Giovanna di Napoli, Neron y Acte, Cami del sol, Der Fackeltanz*; symph. poem *Nova Catalonia*; Span. vln. concerto, Catalan Caprices and *Scherzo fantastique* for vln. and orch., Concerto

grosso *Juventus* for 2 vlns., pf. and orch.; string 4tet; suites for vln. and pf., etc.

Manfred, incid. mus. for Byron's drama by Schumann, Op. 115, comp. 1849; 1st concert perf. of the overture, Leipzig, Gewandhaus, III. 1852. The whole prod. with Byron's play, Weimar, 13. VI. 1852.

Symph. by Tchaikovsky, Op. 58, based on the same, comp. 1885 and perf. Moscow, 6. IV. 1886.

Manfredina, a corruption of the name of the Monferrina which became current in Eng. when that dance was intro.

Mangold, Ger. family of musicians:

1. (Johann) August Daniel M. (b. Darmstadt, 25. VII. 1775; d. Darmstadt, 1842), cellist 1st at the Frankfurt theatre and from 1814 in the Grand-Ducal orch. at Darmstadt.

2. (Johann) Wilhelm M. (b. Darmstadt, 19. XI. 1796; d. Darmstadt, 23. V. 1875), violinist and comp., nephew of prec. Studied with Vogler and under Méhul and Cherubini at the Paris Cons. In court service at Darmstadt from 1819. Comp. operas, overtures, chamber mus., etc.

3. Karl Ludwig Amand M. (b. Darmstadt, 8. X. 1813; d. Oberstdorf, Allgäu, 5. VIII. 1889), cond. and comp., brother of prec. Studied with his father and brother, and later at the Paris Cons. Court mus. director at Darmstadt from 1848.

Works incl. opera *Tannhäuser* and others; cantatas; orchestral pieces: male voice choruses, etc.

Manicorde (Fr.) = clavichord.

Manieren (Ger. plur., lit. 'manners'). In its now obs. mus. sense the word was used for 'Ornaments'.

Mann, Arthur Henry (b. Norwich, 16. V. 1850; d. Cambridge, 19. XI. 1929), Eng. organist, choirmaster and comp. Choir-boy at Norwich Cathedral under Z. Buck. He held var. organist's posts, took the D.Mus. degree at Oxford in 1882, and in 1876 was app. organist and choirmaster at King's Coll., Cambridge.

Works incl. oratorio *Ecce Homo*; Te Deum, services, anthems and other church mus., etc.

Mann, William (Somervell) (b. Madras, 14. II. 1924), Eng. critic, educ. at Winchester and Cambridge. As a member of a numerous mus. family he had much opportunity to play chamber mus. in his youth; later he studied comp. with Seiber and pf. with Ilona Kabos, and in 1948 joined the mus. staff of *The Times*. He pub. a short intro. to Bach (1950), contrib. to the Britten symposium (1952) and to the 5th ed. of Grove's *Dictionary* (1954). He has also written a book on R. Strauss's operas and a trans. of Wagner's *Ring*. He became chief mus. critic of *The Times* in 1960.

Männergesangverein (Ger. lit. 'men's

singing-association'), a male-voice choral society.

Manners, Charles (actually Southcote Mansergh) (b. London, 27. XII. 1857; d. Dundrum, Co. Dublin, 3. V. 1935), Ir. singer and impresario. Studied at the R. Ir. A.M. at Dublin and the R.A.M. in London; later in It. After joining an opera chorus he made his 1st solo stage appearance in 1882. Having married Fanny Moody in 1890 he estab. the Moody-Manners Opera Co. in 1897.

Mannheim School, a group of comps. assoc. with the Electoral court at Mannheim in the mid-18th cent. Under the leadership of Johann Stamitz (1717–57) the court orch. became the most famous of the time, estab. a completely modern style of playing, and placing partic. emphasis on dynamic contrasts, *crescendo* and *diminuendo*, etc. The Mannheim comps., e.g. (in addition to Stamitz) F. X. Richter, Holzbauer, Beck and Cannabich, made notable contribs. to the early development of the symph.

Manns, August (Friedrich) (b. Stolzenberg nr. Stettin, 12. III. 1825; d. London, 1. III. 1907), Ger. cond. At first cellist and violinist in var. bands and orchs. in Ger.; later bandmaster. Went to London as sub-cond. at Crystal Palace, 1854, becoming full cond. in 1855, when he enlarged the orch. Began popular Saturday concerts in 1856 and cond. the Handel Festival, 1883–1900. Knighted 1903.

Manon, opera by Massenet (lib. by Henri Meilhac and Philippe Gille, based on Prévost's novel *Manon Lescaut*), prod. Paris, Opéra-Comique, 19. I. 1884.

Manon Lescaut, ballet by Halévy (scenario by Scribe, based on Prévost's novel, choreography by Jean-Pierre Aumer), prod. Paris, Opéra, 3. V. 1830.

Opera by Auber (lib. by Scribe, based on Prévost's novel), prod. Paris, Opéra-Comique, 23. II. 1856.

Opera by Puccini (lib., in It., by Marco Praga, Domenico Oliva and Luigi Illica, based on Prévost's novel), prod. Turin, Teatro Regio, I. II. 1893.

Mansergh, Southcote. *See* **Manners, Charles.**

Mantova, Jachet da. *See* **Jachet da Mantova.**

Manual (from Lat. *manus* = hand), a keyboard played by the hand, esp. the keyboards of the org. as distinct from the pedals.

Manualiter (late Lat.), a direction formerly found in org. mus. indicating that a passage is to be played on a manual or manuals.

Manuel Venegas, unfinished opera by H. Wolf (lib. by Moritz Hoernes, based on Alarcón's *El niño de la bola*), begun 1897.

Manzoni, Alessandro (1785–1873), It. poet and novelist. *See* **Bianca e Falliero** (Rossini), **Bryllupet ved Como-Søen** (Gläser), **Promessi sposi** (Petrella and Ponchielli).

Manzoni Requiem, the name often given to Verdi's Requiem, comp. in 1873 for the anniversary of the death of Alessandro Manzoni, on which it was 1st perf. at Milan, church of San Marco, 22. V. 1874; repeated at the Teatro alla Scala on 25. V. The 'Libera me' is adapted from that contrib. by V. to the collective Requiem he suggested should be written by var. It. comps. on the death of Rossini in 1868, a plan which did not materialize. That the 'Libera me' was not merely taken over as it stood is proved by the fact that it contains allusions to material occurring earlier in the M. R.

Manzuoli, Giovanni (b. Florence, *c.* 1725; d. Florence, *c.* 1780), It. castrato soprano. Made his It. début in 1748, and later visited Madrid, London and Vienna.

Maometto Secondo (*Mahomet II*), opera by Rossini (lib. by Cesare della Valle, Duke of Ventignano), prod. Naples, Teatro San Carlo, 3. XII. 1820. A Fr. version entitled *Le Siège de Corinthe*, prod. Paris, 9. X. 1826.

Mara (*née* **Schmeling**), **Gertrud Elisabeth** (b. Cassel, 23. II. 1749; d. Reval, 20. I. 1833), Ger. soprano. Taken on tour by her father, a poor musician, as a child prodigy violinist. Her talent as a singer was discovered in 1759 in London, where she had lessons from Paradisi. Sang under Hiller in Leipzig, and made her operatic début in Dresden in 1767. She married the cellist Mara in 1771 and entered the service of Frederick the Great in Berlin, but left in 1780 and appeared with great success in Vienna, Paris, London, etc.

Mara, La (Marie Lipsius). *See* **La Mara.**

Maraca, a perc. instrument used mainly in jazz and swing bands, a rattle made of a dried gourd containing beads, dried seeds or shot.

Marais, Marin (b. Paris, 31. V. 1656; d. Paris, 15. VIII. 1728), Fr. bass violist and comp. Pupil of Chaperon at the Sainte-Chapelle and of viol masters; later member of the royal band and the orch. at the Opéra, where he studied comp. under Lully. In 1725 he retired to devote himself to gardening, but continued to teach. He added a 7th string to the bass viol.

Works incl. operas *Idylle dramatique*, *Alcide* and *Pantomime des pages* (both with Lully's son Louis), *Ariane et Bacchus*, *Alcyone*, *Sémélé*; Te Deum; concertos for vln. and bass; trios for fl., vln. and bass; pieces for 1 and 2 viols; *La Gamme* pieces for vln., viol. and harpsichord, etc.

Marais, Roland (b. ?, c. 1680; d. ?, c. 1750), Fr. vla.-da-gamba player and comp., son of prec. Succeeded his father as solo gamba in the royal band, pub. a *Nouvelle méthode de musique* (1711) and 2 books of pieces for viol.

Marazzoli (or Marazzuoli), Marco (b. Parma, c. 1619; d. Rome, 24. I. 1662), It. singer, harpist and comp. Sang in the Papal Chapel in Rome in the 1630s and was in the service of Christina of Swed. there.

Works incl. operas *Chi soffre speri* (with V. Mazzocchi), *Dal male il bene* (with Abbatini), *La vita umana* and others; oratorios, cantatas; songs, etc.

Marbeck (or Merbecke), John (b. ? Windsor, c. 1510; d. Windsor, c. 1585), Eng. singer, organist and comp. He was lay-clerk and organist at St. George's Chapel, Windsor, from c. 1540. In 1543 he was arrested and in 1544 tried and condemned for heresy, but he was pardoned and allowed to retain his office.

Works incl. Mass and 2 motets (prob. early); carol *A Virgine and Mother*; *The Booke of Common Praier noted*, 1550 (i.e. set to notes), being the 1st mus. setting of the Angl. prayer book (1st version authorized by Edward VI).

Marcabru (b. ?; d. ?), the earliest troubadour of importance (early 12th cent.). The most famous of his 4 surviving songs with tunes is the semi-religious 'Pax in nomine Domini'.

Marcando (It. = marking, accentuating) or

Marcato (It. = marked, accentuated), a direction indicating that a piece or movement is to be played in a decided, energetic manner, or that a part is to be brought out strongly above the accomp. or surrounding parts in a passage.

Marcello, Benedetto (b. Venice, 2. VIII. 1686; d. Brescia, 25. VII. 1739), It. violinist, comp. and author. A pupil of Gasparini and Lotti, he combined his mus. interests with a career in law and the civil service. As well as comp. he wrote the lib. for Ruggeri's opera *Arato in Sparta*, and in 1720 pub. the important satire on contemporary opera *Il teatro alla moda*.

Comps. incl. operas and serenatas *La fede riconosciuta*, *Arianna*, etc.; oratorios *Giuditta*, *Gioàz*, *Il trionfo della poesia e della musica*; Masses, Misereres and other church mus.; *Estro poetico-armonico*, settings of 50 psalm-papaphrases by G. A. Giustiniani; concertos, sonatas, etc. for various instruments, etc.

March, a piece of mus. in strongly emphasized regular metre, usually in 4–4 or 2–4 time, but sometimes in 6–8, primarily intended for use at military parades to keep marching soldiers in step, but also the mus. most often used for processions of var. kinds, incl. those occurring on the stage in operas and other theatre pieces. Funeral M.s also have primarily a processional purpose, and they are considerably slower in pace. M.s of all kinds, however, may occur in sonatas, symphs. or suites and are often labelled *alla marcia* or *alla marcia funebre*.

Marchal, André (b. Paris, 6. II. 1894), Fr. organist, blind from birth. Studied at the Paris Cons. and from 1915 to 1945 was organist in Paris at St. Germain-des-Prés and from 1945 at St. Eustache. He is esp. well known for his improvisations at the org.

Marchand de Venise, Le (*The Merchant of Venice*), opera by Hahn (lib. by Miguel Zamaçoïs, after Shakespeare), prod. Paris, Opéra, 25. III. 1935.

Marchand, Louis (b. Lyons, 2. II. 1669; d. Paris, 17. II. 1732), Fr. organist and comp. A child prodigy, he was organist of Nevers Cathedral at the age of 14 and later of Auxerre Cathedral, before settling in Paris, c. 1698. Organist of various churches there and of the Royal Chapel, 1708–14, he then toured Ger., visiting Dresden in 1717 and there declining to compete with Bach at the org. On his return to Paris he lived mainly by teaching.

Works incl. org. mus., 2 books of harpsichord pieces, etc.

Marchant, Stanley (Robert) (b. London, 15. V. 1883; d. London, 28. II. 1949), Eng. organist, teacher and comp. Studied at the R.A.M. in London, of which he became principal in 1936, succeeding McEwen. He held var. organist's posts. incl. those of asst. and sub-organist at St. Paul's Cathedral, took the D.Mus. degree at Oxford in 1914 and became 1st organist at St. Paul's in 1927. In 1937 he became prof. of mus. at London Univ. Knighted in 1943.

Works incl. Te Deum for the re-opening of St. Paul's (1930), Te Deum for George V's jubilee (1935), etc.

Marchesi (de Castrone), It. family of singers:

1. **Salvatore M.** (b. Palermo, 15. I. 1822; d. Paris, 20. II. 1908), baritone and teacher. He came of a noble family, succeeding later to the title of Marchese della Raiata. Studying law and philosophy at Palermo, he took singing and comp. lessons from Raimondi and later studied at Milan under Lamperti and others. Having fled to Amer. as a political refugee from the 1848 revolutions he made his 1st stage appearance in N.Y. On his return to Eur. he settled in London for a time. He married Mathilde Graumann in 1852. Wrote books on singing, vocal exercises, a number of songs and made It. transs. of var. opera libs.

2. **Mathilde M.** (*née* Graumann) (b. Frankfurt, 24. III. 1821; d. London,

17. XI. 1913), mezzo-soprano and teacher, wife of prec. Began to study singing when her father, a wealthy merchant, lost his fortune in 1843. In 1845 she went to Paris to continue her studies with García, whose pupils she took over when he was incapacitated by an accident. Settled in London in 1849, she sang much at concerts. Soon after her marriage to M. she became prof. of singing at the Vienna Cons., 1854–61; later taught mainly in Paris.

3. Blanche M. (b. Paris, 4. IV. 1863; d. London, 15. XII. 1940), soprano and teacher, daughter of prec. Studying the vln. at first, she took to singing in 1881, appeared in Berlin and Brussels in 1895, in London in 1896, and settled there as teacher and concert singer.

Marchesi, Luigi (Lodovico) (b. Milan, 8. VIII. 1754; d. Inzago, 14. XII. 1829), It. castrato soprano. Pupil of Fioroni in the choir of Milan Cathedral, made his operatic début in Rome in 1773. Later travelled widely, visiting London, 1788–1790.

Marchetti, Filippo (b. Bolognola, Macerata, 26. II. 1831; d. Rome, 18. I. 1902), It. comp. Studied at the Collegio di San Pietro a Maiella at Naples, settled in Rome and later at Milan. Having prod. several successful operas, he ceased to comp. in 1880, became president of the Accademia di Santa Cecilia in Rome, 1881, and director of the Liceo Musicale there, 1885.

Works incl. operas *Gentile da Verano*, *La demente*, *Il paria*, *Romeo e Giulietta* (after Shakespeare), *Ruy Blas* (after Hugo), *Gustavo Wasa*, *Don Giovanni d'Austria*, etc.

Marchettus (b. Padua, ?; d. ?), It. 13th–14th cent. theorist. Lived at Cesena and Verona at some time and was in the service of Rainier, Prince of Monaco. He wrote a treatise on the division of the scale and 2 more on notation, which aroused much opposition.

Marcia (It.) = march.

Maréchal, (Charles) Henri (b. Paris, 22. I. 1842; d. Paris, 10. V. 1924), Fr. comp. Studied at the Paris Cons., where he gained the Prix de Rome in 1870. In 1896 he became inspector of mus. educ.

Works incl. operas *Les Amours de Cathérine*, *La Taverne des Trabans*, *L'Étoile*, *Déidamie*, *Calendal*, *Ping-Sin*, *Daphnis et Chloé*; ballet *Le Lac des aulnes*; incid. mus. for a stage version of Erckmann-Chatrian's *L'Ami Fritz*, of Dostoievsky's *Crime and Punishment*, etc.; oratorios *La Nativité*, *Le Miracle de Naïm*; cantata *Le Jugement de Dieu*; *Esquisses vénitiennes* and *Antar* for orch.; *Les Vivants et les morts* for vocal 4tet and orch., etc.

Marek, Czeslaw (b. Przemysl, 16. IX. 1891), Pol. pianist and comp. Studied at Lwów, at the Acad. of Mus. in Vienna and was also a pf. pupil of Leschetizky there. In 1913–14 he studied comp. with Pfitzner at Strasbourg. He travelled widely as pianist in 1916–28, taught at Lwów and later at Zürich, where he settled.

Works incl. suite and *Sinfonia* for the Schubert centenary, scherzo for orch.; Pol. folksongs with chamber orch.; *Little Suite* for 3 recorders or vlns. and pf. and other school and home mus.; sonata and pieces for vln. and pf.; 2 *Romantic Pieces* for harp, *Triptych*, *Pieces for Children* and other pf. works; choral works; songs, incl. 5 to words by Lenau, etc.

Marenzio, Luca (b. Coccaglio nr. Brescia, 1553; d. Rome, 22. VIII. 1599), It. singer and comp. Studied with Giovanni Contini, organist at Brescia Cathedral, pub. his 1st work in 1581, went to Rome soon afterwards, where he became *maestro di cappella* to Cardinal d'Este, served under Sigismund III in Pol. for 2 years some time between 1588 and 1593, returned to Rome, where he became a singer or (?) organist in the Papal Chapel and came under the patronage of Cardinal Aldobrandini. His madrigals were intro. into Eng. through Yonge's *Musica transalpina* in 1588 and he was in correspondence with Dowland in 1595.

Works incl. Mass, motets, *Sacri concenti*; madrigals (9 vols.), *Villanelle ed arie alla napolitana* (5 vols.), etc.

Marescotti, André (b. Geneva, 30. IV. 1902), Swiss. organist and comp. Studied at Geneva and with Roger-Ducasse in Paris. App. organist and choirmaster at the Sacré-Cœur at Geneva in 1924 and prof. at the Cons. there.

Works incl. *Messe Saint-André*, 2 motets; overture, *Prélude au Grand Meaulnes* and *Aubade* for orch.; pf. pieces; songs, etc.

Margaret at the Spinning-Wheel (Schubert). *See* Gretchen am Spinnrade.

Margherita d'Anjou, opera by Meyerbeer (lib. in It., by Felice Romani, based on a play by René Charles Guilbert de Pixérécourt), prod. Milan, Teatro alla Scala, 14. XI. 1820.

Maria Antonia Walpurga (or Walpurgis) (b. Munich, 18. VII. 1724; d. Dresden, 23. IV. 1780), Ger. comp. Daughter of the Elector of Bavaria, afterwards Emperor Charles VII. Pupil of Giovanni Ferrandini, Porpora and Hasse; married Frederick Christian, electoral prince of Saxony. She was a member of the Arcadian Acad. in Rome under the name of Ermelinda Talèa Pastorella Arcada (pseud. E. T. P. A.).

Works incl. operas *Il trionfo della fedeltà* (with add. mus. by Hasse) and *Talestri, regina delle Amazoni*, etc.

Maria di Rohan, opera by Donizetti (lib. by Salvatore Cammarano), prod. Vienna, Kärntnertortheater, 5. VI. 1843.

Maria di Rudenz, opera by Donizetti (lib. by Salvatore Cammarano), prod. Venice, Teatro La Fenice, 30. I. 1838.

Maria Theresa Symphony, name given to Haydn's symph. No. 48 in C maj., supposedly comp. for a visit of the Empress M. T. to Esterház in 1773.

Maria Tudor, opera by Gomes (lib. by Marco Praga, based on Victor Hugo's tragedy), prod. Milan, Teatro alla Scala, 27. III. 1879.

Mariages samnites, Les, opera by Grétry (lib. by Barnabé Farmian de Rozoy, based on a story by Marmontel), prod. Paris, Comédie-Italienne, 12. VI. 1776.

Mariani, Angelo (b. Ravenna, 11. X. 1821; d. Genoa, 13. VI. 1873), It. cond. and comp. Studied at home at Rimini and under Rossini at the Liceo Filarmonico of Bologna; came out as violinist-cond. at Messina in 1844 and was cond. of the court theatre at Copenhagen, 1847–8. After fighting in the revolutionary army in 1848, he went to the sultan's court at Constantinople, 1849–52, and then became cond. at the Teatro Carlo Felice at Genoa. He appeared in many places in It. and abroad as guest cond. and gave the 1st It. perf. of Wagner's *Lohengrin* at Bologna in 1871.
Works incl. Requiem; hymn for the Sultan of Turkey, cantatas *La fidanzata del guerriero* and *Gli esuli*; orchestral mus.; songs, etc.

Mariazell Mass, the familiar name of Haydn's C maj. Mass orig. entitled *Missa Cellensis.* Comp. in 1782 for Anton Liebe von Kreutzner, who on his ennoblement wished to make a votive offering at the Marian shrine at Mariazell.

Marie, opera by Hérold (lib. by François Antoine Eugène de Planard), prod. Paris, Opéra-Comique, 12. VIII. 1826.

Mariés de la Tour Eiffel, Les (*The Wedded Pair of the Eiffel Tower*), ballet by 5 of 'Les Six': Auric, Honegger, Milhaud, Poulenc and Tailleferre (scenario by Jean Cocteau), prod. Paris, Théâtre des Champs-Élysées, 18. VI. 1921.

Mariette, Auguste Édouard (Mariette Bey) (1821–81), Fr. Egyptologist. Founder of the museum at Cairo. He outlined the lib. for Verdi's *Aida,* drafted in Fr. by Camille du Locle and written in It. by Ghislanzoni.

Marimba, a Mex. perc. instrument of African origin, made of wood, similar to the Xylophone, but larger and with resonance-boxes to each note.

Marimba Gongs, a perc. instrument similar to the Marimba, but with metal plates instead of wooden strips to prod. the notes.

Marin de La Guerre. *See* **La Guerre.**

Marin, José (b. ? Madrid, 1619; d. Madrid, 17. III. 1699), Span. tenor and comp. He sang in the Encarnación convent at Madrid in his younger years, became a highwayman and a priest, fled to Rome after committing murder, was imprisoned, but at the end of his life had a great reputation as a musician.
Works incl. songs with continuo, songs with guitar accomp., etc.

Marin, (Marie-Martin) Marcel de, Viscount (b. Saint-Jean-de-Luz, 8. IX. 1769; d. ?, after 1861), Fr. harpist, violinist and comp., (?) of It. descent. In 1783 he became a member of the Arcadian Acad. in Rome and during the Fr. Revolution settled in London; later at Toulouse.
Works incl. chamber mus., harp sonatas and pieces, vln. sonatas, etc.

Marine Trumpet. *See* **Trumpet Marine.**

Marini, Biagio (b. Brescia, before 1597; d. Venice, 1665), It. violinist and comp. He was employed successively as violinist at Venice, as mus. director at the church of Sant' Eufemia at Brescia, at the courts of Parma and Munich, at Düsseldorf, Ferrara and Milan.
Works incl. psalms, vespers and other church mus.; symphs.; sonatas, dances, etc., for string instruments; vocal and instrumental chamber mus.; madrigals, *canzonets,* etc., for several voices; sacred songs for several voices, etc.

Marino Faliero, opera by Donizetti (lib. by Emanuele Bidera, based on Byron's drama), prod. Paris, Théâtre Italien, 12. III. 1835.

Marinuzzi, Gino (b. Palermo, 24. III. 1882; d. Milan, 17. VIII. 1945), It. cond. and comp. Studied at the Palermo Cons. 1st appeared as cond. at Catania, later worked at Palermo, Madrid, Trieste, Buenos Aires and Chicago. On his return to It. he cond. opera in all the large cities and he was director of the Liceo Musicale at Bologna, 1915–19. He d. by assassination.
Works incl. operas *Barberina, Jacquerie, Palla de' Mozzi;* suites *Siciliana* and *Romana,* symph. poem *Sicania, Elegia, Rito nuziale* for orch.; *Andantino all' antica* for fl., strings and harp., etc.

Mario (Giovanni Matteo), Cavaliere di Candia (b. Cagliari, 17. X. 1810; d. Rome, 11. XII. 1883), It. tenor. 1st appearance, Paris, 1838; 1st visit to London the following year. Married Giulia Grisi.

Mariotte, Antoine (b. Avignon, 22. XII. 1875; d. Izieux, Loire, 30. XI. 1944), Fr. comp. A naval officer at first, he left the Navy in 1897 and became a student at the Schola Cantorum in Paris as a pupil of d'Indy. He cond. at Saint-Étienne and then at Lyons, and became director of the Orleans Cons. in 1920. In 1935–9 he was director of the Opéra-Comique in Paris. He was accused of having plagiarized R. Strauss in his *Salomé*, but the work was written before Strauss's was prod.

Works incl. operas *Salomé* (Oscar Wilde), *Le Vieux Roi, Esther*: *Princesse d'Israël, Léontine Sœurs, Nele Dooryn, Gargantua* (after Rabelais); *Avril, Pâques françaises* and *Toujours* for unaccomp. chorus; *Impressions urbaines* and *Kakemonos* for pf. and orch.; *En montagne* for 3 wind or string instruments with string 5tet or pf.; sonata, *50 Canons expressifs*, suite *Marine, Sonatines d'automne* for pf.; *Intimités, Poème de pitié, Le Vieux Chemin* and other songs, etc.

Maritana, opera by V. Wallace (lib. by Edward Fitzball, based on the play *Don César de Bazan* by Adolphe Philippe d'Ennery and Philippe François Dumanoir), prod. London, Drury Lane Theatre, 15. XI. 1845.

Marivaux, Pierre de (1688–1763), Fr. novelist and dramatist. *See* **Poise** (*Surprise de l'amour*).

Markevich, Igor (b. Kiev, 27. VII. 1912), Rus. comp. and cond. His parents emigrated and lived in Switz., but he went to Paris at the age of 15 as a pupil of Nadia Boulanger. He has been cond. of the Lamoureux Orch., Paris, since 1958.

Works incl. ballets *Rébus* and *L'Envoi d'Icare*; cantata on Milton's *Paradise Lost* and others, *Cantique d'Amour, Nouvel Age*, cantata for soprano and male-voice chorus (Jean Cocteau); *Hymnes*, concerto grosso and sinfonietta for orch.; concerto and partita for pf. and orch.; *Galop* for small orch.; psalm for soprano and orch.; serenade for vln., clar. and bassoon, etc.

Markull, Friedrich Wilhelm (b. Reichenbach nr. Elbing, Prus., 17. II. 1816; d. Danzig, 30. IV. 1887), Ger. pianist, organist and comp. Studied with Schneider at Dessau and was app. organist at St. Mary's Church at Danzig in 1836.

Works incl. operas *Maja und Alpino, Der König von Zion, Das Walpurgisfest*; oratorios *Johannes der Täufer, Das Gedächtnis der Entschlafenen*; Psalm lxxxvi and hymn-tunes; symphs., org. and pf. works; songs, etc.

Marlowe, Christopher (1564–93), Eng. dramatist. *See* **Bowles** (*Dr. Faustus*).

Marmontel, Antoine François (b. Clermont-Ferrand, 16. VII. 1816; d. Paris, 15. I. 1898), Fr. pianist and teacher. Studied under Zimmermann at the Paris Cons. and became prof. of pf. there in 1848. He wrote several books on the pf. and its mus. and comp. instructive pf. works.

Marmontel, Jean François (b. Bort, Limousin, 11. VII. 1723; d. Abloville, Eure, 31. XII. 1799), Fr. author. Librettist

for Grétry, Piccinni, Cherubini and others; defender of Piccinni against Gluck and author of an *Essai sur les révolutions de la musique en France*.

See also **Amitié a l'épreuve** (Grétry), **Antigone** (Zingarelli), **Atys** (Piccinni), **Céphale et Procris** (Grétry), **Clari** (Bishop, from *Laurette*), **Démophoon** (Cherubini), **Didon** (Piccinni), **Mariages samnites** (Grétry), **Zémire et Azor** (Grétry), **Zemire und Azor** (Spohr).

Mârouf, savetier du Caire (*M., the Cobbler of Cairo*), opera by Rabaud (lib. by Lucien Népoty, based on a story in the *Arabian Nights*), prod. Paris, Opéra-Comique, 15. V. 1914.

Marpurg, Friedrich Wilhelm (b. Sechof nr. Seehausen, Brandenburg, 21. XI. 1718; d. Berlin, 22. V. 1795), Ger. theorist and writer on mus. In Paris as secretary to Gen. Bodenburg (?) in 1746 he met, among others, Voltaire and Rameau, and was influenced by the latter's theories. From 1749 he lived mainly in Berlin, where he began a mus. weekly, *Der critische Musicus an der Spree*. This was followed by numerous other critical and theoret. writings, incl. a notable preface to the 2nd ed. of Bach's *Kunst der Fuge*, treatises on fugue, thorough-bass, keyboard playing, etc. He also comp. some songs and keyboard mus.

Marqués y García, Pedro Miguel (b. Palma de Mallorca, 23. V. 1843; d. Palma, 25. II. 1918), Span. violinist and comp. Studied at the Paris Cons. and with Berlioz, and later in Madrid.

Works incl. zarzuela *El anillo de hierro* and many others; 4 symphs., etc.

Marqués Puig, Antonio (b. Barcelona, 16. IX. 1897), Span. pianist and comp. Pupil of Pedrell and others. In 1913 he became mus. critic at Barcelona.

Works incl. opera *Sor Beatriz* (after Maeterlinck); string 4tet; cello and pf. sonata; pf. sonata; songs, etc.

Marquise de Brinvilliers, La, comic opera by Auber, Batton, Berton, Blangini, Boïeldieu, Carafa, Cherubini, Hérold and Paer (lib. by Scribe and Castil-Blaze), prod. Paris, Opéra-Comique, 31. X. 1831.

Marriage of Figaro (Mozart). *See* **Nozze di Figaro**.

Marriage, The (*Zhenitba*), unfinished opera by Mussorgsky (lib. taken from Gogol's comedy, comp. 1864; never perf. in Mussorgsky's lifetime; prod. with pf. accomp., St. Petersburg, 1. IV. 1909; with orch., Petrograd, 26. X. 1917, with Mussorgsky's *Sorotchintsy Fair*.

Marryat, Frederick (1792–1848), Eng. novelist. *See* **Fliegende Holländer** (Wagner).

Marschner, Heinrich (August) (b. Zittau, 16. VIII. 1795; d. Hanover, 14. XII. 1861), Ger. comp. As a boy he played the pf., sang soprano and comp. tentatively without much instruction. In 1813 he was sent to Leipzig to study law, but met Rochlitz, who induced him to take to mus. In 1816 he went to Vienna and Pressburg with a Hung., Count de Varkony, and settled in the latter place, comp. several operas, until 1823, when he became asst. cond. to Weber and Morlacchi at Dresden. In 1827 he became cond. of the Leipzig theatre and from 1831 to 1859 court cond. at Hanover. He married 4 times.

Works incl. operas *Der Kyffhäuserberg, Saidar, Heinrich IV und Aubigné, Der Holzdieb, Lucretia, Der Vampyr, Der Templer und die Jüdin* (after Scott's *Ivanhoe*), *Des Falkners Braut, Hans Heiling, Der Bäbu, Das Schloss am Aetna, Kaiser Adolf von Nassau, Austin, Sangeskönig Hiarne*; incid. mus. to Kleist's *Prinz Friedrich von Homburg* and other plays; overture on 'God Save the King' and other orchestral works; male-voice choruses; sonatas; songs, etc.

Marseillaise. *See* **National Anthems: France** and **Rouget de l'Isle.**

Marsh, John (b. Dorking, 1752; d. Chichester, 1828), Eng. amateur comp. Practised as a lawyer until 1783, when a legacy enabled him to retire and devote his time to mus., in which he was largely self-taught. Cond. concerts in Chichester and elsewhere, and comp. some notable symphs., also concertos, chamber mus., keyboard mus., etc.

Marsick, Martin Pierre Joseph (b. Jupille nr. Liège, 9. III. 1848; d. Paris, 21. X. 1924), Belg. violinist. Studied at the Liège Cons., later with Léonard at the Brussels Cons. and with Massart at the Paris Cons., succeeding the latter as vln. prof. there in 1892. He was also a pupil of Joachim and 1st appeared in 1873 in Paris, where he formed a string 4tet.

Marson, George (b. Worcester, *c.* 1573; d. Canterbury, 3. II. 1632), Eng. organist and comp. He became organist and choirmaster at Canterbury Cathedral *c.* 1598.

Works incl. services, anthem, psalms and other church mus.; madrigal contrib. to *The Triumphes of Oriana*, etc.

Marteau, Henri (b. Rheims, 31. III. 1874; d. Lichtenberg, Franconia, 3. X. 1934), Fr. violinist and comp. Studied vln. with Léonard and others, and appeared in Vienna, Ger. and Switz. at the age of 10. He then continued his studies at the Paris Cons., where Dubois was his comp. master, travelled much as a violinist later and became prof. of vln. at the Geneva Cons., 1900, at the Berlin Hochschule für Musik, 1908, at the Prague Cons., 1921–4, at the Leipzig Cons., 1926–7 and at the Dresden Cons. from 1928.

Works incl. opera *Meister Schwalbe*; cantata *La Voix de Jeanne d'Arc*; vln. concerto, cello concerto; chamber mus., etc.

Martelé (Fr.) } lit. 'hammered', de-
Martellato (It.) } tached, strongly accentuated playing or singing, used esp. for a stroke of the bow prod. such an effect on string instruments.

Martellement (Fr.) = mordent, also the repetition of a single note on the harp.

Martelli, Henri (b. Bastia, Corsica, 25. II. 1895), Fr. comp. Studied at the Paris Cons., Widor being among his masters.

Works incl. opera *La Chanson de Roland*; incid mus.; 3 symphs., symph. poem *Sur la vie de Jeanne d'Arc, Bas-reliefs assyriens* and concerto for orch.; pf. concerto; string 4tet; string 5tet; pf. pieces; songs, etc.

Martenot, Maurice (b. Paris, 14. X. 1898), Fr. scientist and musician. Studied pf. and cello at the Paris Cons. and comp. with Gédalge. After var. apps. as cond. and teacher he opened the École d'Art Martenot at Neuilly. Inventor of the radio-electrical instrument Ondes Musicales, a development of Theremin's, which he prod. in 1928 and is generally known as the Ondes Martenot. In Fr. a number of comps., Honegger, Milhaud, Koechlin and esp. Messiaen (whose sister-in-law Jeanne Loriod is the instrument's foremost living exponent), have written for it.

Martha, oder Der Markt von Richmond (*M., or The Market at R.*), comic opera by Flotow (lib. by Friedrich Wilhelm Riese, pseud. 'W. Friedrich', based on a ballet-pantomime, *Lady Henriette, ou La Servante de Greenwich*, by Jules Henri Vernoy de Saint-Georges, prod. Paris, 21. II. 1844, with mus. by F. Burgmüller and Deldevez), prod. Vienna, Kärntnertor-theater, 25. XI. 1847.

Martin. The Fr. name of a type of baritone voice of exceptional range, derived from Jean Blaise Martin (1768–1837).

Martin, Frank (b. Geneva, 15. IX. 1890), Swiss pianist and comp. Studied with Joseph Lauber at Geneva and in 1928 became prof. at the Institut Jaques-Dalcroze there.

Works incl. operas *The Tempest* (Shakespeare), *Monsieur Pourceaugnac*, oratorio *Le Mystère de la Nativité*; *Six Monologues from 'Jedermann'* (after Hofmannsthal); ballet *Die blaue Blume*; incid. mus. for Sophocles' *Oedipus Coloneus* and *Oedipus Rex* and Shakespeare's *Romeo and Juliet*; Mass for double chorus, oratorios *In terra pax, Golgotha, Cantate sur la Nativité*; symph. suite *Rhythmes, Esquisse*, symph. for orch.; *Petite Symphonie concertante* for harp, harpsichord, pf. and strings; pf. concerto, vln. concerto, cello concerto; *Cornet* (Rilke) for contralto and orch.; pf. 5tet, rhapsody for string 5tet, string 4tet, string trio, pf. trio on Ir. tunes; *Le Vin herbé* for 12 voices, strings and pf. (on the subject of Tristram and Yseult, from Joseph Bédier); 2 vln. and pf. sonatas, etc.

Martin, George (Clement) (b. Lambourne, Berks., 11. IX. 1844; d. London, 23. II. 1916), Eng. organist and comp. Pupil of Stainer and others. After holding var. org. appts. and becoming org. prof. at the R.C.M. in London he became organist of St. Paul's Cathedral in succession to Stainer in 1888. Knighted 1897, D.Mus., Oxford, 1912.

Works incl. Te Deum for Queen Victoria's Diamond Jubilee; services, anthems and other church mus.; songs, part-songs, etc.

Martín y Soler, Vicente (b. Valencia, 18. VI. 1754; d. St. Petersburg, 30. I. 1806), Span. comp. Chorister at Valencia, made his début as an opera comp. in Madrid in 1776, then went to It., where he prob. studied with Padre Martini, and prod. operas successfully in Naples, Turin, Venice, etc. In Vienna, 1758–8, he comp. 3 operas on libs. by da Ponte, the most successful of which, *Una cosa rara* (1786), for a time eclipsed Mozart's *Figaro*. Apart from a visit to London, 1794–5, he lived from 1788 in St. Petersburg, in the service of the Rus. court.

Works incl. operas *Ifigenia in Aulide*, *Ipermestra*, *Andromaca*, *Astartea*, *Partenope*, *In amor si vuol destrezza* (*L'accorta cameriera*), *Vologeso*, *Le burle per amore*, *La vedova spiritosa*, *Il burbero di buon cuore*, *Una cosa rara, o Bellezza ed onestà*, *L'arbore di Diana*, *Gore Bogatyr Kosometovich*, *Melomania* (Rus.), *Fedul and his Children* (Rus. libs. of these 3 by Catherine II), *Il castello d'Atlante*, *La scuola de' maritati*, *L'isola del piacere*, *Le nozze de' contadini spagnuoli*, *La festa del villaggio*; prologue *La Dora festeggiante* for *Vologeso*; several ballets; church mus.; cantatas *La deità benefica* and *Il sogno*, canzonets, canons, etc.

Martinelli, Giovanni (b. Montagno, 22. X. 1885; d. N.Y., 2. II. 1969), It. tenor. After he played the clar. in an army band his voice was discovered and he studied singing in Milan, making his début in 1910. He sang at Covent Garden, 1912–14, 1919 and 1937, but the greater part of his career was spent at the N.Y. Metropolitan Opera from 1913 to 1946. He became one of the most famous tenors of the cent.

Martines, Marianne (b. Vienna, 4. V. 1744; d. Vienna, 13. XII. 1812), Aus. comp. and clavier player of Span. descent. Daughter of the master of ceremonies to the pope's nuncio in Vienna; pupil of Metastasio, Porpora and Haydn.

Works incl. oratorios *Isacco* and *Santa Elena al Calvario*, psalms trans. by Metastasio, Mass, motets, cantatas; symphs.; overtures; concertos; sonatas, etc.

Martini, Giovanni Battista (or Giambattista, known as **Padre Martini)** (b. Bologna, 24. IV. 1706; d. Bologna, 4. X. 1784), It. priest, theorist, teacher and comp. Received a thorough mus. educ. from his father and others in vln., harpsichord, singing and comp. Entered the Franciscan Order in 1721 (priest 1729), and was app. *maestro di cappella* of San Francesco in Bologna in 1725, after which he rarely left his home town. As the most famous teacher and theorist of his time he attracted many distinguished pupils, incl. Mozart, and corresponded with musicians throughout Eur. His most important works are the unfinished hist. of mus. (3 vols., 1757–81) and a treatise on counterpoint (1773–5).

Comps. incl. oratorios *L'assunzione di Salomone*, *San Pietro*, *Il sacrificio d'Abramo*; Masses, motets, psalm settings and other church mus.; stage works; keyboard works, etc.

Martini, Jean Paul Egide (real name Johann Paul Aegidius Schwartzendorf) (b. Freistadt, Upper Palatinate, 1. IX. 1741; d. Paris, 10. II. 1816), Ger. organist and comp., adopted the name of M. on settling in Nancy as a mus. teacher in 1760. In the service of the Duke of Lorraine (the former King Stanislaus of Pol.) at Lunéville, 1761–4, he then went to Paris, where he wrote military mus. and prod. his 1st opera in 1771. After 3 years' absence during the Revolution, he returned to Paris in 1794 to become one of the inspectors of the Cons. (1795) and prof. of comp. (1800). At the Restoration in 1814 he was app. superintendent of the court mus.

Works incl. operas *L'Amoureux de quinze ans*, *Le Fermier cru sourd*, *Le Rendezvous nocturne*, *Henry IV*, *Le Droit du Seigneur*, *L'Amant sylphe*, *Sapho*, *Annette et Lubin*, *Ziméo* and others; 2 Masses, 2 Requiems, *Te Deum*, psalm settings and other church mus.; cantata for the marriage of Napoleon and Marie-Louise; chamber mus.; marches, etc., for military band; songs incl. 'Plaisir d'amour', etc.

Martini il tedesco (It. = M. the Ger.), the It. nickname given to the above.

Martini, Johannes (b. ?; d. ?), Flem. 15th-cent. comp. He is listed with Compère and Josquin in a Milanese register of 1474, and was in the service of Hercules I of Ferrara from 1475. Comp. Masses, motets and *chansons*.

Martini, Padre. *See* Martini, Giovanni Battista.

Martini, Vincenzo (*see* Martín y Soler, Vicente), the Italian form of the Span. comp.'s name.

Martinon, Jean (b. Lyons, 10. I. 1910), Fr. cond. and comp. Studied vln. at the Lyons Cons. and comp. under Roussel at the Paris Cons. He began to produce works shortly before World War II, during which he was imprisoned in Ger., where he wrote several works. After the war he appeared with success as cond. in Europe and S. Amer.

Works incl. opera *Hécube* (lib. by Serge Moreaux after Euripides); Psalm cxxxvi for solo voices, reciter, chorus and orch., *Absolve Domine* for men's chorus and orch.; 4 symphs., *Symphoniette*, *Hymne à la vie*, *Musique d'exil* for orch.; *Concerto lyrique* for string 4tet and orch., *Concerto giocoso* for vln. and orch.; string 4tet, etc.

Martinů, Bohuslav (b. Polička, 8. XII. 1890; d. Liestal, Switz., 28. VIII. 1959), Cz. comp. Studied vln. at the Prague Cons. from 1906 to 1913 while playing in the Prague Phil. Orch. In 1922 he took comp. lessons with Suk at Prague Cons. and from 1923 to 1924 studied with Roussel in Paris, where he lived for a greater part of the time until he fled to U.S.A. in 1941. He remained in Amer. until 1946, when he became prof. of comp. at Prague Cons., returning to U.S.A. in 1948, where he taught at Princeton and the Berkshire Music Center. From 1957 he lived in Switz. His mus. is often neo-classical in style, with an emphasis on rhythm and counterpoint.

Works incl. operas *The Soldier and the Dancer* (after Plautus), *Les Lames du couteau*, *Les Vicissitudes de la vie*, *Journée de bonté*, *The Miracle of Our Lady*, *The Suburban Theatre*, *Alexandre bis*, *Julietta*, *Mirandolina*, *Ariadne*; radio operas *The Voice of the Forest*, *Comedy on a Bridge*; television opera *The Marriage*; ballets *Istar*, *Who is the Most Powerful in the World?*, *Revolt*, *On tourne*, *La Revue de cuisine*, *Échec au roi*, *The Butterfly that Stamped*, *Špaliček*, *Le Jugement de Paris*; Cz. *Rhapsody*, *Bouquet of Flowers*, *Field Mass* for solo voices, chorus and orch.; madrigals for 6 voices; 6 symphs., sinfonia for 2 orchs., symph. poem *Vanishing Midnight*, tone-poem *The Frescoes of Piero della Francesca*, symph. pieces *Half-time*, *La Bagarre*, *La Rapsodie*, overture for the Sokol Festival, *Memorial to Lidice*, Inventions for grand orch., concerto grosso, *Tre Ricercari*, *Les Sérénades* and *Les Rondes* for chamber orch., partita for string orch.; 4 pf. concertos and concertino, concerto for 2 pfs.; vln. concerto, 2 cello concertos, harpsichord concerto and var. other works for instruments and orch., string 4tet and pf. trio with orch.; 7 string 4tets, string 5tet, wind 5tet, pf. 4tet, pf. 5tet and other chamber mus.; 3 vln. and pf. sonatas, 3 cello and pf. sonatas; var. instrumental pieces; *Film en miniature*, *3 Danses tchèques*, *Préludes*, *Esquisses de danse*, *Ritournelles*, *Train-*

Fantôme, etc. for pf.; 2 preludes for harpsichord, etc.

Martucci, Giuseppe (b. Capua, 6. I. 1856; d. Naples, 1. VI. 1909), It. pianist, cond. and comp. Was 1st taught by his father, a bandmaster, and appeared as pianist in his childhood. He then studied at the Naples Cons., 1867–72, and became prof. there in 1874. He travelled widely as pianist, founded the Quartetto Napoletano for the cultivation of chamber mus. and became an orch. cond. In 1886 he was app. director of the Liceo Musicale at Bologna and there prod. the 1st It. perf. of Wagner's *Tristan* in 1888. In 1902 he returned to Naples as director of the Cons.

Works incl. oratorio *Samuele*; 2 symphs., *4 piccoli pezzi* for orch.; pf. concerto in B♭ min.; pf. 5tet, 2 pf. trios; cello and pf. sonata; var. instrumental pieces; variations and fantasy for 2 pfs.; songs, *Pagine sparse*, *Due sogni* and others, etc.

Marty, (Eugène) Georges (b. Paris, 16. V. 1860; d. Paris, 11. X. 1908), Fr. cond. and comp. Studied at the Paris Cons., where he gained the Prix de Rome in 1882. He became successively chorus-master at the Théâtre Eden and the Opéra, director of the vocal ensemble classes at the Cons. and cond. at the Opéra-Comique. In 1901–8 he cond. the Cons. concerts and from 1906 he also gave classical orchestral concerts at Vichy.

Works incl. operas *Le Duc de Ferrare* and *Daria*; pantomime *Lysis*; *Ballade d'hiver*, overture *Balthasar*, suite *Les Saisons*, symph. poem *Merlin enchanté* for orch.; pf. pieces; songs, etc.

Martyre de Saint Sébastien, Le (*The Martyrdom of St. Sebastian*), incid. mus. by Debussy for the mystery play, written in Fr., by Gabriele d'Annunzio, comp. for solo voices, chorus and orch. in 1911 and 1st perf., Paris, Théâtre du Châtelet, 22. V. 1911, in 5 acts, and Opéra, 17. VI. 1922, in 4 acts.

Martyrs, Les, opera by Donizetti (lib. by Scribe, based on Corneille's *Polyeucte*), prod. Paris, Opéra, 10. IV. 1840.

Martzy, Johanna (b. Temesvar, 26. X. 1924), Hung. violinist. Studied at Budapest Acad. from 1932 to 1942, winning the Reményi Prize at 16, and 1st prize at the Concours International d'Exécution in Geneva in 1947, in which year she began her true concert career.

Marvell, Andrew (1621–78), Eng. poet. *See* White (F.) (*Nymph's Complaint*).

Marx, Adolph Bernhard (b. Halle, 15. V. 1795; d. Berlin, 17. V. 1866), Ger. musicologist and comp. Studied law, but gave it up for mus., to which he devoted himself in Berlin, where in 1824 he founded the *Berliner allgemeine musikalische Zeitung*. In 1830 he became prof. of mus. and in 1850 founded a mus. school with Kullak and Stern (later Stern Cons.). He wrote books on the hist. of mus. teaching, on Gluck, Handel, Beethoven, comp., tone-painting, etc.

Works incl. opera *Jery und Bätely* (Goethe); melodrama *Die Rache wartet*; oratorios *Johannes der Täufer, Moses, Nahid und Omar*; instrumental works, etc.

Marx, Joseph (b. Graz, 11. V. 1882; d. Graz, 3. IX. 1964), Aus. comp. Studied in Vienna and in 1922 became director of the Acad. of Mus. there in succession to Ferdinand Löwe. From 1947 he was prof. at Graz Univ.

Works incl. *Autumn Symph., Symph. Night Music, Spring Music* for orch.; romantic concerto for pf. and orch.; several choral pieces; pf. 4tet, fantasy for pf. trio; vln. and pf. sonata, cello and pf. sonata; *c.* 120 songs, etc.

Marx, Karl (b. Munich, 12. XI. 1897), Ger. comp. Studied natural science at first, but met Carl Orff during the 1914–18 war and later studied mus. with him. App. prof. of the Munich Acad. in 1924 and cond. of the Bach Society there in 1928. From 1939 to 1945 he taught at Graz Cons., becoming prof. in 1944, and in 1946 he became prof. at the Hochschule für Musik in Stuttgart. He has been much occupied with school mus.

Works incl. passacaglia for orch.; concertos for pfs., vln., 2 vlns., vla. and fl.; var. choral works, some to words by Rilke; divertimento for wind instruments, string 4tet and other chamber mus.; songs, some to words by Rilke, etc.

Marxsen, Eduard (b. Nienstädten nr. Altona, 23. VII. 1806; d. Altona, 18. XI. 1887), Ger. pianist, organist, teacher and comp. Assisted his father, an organist, until 1830, then studied comp. with Seyfried and pf. with Bocklet in Vienna, returning to settle at Hamburg in 1834 and devoting himself mainly to teaching. Among his pupils was Brahms.

Works incl. *Beethoven's Schatten* for orch.; pf. mus.; songs, etc.

Marziale (It.) = martial, warlike.

Masaniello furioso, oder Die neapolitanische Fischer-Empörung (*M. enraged, or The Neapolitan Fisherman's Revolt*), opera by Keiser (lib. by Barthold Feind), prod. Hamburg, Theater beim Gänsemarkt, VI. 1706.

Masaniello (Auber). *See* **Muette de Portici.**

Masaniello, ou Le Pêcheur napolitain (*M., or The Neapolitan Fisherman*), opera by Carafa (lib. by C. Moreau and A. M. Lafortelle), prod. Paris, Opéra-Comique, 27. XII. 1827. Auber's *Muette de Portici* was prod. at the Opéra 2 months later.

Mascagni, Pietro (b. Leghorn, 7. XII. 1863; d. Rome, 2. VIII. 1945), It. comp. His father, a baker, wished him to study law, but he managed to take lessons in secret at the Istituto Cherubini. On being discovered, he was adopted by an uncle, and soon reconciled with his father by having 2 works perf. at the Istituto. Later Count Florestano de Larderel paid for his further mus. educ. at the Milan Cons., where Ponchielli was among his masters. But he deserted, not wishing to apply himself to solid study, and joined a travelling opera co. After many wanderings and a marriage that forced him to settle at Cerignola nr. Foggia to make a precarious living by teaching, he won the 1st prize in an operatic competition with *Cavalleria rusticana* in 1889, and after its prod. in Rome, 17. V. 1890, he began to accumulate a great fortune, though his many later operas never repeated its success.

Works incl. operas *Cavalleria rusticana, L'amico Fritz, I Rantzau* (both based on Erckmann-Chatrian), *Guglielmo Ratcliff* (after Heine), *Silvano, Zanetto* (Coppée), *Iris, Le maschere, Amica, Isabeau, Parisina* (d'Annunzio), *Lodeletta, Il piccolo Marat, Pinotta, Nerone*; operetta *Si*; incid. mus. for Hall Caine's *The Eternal City*; *Kyrie*, Requiem in memory of King Humbert; cantata for Leopardi centenary (1898), setting of It. trans. of Schiller's *Ode to Joy* for chorus and orch., cantata *In Filanda*; symph. in C min., symph. poem for a film *Rapsodia satanica*, etc.

Maschera, Fiorenzo (b. ? Brescia, *c.* 1540; d. Brescia, ? 1584), It. comp. Succeeded Merulo as organist at Brescia Cathedral in 1557. Comp. instrumental *canzone.*

Mascherata (It. = masquerade), a type of 16th-cent. *villanella* to be sung at masked balls or during fancy-dress processions.

Mascheroni, Edoardo (b. Milan, 4. IX. 1859; d. Milan, 4. III. 1941), It. cond. and comp. He began to study mus. as an adult under Boucheron at Milan. In 1883 he secured an engagement at the Teatro Goldini at Leghorn. Not long after he moved to the Teatro Apollo in Rome, and in 1893 he was chosen by Verdi to cond. the prod. of his *Falstaff* at Milan.

Works incl. operas *Lorenza* and *La Perugina*; 2 Requiems, for solo voices, chorus and orch. and for voices alone (both on the death of Victor Emmanuel I); chamber mus.; album of pf. pieces, etc.

Maschinist Hopkins, opera by Brand (lib. by comp.), prod. Duisberg, 13. IV. 1929.

Mascotte, La (*The Mascot*), operetta by Audran (lib. by Alfred Duru and Henri Charles Chivot), prod. Paris, Bouffes-Parisiens, 28. XII. 1880.

Masculine Cadence, a cadence, or ful

close, the final note or chord of which falls on a strong, accented beat of a bar.

Masefield, John (1878–1967), Eng. poet and novelist. *See* **Gardiner (H. B.)** (*News from Wydah*), **Ireland (J.)** (*Sea Fever*), **Miles** (*Good Friday*), **Shaw (M.)** (*Seaport and Easter*), **Walton** (*Where does the uttered music go?*).

Masini, Angelo (b. Terra del Sole nr. Forlì, 28. XI. 1844; d. Forlì, 29. IX. 1926), It. tenor. His early studies were retarded by poverty. He appeared in opera for the 1st time in 1867, at Modena, and thereafter acquired a wide reputation, partic. in Verdi's operas.

Mask. *See* **Masque.**

Masked Ball, The (Verdi). *See* **Ballo in maschera.**

Masnadieri, I (*The Brigands*), opera by Verdi (lib. by Andrea Maffei, based on Schiller's drama *Die Räuber*), prod. London, Her Majesty's Theatre, 22. VII. 1847. The only opera commissioned by London from Verdi. Jenny Lind and Lablache appeared in it.

Mason, Colin (b. Northampton, 26. I. 1924; d. London, 6. II. 1971), Eng. critic. Studied at the T.C.M. in London, 1944–5, and in Budapest, 7–9, where he learnt Hung. He was app. London mus. critic to the *Manchester Guardian* in 1950 and in 1951 chief critic at Manchester.

Mason, Daniel Gregory (b. Brookline, Mass., 20. XI. 1873; d. Greenwich, Conn., 4. XII. 1953), Amer. comp. and writer on mus., grandson of Lowell Mason and son of a member of the firm of pf. makers Mason & Hamlin. Graduated from Harvard and studied mus. in N.Y., later with d'Indy in Fr. He wrote a number of books on mus.

Works incl. 3 symphs.; prelude and fugue for pf. and orch.; string 4tet on Negro themes, 3 works for string 4tet, pf. 4tet, 3 pieces for fl., harp and string 4tet, *Pastorale* for vln., clar. and pf.; vln. and pf. sonata, clar. and pf. sonata; pf. pieces incl. variations on *Yankee Doodle* in the style of var. comps.; songs, etc.

Mason, Lowell (b. Medfield, Mass., 8. I. 1792; d. Orange, N.J., 11. VIII. 1872), Amer. hymnologist, grandfather of prec. Self-taught in mus. and a bank clerk at Savannah from 1812. He practised any instrument he could lay hands on and with F. L. Abel adapted Gardiner's *Sacred Melodies*, mainly themes from the classics, to the psalms, with the result that in 1827 he was called to Boston to supervise church mus. there. A more important service was his intro. of mus. teaching into schools.

Mason, William (b. Boston, Mass., 24. I. 1829; d. N.Y., 14. VII. 1908), Amer. pianist, son of prec. Studied at Boston, later at the Leipzig Cons. and under Liszt at Weimar. On his return to U.S.A.

he appeared as a soloist and in 1854, with Theodore Thomas and others, he founded chamber mus. concerts.

Mason, William (1724–97), Eng. poet and dramatist. *See* **Arne (T. A.)**, **Caractacus** (Arne), **Giardini** (*Elfrida*), **Wesley (C.)** (*Caractacus*).

Masque, a stage entertainment cultivated in Eng. in the 17th cent. and laying great stress on spectacular presentation, but also incl. songs and dances. It closely resembled the Fr. *ballet de cour*, except that it retained spoken dialogue, which was replaced by recitative in Fr. The subjects, mainly based on It. models, were mythological, heroic or allegorical.

Masques et bergamasques, mus. by Fauré, Op. 112, for an entertainment by René Fauchois prod. Monte Carlo, 10. IV. 1919; Paris, Opéra-Comique, 4. III. 1920, with a Watteau setting and inspired by Verlaine's poetry. It incl. an overture and 3 dances, newly comp., as well as the Pavane, Op. 50, of 1887 and an orchestral version of the Verlaine song *Clair de lune*, Op. 46 No. 2, of the same year, in which the words 'masques et bergamasques' occur.

Mass, the chief ritual of the Rom. Catholic church service, i.e. the celebration of the Eucharist. Only High M. is concerned with mus., Low M. being spoken, not sung. The M. is still sung to plainsong melodies, but from the 14th cent. onwards it has also been treated as a form of mus. comp., as a rule primarily for the purpose of religious service, but sometimes more elaborately for concert use. Ms. orig. written, esp. in the 18th and 19th cents., for church use with orchestral accomp. can now generally be perf. only in the concert room, Pius X's *Motu proprio* of 1903 having forbidden orchs. in church.

The Ordinary of the M. falls into 5 main sections: Kyrie, Gloria, Credo, Sanctus with Hosanna and Benedictus, and Agnus Dei with Dona nobis pacem; these remain invariable throughout the year and are usually all that is set to mus. by comps. The proper of the M. consists of additional matter (Introit, Gradual, Alleluia or Tract, Offertory and Communion), and these are far more rarely found as parts of a M. comp.

The medieval practice of writing the movements of a M. on plainsong melodies, sung by the tenor, was soon extended to the employment of secular tunes. *L'Homme armé* on the Continent and *The Western Wind* in Eng., for ex., were esp. favoured for this purpose. In the course of the 16th cent., however, more and more comps. wrote wholly original Ms., though the practice of borrowing material from motets or *chansons* was also common. Even in later times the treatment of the M. remained essentially polyphonic, though not necessarily throughout. Certain portions, e.g. 'Et vitam venturi saeculi' at the end of the Credo, were almost invariably set as fugues. *See also* **Requiem.**

Mass in B minor (Bach). *See* **B minor Mass.**

Mass of Life, A, setting of words from Nietzsche's *Also sprach Zarathustra* for solo voices, chorus and orch. by Delius, comp. 1904–5, prod. (2nd part only in Ger.) Munich Mus. Festival, 1908; 1st complete perf. (in Eng.), London, 1909.

Massaini, Tiburtio (b. Cremona, before 1550; d. prob. Lodi or Piacenza, after 1609), It. comp. He served as *maestro di cappella* in Salò, Prague, Salzburg, Cremona (from 1595), Piacenza and Lodi successively. Comp. church mus. and 8 books of madrigals.

Massart, Joseph (Lambert) (b. Liège, 19. VII. 1811; d. Paris, 13. II. 1892), Belg. violinist and teacher. Studied under Auguste Kreutzer (1778–1832) in Paris and in 1843 became vln. prof. at the Cons. there.

Massé, Victor (actually Félix Marie) (b. Lorient, 7. III. 1822; d. Paris, 5. VII. 1884), Fr. comp. Studied at the Paris Cons. where Halévy was his comp. master, and gained the Prix de Rome in 1844. He travelled in It. and Ger. after his stay in Rome; in 1860 became chorusmaster at the Paris Opéra and in 1866 prof. of comp. at the Cons.

Works incl. operas and operettas *La Chambre gothique, La Chanteuse voilée, Galathée, Les Noces de Jeannette, La Reine Topaze, La Fiancée du Diable, Miss Fauvette, Les Saisons, La Fée Carabosse, Mariette la promise, La Mule de Pedro, Fior d'Aliza* (after Lamartine), *Le Fils du brigadier, Paul et Virginie* (after Saint-Pierre), *La favorita e la schiava, Le Cousin de Marivaux, Les Chaises à porteurs, Le Prix de famille, Une Loi somptuaire, Les Enfants de Perrette, La Petite Sœur d'Achille, La Trouvaille, Une Nuit de Cléopâtre; Messe solennelle*; cantata *Le Rénégat*; songs, etc.

Massenet, Jules (Émile Frédéric) (b. Montaud nr. Saint-Étienne, 12. V. 1842; d. Paris, 13. VIII. 1912), Fr. comp. Entered the Paris Cons. at the age of 11, studying comp. with A. Thomas and gaining the Prix de Rome in 1863. On his return from Rome in 1866 he married a pf. pupil and had his 1st opera, *La Grand'tante*, prod. at the Opéra-Comique the next year. The 1st really successful opera, *Hérodiade*, was prod. at Brussels in 1881 and *Manon* at the Opéra-Comique in 1884. Prof. of comp. at the Cons., 1878–96.

Works incl. operas *Don César de Bazan, Le Roi de Lahore, Hérodiade, Manon* (after

Prévost), *Le Cid* (after Corneille), *Esclarmonde, Le Mage, Werther* (after Goethe), *Le Portrait de Manon, La Navarraise, Sapho* (after Daudet), *Cendrillon, Grisélidis, Le Jongleur de Notre-Dame, Thaïs* (both after A. France), *Chérubin, Ariane, Thérèse, Bacchus, Don Quichotte* (after Cervantes), *Roma, Panurge* (after Rabelais), *Cléopâtre, Amadis*; ballets *Le Carillon, La Cigale, Espada*; incid. mus. to Leconte de Lisle's *Les Erynnies*, Racine's *Phèdre* and other plays; oratorios *Marie-Magdeleine, Ève, La Vierge, La Terre promise*; cantatas *David Rizzio, Narcisse, Biblis*; 13 orchestral works incl. *Scènes pittoresques, Scènes napolitaines* and 3 other similar suites, symph. poem *Visions*; pf. concerto, fantasy for cello and orch.; *c.* 200 songs; duets; choruses, etc.

Mässig (Ger.) = moderate.

Massimilla Doni, opera by Schoeck (lib. by Armin Rüeger, based on Balzac's novel), prod. Dresden, 2. III. 1937.

Masson, Paul (Marie) (b. Sète, Hérault, 19. IX. 1882; d. Paris, 27. I. 1954), Fr. musicologist and comp. Studied mus. hist. and aesthetics under Rolland and comp. with d'Indy and Koechlin. App. prof. of mus. hist. at the Institut Français at Florence in 1910 and that of Naples in 1919. Lecturer at Grenoble Univ., 1910, and prof. at the Sorbonne in Paris, 1931. His books incl. studies of Florentine carnival songs, Rameau and Berlioz.

Works incl. *Chant des peuples unis* for solo voices, chorus and orch.; *Chants sans paroles, Le Val de Terzolle*, suite *Printemps guerrier, Prélude et Berceuse* for orch., etc.

Master Peter's Puppet Show (Falla). *See* Retablo de Maese Pedro.

Master-Singers. *See* Meistersinger.

Mastersingers of Nuremberg, The (Wagner). *See* Meistersinger von Nürnberg.

Matačič, Lovro von (b. Sušak, 14. II. 1909), Yugoslav cond. As a boy he sang with the Wiener Sängerknaben. Later studying org. and pf. with Dietrich, theory with Walker and comp. and cond. with Herbst and O. Nebdal, making his début as cond. in Cologne in 1919. After apps. in Ljubljana and Zagreb he became director of the Belgrade Opera in 1938. From 1956 to 1958 he was mus. director of the Dresden Opera and in 1961 succeeded Solti at Frankfurt. He has also comp. a quantity of orchestral and incid. mus.

Matassins (Fr.), an old dance of armed men, sometimes called *Mattachins*.

Matelotte (Fr. from *matelot* = sailor), a Dutch sailors' dance similar to the hornpipe, danced in clogs with the sailors' arms linked behind their backs.

Materna, Amalie (b. St. Georgen, Styria, 10. VII. 1844; d. Vienna, 18. I.

1918), Aus. soprano. 1st appeared on the stage at Graz in 1865, then married the Ger. actor Karl Friedrich, with whom she was engaged at one of the minor theatres in Vienna. In 1869 she 1st sang at the Imp. Opera. She was Wagner's 1st Brünnhilde and Kundry at Bayreuth in 1876 and 1882.

Matheus de Sancto Johanne (Mayhuet de Joan) (b. ?, d. ?), Fr. 14th–15th-cent. comp. He served in the chapel of the antipopes at Avignon, 1382–6, and is almost certainly the 'Mayshuet' of the Old Hall MS. Comp. *chansons* and motets.

Mathias, Georges (Amédée Saint-Claire) (b. Paris, 14. X. 1826; d. Paris, 14. X. 1910), Fr. pianist and comp. Studied at the Paris Cons. and was a private pupil of Kalkbrenner and Chopin. In 1862–93 he was pf. prof. at the Cons.

Works incl. symph., 2 overtures; choral works; 2 pf. concertos, 5 pieces for pf. and strings, 6 pf. trios; pf. studies and pieces; songs, etc.

Mathieu, Émile (Louis Victor) (b. Lille, 16. X. 1844; d. Ghent, 20. VIII. 1932), Belg. comp. Studied at the Brussels Cons. Director of a school of mus. at Louvain, where his mother had taught singing, 1881–96, and then until 1924 director of the Ghent Cons.

Works incl. operas *Georges Dandin* (after Molière), *L'Échange, La Bernoise, Richilde, L'Enfance de Roland*; biblical opera *La Reine Vasthi*; ballet *Les Fumeurs de Kiff;* Te Deum and 3 cantatas *Le Hoyoux, Freyir* and *Le Sorbier* for solo voices, chorus and orch.; 6 ballads by Goethe for voice and pf., etc.

Mathis der Maler (*Matthew the Painter*), opera by Hindemith (lib. by comp.), prod. Zürich, 28. V. 1938. The painter is Matthias Grünewald (15th–16th cent.).

Matilde di Shabran, ossia Bellezza e cuor di ferro (. . ., *or Beauty and Heart of Iron*), opera by Rossini (lib. by Jacopo Ferretti), prod. Rome, Teatro Apollo, 24. II. 1821.

Matin, Le, Le Midi, Le Soir et la Tempête (*Morning, Noon, Evening and Storm*), the orig. titles of Haydn's symphs. Nos. 6 in D maj., 7 in C maj. and 8 in G maj., comp. 1761.

Matinsky, Mikhail (b. nr. Moscow, 1750; d. St. Petersburg, *c.* 1820), Rus. librettist and comp. A liberated serf, he was educ. in Moscow and in It. Wrote lib. and mus. of *The St. Petersburg Bazaar* (1779).

Matrimonio segreto, Il (*The Clandestine Marriage*), opera by Cimarosa (lib. by Giovanni Bertati, based on George Colman and David Garrick's play of that name), prod. Vienna, Burgtheater, 7. II. 1792.

Mattachins. *See* Matassins.

Mattei, Filippo, called Pippo, the supposed comp. of the 1st act of the opera

Muzio Scevola (often attrib. to Ariosti), the others being by Bononcini and Handel, is prob. no other than Filippo Amadei.

Mattei, Stanislao (b. Bologna, 10. II. 1750; d. Bologna, 12. V. 1825), It. priest, theorist and comp. Pupil of Padre Martini, whom he succeeded as *maestro di cappella* at the church of San Francesco in Bologna, and later at San Petronio. From 1804 prof. at the newly founded Liceo Filarmonico, his pupils incl. Rossini and Donizetti. He wrote a treatise on playing from figured bass.

Comps. incl. 8 Masses and other church mus.; a Passion; intermezzo *La bottega del libraio,* etc.

Matteis, Nicola (b. ?; d. ?), It. 17th-cent. violinist. Went to Eng. about 1672; pub. 3 collections of vln. mus., 1 of songs and a treatise, *The False Consonances of Musick.*

Matthay, Tobias (b. London, 19. II. 1858; d. Haslemere, Surrey, 15. XII. 1945), Eng. pianist, teacher and comp. of Ger. descent. Studied at the R.A.M. in London, where he became sub-prof. in 1876 and full prof. of pf. in 1880, remaining until 1925, although he had opened his own school of pf. playing in 1900. In 1893 he married Jessie Kennedy, daughter of David Kennedy and sister of Marjorie Kennedy-Fraser. He wrote several books on his own method of pf. playing and comp. much pf. mus., mainly of educ. value.

Mattheson, Johann (b. Hamburg, 28. IX. 1681; d. Hamburg, 17. IV. 1764), Ger. writer on mus., organist and comp. From the age of 9 sang at the Hamburg Opera, and there prod. his 1st opera in 1799. Became friendly with Handel in 1703 and went with him to Lübeck as a candidate to succeed Buxtehude; but both declined on learning that marriage to B.'s daughter was a condition of the post. After some years as tutor, then secretary to the Eng. Legation, he was app. minor canon and mus.-director at Hamburg Cathedral in 1715, but had to resign in 1728 because of deafness. Among his many writings on mus. the most important are *Der vollkommene Capellmeister* (1739), *Grundlage einer Ehrenpforte* (1740) and a treatise on thorough-bass.

Comps. incl. operas *Die Pleiades, Die unglückselige Cleopatra, Henrico IV* and 5 others; 24 oratorios and cantatas; trio sonatas, etc.; keyboard mus., etc.

Matthews, Denis (b. Coventry, 27. II. 1919), Eng. pianist. Studied with Harold Craxton and William Alwyn at the R.A.M., making his début in 1939. He has travelled widely and is esp. noted for his Mozart playing.

Matthisson, Friedrich von (1761–1831), Ger. poet. Remembered chiefly by Beethoven's setting of his *Adelaïde*; Schubert set 26 of his poems. *See also* **Schröter (C.)** (songs).

Mattinata (It.), a morning song, similar to the Fr. *aubade* and the Span. *alborada*.

Mauduit, Jacques (b. Paris, 16. IX. 1557; d. Paris, 21. VIII. 1627), Fr. lutenist and comp. He was, like his father before him, registrar to the courts of justice in Paris, but became famous as a musician. In 1581 he gained the 1st prize at the annual Puy de Musique at Évreux, and he was assoc. with Baïf in his experiments with *musique mesurée*, though after Baïf's death in 1590 he relaxed the rigid subordination of mus. to verbal rhythm in his settings of verse. In 1588 he (?) saved the MSS. of the Huguenot Le Jeune from destruction by the Catholic soldiers, though he was himself a Catholic.

Works incl. Requiem on the death of Ronsard (1585), motets, *chansons, Chansonnettes mesurées* for 4 voices, etc.

Maugars, André (b. ?, *c.* 1580; d. ?, *c.* 1645), Fr. 16th–17th-cent. violist, politician and trans. He lived in Eng. for 4 years *c.* 1620, on his return entered the service of Cardinal Richelieu, became interpreter in Eng. to Louis XIII and trans. Bacon's *Advancement of Learning*. In 1639 he visited Rome and wrote a pamphlet on It. mus. He comp. viol mus. (lost).

Maugham, W(illiam). Somerset (1874–1965), Eng. novelist and dramatist. *See* **Gardner** (*The Moon and Sixpence*), **Goossens** (*East of Suez*).

Maultrommel (Ger. lit. mouth [vulg.] drum) = Jew's harp. The instrument is neither a drum nor a harp.

Maupassant, Guy de (1850–93), Fr. novelist. *See* **Albert Herring** (Britten), **Glière** (*Mam'zelle Fifi*), **Mademoiselle Fifi** (Cui), **Senilov** (*Wild Geese*).

Maurel, Victor (b. Marseilles, 17. VI. 1848; d. N.Y., 22. X. 1923), Fr. baritone. Went to the school of mus. at Marseilles, after studying architecture, and later to the Paris Cons. Made his 1st appearance in 1868, at the Paris Opéra, but was later devoted more to It. opera. He was the 1st Iago in Verdi's *Otello* and the 1st Falstaff.

Maurer, Ludwig (Wilhelm) (b. Potsdam, 8. II. 1789; d. St. Petersburg, 6. XI. 1878), Ger. violinist and comp. Studied under Haak, the leader of Frederick the Great's orch.; made his 1st appearance at a concert given by Mara in Berlin, 1802. In 1824–33 he led the theatre orch. at Hanover and later lived in Rus., mainly at Moscow and St. Petersburg. He was inspectorgeneral of the Imp. orchs., 1841–62.

Works incl. 3 Ger. operas *Der neue Paris, Aloise* and *Die Runenschrift*, and several in Rus. and Fr.; vln. concertos; string 4tets, etc.

Mavra, opera by Stravinsky (lib., in Rus., by Boris Koshno, based on Pushkin's *The Little House at Kolomna*), prod., in Fr. trans. by Jacques Larmanjat, Paris, Opéra, 2, VI. 1922.

Maw, Nicholas (b. 5. XI. 1935), Eng. comp. Studied with L. Berkeley at the R.A.M. from 1955 to 1958 and with Nadia Boulanger in Paris from 1958 to 1959.

Works incl. *Requiem* for soprano and contralto soloists, women's chorus, string trio and string orch.; comic operas *One Man Show* and *The Rising of the Moon*; *Nocturne* for mezzo-soprano and orch., *Scenes and Arias* for solo voices and orch.; *Chamber Music* for fl., clar., horn, bassoon and pf.

Maximilien, opera by Milhaud (lib. by Armand Lunel, trans. from a Ger. lib. by Rudolf Stephen Hoffmann, based on Franz Werfel's play, *Juarez und Maximilian*), prod. Paris, Opéra, 4. I. 1932.

Maxixe, a Brazil. dance similar to the Tango, which had some vogue in Eur. in the 1910s.

May-horn. *See* **Whithorn.**

May Night (*Maïskaya Notch*), opera by Rimsky-Korsakov (lib. by comp., based on a story by Gogol), prod. St. Petersburg, 21. I. 1880.

Mayer, Charles (b. Königsberg, 21. III. 1799; d. Dresden, 2. VII. 1862), Ger. pianist and comp. Was taken to Rus. as a child and became a pupil of Field at Moscow, and after the fire of 1812 in St. Petersburg. He travelled in Fr., Swed., Ger., etc., taught at St. Petersburg from 1819 to 1850, and in 1850 settled at Dresden. He wrote an enormous number of pf. works, incl. a mazurka in F♯ maj. that was for some time thought to be by Chopin.

Mayer, Robert (b. Mannheim, 5. VI. 1879), Ger.-Eng. patron of mus., a business man resident in London since 1896. His importance in Brit. mus. life has been as the founder of the R.M. Concerts for children and Youth and Mus., and other ways of encouraging youthful love of mus. He was knighted in 1939.

Mayhuet de Joan. *See* **Matheus de Sancto Johanne.**

Maynard, John (b. St. Julians, nr. St. Albans, I. 1577; d. ?), Eng. 16th–17th-cent. lutenist and comp. He was connected with the school of St. Julian in Herts., and at some time in the service of Lady Joan Thynne at Cause Castle in Salop.

Works incl. pavans and galliards for the lute; an org. piece; lessons for lute and bass viol for lyra-viol; 12 songs *The XII Wonders of the World*, describing var. characters, for voice, lute and vla. da gamba, etc.

Mayone, Ascanio (b. Naples, after 1550; d. Naples, 1627), It. comp., pupil of Jean de Macque. Comp. madrigals, and solo and chamber instrumental mus.

Mayr, Johann Simon (b. Mendorf, Bavar., 14. VI. 1763; d. Bergamo, 2. XII. 1845), Ger.-It. comp. Educ. at the Jesuit Seminary at Ingolstadt, he later studied with Lenzi in Bergamo and Bertoni in Venice where he settled, at first writing oratorios and church mus. until 1794, when on the success of his opera *Saffo* he turned to the stage. From 1802 to his death he was *maestro di cappella* at Santa Maria Maggiore, and from 1805 taught at the newly founded Inst. of Mus. there, among his pupils being Donizetti.

Works incl. over 60 operas, e.g. *Lodoiska, Che originali, Adelaide di Guesclino, Il carretto del venditore d'aceto, Ginevra di Scozia, I misteri eleusini, Alonso e Cora, Elisa, Adelasia e Aleramo, La rosa rossa e la rosa bianca, Medea in Corinto*; oratorios *Jacob a Labano fugiens, Sisara, Tobiae matrimonium, Davide, Il sacrifizio di Jefte* and others; Passion; Masses, motets and other church mus., etc.

Mayr, Richard (b. Henndorf, nr. Salzburg, 18. XI. 1877; d. Vienna, 1. XII. 1935), Aus. bass-baritone. Studied medicine at Vienna Univ., but left it for the Cons. and made his 1st stage appearance at the Wagner festival theatre at Bayreuth in 1902.

Mayrhofer, Johann (1787–1836), Aus. poet. *See* **Freunde von Salamanka** (Schubert).

47 of his poems were set by Schubert.

Mayseder, Joseph (b. Vienna, 26. X. 1789; d. Vienna, 21. XI. 1863), Aus. violinist and comp. 1st appeared in Vienna, 1800, and later held several important appts., incl. that of chamber musician to the emperor.

Works incl. Mass; 3 vln. concertos; 8 string 4tets, 5 string 5tets, pf. trios and other chamber mus.; vln. duets; pieces and studies for vln., etc.

Mayshuet. *See* **Matheus de Sancto Johanne.**

Mazas, Jacques (Féréol) (b. Béziers, 23. IX. 1782; d. Bordeaux, 26. VIII. 1849), Fr. violinist and comp. Studied under Baillot at the Paris Cons., appeared with a vln. concerto written for him by Auber, travelled widely, lived in Paris 1829–37 and was director of the mus. school at Cambrai, 1837–41.

Works incl. opera *Le Kiosque*; 2 vln. concertos; string 4tets; vln. duets; many vln. pieces, etc.

Mazeppa, opera by Tchaikovsky (lib. by comp. and Victor Petrovich Burenin, based on Pushkin's *Poltava*), prod. Moscow, Bolshoy Theatre, 15. II. 1884.

Symph. poem by Liszt, comp. in 1854 on Victor Hugo's poem and on the basis of one of the *Grandes Études pour le piano*

of *c.* 1838 and their new version, the *Études d'exécution transcendante* of 1851. 1st perf. Weimar, 16. IV. 1854.

Mazur
or   } a Pol. nat. dance dating at
Mazurka } least as far back as the 16th cent. and originating in Mazowsze (Mazovia). It was at first accomp. with vocal mus. The dance-figures are complicated and subject to much variation, not excluding improvisation. The mus. is in moderate 3–4 time orig. in 2 sections of 8 bars each, both repeated; there is a tendency to accentuate the 2nd or the 3rd beat. Its treatment by comps. (e.g. Chopin) often extends and develops it.

Mazzaferrata, Giovanni Battista (b. Como or Pavia, ?; d. Ferrara, 26. II. 1691), It. comp. *Maestro di cappella* at the Accademia della Morte at Ferrara, 1670–1680. His oratorio was perf. at Siena in 1684.

Works incl. oratorio and cantatas; *Salmi concertati* for 3–4 voices; madrigals and canzonets; cantatas for solo voices; 12 sonatas for 2 vlns. and bass, etc.

Mazzinghi, Joseph (b. London, 25. XII. 1765; d. Downside nr. Bath, 15. I. 1844), Eng. pianist, cond. and comp. of It. descent. Pupil of J. C. Bach. At the age of 10 he succeeded his father as organist of the Port. Chapel in London. He then studied further with Bertoni, Sacchini and Anfossi during their stays in Eng. and in 1784 became cond. and comp. to the King's Theatre. He taught much and was mus. master to the Princess of Wales (later Queen Caroline).

Works incl. operas *La bella Arsena* and *Il tesoro*; plays with mus. *A Day in Turkey, Paul and Virginia* (with Reeve, after Saint-Pierre), *The Wife of Two Husbands, The Exile, The Free Knights* and others; several ballets; Mass for 3 voices; 6 hymns; many keyboard sonatas; glees, arias, songs, etc.

Mazzocchi, Domenico (b. Veia nr. Civita Castellana, 8. XI. 1592; d. Rome, 20. I. 1665), It. comp. Was in the service of the Aldobrandini Borghese family for 20 years.

Works incl. operas *La catena d'Adone* and *L'innocenza difesa*; oratorios *Querimonia di S. Maria Maddalena, Il martirio dei SS. Abbundia ed Abbundanzio*; *Musiche sacre*; madrigals, *Dialoghi e sonetti*, etc.

Mazzocchi, Virgilio (b. Veia, 22. VII. 1597; d. Veia, 3. X. 1646), It. comp., brother of prec. *Maestro di cappella* at St. John Lateran in Rome, 1628–9, and then at St. Peter's until his death.

Works incl. opera *Chi soffre speri* (with Marazzoli); psalms for double chorus; *Sacri flores* for 2–4 voices, etc.

Mazzucato, Alberto (b. Udine, 28. VII. 1813; d. Milan, 31. XII. 1877), It. violinist, teacher and comp. Studied at Padua. He became leader of the Scala orch. at Milan in 1859, taught vln. at the Cons. there and became its director in 1872. Ed. of the *Gazzetta musicale*.

Works incl. operas *La fidanzata di Lammermoor* (after Scott), *Esmeralda* (after Hugo) and 6 others, etc.

Mc (for names with this prefix *see* **Mac . . .**).

Me, the name for the Mediant note in any key in Tonic Sol-fa, so pronounced, but in notation represented by the symbol m.

Meadows White, Alice. *See* **Smith, Alice Mary.**

Mean(e). In the old sense of 'middle' the word was formerly used in var. ways; e.g. for voice-parts in vocal comps. lying between the treble and the tenor; for the 2nd instrument in a consort of viols; for the 2nd and 3rd strings on the viol (small and great meane).

Meantone. In tuning the M. system was used for keyboard instruments before Equal Temperament came into general use. It provided for the pure intonation of the key of C maj. and those lying near it at the expense of the more extreme sharp and flat keys; which is the reason why remote keys were rarely used in keyboard comps. before the adoption of Equal Temperament. There was, for ex., a pure F♯ and B♭, but these notes were out of tune when used as G♭ or A♯.

Meares, Richard (b. ?; d. London, *c.* 1722), Eng. instrument maker. Made lutes, viols, etc. in London in the 2nd half of the cent.

Meares, Richard (b. London, ?; d. London, *c.* 1743), Eng. instrument maker and mus. pub., son of prec. He succeeded to his father's business, but enlarged it by selling not only instruments, but mus., books and cutlery, and he began to pub. mus. *c.* 1714, incl. several operas by Handel.

Measure (Amer.) = Bar. In Eng. (poet.) a 'measure' is a regularly rhythmic piece of m., esp. a dance.

Measured Music. *See* **Musique mesurée.**

Medea, play with mus. (melodrama) by G. Benda (text by Friedrich Wilhelm Gotter), prod. Leipzig, 1. V. 1775.

Médecin malgré lui, Le (*Doctor against his Will*), opera by Gounod (lib. a small alteration of Molière's comedy by comp., Jules Barbier and Michel Carré), prod. Paris, Théâtre Lyrique, 15. 1. 1858.

Médée, opera by Marc-Antoine Charpentier (lib. by Thomas Corneille), prod. Paris, Opéra, 4. XII. 1693.

Opera by Cherubini (lib. by François Benoît Hoffman), prod. Paris, Théâtre Feydeau, 13. III. 1797.

Opera by Milhaud (lib. by Madeleine

Milhaud, the comp.'s wife), prod. in Flem. trans., Antwerp, 7. X. 1939.

Meder, Johann Valentin (b. Wasungen o/Werra, V. 1649; d. Riga, VII. 1719), Ger. singer and comp. After var. appts. he became cantor at Reval in 1674 and at Danzig in 1687, later mus. director at Königsberg and Riga Cathedral.

Works incl. operas *Nero* and others: oratorio, motets; trios; org. mus., etc.

Mederitsch, Johann Georg Anton Gallus (also known as Johann Gallus) (b. Vienna, 26. XII. 1752; d. Lwów, 18. XII. 1835), Boh. cond. and comp. He was a theatre cond. at Olomouc and Pest, and later for many years a private mus. teacher in Vienna, Grillparzer being among his pupils.

Works incl. operas *Babylons Pyramiden* (with Winter), *Orkatastor und Illiane*, *Der redliche Verwalter* and others; incid. mus. for Shakespeare's *Macbeth*; Masses; chamber mus., etc.

Medesimo tempo (It. = 'same time'), a direction indicating that a change of metre does not imply a change of pace. The more usual term is *l'istesso tempo* (formerly *lo stesso tempo*).

Mediant, the 3rd degree of the maj. or min. scale, so called because it stands half way between Tonic and Dominant. The names of the degrees of the whole scale are Tonic, Supertonic, M., Subdominant, Dominant, Submediant and Leading-note.

Mediņš, Jānis (b. Riga, 9. X. 1890), Latvian comp. Studied at Riga, joined the orch. and after 2 years in Rus. became cond. at the Nat. Opera at Riga and prof. at the Cons. until 1944. Settled in Sweden in 1948.

Works incl. operas *Fire and Night*, *Gods and Men* and *Tom Thumb*; cantata; 3 symphs., 2 symph. poems and suites for orch.; 2 cello concertos; pf. concerto; instrumental pieces; songs; etc.

Medium, The, opera in 2 acts by Menotti (lib. by the comp.), prod. Columbia Univ., N.Y., 8. V. 1946.

Medtner, Nikolai Karlovich (b. Moscow, 5. I. 1880; d. London, 13. XI. 1951), Rus. comp. Studied pf. under Safonov at the Moscow Cons., gained the Rubinstein Prize there and toured Eur. as pianist in 1901–2, becoming prof. at the Cons. for a year on his return, but then retiring to devote himself to comp. After the Revolution he taught at a school in Moscow and in 1921 went on another tour in the W., but found himself unable to return. He settled in Paris for a time and later in London, which he left temporarily for Warwickshire in 1940.

Works incl. 3 pf. concertos; pf. 5tet; 3 sonatas and 3 nocturnes for vln. and pf.; 12 pf. sonatas and a great number of pieces for pf. incl. *Fairy Tales* Op. 8, 9, 14,

20, 26, 34, 35, 42, 48, 51, *Forgotten Melodies*
Op. 38–40, *Dithyrambs, Novels, Lyric
Fragments, Improvisations, Hymns in Praise
of Toil*, etc.; *Rus. Round Dance* and *Knight-
Errant* for 2 pfs.; sonata-vocalise for
voice and pf.; 17 op. nos. of songs to
words by Pushkin, Tiutchev, Goethe,
Heine, Nietzsche and others, etc.

Meeresstille und glückliche Fahrt (*Calm
Sea and Prosperous Voyage*) a poem by
Goethe, set by Beethoven as a cantata
for chorus and orch. in 1815, Op. 112,
and ded. to the poet; and used by Mendelssohn as the subject for a concert overture,
Op. 27, in 1828. Elgar quotes from the
latter in the Romance of the 'Enigma'
Variations.

Mefistofele, opera by Boito (lib. by
comp., based on Goethe's *Faust*), prod.
Milan, Teatro alla Scala, 5. III. 1868.

Mehta, Zubin (b. Bombay, 29. IV. 1936),
Indian cond., son of the violinist Mehli M.
(b. Bombay 25. IX. 1908). Received 1st
training from his father and in 1954 went
to Vienna, where he studied cond. with
H. Swarowski. In 1958 he won the com-
petition for young conds. in Liverpool and
in 1959 was guest cond. with the Vienna
Phil. Orch. He has since cond. throughout
Eur., and in 1961 became director of the
Los Angeles Phil. Orch. and in 1962 of the
Montreal Symph. Orch.

Méhul, Étienne Nicolas (b. Givet nr.
Mézières, Ardennes, 22. VI. 1763; d. Paris,
18. X. 1817), Fr. comp. Organist in his
home town at the age of 10, he went to
Paris in 1778, where Gluck's operas and
the encouragement of the comp. himself
gave him the ambition to write for the
stage. He took piano lessons from Edelmann, and supported himself by teaching
until *Euphrosine* (1790) estab. him as an
opera comp., after which he became one of
the most notable comps. of the Revolution,
his greatest success being *Joseph* (1807). On
the foundation of the Cons. in 1795 he
became one of its inspectors.

Works incl. operas *Euphrosine et
Coradin, ou Le Tyran corrigé, Cora,
Stratonice, Le Jeune Sage et le vieux fou,
Horatius Coclès, Mélidore et Phrosine, La
Caverne, Doria, Le Jeune Henri, Le Pont
de Lodi, Adrien, Ariodant, Épicure* (with
Cherubini), *Bion, L'irato, ou L'Emporté,
Une Folie, Le Trésor supposé, Joanna,
Héléna, Le Baiser et la quittance* (with
Kreutzer, Boïeldieu and Isouard), *L'Heur-
eux malgré lui, Les Deux Aveugles de
Tolède, Uthal* (without vlns.), *Gabrielle
d'Estrés, Joseph, Les Amazones, Le Prince
Troubadour, L'Oriflamme* (with Paer,
Berton and Kreutzer), *La Journée aux
aventures, Valentine de Milan* (unfinished,
completed by his nephew Louis Joseph
Daussoigne-M., 1790–1875); ballets *Le
Jugement de Paris* (with adds. from

Haydn and Pleyel), *La Dansomanie,
Daphnis et Pandrose, Persée et Andromède*;
incid. mus. to Joseph Chénier's *Timoléon*;
Mass for the coronation of Napoleon I (not
perf.); cantatas *Chanson de Roland,
Chant lyrique* (for the unveiling of Napoleon's statue at the Institut); patriotic
songs *Chant national du 14 juillet, Chant du
départ, Chant du retour*; symphs.; 2 pf.
sonatas, etc.

Mei, Girolamo (b. Florence, 27. V.
1519; d. Florence, VII. 1594), It. theorist.
His 4 surviving works incl. the *Discorso
sopra la musica antica e moderna*, pub.
Venice, 1602.

Meiland, Jacob (b. Senftenberg, Saxony,
1542; d. Hechingen, 31. XII. 1577), Ger.
comp. He learnt mus. as a choir-boy in the
Saxon court chapel at Dresden, studied at
Leipzig Univ., travelled, and was app.
Kapellmeister to the Margrave of Ansbach, whose chapel was dissolved in 1574,
when M. retired to Frankfurt in ill health.
Works incl. Lat. and Ger. motets;
Cantiones sacrae for 5–6 voices; Ger.
songs for 4–5 voices, etc.

Meinardus, Ludwig Siegfried (b. Hook-
siel, Oldenburg, 17. IX. 1827; d. Bielefeld,
10. VII. 1896), Ger. pianist, cond. and
comp. Pupil of Schumann at Leipzig and
of Liszt at Weimar. Taught at Dresden
from 1865 and was critic at Hamburg,
1874–87.
Works incl. operas *Bahnesa* and *Doktor
Sassafras*; oratorios *Simon Petrus, Gideon,
König Salomo, Luther in Worms* and
Odrun; choral ballad; symphs.; chamber
mus., etc.

Meissen, Heinrich von. *See* **Frauenlob.**

Meistersinger (Ger. = Master-Singers),
14th–16th-cent. guilds of poets and
musicians who cultivated poetry and singing in var. Ger. towns, prob. founded at
Mainz in 1311 by Heinrich von Meissen
(Frauenlob). The members passed through
var. stages from apprenticeship to mastery,
and they were middle-class burghers, mer-
chants, tradesmen and artisans, not nobles
like the Minnesinger.

Meistersinger von Nürnberg, Die (*The
Mastersingers of Nuremberg*), mus. drama
by Wagner (lib. by comp.), prod. Munich,
Court Theatre, 21. VI. 1868.

Mel, Rinaldo del (b. Malines, *c.* 1554;
d. ?, *c.* 1598), Flem. comp. He went to
Rome in 1580 after serving at the Port.
court, entered the service of Cardinal
Gabriele Paleotto and (?) studied under
Palestrina. About 1587–91 he was at Liège
in the household of Ernst, Duke of
Bavaria, but he rejoined Paleotto at
Bologna, who app. him *maestro di cappella*
to Magliano Cathedral.
Works incl. motets, *Sacrae cantiones*, a
Litany; madrigals, etc.

Melani, Jacopo (b. Pistoia, 6. VII.

1623; d. Pistoia, 1676), It. comp. His father was a sexton at Pistoia and had 7 other mus. sons. He was *maestro di cappella* of Pistoia Cathedral, 1657–67, and wrote a number of comic operas for Florence.

Works incl. operas *Il potestà di Colognole, Il girello, Il pazzo per forza, Il vecchio burlato, Enea in Italia, Ercole in Tebe, Il ritorno d'Ulisse*, etc.

His brothers were: Atto M. (1626–1714), castrato; Francesco Maria M. 1628–?), castrato and later a monk; Bartolomeo M. (1634–?), singer; Alessandro M. (?–1703), *maestro di cappella* at Bologna, Pistoia and Rome, comp. of 5 operas, motets, oratorios, cantatas, etc.; Antonio M. (?–?), comp. of instrumental mus.; Domenico M. (?–?), castrato; Nicola M. (?–?), castrato.

Melartin, Erkki (b. Käkisalmi, 7. II. 1875; d. Pukinmäki, 14. II. 1937), Fin. comp. Studied at the Helsinki Cons., Wegelius being his comp. master; later in Ger. He became prof. of comp. at the Cons. in 1901, and cond. at Viipuri in 1908–10. He was director of the Cons. in 1911–22.

Works incl. opera *Aino*; ballet *Sininen helmi*; 7 symphs., 5 orchestral suites, symph. poems; vln. concerto; 4 string 4tets; vln. and pf. sonatas; pf. sonata and *c.* 400 pieces; *c.* 300 songs, etc.

Melba, Nellie (actually Helen Mitchell) (b. Burnley nr. Melbourne, 19. V. 1859; d. Sydney, 23. II. 1931), Austral. soprano. Studied singing at an early age, but was not allowed to take it up professionally until her marriage to Captain Charles Armstrong in 1882 enabled her to do so. She appeared in London in 1886, went to Paris for further study with Mathilde Marchesi and made her 1st stage appearance at the Théâtre de la Monnaie in Brussels, 1887, appearing at Covent Garden, London, in 1888. She 1st visited Paris in 1889, Rus. in 1891, It. in 1892 and N. Amer. in 1903.

Melcer, Henryk (b. Kalisz, 21. IX. 1869; d. Warsaw, 18. IV. 1928), Pol. pianist and comp. Studied comp. with Noskowski at Warsaw and pf. with Leschetizky in Vienna, having already appeared in public at the age of 8. He travelled widely as a pianist, and in 1895 became prof. at the Helsinki Cons. Later he taught at Lwów, Warsaw and Vienna and in 1922 became director of the Warsaw Cons.

Works incl. operas *Maria* (Malczewski)

and *Protesilaus and Laodamia* (lib. by Wyspianski); *3 Mus. Thoughts* and *Variations on a Folk Theme* for orch.; 2 pf. concertos; choral ballad *Pani Twardowska*; pf. trio; vln. and pf. sonata; songs with orch. to words by Dehmel, etc.

Melchior, Lauritz (b. Copenhagen, 20. III. 1890), Dan.-Amer. tenor. Studied in Copenhagen, making his début as a baritone in 1913. In 1918, after further studies, he made a second début as a tenor, singing at Covent Garden and Bayreuth in 1924 and at the N.Y. Metropolitan Opera from 1926 to 1950. He was one of the finest Wagner singers of his time.

Melgunov, Julius Nikolaievich (b. Vetluga, Gvt. Kostroma, 11. IX. 1846; d. Moscow, 31. III. 1893), Rus. pianist and musicologist. Studied at the Moscow Cons. and with private teachers, toured in Ger. and Rus., but later devoted himself mainly to folksong research, on which he wrote several treatises.

Melisma (from Gk. = song, plur. *melismata*), an ornament: in plainsong a group of notes sung to a single syllable; in modern mus. any short passage of a decorative nature.

Mell, Davis (b. Wilton nr. Salisbury, 15. XI. 1604; d. London, ?), Eng. violinist and clockmaker. Became a member of the King's Band at the Restoration (1660) and joint master. Wrote viol mus., etc.

Mellers, Wilfrid (Howard) (b. Leamington, 26. IV. 1914), Eng. critic and comp. Studied at Cambridge and began to write criticism in the review *Scrutiny*, of which he became mus. asst. ed. Prof. of mus. at York Univ. since 1964. He has written books on Couperin, Amer. mus. etc.

Works incl. opera *Christopher Marlowe*; *Ricercare* for orch., do. (No. 2) for chamber orch., do. (No. 3) for string orch., *Concerto grosso* for chamber orch.; string 4tet, pf. 4tet, *Eclogue* for string trio; string trio, serenade for ob., clar. and bassoon; cantata for tenor and string, 4tet, *Carmina felium* for soprano and chamber mus.; sonatas for vln. and pf., cello and pf.; sonata and *Epithalamium* for pf.; 3 songs for soprano, 6 poems for tenor, 4 Lat. hymns for voice and pf., etc.

Melodic Minor Scale, a minor scale in which the 6th and 7th are sharpened when ascending and flattened when descending (*see* illustration).

Mélodie (Fr.), lit. a melody or tune, now generally current in Fr. as an exact

MELODIC MINOR SCALE

equivalent of the Eng. 'Song' or the Ger. 'Lied'.

Melodrama, a spoken play or spoken passages in an opera accomp. by a mus. background. Rousseau's *Pygmalion* and Benda's *Ariadne* and *Medea* are early instances of the former, and the 1st version of Humperdinck's *Königskinder* and works by Fibich are later ones; familiar exs. of the latter occur in Beethoven's *Fidelio* and Weber's *Freischütz*.

Melodramma (It. = music drama), a term for 'opera' current in It. from the end of the 18th cent. onwards. *See also* **Melodrama**.

Melody, an intelligible succession of notes defined by pitch and rhythm. In western mus. it is unusual to find Ms. which do not at least imply harmony.

Melusine, overture (Mendelssohn). *See* **Schöne Melusine**.

Melville, Herman (1819–91), Amer. novelist. *See* **Billy Budd** (Britten), **Ghedini** (*Billy Budd*, *Moby Dick*), **Křenek** (*Cantata for Wartime*), **Moore (D.)** (*Moby Dick*).

Mendelssohn, Arnold (Ludwig) (b. Ratibor, 26. XII. 1855; d. Darmstadt, 19. II. 1933), Ger. comp., son of a cousin of Felix M.-Bartholdy. Studied law at Tübingen and mus. in Berlin, and held teaching and cond. apps. at Bonn, Bielefeld, Cologne, Darmstadt and Frankfurt, where Hindemith was his pupil.

Works incl. operas *Elsi, die seltsame Magd* (after Jeremias Gotthelf), *Der Bärenhäuter* and *Die Minneburg*; cantatas; madrigals to words from Goethe's *Werther*; much church mus.; symph. in E♭ maj.; vln. concerto; 2 string 4tets; sonatas for vln. and pf., cello and pf. and pf.; songs, part-songs, etc.

Mendelssohn, Fanny. *See* **Hensel**.

Mendelssohn (-Bartholdy, Jakob Ludwig) Felix (b. Hamburg, 3. II. 1809; d. Leipzig, 4. XI. 1847), Ger. comp. Son of the banker Abraham M. and grandson of the Jewish philosopher Moses M. M.'s branch of the family embraced Christianity and moved to Berlin in 1812. At 6 he had pf. lessons from his mother and at 7 from Marie Bigot in Paris. In 1817, back in Berlin, he learnt comp. from Zelter, whose friend Goethe he visited at Weimar in 1821. Before that, in 1818, aged 9, he appeared at a public chamber concert, and before he was 13 he had written many works, incl. the pf. 4tet Op. 1. His father was wealthy enough to enable him to cond. a private orch. and he wrote his 1st symph. at 15, when he also had pf. lessons from Moscheles during a visit. By 1825 he had ready the short opera *Camacho's Wedding*, prod. at the family's expense in 1827, and at 17 he had written the overture to Shakespeare's *Midsummer Night's Dream* (the rest of the incid. mus. followed

in 1842). In 1829 he cond. Bach's forgotten St. Matthew Passion at the Vocal Acad. and paid the 1st of his 10 visits to Eng., cond. the Phil. Society in London and taking a holiday in Scot., where he gathered impressions for the *Hebrides* overture and the 'Scottish' symph., at which he worked in It. in 1830–1. The 'It.' symph. he finished in 1833, the year he cond. the Lower Rhine Festival at Düsseldorf, where he was engaged to stay as general mus. director. He left, however, for Leipzig, where he was app. cond. of the Gewandhaus concerts in 1835.

During a visit to Frankfurt he met Cécile Jeanrenaud, descendent of a Fr. Huguenot family, whom he married on 28. III. 1837. In IX of the same year he cond. *St. Paul* at the Birmingham Festival. In 1841 he left for Berlin, having been app. director of the mus. section of the Acad. of Arts, and there furnished incid. mus. for several classical plays, Gk., Eng. and Fr. He returned to Leipzig late in 1842 and founded the Cons. there in XI, opening it in IV. 1843. He was still living in Berlin, however, but resumed his conductorship at Leipzig in IX. 1845 and taught pf. and comp. at the Cons. But he was in poor health, and his visit to Eng. to conduct *Elijah* at the Birmingham Festival on 26. VIII. 1846 was his last but one. After the last, in the spring of 1847, the death of his sister Fanny Hensel greatly depressed him, and he went to Switz. too ill to do any work, returning to Leipzig in IX., completely exhausted.

Works incl. operas *Die Hochzeit des Camacho*, *Die Heimkehr aus der Fremde* (*Son and Stranger*) and *Loreley* (unfinished); incid. mus. to Sophocles' *Antigone* and *Oedipus at Colonos*, Shakespeare's *Midsummer Night's Dream*, Racine's *Athalie* and overture to Hugo's *Ruy Blas*; oratorios *St. Paul* and *Elijah*; many choral settings of psalms and other sacred vocal works, *Lobgesang* (*Hymn of Praise*: the 2nd symph. followed by a short cantata), cantata *Lauda Sion*, Goethe's *Erste Walpurgisnacht* for solo voices, chorus and orch.; 5 symphs.; 6 concert overtures, and some miscellaneous orchestral works; 2 concertos and 3 shorter works for pf. and orch.; vln. concerto in E min.; chamber mus. incl. 7 string 4tets, 3 pf. 4tets, 2 string 5tets, 2 pf. trios, string octet, 6tet, 4 pieces for string 4tet, etc.; vln. and pf. sonata, 2 cello and pf. sonatas; a large amount of pf. mus. incl. 48 *Songs without Words*, 3 sonatas, fantasies, characteristic pieces, capriccios, variations, preludes and fugues, studies, etc.; 6 sonatas, 3 preludes and fugues and other pieces for org.; over 80 songs; 12 sets of vocal duets and part-songs; 44 vols. of miscellaneous works left in MS., etc.

Mendès   Mer

Mendès, Catulle (1841–1909), Fr. writer, port and dramatist. He wrote libs. for several comps., incl. Chabrier, Messager, Pierné, Pessard, Massenet and Debussy. Debussy's work, *Rodrigue et Chimène*, was never finished. Married Judith Gautier (1850–1917), with whom he visited Wagner at Triebschen in Switz., 1869. *See also* **Bruneau** (*Chansons à danser* and *Lieds de France*), **Gwendoline** (Chabrier), **d'Indy** (*Médée*), **Leroux** (*Reine Fiammette*), **Vidal** (**P.**) (do.).

Ménestrel (Fr.) = Minstrel.

Ménestrandise (Fr.), in 17th- and 18th-cent. Paris a corporation of *Ménestriers* protected by an official privilege against the encroachment of other musicians on their exclusive right to play for dancing. Couperin wrote a satirical harpsichord suite on it entitled *Les Fastes de la Grande Mxnxstrxndxsx*.

Ménestrier (Fr.), a player of dance-mus., esp. a fiddler.

Mengelberg, (Curt) Rudolf (b. Crefeld, 1. II. 1892; d. Monte Carlo, 13. X. 1959), Dutch comp., cousin of the cond. Willem M. Studied with var. masters incl. Riemann at Leipzig, and in 1935 became director of the Concertgebouw at Amsterdam.

Works incl. *Missa pro pace*, hymn *Op Amstelredam* (Vondel) and other choral and orchestral works; *Symph. Elegy* for orch.; vln. concerto, capriccio for pf. and orch.; symph. variations for cello and orch.; vln. and pf. sonata, numerous songs incl. settings of Verlaine, etc.

Mengelberg, Willem (b. Utrecht, 28. III. 1871; d. Zuort, Switz., 21. III. 1951), Dutch cond. Studied at Cologne, became cond. at Lucerne in 1891 and in 1895 was app. cond. of the Concertgebouw Orch. in Amsterdam. He made this one of the finest orchs. in Europe, but fell under a cloud when he openly declared his sympathy with the Nazi rule during World War II, and went into exile in Switz. In 1933 he had been made Prof. of Mus. at Utrecht Univ.

Mengozzi, Bernardo (b. Florence, 1758; d. Paris, III. 1800), It. tenor and comp. Studied at Florence and Venice, visited London in 1786 and settled in Paris soon after, becoming prof. of singing on the estab. of the Cons. in 1795. Wrote opera *Pourceaugnac* (after Molière) and *c.* 15 others, operettas, etc.

Meno mosso (It. = less moved), a direction indicating that a slower pace is to be adopted.

Menotti, Gian Carlo (b. Cadegliano, 7. VII. 1911), It. comp. Studied comp. with Scalero at the Curtis Inst., Philadelphia. Has written libs. of his own operas and of Barber's *Vanessa*.

Works incl. operas *Amelia goes to the Ball*, *The Telephone*, *The Medium*, *The Consul*, *Amahl and the Night Visitors*, *The Saint of Bleecker Street*, *Maria Golovin*, radio opera *The Old Maid and the Thief*; symph. poem *Apocalypse*; *Pastorale* for pf. and string orch.; pf. concerto, vln. concerto; 4 pieces for string 4tet, *Trio for a House-warming Party* for fl., cello and pf.; *Poemetti*, pf. pieces for children; pieces for carillon, etc. In 1958 he founded the Festival dei Due Mondi at Spoleto.

Mensurable Music, measured or measurable mus. which can be grouped according to regular successions of beats, as distinct from plainsong, which has no measured rhythmic pulse.

Mensural Notation, the mus. notation which, as distinct from Modal N., came into use during the 13th cent. and for the 1st time began to indicate the exact value of notes and rests by its symbols.

Menter, Joseph (b. Deutenkofen, Bavaria, 19. I. 1808; d. Munich, 18. IV. 1856), Ger. cellist. Played in the orch. of the Royal Opera at Munich most of his life.

Menter, Sophie (b. Munich, 29. VII. 1848; d. Stockdorf nr. Munich, 23. II. 1918), Ger. pianist and teacher, daughter of prec. Studied at the Munich Cons., toured 1st at the age of 15, resumed studied with Tausig and Liszt, married Popper in 1872 and became pf. prof. at St. Petersburg, 1883.

Menu, Pierre (b. Paris, 1896; d. Paris, 16. X. 1919), Fr. comp. Studied with Roger-Ducasse at the Paris Cons., but his career was cut short by his early death.

Works incl. sonatina for string 4tet, pf. 4tet; *Dans l'ambiance espagnole* for chromatic harp; songs; etc.

Menuet (Fr.) = Minuet. The word is a diminutive of *menu* = small.

Menuetto (Ger.-It.). The Ger. classics often labelled their minuets thus under the impression that they were using an It. term. The correct It. is *minuetto*, the Ger. *Menuett*.

Menuhin, Yehudi (b. New York, 22. IV. 1916), Amer. violinist and cond. Began studying the vln. aged 4, first with S. Anker and then with L. Persinger. Aged 7 he played the Mendelssohn vln. concerto publicly in San Francisco, then going to Europe for further study with A. Busch and Enesco. He made his London début in 1929 with the Brahms concerto and by 1934 had completed the first of many world tours. He quickly became recognized as one of the world's outstanding musicians and virtuosi; recently he has devoted less time to solo perfs., and concentrated more on cond. (e.g. at the Bath Festival), in which sphere he has also attained eminence. He now lives in London.

Mer, La (*The Sea*), 3 symph. sketches by Debussy, *De l'aube à midi sur la mer*,

422

Jeux de vagues and *Dialogue du vent et de la mer*, comp. in 1903–5 and 1st perf. Paris, 15. X. 1905.

Merbecke, John. *See* **Marbeck.**

Mercadante, (Giuseppe) Saverio (Raffaele) (b. Altamura nr. Bari, IX. 1795; d. Naples, 17. XII. 1870), It. comp. Studied at the Collegio di San Sebastiano at Naples and, having learnt the fl. and vln., became leader of the orch. there. On being dismissed he began to earn his living as a stage comp. After several successes in It. he won favour in Vienna, visited Spain in 1827–9, and in 1833 became *maestro di cappella* at Novara Cathedral in succession to Generali and in 1840 director of the Naples Cons. While at Novara he lost an eye and in 1862 he became totally blind.

Works incl. *c.* 60 operas, e.g. *Violenza e costanza, Elisa e Claudio, Caritea, regina di Spagna, Gabriella di Vergy, I Normanni a Parigi, I briganti, Il giuramento, I due illustri rivali, Elena da Feltre, Il bravo, La Vestale, Leonora, Gli Orazi ed i Curiazi, Virginia*; 20 Masses, motets, psalms, etc.; cantata *L'apoteosi d'Ercole* and others; instrumental pieces; songs, etc.

Mercante di Venezia, Il (*The Merchant of Venice*), opera by Pinsuti (lib. by Giorgio Tommaso Cimino, after Shakespeare), prod. Bologna, Teatro Comunale, 9. XI. 1873.

Mercury, nickname of Haydn's symph. No. 43, in E♭ maj., comp. *c.* 1771.

Méreaux, Nicolas Jean (Le Froid de) (b. Paris, 1745; d. Paris, 1797), Fr. organist and comp. Organist at the Paris churches of Saint-Sauveur and Petits Augustins and of the royal chapel.

Works incl. operas *Le Retour de tendresse, Le Duel comique, Laurette, Alexandre aux Indes, Oedipe à Thèbes*, etc.; oratorio *Samson*; motets, etc.

Meredith, George (1828–1909), Eng. novelist and poet. *See* **Lark Ascending** (Vaughan Williams).

Méric-Lalande,　　Henriette-Clémentine (b. Dunkirk, 1798; d. Chantilly, 7. IX. 1867), Fr. soprano. As the daughter of a provincial opera manager she acquired enough experience to appear on the stage at Naples in 1814, but after a good deal of success she decided in 1822 to take lessons from García and appeared in 1823 at the Opéra-Comique in Paris, marrying the horn player Méric there. She studied further in It., sang there and 1st appeared in London in 1830.

Merighi, Antonia (b. ?; d. ?), It. 18th-cent. contralto. 1st appeared in London in 1720.

Merikanto, Aare (b. Helsinki, 29. VI. 1893; d. Helsinki, 28. IX. 1958), Fin. comp. Studied with Reger and others at Leipzig and with Vassilenko at Mos-

cow. Later became prof. at the Helsinki Cons.

Works incl. ballet *The Abduction of Kylliki* (on a subject from the *Kalevala*); 3 symphs., variations and fugue and several suites for orch.; 4 vln. concertos, 3 pf. concertos, 2 cello concertos, concerto for vln., clar., horn and strings; partita for woodwind and harp; choral works; folk-song arrs., etc.

Merikanto, (Frans) Oskar (b. Helsinki, 5. VIII. 1868; d. Hausjärvi-Oiti, 17. II. 1924), Fin. comp., father of prec. Studied at the Helsinki Cons. and at Leipzig and Berlin. Cond. of the Fin. Opera, 1911–22.

Works incl. operas *Pohjan neiti, Elinan surma, Regina von Emmeritz*; incid. mus. for plays; cantatas, songs, etc.

Mérimée, Prosper (1803–70), Fr. novelist. *See* Büsser (*Carrosse du Saint-Sacrement* and *Colombo*), Carmen (Bizet), **Carrosse du Saint-Sacrement** (Berners), **Colomba** (Mackenzie), **Cui** (*Matteo Falcone*), **Durey** (*L'Occasion*), **Halévy** (*Dame de Pique*), **Périchole** (Offenbach), **Venus** (Schoeck), **Wetzler** (*Basque Venus*).

Merk, Joseph (b. Vienna, 18. I. 1795; d. Vienna, 16. VI. 1852), Aus. cellist. Studied in Vienna, where he became cellist at the Opera in 1818 and prof. at the Cons. in 1823. Wrote mus. for his instrument.

Merkel, Gustav (Adolf) (b. Oberoderwitz, Saxony, 12. XI. 1827; d. Dresden, 30. X. 1885), Ger. organist and comp. Studied at Dresden and became organist at the orphanage church there in 1858, the Kreuzkirche in 1860 and court organist in 1864. He also cond. the Vocal Acad. and was prof. at the Cons.

Works incl. 9 sonatas, preludes and fugues, fantasies, studies, etc., for org.; instrumental pieces with org.; pf. works; songs, etc.

Merker (Ger. lit. marker = judge, adjudicator, umpire), one of the masters among the Ger. Meistersinger, who was elected to judge the competitions for mastership and prizes. Beckmesser is the M. in Wagner's *Meistersinger*.

Merlo, Alessandro (called Alessandro Romano or A. della Viola) (b. Rome, *c.* 1530; d. ?), It. tenor-bass, violist and comp. Pupil of Willaert and Rore. Singer in the Papal Chapel in Rome.

Works incl. motets; madrigals, *Canzoni alla Napolitana, villanelle*, etc.

Merlotti, Claudio. *See* **Merulo.**

Mermet, Auguste (b. Brussels, 5. I· 1810; d, Paris, 4. VII. 1889), Belg. comp. Pupil of Lesueur and Halévy.

Works incl. operas *La Bannière du roi, Le Roi David, Roland à Roncevaux* and *Jeanne d'Arc.*

Merope, opera by Gasparini (lib. by Apostolo Zeno), prod. Venice, Teatro San Cassiano, 26. XII. 1711.

Opera by Graun (lib., in Fr., by Frederick II of Prus.), prod. Berlin, Opera, 27. III. 1756.

Opera by Jommelli (lib. by Zeno), prod. Venice, Teatro San Giovanni Crisostomo, 26. XII. 1741.

Opera by Terradellas (lib. do.), prod. Rome, Teatro delle Dame, Carnival 1743.

Merrick, Frank (b. Clifton, Bristol, 30. IV. 1886), Eng. pianist and comp. Studied 1st with his parents and then with Leschetizky in Vienna, making his London début in 1903. In 1910 he won a Rubinstein Prize in St. Petersburg and from 1911 to 1929 taught at the Royal Manchester Coll. of Mus., after which he became prof. at the R.C.M. In 1928 he won a prize offered by the Columbia Graphophone Co. for completing Schubert's 'Unfinished' symph.

Merrie England, operetta by German (lib. by Basil Hood), prod. London, Savoy Theatre, 2. IV. 1902.

Merrill, Robert (b. Brooklyn, 4. VI. 1917), Amer. baritone. Studied 1st with his mother and then with S. Margolis in N.Y., making his début in 1944 and joining the N.Y. Metropolitan Opera in 1945.

Merriman, Nan (b. Pittsburg, 28. IV. 1920), Amer. mezzo-soprano. Studied in Los Angeles with Alexia Bassian, making her début in Cincinnati in 1942, but her real career began with Toscanini's patronage.

Merry Widow (Lehár). *See* **Lustige Witwe.**

Merry Wives of Windsor. *See* **Falstaff, Lustigen Weiber, Sir John in Love.**

Mersenne, Marin (b. Oizé, Sarthe, 8. IX. 1588; d. Paris, 1. IX. 1648), Fr. monk and mus. theorist. Educ. at Le Mans and La Flèche, he became a Minorite friar, being ordained in 1612. He taught philosophy at Nevers and then studied mathematics and mus. in Paris, Descartes and the elder Pascal being among his colleagues. He corresponded with scholars in Eng., Hol. and It., the last of which he visited 3 times. His treatises incl. *Harmonie universelle, Questions harmoniques, De la nature des sons,* etc.

Mersmann, Hans (b. Potsdam, 6. X. 1891), Ger. musicologist and cond. Studied at Munich, Leipzig and Berlin, last under Kretzschmar. He held var. appts. in Berlin as lecturer, prof. at the Technical Univ., on the staff of the broadcasting organization and as ed. of the magazine *Melos.* His books incl. *Angewandte Musikästhetik, Musik der Gegenwart* and others on modern mus., 3 works on folksong, etc. From 1947 to 1957 he was director of the Hochschule für Musik in Cologne.

Merula, Tarquinio (b. ? Cremona, *c.* 1590; d. Cremona, 10. XII. 1665), It.

comp. Held appts. alternately at Bergamo and Cremona, and was court and church organist at Warsaw in 1624. From 1628 to 1639 he was at Cremona as *maestro di cappella* at the cathedral, and returned to this post in 1652 after an interval at Bergamo.

Works incl. Masses, motets, psalms, *Concerti spirituali* and other church mus.; madrigals, *canzoni* for voices and/or instruments; church sonatas, etc.

Merulo, Claudio (also called Claudio da Correggio; real name Merlotti, b. Correggio, 8. IV. 1533; d. Parma, 5. V. 1604), It. organist, teacher and comp. App. organist at Brescia in 1556 and 2nd organist at St. Mark's, Venice, in 1557, advancing to 1st organist in 1566. In 1584 he left Venice, visited the court of Mantua and became organist to the ducal chapel at Parma.

Works incl. intermezzi for Dolce's *Le Troiane* and Cornelio Frangipani's *La tragedia*; Masses, motets, *Sacrae cantiones,* Litanies; madrigals; toccatas and *ricercari* for org., etc.

Méry, Joseph (1798–1865), Fr. poet. *See* **Franck (C.)** (songs).

Messa di voce (It. setting or placing of the voice), sustained singing of notes or phrases: but *messa* may also mean a *crescendo* followed by a *diminuendo* on a single breath.

Messager, André (Charles Prosper) (b. Montluçon, 30. XII. 1853; d. Paris, 24. II. 1929), Fr. cond. and comp. Studied at Niedermeyer's school in Paris and later under Saint-Saëns. In 1876 he won prizes for a symph. and a cantata and in 1883 he prod. a completion of an operetta *François les Bas-bleus* left unfinished by Firmin Bernicat. He became cond. of the Opéra-Comique and in 1898 its general director; from 1901 to 1906 he was artistic director at Covent Garden, and from 1901 to 1913 joint director of the Opéra. He was also a concert cond. His wife was the Ir. comp. Hope Temple (Dotie Davies, 1859–1938), who had been a pupil of his. He cond. the first perf. of Debussy's *Pelléas et Mélisande* in 1902.

Works incl. operas and operettas *La Fauvette du Temple, La Béarnaise, Le Bourgeois de Calais, Isoline, Le Mari de la reine, La Basoche, Madame Chrysanthème* (after Pierre Loti's novel), *Miss Dollar, Mirette, Le Chevalier d'Harmental, Les P'tites Michu, Véronique, Les Dragons de l'impératrice, Fortunio, Béatrice, Monsieur Beaucaire* (in Eng.), *La Petite Fonctionnaire, L'Amour masqué, Passionnément, Coup de roulis*; ballets *Les Deux Pigeons, Scaramouche, Le Chevalier aux fleurs, Une Aventure de la Guimard* and others; instrumental pieces; pf. duets; songs, etc.

Messanza (It. = mixture). *See* **Quodlibet.**

Messchaert, Johannes (Martinus) (b. Hoorn, 22. VIII. 1857; d. Zürich, 9. IX. 1922), Dutch bass-baritone. Studied with J. Stockhausen. He sang much in Hol., Ger. and elsewhere and toured as interpreter of songs with Julius Röntgen as pianist.

Messe (Fr. and Ger.) = Mass.

Messe solennelle. *See* **Missa solemnis.**

Messiaen, Olivier (Eugène Prosper Charles) (b. Avignon, 10. XII. 1908), Fr. organist and comp., son of the poet Cécile Sauvage. Studied org. under Marcel Dupré, theory under Maurice Emmanuel and comp. under Dukas at the Paris Cons. App. organist of the Trinité in Paris, 1931, and prof. at the École Normale de Musique and the Schola Cantorum. With Baudrier, Jolivet and Lesur he formed the group 'La Jeune France'. In 1940 he was taken prisoner by the Gers. but repatriated later and app. prof. of harmony at the Cons. in 1942 and prof. of mus. and rhythmic analysis in 1947. He married (1) Claire Delbos, (2) Yvonne Loriod. His mus. makes use of bird-song, Eastern rhythms and exotic sonorities. His influence as a teacher has been considerable.

Works incl. *O sacrum convivium* and 2 Liturgies for chorus; *Trois petites liturgies de la Présence Divine* for women's chorus, celesta, vibraphone, Ondes Martenot, pf., perc. and strings; *Les Offrandes oubliées, Hymne au Saint Sacrement, Turangalila-Symphonie, Chronochromie* for orch.; *Et expecto resurrectionem mortuorum* for woodwind, brass and perc., *Réveil des oiseaux* for pf. and orch., *Oiseaux exotiques* for pf. and wind instruments, *Sept Haikai* for pf. and small orch., *Couleurs de la Cité Céleste* for pf. and wind instruments; *Fêtes des belles eaux* for 6 Ondes Martenot; *Quatuor pour la fin du temps* for clar., vln., cello and pf.; theme and variations for vln. and pf.; *Diptyque, Le Banquet céleste, L'Ascension, La Nativité du Seigneur, Apparition de l'église éternelle, Les Corps glorieux, Messe de la Pentecôte, Le Livre d'orgue* for org.; *Fantaisie burlesque, Vingt regards sur l'Enfant Jésus, Île de feu, Catalogue des oiseaux, Cantéyod jayâ* for pf.; *Visions de l'amen* for 2 pfs.; *Poèmes pour Mi* and *La mort du nombre* for voice and orch.; *Chants de terre et de ciel* and *Harawi* for voice and pf., etc.

Messiah (not *The Messiah*), oratorio by Handel (words selected from the Bible by Charles Jennens), perf. Dublin, Music Hall in Fishamble Street, 13. IV. 1742; 1st perf. in Eng. Covent Garden Theatre, London, 23. III. 1743.

Messidor, opera by Bruneau (lib. by Émile Zola), prod. Paris, Opéra, 19. II. 1897. Bruneau had already written operas on subjects from Zola's works (*L'Attaque du moulin* and *Le Rêve*), but this was the 1st for which Zola himself wrote the lib.

Messner, Joseph (b. Schwaz, Tyrol, 27. II. 1893; d. Salzburg, 23. II. 1969), Aus. organist, cond. and comp. Studied in Munich and was app. organist to Salzburg Cathedral in 1922. He also cond. there, incl. the mus. in the cathedral during the Salzburg Festival.

Works incl. operas *Hadassa, Das letzte Recht, Ines, Agnes Bernauer*; 6 Masses, Te Deum and other church mus.; oratorios *Das Leben* and *Die vier letzten Dinge*; 3 symphs., *Symphonische Festmusik* for orch.; *Sinfonietta* for pf. and orch., etc.

Mesto (It.) = sad, gloomy.

Mesuré (Fr.). *See* **Musique mesurée.**

Metamorphosis, the transformation of a theme or motif, esp. rhythmically while the same notes are retained, as for ex. the *idée fixe* of Berlioz, the themes in Liszt's symph. poems, etc. and the *Leitmotive* in Wagner's operas.

Metaphor Aria. *See* **Parable Aria.**

Metastasio (real name Trapassi), **Pietro** (1698–1782), It. poet and librettist. Operas on his libs. *see* **Achille in Sciro, Adriano in Siria, Alessandro nell' Indie, Antigono, Artaserse, Cinesi, Clemenza di Tito, Cleofide, Contesa dei numi, Demetrio, Demofoonte, Démophoon, Didone abbandonata, Eroe cinese, Ezio, Galatea, Innocenza giustificata, Ipermestra, Isola disabitata, Lucio Silla, Olimpiade, Partenope, Rè pastore, Ruggiero, Semiramide riconosciuta, Siface, Siroe, Sogno di Scipione, Tito Vespasiano, Trionfo di Clelia.**

See also **Araia, Arne** (T. A.), **Bioni** (*Pace fra virtu e bellezza*), **Frederick II, Gluck, Martines** (psalms), **Morlacchi** (Passion oratorio), **Poissl, Poro** (Handel), **Reichardt, Rota** (N.), **Wellesz** (*Amor timido*).

Metre, the rhythmic patterns prod. in mus. by notes of varying length combined with strong and weak beats (*arsis* and *thesis*), similar to the different 'feet' (spondees, dactyls, anapaests, trochees, iambics, etc.) in poetry.

Metronome, an instrument invented by Mälzel in 1814 and designed to determine and prescribe the pace of any mus. comp. by the beats of a pendulum. The tempo is indicated by the comp., who prescribes how many time-units of a certain note-value are to occupy 1 minute: e.g. ♩ = 60 shows that there are to be 60 crotchets to the minute.

Metz, Amalarius of. *See* **Amalarius.**

Mewton-Wood, Noel (b. Melbourne, 20. XI. 1922; d. London, 5. XII. 1953), Austral. pianist, studied at the Melbourne Cons., the R.A.M. in London and under Schnabel. He 1st appeared in London in 1940 and made a great impression. His interest in modern comps. and in chamber mus. gave him many special opportunities.

Mexican Composers. See Ayala, Carrillo (J.), Chávez, Morales (M.), Pomar, Ponce, Revueltas, Rolón.

Mey, Lev Alexandrovich (1822–62), Rus. dramatist and trans. See Pskovitianka (Rimsky-Korsakov), Servilia (do.), Tsar's Bride (do.).

Meyer, Bernard van den Sigtenhorst. See Sigtenhorst Meyer.

Meyer, Conrad Ferdinand (1825–98), Swiss poet and novelist. See Kaminski (*Jürg Jenatsch*), Kunz (*Huttens letzte Tage*), Schoeck (*Stille Leuchten*).

Meyer, Ernst Hermann (b. Berlin, 8. XII. 1905), Ger. musicologist and comp. Studied in Berlin and Heidelberg. Lived in London from 1933 to 1948, when he was app. prof. of mus. sociology at the Humbolt Univ., Berlin. His books incl. studies of 17th-cent. instrumental mus. and Eng. chamber mus. from the Middle Ages to Purcell.

Works incl. film and chamber mus., etc.

Meyer, Gregor (b. ?; d. Basle, XI. 1576), Swiss 16th-cent. organist and comp. He was organist at Solothurn Cathedral and supplied Glareanus with comps. exemplifying the correct use of the modes.

Works incl. motets, Kyries, antiphons, etc.

Meyer-Helmund, Erik (b. St. Petersburg, 25. IV. 1861; d. Berlin, 4. IV. 1932), Ger. singer and comp. Studied under his father and later in Berlin: comp. with Kiel and singing with J. Stockhausen. He wrote the words for many of his own songs.

Works incl. operas and operettas *Margitta*, *Der Liebeskampf*, *Trischka*, *Lucullus* and *Heines Traumbilder*, *Taglioni*; ballets *Münchener Bilderbogen*, *Rübezahl*; numerous songs, etc.

Meyer-Lutz, Wilhelm (b. Männerstadt nr. Kissingen, 1822; d. London, 31. I. 1903), Ger. pianist, organist and comp. Pupil of his father, an organist and theorist. He 1st appeared in public as a pianist, at the age of 12, and later, the family having moved to Würzburg, went to the grammar school and the univ. there. In 1848 he settled in Eng., becoming organist to St. Chad's Rom. Catholic Cathedral at Birmingham and later to St. Ann's Church at Leeds and St. George's Cathedral in London. He also cond. for many years at the Surrey and Gaiety Theatres there.

Works incl. operas and operettas *Faust and Marguerite* (after Goethe), *Blonde and Brunette*, *Zaïda*, *Miller of Milburg*, *The Legend of the Lys*; cantata *Herne the Hunter*; theatre and orchestral mus.; string 4tet and other chamber mus., etc.

Meyer von Schauensee, Franz (Joseph Leonti) (b. Lucerne, 10. VIII. 1720; d.

Lucerne, 2. I. 1789), Swiss organist and comp. Studied in Lucerne and Milan, and after a period of military service, 1742–4, returned to Lucerne as a civil servant and musician. Ordained priest in 1752, he became organist of the collegiate church, and in 1762 choirmaster. He founded the Lucerne coll. of mus. in 1760.

Works incl. *Singspiele Hans Hüttenstock* and others; Masses and other church mus.; arias; instrumental mus., etc.

Meyerbeer, Giacomo (actually Jakob Liebmann Beer) (b. Berlin, 5. IX. 1791; d. Paris, 2. V. 1864), Ger. comp. His father Herz Beer, a Jewish banker, gave him every facility to develop his precocious mus. gifts. He was at first trained as a pianist and had some lessons from Clementi during the latter's stay in Berlin. He played in public at the age of 7, but afterwards studied theory and comp. under Zelter, B. A. Weber and Vogler, to whose house at Darmstadt he moved in 1810, being a fellow-student with C. M. von Weber there. His 1st opera was prod. at Munich in 1812 and the 2nd at Stuttgart in 1813. He then went to Vienna and, hearing Hummel play, he retired for further pf. studies, after which he appeared again as a virtuoso.

On Salieri's advice he went to It. to study vocal writing in 1815, and prod. his 1st It. opera at Padua in 1817. In 1823 he tried his luck in Berlin, but without much success, and having prod. *Il crociato* at Venice in 1824, went to Paris for its 1st 1st perf. there in 1826. He settled and spent much time there for the rest of his life. He wrote no new work between 1824 and 1831, among the reasons being his father's death, his marriage and the loss of 2 children. In 1831 *Robert le Diable* made him sensationally fashionable in Paris. In 1842 the King of Prus. app. him General Mus. Director in Berlin. He visited Vienna and London in 1847 and the latter again in 1862, when he represented Ger. mus. at the Internat. Exhib. His health began to fail about 1850.

Works incl. operas *Jephthas Gelübde*, *Alimelek, oder Die beiden Kalifen*, *Romilda e Costanza*, *Semiramide riconosciuta*, *Emma di Resburgo*, *Margherita d'Anjou*, *L'esule di Granata*, *Das Brandenburger Tor*, *Il crociato in Egitto*, *Robert le Diable*, *Les Huguenots*, *Ein Feldlager in Schlesin*, *Le Prophète*, *L'Étoile du Nord*, *Le Pardon de Ploërmel* (*Dinorah*), *L'Africaine*, *Judith* (unfinished); monodrama *Thevelindens Liebe*; incid. mus. to Michael Beer's (his brother's) drama *Struensee*, Blaze de Bury's *Jeunesse de Goethe* and Aeschylus's *Eumenides*; masque *Das Hoffest von Ferrara*; ballet *Der Fischer und das Milchmädchen*; oratorio *Gott und die Natur*; *Stabat Mater*, Te Deum, psalms and other church mus.; several cantatas, incl. 2 for the Schiller centenary, 1859, 7 sacred cantatas (Klopstock) for unaccomp. chorus; March for do., 3 Torch Dances, Coronation March, *Overture in the Form of a March* for the London Exhibition; pf. works; songs, etc.

Meynell, Alice (1849–1922), Eng. poet. *See* **Davies (Walford)** (*Christ in the Universe*).

Meyrowitz, Selmar (b. Bartenstein, E. Prus., 18. IV. 1875; d. Toulouse, V. 1941), Ger. cond. Studied at the Leipzig Cons. and with Bruch in Berlin. His appts. as opera cond. incl. Carlsruhe, N.Y., Prague and Berlin, and later he was a concert cond. in Berlin, Hamburg, Vienna, Rome, etc. In 1933 he emigrated to Paris.

Mezza (It. fem.) = half, as in *mezza voce* = half-voice, a special way of prod. the voice as if under the breath, resulting not only in a soft tone, but in a quality different from that of the full voice.

Mezzo (It. masc.) = half, as in *mezzo-soprano*, a voice half-way between soprano and contralto in range.

mf (abbr.) = *mezzo forte* (half-loud).

Mi, the old name for the note E (*see* **Solmization**), still used in Lat. countries, and in Tonic Sol-fa the Mediant note in any key, repres. by the symbol ⋔, pronounced Me.

Mi contra Fa, a medieval designation of the Tritone (the forbidden interval of the augmented 4th), the Mi being the mediant of the hard hexachord beginning on G.

Miaskovsky, Nikolai Yakovlevich (b. Novogeorgievsk nr. Warsaw, 20. IV. 1881; d. Moscow, 9. VIII. 1950), Rus. comp. Son of a Rus. military engineer stationed in Pol., whence the family moved successively to Orenburg, Kazan and Nizhny-Novgorod, where M. joined the cadet corps. Intended to follow his father's career, he did not finally take to mus. until 1907, when he resigned his commission, though he had comp. many pf. preludes, studied with Glière and Krizhanovsky and entered the St. Petersburg Cons. in 1906, where he studied with Rimsky-Korsakov, Liadov and Wihtol. In 1914–17 he fought on the Aus. front and was badly wounded; in 1921 he became comp. prof. at the Moscow Cons.

Works incl. oratorio *Kirov is with us*; 27 symphs., 2 sinfoniettas, symph. poems *Silence* (after Poe) and *Alastor* (after Shelley), serenade and *Lyric Concertino* for small orch.; vln. concerto; 9 string 4tets; sonata and pf. sonata; 4 pf. sonatas and other pf. pieces; 13 op. nos. of songs, etc.

Miča, František Václav (b. Třebíč, Morav., 5. IX. 1694; d. Jaroměřice, 15. II. 1744), Morav. tenor and comp. Prob. studied in Vienna, and in 1711 entered the

service of Count Questenberg in Jaroměřice, becoming *Kapellmeister* in 1722 and there producing 5 operas of his own and many by other comps. 2 symphs. sometimes attrib. to him, though clearly too modern in style, are the work of his nephew, Jan Adam František M. (1746–1811).

Works incl. operas; cantatas; Passion oratorios; etc.

Michael, Roger (Rogier) (b. Mons, *c.* 1550; d. Dresden, *c.* 1619), Flem. tenor and comp. Studied under his father, Simon M., a musician to the Emperor Ferdinand I. He became a tenor in the electoral chapel at Dresden in 1575 and *Kapellmeister* in 1587, being succeeded in the latter post by Schütz in 1619.

Works incl. introits in the motet style, settings of hymn-tunes in 4 parts and other sacred mus.

Michael, Tobias (b. Dresden, 13. VI. 1592; d. Leipzig, 26. VI. 1657), Ger. comp., son of prec. Studied as a boy chorister under his father in the Dresden court chapel and became mus. director at Sondershausen in 1619. In 1631 he succeeded Schein as cantor of St. Thomas's Church at Leipzig.

Works incl. *Musikalische Seelenlust* containing sacred madrigals for voices and sacred concertos for voices and instruments, other church mus., etc.

Michelangeli, Arturo Benedetti (b. Brescia, 5. VI. 1920), It. pianist. Studied at the Instituto Musicale Venturi in Brescia and at Milan Cons. In 1939 he won the international pf. competition in Geneva. Though he is among the foremost pianists of today, his concert appearances are infrequent and much of his time is taken up with teaching.

Michelangelo (Michelangiolo Buonarroti) (1475–1564), It. painter, sculptor and poet. *See* **Britten** (7 sonnets), **Dallapiccola** (choruses), **Valen** (*Sonetto*), **Wolf (H.)** (3 sonnets).

Micheli, Romano (b. Rome, *c.* 1575; d. Rome, *c.* 1660), It. comp. Studied under Soriano, travelled widely in It., became a priest, held appts. at Modena and Aquileia, and returned to Rome in 1625 as *maestro di cappella* of the church of San Luigi de' Francesi.

Works incl. Masses, motets, psalms; madrigals, canons, etc.

Micinski, Tadeusz (1873–1919), Pol. poet. *See* **Szymanowski** (*Prince Potemkin* and songs).

Mickiewicz, Adam (1798–1855), Pol. poet. *See* **Cui** (songs), **Moniuszko** (ballads), **Rytel** (*Grayna*).

Microphone, the receiver which transmits and amplifies the sounds of a broadcast perf. It can also be used for other than radio or television purposes, e.g. in theatres and public halls for the relaying of speech and song to amplifiers placed at var. points of the building.

Microtones, the small fractional notes into which the mus. scale was divided by the Mex. comp. Julián Carrillo, who invented special instruments for the purpose.

Middle C, the note C in the centre of the keyboard, variously repres. in notation according to the clef used, e.g.:

Middleton, Thomas (1570–1627), Eng. dramatist. *See* **Johnson (R. ii)** (*Witch*), **Locke** (do.).

Midi, Le. *See* **Matin.**

Midsummer Marriage, The, opera by Tippett (lib. by the composer), prod. London, Covent Garden Theatre, 27. I. 1955.

Midsummer Night's Dream, A. *See also* **Songe d'une nuit d'été.**

Incid. mus. by Mendelssohn to Shakespeare's play. Overture comp. in VII–VIII. 1826 and 1st perf. at Stettin in II. 1827; the rest of the mus. comp. in 1842 and used for a stage prod. at Potsdam on 14. X. 1843.

Opera by Britten (lib. from Shakespeare), prod. Aldeburgh, Jubilee Hall, II. VI. 1960.

Mighty Handful, The. *See* **Kutchka.**

Mignon, opera by A. Thomas (lib. by Jules Barbier and Michel Carré, based on Goethe's *Wilhelm Meister*), prod. Paris, Opéra-Comique, 17. XI. 1866.

Mignone, Francisco (b. São Paulo, 3. IX. 1897), Brazil. comp. Studied at São Paulo Cons. and later in Milan, in 1929 becoming prof. at the Nat. Cons. in Rio de Janeiro.

Works incl. operas *O contrantador dos diamantes, El jayon* (= *L'innocence*); ballet *Maracatú de Chico-Rei*; clar. and bassoon concertos; orchestral mus. and songs, etc.

Migot, Georges (Elbert) (b. Paris, 27. II. 1891), Fr. comp. Studied with var. masters, incl. Widor, and made a speciality of medieval mus. In 1917 he made himself known in Paris by giving a concert of his own, and, holding no official post, he relied on his own efforts to keep before the public.

Works incl. opera *Le Rossignol en amour*; ballets *La Fête de la bergère, Le Paravent de laque, Les Aveux et les promesses*; Psalm xix for chorus and orch., *The Sermon on the Mount* for solo voices, chorus, org. and strings; 2 symphs., *Les Agrestides, 3 Guirlandes sonores* for strings; *La Jungle* for org. and orch.; *Le Livre des danseries* for vln., fl. and pf. and other chamber mus.: *Dialogues* for vln. and pf. and cello and pf., *Ad usum Delphini,*

Le Zodiaque, Le Calendrier du petit berger (for children) and other pf. works; *Les Poèmes de Brugnon, Le Cortège d'Amphitrite* and other songs, etc.

Mihalovich, Ödön (Péter Jozsef de) (b. Fericsancze, 13. IX. 1842; d. Budapest, 22. IV. 1929), Hung. comp. Studied with Mosonyi at Budapest, Hauptmann at Leipzig, Cornelius and Bülow in Munich. In 1887 he succeeded Liszt as director of the Mus. Acad. at Budapest, and remained there until 1919.

Works incl. operas *Hagbarth und Signe* and *Wieland der Schmied* (Wagner's lib.) (both in Ger.), *Toldi Szerelme* (*Toldi's Love*) and *Eliána* (after Tennyson's *Idylls of the King*) (both in Hung.); 4 symphs., *Faust* overture (after Goethe), 4 Ballads for orch., etc.

Mihalovici, Marcel (b. Bucharest, 22. X. 1898), Rum. comp. Studied with d'Indy in Paris and joined a group of advanced Fr. and Rus. comps. there after the 1914–18 war.

Works incl. opera *L'Intransigeant Pluton*; ballets *Karagueuz, Divertissement* and others; *Cortège des divinités infernales* (from the opera), *Introduction au mouvement, Notturno* and fantasy for orch.; 3 string 4tets; string trio; vln. and pf. sonata, sonatina for ob. and pf., etc.

Mikado, The, or The Town of Titipu, operetta by Sullivan (lib. by W. S. Gilbert), prod. London, Savoy Theatre, 14. III. 1885.

Mikrokosmos (*Microcosm*), a set of 153 small pf. pieces by Bartók, arr. in progressive order and pub. in 6 vols., setting the player var. problems of modern technique, each piece being written on a partic. principle or system (special rhythms, time-signatures, chords, intervals, atonal or bitonal combs., etc.), comp. 1926–37, pub. 1940.

Milán, Luis (b. Valencia, *c.* 1500; d. Valencia, after 1561), Span. lutenist and comp. He was the son of a nobleman, Don Luis de M., played the vihuela, (?) visited It. and Port.

Works incl. fantasies and pavans for lute, Span. and Port. *villancicos*, Span. ballads and It. sonnets for voice and lute, etc.

Milanese Chant. *See* **Ambrosian Chant.**

Milanollo, (Domenica Maria) Teresa (b. Savigliano nr. Turin, 28. VIII. 1827; d. Paris, 25. X. 1904), It. violinist. Her father, a poor carpenter, succeeded in having her taught at Turin and in taking her to Paris in 1837, where she had a great success, as later in Hol., Eng., etc. Later still she appeared with her sister, after whose early death she retired for a time, and again for good after her marriage to the military engineer Charles Parmentier. She also prod. some comps., mainly for vln.

Milanollo, Maria (b. Savigliano nr. Turin, 19. VII. 1832; d. Paris, 21. X. 1848), It. violinist, sister of prec. She was taught by her sister and appeared with her on tour until her early death.

Milanov (orig. Kunc), **Zinka** (b. Zagreb, 17. V. 1906), Yugoslav soprano. Studied first in Zagreb and then with Ternina, and Carpi in Prague, making her début in Ljubljana in 1927. From 1928 to 1935 she sang in Zagreb and from 1937 her career centred on the N.Y. Metropolitan Opera. She is esp. known for her Verdi singing.

Milder-Hauptmann, (Pauline) Anna (b. Constantinople, 13. XII. 1785; d. Berlin, 29. V. 1838), Aus. soprano. The daughter of a courier in the Aus. diplomatic service, she was brought to Vienna as a child and on the recommendation of Schikaneder studied singing under Tomaselli and Salieri, making her 1st stage appearance in 1803. Beethoven wrote the part of Leonore in *Fidelio* for her and she early became interested in Schubert's songs. In 1810 she married the jeweller Hauptmann. She sang in Mendelssohn's revival of Bach's *St. Matthew Passion* in 1829.

Mildmay, Audrey (b. Hurstmonceaux, 19. XII. 1900; d. London, 31. V. 1953), Eng. soprano. Orig. a member of the Carl Rosa Opera Co., she married John Christie in 1931 and with him founded the Glyndebourne Festival, which opened on 28. V. 1934. In 1947 she and Rudolf Bing began the Edinburgh Festival.

Miles, Philip Napier (b. Shirehampton, Glos., 21. I. 1865; d. King's Weston nr. Bristol, 19. VII. 1935), Eng. comp. Studied at Dresden, also in London, comp. with Parry and pf. with Dannreuther. He was a landed proprietor, but did much good work for mus. at Bristol and in its neighbourhood.

Works incl. operas *Westward Ho!* (after Kingsley), *Queen Rosamond*, *Markheim* (after R. L. Stevenson), *Good Friday* (lib. by John Masefield) and *Demeter*; choral dance *Music Comes*; Keats's *Ode to Autumn* for baritone, ob., clar. and string 4tet; songs, etc.

Milford, Robin (Humphrey) (b. Oxford, 22. I. 1903; d. Lyme Regis, 29. XII. 1959), Eng. comp. Educ. at Rugby and studied mus. at the R.C.M., where his masters were Holst, Vaughan Williams and R. O. Morris.

Works incl. oratorio *A Prophet in the Land*; cantata *Wind, Rain and Sunshine*, *Bemerton Cantatas*, *5 Songs of Escape* for unaccomp.chorus; symph., concerto grosso, double fugue for orch.; vln. concerto, *The Dark Thrush* (on Hardy's poem) for vln. and small orch.; *2 Easter Meditations* for org.; pf. works; songs; part-songs, etc.

Milhaud, Darius (b. Aix-en-Provence, 4. IX. 1892), Fr. comp. Studied vln. and

comp. at the Paris Cons. from 1909, under Gédalge, Widor and d'Indy. His teachers also incl. Dukas. In 1917–19 he was attaché to the Fr. Legation at Rio de Janeiro, where he met Paul Claudel, who collaborated frequently with him as librettist. About 1920 he became a member of 'Les Six', and in 1922 he was repres. for the 1st time at the festival of the I.S.C.M. He emigrated to U.S.A. in 1940, but returned to Paris in 1947, where he taught at the Cons.

Works incl. operas *La Brebis égarée*, *Les Malheurs d'Orphée*, *Esther de Carpentras*, *Le Pauvre Matelot*, *Christophe Colomb*, *Maximilien*, *Bolivar*, minute-operas *L'Enlèvement d'Europe*, *L'Abandon d'Ariane*, *La Délivrance de Thésée*; ballets *L'Homme et son désir*, *Le Bœuf sur le toit* (*The Nothingdoing Bar*), *Les Mariés de la Tour d'Eiffel* (with others), *La Création du monde*, *Salade*, *Le Train bleu*, *La Bien-aimée* (after Schubert and Liszt), *Jeux de printemps*; incid. mus. for works by Claudel: *Protée*, *L'Annonce faite à Marie* and *Oreste* trans. from Aeschylus (*Agamemnon*, *Les Choëphores* and *Les Euménides*) and for Rolland's *14 Juillet* (with 6 others); orchestral works incl. 8 symphs. for large orch., 2 symph. suites, *Suite provençale*, *Sérénade*, *Suite française*, *Jeux de printemps*, *Saudades do Brazil*; 5 symphs. for small orch.; 5 études, *Ballade*, *Le Carnaval d'Aix* and 5 concertos for pf. and orch.; concerto and *Concertino de printemps* for vln. and orch., vla, cello and clar. concertos and concerto for perc. and small orch.; 18 string 4tets, wind 5tet *La Cheminée de Roi René*; 2 vln. and pf. sonatas, 2 sonatas for vla. and pf., sonata for 2 vlns. and pf.; sonata for pf., fl., ob. and clar.; sonatinas for fl. and pf. and clar. and pf.; some smaller instrumental pieces; sonatina for org.; 6 pf. works incl. suite, sonata, *Printemps* (2 vols.), *Saudades do Brazil* (2 vols.), *3 Rag Caprices*; suite *Scaramouche* and *Bal martiniquais* for 2 pfs.; 14 books of songs incl. *Poèmes de Léo Latil*, *Poèmes de Paul Claudel*, *Poèmes juifs*, *Poèmes de Cocteau*, *Les Soirées de Pétrograde*; *Machines agricoles* for voice and 7 instruments, *Catalogue des fleurs* for voice and chamber orch.; 2 psalms for baritone and orch.; Psalm cxxi for male voices; cantata *Cain and Abel*; 4 *Poèmes* for voice and vln., etc.

Military Band, a wind band attached to military regiments and used by them for their ceremonial occasions, but also often engaged to play for the entertainment of the general public in parks, at the seaside, etc. It incl. woodwind, brass and perc.

'Military' Symphony, Haydn's symph. No. 100 in G maj. (No. 8 of the 'Salomon' symphs.), comp. for London in 1794; so called because of the tpt. call and perc. effects found in the 2nd movement.

Millay, Edna St. Vincent (1892–1950), Amer. poet. See **Bliss** (5 *Amer. Songs*), King's Henchman (Deems Taylor), Wagenaar (B.) (songs).

Millico, Giuseppe (b. Terlizzi nr. Modena, 1739; d. Naples, 1802), It. castrato soprano and comp. He was discovered by Gluck, in whose *Le feste d'Apollo* he sang at Parma in 1769. Engaged by the imp. opera in Vienna, he sang the following year in the 1st perf. of Gluck's *Paride ed Elena*. Later visited London, Paris and Berlin, and from 1780 lived in Naples.

Works incl. operas *La pietà d'amore, La Zelinda, Ipermestra, Le Cinesi*; cantata *Angelica e Medoro* (with Cimarosa), etc.

Millöcker, Karl (b. Vienna, 29. V. 1842; d. Baden nr. Vienna, 31. XII. 1899), Aus. cond. and comp. Studied at the Vienna Cons. and became cond. at Graz in 1864 and at the Harmonietheater in Vienna, 1866. In 1869 he was app. cond. at the Theater an der Wien there and prod. operettas for it.

Works incl. operettas *Der tote Gast, Die beiden Binder, Diana, Die Fraueninsel, Ein Abenteuer in Wien, Das verwunschene Schloss, Gräfin Dubarry, Apajune der Wassermann, Der Bettelstudent, Der Feldprediger, Der Vice-Admiral, Die sieben Schwaben, Der arme Jonathan, Das Sonntagskind, Gasparone* and many others; numerous pf. pieces, etc.

Mills, Charles (b. Ashville, N.C., 8. I. 1914), Amer. comp. Studied with a 6 years' scholarship under Copland, Sessions and Roy Harris, 2 years with each, and later devoted himself entirely to comp.

Works incl. mus. for solo dance *John Brown*; 3 symphs., slow movement for string orch.; concertino for fl. and orch., prelude for fl. and strings; Festival Overture for chorus and orch.; *Ars poetica* for unaccomp. chorus; chamber symph. for 11 instruments, chamber concerto for 10 instruments, chamber concertino for woodwind 5tet, 3 string 4tets, pf. trio in D min.; *Sacred Suite* for 2 vlns. and pf., 2 vln. and pf. sonatas, 2 cello and pf. sonatas; 2 sonatas for solo vln., fl. and pf. sonata, dance sonata and sonata for solo fl., ob. and pf. sonata, *Chant and Hymn* for solo ob.; 2 sonatas, 2 suites, 10 sonatinas for pf.; 4 sacred canticles for voice and pf., etc.

Milner, Anthony (b. Bristol, 13. V. 1925), Eng. comp. Studied pf. with H. Fryer and comp. with R. O. Morris and later with Seiber (1944–7). From 1947 to 1962 he taught at Morley Coll., when he was app. to the R.C.M. and then lecturer at King's College, London Univ., in 1965.

Works incl. symph., *Sinfonia Pasquale* for string orch., *April Prologue* for orch.;

cantatas *Salutatio Angelica, The City of Desolation, St. Francis, The Water and the Fire*; Mass for *a cappella* chorus; string 4tet, ob. 4tet, wind 5tet; songs.

Milojević, Miloje (b. Belgrade, 27. X. 1884; d. Belgrade, 16. VI. 1946), Serb. comp. Studied at Belgrade and Munich. Lecturer in mus. aesthetics at Belgrade Univ.

Works incl. symph. poem *Death of the Mother of Jugovich* and *Antique Legend* for solo voices, chorus and orch.; *Serb. Dance* for vln. and pf., *Legend* for cello and pf.; pf. pieces; songs, folksong settings, part-songs, etc.

Milonga, a late 19th-cent. dance of the Arg., similar to the Tango, with which it became fused, or confused, early in the 20th cent., although orig. it was quicker in pace.

Milstein, Nathan (b. Odessa, 31. XII. 1904), Rus. violinist. Studied 1st at Odessa School of Mus. and then in St. Petersburg with Auer at the Cons. At 1st he appeared publicly with the pianist Horowitz, then moved to Paris where he built up his reputation. He is one of the most musicianly among contemporary virtuosi.

Milton, opera by Spontini (lib. by Victor Joseph Étienne de Jouy and Michel Dieulafoy), prod. Paris, Opéra-opera Comique, 27. XI. 1804. A 2nd Milton was planned by Spontini in 1838, when he visited Eng. in the summer to study the environment. It was to be entitled *Miltons Tod und Busse für den Königsmord* (*Milton's Death and Expiation for the King's Murder*) (lib. by Ernst Raupach), but turned into *Das verlorene Paradies* (*Paradise Lost*); it remained unfinished.

Milton, John (b. Stanton St. John nr. Oxford, c. 1563; d. London, III. 1647), Eng. comp., father of John M., the poet. Educ. (?) at Christ Church, Oxford. He is said to have received a gold medal from a Pol. prince for an In Nomine in 40 parts, was cast out by his father as a Protestant, went to London and in 1600 became a member of the Scriveners' Co., marrying Sarah Jeffrey about that time. Having made a fair fortune as a scribe, he retired to Horton (Bucks.) in 1632, but after his wife's death moved to Reading, c. 1640 and back to London in 1643, where he lived with his son John.

Works incl. var. sacred pieces for several voices; madrigal contrib. to *The Triumphes of Oriana*, 4 vocal pieces contrib. to Leighton *Teares or Lamentacions*; 2 tunes for Ravenscroft's Psalter; 5 fancies for viols., etc.

Milton, John (1608–74), Eng. poet, son of prec. See **L'Allegro, Il Penseroso** (Handel), **Bossi** (E.) (*Paradiso perduto*), **Comus** (H. Lawes and T. A. Arne), **Creation** (Haydn, *Paradise Lost*), **Darke**

(*Ring out, ye crystal spheres*), **Davies**
(Walford) (*Ode on Time*), **Festing** (*Song on
May Morning*), **Finzi** (sonnets), **Galliard** (*P.
Lost*), **Gatty** (*Ode on Time*), **Georges**
(*Paradis perdu*), **Harris (C.)** (*Paradise L.,
Il Penseroso* and *L'Allegro*), **Harwood** (*Ode
on a May Morning*), **Horsley (C. E.)**
(*Comus*), **Jackson (W. i)** (*Lycidas*),
Lutyens (*Salutes*), **Mackenzie** (*Temptation*),
Markevich (*Paradise L.*), **Nabokov** (*Sam-
son Agonistes*), **Occasional Oratorio** (Han-
del), **Paine** (*Nativity*), **Parry (H.)** (*Blest
Pair of Sirens* and *L'Allegro ed Il Pen-
seroso*), **Reichardt** (*Morning Hymn*), **Ritter**
(**P.**) (*Verlorene Paradies*), **Rootham** (*Ode
on Christ's Nativity*), **Rubinstein (A.)**
(*Paradise L.*), **Samson** (Handel), **Schneider
(F.)** (*Verlorene Paradies*), **Scott (C.)**
(*Nativity Hymn*), **Smith (J. C.)** (*Paradise
L.*), **Wood (C.)** (*Ode on Time*).

Minacciando (It.) = menacing, threatening.

Mines of Sulphur, The, opera by R. R.
Bennett (lit. by Beverley Cross), prod.
London, Sadler's Wells Theatre, 24. II.
1965.

Mingotti (*née* **Valentini**), **Regina** (b.
Naples, 16. II. 1722; d. Neuburg o/Danube,
1. X. 1808), Aus.-It. soprano, who became
an orphan as a child, was sent to a convent by an uncle at Graz, but had to
leave on his death and married the It.
musician Pietro M. (attached to the
Dresden Opera), who had her taught
singing by Porpora. She made her 1st
stage appearance at Hamburg in 1743. She
appeared in It., Spain., Eng. and Fr.

Minim, in modern notation the white
note with a tail to it, with the value of half
a semibreve or 2 crotchets: ♩. Orig. the
shortest note-value (Lat. *minima*).

Minnesinger or **Minnesänger** (Ger. plur.),
the singers in 12th- and 13th-cent. Ger.
who cultivated minstrelsy on the lines of
that of the Troubadours in Fr., and preceded the Meistersinger, but unlike them
were aristocrats, not middle-class mer-
chants and artisans.

Minor, 1 of the 2 predominant scales (the
other being Maj.) of the tonal system.
There are 2 forms of the M. scale: the
harmonic and the melodic. *See* **Harmonic
Minor, Melodic Minor.**

Minor Intervals, 2nds, 3rds, 6ths and
7ths which are a semitone smaller than
the corresponding Major I.s, e.g.:

Minore (It.) = Minor. In older mus. the
word is often used as a warning in the
course of a comp. which is predominantly
in a maj. key.

Minstrel, orig. the Eng. equivalent of the
Fr. *Jongleur* and the Ger. *fahrender
Sänger*, but in a wider sense any travelling
musician.

Minuet, a dance of Fr. orig. (*menuet*,
from *menu*—small) 1st appearing in
artistic mus. about the time of Lully. It is
in moderately animated 3–4 time and in
its later developments always has a contrasting trio section, after which the 1st
section is repeated. It was not a regular
feature of the suite, but appeared in many
of its examples; on the other hand it was
the only dance form normally retained in
sonatas, 4tets, symphs., etc.

Minuetto (It.). This, not 'Menuetto', is
the correct It. name for the Minuet.

'Minute Waltz', the nickname sometimes
given to Chopin's Waltz in D♭ maj.,
Op. 64 No. 1.

Miolan-Carvalho, Marie. *See* **Carvalho.**

Miracle of the Gorbals, ballet by Bliss
(scenario by Michael Benthall, choreography by Robert Helpmann), prod.
London, Prince's Theatre, 26. X. 1944.

Miracle, The, nickname of Haydn's
symph. No. 96, in D maj. (No. 4 of the
'Salomon' symphs.), written for London
in 1791. The name is due to the story that a
chandelier fell from the ceiling at the 1st
perf., when the audience miraculously
escaped injury; but in fact the accident
occurred at the 1st perf. of symph. No. 102
in B♭ maj. (1794–5).

Mireille, opera by Gounod (lib. by
Michel Carré, based on the poem *Mirèio*
by Frédéric Mistral), prod. Paris, Théâtre
Lyrique, 19. III. 1864.

Mirliton (Fr.), a toy instrument consisting of a simple pipe covered at one end
with parchment or tissue-paper, into which
the player sings, this prod. a reedy tone not
unlike that of a primitive ob. It is similar
to the Eunuch fl. and was also known as
Kazoo in Eng.

Mirror Canon⎫ a Canon or Fugue in
Mirror Fugue⎰
which 2 or more voices are so inverted
that the intervals appear simultaneously
upside down as well as right side up, look-
ing on paper like a reflection in water.

Misón, Luis (b. Barcelona, ?; d. Madrid,
13. II. 1766), Span. woodwind player and
comp. He entered the royal orch. at
Madrid in 1748 as flautist and oboist, became cond. there in 1756 and prod. his
1st *tonadilla* in 1757.

Works incl. numerous *tonadillas*, 3
operas *La festa cinese, El tutor enamorado*
and *El amor a todos vence*; 6 sonatas for
fl. and bass, etc.

Missa (Lat.) = Mass.

Missa, Edmond (Jean Louis) (b. Reims, 12. VI. 1861; d. Paris, 29. I. 1910), Fr. comp. Pupil of Massenet at the Paris Cons., where he received hon. mention for the Prix de Rome in 1881.
Works incl. operas *Juge et partie, Lydia, Le Chevalier timide, La Princesse Nangara, Mariage galant, Dinah* (after Shakespeare's *Cymbeline*), *Ninon de Lenclos, L'Hôte, Babette, Muguette, Maguelone*; operetta *La Belle Sophie* and others; pantomimes; orchestral works; choruses; pf. pieces; songs, etc.

Missa parodia (Lat., lit. 'parody Mass'), a term arising from a mistaken conjunction of the words *Missa* and *parodia* which occur separately on the title-page of a Mass by the 16th-cent. comp. Jacques Paix. His Mass is described as 'Parodia mottetae Domine da nobis auxilium', i.e. it is based on material from the motet cited. Neither in this work nor in any other are the words *Missa* and *parodia* joined together.

Missa pro defunctis (Lat. = Mass for the dead). *See* Requiem.

Missa solemnis (or **solennis**) (Lat.) = Solemn Mass, a title sometimes used by comps. for a Mass of a particularly festive or elaborate kind, e.g. Beethoven's Op. 123. Schubert also used it, and it occurs in Fr. as *Messe solennelle* (e.g. Gounod). The title is now used partic. for Beethoven's work, comp. in 1818–23 and 1st perf. in part, Vienna, 7. V. 1824.

Mistral, Frédéric (1830–1914), Fr. (Provençal) poet. *See* Mireille (Gounod), Widor (*Nerto*).

Misura (It. = measure), time; thus *senza m.* = without time, not strictly in time. Also the It. term for 'bar'.

Mitchell, Donald (Charles Peter) (b. London, 6. II. 1925), Eng. mus. critic. Largely self-taught in mus., though he studied for a year at Durham Univ. (1949–50). He has specialized in late 19th-and 20th-cent. mus., esp. Mahler, Reger and Britten.

Mitford, Mary Russell (1787–1855), Eng. novelist and dramatist. *See* Rienzi (Wagner).

Mitjana y Gordón, Rafael (b. Málaga, 6. XII. 1869; d. Stockholm, 15. VIII. 1921), Span. diplomat, musicologist and comp. Studied with Pedrell and Saint-Saëns. While on diplomatic service in var. countries, esp. in Swed., he was able to find Span. material scattered in foreign libraries to help his researches. He wrote on 16th-cent. Span. mus., on Morales, Victoria, Infantas, Guerrero, etc. and contrib. the vol. on Span. mus. to the *Encyclopédie du Conservatoire* pub. in Paris, His comps. incl. operas, e.g. *La buena guarda.*

Mitridate Eupatore, Il (*Mithridates*

Eupator), opera by A. Scarlatti (lib. by Girolamo Frigimelica Roberti), prod. Venice, Teatro San Giovanni Crisostomo, Carnival 1707.

Mitridate, Rè di Ponto (*Mithridates, King of Pontus*), opera by Mozart (lib. by Vittorio Amadeo Cigna-Santi, based on a tragedy by Racine), prod. Milan, Teatro Regio Ducal, 26. XII. 1770.

Mitropoulos, Dimitri (b. Athens, 1. III. 1896; d. Milan, 2. XI. 1960), Gk. cond., pianist and comp. He studied pf. and comp. at the Athens Cons. and subsequently with Gilson in Brussels and Busoni in Berlin. He cond. the Athens Cons. Orch. from 1929 to 1937, Minneapolis Symph. Orch. from 1937 to 1949, New York Phil. Orch. from 1950 to 1958.
Works incl. opera *Sœur Béatrice*; concerto grosso for orch.; string 4tet, vln. sonata; pf. mus.; songs, etc.

Mixolydian Mode, the scale beginning on G on the white notes of the pf. keyboard.

Mixtures, org. stops controlling a range of pipes with more than 1 note to each key, sounding not only the fundamental note but some of its harmonics.

Mizler (von Kolof), Lorenz Christoph (b. Heidenheim, Württemberg, 25. VII. 1711; d. Warsaw, III. 1778), Ger. mus. writer and ed. One of Bach's pupils at St. Thomas's School, Leipzig; founded the Assoc. for Mus. Science there in 1738 and ed. a periodical, *Neu eröffnete musikalische Bibliothek*, 1736–54.

Mlada, opera-ballet commissioned from Borodin, Cui, Mussorgsky and Rimsky-Korsakov by the Rus. Imp. Theatres in 1872, but never completed (lib. by V. A. Krilov).
Opera by Rimsky-Korsakov (lib. as above), prod. St. Petersburg, 1. XI. 1892.

Młynarski, Emil (b. Kibarty, 18. VII. 1870; d. Warsaw, 5. IV. 1935), Pol. violinist, cond. and comp. Studied at St. Petersburg. Cond. of the Warsaw Phil. Orch. from 1901 to 1905 and director of the Cons. there from 1904 to 1909. Cond. of the Scot. Orch., 1910–15. Resumed his posts in Warsaw in 1919. From 1929 to 1931 taught at the Curtis Inst., Philadelphia.
Works incl. opera *A Summer Night*; *Polonia* symph.; vln. concerto in D min., etc.

Mock Trumpet, an early Eng. name for the clarinet.

Mocke, Marie Félicité Denise. *See* Moke.

Modal Notation, a form of notation in use for vocal mus. in the 12th and early 13th cents., where the rhythm was determined not by the shapes of individual notes but by the various types of ligature in which they were combined according to one or other of the rhythmic modes.

Moderato (It. = moderate), a direction

used either singly or in comb. with words meaning fast or slow.

Moderne, Jacques (b. ? Pinguente, Istria, ?; d. Lyons, ?), Fr. 16th-cent. musician and pub., (?) of It. stock. He became *maître de chapelle* at the church of Notre-Dame du Confort at Lyons and about 1530 estab. a printing-press there, pub. books of Masses, motets and *chansons* between 1532 and 1567, with contribs. by var. comps., incl. himself.

Modes, the scales which became estab. in the Middle Ages and were still accepted, at least in theory, in the 16th cent. They are easily identified by reference to the white notes of the pf. keyboard. They were orig. known by the Gk. words for 1st, 2nd, 3rd and 4th as follows:

1. *Protus*: D-D
2. *Deuterus*: E-E
3. *Tritus*: F-F
4. *Tetrardus*: G-G

A distinction was made between the Authentic M.s, with the compass given above, and the four Plagal M.s which had the same final notes but a different range:

1. A-A (with final D)
2. B-B (with final E)
3. C-C (with final F)
4. D-D (with final G)

plete scheme is as follows (F. = Final, D. = Dominant):

No.	Name	Range	F.	D.
I	Dorian	D-D	D	A
II	Hypodorian	A-A	D	F
III	Phrygian	E-E	E	C
IV	Hypophrygian	B-B	E	A
V	Lydian	F-F	F	C
VI	Hypolydian	C-C	F	A
VII	Mixolydian	G-G	G	D
VIII	Hypomixolydian	D-D	G	C

The frequent intro. of B♭ in medieval mus. tended to change the character of some of the M.s. Thus M.I with B♭ was simply a transposed form of a M. with a final on A, and M. V with B♭ was identical with a scale of C major transposed to F. Hence Glareanus in the 16th cent. proposed that 2 further M.s, with their plagal forms, should be recognized, as follows:

No.	Name	Range	F.	D.
IX	Æolian	A-A	A	E
X	Hypoæolian	E-E	A	C
XI	Ionian	C-C	C	G
XII	Hypoionian	G-G	C	E

Modes, Rhythmic, the rhythms of medieval mus. were classified in 6 patterns (corresponding to poetic rhythms), units of which, in modern notation, were as below;

RHYTHMIC MODES

The whole series was later renumbered and Gk. names were attached, in the belief that the M.s corresponded to ancient Gk. M.s. In each mode a 'reciting note' (now often called 'dominant') was estab. In the Authentic M.s this note is normally a 5th above the final, and in the Plagal M.s a 3rd below the note in the Authentic M.; but where it would logically be B, the note C is substituted. The com-

Mödl, Martha (b. Nuremberg, 22. III. 1912), Ger. soprano. Studied in Nuremberg and made her début in 1942. Sang at Bayreuth in 1951 and has specialized in dramatic roles, esp. Wagner.

Modulation, the art of changing from one key to another in the course of a comp. by means of logical harmonic progressions.

Modus (Lat.). *See* **Modes, Mood.**

Moeran, E(rnest). J(ohn). (b. Heston, Middlesex, 31. XII. 1894; d. Kenmare, Co. Kerry, Ir., 1. XII. 1950), Eng. comp. of Ir. descent. He lived in Norfolk in his childhood, his father, a clergyman, holding a living there. Educ. at Uppingham School and later studied mus. at the R.C.M. in London. After serving in the 1914–18 war, he continued his studies with Ireland. In 1923 he came before the public with a concert of his works given in London, but after some years spent there he retired to Herefordshire.

Works incl. Magnificat and Nunc dimittis, Te Deum and Jubilate, 2 anthems; *Nocturne* for baritone, chorus and orch., *Songs of Springtime* and suite *Phyllida and Corydon* for unaccomp. chorus, *Blue-eyed Spring* for baritone and chorus, madrigals, part-songs and folksong arrs.; symph. in G min., sinfonietta, 2 rhapsodies, symph. impression *In the Mountain Country* for orch., 2 pieces for small orch. *Whythorne's Shadow* and *Lonely Waters*; concertos for pf., vln. and cello; string 4tet in A min., string trio in G maj., pf. trio in D maj., sonata for 2 vlns., vln. and pf. sonata in E min.; prelude for cello and pf., pf. variations and pieces *On a May Morning, Statham River, Windmills, Bank Holiday, Summer Valley*, etc.; songs incl. cycles *Ludlow Town* (A. E. Housman), *7 Poems by James Joyce, 6 Poems by Seamus O'Sullivan*; folksong arrs., etc.

Moeschinger, Albert (b. Basle, 10. I. 1897), Swiss comp. Studied at Berne, Leipzig and Munich, in the latter place under Courvoisier. In 1927 he settled at Berne as prof., but in 1943 he retired to Saas Fee, Ct. Valais, and later to Ascona.

Works incl. motet *Gottes Pfad*, cantata *Angelus Silesius, Das Posthorn* for male chorus and orch., cantata *Tag unseres Volks*, Mass for chorus and org., part-songs and other choral works, 5 symphs. incl. *Symphonie à la gloire de* . . . and suite for orch., variations on a theme by Purcell for strings and perc., divertimento for strings, *Fantasia 1944* for chamber orch.; 3 pf. concertos, vln. concerto; 6 string 4tets, pf. 5tet, wind 5tet on Swiss folksongs, 2 pf. trios; sonata, *Esquisses valaisannes*, variations and humoresques for vln. and pf., 2 cello and pf. sonatas, sonatine for clar. and pf.; 2 sonatinas, toccata, rondo and other works for pf.; *Vision und Verinnerlichung* for 2 pfs.; variations and fugue on a theme by Purcell, intro. and double fugue, *Fuga mystica* and Studies in Canon for org.; songs, etc.

Moffat, Alfred (b. Edinburgh, 4. XII. 1866; d. London, 9. VI. 1950), Scot. comp. and ed. Studied in Berlin and worked there for a time. Settled in London in the 1890s and ed. a large collection of old string mus., incl. many Eng. and Fr. works, also several vols. of Scot., Welsh and Ir. folksongs.

Moffo, Anna (b. Wayne, Penn., 27. VI. 1934), Amer. soprano. Studied at Curtis Institute, Philadelphia, in N.Y. and in Rome, making her début on It. television in 1956.

Mohaupt, Richard (b. Breslau, 14. IX. 1904; d. Reichenau, Aus., 3. VII. 1957), Ger. cond. and comp. Studied at Breslau Univ. He cond. opera at several Ger. towns and later toured as cond. in Rus. His ballet was prod. in Berlin in 1936, but soon afterwards his works were forbidden by the Nazi régime because he did not subscribe to its ideology and refused to divorce his Jewish wife. In U.S.A., 1939–1955.

Works incl. operas *Die Wirtin von Pinsk* and *Boleslav der Schamhafte*, comic opera for children; ballets *Die Gaunerstreiche der Courasche* (after Grimmelshausen) and *Lysistrata* (after Aristophanes), ballet for children; symph., concerto, *Drei Episoden* and *Stadtpfeifermusik* (on Dürer's mural *Nürnberger Stadtpfeifer*) for orch.; pf. concerto, vln. concerto, etc.

Moise (*Moses*), opera by Rossini, Fr. version of *Mosè in Egitto* (lib. by Giuseppe Luigi Balochi and Victor Joseph Étienne de Jouy), prod. Paris, Opéra, 26. III. 1827.

Moiseiwitsch, Benno (b. Odessa, 22. II. 1890; d. London, 9. IV. 1963), Eng. pianist of Rus. birth. He studied at the Imp. Mus. Acad., Odessa, winning the Rubinstein Prize at the age of 9, and from 1904 to 1908 with Leschetizky in Vienna. He first appeared as a soloist in 1908 in London, where he subsequently settled, becoming a British subject in 1937. After World War I he embarked on a series of tours which took him to every continent in the world.

Moissonneurs, Les (*The Reapers*), opera by Duni (lib. by Charles Simon Favart, based on an incident in Thomson's *Seasons*), prod. Paris, Comédie-Italienne, 27. I. 1768.

Mojsisovics, Roderich von (b. Graz, 10. V. 1877; d. Graz, 30. III. 1953), Aus. comp. of Hung. descent. Studied at Graz, Cologne and Munich (with Thuille there), but took a degree in law and became a civil servant. Reger, however, persuaded him to devote himself to mus. He cond. a male chorus at Brno in 1903–5, returned to Styria, became head of the Styrian Mus. Society at Graz in 1912 and settled at Munich in 1935.

Works incl. operas *Tantchen Rosmarin, Messer Ricciardo Minutolo, Der Zauberer, Die Locke, Anno domini, Die roten Dominos, Norden in Not, Much Ado about Nothing* (after Shakespeare); incid. mus. for Sophocles' *Oedipus Rex* and other plays; ballets *Phantastisches Tanzspiel*, *Chorisches Tanzspiel*; incid. mus. to plays; Mass for the Dead, cantata *Eine Weihnachtskantilene*; 5 symphs., 2 overtures, 2 serenades; 2 pf. concertos, vln. concerto; 3 string 4tets, string trio; 2 vln. and pf. sonatas, vla. sonata; 2 org. sonatas, *Festmusik* for org. and brass; *Waldphantasie* for 2 pfs.; org. and pf. pieces, etc.

Moke (or Mocke or Mooke), Marie (Félicité Denise) (b. Paris, 4. VII. 1811; d. Saint-Josse-ten-Noode nr. Brussels, 30. III. 1875), Fr. pianist. Studied under Herz, Moscheles and Kalkbrenner, and toured very successfully. Berlioz fell in love with her before he went to Rome in 1830 and she begame engaged to him, but married Camille Pleyel, as whose wife she made an international reputation. Pf. prof. at the Brussels Cons., for 24 years until 1872.

Mokroussov, Boris (b. Nizhny-Novgorod, 27. II. 1909; d. Moscow, 27. III. 1968), Rus. comp. Pupil of Miaskovsky at the Moscow Cons.

Works incl. opera *Tchapaiev*; incid. mus. for plays; *Song of Stalin* for chorus and orch.; *Anti-Fascist Symph.* and tone poem for orch.; suite for brass band; tromb. concerto; string 4tet; *Pioneer Suite* for pf., etc.

Moldenhauer, Hans (b. Mainz, 13. XII. 1906), Ger., now Amer., musicologist. Studied with Rosbaud, among others, in Mainz and for a time was active as a *répétiteur* and cond. in different Eur. cities. In 1939 he went to the U.S.A., where after further studies he became director and then president of the Spokane (Washington) Cons. and lecturer at the Univ. of Washington. M.'s most important contrib. to scholarship has been his recovery of a large number of Webern MSS. and documents, including some previously unknown works, and their pub.

Molière (Jean-Baptiste Poquelin) (1622–1673), Fr. dramatist. *See* **Ariadne auf Naxos** (*Bourgeois Gentilhomme*, R. Strauss), **Auric** (*Les Fâcheux*), **Austin (R.)** (*Malade imaginaire*), **Bourgeois Gentilhomme** (R. Strauss), **Charpentier (M.-A.)** (*Comtesse d'Escarbagnas* and *Malade i.*), **David (K. H.)** (*Sicilien*), **Festes de l'Amour** (Lully), **Galuppi** (*Vertuose ridicole*), **Grétry** (*Amphitryon*), **Grosz** (*Sganarell*), **Haug** (*Tartuffe*), **Joncières** (*Sicilien*), **Lattuada** (*Preziose ridicole*), **Liebermann** (*School for Wives*), **Listov** (*Bourgeois G.*), **Lully** (*Mariage forcé, Amour médecin, Princesse d'Élide, Sicilien, George Dandin, M. de Pourceaugnac, Amants magnifiques* and *Bourgeois G.*), **Mathieu** (*George Dandin*), **Médecin malgré lui** (Gounod), **Mengozzi** (*Pourceaugnac*), **Mortari** (*Scuola delle mogli*), **Ollone** (*George Dandin*), **Poise** (*Amour médecin*), **Purcell** (*Female Vir-*

tuosos), **Quinault (J. B.)** (*Bourgeois G.* and *Princesse d'Élide*), **Roger-Ducasse** (*Madrigal*), **Sauguet** (*Sicilien*), **Sauzay** (*George Dandin* and *Sicilien*), **Schulhoff (E.)** (*Bourgeois G.*), **Schweitzer** (do.), **Shaporin** (*Tartuffe*), **Signor di Pourceaugnac** (Franchetti), **Szymanowski** (*Bourgeois G.*), **Veretti** (*Medico volante*), **Wagner-Régeny** (*Sganarelle*), **Wolf-Ferrari** (*Amor medico*), **Wolfurt** (*Tanz um den Narren*), **Zich** (*Précieuses ridicules*).

Molinari-Pradelli, Francesco (b. Bologna, 4. VII. 1911), It. cond. Studied in Bologna and Rome, making his début in 1938, rapidly becoming known as one of the leading conds. of It. opera.

Molinaro, Simone (b. Genoa, *c.* 1565; d. ? Genoa, *c.* 1615), It. lutenist, ed. and comp. Pupil of Gostena, his uncle, whom he succeeded as *maestro di cappella* of Genoa Cathedral in 1599. In 1613 he ed. the madrigals of Gesualdo.

Works incl. Masses, motets, Magnificats, sacred concertos; madrigals, canzonets; lute pieces, etc.

Molique, (Wilhelm) Bernhard (b. Nuremberg, 7. X. 1802; d. Cannstadt nr. Stuttgart, 10. V. 1869), Ger. violinist and comp. Pupil of Spohr and of Rovelli at Munich, succeeding him in 1820 as leader of the orch.; after some time in the orch. of the Theater an der Wien in Vienna, he toured widely, became leader in the royal orch. at Stuttgart in 1826, settled in London in 1849 and returned to Ger. in 1866.

Works incl. 2 Masses; oratorio *Abraham*; symph.; 6 vln. concertos; 8 string 4tets, 2 pf. trios, duets for vlns. and fl. and vln.; vln. studies and pieces, etc.

Moll (Ger., from Lat. *mollis* = soft), the Ger. word for Minor.

Molnár, Antal (b. Budapest, 7. I. 1890), Hung. musicologist, critic and comp. Studied at the Budapest Acad. of Mus., collected folk mus. and joined the Waldbauer 4tet as violist. In 1919 he was given a prof.'s post at the Acad. He has pub. a vast number of books and articles on mus. He retired in 1959.

Works incl. incid. mus. for *Sāvitri*; church mus., choral works; variations, suite, overtures and other orchestral works; cello concerto; chamber mus.; pf. and org. works, etc.

Molteni, Benedetta Emilia (b. Modena, 1722; d. ?, *c.* 1780), It. soprano. App. to the court of Frederick II of Prus. in Berlin, 1742–74, where she married J. F. Agricola in 1751.

Molto (It.) = Much, very.

Moments musicals, the title, which in correct Fr. should be *Moments musicaux*, of Schubert's 6 pf. pieces Op. 94, written prob. in 1828.

Mompou, Federico (b. Barcelona, 16. IV. 1893), Span. pianist and comp.

Studied at the Barcelona Cons. and later in Paris, where I. Philipp was his pf. master and Samuel Rousseau taught him comp. He lived at Barcelona again in 1914–21, then settled in Paris, returning to Barcelona in 1941.

Works incl. pf. pieces *6 Impresiones íntimas, Scènes d'enfants, Suburqis, 3 Pessebres, Canço i dansa, Cants magics, Fêtes lointaines, 6 Charmes, Dialogues, 3 Variations, 4 Préludes*; songs *L'hora grisa, Cançoneta incerta, 4 Mélodies, Le Nuage, 3 Comptines*, etc.

Monckton, Lionel (b. London, 18. XII. 1861; d. London, 15. II. 1924), Eng. comp. Educ. at Charterhouse School and Oxford. He began his mus. career by writing some numbers for mus. comedies prod. by George Edwardes, and even after prod. his 1st complete piece of the kind he continued to write songs for others.

Works incl. mus. comedies *The Quaker Girl, The Dancing-Mistress, The Cingalee, The Country Girl*, etc.

'Monday Pops' (Monday Popular Concerts), chamber concerts held at St. James's Hall, London, until its demolition in 1905. Artists of internat. fame appeared and the series was widely celebrated. It is alluded to as a familiar topic in Gilbert & Sullivan's *Mikado*.

Mondo alla roversa, Il, o sia Le donne che comandano (*The World Upside Down, or Women in Command*), opera by Galuppi (lib. by Goldoni), prod. Venice, Teatro San Cassiano, 14. XI. 1750.

Mondo della luna, Il (*The World of the Moon*), opera by Galuppi (lib. by Goldoni), prod. Venice, Teatro San Moisè, 29. I. 1750.

Opera by Haydn (lib. do.), prod. Esterház, 3. VIII. 1777.

Mondonville, Jean Joseph (Cassanea) de (b. Narbonne, XII. 1711; d. Belleville nr. Paris, 8. X. 1772), Fr. violinist and comp. His parents were aristocrats in reduced circumstances, but he succeeded in studying the vln. He settled in Paris in 1733, made his name as a perf. and comp. and appeared at the Concert spirituel in 1737, for which he wrote motets until 1770. In 1744 he became superintendent of the royal chapel and in 1755–62 he was director of the Concert spirituel. During the *guerre des bouffons* in 1752 he was chosen as the representative of the Fr. nat. school opposing the Its. under the patronage of Mme. de Pompadour.

Works incl. operas and opera-ballets *Isbé, Le Carnaval du Parnasse, Titon et l'Aurore, Daphnis et Alcimaduro* (in Provençal), *Les Fêtes de Paphos, Thésée, Psyché, Érigone, Vénus et Adonis, Les Projets de l'Amour*; oratorios *Les Israélites au Mont Oreb, Les Fureurs de Saül, Les Titans*; the *Privelège du Roi* set as a cantata; trio

sonatas for 2 vlns. or fls. and bass; sonatas incl. *Les Sons harmoniques* for vln. and bass; sonatas and pieces for harpsichord with vln. or voice; harpsichord works incl. *Pièces de clavecin en sonates*; org. pieces, etc.

Monferrina (It.), a Piedmontese country dance intro. into Eng. early in the 19th cent.

Mong Kao-Yen (689–740), Chin. poet. *See* Lied von der Erde (Mahler).

Moniuszko, Stanisław (b. Ubiel, Lithuania, 5. V. 1819; d. Warsaw, 4. VI. 1872), Pol. comp. After studying at home, he went to Berlin as a pupil of Rungenhagen, 1837–9, and on his return settled down at Wilno as mus. teacher and organist, prod. the opera *Halka* there in 1848 (revised version prod. in 1858). In 1858 he became cond. at the Opera in Warsaw and later prof. at the Cons.

Works incl. opera *Halka, Flis, Hrabina* (*The Countess*), *Verbum nobile, Straszny Dwór* (*The Haunted Mansion*), *Paria, Beata*; incid. mus. for Shakespeare's *Hamlet* and *Merry Wives of Windsor* and other plays; cantatas *Spectres, Crimean Sonnets*, etc.; 5 Masses, Litanies and other church mus.; overture *Bajka* (*Fairy Tale*); 270 songs, incl. ballads by Adam Mickiewicz, etc.

Monn, Matthias Georg (b. Vienna, 9. IV. 1717; d. Vienna, 3. X. 1750), Aus. organist and comp. Chorister at Klosterneuburg nr. Vienna, he was from *c.* 1738 organist of the Karlskirche in Vienna. His symph. in D maj. of 1740 is the earliest dated symph. to have 4 movements with minuet in 3rd place.

Works incl. 16 symphs.; 10 partitas for string orch.; 6 string 4tets; concertos; keyboard mus.; church mus., etc.

Monna Vanna, opera by Février (lib. Maeterlinck's play with alterations), prod. Paris, Opéra, 13. I. 1909.

Monnikendam, Marius (b. Haarlem, 28. V. 1896), Dutch critic and comp. Studied at the Amsterdam Cons., at Dresden and the Schola Cantorum in Paris. He became a mus. critic in Amsterdam.

Works incl. 3 Masses, Te Deum, psalms for chorus and org.; symph. movement *Arbeid* (*Labour*); concerto for tpt., horn and orch.; chamber mus.; pf. and org. works, etc.

Monochord, a primitive instrument, not for playing, but for measuring the vibration of strings. It has a single string (hence its name) stretched over a long, narrow box. It is at least as old as the 6th cent. B.C., when it was used by Pythagoras, and it was mentioned by Euclid *c.* 300 B.C., but it still occupied scientists in the Middle Ages. It was found that if the string was stopped exactly in the centre, it gave out the higher 8ve on each side, and other intervals were found to sound at proportional points.

Monocorde (Fr. ⎱
Monocordo (It. ⎰ = single string), a direction used in vln. mus. where the comp. wishes a passage to be played on 1 string.

Monodrama, a mus. stage work for a single singer, an opera with a cast of 1, as for ex. Meyerbeer's *Tevelindens Liebe*, Gomis's *Sensibilidad y prudencia* or Schönberg's *Erwartung*. *See also* **Lélio** (Berlioz).

Monody (from Gk. for 'single song'), a term used to describe mus. making its effect with a single melodic part, accomp. or not, instead of a collaboration of var. parts as in Polyphony.

Monophonic, mus. in a single melodic part, without harmony, as distinct from Homophonic, which is melodic mus. accomp. by harmony, or Polyphonic, which is mus. in a number of melodic parts moving simultaneously.

Monopoli. *See* **Insanguine.**

Monothematic, an adj. used for a work based throughout, esp. in the course of more than one movement, on a single dominating theme. Haydn more than once wrote monothematic movements, e.g. the finale of symph. No. 103 in E♭ maj. and the first movement of symph. No. 104 in D maj.

Monpou, (François Louis) Hippolyte (b. Paris, 12. I. 1804; d. Orleans, 10. VIII. 1841), Fr. comp. He was a choir-boy at the church of Saint-Germain-l'Auxerrois in Paris at the age of 5, and at Notre-Dame at 9. In 1817 he entered Choron's school of mus., became organist at Tours Cathedral in 1819, but being unsuccessful there returned to Choron as accompanist. He picked up more instruction at the school, but never became a good technician, and he took to opera from sheer necessity when Choron's school was closed. But he had already made a name for himself by settings of verses by the new poets, who approved of them.

Works incl. operas *Les Deux Reines*, *Le Luthier de Vienne*, *Piquillo*, *Un Conte d'autrefois*, *Perugina*, *Le Planteur*, *La Chaste Suzanne*, *La Reine Jeanne*, *L'Orfèvre*, *Lambert Simnel* (unfinished, completed by Adam); nocturne for 3 voices *Si j'étais petit oiseau* (Béranger); songs to words by Hugo (*Guitare*), Musset and others, etc.

Monro (or **Monroe**), **George** (b. ?; d. London, ? 1731), Eng. organist and comp. He was organist at St. Peter's, Cornhill, in London and played harpsichord at the theatre in Goodman's Fields.

Works incl. incidental mus. to Fielding's *The Temple Beau*; a great number of songs, incl. 'My lovely Celia', etc.

Monsigny, Pierre Alexandre (b. Fauquembergue nr. St. Omer, 17. X. 1729; d. Paris, 14. I. 1817), Fr. comp. He studied the vln. in his youth, but after the death of his father took an official position in Paris in order to support his family. A perf. of *La serva padrona* in 1754 re-awakened his mus. interests, and he took comp. lessons from the double-bass player Gianotti. His first opera was prod. in 1759, and his assoc. with Sedaine as librettist soon consolidated his success. After *Félix* (1777), at the height of his fame, he comp. no more. He lost his fortune during the Revolution, but was given an annuity by the Opéra-Comique.

Works incl. operas *Les Aveux indiscrets*, *Le Maître en droit*, *Le Cadi dupé*, *On ne s'avise jamais de tout*, *Le Roi et le fermier*, *Rose et Colas*, *Aline, reine de Golconde*, *L'Isle sonnante* (after Rabelais), *Le Déserteur*, *Le Faucon*, *La Belle Arsène*, *Félix, ou L'Enfant trouvé*, etc.

Montagnana, Antonio (b. Montagnana, *c.* 1700; d. ?), It. bass. Sang in several of Handel's operas in London, 1731–8.

Montagnana, Domenico (b. ?, *c.* 1690; d. Venice, *c.* 1750), It. vln.-maker. Possibly a pupil of Antonio Stradivari, he worked first at Cremona, and set up a workshop in Venice in 1721.

Monte, Phillippe de (b. Malines, *c.* 1521; d. Prague, 4. VII. 1603), Flem. comp. He lived (?) in Naples, 1542–54, and then in the Netherlands. He was in England (1554–5) as a member of the choir of Philip II of Spain, when he met the Byrd family. In 1558 or before he returned to It. In 1568 he went to Vienna as *Kapellmeister* to the Emperor Maximilian II, after whose death in 1576 he followed the next emperor, Rudolph II, to Prague. He was made a canon of Cambrai Cathedral, but (?) did not reside there.

Works incl. Masses, motets; over 30 books of madrigals, etc. His motet *Super flumina Babylonis* was sent to Byrd in 1583, to which the latter responded with *Quomodo cantabimus* in 1584.

Montéclair, Michel (Pinolet) de (b. Andelot, Haute-Marne, 4. XII. 1667; d. Saint-Denis, 27. IX. 1737), Fr. comp. Studied mus. as a chorister at Langres Cathedral, later sang in other churches and went to It. in the service of the Prince de Vaudémont. After 1702 he settled in Paris and he was double-bass player at the Opéra in 1707–37.

Works incl. operas and opera-ballets, e.g. *Les Festes de l'été* and *Jephté*, ballet mus. for C. F. Pollaroli's opera *Ascanio*; chamber mus., etc.

Montemezzi, Italo (b. Vigasio, 4. VIII. 1875; d. Vigasio, 15. V. 1952), It. comp. Learnt the pf. as a child, then went to Milan to be trained for engineering, but wished to take to mus. He entered the Cons. with some difficulty, but obtained a diploma there in 1900. After the prod. of his 1st opera in 1905 he was able to give all his time to comp. From 1939 to 1949 he was in the U.S.A., after which he returned to It.

Works incl. operas *Giovanni Gallurese*, *Hellera*, *L'amore di tre rè*, *La Nave* (d'Annunzio), *La notte di Zoraima*, *La principessa lontana* (after Rostand's *Princesse lointaine*); *The Song of Songs* for chorus or orch.; symph. poem *Paolo e Virginia* (after Saint-Pierre); elegy for cello and pf., etc.

Montesquieu, Charles (Louis), Baron de La Brède et de Secondat (1689–1755), Fr. philosopher and historian. *See* Otescu (*Temple de Gnide*).

Monteux, Pierre (b. Paris, 4. IV. 1875; d. Hancock, Maine, 1. VII. 1964), Fr. cond. Studied vln. and comp. at Paris Cons., winning first prize for vln. in 1896. Then played vla. in Colonne Orch. and in 1911 began cond. for Diaghilev, giving the world *premières* of, among other works, Stravinsky's *Petrushka*, *The Rite of Spring*, *The Nightingale*, Ravel's *Daphnis and Chloe*, Debussy's *Jeux*. He was cond. of the San Francisco Symph. Orch. from 1936 to 1952. M. conducted all over the world and was recognized as equally fine in both the Fr. and Ger. repertories.

Monteverdi, Claudio (Zuan Antonio) (b. Cremona, V. 1567; d. Venice, 29. XI. 1643), It. comp. Son of a doctor; was a choir-boy at Cremona Cathedral and a pupil of Ingegneri; became an organist and violist and at 16 pub. sacred madrigals, 1583. Entered the service of the Duke of Mantua, Vincenzo Gonzaga, as violist and singer, and there married the harpist Claudia Cataneo. He was in Gonzaga's retinue in the war against the Turks on the Danube and again in Flanders in 1599. He prob. heard Peri's *Euridice* at Florence in 1600, and in 1602 was made mus. master to the court of Mantua. His wife d. after a long illness on 10. IX. 1607, the year M. finished his 1st opera, *Orfeo*. The next, *Arianna*, made him widely famous. When Francesco Gonzaga succeeded his brother in the dukedom in 1612 he quarrelled with M., who left for his native Cremona to wait for a new appt., which came from Venice in 1613, where he was made master of mus. to the republic and worked at St. Mark's. He had by this time written much church mus. and numerous madrigals. In 1630 he took holy orders after escaping the plague at Venice. In 1639 the 2nd public opera theatre in Venice, the Teatro dei SS. Giovanni e Paolo, was opened with M.'s *Adone*, and *Arianna* was revived the same year when the Teatro di San Moisè was inaugurated.

Works incl. operas *Orfeo*, *Arianna* (lost except the *Lament*), *Il combattimento di Tancredi e Clorinda* (after Tasso), *Il ritorno d'Ulisse in patria*, *L'incoronazione di Poppea* and about a dozen lost stage works; ballets *Ballo delle ingrate* and *Tirsi e Clori*; Masses, Magnificats and psalms; *Sancta Maria* for voice and 8 instruments; 40 sacred madrigals; 21 *canzonette* for 3 voices; 9 books of secular madrigals cont. 250; 26 madrigals published in var. collections; 25 *Scherzi musicali* for 1–3 voices, etc.

Monticelli, Angelo Maria (b. Milan, *c.* 1710; d. Dresden, 1764), It castrato soprano. Made his début in Rome in 1730, sang in London, 1741–6, later in Naples, Vienna and, from 1756, in Dresden under Hasse.

Montigny-Rémaury, Fanny (Marcelline Caroline) (b. Pamiers, 22. I. 1843; d. Pamiers, 29. VI. 1913), Fr. pianist. Pupil of her sister Elvire Rémaury, who married A. Thomas, and of Le Couppey at the Paris Cons. She made her 1st appearance in 1862 and married the journalist Léon Montigny in 1866.

Montpellier Manuscript, a large MS. (400 folios) in 8 gatherings, repres. about 100 years of mus. history (1200–1300). It is the largest source of 13th-cent. motets and was written down between *c.* 1280 and *c.* 1310. It is in the library of the Faculté des Médecins, Montpellier, MS. 196.

Montsalvatge (Bassols), Xavier (b. Gerona, 11. III. 1912), Catalan comp. Studied with Morera and Pahissa at Barcelona Cons., winning the Pedrell Prize in 1936.

Works incl. opera *El gato con botas*; 4 ballets; *Sinfonia mediterranea*; *Concerto breve* for pf. and orch., *Poema concertante* for vln. and orch.; orchestral suite *Calidoscopo*; string 4tet; songs.

Mood (Lat. *modus*), the relationship between the Long (♩) and the Breve (■) in mensural notation.

Moodie, Alma (b. Brisbane, 12. IX. 1900; d. Frankfurt 7. III. 1943), Austral. violinist. Studied with César Thomson at Brussels and travelled widely, making her reputation esp. in Ger., where she married a lawyer at Cologne.

Moody, Fanny (b. Redruth, Cornwall, 23. XI. 1866; d. Dundrum, Co. Dublin, 21. VII. 1945). Eng. soprano. Studied with Charlotte Sainton-Dolby and made her 1st stage appearance at Liverpool in 1887. In 1890 she married Charles Manners and in 1897 became his partner in the Moody-Manners Opera Co.

Mooke, Marie Félicité Denise. *See* Moke.

Moonie, William (Walter Beaton) (b. Stobo, Peeblesshire, 29. V. 1883), Scot. comp. Studied at Edinburgh Univ. and at the Hoch Cons. at Frankfurt. In 1908 he

settled at Edinburgh and occupied himself
with teaching, lecturing and org. playing.
Works incl. opera *The Weird of Colbar*;
A Deeside Symph., symph. poem *The
Riders of the Sidhe*, *Springtime-on-Tweed*
for orch.; chorus works; chamber mus.;
instrumental pieces, etc.

Moonlight Sonata, the nickname of
Beethoven's pf. sonata in C♯ min., Op.
27 No. 2, prob. due to a description of the
1st movement by Rellstab.

Moór, Emanuel (b. Kecskemét, 19. II.
1863; d. Vevey, Switz., 21. IX. 1931),
Hung. pianist, comp. and inventor. Studied
at Budapest and Vienna, and toured in
Eur. and Amer. as pianist and cond. Inventor of the Duplex-Coupler pf. Married
the Eng. pianist Winifred Christie.

Works incl. operas *La Pompadour* (after
Musset), *Andreas Hofer*, *Hochzeitsglocken*;
7 symphs.; 4 vln. concertos; chamber
mus.; pf. works, etc.

Moore, Douglas (Stuart) (b. Cutchogue,
N.Y., 10. VIII. 1893; d. Greenport,
Long Island, 25. VII. 1969), Amer. comp.
Studied at Yale Univ. and with Horatio
Parker, Bloch, d'Indy, Tournemire and
Nadia Boulanger. He served in the U.S.
Navy in the 1914–18 war, was organist
and lecturer at Cleveland, 1921–5, and
became assoc. prof. of mus. at Columbia
Univ. in N.Y. in 1926 and later prof.

Works incl. operas *The Devil and
Daniel Webster* and *The Ballad of Baby
Doe*, operetta *The Headless Horseman*,
chamber opera *White Wings*; motet *Dedication* for 6 voices, *Simon Legree* for male
chorus, *Perhaps to dream* for female
chorus; *A Symph. of Autumn*, Overture on
an Amer. Tune, *Pageant of P. T. Barnum*,
Moby Dick (after Herman Melville), *In
Memoriam*, symph. in A for orch.; string
4tet; sonata and *Down East* suite for vln.
and pf.; wind 5tet, clar. 5tet, etc.

Moore, George (1852–1933), Ir. novelist,
essayist and critic. *See* **Grania and Diarmid**
(Elgar).

Moore, Gerald (b. Watford, 30. VII.
1899), Eng. pianist. Studied in Canada and
after a short career as a concert performer
became an accompanist, in which profession he quickly rose to fame as the
most distinguished of his time, playing for
most of the great instrumentalists and
singers and raising his art to a level with
that of his partner. He has also pub. some
valuable books, incl. *The Unashamed
Accompanist*, *Singer and Accompanist* and
Am I too Loud?

Moore, Thomas (1779–1852), Ir. poet.
From about 1802 he began to pub. songs
with words and occasionally mus. by himself, and between 1807 and 1834 he prod.
collections of Ir. tunes with new words of
his own. He also prod., in 1811, an opera
M.P., or The Blue Stocking with mus.

by himself and C. E. Horn. He wrote the
tune as well as the words of 'The Last Rose
of Summer', used by Flotow in *Martha*.
For works used by comps. *see* **Barnett**
(J. F.) (*Paradise and the Peri*), **Bennett**
(W. S.) (do.), **Bishop** (nat. melodies), **Clay**
(*Lalla Rookh*), **David** (Fél.) (do.), **Feramors** (A. Rubinstein), **Horn** (C. E.) (*L.R.*
and *M.P., or The Blue Stocking*), **Jensen**
(songs), **Jongen** (*Lalla R.*), **Kashin** (*Nourmahal*), **Kelly** (*Gypsy Prince*), **Knight**
(J. P.) (songs), **Krizhanovsky** (*Paradise
and the P.*), **Lalla-Roukh** (F. David),
Paradise and the Peri (Schumann), **Spontini** (*Nurmahal* and *Lalla Rookh*), **Stevenson** (J.) (Ir. songs ed.), **Thomas** (G.) (*Light
of the Harem*), **Veiled Prophet** (Stanford),
Zolotarev (*Paradise and the P.*).

Moorehead, John (b. Ir., ?; d. nr. Deal,
III. 1804), Ir. violinist and comp. Studied
in Ir., went to Eng. as a youth and played
at var. provincial theatres, vla. at Sadler's
Wells Theatre in London from 1796, and
vln. at Covent Garden from 1798. He had
already prod. his 1st stage work in 1796
and wrote several more for Covent Garden. In 1802 he became insane and was
confined, entered the Navy on being released, but hanged himself in a fit of madness.

Works incl. stage pieces *Birds of a
Feather*, *Harlequin's Tour* (with Attwood),
Perouse (with Davy), *The Cabinet* (with
Braham, Davy and others), *Family
Quarrels* (with Braham and Reeve), *The
Naval Pillar*, Morton's *Speed the Plough*
and others; pantomimes, etc.

Morales, Cristóbal (b. Seville, *c.* 1500; d.
? Marchena, between 4. IX. & 7. X. 1553),
Span. comp. Studied at Seville under the
cathedral *maestro de capilla* Fernández de
Castilleja. Was *maestro de capilla* at Avila,
1526–30, and some time later went to
Rome, where he was ordained a priest and
became cantor in the Pontifical Chapel,
1535. In 1545 he was given leave to visit
Spain, but did not return, living at Toledo,
Málaga and Marchena, app. *maestro de
capilla* at the former 2 places and serving
in the household of the Duke of Arcos at
the last.

Works incl. Masses, Magnificats, motets, Lamentations and other church mus.;
cantatas for the peace conference at Nice
(1538) and for Ippolito d'Este; madrigals,
etc.

Morales, Melesio (b. Mex. City, 4. XII.
1838; d. Mex. City, 12. V. 1908), Mex.
comp. Studied in his native city, founded
several mus. societies from and in 1880
became director of the Cons.

Works incl. operas *Romeo e Giulietta*
(after Shakespeare), *Ildegonda*, *Gina Corsini*
and *Cleopatra* (all in It.); *Missa di Gloria*
and other church mus.; 2 cantatas, etc.

Morales, Olallo (Juan Magnus) (b.

Almeria, 15. X. 1874; d. Tällberg, 29. IV. 1957), Span. comp. He studied in Swed., his mother's country, and in Berlin. After apps. at Lausanne and Göteborg, he went to Stockholm in 1909 and became teacher at the Cons. in 1917 and prof. in 1921. He wrote criticism and mus.-hist. studies.

Works incl. symph. in G min., overture *Försommar* and other orchestral works; string 4tet, *Berceuse* for fl. and strings, etc.

Morales, Pedro (García) (b. Huelva, 1879; d. Huelva, 9. XII. 1938), Span. poet and comp. Studied at Seville and the R.C.M. in London, where he remained for most of his life.

Works incl. *Esquisse andalouse* for vln. and orch.; *Bagatelle* for vln. and pf.; songs to his own poems, etc.

Moralt, Rudolf (b. Munich, 26. II. 1902; d. Vienna, 16. XII. 1958), Ger. cond. Studied at the Munich Mus. Acad. with W. Courvoisier and Schmid-Lindner, and in 1919 became a *répétiteur* at the Munich State Opera. After a number of posts in var. Ger. opera houses he became 1st cond. at the Vienna State Opera in 1940.

Moravia, Hieronymus de (b. ?; d. ?), 13th-cent. theorist, prob. a Dominican friar living in Paris. His *Tractatus de Musica* is a comprehensive compilation dealing mainly with plainsong, with an extensive tonary attached.

Moravian Composers. *See* **Bohemian Composers**, where the older names are listed for convenience of reference.

Morawski, Eugeniusz (b. Warsaw, 2. XI. 1876; d. Warsaw, X. 1948), Pol. comp. and painter. Studied mus. with Noskowski at the Warsaw Cons. and painting at the Acad. of Art. He lived in Paris as a political refugee in 1905–29 when he returned and in 1930 became director of the Warsaw Cons.

Works incl. ballet *The Merchant of Switez*; 3 symphs., symph. poems *Vae victis*, *Fleurs du mal* (after Baudelaire), *Don Quixote* (after Cervantes), *Nevermore* and *Ulalume* (both after Poe), dance poem *Love* for orch.; hymns for contralto with org., etc.

Mordent, an ornament over a note, indicated by the sign: ♪. The interpretation, depending on the speed of the music and the length of the note, is approximately:

The double M. ♪♪ repeats the same process. *See also* **Pralltriller.**

Mordente (It.) = **Mordent.**

More, Hannah (1745–1833), Eng. philanthropist, religious writer and poet. *See* **Hook** (*Search after Happiness*), **Latrobe** (airs).

Moreau, Jean-Baptiste (b. Angers, *c.*1656; d. Paris, 24. VIII. 1733), Fr. comp. He learnt mus. as a boy chorister at Angers Cathedral and comp. motets as a youth. App. choirmaster at the cathedral of Langres, where he married, and later that of Dijon, and went to Paris during the 1680s. He found his way into the court, for which he began to write stage pieces, and in 1688 he was commissioned to write mus. for Racine's *Esther* for perf. at the young ladies' acad. of Saint-Cyr. This earned him a pension for life and an appt. at Saint-Cyr jointly with the organist Nivers and later with Clérambault. He remained under the patronage of the king and Mme. de Maintenon. He taught both singing and comp., among his pupils for the former being his daughter Claude-Marie M. and for the latter Clérambault, Dandrieu and Montéclair.

Works incl. Requiem, motet *In exitu Israel*, *Cantiques spirituels* (Racine), Te Deum for the king's recovery (1687) and other church mus.; stage divertissements incl. *Les Bergers de Marly*; chorus for Racine's *Athalie*; *Idylle sur la naissance de Notre Seigneur*; drinking-songs, etc.

Morendo (It.) = dying, a direction used where a phrase is intended to die away. It may mean a decrease not only in tone but in pace as well.

Morera, Enric (b. Barcelona, 22. V. 1865; d. Barcelona, 11. III. 1942), Span. comp. Lived in Argentine in his youth and studied mus. at Barcelona and Brussels. He did much work to further interest in Catalan folksong, which influenced his comps.

Works incl. operas *Emporium*, *Bruniselda*, *Don Joan de Serralonga*, *Titayna*, *Tassarba*, *La nit de l'amor*, *La font de l'Albera*, *La fada*; symph. poems; choral works; arrs. of Catalan songs, etc.

Moresca, a Moorish dance of remote antiquity, 1st intro. by the Moors into Spain and popular all over Eur. by the 15th–16th cent. Allied to the Eng. Morris Dance, 'morys' being an obs. Eng. variant of 'Moorish'; at any rate one of the latter's features—bells or jingles tied to the legs—belonged to the M. also.

Moreto y Cavana, Augustín (1618–61), Span. dramatist. *See* **Donna Diana** (Reznicek), **Ferreira**, **Hofmann (H.)** (*Donna D.*), **Laserna**, **Turina** (*La Adúltera penitente*), **Woyrsch** (*Donna D.*).

Morgenstern, Christian (1871–1914), Ger. poet. *See* **Burkhard** (6 Poems), **Toch** (*Egon und Emilie*).

Morhange, Charles Henri Valentin. *See* **Alkan.**

Mori, Nicholas (b. London, 24. I. 1796 or 1797; d. London, 14. VI. 1839), Eng. violinist and m. pub. of It. descent. Pupil of Barthélemon, at whose concerts he played at the age of 8, and later of Viotti. He appeared as soloist at the Phil. Society's concerts and became leader of its orch. In 1819 he married the widow of the mus. pub. Lavenu and became a partner with her son.

Moriani, Napoleone (b. Florence, 10. III. 1808; d. Florence, 4. III. 1878), It. tenor. Made his 1st appearance at Pavia in 1883 and sang in many Eur. cities during the next 14 years.

Mörike, Eduard (Friedrich) (1804–75), Ger. poet. *See* **Dieren (van)** (songs), **Schoeck** (songs), **Sutermeister** (*Jorinde*), **Trapp** (*Letzte König von Orplid*).

2 songs by Brahms, 3 by Schumann, 57 (incl. 4 early) by H. Wolf.

Morillo, Roberto García (b. Buenos Aires, 22. I. 1911), Arg. comp. Studied at home with Aguirre, J. J. Castro and others, also in Paris in 1926–30 and 1936–8. On his return he devoted himself to comp. and criticism.

Works incl. ballet *Harrild*; 2 symphs., Poem for orch.; pf. concerto and overture *Bersarks* for pf. and small orch.; suite *Las pinturas negras de Goya* for pf., vln., cello, fl., clar. and bassoon, 4tet for vln., clar., cello and pf.; suite *Conjuros* and other pf. works, etc.

Morlacchi, Francesco (b. Perugia, 14. VI. 1784; d. Innsbruck, 28. X. 1841), It. cond. and comp. Studied with his father, then at Perugia Cathedral, later with Zingarelli at Loreto and finally with Mattei at Bologna. In 1810 he was app. mus. director of the It. opera at Dresden, where he remained to the end of his life.

Works incl. operas *Il ritratto*, *Enone e Paride*, *Oreste*, *Le Danaidi*, *Raoul de Crequi*, *La capricciosa pentita*, *Il barbiere di Siviglia* (after Beaumarchais), *Boadicea*, *Gianni di Parigi*, *Il Simoncino*, *Donna Aurora*, *Tebaldo ed Isolina*, *La gioventù di Enrico V*, *Il Colombo*, *Francesca da Rimini* (after Dante, unfinished) and *c.* 10 others; *c.* 12 Masses, Requiem for the King of Saxony (1827), Miserere for 16 voices, unaccomp. Mass for the Gk. service and other church mus.; oratorios *Gli angeli al sepolcro*, *La morte di Abele* and *Il sacrifizio d'Abramo*, Passion oratorio (words by Metastasio); cantatas for the coronation of Napoleon as king of It. (1805) and for the taking of Paris (1814); Narration of Ugolino from Dante's *Inferno* for baritone and pf., etc.

Morlaye, Guillaume (b. *c.* 1515; d. after 1560), Fr. amateur comp., a merchant by profession. He lived in Paris and pub.

several books of mus. for lute and for guitar.

Morley, Thomas (b. ? London, 1557; d. London, X. 1602), Eng. comp. Although (?) a Rom. Catholic he was *magister puerorum* at Norwich Cathedral, 1583–7. A pupil of Byrd, he took his B.Mus. degree at Oxford in 1588 and about that time became (?) organist of St. Giles's Church, Cripplegate, in London. Soon afterwards he was organist of St. Paul's Cathedral and in 1592 became a Gentleman of the Chapel Royal. In 1598 both M. and Shakespeare, who were prob. acquainted, appealed against the assessment for taxes, and in 1599 M. contrib. the setting of 'It was a lover and his lass', if not more mus., to the prod. of *As You Like It*. M. obtained a patent for the printing of mus. and mus. paper in 1598, but he had already pub. his treatise, *A Plaine and Easie Introduction to Practicall Musick*, in 1597. He resigned from the Chapel Royal in 1602, (?) owing to ill health.

Works incl. services, anthems and responses, 10 Lat. motets; madrigals (incl. 2 in *The Triumphes of Oriana*), canzonets and balletts for voices; 4 tunes contrib. to *The Whole Booke of Psalmes*; fancies for viols; virginal pieces, etc.

Morning Heroes, symph. for orator, chorus and orch. by Bliss (words by Homer, Li-Tai-Po, Whitman, Robert Nichols and Wilfred Owen), 1st perf. Norwich Festival, 6. X. 1930.

Morris Dance, an old Eng. folk dance, deriving its name from the Moorish *Moresca* (obs. Eng. 'morys' = 'Moorish'), intro. into Eng. about the 15th cent. It partook of a pageant in character and was danced in var. kinds of fancy dress, with jingles tied to the dancers' legs. In some districts elements of the Sword Dance were intro. into it. The mus., a great variety of tunes, was played by a pipe and tabor, or more rarely by a bagpipe or vln.

Morris, Harold (b. San Antonio, Texas, 17. III. 1890; d. N.Y., 6. V. 1964), Amer. pianist and comp. Studied at Texas Univ. and the Cincinnati Cons. He lectured at the Rice Institute at Houston, Texas, and later became a teacher at the Juilliard School of Mus. in N.Y.

Works incl. 3 symphs. (No. 2 on Browning's *Prospice*), symph. poem on Tagore's *Gitanjali*, variations on a Negro spiritual, suite for small orch.; pf. concerto, vln. concerto; 2 string 4tets, pf. 5tet, 2 pf. trios, suite for fl., vln., cello and pf.; vln. and pf. sonatas, etc.

Morris, R(eginald). O(wen). (b. York, 3. III. 1886; d. London, 14. XII. 1948), Eng. teacher and comp. Educ. at Harrow, New Coll., Oxford, and the R.C.M. in

London, where later he became prof. of counterpoint and comp. In 1926 he was app. to a similar post at the Curtis Inst. at Philadelphia, but soon returned to Eng. His books incl. *Contrapuntal Technique in the 16th Century, Foundations of Practical Harmony and Counterpoint, The Structure of Music.*

Works incl. symph. in D maj.; vln. concerto in G min., *Concerto piccolo* for 2 vlns. and strings; fantasy for string 4tet, Motets for string 4tet; songs with 4tet accomp., etc.

Mors et Vita (*Death and [New] Life*), oratorio by Gounod, a sequel to *The Redemption*, prod. Birmingham Festival, 26. VIII. 1885.

Morselli, Ercole Luigi (1882–1921), It. dramatist. *See* **Belfagor** (Respighi).

Mortari, Virgilio (b. Passirana di Lainate nr. Milan, 6. XII. 1902), It. comp. Pupil of Pizzetti. Prof. of comp. at the S. Cecilia Cons. in Rome from 1940. Director of the Teatro La Fenice, Venice, from 1955 to 1959.

Works incl. operas *Secchi e sberlecchi, La scuola delle mogli* (after Molière); rhapsody for orch.; concerto for 4tet and orch., pf. concerto; chamber mus.; partita for vln.; children's songs *Giro, giro, tondo*, etc.

Mortimer, Philip. *See* **Knight, J. P.**

Morton (Mourton in Fr.**), Robert** (b. ?; d. ?, 1475), Eng. musician. He was in the service of the dukes of Burgundy, Philip the Good and Charles the Bold at Dijon, *c.* 1464–78, and had a great reputation as a learned musician. Later in the cent. he may have been a singer at St. Peter's in Rome, named Robertus Anglicus. His works incl. *chansons* for several voices.

Morton, Thomas (1764–1838), Eng. playwright. *See* **Moorehead** (*Speed the Plough*).

Moscheles, Ignaz (b. Prague, 30. V. 1794; d. Leipzig, 10. III. 1870), Boh. pianist and comp. Studied under Dionys Weber at the Prague Cons., played a concerto in public at the age of 14, was sent to Vienna and there took lessons in counterpoint from Albrechtsberger and comp. from Salieri. He made Beethoven's acquaintance when he arr. the vocal score of *Fidelio* in 1814. He then began to travel widely, and in 1821 appeared in Hol., Paris and London. In 1824 he taught Mendelssohn in Berlin; in 1826 he married Charlotte Embden at Hamburg and settled permanently in London. In 1832 he cond. the 1st perf. there of Beethoven's *Missa solemnis*. In 1846 he went to Leipzig at Mendelssohn's invitation to become 1st pf. prof. at the new Cons.

Works incl. 8 symphs.; pf. concertos, e.g. G min. and *Concerto pathétique*; a great

number of pf. works incl. *Sonate mélancolique, Characteristic Studies, Allegro di bravura* and numerous sonatas, variations, fantasies, studies, etc.; *Hommage à Händel* for 2 pfs., etc.

Mosè in Egitto (*Moses in Egypt*). *See also* **Moïse.**

Opera by Rossini (lib. by Andrea Leone Tottola), prod. Naples, Teatro San Carlo, 5. III. 1818.

Moser, Franz (Joseph) (b. Vienna, 20. III. 1880; d. Vienna, 27. III. 1939), Aus. pianist, cond. and comp. Studied at the Vienna Cons. and after var. apps. became prof. at the State Acad. there, chorus master at the Opera and lecturer at the Univ.

Works incl. a Mass; incid. mus.; 4 symphs. and other orchestral works; 4 string 4tets and other chamber mus.; pf. mus.; songs, etc.

Moser, Hans Joachim (b. Berlin, 25. V. 1889; d. Berlin, 14. VIII. 1967), Ger. singer, musicologist and comp., son of Andreas M. (1859–1925), violinist and writer on mus., biog. of Joachim. Studied with his father and later at Berlin, Marburg and Leipzig, and became prof. of musicology at Halle, Heidelberg and later Berlin. His lit. works incl. a hist. of Ger. mus., studies of medieval string mus., Luther's songs, Ger. song, etc., biogs. of Hofhaimer, Schütz and Bach, etc.

Moser, Rudolf (b. Niederzuwil, St. Gall, 7. I. 1892; d. nr. St. Moritz, 20. VIII. 1960), Swiss comp. Studied at Basle, later with Reger, Sitt and Klengel at the Leipzig Cons. and finally under Huber, Suter and others at Basle again, where he became cond. of the Orch. Society and the cathedral choir and prof. at the Cons. He was killed in a climbing accident.

Works incl. operetta *Die Fischerin* (Goethe), radio opera *Pereander und Lykophron*; Odes by Horace for baritone, chorus and orch.; motets and other choral works; suite, concerto grosso and other orchestral works; pf. concerto, 3 vln. concertos, vla. concerto, org. concerto, triple concerto for vln., vla. and cello; 4 string 4tets, pf. trio, string 6tet, instrumental sonatas and pieces; pf. works; songs, etc.

Moses und Aron (*Moses and Aaron*), opera in 2 acts by Schönberg (projected 3rd act never composed; lib. by comp.), concert *première*, Hamburg, 12. III. 1954; 1st stage perf., Zürich, 6. VI. 1957. (The music was comp. 1930–2).

Mosonyi, Mihály (orig. Michael Brand), (b. Frauenkirchen, Wieselburg, IX. 1815; d. Budapest, 31. X. 1870), Hung. comp. Studied at Pozsony (Pressburg) and was mus. master in a noble family in 1835–1842, when he settled at Budapest. He changed his Ger. name of Brand in 1859, when he began to aim at writing Hung. nat. mus.

Works incl. operas *Kaiser Max auf der Martinswand*, *The Fair Ilonka* and *Almos* (both in Hung.); 3 Masses; symphs., symph. poems *Mourning for Széchényi* and *Festival Music* and other orchestral works; 20 pf. pieces in the Hung. manner; 25 Hung. folksong arrs., etc.

Mosso (It.) = moving, in motion, animated.

Mossolov, Alexander Vassilievich (b. Kiev, 10. VIII. 1900), Rus. pianist and comp. His family, which cultivated var. branches of art, moved to Moscow in 1904 and in 1921 he entered the Cons. there, studying under Glière until 1925. He travelled much as pianist and to study folk mus. in central Asia.

Works incl. operas *The Dam*, *The Hero*, *The Signal*; cantatas *Sphinx* (Oscar Wilde) and *Kirghiz Rhapsody*; 6 symphs., symph. poem *The Iron Foundry* (*Music of Machines*), *Turcomanian Suite* and *Uzbek Dance* for orch.; 2 pf. concertos, vln. concerto, harp concerto, 2 cello concertos; string 4tet, *Dance Suite* for pf. trio; vla. and pf. sonata; songs to words by Pushkin Lermontov and Blok; massed choruses, battle songs, etc.

Mosto, Giovanni Battista (b. Udine, ?; d. ?, ? 1596), It. 16th-cent. comp. Pupil of Merulo, *maestro di cappella* of Padua Cathedral, 1580–9, and then in the service of Prince Bathori of Transylvania.

Works incl. church mus.; madrigals, etc.

Moszkowski, Moritz (b. Breslau, 23. VIII. 1854; d. Paris, 4. III. 1925), Pol.-Ger. pianist and comp. Studied at Dresden and Berlin, where he became prof. at Kullak's acad. later on. After a successful career as pianist and comp. he retired to Paris in 1897. He d. in poverty.

Works incl. opera *Boabdil*; ballet *Laurin*; symph. *Jeanne d'Arc*, 2 suites, *Phantastischer Zug* and other pieces for orch.; pf. concerto in E maj., 2 concert pieces for pf. and orch., vln. concerto; scherzo for vln. and pf., 3 pieces for cello and pf.; 3 concert studies, barcarolle and many other pieces for pf.; Span. dances and *Aus aller Herren Landen* for pf. duet; songs, etc.

Motet (Lat. *motetus*, a dim. of Fr. *mot* = word), a form of sacred vocal comp. for several voices arising out of the rhythmical *clausulae* of Organum in the 13th cent. It was at first an elaboration of a given plainsong melody by the contrapuntal addition of other melodies with different words (in Lat., Fr. or both). The earliest M.s were most frequently for 3 voices, *triplum*, *motetus*— hence the name of the species—and *tenor*,

which was the lowest part. In the 15th cent. it became more independent, and gradually developed into an elaborate form of polyphonic sacred comp. set to any Lat. words not incl. in the Mass. In the 16th cent. it was not uncommon to use the mus. material of a M. as the basis for the comp. of a Mass.

Motetus. *See* **Motet.**

Mother Goose (Ravel). *See* **Ma Mère l'Oye.**

Mother of Us All, The, opera by Virgil Thomson (lib. by Gertrude Stein), prod. N.Y., Brander Matthews Theatre, Columbia Univ., V. 1947.

Motif (Fr.). *See* **Motiv, Motive.**

Motion, the succession of notes of different pitch. The word is used only with some adjectival qualification or other:

Conjunct M.: a single part moving by steps of adjoining notes.

Contrary M.: 2 or more parts moving together in different directions.

Disjunct M.: a single part moving by larger than stepwise intervals.

Oblique M.: one part moving when another stands still.

Similar M.: 2 or more parts moving together in the same direction.

Motiv (Ger.)　　**Motive** (Eng.) } a brief melodic or rhythmic figure, too short to be called a theme, sometimes used as a purely abstract subject, sometimes in programme mus. or opera in assoc. with a character, object or idea, in which case it becomes a Leading Motive like the *idée fixe* of Berlioz or the *Leitmotiv* of Wagner.

Moto (It.) = motion, pace.

Moto perpetuo (It. = perpetual motion), a piece exploiting rapid figuration of a uniform and uninterrupted pattern; also called by the Lat. name of *perpetuum mobile*.

Motta, José Vianna da. *See* **Viana da Mota.**

Motteux, Peter Anthony (1663–1718), Eng. playwright and trans. *See* **Arsinoe** (? Clayton), **Finger** (*Loves of Mars and Venus* and *Anatomist*), **Franck (J. W.)** (masque for *Timon of Athens*), **King (R.)** (*Ode for John Cecil*), **Thomyris** (Pepusch, etc.).

Mottl, Felix (Josef) (b. Unter-St.-Veit nr. Vienna, 24. VIII. 1856; d. Munich, 2. VII. 1911), Aus. cond. and comp. Studied at a choir-school and at the Cons. in Vienna, became cond. of the Wagner Society there and in 1876 was engaged by Wagner to cond. the mus. on the stage in the prod. of the *Ring*. In 1881–1903 he was cond. at the ducal court of Carlsruhe, where he directed the symph. concerts and the opera, prod. many unfamiliar works. From 1903 he was cond. in Munich.

Works incl. operas *Agnes Bernauer* (after Hebbel), *Rama* and *Fürst und Sänger*; festival play *Eberstein*; mus. for O. J. Bierbaum's play *Pan im Busch*; string 4tet; songs, etc.

Motto, in mus. a short and well-defined theme usually occurring at the opening of a comp. and used again during its course, in its 1st form or altered, in the manner of a quotation or an allusion to some definite idea. The opening themes in Tchaikovsky's 4th and 5th symphs. are familiar exs.

Motu proprio (Lat. lit. of one's own motion), a decree issued by the Pope personally, esp. that issued by Pius X in 1903 setting down the principles of, and intro. reforms into, the singing of Rom. Catholic church mus.

Moulu, Pierre (b. ? Flanders, *c.* 1500; d. ?, *c.* 1550), Flem. or Fr. 16th-cent. comp. Pupil of Josquin des Prés. Wrote Masses, motets and *chansons*.

Mounsey, Ann (Sheppard) (b. London, 17. IV. 1811; d. London, 24. VI. 1891), Eng. organist and comp. She held var. org. appts. in London churches and in 1843 began a series of classical concerts. In 1853 she married the painter and trans. William Bartholomew (1793–1867), who was also a violinist.

Works incl. oratorio *The Nativity*; pf. and org. mus.; many songs, part-songs, etc.

Mounsey, Elizabeth (b. London, 8. X. 1819; d. London, 3. X. 1905), Eng. organist and comp., sister of prec. She was app. organist of St. Peter's Church, Cornhill, in 1834, aged 14, and remained there until 1882. She also appeared in public as pianist and guitar player.

Works incl. mus. for org., pf. and guitar.

Mount-Edgcumbe, Earl of (Richard Edgcumbe) (b. Plymouth, 13. IX. 1764; d. Richmond, Surrey, 26. IX. 1839), Eng. mus. amateur and comp. Known chiefly by his *Musical Reminiscences*, pub. privately in 1823, mainly of operatic singing in London between 1773–1823.

Works incl. opera *Zenobia*.

Mount of Olives, The (Beethoven). *See* **Christus am Oelberge.**

Mouret, Jean Joseph (b. Avignon, 16. IV. 1682; d. Charenton, 22. XII. 1738), Fr. comp. He entered the service of the Duchess of Maine in Paris about 1707 and in 1714 began to write for the stage. He was director of the Concert spirituel in 1728–1734, also for a time cond. of the Comédie-Italienne. In 1736 he became insane and was taken to the lunatic asylum of Charenton.

Works incl. operas and opera-ballets *Les Festes de Thalie, Ragonde, Ariane, Les Amours des dieux, Le Triomphe des sens,* etc.; Mass, 2 books of motets; cantatas

Cantatilles; 2 *Suites de Symphonies*, 47 divertissements for orch.; 2 books of *Concerts de chambre*; fanfares, etc.

Mourning Symphony (Haydn). *See* **Trauer-Sinfonie.**

Mourning Waltz (Schubert). *See* **Trauerwalzer.**

Mourton, Robert. *See* **Morton.**

Moussorgsky. *See* **Mussorgsky.**

Mouton, Charles (b. ?, 1626; d. ?, *c.* 1700), Fr. lutenist and comp. Lived at Turin in the 1670s, twice visited Paris, and eventually settled there. Wrote lute pieces, etc.

Mouton, Jean (b. Haut-Wignes, *c.* 1459; d. Saint-Quentin, 30. X. 1522), Fr. comp. Pupil of Josquin des Prés. He was in the service of Louis XII and François I, became canon of Thérouanne, which he left prob. on its being taken by the Eng. in 1513, and afterwards of the collegiate church of Saint-Quentin.

Works incl. Masses, motets, psalms, *Alleluia* and *In illo tempore* for Easter, *Noe, noe, psallite* for Christmas, etc.

Mouvement (Fr.) = tempo, pace; also a movement of a sonata, symph., etc.

Mouvements du cœur, 7 songs for bass and pf. in memory of Chopin (poems by Louise de Vilmorin): 1. *Prélude:* Henri Sauguet; 2. *Mazurka:* Francis Poulenc; 3. *Valse:* Georges Auric; 4. *Scherzo Impromptu:* Jean Françaix; 5. *Etude:* Léo Preger; 6. *Ballade* (*Nocturne*): Darius Milhaud; 7. *Postlude: Polonaise:* Sauguet.

Movable Doh, the Tonic or Keynote in the Tonic Sol-fa system which shifts the tonal centre at each modulation into another Key instead of prescribing Accidentals.

Movement, an independent section of a large-scale work such as a symph. or sonata. The term is used even when there is a link with the section that follows, e.g., in Mendelssohn's 'Scotch' symph.

Mozarabic Chant, one of the important branches of early Lat. chant, also called Visigothic, and used in central and S. Spain during the Middle Ages. Liturgically it is assoc. with the Gallican and Ambrosian rites, pre-dating that of Rome and showing similarities with Eastern liturgies. Its mus. is found in MSS. of the 8th–11th cents., but mostly in undecipherable neumes. Only a few melodies survive in readable form. Rom. chant and rite were imposed everywhere by 1076 except in Toledo, and in spite of the attempted revival under Cardinal Francisco de Cisneros (*c.* 1500), little of the mus. tradition has been preserved.

Mozart and Salieri, opera by Rimsky-Korsakov (lib. Pushkin's dramatic poem, set as it stands), prod. Moscow, 7. XII. 1898.

Mozart, (Johann Georg) Leopold (b. Augsburg, 14. XI. 1719; d. Salzburg,

28. V. 1787), Ger. violinist and comp. Educ. at the Jesuit coll. in Augsburg and at Salzburg Univ., he turned entirely to mus. in 1739, and first held a post with Count Thurn-Valsassina und Taxis. In 1743 he entered the service of the Archbishop of Salzburg, later rising to become court comp. (1757) and vice-*Kapellmeister* (1763). Married in 1747 Anna Maria Pertl; of their 7 children the only 2 to survive were Maria Anna and Wolfgang Amadeus. His important vln. tutor, *Versuch einer gründlichen Violinschule*, was pub. in 1756.

Works incl. church mus.; symphs.; divertimenti and descriptive pieces for orch. (incl. 'Mus. sleigh-ride', 'Toy Symphony', etc.); concertos for var. instruments; chamber mus.; sonatas for vln., etc.

Mozart, Maria Anna (Nannerl) (b. Salzburg, 30. VII. 1751; d. Salzburg, 29. X. 1829), Aus. pianist and teacher, daughter of prec. Like her brother Wolfgang Amadeus she developed very early as a clavier player, though not as a comp., and was taken on tour with him by Leopold. Later she taught at Salzburg, in 1784 married Baron von Berchtold zu Sonnenberg, a court councillor at Salzburg and warden of St. Gilgen, where she lived. She returned to Salzburg as teacher on his death in 1801 and in 1820 became blind.

Mozart, Wolfgang Amadeus (Joannes Chrysostomus Wolfgangus Theophilus) (b. Salzburg, 27. I. 1756; d. Vienna, 5. XII. 1791), Aus. comp., brother of prec. He showed early signs of mus. talent, learnt the harpsichord from the age of 3 or 4, and began to comp. under his father's supervision when he was 5. With his sister (then 11) he was taken to Munich in 1762, then to Vienna, where they played at court. Encouraged by their success, Leopold M. set out with the children the following year on a longer tour, which took them first through S. Ger. to Brussels and Paris (arrival 18. XI. 1763). They appeared at court at Versailles, and 4 sonatas for vln. and harpsichord by M. were pub. in Paris. Moving on to London in IV. 1764, they played before the royal family and made a sensation in public concerts. In London M. was befriended by J. C. Bach, 3 of whose sonatas he arranged as pf. concertos, and who also influenced the symphs., etc., he wrote at the time. They left for Hol. on 24. VII. 1765, and after several stops on the journey through Fr. and Switz. returned to Salzburg in XI. 1766. The next months were spent in study and comp., but on 11. IX. 1767 the whole family went to Vienna. There M. comp. his first Mass (C min., K. 139) and prod. the *Singspiel, Bastien und Bastienne,* though

intrigues thwarted the perf. of the opera *La finta simplice*. Returning to Salzburg on 5. I. 1769, M. had barely a year at home before setting out with his father on an extended tour of It.; in Rome he wrote down Allegri's *Miserere* from memory, in Bologna took lessons from Padre Martini and gained election to the Phil. Society with a contrapuntal exercise, in Milan prod. the opera *Mitridate* with great success on 26. XII. 1770. Two further visits to It. followed, both to Milan, for the perfs. of the serenata *Ascanio in Alba* (17. X. 1771) and the opera *Lucio Silla* (26. XII. 1772). Apart from short visits to Vienna (1773) and Munich (for the prod. of *La finta giardiniera*, 1775), most of the next 5 years was spent in Salzburg, his longest period at home since infancy. In IX. 1777, in company with his mother, he embarked on a lengthy journey which took them *via* Mannheim to Paris, where his mother died on 3. VII. 1778. The main object of this trip was to find suitable employment, but being unsuccessful M. returned in I. 1779 to the uncongenial post of court organist at Salzburg.

His serious opera *Idomeneo* was prod. in Munich on 29. I. 1781, but later the same year, on a visit to Vienna with the household of the Archbishop of Salzburg, he gave up his post to settle in Vienna as a freelance, living by teaching and playing in concerts. His Ger. opera *Die Entführung aus dem Serail* was prod. on 15. VII. 1782, and the next month he married Constanze Weber, whose sister Aloysia, a notable singer, he had courted unsuccessfully in Mannheim 4 years before. At the height of his fame as a pianist, 1782–6, he comp. many concertos for his own use, but thereafter was increasingly plagued by financial worries, which his appt. in 1787 as court comp. (a nominal position only) did little to ease. The first of 3 operas on libs. by da Ponte, *Le nozze di Figaro*, was prod. in 1786, followed by *Don Giovanni* (for Prague, 1787) and *Cosi fan tutte* (1790). A visit to Berlin with Prince Lichnowsky in 1789 took him through Leipzig, where he discussed Bach's music with Doles, Bach's successor, and in 1790 he made a fruitless journey to Frankfurt, hoping to earn money as a pianist. After several lean years 1791 was one of overwork, which must have contrib. to his early death: in addition to the last pf. concerto (K. 595), the clar. concerto (K. 622) and several smaller works, he comp. the operas *La clemenza di Tito* (for the coronation of the Emp. Leopold II, prod. Prague 6. IX) and *Die Zauberflöte* (prod. Vienna, 30. IX). the *Requiem*, commissioned anonymously by a mysterious stranger who was the steward of a nobleman wishing to pass the work off as his own, remained unfinished at M.'s death, and was completed later by his pupil Süssmayr.

Works incl. operas *Bastien und Bastienne, La finta semplice, Mitridate, rè di Ponto, Lucio Silla, La finta giardiniera, Il rè pastore, Idomeneo, Die Entführung aus dem Serail, Der Schauspieldirektor, Le nozze di Figaro, Don Giovanni, Così fan tutte, Die Zauberflöte, La clemenza di Tito,* etc.; serenatas *Ascanio in Alba,* etc.; mus. for Gebler's *Thamos, König in Ägypten*; ballet *Les petits riens*; oratorio *La betulia liberata*; cantata *Davidde penitente* (largely arr. of the C min. Mass, K. 425) and various Masonic pieces; 18 Masses, Requiem (unfinished), 4 settings of Vespers, Litanies, offertories, motets and other church mus.; solo arias, songs, etc.; *c.* 50 symphs. and numerous other orchestral pieces, e.g. serenades (incl. *Eine kleine Nachtmusik*), divertimenti, dances, etc.; concertos: 20 for pf. and one each for 2 pfs. and 3 pfs., 5 for vln., 2 for fl., 1 each for clar., bassoon, and for fl. and harp, 4 for horn; *Sinfonia concertante* for vln. and vla., and another for wind instruments; 6 string 5tets; 23 string 4tets; divertimento for string trio; 2 pf. 4tets; 5tet for pf. and wind; clar. 5tet; horn 5tet; ob. 4tet; fl. 4tets; 7 pf. trios; trio for clar., vla. and pf.; *c.* 40 sonatas, etc., for vln. and pf.; 17 sonatas, 15 sets of variations, 2 fantasias, and numerous other works for pf.; 6 sonatas, etc., for pf. duet; sonata, fugue in C min., etc., for 2 pfs.; Adagio and allegro in F maj., and fantasia in F min., for mechanical org. (later arr. for pf. duet), etc.

Mozart, (Franz Xaver) Wolfgang Amadeus (b. Vienna, 26. VII. 1791; d. Carlsbad, 29. VII. 1844), Aus. pianist and comp., son of prec. Pupil of Hummel, Salieri and Vogler. He settled as mus. master at Lwów in 1808, but toured in Aus. and Ger. in 1819–22. He settled in Vienna in 1838.

Works incl. orchestral and chamber mus., etc.

Mozartiana, Tchaikovsky's 4th suite for orch., Op. 61, comp. in 1887. It consists of 4 works by Mozart scored for orch. by Tchaikovsky: jig and minuet for pf., K. 475 and 355, motet *Ave, verum corpus,* K. 618 and variations on a theme by Gluck for pf., K. 455. 1st perf. Moscow, 26. XI. 1887.

mp (abbr.) = *mezzo piano* (half soft).

Mraczek, Joseph Gustav (b. Brno, 12. III. 1878; d. Dresden, 24. XII. 1944), Morav. violinist and comp. Studied at Brno and Vienna, led the theatre orch. at Brno in 1897–1902 and taught the vln. there in 1898–1918. In 1919 he became prof. at the Dresden Cons.

Works incl. operas *Der gläserne Pantoffel, Der Traum* (after Grillparzer), *Herrn*

Dürers Bild and others; symph. poem *Rustans Traum,* symph. burlesque *Max und Moritz* (after Wilhelm Busch), symph. poems *Eva* and *Variété, Oriental Dance Rhapsody,* etc. for orch.; *Oriental Sketches* for chamber orch.; string 4tet, pf. 5tet; pf. pieces; songs, etc.

Much Ado about Nothing. *See also* **Béatrice et Bénédict.**

Opera by Stanford (lib. by Julian Russell Sturgis, after Shakespeare), prod. London, Covent Garden Theatre, 30. V. 1901.

Muck, Carl (b. Darmstadt, 22. X. 1859; d. Stuttgart, 3. III. 1940), Ger. cond. Studied at Heidelberg Univ. and at the Leipzig Univ. and Cons. In 1880 he began a pianist's career, but became cond. at Salzburg, Brno and Graz in succession, at Prague in 1886, and finally in Berlin, at the Royal Opera, in 1892. He cond. Wagner in London and from 1901 at Bayreuth, also the Phil. concerts in Vienna. From 1906 to 1918, with an interruption, he cond. the Boston Symph. Orch. He was arrested as an enemy alien in 1918. He returned to Eur. after the war and cond. in Hamburg from 1922 to 1933.

Mudarra, Alonso de (b. ?, *c.* 1508; d. Seville, 1. IV. 1580), Span. lutenist and comp. He became (?) a canon of Seville Cathedral and pub. a book of lute pieces and songs to the lute incl. variations and dances, settings of passages from Virgil and Ovid and sonnets by Petrarch and Sannazaro.

Mudd, John (b. ?; d. ? Peterborough, VII. 1639), Eng. organist and comp. Organist at Peterborough Cathedral from 1583 to (?) 1629. Wrote services, anthems, etc.

Mudd, Thomas (b. ? London, *c.* 1560; d. ? Peterborough, ? 1632), Eng. comp. He went to St. Paul's School in London and in 1578 to Cambridge as a sizar for the sons of London mercers.

Works incl. services, anthems; dances for 3 viols., etc.

Mudie, Thomas (Molleson) (b. London, 30. XI. 1809; d. London, 24. VII. 1876), Eng. pianist and comp. Entered the R.A.M. in London in 1823, studying pf. with Potter, comp. with Crotch, and cl. with Willman, and was pf. prof. there in 1832–44. In 1844–63 he taught at Edinburgh and also gave pf. recitals there, returning to London in the latter year.

Works incl. symphs., overtures and other orchestral works; pf. 5tet, pf. trio; pf. pieces; songs; settings of Scot. folksongs, etc.

Muette de Portici, La (*The Dumb Girl of Portici*), opera by Auber (lib. by Scribe and Germain Delavigne), prod. Paris, Opéra, 29. II. 1828. Carafa's *Masaniello,* on the same subject, had been prod. at the Opéra-

Comique 2 months earlier. Auber's work is often called *Masaniello*.

Muffat, Georg (b. Mégève, Savoy, V. 1653; d. Passau, 23. II. 1704), Aus. organist and comp. Studied in Paris, with Lully or members of his school. In 1678 he was app. organist to the Archbishop of Salzburg, and after visiting Vienna and Rome went to Passau to become organist to the bishop in 1690.

Works incl. chamber sonatas *Armonico tributo*, *Auserlesene mit Ernst und Lust gemengte Instrumental-Musik*, *Apparatus musico-organisticus* for org. (12 toccatas, chaconne and passacaglia), *Suaviores harmoniae*, 2 vols. for harpsichord, etc.

Muffat, Gottlieb (Theophil) (b. Passau, IV. 1690; d. Vienna, 10. XII. 1770), Ger. organist and comp., son of prec. Pupil of Fux in Vienna from 1704, he entered the service of the court in 1717 and became 1st organist in 1741. Among his pupils were Wagenseil and the Empress Maria Theresa.

Works incl. 72 fugues and 12 toccatas for org., *Componimenti musicali* for harpsichord, etc.

Müglin, Heinrich von. *See* **Heinrich von Müglin.**

Mugnone, Leopoldo (b. Naples, 29. IX. 1858; d. Naples, 22. XII. 1941), It. cond. and comp. Studied at Naples and at the age of 12 wrote a comic opera; a 2nd was prod. in public in 1875. He also began to cond. very young, at 16, but afterwards gained more experience as chorus master and accompanist. In 1890 he was engaged to cond. the prod. of *Cavalleria rusticana* in Rome, and after that he made a brilliant career as operatic and concert cond. He wrote several more comic operas.

Mühlfeld, Richard (b. Salzungen, 28. II. 1856; d. Meiningen, 1. VI. 1907), Ger. clarinettist. In the grand-ducal orch. at Meiningen from 1873. 1st clarinettist at Bayreuth, 1884–96. Brahms wrote the 4 late chamber works with clar. parts, Op. 114, 115, 120 (i and ii) for him.

Mulè, Giuseppe (b. Termini, Sicily, 28. VI. 1855; d. Rome, 10. IX. 1951), It. cellist and comp. Studied at the Palermo Cons., of which he was director from 1922 to 1925, when he became director of the Santa Cecilia Cons. in Rome. He also became secretary to the Fascist syndicate of musicians. He studied Sicilian folksong and found that its roots went back to Gk. mus.; and he wrote much incid. mus. for the perfs. of Gk. plays at Syracuse.

Works incl. operas *La Baronessa di Carini*, *Al lupo!*, *La monacella della fontana*, *Dafni*, *Liolà* (on Pirandello's play), *Taormina*; mus. for Gk. plays: Aeschylus's *Choephori*, *Seven against Thebes*, Euripides' *Bacchae*, *Medea*, *The*

Cyclops, *Hippolytus*, *Iphigenia in Aulis*, *Iphigenia in Tauris*, Sophocles' *Antigone*; incid. mus. for Corradini's *Giulio Cesare*; oratorio *Il cieco di Gerico*; symph. poems *Sicilia canora* and *Vendemmia*; *Tre canti siciliani* for voice and orch.; string 4tet; vln. and cello pieces, etc.

Mulgrave, Earl of (John Sheffield), later Marquess of Normanby and Duke of Buckingham (1684–1721), Eng. poet and playwright. *See* **Galliard** (*Julius Caesar*).

Müller, August Eberhard (b. Northeim, Hanover, 13. XII. 1767; d. Weimar, 3. XII. 1817), Ger. organist and comp. Held appts. at Magdeburg and Leipzig, where he became cantor of St. Thomas's Church in 1804. App. court *Kapellmeister* at Weimar in 1810.

Works incl. 2 operettas; 3 cantatas; 2 pf. concertos, 11 fl. concertos; pf. trio; vln. and pf. sonatas; pf. sonatas, variations, etc.; sonata, suites, chorale variations, etc., for org.; fl. duets and pieces, etc.

Müller-Blattau, Josef (b. Colmar, 21. V. 1895), Ger. musicologist. Studied at Strasbourg, Pfitzner being among his masters. After serving in the 1914–18 war, he finished his studies with Wilibald Gurlitt at Freiburg i/B., became lecturer at Königsberg Univ. in 1922 and prof. in 1928. Later he held a similar post at Frankfurt, 1935–7 and then at Freiburg. His books incl. works on Schütz, Handel, baroque mus., Ger. folk-song and a hist. of Ger. mus.

Müller-Hartmann, Robert (b. Hamburg, 11. X. 1884; d. Dorking, Surrey, 15. XII. 1950), Ger. critic and comp. He was lecturer in mus. theory at Hamburg Univ. in 1923–33 and settled in London in 1937.

Works incl. incid. mus. to Büchner's *Leonce und Lena* and other plays; variations on a Pastoral Theme and other works for orch.; chamber mus., songs, etc.

Müller-Hermann, Johanna (b. Vienna, 15. 1. 1878; d. Vienna, 19. IV. 1941), Aus. comp. She studied with Karel Navrátil, Josef Labor, Zemlinsky and J. B. Foerster, and in 1918 became teacher of theory at the New Vienna Cons.

Works incl. oratorio *Song of Remembrance* (after Whitman) and other choral works, *Deutscher Schwur*, *Der sterbende Schwan*, *Von Minnelob und Glaubenstreu*; symph. in D maj. with chorus; *Heroic Overture*, symph. fantasy *Brand* and other orchestral works; string 4tet, pf. 5tet; vln. and pf. sonata; pf. pieces; songs, etc.

Müller von Kulm, Walter (b. Basle, 31. VIII. 1899), Swiss comp. Studied under Werner Wehrli at Aarau and at the Basle and Zürich Conss. He was a school teacher until 1928, when he devoted himself entirely to mus., teaching at the Basle

Cons. and cond. male choral societies there.

Works incl. opera *Die Probe*, festival opera *Mutterland*; ballet *Die blaue Blume*; symph., *Overture in the Old Style*, mus. with harpsichord and other orchestral works; chamber concerto for vln., concertino for fl.; 4 string 4tets, pf. trio, serenade for 5 wind instruments and other chamber mus.; org. and pf. works; songs, part-songs, etc.

Müller, Wenzel (b. Trnava, Morav., 26. IX. 1767; d. Baden nr. Vienna, 3. VIII. 1835), Aus. cond. and comp. Pupil of Dittersdorf, became cond. at the Brno theatre in 1783, aged 16, and in 1786 at the Leopoldstadt Theatre in Vienna, where he settled until 1808, and again in 1813, being director at the Prague Opera during those years, when his daughter Therese was engaged there. On his return to Vienna he became again cond. of the Leopoldstadt Theatre.

Works incl. nearly 200 operas and mus. plays, e.g. *Das Sonnenfest der Braminen, Die Zauberzither, oder Kaspar der Fagottist, Das Neusonntagskind, Die Schwestern von Prag, Die Teufelsmühle auf dem Wienerberge, Die travestierte Zauberflöte* (a parody of Mozart's *Magic Flute*); Masses; symphs., etc.

Müller, Wilhelm (1794–1827), Ger. poet. *See* **Loder** (*Brooklet*), **Schöne Müllerin** (Schubert), **Winterreise** (do.).

Mulliner Book, The, a large MS. collection of English keyboard mus. dating from *c*. 1550 to 1575, apparently copied by Thomas Mulliner. It contains both organ and virginal pieces, incl. transcriptions of viol and vocal mus., with the names of Blitheman, Shepherd, Redford and Tallis predominating. There are 123 pieces, and 11 more for cittern.

Mullings, Frank (b. Walsall, 10. V. 1881; d. Manchester, 19. V. 1953), Eng. tenor, studied at the Birmingham and Midland School of Mus., appeared at Coventry in *Faust* in 1907 and at a concert in London in 1911. He then specialized in heroic tenor parts in opera, joined the Denhof Co. in 1913 and was engaged by Beecham in 1919, singing Wagnerian parts with great intensity and being esp. impressive as Verdi's Othello.

Munch, Charles (b. Strasbourg, 26. IX. 1891; d. Richmond, Va., 6. XI. 1968), Fr. cond. Studied at Strasbourg Cons. and then went to Paris for further vln. studies with Capet and Berlin with Flesch. From 1919 to 1925 he taught the vln. at Strasbourg Cons. and led the citv orch., becoming leader of the Leipzig Gewandhaus Orch. in 1926. He made his début as cond. in 1932 in Paris and after var. teaching and cond. posts he became cond. of the Boston Symph. Orch. in 1949 and in 1951

director of the Berkshire Mus. Center in Tanglewood.

Münchinger, Karl (b. Stuttgart, 29. V. 1915), Ger. cond. Studied in Leipzig with H. Abendroth and in 1945 founded the Stuttgart Chamber Orch., which soon became known as one of the finest ensembles of its kind.

Munday, Eliza. *See* **Salmon.**

Mundy, John (b. ?; d. Windsor, 1630), Eng. organist and comp. Studied under his father, William M., became a Gentleman of the Chapel Royal in London and succeeded Merbecke as one of the organists of St. George's Chapel, Windsor, about 1585.

Works incl. anthems, *Songs and Psalmes* for 3–5 voices; madrigals (one in *The Triumphes of Oriana*); virginal pieces incl. the 'Weather' fantasia, etc.

Mundy, William (b. ?, *c*. 1529; d. ? London, *c*. 1591), Eng. singer and comp., father of prec. He was a vicar-choral at St. Paul's Cathedral in London and became a Gentleman of the Chapel Royal in 1564.

Works incl. services, anthems, Lat. motets, etc.

Munkittrick, Richard Lansdale. *See* **Talbot, Howard.**

Munzinger, Karl (b. Balstal, Ct. Solothurn, 23. IX. 1842; d. Berne, 16. VIII. 1911), Swiss comp. and cond. Studied at the Leipzig Cons. and became cond. of the Solothurn *Liedertafel* in 1867. He went to Berne 2 years later to take up a similar post, and later became cond. of the Cecilia Society and the symph. concerts and director of the Mus. School. In 1909 he retired and was succeeded in all these posts by Brun.

Works incl. mus. for the festival of the 700th anniversary of the foundation of Berne (1891); Mass; pf. 4tet; choral works with orch.; instrumental pieces; part-songs, etc.

Muradely, Vano (b. Gory nr. Tiflis, 6. IV. 1908), Rus. comp. Studied with Shtcherbatchev at the Tiflis Cons. and with Shekhter and Miaskovsky at that of Moscow. He made a special study of Caucasian folksong, on which some of his work is based.

Works incl. opera *Great Friendship*; 2 symphs.; choral mus.; film mus., etc.

Murciana, a Span. dance from Murcia allied to the Fandango.

Murdoch, William (David) (b. Bendigo, Austral., 10. II. 1888; d. Holmbury St. Mary, Surrey, 9. IX. 1942), Austral. pianist. Studied at Melbourne and the R.C.M. in London. He began his concert career in 1910.

Murger, Henri (1822–61), Fr. novelist. *See* **Bohème** (Leoncavallo and Puccini).

Murino, Aegidius de (b. ?; d. ?), 14th-cent. theorist and comp. of uncertain nationality. He may possibly be the 'Egidius Anglicus' of the MS. Chantilly 1047. His treatise *Tractatus de diversis figuris* is about note-forms and motet comp. 2 motets and 1 *chanson* also survive.

Muris, Johannes de (b. ?; d. ?), 14th-cent. theorist of unknown nationality. He lived for some time in Paris and worked also as mathematician and astronomer. The chief among the mus. treatises attrib. to him is the *Ars novae musicae*, 1319.

Murky Bass, an 18th-cent. term of unknown origin for a bass played in broken octaves on keyboard instruments.

Murray, (George) Gilbert (Aimé) (1866–1957), Eng. prof. of Gk. and translator. *See* **Alkestis** (Boughton), **Drysdale** (*Hippolytus*).

Murrill, Herbert (Henry John) (b. London, 11. V. 1909; d. London, 25. VII. 1952), Eng. comp. Studied at the R.A.M. in London and at Worcester Coll., Oxford. After holding var. organist's posts from 1926, he became prof. of comp. at the R.A.M. in 1933, joined the mus. staff of the B.B.C. in 1936 and became Head of Mus. in 1950.

Works incl. opera *Man in Cage*; 3 hornpipes for orch.; 2 concertos and 3 pieces for cello and orch.; string 4tet; capriccio for cello and pf., *Prelude, Cadenza and Fugue* for clar. and pf.; sonatina, 2 impromptus, 4 studies, *Presto alla giga,* toccatina and canzone, etc., for pf.; *Suite française* for hapsichord or pf.; song-cycle *Self Portrait,* 2 songs (Herrick), etc.; part-songs, etc.

Murschhauser, Franz Xaver Anton (b. Zabern, VI. 1663; d. Munich, 6. I. 1738), Alsat. comp. Pupil of Kerl at Munich, where he became *Kapellmeister* at the church of Our Lady. In 1721, by a remark made in his treatise on comp., *Academia musico-poetica,* he came into conflict with Mattheson.

Works incl. *Vespertinus latriae* for 4 voices and strings; org. books *Octitonium novum organum, Prototypon longobreve organicum, Opus organicum tripartitum,* etc.

Murska, Ilma de (b. Zagreb, 1836; d. Munich, 14. I. 1889), Croatian soprano. Studied with Mathilde Marchesi in Paris and made her 1st appearance at Florence in 1862. After singing in Vienna she 1st appeared in London in 1865.

Musard, Philippe (b. Tours, 1793; d. Auteuil, 31. III. 1859), Fr. violinist and cond. Studied privately with Reicha in Paris, played at masked balls and instituted a series of promenade concerts in the bazaar in the Rue Saint-Honoré. Having come into competition with J. Strauss, jun., as a dance musician during the Viennese comp.'s visit to Paris, he began to devote himself to classical mus.,

and in 1840 was invited to London to give promenade concerts at Drury Lane Theatre, and afterwards at the Lyceum Theatre. He specialized in Quadrilles.

Muset, Colin (b. ?; d. ?), Fr. 12th-cent. trouvère and jongleur. The poems of 15 and the mus. of 8 of his songs are extant.

Musette (Fr.). (1) A form of bagpipe popular in Fr. in the 17th and 18th cents. Also an 8-ft. org. stop of metal pipes with free reeds repro. bagpipe tone. *See also* **Cabrette.**

(2) A piece on a drone bass imitating more or less faithfully the mus. of a bagpipe. It often took the place of a trio section alternating with a Gavotte in classical suites.

Musgrave, Thea (b. Edinburgh, 27. V. 1928), Scot. comp. and pianist. Studied comp. at Edinburgh Univ. and with N. Boulanger in Paris.

Works incl. operas *The Abbot of Drimock, The Decision; Scot. Dance Suite* for orch., *Divertimento* for string orch.; *Perspectives* for small orch.; 3 chamber concertos for var. instruments; *Triptych* for tenor and orch.; *The Five Ages of Man* for chorus and orch.; string 4tet; 2 pf. sonatas; songs.

Music Drama, an alternative term for 'opera' used by comps., notably Wagner, who felt that the older term implies obs. methods and forms for which they had no use.

Music Makers, The, ode for contralto solo, chorus and orch. by Elgar, Op. 69 (poem by Arthur O'Shaughnessy), perf. Birmingham Festival, 1. X. 1912. The work contains a number of mus. quotations from earlier works by Elgar.

Musica falsa (Lat. = false mus.). *See* **Musica ficta.**

Musica ficta (Lat. = false mus.), the practice of inserting accidentals in medieval and Renaissance mus. where these are not present in the notation, on the assumption that they are implied. In order to make harmonic sense between the parts or to avoid awkward intervals such as the Tritone between F and B, the leading-note of the scale was often sharpened and the B often flattened, the latter esp. in the Dorian mode. Also known as *musica falsa.*

Musica figurata (Lat. and It. = figured or decorated mus.), the ornamenting of Plainsong by auxiliary notes or the addition of a Descant sung against a fundamental melody.

Musica mensurata. *See* **Mensurable Music.**

Musica reservata (Lat. = reserved mus.), a 16th-century term applied to mus. intended for connoisseurs and private occasions, partic. vocal mus. which faithfully interpreted the words.

Musica Transalpina, the title of a collection of It. (transalpine) madrigals with Eng. words pub. in London by Nicholas Yonge in 1588, containing 75 pieces, incl. 2 by Byrd, *La verginella*, set to a trans. of 2 stanzas from Ariosto. The It. contribs. incl. Palestrina and Marenzio, and there are also It. madrigals by Flem. comps. incl. Lassus, de Vert and Verdonck. A 2nd vol. followed in 1597, containing 24 works, this time all by It. comps.

Musical. *See* **Musical Comedy.**

Musical Association. *See* **Royal Musical Association.**

Musical Box, a toy instrument made in var. shapes of fancy boxes and containing a cylinder with pins which, turning round by clockwork, twangs the teeth of a metal comb prod. the notes of a mus. scale. The pins are so arranged as to make the pattern of a piece of mus., and several sets of pins can be set in the barrel, only one touching the teeth at a time, a choice of more than one piece being thus producible by the simple device of shifting the barrel slightly sideways. The M. B. industry is centred mainly in Switz.

Musical Comedy (now generally abbr. to 'Musical'), a light mus. stage entertainment similar to operetta, though often inferior to it in quality. As a non-specific term it appears as early as 1765 in a title of a Covent Garden pasticcio, *The Summer's Tale*.

Musical Glasses. *See* **Harmonica.**

Musical Offering (Bach). *See* **Musikalisches Opfer.**

Musical Snuffbox, a special kind of mus. box made esp. in the 18th cent., with a double bottom concealing a mechanical mus. apparatus beneath its normal contents.

Musicians' Company. *See* **Worshipful Company of Musicians.**

Musicology, the scientific and scholarly study of mus. in all its aspects. Hence musicologist, one who pursues such a study.

Musikalische Opfer, Das (*The Musical Offering*), a late work by Bach containing 2 *ricercari*, a fugue in canon, 8 canons and a sonata for fl., vln. and continuo, all based on a theme given to Bach by Frederick II of Prus. during the comp.'s visit to Potsdam in 1747.

Musikalischer Spass, Ein (Ger. = *A Musical Joke*), a work in 4 movements for 2 horns and strings by Mozart, K. 522 (comp. VI. 1787), sometimes also known by such names as 'The Village Band'. But the joke is not at the expense of rustic performers: the work is a parody of a symph. by an incompetent composer.

Musikwissenschaft (Ger. = mus. science) = Musicology.

Musique concrète. *See* **Concrete Music.**

Musique mesurée (Fr. = measured mus.),

a special method of setting words to mus. cultivated in 16th-cent. Fr. by Baïf, Le Jeune, Mauduit and others. The metrical rhythm of the words was based on classical scansion and the mus. rhythm followed this exactly, long syllables being set to long notes, and short syllables to short notes.

Musset, Alfred de (1810–57), Fr. poet and playwright. *See* **Beydts** (*Il ne faut jurer de rien*), **Djamileh** (Bizet), **Edgar** (Puccini), **Fantasio** (Smyth), **Février** (*Carmosine*), **Franck** (**C.**) (songs), **Gnecchi** (*Rosiera*), **Honegger** (*Fantasio*), **Huré** (do.), **Inghelbrecht** (*Nuit vénitienne*), **Messager** (*Fortunio*), **Monpou** (songs), **Moór** (*Pompadour*), **Nottara** (*On ne badine pas avec l'amour*), **Pierné** (do.), **Poise** (*Carmosine*).

Mussorgsky, Modest Petrovich (b. Karevo, Gvt. of Pskov, 21. III. 1839; d. St. Petersburg, 28. III. 1881), Rus. comp. The son of well-to-do landowners, he was sent to St. Petersburg at the age of 10 to prepare for a military school, which he entered in 1852. He joined a regiment in 1856 and he did not seriously think of a mus. career until he met Dargomizhsky and Balakirev in 1857 and began to study under the latter. He resigned his commission in 1858, but never studied systematically. His family's fortune waned after the liberation of the serfs in 1861, but he was in sympathy with that movement and content to live on the small pay he obtained for a government employment. His interest in the common people led him to write realistic songs following the inflections of their speech, and he endeavoured to do the same with his operatic characters. He finished *Boris Godunov* in its 1st form in 1869, but it was rejected by the Imp. Opera and he recast it in 1871–2, this 2nd version being prod. in 1874. He sank more and more into poverty and ruined his health with drink. He d. in hospital from a spinal disease.

Works incl. operas *Salammbô* (after Flaubert, unfinished), *The Marriage* (Gogol, unfinished), *Boris Godunov* (after Pushkin), *Khovanshtchina*, *Sorochintsy Fair* (after Gogol, unfinished); an act for a collective opera, *Mlada* (with Borodin, Cui and Rimsky-Korsakov, afterwards used for other works); incid. mus. for Ozerov's *Oedipus Rex*; *The Destruction of Sennacherib* (after Byron) and *Jesus Navin* for chorus and orch.; 4 Rus. folksongs for male chorus; *Night on the Bare Mountain* for orch. (later used in *Mlada* [with chorus] and further revised) and 3 small orchestral pieces; suite *Pictures at an Exhibition* and 12 small pieces for pf.; over 60 songs incl. cycles *The Nursery*, *Sunless* and *Songs and Dances of Death*, etc.

Mustafà, Domenico (b. Sterpara nr. Foligno, 14. IV. 1829; d. Montefalco nr

Perugia, 18. III. 1912), It. castrato and comp. He was the last male soprano of the Sistine Chapel, which he entered in 1848. He was later *maestro di cappella* there until 1902, when he was succeeded by Lorenzo Perosi.

Works incl. Miserere, *Tu es Petrus, Dies irae* for 7 voices, *Laudate* and other church mus.

Mustel Organ, an instrument invented by Victor Mustel (1815–90) of Paris. It is of the Harmonium type, but contains some improvements, incl. a device by which the top and bottom halves of the keyboard can be separately controlled for dynamic expression.

Muta (It. imper. = change), a direction used in scores where a change is to be made between instruments (e.g. A and B♭ clar. or different horn crooks) or in tunings (e.g. kettledrums, strings of instruments of the vln. family temporarily tuned to abnormal notes), etc. The plur. is *mutano*.

Mutation. *See* **Gamut.**

Mutation Stops, a range of org. stops sounding notes a 12th, 17th, 19th or flat 21st above those of the key pressed down. They are not played alone, but only with other stops which sound their own proper notes, and they fulfil, together with those normal keys, the function of Mixture Stops.

Mute, the name of var. devices of different kinds but all serving to damp the tone of an instrument. The 'soft pedal' of the pf. is a M., but is rarely so called. M.s of string instruments are a kind of fork whose prongs are made to grip the bridge and lessen its vibration, and with it the vibration of the strings. Brass wind instruments have cone-shaped M.s inserted into the bell. Drums can be muted without any special mechanical device, merely by a cloth spread over the head.

Müthel, Johann Gottfried (b. Mölln, Lauenburg, 17. I. 1728; d. Bienenhof nr. Riga, 14. VII. 1788), Ger. organist, harpsichordist and comp. Pupil of Kunzen in Lübeck, app. court organist to the Duke

of Mecklenburg-Schwerin in 1747. On leave of absence to study in 1750 he visited Bach in Leipzig just before Bach's death, also Altnikol in Naumburg, C. P. E. Bach in Berlin and Telemann in Hamburg. From 1755 organist in Riga.

Works incl. concertos, sonatas and miscellaneous pieces for harpsichord, etc.

Muzio, Claudia (b. Pavia, 7. II. 1889; d. Rome, 24. V. 1936), It. soprano. Studied pf. and harp at first, but her teachers discovered great vocal gifts, and she made her 1st stage appearance at Arezzo in 1912. Soon afterwards she 1st visited London and in 1916 N.Y.

Muzio Scevola, Il (*Mucius Scaevola*), opera by Filippo Mattei (or Amadei), Giovanni Bononcini and Handel (lib. by Paolo Antonio Rolli), prod. London King's Theatre, Haymarket, 15. IV. 1721.

My Country (Smetana), *See* **Má Vlast.**

Myers, Rollo H(ugh). (b. Chislehurst, 23. I. 1892), Eng. critic. Educ. privately and at Oxford, and had a year at the R.C.M. in London. Mus. correspondent to *The Times* and *Daily Telegraph* in Paris 1919–34 and on B.B.C. staff in London, 1935–44, Mus. Officer for Brit. Council in Paris, 1945–6. Ed. *Chesterian* from 1947 and *Music To-day* from 1949. Pub. books *Modern Music, Music in the Modern World, Erik Satie, Debussy*; comp. songs.

Mysliveček, Josef (b. nr. Prague, 9. III. 1737; d. Rome, 4. II. 1781), Boh. comp. Studied org. and comp. in Prague, and pub. there in 1760 a set of symphs. named after the first 6 months of the year. Went to study with Pescetti in Venice in 1763, and a year later prod. his first opera in Parma. Between 1767 and 1780 followed *c.* 30 further operas for the principal theatres in It. He also visited Munich, where Mozart, who had already met him in 1772, saw him in 1777.

Works incl. operas *Medea, Il Bellerofonte, Farnace, Demofoonte, Ezio, Il Demetrio*, etc.; oratorio *Abramo ed Isacco* and 3 others; symphs.; concertos; chamber mus.; church mus., etc.

N

Nabokov, Nikolai (b. Lubtcha, 17. IV. 1903), Rus. comp. Studied in Berlin and Stuttgart. He became attached to Diaghilev's Rus. Ballet in the 1920s, and later he settled in U.S.A.
Works incl. opera *The Holy Devil*; ballets *Ode on seeing the Aurora Borealis* and *Union Pacific*; incid. mus. to a dramatic version of Milton's *Samson Agonistes*; symph., *Sinfonia biblica* for orch.; pf. concerto; cantata *Collectionneur d'échos* for soprano, bass, chorus and perc., etc.

Nabucco. *See* below.

Nabucodonosor (*Nebuchadnezzar*: colloquially *Nabucco*), opera by Verdi (lib. by Temistocle Solera), prod. Milan, Teatro alla Scala, 9. III. 1842.

Nacchera (It. = naker[s],) a military kettledrum. The plur. (*nacchere*) = Castanets.

Naccherone (It., as above, with augment. suffix), medieval word for a kettledrum.

Nachbaur, Franz (b. Giessen nr. Friedrichshafen, 25. III. 1835; d. Munich, 21. III. 1902), Ger. tenor. Studied with Lamperti at Milan and others, sang at var. Ger. opera houses and became attached to the Munich Court opera in 1866, creating the part of Walther in Wagner's *Meistersinger* there in 1868.

Nachez, Tivadar (b. Budapest, 1. V. 1859; d. Lausanne, 29. V. 1930), Hung. violinist. Studied at Budapest, with Joachim in Berlin and with Léonard in Paris, where he settled, living in London from 1889. Ed. much vln. mus. and wrote a vln. concerto, a string 4tet and vln. pieces.

Nachschlag (Ger.). *See* **Ornaments**.

Nachspiel (Ger. = afterpiece). *See* **Postlude**.

Nacht in Venedig, Eine (*A Night in Venice*), operetta by J. Strauss, jun. (lib. by F. Zell and Richard Genée), prod. Berlin, Friedrich-Wilhelmstädtisches Theater, 3. X. 1883. Written for the opening of that theatre. 1st Vienna perf. Theater an der Wien, 9. X. 1883.

Nachtanz (*see also* **Proporz**; Ger. lit. after-dance), the quicker dance following a slower one, often with the same mus. in different rhythm in the 15th–16th cents., esp. the Galliard following the Pavan.

Nachtgall, Othmar. *See* **Luscinius**.

Nachtlager von Granada, Das (*The Night-Camp at Granada*), opera by C. Kreutzer (lib. by Karl Johann Braun von Braunthal, based on a play by Friedrich Kind), prod. Vienna, Josefstadt Theatre, 13. I. 1834.

Nachtmusik (Ger. = night mus.), a sere-

nade, e.g. Mozart's *Eine kleine Nachtmusik*.

Nachtstück (Ger., lit. night piece) = Nocturne.

Naderman, François Joseph (b. Paris, c. 1773; d. Paris, 2. IV. 1835), Fr. harpist and comp. Son of a harp maker, he became harpist at the Paris Opéra and in the royal chapel, also harp prof. at the Cons. from 1825.
Works incl. harp concertos; chamber mus. with harp parts; harp solos; also with Duport, nocturnes for cello and harp.

Nadeshda, opera by G. Thomas (lib. by Julian Russell Sturgis), prod. London, Drury Lane Theatre, 16. IV. 1885.

Nagel, Wilibald (b. Mühlheim o/Ruhr, 12. I. 1863; d. Stuttgart, 17. X. 1929), Ger. musicologist. Studied in Berlin, taught mus. hist. at Zürich and settled for a time in Eng. to collect materials for a 2-vol. hist. of Eng. mus. and annals of Eng. court mus. He returned to Ger. in 1896 and taught at Darmstadt from 1898 to 1913. He also wrote a study of Beethoven's pf. sonatas and other works.

Nägeli, Hans Georg (b. Wetzikon nr. Zürich, 26. V. 1773; d. Zürich, 26. XII. 1836), Swiss comp., teacher, author and mus. pub. Studied at Zürich and Berne and began to pub. mus. at Zürich in 1792. In 1803 he began a series entitled *Répertoire des clavecinistes* and incl. in it Beethoven's sonatas Op. 31 Nos. 1 and 2, adding 4 bars to the former, much to the comp.'s annoyance. He estab. the *Schweizerbund* choral society which soon formed branches, and reformed mus. teaching in schools on the lines of Pestalozzi's educ. system. He also wrote on mus. educ. and lectured on mus. in Switz. and Ger.
Works incl. church and school mus.; toccatas and other pf. pieces; 15 books of popular songs, incl. 'Freut euch des Lebens' and 'Lied vom Rhein', etc.

Naich, Hubert (b. ?; d. ?), Flem. 16th-cent. comp. Lived in Rome, where he was a member of the Accademia degli Amici and pub. a book of madrigals there c. 1540.

Nail Violin, an 18th-cent. instrument also called N. Fiddle or N. Harmonica, invented by a Ger. violinist Johann Wilde, living at St. Petersburg. It was a semicircular sound-board studded with nails along the rounded edge, which were scraped with a bow.

Nairn (*née* Oliphant), Carolina, Lady (1766–1845), Scot. poet. *See* **Gow** (4) (*Caller Herrin'*).

Nakers (from Arabic through old Fr. *nacaires*), an old Eng. name for the Kettledrums, which were then much smaller and therefore higher in pitch, and could not have had their tuning altered. In cavalry regiments they were played on horseback, hung on each side of the horse's neck.

Nakhabin, Vladimir Nikolaievich (b. Kharkov, 21. IV. 1910), Rus. comp. Studied under Bogatirev at Kharkov.

Works incl. ballet *The Burgess of Tuscany* (after Boccaccio); *Dnieprostrov* for chorus and orch.; symph., tone-poems *Lenin's Death* and *The Factory*, suite *Springtime* for orch., etc.

Naldi, Giuseppe (b. Bologna, 2. II. 1770; d. Paris, 15. XII. 1820), It. baritone. Studied law at Bologna and Pavia Univs., but turned to mus. and made his 1st stage appearance at Milan at an early age. He sang in London each year in 1806–19.

Namensfeier (*Name[-Day] Celebration*), concert overture by Beethoven, Op. 115, in C maj., comp. 1814, 1st perf. Vienna, Redoutensaal, 25. XII. 1815, cond. by the comp. The name-day was that of the Aus. emperor, which happened to coincide with the completion of the work: it was not comp. specially for that occasion.

Namouna, ballet by Lalo (scenario by Charles Nuitter; choreography by Marius Petipa), prod. Paris, Opéra, 6. III. 1882.

Nanini, Giovanni Bernardino (b. Vallerano, *c.* 1560; d. Rome, 1623), It. comp. Studied under his brother, went to Rome, and in 1599 became *maestro di cappella* at the church of San Luigi de' Francesi there, later at that of San Lorenzo in Damaso.

Works incl. motets, psalms and other church mus., some with org. accomp.; madrigals, etc.

Nanini, Giovanni Maria (b. Tivoli, *c.* 1545; d. Rome, 11. III. 1607), It. tenor and comp., brother of prec. After learning mus. as a choir-boy at Vallerano, he went to Rome as a pupil of Mel, became a singer at the church of Santa Maria Maggiore, *maestro di cappella* at the church of San Luigi de' Francesi in 1575, singer in the Papal Chapel, 1577, and *maestro di cappella* at Santa Maria Maggiore, 1579. He opened a mus. school with the assistance of his brother and Palestrina, supplied mus. to the Sistine Chapel and became *maestro di cappella* there in 1604.

Works incl. motets (e.g. 2 for Christmas, *Hodie nobis caelorum rex* and *Hodie Christus natus est*), psalms and other church mus.; madrigals, canzonets, etc.

Nantier-Didiée, Constance (Betsy Rosabella) (b. Saint-Denis, Île de Bourbon [Réunion], 16. XI. 1831; d. Madrid, 4. XII. 1867), Fr. mezzo-soprano. Studied with Duprez at the Paris Cons. and made her 1st stage appearance at Turin, and in Paris in 1851. Married a singer named Didiée and 1st visited London in 1853.

Napolitana, a light song for several voices, allied to the *villanella* and cultivated at Naples esp. in the 16th and 17th cents.

Nápravník, Eduard Franzevich (b. Byšt nr. Hradec-Králove 24. VIII. 1839; d. Leningrad, 23. XI. 1916), Cz. (naturalized Rus.) cond. and comp. Studied mus. precariously as a child, being the son of a poor teacher, and was left an orphan and destitute in 1853, but succeeded in entering the Org. School in Prague, where he studied with Kittel and others, and became an asst. teacher. In 1861 he went to St. Petersburg as cond. of Prince Yussipov's private orch., became organist and asst. cond. at the Imp. theatres in 1863, 2nd cond. in 1867 and chief cond., succeeding Liadov, in 1869, holding the post until his death. He also cond. concerts of the Rus. Mus. Society.

Works incl. operas *The Nizhni-Novgorodians, Harold, Dubrovsky* and *Francesca da Rimini* (on Stephen Phillips's play); incid. mus. for Alexei Tolstoy's *Don Juan*; ballads for voices and orch. *The Voyevode, The Cossack* and *Tamara* (after Lermontov); 4 symphs., symph. poems *The Demon* (after Lermontov) and *The East*, suite, *Solemn Overture*, marches and nat. dances for orch.; concerto and fantasy on Rus. themes for pf. and orch., fantasy and suite for vln. and orch.; 3 string 4tets, string 5tet, 2 pf. trios, pf. 4tet; vln. and pf. sonata, 2 suites for cello and pf.; string instrument and pf. pieces, etc.

Narciso (*Narcissus*), opera by D. Scarlatti (lib. by Carlo Sigismondo Capece), prod. Rome, private theatre of Queen Maria Casimira of Pol., 20. I. 1714, under the title of *Amor d'un ombra*. Perf. in London, 31. V. 1720, with add. mus. by T. Roseingrave, under the new title.

Nardini, Pietro (b. Leghorn, 12. IV. 1722; d. Florence, 7. V. 1793), It. violinist and comp. Studied at Leghorn and later with Tartini at Padua. Solo violinist at the ducal court of Württemberg at Stuttgart, 1762–5, then settled at Leghorn and in 1769 at Florence as mus. director to the ducal court of Tuscany.

Works incl. 6 vln. concertos; 6 string 4tets; sonatas for vln., 2 vlns., solo and duets for vlns.; trios for fl., vln., and bass, etc.

Nares, James (b. Stanwell, Mdx., IV. 1715; d. London, 10. II. 1783), Eng. organist and comp. Studied with Gates, Croft and Pepusch as a chorister at the Chapel Royal in London, became deputy organist at St. George's Chapel, Windsor, and in 1734 was app. organist of York Minster. Mus.D., Cambridge, 1756, in which year he returned to the Chapel Royal as organist and comp., becoming Master of the Children in succession to Gates, 1757. He pub. treatises on singing and on harpsichord and org. playing.

Works incl. services and anthems; dramatic ode *The Royal Pastoral*; catches, glees and canons; harpsichord lessons; org. fugues, etc.

Narvaez, Luis de (b. ? Granada, ?; d. ?), Span. 16th-cent. lutenist and comp. Wrote lute pieces, motets, etc.

Nasco, Jean (b. ?; d. ? Treviso, 1561), Flem. comp. He was a master of a mus. acad. at Verona in the 1540s and *maestro di cappella* at Treviso Cathedral in the 1550s. Comp. Lamentations, madrigals, *canzoni*, etc.

Nash, Heddle (b. London, 14. VI. 1896; d. London, 14. VIII. 1961), Eng. tenor. He studied in London and after the 1914–1918 war in Milan, where he appeared for the 1st time in Rossini's *Barber of Seville*. He appeared in Eng. for the 1st time at the Old Vic. in 1925. He subsequently sang with the Brit. Nat. Opera Co. and at Glyndebourne, and in oratorio at the Three Choirs Festival and elsewhere. His last appearance in opera was in Benjamin's *A Tale of Two Cities* in 1957.

Nashe, Thomas (1567–1601), Eng. poet and satirist. *See* Dieren (van) (songs), Lambert (C.) (*Summer's Last Will*).

Nasolini, Sebastiano (b. Piacenza, *c.* 1768; d. Venice, 1798, or Naples, 1816), It. comp. Pupil of Bertoni in Venice, in 1787 app. *maestro al cembalo* at the opera in Trieste, and 1788–90 *maestro di cappella* of the cathedral there. From 1790 he devoted himself to opera comp.

Works incl. operas *Nitteti, Andromaca, La morte di Cleopatra, Eugenia, Le feste d'Iside, Merope, La morte di Mitridate, Il medico di Lucca, Gli umori contrari, Il ritorno di Serse*, etc.

Nathan, Isaac (b. Canterbury, 1792; d. Sydney, 15. I. 1864), Eng. singer and comp. Studied Hebrew, etc., at Cambridge, being intended for a Jewish religious career, but turned to mus., studying with D. Corri in London and appearing as a singer at Covent Garden Theatre. In 1841 he went to Austral., settling at Sydney as a singing-master.

Works incl. stage pieces with mus. *Sweethearts and Wives, The Alcaid, The Illustrious Stranger, Merry Freaks in Troublous Times; Hebrew Melodies* and other songs to words by Byron, etc.

National Anthems. The following are the titles (if any), 1st lines (in the orig. language), with names of the authors of the words (W.) and comps. of the tunes (T.) and dates, where known, of the N.A.s of var. countries:

Afghanistan: (T.) Mohammed Farukh.

Albania: 'Rreth flamurit të për bash-kuar'; (W.) A. S. Drenova; (T.) Ciprian Porumbescu.

Andorra: 'El gran Carlemany, mon Paure'; (W.) D. Joan Benlloch i Vivó; (T.) Enric Marfany.

Argentine: 'Oid, mortales, el grito sagrado Libertad'; (W.) Vicente López y Planes, 1813: (T.) José Blas Parera, revised by Juan P. Esnaola.

Armenia: (W.) Sarmen; (T.) Khatchaturian, 1945.

Australia: 'Advance, Australia fair'; (W. & T.) Peter Dodds McCormick, before 1916 (broadcast, but not actually adopted as a N. A., for which 'God save the Queen' is used).

Austria (Imp.): 'Gott erhalte Franz den (or unsern) Kaiser'; (W.) Leopold Haschka; (T.) Haydn, 1797.

— (repub., 1930): *Oesterreichische Bundeshymne*, 'Sei gesegnet ohne Ende'; (W.) Ottokar Kernstock; (T.) as above.

— (do. 1920–9): 'Deutsch-Oesterreich, du herrliches Land, wir lieben dich'; (W.) Karl Renner; (T.) Kienzl, 1920.

— (Patriotic Front): *Lied der Jugend*, 'Ihr Jungen schliesst die Reihen gut'; (W. & T.) Hermann Leopoldi, *c.* 1933.

— (since 1946): 'Land der Berge, Land am Strome'; (W.) Paul Preradović; (T.) Mozart (from Masonic Cantata, K. 623).

Bavaria: 'Bayern, mein Heimatland'; (W.) F. Beck; (T.) F. Lachner, 1848; also 'Gott mit dir, du Land der Bayern'; (W.) Michael Öchsner; (T.) F. M. Kunz.

Belgian Congo. *See* Congo.

Belgium: *La Brabançonne*, 'Après des siècles d'esclavage'; (W.) Louis Alexandre Hippolyte Decht ('Jenneval'), 1830; (T.) François van Campenhout, 1830.

— (Flem.); *De Vlaamsche Leeuw*; (W.) H. van Peene; (T.) Karel Miry. Replaced 1951 by Flem. version of *La Brabançonne*.

Bolivia: 'Bolivianos, el hado propicio'; (W.) José Ignacio de Sanjinés; (T.) Benedetto Vincenti.

Brazil: 'Ouviram do Ypiranga as margens plácidas'; (W.) Joaquim Osório Duque Estrada; (T.) Francisco Manoel da Silva, 1890.

— (earlier): 'Seja um pallio luz'; (W.) M. Albuquerque; (T.) Léopold Miguez.

Bulgaria: *Shoumi Maritza*; (W.) Mereček; (T.) Gabriel Šebek, later version N. Zivkov.

— Since 1946: 'Bulgaria mila'; (W. & T.) var. authors.

Cambodia: 'Som pouk tepda rak sa moha Khsath yeung'; (W.) Chuon. Nat; (T.) traditional, adapted by F. Perruchot and J. Jekyll.

Cameroon: 'O Cameroun, berceau de nos ancêtres'; (W.) René Jam Afame and others, 1928; (T.) Samuel Minkyo Bamba and Moise Nyate, 1928.

Canada: *The Maple Leaf for ever*, 'In days of yore, from Britain's shore'; (W. & T.) Alexander Muir, 1867. 'God save the Queen' used officially.

— (Fr.): 'O Canada: terre de nos aïeux';

(W.) Adolphe Basile Routhier, c. 1880; (T.) C. Lavallée.

Ceylon: 'Namō Namō Mathā': (W. & T.) Ahanda Samarakoon.

Chile; *Dulce patria*, 'Puro Chile es tu cielo azulado'; (W.) Eusebio Lillo, 1847; (T.) Ramón Carnicer, 1828.

China: 'Tsung-kuoh hiung li jüh dschou tiän'; (W. & T.) unknown, 1912. — (democratic): *The Song of Kuomintang*; (W.) Sun Yat-Sen; (T.) Ch'eng Mao-Yün, 1928. — (communist): (T. only, temp.).

Colombia: *Oh! Gloria inmarcesible*, 'Cesó la horrible noche'; (W.) Rafael Nuñez; (T.) Orestes Sindici, c. 1905.

Congo (Belg.): *Vers l'avenir*: *Naar wijden zijd*, 'Le siècle marche': 'De tijd spoedt heen'; (W.) Gentil Théodore Antheunis: (T.) Gevaert 1908.

Costa Rica: 'Noble patria, tu hermosa bandera'; (W.) anon., replaced 1903 by José Maria Zeledón; (T.) Manuel Maria Gutiérrez, 1851, in use from 1853.

Cuba: *Himno Bayamés*, 'Al combate corred bayameses'; (W. & T.) Pedro Figueredo, 1868.

Czechoslovakia: Combination of 'Kde domov můj'; (W.) Josef Kajetán Tyl; (T.) F. Skroup, 1834, and 'Nad Tatrú sa blýská'; (W.) Janko Matúska, 1844; (T.) traditional; 1st officially used 1919.

Denmark: 'Kong Kristian stod ved højen Mast'; (W.) Johannes Ewald 1779; (T.) J. E. Hartmann (from opera *Fiskerne*), 1780; also 'Der er et yndigt Land'; (W.) Adam Oehlenschläger, (T.) H. E. Krøyer, c. 1819; and 'Dengang jeg drog afsted'; (W.) F. Faber; (T.) J. O. E. Horneman, 19th cent.

Dominican Republic: 'Quisqueyanos valientes, alcemos'; (W.) Emilio Prud'-homme, 1883; (T.) José Reyes, 1900.

Ecuador: *Salve! Oh patria, mil veces*, 'Los primoros los hijos del suelo'; (W.) Juan Léon Mera; (T.) Antonio Neumane, 1866.

Egypt: March, 'Ha ni an bé au da to samil ma kam'; (T.) march by Verdi, c. 1872; (W.) added 1940s.

Eire: *Soldier's Song*, 'Seo dhíbh, a cháirde' (We'll sing a song); (W.) Patrick Kearney; (T.) Patrick Heaney, c. 1917, officially adopted 1926.

England. *See* Great Britain.

Esthonia: 'Mu isamaa, mu õnn ja rõõm'; (W.) J. Jànssen, 1865; (T.) Fr. Pacius, 1848.

Ethiopia: 'Ethiopia hoy, dessyibelish'; (W.) by a group of Abyssinian scholars, 1930; (T.) M. K. Nalbadian, 1925.

Faroe Islands: 'Tú alfagra land mítt'; (W.) Símun av Skarði; (T.) Peter Alberg, 1907.

Finland: *Maamme*, 'Oi maamme Suomi synninmaa'; (W.) J. L. Runeberg (orig. in

Swed.), 1843; (T.) Fr. Pacius, as for Esthonia. A 2nd tune by Pacius was also adopted, 1848.

France: *La Marseillaise*, 'Allons, enfants de la patrie' (W. & T.) Rouget de Lisle, 1792.

Germany (Imp.): 'Heil dir im Siegerkranz'; (W.) Heinrich Harries, 1790, adapted by B. G. Schumacher, 1793; (T.) as for Great Britain. — (repub.): 'Deutschland, Deutschland über alles'; (W.) H. A. Hoffmann von Fallersleben, 1841; (T.) Haydn, as for Aus. — (Nazi): *Horst Wessel Lied*, 'Die Fahne hoch, die Reihen dicht geschlossen'; (W.) Horst Wessel; (T.) ? Boh. comic song; in use 1933–45. — (Western Ger.): 'Land des Glaubens, deutsches Land' (W.) Rudolf Alexander Schröder; (T.) Hermann Reutter, before 1950, when it was replaced by Haydn's tune with new words, 'Einigkeit und Recht und Freiheit.' — (democrat. repub.): 'Auferstanden aus Ruinen'; (W.) J. R. Becher; (T.) Hans Eisler, 1949.

Ghana: 'Lift high the flag of Ghana'; (W.) var. authors; (T.) Philip Gbeho, adopted 1957.

Great Britain: 'God save the Queen (King)'; (W. & T.) unknown, 1744–5.

Greece: 'Segnorizo apo ten kopsi tu spatjiu ten tromere': (W.) Dionysios Solomos, 1824; (T.) N. Mántzaros; in use since 1863.

Greenland: 'Nunarput, utor Karssuángoravit'; (W.) Hendrik Lund; (T.) Jonathan Petersen.

Guatemala: 'Guatemala feliz!'; (W.) J. Joaquín Palma'; (T.) Rafael Álvarez in use from 1896.

Haiti: *La Dessalinienne*, 'Pour le pays, pour les ancêtres'; (W.) Justin Lhérisson; (T.) Nicolas Geffrard, 1903.

Hawaii: 'Hawaii ponoi'; (W. & T.) ? Kalakaua, king of H., c. 1880.

Holkar's Dominions. *See* Indore.

Holland. *See* Netherlands.

Honduras: 'Tu bandera es un lampo de cielo'; (W.) Augusto C. Coello; (T.) Carlos Hartling.

Hungary: *Himnusz*, 'Isten àldd meg a Magyart'; (W.) Ferencz Kölcsey, 1823; (T.) Ferencz Erkel, 1845; usually followed by *Szózat*, 'Hazádnak rendületlenül légy hive óh magyar'; (W.) Michael Vörösmarty, 1836; (T.) Benjamin Egressy, 1844.

Iceland: 'Ó Guð vors land'; (W.) Matthias Jochumsson, 1874; (T.) Sveinbjörn Sveinbjörnsson.

India (repub.): 'Jana Gana Mana'; (W. & ? T.) Rabindranath Tagore, officially adopted 1950.

Indore: 'Prabho prarth ana parisa amuchi'; (W.) ?; (T.) Jad.

Indonesia: 'Indonesia tanah airku': (W. & T.) W. R. Supratman, adopted 1949.

Iran: 'Shahhanshahemaw zende baw'; (W.) S. Afsar; (T.) Najmi Moghaddam, c. 1934.

Iraq: Royal Salute (march); (W.) none; (T.) L. Zambaka, 1959.

Ireland (before separation): 'Let Erin remember the days of old'; (W.) Thomas Moore; (T.) traditional, *The Red Fox*.

Isle of Man: 'O Halloe nyn ghooie'; (W.) W. H. Gill, (T.) traditional, adapted by W. H. Gill, 1907.

Israel: *Hatikvah* 'Kol od balevav penimah'; (W.) Naftali Herz Imber; (T.) traditional, adopted by Zionist movement 1907 and taken over by Israel 1948.

Italy: *La marcia reale*; (W.) none; (T.) Giuseppe Gabetti, 1831; sung in southern It.: *Inno di Garibaldi*, 'All' armi, all' armi, si scopron le tombe'; (W.) L. Mercantini; (T.) A. Olivieri, 1858.

— (Fascist): *La Giovinezza*, 'Sù, compagni in forti schiere'; (W.) Marcello Manni; (T.) G. Castaldo after Giuseppe Blanc, 1921.

— (repub.): *Inno di Mameli*, 'Fratelli d' Italia'; (W.) Goffredo Mameli; (T.) Michele Novaro, 1847.

Japan: 'Kimi ga yo'; (W.) 9th cent.; (T.) Hayashi Hirokami, revised by F. Eckert, 1880.

Johore: 'Allah pleharakan Sultan'; (W.) Bin H. Sulieman; (T.) M. Galistan, 1879.

Jordan: "Asha al Maleek'; (W. 'Abdulmun 'im Ar-rifaa'i; (T.) Abdulkadir At-tannir.

Jugoslavia. *See* Yugoslavia.

Kenya: 'Kenya, land of the lion'; (W. & T.) Cynthia Ryan.

Korea: 'Tonghai Moolkwa Paiktusani; (W.) ?; (T.) Eaktai Ahn.

Laos: 'Xadlao tangtèdeumma'; (W.) Maha Phoumi; (T.) Thongdy, 1941.

Latvia: 'Dievs, sveti Latviju'; (W. & T.) Karlis Baumanis.

Lebanon: 'Koullouna lilouatann'; (W.) Raschid Nachleh; (T.) Wadia Sabra, officially adopted 1927.

Liberia: 'Salve, Liberia, salve!'; (W.) President Daniel B. Warner; (T). Olmstead Luca, 1860.

Libya: 'Ya Biladi'; (W.) Al Baschir al Arebi; (T.) Mohammed Abdul Wahab.

Liechtenstein: 'Oben am deutschen Rhein lehnet sich Liechtenstein'; (W.) H. H. Jauch, 1850; (T.) as for Great Britain.

Lithuania: 'Lietuva, tvėynė mūsų'; (W. & T.) Vincas Kudirka, 1918.

Luxemburg: *Ons Hémecht*, 'Wò d'Uolzécht duréch d'Wisen zét'; (W.) Michel Lentz, 1859; (T.) J. A. Zinnen.

Malaya: 'Negara ku'; (W.) var. authors; (T.) traditional.

Malta: *Tifhíra lil Málta*, 'Int sabîha, Málta tâna'; (W.) Giovanni Antonio Vassalla; (T.) Bersaglieri song adapted, 20th cent. After 1942: 'Lil din l'-art Helwa'; (W.) D. K. Psaila; (T.) R. Samut.

Mexico: 'Mexicanos, al grito de guerra'; (W.) Francisco González Bocanegra; (T.) Jaime Nunó, arr. by Bernardino Beltrán, 1854.

Monaco: 'Principauté Monaco'; (W.) Louis Canis; (T.) Bellando de Castro.

Montenegro: (W.) John Soundechitch; (T.) ?; also 'Onam', onamo! za brda ona'; (W.) King Nikola, 1867; (T.) Davorin Jenko.

Nepal: 'Shri mân gumbhira nepâli'; (W. & T.) ?.

Netherlands: 'Wilhelmus van Nassouwe'; (W.) Philip van Marnix, c. 1570; (T.) unknown, 1st pub. 1626; also 'Wien Neerlands bloed in d'aderen vloeit'; (W.) Hendrik Tollens; (T.) Jan Wilms, 1815.

New Zealand: 'God defend New Zealand'; (W.) Thomas Bracken; (T.) John J. Woods, not consistently used until 1940. 'God save the Queen' continues to be officially used.

Newfoundland: 'When sun rays crown thy pine-clad hills'; (W.) Chas. Cavendish Boyle; (T.) Hubert Parry. This does not displace 'God save the Queen'.

Nicaragua: 'Salve a tí Nicaragua'; (W.) Salomón Ibarra Mayorga; (T.) unknown.

Norway: 'Ja, vi elsker dette landet'; (W.) B. Bjørnsson; (T.) R. Nordraak; 1859.

Orange Free State: 'Heft, Burgers, 't lied der vrijheid aan'; (W. & T.) Hamelberg.

Pakistan: 'Pak sarzamin shad bad'; (W.) Abul A. H. Jullunduri, 1951; (T.) Ahmad G. Chagla, 1950.

Panama: 'Alcanzamos por fin la victoria'; (W.) Gerónimo de la Osa; (T.) Santos Jorge, 1903.

Paraguay: 'Paraguayos, República o muerte'; (W. & T.) Francisco Acuña de Figueroa.

Persia. *See* Iran.

Peru: 'Somos libres, seámos lo siempre'; (W.) José de la Torre Ugarte; (T.) José Bernardo Alcedo, 1821.

Phillipine Republic: 'Tierra adorada (*Marcha nacional filipina*); (W.) José Palma; (T.) Julian Felipe, c. 1898.

Poland: 'Jeszcze Polska nie zginęta;' (W.) Jozef Wybicki; (T.) a folksong, 1st sung 1797.

Portugal (royal): 'O patria, O rei, O povo'; (W. & T.) Pedro I of Brazil, formerly Pedro IV of Port., 1822.

— (repub.): 'Herois do mar'; (W.) Lopes de Mendonça, 1890; (T.) Alfredo Keil; used since 1910.

Prussia: 'Borussia'; (W.) G. R. Duncker; (M.) Spontini, 1818; also 'Ich bin ein Preusse'; (W.) Bernhard Thiersch; (T.) A. H. Neithardt, 1826.

Rumania (royal): 'Trăeasca Regele in pace si onor'; (W.) V. Alexandri; (T.) E. A. Hübsch, 1861.

— (repub.): 'Te slăvim Românie'; (W.) E. Frunza & D. Desliv; (T.) Matei Socor.

Russia (imp.): 'Bohze Tsarya khrani'; (W.) W. A. Zhukovsky, 1833; (T.) Lvov, 1833.

— (Soviet to 1944): *L'Internationale*, 'Debout, les damnés de la terre'; (W.) Eugène Pottier (trans. into Rus., last in 1932); (T.) Pierre Degeyter.

— (Soviet, after 1944): *Gymn Sovietskogo Soiusa*; (W.) Sergey Mikhalkov & I. Registan; (T.) A. V. Alexandrov, c. 1942.

Salvador: 'Saludemos la patria orgullosos'; (W.) Juan J. Cañas; (T.) Juan Aberle.

San Marino: 'Onore a te'; (W.) Giosuè Carducci; (T.) Federico Consolo.

Scotland: 'Scots wha ha'e wi' Wallace bled'; (W.) Burns, 1793; (T.) traditional.

Serbia: *Srpska Himna*, 'Bože pravde, ti što spase'; (W.) J. Djordjewič; (T.) Davorin Jenko, 1872.

South Africa (Union): *Die Stem van Suid-Afrika*, 'Uit die blov van on se hemel' (Ringing out from our blue heavens); (W.) C. J. Langehoven; (T.) M. L. de Villiers, 1921, adopted 1938, Eng. trans. 1952.

Spain (royal): *Marcha real*; (W.) none; (T.) unknown Ger. comp., 1770; *Hymno de Riego* (repub.), c. 1860; (W.) ?; (T.) ? Huerta, based on a tune from a sonata by Mateo Albéniz. Used again since 1942.

— (repub.): *Marcha grandera*, adapted, and Ger. Nazi & It. Fascist songs also used.

Sudan: 'Nahnu djundul'lah'; (W.) Ahmed M. Salih; (T.) Murgan.

Surinam: 'Suriname's trotse stromen'; (W.) C. A. Hoekstra; (T.) C. de Puy.

Sweden: 'Du gamla, du fria, du fjällhöga Nord'; (W.) R. Dybeck; (T.) traditional, 1844.

Switzerland: 'Rufst du, mein Vaterland'; (W.) J. H. Wyss, 1811, with Fr. & It. transs.; (T.) as for Great Britain; also *Schweizerpsalm*, 'Trittst im Morgenrot daher'; (W.) L. Widmer; (T.) Josef (Father Alberik) Zwyssig, 1841.

Syria: 'Humat al-diyári 'alaikum salám'; (W.) Khalil Mardam Bey; (T.) brother Fulayfel, officially adopted 1939.

Thailand: *Sanrasoen Phra Barami*; (W.) Prince Narisaranuvadtivongs; (T.) Huvitzen.

Transvaal: 'Kentgij dat volk vol heldenmoed'; (W. & T.) Catherine Félicie van Rees.

Tunisia: 'Älä Khälidî yä dimânälghäwälî djihädälwatan'; (W.) J. E. Ennakache; (T.) Salah el Mahdi.

Turkey: *Istikläl marsi* (March of Independence), 'Korkma sönmez bu safaklarda yüzen al sancak'; (W.) Mehmed Akif Ersoy; (T.) Osman Zeki Üngör, officially adopted 1921.

U.S.A.: *The Star-Spangled Banner*, 'Oh, say, can you see, by the dawn's early light'; (W.) Francis Scott Key, 1814; (T.) John Stafford Smith; officially adopted 1831; earlier 'Hail Columbia'; (W.) J. Hopkinson; (T.) Fyls, c. 1800.

Uruguay: 'Orientales, la patria o la tumba!'; (W.) Fr. Acuña de Figueroa; (T.) F. Quijano & Fr. J. Deballi.

Venezuela: 'Gloria al bravo pueblo'; (W.) Vicente Salias; (T.) Juan Landaeta, after 1810.

Wales: 'Mae hen wlad fy nhadau' (Land of my fathers); (W.) Evan James; (T.) J. James.

Westphalia: 'Ihr mögt den Rhein, den stolzen, preisen'; (W.) ?; (T.) Johann Peters.

Württemberg: 'Preisend mit viel schönen Reden'; (W.) J. Kerner, 1826; (T.) Traditional.

Yugoslavia: A compound of the Serbian hymn 'Bože pravde' (*see* Serbia), the Croatian hymn 'Lijepa naša domovino'; (W.) Antum Mihanoic; (T.) Lichtenegger, and the Slovene hymn 'Naprej zastava Slav'; (W.) Simon Jenko; (T.) Davorin Jenko. Used till 1945, when it was replaced by 'Hej Slaveni'; (W.) ?; (T.) as for Pol. anthem (*see* Poland).

Zanzibar: National March for military band by Donald Francis Tovey.

Nationalism. In mus. N. manifests itself through the endeavour of individual comps. or schools to find some sort of mus. idiom that may be said to express their countries' characteristics, either idiomatically or spiritually. Idiomatic expression of this kind is most usually and easily attained through the adoption, imitation or adaptation of folksong and nat. dances, which however may become more or less strongly coloured by each comp.'s individuality and will certainly be much elaborated in the process of sustained comp. (e.g. Smetana in Cz., Grieg in Norw., Balakirev in Rus., Falla in Spain, Bartók in Hung., etc.). The reflection of a country's spirit in mus. is less definite, more subtle and not so easily perceptible, but there is no doubt that certain comps. have achieved this without consciously resorting to folk mus.; and those who sometimes do so may remain just as strongly nat. when they happen to refrain (e.g. Tchaikovsky and Mussorgsky in Rus. [in different ways], Elgar in Eng., Fauré and Ravel in Fr., Sibelius in Fin., etc.).

Natural, the sign ♮, which restores to its normal position a note previously raised by a ♯ or lowered by a ♭.

Naturale (It. = natural), a direction indicating that a voice or instrument, after perf. a passage in some unusual way (*mezza voce*, muted, etc.), is to return to its normal manner.

Naumann, Johann Gottlieb (b. Blasewitz nr. Dresden, 17. IV. 1741; d. Dresden, 23. X. 1801), Ger. comp. At the age of 16 accomp. the Swed. violinist Wesström to Hamburg, then to It., where he studied with Tartini, Hasse and Padre Martini. Prod. his 1st opera in Venice in 1763, and the following year was app. to the court at Dresden as 2nd comp. of church mus. Revisited It. to prod. operas 1765–8 and 1772–4, and in 1776 became *Kapellmeister* in Dresden, where, apart from visits to Stockholm, Copenhagen and Berlin, he remained till his death.

Works incl. operas *Achille in Sciro*, *La clemenza di Tito*, *Solimano*, *Le nozze disturbate*, *Armida*, *Ipermestra*, *Amphion*, *Cora och Alonzo*, *Gustaf Vasa* (all 3 in Swed.), *Orpheus og Euridice* (in Dan.), *Protesilao* (with Reichardt), *La dama soldato*, *Aci e Galatea* and others; 21 Masses and other church mus.; 13 oratorios, etc.

Navarra, André (b. Biarritz, 13. X. 1911), Fr. cellist. Studied at Toulouse and Paris Cons. and in 1949 became prof. at the Paris Cons.

Navarraise, La (*The Girl of Navarre*), opera by Massenet (lib. by Jules Claretie and Henri Cain, based on the former's story *La Cigarette*), prod. London, Covent Garden Theatre, 20. VI. 1894.

Navarro, Juan (b. Seville, c. 1530; d. Palencia, 25. IX. 1580), Span. comp. After the death of Morales in 1553 he competed unsuccessfully for the post of *maestro de capilla* at Málaga Cathedral, but he later obtained a similar post in Salamanca. He (?) visited Rome in 1590, where his nephew Fernando Navarro Salazar arr. for the pub. of some of his church mus. After his death Passions and Lamentations in plainsong were pub. in Mex., but he probably never lived there.

Works incl. psalms, hymns, Magnificats and other church mus.; madrigals, etc.

Nave, La (*The Ship*), incid. mus. by Pizzetti for Gabriele d'Annunzio's tragedy, prod. Rome, 11. I. 1908.

Opera by Montemezzi (lib. by Tito Ricordi, based on d'Annunzio), prod. Milan, Teatro alla Scala, 1. XI. 1918.

Navrátil, Karel (b. Prague, 24. IV. 1867; d. Prague, 23. XII. 1936), Cz. violinist and comp. Studied in Prague, theory under Guido Adler and vln. under Ondříček.

Works incl. operas *Hermann* and

Salammbô (after Flaubert); Mass in D maj., 2 psalms for chorus; symph. in G min., 5 symph. poems; vln. concerto, 2 pf. concertos; string 4tet in D min., 2 pf. trios, 2 pf. 5tets; vln. sonata, vla. sonata; pf. mus.; songs, etc.

Naylor, Edward (Woodall) (b. Scarborough, 9. II. 1867; d. Cambridge, 7. V. 1934), Eng. organist, musicologist and comp. Studied at Cambridge and the R.C.M. in London, and after 2 organist's appts. there he returned to Cambridge in 1897 to become organist at Emmanuel Coll., taking the Mus.D. degree at the univ. He lectured and wrote on mus., pub. a book on *Shakespeare and Music*.

Works incl. opera *The Angelus*; cantata *Arthur the King*; part-songs; pf. trio in D maj., etc.

Neapolitan Sixth, a chord consisting of a min. 3rd and a min. 6th on the subdominant of the key, which came into vogue in the 17th cent. It occurs most often in a cadential progression in a min. key, e.g.:

which may further be abbr. as follows:

Neate, Charles (b. London, 28. III. 1784; d. Brighton, 30. III. 1877), Eng. pianist and cellist. He became a pupil of Field, who learnt the cello with him under Wm. Sharp, and made his 1st public appearance at Covent Garden Theatre in 1800. He also studied comp. with Woelfl. In 1815 he spent 8 months in Vienna and made friends with Beethoven, and then 5 at Munich for counterpoint lessons with Winter. He taught and perf. for many years in London with much success and wrote mus., mainly for pf.

Nebra, José de (b. ?, c. 1688; d. Madrid, 11. VII. 1768), Span. organist and comp. He became organist at the Convent of the Descalzas Reales in Madrid and 2nd organist at the royal chapel in 1724. After the destruction of the library more in the fire of 24. XII. 1734, he and Literes were commissioned to replace the lost church

Neckniz
Neri

mus. and to restore what had survived. In 1751 he was made vice-*maestro de capilla* under Corselli, who neglected his duties for the comp. of It. operas, and by 1757 he had completely reorganized the court mus. In 1758 he comp. a Requiem for 8 voices, fl. and strings for the funeral of Queen Barbara of Braganza, who had been D. Scarlatti's patroness.

Works incl. *c.* 20 operas: Requiem, Miserere, psalms and other church mus.; *villancico* for 4 voices. etc.

Neckniz. *See* **Sommer, Hans.**

Nebdal, Oskar (b. Tábor, 26. III. 1874; d. Zagreb, 24. XII. 1930), Cz. cond., vla. player and comp. Pupil of Dvořák, member of the Boh. String 4tet and from 1896 cond. of the Cz. Phil. Society in Prague. From 1906 he cond. concerts and opera mainly in Vienna. He comp. light opera *Polenblut* and others; ballets *Pohádka o Honzovi, Princezna Hyacinta, Andersen,* etc.

Neefe, Christian Gottlob (b. Chemnitz, 5. II. 1748; d. Dessau, 26. I. 1798), Ger. cond. and comp. Studied in Leipzig under Hiller, whom he succeeded as cond. of a touring opera co. in 1776. He settled in Bonn in 1779, where he was app. court organist 3 years later. Beethoven was his pupil from the age of 11. The Fr. occupation of Bonn in 1794 cost him his post, and from 1796 he was mus.-director of the Bossann theatre co. in Dessau.

Works incl. operas *Die Apotheke, Adelheid von Veltheim, Amors Guck-kasten, Der Einspruch, Heinrich und Lyda, Sophonisbe, Zemire und Azor* and others: incid. mus. for Shakespeare's *Macbeth*; church mus.; chamber mus., etc.

Nef, Karl (b. St. Gall, 22. VIII. 1873; d. Basle, 9. II. 1935), Swiss musicologist. Studied at the Leipzig Cons. and became lecturer at Basle Univ. in 1901, was critic of the *Basler Nachrichten* in 1897–1925 and ed. of the *Schweizerische Musikzeitung* in 1898–1909. He wrote a number of books on mus. hist., the symph. and the suite, mus. instruments, Beethoven's symphs., etc.

Neidhart von Reuental (b. Bavaria, ?; d. ?, *c.* 1240), Ger. Minnesänger. Went on a crusade in 1217–19 and settled in Aus. on his return. Several songs of his are preserved; many others are attrib. to him.

Nejedlý, Vít(ĕzslav). (b. Smichov, Prague, 22. VI. 1912; d. Dukla Pass, 1. I. 1945), Cz. comp. He learnt much from his father, Zdenĕk N., but also studied with others, incl. Jeremiaš for comp. Having worked as a critic, choirmaster and theatre cond., he followed his father to Rus. in 1939. During the 1939–45 war he served there with the Cz. army and gave concerts to popularize Cz. mus. He d. of typhoid fever.

Works incl. opera *The Weavers*; cantata *The Day*; 3 symphs., *Sinfonietta* and overture to Verhaeren's *L'Aube* for orch.; chamber mus., songs and part-songs, etc.

Nejedlý, Zdenĕk (b. Litomyšl, 10. II. 1878; d. Prague, 9. III. 1962), Cz. musicologist, father of prec. Lecturer at Prague Univ. and prof. from 1905, later in Moscow. His books incl. a hist. of mus. in Boh., works on Fibich, Mahler, Foerster. Novák and Smetana, on Beethoven's 4tets and on Wagner.

Nekrassov, Nikolai Alexeievich (1821–1877), Rus. poet and journalist. *See* **Cui** (songs), **Koval** (songs).

Nelson Mass, the name given to Haydn's Mass in D min., comp. in 1798. It is sometimes said that the fanfares in the Benedictus commemorate Nelson's victory in the battle of the Nile; in fact Haydn cannot have heard the news of the battle until after the Mass was finished. His own title was *Missa in angustiis.*

Nĕmcová, Božena (1820–62), Cz. novelist. *See* **At the Old Bleaching-Ground** (Kovařovic and Horák).

Nenna, Pomponio (b. Bari nr. Naples, *c.* 1550; d. ?, before 1618), It. comp. Lived (?) mainly at Naples and was the teacher of Gesualdo, Prince of Venosa.

Works incl. *responsoria* and other church mus.; madrigals, etc.

Neo-Bechstein Piano, an electrophonic pf. invented by Vierling of Berlin in 1928–33 and further developed by Franco and Nernst, prod. its notes by the conversion of electrical waves into audible sounds.

Neo-Modal, modern mus. using new derivations from the modes, harmonized, transposed or otherwise altered.

Nepomuceno, Alberto (b. Fortaleza, 6. VII. 1864; d. Rio de Janeiro, 16. X. 1920), Brazil. comp. Studied in It., with Herzogenberg at Leipzig and with Guilmant in Paris. He returned to Brazil 1895 and from 1902–16 was director of the Cons. at Rio.

Works incl. operas *Arthemis* and *Abul*; orchestral works; concertos for var. instruments; *Nat. Hymn*; pf. pieces; songs; arrs. of Brazil. folksongs. etc.

Neri, Filippo (St. Philip Neri) (b. Florence, 21. VII. 1515; d. Rome, 26. V. 1595), It. saint. Of importance to mus. for his foundation of the Society of Oratorians in 1564, which cultivated mus. at the oratory of San Girolamo in Rome, for which among others Animuccia and Palestrina worked in his lifetime and which in 1600 prod. Cavalieri's *Rappresentazione di anima e di corpo.* It was from this society that the Oratorio received its name as a mus. form.

Neri, Massimiliano (b. ?; d. ?), It. 17th-cent. organist and comp. He was the 1st organist of St. Mark's, Venice,

460

in 1644, was ennobled by the Emperor Ferdinand II in 1651 and became court organist to the Elector of Cologne in 1664. Comp. motets; sonatas and instrumental *canzoni*, etc.

Nero. *See also* **Nerone.**
Opera by Rubinstein (lib., in Fr. [*Néron*], by Jules Barbier), prod., in Ger., Hamburg, Municipal Theatre, 1. XI. 1879.

Nerone (*Nero*), opera by Boito (lib. by comp.), begun 1879, but left unfinished at Boito's death in 1918. Prod., ed. by Tommasini and Arturo Toscanini, Milan, Teatro alla Scala, 1. V. 1924.

Neruda, Wilma (Wilhelmina) (Norman-Neruda; Lady Hallé) (b. Brno, 21. III. 1839; d. Berlin, 15. IV. 1911), Morav. violinist. Studied under her father, Josef N. (1807–75) and with Jansa, and made her 1st appearance in Vienna with her sister Amalie, a pianist, in 1846. She then went on tour in Ger. and appeared in London in 1849. Afterwards she appeared all over Eur., often with her brother, the cellist Franz N. (1843–1915). In 1864 she played in Paris and married the Swed. comp. Ludvig Norman. In 1888 she became the 2nd wife of Charles Hallé and settled at Manchester.

Nesbet(t), J. (b. ?; d. ?), Eng. 15th-cent. comp. Wrote a 5-part Magnificat (Carver and Eton choirbooks, incomplete in the latter) and a 3-part *Benedicamus* (Pepys MS., Magdalene Coll., Cambridge).

Nesle, Blondel de. *See* **Blondel.**

Nessler, Viktor (Ernst) (b. Baldenheim, Alsace, 28. I. 1841; d. Strasbourg, 28. V. 1890), Ger. comp. Studied theology at Strasbourg, but took to mus. and prod. a Fr. opera there in 1864. He went to Leipzig, became choral and afterwards operatic cond.
Works incl. operas *Fleurette*, *Die Hochzeitsreise*, *Dornröschens Brautfahrt*, *Nachtwächter und Student*, *Am Alexandertag*, *Irmingard*, *Der Rattenfänger von Hameln*, *Der wilde Jäger*, *Der Trompeter von Säckingen* (after Scheffel's poem), *Otto der Schütz*, *Die Rose von Strassburg*; part-songs, etc.

Nešvera, Josef (b. Praskolesy, 24. X. 1842; d. Olomouc, 12. IV. 1914), Cz. comp. Choirmaster at Olomouc Cathedral from 1884.
Works incl. operas *Perdita* (on Shakespeare's *Winter's Tale*), *The Forest Breeze*, *The Cousin*, *Mlynarski* and *Radhošt*; Mass, Passion, *De profundis* and other church mus.; pf. and vln. pieces, etc.

Netchaiev, Vassily Vassilievich (b. Moscow, 28. IX. 1895), Rus. comp. Studied pf. with Goldenweiser and comp. with Vassilenko at the Moscow Cons.
Works incl. operas *Seven Princesses* (after Maeterlinck) and *Ivan Bolotnikov*; incid. mus. to Shakespeare's *Macbeth*,

Sophocles' *Ajax* and other plays; string 4tet, etc.

Neues vom Tage (*News of the Day*), opera by Hindemith (lib. by Marcellus Schiffer), prod. Berlin, Kroll's Opera, 8. VI. 1929.

Neukomm, Sigismund von (b. Salzburg, 10. VII. 1778; d. Paris, 3. IV. 1858), Aus. comp. As a chorister at Salzburg Cathedral he was a pupil of M. Haydn, who in 1798 sent him to J. Haydn in Vienna. In 1806 he went to Swed. and Rus., becoming cond. at the Tsar's Ger. theatre in St. Petersburg. He returned to Vienna in 1809 and went to live in Paris soon after, succeeding Dussek in 1812 as pianist to Talleyrand. From 1816 to 1821 he was *maestro de capilla* to Pedro I of Brazil, with whom he returned to Lisbon, after the revolution, afterwards travelling with Talleyrand. In 1829 he visited London, meeting Mendelssohn, and lived there and alternately in Paris for the rest of his life.
Works incl. opera *Alexander in Indien* and others; many Masses and Requiem for Louis XVI; oratorios *Mount Sinai*, *David* and 6 others; incid. mus. for Schiller's *Braut von Messina*, songs, etc.

Neumann, František (b. Přerov, Morav., 16. VI. 1874; d. Brno, 25. II. 1929), Cz. comp. and cond. After starting a commercial and military career he went to study mus. at the Leipzig Cons. After filling var. chorus-master's and cond.'s posts at Ger. and Cz. theatres, he went to Brno as chief cond. at the Nat. Theatre.
Works incl. operas *Idalka*, *Die Brautwerbung*, *Liebelei* (on Schnitzler's play), *Herbststurm*, *Beatrice Caracci*; melodrama *Pan*; ballets *In Pleasant Pastures*, *The Peri*, *Pierrot*; Masses and motets; symph. poem *Infernal Dance*, suite *The Sunken Bell*, *Morav. Rhapsody*, overtures, etc. for orch.; octet, pf. trio; choruses, songs, etc.

Neumark, Georg (b. Mühlhausen, Thuringia, 16. III. 1621; d. Weimar, 8. VII. 1681), Ger. poet and musician. He pub. a collection of sacred and secular songs, *Musikalische-poetischer Lustwald* in 1657, some set to mus. by himself, incl. the hymn 'Wer nur den lieben Gott lässt walten'.

Neumes, the signs in Eastern chant and Western plainsong (and in some medieval song-books) indicating the single notes or groups of notes to which each syllable was to be sung. Orig. not set on staves, but merely marked above the words and showing neither precise length nor exact pitch, they served as reminders of tunes already known to the singers.

Neusidler, Hans (b. Poszony [Pressburg], *c.* 1509; d. Nuremberg, 2. II. 1563), Hung. or Ger. lutenist. Settled at Nuremberg, where he pub. books of pieces arr. for lute in tablature in 1536, 1540 and 1544.

Neusidler, Konrad (b. Nuremberg, 1541;

d. Augsburg, prob. after 1604), Ger. lutenist, ? son of prec. He lived in Augsburg from 1562.

Neusidler, Melchior (b. Nuremberg, 1531; d. Augsburg, c. 1590), Ger. lutenist, ? brother of prec. He settled in Augsburg in 1551 or 1552. He visited Italy and pub. 2 books of lute mus. at Venice in 1566. In 1574 he pub. at Strasbourg a book of mus. by Josquin, Lassus, Arcadelt, Rore and others arr. for the lute.

Nevada (actually Wixom), **Emma** (b. Alpha nr. Nevada City, Calif., 7. II. 1859; d. Liverpool, 20. VI. 1940), Amer. soprano. Studied with Mathilde Marchesi in Vienna and made her 1st stage appearance in London in 1880, later singing in It., Paris, the Eng. festivals, etc.

Neveu, Ginette (b. Paris, 11. VIII. 1919; d. San Miguel, Azores, 28. X. 1949), Fr. violinist. Appeared with the Colonne Orch. at the age of 7. Studied at the Paris Cons. and with Flesch, and won the highest reputation for virtuosity and passionate musicality. She was killed in an air accident.

Nevin, Arthur (Finlay) (b. Edgeworth, Pa., 27. IV. 1871; d. Sewickley, Pa., 10. VII. 1943), Amer. comp. Studied at Pittsburgh, Boston and Berlin. He taught and cond. in var. Amer. cities, studied Amer.-Indian mus., and on 23. IV. 1910 his *Poia* was the 1st Amer. opera prod. in Berlin.

Works incl. operas *Poia* and *A Daughter of the Forest*, masque *A Night in Yaddo Land*; cantatas; suites for orch. incl. *Lorna Doone* (after Blackmore); string 4tet, pf. trio; suites and pieces for pf.; songs, etc.

Nevin, Ethelbert (Woodbridge) (b. Edgeworth, Pa., 25. XI. 1862; d. New Haven, Conn., 17. II. 1901), Amer. comp., brother of prec. Studied pf. and comp. at Boston and Berlin. Later taught at Boston and in Eur.

Works incl. pantomime *Lady Floriane's Dream*; numerous pf. pieces incl. *Narcissus*; many songs, incl. *The Rosary*, etc.

'New World' Symphony, Dvořák's 9th symph., but called 'No. 5', in E min., Op. 95, with the subtitle *From the New World*, because it was written in U.S.A. Comp. 1893 and 1st perf. N.Y., Phil. Society, 16. XII. 1893.

Newark, William (b. ? Newark-on-Trent, c. 1450; d. Greenwich, XI. 1509), Eng. comp. Became a Gentleman of the Chapel Royal in London, 1477 and, after var. other apps., Master of the Children there in 1493. Comp. part-songs.

Newbolt, Henry (John) (1862–1938), Eng. poet. See **Travelling Companion** (Stanford).

Newlin, Dika, (b. Portland, Oregon, 22. XI. 1923), Amer. musicologist and comp. Studied privately with Sessions and

Schönberg and then taught at Western Maryland Coll. and Syracuse Univ. In 1952 she estab. a mus. dept. at Drew Univ., N.J. Her writings incl. studies of Bruckner, Mahler and Schönberg, translations, partic. of Schönberg's writings. She has also comp. for various media, esp. chamber mus.

Newman, Ernest (actually William Roberts) (b. Liverpool, 30. XI. 1868; d. Tadworth, 7. VII. 1959), Eng. critic and writer on mus. Educ. at Liverpool. Became critic of the *Manchester Guardian*, 1905, the *Birmingham Post*, 1906, the *Observer*, 1919, and the *Sunday Times*, 1920. Books incl. *Gluck and the Opera*, *Hugo Wolf*, *A Musical Critic's Holiday* and several works on Wagner, incl. the largest modern biog.

Newman, John Henry (1801–90), Eng. cardinal and poet. See **Dream of Gerontius** (Elgar).

Newmarch (*née* Jeaffreson), **Rosa (Harriet),** (b. Leamington, 18. XII. 1857; d. Worthing, 9. IV. 1940), Eng. writer on mus. Wrote programme notes for London Queen's Hall concerts, 1908–27. Made special studies of Rus. and Cz. mus. Her books incl. *The Russian Opera* and *The Music of Czechoslovakia*.

Newton, Ivor (b. London, 15. XII. 1892), Eng. pianist and accompanist. Studied in London, Amsterdam and Berlin and then concentrated mainly on accomp., playing for many great artists.

Ney, Elly (b. Düsseldorf, 27. IX. 1882; d. Tutzing, 31. III. 1968), Ger. pianist. Studied with Böttcher and Seiss at Cologne Cons. and then with Leschetitsky and Sauer in Vienna. After winning the Mendelssohn and Ibach Prizes she taught at the Cologne Cons. in 1906 and began a very successful concert career, becoming esp. well known as a Beethoven interpreter.

Nibelung Saga (*Nibelungenlied*), ancient Teutonic epic in the Middle High Ger. dialect. See **Dorn** (*Nibelungen*), **Draeseke** (*Gudrun*), **Ring des Nibelungen** (Wagner), **Sigurd** (Reyer).

Nibelung's Ring, The (Wagner). See **Ring des Nibelungen.**

Nicaraguan Composer. See **Delgadillo.**

Niccolini, Giuseppe (b. Piacenza, 29. I. 1763; d. Piacenza, 18. XII. 1842), It. comp. Studied at the Cons. di Sant' Onofrio, Naples, under Insanguine. Was at first very successful in opera, but was eventually driven from the stage by Rossini. *Maestro di cappella* at Piacenza Cathedral from 1819.

Works incl. operas *I baccanti di Roma*, *Traiano in Dacia*, *Coriolano* and c. 40 others; Masses and other church mus., etc.

Niccolò or **Nicolò.** See **Isouard.**

Nichelmann, Christoph (b. Treuenbrietzen, Brandenburg, 13. VIII. 1717; d.

Berlin, 20. VII. 1762), Ger. harpsichordist and comp. Pupil of Bach at St. Thomas's School, Leipzig; lived at Hamburg and Berlin, being app. 2nd harpsichordist to Frederick the Great in 1744.

Works incl. opera (serenata) *Il sogno di Scipione*; harpsichord concertos; harpsichord sonatas, etc.

Nichols, Robert (Malise Bowyer) (1893–1944), Eng. poet. *See* **Darnton** (*Swansong*), **Dieren (van)** (*Tailor*), **Frankel** (*Aftermath*), **Morning Heroes** (Bliss), **Pastoral** (Bliss).

Nicholson, Richard (b. ?; d. ? Oxford, 1639), Eng. organist and comp. Became choirmaster and (?) organist at Magdalen Coll., Oxford, in 1595, took the B.Mus. there, 1596, and became the 1st Prof. of Mus. there in 1627.

Works incl. anthems, madrigals (1 in *The Triumphes of Oriana*), mus. for viols, 'dialogue' (or song-cycle) for 3 voices 'Joane, quoth John', etc.

Nicholson, Sydney H(ugo). (b. London, 9. II. 1875; d. Ashford, Kent, 30. V. 1947), Eng. organist and church educationalist. Studied at the R.C.M. in London and under Knorr at Frankfurt. Organist of Manchester Cathedral, 1908–18, and Westminster Abbey, 1918–27, when he founded the School of Eng. Church Mus. at Chislehurst, now transferred to Addington. Knighted 1938. His comps. incl. church mus., a comic opera *The Mermaid* (lib. by George Birmingham) and an opera for boys' voices, *The Children of the Chapel*.

Nicodé, Jean Louis (b. Jerczig nr. Poznan, 12. VIII. 1853; d. Langebrück nr. Dresden, 5. X. 1919), Ger.-Pol. cond. and comp., ? of Fr. descent. The family having moved to Berlin in 1856, N. studied there, 1st under his father and from 1869 at the Neue Akademie der Tonkunst. Afterwards he taught there and arr. concerts at which he appeared as pianist, toured in the Balkans with Désirée Artôt and in 1878 became prof. at the Dresden Cons. From 1885 he devoted himself to cond. and comp.

Works incl. symph. ode *Das Meer* for solo voices, male chorus orch. and org.; symph. poems *Maria Stuart* (after Schiller), *Die Jagd nach dem Glück*, *Gloria*, symph. variations, etc., for orch.; romance for vln. and orch.; cello and pf. sonata; sonata and numerous pieces for pf.; songs, incl. cycle *Dem Andenken an Amarantha*; male-voice choruses, etc.

Nicolai, (Carl) Otto (Ehrenfried) (b. Königsberg, 9. VI. 1810; d. Berlin, 11. V. 1849), Ger. cond. and comp. Studied the pf. as a child, but was so unhappy at home that in 1826 he ran away and was sent to Berlin for study under Zelter and Klein by a patron the following year. In 1833 another patron sent him to Rome as organist in the

Prus. Embassy chapel, and there he studied under Baini. He returned there after a year at the Kärntnertortheater in Vienna, 1837–8. He became court *Kapellmeister* in Vienna in 1841 and founded the Phil. concerts there in 1842. In 1847 he became director of the cathedral choir and the Court Opera in Berlin, where he d. of a stroke, 2 months after the prod. of his *Merry Wives of Windsor*.

Works incl. operas *Enrico II* (later *Rosmonda d'Inghilterra*), *Il templario*, *Odoardo e Gildippe*, *Il proscritto* (later *Die Heimkehr des Verbannten*), *Die lustigen Weiber von Windsor* (after Shakespeare); Mass for Frederick William IV of Prus., Requiem, Te Deum; Symph. Festival Overture on 'Ein' feste Burg' for the jubilee of Königsberg Univ., etc.

Nicolai, Philipp (b. Mengeringhausen, 10. VIII. 1556; d. Hamburg, 26. X. 1608), Ger. pastor, poet and amateur musician. In 1599 he pub. a hymnbook, *Freudenspiegel des ewigen Lebens*, containing the tunes of 'Wachet auf' and 'Wie schön leucht' uns der Morgenstern'.

Nicolai, Willem (Frederik Gerard) (b. Leyden, 20. XI. 1829; d. Bloemendaal, 20. IV. 1896), Dutch teacher and comp. Studied at the Leipzig Cons. and from 1852 taught at The Hague Cons., becoming director in 1865.

Works incl. oratorio *Bonifacius*, choral works *The Song of the Bell* (Schiller), *The Swedish Nightingale*, *Jehovah's Wrath* and *Hanske van Gelder*; symph. and overtures; songs, etc.

Nicolau, Antonio (b. Barcelona, 8. VI. 1858; d. Barcelona, 26. II. 1933), Span. teacher, cond. and comp. Studied with Pujol and others, cond. the Sociedad de Conciertos at Barcelona and had a number of distinguished pupils.

Works incl. operas *Costanza* and *El rapto*, choral works *La mort del Escolà*, *Captant*, *Entre flors*, *La Mare de Deu*; symph. poems *El triunfo de Venus* and *Spes*; songs, etc.

Nicolaus de Cracovia (b. ?; d. ?), 16th-cent. Pol. organist and comp., in the service of the royal court. Org. mus. by him is incl. in two MSS.: that of Jan of Lublin (1537–48) and the Cracow Tablature (1548).

Nicolini (Nicola Grimaldi) (b. Naples, IV. 1673; d. Naples, 1. I. 1732), It. castrato. 1st appearance in Rome, about 1694. 1st went to Eng. in 1708 and sang the title role in Handel's *Rinaldo* in 1711. He returned to It. in 1718.

Nicolò or **Niccolò**, the name under which Isouard prod. most of his operas.

Niecks, Frederick (orig. Friedrich) (b. Düsseldorf, 3. II. 1845; d. Edinburgh, 24. VI. 1924), Ger. musicologist. Studied at Düsseldorf and appeared as a violinist

Niedermeyer   Nigg

there, later went to Leipzig Univ. and in 1868 was invited by Mackenzie to join his string 4tet at Edinburgh. He lectured there and in 1891 was app. Reid Prof. of Mus. at the Univ. He wrote books on Chopin, Schumann, the hist. of programme mus., etc.

Niedermeyer, (Abraham) Louis (b. Nyon, Vaud, 27. IV. 1802; d. Paris, 14. III. 1861), Swiss comp. and educationist. Studied in Vienna, Rome and Naples, settled as mus. teacher at Geneva and went to Paris in 1823, settling there after a brief teaching period at Brussels. In Paris he took over Choron's school of mus. and called it École de Musique Religieuse Classique.

Works incl. operas *Il reo per amore, La casa nel bosco, Stradella, Marie Stuart* (after Schiller), *La Fronde*; numerous Masses, motets and anthems; songs to words by Lamartine (e.g. *Le Lac*), Hugo, Deschamps, etc.

Nielsen, Carl (August) (b. Nørre-Lyndelse nr. Odense, 9. VI. 1865; d. Copenhagen. 3. X. 1931), Dan. cond. and comp. Being poor as a youth, he joined a military band at the age of 14, but at 18 succeeded in entering the Copenhagen Cons. as a pupil of Gade. In 1891 he entered the royal orch. and was its cond. in 1908–14. He also became cond. of the Mus. Society and director of the Cons. One of the most remarkable late Romantic symphonists, combining traditional forms with a new and orig. approach to tonality.

Works incl. operas *Saul og David, Maskarade* (after Holberg); incid. mus. for Oehlenschläger's *Aladdin* and many other plays; *Hymnus Amoris* for chorus and orch.; 3 motets for unaccomp. chorus; 6 symphs. (II. *The Four Temperaments*, III. *Espansiva*, IV. *The Inextinguishable*, VI. *Sinfonia semplice*), *Saga-Dream*, symph. rhapsody for orch.; vln. concerto, fl. concerto, clar. concerto; 4 string 4tets and other chamber mus.; 2 vln. and pf. sonatas; *Commotio* for org.; suites and other pf. works; songs, etc.

Nielsen, Hans (b. ? Roskilde, c. 1585; d. ? Copenhagen, ?), Dan. lutenist and comp. After learning mus. as choir-boy in the royal chapel at Copenhagen, he studied with G. Gabrieli at Venice between 1599 and 1606, and in 1606–8 with the Eng. lutenist Richard Howett at Wolfenbüttel. After that he was lutenist at the Dan. court until 1611, when he was dismissed and went to Heidelberg Univ. In 1623 he was app. vice-director of the royal chapel in succession to Pedersøn.

Nielsen, Ludolf (b. Nørre Tvede, 29. I. 1876; d. Copenhagen, II. V. 1939), Dan. cond. and comp. Studied at the Copenhagen Cons., became cond. at the Tivoli and the Palace until 1909.

Works incl. operas *The Clock, Lola* (after Victor Hugo) and *Isbella*; ballet *Lakschmi*; 3 symphs., 3 symph. poems, 2 suites and concert overture for orch.; 3 string 4tets; pf. pieces; songs, etc.

Nielsen, Riccardo (b. Bologna, 3. III. 1908), It. comp. of Scand. descent. Studied at the Liceo Musicale of Bologna and at Salzburg, and was influenced by Casella.

Works incl. incid. mus. for *Maria ed il Nazzareno*; Psalms for male voices and orch.; concerto for orch., symph. for small orch.; capriccio and *Sinfonia concertante* for pf. and orch., vln. concerto; divertimento for bassoon, tpt., vln., vla. and cello, trio for ob., bassoon and horn, Adagio and Allegro for cello and 11 instruments; sonatas for vln. and pf. and cello and pf.; *Musica* for 2 pfs.; sonata and *ricercare*, chorale and toccata on B.A.C.H. for pf.; *Laude di Jacopone da Todi* and *Tre satire di Giusti* for voice and pf., etc.

Niemann, Albert (b. Erxleben, Magdeburg, 15. I. 1831; d. Berlin, 13. I. 1917), Ger. tenor. After a precarious beginning on the stage at Dessau, he was discovered by F. Schneider, the court mus. director, and given some lessons, and was also taught by a singer. He gradually obtained better engagements and was sent to Paris by the King of Hanover to study under Duprez. In 1866–88 he was court opera singer in Berlin and in 1876 Wagner chose him to create the part of Siegmund in the *Ring* at Bayreuth.

Niemann, Walter (b. Hamburg, 10. X. 1876; d. Leipzig, 17. VI. 1953), Ger. comp. and writer on mus. Studied under his father, the pianist and comp. Rudolph Friedrich N. (1838–98) and at Leipzig Univ. and Cons. His books include studies of Scand. mus., virginal and pf. mus., Brahms, Grieg, Sibelius, etc.

Niente (It. = nothing). The word is generally used in connection with *quasi* (so to speak, almost) when extreme softness of tone is required.

Nietzsche, Friedrich (1844–1900), Ger. philosopher and author. *See Also* search Zarathustra (R. Strauss), Ingenhoven (do.), Mass of Life (Delius), Medtner (songs), Rezniček (*Ruhm und Ewigkeit*).

Niewiadomski, Stanisław (b. Soposzyn nr. Lwów, 4. XI. 1859; d. Lwów, 15. VIII. 1936), Pol. critic and comp. Studied with Chopin's pupil Karol Mikuli at Lwów and later in Vienna and Leipzig. He became prof. at the Lwów Cons. and director of the Opera, later prof. at the Cons. and critic in Warsaw. He wrote books on Chopin, Moniuszko, etc.; his comps. are mainly songs and choruses.

Nigg, Serge (b. Paris, 6. VI. 1924), Fr. comp. Studied under Messiaen at the Paris Cons., but in 1946 adopted the 12-

note technique under the influence of Leibowitz, with which he in turn came to disagree 2 years later.
Works incl. melodrama *Perséphone*; symph. movement for orch. *Timour*; *La Mort d'Arthus* for voice and orch.; pf. concerto, *Concertino* for pf., wind and perc.; variations for pf., and 10 instruments; sonata and *Fantaisie* for pf., etc.

Night in May, A (Rimsky-Korsakov). *See* **May Night.**

Night on the Bare Mountain, a work in var. forms by Mussorgsky, more properly called *St. John's Night on the B. M.*, based on the incident of the witches' sabbath in Gogol's story *St. John's Eve*: comp. as a symph. poem for orch. in 1866–7; later used in a version for chor. and orch. and called *Night on Mount Triglav* in 1872 as part of the opera *Mlada* commissioned from M., Borodin, Cui and Rimsky-Korsakov, but never completed; revised version of this used as intro. to Act III of the unfinished opera *Sorotchintsy Fair*, begun in 1875; this last version revised and arranged as an orchestral piece by Rimsky-Korsakov after Mussorgsky's death.

Nightingale, a toy instrument. *See* **Toy Symphony.**

Nightingale, The, opera by Stravinsky (lib. by comp. and Stepan Nikolaievich Mitusov, from Hans Andersen's fairy-tale), prod. Paris, Opéra, 26. V. 1914; revived in the form of a ballet (choreography by Leonid Massin), Paris, Opéra, 2. II. 1920.

Nights in the Gardens of Spain (Falla). *See* **Noches en los jardines de España.**

Nikisch, Arthur (b. Lébényi Szant Miklos, 12. X. 1855; d. Leipzig, 23. I. 1922), Hung.-Ger. cond. Studied in Vienna and played the vln. in the court orch. from 1874–1877. He was cond. at the Leipzig Opera from 1878 to 1889. Subsequent posts incl. the Boston Symph. Orch., 1889–93, Budapest Opera, 1893–5, Leipzig Gewandhaus, from 1895, and the Berlin Phil. Orch.

Nikisch, Mitja (b. Leipzig, 21. V. 1899; d. Venice, 5. VIII. 1936), Hung.-Ger. pianist, son of prec. Studied at the Leipzig Cons. and made his 1st appearance there in 1912.

Nilsson, Birgit (b. Karup, 17. V. 1918), Swed. soprano. Studied in Stockholm, making her début in 1946 and becoming a member of the Swed. Royal Opera in 1947. She is best known as a leading Wagner singer, but is also outstanding in the It. dramatic repertory.

Nilsson, Bo (b. Skellefteå, 1. V. 1937), Swed. comp. Largely self-taught, he belongs to the younger generation of *avant-garde* comps.
Works incl. *Songs on the Death of Children* for soprano and small orch.;

Moments of Time for 10 wind instruments; *Frequencies* for chamber ensemble; *A Prodigal Son* for contralto, alto fl. and chamber ensemble; *Reactions* for perc. 4tet.; *Audiograms* for electronic generators; *Quantities* for pf.

Nilsson, Kristina (Christine) (b. Sjöabol nr. Vexiö, 20. VIII. 1843; d. Stockholm, 22. XI. 1921), Swed. soprano. Studied at Stockholm and Paris, and after several appearances in Swed. received her 1st important stage engagement in Paris in 1864, and 1st went to London in 1867 where she married Auguste Rouzeaud in 1872. In 1887 she married Count Casa Miranda.

Nin (y Castellanos), Joaquín (b. Havana, 29. IX. 1878; d. Havana, 24. X. 1949), Span. pianist, musicologist and comp. Studied at Barcelona and in Paris, where in 1906 he became pf. prof. at the Schola Cantorum. After short periods in Berlin and Cuba, he settled in Brussels and later in Paris again. He ed. much old Span. mus. and wrote 3 books.
Works incl. mimodrama *L'Autre*, ballet *L'Écharpe bleue*; vln. pieces; pf. works; songs, etc.

Nina, o sia La pazza per amore (*Nina, or the Lunatic from Love*), opera by Paisiello (lib. by Giuseppe Carpani, with additions by Giovanni Battista Lorenzi, based on the Fr. lib. by Benoît Joseph Marsollier), prod. Naples, Caserta Palace, for the visit of Queen Maria Carolina of Sicily, 25. VI. 1789; 1st public perf. Naples, Teatro Fiorentino, 1790.

Nina, ou La Folle par amour (do.), ballet by Persuis, partly based on Dalayrac's mus. (choreography by Louis Milon), prod. Paris, Opéra, 23. XI. 1813.
Opera by Dalayrac (lib. by Marsollier), prod. Paris, Comédie-Italienne, 15. V. 1786.

Ninth, the interval a whole tone larger than an 8ve: (maj. N.) or a semitone larger (min. N.), e.g.:

Ninth Symphony (Beethoven). *See* **'Choral' Symphony.**

Nissen, Erika. *See* **Lie-Nissen.**

Nissen, Georg Nikolaus (b. Haderslev, 22. I. 1761; d. Salzburg, 24. III. 1826), Dan. diplomat and author, married Mozart's widow in 1809. His important biog. of Mozart, incorporating many of Mozart's letters, was pub. posthumously in 1828.

Nivers, Guillaume (Gabriel) (b. Melun, *c*. 1631; d. Paris, 30. XII. 1714), Fr. organist, harpsichordist, theorist and comp. Pupil of Chambonnières in Paris and organist of the church of Saint-Sulpice in 1654, also app. organist to the king in 1678 and mus. master to the queen. He wrote a treatise on singing, and others.

Works incl. motets and other church mus.; org. pieces, etc.

No Song, No Supper, opera by Storace (lib. by Prince Hoare), prod. London, Drury Lane Theatre, 16. IV. 1790.

Noble, Dennis (b. 25. IX. 1899; d. Spain, 14. III. 1966), Eng. baritone. Educated as a chorister at Bristol Cathedral, he became a member of Covent Garden Opera in 1938. He sang the solo at the first performance of Walton's *Belshazzar's Feast.*

Noble, (Thomas) Tertius (b. Bath, 5. V. 1867; d. Rockport, Mass., 4. V. 1953), Eng. organist and comp. In 1881 he went to Colchester, where he received his educ. from the rector of All Saints Church, who also made him organist there. In 1886 he entered the R.C.M. in London, studying under Parratt, Bridge and Stanford, and later he joined the staff. After 2 smaller appts. he became organist at Ely Cathedral in 1892 and at York Minster in 1898, but went to N.Y. in 1912 as organist and cond.

Works incl. incid. mus. for Aristophanes' *Wasps*; services and other church mus.; *The Sound of War, Gloria Domini* and other choral works; orchestral works; chamber mus., etc.

Noces (Stravinsky). *See* **Wedding.**

Noces de Jeannette, Les (*Jenny's Wedding*), operetta by Massé (lib. by Jules Barbier and Michel Carré), prod. Paris, Opéra-Comique, 4. II. 1853.

Noches en los jardines de España (*Nights in the Gardens of Spain*), symph. impressions for pf. and orch. by Falla, begun in 1909, finished in 1915. 1st perf. Madrid, IV. 1916. There are 3 movements: 1. *En el Generalife*; 2. *Danza lejana* (*Dance in the distance*); 3. *En los jardines de la Sierra de Córdoba.*

Nocturne (Fr.), a 'night piece' or instrumental serenade, generally of a quiet, lyrical character, but sometimes (as in Chopin) with a more agitated middle section. As a pf. piece it originated with Field, but it existed already as the It. Notturno in the 18th cent., when however it was similar to the Serenade or Divertimento in several movements. The N. in the modern sense is not necessarily slow, soft and sentimental. *Fêtes* in Debussy's work below is a very animated piece; in Vaughan Williams's *London Symph.* the scherzo is a N., i.e. a piece suggesting London's gaiety by night.

Nocturnes, 3 orchestral pieces by Debussy, *Nuages, Fêtes* and *Sirènes*, the last with female chorus, comp. in 1893–9 and 1st perf. Paris, 9. XII. 1900 (Nos. 1 and 2); 27. X. 1901 (complete).

Node (from Lat. *nodus* = knot), the point in a vibrating string at which the vibration becomes cut into segments.

Nodier, Charles (1783–1844), Fr. novelist. *See* **Schmitt (G. A.)** (*Trilby*).

Noël (Fr.) = Christmas carol.

Noël, Victoire. *See* **Stoltz, Rosine.**

Nola, Domenico da (Joan Domenico del Giovane) (b. Nola, Naples, *c.* 1510; d. Naples, 5. V. 1592), It. 16th-cent. comp. *Maestro di cappella* of the church of the Annunciation at Naples. Comp. motets, madrigals, *villanelle*, etc.

Non nobis Domine, a canon for voices, ? by Byrd, often sung in Eng. for 'grace' after public dinners. It is a Riddle C. capable of being sung with the entries in var. positions, also in Inversion.

Nonet, a comp. for 9 instruments, usually in several movements.

Nonnengeige (Ger. = nun's fiddle). *See* **Tromba marina.**

Nono, Luigi (b. Venice, 29. I. 1924), It. comp., whose work has been perf. principally in Ger. He studied with Scherchen, who cond. his *Polifonia-monodia-ritmica* at Darmstadt in 1951. He married a daughter of Schönberg, whose mus. has had a strong influence on him.

Works incl. opera-oratorio *Intolleranza*; *Variazioni canoniche* on a theme of Schönberg's, *Due espressioni* and *Diario polacco '58* for orch.; *Canti* for 13 instruments, *Incontri* for 24 instruments; *Il canto sospeso* and other choral works incl. *La Victoire de Guernica, Epitaph I for F. Garcia Lorca, Cori di Didone*; cantata *Sul ponte di Hiroshima* for soprano and tenor and orch.; *La Fabbrica illuminata* for mezzo-soprano and electronic tape; *Epitaphs II & III for F. Garcia Lorca* (II for fl., strings and perc., III for speaker, speaking chorus and orch.); electronic mus. incl. *Omaggio a Emilio Vedova*, etc.

Noordt, Anthony van (b. ?; d. Amsterdam, 1675), Dutch organist and comp. Organist of the Nieuwe Kerk at Amsterdam in 1659, when he pub. a book of org. works in tablature, incl. variations on Fr. psalm tunes and fugal fantasies.

Norcome, Daniel (b. Windsor, 1576; d. ? Brussels, before 1626), Eng. singer and comp. He went to the Dan. court in his early 20s., but fled from Copenhagen to Ger., Hung. and Venice *c.* 1600. Later he became a lay-clerk at St. George's Chapel, Windsor, but lost that post on turning Rom. Catholic and went to Brussels as an instrumental player to the viceregal chapel.

Works incl. viol pieces; madrigal contrib. to *The Triumphes of Oriana*, etc.

Nordica, Lilian (actually Lillian Norton) (b. Farmington, Me., 12. V. 1857; d. Batavia, 10. V. 1914), Amer. soprano. Studied at Boston and, after successful appearances in U.S.A. and Eng., at Milan, making her 1st stage appearance at Brescia in 1879.

Nordraak, Rikard (b. Christiania, 12. VI. 1842; d. Berlin, 20. III. 1866), Norw. comp. Studied pf. and comp. in Berlin and on his return to Norw. made friends with Grieg and became an enthusiastic exponent of nat. mus.

Works incl. incid. mus. for Bjørnson's *Mary Stuart* and *Sigurd Slembe*; songs incl. a setting of Bjørnson's 'Ja, vi elsker dette landet', now the Norw. nat. anthem.

Noren, Heinrich (Gottlieb) (b. Graz, 5. I. 1861; d. Rottach, 6. VI. 1928), Aus. violinist and comp. Studied in Paris and was orch. leader in Belg., Spain, Rus. and Ger. Later taught at Crefeld, Cologne and Berlin.

Works incl. *Kaleidoskop* variations and *Vita* symph. for orch.; vln. concerto; chamber mus.; instrumental sonatas, etc.

Norma, opera by Bellini (lib. by Felice Romani, based on Louis Alexandre Soumet's tragedy), prod. Milan, Teatro alla Scala, 26. XII. 1831.

Norman, John (b. ?; d. ?), Eng. 15th–16th-cent. organist and comp. He was master of the choristers, St. David's Cathedral, *c.* 1509–*c.* 1522; he was at Eton, 1534–45.

Works incl. Masses, motets, etc.

Norman, (Fredrik Vilhelm) Ludvig (b. Stockholm, 28. VIII. 1831; d. Stockholm, 28. III. 1885), Swed. pianist, cond. and comp. Pub. a book of songs at the age of 11, was left a poor orphan, but enabled by patrons, incl. Jenny Lind, to study at the Leipzig Cons. In 1851 his 1st pf. work was pub. at Schumann's instigation. Returning to Stockholm in 1861, he became cond. of the royal opera, which he cond. until 1879, and was cond. of the symph. concerts to his death. In 1864 he married the violinist Wilma Neruda.

Works incl. incid. mus. to Shakespeare's *Antony and Cleopatra*; 4 symphs., 4 overtures; chamber mus., incl. 6 string 4tets; instrumental sonatas: pf. works; songs, etc.

Norman-Neruda, Wilma. *See* Nordica.

Norris, William (b. ?, *c.* 1675; d. ? Lincoln, *c.* 1710), Eng. singer and comp. Choir-boy in the Chapel Royal in London, later a singer there and choirmaster at Lincoln Cathedral from 1691.

Works incl. services and anthems; Ode for St. Cecilia's Day, etc.

North, Roger (Hon.) (b. Tostock, Suffolk, 3. IX. 1653; d. Rougham, 1. III. 1734), Eng. lawyer and amateur musician, brother of Francis N., Lord Guilford (1637–85), who was also a musician and pub. *A Philosophical Essay on Musick* in 1677. R. N. wrote *Memoires of Musick* incl. the treatise *The Musicall Gramarian*.

Northcote, Sydney (b. Deri, Glam., 3. XI. 1897; d. 16. V. 1968), Eng. educationist, comp. and writer on mus. Studied at the R.C.M. in London and New Coll., Oxford, where he took the D.Mus. in 1932. Prof. at the G.S.M., examiner and festival adjudicator. He wrote a book on *The Ballad in Music* and his comps. incl. choral works, folksong arrs., etc.,

Norton, Lillian. *See* Nordica.

Norwegian Composers. *See* Alnaes, Backer-Grøndahl, Backer-Lunde, Brustad, Egge, Grieg, Haberbier, Halvorsen, Johansen, Kjerulf, Lie, Lindeman, Lund (Signe), Nordraak, Saeverud, Schjelderup, Sinding, Svendsen, Thrane, Valen.

Norwich Festival, a triennial mus. festival estab. at Norwich in 1824, but preceded by festivals held at irregular intervals between 1770 and 1817.

Noskowski, Zygmunt (b. Warsaw, 2. V. 1846; d. Wiesbaden, 23. VII. 1909), Pol. comp. Studied with Moniuszko in Warsaw and with Kiel in Berlin, and after cond. at Constance returned to Pol. in 1881, teaching and cond. at Warsaw, where he became prof. of comp. at the Cons.

Works incl. operas *Livia Quintilla*, *The Judgment*, *The Quarrel about a Frontier Wall*; ballet *The Fire Feast*; *Return* suite for solo voices, chorus and orch., cantata *The Mermaid*, *Veni Creator* for chorus; 3 symphs., variations on a Chopin prelude and 3 overtures for orch.; songs, children's songs, etc.

Nota cambiata (It. = changed note), a term used in two senses in the analysis of 16th-cent. polyphony: (1) a dissonant passing-note on the beat (in Palestrina only on the weak beats); (2) a curling figure (also called 'changing note group') in which a dissonant passing-note (not on the beat) leads to a note a 3rd lower, which then rises one step, e.g.:

(1)

Palestrina, *Missa brevis*

(2)

Palestrina, *Veni sponsa Christi*

Notation, the act of writing down mus.

by means of special symbols, as by specially
devised letters in Gk. mus., by neumes in
the early Middle Ages, in tablature for old
lute and org. mus., in notes according to
the present system, or in the special syllable
form of the Tonic Sol-fa system.

Note sensible (Fr., or **Sensible** [noun])
= Leading-note.

Notker (Balbulus = 'The Stammerer')
(b. ? Switz., *c.* 840; d. St. Gall, 6. IV.
912), Swiss monk and musician at the
monastery of St. Gall. He wrote on mus.
notation, the org. and the perf. of plainsong, and as a comp. contrib. to the development of the Sequence.

Notker Labeo (b. ?, 950; d. St. Gall, 29.
VI. 1022), also known as 'Teutonicus',
Ger. monk at St. Gall. He wrote on mus.
and other subjects, including a short
treatise in Old High Ger. on the measurement of org. pipes.

Notot, Joseph (b. Arras, 1755; d. Eng.,
?), Fr. organist and comp. Was sent to
Paris as a child for his educ., but was
discovered as a wonderful extempore
player on the org. by Leclerc, the organist
of the church of Saint-Germain-des-Prés,
who undertook to teach him. Later he
became organist at Arras, but the Revolution drove him to Eng. and he gave up
mus.

Works incl. 4 symphs.; 3 pf. concertos;
pf. sonatas, etc.

Nottara, Constantine (b. Bucharest,
1890, Rum. violinist and comp. Studied
at the Bucharest Cons. and later in Paris
and Berlin. After playing vln. in the
Charlottenburg opera orch. he returned to
Bucharest as a member of the Phil. Orch.,
formed a string 4tet for the queen and
became prof. at the Cons.

Works incl. operas *On the Highway*
(after Tchekhov) and *On ne badine pas
avec l'amour* (after Musset); ballet *Iris*;
incid. mus. to Euripides' *Hecuba* and
Corneille's *Polyeucte*; *Hymn to Peace* for
chorus and orch.; Rum. and Cz. suites,
Saudades de Portugal, dramatic overture, 5
preludes for orch.; *Poem for vln. and orch.*;
Mircea and Baiazid for baritone and orch.;
instrumental sonatas and pieces; songs,
etc.

Nottebohm, (Martin) Gustav (b. Lüden-
scheid, Westphalia, 12. XI. 1817; d. Graz,
29. X. 1882), Ger. writer on mus. Friend of
Mendelssohn and Schumann at Leipzig;
settled in Vienna, 1846. He compiled
thematic catalogues of Beethoven's and
Schubert's works, wrote a book on the
former's sketches, etc.

Notturno (It. = night piece), the 18th-
cent. forerunner of the Nocturne, not then
a single lyrical instrumental piece, but a
comp. in several movements similar to the
Serenade or Divertimento. In the 19th
cent. it became simply the It. equivalent of

the Nocturne, as for ex. in Mendelssohn's
Midsummer Night's Dream mus.

Nouguès, Jean (b. Bordeaux, 25. IV.
1875; d. Auteuil, 28. VIII. 1932), Fr.
comp. Worked and prod. operas at
Bordeaux at 1st, later in Paris.

Works incl. operas *Le Roy du Papagey*,
Thamyris, *La Mort de Tintagiles* (after
Maeterlinck), *Chiquito*, *Quo vadis?* (after
Sienkiewicz), *L'Auberge rouge* (from Bal-
zac's *Nouveaux Contes philosophiques*), *La
Vendetta*, *L'Aigle*, *L'Éclaircie*, *Dante*,
Jeanne de France, *Le Scarabée bleu*,
Une Aventure de Villon; ballets *La Dan-
seuse de Pompéi* and *Narcisse*; incid.
mus. for Rostand's *Cyrano de Bergerac*;
film mus., etc.

Nourrit, Adolphe (b. Paris, 3. III. 1802;
d. Naples, 8. III. 1839), Fr. tenor. Made
his 1st appearance at the Paris Opéra 1821,
remaining attached to that theatre for 16
years.

Nováček, Ottokar (b. Fehertemplom,
13. V. 1866; d. N.Y., 3. II. 1900), Hung.
violinist and comp. Studied with his
father, later in Vienna and Leipzig. In the
latter city he joined the string 4tet of his
teacher, Brodsky, as 2nd vln. and then as
vla. In 1892 he went to N.Y. and became
vla. leader in Damrosch's orch. In 1899 he
retired for reasons of health and took to
comp.

Works incl. pf. concerto, *Perpetuum
mobile* for vln. and orch.; 3 string 4tets; 8
caprices and other works for vln. and pf.;
pf. mus.; 6 songs to words by Tolstoy,
etc.

Novák, Vítězslav (b. Kamenice, 5. XII.
1870; d. Skuteč, 18. VII. 1949), Cz. comp.
He was the son of a doctor, but lost his
father early and had to support the family
by teaching. While studying law at Prague
Univ. he attended the Cons., studying
pf. with Jiránek and comp. with Dvořák,
who persuaded him to devote himself
wholly to mus. His first works were pub.
with the help of Brahms. He soon made a
career as a distinguished teacher of comp.
and in 1909 was app. prof. at the Cons.
After the 1914–18 war, which restored his
country's independence, he became prof.
of the 'Master School' and was its director
in 1919–22.

Works incl. operas *The Imp of Zvíkov*,
A Night at Karlstein, *The Lantern*, *The
Grandfather's Will*, *The Wood Nymph*;
ballets *Signorina Gioventù* and *Nikotina*;
cantatas *The Storm*, *The Spectre's Bride* and
choral ballads; symph. poems *In the Tatra*,
Eternal Longing, *Toman and the Wood
Nymph*, *De profundis*, overtures *The Corsair* (after Byron), *Maryša*, *Lady Godiva*,
serenade for small orch.; pf. concerto,
2 string 4tets, 2 pf. trios, pf. 4tet, pf. 5tet;
Sonata eroica, *Manfred* (ballad after
Byron), *Songs of Winter Nights*, *Pan*,

Exoticon, 6 sonatinas, *Youth* (children's pieces), etc., for pf.; song cycles *Gypsy Songs, Melancholy, In the Valley of a New Kingdom, Melancholy Songs of Love, Nocturnes, Eroticon,* and other songs; part-songs, etc.

Novelletten (Ger. lit. 'short stories'), a category title used by Schumann for his 8 pf. pieces Op. 21, comp. in 1838, also for No. 9 of the *Bunte Blätter* for pf., Op. 99.

Novello, Clara (Anastasia) (b. London, 10. VI. 1818; d. Rome, 12. III. 1908), Eng. soprano. Studied at the Paris Cons. and 1st appeared at Worcester in 1833. Lived in London but had many successes abroad, esp. in It. and Ger. Married Count Gigliucci in 1843.

Novello, Vincent (b. London, 6. IX. 1781; d. Nice, 9. XIII. 1861), Eng. comp., organist, ed. and pub., father of prec. Founder of the mus. pub. firm of Novello & Co. in London, 1811. Ed. valuable collections of mus. and comp. church mus., cantatas, etc.

November Woods, symph. poem by Bax, comp. 1917, 1st perf. Manchester, Hallé Orch., 18. XI. 1920.

Novotný, Jaroslav (b. Jičín, 28. III. 1886; d. Miass, Ural, 1. VI. 1918), Cz. comp. Studied in Prague, joined the Aus. army during World War I, was a prisoner in Rus., where he wrote much in camp, and was released and killed near the end of the war fighting on the other side with the Cz. legion.

Works incl. string 4tet; choruses; pf. sonata; song cycles *The Eternal Wedding* and *Ballads of the Soul,* etc.

Nowell (from Fr. *Noël*). *See* **Carol.**

Nowowiejski, Feliks (b. Wartenburg, E. Prus., 7. II. 1877; d. Poznań, 23. I. 1946), Pol. cond. and comp. Studied in Berlin and church mus. at Regensburg, afterwards in Fr., Belg. and It. In 1909 he returned to Pol., cond. the Cracow Mus. Society until 1914 and in 1919 became prof. of org. at the Poznań Cons. and cond. orchestral concerts there.

Works incl. operas *Baltic Legend, The Mountain Goblin;* opera-ballet *Leluja;* ballets *Tatra, Polish Wedding;* Masses, motets and psalms; oratorios *Quo vadis?, Beatum scelus, Missa pro pace,* etc.; cantata *Upper Silesian Folk Scene;* symph. poems *Beatrix, Nina,* overture *Polish Wooing, The Prodigal Son, Jerusalem;* 9 symphs. etc. for org., etc.

Noyes, Alfred (1880–1958), Eng. poet. *See* **Coleridge-Taylor** (*Tale of Old Japan*), **Gibbs** (C. A.) (*Highwayman*), **Wood** (T.) (*40 Singing Seamen*).

Nozze d'Ercole e d'Ebe, Le (*The Nuptials of Hercules and Hebe*), opera by Gluck (lib. by ?), prod. Pillnitz nr. Dresden, at the double wedding of Max

Joseph, Elector of Bavaria, and Maria Anna, Princess of Saxony, and Frederick Christian, Prince of Saxony, and Maria Antonia Walpurgis, Princess of Bavaria, 29. VI. 1747.

Opera by Porpora (lib. as above), prod. Venice, 18. II. 1744.

Nozze di Figaro, Le (*The Marriage of Figaro*), opera by Mozart (lib. by Lorenzo da Ponte, based on Beaumarchais's comedy, *La Folle Journée, ou Le Mariage de Figaro*), prod. Vienna, Burgtheater, 1. V. 1786.

Nozze di Teti e di Peleo, Le (*The Nuptials of Thetis and Peleus*), opera by Cavalli (lib. by Orazio Persiani), prod. Venice, Teatro San Cassiano, prob. 24. I. 1639.

Nucius (or **Nux** or **Nucis**), **Joannes** (b. Görlitz, *c.* 1556; d. Himmelwitz, Silesia, 25. III. 1620), Ger. monk and comp. Entered the Cistercian abbey of Rauden, Upper Silesia, and in 1591 became abbot of its offshoot at Himmelwitz. Comp. Masses, motets, etc.

Nuitter (actually Truinet), **Charles (Louis Étienne)** (b. Paris, 24. IV. 1828; d. Paris, 24. II. 1899), Fr. librettist and writer on mus. A lawyer at first, he later devoted himself to the writing and trans. of libs. and of books on opera. In 1865 he became archivist of the Paris Opéra.

Nunc dimittis (Lat. 'Now lettest thou [thy servant] depart [in peace]'). Part of the Evening Service of the Angl. church and often set by comps. as a 2nd part following the Magnificat.

Nursery, The, song cycle by Mussorgsky (words by comp.), comp. 1868–72: 1. *With Nurse;* 2. *In the Corner;* 3. *The Cockchafer;* 4. *With the Doll;* 5. *Going to sleep;* 6. *On the Hobby-Horse;* 7. *The Cat 'Sailor'.*

Nut, the contrivance at the heel of a vln. or other bow at which the hairs are attached and can be stretched by the turn of a screw; also the strip, usually of ebony, at the end of the fingerboard of a string instrument near the pegs, serving to raise the strings clear of the board.

Nutcracker (*Casse-Noisette*), ballet by Tchaikovsky (choreography by Lev Ivanovich Ivanov, based on a tale by E. T. A. Hoffmann), prod. St. Petersburg, Maryinsky Theatre, 18. XII. 1892.

Nux, Joannes. *See* **Nucius.**

Nystroem, Gösta (b. Österhaninge nr. Stockholm, 13. X. 1890; d. Goteborg, 10. VIII. 1966), Swed. comp. and painter. Son of a headmaster who taught him mus. and painting, which he afterwards studied at Stockholm, Copenhagen and Paris, where he lived for 12 years and where d'Indy and Sabaneiev were among his masters for comp. and he came under the influence of Picasso, Braque, Chirico and other modern painters. After some further studies in It.

and Spain he settled at Göteborg and in 1933 became mus. critic of the *Göteborgs Handelstidning*.

Works incl. ballet-pantomime *Maskerade*; incid. mus. to var. plays incl. Shakespeare's *Merchant of Venice* and *The Tempest*; 4 symphs. (*Sinfonia breve, S. espressiva, S. del mare, S. Shakespeariana*), symph. poems *The Arctic Sea, The Tower of Babel,* Lyric Suite and Festival Overture for orch., *Concerto grosso* for string orch.; vln. concerto, vla., concerto, *Sinfonia concertante* for cello and orch.; pf. suites and pieces; songs, etc.

Ocarina

O

Oakeley, Herbert (Stanley) (b. London,
22. VII. 1830; d. Eastbourne, 26. X.
1903), Eng. organist, educationist and
comp. Educ. at Rugby and Oxford,
studied mus. in London, Dresden and
Leipzig. He became Prof. of Mus. at
Edinburgh Univ. in 1865 and Mus.D.
(Cantuar.) in 1871. Knighted 1876.
Works incl. services and anthems;
Jubilee Cantata (1887) and other choral
works, part-songs; Festal and Funeral
Marches for orch.; org. and pf. mus.;
songs, etc.

Obbligato (It. = obligatory, compul-
sory), instrumental part in a work that is
'essential' in the sense that it performs an
important soloistic function.

Obbligo. *See* Con obbligo.

Oberon, König der Elfen (*Oberon, King
of the Fairies*), opera by Wranitzky (lib.
by Karl Ludwig Gieseke, based on Wieland's poem and Friederike Sophie
Seyler's lib. *Hüon und Amande*), prod.
Vienna, Theater auf der Wieden, 7. XI.
1789.

Oberon, or The Elf King's Oath, opera
by Weber (lib. by James Robinson
Planché, based on Wieland's poem and
further back on the medieval Fr. romance
Huon de Bordeaux), prod. London,
Covent Garden Theatre, 12. IV. 1826.

Obertas, a Pol. dance perf. in figures
by couples following a leader. The mus.
is in 3–4 time, not unlike that of the
Mazurka, but wilder in character.

Oberthür, Charles (b. Munich, 4. III.
1819; d. London, 8. XI. 1895), Ger.
harpist and comp. After var. orchestral engagements in Ger. and Switz. he settled
in London in 1844 as perf. and teacher.
Works incl. opera *Floris von Namur*;
Mass *St. Philip Neri*; cantatas *The Pilgrim
Queen, The Red Cross Knight, Lady Jane
Grey*; overture *Rübezahl*, overture for
Shakespeare's *Macbeth* and others; *Loreley*
and concertino for harp and orch.; trios
for harp, vln. and cello, 4tets for harps;
many harp solos, etc.

Oberto, Conte di San Bonifacio, opera
by Verdi (lib. by Antonio Piazza, altered
by Bartolommeo Merelli and Temistocle
Solera), prod. Milan, Teatro alla Scala,
17. XI. 1839, Verdi's 1st opera.

Obertus, Jacobus. *See* Obrecht.

Obey, André (b. 1892), Fr. dramatist.
See **Honegger** (*800 mètres*), **Rape of
Lucretia** (Britten).

Oblique Motion. *See* Motion.

Oboe, a woodwind instrument formerly
called hautboy, held vertically and played
with a double reed. It descended from the
Shawm and was in full use by the 17th

cent., though it was not properly developed
until the 18th and not wholly perfected
until the 19th. 2 O.s, together with 2
horns, were the most constant instruments
in the orch., apart from the strings, in
the 18th cent. The O. has a compass of
about 2½ 8ves:

Also an 8-ft. reed org. stop sometimes
called Hautboy and repro. the tone of
the O.

Oboe d'amore (It. = love ob.), an ob.
tuned a min. 3rd lower and transposing a
min. 3rd down.

Oboe da caccia (It. = hunting ob.), an
ob., tuned a 5th lower and transposing a
5th down. Its parts in old mus. are now
generally played on the Eng. horn, whose
pitch is the same

Oborin, Lev (Nikolayevich) (b. Moscow,
11. IX. 1907), Rus. pianist. Studied at
Moscow Cons. with Igumnov, graduating
in 1926. Taught at the Moscow Cons.
from 1928, becoming prof. in 1935.
Although he has had much success as a
concert performer, he devotes much of his
time to teaching.

Obrecht (or **Hobrecht**), **Jacob** (or
Jacobus Obertus) (b. ? Bergen-op-Zoom,
22. XI. ? 1450; d. Ferrara, 1505), Nether-
lands comp. In 1479 became choirmaster at
Bergen-op-Zoom. Director of the singing-
school at Cambrai, 1484–5, and teacher at
Bruges, 1491–6, though he must have
resided at Antwerp, where he was app.
maître de chapelle at the cathedral in 1491.
Towards the end of his life he went to
It. and was for a time at the court of
Lorenzo de' Medici at Florence.
Works incl. Masses, motets, *chansons*,
etc.

Obukhov, Nikolai (b. Moscow, 22. IV.
1892; d. Paris, 13. VI. 1954), Rus. comp.
Pupil of N. Tcherepnin and Steinberg at the
St. Petersburg Cons. He settled in Paris in
1918 and made further studies with Ravel
and others.
Works incl. mystery *Le Livre de la vie*,
Poèmes liturgiques, etc.

Oca del Cairo, L' (*The Goose of Cairo*),
unfinished opera by Mozart (lib. by
Giovanni Battista Varesco). Prod. in
a version completed with other Mozartian
fragments (lib. by Victor Wilder), Paris,
Fantaisies-Parisiennes, 6. VI. 1867; new
version by Virgilio Mortari (lib. by L.
Cavicchioli), Salzburg, 22. VIII. 1936;
another by Hans Redlich, London,
Sadler's Wells Theatre, 30. V. 1940.

Ocarina, a primitive instrument of the
fl. type with finger-holes, approx. pear-

473

shaped, with a mouthpiece protruding like a fish's fin, and usually made of terracotta.

O'Casey, Sean (1884-1964), Ir. dramatist. *See* **Bush (A.)** (*Star Turns Red*).

Occa, Sophie dall'. *See* **Schoberlechner.**

Occasional Oratorio, oratorio by Handel (lib. from Milton's Psalms completed by ? Thomas Morell), comp. to celebrate the suppression of the Jacobite rebellion, prod. London, Covent Garden Theatre, 14. II. 1746.

Occasione fa il ladro, L' (*Opportunity makes a Thief*), opera by Rossini (lib. by Luigi Prividali), prod. Venice, Teatro San Moisè, 24. XI. 1812.

Ochelly. *See* **Kelly, Michael.**

Ochetto (It.)
Ochetus (Lat.) } *See* **Hocket.**

Ochs, Siegfried (b. Frankfurt, 19. IV. 1858; d. Berlin, 6. II. 1929), Ger. cond. and comp. After a general educ. at Darmstadt and at Heidelberg Univ., he studied mus. in Berlin and founded a choral society in 1882, which in assoc. with the Phil. Orch. became the Philharmonische Chor in 1888. In the 1920s he became prof. at the Hochschule für Musik and cond. the oratorios and other choral concerts there.

Works incl. opera *Im Namen des Gesetzes*; songs, etc.

Ochsenkuhn, Sebastian (b. Nuremberg, 6. II. 1521; d. Heidelberg, 20. VIII. 1574), Ger. lutenist. In the service of Otto Heinrich, Elector Palatine of the Rhine, and his successors. He pub. in 1558 a book of arrs. of motets and Fr. and Ger. songs in lute tablature.

Ockeghem
Ockenheim } *See* **Okeghem**

Octave, an interval embracing 8 notes of a diatonic scale. The upper note having exactly twice the number of vibrations of the lower, the phenomenon results that the 2 appear to be the same, although different in pitch. Also another name for the Principal org. stop.

Octave Flute. *See* **Piccolo.**

Octave Keys. *See* **Speaker Keys.**

Octet, a comp. for 8 instruments, usually in several movements.

Octo Basse (Fr.)
Octobass (Eng.) } a 3-stringed double bass of huge size invented in 1849 by J. B. Vuillaume in Paris, which never became current and is now obs. It was capable of playing extremely low notes, the strings being tuned:

8ve lower⌐

It was extremely unwieldy and its strings were so thick and heavy that they had to be stopped by means of levers and pedals.

Odak, Krsto (b. Siverič, 20. III. 1888; d. Zagreb, 4. XI. 1965), Yugoslav comp. Studied at Munich and with Novák in Prague. In 1922 he was app. prof. at the Acad. of Mus. at Zagreb.

Works incl. opera *Dorrit Dances*; mus. for a Christmas play and other incid. mus.; ballet *The Butterfly and the Moon*; 2 Slav Masses; madrigal and other choruses; 2 symphs., symph. overture for orch.; rhapsodies for vln. and orch.; 4 string 4tets; vln. and pf. sonata; 3 Psalms for baritone and pf., songs, etc.

Ode, a comp. in several movements, with alternating solos and choruses, often of a dedicatory or congratulatory character.

Ode for St. Cecilia's Day, setting by Handel of Dryden's poem, prod. London, Theatre in Lincoln's Inn Fields, 22. XI. 1739.

Odes for St. Cecilia's Day by Purcell; 1. *Laudate Ceciliam* (1683); 2. *Welcome to all the pleasures* (Fishburn; 1683); 3. *Hail, bright Cecilia* (Brady; 1692); 4. *Raise, raise the voice* (?).

Odington, Walter de (or W. of Evesham) (b. ? Oddington, Glos., ?; d. ? Evesham, ?), Eng. 13th-cent. monk, musician and astronomer. He entered the Benedictine monastery at Evesham and wrote a treatise *De speculatione musicae*.

Odnoposoff, Ricardo (b. Buenos Aires, 24. II. 1914), Arg. violinist. A child prodigy, he first appeared in public aged 5. Studied first in Buenos Aires and then in Berlin with Flesch, winning prizes in Vienna and Brussels (1932 and 1937).

Odo (b. ?, 879; d. Tours, 18. XI. 942), Fr. monk and musician. Educ. at the court of Guillaume, Duke of Aquitaine, took holy orders, joined the monastery of Saint-Martin at Tours, and after studying dialectics and mus. in Paris, returned there, then entered the Benedictine monastery of Beaume nr. Besançon, became abbot of that of Cluny nr. Macon, 927-42, but returned to Tours to die. He comp. hymns and antiphons and wrote treatises on mus.

Odzmek, a Slovak dance in quick 2-4 time with a more moderately paced middle section. The 9th of Dvořák's *Slavonic Dances* for pf. duet is an O.

Œdipe, opera by Enesco (lib. by Edmond Fleg, after Sophocles), prod. Paris, Opéra, 10. III. 1936.

Œdipe à Colone (*Oedipus Coloneus*), opera by Sacchini (lib. by Nicolas François Guillard, after Sophocles), prod. Versailles, at court, 4. I. 1786; 1st Paris perf. Opéra, 1. II. 1787.

Oedipus auf Kolonos, incid. mus. by Mendelssohn for Sophocles' tragedy, Op. 93, for male chorus and orch., prod. Potsdam, 1. XI. 1845.

Oedipus Rex, stage oratorio by Stravinsky (lib., in Lat., by J. Daniélou, trans. from Fr. by Jean Cocteau, after Sophocles), prod. Paris, Théâtre Sarah Bernhardt, 30. V. 1927. The parts are sung in costume but without action, and the words are in Lat. in order not to distract the ordinary listener by verbal associations.

Oedipus Tyrannus, incid. mus. by Mendelssohn for Sophocles' tragedy, never perf. and now lost.

Incid. mus. for do. by Stanford, prod. Cambridge, 22–6. XI. 1887.

Oehlenschläger, Adam (1779–1850), Dan. poet and dramatist. *See* **Danning** (*Aladdin*), **Gyrowetz** (do.), **Hartmann (J. P. E.)** (*Golden Horns*), **Heise** (*Palnatoke*), **Horneman** (*Aladdin*), **Nielsen (C.)** (do.).

Offenbach, Jacques (actually Jakob Levy Eberst) (b. Cologne, 20. VI. 1819; d. Paris, 5. X. 1880), Ger.-Fr. comp. His father was cantor at the synagogue of Cologne, but he was sent to Paris early in his youth, studying at the Cons. in 1833–7, perfecting himself in cello playing and then playing in the orch. of the Opéra-Comique even before he left the Cons. In 1850 he

La Fille du tambour-major, La Foire de Saint-Laurent, Geneviève de Brabant, La Grande-Duchesse de Gérolstein, L'Île de Tulipatan, La Jolie Parfumeuse, Madame Favart, Orphée aux enfers, La Périchole, Princess de Trébizonde, Robinson Crusoé (after Defoe), *Vert-Vert, La Vie Parisienne, Voyage dans la lune* (after Verne), *Whittington and his Cat;* ballet *Le Papillon;* incid. mus. for Barrière's *Le Gascon* and Sardou's *La Haine,* etc. A 2nd opera, *The Goldsmith of Toledo* (after a tale by E. T. A. Hoffmann) is a pasticcio from var. operettas, esp. *Le Corsaire noir,* prod. Mannheim, 1919.

Offertory (Lat. *Offertorium*), the 3rd or 4th item of the Proper of the Rom. Mass, following the gospel or the *Credo*. It was orig. an antiphonal chant, sung with a complete psalm and accomp. the offering of bread and wine. In the 10th cent. it became an elaborate responsorial chant provided with complex verses sung by soloists. The verses were later dropped, but the style of what remains is still closer to the Gradual than to the Introit or Communion (*see* illustration).

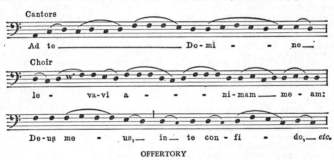

Cantors

Ad te ———————— Do - mi - ne —

Choir

le - va-vi a - - ni - mam — me - am:

De - us me - us, — in - te con - fi - do, — *etc.*

OFFERTORY

became cond. at the Théâtre Français. In 1853 he prod. his 1st operettas and during a quarter of a century he turned out nearly 100 light stage pieces. In 1855 he took over the management of the Théâtre Comte and renamed it the Bouffes-Parisiens. This lasted until 1861, after which he had no theatre of his own until 1873, when he managed the Théâtre de la Gaîté until 1875. In 1876–7 he was in U.S.A., but returned to Paris, where alone he found that his success was permanent. His only large-scale opera, *Les Contes d'Hoffmann,* occupied him for many years, but he left it not quite finished at his death, and it was revised and partly scored by Guiraud.

Works incl. opera *Les Contes d'Hoffmann,* 89 operettas incl. *Barbebleue, Ba-ta-clan, La Belle Hélène, Chanson de Fortunio, Le Docteur Ox* (after Jules Verne),

In the Ang. church it survived as a spoken biblical sentence, occasionally set to mus. The O. was frequently set by 16th-cent. comps., and with instrumental accomp. by Michael Haydn, Mozart, Schubert, etc.

Ogdon, John (Andrew Howard) (b. Manchester, 27. I. 1937), Eng. pianist. Studied at Royal Manchester Coll. of Mus. and in 1962 won the Tchaikovsky Competition in Moscow. He is equally at home in both the classical and modern repertory, and has also pub. a number of comps., incl. a pf. concerto.

Ogiński, Polish noble family of amateur musicians:

1. Prince Michal Kazimierz O. (b. ?, 1731; d. Warsaw, 1803). Studied the vln. with Viotti and also played the harp. He kept a small opera co. and orch. on his estate.

Works incl. a comic opera, incid. mus. for 2 plays, and polonaises for vln. and pf.
2. Prince Michal Kleofas O. (b. Gozuw nr. Warsaw, 25. IX. 1765; d. Florence, 18. X. 1833), nephew of prec. Was taught the pf. by Kozlowski and vln. by Viotti and others. After the 3rd partition of Poland he emigrated, 1st to Turkey, then to Hamburg, Paris (1823) and finally Florence. Works incl. opera *Zélis et Valeur, ou Bonaparte au Caire*; military marches; polonaises and mazurkas for pf., etc.
3. Prince Gabriel O. (b. ?, 1788; d. Lithuania, 1843), remote cousin of prec. Played the vln. but did not comp.

Öglin, Erhard (b. Reutlingen, ?; d. ?), Ger. 15th–16th-cent. mus. pub. He worked in Augsburg, where he pub. an important collection of 4-part songs in 1512.

Ohana, Maurice (b. Gibraltar, 12. VI. 1915), Eng. comp. of Moroccan descent. Studied in Barcelona, Rome and at the Schola Cantorum in Paris. His mus. belongs to the *avant-garde* school.
Works incl. *Chanson de Toile*, opera for marionettes; ballets *Prométhée* and *Paso*; *Les Représentations de Tanit* and *Suite pour un Mimodrame* for small orch.; guitar concerto; concertino for tpt.; *Études Choréographiques* for perc.; pf. mus.; choral mus.; film mus.; etc.

Oiseau bleu, L' (*The Blue Bird*), opera by A. Wolff (lib. taken from Maeterlinck's play), prod. N.Y., Metrop. Opera, 27. XII. 1919.

Oiseau de feu, L'. *See* Firebird.

Oistrakh, David (Fedorovich) (b. Odessa, 30. IX. 1908), Rus. violinist. Began his studies aged 5, entered the Odessa Cons. and graduated in 1926, winning a number of prizes, incl. the Brussels Competition in 1937, which made him internationally famous. Since 1934 he has taught at the Moscow Cons., and also appeared widely as a soloist. He has given the first perfs. of vln. concertos by Miaskovski, Katchachurian and Shostakovich.

Oistrakh, Igor (b. Odessa, 27. IV. 1931), Rus. violinist, son of prec. Studied with his father at the Moscow Cons., graduating in 1955 after winning prizes in Budapest (1949) and Poznan (1952).

Okeghem, Jean de (Joannes) (or Ockeghem, Ockenheim, Hoquegan), (b. ?, *c.* 1425; d. ? Tours, *c.* 1495), Flem. comp. Pupil (?) of Binchois, chorister at Antwerp Cathedral until 1444, in the service of Charles, Duke of Bourbon, at Moulins in 1446–8, and in the service of the Fr. court from *c.* 1452, where he became 1st *maître de chapelle*. Louis XI app. him treasurer of Saint-Martin at Tours, where he lived during the latter part of his life, though he visited Spain in 1469. He had many

distinguished pupils, incl. Josquin Desprez and Pierre de La Rue.
Works incl. Masses, motets; Fr. *chansons*, etc.

Okeland, Robert (b. ?, d. ?), 16th-cent. Eng. comp. He was a member of Eton Coll., 1532–4, and of the Chapel Royal, 1547–8, Mus. of his is preserved in the 'Gyffard' part-books, *c.* 1555.

Olav Trygvason, unfinished opera by Grieg (lib. by Bjørnson), 3 scenes only, perf. in concert form, Christiania, 19. X. 1889; never staged in Grieg's lifetime, but prod. Christiania, 8. X. 1908.

Old Hall Manuscript, a collection of early 15th-cent. church mus. (*c.* 1415–80) copied in several different hands and kept at St. Edmund's Coll., Old Hall nr. Ware (Herts.).

Oldham, Arthur (William) (b. London, 6. IX. 1926), Eng. comp. Studied comp. with Howells and pf. with Kathleen Long at the R.C.M. in London, also privately with Britten. He was for a time mus. director at the Mercury Theatre and to the Ballet Rambert, but later devoted himself wholly to comp.
Works incl. 4 ballets incl. *Bonne-Bouche*, incid. mus. for Ronald Duncan's *This Way to the Tomb*; 6 anthems; orchestral mus.; vln. and pf. sonata; songs, etc.

Oldman, C(ecil). B(ernard). (b. London, 2. IV. 1894; d. London, 7. X. 1969). Eng. bibliog. and musicologist. Educ. at City of London School and Exeter Coll., Oxford. He joined the staff of the Brit. Museum library in 1920, where he was Deputy Keeper of Printed Books from 1943 to 1948 and Keeper from 1948 to 1960. He was active in mus. research, specializing partic. in Mozart, on whom he wrote var. learned studies.

Olé. *See* Polo.

Oleg. *See* Early Reign of Oleg.

Olimpia vendicata (*Olympia revenged*), opera by A. Scarlatti (lib. by Aurelio Aureli), prod. Naples, Palazzo Reale, 23. XII. 1685.

Olimpiade, L' (*The Olympiad*). *See also* Olympie. Lib. by Metastasio.
Opera by Caldara, prod. Vienna, 28. VIII. 1733.
Opera by Cimarosa, prod. Vicenza, 10. VII. 1784.
Opera by Ignazio Fiorillo (1715–87), prod. Venice, Teatro San Samuele, V. 1745.
Opera by Galuppi, prod. Milan, Teatro Regio Ducal, 26. XII. 1747.
Opera by Hasse, prod. Dresden, at court, 16. II. 1756.
Opera by Jommelli, prod. Stuttgart, at court, 11. II. 1761.
Opera by Leo, prod. Naples, Teatro San Carlo, 19. XII. 1737.

Opera by Mysliveček, prod. Naples, Teatro San Carlo, 4. XI. 1778.

Opera by Pergolesi, prod. Rome, Teatro Tordinona, 8. I. 1735.

Opera by Sacchini, prod. Padua, VI. 1763.

Opera by Traetta, prod. Verona, autumn 1758.

Opera by Vivaldi, prod. Venice, Teatro Sant' Angelo, Carnival 1734. (There are at least 30 other settings of this lib. O. is prob. the most frequently comp. work by Metastasio or by any other librettist).

Oliphant (from old Eng. 'olifaunt' = elephant), a bugle-like horn made of an elephant's tusk, used for signalling and hunting in old times, often beautifully carved.

Olivieri-Sangiacomo, Elsa. *See* Respighi.

Ollone, Max (properly Maximilien-Paul-Marie-Félix) **d'** (b. Besançon, 13. VI. 1875; d. Paris, 15. V. 1959), Fr. cond. and comp. Studied under Massenet and Lenepveu at the Paris Cons. and gained the Prix de Rome in 1897. After cond. at Angers, Geneva and Paris (Opéra-Comique, concerts, etc.), and touring as cond., he became prof. at the Cons. in 1939.

Works incl. operas *Le Retour*, *Les Amants de Rimini* (after Dante), *Les Uns et les autres* (on a comedy by Verlaine), *L'Arlequin*, *George Dandin* (after Molière) and *La Samaritaine* (after Rostand); ballet *Le Peuple abandonné*; pantomime *Bacchus et Silène*; oratorio *François d'Assise*, cantatas *Frédégonde*, *Jeanne d'Arc à Domrémy*; fantasy for pf. and orch., *Le Ménétrier* for vln. and orch., string 4tet, pf. trio; songs, etc.

Olmeda de San José, Federico (b. Burgo de Osma, 1865; d. Madrid, 11. II. 1909), Span. musicologist, organist and comp. After 2 other organist's appts. he became organist to the convent of the Descalzas Reales in Madrid, 1893. He wrote on early Span. polyphony and Castilian folksong.

Works incl. church mus.; 4 symphs.; string 4tet; pf. pieces, etc.

Olsen, Ole (b. Hammerfest, 4. VII. 1850; d. Oslo, 9. XI. 1927), Norw. organist, cond. and comp. Studied engineering at Trondhjem, but took to mus., taking any appt. as organist and travelling theatre cond. he could secure. In 1870–4 he consolidated his studies at the Leipzig Cons. and then settled at Christiania where he taught cond. and wrote criticism.

Works incl. operas *Stig Hvide*, *Lajla*, *Klippeøerne* and *Stallo*; incid. mus. to Nordahl Rolfsen's *Svein Urœd*; oratorio *Nidaros*, cantatas *Ludwig Holberg*, *Griffenfelt*, *Broderbud*, *Tourist Cantata*; symph. in G maj., symph. poems *Aasgaardsreien*, *Elf-dans*, etc.

Olthoff, Statius (b. Osnabrück, 1555; d. Rostock, 28. II. 1629), Ger. comp. Became cantor at St. Mary's Church at Rostock in 1579 and there comp. 4-part settings of George Buchananan's Lat. verse paraphrase of the psalms.

Olympians, The, opera by Bliss (lib. by J. B. Priestley), prod. London, Covent Garden Theatre, 29. IX. 1949.

Olympie, opera by Spontini (lib. by Michel Dieulafoy and Charles Brifaut, based on Voltaire's tragedy), prod. Paris, Opéra, 22. XII. 1819.

Olyver (b. ?, d. ?), early 15th-cent. Eng. comp. repres. in the Old Hall MS.

Omar Khayyám (?–1123), Persian scholar and poet. *See* Bantock, Cadman, Ettinger, Lehmann (L. ii), Levidis, Respighi (E.).

O'Mara, Joseph (b. Limerick, 16. VII. 1866; d. ?, 5. VIII. 1927), Ir. tenor. Studied at Milan and made his 1st appearance in London, 1891.

Ombra di Don Giovanni, L' (*Don Juan's Shade*), opera by Alfano (lib. by Ettore Moschino), prod. Milan, Teatro alla Scala, 2. IV. 1914; revived as *Don Giovanni di Mañara*, Florence, V. 1941.

Omphale, opera by Destouches (lib. by Antoine Houdar de la Motte), prod. Paris, Opéra, 10. XI. 1700.

On Hearing the First Cuckoo in Spring, 1 of 2 pieces for small orch. by Delius (the other being *Summer Night on the River*), comp. 1912 and 1911 respectively, 1st perf. Leipzig Gewandhaus, 2. X. 1913. The cuckoo call is heard unobtrusively on the clar. and the main theme is a Norw. folksong, *In Ole Dale*, previously used by Grieg, arr. for pf. in *Norske Folkeviser*, Op. 66 (No. 14).

Ondes Musicales, an electrophonic instrument invented by Maurice Martenot of Paris in 1929, prod. notes from the air graded according to the chromatic scale by a special device, not indeterminate in pitch like those of the Aetherophone or Theremin.

Ondřiček, František (b. Prague, 29. IV. 1859; d. Milan, 13. IV. 1922), Cz. violinist. Pupil of his father and at the Prague and Paris Conss. 1st appeared in London in 1882 and then went on tour. Director of the New Vienna Cons., 1912–19, and then at that of Prague.

Onegin (*née* **Hoffmann**), **Sigrid** (b. Stockholm, 1. VI. 1891; d. Magliaso, Switz., 16. VI. 1943), Swed. contralto of Ger. descent. Studied in Swed. and Ger. and appeared frequently in both countries, also in Eng. Her 1st husband was a great-nephew of Lvov.

O'Neill, Eugene (Gladstone) (1888–1953), Amer. dramatist. *See* Easdale (*Mourning Becomes Electra*), Gruenberg (*Emperor Jones*), Whithorne (*Marco Millions*).

O'Neill, Norman (b. London, 14. III. 1875; d. London, 3. III. 1934), Anglo-Ir. cond. and comp. Great-grandson of Callcott. Studied with Somervell in London and with Knorr at the Hoch Cons. at Frankfurt. In 1899 he married the Fr. pianist Adine Rückert and in 1908 became cond. at the Haymarket Theatre, for which he wrote much incid. mus. In 1919 he became treasurer of the Royal Phil. Society and in 1924 prof. at the R.A.M.

Works incl. incid. mus. for Shakespeare's *Hamlet*, *Henry V*, *Julius Caesar*, *King Lear*, *Macbeth*, *Measure for Measure* and *The Merchant of Venice*, Maeterlinck's *Blue Bird*, Barrie's *Mary Rose* and *A Kiss for Cinderella*, Ibsen's *Pretenders*, Stephen Phillips's *The Lost Heir*: dramatic adaptations of Dicken's *Pickwick* and Scott's *Bride of Lammermoor*, etc.; *Swinburne Ballet* and *Punch and Judy* ballet; concert overtures, variations, *Miniatures* and other works for orch.; choral works; pf. 5tet, 2 pf. trios; Variations and Fugue on an Ir. Air for 2 pfs.; pf. pieces; many songs, etc.

Onslow, (André) George (or Georges) (Louis) (b. Clermont-Ferrand, 27. VII. 1784; d. Clermont-Ferrand, 3. X. 1853), Fr. comp. of Eng. descent. Grandson of the 1st Lord Onslow. He studied pf. with Hüllmandel, Dussek and Cramer while living in London for some years as a young man, but settled at Clermont-Ferrand as a country squire, held regular chamber mus. practices there, studied the cello and went for 2 years to Vienna to study comp. In the 1820s, wishing to write operas, he made further studies with Reicha in Paris, where he lived alternatively.

Works incl. operas *L'Alcade de la Vega*, *Le Colporteur* and *Le Duc de Guise*; 4 symphs.; 36 string 4tets, 36 string 5tets, 2 pf. 6tets, pf. 7tet, nonet for strings and wind, 6 pf. trios; vln. and pf. and cello and pf. sonatas; sonatas for pf. duet; pf. pieces, etc.

Op. (abbr.) = Opus (Lat. = work), a prefix used for the enumeration of a comp's works. It was at first a pub.'s rather than a comp.'s device and in the early 18th cent. (e.g. Handel) was used only for instrumental comps. Later in that cent. it began to become more general, being used for Haydn but not for Mozart, and from Beethoven onward it began to be used regularly, though the number of an O. is not necessarily a guide to the date of its comp.

Open, org. pipes of which the upper end is left open and which, unlike the Stopped pipes, prod. notes corresponding to their full length.

Open Diapason. *See* **Diapason.**

Open Notes, on wind instruments the notes prod. naturally as harmonics as distinct from Stopped Notes prod. by valves, keys or other mechanical means, or by the hand in horn playing; on string instruments any notes prod. by the strings without being stopped by a finger.

Open Strings, the strings of string instruments as played without being stopped by the left hand on the fingerboard.

Opera (It. = work: the same as the Lat. *opus* and orig. used in the same sense), a mus. work for the stage of varying types, originating in the last years of the 16th cent. in It. The dramatic foundation of it is a Libretto, which is set to mus. in var. ways that may be divided into 3 main types: (1) recitative carrying on the action and set mus. numbers such as arias, concerted pieces for several voices, choruses, etc., forming mus. climaxes; (2) similar mus. numbers, but with the action carried on in spoken dialogue instead of recitative; (3) the text set continuously throughout, but often with traces of separate mus. numbers still apparent. The instrumental share in an O. is almost always orchestral.

See also **Action musicale; Azione teatrale; Ballad Opera; Burlesque; Burletta; Comédie lyrique; Commedia per musica; Dramma giocoso; Dramma per musica; Extravaganza; Favola per musica; Festa teatrale; Handlung; Intermezzi; Melodrama; Melodramma; Music Drama; Musical Comedy; Opera-Ballet; Opéra bouffe; O. buffa; Opéra comique; O. seria; Operetta; Pastorale; Sing-Spiel; Singspiel; Tragédie lyrique; Vaudeville.**

Opera-Ballet, a combination of opera and ballet orig. in 17-cent. Fr. and there called *opéra-ballet* from the beginning.

Opéra bouffe (Fr. = comic opera, derived from It. *opera buffa*), a type of Fr. comic opera, or rather operetta, lighter in tone and flimsier in mus. workmanship than an *opéra comique*.

Opera buffa (It. = comic opera), a light type of opera with a comedy lib., partic. of the 18th cent. in It., with dialogue in recitative (accomp. by the harpsichord) and mus. numbers: arias, duets, etc., and (more rarely) choruses.

Opéra comique (Fr. lit. comic opera), an exclusively Fr. type of opera, not always comic and often by no means light, but orig. always with spoken dialogue.

Opera seria (It. = serious opera), a type of 18th-cent. opera, esp. that cultivated by the librettists Zeno and Metastasio, treating mythological or heroic-historical subjects. The mus. treatment is mainly by recitative and arias, more rarely duets and other concerted numbers or choruses.

Operetta (It. = little opera), a light

opera or mus. comedy, normally with spoken dialogue.

Opernball, Der (*The Opera Ball*), operetta by Heuberger (lib. by Victor Léon and Heinrich von Waldberg), prod. Vienna, Theater an der Wien, 5. I. 1898.

Ophicleide (lit. 'keyed snake' from Gk. *ophis*, a snake, and *kleis*, a key), a bass brass instrument similar to the Key Bugle, played with a cup-shaped mouthpiece and having holes covered with keys in the side. It was patented by Halary (i.e. Jean-Hilaire Asté) in Paris in 1821. It had a compass of about 3 8ves. It was gradually superseded by the bass tuba.

Also a 16-ft. reed org. pedal stop of powerful tone.

Opie (*née* **Alderson**), **Amelia** (1769–1853), Eng. novelist, wife of the painter John O. *See* **Agnese di Fitz-Henry** (Paer).

Opieński, Henryk (b. Cracow, 13. I. 1870; d. Morges nr. Lausanne, 21. I. 1942), Pol. musicologist, cond. and comp. Studied pf. with Paderewski, comp. with d'Indy at the Schola Cantorum in Paris and cond. and musicology with Nikisch and Riemann at Leipzig. He formed a vocal society at Lausanne in 1918 and lived in Switz. until his death, except when he was director of the Poznan Cons. in 1920–6. He ed. Chopin's letters and wrote on him, Paderewski, and Pol. mus. in general.

Works incl. operas *Maria* (Malczewski) and *Jacob the Lutenist*; incid. mus. for Calderón's *El principe constante*; oratorio *The Prodigal Son*; cantata *Mickiewicz*; symph. poems *Zymunt August i Barbara* and *Lilla Weneda*; string 4tet; instrumental pieces; songs, etc.

Opitiis, Benedictus de (b. ?, d. ?), 16th-cent. comp. of uncertain nationality. He wrote 2 motets for the entry of the future emperor Charles V into Antwerp in 1515; he was the organist at the church of Our Lady in Antwerp, *c.* 1514–16, and stayed in England, 1516–18. He disappears from records after 1522.

Opitz (von Boberfeld), Martin (1597–1639), Ger. poet. *See* **Dafne** (Schütz), **Loewenstern** (*Judith*).

Oppure (It. = or). *See* **Ossia**. A less common word for the same thing.

Opus (Lat. = work). Its abbr., Op., is used as a prefix to enumerations of a comp.'s works. *See* **Op.**

Oratorio, a vocal work, usually for solo voices and chorus with some kind of instrumental accomp. and generally set to sacred words, often direct from the Bible or paraphrased from it, and at any rate nearly always treating a subject of a sacred character (such notable exceptions as Handel's *Hercules* and Haydn's *Seasons* are not strictly speaking O.s). It originated in the congregation of the Oratorians

founded by St. Philip Neri in the 16th cent., where scenes from Scripture were enacted with mus. In the 17th cent. the O. developed side by side with Opera and was indistinguishable from it in some of its features, except that greater prominence was nearly always given to the chorus. Settings of one of the Evangelists' narratives of the Passion developed a special type of O., esp. in Ger.

Orazi ed i Curiazi, Gli (*The Horatii and the Curiatii*), opera by Cimarosa (lib. by Antonio Simone Sografi), prod. Venice, Teatro La Fenice, 26. XII. 1796.

Opera by Mercadante (lib. by Salvatore Cammarano), prod. Naples, Teatro San Carlo, 10. XI. 1846.

Orchestra (Gk. = dancing-place), orig. the space in the Gk. theatre equivalent to that now occupied by the O. in an opera-house; now the name for the assembly of instrumental players itself. The modern O. originated in the ballets and operas of the early 17th cent. At that time various groups, e.g. strings, brass, were used separately and it was only gradually that they were combined. In the course of the 17th cent. tpts. and timpani, originally ceremonial and military instruments, were intro. into the orch. for festal or heroic mus. By the early 18th cent. fls., obs. and bassoons were normal members of the O., though recorders often appeared as alternatives to the fls., and horns came to be used for mus. of a jovial character. Throughout this time keyboard instruments were used to support and enrich the ensemble. In the course of the 18th cent. clars. were added, though they only gradually became a normal part of the orch., and the keyboard continuo disappeared, except in church mus. Up to this time trombs. were used only in church mus. and in solemn operatic scenes; Beethoven incorporated them in ordinary orchestral mus. The 19th cent. saw the gradual establishment of the piccolo, Eng. horn, bass clar., double bassoon, tuba and harp as normal members of the O. and the replacement of the older horns and tpts. by valve instruments. Until the end of the 18th cent., and sometimes later, the cond. sat at the harpsichord or played 1st vln.

Orchestration (or **Scoring**), the art of setting out a comp. for the instruments of an orch. Methods of O. have changed considerably. Monteverdi in *Orfeo* (1607) used his instruments mainly in groups; Bach chose a particular combination of instruments and retained it throughout a movement or even throughout a work; Haydn, Mozart and Beethoven developed a new art of combining, doubling and contrasting instruments. Modern O. developed mainly from the works of Berlioz, Wagner, Strauss and Debussy, all of whom exploited the characteristic colours of the instruments and their combinations.

Orchestrion, a mechan. instrument, such as Mälzel's 'Panharmonicon', which by var. technical contrivances imitates as nearly as possible the sounds of orchestral instruments.

Orczy, Baroness (1865–1947), Hung.- Eng. novelist. *See* **Arundell** (*Scarlet Pimpernel*), **Schjelderup** (do.).

Ordoñez, Pedro (b. Palencia, *c.* 1500; d. Rome, 1550), Span. singer and comp. In 1539 he went to Rome as a singer in the Pontifical chapel and remained there to his death, attending the Council of Trent in 1545 and again in 1547, when it had moved to Bologna.

Ordre (Fr.), the old Fr. name for the Suite.

Orefice, Giacomo (b. Vicenza, 27. VIII. 1865; d. Milan, 22. XII. 1922), It. comp. Studied at the Bologna Liceo Musicale, Mancinelli being among his masters. In 1909 became prof. of comp. at Milan Cons.
Works incl. operas *Consuelo* (after George Sand), *Chopin* (on mus. by Chopin), *Cecilia, Mosè, Pane altrui, Radda, Il castello del sogno* and others; symph. in D min., *Sinfonia del bosco, Anacreontiche* for orch.; suite for cello and orch.; *Riflessioni ed ombre* for 5tet, pf. trio; 2 vln. and pf. sonatas, cello and pf. sonata; *Preludi del mare, Quadri di Böcklin, Crepuscoli, Miraggi,* etc. for pf.

Orel, Alfred (b. Vienna, 3. VII. 1889; d. Vienna, II. IV. 1967), Aus. musicologist. A lawyer and civil servant at first, he studied mus. with Adler when nearly 30. Later app. prof. at Vienna Univ. and head of the mus. dept. of the municipal library. Author of works on Bruckner and co-ed. with Robert Haas of the ed. of the orig. versions of Bruckner's works.

Orel, Dobroslav (b. Ronov, 15. XII. 1870; d. Prague, 18. II. 1942), Cz. musicologist. Studied theology and taught church mus. at the Prague Cons., later studied comp. with Novák and musicology with Adler. App. prof. at the Komensky Univ. at Bratislava, 1921. Author of studies of old Boh. mus., etc.

Oresteia, trilogy of short operas by Taneiev (lib. by A. A. Venkstern, after Aeschylus), prod. St. Petersburg, 29. X. 1895.

Orestes. *See also* **Leben des Orest.**

Opera by Weingartner (lib. by comp., after Aeschylus), prod. Leipzig, 15. II. 1902.

Orfeide, L', cycle of operas by Malipiero (lib. by comp.), prod. complete, in Ger. trans., Düsseldorf, 30. X. 1925.

I. **La morte delle maschere** (*The Death of the Masks*).

II. **Sette canzoni** (*Seven Songs*), prod. in Fr. trans., Paris, Opéra, 10. VII. 1920.

III. **L'Orfeo, ossia L'ottava canzone** (*Orpheus, or the Eighth Song*).

Orfeo (Monteverdi). *See* **Favola d'Orfeo.**

Orfeo ed Euridice (*Orpheus and Eurydice*), opera by Bertoni (lib. by Ranieri da Calzabigi, written for Gluck), prod. Venice, Teatro San Benedetto. I. 1776.

Opera by Gluck (lib. do.), prod. Vienna, Burgtheater, 5. X. 1762. (For Fr. version *see* **Orphée et Euridice**).

Orfeo, L' (*Orpheus*), opera by Luigi Rossi (lib. by Francesco Buti), prod. Paris, Palais Royal, 2. III. 1647.

Orff, Carl (b. Munich, 10. VII. 1895), Ger. comp. and teacher. Studied at Munich and became prof. of comp. at the Günther School there. He is also a cond. and ed. of old mus.
Works incl. mainly 9 operas, incl. *Carmina Burana* (settings of medieval poetry), *Die Kluge, Catulli Carmina, Antigonae* and *Oedipus der Tyrann* (both Hölderlin, after Sophocles), cantata *Des Turmes Auferstehung* (Franz Werfel); ballet *Der Feuerfarbene*; *Schulwerk* for combinations of popular instruments and similar comps. intended for use by amateurs; incid. mus. for Shakespeare's *Midsummer Night's Dream*, etc.

Organ, the most elaborate instrument playable by a single perf. Its origin lies in remote antiquity, e.g. the syrinx or panpipe. Later the wind was no longer supplied by the player's breath, but by bellows; the pipes were opened and closed by an action of keys, and a keyboard of pedals, played by the feet, was added to control the largest bass pipes. The number of pipes, ranging from 32 ft. down to a fraction of an inch, was enormously increased, and they were made in a growing variety of shapes from different materials, and with different speaking-mechanisms, each range being controlled by stops which could bring it into action or shut it off at the player's will. The number of manuals (hand keyboards) increased to 3 or more, which meant that a greater number of stops drawn before the perf. could be controlled and varied. From the late 19th cent. the bellows, formerly blown by hand, were operated mechan. and devices by which whole ranges of stops could be brought into action in var. combinations were invented, still further increasing the resources already enlarged by the couplers, by which the registration controlled by 2 manuals or by a manual and the pedals could be mechanically united. Expression was added by swell pedals prod. *crescendo* and *diminuendo*, but beyond that the player's hands and feet have no power to vary the tone either in strength or in quality.

Organ-Point (from Ger. *Orgelpunkt*), another term, used mainly in Amer., for Pedal-Point.

Organ Stops. *See* **Acoustic Bass, Acute Mixture, Bass Flute, Bassoon, Bell Gamba, Bombarde, Bombardon, Bourdon, Carillons, Claribel, Claribel Flute, Clarinet, Clarion, Clarion Mixture, Clarionet Flute, Closed Horn, Cor anglais, Cor-de-Nuit, Cor-Oboe, Cornet, Corno di Bassetto, Corno dolce, Cornopean, Cremona, Cymbal, Diapason, Diaphone, Dolcan, Dulciana, Dulciana Mixture, Echo, Fagotto, Fifteenth, Flageolet, Flautina, Flauto traverso, Flute, Flûte à cheminée, Flute Bass, Flûte d'amour, Flute Harmonic, Furniture, Gamba, Gedackt, Geigen Principal, Gemshorn, Grave Mixture, Hautboy, Hohl Flute, Hohlflöte, Horn, Horn Diapason, Keraulophon, Lieblich Flute, Lieblich Gedackt, Major Bass, Mixture, Oboe, Octave, Ophicleide, Piccolo, Posaune, Principal, Quint, Quintaton, Rohr Flute, Rohrflöte, Salicional, Sesquialtera, Sharp Mixture, Suabe Flute, Sub Bass, Sub Bourdon, Super Octave, Tremulant, Tromba, Trombone, Trumpet, Tuba, Twelfth, Unda Maris, Viol d'amour, Viol da Gamba, Viol d'orchestre, Viola, Violin Diapason, Violoncello, Violone, Voix céleste, Vox angelica, Vox humana, Wald Flute.**

Organistrum. *See* **Hurdy-Gurdy.**

Organo pieno (It.)
or
[Pro] Organo pleno (Lat.) } = full org.,
a direction indicating that an org. passage is to be played with the use of the full extent of the instrument's power, or in earlier mus. with a substantial body of tone.

Organum (Lat., lit. 'instrument', also 'organ'), a term (orig. a nickname) for early medieval mus. in parts, either moving wholly or mainly in parallel lines (9th cent.) or independently (11th cent.) or with florid melodies above a slow-moving plainsong (12th cent.).

Orgatron, an electrophonic org. invented by Everett of Michigan in 1934, prod. its notes by amplifying the vibration of harmonium reeds.

Orgelpunkt (Ger. = organ-point). *See* **Pedal-Point.**

Orgeni (actually Görger St. Jörgen (Anna Maria) Aglaia (b. Rima Szombat, 17. XII. 1841; d. Vienna, 15. III. 1926), Aus. soprano. Pupil of Pauline Viardot-García. Made her 1st stage appearance in Berlin, 1865.

Orgue expressif (Fr.) = **Harmonium.**

Orione, o sia Diana vendicata (*Orion, or Diana Avenged*), opera by J. C. Bach (lib. by Giovanni Gualberto Bottarelli), prod. London, King's Theatre, 19. II. 1763. J. C. Bach's 1st opera.

Orlandi, Santi (b. Florence, ?; d. Mantua, VII. 1619), It. comp. He was *maestro di cappella* to Ferdinando Gonzaga at Florence and succeeded Monteverdi as *maestro di cappella* to the Gonzaga family at Mantua in 1612.

Works incl. opera *Gli amori di Aci e Galatea;* 5 books of madrigals, etc.

Orlandini, Giuseppe Maria (b. ?; d. Florence, 24. X. 1760), It. comp. *Maestro di cappella* to the Duke of Tuscany at Florence, and app. to the same post at the cathedral there in 1732.

Works incl. *c.* 50 operas, e.g. *Amore e maestà, Antigona, Il marito giocatore, Nerone,* etc.; oratorios; cantatas; etc.

Orlando (*Roland*), opera by Handel (lib. by Grazio Braccioli, based on Ariosto's *Orlando furioso*), prod. London, King's Theatre, Haymarket, 27. I. 1733.

Orléans, Charles Duc d' (1391–1465), Fr. prince and poet. *See* **Debussy** (*Chansons de France*), **Dieren (van)** (songs).

Ormandy (actually Blau), **Eugene** (b. Budapest, 18. XI. 1899), Amer. cond. of Hung. origin. Studied vln. 1st with his father and then entered the Budapest R.A.M. for further studies with Hubay. He graduated in 1917, becoming leader of the Blüthner Orch. in Berlin. In 1921 he went to the U.S.A., taking various posts both as perf. and cond. In 1931 he was app. permanent cond. of the Minneapolis Symph. Orch., and in 1938 of the Philadelphia Symph. Orch. He was awarded the Fr. *Légion d'honneur* in 1952.

Ornaments. *See also* **Acciaccatura, Appoggiatura, Arpeggio, Mordent, Shake, Turn, Tremolo, Vibrato.**

Apart from the main O.s discussed under the above headings, the following are some of the terms found in old treatises on the subject. Some are now obs., either because the fashion of highly ornamented singing and playing is dead or because great elaboration is not suited to modern instruments:

Eng.:

Acute = Springer.
Backfall = Appoggiatura (from above).
Battery = Arpeggio.
Beat = Appoggiatura (from below).
Close Shake = Vibrato.
Forefall = Appoggiatura (from below).
Half fall, a semitonal Appoggiatura from below on the lute.
Lead (imper.), perform with an Appoggiatura.
Passing Appoggiatura, an unaccented A. inserting a note between 2 notes of a falling 3rd.
Prepare (imper.), perform with an Appoggiatura.
Prepared Shake, a Shake beginning with an Appoggiatura.
Relish = Turn.
Shake = Trill.
Sigh = Springer.
Slide, 2 notes below a principal note leading up to it.
Springer, a short auxiliary note inserted

after a main note, the reverse of an Appoggiatura.

Turned Shake, a Shake followed by a Turn.

Unprepared Shake, a Shake beginning at once on the main note, without an Appoggiatura.

Fr.:

Accent, an Appoggiatura inserting a grace-note between a rising or falling 3rd or repeating the 1st note of a rising or falling 2nd.

Appuyer (verb), perf. with an Appoggiatura.

Aspiration = Springer.

Battement = Mordent.

Brisé = Turn.

Cadence = Shake.

Cadence appuyée = Prepared Shake.

Cadence sans tremblement = Turn.

Chevroté (goaty), the description of a too rapid Shake.

Chute = Appoggiatura (from above or below).

Coulé or Coulade = Appoggiatura (from below) or Slide, in which all the intermediate notes are not clearly articulated.

Doublé = Turn.

Double Cadence = Turn.

Flatté = Slide.

Frappé = Passing Appoggiatura.

Harpègement = Arpeggio, which could be upwards or downwards according to the sign used.

Jeté = Port de voix double.

Martellement = Mordent with note above.

Pincé = Mordent with note below.

Pincé étouffé = Acciaccatura.

Pincé renversé = Shake.

Pincement = Mordent.

Plainte = Springer.

Port de voix = Appoggiatura (from below).

Port de voix double or jeté, a double Appoggiatura with 1 note below and 1 above the principal note.

Roulade, a general term for extended ornamental vocal phrases; more specifically an O. consisting of a descending scale with intermediate notes rising by 1 degree.

Suspension, the delaying of a note a fraction of time.

Tacté = Acciaccatura.

Tour de gosier = Turn.

Trait, a slide similar to the Coulé, but with all the intermediat notes articulated.

Tremblement = Shake.

Tremblement appuyé = Prepared Shake.

Trille = Shake.

Ger.:

Abzug, an Appoggiatura inserting a grace-note between a rising or falling 3rd or repeating the 1st note of a rising or falling 2nd.

Anschlag = Port de voix double.

Anschlagend (adj.), of Passing Appoggiatura.

Bebung = Vibrato.

Beisser = Mordent.

Brechung = Arpeggio.

Doppelschlag = Turn.

Nachschlag = Springer.

Pralltriller See p. 529.

Schleifer = Slide.

Schneller = Mordent with note above.

Triller = Shake.

Vorschlag = Appoggiatura.

Zusammenschlag = Mordent or Acciaccatura.

It.:

Circolo mezzo = Turn.

Groppo = Shake.

Mordente = Mordent.

Portamento = Appoggiatura (for another meaning see main entry).

Ribattuta (from *ribattere* = to strike again). The Eng. name of this O. might lit. be 'Rebound'. It consists of a repetition of 2 alternating adjacent notes several times with increasing speed, the note-values being progressively doubled, until a shake is worked up.

Tatto = Acciaccatura.

Tremoletto = Shake.

Trillo = Shake. *See also* **Vibrato.**

Lat.:

Tremor pressus = Vibrato.

Ornithoparcus (actually Vogelgesang or Vogelsang), **Andreas** (b. Meiningen, ?; d. ?), Ger. 15th–16-cent. mus. scholar. Studied (?) at Tübingen Univ., travelled in many countries and (?) held some post at Wittenberg Univ. Author of the Lat. treatise *Musicae activae micrologus* (1517), which was trans. into Eng. by J. Dowland (1609).

Ornstein, Leo (b. Krementchug, 11. XII. 1895), Rus. pianist and comp., naturalized in U.S.A. Studied at the St. Petersburg Cons., where he appeared as a child prodigy, settled in N.Y. in 1907, studying further at the Inst. of Mus. Art, and made his 1st concert appearance there in 1911.

Works incl. pantomime *Lima Beans*, pantomime ballet; incid. mus. to Aristophanes' *Lysistrata*; symph., 2 Nocturnes, *Nocturne and Dance of the Fates*, symph. poem *The Fog* for orch.; 2 pf. concertos; string 4tet, pf. 5tet; 2 vln. and pf. sonatas, sonata for cello and pf.; choral works; pf. mus., etc.

Orologio, Alessandro (b. Italy, *c.* 1550; d. ? Vienna, 1633), It comp. and instrumentalist. His career took him to Prague, Cassel, Dresden and Wolfenbüttel. He pub. several books of madrigals and canzonets, and a collection of Intradas 'for all kinds of instruments'.

Orpharion, an obs. instrument of the Cittern type. It had 6 or 7 pairs of strings played with a plectrum.

Orphée et Euridice, opera by Gluck (lib. by Pierre Louis Moline, trans from Calzabigi's *Orfeo ed Euridice*, of Gluck's 1st setting of which it is a revised version), prod. Paris, 2. VIII. 1774.

Orphée aux enfers (*Orpheus in the Underworld*), operetta by Offenbach (lib. by Hector Crémieux and Ludovic Halévy), prod. Paris, Bouffes-Parisiens, 21. X. 1858.

Orphéon (Fr.), a Fr. male-voice choral society similar to the Ger. *Liedertafel*.

Orpheus. *See also* **Favola d'Orfeo; Malheurs d'Orphée; Orfeide; Orfeo; Orfeo ed Euridice; Orphée; Orphée aux enfers; Orpheus og Euridice; Orpheus und Eurydike.**

Ballet by Stravinsky (choreography by George Balanshin), prod. N.Y., 29. IV. 1948.

Opera by Keiser (lib. by Friedrich Christian Bressand), prod. Brunswick (Part I: *Die sterbende Eurydice*) ? II. 1699. Hamburg (Part II: *Die verwandelte Leyer des Orpheus*), 1709.

Symph. poem by Liszt, comp. 1853–4, 1st perf. as an intro. to Gluck's *Orfeo*, Weimar, 16. II. 1854, with closing mus. on the same themes after the opera.

Orpheus Britannicus, a collection of vocal mus. by Purcell begun soon after Purcell's death by Henry Playford, who pub. a 1st vol. in 1698 and a 2nd in 1702; also a collection of Purcell's songs pub. by John Walsh in 1735.

Orpheus og Euridice, opera by Naumann (lib. by Charlotte Dorothea Biehl, based on Calzabigi), prod. Copenhagen, 21. I. 1786. The 1st grand opera on a Dan. lib.

Orpheus und Eurydike, opera by Křenek (lib. by Oskar Kokoschka), prod. Cassel, 27. XI. 1926.

Orr, C(harles). W(ilfred). (b. Cheltenham, 31. VII. 1893), Eng. comp. Educ. at Cheltenham Coll. He suffered much from ill-health in his youth and did not begin to study mus. at the G.S.M. in London until 1917. He has lived most of his life quietly at Painswick, Glos., and has never held any official mus. posts; but he did warwork in London during World War II.
Works incl. *A Cotswold Hill Tune* for string orch.; numerous songs, esp. settings of A. E. Housman, also D. G. Rossetti, James Joyce, etc.

Orr, Robin (b. Brechin, 2. VI. 1909), Scot. comp. Studied at the R.C.M. in London and with E. J. Dent at Cambridge, also with Casella at Siena and Nadia Boulanger in Paris. From 1938 to 1956 he was organist and director of studies at St. John's Coll., Cambridge. Prof. of mus. at Glasgow Univ. 1956–64, and at Cambridge since 1964.
Works incl. opera *Full Circle*; symph.

in one movement, divertimento for chamber orch.; 3 Lat. psalms for voice and string 4tet; sonatina for vln. and pf., vln. sonata, vla. sonata; pf. pieces; songs, etc.

Ortigue, Joseph Louis, d' (b. Cavaillon, 22. V. 1802; d. Paris, 20. XI. 1866), Fr. writer on mus. and authority on church mus. Succeeded Berlioz as critic of the *Journal des Débats*, having already contrib. to many other papers since 1829.

Ortiz, Diego (b. Toledo, *c.* 1525; d. ?), Span. comp. He went to Naples about the 1550s to become *maestro de capilla* to the viceroy, the Duke of Alva, where he worked with many other Span. musicians, incl. Salinas. He wrote an important treatise on ornamentation in viol mus., the *Trattado de Glosas*, pub. in 2 eds. (Span. and It.) in Rome, 1553.
Works incl. motets; variations for bass viol, etc.

Orto, Mabriano de (b. ?; d. Nivelles, II. 1529), Flem. singer and comp. His name may have been Dujardin, the It. form being taken when he went to Rome, where he was a singer in the Papal chapel in 1484–94, with Josquin des Prés. Early in the 16th cent. he became chaplain and singer at the court of Philip the Fair of Burgundy.
Works incl. Masses, motets and other church mus.; *chansons*, etc.

Osborne, George Alexander (b. Limerick, 24. IX. 1806; d. London, 16. XI. 1893), Ir. pianist. Studied in Belg. and afterwards taught pf. in Brussels. In 1826 he went to Paris, making further studies with Pixis and Kalkbrenner and becoming a friend of Chopin, Berlioz and Rossini. He settled in London in 1843, where he taught and championed Chopin's work.

O'Shaughnessy, Arthur (William Edgar) (1844–81), Eng. poet of Ir. descent. *See* **Music Makers** (Elgar).

Osiander, Lucas (b. Nuremberg, 16. XII. 1534; d. Stuttgart, 17. IX. 1604), Ger. theologian and comp., son of the reformer Andreas O. He comp. sacred songs and psalms in 4 parts with Ger. words.

Ossia (It., from *o sia* = or be it, or else), a word shown with an alternative passage, usually easier and sometimes more difficult, which may be perf. at will instead of that orig. written down by the comp. Such passages are usually shown in smaller notes above or below the stave. The word may also be used for alternatives where a comp. clearly wrote a passage of pf. mus. for a short keyboard and where it is clear that he would have written it otherwise for a modern pf. It also occurs, like the older *ovvero*, in 2nd alternative titles of mus. works (e.g. 'Così fan tutte, ossia La scuola degli amanti,' etc.).

Ossian. *See* **Macpherson, James.**
Works based on 'Ossian' *see* **Bainton**

(*Oithona*), **Carillo (J.)** (opera), **Coquard** (symph. poem), **Davie, Dupuis (S.)** (*Moïna*), **Gade** (overture), **Goossens** (symph. prelude), **Ippolitov-Ivanov** (symph. poem), **Kunzen** (*O.'s Harfe*), **Lesueur** (opera), **Pavesi** (*Fingallo e Comala*), **Reeve** (*Oscar and Malvina*), **Sobolevsky** (*Komala*), **Uthal** (Méhul), **Whyte** (*Comala*), **Zumsteeg** (*Kolma*).
9 songs by Schubert.

Osterc, Slavko (b. Veržej, 17. VI. 1895; d. Ljubljana, 23. V. 1941), Yugoslav comp. Studied with Jirák and Novák at the Prague Cons., also quarter-tone mus. with Hába. Later he became prof. at the Ljubljana Cons.
Works incl. 3 miniature operas; ballet; children's cantata; 2 string 4tets, trio for wind instruments, nonet; sonata for saxophone and pf.; pf. mus.; songs; quarter-tone comps., etc.

Ostinato (It. = obstinate), a persistently repeated figure in a comp. If it is in the bass, it is called *basso o.* A rhythm also can be called O., and so can some instrumental device, like Tchaikovsky's *pizzicato o.* in the 4th symph.

Ostrčil, Otakar (b. Smíchov nr. Prague, 25. II. 1879; d. Prague, 20. VIII. 1935), Cz. cond. and comp. Studied at Prague Univ. and became prof. of modern languages at the Commercial Acad. there. He had already studied mus., esp. with Fibich, and in 1909 he became cond. of an amateur orch. and in 1914 at the Vinohrady Theatre. He succeeded Kovařovic as cond. of the Nat. Theatre in 1920.
Works incl. operas *The Death of Vlasta*, *Kunala's Eyes*, *The Bud*, *Legend of Erin* and *John's Kingdom*; incid. mus. for Jaroslav Kvapil's play *The Orphan*; *The Legend of St. Zita* for tenor, chorus, orch. and org. and other choral works; symph. in A maj., sinfonietta, 2 suites, symph. poem *The Tale of Šemik*, *Rustic Festival* and *Impromptu* for orch.; *Ballad of the Dead Cobbler* and *Cz. Ballad* for declamation and orch.; string 4tet in B maj., sonatina for vln., vla. and pf.; songs, etc.

Ostrovsky, Alexander Nikolaievich (1823–86), Rus. dramatist. *See* **Arensky** (*Dream on the Volga*), **Blaramberg** (*Tushino* and *Voyevoda*), **Dzerzhinsky** (*Storm*), **Kashperov** (do.), **Káta Kabanová** (Janáček), **Serov** (*Power of Evil*), **Snow Maiden** (Rimsky-Korsakov), **Tchaikovsky** (*Snegurotchka*), **Tcherepnin (N.)** (*Poverty no Crime*), **Voyevoda** (Tchaikovsky).

O'Sullivan, Denis (b. San Francisco, 25. IV. 1868; d. Columbus, Ohio, 1. II. 1908), Amer. baritone of Ir. descent. Studied in Florence, London and Paris. Made his 1st concert appearance in London and his 1st on the stage in Dublin in 1895.

O'Sullivan, Seumas (1879–1958), Ir. poet. *See* **Moeran** (6 poems).

Otello, opera by Verdi (lib. by Boito, after Shakespeare), prod. Milan, Teatro alla Scala, 5. II. 1887.

Otello, ossia Il Moro di Venezia (*Othello, or The Moor of Venice*), opera by Rossini (lib. by Marchese Francesco Berio di Salsa, after Shakespeare), prod. Naples, Teatro Fondo, 4. XII. 1816.

Otescu, Ion Nonna (b. Bucharest, 3. XII. 1888; d. Bucharest, 25. III. 1940), Rum. cond. and comp. Studied at Bucharest and at the Cons. and Schola Cantorum in Paris. On his return he founded what became the Royal Opera at Bucharest, and cond. this as well as the Phil. Orch. He became director of the Royal Acad. of Mus. and of the Opera.
Works incl. operas *Ilderim* (after Carmen Sylva) and *De la matei cetire*; ballets *Ileana Cosinzeana* and *Le Rubis enchanté*; symph. poems *Le Temple de Gnide* (after Montesquieu), *Narcisse* and others, etc.

Othello. *See also* **Otello.**
Concert overture by Dvořák, Op. 93, ref. to Shakespeare's tragedy, comp. 1892 and forming, with *Amid Nature* and *Carnival*, a cycle with thematic connections orig. called *Nature, Life and Love*.

Othmayr, Kaspar (b. Amberg, 12. III. 1515; d. Nuremberg, 4. II. 1553), Ger. clergyman and musician. Studied at Heidelberg Univ. and was a pupil of Lemlin for mus. there. He held church appts. at Heilsbronn and Ansbach, but *c*. 1550 retired to Nuremberg on account of religious controversies, himself being a Lutheran.
Works incl. Lat. motets, Ger. hymns and other scared mus.; an Epitaph on Luther's death; 26 secular songs contrib. to Georg Forster's collection, etc.

Ott, Hans (b. ?; d. Nuremberg, 1546), Ger. mus. ed. His collections, all pub. at Nuremberg, incl. 121 songs (1534) and an important collection of 13 Masses (1539).

Ottava (It.) = Octave.

Ottavino (It. from *ottava* = 8ve), the current It. name of the 8ve fl. elsewhere called Piccolo (from *flauto piccolo* = little fl.).

Otterloo, (Jan) Willem van (b. Winterswijk, 27. XII. 1907), Dutch cond. and comp. Studied at the Amsterdam Cons. under Dresden and others. App. 2nd cond. of the Utrecht Munic. Orch. in 1933 and 1st in 1937.
Works incl. symph., 3 suites and passacaglia for orch.; chamber mus.; pf. and org. works, etc.

Otto, Lisa (b. Dresden, 14. XI. 1919), Ger. soprano. Studied pf. and singing at the Dresden Hochschule für Musik from 1938 to 1940, making her début as a singer in 1941. From 1945 to 1950 she sang at the Dresden State Opera and in 1952 became a member of the Berlin State Opera. She is best known in lighter soubrette roles.

Otto, Stephan (b. Freiberg, Saxony, 1603; d. Schandau, 2. X. 1656), Ger. comp. Studied at Freiberg under Christoph Demantius, and after an appt. at Augsburg he became cantor at his home town in 1632 and at Schandau in 1639. Hammerschmidt was among his pupils.

Works incl. *Kronen-Krönlein*, a collection of sacred vocal pieces in a mixed motet and madrigal style, for 3–8 voices, setting of Luther's hymn 'Ein' feste Burg' for 19 voices, etc.

Ottobi, Giovanni. *See* Hothby.

Ottone, rè di Germania (*Otho, King of Germany*), opera by Handel (lib. by Nicola Francesco Haym), prod. London, King's Theatre, Haymarket, 12. I. 1723.

Otway, Thomas (1652–85), Eng. dramatist. *See* Lenton (*Venice Preserved*).

Oudin, Eugène (Espérance) (b. N.Y., 24. II. 1858; d. London, 4. XI. 1894), Amer. baritone of Fr. descent. Studied law at Yale Univ. and practised in for a time, but during a holiday in London in 1886 decided to turn to mus. He made his 1st stage appearance in N.Y. that year, with Louise Parker, who became his wife on 4. XII. In 1891 he 1st appeared in opera in London as the Templar in Sullivan's *Ivanhoe*.

Oulibicheff. *See* Ulibishev.

Ours, L' (*The Bear*), nickname of Haydn's symph. No. 82 in C maj., comp. for Paris in 1786.

Ouseley, Frederick (Arthur) Gore (b. London, 12. VIII. 1825; d. Hereford, 6. IV. 1889), Eng. organist, comp. and divine. Studied at Oxford, where he took the D.Mus. in 1854 and was app. Prof. of Mus. in 1855. Founder of St. Michael's Coll., Tenbury. He succeeded to his father's baronetcy in 1844. He ed. old mus. and wrote books on technique.

Works incl. *c.* 70 anthems; 4 services, oratorios, *The Martyrdom of St. Polycarp* and *Hagar*; over 30 preludes and fugues, 2 sonatas and other works for org.; 2 string 4tets; part-songs, glees; songs etc.

Ouverture (Fr.) *See* Overture.

Overblowing, the playing of wind instruments in such a way that the upper harmonics are prod. instead of the fundamental notes. Brass instruments prod. a greater number of harmonics than woodwind. O. may occur by accident in org. pipes by too great a pressure of wind, but safety-valve devices have been invented to prevent this.

Overspun, the lower strings of instruments of the vln. family and also those of the pf. are O., i.e. spun round with wire.

Overstrung, strings in pfs. which are made in 2 ranges crossing each other

diagonally to save space and to secure greater length in the strings.

Overtones. *See* Harmonics and Partials.

Overture (from Fr. *ouverture* = opening), an instrumental introductory comp. preceding some other large work, esp. an opera or oratorio; also sometimes an independent comp. for concert use, e.g. Mendelssohn's *Hebrides* and Brahms's *Tragic* O.s. From the time of Lully to that of Handel the O. in its Fr. form had a slow intro. and a fugal *allegro*. often followed by a return to the slow section or by a new slow portion, and in some cases by one or more independent pieces in dance form, in which case it resembled the Suite; hence Bach's O.s are in fact suites with 1st movements in Fr. O. form. The It. O. form differed from the Fr. in the late 17th and 18th cents. by being in several movements approximating more to the early symph., to which in fact it gave birth.

In opera the mus. of the O. had no special relevance to the work itself up to the time of Rameau, and sometimes not afterwards (e.g. Rossini, except his O. to *Guillaume Tell*). Gluck's mature O.s foreshadow the character and atmosphere of the operas to which they belong, and from his time on the actual mus. material of the O. was more often than not drawn from the opera itself to a greater or smaller extent.

Ovid (Publius Ovidius Naso) (43 B.C.– A.D. 17), Rom. poet. *See* Dittersdorf (*Metamorphoses*), **Mudarra, Philémon et Baucis** (Gounod), **Rebikov** (*Metamorphoses*), **Steinberg** (do.).

Ovvero (It. = or rather, or else, lit. from *o vero*, or truly), an earlier word for *ossia*; also found in front of 2nd, alternative titles of mus. works.

Owen, Wilfred (1893–1918), Eng. poet. *See* **Morning Heroes** (Bliss), **War Requiem** (Britten).

Ox Minuet. *Die Ochsenmenuette* is the title of a *Singspiel* by Seyfried, prod. in Vienna in 1823, with mus. arr. from comps. by Haydn. It was based on 2 earlier Fr. works, *Le Menuet du Bœuf, ou Une Leçon de Haydn* (1805) and *Haydn, ou le Menuet du Bœuf* (1812). The title is sometimes mistakenly thought to be the nickname of one of Haydn's minuets.

Oxford Symphony, the name given to Haydn's symph. No. 92 in G maj., comp. 1788. It was not written for Oxford, but received its title after it was perf. there in VII. 1791 when Haydn was given the hon. degree of D.Mus.

Ozaneaux, Jean Georges (1795–1852), Fr. historian and author. *See* Hérold (*Dernier Jour de Missolonghi*).

Ozerov, Vladislav Alexandrovich (1769– 1816), Rus. dramatist. *See* Mussorgsky (*Oedipus in Athens*).

P

p (abbr.). Used in mus. for *piano* = soft, in this form: *p*; sometimes also for the pedal in pf. mus., in this: *P*. In the latter case, however, it is more often *Ped.*

Pabst. Ger. family of musicians:
1. August P. (b. Elberfeld, 30. V. 1811; d. Riga, 21. VII. 1885), organist and comp. He became organist at Königsberg and later director of the Mus. School at Riga. Comp. operas, etc.
2. Louis P. (b. Königsberg, 18. VII. 1846; d. Moscow, after 1903), pianist and comp., son of prec. Studied under his father, made his 1st appearance as pianist in 1862, lived at Liverpool, Riga, Melbourne, founding mus. schools in the latter 2 places, and finally held a professorship in Moscow. Comp. melodramas, pf. works, songs, etc.
3. Paul P. (b. Königsberg, 27. V. 1854; d. Moscow, 9. VI. 1897), pianist and comp., brother of prec. Studied under his father and brother, later under Liszt. Settled in Moscow as prof. at the Cons. Comp. pf. mus., incl. operatic paraphrases.

Pacchierotti, Gaspard (b. Fabriano nr. Ancona, V. 1740; d. Padua, 28. X. 1821), It. castrato soprano. Chorister at Forlì Cathedral, then at St. Mark's, Venice, under Bertoni, he made his operatic début in 1766 and became *primo musico* at the Teatro San Benedetto in Venice. Later sang in Palermo, London, Naples, etc., and retired to Padua in 1792.

Pacchioni, Antonio (Maria) (b. Modena, 5. VII. 1654; d. Modena, 16. VII. 1738), It. priest and comp. Studied at Modena Cathedral, where he became chaplain at the ducal court and later asst. choirmaster. In 1733 he and Pitoni settled a dispute between Martini and Redi about the solution of a canon by Animuccia.
Works incl. Masses and other church mus., oratorios, etc.

Pace (also called Pacius), **Pietro** (b. Loreto, 1559; d. Loreto, 11. IV. 1622), It. comp. Was organist at Pesaro in 1597 and of the Santa Casa at Loreto, 1591–2, and again, 1611–22.
Works incl. mus. for Ignazio Bracci's *L'ilarocosmo, ovvero Il mondo lieto*; Magnificats, motets (with accomp.) and other church mus.; *Arie spirituali* and madrigals with and without accomp., etc.

Pacelli, Asprilio (b. Vasciano nr. Narni, Umbria, *c*. 1570; d. Warsaw, 4. V. 1623), It. comp. Choirmaster of the Ger. Coll. and later of the Vatican basilica in Rome until 1603, when he went to the court of Sigismund III of Pol. at Warsaw, succeeding Marenzio.

Works incl. motets, psalms, *Sacrae cantiones*; madrigals, etc.

Pachelbel, Johann (b. Nuremberg, VIII. 1653; d. Nuremberg, 3. III. 1706), Ger. organist and comp. Studied under Heinrich Schwemmer at home and after holding brief appts. at Altdorf and Regensburg, went to Vienna, *c*. 1671–2. Between 1677 and 1695 he was organist successively at Eisenach, Erfurt, Stuttgart and Gotha, and in 1695 was app. organist at St. Sebaldus's Church at Nuremberg.
Works incl. 94 org. fugues on the Magnificat, org. variations and preludes on chorales; suites for 2 vlns. *Musikalisches Ergötzen*; 6 sets of variations for harpsichord *Hexachordum Apollinis*, etc.

Pachelbel, Wilhelm Hieronymus (b. Erfurt, VIII. 1685; d. Nuremberg, 1764), Ger. organist and comp., son of prec. Pupil of his father. Organist at St. Sebaldus's Church, Nuremberg, from 1719. Comp. org. and harpsichord mus., etc.

Pachmann, Vladimir de (b. Odessa, 27. VII. 1848; d. Rome, 6. I. 1933), Rus. pianist of Aus. descent. Studied 1st under his father, a univ. prof., and later in Vienna, and made his 1st concert appearance in Rus. in 1869. In 1882 he 1st visited London. He became a famous but somewhat eccentric exponent of Chopin.

Pacific 231, symph. movement by Honegger, named after a railway engine and depicting its start and progress, not merely realistically, but, the comp. claims, 'lyrically'. 1st perf. Paris, at a Kussevitsky concert, 8. V. 1924.

Pacini, Giovanni (b. Catania, 17. II. 1796; d. Pescia, 6. XII. 1867), It. comp. Studied 1st under his father, a famous tenor, and later at Bologna and Venice. At the age of 17 he prod. his 1st opera at Venice. He became *maestro di cappella* to Napoleon's widow, the Empress Marie Louise, and in 1834 settled at Viareggio, where he opened a mus. school, later transferred to Lucca. For this he wrote some theoret. treatises.
Works incl. operas *Annetta e Lucindo*, *La sacerdotessa d'Irminsul*, *La schiava in Bagdad*, *La gioventù di Enrico V* (after Shakespeare's *Henry IV*), *L'ultimo giorno di Pompei* (not based on Bulwer-Lytton), *Gli Arabi nelle Gallie*, *Saffo*, *Medea*, *Lorenzino de' Medici*, *La regina di Cipro*, *Il saltimbanco*, *Ivanhoe* (after Scott) and over 60 others; incid. mus. for Sophocles' *Oedipus Rex*; Masses, oratorios, cantata for Dante anniversary and others; string 4tet in C maj., etc.

Paciotti, Pietro Paolo (b. Tivoli, *c*. 1550; d. ? Rome, after 1614), It. 16th-cent. comp. Choirmaster of the Seminario Romano in Rome, 1591. Wrote Masses, motets, madrigals, etc.

Pacius. *See also* **Pace.**

Pacius, Fredrik (b. Hamburg, 19. III. 1809; d. Helsinki, 9. I. 1891), Ger. violinist and comp., naturalized Finn. Pupil of Spohr and Hauptmann at Cassel, violinist in the court orch. at Stockholm, 1828–34, when he became mus. teacher at Helsinki Univ. He remained in the Fin. capital, estab. orchestral concerts there in 1845 and became prof. of mus. at the univ. in 1860.

Works incl. operas *Kung Karls Jakt* and *Loreley*; incid. mus., for Topelius's *Princess of Cyprus*; vln. concerto; cantatas; songs incl. *Suomis Saang* and *Vaart Land*, both adapted as Fin. nat. anthems.

Packe, Thomas (b. ?; d. ?), Eng. 15th–16th-cent. comp. He was a knight and prob. held no official mus. post.

Works incl. Masses, motets and a *Te Deum*.

Paderewski, Ignacy (Jan) (b. Kurylówka, Podolia, 6. XI. 1860; d. New York, 29. VI. 1941), Pol. pianist, comp. and statesman. Studied at the Warsaw Cons. and went on his 1st concert tour in 1877. After teaching in 1878–81 at the Cons. he went to Berlin for further study, finishing with Leschetizky in Vienna, reappearing there and in Paris in 1887. In 1890 he paid his 1st visit to Eng. and in 1891 to U.S.A. During World War I he collected large sums for the Pol. relief fund and in 1919 became the 1st president of the Pol. Republic.

Works incl. operas *Manru* and *Sakuntala* (after Kalidasa); symph. in B min.; concerto in A min. and Pol. Fantasy for pf. and orch.; vln. and pf. sonata; sonata in Eb min. and many other pf. works; songs, etc.

Padilla y Ramos, Mariano (b. Murcia, 1842; d. Auteuil nr. Paris, 23. XI. 1906), Span. baritone. Studied in It. and toured Eur. extensively. Married Désirée Artôt in 1869.

Padlock, The, opera by Dibdin (lib. by Isaac Bickerstaffe, based on a story by Cervantes, *El celoso extremeño*), prod. London, Drury Lane Theatre, 3. X. 1768.

Padmâvati, opera by Roussel (lib., in Fr., by Louis Laloy), prod. Paris, Opéra, 1. VI. 1923.

Padovana (It., i.e. of Padua). The It. name of the Pavan.

Padovano, Annibale. *See* **Annibale.**

Padua, Bartolino da (b. ?, d. ?), It. 14th–15th-cent. comp. Wrote madrigals and *ballate* in the It. *Ars nova* style.

Paer, Ferdinando (b. Parma, 1. VI. 1771; d. Paris, 3. V. 1839), It. comp. Studied with Gasparo Ghiretti at Parma, and at the age of 20 became a cond. at Venice. Having married the singer Riccardi, he was invited to Vienna in 1798, where she was engaged at the court opera, and prod. *Camilla* there. In 1803 he went to Dresden, remaining as opera cond. until

1806, and there prod. *Leonora*, a setting of an It. version of Gaveaux's opera on which Beethoven's *Fidelio* was also based later. In 1807, after accomp. Napoleon to Warsaw and Posen, he was app. his *maître de chapelle* and settled in Paris.

Works incl. *Circe*, *Il tempo fa giustizia a tutti*, *Il nuovo Figaro* (after Beaumarchais' *Mariage de Figaro*), *Il matrimonio improvviso*, *Idomeneo*, *Eroe e Leandro*, *L'intrigo amoroso*, *Il principe di Taranto*, *Camilla*, *o Il sotterraneo*, *La sonnambula*, *Achille*, *Leonora*, *o L'amore conjugale*, *Sofonisba*, *Numa Pompilio*, *Agnese di Fitz-Henry*, *Didone abbandonata*, *Le Maître de chapelle*, *La Marquise de Brinvilliers* (with Auber, Batton, Berton, Blangini, Boïeldieu, Carafa, Cherubini, and Hérold) and over 20 others; oratorios *Il santo sepolcro* and *La passione*, Masses and motets; *c.* 12 cantatas (It., Fr. and Ger.); Bacchanalian symph. for orch., Bridal March for the wedding of Napoleon and Joséphine, etc.

Paesiello. *See* **Paisiello.**

Paganini, Niccolò (b. Genoa, 27. X. 1782; d. Nice, 27. V. 1840), It. violinist and comp. Learnt guitar and vln. from his father, afterwards with the theatre violinist Servetto and the cathedral *maestro di cappella* Giacomo Costa. At the age of 11 he made his 1st appearance as a violinist. As a comp. he profited by the advice of Gnecco, and in 1795 his father sent him to the violinist Alessandro Rolla at Parma. While there he also studied comp. with Gasparo Ghiretti, and in 1797 made his 1st professional tour. After that he became increasingly famous, travelled widely, beginning with Vienna and Paris in 1828–1831, and in the latter year went to Eng. for the 1st time. In 1834 he invited Berlioz in Paris to write a concert work for vla. *Harold en Italie* was the result, but he never played it.

Works incl. 2 vln. concertos (Op. 7 with the *Rondo alla campanella*), variations (e.g. on 'God save the King') and concert pieces for vln. and orch.; 3 string 4tets with a guitar part; 12 sonatas for vln. and guitar; 24 *Capricci* (studies) for vln. solo, etc.

Paganini Rhapsody, a work by Rakhmaninov for pf. and orch. entitled *Rhapsody on a Theme by Paganini*, but actually a set of variations, without opus number, comp. in 1934, 1st perf. Baltimore, 7. XI. 1934. The theme, in A min., from P.'s *Capricci* for unaccomp. vln., is the same as that used by Brahms for the variations below.

Paganini Studies, a set of 6 studies for pf. by Liszt, transcribed from P.'s vln. *Capricci* (except No. 3, which is another version of *La Campanella*), ded. to Clara Schumann. There is an orig. version, *Études d'exécution transcendante d'après Paganini*, written in 1838, and a revised

Paganini Variations

one, *Grandes Études de Paganini*, written in 1851.

2 sets of studies for pf. (6 each) by Schumann on themes from P.'s vln. *Capricci*: Op. 3, written in 1832, and Op. 10, written in 1833.

Paganini Variations, 2 sets of studies for pf. in variation form by Brahms, Op. 35, comp. in 1866, on a theme in A min. from P.'s vln. *Capricci*.

Pagliacci (*Clowns*), opera by Leoncavallo (lib. by comp.), prod. Milan, Teatro dal Verme, 21. V. 1892.

Pagliardi, Giovanni Maria (b. Florence, ?; d. ?), It. 17th-cent. comp. *Maestro di cappella* to the Duke of Tuscany at Florence and in the 1660s at 2 churches in Rome.

Works incl. operas *Caligula delirante, Lisimaco, Numa Pompilio, Attilio Regolo, Il pazzo per forza* and *Il tiranno di Colco*; motets, sacred songs; vocal duets, etc.

Pahissa, Jaime (b. Barcelona, 7. X. 1880), Span. comp. Pupil of Morera.

Works incl. operas *La presó de Lleida, Canigó, Gala Placidia, La Morisca. Marianela, La Princesa Margarida*; orchestral works; pf. pieces, etc.

Paine, John Knowles (b. Portland, Me., 9. I. 1839; d. Cambridge, Mass., 25. IV. 1906), Amer. organist, comp. and teacher. Studied at home and at the Hochschule für Musik in Berlin, gave org. recitals in Ger. and returned to U.S.A. in 1861. He became instructor in mus. at Harvard Univ. in 1862, asst. prof. in 1872 and full prof. in 1875. Hon. D.Mus. of Yale, 1890.

Works incl. opera *Azara*; incid. mus. for Sophocles' *Oedipus Tyrannus* and Aristophanes' *Birds*; Mass in D maj.; oratorio *St. Peter*; cantatas *A Song of Promise, Phoebus arise* (Wm. Drummond), *The Realm of Fancy* (Keats), *The Nativity* (Milton); symphs. in C min. and A maj. (*Spring*), symph. poems *An Island Fantasy* and *The Tempest* (after Shakespeare), overture for Shakespeare's *As you like It*; string 4tet, pf. trio; vln. and pf. sonata; instrumental pieces, etc.

Paintings, etc., Music based on:

Fibich, *Malirske Studie* for pf. (Ruysdael, Brueghel, sen., Fra Angelico, Correggio and Watteau).

Frank, duets from Kate Greenaway's *At the Window.*

Gasco, var. works (Besnard, Carpaccio, Giorgione and Rossetti).

Gipps, *Death on the Pale Horse* (Blake).

Granados, *Goyescas* for pf. and opera (Goya).

Hahn, *Portraits de peintres* for pf. (Cuyp, Potter, van Dyck, Watteau).

Hallén, *The Isle of the Dead* for orch. (Böcklin).

Honegger, *Danse des morts* (Holbein).

Paintings

Huber, Böcklin Symph. (No. 2).

Josten, *Jungle* (Henri Rousseau's 'Forêt exotique').

Kazanly, *Villa by the Sea* for orch. (Böcklin).

Liszt, *Il sposalizio* (Raphael) in *Années de pèlerinage* for pf.

—, *The Battle of the Huns*, symph. poem (Kaulbach).

—, *Totentanz* for pf. and orch. (Orcagna).

Martinů, *The Frescoes of Piero della Francesca* for orch.

Mohaupt, *Stadtpfeifermusik* (Dürer).

Morillo, *Pinturas negras de Goya.*

Mussorgsky, *Pictures at an Exhibition* for pf. (Victor Hartmann).

Orefice, *Quadri di Böcklin* for pf. (6 pictures).

Potter, *The Enigma* (variations in the style of 5 painters).

Rakhmaninov, *The Isle of the Dead*, symph. poem (Böcklin).

Reger, Böcklin suite for orch. (4 pictures).

Respighi, *Trittico Botticelliano* for orch.

Rózycki, orchestral prelude *Mona Lisa Gioconda* (on Leonardo da Vinci's portrait).

Schubert, song *Liebeslauschen* (Schlechta's poem on a picture by Schnorr).

Schulz-Beuthen, *The Isle of the Dead* for orch. (Böcklin).

Tcherepnin (N.), *The Rus. Alphabet*, pf. pieces on Benois's picture-book.

Toch, Serenade *In Spitzwegs Art* for 2 vlns. and vla.

Vaughan Williams, *Job*, masque for dancing (based on Blake's illustrations for the Book of Job); settings by Gwendolen Raverat.

Walton, *Portsmouth Point* and *Dr. Syntax* overtures (Rowlandson).

—, *Scapino* overture (etching by Callot).

Weingartner, *Die Gefilde der Seligen*, symph. poem (Böcklin).

White (Felix), *Astarte Syriaca* for orch. (D. G. Rossetti).

Wood (Haydn), *3 Pictures* for orch. (2 by Luke Fildes and Hal's *Laughing Cavalier*).

Woyrsch, Böcklin suite for orch. (4 pictures).

Zandonai, *Quadri di Segantini* for orch.

In opera S. Arnold's *The Enraged Musician* is based on Hogarth's picture; the finale in Auber's *Marco Spada* repro. Horace Vernet's 'La Confession du bandit'; Rheinberger's *Die sieben Raben* is founded on Schwind's cycle of paintings; Julius Röntgen's *The Laughing Cavalier* is inspired by Frans Hals's picture; Schilling's *Mona Lisa*, intro. the subject of Leonardo da Vinci's portrait; Mraczek's *Herrn Dürers Bild* deals with that master's 'Madonna "am Weisenzaun"'; Hindemith's *Mathis der Maler* is based on

Matthias Grünewald's altar-piece at Colmar; R. Strauss's *Friedenstag* on Velazquez's 'Surrender of Breda'; Stravinsky's *The Rake's Progress* on Hogarth's series (*see also* Gasco). In ballet there is A. Tcherepnin's *Ajanta Frescoes*; Inghelbrecht's *El Greco* uses that master's 'Burial of Count Orgaz'; *The Rake's Progress* by Gavin Gordon is based on Hogarth settings by Rex Whistler.

Paisible (or Peasable), James (b. ? Fr., *c.* 1650; d. London, *c.* VIII. 1721), Eng. musician, ? of Fr. extraction. Member of the King's Band in London.

Works incl. incid. mus. for Shakespeare's *Henry IV* (*The Humours of Sir John Falstaff*), Southerne's adaptation of Aphra Behn's *Oroonoko*, Bancroft's *King Edward III*, Cibber's *She wou'd and she wou'd not* and *Love's Last Shift* and Mme. La Roche Guilhen's *Rare en tout*; duets, sonatas and pieces for fl., etc.

Paisiello, Giovanni (b. Taranto, 9. V. 1740; d. Naples, 5. VI. 1816), It. comp. Pupil of Durante, later of Cotumacci and Abos at the Cons. Sant' Onofrio in Naples 1754–63, where he first comp. some oratorios and church mus. But with *Il ciarlone* (Bologna, 1764) he began his successful career as a comp. of *opera buffa*, and over the next 20 years prod. many works in Modena, Naples, Venice, etc. In the service of the Rus. court at St. Petersburg 1776–84, he there comp., among others, his most famous opera, *Il barbiere di Siviglia* (after Beaumarchais' *Le Barbier de Séville*, 1782), which held the stage until Rossini's setting of the same story (1816). Back in Naples, he was app. *maestro di cappella* and court comp. to Ferdinand IV. Summoned to Paris as mus. director of Napoleon's household in 1802, he remained only a year, and returned to his old post in Naples.

Works incl. *c.* 100 operas, e.g. *Il ciarlone* (after Goldoni's *La pupilla*), *I Francesi brillanti*, *Demetrio*, *Le finte Contesse*, *L'idolo cinese*, *Socrate immaginario*, *La serva padrona*, *Il barbiere di Siviglia* (after Beaumarchais), *Il mondo della luna*, *Il Rè Teodoro in Venezia*, *L'Antigono*, *Nina, ossia La pazza per amore*, *La molinara* (orig. *L'amor contrastato*), *Proserpine*, etc.; oratorios *La Passione di Gesù Cristo*, *Christus*, etc.; cantatas; Masses, 2 Requiems, *Miserere* and other church mus.; symphs.; concertos, etc.; 6 string 4tets, 12 pf. 4tets; keyboard mus., etc.

Paix, Jakob (b. Augsburg, 1556; d. ?, *c.* 1620), Ger. comp., organist at Lauingen in Swabia. He wrote Ger. songs and Lat. church mus., but his chief work was his collection of keyboard music (pub. 1583), incl. orig. comps. as well as highly ornamented arrangements of songs and motets.

Paladilhe, Émile (b. Montpellier, 3.

VI. 1844; d. Paris, 8. I. 1926), Fr. comp. Studied at the Paris Cons. and gained the Prix de Rome in 1860.

Works incl. operas *Le Passant* (lib. by François Coppée), *L'Amour africain*, *Suzanne*, *Diana*, *Patrie* (after Sardou); oratorio *Saintes Maries de la mer*; 2 Masses; symph. and *Fragments symphoniques* for orch.; songs, etc.

Palazol, Berenguier de (b. Palol, Catalonia, ?; d. ?), Catalonian troubadour of the 2nd half of the 12th cent. His 8 surviving songs have Catalan words, but are stylistically akin to those by Provençal comps.

Palester, Roman (b. Sniatyn, 28. XII. 1907), Pol. comp. Studied at Lwów and under Kasimierz Sikorski in Warsaw. For some years he lived in Paris, later settled in Warsaw. During the 1939–45 war he was imprisoned by the Gers.

Works incl. opera *The Living Stones*; ballets *Song of the Earth* and *The End of the World*; incid. and film mus.; Requiem and Psalm v for solo voices, chorus and orch.; 4 symphs., symph. suite, *Symph. Mus.*, *Wedding Celebration*, *Musique polonaise*, variations (overture) and other orchestral works, *Concertino* for saxophone, pf. concerto; *Divertimento* for 6 instruments, 3 string 4tets, sonatinas for 3 clars. and for vln. and cello; sonata for 2 vlns. and pf.; org. toccata; pf. pieces; songs, etc.

Palestrina, Giovanni Pierluigi da (b. Palestrina, (?) 1525; d. Rome, 2. II. 1594), It. comp. Son of Sante Pierluigi, a well-to-do citizen. Became a choir-boy at the cathedral of St. Agapit in his native town. When the Bishop of Palestrina went to the church of Santa Maria Maggiore in Rome in 1534, he took P. with him, and he remained there until he was 14, when his voice broke. After a stay at home he returned to Rome in 1540 and (?) became a pupil of Firmin Le Bel. At 19 he was app. organist and singing-master at St. Agapit's at home. On 12. VI. 1547 he married Lucrezia Gori, who inherited money and property from her father.

P. was app. *maestro di cappella* of the Julian choir in Rome, 1551, and pub. a madrigal and a 1st book of Masses in 1554. Pope Julius III made him a member of the Pontifical Choir in 1555, in spite of the resentment of members at his having been elected without examination. Pope Marcellus II, who succeeded that year, to whom P. ded. the *Missa Papae Marcelli*, intended to reform the church mus. with P.'s help, but d., and under his successor, Paul IV, P. retired from the choir with a pension, becoming *maestro di cappella* at the church of San Giovanni, in the Lateran. When under Pius IV in 1560 that church wished to make economies, P. resigned and was app. the next year *maestro di cappella* at Santa Maria Maggiore.

Before the accession of Pius V in 1566, P. was made director of the new Roman seminary in 1565. The Council of Trent having already laid down some reforms in church mus. in 1563, the new pope, Gregory XIII, in 1577 directed P. and Zoilo to revise the Gradual. P.'s wife having d. in VII. 1580, he applied for admission to the priesthood, but having been made a canon, he renounced his vows and was married again on 28. III. 1581 to Virginia Dormuli, the widow of a prosperous furrier, in whose business he now took a considerable interest. After the accession of the next pope, Sixtus V, there was a scheme to app. P. *maestro di cappella* of the Pontifical Choir, but it was defeated, 1585. Much of P.'s mus. was pub., partic. in the last 10 years of his life, incl. 4 vols. of motets and 6 of Masses; the 7th of the latter was sent to press in I. 1594 when P. was seized with the illness from which he d.

Works incl. 41 Masses for 4 voices, 38 for 5 voices, 22 for 6 voices, 4 for 8 voices; 67 motets for 4 voices, 108 for 5 voices, 34 for 6 voices, 2 for 7 voices, 56 for 8 voices, 6 for 12 voices; 45 hymns for 4 voices; 68 offertories for 5 voices; 12 Lamentations; 7 Litanies; 4 psalms for 12 voices; 1 antiphon; 35 Magnificats; 7 *Cantiones sacrae*; 61 spiritual madrigals; 95 secular madrigals; 12 *Cantiones profanae*, etc.

Palestrina, opera by Pfitzner (lib. by comp.), prod. Munich, 12. VI. 1917.

Paliashvili, Zakharia Petrovich (b. Kutais, 26. VIII. 1871; d. Tiflis, 6. X. 1933), Rus. (Georgian) comp. Studied at the Moscow Cons. under Taneiev, later taught at Tiflis, cond. the orch. and made excursions into eastern Georgia to study its folk mus., on which his work is based.

Works incl. operas *Abessalom and Eteri, Twilight* and *Latavra*; choral works; folksong arrs., etc.

Palindrome, lit. a word or poem reading the same backwards as forwards. In mus. a piece constructed in the same way, more or less loosely, as e.g. the prelude and postlude in Hindemith's *Ludus tonalis*, the same comp.'s 1-act opera *Hin und zurück* or the prelude to Lambert's ballet *Horoscope*. The procedure is that of *Recte et retro* or *Rovescio* on a larger scale.

Pallavicini, Carlo (b. Brescia or Salò, c. 1630; d. Dresden, 26. I. 1688), It. comp. Lived at Salò, married Giulia Rossi at Padua and settled there, prod. operas between 1666 and 1687 at Venice, where he also lived for a time. In 1667–73 he was at the Saxon court at Dresden; 1st as asst. and later as 1st mus. director. In 1674 he was back at Venice, but was recalled to Dresden in 1685 to reorganize the It. opera.

Works incl. *Demetrio, Diocletiano, Enea in Italia, Vespasiano, Nerone, Le amazoni nell' isole fortunate, Messalina, Bassiano, overro Il maggior impossibile, Penelope la casta, Massimo Puppieno, Didone delirante, L'amazone corsara, La Gerusalemme liberata* (after Tasso), *Antiope* (finished by Strungk) and 9 others; a Mass and an oratorio; arias and *canzoni* with instruments; string fantasies, etc.

Pallavicini, Vincenzo (b. Brescia, ?; d. ?), It. 18th-cent. comp. *Maestro di cappella* at the Cons. degl' Incurabili at Venice.

Works incl. opera *Lo speziale* (with Fischietti, lib. by Goldoni), etc.

Pallavicino, Benedetto (b. Cremona, ?; d. Mantua, 6. V. 1601), It. comp. Towards the end of the 16th cent. he was in the service of the Duke of Mantua, succeeded Wert as *maestro di cappella* there in 1596, but was in turn succeeded in 1601, when he retired to the monastery of Camaldoli in Tuscany.

Works incl. Masses, psalms and other church mus.; madrigals, etc.

Palma, Silvestro (b. Ischia, 15. III. 1754; d. Naples, 8. VIII. 1834), It. comp. Studied at Naples and was a pupil of Paisiello.

Works incl. operas *La pietra simpatica, Il geloso di se stesso* and *c.* 15 others; church mus., etc.

Palmer, Robert (b. Syracuse, N.Y., 2. VI. 1915), Amer. comp. Studied at the Eastman School of Mus. at Rochester, N.Y., where he took degrees in 1938–9, also privately with Roy Harris. In 1943 he he became asst. prof. of mus. at Cornell Univ., Ithaca, N.Y.

Works incl. ballet *Ir. Legend* with chamber orch.; symph., elegy *K. 19* and concerto for orch.; concerto for chamber orch.; *Abraham Lincoln Walks at Midnight* (Vachel Lindsay) for chorus and orch.; 3 string 4tets, pf. 4tet, 2 string trios, concerto for fl., vln., clar., Eng. horn and bassoon; vla. and pf. sonata; sonata for 2 pfs.; sonata and 3 preludes for pf., etc.

Palmgren, Selim (b. Björneborg, 16. II. 1878; d. Helsinki, 13. XII. 1951), Fin. pianist, cond. and comp. Studied at the Helsinki Cons., where Wegelius was among his masters, and later with Ansorge in Ger. and Busoni in It. On his return he became cond. of the Fin. Students' Choral Society and later of the Mus. Society at Turku. He also frequently appeared as pianist. Married the singer Maikki Järnefelt, toured Eur. and U.S.A. with her and from 1923 to 1926 was prof. of comp. at the Eastman School of Mus. at Rochester, N.Y.

Works incl. operas *Daniel Hjort* and *Peter Schlemihl* (after Chamisso); incid.

mus. to Kyösti's *Tukhimo* (*Cinderella*); choral works; 5 pf. concertos (II. *The River*; III. *Metamorphoses*; IV. *April*); numerous pf. pieces, etc.

Palotta, Matteo (b. Palermo, 1680; d. Vienna, 28. III. 1758), It. comp., priest and mus. scholar. Studied at Naples, returned to Sicily after being ordained, but was app. one of the court comps. in Vienna in 1733. He wrote treatises on solmization and the modes and comp. Masses, motets and other church mus.

Paminger, Leonhard (b. Aschau, Upper Aus., 29. III. 1495; d. Passau, 3. V. 1567), Aus. comp. Educ. at the monastery of St. Nicholas at Passau, studied in Vienna afterwards, but returned to Passau to become a teacher and later secretary at the monastery. He became a Lutheran.

Works incl. Lat. motets, Ger. hymns, psalms, etc.

Pammelia, the 1st part of a collection of canons, rounds and catches pub. by Ravenscroft in 1609, the 2nd being *Deuteromelia*.

Pan (or Pandean) Pipe, a primitive wind instrument, also called Syrinx, consisting of a bundle of reeds of graded lengths made into pipes giving out a scale of different notes.

Pan Tvardovsky, opera by Verstovsky (lib. by Konstantin Sergeievich Aksakov), prod. Moscow, 5. VI. 1828.

Pan Voyevoda, opera by Rimsky-Korsakov (lib. by I. F. Tiumenev,) prod. St. Petersburg, 16. X. 1904.

Pandean Pipe. *See* Pan Pipe.

Pandora (or Bandora), an obs. string instrument of the Cittern type, with 6 or 7 metal strings. plucked by the fingers and with a flat back.

Pandorina, an obs. string instrument; a small lute.

Pandoura (from Gk.; also from Arab. *tanbur*, Tamboura), an obs. string instrument of the lute type with a long neck and a small body, surviving in var. forms only in the Balkans, Turkey, Egypt and the East.

Pane, Domenico del (b. Rome, ?; d. Rome, 10. XII. 1694), It. singer and comp. Pupil of Abbatini in Rome, went to Vienna in 1650 as a singer in the Imp. chapel, but returned to Rome to join the Papal Chapel in 1654 and became choirmaster there in 1669.

Works incl. Masses on motets by Palestrina, motets of his own; sacred concertos; madrigals, etc.

Panharmonicon. *See* Mälzel and Orchestrion.

Panizza, Ettore (b. Buenos Aires, 12. VIII. 1875; d. Milan, 29. XI. 1967), Arg. cond. and comp. of It. descent. Studied at the Milan Cons. and 1st appeared as cond. in Rome, 1899, 1st visiting London (Covent Garden) in 1907.

Works incl. operas *Il fidanzato del mare*, *Medio evo latino*, *Aurora*, *Bisanzio*, etc.

Pankiewicz, Eugeniusz (b. Siedlce, 15. XII. 1857; d. Tworki, 12. XII. 1898), Pol. pianist and comp. Began to study privately, then at Warsaw and finally at St. Petersburg, where Leschetizky was his pf. master and Rubinstein and Rimsky-Korsakov taught him comp. He finished his studies with Żeleński and Noskowski at the Warsaw Cons., where he became prof. in succession to Paderewski, 1880.

Works incl. *Ballet-Waltzes* for male chorus; variations and other works for pf.; song cycles *Love Stories*, etc., single songs, etc.

Pannain, Guido (b. Naples, 17. XI. 1891), It. mus. critic. Studied at the Naples Cons., where he became prof. later. He also studied philosophy under the influence of Benedetto Croce. App. mus. critic to *Il mattino* at Naples. His books incl. studies of Tinctoris, old It. keyboard mus., the Neapol. school, Bellini and modern mus.

Panny, Joseph (b. Kolmitzberg, 23. X. 1794; d. Mainz, 7. IX. 1838), Aus. violinist and comp. Studied at home and with Eybler in Vienna, made friends with Paganini during his visits there, appeared in Ger., Norw., Paris and London, founded a school of mus. at Weisserling in Alsace and another at Mainz.

Works incl. 3 Masses, Requiem; 3 string 4tets, pf. trios; *Scène dramatique* for the vln. G string (for Paganini) and other solos; choruses; songs, etc.

Panofka, Heinrich (b. Breslau, 3. X. 1807; d. Florence, 18. XI. 1887), Ger. violinist, singing-teacher and comp. Studied at home and with Mayseder in Vienna, where he 1st appeared in public in 1827. After living in Munich and Berlin, he settled by turns in Paris, London and Florence, teaching singing and pub. treatises on the subject. Comp. works for vln. with pf. and with orch.

Panseron, Auguste (Matthieu) (b. Paris, 26. IV. 1795; d. Paris, 29. VII. 1859), Fr. comp. and singing-teacher. Studied at the Paris Cons. and took the Prix de Rome in 1813, making further studies in It. under Mattei. As accompanist at the Opéra-Comique in Paris, he gained much experience in singing and he became prof. at the Cons. in 1826, writing treatises on solfège and singing.

Works incl. operas *La Grille du parc*, *Le Mariage difficile* and *L École de Rome*; 2 Masses for treble voices, motets and canticles *Mois de Marie*; numerous songs, etc.

Pantaleon, an instrument of the Dulcimer type invented by Pantaleon Hebenstreit in the 18th cent. and called P. after him by Louis XIV.

Pantomime (from Gk. = 'all-imitating'), properly a play in dumbshow, but in Eng. since the 18th cent. a popular stage entertainment with mus., deriving from the It. *commedia dell'arte*. It is still based, even if remotely, on fairy-tales, but it has lost the Harlequinade which used to be an indispensable supplement and has become a spectacular extravaganza, often intro. songs popular at the time.

Pantonality, a term less frequently used, but preferred by Schönberg and others for Atonality, i.e. mus. not written in any definite key.

Pantoum (Fr. and Eng. from Malay *pantun*), the title of a movement in Ravel's pf. trio, the form of which is based on the type of Malay verse named P., which has been adopted by Fr. and Eng. poets. A P. is a quatrain, and in Fr. or Eng. poems where more than one such stanza occurs the 2nd and 4th line of each reappear as the 1st and 3rd of the next.

Panufnik, Andrzei (b. Warsaw, 24. IX. 1914), Pol. comp. Studied with Sikorski at the Warsaw Cons. and received a diploma in 1936. Some of his mus. was destroyed in the bombardment of Warsaw. He settled in Eng. in 1954 and from 1957 to 1959 was cond. of the Birmingham Symph. Orch.

Works incl. film mus.; Psalm cxlv for chorus and orch., 4 symphs., symph. variations, symph. studies, Tragic Overutre, Heroic Overture, *Sinfonia sacra* for orch.; tpt. concerto, pf. concerto; pf. trio and other chamber mus.; 5 Pol. folksongs for treble voices, 2 fls., 2 clars. and bass clar.; preludes, mazurkas and other works for pf., etc.

Panum, Hortense (b. Kiel, 14. III. 1856; d. Copenhagen, 26. IV. 1933), Dan. musicologist, who taught at the Copenhagen Cons. from 1907. She pub. studies of mus. hist. and instruments, a mus. lexicon, etc.

Panzacchi, Enrico (1840–1904), It. poet, librettist and writer on mus. *See* Scontrino (*Intima vita*).

Paolo e Francesca, opera by Mancinelli (lib. by Arturo Colautti, after Dante), prod. Bologna, Teatro Comunale, 11. XI. 1907.

Paolo e Virginia, opera by P. C. Guglielmi (lib. by Giuseppe Maria Diodati, based on Bernardin de Saint-Pierre's novel), prod. Naples, Teatro Fiorentino, 2. I. 1817.

Papandopulo, Boris (b. Honnef o/Rhine, 25. II. 1906), Yugoslav cond. and comp. Studied at Zagreb and Vienna, and became choral and orchestral cond. at Zagreb, returning there after teaching at the Mus. School of Split in 1935–8. Since then he has been active as an opera cond.

Works incl. operas *The Sun Flower*, *Amphitryon* and *Rona*; ballet *Gold*; oratorio for

unaccomp. chorus *The Torments of Our Lord Jesus Christ, Laudamus* for solo voices, chorus and orch., *Croatian Mass* for soloists and chorus; 2 symphs., symph. picture *The Overflowing*; 2 pf. concertos; 2 string 4tets and other chamber mus.; pf. mus.; songs, etc.

Papillons (*Butterflies*), a set of short pf. pieces by Schumann, Op. 2, with a finale suggesting the end of a ball in the early morning, with a clock striking 6 and a quotation of the *Grossvatertanz* or *Kehraus*, which also appears in *Carnaval*, for which this smaller work might almost be a kind of preliminary sketch. There is a further connection between the 2, the opening of *Papillons* being quoted in the *Florestan* piece in *Carnaval*. The 1st part of Op. 2 was comp. (before Op. 1) in 1829, the end in 1831.

Papini, Guido (b. Camaiore, Lucca, 1. VIII. 1847; d. London, 3. X. 1912), It. violinist and comp. Made his 1st public appearance at Florence at the age of 13, became leader of the Società del Quartetto there, travelled and 1st visited London in 1874, became vln. prof. at the R. Ir. A.M. at Dublin in 1893 and retired to London in 1896.

Works incl. vln. concerto, cello concerto; vln. duets and trios; many vln. studies and pieces; cello pieces; songs, etc.

Pâque, Guillaume (b. Brussels, 24. VII. 1825; d. London, 2. III. 1876), Belg. cellist. Studied at the Brussels Cons. and after working in Paris and Madrid settled in London in 1851.

Parable Aria (esp. Ger. *Gleichnisarie*) or Metaphor Aria, a type of mainly operatic aria cultivated in the early 18th cent., esp. by Zeno and Metastasio in their libs., where certain abstract conceptions are illustrated by concrete ideas resembling them, e.g. fidelity by a rock in a stormy sea, love by cooing turtle-doves, etc. 'As when the dove' in Handel's *Acis and Galatea* is a P. A. and 'Come scoglio' ('Like a rock') in Mozart's *Così fan tutte* is both verbally and musically a parody of the type. The mus. of a P. A. was usually illustrative of the image chosen by the librettist.

Parabosco, Girolamo (b. Piacenza, 1520 or 1524; d. Venice, 2. IV. 1557), It. comp. He became a pupil of Willaert in Venice, and pub. 2 pieces in the miscellaneous collection of instrumental mus. *Musica Nova* (1540). He succeeded J. Buus as 1st organist at St. Mark's, Venice, a post which he held until his death.

Paradies, Domenico. *See* Paradisi.

Paradis, Maria Theresia von (b. Vienna, 15. V. 1759; d. Vienna, 1. II. 1824), Aus. pianist, organist, singer and comp. She was blind from childhood, but had a great success, which she extended to Paris and London. Mozart wrote the pf. concerto in B♭ maj. (K. 456) for her.

Works incl. operas *Der Schulcandidat, Rinaldo und Alcina*; melodrama *Ariadne und Bacchus*; cantata *Deutsches Monument* (on the death of Louis XVI); pf. trios; sonatas and variations for pf.; songs incl. a setting of Burger's *Lenore*, etc.

Paradise and the Peri (*Das Paradies und die Peri*), a setting for solo voices, chorus and orch. of one of the poems in Thomas Moore's *Lalla Rookh*, trans. into Ger. with alterations, by Schumann, Op. 50; comp. 1st contemplated in 1841, begun II. 1843; 1st perf., Leipzig, 4. XII. 1843.

Paradisi (or **Paradies**), (**Pietro**) **Domenico** (b. Naples, 1707; d. Venice, 25. VIII. 1791), harpsichordist and comp. Pupil of Porpora, lived for many years in London as a teacher.

Works incl. operas *Alessandro in Persia, Il decreto del fato, Fetonte, La forza d'amore*; cantata *Le Muse in gara*; harpsichord sonatas, toccatas, etc.

Parallel Motion, 2 or more parts in counterpoint moving up or down in unchanging intervals.

Paray, Paul (Charles) (b. Tréport, 24. V. 1886), Fr. cond. and comp. Studied with Leroux and others at the Paris Cons. and took the Prix de Rome in 1911. Returning to Paris from imprisonment during the 1914–18 war he became asst. and later successor to Chevillard, whose concerts he continued to cond. until 1933, when he succeeded Pierné as cond. of the Colonne Orch. In 1952 he became cond. of the Detroit Symph. Orch.

Works incl. oratorio *Jeanne d'Arc*; ballet *Artémis troublée*; Mass for the 500th anniversary of the death of Joan of Arc; symph. in C maj.; fantasy for pf. and orch.; string 4tet; vln. and pf. sonata, etc.

Pardon de Ploërmel, Le, opera by Meyerbeer (lib. by Jules Barbier and Michel Carré), prod. Paris, Opéra-Comique, 4. IV. 1859. The work is also known as *Dinorah*.

Parepa-Rosa, Euphrosyne (b. Edinburgh, 7. V. 1836; d. London, 21. I. 1874), Scot. soprano of Wallachian descent. She was taught by her mother, the singer Elizabeth Seguin, and by several famous masters, and made her 1st appearance at Malta at the age of 16, and in London in 1857. Married Carl Rosa in 1867 and was the leading soprano of his opera company.

Paride ed Elena (*Paris and Helen*), opera by Gluck (lib. by Ranieri Calzabigi), prod. Vienna, Burgtheater, 3. XI. 1770.

Paris and Helen (Gluck). *See above.*

Paris Symphonies, a set of 6 symphs. by Haydn commissioned by the Concert de la Loge Olympique in Paris: No. 82 in C

maj. (*L'Ours*), comp. 1786; No. 83 in G min./maj. (*La Poule*), 1785; No. 84 in E♭ maj., 1786; No. 85 in B♭ maj. (*La Reine [de France]*), 1785–6; No. 86 in D maj., 1786; No. 87 in A maj., 1785.

'Paris' Symphony, Mozart's symph. in D maj., K. 297, written in Paris for perf. at the Concert spirituel in 1778. After the 1st perf. Mozart replaced the slow movement by another.

Parish-Alvars, Elias (b. Teignmouth, 28. II. 1808; d. Vienna, 25. I. 1849), Eng.-Jewish harpist and pianist. Studied under Bochsa and others, 1st went on tour, in Ger., in 1831, and later visited It., Aus. and the E. In 1847 he settled in Vienna as chamber musician to the court.

Works incl. harp concertos, fantasies for harp and for harp and pf., etc.

Parisina, opera by Donizetti (lib. by Felice Romani, based on Byron's poem) prod. Florence, Teatro della Pergola, 17. III. 1833.

Opera by Mascagni (lib. by Gabriele d'Annunzio), prod. Milan, Teatro alla Scala, 15. XII. 1913.

Parker, Clifton (b. London, 5. II. 1905), Eng. comp. He was made to go into business, but being anxious to become a musician, he began by copying mus. and laboriously taught himself. In 1936 he joined the Folkestone Municipal Orch. as copyist, arranger, etc., then became pianist to the Ballet Jooss school at Dartington Hall, Totnes, where he married the dancer Yoma Saburgh. In 1941 he settled in London as theatre and film comp.

Works incl. opera *Aucassin and Nicolette*; incid. mus. for Shakespeare's *Othello*, for an adaptation of Tolstoy's *War and Peace* and other plays; mus. for film *Western Approaches* and others, etc.

Parker, Horatio (William) (b. Auburndale, Mass., 15. IX. 1863; d. Cedarhurst, N.Y., 18. XII. 1919), Amer. organist and comp. Studied at Boston and Munich, where he was a pupil of Rheinberger. In 1884 he returned to N.Y. and became an organist and choirmaster, and taught at the Nat. Cons. directed by Dvořák, Later he became organist at Trinity Church, Boston, and in 1894 prof. of mus. at Yale Univ. He visited Eng. several times for perfs. of his works at the festivals and to receive the Mus.D. from Cambridge in 1902.

Works incl. operas *Mona* and *Fairyland*; oratorios *Hora novissima, The Legend of St. Christopher, Morven and the Grail*; *The Holy Child, The Dream of Mary* and other cantatas, choral ballads and songs; church services; symph. in C min., overtures and other orchestral works; org. concerto; string 4tet in F maj.; org. sonata; pf. pieces; songs, etc.

Parlando
or   ⎰ (It. = speaking), a direction
Parlante ⎱
indicating, in instrumental mus., that a passage is to be perf. in a 'speaking' manner, expressively but not sustained or 'sung'; in vocal mus., that the tone is to be reduced to something approximating speech.

Parodies. *See* **Imitations.**

Parratt, Walter (b. Huddersfield, 10. II. 1841; d. Windsor, 27. III. 1924), Eng. organist. Held var. appts. from childhood. Organist of St. George's Chapel, Windsor, 1882–1924, D.Mus. Oxford, 1892; Mus.D., Cambridge, 1910. Prof. of Mus. at Oxford, 1908–18. Knighted 1892.

Parrott, Ian (b. London, 5. III. 1916), Eng. comp. Educ. at Harrow and Oxford, he studied in London at the R.C.M. and with B. Dale. After var. appts. he became Prof. of Mus. at Aberystwyth Univ. in 1950.

Works incl. operas *The Sergeant-Major's Daughter, The Black Ram*; ballet *Maid in Birmingham*; Psalm xci for chorus and orch., cantata *Three Kings have come*; Symph., symph. prelude *El Alamein*, symph. impression *Luxor, Pensieri* for strings; pf. concerto, ob. 4tet, wind 5tet, Fantasy Trio for vln., cello and pf.: instrumental pieces; pf. works; songs, etc.

Parry, (Charles) Hubert (Hastings) (b. Bournemouth, 27. II. 1848; d. Rustington, 7. X. 1918), Eng. comp. and writer on mus. Son of Thomas Gambier P., a distinguished amateur painter and squire at Highnam Court nr. Gloucester. Educ. at Eton and Oxford, studied mus. with Elvey at Eton and with Macfarren and Sterndale Bennett later, also during vacation with Pierson at Stuttgart. He did not make his mark in public until his pf. concerto was played by Dannreuther at the Crystal Palace in 1880 and his choral scenes from Shelley's *Prometheus Unbound* appeared at the Gloucester Festival the same year. Hon. Mus.D., Cambridge 1883, D.Mus., Oxford 1884 and Dublin 1891. After examining for London Univ. and teaching at the R.C.M., he was app. director of the latter in succession to Grove in 1894, remaining until his death. Knighted in 1898 and app. Prof. of Mus. at Oxford in 1900, a post he resigned in 1908. He wrote several books on mus., incl. a study of Bach and a volume of the *Oxford History of Music*.

Works incl. opera *Guinevere*; incid. mus. to Aristophanes' *The Birds, The Frogs, The Clouds* and *The Acharnians*, Aeschylus's *Agamemnon*, Ogilvy's *Hypatia*, Pearl Mary Theresa Craigie's *A Repentance* and Keats's *Proserpine*; oratorios *Judith, Job, King Saul*; 6 motets, 4 *Songs of Farewell* and 2 other motets for chorus; choral

works: scenes from Shelley's *Prometheus Unbound*, ode *The Glories of our Blood and State* (Shirley), ode *Blest Pair of Sirens* (Milton), *Ode on St. Cecilia's Day* (Pope), *L'Allegro ed il Pensieroso* (Milton), ode *Eton* (Swinburne), choric song from Tennyson's *Lotos-Eaters, Invocation to Music* (Bridges), *A Song of Darkness and Light* (Bridges), *The Pied Piper of Hamelin* (Browning), *Ode on the Nativity* (Dunbar), *The Chivalry of the Sea* and *Eton Memorial Ode* (both Bridges). Ode *Persicos odi* (Horace); Magnificat in F maj., 3 Te Deums (the last for George V's coronation) anthem and processional mus. for Edward VII's coronation; 2 madrigals; *c.* 50 partsongs; services, anthems and hymn tunes; *Jerusalem* (Blake) for chorus; 5 symphs., 3 concert overtures, symph. poem *From Death to Life* and *Suite Moderne* for orch., *Lady Radnor's Suite* and *An English Suite* for string orch.; pf. concerto in F♯ min.; string 5tet, 3 string 4tets, 4tet, nonet for wind instruments, 4 pf. trios; sonatas for vln. and pf. and cello and pf., 2 suites and many smaller pieces for vln. and pf.; org. and pf. mus.; over 100 songs incl. 74 in 12 books of *English Lyrics*, etc.

Parry, John (b. ?; d. Ruabon, 7. X. 1782), Welsh harpist. Appeared at Dublin in 1736 and in London and Cambridge in 1746. Handel admired him and Gray wrote his poem *The Bard* on him. He pub. collections of Welsh and other Brit. nat. melodies.

Parry, John (b. Denbigh, 18. II. 1776; d. London, 8. IV. 1831), Welsh clarinettist, bandmaster and comp. Settled in London in 1807 and in 1809 was engaged to comp. songs for Vauxhall Gardens. Later he became a theatre comp. and mus. critic to the *Morning Post* in 1834–48. In the 1820s he cond. Welsh festivals at Wrexham and Brecon.

Works incl. stage pieces *Harlequin Hoax* (lib. by T. Dibdin), *Oberon's Oath, Fair Cheating, The Sham Prince*, etc.; songs and ballads; arrs. of Welsh songs, etc.

Parry, John Orlando (b. London, 3. I. 1810; d. East Molesey, 20. II. 1879), Welsh harpist, pianist, singer and comp., son of prec. Studied with his father and later in It. under Lablache. In 1836 he began a career in London as stage singer, mus. entertainer and mimic of singers. He wrote and arr. comic songs, glees, etc.

Parry, Joseph (b. Merthyr Tydvil, 21. V. 1841; d. Penarth, 17. II. 1903), Welsh comp. In spite of the poorest circumstances, he acquired a mus. educ. and after 2 visits to U.S.A. entered the R.A.M. in London at the age of 27, was app. prof. of mus. at Aberystwyth in 1870 and took the Mus.D. at Cambridge in 1878.

Works incl. operas *Blodwen, Virginia, Arianwen, Sylvia, King Arthur*; oratorios

Emmanuel, Saul of Tarsus and *The Maid of Cefu Idfa, The Prodigal Son, Nebuchadnezzar*; cantata *Cambria* and others; ballad, overtures and other works for orch.; string 4tet; Welsh hymn-tunes; songs, etc.

Parry, Joseph Haydn (b. Pennsylvania, V. 1864; d. London, 29. III. 1894), Welsh pianist and comp., son of prec. Studied under his father and in 1890 became prof. at the G.S.M. in London.

Works incl. operas *Cigarette, Miami, Marigold Farm*; cantata *Gwen*; pf. sonata, etc.

Parsifal, mus.-drama by Wagner (lib. by comp.), prod. Bayreuth, Wagner Festival Theatre, 26. VII. 1882.

Parsley, Osbert (b. ?, 1511; d. Norwich, 1585), Eng. singer and comp. Attached to Norwich Cathedral for 50 years. Comp. services, motets, etc.

Parsons, John (b. ?; d. London, VII. 1623), Eng. organist and comp. Became parish clerk and organist at St. Margaret's Church, Westminster, in 1616, and in 1621 organist and choirmaster of Westminster Abbey. He wrote a Burial Service, which Purcell used in 1685 for the funeral of Charles II.

Parsons, Robert (b. Exeter, ?; d. Newark-on-Trent, 25. I. 1570), Eng. comp., (?) father of prec. He became a Gentleman of the Chapel Royal in London, 1563. He was drowned in the Trent.

Works incl. services, anthems, motets; madrigals; In Nomines for viols or virginal; song *Pandolpho* for a stage play, etc.

Part, the mus. perf. by any single singer or player in a work for a number of perfs.; a single strand of melody in a polyphonic or other comp. in a number of voices, whether perf. by several people or by a single player on a keyboard instrument; also the copy of the mus. from which a single singer or player perfs. in a work for a number of people.

Part du diable, La (*The Devil's Share*), opera by Auber (lib. by Scribe), prod. Paris, Opéra-Comique, 16. I. 1843. The work is sometimes called *Carlo Broschi*, the real name of Farinelli, who is the chief character, sung by a soprano.

Part-Writing, in comp. the way of managing the satisfactory progress of each single part or voice in a texture of any number of parts.

Partbooks, books containing printed or MS. mus. to be sung or played by 1 or 2 perfs. in a work written for a larger number.

Partch, Harry (b. Oakland, Calif., 24. I. 1901), Amer. comp. Largely self-taught, he has experimented with microtonal scales and new instrumental designs.

Works incl. *8 Hitch-hiker Inscriptions*

from a California Highway Railing and *U.S. Highball, a Musical Account of a Transcontinental Hobo Trip* for chorus and instruments; *The Letter, a Depression Message from a Hobo Friend*, for voices and instruments; *Oedipus*, mus. drama; *The Bewitched*, a dance satire; *Revelation in the Courthouse Park*, a mus. tragedy; *Water, Water*, an Amer. ritual.

Parte (It.). *See* **Colla parte.**

Partenope, opera by Handel (lib. by Silvio Stampiglia), prod. London. King's Theatre, Haymarket, 24. II. 1730.

Opera by Hasse (lib. by Metastasio), prod. Vienna, Burgtheater, 9. IX. 1767.

Parthenia, the title of the 1st collection of virginal mus. to be printed in Eng., pub. in 1612–13 and containing 21 pieces by Byrd, Bull and O. Gibbons.

Parthenia inviolata, a companion vol. to the prec. containing 20 pieces for virginals and bass viol.

Parthia, a variant spelling of the Ger. *Partie*, used by Haydn and Beethoven among others. *See* **Partita.**

Partials, in acoustics the constituents (fundamentals and overtones) of a mus. note, i.e. pure tones, not perceived separately save by intent listening or with the aid of a resonator.

Partie (Fr.), a part or voice in a polyphonic comp.

Partie (Ger., also *Parthie*), the old name for Partita or Suite.

Partimenti (It. = divisions), exercises in playing more or less elaborate contrapuntal parts over a figured bass.

Partita (It., lit. = set [as in tennis]), in the 17th and early 18th cent. a variation used in the plural (*partite diverse*) to mean a set of Variations, e.g. by Bach in some of his org. works based on chorales. It also acquired the meaning Suite (Ger. *Partie*) and was so used also by Bach, e.g. in his 6 P.s for harpsichord and his 3 P.s for solo vln. The term has been revived by 20th-cent. comps., e.g. Casella, Dallapicola, Vaughan Williams and Walton. *See also* **Suite.**

Partition (Fr.) } = Score.
Partitur (Ger.) }

Partos, Ödön (b. Budapest, 1. X. 1907), Hung.-Israeli comp. Studied vln. with Hubay and comp. with Kodály. Led various orchs. in Lucerne, Berlin and Budapest between 1925 and 1936, and since 1938 played vla. with the Israel Phil. Orch.

Works incl. *Yis Kor* (*In Memoriam*) for vla. and string orch.; *Song of Praise* for vla. and orch.; symph. fantasy *En Gev*; *Phantasy on Yemeni Themes* for chorus and orch.

Part-song, a comp. for several voices (mixed, female or male) usually less polyphonic than a madrigal.

Pasdeloup, Jules (Étienne) (b. Paris, 15. IX. 1819; d. Fontainebleau, 13. VIII. 1887), Fr. cond. Studied at the Paris Cons. Founder of the Société des Jeunes Artistes du Cons., 1851, and the Concerts Pasdeloup, 1861, at which he prod. many works previously unknown in Fr.

Pashkevich, Vassily Alexeievich (b. ?, c. 1742; d. ?, c. 1800), Rus. violinist and comp. Entered the service of Catherine II in 1763 and became cond. and court comp.

Works incl. operas *The Carriage Accident, Fevey, The Miser, Fedul and his Children* (with Martín y Soler), *The Early Reign of Oleg* (with Sarti and Canobbio), *The Pasha of Tunis*, etc.

Pashtchenko, Andrey Filipovich (b. Rostov-on-Don, 15. VIII. 1883), Rus. comp. Entered the St. Petersburg Cons. in 1914, after receiving private mus. instruction, and studied comp. under Steinberg and Wihtol. He has been active as teacher and mus. organizer, but devoted most of his time to comp. During World War II he remained at Leningrad all through the siege.

Works incl. operas *The Revolt of the Eagles, Emperor Maximilian, The Black Cliff, The Pompadours* (after Saltikov-Shtchedrin's story), *The Stubborn Bride, Radda and Loyko* (after Gorki's story *Makar Tchudra*); film mus.; oratorios *The Liberation of Prometheus* and *Lenin*, Requiem in memory of the heroes of the great war; 9 symphs., *Solemn Polonaise* and *Festive Overture*, symph. poems *The Giants* and *The Bacchantes*, scherzo *Harlequin and Columbine*, Suite in the Classical Style, *Legend* for orch.; 3 pieces for a band of folk instruments; 2 string 4tets; songs, etc.

Pasino (called Ghizzolo Stefano) (b. Brescia, ?; d. ? Salò, ?), It. 17th-cent. comp. Became town organist at Lonato c. 1640 and *maestro di cappella* at Salò in 1651.

Works incl. Masses and motets: sonatas for 2–4 instruments, instrumental *ricercari*, etc.

Paso doble (or Pasodoble; Span. = double step, two-step), a modern Span. dance.

Paspy (Eng. obs.), the old Eng. word for the Passepied.

Pasquali, Francesco (b. Cosenza, ?; d. ? Rome, ?), It. 16th–17th-cent. comp. Studied and worked in Rome.

Works incl. sacred and secular songs, madrigals, etc.

Pasquali, Niccolò (b. ?, c. 1718; d. Edinburgh, 13. X. 1757), It. violinist and comp. Settled at Edinburgh c. 1740, lived at Dublin in 1748–51, but returned to Edinburgh, visiting London in 1752. Wrote treatises on thorough-bass and harpsichord playing.

Works incl. opera *The Triumph of Hibernia*; dirge in Shakespeare's *Romeo and Juliet*; oratorios *Noah* and *David*; 12 overtures for (or with) horns; sonatas for vln. or 2 vlns. and bass; songs contrib. to var. collections, etc.

Pasquini, Bernardo (b. Massa Valdinievole, Tuscany, 7. XII. 1637; d. Rome, 21. XI. 1710), It. harpsichordist, organist and comp. Studied with Loreto Vittori and Cesti. As a young man he settled in Rome and became organist of the church of Santa Maria Maggiore. His *Accademia per musica* was perf. at the Rom. palace of Queen Christina of Swed. in 1687 to celebrate the accession of James II, Corelli leading a string orch. of 150 players.

Works incl. operas *La donna ancora è fedele, Dov' è amore e pietà, La forza d'amore* and 11 others; 13 sonatas and other works for harpsichord, etc.

Passacaglia (prob. from Span. *pasar calle* = to walk the street), orig. an It. or Span. dance, but now an instrumental comp. based on a Ground, i.e. a tune continuing throughout, usually but not necessarily in the bass. The best-known ex. is Bach's for org.; the finale of Brahms's 4th symph., although not so entitled, is also in this form.

Passacaille (Fr.) = Passacaglia.

Passage, any melodic or decorative feature in a comp., esp. if it is conspicuous or calls for brilliant perf.

Passaggio (It.), as above, but used in more specialized senses for Modulations (i.e. passing from key to key) and for florid vocal or instrumental decorations.

Passamezzo (It., prob. a corruption of *passo e mezzo* = pace and a half), a brisk dance of the late 16th and early 17th cents., popular not only in It. but throughout Eur. Its name is prob. due to the fact that it was a more lively form of the Pavane. It consisted basically of variations on a ground bass. The *passamezzo antico* (Shakespeare's 'passy measures pavyn') was in the min. key, the *passamezzo moderno* in the maj. *See also* **Romanesca.**

Passepied (Fr. lit., pass-foot), a Fr. (prob. Breton) dance at least as old as the 16th cent. The mus. is in 3–4 or 3–8 time taken at a moderately running pace. It sometimes occurs in suites, but is not an obligatory part of them.

Passereau (b. ?; d.?), Fr. 16th-cent. comp. His *chansons* were pub. by Attaingnant and others at var. times between 1529 and 1572. The best known of them, 'Il est bel et bon', was arr. for org. by Girolamo Cavazzoni.

Passing Appoggiatura. *See* **Ornaments.**

Passing Notes, incidental notes in one or more parts of a comp. which create a temporary dissonance with the prevailing harmony (*see* illustration).

Pastoral, an anthology by Bliss for mezzo-soprano solo, chorus, fl., drums

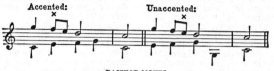

Accented: Unaccented:

PASSING NOTES

Passion Music. The medieval recitation of the gospel story of Christ's Passion was sung, as it still is, by three singers with different vocal ranges. The singer representing the Evangelist had a medium range, Christus a low range, and the singer responsible for the other characters and the crowd (*turba*) a high range. By the 15th cent. the *turba* began to be entrusted to a vocal ensemble, and in the course of the 16th cent. the whole text was sung in a polyphonic setting. In the 17th cent. Lutheran comps. intro. recitative, chorales and instrumental accomp. In the early 18th cent. the incl. of arias set to non-Biblical words turned the Lutheran Passion into an oratorio, indistinguishable in style from opera. Bach's 2 surviving Passions belong to this new category.

Passione, La (*The Passion*), name given to Haydn's symph. No. 49 in F min., comp. 1768.

Pasta (*née* **Negri**) **Giuditta** (b. Saronno nr. Milan, 9. IV. 1798; d. Blavio nr. Como, 1. IV. 1865), It. soprano. Studied at home, at the Milan Cons. and in Paris, made her 1st appearance in 1815 and went to London in 1816. In Paris she was 1st heard at the Théâtre Italien in 1821.

Pasterwitz, Georg (b. Bierhütten nr. Passau, 7. VI. 1730; d. Kremsmünster, 28. I. 1803), Aus. monk, organist and comp. Studied at Kremsmünster Abbey, where he was ordained priest in 1755, and with Eberlin at Salzburg. In 1767–82 he was choirmaster at the abbey, but later lived chiefly in Vienna.

Works incl. opera *Samson*; Masses, Requiem; numerous fugues and other pieces for keyboard instruments, etc.

Pasticcio (It. lit. pie or pasty), a stage entertainment with mus. drawn from existing works by one or more comps. and words written to fit the mus. It was partic. popular in the 18th cent.

Pastor fido, Il (*The Faithful Shepherd*), opera by Handel (lib. by Giacomo Rossi after Guarini's pastoral play), prod. London, Queen's Theatre, Haymarket, 22. XI. 1712.

Pastoral, a light-hearted Eng. madrigal with words of a pastoral character. *See also* **Pastorale.**

and strings (words by Theocritus, Poliziano, Ben Jonson, John Fletcher and Robert Nichols), 1st perf. London, 8. V. 1929.

'Pastoral' Sonata, Beethoven's pf. sonata in D maj., Op. 28, comp. in 1801 and ded. to Joseph, Edler von Sonnenfels. The nickname was not Beethoven's own, but was invented later by the Hamburg pub. Cranz. It suits only the finale.

'Pastoral' Symphony, Beethoven's 6th symph., in F maj., Op. 68, comp. in 1807–8, 1st perf. Vienna, 22. XII. 1808. The title-page bears B.'s own heading of *Symphonie pastorale*, and on the 1st vln. part is the inscription, 'Pastoral-Sinfonie oder Erinnerung an das Landleben (mehr Ausdruck der Empfindung als Mahlerey).' (P. S. or Recollection of Country Life [Expression of Emotion rather than Painting].)

Pastoral Symphony, A, the 3rd symph. by Vaughan Williams, for orch. with a soprano voice (without words), comp. 1920, prod. London, Queen's Hall, 26. I. 1922.

Pastorale (Fr. and It.), a type of 17th-cent. opera, or opera-ballet, with recitatives, airs and choruses, often prod. on special festive occasions and treating pastoral subjects in a courtly and artificial manner, often allegorically. Its origin was the pastoral drama of the 16th cent. In later times P. has been often used as a title for all kinds of comps. of a pastoral character.

Pastorale, La (called *La Pastorale d'Issy*), opera by Cambert (lib. by Pierre Perrin), prod. at Issy nr. Paris, IV. 1659. Long regarded as the 1st Fr. opera (but *see* Triomphe de l'Amour).

Pastorella nobile, La (*The Noble Shepherdess*), opera by P. Guglielmi (lib. by Saverio Zini), prod. Naples, Teatro Nuovo, 19. IV. 1788.

Pastourelle (Fr.), a medieval pastoral song.

Patey (*née* **Whytock**), **Janet** (**Monach**) (b. London, 1. V. 1842; d. Sheffield, 28. II. 1894), Scot. contralto. Studied with John Wass, Mrs. Sims Reeves and Pinsuti, made an early appearance at Birmingham and went on tour in Eng. in 1865, marrying John P. the following year.

Patey, John (**George**) (b. Stonehouse,

Devon, 1835; d. Falmouth, 4. XII. 1901), Eng. baritone, husband of prec. Studied medicine at first, but went to Paris and Milan to learn singing and made his 1st stage appearance in London, 1858. He married Janet Whytock in 1866.

Pathetic Sonata (*Sonate pathétique*), Beethoven's pf. sonata in C min., Op. 13, comp. *c.* 1798 and ded. to Prince Carl von Lichnowsky. The title (in Fr.) is, exceptionally, the comp.'s own.

'Pathetic' Symphony, Tchaikovsky's 6th symph., in B min., Op. 74, comp. 1893 and 1st perf. under the comp., St. Petersburg, 28. X. 1893. The title 'Tragic' Symph. was suggested by the comp.'s brother Modest, but rejected by Tchaikovsky, who afterwards agreed to the adj. 'Pathétique'.

Pathétique. *See* **Pathetic Sonata** (Beethoven).

Patience, or Bunthorne's Bride, operetta by Sullivan (lib. by W. S. Gilbert), prod. London, Opéra-Comique, 25. IV. 1881.

Patiño, Carlos (b. Galicia, ?; d. Madrid, 1683), Span. comp. Was (?) in the service of John IV of Port. early in the cent. and in 1633 became choirmaster in the royal chapel at Madrid.

Works incl. Masses, Benedictus for the funeral of Philip II (1599) and other church mus.; incid. mus. for plays; *villancicos*, etc.

Paton, Mary Ann (b. Edinburgh, X. 1802; d. Chapelthorpe, Yorks., 21. VII. 1864), Scot. soprano. Appeared as a child playing the harp, pf. and vln. and made her 1st stage appearance in London in 1822. Married Lord William Pitt Lennox in 1824, but they separated later. She was the 1st Rezia in Weber's *Oberon* in 1826.

Patrie, overture by Bizet (not for Sardou's play of that name), comp. 1873, 1st perf. Paris, 15. II. 1874.

Patter Song, a type of song, usually comic, the effect of which depends on a rapid, syllabic delivery of the words to quick mus. Many familiar exs. occur in Sullivan's operettas.

Patti, Adelina (Adela Juana Maria) (b. Madrid, 10. II. 1843; d. Craig-y-Nos, Wales, 27. IX. 1919), It. soprano. Made her 1st appearance in N.Y. at the age of 7, and after a brief period of study reappeared there in 1859. She went to London in 1861 and sang at Covent Garden, and in Paris in 1862. She sang for the last time in 1914.

Patti, Carlotta (b. Florence, 30. X. 1835; d. Paris, 27. VI. 1889), It. soprano, sister of prec. Studied pf. with Herz in Paris, but turned to singing and made her 1st appearance in N.Y. in 1861.

Patzak, Julius (b. Vienna, 9. IV. 1898), Aus. tenor. Studied at Vienna Univ. and School of Mus., making his début in Liberec in 1926. From 1927 to 1928

he sang at Brno, from 1928 to 1945 at the Munich State Opera and from 1945 to 1960 at the Vienna State Opera. His fine lyrical voice and great mus. intelligence made him one of the great singers of the century.

Pauke (Ger.; plur. *Pauken*) = Kettledrum.

Paukenmesse (Ger., 'Kettledrum Mass'), the name given to Haydn's Mass in C maj., comp. in 1790. The reason for the unusually prominent timpani, esp. in the *Agnus Dei*, is suggested by Haydn's own title, *Missa in tempore belli* ('Mass in time of war').

Paukenschlag, Sinfonie mit dem (Haydn). *See* **Surprise Symphony.**

Paukenwirbel, Sinfonie mit dem (Haydn). *See* **Drum-Roll Symphony.**

Paul et Virginie. *See also* **Paolo e Virginia.**

Opera by R. Kreutzer (lib. by Étienne Guillaume François de Favières, based on Bernardin de Saint-Pierre's novel), prod. Paris, Comédie-Italienne, 15. I. 1791.

Opera by Massé (lib. by Jules Barbier and Michel Carré, after Saint-Pierre), prod. Paris, Opéra National Lyrique, 15. XI. 1876.

Paulin et Virginie, opera by Lesueur (lib. by Alphonse Du Congé Dubreuil, after Saint-Pierre), prod. Paris, Théâtre Feydeau, 13. I. 1794.

Pauline, opera by Cowen (lib. by Henry Hersee, based on Bulwer-Lytton's *The Lady of Lyons*), prod. London, Lyceum Theatre, 22. XI. 1876.

Paulli, Holger (Simon) (b. Copenhagen, 22. II. 1810; d. Copenhagen, 23. XII. 1891), Dan. violinist, cond. and comp. Made the vln. his principal study, became violinist in the royal orch., leader in 1849 and cond. in 1864, also cond. orchestral and choral societies. In 1866, with Gade and J. P. E. Hartmann, he became one of the directors of the Cons.

Works incl. opera *Lodsen* (*The Pilot*); 13 ballets; overture and other orchestral works; vln. pieces; songs, etc.

Paulus, the Ger. title of Mendelssohn's oratorio *St. Paul.*

Paumann, Conrad (b. Nuremberg, *c.* 1415; d. Munich, 24. I. 1473), Ger. organist and comp. Although blind from birth, he was educ. by the Grundherr family of Nuremberg, learnt the org. and comp. and became organist at St. Sebald's Church in the early 1440s. In 1467 he was app. organist to Duke Albrecht III at Munich. He travelled as org. perf. and also played other instruments.

Works incl. a *Fundamentum organisandi* (*c.* 1450), or 'Principles of Comp.', laid out in keyboard tablature, which exists in several versions; org. arr. of monophonic and polyphonic pieces; and a Ger. song, 'Wiplich figur'.

Paumgartner, Bernhard (b. Vienna, 14. XI. 1887), Aus. musicologist and comp. Studied 1st with his parents, the critic Hans P. and the singer Rosa P., *née* Papier, and afterwards with Bruno Walter. He was director of the Mozarteum at Salzburg, 1917–38, cond. a Mozart orch. there and was one of the organizers of the Salzburg festivals. He has written mainly on Mozart. Works incl. operas *Das heisse Eisen* (after Hans Sachs), *Die Höhle von Salamanca* (after Cervantes), *Rossini in Neapel*, *Aus dem Leben eines Taugenichts* (after Eichendorff's novel); ballet *Pagoden*; incid. mus. to Shakespeare's *King Lear* and *Twelfth Night* (on old Eng. tunes), Goethe's *Faust*, Gozzi's *Turandot*, etc.; *Eine deutsche Weihnachtsmusik* for chorus and orch.; suite in G min., *Overture for a Chivalric Play*, divertimento, etc., for orch.; choruses, songs, etc.

Pause, the prolongation of a note, chord or rest beyond its normal value, indicated by the sign ⌢. In the 18th-cent. concerto it is regularly placed over the $\frac{6}{4}$ chord which precedes the cadenza. In a *da capo* it marks the point at which the piece ends after repetition of the first section. In the Ger. chorale or in comps. based on it, it marks the end of each line and is to be ignored in perf.

Pause (Ger.) = Rest.

Pause del silenzio (*Pauses of Silence*), 7 symph. expressions by Malipiero, prod. Rome, Augusteo, 27. I. 1918.

Pavan (Eng.)　⎫
Pavane (Fr.)　⎬ an old dance, prob. of It.
orig., since one of its It. names is Padovana (i.e. 'from Padua'), dating back to at least the 16th cent. But the name may also come from Lat. *pavo* (peacock), and the real orig. of the dance may be Span. It was normally in common time and moved at a stately pace (*see* illustration).

comp. Studied at the Cons. dei Turchini, Naples, 1795–9, and became very popular as an opera comp.

Works incl. operas *Un avvertimento ai gelosi*, *Fingallo e Comala* (after Ossian), *Ser Marcantonio* and more than 60 others.

Pavillon (Fr.), the bell of a horn, tpt. or tromb. The direction *pavillon en l'air* occurs in scores where the comp. wishes the bell to be raised to increase the power of tone.

Pavillon chinois (Fr. = Chin. pavilion), the instrument hung with bells, etc., known in Eng. as Turkish Crescent or Jingling Johnny.

Pavin (Old Eng.) = Pavan, Pavane.

Paz, Juan Carlos (b. Buenos Aires, 5. VIII. 1897), Arg. comp. Studied in Buenos Aires and was one of the founders of the Grupo Renovación of progressive comps. in 1929, also founded a society for the perf. of new mus.

Works incl. incid. mus. for Ibsen's *Julian the Emperor*; *Canto de Navidad*, *Movimiento sinfónico*, Polytonal Variations, 3 Jazz Movements and passacaglia for orch.; overture for 12 solo instruments; 4tet for vln., clar., bass clar. and saxophone; sonatinas for clar. and pf., fl. and clar., and ob. and bassoon; 3 sonatas, 9 Ballads, 3 Inventions and other works for pf.; var. works in 12-note technique, etc.

Peacock, Thomas Love (1785–1866), Eng. novelist. *See* Maid Marian (Bishop).

Pears, Peter (b. Farnham, 22. VI. 1910), Eng. tenor. Studied at R.C.M. in London and later with Elena Gerhardt. He sang with the B.B.C. and Glyndbourne choruses (1938) and made his stage début in London in 1942. From 1943 to 1946 he was a member of Sadler's Wells Opera Co., but much of his artistic career has been assoc. with Britten's mus. His intelligence and musicianship have made him one of the great *Lieder*-singers of the day.

Pearsall, Robert (Lucas) (b. Clifton,

Byrd

PAVANE

The P. was often followed by a Galliard based on the same thematic material.

Pavane pour une infante défunte (*Pavan for a deceased Infanta*). A pf. piece by Ravel (1899), later orch. (1912).

Pavesi, Stefano (b. Vaprio nr. Crema, 22. I. 1779; d. Crema, 28. VII. 1850), It.

Bristol, 14. III. 1795; d. Wartensee, 5. VIII. 1856), Eng. comp. Studied law and was called to the Bar in 1821, but had already comp. In 1825 he settled at Mainz and studied with Panny there, devoting himself entirely to mus. Another year in Eng., 1829–30, was his last, except for visits; he settled in Ger. for good, although he inherited a property at Willsbridge, Glos., in 1836. He sold this and bought Wartensee Castle on Lake Constance.

Works incl. church mus. (Angl. and Rom.), Requiem; overture and chorus for Shakespeare's *Macbeth*; madrigals, part-songs, etc.

Pearson, Henry Hugh. See **Pierson, Henry Hugh.**

Pearson, Martin. See **Peerson.**

Peasable, James. See **Paisible.**

Peasant a Rogue, The (*Selma Sedlák*), comic opera by Dvořák (lib. by Josef Otakar Veselý), prod. Prague, Cz. Theatre, 27. I. 1878.

Peasant Cantata (*Mer hahn en neue Oberkeet = We have a new magistracy*), a secular cantata by Bach for solo voices, chorus and orch., comp. in 1742, to words in Saxon dialect. The mus. is noticeably rustic and comes as near to the manner of folksong as anything Bach ever wrote.

Pêcheurs, Les (*The Fishermen*), opera by Gossec (lib. by Adrien Nicolas de La Salle d'Offémont), prod. Paris, Comédie-Italienne, 7. VI. 1766.

Pêcheurs de perles, Les (*The Pearl Fishers*), opera by Bizet (lib. by Eugène Cormon and Michel Carré), prod. Paris, Théâtre Lyrique, 30. IX. 1863.

Ped., an abbr. used in the notation of pf. mus. to indicate the use of the sustaining pedal. (The use of the damping pedal is indicated by the words *una corda* [one string], or sometimes its abbr. *u.c.*) The abbr. also occurs in org. mus. written on 2 staves, to indicate which notes or passages are to be played on the pedals.

Pedal. (1) A sustained note in a polyphonic comp., generally but not invariably in the bass. If often occurs at the climax of a fugue.

(2) *See* **Pedals.**

Pedal Board, the keyboard of pedals.

Pedal Harp, the ordinary harp in current use, as distinct from the chromatic harp.

Pedal Notes, the fundamental notes of tromb. and other brass wind instruments, the normal compass of which consists of the upper harmonics.

Pedal Organ, the portion of the org. controlled by the pedals and the stops connected with them.

Pedal Piano, a pf. specially constructed with a keyboard of pedals and used mainly for org. practice at home, very little mus. having been written expressly for it except by Schumann.

Pedal-Point, another name for the Pedal as applied to comp.

Pedalflügel (Ger.), the Ger. name for the Pedal (grand) pf., used for ex. by

Schumann for his works for that instrument.

Pédalier (Fr.), the Fr. name for the pedal keyboard and also for the Pedal Piano.

Pedals, mechanical devices in certain instruments which require manipulation by the feet. P. may actually prod. notes, as in the org.; they may be means of obtaining certain effects of tone, as in the sustaining and damping pf. P.; or they may be used to alter the length, and thus the tuning, of strings, as in the harp.

Pedersøn, Mogens (b. ?, c. 1585; d. ? Copenhagen, 1623), Dan. singer and comp. Pupil of Melchior Borgrevinck in the royal chapel of Christian IV. After a visit to Venice, 1599–1603, he became a singer in the chapel. In 1605–9 he was at Venice again studying pf. with G. Gabrieli. In 1611–14 he was in Eng., but returned to Den. and became vice-director of the chapel in 1618.

Works incl. madrigals for 5 voices, *Pratum spirituale* for voices, etc.

Pedrell, Carlos (b. Minas, 16. X. 1878; d. Montrouge nr. Paris, 3. III. 1941), Uruguayan comp. of Span. descent. Studied at Montevideo, with his uncle Felipe P. at Barcelona in 1898–1900 and then with d'Indy and Bréville at the Schola Cantorum in Paris. In 1906 he went to Buenos Aires, where he held var. official mus. posts and founded the Sociedad Nacional de Música in 1915. In 1921 he settled in Paris.

Works incl. operas *Ardid de amor* and *Cuento de abril*; ballet *Alleluia*; *Une Nuit de Schéhérazade, Danza y canción de Aixa, En el estrado de Beatriz, Fantasia Argentina* and *Ouverture catalane* for orch.; choruses; songs with orch. and with pf., etc.

Pedrell, Felipe (b. Tortosa, 19. II. 1841; d. Barcelona, 19. VIII. 1922), Span. comp. and musicologist, uncle of prec. Studied mus. at home and as a choir-boy at Tortosa Cathedral, but had otherwise little systematic instruction. He began to pub. works in 1871 and prod. his 1st opera in 1874, at Barcelona. From that time he taught mus. hist. and aesthetics at the Madrid Cons., but he settled at Barcelona in 1894, where he worked for the revival of old and the spread of new Span. mus., ed. the complete works of Victoria and a collection of old Span. church mus., also old stage and org. mus., etc.

Works incl. operas *El último Abencerraje* (after Chateaubriand), *Quasimodo* (on Victor Hugo's *Notre-Dame de Paris*), *Cleopatra, Los Pirineos, La Celestina, El Conde Arnau, Visión de Randa* and 4 early light operas; incid. mus. for Shakespeare's *King Lear*; Mass, Requiem and Te

Deum; *Mazeppa, Il Tasso a Ferrara, La Canço Llatina, In captivitatem comploratio, Glosa* and other vocal works; *Festa, Lo cant de los montanyes, Excelsior, I trionfi,* symph. poems *Marcha de la coronación a Mistral, Motinada, Otger* for orch.; string 4tet; *Escenas de niños* for pf. duet; songs *Orientales, Consolations, Canciones arabescas,* etc.

Pedrollo, Arrigo (b. Montebello Vicentino, 5. XII. 1878; d. Vicenza, 23. XII. 1964), It. cond. and comp. Studied under his father and at the Milan Cons.

Works incl. operas *Juana, La veglia* (after Synge's *The Shadow of the Glen*), *L'uomo che ride* (after Victor Hugo), *Delitto e castigo* (after Dostoievsky's *Crime and Punishment*), *L'amante in trappola* and 5 others, 3 mimodramas; 2 *Poemetti* for chorus and orch.; symph.; chamber mus., etc.

Pedrotti, Carlo (b. Verona, 12. XI. 1817; d. Verona, 16. X. 1893), It. cond. and comp. Studied under Domenico Foroni at Verona and prod. his 1st opera there in 1840. From that time until 1845 he was cond. at the It. Opera of Amsterdam, and in 1845–68 he directed the Nuovo and Filarmonico theatres at Verona. In the latter year he settled at Turin, where he became director of the Liceo Musicale, cond. at the Teatro Regio and founded popular orchestral concerts for classical mus. He committed suicide.

Works incl. operas *Lina, Matilde, La figlia dell' arciere, Romea di Montfort, Fiorina, Il parrucchiere della reggenza, Gelmina, Genoveffa del Brabante, Tutti in maschera, Isabella d'Aragona, Mazeppa, Guerra in quattro, Marion Delorme* (after Hugo), *Il favorito, Olema la schiava,* etc.

Peel, (Gerald) Graham (b. nr. Manchester, 9. VIII. 1877; d. Bournemouth, 16.X. 1937), Eng. comp. Educ. at Harrow and Oxford, where he remained to study mus. with Ernest Walker.

Works incl. over 100 songs, many on words by A. E. Housman.

Peele, George (? 1558–? 97), Eng. poet and dramatist. *See* **Finzi** (*Farewell to Arms*).

Peer Gynt, incid. mus. for Ibsen's drama by Grieg, prod. Christiania, 24. II. 1876. Grieg afterwatds arr. 2 orch. suites from it, Op. 46 and 55.

Peerce, Jan (actually Jacob Pincus Perelmuth) (b. N.Y., 3. VI. 1904), Amer. tenor. After beginning his career as a dance-band violinist and singer he was engaged by Radio City Mus. Hall in 1933 and made his operatic début in Philadelphia in 1938. Since then he has sung largely at the N.Y. Metropolitan Opera.

Peerson, Martin (b. March nr. Ely, *c.* 1572; d. London, XII. 1650), Eng. organist and comp. He took the B.Mus. at

Oxford and was soon afterwards app. organist and choirmaster at St. Paul's Cathedral in London.

Works incl. church mus., airs and dialogues for voices, *Mottects or Grave Chamber Musique* for voices and instruments on sonnets from Fulke Greville's *Caelica*; fancies and almains for viols, virginal pieces, etc.

Peeters, Flor (b. Tielen, 4. VII. 1903), Belg. organist and comp. He studied at Mechlin and at Paris (under Dupré and Tournemire). In 1925 he was app. organist of Mechlin Cathedral. He has held teaching posts at the Lemmens Institute, Mechlin, Ghent Cons., Tilburg Cons. (Hol.) and Antwerp Cons., of which he was app. director in 1952. He has also toured widely as a recitalist and ed. several collections of early org. mus.

Works incl. 8 Masses, Te Deum; org. concerto, pf. concerto, concerto for org. and pf.; about 200 org. works; chamber mus.; pf. works; songs; etc.

Péghuilan, Aimeric de (b. Toulouse, ?; d. ?), Fr. troubadour of the 12th–13th cent. 54 poems and 6 melodies have survived.

Peintre amoureux de son modèle, Le (*The Painter in Love with his Model*), opera by Duni (lib. by Louis Anseaume), prod. Paris, Opéra-Comique, 26. VII. 1757.

Pekiel, Bartolomiej (b. ?; d. Cracow, *c.* 1670), Pol. organist and comp. He became organist at the royal chapel in Warsaw *c.* 1633–7 and 2nd director in 1641, succeeding Schacchi to the principal post in 1649. He went to Cracow during the Swed. occupation of Warsaw and in 1657 became director of mus. at the cathedral.

Works incl. Masses and motets, some with Pol. folk tunes as *canto fermo.*

Pèlerins de la Mecque (Gluck). *See* **Rencontre imprévue.**

Pelléas et Mélisande, incid. mus. for Maurice Maeterlinck's play by Fauré, prod. London, Prince of Wales Theatre, 21. VI. 1898.

Incid. mus. for do. by Sibelius, Op. 46, comp. 1905.

Opera by Debussy (lib. Maeterlinck's play, slightly altered), prod. Paris, Opéra-Comique, 30. IV. 1902.

Symph. poem on do. by Schönberg, Op. 5, comp. 1902, prod. Vienna, 26. I. 1905.

Pellegrini, Valeriano. *See* **Valeriano.**

Pellegrini, Vincenzo (b. Pesaro, ?; d. ? Milan, 1631), It. 16th–17th-cent. cleric and comp. He was a canon at Pesaro early in the 17th cent. and *maestro di cappella* at Milan Cathedral in 1611–31.

Works incl. Masses and other church mus.; org. canzonets; instrumental pieces in 3–4 parts; secular canzonets for voices, etc.

Peñalosa, Francisco (b. Toledo, *c.* 1470; d. Seville, 1. IV. 1528), Span. comp. He was (?) choirmaster to Ferdinand the Catholic after 1504 and (?) singer in the Julian Chapel in Rome under Leo X.
Works incl. church mus.; secular songs for several voices, etc.

Penderecki, Krystof (b. Dębica, 23. XI. 1933), Pol. comp. Studied comp. with Malawski and Wiechowicz in Cracow, graduating in 1958. His mus. makes frequent use of aleatory techniques and microtonal clusters, belonging to the present-day *avant-garde.*
Works incl. *St. Luke Passion* for speaker, 2 soloists, chorus and orch.; *Stabat Mater* and *Psalms of David* for chorus and orch.; *Emanations* for 2 string orchs.; *Anaclasis* for strings and perc.; *Threnody for the Victims of Hiroshima* for 52 strings: *Fluorescences* for chamber ensemble.

Penelope. *See* Circe for Keiser's opera.
Opera by Galuppi (lib. by Paolo Antonio Rolli), prod. London, King's Theatre, Haymarket, 12. XII. 1741.

Pénélope, opera by Fauré (lib. by René Fauchois), prod. Monte Carlo, 4. III. 1913; 1st Paris perf., Théâtre des Champs-Élysées, 10. V. 1913.

Penet, Hilaire (b. ?; d. ?), Fr. 16th-cent. singer and comp. He held some clerical post at Poitiers and in 1514 became a singer in the Papal Chapel in Rome, also chamber musician to Leo X.
Comp. Masses, motets, etc.

Penillion, an old form of Welsh song to the harp which was improvised (often the words as well as the mus.) as a counterpoint or descant to the harp part. It is still cultivated, but now tends to rely on tradition rather than improvisation.

Penna, Lorenzo (b. Bologna, 1613; d. Imola, 20. X. 1693), It. monk and comp. Entered the Carmelite order at Mantua and in 1669 became *maestro di cappella* at the Carmelite church of Parma, also a prof. of theology. Later he was app. to Imola Cathedral. He wrote treatises on counterpoint and figured bass.
Works incl. Masses and other church mus.; *correnti francesi* for 4 instruments, etc.

Penny Whistle, a small and rudimentary pipe of the Fife or Recorder type, also known as 'tin whistle', played vertically and having a small range of treble notes controlled by 6 finger-holes.

Penorcon, a 17th-cent. instrument of the Cittern type.

Pentatone (from Gr. = 5 notes), another name for the Pentatonic Scale.

Pentatonic Scale, a scale of 5 notes; actually any 'gapped' scale that omits 2 of the normal 7 notes of the ordinary diatonic scales, but more partic. that represented by the black notes of the pf.

Penthesilea, opera by Schoeck (lib. by comp., based on Kleist's drama), prod. Dresden, 8. I. 1927.
Symph. poem on do. by H. Wolf, comp. 1883–5.

Pepita Jiménez, opera by I. Albéniz (lib., in Eng., by Francis Burdett Money-Coutts, based on a story by Juan Valera), prod. in Span., Barcelona, Liceo, 5. I. 1896.

Pepping, Ernst (b. Duisburg, 12. IX. 1901), Ger. comp. Studied at the Hochschule für Musik in Berlin and devoted himself chiefly to the cultivation of Protestant church mus., being app. prof. at the Kirchenmusikschule at Spandau in 1947.
Works incl. setting of the 90th Psalm, unaccomp. motets, *Te Deum, Spandauer Chorbuch* containing vocal pieces for 2–6 voices for the whole eccles. year; 3 symphs., partita, var. concertos and variations on a theme by Senfl for orch.; 4 pf. concertos, 2 org. concertos; 4 pf. sonatas; chamber mus., songs, etc.

Pepusch, Johann Christoph (John Christopher) (b. Berlin, 1667; d. London, 20. VII. 1752), Ger. comp. and theorist. App. to the Prus. court at the age of 14; emigrated 1st to Hol. and went to Eng. about 1700, where he settled in London for the rest of his life. Married Margherita de l'Épine in 1718. He arranged the mus. of *The Beggar's Opera* for John Gay in 1728.
Works incl. recitatives and songs for a pasticcio opera *Thomyris* and prob. others; incid. mus. for Colley Cibber's *Myrtillo;* mus. for masques *Apollo and Daphne, The Death of Dido, The Union of the Sister Arts, Venus and Adonis;* dramatic ode for the Peace of Utrecht; overture for *The Beggar's Opera* and arrs. for it and its sequel, *Polly,* and another ballad opera, *The Wedding;* services, anthems and Lat. motets; cantatas to words by John Hughes (incl. *Alexis*) and others; odes, concertos, sonatas, etc.

Pepys, Samuel (b. London, 23. II. 1633; d. London, 25. V. 1703), Eng. official, diarist and amateur musician. Educ. at Huntingdon, St. Paul's School in London and Cambridge Univ. He held several government posts and was last secretary to the Admiralty. He kept his diary from I. 1660 to V. 1669. It testifies to his interest in mus. perfs. of all kinds and to his cultivation of mus. in his home. In 1665 he made a setting of the song 'Beauty retire' from Davenant's *Siege of Rhodes,* prod. in 1656 with mus. by H. Lawes, Locke and others. *See also* Coates (A.).

Per arsin et thesin (Lat. = by rise and fall), an obs. description of imitation by contrary motion, since one part goes up where the other goes down (*see* illustration).

Astartea, Medea, L'isola incantata, La clemenza di Tito, Semiramide, Alessandro

Bach, *The Art of Fugue*

PER ARSIN ET THESIN

Perabo, Ernst (b. Wiesbaden, 14. XI. 1845; d. Boston, Mass., 29. X. 1920), Ger. pianist and comp. A very gifted pianist as a child, he was taken to N.Y. in 1852, studied there and from 1858 in Ger., finishing at the Leipzig Cons. He returned to U.S.A. in 1865 and soon afterwards settled at Boston.

Works incl. studies and pieces for pf., e.g. *Pensées* containing an impression of the soliloquies in *Hamlet*, 10 transcriptions from Sullivan's *Iolanthe*, concert fantasies on Beethoven's *Fidelio*, etc.

Percussion, a term used in harmony for the actual incident of a discord, after its Preparation and before its Resolution.

Percussion Instruments. All instruments played by being beaten are called P. I., incl. all varieties of drums, bells, cymbals, triangles, gongs, etc. also some in which the perc. is prod. by the intermediary of a keyboard, such as the Celesta. These last instruments, as also bells, xylophone and kettledrums, prod. notes of definite pitch; others prod. sound without pitch.

Perdendosi (It. = losing itself), a direction indicating that the sound of a note or passage is to become gradually weaker until it fades away.

Peregrine Tone. *See* **Tonus peregrinus.**

Perez, Davide (b. Naples, 1711; d. Lisbon, 30. X. 1778), Span. comp. Studied at the Cons. di Santa Maria di Loreto at Naples and prod. his 1st opera, *La nemica amante*, in 1735. He became *maestro di cappella* to Prince Naselli at Palermo and in 1752 went to Lisbon, where he became attached to the royal chapel and the new Opera opened in 1755.

Works incl. operas *Siroe, I travestimenti amorosi, L'eroismo di Scipione,*

nell' Indie, Demetrio, Demofoonte, Solimano, Ezio and others, many to libs. by Metastasio; *Mattutino de' morti*, Masses and other church mus.; oratorio *Il martirio di San Bartolomeo.*, etc.

Pérez, Juan Ginés. *See* **Ginés.**

Perfall, Karl von (b. Munich, 29. I. 1824; d. Munich, 14. I. 1907), Ger. comp. Studied at Leipzig with Moritz Hauptmann, returned to Munich in 1850 and founded an oratorio society in 1854. Became intendant of the court mus. in 1864 and also of the court theatres in 1867, and was one of Wagner's opponents there.

Works incl. operas *Sakuntala* (after Kalidasa), *Das Konterfei, Raimondin (Melusine)* and *Junker Heinz*; incid. mus. for Shakespeare's *Pericles*; fairy tales for solo voices, chorus and orch. *Dornröschen, Undine* (after Fouqué) and *Rübezahl*; choruses, songs, etc.

Perfect Cadence, a C. which conclusively leads to the common chord of the tonic, either by a step from the Dominant to the Tonic in the bass (Authentic C.) or from the Sub-dominant to the Tonic (Plagal C.). In Eng. the term is generally confined to the former. *See* **Cadence.**

Perfect Fool, The, opera by Holst (lib. by comp.), prod. London, Covent Garden Theatre, 14. V. 1923.

Perfect Intervals, those Is. which do not possess alternative maj. and min. forms, but become Augmented or Diminished by being enlarged or reduced by a semitone, viz. 4ths, 5ths and 8ves, also their repetitions beyond the 8ve, i.e. 11ths, etc.

Pergolesi, Giovanni Battista (b. Jesi nr. Ancona, 4. I. 1710; d. Pozzuoli nr. Naples, 16. III. 1736), It. comp. Studied in Jesi and from 1725 under Greco, Vinci and Durante

504

at the Cons. dei Poveri di Gesù Cristo in
Naples. His earliest works were sacred
pieces, but he made his début as a comp.
for the stage in 1731, and 2 years later
prod. the comic intermezzo *La serva
padrona* (perf. between the acts of his
serious opera *Il prigionier superbo*), which
was to be decisive in the hist. of *opera
buffa*. *Maestro di cappella* to the Prince
of Stigliano from 1732, he entered the
service of the Duke of Maddaloni *c.* 1734,
but returned to Naples the next year, becoming organist to the court. In II. 1736
he retired on grounds of ill health to the
Capuchin monastery in Pozzuoli, where he
completed his last work, the *Stabat
Mater*, just before his death.

Works incl. operas *Salustia*, *Il prigionier
superbo*, *Adriano in Siria*, *L'Olimpiade*, *Lo
frate 'nnamorato Flaminio*; intermezzi *La
serva padrona*, *Livietta e Tracollo*; oratorios
La morte di S. Giuseppe, *La Conversione
di S. Guglielmo d'Acquitania*, *La morte
d'Abel*, etc.; Masses, *Stabat Mater* for
soprano and alto soloists and strings,
settings of *Salve Regina*, and other church
mus.; chamber mus., keyboard mus., etc.
There are also many other works attrib.
to P. which are of doubtful authenticity.

Peri, Jacopo (b. Rome, 20. VIII. 1561;
d. Florence, 12. VIII. 1633), It. singer and
comp. Pupil of Cristoforo Malvezzi,
a canon at the church of San Lorenzo at
Florence and *maestro di cappella* to the
Medici family. P. himself became attached
to their court, later as *maestro di cappella*
and chamberlain. He became a member of
the progressive artists grouped round
Count Giovanni Bardi with Caccini,
Corsi, V. Galilei and the poet Ottavio
Rinuccini. In their mistaken endeavour
to revive Gk. drama with the kind of mus.
they imagined to be genuine Gk., they
stumbled on the invention of opera.

Works incl. operas *Dafne*, *Euridice*,
Tetide, *Adone*, tournament with mus. *La
precedenza delle dame*; parts of operas
(with others) *La guerra d'amore* and *Flora*
(with Gagliano); several ballets; *Lamento
d'Iole* for soprano and instruments,
madrigals, etc.

Péri, La, (ballet (*poème dansé*) by
Dukas, prod. Paris, Théâtre du Châtelet,
22. IV. 1912.

Périchole, La, operetta by Offenbach (lib.
by Henri Meilhac and Ludovic Halévy,
based on Mérimée's *Le Carrosse du
Saint-Sacrement*, prod. Paris, Théâtre des
Variétés, 6. X. 1868.

Périgourdine, a Fr. country dance from
the region of Périgord, known to musicians
from at least the 18th cent. Its mus. is in
6–8 time.

Perkowski, Piotr (b. Ukraine, 17. XI.
1902), Pol. comp. Studied with Statkowski
and Szymanowski at the Warsaw Cons.

and later with Roussel in Paris, where in
1927 he founded a society of young Pol.
comps. with Czapski, Labuński and Wiechowicz. He returned to Pol. and in
1935 became director of the Torun Cons.

Works incl. ballets *Swantewid*, *Klemen-
tyna*; 2 symphs., sinfonietta for small orch.;
pf. concerto, 2 vln. concertos; string 4tet;
instrumental pieces; choral works, songs,
etc.

Perle du Brésil, La (*The Pearl of Brazil*),
opera by Fél. David (lib. by Jules Joseph
Gabriel and Sylvain Saint-Étienne), prod.
Paris, Théâtre Lyrique, 22. XI. 1851.

Perlea, Jonel (b. Ograda, 13. XII.
1900), Rum. cond. Studied in Munich and
Leipzig, making his début in 1923. From
1934 to 1944 he was mus. director of the
Bucharest Opera and has cond. in leading
opera houses both in Eur. and Amer.

Perne, François Louis (b. Paris, 4. X.
1772; d. Paris, 26. V. 1832), Fr. comp.
and mus. scholar. Although he began
humbly as a choral singer and later
double bass player at the Paris Opéra, he
made a career as a serious comp. and
made a close study of Gk. mus. In 1813 he
succeeded Catel as prof. of harmony at the
Cons. and became inspector in 1816 and
librarian in 1819.

Works incl. Masses and other church
mus.; choruses for Racine's *Esther*, etc.

Perosi, Lorenzo (b. Tortona, 20. XII.
1872; d. Rome, 12. X. 1956), It. priest and
comp. Studied at Milan and Ratisbon,
and among other apps. became choirmaster at St. Mark's, Venice, 1894, and
mus. director of the Sistine Chapel in
Rome, 1898. In 1905 he was nominated
perpetual master of the Pontifical Chapel.

Works incl. 25 Masses, Requiem,
Stabat Mater, a Te Deum and much other
church mus.; oratorios *The Transfiguration*,
The Raising of Lazarus, *The Resurrection*,
Moses, *Leo the Great*, *The Last Judgment*
and *Il sogno interpretato*; *Florence*, *Rome*,
Venice and *Bologna* from 10 symphs. on
the names of It. cities planned; org.
works, etc.

Perosi, Marziano (b. Tortona, 20. X.
1875; d. Rome, 2I. I1. 1959), It. comp.,
brother of prec. Pupil of Haberl at Regensburg and of Riemann at Leipzig. Church
musician at Zürich and Vienna, 1906–12,
and organist at the Basilica di Valle
di Pompei in Rome, 1912–21.

Works incl. opera *Pompei* (after Bulwer-
Lytton); oratorio *L'addolorata*; cantata
Spes nostra, symph. poem *Notte e giorno*
for solo voices, chorus and orch.; 3
symphs. for org. and orch., etc.

Pérotin (Perotinus Magnus) (b. ?; d.
? Paris, ?), Fr. 12th-cent. comp. and
scholar. *Maître de chapelle* of the church of
the Blessed Virgin Mary (later Notre-
Dame Cathedral). He is said to have re-

vised the *Liber organi de gradali* of Leoninus, and comp. Organa in as many as
4 parts.

Perotti, Giovanni Agostino (b. Vercelli,
11. IV. 1769; d. Venice, 28. VI. 1855), It.
comp. Studied under his brother G. D. P.
and Mattei, visited Vienna in 1795 and
London in 1798, settled in Venice *c*. 1800,
became 2nd *maestro di cappella* at St.
Mark's, 1812, and 1st in succession to
Furlanetto, 1817.

Works incl. operas, ballets; church
mus., oratorios; pf. sonatas, etc.

Perotti, Giovanni Domenico (b. Vercelli, 1750; d. Vercelli, 1824), It. comp.,
brother of prec. Pupil of G. B. Martini
and *maestro di cappella* of Vercelli Cathedral from 1779. Comp. operas, church
mus., etc.

Perpetual Canon, a canon in which each
part begins again as soon as it is finished,
the other parts being at that moment at
other stages of their progress. Since even a
P. C. must finish sooner or later, however, it is broken off at a point agreed to
by the perfs.

Perpetuum mobile (Lat. = perpetually
in motion). See **Moto perpetuo.**

Perrault, Charles (1628–1703), Fr. poet
and fairy-tale writer. *See* **Cendrillon** (4
operas), **Cenerentola** (2 operas), **Forêt
bleue** (Aubert), **Fourdrain** (opera), **Hérold**
(*Belle au bois dormant*), **Hüe** (*Riquet à la
Houppe*), **Lioncourt** (*Belle au bois dormant*),
Ma Mère l'Oye (Ravel).

Perrin, Pierre (1620–75), Fr. author,
who in 1669–72 prec. Lully in holding
the patent for the management of the
Académie de Musique (Opéra) in Paris.
Librettist for Cambert and others. *See also*
Boësset (J.-B.) (*Mort d'Adonis*), **Pomone**
(Cambert).

Perry, George Frederick (b. Norwich,
1793; d. London, 4. III. 1862), Eng.
violinist, organist, cond. and comp. Learnt
mus. as a choir-boy at Norwich Cathedral
and later became violinist at the theatre
there. Settled in London as cond. of the
Haymarket Theatre, 1822, was organist at
Quebec Chapel and became leader and
later cond. of the Sacred Harmonic Society.

Works incl. opera *Morning, Noon and
Night*; oratorios *The Death of Abel, Elijah
and the Priests of Baal, The Fall of Jerusalem, Hezekiah*, cantata *Belshazzar's
Feast*; church mus.; overture *The Persian
Hunters*; songs for var. plays, etc.

Persée (*Perseus*), opera by Lully (lib.
by Quinault), prod. Paris, Opéra, 18. IV.
1682.

Perseleye, Osbert. See **Parsley.**

Perséphone, melodrama for the stage
or concert-room by Stravinsky (lib. by
André Gide), prod. Paris, Opéra, 30. IV.
1934.

Persiani (*née* **Tacchinardi**), **Fanny** (b.

Rome, 4. X. 1812; d. Neuilly nr. Paris, 3.
V. 1867), It. soprano. Studied under her
father, Niccolò Tacchinardi, and appeared at
his private pupils' theatre near Florence at
the age of 11. Married the comp. Giuseppe P.
in 1830 and made her 1st public stage
appearance at Leghorn in 1832. She 1st
went to Paris in 1837 and to London in
1838.

Persiani, Giuseppe (b. Recanati, 11. XI.
1799; d. Paris, 14. VIII. 1869), It. comp.,
husband of prec. He settled as singing-
master in Paris.

Works incl. operas *Inez di Castro,
Eufemio di Messina* and 8 others.

Persichetti, Vincent (b. Philadelphia, 6.
VI. 1915), Amer. comp. Studied pf. with
A. Jonás and O. Samaroff, comp. with P.
Nordoff and Roy Harris, cond. with Fritz
Reiner. From 1942 to 1948 he taught
comp. at the Philadelphia Cons., and then
at the Juilliard School of Mus. in N.Y.

Works incl. 7 symphs.; ballet *King Lear*;
10 serenades for different instrumental
groups; *The Hollow Men* for tpt. and string
orch.; pf. concerto; 2 pf. 5tets, 2 string
4tets; 9 pf. sonatas, 6 pf. sonatinas; vocal
mus., etc.

Persuis, Louis (Luc Loiseau) de (b.
Metz, 4. VII. 1769; d. Paris, 20. XII.
1819), Fr. violinist and comp. Studied
under his father, member of the mus.
staff at Metz Cathedral, became a violinist
in the theatre orch. and went to Avignon
following an actress with whom he had
fallen in love. There he studied further,
went to Paris, appeared at the Concert
spirituel in 1787, again became a theatre
violinist, in 1793 at the Opéra. In 1795–
1802 he was vln. prof. at the Cons., in
1810–15 court cond. to Napoleon, inspector
of mus. in 1814 and manager of the Opéra
in 1817.

Works incl. operas *La Nuit espagnole,
Estelle, Phanor et Angéla, Fanny Morna,
Le Triomphe de Trajan* (with Lesueur),
Jérusalem délivrée (after Tasso), *Les Dieux
rivaux* (with Berton, R. Kreutzer and
Spontini) and others; ballets *Nina, ou La
Folle par amour* and 5 others (some with
R. Kreutzer); church mus.; cantatas *Chant
de victoire, Chant français* and others, etc.

Persymfans (abbr. of Pervyi Symfonitchesky Ansamble = Rus. for 1st
symph. ensemble), a conductorless orch.
organized in Moscow and making its 1st
appearance there on 13. II. 1922. It was
later discontinued, not from any lack of
success, but because it was found that its
principle involved an enormous amount
of discussion and rehearsing.

Perti, Giacomo (Antonio) (b. nr. Bologna,
6. VI. 1661; d. Bologna, 10. IV. 1756), It.
comp. Studied with his uncle Lorenzo P., a
priest at San Petronio at Bologna, and
later with Petronio Franceschini. After

visits to Venice and Modena in the 1680s, he became *maestro di cappella* at San Pietro at Bologna in 1690 and of San Petronio in 1696.

Works incl. operas *Oreste*, *Marzio Coriolano*, *L'incoronazione di Dario*, *Teodora*, *Il furio Camillo*, *Pompeo*, *Nerone fatto Cesare*, *Penelope la casta*, *Fausta*, *Rodelinda*, *Lucio Vero* and 17 others; *Missa solemnis* for solo voices, chorus and orch., other Masses, motets, etc.; oratorio *Abramo*, 4 Passion oratorios and several others, etc.

Pertile, Aureliano (b. Montagnana, nr. Padua, 9. XI. 1885; d. Milan, 11. I. 1952), It. tenor. Studied with Orefice, making his début in Vincenza in 1911. After further study he sang at the N.Y. Metropolitan Opera from 1921 to 1922, at La Scala, Milan, from 1921 to 1937, and also at Covent Garden from 1927 to 1931. On his retirement he taught at the Milan Cons.

Peruvian Composer. *See* Sas.

Pes (Lat. = foot), in medieval Eng. mus. the lowest part of a vocal comp. in several parts, partic. one that consists of a recurrent figure, as in 'Sumer is icumen in'.

Pesante (It. = heavy, weighty), a direction indicating that a passage is to be played very firmly.

Pesca (It. noun = fishing), a 14th-cent. *caccia* with a text referring to fishing.

Pescatrici, Le (*The Fisher Girls*), opera by Bertoni (lib. by Goldoni), prod. Venice, Teatro San Samuele, 26. XII. 1751.

Pescetti, Giovanni Battista (b. Venice, *c.* 1704; d. Venice, 20. III. 1766), It. comp. A pupil of Lotti, he prod. his first opera, *Nerone detronato*, in Venice in 1725. From 1737 to *c.* 1747 he lived in London, and was for a time mus. director of the Covent Garden and King's theatres. App. 2nd organist at St. Mark's, Venice, in 1762.

Works incl. operas *Gli odi delusi del sangue*, *Dorinda* (both with Galuppi), *Demetrio*, *Diana ed Endimione*, *La conquista del vello d'oro*, *Tamerlano* (with Cocchi) and *c.* 20 others; oratorio *Gionata*: church mus.; harpsichord sonatas, etc.

Pesenti, Michele (b. Verona, *c.* 1475; d. ?, after 1521), It. 15th–16th-cent. priest and comp. Wrote *frottole*, etc.

Pessard, Émile (Louis Fortuné) (b. Paris, 29. V. 1843; d. Paris, 10. II. 1917), Fr. comp. and teacher. Studied at the Paris Cons., where he gained the Prix de Rome in 1866. He later became prof. of harmony there and also inspector of singing in the Paris municipal schools.

Works incl. operas *La Cruche cassée*, *Don Quichotte* (after Cervantes), *Le Capitane Fracasse* (after Gautier), *Tartarin sur les Alpes* (after Daudet), *Les Folies amoureuses* (after Regnard), *Une nuit de Noël*, *La Dame de trèfle*, *Mamzelle Cara-*

bin and others; church mus.; orchestral works; chamber mus.; songs, etc.

Peter Grimes, opera by Britten (lib. by Montagu Slater, based on part of Crabbe's poem *The Borough*), prod. London, Sadler's Wells Opera, 7. VI. 1945.

Peter Ibbetson, opera by Deems Taylor (lib. by comp. and Constance Collier, based on George du Maurier's novel), prod. N.Y., Metropolitan Opera, 7. II. 1931.

Peter Schmoll und seine Nachbarn (*P. S. and his Neighbours*), opera by Weber (lib. by Joseph Turk, based on a novel by Carl Gottlob Cramer), prod. Augsburg, (?) III. 1803.

Peter the Shipwright (Lortzing). *See* Zar und Zimmermann, of which it was the 1st Eng. title.

Peterkin, Norman (b. Liverpool, 21. XII. 1886), Eng. comp. of Scot. and Ir. descent. He is self-taught in mus. He joined the mus. dept. of the Oxford Univ. Press and was its director from 1941–7.

Works incl. chamber mus.; rhapsody and *Twilight Tune* for vln. and pf.; 2 suites and many pieces for pf.; numerous songs, etc.

Peters, C. F., a mus. pub. firm founded at Leipzig in 1814 by Carl Friedrich P. (1779–1827), who bought the Bureau de Musique founded by F. A. Hoffmeister and A. Kühnel in 1800. In 1950 the firm was re-estab. in Frankfurt, where it is directed by Johannes Petschull. The C. F. Peters Corporation, N.Y., is directed by Walter Hinrichsen.

Peters, Roberta (b. N.Y., 4. V. 1930), Amer. soprano. Studied in N.Y. with W. Hermann, making her début at the Metropolitan Opera in 1950, where she has remained as one of America's leading coloratura singers.

Peterson-Berger, (Olof) Wilhelm (b. Ullånger, 27. II. 1867; d. Östersund, 3. XII. 1942), Swed. mus. critic, poet and comp. Studied at the Stockholm Cons. and at Dresden, where he taught at the Mus. School for a time. Later he settled at Stockholm as critic.

Works incl. operas *Ran*, *Arnljot*, *Domesdagsprofeterna* and *Adils och Elisiv*; 5 symphs.: I. *Baneret*, II. *Sunnanfärd*, III. *Same-Åtnam*, IV. *Holmia*, V. *Solitudo*, intermezzo *Carnival in Stockholm* for orch.; ballad *Florez and Blanzeflor* for voice and orch.; many songs, etc.

Petit Chaperon Rouge, Le (*Little Red Riding-Hood*), opera by Boïeldieu (lib. by Emmanuel Guillaume Théaulon de Lambert), prod. Paris, Opéra-Comique, 30. VI. 1818.

Petit Faust, Le, operetta by Hervé (lib. by Hector Crémieux and Adolphe Jaime, a parody of Goethe's drama and esp.

of Gounod's opera), prod. Paris, Fantaisies-Parisiennes, 29. IV. 1869.

Petits Riens, Les (*The Little Nothings*), ballet by Mozart, K. App. 10 (choreography by Jean Noverre), written in Paris and prod. there, Opéra, 11. VI. 1778.

Petrarch (Francesco Petrarca) (1304–1374), It. poet. *See* **Balmer** (Sonnet 103), **Mudarra** (sonnets), **Tommasini** (choral work). There are also 3 sonnets set as songs by Schubert in trans. by A. W. Schlegel and 3 *Sonetti di Petrarca* in Liszt's *Années de Pèlerinage* for pf., arr. in 1846 from earlier settings of the poems for voice and pf. Many settings by It. 16th–17th cent. madrigalists.

Petrassi, Goffredo (b. Zagarolo nr. Rome, 16. VII. 1904), It. comp. Learnt mus. as a child in the singing-school of the church of San Salvatore in Lauro at Rome, but did not study systematically until the age of 21, when he entered the Cons. di Santa Cecilia, gaining comp. and org. prizes there. He also had advice from Casella, and in 1933 he came out as a comp. by a perf. of his orchestral Partita at the Augusteo, which was later given at the S.I.M.C. festival in Amsterdam. His music makes individual use of 12-note methods.

Works incl. operas *Il Cordovano* and *La morte dell' aria*; ballet *Il ritratto di Don Chisciotte* (after Cervantes); incid. mus. for A. Aniante's play *Carmen*; Psalm ix for chorus and orch.; *Il coro dei morti* and *Noche oscura* for chorus; Magnificat for voice and orch.; Partita, Passacaglia, 7 concertos and concert overture for orch.; *Tre Cori* for chamber orch.; pf. concerto; *Lamento d'Arianna* (Rinuccini) for voice and chamber orch., *Introduzione ed Allegro* for vln. and 11 instruments; *Sinfonia, Siciliana e Fuga* for string 4tet; *Preludio, Aria e Finale* for cello and pf.; toccata for pf., *Siciliana e Marcetta* for pf. duet; song cycle *Colori del tempo* and other sings, etc.

Petrella, Enrico (b. Palermo, 1. XII. 1813; d. Genoa, 7. IV. 1877), It. comp. Studied at Naples with Zingarelli and others and prod. his 1st opera, *Il diavolo color di rosa*, there in 1829.

Works incl. operas *Le precauzioni, Elena di Tolosa, La contessa d'Amalfi* (on Feuillet's *Dalila*), *Ione, Marco Visconti, Giovanna II di Napoli, I promessi sposi* (after Manzoni), *Bianca Orsini* and many others, etc.

Petri, Egon (b. Hanover, 23. III. 1881; d. Berkeley, Calif., 27. V. 1962); Amer. pianist of Dutch origin, son of the violinist Henri Wilhelm Petri (1856–1914). He studied both the vln. and the pf. (the latter with Busoni). From 1899 to 1901 he was a violinist in the Dresden Opera orch. He first appeared as a solo pianist in 1902. He taught at the Manchester R.C.M.,

1905–11, and subsequently in Berlin, Poland and Basle. He lived in Poland from 1926 to 1939. In 1939 he settled in the U.S.A., teaching at Cornell Univ., from 1940 to 1947 and at Mills Coll., Oakland, from 1947 to 1957. He excelled as an interpreter of pf. mus. of Liszt and Busoni.

Petridis, Petro (b. Nigdé, Asia Min., 23. VII. 1892), Gk. comp. Studied at Constantinople and in Paris.

Works incl. opera *Zemfyra*; ballet; 5 symphs., dramatic symph. *Digenis Afrikas*, Gk. and Ionian Suites, Elegiac Overture, *Prelude, Aria and Fugue* for orch.; 2 pf. concertos, cello concerto; concerto grosso for wind instruments; pf. trio; 2 *Modal Suites* for pf.; songs, etc.

Petronius (Arbiter) (1st cent. A.D.), Lat. author. *See* **Durey** (*3 Poèmes de Petrone*), **Ireland** (*Satyricon* overture).

Petrov, Ossip Afanassievich (b. Elisavetgrad, 15. XI. 1806; d. St. Petersburg, 14. III. 1878), Rus. bass. Discovered singing in the market at Kursk in 1830, he was brought to St. Petersburg and made his 1st stage appearance there that year. In 1836 he created the part of Ivan Sussanin in Glinka's *Life for the Tsar.*

Petrucci, Ottaviano dei (b. Fossombrone nr. Ancona, 18. VI. 1466; d. Venice, 7. V. 1539), It. mus. printer. He estab. himself at Venice c. 1491 and held a patent for the pub. of mus. in tablature and notes in 1498–1511, when he returned to Fossombrone to continue business there. He issued many famous collections of Masses, motets, *frottole*, etc.

Petrus de Cruce (b. ?; d. ?), Fr. 13th-cent. comp., possibly from Amiens. His mensural theory is expounded in the works of Robert de Handlo and J. Hanboys. 2 motets from the Montpellier MS. can be assigned to him on the authority of the *Speculum Musicum* by Jacobus of Liège.

Petrushka, ballet by Stravinsky (scenario by comp. and Alexander Benois; choreography by Mikhail Mikhailovich Fokin), prod. Paris, Théâtre du Châtelet, 13. VI. 1911.

Petrželka, Vilém (b. Královo Pole, 10. IX. 1889), Cz. comp. He studied with Novák in Prague and Janáček at Brno, became a cond. at Pardubice and in 1919 went to Brno as prof. at the Cons.

Works incl. symph. drama *Sailor Nicholas*; *Hymn to the Sun* for chorus and orch.; 4 symphs., *Eternal Return*, 2 suites, Dramatic Overture for orch.; 4 string 4tets, fantasy and suite for string, 4tet; sonata and *Intimate Hours* for vln. and pf.; pf. pieces; songs; part-songs, etc.

Petto (It.). Chest. Hence *voce di petto* = Chest Voice.

Petyrek, Felix (b. Brno, 14. V. 1892; d. Vienna, 1. XII. 1951), Cz. pianist and comp. Studied with his father, an organist and cond. and with Adler in Vienna for theory, with Godowsky and Sauer for pf. and with Schreker for comp. Later he taught at Salzburg, Berlin, Athens and Stuttgart.

Works incl. operas *Die arme Mutter und der Tod, Der Garten des Paradieses*; pantomime *Comedy*; incid. mus. for Hans Reinhart's *Der Schatten*; *Das heilige Abendmahl*, *Litanei* and other cantatas, 3 sacred madrigals; 6tet; *Kammerlieder* for voice and chamber mus.; vln. and pf. sonata; pieces for 2 fls.; concerto, *Toccata and Fugue* (Mixolydian), *Dreikönigsmusik* (Dorian) and 6 concert studies for 2 pfs.; chorale variations and sonatina, 6 Gk. Rhapsodies, variations on an Aus. soldier's song, 24 Ukrainian folksongs for pf., etc.

Pevernage, André (b. Harlebeke nr. Courtrai, 1543; d. Antwerp, 30. VII. 1591), Flem. comp. After holding an appt. at Courtrai, he moved to Antwerp *c.* 1577 and became choirmaster at the cathedral, holding the post until his early death. Apart from cultivating church mus., he held weekly concerts at his house.

Works incl. *Cantiones sacrae* and other church mus.; madrigals and *chansons*; ode to St. Cecilia, etc.

Peyro, José (b. ?; d. ?), Span. 17th-cent. comp.

Works incl. incid. mus. to Calderón's *El jardin de Falerina* and (?) Lope de Vega's *Selva sin amor*.

Pezzo (It., plur. *pezzi*). A piece of mus.

Pfeifertag, Der (*The Piper's Day*), opera by Schillings (lib. by Ferdinand von Sporck), prod. Schwerin, 26. XI. 1899.

Pfeiffer, Marianne. *See* Spohr.

Pfitzner, Hans (b. Moscow, 5. V. 1869; d. Salzburg, 22. V. 1949), Ger. cond. and comp. The family moved to Frankfurt, where P.'s father, a violinist, became mus. director of the munic. theatre. He studied pf. with Kwast and comp. with Knorr at the Cons. there. In 1893 he gave a 1st concert of his own works in Berlin, and after some teaching and cond. apps. he became prof. at Stern's Cons. there in 1897, 1st cond. at the Theater des Westens in 1903. He also cond. the Kaim orch. at Munich and the Opera at Strasbourg. After the success of his *Palestrina* in 1917 he devoted himself mainly to comp., but wrote many essays and pamphlets attacking modern mus., esp. Busoni, and defending romantic and Germanic ideals.

Works incl. operas *Der arme Heinrich, Die Rose vom Liebesgarten, Christelflein, Palestrina, Das Herz*; incid. mus. to Ibsen's *Feast at Solhaug* and Kleist's *Käthchen von Heilbronn*; cantatas *Von deutscher Seele* (Eichendorff), *Das dunkle*

Reich and others; 3 symphs., scherzo for orch.; pf. concerto, vln. concerto, 2 cello concertos; ballads and songs for voice, and orch.; 3 string 4tets, pf. 5tet, pf. trio; vln. and pf. sonata, cello and pf. sonata; numerous songs, etc.

Phaedra. *See* Fedra.

Phaéton, opera by Lully (lib. by Quinault), prod. Versailles, 9. I. and 1st perf. Paris, 27. IV. 1683.

Symph. poem by Saint-Saëns, 1st perf. Paris, 7. XII. 1873.

Phagotus (= It. *fagotto* = faggot, bundle), a curious instrument, long obs., developed from the Serbian bagpipe by Afranio Albonese of Pavia early in the 16th cent. It consisted of 2 pipes like those of an org., supplied with wind from hand bellows, but their pitch was variable by their being fingered on holes.

Phalèse, Flem. family of mus. printers:
1. **Pierre P.** (b. Louvain, *c.* 1510; d. Louvain, 1573–4), began to pub. mus. at Louvain, *c.* 1545.
2. **Corneille** (or **Cornelius**) **P.** (b. Louvain, ?; d. ?), son of prec., who gave up his share in the business to his brother (3) at an early date.
3. **Pierre P.** (b. Louvain, ?; d. Antwerp, 13. III. 1629), brother of prec., who moved to Antwerp to join his father's partner, Jean Bellère, there.
4. **Madeleine P.** (b. Antwerp, 1586; d. Antwerp, 30. V. 1652), daughter of prec., who continued her father's business in partnership with her sister (5).
5. **Marie P.** (b. Antwerp, 1589; d. Antwerp, *c.* 1674), sister of prec., with whom she continued in partnership and after her death ran the business under her married name of de Meyer.

Phantasy. *See* Fantasy.

Philémon et Baucis, opera by Gounod (lib. by Jules Barbier and Michel Carré, after Ovid), prod. Paris, Théâtre Lyrique, 18. II. 1860.

Philharmonic Pitch. *See* Pitch.

Philharmonic Society, London, *see* Royal Philharmonic Society; Vienna, *see* Gesellschaft der Musikfreunde.

Philidor, Fr. family of musicians:
1. **Jean P.** (b. ?, *c.* 1620; d. Paris, 8. IX. 1679), fifer, oboist, cromorne and tromba marina player, brother of Michel Danican, which was the orig. family name (for reasons of the change of name *see* Danican). He entered the service of Louis XIII about the time of his brother's death, *c.* 1659. Comp. dance mus.
2. **André P.** (b. ?, *c.* 1647; d. Dreux, 11. VIII. 1730), bassoonist, oboist, etc., and comp., son of prec. Entered the royal service as a boy, played all sorts of instruments there, competed with Lully in writing fanfares, marches, etc., and was soon commissioned to provide dances and

Philidor

stage diversions. In 1684 he became librarian of the king's mus. library and made a huge MS. collection of court and church mus.

Works incl. divertissements *Le Carnaval de Versailles*, *Le Mariage de la Couture avec la grosse Cathos*, *La Princesse de Crète*, *La Mascarade du vaisseau marchand*, *Le Jeu d'échecs*, etc.

3. Jacques P. (b. Paris, 5. V. 1657; d. Versailles, 27. V. 1708), oboist, bassoonist, etc., and comp., brother of prec. Entered court service *c.* 1670, the royal chapel in 1683 and the chamber mus., as bassoonist in 1690. Comp. marches, airs for ob., dance mus., etc.

4. Alexandre P. (b. Paris, *c.* 1660; d. ?), cromorne and tromba marina player, brother of prec. He too was in service at court.

5. Anne Danican P. (b. Paris, 11. IV. 1681; d. Paris, 8. X. 1728), oboist and comp., son of 2 by his 1st wife, Marguerite Monginot. Entered court service as oboist in the chamber mus. and the royal chapel, founded the Concert spirituel in Paris, 1725, and later in life superintended the Duchesse de Maine's and the Prince de Conti's private concerts.

Works incl. pastorals *L'Amour vainqueur*, *Diane et Endymion*, *Danaé*, etc.

6. Michel P. (b. Versailles, 2. IX. 1683; d. ?), drummer, brother of prec. In service at court.

7. François P. (b. Versailles, 17. III. 1689; d. ? Versailles, 1717–18), ob., cromorne, tromba marina and bass viol player and comp., brother of prec. In court service, comp. fl. pieces, etc.

8. François André (Danican) P. (b. Dreux, 7. IX. 1726; d. London, 24. VIII. 1795), comp. and chess-player, half-brother of prec., being the son of 2 by his 2nd wife. As a page at court he studied mus. under Campra, and also showed a remarkable precocity for chess, which took him on a tour of Hol., Ger. and Eng. in 1745. Further travels followed, and in 1749 he pub. in London his *Analyse du jeu des échecs*. He returned to Paris in 1754, and there prod. his first *opéra-comique* in 1759, the beginning of a long series of spectacular successes. He continued to visit Eng. as a chess-player, and in 1792 took refuge from the Fr. Revolution in London, where he remained till his death.

Works incl. operas *Blaise le savetier*, *L'Huître et les plaideurs*, *Le Quiproquo*, *Le Soldat magicien*, *Le Jardinier et son seigneur* (after La Fontaine), *Le Maréchal ferrant*, *Sancho Pança dans son île* (after Cervantes), *Le Bûcheron*, *Les Fêtes de la paix*, *Le Sorcier*, *Tom Jones* (after Fielding), *Le Jardinier de Sidon*, *L'Amant déguisé*, *La Nouvelle école des femmes*, *Mélide*, *ou Le Navigateur*, *Le Bon Fils*, *Les Femmes vengées*, *Ernelinde*, *Persée* (after Lully's old

Phillips

lib.), *Thémistocle*, *L'Amitié au village*, *La Belle Esclave*, *ou Valcour et Zeïla*, *Bélisaire* and others; Requiem for Rameau, motet *Lauda Jerusalem* and others; settings of Horace's *Carmen saeculare* and Congreve's *Ode on St. Cecilia's Day*, etc.

9. Pierre P. (b. Paris, 22. VIII. 1681; d. ?, 1. IX. 1731), flautist, violist and comp., son of 3. Was in the royal band, comp. fl. suites, etc.

10. Jacques P. (b. ? Paris, 7. IX. 1686; d. Pamplona, 25. VI. 1726), oboist and drummer, brother of prec. Succeeded his father in the royal service.

11. François P. (b. Paris, 21. I. 1695; d. Paris, 27. X. 1728), oboist, brother of prec. Member of the royal chamber mus.

12. Nicholas P. (b. Versailles, 3. XI. 1699; d. ? Paris, 1769), oboist and violist, brother of prec. In service at court.

Philip, Saint. *See* Neri.

Philippe de Vitry. *See* Vitry.

Philips, Peter (b. ?, 1561; d. Brussels, 1628), Eng. organist and comp. He left Eng. in 1582, prob. because he was a Rom. Catholic, visited It., Fr. and Spain, settled at (?) Antwerp, became a canon at the collegiate church of Soignies and *c.* 1611 was app. organist at the royal chapel in Brussels. In 1621 he became chaplain of the church of Saint-Germain at Tirlemont and *c.* 1623 canon of Béthune, but may not have resided at either place. He was famous as an organist throughout the Netherlands.

Works incl. Masses, motets, hymns, *Sacrae cantiones*; madrigals; fantasies, pavans and galliards for var. instruments; org. and virginal pieces, etc.

Phillipps, Adelaide (b. Stratford-on-Avon, 26. X. 1833; d. Carlsbad, 3. X. 1882), Eng. contralto. The family settled in N. Amer. in 1840, where she 1st appeared as a dancer. On the recommendation of Jenny Lind she turned to mus. and studied singing with Garcia in London in 1854 made her 1st appearance in opera at Milan. Later she sang chiefly in U.S.A.

Phillips, Burrill (b. Omaha, Nebraska, 9. XI. 1907), Amer. comp. Pupil of Howard Hanson at the Eastman School of Mus. at Rochester, N.Y., where he joined the teaching staff later.

Works incl. 1-act opera; ballet *Princess and Puppet*; *Grotesque Dance*, *Selections from Guffey's Reader* and *Courthouse Square* for orch.; concerto for pf. and chamber orch.; 4tet for ob. and strings; trio for tpts.; pf. suite *3 Informalities*, etc.

Phillips, Henry (b. Bristol, 13. VIII. 1801; d. London, 8. IX. 1876), Eng. baritone. Appeared on the stage as a boy, sang in the chorus at Drury Lane Theatre in London and gradually worked his way up as a concert singer. He also sang in opera and prod. table entertainments.

Phillips, Montague (Fawcett) (b. London, 13. XI. 1885; d. Esher, 4. I. 1969), Eng. comp. Studied at the R.A.M. in London.

Works incl. operettas *The Rebel Maid* and *The Golden Triangle*; symph. in C min., sinfonietta, overtures and suites, symph. poem *Boadicea* for orch.; 2 pf. concertos, fantasy for vln. and orch.; songs, etc.

Phillips, Stephen (1868–1915), Eng. poet and dramatist. *See* **Coleridge-Taylor** (4 plays, incid. mus.), **Francesca da Rimini** (Napravnik), **O'Neill** (*Lost Heir*), **Pitt** (*Paolo and Francesca*).

Philosopher, The, nickname of Haydn's symph. No. 22 in E♭ maj., comp. 1764 and containing, exceptionally, parts for 2 cors anglais.

Philtre, Le (*The Love Potion*), opera by Auber (lib. by Scribe), prod. Paris, Opéra, 20. VI. 1831. *See also* **Elisir d'amore**.

Phinot (or **Finot**), **Dominique** (b. ?; d. ?), Fr. 16th-cent. comp.

Works incl. Masses, motets, Magnificats, psalms and other church mus.; *chansons*, etc.

Phoebus and Pan (Bach). *See* **Streit zwischen Phöbus und Pan.**

Phonetics, the science of the physical conditions of speech and song.

Phonograph. *See* **Gramophone.**

Phonology, the science of vocal sound.

Phrase, a small group of notes forming a definite melodic or thematic feature in a comp.

Phrasing, the proper perf. of a Phrase delivered according to the comp.'s prescriptions and, where these are not sufficiently definite, according to the perf.'s taste and feeling. Good P. incl. the observance of tied or detached grouping of notes, the distribution of stresses and inflections, bowing on string instruments, breath control in wind playing and singing and choice of the best fingering in instrumental mus. The problems of breathing also affect, by analogy, the delivery on other than wind instruments.

Phrygian Cadence, a Cadence which owes its name to the fact that in the Phrygian Mode (E–E) the 6th degree of the scale (D) was not sharpened by *musica ficta*, since this would have resulted in an augmented 6th with the note F, and altering F to F♯ would have destroyed the character of the mode. Hence the normal practice was to harmonize the Cadence as follows:

This Cadence was so firmly estab. that it survived the disappearance of the modes and acquired the flavour of a kind of imperfect Cadence on the dominant of A min. Transposed into any key that was required it was widely used in the late 17th and early 18th cent., particularly to mark a transition from one movement to another. This transition was not always harmonically obvious; it was common practice to use it at the end of a slow middle movement in a min. key in order to lead into a final movement in a maj. key. In Bach's 3rd Brandenburg Concerto it is used by itself without any middle movement at all.

Phrygian Mode, the 3rd eccles. mode, represented on the pf. by the scale beginning with the note E played on the white notes.

Physharmonica, a small reed org. invented by Anton Hackel of Vienna in 1818; a forerunner of the Harmonium.

Piacere (It. = pleasure). *See* **A piacere.**

Piacevole (It.), pleasantly, agreeably.

Pianette (corrupt Fr.), a name used in Eng. for a tiny upright pf. similar to the Pianino, but even smaller. It is called Bibi, orig. Bébé, in Fr.

Piangendo (It.), weeping, wailing, plangent.

Pianino, a small upright pf.

Pianissimo (It., superlative = very soft), a direction rarely written out in full, but indicated by the sign *pp* or a multiplication thereof.

Piano (It. adj. = soft). This too is as a rule repres. by a symbol: *p*. The compar. 'softer' for a dynamic direction between *p* and *pp*, etc., has no symbol, but is expressed by the words *più piano* (or *più p*).

Piano (noun), the current abbr. name of the Pianoforte.

Piano-Organ (or Handle-Piano), a mechanical instrument similar to the Barrel Org., in the shape of an upright pf., prod. its notes in the same way by a studded cylinder, but from strings struck by hammers instead of pipes. It was widely used by street musicians in the larger Eng. cities in the late 19th and early 20th cent., esp. in London, of which it was long part of the atmosphere. It was often wrongly called 'barrel org.' and even more incorrectly 'hurdy-gurdy'.

Piano Quartet, the technical term for a 4tet for pf., vln., vla. and cello.

Piano Quintet, a 5tet for pf. and string 4tet.

Piano Score. *See* **Score.**

Piano Trio, a trio for pf., vln. and cello.

Pianoforte (It. lit. soft-loud), a keyboard instrument orig. similar to the harpsichord in appearance, but prod. its sound by striking the strings with hammers (a principle derived from the medieval

Dulcimer) instead of plucking them with quills or leather tongues. Its beginnings go back to It. at the end of the 16th cent., but the 1st inventor who prob. consolidated it in its present form was Bartolommeo Cristofori of Padua, settled in Florence, about the 1st decade of the 18th cent. The table-shaped square pf. came later in the cent. and the upright pf. followed last in the 19th cent. The hammer action was improved by very gradual processes, and Eng. makers contrib. the invention of the iron frame, which was capable of supporting a much greater tension of strings, resulting in more powerful tone.

Pianola, a mechanical device attached to an ordinary pf. whereby the hammers are made to touch the strings not by action of the hand on the keyboard but by air-pressure. This is regulated by a roll of perforated paper running over a series of slits corresponding with the mus. scale and releasing the air only where the holes momentarily pass over the slits. The mechanism is set in motion by pedals like those of a harmonium. Dynamics were at first controlled by action of the player's hands, more or less roughly, according to his skill, but they were later repro. mechanically exactly as played by the recording artist. This, however, left the manipulator with nothing of any interest to do, and no doubt for that reason the P., after enjoying a great vogue in the early 20th cent., has now fallen into neglect.

Pianotron, an electrophonic upright pf. evolved from the Neo-Bechstein grand pf. by Selmer of London in 1938, prod. its notes by the conversion of electrical waves into audible sounds.

Piatigorsky, Gregor (b. Ekaterinoslav, 20. IV. 1903), Rus. cellist. First studied the vln. with his father and then the cello with von Glehn, subsequently playing with various Moscow orchs. He left Rus. in 1921 and went to Berlin, where he studied with J. Klengel and became 1st cello with the Berlin Phil. Orch. Since then he has become known as one of the leading solo performers of today.

Piatti (It. = plates) = Cymbals.

Piatti, Alfredo (Carlo) (b. Bergamo, 8. I. 1822; d. Crocetta di Mozzo, 18. VII. 1901), It. cellist. Studied mus. under his father, a violinist, and cello under his great-uncle Zanetti. He soon entered a theatre orch., came under the notice of Mayr and was sent to study at the Milan Cons., making his 1st public appearance in 1837. He travelled widely later and lived much of his life in London, where he became assoc. with Joachim and played frequently at the Popular Concerts at St. James's Hall. He wrote 2 concertos

and a number of pieces and studies for cello.

Pib-Corn or ⎫
Pibgorn ⎭ (from Welsh = pipe-horn), a primitive wind instrument, made of wood or bone with a bell made of an animal's horn, formerly used by the Welsh and other Celts.

Pibrac (du Faur), Guy (1529–86), Fr. poet. *See* **Boni** (quatrains).

Pibroch, variations for the bagpipe played elaborately on a type of theme called the Urlar.

Picardy Third. *See* **Tierce de Picardie.**

Piccaver, Alfred (b. Long Sutton, Lincs., 25. II. 1884; d. Vienna, 23. IX. 1958), Eng. tenor. He worked as an electrical engineer in N.Y., where he was brought up, and also sang in student perfs. at the Metropolitan Opera School. On a visit to Europe in 1907 he applied for an audition and made his 1st professional appearance at the Prague Opera in the same year. After a period of further study he joined the Vienna Opera in 1910 and remained there until 1937, when he retired and settled in London. He returned to Vienna in 1955 and was active as a teacher.

Picchettato ⎫
Picchiettando ⎬ (It. = knocking, spot-
Picchiettato ⎭ ted), a detached style of bowing in string playing, similar to *spiccato*.

Piccinni, Louis-Alexandre ⎫ *See* end of
Piccinni, Luigi ⎭ paragraph below.

Piccinni, Niccolò (b. Bari, 16. I. 1728; d. Passy nr. Paris, 7. V. 1800), It. comp. Studied at the Cons. di Sant' Onofrio at Naples, Leo and Durante being among his masters. He prod. his 1st opera at Naples in 1754. In spite of Logroscino's exclusive success it was well received and soon followed by other operas, both comic and serious. In 1756 he married the singer Vincenza Sibilla, his pupil. In 1760 he made an enormous success in Rome with *La buona figliuola.* After some years of success there he was ousted by Anfossi and returned to Naples in 1773. In 1776 he was invited to Paris, where he was at first in great difficulties, but was helped by Marmontel, who taught him Fr. and wrote the lib. of his 1st Fr. opera, *Roland,* for him, which was prod. in I. 1778. By this time he had been artificially made into an opponent to Gluck by those who were determined to organize a partisan feud, though neither he nor Gluck had any desire to take a share in this and liked and respected each other. The quarrel of their adherents was heightened by, their being both given an *Iphigénie en Tauride* to set to mus. At the Revolution he left for It., visited Venice and then returned home to Naples, where, however, he was placed under close surveillance and lived in great poverty. In 1798 he at last succeeded in returning to Paris. After a period of comparative affluence, he again fell into poverty, was relieved by a gift from Bonaparte and an inspector's post at the Cons., but became paralysed and finally d. in distress. His son Luigi (1766–1827) and his natural grandson Louis-Alexandre (1779–1850) were both comps. The former wrote operas for Paris and Stockholm, the latter ballets, melodramas, etc., for the Paris theatres.

Works incl. *c.* 120 operas, e.g. *Le donne dispettose, Le Gelosie, Zenobia, Alessandro nell' Indie* (2 versions), *Madama Arrighetta, La buona figliuola, La buona figliuola maritata* (both after Richardson's *Pamela*), *Il cavaliere per amore, Le contadine bizarre, Gli stravaganti, L'Olimpiade, I viaggiatori, La pescatrice, Le finte gemelle, Vittorina* (Goldoni), *Roland, Atys, Iphigénie en Tauride, Didon, Le Faux Lord, Pénélope, Endymion*; oratorio *Jonathan* and 3 others; Mass, psalms and other church mus., etc.

Picco Pipe, a woodwind instrument of the recorder or flageolet type which became fashionable in Eng. on being intro. to London in 1856 by a Sardinian player named Picco.

Piccolo (It., abbr. for *flauto piccolo* = little flute), the small 8ve fl., more usually called *ottavino* in It., similar in shape and technique to the ordinary fl., but smaller in size and standing an 8ve higher in pitch. Its mus. is written an 8ve below the actual sound. Also a 2-ft org. stop repro. P. tone.

Piccolomini, Marietta (b. Siena, 15. III. 1834; d. Florence, 23. XII. 1899), It. soprano. Made her 1st appearance at Florence in 1852 and 1st visited Eng. in 1856.

Pichl, Wenzel (b. Bechyně nr. Tábor, 25. IX. 1741; d. Vienna, 23. I. 1805), Boh. violinist and comp. Studied in Prague and in 1765 became violinist and vice-director of mus. (under Dittersdorf) to the Bishop of Grosswardein. In 1769 he moved to Vienna and thence to Milan in the service of the Archduke Ferdinand, remaining in It. until his return to Vienna in 1796.

According to Pichl's own catalogue, works incl. 12 operas; over 20 Masses; 89 symphs.; *c.* 30 concertos; 172 4tets, 21 5tets, etc.; 148 pieces for barytone, etc.

Pick-Mangiagalli, Riccardo (b. Strakonice, 10. VII. 1882; d. Milan, 8. VII. 1949), Cz.-It. comp. Studied in Prague, Vienna and Milan. In 1936 he succeeded Pizzetti as director of the Milan Cons.

Works incl. operas *Basi e Bote, L'ospite inatteso* and *Notturno romantico*; ballets *Salice d'oro, Il carillon magico, Casanova a*

Venezia, La Berceuse and *Variazioni coreografiche*; mime dramas *Sumitra* and *Mahit*; *Sortileggi* for pf. and orch.; string 4tet; vln. and pf. sonata; pf. works, etc.

Pickwick, opera by Albert Coates (lib. by comp., based on Dickens), prod. London, Covent Garden Theatre, 20. XI. 1936.

Pictures at an Exhibition, a suite of pf. pieces by Mussorgsky, comp. in 1874 in memory of the painter and architect Victor Alexandrovich Hartmann (d. 1873) and illustrating pictures and designs by him shown at a memorial exhibition, organized by V. V. Stassov. Orchestral versions of the work have been made by Henry J. Wood, Ravel and Walter Goehr.

Pictures, Music based on. *See* **Paintings.**

Pieno (It. = full), a direction used esp. in org. mus. in combination, *organo pieno*, meaning either that a figured bass is to be filled with ample harmony or that the instrument is to be played with full registration.

Pierluigi, Giovanni. *See* **Palestrina.**

Pierné, (Henri Constant) Gabriel (b. Metz, 16. VIII. 1863; d. Ploujean, Côtes du Nord, 17. VII. 1937), Fr. cond. and comp. Studied at the Paris Cons. and gained the Prix de Rome in 1882. In 1890 he succeeded Franck as organist of the church of Sainte-Clotilde, became 2nd cond. of Colonne's orch. in 1903 and at Colonne's death in 1910 succeeded him as chief cond.

Works incl. operas *Les Elfes, Pandore, La Coupe enchantée* (after La Fontaine), *La Nuit de Noël, Vendée, La Fille de Tabarin, On ne badine pas avec l'amour* (after Musset), *Fragonard, Sophie Arnould*; ballets *Les Joyeuses Commères de Paris, Bouton d'or, Cydalise et Chèvre-pied, Impressions de Music-Hall, Girations, Images, La Grisi*; pantomimes *Le Collier de saphirs, Le Docteur Blanc, Salomé*; incid. mus. to Shakespeare's *Hamlet*, Rostand's *Princesse lointaine* and other plays; oratorios *Les Enfants de Bethléem, Les Fioretti de Saint François d'Assise*; symph. poem for chorus and orch. *L'An mil; La Croisade des enfants* for children's chorus and orch.; suites, *Ouverture symphonique, Paysages franciscains, Divertissement sur un thème pastoral, Gulliver au pays de Lilliput* (after Swift), etc. for orch.; concerto in C min., *Fantaisie-ballet, Scherzo-caprice, Poème symphonique*, etc. for pf. and orch.; pf. 5tet, pf. trio, *3 Pièces en trio* for vln., vla. and cello, and other chamber mus.; pf. works; songs, etc.

Pierrot lunaire, song-cycle with chamber orch. by Schönberg, Op. 21, consisting of 21 poems by Albert Giraud trans. into Ger. by Otto Erich Hartleben, comp. 1912 and 1st perf. Berlin, 16. X. 1912. The treatment of the voice-part is one of the outstanding exs. of the use of Speech-song (*Sprechgesang*).

Pierson (orig. **Pearson**), **Henry Hugh** (or **Heinrich Hugo**) (b. Oxford, 12. IV. 1815; d. Leipzig, 28. I. 1873), Eng. comp. Educ. at Harrow and Cambridge, studied mus. with Attwood and Corfe, and interrupted a medical course to continue mus. studies at Leipzig, where he met Mendelssohn, Schumann and others. He became Reid Prof. of Mus. at Edinburgh in 1844 in succession to Bishop, but soon resigned and returned to Ger., where he remained, married Caroline Leonhardt and changed the spelling of his name.

Works incl. operas *Der Elfensieg*, *Leila* and *Contarini* (*Fenice*); incid. mus. to Goethe's *Faust* (Part II); oratorio *Jerusalem*; *Macbeth* symph., overtures to Shakespeare's *Twelfth Night*, *Julius Caesar* and *Romeo and Juliet*, funeral march for *Hamlet*; numerous songs; part-songs, etc.

Pierson, Martin. *See* Peerson.

Piéton, Loyset (b. Bernay, Normandy, ?; d. ?, after 1545), Fr. comp. often confused with Compère, both being usually called only by their Christian names. Comp. Masses, motets, psalms, etc.

Pietoso (It. from *pietà* = pity) = pityingly, compassionately.

Pietra del paragone, La (*The Touchstone*), opera by Rossini (lib. by Luigi Romanelli), prod. Milan, Teatro alla Scala, 26. IX. 1812.

Pifa. *See* below.

Piffaro (It. = fife), a small fl.-like pipe, also a shepherd's pipe akin to the ob. or bagpipe. It was often played in It. cities, esp. Rome and Naples, at Christmas time, by pipers from the hills, who seem to have played tunes of the Siciliana type akin to that of the *Pastoral Symph.* in Handel's *Messiah*, which bears the word 'Pifa' in the MS., evidently in reference to the P.

Pifferari (It.), players on the instrument above.

Piggott, Richard. *See* Pygott.

Pigheaded Peasants, The (*Tvrdé Palice*), opera by Dvořák (lib. Josef Štolba), prod. Prague, Czech Theatre, 2. X. 1881.

Pigott, Richard. *See* Pygott.

Pijper, Willem (b. Zeist, 8. IX. 1894; d. Leidschendam, 19. III. 1947), Dutch comp. Studied with Wagenaar and was app. prof. of comp. at the Amsterdam Cons. in 1925; director of the Rotterdam Cons. in 1930.

Works incl. opera *Halewijn*; incid. mus. for *Euripides'* *The Cyclops* and *The Bacchantes*, Sophocles' *Antigone* and Shakespeare's *Tempest*; 3 symphs., 6 Symph. Epigrams for orch., pf. concerto, vln. concerto, cello concerto; 4 string 4tets, 2 pf. trios, 6tet for wind and pf.;

vln. and pf. sonatas; pf. mus.; choruses; songs, etc.

Pilaczyk, Helga (b. Schöningen, 12. III. 1925), Ger. soprano. Studied in Brunswick and Hamburg, making her début at the Brunswick State Theatre in 1951. Since 1954 she has been a member of the Hamburg State Opera. She is best known for her singing of modern mus.

Pilati, Mario (b. Naples, 16. X. 1903; d. Naples, 10. XII. 1938), It. comp. Studied at the Naples Cons. Taught at Cagliari and Milan for some time and then returned to Naples, where he was app. prof. at the Cons. S. Pietro a Maiella.

Works incl. pf. concerto in C maj., suite for pf. and strings; pf. 5tet; vln. and pf. sonatas, etc.

Pilgrim's Progress, The, opera by Vaughan Williams (lib. by the comp. after Bunyan), prod. London, Covent Garden Theatre, 26. IV. 1951. It incorporates most of the comp.'s 1-act opera *The Shepherds of the Delectable Mountains* (prod. London, R.C.M., 11. VII. 1922).

Pilgrims to Mecca, The (Gluck). *See* Rencontre imprévue.

Pilkington, Francis (b. ? Lancashire, c. 1562; d. Chester, 1638), Eng. comp. Took the B.Mus. at Oxford in 1595 and was soon after app. to some post at Chester Cathedral where he remained to his death, becoming a minor canon in 1612.

Works incl. anthems (1 in Leighton's *Teares or Lamentacions*); madrigals and pastorals for 3–6 voices; lute pieces; songs to the lute, etc.

Pimmaglione (*Pygmalion*), opera by Cimadoro (lib. by Antonio Simone Sografi, based on Rousseau's *Pygmalion*), prod. Venice, Teatro San Samuele, 26. I. 1790.

Pimmalione (*Pygmalion*), opera by Cherubini (lib. by Stefano Vestris), prod. Paris, Tuileries, at Napoleon's private theatre, for which it was written, 30. XI. 1809.

Pincé (Fr.) = Mordent.

Pincé étouffé (Fr.) = Acciaccatura.

Pincé renversé (Fr.) = Shake.

Pincement (Fr.) = Mordent.

Pincherle, Marc (b. Constantine, Algeria, 13. VI. 1888), Fr. musicologist. Prof. at the École Normale de Musique in Paris and ed. successively of *Le Monde musical* and *Musique*. His works incl. studies of Corelli, Vivaldi, the vln. and vln. mus.

Pinelli, Ettore (b. Rome, 18. X. 1843; d. Rome, 17. IX. 1915), It. violinist and cond. Studied in Rome and with Joachim at Hanover, organized chamber concerts in Rome and with Sgambati founded the Liceo Musicale there, became vln. prof. and cond. orchestral and choral concerts. Comp. an overture, a string 4tet, etc.

Pinello di Gherardi, Giovanni Battista (b. Genoa, *c.* 1544; d. Prague, 15. VI. 1587), It. comp. After an app. at Vicenza Cathedral he went to Innsbruck in the 1570s as musician to the archduke, to the Imp. chapel in Prague soon afterwards and to the Saxon court at Dresden in 1580 in succession to Scandello, but was dismissed because of differences with other musicians, and returned to Prague.

Works incl. motets, Ger. Magnificats and other church mus.; madrigals and *canzone napoletane*; part-songs, etc.

Pini-Corsi, Antonio (b. Zara, VI. 1859; d. Milan, 22. IV. 1918), It. baritone. Made his 1st appearance at the age of 19 at Cremona and became one of the leading interpreters of comic parts, Verdi choosing him for Ford in his *Falstaff* in 1893.

Pinsuti, Ciro (b. Sinalunga, Siena, 9. V. 1829; d. Florence, 10. III. 1888), It. pianist, singing-teacher and comp. Studied with his father and played the pf. in public as a child, was taken to Eng., studying comp. with Potter, returning to It. in 1845 and becoming a pupil of Rossini at Bologna. From 1848 he was in Eng. again, teaching singing for many years in London and Newcastle-on-Tyne and becoming prof. at the R.A.M. in 1856.

Works incl. operas *Il mercante di Venezia* (after Shakespeare), *Mattia Corvino* and *Margherita*; Te Deum for the annexation of Tuscany to It. (1859); hymn for the International Exhibition in London (1871); 30 pf. pieces; 230 songs; many vocal duets and trios, part-songs, etc.

Pinto, George Frederic (b. London, 25. IX. 1786; d. London, 23. III. 1806), Eng. violinist and comp. His real name was Sanders, but he adopted that of his maternal grandfather. Studied with Salomon and others and appeared at Salomon's concerts from 1796. He then toured in Eng. and Scot. and visited Paris.

Works incl. vln. and pf. sonatas, vln. duets, pf. sonatas, canzonets, etc.

Pinto, Thomas (b. ?, 1714; d. Dublin, 1783), Eng. violinist of It. descent, grandfather of prec. through his 1st wife. In 1766 he married the singer Charlotte Brent as his 2nd wife. He played in London at an early age, later at the Three Choirs Festival, etc., failed in a speculation with Arnold to run Marylebone Gardens and last lived in Scot. and Ir.

Pinza, Ezio (Fortunato) (b. Rome, 18. V. 1892; d. Stamford, Conn., 9. V. 1957), It. bass. He studied at the Bologna Cons. and 1st appeared at Soncino (nr. Milan) in *Norma*, 1914. After the 1914–18 war he sang in Rome and other Italian cities until he joined the Metropolitan Opera, N.Y., in 1926. In 1948 he left the Metropolitan to devote himself to operetta, films and television.

Piozzi, Gabriel(e) (Mario) (b. Brescia, 8. VI. 1740; d. Dymerchion, Denbighshire, 26. III. 1809), It.-Eng. mus. teacher and comp. Settled in Eng. *c.* 1776, and won a good reputation as a singing-teacher and pianist. In 1784 he married Mrs. Hester Thrale, to the displeasure of her friend Dr. Johnson.

Works incl. string 4tets, pf. 4tets, vln. sonatas, canzonets, etc.

Pipe and Tabor, a combination of 2 instruments of a primitive kind, a small pipe of the recorder type, but held with one hand only while the other beats the T., a small drum without snares hung round the player's shoulder or strapped to his waist. The instruments are obs., but have been revived for folk-dancing.

Pipelare, Matthaeus (b. ?; d. ?), Flem. 15th–16th-cent. comp. In 1498 he became master of the choristers at 's-Hertogenbosch. He wrote Masses, motets, and secular works to Fr. and Dutch texts.

Pipo
or ⎱the nickname adopted by Filippo
Pippo ⎰ Amadei.

Pique-Dame, the Ger. title of Tchaikovsky's opera *The Queen of Spades* (*Pikovaya Dama*).

Pirame et Thisbé (*Pyramus and Thisbe*), opera by Rebel and Francœur (lib. by Jean Louis Ignace de La Serre), prod. Paris, Opéra, 17. X. 1726.

Pirandello, Luigi (1867–1936), It. dramatist. *See* **Casella** (*Giara*), **Liuzzi** (*Scamandro*), **Malipiero** (*Favola del figlio cambiato*), **Mulè** (*Liola*).

Pirata, Il (*The Pirate*), opera by Bellini (lib. by Felice Romani), prod. Milan, Teatro alla Scala, 27. X. 1827.

Pirates of Penzance, The, or The Slave of Duty, operetta by Sullivan (lib. by W. S. Gilbert), prod. Paignton, Bijou Theatre, 30. XII. 1879; pirated perf., N.Y., Fifth Avenue Theatre, 31. XII. 1879; 1st London perf., Opéra-Comique, 3. IV. 1880.

Piron, Alexis (1689–1773), Fr. poet and dramatist. *See* **Fernand Cortez** (Spontini), **Rameau** (mus. for 5 plays).

Pirro, André (b. Saint-Dizier, 12. II. 1869; d. Paris, 11. XI. 1943), Fr. musicologist. Studied law and literature in Paris and at the same time picked up as much mus. educ. as he could, attending the org. classes of Franck and Widor. In 1896 he became prof. and a director of the newly opened Schola Cantorum. In 1904 he began to lecture at the École des Hautes Études Sociales and in 1912 succeeded Rolland as prof. of mus. hist. at the Sorbonne. His books incl. studies of Schütz, Buxtehude, Bach (general and org. works), the Fr. clavecinists, Descartes and mus., old Ger. church and secular mus., etc.

Pirro e Demetrio (*Pyrrhus and Demetrius*), opera by A. Scarlatti (lib. by Adriano Morselli), prod. Naples, Teatro San Bartolommeo, prob. 28. I. 1694.

Pisador, Diego (b. Salamanca, ? 1508; d. ?, after 1557), Span. lutenist. Son of a notary attached to the household of the Archbishop of Santiago. He took holy orders but did not enter the church. In 1552 he pub. a book of transcriptions of old Span. songs, portions of Masses by Josquin des Prés, motets by Morales and others, etc. for vihuela.

Pisari, Pasquale (b. Rome, 1725; d. Rome, 27. III. 1778), It. singer and comp., pupil of Gasparini and Biordi. From 1752 he was a singer in the Papal Chapel in Rome, and comp. church mus. in the old *a cappella* style.
Works incl. Masses, motets, etc.

Pisaroni, Benedetta (Rosamunda) (b. Piacenza, 6. II. 1793; d. Piacenza, 6. VIII. 1872), It. contralto. Studied under Marchesi and others and made her 1st appearance at Bergamo in 1811, as a soprano, but changed to contralto on Rossini's advice in 1813.

Pischek (or **Pišek**), **Johann Baptist** (b. Melnik, 14. X. 1814; d. Stuttgart, 16. II. 1873), Cz. baritone. Made his 1st stage appearance at the age of 21 and in 1844 was app. court singer to the King of Württemberg. Paid his 1st visit to Eng. in 1845.

Pisendel, Johann Georg (b. Cadolzburg, Bavar., 26. XII. 1687; d. Dresden, 25. XI. 1755), Ger. violinist and comp. Studied the vln. under Torelli while he was a choir-boy at the chapel of the Margrave of Ansbach and theory under Pistocchi. After studying at Leipzig Univ. he went to Dresden to enter the service of the king of Pol. there in 1712, travelled in Fr., Ger., It. and Aus. with the king, became concert master in 1728 on the death of Volumier and led the opera orch. under Hasse. Wrote concertos and pieces for the vln.

Pisk, Paul A(madeus). (b. Vienna, 16. V. 1893), Aus. musicologist and comp. Studied under Adler at Vienna Univ. and comp. with Schreker and Schönberg. After cond. at var. Ger. theatres, he returned to Vienna, cond. and broadcasting, and became director of the mus. dept. of the Volkshochschule, but left for U.S.A. in 1936 and became prof. of musicology at the Univ. of Texas. In 1963 he joined the staff of Washington Univ., St. Louis. He has ed. old mus. and written on modern Ger. mus.
Works incl. monodrama *Schattenseite*; ballet *Der grosse Regenmacher*; cantata *Die neue Stadt*; Requiem for baritone and orch.; Partita for orch., suite for small orch., *Bucolic Suite* for strings and other orchestral works; string 4tet and other

chamber mus.; pf. mus.; songs with org., etc.

Pistocchi, Francesco (Antonio Mamiliano) (b. Palermo, 1659; d. Bologna, 13. V. 1726), It. singer and comp. The family moved to Bologna in 1661, where he began to comp. at a very early age, entered San Petronio as a choir-boy in 1670 and in 1675 began to appear in opera. In 1679 his 1st opera, for puppets, *Il Leandro* (*Gli amori fatali*), was prod. at Venice. In 1687–94 he was a singer at the ducal court of Parma, and he then became mus. director to the Margrave of Ansbach, returning to Bologna in 1701, founding a singing-school there.
Works incl. operas *Il girello, Narciso, Le pazzie d'amore, Le risa di Democrito* and *Il Leandro*, etc.; oratorios *Il martirio di Sant' Adriano, Maria Vergine addolorata, La fuga di Santa Teresa*; church mus.; vocal duets and trios; airs *Scherzi musicali* to It., Fr. and Ger. words, etc.

Piston (Fr.) = Valve, also an abbr. for *cornet à pistons.*

Piston, Walter (b. Rockland, Me., 20. I. 1894), Amer. comp. Studied at the École Normale de Musique in Paris and at Harvard Univ., also with Nadia Boulanger and others. App. asst. prof. at Harvard in 1926 and prof. from 1944 to 1960.
Works incl. ballet *The Incredible Flutist*; 8 symphs., suite, concerto, Symph. Piece, Prelude and Fugue for orch.; concertino for pf. and chamber orch., clar. concertino, vln. concerto; *Carnival Song* for male chorus and brass instruments; 5 string 4tets, pf. trio, 3 pieces for fl., clar. and bassoon; vln. and pf. sonata, fl. and pf. sonata, suite for ob. and pf., partita for vln., vla. and org., etc.

Pistons, another name for the valves of brass instruments.

Pitch, the exact height (or depth) of any mus. sound according to the number of vibrations that prod. it; also the standard by which notes, with the A above middle C as a starting-point, are to be tuned, a standard which determines at how many vibrations to the second that A is to be taken, as well as every other note in relation to it. P. varied at different times and in different countries. Early in the 19th cent. it was gradually raised, esp. by makers of wind instruments to secure more brilliant effect, but with results dangerous to singers, and in Eng. 2 P.'s were in use, the higher for orch. perf. and the lower Classical or Fr. P. for church and purely vocal mus. The P. with 440 cycles per second is now in general use, even by military bands, which until 1927 used the old Philharmonic P., which was slightly higher. *See* A.

Pitoni, Giuseppe Ottavio (b. Rieti, 18. III. 1657; d. Rome, 1. II. 1743), It. comp.

Studied with Pompeo Natale from an early age, and became a chorister at the churches of S. Giovanni dei Fiorentini and SS. Apostoli in Rome, where he was a pupil of Foggia. After church posts in Monterotondo and Assisi he became *maestro di cappella* at Rieti in 1676, and from the next year to his death at the Collegio San Marco in Rome, later also at the Lateran and St. Peter's.

Works incl. over 200 Masses, 700 psalm settings (incl. a 16-part *Dixit Dominus* still hung at St. Peter's in Holy Week), Magnificats, motets, Litanies, 2 Passions, etc.

Pitt, Percy (b. London, 4. I. 1870; d. London, 23. XI. 1932), Eng. cond. and comp. Educ. in Fr. and studied mus. there and at Leipzig with Reinecke and Jadassohn, and at Munich with Rheinberger. In 1896 he became organist at Queen's Hall in London and in 1902 adviser and cond. at Covent Garden Opera, later director of the Grand Opera Syndicate there, of the B.N.O.C. and in 1922 mus. director of the B.B.C.

Works incl. incid. mus. to Stephen Phillips's *Paolo and Francesca*, Alfred Austin's *Flodden Field* and Shakespeare's *Richard II*; suites *Fêtes galantes* (after Verlaine), *Cinderella*, *Dance Rhythms* and others, overture to Shakespeare's *Taming of the Shrew*, symph. prelude *Le Sang des crépuscules*, sinfonietta and other works for orch.; ballade for vln. and orch., concerto for clar. and orch.; songs with orch., etc.

Pittore e Duca (*Painter and Duke*), opera by Balfe (lib. by Francesco Maria Piave), prod. Trieste, 21. XI. 1854.

Pittore parigino, Il (*The Parisian Painter*), opera by Cimarosa (lib. by Giuseppe Petrosellini), prod. Rome, Teatro Valle, 4. I. 1781.

Più (It. = more), used for var. mus. directions in combinations such as *più allegro* (faster), *più lento* (slower), *più mosso* (more animated), *un poco più* (a little more [of whatever has been happening before]), etc.

Piuttosto (It.) = somewhat, rather, a word used with directions where the comp. wishes to make sure that an indication of tempo or expression is obeyed in moderation.

Piva (It.) = Bagpipe.

Pixérécourt, René Charles Guilbert de (1773–1844), Fr. dramatist and librettist, biog. of Dalayrac, author of melodramas with mus. *See* **Margherita d'Anjou** (Meyerbeer).

Pixis, Johann Peter (b. Mannheim, 10. II. 1788; d. Baden-Baden, 22. XII. 1874), Ger. pianist and comp. Studied with his father, Friedrich Wilhelm P. (*c.* 1760–*c.* 1810), and began to appear as pianist with his brother Friedrich Wilhelm P. (1786–1842), a violinist. Settled at Munich in 1809 and in Paris in 1825, where he became a noted pf. teacher. In 1845 he bought a villa at Baden-Baden and continued to train pupils there. He adopted and trained the singer Franzilla Göhringer (1816–?).

Works incl. operas *Almazinde*, *Bibiana* and *Die Sprache des Herzens*; pf. concertos; sonatas and pieces for pf., etc.

Pizz. (abbr.). *See* **Pizzicato**, for which this abbr. is very commonly used.

Pizzetti, Ildebrando (b. Parma, 20. IX. 1880; d. Rome, 13. II. 1968), It. comp. Son of a pf. teacher. He entered the Parma Cons. in 1895 and wrote several orchestral choral and chamber works before he left in 1901, when he received a diploma for comp. In 1905 he returned to the Cons. to take a course in mus. hist., and in 1908 he was app. prof. of harmony and counterpoint at the Instituto Musicale at Florence, of which he became director in 1917. He removed to Milan in 1924 on his appt. as director of the Cons. Giuseppe Verdi there, and in 1936 he went to Rome to succeed Respighi as prof. of advanced comp. at the Accademia di Santa Cecilia.

Works incl. operas *Fedra*, *Debora e Jaele*, *Lo straniero*, *Fra Gherardo*, *Orseolo*, *L'oro*, *Cagliostro*, *La figlia d'Jorio*, *Assassinio nella cattedrale* (after T. S. Eliot); incid. mus. for *La Nave* and *La Pisanella* (both by d'Annunzio), Feo Belcari's *Sacra rappresentazione di Abraam ed Isacco*, Sophocles' *Trachiniae*, Corrado d'Errico's *Rappresentazione di Santa Uliva*, *Le feste delle Panatenee*, Shakespeare's *As You Like It*; orchestral works; symph. in A maj., dances for Tasso's *Aminta*, 3 symph. preludes for Sophocles' *Oedipus Rex* and *Coloneus*, *Ouverture per una farsa tragica*, *Concerto dell' estate*, *Rondo veneziano*; choral and orchestral works: *L'ultima caccia di Sant' Uberto*, intro. to Aeschylus's *Agamemnon* and *Epithalamium*; film mus.; *Sinfonia del fuoco* for d'Annunzio's *Cabirio* and orchestral and choral mus. for *Scipione l'Africano*; pf. concerto, vln. concerto, cello concerto; *Missa di Requiem* and *De profundis* for unaccomp. chorus, also some smaller sacred and secular works; 2 string 4tets, pf. trio; sonatas for vln. and pf. and for cello and pf.; sonata, *Foglio d'album* and suite *Da un autunno già lontano* for pf.; 2 songs for baritone and pf. 4tet, 3 with string 4tet and 21 with pf., etc.

Pizzicato (It. = pinched), a direction indicating that the strings on instruments of the vln. family are to be played, not with the bow, but by being plucked with a finger of the right hand, or occasionally with fingers of the left hand between bowed notes.

Pizzicato tremolando (It. = pinched and

trembling), an effect 1st used by Elgar in the accomp. cadenza of his vln. concerto, where the orch. strings play chords by thrumming the strings both ways across with the fingers of the right hand.

Plagal Cadence. A C. from the Subdominant to the Tonic. *See* **Cadence.**

Plagal Modes. *See* **Modes.**

Plaidy, Louis (b. Wermsdorf, Saxony, 28. XI. 1810; d. Grimma, Saxony, 3. III. 1874), Ger. pianist, violinist and teacher. Studied at Dresden, worked 1st as violinist but later turned to the pf., appeared with success and was app. by Mendelssohn as prof. at the Leipzig Cons. in 1843. Wrote technical studies for pf.

Plainchant or **Plainsong** } The medieval church mus., still surviving in the services of the Rom. Catholic Church, properly sung in unison, without harmony and with no definitely measured rhythms. Its groupings of notes have, however, a strongly rhythmic character, but it resembles the free rhythm of prose, whereas that of measured mus. is comparable to the rhythm of verse. The old notation on a stave of 4 lines, with square or diamond-shaped notes and Ligatures, is still used for P.

Plainte (Fr. = complaint), a lament or memorial piece, whether vocal or instrumental. *See also* **Ornaments.**

Plamenac, Dragan (b. Zagreb, 8. II. 1895), Amer. musicologist of Croatian origin. Studied law at the Univ. of Zagreb, then comp. with Schrecker, musicology with Adler in Vienna and with Pirro in Paris, taking his doctorate in 1925. In 1939 he went to the U.S.A., becoming Prof. of Musicology at the Univ. of Illinois in 1955. He has pub. a number of studies of pre-classical mus. and has ed. the works of Okeghem.

Planché, James Robinson (b. London, 27. II. 1796; d. London, 30. V. 1880), Eng. dramatist, librettist and critic of Fr. descent. Lived in London and wrote a number of libs. incl. *Maid Marian* for Bishop, *Oberon* for Weber and *The Surrender of Calais*, intended for Mendelssohn and later offered to H. Smart, who left it unfinished.

Plançon, Pol (Henri) (b. Fumay, Ardennes, 12. VI. 1851; d. Paris, 11. VIII. 1914), Fr. bass. Studied with Duprez and Sbriglia in Paris, made his 1st stage appearance at Lyons in 1877, came out in Paris in 1880 and 1st visited London in 1891.

Planets, The, suite by Holst for orch. with org. and (in final section) female chorus. 1. *Mars, the Bringer of War*; 2. *Venus, the Bringer of Peace*; 3. *Mercury, the Winged Messenger*; 4. *Jupiter, the Bringer of Jollity*; 5. *Saturn, the Bringer of Old Age*; 6. *Uranus, the Magician*;

7. *Neptune, the Mystic.* 1st (private) perf. London, Queen's Hall, 29. IX. 1918; 1st public perf., London, 15. XI. 1920. The idea of writing mus. on the P.s was not new: Buxtehude wrote a harpsichord suite on them; but Holst dealt with them from the astrological aspect.

Planquette, (Jean) Robert (b. Paris, 31. VII. 1848; d. Paris, 28. I. 1903), Fr. comp. Studied briefly at the Paris Cons. and then began to make a success with songs perf. at café-concerts. From this he passed on to operettas, the 4th of which, *Les Cloches de Corneville*, was immensely successful in 1877.

Works incl. operettas *Valet de cœur, Le Serment de Mme. Grégoire, Paille d'avoine, Les Cloches de Corneville, Le Chevalier Gaston, Les Voltigeurs de la 32me* (*The Old Guard*), *La Cantinière, Rip van Winkle* (after Washington Irving), *Nell Gwynne, La Crémaillère, Surcouf* (*Paul Jones*), *Capitaine Thérèse, La Cocarde tricolore. Le Talisman, Panurge* (after Rabelais), *Mam'zelle Quat' Sous, Le Paradis de Mahomed*, etc.

Plantade, Charles Henri (b. Pontoise, 14. X. 1764; d. Paris, 18. XII. 1839), Fr. pianist, harpist, cellist and comp. Learnt singing and cello as one of the royal pages and later studied comp. with Langlé, pf. with Hüllmandel and harp with Petrini. Having set up as a teacher of singing and harp, he began to write duets and they gained him access to the stage. He taught singing to Queen Hortense, became *maître de chapelle* at court and prof. at the Cons., and held other posts and distinctions.

Works incl. operas *Palma, ou Le Voyage en Grèce, Zoé, ou La Pauvre Petite, Le Mari de circonstance* and many others; Masses, Requiem, Te Deum, motets, etc.; romances and nocturnes for 2 voices, etc.

Planté, Francis (b. Orthez, Basses Pyrénées, 2. III. 1839; d. Mont-de-Marsan, 19. XII. 1934), Fr. pianist. Appeared as an infant prodigy, studied with Marmontel at the Paris Cons. and reappeared with brilliant success, taking part in Alard and Franchomme's chamber concerts. In 1863–72 he lived retired in the Pyrenees, having been offended by the inattention of the Parisian public, but he began playing again and continued until the war of 1914–18.

Platée (*Plataea*), comic ballet by Rameau (lib. by Jacques Autreau and Adrien Joseph Le Valois d'Orville), prod. Versailles, at court, 31. III. 1745; 1st Paris perf., Opéra, 4. II. 1749.

Platel, Nicolas Joseph (b. Versailles, 1777; d. Brussels, 25. VIII. 1835), Fr. cellist. As the son of a royal chamber musician he was educ. as a page at court, learning the cello from Duport. After some orchestral appts. in Paris and Lyons, he toured in Belg. and Eng., settled at Antwerp and then at Brussels, where he became prof. at the Cons. in 1831. Comp. 5 cello concertos; duets for vln. and cello; cello concertos, etc.

Platerspiel (old Ger., lit. bladder [modern *Blase*] play) = Bladder Pipe.

Plato (*c.* 428–*c.* 348 B.C.), Gk. philosopher. He outlined a system of 'harmony', as understood by the Gks., in *Timaeus* and discussed the nature of the modes, from their supposed moral aspect. in *The Republic. See also* Socrate (Satie).

Platti, Giovanni (b. Venice, *c.* 1700; d. Würzburg, 11. I. 1763), It. harpsichordist and comp. Little is known of his life, but he was from 1722 in the service of the archiepiscopal court in Würzburg. He made important contribs. towards the development of a modern style of keyboard mus.

Works incl. 2 Masses and other church mus.; oratorios, cantatas, etc.; sonatas for fl., cello, etc.; concertos and sonatas for harpsichord and other keyboard mus., etc.

Plautus, Titus Maccius (*c.* 252–184 B.C.), Rom. playwright. *See* Emmanuel (*Amphitryon*), Martinů (*Soldier and Dancer*).

Player-Piano. *See* Pianola.

Playford, Henry (b. London, 5. V. 1657; d. London, *c.* 1709), Eng. bookseller and mus. pub. Succeeded to his father's business in 1684; estab. regular concerts, held 3 times a week at a London coffee-house from 1699, and another series at Oxford in 1701.

Playford, John (b. Norfolk, 1623; d. London, XI. 1686), Eng. bookseller and mus. pub., father of prec. Estab. in London about 1648. His 1st mus. pub., *The English Dancing Master*, appeared in 1650, dated 1651.

Playford, John (b. Stanmore Magna, *c.* 1655; d. London, *c.* 1685), Eng. printer, nephew of prec. Was apprenticed to the printer William Godbid in London and in 1679 went into partnership with his widow, Anne Godbid. He printed the mus. works issued by his cousin Henry.

Plectrum (Lat.), a hard spike of quill or metal with which the strings of certain instruments are made to sound. In the virginals, spinet and harpsichord, the P. is attached to the jack, and when used for instruments of the lute type, such as the cittern and the mandoline, it projects from a metal ring placed on the thumb.

Plein jeu (Fr. = full play), the Fr. equivalent of *Organo pleno* (or *pieno*).

Pleno (Lat. abl. = full). *See* Pieno and Organo pleno.

Pleyel, Camille (b. Strasbourg, 18. XII. 1788; d. Montmorency nr. Paris, 4. V.

1855), Fr. pf. maker, mus. pub. and pianist, husband of Marie Moke. He succeeded to his father's business in 1824 and assoc. himself with Kalkbrenner. Studied mus. with his father and Dussek and pub. some pf. pieces.

Pleyel, Ignaz Joseph (b. Ruppertsthal, Lower Aus., 1. VI. 1757; d. Paris, 14. XI. 1831), Aus. pianist, pf. maker and comp., father of prec. Pupil of Wanhal and Haydn, in 1777 became *Kapellmeister* to Count Erdödy, who gave him leave for further study in Rome. In 1783 he moved to Strasbourg as vice-*Kapellmeister*, succeeding Richter as *Kapellmeister* in 1789. Three years later he visited London as cond. of a rival series of concerts to those given by Salomon and Haydn. Settled in Paris in 1795, and in 1807 founded his pf. factory.

Works incl. 2 operas; 29 symphs. and 5 *sinfonie concertanti*; concertos; 45 string 4tets and much other chamber mus.; pf. sonatas; songs, etc.

Pleyel, Marie. *See* Moke.

Plica (Lat., from *plicare*, to fold), an ornamental passing note indicated in medieval notation by a vertical stroke at the side of the note. Its length was determined by the length of the stroke, its pitch by the context (*see* illustration overleaf).

According to theorists it should be sung with a kind of quavering in the throat, but its convenience as an abbr. led to its frequent employment as a substitute for a written note.

Plummer, John (b. ?, *c.* 1410; d. Windsor, *c.* 1484), Eng. comp. He was a clerk of the Chapel Royal by 1441 and in 1444 became the first official master of its children. In *c.* 1458 he became verger at St. George's Chapel, Windsor, while continuing as a member of the Chapel Royal; the Windsor post he held until 1484. His surviving works consist of 4 antiphons for 2 and 4 voices and part of a Mass.

Pneuma (Gk. = 'breath'), a vocal ornament in Plainsong inserting long cadential phrases on the syllables of certain words, notably 'Alleluia'. The P. were also called by the Lat. name of Jubili, and they developed later into Tropes and Sequences. Sometimes written *pneuma*, by confusion with the word for a Neume.

Pochette (Fr.), a small pocket vln. used by dancing-masters in the 17th and 18th cents., similar to the Kit.

Pochettino (It.), the diminutive of *poco* ('a very little'), sometimes used as a direction.

Pochissimo (It.), the superlative of *poco* ('extremely little').

Poco (It. = little), often used as a qualifying direction where any indication of tempo or expression is to be applied in moderation; e.g. *poco più mosso*, a little faster; *poco rallentando*, slowing down a little; *poco forte*, fairly loud.

Poe, Edgar Allan (1809–49), Amer. poet and novelist. *See* Caplet (2 works), Chute de la Maison Usher (Debussy), Diable dans le beffroi (Debussy), Gilbert (H. F.) (*Island of Fay*), Gnessin (*Conqueror Worm*), Hawley (*Bells* and *Raven*), Holbrooke (*Red Mask*, *Bells*, *Raven*, *Ulalume*, *Masque of Red Death*), Kelley (*Sleeper*), Lualdi (*Diavolo nel campanile*), Miaskovsky (*Silence*), Morawski (*Nevermore* and *Ulalume*), Rakhmaninov (*Bells*), Schmitt (F.) (*Palais hanté*), Séverac (songs), Shapleigh (*Raven*), Tcherepnin (N.) (*Masque of the R.D.*), Vactor (do.),

became librarian to the Phil. Society in Vienna. He wrote on this, on Haydn and Mozart in London, the standard biog. of Haydn (finished by Botstiber), etc.

Pohl, Richard (b. Leipzig, 12. IX. 1826; d. Baden-Baden, 17. XII. 1896), Ger. critic and author. Studied at Göttingen and Leipzig, and was for a time ed. of the *Neue Zeitschrift für Musik*. Wrote mainly on Wagner, also on Berlioz, Liszt, etc., and comp. songs.

Pohl, Vladimir (b. Kiev, 17. I. 1880), Rus. comp. Studied at the Kiev and Moscow Conss., became one of the directors of the Rus. Mus. Society in Moscow, 1905–10, and in 1911 succeeded

Modern equivalent

PLICA

Poet's Love (Schumann). *See* Dichterliebe.

Poglietti, Alessandro (b. ?; d. Vienna, VII. 1683), It. organist and comp. His early career is unknown; he became organist of the Imp. chapel in Vienna, 1661, and was killed during the Turkish siege of the Aus. capital.

Works incl. sacred vocal comps. with instrumental accomp.; toccatas and other works for org.; harpsichord suites incl. *Rossignolo*, *Sopra la ribellione di Ungheria*, another containing a capriccio on the cries of cocks and hens, etc.

Pohjola's Daughter, symph. poem by Sibelius, Op. 49, comp. 1906 and based on an incident in the *Kalevala*; 1st perf. St. Petersburg, Siloti concerts (cond. by comp.), 29. XII. 1906.

Pohl, Carl Ferdinand (b. Darmstadt, 6. IX. 1819; d. Vienna, 28. IV. 1887), Ger. organist, bibliog. and writer on mus. Studied with Sechter in Vienna, was organist at the Protestant church in the Gumpendorf suburb, 1849–55, lived in London, 1863–6, and in the latter year

Rakhmaninov as director of the Empress Maria Mus. Inst. there. Later settled in Paris.

Works incl. ballet *Trois Ballets sur des thèmes de Beethoven*; incid. mus. for plays, etc.

Pohlenz, (Christian) August (b. Sallgast, Lusatia, 3. VII. 1790; d. Leipzig, 10. III. 1843), Ger. organist, teacher and cond. Studied at Leipzig, where he became organist at St. Thomas's Church, cond. of the Gewandhaus concerts before Mendelssohn, etc.

Poi (It. = then), used in directions where some mus. section is to follow another in a way not made immediately obvious by the notation: e.g. after a repeat of an earlier section, *poi la coda* or *e poi la coda*.

Point d'Orgue (Fr. = org.-point), the same as Pedal or Pedal-Point in comp.; also the Pause on a $\frac{6}{4}$ chord marking the traditional place for the insertion of a Cadenza; also the Pause.

Pointing, the distribution of the syllables of the Psalms in Angl. chant according to the verbal rhythm.

Poise, (Jean Alexandre) Ferdinand (b. Nîmes, 3. VI. 1828; d. Paris, 13. V. 1892), Fr. comp. Studied with Adam and others at the Paris Cons. and in 1853 prod. his 1st opera.

Works incl. operas *Bonsoir Voisin*, *Les Charmeurs*, *Polichinelle*, *Le Roi Don Pèdre*, *Le Jardinier galant*, *Les Absents*, *Corricolo*, *Les Trois Souhaits*, *La Surprise de l'amour* (after Marivaux), *L'Amour médecin* (after Molière), *Les Deux Billets*, *Joli Gilles*, *Carmosine* (after Musset); oratorio *Cécile*, etc.

Poisoned Kiss, The, or The Empress and the Necromancer, opera by Vaughan Williams (lib. by Evelyn Sharp), prod. Cambridge Arts Theatre, 12. V. 1936. Much of the score is a satire on var. mus. styles.

Poissl, Johann Nepomuk von (b. Haukenzell, Bavar., 15. II. 1783; d. Munich, 17. VIII. 1865), Ger. comp. Studied with Danzi at Munich and became intendant of the royal orch. and director of the royal opera there.

Works incl. operas *Athalia* (after Racine), *Der Wettkampf zu Olympia* and *Nittetis* (transs. of Metastasio's *Olimpiade* and *Nitteti*), *Zayde* and *c.* 10 others; Mass, *Stabat Mater*, Psalm xcv; oratorio *Der Erntetag*, etc.

Pokrass, Dmitri (b. Kiev, 7. XI. 1899), Rus. comp. The son of a poor cattle drover, he early played the pf. in cinemas to earn a living. In 1914 he was heard by the director of the St. Petersburg Cons., who took him there for study, and he lived on his earnings there playing in restaurants and cinemas. In 1917 he returned to Kiev and in 1919 joined the Red Army, for which he wrote many songs, incl. the *Budenny March*. He attracted the attention of Marshal Voroshilov, who advised him to go to Moscow, where he appeared as cond. and pianist and wrote mus. for var. occasions. In 1926–36 he was mus. director of the Moscow Mus. Hall and of the jazz-band in the railway workers' house of culture, and in 1941 he gained the Stalin Prize for film mus.

Works incl. mus. for many films; popular choruses, army and battle songs, mus.-hall songs, etc.

Polacca (It. = Polonaise). Although P. is the exact It. equivalent of the Polonaise, the word is often more loosely used for pieces in polonaise rhythm, but not necessarily in polonaise form, in which case they are actually, as indeed they are often designated, *alla polacca*.

Polaroli, another form of the surname of Antonio and Carlo Francesco Pollarolo.

Poldini, Ede (b. Budapest, 13. VI. 1869; d. Vevey, 29. VI. 1957), Hung. comp. Studied at Budapest and with Mandyczewski in Vienna.

Works incl. operas *The Vagabond and the Princess*, *Wedding in Carnival-Time* (*Love Adrift*), *Himfy*; ballet *Night's Magic*; *Marionettes* for orch. (orig. pf.); numerous pf. suites and pieces incl. *Arlequinades*, *Morceaux pittoresques*. *Épisodes à la Cour*, *Images*, *Moments musicaux*, *Poupée valsante*, etc.

Poldowski (Irene Regine Wieniawska, later Lady Dean Paul) (b. Brussels, 16. V. 1879; d. London, 28. I. 1932), Pol.-Eng. comp. Daughter of H. Wieniawski. After some private mus. tuition she studied at the Brussels Cons., where Gevaert was her comp. master. Later she went to London and continued studying under Percy Pitt, married Sir Aubrey Dean Paul, and after her marriage studied in Paris, 1st under Gédalge and later, after the death of her 1st child, with d'Indy at the Schola Cantorum.

Works incl. operetta *Laughter*; *Nocturnes* and *Tenements* for orch.; *Pat Malone's Wake* for pf. and orch.; *Suite miniature de chansons à danser* for woodwind; vln. and pf. sonata; *Berceuse de l'enfant mourant* and *Tango* for vln. and pf.; suite *Caledonian Market* for pf.; Fr. and Eng. songs to words by Verlaine, Samain, Blake, etc.

Polidori, John William (1795–1821), Eng. novelist, Byron's secretary and physician. *See* **Vampyr** (Lindpaintner and Marschner).

Polifemo, opera by Giovanni Bononcini (lib. by Attilio Ariosti), prod. Berlin, Lietzenburg Palace, summer 1702.

Poliphant, an obs. string instrument, also called Polyphone, of the lute or cittern type but with anything from 25 to 40 strings, invented *c.* 1600 by Daniel Farrant and played by Queen Elizabeth.

Polish Composers. *See* **Bacewicz, Baird, Brzezinski, Chopin, Durand (Duranowski), Elsner, Felsztyński, Fitelberg (2), Friedman, Górczyński, Joteyko, Kamieński, Karlowicz, Kassern, Kazuro, Koffler, Kolberg, Kondracki, Kurpiński, Labuński, Lipiński, Lutosławski, Maciejewski, Maklakiewicz, Maliszewski, Marek, Melcer, Młynarski, Moniuszko, Morawski, Niewiadomski, Noskowski, Nowowiejski, Ogiński (3), Paderewski, Palester, Pankiewicz, Panufnik, Penderecki, Perkowski, Poldowski, Poniatowski, Poradowski, Radziwill, Rathus, Rogowski, Rózycki, Rytel, Scharwenka (2), Sikorski, Soltys, Statkowski, Stojowski, Surzyński, Szalowski, Szamotulski, Szeligowski, Szulc, Szymanowski, Tansman, Tausig, Waclaw of Szamotuły, Wallek-Walewski, Wiechowicz, Wieniawski (3), Woytowicz, Zarebski, Zarzyycki, Żeleński, Zieleński.**

'Polish' Symphony, Tchaikovsky's 3rd symph., in D maj., Op. 29, finished VIII. 1875 and prod. Moscow, 19. XI. 1875. The finale is in polonaise rhythm.

Politian. *See* **Poliziano.**

Poliuto (later *Martyrs* and *I martiri*), opera by Donizetti (lib. devised by Adolphe Nourrit and written by Salvatore Cammarano, based on Corneille's tragedy *Polyeucte*), finished 1838 for prod. at Naples, but forbidden by censor; prod. in Fr. (trans. by Scribe), Paris, Opéra, 1. IV. 1840.

Poliziano (real name Angelo Ambrogini) (1454–94), It. poet. *See* **Favola d'Orfeo** (Casella), **Isaac** (Monody on Lorenzo de' Medici), **Malipiero** (3 songs), **Pastoral** (Bliss), **Vatielli** (*Favolo di Orfeo*).

Polka, a dance dating from *c.* 1830 and prob. originating in Boh., though the story of its being invented there by a servant-girl, the tune being written down by a musician named Neruda, is not authenticated. It is danced in couples and the mus. is in 2–4 time and divided into regular 2-bar patterns grouped into periods of 8 bars.

Pollarolo, Antonio (b. Venice, 1680; d. Venice, 4. V. 1746), It. comp. Pupil of his father, became asst. *maestro di cappella* at St. Mark's in Venice, 1723, and *maestro di cappella* in 1740.

Works incl. operas *Aristeo, Leucippo e Teonoe, Cosroe, I tre voti* and 10 others; church mus., etc.

Pollarolo, Carlo Francesco (b. Brescia, 1653; d. Venice, 1722), It. organist and comp., father of prec. Pupil of Legrenzi at Venice, became a singer at St. Mark's there in 1665, 2nd organist in 1690 and asst. *maestro di cappella* in 1692. Later taught mus. at the Cons. degli Incurabili.

Works incl. operas *Roderico, La forza della virtù, Ottone, Faramondo, Semiramide, Marsia deluso, Ariodante, Le pazzie degli amanti, Gl' inganni felici, Santa Genuinda* (with Violone and A. Scarlatti) and *c.* 65 others; 12 oratorios; org. mus., etc.

Polledro, Giovanni Battista (b. Piovà nr. Turin, 10. VI. 1781; d. Piovà, 15. VIII. 1853), It. violinist and comp. Pupil of Pugnani. Made his 1st appearance at Turin in 1797 and, after touring widely, was leader of the orchestra at Dresden, 1814–24, and court *maestro di cappella* at Turin from 1824.

Works incl. 2 vln. concertos, chamber mus., symph., Mass, etc.

Pollini, Francesco (Giuseppe) (b. Ljubljana, 1763; d. Milan, 17. IX. 1846), It. pianist and comp. Pupil of Mozart in Vienna and later of Zingarelli at Milan, where he was app. pf. prof. at the Cons. in 1809.

Works incl. *Stabat Mater*; mus. for the stage; many pf. studies and pieces, etc.

Polly, ballad opera, sequel to *The Beggar's Opera* (words by John Gay), pub. 1729, but not allowed to be perf.

Prod. London, with the mus. arr. by Arnold, Little Haymarket Theatre, 19. VI. 1777. Modern version by F. Austin, prod. London, Kingsway Theatre, 30. XII. 1922.

Polo (or **Olé**), a Span. dance with song, native to Andalusia but prob. of Moorish origin.

Polonaise, a Pol. dance of a stately, processional character, dating back to at least the 16th cent. The mus. is in 3–4 time and is characterized by feminine cadences at the end of each section, also often by dotted rhythms. The more primitive exs. were in binary form: 2 sections, each repeated; but later (e.g. Chopin) a trio section developed, after which the main section is repeated.

Polonia, symph. prelude for orch. by Elgar, Op. 76, written for a concert given for the Pol. Relief Fund, London, 6. VII. 1915, and ded. to Paderewski, a quotation from whose *Polish Fantasy* it contains as well as one from Chopin and the Pol. Nat. Anthem.

Polovinkin, Leonid Alexeievich (b. Kurgan, Siberia, 13. VIII. 1894; d. Moscow, 2. II. 1949), Rus. comp. Son of a railway engineer, who moved to Moscow in 1896 with his family. P. was educ. at law at the univ. there, but in spite of many other cultural interests he wished to devote himself to mus. and entered the Cons. in 1915. He taught there later, but devoted himself mainly to comp.

Works incl. operas *The Irish Hero* (after Synge's *Playboy of the Western World*), *The Fisherman and his Wife, The Mirror*; ballet *The Gypsy*; mus. for children's plays; 9 symphs., *Telescopes* (4 parts), overture *1st May* and *Dance-Riddle* for orch.; pf. concerto; suite for woodwind 4tet; pf. trio; instrumental pieces; 5 sonatas, 5 suites *Magnets, Happenings* and others, 24 preludes and other pf. pieces, etc.

Polska, a Swed. folk dance whose mus. is in a brisk 3–4 time and usually in min. keys.

Polyeucte. *See also* **Poliuto.**

Opera by Gounod (lib. by Jules Barbier and Michel Carré, based on Corneille's drama), prod. Paris, Opéra, 7. X. 1878.

Polyphone. *See* **Poliphant.**

Polyphony, mus. which combines 2 or more independent melodic lines.

Polyrhythm, the combination of different rhythmic formations.

Polytonality, the simultaneous combination of 2 or more different keys.

Polytone, a keyboard instrument invented by the Amer. comp. Arthur Fickenscher and patented in Ger. in 1912, prod. 60 notes to the 8ve in 'pure' intonation.

Pomar, José (b. Mex. City, 18. VI. 1880), Mex. comp. He did not begin to study until he was 48, and then at once experimented in var. modern techniques.

Works incl. ballets *Ocho horas* and *Bestia parda* (*The Brown Beast*, a satire on Hitler); Mex. dance *Huapengo* for orch.; prelude and fugue for perc. instruments, etc.

Pommer (Ger.) = Bombard.

Pomo d'oro, Il (*The Golden Apple*), opera by Cesti (lib. by Francesco Sbarra), prod. Vienna, Carnival 1667, for the wedding of the Emperor Leopold I and the Infanta Margherita of Spain. The subject is the judgment of Paris.

Pomone, opera by Cambert (lib. by Pierre Perrin), prod. Paris, Opéra, 3. III. 1671.

Pomp and Circumstance, 5 military marches by Elgar, orig. intended as a set of 6, Op. 39. 1–4 comp. 1901–7, 5 in 1930. 1 contains, as a trio, the tune afterwards used in the *Coronation Ode* to the words 'Land of hope and glory'. The title of the set comes from *Othello*, III. iii: 'Pride, pomp and circumstance of glorious war'.

Pomposo (It. = pompous, stately), a direction used for mus. of a sumptuous character.

Ponce, Manuel (b. Fresnillo, 8. XII. 1882; d. Mex. City, 24. IV. 1948), Mex. comp. Learnt mus. from his sister at first, became cathedral organist at Aguas Calientes and at 14 comp. a gavotte which was later made famous by the dancer Argentina. He entered the Nat. Cons. at Mex. City and in 1905 went to Eur. for further study with Bossi at Bologna and Martin Krause in Berlin. In 1906 he returned home and became prof. at the Nat. Cons. In 1915–18 he lived at Havana and at the age of 43 went to Paris to take a comp. course with Dukas.

Works incl. symph. triptych *Chapultepec*, *Canto y danza de los antiguos Mexicanos*, *Poema elegiaco*, *Ferial* for orch.; pf. concerto, vln. concerto, concerto for guitar and chamber orch.; 3 Tagore songs with orch.; *Sonata en duo* for vln. and vla.; 2 Mex. Rhapsodies and many other pf. works, numerous songs, etc.

Ponchielli, Amilcare (b. Paderno Fasolaro nr. Cremona, 1. IX. 1834; d. Milan, 17. I. 1886), It. comp. Studied at the Milan Cons. and prod. his 1st opera, on Manzoni's *Promessi sposi*, at Cremona in 1856. In 1881 he was app. *maestro di cappella* at Bergamo Cathedral.

Works incl. operas *I promessi sposi*, *La Savoiarda* (*Lina*), *Roderico*, *Bertrand de Born*, *Il parlatore eterno*, *I Lituani* (*Aldona*), *Gioconda* (after Hugo's *Angelo*), *Il figliuol prodigo*, *Marion Delorme* (on Hugo's play), *I Mori di Valenza*; ballets *Le due gemelle* and *Clarina*; cantatas for the reception of the remains of Doni-

zetti and Mayr at Bergamo and in memory of Garibaldi, etc.

Poniatowski, Józef Michal Xawery Franciszek Jan, Prince of Monte Rotondo (b. Rome, 20. II. 1816; d. Chislehurst, 3. VII. 1873), Pol. tenor and comp. Studied at the Liceo musicale at Florence and under Ceccherini. He sang at the Teatro della Pergola there and prod. his 1st opera there in 1839, singing the title-part. After the 1848 Revolution he settled in Paris, but after the Franco-Prussian war he followed Napoleon III to Eng., 1871.

Works incl. operas *Giovanni da Procida*, *Don Desiderio*, *Ruy Blas* (after Hugo), *Bonifazio de' Geremei* (*I Lambertazzi*), *Malek Adel*, *Esmeralda* (after Hugo's *Notre-Dame de Paris*), *La sposa d'Abido* (after Byron's *Bride of Abydos*), *Pierre de Médicis*, *Gelmina* and others; Mass in F maj.; songs incl. *The Yeoman's Wedding Song*, etc.

Poniridy, Georges (b. Constantinople, 8. X. 1892), Gk. comp. Studied with Gilson and others at Brussels and with d'Indy and Gastoué in Paris. Later settled in Athens and studied plainsong and Byzantine mus.

Works incl. opera *Lazarus*; ballet *Dodekamero*; incid. mus.; 3 Byzantine chants for female voices and orch., cantata *Kassiani*; 2 symphs., *Symph. Triptych* for orch.; prelude and fugue for strings; poems for voice, fl., clar., string 4tet and pf.; vln. and pf. sonata; sonata, 3 Attic Suites, preludes and fugues, prelude and gigue, etc., for pf.; songs, etc.

Pons, José (b. Gerona, Catalonia, 1768; d. Valencia, 1818), Span. comp. Studied at Córdoba, became *maestro de capilla* at Gerona and later at Valencia.

Works incl. Misereres and other church mus.; *villancicos* for Christmas with orch. or org., etc.

Pons, Lily (Alice Joséphine Pons) (b. Draguignan, 12. IV. 1904), Fr. coloratura soprano. Studied pf., aged 13, at the Paris Cons., and then singing with A. de Gorostiaga, making her début at Mulhouse in 1928. From 1931 to 1959 she sang at the N.Y. Metropolitan Opera.

Ponsard, François (1814–67), Fr. dramatist. *See* Gounod (*Ulysse*).

Ponselle (actually Ponzillo), **Rosa** (b. Meridan, Conn., 22. I. 1897), Amer. soprano of It. parentage. Studied in N.Y. with W. Thorner and Romani, making her début at the Metropolitan Opera in 1918. She sang there from 1918 to 1937, and at Covent Garden from 1929 to 1931. One of the great singers of the cent., she retired at the height of her powers to teach.

Ponsin, Marie. *See* Roze.

Pont-neuf (Fr. lit. new bridge), a satirical song of the 18th cent. similar to the Vaudeville, sung in public mainly on the P.-N. in Paris.

Ponte, Lorenzo da (actually Emmanuele Conegliano) (b. Ceneda nr. Venice, 10. III. 1749; d. N.Y., 17. VIII. 1838), It. poet and librettist. Of Jewish parentage, he took the name da Ponte at his baptism. Educ. at the theological seminary in Portogruaro, he was ordained in 1773, but led the life of an adventurer, being banished from Venice because of scandal in 1779. App. poet to the Court Opera in Vienna in 1784, he moved to London in 1792, and thence, to escape his creditors, to N.Y. in 1804. He pub. his memoirs in 1823–7. Wrote the libs. of *Le nozze di Figaro*, *Don Giovanni* and *Così fan tutte* for Mozart, others for Bianchi, Martín y Soler, Winter, etc. *See also* **Burbero di buon cuore** (Martín y Soler), **Ratto di Proserpina** (Winter), **Scuola de' maritati** (Martín y Soler), **Una cosa rara** (do.).

Ponticello (It. = little bridge), the bridge of string instruments over which the strings are stretched to keep clear of the body of the instrument. The direction *sul ponticello* (on the bridge) indicates that the bow is to be drawn close to the bridge, which results in a peculiar nasal tone.

Poole, Elizabeth (b. London, 5. IV. 1820; d. Langley, Bucks., 14. I. 1906), Eng. soprano and actress. Appeared as a child actress at the Olympic Theatre and made her 1st appearance in opera at Drury Lane in 1834.

Poot, Marcel (b. Vilvoorde nr. Brussels, 7. V. 1901), Belg. comp. Studied at the Brussels Cons. and with Mortelmans at that of Antwerp. He early became interested in film, radio and jazz mus. In 1935 he founded the group known as Les Synthétistes and in 1930 gained the Rubens Prize and went to Paris to study with Dukas. On his return he held several teaching posts, incl. the Brussels Cons., of which he became director in 1949.

Works incl. operas *Het Ingebeeld Eiland*, *Het Vrouwtje van Stavoren* and *Moretus*; ballets *Paris in verlegenheid* and *Pygmalion*; oratorios *Le Dit du routier* and *Icaros*; 3 symphs. and other orchestral works; chamber mus., etc.

Pope, Alexander (1688–1744), Eng. poet. *See* **Acis and Galatea** (Handel), **Busby** (*Prophecy* and odes), **Greene (M.)** (*Ode on St. Cecilia's Day*), **Jackson (W. i)** (*Dying Christian*), (?) **Semele** (Handel).

Popov, Gavriyl Nikolaievich (b. Novotcherkass, 25. IX. 1904), Rus. comp. Studied at the School of Mus. at Rostov-on-Don and from 1922 at the St. Petersburg Cons., where Steinberg and Shtcherbatchev were his comp. masters.

Works incl. operas *The Slow Horseman* (after Pushkin) and *Alexander Nevsky*;

film mus.; *Heroic Intermezzo* for solo voice, chorus and orch., based on the 2nd opera; 4 symphs., 2 suites for orch.; vln. concerto; 7tet for fl., clar., bassoon, tpt., vln., vla. and double bass; suite and pieces for pf., etc.

Popper, David (b. Prague, 16. VI. 1843; d. Baden nr. Vienna, 7. VIII. 1913), Ger.-Cz. cellist and comp. Studied mus. in general at the Prague Cons. and the cello under Goltermann at Frankfurt, and made his 1st concert tour in Ger. in 1863. In 1868 he became 1st cellist at the Court Opera in Vienna, in 1872 he married Sophie Menter, but the marriage was disolved in 1886, and in 1896 he became cello prof. at the Budapest Cons.

Works incl. 4 cello concertos, *Requiem* for 3 cellos, numerous pieces for cello, etc.

Poradowski, Stefan Bolesław (b. Wloclawek, 16. VIII. 1902; d. Posnań, 6. VII. 1967), Pol. comp. Studied at the Cons. and Univ. of Poznań and in 1930 became prof. at the former and mus. critic.

Works incl. cantatas *Triumph*, *The Song of Spring*, *The Horse of Swiatowid*; 5 symphs., sinfonietta on folk themes, *Lyrical Overture* and other orchestral works; *Antique Suite* for strings; double bass concerto, *Concerto antico* for vla. d'amore and string orch.; string 4tet and *Metamorphoses* for string 4tet, 3 string trios, duets for 2 vlns.; Prelude and Pol. Dance for pf.; songs, part-songs, etc.

Porgy and Bess, opera in 3 acts by Gershwin (lib. by Du Bose Heyward and Ira Gershwin, after the play *Porgy* by Du Bose and Dorothy Heyward), prod. Boston, 30. IX. 1935.

Poro, rè dell' Indie (*Porus, King of the Indies*), opera by Handel (lib. by ?, altered from Metastasio's *Alessandro nell' Indie*), prod. London, King's Theatre, Haymarket, 2. II. 1731.

Porpora, Nicola Antonio (b. Naples, 17. VIII. 1686; d. Naples, 3. III. 1768), It. comp. and singing teacher. Pupil of Greco and Campanile at the Cons. dei Poveri in Naples, where his first opera, *Agrippina*, was prod. in 1708. At first *maestro di cappella* to the Imp. Commandant in Naples, Prince Philip of Hesse-Darmstadt, he was app. singing teacher at the Cons. di S. Onofrio there in 1715, and 10 years later became *maestro* at the Cons. degli Incurabili in Venice. Among his pupils were Farinelli and Caffarelli, and, briefly, Hasse. Travelling as an opera cond., he rivalled Handel in London (1733–6) and Hasse in Dresden (1748–52). In Vienna Haydn was his pupil-valet. P. finally settled in Naples in 1760, remaining there till his death.

Works incl. operas *Basilio, Berenice, Flavio Anicio Olibrio, Faramondo, Eumene,*

Amare per regnare, Semiramide, Semiramide riconosciuta, L'Imeneo, Adelaide, Siface, Mitridate, Annibale, Il trionfo di Camilla, Arianna, Temistocle, Filandro and *c.* 20 others; oratorios *Il martirio di Santa Eugenia* and 8 others; Masses, motets, duets on the Passion and other church mus.; cantatas; vln. sonatas; keyboard mus., etc.

Porporino. See **Uberti.**

Porrino, Ennio (b. Cagliari, Sardinia, 20. I. 1910), It. comp. Studied in Rome with Respighi and others and won a competition at the Academia di Santa Cecilia.

Works incl. operas *Gli Orazi. L'organo di Bambû* and *I. Shardana*; ballets; choral comps., symph. poem *Sardegna*, overture *Tartarin de Tarascon* (after Daudet), concertos, etc.

Porsile, Giuseppe (b. Naples, ? 1672; d. Vienna, 29. V. 1750), It. comp. He was vice-*maestro de capilla* to the Span. court in Barcelona from 1695 (*maestro* 1697), and from 1720 court *Kapellmeister* in Vienna.

Works incl. *c.* 12 operas, e.g. *Meride e Selinunte. Spartaco*; 12 oratorios; serenades, cantatas, canzonets, etc.

Port de voix }
Port de voix double } (Fr. *see* Ornaments). The term P. de v. is also used for Portamento in singing, i.e. passing from 1 note to the next with a very slight effect of scooping.

Porta, Costanzo (b. Cremona, *c.* 1529; d. Padua, 19. V. 1601), It. monk and comp. Pupil of Willaert at Venice. He took orders and became choirmaster at Osimo nr. Ancona, 1552–64, when he went to Padua to take up a similar post at the Cappella Antoniana, the church of the Minorite order to which he belonged, which he left for a time to work at Ravenna and Loreto by turns.

Works incl. Masses, motets, psalms, hymns, introits and other church mus.; madrigals, etc.

Porta, Ercole (b. Bologna, IX. 1585; d. Carpi, 30. IV. 1630), It. organist and comp. Organist at the coll. of San Giovanni in Persiceto in 1609.

Works incl. sacred vocal concertos; secular works; vocal mus., etc.

Porta, Francesco della (b. Monza, *c.* 1590; d. Milan, I. 1666), It. organist and comp. Studied with the organist Ripalta at Monza and became organist and *maestro di cappella* of 3 churches at Milan.

Works incl. motets, psalms; instrumental *ricercari*; *villanelle* for 1–3 voices with instruments, etc.

Porta, Giovanni (b. Venice, *c.* 1690; d. Munich, 21. VI. 1755), It. comp. Worked in Rome 1706–16 in the service of Cardinal Ottoboni, then at the Cons. della pietà in Venice, and also visited

London, where his opera *Numitore* was prod. in 1720. From 1736 to his death he was *Kapellmeister* to the court in Munich.

Works incl. over 30 operas; oratorios; cantatas; 19 Masses and other church mus., etc.

Portamento (It.). The ornament called P. is synonymous with Appoggiatura. In another sense the word means the carrying on from 1 note to another with a very slight effect of scooping.

Portative Organ, a small org. with a single keyboard and 1 range of pipes, which could be carried, placed on a table or suspended from the shoulder by a strap. Representations are frequent in medieval and Renaissance paintings.

Portato (It.), a manner of delivering a mus. phrase somewhere between *legato* and *staccato*.

Portée (Fr.) = Stave.

Porter, Anna Maria (1780–1832), Eng. novelist and playwright. *See* **Busby** (*Fair Fugitives*).

Porter, Cole (b. Peru, Indiana, 9. VI. 1893; d. Santa Monica, Calif., 15. X. 1964), Amer. comp. Studied at Yale and at Harvard Law School and School of Mus. While still a student he became well known for his football songs. In 1916 he joined the Foreign Legion and after the war studied at the Schola Cantorum in Paris. His output consists entirely of musicals, of which the best known are *Kiss me, Kate, Can-Can* and *Silk Stockings.*

Porter, (William) Quincy (b. New Haven, Conn., 7. II. 1897; d. Bethany, Conn., 12. XI. 1966), Amer. comp. Studied at Yale Univ. and School of Mus. with H. Parker and D. S. Smith, later with Bloch and with d'Indy in Paris. He taught at the Cleveland Inst. of Mus. for 2 periods in 1922–32, at Vassar Coll., Poughkeepsie, in 1932–8 and at the New Eng. Cons. at Boston from 1938. He also played vla. in var. string 4tets.

Works incl. incid. mus. for Shakespeare's *Antony and Cleopatra* and T. S. Eliot's *Sweeney Agonistes*; symph., *Poem and Dance* for orch.; *Ukrainian Suite* for strings; *Dance in Three Time* for chamber orch.; vla. concerto harpsichord concerto, concerto for 2 pfs.; *3 Gk. Mimes* for voices, string 4tet and perc.; 9 string 4tets; 2 vln. and pf. sonatas, suite for vla. solo, etc.

Porter, Walter (b. ?, *c.* 1595; d. London, XI. 1659), Eng. comp. He became a Gentleman of the Chapel Royal in London in 1617. At some time, prob. earlier, he was a pupil of Monteverdi. In 1639 he became choirmaster at Westminster Abbey and when the choral service was suppressed in 1644 came under the patronage of Sir Edward Spencer.

Works incl. motets for 2 voices and instruments, psalms (George Sandys's paraphrases) for 2 voices and org.; madrigals and airs for voices and instruments, etc.

Portinaro, Francesco (b. ?; Padua, *c.* 1520; d. ? Padua, after 1578), It. comp. He was assoc. with the *Accademia degli Elevati* in Padua (1557), and later with the d'Este family at Ferrara and Tivoli. His 3 books of motets and 6 of madrigals were pub. at Venice.

Portman, Richard (b. ?; d. ? London, *c.* 1655), Eng. organist and comp. Pupil of O. Gibbons, succeeded Thomas Day as organist of Westminster Abbey in London, 1633. Like W. Porter, who was choirmaster, he lost this post in 1644 and became a mus. teacher.

Works incl. services, anthems; *Dialogue of the Prodigal Son* for 2 voices and chorus, meditations *The Soules Life*; harpsichord mus., etc.

Portogallo. *See* **Portugal.**

Portsmouth Point, concert overture by Walton, inspired by Rowlandson's drawing, 1st perf. I.S.C.M. Festival, Zürich, 22. VI. 1926.

Portugal, Marcus Antonio da Fonseca (called Portogallo in It.) (b. Lisbon, 24. III. 1762; d. Rio de Janeiro, 7. II. 1830), Port. comp. Educ. at the Patriarchal Seminary at Lisbon, where later he became cantor and organist, and learnt

it in 1810, but was unable to return with it in 1821, being incapacitated by a stroke.

Works incl. *Licença pastoril, A Castanheira* and 20 other Port. operas; *La confusione nata della somiglianza, Demofoonte, Lo spazzacamino principe, La donna di genio volubile, Fernando nel Messico, Alceste, La morte di Semiramide, Non irritare le donne, L'oro non compra amore, Il trionfo di Clelia, Il diavolo a quattro, La pazza giornata* (on Beaumarchais's *La Folle Journée* [*Figaro*]) and *c.* 25 other It. operas; church mus.; cantata *La speranza*; songs, etc.

Portugese Composers. *See* **Arneiro, Arroyo, Bomtempo, Cardoso, Carneyro, Carvalho, Coelho, Cruz, Escobar, Freitas, Freitas Branco** (2), **Kastner, Keil, Lima, Lobo, Lusitano, Machado, Magalhães, Portugal, Rebelo, Seixas, Silva Leite, Viana da Mota.**

Posaune (Ger.) = Trombone. Also an 8-ft. and 16-ft. org. stop powerfully repro. tromb. tone.

Positif (Fr.) = Choir Organ.

Positions. (1) The points at which the left hand is placed in order to stop the strings on a string instrument. Since only 4 fingers are available, the hand has to change from one position to another in order to reach higher notes e.g. on the vln. (*see* illustration).

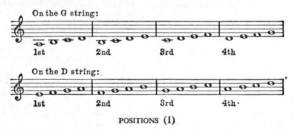

POSITIONS (1)

mus. from João de Sousa Carvalho. He was also a theatre cond. and in 1785 prod. his 1st stage work. In 1792 he went to

(2) The points at which the slide of the tromb. is arrested, e.g. on the B♭ tenor tromb. (*see* illustration).

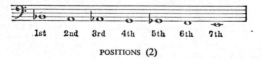

POSITIONS (2)

Naples and began to comp. It. operas in great numbers. In 1800 he returned to Lisbon to become director of the San Carlos Theatre, where he continued to prod. It. operas. In 1807 the Fr. invasion drove the court to Brazil, and he followed

Each position offers a complete series of harmonics and hence provides the instrument with a chromatic compass. *See* **Trombone.**

Positive Organ. A small chamber org.

Postans, Mary. *See* **Shaw.**

Posthorn, a primitive brass instrument akin to the bugle rather than the horn, used by postillions in the 18th and early 19th cent. It had no valves and could therefore prod. only the natural harmonics, which were coarse and penetrating in tone. It was hardly ever used in serious mus., but Bach imitated it in his Capriccio on his brother's departure for harpsichord and Mozart scored parts for 2 in his Ger. Dances, K. 605.

Posthumous (from Lat. *postumus* = last). A work pub. after its comp.'s death is described as P. The common abbr. is Op. posth.

Postillon de Longjumeau, Le, opera by Adam (lib. by Adolphe de Leuven and Léon Lévy Brunswick), prod. Paris, Opéra-Comique, 13. X. 1836.

Postlude
or }the opposite of Prelude or
Postludium
Praeludium: a final piece, esp. an org. piece played after service.

Poston, Elizabeth (b. Highfield, Herts., 24. X. 1905), Eng. comp. Studied at the R.C.M. in London and pf. with Harold Samuel. In 1925 she pub. 7 songs and in 1927 a prize-work, a vln. and pf. sonata was broadcast, and in 1940–5 she was director of mus. in the foreign service of the B.B.C.
Works incl. mus. for radio prods.; choral mus.; songs, etc.

Pot-Pourri (Fr. lit. rotten pot), a medley of preserves, identical with the Span. *olla podrida,* the name of which is applied to selections of themes from var. mus. works, esp. operas or operettas.

Potter (Philip) Cipriani (Hambley) (b. London, 2. X. 1792; d. London, 28. IX. 1871), Eng. pianist and comp. Studied under Attwood, Callcott and Crotch, and had finishing pf. lessons from Woelfl in 1805–10. He became an assoc. of the Phil. Society on its foundation in 1813 and a member when he reached majority, and in 1816 wrote an overture for it, also playing the pf. there that year in a 6tet of his own. In 1817 he went to Vienna, studied with Aloys Förster and met Beethoven. After visiting Ger. and It. he returned to London in 1821, became prof. of pf. at the R.A.M. the next year and principal in succession to Crotch in 1832, but resigned in 1859. In 1855 Wagner cond. one of his symphs. with the Phil. Society.
Works incl. cantata *Medora e Corrado,* Ode to Harmony; 9 symphs., 4 overtures for orch.; 3 pf. concertos, Concertante for cello and orch.; 3 pf. trios, 6tet for pf. and strings; horn and pf. sonata, duo for vln. and pf.; 2 sonatas, *The Enigma* ('Variations in the style of 5 eminent artists'), studies, rondos, toccatas, etc.. for pf.; symph. and

other works for pf. duet; fantasy and fugue for 2 pfs., etc.

Poueigh, (Marie Octave Géraud) Jean (b. Toulouse, 24. II. 1876; d. Olivet, 14. X. 1958), Fr. critic and comp. Studied at the Toulouse Cons. and at that of Paris with Caussade and Lenepveu, later with Fauré, and also had advice from d'Indy. He became mus. critic to *L'Ère nouvelle* and pub. a book on *Musiciens français d'aujourd'hui* under the name of Octave Séré.
Works incl. operas *Le Meneur de louves* and *Perkain;* ballets *Fünn* and *Frivolant; La Ronde du Blé-d'Amour* for chorus and orch.; *Marche triomphante* for orch.; vln. and pf. sonata; *Pointes sèches* for pf.; songs; arrs. of Languedocian and Gascon folksongs, etc.

Pougin, (François Auguste) Arthur (Eugène Paroisse-) (b. Châteauroux, 6. VIII. 1834; d. Paris, 8. VIII. 1921), Fr. musicologist. He had little general educ., but studied vln. with Alard and theory with Réber at the Paris Cons. After working at var. theatres as violinist and cond., he began to write biog. articles on 18th-cent. Fr. musicians and gradually made his way by writing for var. mus. papers, contrib. to dictionaries and writing mus. criticism for several newspapers. He wrote biogs. of Verdi, Campra, Meyerbeer, V. Wallace, Bellini, Rossini, Auber, Adam, Méhul, etc., and studies of Fr. mus. hist., the vln., Rus. mus., etc.

Pouishnov, Lev (b. Odessa, 11. X. 1891; d. London, 28. V. 1959), Rus. pianist. He 1st appeared in public when 5 years old. From 1907 to 1910 he studied at the St. Petersburg Cons. and then toured Eur. as a soloist, subsequently playing also in U.S.A., Austral. and the Far East. He left Rus. in 1920 and settled in Eng., becoming naturalized in 1931.

Poule, La (*The Hen*), the nickname of a symph. by Haydn, No. 83, in G min., (No. 2 of the 'Paris' symphs.), comp. in 1786.

Poulenc, Francis (b. Paris, 7. I. 1899; d. Paris, 30. I. 1963), Fr. comp. Received a classical educ., but was able to take pf. lessons from Ricardo Viñes and to pick up technical knowledge in var. ways. When he was called up for war service in 1918 he had already written 1 or 2 works under the influence of Satie, and on being demobilized he joined the group of 'Les Six' with Auric, Durey, Honegger, Milhaud and Tailleferre, and thus came for a time under the influence of Jean Cocteau.
Works incl. opera *Dialogues des Carmélites;* comic operas *Le Gendarme incompris* and *Les Mamelles de Tirésias* (lib. by Guillaume Apollinaire); ballets *Les Biches* (*The House-Party*) and *Les Animaux modèles* (after La Fontaine); Mass

in G min. and cantatas *Tel jour telle nuit*
and *Figure humaine* (Paul Éluard), cantata *Le Bal masqué* (Max Jacob); *Sécheres-
ses* for chorus and orch.; choruses (unaccomp.), *7 Chansons* (Éluard and Apollinaire), *Poésie et Vérité*; *2 Marches et un
Intermède* for orch.; *Concert champêtre* for
harpsichord and orch., *Marches mili-
taires* for pf. and orch., concerto in D
min. for 2 pfs. and orch., org. concerto;
Aubade for pf. and 18 instruments; *Rapsodie nègre* for fl., clar. and string 4tet,
trio for ob., horn and pf.; sonatas for 2
clars., for clar. and bassoon and for
horn, tpt. and tromb.; vln. and pf. and
cello and pf. sonatas; song cycles with
chamber instruments *Le Bestiaire* (G.
Apollinaire) and *Cocardes* (Cocteau);
*Mouvements perpétuels, Suite, Impromp-
tus, Feuillets d'album, Nocturnes, Suite
française, Villageoises*, etc. for pf.; sonata
for pf. duet; *5 Poèmes de Ronsard*, 8
Pol. Songs, *Banalités* (Apollinaire), *Chansons villageoises* (Éluard), *Fiançailles pour
rire* and other songs, etc.

Pound, Ezra (b. 1885), Amer. poet.
See **Diamond** (*Night Litany*).

Poupée de Nuremberg, La (*The Nuremberg Doll*), opera by Adam (lib. by
Adolphe de Leuven and Léon Lévy
Brunswick), prod. Paris, Théâtre Lyrique,
21. II. 1852.

Poupée, La (*The Doll*), operetta by
Audran (lib. by Maurice Ordonneau),
prod. Paris, Théâtre de la Gaîté, 21. X.
1896.

Poupelinière, Alexandre de la. *See* **La
Poupelinière.**

Poussé (Fr. = pushed), the upstroke
of the bow in the playing of string instruments, the opposite of *tiré* (= drawn).

Pousseur, Henri (b. Malmédy, 23. VI.
1929), Belg. comp. Studied at Brussels
Cons. and took private comp. lessons from
André Souris and Pierre Boulez. In 1958
he founded a studio for electronic mus. in
Brussels.
  Works incl. *3 Chants sacrés* for soprano
and string trio; *Symphonies* for 15 solo
instruments; *Modes* for string 4tet; 5tet
to the memory of Webern; *Seismographs*
for magnetic tape; *Scambi* for tape; *Rimes
pour différentes sources sonores* for orch.
and tape; *Répons* for 7 musicians; *Mobile*
for 2 pfs., etc.

Powell, John (b. Richmond, Virgina, 6.
IX. 1882; d. Charlottesville, Va., 15. VIII.
1963), Amer. pianist and comp. Studied
at Virginia Univ. and with Leschetizky
and Navrátil in Vienna. Made his 1st
appearance in Berlin in 1907 and toured
in Eur. and U.S.A.
  Works incl. *The Babe of Bethlehem* for
chorus and orch.; symph. in A maj.,
Natchez on the Hill, A Set of Three, etc.,
for orch.; concerto and *Rapsodie nègre*

for pf. and orch., vln. concerto; string
4tet; 3 vln. and pf. sonatas; pf. sonata
and pieces; songs, etc.

Powell, Maud (b. Peru, Ill., 22. VIII.
1868; d. Uniontown, Pa., 8. I. 1920),
Amer. violinist. Studied with Schradieck
at Leipzig and Dancla in Paris and made
her 1st appearance in Eng. in 1883.

Power, Leonel (b. ?; d. Canterbury, 5.
VI. 1445), Eng. comp. and theorist. He
wrote a treatise on the singing of descant
and comp. Masses, motets and other
church mus.

pp (abbr.) = *pianissimo* (It. = softest).
Although the sign indicates a superlative,
it can be further multiplied to demand
ever greater softness of tone.

Praeger, Ferdinand (Christian Wilhelm)
(b. Leipzig, 22. I. 1815; d. London, 2. IX.
1891), Ger. pianist and comp. Studied
under his father and settled in London in
1834; wrote a book *Wagner as I knew him*
in 1885 and comp. a symph. prelude to
Byron's *Manfred*, an overture *Abellino*, a
pf. trio, pf. pieces, etc.

Praeludium. *See* **Prelude.**

Praetorius (real name Schulz, Schulze,
Schultz or Schultze), Ger. 16th–17th-
cent. musicians not of the same family,
except 3 and 5:
  1. Godescalcus P. (b. Salzwedel, 28.
III. 1524; d. Wittenburg, 8. VII. 1573),
scholar. Prof. of philosophy at Wittenberg Univ. Pub. in 1557 a vol. *Melodiae
scholasticae* in which he was asst. by M.
Agricola.
  2. Bartholomaeus P. (b. ?; d. ?), comp.
Pub. pavans and galliards in 5 parts in
1616.
  3. Hieronymus P. (b. Hamburg, 10.
VIII. 1560; d. Hamburg, 27. I. 1629),
organist and comp. Pupil of his father,
Jacob P. (or Schultz), organist at St.
James's Church, Hamburg, whom he
succeeded in 1582. He wrote in the Venetian antiphonal choral style.
  Works incl. Masses, motets, Magnificats, *Cantiones sacrae*, hymn-tunes; Lat.
and Ger. songs in 5–20 parts, etc.
  4. Michael P. (b. Kreuzberg, Thuringia,
? 15. II. 1571; d. Wolfenbüttel, 15. II.
1621), organist, comp. and author. He
was mus. director at Lüneburg until
1604, when he was app. organist to the
Duke of Brunswick, who later made him
his mus. director. He wrote the volu-
minous treatise on mus. and instruments
entitled *Syntagma musicum* and comp.
a number of vols. of Lat. and Ger. sacred
and secular songs for several voices, one
entitled *Musae Sionae* and others
named after separate Muses, etc.
  5. Jacob P. (b. Hamburg, 8. II. 1586;
d. ? Hamburg, 21. X. 1651), organist and
comp., son of 3. Pupil of Sweelinck at
Amsterdam; app. organist of St. Peter's

Church, Hamburg, in 1603. Wrote motets, etc.

'Prague' Symphony, Mozart's symph. in D maj., K. 504, comp. in Vienna, XII. 1786 and perf. in Prague, 19. I. 1787, during a visit for the prod. there of *Le nozze di Figaro*.

Pralltriller (Ger.), the rapid repetition of a note, with a note a degree higher in between, indicated by the sign ᴧᴧ:

It is sometimes known as the Inverted Mordent.

Pratella, Francesco (Balilla) (b. Lugo, Romagna, 1. II. 1880; d. Ravenna, 18. V. 1955), It. comp. Studied at the Liceo Musicale of Pesaro, where Mascagni was among his masters. He settled at Milan, where in 1910 he began to make propaganda for futurist mus., on which he lectured and wrote in the more progressive periodicals.

Works incl. operas *Il regno lontano, Lilia, La Sina d'Vargöun, L'aviatore Dro, Il dono primaverile, Fabiano*; children's opera *La ninna nanna della bambola*; incid. mus. to plays; symph. poems on Carducci's ode *La chiesa di Polenta*, 5 symph. poems (*Romagna*), *Inno alla vita* (musica futuristica), 3 dances *La guerra*, etc. for orch.; pf. trio; vln., org. and pf. pieces; songs, etc.

Prati, Alessio (b. Ferrara, 19. VII. 1750; d. Ferrara, 17. I. 1788), It. comp. Pupil of Piccinni at the Cons. di Loreto in Naples, went to Paris in 1779, then to St. Petersburg (1781) and Warsaw (1782). Travelling by way of Vienna (1783) he returned to Ferrara in 1784.

Works incl. *c.* 12 operas, e.g. *L'École de la jeunese, Ifigenia in Aulide*, etc.; Masses and other church mus.; arias and miscellaneous other vocal pieces; symph. and *sinfonia concertante*; concertos; vln. sonatas, etc.

Pré aux clercs, Le (*The Scholars' Meadow*), opera by Hérold (lib. by François Antoine Eugène de Planard), prod. Paris, Opéra-Comique, 15. XII. 1832.

Préamble (Fr. } = preamble), other
Preambulum (Lat. } names for Prelude.

Precentor, a dignitary in an Angl. cathedral, orig. the leading singer in the choir, but also in charge of the vocal

church mus. and superior to the organist. His seat is opposite that of the dean (who takes the Decani side) on the Cantoris side of the chancel.

Preciosa, play with mus. by Weber (lib. by Pius Alexander Wolff, based on Cervantes's story *La Gilanella*), prod. Berlin, Opera House, 15. III. 1821.

Precipitando (It. = precipitately), a direction indicating that an *accelerando* is to be made to increase in pace very rapidly.

Predieri, Luc' Antonio (b. Bologna, 13. IX. 1688; d. Bologna, 1767), It. comp. *Maestro di cappella* of the cathedral at Bologna; went to the court chapel in Vienna, 1738, and became chief *Kapellmeister* there in 1746; but returned to It. in 1751.

Works incl. operas *Il sogno di Scipione* and others, serenades and festival plays for the stage; oratorios, etc.

Preindl, Joseph (b. Marbach, Lower Aus., 30. I. 1756; d. Vienna, 26. X. 1823), Aus. church musician and comp., pupil of Albrechtsberger. App. *Kapellmeister* at St. Peter's, Vienna in 1793, he held the same post at St. Stephen's from 1809. Pub. treatises on singing and on comp.

Works incl. at least 13 Masses, 2 Requiems, Offertories, motets and other church mus.; keyboard mus., etc.

Prelude (from Lat. *praeludium*), an intro. piece played, for ex., before a church service or a mus. perf., or forming the 1st movement of a suite or other sectional work; also one paired with a fugue, to which it forms an intro.; from the 19th cent. onwards sometimes a separate concert work, esp. for pf. (Chopin, etc.) or orch.; and from Wagner onwards the orchestral intro. to an opera where it does not take the form of a detached overture and leads straight into the 1st act.

Prélude à l'Après-midi d'un faune (*Prelude to 'The Afternoon of a Faun'*). An orchestral piece by Debussy intended as a mus. intro. to Stéphane Mallarmé's poem of that name, comp. in 1892–4 and 1st perf. Paris, Société Nationale, 23. XII. 1894.

Ballet on this work (choreography by Vaslav Nizhinsky), prod. Paris, Théâtre du Châtelet, 29. V. 1912.

Préludes, 2 sets of pf. pieces, 12 in each, by Debussy, comp. in 1910–13. Their contents are: I. 1. *Danseuses de Delphes*; 2. *Voiles* (*Sails*, not *Veils*); 3. *Le Vent dans la plaine*; 4. *Les Sons et les parfums tournent dans l'air du soir* (*Sounds and scents whirl in the evening air*: a quotation from Baudelaire); 5. *Les Collines d'Anacapri*; 6. *Des Pas sur la neige* (*Footprints in the snow*); 7. *Ce qu'a vu le vent d'Ouest* (*What the West Wind saw*); 8. *La Fille* *aux cheveux de lin* (*The Flaxen-haired Girl*: based on a Scot. song by Leconte de Lisle); 9. *La Sérénade interrompue*; 10. *La Cathédrale engloutie* (*The Submerged Cathedral*: on the old Breton tale of the sunken city of Ys); 11. *La Danse de Puck* (on Shakespeare's *Midsummer Night's Dream*); 12. *Minstrels* (mus.-hall artists, not troubadours). II. 1. *Brouillards* (*Mists*); 2. *Feuilles mortes* (*Dead Leaves*); 3. *La Puerta del Vino* (a gate at Granada); 4. *Les Fées sont d'exquises danseuses* (*The Fairies are exquisite Dancers*); 5. *Bruyères* (*Heather*); 6. *General Lavine—eccentric* (a mus.-hall character); 7. *La Terrasse des audiences du clair de lune* (*The Terrace of the Moonlight Audiences*; a reference to an account of George V's Durbar in 1912; the piece contains a quotation of the folksong 'Au clair de la lune'); 8. *Ondine*; 9. *Hommage à S. Pickwick, Esq., P.P.M.P.C.* (after Dickens; the piece quotes 'God save the King' in the bass); 10. *Canope* (a Canopic jar holding the ashes of a dead lover); 11. *Les Tierces alternées* (*Alternating Thirds*); 12. *Feux d'artifice* (*Fireworks*; quoting a few notes of the *Marseillaise* at the end).

Préludes, Les, symph. poem by Liszt, comp. 1848, revised early 1850s, 1st perf. Weimar, 28. II. 1854. The title is taken from a poem by Lamartine, with which in fact the mus. has no connection.

Preparation, a term used in harmony for a chord, one note of which will create a dissonance in the chord that follows, e.g.:

Preparation Percussion Resolution

Prepared Shake. *See* **Ornaments.**
Prés, Josquin des. *See* **Josquin.**
Presle, Jacques de la. *See* **La Presle.**
Prestissimo (It.) = extremely fast.
Presto (It. = quick, fast), the direction most commonly used to indicate the fastest speeds in mus. P. is quicker than *allegro*.
Preston, Thomas (b. ?; d. ? Windsor, after 1559), Eng. comp. He was (?) organist and master of the choristers, Magdalen Coll., Oxford, and is recorded as having played at Windsor Chapel in 1558 and 1559. He wrote a large amount of org. mus. for the Latin rite, incl. the Proper of the Mass for Easter Day (incomplete).
Prêtre, Georges (b. Waziers, 14. VIII. 1924), Fr. cond. Studied at Douai and in Paris, making his début in 1946 at the Paris Opéra-Comique. He is equally well

known as a cond. of both classical and modern mus.
Previtali, Fernando (b. Adria, 16. II. 1907), It. cond. and comp. Studied comp., org., pf. and cello at Turin Cons. From 1928 to 1936 he cond. in Florence (Maggio Musicale Fiorentino), from 1936 to 1953 with the Rome Radio Orch., and in 1953 became cond. of the Santa Cecilia Orch.
Works incl. ballet *Alluzinazione*; cantata for chorus and orch.; string 4tet, string trio; songs, etc.
Prévost (d'Exiles), Antoine François (1697–1763), Fr. novelist. For works based on *Manon Lescaut see* **Henze** (*Boulevard Solitude*), **Kleinmichel** (*Schloss de l'Orme*), **Manon** (opera, Massenet), **Manon Lescaut** (ballet, Halévy; operas, Auber and Puccini).
Prévost, Eugène (Prosper) (b. Paris, 23. VIII. 1809; d. New Orleans, 19. VIII. 1872), Fr. comp. and singing-teacher. Studied at the Paris Cons. with Lesueur and others and gained the Prix de Rome in 1831. After prod. works in Paris, he became cond. at the theatre of Le Havre for a time, but left for New Orleans in 1838, where he cond. at the Fr. theatre and taught singing. In 1862 he returned to Paris, but went again to New Orleans in 1867.
Works incl. operas *L'Hôtel des Princes, Le Grenadier de Wagram, Cosimo, Le Bon Garçon, Esmeralda* (after Hugo's *Notre-Dame de Paris*), *L'Illustre Gaspard*; Mass with orch.; cantata *Bianca Capello*, etc.
Prey, Hermann (b. Berlin, 11. VII. 1929), Ger. baritone. Studied at the Berlin Hochschule für Musik with H. Gottschalk. From 1952 to 1953 he sang at the Wiesbaden State Opera, and then became a member of the Hamburg State Opera, also singing frequently in Berlin at the Städtische Oper and at the Vienna State Opera. He is also well known as a *Lieder*-singer.
Price, Leontyne (b. Laurel, Miss., 10. II. 1927), Amer. soprano. Studied at Central State Coll., Ohio, and at the Juilliard School of Mus. in N.Y. (1949–1952), achieving her first success in *Porgy and Bess*. From 1958 to 1959 she sang with the San Francisco Opera Co., and in 1959 became a lyric soprano with the Chicago Opera. She made her début at the N.Y. Metropolitan Opera in 1961 and sang at La Scala, Milan, in 1962.
Prick-Song. From the 15th to the 18th cent. 'to prick' was used to mean 'to write mus. notes'. Hence P.-S. meant written, as opposed to improvised, mus.
Priestley, J(ohn). B(oynton). (b. 1894), Eng. novelist and dramatist. *See* **Arundell** (*Ever since Paradise*), **Britten** (*Johnson over Jordan*), **Olympians** (Bliss).

Prigione di Edimburgo, La (*Edinburgh Gaol*), opera by F. Ricci (lib. by Gaetano Rossi, based on Scribe and Planard's *Prison d'Édimbourg* and further back on Scott's *Heart of Midlothian*), prod. Trieste, 13. III. 1838.

Prima donna (It. = 1st lady), the singer of the leading soprano part in a partic. opera or the leading soprano in an opera co.

Prima Donna, opera by Benjamin (lib. by Cedric Cliffe), prod. London, Fortune Theatre, 23. II. 1949.

Prima vista (It. = 1st sight), sight-reading.

Prima volta (It. = 1st time), a direction sometimes given where a repeated portion of a comp. takes a new turn after the repetition. The join leading to the repeat is then called *P. v.*, while the different one taking the mus. on to its continuation is marked *Seconda volta*. The figures 1 and 2 are commonly used as abbrs. for these terms.

Primavera, Giovanni Leonardo (b. Barletta, Naples, *c.* 1540; d. ?), It. comp. *Maestro di cappella* to the Span. governor of Milan in 1573. Palestrina used his madrigal 'Nasce la gioia mia' as a *cantus firmus* for a Mass, called by that name.

Works incl. madrigals, *Canzoni napoletane* for 3 voices, *villotte* for 3 voices, etc.

Primo (It. = first). P. is often written over the top part in pf. duets, the bottom one being *Secondo*; the word also appears in orchestral scores where the comp. wishes to make sure that a passage is played by only the 1st of a pair or groups of similar intruments.

Primo uomo (It. = 1st man), the singer of the leading male soprano part in an opera or the leading male soprano in an opera company in the 18th cent.

Primrose, William (b. Glasgow, 23. VIII. 1904), Scot. vla. player After studying in Glasgow and at the G.S.M. in London, he studied with Ysaÿe in Belg. from 1925 to 1927, and on his advice took up the vla. From 1930 to 1935 he played with the London String Quartet, and in 1937 was selected by Toscanini to become 1st vla. of the N.B.C. Symph. Orch., with which he remained until 1942. In 1939 he estab. his own string quartet. He also commissioned a vla. concerto from Bartók, of which he gave the 1st perf. in 1949.

Prince Ferelon, or The Princess's Suitors, opera by Gatty (lib. by comp.), prod. London, Old Vic Theatre, 21. V. 1921.

Prince Igor (*Kniaz Igor*), opera by Borodin (lib. by comp. based on a sketch by Stassov), comp. between 1871 and 1887 and left unfinished at Borodin's death in the latter year. Completed and scored by Rimsky-Korsakov and Glazunov. Prod. St. Petersburg, 4. XI. 1890.

Prince of the Pagodas, The, ballet by Britten (choreography by John Cranko), prod. London, Covent Garden, 1. I. 1957.

Princess Ida, or Castle Adamant, operetta by Sullivan (lib. by W. S. Gilbert, a parody of Tennyson's *Princess*), prod. London, Savoy Theatre, 5. I. 1884.

Princesse jaune, La (*The Yellow Princess*), opera by Saint-Saëns (lib. by Louis Gallet), prod. Paris, Opéra-Comique, 12. VI. 1872.

Principal, an open Diapason org. stop which sounds an 8ve higher, 4 ft. in the manuals and 8 ft. in the pedals. Also, in old mus., the lowest tpt. part, in which high and florid notes were not demanded. In modern terminology a P. is the leading player of any group of orchestral instruments.

Prinz von Homburg, Der, opera by Henze (lib. by Ingeborg Bachmann, after Kleist), prod. Hamburg, Staatsoper, 22. V. 1960.

Prior, Matthew (1664–1721), Eng. poet. *See* Arne (T. A.) (*Henry and Emma*), Travers (canzonets).

Prioris, Johannes (b. ?; d. ?), 15th–16th-cent. organist and comp. Organist at St. Peter's in Rome in 1490 and *maître de chapelle* to Louis XII of Fr. in 1507. Wrote Masses, motets, Magnificats, etc.

Prise de Troie, La (Berlioz). *See* Troyens.

Prison d'Édimbourg, La (*Edinburgh Gaol*), opera by Carafa (lib. by Scribe and François Antoine Eugène de Planard, based on Scott's *Heart of Midlothian*), prod. Paris, Opéra-Comique, 20. VII. 1833.

Prisoner in the Caucasus, The (*Kavkasky Plennik*), opera by Cui (lib. by Victor Alexandrovich Krilov, based on Pushkin's poem), prod. St. Petersburg, 16. II. 1883.

Priuli, Giovanni (b. Venice, *c.* 1575; d. ? Vienna, 1629), It. comp. *Kapellmeister* to the Archduke Ferdinand of Aus. at Graz early in the 17th cent.; remained in his service when he became the Emperor Ferdinand II.

Works incl. motets, psalms and other church mus.; madrigals, *Musiche concertate*, *Delicie musicali* for several voices, etc.

Prix de Rome (Fr. Prize of Rome; officially Grand Prix de Rome), a prize instituted in 1803 and offered annually in Paris by the Académie des Beaux-Arts, a branch of the Institut de France, to var. artists, that for mus. going to the successful competitor at the Cons. The holder is entitled to 3 years' study at the Fr. Acad. housed in the Villa Medici in Rome. The work required was formerly a dramatic cantata, but is now a 1-act opera.

Belg. has a similar prize, but without obligatory residence in Rome.

Procopé, Hjalmar (1868–1927), Fin. dramatist. *See* Sibelius (*Belshazzar's Feast*).

Prodana Nevěstá (Smetana). *See* **Bartered Bride.**

Prod'homme, J(acques). G(abriel). (b. Paris, 28. XI. 1871; d. Paris, 18. VI. 1956), Fr. musicologist. Studied in Ger. and lived at Munich in 1897–1900, where he founded a periodical in Fr. and Ger. After his return to Paris he founded the Fr. section of the S.I.M., became its secretary and performed var. other mus. administrative functions, succeeding Bouvet in 1931 as librarian and archivist at the Opéra, and Expert in 1934 as Cons. librarian. He wrote several works both on Beethoven and on Berlioz, also on Mozart, Schubert, Wagner, etc.

Prodoscimo de Beldemandis. *See* **Beldemandis.**

Programme Music, any kind of instrumental mus., esp. orchestral, based on a lit., pictorial, hist., biog., autobiog., descriptive or other extra-mus. subject and not intended to appeal only as mus. pure and simple.

Programme Notes, analyses printed in concert progammes, esp. in Brit., describing the mus. performed. Early exs. in Eng. were those written by Grove for the Crystal Palace concerts.

Progression, the movement of 2 or more chords in succession, either harmonically with all the notes moving simultaneously or polyphonically with each one being part of a continuously moving horizontal melodic line.

Prohaska, Carl (b. Mödling, nr. Vienna, 25. IV. 1869; d. Vienna, 28. III. 1927), Aus. comp. Studied pf. with d'Albert and comp. with Mandyczewski and Herzogenberg, being also befriended by Brahms. He taught at the Strasbourg Cons. in 1894–5 and cond. the Warsaw Phil. Orch. in 1901–1905. In 1908 he became prof. at the Cons. of the Vienna Phil. Society.

Works incl. opera *Madeleine Guimard*; oratorio *Frühlingsfeier*, motet *Aus dem Buch Hiob*, *Lebensmesse*, *Der Feind*, *Infanterie* and other choral works; variations on a theme from Rousseau's *Devin du village*, symph. prelude to Anzengruber's *Das vierte Gebot*, symph. fantasy, serenade, passacaglia and fugue for orch.; string 4tet, string 5tet, pf. trio; sonata and *Allegro con spirito* for vln. and pf.; songs, duets, etc.

Prokofiev, Sergey Sergeyevich (b. Sontsovka, Ekaterinoslav, 23. IV. 1891; d. Moscow, 5. III. 1953), Rus. comp. Began to comp. almost before he could write and tried his hand at an opera at the age of 9. He was sent to Glière for lessons, wrote 12 pf. pieces in 1902 as well as a symph.

for pf. duet, and at 12 set Pushkin's play *A Feast in Time of Plague* as an opera. At the St. Petersburg Cons., which he left in 1914, he studied pf. with Anna Essipova, comp. with Rimsky-Korsakov and Liadov, and cond. with N. Tcherepnin. By that time he had written many works, incl. the 1st pf. concerto, and he then set to work on the *Scythian Suite* for orch. During the war of 1914–18 he lived in London for a time and at its close he went to the U.S.A. by way of Japan. The opera *The Love for Three Oranges* was prod. at Chicago in 1921, and the next year he went to live in Paris and became connected with Diaghilev's Rus. Ballet, which prod. several of his works. In 1933 he settled in Moscow and was induced by the Soviet government to simplify and popularize his style, a tendency which is very noticeable in such works as *Peter and the Wolf* and the quantities of film mus. he wrote there.

Works incl. operas *Magdalene*, *The Gambler* (after Dostoievsky), *The Love for Three Oranges* (after Gozzi), *The Flaming Angel*, *War and Peace* (after Tolstoy), *Betrothed in a Monastery* (after Sheridan's *Duenna*), *Semyon Kotko*; ballets *The Buffoon*, *Le Pas d'acier*, *L'Enfant prodigue*, *Sur le Borysthène*, *Romeo and Juliet* (after Shakespeare), *Cinderella*; *Ode to the Unknown Boy* for soprano, tenor, men's chorus and orch.; orchestral works incl. *Symphonie classique* and 6 other symphs., *Sinfonietta*, *Scythian Suite*, *Symphonic Song*, Rus. Overture *Toast to Stalin* and *Ode to the End of the War*; incid. mus. for *Egyptian Nights* (after Shakespeare and Shaw), *Boris Godunov* and *Eugene Onegin* (both Pushkin); film mus. for *Lieutenant Kizhe*, *The Queen of Spades* (after Pushkin), *Ivan the Terrible*, etc.; 5 pf. concertos, 2 vln. concertos, 2 cello concertos; 2 string 4tets, 5tet for wind and pf., sonata for 2 vlns., *Overture on Hebrew Themes* for clar., string 4tet and pf.; sonata in D maj. for vln. and pf., Ballade for cello and pf.; 9 pf. sonatas, *c.* 25 other op. nos. of pf. pieces, incl. 3 studies, toccata, *Sarcasms*, *Visions fugitives*, *Contes de la vieille grand'mere* and 2 sonatinas; 8 sets of songs (1 without words, 1 to words by Pushkin); *Seven, they are Seven*, for tenor chorus and orch. and some other choral works; cantata for the 29th anniversary of the Oct. Revolution (words by Stalin, Lenin and Marx) for orch., military band, accordion band, percussion and double chorus, etc.

Prolation, the division of the Semibreve into Minims in old notation, where according to the time-signature a semibreve could be equal to 2 minims (min. P) or to 3 (maj. P).

Promenade Concerts, a type of popular

orchestral concert, cultivated espec. at the London Queen's Hall from 1895 until its destruction in 1941, under the direction of Sir Henry Wood, and continued at the Albert Hall. The programmes gradually improved, until they contained all the best orchestral mus. and modern novelties, and a special feature is that the floor of the hall is left bare for people to stand, not to walk about, for which they have neither room nor inclination. In recent years operas and chamber mus. have been included in the programmes. P. C. were not new to London in 1895; they were started by Musard at Drury Lane in 1840 and by Jullien at Covent Garden about the same time.

Promessi sposi, I (*The Betrothed*). *See also* **Bryllupet ved Como-Søen.**
Opera by Petrella (lib. by Antonio Ghislanzoni, based on Manzoni's novel), prod. Lecco, 2. X. 1869; 1st perf. Milan, X. 1872. The prod. at Lecco was given there because it is the scene of Manzoni's book.
Opera by Ponchielli (lib. by ?, based on Manzoni's novel), prod. Cremona, 30. VIII. 1856.

Prométhée (*Prometheus*), open-air spectacle by Fauré (lib. by Jean Lorrain and André Ferdinand Hérold, based on Aeschylus), prod. Béziers, Arènes, 27. VIII. 1900; 1st Paris perf., Hippodrome, 5. XII. 1907.

Prometheus (Beethoven). *See* **Geschöpfe des Prometheus.**
Symph. poem by Liszt, comp. 1850 as an overture to the choruses from Herder's *Prometheus*, perf. Weimar, 28. VIII. 1850; revised 1855 and 1st perf. Brunswick, 18. X. 1855.

Prometheus, the Poem of Fire, symph. work for pf. and orch. by Skriabin, perf. Moscow, 15. III. 1911. The score contains a part for an instrument projecting coloured lights, called *Tastiera per luce,* which was however never perfected.

Prometheus Unbound, setting of Shelley's poem for solo voices, chorus and orch. by Parry, perf. Gloucester Festival, 1880.

Prometheus Variations (Beethoven). *See* **'Eroica' Variations.**

Prophète, Le, opera by Meyerbeer (lib. by Scribe), prod. Paris, Opéra, 16. IV. 1849.

Prophetess, The, or The History of Dioclesian, mus. by Purcell for the play adapted from Beaumont and Fletcher by Thomas Betterton, prod. London, Dorset Gardens Theatre, IV. or V. 1690. Pepusch wrote new mus. for its revival, Lincoln's Inn Fields Theatre, 28. XI. 1724.

Proportio (Lat.). *See* **Saltarello.**

Proportion, the mathematical relationship betwen the numbers of vibrations of different notes, which are exactly in tune

with each other when the ratios between these vibrations are mathematically correct, e.g. a perfect 5th stands in the relation of 2 : 3 in the number of vibrations of its 2 notes. The term P. was also used in old mus. to designate the rhythmic relationships between one timesignature and another (*see* illustration overleaf).

Proporz (Ger.). *See* **Saltarello.**

Proscritto, Il (*The Outlaw*), opera by Nicolai (lib., orig. written for Verdi, by Gaetano Rossi), prod. Milan, Teatro alla Scala, 13. III. 1841.

Prose, another name, chiefly Fr., for the sequence (in the medieval sense of an ornamental interpolation into the mus. of the Mass). After the 9th cent. words began to be added to the sequences, and this is the reason for their being called P.s, since the texts were not orig. in verse.

Prose de l'âne, La, a Fr. 12th-cent. processional with mus. repres. the Flight into Egypt and held annually at Beauvais on 1. I.

Proserpine, opera by Lully (lib. by Quinault), prod. Saint-Germain, 3. II. 1680; 1st Paris perf., 15. XI. 1680.
Opera by Paisiello (lib. by Quinault, revised by Nicolas François Guillard), prod. Paris, Opéra, 29. III. 1803. Paisiello's only Fr. opera.

Proske, Karl (b. Gröbnig, Silesia, 11. II. 1794; d. Regensburg, 20. XII. 1861), Ger. priest and mus. ed. Studied medicine and practised for a time, but was ordained priest in 1826 and became attached in a mus. capacity to Regensburg Cathedral. There and in It. he made his great collection of church mus. entitled *Musica Divina.*

Proust, Marcel (1871–1922), Fr. novelist. *See* **Hartmann (T. de)** (*A l'ombre des jeunes filles*).

Prout, Ebenezer (b. Oundle, 1. III. 1835; d. London, 5. XII. 1909), Eng. theorist and comp. Studied pf. and org. and began to make a career as organist, pf. teacher, mus. ed. and critic. In 1876 he became prof. at the Nat. Training-School for Mus. in London and 3 years later at the R.A.M. He wrote a number of books on harmony, counterpoint, form, orchestration, etc. and comp. cantatas, symphs., org. concertos, chamber mus., etc.

Provenzale, Francesco (b. Naples, ? 1627; d. Naples, 6. IX. 1704), It. comp. Studied (?) at Naples and in 1663–74 taught at the Cons. Santa Maria di Loreto there. He was also *maestro di cappella* at the church of San Gennaro and in the royal chapel.
Works incl. operas *Lo schiavo di sua moglie, Difendere l'offensore* and 6 others; church mus.; 9 cantatas, etc.

Prudent, Émile (Racine Gauthier) (b.

PROPORTION

Angoulême, 3. II. 1817; d. Paris, 14. V. 1863), Fr. pianist and comp. Having no parents, he was adopted by a pf. tuner, entered the Paris Cons. at the age of 10 and afterwards had a hard struggle to make a living, but eventually made his way successfully.

Works incl. concerto-symph. *Les Trois Rêves* and concerto in B♭ maj. for pf. and orch.; pf. trio; *Étude de genre* and many pieces, fantasies and transcriptions for pf., etc.

Prunières, Henry (b. Paris, 24. V. 1886; d. Nanterre, 11. IV. 1942), Fr. musicologist and ed. Studied with Rolland at the Sorbonne, founded the *Revue musicale* in 1920 and was app. ed. of the complete ed. of Lully's works. He wrote books on that comp., on Monteverdi, Cavalli, Fr. and It. opera and ballet, etc., also a hist. of mus. (unfinished).

'Prussian' Quartets, a set of 3 string 4tets by Mozart, comp. in 1789–90 and ded. to the cello-playing King Frederick William II of Prussia. The 4tets (K. 575 in D, K. 589 in B♭, K. 590 in F) are the first 3 of an intended set of 6. All have prominent cello parts.

Psalms. The P. form part of the offices of the Rom. Catholic Church and of the Angl. morning and evening services; in the former they are chanted in Plainsong, in the latter to Chants. P. have also been set by comps. as motets and also as concert works for solo voices, chorus and orch.

Psaltery, an obs. instrument of the Dulcimer type, triangular in shape and with strings stretched across its frame harp-wise, which were played with the bare fingers or with a plectrum. It became extinct during the 17th cent.

Pskovitianka (*The Maid of Pskov*, also known as *Ivan the Terrible*), opera by Rimsky-Korsakov (lib. by comp. based on a play by Lev Alexandrovich Mey), prod. St. Petersburg, 13. I. 1873. Revived with a new prologue-opera, *Boyarina Vera Sheloga*, Moscow, 27. XII. 1898.

Psyche, opera by Locke (lib. by Shadwell), prod. London, Dorset Gardens Theatre, 27. II. 1675.

Psyché, opera by Lully (lib. by Thomas Corneille and Bernard de Fontenelle), prod. Paris, Opéra, 19. IV. 1678.

Suite by Franck for orch. with choral interpolations, comp. 1887–8, 1st perf. Paris, Société Nat., 10. III. 1888.

Puccini. It. family of musicians and opera comps. of Lucca:

1. Giacomo P. (1712–81).
2. Antonio P. (1747–1832), son of prec.
3. Domenico P. (1771–1815), son of prec.
4. Michele P. (1813–64), son of prec.

Puccini, Giacomo (Antonio Domenico Michele Secondo Maria) (b. Lucca, 22. XII. 1858; d. Brussels, 29. XI. 1924), It. comp., son of prec. Although his father d. early, he was given a mus. educ. and at the age of 19 was organist and choirmaster at the church of San Martino and had written a motet. In 1880 his mother managed with the aid of a grant from the queen to send him to the Milan Cons., where he studied comp. 1st under Bazzini and later under Ponchielli. Here he wrote a *Capriccio sinfonico* for orch. Ponchielli urged him to take part in a competition for a 1-act opera advertised by the mus. pub. Sonzogno, and he wrote *Le Villi*; but the prize was won by Mascagni's *Cavalleria rusticana*. *Le Villi*, however, was prod. at Milan in 1884, as a result of which Ricordi commissioned him to write a 2nd opera, *Edgar*, prod. in 1889. It failed but P. had his 1st great success with *Manon Lescaut* at Turin in 1893. The same city brought out *La Bohème* in 1896. His successes now made him immensely wealthy and he bought an estate at Torre del Lago near Lucca, where he lived with Elvira Bonturi, who had left her husband for him, but whom he was unable to marry until much later, when she became a widow. In the last years of his life he suffered from cancer of the throat and d. after an operation undergone at Brussels.

Works incl. operas *Le Villi*, *Edgar*, *Manon Lescaut*, *La Bohème*, *Tosca*, *Madama Butterfly*, *La fanciulla del West*, *La rondine*, *Trittico*: *Il tabarro*, *Suor Angelica* and *Gianni Schicchi*, *Turandot* (unfinished, completed by Alfano); *Scherzo sinfonico* for orch. (later used in *La Bohème*); cantata *Juno*; 2 minuets for strings; a Mass and a motet: *Inno a Roma* for chorus, etc.

Pugnani, Gaetano (b. Turin, 27. XI. 1731; d. Turin, 15. VII. 1798), It. violinist and comp. Pupil of Somis and possibly, later, Tartini, worked for most of his life at the Turin court, and became leader of the orch. in 1770. But he also travelled widely, visiting Paris (1754) and London (1767–70), where his first opera, *Nanetta e Lubino*, was prod. in 1769. His pupils incl. Viotti, Bruni and Conforti.

Works incl. operas *Nanetta e Lubino*, *Issea*, *Tamas Kouli-Kan nell' India*, *Aurora*, *Adone e Venere*, *Achille in Sciro*, *Demofoonte*, *Demetrio a Rodi*, etc.; oratorio *La Betulia liberata*; orchestral suite on Goethe's *Werther*; concertos, sonatas, etc. for vln. and other instrumental mus.

Pugno, (Stéphanie) Raoul (b. Paris, 23. VI. 1852; d. Moscow, 3. I. 1914), Fr. pianist and comp. Studied at the Paris Cons. where after some organist's and choirmaster's posts he became prof. of harmony 1892 and of pf. in 1896. He 1st appeared in London in 1894.

Works incl. operas *Ninetta*, *La Sosie*, *Le Valet de cœur*, *Le Retour d'Ulysse*, *La Vocation de Marius*, *La Petite Poucette*, etc.; ballets *Les Papillons*, *Viviane*, *Le Chevalier aux fleurs* (with Messager); fairy-plays, pantomimes and mimo-drama; incid. mus. for d'Annunzio's *Città morte* (with Nadia Boulanger); oratorio *La Resurrection de Lazare*; sonata and *Les Nuits* for pf.; songs, etc.

Puits d'amour, Le (*The Well of Love*), opera by Balfe (lib. by Scribe and Adolphe de Leuven), prod. Paris, Opéra-Comique, 20. IV. 1843. Balfe's 1st Fr. opera.

Pujol, Joan (b. Barcelona, 1573; d. Barcelona, V. 1626), Span. priest and comp. He was *maestro de capilla* at

Tarragona, 1593–5, Saragossa Cathedral, 1595–1612, and Barcelona, 1612–26.

Works incl. Masses and other church mus.; secular songs, etc.

Pulcinella, ballet by Stravinsky with mus. adapted from Pergolesi (choreography by Leonid Fedorovich Massin), prod. Paris, Opéra, 15. V. 1920. The settings were designed by Picasso.

Pullois, Jean (b. ?; d. 23. VIII. 1478), Flem. comp. He was in 1442 a choir-boy, and later *maître des enfants* at Antwerp Cathedral. In 1447 he became a member of the Burgundian chapel, returning to Antwerp in 1476, having twice visited Rome in the meantime. He wrote mus. for the Mass and secular songs.

Puns. Punning in mus. is rare and can be done only by allusions to mus. which in some way suggests words or ideas outside strictly mus. concepts, as for ex. Fauré's beginning the melody of the song *Lydia* in the Lydian mode or Stanford's accomp. the words 'O, cursèd parry' in *The Critic* (Sheridan) with the opening of Parry's *Blest Pair of Sirens*. Occasionally the sound of some particular instrument can be used punningly: the use of the horns at the end of the aria 'Aprite un po' quegl' occhi' in Mozart's *Figaro*, in which Figaro declares that all women deceive their menfolk, may or may not be a pun on the traditional symbol for the betrayed male.

Punto. See **Stich.**

Puppo, Giuseppe (b. Lucca, 12. VI. 1749; d. Florence, 19. IV. 1827), It. violinist. Studied at the Naples Cons. and made a great success as a youth; visited Paris in 1775, then Span., Port. and Eng. Wrote vln. concertos, studies, duets, etc.

Purcell, Daniel (b. ? London, *c.* 1663; d. London, XI. 1717), Eng. organist and comp., brother of the foll. He was a choirboy in the Chapel Royal and was organist at Magdalen Coll., Oxford, 1688–95, when he came to London and added mus. to his dead brother Henry's *Indian Queen*. After a busy career as comp. of mus. for plays, he became organist of St. Andrew's Church, Holborn, in 1713.

Works incl. mus. for *Brutus of Alba*, Cibber's *Love's Last Shift* and *Love makes a Man*, Durfey's *Cynthia and Endymion*, Lacy's *Sawny the Scot* (based on Shakespeare's *Taming of the Shrew*), Steele's *Funeral* and *Tender Husband*, Farquhar's *The Beaux's Stratagem*, *The Inconstant* and (with Leveridge) *The Constant Couple*, Vanbrugh's *The Relapse* and (with Finger) *The Pilgrim*, an adaptation of Shakespeare's *Macbeth*, and many others; odes for St. Cecilia's Day; mus. for Congreve's *Judgment of Paris* (3rd prize in competition with Eccles, Finger and Weldon); odes; church mus.; sonatas for vln. and bass, and for fl. and bass; sonatas for tpt. and strings; cantatas for 1 voice, etc.

Purcell, Henry (b. ? London, between VI. and 20. XI. 1659; d. London, 21. XI. 1695), Eng. comp., brother of prec. Probably son of Thomas P., musician attached to the court after the Restoration of 1660. He showed genius in early childhood and became a choir-boy at the Chapel Royal (?) in 1669 under Cooke, from 1672 under Humfrey. Left in 1673 and became asst. to the keeper of the king's instruments and the following year, on Humfrey's death, pupil of Blow; tuned the org. and copied parts for Westminster Abbey; app. Composer in Ordinary for the Violins, IX. 1677. Songs of his were pub. from the age of 16. In 1679 he succeeded Blow as organist of Westminster Abbey; the next year he wrote string fantasies in the old polyphonic style and his 1st theatre mus., for Lee's *Theodosius*. Married in (?) 1681 and became a very successful church and theatre comp.; also in 1683, pub. his 1st instrumental sonatas. Made a speciality of welcome-songs for royalty and odes for official occasions. Wrote a coronation anthem for James II, 1685, and played at that of William and Mary, 1689. Prod. the operas *Dido and Aeneas* at a girls' school at Chelsea, (?) 1689, and collaborated with Dryden in *King Arthur*, prod. 1690. Ed. the 12th ed. of Playford's *Introduction to the Skill of Music* (with substantial additions), 1694. Anthem for the funeral service of Queen Mary comp. 1695, the year of his own death.

Works incl. operas and quasi-operas: *Dido and Aeneas*, *The Fairy Queen* (adapted from Shakespeare's *Midsummer Night's Dream*), *King Arthur*, *The Prophetess*, *The Tempest* (adapted from Shakespeare); incid. mus. and songs for plays: Bancroft, *Henry II*, Beaumont and Fletcher, *Bonduca*, *The Double Marriage*, Behn, *Abdelazer*, Congreve, *The Double Dealer*, *The Old Bachelor*, Crowne, *The Married Beau*, *Regulus*, Chas. Davenant, *Circe*, Dryden, *Amphitryon*, *Aureng-Zebe*, *Cleomenes*, *Love Triumphant*, *The Spanish Friar*, *Tyrannic Love*, Dryden and Howard, *The Indian Queen*, Dryden and Lee, *Oedipus*, Durfey, *Don Quixote*, *A Fool's Preferment* (adapt. from Fletcher), *The Marriage-Hater Matched*, *The Richmond Heiress*, *Sir Barnaby Whigg*, *The Virtuous Wife*, Fletcher, *Rule a Wife and Have a Wife*, Gould, *The Rival Sisters*, Lee, *The Massacre of Paris*, *Sophonisba*, *Theodosius*, Molière (adapted Wright), *The Female Vertuosos* (*Les Femmes savantes*), Norton, *Pausanias*, Ravenscroft, *The Canterbury Guests*, Thomas Scott, *The Mock Marriage*, Settle, *Distressed Innocence*, Shadwell,

Epsom Wells, *The Libertine*, Shakespeare (adapted Tate), *King Richard II* (adapted Shadwell), *Timon of Athens*, Southerne, *The Fatal Marriage*, *The Maid's Last Prayer*, *Oroonoko* (adapted from Behn), *Sir Anthony Love*, *The Wives' Excuse*, ?, *The Gordian Knot Untied*; 15 odes for voices and orch.; 9 welcome-songs for voices and orch.; *Yorkshire Feast Song* for voices and orch.; 9 secular cantatas; 66 anthems; 3 services; 26 hymns, psalms, chants and sacred canons; 22 sacred songs; 53 catches; 4 3-part songs; 42 vocal duets; over 100 songs (not counting *c*. 150 in the plays); 13 fantasies and 4 other works for strings; 22 sonatas for 2 vlns. and bass and some other miscellaneous chamber works; 8 suites (lessons) and *c*. 30 other pieces for harpsichord; 3 or 4 voluntaries for org., etc.

Puritani di Scozia, I (*The Puritans of Scotland*), opera by Bellini (lib. by Carlo Pepoli, based on a play by Jacques Ancelot and Xavier Boniface Saintine, *Têtes rondes et Cavaliers*, and farther back on Scott's *Old Mortality*), prod. Paris, Théâtre Italien, 25. I. 1835.

Puschmann, Adam Zacharias (b. Görlitz, 1532; d. Breslau, 4. IV. 1600), Ger. master-singer. Pupil of Hans Sachs at Nuremberg. He pub. in 1574 a treatise on master-singing, containing songs of his own as well as by Sachs, Behaim and others.

Pushkin, Alexander (1790–1837), Rus. poet, dramatist and novelist. *See* Aleko (Rakhmaninov), Assafiev (*Feast in Time of Plague*, Brass Horseman and Fountain of Bakhchissarai), Boris Godunov (Mussorgsky), Cui (*Captive in the Caucasus*, Feast in Time of Plague and songs), Dargomizhsky (*Bacchus' Feast*), Eugene Onegin (Tchaikovsky), Feinberg (songs), Francesca da Rimini (Rakhmaninov), Gaigerova (songs), Golden Cockerel (Rimsky-Korsakov), Ilyinski (*Fountain of Bakhchissarai*), Khrennikov (songs), Koval (*Manor House* and songs), Legend of Tsar Saltan (Rimsky-Korsakov), Leoncavallo (*Zingari*), Lourié (*Feast in Time of Plague* and songs), Makarova (songs), Mavra (Stravinsky), Mazeppa (Tchaikovsky), Medtner (songs), Mossolov (songs), Mozart and Salieri (Rimsky-Korsakov), Popov (*Slow Horseman*), Prisoner in the Caucasus (Cui), Prokofiev (*Feast in Time of Plague*, Boris Godunov, Eugene Onegin, Egyptian Nights, Queen of Spades and songs), Queen of Spades (Tchaikovsky), Russalka (Dargomizhsky), Russlan and Ludmilla (Glinka), Shaporin (*Boris Godunov* and songs), Shebalin (*Mozart and Salieri, Stone Guest* and songs), Shostakovich (songs), Stone Guest (Dargomizhsky), Tcherepnin (N.) (*Golden Fish*), Vassilenko (*Gypsies*), Verstovsky (*Black Shawl*).

Püttlingen, Johann Vesque von. *See* **Vesque von Püttlingen.**

Puy (Fr.), a competitive festival held in Fr. in the Middle Ages by literary and mus. guilds, incl. the Troubadours of the 12th cent. P.s continued to the 16th cent. and the most famous was that of Évreux, held annually on St. Cecilia's Day (22. XI), 1570–1614. Prizes were given and the laureate was called *roy de puy*.

Puy, Jean du. *See* **Du Puy.**

Pyamour, John (b. ?; d. before 4. VII. 1431), Eng. comp. He was a member of the Chapel Royal, 1420–1, and of the chapel of the Duke of Bedford in 1427. Wrote church mus.

Pycard (b. ?; d. ?), Eng. comp., repres. in the Old Hall MS. His mus. is remarkable for its extensive use of canon.

Pygott, Richard (b. ?, *c.* 1485; d. ?

Greenwich, 1552), Eng. comp. He was in Wolsey's private chapel in 1517 as master of the children and in 1524 became a Gentleman of the Chapel Royal. Later he was given a corrody at Coggeshall monastery in Essex and a canonry at Tamworth, but lost some of the benefits at the dissolution of the monasteries, Henry VIII, however, and after him Edward VI, retained his services.

Works incl. Masses, motets, *Salve Regina*; carols, etc.

Pythagoras (b. ?; d. ?), Gk 6th-cent. (B.C.) philosopher. He contrib. to the science of mus. by working out by mathematics the intervals of the scale according to the number of vibrations to each note and by helping to systematize the Tetrachords.

Q

Quadrille, a dance originating from the figured displays of mounted squadrons at tournaments, intro. into the ballet in the 18th cent., where dancers perf. similar figures, and in the 19th cent. passing into the ballroom for the perf. of country dances, 5 in number and each calling for different figures and different mus. Its mus., like that of the Lancers, which evidently had a military orig., soon ceased to use the orig. country-dance tunes and was made up of arrs. of popular songs or more esp. fashionable operatic tunes.

Quadruple Counterpoint, counterpoint in which 4 parts are reversible. *See also* **Triple Counterpoint.**

Quadruplets, groups of 4 notes occurring abnormally in mus. written in a time in which the regular units are divisible by 3.

Quagliai, Paolo (b. Chioggia, *c.* 1555; d. Rome, 16. XI. 1628), It. comp. He was organist at the church of Santa Maria Maggiore in Rome from 1601.
Works incl. dramatic cantata *Carro di fedeltà d'amore*; motets; spiritual and secular madrigals and canzonets; org. and harpsichord works, etc.

Quail, a toy instrument. *See* **Toy Symphony.**

Quantz, Johann Joachim (b. Oberscheden nr. Göttingen, 30. I. 1697; d. Potsdam, 12. VII. 1773), Ger. flautist and comp. As a boy he learned several instruments, and studied comp. with Zelenka in Vienna in 1717. The following year he was app. oboist to the court of August II in Dresden and Warsaw, but later turned to the fl., studying under Buffardin. After travels in It., Fr. and Eng. he returned to Dresden, becoming 1st flautist to the court, until in 1741 he entered the service of Frederick II of Prussia. He was the king's fl. teacher and wrote for him over 500 works for fl. His important treatise, *Versuch einer Anweisung die Flöte traversiere zu spielen*, was pub. in 1752.
Works incl. *c.* 300 concertos and *c.* 200 other works for fl., hymns on poems by Gellert, etc.

Quarles, Francis (1592–1644), Eng. poet. *See* **Britten** (Canticle).

Quart-Geige (Ger. = quarter vln.). *See* **Violino piccolo.**

Quartal Harmony, a harmonic theory, expounded by Yasser and others, which bases the harmonic system on the intervals of the 4th, instead of the 3rd which decisively determines maj. or min. tonalities.

Quarter Note (Amer.), crotchet.

Quarter-tones, intervals half-way between a semitone. They were known to the Greeks and were apparently used in early plainsong but soon came to be abandoned and were not revived in western mus. until the 20th cent. The chief exponent of quarter-tone mus. is Alois Hába; others, e.g. Bartók and Bloch, have used the device, but not systematically.

Quartet, any work or mus. number in a work written for 4 vocal or instrumental parts; more partic. a chamber work for 2 vlns., vla. and cello (string 4tet) or vln., vla., cello and pf. (pf. 4tet). The use of the word Q. without further specification usually suggests a string 4tet.

Quartettsatz (Ger. = quartet movement), the name given to the 1st movement of Schubert's unfinished string 4tet in C min., comp. in XII. 1820 and not perf. until 1. III. 1867, in Vienna. The work was clearly intended to be completed, for Schubert wrote 41 bars of a slow movement in A♭ maj.

Quasi (It. = as it were, so to speak), a qualifying word used in directions suggesting an approximate manner of perf. (e.g. *quasi allegro*) or an apparent contradiction of a time signature by the music's actual effect (e.g. *andante quasi allegro*, meaning that although the beats are moderately slow, the figuration is rapid and will give an effect of quickness). Q. is also used for titles of mus. comps. approximating to some partic. style, e.g. 'Quasi Scherzo', Beethoven's sonatas 'quasi una fantasia', etc.

Quatorze Juillet, Le (*The Fourteenth of July*), play by Romain Rolland, forming part of the trilogy *Le Théâtre de la Révolution* with *Danton* and *Les Loups*, pub. and perf. *c.* 1900–2, collectively pub. 1909. It was prod. in the open air, Paris, Arènes de Lutèce, 14. VII. 1936, with mus. by Auric, Honegger, Ibert, Koechlin, Lazarus, Milhaud and Roussel.

Quatrible (Eng., obs.), the highest part in a 4-part comp.; also the 4th part in Fauxbourdon.

Quattro rusteghi, I (*The Four Boors*), opera by Wolf-Ferrari (lib. by Giuseppe Pizzolato, based on Goldoni's comedy), prod., in Ger., Munich, 19. III. 1906; in Eng. as *The School for Fathers*, London, Sadler's Wells Theatre, 7. VI. 1946.

Quatuor (Fr.), quartet.

Quaver, the black note (♪) of half the time-value of a crotchet or an eighth of a semibreve, symbolized by the figure 8 in time-signatures, e.g. 3–8 indicates barlengths of 3 Q.s.

Queen of Cornwall, The, opera by Boughton (lib. Thomas Hardy's play, with alterations), prod. Glastonbury, 21. VIII. 1924. The subject is Tristram and Iseult.

Queen of Sheba. *See* **Königin von Saba;** **Reine de Saba.**

Queen of Spades, The (*Pikovaya Dama*), opera by Tchaikovsky (lib. by Modest Ilich Tchaikovsky, Tchaikovsky's brother, based on Pushkin's story), prod. St. Petersburg, 19. XII. 1890.

Quentin Durward, opera by Gevaert (lib. by Eugène Cormon and Michel Carré, based on Scott's novel), prod. Paris, Opéra-Comique, 25. III. 1858.

Opera by A. Maclean (lib. by Sheridan Ross, based on Scott), prod. Newcastle-on-Tyne, 13. I. 1920.

Querflöte (Ger.), Transverse Flute.

Quest, The, ballet by Walton (choreography by Frederick Ashton, based on Spenser's *Faery Queen*), prod. London, Sadler's Wells Ballet, 1943.

Quickstep, a military march with quick steps, also the mus. for such a march.

Quiet Don, The (*Tikhi Don*), opera by Dzerhinsky (lib. by comp., based on Mikhail Sholokhov's novel), prod. Leningrad, 22. X. 1935.

Quilter, Roger (b. Brighton, 1. XI. 1877; d. London, 21. IX. 1953), Eng. comp. Educ. at Eton and studied mus. with Knorr at Frankfurt. He never held any official mus. posts.

Works incl. opera *Julia*, radio opera *The Blue Boar*; incid. mus. for Shakespeare's *As You Like It* and the children's fairy-play *Where the Rainbow ends*; *Children's Overture* on nursery tunes, serenade, *3 Eng. Dances*, etc. for orch.; song-cycle *To Julia* (Herrick), songs to words by Shakespeare, Tennyson and others, etc.

Quinault, Jean-Baptiste (Maurice) (b. Paris, ? 1685; d. Gien, 1744), Fr. singer, actor and comp. Sang at the Théâtre Français in Paris 1712–18, and worked as an actor there from 1718. His comps. were almost all written for the Comédie Française. In 1733 he retired to Gien.

Works incl. ballet *Les Amours des déesses* and others; stage divertissements; incid. mus. for Molière's *Bourgeois Gentilhomme* and *La Princesse d'Élide*, etc.

Quinault, Philippe (1635–88), Fr. poet and librettist. *See* Alceste (Lully), **Amadis,** (Lully), **Amadis de Gaule** (J. C. Bach), **Armida** (Mysliveček), **Armide** (Gluck and Lully), **Atys** (Lully and Piccinni), **Cadmus et Hermione** (Lully), **Festes de l'Amour** (Lully), **Floquet** (*Nouvelle Omphale* and *Alceste*), **Isis** (Lully), **Lully** (*Églogue de Versailles*) **Persée** (Lully), **Phaéton** (Lully), **Proserpine** (Lully and Paisiello), **Roland** (Lully and Piccinni), **Thésée** (Lully).

Quinet, Fernand (b. Charleroi, 29. I. 1898), Belg. cellist, cond. and comp. Studied at the Brussels Cons., where he was awarded the Belg. Prix de Rome in 1921. Later became director of the Charleroi Cons., and of the Liège Con. in 1938.

Works incl. *Esquisses symphoniques, Mouvements symphoniques,* etc., for orch.; suite *L'École buissonière* and fantasy for string 4tet, *Charade* for pf. trio, suite for 2 clars. and bass clar.; *Moralités non légendaires* for voice and 18 instruments; vla. and pf. sonata; song-cycle *La Bonne Aventure* and other songs, etc.

Quinible (Eng., obs.), the highest part in a 5-part comp.; also the 5th part in Fauxbourdon.

Quint, a 5⅓-ft. org. stop transposing a 5th upwards; also called Great Q.

Quint de Loup (Fr. = wolf's 5th). *See* Wolf.

Quinta falsa (Lat. = false 5th), another name for the Tritone when it appears as a diminished 5th, not an augmented 4th.

Quintadena⎫ a 16-ft. org. stop governing
Quintatön ⎭ wood or metal pipes with labial openings sounding the 12th together with the fundamental note.

Quinte (Fr.). The word is now used for the interval of the 5th, but was formerly also the name of a string instrument of the viol family, the tenor viol with 5 strings; also later of the vla., another Fr. name of which was Taille.

Quintero, Joaquín Alvarez (1873–1944) and **Serafin Alvarez** (1871–1938), Span. dramatists. *See* Vittadini (*Anima allegra*).

Quintet, any work or mus. number in a work written in 5 vocal or instrumental parts; more partic. a chamber work for 5 instruments, e.g. pf. and string 4tet (pf. 5tet) or 5 string instruments (string 5tet).

Quintoles, another name for Quintuplets.

Quinton (Fr.), a 19th-cent. name for a hybrid string instrument, half viol and half vln.

Quintuple Time. Mus. with 5 beats to the bar, the time-signature of which is 5–4, 5–8, etc., is said to be in Q. T.

Quintuplets, groups of 5 notes occupying a beat or the space of a note of normal duration.

Quintus (Lat. = the fifth), the 5th part in a comp. for 5 or more voices in old mus. It was so called because its range was always equal to that of one of the other parts, so that it could not be described as *cantus, altus, tenor* or *bassus.*

Quire, the old Eng. spelling of Choir.

Quiterne (Fr. and old Eng.) = Cittern.

Quittard, Henri (b. Clermont-Ferrand, 13. V. 1864; d. Paris, 21. VII. 1919), Fr. musicologist. Studied with Franck in Paris, but soon began to specialize in mus. hist. He wrote numerous articles on Fr. mus. of the past and one or two books.

Quo vadis?, opera by Nouguès (lib. by Henri Cain, based on Sienkiewicz's novel), prod. Nice, 9. II. 1909.

Quodlibet (Lat. *quod libet* = as it

pleases), a comp. made up of a medley o tunes, usually familiar songs, in polyphonic combinations. Obrecht's *Missa diversorum tenorum* is an elaborate Q., introducing the melodies of *chansons* by 15th-cent. comps. A more familiar ex. is the Q. at the end of Bach's Goldberg Variations. The Span. term for a Q. was *ensalada*.

Quotations, short passages in mus. works taken from other mus. (*a*) by the same comp., (*b*) by another, or (*c*) traditional, folk or popular tunes, e.g.:

(*a*) Brahms, *Regenlied* in finale of G maj. vln. sonata;

Elgar, a number of themes from earlier works in *The Music Makers*; demons' chorus from *The Dream of Gerontius* in *The Fourth of August* (as a theme for the enemy);

Mozart, 'Non più andrai' from *Figaro* in 2nd finale of *Don Giovanni*;

Prokofiev, March from *The Love for Three Oranges* in ballet *Cinderella*;

Puccini, 'Mimì' theme from *La Bohème* in *Il tabarro*;

Rimsky-Korsakov, theme from *Pskovitianka* (*Ivan the Terrible*) in *The Tsar's Bride* (ref. to Ivan);

Saint-Saëns, theme from *Danse macabre* in *Fossils* section of *Le Carnaval des animaux*;

Schumann, opening of *Papillons*, Op. 1, in *Florestan* piece in *Carnival*, Op. 9;

Smetana, theme assoc. with the Vyšehrad citadel of Prague in *My Country* (symph. poem of that name) ref. to in the later one entitled *Vltava*;

Smyth, *March of the Women* in the overture to *The Boatswain's Mate*;

Strauss, theme from *Guntram* in 'Childhood' section of *Tod und Verklärung*; a number of themes from earlier works in the 'Hero's Works' section of *Heldenleben* and in the dinner mus. in the *Bourgeois Gentilhomme* incid. mus.; *Ariadne auf Naxos* in *Capriccio*; transfiguration theme from *Tod und Verklärung* in *Im Abendrot* ('Last Songs');

Sullivan, *H.M.S. Pinafore* in *Utopia Limited*;

Vaughan Williams, theme from *Hugh the Drover* in vln. conc.

Wagner, 2 themes from *Tristan* in *Meistersinger*, III. i; swan motive from *Lohengrin* in *Parsifal*, I; themes from *Siegfried* in *Siegfried Idyll* (some going back to a projected string 4tet);

Wolf, song, 'In dem Schatten meiner Locken' from *Span. Song-Book* in opera *Der Corregidor*, I.

(*b*) Bax, theme from Wagner's *Tristan* in symph. poem *Tintagel*; passage from Elgar's vln. concerto in G maj. string 4tet ded. to Elgar;

Beethoven, 'Notte e giorno faticar'

from Mozart's *Don Giovanni* in Vars. on a theme by Diabelli, Op. 120;

Berg, theme from Wagner's *Tristan* in suite for string 4tet;

Brahms, 'Batti, batti' from Mozart's *Don Giovanni* in song *Liebe und Frühling*, Op. 3 No. 2;

Bréville, 'Tarnhelm' motive from Wagner's *Ring* in *Portraits de Maîtres* for pf., indicating a transformation between the pieces imitating var. comps.

Britten, theme from Wagner's *Tristan* in *Albert Herring*;

Chabrier, Serenade from Mozart's *Don Giovanni* in song *Ballade des gros dindons*;

Charpentier, theme from Wagner's *Ring* in *Louise*, II;

Chopin, air from Rossini's *Gazza ladra* in Polonaise in B min. ded. to Kolberg (1826);

Debussy, theme from Wagner's *Tristan* in *Golliwog's Cake-Walk* (*Children's Corner*);

Elgar, theme from Mendelssohn's overture *Calm Sea and Prosperous Voyage* in 'Enigma' Variations (*Romance*); Chopin's G min. nocturne and Paderewski's *Polish Fantasy* for pf. and orch. in symph. prelude *Polonia*;

Falla, opening motive from Beethoven's 5th symph. ('Fate knocking at the door') in ballet *The Three-cornered Hat*;

Fibich, var. themes from Mozart's *Don Giovanni* in opera *Hedy* (based on Byron's *Don Juan*);

Křenek, Mendelssohn's *Spring Song* in incid. mus. for Goethe's *Triumph der Empfindsamkeit*;

Mozart, tunes from Martín y Soler's *Una cosa rara* and Sarti's *Fra due litiganti* in 2nd finale of *Don Giovanni*;

Mussorgsky, Handel's 'See the conquering hero' and themes by Famitsin and from Serov's opera *Rogenda* in satirical song *The Peep-Show*; sea motive from Rimsky-Korsakov's *Sadko* in song *The Classicist*;

Noren, 2 themes from Strauss's *Heldenleben* in *Kaleidoskop* suite for orch.;

Offenbach, 'Notte e giorno faticar' from Mozart's *Don Giovanni* in *Tales of Hoffmann*, prologue: 'Che farò' from Gluck's *Orfeo* in *Orphée aux enfers*;

Parry, Chopin's Funeral March from B♭ min. sonata in cantata *The Pied Piper of Hamelin*; var. Q.s in incid. mus. for Aristophanes' *Clouds*;

Rimsky-Korsakov, themes from Mozart's Requiem in opera *Mozart and Salieri*;

Saint-Saëns, themes from overture to Offenbach's *Orphée aux enfers* in *Tortoises* section of *Le Carnaval des animaux* (because Orpheus's lute was made of tortoise-shell), also Berlioz's *Danse des Sylphes* in *Elephants* and a phrase from

Rossini's *Barber of Seville* in *Fossils* in the same work;

Schumann, aria from Marschner's *Der Templer und die Jüdin* in finale of *Études symphoniques*, Op. 13.

Smyth, opening motive from Beethoven's 5th symph. ('Fate knocking at the door') in *The Boatswain's Mate*; song from Méhul's *Joseph* in *Entente cordiale*;

Stanford, a number of themes in opera *The Critic* (incl. opening of Parry's *Blest Pair of Sirens* at the words 'O, cursèd parry');

Strauss, Denza's song *Funiculì, funiculà* in symph. *Aus Italien* (under the impression that it was an It. folksong); giants' motive in Wagner's *Ring* in *Feuersnot*; Wagner's Rhinemaidens' theme in dinner mus. (salmon) of Strauss's *Bourgeois gentilhomme* (*Ariadne*, 1st version); themes by Bull, Legrenzi, Monteverdi and Peerson in *Die schweigsame Frau*; fragment from funeral march in Beethoven's 'Eroica' symph. in *Metamorphosen* for strings;

Stravinsky, waltz by Lanner (played on a barrel-organ) in ballet *Petrushka*;

Sullivan, Bach's great G min. org. fugue in song 'A more humane Mikado never' in *The Mikado*;

Tchaikovsky, song from Grétry's *Richard, Cœur de Lion* in *The Queen of Spades*;

Vaughan Williams, opening theme from Debussy's *L'Après-midi d'un faune* in incid. mus. for Aristophanes' *Wasps*;

Wagenaar, a patchwork of themes from numerous comps. in *Jupiter amans*;

Wagner, *Di tanti palpiti*, from Rossini's *Tancredi*, parodied in the tailors' episode in *Meistersinger* III.

Walton, 2 themes from Rossini's *William Tell* overture in *Façade* (*Swiss Yodelling Song*); theme from Rossini's *Tancredi* overture in *Scapino* overture;

(*c*) Beethoven, 'God save the King' and 'Malbrouk s'en va-t-en guerre' in *The Battle of Victoria*; Rus. folk-songs in Rasumovsky 4tets Op. 59;

Brahms, 'God save the King' (as 'Heil Dir im Siegerkranz') and hymn 'Now thank we all our God' in *Triumphlied*; Ger. students' songs in *Acad. Festival* overture;

Busoni, song *Greensleeves* in *Turandot*.

Chabrier, Rakoczy March in *Le Roi malgré lui*;

Debussy, 'Au clair de la lune' in *Préludes*, II. 7; 'God save the King' in *Hommage à S. Pickwick, Esq.* and *Marseillaise* in *Feux d'artifice* (both in *Préludes*, II); 'Nous n'irons plus au bois' in *Jardins sous la pluie* for pf. and *Rondes de printemps* for orch.

Elgar, Pol. nat. anthem in symph. prelude *Polonia*;

Glazunov, Volga boatmen's song in symph. poem *Stenka Razin*;

Litolff, *Marseillaise* in *Robespierre* overture.

Mendelssohn, chorale *Ein' feste Burg* in Reformation symph.

Meyerbeer, do. in *Les Huguenots*.

Puccini, Amer. nat. anthem in *Madama Butterfly*, I;

Saint-Saëns, Fr. folksongs in *Fossils* section of *Le Carnaval des animaux*;

Schumann, *Marseillaise* in *Faschingsschwank aus Wien* for pf., in ovt. *Hermann und Dorothea* and in song *Die beiden Grenadiere*; old Ger. 'Grossvatertanz' (or 'Kehraus') at the end of *Papillons* and *Carnaval* for pf.

Smyth, 2 Fr. folksongs in *Entente cordiale*, later pub. as *Two Interlinked Fr. Melodies* for fl., ob. and pf.

Stravinsky, Fr. popular song 'Ell' avait une jamb' en bois' in ballet *Petrushka*;

Suppé, Ger. students' songs in overture *Flotte Bursche*.

Tchaikovsky, Rus. nat. anthem and *Marseillaise* in overture *The Year 1812*; Dan. and Rus. nat. anthems in *Danish Overture*; Rus. nat. anthem in *Slav March*, *Coronation March* and *Jurists' March*;

Vaughan Williams, song *Greensleeves* in opera *Sir John in Love*;

Wagner, *Marseillaise* in Fr. song *Les Deux Grenadiers* (trans. from Heine); Ger. folksong 'Schlaf, Kindlein, schlaf' in *Siegfried Idyll*; chorale *Ein' feste Burg* in *Kaisermarsch*;

Weber, 'God save the King' at close of *Jubilee Overture*;

Wolf-Ferrari, 'Grossvatertanz' (*cf.* Schumann) in *I quattro rusteghi*.

(*See also* **Dies irae** for var. Q.s of the plainsong tune).

R

r, the Supertonic note in any key in Tonic Sol-fa notation, pronounced Ray.

R.A.M. (abbr.) = Royal Academy of Music (London).

R.C.M. (abbr.) = Royal College of Music (London).

R.H. (abbr.) = Right Hand.

R.Ir.A.M. (abbr.) = Royal Irish Academy of Music (Dublin).

Raaff, Anton (b. Gelsdorf nr. Bonn, V. 1714; d. Munich, 28, V. 1797), Ger. tenor. Studied in Munich and Bologna, sang much in It. as well as in Ger. and Aus. From 1770 in the service of the Elector Palatine. The first Idomeneo in Mozart's opera of that name.

Rabaud, Henri (Benjamin) (b. Paris, 10. XI. 1873; d. Paris, 11. IX. 1949), Fr. comp. Studied under his father, the cellist Hippolyte R. (1839–1900), and with Gédalge and Massenet at the Paris Cons., where he gained the Prix de Rome in 1894. After his stay in Rome he visited Vienna and travelled elsewhere, and after his return to Paris he became harmony prof. at the Cons. and cond. at the Opéra. In 1920 he succeeded Fauré as director of the Cons., and was in turn succeeded in that post by Delvincourt in 1941.

Works incl. operas *La Fille de Roland, Le Premier Glaive, Mârouf, savetier du Caire, L'Appel de la mer* (after Synge's *Riders to the Sea*), *Rolande et les mauvais garçons*; incid. mus. for Shakespeare's *Merchant of Venice* and *Antony and Cleopatra*; mus. for films *Joueurs d'échecs* and *Le Miracle des loups*; Psalm iv for chorus; 2 symphs., symph. poem *Andromède, La Procession nocturne* (after Lenau's *Faust*), *Le Sacrifice d'Isaac, La Flûte de Pan, Divertissement grec, Divertissement sur des airs russes, Poème sur le livre de Job,* etc., for orch.; string 4tet; songs, etc.

Rabelais, François (c. 1490–1553), Fr. novelist. See **Dieren (van)** (*Propous des Beuveurs*), **Fanelli** (suite), **Ganne** (operetta), **Gargantua** (Mariotte), **Grétry** (*Panurge*), **Massenet** (do.), **Monsigny** (*Île sonnante*), **Planquette** (*Panurge*), **Terrasse** (*Pantagruel*).

Rachmaninoff. See **Rakhmaninov.**

Racine, Jean (1639–99), Fr. poet and dramatist. See **Andromaque** (Grétry), **Athalie** (Mendelssohn and others), **Boïeldieu** (*Athalie*), **Clément (F.)** (*Athalie* and *Esther*), **Cohen** (do., do.), **Coquard** (*Esther*), **Esther** (Handel), **Fauré** (*Cantique*), **Hartmann (T. de)** (*Esther*), **Hervé** (*Nouvel Aladin*), **Honegger** (*Phèdre*), **Ifigenia in Aulide** (Graun), **Iphigénie en Aulide** (Gluck), **Lemoyne** (*Phèdre*), **Lully** (*Idylle*

sur la paix), **Lunssens** (*Phèdre*), **Massenet** (do.), **Mitridate** (Mozart), **Moreau** (*Cantiques spirituels* and *Esther* and *Athalie*), **Perne** (*Esther*), **Poissl** (*Athalia*), **Roseingrave (2)** (*Phaedra and Hippolytus*), **Rossini** (*Ermione*), **Rousseau (M.)** (*Bérénice*), **Saint-Saëns** (*Andromaque*), **Schulz** (*Athalie*), **Thomson (V.)** (*Air de Phèdre*), **Vogler** (*Athalie*).

Rackett, an obs. double-reed instrument, also called Racket, Ranket or Sausage Bassoon. Its long tube was folded many times, so that the actual size of the instrument seemed small.

Radamisto, opera by Handel (lib. by Nicola Francesco Haym, after Tacitus), prod. London, King's Theatre, Haymarket, 27. IV. 1720.

Radcliffe (*née* **Ward**), **Ann** (1764–1823), Eng. novelist. See **Arneiro.**

Radcliffe, Philip (FitzHugh) (b. Godalming, 27. IV. 1905), Eng. scholar, author and comp. Educ. at Charterhouse and King's Coll., Cambridge. In 1947 he was app. univ. lecturer in mus. at Cambridge. His comps. incl. chamber mus., partsongs and songs. He has also written a book on Mendelssohn, and contrib. chapters on the Scarlattis, Corelli and Vivaldi to *The Heritage of Music.*

Raddoppiamento (It. = redoubling) = Augmentation.

Radford, Robert (b. Nottingham, 13. V. 1874; d. London, 3. III. 1933), Eng. bass. Studied at the R.A.M. in London and made his 1st appearance at the Norwich Festival in 1899, and in opera at Covent Garden Theatre in London in 1904.

Radicati, Felice Alessandro (b. Turin, 1775; d. Bologna, 19. III. 1820), It. violinist and comp. Pupil of Pugnani, he toured as a vln. virtuoso in It., Fr. and Eng., then settled in Bologna in 1815 as leader of the munic. orch., *maestro di cappella* at San Petronio and vln. prof. at the Liceo Filarmonico.

Works incl. operas *Riccardo Cuor di Leone, Fedra, Coriolano, Castore e Polluce* and some others; vln. concertos; vln. pieces; arias, etc.

Radiciotti, Giuseppe (b. Iesi, 25. I. 1858; d. Tivoli, 4. IV. 1931), It. musicologist. Studied with his uncle G. Faini, worked in Rome for a time and in 1881 became prof. of mus. hist. at the Liceo at Tivoli. His books incl. studies of Pergolesi, of the mus. hist. of Rome, Senigallia, Urbino and Tivoli, a biog. of Rossini, etc.

Radino, Giovanni Maria (b. ?; d. ?), It. 16th-cent. organist and comp. He was organist at the church of San Giovanni di Verdara at Padua.

Works incl. madrigals for 4 voices; dances for harpsichord or lute, etc.

Radio-Synthetic Organ, an electrophonic org. invented by Abbé Puget of Paris in 1934, prod. its notes by the conversion of electrical waves into audible sounds.

Radnai, Miklós (b. Budapest, 1. I. 1892; d. Budapest, 4. XI. 1935), Hung. comp. Studied at Budapest and Munich, became a prof. at the Budapest Cons., 1919–25, and then director of the Opera there.

Works incl. opera *The Former Lovers*; ballet *The Infanta's Birthday* (after Wilde); Hung. Symph., *Mosaic* suite, 5 poems, *Fairy Tale, Orcan the Hero*, for orch.; pf. trio; instrumental sonatas; pf. works; songs, etc.

Radoux, Charles (Jean Édouard Firmin Paul) (b. Liège, 30. VII. 1877; d. Liège, 30. IV. 1952), Belg. comp. Studied under his father at the Liège Cons. and gained the Belg. Prix de Rome in 1907. He became prof. there in 1911, having acted as asst. since 1905.

Works incl. operas *Oudelette, Le Sanglier des Ardennes, Œdipe à Colone* (after Sophocles) and *Le Poème de Roseclaire*; incid. mus.; Te Deum; *Geneviève de Brabant, Cantate à Grétry* and other choral works; *Danse tzigane, Burlesque, Triptyque champêtre* for orch.; variations for pf. and orch., *Fantaisie* and *Dans les fagnes* for vln. and orch., *Scènes grecques* and *Choral varié* for cello and orch.; pf. pieces; songs, etc.

Radoux, (Jean) Théodore (b. Liège, 9. XI. 1835; d. Liège, 20. III. 1911), Belg. comp., father of prec. Studied at the Liège and Paris Conss. and obtained the Belg. Prix de Rome in 1859. He taught bassoon at the Liège Cons. from 1855 and became its director in 1872.

Works incl. operas *Le Béarnais, La Coupe enchantée* and *André Doria* (unfinished); Te Deum; oratorio *Cain* and cantatas; symph. poems *Ahasvère, Le Festin de Balthasar* and *Godefroid de Bouillon*; overture. *Épopée nationale*; choruses; songs, etc.

Radziwiłł, Antoni (Henryk), Prince (b. Wilno, 13. VI. 1775; d. Berlin, 7. IV. 1833), Ger.-Pol. amateur cellist, singer and comp. He married the sister of another amateur musician, Prince Louis Ferdinand of Prus., and became Prus. governor of the duchy of Posen.

Works incl. incid. mus. to Goethe's *Faust*; *Complaint of Mary Stuart* for voice, pf. and cello, songs with guitar and cello, duets and songs with pf.; part-songs, etc.

Raff, (Joseph) Joachim (b. Lachen, Ct. Zürich, 27. V. 1822; d. Frankfurt, 24–5. VI. 1882), Swiss comp. Studied to become a schoolmaster, but took to mus. and in 1843 had some comps. pub. on Mendelssohn's recommendation. He met Liszt, and

at Cologne in 1846 Mendelssohn, who invited him to become his pupil at Leipzig but d. before this was done. He then wrote criticism at Cologne, studied further at Stuttgart and in 1850 settled at Weimar to be near Liszt. In 1856 he went to Wiesbaden, where he wrote incid. mus. for a drama by Wilhelm Genast and married his daughter Doris, an actress. In 1877 he became director of the Hoch Cons. at Frankfurt.

Works incl. operas *König Alfred, Dame Kobold* (on Calderón's *Dama duende*) and others; incid. mus. for Genast's *Bernhard von Weimar* and other plays; oratorio *Weltende* and other choral works; programme symphs. *An das Vaterland, Im Walde, Lenore* (on Bürger's ballad), *Gelebt, gestrebt . . ., In den Alpen, Frühlingsklange, Im Sommer, Zur Herbstzeit, Der Winter* (unfinished), 2 suites, 3 overtures for orch.; sinfonietta for wind instruments; concerto, suite and *Ode au printemps* for pf. and orch., 2 vln. concertos; cello concerto; 8 string 4tets, string 6tet, string 8tet, 4 pf. trios, 2 pf. 4tets, pf. 5tet; 5 vln. and pf. sonatas; numerous pf. works; vln. pieces, etc.

Ragtime, an Amer. form of syncopated dance mus. of Negro orig. and coming into fashion *c.* 1910, the forerunner of Jazz and Swing.

Raimann, Rezsö (b. Veszprém, 7. V. 1861; d. Vienna, 26. IX. 1913), Hung. comp., mus. director to Prince Esterházy at Totis Castle.

Works incl. operas *Enoch Arden* (after Tennyson), *Imre Kiraly* and others, operettas; incid. mus. to plays; pf. pieces; songs, etc.

Raimondi, Ignazio (b. Naples, *c.* 1737; d. London, 14. I. 1813), It. violinist and comp. After playing vln. in the San Carlo opera orch. in Naples he went to Amsterdam, where he was director of the subscription concerts *c.* 1762–80, after which he settled in London. Works incl. opera *La Muette* (prod. Paris); programme symphs. *The Adventures of Telemachus* and *The Battle*; sinfonie concertanti; string 4tets and other chamber mus., etc.

Raimondi, Pietro (b. Rome, 20. XII. 1786; d. Rome, 30. X. 1853), It. comp. Studied at the Cons. di Pietà de' Turchini at Naples and wandered all over It. in great poverty until he succeeded in prod. an opera at Genoa in 1807. Prod. operas at Rome, Milan, Naples and in Sicily until 1824, became director of the royal theatres there until 1832, when he became prof. of comp. at the Palermo Cons. In 1852 he was app. *maestro di cappella* at St. Peter's in Rome in succession to Basili.

Works incl. operas *Le bizzarrie d'amore, Il ventaglio* and 60 others incl. a serious and a comic one which could be perf. together;

21 ballets; 8 oratorios incl. trilogy *Giuseppe* (incl. *Putifar, Farao* and *Giacobbe* performable separately or together), Masses, Requiems, psalms and other church mus., much of it in very numerous parts; vocal fugues, one in 64 parts and incl. others in 4 parts, 4 of which could be sung together in 16 parts, etc.

Raimund, Ferdinand (1790–1836), Aus. actor and playwright. *See* **Alpenkönig und Menschenfeind** (Blech), **Kreutzer (C.)** (*Verschwender*), **Reiter** (*Bauer als Millionär*).

Raindrop Prelude, Chopin's pf. prelude in D♭ maj., Op. 28 No. 15, written at Valdemosa, Majorca, in 1839 and said to have been suggested by the dripping of raindrops from the roof; hence the continuously repeated A♭ = G♯, which is the dominant both of the main key and of the C♯ min. middle section.

Rainforth, Elizabeth (b. ?, 23. XI. 1814; d. Bristol, 22. IX. 1877), Eng. soprano. Studied under George Perry and T. Cooke and made her 1st stage appearance in London in 1836, and in oratorio the following year.

Rainier, Priaulx (b. Howick, Natal, 3. II. 1903), S. African comp. She studied at Cape Town and after 1920 at the R.A.M. in London; lastly with Nadia Boulanger in Paris. In 1942 she was app. prof. at the R.A.M.

Works incl. *Archaic Songs* for chorus; ballet suite for orch., *Sinfonia da camera* for strings; *Incantation* for clar. and orch.; cello concerto; 3 string 4tets; vla. and pf. sonata; pf. works; songs, etc.

Raison, André (b. ?, before 1650; d. Paris, 1719), Fr. organist. Held posts at the Sainte-Geneviève and Jacobin churches in Paris. Comp. org. mus.

Raitio, Väinö (b. Sortavala, 15. IV. 1891; d. Helsinki, 10. IX. 1945), Fin. comp. Studied the pf. with his mother, later comp. with Melartin and Furuhjelm and in 1916–17 with Ilyinsky in Moscow. Taught comp. at Viipuri in 1932–8, but settled at Helsinki and devoted himself entirely to comp.

Works incl. operas *Jephtha's Daughter, Princess Cecilia* and 3 others; ballet *Waterspout*; symph., 10 symph. poems; pf. concerto; concerto for vln. and cello, Poem for cello and orch.; string 4tet, pf. 5tet; vln. and pf. sonata; songs, etc.

Rake's Progress, The, ballet by Gavin Gordon (choreography by Ninette de Valois, setting by Rex Whistler based on Hogarth), prod. London, Sadler's Wells Theatre, 20. V. 1935.

Opera by Stravinsky (lib. by W. H. Auden and Chester Kallman, based on Hogarth), prod. Venice, 11. IX. 1951. *See also* **Whitaker.**

Rakhmaninov, Sergey Vassilievich (b.

Oneg, Novgorod, 1. IV. 1873; d. Beverley Hills, Calif., 28. III. 1943), Rus. pianist and comp. Son of a captain in the Imp. Guards and descendant of a wealthy and noble family. The family fortune was gravely impaired during his childhood and his parents separated in 1882, R. living with his mother in St. Petersburg. There he continued mus. lessons in a desultory way until Siloti, who was his cousin, advised his mother to send him to Moscow to study under Nikolai Sverev. He went to the Moscow Cons. and lived in Sverev's house for 4 years. Later he went to live with his aunt, whose daughter, Natalia Satin, was later to become his wife. He wrote the 1-act opera *Aleko* while still a student, and the pf. pieces Op. 3, containing the popular C♯ min. prelude, at the age of 19. In 1895 he wrote his 1st (unpub.) symph. and in 1898 he was invited by the Phil. Society in London to appear as pianist and to cond. his orchestral fantasy *The Rock.* In 1905–6 he became cond. of the Imp. Grand Opera at Moscow and in 1909 he visited the U.S.A. for the 1st time, writing the 3rd pf. concerto for the occasion and playing it himself. He had by this time developed into one of the finest pianists of the time and he remained pre-eminent in that respect throughout his life.

He lived in Moscow again from 1910 to 1917 and cond. the Phil. concerts there, 1911–13. During the war of 1914–18 he played much for charity, and at the death of Skriabin, who had been his fellow-pupil under Arensky, he decided to make a tour playing that comp.'s works only. It was from that time on that he became a much-travelled pianist, and finding himself out of sympathy with the Revolution in Rus., he took the opportunity of a concert journey to Scandinavia in 1917 to leave his country for ever. He lived in Paris for a time and then spent most of the rest of his life in Amer., touring there each year from Jan. to Apr. and visiting Eur. as pianist in Oct. and Nov., spending some of the summer months at a small property he had acquired in Switz. on the lake of Lucerne.

Works incl. operas *Aleko, The Miserly Knight, Francesca da Rimini*; choral symph., *The Bells* (Poe), for solo voices, chorus and orch.; cantata, *The Spring*; *Liturgy of St. John Chrysostom* and Vesper Mass; 3 Rus. folksongs for chorus; 5 pf. concertos (1 unpub.) and *Rhapsody on a Theme by Paganini* for pf. and orch.; 3 symphs.; fantasy *The Rock, Caprice bohémien* and symph. poem, *The Isle of the Dead* (after Böcklin's picture) for orch.; *Elegiac Trio* for vln., cello and pf., string 5tet and pf. trio (unpub.); cello and pf. sonata, 2 pieces for vln. and pf. and 2 for cello and pf.; a dozen works for pf. solo, incl. 2 sonatas, variations on themes by Chopin and Corelli and 57 smaller pieces (preludes, *Études-Tableaux*, etc.); 4 works for 2 pfs.; 77 songs, etc.

Rakoczy March, a Hung. nat. tune named after Prince Ferencz Rákóczi, the leader of the revolt against Aus. in 1703–1711. The orig. of the tune is unknown. The Hung. March in Berlioz's *Damnation of Faust* is an orchestral arr. of it and Liszt's 15th Hung. Rhapsody for pf. is based on it. Liszt also made a symph. arr. for orch. and himself transcribed this for pf. duet.

Rallentando (It. = slowing down). The same direction is also expressed by *ritenuto* (held back) or *ritardando* (retarding).

Rameau, Jean Philippe (b. Dijon, 25. IX. 1683; d. Paris, 12. IX. 1764), Fr. comp. and theorist. A pupil of his father, who sent him to study in It. in 1701, he worked first as an organist in Avignon (1702), Clermont-Ferrand (1702–5), Paris (1705–8), Dijon (succeeding his father as cathedral organist in 1709), Lyons (1714) and from 1715 again in Clermont-Ferrand, where he wrote his important treatise, *Traité de l'Harmonie* (pub. 1722). In the latter year he settled in Paris, where he received support from the wealthy patron La Pouplinière. He had previously pub. some harpsichord pieces, but with *Hippolyte et Aricie* (1733) he began at the age of 50 a second career as an opera comp. Though at first opposed by the adherents of Lully's operas, he quickly estab. himself as the leading Fr. comp. for the stage, and during the Guerre des Bouffons was the champion of Fr. mus. against the It. party.

Works incl. operas and opera-ballets *Hippolyte et Aricie, Les Indes galantes, Castor et Pollux, Les Fêtes d'Hébé, Dardanus, Les Fêtes de Polyhymnie, Le Temple de la gloire, Zaïs, Pygmalion, Les Fêtes de l'Hymen et de l'Amour, Platée, Naïs, Zoroastre, Acante et Céphise, Les Surprises de l'amour, Les Paladins, Abaris, ou Les Boréades, Lysis et Délie, Daphnis et Églé, Les Sybarites, La Naissance d'Osiris, Anacréon, La Princesse de Navarre* (lib. by Voltaire), *La Guirlande* and others; incid. mus. for *L'Endriague* and 4 other plays by Piron; cantatas; *Pièces en concert* for vln. or fl. and harpsichord; harpsichord pieces, some adapted from the operas, etc.

Ramin, Günther (b. Carlsruhe, 15. X. 1898; d. Leipzig, 27. II. 1956), Ger. organist, cond. and comp. Studied at the Leipzig Cons. and in 1939 succeeded Straube as cantor of St. Thomas's Church there, the post once held by Bach.

Works incl. motet in 4 parts; vln. and pf. sonata; much org. mus., etc.

Ramis de Pareja, Bartolomé (b. Baeza,

c. 1440; d. ? Rome, after 1491), Span. theorist and comp. He lectured at Salamanca, went to It., living at Bologna in 1480–2 and later in Rome. He wrote a theoret. work in which he devised a way of tuning the monochord and comp. church mus.

Ramler, Karl Wilhelm (1725–98), Ger. poet. *See* **Bach** (J. C. F.) (*Tod Jesu*), **Graun** (K. H.) (do.), **Kreusser** (do.), **Telemann** (*Tod Jesu* and *Auferstehung Christi*, **Veichtner** (*Cephalus und Procris*), **Vogler** (*Ino*).

Ramondon, Lewis (b. ?; d. ? London, c. 1720), Eng. or Fr. bass and comp. He sang in opera in London until c. 1711 and then made a success as a comp. of songs, some contrib. to var. plays.

Ramsay, Allan (1686–1758), Scot. poet. *See* **Gentle Shepherd.**

Ramsey, Robert (b. ?; d. ? Cambridge, ?), Eng. 17th-cent. organist and comp. He took the Mus.B. at Cambridge in 1616 and became organist and master of the children at Trinity Coll. there, 1628–44.

Works incl. services, anthems, motets; madrigals, canons; dialogue between Saul and the Witch of Endor; songs, etc.

Randall, John (b. ? London, 1715; d. Cambridge, 18. III. 1799), Eng. organist, scholar and comp. He was a choir-boy under Gates at the Chapel Royal in London; organist of King's Coll., Cambridge, from 1743 and prof. of mus. there in succession to Greene from 1756, taking the Mus.D. the same year; also organist of Trinity Coll. later.

Works incl. church mus., hymn tunes, setting of Gray's ode for the installation of the Duke of Grafton as Chancellor of the Univ., etc.

Randegger, Alberto (b. Trieste, 13. IV. 1832; d. London, 18. XII. 1911), It. cond., singing-master and comp. Studied at Trieste with L. Ricci, became known locally as a comp. for the church and stage, and in the 1850s settled in London, where he became prof. of singing at the R.A.M. in 1868. He also cond. opera, orchestral and choral concerts and in 1881–1905 the triennial Norwich Festival.

Works incl. operas *Il lazzarone, Bianca Capello, The Rival Beauties;* Masses and other church mus.; cantata *Fridolin,* 150th Psalm, Funeral Anthem for the Prince Consort and other choral works; scena for tenor *The Prayer of Nature;* songs with orch. and with pf., etc.

Randhartinger, Benedikt (b. Ruprechtshofen, Lower Aus., 27. VII. 1802; d. Vienna, 22. XII. 1893), Aus. tenor, cond. and comp. Fellow-pupil of Schubert's at the Seminary in Vienna; sang in the court chapel from 1832 and in 1862 became 2nd cond. there.

Works incl. opera *König Enzio; c.* 20

Masses, c. 600 motets; choruses; chamber mus.; c. 400 songs, etc.

Rands, Bernard (b. Sheffield, 2. III. 1935), Eng. comp. Studied at Univ. Coll., Bangor, and then in It. with Roman Vlad and Dallapiccola. From 1961 to 1970 he was a lecturer at Bangor and was app. lecturer at York Univ. in 1970. Works incl. *Refractions* for 24 performers; *Actions for 6* for fl., vla., cello, harp and 2 perc. players, *Quartet Music* for pf. 4tet; *4 Compositions* for vln. and pf.; *Espressione IV* for 2 pfs.; *3 Aspects* for pf.; *Formants* for harp.

Rangström, Ture (b. Stockholm, 30. XI. 1884; d. Stockholm, 11. V. 1947), Swed. cond., critic and comp. Studied with Lindegren at Stockholm and Pfitzner at Munich, also in Berlin. He settled in Stockholm as critic in 1907 and in 1922–5 cond. the Göteborg Symph. Orch. Works incl. *Kronbruden* (after Strindberg) and *Medeltida* (after Drachman); incid. mus. to Ibsen's *Brand* and Strindberg's *Till Damaskus*; symphs. *August Strindberg in memoriam, Mitt land, Sång under stjärnorna,* symph. poems *Dityramb, Ett midsommarnattstycke, En höstsång, Havet sjunger,* chamber mus.; songs, etc.

Rank, a set of org. pipes of the same quality, partic. a Mixture.

Ranket. *See* Rackett.

Rankl, Karl (b. Gaden, 1. X. 1898; d. St. Gilgen, 6. IX. 1968), Aus. cond. and comp. He studied comp. privately with Schönberg and Webern. He was an opera conductor at Reichenberg from 1925 to 1927, at Königsberg from 1927 to 1928, at the Berlin State Opera from 1928 to 1931, at Wiesbaden from 1931 to 1933, at Graz from 1933 to 1937, at the German Theatre, Prague, from 1937 to 1938, and at Covent Garden, London from 1946 to 1951. From 1952 to 1957 he was cond. of the Scot. Nat. Orch., and in 1957 was app. cond. of the Elizabethan Trust Opera Co. in Australia. Works incl. opera *Deirdre of the Sorrows* (based on Synge's play); 8 symphs.; string 4tet; choruses; songs, etc.

Rant, an old Eng. dance the precise character of which is not known.

Ranta, Sulho (Veikko Juhani) (b. Peräseinäjoki, 15. VIII. 1901), Fin. comp. Studied with Melartin and Krohn at the Helsinki Cons., with Arthur Willner in Vienna, and in Paris. Became prof. at Viipuri Cons. and in 1933 at that of Helsinki. He wrote books on harmony and mus. hist. Works incl. a ballet *Kirsikankukkia*; 5 symphs. incl. *Sinfonia programmatica, Sinfonia piccola* for orch.; pf. concerto; chamber mus.; pf. pieces; songs, etc.

Ranz des Vaches, a Swiss cowherds' song or Alphorn signal by which the cattle is called in June from the valleys to the mountain pastures. There are many different tunes, varying according to the cantons or even districts. They are metrically very irregular and use only the natural notes of the alphorn.

Rape of Lucretia, The, opera by Britten (lib. by Ronald Duncan, based on Livy, Shakespeare and Obey's *Viol de Lucrèce*), prod. Glyndebourne, 12. VII. 1946.

Raphael, Günther (b. Berlin, 30. IV. 1903; d. Herford, 19. X. 1960), Ger. comp. Studied under his father, a church organist, and later with Trapp, R. Kahn and others at the Berlin Hochschule für Musik. In his early 20s he succeeded in having works pub., played by the Busch 4tet, cond. by Wilhelm Furtwängler and others. From 1926 to 1934 he was prof. at the Cons. and church mus. inst. at Leipzig, from 1949 to 1953 at Duisburg Cons., and from 1957 at the Cologne Musikhochschule. Works incl. Requiem, Te Deum, cantata *Vater unser*; 16 motets, Psalm civ and other unaccomp. sacred choral works; 5 symphs., sinfonietta, *Theme, Variations and Rondo,* divertimento, Smetana Suite for orch.; 2 vln. concertos, org. concerto; chamber concerto for cello with wind and strings, much other chamber mus.; org. and pf. works, etc.

Rapimento di Cefalo, Il (*The Abduction of Cephalus*), opera by Caccini (lib. by Gabriele Chiabrera), prod. Florence, Palazzo Vecchio, 9. X. 1600.

Rappresentativo. *See* Stile rappresentativo.

Rappresentazione di anima e di corpo (*Representation of Soul and Body*), a dramatic allegory, words by Agostino Manni, mus. by Emilio de' Cavalieri, prod. Rome, oratory of St. Philip Neri, II. 1600.

Rapsodie espagnole (*Span. Rhapsody*), an orchestral work by Ravel in a Span. manner as cultivated by a typically Fr. comp. with a strong taste for and leanings towards Span. mus.; comp. 1907, 1st perf. Paris, 15. III. 1908.

Raselius (orig. Rasel), **Andreas** (b. Hahnbach nr. Amberg, Upper Palatinate, c. 1563; d. Heidelberg, 6. I. 1602), Ger. clergyman, theorist and comp. Studied at the Lutheran Univ. of Heidelberg, became cantor at Regensburg, 1584–1600, and then mus. director to the Elector Palatine at Heidelberg. Wrote a treatise on the hexachord, set hymn and psalm tunes in 5 parts and comp. Ger. motets.

Rasi, Francesco (b. Arezzo, c. 1575; d. ?), It. singer, poet and comp. He came of a noble family and was a pupil of Caccini at Florence. Musician at the court of Mantua, c. 1600–20.

Works incl. *Musica di camera e di chiesa*; madrigals, songs, etc.

Rasumovsky Quartets, Beethoven's 3 string 4tets, Op. 59 in F maj., E min. and C maj., comp. in 1806 and ded. to the Rus. ambassador to Vienna, Count (later Prince) Andrey Kyrillovich Rasumovsky (1752–1836), by whose domestic 4tet, led by Schuppanzigh, they were 1st perf.

Rataplan (Fr. onomat. = Eng. rub-a-dub), a word imitating the sound of the side-drum and used for mus. pieces, esp. in opera, of a military-march character.

Ratcliff, opera by Andreae (lib. taken from Heine's tragedy *William R.*), prod. Duisburg, 25. V. 1914.

Rathaus, Karol (b. Tarnopol, Galicia, 16. IX. 1895; d. N.Y., 21. XI. 1954), Pol. comp. Studied with Schreker in Vienna and followed him to Berlin when S. became director of the Hochschule für Musik, where R. taught in 1925–33. In 1934 he took refuge from the Nazi regime in London and later settled in U.S.A.

Works incl. opera *Strange Soil*; ballets *The Last Pierrot* and *Lion amoureux*; incid. mus. to Shakespeare's *Merchant of Venice*, Gutzkow's *Uriel Acosta*, Hebbel's *Herodes und Mariamne*, etc.; choral works; 4 symphs., overture, serenade, suites, *4 Dance Pieces*, *Kontrapunktisches Triptychon*, *Jacob's Dream*, *Polonaise symphonique* for orch.; concertino for pf. and orch., suite for vln. and orch., *Little Prelude* for tpt. and strings; 5 string 4tets, 2 trios for vln., clar. and pf., *Little Serenade* for wind instruments and pf.; 2 vln. and pf. sonatas, pf. and org. works, etc.

Ratsche (Ger.), rattle.

Ratswahlkantate, cantata by Bach (BWV. 71) written for the election of the town council of Mühlhausen on 4. II. 1708, and perf. on that day in St. Mary's Church. Bach was at the time organist of St. Blasius's.

Rattle, a noise-prod. toy, a ratchet, occasionally used as a perc. instrument in the modern orch.

Ratto di Proserpina, Il (*The Rape of Proserpine*), opera by Winter (lib. by Lorenzo da Ponte), prod. London, King's Theatre, Haymarket, 3. V. 1804.

Rauchfangkehrer, Der (*The Chimney-Sweep*), Singspiel by Salieri (lib. by Leopold von Auenbrugger), prod. Vienna, Burgtheater, 30. IV. 1781.

Raugel, Félix (Alphonse) (b. Saint-Quentin, 27. XI. 1881), Fr. cond. and musicologist. Studied at the Schola Cantorum in Paris with d'Indy, Roussel and others, founded a Handel Society in 1908 and cond. this as well as the Société Chorale Française later, and was *maître de chapelle* at the church of Saint-Eustache, 1911–28, later of Saint-Honoré-d'Eylau, and founded a Mozart Society

and a choir of his own in 1930–1. Wrote books on orgs. and their mus., Palestrina, Bruckner, etc.

Raupach, Christoph (b. Tondern, Slesvig, 5. VII. 1686; d. ? Straslund, 1744), Ger. organist and writer on mus. Lived at Hamburg for a time and in 1703 became organist at Stralsund.

Raupach, Hermann Friedrich (b. Stralsund, 21. XII. 1728; d. ? St. Petersburg, XII. 1788), Ger. harpsichordist and comp., son of prec. Pupil of his father, he was in the service of the Rus. court at St. Petersburg from 1755. In Paris in 1766 he met Mozart, who arr. some movements from sonatas by R. for piano and string orch.

Works incl. operas *Alceste* and *Good Soldiers* (in Rus.) and *Siroe* (It.); *c.* 15 ballets; vln. sonatas, etc.

Rauzzini, Matteo (b. Camerino, 1754; d. Dublin, 1791), It. comp. and singing-master. Brought out his 1st opera at Munich in 1772, went to Eng. and then to Ir., settling in Dublin as singing-master.

Works incl. operas *I finti gemelli*, *L'opera nuova*, *Il rè pastore*, etc.

Rauzzini, Venanzio (b. Camerino, 19. XII. 1746; d. Bath, 8. IV. 1810), It. castrato soprano, brother of prec. Made his operatic début in Rome in 1765, and two years later entered the service of the court in Munich. In 1772 sang the leading role in Mozart's *Lucio Silla* in Milan, where Mozart also wrote for him the motet *Exsultate, jubilate*. In 1774 he settled in Eng., appearing both as a singer and opera comp. From 1778 he lived increasingly in Bath, where he taught singing and was director of the Assembly Room concerts. Among his pupils were Nancy Storace, John Braham, Mara and Michael Kelly.

Works incl. operas *Piramo e Tisbe*, *L'ali d'amore*, *L'Eroe Cinese*, *Astarto*, *Creusa in Delfo*, *La Regina di Golconda*, *La Vestale*; Requiem; cantatas; It. arias, duets, etc.; string 4tets and other chamber mus.; harpsichord sonatas, etc.

Raval, Sebastián (b. Diocese of Cartagena, Murcia, *c.* 1550; d. Palermo, 25. X. 1604), Span. comp. He went to It. early in his career and served var. patrons at (?) Naples, Urbino, Rome and Palermo. In Rome in 1593 he was challenged through his boastfulness to a contest with Nanini and Soriano, and defeated by them. His last post was that of *maestro de capilla* to the Span. Duke of Maqueda at Palermo.

Works incl. motets, Lamentations; madrigals, canzonets for 4 voices, etc.

Ravel, (Joseph) Maurice (b. Ciboure, Basses-Pyrénées, 7. III. 1875; d. Paris, 28. XII. 1937), Fr. comp. His father was of Swiss and his mother of Basque descent.

They moved to Paris the year of his birth and after some preliminary teaching he entered the Cons. in 1889, studying pf. with Anthiome and later with Bériot, also theory under Pessard from 1891. He comp. a good deal and in 1897 passed to Fauré's class for comp. and to that of Gédalge for counterpoint. In 1899 he had an overture *Schéhérazade* (unpub. and unconnected with the later song-cycle) and the *Pavane pour une infante défunte* in the orig. pf. version perf. by the Société Nationale. During the next 10 years he wrote some of his best works, but his 1st great public success came in 1911, when the Opéra-Comique brought out *L'Heure espagnole*, and the second in 1912, when Diaghilev's Rus. Ballet prod. *Daphnis et Chloé*. During the war of 1914–18 he served in an ambulance corps at the front, but was demobilized owing to ill-health in 1917. In the 1920s he visited London more than once with great success and in 1928 he was made an Hon. D.Mus. of Oxford Univ. In 1935, after a car accident, he began to suffer from a kind of mental paralysis, and he d. after an operation on his brain.

Works incl. opera *L'Heure espagnole*; opera-ballet *L'Enfant et les sortilèges*, ballet *Daphnis et Chloé* and 2 others arr. from pf. works: *Ma Mère l'Oye* and *Adélaïde, ou Le Langage des fleurs = Valses nobles et sentimentales*, also *La Valse* and 2 from orchestral works; *Boléro*; *Rapsodie espagnole* for orch.; concerto for pf. and orch.; pf. concerto for the left hand with orch.; string 4tet, *Introduction et Allegro* for harp, fl., clar. and string 4tet, pf. trio in A min.; sonata for vln. and cello, sonata and *Tzigane* for vln. and pf.; 15 pf. works incl. *Menuet antique*, *Pavane pour une infante défunte*, *Jeux d'eau*, 5 *Miroirs*, Sonatina, *Gaspard de la nuit* (3 pieces after Louis Bertrand's prose poems), suite *Le Tombeau de Couperin*; suite *Ma Mère l'Oye* for pf. duet; 29 songs incl. cycles *Schéhérazade*, *Cinq Mélodies populaires grecques*, *Histoires naturelles*; 3 *Poèmes de Mallarmé* for voice, 2 fls., 2 clars., string 4tet and pf.; *Chansons madécasses* for voice, fl., cello and pf.; *Don Quichotte à Dulcinée* (after Cervantes) for baritone and small orch.; 3 part-songs, etc.

Ravenscroft, Edward (17th cent.), Eng. playwright. *See* Purcell (*Canterbury Guests*).

Ravenscroft, Thomas (b. ? London, c. 1590; d. ? London, c. 1633), Eng. comp. He was a chorister at St. Paul's Cathedral under Edward Pearce, took the Mus.B. at Cambridge in 1607 and in 1618–22 was mus. master at Christ's Hospital.

Works incl. anthems, 48 hymn-tune settings in his Psalter containing 100; madrigals; some of the 4-part songs *The*

Pleasures of 5 usuall Recreations in his treatise on notation *A Briefe Discourse*, are by himself; some of the rounds and catches in the collections *Pammelia*, *Deuteromelia* and *Melismata* are prob. of his own comp.

Ravvivando (It. = reviving), a direction sometimes used to indicate a return to an orig. faster tempo after a slowing-down.

Rawsthorne, Alan (b. Haslingden, Lancs., 2. V. 1905), Eng. comp. He studied dentistry at first but turned to mus. at the age of 20 and in 1926–9 studied at the R. Manchester C.M. In 1932–4 he taught at Dartington Hall, Totnes; but settled in London in 1935 and married the violinist Jessie Hinchliffe. In 1938–9 he had works perf. at the I.S.C.M. festivals in London and Warsaw.

Works incl. ballet *Mme. Chrysanthème* (after Loti); incid. mus. for Shakespeare's *King Lear*; mus. for radio play on Max Beerbohm's *The Happy Hypocrite*; film mus. for *Burma Victory*, *The Captive Heart* and Army films; 2 symphs., *Symph. Studies*, overture *Street Corner* and fantasy-overture *Cortèges* for orch., 2 pf. concertos, 2 vln. concertos, concerto for clar. and strings; 2 string 4tets, Theme and Variations for string 4tet, pf. 5tet; vla. and pf. sonata, Theme and Variations for 2 vlns.; 4 Bagatelles for pf.; *The Creel* suite for pf. duet based on Izaak Walton's *Compleat Angler*; songs *The Enemy Speaks* (C. Day Lewis), *Away Delights* and *God Lyaeus* (John Fletcher), 3 *Fr. Nursery Songs*, etc.

Ray, the name for the Supertonic note in any key in Tonic Sol-fa, so pronounced, but in notation represented by the symbol **r**.

Raymond, ou Le Secret de la Reine (*R.*, or *The Queen's Secret*), opera by A. Thomas (lib. by Adolphe de Leuven and Joseph Bernard Rosier), prod. Paris, Opéra-Comique, 5. VI. 1851.

Raymonda, ballet by Glazunov (choreography by Marius Petipa), prod. St. Petersburg, Maryinsky Theatre, 19. I. 1898.

'Razor' Quartet (*Rasiermesser*), nickname of Haydn's string 4tet in F min., Op. 55, No. 2, comp. ? 1788, so called because Haydn is said to have offered the pub. Bland his best 4tet in return for a good razor.

Re, the old name for the note D in Solmization, still used in Lat. countries, and in Tonic Sol-fa notation the Supertonic in any key, represented by the symbol **r**, pronounced Ray.

Re Lear (*King Lear*), opera by Alberto Ghislanzoni (b. 1897), (lib. by comp., based on Shakespeare), prod. Rome, Teatro Reale, 24. VI. 1937.

For Verdi *see* **King Lear**.

Re pastore, Il (*The Shepherd King*), opera by Bonno (lib. by Metastasio), prod. Vienna, Schönbrunn Palace, 13. V. 1751.

Opera by Gluck (lib. do.), prod. Vienna, Burgtheater, 8. XII. 1756.

Opera by Mozart (lib. do.), prod. Salzburg, 23. IV. 1775.

Re Teodoro in Venezia, Il (*King Theodore at Venice*), opera by Paisiello (lib. by Giovanni Battista Casti), prod. Vienna, Burgtheater, 23. VIII. 1784.

Reading Rota. *See* **Sumer is icumen in.**

Real Fugue. *See* **Fugue.**

Real Sequence. *See* **Rosalia** and **Sequence.**

Realism. (1) Strictly realistic repres. in mus. is not easily attainable. Exs. are the anvils in Wagner's *Rheingold*, the sheep and wind machine in R. Strauss's *Don Quixote* and the nightingale (gramophone record of the bird's song) in Respighi's *Pini di Roma*. Imitations of bells, birds, etc. are very frequent, but usually the more musical they are the less they approach realism.

(2) More generally, a realistic style of It. opera is known as *Verismo*.

Realization, the writing out or playing at sight of the harmony from a Thorough-bass.

Rebab
or }an obs. string instrument of
Rebec(k)
vln. type of Arab orig., the ancestor of the vln. family, though its shape was more like that of the mandoline, which is prob. one of its descendants. It had 3 gut strings and was played with a bow. In Fr. it survived until the 18th cent., but only as a street instrument.

Rebel, Fr. family of musicians:

1. Jean R. (b. ?; d. ? Versailles or Paris, 1692), singer. Was in the service of the court from 1661.

2. Jean-Féry R. (b. Paris, IV. 1661; d. Paris, 2. I. 1747), violinist and comp., son of prec. Pupil of Lully, entered the Opéra orch. as a violinist *c*. 1700 and prod. his 1st opera there in 1703. It failed, but a vln. solo, *Le Caprice*, was so successful that it was long afterwards used as a test piece for ballet dancers. He then wrote similar pieces for a number of ballets, became one of the 24 vlns. at court in 1717 and chamber musician to the king in 1720.

Works incl. opera *Ulysse*; ballet pieces for vln.; vln. sonatas, etc.

3. Anne-Renée R. (b. Paris, 1662; d. Paris, 1722), singer, sister of prec. Appeared in stage pieces at court from the age of 11, became one of the best singers there and married Lalande in 1684.

4. François R. (b. Paris, 19. VI. 1701; d. Paris, 7. XI. 1775), violinist and comp., son of 2. A pupil of his father, he entered

the Opéra orch. at the age of 13, where he met Francœur, with whom he was to collaborate extensively. Three years later he became a member of the 24 Violons du Roi. In 1723 he went with Francœur to Prague for the coronation of Charles VI. They were joint leaders of the Opéra 1733–43, and directors 1757–67, when they were succeeded by Berton and Trial.

Works incl. *Pyrame et Thisbé, Tarsis et Zélie, Scanderbeg, Les Augustales, Le Retour du roi, Zélindor, Le Trophée, Ismène, Les Génies tutélaires, Le Prince de Noisy, Ballet de la Paix* (all with Francœur), *Pastorale héroïque*; Te Deum, De Profundis, cantatas, etc.

Rebelo (Rebello), **João Soares** (or João Lourenço) (b. Caminha, 1609; d. S. Amaro nr. Lisbon, 16. XI. 1661), Port. comp. A fellow-student of King John IV, who promoted him on his accession.

Works incl. psalms, Magnificat, Lamentations, Miserere, etc.

Reber, Napoléon-Henri (b. Mulhouse, 21. X. 1807; d. Paris, 24. XI. 1880), Fr. comp. Studied at the Paris Cons. with Lesueur and others. He was app. prof. of harmony there in 1851 and of comp. in 1862 in succession to Halévy.

Works incl. operas *La Nuit de Noël, Le Père Gaillard, Les Papillotes de M. Benoît, Les Dames capitaines*; 2nd act of ballet *Le Diable amoureux*; cantata *Roland*; 4 symphs., overtures to unpub. operas *Le Ménétrier à la cour* and *Naïm*; 3 string 4tets, string 5tet, pf. 4tet, 7 pf. trios; duets for vln. and pf.; pf. pieces and duets, etc.

Rebhuhn, Paul (b. Waidhofen, *c*. 1500; d. Ölsnitz, after 10. V. 1546), Ger. poet and comp. Wrote dramas, *Susanna* and others, for which he wrote his own incid. mus.

Rebikov, Vladimir Ivanovich (b. Krasnoiarsk, 31. V. 1866; d. Yalta, 1. XII. 1920), Rus. comp. Studied at Moscow and Berlin and later settled in the south of Rus. and founded mus. societies at Odessa and Kishinev.

Works incl. operas and dramatic scenes *The Storm, The Christmas Tree, Thea, The Woman with the Dagger* (based on Schnitzler's play), *Alpha and Omega, The Abyss* (after Andreiev), *Narcissus* (after Ovid's *Metamorphoses*), *Fables* (after Krilov); ballet *Snow-White*; suites for orch. and string orch.; numerous sets of pf. pieces incl. *Rêveries d'automne, Mélomimiques, Aspirer et attendre, Chansons blanches* (on the white keys), etc.

Reboul, Jean (1796–1864), Fr. poet. *See* **Franck (C.)** (songs).

Recapitulation. *See* **Sonata.**

Recherché (Fr. = searched out), the Fr. equivalent of *ricercato*, from which the Ricercare is derived, Beethoven still used this old term, as meaning strict fugal writing, in his *Great Fugue* for string 4tet, Op. 133, which he called a fugue 'tantôt libre, tantôt recherchée.'

Récit (Fr.), in the 17th cent. a term for an accomp. solo, such as a vocal aria, an org. piece with a solo stop, etc. Also = Swell Organ.

Recital, a mus. perf., usually with a miscellaneous programme, given by a single perf. or by one singing or playing an instrument with a pf. accompanist.

Recitation. Works to be recited to a mus. background for orch., pf. or var. instrumental combinations include the following (stage-works [melodramas] by Benda, Rousseau, etc. are not cited here):

Badings, Rs. with orch.
Bemberg, *La Ballade du désespéré.*
Copland, *A Lincoln Portrait.*
Corder, var. poems with pf.
Dieren (van), Baudelaire and Villon poems.
Elgar, *Carillon* and *Le Drapeau belge* (Emile Cammaerts).
Foerster (J. B.), var. poems with pf.
Gilson, *La Mer.*
Goossens, *The Cowl.*
Grieg, *Bergliot* (Bjørnson).
Hawley, poems by Poe and others.
Hauer, R. with voices and chamber orch.
Klose, *Wallfahrt nach Kevlaar* (Heine).
Lier, *The Dyke.*
Liszt, Bürger's *Lenore* and Lenau's *Der traurige Mönch* (Ger.), Jókai's *The Dead Poet's Love* (Hung. and Ger.) and A. Tolstoy's *The Blind Singer* (Rus. and Ger.), all with pf. accomp.
Ostrčil, Ballads with orch.
Prokofiev, *Peter and the Wolf.*
Schillings, Wildenbruch's *Hexenlied.*
Schönberg, Ode to Napoleon (Byron).
Schumann, Hebbel's *Schön Hedwig* and *Ballade vom Heideknaben*; Shelley's *The Fugitives.*
Sibelius, Rydberg's *Skogrået* and Runeberg's *Nights of Jealousy.*
Strauss (R.), Tennyson's *Enoch Arden* and Uhland's *Das Schloss am Meer*, with pf.
Vaughan Williams, *An Oxford Elegy.*

This list does not include works containing a part for a narrator or a dramatic speaking-part, like Berlioz's *Lélio*, Bliss's *Morning Heroes*, Honegger's *Jeanne d'Arc au bûcher* or Vaughan Williams's *Thanksgiving for Victory* (1945).

Recitative, declamation in singing, with fixed notes but without definite metre or time, except where this is imposed by an orchestral accomp. Although the time is free, R. is generally written by convention in 4-4 time, with bar-lines. There are, broadly speaking, 2 kinds of R., as follows:

Recitativo accompagnato (or *stromen-*

tato), a type of recitative accomp. by the orch. R. a. served to modulate to or near the key of the set mus. number, usually an aria, that followed it, and also to give the singer an opportunity for dramatic declamation, aided and abetted by the orch.

Recitativo secco, a 19th-cent. term for a type of recitative accomp. by a keyboard instrument, played from figured bass. Its chief function was to advance the action and to facilitate dialogue. It also served to modulate from the key of one set mus. number to the next.

Recitativo stromentato (It. = instrumentated recitative), another term for *R. accompagnato*, though a distinction was sometimes made between *R. accompagnato*, with a plain orch. accomp., and R.s., with a more independent instrumental participation.

Reciting Note. *See* **Modes.**

Recorder, a woodwind instrument, also known formerly as the English fl. Unlike the fl. it is held vertically and blown into through a mouthpiece in which the air is diverted by an obstructive block called the 'fipple' and prod. a milder tone than that of the fl. R.s were made in 5 different sizes from high treble (sopranino) to bass. In modern times the R. has been revived, mainly for amateur perf., esp. in Eng. and Ger. (*Blockflöte*); but it has also engaged the attention of professionals, and modern works have been written for it. In the early 18th cent. *flauto* by itself always means R.

Recte et retro (Lat. = right way and backwards), a form of canon, also called, in It., *al rovescio*, in which a 2nd entry brings in the tune sung or played backwards. R. et r. is similar to Cancrizans.

Redemption, The, Eng. oratorio by Gounod (words compiled by the comp.), prod. Birmingham Festival, 1882.

Redford, John (b. ?; d. London, 1547), Eng. organist, comp. and playwright. He was a vicar-choral at St. Paul's Cathedral in 1534, when he signed an acknowledgment of Henry VIII's supremacy, and prob. succeeded Thomas Hickman as Almoner and Master of the Choristers there in the same year. His duties certainly included the playing of the org., although the post of organist was not officially recognized at that date. He also supervised the prod. of choir-boy plays with mus.

He comp. a large amount of org. mus. for the liturgy, a few Lat. vocal works, and a play, *Wyt and Science.*

Redi, Tommaso (b. Siena, *c.* 1675; d. Montelupone nr. Loreto, 20. VII. 1738), It. comp. App. *maestro di cappella* of the church of the Santa Casa at Loreto in 1731. In 1733 he had a dispute with Martini of Bologna about the solution of a canon by Animuccia, which was settled by Pacchioni and Pitoni in Martini's favour.

Works incl. Masses and other church mus. etc.

Redlich, Hans (Ferdinand) (b. Vienna, 11. II. 1903; d. Manchester, 27. XI. 1968), Brit. musicologist of Aus. birth. Studied at the Univs. of Vienna, Munich and Frankfurt and took the Ph.D. in 1931. In 1925–9 he was opera cond. at Mainz, but in 1939 he took refuge in Eng. From 1955 to 1962 he was lecturer at Edinburgh Univ. and in 1962 was app. prof. at Manchester Univ. He specialized in Monteverdi, several of whose works he ed. and on whom he wrote 2 books (1932 and 1949, Eng. 1952). He also wrote on modern mus., incl. a book on Alban Berg. 3 comps. are pub., many others in MS.

Redman, Reginald (b. London, 17. IX. 1892), Eng. comp. After an attempt to make a career in banking, he studied mus. at the G.S.M. in London, became organist at Stanmore parish church and mus. master at Harrow preparatory school. 3 years later he went to the B.B.C. as pianist and chorus master, became mus. director of the Welsh region and later of that of the W. of Eng. at Bristol.

Works incl. opera *The Ring of Jade*; mus. for many radio plays; *The Hills of Dream* and *The Dancers of Huai-Nan* for chorus and orch.; nocturne *Moods*, suite *The West Countree* for orch.; *Away on the Hills*, *Introduction and Folk Tune* and *Serenade* for string orch.; cello concerto, concerto for pf. and strings; *Pan's Garden* for chamber orch.; Chin. songs to transs. by Arthur Waley and L. Cranmer-Byng; ed. of Chin. folksongs, etc.

Redoute (Fr., used also in Ger., and derived from It. *ridotto*), a kind of public ball, partic. in the 18th cent.; but carried on into the 19th in Aus. and Ger. where dancers gathered haphazard from all classes of society, usually at assembly halls called *Redoutensäle* in Ger. Comps. of note, esp. in Vienna, often wrote dances for R.s.

Redova ⎫
  or   ⎬ a Boh. dance of unknown age,
Redowa ⎭
but not intro. in western Eur. until near the middle of the 19th cent. The name seems to be a corrupt. of Rejdovák, a dance in moderate triple time, to which var. exs. used by comps. conform; but there is also a Rejdovacka in 2–4 time.

Réduction (Fr.), an arr., esp. from a complex to a simpler score, e.g. an opera 'reduced' to a vocal score or an orchestral work arr. for pf.

Reed Stops, org. stops which control pipes resembling obs., clars. and other reed instruments in having vibrating (metal) tongues, as distinct from Flue Stops, which are tubes with open mouthpieces.

Reed, W(illiam). H(enry). (b. Frome, Somerset, 29. VII. 1876; d. Dumfries, 2. VII. 1942), Eng. violinist and comp. Studied vln. with Sauret and comp. with F. Corder and Prout at the R.A.M. in London. He joined the London Symph. Orch. on its foundation in 1904 and became its leader in 1912; also vln. prof. at the R.C.M. He wrote 2 books on Elgar.

Works incl. symph. poems *The Lincoln Imp* and *Aesop's Fables*, 2 *Somerset Idylls* for small orch., symph. and variations for string orch.; concerto in A min. and rhapsody for vln. and orch.; chamber mus., etc.

Reed, William Leonard (b. London, 16. X. 1910), Eng. comp. Studied at Oxford and at the R.C.M. in London, with Howells for comp. and Lambert for cond. After travelling in Scand. and the Baltic states he was sent on a mus. mission there by the Brit. Council, 1937–9. In 1939 he took the D.Mus. at Oxford.

Works incl. operas *The Vanishing Island* and *The Crowning Experience*; *Recitative and Dance*, scherzo, *3 Dance Movements*, *2 Short pieces* for orch., *Idyll* for small orch.; fantasy for fl., vla. and harp; *Pavane Caprice* and *Child Portrait* for pf., etc.

Reeds, the vibrating tongues prod. the tone of certain woodwind instruments and of org. pipes (in the latter case made of brass). These instruments use so-called 'beating R.', single for clars., saxophones and org. pipes and double for obs., bassoons and bagpipes. There are also 'free R.', used in harmoniums and instruments of the concertina and mouthorg. type.

Reel, a Scot., Ir. and Scand. dance, either of Celtic or Scand. orig. It is perf. with the dancers standing face to face and the mus. is in quick 2–4 or 4–4, occasionally 6–8, time and divided into regular 8-bar phrases. A mus. characteristic of many R.s is a drop into the triad of the subdominant unprepared by modulation.

Reese, Gustave (b. New York, 29. XI. 1899), Amer. musicologist. Studied at N.Y. Univ. and became lecturer in mus. there in 1927 and prof. in 1955. He was assoc. ed. of *The Music Quarterly* and its ed. on the death of Carl Engel in 1944, but resigned in 1945. His work incl. books on *Music in the Middle Ages* and *Music in the Renaissance*.

Reeve, William (b. ? London, 1757; d. London, 22. VI. 1815), Eng. comp. Studied with Richardson, the organist at St. James's Church, Westminster, and was organist at Totnes, Devon, 1781–3. After var. engagements at London theatres, he joined the Covent Garden chorus, and there was asked to complete the ballet-pantomime *Oscar and Malvina* (after Ossian) left unfinished by Shield in 1791 on account of differences with the management. He then became comp. to that theatre and in 1802 part-owner of Sadler's Wells Theatre.

Works incl. pieces for the stage, *The Apparition, Merry Sherwood, Harlequin and Oberon, Harlequin and Quixote* (after Cervantes), *Joan of Arc, Paul and Virginia* (with Mazzinghi, based on Saint-Pierre), *Rokeby Castle* and many others (some with Braham, Davy, Mazzinghi or Moorehead); mus. for Sadler's Wells pantomimes, etc.

Reeves, (John) Sims (b. Woolwich, 26. IX. 1818; d. Worthing, 25. X. 1900), Eng. tenor. Learnt mus. from his father, a musician in the Royal Artillery, studied singing and made his 1st stage appearance at Newcastle-on-Tyne, as a baritone. After further study, incl. Paris and Milan, he came out at the Teatro alla Scala there as a tenor and as such made a 1st London appearance in 1847.

Refice, Licinio (b. Patrica, Rome, 12. II. 1883; d. Rio de Janeiro, 11. IX. 1954). It. priest and comp. He became prof. of church mus. at the Scuola Pontifica in Rome in 1910 and in 1911 cond. at the church of Santa Maria Maggiore.

Works incl. Masses, motets, Requiem, *Stabat Mater* and other church mus.; 2 oratorios, 3 sacred cantatas, 3 choral symph. poems, etc.

'Reformation' Symphony, Mendelssohn's 5th symph., Op. 107, in D min., comp. in 1830 for the tercentenary of the Augsburg Conference. It was not perf. there owing to Rom. Catholic opposition, but prod. Berlin, XI. 1832.

Refrain (from Fr.), a recurrent strain in a song, returning with the same words at the beginning, middle or end of each verse with mus. which may or may not be derived from the 1st strain.

Regal, a small portable reed org., said to have been invented about 1460 by Heinrich Traxdorff of Nuremberg.

Reger, Max (Johann Baptist Joseph Maximilian) (b. Brand, Bavar., 19. III. 1873; d. Leipzig, 11. V. 1916). Ger. comp. 1st learnt mus. from his mother and was so precocious that at the age of 13 he became organist at the Catholic church of Weiden in Bavar., where his parents had moved in 1874. After 3 years there Riemann was consulted about his gifts and invited him to become his pupil at Sondershausen. Reger went there in 1890 and the next year followed his master to Wiesbaden, where he soon became a teacher at the Cons. A period divided between hard work and dissipation led to a serious breakdown, and he lived with his parents at

Weiden again in 1898–1901, writing vast quantities of mus. In the latter year he went to Munich in the hope of making his way as a comp., but posing as a progressive and being in reality a conservative, he made enemies all round and had some success only with his pf. playing. But he began to tour Ger. and also visited Prague and Vienna, and gradually he made his work known; he also made a reputation as a remarkable comp. teacher. In 1907 he settled at Leipzig as mus. director to the Univ. and prof. at the Cons., soon resigning the former post as uncongenial, but retaining the latter for the rest of his life. In 1911 he became cond. of the ducal orch. at Meiningen, with which he went on tour, but this came to an end in 1914, when he went to live at Jena, travelling to Leipzig each week to carry out his duties at the Cons.

Works incl. *Gesang der Verklärten* and Psalm c for chorus and orch.; sinfonietta, serenade, variations on themes by J. A. Hiller and by Mozart, Symph. Prologue to a Tragedy, Comedy Overture, Concerto in the Old Style, Romantic Suite, 4 tone-poems on pictures by Böcklin, etc. for orch.; pf. concerto, vln. concerto, 2 romances for vln. and orch.; 5 string 4tets, string 6tet, clar. 5tet, 2 pf. 4tets, string trio, 2 pf. trios, pf. 5tet; 7 vln. and pf. sonatas, 4 cello and pf. sonatas, 3 clar. and pf. sonatas; 2 sonatas, 2 suites, Fantasy and Fugue on B.A.C.H., Variations and Fugue on orig. theme, chorale preludes, preludes and fugues, Introduction, Passacaglia and Fugue, Symph. Fantasy and Fugue, etc. for org.; Introduction, Passacaglia and Fugue for 2 pfs.; 2 sonatas, Variations and Fugue on theme by Bach and numerous smaller works for pf.; pf. duets; many songs incl. *Schlichte Weisen*; part-songs, etc.

Reggio, Pietro (b. Genoa, ?; d. London, 23. VII. 1685), It. singer, comp. and lutenist. In the service of Queen Christina of Swed. in Rome; later settled at Oxford, where he pub. *A Treatise to sing well any Song whatsoever*, 1677. Comp. motets, song for Shadwell's adaptation of Shakespeare's *Tempest*, songs, duets, etc.

Regino of Prüm (b. ? Altrip nr. Ludwigshafen, c. 850; d. Trier, 915), Benedictine monk and mus. theorist. He was abbot of Prüm, 892–9. He was (?) the 1st to arrange antiphons and responsories according to their mode in a *tonarius.*

Regis, Jean (b. ?; d. Soignies, c. 1485), Flem. comp. He was choirmaster at Antwerp Cathedral and (?) was at some time connected with Dufay.

Wrote Masses, incl. one on *L'Homme armé*, songs in parts, etc.

Register, a certain set of pipes brought into action in org. playing to prod. a particular kind of tone and dynamics; also the different parts of the range of the human voice according to the manner, or supposed manner, of its prod. as 'head R.' or 'chest R.'

Registration, the use of the org. stops by means of which the qualities and power of the instrument, over which the manuals and pedals have no dynamic control, can be altered according to the comp.'s prescription or the perf.'s skill and taste.

Regnard, Jean François (1655–1709), Fr. playwright. *See* **Distratto** (Haydn), **d'Indy** (*Attendez-moi sous l'orme*), **Lattuada** (*Follie d'amore*), **Pessard** (*Folies amoureuses*).

Regnart, François (b. Douai, *c.* 1530; d. ?, *c.* 1600), Flem. comp. Learnt mus. at Tournai Cathedral and studied at Douai Univ.

Works incl. motets; *chansons*: *Poésies de Ronsard et autres* for 4–5 voices, etc.

Regnart, Jacques (b. ? Douai, *c.* 1539; d. Prague, 16. X. 1599), Flem. comp., brother of prec. Went to Vienna and Prague as a pupil to the Imp. chapel at an early age, became a tenor there in the 1560s, and in the 1570s choirmaster and vice-*Kapellmeister*. In 1582–95 he was in the service of the Archduke Ferdinand at Innsbruck, but lived in Prague for the last 5 years of his life.

Works incl. Masses, motets; *Canzone italiane* and Ger. songs for 5 voices, etc.

There were 2 other brothers, Charles and Paschasius, who contrib. motets to a collection in which François and Jacques also appeared, ed. by a 5th brother, Augustin, a canon at Lille.

Régnier, Henri de (1864–1936), Fr. poet. *See* **Roussel (A.)** (songs), **Witkowski**, (songs with orch.).

Regola dell' ottava (It.). *See* **Rule of the Octave.**

Rehfuss, Heinz (Julius) (b. Frankfurt, 25. V. 1917), Swiss bass-baritone. Studied with his father and from 1940 to 1952 sang at the Zürich State Opera. Also well known as a *Lieder*-singer.

Reich, Willi (b. Vienna, 27. V. 1898), Aus. mus. author and ed. Studied at Vienna Univ. and mus. with Berg and Webern. He founded and ed. the review *23* in 1932, but in 1938 went to Switz., settling at Basle. He pub. a study of Berg's *Wozzeck* and worked with Křenek and Theodor Wiesengrund-Adorno on a biog. of the same comp., and later prod. independent works on Schönberg and Berg.

Reicha, Antonín (b. Prague, 26. II. 1770; d. Paris, 28. V. 1836), Boh. theorist, teacher and comp., naturalized Fr. Studied at Wallerstein, Bavar., under his uncle Joseph R. (1746–95), from whose wife he learnt Fr. In 1785 he went to Bonn with his uncle, who became mus. director

there and worked at the electoral court, where he made friends with Beethoven. From 1794 to 1799 he was a mus. teacher in Hamburg. In 1799–1802 he had some success as a comp. in Paris, but went to Vienna, where he remained until 1808 and was patronized by the empress. He then settled in Paris for the rest of his life and became prof. at the Cons. in 1818.

Works incl. operas *Godefroid de Montfort*, *Ouboualdi, ou Les Français en Égypte*, *Cagliostro* (with Dourlen), *Natalie, Sapho*; 2 symphs., *Scènes italiennes* for orch.; 20 string 4tets, 6 string 5tets, Diecetto and Octet for strings and wind, 24 wind 5tets, 6 string trios, duets for vlns. and for fls.; 12 vln. and pf. sonatas; pf. sonatas and pieces, etc.

Reichardt, Johann Friedrich (b. Königsberg, 25. XI. 1752; d. Giebichenstein nr. Halle, 27. VI. 1814), Ger. comp. Studied at Königsberg Univ. and picked up a rather haphazard mus. educ. He travelled widely in 1771–4 and pub. his experiences in *Vertraute Briefe*. After working as a civil servant at Königsberg, he obtained the post of mus. director at the Prus. court in 1776, lived at Berlin and Potsdam, prod. operas and in 1783 founded a Concert spirituel. He also pub. collections of mus. and wrote criticism. After the death of Frederick II he made himself disliked more and more and in 1793 he was dismissed, ostensibly for his sympathy with the Fr. Revolution. He retired to Giebichenstein in 1794, only briefly holding a post at the court of Jérôme Bonaparte at Cassel in 1808. He wrote several books on mus., was a forerunner of Schubert in song comp., married Juliane Benda (1752–83), a singer, pianist and comp., daughter of F. Benda, and had a daughter, Louise (1780–1826), who became a singer and also wrote songs.

Works incl. operas and plays with mus. *Hänschen und Gretchen, Amors Guekkasten, Cephalus und Procris, Le feste galanti, Claudine von Villa Bella* (Goethe), *Erwin und Elmire* (Goethe), *L'Olimpiade* (Metastasio), *Tamerlan* (in Fr.), *Jery und Bätely* (Goethe), *Der Taucher* (after Schiller's ballad), *Brenno, Die Geisterinsel* (after Shakespeare's *Tempest*) and *c.* 12 others; incid. mus. to Shakespeare's *Macbeth*, several plays by Goethe and Kotzebue's *Die Kreuzfahrer*; cantatas *Ariadne auf Naxos, Ino, Morning Hymn* (Milton, trans. Herder) and others; instrumental works; numerous songs, etc.

Reichenau, Berno of (b. ?; d. 1048), Ger. Benedictine monk and mus. theorist. He was 1st a monk at Prüm, and abbot of Reichenau from 1008. He compiled a *tonale*, dealing with the organization of the church chants into modes.

Reicher-Kindermann, Hedwig (b. Munich,

15. VII. 1853; d. Trieste, 2. VI. 1883), Ger. mezzo-soprano, daughter of the baritone August Kindermann (1817–91). Studied with her father, made var. small stage appearances in her youth, 1st appeared as a concert singer at Leipzig in 1871 and on the stage in Berlin in 1874.

Reichmann, Theodor (b. Rostock, 15. III. 1849; d. Marbach, Lake of Constance, 22. V. 1903), Ger. bass. Studied in Ger. and with Lamperti at Milan and made his 1st appearance at Magdeburg in 1869.

Reigen (Ger.) = Roundelay.

Reina Codex, an important source of It. and Fr. 14th–15th-cent. mus., now in the Bibl. Nat. at Paris (n.a. fr. 6771). It also includes 2 keyboard arrs., one of them incomplete, of vocal works by Landini.

Reinach, Théodore (b. Saint-Germain-en-Laye, 3. VII. 1860; d. Paris, 30. X. 1928), Fr. archaeologist and hist. Author of several works on Gk. mus. and of the libs. of Maurice Emmanuel's *Salamine* (after Aeschylus' *Persae*) and Roussel's *La Naissance de la lyre*.

Reincken. *See* **Reinken.**

Reine de Chypre, La (*The Queen of Cyprus*), opera by Halévy (lib. by Jules Henri Verney de Saint-Georges), prod. Paris, Opéra, 22. XII. 1841.

Reine (de France), La (*The Queen of France*), nickname of Haydn's symph. No. 85 in B♭ maj., comp. for Paris in 1785–6.

Reine de Saba, La (*The Queen of Sheba*), opera by Gounod (lib. by Jules Barbier and Michel Carré), prod. Paris, Opéra, 28. II. 1862.

Reinecke, Carl (Heinrich Carsten) (b. Altona, 23. VI. 1824; d. Leipzig. 10. III. 1910), Ger. pianist, cond. and comp. Settled in Leipzig from 1843. App. pianist to the Dan. court, 1846–8 and several times visited Copenhagen. Cond. of the Gewandhaus concerts and prof. of comp. at the Leipzig Cons. from 1860.

Works incl. operas *König Manfred* (after Byron), *Der vierjährige Posten* (after Körner), *Ein Abenteuer Händels, Auf hohen Befehl, Der Gouverneur von Tours*; incid. mus. for Schiller's *Wilhelm Tell*; oratorio *Belsazar*; 2 Masses; cantatas *Haakon Jarl, Die Flucht nach Aegypten*, fairy-tale cantatas for female voices *Schneewittchen, Dornröschen, Aschenbrödel* and others; 3 symphs., overtures *Dame Kobold* (Calderón's *Dama duende*), *Aladdin, Friedensfeier, Zenobia* and other orchestral works; 3 pf. concertos, concertos for vln. and for cello; 4 string 4tets, wind 8tet, 7 pf. trios and other chamber mus.; 3 pf. sonatas and many pieces; songs, etc.

Reiner, Fritz (b. Budapest, 19. XII. 1888; d. N.Y., 15. XI. 1963), Amer. cond. of Hung. orig. He studied in Budapest

and at Jura Univ. He held a number of cond. posts in Eur., incl. Budapest and Dresden, before succeeding Ysaÿe as cond. of the Cincinnati Symph. Orch. in 1922. From 1938 to 1948 he was cond. of the Pittsburgh Symph. Orch., from 1948 at the Metropolitan Opera, N.Y., and from 1953 cond. of the Chicago Symph. Orch. He returned to Eur. from time to time as a guest cond. and in 1955 cond. *Die Meistersinger* for the reopening of the Vienna Opera.

Reiner, Jacob (b. Altdorf, Württemberg, *c.* 1560; d. Weingarten, 12. VIII. 1606), Ger. singer and comp. Learnt mus. at the monastery of Weingarten and later studied with Lassus at Munich. He returned to Weingarten about 1585 and remained there as singer and choirmaster to his death.

Works incl. Masses, motets, Magnificats, 3 Passions; Ger. songs for 3–5 voices, etc.

Reinhold, Frederick Charles (b. London, 1737; d. London, 29. IX. 1815), Eng. bass, son of the Ger. singer Thomas R. (*c.* 1690–1751), who had followed Handel to London. Pupil of his father and chorister at St. Paul's Cathedral and the Chapel Royal. Made his 1st stage appearance, at Drury Lane Theatre, 1755.

Reinken (or Reincken), Johann Adam (Jan Adams) (b. Wilshausen, Alsace, 27. IV. 1623; d. Hamburg, 24. XI. 1722), Ger. organist and comp. Pupil of Heinrich Scheidemann. App. organist of the church of St. Catherine at Hamburg, 1663, where he remained to his death. Bach walked from Lüneburg as a youth and later came from Cöthen to hear him play.

Works incl. chorale preludes, toccatas, fugues, etc. for org.; *Hortus musicus* for 2 vlns., vla. da gamba and bass; keyboard pieces, etc.

Reinthaler, Karl (Martin) (b. Erfurt, 13. X. 1822; d. Bremen, 13. II. 1896), Ger. cond. and comp. After some early mus. training he went to Berlin to study theology, but turned to mus., studying under A. B. Marx. With a grant from Frederick William IV he then studied further in Paris and It.; in 1825 he joined the staff of the Cologne Cons. and in 1858 became cathedral organist and choral cond. at Bremen.

Works incl. operas *Edda, Das Käthchen von Heilbronn* (after Kleist); oratorio *Jephtha*, cantata *In der Wüste*; hymns and other church mus.; symph.; part-songs, etc.

Reissiger, Karl (Gottlieb) (b. Belzig nr. Wittenberg, 31. I. 1798; d. Dresden, 7. XI. 1859), Ger. cond. and comp. Studied under his father, the cantor and comp. Christian Gottlieb R., and with Schicht at St. Thomas's School, Leipzig. Later he studied in Vienna and with Winter at Munich, toured in Hol., Fr. and It. in 1824, and in 1826 succeeded Weber as cond. of the Dresden opera.

Works incl. operas *Dido*, *Libella*, *Turandot* (after Gozzi), *Die Felsenmühle zu Estalières* and others; melodrama *Yelva*; oratorio *David*; Masses, motets and other church mus.; pf. concerto; pf. trios and other chamber mus.; pf. pieces incl. *Danses brillantes* (with that known as *Webers letzter Gedanke*), etc.

Reiter, Josef (b. Braunau, Upper Aus., 19. I. 1862; d. Vienna, 2. VI. 1939), Aus. comp. Studied with his father, an organist. Taught and cond. in Vienna, 1886–1907, was director of the Mozarteum at Salzburg, 1908–11, and cond. at the Hofburgtheater in Vienna, 1917–18.

Works incl. operas *Klopstock in Zürich*, *Der Bundschuh*, *Totentanz* and *Der Tell*; incid. mus. for Raimund's *Bauer als Millionär*; Masses and Requiem; choral works; 6 string 4tets, 2 string 5tets and other chamber mus.; part-songs; *c.* 120 songs, etc.

Reizenstein, Franz (b. Nuremberg, 7. VI. 1911; d. London, 15. X. 1968), Eng. pianist and comp. of Ger. birth. He was very precocious and studied at the State Acad. for Mus. in Berlin in 1930–4, Hindemith being among his masters. The Nazi régime drove him to Eng. in 1934 and he studied with Vaughan Williams at the R.C.M. in London, also pf. with Solomon. From 1958 he taught the pf. at the R.A.M.

Works incl. radio opera *Anna Kraus*; film mus.; oratorio *Genesis*, cantata *Voices of Night*; orchestral mus.; cello; pf. (2) and vln. concertos; chamber mus.; pf. works, etc.

Réjouissance (Fr. = enjoyment), a sprightly movement sometimes found as one of the accessory pieces in old suites.

Relative, the connection between maj. and min. keys with the same key-signature is said to be R. Thus E♭ maj. is the R. maj. of C min. (3 ♭s), B min. the R. min. of D maj. (2 ♯s), etc.

Reliquie (Ger. from Lat. = the relic), a nickname sometimes given to Schubert's unfinished C maj. pf. sonata begun in 1825, of which only the 1st and slow movements were completed. The fragmentary minuet and finale have been completed by Ludwig Stark, by Ernst Křenek and by Willi Rehberg.

Relish (obs.) { (noun), an ornament, a special kind of Turn. (verb) = to ornament.

Rellstab, (Heinrich Friedrich) Ludwig (b. Berlin, 13. IV. 1799; d. Berlin, 27. XI. 1860), Ger. critic, novelist and poet, son of the pub. and critic Johann Karl Friedrich R. (1759–1813). He studied with Ludwig Berger and Bernhard Klein, and

followed his father as mus. critic of the *Vossische Zeiting* and ed. the mus. periodical *Iris im Gebiete der Tonkunst* in 1830–1842. He was imprisoned for libelling Henriette Sontag and attacking Spontini. His books incl. var. mus. studies and several novels on mus. themes. Schubert set 10 of his poems to mus., incl. *Ständchen*. *See* Schwanengesang.

Rémaury, Fanny. *See* **Montigny-Rémaury.**

Reményi (actually Hoffmann), **Eduard** (b. Miskolc, 17. I. 1830; d. San Francisco, 15. V. 1898), Hung. violinist. Studied at the Vienna Cons. with Joseph Böhm and others. He took part in the 1848 Revolution, toured with Brahms in 1852–3 and intro. Hung. gypsy mus. to him, made friends with Liszt at Weimar and afterwards toured widely in Eur. and U.S.A.

Remigius of Auxerre (b. *c.* 841; d. *c.* 908), Benedictine monk and mus. theorist. He was at the monastery of St. Germain in Auxerre from 861. His mus. theory takes the form of a commentary on Martianus Capella.

Remoortel, Edouard van, (b. Brussels, 30. V. 1926), Belg. cond. Studied at Brussels Cons., at Geneva Cons., and then privately with Joseph Krips. In 1951 he became chief cond. of the Belg. Nat. Orch., and in 1958 permanent cond. of the St. Louis Symph. Orch. in the U.S.A.

Renard (Stravinsky). *See* **Fox.**

Renaud, Maurice (Arnold) (b. Bordeaux, 24. VII. 1861; d. Paris, 16. X. 1933), Fr. baritone. Studied at the Conss. of Paris and Brussels, and in 1883 made his 1st stage appearance at the Théâtre de la Monnaie there. In 1890 he 1st sang in opera in Paris and in 1897 in London.

Rencontre imprévue, La (*The Unforeseen Meeting*), later known as *Les Pèlerins de la Mecque* (*The Pilgrims to Mecca*), opera by Gluck (lib. by L. H. Dancourt, based on a vaudeville by Lesage and d'Orneval), prod. Vienna, Burgtheater, 7. I. 1764.

Rendano, Alfonso (b. Carolei nr. Cosenza, 5. IV. 1853; d. Rome, 10. IX. 1931), It. pianist and comp. Studied at Naples and Leipzig, also with Thalberg. Appeared at the Leipzig Gewandhaus in 1872, then in Paris and London, where he remained some time, afterwards becoming pf. prof. at the Naples Cons.

Works incl. opera *Consuelo* (after George Sand); pf. concerto; pf. mus., etc.

Renié, Henriette (b. Paris, 18. IX. 1875; d. Paris, 1. III. 1956), Fr. harpist and comp. She studied harp at the Cons., also comp. with Lenepveu, appearing with great success at an early age.

Works incl. concerto and *Élégie* for harp and orch.; trio for harp, vln. and cello; cello and pf. sonata; pieces for vln. and harp; many harp solos and transcriptions of harpsichord pieces; songs, etc.

Rennes, Catharina van (b. Utrecht, 2. VIII. 1858; d. Amsterdam, 23. XI. 1940), Dutch singer and comp. Studied singing with Richard Hol and Messchaert, also abroad, taught at Utrecht, Hilversum and The Hague, and comp. children's cantatas, many songs, etc.

Renvoysy, Richard de (b. Nancy, *c.* 1530; d. Dijon, 6. III. 1586), Fr. cleric, lutenist and comp. Canon and choirmaster at the Sainte Chapelle of Dijon. He was condemned to death by fire for immorality.

Works incl. psalms; Anacreontic odes for 4 voices, etc.

Reomensis, Aurelianus (Aurelian of Réomé) (b. ?; d. ?), Fr. 9th-cent. Benedictine monk and musician. His theoretical works describe the modal significance of melodic formulae and the correspondence between the rhythm of text and melody.

Repeat, the restatement of a section of a mus. comp., not written out a 2nd time, but indicated by the signs:

In classical mus. the expositions of movements in sonata form are nearly always marked for repetition, and more rarely the working-out and recapitulation also, with or without the coda.

Répétiteur (Fr. = coach), the musician at an opera-house whose function it is to teach the singers their parts before they gather for rehearsal with the conductor.

Repetizione (It.) = Repeat.

Reports (Eng., obs.), an old Eng. term for Imitation.

Reprise (Fr. lit. re-taking = Repetition). Although the Fr. meaning is simply that of Repeat, in Eng. the word is sometimes used in a special sense, indicating the reappearance of the 1st subject in a sonata-form movement at the point where the recapitulation begins.

Requiem, the Mass for the Dead in the Rom. Catholic church service, used generally on All Souls' Day (2. XI) and specifically at funeral services at any time. It may be sung to plainsong or in more or less elaborate mus. settings. Some of the greatest settings, although orig. written to order (Mozart) or intended for a special religious occasion (Berlioz, Verdi), are now fit mainly or solely for concert use, and some were actually written for that purpose (e.g. Dvořák). Britten's *War Requiem* combines the liturgical text with settings of poems by Wilfrid Owen.

Requiem (Brahms). *See* **German Requiem.**

Requiem (Verdi). *See* **Manzoni Requiem.**

Requiem for Rossini, a Mass for the Dead planned by Verdi for perf. in memory of Rossini's death in 1868, his suggestion being that each portion should be written by a different It. comp. of eminence. He himself comp. the 'Libera me' in 1869, and the other contribs. were Bazzini, Cagnoni, Coccia, Mabellini, Pedrotti, Petrella and Ricci. Mercadante was also invited, but was unable to comply on account of blindness and infirmity. The work was never perf. and the comps. all withdrew their contribs. Verdi's was later used, with some alterations, for the Manzoni Requiem of 1873–4.

Rescue Opera, a type of Fr. opera the lib. of which is based on plots, often taken from true happenings (the words *fait historique* sometimes appear in the subtitle), in which the hero or heroine are saved after fearful trials and tribulations. The taste for such works arose during the Revolution. The most familiar exs. are Cherubini's *Les Deux Journées* and Beethoven's *Fidelio,* both with libs. by Bouilly, the latter a Ger. trans. of *Léonore* written for Gaveaux.

Resin. *See* **Rosin.**

Resnik, Regina (b. N.Y., 30. VIII. 1922), Amer. soprano. Studied in N.Y., making her début in Brooklyn in 1942. In 1943 she sang in Mex. and at the N.Y. Metropolitan Opera in 1944. She has also sung in Eur. (Bayreuth in 1953).

Resolution, a term used in harmony for the process by which a discord is made to pass into a concord. *See* **Preparation.**

Reson, Johannes (b. ?; d. ?), early 15th-cent. Fr. comp. He wrote *chansons* and a few sacred works.

Respighi (*née* Olivieri-Sangiacomo), **Elsa** (b. Rome, 24. III. 1894), It. singer and comp. Pupil of Ottorino R. at the Accademia di Santa Cecilia in Rome and later (1919) his wife. She finished the orch. of his opera *Lucrezia* and wrote 3 of her own, also choral works, a symph. poem, a dance suite for orch., songs from the *Rubáiyát* of Omar Khayyám and many others.

Respighi, Ottorino (b. Bologna, 9. VII. 1879; d. Rome, 18. IV. 1936), It. comp., husband of prec. He entered the Liceo Musicale of Bologna as a vln. student in 1891 and received a diploma for vln. in 1899. The previous year he began to study comp. under Luigi Torchi and later under Martucci. In 1900 he became 1st vla. in the Opera orch. at St. Petersburg and the next year studied comp. and orch. with Rimsky-Korsakov. In 1902 he took an additional comp. course with Bruch in Berlin, but returned home in 1903 to join the Mugellini 5tet, of which he remained a member until 1908, when Bologna prod.

his 1st opera. In 1913 he was app. prof.
of comp. at the Accademia di Santa
Cecilia in Rome and toured It. as cond.
of his own works. In 1919 he married his
pupil Elsa Olivieri-Sangiacomo, a comp.
and singer, and from about that time he
began to take a keen interest in old It.
mus. and the church modes. App. director
of the Accademia in 1923, but resigned in
1925, though retaining the comp. professorship.

Works incl. operas *Re Enzo*, *Semi-
rama*, *Belfagor*, *Marie Victoire*, *La campana sommersa* (after Gerhart Hauptmann), *La bella addormentata nel bosco*,
Maria Egiziaca, *La fiamma*, *Lucrezia*
(orch. finished by his wife), also a transcription of Monteverdi's *Orfeo*; ballets
Scherzo veneziano, *La Boutique fantasque*
(mus. adapted from Rossini), *Belkis*,
regina di Saba, *Il ponticello dei sospiri* and
Gli uccelli (adapted from the orchestral
suite to form a triology with *Maria E.* and
Lucrezia); 17 orchestral works incl. the
suites *Fontane di Roma*, *Pini di Roma*,
Vetrate di chiesa, *Trittico Botticelliano*, *Gli*

verse sung by soloists, also called Respond.
Originally this would have taken the form
of a response by the congregation to the
leader or *cantor*. In the 9th cent. it became
an elaborate mus. form demanding
trained soloists and choir. The Gradual,
Alleluia and (for a time) the Offertory of
the Mass were responsorial chants. In the
Offices the most important were the
responsoria prolixa, sung at Mattins. Like
those of the Mass, they became a vehicle
for polyphonic settings, the polyphony
being reserved for the soloists' portions of
the chant. When from the mid-15th cent.
choral polyphony became the norm the
procedure was frequently, though not
invariably, reversed. Late 16th-cent. settings, such as those by Victoria for Holy
Week, assign the entire text to the polyphonic choir.

Rest. All organized mus. consists not
only of notes, but also of R.s, which, like
the notes, take part of the measured
scheme of a comp. and thus have definite
time-values in the same way as the notes.
The symbols are:

Breve   Semibreve   Minim   Crotchet   Quaver   Semiquaver Demisemiquaver

REST

uccelli (bird pieces by old masters), *Feste
romane* and *Sinfonia drammatica*, 2 sets
of old lute airs and dances arr., concerto
in the Mixolydian mode, also 3 works by
Bach arr.; fantasy and toccata for pf. and
orch., concerto in the old style and *Concerto gregoriano* for vln. and orch., Adagio
with variations for cello and orch.; concerto for ob., tpt., vln., double bass, pf.
and strings; 2 string 4tets (2nd in the
Dorian mode), pf. 5tet; sonata in B min.
and 5 pieces for vln. and pf.; 3 Preludes on
a Gregorian melody for pf.; *Aretusa*
for mezzo-soprano and orch.; *La primavera*, for solo voices, chorus and orch.;
eds. of Monteverdi's *Lamento d'Arianna*
and Marcello's *Didone* for voice and orch.;
Il tramonto and *La sensitiva* for voice and
string 4tet; 52 songs, etc.

Respond. *See* **Responsory.**

Responses, in Angl. church mus. the
choral and congregational cadences answering the versicles read or chanted in
monotone by the priest, e.g. the 'Amens' or
'Have mercy upon us . . .' in the Litany.

Responsorial Psalmody, an ancient
method of singing the psalms (borrowed
from the Jews), in which a soloist is
answered by a chorus.

Responsory (Lat. *responsorium*), a chant
involving the response by a choir to a

Dots can be added to rests as they are to
notes.

Resta, Natale (b. Milan, ?; d. ?), It.
18th-cent. comp.

Works incl. opera *Gli tre cicisbei ridicoli*, 1748 (containing the song 'Tre
giorni son che Nina', formerly ascribed
to Pergolesi and later said to be by Ciampi,
under whose direction R.'s opera was
prod. in London, 1749, but more probably
a popular Neapol. air).

Resultant Tones. *See* **Combination Tones.**

Resurrection (Alfano). *See* **Risurrezione.**

Reszke, Édouard de (b. Warsaw, 23.
XII. 1853; d. Garnek, 25. V. 1917), Pol.
bass. Pupil of his brother Jean de R. and
others. Made his 1st appearance in Verdi's
Aida at the Théâtre Italien in Paris, 1876.

Reszke, (Jan Mieczysław) Jean de (b.
Warsaw, 14. I. 1850; d. Nice, 3. IV. 1925),
Pol. tenor, brother of prec. Sang at
Warsaw Cathedral as a child, studied
there and in It. and made his 1st appearance (as a baritone) in 1874, at the Teatro
La Fenice, Venice. He 1st appeared as a
tenor at Madrid in 1879. In 1902 he
retired and devoted himself to teaching.

Retablo de Maese Pedro, El (*Master
Peter's Puppet Show*), marionette opera by
Falla (lib. by comp., based on a chapter
from Cervantes's *Don Quixote*), prod.

Seville, 23. III. 1923, in concert form; 1st stage perf. Paris, 25. VI. 1923.

Retardation, a term sometimes used for a Suspension which resolves upwards, e.g.:

Reti, Rudolf (b. Užice, Serbia, 27. XI. 1885; d. Montclair, N.J., 7. II. 1957), Aus. comp., pianist and critic. Studied at Vienna Cons. A champion of new mus. from the first, he was one of the founders of the I.S.C.M. in 1922. In 1938 he emigrated to the U.S.A. Books incl. *The Thematic Process in Music, Tonality, Atonality and Pantonality.*

Mus. incl. opera *Ivan and the Drum* (after Tolstoy), opera-ballet *David and Goliath*; *The Dead Mourn the Living, Three Allegories* for orch.; pf. concerto; *The Greatest of All* for chorus and orch.; string 4tet; pf. pieces, songs, etc.

Retrograde Motion. *See* **Cancrizans** and **Recte et retro.**

Reubke, Julius (b. Hausneindorf nr. Quedlinburg, 23. III. 1834; d. Pillnitz, 3. VI. 1858), Ger. pianist and comp. Son of the org.-builder Adolf R. (1805–75). Pupil of Liszt at Weimar. His early death cut short a very promising career.

Works incl. org. sonata *The 94th Psalm*; sonata and pieces for pf.; songs, etc.

Reusner, Esajas (b. ?; d. ?), Ger. 17th-cent. lutenist. Pub. a book of sacred songs arr. for the lute in 1645.

Reusner, Esajas (b. Löwenberg, Silesia, 29. IV. 1636; d. Berlin, 1. V. 1679), Ger. lutenist and comp., son of prec. Studied with a Fr. lutenist at the court of the Pol. Princess Radziwill, became lutenist at the court of Liegnitz-Brieg in 1655 and at that of Brandenburg in 1674.

Works incl. 4 books of lute suites, lute arrs. of 100 sacred tunes, etc.

Reuss, August (b. Liliendorf nr. Znaim, Moravia, 6. III. 1871; d. Munich, 18. VI. 1935), Ger.-Morav. comp. Pupil of Thuille at Munich, where he became prof. at the Acad. of Mus. in 1929.

Works incl. opera *Herzog Philipps Brautfahrt*; 2 pantomimes; orchestral prologue to Hofmannsthal's *Der Tor und der Tod*; *Johannisnacht, Judith, Sommer Idylle*, ballet suite for orch.; pf. concerto, serenade for vln. and orch.; 2 string 4tets, pf. 5tet, string trio; instrumental sonatas; choruses; songs and duets, etc.

Reutter, Georg (sen.) (b. Vienna, XI. 1656; d. Vienna, 29. VIII. 1738), Aus. organist and comp. In the service of the Viennese court as theorbo player (1697–1703) and organist (from 1700). App. organist at St. Stephen's Cathedral in 1686, he rose to succeed Fux as 2nd *Kapellmeister c.* 1712, and became 1st *Kapellmeister* in 1715. Comp. principally church mus.

Reutter, (Johann Adam Karl) Georg (jun.) (b. Vienna, IV. 1708; d. Vienna, 11. III. 1772), Aus. organist and comp., son of prec. (There is still considerable confusion between the two.) Pupil of his father and of Caldara, was app. court comp. in Vienna in 1731, and in 1738 succeeded his father as 1st *Kapellmeister* of St. Stephen's Cathedral, where Haydn was his pupil as a chorister. 2nd court *Kapellmeister* 1747, 1st 1751, he held these posts, in plurality with that at St. Stephen's to the detriment of both estabs. He was ennobled in 1740.

Works incl. *c.* 40 operas, e.g. *Archidamia, La forza dell' amicizia* (with Caldara); oratorios *Abel, La Betulia liberata, Gioas,* etc.; 80 Masses; 6 Requiems; over 120 motets, and much other church mus.; symphs.; serenades; chamber mus.; keyboard mus., etc.

Reutter, Hermann (b. Stuttgart, 17. VI. 1900), Ger. comp. Studied under Courvoisier and others at Munich. In 1932 he became prof. at the Musikhochschule at Stuttgart and later became director of the State Hochschule at Frankfurt. In 1956 he became director of the Stuttgart State Cons.

Works incl. operas *Saul, Der verlorene Sohn* (Gide, trans. by Rilke), *Doktor Johannes Faust* (on the old Ger. puppet play), *Odysseus, Die Witwe von Ephesus* and *Die Brücke von San Luis Rey*; ballets *Die Kirmes von Delft,* and *Topsy*; oratorios *Volks-Seele* and *Der grosse Kalender,* cantata *Gesang des Deutschen*; 4 pf. concertos, vln. concerto; chamber mus.; pf. works; song cycle *Weise von Liebe und Tod* (Rilke), etc.

Rêve, Le (*The Dream*), opera by Bruneau (lib. by Louis Gallet, based on Zola's novel), prod. Paris, Opéra-Comique, 18. VI. 1891.

Reverse, Eng. for *Rovescio.*

Revolutionary Study, the nickname of Chopin's study in C min., Op. 10 No. 12, for pf., written at Stuttgart in IX. 1831, where, on his way to Paris, he heard of the taking of Warsaw by the Russ.

Revueltas, Silvestre (b. Santiago Papasquiaro, 31. XII. 1899; d. Mexico City, 5. X. 1940), Mex. violinist and comp. Studied at Mex. City and at St. Edward's Coll., Austin, Texas, also comp. with Felix Borowski at Chicago. App. at Mex.

as violinist in 1920, but continued to study the instrument in 1922 under Kochansky and Ševčik. Later he gave recitals of modern mus. with Chávez as pianist, whom after some theatre appts. he went to assist in cond. the Orquesta Sinfónica at Mex., where he also became prof. at the Cons.

Works incl. mus. for numerous films; *Cuauhnahuac, Esquinas, Ventanas, Alcancías, Colorines, Planos, Caminos, Janitzio, homenaje á García Lorca, El renacuajo paseador, Sensemayá,* etc., for orch.; toccata for vln. and small orch.; 3 string 4tets, *Feria* for string 4tet; pieces for vln. and pf.; *Siete canciones* and other songs, etc.

Revutsky, Lev Nikolaievich (b. Iriovets nr. Poltava, 20. II. 1889), Rus. comp. Pupil of Glière at the Kiev Cons.; began to teach at Kiev in 1924.

Works incl. incid. mus. for plays; film mus.; cantata *Song to Stalin*; 2 symphs.; 2 pf. concertos; war songs, Ukrainian folksong arrs., etc.

Rey, Jean-Baptiste (b. Lauzerte, 18. XII. 1734; d. Paris, 15. VII. 1810), Fr. cond. and comp. A chorister at the Abbey of St. Sernin, he was app. at the age of 17 *maître de chapelle* at the cathedral in Auch, but left to become opera cond. in Toulouse. Later cond. at var. provincial theatres until 1776, when he settled in Paris, becoming chief cond. at the Opéra in 1781. He was a prof. at the Cons. 1799–1802.

Works incl. operas, Masses, motets, *solfèges,* etc.

Reyer, Ernest (actually Louis Étienne Rey) (b. Marseilles, 1. XII. 1823; d. Le Lavandou, Hyères, 15. I. 1909), Fr. comp. Learnt mus. at the Free School of Mus. at Marseilles, but showed no exceptional promise. At the age of 16 he was sent to live with an uncle at Algiers and there began to comp. songs, etc., and in 1847 succeeded in having a Mass perf. at the cathedral. In 1848 he went to Paris and studied with his aunt, the comp. Louise Farrenc. He met Flaubert, Gautier and others, with whom he had an interest in oriental subjects in common, and they provided him with subjects for comps. He became a critic in the 1850s and in 1871 succeeded d'Ortigue as mus. critic to the *Journal des Débats,* becoming a champion of Wagner and the new Fr. school.

Works incl. operas *Maître Wolfram, La Statue, Érostrate, Sigurd* (on the Nibelung Saga), *Salammbô* (after Flaubert); ballet-pantomime *Sacountala* (after Kalidasa); symph. ode *Le Sélam* (words by Gautier), dramatic cantata *Victoire; L'Hymne du Rhin* for soprano, chorus and orch., hymn *L'Union des Arts; Ave Maria, Salve Regina* and *O Salutaris; La*

Madeleine au désert for baritone and orch.; male-voice choruses; pf. pieces; songs, etc.

Rezniček, E(mil). N(ikolaus). von (b. Vienna, 4. V. 1860; d. Berlin, 2. VIII. 1945), Aus. cond. and comp. Studied law at Graz, but at 22, when he was already married to Milka Thurn, a kinswoman of Weingartner's, he went to the Leipzig Cons. to study with Reinecke and Jadassohn. He gained stage experience as theatre cond. in var. towns and finally became military cond. at Prague. From 1896 to 1899 he was successively court cond. at Weimar and Mannheim. In 1906 he was app. prof. at the Klindworth-Scharwenka Cons. in Berlin, where he founded a chamber orch., and later he cond. the Warsaw Opera (1907–8) and the Komische Oper in Berlin (1908–11). He taught at the Hochschule für Musik in Berlin from 1920 to 1926.

Works incl. operas *Die Jungfrau von Orleans* (after Schiller), *Satanella, Emmerich Fortunat, Donna Diana* (after Moreto), *Till Eulenspiegel, Ritter Blaubart, Holofernes* (after Hebbel's *Judith), Satuala, Spiel oder Ernst?, Der Gondoliere des Dogen;* incid. mus. for Strindberg's *Dream Play;* Mass in F maj., Requiem in D min., *Vater unser* for chorus; 4 symphs. (incl. *Schlemihl* [after Chamisso], 'Tragic' and 'Ironic'), 2 symph. suites, Comedy and Idyllic Overtures, fugue in C♯ min. for orch.; serenata for strings; vln. concerto, Intro. and Valse-Caprice for vln. and orch.; *Ruhm und Ewigkeit* (Nietzsche) for tenor and orch.; string 4tet in C♯ min., etc.

rfz, an abbr. used in mus. notation for *Rinforzando.*

Rhapsodie (so-called 'Alto Rhapsody'), a setting of a fragment from Goethe's *Harzreise im Winter* for contralto solo, male chorus and orch. by Brahms, Op. 53, comp. in 1869 and 1st perf. Jena, 3. III. 1870.

Rhapsody (from Gk. *rhapsōidia* = an epic poem, lit. 'songs stitched together'; in Fr. *rapsodie*), in the 18th cent. a poem set to mus. of an improvisatory character. Hence an instrumental piece showing similar freedom. In the 19th cent. and later the term was applied to large-scale comps. in which different elements, sometimes derived from folksong, were strung together, e.g. Liszt's *Hungarian R.s.* Brahms's *R.s* for pf., on the other hand, are self-contained pieces which might equally well be called Capriccio or Intermezzo.

Rhau (or **Rhaw), Georg,** (b. Eisfeld, Franconia, *c.* 1488; d. Wittenberg, 6. VIII. 1548), Ger. comp. and pub. Cantor at St. Thomas's School, Leipzig, until 1520, then schoolmaster at Eisleben and printer at Wittenberg, where he pub. var.

mus. collections incl. works of his own. Wrote vocal works incl. (?) hymn-tunes.

Rheinberger, Joseph (Gabriel) (b. Vaduz, Liechtenstein, 17. III. 1839; d. Munich, 25. XI. 1901), Ger. organist, teacher and comp. He was so precociously gifted that he was app. organist at the parish church of his native place at the age of 7. After some lessons at Feldkirch, he went to the Munich Cons. in 1850, continued to study with F. Lachner on leaving in 1854, supported himself by teaching and in 1859 became pf. prof. at the Cons. He also for a time worked at the Court Opera, and became a church organist and choral cond. When the Cons. was reorganized by Bülow in 1867 he was app. org. and comp. prof. In 1877 he became director of the court church mus. in succession to Wüllner.

Works incl. operas *Die sieben Raben, Der Türmers Töchterlein* and *Das Zauberwort*; incid. mus. for Calderón's *Mágico prodigioso*; numerous Masses, 3 Requiems, *Stabat Mater*, motets; cantatas and choral ballads; symphs. *Wallenstein* (after Schiller) and 'Florentine,' overtures to Shakespeare's *Taming of the Shrew* and Schiller's *Demetrius, Academic (fugal) Overture* for orch.; 2 org. concertos, pf. concerto; 2 string 4tets, 2 pf. trios, pf. 5tet, pf. 4tet, string 5tet; sonatas for vln. and pf., cello and pf., horn and pf.; 20 org. sonatas and many other org. works; numerous pf. works; songs, part-songs, etc.

Rheingold, Das (*The Rhinegold*, Wagner). *See* **Ring des Nibelungen**.

Rhené-Baton (real name René Baton) (b. Courseulles-sur-Mer, Calvados, 5. IX. 1879; d. Le Mans, 23. IX. 1940), Fr. cond. and comp. Studied at the Paris Cons. and worked in Paris, Bordeaux and Angers; in 1916 he returned to Paris as cond. of the Pasdeloup concerts, a post which he retained until 1932.

Works incl. suite for orch.; variations for pf. and orch.; *Suite bretonne* and var. pieces for pf.; songs, etc.

'Rhenish' Symphony, the name of Schumann's 3rd symph., in E♭ maj., Op. 97, begun after a Rhine excursion in IX. 1850. The 4th of the 5 movements is an impression of Cologne Cathedral. 1st perf. Düsseldorf, 6. II. 1851.

Rhys, Philip ap (b. ?; d.?), 16th-cent. Eng. or Welsh organist and comp. He was organist at St. Mary-at-Hill, London, until 1547, when he took over Redford's duties as organist at St. Paul's. He was still organist there in 1559, although Sebastian Westcott had become almoner (Redford's official post) in 1551. He wrote org. mus. for the liturgy, incl. a setting of the Ordinary of the Mass (without the *Credo*).

Rhythm. In a larger sense the word means all that is concerned in mus. with matters dependent on time, such as the metre, the proper division of the mus. into bars, the distribution and balance of phrases, etc. R., however, is not synonymous with metre and may be independent of bar-lines. It also implies the proper perf. of mus. in a natural, living and breathing way, as distinct from a merely mechanical accuracy. What is often called R. in modern dance mus., which is rigidly accurate in time, is therefore not R., but merely a strict application of Time.

Rhythmic Modes. *See* **Modes, Rhythmic**.

Rhythmicon, an instrument invented by Lev Theremin and Henry Cowell for the artificial prod. of rhythms and cross-rhythms.

Riadis (actually Khu), **Emilios** (b. Salonika, I. V. 1886; d. Salonika, 17. VII. 1935), Gk. comp. Studied with Mottl and others at Munich and with Ravel in Paris. Asst. director of the Salonika Cons. from 1918.

Works incl. operas *Le Chant sur le fleuve, Galatea* and *La Route verte*; incid. mus. for Euripides' *Hecuba* and Wilde's *Salome*; Byzantine Mass; *Sunset on Salonika* and other orchestral works; chamber mus.; pf. pieces, etc.

Ribattuta. *See* **Ornaments**.

Ribeca (It.) = Rebec.

Ribible (Eng., obs.), another old word for the Rebec, or for a slightly different instrument of the same type.

Riccardo I, rè d'Inghilterra (*Richard I, King of England*), opera by Handel (lib. by Paolo Antonio Rolli), prod. London, King's Theatre, Haymarket, 11. XI. 1727.

Ricci, Federico (b. Naples, 22. X. 1809; d. Conegliano, 10. III. 1877), It. comp. Studied with Bellini and Zingarelli at the Naples Cons. In 1835 he prod. his 1st opera with his brother Luigi R. at Naples and the 1st of his own at Venice and from 1853 to 1869, after several stage successes, he was mus. director at the Imp. theatres in St. Petersburg.

Works incl. operas *Monsieur de Chalumeaux, La prigione d'Edimburgo* (on Scott's *Heart of Midlothian*), *Un duello sotto Richelieu, Luigi Rolla e Michelangelo, Corrado d'Altamura, Vallombra, Isabella de' Medici, Estella di Murcia, Griselda, I due ritratti, Il marito e l'amante, Il paniere d'amore, Une Folie à Rome, Le Docteur rose* and 4 others in collaboration with Luigi R.; 2 Masses; cantata for the marriage of Victor Emmanuel; songs, etc.

Ricci, Luigi (b. Naples, 8. VII. 1805; d. Prague, ? 21. XII. 1859), It. comp., brother of prec. Studied under Zingarelli at the Naples Cons., where he and Bellini became sub-profs. in 1819. His 1st opera was prod. there in 1823. In 1835, after a number of successful prods., he became cond. of the Opera and mus. director of the cathedral at Trieste. In 1844 he married Lidia Stoltz of Prague, where he was confined in an asylum in 1859, having become hopelessly insane.

Works incl. opera *L'impresario in angustie*, *Il diavolo condannato*, *Il Colombo*, *L'orfanella di Ginevra*, *Chiara di Rosemberg*, *Il nuovo Figaro*, *Un' avventura di Scaramuccia*, *Gli esposti* (*Eran due ed or son tre*), *Chi dura vince*, *Chiara di Montalbano*, *La serva e l'ussaro*, *Le nozze di Figaro* (after Beaumarchais), *Il birraio di Preston*, *La festa di Piedigrotta*, *Il diavolo a quattro* and 14 others incl. 4 in collaboration with F. R.; church mus.; song-books *Mes Loisirs* and *Les Inspirations du thé*, etc.

Operas written jointly by the 2 brothers: *Il colonello*, *Il disertore per amore*, *L'amante di richiamo* and *Crispino e la comare*.

Ricci, Ruggiero (b. San Francisco, 24. VII. 1920), Amer. violinist. Studied with Persinger, making his 1st public appearance aged 8. In 1932–4 he undertook his 1st Eur. tour and in 1957 a world tour.

Ricciardo e Zoraide, opera by Rossini (lib. by Marchese Francesco Berio di Salsa), prod. Naples, Teatro San Carlo, 3. XII. 1818.

Riccio, (Antonio) Teodoro (b. Brescia, *c.* 1540; d. Königsberg or Ansbach, after 1599), It. comp. Choirmaster at a church at Brescia, app. mus. director by the Margrave of Brandenburg-Ansbach, settled there and followed the margrave to Königsberg in 1579, having become a Lutheran, and returned to Ansbach with his patron in 1586. Eccard served under him there from 1581 and succeeded him at his death.

Works incl. motets and other church mus.; madrigals, *Canzoni alla napoletana*, etc.

Ricercare (It. = to search out), a fugal comp., also called *ricercar* or *ricercata*, the instrumental counterpart of the motet or madrigal in the 17th cent., played on keyboard instruments or by a consort of string or wind instruments.

Ricercata. *See* Ricercare.

Richafort, Jean (b. Hainault, *c.* 1480; d. ? Bruges, *c.* 1547), Flem. comp. Pupil of Josquin des Prés. He was choirmaster at the church of Saint-Gilles at Bruges in the 1540s. Wrote Masses, motets, *chansons*, etc.

Richard I (Cœur de Lion) (b. Oxford, IX. 1157; d. ?, 6. IV. 1199), King of Eng. and Fr. trouvère. He was the son of Henry II and his mother was Eleanor of Aquitaine. She intro. the art of the Troubadours to the north of Fr. and this estab. the school of the Trouvères to which R. belonged both as poet and as musician.

According to legend another trouvère, Blondel de Nesle, discovered his place of imprisonment in Aus. in 1192, when he is said to have sung outside the castle of Dürenstein and to have been answered by R. in song from within, a story which furnished the plot for the following opera: **Richard Cœur-de-Lion**, opera by Grétry (lib. by Jean Michel Sedaine), prod. Paris, Comédie-Italienne, 21. X. 1784. Beethoven wrote pf. variations on the song 'Une fièvre brûlante' from it.

Richards, (Henry) Brinley (b. Carmarthen, 13. XI. 1817; d. London, 1. V. 1885), Welsh pianist and comp. Studied at the R.A.M. in London and with Chopin in Paris. Settled in London, where he taught the pf. and lectured on Welsh mus.

Works incl. overture in F min.; addit. songs for Auber's *Diamants de la couronne*; pf. pieces; songs, incl. 'God bless the Prince of Wales'; part-songs, etc.

Richardson, Alan (b. Edinburgh, 29. II. 1904), Scot. pianist and comp. He became B.B.C. pianist in Edinburgh in 1924 and in 1928 went to London to study at the R.A.M. His works are mainly for pf. incl. *The Dreaming Spires*, *Sussex Lullaby*, *Meadowlands*, etc.

Richardson, Ferdinand(o) (real surname Heybourne) (b. ?, *c.* 1558; d. Tottenham, 4. VI. 1618), Eng. comp. Pupil of Tallis. Groom of the Privy Chamber, 1587–1611. Comp. virginal pieces, etc.

Richardson, Samuel (1689–1761), Eng. novelist. *See* Buona figliuola (Piccinni), **Generali** (*Pamela nubile*), Maid of the Mill (Arnold).

Richardson, Vaughan (b. London, ?; d. London, 1729), Eng. organist and comp. Chorister in the Chapel Royal. App. organist of Winchester Cathedral in 1692.

Works incl. services, anthems *O Lord God of my salvation*, *O how amiable* and others; *Song in Praise of St. Cecilia*; *Entertainment for the Peace of Ryswick*; songs for 1–3 voices with instruments, etc.

Richepin, Jean (1849–1926), Fr. poet and dramatist. *See* Chemineau (Leroux), Cui (*Flibustier* and songs), Dupont (*La Glu*), Georges (*Miarka*), Leroux (*Xantho chez les courtisanes*).

Richter, Ferdinand (Tobias) (b. Würzburg, 1649; d. Vienna, 1711), Ger. organist and comp. App. court organist in Vienna, succeeding Poglietti, in 1683, and mus. teacher to the Imp. children.

Works incl. serenatas *L'istro ossequioso* and *Le promesse degli dei*; sacred dramas for the Jesuit Coll.; sonata for 7 instruments and others in 8 parts, *balletti* in 4 and 5 parts; org. toccatas and other works; suites for harpsichord, etc.

Richter, Franz Xaver (b. Holešov, Morav., 1. XII. 1709; d. Strasbourg, 12. IX. 1789), Morav. bass, violinist and comp. App. vice-*Kapellmeister* at the

Abbey of Kempten in 1740, he entered the service of the Mannheim court c. 1747, first as a singer and violinist, later becoming court comp. From 1769 he was mus. director of Strasbourg Cathedral. His work at Mannheim made him a prominent member of that school of symphonists.
Works incl. over 30 Masses; 2 Requiems; 2 Passions; numerous motets, and other church mus.; almost 70 symphs.; concertos; string 4tet and other chamber mus., etc.

Richter, Hans (b. Györ, Hung., 4. IV. 1843; d. Bayreuth, 5. XII. 1916), Aus.-Hung. cond. Studied in Vienna, where he played horn at the Kärntnertortheater, 1862–6. Asst. to Wagner, opera cond. at Budapest and Vienna; 1st to cond. Wagner's *Ring* at Bayreuth, 1876; cond. much in London between 1877 and 1910. Cond. of the Hallé Orch., Manchester, 1900–11.

Richter, Johann Paul Friedrich (called Jean Paul) (1763–1825), Ger. novelist, *See* Heller.

Richter, Sviatislav (Teofilovich) (b. Zhitomir, 20. II. 1914), Rus. pianist. Entered Moscow Cons. in 1937, where he studied with H. Neuhaus, graduating in 1947. He won a national competition in 1945 and was awarded the Stalin Prize in 1949. A magnificent technique and fine musicianship place him in the front rank of modern pianists.

Ricochet (Fr. = rebound), a special kind of *staccato* in vln. mus., prod. by letting the bow bounce on the strings, whereas in ord. *staccato* it remains on the string and is moved in rapid jerks.

Ricordi, Giovanni (b. Milan, 1785; d. Milan, 15. III. 1853), It. mus. pub. Founded the pub. house at Milan c. 1808.

Ricordi, Giulio (b. Milan, 19. XII. 1840; d. Milan, 6. VI. 1912), It. mus. pub., grandson of prec. Became head of the Milan firm on his father's death in 1888. He was also a comp. under his own name and that of J. Burgmein.

Ricordi, Tito (b. Milan, 29. X. 1811; d. Milan, 7. IX. 1888), It. mus. pub., father of prec. Succeeded his father, Giovanni R., in 1853.

Riddle Canon, a form of canon written in a single part with no indication where the subsequent entries of the parts are to occur, the perfs. being left to guess how the mus. fits by solving a riddle.

Riders to the Sea, opera by Vaughan Williams (lib. John Millington Synge's play), prod. London, R.C.M., 1. XII. 1937; 1st public perf. Cambridge, Arts Theatre, 22. II. 1938.

Ridotto. *See* **Redoute.**

Riedel, Carl (b. Kronenberg nr. Elberfeld, 6. X. 1827; d. Leipzig, 3. VI. 1888),

Ger. choral cond. Studied at the Leipzig Cons. after starting life in commerce and founded a choral society there.

Rieder, Ambrosius (b. Döbling nr. Vienna, 10. X. 1771; d. Perchtoldsdorf nr. Vienna, 19. XI. 1855), Aus. comp. Pupil of Albrechtsberger in Vienna, where he became a choirmaster later on.
Works incl. Masses and other church mus.; chamber mus.; org. works, etc.

Riegger, Wallingford (b. Albany, Ga., 29. IV. 1885; d. N.Y., 2. IV. 1961), Amer. comp. Studied in N.Y. and Berlin, with Goetschius, Stillman-Kelley and others. After cond. in Ger., he returned to U.S.A., where he held var. teaching appts.
Works incl. *Amer. Polonaise—Triple Jazz*, Rhapsody, Fantasy and Fugue, Lyric Suite, 2 Dance Suites, Canon and Fugue, etc. for orch.; var. works for dancers; *La Belle Dame sans merci* (Keats) for 4 voices and chamber orch.; 4 symphs.; *Dichotomy* and *Scherzo* for chamber orch.; *Study in Sonority* for 10 vlns.; string 4tet in G min., pf. Trio, *Divertissement* for harp, fl., and cello, 3 Canons for woodwind and other chamber mus.; Suite for solo fl., etc.

Riemann, (Karl Wilhelm Julius) Hugo (b. Grossmehlra nr. Sondershausen, 18. VII. 1849; d. Leipzig, 10. VII. 1919), Ger. musicologist. Studied law at Berlin and Tübingen, mus. at the Leipzig Cons. and later became lecturer at the univ. there, 1878–80, and again, after var. appts. elsewhere, in 1895–1901, when he became prof. Among his many mus.-lit. works are a *Musiklexikon, Handbuch der Musikgeschichte, Opernhandbuch*, works on notation, harmony, phrasing, hist., etc. He ed. many standard works and also comp., mainly teaching pieces for pf.

Rienzi, der letzte der Tribunen (*Rienzi, the Last of the Tribunes*: first called *Cola Rienzi*, . . .), opera by Wagner (lib. by comp., based on Bulwer-Lytton's novel and, further back, on Mary Russell Mitford's play), prod. Dresden, 20. X. 1842.

Ries. Ger. family of musicians:
1. **Johann R.** (b. Benzheim o/Rhine, 1723; d. Cologne, 1784), violinist and trumpeter. Worked at the court of the Elector of Cologne at Bonn.
2. **Franz Anton R.** (b. Bonn, 10. XI. 1755; d. Godesberg, 1. XI. 1846), violinist, son of prec. Pupil of Salomon, he entered the service of the court at Bonn in 1774, becoming 1st vln. after a visit to Vienna in 1779, and mus. director in 1791. Beethoven was his pupil.
3. **Ferdinand R.** (b. Godesberg, XI. 1784; d. Frankfurt, 13. I. 1838), pianist, violinist and comp., son of prec. Pupil of his father for pf. and vln. and of B. Romberg for cello. After a short course in comp.

with Winter at Munich in 1801, he went
to Vienna that year, studying pf. with
Beethoven and comp. with Albrechtsberger and becoming pianist to Counts
Browne and Lichnowsky. Later he lived
by turns in Paris, Vienna, Cassel, Stockholm and St. Petersburg. In 1813–24 he
lived in London, where he married an
Englishwoman and played, taught and
comp. He bought a property at Godesberg
nr. Bonn, but in 1826 went to live at
Frankfurt, where he returned again after
2 years as cond. at Aachen, 1834–6. He
cond. several of the Lower Rhine Festivals.

Works incl. operas *Die Räuberbraut,
Liska* (*The Sorceress*) and *Eine Nacht auf
dem Libanon*; oratorios *Der Sieg des
Glaubens* and *Die Könige Israels*; 6
symphs., 4 overtures; 9 pf. concertos; 14
string 4tets, 6 string 5tets, 3 pf. 4tets, 5
pf. trios, octet, 7tet and other chamber
mus.; 20 duets for vln. and pf.; 10 sonatas
and many other works for pf., etc.

4. Peter Joseph R. (b. Bonn, 6. IV.
1791; d. London, 6. IV. 1882), pianist,
brother of prec. He lived in London, was
a friend of Charles Lamb and worked for a
time in Broadwood's pf. manufacture, also
taught the pf.

5. Hubert R. (b. Bonn, 1. IV. 1802; d.
Berlin, 14. IX. 1886), violinist, brother of
prec. Pupil of his father and Spohr. Held
var. appts. in Berlin from 1824.

6. Louis R. (b. Berlin, 30. I. 1830; d.
London, 3. X. 1913), violinist, son of
prec. Studied under his father and Vieuxtemps, and lived in London from 1853.

7. Adolph R. (b. Berlin, 20. XII. 1837;
d.?, IV. 1899), pianist and comp., brother of
prec. Studied pf. with Kullak and comp.
with Boehmer. Settled in London as pf.
teacher. Comp. pf. works and songs.

8. Franz R. (b. Berlin, 7. IV. 1846; d.
Naumburg, 20. VI. 1932), violinist and
ed., brother of prec. Pupil of his father
and of Massart and Vieuxtemps in Paris.
Appeared in London in 1870, but later
gave up playing and took to mus. pub.
and ed.

Rieti, Vittorio (b. Alexandria, 28. I.
1898), It. comp. Studied with Frugatta at
Milan and Respighi in Rome, but destroyed all his works written up to 1920. In
1939 he became an Amer. citizen.

Works incl. opera *Teresa nel bosco*;
ballets *Noah's Ark, Barabau, Waltz
Academy, The Sleep-walker, Robinson and
Friday* (after Defoe) and *David's Triumph*;
incid. mus. for Pierre Corneille's *L'Illusion
comique* and Giraudoux's *Électre*; 5
symphs.; *Notturno* for strings; concerto for
wind instruments and orch., vln. concerto,
harpsichord concerto, 3 pf. concertos, 2
cello concertos; *Madrigal* for 12 instruments, partita for fl., ob., string 4tet
and harpsichord; sonata for fl., ob.,

bassoon and pf.; *Second Avenue Waltzes*
for 2 pfs., pf. pieces, etc.

Rietz, Eduard (b. Berlin, 17. X. 1802; d.
Berlin, 23. I. 1832), Ger. violinist. Pupil
of his father and of Rode. He joined the
royal orch. in Berlin and founded an orch.
of his own, but suffered from consumption
and had to give up work.

Rietz, Julius (b. Berlin, 28. XII. 1812; d.
Dresden, 12. IX. 1877), Ger. comp. and
cond., brother of prec. Studied under his
father, cello under B. Romberg and others,
and comp. under Zelter. In 1835 he succeeded Mendelssohn as cond. of the opera
at Düsseldorf, and the next year became
town mus. director and cond. the orchestral and choral concerts. In 1847–60
he was cond. of the Vocal Acad. and the
Gewandhaus orch. at Leipzig and taught
comp. at the Cons. In 1860 he was app.
cond. of the Royal Opera, director of
the church chapel and of the Cons. at
Dresden. He ed. works by Bach, Beethoven,
Mendelssohn and Mozart.

Works incl. operas *Der Corsar, Das
Mädchen aus der Fremde* and *Georg Neu-
mark*, operetta *Jery und Bätely* (Goethe);
incid. mus. for Shakespeare's *Hamlet* and
As You Like It, Holtei's *Lorbeerbaum und
Bettelstab* and plays by Goethe, Calderón,
Immermann, etc.; 2 symphs. and 3 over-
tures; *Altdeutscher Schlachtgesang* and
Dithyrambe for male chorus and orch.,
etc.

Rigadoon (Eng.) }
Rigaudon (Fr.) } a Fr. dance, prob.
from the south (Provence or Languedoc),
dating back to the 17th cent. at the latest.
It is in lively common or 2–4 time and
consists of 3 or 4 parts, each repeated, the
3rd being the shortest.

Rigby, George Vernon (b. Birmingham,
21. I. 1840; d. ?), Eng. tenor. Made his
1st appearance in London, in 1861, later
studied at Milan, where he sang in opera,
as also in Berlin and Copenhagen.

Righetti-Giorgi, Geltrude (not Maria
Brighenti). *See* **Giorgi-Righetti**.

Righini, Vincenzo (b. Bologna, 22. I.
1756; d. Bologna, 19. VIII. 1812), It.
singer and comp. A chorister at San
Petronio in Bologna and pupil of Padre
Martini, he made his stage début in Parma
and went as a singer to Prague, where his
Don Giovanni was prod. in 1776, 11 years
before Mozart's opera on the same
subject. App. director of the *opera buffa*
in Vienna in 1780, he was in the service of
the court at Mainz 1787–92, and from 1793
court *Kapellmeister* in Berlin.

Works incl. operas *Il convitato di
pietra* (*Don Giovanni*), *La vedova scaltra,
Demogorgone, Alcide al bivio, Enea nel
Lazio, Il trionfo d'Arianna, Ariadne,
Tigrane, La selva incantata* and *Geru-
salemme liberata* (both after Tasso) and

others; oratorio *Der Tod Jesu*; cantatas, etc.; *Missa solemnis*, Requiem, Te Deum and other church mus.; chamber mus.; keyboard mus.; songs, etc.

Rignold, Hugo (Henry) (b. Kingston-on-Thames, 15. V. 1905), Eng. cond. Taken to Canada as a child, studied vln. in Winnipeg, but returned to study at the R.A.M., vln. with H. Wessely, ob. with L. Goossens and vla. with L. Tertis. After some years as a freelance violinist in London he became cond. of the Palestine Symph. Orch. in 1944 and in 1945–7 of the Cairo Symph. Orch. After a year at Covent Garden he became resident cond. of the Liverpool Phil Orch. from 1948 to 1954, mus. director of the Royal Ballet 1957–60, and from 1960 to 1969 cond. of the Birmingham Symph. Orch.

Rigoletto, opera by Verdi (lib. by Francesco Maria Piave, based on Victor Hugo's play *Le Roi s'amuse*), prod. Venice, Teatro la Fenice, 11. III. 1851.

Riisager, Knudåge (b. Port Kunda, Estonia, 6. III. 1897), Dan. comp. Studied political economy at Copenhagen Univ., but later turned to mus., studying comp. with Peder Gram and Otto Malling, later with Roussel and Le Flem in Paris and finally with Hermann Grabner at Leipzig.

Works incl. opera *Susanne*; ballets *Benzin*, *Cocktail Party* and *Slaraffenland* (*Land of Cockaigne*); incid. mus. to Johannes Jensen's fairy play *Darduse*; chorus works; 4 symphs., variations *Poème mécanique*, *Jabiru T—DOXC* and overture to Holberg's *Erasmus Montanus* for orch.; concerto for tpt. and strings; 5 string 4tets, sonata for fl., clar., vln. and cello, serenade for fl., vln. and cello; vln. and pf. sonata; sonata and var. pieces for pf., songs, etc.

Rilke, Rainer Maria (1875–1926), Ger. poet. *See* Beck (*Lyric Cantata*), Burkhard (song cycle), Foss (L.) (*Parable of Death*), Hindemith (*Marienleben*), Klenau, Martin (F.) (*Cornet*), Marx (K.) (choruses and songs), Reutter (H.) (*Weise von Liebe and Tod* and opera trans. from Gide), Studer (cantata), Webern (songs), Weill (songs with orch.).

Rimbaud, (Jean) Arthur (1854–91), Fr. poet. *See* Britten (*Illuminations*), Lutyens (*O saisons, o châteaux*).

Rimbault, Edward F(rancis). (b. London, 13. VI. 1816; d. London, 26. IX. 1876), Eng. mus. hist. and antiquarian. After beginning his career as an organist he took part in the foundation of the Mus. Antiquarian Society in 1840 and became its secretary, also of the Percy Society, and he ed. old Eng. mus. for both. He also ed. much old church, oratorio, etc., mus. independently, collected a library and wrote several books on the org., the pf., old Eng. vocal mus., etc. Comp. an operetta *The Fair Maid of Islington*, incid. mus., a cantata *Country Life*, songs, etc.

Rimington, A(lexander). Wallace (1854–1918), Eng. painter and prof. of fine arts. Inventor of a 'Colour Organ' first shown in London in 1895.

Rimonte (Ruimonte), Pedro (b. Saragossa, ?; d. ?), Span. 16th–17th-cent. comp. The Infanta Isabella took him to the Netherlands on her marriage to the Archduke Albert, governor of the Netherlands, at whose court at Brussels he became chamber musician in 1603. He returned to Spain in 1614, but was in Brussels again 4 years later.

Works incl. Masses and *Cantiones sacrae*; madrigals and *villancicos*, etc.

Rimsky-Korsakov, Andrey Nikolaievich (b. St. Petersburg, 17. X. 1878; d. Leningrad, 23. V. 1940), Rus. critic and mus. hist. Studied at the Univs. of St. Petersburg, Strasbourg and Heidelberg, and did not turn to mus. until 1913, after his father's death. In 1915 he founded the monthly mus. journal *Muzikalny Sovremennik* (*The Musical Contemporary*) and in 1922 he became ed. of *Muzikalnayu Lietopis* (*Musical Chronicle*). He ed. his father's and Glinka's memoirs, Mussorgsky's letters and documents, Cui's critical writings, his father's correspondence with Tchaikovsky; wrote on Mussorgsky's *Boris Godunov*, the mus. MSS. in the Leningrad Public Library, of which he was curator, etc. He married the comp. Julia Lazarevna Weissberg (1878–1942).

Rimsky-Korsakov, Nikolay Andreievich (b. Tikhvin, Gvt. Novgorod, 18. III. 1844; d. St. Petersburg, 21. VI. 1908), Rus. comp., father of prec. He came of a naval family and his ambition was to become a sailor, though he showed great interest in the Rus. folksongs and church mus. he heard in his childhood, as well as in the operas he knew from pf. selections. In 1856 he was sent to the Naval Coll. at St. Petersburg, where he remained until 1862. He had more pf. lessons during that time and learnt a little theory, but was not taught anything systematic even when in 1861 he met Balakirev and his circle, and came under their influence. He began a symph. in E♭ min., but in 1862 was ordered on a 3-years' cruise. He wrote the slow movement of the symph. off Gravesend and heard opera in London and N.Y., but did not take up mus. again until his return to St. Petersburg in 1865, when he worked more seriously under Balakirev, who cond. the symph. The 1st important works were the symph. poem *Sadko* (1867) and the programme symph. *Antar* (1868). In 1868 he also began his 1st opera, *The Maid of Pskov*, finished in 1872. Meanwhile he had been app. prof. of comp. at the Cons., though in theoret. knowledge he was always little more than 1 lesson ahead of his pupils, and in 1872 he married the pianist Nadezhda Purgold.

App. inspector of naval bands in 1873 and director of the Free School of Mus. in 1874, in succession to Balakirev, until 1881, when he became the latter's asst. in the direction of the Imp. Chapel. He became rather pedantically scholastic during those years, in reaction against his earlier amateurism, but this tendency was counteracted by his interest in Rus. folk mus. and by the influence of Wagner. In 1892–3 he had a serious nervous breakdown and temporarily took a dislike to mus., but his interest revived. In 1905, when he had sided with the 'wrong' party during political disturbances, he was dismissed from the Cons., but there was such a storm of protest that he was reinstated later; but his last opera, based on Pushkin's *Golden Cockerel* (comp. 1906–7), was a satire on official stupidity and its perf. was forbidden. He cond. a festival of Rus. mus. in Paris at Diaghilev's invitation in 1907. In 1908 he suffered from angina and d. 4 days after the marriage of his daughter Nadia to his pupil M. Steinberg.

Works incl. operas *The Maid of Pskov* (*Ivan the Terrible*), *A Night in May*, *The Snow Maiden* (*Snegurotchka*), *Mlada* (based on the collective opera commissioned earlier from him, Borodin, Cui and Mussorgsky), *Christmas Eve*, *Sadko*, *Mozart and Salieri*, *Boyarina Vera Sheloga* (prologue to *The Maid of Pskov*), *The Tsar's Bride*, *The Legend of Tsar Saltan*, *Servilia*, *Kashtchey the Immortal*, *Pan Voievoda*, *The Legend of the Invisible City of Kitezh*, *The Golden Cockerel*; 3 symphs. (2nd *Antar*); symph. poem *Sadko*, concert overtures on Rus. themes and *Rus. Easter*, fantasy on Serbian themes, sinfonietta on Rus. themes, symph. suite *Shahrazad*, *Spanish Capriccio*, *Fairy-Tale*, *On the Tomb* (Belaiev's) and *Dubinushka* for orch.; pf. concerto and fantasy for vln. and orch. (both on Rus. themes); 2 string 4tets (2nd unpub.) and 3 movements for string 4tet contrib. to collective sets by var. comps., string 6tet, 5tet for pf. and wind instruments; 4 cantatas; pf. pieces; many part-songs, songs, vocal duets, 2 collections of Rus. folksongs, etc.

Rinaldo, cantata for tenor solo, male chorus and orch. by Brahms, Op. 50, on a ballad by Goethe, perf. Vienna, 28. II. 1869.

Opera by Handel (lib. by Giacomo Rossi, from a sketch based on Tasso by Aaron Hill), prod. London, Queen's Theatre, Haymarket, 24. II. 1711. Handel's 1st London opera.

Rinaldo di Capua (b. ? Capua or Naples,

c. 1710; d. Rome, after 1770), It. comp., according to Burney the illegitimate son of a Neapol. nobleman. Of more than 30 operas most were prod. in Rome, the first in 1737. But some appeared in Florence and Venice, and in 1752–3 the *Bouffons* in Paris perf. his *La donna superba* and *La zingara*. His last *opera seria* was written in 1758, after which he devoted himself to comic opera. Burney found him living in poor circumstances in Rome in 1770, after which nothing is known.

Works incl. operas *Ciro riconosciuto*, *Vologeso rè de' Parti*, *Mario in Numidia*, *Adriano in Siria*, etc.; intermezzi, etc. *Il bravo burlato*, *La donna superba*, *La zingara*, *Le donne ridicole*, *I finti pazzi per amore*, etc.; *Cantata per la natività della Beata Vergine*, etc.

Rinck, (Johann) Christian Heinrich (b. Elgersburg, Saxe-Gotha, 18. II. 1770; d. Darmstadt, 7. VIII. 1846), Ger. organist, comp. and teacher. Studied at Erfurt under the Bach pupil Kittel. In 1805 he settled at Darmstadt, where he became prof., court organist and ducal chamber musician.

Works incl. *Practical Organ School* and many other works for org.; motets and *Pater noster* for voices and org.; sonatas for pf., vln. and pf., cello and pf.; pf. duets, etc.

Rinf., an abbr. often used for

Rinforzando (It. = reinforcing), a sudden *crescendo* made on a short phrase, similar to the *sforzando*, which is made on a single note or chord.

Ring des Nibelungen, Der (*The Nibelung's Ring*), trilogy of mus.-dramas, with a prologue, by Wagner (lib. by comp. based on the Nibelung Saga):

Das Rheingold (*The Rhinegold*), prod. Munich, Court Opera, 22. IX. 1869.

Die Walküre (*The Valkyrie*), prod. Munich, Court Opera, 26. VI. 1870.

Siegfried, prod. Bayreuth, Wagner Festival Theatre, 16. VIII. 1876.

Götterdämmerung (*The Dusk of the Gods*), prod. Bayreuth, Wagner Festival Theatre, 17. VIII. 1876.

The whole cycle prod. Bayreuth, Wagner Festival Theatre, 13–17. VIII. 1876.

Rinuccini, Ottavio (1562–1621), It. poet and librettist. *See* Arianna (Monteverdi), **Bonini** (*Lamento d'Arianna*), **Camerata**, **Dafne** (Gagliano, Peri and Schütz), **Euridice** (Caccini and Peri), **Petrassi** (*Lamento d'Arianna*).

Rios, Alvaro de los (b. ?; d. ? Madrid, 1623), Span. comp. App. chamber musician to the queen, Margaret of Aus., in 1607.

Works incl. incid. mus. to Tirso de Molina's play *El vergonzoso en palacio*, etc.

Riotte, Philipp Jacob (b. St. Wendel, Saar, 16. VIII. 1776; d. Vienna, 20. VIII. 1856), Ger. cond. and comp. Studied with André at Offenbach, became theatre cond. at Gotha and in 1809 went to Vienna, where he settled, being app. cond. at the Theater an der Wien in 1818. Works incl. operas and operettas *Mozarts Zauberflöte*, *Nureddin*, *Der Sturm* (on Shakespeare's *Tempest*) and many others; ballets; incid. mus.; cantata *Der Kreuzzug*; symph.; 3 clar. concertos; 6 vln. and pf. sonatas; 9 pf. sonatas, pf. piece *The Battle of Leipzig*, etc.

Ripieno (It. adj. = full, noun = filling, stuffing), an instrument subordinate to a soloist or the leader of a section. In the 18th-cent. *concerto grosso* the string players other than the soloists are *ripieni*. Similarly in the brass band a R. cornet is one that comes 2nd to the solo cornet.

Rippe, Albert de (b. Mantua, *c.* 1480; d. Paris, 1551), It. comp., lutenist at the French court from *c.* 1529. Most of his lute mus. was pub. in Paris after his death.

Ripresa (It. = re-taking, repetition), a refrain, esp. in the 14th-cent. It. *ballata.*

Riquier, Guiraut (b. ?; d. ?, 1292), Fr. troubadour. He was the last great exponent of this art. 48 tunes of his songs are extant.

Riseley, George (b. Bristol, 28. VIII. 1845; d. Bristol, 12. IV. 1932), Eng. organist and cond. Held var. organist's posts at Bristol, incl. Colston Hall and the cathedral, started orchestral concerts in 1877, founded the Bristol Choral Society in 1889 and began a triennial Bristol Festival in 1896.

Rising of the Moon, The, opera by Maw (lib. by Beverley Cross and comp.), prod. Glyndebourne, 19.VII.1970.

Risler, (Joseph) Édouard (b. Baden-Baden, 23. II. 1873; d. Paris, 22. VII. 1929), Fr. pianist of Ger. descent. Studied at the Paris Cons. and later in Ger. with d'Albert, Klindworth and others. He was pf. prof. at the Cons. in 1907–9 and toured widely as a recitalist, esp. as an exponent of Beethoven's sonatas.

Rispetto, a type of old It. improvised folk poem of 6–10 (usually 8) inter-rhyming lines, sung to popular tunes.

Rist, Johann (b. Ottensen nr. Hamburg, 8. III. 1607; d. Wedel on Elbe, 31. VIII. 1667), Ger. clergyman, poet and musician. He founded a song school at Hamburg and wrote words for a great number of songs and hymns, some of which he comp. himself.

Ristori, Giovanni Alberto (b. Bologna, 1692; d. Dresden, 7. II. 1753), It. comp. His 1st opera was prod. in Venice in 1713, but 2 years later he moved to Dresden with his father, director of an It. theatrical co. whose mus. director he became in 1717.

App. director of the Polish chapel in Dresden in 1718, he became vice-*Kapellmeister* to the court, under Hasse, in 1750. Works incl. *c.* 20 operas, e.g. *Calandro, Don Chisciotte, Le fate,* etc.; 3 oratorios; 15 cantatas; 15 Masses, 3 Requiems, motets and other church mus., etc.

Risurrezione (*Resurrection*), opera by Alfano (lib. by Cesare Hanau, based on Tolstoy's novel), prod. Turin, Teatro Vittorio Emanuele, 30. XI. 1904.

Ritardando (It.) = retarding. The same direction is also expressed by *rallentando* (slowing down) or *ritenuto* (held back).

Rite of Spring, The, ballet by Stravinsky (scenario by comp. and Nikolay Roerich, choreography by Vaslav Fomich Nizhinsky), prod. as *Le Sacre du printemps,* Paris, Théâtre des Champs-Élysées, 29. V. 1913. There was a riot between partisans and opponents on the first night.

Ritenuto (It.) = held back. The same direction is also expressed by *rallentando* (slowing down) or *ritardando* (retarding).

Ritmo di ... battute (It. = rhythm of ... beats), an indication that the metrical scheme of a piece or movement is to be accented in groups of as many bars as may be shown in this direction between the 2nd and 3rd word, e.g. in the scherzo of Beethoven's 9th symph., where the metre changes between *ritmo di tre battute* and *ritmo di quattro battute.*

Ritornello (It. lit. 'little return'), orig. a refrain and thence, in the early 17th cent., a recurrent instrumental piece played in the course of a mus. stage work; later the instrumental passages between vocal portions of an anthem or aria, from which in turn is derived the meaning of the word R. as applied to the orchestral *tutti* in concertos, esp. in rondos where the same theme returns several times. *See also* Stornello.

Ritorno d'Ulisse in patria, Il (*Ulysses' Return to his Country*), opera by Monteverdi (lib. by Giacomo Badoaro), prod. Venice, Teatro San Cassiano, II. 1641.

Ritter, Alexander (b. Narva, Rus., 2. VI. 1833; d. Munich, 12. IV. 1896), Ger. violinist, cond. and comp. Studied vln. with Franz Schubert of Dresden and later went to the Leipzig Cons. Married Wagner's niece, Franziska Wagner, in 1854, became an ardent Wagnerian, cond. at Stettin in 1856, settled at Würzburg in 1863, ran a mus. shop there in 1875–82 and then joined the ducal orch. at Meiningen under Bülow, whose retirement caused him to move to Munich in 1886. He was a close friend of Richard Strauss. Works incl. operas *Der faule Hans* and *Wem die Krone?*; symph. poems, etc.

Ritter Blaubart (*Knight Bluebeard*), opera by Reznicek (lib. by Herbert Eulenberg), prod. Darmstadt, 29. I. 1920.

Ritter, Christian (b. c. 1650; d. ? Hamburg, after 1725), Ger. organist and comp. Worked at Halle, Dresden, Stockholm and Hamburg. Works incl. Te Deum for double chorus; cantatas incl. *O amantissime sponse Jesu* for soprano and strings; instrumental works, etc.

Ritter, Peter (b. Mannheim, 2. VII. 1763; d. Mannheim, 1. VIII. 1846), Ger. cellist and comp. Studied cello with Danzi, comp. with Vogler, succeeded Danzi in the Mannheim orch. in 1784 and became cond. in 1803.
Works incl. operas *Der Eremit auf Formentara* (Kotzebue), *Die lustigen Weiber* (after Shakespeare's *Merry Wives*) and c. 20 others; plays with mus.; church mus.; oratorio *Das verlorene Paradies* (after Milton); cello concertos; chamber mus.; cello and pf. sonatas, etc.

Rivarde, (Serge) Achille (b. N.Y., 31. X. 1865; d. London, 31. III. 1940), Span.-Amer. (Anglicized) violinist. Studied in U.S.A. and with Dancla at the Paris Cons. After a return to U.S.A., when he gave up playing, he entered the Lamoureux Orch. in Paris, 1885, as leader, leaving in 1891. He made his 1st appearance in London in 1894, settled there and in 1899 became vln. prof. at the R.C.M.

Rivas, Duke of (Angel Pérez de Saavedra) (1791–1865), Span. poet and dramatist. *See* Forza del destino (Verdi).

Rivier, Jean (b. Villemomble, 21. VII. 1896), Fr. comp. He did not study mus. until after World War I in which he was badly injured, entering the Paris Cons. at the age of 26. App. prof. of comp. at the Cons. in 1962.
Works incl. opera *Vénitienne*; Psalm lvi for soprano chorus and orch.; 7 symphs. and other orchestral works; pf. and vln. concertos, chamber mus.; pf. works; songs, etc.

Rizzio, Davide (b. Turin, ?; d. Edinburgh, 9. III. 1566), It. bass and diplomat. In service at the court of Savoy, he visited Scot. in 1561 in the ambassador's suite and remained in the service of Queen Mary with his brother Giuseppe. He arr. masques at court and became her foreign secretary in 1564, but her favour aroused jealousies and he was stabbed to death in Holyrood Palace. Comp. (?) several tunes now regarded as traditional Scot.

Roberday, François (b. Paris, III. 1624; d. Auffargis, 13. X. 1680), Fr. organist and comp. He held appts. as a goldsmith under the Queens Anne of Aus. and Marie-Thérèse, and was one of Lully's teachers.
Works incl. *Fugues et Caprices* for org., etc.

Robert le Diable (*Robert the Devil*), opera by Meyerbeer (lib. by Scribe), prod. Paris, Opéra, 21. XI. 1831.

Roberto Devereux, Conte d'Essex, opera by Donizetti (lib. by Salvatore Cammarano, based on Jacques Ancelot's tragedy *Élisabeth d'Angleterre*), prod. Naples, Teatro San Carlo, 2. X. 1837.
Opera by Mercadante (lib. by Felice Romani, based on Corneille's *Comte d'Essex*), prod. Milan, Teatro alla Scala, 10. III. 1833.

Roberts, John Henry (b. Bethesda, 31. III. 1848; d. Liverpool, 30. VII. 1924), Welsh organist, educationist and comp. Played the org. as a child. Studied with S. S. Wesley and at the R.A.M. in London. He then held org. appts. at Bethesda and Carnarvon and later became director of the Cambrian School of Mus. at Liverpool.
Works incl. hymn tunes, part-songs, etc.

Roberts, Juliane. *See* Walter, Ignaz.

Robertsbridge Manuscript, the earliest known source of keyboard mus., consisting of 2 leaves bound in with an old Robertsbridge Abbey register (British Museum Additional 28,550). It contains 3 *estampies* (the 1st incomplete) showing It. influence, and 3 Lat. motets (the 3rd incomplete), of which the first 2 are arrs. of motets incl. in the Fr. *Roman de Fauvel*. No convincing arguments have been put forward against an Eng. origin for the MS. The date is c. 1325.

Robertson, Alec (b. Southsea, 3. VI. 1892), Eng. musicologist. Studied at the R.A.M. in London and became an organist and choirmaster in 1913. After serving in the 1914–18 war he lectured at L.C.C. evening institutes and in 1920 became lecturer and later head of the Gramophone Co.'s educ. dept. Lived in Rome for 4 years to study plainsong and in 1940 joined the B.B.C. in charge of the mus. talks in the home service. His books incl. *The Interpretation of Plainchant, Art and Religion, Dvořák* and *Requiem: Music of Mourning and Consolation.*

Robertus Anglicus. *See* Morton.

Robeson, Paul (b. Princeton, N.J., 9. IV. 1898), Amer. bass. After studying law at Rutgers and Columbia Univs. he began a career as an actor, becoming esp. well known as Othello. In 1925 he first appeared as a singer, with a recital of negro spirituals, and soon attained world fame, but his career was impeded by his Communist sympathies. In 1952 he was awarded the Stalin Peace Price.

Robin et Marion, Li Gieus de (*The Play of Robin and Marion*), a pastoral play with monophonic mus., by Adam de la Halle, written in Naples between 1283 and his death in 1286 or 1287.

Robin Hood, opera by Macfarren (lib. by John Oxenford), prod. London, Her Majesty's Theatre, 11. X. 1860.

Robin Hood, or Sherwood Forest, opera

by Shield (lib. by Leonard MacNally), prod. London, Covent Garden Opera, 17. IV. 1784.

Robinet (Rubinus) (b. Fcuseran, 30. III. 1415; d. ?, 17. IX. 1478), Fr. comp. His surviving works are a 4-part dance, 'Der bauernschwantz', and 3 textless *chansons*.

Robinson, Anastasia (b. ? It., *c.* 1695; d. Southampton, IV. 1755), Eng. soprano. A pupil of Croft, she made her stage début in 1714 and during the next 10 years sang in many of Handel's operas. Having married the Earl of Peterborough, she retired in 1724.

Robinson Crusoé, operetta by Offenbach (lib. by Eugène Cormon and Hector Crémieux, based distantly on Defoe's novel), prod. Paris, Opéra-Comique, 23. XI. 1867.

Robinson, Elizabeth (b. ? London, *c.* 1700; d. ?), Eng. singer, sister of Anastasia R. She was intended to follow her father as a miniature painter, but studied mus. with Bononcini in London and Rameau in Paris; retired on making a favourable marriage.

Robinson, John (b. ? London, 1682; d. London, 30. IV. 1762), Eng. organist and comp. Chorister in the Chapel Royal, became organist of St. Lawrence, Jewry, and St. Magnus, London Bridge, and in 1727 succeeded Croft as organist of Westminster Abbey. In 1716 he married Wm. Turner's daughter Ann (?–1741), a singer at the It. Opera. Works incl. Double Chant in E♭ maj., etc.

Robledo, Melchior (b. ?; d. Saragossa, 1587), Span. comp. Spent some time in Rome, but returned to Spain in 1569 and became *maestro de capilla* at the old cathedral of Saragossa, where, as at the new one, his work alone was sung with that of Morales, Victoria and Palestrina. Works incl. Masses, motets, etc.

Rocca, Lodovico (b. Turin, 29. XI. 1895), It. comp. Pupil of Orefice. App. director of the Turin Cons. in 1940. Works incl. operas *La morte di Frine*, *La corona del re Gaulo*, *Il Dibuk*, *In terra di leggenda*, *Monte Ivnor* and *L'uragano*; symph. poems *Contrasti*, *Aurora di morte*, *L'alba del malato* and *La foresta delle Samodive*, also *La cella azzura*, *Chiaroscuri* and *Interludio epico* for orch.; chamber mus., etc.

Rochberg, George (b. Paterson, N.J., 8. VII. 1918), Amer. comp. Studied comp. with Szell and L. Mannes (1939–41) in N.Y., and then at the Curtis Inst., Philadelphia, with Scalero and Menotti. In 1950 he was awarded a Fulbright Fellowship and in 1956 a Guggenheim Fellowship. From 1948 to 1954 he taught at the Curtis Inst. Works incl. symph. poem *Night Music*,

2 symphs., *Time-Span, Waltz Serenade, Sinfonia Fantasia* for orch.; *Cantio Sacra* for chamber orch.; string 4tet; clar. sonata; fantasia for vln. and pf.; 2 pf. sonatas, etc.

Rochlitz, Johann Friedrich (b. Leipzig, 12. II. 1769; d. Leipzig, 16. XII. 1842), Ger. mus. critic and poet. Studied under Doles at the St. Thomas School, Leipzig, later theology at the univ. In 1798 he founded the *Allgemeine musikalische Zeitung*, which he ed. until 1818. He also comp., wrote libs. and poems, 3 of which were set by Schubert.

Rockstro (orig. Rackstraw), **William (Smith)** (b. North Cheam, Surrey, 5. I. 1823; d. London, 2. VII. 1895), Eng. organist, comp., theorist and teacher. Studied with Sterndale Bennett and at the Leipzig Cons. From the early 1860s to 1891 he lived at Torquay. He wrote books on hist. and theory, and biogs. of Handel, Mendelssohn and Jenny Lind.

Works incl. oratorio *The Good Shepherd*; madrigal 'O too cruel fair'; songs, etc.

Rode, (Jacques) Pierre (Joseph) (b. Bordeaux, 16. II. 1774; d. Château de Bourbon nr. Damazon, 25. XI. 1830), Fr. violinist and comp. After making great progress as a child, he was sent to Paris in 1787 and became a pupil of Viotti, making his 1st public appearance in 1790. He joined the orch. at the Théâtre Feydeau and in 1794 began to tour abroad, visiting Hol., Ger. and Eng. On his return to Paris he became prof. at the new Cons. and leader at the Opéra. In 1799 he visited Spain, where he met Boccherini. In 1800 he became violinist to Napoleon and in 1803 went to St. Petersburg with Boïeldieu, remaining until 1808. In 1811–13 he travelled in Ger. again, going to Vienna in the latter year, where Beethoven finished the sonata Op. 96 for him. In 1814 he settled in Berlin, where he married, but soon afterwards went to live in retirement near Bordeaux.

Works incl. 13 vln. concertos; many string 4tets; vln. duets; 24 caprices, variations, etc., for vln., etc.

Rodelinda, opera by Handel (lib. by Antonio Salvi, adapted by Nicola Francesco Haym), prod. London, King's Theatre, Haymarket, 13. II. 1725.

Rodelinda, regina de' Longobardi, opera by Graun (lib. by Giovanni Gualberto Bottarelli, altered from Antonio Salvi), prod. Berlin, at court, 13. XII. 1741.

Rodenbach, Georges (1855–98), Belg. dramatist. *See* **Tote Stadt** (Korngold).

Rodgers, Richard (b. N.Y. 28. VI. 1902), Amer. comp. Studied at Columbia Univ (1919–21) and at the Inst. of Mus. Art, N.Y. (1921–3). For 18 years he worked with the librettist Hart, producing

Rodio   Rogers

very successful mus. comedies, incl. *The
Girl Friend* and *The Boy from Syracuse*.
After Hart's death he worked with Oscar
Hammerstein II, producing *Oklahoma*
(1943), which was awarded a Pulitzer
Prize in 1944; also *Carousel, South Pacific*
(1948, Pulitzer Prize 1950), *The King and I*
(1951), *The Flower Drum Song* and many
others.

Rodio, Rocco (b. Bari, *c*. 1535; d.
Naples, shortly after 1615), It. comp. He
wrote church mus. (incl. 10 Masses),
madrigals and instrumental mus., and a
treatise, *Regole di Musica*, pub. Naples,
1600, but known only from its 2nd and
3rd eds. (1609, 1626), ed. by his pupil
Olifante.

Rodolphe, Jean Joseph (orig. Johann
Joseph Rudolph) (b. Strasbourg, 14. X.
1730; d. Paris, 18. VIII. 1812), Fr. horn
and vln. player and comp. Studied horn
and vln. with his father, and from 1746 vln.
with Leclair in Paris. In 1754 he went to
Parma, in 1761 to Stuttgart and in 1767
back to Paris. He studied comp. under
Traetta and Jommelli. In later years he
taught, from 1798 at the Cons.
Works incl. operas *Le Mariage par
capitulation, L'Aveugle de Palmyre* and
Isménor; ballets; horn concertos; vln.
duets; horn pieces, etc.

Rodrigo, Joaquín (b. Sagunto, Prov.
Valencia, 22. XI. 1902), Span. comp. and
critic. He was blind from the age of 3, but
contrived to study mus. and in 1927 he
went to Paris as a pupil of Dukas. He returned to Spain in 1933 and again, after
travels in Eur., in 1936, settling in Madrid
in 1939.
Works incl. *Ausencias de Dulcinea* for
bass, 4 sopranos and orch.; Heroic concerto and other works for orch.; 'Arun-
juez' concerto for guitar, 'Summer'
concerto for vln., cello concerto; songs,
etc.

Rodríguez de Hita, Antonio (b. ? 1724;
d. Madrid, 21. II. 1787), Span. comp. He
was *maestro de capilla* of Palencia Cathedral, and from 1757 of the Convent of the
Incarnation in Madrid. In collaboration
with the poet Ramón de la Cruz he made
important contribs. to Span. opera.
Works incl. operas *Briseida, Las
segadoras de Vallecas, Las labradoras de
Murcia*; hymns for 4 and 8 voices, etc.

Rodwell, George (Herbert Bonaparte) (b.
London, 15. XI. 1800; d. London, 22. I.
1852), Eng. cond., author and comp.
Studied with V. Novello and Bishop and
became mus. director at the Adelphi
Theatre, under his brother's management,
to which he succeeded in 1825. In 1828 he
became prof. at the R.A.M. and in 1831
mus. director at Covent Garden Theatre.
He also wrote plays and novels.
Works incl. stage pieces *The Flying

*Dutchman, The Cornish Miners, The Bottle
Imp, The Earthquake, The Devil's Elixir,
The Lord of the Isles* (after Scott), *The
Sexton of Cologne, The Seven Sisters of
Munich* and a number of others; *Songs of
the Sabbath Eve, Songs of the Birds*, etc.

Rodzinski, Artur (b. Spalato, Dalmatia,
2. I. 1892; d. Boston, 27. XI. 1958),
Yugoslav cond. Studied law at the Univ.
of Vienna, and then mus. at the Vienna
Acad., with E. Sauer, F. Schalk and Schre-
cker. He made his début as a cond. in
Lwów in 1921, then took up posts in
Warsaw. In 1926 he became asst. to
Stokowski and in 1929 permanent cond.
of the Los Angeles Phil. Orch., and of the
Cleveland Orch. in 1933. In 1937 he or-
ganized the N.B.C. Symph. Orch. for
Toscanini and cond. many of its concerts.
From 1943 to 1947 he was permanent cond.
of the N.Y. Phil. Orch. and from 1948 of
the Chicago Symph. Orch.

Rogel, José (b. Orihuela, Alicante, 24.
XII. 1829; d. Cartagena, 25. II. 1901),
Span. cond. and comp. Studied under the
cathedral organist at Alicante, but was
sent to Valencia to study law. There he
pursued further mus. studies under Pascual
Pérez, and after taking his degree in law,
became a theatre cond. He wrote or
collaborated in over 80 stage works, some
with Barbieri.
Works incl. operas and *zarzuelas Loa
a la libertad, El joven Telémaco, Revista
de un muerto, Un viaje de mil demonios, El
General Bumbum*, etc.

Roger-Ducasse (Jean Jules Aimable
Roger Ducasse) (b. Bordeaux, 18. IV.
1873; d. Taillan nr. Bordeaux, 20. VII.
1954), Fr. comp. Studied at the Paris
Cons., where he was a comp. pupil of
Fauré. App. inspector of singing in the
Paris city schools in 1909, and in 1935
succeeded Dukas as comp. prof. at the
Cons.
Works incl. opera *Cantegril*, mimed
drama *Orphée*; *Au Jardin de Marguerite*
and *Ulysse et les Sirènes* for voices and
orch.; motets and secular vocal works incl.
*Sur quelques vers de Virgile, Madrigal sur
des vers de Molière*; *Suite française, Le
Joli Jeu de furet, Prélude d'un ballet,
Nocturne de printemps, Épithalame, Poème
symphonique sur le nom de Fauré* for orch.;
Variations plaisantes for harp and orch.;
pf. works; instrumental pieces; songs, etc.

Roger, Gustave Hippolyte (b. Paris, 17.
XII. 1815; d. Paris, 12. IX. 1879), Fr.
tenor. Studied at the Paris Cons. and made
his 1st appearance, at the Opéra-Comique,
in 1838. In 1849 he transferred to the
Opéra. In 1868 he became prof. at the
Cons.

Rogers, Benjamin (b. Windsor, V.
1614; d. Oxford, VI. 1698), Eng. organist
and comp. Learnt mus. from his father,

Peter R., a lay-clerk at St. George's Chapel, Windsor, and from the organist, Giles. He became himself a lay-clerk, but in 1639 went to Dublin as organist of Christ Church Cathedral. He returned to Windsor in 1641, but in 1644 the choir was disbanded and he taught mus. privately. Mus.B., Cambridge, 1658, and in 1669 D.Mus., Oxford, where he had become organist and choirmaster at Magdalen Coll., in 1664, being dismissed for irregularities in 1685, but given a pension.

Works incl. services and anthems, *Hymnus Eucharisticus* (sung on Magdalen tower at 5 a.m. on 1. V. each year); instrumental pieces; org. works, etc.

Rogers, Bernard (b. N.Y., 4. II. 1893; d. Rochester, N.Y., 24. V. 1968), Amer. comp. Studied at the N.Y. Inst. of Mus. Art and with Bloch at Cleveland. He gained several prizes and distinctions and for a time did mus. journalism. In 1938 he became prof. of comp. at the Eastman School of Mus. at Rochester, N.Y.

Works incl. operas *The Marriage of Aude*, *The Warrior*, *The Veil* and *The Nightingale*; cantatas *The Raising of Lazarus* and *The Exodus*, *Passion* with org. accomp.; 4 symphs., overture *The Faithful*, *3 Eastern Dances*, *2 Amer. Frescoes*, *4 Fairy Tales*, *The Supper at Emmaus*, *The Colours of War*, *The Dance of Salome*, *The Song of the Nightingale*, *The Plains*, *The Sailors of Toulon*, *Invasion* and *Characters from Hans Andersen* for orch.; soliloquies for fl. and strings and bassoon and strings, fantasy for fl., vla. and orch.; *Pastorale* for 11 instruments, string 4tet; *Mus. for an Industrial Film* for 2 pfs., songs. etc.

Rogier, Philippe (b. Arras, c. 1560; d. Madrid, 29. II. 1596), Fr. comp. He must have been sent to Spain as a child, being a choir-boy at Madrid in 1572; member of the royal chapel from 1586, *maestro de capilla* from 1587.

Works incl. Masses, motets, etc.

Rogneda, opera by Serov (lib., in Rus., by Dmitri Vassilievich Averkiev), prod. St. Petersburg, 8. XI. 1865.

Rogowski, Ludomir (Michal) (b. Lublin, 3. X. 1881; d. Dubrovnik, 14. III. 1954), Pol. comp. Studied at the Warsaw Cons. and with Riemann and Nikisch at Leipzig. On his return to Pol. he founded a symph. orch. at Wilno, lived in Paris in 1914–21 and withdrew to a monastery in Yugoslavia in 1926.

Works incl. opera *Tamara* (after Lermontov) and *Prince Marco*; film opera *Un Grand Chagrin de la Petite Ondine*, ballets *St. John's Eve* and *Fairy Tale*; 2 svmphs., suites *Pictures of my Daughter*, *The Seasons*, *Les Sourires*, *Villafranca*,

Phantasmagoria, *Sporting Scene*, *Fantasy Pictures* for orch.; 4tet for 4 cellos, suites for 6 and for 9 instruments and other chamber mus.; instrumental pieces; pf. works; choral songs with and without accomp., etc.

Rohr Flute, a stopped Diapason org. stop of metal pipes prod. 8-ft. tone.

Rohrflöte (Ger. lit. tube flute), the name sometimes used in Eng. for the Rohr F. org. stop.

Roi David, Le, dramatic Psalm by Honegger (lib. by René Morax), prod. Mézières, Switz., open-air Théâtre du Jorat, 11. VI. 1921.

Roi de Lahore, Le (*The King of L.*), opera by Massenet (lib. by Louis Gallet), prod. Paris, Opéra, 27. IV. 1877.

Roi des Violons (Fr. = King of the Violins), the title of the head of the guild of vln. players, the Ménétriers, founded in Paris in 1321. It was not abolished until 1773.

Roi d'Ys, Le, opera by Lalo (lib. by Édouard Blau), prod. Paris, Opéra-Comique, 7. V. 1888. Ys is the submerged city of Debussy's pf. prelude *La Cathédrale engloutie*.

Roi et le fermier, Le (*King and Farmer*), opera by Monsigny (lib. by Jean Michel Sedaine), prod. Paris, Comédie-Italienne, 22. XI. 1762.

Roi l'a dit, Le (*The King has said it*), opera by Delibes (lib. by Edmond Gondinet), prod. Paris, Opéra-Comique, 24. V. 1873.

Roi malgré lui, Le (*King against his Will*), opera by Chabrier (lib. by Émile de Najac and Paul Burani, based on a comedy by Ancelot), prod. Paris, Opéra-Comique, 18. V. 1887.

Rokitansky, Hans von, Freiherr (b. Vienna, 6. III. 1835; d. Laubegg Castle, Styria, 2. XI. 1909), Aus. bass. Studied at Bologna and Milan, made his 1st appearance in Eng. in 1856, in Prague, 1862, and in Vienna, 1863. In 1894 he became prof. at the Vienna Cons.

Rokseth (*née* Rihouet), **Yvonne** (b. Maisons-Laffitte, 17. VII. 1890; d. Strasbourg, 28. VIII. 1948), Fr. musicologist and comp. Studied vln. at the Paris Cons., also org. with Abel Decaux and comp. with d'Indy at the Schola Cantorum. Later she became a private pupil of Roussel. She took degrees in science and letters, and in 1937 was app. Prof. of Mus. at Strasbourg Univ. She ed. old Fr. org. mus. for the Société Française de Musicologie and the Montpellier MS. of 13th-cent. polyphonic mus. Her books incl. studies of 15th–16th-cent. org. mus. and of Grieg; her comps. a Te Deum for chorus, strings and org., a fantasy for pf. and orch. and a string 5tet.

Roland. *See also* **Orlando.**

Opera by Lully (lib. by Quinault), prod. Versailles, at court, 8. I. 1685, 1st Paris perf., 8. III. 1685.

Roland-Manuel, Alexis (b. Paris, 22. III. 1891; d. 2. XI. 1966), Fr. comp. and critic. Pupil of Roussel at the Schola Cantorum in Paris and of Ravel. In 1947 he became a prof. at the Paris Cons. He wrote much criticism and books on Ravel and Falla.

Works incl. operas *Isabelle et Pantalon*, *Le Diable amoureux*; ballets *Le Tournoi singulier*, *L'Écran des jeunes filles*, *Elvire* (on mus. by D. Scarlatti); film mus. *L'Ami Fritz* (after Erckmann-Chatrian), *La Bandéra* and others; oratorio *Jeanne d'Arc*; symph. poems *Le Harem du vice-roi*, *Tempo di ballo*, suite *Pena de Francia* for orch.; suite in the Span. style for harpsichord, ob., bassoon and tpt., string trio; part-songs; songs, etc.

Roldán, Amadeo (b. Paris, 12. VII. 1900; d. Havana, 2. III. 1939), Cuban mulatto comp. Studied vln. in Madrid and comp. at Havana, where in 1924 he became leader and in 1932 cond. of the Phil. Orch. He studied Cuban folk mus., on which all his works are based.

Works incl. ballets *La Rebambaramba* and *El Milagro de Anaquillé*; *Obertura sobre temas cubanos* and *Tres pequeños poemas* for orch.; *3 Toques* for chamber orch.; *Danza negra* for soprano and 7 instruments, *Poema negra* for string 4tet; 6 *Ritmicas* for var. instruments, etc.

Rolfsen, Johan Nordahl (Brun) (1848–1928), Norw. dramatist. *See* **Olsen** (*Svein Uroed*).

Roll, a very rapid succession of notes on drums prod. by quick alternating strokes of the 2 sticks.

Rolla, Alessandro (b. Pavia, 6. IV. 1757; d. Milan, 15. IX. 1841), It. violinist (later esp. vla. player) and comp. Studied with Renzi and Conti, was in the service of the court at Parma 1782–1802, where Paganini was his pupil in 1795. In 1803 he was app. orch. director at the Scala in Milan, in 1805 prof. at the Cons. there.

Works incl. ballets; symphs.; vln. and vla. concertos; string 5tets, 4tets and other chamber mus.; vln. duets, studies, etc.

Rolland, Romain (b. Clamency, Nièvre, 29. I. 1866; d. Vézelay, Yonne, 30. XII. 1944), Fr. musicologist and author. He had a 1st-rate general educ., but devoted himself to mus. and other artistic studies. In 1901 he became president of the mus. section of the École des Hautes Études Sociales and lectured on mus. 1st at the École Normale Supérieure and from 1903 at the Sorbonne. He also contrib. essays on mus. to var. periodicals and wrote plays and other lit. works. From 1913 he lived in Switz., having retired owing to bad health. He returned to Fr. in 1938 in order

not to evade the war, was interned in a concentration camp by the Gers. and released only when he was mortally ill. His works incl. books on Handel and Beethoven, on early opera, *Musiciens d'autrefois*, *Musiciens d'aujourd'hui*, *Voyage musical au pays du passé*, the novel *Jean-Christophe* (10 vols.) with a musician as hero, etc.

For incid. mus. to his plays *see* **Honegger** (*Danton*), **Kabalévsky** (*Craftsman of Clamecy*), **Lopatnikov** (*Danton*), **Quatorze Juillet** (7 comps.), **Tcherepnin (A.)** (*Esprit triomphant*).

Rolle, Johann Heinrich (b. Quedlinburg, 23. XII. 1716; d. Magdeburg, 29. XII. 1785). Ger. organist and comp. Pupil of his father, Christian Friedrich R. (1681–1751), he was app. organist of St. Peter's, Magdeburg, at the age of 17. After legal studies in Leipzig he entered the service of Frederick II of Prus. in 1741, but returned to Magdeburg in 1746 as organist of St. John's, and became municipal mus. director in 1752, succeeding his father.

Works incl. over 20 dramatic oratorios, e.g. *David und Jonathan*, *Der Tod Abels*, *Saul*, etc.; Passion oratorios; cantatas and numerous other church works; instrumental mus., songs, etc.

Rolltrommel (Ger.) = Tenor Drum (more often called *Rührtrommel*).

Rolón, José (b. Ciudad Guzmán, Jalisco, 22. VI. 1883; d. Mex. City, 3. II. 1945), Mex. comp. Studied with his father and later with Moszkowski in Paris, where however he came under the influence of the modern school. He returned to Mex. in 1907 and founded a mus. school at Guadalajara, but at the age of 44 he returned to Paris to study with Dukas and Nadia Boulanger.

Works incl. symph., overture, *El festin de los enanos*, *Scherzo sinfónico*, *Baile Michoacana*, *Zapotlán*, *Cuauhtémoc* for orch.; pf. concerto, etc.

Roma, orchestral suite by Bizet, comp. 1866–8, 1st perf. Paris, 1869.

Roman, Johan Helmich (b. Stockholm, 26. X. 1694; d. Haraldsmåla nr. Kalmar, 19. X. 1758), Swed. comp. Pupil of his father, leader of the court orch. in Stockholm, he entered the royal service in 1611. In Eng. from 1714, he studied with Ariosti and Pepusch and was in the service of the Duke of Newcastle. Returning to Stockholm he became vice-*Kapellmeister* (1721), then *Kapellmeister* (1729). Toured Eng., Fr. and It. 1735–7, became a member of the Swed. Acad. in 1740 and retired in 1745.

Works incl. Mass, motets, psalms; 21 symphs., 6 overtures; concertos; over 20 vln. sonatas, 12 sonatas for fl., vla. da gamba and harpsichord, *Assaggio* for solo vln., etc.

Romance (Eng. and Fr.), a piece or song of a 'romantic' nature, usually moderate in tempo and emotional in style. There is no prescribed form, but it is as a rule fairly short and in the character of a song.

Romance (Fr.), as above, but more often and more specifically a song. In Fr. single-voice songs were called *romances* from about the end of the 18th cent. onward until recently, and the term is still in use, though the more general one now is *mélodie*.

Romanesca, originally the melody of a 16th-cent. Span. song with a simple bass, used as a theme for variations. The bass, of which the simplest form is:

came to be used independently as a ground, as in the *passamezzo*.

Romanticism, a term capable of as vague an application as are Classicism and Modernism. Applied to a period it defines with fair accuracy the greater part of mus. of the 19th cent., from Schubert to Brahms, as well as a good deal of the mus. of the early 20th cent. As a definition of mood and outlook it may be said to describe mus. which is consciously an expression of the comp.'s state of mind, a mood of place, season or time of day, the feeling or content of some other work of art (e.g. a poem or a picture), etc.

Romanze (Ger.) = Romance, in the 1st sense defined above.

Romberg, Andreas (Jakob) (b. Vechta nr. Münster, 27. IV. 1767; d. Gotha, 10. XI. 1821), Ger. violinist and comp. Pupil of his father, Gerhard Heinrich R. (1745–1819). He appeared in string duets with his cousin Bernhard R. at the age of 7 and at 17 played at the Concert spirituel in Paris. In 1790 he joined the electoral orch. at Bonn and in 1793–6 he was in It., Spain and Port. with Bernhard, whom he joined again in Paris in 1800 after visits to Vienna and Hamburg. He returned to the latter place, married and remained for 15 years, after which he became court mus. director at Gotha.

Works incl. operas *Don Mendoce, ou Le Tuteur portugais* (with Bernhard R.), *Das blaue Ungeheuer*, *Der Rabe* (both after Gozzi), *Die Ruinen zu Paluzzi*, *Die Grossmut des Scipio* and others; Te Deum, Magnificat, psalms and other church mus.; setting of Schiller's *Lied von der Glocke* for solo voices, chorus and orch., and other cantatas *The Transient and the Eternal*, *The Harmony of the Spheres*, *The Power of Song*, etc.; 6 symphs. and Toy Symph.; string 4tets and 5tets, etc.

Romberg, Bernhard (b. Dinklage, Oldenburg, 12. XI. 1767; d. Hamburg, 13. VIII. 1841), Ger. cellist and comp., cousin of prec. Pupil of his father Anton R. (1742–1814), appeared at the age of 7 with his cousin and in Paris at 14. In 1790–3 he was in the electoral orch. at Bonn, together with Andreas, also Beethoven, Reicha and F. A. Ries; then, until 1796, he was in It., Spain and Port. with Andreas. After visits to Vienna and Hamburg he taught the cello at the Paris Cons., 1801–3, and in 1804–6 he was cellist in the royal orch. in Berlin, where he was court mus. director in 1815–19, after a tour in Rus., retiring to Hamburg in 1819. In the meantime he had visited London, Paris, Vienna, St. Petersburg, Moscow, etc.

Works incl. operas *Don Mendoce, ou Le Tuteur portugais* (with Andreas R.), *Die wiedergefundene Statue* (after Gozzi), *Der Schiffbruch*, *Alma*, *Ulysses und Circe*, *Rittertreue*; many cello concertos, concerto for 2 cellos; funeral symph. for Queen Louise of Prus.; string 4tets, pf. 4tets and other chamber mus.; cello pieces, etc.

Romberg, Siegmund (b. Szeged, 29. VII. 1887; d. N.Y., 9. XI. 1951), Amer. comp. of Hung. origin. Studied at Univ. of Bucharest and then in Vienna with Heuberger. In 1909 he went to the U.S.A. as an engineer, but later began comp. with great success.

Works incl. operettas *Blossom Time* (after music by Schubert), *The Rose of Stamboul*, *The Student Prince*, *The Desert Song*.

Romeo and Juliet. *See also* **Giulietta e Romeo, Capuleti e Montecchi.**

Fantasy overture by Tchaikovsky, based on Shakespeare's tragedy, comp. at Balakirev's suggestion, 1869–70; perf. Moscow, 16. III. 1870; revised X. 1870.

Opera by John Edmund Barkworth (1858–1929) (lib. by comp. adapted from Shakespeare), prod. Middlesbrough, 7. I. 1916; 1st London perf. Surrey Theatre, 10. IV. 1920.

Roméo et Juliette, opera by Gounod (lib. by Jules Barbier and Michel Carré, after Shakespeare), prod. Paris, Théâtre, Lyrique, 27. IV. 1867.

Opera by Steibelt (lib. by Joseph Alexandre Pierre de Ségur, after Shakespeare), prod. Paris, Théâtre Feydeau, 10. IX. 1793.

Symph. by Berlioz, Op. 17, for solo voices, chorus and orch., based on Shakespeare's tragedy, comp. in 1839, 1st perf. Paris Cons., 24. XI. 1839.

Romeo und Julia, opera by Sutermeister (lib. by comp., after Shakespeare), prod. Dresden, 13. IV. 1940.

Romeo und Julia auf dem Dorfe (*A Village Romeo and Juliet*), opera by Delius (lib. by comp., in Ger., based on a story by Gottfried Keller), prod. Berlin, 21. II. 1907. First perf. in Eng., London, Covent Garden Theatre, 22. II. 1910.

Romeo und Julie, opera by G. Benda (lib. by Friedrich Wilhelm Gotter), prod. Gotha, at court, 25. IX. 1776. The 1st opera to be based on Shakespeare's tragedy.

Romero, Mateo (known as Maestro Capitán) (b. ?; d. Madrid, 10. V. 1647), Span. singer, comp. and priest. He joined the royal chapel at Madrid in 1594. He was a pupil of Rogier and belonged to the Flem. section of the choir. In 1598 he succeeded Rogier as *maestro de capilla*. He was ordained priest in 1609 and retired with a pension in 1633, but was sent on a mus. mission to Port. in 1638.

Works incl. motets and other church mus.; secular songs for 3 and 4 voices, incl. settings of poems by Lope de Vega, etc.

Romilda e Costanza, opera by Meyerbeer (lib. by Giacomo Rossi), prod. Padua, 19. VII. 1817.

Ronald, Landon (b. London, 7. VI. 1873; d. London, 14. VIII. 1938), Eng. cond., pianist and comp., illegitimate son of Henry Russell. Studied at the R.C.M., made his 1st public appearance at the piano in Wormser's *L'Enfant prodigue* and gained experience as asst. cond. to Mancinelli at Covent Garden and accompanist to Melba. Later he cond. symph. concerts and visited Ger., Aus. and It. as cond. In 1910 he was app. principal of the G.S.M. in London. Knighted 1922.

Works incl. incid. mus. to dramatic version of Robert Hichens's *Garden of Allah*; *Birthday Overture* for orch.; *Adonais* (Shelley) for voice and orch.; pf. pieces; songs, etc.

Ronconi. It. family of singers:
1. Domenico R. (b. Lendinara nr. Rovigo, 11. VII. 1772; d. Milan, 13. IV. 1839), made his 1st appearance, at the Teatro La Fenice in Venice, in 1797, later worked at St. Petersburg, Vienna, Paris and Munich. He founded a school of singing at Milan in 1829.
2. Giorgio R. (b. Milan, 6. VIII. 1810; d. Madrid, 8. I. 1890), baritone, son of prec. Pupil of his father, made his 1st appearance at Pavia in 1831. Travelled all over It. and 1st visited London in 1842. Married the singer Elguerra Giannoni and visited many Eur. countries as well as the U.S.A. In 1874 he became prof. of singing at the Madrid Cons.
3. Felice R. (b. Venice, 1811; d. St. Petersburg, 10. IX. 1875), brother of prec. Pupil of his father, taught at Würzburg, Frankfurt, Milan, London and St. Petersburg.

4. Sebastiano R. (b. Venice, V. 1814; d. Milan, I. 1900), baritone, brother of prec. Pupil of his father and made his 1st appearance at Lucca in 1836, and in London later that year. He travelled widely and in 1849 settled at Milan as singingmaster.

Rondeau (Fr.), a medieval song with a refrain. Also, by analogy, in the 17th and 18th cents. an instrumental piece in which one section recurs. *See also* **Rondo**.

Rondelet (Fr.) = Roundelay.

Rondeña, a Span. folksong type of Andalusia, resembling the Fandango, with words in stanzas of 4 lines of 8 syllables.

Rondine, La (*The Swallow*), operetta by Puccini (lib. by Giuseppe Adami, trans. from the Ger. of Alfred Maria Willner and Heinrich Reichert), prod. Monte Carlo, 27. III. 1917. Orig. intended to be set to the Ger. words for the Carl Theater in Vienna, but It. being at war with Aus., this fell through.

Rondo, an instrumental piece or movement in which a theme heard at the beginning recurs between contrasting episodes and at the end. In the late 18th and early 19th cents. the form was combined with sonata form, i.e. the 1st episode, in a related key, was repeated in the tonic key before the last appearance of the R. theme. Thus a simple R. might be in the following form: *ABACADA*, and a sonata R.: *ABACAB'A*, where *C* has the character of a development. Variants of the latter scheme are not uncommon. The final movements of sonatas, symphs., etc. in the period mentioned are often R.s.

Ronga, Luigi (b. Turin, 19. VI. 1901), It. musicologist. Studied at Turin Univ. and at Dresden, became prof. of mus. hist. at the Palermo Cons. in 1926 and later at the Univ. and Accademia di Santa Cecilia in Rome. His works incl. studies of Frescobaldi, Rossini and Wagner, a treatise on mus. hist., etc.

Ronsard, Pierre de (1524–85), Fr. poet. *See* Bertrand (A. de) (*Amours*), Boni (sonnets), Dieren (van) (songs), Dukas (*Sonnet de R.*), Honegger (songs), Poulenc (songs), Regnart (F.) (*chansons*), Roussel (A.) (songs), Séverac (songs), Witkowski (songs with orch.).

Röntgen, Engelbert (b. Deventer, 30. IX. 1829; d. Leipzig, 12. XII. 1897), Dutch violinist. Studied at the Leipzig Cons. and became a member of the Opera and Gewandhaus orchs. there, and in 1869 vln. prof. at the Cons. In 1873 he succeeded David as leader at the Gewandhaus. He married a daughter of a former leader, Moritz Klengel.

Röntgen, Julius (b. Leipzig, 9. V. 1855; d. Utrecht, 13. IX. 1932), Ger. pianist, cond. and comp. of Dutch des-

cent, son of prec. Studied at the Leipzig
Cons., but reverted to Hol., living at
Amsterdam in 1878–1924 as teacher and
cond., becoming director of the Cons.
in 1914. He was a great friend of Grieg,
of whom he wrote a biog.

Works incl. operas *Agnete*, *The Laughing
Cavalier* (on Frans Hals's painting),
Samûm (on Strindberg's play); film mus.;
12 symphs.; 3 pf. concertos; chamber
mus.; arrs. of old Dutch songs and dance,
etc.

Rooke (actually Rourke or O'Rourke),
William Michael (b. Dublin, 29. IX. 1794;
d. London, 14. X. 1847), Ir. violinist,
pianist and comp. He was largely self-
taught, and after an appt. at the Crow
Street Theatre, Dublin, prod. his 1st
opera in London, where he settled in 1821,
working at Drury Lane Theatre and Vauxhall and cond. oratorios at Birmingham.

Works incl. operas *Amilie, or The
Love Test*, *Henrique, or The Love Pilgrim*,
Cagliostro, *The Valkyrie*, etc.

Roos, Robert de (b. The Hague, 10. III.
1907), Dutch comp. Studied with Wagenaar at the Hague Cons. and later with
Isidor Philipp (pf.), Koechlin and Roland-
Manuel (comp.) and Monteux (cond.) in
Paris. He is a government official, but is
highly regarded as a comp.

Works incl. incid. mus. for Vondel's
Joseph at Dothan amd other plays;
dramatic oratorio *On the Ruins*; 2 symphs.
and *Sinfonietta* for orch., *Sinfonia romantica* for chamber orch.; pf. concerto,
vla. concerto, dances for fl. and orch.;
Christmas Song for soprano and orch.;
5 string 4tets, *Adagio and Allegro* for 2
vlns.; 2 pf. sonatas; 5 *Quatrains by Francis
Jammes* for soprano and pf., etc.

Root, according to 19th-cent. theory
the lowest note of a maj. or min. triad, or
of chords in which one or more 3rds are
superimposed on such triads (7ths, 9ths,
11ths, 13ths). Thus the following chord:

Root position

is said to be in R. position. Rearrangements
of the notes of the chord:

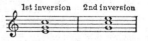

1st inversion   2nd inversion

are described as Inversions. According to
this theory, which takes no account of the
different functions of chords, a 4-note
chord has 3 possible inversions, and so on.

Rootham, Cyril B(radley). (b. Bristol,
5. X. 1875; d. Cambridge, 18. III. 1938),
Eng. organist, educationist and comp.
Studied under his father, the singer,
organist and cond. Daniel R. (1837–1922),
later at St. John's Coll., Cambridge, where
he took the Mus.B. in 1900, and the
R.C.M. in London. In 1901 he went back
to Cambridge as organist and mus.
director at St. John's Coll. and took the
Mus.D. in 1910. He cond. many interesting perfs. with the Cambridge Univ.
Mus. Society and at festivals in the town.

Works incl. opera *The Two Sisters*;
choral and orchestral works *Andromeda*,
Coronach, For the Fallen (Binyon), *Brown
Earth, Ode on the Morning of Christ's
Nativity* (Milton), *City in the West*,
Psalm ciii: 2 symphs. (2nd with choral
finale), rhapsodies *Pan* and on the tune
Lazarus (strings), *Miniature* and *St.
John's* suites for orch.; string 4tet, string
5tet, pf. trio, 7tet for vla., wind and harp;
vln. and pf. sonata, suite for fl. and pf.;
part-songs, etc.

Rooy, Anton(ius Maria Josephus) van
(b. Rotterdam, 1. I. 1870; d. Munich, 28.
XI. 1932), Dutch bass-baritone. Orig.
engaged in commerce, he went to Frankfurt to study singing with Stockhausen,
sang at concerts in Ger. and obtained his
1st stage engagement at the Wagner
festival theatre at Bayreuth in 1897. He
1st visited London as a Wagner singer at
Covent Garden in 1898.

Ropartz, (Joseph) Guy (Marie). *See*
Guy-Ropartz.

Rore, Cyprien de (Cipriano de) (b.
Mechlin, ? 1516; d. Parma, 1565), Flem.
comp. Studied under his fellow-country-
man Willaert at Venice, where he was (?) a
singer, and began to pub. madrigals in
1542. He left Venice *c*. 1550 to enter the
service of Ercole II, Duke of Ferrara.
In 1558 he visited his parents at Antwerp
and the court of Margaret of Aus. in the
Netherlands, into the service of whose
husband, Ottavio Farnese, Duke of
Parma, he passed. He succeeded Willaert
as *maestro di cappella* of St. Mark's,
Venice, in 1563, but returned to Parma in
VII. 1564.

Works incl. Masses, motets, 2 Passions
and other church mus.; madrigals; instrumental fantasies and *ricercari*, etc.

Rosa (orig. Rose), **Carl (August Nikolaus)** (b. Hamburg, 22. III. 1842; d. Paris, 30.
IV. 1889), Ger. violinist and cond. Studied
at the Leipzig and Paris Conss., became
orch. leader at Hamburg and visited Eng.
in 1866 and afterwards the U.S.A., where
he met and in 1867 married Euphrosyne
Parepa (1836–74), with whom he formed
an opera co. which incl. Santley and G.
Ronconi. This he took to Eng. and carried
on as the C. R. Opera Company.

Rosalia, the usual name for the Real
Sequence repeating a phrase higher or

lower, not within the scale of the same key, as in the Tonal Sequence, but by so changing the key that its steps retain exactly the same succession of whole tones and semitones. e.g.:

27. VII. 1918), Amer. cellist. Studied at Curtis Inst., Philadelphia, with F. Salmond and then played in the N.B.C. Orch. under Toscanini and later as 1st cello in the N.Y. Phil. Orch. Since 1951 he has taught at the

ROSALIA

The name derives from an It. popular song, 'Rosalia, mia cara', in which this device occurs.

Rosalie. *See* **Levasseur.**

Rosamond, opera by Arne (lib. by Joseph Addison), prod. London, Theatre in Lincoln's Inn Fields, 7. III. 1733.

Opera by Clayton (lib. do.), prod. London, Drury Lane Theatre, 4. III. 1707.

Rosamunde, incid. mus. by Schubert for a play by Helmina von Chézy, *Rosamunde, Prinzessin von Cypern,* prod. Vienna, Theater an der Wien, 20. XII. 1823. The mus. consists of 3 entr'actes, 2 ballet tunes, a romance for contralto, a chorus of spirits, a shepherd's melody and shepherds' chorus and a hunting-chorus. No overture was specially written for the piece. At the 1st perf. that to the opera *Alfonso und Estrella* was used; later that to the melodrama *Die Zauberharfe* was pub. as *Rosamunde* overture and is still so played.

Rosbaud, Hans (b. Graz, 22. VII. 1895; d. Lugano, 29. XII. 1962), Aus. cond. He studied at the Frankfurt Cons. and began his career as a cond. at Mainz in 1921. His numerous other appts. incl. the Radio Orch. at Baden-Baden, from 1948, the Zürich Opera, 1950–8, and the festivals at Aix-en-Provence and Donaueschingen. He had a unique reputation as an interpreter of contemporary mus.

Rose, the ornamental fretwork soundhole of many flat-bellied string instruments of the lute and guitar type, also of dulcimers, harpsichords, etc., sometimes serving as the makers' trade-mark. Another name for it is Knot.

Rosé, Arnold (Josef) (b. Jassy, Rumania, 24. X. 1863; d. London, 25. VIII. 1946), Aus.-Hung. violinist. He was leader of the opera orch. in Vienna from 1881 to 1938 and founded the R. 4tet in 1882. He married a sister of Mahler.

Rose Cavalier (R. Strauss). *See* **Rosenkavalier.**

Rose et Colas, opera by Monsigny (lib. by Jean Michel Sedaine), prod. Paris, Comédie-Italienne, 8. III. 1764.

Rose, Leonard (b. Washington, D.C.,

Juilliard School of Mus. and the Curtis Inst., and has also pursued a distinguished career as a soloist.

Rose of Castille (*sic*), **The,** opera by Balfe (lib. by Augustus Glossop Harris and Edmund Falconer, based on a Fr. lib., *Le Muletier de Tolède,* by Adolphe Philippe d'Ennery and Clairville, set by A. Adam and prod. 1854), prod. London, Lyceum Theatre, 29. X. 1857.

Rose of Persia, The, or **The Story-Teller and the Slave,** operetta by Sullivan (lib. by Basil Hood), prod. London, Savoy Theatre, 29. XI. 1899.

Roseingrave, Eng. family of musicians:

1. **Daniel R.** (b. ? London, *c.* 1650; d. Dublin, V. 1727), organist and comp. Educ. in mus. as a chorister in the Chapel Royal in London. From 1679–98 he was successively organist of Gloucester, Winchester and Salisbury Cathedrals, and was then app. to St. Patrick's and Christ Church Cathedrals, Dublin.

Works incl. services, anthems, etc.

2. **Thomas R.** (b. Winchester, 1690; d. Dunleary nr. Dublin, 23. VI. 1766), Eng. organist and comp., son of prec. Pupil of his father at Dublin, where he was educ. at Trinity Coll. In 1710 he went to It. where he met A. and D. Scarlatti, making great friends with the latter and travelling with him. He went to London before 1720, when he prod. D. Scarlatti's opera *Narcisco* with interpolations of his own. In 1725 he was app. organist of St. George's church, Hanover Square. He retired in 1741 and moved to Dublin, living prob. with his nephew William R.

Works incl. opera *Phaedra and Hippolytus* (on Edmund Smith's play based on Racine); services and anthems; org. voluntaries and fugues; suites for harpsichord and an intro. piece for his ed. of Scarlatti's sonatas; 12 solos for fl. and harpsichord; 6 It. cantatas, etc.

3. **Ralph R.** (b. Salisbury, *c.* 1695; d. Dublin, 1747), Eng. organist and comp., brother of prec. Studied with his father, who petitioned for him to succeed him as organist of St. Patrick's Cathedral, Dublin, in 1719; but he was app. vicarchoral and not organist till 1726. He also

became organist of Christ Church Cathedral on his father's death.
Works incl. services, anthems, etc.
Rosenberg, Hilding (Constantin) (b. Bosjökloster, 21. VI. 1892), Swed. cond. and comp. Studied at the Stockholm Cons., and at Dresden, Berlin, Vienna and Paris. On his return to Swed. he was cond. of the Stockholm Opera from 1932 to 1934.
Works incl. operas *Journey to America* (incl. *Railway Fugue*), *The Marionettes* (on Benavente's *Los intereses creados*), *The Isle of Felicity* and *The Two Princesses*; choreographic pantomime *The Last Judgment*; ballet *Orpheus in the City*, incid. mus. for Sophocles' *Oedipus Tyrannus*, Euripides' *Medea* and plays by Calderón, Goethe, Musset, O'Neill, Masefield and Obey; film mus.; 6 symphs. (incl. No. 2 *Sinfonia grave*, No. 3 *The 4 Ages of Man*, No. 4 *The Revelation of St. John*), 2 *Sinfonie da chiesa*, *Adagio non troppo*, *3 Fantasy Pieces* for orch.; chamber symph., concerto and suite on Swed. folk tunes for strings, vln. concerto, cello concerto; 12 string 4tets, trios for fl., vln. and vla, and for ob., clar. and bassoon; sonata and suite for vln. and pf., sonatina for fl. and pf., sonata for unaccomp. vln.; pf. suite,etc.
Rosenhain, Jacob (b. Mannheim, 2. XII. 1813; d. Baden-Baden, 21. III. 1894), Ger. pianist and comp. Studied with Kalliwoda, Schnyder von Wartensee and others, and made his 1st appearance as a pianist at Frankfurt in 1832. He visited London in 1837 and then settled in Paris, where he played and taught.
Works incl. operas *Der Besuch im Irrenhause*, *Liswenna* (*Le Démon de la Nuit*), *Volage et jaloux*; 3 symphs.; pf. concerto; 3 string 4tets, 4 pf. trios; 2 cello and pf. sonatas; sonata, studies and pieces for pf.; songs, etc.
Rosenkavalier, Der (*The Rose Cavalier*), opera by R. Strauss (lib. by Hugo von Hofmannsthal), prod. Dresden, Royal Opera, 26. I. 1911.
Rosenmüller, Johann (b. Ölsnitz, Saxony, c. 1619; d. Wolfenbüttel, IX. 1684), Ger. comp. Studied at Leipzig Univ. and in 1642 became asst. master at St. Thomas's School there, studying mus. with the cantor, Tobias Michael, and acting as his deputy when he became infirm. He was marked out for the succession and in 1651 became organist of St. Nicholas's Church; but in 1655 he was imprisoned for a homosexual offence, escaping to Hamburg and later fleeing to Venice, where he settled and was influenced as a comp. by the local style. There J. P. Krieger became his pupil. In 1674 he was recalled to Ger. by an appt. to the court of Duke Anton Ulrich of Brunswick, at Wolfenbüttel.

Works incl. Masses, motets, vesper psalms and Lamentations, Lat. and Ger. motets *Kernsprüche* for 3–7 voices and instruments, Ger. motets and cantatas, hymns, hymn by Albinus 'Straf mich nicht'; *Sonate da camera* for 5 instruments, sonatas for 2–5 instruments, suites of instrumental dances, etc.
Rosenthal, Manuel (orig. **Emmanuel**) (b. Paris, 18. VI. 1904), Fr. cond. and comp. Studied at the Paris Cons., with Ravel and others. He became leader of var. orchs. From 1935 to 1939 and from 1944 to 1946 he cond. the Fr. Nat. Radio Orch. and from 1949 to 1951 the Seattle Symph. Orch.
Works incl. operas *Rayon des soieries* and *Hop Signor!*; operettas *Les Bootleggers* and *La Poule noire*; ballet *Un Baiser pour rien*; oratorio *Saint François d'Assise*; suite *Jeanne d'Arc*, *Fête du vin*, *Les Petits Métiers*, serenade for orch.; sonatina for 2 vlns. and pf.; pf. pieces; songs, etc.
Rosenthal, Moriz (b. Lwów, 18. XII. 1862; d. N.Y., 3. IX. 1946), Pol. pianist, son of a prof. at the Academy of Lwów. He began to learn the pf. at the age of 8 and in 1872 entered the Lwów Cons., where he studied under the director Carl Mikuli. In 1875 the family moved to Vienna, where he continued his studies under Joseffy. He gave his 1st recital there in 1876 and then began to tour, finishing his studies with Liszt and also qualifying in philosophy. In 1895 he 1st appeared in Eng.
Rosetti, Francesco Antonio. See Rösler.
Rosin (also called Resin), a preparation made of gum of turpentine applied to the hair of the bows of string instruments to prod. the required friction on the strings.
Rosina, ballad opera by Shield (lib. by Frances Brooke, based on an episode in Thomson's *Seasons* and Favart's *Les Moissonneurs* with Duni's mus.), prod. London, Covent Garden Theatre, 31. XII. 1782.
Roslavets, Nikolai Andreievich (b. Surai, Gvt. of Tchernigov, 5. I. 1881; d. Moscow, 23. VIII. 1944), Rus. comp. He came of peasant stock, but studied mus. at the Moscow Cons. and attracted attention by his advanced tendencies.
Works incl. cantata *Heaven and Earth* (after Byron); symph., 2 symph. poems; 5 string 4tets, 5tet for ob., 2 vlns., cello and harp, 2 pf. trios; 5 vln. and pf. sonatas, 2 cello and pf. sonatas; many pf. pieces; songs, etc.
Rösler, Franz Anton (b. Litomeřice, c. 1750; d. Ludwigslust, Mecklenburg-Schwerin, 30. VI. 1792), Boh. comp. Destined for the priesthood, he attended the Jesuit Coll. of Olomouc, but in 1773

entered the service of the Prince of Otting-en as double bass player and later became cond. He left for Ludwigslust in 1789 and was court mus. director there to his death. He wrote under the name of Francesco Antonio Rosetti.

Works incl. opera *Das Winterfest der Hirten*; oratorios *Der sterbende Jesus* and *Jesus in Gethsemane*; Requiem for Mozart; 34 symphs.; concertos for pf., vln., fl., ob., clar. and horn; chamber mus.; vln. son-atas, etc.

Rosmene, La, ovvero L'Infedeltà fedele (*R., or Faithful Faithlessness*), opera by A. Scarlatti (lib. by Giuseppe Domenico de Totis), prod. Naples, Palazzo Reale, Carnival 1688.

Rossellini, Renzo (b. Rome, 2. II. 1908), It. comp. Pupil of Sallustio, Setacioli and Molinari.

Works incl. operas *Alcassino e Nicoletta* and *La querra*; ballets *La danza di Dassine* (mus. adapted from *Hoggar* suite) and *La Guerra Racconto d'inverno*; 2 oratorios; film mus.; rhapsodic suite *Hoggar*, *Preludio all' Aminta del Tasso*, *Canti di marzo* and *Ditirambo a Dioniso* for orch.; pf. trio, etc.

Rossello, Franceso. *See* Roussel, Fran-çois.

Rosseter, Philip (b. ?, *c.* 1568; d. London, 5. V. 1623), Eng. lutenist and comp. Worked in London and was assoc. with R. Jones, Kingham and Reeve in the training of the children for the queen's revels; also with Campian, with whom he was on terms of friendship and pub. a book of songs to the lute, some if not all of the words by Campian and half of the mus. by R.

Works incl. *A Booke of Ayres* with lute, orpheoreon and bass viol; *Lessons for the Consort* for 6 instruments by var. comps., etc.

Rossetti, Christina (Georgina) (1830–1894), Eng. poetess of It. descent. *See* Finzi (Children's Songs), Ireland (J.) (*Mother and Child*).

Rossetti, Dante Gabriel (1828–82), Eng. poet and painter of It. descent, brother of prec. *See* Bainton (*Blessed Damozel*), Damoiselle élue (Debussy), Gasco (*Sette torri*), Orr (C. W.) (songs), Vaughan Williams (*Willow Wood*, *Silent Noon* and *House of Life*), Wallace (W.) (*Sister Helen*), White (F.) (*Astarte Syriaca*).

Rossetto, Stefano (b. Nice, ?; d. ?), It. 16th-cent. organist and comp. He lived at Florence in the 1560s as musician to Cardinal de' Medici, was court or-ganist at Munich in 1579–80 and later (?) organist at Novara.

Works incl. motets in 5–6 parts for voice and instruments in different com-binations; madrigal cycle *Il lamento di Olimpia*, other madrigals for 4–6 voices, etc.

Rossi, Giovanni Gaetano (b. Borgo San Donnino nr. Parma, 5. VIII. 1828; d. Genoa, 30. III. 1886), It. cond. and comp. Studied at the Milan Cons. App. leader of the theatre orch. and organist at the court chapel of Parma; director of the Cons. there in 1864–73; cond. of the Teatro Carlo Felice at Genoa, 1873–9.

Works incl. operas *Elena di Taranto*, *Giovanni Giscala*, *Nicolò de' Lapi*, *La Contessa d'Altemberg*; 3 Masses, Re-quiem; oratorio; symph *Saul*, etc.

Rossi, Lauro (b. Macerata, 19. II. 1810; d. Cremona, 5. V. 1885), It. comp. Studied at Naples with Zingarelli and others, and began to prod. operas at the age of 18. He had much success in It. cities until 1835, when he left for Mex. in disgust after a failure. Thence he went as far as India, but returned to Eur. in 1843 and again prod. many operas. In 1870 he succeeded Mercadante as director of the Naples Cons.

Works incl. operas *Le contesse villane*, *Il casino di campagna*, *Costanza ed Orin-galdo*, *La casa disabitata*, *Amelia*, *Leo-cadia*, *Cellini a Parigi*, *Azema di Granata*, *Il borgomastro di Schiedam*, *Il domino nero*, *Bianca Contarini*, *La Contessa di Mons*, *La figlia di Figaro*, *Biorn* (after Shakespeare's *Macbeth*) and 15 others; oratorio *Saul*; Mass; 6 fugues for strings; elegies on the deaths of Bellini and Mer-cadante, etc.

Rossi, Luigi (b. Torremaggiore, 1598; d. Rome, 19. II. 1653), It. singer and comp. He was in the service of Cardinal Bar-berini in Rome from 1641 to 1646. In 1646 he was called to Paris at the instigation of Mazarin and prod. his *Orfeo* in 1647 as one of the 1st It. operas to be given there.

Works incl. operas *Il palagio d'Atlante* (or *Il palazzo incantato*), *L'Orfeo*; oratorio *Giuseppe, figlio di Giacobbe*, cantatas, etc.

Rossi, Michel Angelo (b. ? Rome, *c.* 1600; d. ? Faenza, *c.* 1670), It. organist and comp. Pupil of Frescobaldi. His opera *Erminia sul Giordano*, to a lib. by (?) Giulio Rospigliosi, later Pope Clement IX, was given in Rome in 1633.

Works incl. operas *Erminia sul Giordano* (after Tasso) and *Andromeda*; toccatas and *correnti* for org. or harpsichord, etc.

Rossi, Salomone (b. ?, *c.* 1570; d. ?, Mantua, *c.* 1630), It. comp. He worked at the court of Mantua and enjoyed the privilege of dispensing with the wearing of the yellow badge that stigmatized the Jews in It.

Works incl. mus. for Guarini's *Idropica* and oratorio *Maddalena* (both with Monte-verdi and others); 28 Hebrew psalms for 4–8 voices; madrigals and canzonets; in-strumental works *Sinfonie e gagliarde* and *Sonate*, etc.

Rossignol, Félix Ludger. *See* Joncières.

Rossignol, Le (Stravinsky). *See* **Nightingale.**

Rossini, Gioacchino (Antonio) (b. Pesaro, 29. II. 1792; d. Passy nr. Paris, 13. XI. 1868), It. comp. His father was a horn and tpt. player, his mother a singer in a small way. He learnt pf., singing and harmony early and at 10 sang in churches in Bologna; at 13 he was employed as an accompanist at the theatre; at 15, when he had already tried his hand at an opera and other works, he entered the Bologna Liceo Musicale, studying counterpoint and cello. In 1808 he won a prize with a cantata and in 1810 had his 1st comic opera, *La cambiale di matrimonio,* prod. at Venice. From that time he went from success to success, the 1st great one being *Tancredi* at Venice in 1813, but *Il barbiere di Siviglia* was at first a failure in Rome in 1816. His 1st great foreign success came during a visit to Vienna in 1822, soon after his marriage to the Span. soprano Isabella Colbran, 16. III. *Semiramide,* prod. at Venice in 1823, was his last opera written for the It. stage: he and his wife went to Paris and to London that year, remaining in Eng. until VII. 1824, being well received at court. He wrote a lament on the death of Byron for 8 voices.

On returning to Paris he was app. director of the Théâtre Italien, where he prod. a new and 2 revised works, followed by a Fr. comic opera, *Le Comte Ory,* and finally *Guillaume Tell* (1829) at the Opéra. After that, although only 37, he gave up opera and lived alternatively at Bologna and Paris. In 1832, at Aix-les-Bains, he met Olympe Pélissier, a *demi-mondaine,* and entered into a liaison with her; his separation from Isabella was legalized in 1837, she d. in 1845, and he married Olympe on 21. VIII. 1846. He wrote very little at this time and took 10 years to complete the *Stabat Mater* (1831–41). In 1839 he was commissioned to reform the Liceo Musicale at Bologna, where he had once been a pupil, and he worked there at intervals until 1848, when he left for Florence, to remain until 1855, leaving It. for the last time for Paris that year. In his retirement he wrote many small pieces for the entertainment of his friends and in 1863 the *Petite Messe solennelle*; and his dinner parties, for which he cooked the food himself, were much sought after.

Works incl. operas *La cambiale di matrimonio, L'equivoco stravagante, L'inganno felice, Ciro in Babilonia, La scala di seta, La pietra del paragone, L'occasione fà il ladro, Il signore Bruschino, Tancredi, L'Italiana in Algeri, Aureliano in Palmira, Il Turco in Italia, Sigismondo, Elisabetta, regina d'Inghilterra, Torvaldo e Dorliska, Il barbiere di Siviglia* (after Beaumarchais), *La gazzetta, Otello* (after Shakespeare), *La*

Cenerentola, La gazza ladra, Armida, Adelaida di Borgogna, Mosè in Egitto, Adina, Ricciardo e Zoraide, Ermione (on Racine's *Andromaque), Edoardo e Cristina, La donna del lago* (after Scott), *Bianca e Falliero, Maometto secondo, Matilda di Shabran, Zelmira, Semiramide, Il viaggio a Reims, Le Siège de Corinthe* (Fr. revised version of *Maometto secondo), Moise* (Fr. revised version of *Mosè in Egitto), Le Comte Ory, Guillaume Tell* (after Schiller); 15 cantatas; *Missa solenne, Stabat Mater, La Foi, l'Espérance, la Charité, Petite Messe solenelle* and some shorter sacred pieces; *Soirées musicales* (songs and duets); *Péchés de vieillesse* (small pf. pieces, songs, etc.); a number of works written in his youth incl. the opera *Demetrio e Polibio,* a Mass for male voices, duets for horns, 2 overtures and 5 string 4tets. 6 pasticcios with mus. from his works were prod. in his lifetime, and a modern one is the ballet *La Boutique fantasque* arr. by Respighi from *Péchés de vieillesse,* etc.

Rostal, Max (b. Teschen, 7. VIII. 1905), Aus. violinist of Brit. nationality. Studied with Rosé and Flesch, and in 1927 became leader of the Oslo Phil. Orch. In 1928 he was asst. Flesch in his teaching and from 1930 to 1933 was prof. at the Berlin Hochschule für Musik. Since 1934 he has lived in Eng. and from 1944 to 1958 was prof. at the G.S.M. In 1957 he became a prof. at the Cologne Cons., and in 1958 at Berne. Among his many pupils have been members of the Amadeus Quartet. Although much of his time is spent teaching, his technical excellence and musicianship make him one of the leading violinists of the day.

Rostand, Edmond (1868–1918), Fr. poet and dramatist. *See* **Addinsell** *(Aiglon),* **Aiglon** (Honegger and Ibert), **Cyrano de Bergerac** (Alfano and W. Damrosch), **Gipps** *(Chantecler),* **Hahn** *(Bois sacré),* **Hüe** *(Romanesques),* **Jacobson** *(Woman of Samaria),* **Maclean (A.)** *(Cyrano de B.),* **Montemezzi** *(Princess lointaine),* **Nouguès** *(Cyrano de B.),* **Ollone** *(Samaritaine),* **Pierné** *(Princesse l.),* **Stoessel** *(Cyrano de B.),* **Tcherepnin (N.)** *(Princesse l.),* **Wagenaar (J.)** *(Cyrano de B.),* **Witkowski** *(Princesse l.).*

Rostropovich, Mstislav (Leopoldovich) (b. Baku, 27. III. 1927), Rus. cellist and comp. Studied at the Moscow Cons., where he became a prof. in 1957. He rapidly acquired a world-wide reputation as a soloist. He is also an accomplished pianist.

Rota (Lat. = wheel), another form of the name of the Rote or Rotte; also an old term for a Round, e.g. *Sumer is icumen in,* known as the Reading R.

Rota, Andrea (b. Bologna, *c.* 1553; d. Bologna, VI. 1597), It. comp. He became choirmaster at San Petronio at Bologna in 1583.

Works incl. Masses, motets, *Agnus Dei* (with double canon), *Dixit Dominus* for 8 voices and other church mus.; madrigals, etc.

Rota, Nino (b. Milan, 3. XII. 1911), It. comp. Studied with Pizzetti, Casella and in U.S.A. On his return to Milan he obtained a degree with a treatise on Zarlino and It. Renaissance mus. App. director of the Bari Cons. in 1950.

Works incl. operas *Il principe porcaro* (after Hans Andersen) and *Ariodante* (after Ariosto); oratorio *L'infanzia di San Giovanni Battista*; 2 Masses; 3 symphs., serenade and concerto for orch.; *Invenzioni* for string 4tet, 5tet for fl., ob., vla., cello and harp., *Il presepio* for voice, string 4tet and pf.; sonatas for vln. and pf., vla. and pf. and fl. and harp; songs *Liriche di Tagore, Tre liriche infantili*; film mus., etc.

Rote, an obs. instrument of the lyre type, also called Rota or Rotte, and similar to the Crwth. It was in use up to medieval times.

Rothenberger, Anneliese (b. Mannheim, 19. VI. 1926), Ger. soprano. Studied at Mannheim Musikhochschule and made her début in Coblenz in 1947. In 1956 she became a member of the Deutsche Oper am Rhein, and in 1958 of the Vienna State Opera. She is equally at home in the classical and modern repertory and is one of the most successful singers on the Ger. stage.

Rotte. *See* Rote.

Rouge, Guillaume (? = Guillaume Ruby) (b. ?; d. *c.* 1451), French comp. active at the Burgundian court under John the Fearless and Philip the Good. Comp. *chansons* and a Mass, *Soyez aprantis.*

Rouget de Lisle, Claude Joseph (b. Lons-le-Saulnier, 10. V. 1760; d. Choisy-le-Roi, 26–7. VI. 1836), Fr. soldier, author and musician. Having embarked on a military career, he was stationed at Strasbourg in 1791 and made a name as poet, violinist and singer. He wrote the *Hymne à la liberté,* set by I. Pleyel, that year and words and mus. of the *Marseillaise* in 1792. Similar later pieces of the kind were *Hymne dithyrambique, Le Chant des vengeances, Le Chant des combats, Hymne à la Raison, Hymne du 9 Thermidor* and *Les Héros du Vengeur.* He also wrote libs., incl. *Bayard dans Bresse* for Champein and *Macbeth* (based on Shakespeare) for Chelard.

Roulade. *See* Ornaments.

Round, a kind of Canon best defined by saying that its successive entries consist of complete melodies rather than mere phrases. The entries are thus apt to lie farther apart. Unlike canons, R.s are always sung with the theme in its orig.

position or in the octave, never at other intervals. An older name for the R. was Rota : *Sumer is icumen in,* known as the 'Reading Rota', is a typical early R. A familiar later ex. is in the 2nd finale of Mozart's *Così fan tutte.*

Rounds, round dances, i.e. dances perf. in circles, and hence tunes intended for such dances.

Rousseau, Jean Baptiste (1669–1741), Fr. poet. *See* Floquet (*Gloire du Seigneur*), **Vénus et Adonis** (Desmarets).

Rousseau, Jean-Jacques (b. Geneva, 28. VI. 1712; d. Ermenonville nr. Paris, 2. VII. 1778), Swiss-Fr. philosopher, author and comp. He was a chorister at Annecy Cathedral but had little formal training in mus. Went to Paris in 1741, where he presented a paper to the Académie des Sciences advocating a new system of notation (pub. in 1743 as *Dissertation sur la musique moderne*), and later contrib. mus. articles to Diderot's *Encyclopédie* which were severely criticized by Rameau for their inaccuracy. As secretary to the Fr. ambassador in Venice 1743–4 he became acquainted with It. mus., and during the Guerre des Bouffons sided with the It. party, decrying Fr. mus. in his controversial essay, *Lettre sur la musique française* (1753). His most important comp., the one-act *intermède Le Devin du village,* though in Fr., was supposedly written in tuneful It. style. In 1767 he pub. his valuable *Dictionnaire de musique.* The 'monodrama' *Pygmalion* (1770), only 2 pieces of which were by R., attempted to found a new form, and in its combination of spoken words and mus. was the ancestor of the later melodrama. Among his other writings are 2 essays in support of Gluck.

Comps. incl. operas *Iphis et Anaxerète, La Découverte du nouveau monde, Le Devin du village, Daphnis et Chloé* (unfinished); opera-ballet *Les Muses galantes;* monodrama *Pygmalion; c.* 100 songs, etc., pub. as *Consolations des misères de ma vie,* etc.

Rousseau, Marcel (Auguste Louis; called **Marcel Samuel-R.)** (b. Paris, 18. VIII. 1882; d. Paris, 11. VI. 1955), Fr. comp. Pupil of his father and of Lenepveu. He took the 2nd Prix de Rome in 1905.

Works incl. operas *Tarass-Boulba* (after Gogol), *Le Hulla, Le Bon Roi Dagobert* and *Yamilé sous les cèdres;* ballet *Promenade dans Rome;* incid. mus. for Racine's *Bérénice,* etc.

Rousseau, Samuel (Alexandre) (b. Neuve-Maison, Aisne, 11. VI. 1853; d. Paris, 1. X. 1904), Fr. comp., father of prec. Studied at the Paris Cons., gaining the Prix de Rome in 1878. He became *maître de chapelle* at the church of Sainte-Clotilde and held other mus. offices.

Works incl. operas *Dianora, La Cloche du Rhin, Mérowig, Milia* and *Leone*; Masses, motets and other church mus.; symph. poems *Sabinus, Kaddir, La Florentine*; cantata *La Fille de Jephté* and other choral works; org. and pf. works; instrumental pieces, etc.

Roussel, Albert (b. Tourcoing, 5. IV. 1869; d. Royan, 23. VIII. 1937), Fr. comp. Educ. in Paris for the Navy, but took pf. lessons at the same time. Wrote his 1st comps. while engaged in naval service and voyaging to the E., but he resigned in 1893 to devote himself to mus., studying with Gigout and d'Indy. In 1902 he became prof. at the Schola Cantorum, where he had studied. In the 1914–18 war he served with the Red Cross and later with the transport service, in 1918 retired, broken in health, to Perros-Guirec in Brittany and in 1920 to a villa nr. Varengeville.

Works incl. operas *Padmâvati, La Naissance de la lyre*; operetta *Le Testament de Tante Caroline*; ballets *Le Festin de l'araignée, Bacchus et Ariane, Énée, Les Enchantements d'Alcine* (after Ariosto) and contrib. to *L'Éventail de Jeanne*; incid. mus. to Jean-Aubry's *Le Marchand de sable qui passe*, prelude to Act II of Rolland's *14 Juillet* (with 6 others); Psalm lxxx for tenor, chorus and orch. (in Eng.); 4 symphs. (No. 1 *Le Poème de la forêt*), *3 Évocations* (3rd with chorus), *Pour une fête de printemps, Suite en Fa, Concert, Petite Suite, Rapsodie flamande* for orch.; sinfonietta for strings; *A Glorious Day* for military band; pf. concerto, concertino for cello and orch.; string 4tet, *Divertissement* for wind and pf., serenade for fl., vln., vla., cello and harp, string trio, trios for vln. clar. and pf. and fl., vln. and clar.; 2 vln. and pf. sonatas, *Joueurs de flûte* for fl. and pf.; Impromptu for harp; *Segovia* for guitar; suite *Des heures passent, Rustiques*, suite, sonatina, prelude and fugue (*Hommage à Bach*), etc., for pf.; songs *6 Odes anacréontiques, 2 Poèmes chinois*, 8 poems by Henri de Régnier, 2 poems by Ronsard, *A Flower given to my Daughter* (James Joyce), etc.

Roussel, François (Francesco Rossello) (b. ?; d. ?), Fr. or It. 16th-cent. musician. Succeeded Ferrabosco as master of the children at Santa Maria Maggiore in Rome, 1548–50. In 1572–3 he was *maestro di cappella* at San Giovanni in Laterano there.

Works incl church mus., etc.

Roux, Gaspard Le. *See* Le Roux.

Rovescio. *See* Cancrizans, Palindrome and Recte et retro.

Rovetta, Giovanni (b. Venice, ?; d. Venice, VIII. 1668), It. priest. and comp. Learnt mus. as a choir-boy at St. Mark's in Venice and in 1623 was app. a bass

there. He was ordained priest, became vice-*maestro di cappella* at St. Mark's in 1627 and 1st *maestro di cappella* in succession to Monteverdi in 1644.

Works incl. Masses, motets, psalms, operas, madrigals, etc.

Rowe, Nicholas (1674–1718), Eng. dramatist. *See* Conti (C.) (*Giovanna Shore*), Eccles (*The Biter*), Lenton (*Tamerlane* and *Fair Penitent*).

Rowe, Walter (b. ?; d. ?), Eng. 16th–17th-cent. violinist and comp. He was at Hamburg before 1614, when he was app. violist at the court chapel in Berlin. His son (d. Berlin, 1671) had the same name and occupation.

Works incl. mus. for vla. da gamba.

Rowley, Alec (b. London, 13. III. 1892; d. London, 11. I. 1958), Eng. pianist, teacher and comp. Studied at the R.A.M. in London and became prof. and examiner at Trinity Coll. of Mus. there in 1920.

Works incl. mimed ballet *The Princess who lost a Tune*; *Burlesque Quadrilles* for orch.; 2 pf. concertos (1st with military band), rhapsody for vla. and orch., ob. concerto; suite for chorus (without words); string 4tet, 2 trios for fl., ob. and pf.; many pf. pieces, mainly educ., etc.

Roxelane, La, authentic name of Haydn's symph. No. 63 in C maj., comp. *c.* 1777–80, so called apparently after an old Fr. melody used for variations in the slow movement.

Roy, Adrien Le. *See* Le Roy.

Roy, Bartolomeo (b. Burgundy, ?; d. Naples, 1598), comp. of Fr. origin who lived for a time in Rome, and from 1583 until his death as *maestro di cappella* at the royal palace at Naples. Comp. madrigals and church mus.

Royal Academy of Music, founded in London in 1822 and opened in III. 1823 with Crotch as principal, who was followed by Potter (1832), Charles Lucas (1859), Sterndale Bennett (1866), Macfarren (1875), Mackenzie (1888), McEwen (1924), Stanley Marchant (1936), Reginald Thatcher (1949), Thomas Armstrong (1955), Anthony Lewis (1968).

Royal College of Music, founded in London in 1882 and opened on 7. V. 1883 with Grove as director, who was followed by Parry (1894), Hugh Allen (1918), George Dyson (1938), Ernest Bullock (1953), Keith Falkner (1960).

Royal Musical Association, a society formed to hold lectures on mus. research, to be pub. annually in *Proceedings of the R.M.A.* It was founded in London in 1874 as The Mus. Association and became 'Royal' in 1944. 8 meetings are held annually.

Royal Philharmonic Society, a society formed in London for the cultivation of good orchestral mus. in 1813 by J. B.

Cramer, P. A. Corri and W. Dance. The 1st concert was given at the Argyll Rooms, 8. III. 1813, cond. by Clementi (at the pf.) and led by J. P. Salomon. Among the 1st members were Attwood, Ayrton, Bishop, Horsley, Knyvett, V. Novello, Potter, Shield, G. Smart, Viotti and Webbe, jun. It has continued uninterruptedly until the present day. Among later conds. were Weber, Mendelssohn, Spohr, Wagner, Sullivan, Mackenzie, H. J. Wood, Nikisch, Chevillard, Elgar, Safonov, Bruno Walter, Beecham, Mengelberg, Stanford, Hamilton Harty, Furtwängler, Weingartner and Monteux. Beethoven figured in the programmes from the first and when he was on his deathbed the R. P. S. sent him the sum of £100.

Roze (née Ponsin), Marie (Hippolyte) (b. Paris, 2. III. 1846; d. nr. Paris, 21. VI. 1926), Fr. soprano. Studied at the Paris Cons. and made her 1st appearance, at the Opéra-Comique, in 1865. Later she also sang at the Opéra and in Brussels, and in 1872 she 1st visited London. She remained in Eng. as a member of the Carl Rosa Opera Co. until 1890, when she returned to Paris to settle down as a teacher.

Rozkošný, Josef Richard (b. Prague, 21. IX. 1833; d. Prague, 3. VI. 1913), Cz. pianist and comp. Studied in Prague and toured as pianist in Aus., Hung., It., Serbia and Rum. Later had a great success as a popular opera comp.

Works incl. operas *Nicholas*, *The Rapids of St. John*, *Cinderella*, *Stoja*, *Zavis of Falkenstein*, *Krakonos*, *The Poacher*, *Satanella*, *The Black Lake*; pf. pieces; songs, etc.

Rózsa, Miklos (b. Budapest, 18. IV. 1907), Amer. comp. of Hung. orig. Studied pf. and comp. in Leipzig, and in 1932 settled in Paris, achieving success as a comp. In 1935 he moved to London, where he worked in the film industry and in 1939 settled in Hollywood, U.S.A.

Works incl. *Ballet Hungarica*; symph., *Scherzo, Theme, Variations and Finale* for orch.; concert overture, serenade for chamber orch.; concerto for string orch.; vln. concerto; string 4tet; pf. 5tet, trio for vln., vla. and clar.; film mus., etc.

Rózycki, Ludomir (b. Warsaw, 6. XI. 1883; d. Katowice, 1. I. 1953), Pol. cond. and comp. Studied with Noskowski at the Warsaw Cons. and with Humperdinck in Berlin. In 1912 he became cond. at Lwów, and later lived by turns in Warsaw and Berlin.

Works incl. operas *Bolesław the Bold*, *Medusa*, *Eros and Psyche*, *Casanova*, *Beatrice Cenci*, *The Devil's Mill*; ballet *Pan Twardowski*; symph. poems *Bolesław the Bold*, *Anhelli* and others, prelude *Mona Lisa Giaconda* and ballad for orch.; pf. concerto in G min.; string 4tet, pf. 5tet,

rhapsody for pf. trio; cello and pf. sonata; pf. pieces; songs, etc.

Rub-a-dub. *See* **Rataplan.**

Rubato (It. lit. 'robbed'), a manner of perf. mus. without adhering strictly to time. Var. rules have been estab. at different times, e.g. that what is taken away by hurrying from the time properly occupied by a comp. as written, must be given back elsewhere by slackening, or that in pf. mus. the right hand only may play R. while the left keeps strict time; but R. should be subject, not to rules, but to feeling, and it cannot be taught to those who have either no mus. sense or an exaggerated notion of it.

Rubbra, Edmund (b. Northampton, 23. V. 1901), Eng. comp. Studied at Reading Univ. and the R.C.M. in London, Holst, Vaughan Williams and R. O. Morris being among his masters. Lecturer at Oxford Univ. from 1947 to 1968.

Works incl. opera *Bee-Bee-Bei*; incid. mus. for Shakespeare's *Macbeth*; Canterbury Mass, *Missa in honorem Sancti Dominici*, Festival Te Deum; *La Belle Dame sans merci* (Keats) and *The Morning Watch* (Henry Vaughan) for chorus and orch.; Masses, motets, madrigals and other choral works; 8 symphs., Double and Triple Fugues, *Improvisations on Virginal Pieces by Farnaby* and Festival Overture for orch.; concerto and *Sinfonia concertante* for pf. and orch., rhapsody for vln. and orch., vla. concerto, pf. concerto, *Soliloquy* for cello and small orch.; works for voice and orch.; 3 string 4tets, trio for vln., cello and pf. and other chamber mus.; 5 sonnets by Spenser for voice and string 4tet; 3 sonatas and sonatina for vln. and pf., cello and pf. sonata; pf. and org. mus.; songs, etc.

Rubebe
or   }(Eng., obs.), other old words
Rubible
for the Rebec, or for a slightly different instrument of the same type.

Rubinelli, Giovanni Battista (b. Brescia, 1753; d. Brescia, 1829), It. castrato alto. Made his début in 1771 in Stuttgart, where he was in the service of the Duke of Württemberg, but from 1774 sang in the leading It. opera houses. Visited London in 1786, singing in revivals of operas by Handel. He retired in 1800.

Rubini, Giovanni Battista (b. Romano nr. Bergamo, 7. IV. 1794; d. Romano, 2. III. 1854), It. tenor. He began with small engagements, but made his way to Venice, Naples and Rome, where his successes in opera increased steadily. In 1819 he married the Fr. singer Chomel at Naples, visited Paris for the 1st time in 1825 and London in 1831. In 1843 he toured Hol. and Ger. with Liszt, and went on alone to St. Petersburg.

Rubinstein, Anton Grigorievich (b. Vykhvatinets, Volhynia, 28. XI. 1829; d. Peterhof, 20. XI. 1894), Rus. pianist and comp. of Ger.-Pol. descent. Learnt the pf. from his mother and from a teacher named Villoing at Moscow. He appeared in public at the age of 9 and in 1840 went on tour with his teacher, who took him to Paris and placed him under Liszt for further instruction. He afterwards went to Eng., Hol., Ger. and Swed. and from 1844 to 1846 studied comp. with Dehn in Berlin. After teaching in Vienna and Pressburg he returned to Rus. in 1848, becoming chamber virtuoso to the Grand Duchess Helena Pavlovna. From 1854 onward he again travelled widely as a pianist and in 1858 he was app. imp. mus. director at St. Petersburg, founding the Cons. in 1862.

Works incl. operas and stage oratorios, *Dimitry Donskoy*, *The Siberian Hunters*, *Children of the Heath*, *Feramors* (from Moore's *Lalla Rookh*), *The Tower of Babel*, *The Demon* (after Lermontov), *The Maccabees* (after Otto Ludwig), *Paradise Lost* (after Milton), *Nero*, *The Merchant of Moscow*, *The Shulamite*, *Moses*, *Christus* and others; Songs and Requiem for Mignon from Goethe's *Wilhelm Meister* for solo voices, chorus and pf.; 6 symphs. (2. *Ocean*, 4. *Dramatic*), 4 concert overtures (1 on Shakespeare's *Antony and Cleopatra*, mus. portraits *Faust* (after Goethe), *Ivan the Terrible*, *Don Quixote* (after Cervantes), suite in E♭ maj. for orch.; 5 concertos and *Conzertstück* for pf. and orch.; vln. concerto, 2 cello concertos; 10 string 4tets, string 5tet and 6tet, octet for pf., strings and wind, 5 pf. trios, pf. and wind 5tet, pf. 5tet and 4tet; 3 vln. and pf. sonatas, vla. and pf. sonata, 2 cello and pf. sonatas; instrumental pieces; 4 sonatas, Theme and Variations and many other works for pf.; *Bal costumé* for pf. duet; numerous songs, etc.

Rubinstein, Artur (b. Lódz, 28. I. 1886), Amer. pianist of Pol. birth. After early studies in Pol. he was sent to Berlin, studying pf. with H. Barth and R. M. Breithaupt, comp. with R. Kahn and with Bruch. He made his début aged 12 in a concert cond. by Joachim. He then studied with Paderewski in Switz., and toured the U.S.A. in 1906. In 1946 he became an Amer. citizen. He is best known for his playing of the classical repertory, to which he brings great virtuosity combined with elegance and poetry.

Rubinstein, Nikolai Grigorievich (b. Moscow, 14. VI. 1835; d. Paris, 23. III. 1881), Rus. pianist and comp., of Ger.-Pol. descent, brother of Anton. Studied under Kullak and Dehn in Berlin and after his return to Rus. settled at Moscow, where he founded the Rus. Mus. Society

in 1859 and the Cons. in 1864, to which he invited Tchaikovsky as prof.

Rubsamen, Walter H(oward) (b. N.Y., 21. VII. 1911), Amer. musicologist. Studied at Columbia Coll., N.Y., and at Munich Univ., later joined the mus. dept. of his coll. and in 1938 became lecturer and in 1955 prof. at the Univ. of California at Los Angeles. His works incl. studies of Pierre de La Rue, old It. secular mus., etc.

Ruby, Guillaume. *See* Rouge, Guillaume.

Ruckers. Flem. family of harpsichord makers:

1. Hans R. (b. Mechlin, *c.* 1550; d. Antwerp, *c.* 1625).

2. Joannes R. (b. Antwerp, I. 1578; d. Antwerp, 1642), son of prec.

3. Andries R. (b. Antwerp, VIII. 1579; d. Antwerp, *c.* 1645), brother of prec.

4. Andries R. (b. Antwerp, 1607; d. Antwerp, *c.* 1670), son of prec.

5. Christophel R. (b. Antwerp, *c.* 1620; d. ?), son of ?.

Rückert, Friedrich (1788–1866), Ger. poet. *See* Kindertotenlieder (Mahler), Rudorff (*Gesang an die Sterne*), also 5 other songs by Mahler, 5 by Schubert, 18 by Schumann, 2 by Brahms.

Ruddigore, or The Witch's Curse, operetta by Sullivan (lib. by W. S. Gilbert), prod. London, Savoy Theatre, 22. I. 1887.

Rudersdorff, Hermine (b. Ivanovsky, Ukraine, 12. XII. 1822; d. Boston, 26. II. 1882), Ger. soprano. Learnt mus. from her father, the violinist Joseph R., and singing in Paris, Milan and London. She made her 1st appearance in Ger. at the age of 18, sang in the prod. of Mendelssohn's *Hymn of Praise* at Leipzig in 1840 and then appeared in opera at Carlsruhe and Frankfurt. In 1854 she 1st visited London, where she remained for a number of years, but settled in Boston in the 1870s.

Rudhyar, Dane (actually Daniel Chennevière) (b. Paris, 23. III. 1895), Fr.-Amer. comp. Studied in Paris and settled in U.S.A. in 1916, receiving a comp. prize in 1920.

Works incl. ballet *Dance Poem*; symph. poem *Surge of Fire* and other orchestral works; pf. pieces, mus. for 2 pfs.; songs, etc.

Rudolph (Johann Joseph Rainer) of Habsburg, Archduke (b. Florence, 8. I. 1788; d. Baden nr. Vienna, 24. VII. 1831), Aus. amateur musician. Pupil of Anton Teyber, mus. instructor of the Imp. children, and later, by his own choice, of Beethoven, who wrote the *Missa solemnis* for his installation as Archbishop of Olomouc (1820), though he finished it 2 years too late.

Works incl. sonata for clar. and pf.; variations for pf. on themes by Beethoven and Rossini, etc.

Rudorff, Ernst (Friedrich Karl) (b. Berlin, 18. I. 1840; d. Berlin, 31. XII. 1916), Ger. pianist, teacher and comp.

Ruggiero, a simple bass line, 1st found in the 16th cent., which was widely used for variations. A typical form is:

RUGGIERO

Pupil of Bargiel, Clara Schumann and others, later studied at the Leipzig Univ. and Cons. In 1865 he became prof. at the Cologne Cons. and in 1869–1910 at the Hochschule für Musik in Berlin. He also cond. Stern's Vocal Acad. in 1880–90. Works incl. *Der Aufzug der Romanze* (Tieck) for solo voices, chorus and orch., *Gesang an die Sterne* (Rückert) for chorus and orch.; 3 symphs., 2 sets of variations, ballad, serenade, 3 overtures for orch.; romance for cello and orch.; string 6tet; variations for 2 pfs.; pieces for pf. solo and duet; songs, part-songs, etc.

Rue, Pierre de la. *See* **La Rue.**

Rufer, Josef (b. Vienna, 18. XII. 1893), Aus. writer on mus. Studied with Zemlinsky and Schönberg, becoming Schönberg's asst. in Berlin from 1925 to 1933. In 1945, with H. H. Stuckenschmidt, he founded the periodical *Stimmen*, and from 1956 taught at the Free Univ. in Berlin. His books on mus. incl. *Composition with 12 notes related only to one another* (a study of Schönberg's methods) and the valuable catalogue *The Works of Arnold Schönberg.*

Ruffo, Vincenzo (b. Verona, *c.* 1510; d. Sacile nr. Udine, 9. II. 1587), It. male soprano and comp. App. *maestro di cappella* at Verona Cathedral in 1554 and in 1563 at that of Milan. He occupied a similar post at Pistoia in 1574–9, but returned to Milan.

Works incl. Masses, motets, Magnificat, psalms and other church mus.; madrigals, etc.

Rugby, Honegger's 2nd symph. movement for orch., following *Pacific 231* and succeeded by *Mouvement symphonique No. 3*. It is an impression of a game of football. 1st perf. Paris, Orchestre Symphonique, 19. X. 1928.

Ruggieri. It. family of vln. makers at Cremona and Brescia:

1. Francesco R. (b. ?; d. ?), worked *c.* 1668–1720.

2. Giovanni Battista R. (b. ?; d. ?), worked *c.* 1700–25.

3. Guido R. (b. ?; d. ?) ⎱
4. Vincenzo R. (b. ?; d. ?) ⎰ Worked early 18th cent.

It may orig. have been a dance, though it is found also in vocal settings. *See also* **Romanesca.**

Ruggiero, o vero L'eroica gratitudine (*Ruggiero, or Heroic Gratitude*), opera by Hasse (lib. by Metastasio), prod. Milan, Teatro Regio Ducal, 16. X. 1771. Hasse's last opera.

Ruggles, Carl (b. Marion, Mass., 11. III. 1876), Amer. comp. and painter. Studied at Harvard Univ., with Walter Spalding and others. Afterwards he cond. the Symph. Orch. at Winona, Minnesota, for a time.

Works incl. opera *The Sunken Bell*; *Men and Angels, Men and Mountains, Portals, The Sun Treaders, Evocations* for orch.; concertino for pf. and orch.; *Vox clamans in deserto* for voice and chamber orch.; *Polyphonic Comps.* for 3 pfs., *Evocations* and other works for pf., etc.

Rührtrommel (Ger.) = Tenor Drum.

Ruimonte, Pedro. *See* **Rimonte.**

Ruins of Athens, The, incid. mus. by Beethoven, Op. 113, for a play by Kotzebue written for the opening of the Ger. theatre at Pest, 9. II. 1812. It comprises an overture and 8 numbers, incl. the *Turkish March*, already comp. by Beethoven for his pf. variations, Op. 76, in 1809.

Rule, Britannia, a patriotic song by Arne, now almost a 2nd Brit. nat. anthem, orig. part of the masque *Alfred* prod. I. VIII. 1740, at Cliefden (now Cliveden) House nr. Maidenhead, the residence of Frederick, Prince of Wales.

Rule of the Octave, an 18th-cent. procedure in the treatment of Thorough-bass, esp. in It. (*regola dell' ottava*), providing a series of simple chords of the tonic, dominant and subdominant for the elementary harmonization of a bass formed by a rising diatonic scale.

Rumanian Composers. *See* **Alessandrescu, Andrico, Constantinescu, Cuclin, Dima, Enesco, Golestan, Mihalovici, Nottara, Otescu.**

Rumba, a Cuban dance of African Negro origin, in quick 2–4 time and making much use of Syncopation. It was intro. in Jazz in the 1920s.

Runeberg, Johan Ludvig (1804–77). Swed. poet. *See* **Sibelius** (*Nights of Jealousy*).

Rung, Frederick (b. Copenhagen, 14. VI. 1854; d. Copenhagen, 22. I. 1914), Dan. cond. and comp. Pupil of his father Henrik R. (1807–71), of Gade and others. He went to the Royal Opera, as coach, became asst. cond. in 1884 and succeeded Svendsen as 1st cond. in 1911. He also taught at the Cons. and Horneman's mus. school and cond. choral societies, incl. a madrigal choir founded by him.

Works incl. operas *The Secret Society* and *The Three-Cornered Hat* (after Alarcón's story); ballet *Aditi* and *A Carnival Jest in Venice*; incid. mus. to Holger Drachman's *1001 Nights* and other plays; symph. in D min., rhapsody, *Suite in the Old Style* and *Danse des papillons* for orch.; suite for tpt. and strings, nonet for woodwind, pf. 5tet, 2 string 4tets; pf. pieces; songs, etc.

Rungenhagen, Carl Friedrich (b. Berlin, 27. IX. 1778; d. Berlin, 21. XII. 1851), Ger. comp. and cond. Worked in Berlin, where he became asst. cond. to Zelter of the Voc. Acad. in 1815 and succeeded to the post of 1st cond. in 1833.

Works incl. 4 operas, 3 oratorios; Mass, *Stabat Mater* for female voices and other church mus.; orchestral works; chamber mus.; songs, etc.

Russalka (*The Water-Sprite*), opera by Dargomizhsky (lib. by comp., from Pushkin's dramatic poem), prod. St. Petersburg, 16. V. 1856.

Opera by Dvořák (lib. by Jaromir Kvapil), prod. Prague, Cz. Theatre, 31. III. 1901.

Russell, Henry (b. Sheerness, 24. XII. 1812; d. London, 8. XII. 1900), Eng. singer, organist and comp. Studied at Bologna and with Rossini at Naples, appeared as singer in London in 1828, lived in Canada and U.S.A. (organist at Rochester, N.Y.) in 1833–41 and then gave entertainments in London with Charles Mackay for which he wrote many popular songs. He was the father of Landon Ronald.

Works incl. songs 'Cheer, boys, cheer', 'There's a good time coming', 'A life on the ocean wave' (march of the Royal Marines), etc.

Russian Bassoon, a Serpent made in the shape of a bassoon.

'Russian' Quartets, one of the nicknames of Haydn's 6 string 4tets, Op. 33, comp. in 1781 and ded. to the Grand Duke of Russia. Also known as *Gli scherzi* or *Jungfernquartette*.

Russlan and Ludmila, opera by Glinka (lib. by Valerian Fedorovich Shirkov and Constantin Alexandrovich Bakhturin,

based on Pushkin's poem), prod. St. Petersburg, 9. XII. 1842.

Russolo, Luigi (b. Portogruoro, 1. V. 1885; d. Cerro, 4. II. 1947), It. comp. In 1909 he joined the Futurist movement of Marinetti and formulated a mus. based on noise, about which he pub. a book in 1916, *L'arte dei rumori*. His futurist manifesto of 1913 expanded the orch. to include explosions, clashes, shrieks, screams and groans. He also invented the Russolophone, which could produce 7 different noises in 12 different gradations.

Works incl. *Meeting of the Automobiles and the Aeroplanes, Awakening of a City*.

Rust, Friedrich Wilhelm (b. Wörlitz nr. Dessau, 6. VII. 1739; d. Dessau, 28. II. 1796), Ger. violinist and comp. Pupil of W. F. Bach in Halle, where he studied law, then of F. Benda and C. P. E. Bach in Berlin, later of G. Benda, Pugnani and Tartini in It. 1765–6. He returned to Dessau in 1766, taught at Basedow's *Philanthropin* from its foundation in 1774, and a year later became municipal mus. director.

Works incl. monodramas and duodramas *Inkle und Yariko, Colma,* etc.; cantatas; odes and songs; pf. sonatas and other keyboard mus., etc.

Rust, Wilhelm (b. Dessau, 15. VIII. 1822; d. Leipzig, 2. V. 1892), Ger. pianist, violinist and comp., grandson of prec. Studied with his uncle W. K. R. and F. Schneider and settled in Berlin as pianist organist and teacher. In 1870 he became prof. at Stern's Cons. there and in 1878 organist and 2 years later cantor at St. Thomas's Church, Leipzig. He ed. his grandfather's pf. sonatas, much modernizing them, on the strength of which ed. d'Indy declared F. W. R. to be a prophetic forerunner of Beethoven.

Works incl. pf. and vocal mus.

Rust, Wilhelm Karl (b. Dessau, 29. IV. 1787; d. Dessau, 18. IV. 1855), Ger. pianist and teacher, uncle of prec. and son of F. W. R. Pupil of his father and of Türk at Halle. In 1807 he went to Vienna, where he met Beethoven, and remained there as teacher until 1827, when he returned to Dessau.

Rutini, Fernando (b. Modena, 1767; d. Terracina, XI. 1827), It. comp. Son and pupil of Giovanni Maria R., later *maestro di cappella* at Macerata and Terracina.

Works incl. over 20 operas; cantatas; sonatas, etc.

Rutini, Giovanni Maria (also called G. Marco and G. Placido) (b. Florence, 25. IV. 1723; d. Florence, 7. XII. 1797), It. comp., father of prec. Pupil of Leo and Fago at the Cons. della Pietà dei Turchini in Naples, he went to Prague in 1748, where his first opera was prod. in 1753. Visited Dresden and Berlin, and went to St.

Petersburg in 1758. Returning to It. in 1762, he was *maestro di cappella* to the Crown Prince of Modena 1765–70, and lived mostly in Florence.

Works incl. *c.* 20 operas, e.g. *Semiramide, Il matrimonio in maschera, L'Olandese in Italia*, etc.; cantatas; vln. sonatas; numerous harpsichord sonatas, etc.

Rutscher (Ger. lit. glider). *See* **Galop.**

Ruy Blas, opera by William Howard Glover (1819–75) (lib. by comp., based on Victor Hugo's drama), prod. London, Covent Garden Theatre, 24. X. 1861.

Opera by Marchetti (lib., in It., by Carlo d'Ormeville, based on Hugo), prod. Milan, Teatro alla Scala, 3. IV. 1869.

Overture and chorus for Hugo's drama by Mendelssohn, Op. 95 and Op. 77 No. 3, comp. for a prod. at Leipzig, 9. III. 1839.

Ruygrok, Leonard (b. Utrecht, 8. V. 1889; d. Hilversum, 3. I. 1944), Dutch cellist and comp. Pupil of Wagenaar for comp. He became 1st cellist in the Residentie orch. at The Hague and in 1924 was app. 2nd cond.

Works incl. incid. mus. for plays; film mus. for *Forty Years, 1898–1938* for Queen Wilhelmina's jubilee; 2 symphs., 4 overtures; Poem for vla. and orch., etc.

Ruyneman, Daniel (b. Amsterdam, 8. VIII. 1886; d. Amsterdam, 25. VII. 1963), Dutch comp. He was trained for commerce and self-taught in mus. He made many experiments with comp. and instruments and invented cup-bells with a rich and long-sustained sonority, which he used in several of his works.

Works incl. psycho-symbolic play with vocal and instrumental orch. *The Clown*; scena for tenor and orch. from Kafka's

Der Prozess; symph., partita for strings, *Hieroglyphs* for chamber orch.; 4 string 4tets; sonata in G maj. and *Klaaglied van een Slaaf* for vln. and pf.; 9 sonatas, 3 *Pathemologies* and sonatina for pf.; 2 Sacred Songs (Tagore) and several other sets, etc.

Rydberg, Abraham Viktor (1828–95), Swed. poet. *See* **Sibelius** (*Skogrået*).

Ryelandt, Joseph (b. Bruges, 7. IV. 1870; d. Bruges, 29. VI. 1965), Belg. comp. Pupil of Tinel.

Works incl. opera *Sainte Cécile*; oratorios *La Parabole des vierges, Purgatorium, De Komst des Heeren, Maria, Agnus Dei* and *Christus Rex*, cantatas *Le Bon Pasteur* and *L'Idylle mystique*; 5 symphs., symph. poem *Gethsémani*, 2 overtures for orch.; chamber mus.; 11 pf. sonatas; numerous songs, etc.

Rysanek, Leonie (b. Vienna, 14. XI. 1926), Aus. soprano. Studied in Vienna with Jerger, and later with R. Grossmann, whom she married. She made her début in Innsbruck in 1949. From 1950 to 1952 she sang at the Saarbrucken Opera, and in 1954 became a member of the Vienna State Opera.

Rytel, Piotr (b. Wilno, 20. IX. 1884), Pol. comp. Studied at the Warsaw Cons., and taught there from 1911 to 1952. He was rector of the Zoppot Cons. from 1952 to 1962. For many years he was active as a critic.

Works incl. opera *Ijola*; ballet *Faun and Psyche*; symph., symph. poems *The Corsair* (Byron), *Grażyna* (Mickiewicz), *Dante's Dream, The Holy Grove, The Legend of St. George, An Intro. to a Drama*; pf. concerto, vln. concerto; chamber mus.; pf. works; songs, etc.

S

s, the Dominant note in any key in Tonic Sol-fa notation, pronounced Soh.

Sabaneiev, Leonid Leonidovich (b. Moscow, 19. XI. 1881), Rus. critic and comp. Studied with Taneiev at the Moscow Cons. and at the univ. there. He left Rus. in 1926 and settled eventually in Fr. He wrote on Skriabin, Debussy and Taneiev. Works. incl. ballet *L'Aviatrice*; symph. poem *Flots d'azur*; chamber mus.; songs; pf. mus., etc.

Sabata, Victor de (b. Trieste, 10. IV. 1892; d. Santa Margherita Ligure, 11. XII. 1967), It. cond. and comp. Studied under his father, a chorus master at the Teatro alla Scala, Milan, and at the Cons. there, with Orefice and others. He became cond. at the Scala and at the Royal Opera in Rome, visited U.S.A. in 1938, cond. at Bayreuth in 1939 and became known in London in 1946.

Works incl. operas *Lisistrata* (after Aristophanes), *Il macigno*, *Mille e una notte*; incid. mus. for Shakespeare's *Merchant of Venice*; symph. poems *Juventus*, *La notte di Platon*, *Gethsemani*, suite for orch., etc.

Sabatier, Caroline. *See* Unger.

Sabbatini, Galeazzo (b. ? Pesaro, 1597; d. ? Pesaro, 6. XII. 1662), It. comp. He was *maestro di cappella* at Pesaro in the 1620s and director of chamber mus. to the Duke of Mirandola in the 1630s. He was also at Bergamo some time. In 1628 he pub. a treatise on thorough-bass.

Works incl. Masses, motets, lauds and other church mus.; madrigals, etc.

Sabbatini, Luigi Antonio (b. Albano Laziale nr. Rome, 1739; d. Padua, 29. I. 1809), It. comp. A pupil of Padre Martini and Vallotti, he was *maestro di cappella* of Marino Cathedral 1766, at the Church of the Holy Apostles in Rome 1772, finally from 1786 at S. Antonio in Padua. He pub. a number of treatises on counterpoint, fugue, etc. Comp. chiefly church mus.

Works incl. Masses, motets, psalms, etc.

Sabbatini, Pietro Paolo (b. Rome, *c.* 1600; d. ? Rome, *c.* 1660), It. comp. He was *maestro di cappella* in Rome, from 1630 of the church of San Luigi de' Francesci, and prof. of mus. from 1650, when he pub. a treatise on thorough-bass, etc.

Works incl. psalms, spiritual songs; *villanelle* and *canzonette* for 1–3 voices, etc.

Sabino, Ippolito (b. Lanciano, Chieto, *c.* 1550; d. ?), It. comp. In 1587 he was employed as a musician in the cathedral of his native town. He pub. many collections of church mus. and madrigals; two of the latter contain madrigals by his brother (?) Giovanni Francesco.

Sackville-West

Sacher, Paul (b. Basle, 28. IV. 1906), Swiss cond. Studied with Nef and Weingartner, and in 1926 founded the Basle Chamber Orch., for which he has commissioned works from many distinguished comps. incl. Bartók (Divertimento), Fortner, Henze, Hindemith, Honegger, Ibert, Křenek, Martin, Martinů, Malipiero, Roussel, Strauss, Stravinsky and Tippett. In 1933 he also founded the distinguished chamber ensemble Schola Cantorum Basiliensis.

Sacchini, Antonio Maria Gaspare (b. Florence, 14. VI. 1730; d. Paris, 6. X. 1786), It. comp. Pupil of Durante at the Cons. Santa Maria di Loreto at Naples, where his intermezzo *Fra Donato* was prod. in 1756. He worked first at the Cons., but prod. his 1st serious opera, *Andromaca*, in 1761, and 3 years later gave up his teaching to devote himself to comp. After a time in Rome he went to Venice in 1769 where he became director of the Ospedaletto. Visited Ger., and in 1772 went to London, remaining there 10 years and prod. many operas. Settling in Paris in 1782, he had the support of Marie Antoinette, and there wrote 2 operas which show the influence of Gluck. But (like Gluck before him) he became unwillingly involved in rivalry with Piccinni, and had little success.

Works incl. *c.* 60 operas, e.g. *Alessandro nell' Indie*, *Semiramide*, *Isola d'amore*, *Il Cidde* (after Corneille), *Renaud*, *Tamerlano*, *Perseo*, *Nitetti*, *Montezuma*, *Rosina*, *Dardanus*, *Oedipe à Colone*, etc.; Masses, motets and other church mus.; 2 symphs.; string 4tets, trio sonatas and other chamber mus.; vln. sonatas, etc.

Sachs, Curt (b. Berlin, 26. VI. 1881; d. N.Y., 5. II. 1959), Ger. musicologist. First studied hist. of art at Berlin Univ., graduating in 1904. After some years as an art critic he studied mus. with Kretzschmar and J. Wolf, specializing in the hist. of mus. instruments. In 1919 he became director of the Berlin Museum of Mus. Instruments, and also prof. at Berlin Univ. From 1933 to 1937 he lived in Paris, then moved to N.Y., where he became prof. at the univ. From 1953 he was also prof. at Columbia Univ., in N.Y. His many writings extend not only over the field of mus. instruments but also over many others.

Sachs, Hans (1494–1576), Ger. cobbler, master-singer, poet and playwright. *See* Forster (*Dot Mon*), **Paumgartner** (*Heisse Eisen*), **Wehrli** (do.). He also plays a prominent part in Wagner's *Die Meistersinger*.

Sackbut, the old Eng. name for the tromb.

Sackville-West, Victoria (1892–1964), Eng. poet and novelist. *See* Maconchy (*The Land*).

Sacountala, ballet by Reyer (scenario by Théophile Gautier, based on Kalidasa's drama; choreography by Lucien Petipa), prod. Paris, Opéra, 14. VII. 1858.

Sacrae Cantiones. *See* **Cantiones sacrae.**

Sacre du printemps, Le (Stravinsky). *See* **Rite of Spring.**

Sadko, opera by Rimsky-Korsakov (lib. by comp. and Vladimir Ivanovich Bielsky), prod. Moscow, 7. I. 1898. The mus. is partly based on Rimsky-Korsakov's symph. poem of the same name, Op. 5, comp. 1867, 1st perf. St. Petersburg, 21. XII. 1867.

Sadler's Wells Opera. The Sadler's Wells theatre was built in the 18th cent., when Islington was a village outside London and Sadler's Wells a watering-place and pleasure garden dating back to the end of the 17th cent. It was used for plays and pantomime into the 19th cent., then became a mus.-hall and later fell into disuse, but was acquired as a northern branch of the Old Vic Theatre for the alternate prod. of classical drama and opera, rebuilt and opened on 6. I. 1931. From 1935 plays were confined exclusively to the Old Vic and opera to Sadler's Wells, which became the only permanent repertory opera-house in Brit. for the prod. of opera in Eng. In 1968 the operas were transferred to the Coliseum.

Saeta (Span.), an unaccomp. Andalusian folksong sung during a halt in a religious procession.

Sæverud, Harald (b. Bergen, 17. IV. 1897), Norw. cond. and comp. Studied at Bergen and Berlin, cond. under Clemens Krauss. He returned to Bergen as cond. and received a state pension for comp. in 1933.
  Works incl. *Minnesota Symph.*; 7 symphs.; concertos for ob., cello, vln. and pf.; incid. mus. for Shakespeare's *Rape of Lucrece* and Ibsen's *Peer Gynt*; 50 variations for chamber orch.; pf. pieces, etc.

Saffo (*Sappho*), opera by Pacini (lib. by Salvatore Cammarano), prod. Naples, Teatro San Carlo, 29. XI. 1840.

Safonov, Vassily Ilich (b. Itsiursk, Terek, 6. II. 1852; d. Kislovodsk, Caucasus, 13. III. 1918), Rus. cond. and pianist. Studied at St. Petersburg; prof. at the Cons. there, 1881, and at Moscow, 1885. Became director of Moscow Cons., 1889. Estab. popular concerts there and was cond. of the Moscow branch of the Rus. Mus. Society, 1890–1905. Appeared frequently in London and N.Y.

Saga, A (*En Saga*), symph. poem by Sibelius, Op. 9, comp. in 1891, 1st perf. Helsinki, 1892, revised in 1901. It depicts no partic. incident, but has a distinctly narrative, ballad-like tone.

Sagbut, another spelling of Sackbut.

Sagittarius, the Lat. form of the name of Schütz, sometimes used on his title-pages. Like his Ger. name it = archer.

Sainete (Span.), a type of comedy with mus.

'St. Anne' Fugue, the fugue in E♭ maj. at the end of Pt. III of Bach's *Clavierübung*, so named in Eng. because its subject is identical with the opening of Croft's (?) hymn-tune *St. Anne*.

'St. Anthony' Variations (Brahms). *See* **'Haydn' Variations.**

St. Elizabeth (Liszt). *See* **Legende von der heiligen Elisabeth.**

Saint-Exupéry, Antoine de (1900–44), Fr. aviator and novelist. *See* **Dallapiccola** (*Volo di notte*).

Saint-Foix, (Marie Olivier) Georges (du Parc Poullain) de, Count (b. Paris, 2. III. 1874; d. Aix-en-Provence, 26. V. 1954), Fr. musicologist. Studied law, and mus. at the Schola Cantorum in Paris. He wrote on var. subjects, incl. Beethoven and Boccherini, but mainly on the classification and analysis of Mozart's works in a large 5-vol. work, the 1st 2 vols. in collaboration with Théodore de Wyzewa.

St. Gall, Swiss monastery famous for its MSS. of Gregorian chant, the earliest of which date back to the 10th cent.

Saint-Huberty (actually Clavel), **Antoinette (Cécile)** (b. Toul, *c.* 1756; d. London, 22. VII. 1812), Fr. soprano. Studied with the cond. Lemoyne at Warsaw and made her 1st appearance there, then sang in Berlin and Strasbourg, and 1st appeared in Paris in 1777. In 1790 she married the Comte d'Entraigues, a royalist, with whom she escaped to Lausanne. In 1797 she rescued her husband from prison at Milan. They went 1st to St. Petersburg and then to London, where they settled and were murdered by a servant.

St. James's Hall, a concert hall in London, between Regent Street and Piccadilly (the site of the present Piccadilly Hotel), opening on 25. III. 1858 and sold for demolition in 1905, when the last concert took place on 11. II. It was large enough for an orch., but used also for chamber mus., partic. the Monday Popular Concerts ('Monday Pops'), at which artists of internat. fame appeared.

St. John Passion, Bach's setting of the Passion narrative as told in St. John's Gospel, with interpolated texts after Brockes and chorales, for soloists, chorus and orch., comp. in Cöthen 1722–3 and perf. in St. Thomas's, Leipzig, on Good Friday, 26. III. 1723, as a trial before Bach's election as Cantor.

Saint-Lambert, (? Michel) de (b. ?; d. ? Paris, ?), Fr. 17th–18th-cent. harpsichord player, teacher and author. He lived and taught in Paris, and wrote 2 books, *Les Principes du clavecin* (1702) and *Nouveau Traité de l'accompagnement* (1707).

St. Ludmilla, oratorio by Dvořák, Op.

71 (Cz. words by Jaroslav Vrchlický), comp. 1886 and perf. in the autumn at the Leeds Festival, in an Eng. trans.

St. Martial, the Benedictine abbey at Limoges. Over 20 MSS. originating from here are extant, dating from the 12th cent. They include tropes, sequences and exs. of early polyphony.

St. Matthew Passion, Bach's setting of the Passion narrative as told in St. Matthew's Gospel, with interpolated texts by Picander and chorales, for soloists, chorus and orch., comp. in Leipzig 1728–9 and perf. in St. Thomas's on Good Friday, 15. IV. 1729.

St. Paul, oratorio by Mendelssohn, Op. 36, perf. Düsseldorf, Lower Rhine Festival, 22. V. 1836; in Eng., Liverpool, 7. X. 1836.

St. Philip. *See* **Neri.**

Saint-Pierre, (Jacques Henri) Bernardin de (1737–1814), Fr. naturalist and novelist. For works based on *Paul et Virginie see* **Gavazzeni** (opera), **Lesueur** (do.), **Mazzinghi** (do.), **Montemezzi** (symph. poem), **Paolo e Virginia** (P. C. Guglielmi), **Paul et Virginie** (R. Kreutzer and Massé), **Reeve** (opera).

Saint-Saëns, (Charles) Camille (b. Paris, 9. X. 1835; d. Algiers, 16. XII. 1921), Fr. comp. He began to comp. at the age of 5 and played the pf. well at that age. Gave a public recital in 1846 and entered the Cons. as an org. scholar in 1848, gaining a 1st prize in 1851, when he entered Halévy's class for comp. App. organist at the church of Saint-Merry in Paris, 1853, the Madeleine, 1857, and pf. prof. at the École Niedermeyer in 1861. His 1st 2 symphs. were perf. in 1853 and 1857, he played his 2nd pf. concerto in 1868 and founded the Société Nationale de Musique with Romain Bussine in 1871. He played in Eng. several times from 1871 and toured Spain and Port. in 1880. The biblical opera *Samson et Dalila,* begun in 1868 and prohibited on the Fr. stage on account of its subject, was prod. by him at Weimar in 1877; it was allowed in Paris from 1892, the year he received the hon. Mus. D. at Cambridge. In 1906 he visited the U.S.A., and again in 1916, together with S. Amer.

Works inc. operas *La Princesse jaune, Le Timbre d'argent, Étienne Marcel, Samson et Dalila, Henri VIII, Proserpine, Ascanio, Phryné, Les Barbares, Hélène, L'Ancêtre, Déjanire;* ballet *Javotte;* incid. mus. for Sophocles' *Antigone,* Racine's *Andromaque* and 6 other plays; 3 symphs. (the 3rd with org. and pf. duet), symph. poems *Le Rouet d'Omphale, Phaëton, Danse macabre* (orig. a song), *La Jeunesse d'Hercule,* suite and *Suite algérienne* for orch., other orchestral pieces incl. *Une Nuit à Lisbonne, Jota aragonesa, Ouverture de*

fête; 5 pf. concertos, *Allegro appassionato, Rapsodie d'Auvergne* and *Africa* for pf. and orch., 3 vln. concertos and *Intro. et Rondo capriccioso,* Romance, *Morceau de concert* and *Caprice andalou* for vln. and orch., 2 cello concertos, var. pieces for wind instruments and orch.; *Le Carnaval des animaux* for chamber orch.; 2 string 4tets, pf. 5tet and 4tet, 2 pf. trios, 7tet for pf., strings and tpt.; 2 vln. and pf. sonatas, 2 cello and pf. sonatas, suite for cello and pf., sonatas for ob., clar. and bassoon and pf.; fantasies for harp and for vln. and harp; many smaller instrumental pieces with pf.; 24 op. nos. of pf. mus., 6 op. nos. for pf. duet, 5 op. nos. for 2 pfs. incl. variations on a theme by Beethoven; 7 org. works; Mass, Requiem, 2 Psalms and other church mus. for chorus and orch. (some with solo voices); *Ode à Sainte Cécile* and *La Fiancée du timbalier* for voice and orch.; oratorio *Le Déluge;* several cantatas; many songs, etc.

St. Victor, Adam of (b. ?; d. 1177 or 1192), French monk. In *c.* 1130 he joined the abbey of St. Victor near Paris. He wrote sequences comp. in pairs of metrically regular 3-line stanzas, and was the first important exponent of this type. He apparently comp. the melodies of his sequences.

Saintine, Xavier (Boniface) (1798–1865), Fr. novelist and playwright. *See* **Puritani di Scozia** (Bellini).

Sainton-Dolby (*née* **Dolby**), **Charlotte (Helen)** (b. London, 17. V. 1821; d. London, 18. II. 1885), Eng. contralto and comp. Studied at the R.A.M. in London and made her 1st appearance at a Phil. concert there in 1842. In 1845 Mendelssohn invited her to sing with Jenny Lind at Leipzig, and later she had a success in Fr. and Hol. In 1860 she married Prosper Sainton.

Works incl. cantatas *The Legend of St. Dorothea* and *The Story of a Faithful Soul,* cantata for female voices *Florimel,* etc.

Sainton, Prosper (Philippe Cathérine) (b. Toulouse, 5. VI. 1813; d. London, 17. X. 1890), Fr. violinist and comp., husband of prec. Studied vln. under Habeneck at the Paris Cons., played at the Société des Concerts and the Opéra there, then travelled widely in Eur. and in 1840 became prof. at the Toulouse Cons. In 1844 he visited London and played under Mendelssohn, returning in 1845 to settle down as member of the Beethoven 4tet Society, orch. leader and teacher.

Works incl. 2 vln. concertos and other solos with orch.; variations, romances, operatic fantasies, etc. for vln. and pf., etc.

Saite(n) (Ger.) = string(s).

Saiteninstrumente (Ger.) = string instruments.

591

Sakuntala. *See also* **Leggenda di Sakuntala, Sacountala.**
Opera by Weingartner (lib. by comp., based on Kalidasa's drama), prod. Weimar, 23. III. 1884.

Sala, Nicola (b. Tocco-Caudio nr. Benevento, 7. IV. 1713; d. Naples, 31. VIII. 1801), It. comp. and theorist. Studied with Fago and Leo at the Cons. de' Turchini at Naples and later became a master there, principal in 1787, succeeding Cafaro. In 1794 he pub. *Regole del contrappunto prattico* in 3 vols.
Works incl. operas *Vologeso, Zenobia, Merope* and *Demetrio*; oratorio *Giuditta*; Mass, Litany and other church mus.; Prologues for the birth of kings of Naples, etc.

Salaman, Charles (Kensington) (b. London, 3. III. 1814; d. London, 23. VI. 1901), Eng. pianist, comp., cond. and lecturer. Studied at the R.A.M. in London and under Neate, made his 1st appearance in 1828 and went to Paris for further studies with Herz. On his return to London he played much at concerts and helped to found chamber mus. and choral societies. He also lectured and contrib. to mus. papers. In 1846–8 he cond. in Rome.
Works incl. anthems and Hebrew services; Ode for the Shakespeare commemoration at Stratford-on-Avon (23. IV. 1830); *Rondeau brillant* for pf. and orch.; pf. works; songs in Eng., Hebrew, Gk. and Lat., incl. 'I arise from dreams of thee' (Shelley), etc.

Salammbô, opera by Reyer (lib. by Camille du Locle, based on Flaubert's novel), prod. Brussels, Théâtre de la Monnaie, 10. II. 1890.
Unfinished opera by Mussorgsky (lib. by comp., based on Flaubert), partly comp. in the 1860s.

Salazar, Adolfo (b. Madrid, 6. III. 1890; d. Mexico City, 27. IX. 1958), Span. musicologist and comp. Pupil of Pérez Casas and Falla. He ed. the *Revista Musical Hispano-Americana* in 1914–18 and from 1918 to 1936 was mus. critic to *El Sol* in Madrid. He emigrated to Buenos Aires after the Span. Civil War and lived in Mex. after 1939. His books incl. studies of modern mus., Span. mus., symph. and ballet, etc.
Works incl. symph. poem *Don Juan en los infiernos, Paisajes* and *Tres preludios* for orch.; string 4tet, *Arabia* for pf. 5tet; vln. and pf. sonata; pf. pieces; *Romancilla* for guitar, etc.

Salcional, another name for the Salicional org. stop.

Sales, Pietro Pompeo (b. Brescia, *c.* 1729; d. Hanau, 21. XI. 1797), It. comp. App. *Kapellmeister* to the Prince-Bishop of Augsburg in 1756, he served the Electoral Court in Coblenz in the same

capacity from 1770. Also travelled in It. and Eng. (1776), appearing as a virtuoso gamba-player.
Works incl. operas *Le nozze di Amore e di Norizia, L'Antigono, Achille in Sciro, Il rè pastore,* etc.; oratorios *Giefte, Giuseppe ricognosciuto, La Betulia liberata,* etc.; church mus.; 2 symphs.; concertos; arias, etc.

Salicet, a 4-ft. org. stop similar to the Salicional but an 8ve higher.

Salicional, an 8-ft. open metal org. stop, prod. a soft and slightly stringy tone.

Salieri, Antonio (b. Legnago nr. Verona, 18. VIII. 1750; d. Vienna, 7. V. 1825), It. comp., cond. and teacher. Studied with his brother Francesco S., a pupil of Tartini. Orphaned at 15; his educ. at the school of San Marco in Venice was cared for by the Mocenigo family. There he met Gassmann, who in 1766 took him to Vienna, saw to his further educ. and intro. him at court. On Gassmann's death in 1774 he became court comp. and cond. of the It. opera. Visited It. 1778–80, where his opera *Europa riconosciuta* was prod. at the opening of La Scala, Milan, and Paris (1774 and 1786–7), but from 1788, when he succeeded Bonno as court *Kapellmeister*, lived mostly in Vienna. His intrigues against Mozart were exaggerated into the story that he had poisoned Mozart. He was cond. of the Tonkünstler Society until 1818, and played the continuo in the first perf. of Haydn's *Creation* in 1798. Among his pupils were Beethoven, Schubert, Hummel and Liszt.
Works incl. *c.* 40 operas, e.g. *Armida, La fiera di Venezia, La locandiera, Europa riconosciuta, La scuola de gelosi, La dama pastorella, Der Rauchfangkehrer, Les Danaïdes, Tarare, Les Horaces* (the last 3 for Paris), *La grotta di Trofonio, Il talismano, Palmira, regina di Persia, Falstaff* (after Shakespeare), *Cesare in Farmacusa, Angiolina,* etc.; incid. mus. to Kotzebue's *Die Hussiten vor Naumburg*; Passion oratorio and others; Masses, Requiem, Litanies and other church mus.; cantatas incl. *La riconoscenza* for the 25th anniversary of the Tonkünstler-Societät; 3 symphs. and *sinfonia concertante*; concertos; serenades, etc.; arias, duets, canons and miscellaneous other small vocal pieces, etc.

Salimbeni, Felice (b. Milan, *c.* 1712; d. Ljubljana, VIII. 1751), It. male soprano. Pupil of Porpora, made his 1st appearance in Rome in 1731 and afterwards sang in It., Vienna, Berlin and Dresden, and was one of Hasse's chief interpreters.

Salinas, Francisco de (b. Burgos, 1. III. 1513; d. Salamanca, 13. I. 1590), Span. organist, theorist and folksong investigator. He was the son of an official in the treasury of Charles V and became blind at the age of 10, whereupon his parents decided to let him study mus. He was taken to Rome in 1538, where he met the lutenist Francesco da Milano and became a great admirer of Lassus. In 1558 he became organist to the Duke of Alba, viceroy of Naples, under Ortiz. In 1561 he returned to Spain, became organist at León in 1563 and prof. of mus. at Salamanca Univ., 1567. There he made friends with the poet Luis de León, who wrote a poem on his org. playing. In his treatise *De musica libri septem* (1577) he quotes the tunes of many Span. folksongs.

Salmhofer, Franz (b. Vienna, 22. I. 1900), Aus. cond. and comp. Having learnt mus. as a choir-boy, he studied at the Vienna Acad. under Schreker and others, later taught at Horak's mus. school and in 1929–39 was cond. at the Burgtheater, for which he wrote incid. mus. to over 100 plays. Since 1955 he has been director of the Vienna Volksoper.

Works incl. operas *Dame im Traum, Iwan Sergejewitsch Tarassenko, Das Werbekleid* and several others; ballets *Das lockende Phantom, Der Taugenichts in Wien, Weihnachtsmärchen, Österreichische Bauernhochzeit*; incid. mus. for Shakespeare's *The Tempest, King Lear, Romeo and Juliet, Othello, The Merry Wives of Windsor*, Goethe's *Faust* (pts. I and II), etc.; overture to Maeterlinck's *L'Intruse* and others, *Der geheimnisvolle Trompeter, Fairy-Tale* for orch.; suite for chamber orch.; concertos for cello, vln. and cello and tpt.; string 4tet in F min., pf. 4tet in F min., serenade for string trio, Slavonic Rhapsody and Dance Suite for vln., vla. and guitar; sonatas for vla. and pf. and cello and pf.; songs, etc.

Salmo (It., plur. *salmi*) = psalm.

Salmon (*née* **Munday**), **Eliza** (b. Oxford, 1787; d. London, 5. VI. 1849), Eng. soprano. Studied with John Ashley and made her 1st appearance at a Lenten concert at Covent Garden Theatre in London, 1803. She married James Salmon in 1806 and they settled at Liverpool, but she continued to sing in London and at the festivals until she lost her voice in 1825.

Salmon, Jacques (b. Picardy, ?; d. ?), 16th-cent. Fr. comp. He was in the royal service from 1575 and contrib. to the *Ballet comique de la Royne* (1581). A few *chansons* have also survived.

Salmon, James (b. ?; d. West Indies, ?), Eng. 18th–19th-cent. organist, husband of Eliza S. Studied with his father, James S. (?–1827), vicar-choral at St. Paul's Cathedral in London and lay-clerk at St. George's Chapel, Windsor, and in 1805 settled at Liverpool as organist of St. Peter's Church. In 1813 he enlisted and went to the W. Indies.

Salmon, Thomas (b. London, 24. VI. 1648; d. Mepsal, Beds., VII. 1706), Eng. clergyman and writer on mus. Wrote on notation and temperament. His *Essay on the Advancement of Musick* in 1672 involved him in a controversy with Locke.

Salmond, Felix (b. London, 19. XI. 1888; d. N.Y., 19. II. 1952), Eng. cellist. Studied at the R.A.M. in London, later in Brussels, and made his début in London in 1909. In 1919 he played in the 1st perfs. of Elgar's string 4tet, pf. 5tet and cello concerto. He settled in U.S.A. in 1922 and in 1942 became cello prof. at the Juilliard School in N.Y. He toured extensively.

Salò, Francesco da (b. Brescia, 1565; d. ?), It. vln. maker. Succeeded his father, whose business however he sold after his death, and he seems to have left Brescia in 1614.

Salò, Gasparo da (real name G. di Bertoletti) (b. Salò, V. 1540; d. Brescia, 14. IV. 1609), It. vln. maker, father of prec. He began working at Brescia in the 1560s.

Salomé, opera by Mariotte (lib. Oscar Wilde's orig. in Fr.), prod. Lyons, 30. X. 1908. Comp. earlier than R. Strauss's opera, although prod. later.

Salome, opera by R. Strauss (lib. Hedwig Lachmann's Ger. trans. of Oscar Wilde's play, written in Fr.), prod. Dresden, Royal Opera, 9. XII. 1905.

See also **Tragédie de Salomé**.

Salomon, Johann Peter (b. Bonn, I. 1745; d. London, 28. XI. 1815), Ger. violinist, cond. and comp. Studied at Bonn and joined the electoral orch. in 1758. After a tour in 1765 he became court musician at Rheinsberg to Prince Henry of Prus., who however dissolved his orch. *c.* 1780, when S. went to Paris and thence to London, 1781, where he settled as concert violinist, 4tet player and cond. He gave subscription concerts at the Hanover Square Rooms and invited Haydn to London in 1790 and again in 1794. He wrote 4 Fr. operas and an Eng. one, *Windsor Castle*, for the marriage of the Prince of Wales in 1795, an oratorio *Hiskias*, vln. sonatas, etc.

Salomon Symphonies, the 12 symphs. written by Haydn in 1791–5 for the concerts given by Johann Peter Salomon in London during Haydn's 2 visits to Eng. in 1791–2 and 1794–5. They are Nos. 93–104.

Saltando (It. = springing, bounding), a special way of playing the vln. and other string instruments in such a manner that the bow is made to rebound from the strings.

Saltarello, an It. dance, obviously incl. jumps (*salti*) and in the 16th cent. a kind of after-dance in common time, also called by the Lat. name of *proportio* and the Ger.

one of *Proporz*, the name being due to its using the same mus. as the 1st dance (Passamezzo), but with the 'proportions' (i.e. time) altered; later a Rom. dance in animated 3–4 or 6–8 time, not unlike the Neapol. Tarantella, but using jerky instead of even mus. figuration. In perf. by dancers it gradually increased its pace towards the end.

Saltato (It.) = Saltando.

Salterio (It.) = Psaltery.

Salterio tedesco (It. = Ger. psaltery) = Dulcimer.

Saltikov-Shtchedrin, Mikhail (1826–89), Rus. novelist and satirist. *See* Pashtchenko (*Pompadour*).

Salvayre, Gaston (actually Gervais Bernard) (b. Toulouse, 24. VI. 1847; d. Saint-Ague nr. Toulouse, 16. V. 1916), Fr. organist and comp. Studied at the Paris Cons., A. Thomas being among his masters, and gained the Prix de Rome in 1872. After his stay in Rome he was app. chorus master at the Opéra Populaire at the Théâtre du Châtelet and later he became mus. critic to *Gil Blas*.

Works incl operas *Salah-el-Din, Egmont, Sainte Geneviève, Myrto, Le Bravo, Richard III, La Dame de Monsereau* (after Dumas) and *Solange*; ballets *La Fontaine des fées, L'Odalisque* and *Fandango* and ballet mus. for Grisar's *Amours du Diable*; *Stabat Mater* and Psalm cxiii for solo voices, chorus and orch.; symph. *Le Jugement dernier* (later called *La Résurrection* and *La Vallée de Josaphat*), *Ouverture symphonique*, air and variations for string orch., etc.

Salviucci, Giovanni (b. Rome, 26. X. 1907; d. Rome, 4. IX. 1937), It. comp. and teacher. Giving up legal studies, he studied mus. under Boezi, director of the Cappella Giulia at St. Peter's, and the Accademia di Santa Cecilia, also with Casella and Respighi. He afterwards taught at the Istituto Muzio Clementi in Rome and the Liceo Musicale at Pescara.

Works incl. episode from *Alcestis* (Euripides) for chorus and orch.; symph. poems and suites *Samarith, Saul, Campagna romana, Serena, La Tentazione e la preghiera*, 2 sketches *Villavecchia*, overture in C♯ min., *Sinfonia italiana, Introduzione, passacaglia e finale; Sinfonia da camera* for 17 instruments, *Serenata* for 9 instruments; *Salmo di Davidde* for tenor and chamber orch.; string 4tet; instrumental pieces; songs, etc.

Salzburg Festivals, summer festivals of mus. and drama begun at Salzburg in 1920, mainly at the instigation of the poet Hugo von Hofmannsthal, the producer Max Reinhardt, the cond. Franz Schalk and the comp. Richard Strauss. The mus. perfs. incl. opera, church mus., orchestral concerts, chamber mus. and serenades, a

festival opera-house being built in 1926. Being Mozart's birthplace, Salzburg gave prominence to his works, but cultivated old and modern mus. of many kinds. The S. F. were interrupted in 1944, but resumed in 1945.

Salzedo, Carlos (b. Arcachon, Gironde, 6. IV. 1885; d. Waterville, Me., 17. VIII. 1961), Fr.-Amer. harpist and comp. Studied pf. and harp at the Paris Cons. and went to N.Y. at Toscanini's invitation to become 1st harp at the Metropolitan Opera. Much interested in modern mus., he founded the Internat. Comps.' Guild with Varèse, ed. *Eolus* and cond. many concerts. Prof. of harp at the Juilliard School in N.Y. and the Curtis Inst. at Philadelphia.

Works incl. *The Enchanted Isle* for harp and orch., concerto for harp and 7 wind instruments, *Préambule et Jeux* for harp and chamber orch.; sonata for harp and pf.; many pieces and arrs. for harp, etc.

Samain, Albert (1858–1900), Fr. poet. *See* Bernard (*Polyphème*), Cras (do.), Lioncourt (*Hyalis*), Poldowski (songs).

Samara, Spiro (b. Corfu, 22. XI. 1863; d. Athens, 7. IV. 1917), Gk. comp. Studied at Athens, later with Delibes and others at the Paris Cons. The It. pub. Sonzogno procured him his 1st operatic prod. at Milan. He subsequently prod. other works at Rome, Naples, Florence, Milan and Genoa, with no more than ephemeral success, and the last came out at Athens in 1914.

Works incl. operas *Flora mirabilis, Medgé, Lionella, La martire, La furia domata* (after Shakespeare's *Taming of the Shrew*), *Storia d'amore, Mademoiselle de Belle-Isle, Rhea, La guerra in tempo di guerra, The Princess of Saxony* (in Gk.); suite for pf. duet, pf. pieces; songs, etc.

Samazeuilh, Gustave (Marie Victor Fernand) (b. Bordeaux, 2. VI. 1877; d. Paris, 4. VIII. 1966), Fr. comp. and critic. Pupil of Chausson and after his master's death of d'Indy and Dukas at the Schola Cantorum. His lit. works incl. studies of Rameau and Dukas, transs. of Wagner's *Tristan* and Schumann's *Genoveva*, songs by Wagner and Liszt, etc. He also made pf. arrs. of modern Fr. mus.

Works incl. *Étude symphonique pour 'La Nef'* (Élemire Bourges), *Nuit, Naïades au soir, Le Sommeil de Canope* for orch.; the last also for voice and orch.; string 4tet; sonata and *Fantaisie élégiaque* for vln. and pf.; *Le Chant de la mer* and suite for pf.; serenade for guitar; songs, etc.

Saminsky, Lazare (b. nr. Odessa, 8. XI. 1882; d. Port Chester, N.Y., 30. VI. 1959), Rus.-Amer. comp., cond. and writer on mus. Pupil of Liadov and Rimsky-Korsakov at St. Petersburg Cons. Cond. at Tiflis in 1915–18 and then director of the People's Cons. there. After a period in London, he went to the U.S.A., where he became naturalized. He was one of the founders of the League of Comps. in 1924, became mus. director of the Jewish Temple of Emanu-El, and did much cond. in Amer. and Eur. Author of *Music of Our Day* and *Music of the Ghetto.*

Works. incl. opera-ballets *The Vision of Ariel, Lament of Rachel* and *The Daughter of Jephtha,* chamber opera *Gagliarda of the Merry Plague;* Requiem; 5 symphs., symph. poems *Three Shadows, Pueblo, a Moon Rhapsody* and *Ausonia, 2 Images* for orch.; *By the Rivers of Babylon* for chorus; *Litanies of Women* for mezzo-soprano and small orch.; Sabbath Morning Service and Holiday Service for the synagogue, etc.

Sammarco, Mario (b. Palermo, 13. XII. 1873; d. Milan, 24. I. 1930), It. baritone. Pupil of Antonio Cantelli; made his 1st appearance at Milan and 1st visited London in 1904. He was a director of La Scala, Milan, from 1918.

Sammartini (or San Martini), Giovanni Battista (b. Milan, *c.* 1700; d. Milan, 15. I. 1775), It. comp. He spent his whole life in Milan as a church musician, from 1730 *maestro di cappella* at the convent of Santa Maria Maddelena. Gluck was his pupil 1737–41. He was the most important It. symphonist of his time, and contrib. much towards the founding of a modern style of instrumental mus.

Works incl. 2 operas; 2 oratorios; 3 Masses and other church mus.; over 80 symphs.; *c.* 15 concertos; 6 *concerti grossi;* 6 string 5tets, *c.* 20 4tets, almost 200 trios, and other chamber mus., etc.

Sammartini (or San Martini), Giuseppe (b. Milan, *c.* 1693; d. London, *c.* 1750), It. oboist and comp., brother of prec. Settled in Eng. *c.* 1727, became oboist at the opera, and 1732–44 was director of the Hickford's Room concerts with Arrigoni, then was app. director of chamber mus. to the Prince of Wales.

Works incl. setting of Congreve's masque *The Judgment of Paris;* oratorio *La calunnia delusa; Concerti grossi;* concertos for harpsichord and for vln.; sonatas for 2 fls., 2 vlns., etc. with bass, fl. solos (? all fl. works intended also for ob.), etc.

Sammons, Albert (b. London, 23. II. 1886; d. Southdean, Sussex, 24. VIII. 1957), Eng. violinist. Taught by his father, an amateur, John Saunders and F. Weist-Hill, he 1st played at a London hotel, where Sir Thomas Beecham heard him in 1908 and engaged him as leader of his orch. S. later led the London String 4tet and gradually emerged as a splendid soloist, with works like Elgar's and Delius's concertos in his repertory. He

excelled both in virtuosity and in musicianship.

Samori, opera by Vogler (lib. by Franz Xaver Huber), prod. Vienna, Theater an der Wien, 17. V. 1804. Weber wrote a set of pf. variations, Op. 6, on a theme from it.

Sampson, Richard (b. ?, *c.* 1475; d. Eccleshall, 25. IX. 1554), Eng. comp. He was a Canon of St. Paul's Cathedral, and Dean of the Chapel Royal from 1523, later becoming Bishop of Chichester. In 1511 he had travelled to Antwerp, where he probably met Benedictus de Opitiis, who in 1516 became court organist to Henry VIII. Comps. by the two men are incl. in a MS. (Brit. Mus. Roy. 11 Ex. xi) dated 1516, including two by Sampson: *Psallite felices,* in praise of the king, and a Marian antiphon, *Quam pulchra es.*

Samson, oratorio by Handel (lib. by Newburgh Hamilton, based on Milton's *Samson Agonistes, Hymn on the Nativity* and *At a Solemn Musick*), prod. London, Covent Garden Theatre, 18. II. 1743.

Samson et Dalila, opera (orig. oratorio) by Saint-Saëns (lib. by Ferdinand Lemaire), prod. Weimar, in Ger., 2. XII. 1877; not perf. in Paris until 31. X. 1890, and at the Opéra 23. XI. 1892, having been at first forbidden on account of its biblical subject.

Samuel, Harold (b. London, 23. V. 1879; d. London, 15. I. 1937), Eng. pianist. Studied under Dannreuther and Stanford at the R.C.M. in London, where he became pf. prof. later. He made a speciality of Bach's keyboard works, but he also excelled as a chamber mus. player.

Samuel-Rousseau. *See* **Rousseau, Marcel.**

San Martini. *See* **Sammartini.**

Sances, Giovanni Felice (b. Rome, *c.* 1600; d. Vienna, 24. XI. 1679), It. tenor and comp. He went to Vienna as a singer in the Imp. Chapel in 1637, became vicemus. director in 1649 and 1st mus. director in 1669.

Works incl. operas *Apollo deluso* (with the Emperor Leopold I), *Aristomene Messenio* and others; oratorios; cantatas for solo voice, *Capricci poetici, Trattenimenti musicali per camera,* etc.

Sánchez de Fuentes y Peláez, Eduardo (b. Havana, 3. IV. 1874; d. Havana, 9. IX. 1944), Cuban comp. and mus. hist. He wrote several books on the hist. of Cuban folk mus.

Works incl. operas *Dolorosa, Doreya* and 3 others, operettas and *zarzuelas;* oratorio *Novidad;* suite *Bocetos cubanos,* symph. prelude *Temas del Patio* for orch.; vocal *habanera Tú espera,* etc.

Sancho Pança dans son île (*Sancho Panza on his Island*), opera by Philidor (lib. by Antoine Alexandre Henri Poisinet, based on Cervantes's *Don Quixote*), prod. Paris, Comédie-Italienne, 8. VII. 1762.

Sancho Panza, opera by Jaques-Dalcroze (lib. by Robert Yve-Plessis, based on Cervantes's *Don Quixote*), prod. Geneva, 13. XII. 1897.

Sancio Panza, governatore dell' isola Barattaria (*Sancho P., Governor of the Isle of Barataria*), opera by Caldara (lib. by Giovanni Claudio Pasquini, based on Cervantes's *Don Quixote*), prod. Vienna, Burgtheater, 27. I. 1733. W. S. Gilbert borrowed the name of the island for Sullivan's *Gondoliers*.

Sancta Civitas (*The Holy City*), oratorio by Vaughan Williams (words from the Bible, etc.) for solo voices, chorus and orch., 1st perf. Oxford, 7. V. 1926.

Sanctus, the fourth chant of the Ordinary of the Rom. Mass. Its text is founded on Isaiah vi. 3 and Matthew xxi. 9, and it was incorporated into the Lat. liturgy at least as early as the 6th cent. in Gaul. The earliest known melody is that of Mass XVIII (Vatican edition). It is basically syllabic; it forms a natural continuation from the mus. of the Preface which precedes it; it is psalmodic in structure; and its last phrase echoes the *Per omnia saecula saeculorum* formula which occurs 3 times during the Preface and Canon of the Mass. The ex. shows part of the Preface and the whole Sanctus:

Later settings are more complex: a total of 231 melodies has been catalogued. The S. was set in polyphony from the 13th cent., and became an integral part of all settings of the Ordinary of the Mass.

Sand, George (Aurore Dudevant, *née* Dupin) (1804–76), Fr. novelist. *See* **Fourdrain** (*Claudie* and *Mare au Diable*), **Hillemacher** (*Claudie*), **Kashperov** (*Consuelo*), **Orefice** (do.), **Rendano** (do.).

Sandberger, Adolf (b. Würzburg, 19. XII. 1864; d. Munich, 14. I. 1943), Ger. musicologist and comp. Studied in a number of Eur. centres and in 1894 became lecturer in mus. at Munich Univ. and was prof. in 1900–29, being at the same time curator of the mus. dept. of the State Library. He was chief ed. of the incomplete ed. of Lassus and the *Denkmäler der Tonkunst in Bayern*, and his books incl. studies of the Bavarian court chapel under Lassus, of Cornelius, etc.

Works incl. operas *Ludwig der Springer* and *Der Tod des Kaisers*; symph. poem *Viola* (on Shakespeare's *Twelfth Night*), symph. prologue *Riccio*; chamber mus.; pf. works; songs; etc.

Sanderson (or **Saunderson**), **James** (b. Washington, Durham, IV. 1769; d. London, *c.* 1841), Eng. violinist and comp. He was self-taught and in 1783 obtained an engagement as violinist at the Sunderland theatre. Later he taught at Shields,

SANCTUS

became leader at the Newcastle-on-Tyne theatre, 1787, and at Astley's Amphitheatre in London, 1788. He began to write stage pieces and in 1793 went as mus. director and comp. to the Royal Circus (Surrey Theatre).

Works incl. stage pieces and pantomimes *Harlequin in Ireland, Blackbeard, Cora, Sir Francis Drake, The Magic Pipe, Hallowe'en* and many others; instrumental interludes for Collins's *Ode to the Passions*; vln. pieces; many popular songs, etc.

Sanderson, Sibyl (b. Sacramento, Calif., 7. XII. 1865; d. Paris, 15. V. 1903), Amer. soprano. Studied at the Paris Cons. and made her 1st stage appearance at The Hague in 1888, in Massenet's *Manon*. She was later chiefly assoc. with that comp.'s operas, making her 1st Paris appearance in his *Esclarmonde* in 1889.

Sandrin (Pierre Regnault) (b. ?; d. after 1561), Fr. comp. He was a member of the royal chapel, 1543–60, during which time he also travelled to It. He comp. only *chansons*, of which the majority were pub. by Attaingnant.

Sandys, George (1578–1644), Eng. trans. *See* Porter (W.) (psalms).

Sanglot (Fr. = sob), a vocal ornament, esp. an appoggiatura, sung to some plaintive word such as 'Hélas'.

Sannazaro, Jacopo (1458–1530), It. poet. *See* Mudarra (sonnets).

Santa Cruz, (Wilson) Domingo (b. La Cruz, 5. VII. 1899), Chilean comp., teacher and critic. Studied at Santiago de Chile and Madrid. In 1918 he founded a Bach Society at Santiago and in 1932 became dean of the Fine Arts Dept. at the Univ. of Chile and rector of the univ. from 1948 to 1951.

Works incl. 3 symphs.; *5 Piezas brevas* for string orch.; 3 string 4tets; 3 vln. and pf. pieces; pf. works; songs, etc.

Santa Maria, Tomás de (b. Madrid, *c.* 1515; d. Valladolid, 1570), Span. monk and organist. He joined a Dominican monastery and in 1565 pub. a treatise on playing polyphonic fantasies on keyboard instruments and lutes.

Santi, Angelo de (b. Trieste, 12. VII. 1847; d. Rome, 28. I. 1922), It. priest and mus. scholar. He entered the Jesuit Order as a youth and graduated at Innsbruck. He advocated reforms in Rom. church mus. to the Popes Leo XIII and Pius X, and it was owing to his recommendations that the latter issued the *Motu proprio* of 1903.

Santini, Fortunato (b. Rome, 5. I. 1778; d. Rome, 1862), It. priest, mus. scholar and comp. He studied mus. with Jannaconi and after being ordained in 1801 began to make an immense collection of old mus., scoring it from parts in var. mus. libraries. He made friends with Mendelssohn and

through him intro. many works by Bach into It., as well as other Ger. sacred mus.

Works incl. Requiem for 8 voices, Masses and other church mus., etc.

Santley, Charles (b. Liverpool, 28. II. 1834; d. London, 22. IX. 1922), Eng. bass-baritone. Learnt mus. as a choir-boy and at first appeared as an amateur singer, but went to Milan in 1855 to study with Gaetano Nava, made a stage appearance at Pavia and in 1857 returned to Eng., continuing his studies with Manuel García in London, where he 1st appeared on 16. XI. He soon sang in opera, oratorio and at the great festivals with enormous success. He toured the U.S.A. in 1871 and Austral. in 1890. In 1907 he celebrated his 50th anniversary as a singer and was knighted.

Santoliquido, Francesco (b. San Giorgio a Cremano, Naples, 6. VIII. 1883), It. comp. Studied at the Liceo di Santa Cecilia in Rome, cond. his student work, *Crepuscolo sul mare*, at Nuremberg in 1909 and prod. his 1st opera at Milan in 1910. He then went to live in Tunisia, in the small Arab village in Hammamek, where he became interested in the study of native mus.

Works incl. operas *La favola di Helga, Ferhuda, L'ignota* and *La porta verde*, mimed drama *La baiadera della maschera gialla*; symph. in F maj., *Crepuscolo sul mare, Il profumo delle oasi sahariane, La morte di Tintagiles* (after Maeterlinck), *Paesaggi, Acquarelle* for orch.; *Due acqueforti tunisine, Ex humo ad sidera*, etc. for pf.; songs on Jap. and Persian poetry, etc.

Sanzogno, Nino (b. Venice, 13. IV. 1911), It. cond. and comp. Studied with Malipiero and Scherchen, and then played vln. in the Guarnieri 4tet, later becoming cond. at La Fenice opera house in Venice and at La Scala, Milan.

Works incl. symph. poems *The 4 Horsemen of the Apocalypse, Vanitas*; concertos for vla., cello; songs.

Sapho, opera by Gounod (lib. by Émile Augier), prod. Paris, Opéra, 16. IV. 1851. Gounod's 1st opera.

Opera by Massenet (lib. by Henri Cain and Arthur Bernède, based on Daudet's novel, prod. Paris, Opéra-Comique, 27. XI. 1807. The heroine is not the Gk. poet Sappho.

Sappho. *See also* Saffo, Sapho.

Opera by Hugo Kaun (1863–1932) (lib. by comp. based on Grillparzer's play), prod. Leipzig, 27. X. 1917.

Saraband (Eng.) } a dance, poss. orig. **Sarabande** (Fr.) } in Spain in the 16th cent. Its name was formerly supposed to be derived from a dancer called Zarabanda, but it is very

Sarasate   Sarrusophone

likely of more remote eastern orig. It was
intro. to the Fr. court in 1588 and in 17th-
cent. Eng. became a country dance. The
mus. is in slow 3–2 time with, as a rule, a
peculiar rhythm of a minim, dotted minim
and crotchet in the 1st bar, e.g.:

1914. He served in World War I and in
1919 took his D. Mus. at Durham. He
made his début as a cond. at a Promenade
Concert in a work of his own in 1921.
Later he taught at the R.C.M. and cond.
in many parts of the world, incl. a period

SARABANDE

Bach, *English Suite, No.6*

The S. was one of the 4 regular movements in the 17th and 18th-cent. Suite,
together with the Allemande, Courante
and Gigue (Jig).

**Sarasate (y Navascues), Pablo (Martín
Melitón)** (b. Pamplona, 10. III. 1844;
d. Biarritz, 20. XI. 1908), Span. violinist
and comp. Pupil of Alard at the Paris
Cons. He soon began to make a remarkable career as a virtuoso, at first in Fr. and
Spain, later all over Eur. and Amer. He
1st appeared in London in 1861.

Works incl. romances, fantasies, 4 books
of Span. Dances, etc. for vln.

Sardana, a Span. dance of Catalonia
revived in the middle of the 19th cent. and
perf. to pipe and drum.

Sardou, Victorien (1831–1908), Fr.
playwright. *See* **Duchess of Dantzic**
(Caryll), **Fedora** (Giordano), **Giordano**
(*Mme. Sans-Gêne*), **Leroux** (*Cléopâtre* and
Théodora), **Offenbach** (*Haine*), **Paladilhe**
(*Patrie*), **Saint-Saëns** (*Barbares*), **Soloviev**
(*Cordelia*), **Strauss (J. ii)** (*Karneval in
Rom*), **Tosca** (Puccini), **Webber** (*Fiorella*).

(Bizet's *Patrie* overture has no connection with S.'s play.)

Sargent, (Harold) Malcolm (Watts) (b.
Stamford, Lincs., 29. IV. 1895; d. London,
3. X. 1967), Eng. cond. Studied at the
Royal Coll. of Organists, winning the
Sawyer Prize in 1910. From 1911 to 1914
he was asst. organist at Peterborough
Cathedral, after which he become organist
at Melton Mowbray parish church in

with the Diaghilev ballet co. from 1927 to
1930. In 1928 he became chief cond. of the
Royal Choral Society and from 1950 to
1957 chief cond. of the B.B.C. Symph.
Orch., and of the Promenade Concerts
until his death. He was knighted in 1947.

Šárka (Smetana). *See* **Má Vlast.**
Opera by Fibich (lib. by Anežka
Schulzová), prod. Prague, Cz. Theatre,
28. XII. 1897.

Saroyan, William (b. 1908), Armenian-
Amer. playwright and novelist. *See*
Bowles (*My Heart's in the Highlands* and
Love's Old Sweet Song).

Sarro (or Sarri), Domenico (b. Trani,
Naples, 24. XII. 1679; d. Naples, 25. I.
1744), It. comp. Pupil of Durante at the
Cons. S. Onofrio in Naples, he became
vice-*maestro di cappella* to the court in 1703.
He lost his post in 1707 but returned in
1725, succeeding Mancini as *maestro di
cappella* in 1737.

Works incl. *c.* 50 operas, e.g. *Didone
abbandonata* (the first setting by any comp.
of a lib. by Metastasio); 4 oratorios;
cantatas, etc.; much church mus.; instrumental mus.

Sarrusophone, a brass wind instrument
with a double-reed mouthpiece invented
in 1856 by Sarrus, a bandmaster in the Fr.
army, intended to be made in var. sizes to
cover a whole range of tone replacing obs.
and bassoons in military bands. In the
orch. only the contrabass has been used,
mainly by Fr. comps.

Sarselli, Elisabeth. *See* **Wendling.**

Sarti, Giuseppe (b. Faenza, XI. 1729; d. Berlin, 28. VII. 1802), It. cond. and comp. Pupil of Vallotti in Padua and of Padre Martini in Bologna, he was organist of Faenza Cathedral 1748–51, then mus. director of the theatre there in 1752 and prod. his 1st opera the same year. In 1753 he went to Copenhagen as cond. of the Mingotti opera co., and 2 years later was app. *Kapellmeister* to the Dan. court, staying there, except for 3 years in It. 1765–8, until 1775. Director of the Ospedaletto Cons. in Venice 1775–9, he was then *maestro di cappella* of Milan Cathedral, where Cherubini was his pupil. App. mus. director to the Rus. court in 1784, he travelled to St. Petersburg *via* Vienna, there meeting Mozart, who quoted the aria 'Come un agnello' from his opera *Fra due litiganti* in the supper scene in *Don Giovanni*. He prod. a number of operas in Rus., incl. *Oleg* on a lib. by the empress, and stayed there until 1802, founding a mus. school in the Ukraine and becoming director of the Cons. in St. Petersburg in 1793. He then intended retiring to It., but d. in Berlin on the way.

Works incl. operas (libs. in It., Dan., Fr. and Rus.), e.g. *Pompeo in Armenia, Il rè pastore, La giardiniera brillante, Farnace, Le gelosie villane, Fra due litiganti, Medonte, Giulio Sabino, I finti eredi, Armida e Rinaldo, Oleg* (Rus., with Pashkevich and Canobbio), etc.; 2 Rus. oratorios; Requiem for Louis XVI; Masses, *Te Deum* and other church mus.; keyboard mus., etc.

Sarto, Johannes de (b. ?; d. ?), early 15th-cent. comp. He was apparently a member of the Imp. Chapel. He wrote a number of motets.

Sartorio, Antonio (b. Venice, c. 1620; d. Venice, 5. I. 1681), It. comp. He was mus. director at the Court of Brunswick from 1666 to 1675 and then vice-*maestro di cappella* at St. Mark's, Venice, preceding Legrenzi.

Works incl. operas *Seleuco, La prosperità di Elio Seiano, La caduta di Elio Seiano, Adelaide, Orfeo* and 10 others; psalms and motets; cantatas for chorus and for solo voices; canzonets, etc.

Sartorius (= Schneider), **Paul** (b. Nuremberg, XI. 1569; d. Innsbruck, 28. II. 1609), Ger. organist and comp. He was organist to the Archduke Maximilian of Aus. in 1599 and lived at Nuremberg.

Works incl. Masses, *Sonetti spirituali* for 6 voices, motets, madrigals, *Neue teutsche Liedlein*, etc.

Sarum Use, the liturgy in use at Salisbury before the Reformation, differing in some respects from that of Rome and widely spread through medieval Eng. until it was abolished in 1547, though revived from 1553–9.

Sas Orchassal, André (b. Paris, 6. IV. 1900), Belg.-Fr.-Peruvian comp. Studied in Brussels and went to Peru in 1924 as vln. teachei at the Nat. Acad. of Mus. at Lima. He married the Peruvian pianist Lily Rosay and with her founded a private mus. school in 1929. He has done extensive research into Peruvian folklore and frequently used folk-tunes in his comps.

Works incl. *Himno al sol, Himno y danza* and *Poema Indio* for orch.; *Rapsodia peruana* for vln. and orch; *Quenas* for voice, fl. and harp; *Sonatina india* for fl. and pf.; works for vln. and pf.; pf. pieces; songs; etc.

Sass (Saxe), Marie (Constance) (b. Ghent, 26. I. 1838; d. Auteuil nr. Paris, 8. XI. 1907), Belg. soprano. Pupil of Delphine Ugalde, had her 1st stage perf. in Paris in 1859 and went to the Opéra in 1860, where the following year she sang Elisabeth in the Fr. version of Wagner's *Tannhäuser*. She d. insane.

Satanella or The Power of Love, opera by Balfe (lib. by Augustus Glossop Harris and Edmund Falconer, based on Lesage's *Diable boiteux*), prod. London, Covent Garden Theatre, 20. XII. 1858.

Satie, Erik (Alfred Leslie) (b. Honfleur, 17. V. 1866; d. Paris, 1. VII. 1925), Fr. comp. He was brought up in a mus. home, his father being a comp. and mus. pub. in Paris and his mother, of Scot. orig., a minor comp. of pf. pieces under the name of Eugénie Satie-Barnetsche. He spent only a year at the Paris Cons. and later made a precarious living by playing at cafés, writing mus. for the Montmartre song-writer Hypsa and the mus.-hall singer Paulette Darty. Through his friendship with Debussy, c. 1890, he came into contact with intellectual circles. He also studied at the Schola Cantorum under d'Indy and Roussel at the age of 40. He continued to pub. small pf. works under eccentric titles. In later years he came into touch with Jean Cocteau and estab. a school at Arcueil where he exercised some influence on younger comps.

Works incl. symph. drama *Socrate*; incid. mus. for Péladan's *Le Fils des étoiles*; ballets *Parade, Relâche* and *Mercure*; operettas *Geneviève de Brabant* (for marionettes), *Pousse-l'Amour* and *Le Piège de Méduse*; pantomime *Jack in the Box* (orch. by Milhaud); *Messe des pauvres* for voices and org.; pf. pieces *Ogives, 3 Sarabandes, 3 Gymnopédies, 3 Gnossiennes, Danses gothiques, Sonneries de la Rose-Croix, Pièces froides, Préludes en tapisserie, 3 Préludes flasques, Descriptions automatiques, Embryons desséchés, Croquis et agaceries d'un gros bonhomme en bois, Chapitres tournés en tous sens, Vieux*

Sequins et vieilles cuirasses, Heures séculaires et instantanées, 3 Valses du précieux dégoûté, Avant-dernières pensées, etc.; *3 Morceaux en forme de poire, Aperçus désagréables* and *En habit de cheval* for pf. duet; 4 sets of songs, etc.

Satz (Ger. lit. 'setting') = Movement; also texture, lay-out or general contrivance in comp.

Saudades (Port. plur.: *saudade* = longing for the past, nostalgia). The word has been used by Warlock for a set of songs and by Milhaud for 2 vols. of pf. pieces, *S. do Brasil.*

Sauer, Emil (George Konrad) (b. Hamburg, 8. X. 1862; d. Vienna, 28. IV. 1942), Ger. pianist and comp. Studied with N. Rubinstein at the Moscow Cons. and later with Liszt. Began to tour Eur. in 1882 and 1st visited Eng. in 1894. From 1901, with certain intervals, he directed a master class at the Vienna Cons.

Works incl. 2 pf. concertos; 2 sonatas, 24 concert studies, *Suite moderne* and many pieces for pf.

Sauguet, Henri (actually Jean Pierre Poupard) (b. Bordeaux, 18. V. 1901), Fr. comp. and critic. Studied pf. and org. at Bordeaux, then became a pupil of J. Canteloube at Montauban and in 1922 of Koechlin in Paris. Intro. by Milhaud to Satie, he joined the latter's school at Arcueil. In 1936 he succeeded Milhaud as mus. critic to *Le Jour-Écho de Paris.*

Works incl. operas *La Chartreuse de Parme* (after Stendhal) and *La Gageure imprévue* (Sedaine), operettas *Le Plumet du colonel* and *La Contrebasse*; ballets *La Chatte, David, La Nuit, Fastes* and *Les Forains*; incid. mus. for Molière's *Le Sicilien,* Roger Ferdinand's *Irma,* Pierre Emmanuel's *Les Lépreux* and other plays; 3 symphs. incl. *Symphonie expiatoire* (in memory of war victims); pf. concerto; *La Voyante* for soprano and chamber orch.; 2 string 4tets; sonatina for fl. and pf.; sonata in D maj. and other works for pf.; songs to poems by Tagore; film mus., etc.

Saul, oratorio by Handel (lib. by Charles Jennens), prod. London, King's Theatre, 16. I. 1739.

Saunders, John (b. London, 23. XII. 1867; d. London, 7. X. 1919), Eng. violinist. Studied at the G.S.M. in London, became an orch. player and in 1910 leader of the Royal Phil. Society; but he chiefly cultivated chamber mus., esp. at the South Place Concerts, where he played regularly from 1891 to 1919.

Saunderson, James. *See* **Sanderson.**

Sauret, Émile (b. Dun-le-Roi, 22. V. 1852; d. London, 12. II. 1920), Fr. violinist and comp. Pupil of Bériot. He began to travel at an early age, 1st visited London in 1862, played much at the Fr.

court in the last years of the 2nd Empire, visited the U.S.A. twice in 1872–6, studied comp. with Jadassohn at Leipzig and appeared with Liszt. In 1872 he married Teresa Carreño, but they were divorced before long. In 1891 he succeeded Sainton as vln. prof. at the R.A.M. in London and in 1903 he took up a similar post at Chicago.

Works incl. 2 concertos, *Ballade, Légende*; serenade for vln. and orch.; many vln. pieces, studies and arrs., etc.

Sausage Bassoon. *See* **Racket.**

Sautillé (Fr. = springing, bounding), a special way of playing the vln. and other string instruments in such a manner that the bow is made to rebound from the strings.

Sauzay, Charles Eugène (b. Paris, 14. VII. 1809; d. Paris, 24. I. 1901), Fr. violinist and comp. Studied at the Paris Cons., Baillot and Reicha being among his masters. He joined Baillot's 4tet and married his daughter, became court violinist in 1840 and prof. at the Cons. in 1860.

Works incl. incid. mus. for Molière's *George Dandin* and *Le Sicilien*; string trio, pf. trio; vln. and pf. pieces; *Études harmoniques* for solo vln.; songs, etc.

Savart, Félix (b. Mézières, 30. VI. 1791; d. Paris, 17. III. 1841), Fr. scientist. Orig. a physician, he gave up practice in order to investigate sound-waves, becoming a lecturer in physics at the Collège de Fr. in Paris in 1819. He made inventions in connection with vibrations and wrote a number of treatises.

Savile, Jeremy (b. ?; d. ?), Eng. 17th-cent. comp. Contrib. songs to *Select Musicall Ayres and Dialogues* in 1653. Comps. incl. part-song *The Waits,* song 'Here's a health unto His Majesty', etc.

Sāvitri, opera by Holst (lib. by comp., based on an episode in the *Mahabharata*), prod. London, Wellington Hall, 5. XII. 1916; 1st public perf. London, Lyric Theatre, Hammersmith, 23. VI. 1921.

Savonarola, opera by Stanford (lib. by Gilbert Arthur à Beckett), prod., in Ger. (trans. by Ernst Frank), Hamburg, 18. IV. 1884.

Savorini, Eugenia. *See* **Tadolini.**

Sawallisch, Wolfgang (b. Munich, 26. VIII. 1923), Ger. cond. Studied at the Munich Hochschule für Musik with J. Haas, making his début in Augsburg in 1947, where he remained until 1953, when he became mus. director at the opera in Aachen. From 1957 to 1959 he cond. at the Wiesbaden opera and from 1959 to 1963 in Cologne. Since 1957 he has also cond. at Bayreuth.

Sax. Belg. family of instrument makers:
1. Charles Joseph S. (b. Dinant, 1. II. 1791; d. Paris, 26. IV. 1865). He set up in business at Brussels, made wind instru-

ments and prod. several inventions, esp. in connection with horns and other brass instruments.

2. Adolphe (actually Antoine Joseph) S. (b. Dinant, 6. XI. 1814; d. Paris, 4. II. 1894), son of prec. Studied fl. and clar. at the Brussels Cons. and worked with his father, made several improvements in wind instruments and estab. himself in Paris in 1842. His chief inventions are the Saxhorn and the Saxophone.

3. Alphonse S. (b. ?; d. ?), brother of prec. He made some inventions in connection with the valves of brass instruments

Works incl. operas *Il ratto di Helena, Narciso trasformato, Armida abbandonata, Enea, Le nozze d'Amore e di Psiche* and *Circe delusa*; Masses; oratorio *S. Cecilia*; madrigals, etc.

Scala di seta, La (*The Silken Ladder*), opera by Rossini (lib. by Gaetano Rossi, based on Planard's lib. *L'Échelle de soie* set by Gaveaux), prod. Venice, Teatro San Moisè, 9. V. 1812.

Scala enigmatica (It. = enigmatic scale; also *enimmatica*), Verdi's term for the curious scale on which he constructed his *Ave Maria* for 4 voices comp. *c*. 1889:

SCALA ENIGMATICA

and estab. himself independently in Paris, but did not succeed.

Saxe, Marie. *See* **Sass.**

Saxhorn, a brass wind instrument allied to the Bugle, but with valves, invented by Adolphe Sax and patented by him in 1845. It is played with a cup mouthpiece and made in 7 different pitches, covering between them a range of some 5 8ves: soprano in Eb, alto in Bb (both also called Flügelhorns), tenor in Eb, baritone in Bb (both also called Althorns), bass in Bb (Euphonium), bass tuba in Eb (Bombardon) and contrabass in Bb. They are rarely used in the orch., but are regular constituents of military and brass bands.

Saxophone, a wind instrument made of brass, but with woodwind characteristics, invented by Adolphe Sax *c*. 1840 and patented by him in 1846. It is played through a mouthpiece with a single reed of the clar. type and the notes are controlled by keys. It is made in 5 or 6 pitches: sopranino in Eb (rare), soprano in Bb, alto in Eb, tenor in Bb (these 2 the most common), baritone in Eb and bass in Bb. It is less common in the orch. than in military and jazz bands, where it is regularly used.

Sayers, Dorothy (1893–1957), Eng. novelist and dramatist. *See* **Hopkins** (*Just Vengeance*).

Saynète (Fr.) = Span. **Sainete.**

Sayve (Sainne, Saibe, etc.), **Lambert de** (b. ? Liège, 1549; d. Linz, 1614). He was a pupil of Philippe de Monte, and succeeded him as Imp. *Kapellmeister* in 1603. Wrote motets, Masses, *canzoni* and Ger. songs.

Scacchi, Marco (b. Rome, *c*. 1602; d. Gallese nr. Rome, *c*. 1685), It. comp. Pupil of G. F. Anerio. In 1628 he was app. director of mus. to the court at Warsaw, whence he returned to It. in 1648. He intro. It. opera to Warsaw, Danzig and Vilna. He wrote some theoret. tracts.

Scala Theatre (Teatro alla Scala), the great opera-house at Milan, built, after the destruction by fire of the Teatro Regio Ducal in 1776, on the site of the church of Santa Maria alla Scala and opened 3. VIII. 1778. It was reconstructed in 1867 and the stage was re-equipped in 1921. During the 1939–45 war it was damaged, but not irreparably.

Scalabrini, Paolo (b. ? Bologna or Lucca, *c*. 1713; d. Lucca, 23. II. 1806), It. comp. Went to Copenhagen in 1747 as cond. of the Mingotti opera co., and stayed there as mus. director to the Dan. court 1748–53 and again 1775–81, when he retired to It. He was among the 1st to write an opera to Dan. words.

Works incl. Dan. operas *Love rewarded, or The Faithful Lovers, The Oracle, Love without Stockings,* and *c*. 20 It. operas; oratorio *Giuseppe riconosciuto*; symphs., etc.

Scalchi, Sofia (b. Turin, 29. XI. 1850; d. Rome, 22. VIII. 1922), It. contralto. Studied with Boccabadati and made her 1st stage appearance at Mantua in 1866. She 1st visited Eng. in 1868 and sang regularly in London until 1890; also travelled widely in Eur. and 1st went to U.S.A. in 1882.

Scale (from Lat. and It. *scala* = ladder), succession of adjoining notes whether proceeding in ascent or descent. For possible varieties see illustration overleaf. *See also* **Scala enigmatica.**

Scandello (or **Scandellus**), **Antonio** (b. Bergamo, 17. I. 1517; d. Dresden, 18. I. 1580), It. comp. He is 1st heard of as a member of the Saxon court chapel at Dresden in 1553, but he often returned to Brescia for visits, as in 1567, when he and his family took refuge there during the plague at Dresden. Among the court musicians was his brother Angelo S., and also employed at the court was the It.

painter Benedetto Tola, whose daughter Agnese became S.'s 2nd wife in 1568, in which year he was app. *Kapellmeister* in place of Matthieu Le Maistre, whose asst. *Kapellmeister* he had been for 2 years. He became involved in quarrels with the Ger. court musicians and the Flem. singers because the Its. received higher pay.

Works incl. Masses, motets, setting for voices of the Passion and Resurrection narrative according to St. John, hymn

Swed. (1680–3). He also held a similar post at the church of San Gerolamo della Carità before moving to Naples as cond. of the San Bartolomeo opera house (1683–4) and *maestro di cappella* to the court (1684), remaining there for almost 20 years. In Florence 1702–3 he found a patron in Ferdinand (III) de' Medici, for whom he continued to write operas later, but 1703–8 lived mostly in Rome, working first as asst. (1703) then as chief *maestro di cappella* (1707) at the church of Santa

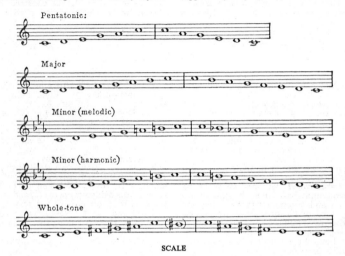

Pentatonic:

Major

Minor (melodic)

Minor (harmonic)

Whole-tone

SCALE

tunes for several voices and other church mus.; madrigals, epithalamia, *canzoni napoletane* for 4 voices, sacred and secular Ger. songs for several voices and instruments; lute mus., etc.

Scandinavian Composers. *See* **Danish, Norwegian, Swedish.**

Scaria, Emil (b. Graz, 18. IX. 1838; d. Blasewitz nr. Dresden, 22. VII. 1886), Aus. bass. Studied at the Vienna Cons. and made his 1st stage appearance at Budapest in 1860. In 1862 he visited London to study under Manuel García and sang at the Crystal Palace. In 1876 he sang Wotan in Wagner's *Ring* at Bayreuth and in 1882 Gurnemanz in *Parsifal* there.

Scarlatti. It. family of musicians:

1. **(Pietro) Alessandro (Gaspare) S.** (b. Palermo, 2. V. 1660; d. Naples, 24. X. 1725), comp. At the age of 12 he moved with his parents to Rome, where the success of his first opera, *Gli equivoci nel sembiante* (1679), won him the appt. of *maestro di cappella* to Queen Christina of

Maria Maggiore, and receiving support from Cardinal Ottoboni, who made him his private *maestro di cappella*. In Rome he was restricted by eccles. opposition to opera, but, in addition to operas for Florence, comp. numerous oratorios, serenatas, cantatas, etc. After a brief visit to Venice in 1707 he was recalled to his old post in Naples at the end of the following year, and was knighted in 1715. He again lived chiefly in Rome 1717–22, but then returned finally to Naples. Among his pupils were his son Domenico S. (5. below), Geminiani and Hasse.

Works incl. 115 operas, incl. *Gli equivoci nel sembiante, L'honestà negli amori, Il Pompeo, Olimpia vendicata, La Rosmene, La Statira, Gli equivoci in amore, Pirro e Demetrio, La caduta de' decemviri, Il prigioniero fortunato, L'Eraclea, Il Mitridate Eupatore, Il Tigrane, Il trionfo dell' onore, Marco Attilio Regolo, La Griselda,* etc.; oratorios *La Maddalena pentita, Giuditta, San Filippo Neri,* etc.;

Passion; 16 extant Masses, incl. 5 with orch.; *Salve Regina, Stabat Mater, motets* and other church mus.; over 600 cantatas; 12 *Sinfonie da concerto grosso*; concertos; chamber mus.; keyboard mus., etc.

2. Francesco S. (b. Palermo, 5. XII. 1666; d. ? Dublin, *c.* 1741), violinist and comp., brother of prec. He became violinist to the court at Naples on Alessandro S.'s appt. as *maestro di cappella* in 1684, and later worked in Palermo. In Vienna in 1715 Fux unsuccessfully recommended him for appt. at court. He was in London 1619–24, and later prob. went to Dublin.

Works incl. operas; church mus.; cantatas, arias, etc.

3. Tommaso S. (b. Palermo, *c.* 1671; d. Naples, 1. VIII. 1760), tenor, brother of prec. Lived in Naples, where he studied at the Cons. di S. Onofrio and sang in the operas of his brother Alessandro S.

4. Pietro Filippo S. (b. Rome, 5. I. 1679; d. Naples, 22. II. 1750), organist, nephew of prec., son of 1. Pupil of his father, he was *maestro di cappella* of Urbino Cathedral 1705–8, then moved to Naples, where he became supernumerary, in 1712 chief, organist of the court chapel. Of his comps. only 6 toccatas survive.

5. (Giuseppe) Domenico S. (b. Naples, 26. X. 1685; d. Madrid, 23. VII. 1757), harpsichordist and comp., brother of prec. Pupil of his father, in 1701 he was app. organist and comp. to the court at Naples, where his operas *L'Ottavia ristituita al trono* and *Il Giustino* were prod. in 1703. Sent by his father to Venice in 1705, he travelled by way of Florence, where he presented himself to Alessandro's patron, Ferdinando de' Medici. In Venice he met Gasparini, and prob. studied with him. Moving to Rome, he is said to have engaged with Handel in a contest in harpsichord and org. playing, arranged by Cardinal Ottoboni. He was *maestro di cappella* to Queen Maria Casimira of Pol. in Rome 1709–14, and of the Cappella Giulia 1714–19, but the next year went to the Port. court in Lisbon. Back in Th. 1724–9, he then went to Seville (later Madrid) in the service of the Span. court, where he remained until his death.

Works incl. operas *La silvia, Tolomeo ed Alessandro, L'Orlando, Tetide in Sciro, Ifigenia in Aulide, Ifigenia in Tauride, Amor d'un' ombra, Ambleto,* etc.; oratorios; church mus.; cantatas, etc.; *c.* 600 one-movement harpsichord pieces (30 of them pub. in his lifetime under the title *Essercizi*), now commonly called sonatas.

6. Giuseppe S. (b. Naples, *c.* 1718; d. Vienna, 17. VIII. 1777), comp., cousin (?) of prec. Wrote operas for the It. stage,

possibly spent some time in Spain, and settled in Vienna in 1757.

Works incl. operas *Merope, Dario, I portentosi effetti della Madre Natura* (lib. by Goldoni), *L'isola disabitata, L'amor geloso,* etc.; arias; cantatas; keyboard mus., etc.

Scarlet Letter, The, opera by W. Damrosch (lib. by George Parsons Lathrop, based on Hawthorne's novel), prod. Boston, 10. II. 1896.

Scarron, Paul (1610–60), Fr. author and poet. *See* **Lächerliche Prinz Jodelet** (Keiser).

Scena (It. = stage, or scene, i.e. the subdivision of an act in a dramatic piece), a technical term for operatic solo numbers on a large scale, usually a recitative followed by one or more aria-like sections; also similar pieces designed for concert perf.

Scenario (It.), the sketch or rough draft for the plot of an opera lib. or for the story of a ballet, etc.

Scenes from Goethe's 'Faust' (Schumann). *See* **Szenen aus Goethe's 'Faust'.**

Schachbrett (Schachtbrett), prob. an early form of harpsichord. It is mentioned in Cersne von Minden's *Minneregeln* of 1404. The name does not, apparently, mean 'chessboard' but derives from an old Germanic word *Schacht,* meaning spring or quill (*cf.* Eng. 'jack').

Schack (orig. Žák), **Benedict** (b. Miřovice, II. 1758; d. Munich, 11. XII. 1826), Boh. tenor and comp. A member of Schikaneder's opera co., he was the 1st Tamino in Mozart's *Magic Flute.* Mozart wrote pf. variations on a song prob. by him, 'Ein Weib ist das herrlichste Ding' (K.613).

Works incl. *Singspiele* (some with Gerl and others), *Der dumme Gärtner, Der Stein der Weisen. Der Fall ist noch weit seltner* (sequel to Martín y Soler's *Una cosa rara*), etc.; also church mus.

Schadaeus, Abraham (b. Senftenberg, 1566; d. Finsterwalde, 10. X. 1626), Ger. comp. He became *Rektor* of the *Lateinschule* in Speyer in 1603. His *Promptuarium musicum,* a collection of motets, was pub. in Strasbourg in 3 parts, in 1611, 1612 and 1613. A *bassus generalis* was added by his friend Caspar Vincentius. (A 4th part, 1617, was entirely by Vincentius.)

Schaeffner, André (b. Paris, 7. II. 1895), Fr. musicologist. Studied at the Schola Cantorum in Paris and after 1920 became mus. critic to var. periodicals. His books incl. studies of the origin of mus. instruments and of Stravinsky. In 1929 he became director of the ethnomusicological section of the Musée de l'Homme in Paris.

Schäfer, Dirk (b. Rotterdam, 25. XI. 1873; d. Amsterdam, 16. II. 1931), Dutch pianist and comp. Studied at the

Cologne Cons. and in Berlin. He 1st settled at The Hague and in 1904 at Amsterdam.

Works incl. *Suite pastorale* and *Javaansche Rhapsodie* for orch.; string 4tet, pf. 5tet; vln. and pf. sonatas; pf. works, etc.

Schäffer, Bogusław (b. Lwów, 6. VI. 1929), Pol. comp. Studied in Cracow with A. Malawski and musicology in Warsaw with Jachimecki. For some of his works he has evolved a graphical notation.

Works incl. *Scultura* for orch.; *Monosonata* for 24 string instruments; *Topofonica* for 40 instruments; *Equivalenze sonore* for perc. instruments; concerto for harpsichord, perc. and orch.; *4 Movements* for pf. and orch.; *Tertium datum* for clavichord and chamber orch.

Schaffrath, Christoph (b. Hohenstein nr. Dresden, 1709; d. Berlin, 17. II. 1763), Ger. harpsichordist, organist and comp. In 1733, when in the service of a Pol. prince, he competed unsuccessfully with W. F. Bach for the post of organist at St. Sophia's Church at Dresden, but in 1736 he became chamber musician to the crown prince of Prus. and remained with him when he acceded as Frederick II.

Works incl. symphs. and overtures for orch.; harpsichord and vln. concertos; chamber mus., etc.

Schale, Christian Friedrich (b. Brandenburg, 10. III. 1713; d. Berlin, 2. III. 1800), Ger. organist and comp. Pupil of C. F. Rolle in Magdeburg, he entered the service of Frederick II of Prus. in 1741 and became organist of Berlin Cathedral in 1763. Comp. mostly keyboard mus.

Schalk, Franz (b. Vienna, 27. V. 1863; d. Edlach, 2. IX. 1931), Aus. cond. Pupil of Bruckner and, after var. engagements, chief cond. at the Vienna Court Opera in succession to Ferdinand Löwe, and director (partly with R. Strauss) from 1918 to 1929. He 1st visited Eng. in 1898. He was responsible for a radical revision of Bruckner's symphs.

Schalmei (Ger.) = Shawm.

Schantz, Johan Filip von (b. Ulvila, 17. I. 1835; d. Helsinki, 24. VII. 1865), Fin. cond. and comp. Studied law at Helsinki Univ. and, after involving himself in political demonstrations during the Crimean War in 1855, at Stockholm and at the Leipzig Cons. In 1860 he returned home as cond. of the orch. attached to the new theatre, but left for Stockholm in 1863 with part of the orch. after a disagreement with the management. He cond. concerts also at Göteborg and Copenhagen, but later returned to Helsinki in poor health.

Works incl. symph. poem *Kullervo* (on the *Kalevala*); part-songs, songs, folksong settings, etc.

Scharwenka, (Ludwig) Philipp (b. Szamotuly, Poznań 16. II. 1847;. d. Bad Nauheim, 16. VII. 1917), Ger.-Pol. comp. and teacher. On the family's removal to Berlin he studied mus. at Kullak's school there and remained as teacher until 1881, when he joined his brother's newly opened Cons., which he directed in 1891 on the latter's departure for Amer., together with Hugo Goldschmidt. In 1880 he married the violinist Marianne Stresow (1856–1918).

Works incl. 2 symphs., serenade, Festival Overture, *Liebesnacht*, *Arcadian Suite*, symph. poems *Frühlingswogen* and *Traum und Wirklichkeit*; vln. concerto; *Herbstfeier* and *Sakuntala* (after Kalidasa) for solo voices, chorus and orch.; pf. trio in C♯ min.; 3 concert pieces for vln. and pf., vln. and cello studies; *Album polonais*, 3 sonatas and many other works for pf., etc.

Scharwenka, (Franz) Xaver (b. Szamotuly, Poznań, 6. I. 1850; d. Berlin, 8. XII. 1924), Ger.-Pol. pianist, comp. and teacher, brother of prec. Studied at Kullak's school of mus. in Berlin, where the family had settled in 1865, and made his 1st appearance as a pianist there in 1869. Later he travelled widely, paying his 1st visit to Eng. in 1879. In 1881 he opened a Cons. of his own in Berlin, which in 1893 became amalgamated with Klindworth's. In 1891–8 he lived mainly in N.Y., where he had opened a branch of his school.

Works incl. opera *Mataswintha* (on Felix Dahn's novel *Ein Kampf um Rom*); symph. in C min.; 4 pf. concertos; pf. 4tet, 2 pf. trios; 2 cello and pf. sonatas; Theme and Variations, Pol. dances and numerous other works for pf., etc.

Schat, Peter (b. Utrecht, 5. VI. 1935), Dutch comp. Studied in Utrecht and The Hague, and then with Seiber and Boulez. He is well known as an experimental comp.

Works incl. *Mosaics* for orch.; *Cryptogamen* for baritone and orch.; *Signalement* for 6 perc. instruments and 3 double basses; *Improvisations and Symphonies* for wind 5tet; *Labyrinth*, work for 'musical theatre' with 'happenings'.

Schauspieldirektor, Der (*The Impresario*), play with mus. by Mozart (lib. by Gottlieb Stephanie, jun.), prod. Vienna, Schönbrunn Palace, at court, 7. II. 1786; 1st Vienna perf., Kärntnertortheater, 18. II. 1786.

Schechner, Anna (Nanette) (b. Munich, 1806; d. ? 29. IV. 1860), Ger. soprano. Pupil of Weber and studied in It. 1st appeared in Munich and in 1826 in Vienna. She married the painter Karl Waagen in 1832.

Scheffel, Joseph Victor von (1826–86), Ger. poet and novelist. *See* Henschel (*Trompeter von Säckingen*), Jensen (*Gaudeamus*), Scholz (*Trumpeter von Säck-*

ingen), **Schreker** (*Ekkehard*), **Trompeter von Säckingen** (Nessler).

Scheherazade (Ravel and Rimsky-Korsakov). *See* **Shéhérazade** and **Shahrazad.**

Scheibe, Johann Adolph (b. Leipzig, V. 1708; d. Copenhagen, 22. IV. 1776), Ger. writer on mus., critic and comp. Studied law at Leipzig Univ. and in 1736 settled in Hamburg, where he ed. the periodical *Der critische Musikus* (1737–40), in which he attacked Bach. He was *Kapellmeister* to the Margrave of Brandenburg-Culmbach 1739–44, and cond. of the court opera in Copenhagen 1744–8.

Works incl. one opera; cantatas; Masses and other church mus.; instrumental mus.; songs, etc.

Scheidemann. Ger. family of organists and comps.:

1. **David S.** (b. Hamburg, ?; d. Hamburg, ?), organist in Wohrden and subsequently at St. Catherine's Church, Hamburg. Pub. a hymn-book with H. and J. Praetorius and Joachim Decker in 1604, with the tunes in the soprano part, not, as earlier, in the tenor.

2. **Heinrich S.** (b. Wöhrden, *c.* 1596; d. Hamburg, 1663), son of prec. Pupil of his father and later of Sweelinck at Amsterdam. In 1625 he succeeded his father as organist at St. Catherine's Church, Hamburg, where on his death he was himself succeeded by Reinken, who was his pupil, as were Fabricius and Weckmann. He contrib. to Part V of Rist's hymn-book *Neue himmlische Lieder* (1651).

Works incl. church mus.; org. pieces, etc.

Scheidemantel, Karl (b. Weimar, 21. I. 1859; d. Weimar, 26. VI. 1923), Ger. baritone. Studied with Bodo Borchers and made his 1st stage appearance at Weimar in 1878. After further study with Stockhausen he became famous, mainly as a Wagner singer. He 1st visited London in 1884 and was 1st engaged at the Bayreuth Wagner theatre in 1886. From 1920 to 1922 he was director of the Dresden Landesoper. He wrote 2 books on singing.

Scheidler, Dorette. *See* Spohr.

Scheidt, Samuel (b. Halle, 1587; d. Halle, 30. III. 1654), Ger. organist and comp. Organist at St. Maurice's Church, Halle, 1603. Pupil of Sweelinck at Amsterdam. He returned to Halle in 1609, and became court organist to the Margrave of Brandenburg, in his capacity as Protestant administrator of the archbishopric of Magdeburg, and *Kapellmeister* in 1619. He lost his appt. in 1625 as a result of the 30 Years War. His *Tabulatura nova* for the org. was printed in score, not in the old Ger. Tablature.

Works incl. *Cantiones sacrae* for 8 voices;

sacred concertos for 2–12 voices with instruments; pavans and galliards for 4–5 voices; *Liebliche Krafft-Blümlein* for 2 voices and instruments; org. accomps. for or transcriptions of 100 hymns and psalms; *Tabulatura nova* containing a great variety of org. pieces in 3 vols., etc.

Schein, Johann Hermann (b. Grünhain, Saxony, 20. I. 1586; d. Leipzig, 19. XI. 1630), Ger. comp. After the death of his father, a Lutheran pastor, he went to Dresden as a choir-boy in the court chapel in 1599, to the grammar-school at Schulpforta in 1603 and to Leipzig Univ. in 1607. In 1615 he was app. *Kapellmeister* at the court of Weimar and in 1616 became cantor at St. Thomas's School, Leipzig, on the death of Calvisius, remaining there until his death.

Works incl. *Cantiones sacrae* for 5–12 voices; 2 vols. of sacred concertos for 3–5 voices with instruments; *Fontana d'Israel* containing biblical words set for 4–5 voices and instruments; *Cantional* hymn-book with *c.* 80 tunes of his own; songs for 5 voices, *Venus-Kränzlein, Studenten-Schmaus* and *Diletti pastorali*; instrumental dances *Banchetto musicale*; songs with instruments *Musica boscareccia*; wedding and funeral cantatas, etc.

Schelble, Johann Nepomuk (b. Hüfingen, Black Forest, 16. V. 1789; d. Frankfurt, 7. VIII. 1837), Ger. singer, teacher and cond. Studied with Vogler and others, lived and sang in Vienna in 1813–16 and then settled at Frankfurt, where he taught and founded the Caecilian Society in 1818.

Schelle, Johann (b. Geissing nr. Meissen, 6. IX. 1648; d. Leipzig, 10. III. 1710), Ger. organist and comp. He was a choir-boy at Dresden, Wolfenbüttel and Leipzig. Studied at Leipzig, became cantor at Eilenburg and in 1677 cantor at St. Thomas's Church, Leipzig.

Works incl. cantatas, songs, etc.

Schellen (Ger.) = Jingles.

Schellenbaum (Ger. lit. jingle-tree) = Chinese Pavilion, Jingling Johnny, Turkish Crescent.

Schellentrommel (Ger. lit. drum with jingles) = Tambourine.

Schelling, Ernest (b. Belvidere, New Jersey, 26. VII. 1876; d. New York, 8. XII. 1939), Amer. pianist and comp. After coming out as a wonder child at Philadelphia at the age of 4, he studied at the Paris Cons., also in Vienna with Leschetizky for pf. and Bruckner for comp., as well as elsewhere with Paderewski, Moszkowski and others. He toured widely, joined the Amer. army in 1918 and later lectured on the orch. to children.

Works incl. symph. in C min., *Symph. Legend*, fantasy *A Victory Ball* and *Morocco* for orch.; *Fantastic Suite* and *Impressions from an Artist's Life* for pf.

and orch., vln. concerto; *Divertimento* for pf. 5tet and other chamber mus.; pf. pieces; songs, etc.

Schelomo, rhapsody for cello and orch. by Bloch, comp. 1915. 1st perf. N.Y., 3. V. 1916.

Schemelli, Georg Christian (b. Herzberg, *c.* 1678; d. Zeitz, 5. III. 1762), Ger. musician and mus. ed. Pupil at St. Thomas's school, Leipzig, cantor at the palace of Zeitz. His *Musicalisches Gesang-Buch*, ed. by Bach, was pub. in 1736. To some of the hymns in it Bach wrote chorale preludes.

Schenck, Johan(n) (b. Elberfeld, II. 1656; d. ?), Ger. or Dutch vla. da gamba player and comp. He worked at the electoral court at Düsseldorf and in Amsterdam.

Works incl. opera *Ceres en Bacchus*; chamber sonatas for 2 vlns., vla. da gamba and bass, vla. da gamba sonatas and suites, etc.

Schenk, Johann Baptist (b. Wiener Neustadt, 30. XI. 1753; d. Vienna, 29. XII. 1836), Aus. comp. Pupil of Wagenseil 1774–7, he made his public début as an opera comp. in 1785. Beethoven was his pupil in 1793, and he was also a friend of Mozart and Schubert.

Works incl. *Singspiele*: *Die Weinlese, Die Weihnacht auf dem Lande, Achmet und Almanzine, Der Dorfbarbier, Die Jagd, Der Fassbinder*, etc.; Masses and other church mus.; cantatas *Die Huldigung* and *Der Mai*; 10 symphs.; 4 harp concertos; string 4tets and trios; songs, etc.

Schenker, Heinrich (b. Wisniowczyki, 19. VI. 1867; d. Vienna, 13. I. 1935), Pol.-Aus. theorist. Studied with Bruckner at the Vienna Cons. and on Brahms's recommendation pub. some early comps. He taught a number of pupils privately and in his literary works, incl. *Neue musikalische Theorien und Phantasien* and *Das Meisterwerk in der Musik*, laid down his extremely minute method of analysing masterpieces.

Scherchen, Hermann (b. Berlin, 21. VI. 1891; d. Florence, 12. VI. 1966), Ger. cond. Self-taught in mus., he played the vla. in the Blüthner Orch. from 1907 to 1910, also playing with the Berlin Phil. Orch. He made his début as a cond. in 1912 with Schönberg's *Pierrot lunaire*, and in 1914 became cond. of the Riga Symph. Orch., being interned in Rus. during World War I. After the war he founded the Neue Musikgesellschaft and edited the periodical *Melos* (1920–1). From 1928 to 1933 he was cond. of the Königsberg Radio Orch. He was esp. well known as a cond. of new mus., the cause of which he championed throughout his life.

Scherer, Sebastian Anton (b. Ulm, X. 1631; d. Ulm, 26. VIII. 1712), Ger.

organist and comp. He rose through var. posts to that of organist of Ulm Cathedral in 1671.

Works incl. Masses, motets and psalms; sonatas for 2 vlns. and bass; org. pieces; suites for lute, etc.

Schering, Arnold (b. Breslau, 2. IV. 1877; d. Berlin, 7. III. 1941), Ger. musicologist. Studied at Leipzig Univ., where in 1907 he became lecturer and later prof. of mus. From 1909 he also lectured at the Cons. In 1920 he became prof. at Halle Univ. and in 1928 at Berlin Univ. His books incl. studies of the early vln. concerto, the develop. of the oratorio and sonata, the perf. of old mus., early org. and chamber mus. and a series of attempts to prove that Beethoven's sonatas and 4tets are based on Shakespeare's plays and other dramatic works.

Scherz, List und Rache (*Jest, Cunning and Revenge*), operetta by Bruch (lib. by Goethe, altered by Ludwig Bischoff), prod. Cologne, 14. I. 1858.

Opera by Philipp Christoph Kayser (1755–1823) (lib. do.), comp. 1785–6, not perf.

For other settings *see* **Goethe.**

Scherzando (It. = playful, humorous, skittish), a direction written by comps. over passages intended to be perf. in that manner. It may also be used as an adj. in tempo directions, e.g. *allegretto scherzando*.

Scherzevole (It., accent on 2nd syll.), the same as the prec., but less frequently used.

Scherzetto, a small Scherzo.

Scherzi, Gli (*The Jokes*), one of the nicknames of Haydn's 6 string 4tets, Op. 33, comp. 1781. Also known as the 'Rus.' 4tets or *Jungfernquartette*.

Scherzino, a small Scherzo. This term, like Scherzetto, is used only for short instrumental pieces of the scherzo type, not for movements in Scherzo form.

Scherzo, one of the 2 middle movements, more usually the 3rd, of a 4-movement symph., sonata or other sonata-form work, where it displaced the Minuet. It does not occur regularly before the early 19th cent., being estab. mainly by Beethoven and Schubert; but the term S. dates back to the 17th cent., when It. canzonets were often called 'scherzi musicali' and instrumental pieces were also sometimes pub. under that title. (For an early use of the name *see* Haydn's work above.) The S., having arisen from the minuet, is normally in fast triple time, generally 3–4 with one beat in a bar, and it has as a rule a contrasting trio section. But exs. in duple or quadruple time occur, e.g. in Beethoven's Eb maj. pf. sonata, Op. 31 No. 3, in Mendelssohn and Schumann. Sometimes the trio occurs twice, e.g. in Beethoven's 7th symph., or there may be, esp. in

Schumann, 2 different trios. A coda, often based on the trio, is neither normal nor unusual. There are very successful S.s which do not conform to the classical pattern, e.g. Chopin's.

Scherzoso (It.) = Scherzando, but less frequently used.

Scheurleer, Daniel (François) (b. The Hague, 13. XI. 1855; d. The Hague, 6. II. 1927), Dutch musicologist. A banker by profession, he made a collection of mus., mus. books and instruments and was a member of several important Dutch mus. societies. His writings incl. books on mus. in the Netherlands, Mozart, Berlioz, Liszt, etc.

Schiavetto, Giulio (b. ?; d. ?), It. comp., active in Dalmatia during the 2nd half of the 16th cent. His madrigals and motets, pub. in Venice in 1563 and 1565 respectively, were dedicated to Gerolamo Savorgnano, bishop of Šibenik.

Schibler, Armin (b. Kreuzlingen, Lake Constance, 20. XI. 1920), Swiss comp. Studied mus. while at school at Aarau and then at the Zürich Cons. In 1942 he became a pupil of Burkhard.

Works incl. oratorio *Media in vita*; operas *Der spanische Rosenstock*, *The Devil in the Winter Palace*, *The Feet in the Fire*; 3 chamber ballets; cantatas *Marignano*, *Vision des Mittelalters*, *Die Hochzeit* (Gotthelf) and *Cantata domestica*; 3 symphs., symph. variations, toccata and fugue for string orch.; vln. concerto, pf. concerto, horn concerto, trombone concerto, perc. concerto, fantasy for vln. and orch; concerto for vln., cello and strings; toccata, interlude and fugue for wind instruments; pf. 4tet; 4 string 4tets; vln. and pf. sonata; toccata for org.; *Circulus Fugae* for pf.; songs, etc.

Schicht, Johann Gottfried (b. Reichenau nr. Zittau, 29. IX. 1753; d. Leipzig, 16. II. 1823), Ger. harpsichordist and comp. Studied law at Leipzig Univ. but turned to mus. and was engaged as harpsichordist by J. A. Hiller for his concerts, later succeeding him as their cond. In 1810 he was app. cantor at St. Thomas's Church.

Works incl. 3 oratorios, church mus., chamber works, etc.

Schick, Ernst (b. The Hague, X. 1756; d. Berlin, 10. II. 1815), Dutch or Ger. violinist. Married the singer Margarete Luise Hamel in 1791 and was engaged for the Berlin Court Opera in 1793. He estab. chamber concerts there with Bohrer.

Schick (*née* Hamel), **Margarete Luise** (b. Mainz, 26. IV. 1773; d. Berlin, 29. IV. 1809), Ger. soprano. Studied at Würzburg and with Righini at Mainz, where she made her 1st stage appearance in 1788. In 1791 she married Ernst Schick and in 1793 they were both engaged by Frederick William II of Prus. and went to Berlin.

Schicksalslied (*Song of Destiny*), a setting by Brahms for chorus and orch. of a poem in Hölderlin's *Hyperion*, Op. 54, comp. in 1871.

Schiedermair, Ludwig (b. Regensburg, 7. XII. 1876; d. Bensberg nr. Cologne, 30. IV. 1957), Ger. mus. scholar. Studied with Sandberger and Beer-Walbrunn at Munich, where he took a degree in 1901. After further studies with Riemann and Kretzschmar in Berlin he became lecturer at Marburg and in 1914 prof. of mus. at Bonn. Univ. There he became director of the Beethoven Archives, and among his books are bibliog. works on Beethoven and an ed. of Mozart's letters with an iconographical vol.

Schikaneder, (Johann Josef) Emanuel (b. Straubing, 1. XI. 1751; d. Vienna, 21. IX. 1812), Ger. actor, singer, playwright and theatre manager. Settled in Vienna in 1784. Author (or ? part-author with Ludwig Gieseke) of the lib. of Mozart's *Magic Flute*, which he prod. with himself as Papageno. He also wrote libs. for Schack, Gerl, Süssmayr, Woelfl, Seyfried, Winter and others.

Schiller, (Johann Christoph) Friedrich von (1759–1805), Ger. poet and dramatist. *See* Assafiev (*Fiesco* and *Don Carlos*), Balfe (*Joan of Arc*), Berneker (*Bride of Messina*), Boughton (*Invincible Armada*), Bride of Messina (Fibich), Briganti (Mercadante), Bruch (*Lied von der Glocke* and *Macht des Gesanges*), Carafa (*Jeanne d'Arc*), Costa (*Don Carlos*), 'Choral' Symphony (Beethoven), Denza (*Wallenstein*), Don Carlos (Verdi), Faisst (*Macht des Gesanges*), Foerster (J. B.) (*Maria Stuart*), Giovanna d'Arco (Verdi), Guillaume Tell (Rossini), Hellmesberger (3) (*Bürgschaft*), Hiller (F.) (*Demetrius*), Holstein (*Braut von M.*), Ideale (Liszt), d'Indy (*Piccolomini*, *Wallenstein*), Joachim (*Demetrius*), Lachner (F.) (*Bürgschaft*), Lachner (V.) (*Turandot*), Lalo (*Fiesque*), Liadov (*Bride of M.*), Lindpaintner (*Lied von der Glocke*), Luisa Miller (Verdi), Macfarren (G.) (*Don Carlos*), Maid of Orleans (Tchaikovsky), Mascagni (*Ode to Joy*), Masnadieri (Verdi), Mermet (*Jeanne d'Arc*), Naenia (Brahms and Goetz), Neukomm (*Braut von M.*), Nicodé (*Maria Stuart*), Nicolai (W.) (*Song of the Bell*), Niedermeyer (*Marie Stuart*), Reichardt (*Taucher*), Reinecke (*Wilhelm Tell*), Rezniček (*Jungfrau von Orleans*), Rheinberger (*Wallenstein* and *Demetrius*), Romberg (A.) (*Lied von der Glocke*), Schillings (*Verklärten*), Scholz (*Lied von der Glocke*), Schröter (C.) (*Taucher* and *Würde der Frauen*), Schulz-Beuthen (*Wilhelm Tell*), Sechter (*Braut von M.*), Seyfried (*Räuber* and *Jungfrau von O.*), Shaporin (*Robbers*), Shebalin (*Robbers* and *Mary Stuart*), Smetana (*Wallenstein's Camp*), Söderman

(*Maid of Orleans*), **Suppé** (*Wallensteins Lager*), **Tomašek** (*Wallenstein, Maria Stuart, Braut von M.* and songs), **Vaccai** (*Giovanna d'Arco* and *Sposa di Messina*), **Vierling** (*Maria S.*), **Wallenstein** (d'Indy), **Weber (B. A.)** (*W. Tell*), **Weber (C. M. v.)** (*Turandot*), **Weinberger** (*Wallenstein*), **White (M. V.)** (*Ich habe gelebt*), **Zajc** (*Amelia*), **Zumsteeg** (*Räuber, Wallensteins Lager* and *Ritter Toggenburg*). 42 songs by Schubert.

Schillinger, Joseph (b. Kharkov, 31. VIII. 1895; d. N.Y., 23. III. 1943), Rus., later Amer., comp. and theoretician. Studied at St. Petersburg Cons. with Tcherepnin, among others, and then taught at Kharkov Mus. Acad. from 1918 to 1922, and from 1926 to 1928 in Leningrad. In 1929 he settled in the U.S.A., teaching a mathematical method of his own; among his many pupils was Gershwin. He pub. his system in a number of books, and also some comps. incl. *March of the Orient; First Airphonic Suite* for theremin, orch. and pf.; pf. pieces, etc.

Schillings, Max von (b. Düren, Rhineland, 19. IV. 1868; d. Berlin, 23. VII. 1933), Ger. cond. and comp. Studied at Bonn and Munich, where he settled, taking part in the Wagner perfs. at Bayreuth. In 1908 he went to Stuttgart, where he gradually rose to the post of general mus. director of the Court Opera. In 1919 he went to Berlin as director of the State Opera.

Works incl. operas *Ingwelde, Der Pfeifertag, Moloch* (after Hebbel) and *Mona Lisa*; incid. mus. for Aeschylus's *Orestes* and Goethe's *Faust*; symph. fantasies *Meergruss* and *Seemorgen*, symph. prologue, *Oedipus* (after Sophocles) for orch.; recitations with orch. incl. Wildenbruch's *Hexenlied*; vln. concerto, *Zwiegespräch* for vln., cello and small orch.; *Hochzeitslied* for solo voices, chorus and orch.; *Dem Verklärten* (Schiller) and *Glockenlieder* for solo voice and orch.; string 4tet in E. min., string 5tet in E♭ maj.; improvisation for vln. and pf., etc.

Schindler, Anton (b. Meedl nr. Neustadt, Morav., 13. VI. 1795; d. Bockenheim nr. Frankfurt, 16. I. 1864), Aus. violinist and writer on mus. Studied in Vienna, met Beethoven in 1814, played at his concerts and later became his factotum and early biog. He was successively leader of the orch. at the Josephstadt Theatre and the Kärntnertortheater, and later mus. director at Münster and Aachen.

Schipa, Tito (actually Raffaele Attilio Amadeo) (b. Lecce, 2. I. 1889; d. N.Y., XII. 1965), It. tenor. First studied comp., producing some songs and pf. pieces. Then studied singing, making his début in

Vercelli in 1911. From 1920 to 1932 he was a member of the Chicago Civic Opera and from 1932 to 1935 sang at the N.Y. Metropolitan. He lived in the U.S.A. until 1941, when he returned to It.

Works incl. operetta *La Principessa Liana*; a Mass; a Hosanna.

Schippers, Thomas (b. Kalamazoo, 9. III. 1930), Amer. cond. First appeared in public aged 6, at the pf., and became a church organist aged 14. From 1944 to 1945 he studied at the Curtis Inst. in Philadelphia and from 1946 to 1947 privately with O. Samaroff. He also studied at Yale Univ. and the Juilliard School of Mus., and made his début as a cond. with the Lemonade Opera Co. in 1948. After appearances with the N.Y. City Opera Co. and the N.Y. Phil. Orch., he appeared at the N.Y. Metropolitan and La Scala, Milan, in 1955.

Schira, Francesco (b. Malta, 21. VIII. 1809; d. London, 15. X. 1883), It. cond. and comp. Studied at the Cons. of Milan and prod. his 1st opera there in 1832, on the strength of which he was engaged as cond. and comp. for the Opera at Lisbon, where he also taught at the Cons. In 1842 he left for Paris in the hope of obtaining a Fr. lib., but met the manager of the Princess's Theatre in London, who engaged him as cond. In 1844 he went to Drury Lane as Benedict's successor and in 1848 to Covent Garden. He remained in London to his death. In 1873 the Birmingham Festival commissioned a cantata from him.

Works incl. operas *Elena e Malvina, I cavalieri di Valenza, Il fanatico per la musica, Kenilworth* (in Eng., after Scott), *Mina, Theresa, the Orphan of Geneva, Niccolo de' Lapi, Selvaggia, Lia,* operetta *The Ear-Ring*; cantata *The Lord of Burleigh* (after Tennyson); vocal trios and duets; songs, etc.

Schiske, Karl (b. Györ, 12. II. 1916; d. Vienna, 16. VI. 1969), Aus.-Hung. comp. Studied with Ernst Kanitz and devoted himself wholly to comp., without holding any appt., after taking the Ph.D. in 1942.

Works incl. oratorio *Vom Tode* and other choral pieces; 4 symphs. and other orchestral works; pf. concerto, vln. concerto; 2 string 4tets, clar. 5tet, wind 5tet; vln. and pf. sonata; pf. works; org. variations; songs, etc.

Schjelderup, Gerhard (Rosenkrone) (b. Christiansand, 17. XI. 1859; d. Benediktbeuren, Bavar., 29. VII. 1933), Norw. comp. Studied in Paris and later with Mottl at Carlsruhe. He prod. his operas at first in Ger. and Prague. He wrote a hist. of Norw. mus. and biogs. of Grieg and Wagner.

Works incl. operas *Sunday Morning, Norwegian Wedding, Spring Night, The*

Scarlet Pimpernel (after Orczy), *Storm Birds* and others; incid. mus. to Gjellerup's *Offerildene* and other plays; 2 symphs., symph. poem *Brand* (after Ibsen), Christmas and Norw. Suites for orch.; string 4tet, pf. trio; songs, etc.

Schläger (Ger. lit. beaters), sometimes used in scores, etc. as an abbr. for the following. Also in the sing. a popular song.

Schlaginstrumente (Ger. lit. beaten instruments) = Percussion instruments.

Schlagobers (*Whipped Cream* in Viennese dialect), ballet by R. Strauss (choreography by Heinrich Kröller), prod. Vienna, Opera, 9. V. 1924.

Schlagzither (Ger. lit. striking-zither), a zither the strings of which are struck with hammers, i.e. a dulcimer rather than a zither.

Schlegel, August Wilhelm von (1767–1845), Ger. poet, critic and trans. *See* **Fierrabras** (Schubert), **Hark, hark, the lark** (Schubert).

7 poems by S. set as songs by Schubert.

Schleifer (Ger.). *See* **Ornaments**.

Schleppen (Ger. = to drag), sometimes used by Ger. comps. as a negat. imper., *nicht schleppen* = 'do not drag'.

Schlesinger, Kathleen (b. Hollywood nr. Belfast, 27. VI. 1862; d. London, 18. IV. 1953), Brit. mus. research scholar. Made a special study of instruments and contrib. articles on them to the *Encyclopaedia Britannica* and a chapter to the *Oxford Hist. of Music*. Her original scientific investigations into the pipe instruments of ancient Greece resulted in the book *The Greek Aulos*.

Schlick, Arnolt (b. ? Heidelberg, before 1460; d. ? Heidelberg, after 1521), Ger. organist, comp. and theorist. His early life was spent in Heidelberg, but he subsequently travelled widely: to Frankfurt in 1486, where he played the org. during the festivities for the coronation of Maximilian I; to Hol. in 1490; to Strasbourg (many times); to Worms in 1495, where he met Sebastian Virdung; and subsequently to Speyer, Hagenau and elsewhere. During these journeys he gained an enormous reputation for testing new orgs. He was blind, prob. from infancy.

In 1511 he pub. his *Spiegel der Orgelmacher und Organisten*, a treatise on org. building and playing. The *Tabulaturen etlicher lobgesang und lidlein* (Mainz, 1512) followed; it was the first printed book of keyboard mus. to appear in Ger., and contained liturgical org. mus., lute pieces and songs with lute. He also wrote mus. for the coronation of Charles V in Aachen, 1520.

Schlick, Johann Konrad (b. ? Münster, 1748; d. Gotha, 12. VII. 1818), Ger. cellist and comp. He worked in the episcopal chapel at Münster, and in 1777 entered the service of the court in Gotha. He married the violinist Regina Strinasacchi in 1785.

Works incl. concertos; string 5tets and 4tets; pf. trios; cello sonatas; guitar pieces, etc.

Schloezer, Boris Feodorovich de (b. Vitebsk, 8. XII. 1884), Rus. mus. critic. His sister Tatiana married Skriabin, on whom he wrote at first. In 1920 he settled in Paris and wrote criticism both in Rus. and Fr. His books incl. works on Skriabin and Stravinsky.

Schlusnus, Heinrich (b. Braubach, 6. VIII. 1888; d. Frankfurt, 19. VI. 1952), Ger. baritone. Studied with Bachner in Berlin and made his début in Frankfurt in 1912 as a concert singer, and as an opera singer in Hamburg in 1915. From 1915 to 1917 he was a member of the Nuremberg Opera, and from 1917 to 1945 of the Berlin State Opera.

Schlüssel (Ger. lit. key) = Clef.

Schmedes, Erik (b. Gjentofte nr. Copenhagen, 27. VIII. 1866; d. Vienna, 23. III. 1931). Dan. tenor. Studied in Ger. and Aus. and with Padilla in Paris; made his 1st stage appearance at Wiesbaden in 1891. From 1898 to 1924 he sang at the Vienna Court Opera, and in 1899 he was 1st engaged for the Wagner theatre at Bayreuth.

Schmeltzl, Wolfgang (b. Kemnat, Upper Palatinate, *c.* 1500; d. ?, *c.* 1560), Ger. comp. He became cantor at Amberg and married there, but later became a Catholic priest and left his family. He was a schoolmaster in Vienna in 1540.

Works incl. a book of songs, quodlibets and folksong settings for 4–5 voices, etc.

Schmelzer (von Ehrenruff), Andreas (Anton) (b. Vienna, 26. XI. 1653; d. Vienna, 13. X. 1701), Aus. violinist and comp. He was in the service of the Aus. court in 1671–1700.

Works incl. ballet mus. for more than 30 of Draghi's operas.

Schmelzer, (Johann) Heinrich (b. Vienna, *c.* 1623; d. Vienna, 30. VI. 1680), Aus. comp., father of prec. He was chamber musician at the Aus. court in Vienna from 1649, asst. cond. from 1671 and 1st cond. from 1679.

Works incl. ballet mus. for *c.* 40 operas by Draghi and others; *Missa nuptialis* and other church mus.; instrumental sonatas; tpt. fanfares, etc.

Schmetternd (Ger. = brassy, brazen, clanging). The term is prescribed, like the Fr. *cuivré*, when that kind of tone is required of brass instruments, esp. horns.

Schmid(t), Bernhard the Elder (b. ? Strasbourg, 1535; d. there, 1592), Ger. comp. and poet. He pub. a collection of mus. arr. for org. in 2 parts: the 1st contained motets, the 2nd secular songs and dances (Strasbourg, 1577).

Schmid(t), Bernhard the Younger (b. Strasbourg, III. 1567; d. there, ? 1625), Ger. comp., son of prec. His own collection of org. arrs., highly ornamented, was pub. at Strasbourg in 1607.

Schmidt, Bernhard. *See* **Smith, Bernard.**

Schmidt, Franz (b. Pressburg, 22. XII. 1874; d. Perchtoldsdorf, 11. II. 1939), Aus. cellist, pianist and comp. Studied at the Vienna Cons. and in 1896 became cellist in the Court Opera orch. He left in 1910 to become pf. prof. at the Vienna Mus. Acad., of which he became director in 1925. He also appeared as concert pianist.

Works incl. operas *Notre-Dame* (after Hugo) and *Fredegundis*; oratorio *Das Buch mit den sieben Siegeln*; 4 symphs., chaconne and *Variations on a Hussar's Song* for orch.; variations on a theme by Beethoven for pf. and orch.; string 4tet, pf. 5tet; 7 org. works, etc.

Schmidt, Gustav (b. Weimar, 1. IX. 1816; d. Darmstadt, 11. II. 1882), Ger. cond. and comp. Studied with Hummel and others at Weimar and with Mendelssohn at Leipzig. He began as opera cond. at Brno and then served in the same capacity in several Ger. towns, last at Darmstadt.

Works incl. operas *Prinz Eugen der edle Ritter, Weibertreue, La Réole, Alibi*; incid. mus. for a play based on Dickens's *Christmas Carol*; male-voice choruses; songs, etc.

Schmidt-Isserstedt, Hans (b. Berlin, 5. V. 1900), Ger. cond. Studied with Schrecker and also at the Univ. of Cologne, graduating in 1923. He began his career at the Wuppertal opera and then from 1928 to 1931 cond. at Rostock, from 1931 to 1933 at Darmstadt, and from 1935 to 1942 was principal cond. at the Hamburg State Opera. He was director of the Ger. Opera in Berlin from 1942 to 1945 and since then has been chief cond. of the North Ger. Radio Symph. Orch.

Schmidt, Johann Christoph, sen. and **jun.** *See* **Smith, John Christopher.**

Schmitt, (Georg) Aloys (b. Hanover, 2. II. 1827; d. Dresden, 15. X. 1902), Ger. cond., pianist and comp. Pupil of his father, the pianist and comp. Aloys S. (1788–1866). He toured widely in Eur. as pianist and after var. cond.'s posts settled at Dresden in 1893 as director of the Mozart Society. He married the singer Cornelia Czany (1851–1906) and completed and ed. Mozart's unfinished C min. Mass.

Works incl. opera *Trilby* (adapted from Nodier by Scribe), *Das Wunderwasser* and *Maienzauber*; incid. mus. for plays; overtures and other orchestral works; concert piece for ob. and orch.; string 4tets, pf. trios; pf. pieces; songs, etc.

Schmitt, Florent (b. Blamont, 28. IX. 1870; d. Neuilly-sur-Seine, 17. VIII. 1958), Fr. comp. Studied mus. at Nancy

from 1887 and in 1889 was sent to the Paris Cons., where he was 1st a pupil of Dubois and Lavignac and afterwards of Massenet and Fauré for comp. Won the Prix de Rome in 1900 and wrote his 1st mature works during his 3 years in Rome. Director, Lyons Cons. 1922–4.

Works incl. ballets *La Tragédie de Salomé, Le Petit Elfe Ferme-l'œil, Reflets, Ourvasi* and *Oriane et le Prince d'Amour*; incid. mus. for Shakespeare's *Antony and Cleopatra* (trans. by Gide); film mus. for an adaptation of Flaubert's *Salammbô*; Psalm xlvi for soprano solo, chorus, org. and orch.: symph. study *Le Palais hanté* (after Poe), symph., *3 Rapsodies, Ronde burlesque, Çançunik, Kermesse-Valse, Symphonie concertante* and *Suite sans esprit de suite* for orch.; *Légende* for saxophone and orch., *Final* for cello and orch.; pf. 5tet, *Lied et Scherzo* for double wind 5tet, *Andante et Scherzo* for chromatic harp and string 4tet, *Suite en Rocaille* for strings, fl. and harp, *Sonatine en trio* for fl., clar. and harpsichord (or pf.), string 4tet, string trio; *Sonate libre* for vln. and pf.; instrumental pieces; *c*. 25 works for pf.; 6 works for pf. duet; *3 Rapsodies* for 2 pfs.; part-songs; 8 op. nos. of songs, etc.

Schmittbauer, Joseph Aloys (b. ? Bamberg, 8. XI. 1718; d. Carlsruhe, 24. X. 1809), Ger. comp. Pupil of Jommelli, he was *Kapellmeister* of Cologne Cathedral 1775–7, and at the court at Carlsruhe from 1777 to his retirement in 1804.

Works incl. operas *L'isola disabitata, Lindor und Ismene, Herkules auf dem Oeta, Betrug aus Liebe*, etc.; much church mus.; cantatas; symphs.; concertos; chamber mus., etc.

Schmuck, Margarete. *See* **Stockhausen (J.).**

Schnabel, Artur (b. Lipnik, Aus., 17. IV. 1882; d. Axenstein, Switz., 15. VIII. 1951), Aus. pianist and comp. Studied pf. with Essipova and Leschetizky, mus. in general with Mandyczewski in Vienna. He married the singer Therese Behr in 1905, travelled very extensively and made a great reputation for himself as a thoughtful interpreter, partic. of Beethoven, Schubert and Brahms. He taught in Berlin, but was forced by the Nazi rule to leave in 1933; settled in U.S.A. in 1939, but later returned to Eur.

Works incl. symph. and other orchestral mus.; pf. concerto; string 4tet and other chamber mus.; pf. pieces, etc.

Schnabelflöte (Ger. lit. beak fl., from Fr. *flûte à bec*) = Recorder.

Schnadahüpfeln (Aus. dialect), folk dances, often sung with words, of the *Ländler* or slow waltz type as a rule, belonging to the Tyrol or other Aus. mountain regions.

Schnéevoigt, Georg (Lennart) (b.

Viipuri, 8. XI. 1872; d. Malmö, 28. XI. 1947), Fin. cond. Studied in Helsinki, Leipzig, Dresden and Vienna, became cellist in the Helsinki orch. and in 1901 decided to make cond. his whole career. He held several appts. abroad and toured extensively. From 1930 to 1947 he cond. the Malmö Symph. Orch., and from 1932 to 1941 was permanent cond. of the Fin. Nat. Orch. in succession to Kajanus.

Schneeweiss, Amalie. *See* Weiss.

Schneider. (Johann Christian) Friedrich (b. Alt-Waltersdorf nr. Zittau, 3. I. 1786; d. Dessau, 23. XI. 1853), Ger. cond., teacher and comp. Studied at Zittau and at Leipzig while a student at the Univ. He advanced through several posts there to that of organist at St. Thomas's Church and cond. at the municipal theatre. In 1821 he moved to Dessau, where he was app. *Kapellmeister* to the ducal court. There he founded a vocal acad. and a mus. school.

Works incl. 7 operas; oratorios *Die Höllenfahrt des Messias, Das Weltgericht, Die Sündflut, Das verlorene Paradies* (after Milton), *Das befreite Jerusalem, Gethsemane und Golgatha* and several others; 14 Masses and other church mus.; 25 cantatas; 23 symphs., overture on 'God save the King'; 6 concertos; 60 sonatas; 400 male-voice part-songs; 200 songs, etc.

Schneider, Johann Gottlob (b. Alt-Gersdorf, 28. X. 1789; d. Dresden, 13. IV. 1864), Ger. organist and comp., brother of prec. Studied at Leipzig and became organist to the Univ. there, remaining until 1825, when he became court organist at Dresden. His fame was enormous and he had many distinguished pupils, incl. Mendelssohn, Schumann and Liszt.

Works incl. fantasy and fugue in D min., and others for org.

Schneider, Max (b. Eisleben, 20. VII. 1875; d. Halle, 5. V. 1967), Ger. musicologist. Studied with Kretzschmar and Riemann at Leipzig Univ. and comp. with Jadassohn. After a cond. appt. at Halle and a teaching post in Berlin, he became prof. of mus. at Breslau, returning to Halle in the same capacity in 1928. In 1935 he succeeded Einstein as ed. of the *Zeitschrift für Musikwissenschaft*. His writings were mainly on the Bach family and he ed. works by Schütz, Keiser, Telemann and others.

Schneider, Paul. *See* Sartorius.

Schneiderhahn, Wolfgang (b. Vienna, 28. V. 1915), Aus. violinist. Studied with Ševčic and Pisek in Prague and with Winkler in Vienna. In 1932 he became leader of the Vienna Symph. Orch. and in 1936 joined the Vienna State Opera Orch., becoming prof. at the State Acad. and leader of the Vienna Phil. Orch. From 1938 to 1951 he led his string 4tet, and

from 1949 to 1960 a pf. trio. In 1948 he married the soprano Irmgard Seefried.

Schneider-Trnavský, Mikuláš (orig. Schneider [of Trnava]) (b. Trnava, 24. V. 1881; d. Bratislava, 28. V. 1958), Slovak comp. Studied at the Budapest, Vienna and Prague Conss. and became mus. inspector at Trnava.

Works incl. operetta *Bellarosa*; church mus.; *Dumka and Dance* for orch.; pf. 5tet; vln. and pf. sonata; choruses; songs; arrs. of Slovak folksongs, etc.

Schneller (Ger. noun). *See* Ornaments.

Schnitzler, Arthur (1862–1931), Aus. novelist. *See* Neumann (*Liebelei*), Rebikov (*Woman with the Dagger*).

Schnorr von Carolsfeld, Ludwig (b. Munich, 2. VII. 1836; d. Dresden, 21. VII. 1865), Ger. tenor. Studied at Dresden, Leipzig and Carlsruhe, where he was engaged at the Opera and married the soprano Malwina Garrigues (1825–1904). In 1860 they were engaged by the Dresden Court Opera. He was Wagner's 1st Tristan at the Munich prod. in 1865.

Schnorr von Carolsfeld, Malwina. *See* Garrigues.

Schnyder von Wartensee, (Franz) Xaver (Joseph Peter) (b. Lucerne, 18. IV. 1786; d. Frankfurt, 27. VIII. 1868), Swiss pianist and comp. He appeared early as a pianist at Lucerne and although intended for the civil service, studied assiduously, visiting Zürich to be in touch with Nägeli in 1810–11 and in 1812 Vienna, where he met Beethoven and others. Finding himself disappointed in the expectation of a good heritage in 1815, he went to teach at Pestalozzi's model school at Yverdon and in 1817 went to Frankfurt as pf. teacher at an inst. for young ladies. He remained there for the rest of his life, except for visits to Switz., founded a choral society and periodically attended the Swiss mus. festivals.

Works incl. opera *Fortunat*, operetta *Heimweh und Heimkehr*; 4 symphs. (1 unfinished), overture in C min. and other orchestral works; variations for pf. and orch., concerto for 2 clars.; choral works; many pf. works; part-songs; songs, etc.

Schoberlechner, Franz (b. Vienna, 21. VII. 1797; d. Berlin, 7. I. 1843), Aus. pianist and comp. He played a pf. concerto by Hummel, comp. for him, at the age of 10 and was sent to Vienna by Prince Esterházy to study with Förster. In 1814 he went to It. and in 1823 to Rus., marrying the singer Sophie dall' Occa there in 1824. After 4 years in St. Petersburg they retired to a villa near Florence in 1831.

Works incl. operas *I virtuosi teatrali, Il Barone di Dolzheim* and *Rossane*; 2 pf. concertos; chamber mus.; sonatas and other works for pf., etc.

Schoberlechner (*née* dall' Occa), **Sophie**

Schobert   Schönberg

(b. St. Petersburg, 1807; d. St. Petersburg,
I. 1864), Rus. singer of It. descent, daughter
of a singing-master, with whom she
studied. She married Schoberlechner in
1824, sang at concerts at first, but in 1827
was engaged by the Imp. Opera in St.
Petersburg. She retired with her husband
in 1831, but returned to Rus. later.

Schobert, Johann (Jean) (b. ? Silesia or
Nuremberg, c. 1720; d. Paris, 28. VIII.
1767), Ger. harpsichordist and comp. He
lived in Paris, in the service of the Prince of
Conti from c. 1720, but d. young, with
some of his family and friends, as a result
of fungus poisoning. Mozart arr. one of
his sonata movements as the 2nd movement of the concerto K.39.

Works incl. *opéra comique Le Garde-
Chasse et le braconnier*; 6 harpsichord
concertos; 6 *Sinfonies* for harpsichord,
vln. and 2 horns; pf. 4tets (with 2 vlns.);
pf. trios; sonatas for pf. and vln.; sonatas
for harpsichord, etc.

Schoeck, Othmar (b. Brunnen, 1. IX.
1886; d. Zürich, 8. III. 1957), Swiss comp.
He was at first undecided whether to follow
his father's calling of a painter, but at 17
went to the Zürich Cons. to study with
Niggli and others, finishing with Reger at
the Leipzig Cons. In 1907–17 he cond.
choral societies at Zürich and remained
there when app. cond. of the St. Gall
symph. concerts that year. The univ.
conferred an hon. doctor's degree on him
in 1928.

Works incl. operas *Don Ranudo* (after
Holberg), *Venus* (after Mérimée), *Penthesi-
lea* (after Kleist), *Vom Fischer und syner
Fru* (after Grimm), *Massimilla Doni* (after
Balzac), *Das Schloss Dürande* (after
Eichendorff), operetta *Erwin und Elmire*
(Goethe), *scena* and pantomime *Das
Wandbild*; *Der Postillon* (Lenau) for tenor
solo, chorus and orch., *Dithyrambe*
(Goethe) for double chorus and orch.;
Trommelschläge (Whitman's *Drum Taps*)
for chorus and orch., *Für ein Gesangfest
im Frühling* (Keller) for male voices and
orch.; serenade for small orch., praeludium
for orch., pastoral intermezzo *Somernacht*
(after Keller) for strings, suite for strings;
Lebendig begraben (Keller), song-cycle for
baritone and orch.; vln. concerto, cello
concerto, horn concerto; 2 string 4tets;
2 vln. and pf. sonatas, sonata for bass clar.
and pf.; song-cycles *Elegie* with chamber
orch., *Gaselen* (Keller) with 6 instruments,
Wandersprüche (Eichendorff) with 4 instruments, *Notturno* with string 4tet; pf.
pieces; song-cycles *Wandsbecker Liederbuch* (Matthias Claudius), *Unter Sternen*
(Keller), *Das stille Leuchten* (C. F. Meyer)
and numerous sets of songs to words by
Eichendorff, Goethe, Hafiz, Hebbel, Heine,
Keller, Lenau, Mörike, Uhland and
others, etc.

Schoeffler, Paul (b. Dresden, 15. IX.
1897), Ger., later Aus., baritone. Studied
in Dresden, Berlin and Milan, making his
début in Dresden in 1925, where he remained until 1937, when he was engaged
by the Vienna State Opera. He also sang
at Covent Garden between 1934 and 1939
and 1949 and 1953 and at the N.Y.
Metropolitan between 1949 and 1956. He
was esp. well known in the role of Hans
Sachs.

Schoelcher, Victor (b. Paris, 21. VII.
1804; d. Houilles, 24. XII. 1893), Fr.
politician and writer on mus. He lived in
exile in London during the reign of
Napoleon III and worked on Handel research, part of the result of which he
published in an Eng. biog. in 1857. He
also made a collection of mus. which he
presented to the Paris Cons.

Schoenberg. *See* Schönberg.

Scholes, Percy A(lfred). (b. Leeds, 24.
VII. 1877; d. Vevey, Switzerland, 31. VII.
1958), Eng. critic, mus. author and ed.
He became mus. critic to the *Evening
Standard* and the *Observer* in London,
founded and ed. the *Music Student* and
Music and Youth, in 1923 became mus.
critic to the B.B.C., but later settled in
Switz., where he lived until the outbreak
of the 1939–45 war and twice after it. He
was a D.Litt. of Lausanne and Oxford
Univs. and an hon. D.Mus. of Oxford.
He wrote many books to further the
popularity and appreciation of mus. and
compiled a dictionary, *The Oxford Companion to Music*.

Scholz, Bernhard (b. Mainz, 30. III.
1835; d. Munich, 26. XII. 1916), Ger.
cond. and comp. Pupil of Ernst Pauer for
pf. and of S. W. Dehn for theory. He was
app. teacher at the Royal School of Mus.
at Munich in 1856, was cond. at the
Hanover Court Theatre in 1859–65, then
worked at Berlin and Breslau, and in 1883
succeeded Raff as director of the Hoch
Cons. at Frankfurt.

Works incl. operas *Carlo Rosa*,
Zietensche Husaren, *Morgiane*, *Golo* (after
Tieck), *Der Trompeter von Säckingen*
(after Scheffel), *Die vornehmen Wirte*,
Ingo, *Anno 1757* and *Mirandolina* (Goldoni); Requiem; setting of Schiller's *Lied
von der Glocke* for solo voices, chorus
and orch.; symph. *Malinconia*, overture to
Goethe's *Iphigenie*, overture *Im Freien*
and other orchestral works; pf. concerto;
2 string 4tets, pf. 5tet; songs, etc.

Schönberg, Arnold (b. Vienna, 13. IX.
1874; d. Los Angeles, 13. VII. 1951), Aus.
comp. He played vln. as a boy and cello
as a youth, and at 16 decided to become a
musician, studying counterpoint with
Zemlinsky, but being otherwise self-
taught. About the turn of the century he
earned his living by scoring operettas, but

his own comps. of that period were the string 6tet *Verklärte Nacht* and the *Gurrelieder*. He married Mathilde von Zemlinsky, his teacher-friend's sister, and in 1901 became cond. of an artistic cabaret in Berlin and a little later teacher at Stern's Cons. there. Back in Vienna in 1903, he gradually changed his style and his Chamber Symph. created a riot in 1906, but Mahler took his part. In 1911 he returned to Berlin, and by that time he had adopted atonality and also took to painting in an advanced manner. After the war of 1914–18, during which he did garrison duty, he settled at Mödling nr. Vienna, but in 1920 taught at Amsterdam, where he had begun to attract attention. In 1923 his wife d. and in 1926 he was recalled to Berlin to teach at the Prus. Acad. of Arts, where he remained until 1933 and married a sister of the violinist Rudolf Kolisch. The Nazi régime drove him from Ger. and he settled in U.S.A., teaching in Boston and N.Y., 1933–4, and later in Los Angeles, where he was app. prof. at the Univ. of California in 1936, retiring in 1944. In 1947 he was elected a member of the Amer. Acad. of Arts and Letters.

Works incl. operas *Von heute auf morgen* and *Moses und Aron*, monodrama *Erwartung*, drama with mus. *Die glückliche Hand*; symph. poem *Pelleas und Melisande* (after Maeterlinck), 5 pieces for orch., variations for orch.; pf. concerto, vln. concerto; *Gurre-Lieder* (to words trans. from Jacobsen), for solo voices, chorus and orch.; Byron's *Ode to Napoleon* for reciter, pf. and string orch.; *Pierrot lunaire* for speech-song and chamber orch.; *Friede auf Erden* for chorus; *Verklärte Nacht* for string 6tet; 4 string 4tets (2nd with a voice part); 2 chamber symphs.; serenade for low voice and chamber orch.; 5tet for wind instruments; sonata for vln. or clar. and pf.; variations for org.; 16 pf. pieces and suite for pf.; 10 songs with orch. and 39 with pf. incl. cycle *Das Buch der hängenden Gärten* (Stefan George); *Herzgewächse* for soprano with celesta, harmonium and harp; books: *Harmonielehre* and a treatise on counterpoint, etc.

Schöne Melusine, Die (*The Fair Melusina*), concert overture by Mendelssohn, Op. 32, comp. in 1833 after a perf. in Berlin of K. Kreutzer's opera *Melusina*, with a lib. by Grillparzer orig. written for Beethoven.

Schöne Müllerin, Die (*The Fair Maid of the Mill*), song cycle by Schubert (poems by Wilhelm Müller), comp. 1823.

School for Fathers, The (Wolf-Ferrari). *See* **Quattro rusteghi.**

Schoolmaster, The, nickname of Haydn's symph. No. 55 in E♭ maj., comp. in 1774.

Schop, Johann (b. *c*. 1590; d. Hamburg, 1667), Ger. lutenist, violinist, trombonist and comp. Court musician at Wolfenbüttel and Copenhagen; became director of the town council mus. at Hamburg. Works incl. hymn tunes, sacred concertos; occasional odes; instrumental pavans, galliards and almains, etc.

Schöpfungsmesse (Creation Mass), the nickname of Haydn's Mass in B♭ maj. of 1801, where a theme from *The Creation* is used in the 'Qui tollis'.

Schorr, Friedrich (b. Nagyvarad, 2. IX. 1888; d. Farmington, Conn., 14. VIII. 1953), Aus.-Hung. baritone. Studied in Vienna and made his début at Graz in 1910, as Wotan, a part he made peculiarly his own. He 1st appeared in London and N.Y. in 1924 and from 1925 he was for several years the Wotan in the Bayreuth Wagner perfs.

Schott, Anton (b. Castle Staufeneck, Swabia, 24. VI. 1846; d. Stuttgart, 6. I. 1913), Ger. tenor. Pupil of Pischek and Agnes Schebest, made his 1st stage appearance at Frankfurt in 1870.

Schottisch (Ger. = Scottish), a ballroom dance fashionable in the 19th cent. intro. to Eng. in 1848, not identical with the *Écossaise*. In Eng. it is usually called by its plur., *Schottische*. The mus. is in 2–4 time, much like that of the Polka, but played rather slower.

Schrade, Leo (b. Allenstein, 13. XII. 1903; d. Speracedes, 21. IX. 1964), Ger. musicologist. He studied at several Ger. univs. and taught at Königsberg Univ. from 1929 to 1932 and at Bonn Univ. from 1932 to 1937, when he left Ger. and settled in U.S.A. He taught at Yale Univ. from 1938 to 1958, becoming prof. in 1948. From 1958 he was prof. at Basle Univ. His studies ranged widely over medieval, Renaissance and Baroque mus. and incl. a book on Monteverdi and eds. of the works of Philippe de Vitry, Machaut, Landini and other 14th-cent. comps.

Schreker, Franz (b. Monaco, 23. III. 1878; d. Berlin, 21. III. 1934), Aus. cond. and comp. Studied under Fuchs in Vienna, founded the Phil. Choir there in 1911 and taught at the Imp. Acad. of Mus. until his appt. as director of the Acad. of Mus. in Berlin in 1920.

Works incl. operas *Flammen, Der ferne Klang, Das Spielwerk und die Prinzessin, Die Gezeichneten, Der Schatzgräber, Irrelohe, Der singende Teufel, Der Schmied von Gent*; ballets *Der Geburtstag der Infantin* (after Wilde), *Der Wind* and *Rokoko*; Romantic Suite, Fantastic Overture, overture *Ekkehard* (after Scheffel), Dance Suite for orch.; chamber symph. for 23 instruments; Psalm cxvi and *Swan Song* for chorus and orch.; vln. and pf. pieces; songs, etc.

Schröder-Devrient, Wilhelmine (b. Hamburg, 6. XII. 1804; d. Coburg, 26. I. 1860), Ger. soprano. She learnt much from her parents, the baritone Friedrich S. (1744–1816) and the actress Antoinette Sophie Bürger, and when still in her teens appeared as a classical actress at the Burgtheater in Vienna, where she made her 1st operatic appearance in 1821. In 1822 she greatly pleased Beethoven as Leonore in the revival of *Fidelio.* In 1823 she was engaged by the Dresden Court Opera and soon afterwards married the actor Karl Devrient, from whom she separated in 1828. In 1830 she 1st sang in Paris and in 1832 in London. She worked long enough to appear in the early Wagner operas.

Schroeter, Christoph Gottlieb (b. Hohnstein, Saxony, 10. VIII. 1699; d. Nordhausen, 20. V. 1782), Ger. musician. He was educ. in theology as well as mus. and in 1721 invented a hammer action to apply to the harpsichord, but was similarly pated in the actual invention of the pf. by Cristofori.

Schroeter, Leonhard (b. ? Torgau, *c.* 1540; d. ? Magdeburg, ? 1595), Ger. comp. Succeeded Gallus Dressler as cantor of Magdeburg Cathedral in 1564.

Works incl. Ger. Te Deum for double choir, *Hymni sacri* for 4–5 voices, *Weihnachts-Liedlein* for several voices, etc.

Schröter, Corona (Elisabeth Wilhelmine) (b. Guben, 14. I. 1751; d. Ilmenau, 23. VIII. 1802), Ger. singer, actress and comp. She learnt mus. from her father, the oboist Johann Friedrich S., lived in Warsaw and Leipzig as a child, appeared in the latter town at the age of 14. Between 1772 and 1774 she was in London with her family, but Goethe invited her to the court of Weimar in 1776, where she appeared in his plays and comp. the mus. for his play *Die Fischerin,* which incl. a setting of *Erl King* by her. She retired in 1786 to teach, paint and comp.

Works incl. play with mus. *Die Fischerin;* songs, incl. settings of Goethe's *Der neue Amadis* and *Erlkönig,* Schiller's *Der Taucher* and *Würde der Frauen,* poems by Herder, Klopstock, Mathisson, etc.

Schröter, Johann Samuel (b. Warsaw, *c.* 1752; d. London, 2. XI. 1788), Ger. pianist and comp. Pupil of his father, he made his début as a pianist in Leipzig in 1767, and in 1772 went on tour with his father and sister to Hol. and Eng., where he appeared at one of the Bach-Abel concerts. Settling in Eng., he succeeded J. C. Bach as mus. master to the queen in 1782. It was his widow with whom Haydn had an autumnal affair during his 1st visit to London.

Works incl. keyboard concertos, sonatas, etc.; pf. 5tets and trios, etc.

Schubart, Christian Friedrich Daniel (b.

Obersontheim, Swabia, 24. III. 1739; d. Stuttgart, 10. X. 1791), Ger. author, ed. and musician. Lived as organist and teacher in Geislingen and Ludwigsburg, later in Augsburg, where he ed. the *Deutsche Chronik* (from 1774), and Ulm, and from 1787 was poet to the court and theatre in Stuttgart. He was the author of *Die Forelle, An den Tod* and *Grablied auf einen Soldaten,* all set to mus. by Schubert. His autobiog. was pub. in 1791–3. Also comp. keyboard mus. and songs.

Schubaur, Johann Lukas (b. Lechfeld, Swabia, XII. 1749; d. Munich, 15. XI. 1815), Ger. comp. Had a distinguished career as a doctor, but was also a successful *Singspiel* comp. (from 1783).

Works incl. *Singspiele Die Dorfdeputierten, Das Lustlager, Die treuen Köhler,* etc.

Schubert, Franz (Peter) (b. Vienna, 31. I. 1797; d. Vienna, 19. XI. 1828), Aus. comp. Son of a schoolmaster who cultivated mus. in his household. Began to learn pf. and vln. early and received lessons from Michael Holzer at the age of 9, learning also org. and counterpoint. Admitted to the Seminary for choristers in the Imp. Chapel in 1808, played vln. in the orch. there and sometimes cond. as deputy. At 13 he wrote a fantasy for pf. duet and sketched other works, and in 1811 comp. his 1st song. Played vla. in the string 4tet at home. His mother d. in 1812 and the father married again in 1813, when S. wrote the 1st symph. and left the Seminary, continuing studies under Salieri. At 17 he became asst. teacher in his father's school, but disliked teaching; comp. the G maj. Mass, the 2nd and 3rd symphs. and several dramatic pieces. In 1816 he left the school and joined his friend Schober in rooms, gathering a circle of literary and artistic rather than mus. friends round him and in 1817 meeting the singer Michael Vogl, who took a great interest in his songs and succeeded in getting his play with mus., *The Twin Brothers,* prod. in VI. 1820. His reputation grew beyond his own circle, but pubs. failed to recognize him until his friends had 20 songs pub. at their own expense in 1821.

He lived in Vienna all his life, except for some summer excursions and 2 visits to Hung. as domestic musician to the Esterházy family on their country estate at Zséliz, 1818 and 1824. He never held an official appt. and failed to stabilize his financial position, but earned enough casually to lead a modest if improvident and Boh. existence. His industry was phenomenal. His death was due to typhoid fever.

Works incl. operas *Alfonso und Estrella, Fierrabras* [*sic*]*, Des Teufels Lustschloss,*

Die Verschworenen (*Der häusliche Krieg*), operettas *Die Freunde von Salamanka*, *Fernando*, *Der Spiegelritter*, *Der vierjährige Posten*, *Die Zwillingsbrüder*, melodrama *Die Zauberharfe*, incid. mus. *Rosamunde*; 7 Masses and *c*. 20 other church works; over 70 choral works with orch., pf. or without accomp.; 9 symphs. (2 unfinished) and var. miscellaneous orchestral works, incl. 2 overtures in the It. style; octet, pf. 5tet (*Trout*), string 5tet, 15 string 4tets (1 unfinished), 2 pf. trios and var. other chamber works; fantasy, *Rondo brillant*, sonata and 3 sonatinas for vln. and pf.; over 30 works for pf. duet; 21 pf. sonatas (some unfinished) and numerous other pf. works incl. 8 Impromptus, *Moments musicaux* and many dances; 606 songs incl. cycles *Die schöne Müllerin* and *Die Winterreise* (the 3rd, *Schwanengesang*, was so named by the pub.), 71 settings of Goethe, 42 of Schiller, 8 trans. of Scott, 3 trans. of Shakespeare, etc.

Schuch, Ernst von (b. Graz. 23. XI. 1846; d. Dresden, 10. V. 1914), Aus. cond. Studied at Graz and Vienna, had his 1st cond. engagement at Breslau, and after several others went to Dresden in 1872 and was made court mus. director the next year. He also cond. the symph. concerts of the Royal (later State) Orch.

Schuch-Proska, Clementine (b. Vienna, 12. II. 1853; d. Kötzschenbroda nr. Dresden, 8. VI. 1932), Aus. soprano, wife of prec. Pupil of Mathilde Marchesi at the Vienna Cons., was engaged by the Dresden Court Opera in 1873 and married Schuch there in 1875.

Schuh, Willi (b. Basle, 12. XI. 1900), Swiss musicologist. Studied under Courvoisier and Sandberger at Munich and Ernst Kurth at Berne, where he took a doctor's degree in 1927. He became a critic at Zürich. From 1930 to 1944 he taught at the Zürich Cons. His works incl. studies of Schütz, Swiss folk and early mus., Schoeck, etc.

Schuhplattler (Ger.), a Bavar. country dance with mus. in moderate 3–4 time similar to that of the Ländler. The dancers are men only and they strike their palms on their knees and soles.

Schulhoff, Erwin (b. Prague, 8. VI. 1894; d. Wülzburg, Ger., 18. VIII. 1942), Cz. pianist and comp. Studied at the Prague, Vienna, Leipzig and Cologne Conss. He d. in a concentration camp.

Works incl. operas *Don Juan's Destination* and *Flames*; ballets *Ogelala* and *Moonstruck*; incid. mus. to Molière's *Bourgeois gentilhomme*; 2 symphs.; pf. concerto; chamber mus.; pf. works, etc.

Schulhoff, Julius (b. Prague, 2. VIII. 1825; d. Berlin, 13. III. 1898), Cz. pianist and comp., great-greatuncle of prec. Settled in Paris from 1842 until the 1848

Revolution, then toured, and finally lived at Dresden and Berlin. Comp. drawing-room mus. for his instrument, also a sonata in F min. and 12 studies.

Schuller, Gunther (b. N.Y., 22. XI. 1925), Amer. comp. and horn player. After playing horn in the Cincinnati Symph. Orch., he joined the N.Y. Metropolitan Orch. He is now prof. of comp. at the New Eng. Cons., Boston, Mass.

Works incl. *Seven Studies on Themes of Paul Klee*, *Three Studies in Texture* for orch.; ballet *Variants*; symph.; concertos for cello, horn, pf.; *Fantasia concertante* for 3 trombs. and pf.; 4tet for 4 double basses; 5 pieces for 5 horns.

Schuloper (Ger. = school opera), a Ger. work of a special type of the 20th cent. with a didactic purpose; the same as a *Lehrstück*, but invariably intended for the stage.

Schultheiss, Benedict (b. ?, *c*. 1650; d. Nuremberg, 1. III. 1693), Ger. organist and comp. Pupil of his father, Hieronymus S. (1600–69). He was app. organist of the church of St. Giles at Nuremberg.

Works incl. hymn tunes; harpsichord pieces, etc.

Schultz (or **Schulz**), prob. the Ger. form of the name of the musicians calling themselves Praetorius.

Schultz, Helmut (b. Frankfurt, 2. XI. 1904; d. Waldburg, 19. IV. 1945), Ger. mus. scholar. Studied with Theodor Kroyer at Leipzig and took a doctor's degree in 1930. He became lecturer at Leipzig Univ. in 1932 and prof. in 1933. He ed. works by Haydn and the early works of Hugo Wolf, and his literary works incl. studies of the madrigal, old instruments, etc.

Schulz-Beuthen, Heinrich (b. Beuthen, Silesia, 19. VI. 1838; d. Dresden, 12. III. 1915), Ger. comp. Studied at the Leipzig Cons., taught at Zürich in 1866–80, at Dresden in 1880–93, in Vienna in 1893–5, and at the Dresden Cons. from 1895.

Works incl. operas *Aschenbrödel*, *Die Verschollene* and 3 others; Christmas play *Die Blume Wunderhold*; Requiem, 6 Psalms and other choral works; 8 symphs. (No. 6 on Shakespeare's *King Lear*), symph. poems on Schiller's *Wilhelm Tell*, on Böcklin's picture 'The Isle of the Dead', on Grillparzer's *Des Meeres und der Liebe Wellen* and others, 2 suites, 2 scenes from Goethe's *Faust*, serenade and other works for orch.; pf. concerto; wind octet, string 5tet and trio; 2 sonatas and pieces for pf.; numerous songs, etc.

Schulz, Johann Abraham Peter (b. Lüneburg, 31. III. 1747; d. Schwedt, 10. VI. 1800), Ger. author, cond. and comp. A pupil of Kirnberger, he travelled in Aus., It. and Fr. in 1768, and after holding a post in Pol. returned in 1773 to Berlin, where he collaborated in Kirnberger and Sulzer's encyclopaedia. Cond. at the Fr. theatre in Berlin 1776–8, he was court comp. to Prince Heinrich of Prus. at Rheinsberg 1780–7, then at the Dan. court in Copenhagen until his return to Ger. in 1795. Wrote a number of theoret. works, incl. (with Kirnberger) a treatise on harmony.

Works incl. operas (Fr.) *Clarisse, La Fée Urgèle* (after Voltaire), *Le Barbier de Séville* (after Beaumarchais) and *Aline, reine de Golconde* (Dan.), *The Harvest Home, The Entry* and *Peter's Wedding*; Ger. melodrama *Minona*; incid. mus. for Racine's *Athalie* and other plays; *Christi Tod, Maria und Johannes* and other sacred works; chamber mus., *Lieder im Volkston* and many other songs.

Schuman, William H(oward). (b. N.Y., 4. VIII. 1910), Amer. comp. Studied at Columbia Univ. and at the Mozarteum, Salzburg. In 1936 he was app. teacher at the Columbia Univ. summer school and in 1938 at the Sarah Lawrence Coll. in N.Y. In 1945 he succeeded Carl Engel as director of mus. pubs. in the house of Schirmer in N.Y. and Ernest Hutcheson as president of the Juilliard School of Mus. Director of the Lincoln Center, N.Y., 1961.

Works incl. baseball opera *The Mighty Casey*; ballets *Choreographic Poem, Undertone, Night Journey*; incid. mus. for Shakespeare's *Henry VIII*; film mus. for *Steeltown*; 2 secular cantatas for chorus and orch.; 8 symphs., *Amer. Festival* and *William Billings* overtures, *Prayer in Time of War* and *Side-Show* for orch.; symph. for string orch.; *Judith* (choreographic poem); *Newsreel* for military band; pf. concerto, vln. concerto; 4 *Canonic Choruses, Pioneers, Requiescat* (without words), etc., for unaccomp. chorus; 4 string 4tets, canon and fugue for pf. trio; quartettino for 4 bassoons; *Three-Score Set* for pf., etc.

Schumann (*née* Wieck), **Clara (Josephine)** (b. Leipzig, 13. IX. 1819; d. Frankfurt, 20. V. 1896), Ger. pianist and comp. Pupil of her father, Friedrich Wieck, made her 1st public appearance at the age of 9 in 1828 and gave her own 1st concert at the Leipzig Gewandhaus on 8. XI. 1830. In 1837 she was in Vienna for some time. Her engagement to Schumann was violently opposed by her father, but they married after many difficulties on 12. IX. 1840. She appeared less frequently during her married life, but after S.'s death in 1856 she was obliged to do so continuously and to teach. She went to live in Berlin with her mother, who had married Bargiel, but in 1863 she settled at Baden-Baden and in 1878 became chief pf. prof. at the Hoch Cons. at Frankfurt.

Works incl. pf. concerto in A min.; pf.

trio in G. min.; variations on a theme by Robert S. and *c.* 12 other op. nos. for pf.; several sets of songs, etc.

Schumann, Elisabeth (b. Merseburg, 13. VI. 1888; d. N.Y., 23. IV. 1952), Ger. soprano. Studied at Dresden, Berlin and Hamburg, at the last she made her stage début in 1909 and remained attached to the Opera until she joined the Vienna Opera in 1919. She toured the U.S.A. in 1921 with Strauss and 1st appeared at Covent Garden, London, in 1924. In 1938 she settled in U.S.A. and taught at the Curtis Inst. in Philadelphia, becoming an Amer. citizen in 1944.

Schumann, Georg (Alfred) (b. Königstein o/Elbe, 25. X. 1866; d. Berlin, 23. V. 1952), Ger. violinist, organist, cond. and comp. Studied with his father, later at Dresden and at the Leipzig Cons. After var. appts. at Danzig and Bremen, he became prof. and director of the Vocal Acad. in Berlin, 1900. In 1913 he succeeded Bruch as prof. of comp. at the Acad. of Arts.

Works incl. oratorio *Ruth; Amor und Psyche, Totenklage* and *Sehnsucht* for chorus and orch.; 2 symphs., Variations and Double Fugue on a Merry Theme, serenade, overture *Liebesfrühling* for orch.; Symph. Variations on a Chorale for org. and orch.; 2 pf. 5tets, 2 pf. trios; 2 vln. and pf. sonatas, cello sonata; variations and fugue on a theme by Beethoven for 2 pfs., etc.

Schumann-Heink (*née* Rössler), **Ernestine** (b. Lieben nr. Prague, 15. VI. 1861; d. Hollywood, Calif., 16. XI. 1936), Cz.-Ger.-Amer. contralto. Studied with Marietta Leclair at Graz and made her 1st stage appearance at Dresden in 1878. In 1892 she paid her 1st visit to London and in 1896 made her 1st appearance at the Wagner theatre at Bayreuth. She settled in U.S.A. after 1898, though continuing to appear in Eur., and was naturalized in 1908.

Schumann, Robert (Alexander) (b. Zwickau, Saxony, 8. VI. 1810; d. Endenich nr. Bonn, 29. VII. 1856), Ger. comp. Son of a bookseller and pub. Began to learn the pf. from a schoolmaster and organist at the age of 8 and played well by the time he was 11, besides studying all the mus. found at his father's shop, where he also developed a literary taste. He played at school concerts and private houses and made such progress in improvisation and comp. that in 1825 Weber was approached to teach him, but could not, being busy preparing *Oberon* for London and expecting to go there. S.'s father d. in 1826, and in 1828 he was sent to Leipzig Univ. to study law. There he met Wieck, from whom he took pf. lessons, neglecting his legal studies, as he did again when in 1829 he moved to Heidelberg Univ., where he came under the influence of Thibaut. Back at Leipzig in 1830, he lodged at Wieck's house, wrote his 1st pub. works (Op. 1 and 7) and the next year went to the St. Thomas cantor, Weinlig, for instruction, but left him for the younger Dorn. In 1832 he permanently injured his hand by a mechanical contrivance he had invented for finger-development and thus had to give up a pianist's career for that of a comp.

With a circle of young intellectuals he founded the *Neue Zeitschrift für Musik* in 1833, and the circle calling itself the 'Davidsbündler'. He fell in love with Ernestine von Fricken in 1834, but the engagement was broken off next year. In 1836 Wieck's daughter Clara, already a remarkable pianist, was 17 and she and S. fell seriously in love. The father violently opposed a match and in 1839 they took legal proceedings against him; he failed to yield, but they married on 12. IX. 1840, the day before she came of age. In 1843 S. suffered a crisis of mental exhaustion and he had a more serious breakdown after a tour in Rus. with Clara in 1844, at the end of which year they settled at Dresden.

Although his nervous complaint grew more marked after periods of recovery, he accepted the conductorship at Düsseldorf, incl. subscription concerts, choral practices and church mus., in 1850, a post for which he proved quite unfit. The committee tactfully suggested his resignation in 1852, but with Clara's injudicious support he obstinately refused to withdraw. Signs of a mental collapse grew more and more alarming and his creative work progressively less convincing, and in II. 1854 he threw himself into the Rhine. On being rescued he was sent at his own request to a private asylum at Endenich, where he d. more than 2 years later.

Works incl. *Genoveva*; incid. mus. to Byron's *Manfred*; 15 works for chorus and orch. with or without solo voices, incl. *Das Paradies und die Peri*, *Vom Pagen und der Königstochter* (Geibel); *Das Glück von Edenhall* (Uhland); *Requiem für Mignon* and scenes from Goethe's *Faust*; 4 symphs.; *Overture, Scherzo and Finale* for orch.; 5 concert overtures; concertos for pf., vln. and cello, 2 short works for pf. and orch., fantasy for vln. and orch. and *Concertstück* for 4 horns and orch.; 3 string 4tets, 3 pf. trios, pf. 4tet, pf. 5tet, *Fantasiestücke* and *Märchenerzählungen* for pf. trio (the latter with clar. and vla.); 2 vln. and pf. sonatas; sets of pieces for horn, clar., ob., vla. and cello with pf.; 36 op. nos. of pf. mus. incl. *Papillons*, 6 *Intermezzi*, *Davidsbündlertänze*, *Carnaval*, 3 sonatas, *Fantasiestücke* (2 sets), *Études symphoniques*, *Kinder-*

scenen, Kreisleriana, Humoreske, Nachtstücke, Faschingsschwank aus Wien, 3 romances, *Album für die Jugend, Waldscenen, Bunte Blätter, Albumblätter*; 4 works for pf. duet (33 pieces); *Andante and Variations* for 2 pfs.; Studies and Sketches for pedal pf.; 6 org. fugues; 35 op. nos. of songs (some containing numerous pieces), incl. the cycles *Frauenliebe und Leben* and *Dichterliebe*, also *Liederkreise* (Heine and Eichendorff) and *Myrthen*; 3 pieces for declamation and pf.; 4 op. nos. of vocal duets, 1 of vocal trios, 4 of vocal 4tets; 14 op. nos. of part-songs, etc.

Schünemann, Georg (b. Berlin, 13. III. 1884; d. Berlin, 2. I. 1945), Ger. musicologist and flautist. Studied at Stern's Cons. in Berlin and with Kretzschmar at the univ., where he took a Ph.D. degree in 1907. He was 1st active as fl. virtuoso and critic, but in 1919 became lecturer and in 1923 prof. in Berlin Univ., and in 1932 director of the Hochschule für Musik. In 1933 he succeeded Curt Sachs, who resigned under the Nazi régime, as director of the collection of ancient instruments and in 1935 became head of the Prus. State Library's mus. dept. Among his works are studies of the hist. of cond., Ger. choral mus., mus. autographs and a biog. of Zelter.

Schunke, Ludwig (b. Cassel, 21. XII. 1810; d. Leipzig, 7. XII. 1834), Ger. pianist. Pupil of Kalkbrenner and Reicha in Paris. At Leipzig at the end of his short life and an intimate friend of Schumann's. Left some promising work for pf.

Schuppanzigh, Ignaz (b. Vienna, 20. XI. 1776; d. Vienna, 2. III. 1830), Aus. violinist. Worked in Vienna; director of the Augarten concerts, founder of a 4tet of his own and that of Prince Rasumovsky. He was the 1st to lead 4tets by Beethoven and Schubert.

Schürmann, Georg Caspar (b. Idensen, Hanover, c. 1672; d. Wolfenbüttel, 25. II. 1751), Ger. singer and comp. He was 1st engaged at the Hamburg opera in 1693–7, then at Wolfenbüttel, entered the service of the Duke of Brunswick, who sent him to It. for further study and gave him leave in 1702–7 to enter the service of the Duke of Meiningen, after which he remained at Wolfenbüttel to his death.

Works incl. operas *Télémaque* (after Fénelon), *Heinrich der Vogler, Die getreue Alceste* (after Euripides), *Ludovicus Pius* and c. 16 others; New Year cantata, etc.

Schusterfleck (Ger. cobbler's patch), a playful Ger. description of a technical device, esp. the Rosalia, used as an easy subterfuge in comp. Beethoven called Diabelli's waltz, on which he wrote the variations Op. 120, a S.

Schütt, Eduard (b. St. Petersburg, 22.

X. 1856; d. Obermais nr. Meran, 26. VII.
1933). Ger. pianist and comp. Studied at
the St. Petersburg and Leipzig Conss. and
settled in Vienna in 1878.
Works incl. opera *Signor Formica*;
serenade for string orch.; 2 pf. concertos;
variations for 2 pfs.; many pf. pieces and
arrs.; songs, etc.

Schütz, Heinrich (b. Köstritz, Saxony,
4. X. 1585; d. Dresden, 6. XI. 1672),
Ger. comp. Learnt mus. as a choir-boy in
the chapel of the Landgrave of Hesse-Cassel, studied law at Marburg Univ. and mus.
under G. Gabrieli at Venice, 1609–12.
He returned to Cassel as court organist,
but left for Dresden in 1614, with an appt.
as mus. director to the Elector Johann
Georg of Saxony. He did much there to
estab. the fashion for It. mus. and musicians, but although he had written It.
madrigals at Venice, he set his own works
to Ger. or Lat. words. In 1627 he wrote the
1st Ger. opera, *Dafne*, on a trans. of
Rinuccini's lib. by Martin Opitz, for the
marriage of the elector's daughter to the
Landgrave of Hesse-Darmstadt. After the
death of his wife in 1628, he again went to
It. in 1629. In 1633, the 30 Years War
having disorganized the Dresden court
chapel, he obtained leave to go to Copenhagen, and he spent the years until 1641
there and at other courts. Returning to
Dresden, he did not succeed in reorganiz-
ing the court mus. satisfactorily until the
later 1640s. In the 1650s he became much
dissatisfied with the new tendencies among
the It. court musicians and had many
quarrels with Bontempi, but did not succeed in obtaining his release, and after
some improvements later on he remained
at the Saxon court for the rest of his
life.
Works incl. opera *Dafne* (lost); ballet
Orpheus und Euridice (lost); motets,
Cantiones sacrae, psalms, sacred symphs.
and concertos for voices and instruments
and other church mus.; Christmas,
Passion and Resurrection oratorios, *The 7
Words of Christ*; It. madrigals; *Exequien*
(funeral pieces) for 6–8 voices, Elegy on the
death of the electress of Saxony, etc.

Schützendorf, Leo (b. Cologne, 7. V.
1886; d. Berlin, 18. XII. 1931), Ger.
baritone. After singing in Düsseldorf,
Vienna and Wiesbaden he joined the
Berlin State Opera in 1920, where he
created the role of Wozzeck in 1925. His
brothers Guido, Alfons and Gustav were
also successful singers.

Schuyt, Cornelis (b. Leyden, 1557; d.
there, 9 or 10. VI. 1616), Flem. comp. He
travelled to It. to study mus., returning in
1581. He held a succession of org. appts.
in the Netherlands. He pub. several books
of madrigals and a book of instrumental
pieces.

Schwanda (Švanda) the Bagpiper. *See*
Švanda Dudák.

**Schwanenberg (Schwanenberger), Jo-
hann Gottfried** (b. Wolfenbüttel, 28. XII.
1740; d. Brunswick, 5. IV. 1804), Ger.
comp. Pupil of Hasse. He was app. court
cond. at Brunswick in 1762.
Works incl. operas *Romeo e Giulia*
(after Shakespeare), *Adriano in Siria*,
Solimano, *Zenobia* and *c.* 10 others;
symphs.; pf. concertos; pf. sonatas, etc.

Schwanengesang (*Swan Song*), song
cycle by Schubert, containing the last
songs written by him in 1828, incl. 7 settings
of Rellstab, 6 of Heine (his only settings of
that poet) and Seidl's *Pigeon Post* (*Die
Taubenpost*). The idea of a cycle was
actually Schubert's, but not, of course, the
title, which was invented by the pub. as an
allusion to the comp.'s death, and the
inclusion of Seidl's song was also the
pub.'s afterthought.

Schwartzendorf, Johann Paul. *See*
Martini, Giovanni Paolo.

Schwarz, Joseph (b. Riga, 1880; d.
Berlin, 10. XI. 1926), Baltic baritone. He
was a member of the Vienna Volksoper and
later of the Berlin Court (afterwards State)
Opera; also sang in London and N.Y.

Schwarz, Rudolf (b. Vienna, 29. IV.
1905), Aus., later Eng., cond. Studied pf.
and vln., playing vla. in the Vienna Phil.
Orch. In 1923 he became an asst. cond.
at the Düsseldorf Opera and from 1927 to
1933 cond. at the Carlsruhe Opera, after
which he became mus. director of the
Jewish Cultural Union in Berlin until 1941,
when he was sent to Belsen concentration
camp. He survived and went to Swed. in
1945 and then Eng., where he became
cond. of Bournemouth Symph. Orch. from
1947 to 1951, Birmingham Symph. Orch.
from 1951 to 1957, and B.B.C. Symph.
Orch. from 1957 to 1962.

Schwarzkopf, Elisabeth (b. Jarotschin,
nr. Poznań, 9. XII. 1915), Ger. soprano.
Studied in Berlin with M. Ivogün, making
her début at the Berlin State Opera in
1938. In 1943 she joined the Vienna
State Opera. She is esp. well known for her
singing of Mozart and R. Strauss, and also
created the role of Anne Truelove in
Stravinsky's *The Rake's Progress*. She is
equally famous as a *Lieder*-singer.

Schweigsame Frau, Die (*The Silent
Woman*), opera by R. Strauss (lib. by
Stefan Zweig, based on Ben Jonson's
Epicoene), prod. Dresden, 24. VI. 1935.

Schweitzer, Albert (b. Kaysersberg,
Upper Alsace, 14. I. 1875; d. Lambaréné,
4. IX. 1965), Alsat. theologian, medical
missionary, organist and mus. scholar.
Studied org. at Strasbourg and with Widor
in Paris. He was lecturer in theology at
Strasbourg Univ. in 1902–12 and later
undertook medical missions in Central

Africa, where he spent most of his life, visiting Eur. periodically and giving org. recitals of Bach's works. Author of a work on Bach pub. in Fr. in 1905 and in an enlarged Ger. ed. in 1908. He was awarded the Nobel Peace Prize in 1952.

Schweitzer, Anton (b. Coburg, VI. 1735; d. Gotha, 23. XI. 1787), Ger. cond. and comp. Studied with Kleinknecht in Bayreuth and in It. 1764–6, and was app. cond. and comp. to the court in Hildburghausen in 1766. Cond. of the Seyler opera troupe 1769, he was at Weimar 1772–4 and Gotha from 1774 to his death, succeeding G. Benda as court cond. there in 1780.

Works incl. *Singspiele* and operas *Walmir und Gertraud, Die Dorfgala, Alceste* (lib. by Wieland), *Rosamunde* (do.), etc.; monodramas *Pygmalion* (after Rousseau), *Polyxena*; dramatic prologues *Elysium, Apollo unter den Hirten,* etc.; incid. mus. to Goethe's *Clavigo,* Molière's *Le Bourgeois Gentilhomme,* etc.; ballets; cantatas; symphs., etc.

Schweizerfamilie, Die (*The Swiss Family*), opera by Weigl (lib. by Ignaz Franz Castelli), prod. Vienna, Kärntnertortheater, 14. III. 1809.

Schwemmer, Heinrich (b. Gumbertshausen, Franconia, 28. III. 1621; d. Nuremberg, 26. V. 1696), Ger. comp. Studied with Kindermann at Nuremberg, where he became a master at a school in 1650 and in 1656 choirmaster at the church of Our Lady. Among his pupils were J. Krieger and Pachelbel.

Works incl. wedding and funeral anthems, motets, hymn tunes and other church mus., etc.

Schwenke, Christian Friedrich Gottlieb (b. Wachenhausen, Harz, 30. VIII. 1767; d. Hamburg, 27. X. 1822), Ger. organist, cond., comp. and ed. Pupil of his father, Johann Gottlieb S. (1744–1823) and of Kirnberger and Marpurg in Berlin, he succeeded C. P. E. Bach as municipal mus. director in Hamburg in 1789. His sons Johann Friedrich S. (1792–1852) and Karl S. (1789–after 1870), as well as the former's son, Friedrich Gottlieb S. (1823–96), were also musicians.

Works incl. mus. for the stage; 2 oratorios; cantatas; church mus.; settings of odes by Klopstock; ob. concerto; 6 org. fugues; pf. sonatas, etc. Also ed. Bach's '48', Mozart's Requiem, etc.

Schwindel, Friedrich (b. Amsterdam, 3. V. 1737; d. Carlsruhe, 7. VIII. 1786), Dutch or Ger. violinist, flautist, harpsichordist and comp. He was at The Hague when Burney stayed there in 1770, later at Geneva and Mulhouse, and finally at Carlsruhe as mus. director to the Margrave of Baden. As a symphonist he belonged to the Mannheim school.

Works incl. operas *Das Liebesgrab* and *Die drei Pächter*; Mass in E♭ maj.; symphs.; 4tets, trios, etc.

Schytte, Ludvig Theodor (b. Aarhus, Jutland, 28. IV. 1848; d. Berlin, 10. XI. 1909), Dan. pianist and comp. He was in business as a chemist, but took to mus. in 1870, studying with Gade and others in Copenhagen and later with Taubert in Berlin and Liszt at Weimar. In 1887 he settled in Vienna as concert pianist and teacher.

Works incl. monodrama *Hero,* operettas *Der Mameluk* and *Der Student von Salamanca*; pf. concerto; numerous pf. works, incl. a sonata and *Naturstimmungen; Pantomimen,* etc., for pf. duet; song-cycle *Die Verlassene* and other songs, etc.

Scioltezza (It.) = Freedom, independence, looseness.

Sciolto (It.) = Free, independent, unfettered.

Scipione (*Scipio*), opera by Handel (lib. by Paolo Antonio Rolli, based on Apostolo Zeno's *Scipione nelle Spagne*), prod. London, King's Theatre, Haymarket, 12. III. 1726.

Sciutti, Graziella (b. Turin, 17. IV. 1932), It. soprano. Studied in Rome, making her début at Aix-en-Provence in 1951. She is esp. well known in soubrette roles.

Scola de' maritati, La (*The School for the Married*), opera by Martín y Soler (lib. by Lorenzo da Ponte), prod. London, King's Theatre, Haymarket, 27. I. 1795.

Scontrino, Antonio (b. Trapani, Sicily, 17. V. 1850; d. Florence, 7. I. 1922), It. double bass player and comp. Although the son of a poor carpenter, his father running a primitive but enthusiastic amateur orch. in which he played double bass parts on an adapted cello. In 1861 he went to the Palermo Cons. and in 1870 began to tour as a double bass virtuoso. In 1876 he prod. his 1st opera, having studied for another 2 years at Munich. In 1891 he became prof. at the Palermo Cons. and in 1892 at the Reale Istituto Musicale at Florence.

Works incl. operas *Matelda, Il progettista, Il sortilegio, Gringoire* (after Banville's play) and *La cortigiana*; incid. mus. for d'Annunzio's *Francesca da Rimini*; motet *Tota pulchra, O Salutaris, Salve Regina* and other church mus.; *Sinfonia marinesca* and *Sinfonia romantica* for orch.; 3 string 4tets and prelude and fugue for string 4tet; pieces for vln., cello and double bass; pf. pieces; song cycles *La Vie intérieure* (Sully-Prud'homme) and *Intima vita* (Panzacchi) and many other songs, etc.

Scordatura (It. = mistuning), tuning of the vln. or other string instruments temporarily to other intervals than the normal perfect 5ths, etc., for the purpose of facilitating the playing of chords with certain intervals or altering the instrument's tone-quality. The mus. is still written as for the normal tuning (and fingering), so that the instrument becomes to that extent a transposing instrument.

Score, the copy of any mus. written in several parts on separate staves, with the coincident notes appearing vertically over each other. Complete orchestral or choral S.s showing all the parts are given the name of Full S.; arrs. of operas, oratorios, etc., for voices and pf. are Vocal S.s; arrs. for pf. only are Piano S.s; comps.' sketches reduced to a few staves, to be elaborated and fully written out later, are known as Short S.s. The usual lay-out of orchestral S.s is in groups of var. types of instruments, with the treble instruments of each group at the top and the bass instruments at the bottom. The order is as a rule woodwind at the top, brass in the middle and strings at the bottom. Harps, perc. and any other extras are placed between brass and strings.

Scoring. *See* **Orchestration.**

Scorrevole (It.) = scurrying, fluent.

Scotch Snap, the technical name for rhythmic figures inverting the order of dotted notes, the short note coming 1st instead of last, e.g.:

O'Neill and Quilter were there at the same time. In 1898 he settled at Liverpool as pianist and gave some lessons, and soon after the turn of the cent. he began to become known as a comp. in London, having some works perf. and soon afterwards a number of songs and pf. pieces pub. In 1913 Alma Mahler, the comp.'s widow, invited him to Vienna, where he gave some perfs. During the 1914–18 war some works were prod. in Eng. and in 1925 the opera *The Alchemist* was given, in Ger., at Essen.

Works incl. opera *The Alchemist* and others (unpub.); ballet *The Incompetent Apothecary*; *La Belle Dame sans merci* (Keats), *Nativity Hymn* (Milton), *Let us now praise famous men* for chorus and orch.; *Aubade, Christmas Overture,* 2 *Passacaglias on Ir. Themes, Rhapsody,* 3 *Symph. Dances,* 2 symphs. for orch.; pf. concerto, vln. concerto; *Fair Helen of Kirkconnel* for baritone and orch.; 3 string 4tets, pf. 5tet, pf. 4tet, pf. trio; sonata, *Tallahassee* suite and var. pieces for vln. and pf.; pieces for vla., cello and fl. with pf., sonata, 4 suites, *Impressions from the Jungle Book* (after Kipling) and *c.* 100 pieces for pf.; *Idyll* for voice and fl., *Idyllic Fantasy* for voice, ob. and cello; *c.* 80 songs, etc.

Scott, Francis George (b. Hawick, 25.

SCOTCH SNAP   Handel, *Alcina*

Its name in Eng., which is also Scots Catch, is no doubt due to the fact that the S. S. is a feature in the Scot. Strathspey. It was popular in It. in the 17th and 18th cents. and was called by Ger. writers the 'Lombardy rhythm'.

'Scotch' Symphony. *See* **'Scottish' Symphony.**

Scots Catch. *See* **Scotch Snap.**

Scott, Cyril (Meir) (b. Oxton, Ches., 27. IX. 1879; d. Eastbourne, 31. XII. 1970), Eng. comp. and poet. He played the pf. and began to comp. as a child and was sent to the Hoch Cons. at Frankfurt at the age of 12. Later he studied pf. under Steudner-Welsing at Liverpool and returned to Frankfurt for comp. studies with Iwan Knorr. Grainger,

I. 1880; d. Glasgow, 6. XI. 1958), Scot. comp. Educ. at Hawick and Edinburgh Univ., took the B.Mus. at Durham Univ. and later studied with Roger-Ducasse in Paris. In 1925 he became lecturer in mus. at the Jordanhill Training-Coll. for Teachers.

Works incl. overture *Renaissance*, dance suite *The Seven Deadly Sins* (after Dunbar) for orch., *Lament for the Heroes* for string orch.; *The Ballad of Kynd Kittock* (Dunbar) and Scot. ballad *Edward* for baritone and orch.; 55 songs in 5 vols. of *Scottish Lyrics* (poems by Dunbar, Wm. Drummond, Burns, Allan Cunningham and others), *c.* 50 other songs (Scot. and Eng. poets), 4 Fr. and 4 Ger. songs; 14 part-songs, etc.

Scott, Marion M(argaret). (b. London, 16. VII. 1877; d. London, 24. XII. 1953), Eng. musicologist. Studied at the R.C.M. in London, 1896–1904, with which she afterwards remained assoc. as sec. of the R.C.M. Union and ed. of the *R.C.M. Magazine*. She wrote criticism for var. periodicals and many articles, notably on Haydn, in whose work she specialized and on whom she was engaged in writing a large work. She also contributed the vol. on Beethoven to the Master Musicians Series.

Scott, Thomas (b. Campbellsburgh, Kentucky, 28. V. 1912; d. N.Y., 12. VIII. 1961), Amer. comp. Although obliged to earn his living in commerce and radio, he studied comp. privately with Harrison Kerr in N.Y.

Works incl. opera *The Fisherman*; symph., *Horn and Chantey* and *Johnny Appleseed* for orch.; *Appalachian Suite* for string orch.; 2 string 4tets; sonatina for pf.; songs; var. Amer. folksong arrs., etc.

Scott, Walter (1771–1832), Scot. poet and novelist. *See* Adam (*Richard en Palestine*), Amy Robsart (de Lara), Berlioz (*Rob Roy* overture), Bishop (do., *Heart of Midlothian*, *Montrose*, *Kenilworth* and *Waverley*), Bruch (*Feuerkreuz*), Bruden fra Lammermoor (Bredal), Buck (D.) (*Marmion*), Carafa (*Fiancée de Lammermoor*, *Prison d'Édimbourg* and *Elisabetta in Derbyshire*), Corder (*Bridal of Triermain*), Costa (*Kenilworth*, ballet), Dame blanche (Boïeldieu: *Guy Mannering* and *Monastery*), Donizetti (*Castello di Kenilworth* and *Lucia di Lammermoor*), Donna del lago (Rossini), Eve of St. John (Mackenzie), Flotow (*Rob Roy*), Gomis (*Revenant*), Grisar (*Sarah*), Holstein (*Waverley*), Horn (C. E.) (*Peveril of the Peak*), Ivanhoe (Sullivan), Jeanie Deans (MacCunn), Jensen (*Donald Caird* and songs), Jolie Fille de Perth (Bizet), Klein (*Kenilworth*), Koven (*Robin Hood* and *Rob Roy*). Lady of the Lake (Schubert), Leicester (Auber), Lucia di Lammermoor (Donizetti), Macbeth (*Bruce* [*Lord of the Isles*]), MacCunn (*Lay of the Last Minstrel*, 'Land of the mountain and the flood'), Macfarren (G.) (*Lady of the Lake*), Mackenzie (*Marmion*), Mazzucato (A.) (*Fidanzata di Lammermoor*), O'Neill (*Bride of Lammermoor*), Pacini (*Ivanhoe*), Prigione d'Edimburgo (F. Ricci), Prison d'Édimbourg (Carafa), Puritani (Bellini), Quentin Durward (Gevaert and A. Maclean), Rodwell (*Lord of the Isles*), Schira (*Kenilworth*), Sullivan (do., and *Marmion*), Talismano (Balfe), Templario (Nicolai), Templer und die Jüdin (Marschner), Vesque von Püttlingen (*Donna del lago*), Waverley (Berlioz), Weyse (*Feast at Kenilworth*), Whitaker (*Guy Mannering*), Whyte (I.) (*Marmion*), Wood (Haydn) (*Lochinvar* [*Marmion*]).

8 songs by Schubert (in Ger. trans.).

Scotti, Antonio (b. Naples, 25. I. 1866; d. Naples, 26. II. 1936), It. baritone. Pupil of Signora Trifari-Paganini (?–1908). Made his 1st appearance at Malta in 1889 and 1st visited London, after successful tours in It., Spain and S. Amer., in 1899.

Scottish Composers. *See* Carver, Chisholm, Davie, Drysdale, Gordon, Gow, Hamilton, Holden (J.), Johnson (R.), Linstead, Macbeth, MacCunn, McEwen, M'Gibbon, Mackenzie, Mackintosh, M'Leod, Macpherson, McQuaid, Moffat, Orr (R.), Scott (F. G.), Skinner, Smith (R. A.), Stephen, Wallace (W.), Whyte.

'Scottish' Symphony, Mendelssohn's 3rd symph., Op. 56, in A min. and maj., begun in It. in 1831 and finished in Berlin, 20. I. 1842; perf. Leipzig, Gewandhaus, 3. III. 1842.

Scotto, Renata (b. Savona, 24. II. 1934), It. soprano. Studied in Milan with Ghiradini and Clopart, making her début at the Milan Nat. Theatre in 1953.

Scriabine. *See* Skriabin.

Scribe, Eugène (1791–1861), Fr. playwright and librettist. *See* Adriana Lecouvreur (Cilèa), Africaine (Meyerbeer), Alexandrov (A. N.) (*Adrienne Lecouvreur*), Ali Baba (Cherubini), Ballo in maschera (Verdi), Châlet (*Adam*), Cheval de bronze (Auber), Comte Ory (Rossini), Dame blanche (Boïeldieu), Diamants de la Couronne (Auber), Domino noir (Auber), Don Sébastien (Donizetti), Elisir d'amore (do.), Étoile du Nord (Meyerbeer), Favorite (Donizetti), Fra Diavolo (Auber), Gustave III (do.), Huguenots (Meyerbeer), Juive (Halévy), Leicester (Auber), Lortzing (*Yelva*), Maçon (Auber), Manon Lescaut (Auber), Marquise de Brinvilliers (8 comps.), Martyrs (Donizetti), Muette de Portici (Auber), Part du diable (Auber), Philtre (Auber), Prophète (Meyerbeer), Puits d'Amour (Balfe), Robert le Diable (Meyerbeer), Schmitt (A.) (*Trilby*), Setaccioli (*Adrienne Lecouvreur*), Shebalin (*Glass of Water*), Vêpres siciliennes (*Verdi*).

Scrittura (It. lit. writing). In It. operatic circles the term is used for a commission to comp. an opera.

Scudo, Pietro (Pierre) (b. Venice, 8. VI. 1806; d. Blois, 14. X. 1864), It. critic who wrote in Fr. Educ. in Ger. but settled in Paris in boyhood and unsuccessfully tried to become a singer. Later became a critic and joined the *Revue des Deux Mondes*.

Sculthorpe, Peter (b. Launceston, Tasmania, 1929), Austral. comp. Studied at Melbourne Univ. Cons. and Oxford. Lecturer at Sydney Univ.

Works incl. mus. for the theatre; *Sun Music I* for orch.; *Irkanda IV* for strings and perc.; *Sun Music II* for chorus and perc.; 7 string 4tets, string trio, pf. trio; sonata for vla. and perc.; pf. sonatina, etc.

Scuola   Seefried

Scuola. *See* **Scola.**

Scylla et Glaucus, opera by Leclair (lib. by d'Albaret), prod. Paris, Opéra, 4. X. 1746.

Sea Drift, setting of a poem by Walt Whitman for baritone solo, chorus and orch. by Delius, comp. 1903, 1st perf., in Ger., Essen Mus. Festival, 24. V. 1906; in Eng., Sheffield Festival, 1908.

Sea Pictures, song cycle for contralto and orch. by Elgar, Op. 37: 1. *Sea Slumber Song* (Roden Noel); 2. *In Haven* (Alice Elgar); 3. *Sabbath Morning at Sea* (Elizabeth Barrett Browning); 4. *Where Corals lie* (Richard Garnett); 5. *The Swimmer* (A. L. Gordon); 1st perf., Norwich Festival, 1899.

Sea Symphony, A, the 1st symph. by Vaughan Williams, for solo voices, chorus and orch. (words by Walt Whitman), perf. Leeds Festival, 1910.

Seal Woman, The, opera by Bantock (lib. by Marjorie Kennedy Fraser), prod. Birmingham, Repertory Theatre, 27. IX. 1924. A Celtic folk opera containing many traditional Hebridean tunes.

Searle, Humphrey (b. Oxford, 26. VIII. 1915), Eng. comp. and writer on mus. Educ. at Winchester Coll. and Oxford, he studied mus. with Ireland at the R.C.M. in London and in Vienna under Webern. In 1938 he joined the B.B.C. and in 1947 became Hon. Sec. to the I.S.C.M. He served in the army in 1940–6.

Works incl. operas *The Diary of a Madman* (after Gogol), *The Photo of the Colonel* (after Ionesco), *Hamlet* (Shakespeare); ballets *The Great Peacock*, *Dualities*; *Gold Coast Customs* and *The Shadow of Cain* (Edith Sitwell) and *The Riverrun* (James Joyce) for speakers, chorus and orch.; 5 symphs., 2 suites and *Highland Reel* for orch.; 2 nocturnes and 2 suites for chamber orch.; pf. concerto; *Intermezzo* for chamber ensemble, 5tet for horn and strings; 4tet for vln., vla., clar. and bassoon; sonata, *Vigil* and *Ballad* for pf.; 2 Housman songs, etc.

Seasons, The, ballet by Glazunov (choreography by Marius Petipa), prod. St. Petersburg, Maryinsky Theatre, 20. II. 1900.

Oratorio (*Die Jahreszeiten*) by Haydn (Ger. words by Gottfried van Swieten, based on Thomson's poem), comp. 1798–1801; prod. Vienna, Schwarzenberg Palace, 24. IV. 1801.

Sebastiani, Johann (b. Weimar, 30. IX. 1622; d. Königsberg, spring 1683), Ger. comp. Studied prob. in It., went to Königsberg *c.* 1650, where he became cantor in 1661 and mus. director at the electoral church in 1663, retiring in 1679.

Works incl. a Passion for voices and strings; sacred concertos for voices and instruments and other church mus.; wedding and funeral cantatas; sacred and secular songs *Parnass-Blumen*, etc.

Sec (Fr. = dry), a term used by modern Fr. comps., esp. Debussy, where a note or chord is to be struck and released again abruptly without any richness of tone.

Secco (It. = dry). *See* **Recitativo secco,** for which it sometimes serves as an abbr.

Sechter, Simon (b. Friedberg, Boh., 11. X. 1788; d. Vienna, 10. IX. 1867), Boh.-Aus. theorist, organist and comp. Settled in Vienna in 1804 and continued mus. studies there, wrote pf. accomps. for Dragonetti's double bass concertos in 1809, while the It. player took refuge in Vienna, and in 1812 became teacher of pf. and singing at the Inst. for the Blind. In 1825 he succeeded Worzischek as court organist. In 1850 he became prof. at the Cons. He wrote several theoret. works.

Works incl. opera *Ali Hitsch-Hatsch*; Masses, Requiem and other church mus.; oratorios and cantatas; choruses from Schiller's *Braut von Messina*; chorale preludes, fugues, etc. for org.; variations, fugues and other works for pf., etc.

Second, the interval between 2 adjacent notes on the stave, e.g.:

Second Subject. *See* **Sonata.**

Secondo (It. = second), the part of the 2nd player in a pf. duet, that of the 1st being called Primo. Also as an adj., applied to the 2nd player of a pair or a group, e.g. *clarinetto secondo.*

Secret, The (*Tajemství*), opera by Smetana (lib. by Eliška Krásnohorská), prod. Prague, Czech Theatre, 18. IX. 1878.

Sedaine, Michel Jean (1719–97), Fr. playwright and librettist. *See* **Aline, Reine de Golconde** (Berton and Monsigny), **Aucassin et Nicolette** (Grétry), **Blaise le savetier** (Philidor), **Déserteur** (Monsigny), **Diable à quatre** (Philidor), **Félix** (Monsigny), **Grétry** (*Raoul Barbe-bleue*), **Guillaume Tell** (Grétry), **Jagd** (J. A. Hiller), **Richard Cœur de Lion** (Grétry), **Roi et le fermier** (Monsigny), **Rose et Colas** (do.).

Sedie, Enrico delle. *See* **Delle Sedie.**

Sedley, Charles (? 1639–1701), Eng. poet and dramatist. *See* **Clarke (J.)** (*Antony and Cleopatra*).

Seefried, Irmgard (b. Königfried, Bavar., 9. X. 1919), Ger. soprano. Studied singing at the Augsburg Cons. and after her first engagement at Aachen (1939–43) joined the Vienna State Opera. She is esp. well known as a Mozart singer, and also in *Lieder*. In 1948 she married the violinist Wolfgang Schneiderhahn.

Seeger, Charles (Louis) (b. Mex. City, 14. XII. 1886), Amer. cond., teacher and comp. Studied at Harvard Univ. After cond. at the Cologne Opera in 1910, he was Prof. of Mus. at California Univ., 1912–19, where since 1958 he has been engaged in research. Author of books on theory and ethnomusicology.
Works incl. masques *Derdra* and *The Queen's Masque*; overture *Shadowy Waters* for orch.; chamber mus.; vln. and pf. sonata; numerous songs, etc.

Seegr, Joseph (Ferdinand Norbert) (b. Řepín, nr. Mělník, 21. III. 1716; d. Prague, 22. IV. 1782), Boh. organist and comp. Studied in Prague and became singer, violinist and organist at several churches there. On hearing him play, Joseph II offered him a court appt. in Vienna, but he d. before he could take it up.
Works incl. Masses, psalms, litanies and other church mus.; toccatas and fugues for org., etc.

Seger, or Segert. *See* **Seegr.**

Segni, Giulio (Giulio da Modena) (b. Modena, 1498; d. Rome, 24. VII. 1561), It. comp. After a short period as organist of St. Mark's, Venice, (1530–3) he entered the service of Pope Clement VII. Comp. 3 *ricercari à 4* (pub. in *Musica Nova*, 1540) and other instrumental works.

Segno (It. = sign). *See* **Dal segno.**

Segovia, Andrés (b. Linares, 17. II. 1893), Span. guitarist. Self-taught, he 1st appeared in public aged 14. Since his 1st concert in Paris in 1924 he has been regarded as foremost among modern guitarists, and many comps. have written works esp. for him.

Segreto di Susanna, Il (*Susanna's Secret*), opera by Wolf-Ferrari (lib. by Enrico Golisciani), prod. Munich, Court Opera, in Ger. trans. by Max Kalbeck, 4. XII. 1909.

Segue (It. = follows), an indication, like *attacca*, that a piece, number or section is to be played or sung immediately after another one. In MSS. the word is sometimes used instead of *V.S.* (*volti subito*) where a blank space is left at the bottom of a page to avoid turning over during the perf. of what follows on the next.

Seguidilla, a Span. dance dating back to at least the 16th cent. and 1st heard of in La Mancha, though poss. of earlier Moorish orig. The orig. form was the S. Manchega, but when the dance spread over Spain others developed: the S. Bolera—slow and stately; the S. Gitana—slow and sentimental. The S. is usually played on guitars, often with castanet accomp. and sometimes with vln. or fl. Frequently popular verses are sung to the S. consisting of *coplas* (couplets) of 4 lines followed by *estribillos* (refrains) of 3 lines.

Seguin, Arthur (Edward Shelden) (b. London, 7. IV. 1809; d. N.Y., 9. XII. 1852),

Eng. bass. Studied at the R.A.M. in London and made his 1st appearance at the Exeter Festival in 1829, 1st came out in opera at Covent Garden Theatre in London in 1833 and visited U.S.A. in 1838, settling later in N.Y. He married the soprano Ann Childe (1814–88).

Sehnsuchtswalzer (attrib. to Beethoven). *See* **Trauerwalzer.**

Seiber, Mátyás (b. Budapest, 4. V. 1905; d. Transvaal, 24. IX. 1960), Hung. cellist, cond. and comp. Studied with Kodály at the Budapest Acad. of Mus. Travelled abroad, incl. N. and S. Amer., from 1928–33 taught in the newly estab. jazz class at Hoch's Cons. in Frankfurt, also cellist in a string 4tet there and cond. at a theatre and of a workers' chorus. In 1935 he settled in London, as choral cond. and film comp., and joined the teaching staff at Morley Coll.
Works incl. opera *Eva plays with Dolls*, 2 operettas; incid. mus. for plays; film and radio mus.; *Missa brevis* for unaccomp. chorus; cantata *Ulysses* (chapter from James Joyce); 2 Besardo Suites (from 16th-cent. lute tablatures), *Transylvanian Rhapsody* for orch.; *Pastorale* and *Burlesque* for fl. and strings; *Fantasia concertante* for vln. and strings, *Notturno* for horn and strings; concertino for clar. and strings; 4 Gk. songs for voice and strings; 3 string 4tets, wind 6tet, 5tet for clar. and strings, duo for vln. and cello; fantasy for cello and pf., vln. pieces; pf. works; songs, choruses, folksong arrs., etc.

Seidl, Anton (b. Pest, 7. V. 1850; d. N.Y., 28. III. 1898), Hung.-Ger. cond. Studied at the Leipzig Cons. from 1870 and 2 years later went to Bayreuth as Wagner's asst. Cond. at the Leipzig Opera, 1879–82, afterwards toured and cond. Ger. opera at the Metropolitan Opera House in N.Y. from 1885 to his death.

Seiffert, Max (b. Beeskow o/Spree, 9. II. 1868; d. Slesvig, 13. IV. 1948), Ger. musicologist. Studied with Spitta in Berlin and took a doctor's degree in 1891. In 1904–14 he was ed. of the pubs. of the I.M.S. and in 1918 became ed. of the *Archiv für Musikwissenschaft*. He held 2 professorships in Berlin and in 1935 became director of the State Institute for Ger. Mus. Research. He ed. much old mus., incl. the complete works of Sweelinck and several vols. of the Aus., Ger. and Bavar. *Denkmäler*.

Seises (from Span. *seis* = six), choirboys in Span. cathedrals and churches (now Seville Cathedral only) perf. liturgical dances before the altar, orig. in groups of 6.

Seixas, (José Antonio) Carlos de (b. Coimbra, 11. VI. 1704; d. Lisbon, 25. VIII. 1742), Port. organist and comp. Pupil of his father, whom he succeeded

as organist at Coimbra Cathedral in 1718, he was from 1720 to his death organist to the court in Lisbon, at first serving under D. Scarlatti.
Works incl. church mus.; symph. and overture; toccatas, sonatas, etc. for org. and harpsichord, etc.

Séjan, Nicolas (b. Paris, 19. III. 1745; d. Paris, 16. III. 1819), Fr. organist and comp. Pupil of his uncle N.-G. Forqueray, he was organist of various Paris churches from 1760, succeeding Daquin at Notre Dame in 1772 and Armand-Louis Couperin at the chapel royal in 1789. At the Revolution he lost his post, but returned to it in 1814, having been meanwhile prof. at the Cons. and organist at the Invalides.
Works incl. 3 pf. trios; 6 vln. and pf. sonatas; keyboard mus., etc.

Sekles, Bernhard (b. Frankfurt, 20. VI. 1872; d. Frankfurt, 15. XII. 1934), Ger. comp. Studied at the Hoch Cons. at Frankfurt, under Knorr and others, cond. for a time at Heidelberg and Mainz and then joined the teaching-staff at his former school.
Works incl. operas *Schahrazade* (after the *Arabian Nights*) and *Die zehn Küsse*, burlesque *Die Hochzeit des Faun*, dance play *Der Zwerg und die Infantin* (after Wilde); symph. poem *Aus den Gärten der Semiramis*, *Kleine Suite*, *Die Temperamente* for orch.; passacaglia and fugue for org. and orch.; serenade for 11 instruments; passacaglia and fugue for string 4tet; cello and pf. sonata; pf. pieces; songs, etc.

Se'ection. *See* **Pot-Pourri.**

Selle, Thomas (b. Zörbig, Saxony, 23. III. 1599; d. Hamburg, 2. VII. 1663), Ger. comp. Was rector and cantor at var. places, finally at the Johanneum in Hamburg from 1641.
Works incl. Passion mus., motets, sacred concertos; madrigals; sacred and secular songs, etc.

Selneccer, Nikolaus (b. Hersbruck nr. Nuremberg, 6. XII. 1528; d. Leipzig, 12. V. 1592), Ger. theologian and organist. Court preacher at Dresden, 1557–61, later held var. posts at Jena, Leipzig and Wolfenbüttel. Wrote words and mus. of many chorales, of which he pub. an important book, containing the work of others and his own, in 1587.

Selva, Blanche (b. Brive, Corrèze, 29. I. 1884; d. Saint-Amand, Tallende, 3. XII. 1942), Fr. pianist. Studied with d'Indy at the Paris Schola Cantorum and at Strasbourg and Prague. She specialized in modern Fr. and Cz. mus.

Sembrich, Marcella (actually Praxede Marcelline Kochanska) (b. Wisniewczek, Galicia, 15. II. 1858; d. N.Y., 11. I. 1935), Pol. soprano. Pupil of her father, Kasimir Kochanski (S. being her mother's name),

and appeared at the age of 12 as pianist and violinist. In 1875 she began to study singing with Rokitansky in Vienna and then with Lamperti at Milan and Richard Lewy in Ger. In 1877 she made her 1st stage appearance at Athens. In 1880 she 1st visited London and later sang mainly at the Metropolitan Opera in N.Y., where she settled.

Semele, opera-oratorio by Handel (lib. by Congreve with anonymous alterations), perf. London, Covent Garden Theatre, 10. II. 1744. Congreve's lib. was originally intended for an opera.

Semellum. *See* **Gemellum.**

Semet, Théophile (b. Lille, 6. IX. 1824; d. Corbeil nr. Paris, 15. IV. 1888), Fr. comp. Studied at the Lille and Paris Conss., Halévy being among his masters. In 1850 he prod. his 1st stage piece, a vaudeville on George Sand's *La Petite Fadette*, but in 1857 began to have operatic successes. He was a perc. player in the Paris Opéra orch.
Works incl. operas *Nuits d'Espagne*, *La Demoiselle d'honneur*, *Gil Blas* (after Lesage), *Ondine* and *La Petite Fadette* (a new operatic version); ballet *Les Pirates de la Savane*; songs for the play *Constantinople*; cantata; part-songs; songs, etc.

Semi-Chorus, a group of singers detached from a chorus for the purpose of obtaining antiphonal effects or changes of tone-colour. It does not often lit. consist of half the voices, but is more usually a much smaller contingent.

Semibreve, the largest note-value now in current use, called 'whole note' in Amer. It is the value of the old Breve, and is represented by the symbol ○.

Semicroma (It.) = Semiquaver.

Semiquaver, the note-value of half a Quaver, and one 16th of a Semibreve, represented by the symbol ♪.

Semiramide (*Semiramis*), opera by Rossini (lib. by Giacomo Rossi, based on Voltaire's tragedy), prod. Venice, Teatro La Fenice, 3. II. 1823.

Semiramide riconosciuta (*Semiramis Recognized*), opera by Gluck (lib. by Metastasio), prod. Vienna, Burgtheater, 14. V. 1748.
Opera by Hasse (lib. do.), prod. Venice, Teatro San Giovanni Crisostomo, 26. XII. 1744.
Opera by Vinci (lib. do.), prod. Rome, Teatro delle Dame, 6. II. 1729.

Sémiramis, opera by Catel (lib. by Philippe Desriaux, after Voltaire), prod. Paris, 4. V. 1802.

Semiseria (It. fem. = half-serious), the term for a hybrid between *opera seria* and *opera buffa.*

Semitone, the smallest interval normally used in Western mus. Except for adjustments of leading-notes (*see* **Musica ficta**) only 2 S. intervals occur in any of the

Modes and in the Diatonic Scales, the others being whole tones; in the chromatic scales all the intervals are S.s. *See* **Scale.**

Semplice (It. = simple), a direction indicating that a passage or whole comp. is to be perf. in an unaffected or not over-expressive manner.

Sempre (It.) = Always, ever.

Senallié (Senaillé), **Jean Baptiste** (b. Paris, 23. XI. 1687; d. Paris, 8 or 15. X. 1730), Fr. violinist and comp. Studied under his father, Jean S., a member of the royal orch. and with the latter's colleague there, Queversin; later with Corelli's pupil Anet and with Vitali at Modena, where he was app. to the ducal court. He returned to Paris in 1720 and received an appt. at court under the regent, the Duke of Orleans, later confirmed under Louis XV.

Works incl. sonatas for unaccomp. vln.; vln. sonatas with bass; pieces for vln. and harpsichord, etc.

Senancour, Étienne Pivert de (1770–1846), Fr. man of letters. *See* Liszt (*Années de pèlerinage*).

Senesino (i.e. the Sienese). The nick-name of the singer below was sometimes also given to Tenducci, another native of Siena.

Senesino (real name Francesco Bernardi) (b. Siena, *c.* 1680; d. Siena, *c.* 1750), It. male soprano. Studied with Bernacchi at Bologna. Attached to the court opera at Dresden in 1719 and there invited by Handel to London, where he 1st appeared in 1720.

Senfl, Ludwig (b. Basle, *c.* 1490; d. Munich, *c.* 1543), ? Swiss comp. Pupil of Isaac in Vienna and his successor as *Kapellmeister* to Maximilian I, which post he held until the emperor's death in 1519. In 1520 he went to Augsburg and some time after that to Munich, where he settled, (?) in some connection with the ducal court. In 1530 he was in correspondence with Luther.

Works incl. Masses, Magnificats, motets and other church mus.; odes by Horace for voices; *c.* 150 Ger. songs, etc.

overture *In Autumn*, symph. poems *The Wild Geese* (after Maupassant), *The Mtsyrs* (after Lermontov), *Pan*, *The Scythians* and *Variations on a Chant of the Old Believers* for orch.; *Chloe forsaken* for voice and orch.; cantata *John of Damascus*; 3 string 4tets; poem for cello and pf., scherzo for fl. and pf., etc.

Sennet (Eng., obs.), a word found in stage-directions of Eng. plays of the Elizabethan period where the author asks for mus. to be played on or off the stage. It is prob. either a variant of 'signet' = 'sign' or a corrup. of *sonata*.

Sensible (Fr. noun, or *note sensible*) = Leading-note.

Senza (It.) = without.

Septave, an org. builders' term for the diatonic notes counted upwards from the keynote of a scale, excluding that note.

Septet, any work or number in a work, written in 7 parts for voices or instruments.

Septimole
or } a group of 7 notes to be
Septuplet
fitted into a beat or other time-unit in which its number is irregular.

Sequence. (1) A development of the long vocalizations at the end of the Alleluia in the Mass. In the late 9th or early 10th cent. words were fitted to these melodies on the principle of one syllable to a note. Since the melodies were in no regular rhythm the texts were not in verse and were in fact known in Fr. as *prosae*. The S. was so called because it followed (Lat. *sequor* = I follow) the Alleluia, which in turn followed the Gradual. In the course of time new melodies were written and rhyming verse came to be adopted for the texts. At the Council of Trent in the 16th cent. all but 4 S.s were abolished: *Victimae paschali* (Easter), *Veni, sancte spiritus* (Whitsun), *Lauda Sion* (Corpus Christi) and *Dies irae* (Requiem Mass). *Stabat mater* (Seven Dolours) (13th cent.), not orig. liturgical, was admitted as a S. in the 18th cent.

(2) The repetition of a melodic figure at a higher or lower degree of the scale, e.g.:

SEQUENCE   Handel, *Acis and Galatea*

Senilov, Vladimir Alexeievich (b. Viatka, 8. VIII. 1875; d. St. Petersburg, 18. IX. 1918), Rus. comp. Studied law at first, but went to Leipzig for mus. studies under Riemann and later worked under Glazunov and Rimsky-Korsakov at the St. Petersburg Cons.

Works incl. operas *Vassily Buslaiev* and *Hippolytus* (after Euripides), mus. action *George the Bold*; symph. in D maj.,

Serafin, Tullio (b. Rottanova di Cavarzere nr. Venice, 8. XII. 1878; d. 2. II. 1968), It. cond. Studied at the Milan Cons., making his début in 1900 in Ferrara, in 1909 becoming cond. at La Scala, Milan. From 1924 he was one of the chief conds. at the N.Y. Metropolitan, returning to It. in 1935, where he cond. mostly in Milan and Rome. He also appeared in London and Paris.

Serafino, Giorgio (b. ?; d. ?), It. 18th-cent. vln. maker, who worked at Venice.

Serafino, Santo (b. ?; d. ?), It. 17th–18th-cent. vln. maker, uncle of prec. He worked at Udine, *c.* 1678–98, and then at Venice until *c.* 1735.

Seraglio, The (Mozart). *See* **Entführung aus dem Serail.**

Serbian Composers. *See* **Yugoslav Composers.**

Séré, Octave. *See* **Poueigh, Jean.**

Serenade, evening song or evening mus., whether for one or more voices or for instruments. In the 18th cent. it took the form of a suite.

'Serenade' Quartet, nickname of a string 4tet formerly known as Haydn's Op. 3, No. 5, but now thought to be by Roman Hofstetter.

Serenata (It.), actually the It. word for Serenade (as above), but used in Eng. with a specific meaning for 18th-cent. works, often of an occasional or congratulatory type, either prod. on the stage as small topical and allegorical operas or at concerts (and even then sometimes in costume) in the manner of a secular cantata.

Serf, The, opera by G. Lloyd (lib. by William Lloyd, the comp.'s father), prod. London, Covent Garden Theatre, 20. X. 1938.

Seria (It. fem. = serious). *See* **Opera seria.**

Series. *See* **Tone-Row.**

Sérieyx, Auguste (Jean Marie Charles) (b. Amiens, 14. VI. 1865; d. Montreux, 19. II. 1949), Fr. comp. Studied with Gédalge and d'Indy, and assisted in the writing of the latter's *Cours de Composition*. From 1900 to 1914 he was prof. of comp. at the Schola Cantorum in Paris.

Works incl. Masses and motets; cantata *Salvete cedri Libani*; *La Voie lactée* for chorus and orch.; vln. and pf. sonata; org. and pf. pieces; songs; etc.

Serious Songs (Brahms). *See* **Vier ernste Gesänge.**

Serkin, Rudolf (b. Eger, Boh., 28. III. 1903), pianist of Rus. parentage. He studied in Vienna, pf. with R. Robert and comp. with J. Marx and Schönberg. Although making his début aged 12, it was not until 1920 that he began his true concert career. He appeared frequently with the violinist A. Busch and married Busch's daughter. From 1939 he taught at the Curtis Inst. in Philadelphia. He excels partic. in the Viennese classics. His son Peter (b. N.Y., 24. VII. 1947) is also a successful concert pianist.

Sermisy, Claudin de (b. ?, *c.* 1490; d. ? Paris, 13. IX. 1562), Fr. comp. In 1508–14 he was attached to the Sainte-Chapelle in Paris and in 1515 became a singer in Louis XII's royal chapel, just before that king's death, and later he succeeded Antoine de Longueval as master of the choir-boys. In 1533 he was made a canon of the Sainte-Chapelle, with a living and a substantial salary attached to it; but his duties there were light and he remained in the royal chapel, with which, under François I, he visited Bologna, where his choir competed with the Papal choir before Leo X, in 1515. In 1520, with the same king, he met Henry VIII at the Field of the Cloth of Gold, a similar meeting following in 1532 at Boulogne; and on both occasions the Fr. and Eng. choirs sang together.

Works incl. Masses, motets; over 200 *chansons* for several voices, etc.

Serocki, Kamiriez (b. Torun, 3. III. 1922), Pol. comp. Studied at Lodz and later with N. Boulanger (1947–8). From 1950 to 1952 he appeared in Europe as a pianist, but has since devoted himself to comp. in a modernist idiom.

Works incl. 2 symphs., *Triptych* for orch.; pf. concerto, tromb. concerto; choral mus.; *Episodes* for strings and 3 perc. groups, *Segmenti* for chamber ensemble and perc.; chamber mus., etc.

Serov, Alexander Nikolaievich (b. St. Petersburg, 23. I. 1820; d. St. Petersburg, 1. II. 1871), Rus. comp. and critic. Studied law, but found time to cultivate mus., which eventually, after a career as a civil servant, he took up professionally. He studied cello and theory from *c.* 1840 and began an opera on Shakespeare's *Merry Wives* in 1843, but was reduced to a correspondence course of mus. instruction when transferred to Simferopol. He became a mus. critic and in 1858, when he returned from a visit to Ger. as an ardent admirer of Wagner, he began to attack the Rus. nat. school of comps., but found a powerful opponent in Stassov. He was over 40 when he began his 1st opera. He married the comp. Valentina Semionovna Bergman (1846–1927), who wrote some operas of her own, incl. *Uriel Acosta* (based on Gutzkow's play). When he d. from heart disease, he had just begun a 4th opera on Gogol's *Christmas Eve Revels*.

Works incl. operas *Judith*, *Rogneda*, *The Power of Evil* (after Ostrovsky's play; orch. finished by Soloviev); incid. mus. to Nikolai Pavlovich Zhandr's tragedy *Nero*; *Stabat Mater* and *Ave Maria*; *Gopak, Dance of the Zaporogue Cossacks* and other orchestral works, etc.

Serpent, an obs. wind instrument, formerly the bass of the Cornett family, with a long winding wooden tube covered with leather and played with a cup-shaped mouthpiece. It prob. originated late in the 16th cent. and was used both in bands and in churches, but fell out of use in the 19th cent.

Serpentone (It.) = **Serpent.**

Serpette, (Henri Charles Antoine) Gaston (b. Nantes, 4. XI. 1846; d. Paris, 3. XI. 1904), Fr. comp. He was orig. a lawyer, but studied with A. Thomas at the Paris Cons. and took the Prix de Rome in 1871. Returning from Rome in 1874, he hoped to prod. a work at the Opéra-Comique, but failed and took to writing light pieces for the Bouffes-Parisiens.

Works incl. operettas *La Branche cassée*, *La Petite Muette*, *Cendrillonnette*, *La Demoiselle du téléphone*, *La Dot de Brigitte*, *Le Capitole*, *Le Carnet du diable*, *Shakespeare* and others: cantata *Jeanne d'Arc*, etc.

Serrano y Ruiz, Emilio (b. Victoria, Alava, 15. III. 1850; d. Madrid, 9. IV. 1939), Span. pianist and comp. He became court pianist to the Infanta Isabella, director of the Royal Opera in Madrid and prof. at the Cons.

Works incl. operas *Mitridate, Giovanna la pazza, Irene de Otranto, Gonzalo de Córdoba* and *La maja de Rumbo*; symph. poem *La primera salide de Don Quijote* (after Cervantes), etc.

Serrao, Paolo (b. Filadelfia, Catanzaro, 1830; d. Naples, 17. III. 1907), It. comp. Studied at the Naples Cons. and became a prof. there in 1863.

Works incl. operas *Pergolesi, La duchessa di Guisa, Il figliuol prodigo, L'impostore, Leonora de' Bardi*; oratorio *Gli Ortonesi in Scio*, Passion *Le tre ore d'agonia*; Mass, Requiem and other church mus.; funeral symph. for Mercadante; overture for orch.; pf. pieces, etc.

Serré (Fr. = tightened), a direction sometimes used by Fr. comps. for *stringendo*.

Serres, (Marie François) Louis (Arnal) de (b. Lyons, 8. XI. 1864; d. Nérondes, Loire, 25. XII. 1942), Fr. organist and comp. Studied at the Paris Cons., Franck being his org. master. After studying with him privately for another 5 years, he became org. prof. at the Schola Cantorum and organist at the Ir. Chapel.

Works incl. Fr. and Lat. motets, *Ave*, *verum corpus* and other church mus.; *Nuits d'été, Le Jour des morts*, etc. for chorus and orch.; *Les Caresses*, etc. for orch.; *Les Heures claires* for voice and orch.; songs, etc.

Serse (*Xerxes*) (*see also* **Xerse**), opera by Handel (lib. by Niccolò Minato, altered), prod. London, King's Theatre, Haymarket, 15. IV. 1738. It contains the famous so-called *Largo*, 'Ombra mai fù'. The original lib. was that for Cavalli's *Xerse* (1654).

Serva padrona, La (*The Maid as Mistress*), intermezzi by Paisiello (lib. by Gennaro Antonio Federico), prod. St. Petersburg, Hermitage, at court, 10. IX. 1781.

Intermezzi by Pergolesi (lib. do.), prod. Naples, Teatro San Bartolommeo, between the acts of P.'s serious opera *Il prigionier superbo*, 28. VIII. 1733.

Servais, (Adrien) François (b. Hal nr. Brussels, 6. VI. 1807; d. Hal nr. Brussels, 26. XI. 1866), Belg. cellist and comp. Studied with Platel at the Brussels Cons., visited Paris and London, later toured all over Eur. and in 1848 became prof. at the Cons.

Works incl. 3 cello concertos and 16 fantasies for cello and orch.; duets for vln. and cello; many cello studies and pieces, etc.

Servais, Joseph (b. Hal nr. Brussels, 28. XI. 1850; d. Brussels, 29. VIII. 1885), Belg. cellist, son of prec. Pupil of his father, with whom he travelled afterwards. In 1868–70 he was at the court of Weimar, in 1875 made his 1st appearance in Paris, and eventually settled at Brussels.

Service. As a mus. term the word implies the setting of those parts of the services of the Angl. Church which lend themselves to mus. treatment, i.e. Morning Prayer, Evening Prayer (Magnificat and Nunc dimittis) and Communion.

Servilia, opera by Rimsky-Korsakov (lib. by comp., based on a play by Lev Alexandrovich Mey), prod. St. Petersburg, 14. X. 1902.

Sesquialtera (Lat., short for *pars sesquialtera* = a quantity $1\frac{1}{2}$ times as much). (1) In mensural notation the proportion 3 : 2. *See* **Proportion**.

(2) An org. mixture stop, normally of 2 ranks, $2\frac{2}{3}$ ft. and $1\frac{3}{5}$ ft.

Sessions, Roger (b. Brooklyn, N.Y., 28. XII. 1896), Amer. comp. Studied at Harvard Univ. and later at Yale Univ. with H. Parker, also with Bloch in N.Y. and Cleveland. In 1917–21 he taught at Smith Coll., Northampton, Mass. and in 1921–5 was head of the theoret. dept. of the Cleveland Inst. of Mus. He lived in It. and Ger. in 1925–33, then taught for 2 years at Boston Univ. and afterwards at var. places. He is now prof. at Princeton Univ.

Works incl. operas *Lancelot and Elaine* (after Tennyson), *The Trial of Lucullus* and *Montezuma*; incid. mus. for Andreiev's *The Black Maskers* and Gozzi's *Turandot* (trans. by Vollmöller); *Turn O Libertad* (Whitman) for chorus and pf. duet; 5 symphs., 3 dirges for orch.; mus. for 4 trombs. and tuba; vln. concerto, pf. concerto; 2 string 4tets, pf. trio, duo for vln. and pf.; sonata and 3 chorale preludes for org.; 2 sonatas and pieces for pf.; songs to words by James Joyce and others, etc.

Sestet, in mus. an obs. form of the word **Sextet**.

Set, an old Eng. name for the Suite.

Setaccioli

Sf.

Setaccioli, Giacomo (b. Corneto Tarquinia, 8. XII. 1868; d. Siena, 5. XII. 1925), It. comp. Studied at the Academia di Santa Cecilia in Rome and became a prof. there in 1922, but moved to Florence in 1925 on being app. director of the Cherubini Cons. there.

Works incl. operas *La sorella di Mark*, *L'ultimo degli Abenceragi* (after Chateaubriand), *Il mantellaccio* and *Adrienne Lecouvreur* (after Scribe); Requiem for Humbert I, *Cantica* for solo voices, chorus and orch., motets, *Quadro sinfonico* for chorus, org. and orch.; symph. in A maj., symph. poems, fugue, etc. for orch.; Concert Allegro for pf. and orch., suite for harp and strings; string 4tet, nonet for wind instruments; sonata for clar. and pf.; org. prelude and fugue; pf. pieces; songs, etc.

Sett, an old Eng. name for the Suite.

Sette canzoni (*Seven Songs*). opera by Malipiero (lib. by comp.), prod., in Fr. version by Henry Prunières, Paris, Opéra, 10. VII. 1920. Part II of the operatic cycle *L'Orfeide*.

Settle, Elkanah (1648–1724), Eng. poet and dramatist. *See* Clarke (J.) (*World in the Moon*, with D. Purcell), **Fairy Queen** (Purcell), **Finger** (*Virgin Prophetess*), **Purcell** (*Distressed Innocence*), **Turner** (*Pastor fido*, from Guarini).

Ševčík, Otakar (b. Horaždovice, 22. III. 1852; d. Pisek, 18. I. 1934), Cz. violinist and teacher. Studied at the Prague Cons. and became leader at the Mozarteum at Salzburg and gave concerts in Prague. In 1873 he settled in Vienna, was prof. at the Mus. School at Kiev in 1875–92 and then became chief vln. prof. at the Prague Cons. He wrote a vln. method in 4 vols. and in 1903 formed a string 4tet.

Seven Words of the Saviour on the Cross, The (or *The Seven Last Words*). 1. Orchestral work by Haydn consisting of 7 slow movements, commissioned by Cadiz Cathedral in 1785 as mus. meditations for a 3-hour service on Good Friday. Later arr. by Haydn for string 4tet (Op. 51, 1787) and as a choral work (1796).

2. Oratorio by Schütz (words from the 4 Gospels plus 2 verses of a chorale), comp. 1645.

Seventh, the interval between 2 notes lying 7 degrees of a diatonic scale apart, e.g.:

Maj.   Min.   Diminished

Séverac, (Joseph Marie) Déodat de (b. Saint-Félix de Caraman, Lauraguais,

20. VII. 1873; d. Céret, Pyrénées Orientales, 24. III. 1921), Fr. comp. Studied at the Toulouse Cons. and the Schola Cantorum in Paris, with Magnard and d'Indy. He returned to the S. of Fr. and devoted himself entirely to comp., neither his health nor his taste permitting him to hold any official mus. position.

Works incl. opera *Le Cœur du moulin*; ballet *La Fête des vendanges*; incid. mus. for Sicard's *Héliogabale* and for Verhaeren's *Hélène de Sparte*; *Ave, verum corpus* and other church mus.; *Chant de vacances* for chorus; *Nymphes au crépuscule* (unpub.), *Didon et Énée* (lost) and other unpub. orchestral works; *Sérénade au clair de lune* for fl., string 5tet and pf. and unpub. chamber mus.; suite for org.; *Le Soldat de plomb* for pf. duet; *Le Chant de la terre*, *En Languedoc*, *Baigneuses au soleil*, *Cerdaña*, *En vacances* for pf.; 19 songs to poems by Ronsard, Verlaine, Maeterlinck, Poe and others, and poems in *langue d'oc*.

Sevillana (Span.), an Andalusian folksong type similar to the Seguidilla and orig. confined to Seville.

Sextet, any work, or number in a work, written in 6 parts for voices or instruments.

Sextolet, a group of 6 notes, or double Triplet, when used in a comp. or movement whose time-unit is normally divisible into 2, 4 or 8 note-values.

Sextus, in old vocal mus. the 6th part in a comp. for 6 or more voices, always equal in compass to one of the voices in a 4-part comp.: soprano, alto, tenor or bass.

Seyfried, Ignaz Xaver von (b. Vienna, 15. VIII. 1776; d. Vienna, 27. VIII. 1841), Aus. cond., teacher and comp. Orig. intended for a legal career, he turned to mus., and was a pupil of Mozart and Kozeluch for pf., Albrechtsberger and Winter for comp. From 1797 to 1828 he was cond. and comp. to Schikaneder's theatre (from 1801 known as the Theater an der Wien). After his retirement he comp. almost exclusively church mus.

Works incl. over 100 operas, *Singspiele*, etc., e.g. *Der Löwenbrunnen, Der Wundermann am Rheinfall, Die Ochsenmenuette* (pasticcio arr. from Haydn's works), *Ahasverus* (arr. from piano works of Mozart), etc.; biblical dramas; incid. mus. to Schiller's *Die Räuber* and *Die Jungfrau von Orleans*, etc.; Masses, Requiem, motets and other church mus.; *Libera me* for Beethoven's funeral, etc. Also ed. Albrechtsberger's theoret. works and pub. an account of Beethoven's studies in figured bass, counterpoint and comp. (1832).

Sf. (abbr.) = *Sforzando*.

Sfogato (It. = airy), sometimes used as a direction by comps., e.g. Chopin, to indicate a delicate and ethereal perf. of certain passages; also as an adj., esp. 'soprano s.' = light soprano.

Sforzando ⎤
or   ⎬ (It. = forced, reinforced),
Sforzato ⎦
a direction indicating that a note or chord is to be strongly emphasized by an accent

Sfumato (It.), dissolved, blended (as in the colours of a painting).

Sfz. (abbr.) = *Sforzando.*

Sgambati, Giovanni (b. Rome, 28. V. 1841; d. Rome, 14. XII. 1914), It. pianist and comp. Studied at Trevi in Umbria and in Rome and was a pupil of Liszt; later estab. important orch. and chamber concerts for the cultivation of serious mus. in the It. capital. In 1869 he visited Ger. and 1st heard works by Wagner, whom he met in Rome in 1876 and who induced his pub., Schott, to bring out some of S.'s works. In 1882 he 1st visited Eng.

Works incl. Requiem; symphs. in D and

suite, studies and other works for pf.; songs, etc.

Shadwell, Thomas (*c.* 1642–92). Eng. poet and playwright. *See* **Franck (J. W.)** (masque for *Timon of Athens*), **Grabu** (*Timon of A.*), **King (R.)** (*Ode on St. Cecilia's Day*), **Locke** (*Tempest*), **Psyche** (Locke), **Purcell** (*Timon of Athens* and *Libertine*), **Reggio** (song 'Arise ye subterranean winds', *Tempest*), **Turner** (*Libertine*).

Shagbut, another spelling of Sackbut.

Shahrazad (*Sheherazade*), symph. suite by Rimsky-Korsakov on the subject of the story-teller in the *Arabian Nights* and of some of the tales, Op. 35, finished summer 1888 and prod. St. Petersburg, 3. XI. 1888. Ballet based on it (choreography by Mikhail Fokin, settings by Leon Bakst), prod. Paris, Opéra, 4. VI. 1910. *See also* **Shéhérazade.**

Shake, a mus. ornament consisting of the rapid alternation of the note written down with that a whole tone or semitone above, according to the key in which the piece is written, or according to the comp.'s notation, e.g.:

SHAKE

Eb maj., *Epitalamio sinfonico*, overture *Cola di Rienzi* and Festival Overture for orch.; pf. concerto in G min.; string 4tet, 2 pf. 5tets; prelude and fugue, *Fogli volanti*, *Pièces lyriques*, *Mélodies poétiques*,

Shakespeare, William (1564–1616), Eng. poet and dramatist. *See:*

All's Well that Ends Well: **Linley** (W.) (song 'Was this fair face').

Antony and Cleopatra: **Amours d'Antoine**

629

et de Cléopatre (ballet, R. Kreutzer), Antonio e Cleopatra (opera, Malipiero), Barber (opera), Come, thou monarch of the vine (Schubert [also set by Bishop and W. Linley]), Hopkins (A.) (incid. mus.), Jacobson (do.), Klenovsky (do.), Norman (L.) (do.), Porter (Q.) (do.), Prokofiev (play, *Egyptian Nights*), Rabaud (incid. mus.), Rubinstein (A.) (overture), Smyth (overture).

As You Like It: Arne (songs), Bishop (incid. mus.), Castéra (2 choruses), Farkas (F.) (incid. mus.), German (do.), Morley (? do.), Paine (overture), Pizzetti (incid. mus.), Quilter (do.), Rietz (do.), Toch (do.), Veracini (opera *Rosalinda*), Walton (film mus.), Wetzler (incid. mus.).

Comedy of Errors, The: Bishop (incid. mus.), Equivoci (opera, Storace), Fogg (overture), Goldschmidt (B.) (overture), Krejči (opera, *Confusion at Ephesus*), Shaporin (incid. mus.).

Coriolanus: Höffer (incid. mus.), Lux (scene), Mackenzie (incid. mus.). [Beethoven's overture [not for Shakespeare], *see* Coriolan.)

Cymbeline: Arne (incid. mus.), Aylward (do.), Boyce (do.), Dietrich (A.) (do.), Hark, hark, the lark (Schubert [also set by Aylward, Thomas Chilcot, B. Cooke, Kücken, G. Macfarren, etc.]), Lambert (C.) (Dirge), Missa (opera *Dinah*), Sobolewski (opera *Imogene*), Tiessen (incid. mus.).

Hamlet: Ambleto (operas, Gasparini and D. Scarlatti), Amleto (opera, Faccio), Berlioz (funeral march), Bishop (incid. mus.), Blacher (symph. poem), Bourgault-Ducoudray (*Enterrement d'Ophélie* for orch.), Bridge (Lament for strings), Ferrari (G.) (incid. mus.), Gade (overture), German (symph. poem), Hamlet (operas, Hignard and A. Thomas; incid. mus., Tchaikovsky; symph. poem, Liszt), Haydn (incid. mus.), Henschel (do.), Honegger (do.), Jacobson (do.), Joachim (overture), Joncières (incid. mus.), Lambert (C.) (do.), Lazzari (*Ophélie* for orch.), Lekeu (symph. study), MacDowell (symph. poem), Macfarren (G.) (overture), Moniuszko (incid. mus.), O'Neill (do.), Perabo (pf. pieces), Pierné (incid. mus.), Pierson (H. H.) (funeral march), Rietz (incid. mus.), Searle (opera), Shostakovich (incid. mus.), Stenhammar (do.), Taneiev (A. S.) (overture), Tchaikovsky (incid. mus. and overture-fantasy), Thomson (V.) (incid. mus.), Tiessen (do.), Vogler (incid. mus.), Walton (film mus.), Woyrsch (overture), Zumsteeg (incid. mus.). 5 songs for Ophelia set by Brahms in 1873; 'To be or not to be' noted for Pepys by one Cesare Morelli, prob. ordered by Pepys from some comp., (?) Locke.

Henry IV, 1 and *2:* At the Boar's Head (opera, Holst), Bishop (incid. mus.),

Corbett (do.), Falstaff (symph. study, Elgar), Gioventù di Enrico V (opera on *Henry IV*, Pacini), Joachim (overture), Paisible (incid. mus.), Williams (G.) (symph. impressions *Owen Glendower*).

Henry V: Boughton (Agincourt scene), Falstaff (symph. study, Elgar), Macfarren (W.) (overture), O'Neill (incid. mus.), Smith (D. S.) (overture *Prince Hal*), Walton (film mus.).

Henry VIII: German (incid. mus.), Hatton (do.), Henry VIII (opera, Saint-Saëns), Schuman (incid. mus.), Sullivan (do.).

Julius Caesar: Blitzstein (incid. mus.), Castelnuovo-Tedesco (overture), Doret (incid. mus.), Falchi (overture), Frankel (film), Galliard (incid. mus. for Mulgrave's adaptation), García Roblez (opera), Giulio Cesare (opera, Malipiero), Jacobson (incid. mus.), Lunssens (symph. poem), O'Neill (do.), Pierson (H. H.) (overture).

King John: Castelnuovo-Tedesco (overture).

King Lear: André (J.) (incid. mus.) Balakirev (incid. mus.), Barraine (do.), Bazzini (do.), Berlioz (overture), Dukas (do.), Hatton (incid. mus.), King Lear (overture, Berlioz; incid. mus., Haydn; sketched opera, Verdi), O'Neill (incid. mus.), Paumgartner (do.), Pedrell (F.) (do.), Rawsthorne (do.), Re Lear (opera, Ghislanzoni), Salmhofer (do.), Schulz-Beuthen (symph.), Shaporin (incid. mus.), Shostakovich (do.), Weingartner (symph. poem).

Love's Labour's Lost: Bishop (incid. mus.), Cusins (overture), Finzi (incid. mus.), also songs by Arne, Braham, Thomas Chilcot, Leveridge, G. Macfarren, H. Parry, J. C. Smith, etc.

Macbeth: Aspelmayr (pantomime), Assafiev (incid. mus.), Bantock (do.), Braunfels (do.), Brüll (overture), Bush (A.) (incid. mus.), Dupuis (S.) (symph. poem), Eccles (J.) (incid. mus.), Fisher (J. A.) (do.), Frankel (film), Gatty (opera), Hatton (incid. mus.), Jacobson (do.), Kelley (do.), Khatchaturian (do.), Le Flem (choreographic drama), Leveridge (incid. mus.), Macbeth (incid. mus., Locke; operas, Bloch, Chelard, Collingwood, Taubert, Verdi; overture, Spohr; symph. poem, R. Strauss), Mederitsch (incid. mus.), Neefe (do.), Netchaiev (do.), Oberthür (overture), O'Neill (incid. mus.), Pearsall (choruses), Pierson (H. H.) (symph.), Purcell (D.) (incid. mus.), Reichardt (do.), Rossi (Lauro) (opera *Biorn*), Rubbra (incid. mus.), Smetana (pf. pieces), Sullivan (do.), Sutor (do.), Tcherepnin (N.) (witches' scene for orch.), Walton (incid. mus.), Zumsteeg (do.).

Measure for Measure: Kabalevsky (incid. mus.), Liebesverbot (Wagner), O'Neill (incid. mus.), Wilson (J.) (song 'Take, O

take' [also set by Bishop, Galliard, G.
Giordani, W. Linley, G. Macfarren, H.
Parry, etc.]).
Merchant of Venice, The: Arne (T. A.)
(incid. mus.), Assafiev (do.), Castelnuovo-
Tedesco (overture), Fauré (incid. mus.
Shylock), Foerster (J. B.) (opera *Jessica*),
Greenwood (incid. mus.), Hatton (do.),
Humperdinck (do.), Macfarren (G.) (over-
ture), Marchand de Venise (opera, Hahn),
Mercante di Venezia (opera, Pinsuti),
Nystroem (incid. mus.), O'Neill (do.),
Rabaud (do.), Rathaus (do.), Sabata (do.),
Simon (A.) (do.), Sullivan (do.), Taub-
mann (opera *Porzia*), Vaughan Williams
(*Serenade to Music*), White (F.) (overture
Shylock).
Merry Wives of Windsor, The: Adam
(opera *Falstaff*), Dittersdorf (opera), Fal-
staff (operas, Balfe, Salieri and Verdi),
Horn (C. E.) (songs), Kaun (opera *Falstaff*),
Lustigen Weiber von Windsor (opera,
Nicolai), Moniuszko (incid. mus.), Ritter
(P.) (opera), Salmhofer (incid. mus.), Sir
John in Love (opera, Vaughan Williams),
Sullivan (incid. mus.).
Midsummer Night's Dream, A: Arne
(M.) (songs), Arundell (incid. mus.),
Aylward (songs), Bishop (incid. mus.),
Burney (songs), Castelnuovo-Tedesco (over-
ture), Cooke (T.) (songs), Fairies (opera,
J. C. Smith), Fairy Queen (Purcell), Green-
wood (incid. mus.), Hüe (opera *Titania*),
Křenek (incid. mus.), Lampe (*Pyramus
and Thisbe*), Leigh (incid. mus.), Leveridge
(*Pyramus and Thisbe*), Mancinelli (opera
Sogno di una notte d'estate), Midsummer
Night's Dream (opera, Britten; incid. mus.,
Mendelssohn), Orff (do.), Preludes (De-
bussy, I. 11), Suppé (incid. mus.), Vreuls
(opera), Wolf (E. W.) (opera *Zauberir-
rungen*), Wolf (H.) (*Elfenlied*).
Much Ado about Nothing: Béatrice et
Bénédict (opera, Berlioz), German (incid.
mus.), Godard (do.), Hahn (do.), Khren-
nikov (incid. mus.), Korngold (incid. mus.),
Mojsisovics (opera), Much Ado (opera,
Stanford), Stransky (opera *Beatrice and
Benedick*). Settings of 'Sigh no more' by
Arne, Balfe, W. Linley, G. Macfarren,
J. C. Smith, Sullivan, etc.
Othello: Ambros (overture), Assafiev
(incid. mus.), Bortkievich (symph. poem),
Coleridge-Taylor (do.), Esposito (over-
ture), Fibich (symph. poem), Hadley
(H.) (overture), Krein (A.) (ballet), Krug
(prelude), Lenton (incid. mus.), Macfarren
(W.) (overture), Otello (operas, Rossini
and Verdi), Othello (overture, Dvořák),
Parker (C.) (incid. mus.), Salmhofer
(do.), Shostakovich (do.), Zumsteeg (do.).
Settings of Drinking Song by Humfrey
and W. Linley; of Willow Song by Bishop,
Giordani, J. Hook, W. Linley, Shield,
Sullivan, etc.
Pericles: Perfall (incid. mus.).

Rape of Lucrece, The: Rape of Lucretia
(Britten), Sæverud (suite).
Richard II: Ames (incid. mus.), Hatton
(do.), Pitt (do.), Purcell (do.).
Richard III: German (incid. mus.),
Smetana (symph. poem), Volkmann (incid.
mus.).
Romeo and Juliet: Arne (T. A.) (incid.
mus.), Blacher (scenic oratorio), Bedford
(love scene), Boyce (incid. mus.), Campo
(opera), Capuleti ed i Montecchi (opera,
Bellini), Dalayrac (opera, *Tout pour
l'amour*), Farkas (F.) (incid. mus.),
German (do.), Giulietta e Romeo (operas,
Vaccai, Zandonai and Zingarelli), Hol-
brooke (symph. poem, *Queen Mab*),
Holmes (A.) (symph.), d'Ivry (opera *Amants
de Vérone*), Lambert (C.) (ballet), Lunssens
(symph. poem), Macfarren (G.) (overture),
Marchetti (opera), Martin (F.) (incid.
mus.), Morales (M.) (opera), Pasquali
(N.) (dirge), Pierson (H. H.) (incid. mus.),
Prokofiev (ballet), Romeo and Juliet
(opera, Barkworth; fantasy-overture,
Tchaikovsky), Roméo et Juliette (operas,
Gounod and Steibelt; symph., Berlioz),
Romeo und Julie (opera, G. Benda),
Salmhofer (incid. mus.), Schwanberg
(opera), Stenhammar (incid. mus.), Suter-
meister (opera), Svendsen (overture),
Thomé (incid. mus.).
Songs: Castelnuovo-Tedesco (all the
songs in the plays), Finzi, Macfarren (G.),
Quilter, Schubert (3 songs in Ger. trans.),
Strauss (R.), Westrup.
Sonnets: Cooke (A.), Dieren (van),
Ketting.
Taming of the Shrew, The: Addinsell
(incid. mus.), Bossi† (R.) (opera *Volpino
il calderaio*), Braham, Castelnuovo-Tedesco
(overture), Macfarren (W.) (do.), Maclean
(A.) (opera), Pitt (overture), Purcell
(D.) (incid. mus.), Rheinberger (overture),
Samara (opera *Furia domata*), Sly (opera,
Wolf-Ferrari), Wagenaar (J.) (overture),
Widerspänstigen Zähmung (opera, Goetz).
Tempest, The: Arensky (incid. mus.),
Arne (do.), Arnold (M.) (do.), Arundell
(do.), Berkeley (incid. mus.), Bliss (do.),
Boyce (do.), Chausson (do.), Corder
(overture *Prospero*), Davy (J.) (incid.
mus.), Farwell (masque *Caliban*), Fibich
(opera and symph. poem), Fisher
(incid. mus.), Frank (opera *Sturm*),
Gatty (opera), Halévy (do.), Honegger
(orch. preludes), Humfrey (incid. mus.),
Humperdinck (do.), Johnson (R. ii)
(songs), Kunzen (opera *Stormen*), Lattuada (opera), Linley (3) (incid. mus.),
Locke (do.), Martin (F.) (opera), Nystroem
(incid. mus.), Paine (symph. poem),
Pijper (incid. mus.), Reichardt (opera
Geisterinsel), Riotte (opera), Salmhofer
(incid. mus.), Smith (J. C.) (opera),
Stucken (incid. mus.), Sullivan (do.),
Sutermeister (opera *Zauberinsel*), Taubert

(incid. mus.), **Tempest** (do., Sibelius; operas, Fibich, Gatty, Purcell, etc.; symph. fantasy, Tchaikovsky, **Tempesta** (opera, Halévy), **Tiessen** (incid. mus.), **Unger (H.)** (do.), **Vierling** (overture), **Weingartner** (incid. mus.), **Wellesz** (suite *Prosperos Beschwörungen*), **Wessely (C. B.)** (incid. mus.), **Wood** (Ralph, do.), **Zumsteeg** (opera *Geisterinsel*).

Timon of Athens: **Farkas (F.)** (incid. mus.), **Franck (J. W.)** (masque), **Grabu** (incid. mus.), **Lunssens** (symph. poem), **Purcell** (do.), **Sullivan** (overture), **Trapp** (incid. mus.).

Titus Andronicus: **Clarke (J.)** (incid. mus.).

Troilus and Cressida: Song 'O heart, heavy heart' set by Matthew King.

Twelfth Night: **Arne** (songs), **Bishop** (incid. mus.), **Bowles** (do.), **Braunfels** (do.), **Castelnuovo-Tedesco** (overture), **Clay** (incid. mus.), **Dale** (songs), **Filippi** (opera *Malvolio*), **Humperdinck** (incid. mus.), **Koreshtchenko** (do.), **Mackenzie** (overture), **Paumgartner** (incid. mus.), **Pierson (H. H.)** (overture), **Sandberger** (symph. poem *Viola*), **Stenhammar** (incid. mus.), **Taubert** (opera *Cesario*), **Tausch** (incid. mus.), **Vernon** (songs), **Viola** (Holenia and Smetana), **Weis (K.)** (opera *Viola = The Twins*), **Widor** (incid. mus.). 'Come away, death' set for 3 female voices by Brahms; 'She never told her love' set for 1 voice by Haydn.

Two Gentlemen of Verona: **Bishop** (incid. mus.), **Vernon** (songs), **Who is Silvia?** (Schubert [also set by Leveridge, W. Linley, G. Macfarren, S. Webbe, etc.]).

Winter's Tale, A: **Barnett (J. F.)** (overture), **Boyce** (incid. mus.), **Castelnuovo-Tedesco** (overture), **Ehlert** (do.), **Flotow** (incid. mus.), **Hermione** (opera, Bruch), **Humperdinck** (incid. mus.), **Larsson** (do.), **Macfarren (W.)** (overture), **Nešvera** (opera *Perdita*), **Sokolov** (incid. mus.), **Suk** (overture), **Wilson (J.)** (song 'Lawn as white as driven snow'), **Wintermärchen** (opera, Goldmark).

See also **Jirák** (overture to a comedy), **Linley** (3) (ode on the witches), **Speaight** (fairy characters for string 4tet), **Zilcher** (incid. mus. for var. plays).

Shakespeare, William (b. Croydon, 16. VI. 1849; d. London, 1. XI. 1931), Eng. tenor, teacher and comp. Studied under Molique in London and later at the R.A.M. with Sterndale Bennett, afterwards with Reinecke at the Leipzig Cons., where he prod. his symph. Later he studied singing with Lamperti at Milan. In 1875 he returned to London and made his name as a concert singer, and in 1878 became prof. of singing at the R.A.M. He wrote several books on singing.

Works incl. symph. in C min., 2 over-

tures for orch.; concerto and *Capriccio* for pf. and orch.; 2 string 4tets, pf. trio; pf. pieces; songs, etc.

Shaliapin, Feodor Ivanovich (b. Kazan, 11. II. 1873; d. Paris, 12. IV 1938), Rus. bass-baritone. After a childhood spent in poverty, he joined a provincial opera co. and in 1892 studied singing at Tiflis. In 1894 he made his 1st appearance at St. Petersburg and began to become famous when he was engaged for Mamontov's Private Opera at Moscow in 1896. He sang at Milan in 1901 and 1904 and was engaged for Paris and London by Diaghilev in 1913. He left Rus. in 1920 and from 1921 to 1925 sang at the Metropolitan Opera, N.Y.

Shalm. *See* **Shawm.**

Shamus O'Brien, opera by Stanford (lib. by George H. Jessop, based on a poem by Joseph Sheridan Le Fanu), prod. London, Opera Comique, 2. III. 1896.

Shanewis (*The Robin Woman*), opera by Cadman (lib. by Nelle Richmond Eberhart), prod. N.Y., Metropolitan Opera, 23. III. 1918.

Shankar, Ravi (b. Benares, 7. IV. 1920), Indian sitar-player and comp. Studied with his brother and began his career as a dancer before studying the sitar seriously and becoming a great virtuoso. He has frequently perf. in both Eur. and Amer. His comps. incl. the score to the film 'Pather Panchali' and a ballet after Tagore, *Samanya Kshati*.

Shanty (possibly from Fr. *chantez*, imper. of *chanter*, 'to sing'), a sailors' song with the quite definite character of a labour song, sung to lighten some hard manual task by aiding the rhythmic motions in the act of pumping, hauling ropes, hoisting sails and the like.

Shapleigh, Bertram (b. Boston, 15. I. 1871; d. Washington, 2. VII. 1940), Amer. comp. Studied medicine, but was a pupil of Chadwick, MacDowell and others for mus. He bought an estate in Eng., but returned to U.S.A. in 1915 after its destruction by fire.

Works incl. 2 operas, 5 1-act operas; Mass in D maj. and other church mus.; cantata on the Song of Solomon, *The Raven* (Poe) and *Mirage* for chorus and orch.; works for unaccomp. chorus; 2 symphs., 2 suites, symph. prelude, 3 Consolations, etc., for orch.; poem for cello and orch.; instrumental pieces; pf. works, etc.

Shaporin, Yuri Alexandrovich (b. Glukhov, 8. XI. 1887; d. Moscow, XII. 1966), Rus. comp. Educ. at St. Petersburg, where he graduated in law at the univ. In 1913 he entered the Cons. there, studying under Sokolov, Steinberg and N. Tcherepnin. On leaving he became interested in stage mus. and founded the Great Dramatic

Theatre with Gorky and Blok. In 1937 he moved to Moscow.

Works incl. opera *The Decembrists* (lib. by Alexey Tolstoy); incid. mus. for Shakespeare's *King Lear* and *Comedy of Errors*, Schiller's *Robbers*, Molière's *Tartuffe*, Pushkin's *Boris Godunov*, Beaumarchais's *Marriage of Figaro*, Turgenev's *The Nest of Gentlefolk* (*Liza*), Labiche's *The Italian Straw Hat*, etc.; film mus. incl. *General Suvarov*; symph. cantata *On the Kulikov Field*; symph. in E min., suite *The Flea* for orch., 2 suites for pf.; song cycles to words by Pushkin and Tiutchev, and other songs, etc.

Sharp, the sign ♯, which raises a note by a semitone; also an adj. describing out-of-tune intonation on the S. side.

Sharp, Cecl (James) (b. London, 22. XI. 1859; d. London, 23. VI. 1924), Eng. folksong collector. Educ. at Uppingham and Clare Coll., Cambridge. After living in Austral. in 1889–92, he returned to London and in 1896 became principal of the Hampstead Cons. In 1899 he began to collect folksongs and dances, later he joined the Folksong Society and in 1911 founded the Eng. Folk-Dance Society. In 1916–18 he visited the U.S.A. to collec songs in the Appalachian mountains, where many Eng. songs were still preserved in the primitive form by descendants of the 17th-cent. emigrants.

Sharp Mixture, an org. Mixture stop sounding the higher harmonics above the fundamental notes.

Shaw, Geoffrey (Turton) (b. London, 14. XI. 1879; d. London, 14. IV. 1943), Eng. church musician and educationist. He was a choir-boy at St. Paul's Cathedral in London and later studied with Stanford and Chas. Wood at Cambridge. After some years as organist in London, he became Staff Inspector of Mus. to the Board of Educ., and he did much adjudicating at mus. festivals.

Shaw, George Bernard (b. Dublin, 26. VII. 1856; d. Ayot St. Lawrence, Herts., 2. XI. 1950), Ir. critic, dramatist, novelist and political author. Settled in London early in his career and wrote mus. criticism for the *Star* and the *World*, 1890–4. *See also* **Arundell** (*St Joan*), **Auric** (*Caesar and Cleopatra*), **Bliss** (do.), **Chagrin** (*Heartbreak House*), **Chocolate Soldier** (Straus), **Honegger** (*Pygmalion*), **Lilien** (*Grosse Katharina*), **Prokofiev** (*Egyptian Nights* [*Caesar and Cleopatra*]), **Walton** (*Major Barbara*).

Shaw, Martin (Fallas) (b. London, 9. III. 1875; d. Southwold, 24. X. 1958), Eng. organist and comp., brother of Geoffrey S. Studied at the R.C.M. in London, was organist at several London churches, founded the Purcell Operatic Society in 1900, ed. var. vocal pubs., incl.

the hymn-book *Songs of Praise* with Vaughan Williams, and in 1935 became mus. director to the diocese of Chelmsford.

Works incl. opera *The Thorn of Avalon*, ballad operas *Mr. Pepys* and *Waterloo Leave* (Clifford Bax), operetta *Philomel*; pageant *Judgment at Chelmsford*; Lenten oratorio *The Redeemer*, choral works *The Seaport* and *Easter* (Masefield), *Sursum corda* (Binyon), *The Rock* (T. S. Eliot), 2 motets for double chorus; *The Ungentle Guest* for baritone, string 4tet and harp, *Water Folk* for baritone, string 4tet and pf.; sonata for fl. and pf.; *c.* 100 songs, part-songs, incl. *Budmouth Dears* (Hardy), etc.

Shaw (*née* Postans), Mary (called Mrs. Alfred Shaw) (b. Lea, Kent, 1814; d. Hadleigh Hall, Suffolk, 9. IX. 1876), Eng. contralto. Student at the R.A.M. in London and then pupil of G. Smart. She made her 1st appearance in 1834 and the following year married the painter Alfred S. In 1838 she sang at the Gewandhaus, Leipzig, under Mendelssohn, and the next year at the Scala, Milan.

Shawe-Taylor, Desmond (b. Dublin, 29. V. 1907), Ir. critic. He was educated at Shrewsbury and Oxford, became a literary critic at first, but in 1945 became mus. critic to the *New Statesman and Nation* and in 1959 to the *Sunday Times*, in succession to Ernest Newman. He is esp. interested in singing and the gramophone. His books are *Covent Garden* ('World of Music' series, 1948) and, with Edward Sackville-West, *The Record Guide* (1951) and *The Record Year* (1952).

Shawm (or Shalm), a primitive woodwind instrument, the forerunner of the ob., with a double-reed mouthpiece and a wide bell. The largest types had bent tubes to their mouthpieces and thus approximated more to the bassoon.

Shchedrin, Rodion (b. Moscow, 16. XII. 1932), Rus. comp. Studied at Moscow Cons. with Shaporin, graduating in 1955.

Works incl. opera *Not for Love Alone*; ballet *The Little Hump-backed Horse*; pf. concerto; pf. 5tet, 3 string 4tets; songs.

Shcherbatchev, Andrey Vladimirovich (b. Manuilovo, Gvt. of Poltava, 20. I. 1869; d. Kiev, 14. II. 1916), Rus. comp. Studied under Blumenfeld, Liadov and Rimsky-Korsakov at the St. Petersburg Cons.

Works incl. march for orch.; pf. sonata and pieces; songs, etc.

Shcherbatchev, Vladimir Vassilievich (b. Warsaw, 24. I. 1889; d. Leningrad, 5. III. 1952), Rus. comp. Studied with Steinberg, Liadov and Wintol at the St. Petersburg Cons., and later became prof. at the Leningrad Cons.

Works incl. opera *Anna Kolossova*; film mus. *The Tempest*; 5 symphs. (No. 4 choral), suite and other orchestral works;

nonet for voice and instruments and other chamber mus.; 2 pf. sonatas and other pf. works, etc.

She Stoops to Conquer, opera by Macfarren (lib. by Edward Fitzball, based on Goldsmith's comedy), prod. London, Covent Garden Theatre, 11. II. 1864.

Shebalin, Vissarion Yakovlevich (b. Omsk, 11. VI. 1902; d. Moscow, 29. V. 1963), Rus. comp. Son of a teacher; received his 1st mus. training at the Omsk School of Mus., entered the Moscow Cons. as a pupil of Miaskovsky in 1923 and stayed there as a prof. in 1928., as well as teaching at the Gnessin School of Mus. Director of the Moscow Cons. 1942–8.

Works incl. opera *Sun over the Steppes*, comic opera *The Embassy Bridegroom*; incid. mus. for Schiller's *Robbers* and *Mary Stuart*, Pushkin's *Mozart and Salieri* and *The Stone Guest* (Don Juan), Lermontov's *Masquerade*, Scribe's *A Glass of Water*, etc.; film mus.; symph. cantata *Lenin* for solo voices, chorus and orch.; 5 symphs., 2 suites and 2 overtures for orch.; vln. concerto, concertinos for vln. and strings and for harp and small orch.; 9 string 4tets, string trio; sonatina for vln. and vla., a suite for solo vln.; 2 pf. sonatas and 3 sonatinas; songs (Pushkin, Heine, etc.), popular choruses and war songs, etc.

Shedlock, John S(outh). (b. Reading, 29. IX. 1843; d. London, 9. I. 1919), Eng. mus. scholar and critic. Studied at London Univ., with Lalo in Paris and elsewhere abroad. He settled in London and taught, and in 1879 he became mus. critic to the *Academy* and in 1901 to the *Athenaeum*. He wrote works on Beethoven's sketch-books and pf. sonatas and another on *The Pianoforte Sonata*.

Sheffield, John. *See* Mulgrave, Earl of.

Sheffield Musical Festival. Founded in 1895, cond. by Henry Coward, held triennially from 1896 to 1911, but interrupted by World War I in 1914; revived in 1933, but again stopped by the 1939–45 war.

Sheherazade (Rimsky-Korsakov). *See* Shahrazad.

Shéhérazade, song-cycle with orch. by Ravel (poems by Tristan Klingsor), comp. 1903 on the basis of an unpub. overture of the same name of 1898. There are 3 songs: *Asie, La Flûte enchantée* and *L'indifférent*. 1st perf. Paris, 17. V. 1904.

Shekhter, Boris Semionovich (b. Odessa, 20. I. 1900; d. Moscow, 16. XII. 1961), Rus. comp. Pupil of Miaskovsky at the Moscow Cons. Later he made a close study of Turcomanian folk mus., and based some of his works on it.

Works incl. operas *The Year 1905* (with Davidenko) and *The Son of the People*; suite *Turkmenia* for orch., symph.

Dithyramb for the celebrations of the 20th anniversary of the Rus. Revolution; pf. concerto; song cycles, etc.

Shelbye, William (b. ?; d. ?), Eng. comp. and organist. He was organist at Canterbury Cathedral, 1547–53. A *Felix namque* and *Miserere* are in the Mulliner Book (*q.v.*).

Shelley, Percy Bysshe (1792–1822), Eng. poet. *See* Barber (scene for orch.), Brian (*Prometheus*), Chadwick (*Adonais*), Coke (*Cenci*), Davis (J. D.) (do.), Dieren (van) (do. and songs), Gatty (odes), Gnessin (symph. fragment), Goldschmidt (B.) (*Beatrice Cenci*), Miaskovsky (*Alastor*), Prometheus Unbound (H. Parry), Ronald (*Adonais*), Salaman ('I arise from dreams') Tiersot (*Hellas*), White (M. V.) (songs).

Shenshin, Alexander Alexeievich (b. Moscow, 18. XI. 1890), Rus. comp. Studied philology in Moscow and became a teacher of hist. and Lat. Only then did he begin to study mus. with Gretchaninov and Glière, and in 1912 he pub. his 1st work.

Works incl. opera *O'Tao* and other works for the stage; song cycles *From Jap. Anthologies* and other songs, etc.

Shepherd, Arthur (b. Paris, Idaho, 19. II. 1880; d. Cleveland, 12. I. 1958), Amer. cond. and comp. Studied at the New Eng. Cons. at Boston, where after a period of teaching at Salt Lake City he was prof. at the New Eng. Cons., Boston, from 1908 to 1917, when he joined the army. From 1920 to 1926 he was asst. cond. of the Cleveland Symph. Orch., and from 1927 to 1950 at Western Reserve Univ.

Works incl. 2 symphs. incl. *Horizons, Choreographic Suite* for orch.; fantasy for pf. and orch.; vln. concerto; 3 string 4tets; *Triptych* (from Tagore's *Gitanjali*) for voice and string 4tet; vln. and pf. sonata; 2 pf. sonatas and pieces; songs, etc.

Shepherd, John. *See* Sheppard.

Shepherd's Pipe. A rustic wind instrument akin to the ob., the Fr. Musette, played with a double reed, like the chanter of a bagpipe, but usually used separately.

Shepherds of the Delectable Mountains, The, opera by Vaughan Williams (lib. by comp., based on Bunyan's *Pilgrim's Progress*), prod. London, R.C.M., 11. VII. 1922. *See also* Pilgrim's Progress.

Sheppard, John (b. ? London, ?; d. ?, ? 1563), Eng. comp. Learnt mus. as a choir-boy at St. Paul's Cathedral in London under Thomas Mulliner. In 1542 he became organist and choirmaster at Magdalen Coll., Oxford, and later was in Queen Mary's Chapel Royal.

Works incl. Masses *The Western Wynde, The French Masse, Be not afraide* and *Playn Song Mass for a Mene*, motets, 2 Te Deums, 2 Magnificats, anthems, etc.

Shera, F(rank). H(enry). (b. Sheffield,

4. V. 1882; d. Sheffield, 21. II. 1956), Eng. mus. scholar. Studied at the R.C.M. in London and after taking var. degrees was director of mus. at Malvern Coll. from 1916 to 1926, and from 1928 to 1950 prof. of mus. at Sheffield Univ. He pub. studies of Debussy and Ravel, Elgar's instrumental works and a book on *Musical Groundwork*.

Sheridan, Richard Brinsley (1751–1816), Eng. dramatist. *See* **Arundell** (*St. Patrick's Day*), **Barber** (*School for Scandal*), **Critic** (Stanford), **Duenna** (Linley), **Dussek** (*Pizarro*), **Gerhard** (*Duenna*), **Giordani** (T.) (*Critic*), **Hatton** (*Duenna*), **Kabalevsky** (*School for Scandal*), **Kelly** (*Pizarro*), **Klenau** (*School for Scandal*), **Linley** (**1** and **3**) (*Duenna*), **Linley** (**1**) (*School for Scandal, Robinson Crusoe* and *Monody on the Death of Garrick*), **Prokofiev** (*Betrothed in a Monastery*).

Sherrington, Helen. *See* **Lemmens-Sherrington.**

Sheryngham, ? (b. ?; d. ?), Eng. 15th–16th-cent. comp.
Works incl. a carol for 4 voices, 'My wofull hart', and a 2-part madrigal.

Shield, William (b. Swalwell, Co. Durham, 5. III. 1748; d. Brightling, Sussex, 25. I. 1829), Eng. violinist and comp. Orphaned at the age of 9, he was apprenticed to a shipbuilder, but studied mus. with Avison in Newcastle, where he also appeared as a solo violinist and led the subscription concerts from 1763. After engagements in Scarborough and Stockton-on-Tees he went to London as 2nd vln. of the Opera orch. in 1772, becoming principal vla. the following year. After the success of his first opera, *The Flitch of Bacon* (1778), he was app. comp. to Covent Garden Theatre (1778–91 and again 1792–1807). In 1791 he met Haydn in London, and visited Fr. and It. Two treatises, on harmony and thorough-bass, were pub. in 1800 and 1817, in which year he was app. Master of the King's Mus.
Works incl. over 50 works for the stage, e.g. *The Flitch of Bacon, Rosina, Robin Hood, Richard Cœur de Lion, The Marriage of Figaro* (after Beaumarchais), *Aladdin, The Woodman, The Travellers in Switzerland, Netley Abbey, The Italian Villagers*, etc.; string 4tets and trios; vln. duets; songs, etc.

Shift, the change from one position to another in string and tromb. playing, in the former case by moving the left hand to a different position on the fingerboard, in the latter by lengthening or shortening the slide to alter the length of the tube.

Shifting Pedal. *See* **Damping Pedal.**

Shimmy, an Amer. ballroom dance that became popular after the 1914–18 war

and was accomp. by jazz mus.; a fast movement of the Foxtrot type.

Shirinsky, Vassily Petrovich (b. Ekaterinodar, 17. I. 1901; d. Moscow, 16. VIII. 1965), Rus. violinist and comp. Studied at the Moscow Cons. and became a member of that institution's string 4tet.
Works incl. 2 symphs. and suite for orch.; 4 string 4tets, pf. 5tet; vln. and pf. sonata, vla. and pf. sonata; sonata and pieces for pf.; songs, etc.

Shirley, James (1596–1666), Eng. dramatist. *See* **Coleman** (E.) (*Ajax and Achilles*), **Cupid and Death** (Locke and C. Gibbons), **Parry** (H.) (*Glories of our Blood and State*), **Triumph of Peace** (W. Lawes and Ive).

Shofar, an ancient Jewish wind instrument made of a ram's horn, still used in the synagogue.

Sholokhov, Mikhail Alexandrovich (b. 1905), Rus. novelist. *See* **Dzerzhinsky** (*Ploughing the Fallows*, also called *Virgin Soil Upturned*), **Quiet Don** (Dzerzhinsky).

Shore. Eng. family of musicians:
1. **Mathias S.** (b. ?; d. London, 1700), trumpeter. In the service of the court of James II and William and Mary in the post of Sergeant Trumpeter.
2. **William S.** (b. London, *c.* 1665; d. London, XII. 1707), trumpeter, son of prec. Succeeded his father in his post.
3. **Catherine S.** (b. London, *c.* 1668; d. London, *c.* 1730), singer and harpsichordist, sister of prec. Pupil of Purcell; married Colley Cibber in 1693.
4. **John S.** (b. London, *c.* 1662; d. London, 20. XI. 1752), trumpeter and lutenist, brother of prec. Succeeded in his brother's post in 1707.

Short Octave. On old keyboard instruments the notes governed by the extreme bottom keys were sometimes not tuned to the ordinary scale, but to a selection of lower notes more likely to be frequently required, e.g.:

The bottom octave so tuned was called the S. O.

Short Score. *See* **Score.**

Shostakovich, Dimitri (b. St. Petersburg, 25. IX. 1906), Rus. comp. Entered the Cons. there in 1919 and studied with Nikolaiev, Steinberg and Glazunov. He left in 1925, having already written a great many works. The 1st symph., which dates from that year, was prod. in 1926. He quickly made his mark, but came into conflict with Soviet authority in 1930, when his opera, *The Nose*, based on a story by Gogol, was denounced as bourgeois and decadent. The next, *A Lady Macbeth of Mtsensk*, prod. in 1934, was even more violently attacked in 1936 and had to be withdrawn. Thereafter, however, he suited his manner to the government's requirements, which in turn became somewhat modified, and estab. himself as the leading comp. of the day, gaining the Stalin Prize with his pf. 5tet in 1941.

Works incl. operas *The Nose* and *A Lady Macbeth of Mtsensk*; ballets *The Golden Age*, *The Bolt*, *The Limpid Stream* and *The Golden Key*; incid. mus. to several plays incl. Shakespeare's *Hamlet*, *King Lear* and *Othello*, Piotrovsky's *Rule*, *Britannia* and an adaptation from Balzac's *Human Comedy*; cantata *The Execution of Stefan Razin*; mus. to *c.* 14 films; 13 symphs. (No. 7 *Leningrad Symph.*); concerto for pf., tpt. and strings; pf. concerto, vln. concerto; 2 cello concertos; 2 pieces for string 8tet, 12 string 4tets, pf. 5tet; vln. sonata, cello sonata; 2 sonatas, 24 Preludes and fugues and many pieces for pf.; songs incl. cycle to Jap. poems, 4 poems by Pushkin, etc.

Shuard, Amy (b. London, 19. VII. 1924), Eng. soprano. Studied at Trinity Coll. of Mus. in London, making her début in Johannesburg in 1949. She is well known as a dramatic singer, esp. in Wagner. Since 1954 she has sung at Covent Garden.

Shudi, Burkat (Burkhardt Tschudi) (b. Schwanden, Glarus, 13. III. 1702; d. London, 19. VIII. 1773), Swiss (anglicized) harpsichord maker. He settled in London as a cabinet maker in 1718, joined the harpsichord maker Tabel and set up on his own account in the 1730s. *See also* **Broadwood.**

Si, the old name for the note B (*see* **Solmization**), still used in Lat. countries, and in Tonic Sol-fa the leading note in any key, represented by the symbol **t,** pronounced Te.

Si j'étais roi (*If I were King*), opera by Adam (lib. by Adolphe Philippe d'Ennery and Jules Brésil), prod. Paris, Théâtre Lyrique, 4. IX. 1852.

Sibelius, Jean (Johan Julius Christian) (b. Tavastehus, 8. XII. 1865; d. Järrenpää nr. Helsinki, 20. IX. 1957), Fin. comp. Son of a surgeon. Having been given a classical educ., he was intended for the law, entering Helsinki Univ. He learned pf. and vln. as a child and tried comp. long before he had any theoret. instruction. While studying law he managed to take a special course under Wegelius at the Cons. and in 1885 went there altogether, giving up the univ. He left in 1889 and had a string 4tet and a suite for string orch. perf. in public. With a government grant he went to study counterpoint with

A. Becker in Berlin and later orch. with Fuchs in Vienna, where he also consulted Goldmark. When he returned home he became a passionate nationalist, studying the *Kalevala* and other Fin. literature for subjects for his works, the 1st being *Kullervo*, prod. at Helsinki on 28. IV. 1892, the year in which he married Aino Järnfelt, sister of the comp. of that name, and was asked by Kajanus to write an orchestral work for perf. at the Cons., a request to which he responded with *A Saga*. His only opera, *The Maiden in the Tower*, had a single perf. in 1896, but like *Kullervo* remained unpub.

An annual grant was voted to S. by the government in 1897 and increased in 1926, and he was thus enabled to devote himself entirely to comp. without having to fill any official or administrative post. He gradually made his way abroad, but not in every country. Much of his work was pub. in Ger., but not widely perf. there; in Eng. he became much better known after the perf. of the 4th symph. at the Birmingham Festival in 1912, and in Amer. after his visit in 1914, when Yale Univ. conferred a doctor's degree on him. During the Rus. Revolution after the 1914–18 war there was much unrest in Fin., and S.'s country home at Järvenpää was invaded; but he spent most of his life there quietly, devoted wholly to comp.

Works incl. opera, *The Maiden in the Tower* (unpub.); incid. mus. to Adolf Paul's *King Christian*, Arvid Järnefelt's *Kuolema* (incl. *Valse triste*), Maeterlinck's *Pelléas et Mélisande*, Hjalmar Procopé's *Belshazzar's Feast*, Strindberg's *Svanevit*, Paul Knudsen's *Scaramouche*, Hofmannsthal's version of *Everyman*, Shakespeare's *Tempest*; 7 symphs., *Kullervo*, with solo voices and chorus (unpub.), symph. poem *A Saga*, *Karelia* overture and suite, *Rakastava* for strings and timpani, *Spring Song*, 4 Legends (*Lemminkäinen* and the *Maidens of Saari*, *The Swan of Tuonela*, *Lemminkäinen in Tuonela*, *Lemminkäinen's Homefaring*), 2 suites of *Scènes historiques*, tone-poem *Finlandia*, 2 pieces *The Dryads* and *Dance Intermezzo*, symph. fantasy *Pohjola's Daughter*, dance intermezzo *Pan and Echo*, tone-poem *Night-Ride and Sunrise*, funeral march *In Memoriam*, tone-poems *The Bard* and *Luonnotar*, symph. poems *The Oceanides* and *Tapiola*, a number of smaller orchestral pieces; vln. concerto; string 4tet *Voces intimae*; sonatina and many smaller pieces for vln. and pf.; *Malinconia* and 2 *Serious Pieces* for cello and pf.; 18 op. nos. of pf. works incl. sonata in F maj., *Pensées lyriques*, *Kyllikki*, 3 sonatinas; 2 org. pieces; choral works with orch. (with or without solo voices): *Impromptu* (female chorus), *The Origin of Fire*, *The Ferryman's Bride*,

The Captive Queen; a number of part-songs; 85 songs; Rydberg's *Skogsrået* and Runeberg's *Nights of Jealousy* for recitation and instrumental accomp.; a large number of miscellaneous works, many unpub., etc.

Siboni, Erik (Anton Valdemar) (b. Copenhagen, 26. VIII. 1828; d. Copenhagen, 22. II. 1892), Dan. pianist, organist and comp. of It. origin. Studied at Copenhagen, J. P. E. Hartmann being among his masters, and with Moscheles and Hauptmann at Leipzig. He fought on the Dan. side in the war of Slesvig-Holstein in 1848. In 1851–3 he continued his studies with Sechter in Vienna. After his return to Copenhagen he settled as a mus. teacher, among his pupils being Princess Alexandra. In 1864–83 he was prof. of the Royal Acad. at Sorø.

Works incl. operas *Loreley* and *Carl den Andens Flugt*; Psalm cxi, *Stabat Mater*, cantatas *The Battle of Murten* and *The Assault of Copenhagen* for solo voices, chorus and orch.; 2 symphs. and other orchestral works; pf. concerto; string 4tets, pf. 4tet, pf. trio; vln. and pf. and cello, and pf. sonatas; duet for 2 pfs.; pf. pieces; songs, etc.

Siboni, Giuseppe (b. Forlì, 27. I. 1780; d. Copenhagen, 29. III. 1839), It. tenor, father of prec. He made his 1st appearance at Florence in 1797, and having appeared elsewhere in It., went to Prague, London, Vienna and St. Petersburg, settling at Copenhagen in 1819, where he became director of the Royal Opera and the Cons.

Siccardi, Honorio (b. Buenos Aires, 13. IX. 1897), Arg. comp. Studied at Buenos Aires and in It. with Malipiero. After his return home he took part in the foundation of the Grupo Renovación in 1933.

Works incl. symph. suite for orch., ballet suite for wind and perc.; 3 cantatas on Aeschylus's *Prometheus*; pf. pieces; songs, etc.

Sicher, Fridolin (b. Bischofszell, Switz., 6. III. 1490; d. there, 13. VI. 1546), Ger. comp. and arr. He compiled a MS. (St. Gall, MS. 530) incl. comps. by himself and arrs. of vocal works by others.

Sicilian Vespers (Verdi). *See* **Vêpres siciliennes.**

Siciliana or **Siciliano** } (It.), a piece or song in dotted 6–8 rhythm derived from a Sicilian dance. It is rather slow, and indeed may form the slow movement of a sonata or suite. Arias in S. rhythm were common in the 18th cent.

Sicilienne (Fr.) = Siciliana, Siciliano.

Side Drum, the military drum, which is the smallest drum used in the orch., covered with a skin at either end and having a snare of catgut string stretched over the lower one, to produce a rattling sound when the upper one is struck by a pair of hard wooden drumsticks. Single strokes on the S. D. are ineffective: it is usually made to prod. small patterns of repeated notes or more or less prolonged rolls. Its tone is bright and hard, without definite pitch. It can be muted by relaxing the tension of the snare.

Sidney, Philip (1554–86), Eng. poet. *See* **Tessier (C.)** (*Astrophel and Stella*).

Siefert, Paul (b. Danzig, 1586; d. Danzig, 6. V. 1666), Ger. organist and comp. Pupil of Sweelinck at Amsterdam. After serving in the royal chapel of Sigismund III at Warsaw, he became organist at St. Mary's Church, Danzig, *c.* 1620.

Works incl. Te Deum, psalms for 4–8 voices and other church mus.; org. pieces, etc.

Siège de Corinthe (Rossini). *See* **Maometto II.**

Siege of Belgrade, The, opera by Storace (lib. by James Cobb), prod. London, Drury Lane Theatre, 1. I. 1791.

Siege of Rhodes, The, opera by Locke, H. Lawes, H. Cooke, Coleman and Hudson (lib. by William Davenant), prod. London, Rutland House, IX. 1656. The 1st Eng. opera.

Siege of Rochelle, The, opera by Balfe (lib. by Edward Fitzball, based on the Comtesse de Genlis's novel), prod. London, Drury Lane Theatre, 29. X. 1835.

Siegel, Rudolf (b. Berlin, 12. IV. 1878; d. Munich, 4. XII. 1948), Ger. cond. and comp. Pupil of Humperdinck and of Thuille at Munich. He cond. at Berlin, 1912–14, Königsberg, 1914–17 and Crefeld, 1919–30.

Works incl. opera *Herr Dandolo*; *Heroische Tondichtung* and other works for orch.; choruses; *Deutsche Volkslieder* and other songs, etc.

Siegfried (Wagner). *See* **Ring des Nibelungen.**

Siegfried Idyll, a symph. piece for small orch. by Wagner, comp. at Triebschen on the Lake of Lucerne in XI. 1870 and perf. on Cosima Wagner's birthday, 25. XII, on the staircase of the villa. It was therefore at first entitled *Triebschener Idyll* and called 'Treppenmusik' in the family circle. The thematic material is taken from *Siegfried*, except the Ger. cradle song 'Schlaf, Kindlein, schlaf', but some of it, even though incl. in *Siegfried*, dates back to a string 4tet of 1864.

Siegl, Otto (b. Graz, 6. X. 1896), Aus. violinist, cond. and comp. Studied vln. with E. Kornauth and comp. with Mojsisovics in Vienna. Joined the Vienna Symph. Orch. as a violinist, worked at the Graz

Opera and then went to Ger., becoming mus. director at Paderborn, at the same time cond. and teaching at Bielefeld and Essen. In 1933 he became comp. prof. at the Cologne Cons., returning to Vienna in 1948.

Works incl. fairy opera *Der Wassermann*; mus. for 2 puppet plays; oratorios *Das Grosse Halleluja* (Claudius), *Eines Menschen Lied, Klingendes Jahr, Trostkantate, Mutter Deutschland*; *Missa Mysterium Magnum*; *Verliebte alle Reime* for chorus; 3 symphs., sinfonietta, *Lyrische Tanzmusik, Festliche Ouvertüre, Pastoralouvertöre, Concerto grosso antico, Galante Abendmusik, Festmusik und Trauermusik* for orch.; pf. concerto, vln. concerto, concerto for string 4tet and string orch.; chamber mus.; songs, etc.

Sienkiewicz, Henryk (1846–1916), Pol. novelist. *See* Quo vadis? (Nouguès).

Siepi, Cesare (b. Milan, 10. II. 1923), It. bass. Studied at Milan Cons., making his début in 1941. From 1946 he sang at La Scala, Milan, and since 1950 has been a leading member of the N.Y. Metropolitan Opera.

Sierra, Gregorio Martinez (1882–1947), Span. dramatist. *See* Turina (*Margot, Jardin de oriente* and *Navidad*).

Siface (Giovanni Francesco Grossi) (b. Uzzanese Chiesina nr. Pescia, 12. II. 1653; d. nr. Ferrara, 29. V. 1697), It. male soprano. Became singer at the Papal Chapel in Rome, 1675, and went to Eng. about 1679. Sang at the court of James II, but soon returned to It. Purcell wrote a harpsichord piece, *Sefauchi's Farewell*, on his departure. He was murdered on a journey.

Siface (*Syphax*), opera by Feo (lib. by Metastasio), prod. Naples, Teatro San Bartolommeo, 13. V. 1723.

Opera by Porpora (lib. do.), prod. Milan, Teatro Regio Ducal, 26. XII. 1725.

Sigh. *See* Ornaments.

Signature. *See* Key Signature; Time Signature.

Signature Tune, a favourite song or dance tune of a popular kind by which perfs., esp. dance bands and light orchs., identify themselves, partic. when they broadcast and are invisible to their audiences.

Signor Bruschino, Il, ossia Il figlio per azzardo (*Mr. B., or The Son by Accident*), opera by Rossini (lib. by Giuseppe Maria Foppa), prod. Venice, Teatro San Moisè, I. 1813.

Signor di Pourceaugnac, Il, opera by Franchetti (lib. by Ferdinando Fontana, based on Molière's comedy, *Monsieur de P.*), prod. Milan, Teatro alla Scala, 10. IV. 1897.

Sigtenhorst Meyer, Bernhard van den

(b. Amsterdam, 17. VI. 1888; d. The Hague, 17. VII. 1953), Dutch pianist and comp. Studied with Zweers, D. de Lange and others and later in Paris, afterwards travelling to Java and the Far East. He returned to Amsterdam, but moved to The Hague, where he lived for many years. Ed. of works by Sweelinck and author of books on him.

Works incl. incid. mus. to Tagore's play *The King's Letter*; oratorio *The Temptation of Buddha, Stabat Mater, Hymn to the Sun* (St. Francis of Assisi); 2 string 4tets; vln. and pf. sonata; sonata and *c.* 12 other op. nos. of pf. pieces; several op. nos. of songs, etc.

Sigurd, opera by Reyer (lib. by Camille du Locle and Alfred Blau, based on the Nibelung Saga), prod. Brussels, Théâtre de la Monnaie, 7. I. 1884.

Siklós, Albert (b. Budapest, 26. VI. 1878; d. Budapest, 3. IV. 1942), Hung. cellist, musicologist and comp. Studied at the Hung. Mus. School in Budapest and appeared as cellist in 1891, as lecturer in 1895 and began to comp. seriously in 1896, when he finished a cello concerto, a symph. and an opera. He held distinguished teaching-posts in Budapest and was app. prof. in 1913.

Works incl. 3 operas, 2 ballets, choral and a vast number of orchestral works, concertos, chamber and much pf. mus., etc., also 10 books of songs.

Sikorski, Kazimierz (b. Zürich, 28. VI. 1895), Pol. comp. Studied at the Chopin High School in Warsaw and later in Paris. In 1926 he became prof. at the Poznań Cons., and in 1927 at the Warsaw Cons. In 1936 he was one of the founders of the Society for the Pub. of Pol. Mus.

Works incl. Psalm vii for chorus and orch.; 2 symphs. and symph. poem for orch.; 3 string 4tets, string 6tet; songs; part-songs, etc.

Silas, Édouard (b. Amsterdam, 22. VIII. 1827; d. London, 8. II. 1909), Dutch pianist, organist and comp. Studied at Amsterdam, made his 1st appearance there at the age of 10, took further lessons with Lacombe and Kalkbrenner in Paris, where he entered the Cons. to study org. with Benoist and comp. with Halévy. In 1850 he settled in London as church organist, concert pianist and teacher.

Works incl. opera *Nitocris*; oratorio *Joash*; Mass for voices and org.; symph. in A maj. and *Mythological Pieces* for orch.; concerto in D min., fantasy and elegy for pf. and orch.; org. pieces; suite in A min. and pieces for pf., etc.

Silbermann. Ger. family of org. builders and harpsichord makers.

1. **Andreas S.** (b. Kleinbobritzsch nr. Frauenstein, Saxony, 16. V. 1678; d. Strasbourg, 16. III. 1734), son of the

carpenter Michael S. Worked with Casparini in Görlitz 1797–c. 99. settled in Strasbourg in 1721 and built the cathedral org. there in 1713–16.

2. Gottfried S. (b. Kleinbobritzsch, 14. I. 1683; d. Dresden, 4. VIII. 1753), brother of prec. At first apprenticed to a bookbinder, he joined his brother Andreas in Strasbourg in 1702, staying there till 1710. He then settled in Freiberg, where he built the cathedral org. (1711–14), and d. while at work on a new org. for the Dresden court. He also built harpsichords and clavichords (one of them commemorated by a piece by C. P. E. Bach entitled 'Farewell to my Silbermann Clavichord'), and was the first Ger. to make pfs.

3. Johann Andreas S. (b. Strasbourg, 26. VI. 1712; d. Strasbourg, 11. II. 1783), son of 1. He built 54 orgs.

4. Johann Daniel S. (b. Strasbourg, 31. III. 1717; d. Leipzig, 9. V. 1766), brother of prec. Worked with his uncle, 2, whose org. at Dresden he finished.

5. Johann Heinrich S. (b. Strasbourg, 24. IX. 1727; d. Strasbourg, 15. 1. 1799), brother of prec. He made harpsichords and pfs., some with pedal boards.

Silcher, Friedrich (b. Schnaith nr. Schorndorf, Württemberg, 27. VI. 1789; d. Tübingen, 26. VIII. 1860), Ger. cond. and comp. Pupil of his father and others. He became a schoolmaster, but in 1815 went to Stuttgart as cond. and in 1817 to the Univ. of Tübingen in the same capacity. Some of his songs have become what in Ger. are called folksongs.

Works incl. 2 hymn-books (3 and 4 voices), collections of songs, some arr., some comp. by himself, incl. *Aennchen von Tharau, Loreley* (Heine), *Morgen muss ich fort, Zu Strassburg auf der Schanz,* etc.

Silent Woman (R. Strauss). *See* **Schweigsame Frau.**

Silk, Dorothy (b. Alvechurch, Worcs., 1884; d. Alvechurch, 30. VII. 1942), Eng. soprano. Studied at Birmingham and in Vienna, giving her 1st recital in London in 1920. She specialized in Bach and earlier comps., but also studied modern works.

Siloti, Alexander (Ilyich) (b. nr. Kharkov, 9. X. 1863; d. N.Y., 8. XII. 1945), Rus. pianist. Studied at the Moscow Cons. under Tchaikovsky, N. Rubinstein and others, later with Liszt. He 1st appeared at Moscow in 1880 and later travelled widely. He left Rus. in 1919 and lived in U.S.A. at the end of his life. From 1925 to 1942 he taught at the Juilliard School in N.Y.

Silva, Andreas de (Silvanus or Sylvanus) (b. ?; d. ?), ? Flem. 15th–16th-cent. singer and comp. Sang in the Papal Chapel in Rome early in the 16th cent. and later

was prob. in the service of the Duke of Mantua.

Works incl. Masses, motets; madrigals, etc.

Silva Leite, António Joaquim da (b. Oporto, 23. V. 1759; d. Oporto, 10. I. 1833), Port. comp. Pupil of the It. Girolamo Sartori (?), he was *maestro de capilla* at Oporto Cathedral from 1814.

Works incl. It. operas *Puntigli per equivoco* and *Le astuzie delle donne; Tantum ergo* with orch ; sonatas and studies for guitar, etc. A projected anthology of org. mus. was never finished.

Silvana, opera by Weber (lib. by Franz Karl Hiemer, altered from Steinsberg's *Waldmädchen*), prod. Frankfurt, 16. IX. 1810. Weber's 2nd version of *Das Waldmädchen* of 1800.

Silvani, Giuseppe Antonio (b. Bologna, 21. I. 1672; d. Bologna, before 1727), It. comp. and mus. pub. *Maestro di cappella* at the church of San Stefano at Bologna, 1702–25. He inherited Marino S., his father's (?), mus. pub. business.

Works incl. Masses, motets, Lamentations, *Stabat Mater,* Litanies, sacred cantatas and other church mus. for voices with string or org. accomp.

Silveri, Paolo (b. Ofena nr. Aquila, 28. XII. 1913), It. baritone. Made his début in Rome in 1944 and sang at Covent Garden from 1947 to 1949 and at the N.Y. Metropolitan Opera from 1950 to 1953. After a brief period as a tenor in 1959 he reverted to baritone in 1960.

Silvestri, Constantin (b. Bucharest, 31. V. 1913; d. London, 23. II. 1969), Rum. cond., comp. and pianist. Studied at the Bucharest Cons., making his début as a pianist in 1924 and as a cond. in 1930. He became cond. at the Bucharest Opera in 1935 and of the Bucharest Phil. Orch. in 1945. From 1961 he conducted the Bournemouth Symph. Orch.

Works incl. *Music for Strings, Three Pieces for String Orchestra;* 2 string 4tets; 2 sonatas for vln. and pf.; sonatas for harp, fl., clar., bassoon.

Simes, William. *See* **Simmes.**

Similar Motion. *See* **Motion.**

Simile (It. = like), an abbr. often used to indicate that certain passages are to be perf. in the same way as similar passages occurring before.

Simionato, Giulietta (b. Forlì, 15. XII. 1910), It. mezzo-soprano. Studied in Florence, winning a prize at a competition there in 1933. Since then has sung in Eur. and Amer., incl. Covent Garden in 1952.

Simmes (or **Simes** or **Sims**), **William** (b. ?; d. ?), Eng. 16th–17th-cent. comp.

Works incl. anthems; fantasies for viols, etc.

Simon, Antoine (Antony Yulievich)

(b. Fr., 5. VIII. 1850; d. St. Petersburg, I. II. 1916), Fr. cond. and comp. Studied at the Paris Cons. and in 1871 settled at Moscow, where he became cond. of the Théâtre-Bouffe. In the 1890s he became pf. prof. at the Phil. Mus. School and superintendent of the orch. of the Imp. theatres.

Works incl. operas *Rolla*, *The Song of Love Triumphant* (after Turgenev), *The Fishers* (after Hugo); mimed drama *Esmeralda* (after Hugo's *Notre-Dame*); ballets *The Stars* and *Living Flowers*; incid. mus. for Shakespeare's *Merchant of Venice*; Mass; suite, *Triumphal Overture* on Rus. themes, overture-fantasy on Malo-Rus. themes, symph. poems *The Midnight Review* and *La Pêcheresse* for orch.; concertos for pf. and for clar.; string 4tets, 2 pf. trios and other chamber mus.; vln. and pf. pieces; pieces for 1 and 2 pfs.; *c*. 80 songs, etc.

Simon Boccanegra, opera by Verdi (lib. by Francesco Maria Piave, based on a Span. drama by Antonio García Gutiérrez), prod. Venice, Teatro La Fenice, 12. III. 1857; revised version, with the lib. altered by Boito, prod. Milan, Teatro alla Scala, 24. III. 1881.

Simon, Simon (b. Vaux-de-Cernay nr. Rambouillet, *c*. 1720; d. ? Versailles, after 1780), Fr. harpsichordist and comp. Pupil of Dauvergne. He was app. harpsichord master to the queen and the royal children at Versailles.

Works incl. 3 books of harpsichord pieces, pieces and sonatas for harpsichord with vln., etc.

Simonetti, Achille (b. Turin, 12. VI. 1857; d. London, 19. XI. 1928), It. violinist and comp. Pupil of Pedrotti for comp. and later of Sivori at Genoa for vln. Having appeared as a concert artist, he went to Paris for further study with Dancla and Massenet. Later he settled in London as perf., teacher and member of the London Trio.

Works incl. 2 string 4tets; 2 vln. and pf. sonatas, vln. pieces, etc.

Simoutre, Nicolas Eugène (b. Mirecourt, 19. IV. 1839; d. Geneva, I. 1908), Fr. vln. maker. After working with var. masters in Paris and Strasbourg, he settled in business at Basle in 1859.

Simple Intervals, any Intervals not larger than an 8ve, those exceeding that width being called Compound I.

Simple Time, any mus. metre in which the beats can be subdivided into two, e.g. 2–4, 3–4, 4–4. *Cf*. **Compound Time**.

Simpson, Christopher (b. Yorkshire, ?; d. ? Scampton, Lincs. or London, 1669), Eng. vla. da gamba player, theorist and comp. He joined the royalist army under the Duke of Newcastle in 1643 and endured much hardship, but later came under the patronage of Sir Robert Bolles,

at whose residences at Scampton and in London he lived in comfort, teaching the children of the family and taking charge of the domestic mus.-making. He wrote an instruction book for the vla. da gamba, *The Division Violinist*. He bought a house and farm at Pickering, Yorks., but d. (?) at one of Sir John Bolles's houses. He wrote another treatise, *The Principles of Practicle Musick* and annotations to Campion's *Art of Descant*.

Works incl. *Months and Seasons* for a treble and 2 bass viols., fancies and consorts for viols, suite in 3 parts for viols, divisions (variations) and pieces for vla. da gamba, etc.

Simpson, Robert (b. Leamington, 2. III. 1921), Eng. comp. and mus. critic. Studied privately with Howells and took D.Mus. at Durham in 1952. He is active in the B.B.C. and as a writer on mus., esp. that of Bruckner, Nielsen and Sibelius.

Works incl. 3 symphs., overture for orch.; fantasia for strings; 3 string 4tets; pf. mus., etc.

Simpson, Thomas (b. Milton nr. Sittingbourne, ? III. 1582; d. ?), Eng. 16th–17th-cent. violist and comp. Settled in Ger. early in the 17th cent., was in the service of the Elector Palatine in 1610, in that of the Prince of Holstein-Schaumburg in 1617–21, and afterwards at the Dan. court in Copenhagen.

Works incl. pavans, galliards and other dances for viols; songs with instruments, etc.

Sims, William. *See* **Simmes**.

Sin' (It. abbr.). *See* **Sino**.

Sinclair, John (b. nr. Edinburgh, 9. XII. 1791; d. Margate, 23. IX. 1857), Scot. tenor. Studied at Aberdeen and 1st appeared in London in 1810. In 1819 he visited Paris, studied in It. and sang there with success until 1823.

Sinding, Christian (b. Kongsberg, 11. I. 1856; d. Oslo, 3. XII. 1941), Norw. pianist and comp. Studied at Leipzig, Berlin and Munich. He settled at Oslo as pianist and comp.

Works incl. opera *The Holy Mountain*; 4 symphs. and *Rondo infinito* for orch.; pf. concerto in D♭ maj., 2 vln. concertos; string 4tet, pf. 5tet, pf. trio; sonatas and suite for vln. and pf.; variations for 2 pfs.; suite, studies and numerous pieces for pf.; songs, etc.

Sinfonia (It.) = Symphony. In the early 18th cent. the S. was simply an instrumental piece in an opera or other vocal work, esp. the Overture; it is in fact out of the latter that the symph. developed.

Sinfonia concertante, a work in symph. form with 1 or more solo instruments, similar to a concerto. Familiar exs. are Mozart's K. 364 for vln., vla. and orch.

of 1779 and K. App. 9 for ob., clar., horn and bassoon with orch. of 1778.

Sinfonia domestica (R. Strauss). *See* **Symphonia domestica**.

Sinfonietta (It. = little sym.), a work in symph. form, but of smaller dimensions and usually lightly scored.

Singakademie (Ger. lit. singing-academy = vocal academy), the special name of certain choral societies in Ger. and Aus.

Singspiel (Ger. = song play), orig. a trans. of the It. *dramma per musica*, i.e. opera. In the course of the 18th cent. the term was restricted to comic opera with spoken dialogue, e.g. Mozart's *Die Entführung*.

Sinigaglia, Leone (b. Turin, 14. VIII. 1868; d. Turin, 16. V. 1944), It. comp. Studied at the Turin Cons. and with Mandyczewski in Vienna. After his return home he settled down to comp. and folksong collecting.

Works incl. suite *Piemonte* overture to Goldoni's *Le baruffe chiozzote*, *Danze piemontesi* for orch.; concerto, *Rapsodia piemontese* and romance for vln. and orch.; string 4tet in D maj., concert study and variations on a theme by Brahms for string 4tet; variations on Schubert's *Heidenröslein* for ob. and pf., 2 pieces for horn and pf., pieces for vln., cello, etc.; settings of Piedmontese folksongs, etc.

Sinkapace. *See* **Cinquepace**.

Sino (It. = till, until, or abbr. *sin'* when followed by a vowel), a word used in such directions as that indicating a repeat *sin' al fine* (until the end) or *sin' al segno* . . . (to the sign . . .), etc.

Siqueira, José (b. Conceição, 24. VI. 1907), Brazil. comp. Pupil of his father, a bandmaster, and studied at Rio de Janeiro. In 1940 he became director of the Brazil. Orch. and cond. of broadcast concerts.

Works incl. symph. in D min., 2 overtures, 3 symph. poems, 3 symph. preludes, suite for orch., 5 pieces for strings, *Frevo* for brass band; *Elegia* for cello and orch.; string 4tet, pf. trio; vln. and pf. sonata; instrumental pieces; pf. mus.; songs, etc.

Sir John in Love, opera by Vaughan Williams (lib. selected by comp. from Shakespeare's *Merry Wives of Windsor*), prod. London, R.C.M., 21. III. 1929.

Sirmen (*née* **Lombardini**), **Maddalena** (b. Venice, ? 1735; d. ?), It. violinist, singer and comp. Studied at the Cons. dei Mendicanti at Venice and vln. with Tartini at Padua. In 1760 she began to tour in It. and at Bergamo she met Ludovico Sirmen, a violinist and cond. at the church of Santa Maria Maddalena there, and married him. They visited Paris in 1768 and in 1771 she 1st appeared in London, where she also played the harpsichord.

Works incl. 6 vln. concertos; 6 string 4tets, 6 trios for 2 vlns. and cello; 6 duets and 6 sonatas for 2 vlns., etc.

Siroe, rè di Persia (*Siroes, King of Persia*), lib. by Metastasio.
Opera by Handel, prod. London, King's Theatre, Haymarket, 17. II. 1728.
Opera by Hasse, prod. Bologna, Teatro Malvezzi, 2. V. 1733.
Opera by Pérez, prod. Naples, Teatro San Carlo, 4. XI. 1740.
Opera by Vinci, prod. Venice, Teatro San Giovanni Crisostomo, I. 1726.

Sirola, Božidar (b. Žakanj, 20. XII. 1889; d. Zagreb, 10. IV. 1956), Yugoslav comp. Studied at Zagreb and in Vienna, where he took a doctor's degree. Later he was app. director of the Mus. Acad. at Zagreb.

Works incl. operas *A Story from Stanac*, *The Wandering Scholar* and 3 others; ballet *Shadows*; incid. mus. to plays; 3 oratorios; symph., suite and overtures for orch.; 13 string 4tets, 3 pf. trios; songs, etc.

Sirvente (Prov.), a Provençal Troubadour song the words of which were in *terza rima*.

Sistrum, an ancient instrument, prob. orig. in Egypt, played like a rattle. It had a metal frame fitted to a handle and metal bars or loops were loosely hung on the frame and made to strike against it by shaking the instrument.

Sitt, Hans (b. Prague, 21. IX. 1850; d. Leipzig, 10. III. 1922), Cz.-Ger. violinist, teacher and ed. Studied at the Prague Cons., became leader at Breslau, 1867, and cond. at Breslau and Prague, 1870–3, Chemnitz, 1873–80, and Nice. He returned to Leipzig, where he joined Brodsky's 4tet as violist. He was prof. of vln. at the Leipzig Cons, 1883–1921. He ed. much vln. mus.

Works incl. 3 vln. concertos, vla. concerto, 2 cello concertos, chamber mus., vln. studies and pieces, songs, etc.

Sitwell, Edith (1887–1964), Eng. poet and essayist. *See* **Façade** (Walton), **Searle** (*Gold Coast Customs* and *Shadow of Cain*), **Tippett** (*Weeping Babe*), **Walton** (songs).

Sitwell, Osbert (1892–1969), Eng. poet, essayist and novelist, brother of prec. *See* **Belshazzar's Feast** (Walton), **Lutyens** (*Winter the Huntsman*).

Sitwell, Sacheverell (b. Scarborough, 1897), Eng. poet and essayist, brother of prec. Educ. at Eton and Balliol Coll., Oxford. Mentioned here as the author of biog. books on D. Scarlatti, Mozart, Liszt and Offenbach. *See also* **Triumph of Neptune** (Berners).

Sivori, (Ernesto) Camillo (b. Genoa, 25. X. 1815; d. Genoa, 19. II. 1894),

It. violinist and comp. Pupil of Paganini, who wrote his works for 4tet with guitar for him and, going on tour, sent him to another master, Giacomo Costa, and later to Dellepiane, with whom he went on tour, making his 1st appearance at Turin in 1827. They went on to Fr. and London, but in 1829 S. returned to Genoa to study comp. with Giovanni Serra. He then travelled widely in Eur. and N. and S. Amer. until 1870.

Works incl. 2 concertos, *Tarantelle napolitaine*, etc. for vln. and orch.; duet for vln. and double bass (with Bottesini); 2 *Duos concertants* for vln. and pf.; 3 *Romances sans paroles*, *Andante spianato* and numerous other pieces and fantasies on operatic airs for vln. and pf.; vln. studies, etc.

Six-Four Chord. *See* **Sixth.**

Six, Les, a group of Fr. comps. who in their youth gathered together, under the leadership of Satie and Jean Cocteau, for the furtherance of their interests and to some extent those of modern mus. in general. It was formed in Paris in 1917 and its active comp. members were Auric, Durey, Honegger, Milhaud, Poulenc and Tailleferre; the chief perfs. were the singer Jane Bathori and the pianist Andrée Vaurabourg, the latter becoming Honegger's wife. The group gradually lost its solidarity during the 1920s.

Sixth, the interval between 2 notes lying 6 degrees of a diatonic scale apart, e.g.:

Maj.   Min.   Augmented

The so-called 'chord of the 6th' (maj. or min.) consists of a 3rd with a 4th above it, e.g.:

Maj.   Min.

The '6–4 chord' consists of a 4th with a 3rd above it, e.g.:

Maj.   Min.

Chords of the augmented 6th are known in 3 forms, *see* **French Sixth, German Sixth, Italian Sixth.**

Sjögren (Johan Gustaf) Emil (b. Stockholm, 16. VI. 1853; d. Stockholm, 1. III. 1918), Swed. comp. Studied at the Stock-

holm Cons. and later in Berlin, also came under the influence of Lange-Müller during a stay of 6 months at Meran. In 1891 he became organist at St. John's Church, Stockholm, but devoted most of his time to teaching and comp.

Works incl. 5 vln. and pf. sonatas; org. works; 2 pf. sonatas, *Erotikon, Novellettes* and numerous other works for pf.; songs, etc.

Skalkottas, Nicos (b. Chalkis, Euboea, 8. III. 1904; d. Athens, 19. IX. 1949), Gk. comp. Studied at the Athens Cons. and with Economidis, later in Ger. with Schönberg, Weill and Jarnach, living there for 12 years. From 1933 he lived in Athens.

Works incl. 2 ballets, 36 Gk. Dances, *Sinfonietta*, overture *The Return of Ulysses* and 2 suites for orch.; concerto and symph. for wind instruments, 3 pf. concertos, vln. concerto, cello concerto, concerto for vln. and vla., concerto for 2 vlns.; 4 string 4tets and other chamber mus., etc.

Skelton, John (? 1460–1529), Eng. poet. *See* **Cornyshe, Five Tudor Portraits** (Vaughan Williams).

Škerjanc, Lucijan (b. Graz, 17. XII. 1900), Yugoslav pianist, cond. and comp. Studied in Prague, Vienna (J. Marx), Basle and Paris (d'Indy), taught and cond. at Ljubljana, but later retired to devote himself to comp.

Works incl. cantatas, 5 symphs. and other orchestral works, vln. and pf. concertos, 5 string 4tets, etc.

Skilton, Charles Sanford (b. Northampton, Mass., 16. VIII. 1868; d. Lawrence, Kans., 12. III. 1941), Amer. comp. Studied at Yale Univ. and in Ger. In 1903 he was app. Prof. of Mus. at Kansas Univ. and there made a study of Indian tribal tunes.

Works incl. operas *Kalopin, The Sun Bride, The Day of Gayomair*; incid. mus. for Sophocles' *Electra* and Barrie's *Mary Rose*; oratorio *The Guardian Angel* and cantatas; *Primeval Suite* and other suites and overtures for orch.; 2 *Indian Dances* for string 4tet; vln. and pf. sonata; org. and pf. works, etc.

Skinner, James Scott (b. Banchory-Ternan, 5. VIII. 1843; d. Aberdeen, 17. III. 1927), Scot. violinist and comp. He joined an orch. for orphaned children, studied with Charles Rougier at Manchester, then settled at Aberdeen as a dancing-master and wrote popular dance mus., mainly based on Scot. reels, strathspeys and other nat. dances and airs.

Skjöldebrand, Anders Fredrik (1757–1834), Swed. dramatist. *See* **Vogler** (*Hermann von Unna*).

Skočná, a Cz. dance in quick 2–4 time in which 3-bar phrases are a feature.

The 5th, 7th and 11th of Dvořák's *Slavonic Dances* for pf. duet are S.s.

Skolie (Ger. from Gk. *skolion* = a song sung by an irregular succession of guests at a banquet), a drinking-song, the title given to 2 of Schubert's songs: 'Lasst im Morgenstrahl' (words by Deinhardstein) and 'Mädchen entsiegelten' (words by Mathisson).

Skriabin, Alexander Nikolaievich (b. Moscow, 6. I. 1872; d. Moscow, 27. IV. 1915), Rus. pianist and comp. Giving up a military career, he studied pf. with Safonov and comp. with Taneiev at the Moscow Cons., where he became prof. of pf. in 1898 after touring successfully in western Eur. He gave up that post in 1904 to devote himself entirely to comp. and occasional appearances as pianist. He visited Eng. on several occasions, notably in 1913 and 1914.

Works incl. 3 symphs., *Rêverie* and *Poem of Ecstasy* for orch.; pf. concerto in F♯ min., *Prometheus: a Poem of Fire* for orch., pf. and org. (and a projected colour org.); 10 pf. sonatas and 58 op. nos. of other pf. works, incl. preludes, impromptus, studies, mazurkas, nocturnes, *Tragic Poem*, *Satanic Poem*, *Vers la flamme*, prelude and nocturne for the left hand, etc.

Škroup, František Jan (b. Osice nr. Pardubice, 3. VI. 1801; d. Rotterdam, 7. II. 1862), Boh. comp. Studied law, but was from 1827 2nd and in 1837–57 1st cond. at the Nat. Theatre in Prague; from 1860 cond. at the Opera of Rotterdam. Comp. the 1st Cz. opera and the nat. anthem.

Works incl. operas *Drátenik* (*The Tinker*), *The Marriage of Libuša*, *Oldřich and Božena*, *Drahomíra* and some other Cz. and Ger. operas; incid. mus. to Tyl's *Fidlovačka*; 3 string 4tets and other chamber mus.; songs, etc.

Skuherský, František Zdeněk (b. Opočno, 31. VII. 1830; d. Budějovice, 19. VIII. 1892), Boh. comp. and teacher. He gave up medical studies for mus., which he studied under Kittl and Pitsch, the directors of the Prague Cons. and Org. School respectively. In 1854–65 he was cond. at Innsbruck, but returned to Prague as director of the Org. School in the latter year. He was also active as pianist and as lecturer at the Cz. Univ., and he took part in the reform of church mus. after studying it in Rome and Regensburg. He wrote several theoret. treatises.

Works incl. operas *Samo*, *Vladimir: God's Chosen*, *Lora*, *Rector and General* and *The Love Ring*; symph. poem *May* and 3 fugues for orch.; string 4tet, pf. 5tet, pf. trio, etc.

Skyscrapers, ballet by Carpenter (choreography by Heinrich Kröller), prod. Monte Carlo, Rus. Ballet, 1925; 1st Amer. perf. N.Y., Metropolitan Opera, 19. II. 1926.

Slancio (It. = dash, impetuosity), usually used in the form of *con* (with) *s*.

Sleeping Princess, The, ballet by Tchaikovsky (choreography by Marius Petipa), prod. St. Petersburg, Maryinsky Theatre, 15. I. 1890; new version, with add. orchs. by Stravinsky and adds. to the choreography by Bronislava Nizhinska, London, Alhambra Theatre, 2. XI. 1921.

Slentando (It.) = Gradually decreasing in pace.

Slezak, Leo (b. Šumperk, 18. VIII. 1873; d. Egern, Bavar., 1. VI. 1946), Morav. tenor. He studied engineering, but had his voice trained at the same time and in 1896 made his 1st stage appearance at Brno. He was a member of the Vienna State Opera from 1901 to 1926. He studied further with J. de Reszke in Paris in 1908. After retiring from the stage he made a successful career as a film actor. He pub. several autobiog. works.

Slide (*see* **Ornaments**), also the device of passing from one note to another on string instruments by moving the finger along the string instead of lifting it to make way for another finger; also the movable part of the tube of the tromb. by which the positions, and therefore the notes, are altered, as well as mechanisms on other wind instruments by which the pitch can be adjusted by a change in the length of the tube.

Slide Trumpet. See **Tromba da tirarsi.**

Śliwiński, Josef (b. Warsaw, 15. XII. 1865; d. Warsaw, 4. III. 1930), Pol. pianist. Studied with Strobl at Warsaw, Leschetizky in Vienna and A. Rubinstein in St. Petersburg. Made his 1st public appearance in 1890 and 1st visited Eng. in 1892.

Slonimsky, Nicolas (orig. Nikolai) (b. St. Petersburg, 27. IV. 1894), Rus. musical author and comp. Studied at the St. Petersburg Cons. and in 1923 settled in U.S.A., becoming a naturalized Amer. in 1931. He compiled a survey, *Music since 1900*.

Works incl. *Fragment from Orestes* (Euripides) for orch. (in quarter-tones); *Suite in Black and White* for pf., etc.

Slovak Composers. See **Czech** (for Czechoslovak) **Composers.**

Slow Movement, the slowest of the movements in a mus. comp. in several parts, esp. a symph., sonata or chamber work. It may, however, be slow only relatively to the other movements.

Slur, an arching stroke in mus. notation drawn over a group of notes and indicating that they are to be played *legato*. It is also used in vocal mus. where 2 or more notes are to be sung to the same syllable. *See also* **Tie.**

Sly (i.e. Christopher Sly), opera by Wolf-Ferrari (lib. by Giovacchino Forzano, based on the prologue of Shakespeare's *Taming of the Shrew*), prod. Milan, Teatro alla Scala, 29. XII. 1927.

Smanioso (It.) = Furious, rabid, frenzied.

Smareglia, Antonio (b. Pola, Istria, 5. V. 1854; d. Grado nr. Trieste, 15. IV. 1929), It. comp. He was sent to Vienna to study engineering, but on hearing works by the great masters there he left for Milan in 1872 and studied comp. under Faccio at the Cons. He prod. his 1st opera there in 1879, but he never had any real success, in spite of the good quality of his work, and in 1900 he went blind.

Works incl. operas *Preziosa, Bianca da Cervia, Rè Nala, Der Vasall von Szigeth, Cornelius Schutt, Nozze istriane, La Falena, Oceàna, L'Abisso*; symph. poem *Leonore*, songs, etc.

Smart, George (Thomas) (b. London, 10. V. 1776; d. London, 23. II. 1867), Eng. organist, comp. and cond. He was sent by his father, George S., a mus. pub., to become a choir-boy at the Chapel Royal under Ayrton, and later became a comp. pupil of Arnold. He became an organist, teacher and cond., was one of the orig. members of the Phil. Society in 1813 and succeeded Charles Knyvett as organist of the Chapel Royal in 1822. In 1825 he went to Dresden with Charles Kemble to engage Weber to write *Oberon* for Covent Garden, and it was at his house that Weber stayed during the prod. in 1826 and d. in the night of 4–5. VI. S. was knighted in 1811, and became a favourite festival cond.

Works incl. anthems, chants and other church mus.; canons and glees, etc.

Smart, Henry (Thomas) (b. London, 26. X. 1813; d. London, 6. VII. 1879), Eng. organist and comp., nephew of prec. Learnt mus. from his father, the violinist Henry S. (1778–1823) and later under W. H. Kearns; but was largely self-taught. After an organist's appt. at Blackburn in 1831–6 he returned to London and was successively organist at several churches until he became blind in 1864.

Works incl. operas *Berta, or The Gnome of the Hartzberg, Undine* and *The Surrender of Calais* (last 2 unfinished); cantatas *The Bride of Dunkerron, King René's Daughter* (after Herz), *The Fishermaidens* and *Jacob*; festival anthems *Sing to the Lord* and *Lord, thou hast been our refuge*; org. works; part-songs, etc.

Smert, Richard (b ? Devonshire; d. ?), Eng. 15th-cent. comp. Carols of his for 2 voices and 3-part chorus, some written with **John Truelove,** are preserved. He

was a vicar-choral of Exeter Cathedral, 1428–c. 1465. It is possible, however, that he was the owner of the MS., or the author of the words, rather than the comp. of the mus.

Smetana, Bedřich (b. Litomyšl, Boh., 2. III. 1824; d. Prague, 12. V. 1884), Cz. comp. Son of a brewer. He played pf. and vln. at a very early age and was soon able to play in the domestic string 4tet. He was educ. in Ger. and all his life, in spite of his mus. nationalism, spoke and wrote Cz. like a foreigner. He was sent to school 1st in Prague and then at Pilsen. His father opposed a mus. career, but he was in the end allowed to study mus. in Prague, though with a very small allowance. In 1844 he obtained the post of mus. master in Count Thun's family, which helped to support him till 1847. In 1848 he took part in the revolution against Aus., married the pianist Kateřina Kolařová, estab. a school of mus. for which Liszt supplied funds, and was recommended by the latter to the Leipzig pub. Kistner.

In 1856 he went to Göteborg in Swed., where at first he taught but later became cond. of the new Phil. Society and gave pf. and chamber mus. recitals. He returned to Prague in 1859 because the northern climate did not suit his wife, who d. at Dresden on the way back, 19. IV. He married Bettina Ferdinandova in VII. 1860 and returned to Swed. in the autumn, but finally returned to Prague in the spring of 1861. After a long tour in Ger., Hol. and Swed. to collect funds, he settled in the Cz. capital in 1863 and opened another school of mus., this time with distinctly nat. tendencies, and became cond. of the choral society Hlahol. His work too was now becoming thoroughly Cz. in character, and he began to prod. Cz. operas in the nat. theatre estab. in 1864, of which he became cond. in IX. 1866. In 1874 he suddenly became totally deaf, but still comp. operas as well as the string 4tet *From my Life* and the cycle of symph. poems *My Country*. In 1883 he became insane and in IV. 1884 he had to be taken to an asylum, where he d.

Works incl. operas *The Brandenburgers in Bohemia, The Bartered Bride, Dalibor, Libuše, Two Widows, The Kiss, The Secret, The Devil's Wall, Viola* (based on Shakespeare's *Twelfth Night*, unfinished); 3 concert overtures; symph. poems *Richard III* (after Shakespeare), *Wallenstein's Camp* (after Schiller), *Haakon Jarl*; cycle of symph. poems *My Country* containing *Vyšehrad, Vltava, Šárka, In the Bohemian Woods and Fields, Tábor, Blaník*; Festival March for orch.; pf. trio in G min., 2 string 4tets (1st *From my Life*); 8 op. nos. of pf. works and many miscellaneous pf.

pieces incl. *Wedding Scenes, Scenes from Macbeth*, Cz. dances, etc.; a cantata and a number of part-songs; 3 books of songs, etc.

Smijers, Albert (Anton) (b. Raamsdonksveer, 19. VII. 1888; d. Utrecht, 15. V. 1957), Dutch musicologist. Ordained priest in 1912. Pupil of Anton Averkamp at Amsterdam and of Adler in Vienna, where he took a doctor's degree. He taught mus. hist. at the Amsterdam Cons., 1929–1934, and became prof. of mus. science at Utrecht Univ. in 1930. His works incl. a catalogue of Dutch mus. in It. libraries and he ed. the complete works of Josquin Desprez as well as old Dutch and Flem. mus.

Smith, Alice Mary (b. London, 19. V. 1839; d. London, 4. XII. 1884), Eng. comp. Pupil of Sterndale Bennett and Macfarren. Married Frederick Meadows White, Q.C., in 1867.

Works incl. masque *Pandora*; cantatas on Kingsley's *Ode to the North-East Wind, Song of the Little Baltung* and *Red King*, Collins's *Ode to the Passions*; 2 symphs., 4 overtures, for orch.; clar. concerto, *Introduction and Allegro* for pf. and orch.; 3 string 4tets, 4 pf. 4tets, pf. trio; songs, duets, part-songs, etc.

Smith, Bernard (Bernhard Schmidt) (b. Ger., 1629; d. London, II. 1708), Ger. org. builder. Settled in Eng. from 1660. His 1st Eng. org. was at the Chapel Royal in London. App. organist at St. Margaret's Church, Westminster, after building the org. there. He also built orgs. at Durham Cathedral and St. Paul's Cathedral, London. Known as Father Smith.

Smith, Carleton Sprague (b. N.Y., 8. VIII. 1905), Amer. critic, musicologist and flautist. Studied at Harvard Univ. and in Vienna. After a year as critic to the *Boston Transcript*, he became chief librarian of the mus. section of the N.Y. Public Library and lecturer in mus. hist. at Columbia Univ. In 1938 he was president of the Amer. Musicological Society.

Smith, David Stanley (b. Toledo, Ohio, 6. VII. 1877; d. New Haven, Conn., 17. XII. 1949), Amer. comp., cond. and teacher. Studied with H. Parker at Yale Univ. and later in London, Munich and Paris. In 1903 he became instructor and later prof. of mus. at Yale.

Works incl. *Rhapsody of St. Bernard* for solo voices, chorus and orch., *The Fallen Star* for chorus and orch., *The Vision of Isaiah* for chorus; anthems; part-songs; 4 symphs., *A Poem of Youth*, suite *Impressions, Epic Poem, 1929—A Satire*, overtures *Prince Hal* (on Shakespeare's *Henry IV*) and *Tomorrow*, etc. for orch.; *Fête galante* for fl. and orch.; *Cathedral Prelude* for org. and orch.,

Rondo appassionato for vln. and orch.; 10 string 4tets, pf. 5tet; sonatas for vln. and pf. and cello and pf., *Sonata pastorale* for ob. and pf.; songs, etc.

Smith, Edmund (1672–1710), Eng. playwright. See **Roseingrave** (2) (*Phaedra and Hippolytus*).

Smith, John Christopher (b. Ansbach, 1712; d. Bath, 3. X. 1795), Ger. (anglicized) organist and comp., son of Johann Christoph Schmidt of Ansbach, who went to London as Handel's treasurer and copyist. J. C. S. became a pupil of Handel, and later of Pepusch and T. Roseingrave. In 1746–8 he travelled on the Continent and in 1754 became organist of the Foundling Hospital. He acted as Handel's amanuensis during the comp.'s blindness.

Works incl. operas *Teraminta, Ulysses, Issipile, Ciro riconosciuto, Dario, The Fairies* (from Shakespeare's *Midsummer Night's Dream*), *The Tempest* (after Shakespeare); *Rosalinda, The Enchanter, or Love and Magic* (Garrick); oratorios *David's Lamentation over Saul and Jonathan, Paradise Lost* (after Milton), *Rebecca, Judith, Jehoshaphat, The Redemption*; Burial Service; instrumental works, etc.

Smith, John Stafford (b. Gloucester, III. 1750; d. London, 21. IX. 1836), Eng. organist, tenor and comp. Pupil of his father, Martin S., organist at Gloucester Cathedral, and later of Boyce and Nares in London, where he was a chorister in the Chapel Royal. He became a Gentleman of the Chapel Royal in 1784, organist of Gloucester Cathedral in 1790 and in 1802 of the Chapel Royal in succession to Arnold, succeeding Ayrton as Master of the Children in 1805. He assisted Hawkins in his *History of Music*.

Works incl. anthems, glees, catches, canons, madrigals, part-songs; songs incl. *Anacreon in Heaven* (now *The Star-spangled Banner*), etc.

Smith, Robert (b. ?, *c*. 1648; d. ? London, 22. XI. 1675), Eng. comp. Chorister at the Chapel Royal in London under Cooke; became Musician in Ordinary to the King on the death of Humfrey in 1674.

Works incl. incid. mus. for numerous plays (some with Staggins and others); mus. for strings; harpsichord pieces; songs, duets, etc.

Smith, Robert Archibald (b. Reading, 16. XI. 1780; d. Edinburgh, 3. I. 1829), Scot. comp. and pub. Although b. in Eng., he was the son of a Scot. silk-weaver, who returned to Paisley in 1800. In 1807 he became precentor at the Abbey church there and in 1823 leader of the psalmody at St. George's Church, Edinburgh. He pub. from 1820 *The Scottish Minstrel*, ed. by Lady Nairn and others, to which he contrib. tunes of his own. He also pub. other collections, incl. *Select Melodies of*

All Nations and *Sacred Harmony of the Church of Scotland.* Works incl. anthems; songs, duets, etc.

Smith, (Edward) Sydney (b. Dorchester, 14. VII. 1839; d. London, 3. III. 1889), Eng. pianist and comp. Studied at Leipzig and settled as pf. teacher in London in 1859. He wrote numerous drawing-room pieces for pf.

Smolensky, Stepan Vassilievich (b. Kazan, 1848; d. Kazan, 6. VIII. 1909), Rus. musicologist. He made a special study of Rus. church mus. and in 1889 became director of the Synodal school and choir and prof. at the Cons. in Moscow. In 1901–3 he was director of the Imp. court chapel. He collected MSS. of old church mus. and wrote several works on the subject.

Smollett, Tobias (George) (1721–71), Eng. novelist and playwright. *See* **Alceste** (Handel).

Smorzando (It. = toning down), a direction indicating that a passage is to be perf. with an effect of calming down or fading away.

Smyth, Ethel (Mary) (b. London, 23. IV. 1858; d. Woking, 9. V. 1944), Eng. comp. Studied at the Leipzig Cons. and then privately there with Herzogenberg. She had some works perf. there and after her return to Eng. one or two appeared in London, incl. the Mass in 1893. Her earlier operas were prod. in Ger. She lived much abroad, but in 1910 received the hon. D.Mus. degree from Durham Univ. and about that time joined actively in the movement for women's suffrage. In her later years she lived at Woking in Surrey and, regarding herself as neglected on account of her sex, comp. less and less, but wrote a number of autobiog. books. She received the honour of a D.B.E. in 1922. During her last years she suffered much from deafness and distorted hearing. Works incl. operas *Fantasio* (after Musset), *The Forest, The Wreckers, The Boatswain's Mate* (after W. W. Jacobs), *Fête galante, Entente cordiale*; Mass in D maj.; *The Prison* for solo voices, chorus and orch.; *Sleepless Dreams, Hey Nonny No!* and *March of the Women* for chorus and orch.; overture to Shakespeare's *Antony and Cleopatra*, serenade, etc. for orch.; concerto for vln., horn and orch.; 3 Anacreontic Odes for voice and orch.; string 5tet, string 4tet; sonatas for vln. and pf. and cello and pf.; 3 songs with fl., harp, strings and perc.; songs, etc.

Smythe, William (b. *c.* 1550; d. Durham, *c.* 1600), Eng. comp. He was a min. canon and later master of the choristers (1594–1598) at Durham Cathedral. He wrote a number of works for the Angl. church, not to be confused with those by his later namesake, 'William Smith of Durham'.

Snap. *See* **Scotch Snap.**

Snares, gut strings stretched over one of the heads of some types of drum, esp. the Side-drum, adding brilliance to their tone by vibrating against the skin as the drum is struck. If that effect is not required, the S.s can be temporarily slackened.

Snow Maiden, The (*Snegurotchka*), opera by Rimsky-Korsakov (lib. by comp. based on a play by Alexander Nikolaievich Ostrovsky), prod. St. Petersburg, 10. II. 1882.

Snow, Valentine (b. ? London, ?; d. London, XII. 1770), Eng. trumpeter. Son of (?) Moses S., a Gentleman of the Chapel Royal in London and lay-vicar at Westminster Abbey. In 1753 he succeeded John Shore as Sergeant Trumpeter to the King. Handel wrote the tpt. obbligato parts in his oratorios for him.

Soave (It.) = Sweet, tender.

Sob, a trick in lute-playing prod. a peculiar effect of deadening the tone by immediately lightening the pressure of the finger on the string after it has been struck.

Sobolewski, (Friedrich) Eduard (b. Königsberg, 1. X. 1808; d. St. Louis, 23. V. 1872), Ger.-Pol. cond. and comp. He was cond. at the Königsberg Theatre in succession to Dorn, 1830–6. Later he lived at Weimar and in 1859 he emigrated to U.S.A., where he became cond. to the St. Louis Phil. Society. Works incl. operas *Komala* (after Ossian), *Imogene* (after Shakespeare's *Cymbeline*), *Velleda, Salvator Rosa* and *Mohega*; oratorio *The Saviour*; symphs., symph. poems, etc.

Sobrino, Carlos (b. Pontevedra, 25. II. 1861; d. London, 17. I. 1927), Span. pianist. Studied at the Madrid Cons. and with A. Rubinstein, later toured widely in Eur., sometimes in partnership with Sarasate or Ysaÿe. He settled in London and in 1905 became pf. prof. at the G.S.M.

Socrate (*Socrates*), symph. drama by Satie (lib. taken from Victor Cousin's Fr. trans. of Plato's *Dialogues*), prod. Paris, 14. II. 1920 and perf. Prague, festival of the I.S.C.M., V. 1925.

Söderman, (Johan) August (b. Stockholm, 17. VII. 1832; d. Stockholm, 10. II. 1876), Swed. comp. Learnt mus. from his father, a theatre cond., at 18 went to Fin. as director of mus. to a Swed. co. of musicians, and in 1852 prod. his 1st operetta at Helsinki. After a period of study at Leipzig he was app. chorus master at the Royal Opera at Stockholm in 1860 and 2nd cond. in 1862. Works incl. operetta *The Devil's First Lesson* and others; incid. mus. to Schiller's *Maid of Orleans*, Topelius's *Regina* and other plays; Mass for solo voices, chorus and orch.; *Swed. Wedding* for female voices, cantatas and part-songs; vocal settings of Bellman's rhapsodies; *Circassian Dance* and concert overture for orch.; sacred songs and hymns with org.; ballads and songs for voice and pf., etc.

Söderström, Elisabeth (b. Stockholm, 7. V. 1927), Swed. soprano. Studied in Stockholm, making her début there in 1948. Her highly successful career has taken her to Salzburg, Glyndebourne, Covent Garden and the N.Y. Metropolitan.

Sofonisba, La, opera by Caldara (lib. by Francesco Silvani), prod. Venice, Teatro S. Giovanni Crisostomo, XII. 1708.

Opera by Gluck (lib. do., with airs from different libs. by Metastasio), prod. Milan, Teatro Regio Ducal, I. 1744.

Soft Pedal, the popular name for the Damping Pedal of the pf.

Soggetto (It.) = Subject, in the mus. sense, esp. the subject of a fugue.

Soggetto cavato (It. = extracted subject), in the 15th cent. and thereabouts a vocal theme sung to a melody formed from the vowels of a sentence converted by the comp. into mus. notes of the hexachord: a = fa or la, e = re, i = mi, o = do, u = ut.

Sogno di Scipione, Il (*Scipio's Dream*), dramatic serenade by Mozart (lib. by Metastasio), prod. Salzburg, at the installation of the new archbishop, Hieronymus von Colloredo, 1. V. 1772.

Dramatic serenade by Predieri (lib. do.), prod. Laxenburg, nr. Vienna, 1. X. 1735.

Soh, the name for the Dominant note in any key in Tonic Sol-fa, so pronounced, but in notation represented by the letter **s.**

Sohier, Mathieu (b. Noyen, ?; d. ?, *c.* 1560), Fr. comp. He was master of the choristers at Notre-Dame, Paris, from 1533, and later canon of St.-Denis-du-Pas. Comp. Masses, motets and *chansons.*

Soir et la Tempête, Le. *See* Le Matin.

Sokalsky, Peter Petrovich (b. Kharkov, 26. IX. 1832; d. Odessa, 11. IV. 1887), Rus. scholar, author and comp. Studied at Kharkov Univ., collected folksongs, was sec. to the Rus. Consulate in N.Y., 1857–1860, and then became a newspaper ed. at Odessa.

Works incl. operas *Maria* (*Mazeppa*), *A Night in May* (after Gogol), *The Siege of Dubno* (after Gogol's *Taras Bulba*), etc.

Sokolov, Nikolai Alexandrovich (b. St. Petersburg, 26. III. 1859; d. Leningrad, 27. III. 1922), Rus. comp. Studied with Rimsky-Korsakov and others at the St. Petersburg Cons. where he became prof. in 1896.

Works incl. ballet *The Wild Swans,* incid. mus. to Shakespeare's *Winter's Tale* and Tolstoy's *Don Juan*; elegy for

orch.; 3 string 4tets; vln. and cello pieces with pf.; part-songs; *c.* 80 songs, etc.

Sol, the old name for the note G (*see* **Solmization**), still used in Lat. countries, and in Tonic Sol-fa notation the Dominant note in any key represented by the symbol **s** pronounced Soh.

Sol-fa. *See* **Solmization** and **Tonic Sol-fa.**

Solage (b. ?; d. ?), late 14th-cent. Fr. comp. Wrote several *chansons,* found in Chantilly, Musée Condé, MS. 1047.

Soléa (Span., plur. *soléares*), a Span. folksong of Andalusia with words in 3-line stanzas of 8 syllables, the 1st and 3rd of which rhyme.

Soler, Antonio (b. Olot, Catalonia, 3. XII. 1729; d. Escurial Palace, 20. XII. 1783), Span. friar, organist and comp. A chorister at Montserrat, he was *maestro de capilla* at Lérida Cathedral and entered the Escurial monastery in 1752, becoming organist and choirmaster there the following year. He was prob. a pupil of D. Scarlatti 1752–7. His treatise *Llave de la Modulación* was pub. in 1762.

Works incl. incid. mus. for plays by Calderón and others; Masses, motets and other church mus.; 5tets for org. and strings; org. concertos; harpsichord sonatas, etc.

Solerti, Angelo (b. Savona, 20. IX. 1865; d. Massa Carrara, 10. II. 1907), It. musicologist. He wrote several works on the origins of dramatic mus. in the early 17th cent.

Solfège (Fr.) } an elementary method
Solfeggio (It.) } of teaching sight-reading and of ear-training, practised mainly in Fr. and It. The names of the notes ('Do, re, mi', etc.) are pronounced while the notes are sung unaccomp. and the intervals have thus to be learnt by ear.

Soli (It. plur. of **Solo**). The word designates a group of solo perfs. as distinct from the whole vocal or orchestral body employed in a work.

Solié (orig. Soulier), **Jean-Pierre** (b. Nîmes, 1755; d. Paris, 6. VIII. 1812), Fr. singer, cellist and comp. A chorister at Nîmes Cathedral, he learnt the cello from his father and played in local theatres. He made his début as a singer in 1778 and from 1787 was at the Opéra-Comique in Paris, rising to become leading baritone. Many of Méhul's roles were written for him. From *c.* 1790 he also had success as an opera comp.

Works incl. 33 *opéras-comiques,* e.g. *Jean et Geneviève, Le Jockey, Le Secret, Le Chapitre second, Mademoiselle de Guise, Le Diable à quatre, Les Ménestrels,* etc.

Solmization (from Lat. *solmisatio*), the designation of the mus. scales by means of syllables, at the same time indicating

Solo

Mutation according to the Gamut. The notes of the Gk. Tetrachords were already designated by syllables, but Guido d'Arezzo in the 11th cent. replaced them by the Hexachords and used the Lat. syllables Ut, Re, Mi, Fa, Sol, La for their 6 notes, Si being added later for the 7th and Ut being replaced by Do in It. and elsewhere, though still largely retained in Fr. These syllables, as in modern Tonic Sol-fa with movable Doh, were not immutably fixed

(*Triolets of the North*), **Gnessin** (songs), **Tcherepnin** (N.) (*Vanka the Chancellor*).

Solomon, oratorio by Handel (lib. ? by Newburgh Hamilton), perf. London, Covent Garden Theatre, 17. III. 1749.

Solomon (actually Solomon Cutner) (b. London, 9. VIII. 1902), Eng. pianist. Made his first public appearance at Queen's Hall aged 8, in Tchaikovsky's 1st pf. concerto, and then studied in Paris, beginning his true career in 1923. His

SOLMIZATION

to C, D, E, F, G, A, but could be transferred by Mutation to other degrees of the scale, so long as the semitone always occurred between Mi and Fa. The so-called 'natural hexachord' beginning on C could thus be changed to the 'hard hexachord' beginning on G, in which case Mi–Fa corresponded with B–C, or to the 'soft Hexachord' beginning on F (*see* **Hexachord**). The syllables were derived from a hymn of the year 770 for the festival of St. John the Baptist, the lines of the plainsong of which began on the successive notes of the hexachord:

UT queant laxis
REsonare fibris
MIra gestorum
FAmuli tuorum
SOLve polluti
LAbii reatum
Sancte Ioannes.

The 7th syllable, Si, was derived from the initial letters of the last line.

Solo (It. = alone), as a noun, a piece or part of a comp. sung or played by a single perf., with or without accomp. The word is also used adjectivally in directions given in It., e.g. *violino solo* (to be played by one vln. alone), *voce sola* (voice unaccomp.), etc.

Solo Organ, one of the manuals of an org. governing mainly Solo Stops.

Solo Stops, org. stops controlling a range of pipes of strikingly characteristic tone generally used for single melodic lines rather than in chords.

Sologub, Feodor Kuzmich (real name Teternikov) (1863–1927), Rus. poet, novelist and playwright. *See* **Dukelsky**

brilliant technique and musicianship made him outstanding among modern pianists.

Soloviev, Nikolai Feopemptovich (b. Petrozavodsk, 9. V. 1846; d. Petrograd, 27. XII. 1916), Rus. comp. Began by studying medicine, but turned to mus. and entered the St. Petersburg Cons., Zaremba being among his masters. He became prof. there in 1874. In 1871 Serov, when dying, charged him with the orch. of his opera *The Power of Evil*. He was also a critic and collector of folksongs.

Works incl. operas *Cordelia* (after Sardou's *La Haine*), *Vakula the Smith* (on Gogol's *Christmas Eve*) and *The Cottage of Kolomua*; cantata for the bicentenary of Peter the Great; symph. poem *Russians and Mongols* and Fantasy on a Folksong for orch.; pf. pieces; songs, etc.

Solti, Georg (b. Budapest, 21. X. 1912), Hung. cond. and pianist. Studied at the Budapest Cons., pf. with Dohnányi and comp. with Kodály and Bartók. From 1930 to 1939 he cond. at the Budapest Opera and then went to Switz., where he was active both as pianist and cond., winning first prize for pf. at the Concours Internationale at Geneva in 1942. In 1946 he became cond. at the Munich State Opera and in 1952–61 director of the Frankfurt Opera. In 1959 he made his début at Covent Garden, of which he was director from 1961 to 1971. He has also made many highly successful recordings, among them the complete *Der Ring des Nibelungen*.

Soltys, Adam (b. Lwów, 4. VII. 1890), Pol. cond. and comp. Studied at Lwów Cons., the Berlin Hochschule für Musik and the Kunstakademie, and Berlin Univ. Prof. at Lwów Cons. from 1921 (director, 1930–9) and cond. of the symph. orch.

Works incl. 2 symphs., symph. poem *Słowianie* (*The Slavs*); chamber mus.; variations for pf.; songs, etc.

Sołtys, Mieczysław (b. Lwów, 7. II. 1863; d. Lwów, 12 XI. 1929), Pol. cond. and comp., father of prec. Studied in Vienna and Paris, where he was a pupil of Saint-Saëns. He returned to Lwów in 1891 and became director of the Cons. and cond. of the Mus. Assoc.

Works incl. operas *The Republic of Babin, Maria* (on Antoni Malczewski's poem), *Panie Kochanku* and others; oratorios; symph., symph. poem *The Fugitive*, etc.

Sombrée (Fr. = darkened), the Fr. adj. for the term Veiled Voice (*voix s.*).

Sombrero de tres picos, El (*The Three-cornered Hat*), ballet by Falla (scen. by Martínez Sierra, based on Alarcón's story; choreography by Leonid Fedorovich Massin), prod. London, Alhambra Theatre, 22. VII. 1919. The setting and dresses were designed by Picasso.

Somervell, Arthur (b. Windermere, 5. VI. 1863; d. London, 2. V. 1937), Eng. comp. and educationist. Educ. at Uppingham School and King's Coll., Cambridge, where he studied comp. with Stanford, going later to Kiel in Berlin, to the R.C.M. in London in 1885 and to Parry as a private pupil in 1887. In 1894 he became prof. at the R.C.M. and in 1901 an inspector of mus. in schools, which led to his appt. as official Inspector of Mus. to the Board of Educ., which he resigned in 1928. Knighted 1929.

Works incl. Masses in C min. and D min. (the latter for male voices), anthem *Let all the world*, oratorio *The Passion of Christ*, cantatas *A Song of Praise, The Power of Sound, The Forsaken Merman* (Matthew Arnold), *Ode to the Sea* and others; symph. in D min. *Thalassa*, ballad *Helen of Kirkconnell*, suite *In Arcady* for orch.; symph. variations *Normandy* for pf. and orch., concerto in G min. and *Concertstück* for vln. and orch.; clar. 5tet; vln. and pf. sonata; Variations on an Original Theme for 2 pfs.; vln. pieces; pf. pieces; song cycles *Maud* (Tennyson), *A Shropshire Lad* (A. E. Housman), *James Lee's Wife, A Broken Arc* (both Browning) and *Love in Springtime*, and other songs; part-songs, etc.

Somis, Giovanni Battista (b. Turin, 25. XII. 1686; d. Turin, 14. VIII. 1763), It. violinist and comp. Pupil of Corelli in Rome and (?) Vivaldi at Venice. Returning to Turin, he was app. violinist to the King of Piedmont and leader of the royal orch. About 1733 he lived in Paris for a time.

He taught many famous pupils, incl. Leclair, Giardini and Pugnani.

Works incl. vln. concertos; sonatas, etc.

Somis, Lorenzo (b. Turin, 11. XI. 1688; d. Turin, 29. XI. 1775), It. violinist and comp., brother of prec. Lived in Turin as violinist in the royal orch. Comp. vln. sonatas, etc.

Sommeils (Fr., plur. of *sommeil* = sleep), quiet airs in old Fr. operas supposed to induce sleep.

Sommer, Hans (actually Hans Friedrich August Zincken, sometimes anag. 'Neckniz') (b. Brunswick, 20. VII. 1837; d. Brunswick, 28. IV. 1922), Ger. comp. Studied at Göttingen Univ. and became prof. of physics there. In 1875 he became director of the Technical High School at Brunswick, settled in Berlin in 1885, at Weimar in 1888, and in 1898 returned to Brunswick. He had been comp. as an amateur since before 1865, when he prod. his 1st opera.

Works incl. operas *Der Nachtwächter, Loreley, Saint-Foix, Der Meermann, Augustin Münchhausen, Rübezahl, Riquet mit dem Schopf* and *Der Waldschratt*; song cycles from Julius Wolff's *Der Wilde Jäger* (*Mädchenlieder*), *Hunold Singuf* and *Tannhäuser*, from Carmen Sylva's *Sappho* and many other songs, etc.

Son and Stranger (Mendelssohn). *See* **Heimkehr aus der Fremde.**

Sonata (It. and Eng.), a term designating both a type of comp. and a mus. form. The classical S. is normally a comp. in 3 or 4 movements, the 1st of which is with few exceptions in S. form, and often the last, though that is at least as frequently a Rondo. The word is derived from *suonare* or *sonare* = 'to sound': a S. is thus orig. simply 'a thing sounded', i.e. played, as distinct from a Cantata (from *cantare*), 'a thing sung'. But in the 17th cent. the S. developed into the two types described hereunder, the S. da camera and the S. da chiesa. In the 18th cent. the 1-movement S. of D. Scarlatti began to approximate to the modern 1st-movement form, while other works of the kind, esp. in Ger., still approximated to the Suite, from which indeed the mature S. borrowed the minuet (later developed into the Scherzo), but often dropped it in favour of a 3-movement comp.: 1st movement in S. form, slow movement, and finale in S. or rondo form.

The modern 1st-movement form, developed through C. P. E. Bach and some of his contemporaries, reached full maturity in the hands of Haydn, Mozart and others, and was greatly strained by the innovations of Beethoven, e.g. in his type of S. quasi una fantasia and late works, which admitted fugal developments and variations.

After Beethoven the S. became often so much modified as to lose its classical shape, e.g. in the hands of Schumann and Chopin, to whom it was uncongenial, or in those of Liszt, who intro. his principle of thematic transformation (as distinct from development) into it.

The S. form in its fully matured but not sophisticated manifestations shows the following main outlines: a single movement in 2 principal sections, the 1st called the Exposition, ending in another key than that of the tonic. Two main thematic groups make up its material, with room for subsidiary themes and connecting bridge passages. These groups are traditionally described as First and Second Subjects. The 1st is in the tonic key, the 2nd in a related key (e.g. the dominant in a movement in a maj. key and the relative maj. in one in a min. key). The 2nd section begins with a Development, which, as its name suggests, develops some of the foregoing material in new ways, but may also partly or even exclusively intro. new matter (e.g. Mozart). This Development leads to the Recapitulation, where the opening of the movement, i.e. the 1st subject, returns as before, though possibly with varied treatment; the 2nd subject also appears in the tonic key, maj. or min., and in the latter case it is often in min. even if in the 1st section it appeared in maj. All this necessitates a new modulatory transition between 1st and 2nd subjects. The movement may end in the tonic exactly as the 1st section ended in another key; but there may be a Coda added, either a very brief tail-piece of a merely ceremonial nature or a more developed section which may further work upon the foregoing material, as often in the case of Beethoven. Not only works so called are S.s, but also chamber mus. of the normal classical type and symphs.

Sonata da camera (It. = chamber sonata), an instrumental work of the late 17th and early 18th cent. of the Suite or Partita type in several movements, mainly in dance forms, but always for more than 1 instrument, most usually 2 vlns. with continuo for bass viol or cello with a keyboard instrument, generally harpsichord. Unlike the sonata da chiesa, the S. d. camera usually had a quick 1st movement.

Sonata da chiesa (It. = church sonata), an instrumental work of the late 17th and early 18th cent., frequently, though not invariably, in 4 movements (slow intro., fugal *allegro*, slow *cantabile* movement and quick finale), written for more than 1 instrument, most usually 2 vlns. with continuo for bass viol or cello with a keyboard instrument, which if played in church must have been generally the org.

Sonata quasi una fantasia (It. = sonata, as it were a fantasy), a term invented by Beethoven for some of his sonatas in which he began to modify the form freely, the 2 works of Op. 27 for pf. being the 1st of the kind.

Sonate (Fr. and Ger.) = Sonata.

Sonate pathétique (Beethoven). *See* **Pathetic Sonata.**

Sonatina (It. dim. of sonata = little sonata), a work of the sonata type in a condensed form or easy to play. The 1st movement of a S. usually contains the normal 1st and 2nd subjects, though as a rule they are less extended, but it may have only a rudimentary working-out section and coda or none at all. The key-scheme for the reappearance of the 2 subjects in the 2nd section, however, will be similar to that in a sonata. S.s have often been written for teaching purposes, esp. for the pf.

Song, strictly speaking any poem set to mus. for a single voice, with or without an accomp., is a S., but the species is distinct from other forms of vocal comp. such as the aria, the ballad, the couplet, etc. A S. may either be set to a repetition of the same tune, or be set continuously, the mus. developing throughout in a manner calculated to illustrate the progress of the words.

Song Cycle, a series of songs set as a rule to a number of poems with a connected narrative or some other unifying feature. Schubert's *Fair Maid of the Mill* and *Winter Journey*, for ex., are thus S. Cs properly speaking, while his *Swan Song* is not. An earlier example is Beethoven's *An die ferne Geliebte*: later ones are Schumann's *Dichterliebe* and *Frauen-Liebe und Leben*, Fauré's *La Bonne Chanson*, Debussy's *Chansons de Bilitis* and Vaughan William's *On Wenlock Edge*.

Song of Destiny (Brahms). *See* **Schicksalslied.**

Song of the Earth (Mahler). *See* **Lied von der Erde.**

Song of Triumph (Brahms). *See* **Triumphlied.**

Songe d'une nuit d'été, Le (*The Dream of a Midsummer Night*), opera by A. Thomas (lib. by Joseph Bernard Rosier and Adolphe de Leuven, not based on Shakespeare's play), prod. Paris, Opéra-Comique, 20. IV. 1850. Shakespeare, Queen Elizabeth and Falstaff appear in it as characters.

Songs and Dances of Death, song cycle by Mussorgsky (poems by A. A. Golenishtchev-Kutuzov), comp. 1875–7: 1. *The Peasant's Lullaby*; 2. *Serenade*; 3. *Trepak*; 4. *The Field Marshal.*

Songs without Words (Mendelssohn). *See* **Lieder ohne Worte.**

Sonnambula, La (*The Sleepwalker*), opera by Bellini (lib. by Felice Romani), prod. Milan, Teatro Carcano, 6. III. 1831.

Sonneck, Oscar (George Theodore) (b. Jersey City, N.J., 6. X. 1873; d. N.Y., 30. X. 1928), Amer. musicologist of Ger. descent. Educ. at Frankfurt and Heidelberg and Munich Univs. Head of the mus. division of the Library of Congress at Washington, 1902–17, and ed. of the *Musical Quarterly* from 1915 to his death. Pub. a catalogue of early opera libs. and lists of Stephen Foster's and Mac-Dowell's works, wrote books on Beethoven and a number on early Amer. mus.

Sonore (Fr. = sonorous), an indication that a passage is to be played or sung with full tone. The It. term is *sonoro*.

Sons bouchés (Fr.) = stopped notes, in horn playing.

Sons, Maurice (b. Amsterdam, 13. IX. 1857; d. London, 28. IX. 1942), Dutch violinist. Studied at the Brussels Cons. with Wieniawski and others, and with Rappoldi at Dresden. After an appt. in Switz. he settled in Scot. as leader of the Scot. Orch. and in 1904 removed to London to become leader of the Queen's Hall Orch., where he remained until 1927. He was vln. prof. at the R.C.M., 1903–37.

Sontag, Henriette (Gertrud Walpurgis) (b. Coblenz, 3. I. 1806; d. Mex. City, 3. VI. 1854), Ger. soprano. The daughter of actors, she appeared on the stage as a child, but in 1815 entered the Prague Cons. as a singing-student, and in 1821 made a very successful stage appearance as an understudy. She was then taken to Vienna for further study and at once appeared there in It. and Ger. opera, Weber choosing her to sing the title-part in *Euryanthe* in 1823. She 1st visited Paris in 1826 and London in 1828. She married Count Rossi, a diplomat of the Sardinian court, and retired, living with him at var. courts in Hol., Ger. and Rus., but after the 1848 revolutions she reappeared on the stage, esp. in Eng. and U.S.A.

Sophocles (497 or 495–405 B.C.), Gk. dramatist. *See* **Antigone** (incid. mus., Mendelssohn; operas, Honegger, Zingarelli), **Arundell** (*Electra*), **Assafiev** (*Oedipus Rex*), **Bantock** (*Electra*), **Bennett** (W. S.) (*Ajax*), **Champein** (*Electra*), **Commer** (do.), **Diepenbrock** (do.), **Dupuis** (A.) (*Oedipus Coloneus*), **Elektra** (R. Strauss), **Gabrieli** (A.) (*Oe. Tyrannus*), **Gnessin** (do. and *Antigone*), **Hadley** (P.) (*Antigone*), **Hauer, Honegger** (do. and *Oe. Rex*), **Hopkins** (A.) (*Oe. Rex*), **Hüttenbrenner** (A.) (*Ödipus auf Kolonos*), **Ilynsky** (*Oe. Rex* and *Philoctetes*), **Krejči** (*Antigone*), **Lassen** (*Oe.*), **Lemoyne** (*Électre*), **Leoncavallo** (*Edipo rè*), **Lier** (*Ajax*), **Martin** (F.)

(*Oe. Rex*), **Mojsisovics** (*Oe. Rex*), **Mulè** (*Antigone* and *Satyr*), **Œdipe** (Enesco), **Œdipe à Colone** (Sacchini), **Oedipus Coloneus** (Mendelssohn), **Oedipus Rex** (Stravinsky), **Oedipus Tyrannus** (Mendelssohn and Stanford), **Orff** (*Antigonae* and *Oedipus Tyrann*), **Pacini** (*Oe. Rex*), **Paine** (*Oe. Tyrannus*), **Pijper** (*Antigone*), **Pizzetti** (*Trachiniae, Oe. Rex and Coloneus*), **Radoux** (C.) (*Œdipe à Colone*), **Ropartz** (*Oe. Col.*), **Saint-Saëns** (*Antigone*), **Schillings** (*Oe.*), **Skilton** (*Electra*), **Tiessen** (*Antigone*), **Zingarelli** (*Edipo a Colono*).

Sopra (It. = above). The word is used in pf. mus. to indicate in passages for crossed hands whether the right is to go above the left or *vice versa. See also* **Come sopra.**

Sopranino, as an adj. indicates the highest member of a family of wind instruments, e.g. S. recorder, S. saxophone.

Soprano, the highest female voice, with approx. the following compass:

but often extended further in florid operatic arias requiring dexterity. Up to the end of the 18th cent. there were also artificial male S.s, prod. by castration. Boy sopranos are more often described as Trebles. Some instruments made in var. ranges use the word S. as a prefix for those types which roughly equal the compass of the S. voice (e.g. S. saxophone).

Soprano Clef, the C clef so used as to indicate that middle C stands on the bottom line of the stave:

Sor (or Sors), Fernando (b. Barcelona, 13. II. 1778; d. Paris, 10. VII. 1839), Span. guitarist and comp. Educ. at the Escalonía at Montserrat, prod. his first opera at the age of 19, went to Paris and *c.* 1815 to London, where he played and taught the guitar, returning to Paris in 1823.

Works incl. ? 5 operas, e.g. *Telemaco nell' isola di Calipso*; 6 ballets; guitar pieces and studies, etc. His guitar tutor was pub. in 1830.

Sorabji, Kaikhosru Shapurji (orig. Leon Dudley) (b. Chingford, Essex, 14. VIII. 1892), Parsee pianist and comp. He has lived in Eng. all his life and has Eur. blood in him through a Span. mother. Except for the pf., he was mainly self-taught, but was fortunate enough to be able to give all his time to mus. studies. He appeared as pianist in his own works in London, Paris and Vienna, and has also written criticism, incl. a book *Around Music*.

Works incl. 2 symphs. for orch., pf., org. and chorus; *Chaleur* and *Opusculum* for orch.; 5 pf. concertos, symph. variations for pf. and orch.; 2 symphs. for org.; 2 pf. 5tets; 5 sonatas, *Opus clavicembalisticum*, *Le Jardin parfumé*, *Fantaisie espagnole*, *In the Hothouse*, *Prelude*, *Interlude and Fugue*, *Valse-Fantaisie*, *Fantasia Hispanica*, 3 toccatas, symph., variations on *Dies irae* for pf.; *3 Poèmes* (Verlaine and Baudelaire), *Fêtes galantes* (Verlaine) for voice and pf., etc.

Sorcerer, The, operetta by Sullivan (lib. by W. S. Gilbert), prod. London, Opera Comique, 17. XI. 1877.

Sorcerer's Apprentice, The (Dukas). *See* **Apprenti sorcier.**

Sordino (It. from *sordo* = deaf) (*See* **Mute**), also the It. name for the Kit.

Soriano, Francesco (b. Soriano sul Cimino, 1549; d. Rome, I. 1620), It. comp. Became a choir-boy at St. John Lateran in Rome and studied with var. masters incl. G. B. Nanini and Palestrina. After a 1st appt. he went to the court of Mantua, 1583–6, and then became *maestro di cappella* in Rome, by turns at Santa Maria Maggiore, St. John Lateran and in 1603 St. Peter's.

Works incl. Masses, motets, psalms, Magnificat, a Passion and other church mus.; madrigals, etc.

Sorochintsy Fair (*Sorochinskaya Yarmarka*), unfinished opera by Mussorgsky (lib. by comp., based on Gogol's *Evenings on a Farm near Dakanka*), comp. begun 1875; revised by Liadov for concert perf., 1904; perf. in orig. form, St. Petersburg, Comedia Theatre, 30. XII. 1911; a version by Sakhnovsky prod. Moscow, Free Theatre, 3. XI. 1913; version by Cui with mus. of his own added prod. St. Petersburg, Musical Drama Theatre, 26. X. 1917; version by N. Tcherepnin prod. Monte Carlo, 17. III. 1923 (in Fr.); another version made by Shebalin in 1931 was prod. Leningrad, Little Opera Theatre, 21. XII. 1931.

Sors, Fernando. *See* **Sor.**

Sortita (It. from *sortire* = to come out), the aria sung by a principal character in an 18th-cent. opera at his 1st entry on the stage.

Sosarme, rè di Media (*Sosarmes, King of the Medes*), opera by Handel (lib. by ?, based on Matteo Noris's *Alfonso primo*), prod. London, King's Theatre, Haymarket, 15. II. 1732.

Sostenendo ⎱ (It.), less frequently used
Sostenente ⎰ forms of

Sostenuto (It. = sustained), a direction which may mean either that a note or notes

are to be held to their full value (as with *tenuto*) or that a passage is to be played broadly, though not exactly slowed down (as with *ritenuto*).

Soto de Langa, Francisco (b. Langa nr. Osma, 1534 or 1538; d. Rome, 25. IX. 1619), Span. priest, male soprano and arranger. He entered the Papal choir in Rome in 1562, joined the Oratory of St. Philip Neri and continued to sing to the end of his long life. He adapted 5 books of *laudi spirituali* for 3 and 4 voices, using It. folksongs and var. It. and Span. comps.

Sotto voce (It. = under the voice), a direction indicating that a passage is to be perf. in an undertone. As the term indicates, it was orig. applied to vocal mus., but it became current for instrumental mus. also.

Soubies, Albert (b. Paris, 10. V. 1846; d. Paris, 19. III. 1918), Fr. musicologist. After studying law, he entered the Paris Cons., became a critic and contrib. to mus. journals, and pub. a number of books incl. a hist. of mus. divided into several vols. for var. countries, studies of opera in Paris, of Wagner (with Malherbe), etc.

Soubrette (Fr. from Prov. *soubret* = coy), a stock figure in opera given to a singer with a light soprano voice and impersonating characters of the type of servants, young confidantes, girls usually connected with the sub-plot, etc. (e.g. Despina in Mozart's *Così fan tutte*, Aennchen in Weber's *Freischütz*). Occasionally the S. may assume a principal part (e.g. Serpina in Pergolesi's *Serva padrona*, Susanna in Mozart's *Figaro*, etc).

Soulier, Jean Pierre. *See* **Solié.**

Soumet, Alexandre (1788–1845), Fr. poet and dramatist. *See* **Norma** (Bellini).

Sound-Board, a resonant wooden part of var. instruments, incl. org., pf., dulcimer, cimbalom, etc. which adds to the volume of tone by vibrating with the notes.

Sound-Holes, the holes in the tables of string instruments, also in the sound-boards of harpsichords, etc. In instruments of the vln. family they take the shape of *f* holes or something approximating to them; in keyboard instruments as well as lutes, guitars, etc., usually the shape of a 'Rose'.

Sound-Post, the piece of pine wood standing upright between the table and the back of string instruments, inserted partly to support the pressure of the strings on the bridge, but mainly to act as the chief distributor of the vibrations.

Sounding-Board. *See* **Sound-Board.**

Soupir (Fr. = sigh) = crotchet rest.

Sourdine (Fr. from *sourd* = deaf) (*See* **Mute**), also an obs. instrument of the bassoon type, which derived its name from the fact that its tone was muffled. It was

known as *Sordun* in Ger. and *sordone* in
It.

Šourek, Otakar (b. Prague, 10. X. 1883;
d. Prague, 15. II. 1956), Cz. mus. critic.
Although an engineer by profession, he
became critic to 2 Prague newspapers
and pub. important works, mainly on
Dvořák, incl. a thematic catalogue and a
large 2-vol. life and study of the works.

Souris, André (b. Marchienne-au-Pont,
10. VII. 1899), Belg. comp. He worked
under the influence of Fr. impressionism
at first, but from 1926 endeavoured to prod.
in mus. some equivalent to the surrealist
painters.

Works incl. incid. mus. for *Le Dessous
des cartes*; *Musique* for orch.; fanfare
Hommage à Babeuf; *Petite Suite* for 4
brass instruments; *Quelques airs de
Clarisse Juranville* for contralto and pf., etc.

Sousa, John Philip (b. Washington, 6.
XI. 1854; d. Reading, Pa., 6. III. 1932),
Amer. bandmaster and comp. After some
years' experience as an orch. violinist he
became master of the U.S. Marine Corps
band in 1880 and in 1892 formed a band of
his own.

Works incl. operetta *El Capitán* and
others; military marches, dances, incl.
The Washington Post, etc.

Sousaphone, a brass instrument of the
Tuba type made for Sousa's band in 1899
with a bell opening towards the audience.

Sousedská, a Boh. country dance in
slow triple time. The 3rd, 4th and 16th of
Dvořák's *Slavonic Dances* for pf. duet are
S.s.

Souter Liedekens (Dutch = little psalter
songs), metrical psalms sung in Hol. to
popular tunes, trans. and provided with
appropriate melodies by (prob.) Willem
van Zuylen van Nyevelt. The 1st complete
collection, printed by Symon Cock at
Antwerp in 1540, contained 159 texts;
Psalm cxix was in 4 sections, and the Te
Deum and 5 canticles were incl. Clemens
non Papa later arr. the whole collection
for 3 voices, pub. in Antwerp as the 4th–
7th of Susato's *Musyck Boexken* (little
music books) in 1556–7. 10 settings are by
Susato himself, perhaps because of
Clemens' premature death. The 8th–11th
books contained another complete setting,
the work of Gerhard Mes.

South American Composers. *See* Argentine, Brazilian, Chilean, Colombian,
Uruguayan.

South Place Concerts. *See* Walthew.

Southerne, Thomas (1660–1746), Ir.
playwright. *See* Courteville (2) (*Oroonoko*),
Paisible (do.), Purcell (*Fatal Marriage,
Maid's Last Prayer, Sir Anthony Love* and
Wives' Excuse), Stanley (*Oroonoko*).

Southey, Robert (1774–1843), Eng. poet.
See Bantock (*Processional* and *Jaga-
Naut*).

Sowerby, Leo (b. Grand Rapids, Mich.,
1. V. 1895; d. Fort Clinton, Ohio, 7.
VII. 1968), Amer. pianist and comp.
Studied at the Amer. Cons. of Chicago,
where he taught later. He served as bandmaster in Eur. during the 1914–18 war and
in 1922 won the Amer. Prix de Rome. He
appeared as pianist in U.S.A., Eng., It
and Aus. He was organist of St. James'
Episcopal Cathedral in Chicago from 1927
to 1962.

Works incl. oratorio *Christ Reborn*,
cantata *Great is the Lord* and Te
Deum for mixed chorus and org.;
4 symphs., suite *From the Northland*,
overture *Comes Autumn Time*, *Irish
Washerwoman*, *Money Musk*, *Set of Four*,
symph. poem *Prairie*, *Theme in Yellow*
for orch.; sinfonietta for strings; rhapsody
for chamber orch.; *Sinconata* for jazz
orch.; 2 pf. concertos, org. concerto,
2 cello concertos, vln. concerto, ballad
King Estmere for 2 pfs. and orch., *Medieval
Poem* for org. and orch.; 2 string 4tets,
wind 5tet, serenade for string 4tet; sonata
and suite for vln. and pf.; symph., sonata
and suite for org.; *Florida Suite* and other
pf. works; songs; etc.

Spacing, the distribution of the notes of
chords beyond the range of an 8ve in such
a way that they come within reach of the
voices or instruments employed and at the
same time prod. a variety of mus. effects.

Spagna, La, a 15th-cent. *basse danse*
tune originating in Castile.

Spagnoletti, Paolo (real surname ?
Diana) (b. Cremona, 1768; d. London,
23. IX. 1834), It. violinist. Studied at
Naples and settled in London in 1802 as
orch. leader, teacher and soloist. He wrote
some vln. pieces and songs.

Spagnoletto (or **Spagnoletta**), an It.
dance of Span. orig.

Spalding, Albert (b. Chicago, 15. VIII.
1888; d. N.Y., 26. V. 1953), Amer. violinist
and comp. Studied at Bologna and Paris
and made his 1st appearance at the latter
in 1905. After touring widely in Eur. he 1st
appeared in N.Y. in 1908.

Works incl. suite for orch.; 2 vln.
concertos; string 4tet in E min.; sonata
and suite for vln. and pf., *Etchings* and
other works for vln. and pf.; pf. pieces;
songs; etc.

Spanisches Liederbuch (*Span. Song
Book*), H. Wolf's settings of Span. poems
in Ger. trans. by Emanuel Geibel and
Paul Heyse, comp. X. 1889–IV. 1890.
There are 10 sacred and 34 secular poems
in his set.

Spanish Lady, The, unfinished opera by
Elgar (lib. by Barry Jackson, based on
Ben Jonson's play *The Devil is an Ass*).
Begun 1932–3; only a number of sketches
are left.

Spanish Viol (or **Vial**) = Cittern.

Špasírka   Spiegato

Špasírka, a Cz. dance in alternating slow and quick 4–8 time. The 13th of Dvořák's *Slavonic Dances* for pf. duet is a S.

Spataro, Giovanni (b. Bologna, ? 1458; d. there, 17. I. 1541), It. comp. and theorist. He was a pupil of Ramos de Pareia and corresponded with Pietro Aron. He was involved in a protracted controversy with Gafurius, against whom 2 of his printed treatises are directed. He comp. a number of sacred works.

Speaight, Joseph (b. London, 24. X. 1868; d. Cheshunt, 20. XI. 1947), Eng. pianist and comp. Studied with Ernst Pauer and Orlando Morgan at the G.S.M. in London, became a prof. there in 1894 and at Trinity Coll. of Mus. in 1919.

Works incl. 2 symphs., 3 symph. poems, 3 suites for orch.; pf. concerto; 5 string 4tets, 3 string 5tets, *Shakespeare Fairy Characters* for string 4tet; instrumental pieces; pf. works; part-songs; songs, etc.

Speaker Keys, extra keys fitted to reed wind instruments to facilitate the prod. of harmonic notes: e.g. 2 on the ob. prod. octaves (also known as Octave Keys) and 1 on the clar. prod. 12ths.

Speaking-Length, that portion of an org. pipe in which the air vibrates to prod. the note.

Specht, Richard (b. Vienna, 7. XII. 1870; d. Vienna, 18. III. 1932), Aus. writer on mus. Studied architecture, but encouraged by Brahms and others took up mus. criticism, joined the staff of *Die Zeit* and in 1909 founded *Der Merkur* with Bittner and Richard Bakta. His books incl. studies of Brahms, J. Strauss, R. Strauss, Mahler, Puccini, Bittner, Rezniček, the Vienna Opera, etc.

Species, the var. types of Counterpoint taught in academic contrapuntal instruction.

Specification, the detailed list of the pipes, stops, keyboards and mechanisms of an org. given to the builder or used to describe the instrument.

Spectre's Bride, The (actually *The Wedding-Shift*), dramatic cantata by Dvořák, Op. 69 (Cz. words by K. J. Erben), comp. 1884, perf. in Eng., Birmingham Festival, VIII. 1885.

Speech-Song (Ger. *Sprechgesang*), a term for a kind of singing that approximates to speech and touches the notes, indicated by special signs, without intoning them clearly at the proper pitch. It is used esp. by Schönberg (e.g. in *Pierrot lunaire*) and his disciples (e.g. Berg in *Wozzeck* and *Lulu*).

Spelman, Timothy Mather (b. Brooklyn, N.Y., 21. I. 1891), Amer. comp. Studied in N.Y., at Harvard Univ. and with Courvoisier at the Munich Cons.

Works incl. operas *La Magnifica, The*

Sea Rovers, Babakan and *The Sunken City*; pantomimes *The Romance of the Rose* and *Snowdrop*; *Litany of the Middle Ages* for soprano, women's chorus and orch., *Pervigilium Veneris* for soprano, baritone, chorus and orch.; symph. in G min., symph. poem *Christ and the Blind Man*, suites *Barbaresques* and *Saints' Days* for orch.; *Dawn in the Woods* for vln. and orch.; *Eclogue* and *In the Princess's Garden* for chamber orch.; 5 *Whimsical Serenades* for string 4tet, *Le Pavillon sur l'eau* for 5 instruments; Span. and *Barbaresques* suite for pf., etc.

Spender, Stephen (b. 1909), Eng. poet. *See* Barber (choruses.).

Spendiarov, Alexander Afanasievich (b. Kakhovka, Crimea, 1. XI. 1871; d. Erivan, 7. V. 1928), Rus. comp. Studied with Klenovsky at Moscow and with Rimsky-Korsakov in St. Petersburg. In 1924 he settled at Erivan, Armenia, and began to write mus. based on Armenian folksong.

Works incl. opera *Almast*; memorial cantata for Stassov; *Crimean Sketches*, symph. poem *The Three Palm Trees* (after Lermontov), *Erivan Sketches* for orch., etc.

Spenser, Edmund (? 1552–99), Eng. poet. *See* Darke (*Hymn of Heavenly Beauty*), Davies (Walford) (*High Heaven's King*), Dieren (van) (*Fayre eies*), Greene (M.) (*Amoretti*), Quest (Walton), Rubbra (5 sonnets).

Speyer, Wilhelm (b. Offenbach, 21. VI. 1790; d. Offenbach, 5. IV. 1878), Ger. violinist and comp. Studied at Offenbach with Thieriot and André and with Baillot in Paris. He became a merchant at Frankfurt, but continued to comp.

Works incl. string 4tets and 5tets; vln. duets; numerous songs, etc.

Speziale, Lo (*The Apothecary*), opera by Haydn (lib. by Goldoni), prod. Esterház, autumn 1768.

Sphaerophon (Ger. from Gk.), an electrophonic instrument invented by Jörg Mager in 1921, prod. notes from the air graded according to the chromatic scale, not indeterminate in pitch like those of the Aetherophone or Theremin. In 1928 Mager improved it by applying a keyboard to it and called it *Klaviatur Sphaerophon*.

Spianato (It.) = smoothed, level.

Spiccato (It. = articulated), a direction indicating a special kind of bowing on instruments of the vln. family, possible only in rapid passages of notes of equal duration, which are played with the middle of the bow and a loose wrist, allowing the bow to rebound off the strings after each note.

Spiegando (It. = spreading, unfolding) ⎫
Spiegato (It. = spread, unfolded) ⎬ = increasing.

Spieloper (Ger. = play-opera), a type of light Ger. opera of the 19th cent. the subject of which is a comedy and the mus. numbers of which are interspersed with dialogue.

Spies, Hermine (b. Löhneberger Hütte nr. Weilburg, Nassau, 25. II. 1857; d. Wiesbaden, 26. II. 1893), Ger. contralto. Studied at the Weisbaden Cons., in Berlin and with Stockhausen at Frankfurt. She sang while a student at the Mannheim Festival in 1880, made her 1st professional appearance at Wiesbaden in 1882, later travelled widely and visited London in 1889. She married a lawyer at Wiesbaden in 1892. Brahms was one of her warmest admirers.

Spinaccino, Francesco (b. Fossombrone, ?; d. Venice, ?), It. 15th–16th-cent. lutenist. Pub. 4 books of arrs. of songs, *ricercari* and dances in lute tablature.

Spindler, Fritz (b. Wurzbach, Lobenstein, 24. XI. 1817; d. Niederlössnitz nr. Dresden, 26. XII. 1905), Ger. pianist and comp. Pupil of Schneider at Dessau, settled at Dresden as concert perf. and teacher.
Works incl. 2 symphs.; pf. concerto; pf. trios; studies and numerous drawing-room pieces for pf.

Spinelli, Nicola (b. Turin, 29. VII. 1865; d. Rome, 17. X. 1909), It. pianist, cond. and comp. Studied at Florence, Rome and Naples, pupil of Mancinelli and Sgambati. His 2nd opera, *Labilia*, came 2nd to Mascagni's *Cavalleria rusticana* in the competition for the Sonzogno Prize in 1889. He suffered from a mental complaint during his last years.
Works incl. operas *Labilia, A basso porto*, etc.

Spinet, a small harpsichord, pentagonal in shape and with a single manual. Its name may derive from the It. *spina* = thorn, ref. to the plectra with which the strings were plucked.

Spirit of England, The, 3 cantatas for soprano solo, chorus and orch. by Elgar, Op. 80, *The Fourth of August, To Women* and *For the Fallen* (poems by Laurence Binyon), comp. in 1916–17 and perf. (II and III) London, 7. V. 1916 and (I–III) London, 24. XI. 1917.

'Spirit' Trio (Beethoven). *See* **'Ghost' Trio.**

Spiritoso (It. = spirited), a direction indicating that a comp., movement or passage is to be perf. briskly and energetically.

Spiritual, a negro song of the southern states of U.S.A., with religious words and folksong tunes. One of the chief influences from which jazz and swing have sprung. It has influenced many serious Amer. comps. and even Eur. ones.

Spitta, (Julius August) Philipp (b. Wechold, Hanover, 7. XII. 1841; d.

Berlin, 13. IV. 1894), Ger. musicologist. Studied at Göttingen Univ. and in 1875 became prof. of mus. hist. at Berlin Univ. He also taught the subject at the Hochschule für Musik, of which he became director in 1882. He was joint ed. with Adler and Chrysander of the *Vierteljahrsschrift für Musikwissenschaft*, and ed. the complete works of Schütz and the org. works of Buxtehude. His chief lit. work is his book on Bach in 2 vols.

Spitteler, Karl (1845–1924), Swiss poet. *See* **Courvoisier.**

Spitzflöte (Ger. = point-fl.), a 2-ft., 4-ft. (most usually) and 8-ft. org. stop governing tapering pipes with a thin, fl.-like but rather reedier tone.

Spofforth, Reginald (b. Southwell, 1768 or 1770; d. London, 8. IX. 1827), Eng. comp. Pupil of his uncle Thomas S., organist of Southwell Minster and of B. Cooke in London, where he settled. He gained several of the Glee Club's prizes.
Works incl. farce with mus. *The Witch of the Wood, or The Nutting Girls,* adds. to Salomon's *Windsor Castle*; many glees, incl. 'Hail, smiling morn', etc.

Spohr, Louis (b. Brunswick, 5. IV. 1784; d. Cassel, 22. X. 1859), Ger. violinist and comp. He 1st learnt mus. from his parents, who were both mus., although his father was a physician. They lived at Seesen in his childhood, and he was afterwards taught by 2 amateurs, but sent to school and for further mus. studies to Brunswick. He played a vln. concerto of his own at a school concert and at 14 went to Hamburg trying to gain a hearing. He failed and on his return petitioned the duke for assistance and was sent to Franz Eck for lessons, the duke paying half the expenses for his accompanying that violinist on his travels. They went to Rus. in 1802, where he met Clementi and Field. He practised and comp. much at that time, returned to Brunswick in 1803, heard Rode there and entered the ducal orch. In 1804 he visited Berlin and played there with Meyerbeer, aged 13. In 1805 he became leader in the Duke of Gotha's orch. and married the harpist Dorette Scheidler, with whom he toured much. After prod. his 3rd opera at Hamburg in 1811, he visited Vienna in 1812, becoming leader at the Theater an der Wien and staying until 1815. After prod. *Faust* in Prague, he travelled in It., 1816–17 and then became cond. at the Frankfurt opera 1817–19. In 1820 he 1st visited London and Paris, meeting Cherubini, R. Kreutzer, Viotti and others.

After a visit to Dresden he became court mus. director at Cassel on 1. I. 1822, having accepted the post declined by Weber, who had recommended him in his place. He remained there for the rest of his life, but continued to travel. In 1831 he finished his *Vln. School*, in 1834 his wife d., and in 1836 he married the pianist Marianne Pfeiffer. In 1839 he revisited Eng. for the perf. of *Calvary* at the Norwich Festival, and was commissioned to write an Eng. oratorio, *The Fall of Babylon* for the next festival of 1842, in which year he prod. Wagner's *Flying Dutchman* at Cassel. He was not allowed leave to go to Eng. for the oratorio, but went during his summer vacation in 1843, when he appeared before Queen Victoria and Prince Albert and toured Eng. and Wales. During the 1848 revolutions he showed liberal leanings and so annoyed the elector that he was refused leave of absence, and having taken his vacation without leave, he became involved in a long law-suit, which he lost after 4 years. In 1852 he adapted *Faust* with recitatives for a prod. in It. in London and in 1863 he prod. Wagner's *Tannhäuser* at Cassel. He was pensioned off against his will in 1857.

Works incl. operas *Die Prufüng*, *Alruna*, *Der Zweikampf mit der Geliebten*, *Faust*, *Zemire und Azor*, *Jessonda*, *Der Berggeist*, *Pietro von Albano*, *Der Alchymist*, *Die Kreuzfahrer*; oratorios *Das jüngste Gericht*, *Die letzten Dinge* (both *The Last Judgment*), *Des Heilands letzte Stunden* (*Calvary*), *The Fall of Babylon*; Mass, psalms, hymn *St. Cecilia*, cantata *Vater unser* (Klopstock); 9 symphs. (4. *Die Weihe der Töne*, 6. Hist. Symph., 9. *The Seasons*), 5 overtures (incl. one on Shakespeare's *Macbeth*); 17 vln. concertos (8. *In modo d'una scena cantante*) and concertinos, concert pieces for vln. and orch.; 4 clar. concertos; 33 string 4tets, 4 double string 4tets, 8 string 5tets, 2 string 6tets, 7tet for pf., strings and wind, octet for strings and wind, nonet for do., 5 pf. trios; pieces, variations, pot-pourris, etc. for vln.; vln. duets; sonatas for vln. and harp; harp pieces; songs; part-songs, etc.

Sponga or **Spongia** } *See* **Usper.**

Spontini, Gaspare (Luigi Pacifico) (b. Maiolati nr. Jesi, 14. XI. 1774; d. Maiolati, 24. I. 1851), It. comp. His parents, who were poor peasants, and an uncle destined him for the priesthood, but he ran away to Monte San Vito, where another uncle allowed him to study mus., and when he had advanced sufficiently, he returned home and was allowed to study at the Cons. de' Turchini at Naples from 1791, Sala and Tritto being among his masters. In 1795 he became a pupil-teacher. In 1796 he prod. his 1st opera in Rome, having run away from the Cons., but he was readmitted at the intercession of Piccinni, from whom he learnt much. He now prod. one opera after another, and in 1798 went

to Palermo with the Neapol. court, which took refuge there and app. him mus. director in the place of Cimarosa, who refused to leave Naples. In 1803 he left for Paris, where he taught singing and tried his hand at Fr. comic opera, but made his 1st real success with the serious opera *La Vestale* in 1807. He was app. comp. to the Empress Joséphine and in 1810 became director of the It. opera at the Théâtre de l'Impératrice. In 1812 he was dismissed, but the Bourbon restoration in 1814 reinstated him. He soon sold his post to Angelica Catalani, however.

In 1820 he was summoned to the court of Frederick William III in Berlin as general mus. director to the Prus. court. He was not on good terms with the intendant, Count Brühl, though he succeeded in intro. excellent reforms at the court opera; but his success was obscured in 1821 by that of Weber's *Freischütz*, which aroused an appetite for Ger. opera, as distinct from foreign opera set to Ger. words. In 1822–1823 he visited Dresden, where he met Weber, also Vienna and Paris. In 1838 he spent the summer in Eng. to study Eng. hist. and local colour for a new opera on the subject of Milton, differing from his early one, which however was never finished; neither was an earlier work, *Les Athéniennes*. On the king's death in 1840 his position became more and more difficult, partly through his own fault, for he quarrelled with the new intendant, Count Redern, and became involved in a law-suit, and after much trouble and threatened imprisonment he left Berlin in VII. 1842. He went to live in Paris, visited Dresden in 1844 to cond. a perf. of *La Vestale* rehearsed for him by Wagner, became deaf in 1848 and returned to his birthplace, founding a mus. school at Jesi.

Works incl. operas *I puntigli delle donne*, *Adelina Senese*, *L'eroismo ridicolo*, *Il finto pittore*, *La finta filosofa*, *La fuga in maschera* and 8 other It. operas, *La Petite Maison*, *Julie, ou Le Pot de fleurs*, *Milton* (in Fr.), *La Vestale*, *Fernand Cortez*, *Olympie* (Fr., revised in Ger. as *Olympia*), *Pélage, ou Le Roi de la paix*, *Nurmahal* (Ger., after Moore's *Lalla Rookh*), *Alcidor*, *Agnes von Hohenstaufen*, *Les Dieux rivaux* (with Berton, R. Kreutzer and Persuis); festival play with mus. on Moore's *Lalla Rookh* (orig. version of the opera); ballet for Salieri's *Les Danaïdes*; *Domine salvum fac* and other church mus.; cantata *L'eccelsa gara* for the victory of Austerlitz, coronation cantata for Nicholas I of Rus.; vocal duets and trios; songs with pf. or harp. *Sensations douces*, etc.

Spontone, Bartolommeo (b. Bologna, VIII. 1530; d. Treviso, 1592), It. comp. Pupil of Nicola Mantovano and Morales, singer and in 1577–83 *maestro di cappella* at San Petronio at Bologna, and in 1584–6 at Santa Maria Maggiore, Bergamo. Comp. Masses, madrigals, etc.

Sponza. *See* **Usper.**

Sporer, Thomas (b. *c*. 1490; d. Strasbourg, ? 1534), Ger. comp. Wrote songs with accomp., then rare, but cultivated by Isaac, Hofhaimer, Senfl and others beside S.

Spourni, Dorothea. *See* **Wendling.**

Sprechgesang (Ger.). *See* **Speech-Song.**

'Spring' Sonata, the familiar nickname given to Beethoven's vln. and pf. sonata in F maj., Op. 24, comp. 1801.

'Spring' Symphony, Schumann's orig. name for his 1st symph., in B♭ maj., Op. 38, finished II. 1841 and 1st perf. at Leipzig by Mendelssohn, 31. III. 1841. Also the title of a choral work by Britten, 1st perf. at Amsterdam, 9. VII. 1949.

Springdans, or **Springer** (Norw.), a folk dance of Norw. in animated 3–4 time with a tune over a drone-bass.

Springer. *See* **Ornaments.**

Springer, Max (b. Schwendi, Württemberg, 19. XII. 1877; d. Vienna, 20. I. 1954), Ger. organist, comp. and writer on church mus. Educ. at Benedictine monasteries in Cz. and Aus. and later studied mus. in Prague. App. prof. of church mus. at the Vienna Acad. Author of books on plainsong and other church subjects.

Works incl. Christmas Mass, Easter Mass, Crescenzia Mass, Te Deum, *Lauda Sion*, Psalm cl, *Resurrection, Evening at Golgotha* and other sacred vocal works; 4 org. sonatas, 3 pastorals, 4 preludes, 8 postludes and other org. works; 4 symphs.; string 5tets, pf. 5tet; pf. pieces; songs, etc.

Sprung Rhythm, a term invented by Gerard Manley Hopkins for displacements of metrical stresses in poetry, not new to his verse, but exploited by him consciously and with great persistence and variety; and transferred to mus. terminology by Michael Tippett in the prefatory notes to his 2nd string 4tet, where S. R. is used with a deliberation similar to Hopkins's in the finale. It is no new thing to mus., where it may be said to incl. such devices as syncopation, transference of stresses to weak beats or by tying notes over bar-lines or beats, the omission of rhythmic units by rests or the addition of them by triplets, etc.

Squarcialupi, Antonio (b. Florence, 27. III. 1416: d. Florence, 6. VII. 1480), It. comp. and organist. He was organist at Florence Cathedral from 1436 until his death, and was a friend of Dufay. No comps. have survived. He was the owner of a MS. now in the Laurentian Library at Florence (Med. Pal. 87), containing a large repertory of It. 14th- and 15th-cent. mus. It has been ed. by Johannes Wolf (Lippstadt, 1955).

Squire, W(illiam). Barclay (b. London, 16. X. 1855; d. London, 13. I. 1927), Eng. musicologist, Educ. at Frankfurt and Pembroke Coll., Cambridge, where he took the M.A. in 1902. In 1885 he took charge of the dept. of printed mus. in the British Museum. He was also a critic and the author of the lib. of Stanford's opera *The Veiled Prophet*, hon. sec. of the Purcell Society and one of the hon. secs. of the I.M.S. He pub. catalogues for the British Museum and the R.C.M., ed. Purcell's harpsichord mus. and other works, and with Fuller-Maitland the *Fitzwilliam Virginal Book*.

St. *See* **Saint** for names combined with it, e.g. Saint-Saëns.

Stabat Mater, a medieval Lat. sacred poem, prob. by Jacopone da Todi, not orig. liturgical, but increasingly used for devotional purposes until it was admitted as a Sequence to the Rom. missal in 1727.

Stabile, Annibale (b. Naples, *c*. 1535; d. Rome, IV. 1595), It. comp. Pupil of Palestrina in Rome, where he became *maestro di cappella* at the Lateran. From 1579 to 1590 he held a similar post at the Ger. Coll. there, in 1591 at the church of Santa Maria Maggiore.

Works incl. motets, Litanies and other church mus.; madrigals, etc.

Stabile, Mariano (b. Palermo, 12. V. 1888; d. Milan, 11. I. 1968), It. baritone. Studied in Rome and made his 1st appearance on the stage at Palermo in 1911. His internat. reputation dated from his perf. in the title role of Verdi's *Falstaff* at La Scala, Milan in 1922. He appeared several times in opera at Covent Garden, Glyndebourne and Salzburg.

Staccato (It. = detached), a special manner of perf. mus. phrases without slurring the notes together, articulating each separately. The S. actually shortens the value of each note as written by the insertion of a minute pause, so that for ex. crotchets marked S. become something like dotted quavers followed by a semi-quaver rest. The notation of S. is a dot placed over each note or chord to be so perf.

Staden, Johann (b. Nuremberg, 1581; d. Nuremberg, XI. 1634), Ger. organist and comp. He was in the service of the Margrave of Kulmbach and Bayreuth in 1603–16, after which he became organist of St. Lorenz's Church at Nuremberg and soon afterwards of St. Sebald's Church.

Works incl. motets for voices alone, motets with instrumental thorough-bass, sacred concertos for voices and instruments; *Hausmusik* for voices and instruments with Ger. words; sacred and secular songs with continuo for org. or lute; secular songs for 4–5 voices; instrumental pavans, galliards, *canzoni*, etc.

Staden, Sigmund Gottlieb (or Theophilus) (b. ? Kulmbach, 1607; d. Nuremberg, 30. VII. 1655), Ger. organist, violist and comp., son of prec. Pupil of his father, then of Jacob Baumann at Augsburg, 1620, and for *viola bastarda* of Walter Rowe in Berlin, 1626. In 1627 he became town musician at Nuremberg and in 1634 organist of St. Lorenz's Church, whose organist, Valentin Dretzel, succeeded his father at St. Sebald's. In 1636 he pub. a book on singing.

Works incl. opera *Seelewig*; hymntunes for 4 voices; *Seelenmusik* containing hymn-tunes for 4 voices with thoroughbass for domestic use; songs with figured bass, etc.

Stader, Maria (b. Budapest, 5. XI. 1915), Swiss soprano. Studied at Carlsruhe with H. Keller, I. Darigo at Zürich and Lombardi in Milan, in 1939 winning 1st prize at an internat. singing competition in Geneva. She is well known as an opera and concert singer, esp. of Mozart, and teaches at the Zürich Acad. of Mus.

Stadler, Anton (b. ? 1753; d. Vienna, 15. VI. 1812), Aus. clarinettist. Lived in Vienna and there became acquainted with Mozart, who wrote for him, e.g. the clar. trio (K.498), 5tet (K.581) and concerto (K.622).

Stadler, Maximilian (b. Melk, 7. VIII. 1748; d. Vienna, 8. XI. 1833), Aus. priest, organist and comp. Pupil of Albrechtsberger, he entered the Benedictine monastery of Melk in 1766 (priest 1772), became prior there in 1784, abbot of Lilienfeld (1786) and of Kremsmünster (1789). In 1796 he settled in Vienna, and after working as a parish priest 1803–15 returned there to devote himself entirely to mus. A friend of Mozart, he completed some of the latter's unfinished works, and wrote in defence of the authenticity of the Requiem.

Works incl. Masses, 2 Requiems, Te Deum, 3 Magnificat settings and other church mus.; oratorio *Die Befreyung von Jerusalem*; mus. for Collin's tragedy *Polyxena*; cantatas *Frühlingsfeyer* (Klopstock), etc.; org. sonatas and fugues; pf. mus., etc.

Stadlmayr, Johann (b. ? Freising, Bavaria, ?; d. Innsbruck, 12. VII. 1648), Ger. comp. He was in the service of the Archbishop of Salzburg early in the 17th cent., and *Kapellmeister* of the Archdukes Maximilian and Leopold in 1610 and 1625 and of the Archduchess Claudia in 1636, at Innsbruck.

Works incl. Masses, Magnificats, Marian canticles, introits, hymns, psalms and other sacred mus., some with instruments, etc.

Staempfli, Edward (b. Berne, 1. II. 1908), Swiss comp. Studied medicine at first but gave it up for mus., which he studied with Jarnach at Cologne and with Dukas in Paris.

Works incl. ballets *Das Märchen von den zwei Flöten* and *Le Pendu*; cantata *Filles de Sion* for solo voices, chorus and orch.; 3 symphs., 4 *Sinfonie concertanti* and other orchestral works; 3 pf. concertos, 2 vln. concertos, concerto for 2 pfs. and strings; mus. for 11 instruments, concerto for pf. and 8 instruments, 5 string 4tets, 5tet for wind, 4tet for fl. and strings, pf. trio, string trio and other chamber mus.; pf. pieces; songs, etc.

Staff Notation, the ordinary mus. notation, so called to distinguish it from the notation used for Tonic Sol-fa.

Staggins, Nicholas (b. ? London, 1645; d. Windsor, 13. VI. 1700), Eng. comp. Pupil of his father, Isaac S. (d. 1684). Charles II app. him Master of the King's Band in 1674. He took the Mus.D. degree at Cambridge in 1682, becoming prof. of mus. there in 1684. He advanced to the post of Master of the King's Mus., but was succeeded in it by Eccles in 1698.

Works incl. masque *Calisto, or The Chaste Nimph* (Crowne); incid. mus. for Etheredge's *The Man of Mode*, Lee's *Gloriana*, Dryden's *Conquest of Granada* and *Marriage à la Mode* and Shadwell's *Epsom Wells* (last 2 with Robert Smith); odes for the birthday of William III; songs, etc.

Stagione (It. = season). The term is used esp. for an opera season.

Stahlspiel (Ger. lit. = steel-play), a perc. instrument with tuned steel plates or bars which are played with hammers. It is known in Eng. military bands as Lyra, being made for them in the shape of a lyre. The modern Glockenspiel, being also made of steel bars, and no longer of actual bells, is now to all intents and purposes the same instrument. There is also an org. stop controlling steel bars named S.

Stainer, Jacob (b. Absam nr. Hall, 14. VII. 1621; d. ?, 1683), Aus. vln. maker. He learnt his craft at Innsbruck and (?) with one of the Amati family at Cremona or (?) with Vimercati at Venice. He began to work on his own account at Absam c. 1640.

Stainer, John (b. London, 6. VI. 1840; d. Verona, 31. III. 1901), Eng. organist and comp. He became a choir-boy at St. Paul's Cathedral at the age of 7 and before long was able to deputize at the org. After working under var. masters and receiving an organist's appt. in the City of London, he was app. by Ouseley organist of St. Michael's Coll., Tenbury, in 1856. In 1860 he went to Oxford as an undergraduate at St. Edmund Hall and organist to Magdalen Coll., then became organist to the Univ. in succession to Elvey and in 1865 took the D.Mus. degree.

In 1872 he returned to London as organist at St. Paul's Cathedral. His many posts incl. those of univ. examiner and prof. at the Nat. Training School for Mus., where he succeeded Sullivan as principal in 1881. In 1888, having resigned from St. Paul's Cathedral through failing eyesight, he was knighted and in 1889 became Prof. of Mus. at Oxford. He wrote on mus. in the Bible, and ed. *Early Bodleian Music, Dufay and his Contemporaries*, etc.

Works incl. oratorios *Gideon* and *The Crucifixion*; *Sevenfold Amen*, services and anthems; cantatas *The Daughter of Jairus* and *St. Mary Magdalen*, etc.

Stamaty, Camille (Marie) (b. Rome, 13. III. 1811; d. Paris, 19. IV. 1870), Fr. pianist and comp. of Gk. descent. After the death of his father, his mother returned to Fr., taking him 1st to Dijon and then to Paris and teaching him mus. In 1828 he became a civil servant, but continued to cultivate mus., studying the pf. with Kalkbrenner and others, though his public appearances were restricted by severe rheumatism. He taught successfully, but sought further study with Mendelssohn at Leipzig in 1836–7. He had many distinguished pupils, incl. Saint-Saëns.

Works incl. pf. concerto; sonatas, variations on an orig. theme, numerous studies (one set on Weber's *Oberon*), exercises, transcriptions for pf., etc.

Stamitz. Boh. family of musicians:

1. Johann Wenzel Anton S. (b. Německý Brod, 17. or 19. VI. 1717; d. Mannheim, 27. III. 1757), violinist and comp. He entered the service of the Electoral court at Mannheim in 1741, became principal violinist in 1743 and later mus. director. Under him the orch. became the most famous in Eur., called by Burney 'an army of generals'. He was the founder and most important member of the Mannheim school of symphonists.

Works incl. 74 symphs., concertos for vln., harpsichord, fl., ob., clar.; trio sonatas and other chamber mus.; vln. sonatas, etc.

2. Carl S. (b. Mannheim, 7. V. 1745; d. Jena, 9. XI. 1801), violinist and comp., son of prec. Pupil of his father, entered the Mannheim orch. as 2nd vln. in 1762, then went to Strasbourg (1770), Paris and London, appearing as a virtuoso on the vln. and vla. d'amore. He continued to travel widely, visiting Prague in 1787 and Rus. in 1790, until in 1794 he settled in Jena as mus. director to the univ.

Works incl. operas *Der verliebte Vormund* and *Dardanus*; c. 80 symphs. and *sinfonies concertantes*; concertos; chamber mus., etc.

3. Johann Anton S. (b. Mannheim, 24. XI. 1754; d. Paris, before 1809), violinist and comp., brother of prec.

Pupil of his father and of Cannabich, in 1770 he went with his brother Carl S. to Paris, where he settled as violinist in the court orch. Kreutzer was his pupil.

Works incl. 12 symphs.; concertos for vln., vla., fl., ob., etc.; chamber mus., etc.

Stanchinsky, Alexey Vladimirovich (b. Government Vladimir, 1888; d. Crimea, 6. X. 1914), Rus. comp. He studied at the Moscow Cons., also comp. with Zhilayev and Taneiev, showed great brilliance in a number of pf. works, but soon ceased to write owing to attacks of insanity, and d. early, perhaps by suicide.

Works (all for pf.) incl. 2 sonatas, numerous preludes, several studies, etc.

Ständchen (Ger.) = Serenade.

Standfuss, J. C. (b. ?; d. ? Hamburg, c. 1759), Ger. violinist and comp. At one time a member of Koch's opera troupe in Leipzig, he was the 1st to prod. a Ger. *Singspiel*, in adapting Coffey's *The Devil to Pay* as *Der Teufel ist los* (1752). Coffey's sequel *The Merry Cobbler* was similarly arr. as *Der lustige Schuster* in 1759. His 3rd *Singspiel* was *Der stolze Bauer Jochem Tröbs*.

Stanford, Charles Villiers (b. Dublin, 30. IX. 1852; d. London, 29. III. 1924), Ir. comp. In 1870 he became choral scholar at Queens' Coll., Cambridge, and in 1873 organist of Trinity Coll., where he took classical honours the next year; also cond. of the Cambridge Univ. Mus. Society. In 1874–6 he studied with Reinecke at Leipzig and Kiel in Berlin, and in the latter year Tennyson suggested him as comp. of incid. mus. for his *Queen Mary*. D.Mus. at Oxford 1883 and Mus.D. at Cambridge 1888, where he had succeeded Macfarren as Prof. of Mus. in 1887. He was also cond. of the Bach Choir in London and prof. of comp. at the R.C.M., where he cond. the orchestral and opera classes. Knighted 1901.

Works incl. operas *The Veiled Prophet of Khorassan, Savonarola, The Canterbury Pilgrims* (after Chaucer), *Shamus O'Brien* (after Le Fanu), *Much Ado About Nothing* (on Shakespeare), *The Critic* (on Sheridan), *The Travelling Companion*; incid. mus. for Tennyson's *Queen Mary* and *Becket*, Aeschylus' *Eumenides*, Sophocles' *Oedipus Tyrannus*, Binyon's *Attila* and Louis N. Parker's *Drake*; 7 symphs.; 5 Ir. rhapsodies, 3 concert overtures, serenade and Ir. dances for orch.; 3 pf. concertos, 2 vln. concertos, cello concerto, clar. concerto, suite for vln. and orch., Variations on an Eng. Theme for pf. and orch.; 8 string 4tets, 2 string 5tets, 2 pf. trios, 2 pf. 4tets, pf. 5tet, serenade for 9 instruments; 2 sonatas for vln. and pf., 2 sonatas for cello and pf., clar. and pf. sonata, some smaller instrumental pieces with pf.; pf. works incl. suite, toccata, sonata, 3 *Dante Rhapsodies*; 11 org. works incl. 5 sonatas; oratorios *The Three Holy Children, Eden*; Mass, Requiem, Te Deum, *Stabat Mater*, Magnificat; 2 psalms, 6 services, 3 anthems; choral ballads *The Revenge* (Tennyson), *Phaudrig Crohoore* (Le Fanu), *The Last Post* (Henley), etc.; works for solo voice and chorus (with or without orch.); *3 Cavalier Songs* (Browning), *The Bard* (Gray), *Songs of the Sea, Songs of the Fleet*; a number of part-songs; 20 op. nos. of songs (*c.* 100), incl. Heine's *Die Wallfahrt nach Kevlaar* and cycles *A Child's Garland* (Stevenson), poems by Robert Bridges, *An Irish Idyll, Songs of Faith, Cushendall*; vocal 4tets from Tennyson's *Princess*; 5 collections of Ir. folksongs ed., incl. the Petrie Collection in 3 vols., etc.

Stanley, John (b. London, 17. I. 1713; d. London, 19. V. 1786), Eng. organist and comp. He was blind from the age of 2, but became a pupil of Greene and held var. organist's appts. in London later. In 1759 he joined John Christopher Smith to continue Handel's oratorio concerts, and when Smith retired in 1774, he continued with T. Linley. In 1779 he succeeded Boyce as Master of the King's Mus.

Works incl. opera *Teraminta*; dramatic cantata *The Choice of Hercules*; mus. for Lloyd's *Arcadia, or The Shepherd's Wedding* and *Tears and Triumphs of Parnassus* and Southerne's *Oroonoko*; oratorios *Jepthah, Zimri* and *The Fall of Egypt*; 12 cantatas to words by John Hawkins; 6 concertos for strings; solos for fl. or vln.; cantatas and songs for voice and instruments, etc.

Stanton, W(alter). K(endall). (b. Dauntsey, Wilts., 29. IX. 1891), Eng. comp. and educationist. Learnt mus. as choir-boy at Salisbury Cathedral and was educ. at Lancing Coll. and Merton Coll., Oxford, where he took the D.Mus. degree in 1935. In 1924 he succeeded Dyson as director of mus. at Wellington Coll. and in 1927–37 he also directed the mus. at Reading Univ. and cond. perfs. in that town. In 1937 he became director of mus. to the Midland Region of the B.B.C. at Birmingham, resigning in 1945, and from 1947 to 1958 he was Prof. of Mus. at Bristol Univ.

Works incl. motets for double choir *The Spacious Firmament* (Addison) and *Sing we triumphant hymns*, etc.

Stappen, Crispinus van (b. ?, ? 1470; d. Cambrai, 10. III. 1533), Fl. comp. He became a singer at the Ste. Chapelle, Paris, in 1492, and shortly afterwards, until 1507, at the Papal Chapel in Rome. In 1524–5 he was *maestro di cappella* at the Casa Santa, Loreto. He held a canonry at Cambrai from 1504. He comp. sacred and secular works, incl. a *strambotto* in praise of Padua.

Stapylton, Robert (1599–1669), Eng. playwright. *See* **Locke** (*Stepmother*).

Starck, Ingeborg (b. St. Petersburg, 24. VIII. 1840; d. Munich, 17. VI. 1913), Swed. pianist and comp. Pupil of Henselt at St. Petersburg and of Liszt at Weimar. She made a long concert tour in 1858–9 and in 1862 married Hans von Bronsart (1830–1913), who later became intendant of the court theatre at Hanover.

Works incl. operas *Die Göttin von Sais, Jery und Bätely* (Goethe), *König Hiarne, Manfred* (after Byron), *Die Sühne*; pf. concerto; *Kaiser Wilhelm Marsch*; chamber mus.; pf. pieces; songs, etc.

Starker, Janos (b. Budapest, 5. VII. 1924), Hung. cellist. Studied at Budapest Acad. of Mus., becoming 1st cello in the Budapest Opera orch. In 1946 he settled in the U.S.A., playing with the Dallas Symph. Orch., the orch. of the N.Y. Metropolitan and the Chicago Symph. Orch. In 1958 he became prof. at Indiana Univ., Bloomington. As a soloist he has toured widely both in Eur. and Amer.

Starokadomsky, Mikhail (b. Brest-Litovsk, 13. VI. 1901; d. Moscow, 24. IV. 1954), Rus. comp. Studied at the Moscow Cons. under Vassilenko, Miaskovsky and Catoire.

Works incl. opera *Sot*; oratorio *Simon Proshakov*; symph., concerto and 2 suites for orch.; org. concerto, vln. concerto, 2 string 4tets; pf. sonata, etc.

Starzer, Josef (b. Vienna, 1726; d. Vienna, 22. IV. 1787), Aus. violinist and comp. Violinist at the Fr. theatre in Vienna from 1752, he was court comp. and leader of the orch. in St. Petersburg 1758–? 1768. Back in Vienna he comp. mus. for Noverre's ballets, and was active in the Tonkünstler-Soc., for whose concerts he re-orch. Handel's *Judas Maccabeus* in 1779. From 1783 increasing corpulence enforced his retirement.

Works incl. *Singspiele Die drei Pächter* and *Die Wildschützen*; ballets *Roger et Bradamante, Adèle de Ponthieu, Gli Orazi e gli Curiazi* (all with Noverre) and many others; oratorio *La Passione di Gesù Cristo*; symphs., divertimenti, etc. for orch.; vln. concerto; chamber mus., etc.

Stassov, Vladimir Vassilievich (b. St. Petersburg, 14. I. 1824; d. St. Petersburg, 23. X. 1906), Rus. scholar and art critic. Educ. at the School of Jurisprudence and joined the Imp. Public Library in 1845. He studied in It. from 1851 to 1854, after which he returned to the Library and in 1872 became director of the dept. of fine arts there. He was the 1st lit. champion of the Rus. nationalist school of comps.

Statkowski, Roman (b. Szczypiórno nr. Kalisz, 5. I. 1860; d. Warsaw, 12. XI. 1925), Pol. comp. Studied with Żeleński at Warsaw and with Soloviev at St. Petersburg. On the death of Noskowski in 1909 he was app. prof. of comp. at the Warsaw Cons.

Works incl. operas *Philaenis* and *Maria* (after Malczewski); fantasy, polonaise and other works for orch.; 6 string 4tets; vln. and pf. pieces; *Krakowiak* and other works for pf.; songs, etc.

Staudigl, Joseph (b. Wöllersdorf, 14. IV. 1807; d. Döbling nr. Vienna, 28. III. 1861), Aus. bass. Learnt mus. as a novice at the monastery of Melk, but ran away to Vienna in 1827 and entered the chorus of the Kärntnertortheater, where he soon rose through small parts to a position of eminence. He 1st visited Eng. in 1846, when he created the title part in Mendelssohn's *Elijah* at the Birmingham Festival. He d. insane.

Stave, the 5 horizontal lines on which mus. is written.

Stavenhagen, Bernhard (b. Greiz, Reuss, 25. XI. 1862; d. Geneva, 26. XII. 1914), Ger. cond. and pianist. Studied with Kiel and Rudorff in Berlin and with Liszt at Weimar, where he became court pianist in 1890 and mus. director in 1895. After a similar post in Munich, he returned to Weimar, but in 1907 went to Switz. and settled at Geneva as cond. He wrote 2 concertos and pieces for pf. and songs, etc.

Stcherbatchev. See **Shcherbatchev.**

Steber, Eleanor (b. Wheeling, W.Va., 17. VII. 1916), Amer. soprano. Studied at the New Eng. Cons. and with P. Althouse in N.Y. After winning a N.Y. Metropolitan radio competition in 1940, she made her début there in the same year. She created the title role in Barber's *Vanessa.*

Steele, Richard (1672–1729), Ir. essayist and dramatist. See **Croft** (*Lying Lover*), **Inkle and Yarico** (Arnold), **Rust (F. W.)** (*Inkle und Yariko*).

Stefan, Paul (b. Brno, 25. XI. 1879; d. N.Y., 12. XI. 1943), Aus. writer on mus. Studied at Brno, at Vienna Univ. and with Graedener and Schönberg. Settled in Vienna as mus. critic and correspondent and in 1921 founded the *Musikblätter des Anbruch.* In 1938 he left Aus. owing to the Nazi régime and went to Switz., later to U.S.A. He wrote books on mus. in Vienna, on Schubert, Dvořák, Mahler, Schönberg, Toscanini, Bruno Walter, etc.

Steffani, Agostino (b. Castelfranco, 25. VII. 1654; d. Frankfurt, 12. II. 1728), It. diplomat and comp. Learnt mus. as a choirboy at Padua and was taken to Munich, where he studied mus. under Kerl at the expense of the Elector Ferdinand Maria. After further studies in Rome, 1673–4, he returned to Munich and became court organist in 1675; having also studied mathematics, philosophy and theology he was ordained priest in 1680. He was

made director of the court chamber mus., but in 1688 the younger Bernabei was app. general mus. director on the death of his father, and S., disappointed of the post, left Munich. After a visit to Venice he went to the court of Hanover, where the post of mus. director was offered him, and there he also filled other posts, incl. diplomatic ones. The philosopher Leibniz, who was also at the court, sent him on a diplomatic mission to var. Ger. courts in 1696; in 1698 he was ambassador to Brussels, and on the death of the Elector Ernest Augustus transferred his services to the Elector Palatine at Düsseldorf. In 1706 he was made a nominal bishop. In 1708–9 he was on a diplomatic mission in It., where he met Handel, who went into service at the Hanoverian court at his suggestion. In 1722–5 he lived at Padua and in 1727 he was elected hon. president of the London Acad. of Vocal Mus. In 1727 he went to It. for the last time. He d. at Frankfurt during a diplomatic visit.

Works incl. operas *Marco Aurelio, Solone, Servio Tullio, Alarico il Baltha, Niobe, Enrico Leone, La lotta d'Hercole con Achelao, La superbia d'Alessandro, Orlando generoso, Le rivali concordi, La libertà contenta, I trionfi del fato, Baccanali, Briseide, Arminio, Enea* and *Tassilone*; mus. for a tournament *Audacia e rispetto*; motets, vesper psalms for 8 voices, *Stabat Mater* for 6 voices, strings and org., *Confitebor* for 3 voices and strings and other church mus.; madrigals; vocal chamber duets with bass; chamber sonatas for 2 vlns., vla. and bass, etc.

Steffkins. Family of lutenists and violists of Ger. origin settled in London ? in the 17th cent.:

1. **Dietrich** (or **Theodore**) S. (b. ?; d. ?, 1674) teacher of the lute and vla. da gamba and member of Charles I's band. He lived in Hamburg during the Commonwealth, returning in 1660 to serve under Charles II. He was much admired by John Jenkins.

2. **Frederick William** S. (b. London, ?; d. ? London, ?), son of prec. Violist in the royal service after the Restoration.

3. **Christian** S. (b. London, ?; d. ? London, ?), brother of prec. Violist in the royal service.

Steg (Ger.), the bridge of a string instrument.

Steggall, Reginald (b. London, 17. IV. 1867; d. London, 16. XI. 1938), Eng. organist and comp. Studied with his father, Charles S. (1826–1905), and at the R.A.M., where he became org. prof. in 1895. In 1886 he was app. organist at St. Anne's Church, Soho, and in 1905 succeeded his father as organist of Lincoln's Inn chapel.

Works incl. Mass, services and anthems;

symph., variations on an orig. theme, fantasy overture for orch.; vocal scenas with orch. *Elaine* and *Alcestis*; org. pieces, etc.

Stegmann, Carl David (b. Dresden, 1751; d. Bonn, 27. V. 1826), Ger. tenor, cond. and comp. Studied with Homilius and others at Dresden, and after singing and cond. at var. opera houses in Ger., he became cond. at the Hamburg theatre in 1798, retiring to Bonn in 1811.

Works incl. operas *Heinrich der Löwe, Der Triumph der Liebe, Erwin und Elmire* (Goethe) and many others; concertos, etc.

Steibelt, Daniel (b. Berlin, 22. X. 1765; d. St. Petersburg, 2. X. 1823), Ger. pianist and comp. He learnt much about keyboard instruments in his childhood, being the son of a harpsichord and pf. maker, and studied mus. with Kirnberger. After serving in the army, he made his 1st appearance as pianist and comp. in Paris during the late 1780s. At the end of 1796 he visited London, where he remained until 1799 and married an Englishwoman. He visited Hamburg, Dresden, Prague, Berlin and Vienna, where he had an encounter with Beethoven at the pf., and in VIII. 1800 again settled in Paris, but spent as much of his time in London. In 1808 he left for the court at St. Petersburg, where he became director of the Fr. Opera on the departure of Boïeldieu in 1810.

Works incl. operas *Roméo et Juliette* (after Shakespeare), *La Princesse de Babylone, Cendrillon, Sargines* and *Le Jugement de Midas* (unfinished); ballets *Le Retour de Zéphyr, Le Jugement du berger Paris, La Belle Laitière, La Fête de l'empereur*; intermezzo *La Fête de Mars* for the victory at Austerlitz; incid. mus.; 5 pf. concertos; 50 studies and numerous pieces and transcriptions for pf., etc.

Steigleder, Hans Ulrich (b. Schwäbisch-Hall, III. 1593; d. Stuttgart, 10. X. 1635), Ger. organist and comp. After an appt. as organist at Lindau on Lake Constance, he became organist at a monastery at Stuttgart in 1617 and musician to the court of Württemberg.

Works. incl *ricercari* and variations on a Lord's Prayer hymn-tune for org., etc.

Stein. Ger. family of pf. makers:
1. **Johann Andreas S.** (b. Heidelsheim, 6. V. 1728; d. Augsburg, 29. II. 1792), org. builder and pf. maker. Learnt his craft from his father, Johann Georg S. (1697–1754), worked with J. A. Silbermann in Strasbourg and settled in Augsburg in 1751. Mozart preferred his pfs. above all others.
2. **Maria Anna (Nanette) S.** (b. Augsburg, 2. I. 1769; d. Vienna, 16. I. 1833), pianist and pf. maker, daughter of prec.

She played to Mozart as a child during his visit to Augsburg in 1777, and on her father's death in 1792 carried on the business with her brother, 3, but married Andreas Streicher in 1794 and moved with him to Vienna, where they estab. a new firm, jointly with 3. Later she and her husband became friends of Beethoven.
3. **Matthäus Andreas S.** (b. Augsburg, 12. XII. 1776; d. Vienna, 6. V. 1842), pf. maker, brother of prec. He accomp. his sister and her husband to Vienna in 1793 and joined their firm, but estab. himself independently in 1802.
4. **Andreas Friedrich S.** (b. Augsburg, 26. V. 1784; d. Vienna, 5. V. 1809), pianist and comp., brother of prec. Went to Vienna as a child with his sister and brother, and studied pf. playing, also comp. with Albrechtsberger. He appeared in public frequently, esp. with Mozart's concertos.

Works incl. 3 operettas; pantomime *Die Fee Radiante*; vln. concerto; pf. trio; pf. sonata; songs; etc.
5. **Karl Andreas S.** (b. Vienna, 4. IX. 1797; d. Vienna, 28. VIII. 1863), comp. and pf. maker, nephew of prec., son of 3. Pupil of Förster. He 1st devoted himself to comp., but later mainly to his father's factory, to which he succeeded.

Works incl. comic opera *Die goldene Gans*; 2 overtures; 2 pf. concertos, etc.

Stein, Erwin (b. Vienna, 7. XI. 1885; d. London, 19. VII. 1958), Aus. musicologist. Pupil of Schönberg. After cond. at var. places, he joined the Universal Ed. in Vienna, but settled in London after the Anschluss. He wrote much on Schönberg.

Stein, Gertrude (1874–1946), Amer. author. *See* Berners (*Wedding Bouquet*), **Bowles** (*Letter to Freddy*), **Mother of us all** (V. Thomson), **Thomson** (V.) (*4 Saints in 3 Acts, Capital, Capitals* and *Mother of us all*).

Steinbach, Emil (b. Lengenrieden, Baden, 14. XI. 1849; d. Mainz, 6. XII. 1919), Ger. cond. and comp. Studied at the Leipzig Cons. and became cond. and theatre director at Mainz. Comp. orchestral works, chamber mus., songs, etc.

Steinbach, Fritz (b. Grünsfeld, Baden, 17. VI. 1855; d. Munich, 13. VIII. 1916), Ger. cond. and comp., brother of prec. Studied with his brother and at the Leipzig Cons. After working as 2nd cond. at Mainz in 1880–6, he went to the court of Meiningen, with whose orch. he visited London in 1902, when he succeeded Wüllner as municipal cond. and director of the Cons. at Cologne. His works incl. a 7tet and a cello sonata.

Steinberg, Maximilian Osseievich (b. Wilno, 4. VII. 1883; d. Leningrad, 6. XII. 1946), Rus. comp. Studied at St. Petersburg Univ. and Cons. Pupil (and later son-in-law) of Rimsky-Korsakov, also of Liadov and Glazunov. He became prof. at the Leningrad Cons.

Works incl. ballets *Midas* (after Ovid) and *Till Eulenspiegel*; incid. mus.; oratorio *Heaven and Earth* (after Byron); 4 symphs., dramatic fantasy on Ibsen's *Brand*, overture to Maeterlinck's *La Princesse Maleine* and other orchestral works; vln. concerto; 2 string 4tets; songs incl. 2 Tagore cycles, folksong arrs., etc.

Steinberg, William (b. Cologne, 1. VIII. 1899), Amer. cond. of Ger. origin. After an early start in comp. he studied at Cologne Cons., graduating in 1920 and becoming asst. to Klemperer at the Cologne Opera and in 1924 its principal cond. In 1925 he went to the Ger. Theatre in Prague and in 1929 became mus. director of the Frankfurt Opera. In 1933 he was removed from this post by the Nazis and became connected with the Jewish Cultural Society, from 1936 to 1938 cond. the Palestine Symph. Orch. and in 1938 the N.B.C. Symph. Orch. in Amer. From 1945 he cond. the Buffalo Phil. Orch. and from 1952 the Pittsburgh Symph. Orch.

Steinway (orig. Steinweg), a firm of pf. makers in N.Y., founded in 1849 by Heinrich Engelhard Steinweg (1797–1871) at Brunswick, who emigrated with 5 sons and estab. himself in 1853. Branches of the firm were later set up in London, Hamburg and Berlin.

Stem, the stroke attached to the heads of all notes of smaller value than a semibreve.

Stendhal (Henri Beyle) (1783–1842), Fr. critic and novelist. Wrote a biog. of Rossini, letters on Haydn (partly plagiarized from Carpani), etc. *See* Chartreuse de Parme (Sauguet).

Stenhammar, (Karl) Wilhelm (Eugen) (b. Stockholm, 7. II. 1871; d. Stockholm, 20. XI. 1927), Swed. pianist, cond. and comp. Pupil of his father, the comp. Per Ulrik S. (1829–75), and later of Sjögren and others; also studied in Berlin. He became cond. of the royal orch. at Stockholm and also cond. at Göteborg.

Works incl. operas *The Feast of Solhaug* (based on Ibsen) and *Tirfing*; incid. mus. to Shakespeare's *Twelfth Night*, *Hamlet* and *Romeo and Juliet*, Strindberg's *Ett drömspel*, Gozzi's *Turandot*, Tagore's *Chitra* and other plays; cantatas *The Princess and the Page*, *Snöfrid*, *Hemmarschen* and *Sången*; 2 symphs., svmph. overture *Excelsior*, *Prelude and Bourrée*, serenade in F maj., for orch.; 2 pf. concertos, *2 Sentimental Romances* for vln. and orch.; 6 string 4tets, pf. 4tet; vln. and pf. sonata; 4 sonatas and fantasy for pf.; part-songs incl. *Sverige*; songs, etc.

Stenka Razin, symph. poem by Glazu-

nov, Op. 13, comp. 1884, 1st perf. St. Petersburg, 1885. It contains the tune of the Volga boatmen's song *Ey ukhnem*.

Stentando (It. = toiling, labouring), a direction indicating a dragging delivery of a passage.

Štěpán, Vaclav (b. Pečky, 12. XII. 1889; d. Prague, 24. XI. 1944), Cz. pianist, critic and comp. Studied with Novák and others and became prof. of mus. aesthetics at the Prague Cons. His literary works incl. a study of *Musical Symbolism of Programme Music* and his comps. a poem *Life's Halcyon Days* for cello and pf.

Stepanian, Aro (b. Elisabetopol, 1897), Rus. comp. He began to teach mus. in the Armenian school of his native town and later of Alexandropol before he was 20; then studied at the Moscow School of Mus. under Glière and Gnessin and at the Leningrad Cons. under Shcherbatchev. Settled as prof. of mus. at Everan in Rus. Armenia, the folksongs of which he studied.

Works incl. operas *Nazar the Brave*, *David Sassunsky* and *The Dawn*; 3 symphs., symph. poem *To the Memory of Twenty-six Commissars*; chamber mus.; instrumental pieces; songs, etc.

Stephan, Rudi (b. Worms, 29. VII. 1887; d. Gorlice, Galicia, 29. IX. 1915), Ger. comp. Studied at Worms, with Sekles at Frankfurt and at Munich. He fell in battle near Gorlice.

Works incl. opera *Die ersten Menschen*; ballad *Liebeszauber* (Hebbel) for baritone and orch.; *Music for Orch.*; *Music for Fiddle and Orch.*; *Music for 7 Stringed Instruments* (incl. pf. and harp); pf. pieces; songs, etc.

Stephen, David (b. Dundee, 25. VIII. 1869; d. nr. Edinburgh, 9. III. 1946), Scot. pianist, organist and comp. Studied in London, returned to Scot. and became organist at Dundee and then at Glasgow, and was mus. director to the Carnegie Trust at Dunfermline, 1903–27. Ed. of a *Collection of Scot. Songs*.

Works incl. cantata *The Abbot's Bell*, ballad for chorus and orch. *Sir Patrick Spens*; symph., sinfonietta, *Hebridean Rhapsodie* and *Coronach*; fantasy pf. 5tet; vln. and pf. sonata, etc.

Stephens, Catherine (b. London, 18. IX. 1794; d. London, 22. II. 1882), Eng. soprano. 1st appeared in It. opera in 1812, in London, and at Covent Garden in 1813.

Stephens, James (1882–1950), Ir. novelist and poet. *See* Barber (choruses), Busch (W.), (songs).

Sterkel, Johann Franz Xaver (b. Würzburg, 3. XII. 1750; d. Würzburg, 21. X. 1817), Ger. priest, pianist and comp. Educ. at Würzburg Univ., he was ordained priest in 1774, and in 1778 became chaplain and musician at the court in Mainz. After a visit to It. in 1782, where he met Padre Martini, he returned to Mainz, becoming mus. director to the court in 1793. Lived in Regensburg 1802–10, then in Aschaffenburg, and finally retired to Würzburg in 1815.

Works incl. opera *Farnace*; 10 symphs., 2 overtures for orch.; 6 pf. concertos; string 5tet, pf. 4tet, 6 string trios; sonatas for pf. solo and duet, pf. pieces, variations, etc.; Ger. songs, It. canzonets; vocal duets, etc.

Sterling, Antoinette (b. Sterlingville, N.Y., 23. I. 1850; d. London, 9. I. 1904), Amer. contralto. Studied in N.Y. and made her 1st appearance in Eng. in 1868. After a visit to Ger. and further studies with Pauline Viardot-García and Manuel García, she sang in U.S.A. and London, where she settled and married John MacKinlay. Mother of the folksong singer Jean Sterling MacKinlay and the baritone Sterling MacKinlay.

Stern, Isaac (b. Kemenetz, 21. VII. 1920), Amer. violinist of Rus. origin. Brought to San Francisco as a child, he received his first mus. training at home, later studying the vln. with N. Blinder and L. Persinger and making his début in San Francisco, aged 11. He has toured widely and is one of the most musical and successful of modern virtuosi.

Stern, Julius (b. Breslau, 8. VIII. 1820; d. Berlin, 27. II. 1883), Ger. cond. and educationist. Studied in Berlin, Dresden and Paris, and after a career as choral cond. opened a Cons. in Berlin with Kullak and Marx, who later withdrew from it.

Stern, Leo(pold Lawrence) (b. Brighton, 5. IV. 1862; d. London, 10. IX. 1904), Eng. cellist. After beginning a career as chemist, he studied at the R.A.M. in London and with J. Klengel and Davidov at Leipzig, making his 1st appearance in London in 1886.

Sterndale Bennett. *See* **Bennett, William Sterndale.**

Stesso tempo, Lo (It., more frequently *l'istesso tempo* = the same pace), a direction given where a change is indicated in the time-signature, but the comp. wishes the mus. to continue at the same pace or beat.

Steuermann, Eduard (b. Sambor nr. Lwów, 18. VI. 1892; d. N.Y., 11. XI. 1964), Pol. pianist. Studied pf. with Busoni and comp. with Schönberg (1911–14). Later taught at the Paderewski School in Lwów and from 1932 to 1936 at the Jewish Cons. in Cracow. In 1937 he settled in the U.S.A. He ded. himself to the cause of modern mus., esp. that of Schönberg, from whose orchestral works he made pf. scores.

Stevens, Bernard (b. London, 2. III. 1916), Eng. comp. Studied at Cambridge

with E. J. Dent and Rootham and at the R.C.M. in London with R. O. Morris. He gained the Leverhulme Scholarship and Parry Prize for comp. In 1940–6 he served in the army. App. prof. of comp. at the R.C.M., 1948.

Works incl. film mus.; cantata *The Harvest of Peace* and other choral works; symph., *Symph. of Liberation* and Fugal Overture for orch., *Ricercar* and *Sinfonietta* for strings, overture *East and West* for wind band; vln. concerto, cello concerto; string 4tet, pf. trio, theme and variations for string 4tet, *Fantasia* for 2 vlns. and pf.; vln. and pf. sonata; pf. mus.; songs, etc.

Stevens, Denis (William) (b. High Wycombe, 2. III. 1922), Eng. musicologist. He studied at Oxford in 1940–2 and 1946–1949, and after playing in orchs. was a member of the B.B.C. mus. dept. in London from 1950–4. He has ed. the Mulliner Book in *Musica Britannica* and other works and pub. books on Tomkins and Tudor church mus. He is now a prof. at Columbia Univ., N.Y.

Stevens, Richard (John Samuel) (b. London, 27. III. 1757; d. London, 23. IX. 1837), Eng. organist and comp. Learnt mus. as a choir-boy at St. Paul's Cathedral and became organist of the Temple Church in 1786, also at the Charterhouse in 1796, and was app. Gresham Prof. of Mus. in 1801.

Works incl. harpsichord sonatas; glees; songs, etc.

Stevens, Risë (b. N.Y., 11. VI. 1913), Amer. mezzo-soprano. Studied in N.Y. at the Juilliard School of Mus., and with Gutheil-Schoder in Vienna, making her début in Prague in 1936. Since 1938 she has sung at the N.Y. Metropolitan and also in Europe. Among her most distinguished roles is that of Carmen.

Stevenson, John (Andrew) (b. Dublin, XI. 1761; d. Kells, Co. Meath, 14. IX. 1833), Ir. organist and comp. Learnt mus. as a chorister at Christ Church and St. Patrick's Cathedrals at Dublin and later became vicar-choral at both. In 1814 he was app. organist and mus. director at the Castle Chapel. Knighted in 1803.

Works incl. operas *The Contract* (with Cogan) and *Love in a Blaze*; mus. for O'Keeffe's farces *The Son-in-Law, The Dead Alive* and *The Agreeable Surprise*, mus. for other stage pieces; oratorio *Thanksgiving*; services and anthems; glees, canzonets and duets; songs; accomps. for Ir. songs ed. with words by Thomas Moore, etc.

Stevenson, Robert (b. ?; d. ? Chester, ?), Eng. 16th-cent. comp. Took the B.Mus. and D.Mus. degrees at Oxford in 1587 and 1596 and was organist at Chester Cathedral, 1570–99.

Works incl. services, anthems, Miserere for 6 voices, etc.

Stevenson, Robert Louis (1850–94), Scot. poet, novelist and essayist. *See* **Gilbert (H. F.)** (*Pirate Song*), **Hill (E. B.)** (suites), **Hughes (G.)** (songs), **Miles** (*Markheim*), **Stanford** (*Child's Garland*), **Vaughan Williams** (*Songs of Travel*).

Stewart, Robert (Prescott) (b. Dublin, 16. XII. 1825; d. Dublin, 24. III. 1894), Ir. organist and comp. Learnt mus. as a chorister at Christ Church Cathedral, Dublin, and became organist there and at Trinity Coll. in 1844; also cond. of the choral society at Dublin Univ. in 1846, where he became prof. of mus. in 1861. Knighted in 1872. Ed. the Ir. *Church Hymnal* in 1876.

Works incl. Fantasy on Ir. Airs for chorus, org. and orch., cantata *A Winter Night's Wake* and *The Eve of St. John*, *Ode on Shakespeare* and Ode for Cork Exhibition; org. works; glees, etc.

Stiastný, Jan (b. Prague, 1764; d. Mannheim, *c.* 1820), Cz. cellist and comp. Studied at Prague, together with his brother, Bernard Wenzel S. (1760–1835), also a cellist, later lived by turns at Frankfurt, Nuremberg and Mannheim, and became known both in London and Paris.

Works incl. concertino and Andante for cello with fl. and strings; trio for cello with vla. and 2nd cello; duets for 2 cellos; cello pieces and studies, etc.

Sticcado-Pastrole, a glass dulcimer popular in Eng. in the 18th cent.

Stich, Johann Wenzel (called Punto) (b. Žehušice nr. Časlav, 28. X. 1746; d. Prague, 16. II. 1803), Boh. horn player and comp. Studied in Prague, Munich and Dresden, held posts in var. court orchs., and made a great reputation as a travelling virtuoso under the name of Punto. Beethoven's horn sonata, Op. 17, was written for him.

Sticheron. *See* **Byzantine Chant.**

Stich-Randall, Teresa (b. W. Hartford, Conn., 24. XII. 1927), Amer. soprano. Studied at Hartford School of Mus., making her début aged 15. In 1951 she won a singing competition at Lausanne and in 1952 joined the Vienna State Opera. She is esp. well known as a Mozart singer.

Stiedry, Fritz (b. Vienna, 11. X. 1883; d. Zürich, VIII. 1968), Aus. cond. Studied law at Vienna Univ. and mus. theory at the Vienna Cons. From 1907 to 1908 he was asst. to E. von Schuch in Dresden and from 1914 to 1923 was principal cond. at the Berlin State Opera. From 1923 to 1925 he cond. in Vienna at the Volksoper and from 1928 to 1933 at the Berlin Städtische Oper. Forced to leave Germany by the Nazis, he cond. in Leningrad from 1933 to 1937 and in 1938 settled in the

U.S.A., from 1946 to 1958 cond. at the N.Y. Metropolitan. He was esp. distinguished as a Wagner cond., and also in modern mus.

Stiehl, Heinrich (Franz Daniel) (b. Lübeck, 5. VIII. 1829; d. Reval, 1. V. 1886), Ger. organist, cond. and comp. Studied with his father, Johann Dietrich S. (1800–72), organist at Lübeck, and at Weimar and Leipzig. He lived by turns in Rus., Aus., It., Eng., Ir., and Eng. and Rus. again, working as organist, cond. and teacher. His brother Karl Johann Christian S. (1826–1911) was an organist and cond.

Works incl. operas *Der Schatzgräber* and *Jery und Bätely* (Goethe); *The Vision* and other orchestral pieces; string 4tets, 3 pf. trios; cello and pf. sonata; *Sonata quasi fantasia* and other pf. works, etc.

Stierhorn (Ger. = bull horn), a primitive wind instrument, made of a bull or cow horn, sounding a single note of rough quality. Wagner used it for the watchman in *The Mastersingers*.

Stiffelio, opera by Verdi (lib. by Francesco Maria Piave), prod. Trieste, 16. XI. 1850.

Stile rappresentativo (It. = representative style), a term used by It. musicians of the new monodic school in the early years of the 17th cent. to describe the new vocal style of declamatory, recitative-like dramatic mus. which tried to imitate human speech as closely as possible and thus endeavoured to 'represent' dramatic action in a naturalistic way.

Still, William Grant (b. Woodville, Miss., 11. V. 1895), Amer. Negro comp. Educ. at Wilberforce Univ. and studied mus. at Oberlin Cons., later with Chadwick at Boston and with Varèse.

Works incl. opera *Blue Steel*; ballets *La Guiablesse* and *Sahdji*; *Lenox Avenue* for radio announcer, chorus and orch.; 4 symphs., incl. *Afro-Amer. Symph.*, *Africa, Poem, Phantom Chapel* for strings and other orchestral works; *Kaintuck* for pf. and orch.; *From the Black Belt* and *Log Cabin Ballads* for chamber orch., etc.

Stimme (Ger. = voice and part), not only the human voice, but also any part, vocal or instrumental, in a comp., esp. a polyphonic one; also the copy of an orchestral, vocal or chamber mus. part used for perf.

Stimmführung (Ger.) = part-writing.

Sting, an old term describing the effect of Vibrato in lute playing.

Stirling, Elizabeth (b. Greenwich, 26. II. 1819; d. London, 25. III. 1895), Eng. organist and comp. Studied with Macfarren and others and in 1839, having given very successful org. recitals, she was app. organist at All Saints' Church, Poplar, later going to St. Andrew's Undershaft,

1858–80. She married the organist Frederick Albert Bridge in 1863.
Works incl. Psalm for 5 voices and orch.; org. fugues and other pieces; songs, duets, part-songs, etc.

Stivori, Francesco (b. ?; d. ?), It. 16th–17th-cent. organist and comp. Pupil of Merulo. He became town organist at Montagnana in 1579 and was later in the service of the Archduke Ferdinand of Aus. until 1605.
Works incl. Masses, Magnificat, *Sacrae cantiones*; madrigals; instrumental *ricercari*, etc.

Stobaeus, Johann (b. Graudenz, W. Prus., 6. VII. 1580; d. Königsberg, 11. IX. 1646), Ger. bass and comp. While attending the Univ. at Königsberg, he studied mus. with Eccard, and after holding various minor appts. there became *Kapellmeister* to the Elector of Brandenburg in 1626.
Works incl. *Cantiones sacrae* for 5–10 voices, Magnificats for 5–6 voices, 5-part settings of hymn-tunes, Prus. Festival Songs for 5–8 voices (with Eccard); sacred and secular occasional comps., etc.

Stock-and-Horn, a primitive Scot. instrument, similar to the Pibgorn, made of wood or bone fitted with a cow horn. It was played like the chanter of a bagpipe, with a single reed. A different instrument from the Stockhorn, which was a forester's horn.

Stock, Frederick (Friedrich August) (b. Jülich, 11. XI. 1872; d. Chicago, 20. X. 1942), Ger.-Amer. violinist, cond. and comp. Studied with his father, a bandmaster, and at the Cologne Cons., later with Humperdinck, Jensen and Wüllner. He joined the Cologne orch. as a violinist in 1890, but settled at Chicago in 1895 in the same capacity, becoming asst. cond. to Theodore Thomas and succeeding him as cond. in 1905.
Works incl. *Psalmic Rhapsody* for solo voice, chorus and orch.; 2 symphs., symph. poem *Life*, variations, *Symph. Sketches* and 3 overtures for orch.; vln. concerto; chamber mus.; vln. pieces; pf. pieces; songs, etc.

Stockflöte (Ger. = stick fl.). *See* Czakan.

Stockhausen, Julius (b. Paris, 22. VII. 1826; d. Frankfurt, 22. IX. 1906), Ger. baritone. Pupil of his mother and later of Manuel García in Paris for singing and Hallé and Stamaty for pf. He made his 1st important concert appearance at Basle in 1848, visited Eng. the next year and then divided his attention between Fr. opera and Ger. song. From 1862–9 he was director of the Phil. Concerts in Hamburg. In 1869 he became chamber singer to the King of Württemberg, but left Stuttgart in 1874, teaching by turns at Berlin and Frankfurt.

Stockhausen, Karlheinz (b. Mödrath nr. Cologne, 22. VIII. 1928), Ger. comp. He studied at the Cologne Musikhochschule and in Paris with Messiaen and Milhaud. Since 1953 he has worked intensively at the studio for electronic mus. of the W. Ger. Radio at Cologne. He is one of the most enterprising of the comps. creating electronic mus. but has also written mus. for traditional media.
Works incl. *Carré* for 4 orchs. and 4 choruses, *Momente I and II* for soprano, 4 choral groups and 13 players, *Mikrophonie II* for chorus, Hammond org. and ring modulators; *Gruppen* for 3 orchs., *Mixtur* for 5 orchestral groups, ring modulators and loudspeakers; *Kreuzspiel* for ob., bass clar., pf. and perc., *Zeitmasse* for 5 woodwind instruments; *Kontra-Punkte* for 10 instruments; *Zyklus* for perc.; *Mikrophonie I* for gong, 2 microphones, 2 filters and potentiometers; *Gesang der Jünglinge* for treble and electronic mus.; *Elektronische Studien*; *Kontakte* for electronic sounds, pf. and perc.; *Plus/minus* 2×7 pages for elaboration; *Originale* (mus. theatre); *Klavierstücke*, etc.

Stockhausen (*née* Schmuck), **Margarete** (b. Gebweiler, 1803; d. Colmar, 6. X. 1877), Ger. soprano, mother of Julius S. and wife of the harpist and comp. Franz S. (1792–1868). Studied with Catrufo in Paris and 1st toured with her husband in 1825.

Stockhorn. *See* Stock-and-Horn.

Stockmarr, Johanne (b. Copenhagen, 21. IV. 1869; d. Copenhagen, 2. II. 1944), Dan. pianist. Studied in Copenhagen and Paris; app. court pianist to the King of Den.

Stodart, a firm of Eng. 18th–19th-cent. harpsichord and pf. makers, founded *c.* 1776 by Robert S., carried on by his son William S., whose workman William Allen invented the metal frame for the pf., and later by his grandson Malcolm S.

Stoessel, Albert (Frederic) (b. St. Louis, 11. X. 1894; d. N.Y., 12. V. 1943), Amer. violinist, cond. and comp. Studied at home and later at the Hochschule für Musik in Berlin. On his return to Amer. he appeared as solo violinist, served as a bandmaster during the 1914–18 war and in 1922 succeeded W. Damrosch as cond. of the Oratorio Society of N.Y. and director of mus. at the Chautauqua Institution. In 1930 he became director of the opera and orch. at the Juilliard Graduate School there.
Works incl. opera *Garrick*; *Hispania* and *Early Americana* suites, *Suite antique*, symph. portrait *Cyrano de Bergerac* (after Rostand), Concerto grosso, etc. for orch.; *Suite antique* arr. for 2 vlns. and pf.; vln. and pf. sonata and pieces, etc.

Stoelzel. *See* Stölzel.

Stojowski, Zygmunt (Denis Antoni) (b. Strzelce, 14. V. 1869; d. N.Y., 5. XI. 1946), Pol. pianist and comp. Studied with Żeleński at Cracow, then with Diémer, Dubois, Delibes and Massenet in Paris, and finally, on his return, with Gorski and Paderewski. After touring Eur. as a pianist he settled in N.Y. in 1905 and became head of the pf. dept. at the Inst. of Mus. Art in 1911.

Works incl. *A Prayer for Poland* for chorus, org. and orch., cantata; symph. in D min.; pf. concertos, *Symph. Rhapsody* for pf. and orch., Concerto and Romanza for vln. and orch., cello concerto; chamber mus.; instrumental sonatas; pf. pieces; songs, etc.

Stokem, Johannes (also Stokhem, etc.) (b. c. 1440; d. c. 1500), Flem. comp. He was prob. born and spent his early life nr. Liège. He was in the service of Beatrice of Hung. in the early 1480s and a singer in the Papal Choir, 1487–9. He was a friend of Tinctoris, who sent him portions of his 12th treatise (all that survives) with a letter. A few sacred and secular works survive, incl. 4 *chansons* printed in Petrucci's *Odhecaton A* (1501).

Stokowski, Leopold (Antonin Stanisław Bolesławowicz) (b. London, 18. IV. 1882), Amer. cond., the son of a Pol. father and an Irish mother. Studied at the R.C.M. and took the B.Mus. at Oxford. In 1900 he became organist at St. James's Church, Piccadilly, and later studied in Paris and Munich. From 1905 to 1908 he was organist in N.Y., and in 1908 cond. in London, in 1909 becoming cond. of the Cincinnati Symph. Orch., and of the Philadelphia Symph. Orch. in 1912, where he intro. much modern mus. In 1931 he gave the Amer. *première* of Berg's *Wozzeck* and from 1942 to 1943 cond. the N.B.C. Symph. Orch. with Toscanini. In 1945 he became mus. director of the Hollywood Bowl and in 1949–50 of the N.Y. Phil. Orch., taking over the Houston Symph. Orch. in 1955. He has been thrice married, acted in films, made many arrs. of mus. and is one of the most colourful and gifted executants of the cent.

Stollen (Ger. = props). The songs of the Ger. Minnesinger and Meistersinger were usually divided into 3 sections: 2 S. of equal length often sung to the same and always to very similar mus. and an *Abgesang* (after-song) forming a concluding section of unspecified length and with different though relevant mus. The 2 S. together were called the *Aufgesang* (fore-song). The whole form was called a *Bar*.

Stoltz, Rosine (actually Victorine Noeb) (b. Paris, 13. II. 1815; d. Paris, 28. VII. 1903), Fr. mezzo-soprano. Studied at Choron's school, became a chorus singer after the 1830 Revolution, made a 1st appearance as a soloist at Brussels in 1832 and from 1837 to 1847 sang at the Paris Opéra.

Stoltzer, Thomas (b. Schweidnitz, Silesia, c. 1486; d. Ofen, 1526), Ger. comp. Became *Kapellmeister* to King Louis of Boh. and Hung. at Buda, but left after the battle of Mohács in 1526 (if he was not killed in it) and (?) took up a post in the service of Duke Albert of Prus. at Königsberg.

Works incl. Lat. motets and psalms, Lat. hymns for 4–5 voices, Psalm xxxvii in Luther's Ger. trans. for 3–7 voices in motet form and 4 others; Ger. sacred and secular songs, etc.

Stolz (orig. Stolzová), **Teres(in)a** (b. Kostelec nad Labem, 2. VI. 1834; d. Milan, 22–3. VIII. 1902), Boh.-It. soprano. Studied under Lamperti at Milan and made her 1st stage appearance in 1860. She was Verdi's 1st Aida at Milan and the soprano in the 1st perf. of his Requiem.

Stolze, Gerhard (b. Dessau, 1. X. 1926), Ger. tenor. Studied in Dresden and made his début there in 1949. Since 1951 he has sung at Bayreuth and since 1957 at the Vienna State Opera. He is a highly dramatic character singer, specializing in more modern roles.

Stölzel, Gottfried Heinrich (b. Grünstädtel, Saxony, 13. I. 1690; d. Gotha, 27. XI. 1749), Ger. comp. Studied at Leipzig Univ., taught in Breslau 1710–12, and visited It. 1713–14, meeting Gasparini, Vivaldi and others. Lived in Prague, Bayreuth and Gera, and from 1719 was *Kapellmeister* to the court at Gotha.

Works incl. 22 operas, e.g. *Narcissus, Orion, Venus und Adonis*, etc.; oratorios; Masses, motets, etc.; Passions; *concerti grossi*; trio sonatas, etc.

Stonard, William (b. ?; d. Oxford, 1630), Eng. organist and comp. In 1608 he took a degree at Oxford and became organist of Christ Church Cathedral there, retaining the post until his death.

Works incl. services, anthems; catch 'Ding dong bell', etc.

Stone Guest, The (*Kamennyi Gost*), opera by Dargomizhsky (lib. Pushkin's drama, set unaltered), not perf. in the comp.'s lifetime; prod. St. Petersburg, 28. II. 1872.

Stone, Robert (b. Alphington, Devon, 1516; d. London, 2. VII. 1613), Eng. comp. He learnt mus. as a chorister at Exeter Cathedral, but c. 1543 went to London to enter the Chapel Royal, of which he became a Gentleman. Comp. a setting of the Lord's Prayer, part of his Morning Service.

Stonerd or **Stonnard, William.** *See* **Stonard.**

Stonings (Stoninge), Henry (b. ?; d. ?), Eng. comp. of the 2nd half of the 16th cent. Wrote (?) a Lat. Magnificat; also *In nomines* and other works for strings. His first name is known only from a statement by Hawkins, and it is possible that the Magnificat, at least, may be by Oliver Stonyng (*q.v.*).

Stonyng, Oliver (b. ?; d. ?), Eng. 16th-cent. comp. He was a fellow of Eton Coll., 1530–47, and precentor, 1533–5. He comp. (?) a Lat. Magnificat (Brit. Mus. Add. MSS. 17802–5).

Stopped. Org. pipes the upper end of which is closed are said to be S. pipes. They prod. notes similar in pitch to those of Open pipes of twice their length.

Stopped Diapason. *See* **Diapason.**

Stopped Notes, on wind instruments the N.s not prod. naturally as harmonics, but by valves, keys or other mechanical means, or sometimes by the hand in horn playing. On string instruments any N.s not prod. on open strings.

Stopping, the placing of the left-hand fingers on the strings of string instruments to change the pitch of the notes of the open strings. The playing of 2 notes in this way simultaneously is called Double S., but the term is also used loosely for playing of chords with more than 2 notes. S. is also a device in horn playing: the placing of the hand in the bell to prod. a special quality of sound and formerly, before the invention of the valves, to change the pitch of some notes.

Stops, the devices by which the registration of the org. can be regulated and altered. *See* **Organ Stops** for ref. to their names to be found under separate headings. The larger kinds of harpsichords also had S.s prod. different qualities of tone and different pitches.

Storace, Ann Selina (Nancy) (b. London, 27. X. 1765; d. London, 24. VIII. 1817), Eng. soprano. Pupil of Rauzzini in London and of Sacchini in It., sang leading roles in Florence, Milan and Venice, and in 1784 was engaged as *prima donna* at the Vienna opera, where she was the first Susanna in Mozart's *Nozze di Figaro* (1786). She returned to London in 1787.

Storace, Stephen (b. London, 4. IV. 1762; d. London, 19. III. 1796), Eng. comp., brother of prec. Studied at the Cons. di S. Onfrio in Naples, in c. 1784 went to Vienna, where he prod. 2 operas and became friendly with Mozart, and returned to London with his sister in 1787, becoming comp. to Sheridan's co. at the Drury Lane Theatre.

Works incl. operas *Gli sposi malcontenti*, *Gli equivoci* (after Shakespeare's *Comedy of Errors*), *La cameriera astuta, The Haunted Tower, No Song, No Supper, The Siege of Belgrade, The Pirates, Dido:*

Queen of Carthage, The Cherokee, The Iron Chest (Colman), *Mahmoud, or The Prince of Persia* (unfinished, completed by Kelly and Ann S.) and others; ballet *Venus and Adonis,* etc.

Storm, Theodor (1817–88), Ger. poet and novelist. *See* **Vrieslander** (songs).

Stornello (It., prob. corrupt. of *Ritornello*, which is also used in the same sense), an old It. form of popular song set to verses of 3 lines, the 1st and 3rd of which rhyme, as in *terza rima.*

Strada, Anna Maria (also known by her married name of S. del Pò) (b. ?; d. ?), It. soprano. Brought to London by Handel in 1729, she sang in several of his operas, remaining in Eng. till 1738.

Stradal, August (b. Teplice, 17. V. 1860; d. Schönlinde, 13. III. 1930), Sudeten-Ger. pianist. Studied pf. with Anton Door and Leschetizky and theory with Nottebohm and Bruckner in Vienna. In 1884 he took a finishing course with Liszt and in 1893 he joined the staff of Horak's Cons. in Vienna, later touring extensively. He made c. 250 arrs. of important classical works.

Stradella (Flotow). *See* **Alessandro Stradella.**

Stradella, Alessandro (b. Rome, 1. X. 1644; d. Genoa, 25. II. 1682), It. singer, violinist and comp. Of noble birth, he never held any official posts, and most of what is known of his career seems to be based on legend rather than fact. He prod. operas and oratorios in Rome, Modena and Genoa. He (?) entered the service of the Duchess of Savoy and regent of Piedmont, Marie de Nemours, at Turin. He had numerous love affairs, the last of which led to his assassination.

Works incl. operas *La forza dell' amor paterno, Doriclea, Il trespolo tutore balordo, Il Floridoro*; motets and other church mus.; oratorio *San Giovanni Battista* and others; sacred and secular cantatas; serenade *Qual prodigio che io miri* and others; madrigals; concerto for strings, etc.

Stradivari (Latinized Stradivarius), It. family of vln. makers:

1. Antonio S. (b. ?, ? 1644; d. Cremona, 18. XII. 1737), founder of the workshop at Cremona in the 1660s, after (?) serving an apprenticeship to Nicolo Amati.

2. Francesco S. (b. Cremona, 1. II. 1671; d. Cremona, 11. V. 1743), son of prec. He carried on his father's craft with

3. Omobono S. (b Cremona, 14. XI. 1679; d. Cremona, 8. VI. 1742), brother of prec.

Straeten, Edmond van der (b. Oudenarde, 3. XII. 1826; d. Oudenarde, 25. XI. 1895), Belg. musicologist. Studied law at Alost and Ghent, but on returning home cultivated mus. hist. He became sec. to

Fétis for the purpose of studying with him and contrib. to his Dictionary. He also acted as critic and wrote books on Flem. mus., incl. *La Musique aux Pays-bas* in 8 vols. He also comp. incid. mus. and a Te Deum.

Straeten, Edmund (Sebastian Joseph) van der (b. Düsseldorf, 29. IV. 1855; d. London, 17. IX. 1934), Ger. cellist and writer on mus. He settled in London in 1881 and wrote and lectured much on old string instruments. His works incl. a *History of the Violoncello.*

Strambotto (It.), a form of verse used by the comps. of *frottole* in the 15th–16th cents. It had 8 lines (*ottava rima*), the 1st 6 rhyming alternately and the last 2 consecutively.

Strangways, A. H. Fox. *See* Fox Strangways.

Straniera, La (*The Stranger*), opera by Bellini (lib. by Felice Romani), prod. Milan, Teatro alla Scala, 14. II. 1829.

Stransky, Josef (b. Hupoleč, 9. IX. 1872; d. N.Y., 6. III. 1936), Cz. cond. and comp. Studied medicine at 1st, but turned to mus., studying under Fibich and Dvořák in Prague and Fuchs and Bruckner in Vienna. He became cond. of the Ger. Opera in Prague, then of the Hamburg Opera, 1909, and in 1911–22 cond. the N.Y. Phil. Society, following Mahler.

Works incl. opera *Beatrice and Benedick* (after Shakespeare's *Much Ado*), operetta *The General*; symphs.; chamber mus.; songs, etc.

Strascinando (It.), dragging, slurring.

Strathspey, a Scot. folk dance in quick common time, similar to the Reel, but with dotted rhythms. The name derives from the strath (valley) of Spey and is 1st heard of in 1780, though dances of the kind are much older.

Straube, (Montgomery Rufus) Karl (Siegfried) (b. Berlin, 6. I. 1873; d. Leipzig, 27. IV. 1950), Ger. organist and cond., son of a Ger. father and an Eng. mother. Studied with his father, an organist and harmonium maker, and with Heinrich Reimann among others. He was app. organist of Wesel Cathedral in 1897 and of St. Thomas's, Leipzig, in 1902. There he became cond. of the Bach Society in 1903, prof. of org. at the Cons. in 1907, and cantor of St. Thomas's in 1918. He travelled all over Eur. with the choir of St. Thomas's. He pub. many eds. of org. and choral mus. of the past. He was made an hon. Ph.D. of Leipzig Univ. in 1923.

Straus, Ludwig (b. Pressburg, 28. III. 1835; d. Cambridge, 23. X. 1899), Aus. violinist. Studied at the Vienna Cons. and made his 1st appearance there in 1850. In 1855 he made a tour incl. It. and in 1857 another in Ger. and Swed., with Piatti. In 1860 he 1st visited Eng. and in 1864

settled in Manchester as leader of the Hallé Orch., and in 1888 in London.

Straus, Oscar (b. Vienna, 6. III. 1870; d. Ischl, 11. I. 1954), Aus. cond. and comp. Studied with Graedener and Bruch in Berlin and became theatre cond. at var. towns. He then settled in Berlin and in 1927 in Vienna and subsequently in Paris. In 1940 he emigrated to the U.S.A., returning to Europe in 1948.

Works incl. operas *Die Waise von Cordova* and *Das Tal der Liebe*; operettas *Ein Walzertraum* (*A Waltz Dream*), *Der tapfere Soldat* (*The Chocolate Soldier*, after Shaw's *Arms and the Man*), *Love and Laughter*, *The Last Waltz*, *Riquette* and others; overture to Grillparzer's *Der Traum ein Leben*, serenade for string orch., etc.

Strauss. Aus. family of musicians:

1. Johann (Baptist) S. (b. Vienna, 14. III. 1804; d. Vienna, 25. IX. 1849), violinist, cond. and comp. His parents were innkeepers and apprenticed him to a bookbinder, but he learnt the vln. and vla. and was eventually allowed to study with Seyfried. He played vla. in private string 4tets, at 15 managed to join Pamer's orch. at the Sperl, a place of entertainment, mus. and dancing, then Lanner's band, in which he became deputy cond. In 1825 he and Lanner parted and he began a rival band, for which he comp. dances, esp. waltzes, which had by that time become fashionable. He was invited to return to the Sperl, which had enlarged the orch., and in 1833 began travelling abroad with a visit to Pest. By 1837 he had been to Ger., Hol., Belg., Fr., Eng. and Scot. He added the quadrille to the mus. of the Viennese ballrooms, having picked it up in Paris, and made a great hit with the *Radetzky Marsch*. He toured again and was then made cond. of the court balls.

Works incl. 150 waltzes (*Täuberl, Kettenbrücken, Donaulieder Walzer*, etc.), 35 quadrilles, 28 galops, 19 marches, 14 polkas, etc.

2. Johann S. (b. Vienna, 25. X. 1825; d. Vienna, 3. VI. 1899), violinist, cond. and comp., son of prec. He was not allowed to follow his father's profession, but learnt the vln. and studied secretly with Drechsler and others. In 1844 he appeared as cond. at Dommayer's hall in the Hietzing suburb, and his father capitulated. After the latter's death he amalgamated his orch. with his own, toured in Aus., Pol. and Ger. and in 1855–65 visited St. Petersburg in the summer. In 1863 he became cond. of the court balls.

Works incl. operettas *Indigo und die vierzig Räuber, Der Karneval in Rom, Die Fledermaus, Cagliostro in Wien, Prinz Methusalem, Blindekuh, Das Spitzentuch der Königin, Der lustige Krieg, Eine Nacht in Venedig, Der Zigeunerbaron, Simplizius, Ritter Pázmán, Fürstin Ninetta, Jabuka, Waldmeister, Die Göttin der Vernunft*; ballet *Aschenbrödel; Traumbilder* for orch.; a large number of waltzes (*An der schönen blauen Donau, Tausend und eine Nacht, Wiener Blut, Künstlerleben, Man lebt nur einmal, Morgenblätter, Geschichten aus dem Wiener Wald*, etc.), polkas, galops and other dances, etc.

3. Josef S. (b. Vienna, 22. VIII. 1827; d. Vienna, 21. VII. 1870), cond. and comp., brother of prec. He became an architect at his father's wish, but secretly studied mus. and during an illness of 2 cond. his band with success. He then formed his own band and wrote 283 dances for it. He d. after a visit to Warsaw, where he injured his hand in a fall on the platform at his last concert.

4. Eduard S. (b. Vienna, 15. III. 1835; d. Vienna, 28. XII. 1916), cond. and comp., brother of prec. Studied harp and comp. and appeared as cond. in 1862. After 1865 he took 2's place at the summer concerts in St. Petersburg and in 1870 became cond. of the court balls. He toured much, appearing at the Inventions Exhibition in London in 1885. His works incl. over 300 dances.

Strauss, Christoph (b. Vienna, *c*. 1580; d. Vienna, VI. 1631), Aus. organist and comp. He entered the service of the court in 1594 and in 1601 became organist at the church of St. Michael. In 1617–19 he was court cond. and afterwards *Kapellmeister* at St. Stephen's Cathedral.

Works incl. Masses, Requiems, motets for voices and instruments, etc.

Strauss, Richard (Georg) (b. Munich, 11. VI. 1864; d. Garmisch-Partenkirchen, 8. IX. 1949), Ger. comp. and cond. His father, Franz S. (1822–1905), was horn player at the Court Opera in Munich, but had married into the wealthy brewers' family of Pschorr. S. began to comp. at the age of 6 and at 10 wrote his 1st two pub. works, the *Festival March* and the serenade for wind instruments. In 1880 he finished a symph. in D min. and the next year his A maj. string 4tet was perf. in public. He entered Munich Univ. in 1882, but left it in 1883, went to Berlin for a short period of study, but became asst. cond. to Bülow at Meiningen very soon after. A member of the orch., Alexander Ritter, turned his classical leanings into admiration for Berlioz, Wagner and Liszt. In 1885 Bülow resigned and S. became 1st cond. at Meiningen. In spring 1886 he visited It. and afterwards wrote the symph. *Aus Italien*, prod. at Munich in spring 1887, when he became sub-cond. at the Opera there. *Macbeth*, his 1st symph. poem, was comp. that year. In 1889 he became asst. cond. to Lassen at the Weimar Court

Opera and in 1891 Cosima Wagner invited him to cond. *Tannhäuser* at Bayreuth.

Under Wagner's influence he wrote his 1st opera, *Guntram*, most of it during a tour in the Mediterranean undertaken to counteract threatening lung trouble. It was prod. at Weimar on 10. V. 1894. The heroine was sung by Pauline de Ahna, whom he married in June, and he was that year app. cond. of the Berlin Phil. Orch. in succession to Bülow. After the prod. of *Salome* at Dresden in 1905 S. began his series of operas written with Hugo von Hofmannsthal as librettist with *Elektra*, prod. there in 1909, and about that time he bought a country house at Garmisch in the Bavar. highlands, where all his later works were written. After Hofmannsthal's death in 1929 S., who had already written a lib. of his own for *Intermezzo*, prod. at Dresden, 1924, worked with Stefan Zweig on *Die schweigsame Frau* (based on Ben Jonson's *Epicoene*), which was prod. at Dresden in 1935 but quickly withdrawn on a trumped-up excuse because Zweig, as a Jew, had to be boycotted by the Nazi party. Strauss thereupon resigned his appt. as president of the Reichs-Musikkammer and was himself under a cloud for a time, but had long been too important a figure in Ger. mus. life to be ignored.

Works incl. operas *Guntram, Feuersnot, Salome, Elektra, Der Rosenkavalier, Ariadne auf Naxos, Die Frau ohne Schatten, Intermezzo, Die ägyptsiche Helena, Arabella, Die schweigsame Frau, Friedenstag, Daphne, Die Liebe der Danae, Capriccio*; ballets *Josephs-Legende, Schlagobers*; incid. mus. to Molière's *Le Bourgeois Gentilhomme* (orig. connected with *Ariadne auf Naxos*); 2 symphs.: F min. and *Aus Italien*; symph. poems *Macbeth, Don Juan, Tod und Verklärung, Till Eulenspiegels lustige Streiche, Also sprach Zarathustra, Don Quixote, Ein Heldenleben, Symphonia domestica, Eine Alpensinfonie*; other orchestral works: *Festival March*, 2 serenades for wind instruments, 2 military marches, *Festliches Praeludium, Japanische Festmusik*, divertimento on pieces by Couperin; vln. concerto, ob. concerto, 2 horn concertos, *Burleske* for pf. and orch., *Parergon zur Symphonia domestica* for pf. left hand and orch.; string 4tet in A maj., pf. 4tet in C min., 2 sonatinas for wind instruments, *Metamorphosen* for 23 solo string instruments; sonatas for vln. and pf. and cello and pf.; 11 songs with orch. incl. 3 Hymns by Hölderlin; 26 op. nos. of songs (*c*. 150) incl. cycles *Schlichte Weisen* (Felix Dahn), *Mädchenblumen, Krämerspiegel* and 6 songs by Shakespeare and Goethe; pf. sonata, 9 pf. pieces; Tennyson's *Enoch Arden* and Uhland's *Das Schloss am Meer* for recitation and pf.

Stravaganza (It. = extravagance), a word sometimes used for a comp. of a freakish nature.

Stravinsky, Igor (Feodorovich) (b. Oranienbaum nr. St. Petersburg, 17. VI. 1882; d. New York, 6. IV. 1971), Rus. comp. His father was a bass at the Imp. Opera. In 1903 S. met Rimsky-Korsakov at Heidelberg and played him his early comps., but did not become his pupil until 1907, by which time he had finished a pf. sonata, begun a symph. and married his 2nd cousin, Nadezhda Sulima, 11. I. 1906. In 1908 he had the symph. perf. and wrote *Fireworks* for orch. for the marriage of Nadia Rimsky-Korsakov and M. Steinberg, and a *Funeral Chant* on Rimsky-Korsakov's death. The perf. of the *Fantastic Scherzo* in 1909 drew Diaghilev's attention to S., who was commissioned to write *The Fire-Bird* for the Rus. Ballet. It was prod. in Paris in 1910, and S. began to become known in western Eur. *Petrushka* followed in 1911 and *The Rite of Spring* in 1913, both prod. in Paris, where the latter provoked a riot of protest and fanatical partisanship. In 1914 S. went to Rus. for the last time; he never returned after the 1914–18 war and the Revolution. He settled in Switz., on the Lake of Geneva. From 1914 he became as well known in London as in Paris, and in 1925 he 1st made a tour in U.S.A. In 1934 he became a Fr. citizen, but from 1939 he lived mostly in Amer.

Works incl. operas *The Nightingale* (afterwards a ballet), *Mavra*, *The Rake's Progress* (Auden, after Hogarth); opera-oratorio *Oedipus Rex*; ballets *Fire-Bird*, *Petrushka*, *The Rite of Spring*, *The Fox*, *The Bees*, *The Wedding*, *Pulcinella*, *Apollo Musagetes*, *The Fairy's Kiss*, *Card-Party*, *Orpheus*; play with mus. *The Soldier's Tale*; melodrama *Persephone*; *The Flood*; Mass, cantata *Babel*; symph. in Eb maj., symph. in C maj., symph. in 3 movements, *Fantastic Scherzo*, *Fireworks*, *Symphonies for Wind Instruments*, *4 Études*, *Scènes de ballet*, *Ode*; *4 Norw. Moods*; 2 suites for small orch., *Ragtime* and *Danses concertantes* for chamber orch., *Polka* for circus elephants; concerto for 16 instruments (*Dumbarton Oaks*); concerto for pf. and wind instruments, pf. concerto, *Ebony Concerto* for jazz band, *Capriccio* for pf. and orch., *Movements* for pf. and orch., vln. concerto; songs for mezzo-soprano and orch. *Le Faune et la bergère*, cantata for voice and orch. *The King of the Stars*; *Funeral Chant on the Death of Rimsky-Korsakov* for chorus and orch., *Symph. of Psalms* for chorus and orch., *Canticum sacrum*, *Threni*; 3 pieces and concertino for string 4tet, octet for wind instruments, *Duo concertant* for vln. and pf.; 3 pieces for clar. solo, *Elegy* for vla.

solo; 3 poems from the Jap. for soprano and 9 instruments, *Pribaoutki* for voice and 3 instruments, *The Cat's Cradle-Songs* for voice and 3 clars.; 2 sonatas, 4 études, serenade, *Piano Rag-Music* and *The Five Fingers* for pf; 2 sets of easy pieces for pf. duet; concerto and sonata for 2 pfs.; étude for pianola; *The Saucer*, 4 Rus. peasant songs for female voices; 14 songs, etc.

Straw Fiddle. *See* Strohfiedel.

Streich, Rita (b. Barnaul, Rus., 18. XII. 1920), Ger. soprano of Rus.-Ger. parentage. Studied 1st in Augsburg and then with M. Ivogün and Erna Berger in Berlin and later with Domgraf-Fassbänder, making her début in 1943. From 1946 to 1950 she sang at the Berlin State Opera and from 1950 at the Berlin Städtische Oper. In 1953 she joined the Vienna State Opera and made her début in London in 1954. She is best known for her singing of Mozart and R. Strauss coloratura roles.

Streicher (Ger., plur.), strings, as in Eng. for string instruments.

Streicher. Ger. family of pf. makers:
1. **Johann Andreas S.** (b. Stuttgart, 13. XII. 1761; d. Vienna, 25. V. 1833), mus. teacher in Vienna and founder there of a pf. manufacture after 1794, when he married
2. **Maria Anna (Nanette) S.** (*née* Stein) (b. Augsburg, 2. I. 1769; d. Vienna, 16. I. 1833.) *See* Stein, family, 2.
3. **Johann Baptist S.** (b. Vienna, 3. I. 1796; d. Vienna, 28. III. 1871), son of above. He succeeded his parents in business, and from him it descended to his son Emil.

Streicher, Theodor (b. Vienna, 7. VI. 1874; d. Wetzelsdorf nr. Graz, 28. V. 1940), Aus. comp., great-grandson of J. A. and M. A. S. Studied in Vienna, Dresden and Bayreuth.

Works incl. *Mignons Exequien* (after Goethe's *Wilhelm Meister*) for chorus, children's chorus and orch., *Die Schlacht bei Murten* for chorus and orch.; *Kleiner Vogel Kolibri* for chamber orch.; *Um Inez weinten* for soprano and orch.; *Die Monologe des Faust* (after Goethe) for string 6tet; many songs, etc.

Streichinstrumente (Ger.), string instruments.

Streichzither (Ger. lit. stroke-zither), a var. of Zither played with a vln. bow instead of being plucked with the fingers or with a plectrum.

Streit zwischen Phöbus und Pan, Der (*The Dispute between Phoebus and Pan*), secular cantata by Bach, written in 1731 and (?) satirizing Johann Adolf Scheibe, ed. of *Der critische Musikus*, in the part of Midas.

Strepitoso (It. = noisy), a direction suggesting a forceful and spirited perf., but more often used in the sense of a climax growing in force and speed.

Strepponi, Giuseppina (b. Lodi, 8. IX. 1815; d. Busseto, 14. XI. 1897), It. soprano, daughter of the comp. Feliciano S. (1797–1832). Studied at the Milan Cons. and made her 1st appearance in 1835, at Trieste. Verdi's 2nd wife, previously his mistress.

Stretta (It. lit. pressure, tightening, squeezing), a passage, usually at the end of a comp., esp. an operatic finale, in which the tempo is accelerated either gradually or by sections and so makes a climax.

Stretto (It. lit. narrow, tightened, squeezed), a device in fugal writing whereby the entries of the subject are drawn more closely together in time. Instead of following each other voice by voice, each waiting until the last has been fully stated, in S. they are made to overlap, the 2nd coming in before the end of the 1st, and so on, e.g.:

Strinasacchi, Regina (b. Ostiglia nr. Mantua, 1764; d. Dresden, 1839), It. violinist and guitar player. Studied at the Cons. della Pietà in Venice, toured It. 1780–3, and in 1784 visited Vienna, where Mozart wrote for her the vln. sonata in B♭ maj., K. 454. She married the cellist J. C. Schlick in 1785.

Strindberg, August (1849–1912), Swed. novelist and dramatist. *See* **Foerster (J. B.)** (*Journey of Fortunate Peter*), **Rangström** (*Kronbruden* and *Til Damaskus*), **Rezniček** (*Dream Play*), **Röntgen (J.)** (*Samûm*), **Sibelius** (*Svanevit*), **Stenhammar** (*Drömspel*), **Tiessen** (*Advent*), **Vladigerov** (*Dream Play*), **Weismann** (3 operas).

String Quartet, a chamber combination consisting of 2 vlns., vla. and cello.

Stringendo (It. from verb *stringere* = to tighten), a direction indicating that a passage is to be perf. with increasing speed and mounting excitement.

Strings, the cords, usually of gut (vln.

STRETTO   Bach, '48', Bk. I, no. 1.

Stretto maestrale (It. lit. masterly S.), a S. in which the fugal subject not only appears in close, overlapping entries, but is carried through from beginning to end at each entry.

Strict Counterpoint, the traditional name for counterpoint written according to the rules of the Species.

Striggio, Alessandro (b. Mantua, *c.* 1535; d. Mantua, *c.* 1595), It. organist, lutenist, violist and comp. He was in the service of Cosimo de' Medici at Florence, *c.* 1560–70, and subsequently visited several Eur. courts. He returned to Mantua, (?) to the court of Duke Guglielmo Gonzaga.

Works incl. Masses, motet in 40 parts for voices and instruments; madrigal comedy *Il cicalamento delle donne al bucato*; intermezzi for perf. between the acts of plays; madrigals; var. works for voices and instruments in many parts, etc.

Striggio, Alessandro (b. Mantua, 1573; d. Venice, 6. VI. 1630), It. librettist, son of prec. He was secretary to the Duke of Mantua. Author of the text of Monteverdi's *Orfeo*.

family, harps, etc.) or wire (lute, vln. and guitar families, pfs., etc.) by means of which the notes are prod. on such instruments. The term S. is also used to designate string instruments collectively, esp. those of the vln. family in the orch.

Strisciando (It. lit. sliding), smooth, also *glissando*.

Strogers, E. (properly E. Strowger), early 16th-cent. Eng. comp. Wrote a *Miserere* for org. (Brit. Mus. Add. MS. 29996).

Strogers, Nicholas (b. ?; d. ?), Eng. 16th–17th-cent. organist and comp., (?) son of prec.

Works incl. motets, services and other church mus.; madrigals; *In nomines* for strings; org., lute and virginal pieces, etc.

Strohfiedel (Ger. lit. straw fiddle), a 16th-cent. perc. instrument similar to the xylophone.

Stromentato (It. = instrumented, orchestrated, scored). The word is assoc. mainly with recitative (*recitativo stromentato*), where it implies a more or less independent orchestral accomp.

Strong, G(eorge). Templeton (b N.Y., 26. V. 1856; d. Geneva, 27. VI. 1948), Amer. comp. Studied at the Leipzig Cons., became a member of the Liszt circle, was in close touch with MacDowell while living at Wiesbaden in 1886–9, and after teaching at Boston in 1891–2 settled in Switz. on the Lake of Geneva, living 1st at Vévey and later in Geneva.

Works incl. *Knights and Dryads* for solo voices, chorus and orch.; 2 cantatas for solo voices, male chorus and orch.; 3 symphs.: *Sintram* (after Fouqué), *In the Mountains* and *By the Sea*, symph. poem *Undine* (after Fouqué); *2 Amer. Sketches* for vln. and orch.; trio for 2 vlns. and vla. *A Village Music-Director* and other chamber mus., etc.

Strophic Bass, an instrumental bass part used without change throughout a series of verses of a song or chorus the upper parts of which vary at each occurrence; or a similar device in instrumental mus.

Strophic Song, the simplest form of song, structurally considered, in which each verse of a poem is set to the same mus.

Strowger. *See* Strogers.

Strozzi, Barbara (b. Venice, *c.* 1620; d. ?), It. singer and comp. Adopted daughter of the poet Giulio S. Comp. madrigals, cantatas, sacred songs with continuo, duets, ariettas, etc.

Strozzi, Gregorio (b. San Severino, ?; d. ? Naples, *c.* 1690), It. priest, organist and comp. Studied with Sabino in Naples, and succeeded him as organist of the Church of the Madonna there.

Works incl. responsories, Lamentations, psalms, motets, etc.; *Capricci da sonare Cembali et Organi.*

Strungk (or Strunck), Delphin (b. ?, 1601; d. Brunswick, X. 1694), Ger. organist and comp. He was, after 1630, successively organist at Wolfenbüttel, Celle and Brunswick.

Works incl. mus. for the Duke of Brunswick in 5 vocal and 8 instrumental parts; var. vocal works with instruments; chorale preludes and other works for org., etc.

Strungk, Nikolaus Adam (b. Brunswick, XI. 1640; d. Dresden, 23. IX. 1700), Ger. violinist, organist and comp., son of prec. Pupil of his father, for whom he deputized at the org. at Brunswick from the age of 12. While at Helmstadt Univ. he learnt the vln. at Lübeck during vacations. In 1660 he joined the court orch. at Wolfenbüttel, then at Celle, and in 1665 went to the court of Hanover. After a period at Hamburg from 1678, two visits to Vienna and one to It., he returned to Hanover, 1682–6, but in 1688 he went to Dresden as chamber organist and 2nd *Kapellmeister* to the Saxon court in succession to Ritter, and succeeded Bernhard as 1st *Kapellmeister* in 1692. In 1693 he opened an opera-house at Leipzig, where he prod. his later stage works and where his daughters Philippine and Elisabeth sang.

Works incl. operas *Der glückseligsteigende Sejanus, Der unglücklichfallende Sejanus, Esther, Doris, Semiramis, Nero, Agrippina* and others, completion of Pallavicini's *L'Antiope*; oratorio *Die Auferstehung Jesu*; ricercare on the death of his mother; sonatas and chaconnes for vln. or vla. da gamba; sonatas for 2 vlns. and vla. and for 6 strings; airs and dances for recorders, etc.

Strunz, Jacob (b. Pappenheim, 1783; d. Munich, 23. V. 1852), Ger. comp. Pupil of Winter at Munich. He travelled all over Eur. in 1798–1845 and also visited Egypt; then settled at Munich for the rest of his life. He was a friend of Meyerbeer, Berlioz and Balzac, who ded. his story *Massimilla Doni* to him.

Works incl. operas *Le Maître de chapelle* and *Les Courses de Newmarket*; several ballets; incid. mus. (the 1st) for Hugo's *Ruy Blas*; 3 string 4tets; songs, etc.

Stuart, Leslie (actually Thomas Barrett) (b. Southport, 15. III. 1866; d. Richmond, Surrey, 27. III. 1928), Eng. comp.

Works incl. operettas *Florodora, The Silver Slipper, The School Girl, The Belle of Mayfair, Havana, Captain Kidd, The Slim Princess, Peggy*, etc.

Stück (Ger. = piece), a piece of mus.

Stuck, Jean Baptiste (usually called Batistin) (b. Florence, *c.* 1680; d. Paris, 9. XII. 1755), Fr. cellist and comp. of Ger. origin. He went to Fr. at an early age and was the 1st cellist in the Paris Opéra orch., also court musician to the Duke of Orleans.

Works incl. operas *Rodrigo in Algieri* (with Albinoni), *Méléagre, Mantho la fée* and *Polidore*; many court ballets; cantatas, airs, etc.

Stucken, Frank (Valentin) van der (b. Fredericksburg, Texas, 15. X. 1858; d. Hamburg, 18. VIII. 1929), Amer. cond. and comp. of Ger. and Belg. descent. Studied in Eur. with Benoît, Reinecke, Grieg and others. In 1884–95 he cond. a male-voice choir in N.Y., where he also cond. orchestral concerts. In 1895–1903 he was director of the Cincinnati Coll. of Mus. and from the same year to 1907 he cond. the Symph. Orch. there. After 1908 he lived much in Eur.

Works incl. opera *Vlasda*; incid. mus. to Shakespeare's *Tempest*; prologue to Heine's *William Ratcliff*, symph. prologue *Pax triumphans, Louisiana* festival march and other orchestral works; choral works; songs, etc.

Stuckenschmidt, Hans Heinz (b. Strasbourg, 1. XI. 1901), Ger. musicologist.

Studied pf., vln. and comp. in Berlin, and also analysis with Schönberg. He has held many posts as mus. critic and since 1948 has taught at the Technical Univ. in Berlin. He is esp. well known as a writer on 20th-cent. mus., incl. Schönberg and the Viennese School.

Studer, Hans (b. Muri nr. Berne, 20. IV. 1911), Swiss comp. Studied at the Univ. and Cons. of Berne, later became mus. teacher at women's training-colls. at Berne and Thun.

Works incl. oratorio *Die Leiden Hiobs*, cantata (Rilke); suite for string orch.; variations for cello and orch., concerto for fl., ob. and strings; string 4tet, *Divertimento* for fl., ob., horn and double bass; org. works, etc.

Study, an instrumental piece, usually for a single instrument, written mainly for the purpose of technical exercise and display, but not necessarily devoid of expression and high artistic quality. The Fr. word *étude* is more often used for it.

Stump, an obs. string instrument of the Cittern type invented *c*. 1600 by Daniel Farrant. No details of it are known.

Stumpf, Carl (b. Wiesentheid, 21. IV. 1848; d. Berlin, 29. XII. 1936), Ger. mus. scientist and psychologist. Studied at Göttingen Univ. and held professorships at Würzburg, Prague, Halle, Munich, and from 1893 in Berlin. He collaborated with Hornbostel in ed. the *Beiträge zur Akustik und Musikwissenschaft* and wrote much on the psychological aspects of acoustical phenomena.

Stuntz, Joseph (Hartmann) (b. Arlesheim nr. Basle, ? 23. VII. 1793; d. Munich, 18. VI. 1859), Swiss cond. and comp. Studied with Winter at Munich and Salieri in Vienna. He spent 3 years in It. and in 1825 succeeded Winter as 1st cond. of the Royal Opera at Munich.

Works incl. operas *La rappresaglia*, *Costantino*, *Argene e Dalmiro*, *Elvira e Lucindo*, *Heinrich IV zu Givry* (after Voltaire's *Charlot*) and *Maria Rosa*; ballets; church mus.; cantatas and partsongs, symph. in D min. and concert overtures; songs, etc.

Sturgeon, Nicholas (b. ?, *c*. 1390; d. London, 31. V. 1454), Eng. comp. He was a scholar of Winchester Coll., 1399, aged 8–12. In 1442, after serving as a clerk of the Chapel Royal, he became a canon of Windsor and precentor of St. Paul's Cathedral. He contrib. to the Old Hall MS. during the second phase of its existence, when it was in use at the Chapel Royal.

Sturton, Edmund (b. ?; d. ?), Eng. 15th–16th-cent. comp. He was (?) clerk and instructor of the choristers at Magdalen Coll., Oxford, 1509–10. He wrote an *Ave Maria* and *Gaude virgo mater*, the latter in the Eton Choirbook.

Sturzenegger, Richard (b. Zürich, 18. XII. 1905), Swiss cellist and comp. He studied at the Zürich Cons. and with Alexanian, Casals and Nadia Boulanger in Paris. Later he joined the Dresden Opera orch. and studied further with Feuermann for cello and Toch for comp. He settled as cello prof. in Berne.

Works incl. cantatas and other choral works; theatre mus.; 3 cello concertos, chamber mus., etc.

Styrienne (Fr.), in drawing-room mus. what is supposed to be a Styrian dance, but not more genuinely so than the Écossaise is a Scot. one. It is usually in moderate 2–4 time and in a min. key.

Suabe Flute, a 4-ft. org. stop similar in tone to the Claribel, but smaller in scale and with the lips of its pipes inverted.

Sub, a prefix denoting transposition an 8ve lower, like Contra or Double, used for certain org. stops.

Sub Bass, another name for the Bourdon org. stop.

Sub Bourdon, a Bourdon org. stop prod. 32-ft. tone.

Subdiapente (*see also* **Diapente**; from Lat. and Gk.), a 5th lower. The term is used esp. for canons at the 5th.

Subdiatessaron (from Lat. and Gk.), a 4th lower.

Subdominant, the 4th degree of the maj. or min. scale. For the S. chord see **Cadence**.

Subito (It.) = at once, immediately.

Subject, a theme used as a principal feature in a mus. comp., esp. in a Fugue, where it is brought in a number of times, voice by voice, or in a Rondo, where it is a recurrent main theme returning after a series of episodes. In sonata form 1st and 2nd S.s are the main structural features, but there they are thematic groups more often than single themes.

Submediant, the 6th degree of the maj. or min. scale, so called because it is the opposite of the Mediant, i.e. it is a 3rd below instead of above the Tonic. The S. of a maj. scale is the tonic of its relative min.

Subsemitonium (Lat. = under-semitone), the old name for the Leading-note, esp. when used in the Modes by sharpening the 7th of the scale.

Subtonium (Lat. = under-[whole] tone), the old name for the 7th degree of the Modes, except the Lydian (and later the Ionian), so called because it was a whole tone below the final, though it was often sharpened in perf. according to the principle of Musica ficta.

Sucher, Josef (b. Döbör, Hung., 23. XI. 1844; d. Berlin, 4. IV. 1908), Aus.-Hung. cond. and comp. Learnt mus. as choirboy of the Aus. court chapel at the Löwenburg seminary in Vienna and later studied with Sechter. After var. cond. appts.

at Viennese theatres, incl. the Court Opera, he went to Leipzig as cond. of the municipal theatre in 1876. In 1877 he married the singer Rosa Hasselbeck. He was cond. of the court opera in Berlin from 1888 to 1899.

Works incl. opera *Ilse*; Masses and cantatas, overtures for orch.; song cycle *Ruheort*, etc.

Sucher (*née* **Hasselbeck**), **Rosa** (b. Velburg, Bavar., 23. II. 1849; d. Eschweiler nr. Aachen, 16. IV. 1927), Ger. soprano, wife of prec. She made her 1st appearance at Trier and advanced rapidly to more important opera houses, going with her husband to Hamburg in 1879, where he became cond. of the Opera. They visited Eng. in 1882 and in 1886 she sang Isolde at the Wagner Theatre at Bayreuth.

Suchon, Eugen (b. Pezinok, 25. IX. 1908), Slovak comp. Studied at Bratislava Cons. from 1927 to 1931 and then in Prague with Novák from 1931–3. From 1933 to 1941 he taught at the Bratislava Acad. of Mus. and from 1941 to 1947 was prof. at the State Cons. From 1947 to 1953 he was prof. at the Slovak Univ. and from 1953 at the Pedagogic High School in Bratislava.

Works incl. opera *The Whirlpool*; serenades for strings, for wind 5tet; choral mus.; pf. 4tet, pf. pieces.

Suckling, Norman (Charles) (b. Forest Gate, Essex, 24. X. 1904), Eng. scholar, pianist, comp. and writer on mus. Educ. at Bancroft's School and Queen's Coll., Oxford. He taught at Liverpool and was lecturer in Fr. at King's Coll., Newcastle-on-Tyne from 1943 to 1969. His writings incl. a book on Fauré and his comps. a chamber opera *Avalon*, a Mass for 8 voices and an intro. and scherzo for string 4tet.

Sue, Eugène (1804–57), Fr. novelist. *See* Halévy (*Juif errant*).

Suggia, Guilhermina (b. Oporto, 27. VI. 1888; d. Oporto, 31. VII. 1950), Port. cellist. She played in the Oporto orch. and a string 4tet before she was 13, in 1904 was sent to Leipzig to study with Klengel, appeared there under Nikisch and lastly studied with Casals, to whom she was married from 1906 to 1912, in Spain. She lived in London for many years, but returned to Port. some years before her death.

Suite, a form of instrumental mus. consisting of a number of movements, orig. dances, but now any pieces the comp. desires, incl. chosen numbers from operas, ballets, etc. In the late 17th cent. a tradition was estab. of incl. 4 regular dance movements: Allemande, Courante, Sarabande and Gigue (to give the Fr. names as the most frequently used). These were almost invariably in the same key, prob. because S.s were often written for lutes,

which had to be newly tuned for each key. Other dances could be added at will, such as the Gavotte, Minuet, Bourrée, Rigaudon, Hornpipe, etc., and the whole could be preceded by a Prelude (e.g. Purcell, Bach's Eng. S.s, etc.). There could also be fancy pieces with a var. of titles, as in Bach's Partitas (*partita* being another name for S.) and more esp. in the S.s by Fr. comps., e.g. those by Couperin. The chief features inherited from the S. by the sonata were the binary form of the dances, which became the exposition, working-out and recapitulation of the sonata form, and the minuet, which was retained partic. in symphs. and in the 19th cent. turned into the scherzo.

Suivez (Fr. imper. = follow), a direction used in two senses: (1) to indicate that one movement of a comp. is to follow the preceding one immediately (equivalent to It. *attacca*); (2) to indicate that accompanying parts are to follow a vocal or other solo part moving independently of the prescribed rhythm or tempo (equivalent to It. *colla parte*).

Suk, Josef (b. Křečovice, 4. I. 1874; d. Benešov nr. Prague, 29. V. 1935), Cz. violinist, violist and comp. Studied with Dvořák in Prague and in 1898 became his son-in-law. In 1892 he formed the Boh. String 4tet with Karel Hofmann, Oscar Nedbal and Otto Berger, playing 2nd vln. He began to comp. early and in 1922 became prof. of comp. at the Prague Cons., of which he was director in 1924–6. Much of his mus. was influenced by personal experiences, esp. the death of his wife in 1905, e.g. the pf. pieces *About Mother* written for his infant son, and by that of Dvořák, e.g. the *Asrael* symph., which refers to those 2 deaths.

Works incl. Mass in B♭ maj.; incid. mus. for Julius Zeyer's *Radúz and Mahulena*; *Epilogue* for baritone solo, women's chorus and orch.; symphs. in E maj. and *Asrael*, symph. poems *Prague*, *A Summer Tale* and *Maturity*, Dramatic Overture and overture to Shakespeare's *Winter's Tale*, *A Tale* and *Under the Apple-trees* for orch.; serenade and meditation on a chorale for string orch.; fantasy for vln. and orch.; 2 string 4tets, pf. 4tet, pf. trio, elegy for vln. and cello with string 4tet, harmonium and harp; *Ballade and Serenade* for cello and pf.; instrumental pieces; sets of pf. pieces *Moods*, *Spring*, *Summer Impressions*, *About Mother*, *Things Lived and Dreamed*, *Slumber Songs*, *Pol. Fantasy* and other pf. pieces; part-songs with and without pf., etc.

Suk, Joseph (b. Prague, 8. VIII. 1929), Cz. violinist. Grandson of prec. and great-grandson of Dvořák. Studied at Prague Cons. with J. Kocian, graduating in 1950.

Suk, Váša (b. Kladno, 1. XI. 1861; d.

Moscow, 12. I. 1933), Cz. violinist, cond. and comp. Studied at the Prague Cons. and became violinist and cond. successively at Warsaw, Kiev and Moscow.

Works incl. opera *The Forest King*; symph. poem *Jan Hus*; serenade for string orch., etc.

Sul ponticello (It.) = on the bridge, a direction in mus. for bowed string instruments to play a passage very near (not actually on) the bridge to prod. a peculiar nasal and rustling sound.

Sul tasto (It.), a direction indicating that a passage of string mus. is to be played with the bow over the finger-board.

Sullivan, Arthur (Seymour) (b. London, 13. V. 1842; d. London, 22. XI. 1900), Eng. comp. Son of a bandmaster and prof. at the Royal Military School of Mus., entered the Chapel Royal in 1854 and was taught by Helmore. In 1856 he gained the Mendelssohn scholarship at the R.A.M., where he studied under Sterndale Bennett, Goss and O'Leary. The scholarship entitled him to a course of study at the Leipzig Cons., where he studied comp., cond. and pf., returning in 1861 to London, where he became organist at St. Michael's Church, Chester Square. He 1st made his mark as comp. with incid. mus. to Shakespeare's *Tempest*. His 1st operetta, *The Sapphire Necklace*, was prod. in 1864 and the 1st for which Gilbert wrote the lib. in 1871. After that he and Gilbert repeated their joint triumphs until 1889, when they reached their climax in *The Gondoliers*. S. taught and cond. intermittently; he had been app. prof. of comp. at the R.A.M. in 1866. The following year he and Grove went to Vienna and discovered a pile of forgotten MSS. of Schubert's works. He was knighted in 1883.

Works incl. opera *Ivanhoe*; operettas (with Gilbert as librettist) *Thespis, or The Gods Grown Old, Trial by Jury, The Sorcerer, H.M.S. Pinafore, The Pirates of Penzance, Patience, Iolanthe, Princess Ida, The Mikado, Ruddigore, The Yeomen of the Guard, The Gondoliers, Utopia Limited, The Grand Duke*; other operettas: *The Sapphire Necklace, Cox and Box, The Contrabandista, The Zoo, Haddon Hall, The Chieftain* (adapted from *The Contrabandista*), *The Beauty Stone, The Rose of Persia, The Emerald Isle* (unfinished, completed by German); ballets *L'Île enchantée* and *Victoria and Merrie England*; incid. mus. to Shakespeare's *Tempest, Merchant of Venice, Merry Wives of Windsor, Henry VIII* and *Macbeth*, Tennyson's *The Foresters* and Comyns Carr's *King Arthur*; choral works: *Kenilworth* (after Scott), *The Prodigal Son, On Shore and Sea, The Light of the World, The Martyr of Antioch, The Golden*

Legend, Festival Te Deum, Exhibition Ode, Imperial Institute Ode; Te Deum, Jubilate and Kyrie in D; ode 'I wish to tune my quiv'ring lyre' for baritone and orch.; services, anthems and hymn-tunes (incl. 'Onward, Christian Soldiers'); symph. in E maj.; overtures *In Memoriam, Di ballo*, to Shakespeare's *Timon of Athens* and *Marmion* (after Scott); *Procession March, Princess of Wales March, Imperial March*; cello concerto; romance for string 4tet; var. pf. pieces; song cycle *The Window* (Tennyson), a number of songs incl. 'Orpheus with his lute', *The Lost Chord* and Kipling's *The Absent-minded Beggar*, etc.

Sully-Prudhomme, Armand (1839–1907), Fr. poet. *See* Franck (C.) (songs), Scontrino (*Vie intérieure*). 3 songs by Fauré.

Sulzer, Salomon (b. Hohenems, Vorarlberg, 30. III. 1804; d. Vienna, 17. I. 1890), Aus. baritone, Jewish cantor and ed. He was placed in charge of the mus. at the new Vienna synagogue in 1825 and studied with Seyfried. He ed. a collection of Jewish hymns and commissioned var. comps. to contribute to it. Schubert's setting of Psalm xcii in Moses Mendelssohn's trans. for baritone and male chorus originated in this way. In 1844–7 S. was prof. of singing at the Vienna Cons.

Sumer is icumen in (Summer has come), an Eng. song in parts, dating from *c.* 1240 and known as the Reading Rota (round). It is a canon for 4 voices and there are 2 additional bass voices adding a Pes or Ground-bass, also in canon. In the MS. the tune is also provided with Lat. words, beginning *Perspice, Christicola*, but the accompanying voices (or Pes) merely have 'Sing cuccu nu' in both versions, though the mus. they sing is actually part of an Easter antiphon.

Summation Tones. *See* **Combination Tones.**

'Sun' Quartets, the nickname of the 6 string 4tets Op. 20 by Haydn, comp. in 1772.

Sunderland (*née* Sykes), **Susan** (b. Brighouse, Yorks, 30. IV. 1819; d. Brighouse, 6. V. 1905), Eng. soprano. The daughter of a gardener, she was discovered by accident, induced to join the Halifax Choral Society and, after a 1st appearance at Bradford in 1838, given a few months' training in London. She at first sang in Yorkshire only, but in 1849 came out in London.

Sunless, song cycle by Mussorgsky (words by A. A. Golenishchev-Kutuzov), comp. 1874: 1. *Between four walls*; 2. *Thou didst not know me in the crowd*; 3. *The idle, noisy day is ended*; 4. *Boredom*; 5. *Elegy*; 6. *On the River*.

Suor Angelica (Puccini). *See* **Trittico.**

Super, a prefix denoting transposition an 8ve higher, used for certain org. stops.

Super Octave, an org. term denoting transposition an 8ve higher in the case of Couplers and 2 8ves higher in the case of pipes.

Supertonic, the 2nd degree of the maj. or min. scale, so called because it stands above the Tonic.

Supervia, Conchita (b. Barcelona, 8. XII. 1899; d. London, 30 III. 1936), Span. mezzo-soprano. She 1st appeared in London in the 1920s as a concert singer, excelling in Span. songs as well as in arias from the parts written by Rossini for his wife, Isabella Colbran; later she appeared in some of these parts, as well as in *Carmen*, at Covent Garden. She became Eng. by marriage.

Suppé, Franz von (full name Francesco Ezechiele Ermenegildo Suppe Demelli) (b. Spalato [Split], 18. IV. 1819; d. Vienna, 21. V. 1895), Aus. (Dalmatian) cond. and comp. of Belg. descent. He showed a talent for comp. early, prod. a Mass and a comic opera *Der Apfel* at Zara in 1834; but he was sent to Padua Univ. by his father to study medicine. On his father's death, however, he settled in Vienna with his mother, studied with Seyfried and cond. at var. Viennese and provincial theatres, incl. the Josephstadt, Wieden and Leopoldstadt Theatres in Vienna from 1841 to his death.

Works incl. operettas *Das Mädchen vom Lande, Das Pensionat, Paragraph 3, Zehn Mädchen und kein Mann, Flotte Bursche* (with an overture on students' songs), *Die schöne Galatee, Leichte Kavallerie* (*Light Cavalry*), *Fatinitza, Boccaccio, Donna Juanita, Die Afrikareise* and several others; farces; ballets; incid. mus. to Elmar's *Dichter und Bauer* (*Poet and Peasant*), Shakespeare's *Midsummer Night's Dream,* Schiller's *Wallensteins Lager* and others (more than 200 stage works); Mass, Requiem (*L'estremo giudizio*), etc.

Supprimez (Fr. imper. = suppress), a direction in org. mus. indicating the putting out of action of stops.

Suriani
Suriano } Alternative spellings of the
Surianus
name of Francesco Soriano.

'Surprise' Symphony, Haydn's symph. No. 94 in G maj., comp. for London in 1791, so called after the sudden loud interruption after 16 quiet bars at the beginning of the slow movement. Known in Ger. as 'Symphonie mit dem Paukenschlag' (Symph. with the Drum-beat).

Surzyński, Józef (b. Szrem nr. Poznań, 15. III. 1851; d. Koscian, 5. III. 1919), Pol. priest and comp. Studied at Regensburg and Leipzig, later taking holy orders in Rome. In 1882 he became director of the cathedral choir at Poznań and in 1894

provost at Koscian. He ed. the *Monumenta Musices Sacrae in Polonia* and *Musica Ecclesiastica.*

Works incl. numerous Masses, hymns and other church mus., *Polish Songs of the Catholic Church,* etc.

Susanna, oratorio by Handel (lib. by ?), perf. London, Covent Garden Theatre, 10. II. 1749.

Susanna's Secret (Wolf-Ferrari). *See* **Segreto di Susanna.**

Susato, Tielman (b. *c.* 1500; d. ? Antwerp, between 1561 and 1564), Flem. mus. pub., ed. and comp. He worked in Antwerp and was the outstanding Dutch mus. pub. of his time. His 11 *Musyck Boexken* (little mus. books) contained Dutch songs, dance mus. and the *Souter Liedekens* of Clemens non Papa and Gerhard Mes. He also pub. vols. of Masses, motets and *chansons* by the leading comps. of his day. Many of these incl. works by himself.

Suspension (Eng.), the sustaining of a note which forms part of a consonant chord so that it creates a dissonance with one or more of the notes of the next chord: the dissonant note then descends ('resolves' is the technical term) to the next note below so as to turn the dissonance into a consonance, e.g.:

In normal 16th-cent. practice the suspended note is first heard on a weak beat, the dissonance occurs on a strong beat, and the resolution follows on a weak beat: this practice was largely followed by later comps., who extended the idea by resolving the dissonant note upwards (also known as retardation) as well as downwards. S.s can occur simultaneously in more than one part, and the effect is the same if the note which is to create the dissonance is repeated instead of being tied over.

Suspension (Fr.). *See* **Ornaments.**

Suspirium (Lat. = sigh), the old name for the Minima (minim) rest.

Susskind, Walter (b. Prague, 1. V. 1913), Eng. cond. of Cz. origin. Studied comp. with J. Suk and A. Hába, cond. with Szell, making his début at the German Opera House in Prague in 1932. From 1942 to 1945 he cond. with the Carl Rosa Opera Co. and then at Sadler's Wells in 1946. From 1946 to 1952 he was also cond. of the Scot. Nat. Orch., and from 1954 to 1956 he cond. in Austral., becoming cond.

of the Toronto Symph. Orch. from 1956 to 1965. In 1968 he took over the St. Louis Symph. Orch. in Amer.

Süssmayr, Franz (Xaver) (b. Schwanenstadt, Upper Aus., 1766; d. Vienna, 16. IX. 1803), Aus. comp. Educ. at the monastery of Kremsmünster and pupil of Salieri and Mozart in Vienna. He asst. Mozart with *La clemenza di Tito* (prob. the recitatives) and completed his unfinished Requiem. In 1792 he became cond. of the Kärntnertortheater.

Works incl. operas *Moses, L'incanto superato, Der Spiegel von Arkadien, Il Turco in Italia, Idris und Zenide, Die edle Rache, Die Freiwilligen, Der Wildfang* (after Kotzebue), *Der Marktschreier, Soliman II* (after Favart), *Gulnare, Phasma* and others; 2 ballets; Masses and other church mus.; cantatas *Der Retter in Gefahr* and *Der Kampf für den Frieden*; clar. concerto; serenades for fl., vla. and horn and for vln., guitar and Eng. horn; instrumental pieces, etc.

Sustaining Pedal, the so-called 'loud' P. of the pf., not used to prod. greater volume of tone, but to sustain any notes struck after it has been depressed, even after the fingers have left the keys, until it is released again.

Suter, Hermann (b. Kaiserstuhl, Aargau, 28. IV. 1870; d. Basle, 22. VI. 1926), Swiss cond. and comp. Studied with Huber and others at Basle and at the Conss. of Stuttgart and Leipzig. In 1892 he became cond. of a male choral society at Zürich, was invited to several other posts of the kind, and in 1896 became prof. at the Cons. In 1902 he moved to Basle, where he cond. the mixed and male choral societies as well as the orchestral concerts. In 1918–21 he was director of the Cons.

Works incl. *Die erste Walpurgisnacht* (Goethe) and *Le Laudi di San Francesco d'Assisi* for solo voices, chorus and orch.; symph. in D min.; vln. concerto; 3 string 4tets, string 6tet; choral works with and without accomp.; songs, etc.

Sutermeister, Heinrich (b. Feuerthalen, Ct. Schaffhausen, 12. VIII. 1910), Swiss comp. Studied philology at Paris and Basle, where he entered the Cons., later studying with Courvoisier, Pfitzner and others at Munich. In 1934 he settled at Berne, at 1st as operatic coach at the municipal theatre. In 1963 appo. prof. of comp. at the Hochschule für Musik in Hanover.

Works incl. operas *Romeo und Julia* and *Die Zauberinsel (The Tempest)* (both based on Shakespeare), *Niobe, Raskolnikov* (on Dostoievsky's *Crime and Punishment*), radio opera *Die scharze Spinne* (after Jeremias Gotthelf); ballet *Das Dorf unter dem Gletscher*; Christmas radio play *Die drei Geister* (after

Dickens*)*; incid., film and radio mus.; chamber oratorio *Jorinde und Jorindel* (after Mörike); *Baroque Songs* for tenor, women's chorus and instruments, songs for chorus; *Cantata 1944* for contralto, small chorus and pf.; Requiem and other cantatas; *7 Liebesbriefe* for tenor and orch.; divertimento for string orch.; 3 pf. concertos, cello concerto; 3 string 4tets, string trio and other chamber mus.; pf. and org. pieces; songs, etc.

Sutherland, Joan (b. Sydney, 7. XI. 1926), Austral. soprano. Studied 1st in Austral. and then at the R.C.M. in London with C. Carey. She made her London début at Covent Garden in 1952 and in 1959 obtained internat. acclaim in *Lucia di Lammermoor* at that opera house. She has since estab. herself as one of the leading coloratura sopranos of the day.

Sutor, Wilhelm (b. Edelstetten, Bavar., *c.* 1774; d. Linden nr. Hanover, 7. IX. 1828), Ger. tenor and comp. Studied singing with Valesi and others, settled at Stuttgart in 1800 and from 1818 was mus. director at the court of Hanover.

Works incl. opera *Apollos Wettgesang* and 4 others; incid. mus. to Shakespeare's *Macbeth*; oratorio and cantatas; partsongs; songs, etc.

Sutton, John (b. ?; d. ?), Eng. 15th-cent. comp. He was a fellow of Magdalen Coll., Oxford, 1476, and of Eton, 1477–*c.* 1479. He (?) obtained the Mus.B. at Cambridge, 1489. A *Salve regina* for 7 voices is in the Eton Choirbook.

Švanda Dudák (*Shvanda the Bagpiper*), opera by Adalbert Hřimalý (1842–1908) (lib. by Karel Želenský, based on a folk-tale by Josef Kajetán Tyl), prod. Pilsen, 20. I. 1896.

Opera by Weinberger (lib. by Miloš Kareš, source as above), prod. Prague, Cz. Theatre, 27. IV. 1927.

Svanholm, Set (b. Västerås, 2. IX. 1904; d. Saltsvoe-Duvnaes, 4. X. 1964), Swed. tenor. Studied at Stockholm Cons. with Forsell, making his début in Stockholm in 1930 as a baritone. After further study he developed a tenor voice, making a second début in 1936. In 1942 he first sang at Bayreuth and from 1946 to 1956 at the N.Y. Metropolitan, then becoming intendant of the Stockholm Opera House until 1963. He was best known as a heroic tenor, esp. in the works of Wagner.

Svendsen, Johan (Severin) (b. Christiania, 30. IX. 1840; d. Copenhagen, 14. VI. 1911), Norw. comp. Learnt mus. from his father, a bandmaster, and at first adopted that profession himself. But, playing several instruments, he joined the orch. at the Christiania theatre, began extensive travels in Swed. and Ger. in 1861 and studied at the Leipzig Cons. from 1863 to 1867. After travelling in Scand. and

Scot. in 1867, he settled in Paris in 1868. In 1870–1 he was in Ger. again, mainly at Leipzig and Weimar, and in 1872–7 he taught and cond. at Christiania. After visits to Munich, Rome, London, and Paris, he became court cond. at Copenhagen, 1883–1908.

Works incl. incid. mus. to Coppée's *Le Passant*; 2 symphs., overture to Bjørnson's *Sigurd Slembe*, *Carnaval à Paris*, *Carnaval des artistes norvégiens*, 4 Norw. Rhapsodies, legend *Zorahayda*, overture to Shakespeare's *Romeo and Juliet*, etc. for orch.; vln. concerto and romance, cello concerto; string 4tet, string 5tet, string octet; Marriage Cantata; songs, etc.

Swain, Freda (b. Portsmouth, 31. X. 1902), Eng. pianist and comp. Studied at the Tobias Matthay Pf. School in London and at the R.C.M., comp. with Stanford and pf. with Arthur Alexander, to whom she was married in 1921. In 1924 she became prof. at the R.C.M.

Works incl. *Pastoral Fantasy* for orch.; pf. concerto (*Airmail*), *The Harp of Aengus* (after Yeats) for vln. and orch.; string 4tet *Norfolk*; vln. and pf. sonatas in C min. and *The River*, cello and pf. sonata, duets for 2 vlns., *Danse barbare* for vln. and cello; scherzo for 3 pfs., sonata-poem *The Sea*, sonata in F min., *Sonata-Saga*, *Tetrad*, sonatina *The Skerries* and a number of pieces for pf.; songs to poems by Burns, Bridges, Housman, Coppard and others, etc.

Swan Lake, The, ballet by Tchaikovsky (choreography by Marius Petipa and L. I. Ivanov), prod. Moscow, Bolshoy Theatre, 4. III. 1877.

Swan of Tuonela, The, symph. legend by Sibelius, Op. 22, one of 4 on subjects from the *Kalevala*, comp. in 1893–5, 1st perf. Helsinki, 1895.

Swan Song (Schubert). *See* **Schwanengesang.**

Swarowsky, Hans (b. Budapest, 16. IX. 1899), Aus. cond. Studied with Schönberg, Webern and R. Strauss, and then devoted himself mainly to cond., being active at opera houses in Stuttgart, Hamburg, Berlin and Zürich. From 1944 to 1945 he cond. the Cracow Phil. Orch., the Vienna Symph. Orch. from 1947 to 1950, and was director of the Graz Opera from 1947 to 1950.

Swedish Composers. *See* Agrell, Ahlström, Alfvén, Andrée, Aulin, Atterberg, Bäck, Berg (N.), Berwald, Björkander, Blomdahl, Broman, Düben, Frigel, Frumerie, Geijer, Hallén, Hallström, Koch, Larsson, Lindberg, Lindblad (2), Morales (O.), Norman, Nystroem, Peterson-Berger, Rangström, Roman, Rosenberg, Sjögren, Söderman, Starck, Stenhammar, Wennerberg, Wiklund, Wirén.

'Swedish Nightingale, The', the nickname given to Jenny Lind.

Sweelinck, Jan Pieterszoon (b. Deventer, *c.* V. 1562; d. Amsterdam, 16. X. 1621), Dutch organist, harpsichordist and comp. Studied under his father, Pieter S., who became organist at the Old Church at Amsterdam in 1566, and others. His father d. in 1573 and he succeeded to his post between 1577 and 1580, holding it to his death. He had many famous pupils, some from foreign countries, and his org. playing was celebrated; he was also a highly skilled harpsichordist. The poet Vondel wrote an epitaph on his death.

Works incl. 4 books of psalms for 4–8 voices, *Cantiones sacrae* for several voices; org. fantasias, toccatas and chorale variations; harpsichord pieces; *chansons* for 5 voices, *Rimes françoises et italiennes*.

Swell, a device on the harpsichord and the org. for the artificial prod. of *crescendo* and *diminuendo*, which these instruments are incapable of prod. by touch. It took var. forms, the most successful being a contrivance in the form of a slatted blind (hence the name Venetian S.), which, opening and shutting by means of a pedal, increased or reduced the volume of tone.

Swell Box, a box enclosing a number of org. pipes and fitted with a Venetian S. device. In modern orgs. there are S. B.s for the Swell, Choir and Solo manuals.

Swell Organ, one of the manuals of the org., the pipes being enclosed in a S. Box.

Swell Pedal, an org. pedal controlling the S. Box.

Swieten, Gottfried (Bernhard) van (b. Leyden, 29. X. 1733; d. Vienna, 29. III. 1803), Aus. diplomat and amateur musician of Dutch descent. Came to Vienna with his family in 1745 and in 1755 entered the diplomatic service. He held posts in Brussels, Paris and Warsaw, and visited Eng. in 1769, but spent much of his time on mus., and comp. 2 *opéras comiques* and some symphs. As ambassador in Berlin 1770–7 he became acquainted with the works of the Bach family and of Handel, and on his return to Vienna did much to promote interest in their mus. He commissioned 6 symphs. from C. P. E. Bach, and Mozart's arrs. of Handel oratorios were made for the concerts he organized. He was librettist of Haydn's *Creation* and *Seasons*, and a patron of the young Beethoven, who ded. his 1st symph. to him.

Swift, Jonathan (1667–1745), Anglo-Ir. novelist and satirist. *See* Kelley (*Gulliver*), Pierné (do.).

Swinburne, Algernon Charles (1837–1909), Eng. poet. *See* Bainton (*Before Sunrise*), Bantock (*Atalanta in Calydon*), Grainger (*Bride's Tragedy*), Parry (H.) (*Eton*), Wood (C.) (*Ode on Music*).

Swing, a development of Jazz which

became known during the 1930s. It relies
on improvisation on the part of individual
members of a dance band to a much greater
extent than jazz.

Swingler, Randall, Eng. poet. *See*
Bush (A.) (choral work and pf. concerto).

Swinstead, Felix (Gerald) (b. London,
25. VI. 1880; d. Southwold, 14. VIII.
1959), Eng. pianist, teacher and comp.
Studied at the R.A.M. in London, where
he became pf. prof. in 1910. He gave
recitals and toured in the Dominions in
1902–12, wrote a treatise on pf. playing
and became an examiner to the Assoc.
Board of the Royal Schools of Mus.
  Works incl. Scarlatti Suite for pf.
and strings; pieces for vln. and pf.; *c.* 250
studies and pieces for pf., etc.

Swiss Composers. *See* Albicastro, An-
dreae, Attenhofer, Bachofen, Balmer, Bar-
blan, Baumgartner, Beck, Bernard, Binet,
Blanchet, Bloch, Bovy-Lysburg, Brun,
Burkhard, Courvoisier, David **(K. H.),**
Doret, Du Puy, Egli, Ferrari, Frey, Haug,
Hegar, Honegger, Huber **(2),** Jaques-
Dalcroze, Klose, Kunz, Lang, Marescotti,
Martin **(F.),** Meyer **(G.),** Meyer von
Schauensee, Moeschinger, Munzinger,
Nägeli, Niedermeyer, Raff, Schnyder von
Wartensee, Schoeck, Senfl **(?),** Staempfli,
Studer, Stuntz, Sturzenegger, Suter, Suter-
meister, Vogler **(C.),** Vuataz, Wannen-
macher, Wehrli, Zwyssig.

Syberg, Franz (Adolf) (b. Kerteminde
nr. Odense, 5. VII. 1904), Dan. organist
and comp. His father, the painter Fritz S.,
sent him to study at the Leipzig Cons.,
and later he became a private pupil of
Karg-Elert. In 1930 he returned to Den.
to study org. with Peder Thomsen in
Copenhagen, and in 1933 he became
organist at Kerteminde.
  Works incl. incid. mus. to Büchner's
Leonce and Lena and the marionette
comedy *Uffe hin Spage*; symph.; concertino for ob. and strings; string 4tet, string
trio, 5tet for fl., clar., vln., vla. and cello;
suite for org., etc.

Sygar, John (b. ?; d. ?), Eng. 15th-cent.
comp. He was a singer and chaplain at
King's College, Cambridge, in 1499–1501
and 1508–15, and contrib. a Magnificat
(now incomplete) to the Eton Choirbook.

Sykes, Susan. *See* Sunderland.

Sylphides, Les, ballet with mus. adapted
from Chopin (choreography by Mikhail
Mikhailovich Fokin), prod. Paris, Théâtre
du Châtelet, 2. VI. 1909.

Sylva, Carmen. *See* Carmen Sylva.

Sylvana (Weber). *See* Silvana.

Sylvia, ou La Nymphe de Diane, ballet
by Delibes (scenario by Jules Barbier
and Baron de Reinach, choreography by
Louis Mérante), prod. Paris, Opéra, 14. VI.
1876.

Symonds, John Addington (1840–93),

Eng. essayist and poet. *See* **Griffes** (*These
Things shall be*), **Ireland** (do.).

Sympathetic Resonance, an acoustical
phenomenon observed in resonant bodies,
such as a string, a glass, a tuning-fork,
etc., which will vibrate and give forth a
faint sound without being touched, if
their fundamental note is sung or played
on an instrument near them.

Sympathetic Strings, a set of strings
in certain types of bowed instruments
vibrating in accord with those actually
touched by the bow.

Sympathetic Tone   ⎫
Sympathetic Vibration ⎬ *See* **Sympathe-**
tic Resonance.   ⎭

Symphonia (Lat.), lit. = symphony, esp.
in the earlier sense of any piece of mus. in
which instruments play together in
consort; also an obs. instrument, possibly
a kind of Bagpipe and, in a later sense, a
Clavichord. *See also* **Sinfonia** (the It.
term).

Symphonia domestica (*Domestic Symph.*),
a symph. by R. Strauss, Op. 53, comp.
1903, 1st perf. N.Y., 31. III. 1904. Like
Heldenleben the work is autobiog., but
describes the comp.'s private life, while
the earlier work showed him as a public
figure.

Symphonic Poem, a type of orch. work
coming under the category of Programme
Mus., i.e. descriptive of lit. subjects,
actual events in hist. or contemporary
life, landscapes and natural phenomena,
paintings, etc. The term S. P. was the
invention of Liszt, who wrote 13 works of
the kind.

Symphonic Study, a term invented by
Elgar for his *Falstaff*, prob. because it is
intended to be as much an outline of the
Falstaff's character as a description of the
events surrounding him.

Symphonie concertante (Fr.). *See* **Sinfonia
concertante.**

Symphonie fantastique, a symph. by
Berlioz, Op. 14, comp. in 1830, revised in
It. and 1st perf. Paris, 5. XII. 1830, and
with its sequel, *Lélio*, Paris, 9. XII. 1832.
Berlioz gave it a programme arising out of
his disappointed love for Henrietta
Smithson and representing the crazy
dreams of a poet crossed in love who has
taken poison.

Symphonie funèbre et triomphale, a
symph. by Berlioz, Op. 15, for military
band, strings and chorus, comp. in 1840
by order of the Fr. government and perf.
at the 10th anniversary of the 1830
Revolution, Paris, 28. VII. 1840.

Symphony, orig. a piece of mus. for
several perfs., e.g. Schütz's *Symphoniae
sacrae* (1629–50), which are for voices and
instruments. In 17th-cent. It. a S. (*sinfonia*)
was an instrumental movement, partic. the
overture, in an opera or similar work. The

term was still used in this sense in the early part of the 18th cent., e.g. in Bach's cantatas. The development of the opera overture into a work in 3 movements in the time of A. Scarlatti led to the comp. of similar works independent of the theatre. S.s of this kind were written in the 18th cent. not only in It. but also in Vienna and partic. in Mannheim. The Ger. and Aus. S. came to incorporate elements of the Suite (Minuet) and the Divertimento. The originality of Haydn's S.s owed much to his isolation from the world at Esterház. Mozart, more cosmopolitan, was influenced as a boy by the elegance of J. C. Bach's S.s but rapidly developed a style of his own. Dramatic elements are to be found in the S.s of C. P. E. Bach, Haydn and Beethoven, and programmatic features in those of Spohr, Berlioz and Liszt. The problem of integrating symph. structure and Romantic expression was solved most successfully by Brahms. The Scherzo came to replace the Minuet in the S.s of Beethoven, whose use of voices in his 9th S. was followed by Mendelssohn (*Lobgesang*), Mahler and others. The linking of movements into a continuous whole, practised by Schumann and Mendelssohn, has been followed by a number of later comps., e.g. Sibelius. Thematic relationships between movements occur in the S.s of Franck, Tchaikovsky and Elgar among others. A S. is not necessarily a heavily serious or weighty comp.: Prokofiev's *Symphonie classique* and Shostakovich's 9th S. are both light-hearted works.

Sympson, Christopher. *See* **Simpson.**

Syncopation, a displacement of the mus. accent to weak beats or off-beats in the bar, where they are normally expected to lie on the 1st beat and, less pronounced, on the other main divisions of the bar, e.g.:

Handel, *Water Music*

SYNCOPATION

The effect is that of a syncope (i.e. missing a heart-beat): hence the name.

Synge, John Millington (1871–1909), Ir. dramatist. *See* **Gilbert (H. F.)** (*Riders to the Sea*), **Pedrollo** (*Veglia*), **Polovinkin** (*Irish Hero*), **Rabaud** (*Appel de la mer*), **Riders to the Sea** (Vaughan Williams).

Syrian Chant, the earliest of the independent branches of Christian chant. Its language was the E. Aramaic dialect, also called Syriac. In addition to the cantillation of the lessons and the singing of psalms, common to all liturgies, a repertory

of hymns emerged, anticipating in some cases the forms of Byzantine chant (*q.v.*). The *memrâ* was a poetical homily, sung to a recitative formula. The *madrâshâ* was a strophic hymn sung by a soloist, with a refrain sung by the choir (*cf.* Byzantine *kontakion*). The *sogîthâ* was a poem of dramatic character. Lesser forms, inserted between the verses of psalms, are comparable to the *troparion* and *sticheron* of the Byzantine liturgy. The outstanding poet was St. Ephraem (306–73). Apart from some indecipherable cantillation formulae the mus. of the early S. church has not survived; and it is impossible to say how closely what is sung today resembles it.

Syrinx. *See* **Pan Pipe.**

Syrmen, Maddalena (sometimes so spelt). *See* **Sirmen.**

System. In Eng. a S. is a number of mus. staves required for the scoring of a comp., e.g. 2 for a pf. work, 1+2 for a song, 4 for a 4tet, etc., up to any number needed for an orchestral full score. Such a S. is connected on the left-hand side of the page by var. kinds of braces or brackets; an open space between these shows that the next S. begins lower down on the same page.

Szabados, Béla Antal (b. Pest, 3. VI. 1867; d. Budapest, 15. IX. 1936), Hung. comp. Studied with Volkmann, became leader in the orch. of the Budapest Acad. of Mus. and was from 1927 to his death director of the Nat. Cons. there.

Works incl. operas *Aunt is asleep, The Simpleton, Mária* (with Szendy), *Fanni,* operettas; chamber mus.; songs, etc.

Szabelski, Bolesław (b. Radoryż, 3. XII. 1896), Pol. comp. Studied with Szymanowski and Statkowski at the Warsaw Cons., and from 1945 taught comp. and org. at the Kattowice Cons.

Works incl. 4 symphs., sinfonietta, *Concerto grosso* for orch.; concertino and concerto for pf. and orch.; 2 string 4tets; Magnificat for soprano, chorus and orch.; pf. and org. mus.

Szábo, Ferencz (b. Budapest, 27. XII. 1902; d. Budapest, XI. 1969), Hung. comp. Pupil of Bartók and Kodály at the Budapest Cons. Settled in Rus. in 1932, returning to Hung. after the war and becoming director of the Budapest High School for Mus. in 1957.

Works incl. *Song Symph.*, symph. poems *Class Struggle* and *November 7th,* suite *The Collective Farm*; 2 string 4tets, 3 pf. trios; mass songs incl. *A Song of Voroshilov*; songs, etc.

Szałowski, Antoni (b. Warsaw, 21. IV. 1907), Pol. comp. Studied with his father, a vln. prof. at the Warsaw Cons., also pf. with 2 masters and comp. with Sikorski; later with Nadia Boulanger in Paris, where he settled.

Works incl. symph., symph. variations; capriccio and overture for string orch.; pf. concerto; 3 songs with orch.; 4 string 4tets; trio for ob., clar. and bassoon; suite for vln. and pf., sonatina for clar. and pf.; vln. and pf. pieces; partita for solo cello; sonata, 2 sonatinas and other works for pf., etc.

Szamotulczyk, Wacław (Wacław of Szamotuly) (b. Szamotuly nr. Poznań, *c.* 1525; d. ? Pińczów on the Nida, 1560), Pol. comp. He studied at Poznań and at Cracow Univ., and in 1547 became comp. to the king. He comp. much church mus., some of it pub. by Berg and Neuber of Nuremberg.

Szántó, Tivadar (or Theodor) (b. Vienna, 3. VI. 1877; d. Budapest, 7. I. 1934), Hung. pianist and comp. Studied in Vienna and Budapest, and with Busoni in Berlin. Lived in Paris in 1905–14, in Switz. in 1914–21 and then settled at Budapest. He revised Delius's C min. pf. concerto, which is ded. to him.

Works incl. opera *Typhoon* (after Lengyel's play); symph. *Land and Sea, Japan Suite* and other suites, symph. rhapsody for orch.; vln. and pf. sonata; Variations on a Hung. Folksong, *Essays in Japanese Harmony* and other works for pf., etc.

Székely, Zoltán (b. Kocs, 8. XII. 1903), Hung. violinist and comp. Studied vln. with Hubay and comp. with Kodály at Budapest. After touring as soloist he formed the Hung. String 4tet in 1935.

Works incl. string 4tet; sonata for unaccomp. vln., duet for vln. and cello, etc.

Szeligowski, Tadeusz (b. Lwów, 13. IX. 1896; d. Poznań, 10. II. 1963), Pol. comp. Studied at Lwów and Cracow, later with Nadia Boulanger in Paris. He taught at Poznań, Lublin, Wilno and Warsaw. He made special studies of folksong and old church mus.

Works incl. incid. mus. for plays, e.g. Maeterlinck's *Blue Bird*; 2 psalms for solo voices, chorus and orch.; concerto, *Phantaisie rapsodique*, suite *St. Casimir Fair* for orch.; clar. concerto, pf. concerto; 2 string 4tets; *Lithuanian Song* for vln. and pf.; *Children's Album* for pf.; *Green Songs, Flower Allegories* and other songs, etc.

Szell, Georg (b. 7. VI. 1897; d. Cleveland, 29. VII. 1970), Hung. cond. and pianist. A child prodigy, he studied with R. Robert in Vienna, playing

a work of his own with the Vienna Symph. Orch. aged 11. He studied comp. with J. B. Foerster, Mandyczewski and Reger, and then, through the influence of R. Strauss, he obtained a cond. post in Strasbourg, which he held from 1917 to 1918, having already made his début in Berlin in 1914. After further posts in Prague, Darmstadt and Düsseldorf he became 1st cond. at the Berlin State Opera from 1924 to 1930, also teaching at the Berlin Hochschule für Musik from 1927 to 1930. From 1930 to 1936 he again cond. in Prague, taking over the Scot. Nat. Orch. from 1937 to 1939, when he went to the U.S.A. There he was guest cond. with the N.B.C. Symph. Orch. from 1941 to 1942, cond. at the N.Y. Metropolitan from 1942 to 1945, and from 1943 to 1956 frequent guest cond. with the N.Y. Phil. Orch. In 1946 he became permanent cond. of the Cleveland Phil. Orch.

Szendy, Arpád (b. Szarvas, 11. VIII. 1863; d. Budapest, 10. IX. 1922), Hung. pianist and comp. Studied under Liszt and others at the Budapest Acad. of Mus., where he became prof. of pf. in 1890 .

Works incl. *Mária* (with Szábados); fantasy for pf. and orch.; 2 string 4tets; sonata in B min., *Aphorisms on Hung. Folksongs* and other works for pf., etc.

Szenen aus Goethes 'Faust', a setting of a number of scenes from Goethe's drama for solo voices, chorus and orch. by Schumann, comp. begun with a setting of the final chorus, VIII. 1844, resumed 1849, completed without the overture, 1850, overture added 1853.

Szeryng, Henryk (b. Warsaw, 22. XI. 1918), Pol. violinist. Studied with W. Hess and with Flesch in Berlin, emigrating to the U.S.A. in 1933. From 1948 he taught as prof. in Mex. City.

Szigeti, Joseph (b. Budapest, 5. IX. 1892), Hung., now Amer., violinist. Studied in Budapest with Hubay, and received advice from Joachim and Busoni, making his début in 1905. From 1917 to 1925 he was prof. at the Geneva Cons., settling in the U.S.A. in 1926. He gave the 1st perf. of vln. concertos by Busoni and Bloch, and has done much for the cause of modern mus.

Szulc, Józef (Zygmunt) (b. Warsaw, 4. IV. 1875; d. Paris, 10. IV. 1956), Pol. pianist and comp. Studied with Noskowski at the Warsaw Cons. and later with Moszkowski in Paris. On the advice of Paderewski he began a career as concert pianist, but later devoted himself to comp. He settled in Paris.

Works incl. Fr. operettas *Une Nuit d'Ispahan, Flup!, Divin Mensonge, Flossie, Le Garçon de chez Prunier, Le Coffre-fort vivant* and others; overture for orch.; vln. and pf. sonata; songs, etc.

Szymanowska (*née* **Wolowska**), **Maria** (b. Warsaw, 14. XII. 1789; d. St. Petersburg, 24. VII. 1831), Pol. pianist. Pupil of Field at Moscow. In 1821 she met Goethe, who fell in love with her, and later she intro. to him the Pol. poet Adam Mickiewicz, who married one of her daughters. She comp. some pf. pieces and songs.

Szymanowski, Karol (b. Timashovka, Ukraine, 6. X. 1882; d. Lausanne, 29. III. 1937), Pol. comp. Learnt mus. privately as a child and comp. a set of pf. preludes, Op. 1, in 1900. In 1903 he entered the Warsaw Cons., studying with Noskowski, and at the Lwów Chopin Festival won a 1st prize with a C min. pf. sonata in 1905. Lived in Berlin for a time from 1906 and worked on behalf of Pol. mus. As an aristocrat he lost his property in the 1914–1918 war and was imprisoned in Rus., but escaped to Warsaw, where in 1922 he became prof. of comp. and director of the State Cons. His last years were marred by illness and he had to go to a sanatorium in Switz., where he d.

Works incl. operas *Hagith* and *King Roger*; ballets *Mandragora* (also incid. mus. to Molière's *Le Bourgeois Gentilhomme*) and *Harnasie*; incid. mus. to Miciński's *Prince Potemkin*; 3 symphs.; *Sinfonia concertante* for pf. and orch.; 2 vln. concertos; *Penthesilea* (Wyspiański) for soprano and orch.; *Hafiz Love Songs* for voice and orch.; *Stabat Mater*, *Veni Creator* and *Litany* for solo voices, chorus and orch.; 2 string 4tets; pf. trio; numuous vln. and pf. pieces; 3 sonatas and many other works for pf.; many songs incl. cycles *Songs of the Infatuated Muezzin* (J. Iwaszkiewicz), *Slopiewnie* (Julian Tuwim), *Children's Rhymes* (J. Illakowicz) and settings of poems by Kasprowicz, Miciński, James Joyce, Tagore and others, etc.

T

t, the leading-note in Tonic Sol-fa notation, pronounced Te.

Tabarro, Il (Puccini). *See* **Trittico.**

Tablature, var. old systems of writing down mus., esp. for org. (for the left hand only or for both hands) and for lute, without notes, but by means of letters or numbers. The only modern instruments for which a T. notation is now normally in use are the Ukelele and similar guitar types. (For the old Ger. Mastersingers' T. *see* **Tabulatur.**)

Table (Fr.). (1) The belly of a string instrument. (2) The sounding-board of the harp. *Près de la table* is an instruction to play near the sounding-board, prod. a metallic sound. (3) *Musique de table. See* **Tafel-Musik.**

Table Entertainment, an 18th-cent. Eng. entertainment, only partly mus. in character, given by a single perf. sitting at a table and telling stories and jokes, giving displays of mimicry, singing songs, etc. The 1st T. E.s on record are those of George Alexander Steevens at Dublin in 1752. Dibdin began a series in London in 1789 and continued for 20 years, intro. most of his songs in this way.

Tableau parlant, Le (*The Speaking Picture*), opera by Grétry (lib. by Louis Anseaume), prod. Paris, Comédie-Italienne, 20. IX. 1769.

Tabor, a small drum with a high, narrow body and small drum-heads made of animal skin, sounding an indefinite pitch and struck with drum-sticks. It was rarely used alone, but accomp. a pipe of a primitive Fife or Recorder type, similar to the modern Tin Whistle. It is occasionally used in the modern orch. to prod. a dry, dull, percussive sound, and has been revived for folk-dancing.

Tabor (Smetana). *See* **Má Vlast.**

Taboret, a small Tabor.

Tabourin (Fr., obs.) = Tabor.

Tabourot, Jehan (anag.). *See* **Arbeau.**

Tabrete (Eng., obs.) = Drum.

Tabulatur (Ger. = Tablature). In one sense the Ger. word differs from the Eng., meaning the table of rules for the instruction and guidance of the Mastersingers.

Tacchinardi, Niccoló (b. Leghorn, 3. IX. 1772; d. Florence, 14. III. 1859), It. tenor. He studied literature and art at first, but learnt the vln., joined the orch. at the Florence Opera in 1789, and in 1794 began to appear as a singer. He soon sang in the principal theatres of It. and in 1811–14 visited Paris, then settled at Florence in the service of the Grand Duke of Tuscany.

Tacet (Lat. = is silent), an indication in old vocal part-books and later in orchestral parts to show that a voice or instrument has finished its part in a work, although the work itself is still continuing. In that case the wording is usually *tacet al fine* (T. to the end). But the word T. alone may also stand below a certain number or section of a work to show that the voice or instrument in question does not perform during that portion of the mus., though it will come in again later.

Taci
Taciasi } (It.) = Tacet.

Tacitus, Cornelius (*c.* 55–120), Rom. hist. *See* **Incoronazione di Poppea** (Monteverdi), **Radamisto** (Handel).

Taddei, Giuseppe (b. Genoa, 26. VI. 1916). It. baritone. Made his début in Rome in 1936. He is esp. well known as a dramatic Verdi singer, and also in *buffo* roles.

Tadolini, Giovanni (b. Bologna, *c.* 1785; d. Bologna, 29. XI. 1872), It. singer and comp. Studied comp. with Mattei and singing with Babini, and in 1811 was engaged by Spontini as accompanist and chorus master at the Théâtre des Italiens in Paris, leaving in 1814, but going there again in 1830–9, after living in It. and comp. operas in between. He married the soprano Eugenia Savorini (1809–after 1848).

Works incl. operas *Le bestie in uomini, La principessa di Navarra, Il credulo deluso* (*Il finto molinaro*), *Tamerlano, Moctar, Mitridate, Almanzor*; canzonets, incl. *Eco di Scozia* with horn obbligato, etc.

Tafel-Musik (Ger. = table mus.), mus. perf. at or after dinner (Fr. *musique de table*).

Taffanel, (Claude) Paul (b. Bordeaux, 16. IX. 1844; d. Paris, 22. XI. 1908), Fr. flautist. Studied at the Paris Cons. and was 1st fl. at the Opéra in 1864–90. In 1879 he founded the Société des Instruments à Vent, and in 1890 became one of the conds. of the Opéra and the Concerts du Cons.

Tag, Christian Gotthilf (b. Bayerfeld, Saxony, 2. IV. 1735; d. Niederzwönitz nr. Zwickau, 19. VI. 1811), Ger. comp. Pupil of Homilius at Dresden. In 1755 he became cantor at Hohenstein, Saxony.

Works incl. 11 Masses, motets; 72 cantatas; symphs. for org. and orch.; songs, etc.

Tageweisen (Ger. = day tunes), songs formerly used in Ger. to announce the break of day from church towers or by night-watchmen in the streets. They were often folksongs and some have passed into currency as hymns for the Lutheran church.

Taglia, Pietro (b. ?, d. ?), It. 16th-cent. comp., active at Milan. Comp. 3 books of madrigals (1555, 1557, 1564).

Tagliapietra, Gino (b. Ljubljana, 30. V. 1887; d. Venice. 8. VIII. 1954), It. pianist and comp. Studied with Julius Epstein in Vienna and with Busoni in Berlin. In 1906 he was app. prof. of pf. at the Liceo Benedetto Marcello at Venice. He pub. an anthology of keyboard mus. in 18 vols.

Works incl. ballet *La bella addormentata nel bosco*; Requiem and other choral works; pf. concerto; pf. pieces and studies, etc.

Tagliapietra, Giovanni (b. Venice, 24. XII. 1846; d. N.Y., 11. IV. 1921), It. baritone. Studied architecture at Venice and Padua, but later took to singing, toured in It. and S. Amer. and in 1874 settled in N.Y.

Tagliato (It. = cut), a term, now obs., for the vertical stroke through the time-signature C, indicating *Alla breve* time.

Tagliavini, Ferrucio (b. Reggio, 14. VIII. 1913), It. tenor. Studied at Parma Cons. and won 1st prize in a singing competition in Florence in 1938, which enabled him to study in that city with A. Bassi, where he made his début in 1939. He soon estab. himself as a leading *bel canto* singer, appearing at the N.Y. Metropolitan from 1947 to 1954 and at Covent Garden in 1950.

Täglichsbeck, Thomas (b. Ansbach, 31. XII. 1799; d. Baden-Baden, 5. X. 1867), Ger. violinist and comp. Studied in Munich and became deputy cond. to Lindpainter there in 1820. From 1827 he was mus. director to the Prince of Hohenzollern-Hechingen until the 1848 Revolution. He toured frequently during this period as soloist and as cond.

Works incl. operas *Webers Bild, König Enzio*; Mass, Psalm; 4 symphs.; vln. concertos; pf. trio; part-songs, etc.

Taglietti, Giulio (b. Brescia, *c.* 1660; d. ?), It. comp. *Maestro di cappella* of the Jesuit coll. of Sant' Antonio at Brescia. Comp. numerous works for 2 vlns. and bass with org. or harpsichord, vln. sonatas with bass, etc.

Tagore, Rabindranath (1861–1941), Indian poet. *See* **Barraine** (songs), **Carpenter** (*Gitanjali*), **Cras**, **Durey**, **Fogg** (*Hillside* and *Songs of Love and Life*), **Fourestier**, **Janáček** (*Wandering Madman*), **Morris (H.)** (*Gitanjali*), **Ponce** (3 songs), **Rota (N.)** (songs), **Ruyneman** (sacred songs), **Sauguet** (songs), **Shankar** (*Samanya Kshati*), **Shepherd (A.)** (*Triptych*), **Sigtenhorst Meyer** (*King's Letter*), **Stenhammer** (*Chitra*), **Szymanowski** (songs), **Tiessen** (*Post Offie*).

Tailer, John (also Taylor, etc.) (b. ?; d. ? London, ? *c.* 1569), Eng. comp. In 1557 he was (?) master of the choristers at St. Mary Woolnoth, and later at Westminster Abbey. A *Christus resurgens* (Christ Church, Oxford, MSS. 948–8) is prob. by him; it may however be by Thomas Taylor, who obtained the B.Mus. at Oxford, 1531.

Taille (Fr. = cut, edge), the tenor part in a vocal and instrumental ensemble, applied partic. in the 17th and 18th cents. to the vla. and the *oboe da caccia*.

Tailleferre, Germaine (b. Parc Saint-Maur nr. Paris, 19. IV. 1892), Fr. comp. Studied in Paris and joined the group of 'Les Six', 1st appearing as a comp. in public in 1920. She lived in U.S.A. from 1942 to 1946.

Works incl. opera *Il était un petit navire*; ballet *Le Marchand d'oiseaux*; *Pastorale* for small orch.; pf. concerto and ballade for pf. and orch.; string 4tet; 2 vln. and pf. sonatas; *Jeux de plein air* for 2 pfs.; songs, etc.

Tal (actually Grünthal), **Joseph** (b. Pinne, nr. Poznań, 18. IX. 1910), Israeli comp. Studied in Berlin with Tiessen and Trapp, settling in Palestine in 1934. In 1937 he became prof. of comp. and pf. at the Jerusalem Cons. and in 1950 lecturer at the Hebrew Univ. there, also being director of the Cons. from 1948 to 1955.

Works incl. operas *Saul in En-Dor*, *Amon and Tamar*; 2 symphs.; *Exodus*, choreographic poem for orch.; *Visions* for string orch.; 5 pf. concertos, vla. concerto; symph. cantata *A Mother Rejoices*; sonatas for vln., ob.; pf. pieces; songs; electronic mus.

Talbot, Howard (actually Richard Lansdale Munkittrick) (b. Yonkers, N.Y., 9. III. 1865; d. Reigate, 12. IX. 1928), Amer. (anglicized) comp. Studied with Parry at the R.C.M. in London.

Works incl. mus. comedies *Wapping Old Stairs, Three Little Maids, The Girl behind the Counter, The Belle of Brittany, The Arcadians, The Mousmé, The Pearl Girl, A Lucky Miss, My Lady Frayle, Mr. Manhattan* and others.

Talea (Lat. = a cutting), the name given to the repeated rhythmic pattern used in isorhythmic motets. *See* **Isorhythm**.

Tales of Hoffmann (Offenbach). *See* **Contes d'Hoffmann**.

Tálich, Václav (b. Kroměřiž, 28. V. 1883; d. Beroun, nr. Prague, 16. III. 1961), Cz. cond. He studied with his father and was a pupil of Ševčík for the vln. at the Prague Cons. He held various posts as violinist, cond. and teacher from 1904 to 1919, when he was app. cond. of the Cz. Phil. Orch. He retained this post till 1941 and was also director of the National Opera at Prague from 1935 to 1945. Post-war conditions made his position in Prague impossible and he moved to Bratislava. His merits were finally recognized by the government in the last years of his life.

Talismano, Il, unfinished opera by Balfe, completed by Macfarren (lib. *The Knight of the Leopard*, based on Scott's *Talisman*, by Arthur Matthison; It. trans. by

Giuseppe Zaffira), prod. London, Her Majesty's Theatre, 11. VI. 1874.

Tallis, Thomas (b. ? Leicestershire, *c.* 1505; d. Greenwich, 23. XI. 1585), Eng. organist and comp. He may have been educ. in the Chapel Royal or at St. Paul's Cathedral in London, and held a post at Waltham Abbey before its dissolution in 1540, prob. as choirmaster or organist. He became a Gentleman of the Chapel Royal *c.* 1537. In 1557 Queen Mary granted him, jointly with Richard Bowyer, Master of the Children in the Chapel Royal, a lease of the manor of Minster, Thanet, and at her death he passed into the service of Elizabeth, who in 1575 granted him, jointly with Byrd, a patent for the sole right to print mus. and mus. paper in Eng.; but 2 years later, not finding this immediately profitable, they petitioned for an annual grant, which was sanctioned. The 2 masters were then joint organists at the Chapel Royal. In his last years he and his wife Joan, whom he had married in 1552, lived at their own house at Greenwich.

Works incl. 2 Masses, 2 Lat. Magnificats, Lamentations for 5 voices, over 50 Lat. motets, incl. *Spem in alium* in 40 parts; services, psalms, Litanies, *c.* 30 anthems and other Eng. church mus.; secular vocal pieces; 2 In Nomines for strings, 1 for lute; org. and virginal pieces, etc.

Talon (Fr.), the heel (or nut) of the bow of a string instrument.

Tam-Tam (onomat.) = Gong.

Tamagno, Francesco (b. Turin, 28. XII. 1850; d. Varese, 31. VIII. 1905), It. tenor. At first a baker's apprentice and locksmith, he studied at the Turin Cons., sang in the opera chorus there, studied further with Pedrotti at Palermo and made his 1st appearance there in 1873. Verdi's 1st Othello.

Tamara, symph. poem by Balakirev, based on a poem by Lermontov (sometimes called *Thamar* in Eng.), begun 1866, finished 1882; 1st perf. St. Petersburg, Free School of Mus., 1882. Ballet on this work (choreography by Mikhail Fokin, setting by Leon Bakst), prod. Paris, Théâtre du Châtelet, 20. V. 1912.

Tamberlik, Enrico (b. Rome, 16. III. 1820; d. Paris, 13. III. 1889), It. tenor, (?) of Turkish descent. At first intended for a lawyer, he made his 1st stage appearance at Naples in 1841, sang in Port. and Spain and in 1850 1st appeared in London.

Tambour (Fr.) = Drum.

Tambour de Basque (Fr.) = Tambourine.

Tamboura. *See* **Pandora.**

Tambourin (Fr.) = Tabor. The T. du Béarn was a zither with strings sounding only tonic and dominant and struck by a stick. Hence T. was used to mean a dance with a drone bass.

Tambourine, a small, shallow drum with a single skin stretched over the edge of one side of its rim, into which jingles are loosely set to add their noise when the skin is struck or rubbed by the hand or to resound separately when the instrument is shaken.

Tamburini, Antonio (b. Faenza, 28. III. 1800; d. Nice, 9. XI. 1876), It. baritone. Was at first taught the horn, but appeared in opera at the age of 18, at Bologna. He 1st sang in London in 1832 and later spent 10 years in Rus.

Tamburino (It.) = Tambourine.

Tamburo (It. = drum). The term is used in scores, with var. adjectival qualifications, for any kind of drum except the Kettledrums, which are called *timpani* in It.

Tamerlano (*Tamburlane*), opera by Handel (lib. by Agostino Piovene, adapted by Nicola Francesco Haym), prod. London, King's Theatre, Haymarket, 31. X. 1724.

Taming of the Shrew, The. *See* **Sly; Widerspänstigen Zähmung.**

Tampon (Fr.), a drum mallet with 2 heads, one at each end of the stick, sometimes used, esp. by 19th-cent. Fr. comps., to prod. rolls on the Bass Drum, the 2 heads being made to hit the drum-head alternately by rapid rotary motions of the wrist.

Tampur, a Caucasian instrument of the lute type, but played with a bow. It has 3 strings.

Tancredi (*Tancred*), opera by Rossini (lib. by Gaetano Rossi, based on Tasso's *Gerusalemme liberata* and Voltaire's tragedy *Tancrède*), prod. Venice, Teatro La Fenice, 6. II. 1813. Rossini's 1st serious opera.

Taneiev, Alexander Sergeievich (b. St. Petersburg, 17. I. 1850; d. Petrograd, 7. II. 1918), Rus. comp. Entered state service after studies at St. Petersburg Univ., but also studied mus. there and at Dresden, and came under the influence of the Balakirev circle.

Works incl. operas *Cupid's Revenge* and *The Snowstorm*; 3 symphs., symph. poem *Alesha Popovich*, overture to Shakespeare's *Hamlet*, 2 suites for orch.; 3 string 4tets; pieces for vln. and pf. and for pf.; songs, part-songs, etc.

Taneiev, Sergey Ivanovich (b. Gvt. of Vladimir, 25. XI. 1856; d. Djudkowa, 19. VI. 1915), Rus. comp. Studied at the Moscow Cons., intending at 1st to become a pianist, but also studying comp. with Tchaikovsky. In 1876 he toured Rus., in 1877–8 visited Paris, and after playing in the Baltic Provinces became prof. of orch. at the Moscow Cons., in 1881 chief prof. of pf. on N. Rubinstein's death and in 1885 director, succeeding Hubert. He was followed by Safonov in 1889 and concentrated on teaching counterpoint and fugue.

Works incl. operatic trilogy *Oresteia* (based on Aeschylus); cantata *John of Damascus* for solo voices, chorus and orch.; 4 symphs., Overture on Rus. Themes for orch.; concert suite for vln. and orch.; 6 string 4tets, pf. 4tets, 2 string trios, pf. trio; prelude and fugue for 2 pfs.; *c.* 40 songs to words by Tiutchev and others; part-songs, etc.

Tañer (Span. = to touch), a 16th-cent. lute prelude with which the strings were 'touched', or tried; equivalent to a Toccata.

Tangents, the screwdriver-shaped pins striking the wire strings in the Clavichord. The strings continue to sound while the T.s touch them, and their tone can thus be made to vibrate like a vln. *vibrato* by shaking the finger on the key.

Tango, a dance of Central African orig., imported by Negro slaves into Cuba, Haiti and Mex. and thence taken with them when they migrated to the Arg. and Uruguayan shores of the River Plate, where it became indigenous. It is thus not of Arg. orig., but became mainly Arg. during the 19th cent. until, *c.* 1910, it came into the Eur. ballrooms and was taken up by the jazz bands. It is in 2–4 time, like the Span. Habanera, but faster in pace, and is accomp. with a rhythm of 4 quavers, the 1st of which is dotted.

Tannhäuser und der Sängerkrieg auf der Wartburg (*Tannhäuser and the Singers' Contest at the Wartburg*), opera by Wagner (lib. by comp.), prod. Dresden, 19. X. 1845.

Tansman, Alexander (b. Lodz, 12. VI. 1897), Pol. comp. Studied at home and then at Warsaw, and in 1919 took 2 prizes for comp. He settled in Paris, but travelled extensively as pianist and cond. Married the Fr. pianist Colette Cras.

Works incl. operas *La Nuit Kurde*, *La Toison d'or*, *Le Serment* and *Sabbataï Lévi*, *le faux Messie*; ballets *Sextuor* and *La Grande Ville*; 8 symphs., *Sinfonietta*, symph. overture, *Toccata*, *Sonatine transatlantique*, *4 Danses polonaises*, *Triptyque*, *Partita*, *2 Pièces*, *Études symphoniques*, serenade, *Rapsodie polonaise* and suites for orch.; variations on a theme by Frescobaldi for strings; 2 concertos and *Concertino* for pf. and orch.; 8 string 4tets, mazurka for 9 instruments, *Divertimento* for ob., clar., tpt., cello and pf., *Danse de la sorcière* for 5 wind instruments and pf.; *Sonata quasi una fantasia* for vln. and pf.; 5 sonatas and other pf. works; songs, etc.

Tapiola, symph. poem by Sibelius, Op. 112, comp. in 1926 for the Symph. Society in N.Y. The title is the old mythological name of Fin., derived from the forest god Tapio, who appears in the *Kalevala*. 1st perf. N.Y., 26. XII. 1926.

Tapissier, Jean (b. ?; d. ?), Fr. 14th–15th-cent. comp. He (?) lived in It. for some time. Comp. church mus.

Tappert, Wilhelm (b. Ober-Thomaswaldau, Silesia, 19. II. 1830; d. Berlin, 27. X. 1907), Ger. mus. scholar. Studied with Dehn and Kullak in Berlin and after 8 years as teacher and critic at Glogau settled in Berlin in 1866, where he taught at Tausig's pf. school and wrote numerous mus.-lit. works, incl. a Wagner Lexicon and other works on Wagner, studies of notation, old lute mus., the settings of Goethe's *Erl King* (51), etc. He also comp. pf. pieces, incl. 50 Studies for the left hand, songs, etc.

Tarantella, an It. dance deriving its name from Taranto, formerly sometimes sung, but now purely instrumental. It is in quick 6–8 time, increasing its speed progressively towards the end, and consists of alternating maj. and min. sections. It was danced by a couple, or in couples, who often accompanied the mus. with timbrels. 2 superstitions were connected with it: (1) that the bite of the tarantula caused a kind of madness which made people dance it; (2) that the dance was a remedy against such madness.

Tarantino, Il. *See* Fago.

Tarare, opera by Salieri (lib. by Beaumarchais), prod. Paris, Opéra, 8. VI. 1787. It became known later under the It. title of *Axur, re d'Ormus*.

Tarchi, Angelo (b. Naples, *c.* 1759; d. Paris, 19. VIII. 1814), It. comp. Studied at the Cons. dei Turchini at Naples with Fago and Sala. He visited London in 1789 and wrote the operas *Il disertore* and *La generosità d'Alessandro* for the King's Theatre. Later he lived in Paris.

Works incl. over 40 It. and 7 Fr. operas, etc.

Tardando (It. = delaying), a direction indicating that a passage is to be played in a lingering manner.

Tarditi, Orazio (b. Rome, 1602; d. Forlì, 18. I. 1677), It. monk, organist and comp. He was organist at var. It. towns and from 1647–70 *maestro di cappella* at Faenza Cathedral.

Works incl. Masses, motets, madrigals, canzonets, etc.

Tarenghi, Mario (b. Bergamo, 10. VII. 1870; d. Milan, 21. IX. 1938), It. pianist and comp. Studied at the Milan Cons. and later became director of a school of mus. there.

Works incl. operas *Marcella*, *Gara antica*, *La notte di Quarto*, *Piero Vidal*; *Stabat Mater*; choral works; string 4tet in G min.; variations on themes by Chopin and Schumann for 2 pfs., variations on *Santa Lucia* for pf. duet; numerous works for pf. solo, etc.

Tárogató, a Hung. instrument, formerly a double-reed instrument akin to the Shawm; now fitted with a clar. mouthpiece and hence sounding more like a Saxophone.

Tarp, Svend Erik (b. Jutland, 6. VIII. 1908), Dan. comp. Studied at the Copenhagen Cons., later at Munich and Innsbruck. On his return home he 1st earned a living in Copenhagen by playing dance mus. and teaching, but about 1930 he began to come forward as a comp., mainly with chamber mus. In 1937–42 he taught at the Cons.

Works incl. opera *Prinsessen in det fjerne*, 2 ballets; incid. mus.; *Te Deum* and *Christmas oratorio*; 3 symphs., suites and other orchestral works; chamber and pf. mus., etc.

Tartaglione, Ippolito (b. Modena, 1539; d. Naples, VII. 1582), It. comp. He was successively *maestro di cappella* at Santa Maria Maggiore in Rome and, from *c.* 1576, at Naples Cathedral.

Works incl. Masses and motets for 3 and 4 choruses, etc.

Tartini, Giuseppe (b. Pirano, Istria, 8. IV. 1692; d. Padua, 26. II. 1770), It. violinist and comp. Intended for the Church, he went to Padua Univ., but was forced to flee after his runaway marriage with Elisabetta Premazore in 1710, and supported himself as an orchestral violinist. Taking refuge at the Franciscan Monastery at Assisi, he was a vln. pupil of Černohorský, but a meeting with Veracini in Venice in 1716 convinced him of his technical inadequacy, and he went to Ancona for further study. In 1721 he was app. principal violinist at the Basilica of Sant' Antonio, where apart from a period in the service of Count Kinsky in Prague (1723–6) and occasional travels elsewhere, he remained till his death. In 1728 he estab. a school of vln. playing in Padua, where his pupils included Nardini and Pugnani. He discovered combination tones (*q.v.*) and commended their use to his pupils as a guide to true intonation. From 1750 he increasingly withdrew from comp. to devote himself to theoret. study, and pub. a number of treatises incl. *Trattato di musica* (1754).

Works. incl. *Miserere* (said to have been comp. for Pope Clement XII) and other church mus.; over 100 vln. concertos; vln. sonatas, trio sonatas, etc.

Taschengeige (Ger., lit. pocket fiddle). *See* **Kit.**

Taskin, Émile Alexandre (b. Paris, 18. III. 1853; d. Paris, 5. X. 1897), Fr. baritone. Studied at the Paris Cons. and was a member of the Opéra-Comique in 1879–94. Grandson of the organist and comp. Henri Joseph T. (1779–1852), great-grandson of Pascal Joseph T. (1750–1829), keeper of the royal instruments, and great-great-grandson of the instrument maker Pascal T. (1723–93).

Tasso, lamento e trionfo (*Tasso's Lament and Triumph*), symph. poem by Liszt, based on a poem by Byron, comp. 1849, perf. Weimar, 28. VIII. 1849, as an overture to Goethe's drama *Tôrquato Tasso*, revised 1850–1 with a new middle section and 1st perf. Weimar, 19. IV. 1854.

Tasso, Torquato (1544–95), It. poet. *See* **Armida** and **Armide** (11 operas on *Gerusalemme liberata*), **Belli (D.)** (*Aminta*), **Caccini (F.), Campra** (*Tancrède*), **Gavazzeni** (*Aminta*), **Lenepveu** (*Renaud dans les jardines d'Armide*), **Madrigal Opera** (*Aminta*), **Monteverdi** (*Combattimento di Tancredi e Clorinda*), **Pallavicini (C.)** (*Gerus. lib.*), **Persuis** (*Jérusalem délivrée*), **Pizzetti** (*Aminta*), **Righini** (*Gerus. lib.*), **Rinaldo** (Handel), **Rossellini** (*Aminta*), **Rossi (M. A.)** (*Erminia sul Giordano*), **Tancredi** (Rossini).

Tastar (It., from *tastare* = to touch), a 16th-cent. lute prelude with which the strings were 'touched', or tried; equivalent to a Toccata.

Tasten (Ger.) = Keys (of a keyboard).

Tastiera per luce (It. = keyboard for light), an instrument appearing in the score of Skriabin's *Prometheus*, designed to throw differently coloured lights. It was never perfected for practical use.

Tasto (It.), key (of keyboard instruments); also fingerboard (of string instruments).

Tasto solo (It. = key alone), a direction indicating that in a comp. with a thoroughbass the bass notes are for the moment to be played alone on the keyboard instrument used, without any harmony above them.

Tate, Nahum (1652–1715), Ir. poet. *See* **Dido and Aeneas** (Purcell).

Tate, Phyllis (b. Gerrards Cross, 6. IV. 1911), Eng. comp. Studied comp. with Harry Farjeon at the R.A.M. in London, 1928–32. Several of her works were perf. when she was still a student, and in 1933 her cello concerto was her 1st work heard at a public concert.

Works incl. opera *The Lodger*; operetta *The Policeman's Serenade* (A. P. Herbert); symph. and suite for orch., *Valse lointaine* and prelude, interlude and postlude for chamber orch.; cello and saxophone concertos; *Divertimento* for string 4tet. sontata for clar. and cello, *Nocturne* (Sidney Keyes) for 4 voices, string 5tet, celesta and bass clar.; *London Waits* for 2 pfs.; *Songs of Sundry Natures* on Elizabethan poems for voice and pf., songs to words by Blake, W. H. Davies, Hardy, Hood, Tennyson and others, *The Phoenix and the Turtle* for tenor and instrumental ensemble, etc.

Tatto (It. obs.) = Acciaccatura.

Tauber, Richard (actually Ernst Seiffert) (b. Linz, 16. V. 1892; d. London, 8. I. 1948), Aus. tenor and cond. Studied at Freiburg i/B. and made his 1st stage

Taubert

appearance at Chemnitz in 1913. About 1925 he took largely to operetta and in 1931 he 1st appeared in Eng., where he remained.

Taubert, (Karl Gottfried) Wilhelm (b. Berlin, 23. III. 1811; d. Berlin, 7. I. 1891), Ger. pianist, cond. and comp. Pupil of Ludwig Berger for pf. and of Klein for comp., and student at Berlin Univ. He became Prus. court pianist, in 1841 cond. of the Royal Opera and in 1845 court mus. director.

Works incl. operas *Die Kirmess, Der Zigeuner, Marquis und Dieb, Joggeli, Macbeth* (after Shakespeare) and *Cesario* (on Shakespeare's *Twelfth Night*); incid. mus. to *Medea* (Euripides), *The Tempest* (Shakespeare) and other plays; 3 Psalms and other church mus.; 4 cantatas; 4 symphs., Festival Overture for orch.; 3 string 4tets, 2 pf. trios; 6 vln. and pf. sonatas; 6 pf. sonatas and many pieces; *c.* 300 songs incl. *Kinderlieder*; duets, part-songs, etc.

Taubmann, Otto (b. Hamburg, 8. III. 1859; d. Berlin, 5. VII. 1929), Ger. cond., critic and comp. Studied at the Dresden Cons. and became cond. and critic in several towns, settling in Berlin in 1895, where he was prof. at the Hochschule für Musik from 1920 to 1925.

Works incl. opera *Porzia*; *Deutsche Messe* and other choral works; symph.; string 4tet, etc.

Tausch, Julius (b. Dessau, 15. IV. 1827; d. Bonn, 11. XI. 1895), Ger. cond. and comp. Pupil of Schneider at Dessau and at the Leipzig Cons. He became cond. of the Künstlerliedertafel at Düsseldorf in 1847, and succeeded Schumann as cond. of the Mus. Society in 1855.

Works incl. incid. mus. to Shakespeare's *Twelfth Night*; Festival Overture for orch.; pf. pieces; songs, etc.

Tausig, Carl (b. Warsaw, 4. XI. 1841; d. Leipzig, 17. VII. 1871), Pol. pianist and comp. of Boh. origin. Pupil of his father, the pianist Aloys T. (1820–85), and of Liszt at Weimar. In 1858 he made his 1st appearance at a concert cond. by Bülow in Berlin, then toured, settled at Dresden and in 1862 in Vienna, where he gave concerts with programmes of modern mus. In 1865 he married, settled in Berlin and opened a school of advanced pf. playing.

Works incl. symph. poems; pf. concerto; concert studies, exercises, bravura pieces and numerous transcriptions for pf., etc.

Taverner, John (b. ? Tattershall, Lincs., *c.* 1495; d. Boston, Lincs., 25. X. 1545), Eng. organist and comp. In 1526 he was app. master of the choristers at Wolsey's new coll. (Cardinal Coll., later Christ Church) at Oxford and organist at St. Frideswide's Church (later Cathedral)

Tchaikovsky

attached to it. In 1528 he was imprisoned for heresy and in 1530 he left the Coll. or was dismissed, the rest of his career being devoted to the activities of an agent in Thomas Cromwell's pay. He gave up mus., settled at Boston and there took part in the fanatical destruction of church property.

Works incl. 8 Masses (*The Western Wind*, etc.), 28 Lat. motets 3 Magnificats and other church mus.; In Nomines for strings, etc.

Tayber, Anton and **Franz.** *See* **Teyber.**

Taylor, (Joseph) Deems (b. N.Y., 22. XII. 1885; d. N.Y., 3. VII. 1966), Amer. comp. and critic. Studied at the Ethical Culture School and the Univ. in N.Y., received pf. lessons, but was self-taught in other mus. subjects. Having done a good deal of mus. editing, he became mus. critic to the *N.Y. World* in 1921, but from 1925 devoted himself to comp.

Works incl. operas *The King's Henchman, Peter Ibbetson* (after George du Maurier) and *Ramuntcho* (after Loti); incid. mus. for Thornton Wilder's *Lucrece* and other plays; symph. poems *The Siren Song* and *Jurgen* (after J. Branch Cabell), suites *Through the Looking-Glass* (after Lewis Carroll) and *Circus Day*; *Lucrece* suite for string 4tet; choral works, etc.

Taylor, Samuel Coleridge. *See* **Coleridge-Taylor.**

Tchaikovsky, Peter Ilyich (b. Kamsko-Votinsk, 7. V. 1840; d. St. Petersburg, 6. XI. 1893), Rus. comp. His father, an inspector of mines, allowed him to have mus. lessons from the age of 4, and at 6 he played well. The family moved to St. Petersburg in 1848; he received more systematic teaching there and in 1850 was sent to the School of Jurisprudence, which he left in 1859 to become a clerk in the Ministry of Justice. He approached mus. as an amateur, but in 1862 entered the newly opened Cons., having already studied with Zaremba, and had lessons in orch. from A. Rubinstein. N. Rubinstein, having opened a similar Cons. at Moscow, engaged him as prof. of harmony in 1865, and there he began to comp. seriously and professionally. In 1868 he met Balakirev and his circle of nationalist comps. in St. Petersburg, but remained aloof from them.

His operas gained him recognition. The 2nd symph., a distinctly nationalist work, was prod. in 1873, and the B♭ min. pf. concerto, already done abroad by Bülow, was 1st played by Taneiev at Moscow in 1875. In 1876 began a correspondence with Nadezhda von Meck, the widow of a wealthy engineer, who greatly admired his work and made him an allowance to free him from financial anxiety, but never met him face to face. In

1877 he married Antonina Ivanovna Miliukov, whom he left less than a month after the wedding, on the verge of a mental collapse. After some months in Switz. and It., he resigned the post at the Moscow Cons. and lived in the country, wholly devoted to comp. In 1888 he made a 1st international tour as cond. of his own works, which became known in many countries. In 1890 he had a misunderstanding with Nadezhda von Meck which brought their friendship by correspondence to an end; but he was by that time quite able to earn his own living.

He visited the U.S.A. in 1892 and London in the summer of 1893, when the Mus.D. degree was conferred on him by Cambridge Univ. On his return to Rus., where the 6th symph. ('Pathetic') was perf. at St. Petersburg on 28. X, he rashly drank a glass of unboiled water and developed cholera, from which he d.

Works incl. operas *The Opritchnik, Vakula the Smith* (afterwards *Tcherevichki* or *Oxana's Caprices*), *Eugene Onegin, Joan of Arc, Mazeppa, The Sorceress, The Queen of Spades, Iolanta* and 3 partly lost early works; incid. mus. to Ostrovsky's *Snegurochka* and Shakespeare's *Hamlet*; ballets, *The Swan Lake, The Sleeping Beauty* and *The Nutcracker*; 6 symphs.; 4 suites for orch.; miscellaneous works incl. fantasy-overture *Romeo and Juliet*, symph. fantasies *The Tempest* and *Francesca da Rimini, Capriccio italien*, serenade for string orch., overture *The Year 1812*, fantasy-overture *Hamlet*, symph. ballad *The Voyevoda*; 3 pf. concertos (3rd unfinished), vln. concerto, *Variations on a Rococo Theme* for cello and orch. and some smaller pieces for solo instruments and orch.; string 6tet *Souvenir de Florence*, 3 string 4tets, pf. trio; 17 op. nos. of pf. comps. incl. 6 pieces on 1 theme, sonata in G maj., *The Seasons*; 50 Rus. folksongs for vocal duet; 13 op. nos. of songs (nearly 100); 6 vocal duets; 3 cantatas; some church mus.; part-songs, etc.

Tchang-Tsi (*c.* 11th cent.), Chin. poet. *See* **Lied von der Erde** (Mahler).

Tchekhov, Anton Pavlovich (1860–1904), Rus. dramatist and novelist. *See* **Nottara** (*On the Highway*), **Bear** (Walton).

Tcherepnin, Alexander Nikolaievich (b. St. Petersburg, 21. I. 1899), Rus. comp. Studied under his father, Nikolai T., Sokolov and others, learning the pf. from Anna Essipova. He appeared as a boy pianist and began to pub. his works, but in 1921 settled in Paris with his father, studying comp. with Gédalge and pf. with Philipp at the Cons. From 1925 and 1938 he taught in Paris, and from 1949 at DePaul Univ. in Chicago.

Works incl. operas *Ol-Ol* (after Andreiev) and *Die Hochzeit der Sobeide*

(after Hofmannsthal); ballets incl. *The Frescoes of Ajanta* and (with Honegger and Harsányi) *Shota Roustaveli*; incid. mus. for Wilde's *Salome*, Rolland's *L'Esprit triomphant* and Hauptmann's *Hannele*; cantata *Le Jeu de la Nativité*; 4 symphs., 3 pieces for chamber orch., 5 pf. concertos, *Rapsodie géorgienne* for cello and pf., *Concerto da camera* for fl., vln. and small orch.; 2 string 4tets, pf. trio; vln. and pf. sonata, 3 cello and pf. sonatas; sonata, studies and pieces for pf.

Tcherepnin, Nikolai Nikolaievich (b. St. Petersburg, 14. V. 1873; d. Issy-les-Moulineaux nr. Paris, 26. VI. 1945), Rus. cond. and comp. He gave up a legal career at the age of 22 and studied at the St. Petersburg Cons. with Rimsky-Korsakov and others. Having appeared as pianist, he became cond. of the Belaiev concerts in 1901, and then became cond. of opera at the Maryinsky Theatre. In 1908 he joined Diaghilev and cond. Rus. opera and ballet in Paris and elsewhere, remaining with the company until 1914, when he returned to Petrograd, to become director of the Cons. at Tiflis in 1918. In 1921 he settled in Paris.

Works incl. operas *Vanka the Chancellor* (after Sologub) and *Poverty no Crime* (after Ostrovsky); ballets *Armida's Pavilion, Narcissus, A Russian Fairy-Tale, The Romance of a Mummy* (after Gautier), *The Masque of the Red Death* (after Poe), *The Tale of the Princess Ulyba, Dionysius*; symph., sinfonietta, symph. poems *Narcissus and Echo* and *The Enchanted Kingdom*, witches' scene from *Macbeth*, suite *The Enchanted Garden*, overture to Rostand's *La Princesse lointaine*, 6 pieces on Pushkin's *The Golden Fish* for orch.; pf. concerto in C$\sharp$ min., lyric poem for vln. and orch.; string 4tet in A min.; pf. pieces on Benois's picture-book *The Russian Alphabet* and other pf. works; songs, etc.

Tcherevichki (Tchaikovsky). *See* **Vakula the Smith.**

Tchishko, Oles (b. nr. Kharkov, 2. VII. 1895), Rus. singer, cond. and comp. Son of a peasant, he learnt mus. mainly in the choir-school and picked up Ukrainian folksongs. He studied briefly at the Kharkov Cons. Working mainly as singer and cond., he nevertheless comp. an opera, *Judith*, which he went to Leningrad to show to Glazunov, who approved of it. In 1927 he sang in popular opera at Odessa, but returned to Leningrad in 1931 to continue his comp. studies.

Works incl. operas *Judith, Imprisoned by Apple Orchards, Mutiny on the Battleship Potemkin*; overture *Red Army Days, Ukrainian Capriccio, Suite for Dancing*, suite *Youth*, etc., for orch.; Ukrainian songs arr. for chorus and orch., etc.

Te, the name for the leading-note in any

key in Tonic Sol-fa, so pronounced, but in notation represented by the symbol **t**.

Te Deum laudamus (*We praise thee, O God*), Lat. hymn or psalm in 'rhythmical prose', prob. by Nicetas of Remesiana (*c.* 400). It is in 3 sections: a hymn to the Trinity, a hymn to Christ, and a series of prayers. The 1st part is set to a psalmodic formula ending on G, and the 2nd to a similar formula ending on E, but concluding with a more extended melody in the same mode to the words 'Aeterna fac'. The 3rd part makes further use of these last 2 melodies.

The Te Deum was set in polyphony during the Middle Ages, esp. in England, for voices or org. in alternation with the plainsong. It became a normal part of the Angl. 'Morning Service' and it has also been set in Eng. for occasions of rejoicing (e.g. by Handel, Walton). The Latin text has often been set with orchestral accomp., e.g. by Haydn (2), Berlioz, Bruckner and Kodály.

Teares and Lamentacions of a Sorrowfull Soul, The. *See* Leighton.

Tebaldi, Renata (b. Pesaro, 1. II. 1922), It. soprano. Studied at Parma Cons., and then with Carmen Melis from 1939 to 1942, making her début in Rovigo in 1944. She sang at the re-opening of La Scala, Milan, in 1946 under Toscanini and at Covent Garden in 1950. She is known as one of the best Verdi and Puccini singers of the day.

Tedesca (fem.)
Tedesco (masc.) } (It.) = German. The term *alla tedesca* means 'in the Ger. manner', but more partic. indicates a piece or movement in rather slow waltz time, in the character of the *Deutscher* or *Ländler*.

Tegnér, Esias (1782–1846), Swed. poet. *See* Bruch (*Frithjof*), Dubois (do.), Fervaal (d'Indy), Hofmann (H.) (*Frithjof*), Zöllner (do.).

Telemaco, Il, ossia L'isola di Circe (*Telemachus, or Circe's Island*), opera by Gluck (lib. by Marco Coltellini), prod. Vienna, Burgtheater, 30. I. 1765.

Telemann, Georg Philipp (b. Magdeburg, 14. III. 1681; d. Hamburg, 25. VI. 1767), Ger. comp. Educ. at Magdeburg and Hildesheim, and at Leipzig Univ., where he read law, he seems to have been largely self-taught in mus. In Leipzig he founded a student *Collegium musicum* and was app. organist of the New Church (St. Matthew's) in 1704, but the same year moved to Sorau as *Kapellmeister* to Count Promnitz. In the service of the court at Eisenach 1708–12 (*Kapellmeister* from 1709) he made the acquaintance of Bach in nearby Weimar, then worked in Frankfurt until his app. in 1721 as Cantor of the Johanneum and municipal mus. director in Hamburg,

where he stayed for the rest of his life. In 1722 he declined the post of Cantor of St. Thomas's, Leipzig, and Bach was app. He travelled a good deal, several times visiting Berlin, and in 1737 made a successful visit to Paris.

Works incl. *c.* 45 operas, e.g. *Der gedultige Socrates, Der neumodische Liebhaber Damon, Miriways, Pimpinone, Emma und Eginhard*, etc.; oratorios *Die Tageszeiten, Die Auferstehung und Himmelfahrt Christi, Der Tag des Gerichts*, etc.; Passion oratorios (Brockes and Ramler); 46 liturgical Passions; 12 sets of cantatas for the church's year; motets, psalms, etc.; large quantities of instrumental mus.: concertos, orchestral suites, trio sonatas and other chamber mus., keyboard mus., etc.

Telharmonium, an electrophonic instrument invented by the Amer. scientist Thomas Cahill early in the 20th cent., prod. its notes by means of electromagnets and capable of imitating var. instruments.

Tellefsen, Thomas (Dyke Acland) (b. Trondhjem, 26. XI. 1823; d. Paris, 6. X. 1874), Norw. pianist and comp., (?) godson of Thomas Dyke Acland, M.P. for N. Devon, who travelled much in Norw. He was a pupil of Chopin in Paris and visited Eng. with him in 1848. He frequently played there later and ed. Chopin's works in Paris.

Works incl. 2 pf. concertos; chamber mus.; sonata for 2 pfs., sonata and miscellaneous pieces for pf., etc.

Tema (It.) = Theme.

Temistocle (*Themistocles*), opera by Porpora (lib. by Apostolo Zeno), prod. Vienna, 1. X. 1718.

Temperament (*see also* **Equal Temperament**), a term used to designate the tuning of the mus. scale in such a way as to prod. satisfying intonation in some way not according to the natural harmonics.

Tempest, The, incid. mus. by Sibelius, Op. 109, comp. for prod. of Shakespeare's play at the Theatre Royal, Copenhagen, 1926.

Opera by Fibich (lib. by Jaroslav Vrchlický, based on Shakespeare), prod. Prague, Cz. Theatre, 1. III. 1895.

Opera by N. Gatty (lib. by Reginald Gatty, based on Shakespeare), prod. London, Surrey Theatre, 17. IV. 1920.

Symph. fantasy by Tchaikovsky, after Shakespeare, suggested by Stassov, begun VIII. 1873, 1st perf. Moscow, XII. 1873.

Tempest, The, or The Enchanted Island, opera adapted from Shakespeare by Thomas Shadwell, with mus. by (?) Locke, Humfrey, Reggio, James Hart, G. B. Draghi and Banister, prod. London, Dorset Gardens Theatre, 30. IV. 1674.

Opera adapted from Shakespeare by

Shadwell, with mus. by Purcell, comp. (?) 1695.

Tempesta, La, opera by Halévy (lib. by Scribe, orig. written in Fr. for Mendelssohn, based on Shakespeare's *Tempest* and trans. into It.), prod. London, Her Majesty's Theatre, 8. VI. 1850.

Templario, Il (*The Templar*), opera by Nicolai (lib. by Girolamo Maria Marini, based on Scott's *Ivanhoe*), prod. Turin, Teatro Regio, 11. II. 1840.

Temple Block *See* **Chinese Block.**

Temple, Hope. *See* **Messager.**

Templer und die Jüdin, Der (*The Templar and the Jewess*), opera by Marschner (lib. by Wilhelm August Wohlbrück, based on Scott's *Ivanhoe*), prod. Leipzig, 22. XII. 1829.

Templeton, John (b. Riccarton, Kilmarnock, 30. VII. 1802; d. New Hampton, 2. VII. 1886), Scot. tenor. Appeared as a child singer at Edinburgh, studied there and in London, and made his 1st stage appearance at Worthing in 1828. In 1831 he became known in London and in 1833 Malibran engaged him as her partner.

Tempo (It. lit. time) = Pace, the speed of any mus. comp., determined, not by the note-values, which are relative, but by the directions set above the stave at the opening of a piece or section (e.g. *allegro, andante, adagio*, etc.). The exact pace can be estab. only by means of Metronome marks (e.g. ♩ = 96, i.e. 96 crotchets to the minute, etc.). In It. T. also means a movement of a sonata, symph., etc.

Tempo giusto (It.) = Strict time, also the right speed.

Tempo ordinario (It. = common time, ordinary pace), either (1) moderate speed or (2) 4 beats in a bar (C), as opposed to *Alla breve* (₵), where there are 2 beats in a bar.

Tempo primo (It. lit. 1st time = 1st tempo), after a change of tempo the direction *t. p.* means that the pace 1st indicated is to be resumed.

Tempo rubato. *See* **Rubato.**

Tempus imperfectum ⎫
Tempus perfectum ⎭ (Lat. = imperfect and perfect time). *See* **Time Signature.**

Ten. (abbr.) = *tenuto*.

Tenaglia, Antonio Francesco (b. Florence, ?; d. ?), It. 17th-cent. comp. Studied and lived in Rome.

Works incl. opera *Clearco*; madrigals; arias and duets, etc.

Tenducci, Giusto Ferdinando (b. Siena, c. 1736; d. Genoa, 25. I. 1790), It. castrato soprano and comp. Made his début in Naples, then went to London in 1758, remaining there, apart from visits to Ir. (1765–8) and Scot. (1768–9), until 1791, when he returned to It. He pub. a treatise on singing, comp. songs, harpsichord

sonatas, etc., and compiled song collections, etc. He was thrice married.

Tenendo (It. = holding) = Sustaining, without hurrying.

Teneramente (It.) = Tenderly.

Tenerezza (It.) = Tenderness.

Tenero (It.) = Tender, gentle.

Tenete (It. imper.), hold, sustain.

Tennyson, Alfred, Lord (1809–92), Eng. poet. *See* **Clutsam** (*Lady of Shalott*), **Delius** (*Maud*), **Gerster** (O.) (*Enoch Arden*), **Hadley** (P.) (*Mariana*), **Jacobson** (*Lady of Shalott*), **Jensen** (songs), **Lahee** (*Sleeping Beauty*), **Lehmann** (L. ii) (*In Memoriam*), **Macfarren** (G.) (songs), **Mihalovich** (*Eliána*), **Novák** (*Lady Godiva*), **Parry** (H.) (*Lotos-Eaters*), **Quilter** (songs), **Raimann** (*Enoch Arden*), **Schira** (*Lord of Burleigh*), **Sessions** (*Lancelot and Elaine*), **Somervell** (*Maud*), **Stanford** (*Queen Mary, Becket, Revenge* and *Princess*), **Strauss** (R.) (*Enoch Arden*), **Sullivan** (*Foresters* and *The Window*), **Tate** (songs).

Tenor, the highest male voice prod. naturally, i.e. not in falsetto, like the male alto. It is so called (from Lat. *teneo* = 'I hold') because it 'held' the plainsong theme in early polyphonic comps. using a *Cantus firmus*. The compass is approx.:

The word T. was formerly also used for the vla.

Tenor Clef, the C clef so used as to indicate that middle C stands on the 4th line of the stave:

It was formerly used for the tenor voice but is now used only for the tenor tromb. and the higher reaches of the bassoon, cello and double bass.

Tenor Cor, a military-band brass instrument invented c. 1860 to provide a better substitute for the horn than had been found in the Saxhorn. It is in the circular form of a horn, though half the length, and has valves. It is made in F, with an extra slide to change it to E♭.

Tenor Drum, a drum with 2 skins stretched over either end, similar in shape to the side drum and bass drum, but of intermediate size. It prod. a duller sound than that of the side drum, having no snares, but gives out clearer notes, though of indefinite pitch, than the bass drum.

Tenor Horn, a brass valve wind instrument of the Saxhorn type, made in var. tunings and compasses.

Tenor Tuba, another name for the Euphonium.

Tenor Viol. *See* **Viol.**

Tenor Violin, obs. name for the vla. A small cello, tuned a 5th or a 4th above the normal cello, was sometimes known as a T.V.

Tenore (It.) = Tenor.

Tenore robusto (It. = robust tenor), one of the categories of operatic voices: a tenor capable of sustaining parts of a heroic type; equivalent to the Ger. *Heldentenor.*

Tenoroon, an obs. instrument of the bassoon type, smaller and tuned higher than the bassoon.

Tenson, a Troubadour, Trouvère or Minnesinger song the words of which took the form of a dispute.

Tenuta (It.) = Fermata.

Tenuto (It. = held), a direction usually marked *ten.*, indicating that the note or notes to which it applies are to be sustained to their full value, or even an almost imperceptible fraction beyond, but not so much as to give the different effect of *ritenuto*: the meaning is 'held', not 'held back'.

Ternary. A vocal or instrumental piece in 3 distinct sections, the 3rd of which is a repetition of the 1st, is said to be in T. form. The middle section is usually a contrast, sometimes based on similar but more often on different thematic material, but always relevant in style if not in mood. In vocal mus. *da capo* arias and in instrumental mus. minuets or scherzos with trios are outstanding exs. of T. form.

Ternina, Milka (b. Vezisce, Croatia, 19. XII. 1863; d. Zagreb, 18. V. 1941), Yugoslav soprano. Studied at home from the age of 12 and in 1880–2 in Vienna. She appeared at Zagreb when still a student, then sang light parts at Leipzig, rising gradually through greater parts at Graz and Bremen to the Court Opera at Munich, to which she was attached in 1890–9. In 1895 she 1st sang in London, making her 1st appearance at Covent Garden in 1898, and the next year, having become one of the great Wagner singers, she was engaged for Bayreuth.

Terpander (7th cent. B.C.), Gk. poet and musician. He won a prize at the mus. festival in Sparta between 676 and 672 B.C. His contribs. to mus. are uncertain, but are said to have incl. the comp. of drinking-songs, the increase of the lyre strings from 4 to 7 and the intro. of new metres into poetry and consequently into mus.

Terradeglias, Domenico, the It. form of the name of

Terradellas, Domingo Miguel Bernabé (b. Barcelona, II. 1713; d. Rome, 20. V. 1751), Span. comp. Pupil of Durante at the Cons. dei Poveri di Gesù at Naples 1732–8, he there comp. 2 oratorios and prod. his 1st opera in 1739 in Rome, where he was

maestro di cappella at the Span. church 1743–5. He visited London (1746–7) and Paris, then returned to Rome.

Works incl. operas *Astarto, Gli intrighi delle cantarine, Cerere, Merope, Artaserse, Semiramide riconosciuta, Mitridate, Bellerofonte, Imeneo in Atene, Didone, Sesostri, rè d'Egitto*; oratorios, *Giuseppe riconosciuto* and *Ermenegildo martire*; Masses, motets and other church mus., etc.

Terrasse, Claude (Antoine) (b. Grand Lemps nr. Grenoble, 27. I. 1867; d. Paris, 30. VI. 1923), Fr. organist and comp. He studied at the Lyons Cons. and then at Niedermeyer's school in Paris, afterwards privately with Gigout. After living obscurely as an organist at Auteuil and a pf. teacher at Arcachon, he began to comp. and settled in Paris in 1895 as organist of the Trinité.

Works incl. opera *Pantagruel* (after Rabelais), operettas *La Fiancée du scaphandrier, Chonchette, Le Sire de Vergy, Monsieur de la Palisse, L'Ingénu libertin, Le Coq d'Inde, Le Mariage de Télémaque, Les Transatlantiques, La Petite Femme de Loth* (Tristan Bernard), *Les Travaux d'Hercule, Cartouche, Le Cochon qui sommeille, Faust en ménage, Le Manoir enchanté* and several others; incid. mus. for var. comedies; mus. for Théophile Gautier's and Théodore de Banville's *Matinées poétiques; Trio bouffe* for strings, *Sérénade bouffe* for pf. and strings; songs, etc.

Terry, Charles Sanford (b. Newport Pagnell, Bucks., 24. X. 1864; d. Westerton of Pitfodels nr. Aberdeen, 5. XI. 1936), Eng. hist. and mus. biog. He was app. prof. of hist. at Aberdeen Univ. in 1903. He also did invaluable work for mus. by writing an authoritative biog. of Bach as well as numerous detailed studies of var. aspects of his work, and a biog. of J. C. Bach.

Terry, Richard (Runciman) (b. Ellington, Northumberland, 3. I. 1865; d. London, 18. IV. 1938), Eng. organist and musicologist. After var. appts. he became organist and choirmaster at Downside Abbey in Somerset in 1896 and at Westminster Cathedral in London in 1901, where he remained until 1924. He did great work there in enforcing services of the Rom. church according to the highest mus. standards and traditions, and he wrote on and ed. much church mus. He also had a specialist's knowledge of sea shanties and carols. Knighted in 1922.

Tertis, Lionel (b. W. Hartlepool, 29. XII. 1876), Eng. vla. player. First studied vln. at Leipzig Cons. and the R.A.M., and then took up the vla. at the suggestion of Alexander Mackenzie, playing with various string 4tets. This, and his appearances as a soloist, made him one of the most famous violists of his time. He also intro. a new vla. called the 'Tertis Model'. He retired from the concert platform in 1936, but re-emerged during the 1939–45 war.

Terzet (Eng.) } a comp. for 3 voices or
Terzetto (It.) } for instruments in 3 parts. Both terms are obs. in Eng. usage, and are better replaced by Trio.

Terzina (It.) = Triplet.

Teseo (*Theseus*), opera by Handel (lib. by Nicola Francesco Haym), prod. London, Queen's Theatre, Haymarket, 10. I. 1713.

Tesi-Tramontini, Vittoria (b. Florence, 13. II. 1700; d. Vienna, 9. V. 1775), It. contralto. Made her 1st appearance at a very early age. In 1719 she was at Dresden, later in Vienna. It is one of the well-known and purely fictitious Handel stories that he fell in love with her at Florence when his *Rodrigo* was prod. there in 1707: the date of her birth refutes it effectively.

Tess, opera by F. d'Erlanger (lib., in It., by Luigi Illica, based on Thomas Hardy's *Tess of the D'Urbervilles*), prod. Naples, Teatro San Carlo, 10. IV. 1906.

Tessarini, Carlo (b. Rimini, 1690; d. ?, after 1766), It. violinist and comp. He is said to have been (?) a pupil of Corelli, worked as a violinist in Venice at St. Mark's (from 1720) and SS. Giovanni e Paolo, obtained a post at Urbino Cathedral in 1733 but left the same year to enter the service of Cardinal Schrattenbach in Brno, returning to Urbino in 1738. He visited Hol. in 1747 and 1762, and prob. also Paris.
Works incl. *Concerti grossi*; vln. concertos; *sinfonie*; vln. sonatas and duets; trio sonatas, etc. Also wrote a treatise on vln. playing (1741).

Tessier, André (b. Paris, 8. III. 1886; d. Paris, 2. VII. 1931), Fr. musicologist. Studied law, literature and art, and after attending Rolland's lectures took to musicology in 1919. He wrote mainly on old Fr. mus., incl. a book on Couperin, and took part in the complete eds. of Lully and Couperin.

Tessier, Charles (b. Pézénas, Hérault, *c.* 1550; d. ?), Fr. lutenist and comp. He may have been at the court at Cassel and visited Eng. for some time in the 1590s, dedicating a book of *chansons* to Lady Penelope Rich (Sidney's Stella).
Works incl. *chansons* for 4–5 voices, *Airs et villanelles* for 3–5 voices, setting of the 8th song in Sidney's *Astrophel and Stella*, etc.

Tessitura (It. lit. texture), the prevailing range of a voice part in a comp. It may be high, low or normal for the voice required.

Testudo (Lat. = tortoise), a Lat. name for the Gk. lyre, which was often made of

tortoiseshell; transferred to the lute in 16th-cent. Lat.

Tetrachord (from Gk. = having 4 strings), a descending scale of 4 notes embracing the interval of a perfect 4th, e.g.:

Tetrazzini, Luisa (b. Florence, 29. VI. 1871; d. Milan, 28. IV. 1940), It. soprano. Studied with Ceccherini at the Florence Liceo Musicale and with her sister Eva (1862–1938), the wife of the cond. Cleofante Campanini. She made her 1st appearance at Florence in 1895, then toured, 1st in It. and later in Eur., Mex. and S. Amer. In 1907 she 1st appeared in London, in 1908 in U.S.A.

Teufel ist los, Der, oder Die verwandelten Weiber (*The Devil to pay*, or *The Women metamorphosed*), *Singspiel* by J. C. Standfuss (lib. by Christian Felix Weisse, based on Coffey's *Devil to pay*), prod. Leipzig, 6. X. 1752. *See also* **Verwandelten Weiber** (J. A. Hiller).

Teufels Lustschloss, Das (*The Devil's Pleasaunce*), opera by Schubert (lib. by August von Kotzebue), comp. in 1814 but not perf.

Teutsche (Ger., obs.). *See* **Deutsche Tänze**.

Teyber, Anton (b. Vienna, 8. IX. 1754; d. Vienna, 18. XI. 1822), Aus. comp. App. court comp. to the Imp. Chapel in 1793 and mus. teacher to the royal family.
Works incl. melodrama *Zermes und Mirabella*; oratorio *Joas*; Passion, Masses and other church mus.; symphs.; chamber mus., etc.

Teyber, Franz (b. Vienna, 15. XI. 1756; d. Vienna, 22. X. 1810), Aus. cond., organist and comp., brother of prec. Cond. of Schikaneder's company and late in his life app. court organist.
Works incl. operas and *Singspiele*, *Adelheid von Veltheim*, *Laura Rossetti*, *Die Dorfdeputierten*, *Alexander*, *Der Schlaftrunk* and others; oratorio; church mus.; songs, etc.

Teyte (orig. Tâte), **Maggie** (b. Wolverhampton 17. IV. 1888), Eng. soprano. Studied at the R.C.M. and then in Paris with Jean de Reszke (1903–7), making her début in Monte Carlo in 1907. She appeared with Debussy in song recitals and was selected by him to succeed Mary Garden as Mélisande.

Thaïs, opera by Massenet (lib. by Louis Gallet, based on the novel by Anatole France), prod. Paris, Opéra, 16. III. 1894. It contains the popular *Méditation* as an orchestral interlude.

Thalberg, Sigismond (b. Geneva, 7. I. 1812; d. Posilipo, 27. IV. 1871), Aus.

pianist and comp. Illegitimate son of Count Moritz Dietrichstein and Baroness Wetzlar. When he was 10 his father sent him to school in Vienna, where he later studied pf. with Hummel and theory with Sechter. He soon played at private parties, appeared at Prince Metternich's house in 1826 and in 1830 made his 1st tour, in Ger., having by this time begun to pub. comps. In 1835 he made further studies with Pixis and Kalkbrenner in Paris, and in 1836 1st appeared in London.

Works incl. operas *Florinda* and *Cristina di Suezia*; pf. concerto; pf. sonata, studies, nocturnes, romances and numerous other pieces for pf., operatic fantasies and other transcriptions for pf.; over 50 Ger. songs, etc.

Thalberg, Zaré (actually Ethel Western) (b. Derbyshire, 16. IV. 1858; d. London, 1915), Eng. soprano and actress. Pupil of Thalberg, whose name she adopted; also studied in Paris and Milan, and made her 1st London appearance at Covent Garden Theatre in 1875. She soon lost her voice, after some successful appearances on the Continent, and became an actress under her own name.

Thamar (Balakirev). *See* **Tamara**.

Thamos, König in Aegypten (*Thamos, King of Egypt*), incid. mus. by Mozart (K.345) to Tobias Philipp von Gebler's play, comp. 1779 (2 choruses already 1773), not prod. in Mozart's lifetime except in an adaptation to another play, Plümicke's *Lanassa*.

Thayer, Alexander Wheelock (b. S. Natick, Mass., 22. X. 1817; d. Trieste, 15. VII. 1897), Amer. biog. Studied law at Harvard Univ. and in 1849 went to Ger., living at Bonn and Berlin, also to Prague and Vienna, collecting material for a Beethoven biog. After some journalistic activities in N.Y. and Boston, he again went to Eur. in 1854–6 and for a 3rd time in 1858, eventually becoming U.S. consul at Trieste. The 4th vol. of his biog., left unfinished, was completed by Hermann Deiters in a Ger. ed. of the work. An Eng. ed. was pub. in 1921 by Krehbiel and a revision of this by Elliot Forbes in 1964.

Théâtre de la Révolution (Rolland). *See* **Quatorze Juillet**.

Theile, Johann (b. Naumburg, 29. VII. 1646; d. Naumburg, VI. 1724), Ger. comp. Learnt mus. as a youth at Magdeburg and Halle, and later studied at Leipzig Univ., where he took part in the students' perfs. as singer and vla. da gamba player. He then became a pupil of Schütz at Weissenfels and taught mus. at Stettin and Lübeck. In 1673–5 he was *Kapellmeister* to the Duke of Holstein at Gottorp, but fled to Hamburg during the Dan. invasion. In 1676 he completed unsuccessfully for the post of cantor at St. Thomas's Church, Leipzig. He was the 1st comp. to contrib.

to the repertory of the newly opened opera at Hamburg in 1678. In 1685 he succeeded Rosenmüller as mus. director at Wolfenbüttel and in 1689 he was app. to a similar post at Merseburg. In his last years he lived in retirement at his birthplace.

Works incl. operas *Adam und Eva* and *Orontes*; 23 Masses, 8 Magnificats, 12 psalms for 4–11 voices; Passion according to St. Matthew, church cantatas, etc.

Theinred (b. ?, d. ?), 12th-cent. Eng. mus. theorist and monk of Dover Priory. His treatise, a study of intervals and proportions, is known only from an early 15th-cent. copy (Oxford, Bodleian Library, MS. Bodley 842). It includes a diagram of the different forms of alphabetical notation, and a section on the measurement of org.-pipes.

Theme, a mus. idea, generally melodic, sufficiently striking to be memorable and capable of being developed or varied in the course of a comp. A T. is generally complete in itself, whereas a Motive is a figure which contrib. something to a larger conception; but a precise distinction between the two is impossible in practice.

Theocritus (3rd cent. B.C.), Gk. poet. *See* **Durey** (*Épigrammes de Théocrite*), **Pastoral** (Bliss).

Theodora, oratorio by Handel (lib. by Thomas Morell), prod. London, Covent Garden Theatre, 16. III. 1750.

Theorbo, a bass lute of large size with a double neck on which only the upper strings are stretched over a fingerboard, the bass strings being at the side of it and capable only of prod. single notes, except by retuning. The number of strings varied from 14–17. It was used mainly for accompanying singers.

Theremin (*see also* **Aetherophone**), an electrophonic instrument invented by Lev Theremin (b. 1896) of Leningrad in 1920. It was incapable of detaching notes, so that all intervals were linked together by a wailing *portamento*, like that of a siren; but later on T. invented another instrument shaped like a cello on which notes could be prod. detached from each other by means of a cello fingerboard.

Theresienmesse (*Theresa Mass*), Haydn's Mass in B♭ maj. (Collected Ed. No. 10), comp. in 1799. Despite its name, it seems to have no connection with Maria Theresa, wife of the Emperor Franz II.

Thésée (*Theseus*), opera by Lully (lib. by Quinault), prod. at Saint-Germain, 12. I. 1675; 1st Paris perf., IV. 1675.

Thesis. *See* **Metre**.

Thespis, or The Gods Grown Old, operetta by Sullivan (lib. by W. S. Gilbert), prod. London, Gaiety Theatre, 26. XII. 1871. Sullivan's 1st work comp. in assoc. with Gilbert.

Thétis et Pélée (*Thetis and Peleus*), opera

by Colasse (lib. by Bernard de Fontenelle), prod. Paris, Opéra, 11. I. 1689.

Thibaud, Jacques (b. Bordeaux, 27. IX. 1880; d. Mont Cemet nr. Barcelonette, 1. IX. 1953), Fr. violinist. Studied at the Paris Cons. and took a 1st prize in 1896, but was at 1st obliged to play in a café. Colonne heard him and engaged him for his orch. and by 1898–9 he was estab. as a concert artist. He travelled widely, excelled in Mozart and gave much time to chamber mus., forming a trio with Casals and Cortot. He was killed in an aeroplane crash.

Thibaut IV (b. Troyes, 30. V. 1201; d. Pamplona, 7. VII. 1253), king of Navarre and a trouvère, 63 of whose songs are still extant.

Thibaut, Anton Friedrich Justus (b. Hameln, 4. I. 1774; d. Heidelberg, 28. III. 1840), Ger. scholar and musicologist. Studied law at Göttingen and became prof. of jurisprudence at Kiel, Jena and in 1805 at Heidelberg. He founded a society for the study and practice of Palestrina and other old It. church mus., collected folksongs of all nations and pub. in 1824 a treatise *Über Reinheit der Tonkunst.*

Thillon (*née* Hunt), **Sophie Anne** (b. ? Calcutta or London, 1819; d. Torquay, 5. V. 1903), Eng. soprano. She was taken to Fr. for study at the age of 14 and married one of her masters, the Havre cond. Claude Thomas T. After appearing in the provinces she came out in opera in Paris, 1838, studied with Auber and sang with great success in his and other comps.' operas. In 1844 she made her stage début in London and sang much there during the next 10 years, also at Brussels and in U.S.A.

Thiman, Eric (Harding) (b. Ashford, Kent, 12. IX. 1900), Eng. organist and comp. Studied mus. privately, obtained the F.R.C.O. in 1921 and the London Mus.D. in 1927. In 1930 he was app. prof. at the R.A.M. Organist and choirmaster at the City Temple.

Works incl. anthems and other church mus.; org. accomps. in varied harmony and free part-writing to hymns; part-songs, etc.

Third, the interval between 2 notes lying 3 degrees of a scale apart, e.g.:

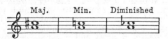

Maj.   Min.   Diminished

Thirion, Louis (Marie Joseph) (b. Baccarat, Meurthe-et-Moselle, 18. II. 1879), Fr. organist, pianist and comp. Pupil of Ropartz at the Nancy Cons., where he became prof. of org. and pf. in 1898.

Works incl. 2 symphs.; string 4tet, pf.

trio; sonatas for vln. and pf. and cello and pf.; sonata, impromptu, *Rêves* and other works for pf.; instrumental pieces, etc.

Thoma, Therese. *See* Vogl.

Thomas, (Charles Louis) Ambroise (b. Metz, 5. VIII. 1811; d. Paris, 12. II. 1896), Fr. comp. Learnt mus. from his father as a child and in 1828 entered the Paris Cons., where he gained the Prix de Rome in 1832. He also privately studied pf. with Kalkbrenner and comp. with Lesueur. Soon after his return from Rome he began to win operatic successes in Paris. In 1852 he became prof. at the Cons. and in 1871 director in succession to Auber.

Works incl. operas *La Double Échelle, Le Perruquier de la Régence, Le Panier fleuri, Carline, Le Comte de Carmagnola, Le Guerillero, Angélique et Médor, Mina, Le Caïd, Le Songe d'une nuit d'été* (not Shakespeare), *Raymond, La Tonelli, La Cour de Célimène, Psyché, Le Carnaval de Venise, Le Roman d'Elvire, Mignon* (after Goethe's *Wilhelm Meister*), *Gille et Gillotin, Hamlet* (after Shakespeare), *Françoise de Rimini* (after Dante); ballets *La Gipsy, Betty* and *La Tempête; Messe solennelle, Messe de Requiem,* motets; cantata *Hermann et Ketty,* cantatas for the unveiling of a Lesueur statue and for the Boïeldieu centenary; fantasy for pf. and orch.; string 4tet, string 5tet, pf. trio; pf. pieces; 6 It. songs; part-songs, etc.

Thomas and Sally, or The Sailor's Return, opera by Arne (lib. by Isaac Bickerstaffe), prod. London, Covent Garden Theatre, 28. XI. 1760.

Thomas, Arthur Goring (b. Ratton Park, Sussex, 20. XI. 1850; d. London, 20. III. 1892), Eng. comp. Educ. for the civil service, but studied mus. after he came of age, with Émile Durand in Paris and with Sullivan and Prout at the R.A.M. in London. Later he went to Bruch in Berlin for orch. He began to work on an opera to a lib. by his brother, *Don Braggadocio,* and although he did not finish it, he persevered and eventually received a commission from the Carl Rosa Opera Co. He became insane in 1891.

Works incl. operas *The Light of the Harem* (after Thomas Moore), *Esmeralda* (after Hugo's *Notre-Dame de Paris*), *Nadeshda* and *The Golden Web*; anthem *Out of the Deep* for soprano, chorus and orch.; cantatas *The Sun Worshippers* and *The Swan and the Skylark; Suite de Ballet* for orch.; songs, duets, etc.

Thomas, John (b. Bridgend, Glam., 1. III. 1826; d. London, 19. III. 1913), Welsh harpist, cond. and comp. Studied at the R.A.M. in London and later became harp prof. there, harpist at the opera in Her Majesty's Theatre and in 1872 harpist to Queen Victoria. But he took great interest in mus. in Wales and in 1861, at the Aberdare Eisteddfod, was nominated chief of the Welsh minstrels.

Works incl. cantatas *Llewelyn* and *The Bride of Neath Valley*; symph., overtures; 2 horn concertos; many harp studies and pieces, etc.

Thomas, Kurt (b. Tonning, Schleswig-Holstein, 25. V. 1904), Ger. comp. Studied at Barmen, at the Leipzig Cons. and privately with Arnold Mendelssohn; he was also influenced by Karl Straube at Leipzig. Active as a teacher and choral conductor in several Ger. cities.

Works incl. Mass in A min.; St. Mark Passion, Easter Oratorio; Psalm cxxxvii for double chorus; pf. concerto; pf. trio in D min.; vln, and pf. sonata in E min., etc.

Thomas, Theodore (b. Esens, E. Friesland, 11. X. 1835; d. Chicago, 4. I. 1905), Ger.-Amer. cond. He was taken to U.S.A. in 1845 and became a professional violinist; appeared in N.Y., with an orch. formed by himself, in 1862; organized the Cincinnati Mus. Festival in 1873 and became cond. of the N.Y. Phil. Society in 1877 and of the Chicago Symph. Orch. in 1891.

Thomé, Francis (actually Joseph François Luc) (b. Port Louis, Mauritius, 18. X. 1850; d. Paris, 16. XI. 1909), Fr. comp. Studied at the Paris Cons. He afterwards settled down as a private teacher of mus.

Works incl. operas and operettas *Martin et Frontin*, *Barbe-Bleuette*, *Endymion et Phœbé*, *Le Caprice de la reine*, *Le Papillon*, *Le Trottin*, *Mademoiselle Pygmalion*; ballets *Djemmah*, *La Folie parisienne*, *La Bulle d'amour*; incid. mus. to plays, incl. Shakespeare's *Romeo and Juliet*, and mystery *L'Enfant Jésus*; *Hymne à la nuit* for chorus; *Simple Aveu* for pf. with many arrs., etc.

Thompson, Herbert (b. Leeds, 11. VIII. 1856; d. Leeds, 6. V. 1945), Eng. mus. and art critic. Educ. at Wiesbaden and St. John's Coll., Cambridge, where he came under the influence of Stanford. In 1886–1936 he was mus. and art critic to the *Yorkshire Post* at Leeds.

Thompson, Oscar (b. Crawfordsville, Ind., 10. X. 1887; d. N.Y., 3. VII. 1945), Amer. mus. critic. In 1937 he succeeded W. J. Henderson as mus. critic of the *N.Y. Sun*. He was the author of several books on mus. and the ed. of the *International Cyclopedia of Music*.

Thompson, Randall (b. N.Y., 21. IV. 1899), Amer. comp. He studied at Harvard Univ. and among his mus. masters was Bloch. He lived in Rome in 1922–5, was asst. prof. of mus. at Wellesley Coll. and was later app. to study mus. conditions at the Amer. colls., becoming prof. of mus. at California Univ. in 1937 and director of the Curtis Inst. at Philadelphia in 1939. Prof. at Harvard Univ. since 1948.

Works incl. opera *Solomon and Balkis*

(after Kipling's *Just So Stories*); incid. mus. for Labiche's *The Italian Straw Hat*; 3 symphs., *Pierrot and Cothurnus* and *The Piper at the Gates of Dawn*, for orch.; *Jazz Poem* for pf. and orch.; *Passion according to St. Luke*, cantata *The Testament of Freedom*, *Odes of Horace* for unaccomp. chorus, *Rosemary* for women's chorus, *Americana* for mixed chorus and pf.; 2 string 4tets, one on Kenneth Grahame's *The Wind in the Willows*, sonata and suite for pf.; songs, etc.

Thomson, César (b. Liège, 17. III. 1857; d. Lugano, 21. VIII. 1931), Belg. violinist. Studied at the Liège Cons., where in 1882 he became vln. prof., after a career as virtuoso that took him to It., Ger., etc. In 1897 succeeded Ysaÿe at the Brussels Cons. He taught in N.Y. from 1924 to 1927.

Thomson, George (b. Limekilns, Dunfermline, 4. III. 1757; d. Leith, 18. II. 1851), Scot. official and mus. collector. Pub. collections of nat. Scot., Welsh and Ir. airs arr. by Haydn, Beethoven, Kozeluch, Weber, Bishop and others.

Thomson, James (1700–48), Scot. poet. *See* **Alfred** (*Arne*), **Moissonneurs** (Duni), **Rosina** (Shield), **Seasons** (Haydn).

Thomson, Virgil (b. Kansas City, 25. XI. 1896), Amer. comp. Studied at Harvard Univ. and comp. with Rosario Scalero and Nadia Boulanger. He was asst. mus. instructor at Harvard in 1920–5 and organist at King's Chapel in Boston from 1923 to 1924, then lived in Paris until 1932, when he became critic to several papers and periodicals in the U.S.A.

Works incl. operas *Four Saints in Three Acts* and *The Mother of us all* (libs. by Gertrude Stein); ballet *The Filling-Station*; incid. mus. for Euripides' *Medea*, Shakespeare's *Hamlet* and other plays; film mus.; 2 symphs., suite *The Plough that Broke the Plains*, 2 *Sentimental Tangoes*, *Portraits*, Symph. on a Hymn-Tune; *Sonata da Chiesa* for orch.; *Oraison funèbre* (Bossuet) for tenor and orch.; 2 *Missae breves*, 3 psalms for women's voices, *Capital*, *Capitals* (Gertrude Stein) for men's chorus and pf.; 2 string 4tets, 5 *Portraits* for 4 clars.; *Stabat Mater* for soprano and string 4tet, 5 *Phrases from the Song of Solomon* for soprano and perc.; *The 40 Portraits* for vln. and pf., sonata for vln. and pf.; *Gospel Hymns*, variations and fugues for org.; 4 pf. sonatas, 5 inventions for pf.; *Synthetic Waltzes* and 5 *Inventions* for 2 pfs.; 3 *Portraits* for harpsichord; *Air de Phèdre* (Racine) and other Fr. songs, etc.

Thomyris, Queen of Scythia, pasticcio arranged by Pepusch from mus. by A. Scarlatti, G. Bononcini, Steffani, Gasparini and Albinoni (lib. by Peter Anthony Motteux), prod. London, Drury Lane Theatre, 1. IV. 1707.

Thorne, John (b. ?; d. York, 7. XII. 1573), Eng. organist, comp. and poet. He was employed at St. Mary-at-Hill, London, in 1540, when he was evidently in the circle of Redford, Ap Rhys and others. He was organist of York Minster from c. 1550

over which they wrote figures or accidentals indicating what the harmony above that bass was to be, but not how it was to be spaced or distributed. The following ex. shows (a) the use of figures and accidentals and (b) the implied harmony:

Bach, *Cantata 140*

THOROUGH-BASS

until his death. A motet, *Stella caeli*, was copied by John Baldwin, and an org. offertory, *Exsultabunt Sancti*, is also extant. Poems by him are incl. in the same MS. as Redford's *Play of Wit and Science* (Brit. Mus., Add. MS. 15233) and in the *Paradyse of Daintie Devices* (1576).

Thorough-Bass, a system of shorthand notation for keyboard instruments that came into use during the early part of the 17th cent. and persisted until c. the middle of the 18th (in church mus. later still). Comps., instead of writing out the full harmony they required for an accomp. provided only a single bass-line, under or

T.-B.s were not always completely figured, and sometimes not at all. The It. term is *basso continuo*.

Thousand and One Nights. *See* **Arabian Nights.**

Thrane, Waldemar (b. Christiania, 8. X. 1790; d. Christiania, 30. XII. 1828), Norw. comp. Learnt mus. at home, his parents being keen amateurs at whose house many musicians met. Although intended for commerce, T. continually exercised himself in mus. and in 1825 wrote the 1st Norw. opera, which however was not staged until 1850. He also studied Norw. folk mus.

Works incl. opera *Fjeldeventyret* (*The Mountain Adventure*); overtures for orch.; choral works, etc.

Three Choirs Festival, a mus. festival, founded in 1724, centred on the combined cathedral choirs of Gloucester, Worcester and Hereford, and held annually at each town in turn in the week beginning with the first Sunday in Sept. The programmes are predominantly choral, but orch. and chamber mus. concerts are also given. New works by Eng. comps. have been a traditional feature of the festival.

Three-Cornered Hat. *See* **Sombrero de tres picos;** *also* **Corregidor.**

Three Musketeers, The (I. de Lara). *See* **Trois Mousquetaires.**

Thuille, Ludwig (b. Bozen, 30. XI. 1861; d. Munich, 5. II. 1907), Aus. comp. Learnt mus. from his father, an amateur, on whose death he was sent as a choir-boy to the monastery of Kremsmünster. At the age of 15 he began to study with Joseph Pembaur in Innsbruck, and in 1879 he went to the Mus. School at Munich, where Rheinberger was among his masters. In 1883 he became prof. at the Munich school, and there was influenced by R. Strauss and Alexander Ritter, who wrote the lib. for his 1st opera, the 2 later ones being by Otto Julius Bierbaum. Apart from teaching and comp., he also cond. the male-voice choir Liederhort.

Works incl. operas *Theuerdank*, *Lobetanz* and *Gugeline*; *Romantic Ovt.* (orig. for *Theuerdank*) for orch.; *Weihnacht im Walde* for male chorus, *Traumsommernacht* and *Rosenlied* for female chorus; pf. 5tet, 6tet for wind and pf.; cello and pf. sonata; pf. pieces; songs, etc.

Thump (old Eng.) = plucking of strings (*pizzicato*); also a piece employing *pizz.*

Thursfield (*née* Reman), **Anne** (b. N.Y., 28. III. 1885; d. London, 5. VI. 1945), Eng. mezzo-soprano. Educ. in mus. mainly in Berlin, but sang other languages as brilliantly as Eng. and Ger., partic. excelling in Fr. She specialized in song recitals chosen with enterprise and taste, and perf. with keenly intelligent interpretation.

Thus spake Zarathustra (R. Strauss). *See* **Also sprach Zarathustra.**

Thyl Uylenspiegel. *See* **Till Eulenspiegel.**

Tibbett, Lawrence (b. Bakersfield, Calif., 16. XI. 1896; d. N.Y., 15. VII. 1960), Amer. baritone. He studied singing after serving in the Navy in the 1914–18 war and 1st appeared at the Metropolitan Opera, N.Y., in 1923. In addition to a successful career in opera he became popular as a film actor.

Tiburtino, Giuliano (b. ?, d. ?), It. 16th-cent. comp. and violinist. In 1545 he was in the service of Pope Paul III. 12 *ricercari* and one fantasia for instrumental

ensemble were incl. in a pub. of 1549 which also incl. works by Willaert and Rore.

Tichatschek (Tichaček), Joseph (Aloys) (b. Ober-Weckelsdorf, Boh., 11. VII. 1807; d. Blasewitz nr. Dresden, 18. I. 1886), Cz. tenor. Studied medicine at first, but learnt singing and in 1830 joined the chorus at the Kärntnertortheater in Vienna, then sang small parts, and made his 1st stage appearance at Graz. He was a member of the Dresden opera from 1838 until he retired in 1870 and was Wagner's 1st Rienzi and Tannhäuser.

Tie, an arching stroke used to connect 2 notes of the same pitch (or a group of such notes in chords), indicating that the 2nd note of the pair is not to be sounded.

Tieck, (Johann) Ludwig (1773–1853), Ger. poet, novelist, critic and trans. *See* **Magelone Romances** (Brahms), **Genoveva** (Schumann), **Rudorff** (*Aufzug der Romanze*), **Scholz** (*Golo*).

Tiefland (*The Lowland*), opera by d'Albert (lib. by Rudolf Lothar based on a Catalan play, *Terra baixa*, by Angel Guimerá), prod. Prague, Ger. Theatre, 15. XI. 1903.

Tiento (Span.), a 16th-cent. type of org. piece similar to the Ricercare.

Tierce, an obsolete term for the interval of the 3rd, maj. or min. It survives, however, as the technical term for one of the tones of a church bell, a min. 3rd above the note of the bell. Also an org. stop sounding 2 8ves and a maj. 3rd above the note played.

Tierce de Picardie (Fr. = Picardy 3rd), the maj. 3rd intro. into the final chord of a comp. in a min. key. The maj. 3rd corresponds to a natural harmonic, the Tierce (*see above*), but the min. 3rd does not: it was therefore for a long time considered, if not an actual dissonance, at any rate not a finally satisfactory ingredient in a concluding chord, for which reason the T. d. P. was often substituted. The orig. of the name is not known.

Tiersot, (Jean Baptiste Élisée) Julien (b. Bourg-en-Bresse, 5. VII. 1857; d. Paris, 10. VIII. 1936), Fr. musicologist and comp. Studied at the Paris Cons., Massenet and Franck being among his masters. He became asst. librarian there in 1883 and librarian in 1910. He wrote many books and articles on Fr. and other folksongs, Rouget de Lisle, Berlioz, Gluck, J. J. Rousseau, Smetana, mus. in Molière's works, Bach, etc., and collected folksongs, some with d'Indy. He was prof. at the École des Hautes Études Sociales and president of the Société Française de Musicologie.

Works incl. incid. mus. to Corneille's *Andromède*; *Hellas* (Shelley) and *Chansons populaires françaises* for chorus and orch.; rhapsody on Bresse folksongs, symph. legend *Sire Halewyn* and *Danses populaires françaises* for orch., etc.

Tiessen, Heinz (b. Königsberg, 10. IV. 1887), Ger. cond. and comp. Studied in Berlin, was critic to the *Allgemeine Musikzeitung* in 1912–17, in 1918 became cond. of the Berlin Volksbühne and in 1920 of the univ. concerts. He also did choral cond. and from 1925 to 1945 and from 1949 to 1955 was prof. at the Hochschule für Musik.

Works incl. ballet *Salammbô* (after Flaubert); incid. mus. to Sophocles' *Antigone*, Shakespeare's *Tempest, Hamlet* and *Cymbeline*, Grabbe's *Don Juan und Faust*, Immermann's *Merlin*, Tagore's *Post Office*, Strindberg's *Advent* and other plays; 3 *Liebeslieder* for chorus; symph. in F min.; *Totentanz* for vln. and orch.; string 5tet, *Spring Mus.* for fl., clar., horn and string 4tet, *Kleine Schularbeit* for wind instruments; Little Suite for 2 vlns., duo for vln. and pf.; *Nature Trilogy, Kleine Schularbeit* and other pieces for pf.; songs, etc.

Tietjens, Therese (Cathline Johanna Alexandra) (b. Hamburg, 17. VII. 1831; d. London, 3. X. 1877), Hung. soprano of Ger. birth and Belg. descent. Made her 1st appearance at Hamburg in 1849; paid her 1st visit to Eng. in 1858, remaining there for good except for her appearances abroad.

Tigrane, Il (*Tigranes*), opera by Gluck (lib. by Francesco Silvani, altered by Goldoni), prod. Crema, 9. IX. 1743.

Opera by Hasse (lib. by Francesco Silvani), prod. Naples, Teatro San Bartolommeo, 4. XI. 1729.

Opera by A. Scarlatti (lib. by Domenico Lalli), prod. Naples, Teatro San Bartolommeo, 16. II. 1715.

Tigrini, Orazio (b. ? Arezzo, *c.* 1535; d. there, 15. X. 1591), It. comp. He appears to have spent his entire mature life in Arezzo, and was *maestro di canto* 1st at S. Maria della Pieve and then at the cathedral. He pub. 2 books of madrigals and a treatise, *Il Compendio della Musica* (1588).

Till Eulenspiegel (*Tyl Owlglass*), a 15th-cent. Low Ger. folk-tale of unknown authorship. For operas on the subject *see* **Blockx, Braunfels, Kistler, Lothar** and **Reznicek**; for a ballet *see* **Steinberg**; for a symph. poem (R. Strauss) *see* below, for a cantata *see* **Vogel (V.).**

Till Eulenspiegels lustige Streiche (*Tyl Owlglass's Merry Pranks*), symph. poem by R. Strauss, Op. 28, based on the old Low Ger. folk-tale, comp. 1894–5, 1st perf. Cologne, 5. XI. 1895.

Tillyard, Henry (Julius Wetenhall) (b. Cambridge, 18. XI. 1881; d. Cambridge, 2. I. 1968), Eng. mus. scholar. Studied at Cambridge Univ. in 1900–4 and at the Eng. schools in Athens and Rome in 1904–7. He specialized in the study of Byzantine mus., on which he wrote a good deal, and was prof. successively at Johannesburg, Birmingham and Cardiff.

Timbales (Fr.) = Kettle-drums.

Timbre (Fr. lit. Chime-bell). In mus. the word is used, in Eng. as well as Fr., for Tone-colour.

Timbrel, the old Eng. name for the Tambourine.

Time. The physical conditions in which all the arts have their existence, so far as they become communicable to the human senses, are either space (painting, sculpture, etc.) or T., or both (drama and in a sense all literature). Mus. exists in T., and has therefore to be written down in symbols repres. certain divisions of T. in which it is to be made audible. T. must not be confused with Tempo or pace, which determines the speed at which a comp. should go; the T. of a comp. is its division into units of notes or rests, and their subdivisions. A piece in 3–4 T., for ex., has 3 crotchets to a Bar and normally a metrical stress on the 1st Beat after the bar-line; and it makes no difference to this fundamental T. whether 2 crotchets are replaced by a Minim, or whether one is displaced by a rest or divided into smaller fractions in any pattern of notes. The T. of a piece or movement remains fixed until the comp. changes the Time Signature. T. is called 'simple' when the beats are divisible by 2, e.g. 2–4, 3–4, 4–4, 'compound' when they are divisible by 3, e.g. 6–8, 9–8, 12–8. Where there are 5 beats in the bar the listener, and often the comp., tends to regard them as 2+3 or 3+2: bars with 7, 11 or 13 beats will divide in a similar way.

Time Signature, the sign at the beginning of a comp. indicating the time-divisions governing the metre of the piece. The T. S. is shown in the shape of a fraction, but does not represent a mathematical fraction: it is a symbol showing in the lower figure the unit of the note-values into which each bar is divided and in the upper figure the number of such note-values contained in a bar: e.g. $\frac{3}{4}$ means that there are 3 crotchets to the bar, with either 3 beats or (in fast time) 1 beat to the bar; $\frac{6}{8}$ is 6 quavers to the bar, with 2 basic beats; $\frac{2}{2}$ is 2 minims to the bar, etc. There are also 2 conventional abbrs., which are signs surviving from the old notation, where the T. S.s were a full circle for Perfect Time (*tempus perfectum*) and a broken circle resembling letter C for Imperfect Time (*tempus imperfectum*). The broken circle has survived as indicating $\frac{4}{4}$ time and as ¢ indicating *alla breve* time, i.e. $\frac{4}{4}$ taken at double speed and beaten in 2's.

Timmermans, Armand (b. Antwerp, 20. I. 1860; d. Antwerp, 12. VII. 1939), Belg. comp. Studied under P. Benoît at the Antwerp Cons. and later devoted himself to comp. and criticism. He wrote under the name Jules Danvers.

Works incl. operas *Marguerite*, *Misères de la guerre* and *Vae victis*; cantatas *21 Juillet* and *Van Dyck*; instrumental works; songs, etc.

Timpan (or Timpe, from Lat. *tympanum*), a kind of Psaltery, now obs., but used in the Brit. Isles in medieval times. It had wire strings stretched on a frame and they were plucked by the fingers or a plectrum, later struck with a rod.

Timpani (It.) = Kettle-drums.

Timpe. *See* **Timpan.**

Tin Whistle, a small and rudimentary pipe of the Fife or Recorder type, also called 'penny whistle', played vertically and having a small range of high notes controlled by 6 finger-holes.

Tinctoris, Joannes de (b. prob. Nivelles, *c.* 1436; d. Nivelles or Naples, before 12. X. 1511), Flem. priest and mus. scholar. Studied both law and theol., was ordained priest and became a canon of Poperinghe. He went to It. and in 1476 was in the service of the king of Naples, Ferdinand of Aragon. He founded a school of mus. and between 1484 and 1500 was in the Papal Chapel in Rome. He wrote a number of important theoret. works and comp. Masses, motets and *chansons.*

Tinel, Edgar (b. Sinay, 27. III. 1854; d. Brussels, 28. X. 1912), Belg. comp. Studied with Gevaert and others at the Brussels Cons. and gained the Belg. Prix de Rome in 1877. In 1881 he became director of the institute of church mus. at Malines in succession to Lemmens, in 1889 mus. inspector of the state schools and in 1896 prof. of counterpoint at the Brussels Cons. in succession to H. Kufferath, and director in 1909.

Works incl. sacred mus.-dramas *Godoleva* and *Katharina*; incid. mus. to Corneille's *Polyeucte*; oratorio *Franciscus*; 2 Te Deums, Mass for the Holy Virgin of Lourdes, Alleluia for chorus and org.; sacred songs for mixed chorus; cantatas *Klokke Roeland*, *Kollebloemen* and *De drie Ridders*; 4 nocturnes for voices and pf., etc.

Tintore, Giovanni del. *See* **Tinctoris.**

Tiorba (It.) = Theorbo.

Tippett, Michael (Kemp) (b. London, 2. I. 1905), Eng. comp. Studied with C. Wood and R. O. Morris at the R.C.M. in London. He became cond. of educational organizations under the London County Council and mus. director at Morley Coll., a post formerly held by Holst. Hon. D.Mus., Oxford, 1967. Knighted 1966.

Works incl. operas *The Midsummer Mar-*riage, *King Priam,* *The Knot Garden*; oratorios *A Child of our Time* for solo voices, chorus and orch. and *The Vision of St. Augustine* for baritone, chorus and orch., *A Song of Liberty* (from Blake's *Marriage of Heaven and Hell*) for chorus and orch.; anthem *Plebs angelica* for double chorus, motet, *The Weeping Babe* (Edith Sitwell) for soprano and chorus; 2 symphs., concerto for double string orch., concerto for orch. *Fantasia concertante* on a theme by Corelli; fantasy on a theme by Handel for pf. and orch., pf. concerto; 3 string 4tets; pf. sonata; *Boyhood's End* cantata for tenor and pf. (from W. H. Hudson's *Far Away and Long Ago*); part-songs *The Source* and *The Windhover* (Hopkins), etc.

Tirade (Fr. = pulling or dragging), an ornamental scale passage between 2 notes of a melody or 2 chords.

Tirana, a Span. dance of Andalusia in 6–8 time, usually danced to guitar mus. and accomp. by words in 4-lined *coplas.*

Tirarsi (It. = to draw itself, to pull itself), a *tromba da tirarsi* is a tpt. with a slide.

Tirasse (Fr.) = (Org.) Coupler.

Tirata (It.) = Fr. *Tirade.*

Tiré (Fr. = drawn), the downstroke of the bow in the playing of string instruments, the opposite of *poussé* (= pushed).

Tirso de Molina (Gabriel Tellez) (1571–1648), Span. dramatist. *See* **Assafiev** (*Don Juan*), **Braunfels** (*Don Gil*), **Don Giovanni Tenorio** (Gazzaniga), **Rios** (*Vergonzoso en palacio*).

Titelouze, Jean (b. Saint-Omer, *c.* 1563; d. Rouen, 24. X. 1633), Fr. priest, organist and comp. He became a canon at Rouen Cathedral in the 1580s; often visited Paris to inaugurate new orgs., incl. that at Notre-Dame in 1610.

Works incl. 3 or 4 Masses; Magnificats and hymns for org., etc.

Titiens, Therese. *See* **Tietjens.**

Tito Vespasiano, ovvero La clemenza di Tito (*Titus Vespasian, or The Clemency of Titus*), opera by Caldara (lib. by Metastasio, partly based on Corneille's *Cinna*), prod. Vienna, 1734.

Opera by Hasse (lib. do.), prod. Pesaro, Teatro pubblico, 24. IX. 1735.

Titov. Rus. family of amateur musicians:

1. **Alexey Nikolaievich T.** (b. St. Petersburg, 24. VI. 1769; d. St. Petersburg, 20. XI. 1827), managed the Imp. Opera for some time before the death of Catherine the Great in 1796 and became a major-general in the cavalry guards. Comp. *c.* 20 operas, vaudevilles, melodramas and other stage works. He is sometimes confused with his brother,

2. **Sergey Nikolaievich T.** (b. ?, 1770; d. ?), who wrote incid. mus. for 2 or 3 plays.

3. **Nikolai Alexeievich T.** (b. St. Peters-

burgh, 10. V. 1800; d. St. Petersburg, 22.
XII. 1875), son of 1. Like his father, he
was in the cavalry guard and rose to the
rank of lieut-gen. He came under the
influence of Glinka and Dargomizhsky.
Comp. popular marches, pf. mus. and
c. 60 songs.

Tiutchev, Feodor Ivanovich (1803–73),
Rus. poet. *See* **Medtner** (songs), **Shaporin**
(songs), **Taneiev (S.)** (songs).

Toccata (from It. *toccare* = lit. to
touch, fig. to play), orig., in the 17th cent.,
simply 'a thing to play', as distinct from
cantata, 'a thing to sing'. But it soon
acquired a sense of touching an instrument
for the purpose of trying or testing it,
which meant that it usually contained
scales, shakes and other brilliant figuration; often interspersed with slow chordal
passages. Modern T.s usually lay stress on
brilliance and rapid execution alone, and
are often more or less uniform in figuration
throughout.

Tocchi, Gianluca (b. Perugia, 10. I.
1901), It. comp. Studied with Respighi in
Rome, where in 1930 he gained a comp.
prize. Prof. of comp. at the Cons. di Santa
Cecilia, Rome, from 1959.
Works incl. symph. poem *Il destino*
(after Maeterlinck), *Rapsodia romantica*,
Quadro sonoro, impressions *Record*, suite
Film for orch.; concerto for jazz orch.;
Tre canzoni alla maniera popolare italiana
for voice and pf., etc.

Toch, Ernst (b. Vienna, 7. XII. 1887;
d. Los Angeles, 1. X. 1964), Aus. pianist
and comp. Studied medicine and philosophy at first and was self-taught in mus.,
but in 1909 was awarded the Frankfurt
Mozart prize and studied there under
Willy Rehberg, being appt. pf. prof. at the
Mannheim Hochschule für Musik in 1913.
He served in the 1914–18 war, settled in
Berlin in 1929, but emigrated in 1932,
visiting the U.S.A., then London for a
time, to settle permanently in U.S.A. in
1934, 1st teaching in N.Y. for 2 years and
then moving to Hollywood as film comp.
and teacher.
Works incl. operas *Wegwende*, *Die
Prinzessin auf der Erbse*, *Egon und Emilie*,
Der Fächer; incid. mus. for Euripides'
Bacchantes, Shakespeare's *As You Like It*,
Zweig's *Die Heilige aus U.S.A.* and other
plays; mus. for radio play *The Garden of
Jade* and others; film mus. for *Catherine
the Great*, *The Private Life of Don Juan*,
etc.; Passover Service; cantata *Das Wasser*;
Der Tierkreis for unaccomp. chorus; 4
symphs., *Bunte Suite*, *Kleine Theater Suite*,
Big Ben, *Pinocchio* overture (after Collodi's
story) for orch.; *Spiel* for wind band;
concerto and symph. for pf. and orch.;
Poems to Martha for baritone and strings;
8 string 4tets, pf. 5tet, string trio, divertimento for vln. and vla.; 2 vln. and pf.

sonatas; sonata, 50 studies and *c.* 12 op.
nos. of pf. pieces, etc.

Tod und das Mädchen (*Death and the
Girl*), song by Schubert on words by
Matthias Claudius, comp. in 1817. The
latter part was adapted as a theme for
variations in the 2nd movement of his
D minor 4tet (1826), which is for that
reason commonly known by the same
name.

Tod und Verklärung (*Death and Transfiguration*), symph. poem by R. Strauss,
Op. 24, comp. 1888–9, 1st perf. Eisenach,
21. VI. 1890.

Todi, Jacopone da (?–1306), It. poet,
prob. author of the Lat. verses of the
Stabat Mater. *See* **Nielsen (R.)** (*Laude*).

Todi (*née* d'Aguiar), **Luiza Rosa** (b.
Setubal, 9. I. 1753; d. Lisbon, 1. X. 1833),
Port. mezzo-soprano. A pupil of Perez,
she made her début as an actress in 1768
and as a singer 2 years later, was at the It.
opera in London 1770–7, then went to
Madrid, where she had her 1st big success
in Paisiello's *Olimpiade* in 1777. She visited
Paris, Berlin and Turin, sang at the opera
in St. Petersburg 1784–7, and subsequently
in Prague and in several It. cities. She
retired to Lisbon in 1803.

Toeschi, Carlo Giuseppe (b. Romagna,
c. 1724; d. Munich, 12. IV. 1788), It.
comp. and violinist. Attached to the
Mannheim school of early symphonists,
and its only It. member. He became
violinist in the court orch. there in 1752
and leader in 1759; later he followed the
court to Munich.
Works incl. ballet mus. for var. operas
by other comps.; symphs.; chamber mus.,
etc.

Tofts, Catherine (b. ?; d. Venice, 1756),
Eng. soprano. She was one of the first
Eng. singers to appear in It. opera in
London in 1705, but went mad in 1709.
At least temporarily recovered, she married
Joseph Smith, and accomp. him on his
appt. as Eng. consul in Venice.

Togni, Camillo (b. Gussago, Brescia,
18. X. 1922), It. comp. and pianist.
Studied comp. with Casella in Rome from
1939 to 1943 and pf. with Michelangeli.
He also graduated in philosophy from
Pavia Univ. in 1948.
Works incl. Variations for pf. and
orch.; *Psalmus cxxvii* for voices, vln.,
vla. and cello; *Choruses after T. S. Eliot*
for chorus and orch.; Fantasia concertante
for fl. and string orch.; *Tre Studi per
'Morts sans sepulture' di J. P. Sarte* and
Helian di Trakl for soprano and pf.;
Ricerca for baritone and 5 instruments;
fl. sonata.

Toinon et Toinette, opera by Gossec (lib.
by Jean Auguste Julien Des Boulmiers),
prod. Paris, Comédie-Italienne, 20. VI.
1767.

Tolomeo, Rè di Egitto (*Ptolemy, King of Egypt*), opera by Handel (lib. by Nicola Francesco Haym), prod. London, King's Theatre, Haymarket, 30. IV. 1728.

Tolstoy, Alexey Constantinovich, Count (1817–75), Rus. poet and dramatist. *See* Ilyinsky (*Tsar Feodor*), Kalinnikov (*Tsar Boris*), Lourié (*Alphabet*), Nápravnik (*Don Juan*), Shaporin (*Decembrists*), Sokolov (*Don Juan*).

Tolstoy, Lev Nikolaievich, Count (1828–1910), Rus. novelist and social reformer, distant relative of prec. *See* Anna Karenina (Hubay), Janáček (*Kreutzer Sonata*), 'Kreutzer' Sonata (Beethoven), Lambert (C.) (*Anna Karenina*, film), Nováček (songs), Parker (C.) (*War and Peace*), Risurrezione (Alfano), Vassilenko (*3 Bloody Battles*), War and Peace (Prokofiev).

Tom Jones, opera by Philidor (lib. by Antoine Alexandre Henri Poinsinet, based on Fielding's novel), prod. Paris, Comédie-Italienne, 27. II. 1765.

Operetta by Ed. German (lib. by Alexander M. Thompson and Robert Courtneidge, lyrics by Charles H. Taylor, based on Fielding's novel), prod. Manchester, 30. III, and London, Apollo Theatre, 17. VI. 1907.

Tomášek, Václav Jan (Wenzel Johann) (b. Skuč, 17. IV. 1774; d. Prague, 3. IV. 1850), Boh. organist, pianist and comp. His father having been reduced to poverty, he was educ. at the expense of 2 elder brothers. He became a choir-boy at the monastery of Jihlava, which he left in 1790 to study law and philosophy in Prague. He also studied the great theoret. treatises on mus. assiduously, as well as any mus. he could lay hands on, and estab. a reputation as teacher and comp. before the end of the cent. Count Bucquoi von Longueval offered him a well-paid post in his household, to which he remained attached even after his marriage to Wilhelmine Ebert in 1823. He often visited Vienna and met Beethoven in 1814, and he played his settings of Goethe's poems to the poet at Eger. He pub. his autobiog. in instalments during 1845–50.

Works incl. opera *Seraphine* and 2 not prod.; 3 Masses, 2 Requiems and other church mus.; vocal scenes from Goethe's *Faust* and Schiller's *Wallenstein*, *Maria Stuart* and *Die Braut von Messina*; symph.; pf. concerto; string 4tets, pf. trio; 5 pf. sonatas, *Elegie auf eine Rose* (after Hölty), 7 sets of *Eclogues* and 2 of *Dithyrambs* and many other works for pf.; numerous songs to words by Goethe, Schiller and others, etc.

Tomasi, Henri (b. Marseilles, 17. VIII. 1901), Fr. cond. and comp. Studied at the Paris Cons. and in 1927 gained the Prix de Rome. On his return from Rome in 1930 became cond. of the nat. wireless

station. Cond., Monte Carlo Opera, 1946–50. Works incl. operas *Don Juan de Mañara* and *Sampiero Corso*; ballets *La Grisi*, *La Rosière du village* and *Les Santons*; symph., *Scènes municipales, Chants laotiens, Petite Suite médiévale, Deux Danses cambodgiennes, Danses brésiliennes* for orch.; capriccio for vln. and orch.; fl. concerto, tpt. concerto, vla. concerto; saxophone concerto, horn concerto; *Ajax* and *Chants de Cyrnos* for chorus and orch., etc.

Tomasini. It.-Aus. family of musicians:

1. Luigi T. (b. Pesaro, 22. VI. 1741; d. Esterház, 25. IV. 1808), violinist and comp. Member of the orch. at Eisenstadt, from 1757, and later at Esterház, where he became leader in 1761. Wrote vln. concertos, string 4tets, divertimenti for barytone, vln. and cello, etc.

2. Anton(io) T. (b. Eisenstadt, 1775; d. Eisenstadt, 12. VI. 1824), violist, son of prec. He played in Esterházy's orch. as an amateur from 1791 and became a regular member in 1796.

3. Luigi T. (b. ?, c. 1780; d. Neustrelitz, 1858), violinist, brother of prec. Travelled as a virtuoso, became a member of the Esterházy orch. in 1796, and in 1808 entered the service of the court of Neustrelitz, becoming *Konzertmeister* in 1725.

Tombeau (Fr. = tomb[stone]), a commemorative comp., esp. in 17th-cent. Fr. mus.

Tombeau de Couperin, Le (*C.'s Tomb*), suite for pf. by Ravel in the form of a suite such as C. might have written, but resembling him in spirit rather than in style, Ravel's idiom being as modern as that of any of his works. It was comp. in 1914–17 and consists of 6 movements: *Prélude, Fugue, Forlane, Menuet, Rigaudon* and *Toccata*. The comp. orch. it in 1919, without the fugue and toccata; 1st perf. in that version, Paris, 8. XI. 1920.

Tombelle, Antoine de la. *See* La Tombelle.

Tomkins. Eng. family of musicians:

1. Thomas Farington T. (b. Lostwithiel, Cornwall, c. 1545; d. Gloucester, c. 1627), organist. He became organist and choirmaster at St. David's Cathedral, later lived at Gloucester in var. church posts and in 1625 became precentor at the cathedral. He married 1st Margaret Poher (or Pore), mother of 2 and 3, and later Ann Hargest, mother of 4–6.

2. Thomas T. (b. St. David's, c. 1570; d. at sea, 1591), singer, son of prec. He became a lay-clerk, but was expelled for misdemeanour and went to sea, losing his life in Grenville's action in the *Revenge*.

3. Thomas T. (b. St. David's, 1572; d. Martin Hussingtree nr. Worcester, VI.

1656), organist and comp., brother of prec. Pupil of Byrd, app. organist of Worcester Cathedral *c.* 1596. He married a widow Alice Pattrick (*née* Hassard) and in 1607 took the B.Mus. at Oxford. Although remaining at Worcester until the 2nd siege of 1646, he became one of the organists in the Chapel Royal in 1621 and in 1625 wrote mus. for Charles I's coronation. His last 10 years were spent at Martin Hussingtree, where the manor house was the property of the wife of his son Nathaniel (7).

Works incl. 7 services, *c.* 100 anthems; madrigals and balletts for 3–6 voices; mus. for viols; virginal pieces, etc.

4. John T. (b. St. David's, *c.* 1586; d. London, 27. IX. 1638), organist and comp., half-brother of prec. Educ. at King's Coll., Cambridge, where he became organist in 1606. In 1619 he went to London as organist of St. Paul's Cathedral, and in 1625 he became a Gentleman Extraordinary of the Chapel Royal, with a reversion of the next vacant organist's post.

Works incl. anthems; variations on 'John come kiss me now' for virginal, etc.

5. Giles T. (b. Gloucester, *c.* 1604; d. Salisbury, IV. 1668), organist and virginalist, brother of prec. In 1624 he succeeded Matthew Barton in his brother's former post as organist of King's Chapel, Cambridge, but in 1629 went to Salisbury Cathedral as organist and choirmaster, and in 1630, though remaining at Salisbury, he succeeded Dering as Musician for the Virginals to Charles I.

6. Robert T. (b. ?; d. ?), comp., brother of prec. He became a musician to Charles I in 1633 and remained in the royal household until 1641 or later. Comp. anthems, etc.

7. Nathaniel T. (b. Worcester, 1599; d. Martin Hussingtree nr. Worcester, 20. X. 1681), amateur musician, son of 3. He joined the choir of Worcester Cathedral in 1629 and (?) saw his father's *Musica Deo Sacra* through the press in 1668.

Tommasini, Vincenzo (b. Rome, 17. IX. 1878; d. Rome, 23. XII. 1950), It. comp. Studied at the Liceo di Santa Cecilia in Rome and became an associate of the Accademia di Santa Cecilia. He travelled much before 1910 and then settled down to comp.

Works incl. operas *Medea* and *Uguale Fortuna*; ballet *The Good-humoured Ladies* (on mus. by D. Scarlatti); choral works on Dante, Petrarch and others; overture to Calderón's *Life is a Dream*, *Poema erotico*, prelude to Baudelaire's *Hymne à la beauté*, suite, *Chiari di luna*, *Il beato regno*, *Paesaggi toscani* for orch.; 2 string 4tets; vln. and pf. sonata, etc.

Ton (Ger. lit. tone, sound). In its obs. sense the word was used by the Ger.

Minnesinger for the words and melody of their songs, and by the Meistersinger for the melody alone. The latter used all kinds of adjectives, sometimes of extreme oddity, to differentiate the numerous tunes. (Specimens of such names appear in Wagner's *Meistersinger*, where a T. is also called a *Weis* (= *Weise* = tune).)

Tonada (Span.), a type of Castilian ballad at least as old as the 16th cent.

Tonadilla (Span., der. from above), a stage interlude for a few singers intro. in the 18th cent.

Tonal Fugue. *See* **Fugue.**

Tonal Sequence. *See* **Sequence.**

Tonale *or* **Tonarium** (Lat.). Medieval theoret. work dealing with the arr. of chants according to their mode, and esp. of the antiphons and the choice of psalm-tone to go with them. The earliest known is by Regino of Prüm (*c.* 900).

Tonality, synonymous with Key, but also meaning, more specifically, the feeling of a definite key suggested by a comp. or passage. In modern mus. terminology 2 antithetical derivatives of the word have appeared. *See* **Atonality** and **Polytonality.**

Tonarium. *See* **Tonale.**

Tonart (Ger. = tone species), key, tonality or mode.

Tondichtung (Ger.) = Tone-poem, symph. poem.

Tone. (1) In Eng. the term is used for pure mus. notes not charged with harmonics, each harmonic being itself a T.; also for the quality of a mus. sound, esp. with ref. to perf. In Amer. T. is used synonymously with 'note', and 'note' is normally reserved for the written symbol.

(2) The interval between the 1st and 2nd degrees of the maj. scale, also between the 2nd and 3rd, 4th and 5th, 5th and 6th, and 6th and 7th.

(3) A melodic formula to which a psalm is sung in plainsong.

Tone-Colour. T.-C., or timbre, is a convenient term for the sound of an instrument or voice as regards the peculiar quality prod. by it; also for combinations of such sounds.

Tone-Poem. *See* **Symphonic Poem.**

Tone-Row, a trans. of the Ger. *Tonreihe*, to designate the 'rows' of 12 notes on which comps. in Twelve-note mus. are based. Also known in Eng. as 'series'.

Tonelli (actually De' Pietri), **Antonio** (b. Carpi, 19. VIII. 1686; d. Carpi, 25. XII. 1765), It. cellist and comp. Learnt mus. from his parents, who were both good amateurs, then studied with the choirmaster of Carpi Cathedral and at Bologna and Parma, where the duke became his patron. He spent 3 years at the Dan. court, returned to his home town and became choirmaster at the cathedral in 1730, but resigned in the 1740s and spent some of his

Tongattung

time in other towns and on tour, returning to his post in 1757.

Works incl. operas *L'enigma disciolto* and *Lucio Vero*; intermezzi *Canoppo e Lisetta*; oratorio *Il trionfo dell' umiltà di S. Filippo Neri* and others; church mus.; cantatas; a *Canzonieri* against nuns, etc.

Tongattung or **Tongeschlecht** (Ger. = tone species), the species of tonality, maj. or min., or else modal, in which a comp. is written.

Tonguing, the act of using the tongue in the playing of wind instruments.

Tonic, the Keynote: the note on which the scale begins and ends which determines the key of a piece of mus. in maj. or min. or defines the mode. F, for ex., is the tonic of a piece in the Lydian mode or in F maj. or min. A Lydian piece, whether harmonized or not, will end on the note F, which is therefore also called the Final; one in F maj. or min. will usually end on the maj. or min. common chord of its tonic, F.

Tonic Sol-fa, a system of mus. notation without staves and notes, invented by John Curwen in the middle of the 19th cent. on a basis of the principles of Solmization and Solfeggio, and now widely used in Brit. and the dominions by choral singers, for whom it simplifies the sight-reading of mus.

T. S.-f. notation is based on the old syllabic system of Do (Ut), Re, Mi, etc. and takes the following form: d, r, m, f, s, l, t, the names of the notes being Doh, Ray, Me, Fah, Soh, Lah, Te. The substitution of 'Te' for the old 'Si' was made to avoid the duplication of the letter 's' in the abbrs. The range of voices being limited, upper and lower 8ves can be sufficiently indicated by a simple stroke placed behind the letters in a higher or lower position, thus: d' and d,. Accidentals are indicated by the addition of a letter 'a' (ra, ma, etc., or exceptionally 'u' for du) for flats and 'e' (de, re, etc., or exceptionally 'y' for my) for sharps. But accidentals appear comparatively rarely now that the system of the 'movable Doh' has been adopted. This is a system of transposition according to which everything is, except for some very short incidental modulations, sung from a notation that looks as though the mus. were always in C maj. or A min.

The actual key is indicated at the beginning of a piece, so that singers know at once, for ex., if the comp. is in A maj., that their **d** is to be read as A, their **r** as B, etc. If the piece modulates to another key, a change is indicated, so that temporarily **d** may become any other note of the scale, etc.; but in maj. keys it will always remain the tonic, in whatever key the mus. moves, **s** always the dominant, **f** always the subdominant, etc., while in min. keys **l** will be

Tonus peregrinus

the tonic, **m** the dominant, **r** the subdominant, etc. (A special syllable, 'ba', is used for the sharp 6th in the melodic min. scale.) The time divisions are indicated by short barlines, and there are subdivisions between these. The way in which the notes fill these spaces determines their time-values, though there are special signs for dotted notes, triplets, etc. A blank space means a rest, dashes after a note mean that it is to be held beyond the space it occupies over one or more of the following time-divisions.

The merits of T. S.-f. have always been subject to controversy, no doubt because there is much to be said on either side. Its great defect is that it is insufficient for any general study of mus. as an art and that it is apt to keep choral singers from expanding their mus. experience. Its advantages to instrumental players, even where it might be applicable, as in the case of non-harmonic instruments, are very slight, since it is not so much easier to learn than staff notation, nor so flexible in picturing the comp.'s intentions. For choralists it has not only the merit of simplicity, but the greater one of teaching them a sense of Relative Pitch as well as removing all difficulties connected with Transposition.

Tonkunst (Ger.) = the art of mus.

Tonkünstler-Societät ('Musicians' Society'), a musicians' benevolent society in Vienna, founded in 1771, which gave charity perfs. twice yearly, in Lent and Advent. These were the first truly public concerts in Vienna. Haydn's oratorio *Il ritorno di Tobia* and Mozart's cantata *Davidde Penitente* (adapted from the C min. Mass) were written for the society, though both comps. were refused membership.

Tonleiter (Ger. lit. tone-ladder) = Scale.

Tonos (Span. plur.), short vocal pieces for several voices sung at the opening of plays in 17th-cent. Spain.

Tonreihe. *See* Tone-Row.

Tonsatz (Ger. lit. 'tone-setting') = Composition. *See also* **Satz.**

Tonstück (Ger. = tone-piece), a comp., a piece of mus.

Tonus lascivus (Lat. = playful, frolicsome, wanton tone), the medieval name for what later became the Ionian mode and the maj. scale, not recognized as a church mode at the time, but often used for secular songs by minstrels and not unknown in plainsong melodies.

Tonus peregrinus (Lat. = foreign tone), a plainsong chant which, unlike the 8 regular psalm tones, had 2 reciting notes, one in the 1st half of the chant and another in the 2nd (*see* illustration opposite). For this reason it was described as 'foreign' and was reserved for the psalm 'In exitu Israel' ('When Israel came out of Egypt'). So far as its tonality is concerned it is in

Topelius   Toscanini

Mode I with flattened B. The melody was also sung in the Lutheran church: Bach uses it in his Magnificat and also in the Cantata *Meine Seel' erhebt den Herren* (a setting of the Ger. Magnificat).

Ir. clergyman, organist and comp. Learnt mus. as a choir-boy in Christ Church Cathedral, Dublin, became an organist and after prod. church mus. and an oratorio before he was 20 went for further

In_ ex-i-tu Is-ra-el de Ae-gy-pto, do-mus Ja-cob.de po-pu-lo bar-ba-ro:_

TONUS PEREGRINUS

Topelius, Zakris (1818–98), Fin. novelist and dramatist. *See* **Merikanto (O.)** (*Regina von Emmeritz*), **Pacius** (*Princess of Cyprus*), **Söderman** (*Regina*).

Torchi, Luigi (b. Mordano, 7. XI. 1858; d. Bologna, 18. IX. 1920), It. musicologist. Pupil of Serrao at Naples and of Jadassohn and Reinecke at Leipzig. Returning to It. in 1884, he became prof. of mus. hist. and aesthetics at the Liceo Rossini at Pesaro. In 1891 he took up a similar-post at the Liceo Musicale of Bologna. He wrote much on Wagner, also on old It. instrumental and vocal mus., and ed. *L'arte musicale in Italia*, a collection of 14th–18th-cent. mus.

Tordion. *See* **Cinquepace.**

Torelli, Giuseppe (b. Verona, 22. IV. 1658; d. Bologna, 8. II. 1709), It. violinist and comp. Prob. a pupil of Perti in Bologna, he played in the orch. of San Petronio there 1686–96, then went to Vienna, and was *Konzertmeister* at the court of the Margrave of Brandenburg 1697–9. He returned to Bologna in 1701. With Corelli he was one of the most important comps. in the hist. of the early concerto.

Works incl. *Concerti grossi*; vln. concertos; *sinfonie* [concertos] for tpt. and orch., etc.

Tornada (Span.), the refrain which is a feature of many old Catalan songs.

Törne, Bengt de (b. Helsinki, 22. XI. 1891; d. Helsinki, 1967), Fin. comp. Studied with Furuhjelm at the Helsinki Cons. and later privately with Sibelius, on whom he wrote a book. Kajanus allowed him to try out his orchestral works with the Fin. State Orch.

Works incl. 4 symphs., 3 sinfoniettas; 6 symph. poems; vln. concerto, pf. concerto; chamber mus.; pf. pieces, etc.

Tornov, a pseud. used by C. M. Loeffler for his earliest, later discarded, works derived from the pseud. 'Tornow' used by his father as an author.

Torquato Tasso, operas by Donizetti (lib. by Jacopo Ferretti), prod. Rome, Teatro Valle, 9. IX. 1833.

Torrance, George William (b. Rathmines, Dublin, 1835; d. Kilkenny, 20. VIII. 1907),

study to Leipzig in 1856. In 1859 he entered Dublin Univ. to study theol. and was ordained in 1865–6. In 1869–97 he lived in Australia, but took the Mus.D. at Dublin in 1879.

Works incl. opera *William of Normandy*; oratorios *Abraham, The Captivity* (words by Goldsmith) and *The Revelation*; 2 settings of Te Deum and Jubilate, hymn tunes and other church mus.; madrigal 'Dry be that tear', etc.

Torrefranca, Fausto (b. Monteleone Calabro, 1. II. 1883; d. Rome, 26. XI. 1955), It. musicologist. Studied at Turin and in Ger. In 1913 he became lecturer in mus. at Rome Univ., and in 1914 lecturer in mus. hist. at Naples Cons., and librarian there in 1915. In 1924 he was librarian at Milan Cons., and at the same time taught at the Catholic Univ. until 1935. In 1941 he became prof. of mus. at Florence Univ. He wrote studies of the It. origins of mus. romanticism, of Verdi, Puccini and Strauss, and of more general aesthetic subjects.

Torri, Pietro (b. Peschiera, Verona, *c.* 1650; d. Munich, 6. VII. 1737), It. comp. Pupil of Steffani. He became court organist at Bayreuth in 1667 and at Munich in 1689, visiting *Kapellmeister* at Hanover in 1696, and returned to Munich in 1703 as director of the chamber mus., becoming mus. director in 1715. Like Abaco, he followed the Elector Max Emanuel into exile at Brussels.

Works incl. operas *Merope, Lucio Vero, Griselda* and *c.* 20 others; oratorio *Les Vanités du monde*; chamber concerto; chamber duets, etc.

Torvaldo e Dorliska, opera by Rossini (lib. by Cesare Sterbini), prod. Rome, Teatro Valle, 26. XII. 1815.

Tosca, La, opera by Puccini (lib. by Giuseppe Giacosa and Luigi Illica, based on Sardou's drama), prod. Rome, Teatro Costanzi, 14. I. 1900.

Toscanini, Arturo (b. Parma, 25. III. 1867; d. N.Y., 16. I. 1957), It. cond. Studied at the Conss. of Parma and Milan and began his career as a cellist. At a perf. of *Aida* in Rio de Janeiro, when the cond. was taken ill, he cond. the work from memory at a moment's notice. Engagements followed in It. and such was his success that in 1898 he was app. chief cond. at the Milan Scala and in 1907 of the Metropolitan in N.Y. He cond. opera and concerts all over Europe, incl. opera at Bayreuth and Salzburg. For some years he cond. in N.Y. the N.B.C. Orch., which he formed himself.

Toselli, Enrico (b. Florence, 13. III. 1883; d. Florence, 15. I. 1926), It. pianist and comp. Studied with Sgambati and Martucci. He made his name chiefly with the song *Serenata* and in 1907 created a sensation by his marriage to the former Crown Princess Luisa of Saxony.

Works incl. operetta *La principessa bizzarra* (lib. by his wife) and some others; symph. poem *Fuoco* (after d'Annunzio); chamber mus.; pf. pieces; songs, etc.

Tosi, Giuseppe Felice (b. Bologna, 1630; d. ?), It. comp. Organist at San Petronio at Bologna, and later *maestro di cappella* at San Giovanni in Monte and the cathedral of Monte di Ferrara.

Works incl. operas; *salmi concertati* and other church mus.; chamber cantatas, etc.

Tosi, Pier Francesco (b. Bologna, c. 1653; d. Faenza, IV. 1732), It. castrato, teacher and comp., son of prec. He learnt mus. from his father and travelled much until 1682, when he settled as singing-master in London. From 1705 to 1711 he was comp. at the Imp. court in Vienna. After a further visit to London he finally returned to It. and was ordained in 1730. He pub. a book on florid singing, and comp. an oratorio and cantatas for voice and harpsichord, etc.

Tosti, (Francesco) Paolo (b. Ortona sul Mare, Abruzzi, 9. IV. 1846; d. Rome, 2. XII. 1916). It. singing-master and comp. Studied at Naples under Mercadante and others from 1858 and was app. a student-teacher, remaining until 1869. During a long illness at home he wrote his 1st songs. He then went to Rome, where Sgambati helped him to give a concert and Princess Margherita of Savoy (afterwards queen of It.) app. him her singing-master. In 1875 he 1st visited London, returning each year until 1880, where he remained as singing-master to the royal family. Knighted in 1908.

Works incl. It., Eng. and Fr. songs, e.g. *Non m'ama più*, *Lamento d'amore*, *Aprile*, *Vorrei morire*, *Forever*, *Good-bye*, *Mother*, *At Vespers*, *That Day*, *Mattinata*, *Serenata*; *Canti popolari abruzzesi* for vocal duet, etc.

Tote Stadt, Die (*The Dead City*), opera by Korngold (lib. by Paul Schott, based on Georges Rodenbach's play *Bruges-la-morte*), prod. Hamburg and Cologne, 4. XII. 1920.

Toten Augen, Die (*The Dead Eyes*), opera by d'Albert (lib. orig. Fr. by Marc Henry,

Ger. trans. by Hanns Heinz Ewers), prod. Dresden, 5. III. 1916.

Touch (modern), the way of approaching the keys in pf. playing to prod. good, varied and significant tone. Scientists have recently denied the possibility of varying the quality of tone by anything but weight, since it is obviously impossible to transmit to the hammers and strings anything but degrees of strength by the intermediary of the action, which is not susceptible to any but a mechanical response to the player's hand. This is quite true so long as it is said of single notes only, but not of combinations of notes, which are capable of varying enormously in quality in countless different ways by the slightest inequalities in the strength of the constituent notes or by the minutest inaccuracies of synchronization. It is these infinitesimal inequalities and inaccuracies which account for subtleties of T., and although they are in the last resort mechanical, they do express the player's interpretative intentions and translate themselves into aesthetic values.

Touch (old). As a verb the word, up to c. the early 17th cent. meant simply to 'sound' an instrument, exactly as *toccare* does in It.; as a noun ('a touch' or 'touche') it was equivalent to Toccata. *See* **Tucket.**

Touche (Fr.) = Key (of pf. etc.); Fingerboard (of string instruments). Also an instrumental piece (= Toccata).

Tour de gosier (Fr. = turn of the gullet), a vocal ornament resembling the Turn.

Tour de Nice, La (Berlioz). *See* **Corsaire, Le.**

Tourdion. *See* **Cinquepace.**

Tourel, Jennie (b. Montreal, 26. VI. 1910), Fr.-Canadian mezzo-soprano of Rus.-Fr. parentage. Studied in Paris with Anna El-Tour, whose name she adopted in anagram form, making her début at the Paris Opéra Comique in 1933. She created the role of Baba the Turk in Stravinsky's *The Rake's Progress.*

Tournai, Mass of, an early 14th-cent. polyphonic setting of the Ordinary of the Mass, incl. *Ite missa est.* It is prob. not the work of a single comp., nor is it necessarily from Tournai, where the MS. now is, but was prob. written at least in part in the S. of Fr.

Tournemire, Charles (Arnould) (b. Bordeaux, 22. I. 1870; d. Arcachon, 3. XI. 1939), Fr. organist and comp. Studied at the Paris Cons. and later with d'Indy. In 1898 he was app. to Franck's former organist's post at the church of Sainte-Clotilde. Later he became prof. of chamber mus. at the Cons. and travelled much as org. recitalist on the Continent.

Works incl. operas *Les Dieux sont morts* and *Nittetis*; *Le Sang de la Sirène* for solo voices, chorus and orch.; 8 symphs.; pf.

4tet, pf. trio and other chamber mus.; *Pièces symphoniques*, *Triple Choral*, *L'Orgue mystique*, *Petites Fleurs musicales* and other org. works; pf. pieces; songs, etc.

Tourte, François (b. Paris, 1747; d. Paris, IV. 1835), Fr. bowmaker. He learnt his craft from his father and set up in business with his elder brother Xavier, but they quarrelled and set up each for himself. He made great improvements in the vln. bow, esp. after 1775.

Tovey, Donald Francis (b. Eton, 17. VII. 1875; d. Edinburgh, 10. VII. 1940), Eng. mus. scholar, pianist and comp. He was privately educ. and taught the pf. early, playing it astonishingly as a child and memorizing Bach and other classics. Before he was 10 he had begun to comp. and was allowed to study counterpoint with Parratt, and at 13 he was a pupil of Parry. He went to Balliol Coll., Oxford, in 1894, after giving a concert with Joachim at Windsor, and there he distinguished himself by brilliant scholarship and by taking a leading part in the univ.'s mus. life. In 1900–1 he gave pf. recitals at St. James's Hall in London, and in 1901–2 in Berlin and Vienna. In 1914 he was app. Reid Prof. of Mus. at Edinburgh Univ., a post he held to his death, and also cond. the Reid orchestral concerts there. He wrote many of the mus. articles in the *Encyc. Brit.* and several books, incl. 6 vols. of *Essays in Musical Analysis*. Knighted in 1935.

Works incl. opera *The Bride of Dionysus*; incid. mus. for Maeterlinck's *Aglavaine et Sélysette*; symph. in D maj.; suite for wind band; pf. concerto, cello concerto; 2 string 4tets, *Aria and Variations* for string 4tet, 2 pf. trios, pf. 4tet, pf. 5tet, *Variations on a Theme by Gluck* for fl. and string 4tet; *Sonata eroica* for vln. solo, sonata for cello solo, vln. and pf. sonata, cello and pf. sonata, clar. and pf. sonata, divertimento for ob. and pf., sonata for 2 cellos; pf. pieces; *Balliol Dances* for pf. duet; songs; conjectural completion of Bach's *Art of Fugue*, etc.

Toy Symphony, piece by Leopold Mozart (formerly attrib. to Haydn) with parts for toy instruments (cuckoo, quail, nightingale, etc.). Similar works have been written by Mendelssohn, A. Romberg and others, most recently by Malcolm Arnold.

Toye (old Eng.), a piece of light, playful character.

Toye, (John) Francis (b. Winchester, 27. I. 1883; d. Florence, 31. X. 1964), Eng. mus. critic and comp. Studied with S. P. Waddington and Edward J. Dent, and after a varied journalistic experience became critic to the *Morning Post* in 1925. He became director of the Brit. Inst. at Florence in 1939, returned to Eng. at the outbreak of war with It. and later went to

Rio de Janeiro as representative of the Brit. Council. He later returned to Florence. His books incl. critical biogs. of Rossini and Verdi.

Works incl. masque *Day and Night* (with his brother); songs, etc.

Toye, Geoffrey (b. London, 17. II. 1889; d. London, 11. VI. 1942), Eng. cond. and comp., brother of prec. Studied at the R.C.M. in London and became a theatre cond.; later also cond. orchestral concerts and founded Lloyd's Choir.

Works incl. opera *The Fairy Cap*; masque *Day and Night* (with his brother); ballet *The Haunted Ballroom*; radio opera *The Red Pen* (A. P. Herbert); symph.; Chin. songs *The Sad Heart* and other songs, etc.

tr (abbr.) = Trill, Shake.

Trabaci, Giovanni Maria (b. Montepeloso [now Irsina], *c.* 1575; d. Naples, 31. XII. 1647), It. organist and comp. He was app. organist in the royal chapel at Naples in 1603 and *maestro di cappella* in 1614.

Works incl. Masses, motets, psalms; madrigals; toccatas, *ricercari* and other org. pieces, etc.

Tract, a chant with penitential words, sung after the Gradual in the Mass in Lent (in place of the Alleluia). T.s are the only surviving examples in the regular chants of the Mass of 'direct psalmody', sung without antiphon or respond. They occur only in modes 2 and 8, and it is possible that those of mode 2 were orig. Graduals. Their structure is that of a highly elaborated psalm-tone. The number of verses ranges from 2 to 14.

Traetta, Tommaso Michele Francesco Saverio (b. Bitonto, Bari, 30. III. 1727; d. Venice, 6. IV. 1779), It. comp. Pupil of Porpora and Durante at the Cons. di Santa Maria di Loreto in Naples 1738–48, he 1st worked as a comp. of church mus., but after the success of *Farnace* (1751) soon estab. himself as an opera comp. *Maestro di cappella* and singing teacher at the court of the Infante Felipe of Spain in Parma 1758–65, he was director of the Cons. dell' Ospedaletto in Venice 1765–8, then went to St. Petersburg as mus. director at the court of Catherine II of Rus. He returned to It. in 1775, visited London in 1777, and finally lived in Venice.

Works incl. over 40 operas, e.g. *Farnace*, *Didone abbandonata*, *Ippolito ed Aricia*, *I Tindaridi*, *La Francese a Malghera*, *Armida*, *Ifigenia in Tauride*, *Le serve rivali*, *Amore in trappola*, *Antigona*, *Merope*, *Germondo*, *Il cavaliere errante*, etc.; oratorio *Rex Salomone*; Passion; *Stabat Mater* and other church mus.; divertimenti for 4 orchs. *Le quattro stagioni e il dodici mesi dell' anno*; sinfonie, etc.

Tragédie de Salomé, La, ballet by Florent Schmitt (choreography by Guerra), prod. Paris, Théâtre des Arts, 9. XI. 1907.

Tragédie lyrique (Fr.), a 17th-cent. term for Fr. opera of a serious character.

Tragic Overture (*Tragische Ouvertüre*), an overture by Brahms, Op. 81, comp. in 1880 as a companion-piece to the *Academic Festival Overture*, written as an acknowledgment of the hon. degree of doctor of philosophy conferred on him by Breslau Univ. in 1879. 1st perf. Vienna, 26. XII. 1880.

'Tragic' Symphony, Schubert's 4th symph., in C min., comp. 1816, 1st pub. perf. Leipzig, 19. XI. 1849. The title was added to the score by the comp.

Traherne, Thomas (? 1636–74), Eng. theol. writer and poet. *See* **Finzi** (*Dies natalis*).

Traînée (Fr.), another name for the *chute. See* **Ornaments.**

Trait. *See* **Ornaments.**

Tranchell, Peter (Andrew) (b. Cuddalore, Brit. India, 14. VII. 1922), Eng. comp. Educated at Clifton and Cambridge, where he was a mus. scholar at King's Coll. in 1946–9. In 1950 he became asst. lecturer in the univ. and in 1953 lecturer.

Works incl. opera *The Mayor of Casterbridge* (after Thomas Hardy); mus. comedy *Zuleika* (after Max Beerbohm); 2 ballets; incid. mus.; choral works; chamber mus.; pf. and org. works; songs, etc.

Tranquillo (It.) = Quiet, calm, tranquil. The adv., more rarely used as a direction, is *tranquillamente.*

Transcription, an arr. of a mus. comp. for some other medium than that intended by the comp. Strictly speaking, a T. differs from an arr. by not merely repro. the orig. as closely as possible, but by intro. more or less imaginative changes which may be supposed to conform to the comp.'s own procedure if he had written for the different medium.

Transitions, passages in a mus. comp. between 2 salient thematic features, more often than not modulating from one key to another. In a movement in sonata form the crux of the comp. often lies in the T. between 1st and 2nd subjects and in the different turn it takes in the Exposition and Recapitulation.

Transposing Instruments. Many wind instruments are built in fundamental tunings in which the maj. scale without key signature, written as C maj., actually sounds higher or lower. A clar. in B♭, for ex., will automatically play the scale of that key when the mus. is written in C maj.; or, conversely stated, if it is to play a piece in F maj., the mus. must be written in G maj., and so on. A horn in F will transpose a 5th down, a tpt. in F a 4th up, and both will play for, ex., in E♭ if their mus. is written in B♭, but the former an octave lower than the latter. Among the most common orch. instruments Eng. horns, clars., horns and tpts.

are T. I.s; fls., obs., bassoons and trombs. are not. In brass bands all the instruments except the bass tromb. are T. I.s.

Transposing Keyboards, contrivances of var. sorts to shift the manuals of keyboard instruments so that the mus. played becomes automatically higher or lower, saving the players from acquiring the art of transposing at sight. Such keyboards appeared on some orgs. as early as the 16th cent. and several inventions of the kind were made for the pf. late in the 18th and throughout the 19th cents.

Transposition, the process, either in comp. or perf., of turning a piece or passage from one key into another in such a way that the mus. remains exactly the same except for the change in pitch. It follows that all Accidentals arising incidentally in the course of the mus. (i.e. not contained in the key signature) still remain accidentals, e.g. *see* illustration opposite. In a piece transposed from E maj. up to F maj., for ex., an incidental A♯ will become B♮, and incidental F♮ will be G♭, and so on. Accompanists are often required to transpose at sight when a song is too high or low for a singer's voice, and occasionally the instrumental parts of a whole orch. have to be transposed in the same way for similar reasons. Horn players, using today an F-B♭ horn, regularly have to transpose at sight older horn parts written for horns in C, D, E♭, etc.

Transverse Flute, the modern fl. held horizontally, as distinct from the fls. of the Recorder type, which are held vertically.

Trapassi. *See* **Metastasio.**

Trapp, Max (b. Berlin, 1. XI. 1887), Ger. comp. Studied comp. with Juon and pf. with Dohnányi at the Berlin Hochschule für Musik, became pf. prof. there in 1920 and prof. of advanced comp. in 1924. He also taught at Dortmund.

Works incl. marionette play *Der letzte König von Orplid* (after Mörike); incid. mus. to Shakespeare's *Timon of Athens*; 7 symphs., 2 concertos, 2 divertimenti, symph. suite, *Notturno* for orch.; pf. concerto, vln. concerto, cello concerto, 2 string 4tets, pf. 5tet, 3 pf. 4tets; variations for 2 pfs.; sonatina for pf., etc.

Traquenard (Fr. lit. trap, snare; also racking-pace [of horses]), a 17th-cent. dance the dotted rhythm of which refers to the 2nd sense of the word.

Trascinando (It.) = Dragging.

Trattenuto (It.) = Held back (in pace).

Traubel, Helen (b. St. Louis, 20. VI. 1899), Amer. soprano. Studied in St. Louis and made her début there in 1925. In 1939 she began a long career at the N.Y. Metropolitan, which lasted until 1953. She also appeared in night clubs, which led to her resignation from the Metropolitan, where she had become the leading Wagner soprano, and pub. some successful detective novels.

Trauer-Ode (*Funeral Ode*), Bach's cantata No. 198, written on the death of the Electress Christiane Eberhardine of Saxony and perf. at the memorial ceremony at Leipzig, 17. X. 1727.

Trauer-Sinfonie (*Mourning Symph.*), the nickname of a symph. by Haydn, No. 44, in E min., comp. *c.* 1771.

Trauermarsch (Ger.) = Funeral March.

Trauerwalzer (*Mourning Waltz*), the title given by the pub. to Schubert's waltz for pf., Op. 9 No. 2, in 1821, a piece later wrongly attrib. to Beethoven. Schubert,

Paul's Church, Covent Garden, and later at Fulham church. In 1737 he succeeded Jonathan Martin as organist in the Chapel Royal.

Works incl. services, anthems, Te Deum; *The Whole Book of Psalms* for 1–5 voices with continuo; 18 canzonets for 2–3 voices to words by Matthew Prior and others; org. voluntaries; harpsichord pieces, etc.

Traversa (It. = transverse), an abbr. sometimes used in old scores for the *flauto traverso*, the modern fl. played sideways, as distinct from fls. of the Recorder type, which are held vertically.

Traversière (Fr. fem. = transverse). The

Bach, *St John Passion*

TRANSPOSITION

who wrote it in 1816, disapproved of the title. The attrib. to Beethoven occurred in 1826, when Schott of Mainz brought out a *Sehnsuchtswalzer* (also called *Le Désir*) under his name, although it was a compound of Schubert's piece and Himmel's *Favoritwalzer*.

Trautonium, an electrophonic instrument invented by Friedrich Trautwein of Berlin in 1930, prod. notes from the air graded according to the chromatic scale by means of a special device, not indeterminate in pitch like those of the Aetherophone or Theremin.

Travelling Companion, The, opera by Stanford (lib. by Henry Newbolt, based on a story by Hans Andersen), pub. 1919, but not perf. in Stanford's lifetime: prod. Liverpool 30. IV. 1925.

Travers, John (b. ?, *c.* 1703; d. London, VI. 1758), Eng. organist and comp. Learnt mus. as a choir-boy at St. George's Chapel, Windsor, and later studied with Greene and Pepusch in London, where in his early 20s he became organist at St.

flûte traversière was the Fr. name for the *flauto traverso*, or Transverse fl.

Traviata, La (*The Lady Gone Astray*), opera by Verdi (lib. by Francesco Maria Piave, based on the younger Dumas's *La Dame aux camélias*), prod. Venice, Teatro La Fenice, 6. III. 1853.

Traybenraiff, Peter. *See* **Tritonius.**

Tre corde (It. = 3 strings), a direction in pf. mus. indicating that after the use of the left pedal (*una corda*) normal playing is to be resumed.

Tre giorni son che Nina ('It was three days ago that Nina . . .'), song formerly attrib. to Pergolesi, now thought to be by (?) Ciampi or Natale Resta.

Trebelli (real name Gilbert), **Zelia** (b. Paris, 1838; d. Étretat, 18. VIII. 1892), Fr. mezzo-soprano. She began serious mus. studies, incl. pf., at the age of 6, and at 16 was allowed to take a course in singing. She made her 1st stage appearance at Madrid in 1859, travelled in Ger., in 1860–1 with Merelli's It. co. and 1st visited London in 1862.

Treble, the highest voice in a vocal comp. in several parts, derived from the Lat. *triplum*, which was the top part of the earliest 3-part Motets. It is the normal term for a boy's voice.

Treble Clef, the G clef (being a modification of that letter and indicating the position of the note G on the stave), the higher of the 2 clefs used for pf. mus., also replacing the former different C clefs used for soprano, alto and tenor voices: it is now generally represented by:

If used for the tenor, it is understood that the voice sounds an 8ve lower:

The G clef on the 1st line (now obs.) was known as the Fr. vln. clef.

Treble Viol, the smallest of the normal members of the viol family, tuned:

Tree, Ann Maria (b. London, VIII. 1801; d. London, 17. II. 1862), Eng. mezzo-soprano and actress. Studied singing with Lanza and T. Cooke, joined the chorus at Drury Lane Theatre and made her 1st important stage appearances at Bath in 1818 and in London in 1819. Later she became a good Shakespearian actress as well as a stage singer.

Tregian, Francis (b. ? Cornwall, *c.* 1574; d. London, 1619), Eng. amateur musician. He was the eldest of a large, highly cultivated Rom. Catholic family, and travelled extensively abroad, returning finally in 1605. He was imprisoned in the Fleet in 1613, where he d. He copied (prob. for the most part in prison) 2 collections of vocal works (the 'Sambrook MS.' in New York, and Brit. Mus., Egerton MS. 3665) and the famous *Fitzwilliam Virginal Book*. The 2 latter contain a few of his own comps.

Treibenreif, Peter. *See* **Tritonius.**

Tremando } **Tremante** } (It.) = trembling, quivering; played with *tremolo*.

Tremblement (Fr.) = Shake.

Tremblement appuyé (Fr.). *See* **Ornaments.**

Tremolando (It. = trembling), a direction sometimes used instead of the conventional notation for string Tremolo, or for a passage to be sung in a tremulous voice.

Tremoletto (It. obs.) = Shake.

Tremolo (It. noun = quivering). (1) The rapid repetition of a single note. In 17th-cent. It. the vocal T. (now generally known as *vibrato*) was called *trillo*. On wind instruments this type of T. is prod. by the breath, on the org. by a mechanical device (*see* **Tremulant**), on bowed string instruments by a rapid movement of the bow, notated thus:

(2) The rapid alternation of 2 or more notes, prod. on wind instruments, the org., the pf. and bowed string instruments by the fingers, notated thus:

Tremor pressus (Lat.) = Vibrato.

Tremulant, a mechanical device on the org., operated by a draw-stop, for prod. *vibrato*.

Trench, (Frederick) Herbert (1865–1923), Eng. poet. *See* Holbrooke (*Apollo and the Seaman*).

Trenchmore, an Eng. country dance 'longways for as many as will', known in the 16th and 17th cents. and intro. into the court and noble houses as a kind of democratic dance in which masters and servants could take part together and strict class distinctions were temporarily relaxed.

Trend, J(ohn). B(rande). (b. Southampton, 17. XII. 1887; d. Cambridge, 20. IV. 1958), Eng. scholar. Educ. at Charterhouse and Cambridge. He specialized in Span. and became prof. of the subject at Cambridge Univ. in 1933. He wrote learned articles and books on Span. mus. subjects.

Trent, Council of. *See* **Council of T.**

Trent Codices, 7 MSS. (Trent, 87–93) of 15th-cent. mus., compiled 1440–80. The 1st 6 were bought by the Aus. Government in 1891, and a selection appeared in 6 vols. of the series *Denkmäler der Tonkunst in Österreich*. They became the property of Italy after World War I, and in 1920 the 7th MS. was found.

Trento, Vittorio (b. Venice, 1761; d. ?, ? 1833), It. comp. Pupil of Bertoni. In the last decade of the 18th cent. he visited London as cond. at the King's Theatre and in 1806 became impresario at Amsterdam, going to Lisbon in the same capacity soon after. After a further visit to London he returned to Venice before his death.

Works incl. operas *La finta ammalata, Quanti casi in un giorno, Teresa vedova, Ifigenia in Aulide, Climene* and *c.* 35 others; ballet *Mastino della Scala* and more than 50 others; oratorios *The Deluge*, *The Maccabees* and others, etc.

Trepak, a Rus. dance of Cossack origin in animated 2–4 time.

Treu, Daniel Gottlieb (b. Stuttgart, 1695; d. Breslau, 7. VIII. 1749), Ger. violinist and comp. Pupil of Cousser and from 1716 of Vivaldi in Venice, where he was called, by lit. trans. of his name, Fedele. In 1725 he went to Breslau as cond. of an It. opera company, in 1727 to Prague as mus. director and in 1740 into the service of Count Schaffgotsch at Hirschberg.

Works incl. operas *Astarto, Ulisse, Don Chisciotte* and others; cantatas; orchestral mus., etc.

Triad, a chord composed of 2 superimposed thirds, e.g.:

Maj.   Min.   Augmented   Diminished

TRIAD

les effets, Le Congrès des rois (with other comps.) and *Le Siège de Lille*.

Trial by Jury, one-act opera by Sullivan (lib. by W. S. Gilbert), prod. London, Royalty Theatre, 25. III. 1875.

Triangle, a perc. instrument consisting of a simple steel bar in 3-cornered form with an open end, hooked so that it can be suspended to hang freely. It is struck with a short steel rod and prod. a bright tinkling sound of no definite pitch.

Tricinium (Lat.), an obs. term for a song in 3 parts.

Tridentine Council. *See* **Council of Trent.**

Trihoris, an old Fr. dance of Lower Brittany, also called Trihory, Triori or Triory, allied to the Branle.

Trill. *See* **Shake.**

Trial, a Fr. term for a special type of operatic tenor voice of a high, thin, rather nasal quality suited to comic parts, derived from Antoine T. below.

Trial. Fr. family of musicians:

1. **Jean Claude T.** (b. Avignon, 13. XII. 1732; d. Paris, 23. VI. 1771), comp. Studied vln. with Garnier at Montpellier, settled in Paris, where he became a friend of Rameau, was app. cond. at the Opéra and later of the private orch. of the Prince de Conti, whose influence procured him the joint directorship of the Opéra with Berton.

Works incl. operas *Ésope à Cythère* (with Vachon), *La Fête de Flore, Silvie* (with Berton), *Théonis* (do.) and *Renaud d'Ast* (with Vachon); cantatas; overture and divertissements for orch., etc.

2. **Antoine T.** (b. Avignon, 1736; d. Paris, 5. II. 1795), tenor, brother of prec. He was educ. as a church singer, but went on the stage, toured in the provinces and in 1764 appeared for the 1st time in Paris. He took part in the Revolution, lost his reason and poisoned himself.

3. **Marie Jeanne T.** (*née* Milon) (b. Paris, 1. VIII. 1746; d. Paris, 13. II. 1818), soprano, wife of prec. Made her 1st stage appearance in 1766.

4. **Armand (Emmanuel) T.** (b. Paris, 1. III. 1771; d. Paris, 9. IX. 1803), pianist and comp., son of 2 and 3. He began to comp. at an early age, married Jeanne Méon, an actress at the Théâtre Favart, and d. from the effects of a wild life.

Works incl. operas *Julien et Colette, Adélaïde et Mirval, Les Deux Petits Aveugles*; revolutionary pieces *La Cause et*

Trille (Fr.)   ⎫
Triller (Ger.)   ⎬ = **Shake.**

Trillo (It.) = **Shake.** *See also* **Vibrato.**

Trillo del diavolo, Il (*The Devil's Trill*), Tartini's vln. sonata written at Assisi *c.* 1714, said to have been inspired by a dream in which he bargained with the devil for his soul in return for mus. inspiration, the devil playing the vln. to him. He related that on waking he immediately wrote down what he had heard, but that the mus. as written fell far short of the dream devil's perf. The work is in 4 movements, written for vln. and continuo; the famous trill is in the finale. An opera on the story of the sonata was written by Falchi.

Trinity College of Music, a school of mus. in London incorporated in 1875. Its principal is Myers Foggin.

Trio. (1) A comp. or movement for 3 vocal or instrumental parts: more partic. a chamber work for 3 instruments, esp. vln., cello and pf. (pf. T.) or vln., vla. and cello (string T.).

(2) The alternative section in a minuet, scherzo, march or similar movement, so called because orig. such sections were written for 2 obs. and bassoon.

Trio Sonata, the medium predominantly used for chamber mus. with a keyboard Continuo part in the later 17th and early 18th cent. T. S.s were most usually written for 2 vlns. and bass viol or cello, with background supplied by a harpsichord or other keyboard instrument played from the figured bass part.

Triomphe de l'Amour sur des bergers et bergères, Le (*The Triumph of Love over Shepherds and Shepherdesses*), opera by La

Guerre (lib. by Charles de Beys), prod. Paris, Louvre, 22. I. 1655. The 1st Fr. opera.

Trionfi del fato, I, ovvero Le glorie d'Enea (*The Triumphs of Fate, or The Glories of Aeneas*), opera by Steffani (lib. by Ortensio Mauro), prod. Hanover, Court Opera, XII. 1695.

Trionfo dell' onore, Il (*The Triumph of Honour*), opera by A. Scarlatti (lib. by Francesco Antonio Tullio), prod. Naples, Teatro dei Fiorentini, autumn 1718.

Trionfo di Camilla, Il (*Camilla's Triumph*), opera by M. A. Bononcini (lib. by Silvio Stampiglia), prod. Naples, Teatro San Bartolommeo, (?) XII. 1696.

Opera by Leo (lib. do.), prod. Rome, Teatro Capranica, 8. I. 1726.

Trionfo di Clelia, Il (*Clelia's Triumph*), opera by Gluck (lib. by Metastasio), prod. Bologna, Teatro Comunale, 14. V. 1763.

Opera by Hasse (lib. do.), prod. Vienna, Burgtheater, 27. IV. 1762.

Opera by Jommelli (lib. do.), prod. Lisbon, Teatro d'Ajuda, 6. VI. 1774.

Trionfo di Dori, Il (*The Triumph of Doris*), collection of It. madrigals pub. by Gardano of Venice in 1592. It contains 29 6-part madrigals on var. poems all ending with the line 'Viva la bella Dori', which suggested the similar uniform final line in the Eng. collection modelled on this, *The Triumphes of Oriana*. The comps., all represented by 1 piece only, incl. Anerio, Asola, Baccusi, Croce, G. Gabrieli, Gastoldi, Marenzio, Palestrina, Striggio and Vecchi.

Triori or **Triory** } *See* **Trihoris.**

Tripla, an old term for triple time in old Mensurable mus., but also the figure 3 shown in the time-signature and later, when the device of the Triplet came into use, the figure 3 set over a group of notes. Also a dance in quick triple time.

Triple Concerto, a concerto with 3 solo parts, e.g. Bach's 2 concertos for 3 harpsichords and strings or Beethoven's concerto for vln., cello and pf. and orch.

Triple Counterpoint, counterpoint in which 3 parts are reversible, each being capable of appearing at the top, in the middle or at the bottom.

Triple Time, 3 beats in a bar, e.g. 3–4.

Triplet, a group of 3 notes perf. in the time of 2 and indicated by the figure 3, e.g.:

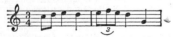

Rests instead of notes may form part of T.s.

Triplex (Lat. = triple) = **Triplum.**

Triplum (Lat. = the third), the highest

of the orig. 3 voices in the Motet, and thus the origin of the Eng. word Treble.

Tristan und Isolde, mus.-drama by Wagner (lib. by comp., based on the Tristram and Iseult legend), prod. Munich, Court Opera, 10. VI. 1865.

Tristitiae remedium (*The Remedy for Sadness*), a MS. collection of motets, anthems and madrigals by Eng. and It. comps. (Byrd, Croce, Milton, Peerson, Tallis, Tye, etc.) made by the clergyman Thomas Myriell of Barnet in 1616.

Tristram and Iseult. *See* **Queen of Cornwall; Tristan und Isolde.**

Tritone, the interval of the augmented 4th (e.g. F–B, progressing upwards). *See* **Diabolus in Musica.**

Tritonius, Petrus (actually Peter Treibenreif or Traybenraiff) (b. Bozen or Sterzing, ?; d. ?), Aus. 15th–16th-cent. comp. and scholar. Studied at Padua Univ. and later became teacher of Lat. and (?) mus. at the cathedral school of Brixen. He was invited to settle in Vienna by Conrad Celtes, a prof. there whom he had met in It., and joined the lit. and humanist society founded by that scholar, making his setting of Horatian odes for it. Senfl later took the tenor parts of these as a *cantus firmus* for his own settings, and Hofhaimer imitated T.'s settings. On the death of Celtes in 1508 T. returned to the Tyrol and became director of the Lat. school at Bozen; but in 1521 he retired to Schwatz nr. Innsbruck.

Works incl. hymns in 4 parts; odes by Horace and other Lat. poems set in 4 parts, etc.

Trittico (*Triptych*), cycle of 3 1-act operas by Puccini, prod. New York, Metropolitan Opera, 14. XII. 1918.

I. **Il Tabarro** (*The Cloak*) (lib. by Giuseppe Adami, based on Didier Gold's *Houppelande*).

II. **Suor Angelica** (*Sister A.*) (lib. by Giovacchino Forzano).

III. **Gianni Schicchi** (lib. by do., based on the story of a rogue who is mentioned in Dante's *Divina commedia*).

Tritto, Giacomo (b. Altamura nr. Bari, 2. IV. 1733; d. Naples, 16. IX. 1824), It. comp. Pupil of Cafaro at the Cons. dei Turchini in Naples, he later taught there and in 1806 became co-director (with Paisiello and Fenarolo). From *c.* 1780 he comp. over 50 operas. He also wrote treatises on thorough-bass and counterpoint.

Works incl. operas *La fedeltà in amore*, *Il convitato di pietra* (on the Don Giovanni story), *Arminio*, *La canterina*, *Gli Americani*, *Marco Albinio*, etc.; Masses and other church mus., etc.

Triumph of Neptune, The, ballet by Lord Berners (scenario by Sacheverell Sitwell, choreography by George Melitonovich Balanshin), prod. London, Lyceum Theatre, 3. XII. 1926. The settings were based on B. Pollock's 'penny plain, twopence coloured' toy theatre designs.

Triumph of Peace, The, masque by James Shirley with mus. by W. Lawes and Simon Ive, prod. at the Banqueting House in Whitehall, 3. II. (Candlemas), 1634.

Triumphes of Oriana, The, an Eng. collection of madrigals written in honour of Queen Elizabeth, ed. by Morley and pub. in 1601. It was modelled on the It. collection of *Il Trionfo di Dori* of 1592 and contains a similar series of different poems all ending with the same line, 'Long live fair Oriana'. There are 25 pieces by 23 Eng. comps.: Bennet, Carlton, Cavendish, Cobbold, Este, Farmer, E. Gibbons (2), Hilton, Holmes, Hunt, E. Johnson, R. Jones, Kirby, Lisley, Marson, Milton, Morley (2), Mundy, Nicolson, Norcome, T. Tomkins, Weelkes, Wilbye. A madrigal by Bateson intended for the collection arrived too late and was incl. in his own *First set of English Madrigals* (1604).

Triumphlied (*Song of Triumph*), a setting by Brahms of words from the Revelation of St. John for 8-part chorus, orch. and org. *ad lib.*, Op. 55, comp. in spring 1871 to celebrate the Ger. victory in the Franco-Prus. war; 1st perf. Carlsruhe, 1872.

Triumphs of Oriana. *See* **Triumphes of Oriana.**

Troilus and Cressida, opera in 3 acts by Walton (lib. by C. Hassall, after Chaucer), prod. Covent Garden, 3. XII. 1954.

Trois Fermiers, Les (*The Three Farmers*), opera by Dezède (lib. by Jacques Marie Boutet de Monvel), prod. Paris, Comédie-Italienne, 24. V. 1777.

Trois Mousquetaires, Les (*The Three Musketeers*), opera by Isidore de Lara (lib. by Henri Cain and Louis Payen, based on Dumas, sen.), prod. Cannes, 3. III. 1921.

Tromba (It.) = Trumpet, also one of the names for the Trumpet org. stop (8 ft.). *See also* **Clarino.**

Tromba da tirarsi (It. lit. tpt. to draw itself [out] = tpt. to be drawn), the Slide tpt., an obs. instrument of the tpt. type. It was used in Ger. in the 18th cent. and had the advantage before the invention of valves of being capable of prod. more notes than the fundamental harmonics by the temporary changes in the length of the tube, as in the tromb. It never attained a wide currency.

Tromba marina (It.). *See* **Trumpet Marine.**

Trombetti, Ascanio (b. Bologna, XI. 1544; d. Bologna, IX. 1590), It. comp. In the service of the Signoria of Bologna. Works incl. motets in 5–12 parts for voices and instruments; madrigals for 4–5 voices, *napolitane* for 3 voices, etc.

Tromboncino, Bartolommeo (b. ? Verona, *c.* 1470; d. ? Venice, after 1535), It. 15th–16th-cent. comp. At the ducal court of Mantua, 1487–95, then at Venice, Vicenza, Casale, at Mantua again in 1501–13, and then at Ferrara. Works incl. Benedictus for 3 voices, 9 Lamentations and other church mus.; *frottole* for 4 voices, etc.

Trombone, a brass wind instrument, developed from the medieval Sackbut, made in 4 basic sizes: alto, tenor, bass and contrabass, the 1st of which is now rarely used, parts written for it being played on the tenor T., while the last hardly ever appears in the orch., except in Wagner's *Ring*. The instrument's most characteristic feature is the slide, by means of which the tube can be adjusted to different lengths in 7 positions, so that all the notes of the chromatic scale can be prod. as natural harmonics. The T. was thus a chromatic instrument long before the horn and tpt. became so by the invention of the valves. The intonation, as in string instruments, is not fixed, but depends entirely on the player's ear and skill. Many notes are, of course, available in more than one position (as different harmonics), so that the player often has the choice between an easier and a more difficult way of passing from note to note. A strict *legato* between notes in different positions is not possible, as the breath has to be interrupted during the change of the slide to avoid an unpleasant scoop; but this scoop, which is usually designated by the term *glissando*, can be used as a special effect.

The compass of the alto T. in E♭ is:

of the tenor in B♭:

of the bass in F:

The compass of the contrabass lies an 8ve below the tenor's. The tenor-bass, a combined instrument in B♭ with a switch lowering the pitch a 4th to F, is widely used at the present day. The length of the slide makes it impossible to play the lowest note (B♮) of the bass T. on this instrument: the compass therefore starts from C and goes as high in the tenor range as the player can manage:

All T.'s except the contrabass can play 2 or 3 'pedal' notes an 8ve below the normal bass notes, e.g. on the tenor T.:

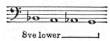

8ve lower⸻|

In the 19th cent. valve T.s were invented and gained favour in military and brass bands as being easier to play, though their tone is inferior. The valve T. never gained a firm footing in the orch.

Trombone Stop, a 16-ft. org. reed stop of powerful tone.

Trommel (Ger.) = Drum.

Trommelbass (Ger. lit. drum bass), a technical term for the notes of a bass part divided up into groups of repeated even quavers, a device used esp. in the 18th cent. to give a kind of artificial animation to mus.

Trompeter von Säckingen, Der (*The Trumpeter of S.*), opera by Nessler (lib. by Rudolf Bunge, based on Scheffel's poem), prod. Leipzig, 4. V. 1884.

Tronco (It. = truncated, cut off, interrupted), a direction indicating that a note or chord is to cease abruptly.

Troparion. See **Byzantine Chant.**

Trope. The verb 'to trope' meant to insert Tropes into eccles. chanting. The process was also called 'farcing' (i.e. larding). See **Tropes.**

Tropen (Ger. = tropes). The term, which does not refer to the old Tropes, was used by Josef Hauer for his own version of the system of Twelve-Note Mus. He divided the possible combinations of the 12 notes of the chromatic scale, which run into hundreds of millions, into 44 main groups, and these are what he called T., and he further divided each row of 12 notes into 2 halves of 6, which form 2 fundamental chords, whatever the order in which each 6 may appear. The T. for him were equivalent to keys in the diatonic system, and a change from one T. to another is equivalent to modulation.

Troper, a book or collection containing Tropes, e.g. the 11th-cent. Winchester T.s, which contain tropes used at Winchester Cathedral.

Tropes, interpolations into liturgical chants dating from the 8th or 9th cent. and prob. of Byzantine orig. They were at first vocalized as purely mus. ornamentations or sung on syllables of certain words, esp. 'Alleluia', but later they became so

important that special words were newly written for them. Sometimes new words came 1st and demanded new mus.; thus the Sequence, which began merely as a special kind of trope, developed into a poetical form with mus. setting.

Troppo (It. = too much). The word is often used in the negative in mus. directions; *non troppo* = not too much, or *ma non troppo* = but not too much.

Troubadour (Fr., from Prov. *trobador* [? from Lat. *tropus*]), a poet-musician of southern Fr. in the 11th–13th cents. T.s always wrote their own poems and probably the tunes as well: some 280 melodies are still extant. The poems were usually *poésies courtoises* (mainly love-songs, but also incl. satires, etc.), while story-telling *chansons à personnages*, though also cultivated by them, belonged chiefly to the northern Trouvères. Only the melodies were written down in a notation which showed the pitch but not, as a rule, the rhythm of the notes, the latter being either committed to memory or else determined by the poetic metre, a question that has never been solved beyond controversy. Neither is it known how the songs were accomp.: prob. on instruments of the harp or lute type, either by the T.s themselves or by attendants, for the T.s were not poor wandering musicians but gentlemen whose audiences were at courts and noble houses.

Troubadour, The (Verdi). See **Trovatore.**

Trouluffe. See **Truelove.**

'**Trout**' **Quintet,** a 5tet in A maj. for vln., vla., cello, double bass and pf. by Schubert, Op. 114, comp. summer 1819 during an excursion to Upper Aus.; so called because the 4th of the 5 movements is a set of variations on his song *The Trout* (*Die Forelle*).

Trouvère (Fr., from old Fr. *trovere* or *troveur*), a poet-musician of northern Fr. in the 12th and 13th cents. The T.s cultivated an art similar to that of the Troubadours in southern Fr. The art was encouraged in the N. by Eleanor of Aquitaine, who married Louis VII in 1137: *c.* 1,700 melodies have been preserved. The poems include *chansons à personnages* (narrative songs), *poésies courtoises* (courtly poems, mainly love-songs) and crusaders' songs. The notation and manner of perf. of the songs was similar to that of the Troubadours.

Trovatore, Il (*The Troubadour* or *The Minstrel*), opera by Verdi (lib. by Salvatore Cammarano, based on a Span. play, *El trovador*, by Antonio García Gutiérrez), prod. Rome, Teatro Apollo, 19. I. 1853.

Troyens, Les (*The Trojans*), opera by Berlioz in 2 parts (lib. by comp., after Virgil): I. **La Prise de Troie** (*The Taking of Troy*), prod. Carlsruhe (in Ger.), 6. XII.

1890; II. **Les Troyens à Carthage,** prod. Paris, Théâtre-Lyrique, 4. XI. 1863, and later at Carlsruhe (in Ger.), 7. XII. 1890 (the 1st perf. of the complete work). The 1st perf. of the complete work in Fr. was at Brussels, 26. and 27. XII. 1906.

Truelove (Trouluffe), John, (b. ?; d. ?), Eng. 15th-cent. comp. He was a canon of St. Probus, attached to Exeter Cathedral, 1465–78. He appears to have been assoc. with Richard Smert (*q.v.*) in the comp. of carols.

Trugschluss (Ger. = deceptive ending in mus. [false conclusion in logic]). The Ger. term for Interrupted Cadence.

Truinet, Charles. *See* **Nuitter.**

Trummscheit, also **Trumbscheit** or **Trumscheit** (Ger., prob. from *tromba* = trumpet and *Scheit* = a piece of wood). *See* **Tromba marina.**

Trumpet, a brass wind instrument of ancient origin. Until the invention of the valves in the 19th cent. the T. was capable of prod. only the natural harmonic notes, for which reason, combined with that of its incisive and carrying tone, it was found useful for fanfares, and for military purposes was often combined with kettledrums, a practice clearly reflected in the scores of classical orch. works up to the early 19th cent. In order to make it possible to play in different keys, crooks were used, as with the horn. The valves made the T. a chromatic instrument. The T.s in modern use are usually in C or Bb, the written compass being:

sounding on the Bb T.:

A T. in D is used for 17th- and 18th-cent. works and has been employed also by modern comps.: its sounding compass is:

A still smaller T. in F (with a compass a min. 3rd higher than that of the D T.) has been made for the perf. of Bach's 2nd Brandenburg concerto, and there is also one in high Bb (with a compass an 8ve

higher than that of the normal Bb T.). *See also* **Bach Trumpet, Bass Trumpet, Clarino, Principal** and **Tromba da tirarsi.**

Trumpet Marine, an obs. and primitive string instrument with a single string and thus allied to the Monochord, played with a bow. It was used mainly for popular mus.-making, esp. in Ger., but also in nunneries, as the Ger. name *Nonnengeige* (nun's fiddle) indicates. It was also called *Trummscheit* (trumpet [*tromba*] wood) or *Brummscheit* (humming wood), and the It. and Eng. names connecting it with a tpt. were doubtless due to its penetrating tone. The adj. 'marine' is said (uncertainly) to have come either from It. because of the instrument's resemblance to the speaking-tpt. on It. ships or from Fr. because a 15th-cent. trumpeter name Marin or Maurin improved the instrument. The instrument prod. harmonics very easily and, like the old tpt., often restricted itself to them, its normally prod. notes being very poor and coarse in quality.

Trumpet Stop, an 8-ft. reed org. stop repro. tpt. tone.

Trumpet Voluntary, in the late 17th cent. a piece, not for tpt., but an org. voluntary the tune of which was played on the tpt. stop. The ex. still familiar is that by J. Clarke, long wrongly attrib. to Purcell, popularized by Sir Henry Wood's orch. arr. The tune was also known as *The Prince of Denmark's March*: it is therefore unlikely to have been Clarke's own, but was prob. merely arr. by him for such an org. piece, evidently from a tune favoured by Queen Anne's consort, Prince George of Denmark.

Trumscheit. *See* **Trummscheit.**

Trunk, Richard (b. Tauberbischofsheim, Baden, 10. II. 1879; d. 2. VI. 1968), Ger. comp. Studied with Knorr at the Hoch Cons., Frankfurt o/M. and with Rheinberger at the Munich Avad. He settled there as choral cond. and critic, but spent 1912–14 in N.Y. as cond. of the Arion choral society. From 1925 to 1934 he was director of the Rheinische Musikschule at Cologne, but he returned to Munich as president of the Akademie der Tonkunst, succeeding Hausegger.

Works incl. operetta *Herzdame*: male-voice choruses, e.g. cycle from *Des Knaben Wunderhorn,* poems by Goethe, etc.; serenade for string orch.; string 4tet; pf. 5tet; romance for vln. and pf.; several sets of songs, etc.

Tsar and Carpenter (Lortzing). *See* **Zar und Zimmermann.**

Tsar Saltan (Rimsky-Korsakov). *See* **Legend of Tsar Saltan.**

Tsar's Bride, The (*Tsarskaya Nevesta*), opera by Rimsky-Korsakov (lib. by I. F. Tumenev, based on a play by Lev

Alexandrovich Mey), prod. Moscow, Imp. Opera, 3. XI. 1899.

Tschaikowski. *See* **Tchaikovsky,** the usual Eng. transliteration of the name.

Tschudi, Burkhardt. *See* **Shudi, Burkat.**

Tuba. (1) An ancient Rom. military tpt. (2) The bass instrument of the saxhorn family, used in the orch. as the bass of the brass instruments. The orchestral instrument is normally in F (non-transposing) with 4 valves and the following compass:

8 ve lower⌋

Military and brass bands also use tubas in E♭ and low B♭. *See also* **Bombardon, Euphonium** and **Wagner Tubas.**

Tuba major
or } (or **Tuba** for short), an
Tuba mirabilis

8-ft. org. reed stop of great power, similar in tone to the tpt.

Tubular Bells, metal tubes tuned to the mus. scale and used for bell effects in the orch., real bells being cumbersome and difficult to play with precision.

Tubuphone, a perc. instrument the notes of which are prod. by metal tubes set in rows like a pf. keyboard, but struck with hammers.

Tuck (old Eng.), the sound of a drum, drum-tap.

Tucke, John (b. ?; d. ?), Eng. 16th-cent. mus. theorist. He was a fellow of New Coll., Oxford, 1500–7; master of the choristers, Higham Ferrers, from 1507, and at Gloucester Cathedral from 1515. He was the compiler and part-author of an important collection of treatises now in the Brit. Mus. (Add. MS. 10,336).

Tucker, Richard (b. N.Y., 28. IV. 1914), Amer. tenor. Studied in N.Y. with P. Althouse, making his début at the N.Y. Metropolitan in 1945, and remaining there as its leading tenor.

Tucker, William (b. ?; d. London, 28. II. 1679), Eng. comp. Gentleman of the Chapel Royal in London, and minor canon and precentor of Westminster Abbey from 1660.
Works incl. services, anthems, etc.

Tucket (Eng. obs.), a word found in stage directions of Eng. plays of the Elizabethan period where the author asks for a fanfare to be played on or off the stage ('tucket within'). It was connected with Fr. *toucher* and It. *toccare* = to touch, and thus prob. with 'toccata', just as 'sennet', which meant much the same thing, may have been with 'sonata'.

Tuczek (or Tuček), Vincenz (b. Prague, 2. II. 1773; d. ?, 1821), Boh. tenor, cond.

and comp. After working as singer and cond. at theatres in Prague and Vienna he was *Kapellmeister* to the Duke of Courland in Sagan 1797–9, then mus. director at the Silesian nat. theatre in Breslau (1799) and at the Leopoldstädtertheater in Vienna (1806–9). Later he also worked in Budapest.
Works incl. operas and *Singspiele Daemona, Lanassa, Der Zauberkuss,* etc.; Masses and other church mus.; cantatas, etc.

Tuczek - Herrenburg, Leopoldine (b. Vienna, 11. XI. 1821; d. Baden nr. Vienna, 20. X. 1883), Boh. soprano, granddaughter of prec. Pupil of Josephine Fröhlich at the Vienna Cons. and of It. masters. She appeared on the stage as a child and made her 1st important operatic appearance *c.* 1840. In 1841–61 she was at the Berlin Court Opera.

Tuder, John (b. ?; d. ?), Eng. 15th-cent. comp. Responsories, Lamentations and the hymn *Gloria laus* are incl. in the 'Pepys' MS. of *c.* 1465 (Magdalene Coll., Cambridge); carols by 'Tutor' are in the 'Fayrfax Book' of *c.* 1500.

Tudor, David (b. Philadelphia, 26. I. 1926), Amer. pianist. Studied pf. and comp. with S. Wolpe. Best known for his close assoc. with John Cage, much of whose mus. he perfs. or helps to realize.

Tudway, Thomas (b. ? Windsor, *c.* 1650; d. Cambridge, 23. XI. 1726), Eng. comp. and organist. Became chorister in the Chapel Royal in London soon after the Restoration (1660) and lay vicar at Windsor in 1664; app. organist at King's Coll., Cambridge, 1670, and Prof. of Mus. in the univ. there, 1705, in succession to Staggins. In 1714–20 he compiled a large collection of Eng. cathedral mus. in 6 vols.
Works incl. services, anthems, etc.

Tulou, Jean Louis (b. Paris, 12. IX. 1786; d. Nantes, 23. VII. 1865), Fr. flautist and comp. 1st learnt mus. from his father, Jean Pierre T. (1749–99), a bassoonist, and studied at the Paris Cons. He played successively in the orchs. of the Théâtre Italien and the Opéra and in 1829 became fl. prof. at the Cons., leaving in 1856 to take to fl. manufacture.
Works incl. fl. concertos, fl. duets and trios, variations, fantasies and other pieces for fl. and pf., test pieces for fl., etc.

Tuma, Franz Ignaz Anton (b. Kostelec, 2. X. 1704; d. Vienna, 30. I. 1774), Boh. vla. da gamba player and comp. Came to Vienna *c.* 1727, studied with Fux, was in the service of Count Kinsky 1731 (or earlier) to 1741, and *Kapellmeister* to the Dowager Empress Elisabeth Christina 1741–50. He retired to a monastery in 1768.
Works incl. numerous Masses, motets and other church mus., etc.

Tunder, Franz (b. Burg auf Fehmarn,

Tune

1614; d. Lübeck, 5. XI. 1667), Ger. organist and comp. In 1632 he was app. court organist at Gottorp and in 1641 organist of St. Mary's Church at Lübeck, where he prec. Buxtehude, who had to marry his daughter in order to secure the post. He greatly improved the church mus. and also instituted the 'Evening Music' (*Abendmusiken*) which soon became famous beyond the town.

Works incl. church cantatas, sacred arias with strings and org.; chorale variations for org., etc.

Tune, another word for Melody, more colloquial and therefore often considered vulgar. 'In tune' means accurate intonation, 'out of tune' the opposite. 'To tune' is to adjust the intonation of an instrument.

Tuning-Fork, a small and simple instrument in the form of a metal fork with 2 long prongs, said to have been invented by the trumpeter John Shore in 1711. It not only retains pitch accurately, but gives out a pure sound free from harmonic upper partials.

Tunsted, Simon (b. ? Norwich, ?; d. ? Bruisyard, Suffolk, ? 1369), Eng. priest and mus. scholar. He took his name from father's birthplace in Norfolk, became a min. friar of the Franciscan Order at Oxford, studied theol., mus. and astronomy, became regent of the Minorites, and head of their order in 1360. The mus. treatise *De quatuor principalibus musice* (1351) is falsely attrib. to him.

Tuotilo (or **Tutilo**) (b. ?; d. St. Gall, 27. IV. 915), ? Swiss monk and musician at the monastery of St. Gall. He played and taught all the instruments of the period and comp. church mus., incl. (?) the Christmas trope *Hodie cantandus est nobis puer*.

Turanda, opera by Bazzini (lib. by Antonia Gazzoletti, based on Gozzi's play *Turandot*), prod. Milan, Teatro alla Scala, 13. I. 1867.

Turandot. See also **Turanda**.

Incid. mus. for Schiller's Ger. version of Gozzi's play by Weber, Op. 37, comp. in 1809 and incl. the *Overtura cinese* (*Chin. Overture*), comp. on a Chin. theme in 1805.

Opera by Busoni (Ger. lib. by comp. based on Gozzi's play), prod. Zürich, 11. V. 1917, together with another short opera *Arlecchino*. The mus. of *Turandot* was elaborated from incid. mus. for Max Reinhardt's prod. of Karl Vollmöller's version of Gozzi's play, prod. Berlin, Deutsches Theater, 27. X. 1911.

Opera by Herman Severin Løvenskjold (1815–70) (Dan. lib. by Hans Haagen Nyegaard, based on Gozzi's play), prod. Copenhagen, 3. XII. 1854.

Opera by Puccini (It. lib. by Giuseppe

Turini

Adami and Renato Simoni, based on Gozzi's play), left unfinished by Puccini and completed by Alfano; prod. Milan, Teatro alla Scala, 25. V. 1926.

See also **Danzi, Jensen, Reissiger** and **Vesque von Püttlingen.**

Turba (Lat. = crowd), the chorus in settings of the Passion representing priests, people, disciples, etc.

Turca (It. fem. = Turkish). The word is used in the combination *alla turca* (in the Turkish manner) by Mozart for the finale of the A maj. pf. sonata (K. 331) and by Beethoven for the *Marcia a. t.* in *The Ruins of Athens*, which is the theme of the pf. variations Op. 76.

Turco in Italia, Il (*The Turk in Italy*), opera by Rossini (lib. by Felice Romani), prod. Milan, Teatro alla Scala, 14. VIII. 1814.

Tureck, Rosalyn (b. Chicago, 14. XII. 1914), Amer. pianist. Made her début aged 11 with the Chicago Symph. Orch., and then studied with O. Samaroff at the Juilliard School of Mus., graduating in 1936. From 1943 she taught at the school, also becoming well known for her playing of Bach.

Turgenev, Ivan (1818–83), Rus. novelist and dramatist. *See* **Ippolitov-Ivanov** (*Assia*), **Kastalsky** (*Clara Milich*), **Shaporin** (*Gentlefolk*), **Simon** (A.) (*Song of Love Triumphant*), **Viardot-García** (operettas).

Turges, Edmund (b. ?; d. ?), Eng. 15th–16th-cent. comp. Son of (?) John T., harper to Queen Margaret. He was at King's Coll., Cambridge, in 1522, not as a student, but prob. as a master of some kind, for he had already written a part-song for the marriage of Prince Arthur and Catherine of Aragon in 1501.

Works incl. Masses, Magnificats, anthems, part-songs, etc.

Turina, Joaquín (b. Saville, 9. XII. 1882; d. Madrid, 14. I. 1949), Span. comp. Studied at Seville and Madrid, later with d'Indy at the Schola Cantorum in Paris. He devoted much time to teaching as well as comp. and wrote a small treatise, *Enciclopedia abreviada de la música.*

Works incl. operas *Margot* and *Jardin de oriente* (libs. by G. Martínez Sierra); incid. mus. for Moreto's *La adúltera penitente*, Martínez Sierra's *Navidad* and other plays; *La procesión del Rocío, Danzas fantásticas, Sinfonía sevillana, Ritmos* and other works for orch.; string 4tet, pf. 5tet, *Escena andaluza* for vla., pf. and string 4tet; *Poema de una Sanluquena* for vln. and pf.; suites *Rincones sevillanos* and *Sevilla* and other works for pf.; songs, etc.

Turini, Francesco (b. Prague, c. 1590; d. Brescia, 1656), It. comp. His father Gregorio T. was cornett player and comp. to the Emperor Rudolph II in Prague, but

d. early, whereupon the emperor sent T. to Venice and Rome to study mus. and later made him his chamber organist. He left Prague in 1624 to become cathedral organist at Brescia.

Works incl. Masses and motets; madrigals, canons, etc.

Türk, Daniel Gottlob (b. Claussnitz nr. Chemnitz, 10. VIII. 1750; d. Halle, 26. VIII. 1813), Ger. theorist and comp. Studied under his father and under Homilius at Dresden. Later he went to Leipzig Univ., where he became a pupil and friend of J. A. Hiller, who procured him appts. as violinist at the Opera and the orchestral concerts. In 1776 he became organist at St. Ulrich's Church at Halle, in 1779 mus. director of the univ. and in 1787 organist at the church of Our Lady. He wrote treatises on org. and clavier playing, thorough-bass and temperament.

Works incl. opera *Pyramus und Thisbe*; cantata *Die Hirten bei der Krippe zu Bethlehem*; pf. sonatas and pieces, etc.

Turkish Crescent. *See* **Chinese Pavilion.**

Turn. An ornament indicated by the sign ∞ and interpreted as follows:

Turner, W(alter). J(ames). (b. Shanghai, 13. X. 1889; d. London, 18. XI. 1946), Eng. poet, novelist and mus. critic. Studied mus. with his father, became organist at Melbourne and later studied at Dresden, Munich and Vienna. He pub. books of miscellaneous mus. essays, works on Mozart, Beethoven, Berlioz and Wagner, *Eng. Music* for the *Britain in Pictures* series ed. by him, etc.

Turner, William (b. Oxford, 1651; d. London, 13. I. 1740), Eng. tenor and comp. Chorister at Christ Church, Oxford, and later in the Chapel Royal in London, where he joined Blow and Humfrey in comp. the so-called 'club anthem'. Later became singer successively at Lincoln Cathedral, St. Paul's Cathedral and Westminster Abbey. Mus.D., Cambridge, 1696. The singer Ann T. (?–1741), wife of John Robinson, was his youngest daughter.

Works incl. services, anthems (1 for Queen Anne's coronation); masque *Presumptuous Love*; songs for Durfey's *A Fond Husband* and *Madam Fickle*, Shadwell's *The Libertine*, Settle's *Pastor fido* and other plays; catches, songs, etc.

TURN

Turn of the Screw, The, opera in a prologue and 2 acts by Britten (lib. by Myfanwy Piper, after Henry James), prod. Venice, 14. IX. 1954, and in London, 6. X. 1954.

Turned Shake. *See* **Ornaments.**

Turner, Ann. *See* **Robinson, John** and **Turner, William.**

Turner, Eva (b. Oldham, 10. III. 1892), Eng. soprano. Studied at R.A.M. and joined the Carl Rosa Opera chorus in 1916 and then sang with them until 1924. She then sang at La Scala, Milan, with Toscanini. She was well known as a dramatic singer in Verdi and Wagner. One of her most famous roles was that of Puccini's Turandot. She was created D.B.E. in 1962.

Turnhout, Gérard de (real name Jacques Gheert) (b. Turnhout, *c.* 1520; d. Madrid, 15. IX. 1580), Flem. singer and comp. He became a church singer at Antwerp in 1545 and *maître de chapelle* of the cathedral in 1562. In 1572 he was called into the service of Philip II at Madrid.

Works incl. Masses and motets; *chansons*, etc.

Turnhout, Jean de (b. *c.* 1545; d. after 1618), Flem. comp., brother or nephew of prec. He became *maître de chant* at St.-Rombaut, Malines, in 1577, and later at the viceregal court at Brussels. He pub. madrigals and sacred Lat. works.

Tusch (Ger.) = Fanfare. The word is prob. derived from Fr. *touche* (with the same source as the It. *toccare* and *toccata*) and is thus related to the Eng. Tucket.

Tut, a device in lute-playing: the damping of a note by a finger not used for stopping.

Tutchev. *See* **Tiutchev.**

Tutilo. *See* **Tuotilo.**

Tutti (It. = all), a term used, in the 1st place, to designate the singing and playing together of all the forces engaged in a mus. perf.; but it is also used for the purely orchestral passages in a concerto, where the solo instrument is silent, whether the whole orch. happens to be playing or only part of it. Used as a noun, the word means any passage in an orchestral work in which the whole force is employed, esp. when playing at full strength.

Tvisöngur (Icelandic = twin songs), ancient songs of Iceland, dating back beyond the 15th cent., sung in 2 parts in a primitive kind of counterpoint akin to Organum.

Twain, Mark (pseud. of Samuel Langhorne Clemens) (1835–1910), Amer. novelist. *See* **Foss (L.)** (*Jumping Frog*).

Twelfth, a 2⅔-ft. org. stop prod. notes 12 diatonic degrees above those played.

Twelfth Mass, a work pub. by Vincent Novello as No. 12 in his ed. of Mozart's Masses, and long popular under this attribution. It is unquestionably spurious, poss. being the work of one Carl Zulehner, who sold the MS. to Simrock, the orig. pub.

Twelve-Note Music, the system of comp. on which the later works by Schönberg and the mus. of some of his disciples (e.g. Berg, Křenek, Pisk, Webern) are based, as well as that of a growing school with adherents in var. countries. It abolishes keys and with them the predominance of certain notes in a scale (tonic, dominant, subdominant and mediant), using instead the 12 notes of the chromatic scale, each of which has exactly the same importance as any other. This rules out, in principle, any feeling of tonality, though in more recent T.-N. M. tonal implications are often evident, and also discards the resource of modulation, so important to mus. structure in the classical sense.

In order to make sure that no note assumes an even temporary predominance, the rule has been estab. that a 'series' must consist of all the 12 notes of the chromatic scale, and that each note must appear only once in its course (transposition into any 8ve being allowed); but this does not mean that all melodic patterns of T.-N. M. are necessarily of the same length, for they may be given any rhythmic shape the comp. desires, and these shapes may be varied throughout a work, though the order of the notes, once determined at his desire, may not. Notes may, however,

appear simultaneously as well as successively. Moreover, 3 ways of achieving melodic as distinct from rhythmic or harmonic variety are open to the comp.: he may (1) restate his theme inverted (i.e. turned upside down), (2) in reverse or *cancrizans* (i.e. turned backwards) or (3) inverted and reversed at the same time.

In the years since 1945 the '12-note system' has found almost universal acceptance among comps. of the younger generation, and among already estab. figures Stravinsky is an outstanding convert, his more recent mus. being indebted to Webern. Although the techniques of Schönberg and Webern have to a greater or lesser extent been superseded, their basic concepts are still recognized as one of the most practical and satisfying ways of organizing totally chromatic mus. In addition, the sound world intro. by the Viennese comps., free from tonal ties, has resulted in a completely new attitude toward aural experience. The work of Schönberg and his pupils has proved one of the great liberating forces in the hist. of mus.

Among the comps. who have made use of the '12-note system' are Berio, Blacher, Boulez, Britten, Cage, Castiglioni, Dallapiccola, Davies (P. M.), Fortner, Goehr (A.), Hartmann, Haubenstock-Ramati, Henze, Kagel, Leibowitz, Ligeti, Lutoslawski, Lutyens, Maderna, Martin, Messiaen, Nigg, Nono, Pousseur, Searle, Seiber, Stockhausen, Stravinsky, Xenakis.

Twilight of the Gods, The (Wagner, better *Dusk of the Gods*). *See* **Ring des Nibelungen.**

Twin Songs. *See* **Tvisöngur.**

Two Sisters, The, opera by Rootham (lib. by Marjorie Fausset, based on the ballad *The Twa Sisters of Binnorie*), prod. Cambridge, 14. II. 1922.

Two Widows (*Dvě Vdovy*), opera by Smetana (lib. by Emanuel Züngel, based on a Fr. comedy by Pierre Jean Félicien Mallefille), prod. Prague, Cz. Theatre, 27. III. 1874.

Tye, Christopher (b. ? Ely or Cambridge, *c.* 1500; d. ? Doddington, ? III. 1573), Eng. comp. and poet. Learnt mus. (?) as a choir-boy in King's Coll. chapel, Cambridge, and was certainly a lay-clerk there in 1537. In 1541 or 1542 he was app. choir-master at Ely Cathedral and in 1545 he took the Mus.D. at Cambridge. He may have been mus. master to Edward VI in 1544–50, and he was made a Gentleman of the Chapel Royal. In 1561 he resigned his post at Ely and was succeeded by R. White, (?) his son-in-law, and, having been ordained accepted the living at Doddington-cum-Marche in the Isle of Ely, and for some time later he held 2 other livings in the neighbourhood, but had to resign them, as well as Doddington, on account of carelessness in the matter of payments due. But he was at the latter place until the year before his death. He wrote a good deal of verse in his later years.

Works incl. Masses, motets, services, anthems, *The Actes of the Apostles* in Eng. metrical versions set for 4 voices; In Nomines for instruments, etc.

Tyes, J. (b. ?; d. ?), Eng. 15th-cent. comp. 2 pieces are preserved in the Old Hall MS.

Tyl, Josef Kajetan (1808–56), Cz. dramatist. *See* **Kovařovic** (*Wood Nymph*), **Škroup** (*Fidlovačka*), **Švanda Dudák** (Hřimalý and Weinberger).

Tyl Owlglass. *See* **Till Eulenspiegel.**

Tymbal (from Fr. *timbale*), an early Eng. name for the kettledrum.

Tympanon (Fr.) = Dulcimer.

Tympanum (Lat.). *See* **Timpan.**

Tyndall, John (b. Leighlin Bridge, Co. Carlow, 2. VIII. 1820; d. Hindhead, Surrey, 4. XII. 1893), Ir. physicist. His contrib. to mus. is a book containing acoustical investigations and entitled *Sound*.

Typophone (Fr.) = Dulcitone.

Typp(e), William (b. ?; d. ?), Eng. 15th-cent. comp. He was precentor of Fotheringay Coll. (Northants) in 1438. 7 pieces are in the Old Hall MS., incl. an isorhythmic setting of the Credo.

Tyrolienne (Fr. fem. = Tyrolese), a country dance similar to the *Ländler* or slow waltz, supposed to be native of the mountain regions of the Tyrol, but really an artificial growth intro. into ballets and operas and loosely based on melodic figurations imitating var. forms of Yodel. T.s also became fashionable in the form of pf. pieces and songs, etc.

Tyrwhitt, Gerald. *See* **Berners, Lord.**

Tzigane (Fr., or *tsigane*), a gypsy or musician of the bohemian world of Paris. The title of a rhapsody for vln. and pf. by Ravel comp. in 1924.

U

U. C. An abbr. occasionally used for *una corda* (one string), indicating the use of the damping Pedal in pf. mus.

Uberti, Antonio (b. Verona, 1697; d. Berlin, 20. I. 1783), It. castrato of Ger. origin. Pupil of Porpora and known as Porporino. He sang in It. opera in Ger. and became chamber singer to Frederick II of Prus. Among his pupils was Mara.

Uberti, Fazio degli (14th cent.), It. poet. *See* **Malipiero** (*Peccati mortali*).

Uccellatori, Gli (*The Birdcatchers*), opera by Gassmann (lib. by Goldoni), prod. Venice, Teatro San Moisè, Carnival 1759.

Uccellini, Marco (b. ? Forlimpopoli, *c.* 1603; d. Forlimpopoli, 10. IX. 1680), It. violinist and comp. Master of instrumental mus. at the ducal court of Modena from 1645 to 1662 and *maestro di cappella* at Modena Cathedral from 1647 to 1665.

Works incl. opera *Gli eventi di Filandro ed Edessa*; prologues *La nave d'Enea* and *Giove di Elide fulminato*; psalms and litanies for voices and instruments; *Composizioni armoniche* and *Sinfonici concerti* for vln. and other instruments, *Sinfonie boscareocie* and sonatas for vln. and bass, etc.

Ugalde (*née* **Beaucé**), **Delphine** (b. Paris, 3. XII. 1829; d. Paris, 19. VII. 1910), Fr. soprano. Pupil of her mother, of Moreau-Sainti and prob. of Laure Cinti-Damoreau. Married the Span. musician Ugalde and made her 1st stage appearance at the Paris Opéra-Comique in 1848.

Ugarte, Floro (b. Buenos Aires, 15. IX. 1884), Arg. Comp. Studied with Fourdrain in Paris and became a private mus. teacher on his return in 1913 and prof. at the Nat. Cons. at Buenos Aires in 1924. He also became mus. director of the Teatro Colón, resigning in 1943.

Works incl. opera *Saika* and others; symph. poems and suites for orch.; instrumental pieces, etc.

Ugolini, Vincenzo (b. Perugia, *c.* 1570; d. Rome, 6. V. 1638), It. comp. Pupil of Bernardino Nassini. *Maestro di cappella* at the church of Santa Maria Maggiore in Rome, 1592–1603. He then retired after a severe illness, but in 1609 became *maestro di cappella* at Benevento Cathedral and returned in 1616 to Rome, where after some other appts. he became Soriano's successor in the Julian Chapel in 1620 and *maestro di cappella* of San Luigi dei Francesi in 1631, a post he had held in 1616–20.

Works incl. Masses, motets, psalms and other church mus.; madrigals, etc.

Ugolino of Orvieto (b. ?, *c.* 1380; d. Ferrara, 1457), It. comp. and theorist. His *Declaratio musicae disciplinae* is mainly a practical handbook for the perf. musician of his day.

Uhland, Johann Ludwig (1787–1862), Ger. poet. *See* **Black Knight** (Elgar), **Humperdinck** (*Glück von Edenhall*), **Schoeck** (songs), **Schumann** (*Glück von E.*), **Strauss (R.)** (*Schloss am Meer*).

Uhlig, Theodor (b. Wurzen nr. Leipzig, 15. II. 1822; d. Dresden, 3. I. 1853), Ger. violinist, author and comp. of theoret. works. Pupil of Schneider at Dessau. He entered the royal orch. at Dresden in 1841 and became an intimate friend of Wagner there.

Uilleann Pipes. *See* **Union Pipes.**

Ukelele (lit. 'the jumping flea'), the Hawaiian guitar, intro. to the Sandwich Islands by the Port. in 1877 and more recently into Eur. as a popular instrument. It has 4 gut strings and can be played from a notation resembling the old lute tablature.

'Ukrainian' Symphony (Tchaikovsky). *See* **'Little-Russian' Symphony.**

Ulibishev, Alexander Dimitrievich (b. Dresden, 2. IV. 1794; d. nr. Nizhny-Novgorod, 2. II. 1858), Rus. writer on mus. and amateur musician. As the son of a nobleman he served in the army and then lived in retirement on his estate. He was a good violinist and 4tet player. He made a special study of Mozart and pub. a work in 3 vols. on him, but disliked the late works of Beethoven and attacked Lenz's book on that composer.

Ullmann, Viktor (b. Těšín, 1. I. 1898), Sudeten-Ger. comp. Pupil of Schönberg in Vienna, later theatre cond. at Aussig and mus. teacher in Prague.

Works incl. operas *Peer Gynt* (after Ibsen) and *Der Sturz des Antichrist*; variations and double fugue on a theme by Schönberg for orch.; 8tet, 2 string 4tets, etc.

Ullrich, Hermann (b. Mödling nr. Vienna, 15. VIII. 1888), Aus. comp. and critic. Studied in Vienna and at the Mozarteum at Salzburg. Lived in London, 1939–46. He was by profession a judge until 1958 but for many years was active as a mus. critic.

Works incl. ballet-pantomime *Der erste Ball*; symph. in F maj., symph. prologue to Machiavelli's *Mandragola*, symph. poem on Hauptmann's *Hanneles Himmelfahrt*, Little Suite in the Old Style for orch.; Variations on a Romantic Theme for chamber orch.; mus. for string 4tet, fantasy for vln., horn and pf., etc.

Ulrich, Hugo (b. Oppeln, Silesia, 26. XI. 1827; d. Berlin, 23. V. 1872), Ger. comp. and teacher. He lost his parents at the age of 12 and was sent to school at Breslau and Glogau. In 1846 he went to Berlin and was helped by Meyerbeer to study with Dehn. He had some success with his comps., lived in It. for some years from 1855, but was driven back to Berlin by poverty, taught there at Stern's Cons., but soon preferred to lead a precarious existence by making arrs. and picking up other casual work.

Works incl. opera *Bertrand de Born* (unfinished); symph. in B min., *Symphonie triomphale* and 3rd symph. (unfinished), 2 overtures for orch ; string 4tet, pf. trio; pf. pieces, etc.

Ultimo giorno di Pompei, L' (*The Last Day of Pompeii*), opera by Pacini (lib. by Andrea Leone Tottola, not founded on Bulwer-Lytton's novel, which was not then pub.), prod. Naples, Teatro San Carlo, 19. XI. 1825. Perf. London in 1831, it may have been heard by Bulwer-Lytton.

Ulysses (*see also* Circe and **Penelope**), opera by Keiser (lib. by Friedrich Maximilian Lersner), prod. (in Ger.) Copenhagen, at court, XI. 1722.

Umbreit, Karl Gottlieb (b. Rehstadt nr. Gotha, 9. I. 1763; d. Rehstadt, 28. IV. 1829), Ger. organist and comp. Pupil of Kittel. He was app. organist at Sonneborn, Coburg, and became a famous org. teacher.

Works incl. chorales, chorale preludes, preludes and fugues, etc. for org.

Umělécká Beseda (Cz. = Society of Arts), an assoc. founded in Prague in 1863 for the encouragement of the arts, esp. nat. Cz. mus.

Umlauff, Ignaz (b. Vienna, 1756; d. Vienna, 8. VI. 1796), Aus. comp. He became a vla. player in the orch. of the court opera in 1772, and on the foundation of the nat. *Singspiel* theatre by Joseph II in 1778 became its director, the inaugural work being his *Die Bergknappen*. From 1789 he was Salieri's deputy as *Kapellmeister* of the court chapel. He also took part with Mozart in the perfs. of Handel's oratorios organized by Gottfried van Swieten.

Works incl. *Singspiele Die Insel der Liebe, Die Bergknappen, Die Apotheke, Die schöne Schusterin oder die pucegefarbenen Schuhe, Das Irrlicht, Welches ist die beste Nation?, Die glücklichen Jäger, Die Ringe der Liebe* (sequel to Grétry's *Zémire et Azor*); incid. mus. for *Der Oberamtmann und die Soldaten* (after Calderón), etc.; church mus., etc.

Umlauff, Michael (b. Vienna, 9. VIII. 1781; d. Baden nr. Vienna, 20. VI. 1842), Aus. cond. and comp., son of prec. Pupil of his father, became a violinist at the Opera and was cond. of the 2 court theatres in 1810–25 and again from 1840. On and after the revival of *Fidelio* in 1814 he asst. Beethoven, who was then too deaf to hear the orch., to conduct some of his maj. works.

Opera *Das Wirtshaus in Granada*, play with mus. *Der Grenadier*; 12 ballets; church mus.; pf. sonatas, etc.

Un ballo in maschera (Verdi). *See* Ballo in maschera, *also* Gustave III (Auber).

Un giorno di regno (Verdi). *See* Giorno di regno.

Un poco (It. = a little), a qualifying direction used where any indication of tempo or expression is to be applied in moderation. Often used in the abbr. form *poco*.

Una corda (It. = one string), a direction used by Beethoven and others in pf. mus. to indicate the use of the Damping Pedal, which so shifts the hammers that they touch only a single string for each note, instead of 2 or 3.

Una cosa rara, o sia Bellezza ed onestà (*A Rare Thing, or Beauty and Honesty*), opera by Martín y Soler (lib. by Lorenzo da Ponte, based on a story by Luis Vélez de Guevara), prod. Vienna, Burgtheater, 17. XI. 1786. Mozart quotes an air from it in the finale of the 2nd act of *Don Giovanni*.

Unda Maris (Lat. lit. sea-wave), an org. stop similar to the Voix céleste.

Undina, opera by Lvov (lib., in Rus., by Count Vladimir Alexandrovich Sollogub based on a Fr. lib. *La Marquise*, by Jules Henri Vernoy de Saint-Georges), prod. St. Petersburg, 20. IX. 1848.

Undine, opera by Karl Friedrich Girschner (1794–1860) (lib. by Friedrich de la Motte Fouqué, based on his own story of that name), prod. Danzig, 20. IV. 1837.

Opera by E. T. A. Hoffmann (lib. do.), prod. Berlin, Schauspielhaus, 3. VIII. 1816.

Opera by Lortzing (lib. by comp., based on Fouqué), prod. Magdeburg, 21. IV. 1845.

Unequal Temperament, a system of tuning, esp. on old keyboard instruments, in which some of the accidentals were treated as sharps according to Just Intonation and some as flats (e.g. F$\sharp$, not G$\flat$; B$\flat$, not A$\sharp$). An attempt was thus made to make some of the more frequently used keys come nearer to just intonation than is possible in the tempered scale of the modern pf., but the result was also that the more extreme sharp and flat keys were out of tune. This is one of the reasons why these keys were rarely used by old comps.

Unequal Voices. A comp. for several voices which do not lie within the same compass is said to be for U. V.

Unfinished Symphony, Schubert's symph. in B min., of which 2 movements only survive, but which he clearly intended to carry on, since he sketched a scherzo and scored the first 9 bars. He wished to dedicate a work to the Graz Mus. Society in 1822, and sent it off to Anselm Hüttenbrenner, director of the Society. Hüttenbrenner kept it until 1865, when he gave it to the cond. Johann Herbeck, who gave the 1st perf. of the 1st 2 movements in Vienna, 17. XII. 1865. These movements, all that Herbeck had received, were pub. in the following year. It is possible that Schubert never finished the work, but it is also possible that Hüttenbrenner lost or mislaid the rest of the scherzo and the whole of the finale. It has been suggested that the B min. entr'acte from *Rosamunde* (1823) was orig. the finale of the symph., but this cannot be proved. As it stands, the symph. has the disadvantage of beginning in one key and ending in another.

Other U. S.s are Schubert's in E min. and maj. (1821), Bruckner's No. 9, Borodin's No. 3 and Mahler's No. 10.

Unger, Caroline (b. Vienna, 28. X. 1803; d. nr. Florence, 23. III. 1877), Aus. contralto. Pupil of Aloysia Lange, Mozart's sister-in-law, and Vogl in Vienna, where she made her 1st stage appearance in 1821. She sang the contralto part, with Sontag as soprano, in the 1st perf. of Beethoven's *Missa solemnis* in 1824. Later she sang in It. and Paris. In 1840 she married François Sabatier and retired in 1843.

Unger, Georg (b. Leipzig, 6. III. 1837; d. Leipzig, 2. II. 1887), Ger. tenor. Studied theol. at first, but took to singing and made his 1st stage appearance at Leipzig in 1867. He was Wagner's 1st Siegfried in the prod. of the *Ring* at Bayreuth in 1876.

Unger, (Gustav) Hermann (b. Kamenz, Saxony, 26. X. 1886; d. Cologne, 31. XII. 1958), Ger. comp. Studied in Munich and later with Reger at Meiningen. Taught for more than 30 years in Cologne.

Works incl. opera *Richmondis* and *Der Zauberhandschuh*; incid. mus. for Shakespeare's *Tempest*, Kleist's *Penthesilea*, Hofmannsthal's *Der Tod und der Tor*, Hauptmann's *Hannele*, Unruh's *Heinrich aus Andernach* and many other plays; *Der Gott und die Bajadere* (Goethe) and *Old Ger. Songs* for chorus and orch.; 2 symphs., symph. suite, suites *Night* and *Rustic Scenes*, *Pictures from the Orient* for orch.; divertimento for string 4tet, string trio, trio for clar., vla. and pf.; variations for 2 pfs.; pf. pieces; songs, part-songs, etc.

Unger, Max (b. Taura, Saxony, 28. V. 1883; d. Zürich, 1. XII. 1959), Ger. cond., painter and musicologist. Studied at Chemnitz and at the Leipzig Cons., also attending Riemann's lectures at the Univ. After a visit to London to collect material for a work on Clementi, he ed. the *Neue Zeitschrift für Musik* in 1919–20 and in 1932 visited Zürich to study Hans Bodmer's Beethoven collection, of which he pub. a catalogue. He also wrote var. works on Beethoven research and one on Mendelssohn's relations with Eng.

Ungherese (It.) = Hungarian. 'All' u.' = in the Hung. manner.

Union Pipes, Ir. bagpipes, also known wrongly as Uilleann P.s, a corrupt. of their name supposed to be Celtic, but actually meaningless.

Unison, 2 notes sounding together at the same pitch, or successions of notes so perf.

Unprepared Shake. *See* **Ornaments.**

Unruh, Fritz von (b. 1885), Ger. dramatist. *See* **Unger (H.)** (*Heinrich aus Andernach*).

Unterbrochene Opferfest, Das (*The Interrupted Sacrificial Feast*), opera by Winter (lib. by Franz Xaver Huber), prod. Vienna, Kärntnertortheater, 14. VI. 1796.

Up Bow, the motion of the bow in the playing of string instruments in the direction from the point to the heel.

Upbeat, an unstressed note or group of notes beginning a comp. and standing before the 1st bar-line, which indicates the 1st main accent. The word derives from the act of beating time in cond., where opening notes before the bar-line are indicated by an upward motion.

Upper Partials. *See* **Partials.**

Upright Piano, the ord. domestic pf. with its strings placed vertically, not horizontally as in the grand pf.

Urbani, Pietro (b. Milan, 1749; d. Dublin, XII. 1816), It. singer, mus. pub. and comp. After a period in London he went to Glasgow in 1780 and to Edinburgh in 1784, singing Scot. songs and later pub. them with his own accomps., with words by Burns, with whom he made friends, and others. Towards the end of the cent. he became a mus.-seller and pub., but *c.* 1810 he failed and went to Dublin, where he d. in poverty.

Works incl. operas *Il Farnace*, *Il trionfo di Clelia* and others; Scot. songs with accomps., etc.

Urbani, Valentino. *See* **Valentini.**

Urhan, Chrétien (b. Montjoie nr. Aix-la-Chapelle, 16. II. 1790; d. Belleville nr. Paris, 2. XI. 1845), Belg. violinist, violist and comp. Learnt the vln. from his father, was heard by the Empress Joséphine and sent by her to Paris with a recommendation to Lesueur. He joined the Opéra orch. in 1814, becoming leader in 1823 and solo vln. in 1836. He played much in public, incl. the vla. and vla. d'amore, also in chamber mus.

Works incl. 2 string 5tets, 2 5tets for 3 vlas., cello and double bass (with drums *ad lib.*) and other chamber mus.; vln. and pf. pieces; pf. works, incl. duets; songs and duets, etc.

Uribe Holguín, Guillermo (b. Bogotá, 17. III. 1880), Colombian comp. Studied at home and with d'Indy at the Schola Cantorum in Paris. In 1910 he became director of the Nat. Cons. at Bogotá, where he founded and cond. symph. concerts.

Works incl. Requiem; 7 symphs., *Sinfonía del terruño*, *3 Danzas*, *Carnavalesca*, *Marche funèbre*, *Marche de fête*, *Suite típica* for orch.; concerto and *Villanesca* for pf. and orch., 2 vln. concertos; 3 string 4tets, pf. 4tet, 2 pf. 5tets; 5 vln. and pf. sonatas, 2 cello and pf. sonatas; pf. pieces, incl. 300 folk dances; songs; etc.

Urio, Francesco Antonio (b. Milan, *c.* 1660; d. Milan, ?), It. priest and comp. A Franciscan monk, he was *maestro di cappella* at SS. Apostoli in Rome in 1690, seven years later at the Frari church in Venice, and finally from 1715 at S. Francesco in Milan.

Works incl. Te Deum (once attrib. to Handel, who borrowed from it for his *Dettingen Te Deum, Saul, Israel in Egypt* and *L'Allegro*); oratorios; motets and psalms for voices and instruments, etc.

Urlar, the name of the themes on which the bagpipe variations of the Pibroch are founded.

Urlus, Jacques (b. Hergenrath, 6. I. 1867; d. Noordwijk-aan-Zee, 6. VI. 1935), Dutch tenor. Studied at the Amsterdam Cons. and made his 1st appearance at Utrecht in 1887. He then studied opera and made his stage début there in 1894. Becoming a Wagnerian singer, he was soon invited to Bayreuth, and in 1910 he 1st visited London. He pub. his autobiog. in 1930.

Uruguayan Composers. *See* Broqua, Pedrell (C.).

Usandizaga, José María. (b. San Sebastián, 31. III. 1887; d. Yanthi, 5. X. 1915), Basque comp. Studied at the Schola Cantorum in Paris.

Works incl. operas *Mendy-Mendiyan, Las Golondrinas* and *La Llama*; works for chorus and orch.; string 4tet, etc.

Usiglio, Emilio (b. Parma, 8. I. 1841; d. Milan, 7. VII. 1910), It. cond. and comp. Pupil of Mabellini.

Works incl. operas *Le educande di Sorrento, Le donne curiose* (after Goldoni) and 6 others; many ballets; chamber mus., etc.

Usper, Francesco (real name Spongia, Sponga or Sponza) (b. Parenzo, ?; d. Venice, 1641), It. priest, organist and comp. In the 1610s he became organist at the church of San Salvatore at Venice, in 1621 he deputized for Grillo as organist at St. Mark's and in the 1620s he became principal of the school of St. John the Evangelist.

Works incl. Masses, motets, psalms, etc.

for voices with instruments, vesper psalms for 4–8 voices and bass, some for double choir; *La battaglia* for voices and instruments, madrigals; *ricercari* and *arie francesi* in 4 parts, etc.

Ut, the old name for the note C, still used in Fr., but elsewhere replaced by Do. For its origin *see* Solmization.

Utenthal, Alexander (b. ? *c.* 1535; d. Innsbruck, 8. V. 1581), Flem. comp. Learnt mus. as a choir-boy in the Archduke Ferdinand's chapel in Prague, and in 1568 became a singer in his chapel at Innsbruck. In 1573 he received the title of court comp. and soon afterwards became 2nd *Kapellmeister*. On the death of Scandello at Dresden in 1580 he was offered the post of *Kapellmeister* to the Saxon court, but declined it.

Works incl. Masses, motets, *Sacrae cantiones*; secular Fr. and Ger. songs for voices and instruments, etc.

Uthal, opera by Méhul (lib. by Jacques Maximilien Benjamin Bins de Saint-Victor, based on Ossian), prod. Paris, Opéra-Comique, 17. V. 1806. The work is scored without violins.

Utility Music. *See* Gebrauchsmusik.

Utopia (Limited), or The Flowers of Progress, operetta by Sullivan (lib. by W. S. Gilbert), prod. London, Savoy Theatre, 7. X. 1893.

Utrecht Te Deum and Jubilate, a T. D. and J. by Handel, comp. for the celebration of the Peace of Utrecht and perf. London, St. Paul's Cathedral, 7. VII. 1713.

Uttendal, Alexander. *See* Utenthal.

Uttini, Francesco Antoni Baldassare (b. Bologna, 1723; d. Stockholm, 25. X. 1795), It. singer and comp. Pupil of Perti and Padre Martini in Bologna, he was elected a member of the Phil. Acad. there in 1743 and became president in 1751. As cond. of the Mingotti opera troupe he travelled to (?) Madrid and Copenhagen (1754–4), and in 1755 settled in Stockholm, becoming mus. director to the court in 1767. He visited London the following year.

Works incl. 13 It. and 5 Fr. operas; Swed. operas *Thetis och Pelée* and *Aline*; incid. mus. to Racine's *Athalie* and *Iphigénie*, etc.; Passion oratorio (Metastasio); symphs.; trio sonatas; harpsichord sonatas, etc.

Valen

V

V.S. (abbr.) = *volti subito* (It. = turn at
once). This is often written at the foot of a
right-hand page in MS. mus. as an indication that a quick turn is necessary in order
to be ready for what follows on the next
page.

Vaccai, Nicola (b. Tolentino, 15. III.
1790; d. Pesaro, 5. VIII. 1848), It. comp.
He went to school at Pesaro, then studied
law in Rome, but at the age of 17 or 18
gave it up for mus. and studied counterpoint with Jannaconi. In 1811 he went to
Paisiello at Naples for dramatic comp. and
in 1815 prod. his 1st opera there. He then
lived at Venice for 7 years, prod. 2 operas
there, afterwards taught singing at Trieste
and Vienna, in 1824 prod. 2 operas at
Parma and Turin and in 1825 had his
greatest success, at Milan, with a work on
Shakespeare's *Romeo and Juliet*. In 1829–
31 he lived in Paris and afterwards briefly
in London, which he visited again in 1833–
1834. In 1838 he succeeded Basili as director
of the Milan Cons., retiring to Pesaro in
1844.
Works incl. operas *I solitari di Scozia,
Pietro il grande, La pastorella feudataria,
Giulietta e Romeo Marco Visconti, Giovanna Grey, Virginia, Giovanna d'Arco, La
sposa di Messina* (both after Schiller) and
others; church mus.; cantata on the death
of Malibran and others; *Ariette per camera*
for voice and pf., etc.

Vaccari, Francesco (b. Modena, 1773; d.
Lisbon, after 1823), It. violinist. Pupil of
Nardini at Florence. He soon began to play
with great success all over It., then went to
Spain, and later appeared in Paris, Ger.,
London, Spain and Port. Wrote vln. mus.,
incl. variations on 'God save the King'.

Vachon, Pierre (b. Arles, VI. 1731; d.
Berlin, 7. X. 1803), Fr. violinist and comp.
Studied in Paris, where he appeared at the
Concert spirituel from 1756. Principal
violinist in the orch. of the Prince of Conti
1761, he visited Eng. in 1772 and c. 1775,
and later settled in Berlin, where he was
app. *Konzertmeister* to the court in 1786.
Works incl. operas *Les Femmes et le
secret, Sara, ou La Fermière écossaise,
Hippomène et Atalante, Ésope à Cythère,
Renaud d'Ast* (both with J. C. Trial); vln.
concertos.; chamber mus.; sonatas for vln.
and bass, etc.

Vacqueras, Beltrame (also known as
Bertrandus or Bernardus de Crassia) (b. ?;
d. ?), Span. 15th–16th-cent. singer and
comp. He was in the Papal Chapel in Rome
in 1483–1507. Comp. Masses, motets,
psalms, *chansons*, etc.

Vactor, David van (b. Plymouth,
Indiana, 8. V. 1906), Amer. flautist and
comp. Studied at the North Western Univ.
School of Mus., later fl. with Moyse and
comp. with Dukas in Paris. On his return
to Amer. he joined the teaching staff of his
univ.
Works incl. ballet *The Play of Words*; 2
symphs., symph, prelude to Poe's *Masque
of the Red Death*, overture *Cristobal Colón*,
Overture to a Comedy, 5 small pieces,
passacaglia and fugue for orch.; chaconne
for string orch.; *Concerto grosso* for 3 fls.
and harp, fl. concerto, vln. concerto; 5tet
for fl. and strings, suite for 2 fls., *Nachtlied*
for soprano and string 4tet, etc.

Vaet, Jacobus (b. Courtrai or Harelbeke,
1529; d. Vienna, 8. I. 1567), Flem. comp.
He was choirmaster to Maximilian, King
of Boh., in the 1560s and in 1564 became
chief mus. director in Vienna, a post
formerly held by Jachet Buus, when his
patron became the Emperor Maximilian II.
Works incl. Masses, motets, Magnificats, Te Deum for 8 voices and other
church mus.; *chansons*, etc.

Vagans (Lat. = wandering, vagrant), the
name given in 15th- and 16th-cent. polyphonic mus. to a part which is mainly
designed to complete the harmony. It
frequently goes above and below the part
nearest to it.

Vagierender Akkord. *See* **Vagrant Chord.**

Vagrant Chord, a term coined in Ger.
(as above) by Schönberg to describe chromatic chords which confuse or lead away
from any definite key-centre.

Vaisseau-fantôme, Le (*The Phantom
Vessel*), opera by Dietsch (lib. by Bénédict
Henri Révoil and Paul Henri Foucher,
founded on Wagner's scenario for *The
Flying Dutchman*, intended for an opera
of his own to be prod. at the Opéra, which
however accepted the lib. only and had it
set by Dietsch), prod. Paris, Opéra, 9. XI.
1842.

Vakula the Smith (*Vakula Kuznets*), opera
by Tchaikovsky (lib. by Yakov Petrovich
Polonsky, based on Gogol's *Christmas
Eve*), prod. St. Petersburg, 6. XII. 1876;
revised version entitled *Tcherevitchki* (*The
Little Shoes*), prod. Moscow, 31. I. 1887. It
is also known as *Oxana's Caprices*.

Valdengo, Giuseppe (b. Turin, 24. V.
1914), It. baritone. Studied in Turin,
making his début in Parma in 1936. He is
best known for his recorded perfs. of
Verdi's Iago and Falstaff under Toscanini.

Valen, Fartein Olav (b. Stavanger, 25.
VIII. 1887; d. Valevåg, 14. XII. 1952),
Norw. comp. Studied languages at Oslo
Univ., but later entered the Cons., finishing
his studies with Reger at the Hochschule
für Musik in Berlin. In 1925–35 he was in
the mus. dept. of the library of Oslo Univ.,
but was then made the recipient of a government grant for comp.
Works incl. 3 sets of Motets and other

choral works; 5 symphs., *Sonetto di Michelangelo*, *To Hope* (after Keats), *Pastorale*, *Epithalamion*, *Le Cimetière marin* (after Paul Valéry), *La isla en las calmas*, *Ode to Solitude* for orch.; pf. concerto; vln. concerto; 6 works for soprano and orch.; 2 string 4tets, pf. trio, serenade for 5 wind instruments; vln. and pf. sonata; 2 sonatas, variations and other works for pf.; org. mus.; songs, etc.

Valente, Antonio (b. ?, d. ?), It. 16th-cent. comp., active in Naples. Blind from his youth he was organist of S. Angelo a Nilo from 1565 to 1580. He pub. 2 collections of keyboard mus., in 1576 and 1580.

Valentini (Valentino Urbani) (b. ?; d. ?), It. 17th–18th-cent. castrato (contralto). 1st went to London in 1707.

Valentini, Giovanni (b. Venice, *c.* 1583; d. ? Vienna, IV. 1649), It. organist and comp. In 1614 he was organist to the Archduke Ferdinand at Graz, and on his patron's succession to the title of Emperor Ferdinand II in 1619 remained in his service, becoming *Kapellmeister* in 1629 and continuing in this employment under Ferdinand III.

Works incl. Masses, motets and other church mus.; madrigals, *Musiche a 2 voci*, etc.

Valentini, Giuseppe (b. ? Rome, 1681; d. Florence, *c.* 1746), It. comp. In the service of the Grand Duke of Tuscany at Florence from *c.* 1735.

Works incl. opera *La costanza in amore*; oratorios *Absalone* and *S. Alessio*; Concerti grossi; symphs., *Bizarrie*, 12 fantasies, *Idee per camera* and 12 sonatas for 3 string instruments and bass; chamber sonatas and *Alletamenti* for vln., cello and bass, etc.

Valentini, Pietro Francesco (b. Rome, *c.* 1570; d. Rome, 1654), It. comp. Pupil of G. M. Nanini in Rome.

Works incl. operas (*favole*) *La mitra* and *La trasformazione di Dafne*; motets, litanies and other church mus.; *Canzonetti spirituali* and *Musiche spirituali* for the Nativity; madrigals and canons; *canzoni* and arias for 1–2 voices, etc.

Valenzuela, Pedro (b. ?; d. ?), Span. 16th-cent. comp. He lived in It., was cantor at St. Mark's, Venice, and cond. to the Phil. Acad. at Verona.

Works incl. madrigals, etc.

Valera y Alcalá Galiano, Juan (1824–1905), Span. novelist. *See* **Pepita Jiménez** (Albéniz).

Valeriano (surname Pellegrini) (b. ?; d. ?), It. countertenor. He was in Eng. 1712–1713 and sang in the first perfs. of Handel's *Il pastor fido* and *Teseo*.

Valéry, Paul (1871–1945), Fr. poet. *See* **Bernard (R).** (*Prélude au cimetière marin*), **Fourestier** (*Orchestique*), **Honegger** (*Amphion* and *Sémiramis*), **Valen** (*Cimetière marin*).

Valesi (real name Wallishauser), **Johann Evangelist** (b. Unterhattenhofen), Bavaria, 28. IV. 1735; d. Munich, 1811), Ger. singer. Chamber singer to the Elector of Bavar. from 1756, later studied in It. and sang there with success. Weber was his pupil for a short time in 1798.

Valkyrie, The (*Die Walküre*, Wagner). *See* **Ring des Nibelungen.**

Vallas, Léon (b. Roanne, Loire, 17. V. 1879; d. Lyons, 9. V. 1956), Fr. musicologist. Studied medicine and literature at Lyons Univ. and in 1903 founded a mus. paper there which in 1912 became the *Revue française de musique*, and in 1920 started the *Nouvelle Revue musicale*. He lectured on mus. hist. at Lyons Univ. in 1908–11, at the Cons. there in 1912–31 and at the Sorbonne in Paris in 1929–30. In 1939 he became mus. director of the radio station at Lyons and president of the Société Française de Musicologie. His books incl. studies of the hist. of mus. at Lyons, of d'Indy, and 2 works on Debussy.

Valledor, Jacinto (b. Cadiz, *c.* 1744; d. Madrid, 1809), Span. comp. Settled in Madrid and wrote *tonadillas* and other works for the stage, incl. *La decantada vida y muerte del General Mambrú*, etc.

Vallotti, Francesco Antonio (b. Vercelli, 11. VI. 1697; d. Padua, 10. I. 1780), It. organist, teacher and comp. He became 3rd organist at the church of Sant' Antonio at Padua in 1722 and in 1730. He wrote a learned treatise, *Della scienza teoretica e pratica della moderna musica*.

Works incl. motets, Requiem for Tartini and other church mus., etc.

Valls, Josep (b. Barcelona, 1904), Span. comp. Educ. at the Orfeo Català. In 1920 he decided to make mus. his career, studied under Joan Salvat, then at the Barcelona Cons. and finally with d'Indy at the Schola Cantorum in Paris.

Works incl. symph. *The Song of Deborah*; concerto for string 4tet and orch., variations for pf. and orch.; string trio; *La inutil ofrena* for voice, fl. and cello; sonatina for pf.; songs, etc.

Valse. *See* **Waltz.**

Valse à deux temps (Fr. = waltz in two-time). The term is not strictly accurate, since a waltz must always be in triple time; but it describes a type of waltz in which each note of the melody takes the time of 2 beats, each 3 notes thus occupying 2 bars and falling alternately on beats 1, 3 and 2 in cross-rhythm. Familiar exs. occur in the waltz in Gounod's *Faust*, many of Tchaikovsky's waltzes (*Eugene Onegin*, the ballets, and *Christmas* in *The Seasons* for pf.), Liadov's *Musical Box*, etc. This rhythm is a special feature of the Boh. dance known as the Furiant, such as that in Smetana's *Bartered Bride* (Act II) and

Dvořák's *Slavonic Dance* in G min., Op.
No. 8.

Valse Boston. *See* **Boston.**

Valse, La, choreographic poem for orch.
by Ravel, finished 1920 and 1st perf. Paris,
12. XII. 1920. It imitates or parodies the
style of J. Strauss's waltzes and has several
times served for ballets, as its description
shows that it was intended to do.

Valses nobles et sentimentales, a set of
waltzes by Ravel, comp. in 1911 and afterwards scored for orch. The title is derived
from Schubert, who pub. 2 sets: *Valses
nobles,* Op. 77, and *Valses sentimentales,*
Op. 50. Ravel's work was turned into a
ballet, *Adélaïde, ou Le Langage des fleurs,*
prod. Paris, 22. IV. 1912.

Valverde, Joaquín (b. Badajoz, 27. II,
1846; d. Madrid, 17. III. 1910), Span. flautist,
cond. and comp. He played the fl. in
theatre orchs., became theatre cond. at
Madrid in 1871 and fl. prof. at the Cons. in
1879.

Works incl. several operettas (with
Chueca), partic. *La gran vía,* etc.

Valves, the keys added to brass wind
instruments, invented early in the 19th cent.
to make it possible for horns, tpts., cornets,
etc. to prod. the complete chromatic scale
instead of only the natural harmonics. V.s
are fitted to all members of the Saxhorn
family and have also been used for the
tromb. as a substitute for the slide.

Vampyr, Der (*The Vampire*), opera by
Lindpaintner (lib. by Cäsar Max Heigel,
based on John William Polidori's story,
pub. in 1819 and thought to be by Byron,
and more directly on a Fr. melodrama by
Charles Nodier, Pierre François Adrien
Carmouche and Achille de Jouffroy), prod.
Stuttgart, 21. IX. 1828.

Opera by Marschner (lib. by Wilhelm
August Wohlbrück, based on the sources
above), prod. Leipzig, 29. III. 1828.

**Van Rooy, Anton (Antonius Maria
Josephus)** (b. Rotterdam, 1. I. 1870; d.
Munich, 28. XI. 1932), Dutch baritone.
Studied with J. Stockhausen in Frankfurt
and in 1897 sang Wotan at Bayreuth. From
1898 to 1908 he sang at the N.Y. Metropolitan, Covent Garden and Bayreuth, and
then became a regular member of the
Frankfurt State Opera. He was best known
as a Wagner singer.

Vanbrugh, John (1664–1726), Eng. drama-
tist and architect of Flem. descent. *See*
Carey (*The Provoked Husband*) **Finger**
(*Pilgrim*), **Leveridge** (*Aesop*), **Purcell (D.)**
(*Pilgrim* and *Relapse*).

Vanessa, opera by Barber (lib. by Gian-
Carlo Menotti), prod. N.Y., Metropolitan
Opera, 15. I. 1958.

Vanhal (or Wanhal), Johann Baptist (b.
Nechanice, 12. V. 1739; d. Vienna, 26. VIII.
1813), Boh. comp. Came to Vienna in 1760
and studied there with Dittersdorf,

travelled in It. 1769–71, and lived on the
estate of Count Erdödy in Hung. 1772–80.
Back in Vienna, he supported himself as a
freelance comp.

Works incl. 2 operas; over 50 Masses and
much other church mus.; *c.* 100 symphs.;
c. 100 string 4tets, etc.

Vaqueras, Bertrandus (or Bernardus) (b.
c. 1450; d. after 1507), Span. (?) comp. He
was a singer in the Papal Chapel, 1483–
1507. Comp. church mus.

Varèse, Edgard (b. Paris, 22. XII. 1885;
d. N.Y., 6. XI 1965), Fr. (Americanized)
comp. Pupil of d'Indy and Roussel at the
Schola Cantorum in Paris and of Widor at
the Cons. He cond. choral and orchestral
mus. in Paris, Berlin and Prague until 1914,
when he joined the Fr. army to take part
in the 1st world war; but he was discharged
for reasons of health in 1915 and settled in
U.S.A. in 1916. He did much to advance
the cultivation of modern mus. in N.Y. and
joined Salzedo in 1921 to found the Internat. Comps. Guild. V. is an important
figure in the field of 20th-cent. experimental
mus., dispensing with thematic development and instead working with different
types of 'noise', either purely instrumental
(*Arcana,* 1927) or combined with tape-
recorded sounds (*Déserts,* 1954), or derived
from perc. (*Ionisation,* 1931). His influence
on modern European and Amer. mus. has
been considerable.

Works incl. symph. with chorus;
Amériques, Arcana and *Espaces* for orch.;
symph. poem *Nuit* with electronic sound;
Hyperprism for wind and perc., *Ionisation*
for perc.; *Intégrales* for chamber orch.;
Metal for soprano and orch.; *Equatorial*
for baritone, brass, org., perc. and theremin, etc.

Varesi, Felice (b. Calais, 1813; d. Milan,
13. III. 1889), It. baritone. Studied at
Milan. He was Verdi's 1st Macbeth in
1847, 1st Rigoletto in 1851 and 1st Ger-
mont, père, in 1853. He 1st visited London
in 1864.

Varga, Tibor (b. Györ, 4. VII. 1921),
Hung. violinist. Studied at Budapest Mus.
Acad. with Hubay and later with Flesch.
From 1939 to 1943 he studied philosophy at
Budapest Univ., and since 1949 he has
been prof. of vln. at the Detmold Mus.
Acad. He is best known for his playing of
modern mus.

Variations, varied treatments of a
theme sometimes with a restatement of the
theme in its 1st form at the end (e.g. Bach's
'Goldberg' V.s), sometimes with a more
elaborate final section, such as a fugue (e.g.
Beethoven's 'Eroica' V.s for pf. or Brahms's
Handel V.s for pf.), or a passacaglia (e.g.
Brahms's Haydn V.s for 2 pfs. or orch.).
There is at least one instance (d'Indy's
Istar) where the theme does not appear in
its primitive form until the end. Historically

the V. principle goes back as far as instrumental mus., but sets of V.s 1st emerge in the course of the 16th cent., esp. in Eng. and Spain. The Eng. virginal comps. wrote sets on popular tunes for their instrument and another favoured medium for V.s was the lute. In 17th-cent. Eng. V.s were called Divisions, because they split up the theme into smaller rhythmic patterns, and they could be based on a Ground, i.e. an unchanging bass.

The later hist. of the form continues to show the 2 different tendencies of (1) varying the tune and (2) maintaining the foundation of the same bass, with greater or lesser incidental changes while the superstructure can be handled very freely and need not keep to the melodic line of the theme at all. Mozart's V.s, for ex., are predominantly melodic, and so are Beethoven's earlier sets, but the latter reverts to the 'ground' type by keeping chiefly to the harmonic framework in such a work as the 'Diabelli' V.s, and in the 32 V.s for pf. he keeps so close to the bass that the work is more like a Passacaglia, which is true also of the finale of Brahms's 4th symph. In Elgar's 'Enigma' V.s for orch., each of which represents a portrait of one of the comp.'s friends, and in R. Strauss's *Don Quixote*, the form is complicated by an element of Programme Mus.

Variations on a Russian Theme, a set of pf. variations on a Rus. folksong by Blumenfeld, Glazunov, Liadov, Rimsky-Korsakov, Sokolov, Wihtol and Winkler.

Variations on a Theme by Goossens, a set of orchestral variations by Amer. comps.: Bloch, Copland, Creston, Fuleihan, Roy Harris, Piston, Bernard Rogers, Sessions, Deems Taylor; with finale by Goossens himself.

Variations on a Theme by Handel (Brahms). *See* 'Handel' Variations.

Variations on a Theme by Haydn (Brahms). *See* 'Haydn' Variations.

Varlamov, Alexander Egorovich (b. Moscow, 27. XI. 1801; d. St. Petersburg, X. 1848), Rus. comp. Learnt mus. as a choir-boy in the court chapel at St. Petersburg, where Bortniansky became interested in his mus. educ. He left in 1819 and went to The Hague as mus. director of the Rus. embassy chapel and became attached to the court of the Princess of Orange, Anna Pavlovna, who was a Rus. Returning home in 1823, he settled at Moscow, where he taught, and he spent his last years alternately there and at St. Petersburg.

Works incl. 223 songs, e.g. *The Red Sarafan*, etc.

Varnay, Astrid (b. Stockholm, 25. IV. 1918), Amer. soprano of Aus.-Hung. parentage. Both her parents were singers. She studied 1st with her mother and then with H. Weigert, whom she married in

1944. She made her début at the N.Y Metropolitan in 1941, where she remained as a leading Wagner and Strauss singer until 1956. Since 1951 she has also appeared at Bayreuth, and has also sung at Covent Garden.

Varney, Louis (b. New Orleans, 30. V. 1844; d. Cauterets, 20. VIII. 1908), Fr. comp. Pupil of his father.

Works incl. operettas *Les Mousquetaires au couvent*, *Les Forains*, *Le Pompier de service*, *Les Demoiselles de Saint-Cyr* and over 30 others, etc.

Varney, Pierre (Joseph Alphonse) (b. Paris, 1. XII. 1811; d. Paris, 7. II. 1879), Fr. cond. and comp., father of prec. Studied at the Paris Cons. and became cond. at var. theatres there, also at different times at The Hague, Ghent, Rouen and Bordeaux. In 1848 he set Dumas's words for the Chant des Girondins, 'Mourir pour la patrie'. He also wrote operas and operettas.

Varsoviana (It.)
   or   } an alleged Pol.
Varsovienne (Fr.) }
dance, but prob. of Fr. orig., appearing 1st in Paris in the middle of the 19th cent. It is in 3–4 time and resembles the Mazurka. The name derives from Warsaw.

Varvoglis, Mario (b. Brussels, 10. XII. 1885), Gk. comp. Studied painting at first, then mus. in Paris with Leroux and Caussade from 1904 and d'Indy from 1913, making his 1st successes there. He returned to Greece in 1922, became prof. at the Athens Cons. and in 1924 at the Hellenic Cons., of which he became director with Evangelatos in 1947.

Works incl. 1-act opera *The Afternoon of Love*; incl. mus. to classical Gk. plays; *Pastoral Suite*, *Meditation* and prelude, chorale and fugue on B. A. C. H. for strings; chamber mus.; pf. works; songs, etc.

Vasquez, Juan (b. Badajoz, ?; d. ?), Span. 16th-cent. comp. Studied at Seville. *See* Vázquez.

Vassilenko, Sergey Nikiforovich (b. Moscow, 30. III. 1872; d. Moscow, 11. III. 1956), Rus. comp. After receiving private lessons from Gretchaninov and Konius, and studying law, he entered the Moscow Cons. in 1895, studying comp. with Taneiev and Ippolitov-Ivanov. In 1905 he taught there and was soon app. full prof. He organized and cond. hist. concerts.

Works incl. operas *The Legend of the Holy City of Kitezh*, *The Son of the Sun*, *Christopher Columbus*, *Suvarov*, etc.; ballets *Joseph the Beautiful*, *The Gypsies* (after Pushkin), etc.; 5 symphs., *Epic Poem*, symph. poem on Oscar Wilde's *The Garden of Death* and others and suite *In the Sun* and others, *Three Bloody Battles* (after Tolstoy) and other orchestral works; vln. concerto; cantata for the 20th anniversary of the Oct. Revolution; 4 string 4tets, woodwind 4tet, pf. trio and other chamber mus.; vla. and pf. sonata; songs, folksong arrs., etc.

Vaterländischer Künstlerverein (Ger. = *Patriotic Artists' Association*), the title of Part II of the variations commissioned by Cappi and Diabelli of Vienna to be written by Beethoven and others on a waltz by Diabelli. Beethoven eventually wrote 33 variations instead of 1, and they were pub. separately as Part I in 1824, Part II following with contribs. by Czerny, Hummel, Kalkbrenner, C. Kreutzer, Liszt (aged 11), Moscheles, W. A. Mozart, jun., the Archduke Rudolph, Schubert, Sechter and *c.* 40 others.

Vatielli, Francesco (b. Pesaro, 1. I. 1877; d. Portogruaro, Udine, 12. XII. 1946), It. musicologist and comp. Studied philosophy at Bologna Univ., but took a private course in mus. as well, later entered the Pesaro cons. and became a pupil of Mascagni. In 1905 he joined the staff of the Liceo Musicale of Bologna. His books incl. hist. studies of mus. at Pesaro and Bologna, 1 of 16th-cent. song-books, etc. He ed. much old It. mus.

Works incl. incid. mus. for Poliziano's *Favola di Orfeo*; pf. pieces; songs, etc.

Vaudeville (Fr.), a term with var. meanings and of uncertain origin. Le Roy, in his *Airs de Cour* of 1571, says that such songs were formerly called 'voix de ville' (town voices); but the form 'vau de Vire' is also known, which may have referred to the valley of Vire in Normandy, the home of Olivier Basselin (*c.* 1400–50), a comp. of such songs. In 18th-cent. Fr. V.s were at first satirical songs, then songs with words set to popular tunes used in comedies with mus. (*comédies mêlées de vaudevilles*), as in the Eng. ballad opera (songs specially comp. being called *ariettes*). In time V.s in Fr. became songs sung at the end of spoken stage pieces, taken up verse by verse by all the characters and sometimes by the chorus, and this device was sometimes intro. into opera, in Fr. and elsewhere, as for ex. at the end of Rousseau's *Devin du village* and Mozart's *Entführung aus dem Serail*. The next step from this was to call a whole light mus. stage entertainment a V.

Vaughan, Henry (1622–95), Anglo-Welsh poet. *See* **Rubbra** (*Revival* and *Morning Watch*).

Vaughan Thomas, David (b. Ystalyfera, 15. III. 1873; d. Johannesburg, 15. IX. 1934), Welsh comp. Studied mus. at Swansea before going to Oxford; then taught mathematics and mus. at var. schools. He settled at Swansea, where he had great influence on mus. life. As an overseas examiner he visited the dominions and died in S. Africa during one of his tours.

Works incl. many cantatas, anthems and part-songs; orch. mus.; 2 string 4tets; vln. and pf. sonata; many songs in Welsh and Eng., etc.

Vaughan Williams, Ralph (b. Down Ampney, Glos., 12. X. 1872; d. London, 26. VIII. 1958), Eng. comp. Son of a clergyman, he was educ. at Charterhouse School, 1887–90, and Trinity Coll., Cambridge, 1892–5, the intervening years being devoted to study at the R.C.M. in London, where he returned for another year after Cambridge. He learnt pf. and org. for the sake of usefulness, but was from the 1st determined to be a comp. But on leaving the R.C.M. in 1896 he became organist at S. Lambeth Church in London and saved enough money to gain further experience by study abroad, 1st at the Akademie der Künste in Berlin, under Bruch, and in 1909 with Ravel, who was younger than himself, in Paris. In 1901 he took the Mus.D. at Cambridge. In 1904 he joined the Folk-Song Society and began to take an active share in the recovery and study of old country tunes, collecting some in Norfolk. His 1st great public success he made with *Towards the Unknown Region* at the Leeds Festival in 1907. In the 1914–18 war he first served as a private in Macedonia and Fr., but later rose to officer's rank, and after the declaration of peace he was app. prof. of comp. at the R.C.M. He was often repres. at the festivals of the I.S.C.M. and in 1935 he had the Order of Merit conferred on him.

Works incl. operas *Hugh the Drover*, *Sir John in Love* (on Shakespeare's *Merry Wives*), *The Poisoned Kiss*, *Riders to the Sea* (Synge) and *The Pilgrim's Progress* (after Bunyan); ballets *Old King Cole* and *On Christmas Night* (after Dickens), masque *Job* (on Blake's illustrations); incid. mus. for Aristophanes' *Wasps*; film mus. incl. *49th Parallel* and *Scott of the Antartic*; 3 motets, Mass in G min., *Te Deum* in G maj., Angl. services, *Festival Te Deum*, hymn tunes; choral works: *Toward the Unknown Region* (Whitman), *Willow Wood* (D. G. Rossetti), *A Sea Symph.* (Whitman), *5 Mystical Songs* (George Herbert), *Fantasia on Christmas Carols, Flos Campi* (Song of Solomon), *Sancta Civitas, Benedicite, Magnificat, Dona nobis pacem, Five Tudor Portraits* (Skelton), *The Sons of Light* (Ursula Wood), *Oxford Elegy* (Matthew Arnold); *Serenade to Music* for 16 solo voices and orch. (from Shakespeare's *Merchant of Venice*); orch. works: *Norfolk Rhapsody, In the Fen Country, Fantasy on a Theme by Tallis* (strings), *A London Symph., A Pastoral Symph.*, symphs. Nos. 4–9, 5 variations on *Dives and Lazarus*, fantasy on *Greensleeves, 2 Hymn-Tune Preludes* (small orch.), *Concerto grosso* (strings), *Sinfonia antartica* (No. 7); *Folksong Suite* for military band; *The Lark*

Ascending (after Meredith) for vln. and pf., *Concerto accademico* for vln. and strings, pf. concerto (later version for 2 pfs.), suite for vla. and orch., concerto for ob. and strings, *Romance* for mouth org. and orch., tuba concerto; 2 string 4tets, fantasy 5tet for strings, *On Wenlock Edge* (Housman) for tenor, string 4tet and pf.; suite for pf., intro. and fugue for 2 pfs.; 3 preludes on Welsh hymn-tunes and prelude and fugue for org.; many songs incl. cycle *The House of Life* (D. G. Rossetti [incl. *Silent Noon*]), *Songs of Travel* (Stevenson), 8 Housman songs; numerous part-songs; folksong arrs., etc.

Vaurabourg, Andrée (b. Toulouse, 8. IX. 1894), Fr. comp. Studied at the Toulouse Cons. and in Paris, with Widor, Nadia Boulanger and others, also pf. with Pugno in 1908–13. She became attached as perf. to the group of 'Les Six' and married Honegger.

Works incl. *Prélude* and *Intérieur* for orch.; vln. and pf. sonata; songs, etc.

Vautor, Thomas (b. ? Leicestershire, *c.* 1590; d. ?), Eng. comp. Educ. at Lincoln Coll., Oxford, where he took the B.Mus. in 1616. He was for many years in the service of Sir George Villiers, father of the later Duke of Buckingham, at Brooksby, and later of his widow at Goadby. Comp. madrigals, pub. 1619.

Vavrinecz, Mauritius (b. Czegléd, 18. VII. 1858; d. Budapest, 5. VIII. 1913), Hung. comp. Studied at the Budapest Cons. and with Volkmann and in 1886 became mus. director of Budapest Cathedral.

Works incl. operas *Ratcliff* (after Heine) and *Rosamunde*; 5 Masses, Requiem, *Stabat Mater*; oratorio *Christus*; overture to Byron's *Bride of Abydos*, Dithyramb for orch., etc.

Vázquez, Juan (b. Badajoz, *c.* 1500; d. ? Seville, *c.* 1560), Span. comp. He was employed at Badajoz Cathedral, 1545–51, and was later in the service of (? Count) Juan Bravo. He was an important exponent of the *villancico* (*q.v.*), and also comp. church mus.

Veale, John (b. Shortlands, Kent, 15. VI. 1922), Eng. comp. Educ. at Repton and Oxford, he was at 1st self-taught in mus., but later studied with Wellesz at Oxford and Roy Harris in U.S.A.

Works incl. 2 symphs., *The Masque of Hope*, film mus., clar. concerto, *Elegy for fl.,harp* and strings, string 4tet, etc.

Vecchi, Lorenzo (b. Bologna before 1564; d. Bologna, 7. III. 1628), It. comp. He was a pupil at San Petronio at Bologna, where he became *maestro di cappella* in 1605. Comp. Masses, Requiem and other church mus.

Vecchi, Orazio (b. Modena, XII. 1550; d. Modena, 19. II. 1605), It. comp. He took holy orders and was made a canon at Correggio in 1586 and archdeacon in 1591; but he deserted to Modena and was deprived of his office in 1595. In 1596 he became *maestro di cappella* of Modena Cathedral and in 1598 at the ducal court. He became famous, being summoned to the court of the Emperor Rudolph II at one time and invited to comp. mus. for the king of Pol. In 1604 his pupil Geminiano Capi-Lupi intrigued successfully against him and supplanted him in his post.

Works incl. madrigal comedy *L'Amfiparnaso*; Masses, motets, lamentations and other church mus.; madrigals, canzonets, etc.

Vecchi, Orfeo (b. Milan, *c.* 1540; d. Milan, *c.* 1603), It. comp. *Maestro di cappella* of the church of Santa Maria della Scala at Milan.

Works incl. Masses, motets, psalms, Magnificats, *Cantiones sacrae* and other church mus.; madrigals, etc.

Vecsey, Franz von (b. Budapest, 23. III. 1893; d. Rome, 6. IV. 1935), Hung. violinist. Studied with Hubay and Joachim, and made a concert tour at the age of 10. He lived mainly in Ger.

Veerbecke di Fiandra (= of Flanders). *See* **Weerbecke**.

Vega (Carpio), Félix Lope de (1562–1635), Span. poet and dramatist. *See* **Casal y Chapí, Khatchaturian** (*Widow of Valencia*), **Krein (A.)** (*Laurencia*), **Laserna, Peyra** (*Selva sin amor*), **Romero** (songs), **Vives** (*Doña Francisquita*), **Wolf-Ferrari** (*Dama boba*).

Veichtner, Franz Adam (b. Regensburg, 10. II. 1741; d. Klievenhof, Courland, 3. III. 1822), Ger. violinist and comp. Pupil of F. Benda for vln. and of Riepel for comp., he was in the service of Count Kaiserling at Königsberg 1763–4, *Konzertmeister* to the Duke of Courland in Mitau 1765–95, then in St. Petersburg as chamber musician to the Rus. court until his retirement in 1820.

Works incl. *Singspiel* and operas *Scipio, Cephalus und Prokris* and *Cyrus und Cassandana*; *c.* 60 symphs.; vln. concerto; 3 string 4tets; 24 fantasias on Rus. songs for vln. and bass; 24 vln. sonatas, etc.

Veilchen, Das (*The Violet*) song by Mozart, K. 476: his only setting of a poem by Goethe, comp. 8. VI. 1785.

Veiled Prophet of Khorassan, The, opera by Stanford (lib. by William Barclay Squire based on Moore's *Lalla Rookh*), prod., in Ger., Hanover, Court Theatre, 6. II. 1881; 1st London perf., in It., Covent Garden Theatre, 26. VII. 1893.

Velasco Maidana, José Maria (b. Sucre, 4. VII. 1901), Boliv. comp. Studied vln. and comp. at Buenos Aires and investigated Bolivian folk mus. after his return home and became cond. of the Nat. Symph. Orch.

Works incl. ballet *Amerindia*; symph. legend *Cory Wara*, overture *Los hijos del sol*, symph. poem *Vida de Cóndores*, *Los Huacos*, *Los Khusillos* and *Cuento brujo* for orch., etc.

Velluti, Giovanni Battista (b. Montolmo [now Panusula] nr. Ancona, 28. I. 1780; d. San Brusone, II. 1861), It. castrato (one of the last). Made his 1st stage appearance at Forlì in 1800. In 1812 he visited Vienna and in 1825 London.

Veloce (It. = quick, swift, rapid, fluent). The direction does not so much indicate increased speed, though it may include that meaning, as smoothness of rapid figuration.

Venatorini, the name sometimes given by the Its. to Mysliveček.

Vendemmia, La (*The Vintage*), opera by Gazzaniga (lib by Giovanni Bertati, partly based on an earlier lib. of the same name by Goldoni), prod. Florence, Teatro della Pergola, 15. V. 1778.

Vendredis, Les, a set of pieces for string 4tet by Artsibushev, Blumenfeld, Borodin, Glazunov, Kopylov, Liadov, M. d'Osten-Sacken, Rimsky-Korsakov, Sokolov and Wihtol, written for Friday chamber-mus. reunions in St. Peterburg.

Venegas de Henestrosa, Luys (b. Hinestrosa, *c.* 1505; d. Toledo, after 1557), Span. 16th-cent lutenist and comp. He pub. a book of variations and transcriptions in a special tablature suitable for keyboard instruments, harps, lutes and guitars.

Venetian Swell, a device in the org. resembling a Venetian blind, the slats of which can be opened and shut gradually and thus, letting through a greater or smaller volume of tone, create an artificial *crescendo* or *diminuendo*.

Venosa, Prince of. *See* Gesualdo.

Ventadorn, Bernart de (b. ?; d. ?, 1195), Fr. troubadour. 45 of his poems and 19 of his melodies have been preserved.

Ventil (Ger.) = Valve.

Vento, Ivo de (b. ?; d. Munich, 1575), (?) Flem. comp. In *c.* the 1560s he was app. *Kapellmeister* to Duke William of Bavaria at Landshut and in 1569 he became organist in the ducal chapel at Munich under Lassus.

Works incl. motets; Ger. sacred and secular songs for several voices, etc.

Vento, Mattia (b. Naples, 1735; d. London, 22. XI. 1776), It. comp. Prod. operas in Rome and Venice, and settled in London in 1763.

Works incl. operas *La finta semplice*, *La Egiziana*, *Leucippo*, *Demofoonte*, *Sofonisba*, *La conquista del vello d'oro*, *Artaserse*, *Il bacio*, *La Vestale*; cantata *Threnodia augustilia* (Goldsmith) on the death of George III's mother; trio sonatas; vln. sonatas; keyboard mus.; songs; etc.

Venturi (del Nibbio), Steffano (b. ? Venice,

?; d. ? Venice, ?), It. 16th-cent. comp. Wrote part of the choruses in Caccini's *Rapimento di Cefalo*, motets, madrigals, etc.

Venturini, Francesco (b. ?; d. Hanover, 18. IV. 1745), (?) Fr. or It. violinist and comp. Pupil of J. B. Farinelli at Hanover, where he joined the electoral chapel in 1698 and succeeded his master as head of the instrumental mus. in 1713, later becoming court *Kapellmeister*. He is said also to have been at the court of Württemberg at Stuttgart.

Works incl. chamber concertos, 4 vln. concertos, overtures for 8 and for 5 instruments, vln. sonatas. etc.

Venus, opera by Schoeck (lib. by Armin Rüeger, on Mérimée's story *La Vénus d'Ille*), prod. Zürich, 10. V. 1922.

Venus and Adonis, masque by Blow (lib. unknown), prod. London, at court, *c.* 1684.

Vénus et Adonis, opera by Desmarets (lib. by Jean Baptiste Rousseau), prod. Paris, Opéra, 17. III. 1697.

Vêpres siciliennes, Les (*The Sicilian Vespers*), opera by Verdi (lib. by Scribe and Charles Duveyrier), prod. Paris, Opéra, 13. VI. 1855. Verdi's 1st Fr. opera, the only other set to Fr. words being *Don Carlos*. Prod. in It., as *Giovanna di Guzman*, Milan, Teatro alla Scala, 4. II. 1856, but later called *I vespri siciliani* there.

Veprik, Alexander Moiseievich (b. Balta, 23. VII. 1899), Rus. comp. Studied with Reger at Leipzig, with Kalafati and Zhitomirsky at St. Petersburg and with Miaskovsky at Moscow. He also had some lessons from Janáček.

Works incl. 5 Episodes for chorus and orch.; *Songs and Dances of the Ghetto*, *A Song of Mourning*, *A Song of Joy* for orch.; *Songs of Death* for vla. and pf.; 2 pf. sonatas, etc.

Vera costanza, La (*True Constancy*), opera by Anfossi (lib. by Francesco Puttini), prod. Rome, Teatro delle Dame, 2. I. 1776.

Opera by Haydn (lib. do., altered by Pietro Travaglia), prod. Esterház, spring 1779.

Vera Sheloga (Rimsky-Korsakov). *See* Pskovitianka.

Veracini, Antonio (b. Florence, 17. I. 1659; d. Florence, 25. X. 1733), It. violinist and comp. Was in the service of the Grand Duchess Vittoria of Tuscany at Florence.

Works incl. 4 oratorios; *Sonate da chiesa* for vln., cello and continuo, *Sonate da camera* for vln. and violone or archlute and continuo, sonatas for 2 vlns. and do., etc.

Veracini, Francesco Maria (b. Florence, 1. II. 1690; d. Florence, 31. X. 1768), It. violinist and comp., nephew of prec. Pupil of his uncle and later of Casini and Gasparini in Rome, poss. also of Corelli, he began touring as a virtuoso in 1711, and visited Eng. in 1714. Returning *via* Ger. to It., he demonstrated his superiority over Tartini (2 years his junior) in a contest in Venice in 1716. The following year he entered the service of the Elector of Saxony in Dresden, where he is said to have attempted suicide in 1722, but left for Prague in 1723, then returned to It. In 1735 he went again to London, where he prod. his first opera, *Adriano in Siria*, followed by several others (1735–44), but as a violinist was overshadowed by Geminiani. He prob. lived in Pisa *c.* 1750–5, then retired to Florence.

Works incl. operas *Adriano in Siria*, *La clemenza di Tito*, *Partenio*, *Rosalinda* (after Shakespeare's *As You Like It*), *L'errore di Salomone*; cantatas *Nice e Tirsi* and *Parla a ritratto dell' amante*; vln. sonatas; canons, arias, etc.

Verbonnet, Jean (b. ?; d. ?), Flem. 15th–16th-cent. comp.

Works incl. Masses, *Salve Regina* and other church mus.; *Dulces exuviae* from Virgil's *Aeneid* for 4 voices; songs for several voices, etc.

Verbunkos, an 18th-cent Hung. recruiting dance for soldiers, who perf. it in full uniform with swords and spurs. Like the later Csárdás, to which it is related, it contained a slow (*lassú*) and quick (*friss*) section.

Vercore. See Werrekoren.

Verdelot, Philippe (b. ?; d.? Florence, before 1552), Flem. singer and comp. He went to It., prob. at an early age, lived at Rome and was a singer at St. Mark's, Venice, and between 1530 and 1540 mus. master at the church of San Giovanni at Florence.

Works incl. Masses, motets; *c.* 100 madrigals, etc.

Verdi, Giuseppe (Fortunino Francesco) (b. Le Roncole nr. Busseto, 10. X. 1813; d. Milan, 27. I. 1901), It. comp. Son of a poor innkeeper and grocer. He heard his 1st mus. from strolling musicians in the village and at the local church, where he became a choir-boy at the age of 7 and was taught by the organist in whose place he was app. in 1823. At 11 he was sent to Busseto and went to school there, walking home twice a week to carry on the organist's duties. Barezzi, a friend of V.'s father at Busseto, took him into his house in 1826, and he learnt much from the cathedral organist Provesi. He had an overture perf. and comp. for military band in 1828, and the next year he wrote a symph. and deputized for Provesi. In 1831 he was sent to Milan with a scholarship and some financial help from Barezzi, but rejected by the Cons. as over entrance age. He studied with Lavigna, the *maestro al cembalo* at the Scala Theatre. When Provesi d. in 1833 he tried for the post of cathedral organist, and when it was

given to an inferior musician the Phil. Sociiety made him an allowance. In 1836 he married Barezzi's daughter, Margherita, by whom he had 2 children, but both mother and children d. between 1838 and 1840. Meanwhile he had comp. his 1st opera, *Oberto*, prod. at the Scala, 17. XI. 1839.

A 2nd (comic) opera, *Un giorno di regno*, was a failure, having been comp. at the time of his bereavement; but *Nabucco*, prod. there in 1842, had a great success. In the cast was Giuseppina Strepponi, who lived with V. from 1848 and in 1859 became his 2nd wife. He now went from strength to strength as an operatic comp. and his fame spread beyond Milan: *Ernani* was prod. at Venice in 1844, *I due Foscari* in Rome, 1844, *Alzira* at Naples, 1845 and *Macbeth* at Florence, 1847. Meanwhile *Ernani* had gone to Paris in 1846 and London commissioned *I masnadieri*, prod. there on 22. VII. 1847. Operas growing in mastery followed almost annually until 1871 and in his old age, after a long interval, he prod. his 2 great Shakespearian master-pieces. Apart from these prods. and frequent travels to var. Eur. countries V.'s life was uneventful, spent mostly at his estate of Sant' Agata nr. Busseto, which he bought in 1848.

An opera on Shakespeare's *King Lear*, at which he worked intermittently, was never completed; otherwise all his plans materialized once they had taken definite shape. Fr., Rus. and Egypt offered him special commissions and his fame spread all over the world. He repres. It. at the Internat. Exhibition in London in 1862 and wrote a *Hymn of the Nations*. In 1868 he suggested a Requiem for Rossini, to be written by var. It. comps., but the plan came to nothing. He used his contrib. in 1873 for a Requiem of his own commemorating the death of Manzoni. *Otello* was prod. at the Scala, Milan, 5. II. 1887, and *Falstaff* at the same theatre, 9. II. 1893, when he was in his 80th year. Giuseppina d. in 1897 and he was himself growing very weak, but still wrote some sacred pieces for chorus and orch. in 1898–9.

Works incl. operas *Oberto* : *Conte di San Bonifacio*, *Un giorno di regno*, *Nabucodonosor* (*Nabucco*), *I Lombardi alla prima crociata*, *Ernani*, *I due Foscari*, *Giovanna d'Arco*, *Alzira*, *Attila*, *Macbeth*, *I masnadieri*, *Jérusalem* (Fr. revised version of *I Lombardi*), *Il corsaro*, *La battaglia di Legnano*, *Luisa Miller*, *Stiffelio*, *Rigoletto*, *Il trovatore*, *La traviata*, *Les Vêpres siciliennes*, *Simon Boccanegra*, *Aroldo* (revision of *Stiffelio*), *Un ballo in maschera*, *La forza del destino*, *Don Carlos*, *Aida*, *Otello*, *Falstaff*; choral works *Inno delle nazioni*, Requiem, *Pater noster*, *Ave Maria*, *Stabat Mater*, *Lauda alla Vergine Maria*, *Te Deum*; *Ave Maria* for soprano and strings; 16 songs; 1 part-song; string 4tet, etc.

Verdi, Giuseppina. *See* **Strepponi.**

Verdonck, Cornelis (b. Turnhout, 1563; d. Antwerp, 4. VII. 1625), Flem. singer and comp. In the service of Corneille Pruenen, treasurer and later sheriff of Antwerp until 1598, when on the death of his patron he served 2 of his nephews. He (or ? a relative) was singer at the Span. court in Madrid for a time.
Works incl. Magnificat, *Ave Maria* and other church mus.; madrigals for 4–9 voices, *Poésies françoises* for 5–10 voices, etc.

Verecoren, *See* **Werrekoren.**

Veress, Sándor (b. Kolozsvár, Transylvania, 1. II. 1907), Hung. pianist and comp. Learnt the pf. from his mother and later entered the Budapest Cons. He also studied with Bartók and Kodály. In 1929 he studied at the Ethnological Museum and began collecting folksongs. He settled at Budapest as teacher of pf. and comp. and asst. to Bartók at the Scientific Acad. of Folk Mus.
Works incl. ballet *The Magic Flute*; 2 symphs. and divertimento for orch.; vln. concerto; cantata and folksong arrs. for unaccomp. chorus; 2 string 4tets, string trio, trio for ob., clar. and bassoon; vln. and pf. sonata, cello and pf. sonata; 2 pf. sonatas, etc.

Veretti, Antonio (b. Verona, 20. II. 1900), It. comp. Studied at Bologna and took a diploma, also a newspaper prize in 1927 for the opera *Il medico volante* (after Molière). In 1943 he became director of the Cons. della G.I.L. in Rome and in 1950 of the Pesaro Cons.
Works incl. opera *Il favorito del re*; ballets *Il galante tiratore* and *Una favola di Andersen*; film mus.; oratorio *Il figliol prodigo*, *Sinfonia sacra* for men's chorus and orch.; *Sinfonia italiana, Sinfonia epica* and *Ouverture della Campanella* for orch., etc.

Verga, Giovanni (1840–1922), It. novelist and playwright. *See* **Cavalleria rusticana** (Mascagni).

Verhaeren, Émile (1855–1916), Belg. poet and dramatist. *See* **Dobroven** (*Philip II*), **Goossens** (do.), **Nejedlý** (V.) (*L'Aube*), Séverac (*Hélène de Sparte*).

Verheyen, Pierre (b. Ghent, *c.* 1750; d. Ghent, 11. I. 1819), Belg. tenor and comp. Pupil of the organist of St. Baron in Ghent, he abandoned his univ. career to become a singer in the choir there, and in 1779 was app. principal tenor at Bruges Cathedral, but soon after joined a travelling opera company. Later he returned to Ghent, where he became comp. to the archbishop and (from 1790) mus. director at the church of St. Pharaïlde.
Works incl. opera *Arlequin magicien, Les*

Chevaliers, ou Le Prix de l'arc and *De Jachtpartij van Hendrik IV*; Masses, psalms, Requiem for Haydn, Te Deum and other church mus.; cantata *La Bataille de Waterloo*, etc.

Verhulst, Johannes (Josephus Herman) (b. The Hague, 19. III. 1816; d. The Hague, 17. I. 1891), Dutch comp. and cond. Studied at The Hague Royal School of Mus. and after some work as violinist at the Opera at Cologne went to Leipzig in 1838 and became cond. of the Euterpe concerts at Mendelssohn's invitation. In 1842 he returned to The Hague as court mus. director and also cond. important mus. societies at Amsterdam and Rotterdam.
Works incl. Requiem for male voices and other church mus.; symphs., overtures, intermezzo *Greetings from Afar* for orch.; string 4tets; songs; part-songs, etc.

Verismo (It. = realism), a term used to classify It. opera of a supposedly 'realistic' order, incl. the works of Puccini, Mascagni, Leoncavallo, Giordani, Zandonai, etc.

Verklärte Nacht (*Transfigured Night*), string 6tet by Schönberg, Op. 4, comp. IX. 1899, arr. for string orch. *c.* 1917, revised 1943. It was inspired by a poem in Richard Dehmel's *Weib und die Welt*.

Verlaine, Paul (1844–96), Fr. poet. *See* **Fauré** (*Bonne Chanson*), **Charpentier** (*Impressions fausses*), **Debussy** (*Ariettes oubliées* and *Fêtes galantes*), **Dieren** (van) (songs), **Durey** (songs), **Fauré** (songs), **Hartmann** (T. de) (*Paysages tristes*), **Lazzari** (*Effet de nuit*), **Mengelberg** (R.) (songs), **Ollone** (*Les Uns et les autres*), **Pitt** (*Fêtes galantes*), **Poldowski** (songs), **Séverac** (songs), **Sorabji** (songs).
18 songs by Debussy, 17 by Fauré.

Vermeulen, Matthijs (b. Helmond, 8. II. 1888), Dutch comp. and critic. Studied with Diepenbrock and from 1908 to 1921 was a mus. critic, when he settled in Paris, where he remained until 1946, after which he returned to Amsterdam.
Works incl. 7 symphs.; chamber mus.; songs, etc.

Vermont, Pierre (b. ?; d. Paris, 1532), Flem. 16th-cent. singer and comp. He sang in the Papal Chapel in Rome from 1528 to 1530, then in the royal chapel in Paris. Comp. motets, *chansons* for several voices, etc. His brother (?) Pernot V. (d. *c.* 1558) comp. a few *chansons*.

Verne, Adela (b. Southampton, 27. II. 1877; d. London, 5. II. 1952), Eng. pianist of Ger. descent. Pupil of her sister Mathilde and Marie Schumann, also taught intermittently by Paderewski. She appeared with great distinction until compelled to withdraw by ill-health, and was a brilliant teacher. *See also* **Wurm.**

Verne, Jules (1828–1905), Fr. novelist. *See* **Hignard** (3 operas, libs. written by

Carré), **Offenbach** (*Docteur Ox* and *Voyage dans la lune*).

Verne, Mathilde (b. Southampton, 25. V. 1865; d. London, 4. VI. 1936), Eng. pianist, sister of Adela Verne. Pupil of Clara Schumann at Frankfurt. She taught and played much in London, organized midday chamber concerts, and in 1909 opened a school for pf. playing.

Vernizzi, Ottavio (b. Bologna, *c.* 1580; d. Bologna, IX. 1649), It. organist and comp. Organist at San Petronio at Bologna from *c.* 1603 to his death.

Works incl. *Intermezzi della coronazione di Apollo per Dafne* and 4 other intermezzi for plays by Silvestro Branchi; motets, *Concerti spirituali*, etc.

Vernon, Joseph (b. Coventry, *c.* 1738; d. London, 19. III. 1782), Eng. actor, tenor and comp. He was a choir-boy at St. Paul's Cathedral in London and 1st appeared on the stage as a boy soprano in 1751, and as a tenor in 1754. Later he became famous chiefly as a singing actor in Shakespeare, Sheridan's *Duenna* and *School for Scandal*, where Linley's song was comp. for him, etc.

Works incl. pantomime *The Witches*; songs for Shakespeare's *Two Gentlemen of Verona* and *Twelfth Night* and for Garrick's *The Irish Widow* and *Linco's Travels*; ballads, etc.

Véronique, operetta by Messager (lib. by Albert Vanloo and Georges Duval), prod. Paris, Bouffes-Parisiens, 10. XII. 1898.

Vers mesurés (Fr. = measured verses), the words of *Musique mesurée*.

Verschiebung (Ger. lit. shift) = Damping pedal: the left (called 'soft') pedal of the pf.

Verschworenen, Die, oder Der häusliche Krieg (*The Conspirators, or Domestic Warfare*), operetta by Schubert (lib. by Ignaz Franz Castelli, based on Aristophanes' *Lysistrata*), never perf. in S.'s lifetime; prod. Frankfurt, 29. VIII. 1861. An Eng. version of the lib., *War in the Household*, by Marian Miller, was set by Henry Hiles (1826–1904) and pub. in 1884.

Verse Anthem. *See* **Anthem.**

Verset (Fr.)　⎱
Versetto (It.)　⎰ a short org. piece, often but not necessarily fugal and frequently containing some reference to a given plainsong tune. The name is derived from the former practice in the Rom. Catholic service of replacing every other sung verse of psalms, etc. by interludes on the org., to relieve the supposed monotony of plainsong.

Versunkene Glocke, Die (*The Submerged Bell*), opera by Respighi (lib., in It. [*La campana sommersa*], by Claudio Guastalla, based on Gerhart Hauptmann's play), prod. in Ger., Hamburg, 18. XI. 1927.

Opera by Zöllner (lib. by comp., based

on Gerhart Hauptmann's play), prod. Berlin, Theater des Westens, 8. VII. 1899.

Vert, Jacques de. *See* **Wert.**

Vertical, an adj. applied to the combination of simultaneous sounds, as seen on the page, in contrast to the horizontal appearance of notes in succession.

Vertovsky, Alexis Nikolaievich (b. Govt. of Tambov, 2. III. 1799; d. Moscow, 17. XI. 1862), Rus. comp. Studied civil engineering at St. Petersburg, but picked up mus. training at the same time, studying theory, singing, vln. and pf., the latter with Field and Steibelt. As a rich man's son he remained an amateur, but prod. his 1st operetta at the age of 19. In 1824 he was app. inspector of the Imp. Opera at Moscow, where in 1828 he prod. his 1st opera. In 1842 he married the famous actress Nadezhda Repin.

Works incl. *Pan Tvardovsky, Vadim, Askold's Tomb, Homesickness, The Valley of Tchurov* and *Gromoboy* (after Zhukovsky); 22 operettas; cantatas, melodramas and dramatic scenas; 29 songs, incl. Pushkin's *The Black Shawl*, etc.

Verwandelten Weiber, Die, oder Der Teufel ist los, *Singspiel* by J. A. Hiller (lib. by Christian Felix Weisse, based on Coffey's *The Devil to Pay*), prod. Leipzig, 28. V. 1766. *See also* **Teufel ist los** (Standfuss).

Vespers (from Lat. *vespera,* evening), the service preceding Compline in the Office of the Rom. Church. It incl. psalms with their antiphons, a hymn and the Magnificat. A number of comps. have made elaborate settings for voices and instruments of all or part of the texts, notably Monteverdi and Mozart.

Vespri siciliani, I (Verdi). *See* **Vêpres siciliennes.**

Vesque von Püttlingen, Johann (pseudo. J. Hoven) (b. Opole, 23. VII. 1803; d. Vienna, 29. X. 1883), Aus. comp. of Belg. descent. He was b. at the residence of Prince Alexander Lubomirsky. The family moved to Vienna in 1815 and he studied mus. there with Leidesdorf, Moscheles and Worzischek. In 1822 he entered Vienna Univ. and in 1827 the civil service. In 1829 he exercised himself in opera by setting the lib. of Rossini's *Donna del lago* (based on Scott) and in 1833 he studied counterpoint with Sechter.

Works incl. opera *Turandot* (after Gozzi), *Jeanne d'Arc, Liebeszauber* (after Kleist's *Käthchen von Heilbronn*), *Ein Abenteuer Carl des Zweiten, Der lustige Rat* and 2 unfinished; 2 Masses, etc.

Vestale, La, opera by Mercadante (lib., in It., by Salvatore Cammarano), prod. Naples, Teatro San Carlo, 10.I II. 1840.

Opera by Spontini (lib., in Fr., by Victor Jacques Étienne de Jouy, ? based on Winckelmann's *Monumenti antichi inediti*), prod. Paris, Opéra, 16. XII. 1807.

Vestris (*née* **Bartolozzi**), **Lucia Elizabeth** (or **Eliza Lucy**) (b. London, 3. I. or 2. III. 1797; d. London, 8. VIII. 1856), Eng. actress and contralto of It. descent, daughter of Gaetano B. and granddaughter of the engraver Francesco B. Studied singing with Domenico Corri, married the dancer Auguste Armand V. (1788–1825) in 1813 and in 1815 made her 1st stage appearance in London. She was Fatima in the prod. of Weber's *Oberon* in 1826.

Vezzoso (It.) = Charming, graceful.

Via (It. imper. = away), a direction to remove pedals, mutes (*via sordini*), etc.

Viadana (real name Lodovico Grossi) (b. Viadana, *c.* 1560; d. Gualtieri o/Po, 2. V. ? 1627), It. comp. Pupil of Porta and before 1590 app. *maestro di cappella* at Mantua Cathedral. In 1596 he joined the Franciscan order, in 1609 became *maestro di cappella* at Concordia, in 1612 at Fano Cathedral; in 1615 went to live at Piacenza, whence he retired to the Franciscan monastery at Gualtieri.

Works incl. Masses, psalms and other church mus.; 100 *Concerti ecclesiastici* for 1–4 voices with org. continuo; madrigals, canzonets, etc.

Viaggiatori felici, I (*The Happy Travellers*), opera by Anfossi (lib. by Filippo Livigni), prod. Venice, Teatro San Samuele, X. 1780.

Viaggio a Reims, Il, ossia L'albergo del giglio d'oro (*The Journey to Rheims, or the Golden Lily Inn*), opera by Rossini (lib. by Giuseppe Luigi Balochi), prod. Paris, Théâtre-Italien, 19. VI. 1825.

Vial
Viall }alternative old names of the Viol.

Viana da Mota, José (b. São Tomé, 22. IV. 1868; d. Lisbon, 31. V. 1948), Port. pianist and comp. Studied at the Lisbon Cons. and with the Scharwenka brothers in Berlin, later with Liszt at Weimar and Bülow at Frankfurt. He began to tour Eur. and S. Amer. in 1902, was app. Prus. court pianist and taught at Geneva in 1915–17. He was director of the Lisbon Cons. from 1919 to 1938.

Works incl. *Lusiads* (Camoens) for chorus and orch.; symph.; string 4tet; *Port. Scenes, Port. Rhapsodies,* etc. for pf.: songs, etc.

Viardot-Garcia, (Michelle Ferdinande) Pauline (b. Paris, 18. VII. 1821; d. Paris, 17–18. V. 1910), Fr. mezzo-soprano and comp. of Span. descent, daughter of Manuel García and sister of Maria Malibran. Pupil of her father, also studied pf. Made her 1st appearance as a singer at Brussels in 1837 and 1st visited London in 1839. In 1841 she married the opera manager and critic Louis V. (1800–83). She comp. operettas, *Le Dernier Sorcier, L'Ogre* and *Trop de femmes,* to libs. by Turgenev, songs, etc.

Viardot, Louise. *See* **Héritte-Viardot.**

Vibraphone, an electrophonic instrument the resonators of which are kept vibrating by an electric current, so that the notes struck give out an oscillating sound.

Vibrato (It. = vibrating, oscillating), a special mus. effect prod. on a single note, though often with minute alternations in pitch. In vocal mus. of the early 17th cent. it was called *trillo* in It., which meant a rapid repeating of the same note on one syllable. On the Clavichord a V. effect is possible by shaking the finger on the key without releasing it. On string instruments a warmer and more vibrant tone is prod. by shaking the fingers of the left hand on the fingerboard while pressing down the string. On the org. a similar effect is made possible by the use of the Tremulant. V. on wind instruments is prod. by the breath.

Vicente de Olivença. *See* **Lusitano.**

Vicente, Gil (1470–1540), Port. dramatist. *See* **Badajoz** (*Dom Duardos*).

Vicentino, Nicola (b. Vicenza, 1511; d. Milan, 1576), It. keyboard player and theorist. Pupil of (?) Willaert at Venice. He entered the service of Ippolito d'Este, cardinal of Ferrara, with whom he went to live in Rome. He sought to revive the Ger. modes in his madrigals, invented an instrument he called the archicembalo and pub. a treatise, *L'antica musica ridotta alla moderna prattica,* which involved him in a controversy with Lusitano, in which he was defeated. He returned to Ferrara with his patron and became his *maestro di cappella.*

Vickers, Jon (b. Prince Albert, Saskatchewan, 29. X. 1926), Canad. tenor. Studied at the Toronto Cons. and made his debut at the Stratford Festival, 1956. 1st appeared at Covent Garden, 1957, at Bayreuth, 1958, at the N.Y. Metropolitan, 1959. He is notable partic. for his singing in Wagner and Verdi.

Victoria, Tomás Luis de (not Vittoria, which is merely the It. form of the name) (b. Avila, 1548; d. Madrid, 27. VIII. 1611), Span. comp. Studied (?) with Escobedo at Segovia. He may have been in touch with St. Teresa, also a native of Avila. In 1565 he received a grant from Philip II and the following year went to Rome, where he became a priest and singer at the Ger. Coll. He became choirmaster there in 1571. In 1578 he resigned, having been app. chaplain to the dowager empress Maria, Philip II's sister, who returned to Spain in 1581 and was followed there by V. in (?) 1583. In 1586 he became choirmaster at the convent of the Descalzas Reales in Madrid, where the empress lived and her daughter, the Infanta Margaret, became a nun. On the death of the empress in 1603 he wrote an *Officium defunctorum* (Requiem Mass) for 6 voices.

Works incl. 18 Masses, 2 Requiems, 44 motets, office for Holy Week, 18 Magnificats, 34 hymns, 10 psalms, 10 antiphons, etc.

Victorinus, Georgius (b. ?; d. ?), Ger. 16th–17th-cent. monk and comp. He became mus. prefect at the Jesuit monastery of St. Michael, where a sacred play with mus. by him was perf. in 1597. Other works incl. Magnificat for 6 voices, 3 Litanies, *c.* 20 sacred songs, etc.

Victory, opera by R. R. Bennett (lib. by Beverley Cross, after Conrad), prod. London, Covent Garden Theatre, 13. IV. 1970.

Vida breve, La (*Life is Short*), opera by Falla (lib., in Span., by Carlos Fernández Shaw), prod. Nice, in Fr., trans. by Paul Milliet, 1. IV. 1913.

Vidal, Louis (Antoine) (b. Rouen, 10. VII. 1820; d. Paris, 7. I. 1891), Fr. cellist and mus. hist. He is said to have studied cello with Franchomme in Paris and became a friend of Vuillaume, from whom he learnt much about string instruments. His lit. works incl. studies of the hist. of string instruments, the old Paris corporations of musicians, the bibliog. of chamber mus., etc.

Vidal, Paul (Antonin) (b. Toulouse, 16. VI. 1863; d. Paris, 9. IV. 1931), Fr. cond. and comp. Studied at the Paris Cons., where he took the Prix de Rome in 1883. In 1889 he became asst. choral master at the Opéra, *répétiteur* in 1898 and cond. in 1906. He also became a prof. at the Cons.

Works incl. operas *Burgonde* and *Guernica*, operetta *Eros*; ballets *La Maladetta* and *Fête russe*, also one on mus. by Chopin, orch. with Messager; pantomimes *Pierrot assassin* and *Colombine pardonnée*; mystery plays *Noël* and *Les Mystères d'Éleusis*; incid. mus. for Banville's *Le Baiser*, Mendès's *La Reine Fiammette* and other plays; motets; cantata *Ecce sacerdos magnus*; old dances arr. for orch., etc.

Vidal, Peire (b. ?; d. ?, *c.* 1215), Fr. troubadour, 50 of whose poems and 12 of whose tunes are preserved.

Vie parisienne, La (*Life in Paris*), operetta by Offenbach (lib. by Henri Meilhac and Ludovic Halévy), prod. Paris, Théâtre du Palais-Royal, 31. X. 1866.

Vielle (Fr.) = Hurdy-gurdy. In medieval Fr. = Fiddle.

Vielle organisée (Fr. = 'organed' [not 'organized'] hurdy-gurdy; It. *lira organizzata*), A hurdy-gurdy (*vielle*) into which are incorporated one or two sets (stops) or organ pipes. These can be made to sound separately or together, or shut off at will. Haydn wrote 5 concertos for 2 of these instruments.

Vier ernste Gesänge (*Four Serious Songs*), settings by Brahms for bar. and pf. of words from the Bible, Op. 121, comp. V.

1896. The corresponding passages in Eng. are *One thing befalleth*, *So I returned*, *O death, how bitter is thy sting*, *Though I speak with the tongues of men and of angels*.

Vierdanck, Johann (b. ?, *c.* 1605; d. Stralsund, III. 1646), Ger. organist and comp. Learnt mus. as a choir-boy in the court chapel at Dresden where he subsequently served as an instrumentalist, From *c.* 1634 he was organist at St. Mary's Church, Stralsund.

Works incl. sacred concertos for 2–9 voices; dances for 2 vlns., viol and continuo, capriccios, canzonets and sonatas for 2–5 instruments with and without continuo, etc.

Vierjährige Posten, Der (*The Four Years' Sentry*), comic opera by Schubert (lib. by Theodor Körner), comp. 1815, but never perf. in Schubert's lifetime. Prod. Dresden, Opera, 23. IX. 1896.

Vierling, Georg (b. Frankenthal, Bavaria, 5. IX. 1820; d. Wiesbaden, 1. V. 1901), Ger. organist and cond. Studied under his father, Jacob V. (1796–1867) a schoolmaster and organist, later at Darmstadt and Berlin. In 1847 he became organist and choral cond. at Frankfurt on Oder. Later he went to Mainz for a short time and then settled in Berlin, where he became royal mus. director in 1859 and prof. of the Acad. in 1882.

Works incl. cantatas for chorus and orch. *Hero and Leander*, *The Rape of the Sabines*, *Alaric's Death* and *Constantine*; symph., overtures to Shakespeare's *Tempest*, Schiller's *Maria Stuart* and others; pf. trio; *O Roma nobilis* for unaccomp. chorus; part-songs; pf. pieces; songs; etc.

Vierling, Johann Gottfried (b. Metzels nr. Meiningen, 25. I. 1750; d. Schmalkalden, 22. XI. 1813), Ger. organist and comp. Studied at Schmalkalden with the organist Fischer, whom he succeeded as church organist there, but interrupted his office to study further with C.P.E. Bach at Hamburg and Kirnberger in Berlin. He wrote treatises on thorough-bass and on preluding to hymns.

Works incl. *Singspiel Empfindung und Empfindelei*; chorale book; 2 cycles of cantatas for the church's year and other church mus.; pf. 4tet; 2 pf. trios; 6 pf. sonatas, etc.

Vierne, Louis (b. Poitiers, 8. X. 1870; d. Paris, 2. VI. 1937), Fr. organist and comp. Pupil of Franck and Widor at the Paris Cons. Although blind, he became asst. organist to Widor at the church of Saint-Sulpice and later organist at Notre-Dame, where he d. at his post.

Works incl. Mass with orch.; symph.; string 4tets; sonatas for vln. and pf. and cello and pf.; 6 symphs., 24 *Pièces en style libre*, 24 *Pièces de fantaisie* and other works for org., etc.

Vieuxtemps, Henri (b. Verviers, 17. II. 1820; d Mustapha-lez-Alger, Algiers, 6. VI. 1881), Belg. violinist and comp. Learnt the vln. at home and at the age of 6 was able to play a concerto by Rode, At 7 he was taken on tour by his father and heard by Bériot, who offered to teach him at Brussels. In 1828 his master took him to Paris and prod. him there. In 1833 he went on tour in Ger. and Aus., remaining in Vienna to study counterpoint with Sechter. In 1834 he 1st visited London, where he met Paganini, and the following year he studied comp. with Reicha in Paris. He afterwards travelled long and extensively in Eur. and in 1844 went to U.S.A. In 1845 he married the Viennese pianist Josephine Eder. In 1846–52 he was vln. prof. at the St. Petersburg Cons. In 1871–3 he taught at the Brussels Cons., but was lamed by a stroke.

Works incl. 6 vln. concertos, *Fantaisie-Caprice* and *Ballade et Polonaise*, etc. for vln. and orch.; vln. and pf. sonata; cadenzas for Beethoven's vln. concerto, etc.

Vigny, Alfred de (1797–1863), Fr. poet, novelist and dramatist. *See* **Gounod** (*Cinq-Mars*), **Leoncavallo** (*Chatterton*).

Vihuela (Span.), the Span. lute, but made in the shape of a guitar. It dates back to at least the 13th cent., but became obs. about the 16th. It usually had 6 strings tuned in 4ths, but with an interval of a 3rd between the 2 middle ones.

Vihuela de arco (Span = bowed V.), actually an instrument of the viol rather than strictly the V. type.

Vihuela de Flandres (Span = Flem. V.), the Span. name for the ordinary lute, which was an outlandish instrument in Spain, played by foreigners.

Vihuela de mano (Span. = hand V.), a V. plucked with the fingers. The most commonly used type.

Vihuela de péndola (Span. = plectrum V.), a V. the strings of which were plucked with a plectrum.

Vila, Pedro Alberto (b. ? Barcelona, 1517; d. Barcelona, 16. XI. 1582), Span. organist and comp. Became a priest and canon of Barcelona Cathedral.

Works incl. madrigals, org. mus., etc.

Vilar, José Teodor (b. Vich nr. Barcelona, 10. VIII. 1836; d. Barcelona, 21. X. 1905), Span. cond. and comp. Studied with the cathedral organist Ramón Vilanova (1801–70) at Barcelona and in 1859 went to Paris to study pf. with Herz and comp. with Bazin and Halévy. Returning home in 1863, he became cond. at one of the minor theatres and later at the principal theatre. He also did much teaching.

Works incl. zarzuelas *La romeria de Racasens*, *L'ultimo rey de Magnolia*, *El pescador de San Pol*, *Una prometensa*, *La rambla de las flores*, *Pot mes qui piuta*, *La lluna en un cove*, *L'esca del pecat*, *La torre del amor*, etc.

Vilbac, Alphonse (Charles Renaud) de (b. Montpellier, 3. VI. 1829; d. Brussels, 19. III. 1884), Fr. organist, pianist and comp. Studied at the Paris Cons., Halévy being among his masters, and gained the Prix de Rome in 1844. He was organist of St. Eugène, Paris, from 1855 to 1871. After an early success he was unfortunate, made a precarious living by arrs. and other hack-work, became almost blind and d. in poverty.

Works incl. operettas *Au Clair de la lune* and *Don Almanzor*; *Messe solennelle*; cantata *Le Renégat de Tanger*; *Pompadour Gavotte*, *Chant cypriote*, *Marche serbe*, etc. for orch.; pf. pieces, etc.

Vilda, Maria. *See* **Wilt, Marie.**

Villa-Lobos, Heitor (b. Rio de Janeiro, 5. III. 1887; d. Rio de Janeiro, 17. XI. 1959), Brazil. comp. He studied the cello at 1st, but became a pianist and for some time toured as a concert artist. In 1912 he began to explore his country's folk mus. and in 1915 gave the 1st concert devoted to his own works at Rio de Janeiro. A government grant enabled him to live in Paris for a few years from 1923, but on his return he did much useful work as cond. and mus. educationist, being app. director of mus. educ. for the schools in the capital in 1930. In 1929 he pub. a book on Brazil. folk. mus., *Alma do Brasil*.

Works incl. operas *Izaht*, *Jesus*, *Zoé* and *Malazerte*; ballet *Uirapúrú*; oratorio *Vidapura*; 14 works entitled *Chôros* cast in a new form and consisting of 4 for orch., 1 for pf. and orch., 1 for 2 pfs. and orch., 2 for chorus and orch. and 6 for var. combinations and solo instruments; orchestral works incl. symph. poem *Amazonas*, *Bachianas Brasileiras* (9 suites in the spirit of Bach), 12 symphs.; 5 pf. concertos, 2 cello concertos, harp concerto; nonet for wind, harp, perc. and chorus, 5tet for wind instruments; 16 string 4tets, 3 pf. trios; 4 sonata-fantasies for vln. and pf.; a very large number of pf. works; songs, etc.

Village Coquettes, The, opera by Hullah (lib. by Dickens), prod. London, St. James's Theatre, 6. XII. 1836.

Village Romeo and Juliet (Delius). *See* **Romeo und Julia auf dem Dorfe.**

Villalba Muñoz, Luis (b. Valladolid, 22. IX. 1873; d. Madrid, 9. I. 1921), Span. mus. hist. He entered the Augustinian order and was ordained priest, retiring as a monk to the Escurial, but renounced the order not long before his death and went to live in Madrid. He wrote a book on Span. 15th–16th-cent. org. mus., ed. old lutenist songs and org. works, and transcribed much other old Span. mus.

Villancico (Span.), a type of verse with a

refrain and a complex rhyme-scheme; also the mus. to which such poems were set, at first tunes without harmony, later pieces similar to madrigals; sometimes a comp. for solo voices, strings and org. to sacred words, esp. connected with the Nativity.

Villanella (It. lit. country girl), an It. part-song of the middle 16th to the earlier 17th cent., set to rustic words and light in character.

Villanella rapita, La (*The Ravished Country Girl*) opera by Bianchi (lib. by Giovanni Bertati, based on Jean Michel Favart's *Le Caprice amoureux*), prod. Venice, Teatro San Moisè, autumn 1783. Mozart wrote an additional 4tet and a trio for the Vienna perf., 25. XI. 1785.

Villanelle (Fr.). In Fr. mus. a V. is not the equivalent of the It. *Villanella* and the Span. *Villancico*, but a vocal setting of a poem in V. form, which consists of stanzas of 3 lines, the 1st and 3rd lines of the opening stanza being repeated alternately as the 3rd line of the succeeding stanzas.

Villi, Le (*The Witches*), opera by Puccini (lib. by Ferdinando Fontana), prod. Milan, Teatro dal Verme, 31. V. 1884.

Villiers de l'Isle Adam, Auguste, Count (1840–89), Fr. poet. *See* Dieren (van) (songs), **Georges** (*Nouveau Monde* and *Axël*), **Wieniawksi (A.)** (*Évasion*).

Villiers, George, Duke of Buckingham (1628–87), Eng. courtier and author. *See* Smith, J. C. (*Chances*).

Villon, François (1431–*c.* 1489), Fr. poet. *See* **Cartan, Debussy** (3 ballads), **Dieren** (van) (recitations).

Villota } \
  or   } a type of *frottola* of no struc- \
Villotta } \
tural regularity, originating in the late 15th cent.

Vilmorin, Louise de. *See* **Mouvements du cœur.**

Vinaccesi, Benedetto (b. Brescia, *c.* 1670; d. Venice, 1719), It. comp. He was *maestro di cappella* to Prince Francesco Gonzaga di Castiglione, but in 1704 was app. 2nd organist at St. Marks', Venice, in 1704 taking on the addit. duties of choirmaster at the girls' Cons. dell' Ospedaletto.

Works incl. operas *L'innocenza giustificata, Gli amanti generosi* and *Gli sponsali di giubilo;* 2 oratorios; motets and other church mus.; *Sonate da chiesa, Sfere armoniche* for 2 vlns., cello and org. continuo, etc.

Vincent, Thomas (b. London, *c.* 1720; d. London, 10. V. 1783), Eng. oboist and comp. Pupil of Sammartini. He entered the king's band as oboist in 1735.

Works incl. solos for ob., fl. or vln. with harpsichord continuo; harpsichord lessons, etc.

Vincentius, Caspar (b. St. Omer, ? 1580; d. Würzburg, 1624), Flem. comp. He was

a choir-boy at the Imp. chapel in Vienna 1594–7, and town organist at Speyer, 1602–4, where he (?) met Schadaeus. He later held appts. at Worms and Würzburg. He provided a *bassus generalis* to the 3 vols. of Schadaeus' *Promptuarium musicum,* and later added a 4th part of his own (1617).

Vinci, Leonardo (b. Strongoli, Calabria, ? 1690 or 1696; d. Naples, 27. V. 1730), It. comp. Pupil of Greco at the Cons. dei Poveri di Gesù Cristo in Naples, estab. himself 1st as a comp. of Neapol. dialect operas (from 1719) and prod. his 1st *opera seria* in 1722. App. as an acting *maestro di cappella* at court in 1725, he was from 1728 *maestro* at his old Cons., where Pergolesi was among his pupils.

Works incl. opera *Lo cecato fauzo, Le zite 'n galera* (both in Neapol. dialect), *Silla dittatore, La mogliera fedele, Astianatte, Siroe, La caduta dei decemviri, Artaserse* and *c.* 30 others.

Vinci, Leonardo da (b. Vinci nr. Empoli, 15. IV. 1452; d. Amboise nr. Paris, 2. V. 1519), It. painter, scientist, inventor and musician. In this last capacity he excelled as singer, lutenist and violist, made improvements in the viols and invented a new kind of lute.

Vinci, Pietro (b. Nicosia, Enna, *c.* 1535; d. Nicosia, *c.* 1584), It. comp. He became *maestro di cappella* at the church of Santa Maria Maggiore at Bergamo in the 1570s and in 1581 took on a similar post at his birth-place.

Works incl. Masses, motets; madrigals, etc.

Viñes, Ricardo (b. Lérida, 5. II. 1875; d. Barcelona, 29. IV. 1943), Span. pianist. Studied and lived in Paris, where he did much useful work for modern Fr. and Span. mus.

Vingt-quatre Violons du Roy (Fr. = The King's 24 Vlns.), the Fr. court string band of the 17th cent., used for ballets, court balls, dinners, etc., and incl. all the instruments of the vln. family. A similar string orch. was founded, on the Fr. model, by Charles II in London after his restoration in 1660.

Vinning, Louisa (b. Kingsbridge, Devon, 10. XI. 1836; d. London, 1904), Eng. soprano and harpist. She sang on the stage at Plymouth as a small child and appeared as singer and harpist in 1840–2 under the name of 'The Infant Sappho'. Having studied singing with Frank Mori, she made her 1st appearance in London in 1856, when she took an indisposed singer's part in *Messiah* at a moment's notice.

Viol, the generic name of a family of bowed string instruments. The It. name was *viola da gamba* (leg viol). V.s 1st appeared in the 15th cent. and were in vogue until near the end of the 17th, disappearing completely, apart from the bass viol, in the 18th. The main representatives were the

Viol d'amour

treble, the tenor and the bass, all of which were tuned on the same plan, i.e.:

Treble

Tenor

Bass

VIOL

The double bass of the family was called *violone*.

See also **Treble Viol**, **Viola da gamba** and **Violone**.

Viol d'amour, an 8-ft. open Diapason org. stop, similar to the Violin Diapason, prod. an imitation of string tone.

Viol de Gamboys (old Eng.) = Viola da gamba.

Viol di Gamba, an 8-ft. org. stop repro. string tone.

Viol d'orchestre, an 8-ft. org. stop of the Gamba type prod. an imitation of energetic string tone.

Viol Lyra Way. *See* **Lyra Viol**.

Viola, opera by Hans Holenia (b. 1890) (lib. by Oskar Widowitz, based on Shakespeare's *Twelfth Night*), prod. Graz, 17. XI. 1934.

Unfinished opera by Smetana (lib. by Eliška Krasnohorská, on Shakespeare's *Twelfth Night*), begun 1883.

Viola, the tenor instrument of the vln. family. It has 4 strings tuned as follows:

It is the regular middle part in the string section of the orch. and in the string 4tet, etc. Also an 8-ft. open Diapason org. stop similar to the Violin Diapason. *See also* **Viola da braccio**, **Viola da gamba**.

Viola, Alfonso della (b. Ferrara, *c.* 1508; d. Ferrara, *c.* 1570), It. comp. *Maestro di cappella* at the court of Ercole d'Este (II), Duke of Ferrara, where he prod. plays with mus. on the stage almost amounting to operas. He remained in the service of the next Duke, Alfonso II.

Viola alta (It. = high vla.), an exceptionally large vla. designed by Hermann Ritter and made by Hörlein of Würzburg in the 1870s for use in the orch. at the Wagner festivals at Bayreuth. In 1898 a

Viola pomposa

5th string was added, tuned to the E of the highest vln. string.

Viola bastarda (It. lit. bastard viol), the It. name for the Lyra Viol, called *bastarda* because it was midway in size between the Tenor Viol and the Bass Viol.

Viola da braccio (It. = arm viol), in the 16th and early 17th cent. the generic name for members of the vln. family, since the smaller instruments were played on the arm and not, as was the case with the *viola da gamba* family, on or between the legs. Since the cello was the bass of the family it was known, illogically, as *bassa viola da braccio*. The treble instrument came to be known exclusively by the diminutive *violino*, and *viola da braccio* was reserved for the alto or tenor, shortened to *viola* in It. and corrupted into *Bratsche* in Ger.

Viola da gamba (It. = leg viol), the generic name for the members of the viol family, all of which, small or large, are played on or between the legs. Unlike the vln. family they have flat backs, sloping shoulders, 6 strings and frets. The smaller instruments of the family gradually went out of use in the course of the 17th cent., but the bass was retained as a solo instrument and for continuo playing. Hence in the 18th cent. *viola da gamba* normally means the bass viol. Exs. of its use are Bach's 3 sonatas with harpsichord and the obbligatos in the St. Matthew Passion. All the members of the family have been successfully revived in modern times. For the tuning *see* **Viol**.

Viola da spalla (It. = shoulder vla.), a portable cello used mainly by wandering musicians in the 17th and 18th cents., held by a shoulder strap. Also an alternative name for the cello.

Viola d'amore (It. lit. love viol), (1) In the 17th cent. a vln. with wire strings. (2) A bowed string instrument of the viol type with 7 strings and from 7 to 14 sympathetic strings not touched by the bow but vibrating with those actually played. There was no standard tuning.

Viola di bordone (It. = drone viol), an alternative name for the Barytone.

Viola, Francesco della (b. Ferrara, ?; d. Ferrara, III. 1568), It. 16th-cent. comp., brother of Alfonso d. V. Pupil of Willaert and later *maestro di cappella* to Alfonso d'Este (II), Duke of Ferrara, with whom he visited Venice in 1562.

Works incl. Masses, motets, madrigals, songs, etc.

Viola pomposa, a special type of bowed

string instrument of the vln. family, very rarely used. It seems to have had 5 strings, the lower 4 tuned like the vla. and the 5th tuned to the E of the vln.

Violet, the Eng. name sometimes given to the Viola d'amore.

Violet, The (Mozart). *See* **Veilchen.**

Violetta, 18th-cent. name for the vla.

Violetta marina (It. lit. little marine viol), a special type of Viol, allied to the Viola d'amore, like which it has sympathetic strings.

Violetta piccola (It. small little viol), an obs. name for the treble viol and the vln.

Violin, the principal modern bowed string instrument, to whose family belong also the Viola, Violoncello and Double Bass. The V. has 4 strings tuned :

It began to displace the Viol in the 17th cent. and completely superseded it in the 18th. *See also* **Basse-contre, Cellone, Cinquième, Dessus, Double Bass, Hardanger Fiddle, Haute-contre, Kit, Quinton, Taille, Tenor Violin, Viola, Viola alta, Viola da braccio, Viola da spalla, Viola pomposa, Violino piccolo, Violon d'amour, Violoncello, Violoncello piccolo, Violotta.**

Violin Diapason, an 8-ft. open Diapason org. stop prod. an imitation of string tone.

Violino piccolo (It. = little vln.), a small string instrument of the vln. family with 4 strings tuned either:

or:

and thus standing a 4th or a minor 3rd above the vln. in pitch.

Violins of St. Jacques, The, opera by Williamson (lib. by William Chappell), prod. London, Sadler's Wells, 29. XI. 1966.

Violon d'amour (Fr. lit. love vln.), the member of the modern string family corresponding to the Viola d'amore of the Viol family, used in the 18th cent., but now obs. It had 5 strings, tuned:

and 6 sympathetic strings, not touched by the bow but vibrating with those actually played.

Violoncello, the bass instrument of the vln. family. It has 4 strings tuned:

Its upward range is considerable. In the 17th and 18th cents. it was also made with 5 strings, i.e. with an E string a 5th above the A. Also an 8-ft. org. stop prod. an imitation of string tone an octave above that of the Violone.

Violoncello piccolo, a small cello on which the playing of high passages was easier than on the normal cello. A familiar example of its use is the obbligato in Bach's aria 'Mein gläubiges Herze' ('My heart ever faithful') in the Cantata *Also hat Gott die Welt geliebt* ('God so loved the world').

Violone, the double bass of the Viol family, similar to the Bass Viol but larger, with 6 strings similarly tuned an 8ve lower. The name was also applied to the double bass of the vln. family. Also a 16-ft. org. stop prod. an imitation of bass string tone.

Violotta, a modern string instrument of the vln. family invented by Alfred Stelzner (d. 1906) of Dresden. It has 4 strings tuned so as to stand in pitch between the vla. and the cello:

Viotti, Giovanni Battista (b. Fontanetto da Po, Piedmont, 12. V. 1755; d. London, 3. III. 1824), It. violinist and comp. Pupil of Pugnani, joined the court orch. at Turin in 1775, but obtained leave of absence in 1780 to go on tour with Pugnani. (A supposed meeting with Voltaire, who d. in 1778, is apparently apocryphal.) Visited Switz., Dresden, Berlin, Warsaw, St. Petersburg and in 1782 arrived in Paris, where he stayed 10 years. He played at the Concert spirituel, was solo violinist to Marie Antoinette 1784–6, cond. some concerts of the Loge Olympique (for which Haydn wrote his 'Paris' symphs.), and from 1788 was involved in the foundation of a new opera co. at the Théâtre de Monsieur. In 1792 he went to London, where he played in Salomon's concerts and became acting manager and leader of the orch. at the King's Theatre opera, but was forced to leave Eng. for political reasons in 1798, and lived nr. Hamburg, writing his autobiog. Returning to London in 1801, he withdrew almost completely from mus. and entered the wine trade, but twice visited Paris (1802 and 1814) and in 1819 became director of the Opéra there, finally returning to London in 1823.

Works incl. 29 vln. concertos; 2 *Symphonies concertantes* for 2 vlns. and orch.; 10 pf. concertos; 21 string 4tets; 36 string trios; vln. duets, sonatas etc.; 9 pf. sonatas, etc.

Virdung, Sebastian (b. Amberg, Upper Palatinate, *c.* 1465; d. ?), Ger. cleric and writer on mus. He was a priest at Eichstätt and in 1511 pub. at Basle his book on mus. instruments, *Musica getutscht und auszgezogen*, ded. to the Bishop of Strasbourg.

Virelai (Fr., from *virer*, to turn, and *lai*, a song), a type of medieval Fr. song with a refrain before and after each verse.

Virgil (Publius Vergilius Maro) (70–19 B.C.), Rom. poet, *See* **Dido and Aeneas** (Purcell), **Énée et Lavinie** (Colasse and Dauvergne), **Freitas** (eclogue), **Lissenko** (*Aeneid*), **Loeffler** (*Pagan Poem*), **Malipiero** (*Vergilii Aeneis*), **Mudurra, Roger-Ducasse, Troyens** (Berlioz), **Verbonnet** (*Dulces exuviae*).

Virginal, the Eng. stringed keyboard instrument of the 16th and 17th cents., often called 'virginals' or 'a pair of virginals'. Except in shape, which was rectangular, it did not differ essentially from the harpsichord. It was generally placed on a table or a suitable stand. Before the Restoration, however, the name was used indiscriminately of any instrument of the harpsichord family. The most likely explanation of its name is that it was the instrument most often played by girls. There are several MS. collections of V. mus. by Eng. comps., incl. *The Fitzwilliam Virginal Book, My Lady Nevell's Book, Will Forster's Book, Benjamin Cosyn's Book* and *Elizabeth Rogers's Book*.

Virginia, opera by Mercadante (lib. by Salvatore Cammarano, based on Alfieri's tragedy), prod. Naples, Teatro San Carlo, 7. IV. 1866.

Virtuosity (der. from Virtuoso, below), the manner of perf. with complete technical mastery.

Virtuoso (It., from Lat. *virtus* = excellence), in mus. an executive artist who has achieved complete mastery over the medium in which he perfs.

Visé, Jean Donneau de (1640–1710), Fr. dramatist. *See* **Charpentier (M.-A.)** (3 plays, 2 with Corneille).

Visée, Robert de (b. ?, *c.* 1660; d. ?, *c.* 1725), Fr. lutenist, guitarist and comp. He was guitar and theorbo player to the dauphin and chamber musician to the king from near the end of the 17th cent. to 1720.

Works incl. guitar pieces, trios for lute, theorbo and bass, songs, etc.

Vitali, Filippo (b. Florence, *c.* 1590; d. Florence, 1653). It. priest, tenor and comp. He worked at Florence until 1631, when he was called to Rome as singer in the Papal chapel. While there he became attached to the household of Cardinal Francesco Barberini; but in 1642 he returned to Florence to become *maestro di cappella* to the Duke of Tuscany and at San Lorenzo. In 1653 he became a canon there.

Works incl. mus.-drama *L'Aretusa*; incid. mus. to Jacopo Cicognini's comedy *La finta Mora*; psalms for 5 voices, hymns, *Sacrae cantiones* and other church mus.; madrigals; var. works for voices and instruments in several parts, etc.

Vitali, Giovanni Battista (b. Cremona, 18. II. 1632; d. Modena, 12. X. 1692), It. violist and comp. Pupil of Maurizio Cazzati, *maestro di cappella* of San Petronio at Bologna, where V. himself was a string player from 1666. In 1673 he became *maestro di cappella* of the Santissimo Rosario, and in 1674 he went to Modena as master of the ducal chapel. His oratorio on Monmouth was prod. there in 1686, the year after Monmouth's execution.

Works incl. psalms for 2–5 voices and instruments; oratorios *Agar, Gefte, Il Giona* and *L'ambitione debellata, ovvero La caduta di Monmouth*; cantata *L'alloro trionfante*; numerous dances for several instruments; sonatas for 2 vlns. and continuo and others for var. instrumental combinations, etc.

Vitali, Tommaso (Antonio) (b. Bologna, 7. III. 1663; d. Modena, 9. V. 1745), It. violinist and comp., son of prec. Pupil of his father, later member of the court chapel at Modena under him. He taught the vln. to distinguished pupils, incl. E. Abaco and Senallié.

Works incl. pf. trios; sonatas for 2 vlns. and continuo.

Vitry, Philippe de (b. Paris, 31. X. 1291; d. Paris, 2. VI. 1361), Fr. diplomat, priest, mus. theorist, poet and comp. He was secretary to Charles IV and Philip VI of Fr., in 1350 arr. a meeting between the king and the pope at Avignon and was soon afterwards created Bishop of Meaux. His poetry was much esteemed, Petrarch writing him a letter of appreciation. A few motets by him survive. He wrote a treatise on the change from the old (*ars antiqua*) to the new mensural notation (*ars nova*).

Vittadini, Franco (b. Pavia, 9. IV. 1884; d. Pavia, 30. XI. 1948), It cond. and comp. Studied at the Milan Cons., became cond. at Varese and later settled at Pavia, where he became director of the Istituto musicale.

Works incl. operas *Il mare di Tiberiade, Anima allegra* (after the Quintero brothers), *Nazareth* (after Lagerlöf), *La Sagredo* and *Caracciolo*; ballets *Vecchia Milano, Le dame galanti* and *Fiordisole*; 10 Masses and motets; oratorio *Il natale di Gesù, Le sette parole di Cristo* for chorus; symph. poem *Armonie della notte*; org. works, etc.

Vittori, Loreto (b. Spoleto, I. 1604; d. Rome, 23. IV. 1670), It. castrato and comp. Studied with Soto, Nanini and Soriano in Rome and lived for a time at the court of Cosimo II de' Medici at Florence, but returned to Rome and entered the Papal Chapel in 1622. Among his pupils were Queen Christina of Swed., during her residence in Rome, and Pasquini.

Works incl. opera *La Galatea*; plays with mus. *La fiera di Palestrina* and *Le zitelle canterine*; oratorios *Santa Irene*, *la pellegrina costante* and *Sant' Ignazio di Loiola*; cantatas, arias, etc.

Vittoria, Tommaso Lodovico da. *See* Victoria, Tomás Luis de.

Vitzthumb, Ignaz (b. Baden nr. Vienna, 20. VII. 1723; d. Brussels, 23. III. 1816), Aus. cond. and comp. Studied in Vienna and settled in Brussels in the service of Prince Charles of Lorraine. He cond. at Ghent, Amsterdam and at the Théâtre de la Monnaie in Brussels, but lost his posts and pension during the Revolution and d. in poverty.

Works incl. comic operas *Le Soldat par amour*, *La Foire de village*, etc., Masses, motets and other church mus.; Fr. cantatas symphs., etc.

Vivace (It.) = lively, animated.

Vivacissimo (It. superl.) = most lively, etc.

Vivaldi, Antonio (Lucio) (b. Venice, 4. III. 1678; d. Vienna, VII, 1741), It. violinist and comp. Pupil of his father Giovanni Battista V., a violinist at St. Mark's, Venice, and poss. also of Legrenzi, he entered the church in 1693 and was ordained priest in 1703 (being commonly known as 'il prete rosso'—'the red [-haired] priest'), but soon afterwards was given dispensations from priestly duties. He was assoc. with the Cons. dell' Ospedale della pietà in Venice 1703–40 (*maestro di violino* 1711), for which he wrote oratorios and instrumental mus., but was frequently absent. His 1st opera was prod. in Vicenza in 1713, followed by many others in Venice, Florence, Munich, Parma, Milan, etc. He was in Mantua as *maestro di cappella* to the Margrave Philip of Hesse-Darmstadt 1720–3, and prob. toured Europe *c*. 1729, but of his extensive travels throughout his career almost nothing is known. Returning to Venice in 1739, he sold a large quantity of his mus. there the following year and moved to Vienna, where he d. in poverty. One of the most prolific comps. of his day, he was partic. influential through his concertos, several of which were transcribed by Bach.

Works incl. *c*. 50 operas, e.g. *Ottone in Villa*, *L'Olimpiade*, *La fida ninfa*, *Griselda*, etc.; Lat. oratorio *Juditha* and others; *Gloria* for voices and orch., and other church mus.; cantatas; over 200 vln. concertos and numerous others for 2–4 vlns., fl., piccolo, clar., ob., bassoon, etc., *c*. 450 in all; vln. sonatas and other chamber mus., etc.

Vives, Amadeo (b. Collbató nr. Barcelona, 18. XI. 1871; d. Madrid, 1. XII. 1932), Span. comp. Prof. of comp. at the Madrid Cons.

Works incl. operas and *zarzuelas Don Lucas del Cigarral*, *Euda d'Uriach*, *Maruxa*, *Balada de carnaval*, *Doña Francisquita* (on Lope de Vega's *La discreta enamorada*) and *c*. 60 others; *Canciones epigramáticas* for voice and pf., etc.

Vivo (It.) = Lively, animated, the same as *vivace*, but more rarely used.

Vlad, Roman (b. Cernauti, 29. XII. 1919), It. comp. of Rum. birth. Studied at the Cernauti Cons. but in 1938 settled in Rome, where he finished studies under Casella. He is the author of books on Dallapiccola and Stravinsky.

Works incl. radio opera *Il dottore di vetro*, ballets *La strada sul caffè* and *La dama delle camelie* (after Dumas); film mus.; *De profundis* for soprano, chorus and orch.; *Divertimento* for 11 insts.; *Studi dodecafonici* for pf., etc.

Vladigerov, Pancho (b. Zürich, 18. III. 1899), Bulg. comp. Studied with Juon and Georg Schumann in Berlin and at the Sofia Cons.

Works incl. opera *Tsar Kaloyan*; incid. mus. for Strindberg's *A Dream Play*; Bulg. Rhapsody *Vardar*; vln. concerto; pf. concerto; pf. trio; vln. and pf. sonata; pf. pieces; songs, etc.

Vltava (Smetana). *See* Má Vlast.

Vocal Score. *See* Score.

Vocalise (Fr.)
Vocalizzo (It.) } any kind of vocal exercise without words, also sometimes in recent years a comp. for voice without words for concert perf. (the most ambitious being Medtner's *Sonata-V.*); also used as a synonym for Solfège and Solfeggio.

Voce di gola (It.) = Throat voice; voice of a guttural quality.

Voce di petto (It.) = Chest Voice.

Voce di testa (It.) = Head Voice.

Vogel, Charles (Louis Adolphe) (b. Lille, 17. V. 1808; d. Paris, 11. IX. 1892), Fr.-Belg. comp. of Ger. descent. Studied at the Paris Cons.

Works incl. opera *Le Podestat*, *Le Siège de Leyde*, *La Moissonneuse*, *Rompons*, *Le Nid de cigognes*, *Gredin de Pigoche*, *La Filleule du roi*; oratorio *Le Jugement dernier*; symphs; string 4tets, string 5tets, songs incl. *Les Trois Couleurs*, etc.

Vögel, Die (*The Birds*), opera by Braunfels (lib. by comp., based on the comedy by Aristophanes), prod. Munich, 4. XII. 1920.

Vogel, (Johannes) Emil (Eduard Bernhard) (b. Wriezen, 21. I. 1859; d. Nikolassee nr. Berlin, 18. VI. 1908), Ger. mus. scholar. Studied at Berlin Univ. and privately. In 1883 he went to It. as asst. to F. X. Haberl. From 1893 to 1901 he was librarian of the Musikbiliothek Peters and ed. of the Peters Jahrbücher. He pub. *Claudio Monteverdi, Marco Gagliano, Bibliothek der gedruckten Vokalmusik Italiens aus den Jahren 1500–1700*, etc.

Vogel, Johann Christoph (b. Nuremberg, III. 1758; d. Paris, 27. VI. 1788), Ger. comp. Pupil of Riepel at Regensburg, went to Paris in 1776 and there became an enthusiastic supporter of Gluck, to whom he ded. his first opera, *La Toison d'or* (1786).

Works incl. operas *La Toison d'or* and *Démophon*; symphs. ; *symphonies concertantes* for wind instruments and orch., etc.

Vogel, Vladimir Rudolfovich (b. Moscow, 29. II. 1896), Rus. comp. of Ger. descent. Studied in Rus., later with Tiessen and Busoni in Berlin.

Works incl. cantatas *Thyl Claes* (after *Till Eulenspiegel*) and *The Fall of Wagadus* for solo voices, chorus and 5 saxophones; *Sinfonia fugata, 2 Studies, Devise, Tripartita* for orch.; vln. concerto, cello concerto; string 4tets, *Composition* and *Chaconne, Étude and Toccata* for pf.; *Composition* for 2 pfs., etc.

Vogelgesang. *See* **Ornithoparcus.**

Vogelhändler, Der (*The Bird Dealer*), operetta by Zeller (lib. by Moritz West and Ludwig Held), prod. Vienna, Theater an der Wien, 10. I. 1891.

Vogelsang. *See* **Ornithoparcus.**

Vogelweide, Walther von der (b. ? Tyrol or Switz., *c.* 1170; d. ? Würzburg, *c.* 1230), Ger. poet, minnesinger and comp. Pupil of Reinmar von Hagenau in Aus. He was in service at the Aus. court in Vienna, then led a wandering life in Ger. and after 1220 prob. lived at an estate given to him at Würzburg. Only a few of his tunes have been preserved.

Vogl, Heinrich (b. Au nr. Munich, 15. I. 1845; d. Munich, 21. IV. 1900), Ger. tenor and comp. Began his career as a schoolmaster, but learnt singing from F. Lachner at Munich, also studied acting. He made his 1st stage appearance there in 1865. He married the soprano Therese Thoma (1845–1921) in 1868. He appeared in the 1st 2 parts of Wagner's *Ring* at Munich in 1869–70 and in the prod. of the whole work at Bayreuth in 1876.

Works incl. opera *Der Fremdling* and songs.

Vogl, Johann Michael (b. Ennsdorf nr. Steyr, 10. VIII. 1768; d. Vienna, 19. XI. 1840), Aus. baritone. Educ. at the monastery of Kremsmünster and Vienna Univ., he was engaged by Süssmayr in 1794 and made his 1st appearance as a court opera singer in 1795. He met Schubert in 1816 and

was the 1st important artist to sing his songs in public. He retired from the stage with a pension in 1821 and devoted himself to songs.

Vogl (*née* **Thoma**), Therese (b. Tutzing, Bavar., 12. XI. 1845; d. Munich, 29. IX. 1921), Ger. soprano. Studied at the Munich Cons. and made her 1st stage appearance at Carlsruhe in 1865. In 1868 she married Heinrich V.

Vogler, Carl (b. Oberrohrdorf, Aargau, 26. II. 1874; d. Zürich, 17. VI. 1951), Swiss comp. Studied at Lucerne, with Hegar and others at Zürich and with Rheinberger and others at Munich. In 1915 he became prof. at the Zürich Cons. and in 1919 joint director with V. Andreae.

Works incl. operas *Rübezahl* and *Fiedelhänschen*, play with mus. *Mutter Sybille*; org. works; songs and part-songs, etc.

Vogler, Georg Joseph (known as Abbé V.) (b. Pleichach nr. Würzburg, 15. VI. 1749; d. Darmstadt, 6. V. 1814), Ger. comp., teacher and theorist. Son of an instrument maker and violinist, he studied theology at Würzburg and Bamberg Univs., went to Mannheim in 1771, becoming court chaplain the following year, and in 1773 received a scholarship from the Elector to go to It. Studied with Padre Martini in Bologna and Palotti in Padua, and in 1775 returned to Mannheim as vice-*Kapellmeister*. Mozart met him there in 1778 and disliked him. When the electoral court moved to Munich in 1778 V. at first remained in Mannheim, but later followed, becoming *Kapellmeister* in 1784. He was *Kapellmeister* to the Swed. court in Stockholm 1786–99, but was able to travel extensively, going as far afield as N. Africa and Greece. After leaving Stockholm he lived successively in Copenhagen, Berlin, Prague, Vienna and Munich, until in 1807 he was app. *Kapellmeister* to the Grand Duke of Hesse-Darmstadt. A notable teacher, his pupils incl. Weber and Meyerbeer, and he wrote a number of theoret. works.

Works incl. operas *Albert III von Bayern, Erwin und Elmire* (Goethe), *La Kermesse, Castore e Polluce, Gustav Adolph och Ebba Brahe, Samori* and others, operetta *Der Kaufmann von Smyrna*; ballet *Rendezvous de chasse*; incid. mus. to Shakespeare's *Hamlet*; choruses for Racine's *Athalie* and Skjöldebrand's *Hermann von Unna*; Masses, motets, psalms and other church mus.; cantata *Ino* (Ramler); symphs.; several pf. variations for pf. and orch.; pf. trios and much other chamber mus.; pf. and vln. sonatas; pf. sonatas and variations, etc.; 6 sonatas for 2 pfs.; choral works, etc.

Voice-Leading, an Amer. trans. of **Stimmführung.**

Voices, the parts in a polyphonic comp., even those for instruments.

747

Voicing, the prod. of particular qualities of tone by mechanical means in org. construction, and more partic. the control of the tone of a whole range of pipes governed by a single stop in such a way that the tone-colour is exactly the same throughout.

Voix céleste (Fr. = heavenly voice), an 8-ft. org. stop with 2 pipes to each note, one tuned slightly sharper than the other, so that they prod. a quivering effect.

Volata (It. lit. flight), a run or other rapid passage.

Volbach, Fritz (b. Wippelfürth, Rhineland, 17. XII. 1861; d. Wiesbaden, 30. XI. 1940), Ger. cond. and comp. Studied at the Cologne Cons. He joined the staff of the Royal Inst. of Church Mus. in Berlin, 1886, became mus. director at Mainz in 1892 and prof. of mus. at Tübingen Univ. in 1907, moving to that of Münster in 1919.

Works incl. opera *Die Kunst zu lieben*: ballads for male voices and orch. *Der Troubadour, Am Siegfrieds-Brunnen, König Laurins Rosengarten*; *Raffael* for chorus, orch. and org., *Hymne an Maria* (Dante) for chorus, solo instruments and org.; symph. in B min., symph. poems *Es waren zwei Königskinder* and *Alt Heidelberg*; *Easter* for org. and orch.; pf. 5tet for wind and pf.; song cycle *Vom Pagen und der Königstochter* (Geibel), etc.

Volkert, Franz (b. Vienna 12. II. 1767; d. Vienna, 22. III. 1845), Aus. organist, cond. and comp. Settled in Vienna as organist in 1806 and became cond. at the Theater an der Wien.

Works incl. *c.* 150 mus. pieces for the stage (farces, melodramas, pantomimes, etc.); graduals and other church mus.; pf. trios; variations for pf.; songs, etc.

Volkmann, (Friedrich) Robert (b. Lommatzsch, Saxony, 6. IV. 1815; d. Budapest, 29. X. 1883), Ger. comp. Pupil of his father. a schoolmaster and cantor, and of another local musician for string instruments. In 1836 he went to Leipzig for further study, was a private mus. tutor in Prague, 1839–1841, lived and taught at Budapest in 1841–1854 and in Vienna in 1854–78, when he became prof. of comp. at the Nat. Mus. Acad. in Budapest.

Works incl. incid. mus. for Shakespeare's *Richard III*; 2 Masses for male voices; 2 symphs., 2 serenades, Festival Overture for orch.; *Concertstück* for pf. and orch.; cello concerto, serenade for cello and strings; 6 string 4tets, 2 pf. trios and other chamber mus.; 2 sonatinas for vln. and pf., vln. and pf. pieces, cello and pf. pieces; sonata and *c.* 20 other op. nos. for pf.; several pf. duet works; 9 op. nos. of songs, etc.

Volkonsky, Andrey (b. Geneva, 14. II. 1933), Rus. comp. Studied pf. with Lipatti and comp. with N. Boulanger in Paris, and

in 1948 went to Moscow to study with Shaporin. He is a modernist among Rus. comps., using a form of the 12-note system.

Works incl. cantata *The Image of the World*; *The Lament of Shaza* for soprano and chamber orch.; concerto for orch.; pf. 5tet.; vla. sonata, etc.

Volkslied (Ger. = Folksong). Although Ger. possesses a treasury of old folksongs, many of which became hymns for the Lutheran church, the term V. no longer exclusively or even principally designates them: what Gers. now mean by V. is a type of popular song, such as Silcher's *Loreley*, the comps. of which are known (which is not the case with genuine folksongs), and which have passed into general currency.

Volkstümlich (Ger. adj. from *Volkstum* = folk matters, folklore), a word used in Ger. to describe popular mus. that has become or is likely to become part of the nation's mus. heritage, without actually belonging to folk mus.

Vollerthun, Georg (b. Fürstenau nr. Danzig, 29. IX. 1876; d. Straussberg, 15. IX. 1945), Ger. cond. and comp. Pupil of Tappert, Gernsheim and others. He cond. at var. towns, lived in Paris in 1908–10 and in 1933 became prof. at the Hochschule für Musik in Berlin.

Works incl. operas *Veeda, Islandsaga* and *Der Freikorporal* (after Gustav Freytag); songs and duets, etc.

Volo di Notte (*Night Flight*), opera in 1 act by Dallapiccola (lib. by the comp., after St.-Exupéry), prod. Florence, 18. V. 1940.

Volta (It. = time, turn, jump). The word is used in such mus. directions as *prima volta* (first time), *seconda volta* (second time), *ancora una volta* (once again). It is also the name of an old dance incl. a characteristic jump. *See* **Lavolta.**

Voltaire, François Marie Arouet de (1694–1778), Fr. man of letters, philosopher and dramatist. *See* **Alzira** (*Verdi*), **Castelnuovo-Tedesco** (*Candide*), **Fée Urgèle** (*Duni*), **Knipper** (*Candide*), **Lefèbvre** (*Zaïre*), **Olympie** (Spontini), **Semiramide** (Rossini), **Sémiramis** (Catel), **Stuntz** (*Heinrich IV*), **Tancredi** (Rossini), **Woelfl** (*Alzire*).

Volte (Fr. for the It. dance). *See* **Lavolta.**

Volti subito. *See* **V.S.**

Volumier, Jean Baptiste (b. ? Spain, *c.* 1670; d. Dresden, 7. X. 1728), Flem. violinist, dulcimer player and comp. Educ. at the Fr. court and in 1692 transferred to that of Prus. in Berlin. where he became leader of the orch, and director of the dance mus. In 1709 he went to Dresden as mus. director to the Saxon court.

Works incl. ballets, divertissements, dances, etc.

Voluntary, an org. piece intended for use in church, but not part of the service. In modern practice it is used only at the beginning and esp. at the end of a service, in the latter case often serving to play the congregation out.

Vom Blatt (lesen, spielen) (Ger. lit. [to read, play] from the leaf or sheet = at sight), sight-reading.

Vomáčka, Boleslav (b. Mladá Boleslav, 28. VI. 1887; d. Prague, 1. III. 1965), Cz. critic and comp. Studied law, and mus. with Novák at the Prague Cons. He was a solicitor until 1919, when he entered the Ministry of Social Welfare. He also worked as critic with 2 newspapers and was ed. of the monthly *Listy Hudební Matice.*

Works incl. opera *The Waterman*; symph., symph. poem *Mládí* (*Youth*) and chaconne for orch.; vln. and pf. sonata; sonata and cycle *The Quest* for pf.; song cycle; partsongs, etc.

Von Heute auf Morgen (*From today until tomorrow*), opera in 1 act by Schönberg (lib. by 'Max Blonda' = the comp.'s wife Gertrud), prod. Frankfurt, 1. II. 1930.

Vondel, Joost van den (1587–1679), Dutch poet and dramatist. *See* **Diepenbrock, Mengelberg (R.), Roos** (*Joseph at Dothan*), **Zweers** (*Gysbrecht van Amstel*).

Voormolen, Alexander (b. Rotterdam, 3. III. 1895), Dutch critic and comp. Studied in Paris and was much influenced by Ravel. On his return home he became mus. critic to the *Nieuwe Rotterdamsche Courant.*

Works incl. melodrama *Beatrijs*; ballets *Baron Hop, Le Roi Grenouille* and *Diana*; sinfonietta; variations for vln. and orch., concerto for 2 obs. and orch., concerto for 2 harpsichords and strings; chamber mus., etc.

Vopelius, Gottfried (b. Herwigsdorf nr. Zittau, 28. I. 1635; d. Leipzig, 3. II. 1715), Ger. comp. App. cantor of St. Nicholas's Church, Leipzig, 1677. Compiled a book of chorales (1682) and harmonized many, besides writing tunes for some.

Vorhalt (Ger.) = Suspension.

Voříšek (Worzischek), Jan Hugo (b. Vamberk, 11. V. 1791; d. Vienna, 19. XI. 1825), Boh. pianist and comp. Pupil of his father, a schoolmaster, and later of Tomašek. He went to Vienna in 1813 and when Hummel left he recommended V. as pf. teacher to all his pupils. He became pianist and cond. to the Phil. Society and in 1823 court organist.

Works incl. church mus.; symph.; duet for cello and pf.; divertissement for 2 pfs.; pf. music, etc.

Vörösmarty, Mihály (1800–55), Hung. poet and dramatist. *See* **Weiner** (*Csongor and Tünde*).

Vorschlag. *See* **Ornaments.**

Vorspiel (Ger. lit. foreplay) = Prelude.

Vortrag (Ger.) = Delivery, performance, interpretation.

Vortragsbezeichnungen or **Vortragszeichen** } Ger., indications of perf., directions, expression marks.

Vos, Laurent de. *See* **Voz.**

Vox angelica or **Vox coelestis** } an 8-ft. open metal org. stop of very delicate tone. The term is also sometimes used for the Voix céleste stop where one of the 2 sets of pipes is tuned slightly flat instead of sharp.

Vox humana, an 8-ft. reed org. stop prod. an imitation of the human voice.

Voyevoda, opera by Tchaikovsky (lib. by comp. and Alexander Nikolaievich Ostrovsky, based on a play by the latter), prod. Moscow, 11. II. 1869.

Voz (or Vos), Laurent de (b. Antwerp, 1533; d. Cambrai, I. 1580), Flem. comp. Brother of the painter Martin de Vos. Worked at Antwerp Cathedral and was app. mus. director and choirmaster at Cambrai Cathedral by the archbishop Louis de Berlaymont. When the latter's place was usurped by Inchy, V. comp. a motet compiled from words from the Psalms in such a way as to attack the latter, who had him hanged without a trial.

Works incl. motets, *chansons*, etc.

Vrchlický, Jaroslav (1853–1912), Cz. poet and playwright. *See* **Fibich** (*Night at Karlstein*), **Foerster (J. B.)** (*Samson*), **St. Ludmilla** (Dvořák).

Other mus. works based on his writings are: Dvořák, opera *Armida*; Fibich, operatic trilogy *Hippodamia* and melodramas *Haakon* and *Queen Emma*; Foerster (J. B.), melodramas *The Three Riders* and *The Legend of St. Julia*; Janáček, choral work *Amarus*; Novák, opera *A Night at Karlstein.*

Vreuls, Victor (b. Verviers, 4. II. 1876; d. Brussels, 26. VII. 1944), Belg. cond., violist and comp. Studied at the Verviers school of mus. and the Liège Cons., later with d'Indy in Paris. He became prof. of vla. and harmony at the Schola Cantorum there and in 1906 director of the Luxembourg Cons.

Works incl. operas *Olivier le simple* and *Un Songe d'une nuit d'été* (after Shakespeare); symph. with solo vln., 3 symph. poems, overture and prelude for orch.; cantata and *Triptyche* for chorus; songs and instrumental pieces with orch.; string 4tet; pf. 4tet, 2 pf. trios; 2 sonatas for vln. and pf., sonata and *Poème* for cello and pf.; songs, etc.

Vrieslander, Otto (b. Münster, 18. VII. 1880; d. Tegna, 16. XII. 1950), Ger. musicologist and comp. Studied at the Cologne Cons. Settled at Munich in 1906 and went to live at Locarno in Switz. in 1920. As a musicologist he was a pupil of Schenker, whose unfinished *Harmonielehre* he completed. He also wrote on C. P. E. Bach and ed. some of his works.

Works incl. songs from *Des Knaben Wunderhorn*, on Giraud's *Pierrot lunaire* and to words by Goethe, Keller, Theodor Storm, etc.

Vuataz, Roger (b. Geneva, 4. I. 1898), Swiss comp. Studied at the Geneva Cons., Barblan and Jaques-Dalcroze being among his masters. In 1918 he became organist to the Fr. Protestant church there. He was cond. of several choirs and prof. at the Acad. de Musique. In 1928–34 he was also mus. critic to the *Journal de Genève* and mus. director of Radio Geneva from 1942 to 1963.

Works incl. stage works *Mil-six-cent-deux* and *Le Mystère d'Abraham*; oratorio *Abraham*; motets, psalms; *Le Rhône* for tenor and chorus, *La Flûte de roseau* for chorus; *Deux pièces brèves* and *Petit Concert* for orch.; *Suite sur deux thèmes populaires anciens* for 15 instruments, *Géométrie* and *Musique* for 5 instruments and other chamber mus.; org. and pf. works, etc.

Vučković, Vojislav (b. Pirot, Serbia, 18. X. 1910; d. Belgrade, 25. XII. 1942), Yugoslav cond., musicologist and comp. Studied in Prague and became prof. and cond. at Belgrade. He was murdered by the Nazi police.

Works inc. several choral comps.; 2 symphs., 3 symph. poems; string 4tet; 2 songs for soprano and wind instruments, etc.

Vuert, Giaches. *See* Wert.

Vuillaume, Jean Baptiste (b. Mirecourt, Vosges, 7. X. 1798; d. Paris, 19. II. 1875), Fr. vln. maker. Estab. independently in Paris, 1828.

Vuillermoz, Émile (b. Lyons, 23. V. 1878; d. Paris, 2. III. 1960), Fr. mus. critic and author. Studied law and literature at Lyons Univ. and mus. at the Paris Cons., where Fauré was among his masters. He gave up comp. to become critic to the *Mercure musical* and from 1911 ed. the journal of the Société Musicale Indépendante. Among his books are studies of

modern mus., 50 years of Fr. mus. and Ravel.

Vukdragović, Mihailo (b. Okučani, Serbia, 8. IX. 1900), Yugoslav cond. and comp. Studied in Belgrade and Prague, returning to the former, where he has held var. important posts: director of the Stankovič Mus. School and mus. director of Radio Belgrade, prof. at Belgrade Acad. of Mus., etc.

Works incl, incid. and film mus.; cantata and choral songs; *Symph. Meditations* and symph. poem *The Road to Victory;* 2 string 4tets; songs, etc.

Vulpius, Melchior (b. Wasungen, Henneberg, *c.* 1570; d. Weimar, 7. VIII. 1615), Ger. comp. He became cantor at Weimar in 1602 and remained there to his death. He harmonized many hymn tunes not his own and wrote a treatise, *Musicae compendium*. Goethe's wife was prob. a descendant of his.

Works incl. *Sacrae cantiones* for 5–8 voices, canticles, hymns for 4–5 voices and other sacred mus.; Passion oratorio according to St. Matthew, etc.

Vuota (It. fem. adj. = void, empty), a direction to string players to play a note or notes on an open string. Also the equivalent of G.P. = general pause.

Vycpálek, Ladislav (b. Vršovice nr. Prague, 23. II. 1882), Cz. comp. Studied philosophy at Prague Univ., took a doctor's degree in it, and became secretary to the Univ. library. He also studied comp. with Novák at the Cons.

Works incl. cantata *The Last Things of Man*; song-cycles *Quiet Reconcilement, Visions, In God's Hands*, Morav. ballads and folksongs; pf. pieces; chamber mus.; choruses for mixed and male voices, etc.

Vyšehrad (Smetana). *See* Má Vlast.

Vyvyan, Jennifer (b. Broadstairs, 13. III. 1925), Eng. soprano. Studied at R.A.M. and then with F. Carpi in Switz., making her début with the English Opera Group in 1947. She created the roles of Penelope Rich in *Gloriana*, the Governess in *The Turn of the Screw* and Tytania in *A Midsummer Night's Dream*, all by Britten.

W

Wächter, Eberhard (b. Vienna, 8. VII. 1929), Aus. baritone. Studied in Vienna, making his début there in 1953, and a year later became a member of the Vienna State Opera. He is also well known as a *Lieder*-singer.

Wächterlieder (Ger. = watchmen's songs), songs formerly used in Ger. by night watchmen in the streets to announce the hours and by fire-watchers on church towers to proclaim festival days, etc. They were often folksongs and some have passed into currency as hymns for the Lutheran church.

Wacław of Szamotuły. *See* **Szamotulczyk.**

Waddell, Helen (b. 1889), Ir. poet and playwright. *See* **Barber** (choruses).

Waelrant, Hubert (b. Tongerloo, N. Brabant, *c.* 1517; d. Antwerp, 19. XI. 1595), Flem. comp. He (?) went to study with Willaert at Venice, and by 1544 was a singer at Notre-Dame, Antwerp, where 3 years later he estab. a school of mus. In *c.* 1554-8 he was assoc. with J. de Laet as mus. pub.

Works incl. motets, madrigals, *chansons*. etc.

Waffenschmied (von Worms), Der (*The Armourer* [*of Worms*]), opera by Lortzing (lib. by comp., based on Friedrich Julius Wilhelm Ziegler's comedy *Liebhaber und Nebenbuhler in einer Person*), prod. Vienna, Theater an der Wien, 31. V. 1846. Weigl's opera *Il rivale di se stesso* (*His Own Rival*), prod. Milan 1808, was based on the same play.

Wagenaar, Bernard (b. Arnhem, 18. VII. 1894), Dutch-Amer. comp. Studied with his father, Johan W., and at the Utrecht Cons. and learnt the vln. and keyboard instruments. In 1921 he settled in N.Y. and joined the N.Y. Phil. Orch. and from 1927 taught at the Juilliard Graduate School there.

Works incl. chamber opera *Pieces of Eight*; 4 symphs., sinfonietta, divertimento, *Feuilleton*, etc. for orch.; vln. concerto, triple concerto for fl., harp and cello; 3 string 4tets, concertino for 8 instruments; vln. and pf. sonata, sonatina for cello; 3 Chin. songs for voice, fl., harp and pf.; pf. sonata; Eclogue for org.; songs, incl. settings of Edna St. Vincent Millay, etc.

Wagenaar, Johan (b. Utrecht, 1. XI. 1862; d. The Hague, 17. VI. 1941), Dutch comp., father of prec. Studied with Richard Hol and with Herzogenberg in Berlin. App. organist at Utrecht Cathedral in 1888 and director of the Cons. there in 1904, also cond. of a choral society. In 1919 he became director of the Royal Cons. at The Hague, retiring in 1937 in favour of S. Dresden.

Works incl. operas *The Doge of Venice*, *The Cid* (after Corneille) and *Jupiter amans*; overtures to Shakespeare's *Taming of the Shrew*, Goldoni's *Philosophical Princess*, Kleist's *Amphitryon* and Rostand's *Cyrano de Bergerac*, overture *Saul and David*, funeral march and waltz suite for orch.; fantasy on Dutch folksongs for male chorus and orch., female choruses with pf.; vln. and pf. pieces; pf. pieces; songs, etc.

Wagenseil, Georg Christoph (b. Vienna, 15. I. 1715; d. Vienna, 1. III. 1777), Aus. comp. Studied in Vienna with Fux and others and in 1735, on that master's recommendation, received a court scholarship, becoming court comp. in 1739. In 1741-1750 he was organist to the dowager empress and he was app. mus. master to the Empress Maria Theresa and her daughters. Mozart at the age of 6 played one of W.'s concertos at court and W. turned pages for him.

Works incl. operas *Ariodante*, *Le cacciatrici* and *c.* 10 others; oratorios *La redenzione* and *Gioas, rè di Giuda*; nearly 20 Masses, Requiem, motets and other church mus.; symphs.; pf. concertos; divertimenti for pf. solo, etc.

Wagenseil, Johann Christoph (b. Nuremberg, 26. XI. 1633; d. Altdorf, 9. X. 1708), Ger. hist. and librarian. Wrote a book on the art of the Meistersinger, pub. in 1697, which served Wagner as a source for *The Mastersingers*.

Waghalter, Ignaz (b. Warsaw, 15. III. 1882; d. N.Y., 7. IV. 1949), Pol.-Ger. cond. and comp. Pupil of Gernsheim. He cond. opera in Berlin and Essen, 1907-1923, and in 1925 cond. the State Symph. Orch. in N.Y., returning to Berlin later and going to Prague in 1933. He settled in N.Y. in 1938.

Works incl. operas *Der Teufelsweg*, *Mandragola* (after Machiavelli), *Jugend*, *Der späte Gast* and *Sataniel*, operettas; vln. concerto; string 4tet; vln. and pf. sonata, etc.

Wagner, Johanna (b. Seelze, nr. Hanover, 13. X. 1826; d. Würzburg, 16. X. 1894), Ger. soprano, adopted daughter of Albert W. (1799-1874), brother of Richard W., who engaged her for the Royal Opera at Dresden, where she was the 1st Elisabeth in his *Tannhäuser* in 1845. In 1847 she went to Paris to study with García. In 1859 she married an official named Jachmann.

Wagner, Peter (Josef) (b. Kürenz nr. Trèves, 19. VIII. 1865; d. Fribourg, Switz., 17. X. 1931), Ger. musicologist. Studied at Strasbourg Univ. and later in Berlin. In 1897 he became prof. at the

Univ. of Fribourg, where he founded a Gregorian coll. in 1901. His works incl. a hist. of the Mass and studies of medieval and Gregorian mus.

Wagner-Régeny, Rudolf (b. Szasz-Régen, 28. VIII. 1903; d. Berlin, 18. IX. 1969), Hung. comp. of Ger. descent. Studied at Leipzig and Berlin.

Works incl. operas *Der Günstling* (on Büchner's version of Victor Hugo's *Marie Tudor*), *Der nackte König* (on Andersen's *The Emperor's New Clothes*), *Moschopulos*, *Sganarelle* (after Molière), *Esau und Jakob*, *La Sainte Courtisane*, *Die Bürger von Calais* (Georg Kaiser) and *Das Bergwerk zu Falun* (Hofmannsthal); ballet *Der zerbrochene Krug* (after Kleist's comedy), etc.

Wagner, (Wilhelm) Richard (b. Leipzig, 22. V. 1813; d. Venice, 13. II. 1883), Ger. comp. and author. Son of a clerk to the city police, who d. 6 months after W.'s birth. His mother removed to Dresden and married the actor and painter Ludwig Geyer in 1815, who in turn d. in 1821. W. learnt the pf. but tried to read vocal scores of operas instead of practising and also acquired knowledge of opera from 2 elder sisters who were both stage singers. He wrote poems and a tragedy at the age of about 13 and at 14 went to school at Leipzig, where the family had returned. There he heard Beethoven's works and tried to imitate them in comps. of his own. In 1830 Dorn perf. an overture of his in the theatre, but it was received with scorn as a very crude work. He then studied harmony and counterpoint with Weinlig at St. Thomas's School and entered the univ. in 1831. At 19 he began an opera, *Die Hochzeit*, but on the advice of his sister abandoned it for *Die Feen*. The libs., as always later on, were written by himself.

He became chorus master at the theatre of Würzburg in 1833 and cond. of a summer theatre at Lauchstädt, the co. of which was at Magdeburg in winter, where he went with it. Minna Planer (1809–66) was there as an actress, and he married her on 24. XI. 1836, at Königsberg, where she had a new engagement. The Magdeburg company had been dissolved soon after a disastrous prod. of W.'s 3rd opera, *Das Liebesverbot*, on 29. III. 1836. The Königsberg theatre also went into liquidation just after W. had been app. cond. but in the summer of 1837 he became cond. at Riga. In I. 1839 his post was given to Dorn and he decided to go to Paris by sea. A very stormy voyage took them as far as the coast of Norw. and then to Eng., and they did not reach Paris until September, in desperate straits. They spent nearly all the time there until IV. 1842 in wretched poverty, but W., in such time as he could spare from hack-work, had managed to finish both *Rienzi* and *The Flying Dutch-*

man, the former of which had been accepted by Dresden and was prod. there on 20. X. 1842, the latter work following on 2. I. 1843, W. being app. 2nd cond. at the court opera. *Tannhäuser* was finished in IV. 1845 and prod. on 19. X.

When the Fr. Revolution of 1848 spread its influence across Eur., W. showed sympathy with liberal ideas, and when the revolt at Dresden failed in V. 1849 he had to fly and a warrant for his arrest was issued, should he be found in Saxony. Not deeming the rest of Ger. safe, he went to Switz. There, at Zürich, he worked on the lib. and mus. for the *Nibelung's Ring* cycle, which was interrupted by *Tristan and Isolde*, written under the influence of Mathilde Wesendonk, the wife of a friend and benefactor with whom he was more and more deeply in love. In 1858 Minna created a scene and Mathilde decided to stay with her husband, W. going to Venice and later to Lucerne, where *Tristan* was finished in VIII. 1859. In 1860 a revised version of *Tannhäuser*, with a ballet, was commissioned by the Paris Opéra, and W. complied so far as his artistic conscience would let him, which was not enough for the patrons, who saw to it that after the prod. on 13. III. 1861 the work should fail disastrously. W. next went to Vienna, where he heard *Lohengrin* for the 1st time, though it had been prod. by Liszt at Weimar in 1850.

In 1862 he settled at Biebrich on the Rhine to work on *The Mastersingers*, but was in Vienna again by the end of the year, staying there until III. 1864, when he was pursued by his creditors and threatened with imprisonment. At the critical moment he was invited by Ludwig II of Bavar. to join his court at Munich as friend and artistic adviser, and he ensured that Hans von Bülow was app. cond. Bülow's wife, Cosima (1837–1930), was Liszt's daughter, and she and W. soon fell deeply in love. This created a scandal which was fully exploited by his enemies, the courtiers and officials who feared his influence on the youthful and idealistic king, and soon after the prod. of *Tristan*, 10. VI. 1865, W. was obliged to go into exile once more. He chose Triebschen on the lake of Lucerne in Switz., where Cosima joined him in III. 1866. Bülow divorced her in 1870 and on 25. VIII she married W., whose 1st wife had d. 25. I. 1866.

After the prod. of *The Mastersingers*, 21. VI. 1868, at Munich, W. quietly continued work on the *Ring* cycle, dropped so many years before, and planned a festival theatre to be erected by subscription at Bayreuth in Bavaria. The family took a house there in 1874; rehearsals began the following year, and the four works were prod. on 13–17. VIII. 1876. *Parsifal* followed, after a slow process of comp. much interrupted by illness and by holidays in It. for his health, on 26. VII. 1882. W. left for Venice in September, greatly exhausted and subject to frequent heart attacks, from one of which he d.

Works incl. operas *Die Hochzeit* (unfinished), *Die Feen*, *Das Liebesverbot*, *Rienzi*, *Der fliegende Holländer*, *Tannhäuser*, *Lohengrin*, *Tristan und Isolde*, *Die Meistersinger von Nürnberg*, *Der Ring des Nibelungen* (comprising *Das Rheingold*, *Die Walküre*, *Siegfried* and *Götterdämmerung*), *Parsifal*; symph., 9 concert overtures (2 unpub.), incl. *Eine Faust Ouvertüre* (after Goethe), 3 marches for orch., *Siegfried Idyll* for small orch.; several choral works; a number of songs, incl. 7 from Goethe's *Faust*, 5 poems by Mathilde Wesendonk and 6 settings of Fr. poems; a sonata and some smaller pf. works; string 4tet (unpub.), etc.

For settings of his libs. by other comps. *see* Bella (*Velaned the Smith*), Bianca und Giuseppe (Kittl), Mihalovich (*Wieland der Schmied*), Vaisseau-fantôme (Dietsch).

Wagner, (Helferich) Siegfried (Richard) (b. Triebschen, Switz., 6. VI. 1869; d. Bayreuth, 4. VIII. 1930), Ger. cond. and comp., son of prec. Although intended for an architect, he studied mus. with Humperdinck and Kneise, and gained much experience by assisting at the Wagner festival perfs. at Bayreuth, some of which he cond. after 1896. When his mother, Cosima W., became too old to manage the affairs of the theatre, he took its direction in hand in 1909.

Works incl. operas *Der Bärenhäuter*, *Herzog Wildfang*, *Der Kobold*, *Bruder Lustig*, *Sternengebot*, *Banadietrich*, *An allem ist Hütchen schuld*, *Schwarzschwanenreich*, *Sonnenflammen*, *Der Schmied von Marienburg*, *Der Friedensengel*, *Der Heidenkönig* and 3 others not perf. or pub.; symph, poem *Sehnsucht*; vln. concerto, fl. concerto, etc.

Wagner, Wieland (Adolf Gottfried) (b. Bayreuth, 5. I. 1917; d. Munich, 17. X. 1966), Ger. producer, son of prec. Studied painting in Munich, also mus. and stage prod. He designed sets for *Parsifal* at Bayreuth in 1937. His first prods. were at Nuremberg in 1942–4. From the reopening of the Bayreuth theatre in 1951 till his death he was in charge of prod. He was also invited to prod. operas in other Eur. cities.

Wagner, Wolfgang (Manfred Martin) (b. Bayreuth, 30. VIII. 1919), Ger. prod., brother of prec. Studied prod. at the Berlin Staatsoper, where he prod. one of his father's operas in 1944. He was assoc. with his brother at Bayreuth from 1951 and himself prod. operas there from 1953.

Wagner Tubas, brass wind instruments devised by Wagner for his *Ring des Nibelungen*, which requires 5, but only 3 different kinds: 2 tenor T.s not unlike the Euphonium, but with funnel-shaped mouthpieces, with the following compass:

2 bass T.s:

and a double bass T. an 8ve lower still.

Wailly, (Louis Auguste) Paul (Warnier) de (b. Amiens, 16. V. 1854; d. Paris, 18. VI. 1933), Fr. comp. He studied law, but became a pupil of Franck for comp. Works incl. dramatic oratorio *L'Apôtre*; *Hylas*, *idylle antique* for voices and orch.; church mus.; 3 symphs.; pf. 5tet, 8tet and other chamber mus.; instrumental sonatas; 26 harmonium pieces; songs; etc.

Waisenhaus, Das (*The Orphanage*), opera by Weigl (lib.? by Georg Friedrich Treitschke), prod. Vienna, Kärntnertortheater, 4. X. 1808.

Wait, an obs. instrument of the ob. type, similar to the Shawm, used in Eng. by the Christmas Waits and, in the 13th cent., by the keepers of the City of London gates and other town gates for the purpose of signalling 'All's well', etc.

Waits, orig. the keepers of town gates, in the 15th–16th cents. salaried bands employed to play at var. functions, afterwards amateur singers and players perf. outside the houses of the more substantial citizens for rewards in money and refreshment at Christmas-tide; also the name of pieces sung and played on these occasions.

Wakefield, (Augusta) Mary (b. Sedgwick nr. Kendal, 19. VIII. 1853; d. Grange-over-Sands, Lancs., 16. IX. 1910), Eng. amateur contralto, pianist and comp. In 1885 she started the 1st competitive festival at her home at Sedgwick, which was later transferred to Kendal and became the Westmorland Mus. Festival.

Wald Flute, a 4-ft. and 8-ft. org. stop similar to the Claribel, but with the mouths of the pipes inverted.

Waldhorn (Ger. = forest horn), the Ger. name for the horn without valves, prod. only the natural harmonics (It. *corno da caccia*).

Waldmädchen, Das (*The Woodland Maid*), opera by Weber (lib. by Carl Franz von Steinsberg), prod. Freiberg, Saxony, 23. XI. 1800. The 1st version of *Silvana*.

Waldmann, Maria (b. Vienna, 1844; d.

Ferrara, 6. XI. 1920), Aus. mezzo-soprano. The 1st Amneris in the Milan prod. of Verdi's *Aida* and the mezzo-soprano in the 1st perf. of his Requiem. She married Duke Galeazzo Massari of Ferrara and retired from the stage.

Waldstein, Ferdinand (Ernst Joseph Gabriel), Count (b. Vienna, 24. III. 1762; d. Vienna, 26. V. 1823), Boh. mus. amateur. Patron of Beethoven, whom he met in the early days at Bonn and knew later in Vienna.

'Waldstein' Sonata, Beethoven's pf. sonata in C maj., Op. 53, comp. in 1804, so called (not by Beethoven) because it is ded. to the above.

Waldteufel (actually Lévy), **(Charles) Émile** (b. Strasbourg, 9. XII. 1837; d. Paris, 12. II. 1915), Fr. (Alsat.) pianist and comp. Studied at the Paris Cons. He joined a pf. factory and was later app. pianist to the Empress Eugénie. He had a great success as a comp. of waltzes.

Works incl. many hundreds of waltzes and other dances, incl. a waltz on Chabrier's *España.*

Waley, Simon (Waley) (b. London, 23. VIII. 1827; d. London, 30. XII. 1875), Eng. pianist and comp. Studied with Moscheles, Sterndale Bennett and others and began to comp. as a boy. He often perf. in public, but was also a member of the Stock Exchange.

Works incl. Psalms cxvii and cxviii for the synagogue; pf. concerto; 2 pf. trios; many studies and pieces for pf.; pf. duets; songs and duets, etc.

Walker, Ernest (b. Bombay, 15. VII. 1870; d. Oxford, 21. II. 1949), Eng. pianist, teacher, musicologist and comp. Educ. at Balliol Coll., Oxford, where he took the D.Mus. in 1898 and remained as teacher at the univ., examiner and, in 1901–25, mus. director at Balliol. His books incl. *A History of Music in England.*

Works incl. incid. mus. to Euripides' *Rhesus; Stabat Mater, Ode to a Nightingale* (Keats) for solo voice, chorus and orch., *Hymn to Dionysus* (Euripides) and *Neptune's Empire* (Campion) for chorus and orch.; concert overture in F min., *Fantasy on a Norfolk Folksong* for orch.; fantasy for string 4tet, pf. 5tet, 5tet for horn and strings, 2 pf. 4tets, pf. trio; variations for pf. (left hand), clar. and string trio; variations on a theme by Joachim for vln. and pf., variations for vla. and pf., cello and pf. sonata; waltzes for 2 pfs.; songs from *England's Helicon* for vocal 4tet and pf.; pf. pieces; songs, etc.

Walker, Frank (b. Gosport, Hants., 10. VI. 1907; d. Tring, 4. III. 1962), Eng. writer on mus. Educ. at Portsmouth Grammar School, engaged in an electrotechnical career and during World War II was attached to the Royal Corps of Signals

in It. His researches there resulted in his 2nd book, *The Man Verdi,* the 1st being a biog. of Hugo Wolf.

Walküre, Die (*The Valkyrie,* Wagner). *See* **Ring des Nibelungen.**

Wallace, Lewis (1827–1905), Amer. general, politician and novelist. *See* **Kelley** (*Ben Hur*).

Wallace, (William) Vincent (b. Waterford, 11. III. 1812; d. Château de Bagen nr. Vieuzos, Hautes-Pyrénées, 12. X. 1865), Ir. comp. Pupil of his father, a bandmaster and bassoon player, who moved to Dublin, where W. played the org. and vln. in public as a boy. In 1831 he married Isabella Kelly, but they separated in 1835 and he lived with the pianist Hélène Stoepel, by whom he had 2 sons. In 1834 he appeared at Dublin with a vln. concerto of his own. Between 1835–45 he was in Australia and elsewhere abroad, but went to London in the latter year and was induced to comp. *Maritana.* After a successful operatic career, incl. a visit to S. Amer. in 1849 and 14 years in Ger., a commission from the Paris Opéra which he was unable to finish owing to failing eyesight, and another visit to S. and N. Amer. in 1850–3, his health broke down and he was ordered to the Pyrenees.

Works incl. operas *Maritana, Matilda of Hungary, Lurline, The Maid of Zürich* (unpub.), *The Amber Witch, Love's Triumph, The Desert Flower, Estrella* (unfinished), operettas *Gulnare* and *Olga;* cantata *Maypole;* vln. concerto; pf. mus., etc.

Wallace, William (b. Greenock, 3. VII. 1860; d. Malmesbury, Wilts., 16. XII. 1940), Scot. ophthalmic surgeon, mus. author and comp. Educ. at Edinburgh and Glasgow Univs. and in Vienna as an eye specialist, began to practise in 1888, but gave up his profession for mus. except during the war of 1914–18. In 1889 he entered the R.A.M. in London for a brief course in comp. and later he became successively secretary and trustee of the Phil. Society. His books incl. *The Threshold of Music, The Musical Faculty, Richard Wagner as he lived* and *Liszt, Wagner and the Princess.*

Works incl. opera *Brassolis;* symph. *Koheleth* for chorus and orch.; symph. *The Creation,* symph. poems *The Passing of Beatrice* (after Dante's *Paradiso*), *Anvil or Hammer* (after Goethe's *Koptisches Lied*), *Sister Helen* (after D. G. Rossetti), *To the New Country, Wallace, A.D. 1305–1905, Villon,* suite *The Lady from the Sea* (after Ibsen), symph. prelude to Aeschylus's *Eumenides,* overture *In Praise of Scottish Poesie, A Scots Fantasy* for orch., 2 suites for small orch.; pf. trio in A maj.; *Spanish Songs* for vocal 4tet; song cycles *Freebooter Songs, Jacobite Songs, Lords of the Sea* and other songs, etc.

Wallek-Walewski, Bolesław (b. Lwów, 1885; d. Cracow, 9. IV. 1944), Pol. cond. and comp. Studied at his home town, at Cracow with Żeleński and Szopski, and with Riemann at Leipzig. On returning to Lwów he became choral and operatic cond. and director of the Cons.

Works incl. operas *Destiny* and *Jontek's Revenge* (a sequel to Moniuszko's *Halka*); oratorio *Apocalypse*; Masses, Requiem, motets, psalms and other church mus.; scherzo *Bawel and Gawel* for orch.; male-voice choruses; folksong arrs., etc.

Wallenstein, 3 symph. poems by d'Indy, Op. 12, after Schiller's dramatic trilogy, comp. 1873–9: 1. *Le Camp de W.*; 2. *Max et Thécla* (1st called *Piccolomini*); 3. *La Mort de W.* 1st complete perf. Paris, 26. II. 1888.

Wallenstein, Alfred (b. Chicago, 7. X. 1898), Amer. cond. and cellist. Of Ger. parentage, he studied medicine at Leipzig Univ., and also the cello with J. Klengel (1920–1). Returning to the U.S.A. he became 1st cello with the Chicago Symph. Orch. (1922–9) and then with the N.Y. Phil. Orch. until 1936. He made his début as a cond. in 1931 and from 1943 to 1956 was cond. of the Los Angeles Phil. Orch., in 1952 also becoming mus. director of the Hollywood Bowl.

Waller, Edmund (1606–87), Eng. poet and dramatist. *See* **Grabu** (*Maid's Tragedy*).

Walliser, Christoph Thomas (b. Strasbourg, 17. IV. 1568; d. Strasbourg, 26. IV. 1648), Ger. comp. Pupil of Vulpius and others. In 1599 he became a teacher at the Acad. and later mus. director of 2 churches at Strasbourg.

Works incl. incid. mus. for Aristophanes' *The Clouds* and other plays; *Ecclesiodae* containing psalms for 4–6 voices or instruments, *Ecclesiodae novae* incl. Te Deum, litany, etc., for 4–7 voices, Ger. psalms for 5 voices and other church mus.

Wallishauser. *See* **Valesi.**

Wally, La, opera by Catalani (lib. by Luigi Illica, based on Wilhelmine von Hillern's novel *Die Geyer-Wally*), prod. Milan, Teatro alla Scala, 20. I. 1892.

Walmisley, Thomas (Attwood) (b. London, 21. I. 1814; d. Hastings, 17. I. 1856), Eng. organist and comp. Learnt mus. from his father, the glee comp. and teacher, Thomas Forbes W. (1783–1866), and studied with his godfather, Attwood. After 3 years as organist at Croydon, he became organist of Trinity and St. John's Colls., Cambridge, in 1833, where he also devoted himself to the study of mathematics and wrote poetry. In 1836 he became Prof. of Mus., but did not take the Mus.D. degree until 1848.

Works incl. services and anthems; 3 odes for the installation of univ. chancellors; madrigal *Sweete Floweres*; duets for ob. and pf.; organ works; songs, etc.

Walsh, John (b. ?, 1665–6; d. London, 13. III. 1736), Eng. mus. pub. and instrument maker. Founded his pub. house in London *c*. 1690 and in 1692 became instrument maker to the king. Pub. much of Handel's mus.

Walsh, John (b. London, 23. XII. 1709; d. London, 15. I. 1766), son of prec., succeeded his father as mus. pub.

Walsworth, Ivor (b. London, 31. XII. 1909), Eng. comp. He studied at the R.A.M. in London and, after winning the Mendelssohn Scholarship, in Ger., Hung. and Aus. He joined the B.B.C. mus. staff in 1936 and was app. Transcription Mus. Organizer in 1957.

Works incl. 4 symphs.; cello concerto; 2 string 4tets, pf. 4tet, pf. trio, sonatas for pf., vln., fl. and recorder; electronic mus., etc.

Walter (actually **Schlesinger**), **Bruno** (b. Berlin, 15. IX. 1876; d. Beverly Hills, Calif., 17. II. 1962), Ger. cond. and pianist. He studied at the Stern Cons. in Berlin and made his 1st appearance as a cond. at Cologne in 1894. After appts. as an opera cond. at Hamburg, Breslau, Pressburg, Riga, Berlin and Vienna (1901–12) he was director of the Munich Opera from 1913 to 1922. He also cond. the Vienna Singakademie, 1911–12. From 1925 to 1933 he was director of the Städtische Oper, Berlin, and from 1929 to 1933 of the Gewandhaus concerts in Leipzig, in succession to Furtwängler. He 1st appeared in England in 1909 and was the regular cond. of the German seasons at Covent Garden from 1924 to 1931. He was also active during this period as cond. at the Salzburg festival. He was compelled to leave Ger. in 1933 and was artistic director of the Vienna Opera from 1936 to 1938. After the *Anschluss* he emigrated to France in 1938 and to U.S.A. in 1939, where he lived till his death. From 1941 he cond. frequently at the N.Y. Metropolitan Opera, and from 1948 returned to Europe as a guest cond. As a cond. he excelled in the works of Mozart and of Romantic comps., especially Mahler, of whose *Lied von der Erde* and 9th symph. he gave the first perf. As a pianist he accomp. many of the famous singers of his time, incl. Lotte Lehmann and Kathleen Ferrier, and also appeared as soloist in Mozart's concertos. He pub. a study of Mahler, an autobiography (*Theme and Variations*) and 3 vols. of essays.

Walter, Gustav (b. Bilin, 11. II. 1834; d. Vienna, 30. I. 1910), Boh.-Aus. tenor. Studied at the Prague Cons., appeared there and at Brno, and in 1856 made his 1st appearance in Vienna, where he settled.

Walter, Ignaz (b. Radovice, Boh., 31. VIII. 1755; d. Regensburg, 22. II. 1822), Boh. tenor and comp. Pupil of Starzer in Vienna, he made his début as a singer there in 1780, later became mus. director of the Grossman opera co. and (1804) of the opera in Regensburg.

Works incl. *Singspiele Doktor Faust* (after Goethe), *Der Spiegelritter* and others; *Cantata sacra* for the coronation of the Emperor Leopold II; memorial mus. for Schiller, etc.

Walter of Evesham. *See* **Odington.**

Waltershausen, Hermann (Wolfgang Sartorius) von (b. Göttingen, 12. X. 1882; d. Munich, 13. VIII. 1954), Ger. comp. and mus. author. Studied at Strasbourg, lost his right arm and foot in a game and learnt to play the pf. and cond. with the left hand. He further studied at Munich from 1901 and attended Sandberger's lectures at the univ., founded a mus. school in 1917 and in 1920 became prof. at the Munich State Acad. of Mus., being app. director in 1922. His books incl. works on mus. style, opera, modern comps., R. Strauss, etc.

Works incl. operas *Oberst Chabert* (after Balzac), *Pellegrino, Else Klapperzehen, Richardis, Die Rauensteiner Hochzeit, Die Gräfin von Tolosa; Apocalyptic Symph., Hero and Leander, Partita on 3 Hymn-tunes,* comedy overture, *Passion and Resurrection Music* for orch.; *Krippenmusik* for harpsichord and chamber orch.; pf. works; songs, etc.

Walther, Johann (b. Thuringia, 1496; d. Torgau, 25. III. 1570), Ger. bass and comp. He sang in the service of the Elector of Saxony and in 1548 organized and directed the singers of the court chapel at Dresden. In 1554 he retired to Torgau with a pension. He was a friend of Luther and in 1524 went to Wittenberg to assist him in framing the Ger. Protestant Mass.

Works incl. Magnificat, Ger. hymns for 4 voices, sacred songs, some with words by Luther; instrumental pieces, etc.

Walther, Johann Gottfried (b. Erfurt, 18. IX. 1684; d. Weimar, 23. III. 1748), Ger. comp., organist and lexicographer. Pupil of J. B. Bach (*see* Bach, No. 21) at Erfurt, where in 1702 he became organist at St. Thomas's Church. In 1707 he was app. town organist at Weimar, where he was in close touch with J. S. Bach, his kinsman. He pub. a *Musicalisches Lexicon* in 1732.

Works incl. much org. mus., incid. preludes and fugues, variations of chorales, etc.; concerto for harpsichord solo, etc.

Walther, Johann Jakob (b. Witterda nr. Erfurt, *c.* 1650; d. Mainz, 2. XI. 1717), Ger. violinist and comp. In the service of the Elector of Saxony and later that of Mainz. Comp. *Scherzi* for vln. and con-

tinuo and *Hortulus Chelicus* for solo vln. and strings containing realistic effects.

Walther von der Vogelweide. *See* **Vogelweide.**

Walthew, Richard (Henry) (b. London. 4. XI. 1872; d. East Preston, Surrey, 14. XI. 1951), Eng. pianist and comp. Studied at the G.S.M. and later at the R.C.M. in London, Parry being his comp. master at the latter. He became much interested in cond. amateur mus. societies and esp. in the South Place Concerts held on Sunday evenings in the City of London, where the finest chamber mus. could be heard free (with a collection) and where he often appeared as pianist.

Works incl. operettas *The Enchanted island* and *The Gardeners*; cantatas *Ode to a Nightingale* (Keats), *The Pied Piper* (Browning) and others; variations in B maj. and overture to Erckmann-Chatrian's *Friend Fritz* for orch.; pf. concerto, *Caprice-Impromptu* for vln. and orch.; 3 string 4tets, pf. trio, trio for vln., clar. and pf., pf. 5tet, pf. 4tet, 5tet for clar. and strings, *5 Diversions* and *Prelude, Sarabande and Fugue* for string trio and other chamber mus.; sonata and serenade-sonata for vln. and pf., cello and pf. sonata: songs, vocal duets and 4tets; part-songs, etc.

Walton, Izaak (1593–1683), Eng. author. *See* **Rawsthorne** (*Creel*).

Walton, William (Turner) (b. Oldham, Lancs., 29. III. 1902), Eng. comp. Showed great precocity of talent at home and was sent to Christ Church Cathedral, Oxford, as a choir-boy, later becoming an undergraduate at Christ Church. He had some comp. lessons from Hugh Allen, but after the age of 16 was self-taught, though he later received some advice from Busoni and others. In 1923 he appeared for the 1st time at the I.S.C.M. festival, at Salzburg, where his 1st string 4tet was perf. He settled in London and was in close touch with the literary family Edith, Osbert and Sacheverell Sitwell. In 1934 his symph. in B♭ min. was perf. in London before it was completed and the finale was added the next year. In 1938 he went to U.S.A. to confer with Jascha Heifetz about the solo part of the vln. concerto, which is ded. to him. During the 1939–45 war he wrote mus. for official films. Knighted in 1951.

Works incl. operas *Troilus and Cressida* (after Chaucer) and *The Bear* (after Tchekhov); ballet *The Quest* (after Spenser), incid. mus. for Shakespeare's *Macbeth*; film mus. for *As You Like It, Henry V* and *Hamlet* (Shakespeare), *Major Barbara* (Shaw), *The First of the Few* (incl. *Spitfire* prelude); radio mus. for *Christopher Columbus* (Louis MacNeice); Coronation Te Deum (1953); Gloria; cantatas *Belshazzar's Feast* (Bible, arr. by Osbert Sitwell) and *In Honour of the City* of London (Dunbar); *Where does the uttered music go?* (Masefield) for unaccomp. chorus; overtures *Doctor Syntax* (on Wm. Combe), *Portsmouth Point* (on Rowlandson's drawing) and *Scapino*, *Siesta* for small orch., 2 symphs., Coronation Marches *Crown Imperial* and *Orb and Sceptre*, *Johannesburg Festival Overture*, *Partita*; *Sinfonia concertante* for pf. and orch., vln. concerto, vla. concerto, cello concerto; 2 string 4tets, pf. 4tet, *Façade* (Edith Sitwell) for speaker and chamber mus.; toccata and sonata for vln. and pf.; pf. duets for children; songs, etc.

Waltz (*see also* **Valse à deux temps**), a ballroom dance coming into fashion in the earlier 19th cent. and developing from the Ger. dances (*Deutsche*) and the Aus. *Ländler*, Beethoven, Weber and Schubert being among the 1st comps. to cultivate it seriously, and the elder J. Strauss and Lanner among the 1st ballroom comps. to develop its vogue in Vienna, whence it rapidly spread all over Eur. It is in 3–4 time, varying in pace at different times and in different countries, but usually rather leisurely, and its most typical feature is a bass note on the 1st beat followed by 2 repeated chords of the upper harmony of that bass on the 2nd and 3rd.

Waltz Dream (Straus). *See* **Walzertraum.**

Waltz, Gustavus (b. ?; d. ? London, c. 1753), Ger. bass and minor comp. He is said, on scanty evidence, to have been for a time Handel's cook in London. In 1732 appeared as Polypheme in Handel's *Acis and Galatea* and then, until 1751, in many operas and oratorios.

Walzer (Ger.) = Waltz.

Walzertraum, Ein (*A Waltz Dream*), operetta by Straus (lib. by Felix Dörmann and Leopold Jacobson), prod. Vienna, Carl Theatre, 2. III. 1907.

Wand of Youth, The, 2 orchestral suites by Elgar, Opp. 1a and b, which are all that remains of mus. written for a play in his childhood, 1869, revised and scored in the present form in 1907.

'Wanderer' Fantasy, Schubert's fantasy in C maj. for pf., Op. 15, comp. Nov. 1822. It is so called because it contains material from his song *The Wanderer* written in 1816.

Wang-Wei (699–759), Chin. poet and painter. *See* **Lied von der Erde** (Mahler).

Wanhal. *See* **Vanhal.**

Wannenmacher, Johannes (b. Neuenburg o/Rhine, c. 1485; d. Bern, 1551), Swiss priest and comp. He was app. cantor of the collegiate foundation of St. Vincent at Berne in 1510, but left in 1514 after a dispute and went to Ger. as canon and cantor at Freiburg, Baden. After a brief return to Switz., in 1519, when he went to Sion (Valais), he went back to Freiburg,

but having come under the influence of the Swiss reformer Zwingli, embraced Protestantism in 1530, was tortured and banished, returned to Berne and, finding no employment there, became town clerk at Interlaken.

Works incl. Psalm cxxxvii for 3–6 voices, motets; Ger. sacred and secular songs, etc.

War and Peace, opera by Prokofiev (lib. by Mira Mendelson, based on Tolstoy's novel), perf. in concert, Moscow, 17. X. 1944.

War Requiem, choral work by Britten, Op. 66 (text of the Requiem Mass, together with poems by Wilfred Owen), 1st perf. Coventry Cathedral, 30. V. 1962.

Ward, David (b. Dumbarton, 3. VII. 1922), Scot. bass. Studied at the R.C.M. with C. Carey and then with H. Hotter. After singing with the Sadler's Wells Chorus (1952) he made his début as soloist in 1953. Since 1960 he has sung regularly at Covent Garden, and has also appeared at Bayreuth.

Ward, John (b. Canterbury, IX. 1571; d. ?, 1638), Eng. 16th–17th-cent. comp. He was in the service of Sir Henry Fanshawe, Remembrancer of the Exchequer, at Ware Park, Herts., and in London.

Works incl. services and anthems; madrigals; fantasies for viols, etc.

Warlich, Reinhold von (b. St. Petersburg, 24. V. 1879; d. N.Y., 10. XI. 1939), Ger. baritone. Studied mus. generally at the Hamburg Cons. and singing at Florence and Cologne. Made his 1st appearance at Florence in 1899.

Warlock, Peter. For biog. *see* **Heseltine, Philip.**

Works incl. *3 Dirges by Webster* and other choral works; *An Old Song* and *Serenade* for string orch.; *The Curlew* for tenor, fl., Eng. horn and string 4tet, *Corpus Christi* and *Sorrow's Lullaby* (Beddoes) for soprano, baritone and string 4tet; *Capriol* suite for full or string orch. on dances from Arbeau's *Orchésographie*; c. 90 songs, many on Elizabethan and Jacobean poems, etc.

Warner, H(arry). Waldo (b. Northampton, 4. I. 1874; d. London, 1. VI. 1945), Eng. violist and comp. He went to London with his family in 1880 and entered the G.S.M. in 1888, later became a prof. there, but resigned in order to be able to travel with the London String 4tet, which he had joined as vla. in 1907. He was also principal vla. in 2 of the great London orchs.

Works incl. opera *The Royal Vagrants*; *3 Elfin Dances* and other suites for orch.; string 4tet in C min., 3 fantasy string 4tets, *The Pixy Ring* for string 4tet, rhapsody for vla. and string 4tet, 3 pf. trios; vln. and pf. sonata, vla. and pf. sonata; pieces for vln., vla. and cello with pf.; numerous songs and part-songs, etc.

Warren (actually Warenoff), **Leonard** (b. N.Y., 21. IV. 1911; d. N.Y., 4. III. 1960), Amer. baritone. Studied in N.Y. and Milan, making his début at the N.Y. Metropolitan in 1939. He was esp. well known as a Verdi singer. His death occurred during a perf. of *La forza del destino* at the Metropolitan.

Warton, Joseph (1722–1800), Eng. critic and poet. *See* **Callcott, Crotch.**

Wasielewski, Joseph (Wilhelm) von (b. Gross Leesen nr. Danzig, 17. VI. 1822; d. Sondershausen, 13. XII. 1896), Ger.-Pol. violinist, cond. and writer on mus. Pupil of Mendelssohn and others at Leipzig, then living at Düsseldorf, Bonn, Dresden and Sonderhausen. His books incl. a biog. of Schumann, works on the vln. and its masters, the cello, the hist. of instrumental mus., mus. princes, etc.

Wasps, The, incid. mus. for Aristophanes' comedy by Vaughan Williams, 1st perf. Cambridge, in Gk., by undergraduates, 1919.

Wassermann, Jakob (1873–1934), Ger. novelist and essayist. *See* **Wellesz** (*Prinzessin Girnara*).

Water Carrier, The (Cherubini). *See* **Deux Journées.**

Water Music, a set of instrumental pieces by Handel, 1st perf. London, *c.* 1715, on a boat following the royal barge on the Thames. The mus. is said to have reconciled George I to Handel after the latter's desertion from the court of Hanover, but the story is doubtful.

Water Organ. *See* **Hydraulis.**

Watkin-Mills, Robert (b. Painswick, Glos., 5. III. 1856; d. Toronto, XII. 1930), Eng. baritone. Studied in London and Milan, and made his 1st appearance at the Crystal Palace in London in 1884. He had much success at concerts and festivals, visited the dominions and U.S.A. in 1894 and finally settled at Toronto.

Watson, Thomas (b. London, *c.* 1557; d. London, 1592), Eng. scholar and amateur musician. He pub. in 1590 *The first sett of Italian Madrigalls Englished,* the successor of N. Yonge's *Musica Transalpina* (1588) and with it the foundation of the native Eng. school of madrigalists.

Waverley, overture by Berlioz, Op. 1b, inspired by Walter Scott, 1st perf. Paris, 26. V. 1828.

Webbe, Samuel (b. ?, 1740; d. London, 25. V. 1816), Eng. comp. From 1776 he held posts at var. foreign embassies in London. He was awarded a prize by the Catch Club in 1766 and became its secretary in 1794. He was also librarian of the Glee Club from 1787. Comp. principally glees, catches, etc., also church mus.

Webbe, Samuel (b. London, *c.* 1770; d. Liverpool, 25. XI. 1843), Eng. pianist, organist and comp., son of prec. Pupil of his father. He obtained the Catch Club prize in 1794 and others later. He settled at Liverpool in 1798, returning briefly to London in 1817 to teach jointly with Logier and became organist of the Span. embassy chapel, but he returned to Liverpool, where he held several church organist posts.

Works incl. operatic farce *The Speechless Wife;* motets, glees, songs, etc.

Webber, Amherst (b. Cannes, 25. X. 1867; d. London, 25. VII. 1946), Eng. comp. Studied with Nicodé at Dresden and with Guiraud at the Paris Cons. Later he became a coach at Covent Garden Opera in London and the Metropolitan Opera in N.Y.

Works incl. opera *Fiorella* (lib. by Sardou); symph.; Eng. and Fr. songs, etc.

Weber, Aloysia (b. Zell, Baden, 1761; d. Salzburg, 8. VI. 1839), Ger. soprano, 2nd daughter of Fridolin W. Mozart, who eventually married her sister Constanze W., fell in love with her in Mannheim in 1778 and later wrote for her the part of Constanze in *Die Entführung.* She married the actor Joseph Lange in 1780.

Weber, Bernhard Anselm (b. Mannheim, 18. IV. 1764; d. Berlin, 23. III. 1821), Ger. pianist, cond. and comp. Pupil of Vogler, he was mus. director of the Grossmann opera troupe in Hanover 1787–90, then toured Scand. with his old teacher, and cond. at the court opera in Berlin from 1792 (*Kapellmeister* 1804).

Works incl. operas and *Singspiele,* e.g. *Mudarra* and *Die Wette;* incid. mus. to Schiller's *Wilhelm Tell, Die Jungfrau von Orleans* and *Wallerstein* and other plays; 2 melodramas; songs, etc.

Weber, Bernhard Christian (b. Wolferschwenda, Thuringia, 1. XII. 1712; d. Tennstedt nr. Erfurt, 5. II. 1758), Ger. organist and comp. App. organist at Tennstedt in 1732. It was long claimed that he anticipated Bach by writing a set of preludes and fugues for keyboard in all the keys, entitled *Das wohltemperierte Clavier,* but he actually was an imitator, the work, wrongly dated 1689 (23 years before his birth), being in fact written *c.* 1745–50.

Weber, Carl Maria (Friedrich Ernst) von (b. Eutin nr. Lübeck, XI. 1786; d. London, 4–5. VI. 1826), Ger. comp. Son of a town and travelling theatre musician of good family but in poor circumstances. He was taken about the country in his childhood and received a desultory educ., but his father, anxious to make a prodigy of him, taught him all the mus. he knew. When at last they settled down at Salzburg, the boy, aged 10, became a pupil of Michael Haydn. After his mother's death in III. 1798 he was taken to Vienna and Munich. There he studied under Valesi (Wallishauser) and Kalcher, and at 13 was a good enough pianist to appear at concerts. By 1800 he had comp. a good deal of juvenile mus. and learned lithography with Senefelder; but the wandering life was resumed and he was reduced to continuing his studies with the aid of theoret. books.

At Augsburg in 1803 he succeeded in having his opera *Peter Schmoll und seine Nachbarn* prod. In Vienna again in 1803–4, he became Vogler's pupil for a time, and his master recommended him for a conductorship at Breslau, where he went in the autumn of 1804. In 1806 he became domestic musician to Duke Eugen of Württemberg, who, on being obliged to dismiss his musicians, recommended W. as private secretary to his younger brother Ludwig. He settled at Stuttgart in VII. 1807, where he led a rather dissolute life and incurred the displeasure of the king, his patron's elder brother. In 1810 he was banished from the kingdom on a trumped-up charge and went to Mannheim and later to Darmstadt, where he resumed his studies with Vogler more seriously.

After much travelling he secured the conductorship at the Ger. theatre in Prague in 1813. In XII. 1816 he was app. cond. of the Dresden court opera, where he did much to estab. Ger. opera in the face of the strong opposition of Morlacchi and other Its. On 4. XI. 1817 he married the opera singer Caroline Brandt, who was still at Prague, and took her to Dresden after a concert tour. On 4. V. 1821 his most famous opera, *Der Freischütz*, was prod. in Berlin, and *Euryanthe* followed in Vienna on 25. X. 1823. In 1824 the Covent Garden Theatre in London commissioned an Eng. opera from him, and he took Eng. lessons to make a success of *Oberon*. He suffered badly from a severe disease of the throat and felt unfit to visit London, but in order to keep his family from want he took the risk in II. 1826, visiting Paris on the way. He arrived in London on 5. III., cond. works of his own at a Phil. concert and prod. *Oberon* on 12. IV. Although he felt increasingly ill, he still cond. the succeeding perfs. and appeared at several concerts. Utterly worn out early in June he made preparations for a hasty return home, but d. during the night at the house of his host, George Smart.

Works incl. operas *Die Macht der Liebe und des Weins* (lost), *Das Waldmädchen* (fragment, early version of *Silvana*), *Peter Schmoll und seine Nachbarn*, *Rübezahl* (fragments only), *Silvana*, *Abu Hassan*, *Der Freischütz*, *Die drei Pintos* (fragment, later finished by Mahler), *Euryanthe*,

Oberon; 32 other works for the stage incl. incid. mus. to Schiller's trans. of Gozzi's *Turandot*, P. A. Wolff's *Preciosa* and extra songs, arias and other interpolations for plays; 7 cantatas; 3 Masses and 2 offertories; 13 orchestral works, incl. overtures, etc.; 22 works for solo instruments and orch., incl. 2 pf. concertos, *Concertstück* for pf. and orch., concertino for clar. and orch., 2 clar. and 1 bassoon concertos; 5tet for clar., 2 vlns., vla. and cello; 27 pf. works incl. 8 sets of variations, 4 sonatas, *Momento capriccioso*, *Rondo brillante*, *Aufforderung zum Tanz* (*Invitation to the Dance*); 64 songs, part-songs, etc., similar vocal pieces, etc.

Weber, Constanze. *See* **Mozart.**

Weber, (Friedrich) Dionys(us) (b. Velichov, 9. X. 1766; d. Prague, 25. XII. 1842), Boh. teacher and comp. Pupil of Vogler. He was one of the founders and the 1st director of the Prague Cons. and wrote several theoret. treatises. He gave the 1st perf. of Wagner's C maj. symph. in 1832.

Works incl. operas; military band mus., etc.

Weber, Fridolin (b. Zell, Baden, 1733; d. Vienna, 23. X. 1779), Ger. singer and violonist, father of Aloysia, Constanze (Mozart) and Josepha W. In the service of the electoral court at Mannheim, later lived in Vienna.

Weber, Gottfried (b. Freinsheim nr. Mannheim, 1. III. 1779; d. Kreuznach, 21. IX. 1839), Ger. comp. and theorist. He pursued a lawyer's profession at Mannheim (1804), Mainz (1812) and Darmstadt (1818). In 1810 his family provided refuge for their namesakes, C. M. v. Weber and his father, after the former's banishment from Stuttgart, and they formed a mus. and cultural society. W. wrote a number of theoret. books.

Works incl. 3 Masses and other church mus.; instrumental sonatas and pieces; songs with pf. and guitar, etc.

Weber, Josepha (b. Zell, Baden, 1759; d. Vienna, 29. XII. 1819), Ger. soprano, eldest daughter of Fridolin W. Pupil of Righini, she joined Schikaneder's opera co. in Vienna, and was the 1st Queen of the Night in Mozart's *Die Zauberflöte* (1791).

Webern, Anton (von) (b. Vienna, 3. XII. 1883; d. Mittersill, Salzburg, 15. IX. 1945), Aus. comp. Studied musicology with Adler and took the Ph.D. degree at Vienna Univ. in 1906. He became a pupil of Schönberg for comp. He cond. for a time at Ger. provincial theatres and in Prague. After the war of 1914–18 he settled at Mödling nr. Vienna and devoted himself to teaching and comp., though he still cond., esp. the modern perfs. of the Verein für musikalische Privataufführungen and the workers' symph. concerts. He also cond.

in London and Barcelona, and in all the Ger.-speaking countries. Much of his life was quiet and contemplative. His death was the result of a tragic misunderstanding (he was shot by an Amer. soldier). Although almost entirely unrecognized during his lifetime, W.'s mus. has proved very influential in the years since 1945, introd. new concepts of sound, rhythm and quasi-mathematical organization. It is almost as much through his work as through Schönberg's that the '12-tone system' has come to find so wide an acceptance.

Works incl. *Das Augenlicht* and Cantatas Nos. 1 and 2 for chorus and orch.; 2 songs (Goethe) for chorus and chamber orch.; symph., passacaglia, variations, 6 pieces, 5 pieces for orch.; concerto for 9 instruments; string 4tet, 5 movements and *6 Bagatelles* for string 4tet, 4tet for vln., clar., saxophone and pf., string trio; 2 songs (Rilke) for voice and chamber mus., 4 and 6 songs for do., 5 canons for voice, clar. and bass clar.; *3 geistliche Volkslieder* for voice, vln., clar. and bass clar., 3 songs with clar. and guitar, *5 geistliche Lieder* for voice and 5 instruments; 4 pieces for vln. and pf., 3 little pieces for cello and pf.; variations for pf.; songs to words by Rilke, Stephan George and others; 'Entflieht auf leichten Kähnen' (George) for unaccomp. chorus, etc.

Webers letzter Gedanke (known in Eng. as *Weber's Last Waltz*). See **Reissiger**.

Webster, John (? 1580–? 1625), Eng. dramatist. See **Britten** (*Duchess of Malfi*), **Warlock** (*3 dirges*).

Wechseldominante (Ger. = change dominant), the Ger. technical term for the dominant of the dominant of any key: e.g. E maj. or min. as related to the key of D maj. or min., A being dominant to D, and E to A.

Wechselnote (Ger. lit. change note, changing note). See **Nota cambiata**.

Wecker, Georg Kaspar (b. Nuremberg, IV. 1632; d. Nuremberg, 20. IV. 1695), Ger. organist and comp. Pupil of his father, an instrumental perf., and Erasmus Kindermann. He was organist at var. Nuremberg churches from the age of 19

Weckerlin, Jean Baptiste (Théodore) (b. Guebwiller, Alsace, 29. XI. 1821; d. Trottberg nr. Guebwiller, 20. V. 1910), Fr. comp. and ed. Studied at the Paris Cons. Although unsuccessful, he was determined to make his way as a musician, collected much old Fr. mus. and in 1863 became archivist of the Société des Compositeurs de Musique, whose library he estab. In 1869 Auber invited him to the Cons. library, of which he became head librarian in 1876. He ed. many collections of old Fr. songs and other mus.

Works incl. opera *L'Organiste dans l'embarras* and 5 others (some in Alsat. dialect); *Roland* for solo voices, chorus and orch.; Mass and motets; symph. and suite for orch.; ichamber mus.; songs, etc.

Weckmann, Matthias (b. Niederdorla, Thuringia, 1621; d. Hamburg, 24. II. 1674), Ger. organist and comp. He became a pupil of Schütz as a choirboy in the electoral chapel at Dresden and in 1637 was sent at the elector's expense to study further with J. Praetorius at Hamburg. In 1641 he became court organist at Dresden, where he remained until 1655, except for a visit to Nyjøbing in the service of the crown prince of Den., some time before 1647. He then became organist at St. James's Church, Hamburg. He organized a concert society (*Collegium musicum*) with Scheidemann, Selle, Schop and other Hamburg musicians and during a visit to Dresden competed as an organist with Froberger.

Works incl. sacred concertos for voices and instruments; org. mus., etc.

Wedding, The, ballet by Stravinsky (choreography by Bronislava Nizhinska), prod. Paris, Théâtre Gaité-Lyrique, 13. VI. 1923. The work is scored for chorus (Rus. words), 4 pfs. and perc. It is more generally known as *Les Noces*.

Wedekind, Frank (1864–1918), Ger. dramatist. See **Ettinger** (*Frühlingserwachen*), **Lulu** (Berg).

'Wedge' Fugue, Bach's E min. org. fugue, BWV. 548, so called because of the progressively widening intervals of its subject:

'WEDGE' FUGUE

and in 1686 was app. to the principal one, St. Sebald's. J. Krieger and Pachelbel were among his pupils.

Works incl. 18 sacred concertos (church cantatas) for voices and instruments; org. mus., etc.

Weelkes, Thomas (b. ?, *c.* 1575; d. London, 30. XI. 1623), Eng. comp. He may have been in the service of George Phillpot at Thruxton nr. Andover in his early years and then was in that of Edward Darcye, Groom of the Privy Chamber. In

1600 he was organist at Winchester Coll. and in 1602 he took the B.Mus. at Oxford, soon afterwards becoming organist of Chichester Cathedral. He remained there to the end, but d. during a visit to London.

Works incl. services and numerous anthems; 2 books of madrigals, ballets, *Ayeres or Phantasticke Spirites* for 3 voices; 2 vocal pieces contrib. to Leighton's *Teares or Lamentacions*; In Nomines for 4–5 viols and other pieces for 5 viols.

Weerbecke, Gaspar van (b. Oudenarde, *c.* 1440; d. ?, after 1515), Flem. singer, priest and comp. Pupil of the *maîtrise* at Oudenarde and of Okeghem. He took holy orders at Tournai and went to It. in the 1470s and became *maestro di cappella* at Milan Cathedral and a singer at the ducal court. He was in Rome as a singer at the Papal Chapel in 1481–9, but in 1488 prod. mus. for allegorical plays given at the marriage of Galeazzo Sforza, Duke of Milan, to Isabella of Aragon. He visited his home-town in 1490 and was received with honours.

Works incl. Masses, motets, *Stabat Mater* and other church mus.; mus. for plays, etc.

Wegelius, Martin (b. Helsinki, 10. XI. 1846; d. Helsinki, 22. III. 1906), Fin. teacher and comp. Studied at Helsinki Univ. and also had mus. lessons there, later studied mus. in Vienna, Leipzig and Munich. Returning home in 1878, he took an active part in the mus. life of the Fin. capital as critic and lecturer, and in 1882 founded the Cons., of which he became the 1st director. Among his pupils there were Sibelius, Melartin, Järnefelt and others.

Works incl. cantata in memory of Runeberg; orchestral works; songs, etc.

Wehrli, Werner (b. Aarau, 8. I. 1892; d. Lucerne, 27. VI. 1944), Swiss comp. Studied natural science at Munich Univ., but turned to mus. and joined the Zürich Cons. Later became a pupil of Knorr at the Hoch Cons. at Frankfurt. In 1918 he settled in his native town as teacher and cond.

Works incl. operas *Das heiss Eisen* (Hans Sachs), *Das Vermächtnis*, festival operas *Die Schweizer*, *Die Brücke*, *Das Weltgericht*, play with mus. *Der Märchenspiegel*; oratorios *Ein weltliches Requiem* and *Wallfahrt*; sinfonietta and variations for orch.; *Pantomime* for chamber orch.; 3 string 4tets, 2 pf. trios and other chamber mus.; pf. and org. works; songs, partsongs, etc.

Weichsel, Carl and Elizabeth. *See* Billington.

Weideman(n), Carl Friedrich (Charles Weideman) (b.?; d. London, 1782), Ger. flautist and comp. Settled in London *c.* 1726. He was concerned with Festing in

the foundation of the Royal Society of Musicians in 1739 and in 1778 became cond. of the royal orch. He comp. concertos, solos, duets, trios and 4tets for fl.

Weigl, Joseph (Franz) (b. Bavar., 19. III. 1740; d. Vienna, 25. I. 1820), Ger. cellist. He joined Prince Esterházy's orch. at Eisenstadt under Haydn in 1761, but left in 1769 for the Vienna Court Opera and joined the Imp. Chapel there in 1792.

Weigl, Joseph (b. Eisenstadt, 28. III. 1766; d. Vienna, 3. II. 1846), Aus. comp., son of prec. and godson of Haydn. Pupil of Albrechtsberger and Salieri, he was the latter's deputy at the court opera in Vienna from 1790 and succeeded him as cond. and comp. in 1792. He visited It. to prod. operas 1807–8 and again in 1815, but shortly afterwards withdrew from opera comp. and wrote mainly church mus. He became vice-*Kapellmeister* at court in 1827.

Works incl. over 30 operas, e.g. *Die betrogene Arglist*, *Das Waisenhaus*, *Der Bergsturz*, *Die Schweizerfamilie*, *La Principessa d'Amalfi*, *Cleopatra*, *Il rivale di se stesso*, *L'imbroscata*, etc.; 18 ballets; incid. mus.; 11 Masses and other church mus.; cantatas, arias, songs, etc.

Weigl, Karl (b Vienna, 6. II. 1881; d. N.Y., 11. VIII. 1949), Aus. comp. Studied musicology at Vienna Univ., worked as asst. cond. under Mahler at the Vienna Opera, became a teacher at the New Vienna Cons. in 1918 and later lecturer at the univ. in 1938, becoming an Amer. citizen in 1943 and teaching successively at Hartford, Brooklyn and Boston.

Works incl. cantata *Weltfeier* for solo voices, chorus, orch. and org.; 6 symphs.; var. concertos; 8 string 4tets; cello and pf. sonata; songs with pf. and with chamber accomp., etc.

Weigl, Thaddäus (b. Vienna, 1776; d. Vienna, 10. II. 1844), Aus. comp. and pub., son and brother of J. Weigl I and II. Pupil of his father, was for a time cond. at the court theatres, but in 1801 became a mus. pub.

Works incl. opera *Der Jahrmarkt zu Grünewald* and others; ballet *Cyrus und Thomyris* and others, etc.

Weihe des Hauses, Die (*The Consecration of the House*), overture by Beethoven, Op. 124, C. maj., written in 1822 for the opening of the Josefstadt Theatre in Vienna, and perf. there in 3. X., cond. by the comp.

Weill, Kurt (b. Dessau, 2. III. 1900; d. N.Y., 3. IV. 1950), Ger. comp. Studied locally at first, later with Humperdinck and Busoni in Berlin. He had his 1st stage success at the age of 26. His modern version of Gay's *Beggar's Opera* (*Die Dreigroschenoper*) made an enormous hit in 1928, but the Nazi regime condemned his works in 1933 as both Jewish and decadent, and he left Ger. He visited London in 1935 for the prod. of an Eng. operetta, *A Kingdom for a Cow*, but went the same year to settle in U.S.A.

Works incl. operas and operettas *Der Protagonist*, *Der Silbersee*, *Der Zar lässt sich photographieren* (libs. by Georg Kaiser), *Royal Palace*, *Die Dreigroschen oper*, *Happy End*, *Mahagonny*, *Der Jasager*, *Die Bürgschaft* (several on libs. by Bert Brecht), *Marie galante*, *A Kingdom for a Cow*, *Johnny Johnson*, *Knickerbocker Holiday*, *The Firebrand*; biblical mus. drama *The Eternal Road*; ballet *Die sieben Todsünden* (*Anna Anna*); cantatas *Der neue Orpheus* and *Der Lindberghflug*; 2 symphs., *Fantasia*, *Passacaglia und Hymnus*, *Divertimento* and *Quodlibet* for orch.; concerto for vln. and wind band; string 4tet; works for voices and chamber orch., songs (Rilke) with orch., etc.

Weinberger, Jaromír (b. Prague, 8. I. 1896; d. St. Petersburg, Fla., 8. VIII. 1967), Cz. comp. Studied with Hofmeister and Kricka in Prague and with Reger in Ger. Prof. of comp. at the Cons. of Ithaca, N.Y., 1922–6; returned to Eur. to cond. and teach. Settled in U.S.A. in 1938.

Works incl. operas *Švanda the Bagpiper*, *The Beloved Voice*, *The Outcasts of Poker Flat* (after Bret Harte) and *Wallenstein* (after Schiller); pantomime *The Abduction of Eveline*; incid. mus. for Shakespeare and other plays; *Don Quixote* (after Cervantes), variations on the Eng. folksong, 'Under the spreading chestnut tree', *Lincoln Symph.*, *Czech Rhapsody* for orch.; works for org., pf., vln. etc.

Weiner, Leo (b. Budapest, 16. IV. 1885; d. Budapest, 13. IX. 1960), Hung. comp. Studied at the Nat. Acad. of Mus. in Budapest, where he became a prof. in 1908.

Works incl. ballet on and incid. mus. for Vörösmarty's *Csongor and Tünde*; 2 divertimentos, scherzo, serenade and humoresque *Carnival* for orch.; *Pastoral, Fantasy and Fugue* for strings; 2 vln. concertos; 3 string 4tets, string trio; 2 vln. and pf. sonatas; pf. works, etc.

Weingartner (Paul) Felix (von) (b. Zara, Dalmatia, 2. VI. 1863; d. Winterthur, Switz., 7. V. 1942), Aus. cond. and comp. Studied at Graz, at the Leipzig Cons. and under Liszt at Weimar, where he prod. his 1st opera in 1884. He became cond. at Königsberg, Danzig, Hamburg and Mannheim before 1891, when he was app. cond. of the Court Opera in Berlin and cond. of the symph. concerts. In 1898 he left for Munich to become cond. of the Kaim orch. and in 1908 he succeeded Mahler as chief cond. at the Vienna Court Opera. After 1911 he frequently changed his sphere of activity, cond. much abroad, esp. in Fr., Eng. and U.S.A. The last years

of his life he spent, still actively, in Switz., esp. at Basle. He was 5 times married. He wrote books on cond., on Beethoven's symphs., etc.

Works incl. operas *Sakuntala* (after Kalidasa), *Malawika*, *Genesius*, *Orestes* trilogy (after Aeschylus), *Kain und Abel*, *Dame Kobold* (after Calderón), *Die Dorfschule*, *Meister Andrea*, *Der Apostat*; incid. mus. for Shakespeare's *Tempest* and Goethe's *Faust*; 6 symphs., symph. poems *King Lear* (after Shakespeare) and *Die Gefilde der Seligen* (after Böcklin's picture), *Lustige Ouvertüre*, overture *Aus schwerer Zeit*; serenade for string orch.; vln. concerto; 3 string 4tets, string 5tet, 5tet for clar., strings and pf., 6tet for strings and pf.; 2 vln. and pf. sonatas; pf. pieces; numerous songs, etc.

Weinlig, Christian Theodor (b. Dresden, 25. VII. 1780; d. Leipzig, 6. III. 1842), Ger. theorist and comp. Pupil of his uncle, Christian Ehregott W. (1743–1813), cantor of the Kreuzschule at Dresden. He succeeded Schicht as cantor of St. Thomas's School at Leipzig in 1823. Schumann and Wagner were his pupils for a short time. He wrote a treatise on fugue and comp. an oratorio, 2 Ger. Magnificats, church cantatas, etc.

Weis, Flemming (b. Copenhagen, 15. IV. 1898), Dan. comp. A member of a mus. cultivated family, he began to comp. as a child. In 1916 he entered the Copenhagen Cons. and in 1920 finished his studies at Leipzig. He has been active on behalf of contemporary mus. and also as a mus. critic.

Works incl. *The Promised Land* for chorus and orch.; 3 symphs., symph. overture and *In temporis vernalis* for orch.; *Introduction grave* for pf. and strings, 5 string 4tets and other chamber mus.; sonatas for var. instruments, suite and sonatina for pf.; songs, etc.

Weis, Karel (b. Prague, 13. II. 1862; d. Prague, 4. IV. 1944), Cz. cond. and comp. Studied at the Prague Cons. and with Skuherský and Fibich at the Org. School. After var. posts as organist, teacher and orch. player (vln. and horn), he became cond. at the Nat. Theatre at Brno in 1886, but from 1888 devoted himself to comp.

Works incl. operas *Viola* (after Shakespeare's *Twelfth Night*; later called *The Twins*), *The Polish Jew* (after Erckmann-Chatrian), *The Attack on the Mill* (after Zola), *The Blacksmith of Lesetin*, operettas *The Village Musicians* and *The Revisor* (after Gogol's comedy); choral scene *Triumfator*; symph. poem *Helios and Selene*; string 4tet; vln. and pf. sonata; pf. pieces; folksong arrs., etc.

Weisgall, Hugo (b. Ivaničice, Czechoslovakia, 13. X. 1912), Amer. comp. of

Cz. origin. His family settled in the U.S.A. in 1920. He studied at the Peabody Cons., Baltimore, and later with Sessions in N.Y. and R. Scalero at the Curtis Inst. in Philadelphia. From 1946 to 1947 he was cultural attaché to the Amer. embassy in Prague and has taught at various schools of mus.

Works incl. operas *Night*, *Lillith*, *The Tenor*, *6 Characters in Search of an Author* (after Pirandello), *Athaliah*; ballets *Quest*, *One Thing is Certain*, *Outpost*; overture in F maj. for orch.; choral mus.; songs, etc.

Weismann, Julius (b. Freiburg i/B., 26. XII. 1879; d. Singen, Bodensee, 22. XII. 1950), Ger. comp. Studied at Munich, with Herzogenberg in Berlin and again at Munich with Thuille.

Works incl. operas *Schwanenweiss*, *Traumspiel*, *Gespenstersonate* (all after Strindberg), *Leonce und Lena* (Georg Büchner), *Landsknechte*, *Regina del Lago*, *Die pfiffige Magd* (after Holberg); 3 symphs., 3 pieces for orch., 3 sinfoniettas; 4 vln. concertos, 3 pf. concertos, cello concerto; 11 string 4tets, 2 pf. trios; sonata for vln. solo, 5 vln. sonatas, 2 cello sonatas, variations for ob. and pf.; choral works; variations for 2 pfs.; 7 op. nos. of pf. pieces; 15 op. nos. of songs, etc.

Weiss, Adolph (b. Baltimore, 12. IX. 1891), Amer. comp. of Ger. parentage. Studied pf., vln. and bassoon, and at the age of 16 played 1st bassoon with the Rus. Symph. Orch. of N.Y. and then in the N.Y. Phil. Orch. under Mahler. He then studied comp. at Columbia Univ. with C. Rybner and later with Schönberg in Vienna.

Works incl. *I Segreti* and *American Life* for orch.; *The Libation Bearers*, choreographic cantata for soloists, chorus and orch.; theme and variations for orch.; tpt. concerto; 3 string 4tets; much mus. for small ensembles, incl. wind instruments; songs; pf. mus., etc.

Weiss (actually Schneeweiss) **Amalie** (b. Marburg, Styria, 10. V. 1839; d. Berlin, 3. II. 1898), Aus. contralto. Made her 1st stage appearance at Troppau in 1853, was later engaged in Vienna and Hanover, and at the latter place married Joachim in 1863. She then appeared only as a concert singer. They separated in 1884.

Weiss, Franz (b. Glatz, Silesia, 18. I. 1778; d. Vienna, 25. I. 1830), Aus. violist and comp. Settled in Vienna and became the vla. player in Prince Rasumovsky's 4tet founded in 1808.

Works incl. symph. for fl., bassoon and tpt. with orch., variations for vln. and orch.; string 4tet; duets for vlns. and for fls.; pf. sonatas, etc.

Weiss, Sylvius Leopold (b. Breslau, 12. X. 1686; d. Dresden, 15. X. 1750), Ger. lutenist and comp. He was in the service of the Pol. Prince Alexander Sobieski, with

whom he went to Rome *c.* 1708, later at the courts of Hesse-Cassel, Düsseldorf, and from 1718 Dresden, where he worked with Lotti, Hasse, Porpora, Hebenstreit, Pisendel and others, and was sent to Vienna with a visiting Saxon orch. that year. In 1723 he played in Prague with Quantz and H. Graun in Fux's coronation opera *Costanza e fortezza*. Comp. lute mus.

Weissberg, Julia Lazarevna (b. Orenburg, 25. XII. 1878; d. Leningrad, 1. III. 1942), Rus. comp. Studied at the St. Petersburg Cons., under Krizhanovsky, Rimsky-Korsakov and Glazunov, but was expelled for taking part in a demonstration against the director, Bernard. In 1907–12 she made further studies in Ger. She married Andrey Rimsky-Korsakov.

Works incl. operas *The Little Mermaid* (after Hans Andersen) and *Gulnara* (from the *Arabian Nights*); cantata *The Twelve* (Alex. Blok); symph. fantasy, symph. poem *In the Night*, *Ballad* and *A Tale* for orch.; songs with orch. *Rautendelein* (from Hauptmann's *The Sunken Bell*); *Chinese Songs* and others for voice and pf.; folksong arrs., etc.

Weissenburg, Hainz. *See* **Albicastro.**

Weissensee, Friedrich (b. Schwerstedt, Thuringia, *c.* 1560; d. Altenweddingen, 1622), Ger. clergyman and comp. Studied (?) at Venice and became rector of a Lat. coll. at Gebesee, *c.* 1590, and of the town school of Magdeburg in 1596. About 1602 he became rector at Altenweddingen.

Works incl. motets, etc.

Weisshan (or Winsheim), Abraham (b. ?; d. ?), Ger. 16th–17th-cent. lutenist and comp. In 1568 he went into service at the Saxon court at Dresden, where he still was in 1611.

Works incl. a collection of lute preludes, fantasies and dances *Silvae musicalis libri VII*, etc.

Weissmann, Adolf (b. Rosenberg, Silesia, 15. VIII. 1873; d. Haifa, 23. IV. 1929), Ger. mus. critic and author. Studied in Cz., Ger., Aus. and Switz. He became mus. critic to several Berlin papers and periodicals, but d. on a lecturing-tour in Palestine. His books incl. studies of Bizet, Chopin, Puccini and Verdi, the virtuoso, the prima donna and the cond., the hist. of mus. in Berlin, modern mus. conditions, etc.

Welcome-Odes
or   } cantatas by Purcell
Welcome-Songs
for the return to London of Charles II and James II on var. occasions. One, of 1682, is addressed to James as Duke of York, before his accession.

Weldon, George (b. Chichester, 5. VI. 1906; d Cape Town, 17. VIII. 1963), Eng. cond. Studied at the R.C.M. with Sargent, and cond. various provincial orchs., in

1943 becoming cond. of the City of Birmingham Symph. Orch., which post he held until 1950.

Weldon, John (b. Chichester, 19. I. 1676; d. London, 7. V. 1736), Eng. organist and comp. Educ. at Eton, where he studied mus. under the coll. organist John Walton, and later became a pupil of Purcell in London. In 1694 he was app. organist of New Coll., Oxford, and in 1700 gained the 1st prize for the setting of Congreve's masque *The Judgment of Paris* against Eccles, Finger and D. Purcell. In 1701 he became a Gentleman of the Chapel Royal and in 1708 organist there on the death of Blow; he also became organist of St. Bride's and (1726) St. Martin's-in-the-Field churches.

Works incl. masque *The Judgment of Paris*; songs for Cibber's *She would and she would not* and other plays; anthems; songs, etc.

Welitsch (actually Velichkova), **Ljuba** (b. Borisovo, 10. VII. 1913), Bulg. soprano. Played the vln. as a child, studied philosophy at Sofia Univ., and then studied singing in Vienna with Lierhammer, making her début in Sofia in 1936. She has since sung all over the world and is a dramatic singer of great power, her most famous role being Strauss's Salome.

Well-tempered Clavier. *See* **Wohltemperierte Clavier, Das.**

Wellesz, Egon (b. Vienna, 21. X. 1885), Aus. musicologist and comp. Studied with Schönberg, Bruno Walter and others in Vienna, also musicology with Adler at the univ., where he graduated Ph.D. in 1908. In 1913 he became lecturer in mus. hist. there and prof. from 1930 to 1938. He specialized in Byzantine and modern mus., ed. and wrote on the former and pub. works on Schönberg, Cavalli and the Venetian opera, modern orch., etc. In 1932 he received the hon. D.Mus. from Oxford Univ. and in 1938 he settled there, becoming lecturer in 1943 and Reader from 1948 to 1956. He is a member of the ed. board of the *New Oxford History of Music* and ed. of Vol. I, and one of the eds. of *Monumenta Musicae Byzantinae*. His books include *A History of Byzantine Music* and *Eastern Elements in Western Chant*. C.B.E. 1957.

Works incl. operas *Die Prinzessin Girnara* (Jacob Wassermann), *Alkestis* (Hofmannsthal) and *Die Bacchantinnen* (both after Euripides), *Opferung des Gefangenen, Scherz, List und Rache* (Goethe's lib.), *Incognita* (on Congreve's story); ballets *Das Wunder der Diana, Persian ballet, Achilles auf Skyros* and *Die Nächtlichen*; unaccomp. choruses to old Eng. poems; *Gebete der Mädchen zu Maria* for soprano, chorus and orch.; 8 symphs., symph. poem *Vorfrühling*, symph.

suite *Prosperos Beschwörungen* (after Shakespeare's *Tempest*), Festival March for orch.; *Amor timido* (Metastasio) and *Lied der Welt* (Hofmannsthal) for soprano and orch., *Leben, Traum und Tod* (Hofmannsthal) for contralto and orch.; dance suite for vln. and chamber orch.; pf. concerto, vln. concerto; 3 Masses, motets, cantata *Mitte des Lebens*; *The Leaden Echo and the Golden Echo* (Gerard Manley Hopkins) for soprano, clar., vla., cello and pf.; 9 string 4tets, string 5tet; clar. 5tet; octet; solo sonatas for vln., cello, ob., clar., etc.; pf. pieces; songs, etc.

Wellingtons Sieg (Beethoven). *See* **Battle of Vittoria.**

Wells, H(erbert). G(eorge). (1866–1946), Eng. novelist. *See* **Bliss** (*Things to come*).

Welsh Composers. *See* **Parry** (4), **Richards, Roberts, Thomas, Williams (G.).**

Wendling (*née* Spurni), **Dorothea** (b. Stuttgart, 21. III. 1736; d. Munich, 20. VIII. 1811), Ger. soprano. Worked at the court of Mannheim and Munich; wife of J. B. Wendling.

Wendling (*née* Sarselli), **Elisabeth Augusta** (b. Mannheim, 20. II. 1746; d. Munich, 10. I. 1786), Ger. soprano, sister-in-law of prec. Attached to the courts of Mannheim and Munich; married the violinist Franz Anton W. in 1764.

Wendling, Johann Baptist (b. Rappoltsweiler, Alsace, 17. VI. 1723; d. Munich, 27. XI. 1797), Ger. flautist, brother-in-law of prec. In the service of the court at Mannheim from *c.* 1751 to 1752, also travelled widely. He married the singer Dorothea Spurni in 1752.

Wennerberg, Gunnar (b. Lidköping, 2. X. 1817; d. Leckö, 22. VIII. 1901), Swed. poet and comp. Educ. at Uppsala Univ. He became a lawyer and was self-taught in mus.

Works incl. oratorio *The Birth of Christ, Stabat Mater*, psalms for solo voices, chorus and orch.; *Gluntarne* (students' songs) for male-voice duet, *Songs of Freedom*, etc.

Wenzinger, August (b. Basle, 14. XI. 1905), Swiss cond., cellist and gambaplayer. Studied 1st at the Basle Cons., until 1927, and then with P. Jarnach in Cologne until 1929. Then played cello with various orchs., and since 1934 has taught at the Schola Cantorum Basiliensis. He is esp. well known as a cond. of baroque mus. (and earlier), using period instruments.

Werba, Erik (b. Baden, near Vienna, 23. V. 1918), Aus. pianist, and comp. Studied with J. Marx, Wellesz and Schenk, graduating in 1940. In 1948 he became prof. at the Vienna State Acad.

Works incl. *Singspiele*, chamber mus. and songs.

Werckmeister, Andreas (b. Beneckenstein, 30. XI. 1645; d. Halberstadt, 26. X.

1706), Ger. organist and theorist. Organist at Hasselfelde, Quedlinburg and Halberstadt in succession. Wrote theoret. works, esp. on the tuning of orgs. and claviers.

Werfel, Franz (b. Prague, 10. IX. 1890; d. Beverly Hills, Calif., 26. VIII. 1945), Aus. novelist and playwright. Studied at Prague and Leipzig Univ. His works incl. a novel on Verdi and transs. of many of Verdi's operas. *See* **Grosz** (*Spiegelmensch*), **Maximilien** (Milhaud), **Orff** (*Turmes Auferstehung*).

Werner, Gregor Joseph (b. ?, 1695; d. Eisenstadt, 3. III. 1766), Aus. cond. and comp. App. mus. director to the Esterházy family in 1728; predecessor of Haydn there and his superior for 5 years from 1761.

Works incl. 65 Masses, 3 Requiems and other church mus.; 18 oratorios; symphs.; string 4tet, 6 fugues for string 4tet (pub. by Haydn); sonatas, etc., for 2 vlns. and bass, etc.

Werrekoren (or **Verecoren**), **Hermann Matthias** (b. ?; d. ?), Flem. 16th-cent. comp. He was in service in It., prob. Milan or Pavia (but the biog. is very uncertain, and there may have been more than 1 comp. of the name).

Works incl. motets for 5 voices, 4-part song on the battles of Bicocca and Pavia, in which Francesco Sforza gained the mastery of Milan, motets, etc.

Wert, Giaches (or **Jaches**) **de** (b. Weert, 1535; d. Mantua, 6. V. 1596), Flem. comp. Was sent to It. as a choir-boy when a small child and at 9 became a member of the choir of the Novellara at Reggio. He began to pub. madrigals towards the end of the 1550s and *c.* 1560 went into service at the ducal court of Mantua under Guglielmo Gonzaga. He was also attached to the church of Santa Barbara, where he succeeded Giovanni Contino as *maestro di cappella* in 1565. In 1566 he accomp. the duke to Augsburg and there declined an offer from the Emperor Maximilian II. In 1567 he visited Venice with the court and later Ferrara under Alfonso (II) d'Este. About that time he suffered much from the intrigues of the It. musicians, who disliked him as a foreigner, and in 1570 one of them, Agostino Bonvicino, was dismissed for a love-affair with his wife. In 1580 he and his family were given the freedom of the city of Mantua in perpetuity.

Works incl. motets, 11 books of madrigals for 5 voices, 1 for 4 voices, canzonets, *villanelle*, etc.

Werther, opera by Massenet (lib. by Édouard Blau, Paul Milliet and Georges Hartmann, based on Goethe's novel), prod., in Ger., Vienna, Opera, 16. II. 1892; 1st Paris perf., Opéra-Comique, 16. I. 1893.

Wesley, Charles (b. Bristol, 11. XII. 1757; d. London, 23. V. 1834), Eng. organist and comp. Pupil of Kelway and Boyce in London and later organist at var. churches and chapels. He also appeared in public as harpsichordist.

Works incl. incid. mus. for Mason's *Caractacus*; Concerto grosso; org. or harpsichord concertos; string 4tets; anthems, hymns, harpsichord pieces; songs, etc.

Wesley, Samuel (b. Bristol, 24. II. 1766; d. London, 11. X. 1837), Eng. organist, cond. and comp., brother of prec. and nephew of John W. Like his brother he showed precocious mus. gifts at a very early age. At 6 he was taught by the organist of the church of St. James, Barton, Bristol, at 8 he finished the oratorio *Ruth* and soon after appeared at the org. as a prodigy. In 1784 he became a Rom. Catholic and in 1787 injured his head in an accident, with the result that he periodically fell into strange behaviour for the rest of his life. He did much work to spread a knowledge of Bach in Eng. and ed. some of his works. He cond. the Birmingham Festival in 1811, lectured at the Royal Institution and gave frequent org. recitals, but had periodically to retire for several years. Shortly before his death he met Mendelssohn and they played the org. to each other.

Works incl. oratorios *Ruth* and *The Death of Abel*; 4 Masses, numerous Lat. and Eng. anthems incl. 'In exitu Israel', 'Exultate Deo', 'Dixit Dominus', 'All go unto one place', 'Behold how good', 'Hear, O thou shepherd' (some with org.), Morning and Evening Service in F maj. and other church mus.; Ode on St. Cecilia's Day; 4 symphs. (1 unfinished) and overtures; org. and vln. concertos; 2 string 4tets and other chamber mus.; org. fugues, voluntaries, etc.; numerous pf. works; glees, songs and duets, etc.

Wesley, Samuel Sebastian (b. London, 14. VIII. 1810; d. Gloucester, 19. IV. 1876), Eng. organist and comp., illegitimate son of prec. Pupil of his father and choir-boy in the Chapel Royal from 1820. In 1826 he was app. organist of a London church and by 1830 he held similar posts at 2 more. In 1832 he became organist of Hereford Cathedral, in 1835, when he married, of Exeter Cathedral; in 1842–9 he was organist of Leeds Parish Church, in 1849–1865 of Winchester Cathedral and then until his death of Gloucester Cathedral. He took the D.Mus. at Oxford in 1839 and became org. prof. at the R.A.M. in London in 1850.

Works incl. 5 services, 24 anthems, Psalm c, 2 settings of 'By the waters of Babylon' with soprano and with contralto solo, chants and hymn tunes; org. works; *Ode to Labour* and *The Praise of*

Music for chorus; 3 glees; 9 songs (2 with cello *ad lib.*); pf. pieces, etc.

Wessely, (Carl) Bernhard (b. Berlin, 1. IX. 1768; d. Potsdam, 11. VII. 1826), Ger. cond. and comp. Pupil of J. A. P. Schulz. He was cond. at the Berlin Nat. Theatre, 1788–95, and in 1796–1802 at Prince Heinrich's private theatre at Rheinsberg. After the prince's death he became a civil servant at Potsdam, where he founded a society for the perf. of classical mus.

Works incl. operas *Psyché, Louis XI* and *L'Ogre*; prologue *Die Freuden des Herbstes*; ballet *Die Wahl des Helden*; incid. mus. to Shakespeare's *Tempest*, Kotzebue's *Sonnenjungfrau* and other plays; cantatas on the deaths of Moses Mendelssohn and Prince Henry of Prus.; string 4tets; songs, etc.

Wessely, Hans (b. Vienna, 23. XII. 1862; d. Innsbruck, 29. IX. 1926), Aus. violinist. Studied at the Vienna Cons. and made his 1st appearance at the age of 21. In 1888 he visited Eng., becoming prof. at the R.A.M. in London in 1889 and remaining for almost the rest of his life. He formed a string 4tet.

Western, Ethel. *See* Thalberg, Zaré.

Westrup, Jack (Allan) (b. London, 26. VII. 1904), Eng. musicologist, critic and comp. Educ. at Dulwich Coll. and Balliol Coll., Oxford, where as an undergraduate he ed. Monteverdi's *Orfeo* and *Incoronazione di Poppea* for perf. by the Oxford Univ. Opera Club. He taught classics at Dulwich Coll. from 1928 to 1934, and was an asst. mus. critic to the *Daily Telegraph* from 1934 to 1940. From 1941 to 1944 he was lecturer in mus. at King's Coll., Newcastle-on-Tyne, from 1944 to 1946 prof. of mus. at Birmingham Univ. and from 1947 to 1971 prof. at Oxford. He is chairman of the ed. board of the *New Oxford History of Music* and ed. of Vol. VI. Ed. of *Music and Letters* since 1959. His literary work incl. a book on Purcell and an intro. to mus. hist. Knighted in 1961.

Works incl. motet 'When Israel came out of Egypt' for unaccomp. double chorus; part-song *Weathers*; passacaglia for orch.; divertimento for bassoon, cello and pf., 3 Shakespeare songs, incid. mus., etc.

Wetz, Richard (b. Gleiwitz, 26. II. 1875; d. Erfurt, 16. I. 1935), Ger. comp. He was very precociously gifted, began to comp. at the age of 8 and was almost wholly self-taught, though he studied a little with Thuille at Munich. In 1906 he settled at Erfurt, where he became cond. of orch. and choral societies and prof. at the Thüringische Musikakademie. From 1916 he also taught at Weimar.

Works incl. operas *Das ewige Feuer* and *Judith*; Christmas Oratorio, Requiem, Psalm iii and other choral works; 3

symphs. and *Kleist Overture* for orch.; vln. concerto; 2 string 4tets; vln. and pf. sonata; 21 op. nos. of songs, etc.

Wetzler, Hermann Hans (b. Frankfurt, 8. X. 1870; d. N.Y., 29. V. 1943), Ger.-Amer. cond. and comp. Spent his childhood in U.S.A., but in 1882 went to study at the Hoch Cons. at Frankfurt under Scholz, Knorr, Humperdinck, Clara Schumann and others. In 1897–1901 he was organist at a N.Y. church. In 1903 he organized symph. concerts there, but in 1905 returned to Ger. and became cond. at var. opera houses. About 1930 he retired to Ascona, Switz., and in 1940 settled in U.S.A.

Works incl. operas *The Basque Venus* (after Mérimée); incid. mus. to Shakespeare's *As You Like It*; Magnificat for soprano, chorus and org.; *Symph. Fantasy, Visions, Assisi* for orch.; *Symphonie concertante* for vln. and orch.; Easter mus. for wind instruments and org.; variations for ob., clar and strings; *Scot. Songs* and 6 other op. nos. of songs, etc.

Weyse, Christoph Ernst Friedrich (b. Altona, 5. III. 1774; d. Copenhagen, 8. X. 1842), Ger.-Dan. pianist and comp. Pupil of Schulz at Copenhagen from 1789. He settled there as organist and mus. teacher. He also collected and ed. Dan. folksongs.

Works incl. operas *The Sleeping-Draught, Faruk, The Cave of Adullam, An Adventure in Rosenborg Gardens, Floribella, The Feast at Kenilworth* (after Scott), operettas; 4 symphs.; *c.* 30 cantatas; org. and pf. works; Dan. folksongs, etc.

Whichello, Abiell (b. ?; d. ? London, *c.* 1745), Eng. organist and comp. He was organist at the church of St. Edmund the King in London, taught the harpsichord and appeared at Thomas Britton's concerts.

Works incl. cantatas *Apollo and Daphne* and *Vertumnus and Pomona*; harpsichord lessons; songs, etc.

Whiffle (old Eng.) = Fife.

Whiffler (old Eng.), a piper, esp. on the Fife.

Whitaker, John (b. ?, 1776; d. London, 4. XII. 1847), Eng. organist, comp. and mus. pub. He was organist at the church of St. Clement, Eastcheap, in London and a partner in the mus. pub. firm of Button and W. He was in request as a comp. of mus. for the Sadler's Wells Theatre pantomimes, incl. the song 'Hot Codlins' sung by the clown Grimaldi.

Works incl. stage pieces *The Outside Passenger* (with Corri and Reeves), *A Chip of the Old Block, A Friend indeed, Three Miles from Paris, A Figure of Fun, The Apprentice's Opera, The Rake's Progress* and others; songs for a stage adaptation of Scott's *Guy Mannering*; anthem and other sacred mus.; settings of Eng. transs. of

Anacreon's Odes and Aesop's Fables; 12 pedal exercises for org., etc.

Whitbroke, William (b. ?; d. ?), Eng. 16th-cent. cleric and comp. He was educ. at Cardinal Coll., (later Christ Church) Oxford, where he was ordained priest in 1529. In 1531 he was app. sub-dean at St. Paul's Cathedral in London and soon afterwards also vicar of All Saints' Church at Stanton, Suffolk, where he may have retired on leaving St. Paul's in 1535.

Works incl. Mass for 4 voices, Magnificat and other church mus.

White, Alice Meadows. See **Smith, Alice Mary.**

White, Eric Walter (b. Bristol, 10. IX. 1905). Studied at Balliol College, Oxford, and was active in various non-mus. posts, in 1946 becoming a member of the Arts Council for Great Britain. He has written books on Stravinsky, Britten and Eng. opera.

White, Felix (Harold) (b. London, 27. IV. 1884; d. London, 31. I. 1945), Eng. pianist and comp. Learnt the pf. from his mother, but was otherwise self-taught. He was almost wholly devoted to comp., but in 1931 he joined the London Phil. Orch. as celesta and pf. player, and he also did transs. of mus. works, editing, etc.

Works incl. anthems; symph. poems *Astarte Syriaca* (D. G. Rossetti's picture) and *The Deserted Village* (after Goldsmith), overture *Shylock* (after Shakespeare's *Merchant of Venice*), serenade for string orch.; *The Nymph's Complaint for the Death of her Fawn* (Marvell) for voice, ob., vla. and pf., *Four Proverbs* for fl., ob., vln., vla. and cello, *Arietta* for string trio; pieces for var. instruments and pf.; *A Dickens Notebook* for pf.; many songs; part-songs, etc.

White, Maude Valérie (b. Dieppe, 23. VI. 1855; d. London, 2. XI. 1937), Eng. comp. After some preliminary lessons from Rockstro and others, she entered the R.A.M. in London and became a comp. student under Macfarren. After a period spent in S. America for her health, she finished her studies in Vienna.

Works incl. Mass for solo voices, chorus and orch.; 'Ich habe gelebt' (Schiller) for soprano and orch.; vocal 5tet 'Du bist wie eine Blume' (Heine); pf. pieces, numerous Eng., Fr. and Ger. songs to words by Herrick, Shelley, Byron, Hugo, Heine, etc.

White, Paul (b. Bangor, Maine, 22. VIII. 1895), Amer. violinist, cond. and comp. Studied at the New Eng. Cons., also comp. with Chadwick, v. with E. Ysaÿe and cond. with Goossens, whose orch. at Cincinnati he joined. Later became cond. of the Civic and Eastman School orchs. at Rochester, N.Y., and in 1938 became a member of the faculty of the latter.

Works incl. *Voyage of the Mayflower*

for chorus and orch.; symph. in E min., *Lyric Overture, Pagan Festival* and *To Youth* overtures, *Feuilles symphoniques, 5 Miniatures* for orch.; sinfonietta and *Old-fashioned Suite for strings*; poem for vln. and orch.; *Little Romance* and *Tune and Variations* for chamber orch., *Fantastic Dance* for woodwind; string 4tet; vln. and pf. sonata.

White (or Whyte), Robert (b. ? London, c. 1530; d. London, XI. 1574), Eng. comp. He was prob. the son of a London org. builder, also named Robert W., and took the Mus.B. degree at Cambridge in 1560. In 1561 he succeeded Tye as choirmaster at Ely Cathedral. He married Ellen Tye, prob. a daughter of that comp., in 1565 and left Ely in 1566, succeeded by John Farrant, to become choirmaster of Chester Cathedral until c. 1570, when he went to London to take up a similar post at Westminster Abbey. Nearly the whole of his family succumbed to the plague of 1574, himself incl.

Works incl. 20 Lat. motets and services; Eng. anthems; In Nomines for viols and arr. for lute; org. piece *Ut re mi fa sol la*; secular songs for several voices, etc.

White, Terence. See **Gervais.**

White, William (b. Durham, c. 1580; d. ?), Eng. 16th–17th-cent. singer and comp. He was a singer at Westminster Abbey in London.

Works incl. verse anthem in 2 parts, 'Almighty Lord' and 'Bend down'; fantasies and pavans for viols, etc.

Whitehill, Clarence (b. Marengo, Iowa, 5. XI. 1871; d. N.Y., 19. XII. 1932), Amer. bass-baritone. Studied at Chicago and Paris and made his 1st stage appearance at Brussels in 1899. After 1st singing in N.Y. in 1900 he made further studies with Stockhausen at Frankfurt and learnt Wagnerian parts with Cosima Wagner at Bayreuth.

Whitehouse, W(illiam). E(dward). (b. London, 20. V. 1859; d. London, 12. I. 1935), Eng. cellist. Studied at the R.A.M. in London, Piatti being among his masters, and joined the teaching-staff there in 1882. He travelled with Joachim and became a member of several chamber-mus. organizations.

Whithorn, a primitive Eng. instrument of the ob. type, also called May-horn, made of willow bark with a double reed of material from the same tree. It was formerly used in Oxfordshire for the Whit-Monday hunt.

Whithorne (real name Whittern), **Emerson,** (b. Cleveland, Ohio, 6. IX. 1884; d. Lyme, Conn., 25. III. 1958), Amer. pianist and comp. Studied at Cleveland and began to appear as pianist at the age of 15, but later had further lessons from Leschetizky in Vienna, where he also studied comp.

with Fuchs. He lived in London, 1907–15, returned to U.S.A., settled at St. Louis, 1915–20, then in N.Y.

Works incl. ballet *Sooner or later*; incid. mus. for Eugene O'Neill's *Marco Millions*; 2 symphs., symph. poems *The Rain, La Nuit, The Aeroplane, Fata Morgana, The Dream Pedlar, The Moon Trail*, suite *New York Days and Nights, Fandango* for orch.; poem for pf. and orch., vln. concerto; *Saturday's Child* for 2 voices and orch.; string 4tet, pf. 5tet, Gk. *Impressions* for string 4tet; *The Grim Troubadour* for voice and string 4tet; vln. and pf. sonata; suites *New York Days and Nights* and *El camino real* and other works for pf.; songs, etc.

Whitlock, Percy (William) (b. Chatham, 1. VI. 1903; d. Bournemouth, 1. V. 1946), Eng. organist and comp. Learnt mus. as a choir-boy at Rochester Cathedral and later studied at the G.S.M. and the R.C.M. in London. Asst. organist at Rochester Cathedral, 1921–30 and organist at Chatham and Borstal, from 1932 borough organist at Bournemouth.

Works incl. services, anthems, motets and hymn-tunes; mus. for a Rochester pageant; symph. for org. and orch.; sonata in C min., *Plymouth Suite* and other works for org., etc.

Whitman, Walt(er) (1819–92), Amer. poet. *See* Bacon (songs with orch.), Bell (symph.), Bonner (*Whispers of Heavenly Death*), Brian (*For Valour*), Bryson (*Drum Taps*), Carpenter (*Sea Drift*), Coleridge-Taylor (do.), Converse (*Mystic Trumpeter* and *Night and Day*), Farwell (symbolistic study), Harris (R.) (suite), Harty (*Mystic Trumpeter*), Henze (chamber cantata), Holst (*Ode to Death*), Kelley (*My Captain*), Loeffler (*Beat! Beat! Drums!*), Morning Heroes (Bliss), Müller-Hermann (*Song of Remembrance*), Schoeck (*Trommelschläge*), Sea Drift (Delius), Sea Symphony (Vaughan Williams), Sessions (*Turn O Libertad*), Vaughan Williams (*Toward the Unknown Region*), Wood (C.) (*Dirge for 2 Veterans* and *Ethiopia Saluting the Colours*).

Whittaker, W(illiam). G(illies). (b. Newcastle-on-Tyne, 23. VII. 1876; d. Orkney Isles, 5. VII. 1944), Eng. educationist, cond., ed. and comp. Taught and cond. choirs at Armstrong and King's Colls., Newcastle-on-Tyne, and founded a Bach Choir there. In 1929 he was app. prof. of mus. at Glasgow Univ. and principal of the Scot. Acad. of Mus. there. He ed. much old mus. and pub. miscellaneous essays and a work on Bach's cantatas.

Comps. incl. overture and choruses for Aeschylus's *Choephorae, A Lykewake Dirge* for chorus and orch.; pf. 5tet *Among the Northumbrian Hills*; part-songs and folksong arrs., etc.

Whittle and Dub, an old Eng. name for the Pipe and Tabor.

Who is Silvia ?, song by Schubert from Shakespeare's *Two Gentlemen of Verona*, trans. by Eduard von Bauernfeld as *An Silvia* and comp., in Ger., in 1826.

Whole-tone Scale, a mus. scale progressing by steps of nothing but whole tones. Only 2 such scales are possible, i.e.:

but they can of course begin at any point, there being no feeling of tonality or of any keynote; neither is there, consequently, any possibility of modulation, and the chances of harmonizing whole-tone mus. are limited. The accidentals may, of course, be equally well written as sharps or flats.

Whytbroke. *See* Whitbroke.

Whyte, Ian (b. Dunfermline, 13. VIII. 1901; d. Glasgow, 27. III. 1960), Scot. cond. and comp. Studied at the Carnegie Dunfermline Trust school of mus. and later at the R.C.M. in London, where Stanford and Vaughan Williams were his comp. masters. In 1923 he became mus. director to Lord Glentanar at Aboyne, Aberdeenshire, where he prod. operas, and in 1931 he was app. Scot. regional mus. director by the B.B.C.

Works incl. opera *Comala* (after Ossian); ballet *Goblin Ha*; incid. mus. for broadcast plays incl. an adaptation of Scott's *Marmion*; film mus. *Bonnie Prince Charlie*; 6 psalms for chorus and orch.; 2 operettas *The Forge* and *The Tale of the Shepherds* for solo voices, chorus and strings., *The Beatitudes* and sonnet by Wordsworth for chorus and strings; 2 symphs., overtures *The Treadmill* and *Bassoon Factory*, Festival March for orch.; pf. concerto; pf. 5tet; vln. and pf. sonatas, etc.

Whyte, Robert. *See* White.

Whythorne, Thomas (b. ?, 1528; d. ?, VIII. 1596), Eng. comp. He travelled in It. and elsewhere on the Continent and pub. his 1st book of mus. in 1571 and his 2nd in 1590. His autobiography was pub. in 1961.

Works incl. psalms and secular songs for 2–5 voices or solo voice with instruments, etc.

Wichello, Abiell. *See* Whichello.

Widdop, Walter (b. Norland nr. Halifax, 19. IV. 1892; d. London, 6. IX. 1949), Eng. tenor. He appeared as a Wagnerian singer with the B.N.O.C. in the 1920s and was almost alone among Eng. tenors to fill heroic parts of this kind. He appeared at Barcelona (1927), in Hol. and Ger., also sang in oratorio.

Widerspänstigen Zähmung, Der (*The Taming of the Shrew*), opera by Götz (lib. by Johann Viktor Widmann, after Shakespeare), prod. Mannheim, 11. X. 1874.

Widmann, Erasmus (b. Swäbisch Hall, IX. 1572; d. Rothenburg, 31. X. 1634), Ger. org. and comp. He wrote Lat. and Ger. sacred works, secular Ger. songs and dance mus., *canzone*, etc. for instruments.

Widor, Charles Marie (Jean Albert) (b. Lyons, 21. II. 1844; d. Paris, 12. III. 1937), Fr. organist, teacher and comp. Studied under his father, an organist at Lyons, and later with Lemmens and Fétis in Brussels. In 1870 he became organist of the church of Saint-Sulpice in Paris, and in 1890 succeeded Franck as org. prof. at the Cons., and became prof. of comp. in succession to Dubois in 1896.

Works incl. operas *Maître Ambros*, *Les Pêcheurs de Saint-Jean*, *Nerto* (after Mistral); ballet *La Korrigane*; pantomime *Jeanne d'Arc*; incid. mus. to *Conte d'Avril* (adaptation of Shakespeare's *Twelfth Night*) and Coppée's *Les Jacobites*; Mass for double chorus and 2 orgs., Psalm cxii for chorus, orch. and org.; 2 symphs., symph. poem *Une Nuit de Valpurgis*; symph. for org. and orch., concertos for pf., vln. and cello; pf. 5tet, pf. trio; vln. and pf. sonata, suite for fl. and pf.; 6 duets for pf. and org.; 10 symphs. and pieces for org.; pf. works; songs, etc.

Wiechowicz, Stanisław (b. Kroszyce, 27. XI. 1893; d. Cracow, 12. V. 1963), Pol. cond., critic and comp. Studied at Cracow, Dresden, Leningrad and Paris and settled at Poznan as cond. and critic. He was awarded the Pol. State prize for mus. in 1939. Taught at the Cracow Cons. from 1945.

Works incl. Romantic Cantata for chorus and orch. and other choral works; *Slavonic Day* for chorus and wind band; symph. poems *Indian Summer*, *Chmiel* and other orchestral works; *Pastoralki* (Pol. Christmas songs) and other songs; part-songs, folksong arrs., etc.

Wieck, Clara. *See* Schumann.

Wieck, Friedrich (b. Pretzsch nr. Torgau, 18. VIII. 1785; d. Dresden, 6. X. 1873), Ger. pianist and teacher of his instrument, father of Clara Schumann. Taught at Leipzig and Dresden, and had Schumann and Bülow among his pupils.

Wiegand, Carl Friedrich (1877–1942), Swiss dramatist. *See* Jelmoli (*Marignano*).

Wiegenlied (Ger. = cradle song), a title often given by Ger. comps. to vocal lullabies or to instrumental pieces in their manner.

Wieland, Christoph Martin (1733–1813), Ger. poet. *See* Oberon (Weber and Wranitzky), Schweitzer (Anton) (4 operas), Wolf (E. W.) (*Seraphina*).

Wieniawski, Adam (Tadeusz) (b. Warsaw, 27. XI. 1876; d. Bydgoszcz, 27. IV. 1950), Pol. comp. Studied with Noskowski and others at Warsaw, later with Bargiel in Berlin and d'Indy and Fauré in Paris. He served at the Fr. front in the 1914–18 war, returned to Warsaw and in 1928 became director of the Mus. Soc. and the Chopin High School of Mus.

Works incl. operas *Megae* and *Escape* (on Villiers de l'Isle-Adam's *L'Évasion*); ballets *A Celebration at Herod's*, *Acté in Jerusalem* and *Lalita*; suite for orch.; concertino for pf. and orch.; 2 string 4tets; songs; folksong arrs., etc.

Wieniawski, Henryk (b. Lublin, 10. VII. 1835; d. Moscow, 31. III. 1880), Pol. violinist and comp., uncle of prec., father of Poldowski. Was sent to the Paris Cons. at the age of 8 and in 1846 allowed to make his 1st tour, in Pol. and Rus. From 1850 he travelled with his brother Józef and in 1860 was app. solo violinist to the Tsar, living in St. Petersburg most of his time until 1872, when he toured the U.S.A. with A. Rubinstein. In 1875 he succeeded Vieuxtemps as 1st vln. prof. at the Brussels Cons. But he travelled again towards the end of his life, in spite of serious ill-health, which caused his sudden death in Rus.

Works incl. 2 vln. concertos; *Souvenir de Moscou*, *Le Carnaval russe*, *Légende* and numerous other pieces, fantasies and studies for vln., etc.

Wieniawski, Józef (b. Lublin, 23. V. 1837; d. Brussels, 11. XI. 1912), Pol. pianist and comp., brother of prec. Studied at the Paris Cons. He began to tour Eur. with his brother Henryk in 1850 and became prof. of pf. successively at Moscow and Brussels.

Works incl. chamber mus., pf. pieces, etc.

Wihan, Hanuš (b. Police, 5. VI. 1855; d. Prague, 1. V. 1920), Cz. cellist. Studied at the Prague Cons. and made his 1st appearance in Berlin, 1876. Solo cellist in the Munich court orch., 1880, and prof. at Prague Cons., 1888. Founded the Cz. String 4tet in 1892. Dvořák's cello concerto is ded. to him.

Wihtol, Joseph (b. Wolmar, 26. VI. 1863; d. Lübeck, 24. IV. 1948), Latvian comp. Studied with Rimsky-Korsakov and others at the St. Petersburg Cons., where in 1886 he became prof. of theory. In 1918 he returned to Latvia and took an important share in its mus. independence as a separate nation, becoming director of the Nat. Opera at Riga and director of the Latvian Cons.

Works incl. mus. for fairy play *King Brussubard*; symph., symph. poem *The Feast of Ligo*, Latvian overture *Spriditis*, dramatic overture for orch.; fantasy on Latvian folksongs for cello and orch.;

string 4tet; 5 pf. sonatas; part songs, folk-song arrs., etc.

Wiklund, Adolf (b. Långserud, Värmland, 5. VI. 1879; d. Stockholm, 3. IV. 1950), Swed. pianist, cond. and comp. Studied at the Stockholm Cons. and later travelled in Fr., It. and Ger., becoming a pupil of Kwast in Berlin. After cond. opera in Ger., he became 2nd cond. at the Stockholm Opera in 1911 and was app. court cond. in 1923.

Works incl. symph., symph. poem *Sommar*, concert overture for orch.; 2 concertos and *Conzertstück* for pf. and orch.; string 4tet; 2 vln. and pf. sonatas; pf. pieces; songs, etc.

Wilbye, John (b. Diss, Norfolk, III. 1574; d. Colchester, IX. 1638), Eng. comp. His father, a tanner and landowner, seems to have given him a good educ. He was patronized by the Cornwallis family at Brome Hall and *c.* 1595 went into the service of their son-in-law, Sir Thomas Kytson, at Hengrave Hall nr. Bury St. Edmunds, and was frequently in London with the family. After the death of his patron he remained in the service of his widow, who d. in 1628, whereupon he went to Colchester to join the household of her daughter, Lady Rivers. He never married and was well-to-do, having been granted a lease of a sheep-farm by Kytson and gradually acquiring property at Diss, Bury St. Edmunds and elsewhere.

Works incl. 2 sacred vocal pieces contrib. to Leighton's *Teares and Lamentacions*; 2 books of (64) madrigals, madrigal *The Lady Oriana* contrib. to *The Triumphes of Oriana*; 3 fantasies for viols (incomplete); lute lessons (lost), etc.

Wilcken, Anna Magdalena. *See* **Bach** family, 29.

Wilde, Oscar (O'Flaherty) (1856–1900), Ir. poet, dramatist and novelist. *See* Bantock (*Salome*), Benjamin (*Ideal Husband*), Bossi (R.) (*Rosa rossa*), Carpenter (*Birthday of the Infanta*), Fortner (*Weisse Rose*, Glazunov (*Salome*), Ibert (*Ballad of Reading Gaol*), Krein (A.) (*Salome*), Křička (*Gentleman in White*), Lutyens (*Birthday of the Infanta*), Mossolov (*Sphinx*), Radnai (*Birthday of the Infanta*), Riadis (*Salome*), Salome (R. Strauss), Salomé (Mariotte), Schreker (*Geburtstag der Infantin*), Sekles (*Zwerg und die Infantin*), Tcherepnin (A.) (*Salome*), Vassilenko (*Garden of Death*), Zemlinsky (*Florentinische Tragödie* and *Zwerg*).

Wildenbruch, Ernst von (1845–1909), Ger. poet and dramatist. *See* Hummel (F.) (incid. mus. for plays), Schillings (*Hexenlied*), Zöllner (*Überfall*).

Wilder, Philip van (b. ?; d. ?), Flem. lutenist and comp. App. lutenist to Henry VIII in 1538 and later became gentleman of the privy chamber to Edward VI. Comp. motets, anthems, etc.

Wilder, Thornton (Niven) (b. 1897), Amer. playwright. *See* **Taylor (Deems)** (*Lucrece*).

Wilder, (Jérôme Albert) Victor (van) (b. Wetteren nr. Ghent, 21. VIII. 1835; d. Paris, 8. IX. 1892), Belg. poet, mus. critic and trans. Studied law and philosophy at Ghent Univ. and mus. at the Cons. Later settled in Paris as critic, made many Fr. transs. of great works, incl. Handel's *Messiah* and Wagner's later operas, and pub. books on Mozart and Beethoven.

Wildroe, Philip de. Another form of the name of Philip van Wilder.

Wildschütz, Der, oder Die Stimme der Natur (*The Poacher, or The Voice of Nature*), opera by Lortzing (lib. by comp. based on a play by Kotzebue), prod. Leipzig, 31. XII. 1842.

Wilhelm, Carl (b. Schmalkalden, 5. IX. 1815; d. Schmalkalden, 16. VIII. 1873), Ger. cond. and comp. He cond. a male-voice choral society at Crefeld in 1840–65, and in 1854 set the words of Max Schneckenburger's *Die Wacht am Rhein* as a patriotic song, for which he received a pension in 1871.

Wilhelmj, August (Emil Daniel Ferdinand Victor) (b. Usingen, Nassau, 21. IX. 1845; d. London, 22. I. 1908), Ger. violinist. Made his 1st public appearance in 1854 and in 1861 was sent by Liszt to Leipzig to study with David at the Cons. In 1865 he began to travel and in 1866 1st visited London, where in 1894 he settled as vln. prof. at the G.S.M.

Wilkinson, Robert (b. ?; d. ?), Eng. 15th–16th-cent. comp. Comp. 2 settings of *Salve Regina* for 5 and 9 voices, 'Jesus autem transiens' (Apostles' Creed) for 13 voices in canon, 'O virgo prudentissima', etc.

Wilkinson, Thomas (b. ?; d. ?), Eng. 16th–17th-cent. comp. He may have been a singer at Durham Cathedral and he contrib. 3 anthems to Myriell's *Tristitiae remedium* in 1616.

Works incl. services, 18 anthems, madrigals, pavans for viols, etc.

Willaert, Adrian (b. ? Bruges, *c.* 1490; d. Venice, 17. XII. 1562), Flem. comp. Educ. for law, he was sent to Paris for further study, but turned to mus. and became a pupil of Mouton or Josquin des Prés. After a return home he went to It., visiting Venice, Rome and Ferrara, then went into the service of King Lewis of Boh. and Hung., who d. in 1526, when W. returned to It., becoming *maestro di cappella* at St. Mark's, Venice, in 1527, and founding a singing-school there. He revisited Flanders in 1542 and 1556.

Works incl. Masses, motets, Magnificat, set of motets on the hist. of Susanna, psalms, hymns; madrigals, *canzoni, villanesche*; instrumental fantasies and *ricercari*, etc.

Willan, Healey (b. London, 12. X. 1880; d. Toronto, II. 1968), Eng.-Canadian organist and comp. Began his career as church organist in London, but emigrated to Toronto, where he became lecturer at the univ. in 1914 and mus. director to the Hart House Players in 1919. In 1920 he became vice-principal of the Cons. and later prof. at the univ.

Works incl. incid. mus. to plays; church mus.; war elegy *Why they so softly sleep, Apostrophe to the Heavenly Hosts* and *Coronation Te Deum* for chorus and orch.; 2 symphs.; *Marche solennelle* for orch.; preludes and fugues, *Epilogue, Introduction, Passacaglia and Fugue* and other works for org.; songs to words by Yeats and others, etc.

William of Newark (b. Newark-on-Trent, ?; d. ? London, 1509), Eng. comp. Predecessor of Cornyshe as Master of the Children in the Chapel Royal. A madrigal and 7 songs are preserved.

William Ratcliff. *See also* **Guglielmo Ratcliff** and **Ratcliff.**

Opera by Cui (lib. by Alexey Nikolaievich Pleshtcheiev, based on Heine's drama), prod. St. Petersburg, 26. II. 1869.

Opera by Dopper (lib. by ?, based on Heine), prod. Weimar, 19. X. 1909.

Opera by Emilio Pizzi (1861–1931) (lib. by Angelo Zanardini, based on Heine), prod. Bologna, Teatro Comunale, 31. X. 1889.

William Tell. *See* **Guillaume Tell** for Rossini's opera; **Schiller** for other works.

Williams, Alberto (b. Buenos Aires, 23. XI. 1862; d. Buenos Aires, 17. VI. 1952), Arg. pianist, cond., poet and comp. of Eng. and Basque descent. Studied at the Buenos Aires Cons. and later in Paris, where he studied pf. with the Chopin pupil Mathias, harmony with Durand, counterpoint with Guiraud and comp. with Franck. In 1889 he returned home, where he gave pf. recitals, cond. symph. concerts and founded the Buenos Aires Cons.

Works incl. 2 symphs. (No. 2 *La bruja de las montanas*) and other orchestral works; choruses; works for vln. and pf. and cello and pf.; *El rancho abandonado* and other pieces; songs, etc.

Williams, Anna (b. London, 6. VIII. 1845; d. London, 3. IX. 1924), Eng. soprano. Studied in London, took a prize at the Crystal Palace in 1872, went to Naples to finish her studies with Scafati and in 1874 made her 1st important appearance in London.

Williams, (John) Gerrard (b. London, 10. XII. 1888; d. Oxted, Surrey, 7. III. 1947), Eng. comp. Studied architecture at first, but picked up any mus. experience

he could in choirs and orchs., etc. He began as a self-taught comp. in 1911, but in 1913 had some lessons from Walthew.

Works incl. ballad opera *Kate, the Cabin Boy*, operetta *The Story of the Willow-pattern Plate* and others; ballet *The Wings of Horus*; suites *Pot Pourri* and *Miniatures* for orch.; 2 string 4tets; preludes, *Side-shows*, etc. for pf.; many songs, etc.

Williams, Grace (b. Barry, Glam., 19. II. 1906), Welsh comp. Educ. at Cardiff Univ., where she took the B.Mus. in 1926; studied with Vaughan Williams at the R.C.M. in London, 1926–30, and with Wellesz in Vienna, 1930–1.

Works incl. *Hymn of Praise* (*Gogonedawg Arglwydd* from 12th-cent. Black Book of Carmarthen) for chorus and orch.; Welsh overture *Hen Walia*, legend *Rhiannon*, Fantasy on Welsh Nursery Rhymes, symph. impressions *Owen Glendower* (after Shakespeare's *1 Henry IV*), *Penillion*; vln. concerto; 2 psalms for soprano and orch., *The Song of Mary* (Magnificat) for soprano and orch.; *Sinfonia concertante* for pf. and orch.; elegy and *Sea Sketches* for string orch.; songs to words by Herrick, Byron, Belloc, D. H. Lawrence, etc.; arrs. of Welsh folksongs, etc.

Williams, Ralph Vaughan. *See* **Vaughan Williams.**

Williamson, Malcolm (b. Sydney, 21. XI. 1931), Aus., now Eng., comp. Studied with Eugene Goossens at the Sydney Cons. and with Lutyens in London, where he later became an organist.

Works incl. operas *English Eccentrics, The Violins of St. Jacques*; concerto for org. and orch., 3 pf. concertos, vln. concerto; *Santiago de Espado*, overture for orch.; 3 pf. sonatas, etc.

Willner, Arthur (b. Teplice, 5. III. 1881; d. London, 7. IV. 1959), Ger.-Cz. comp. Studied at the Leipzig Cons. and later with Rheinberger and Thuille at Munich. In 1903 he joined the staff of the Stern Cons. in Berlin, of which he became deputy director; in 1924 he settled in Vienna and in 1938 in London.

Works incl. symph. in A min., suite of fugues, *The Instruments present themselves* for orch.; pf. concerto, cello concerto, *Bagpipes* and suite for pf. and strings, concerto for 2 vlns. and strings; 5 string 4tets, 12 fugues *Circle of Life* for string 4tet; 4 sonatas, 3 sonatinas and suite for vln. and pf.; var. instrumental pieces; pf. duets, 4 sonatas, variations, *Tanzweisen, A travers les siècles, Sketches, Neues Notenbuch, La Voix du piano* and other works for pf.; songs, etc.

Wilm, Nikolai von (b. Riga, 4. III. 1834; d. Wiesbaden, 20. II. 1911). Latvian comp. Studied at the Leipzig Cons. In 1857 became 2nd cond. at the Riga municipal theatre and in 1860 went to St. Petersburg

as prof. at the Nikolai Inst. He lived
at Dresden in 1875–8 and then at Wiesbaden.

Works incl. motets; string 4tet, string
6tet; 2 sonatas and 2 suites for vln. and pf.,
sonata for cello and pf.; numerous pf.
pieces; songs; part-songs, etc.

Wilson, John (b. ? Faversham, 5. IV.
1595; d. London, 22. II. 1674), Eng.
lutenist, singer and comp. Contrib., (?)
with Coperario and Lanier, to *The Maske
of Flowers*, perf. at Whitehall in 1614. He
became one of the king's musicians in
1635. Lived at Oxford during the Civil
War and took the D.Mus. there in 1645;
soon afterwards was in private service in
Oxfordshire, but in 1656–61 was Prof. of
Mus. at Oxford Univ.; then returned to
London to be at or near the restored court
and became a Gentleman of the Chapel
Royal in 1662 in succession to H. Lawes.

Works incl. mus. for Brome's *The
Northern Lass*, songs for *The Maske of
Flowers*; anthem 'Hearken, O God';
Psalterium Carolinum for 3 voices and
continuo; Elegy on the Death of Wm.
Lawes; *Cheerful Ayres* for 3 voices; airs
and dialogues with lute; songs incl.
Shakespeare's 'Take, O take those lips
away' and 'Lawn as white as driven snow';
catches, etc.

Wilt (*née* Liebenthaler), **Marie** (b.
Vienna, 30. I. 1833; d. Vienna, 24. IX. 1891),
Aus. soprano. An orphan, she was brought
up by foster-parents and married the architect Franz Wilt. After singing at concerts,
she was advised by Désirée Artôt to go on
the stage, studied with Gänsbacher and
Wolf, and made her 1st stage appearance
at Graz in 1865. In 1866 she sang in It.
opera in London as Maria Vilda.

Winchester Tropers. *See* **Troper.**

Winckelmann, Johann Joachim (1717–
1768), Ger. archaeologist and author.
See **Vestale** (Spontini).

Wind Machine (Aeoliphone), a stage
property used by R. Strauss in *Don
Quixote*, Ravel in *Daphnis et Chloé* and
Vaughan Williams in *Sinfonia antarctica*.
It is a barrel covered with silk, the friction
of which on being turned prod. a sound
like a whistling wind.

Windgassen, Wolfgang (b. Annemasse,
26. VI. 1914), Ger. tenor. Studied with his
father and at the Hochschule für Musik in
Stuttgart. From 1939 he sang in Pforzheim and since 1951 has been a member of
the Stuttgart Opera. W. is the leading
heroic tenor of the post-war years, excelling
in Wagnerian roles.

Winkler, Alexander Adolfovich (b. Kharkov, 3. III. 1865; d. Besançon, 6. VIII.
1935), Rus. pianist and comp. Studied at
Kharkov, with Duvernoy in Paris and with
Leschetizky in Vienna. After teaching at
the Kharkov School of Mus. he became

prof. at the St. Petersburg Cons. in 1896.
He left Rus. for Fr. in 1924.

Works incl. overture *En Bretagne*, variations on Rus. and Fin. folksongs for orch.;
3 string 4tets, string 5tet, pf. 4tet, pf. trio;
vla. and pf. sonata; variations and fugue
on a theme by Bach for 2 pfs.: variations
and fugue on an orig. theme and other
works for pf.; songs, etc.

Winsheim, Abraham. *See* **Weisshan.**

Winter Journey (Schubert). *See* **Winterreise.**

Winter, Peter (von) (b. Mannheim, VIII.
1754; d. Munich, 17. X. 1825), Ger. comp.
Played as a boy in the court orch. at Mannheim, where he was a pupil of Vogler and
met Mozart in 1778. Moved with the court
to Munich, but went to Vienna 1780–1
and studied with Salieri. On his return to
Munich he prod. the first of his many
operas, *Helena und Paris*, became vice-
Kapellmeister to the court in 1787 and
Kapellmeister in 1798, but was periodically
absent on tour.

Works incl. operas *Helena und Paris,
Der Bettelstudent, I fratelli rivali, Das
unterbrochene Opferfest, Das Labyrinth*
(sequel to Mozart's *Magic Flute*), *Maria
von Montelban, Tamerlan, La grotta di
Calipso, Il trionfo dell' amor fraterno,
Il ratto di Proserpina, Zaira, Colmal,
Maometto II, Scherz, List und Rache* and
Jery und Bätely (both libs. by Goethe) and
c. 20 others; ballets *Heinrich IV, Inez de
Castro, La Mort d'Hector* and 6 others;
Masses and other church mus.; oratorios
Der Sterbende Jesus, La Betulia liberata
and others; cantata *Timoteo, o Gli effetti
della musica* and others; symphs. and over-
tures; concerted pieces for var. instuments;
songs, part-songs, etc.

'Winter Wind' Study, the nickname
sometimes given to Chopin's pf. Study in
A min., Op. 25 No. 11.

Wintermärchen, Ein (*A Winter's Tale*),
opera by Goldmark (lib. by Alfred Maria
Willner, after Shakespeare), prod. Vienna,
Opera, 2. I. 1908.

Winterreise, Die (*The Winter Journey*),
song cycle by Schubert (poems by Wilhelm
Müller), comp. Part i, II. 1827; Part ii, X.
1827.

Winter's Tale. *See* **Hermione; Wintermärchen.**

Wipo (Wigbert) (b. Solothurn, *c*. 995;
d. in the Bavar. Forest, *c*. 1050), Ger. poet
and priest, who ended his life as a hermit.
He is the reputed author (and perhaps
adaptor of the music) of the sequence
Victimae paschali.

Wirbel (Ger.), a roll on any kind of
drum.

Wirbeltrommel (Ger. = rolling-drum) =
Tenor Drum (more often called *Rührtrommel*).

Wirén, Dag (b. Noraberg, Örebro län,

15. X. 1905), Swed. critic and comp.
Studied at the Stockholm Cons. In 1932
he received a stage grant and continued
his studies with Sabaneiev in Paris. On his
return he became a mus. critic at Stockholm.

Works incl. 4 symphs., sinfonietta;
serenade for strings; cello concerto, vln.
concerto, pf. concerto; 3 string 4tets, 2 pf.
trios; 2 sonatinas for cello and pf.; pf.
pieces; songs.

Wise, Michael (b. ? Salisbury, c. 1648;
d. Salisbury, 24. VIII. 1687), Eng. counter-
tenor and comp. Choir-boy at the Chapel
Royal in London in 1660. In 1663 he
became a lay-clerk at St. George's Chapel,
Windsor, and in 1668 organist and choirmaster of Salisbury Cathedral. He was
admitted a Gentleman of the Chapel Royal
in 1676, but retained his post at Salisbury
until 1685, when at the time of the coronation of James II he was suspended, probably for some political opposition to the
new king. In 1687 he became almoner and
choirmaster at St. Paul's Cathedral in
London, but he still visited Salisbury,
where his wife had remained. After a dispute with her at night he left the house and
was killed in a quarrel with a watchman.

Works incl. services and anthems;
catches; duet *Old Charon*, etc.

'Witch' or **'Witches' Minuet** (Ger. *Hexen-
menuett*), the nickname sometimes given
to the minuet in Haydn's D min. string
4tet, Op. 76 No. 2.

Witkowski, Georges (Martin) (b. Mos-
taganem, Algeria, 6. I. 1867; d. Lyons,
12. VIII. 1943), Fr. comp. Educ. for a
military career, but turned to mus. and
studied with d'Indy. Leaving the army, he
cond. choral and orchestral concerts at
Lyons and was director of the Cons. there
from 1924 to 1941.

Works incl. operas *Le Maître à chanter*,
La Princesse lointaine (after Rostand's
play); *Poème de la maison* for solo voices,
chorus and orch.; 2 symphs.; prelude,
variations and finale *Mon lac* for pf. and
orch., *4 Poèmes* and *Introduction et Danses*
for vln. and orch.; songs with orch. on
poems by Ronsard, H. de Régnier and
others; string 4tet, pf. 5tet; song cycle
Poèmes de l'amour, etc.

Witt, Christian Friedrich (b. Altenburg,
c. 1660; d. Altenburg, 13. IV. 1716), Ger.
comp. Court mus. director at Altenburg.

Works incl. *Psalmodia sacra*, cantatas;
Fr. overtures and suites for orch.; org. and
harpsichord works, etc.

Wittgenstein, Paul (b. Vienna, 5. XI.
1887; d. Manhasset, N.Y., 3. III. 1961),
Aus. pianist. He was a pupil of Leschetizky
in Vienna and gave his 1st recital in 1913.
He lost his right arm in the 1914–18 war
and devoted the rest of his career to playing works for the left hand only. Among

the comps. who wrote works for him were
Strauss (*Parergon zur Symphonia domestica*), Ravel (concerto in D maj.), Korngold
(concerto in C♯ maj.) and Britten (*Diversions on a Theme*).

Woelfl, Joseph (b. Salzburg, 24. XII.
1773; d. London, 21. V. 1812), Aus.
pianist and comp. Pupil of L. Mozart and
M. Haydn at Salzburg, where he was a
choir-boy at the cathedral. In 1790 he went
to Vienna and c. 1792 made his 1st public
appearance, at Warsaw. He soon made his
name as a virtuoso and after prod. some
stage works in Vienna married the actress
Therese Klemm in 1798 and went on a long
tour in Boh. and Ger. In 1801–5 he lived
in Paris, where he prod. 2 more operas,
and then settled in London.

Works incl. operas *Der Höllenberg*,
Das schöne Milchmädchen, *Der Kopf ohne
Mann*, *Liebe macht kurzen Prozess* (with
others), *L'Amour romanesque*, *Fernanda, ou
Les Maures*; ballets *La Surprise de Diane*
and *Alzire* (on Voltaire's play); symph.;
The Calm and other pf. concertos; chamber
mus.; *Non plus ultra* and other pf. sonatas,
var. pf. works, etc.

Wohltemperierte Clavier, Das (*The Well-
tempered Clavier*, see also **Weber, B. C.**).
Two sets of preludes and fugues by Bach
for keyboard (not exclusively clavichord,
as has sometimes been inferred from a misunderstanding of the title), finished in 1722
and 1744 respectively. Each set consists of
a cycle of 24 preludes and fugues in all the
maj. and min. keys in ascending order.
The 2 books together are commonly known
in Eng. as 'the 48'.

Wolf, a technical term for a jarring
sound prod. between certain intervals on
keyboard instruments tuned in meantone temperament or on string instruments
by defective vibration on a certain note or
notes.

Wolf, Ernst Wilhelm (b. Grossgehringen
nr. Gotha, II. 1735; d. Weimar, XI. 1792),
Ger. comp. He was leader and from 1768
court cond. at Weimar.

Works incl. operas *Die Dorfdeputierten*
(after Goldoni), *Das grosse Los*, *Der
Eremit auf Formentara* (Kotzebue), *Die
Zauberirrungen* (after Shakespeare's *Midsummer Night's Dream*), *Erwin und Elmire*
(Goethe) and others; monodrama *Polyxena*; cantata *Seraphina* (Wieland); church
mus.; oratorios, Easter cantatas (Herder);
symphs.; string 4tets and other chamber
mus.; songs, etc.

Wolf-Ferrari, Ermanno (b. Venice, 12.
I. 1876; d. Venice, 21. I. 1948), It.-Ger.
comp. He was sent to Rome to study art
by his Ger. father, a painter, but turned to
mus. and studied with Rheinberger at
Munich. In 1899 he went to Venice and
succeeded in having his oratorio perf. and
in 1900 brought out his 1st opera, after

which his stage successes were frequently repeated. Many of his operas were 1st prod. in Ger. In 1902–12 he was director of the Liceo Benedetto Marcello at Venice. Works incl. operas *Cenerentola*, *Le donne curiose*, *I quattro rusteghi*, *Il segreto di Susanna*, *I gioielli della Madonna*, *Amor medico* (after Molière), *Gli amanti sposi*, *Das Himmelskleid*, *Sly* (after Shakespeare's *Taming of the Shrew*), *La vedova scaltra*, *Il campiello*, *La dama boba* (after Lope de Vega), *Gli dei a Tebe*; cantatas *La Sulamita* and *La vita nuova* (after Dante); vln. concerto; chamber symph. for strings, woodwind, pf. and horn; pf. 5tet, pf. trio; 2 vln. and pf. sonatas; org. pieces; cello pieces; *Rispetti* for soprano and pf., etc.

Wolf, Hugo (Philipp Jakob) (b. Windischgraz [now Slovenjgradec], 13. III. 1860; d. Vienna, 22. II. 1903), Aus. comp. His father, a leather merchant, encouraged his early gifts by teaching him pf. and vln. After visiting var. schools, he was allowed to enter the Vienna Cons. in 1875, but left it the following year, preferring to pick up his own instruction where he could. From 1877, his father having incurred great losses in business, he was obliged to earn his own living by teaching. He often lived in great poverty, but when his pride would allow, he was befriended by var. mus. families, while Schalk and Mottl took a professional interest in him. In 1881 he was engaged as 2nd cond. at Salzburg under Muck, but was found to be temperamentally so unfitted for the post that the engagement was terminated within 3 months. From 1884 to 1887 he was mus. critic for the Vienna *Salonblatt*, but here again his irascibility and his intolerance, which saw no fault in Wagner and no good at all in Brahms, for ex. In 1897 his mind became unhinged and he was sent to a sanatorium. He was discharged as cured in I. 1898, but had a relapse and was taken to an asylum in a hopeless condition in December, remaining there until his death.

Works incl. operas *Der Corregidor* and *Manuel Venegas* (unfinished); incid. mus. to Ibsen's *The Feast at Solhaug*; 48 early songs, 53 songs to words by Mörike, 20 to words by Eichendorff, 51 to words by Goethe, *Italian Song-Book* (46 songs), *Spanish Song-Book* (44 songs), 31 songs to words by var. poets, incl. 6 by Gottfried Keller and 3 sonnets by Michelangelo; symph. poem *Penthesilea* (after Kleist); *Italian Serenade* for small orch. or string 4tet; string 4tet in D min.; *Christnacht* for solo voices, chorus and orch., *Elfenlied* from Shakespeare's *Midsummer Night's Dream* for soprano, chorus and orch., *Der Feuerreiter* and *Dem Vaterland* for chorus and orch.; 6 part-songs, etc.

Wolf, Johannes (b. Berlin, 17. IV. 1869; d. Munich, 25. V. 1947), Ger. musicologist. Studied with Spitta in Berlin and took a doctor's degree at Leipzig in 1893. In 1908 he became prof. of mus. at Berlin Univ. and in 1915 librarian of the mus. section of the Prus. State Library, where he succeeded Altmann as director in 1928. He specialized in and wrote on early mus., old mus. treatises and old notations.

Wolfe, Humbert (1885–1940), Eng. poet. *See* Holst (songs).

Wolff, Albert (Louis) (b. Paris, 19. I. 1884; d. II. 1970), Fr. cond. and comp. Studied at the Paris Cons., became chorus master at the Opéra-Comique in 1908 and cond. in 1911, succeeded Messager as chief cond. in 1922. In 1928–34 he cond. the Lamoureux concerts and later the Pasdeloup concerts.

Works incl. opera *L'Oiseau bleu* (after Maeterlinck), etc.

Wolff, Christian (b. Nice, Fr., 8. III. 1934), Amer. comp. who came to the U.S.A. in 1941. Studied with Cage, and also classical languages at Harvard Univ., obtaining his Ph.D., and in 1962 becoming a lecturer there in classics. His mus. makes use of a strictly mathematical basis, particularly as regards rhythms and rests, while also including chance elements.

Works incl. *Nine* for 9 instruments; *For 6 or 7 players*; *Summer* for string 4tet; *In Between Pieces* for 3 players; *For 5 or 10 Players*; *For 1, 2 or 3 people*; 7tet for any instruments; *For Pianist*; *For Piano I, II*; *Duo for Pianists I and II*; *Duet I* for pf., 4 hands; *Duet II* for horn and pf.

Wolff, Erich (b. Vienna, 3. XII. 1874; d. N.Y., 20. III. 1913), Aus. pianist and comp. Studied at the Phil. Society Cons. in Vienna and became an accompanist.

Works incl. ballet *Zlatorog*; vln. concerto; string 4tet; numerous songs, etc.

Wolff, Pius Alexander (1784–1828), Ger. actor and playwright. *See* Eberwein (*Preciosa*), Preciosa (Weber).

Wolfram of Eschenbach (b. *c.* 1170, d. *c.* 1220), Ger. Minnesinger. He took part in a singing contest at Wartburg in 1207. Several of his melodies survive, and he wrote an epic, *Parzival*, which was a source for Wagner's *Parsifal*.

Wolfrum, Philipp (b. Schwarzenbach, Bavar., 17. XII. 1854; d. Samaden, Switz., 8. V. 1919), Ger. organist and comp. Studied at Munich with Rheinberger and others, later became organist and mus. director to Heidelberg Univ., and also cond. choral perfs.

Works incl. oratorio *Weihnachtsmysterium*, *Das grosse Hallelujah* (Klopstock) for male chorus, hymns *Der evangelische Kirchenchor* for chorus, *Festmusik* for baritone and male chorus; string 4tet, pf. 5tet, string trio; cello and pf.

sonata; 3 sonatas, 57 preludes, *3 Tondicht-ungen*, etc. for org.; pf. pieces; songs, etc.
Wolfurt, Kurt von (b. Lettin, Latvia, 7. IX. 1880; d. Munich, 25. II. 1957), Ger.-Baltic comp. Studied at the Leipzig Cons. and privately with Reger. After cond. at var. places, he lived in Rus. during the 1914–18 war and then in Berlin, where he taught from 1932 to 1945. From 1945 to 1949 he taught at Göttingen Univ. and from 1949 to 1952 in S. Africa. He wrote books on Mussorgsky and Tchaikovsky.

Works incl. operas *Der Tanz um den Narren* (after Molière) and *Dame Kobold* (after Calderón); Christmas Oratorio, rhapsody from Goethe's *Faust* and other choral works; triple fugue, concerto grosso, divertimento, serenade, variations and characteristic pieces on a theme by Mozart for orch.; mus. for strings and drums; pf. concerto, cello concerto, org. concerto; string 4tet; pf. pieces; songs, etc.

Wolkenstein, Oswald von (b. Schöneck Castle, Tyrol , *c.* 1377; d. Meran, 2, VIII. 1445), Aus. Minnesinger. Led a very adventurous life, travelled much, even as far as Asia and Africa. From 1415 he was in the service of King (later Emperor) Sigismund and was sent to Spain and Port. on diplomatic missions. In 1421–7 he involved himself in much strife and was twice imprisoned in his endeavour to extend his land by encroaching on that of his neighbours.

Works incl. songs of love, spring, travel, etc. for 1–3 voices (to his own words).

Wolowska, Maria. *See* **Szymanowska.**

Wolpe, Stefan (b. Berlin, 25. VIII. 1902), Amer. comp. of Rus. and Aus. parentage. Studied with Juon and Schrecker in Berlin and in 1933–4 with Webern, after which he went to Palestine and in 1938 settled in the U.S.A.

Works incl. operas *Schöne Geschichten* and *Zeus und Elida*; ballet *The Man from Midian*; symph., symph. for 21 instruments, Passacaglia and 2 Fugues for orch.; cantatas *The Passion of Man, On the Education of Man, About Sport, Unnamed Lands, Israel and his Land*; chamber mus., etc.

Wolstenholme, William (b. Blackburn, 24. II. 1865; d. London, 23. VII. 1931), Eng. organist and comp. Precociously gifted, although blind, he was trained in mus. at the Coll. for the Blind at Worcester, where Elgar taught him the vln. He cultivated the org. and pf. especially, became church organist at Blackburn in 1887, and from 1902 at var. churches in London. In 1908 he toured the U.S.A. as a recitalist.

Works incl. church mus.; orchestral and military band works; chamber mus.; *c.* 100 works for the org., incl. sonatas, fantasy, prelude and fugue, etc.; pf. pieces, etc.

Wolzogen, Ernst von (b. Breslau, 23. IV. 1855; d. Munich, 30. VII. 1934), Ger. writer. Studied at the Univs. of Strasbourg and Leipzig. With O. J. Bierbaum and F. Wedekind he estab. the satirical cabaret *Das Überbrettl* in Berlin in 1901, for which O. Straus and Schönberg provided some of the mus. The cabaret lasted two successful years, before finally closing. He was the author of the lib. of R. Strauss's *Feuersnot.*

Wolzogen, Hans (Paul) von (b. Potsdam, 13. XI. 1848; d. Bayreuth, 2. VI. 1938), Ger. writer on mus. He was called to Bayreuth by Wagner in 1877 to become ed. of the *Bayreuther Blätter*, and wrote several works of analysis and propaganda on Wagner's mus.-dramas.

Woman's Life and Love (Schumann). *See* **Frauenliebe und Leben.**

Women Composers. Most of the following will be found entered in detail in their proper alphabetical places:

Andrée, Elfrida (1841–1929), Swed.
Backer-Grøndahl, Agathe (1847–1907), Norw.
Barraine, Elsa (b. 1910), Fr.
Beach, Amy Marcy (1867–1944), Amer.
Bergman, Valentina Semenovna (wife of Serov) (1846–1927), Rus.
Bertin, Louise Angélique (1805–77), Fr.
Boulanger, Lili (1893–1918), Fr.
Boulanger, Nadia (b. 1887), Fr.
Bourges, Clémentine de (?–*c.* 1561), Fr.
Bright, Dora (1864–1951), Eng.
Bronsart, Ingeborg von. *See* Starck.
Caccini, Francesca (1581–?), It.
Candeille, Amélie Julie (1767–1834), Fr.
Chaminade, Cécile (1857–1944), Fr.
Clarke, Rebecca (b. 1886), Eng.
Coccia, Maria Rosa (1759–1833), It.
Coleridge-Taylor, Avril (b. 1903), Eng.
Delbos, Claire (wife of Messiaen) (b. *c.* 1910), Fr.
Farrenc, Louise (1804–75), Fr.
Gaigerova, Varvara (b. 1903), Rus.
Gipps, Ruth (b. 1921), Eng.
Glanville-Hicks, Peggy (b. 1912), Austral.
Grétry, Lucile (1773–93), Fr.
Harvey, Mary (Lady Dering) (1629–1704), Eng.
Hensel (*née* Mendelssohn), Fanny (1805–47), Ger.
Héritte-Viardot, Louise (1841–1918), Fr.
Hildegard, Saint (1098–1179), Ger.
Holmès, Augusta (1847–1903), Ir.-Fr.
Holst, Imogen (b. 1907), Eng.
Hopekirk, Helen (1856–1945), Scot.-Amer.
Howell, Dorothy (b. 1898), Eng.
Kaprálová, Vitězslava (1915–40), Cz.
La Guerre (*née* Jacquet), Elisabeth de (*c.* 1666–1729), Fr.
Lebrun, Francesca (1756–91), Ger.
Lehmann, Liza (1862–1918), Eng.

Loder, Kate (1825–1904), Eng.
Lucas, Mary Anderson (1882–1952), Eng.
Lund, Signe (1868–1950), Norw.
Lutyens, Elisabeth (b. 1906), Eng.
Maconchy, Elizabeth (b. 1907), Eng.
Makarova, Nina (b. 1908), Rus.
Maria Antonia Walpurgis, Electress of Saxony (1724–80), Ger.
Martinez, Marianne (1744–1812), Aus.
Mezari, Maddalena (16th-cent.), It.
Mounsey, Ann Sheppard (1811–91), Eng. ⎫
Mounsey, Elizabeth (1819–1905), Eng. ⎬ sisters.
⎭
Müller-Hermann, Johanna (1878–1941), Aus.
Musgrave, Thea (b. 1928), Scot.
Nascimbeni, Maria Francesca (17th-cent.), It.
Paradies, Marie Therese von (1759–1824), Aus.
Poldowski (Lady Dean Paul) (1879–1932), Pol.-Eng.
Poston, Elizabeth (b. 1905), Eng.
Rainier, Priaulx (b. 1903), S. African.
Renié, Henriette (1875–1956), Fr.
Rennes, Catherina van (1858–1940), Dutch.
Respighi (née Olivieri-Sangiacomo), Elsa (b. 1894), It.
Rokseth, Yvonne (1890–1948), Fr.
Sainton-Dolby, Charlotte (1821–85), Eng.
Schröter, Corona (1751–1802), Ger.
Schumann (née Wieck), Clara (1819–1896), Ger.
Sirmen (née Lombardini), Maddalena (? 1735–?), It.
Smith, Alice Mary (1839–84), Eng.
Smyth, Ethel (1858–1944), Eng.
Starck, Ingeborg (1840–1913), Swed.
Stirling, Elizabeth (1819–95), Eng.
Strozzi, Barbara (17th cent.), It.
Swain, Freda (b. 1902), Eng.
Tailleferre, Germaine (b. 1892), Fr.
Tate, Phyllis (b. 1911), Eng.
Temple, Hope (wife of Messager (1859–1938), Ir.-Fr.
Vaurabourg, Andrée (wife of Honegger) (b. 1894), Fr.
Viardot-García, Pauline (1821–1910), Span.-Fr.
Wakefield, Mary (1853–1910), Eng.
Weissberg, Julia Lazarevna (wife of Andrey Rimsky-Korsakov) (1878–1942), Rus.
White, Maude Valérie (1855–1937), Eng.
Williams, Grace (b. 1906), Welsh.
Wurm, Mary (1860–1938), Anglo-Ger.
Wood, Anthony (à) (b. Oxford, 17. XII. 1632; d. Oxford, 29. XI. 1695), Eng. antiquarian. Educ. at Merton Coll., Oxford, where he took the M.A. in 1655. He wrote several works on the hist. of Oxford and compiled biog. particulars of musicians.

Wood, Charles (b. Armagh, 15. VI. 1866; d. Cambridge, 12. VII. 1926), Ir. mus. scholar, teacher and comp. Learnt mus. from the organist of Armagh Cathedral, where his father was lay vicar, and in 1883–1887 studied at the R.C.M. in London, where he became prof. in 1888. From 1888 to 1894 he cond. the Univ. Mus. Society at Cambridge, where he took the Mus.D. in 1894. In 1897 he became mus. lecturer to the Univ. and in 1924 succeeded Stanford of Prof. of Mus.

Works incl. opera *The Pickwick Papers* (after Dickens); incid. mus. to Euripides' *Ion* and *Iphigenia in Tauris*; *Ode to the West Wind* and *The Song of the Tempest* for solo voices, chorus and orch.; *Ode on Mus.* (Swinburne), *Ode on Time* (Milton), *Dirge for Two Veterans* (Whitman), *Ballad of Dundee* for chorus and orch.; Passion according to St. Mark; services, motets, anthems, psalm-tunes; symph. variations on *Patrick Sarsfield*; 8 string 4tets; 16 org. preludes; songs incl. *Ethiopia saluting the Colours* (Whitman), etc.

Wood, Haydn (b. Slaithwaite, Yorks., 25. III. 1882; d. London, 11. III. 1959), Eng. violinist and comp. Having appeared as a child prodigy, he studied vln. with Arbós and comp. with Stanford at the R.C.M. in London, the former also with Thomson in Brussels.

Works incl. cantata *Lochinvar* (from Scott's *Marmion*); rhapsodies, overtures, picturesque suites, variations and other works for orch.; concertos for vln. and for pf.; fantasy string 4tet; instrumental pieces, over 200 songs, etc.

Wood, Henry J(oseph). (b. London, 3. III. 1869; d. Hitchin, Herts., 19. VIII. 1944), Eng. cond. He showed precocious gifts, esp. as an organist, and gave recitals and held church appts. as a boy. In 1889 he had his 1st experience as a cond., in opera, in which he toured for the next few years. In 1895 he was engaged by Robert Newman to take charge of the Promenade Concerts at the newly-built Queen's Hall, and he remained in charge of them for 50 years to the end of his life, celebrating their half-century just before his death. He began modestly with popular programmes, but soon perf. almost all the important orchestral mus. ever written, always incl. many of the latest foreign and Eng. novelties as soon as they appeared. He also cond. many mus. festivals. In 1898 he married the Rus. soprano Olga Urussov, who d. in 1909, and in 1911 Muriel Greatorex. Knighted in 1911.

Wood, Hugh (b. Wigan, 27. VI. 1932), Eng. comp. Studied comp. with A. Milner, I. Hamilton and Seiber. Taught at Morley College from 1959 to 1962, and then at the R.A.M.

Works incl. *Scenes from Comus* for

soprano, tenor and orch.; 2 string 4tets; trio for fl., vla. and pf.; pf. mus., etc.

Wood, Ralph (b. London, 31. V. 1902), Eng. comp. Engaged in business, he studied privately with Walthew, Howells and Gordon Jacob and began to appear in public with articles on mus. at 1st, but later made his mark mainly as a comp.

Works incl. incid. mus. for Shakespeare's *Tempest*; sev. choral works; 2 symphs., symph. variations, suite for small orch., *5 Dramatic Studies* and other works for orch.; 2 string 4tets, string 6tet, pf. 4tet, pf. trio, *Divertimento* for clar. and string, 4tet; vocal chamber mus.; pf. works; songs, etc.

Wood, Thomas (b. Chorley, Lancs., 28. XI. 1892; d. Bures, Essex, 19. XI. 1950), Eng. comp. and author. As the son of a master mariner he spent much of his youth at sea; but he was passionately interested in mus., was sent to Exeter Coll., Oxford, in 1913 and to the R.C.M., London, in 1918, where Stanford was his comp. master. He was mus. director at Tonbridge School in 1918–24, took the D.Mus. at Oxford in 1920 and in 1924–8 was lecturer and precentor at Exeter Coll. there. Owing to poor eyesight he retired to Essex in the latter year and devoted his time to comp., authorship and travel. These last 2 preoccupations produced 2 books, *Cobbers* and *True Thomas*.

Works incl. cantatas *Forty Singing Seamen* (Alfred Noyes), *Master Mariners*, *Merchantmen*, *The Ballad of Hampstead Heath* (Flecker); *c.* 30 part-songs; *In the Hill Country* for org.; pf. pieces, etc.

Woods, Michael (b. ?; d. ?), Eng. 16th-cent. organist and comp. Was organist of Chichester Cathedral in the middle of the cent. and wrote motets.

Woodson, Leonard (b. Winchester. ?; d. ? Eton, *c.* 1641), Eng. organist, singer and comp. He was in the choir at St. George's Chapel, Windsor, early in the 17th cent. and became organist of Eton Coll. in 1615.

Works incl. Te Deum and other church mus.; mus. for viols.; songs, etc.

Woodson, Thomas (b. ?, d. ?), Eng. 16th–17th cent. comp. In 1581 he became a member of the Chapel Royal, his place being taken by William West in 1605. Comp. 40 canonic settings of the plainsong *Miserere* for keyboard, only 20 of which survive. The single *Miserere* at Christ Church, Oxford (MS. 371), ascribed to 'Wodson', is prob. by an earlier comp.

Woodward, Richard (b. Dublin, 1744; d. Dublin, 22. XI. 1777), Ir. organist and comp. Learnt mus. as a choir-boy at Christ Church Cathedral, Dublin, where his father, Richard W., was vicar-choral, and in 1765 he was app. organist there. He

took the Mus.D. at Trinity Coll., Dublin, in 1771.

Works incl. services, anthems, chants and other church mus.; catches and canons; songs, etc.

Wooldridge, H(arry). E(llis). (b. Winchester, 28. III. 1845; d. London, 13. II. 1917), Eng. painter and mus. scholar. He was Slade Prof. of Fine Arts at Oxford from 1895–1904, but made a special study of medieval mus. His chief works are the 1st 2 vols. of the *Oxford History of Music*.

Wooldridge, John (b. Japan, 18. VII. 1911), Eng. comp. Educ. at St. Paul's School in London and Magdalen Coll., Oxford, later studied mus. and in IX. 1939 joined the R.A.F., in which he served through World War II.

Works incl. *A Solemn Hymn for Victory* for orch., etc.

Wordless Songs. Unlike Mendelssohn's *Songs without Words*, which are pf. pieces, W. S. are here understood as songs with voice and accomp. to be sung merely on vowels. Exs. are Medtner's *Sonata-Vocalise*, Ravel's *Vocalise en forme d'Habanera*, Cyril Scott's *Pastorale*, Stravinsky's *Pastorale*, etc.

Wordsworth, William (1770–1850), Eng. poet. *See* Davies (Walford) (orchestral suite), Finzi (*Intimations of Immortality*), Whyte (I.) (sonnet).

Wordsworth, William B(rocklesby). (b. London, 17. XII. 1908), Eng. comp., a direct descendant of the poet's brother. He became interested in mus. as a child, but did not begin to study seriously until he was 20. Finding work for the Mus.D. fruitless, he became a pupil of Tovey in 1935. During the 1939–45 war he took to farming, but after that devoted himself entirely to comp.

Works incl. oratorio *Dies Domini*, dirge *The Houseless Dead* (D. H. Lawrence) for baritone, chorus and orch., *Hymn of Dedication* (Chesterton) for chorus and orch.; 5 symphs., theme and variations, *3 Pastoral Sketches* for orch., *Sinfonia* and *Canzone and Ballade* for strings; pf. concerto, cello concerto; 6 string 4tets; string trio; 2 sonatas for vln. and pf., 2 sonatas for cello and pf.; sonata and suite for pf.; 3 hymn-tune preludes for org.; *4 Sacred Sonnets* (Donne) and other songs; rounds for several voices, etc.

Worgan, John (b. London, 1724; d. London, 24. VIII. 1790), Eng. organist and comp. Pupil of T. Roseingrave. App. organist of the church of St. Andrew Undershaft *c.* 1749 and of Vauxhall Gardens *c.* 1751 in succession to his brother James W. (*c.* 1715–53), to which he was also attached as comp. until 1761, and again in 1770–4. He took the Mus.D. in 1775. He became famous as an org. recitalist.

Works incl. oratorios *The Chief of Maon, Hannah, Manasseh* and *Gioas* (unfinished); anthem for a victory, psalmtunes; serenata *The Royal Voyage*, dirge in memory of Frederick, Prince of Wales; ode on the rebellion of 1745; org. pieces; harpischord lessons; glees; songs, etc.

Working-out (or Development), the 2nd section of a movement in sonata form, following the exposition, where the thematic material is subjected to var. developments, according to the comp.'s fancy. The usual procedure is to develop the 1st or 2nd subjects or both, but subsidiaries may be used as well, or instead, and new matter may be intro. at will.

Wormser, André (Alphonse Toussaint) (b. Paris, 1. XI. 1851; d. Paris, 4. XI. 1926), Fr. comp. Studied at the Paris Cons. and obtained the Prix de Rome in 1875.

Works incl. operas *Adèle de Ponthieu* and *Rivoli*; pantomimes *L'Enfant prodigue* and *L'Idéal*; ballet *L'Étoile*; cantata *Clytemnestre*; symph. poems *Lupercale* and *Diane et Endymion, Suite tzigane* for orch.; *Gigue* for vln. and orch.; *Amour* poem for voice and orch.; pf. pieces; songs, etc.

Worshipful Company of Musicians of London, The, an assoc. dating back to the Middle Ages, but not formally incorporated by royal charter until 1604, under James I, though minstrels had already been allowed to form themselves into guilds by Edward IV in 1469. Among its present functions is the award of prizes and scholarships.

Worzischek (or Worzišek), J(oh)an(n). *See Voříšek.*

Wotquenne, Alfred (Camille) (b. Lobbes, Hainault, 25. I. 1867; d. Antibes, 25. IX. 1939), Belg. mus. bibliog. Studied at the Brussels Cons. and became its librarian in 1894. He pub. its catalogue, bibliogs. of C. P. E. Bach, Galuppi, Gluck and Luigi Rossi, etc.

Woyrsch, Felix (b. Troppau, 8. X. 1860; d. Altona, 20. III. 1944), Ger.-Cz. cond. and comp. He was self-taught in mus. and went to Altona in 1887 as chorus and orch. cond.

Works incl. operas *Der Pfarrer von Meudon, Der Weiberkrieg, Wikingerfahrt*; incid. mus. to Moreto's *Donna Diana*; motets and other church mus.; Passion Oratorio; works for male chorus and orch.; 6 symphs., prologue to Dante's *Divina commedia*, Böcklin suite, theme and variations, overture to Shakespeare's *Hamlet* for orch.; vln. concerto; 4 string 4tets, string 6tet, pf. 5tet, 2 pf. trios and other chamber mus.; org. and pf. pieces; numerous songs, etc.

Woytowicz, Bolesław (b. Dunajowce, Podolia, 5. XII. 1899), Pol. pianist and comp. Began by studying mathematics and philosophy at Kiev Univ. and law at

Warsaw Univ., but coming of a mus. family, turned to the pf., which he studied at the Chopin High School at Warsaw, where he later became a teacher. He next took to comp., studying 1st with Szopski, Maliszewski and others, and in 1930 with Nadia Boulanger in Paris.

Works incl. concertino, concert suite, *Poème funèbre* on the death of Pilsudski, 2 symphs., incl. variations in the form of a symph. for orch.; pf. concerto; 2 string 4tets, trio for fl., clar. and bassoon, *Cradle Song* for soprano, clar., bassoon and harp; variations and other works for pf., etc.

Wozzeck, opera by A. Berg (lib. by comp. from Georg Büchner's drama of 1836), prod. Berlin, Opera, 14. XII. 1925. Opera by M. Gurlitt (lib. do.), prod. Bremen, 22. IV. 1926.

Wranitzky, Anton (b. Nova Říše, 13. VI. 1761; d. Vienna, 6. VIII. 1820), Morav. violinist and comp. Pupil of Haydn, Mozart and Albrechtsberger, he was *Kapellmeister* to Prince Lobkowitz from 1794, and later mus. director at the Theater an der Wien in Vienna.

Works incl. symphs., concertos, serenades; string 4tets, 5tets, 6tets, and other chamber mus., etc.

Wranitzky, Paul (b. Nova Říše, 30. XII. 1756; d. Vienna, 26. IX. 1808), Morav. violinist and comp., brother of prec. Pupil of (?) J. M. Kraus and Haydn in Vienna, in the 1780s he was in the service of Count Esterházy (not Prince E., Haydn's employer) and from *c.* 1790 leader of the court opera orch. in Vienna.

Works incl. operas and *Singspiele*, e.g. *Oberon, König der Elfen, Das Fest der Lazzaroni*, etc.; ballet divertissements *Das Waldmädchen, Die Weinlese, Zemire und Azore, Das Urteil von Paris*; symphs.; string 4tets and 5tets; pf. 4tets; vln. sonatas and large numbers of other instrumental works; over 200 canons; vocal duets, trios, etc.; church mus., etc.

Wreckers, The, opera by Ethel Smyth (lib. orig. in Fr., *Les Naufrageurs*, by Henry Brewster), prod., in Ger., as *Strandrecht*, Leipzig, 11. XI. 1906; 1st perf. in Eng., London, His Majesty's Theatre, 22. VI. 1909.

Wrest (noun), the old Eng. term for a tuning-key, from the verb meaning to twist or wrench. The tuning-pins of the pf. are still called wrest-pins and the board into which they are inserted is the wrestplank.

Wryght, Thomas (b. ?, d. ?), Eng. 16th-cent. comp. He was a member of the Chapel Royal, 1547–8; his *Nesciens mater* is in the 'Gyffard' part-books (*q.v.*).

Wüllner, Franz (b. Münster, 28. I. 1832; d. Braunfels, 7. IX. 1902), Ger. pianist, cond. and comp. Studied at home and at Frankfurt, and appeared as pianist at

Brussels in 1852–3, where he enlarged his experience by meeting Fétis, Kufferath and other musicians. He then made a tour in Ger., settled at Munich in 1854 and in 1856 became pf. prof. at the Cons. In 1858–1864 he was mus. director at Aachen, where he did much choral and orchestral cond., but he returned to Munich as court mus. director, reorganized the court church mus. and became cond. of the court opera in 1869 in succession to Bülow. In 1877–1882 he was court mus. director at Dresden, succeeding Rietz, and from 1884 director of the Cons. at Cologne in succession to F. Hiller and cond. of the Gürzenich concerts.

Works incl. Masses, motets, *Stabat Mater*, Miserere; Psalm cxxv for chorus and orch.; choral works with and without orch.; cantata *Heinrich der Finkler* for voice and orch.; chamber mus.; pf. pieces and duets; songs, etc.

Wurm, Mary (b. Southampton, 18. V. 1860; d. Munich, 21. I. 1938), Eng. pianist and comp. of Ger. parentage, sister of Adela and Mathilde Verne. Studied at the Stuttgart Cons., also with Clara Schumann and Raff at Frankfurt, and made her 1st appearance in London in 1882.

Works incl. overture for orch.; pf. concerto; string 4tet; cello and pf. sonata; pf. pieces, etc.

Wycherley, William (? 1640–1716), Eng. dramatist. *See* **Banister** (*Gentleman Dancing-Master*), **Humfrey** (*Love in a Wood*).

Wyk, Arnold van (b. nr. Calvinia, Cape Province, 26. IV. 1916), S. African comp. Began to learn the pf. at 12 and, after working in an insurance office at Capetown, entered Stellenbosch Univ. in 1936. In 1937 he was commissioned to write mus. for the centenary of the Voortrekkers and in 1938 he went to live in London, having gained the Performing Right Society's scholarship. He studied comp. with Theodore Holland and pf. with Harold

Craxton at the R.A.M., joined the B.B.C. for a short time and later devoted himself to comp.

Works incl. 2 symphs., suite for small orch. on African tunes *Southern Cross*; *Saudade* for vln. and orch.,; string 4tet, 5 elegies for string 4tet; 3 improvisations on a Dutch folksong for pf. duet., etc.

Wylde, John (b. ?, d. ?), Eng. 15th-c. mus. theorist, precentor of Waltham Abbey nr. London. He wrote a summary of Guido d'Arezzo's theoret. work, entitled *Musica Gwydonis monachi*. This stands at the head of a collection compiled by him (Brit. Mus., Lansdowne MS. 763) which later belonged to Tallis, whose signature it bears.

Wynne, Sarah (Edith) (b. Holywell, Flintshire, 11. III. 1842; d. London, 24. I. 1897), Welsh soprano. Studied at Liverpool, at the R.A.M. in London and at Florence. Made her 1st London appearance in 1862.

Wynslate, Richard (b. ?, d. ?), Eng. 16th-cent. comp. He was a singer at St. Mary-at-Hill, London, 1537–8, and master of the choristers, Winchester Cathedral, 1540–72. An org. piece, *Lucem tuam*, has survived.

Wyspiański, Stanisław (1869–1907), Pol. painter and dramatist. *See* **Melcer** (*Protesilaus and Laodamia*), **Szymanowski** (*Penthesilea*).

Wyzewa, (orig. Wyzewski), **Théodore de** (b. Kaluszik, 12. IX. 1862; d. Paris, 17. IV. 1917), Fr. musicologist of Polish parentage. He lived in France from 1869. In 1884 he founded the *Revue Wagnérienne* with Édouard Dujardin and in 1901 the Société Mozart with Boschot. He became a political and literary journalist, but also wrote articles on mus. and trans. var. lit. works from Eng. and Rus. His chief work is his study of Mozart, of which he completed 2 vols. in collaboration with Georges de Saint-Foix.

X

Xenakis, Yannis (b. Athens, 29. V. 1922), Gk. comp. First studied engineering and worked for some years as an architect with Le Corbusier, at the latter's invitation, in Paris. He also studied mus. with Honegger, Milhaud and Messiaen, and evolved a method of comp. using the mathematics of chance and probability and also employing computers (sometimes referred to as 'stochastic' mus.). His ideas have exercised considerable influence on other comps.
Works incl. *Metastasis* for orch.; *Pithoprakta* for string orch.; *Achorripsis* for 21 instruments; electronic comps. incl. *Diamorphosis, Orient-Occident*; *Morsima-Amorsima* (1) for 4 players, (2) for 10 players; *Stratégie* for two opposing orchs.; *Eonta* for pf. and brass instruments, etc.

Xerse (*Xerxes*). *See also* **Serse.**
Opera by Cavalli (lib. by Niccolò Minato), prod. Venice, Teatro dei SS. Giovanni e Paolo, 12. I. 1654.

Xylophone (from Gk. *xulon*, wood, and *phōnē*, sound), a perc. instrument with a series of wooden bars suspended over resonators and tuned in a chromatic scale. It is played with hammers and makes a dry, rattling but perfectly clear and richly sonorous sound. It is made in var. sizes.

Xylorimba, a perc. instrument, a small Marimba made in Amer.

Xyndas, Spyridon (b. Corfu, 8. VI. 1814; d. Athens, 25. XI. 1896), Gk. comp.
Works incl. It. operas *Anna Winter, I due rivali, Il Conte Giuliano, Il candidato al parlamento* and others; pf. pieces; many songs, etc.

Y

Yaniewicz. *See* **Janiewicz.**

Yasser, Joseph (b. Lodz, 16. IV. 1893), Pol.-Amer. organist and musicologist. Studied at the Moscow Cons. and became org. prof. there, also organist at the chief theatres. Later he lectured, cond. and gave many org. recitals in Rus., China and U.S.A., where he settled in 1927 as organist to the N.Y. synagogue and became a naturalized citizen. He made a special study of the mus. scales and the harmonic implications of the old and exotic ones. His books incl. *A Theory of Evolving Tonality* and *Medieval Quartal Harmony*.

Year 1812, The, festival overture by Tchaikovsky, Op. 49, written for the commemoration of the 70th anniversary of Napoleon's retreat from Moscow and 1st perf. during the Moscow Arts and Industrial Exhibition, 20. VIII. 1882, at the consecration of the Cathedral of the Redeemer in the Kremlin.

Yeats, W(illiam). B(utler). (1865–1939), Ir. poet. *See* **Barber** (songs), **Berger** (*Words for Music, Perhaps*), **Bryson** (*Cloak, Boot and Shoes*), **Dunhill** (*Cloths of Heaven*), **Edwards (J.)** (*Land of Heart's Desire*), **Egk** (*Irische Legende*), **Grania and Diarmid** (Elgar), **Hadley (P.)** (*Ephemera*), **Kalomiris** (*Haunted Waters*), **Loeffler** (*Wind among the Reeds*), **Swain** (*Harp of Aengus*).

Yeomen of the Guard, The, or The Merryman and his Maid, operetta by Sullivan (lib. by W. S. Gilbert), prod. London, Savoy Theatre, 3. X. 1888.

Yodel, a peculiar, primitive but elaborate form of song in Switz., Tyrol, Styria, etc., usually sung by men in Falsetto, with rapid changes to chest voice, very free in rhythm and metre and using as a rule the restricted scale of the natural harmonics of instruments like the Alphorn. The Y. is thus very prob. derived or copied from the Ranz des Vaches.

Yonge, Nicholas (b. Lewes, ?; d. London, X. 1619), Eng. singer and mus. ed. Worked in London and pub. in 1588 a vol. of It. madrigals with Eng. trans. entitled *Musica transalpina.*

Yorkshire Feast Song, The, an ode or cantata by Purcell, 'Of old when heroes', for 2 altos, tenor, 2 basses, 5-part chorus, recorders, obs., tpts. and strings, words by Thomas Durfey, written in 1690 for the annual reunion of Yorkshiremen in London, intended to be held that year on 14. II, but postponed to 27. III. owing to parliamentary elections.

Youll, Henry (b. ?; d. ?), Eng. 16th–17th-cent. comp. Pub. a book of canzonets and balletts for 3 voices in 1608.

Young, Alexander (b. London, 18. X. 1920), Eng. tenor. Studied in London, Naples and Vienna. After singing in the Glyndbourne chorus and some smaller parts, he became one of the leading Eng. operatic and concert singers. One of his best-known roles is that of Tom Rakewell in *The Rake's Progress,* which he recorded under the comp.'s baton.

Young, Cecilia (b. London, 1711; d. London, 1. X. 1789), Eng. soprano, daughter of Charles Y., organist of All Hallows, Barking, in London, married Arne in 1737.

Young, Isabella (b. ?; d. ?), Eng. singer, sister of prec., married Lampe in 1738.

Young, La Monte (b. Bern, Idaho, 14. X. 1935), Amer. comp. Studied at Univ. of California, Los Angeles from 1956 to 1957 and at Berkeley from 1957 to 1960. In 1959 he also studied with Stockhausen, and then lectured for a time on guerrilla warfare at the N.Y. School for Social Research.

Works incl. *The Tortoise Droning Selected Pitches From the Holy Numbers for the Two Black Tigers, the Green Tiger and the Hermit; The Tortoise Recalling the Drone of the Holy Numbers as They Were Revealed in the Dreams of the Whirlwind and the Obsidian Gong, Illuminated by the Sawmill, the Green Sawtooth Ocelot and the High-Tension Line Stepdown Transformer* (both works staged with voice, gong and strings); pf. mus., etc.

Young, Percy M(arshall). (b. Northwich, Ches., 17. V. 1912), Eng. mus. educationist, cond. and writer on mus. Educ. at Christ's Hospital and Cambridge, where he was org. scholar at Selwyn Coll. and took the M.A. and Mus.B. degrees. Mus.D. at Trinity Coll., Dublin. In 1934 he became director of mus. at the Teachers' Training Coll., Belfast, in 1937 mus. adviser to the Stoke-on-Trent Educ. Committee, in 1945 director of mus. studies at Wolverhampton Technical Coll. Pub. part-songs and var. collections for children, articles in mus. periodicals and a large number of books.

Young, Polly or Mary (b. London, 1749; d. London, 20. IX. 1799), Eng. singer, niece of Cecilia Y. She appeared in opera in London and married Barthélemon in 1766.

Young, Thomas (b. Canterbury, 1809; d. London, 12. VIII. 1872), Eng. alto. Educ. as a choir-boy at Canterbury Cathedral where he became an alto in 1831. In 1836 he went to London to join the choir at Westminster Abbey and in 1848 he became 1st alto at the Temple Church. He also frequently sang at concerts.

Young, William (b. ?; d. London, 21.

XII. 1671), Eng. violist, violinist, flautist and comp. He was in the service of the Archduke Ferdinand Karl (probably in the Netherlands), but returned to Eng. to join the king's band in 1660. From 1664 he and others were also allowed to play for Killigrew at the theatre.

Works incl. 21 sonatas for 3–5 instruments with appended dances, 3-part fantasies for viols, pieces for lyra viol, for vla. da gamba; airs for 2 treble viols and bass, etc.

Yradier, Sebastian (b. Sauciego, Álava, 20. I. 1809; d. Vitoria, 6. XII. 1865), Span. comp. He was in Paris for a time as singing-master to the Empress Eugénie and later lived in Cuba for some years. Wrote popular Span. songs, incl. *La Paloma* and the melody which formed the basis of the Habanera in Bizet's *Carmen*.

Yrvid, Richard *See* Ivry

Ysaÿe, Eugène (Auguste) (b. Liège, 16. VII. 1858; d. Brussels, 12. V. 1931), Belg. violinist, cond. and comp. Studied with his father, Nicolas Y., then at the Liège Cons. and later with Wieniawski and Vieuxtemps. Having already appeared in public in 1865, he played at Pauline Lucca's concerts at Cologne and Aachen, where he met F. Hiller and Joachim, and later, at Frankfurt, he came into touch with Raff and Clara Schumann. In 1886–98 he was vln. prof. at the Brussels Cons. and founded and cond. orchestral concerts in the Belg. capital. He toured extensively, 1st visiting Eng. in 1889 and U.S.A. in 1894.

Works incl. opera *Piér li Houïeu* (in Walloon dialect); vln. concertos; *Poème élégiaque*, mazurkas and other pieces for vln. and pf., etc.

Ysaÿe, Théo(phile) (b. Verviers, 2. III. 1865; d. Nice, 24. III. 1918), Belg. pianist and cond., brother of prec. Studied at the Liège Cons., with Kullak in Berlin and with Franck in Paris. He often appeared at concerts with his brother and also gave recitals of his own.

Works incl. Requiem; symph., symph. poems, fantasy, *Suite wallonne* for orch.; pf. concerto; pf. 5tet, etc.

Yugoslav Composers *See* Baranović, Gostovac, Lhotka, Lisinski, Miloyevich, Odak, Osterc, Papandopulo, Sirola, Skerjanc, Vučković, Vukdragovic, Zajc.

Yurovsky, Vladimir Mikhailovich (b. Tarastcha, Uzbekistan, 20. III. 1915), Rus. comp. Pupil of Miaskovsky at the Moscow Cons.

Works incl. opera *Concerning Opanas*; symph., symph. suite *Moscow Carnival* for orch.; vln. concerto; songs, etc.

Yussupov, Nikolai Borisovich, Prince (b. St. Petersburg, 1827; d. Baden-Baden, 3. VIII. 1891), Rus. amateur violinist and comp. Studied vln. with Vieuxtemps and later kept a private orch. in his palace, wrote a book on the vln. and planned another on mus. hist. with special reference to Rus.

Works incl. ballet *Ballet d'Espagne*; symph. with vln. solo *Gonzalvo de Córdova*; vln. concerto, etc.

Yvain, Maurice (Pierre Paul) (b. Paris, 12. II. 1891; d. Paris, 28. VII. 1965), Fr. comp. Studied at the Paris Cons. He served in the army during the 1914–18 war, resuming his studies later, devoting his whole attention to the comp. of operettas, the 1st of which, *Ta bouche*, was an immediate success in 1921 and was followed by many others, also a ballet *Vent*.

Z

Zacconi, Lodovico (b. Pesaro, 11. VI. 1555; d. nr. Pesaro, 23. III. 1627), It. priest and mus. theorist. He went to live at Venice, joined the monastic order of St. Augustine and was *maestro di cappella* at its church. In 1593, at the invitation of the Archduke Charles, he went to Vienna, where he became court mus. director and remained until 1619, when he returned to Venice. He wrote a large treatise in 4 vols., *Prattica di musica.*

Zach, Jan (b. Čelákovice nr. Prague, 13 XI. 1699; d. ?, 1773), Boh. organist and comp. Worked as a violinist and organist in Prague, where he came under the influence of Černohorsky, later left for Ger. and in 1745 was app. *Kapellmeister* to the Electoral court in Mainz. Dismissed *c.* 1756, he spent the rest of his life travelling, without permanent employment.
Works incl. *c.* 40 Masses, 4 Requiems, *Stabat Mater* and other church mus.; symphs. and partitas for orch.; chamber mus.; org. mus., etc.

Zachara da Teramo, Antonio (b. ?; d. ?), It. 14th–15th-cent. comp. Nothing is known of his life. A number of *ballate* and sacred works are extant.

Zacharias, Magister (b. ?; d. ?), It. 14th–15th-cent. comp. He (?) concluded his career as a singer for Alexander V and John XXII, *c.* 1410. A few secular works have survived. He may be the 'Zacar' of the Old Hall MS.

Zacharie da Brindisi, Nicola (b. ?; d. ?), It. 15th-cent. comp., son of prec. (?). He was a member of the papal chapel in 1420 and 1434. A few sacred and secular pieces have survived.

Zachau, Friedrich Wilhelm (b. Leipzig, XI. 1663; d. Halle, 14. VIII. 1712), Ger. organist and comp. Pupil of his father, a town musician, under whom he learnt to play all the current instruments. The family moved to Eilenburg in 1676 and in 1684 he was app. organist at the church of Our Lady of Halle, where Handel in due course became his pupil.
Works incl. church cantatas, org. pieces, etc.

Zádor, Jenö (b. Bátaszék, 5. XI. 1894), Hung. comp. Studied with Heuberger in Vienna and Reger at Leipzig, also took a course in musicology and graduated with the Ph.D. in 1921. In 1921 he became prof. at the new Vienna Cons. and in 1934 at the Budapest Acad. of Mus. In 1939 he settled in the U.S.A. and devoted himself largely to the orchestration of film mus. by other comps.
Works incl. operas *Diana, The Island of the Dead, Asra* and others; romantic symph., dance symph., variations on a Hung. folksong, carnival suite, Hung. capriccio, etc.; chamber mus.; pf. works; songs, etc.

Zagwijn, Henri (b. Nieuwer-Amstel nr. Amsterdam, 17. VII. 1878; d. 's Gravenhage, 25. X. 1954), Dutch comp. He was mainly self-taught, settled at Rotterdam and became a teacher at the Cons. there.
Works incl. *The Sorcerer's Apprentice* (Goethe) and *The Course of the Year* for chorus and orch.; overtures *Wijdingsnacht* and *Opstanding* for orch.; chamber mus.; songs, etc.

Zaide, unfinished opera by Mozart (lib., in Ger., by Johann Andreas Schachtner), begun 1779, 1st prod. Frankfurt, 27. I. 1866.

Zajc, Ivan (better known as Giovanni von Zaytz) (b. Rijeka [Fiume], 3. VIII. 1832; d. Zagreb, 16. XII. 1914), Croatian cond. and comp. Pupil of his father, a bandmaster in the Aus. army and of Lauro Rossi at the Milan Cons. He lived at Fiume and Vienna and was from 1870 cond. at the theatre and director of the Cons. at Zagreb.
Works incl. 15 Croatian operas, It. opera *Amelia* (after Schiller's *Räuber*) and others, 15 Ger. and Croatian operettas; oratorio *The Fall of Man*; church mus.; songs, etc.

Zak, Benedict. See Schack.

Zampa, ou La Fiancée de marbre (*Z., or The Marble Betrothed*), opera by Hérold (lib. by Anne Honoré Joseph Mélesville), prod. Paris, Opéra-Comique, 3. V. 1831.

Zampogna (It.), the Calabrian bagpipe.

Zandonai, Riccardo (b. Sacco, Trentino, 28. V. 1883; d. Pesaro, 5. VI. 1944), It. comp. Studied at Roveredo and later at the Liceo Musicale of Pesaro, where Mascagni was director. He left in 1902 and at Milan met Boito, who intro. him to the pub. Ricordi, by whom his 1st opera was commissioned.
Works incl. operas *Il grillo sul focolare* (after Dickens's *Cricket on the Hearth*), *Conchita* (after Louÿs's *La Femme et le pantin*), *Melenis, La via della finestra, Francesca da Rimini* (on d'Annunzio's play), *Giuletta e Romeo* (after Shakespeare), *I cavalieri di Ekebù* (after Selma Lagerlöf), *Giuliano, La farsa amorosa, Una partita*; film mus. for *Princess Tarakanova*; Requiem, *Pater noster* for chorus, org. and orch.; *Ballata eroica, Fra gli alberghi delle Dolomiti, Quadri di Segantini, Rapsodia trentina,* overture *Colombina* for orch.; *Concerto romantico* for vln. and orch.; serenade and *Concerto andaluso* for cello and orch.; string 4tet; songs, etc.

Zanella, Amilcare (b. Monticelli d'Ongina nr. Piacenza, 26. IX. 1873; d. Pesaro, 9. I. 1949), It. pianist, cond. and comp. Studied at Cremona and Parma. After

cond. an opera co. in S. Amer. he became
director of the Parma Cons. in 1903 and 2
years later succeeded Mascagni as director
of the Liceo Musicale at Pesaro.
Works incl. operas *Aura, Sulamita, Il
revisore* (after Gogol) and others; Requiem; symph. poem *Vita* and other
orchestral works; chamber mus.; pf.
works; songs, etc.
Zannetti, Francesco (b. Volterra, 28.
III. 1737; d. Perugia, 31. I. 1788), It.
comp. Pupil of Clari in Pisa, he became
maestro di cappella at Perugia Cathedral
in 1760, remaining there till his death.
Works incl. 7 operas; oratorios;
Masses, Requiems and other church mus.;
string 5tets, string trios, trio sonatas, etc.
Zanettini. *See* **Gianettini.**
Zapateado, a Span. dance for a single
perf., in 3–4 time and with the rhythmic
accents marked by stamping of the heels.
Zapfenstreich (Ger.) = Tattoo.
**Zar und Zimmermann, oder Die zwei
Peter** (*Tsar and Carpenter, or The Two
Peters*), opera by Lortzing (lib. by comp.
based on a Fr. play by Anne Honoré
Joseph Mélesville, Jean Toussaint Merle
and Eugène Cantiran de Boirie), prod.
Leipzig, 22. XII. 1837.
See also **Borgomastro di Saardam.**
Zarathustra (R. Strauss). *See* **Also
sprach Zarathustra.**
Zarebski, Juliusz (b. Żytomierz, 28. II.
1854; d. Żytomierz, 15. IX. 1885), Pol.
pianist and comp. He appeared in public
at the age of 10 with works of his own,
studied later at the Vienna and St. Petersburg Conss., and with Liszt in Rome. He
travelled widely and became pf. prof. at the
Brussels Cons. in 1879, but had to leave
shortly afterwards because he suffered from
consumption.
Works incl. pf. 5tet in G min.; polonaises, mazurkas, studies, waltzes, Pol.
suite, etc. for pf.; Pol. folk dances for pf.
duet *A travers Pologne,* etc.
Zaremba, Nikolai Ivanovich (b. Gvt. of
Vitebsk, 15. VI. 1821; d. St. Petersburg,
8. IV. 1879), Rus. theorist. Prof. at the St.
Petersburg Cons. from its foundation in
1859: succeeded A. Rubinstein as director
from 1867 to 1871.
Works incl. oratorio *St. John the
Baptist.*
Zarlino, Gioseffe (b. Chioggia, 1517;
d. Venice, 4. II. 1590), It. theorist and
comp. Studied theol. and received minor
orders in 1539, but was learned also in
philosophy, sciences and languages. He
settled at Venice in 1541, became a fellow-
student with Rore under Willaert and, in
1565 became 1st *maestro di cappella* at St.
Mark's. In 1583 he was offered the bishop-
ric of Chioggia, but declined it, preferring
to remain at St. Mark's. He wrote 2 large
treatises, the 3-vol. *Istituitioni armoniche*

and *Dimostrationi armoniche,* for which he
was attacked by V. Galilei, whereupon he
issued another vol., *Sopplimenti musicali,* a
4th, non-mus., being added to the complete ed. later.
Comps. incl. dramatic piece *Orfeo*;
Mass for the foundation of the church of
Santa Maria della Salute and other
church mus.; pageant for the victory of
Lepanto, etc.
Zarzuela (Span.), a light Span. mus.
stage play or comic opera, usually in 1 act
but sometimes in 2, generally of a satirical
but occasionally tragic nature, and often
a skit on a spoken play. The mus. is as a
rule strongly nat. The libs. have spoken
dialogue and allow improvised interpolations, in which even the audience
sometimes joins.
Zarzycki, Aleksander (b. Lwów, 21. II.
1834; d. Warsaw, 1. XI. 1895), Pol.
pianist and comp. Studied in Paris, 1856–
1861. Settled in Warsaw in 1866 and became director of the Cons. in 1879.
Works incl. pf. concerto; numerous
vln. pieces, etc.
Zauberflöte, Die, opera by Mozart (lib.
by Emmanuel Schikaneder, ? with the aid
of Karl Ludwig Giesecke), prod. Vienna,
Theater auf der Wieden, 30. IX. 1791.
Winter's opera *Das Labyrinth* is a sequel
to it. There is also an unfinished lib. by
Goethe intended for a sequel.
Zauberharfe, Die (*The Magic Harp*),
magic play with mus. by Schubert (lib.
by Georg Ernst von Hofmann), prod.
Vienna, Theater an der Wien, 19. VIII.
1820.
Zauberoper (Ger.). *See* **Magic Opera.**
**Zauberzither, Die, oder Caspar der
Fagottist** (*The Magic Zither, or Jasper the
Bassoonist*), *Singspiel* by Wenzel Müller,
prod. Vienna, Leopoldstadt Theatre, 8.
VI. 1791. The plot shows close resem-
blances to that of Schikander's lib. for
Mozart's *Magic Flute,* which may have
been borrowed from it or based on the
same source.
Zaytz, Giovanni von. *See* **Zajc.**
Zecchi, Adone (b. Bologna, 23. VII.
1904), It. comp. Pupil of Alfano. He
founded a chamber orch. in 1930 and
began to tour It. with it. He taught at
Ravenna from 1939 to 1942, and at the
G. B. Martini Cons. at Bologna from 1942
to 1965, subsequently becoming its director.
Works incl. *Partita* and *Due preludi* for
orch.; *Giovane pastore* and *Arpège* for
soprano and orch.; *Dittico campestre*
for ob. and strings; 2 vln. and pf. sonatas;
songs, etc.
Zeckert, Joseph. *See* **Seegr.**
Želenka, Jan Dismas (b. Lounovice, 16.
X. 1679; d. Dresden, 23. XII. 1745), Boh.
comp. Studied at Prague, was double bass
player in the court band at Dresden from

1710 and went to Vienna to study under Fux in 1716; then went to It. but returned to Dresden to collaborate with Heinichen, whom he succeeded as director of the church mus. in 1729.

Works incl. Lat. *Melodrama de Sancto Wenceslao*; oratorios *I penitenti al sepolcro*, *Il serpente di bronzo* and *Gesù al Calvario*; 20 Masses, motets, psalms and other church mus.; Lat. cantatas, etc.

Żeleński, Władysław (b. Grodkowice, 6. VII. 1837; d. Cracow, 23. I. 1921), Pol. teacher and comp. Studied at Prague Univ., also mus. (with Krejči) there and later in Paris. He became prof. at the Warsaw Cons. in 1872 and director of the Cracow Cons. in 1881.

Works incl. operas *Konrad Wallenrod*, *Goplana*, *Janek*, *Balandina* and *An Old Story*; Masses and motets; cantatas; 2 symphs., *Woodland Echoes*, concert overture *In the Tatra* and other orchestral works; pf. concerto; 4 string 4tets, pf. 4tet, variations for string 4tet, 6tet for strings and pf., pf. trio; vln. and pf. sonata; pf. pieces, etc.

Zeller, Carl (Johann Adam) (b. St. Peter-in-der-Au, 19. VI. 1842; d. Baden, nr. Vienna, 17. VIII. 1898), Aus. comp. He was a choir-boy in the Imp. chapel in Vienna and studied law at the univ. He also had counterpoint lessons from Sechter. He made his career in the civil service but was continuously active as a comp.

Works incl. operettas *Der Vogelhändler*, *Der Obersteiger*, *Der Vagabund* and many others.

Zelmira, opera by Rossini (lib. by Andrea Leone Tottola, based on a Fr. tragedy by Pierre Laurent Buirette de Belloy), prod. Naples, Teatro San Carlo, 16. II. 1822.

Zelter, Carl Friedrich (b. Berlin, 11. XII. 1758; d. Berlin, 15. V. 1832), Ger. cond., teacher and comp. Having completed his training as a master mason he joined his father's firm, and abandoned the trade completely only in 1815, but meanwhile was active as a musician. Pupil of Schultz and Fasch, he succeeded the latter as cond. of the Berlin Singakademie in 1800, founded the Berliner Liedertafel in 1809, the same year became prof. at the acad., and in 1822 founded the Royal Inst. of Church Mus. Among his pupils were Nicolai, Loewe, Meyerbeer and Mendelssohn, whose plans to revive Bach's *St. Matthew Passion* in 1829 he at first opposed but later approved. In the Singakademie he had himself done much to revive interest in Bach's mus. He was a personal friend of Goethe, many of whose poems he set. Comp. principally songs, also church mus., cantatas, instrumental mus., etc.

Zémire et Azor, opera by Grétry (lib. by Marmontel), prod. Fontainebleau, at court, 9. XI. 1771; 1st Paris perf., Théâtre Italien, 16. XII. 1771.

Zemire und Azor, opera by Spohr (lib. by Johann Jakob Ihlee, based on that by Marmontel) prod. Frankfurt, 4. IV. 1819. The familiar song 'Rose, softly blooming' is in this work.

Zemlinsky, Alexander von (b. Vienna, 4. X. 1872; d. Larchmont, N.Y., 16. III. 1942), Aus. cond. and comp. Studied at the Vienna Cons. He became cond. at the Vienna Volksoper in 1906 and at the Court Opera in 1908, later at Mannheim and in Prague, where he cond. the Ger. Opera; finally in 1927–32, he was one of the conds. at the Berlin State Opera. He returned to Vienna in 1933 and later emigrated to the U.S.A. Schönberg was among his pupils and married his sister.

Works incl. operas *Sarema*, *Es war einmal*, *Kleider machen Leute* (Gottfried Keller), *Eine florentinische Tragödie*, *Der Zwerg* (both after Oscar Wilde), *Der Kreidekreis* (after Klabund); lyric symph., etc.

Zenatello, Giovanni (b. Verona, 22. II. 1876; d. N.Y., 11. II. 1949), It. tenor. 1st appeared as a baritone at Naples, but changed to tenor. He then studied at Milan, appeared in It., S. Amer. and U.S.A., and 1st in London in 1905. He created the role of Pinkerton in Puccini's *Madama Butterfly*. He married Maria Gay in 1913.

Zeno, Apostolo (1668–1750), It. poet and librettist. Operas on his libs. *see* Alessandro Severo (Lotti), Ambleto (Gasparini and D. Scarlatti), Astarto (G. B. Bononcini), Faramondo (Handel), Ifigenia in Aulide (Caldara), Lucio Papiro (do. and Hasse), Lucio Vero (Pollarolo and Sacchini), Merope (Gasparini, Jommelli and Terradellas), Scipione (Handel), Temistocle (Porpora).

Zenta, Hermann. See Holmès, Augusta.

Zeyer, Julius (1841–1901), Cz. poet and dramatist. *See* Janáček (*Šarka*), Ostrčil (*Kunala's Eyes*), Suk (*Radúz and Mahulena*).

Zhelobinsky, Valery Viktorovich (b. Tambov, 12. III. 1913; d. Leningrad, 13. VIII. 1946), Rus. pianist and comp. He played the pf. extremely well as a child and taught it; was sent to the School of Mus. at Tambov, which he left at 15 for the Leningrad Cons., where he was a pupil of Shcherbatchev.

Works incl. operas *The Peasant from Kamarinsk*, *Her Name-day* and *Mother* (based on Gorsky's novel); ballet *Party Ticket*; incid. and film mus.; 6 symphs.; 3 pf. concertos; chamber mus.; 24 preludes for pf.; songs, etc.

Zhiganov, Nazib Gaiazovich (b. Uralsk, 15. VIII. 1911), Rus. comp. He lost his parents during the Revolution and was brought up in an orphanage, later studying comp. with Litinsky.

Works incl. operas *A Fugitive* and *Irik*; cantata for the 15th anniversary of the Tartar Soviet Republic estab. in 1920; chamber mus.; pf. pieces, etc.

Zhivotov, Alexei Semionovich (b. Kazan, 14. XI. 1904), Rus. comp. Pupil of Shcherbatchev at the Leningrad Cons.

Works incl. opera *Enny*; symph. suite and jazz suite for orch.; symph. cycle for voice and orch.; nonet, etc.

Zhukovsky, Vassily Andreievich (1783–1852), Rus. author and trans. *See* Maid of Orleans (Tchaikovsky), Verstovsky (*Gromonoy*).

Ziani, Marc' Antonio (b. Venice, *c.* 1653; d. Vienna, 22. I. 1715), It. comp. *Maestro di cappella* at the church of Santa Barbara and cond. at the theatre at Mantua in 1686. He went to Vienna, where became vice-mus. director in 1700 and 1st mus. director in 1711.

Works incl. operas *Alessandro magno in Sidone*, *Damira placata*, *Meleagro*, *Chilonida* and 41 others; Masses, motets and other church mus.; oratorios, cantatas, etc.

Ziani, Pietro Andrea (b. Venice, *c.* 1620; d. Naples, 12. II. 1684), It. comp., uncle of prec. He was organist at Venice, then at Santa Maria Maggiore, Bergamo, visited Vienna and Dresden in 1660–7 and became organist at St. Mark's, Venice, in succession to Cavalli in 1669. He went to Naples on failing to be app. *maestro di cappella* in 1676, becoming a teacher at the Cons. di Sant' Onofrio and in 1680 royal *maestro di cappella*.

Works incl. operas *Le fortune di Rodope e di Damira*, *L'Antigona delusa da Alceste* and 21 others; Masses, psalms, oratorios; instrumental sonatas; org. pieces, etc.

Zich, Otakar (b. Králové Městec, 25. III. 1879; d. Oubĕnice nr. Benešov, 9. VII. 1934), Cz. comp. He was at 1st a secondary schoolmaster, but took a degree at the Univ. of Brno and was app. prof. of aesthetics there. He also collected folksongs.

Works incl. operas *The Painter's Whim*, *The Sin* and *Les Précieuses ridicules* (after Molière); *The Ill-fated Marriage* and *Polka Rides* for chorus and orch.; songs, etc.

Zichy, Géza, Count (b. Sztára Castle, 22. VII. 1849; d. Budapest, 14. I. 1924), Hung. pianist, poet and comp. Pupil of Volkmann and Liszt at Budapest. He lost his right arm as a boy of 14 in a hunting accident and wrote much pf. mus. for the left hand. He became president of the Hung. Acad. of Mus. and the Nat. Cons.

Works incl. operas *Castle Story*, *Alár*,

Master Roland, trilogy *Rákóczi* (*Nemo*, *Rákóczi Ferenc* and *Rodostó*); ballet *Gemma*; pf. concerto for the left hand; sonata, 6 studies, etc. for the left hand and other pf. mus.; songs, etc.

Ziehharmonika (Ger. lit. draw-harmonica) = Accordion.

Zieleński, Mikolaj (b. ?; d. ?), Pol. 17th-cent. organist and comp. Comp. offertories and communions for the service of the whole year.

Zigeunerbaron, Der (*The Gypsy Baron*), operetta by J. Strauss, jun. (lib. by Ignaz Schnitzer, based on another by Mór Jókai founded on his own story *Saffi*), prod. Vienna, Theater an der Wien, 24. X. 1885.

Zilafone (It.), obs. = Xylophone.

Zilcher, Hermann (b. Frankfurt, 18. VIII. 1881; d. Würzburg, 1. I. 1948), Ger. comp. Studied at the Hoch Cons. at Frankfurt, became prof. at the Acad. of Mus. at Munich in 1908 and in 1920 director of the Würzburg Cons.

Works incl. opera *Doktor Eisenbart*; incid. mus. for plays by Shakespeare, Dehmel's children's play *Fitzbutze* and Hauptmann's *Die goldene Harfe*; oratorio *Liebesmesse*; 5 symphs., *Tanzphantasie* and other works for orch.; pieces for solo instruments and orch.; chamber mus.; pf. pieces; songs, etc.

Zillig, Winfried (b. Würzburg, 1. V. 1905; d. Hamburg, 1963), Ger. comp. and cond. Studied with Schönberg in Vienna and from 1927 to 1928 was asst. to Kleiber at the Berlin State Opera. From 1928 to 1947 he cond. in various Ger. theatres, becoming director of mus. at the radio station, 1st in Frankfurt and then in Hamburg. He also made a performing version of Schönberg's unfinished oratorio *Die Jakobsleiter*.

Works incl. operas *Die Windesbraut*, *Troilus und Cressida*, *Das Opfer*, television opera *Bauernpassion*, radio opera *Die Verlobung von St. Domingo*; vln. and cello concertos; 4 serenades for var. instrumental groups; choral mus.; songs, etc.

Zimbalist, Efrem (b. Rostov on the Don, 9. IV. 1889), Rus. comp. and violinist. Studied first with his father and then with L. Auer at the St. Petersburg Cons. from 1901 to 1907, making his début in Berlin in 1907. In 1911 he emigrated to the U.S.A., and in 1941 became director of the Curtis Inst. in Philadelphia, which had been founded by his wife.

Works incl. opera *Landara*; *Amer. Rhapsody* for orch.; concerto and 3 Slavonic Dances for vln. and orch.; string 4tet; vln. sonata etc.,

Zimbalon (incorrect spelling). *See* Cimbalom.

Zimmerman, Bernd Alois (b. Bliesheim, nr. Cologne, 20. III. 1918; d. Grosskönigsdorf, 10. VIII. 1970), Ger. comp. Studied in Cologne with Lemacher and P. Jarnach, and also studied linguistics and philosophy at the Univs. of Bonn, Cologne and Berlin. From 1950 to 1952 he taught at Cologne Univ. (mus.) and from 1958 at the Hochschule für Musik in Cologne.

Works incl. opera *Die Soldaten*; ballets *Kontraste* and *Alagoana*; cantata *Lob der Torheit*; 4 symphs.; concertos for vln., ob. and cello; concerto for string orch.; vln. sonata, etc.

Zimmermann, Pierre (Joseph Guillaume) (b. Paris, 17. III. 1785; d. Paris, 29. X. 1853), Fr. pianist, teacher and comp. Studied at the Paris Cons., where he became a pupil-teacher in 1811, asst. master in 1817 and prof. of pf. in 1820. Gounod married a daughter of his. He wrote a treatise, *Encyclopédie du pianiste*.

Works incl. operas *L'Enlèvement* and *Nausicaa*; pf. works, etc.

Zincken, Hans Friedrich August. *See* Sommer, Hans.

Zingara, La (*The Gypsy*), intermezzo by Rinaldo di Capua (lib. by ?), prod. (prob. not for the 1st time) Paris, Opéra, 19. VI. 1753.

Zingarelli, Nicola Antonio (b. Naples, 4. IV. 1752; d. Torre del Greco, 5. V. 1837), It. comp. Studied at the Cons. S. Maria di Loreto in Naples, where his intermezzo *I quattro pazzi* was prod. in 1768. Leaving the Cons. in 1772 he at 1st worked as an organist, but with *Motezuma* (Naples, 1781) began his career as an opera comp., and 1785–1803 prod. works in all the main It. cities and also in Paris. He was app. *maestro di cappella* at the cathedral in Milan in 1793, Loreto 1794, and in 1804 succeeded Guglielmi at St. Peter's, Rome, from about this time onwards devoting himself chiefly to church mus. He became director of the Real Collegio di Musica in Naples in 1813, and *maestro di cappella* of the cathedral there in 1816.

Works incl. 37 operas, e.g. *Motezuma*, *Armida*, *Antigono*, *Ifigenia in Aulide*, *Antigone*, *Il mercato di Monfregoso*, *Artaserse*, *Quinto Fabio*, *Gli Orazi e Curazi*, *Giulietta e Romeo* (after Shakespeare), *Andromeda*, *La morte di Mitridate*, *I veri amici*, *Il ratto delle Sabine*, *Edipo a Colono* (after Sophocles), *Berenice regina d'Armenia* and *c.* 20 others; oratorios *La Passione*, *Gerusalemme distrutta*, *La riedificazione di Gerusalemme* and others; many cantatas; numerous Masses, Requiems and other church mus.; canon for 8 voices; *Partimenti* and *Solfeggi* for vocal exercise, etc.

Zingaresa (It. noun) ⎱ words used to des-
Zingarese (It. adj.) ⎰

cribe mus. in, or supposed to be in, a gypsy manner. The adj. is used in the form of *alla z.*

Zingari, Gli (*The Gypsies*), opera by Leoncavallo (lib. by Enrico Cavacchioli and Guglielmo Emanuel, after Pushkin), prod. London, Hippodrome, 16. IX. 1912.

Zink (Ger.) = Cornett.

Zipoli, Domenico (b. Prato, 16. X. 1688; d. Córdoba, Arg., 2. I. 1726), It. comp. Pupil (?) of A. Scarlatti in Naples and Pasquini in Rome, where he became organist of the Jesuit church, he entered the Jesuit Order and in 1717 went to S. Amer. as a missionary.

Works incl. 2 oratorios; church mus.; keyboard mus. (2 vols. of *Sonate d'intavolatura* pub. in 1716), etc.

Zítek, Otakar (b. Prague, 5. XI. 1892; d. Bratislava, 28. IV. 1955), Cz. critic and comp. Pupil of Novák and Adler. Prof. at the Brno Cons., etc. He wrote a book on modern opera.

Works incl. operas *The Sublime Heart* and *The Fall of Peter Králenec*; church mus.; cello sonata; song cycles, etc.

Zither (Ger. from Gk. *kithara*), a string instrument of the Dulcimer type, although etymologically connected with the Cittern, which it does not resemble. It has many strings (27–40) stretched over a flat sound-box, and is played with the tips of the finger, the bass strings alone being struck with a plectrum fixed to the thumb by a ring.

Znamenny Chant (from Rus. *znamia* = neume), the chant of the Rus. Orthodox church in use from the 12th to the 17th cent., when it began to decline.

Zoilo, Annibale (b. Rome, *c.* 1537; d. Loreto, 1592), It. singer and comp. *Maestro di cappella* at the churches of St. John Lateran and San Luigi in Rome, singer in the Papal Chapel from 1570 to *c.* 1582, and *maestro di cappella* of the Santa Casa at Loreto in 1584–92.

Works incl. Masses; madrigals; songs, etc.

Zoilo, Cesare (b. Rome, *c.* 1584; d. ?., after 1622), It. comp. (?) son of prec. Comp. motets, madrigals, etc.

Zola, Émile (1840–1902), Fr. novelist. *See* Attaque du moulin (Bruneau, *Soirées de Médan*), Bruneau (*Kérim*, *Ouragan*, *Enfant-roi*, *Lazare*, *Naïs Micoulin*, *4 Journées* and *Faute de l'Abbé Mouret*), Gurlitt (M.) (*Nana*), Messidor (Bruneau), Rêve (do.), Weis (K.) (*Attack on the Mill*).

Zöllner, Heinrich (b. Leipzig, 4. VII. 1854; d. Freiburg, 4. V. 1941), Ger. cond. and comp., son of the comp. Carl Friedrich Z. (1800–60). Studied at the Leipzig Cons. App. teacher at Dorpat Univ. (Tartu, Estonia) in 1878, cond. at Cologne, lived in U.S.A. in 1890–8, became mus. director of Leipzig Univ. in succession to Kretzschmar until 1906, cond. the Flem. Opera at Antwerp from 1907 and retired to Freiburg in 1914.

Works incl. operas *Frithjof* (after Tegnér), *Faust* (on part of Goethe's orig. text), *Der Überfall* (on a story by Wildenbruch), *Die versunkene Glocke* (on Hauptmann's play) and others; festival cantata *The New World* and others; 5 symphs., overture *Under the Starry Banner*, etc.

Zolotarev, Vassily Andreievich (b. Taganrog, 7. III. 1873; d. Moscow, 25. V. 1964), Rus. comp. He was a choir-boy in the court chapel at St. Petersburg, learnt the vln., but had to give it up because of an injury to his hand, also studied comp. with Liadov and Balakirev, later with Rimsky-Korsakov at the Cons. Later he became prof. at the Moscow Cons., but in 1925 went to live in the Caucasus, returning to Moscow, after var. teaching appts., in 1941.

Works incl. opera *The Decembrists*; cantata *Paradise and the Peri* (after Thomas Moore); 7 symphs., overture *A Rustic Festival*; 6 string 4tets, string 5tet, pf. 4tet, pf. trio; pf. sonata and pieces; songs, etc.

Zopfstil (Ger., lit. 'pigtail style'), derogatory term sometimes applied to the formal courtly style of the later 18th cent.

Zoppa (It. = limp), a strong accent on a 2nd note off the beat or a long note following a short one, as in the Scotch snap. The motion of a mus. piece in such a rhythm is called *alla z.*

Zoroastre, opera by Rameau (lib. by Louis de Cahusac), prod. Paris Opéra, 5. XII. 1749.

Zorrilla y Moral, José (1817–93), Span. poet and dramatist. *See* **Don Giovanni** (Lattuada).

Zortziko (Basque) ⎫ a Basque dance-song
Zorzico (Span.) ⎭
of remote orig., now in 5–8 time, but prob. in 6–8 before the 19th cent.

Zuccalmaglio, Anton Wilhelm Florentin von (b. Waldbröl, 12. IV. 1803; d. Nachrodt, Westphalia, 23. III. 1869), Ger. critic and folksong collector. He was a contributor to Schumann's *Neue Zeitschrift für Musik* and with A. Kretschmer ed. 2 vols. of Ger. folksong, some of which were comp. by himself.

Zuffolo (It.), a whistle or pipe of a flageolet type.

Zumpe, Hermann (b. Oppach, 9. IV. 1850; d. Munich, 4. IX. 1903), Ger. cond. and comp. Educ. at a seminary at Bautzen to become a schoolmaster, but he was so taken up with mus. that he went to Leipzig in 1871, where he taught in a school and studied with A. Tottmann. In 1872–6 he asst. Wagner at Bayreuth and then succeeded in securing one post as theatre

cond. after another, until in 1891 he became court mus. director at Stuttgart. In 1895–7 he cond. the Kaim orch. at Munich and then became court cond. at Schwerin, from 1901 at Munich.

Works incl. operas *Anahra, Die verwunschene Prinzess, Das Gespenst von Horodin* and *Sawitri* (from the Mahabharata, unfinished), operettas *Farinelli, Karin* and *Polnische Wirtschaft*, etc.

Zumsteeg, Johann Rudolf (b. Sachsenflur, Baden, 10. I. 1760; d. Stuttgart, 27. I. 1802), Ger. comp. Fellow-pupil and friend of Schiller at the Karlschule in Stuttgart, he entered the service of the court there as a cellist in 1781, becoming *Konzertmeister* in 1792. His extended ballads were esp. influential, some being later used as models by Schubert.

Works incl. operas *Das tartarische Gesetz, Le delizie campestri o Ippolito e Aricia, Armida, Die Geisterinsel, Das Pfauenfest* and others; melodrama *Tamira*; incid. mus. to *Hamlet, Macbeth,* Schiller's *Räuber* and other plays; cantatas; Masses and other church mus.; 10 cello concertos; songs and ballads *Lenore* (Bürger), *Colma* (Ossian), *Die Büssende, Ritter Toggenburg* (Schiller), *Die Entführung,* etc.

Zur Mühlen, Raimund von (b. Livonia, 10. XI. 1854; d. Steyning, Sussex, 9. XII. 1931), Ger. baritone. Educ. in Ger., he began to learn singing at the Hochschule für Musik in Berlin, later went to Stockhausen at Frankfurt and Bussine in Paris. He 1st visited London in 1882, frequently returned and finally settled in Eng., where he was much sought after as a teacher of singing.

Zusammenschlag (Ger.) = Acciaccatura or Mordent.

Zvonař, Josef (Leopold) (b. Kublov nr. Beroun, 22. I. 1824; d. Prague, 23. XI. 1865), Cz. theorist and comp. He studied at the Org. School in Prague and taught there from 1844 to 1860. He was one of the founders of the Hlahol choral society. He wrote several educ. treatises and a vol. on early Cz. mus.

Works incl. opera *Zàboj*; Masses, 2 Requiems; humorous choruses; chamber mus.; org. sonatas; pf. mus.; songs, etc.

Zweers, Bernard (b. Amsterdam, 18. V. 1854; d. Amsterdam, 9. XII. 1924), Dutch comp. Self-taught at 1st and later a pupil of Jadassohn at Leipzig. On his return to Amsterdam he cond., becoming prof. at the Cons. in 1895.

Works incl. incid. mus. to Vondel's *Gijsbrecht van Amstel,* choral works; 3 symphs. (3rd *To my Fatherland*), etc.

Zweig, Stefan (1881–1942), Aus. novelist and dramatist. *See* **Schweigsame Frau** (R. Strauss), **Toch** (*Heilige aus U.S.A.*).

Z. intended to write the lib. for R. Strauss's *Friedenstag,* suggested to him by

Joseph Gregor; but the Nazi régime making his appearance on any Ger. stage impossible after 1933, this was afterwards undertaken by Gregor himself.

Zwillingsbrüder, Die (*The Twin Brothers*), play with mus. by Schubert (lib. by George Ernst von Hofmann), prod. Vienna, Kärntnertortheater, 14. VI. 1820.

Zwischendominante (Ger. lit. betweendominant). *See* **Interdominant.**

Zwischenspiel (Ger.) = Interlude.

Zwyssig, (Johann) Joseph (Father Alberik) (b. Bauen, Uri, 17. XI. 1808; d. Mehrerau nr. Bregenz, 18. XI. 1854), Swiss priest, organist and comp. Educ. at the monastery school of Wettingen, ordained priest and became mus. teacher and cathedral organist and cond. After the dissolution of the monastery he led a precarious existence, but was in demand as an authority on the org.

Works incl. Masses, offertories and other church mus.; choruses incl. the patriotic *Schweizerpsalm* 'Trittst im Morgenrot daher'; songs, etc.